SPECS: The Comprehensive Foodservice Purchasing and Specification Manual

DEDICATED

to

the memory of

Jerimiah J. Wanderstock

The finest human being
our industry ever had; we
who were touched by him
were changed forever.

SPECS: The Comprehensive Foodservice Purchasing and Specification Manual

RAYMOND B. PEDDERSEN

Jule Wilkinson, Editor

Published by

CBI Publishing Company, Inc.
51 Sleeper Street
Boston, Massachusetts 02210

Library of Congress Cataloging in Publication Data

Peddersen, Raymond B
   SPECS : the comprehensive foodservice purchasing
and specification manual.

   Bibliography: p.
   Includes index.
   1. Food service. 2. Purchasing. I. Title.
TX911.3.P8P4   658.7'2   76-56460
ISBN 0-8436-2084-6

Third printing

ISBN 0-8436-2084-6

Printed in the United States of America

Printing(last digit): 9 8 7 6 5 4 3 2

ABOUT THE AUTHOR

Raymond B. Peddersen is a prominent hospital foodservice director. Mr. Peddersen, co-author of *Increasing Productivity in Foodservice*, Cahners Books 1973, is a frequent innovator, author, and lecturer on every phase of foodservice. SPECS is a result of his codifying the procurement needs in his many years in hotel, restaurant, fast food, contract, and institutional foodservice. He attended the University of Utah and Cornell University School of Hotel Administration and is a member of the Society for the Advancement of Food Service Research, American Society for Hospital Food Service Administrators of the American Hospital Association, and the Food Service Executives Association.

CONTENTS

Forward viii

Introduction ix

Acknowledgements xi

1. Purchasing Policies 1

    What SPECS tells you 1
    The Purchasing Function: What is it? 3
    How to Write a Purchasing Manual 3
    What to Charge? 6
    Ethics 8
    Purchasing Systems 9
    Techniques for Purchasing 39
    Accounting System 51

2. Meat 69
    Cut It or Buy It 84
    How much to Order? 86
    How much to Pay? 89
    How much to Charge 92
    Writing Meat Specifications 93
    Institutional Meat Purchase Specifications . . 94
    Beef 106
    Lamb 143
    Veal and Calf 156
    Pork 172
    Sausage 189
    Cured and Smoked Pork 226

3. Poultry 239
    Rabbits 257

4. Eggs 261

5. Dairy Products 271
    Milk 271
    Cheese 290
    Butter 299
    Frozen Desserts 308

6. Fish and Shellfish 311
    Fresh Water 312
    Salt Water 315
    Canned 358

7. Convenience Foods 311
    Code of Recommended Practices 368
    Federal Standards 373

8. Kosher Products 403

9. Produce 469
    Fresh Fruits and Vegetables 470
    Canned Fruits and Vegetables 487
    Fruits, Specifications 500
    Vegetables, Specifications 676
    Juices, Specifications 847
    Jams and Jellies, Specifications 867

10. Miscellaneous Groceries 881
    Beverages 882
    Cereals, Grains and Flours 886
    Dressings 894
    Fats and Oils 895
    Legumes 905
    Nuts 906
    Spices and Herbs 931

11. Quality Controls and Federal Regulations . . . 945

12. Storage and Handling 987

    Appendix   I - Food Purchasing Guide for
                  Group Feeding 1027

    Appendix II - Specifications 1075

    Appendix III - Specifications 1104

    Appendix IV - Common and Scientific Names 1152

    Index 1158

FOREWORD

Cost control in the foodservice business becomes increasingly important as the individual operation grows. The independent operator sometimes expands without sufficient depth in management, and the owner's attention is concentrated on problem areas not concerned with food purchasing. The institutional and chain purchasing agent becomes embroiled in so many details as expansion develops that he may well lose sight of important money saving factors related to the actual purchasing of food. Often the operator will concentrate on labor costs, portion control, energy consumption and many other equally important factors of the business. Yet, in the area of food purchasing, his knowledge may be limited, and he is inclined to depend on his suppliers to know his needs. In this situation he finds it easier to place an order rather than to do a conscientious purchasing job.

Normally, chains do have more sophisticated methods for purchasing than most independents, however, this book should have a very important place in the library of every foodservice operator. The author has condensed valuable information about food products into a readable and very useful form, providing a book that can be used as a learning and teaching manual as well as a constant source of reference.

An operator or a purchasing agent must know what is available in the market, as well as the actual needs of his own operation. If he lacks this information, he may be buying a quality of merchandise either inferior or superior to his actual requirements.

The old Latin expression, "Caveat Emptor" or "Buyer Beware," certainly applies to the foodservice operator, but he can only blame himself if he is not knowledgeable as to his exact needs and does not purchase through use of specifications. The final step, of course, is that he must be sure that he receives what he orders.

With competition for the food dollar increasing at such a rapid rate, people involved with the purchasing of food will undoubtedly find the chapters of this book a most important means towards improving that bottom line.

Don Roth
Blackhawk Restaurants
Chicago, Illinois

INTRODUCTION

Why SPECS? The industry has needed a book like this for a long time. SPECS is the first and only book that puts into one volume all the comprehensive and basic elements of foodservice purchasing for today's busy foodservice director. It answers the need for a single authoritative reference on food purchasing.

Raymond Peddersen, with the skill of a surgeon, has taken food product specifications and formulated them into practical foodservice terminology. Presented in an easy, readable style, his book contains complete information on purchasing procedures, federal food regulations, inventory control, and budgeting.

The book develops a unique plan of combining all elements of food purchasing — such as resourcefulness, cost control, and seasonal buying — to produce the greatest economic savings. As rising food costs continue to be a problem, this system of controls will help the buyer to work within his budget. SPECS addresses itself to modern communications and transportation systems and shows their impact on food price and quality.

The author develops food purchasing not as a separate function, but incorporates it into the total foodservice operation. Because he is very sensitive to the polarities and ambiguities of food purchasing, he stresses solid purchasing principles and shows the foodservice director how to write specifications that will be most effective in his own particular situation.

Brother Herman Zaccarelli
Director
Hotel, Hospitality, Foodservice
Continuing Education Institute
Purdue University

ACKNOWLEDGMENTS

This book has been written to answer a need that the author has perceived to be vital for a number of years. There are, to be sure, food purchasing books available. Some are very limited in the information supplied; some are laborious texts; some are food production texts with data presented to be used to purchase categories of food products. The intent here has been to provide that data, and where a deeper understanding of an individual product is required to clarify the product specification, also to include specific information. In our industry the user (operator) is most often the buyer; this book has been written with the assumption that the reader knows his business but needs a source of reference as well as a source of specifications which may be used when preparing his operation's own specifications manual, bid sheets, and contract documents. The appendices present models of those items.

I have been a cook and remember well the frustrations of trying to prepare a proper product with inappropriate supplies; had any of my superiors owned and used a book such as this, the problems would have been lessened or eliminated. I have been a manager/buyer in foodservice operations—hotels, quality restaurant, fast food operations, schools and colleges, inplant industrial, office buildings, coffee shops, cafeterias, and hospitals. In every operation I have seen and felt the need for uniform specifications.

It was from this personal need that this work started in November, 1971. It is hoped that these years of effort have resulted in the inclusion of all that the reader needs for his work. Where the work falls short of the need will be known only to the reader; your comments and suggestions will be invaluable in the preparation of revisions of this work.

I cannot and do not hold myself out to be the "expert" on the material in this book. I have tried to reduce an enormous volume of Federal Standards and material from foodservice industry publications (see the bibliographies) to a workable size. The page layout, type design, indexing, and section tabs were selected to make this a "desk-top" reference. This looks like a "telephone book" of specifications; it is intended to be.

No work of this scope can be done alone. There are many to whom a debt of gratitude is owed. They are listed here as well as can be recalled; forgiveness is begged of anyone inadvertently excluded.

As has been the case with a great many important books in our industry, Jule Wilkinson, Book Editor for *Institutions/Volume Feeding Magazine* got me into writing books and started this project rolling. Jule has done a massive editing job, giving the book flow and clarity. Had Jule not been there, this book could not be here. She is gentle, cooperative and helpful all the time; firm, insistent, and flexible when I stray from the need a book is suppose to serve.

I would like to also express my thanks to Charys Pinney, Joan Kocher, and Bridget Janus for so ably handling the innumerable details that are required to produce a book of this comprehensiveness and complexity.

Brother Herman Zaccarelli was supposed to co-author this work. Herman had the original contract to which he added me and from which uncontrollable circumstances forced him to withdraw. Herman supplied the concept as well as a stream of resource material. Herman gave love, friendship, support, and joy.

Marshall Neale and the American Spice Trade Association provided much of the spice information. Marshall has always been most cooperative.

Jacques Block, C.F.E., Director of Food Services, has allowed use of his excellent *Montefiore Hospital Food Purchasing Manual* in the appendix. The reader may use this manual as a model.

Thanks to the Coffee Brewing Institute for materials used in "Beverages."

Thanks to James Myers and his *Cooking for Profit* for the use of Robert Petrie's "Food Cost and the 40 Thieves."

Thanks to James Farrell and *Health Institutions Purchasing* for the material on purchasing manuals which appears in the first chapter.

Thanks to *Institutions/Volume Feeding Magazine* for much

of the information on convenience foods, as well as to the National Frozen Foods Association for their information on frozen foods.

The "Meat" section would not be as useful as it is if the National Live Stock and Meat Board had not lent the use of their information, publications, and, especially, many photographs, which appear in the Meat chapter.

Thanks to the National Dairy Council for materials used in "Milk."

Thanks to the Oscar Mayer Co. for all the material on sausage which has been reproduced here and for the use of sausage photographs.

Thanks to Schrieber Caterers for the use of their material to begin the Kosher section; to Rabbi Berel Wein for use of the Ⓤ Catalogue and to *The Jewish Homemaker* for use of the Ⓚ Catalogue.

R.A. Seeling and the United Fresh Fruit and Vegetable Association have allowed me to use a great amount of information from their excellent *Fruit and Vegetable Facts and Pointers*. What is used here is just the tip of their iceberg; the serious buyer should certainly subscribe to their series.

Thanks to my mother, Beverly Peddersen, who sought out many publications for me.

I owe tremendous gratitude to Pat Niehaus who spent a summer vacation working with me in compiling the information and helping to put it together for use in this book. Leslie Harris did much of the abbreviating of Federal Specifications; I thank her, too.

Judi Weiner Pedderson cheered this project at its conception and, under different circumstances, gave scores of hours to professionally proofreading the manuscript, unsplitting infinitives, undangling participles, chasing gerunds that ran away, unmixing metaphors, dotting i's, inserting commas, and making the first rough copy make sense.

Justin Friedman of Huttenbauer Meat Co. and Wally Frank of Regency Meats gave many hours of consultation on the meat sections.

Steve Laine and Bob McMillan gave me access to quantities of data at the U.S. Department of Agriculture. Because of them the information provided here is the most current available.

Dennis Singleton and Debbie Radford worked weekends at home on some of my other projects; that gave me those weekends for this one.

The people who type are unsung heroes. Without Sheila Aytes, Marian Goldberg, Fran Ruggerri, Sandy Tracey, John Treece, and Annette Rosemond there would be no book.

Everyone has someone who has the faith to provide inspiration and strength. Bruce Smith gave me a start. Fran and Maury Gleckman believed in me. Jimmy Jones and Bob Brice gave me a reason to start.

Ira Goodwin, former Administrator of Hillside Hospital, and Richard Squire, Administrative Director at The Jewish Hospital of Cincinnati, were understanding in letting me take abnormally long periods of vacations to work on this book. Both fine gentlemen understood the value of this project.

Abraham Maslow detailed the need to self-actualize. He believed that we owe ourselves a continual quest for a great book. I never met Dr. Maslow but I owe him many debts of gratitude.

Shaari Ann Peddersen sacrificed many weekends with her daddy for this book. She was the perennial "go-for" this and "go-for" that little girl. Her daddy will try to make up for her patience now.

Gloria Gaugler Peddersen, R.D., has not been sure whether she married a man or manuscript. Certainly, giving up nights, weekends, movies, dances, camping trips, hikes, skiing, sleep, and one-third of the house for this book could not have been her idea of the perfect honeymoon. She was patient, and she helped write part of this book. Now the reader has the manuscript, and Gloria has her man.

There are undoubtedly some that I have inadvertently forgotten here; my appreciation, and my apologies.

Raymond B. Peddersen
Salt Lake City, Utah
February, 1977

PURCHASING POLICIES

Why SPECS Was Written

THE FUNCTION of purchasing is common to all industries. But, as in so many other functions, foodservice purchasing is different.

In many industries the purchasing function stands alone. But in foodservice the quality and the quantity of materials purchased are both the beginning and the end of the circle of total operation. Purchasing must be tightly interrelated.

To put it another way, it is *not* possible to prepare high quality food from low quality ingredients, but it *is* possible to prepare low quality food from high quality ingredients.

What SPECS Tells You, What It Doesn't Tell You, and Why

Items purchased for industrial use, such as nuts and bolts, carry exacting specifications. There are, of course, definite measures which can be applied to nuts and bolts—percentages of different metals in the alloy, physical size, type and depth of threads, and so on. It is commonly believed that equally definite measures can not be applied to foods. That belief is wrong.

This book was written to promote the use of exacting standards in foodservice purchases. Its intent is to help both operator and student know the difference between those ill-defined terms "high" quality and "low" quality, and to bring forward substantially all the knowledge available at the time on measures of quality in foods without presenting the reader with more data than is necessary.

Various agencies and departments of the federal government have established detailed specifications for virtually any type of raw product in the marketplace. The mass of these specifications runs to many thousands of printed pages, with the specification for an individual product often requiring eight or more pages.

These standards and the controls were established by the government to substantially protect citizens from hazardous practices on the part of food processors and generally assure disease-free and unadulterated products. As foodservice operators, we do not need to know all the details about every product, but we do need to know the most important ones to do the best job in purchasing food for preparation. To that end the author has included only the most pertinent details on the very broad range of food and food products availabe in the United States.

The function of this book is akin to that of a dictionary. You keep a dictionary at hand so that you may readily check the spelling or meaning of a word. This book should be a ready reference to the minimum standards by which you can measure the foods you specify for purchase and inspect them at point of receipt. These specifications are the means to assure that your foodservice operation is getting a full dollar's value for every dollar spent.

Obviously food preparation, regardless of quality level, demands far more knowledge than the specifications for raw food. There are many excellent texts on the preparation, production, and service of food. This book does not pretend to be one of them. It is, rather, a companion to any of the excellent texts listed in the bibliography. Wherever the text can be made clearer, or the operator aided in preparation phases by illustrations or charts, an effort has been made to include those materials.*

For those who seek more detailed and complete information, the bibliographies are sources of such information within the federal government. In addition, the federal specification numbers from which abbreviated specifications are derived are included.

The listing of raw, canned, frozen, and dehydrated products is hopefully complete. The data on these has been abbreviated for the above reasons as well as for space.

CAVEAT EMPTOR is a Latin phrase meaning "Let the buyer beware." The foodservice buyer must beware of many things, to be sure, but that which he must beware of most is his own error. Products should be purchased for the use intended. The smart food buyer buys foods that are no better (and no worse) than his need calls for.

There is no reason to buy U.S. No. 1 tomatoes (perfect color, perfect firmness, etc.) when slices from those tomatoes are going to be hidden within a closed sandwich or smothered with a cheese sauce on an open-faced sandwich. A U.S. No. 2 tomato would serve equally well. Conversely, only a U.S. No. 1 tomato should be used where tomato wedges or slices are open to sight and part of the merchandising.

A second example of improper buying would be specifying canned cling peaches with a score of 90 points or better (USDA Grade A) for service on salad plates or for broiling as a garnish. A sensible quality level then would be 84 points (USDA Grade B) for the salad because the allowable defects in the "B" are few and not very visible, while the price difference is usually substantial between the two grades. For broiling, peaches with a score of 70 points (USDA C) would be acceptable because the allowable blemishes in this less expensive grade will be overridden by the physical damage done in broiling.

While information is included within this book about all the

*Unless otherwise noted, all photographs and illustrations in this book were furnished by the United States Department of Agriculture.

available food product grades, details are provided only on those grades the author recommends for the vast majority of foodservice operations. In some cases, such as meat, it has been possible to list the recommended cooking methods or the dishes commonly prepared from the food item as purchased. In these cases the cooking method will determine the grade to be purchased. (In beef it is best to use high yield grade numbers such as "Yield Grade 1" and "Yield Grade 2" for cuts which will be cooked by dry heat methods as the 1975 changes in the grades brought the "Choice" range deep down into the former "Good" grade.)

HOW TO USE THIS BOOK

The purveyor and the operator must be able to communicate in the same language. Just as it is the buyer's job to know what he is buying, it is the purveyor's job to know what he is selling. The buyer who fails to specify exactly what he wants deserves to get a product other than that which he wanted. He has cheated himself. The purveyor who delivers a product inferior to that which was specified by the buyer has cheated the operator.

Generally, the purveyors to operators are middlemen who purchase from a source closer to the farm, as it were. In order to purchase products to sell to operators the distributor must, himself, know specifications. The reader is cautioned to avoid buying from any purveyor who does not demonstrate knowledge of federal specifications, and willingness to comply with specifications and requests for evidence of grade such as grade stamps and grade certificates.

It is not practical to provide a purveyor with full oral or written specifications every time a quotation is taken or an order placed. It is important that both the buyer and the purveyor know they are contracting for the same product. Because so much food purchasing is done by telephone, it is important that an operator provide purveyors with detailed specifications for his operation. There are three ways in which this can be done.

Method 1: Provide purveyors with a listing of food items you may purchase from them. Refer to the page number and paragraph in which each specification is detailed in this book.

Method 2: The specifications in this manual are presented in such a manner to facilitate their use as models. (Photocopying individual pages is expressly forbidden by the publisher.)

Method 3: Provide purveyors with a complete specification for each item you may purchase from them.

This book should be your desk-top reference manual. When you have a question, reach for the *SPECS*.

The Purchasing Function: What is it?

Purchasing food and supplies is somewhat unique in that it goes beyond specifying products and placing orders. In foodservice the functions related to purchasing are generally done by the same people who do the purchasing. While a large volume operation might be an exception, most foodservice operations are not large volume. This section discusses those related functions.

FORECASTING. If you do not know how many you are going to serve, you cannot know how much to buy. Therefore, you must predict how much will be served.

Some foodservice operators have been making good predictions for a long time. Others have made bad predictions for a long time. The former enjoy good controls, fewer headaches, and predictable operating expenses. The latter spend a lot of time figuring out what to serve when they run out, or how to re-use leftovers. Bad forecasting is bad business.

A card which gives a history of food portions served can be used as a record to indicate the percentage of sales on one item compared to competing menu items. In almost every operation the consumption pattern of one item of a class (entrees, desserts, etc.), as opposed to any number of competing menu items of that class, will be fairly consistent.

Also, in most operations there is a pattern as to the total number of customers served. In a restaurant this may be a function of the day of the week, or the season of the year, or both; in an institution, it may reflect many factors.

By keeping careful sales records with customer count patterns, the operator will usually be able to closely estimate (forecast) the number of customers expected on any given day. When this figure is multiplied by the usual consumption percentage of any given menu item, the result is an estimate of the number of portions needed.

In practice it is applied like this. Assume a standardized recipe for 100 portions of Roast Beef that calls for 30 lb. of IMPS No. 167-Knuckle. If the forecast is for 357 portions, then the buyer will know to purchase 3.57 x 30 lb. or 107 lb. (+ 1.6 oz.) of IMPS No. 167-Knuckle.

A more sophisticated system is to use these records to calculate a moving average. A moving average is simply the average number of portions served over a certain period of time. The simplest to calculate is one based on 10 serving times. To calculate the moving average:

(a) add up the number of portions served the last 10 consecutive times the item has been served.

(b) divide the total by 10.

(c) next time the item is served, subtract from the total (a) the number of portions served 11 times ago, and add the number of portions served this time.

(d) divide the new total (c) by 10.

(e) repeat (c) and (d) each time the item is served.

The moving average may then be used as your forecast.

How to write a purchasing manual[1]

A purchasing manual is not a frill or window dressing, it is an aid to better management. The *Guide to Purchasing*, of the National Association of Purchasing Management, declares that no purchasing manager has an excuse for not having at least an informal statement of purchasing policy and a collection of purchasing procedures.

A good manual can provide continuity and consistency which are otherwise hard to maintain. It can help to train and integrate new employees quickly. If purchasing is being centralized for the first time, a manual serves to clarify the value and authority of the function and its relations to other departments.

Much has been written about constructing purchasing manuals. Most of the advice deals with massive and elaborate

[1.]Substantially reprinted by permission of *Health Institutions Purchasing*.

manuals requiring time and manpower. In fact, many instructions on writing purchasing manuals are longer than the manual itself needs to be.

This section is a practical guide to the purposes, contents, and preparation of purchasing manuals. It emphasizes the "how," and then backs it up with some of the "why." The approach is based on the classic management formula: Plan—Do—Control.

Planning a purchasing manual means, essentially, deciding on its contents. These fall in two basic categories:

Policies are broad statements of purchasing's major objectives and relationships, often intended as much for the information of an outside audience—top administration, department heads, suppliers—as for purchasing itself.

Procedures, by contrast, are rather detailed outlines of the methods and routines that purchasing uses to achieve its objectives. They concern internal operations almost entirely.

This distinction is not always perfectly clear in manuals. Because there are two different audiences there should be, ideally, two purchasing manuals, allowing for flexibility in preparation and circulation. But the most realistic way to attack the problem is to consider policies and procedures as two separate parts of one manual.

THE POLICY SECTION

The policy section should contain essentially a foreword-endorsement from top administration, expressing its support for the authority of the purchasing function, and as many specific policies as are appropriate.

Endorsement by the administration gives you the one element crucial to the success of any program: management commitment. The endorsement is evidence that the policies in the manual are not being forced for purchasing's convenience, but to further the overall policies and objectives of the operation. By adding the administration's authority, the endorsement makes observance of the policies, and general acceptance of purchasing's role, far more likely.

The objectives, scope, and responsibility of purchasing can be stated briefly or in some detail, in a single section or several. The author recommends these be treated briefly and generally in one section—perhaps titled "The Role of the Purchasing Department,"—with separate, subtitled paragraphs for each topic. The topics are related. None can be totally understood without some reference to the other aspects of purchasing's role. Therefore, keep them together.

If you start going into detail here, you inevitably slip over into consideration of specific policies. You can avoid duplication and confusion, and make the manual easier to use, if you save the details for the sections on specific policies.

Two other helpful, although not essential, items frequently appear in policy manuals. If they are used, they should be placed near the beginning.

One is an organization chart. It should show at least the reporting relationship of the purchasing manager to the administration and the basic organization. Larger segments of the total organization should be included only if they helps clarify purchasing's role.

The second popular option is a code of ethics. Ethical questions arise frequently in purchasing, and few manuals ignore them completely. Many deal with them under specific policies such as acceptance of gifts, conflict of interest, and the like.

To determine what specific policies a manual should cover, keep in mind what a policy is supposed to do. It represents a solution or a decision involving a problem or question that is so common as to require action repeatedly. By framing a policy, you provide a generalized solution and thus avoid a long process every time the problem comes up. Therefore, identifying such problems is the first step in formulating policy.

Every purchasing function has its own special problems. However, some are so common that they should be dealt with in every manual. Most of these deal with three basic kinds of questions: authority, supplier relations, and ethics. (Because of the nature of purchasing, some of the questions might be in one or more categories.) There are also a few miscellaneous questions.

Perhaps the best way to deal with them here is simply to list the questions that ought to be resolved by specific policy statments, if they are not settled by the general statement of policy. For example:

Which signature is required on a requisition?

What are purchasing's responsibilities and authority to challenge need or specifications?

Who may initiate or maintain contacts with suppliers or potential suppliers?

What are the criteria of supplier selection?

When is competitive bidding required?

Who takes part in negotiation?

Who may commit funds for supplies and equipment? What limits, if any, are there to this authority?

What authority or responsibilities does purchasing share with other departments?

What is the policy on cooperative purchasing arrangements?

Are there limits on sales calls?

Who handles requests for samples or literature?

What are the limits on accepting gifts or entertainment from suppliers?

What rules govern potential conflicts of interest?

Will the purchasing department make personal purchases for employees and staff members?

In what committees or organizations, inside or outside, is purchasing represented?

This list is by no means complete, but it indicates the general type of problems that it is useful to settle by policy.

It is reasonable, but not essential, to formulate policy before procedures. In some cases, however, a newly hired purchasing manager may find it necessary to straighten out systems and procedures first and be content for a while with just the sketchiest statement of policy. Treating the two areas as separate, although related, permits this flexibility.

THE PROCEDURES SECTION

The procedures section of a manual can also be prepared according to the Plan—Do—Control formula. We will begin with the planning phase.

Once again, keep in mind the way the manual will be used. Ideally, it should enable an intelligent stranger to perform the routines necessary to keep the supply cycle going—at least competently.

Some purchasing managers begin a procedures manual with job descriptions. If your operation requires these, or if preparing them will help clarify your thinking, go ahead. However, it takes a lot ot time to make up a really true and helpful job description. And if systems and procedures are described accurately and completely, the roles of all purchasing employees should be clear enough to make job descriptions a luxury.

Perhaps more useful is a simple calendar of each employee's typical work week. It should highlight recurring events that are assigned specific time slots: supplier calls, meetings of committees, supply distribution days, inventory report deadlines, and the like. Such a calendar is easier both to prepare and to grasp than a job description. It simplifies employment and insures that no important task will be overlooked because the employee is sick or on vacation.

The heart of the procedures manual is the detailed descriptions of systems and routines. A good way to plan this section is to think through the procurement cycle, jotting down each major action. Then write a description, in sequence, of sub-events.

Many of these actions can be coordinated with forms or records. A copy of each should be included. Events in the procurement cycle, and forms involved, might include:

DETERMINATION OF NEED. Requisition or other request to purchase; reorder point on inventory records.

SUPPLIER SELECTION. Supplier, product, or buy-history file; invitation-to-bid form.

ORDERING. Purchase order; list or file of blanket orders in force; special forms for lease, rental, trial, or other non-purchase procurement; inventory file; outstanding order file.

DELIVERY. Receiving report; inventory records.

In cataloging these events, be conscious of the questions of who, what, when, where and how. Play down the "why" aspects unless they emphasize or clarify something that otherwise might be overlooked.

Instructions for purchase orders should specify: Who actually prepares them? Who signs them (do some require more than one signature)? What data are required, and where are they to be found? When are they prepared—under what circumstances, at what time of day or week, and about how long before expected need? Where—to what offices or files—do copies go?

Some purchases are exceptional. They may be one-time, small-value orders, paid from petty cash; rush orders taking special attention; emergency orders placed outside normal office hours; orders for capital items. Special procedures for handling these situations should be included.

The arrangement of this material could follow any of several patterns. Perhaps the best is first to cover fully the most standard procedure. Then, for exceptions, give instructions only to cover differences in procedure. For steps that are the same for all types of purchase, refer the user to the standard procedure by page and numbered paragraph.

Here is a sample statement of purchasing objectives, scope, and responsibility that might be found in a purchasing manual.

THE ROLE OF PURCHASING

1. Objectives. The primary objective of the purchasing department is to assure availability of supplies and equipment in quantity and quality consistent with set standards, at the most favorable prices consistent with those standards. The secondary objective is to assure that the supply cycle is accomplished at minimum administrative cost.

2. Scope. The policies and procedures established by the purchasing department for procurement shall be standard.

3. Authority and limitations. Consistent with Item 2, only Purchasing has the authority to commit the organization spending of funds for supplies and equipment. In the case of high cost or capital items, this authority is subject to approval by the chief administrator. Purchasing has the authority to question any and all aspects of a requisition, including need and specifications.

4. Responsibility. Purchasing shall maintain systems, procedures, and records adequate to meet its objectives. It shall evaluate these, and its over-all performance, periodically, in the interests of improvement. It shall prepare such reports and other data as the administration directors.

5. Relationships with other departments. Purchasing shall cooperate fully in filling the procurement needs of all departments. To this end it shall seek all information relevant to good procurement, and share it as dictated by the best interests of the organization. It shall exercise its authority in those interests, and shall not infringe on the authority of other departments.

6. Relations with suppliers. In dealing with suppliers, Purchasing shall pursue the good of the organization vigorously, within the bounds of fairness, courtesy, and good commercial practice.

What To Charge?
SALES ANALYSIS—PERCENTAGE WEIGHTING

Evaluating sales by menu item is essential to determine not only what to charge, but also what should—and should not—be on the menu. The only way to make a sales analysis is to physically tabulate the number of portions served on each item over a specific period of time. The period of time chosen should be no less than a week but need be no longer than a month. To illustrate, let us use a one-week period and a menu of 100 items.

Step 1. Tabulate the number of sales of each item for one week.

Step 2. Multiply the total of each item by its selling price. (1700 coffee at $.15 each = $255.00)

Step 3. Add totals for each of the 100 menu items from Step 2 together. This grand total should equal the total sales dollar for the week.

Step 4. Divide each of the totals in Step 2 by the grand total from Step 3. The quotient of this division is the percentage of the total sales dollar represented by each item. (Example: If coffee sales are $225.00 and grand total sales are $2550.00, then coffee sales represent 10 percent of total sales.)

Step 5. Multiply the number of each item sold (from Step 1) by the item's food cost. (1700 coffee at $.021 food cost = $35.70)

Step 6. Add the 100 totals of the food costs from Step 5 together. This figure will be less than your total food cost (from inventory) for the week because of food items used which are not part of the menu item food cost. (Cream and sugar for coffee, condiments, etc.) Divide this total rough food cost by the actual total food cost (from inventory).

Example: $\dfrac{\text{Rough Food Cost} - \$728.75}{\text{Actual Food Cost} - \$765.00} = 95.3 \text{ percent}$

The difference of 4.7 percent (100.0 percent - 95.3 percent) should be added to the food cost of each menu item. This is done by multiplying each Step 5 figure by 1.047. Now this grand total should equal the actual food cost. (Coffee $.021 x 1.047 = $.022)

Step 7. Divide the food cost of each item by its selling price. The result of this division is the *food cost percentage* of that item. (Coffee: $.022 ÷ $.15 = .1466 or 14.7 percent)

Step 8. Divide the total food cost from Step 6 by the grand total sales from Step 3. The result of this division is the *average food cost percentage* for all items.

Example: $765 (total food cost) ÷ $2550 = .30 or 30 percent.

ADJUSTING PRICES

There are several things that can be done with these figures.

Break-Even Operations. In institutions where the objective is to break even on foodservice operating costs, but not make a profit, the selling price must absorb labor and other overhead expenses. If, in our example operation, total operating costs are 10 percent greater than current sales, then the operator has two choices:

(a) Raise the selling price of each item by 10%. This is often impractical as, for instance, charging $.16½ for a cup of coffee. Or,

(b) Raise the selling price of only enough items to generate a 10% gain in total dollar sales. In the example operation, the total sales were $2550 and the total operating costs $2805. The 10% difference ($255) may be obtained by adding $.05 or $.10 to the price of items with above average sales (step 1) to result in additional revenue of $255. Which items are best for this?

It is likely that the items with the highest food cost percentage will be the entrees and that entrees will account for 30 percent to 50 percent of the total number of items sold. Because meat is the major component of most entrees, and because meat prices generally rise faster than staple items, it is advisable to raise entree prices first and then, if necessary, resort to raising the price of other items.

Another point in favor of raising entree prices is that most customers order entrees, while fewer customers eat entrees and several other items. If the price of a beverage, appetizer, or dessert item goes up, the customer may eliminate those but rarely will eliminate the entree.

Profit-Making Operations. If the objective is to make a profit, then the sales objective must include the total costs of operation plus the profit. If the objective is a 10 percent profit and the total sales are $2550, then selling prices must be similarly altered to bring in total sales of $2805.

Lowering the Food Cost Percentage Without Raising Prices. Presuming that purchasing procedures, specifications, and recipes are at the most economical level, you can use the date derived from Steps 1-8.

Isolate those items which represent an insignificant number of sales, or sales dollars or a food cost percentage well above the average. These are the candidates to be taken off the menu. Replace them with more popular items or items having a lower than average food cost percentage.

PROJECTING FOOD COST AND SALES PRICES FOR A NEW OPERATION.

Step 1. Write the menu for the operation.

Step 2. Write the recipe cards for each item.

Step 3. Obtain current market prices for all recipe items; cost out each recipe.

Step 4. Forecast the number of menu items which will be sold for a one-week period.

Step 5. Using the methods explained in Steps No. 5 and 6 under "Sales Analysis" on page 6, determine the total food cost dollars.

Step 6. Make a forecast of the total non-food operating costs and add to this the total food cost dollars. This figure is the *total operating cost.*

Step 7. Use the procedures explained above in "Break-even Operations" and/or "Profit Making Operations" to establish the selling price of each menu item. Add another 10 percent to cover the cost of items not in the recipes (cream and sugar for coffee, condiments, etc.) and 1 percent to 1½ percent for each month until opening day to cover raw food price increases.

ALLOWING FOR RAW FOOD PRICE INCREASES

One of the best indicators of wholesale level raw food price increases is the *Wholesale Food Price Index* published by Dun and Bradstreet (D&B). A letter to their offices (99 Church St., New York, N.Y.) will bring you a copy of the price increase history for the past several years. Use this history as a general guide to price increases in the future. If you plan to adjust prices annually, add one-half your prediction of the one-year-hence price levels to the menu prices now. This should give you a break-even on price increases, assuming they rise at a fairly even pace over the year.

Another method of determining food price increases has been developed at Stanford University. This is represented as Figure No. 1.

ETHICS—MORALITY—MONEY

Food purveyors operate on a small profit margin. They are selling merchandise which is perishable; if the stock is not sold while it is fresh, it will (a) deteriorate and have to be sold at a discount or (b) spoil and have to be discarded. Such conditions tend to make food purveyors fiercely competitive.

Food buyers are purchasing merchandise which can vary considerably in quality and therefore in price. The price difference between grades is often as great as 20 percent.

The avenue to dishonesty in food purchasing and purveying is paved with temptation. It is not difficult for a purveyor to arrange kickbacks to food buyers in exchange for an operation's exclusive business. The food buyer who accepts such an arrangement has no choice but to accept whatever is shipped to the operation, without complaint. More seriously, he has committed a felony by accepting a bribe.

There is no excuse for the purveyor who offers a bribe; he should be reported to his trade association and to the attorney general of the state. Likewise, there is no excuse for the food buyer who solicits a bribe; he should be reported to his employer and drummed out of the foodservice industry. This is a direct form of theft.

FIGURE 1

EXAMPLE USING SAMPLE DATA

Following step by step using January 1971 and April 1971 data:

1. Determine unit price per item.
Top round roast unit price for January 1971 is $1.02.

2. Determine cost factor per item.
Top round roast unit price x DWF (dollar weight factor) = CF (cost factor)
$1.02 x $7.289   = $7.435

3. Determine cost factor by product group.

A. Beef

Top round roast	$ 7.435
Beef stew	2.103
Ground beef	5.797
BEEF TOTAL	$ 15.335

B. Meat, Poultry & Fish

Beef	$ 15.335
Veal	3.643
Lamb	.421
Pork	7.343
Other	.508
Poultry	6.102
Fish	12.019
MEAT, POULTRY & FISH TOTAL	$ 45.371

C. Entire Market Basket

Meat, Poultry & Fish	$ 45.371
Dairy Products, Fats & Oils	162.608
Cereal & Bakery Products	15.531
Fruits & Vegetables	117.887
Miscellaneous	8.221
Paper Goods	85.687
ENTIRE MARKET BASKET TOTAL	$435.305

4. Determine relative and percentage price change

Item/Group		
	$\dfrac{\text{April 71 CF - Jan 71 CF}}{\text{Jan 71 CF}}$	= Relative Change
Beef	$\dfrac{\$16.296 - \$15.335}{\$15.335}$	= .0627
	Relative change x 100 .0627 x 100	= % change = 6.27%
TOTAL	$\dfrac{439.829 - 435.303}{435.305}$ x 100	= 1.04%

There are other, more subtle forms of theft. Consider these possibilities:

1. All the major food purveyors of any given type of product (such as fresh fruits and vegetables); may agree to set a floor, or minimum, price on certain products or all products. Except on floor prices set by manufacturers of certain products in states having Fair Trade Practice laws, such price fixing is illegal.

2. The purveyors of a given type of product establish territories. Each company gets a section which the other companies agree to respect. Such arrangements may or may not be illegal, but they restrict the food buyer's ability to buy the best product at the best possible price.

Bribes can take forms other than money. For instance:

1. The premium offer. The buyer selects a gift from a sales incentive catalog in exchange for points earned. This is a perfectly honest marketing technique. And it is ethical to participate in such program if (a) the price or the price plus the value of the premium is the best available on the specified product, and (b) the premium is to be owned and used exclusively by the operation that is paying for the food purchased. The problem with premium programs is that the catalogs usually contain 90 percent or more consumer products which would seem to tempt the buyer to use his position to obtain premiums for personal use. The cost of these premium programs, of course, is reflected in the price of the food products purchased.

2. The offer to purchase foods for personal use at discount prices. If all purveyors of a class extend this privilege, then there is nothing wrong in this. If the buyer's ability to make such purchases is limited to one or two purveyors of a class, then the buyer may be tempted to play "favorites."

3. Christmas and/or Birthday presents. In some areas this is a common practice from purveyors to food buyers. Such presents usually take the form of liquor, perfume, clocks, and other inexpensive items. The acceptance of such gifts may not influence the buyer, but the cost is inevitably passed on. Acceptance of such gifts is bad policy.

4. The Donation. Restaurants and institutions that ask purveyors to donate food or money to employee parties, annual picnics, favorite charities, or to the institution itself are, in essence making such contributions a condition of doing business with them. The cost of such donations is inevitably passed on in purchase prices. A request for such contribution is a form of asking for a kickback and should be discouraged.

Figure No. 2 is an example of a letter which may be used to set the tone of the buyer-purveyor relationship and to contract the penalties for dishonest practices.

PURCHASING SYSTEMS. The relationship between the buyer and the purveyor must be one of trust and confidence. There are shady practices to be avoided on both sides. Some purveyors deliver supplies which are inferior to those ordered. This will continue until the buyer stops the practice by rejecting shipments that do not meet the specifications.

To be sure, purveyors who attempt this should be condemned for failing to keep faith with the buyer. On the other hand, the buyer should be condemned for failure to verify that the product received is the product that was ordered.

Specifications are of no use if they are applied only to the buying and no further. The person(s) responsible for receiving food must be as thoroughly familiar with the buying specifications as the buyer. The receiving person(s) must have reference materials readily available in the receiving area. These materials should include the two volumes of the *Meat Buyers Guide* (National Assn. of Meat Purveyors), this book, and any other references which contain clear and concise descriptions and pictures of foods.

Single Source Buying. This occurs frequently when the buyer simply orders what he needs from one purveyor and is billed at a rate over which he has no control. The products received may be of acceptable quality or better, but the buyer has no means of determinging the price paid is a fair market price.

Competitive Buying. This process means taking bids from two or more purveyors for any given item. The taking of bids may be done by telephone, by mail, or in person. All these methods require copies of the specifications to be in the hands of the purveyor.

When taking bids by telephone, the buyer must have a

FIGURE 2

LDS HOSPITAL

---

325 Eighth Ave., Salt Lake City, Utah 84143 / 801-322-5761
David B. Wirthlin, Administrator

In the interest of establishing a purchasing policy which is fair and equitable to both the LDS Hospital and its suppliers the following policies are hereby established:

In re: purveyors:

1. No remuneration of any kind shall be made to our employees nor their relatives. This includes specie, gifts, loans, scholarships, merchandise and all forms of gratuities.

2. Promotions and gratuities related to promotions offered to all clients such as sporting event tickets shall be allowed as long as the value does not exceed $20.00.

3. Violation of the above policies will result in permanent suspension of all dealings with the purveyor.

In re: LDS Hospital employees:

4. Violation of the provisions listed in 1 and 2 above will result in immediate termination of employment and prosecution to the full extent of the law.

---

means of recording these bids. Commercial forms, such as shown in Figure No. 3 may be used or the buyer can construct his own. Telephone bids are common in foodservice because of the short life span of products. Most operators prefer to order quantities close to their needs as often as they can, and so will take telephone bids and place orders for following day delivery. There are financial pitfalls in this practice which are discussed later in the section on financial controls.

Mail bidding takes place when the buyer can forecast needs far enough ahead to allow the sending and receipt of bids by mail. Figure No. 4 is a cover sheet to a bid which gives instructions to the purveyor in preparing the bid. Figure No. 5 is one page of a mail bid for groceries. Note that the instruction sheet is very clear about the cut-off time on receipt of the completed bids.

SELECTING SOURCES. Telephone or mail bids may be compiled on a form such as shown in Figure No. 6. The most straightforward method is to assign the order for each product to the purveyor who has submitted the lowest bid on the item. When there are enough of these going to each purveyor, this is possible.

Note, however, that it costs a purveyor a lot of money to deliver. His delivery expenses (drivers, trucks, fuel, etc.) divided by his number of deliveries typically reveals a cost-per-stop of at least $10, and sometimes as much as $50. It is unfair to expect a purveyor to deliver orders of a dollar amount less than enough to make a *fair* profit. Thus, in the interest of good business relations, the buyer should not place a very small order with a purveyor but should, instead, award those items to the next lowest bidder.

Whatever the mode of taking bids, there must be a means of placing the order. Throughout the foodservice industry, it is common practice to place orders by telephone. There is no argument that this is efficient. What is wrong with this practice is that telephone orders give no written record (or confirmation) of orders against which food received can be checked for quantity and quality. When telephone orders are given, the purveyor should write the specification that was bid onto the invoice.

Also, it is essential that the invoice or a substantial copy of the invoice, called a shipping ticket, accompany the delivery. The invoice must be checked against the buyer's quotation sheet to verify quantity and price. The food received must be checked against the invoice, the quotation sheet, and the specification book to verify that the quantity billed is the quantity received, and that the quality received is identical to that specified. *Never accept a delivery without verifying weight, quality and price.*

A better method of placing orders is with a purchase order (Figure No. 7). The purchase order names the product, gives the specification or a reference to its number in the buyer's specification manual, and includes the price that has been agreed upon. A good purchase order will have at least three parts: a copy for the purveyor, a receiving copy (Figure No. 8) to be used by the buyer in receiving the order, and a copy which is attached to the invoice (Figure No. 9) and used to pay the purveyor.

SYSTEMS CONTRACTING. It is the buyer's duty to obtain the specified product at the best possible price from purveyors that can be relied upon. Food passes through many hands before it reaches the foodservice operator. The different owners of the product, at one time or another, might include the farmer, the pre-processor (slaughterhouse), the processor (butcher, canner), the regional or national distributor, and the local distributor.

Each time the food changes hands, the new handler (owner) must make a profit. The further back on this line the food buyer can purchase, the less add-on costs will be reflected in the price.

Buying "closer to the farm" usually means having to buy very large quantities of a single item either immediately or over a predetermined period of time. In many areas, there are individual operators who have formed buying organizations to purchase for the group.

Frequently, individual buyer can buy in quantities larger than he can stock, at guaranteed prices by

    (a) Soliciting bids from several local purveyors, or

    (b) making a purchase from a national distributor and then making financial arrangements with a local distributor to warehouse and ship the product on a routine as-needed basis.

Many processing companies maintain warehouses and also sell to local distributors. It often takes no more than a phone call to eliminate one layer of handling costs. The difference can be 10 percent to 20 percent in buying price.

Such items as milk, ice cream, and bread are not easily bought on day-to-day or week-to-week bids. In selecting purveyors for these daily delivery products the buyer should solicit fixed price bids for a period of six months or a year, and award "sole-purveyor" contracts. Such contracts should be in writing and should specify any procedure for raising or lowering the contracted prices.

Other dairy products, such as cheese, butter, and eggs can also be contracted for longer periods than week-to-week bids. Most major marketing areas have a publication which gives the wholesale prices being quoted on these items. In the New York City area, such a market guide is published by Urner Barry (Figure No. 10.) A contract for cheese, butter, eggs, even poultry, may be bid for and taken on a basis of a percentage above the prices quoted on the sheet.

Such a contract might specify that the eggs purchased would be priced 6 cents per dozen higher than the highest price quoted for the particular grade and size on the market sheet. The contract might also allow for cheaper prices for larger quantity purchases such as 6 cents over market price when 10 cases or less are purchased, dropping to 5 cents over market price for 11 cases or more, and so forth.

Contracts like this simplify an operator's business because they guarantee the source of supply, fix the buy-price to the wholesale market, and limit the number of purveyors. For the purveyor, such a contract guarantees that he will receive a price which includes his purchase and handling costs, and a fair profit.

Figure No. 11 is a copy of the *Meat Service Report* which is published weekly in Chicago. It is possible to write a systems contract with meat purveyors based on such reports as this.

There are several market reports which wholesale purveyors use as supply and pricing guidelines. Some, such as the USDA's (Figure No. 12) are free; others, such as those mentioned earlier, are available only by subscription. The volume food buyer should learn which publications local purveyors use as market guides and obtain subscriptions to these.

FORM 1291 COPYRIGHT 1968 **FIGURE 3—** Inventory and Quotation List

AMERICAN HOTEL REGISTER CO., 226 W. ONTARIO ST., CHICAGO, ILL. 60610

ARTICLE	QTY. ON HAND	QTY. NEEDED	QUOTATIONS			ARTICLE	QTY. ON HAND	QTY. NEEDED	QUOTATIONS			ARTICLE	QTY. ON HAND	QTY. NEEDED	QUOTATIONS		
BEEF						**PORK (Cont.)**						**SHELL FISH**					
Brisket						Ham, Corned						Abalone					
Chipped Beef						Ham, Fresh						Clams					
Chuck						Ham, Polish											
Corned Beef						Ham, Smoked											
						Ham, Virginia						Crabs					
Fillets						Ham, Westphalia											
Foreshank																	
Flank												Crawfish					
Ground Beef						Head Cheese						Lobster					
Kidney						Hock											
Liver						Lard											
Loin, Short						Loin											
Ox Tails						Phila. Scrapple						Mussels					
Ribs						Pig's Feet						Oysters					
Shank						Antelope						Roe					
Shoulder						Duck						Smelt					
Spring Lamb												Sole					
Spring Rack																	
Tongues																	
						Grouse						Squid					
						Partridge						Sturgeon					
						Pheasant						Swordfish					
PORK						Quoil						Trout, Brook					
Bacon						Rabbit						Trout, Lake					
						Snipe											
						Venison						Tuna					
Bologna												Turbot					
Butt, Smoked												Whale Meat					
												Whitefish					

# of Fresh and Refrigerated Items

DATE _____

ARTICLE	QTY ON HAND	QTY NEEDED	QUOTATIONS				ARTICLE	QTY ON HAND	QTY NEEDED	QUOTATIONS				ARTICLE	QTY ON HAND	QTY NEEDED	QUOTATIONS		
VEGETABLES							**VEGETABLES (Cont.)**							**CHEESE**					
Artichokes							Tomatoes							American					
Asparagus																			
Asparagus Tips														Bel Paese					
														Bleu					
Beans, Green							Turnips, White							Brick					
Beans, Lima							Turnips, Yellow							Brie					
Beans, Wax							Watercress							Camembert					
														Cheddar					
Beets														Cheshire					
Beet Tops														Cottage					
Broccoli														Cream					
Brussels Sprouts																			
Cabbage, Green																			
Cabbage, Red							**FRUIT**												
...toes							Quinces												
							Raspberries												
Pumpkin																			
Radish							Strawberries												
Rhubarb																			
Romaine							Tangerines												
Sage							Watermelons												
Sauerkraut																			
Shallots																			
Sorrel																			
Spinach																			
Squash							**EGGS**												
Tarragon																			
Thyme																			

FIGURE 4

THE JEWISH HOSPITAL

Cincinnati, Ohio 45229

TELEPHONE (513) 872-3220

INVITATION TO BID

Attached please find quotation sheets which must be returned to:

> Mr. Kevin Malloy
> Purchasing Department
> The Jewish Hospital
> Cincinnati, Ohio   45229

no later than 12:00 noon on March 24, 1975.

This bid represents a four week supply of staple supplies which will be scheduled for a single shipment between March 31 through April 4, 1975. We have listed the estimated order quantity. Do not submit quotations on those items which you cannot supply in the estimated quantities on March 24, 1975.

All orders will be considered complete upon delivery. In the event shortages do occur, we do request prompt notification from our vendors as to those items which will not be available on your previously scheduled delivery day. These items will then be re-evaluated as to their availability from other sources and new orders will be placed in an effort to obtain these products as soon as possible.

Where specific quality specifications have not been listed the specifications will be assumed to be no less than a U.S.D.A. score of 90 points. Where brand names are specified they must be supplied. The specified pack is the required pack. Do not bid on those items which you carry in other than the specified pack.

Please direct any questions to the writer.

SUBMITTED BY

DATE

PRICES WILL REMAIN IN EFFECT UNTIL

DATE

PRODUCT	PACK	USDA GRADE MIN. SCORE	MIN. NET MIN. DRAINED WT.	SIZE OR COUNT	REMARKS
ASPARAGUS, Spears	6/#5	Fancy 92/103 oz net	50½ oz.	54/80	All Green, Mammoth.
BEANS, BAKED Vegetarian	6/#10	Fancy 85			White beans, in tomato sauce.
BEANS, GREEN N. West Blue Lake	6/#10	XStd. 82/101 oz net	61 oz.	4 or 5 sieve	Pound. Variety.
BEETS Sliced	6/#10	Fancy 90/104 oz net	68 oz.	2½" Max. Diam.	
BEETS Whole	6/#10	Fancy 90/104 oz net	68 oz.	74/124	No softness, peel or black spots.
CARROTS, WHOLE "Belgian"	6/#10	Fancy 90/105 oz net	69 oz.	290/350	Orange-Yellow; no green
CORN, WHOLE Kernel	6/#10	Fancy 90/106 oz net	70 oz.		Golden. Brine pack.
MUSHROOMS, Whole, Button	24/#8Z	Fancy 85/16 oz net	8 oz.		Formosa; cream colored.
OKRA, CUT	6/#10	XSTD. 85/99 oz net	60 oz.		½" to 1" pods.
PEAS, Sweet	6/#10	XSTD. 82/105 oz net	71 oz.	4 or 5 sieve	
PEPPERS, Green Diced	6/#10				
PEPPERS, Red Diced	6/#10				
POTATOES, DEHY. Pearls.	6/#10				Without milk, vit. C added. Packed by Amer. Potato Comp. only. (Whip brand)
POTATOES, DEHY Sliced	6/4#				
POTATOES, INST. w/o milk, Vit. C added	6/#10				Packed by the Amer. Potato comp. only.
POTATOES, Sweet Mashed	6/#10	A 85	72 oz.		Golden type Brix 25°

RETURN TO:
Raymond B. Peddersen
Director of Food Services
The Jewish Hospital
Cincinnati, Ohio 45229

FIGURE 5
THE JEWISH HOSPITAL
FOOD QUOTATIONS

PAGE 1

_____ COMPANY

PACK	ITEM	ESTIMATED ORDER QUANTITY		JEWISH HOSPITAL FOOD ITEMS FILE NO.	YOUR BID
6/10	ASPARAGUS SPEARS FCY. 54/80 CT	0		33035	
6/10	BEAN GREEN STD. 4/5 SVE 61/ZD/WT	3		33095	
6/10	BEAN DARK RED KIDNEY/SAUCE FCY.	0		33185	
6/10	BEAN SPROUTS	3		33215	
6/10	BEETS SLD. FCY. 2.5 IN. MAX	7		33245	
6/10	CABBAGE RED	3		33299	
6/10	CORN CREAM STYLE FCY. GLON	0		33335	
6/10	MUSHROOM PIECES	2		33395	
6/10	PEPPERS GREEN DICED	4		33560	
6/10	PEPPERS RED DICED	0		33562	
6/10	PEPPERS GREEN HALVES	3		33565	
24/2½ lb.	PIMENTOS BROKEN FCY.	2		33575	
6/10	SAUERKRAUT FCY. 2.5 PCT SALT MAX	4		33725	
6/10	TOMATO PUREE FCY. 12 PCT SDS	9		33780	
6/10	TOMATO PASTE FCY. 33 PCT SDS	2		33782	
6/10	TOMATO WHOLE X STD 68/ZD/WT	0		33785	

JOHN	KARLA	MR. DATILLO	DON	MARY	JANE	MR ADDINGTON	LEN KELLUMS	
58241	58372	58856	58857	58858	58859	58860	58861	
WED	Wed	WED	TUES	TUES			WED	
8:00	8:00	PM	PM	8:00	1:00	AM	PM	
16 ✓		7 ✓	11 ✓		42 ✓	109 ✓	13 ✓	
THOMAS	SEXTON	SQUERI	EBERLE	NIEHAUS	LEFFETT	KRAFT	LYNCH	
9.44	8.82	9.69	8.35	9.73	8.64	—	8.80	
5.78	6.20	7.45	7.38	7.50	—	—	—	
8.80	8.33	8.69	—	8.69	8.94	9.15	8.15	
—	11.61	9.49	10.27	9.70	10.00	—	9.60	
27.61	26.89	29.63	25.96	32.95	26.95	—	26.20	
—	14.08	—	13.17	14.70	13.50	—		
12.53	12.36	12.92	11.46	13.35	11.84	—	—	
—	32.02	—	—	—	35.00	—	—	
7.98	8.14	8.16	9.21	8.25	8.52	8.65	8.10	
11.51	11.90	11.29	10.58	10.73	10.17	12.05	11.30	
16.50	23.92	21.19	20.35	21.93	20.50	—	19.90	
11.62	10.43	9.34	10.41	11.35	9.95	—	10.70	

			FIGURE 6					
QUOTATION SHEET		DAY ORDERED:						
HILLSIDE HOSPITAL FOOD SERVICE		FOR DELIVERY ON:						
			COMPANY		COMPANY		COMPANY	
ITEM	QUAN	UNIT PR	AMOUNT	UNIT PR	AMOUNT	UNIT PR	AMOUNT	

ONE-STOP SHOPPING. One-stop shopping means purchasing all food and supply needs from one purveyor. The advantages of such an arrangement are several:

(a) one order to place;
(b) one delivery to receive, and
(c) one bill to pay.

One-stop shopping can reduce the purchasing, receiving, and accounting functions enough to generate substantial savings.

On the other hand, buying from a one-stop purveyor has the disadvantages of (a) no source of supply if the one-stop purveyor has a disaster or labor difficulties; (b) no alternative source should goods delivered be other than specified, and (c) no price competition.

Despite these disadvantages, many operators have found that the advantages, financially, outweigh the disadvantages.

It is the writer's opinion that one-stop food shopping will be the accepted and prevailing mode of purchasing before the end of the twentieth century. One-stop companies are likely to develop from the merger of several small purveyors. This trend can be seen in the merger of fresh produce with frozen produce houses who then pick up distribution of frozen entrees, baked goods, and meat lines, and then merge with a general groceries and canned goods purveyor.

In almost any city of over 250,000 people, it is possible to purchase 75 percent or more of your needs from any of several large general variety purveyors. We are but a few short steps away from the time when these companies will realize the potential of one-stop shopping and, learning from the mistakes of the pioneers in the field, develop competitive one-stop shopping services in cities across the country.

COOPERATIVE BUYING. A cooperative has been defined as an association of persons who have voluntarily joined together to achieve a common economic end through the formation of a democratically controlled business organization, making equitable contributions to the capital required, and accepting a fair share of the risks and benefits of the undertaking.

Is buying through a Central Agency a practical possibility? Should you wish to consider such a proposition, it is well to ask the following questions:

1. What is a Central Agency?
2. Is it a possibility?
3. Is it practical?

First, a Central Agency is a source through (or from) which many or most of the items you purchase may be obtained, be they perishable or durable.

As for the second question, the context of possibility here suggests something that can or may exist or happen, or is in our power to do. This assertion of possibility should come before the third question as to its practicability. If it is possible to have a Central Agency, it is then wise to consider whether or not it is practical to operate such an agency.

Having defined the premises, let us now turn to how such an agency should be run, to better gauge if it is a "practical possibility."

Research. Setting up a Central Agency entails a great deal of research and organization to achieve the most suitable type of agency through which member institutions can purchase their requirements. The appointment of a sub-committee to investigate all aspects of such an agency appears to be the logical approach. It needs to be stressed that the most important ingredient necessary to achieve the most efficient and profitable results is *loyalty.*

If the agency is to function in the best interests of all, then every constituent member must, at all times, give the highest degree of loyalty to the aims and objects of the agency. Otherwise, its future could be jeopardized.

The agency should be set up as a cooperative. The desire to see a Central Agency brought into existence, is only the first step. Beyond that there are fundamental requirements to achieve this end.

The first and most important of these is *finance*. A cooperative trading agency requires substantial initial capital. Consider, for instance:

Premises have to be acquired, whether purchased, leased, or rented.

Warehousing, showrooms, and office areas have to be created.

Goods have to be purchased for resale, and these goods have to be paid for.

Wages have to be paid.

Vehicles have to be purchased or leased, with subsequent delivery costs to be incurred.

And, of course, there are the ongoing operating expenses to be met.

All these items require initial capital. Therefore, the first consideration, is the financial structure. Under the cooperative system, all those interested would become shareholders and subscribe for an agreed number of shares. If 30 members subscribed for one $5,000 share each, then the actual initial capital would be $150,000 to get the project off the ground.

A preliminary formation meeting would then be held. Here the name of the agency could be decided upon, rules adopted, directors elected, and the various other officers appointed.

Subject to trading only with its own members the net profits of such an agency would be subject to federal income tax only on the amount remaining after deducting the rebates on purchases.

The directors decide the basis of mark-up on the goods purchased for resale. Obviously the difference between the purchase price and the selling price must be sufficient to pay wages and all operating expenses and leave "something over" if the agency is to function.

If the margin between buying and selling is steady, the agency should prosper. As sales rise the proportion for overhead should grow less, which brings us back to the question of loyalty. The members of the agency must insure that as large a share as possible of their requirements are purchased through their own agency for it to be effective.

FIGURE 7

THE JEWISH HOSPITAL

CINCINNATI OHIO 45229

PHONE: (513) 872-3325

58372

THIS NUMBER TO APPEAR
ON EVERY PACKAGE
AND COMMUNICATION

CHARGE ACCOUNT NO.

DATE OF ORDER	TO BE DELIVERED BY	TERMS	304-6394

TO BE SHIPPED F.O.B. JEWISH HOSPITAL

IMPORTANT — ADDRESS ALL SHIPMENTS, INVOICES
& COMMUNICATIONS TO

↓

THE JEWISH HOSPITAL
PURCHASE & ISSUANCE DEPT.
CINCINNATI, OHIO 45229

QUANTITY	UNIT	ARTICLE		PRICE	PER	AMOUNT
2	cs.	Pimentos Broken fcy.	#33575	32.02	cs.	
1	cs.	Waterchestnuts sl.	#33830	22.96	cs.	
1	cs.	Apple rings spiced fcy.	#34045	13.20	cs.	
4	cs.	Cherries dark sweet pitted	#34245	25.28	cs.	
3	cs.	Fruit cocktail fcy.	#34455	14.59	cs.	
12	cs.	Peach cling sliced heavy syrup	#34705	13.04	cs.	
3	cs.	Pear sliced heavy syrup fcy.	#34786	15.72	cs.	
OUT— (3)	cs.	Pineapple chunks fcy.	#34815	15.39	cs.	B/o
3	cs.	Pineapple slice mini fcy. hvy syr.	#34885	17.62	cs.	
12	cs.	Pineapple juice unswt fcy	#35550	6.48	cs.	
1	cs.	Chives dehy.	#36065	17.37	cs.	
6	cs.	Rice wild	#41880	23.39	cs.	
5	cans	Chili powder	#43140	1.61	can	
5	qts.	Extract Vanilla pure bourbon	#43400	7.14	qt.	
2	cs.	Pure honey	#48165	26.65	cs.	
OUT— (1)	cs.	Strawberry Jelly	#48252	46.24	cs.	B/o

QUANTITY	UNIT	ARTICLE		PRICE	PER	AMOUNT
1	cs.	Cherry dark water pack	#51010	16.96	cs.	
3	cs.	Cherry Royal Ann water pack	#51015	16.17	cs.	
6	cs.	Pear Bartlett half water pack	#51050	17.93	cs.	
2	cs.	Plums purple water pack	#51060	13.01	cs.	
10	cs.	Asparagus spears salt free	#51100	21.68	cs.	
3	cs.	Chick peas, Garbanzo beans		9.60	cs.	
3	cs.	Kumquats		27.76	cs.	
5	cs.	Oranges Japanese Mandarin		21.63	cs.	
3	cs.	Instant chicken bouillon, Individual packets		16.49	cs.	
3	cs.	Instant beef bouillon, Individual packets		16.49	cs.	
3	cs.	Soup Minestrone		12.39	cs.	
1	qt.	Pure lemon flavoring		3.98	qt.	
2	cs.	Mixed nuts		27.56	cs.	
1	cs.	Strawberry pie filling		23.83	cs.	
1	cs.	Apple pie filling		18.28	cs.	
1	cs.	Cherry pie filling		22.75	cs.	
1	cs.	Lemon pie filling		17.76	cs.	
1	cs.	Strawberry glaze		14.86	cs.	

DELIVER TO   NOTIFY   REFERENCE

_____
DIRECTOR OF DIETARY

_____
DIRECTOR OF PURCHASES

THE SIGNEE GUARANTEES ALL PRICES ON THIS PURCHASE ORDER. NONE ARE SUBJECT
TO CHANGE WITHOUT THE AUTHORIZATION OF THE DIRECTOR OF FOOD SERVICE.

PURCHASING DEPT.

FIGURE 8
RECEIVING REPORT

THE JEWISH HOSPITAL
CINCINNATI, OHIO 45229

RECEIVING REPORT NO.

58372

	CHARGES	CARRIER	CONDITION ✓			NO. PKGS	ORDER:	PARTIAL ☐	DATE	
COLLECT PREPAID $			GOOD	DAM-AGED	SHORT	3		COMPLETE ☐	3-12-74	

DATE OF ORDER	TO BE DELIVERED BY	TERMS	304-6394

RECEIVED FROM●

REC'D	QUANTITY	UNIT	ARTICLE			AMOUNT
2	2	cs.	Pimentos Broken fcy.	#33575	32.02 cs.	
1	1	cs.	Waterchestnuts sl.	#33830	22.96 cs.	
1	1	cs.	Apple rings spiced fcy.	#34045	13.20 cs.	
4	4	cs.	Cherries dark sweet pitted	#34245	25.28 cs.	
3	3	cs.	Fruit cocktail fcy.	#34455	14.59 cs.	
12	12	cs.	Peach cling sliced heavy syrup	#34705	13.04 cs.	
3	3	cs.	Pear sliced heavy syrup fcy.	#34786	15.72 cs.	
OUT	3	cs.	Pineapple chunks fcy.	#34815	15.39 cs.	
3	3	cs.	Pineapple slice mini fcy. hvy syr.	#34885	17.62 cs.	
12	12	cs.	Pineapple juice unswt fcy.	#35550	6.48 cs.	
1	1	cs.	Chives dehy.	#36065	17.37 cs.	
6	6	cs.	Rice wild	#41880	23.39 cs.	
5	5	cans	Chili powder	#43140	1.61 can	
5	5	qts.	Extract Vanilla pure bourbon	#43400	7.14 qt.	
2	2	cs.	Pure honey	#48165	26.65 cs.	
OUT	1	cs.	Strawberry Jelly	#48252	46.24 cs.	
1	1	cs.	Cherry dark water pack	#51010	16.96 cs.	
3	3	cs.	Cherry Royal Ann water pack	#51015	16.17 cs.	

REC'D	QUANTITY	UNIT	ARTICLE		AMOUNT
6	6	cs.	Pear Bartlett half water pack	#51050	17.93 cs.
2	2	cs.	Plums purple water pack	#51060	13.01 cs.
7	10	cs.	Asparagus spears salt free	#51100	21.68 cs.
3	3	cs.	Chick peas, Garbanzo beans		9.60 cs.
3	3	cs.	Kumquats		27.76 cs.
5	5	cs.	Oranges Japanese Mandarin		21.63 cs.
3	3	cs.	Instant chicken bouillon, Individual packets		16.49 cs.
3	3	cs.	Instant beef bouillon, individual packets		16.49 cs.
3	3	cs.	Soup Minestrone		12.39 cs.
1	1	qt.	Pure lemon flavoring		3.98 qt.
2	2	cs.	Mixed nuts		27.56 cs.
1	1	cs.	Strawberry pie filling		23.83 cs.
1	1	cs.	Apple pie filling		18.28 cs.
1	1	cs.	Cherry Pie filling		22.75 cs.
1	1	cs.	Lemon pie filling		17.76 cs.
1	1	cs.	Strawberry glaze		14.86 cs.

DELIVER TO	NOTIFY	REFERENCE	TOTAL	
RECEIVING CLERK Lana	DELIVERED TO Dietary	RECEIVED	DATE	CHGE. ACCT. 304-6394

REQUISITIONING DEPT.

P.O. Box

14150 CINCINNATI, OHIO 45214

FIGURE 9

JOHN SEXTON & CO.
Quality Foods

PHONE

793-3200 A-513

786-1415 A-317

INVOICE DATE & NUMBER			PAGE			
03	12	75	24748	1		SP
1972	11204	40	3			SB
ROUTE	ACCOUNT	LOAD	STOP	SEG.		

SPECIAL INSTRUCTIONS:

PO 58372 WED AM

SHIP TO

JEWISH HOSPITAL
PURCHASE & ISSUANCE
DEPT
BURNET AVE
CINCINNATI OH
45229

SOLD TO

JEWISH HOSPITAL
PURCHASE & ISSUANCE
DEPT
BURNET AVE
CINCINNATI OH
45229

DUP INV - DOCK OFF HARVEY AVE   CALL ON OUTS

AISLE	SLOT	QUAN.	CNTR.	DESCRIPTION	PACK	SIZE	PRICE	EXTENSION	PROD. CODE	
A	06-10	3	CS SB	FRUIT COCKTAIL	6	10	14.59	43.77	02931	141
A	82-10	12	CS SB	PEACH AMB Y C SLICED	6	10	13.04	156.48	04119	564
B	27-10	1	CS SR	APPLE RINGS SPICE RED	6	10	13.20	13.20	02089	50
B	55-10	5	CS SR	ORANGES MANDARIN	6	10	21.63	108.15	36822	240
B	83-10	12	CS SR	PINEAPPLE JUICE	12	46 OZ	6.48	77.76	18614	528
C	64-10	3	CS SB	PINEAPPLE 115/120 MAY	6	10	17.62	52.86	06445	144
STOCK OUT			CS SR	PINEAPPLE CHUNKS XHS	6	10	15.39	STOCK OUT	3	
D	08-20	2	CS SG	PIMIENTOS BROKEN IMP	24	28 OZ	32.02	64.04	37770	100
D	31-20	1	CS SR	STRAWBERRY PIE FILLING	6	10	23.83	23.83	07641	46
D	34-10	3	CS SB	PEARS BART SLICED	6	10	15.72	47.16	05595	141
D	38-10	1	CS SR	LEMON PIE FILLING RTU	6	10	17.76	17.76	03616	50
D	40-20	1	CS SR	APPLE PIE FILLING RTU	6	10	18.28	18.28	00083	49
E	07-10	4	CS SB	CHERRIES BING PITTED	6	10	25.28	101.12	01545	188
E	07-20	1	CS SR	CHERRY PIE FILLING	6	10	22.75	22.75	01743	56
E	16-10	3	CS SR	KUMQUATS 70/75	12	5	27.76	83.28	03590	138
E	40-10	3	CS SR	BEANS GARBANZO	6	10	9.60	28.80	08896	141
F	01-20	2	CS SR	PLUMS PRUNE DIETETIC	6	10	13.01	26.02	16287	90
F	28-10	3	CS SR	BEEF INST BOUIL PKT	6	100	16.49	49.47	33779	27
F	28-20	3	CS SR	CHICKEN INST BOUL PKT	6	100	16.49	49.47	33787	27
F	29-20	2	CS SR	HONEY PURE	6	5 LB	26.65	53.30	34074	76

AISLE	SLOT	QUAN.	CNTR.	DESCRIPTION	PACK	SIZE	PRICE	EXTENSION	PROD. CODE	
F	40-20	6	CS SR	PEARS BART DIET 30/35	6	10	17.93	107.58	16345	288
F	67-10	7	CS SR	ASPARAGUS DIET M/L GN	24	300	21.68	151.76	17020	217
	PART OUT		CS SR	ASPARAGUS DIET M/L GN	24	300	21.68	PART OUT	3P	
F	71-20	1	CS SR	CHERRIES BING DIETETC	24	303	16.96	16.96	16139	30
F	77-20	3	CS SR	CHERRIES R ANN DIET	24	303	16.17	48.51	16154	90
H	07-20	1	CS SR	WATER CHESTNUTS SLICD	24	30 OZ	22.96	22.96	44917	55
H	17-10	2	CS SR	NUTS SALTED MIXED	12	1 LB	27.56	55.12	72702	34
H	18-20	6	CS PL	RICE WILD MIX U BEN	6	36 OZ	23.39	140.34	73445	96
J	30-10	1	CS SR	GLAZE STRAWBERRY	6	10	14.86	14.86	87734	45
L	11-10	1	CS SR	CHIVES FREEZE DRIED	12	1 OZ	17.37	17.37	31211	5
L	34-20	3	CS SR	SOUP MINESTRONE	12	5	12.37	37.11	91488	135
	STOCK OUT		CS SR	JELLY STRAWBERRY	6	10	46.24	STOCK OUT	1	
M	08-40X	5	EA SR	CHILI POWDER	1	16 OZ	1.61	8.05	29041	5
M	10-10	5	EA SR	EXTRACT VANILLA PURE	1	QT	7.14	35.70	82347	15
M	14-10	1	EA SR	EXTRACT LEMON PURE	1	QT	3.98	3.98	82313	3
		1		REPACK CASE						

*** INVOICE SUB-TOTALS ***

PCS	WGT	AMT	
107	3814		1697.80 PROCESSED FOODS

TOTAL PIECES		TOTAL WEIGHT	PLEASE PAY		TERMS NET
103	*Jn Jntosh*	3814	→ THIS AMOUNT	697.80	

DUPLICATE INVOICE

NOTE: ALL SHORTAGES AND DAMAGES MUST BE NOTED AT TIME OF RECEIPT

FIGURE 10

FIRST CLASS MAIL
U. S. POSTAGE
PAID
PERMIT No. 34

JERSEY CITY, N.J.
JULY 22 1976

The Urner Barry Market

Producers' Price

34 EXCHANGE PLACE
JERSEY CITY, N. J. 07302

ESTA...RE THAN A CENTURY OF MARKET REPORTING SERVICE

PUBLISHED... SUNDAYS AND HOLIDAYS BY URNER BARRY PUBLICATIONS, INC.

N. J. P... .Y. PHONE: 212 - 349 - 0240   CALIF PHONE: 415 - 472 - 2090

...right 1976 By Urner Barry Publications, Inc.

Editor: PAUL B. BROWN, Associate Editors: JOHN M. CARTER,
MICHAEL E. O'SHAUGHNESSY, DAVID P. REESMAN

THURSDAY, JULY 22, 1976

SPOT EGG SITUATION

Despite some reports of a decline in cartoned egg sales, stocks of large are short of full trade requirements. Scattered promotional activity is indicated for next week and there ... ...mmitments for Canada scheduled for ...ery through next week. Offerings of large ...or delivery into mid-week are limited. Supplies of mediums are in good balance although gradual accumulations are noted. Pullets continue in slow sale for export and some supplies clear to breakers. Offerings of heavy breaking stock are limited. Midwest breakers are very aggressive.

On Egg Clearinghouse today 1 load Class I sold 60¢ Southeast; 1 load 62¢ Northeast and 1 load 61¢ Northeast; 1 load Class IV sold 36¢ South Central; 1 load graded large sold 64 1 2¢ Southwest and 1 load Breaking Stock sold 47¢ Southeast.

FROZEN & DRIED EGGS

Asking prices are fully sustained under firm raw product costs. Stocks are ...ght.

...lk, sug...	...1.00	
No color....	70.00-71.50	69.50-70.50
Yolk, salt, 43% solids-		
No color...	68.00-71.50	67.50-68.50
Blend-		
30-32% egg solids	53.50-57.00	51.50-52.00
27-29% egg solids	50.50-53.50	49.00-50.00

EGG SOLIDS   Lcl Sales

Whole plain	1.78-1.83
Yolk	1.79-1.84
Albumen, pan dried	-
Albumen, spray	1.85-1.89

LIQUID EGGS   Tank Carlot

Whole, per lb, track	39.00-39.50
Pasteurized, per lb, track	40.50-41.00
Whites, per lb, track	18.00-18.50
Pasteurized, per lb, track	18.75-19.50
Yolk, 45% solids, per lb, track	-
43% solids, per lb track	-

Fats & Oils

MARGARINE
Less Carlots

Sales by First Receiver - Cents per lb.-
Vegetable Oil, 1 lb. Solids	29.00-30.00
Vegetable Oil, 1 lb. Quarters	30.00-31.00
Blended, 1 lb solids	28.00-29.00
1 lb. Quarters	29.00-30.00

Trucklots - Delivered East - Cents per lb.-
Vegetable Oil, 1 lb. Solids	27.00-
Vegetable Oil, 1 lb Quarters	28.00-
Corn Oil, 1 lb Quarters	36.00-

SOYBEAN OIL FUTURES

Chicago Board of Trade futures trading for previous day.

Deliv.	Open	High	Low	Close	Prev. Close
July	21.25	21.40	20.80	20.90	21.00
Aug	21.40	21.50	20.20	20.30	20.10

NOTICE

In the past we have tried to have our Egg Quotations ready for release no later than 11:15 A.M. Eastern Time. Presently our evaluation includes our telephone canvass, analysis of reports and statistics (military purchases, inventory reports, futures trading, etc.) and Egg Clearinghouse trading. Complete information is not possible much before 11:15 A.M. Eastern Time. Our release time for the Egg Quotations will consequently be delayed until 11:25 Eastern Time. This will be on both outgoing and incoming calls.

*   *   *

TUESDAY, JULY 20, 1976

FRESH VEGETABLES

ARRUGULA	
NJ 5 9 bu cr 24s	-3 50
ARTICHOKES	
Ca ctns var sz...	-9 00
BASIL	
NYLI 1 1 9 bu cr	
bch 20s	-6 00
BEANS Gr-	
Bu cr & bu hprs-	
NC bu hprs	5 00-5 50
NJ bu bkt	-8 00
NY LI bu hprs	8 00-9 00
NYLI wax	-9 00
Pa bu ctns	5 00...
NYLI	...3 00
NYLI red	
CARROTS	
Ca bch 24s	6 50-7 00
Ca 50 lb sk 1se lg	6 00-6 50
Ca 48-1 lb sk &	
ctns...	6 50-7 00
CAULIFLOWER	
Ca Flt Flm ctns 12s	8 00-8 50
CELERY Pascal cr	
Ca 2s	8 00-9 00
Ca 2 1/2s...	8 50-9 00
Ca hearts flm wrap	
18s...	-8 00
Oh 2-2 1/2 dz	-6 00
CHICORY (endive)	
NJ 1 1/9 bu cr	3 50-4 00
CHINESE CABBAGE	
Oh 1 1/9 bu cr	-5 00
COLLARDS	
NJ 1 1/9 bu cr	2 50-3 50
CORN SWEET	
Yel 4 1/2 - 5 dz-	
NJ...	6 00-7 00
Va white sm	5 00-5 50
CUCUMBERS	
Waxed med sz	
Md 1 1/9 bu cr	5 00-6 00
NJ 1 1/9 bu bkt	5 00-6 00
Va 1 1/9 bu ctn	5 00-5 50
Kirby ty-	
NJ bu bkt	9 00-1000
NYLI bu bkt	-7 00
DANDELION	
NJ pear box & bu	
cr 12-15s	2 50-3 00
DILL	
NJ 5/9 bu cr 24s	-6 00
EGGPLANTS-	
Fl bu ctn & hprs	-5 00
Ga 1 1/9 bu cr	5 50-6 00
NJ 1/2 bu bkt	

...S IARD	
NY...3 bu cr	-2 50
ONIONS 50 lb bags-	
Ca stockton yel lg	5 00-5 25
Co repacker	6 50-7 00
Tx grano lg	5 00-5 25
White Boilers 25s-	
NM...	7 50-8 00
Tx...	
Red Type-	
Ca lg 40 lb ctns	-
Italy per lb red	
string...	28- 30
PARSLEY	
Curly-	
NJ by 1 1 9 bu	
cr...	7 00-...
Ga 1...	
finger hots	-7 00
NC 1 1/9 bu cr	5 50-6 00
NC cubans lg	5 00-5 50
NC long hots	
bu hprs...	4 00-5 00
NJ 1 1/9 bu cr lg	6 50-7 00
NJ cuban bu bkts	8 00-9 00
POTATOES	
50 lb sacks -	
Ca LW ctns	5 00-5 50
Ca RR ctns	-6 00
Ca Cent Rus ctns	6 50-7 00
Del RW	3 25-3 50
Id us baled 10-5 lb	
sk USI...	-
NJ RW	3 00-3 25
Va RW	3 25-3 50
Repacked locally-	
Long white tissue	
wrap...	-8 50
Foil wrap...	9 00-9 50
RADISHES	
NY Org. Co 30-6 oz	
bags...	-4 00
Oh 30-6 oz red	4 00-4 50
Oh 16 qt bkt 24 bch	4 25-4 75
RUTABAGAS	
Ca 50 lb sk	-4 50
SPINACH	
Co bu bkt	6 50-7 00
SQUASH	
NJ 1/2 bu bkt	
Ital sm...	-4 00
NJ Yel strt	
nk sm...	-3 75
NC 1 1/9 bu cr	
acorn med	4 50-5 00
Va long grn	
bu ctn	7 00-8 00
SWEET POTATOES	

FRESH FRUITS

APPLES	
Controlled storage-	
US fcy-	
Wash gold del	
cell pk	-9 00
Wash Red del tr pk	-9 00
New Crop-	
NJ 1 1 8 bu lodi	-3 50
NY Hud Val 1 1/8	
bu cr lodi	-4 00
AVOCADOS	
Ca ctns	-1000
Fl ctns	-7 50
BANANAS	
40 lb ctns..	6 00-6 50
lb bagged..	6 00-6 50
Cooking	
DO...	
Nicarag...	
GRAPES	
Az 22 lb-	
Exotic	-1000
Thompson sdls	-1200
HONEYDEWS	
Ca ctns	4 75-6 50
LEMONS	
Ca ctns	-8 50
LIMES	
Fl 20 lb ctns sdls	-4 00
MANGOES	
Fl atkins ctns	-5 75
Mex wd flt	-
NECTARINES	
Ca 2 lyr-	
Early sun grands	-8 50
25 lb ctns-	
Early sun grand	-7 50
Independence	-6 50
ORANGES	
Ca val ctns	-7 00
Fl 4/5 bu cr pope	
summer	-6 00
PEACHES	
2 in min-	
Ga blake	-8 00
NJ Jersey land	-5 00
NJ Red Haven	-6 00
PINEAPPLE	
Hi 5s..	5 75-6 00
Mex 10s...	-
PLUMS	
Ca 28 1h ctn-	
Eldorado	-1500
Frontier	-1400
Laroda	-1550
RASPBERRIES	

BUTTER
URNER BARRY QUOTATIONS

Based on extensive country-wide trade reports and other terminal market wholesale transactions.

TRUCKLOTS BULK Deliv. East (Spot Mkt.)	SALT	SALES FROM WAREHOUSE	
		1 Pound Solids	1 Pound Quarters
$1.12	....93 Score (AA)....	$1.16-1.20	$1.19-1.23
1.11.5	....92 Score (A)....	1.15-1.19	1.18-1.22
1.10.5	....90 Score (B)......	1.14-1.18	1.15-1.21

MIDWEST
LOADS & POOL LOADS DELIVERED (bulk)

93 Score	92 Score	90 Score
$1.10	$1.09.50	$1.08.50

IMPORTED
LOADS & POOL LOADS (bulk)

Finest	1 st's	2nds
—	—	—

CHEESE

CHEDDARS - Whole Milk - lbs.

	Ex Sharp	Sharp	Medium	Mild
Blocks	$1.37-1.45	$1.20-1.25	$1.14-1.24	$1.08-1.18
Daisies	—	—	1.19-1.25	1.16-1.26
Splits	—	1.32-1.37	1.19-1.25	1.20-1.28
Midgets	1.46-1.52	1.29-1.33	1.21-1.29	1.19-1.29
Flats	1.41-1.51	1.29-1.34	1.25-1.30	—

5 lb - Proc. Cheddar -	
Known Brands	$1.02-1.07
Other Brands	1.01-1.06
Muenster	1.08-1.18

DOM. BLOCKS Trucklots -	
Sharp, white	—
Sharp, colored	—

OTHER VARIETIES

DOMESTIC		IMPORTED	
Blue	$1.40-1.45	Argentine, Sardo	$1.10-1.20
Edam	1.25-1.35	Reggianito	1.10-1.20
Gorganzola	1.47-1.62	Denmark, Blue	1.55-1.65
Mozzarella		France, Roquefort	2.90-3.10
		Holland, Edam	1.58-1.68

SWISS - Cuts

DOMESTIC —	
Grade A	$1.42-1.47
Grade B	

Sept	21.50	21.60	20.30	20.30	21.15
Oct	21.65	21.65	20.40	20.50	21.20
Dec	21.85	21.85	20.60	20.70	21.45
Jan	21.90	21.90	20.60	20.70	21.40
Mar	21.75	21.75	20.65	20.70	21.40
May	21.75	21.75	20.70	20.75	21.40
July	21.95	21.95	20.70	20.75	21.40

CONCENTRATED MILK

*Evaporated Whole Milk Case (Carlot) —
Known brands 48 14 1,-2-oz.
tins................................ $14.35-14.40
Other brands 48 14 1/2-oz.
tins........................... 13.60-13.75

*Prices usually subject to 2% discount 10 days.

Dry whole milk spray 28 to 28 1/2% —
Known brands, trucklots lb..... ¢80.00-82.00
Other brands, trucklots lb..... ¢79.50-80.50
Dry whole milk, spray 26% —
Known brands, trucklots, lb.... ¢79.00-81.00
Other brands, trucklots, lb.... ¢78.00-80.00
#Dry skimmilk spray, bags - high heat—
Extra grade, trucklots, lb...... ¢63.00-64.00
Ungraded trucklots, lb.......... —
Dry skimmilk, spray bags - medium heat —
Extra grade, trucklots, lb...... ¢63.00-64.00
Ungraded trucklots, lb.......... —
#Dry skimmilk, spray - low heat—
Grade A, trucklots, lb......... ¢64.00-64.50
Extra grade, trucklots, lb..... ¢64.00-64.50
#Dry sweet cream buttermilk spray, bags —
Trucklots, known brands, lb.... ¢63.00-65.00
Trucklots, other brands......... ¢62.00-

Ital sm..	6 50-7 50	50 lb ctn -	
ESCAROLE		Ala cent	-8 50
NJ bu cr	3 50-4 00	LA Cent USI	-9 00
NYLI 1 1/9 bu cr	3 50-4 00	NC 50 lb ctn PR & Jewel USI	6 50-7 00
ESCHALOTS		SWISS CHARD	
NJ per qt	1 50-2 00	NJ bu cr 12s	-3 50
NJ 1 lb flm bg	-1 40	TOMATOES	
GARLIC		BREAKERS & RIPERS-	
Ca white super jbo	60- 65	30 lb ctns-	
Mex white giant	- 50	Ca 30 lb ex lg	-8 50
GREEN ONIONS		Md ctns	-5 00
Ca 48s..	5 00-6 00	NJ lg...	-8 00
NJ 4/5 bu cr 36s	3 00-3 50	CHERRY	
HANOVER SALAD		Ca 12s	-6 00
NJ 1 1/9 bu cr	-3 50	NJ...	-5 00
HORSERADISH		PLUM	
Mo 50 lb sk unwshd	-3500	Oh grn hse 8 lb ⌐	
KALE		bkt lg	3 00-3 50
NJ 16 in cr	-3 50	12 qt bkt pink-	
KOHLRABI		Va....	-4 50
NJ 1 1/9 bu cr 12s	-3 50	REPACKED LOCALLY	
LEEKS		20 lb ctn	5 50-9 00
NJ 4/5 bu cr 12s	6 50-7 00	25 lb ctn...	7 00-1125
LETTUCE		TURNIPS	
Iceberg 24s cr-		Ca 25 lb sk purp	
Ca...	7 00-7 50	top...	-4 50
NYLI 16 in cr 18s	-2 50		
NY Org. Co	-4 00	NJ 16 in cr bchd	-3 50
Bibb -		TURNIP TOPS	
Oh 12 qt bkt	2 50-3 00	NJ 1 1/9 bu cr bchd	—
Boston-		WATERCRESS	
NJ cr		Pa...	23- 25
Oh 24 qt bkt 16s		YAMS	
Leaf-		Colombia 50 lb ctn	
Oh grn hse 24 qt bkt 10 lb...	2 50-3 00	negro	1500-1550
NJ 24 qt bkt			
Romai			

RASPBERRIES	
Ca 12-1/2 pt flm cov per..	1 25-1 50
STRAWBERRIES	
12 pt trays per pt-	
Ca lg	-1 00
WATERMELONS	
Fl long gray 30 lb	-4 1/2
Ga jubilee 36-38 lb	7 1/2-8
SC long gray 26 lb	5 1/2-6

NUTS

ALMONDS	
Ca per lb...	- 65
BRAZIL NUTS	
Brazil per lb.	- 60
FILBERTS	
Or per lb jbo..	- 70
Ore per lb lg	- 65
PEANUTS	
Fl bu hprs grn in shell	1100-1300
Va raw...	- 40
Va roasted	- 48
Va roasted jbo	- 54
PECANS	
Ga stuarts per lb	- 75
WALNUTS	
Ca jbo...	- 54
Ca lg...	- 50

BEANS & PEAS

BEANS	
Domestic 100 lbs-	
Black turtle	20 00

FRESH GRADE EGGS
URNER BARRY QUOTATIONS

Spot Market	5-Day Average	WHITES	SELLING PRICES CARTONED EGGS Store-door - Delivery - 10-Cs. Min.	Warehouse Delivery Trucklot
------	------	....Jumbos....	79.0-80.0	-------
72.0	70.4	..Extra large..	72.5-76.0	70.0-71.0
69.0	67.4	.....Large......	70.5-72.5	66.5-68.0
61.0	60.2	..Mediums...	62.5-65.5	58.0-60.0
44.0	44.0	....Pullets....	44.0-46.0	41.0-42.0
31.0	31.0	...Peewees...	--------	-------
62.0	60.4	Off grade lg	--------	-------
69.0	67.4	Brown large	68.0-70.0	66.0-70.0

BREAKING STOCK
General Trading Prices

Nest Run, 52 lb, material included, delivered:
Northeast...... $13.95-14.25
53-54 lb....
Midwest...... 14.40-14.70
53-54 lb....
Southeast.... 13.20-13.80
53-54 lb....
Nest Run, 45-46 lb —
All Sections....
Undergrades - B's,C's
stains, 50-51 lb, picked
up, mat. exch.... 43.0
5 day average.. 41.8
Checks - 49-50 lb, picked
up, mat. exch..... 41.0
5 day average.. 39.8

Egg Futures

Chicago Mercantile Exchange Futures complete sales of previous day.

FRESH SHELL EGGS
GRADED LOOSE

Deliv.	Comm. Sales	Open	High	Low	Last
July	13	8	59.75	61.00	59.05	61.00
Aug	253	51	58.35	58.75	57.80	58.25
Sept	1,531	282	59.85	60.40	59.65	60.05
Oct	17	3	57.75	58.00	57.75	58.00
Nov	502	61	61.60	61.70	60.50	61.10
Dec	1,044	205	62.85	63.25	61.90	62.15

Out-of-town egg markets

BOSTON - July 22 - Market quiet.

Note - These quotations currently are arrived at by adding 12¢ to the reported trading prices, delivered buyers, of nest run packs.

This tabulation has been developed by William P. Curtin and is presented for the convenience of our subscribers.

	White	Brown
Jumbos, (2.6 oz. min per egg)	87	87
Ex Large, 50 lbs................	74	77
Large, 46 lbs...................	70	71
Mediums, 40 lbs................	64	64
Pullets, 36 lbs.................	44	44

THURSDAY, JULY 22, 1976

FLUID MILK & CREAM

Fluid milk production noticeably lower. Bottling demand fairly good, especially so, considering the normal summer vacation activity. There is, of course, diversion to manufacturers.

Fluid cream offerings tapering off a bit and in balance with a good demand. Ice cream production up to new seasonal high.

Undertone on most concentrated milk items steadier. Supplies ample. Demand fair to occasionally good.

FLUID MILK
TRUCKLOTS DELIVERED MET. NEW YORK
Bottling quality per 40 qt unit $ 9.70- 9.90
Bottling quality per Cwt 11.41-11.65

FLUID CREAM
DELIVERED METROPOLITAN NEW YORK
Per lb. Solids (SNF) in tanklots ¢64.00-66.00

CONDENSED SKIM MILK
CLASS II or MANUFACTURING
SPOT SALES DELIVERED MET. NEW YORK
Butterfat per lb in tanklots $1.37-1.45
Per 24 qt unit (small lots) —

SPOT SALES DELIVERED PHILADELPHIA
Butterfat per lb in tanklots $1.37-1.45
Per 24 qt unit (small lots) —

SPOT SALES DELIVERED BOSTON
Butterfat per lb in tanklots $1.37-1.45
Per 24 qt unit (small lots) —

USDA Dairy Support Purchases

CCC WEEKLY DAIRY SUPPORT PURCHASES

Wk. End.	Butter	Cheese	Nonfat Dry
June 14	—	2,049,600	6,338,554
Lst Yr	1,361,875	2,162,224	20,333,203
June 21	—	—	7,208,034
Lst Yr	476,722	1,081,675	16,867,537
June 28	—	2,654,400	7,333,720
Lst Yr	1,237,572	1,973,857	15,701,258
July 5	—	—	5,068,492
Lst Yr	100,583	536,634	14,528,506
July 12	—	—	12,899,423
Lst Yr	166,968	75,426	11,423,709
July 19	—	—	8,182,571
Lst Yr	—	—	6,606,972

Purchases since April 1

1976-77	—	10,382,400	100,011,001
1975-76	33,297,849	21,304,842	261,435,945

[Cont.]

FIGURE 10—[Cont.]

DRESSED POULTRY

TURKEYS

Ready to Cook (R.T.C.) Frozen Grade A or Comparable Quality —

YOUNG HENS# heavy breeds	Carlots and Truck Loads	L.C.L. (sales from stores & warehouses) 25 box min)
8 to 10 lbs. each per lb.	50.00-	52.00-54.00
10 to 12 lbs......	50.00-	52.00-54.00
12 to 14 lbs......	50.00-	52.00-54.00
14 to 16 lbs......	50.00-	52.00-54.00
16 lbs. and over	50.00-	52.00-54.00

YOUNG TOMS# - - Heavy breeds — 14 to 16 lbs each

per lb.	49.00-	51.00-53.00
16 to 18 lbs......	49.00-	51.00-53.00
18 to 20 lbs......	49.00-	51.00-53.00
20 to 22 lbs......	49.00-	51.00-53.00
22 to 24 lbs......	52.00-	54.00-56.00
24 to 26 lbs......	57.00-	59.00-61.00
26 to 28 lbs......	62.00-	64.00-66.00
28 to 30 lbs......	65.00-	67.00-69.00
30 to 32 lbs......	67.00-	69.00-71.00
32 to 34 lbs......	67.00-	69.00-71.00
34 lbs. and over..	71.00-	73.00-75.00

FRYER-ROASTERS # –

3 to 5 lbs. each, lb.	52.00-	54.00-56.00
5 to 7 lbs...........	52.00-	54.00-56.00
7 to 9 lbs...........	52.00-	54.00-56.00

#Some nationally advertised marks of hens, fryer-roasters and consumer size toms sell at 3-5¢ premium.

---

*Various premiums paid for low Bact., Staph. and Coliform count as well as fresh product.

COMMINUTED MEAT* T/L

---TURKEY---

Comminuted meat, Salmonella free, under 15% fat, low E. Coli., Straph & rancidity........................	.24
Comminuted meat, (low fat, no skin)	.21
Comminuted turkey, (higher fat, some skin)............	.19

---CHICKEN---

Comminuted chicken meat, (under 15% fat)......................	.24
Comminuted chicken, (approx 23% fat).................	.18

---BEEF---

Low fat under 18%.................	.49
Regular fat over 18%.................	—

---PORK---

Low fat, under 30%.................	.44
Regular, over 30%.................	—

----

*Various premiums paid for low Bact., Staph. and Coliform count as well as fresh product.

RAW TURKEY PARTS

Chilled.............................. 93- 97

Southern Iced Chickens

NORTHEASTERN AREA

Trucklot prices delivered warehouse New York Metropolitan Area - based on current negotiations (deliveries 3 - 7 days).

TODAY'S QUOTATIONS

Plant A Jumble pack 2 lbs. and up	40.00
Plant A sized 2-3 1/2 lbs.........	40.50
U.S. Grade A sized 2-3 1/2 lbs.....	41.00

FIVE DAY AVERAGE QUOTATIONS

Average of lowest quotation for last five business days, including today:

Plant A Jumble Pack 2 lbs and up	41.40
Plant A sized 2-3 1/2 lbs.........	41.90
U.S. Grade A sized 2-3 1/2 lbs.....	42.40

MIDWESTERN AREA

Trucklot prices delivered warehouse Chicago Metropolitan Area - based on current negotiations (deliveries 3 - 7 days).

TODAY'S QUOTATIONS

U.S. Grade A, 2 1/2-3 lbs........ 40.00

FIVE DAY AVERAGE QUOTATIONS

U.S. Grade A, 2 1/2-3 lbs........ 41.80

Pre-Packaged Fresh Chickens

	Dealers Dock Delivery Charges Range 1-2 Cents Per Lb.	Prices Paid Resales At Varying Premiums		Prices Paid by Resales At Varying Premiums
Breasts..........	78.00-79.00	4 lbs.........	49.00	4 lbs....... 35.00
Legs.............	56.00-57.00	4 1/2 lbs.....	51.00	4 1/2 lbs.. 39.00
Wings...........	49.00-50.00	5 lbs.........	58.00	5 lbs...... 41.00
Backs & Necks..	13.00-14.00	5 1/2 lbs.....	59.00	5 1/2 lbs.. 41.00
Livers..........	40.00-45.00	6 lbs.........	60.00	6 lbs...... 41.00
Hearts..........	40.00-45.00	6 1/2 lbs.....	61.00	6 1/2 lbs.. 41.00
Gizzards........	40.00-45.00	7 lbs.........	62.00	7 lbs...... 41.00

BONELESS SKINLESS CHICKEN BREAST All Prices F.O.B. Dealers Dock - Delivery Charges Range 1-2 Cents Per Lb.   1 55-1 60

CANNER PACKED TURKEYS - Carlot or Trucklots
NO NECK - NO GIBLETS

DELIVERED EASTERN AREAS			DELIVERED MIDWESTERN AREAS	
Line Run*	Regular Pak+	—YOUNG TOMS—	Line Run*	Regular Pak+
46.00	45.00	.... 14 to 17 lbs.......	44.00	43.00
50.00	49.00	....17 to 20 lbs.......	47.00	46.00
52.00	51.00	.... 20 lbs & up.......	49.00	48.00
—	—	... Breeder Hens.....	—	39.00
		—YOUNG HENS—		
—	41.00	.... 10 to 14 lbs Avg...	—	39.50

*( ) % A, balance may be B's, C's or P.M.'s.   +B's, C's, & P.M.'s (Procurement II)

TURKEY BREASTS - Trucklots - Cents per Lb.

CONSUMER PACKAGED		BASTED & NETTED
Ribs, Some Neck Skin	First Portion Wing Meat, Back Partially Removed, Ribs In, Some Neck Skin	First Portion Wing Meat, Back Partially Removed, Ribs In, Some Neck Skin

FOWLS

READY TO COOK -- L. C. L.

--- Whole Frozen---		Cut-Up
Institutional Pack	Retail Pack	Tray-Pack
4-4 ½ lbs... 45.0-47.0	47.0-48.0	48.0-49.0
4 ½-5 lbs... 45.0-47.0	47.0-48.0	48.0-49.0
5 lbs. & over.. 45.0-47.0	47.0-48.0	48.0-49.0

FOWLS

READY TO COOK -- T/L

--- Whole Frozen ---

5-7 lbs........................ 45.0

CANNER PACKED FOWLS

CARLOT or TRUCKLOTS

FRESH

WITH NECK - NO GIBLETS

DELIVERED NORTHEAST

3.5 lbs. & up................. 34.0

FROZEN

DELIVERED MIDWESTERN AREAS

65 lbs./box, 2 lb. 4 oz & up..... 33.5

----

*Fresh sell at 1/2¢ premium.

DUCKS

Resales by First Receivers

Long Island-Frozen- R. T. C.	Grade A
5 1/2 lbs. and over each, per lb.	79.0-81.0
5 to 5 1/2 lbs.	79.0-81.0
4 to 5 lbs.	79.0-81.0

...

16 ozs per...	94.0
18 ozs per head	96.0-1.05
20 ozs per head	98.0-1.05
22 ozs per head	99.0-1.05
24 ozs per head	1.00-1.07
25-32 ozs per lb.	67.0-71.0

ROASTERS

3-4 lbs each, per lb.	—
4-5 lbs	61.0-63.0
5-6 lbs	65.0-67.0
6-7 lbs	67.0-70.0

CAPONS

Frozen -- R. T. C. -- Grade A

Truckloads	L.C.L. (Sales from stores 25 box min.)
5 to 6 lbs., each per lb.	—
6 to 7 lbs.	—
7 to 8 lbs.	—
8 lbs. and over	—

"Plant Grade A", sewn*

5 to 6 lbs. each per lb.	—
6 to 7 lbs.	—
7 to 8 lbs.	—
8 lbs. & over	—

*NOTE:- "Plant Grade B" (unsown) sell for 5-10¢ discount.

Iced R. T. C.

7 lbs. & up............ | — |

GEESE

Frozen - R. T. C.

Midwestern	Truckloads	L.C.L. (Sales from stores 25 box min.)
6 to 8 lbs., per lb	—	—
8 to 10 lbs., per lb.	—	—
10 to 12 lbs.	—	—
12 to 14 lbs.	—	—
14 lbs and up	—	—

FROZEN READY-TO-COOK YOUNG TOMS

	Bulk Carlots & Truckloads	L.C.L. (sales from stores & warehouses)	
		Bulk Pack	Consumer* Pack
Drums...23.0		27.0-29.0	31.0-35.0
Wings-			
Whole... 25.0		27.0-29.0	33.0-37.0
Drumette...30.0		37.0-40.0	39.0-41.0
Portion (V) 21.0		25.0-28.0	29.0-33.0
Thigh-			
Bone In.....48.0		—	60.0-65.0
Necks...... 12.5		18.0-22.0	25.0-29.0
Gizzards-			
Natural..... 18.0		33.0-35.0	39.0-46.0
Tails........ 18.0		26.0-28.0	28.0-32.0
Livers....... 21.0#		—	—
Hearts....... 18.0		—	—
Hindquarters-			
W/O Gibs-			
Toms... 26.5		—	37.0-41.0
Hens... 26.5		—	37.0-41.0
Western Style —			
Part Gibs-			
Toms... —		—	34.0
Hens... —		—	34.0

*Grade "A" or Comparable Quality.
#German export orders sell for 10-15¢ more.

CHICKEN PARTS

Quick-Frozen 2 pound
Consumer Packages - (cents per lb.)

| Gizza... | Hearts | 50.0-55.0 |

FOWL FAT

Raw fat, institutional packages, per lb.	—
Rendered institutional packages, per lb.	—
Rendered fat, govt. inspected-	
13 oz. jars, per doz.	9 50-10 50
7 oz. jars, per doz.	10 50-11 50
25 lb. can.	30- 35

GAME-DOMESTIC-Not Shot

Quotations based on reported sales to restaurants, hotels and other users.

Pheasants-

In feather, per lb.	1 60-1 80
R.T.C. 1 2 to 3 1 2 lbs.	1 60-1 80

Chukar Partridges-

In feather, 1 1-1 4 lbs.	3 75-3 95
R. T. C., 1 lb each, per lb.	3 75-3 95

Quail-

In feather, 5-7 ozs.	1 30-1 40
R.T.C. 4-5 each, per head	1 30-1 40
R.T.C. 5-6 each, per head	1 40-1 60

Mallard Ducks-

In feather, 2 to 3 lbs.	1 85-1 95
R.T.C. 1 1 2 to 3 lbs.	1 85-1 95

Venison (Hide on hog-dressed)

| 50 lbs and up per lb. | 1 50-1 80 |

IMPORTED

Scotch Grouse-
Ready to Cook - frozen -

| 3 4 lbs. each per lb. | 4 50-5 50 |

YOUNG GUINEAS

R. T. C. - frozen -

1 3 4 lbs. each, per lb.	1 90-2 10
2 lbs. each, per lb.	1 90-2 10
2 1 4 lbs.	1 90-2 10

U. S. Grade A
From Mid-Atlantic Area
Trucklot Prices-Delivered warehouse New York
Metropolitan Area (Delivery 1-7 days)

2-3 lbs - Whole Chix, bagged	45.50
2-3 lbs - Cut-up Chi.	49.00
Roasters	51.00

-------- PARTS --------

Breasts...... 81.00	Legs....... 62.00
Drumsticks 69.00	Thighs...... 62.00
Wings...... 52.00	Livers....... 50.00
Backs & Necks......	19.00
Gizzards & Hearts	45.00

* * *

IMPORTED BEEF FUTURES

New York Mercantile Exchange clearing House futures trading for previous day.

Deliv	Comm	Sales	Open	High	Low	Last
Nov	51	4	69.80	69.80	69.60	69.60

PORK BELLIES FUTURES

Latest day's trades in 2-14 lb Frozen Pork Bellies, 30,000-lb. carlots on Chicago Mercantile Exchange Clearing House:

Deliv.	Comm.	Sales	Open	High	Low	Last
July	588	156	64.10	65.70	64.10	65.70
Aug	4,694	2,880	61.70	63.35	61.70	63.35
Feb	2,486	940	59.50	60.25	59.40	60.20
Mar	809	82	59.60	60.40	59.40	60.20
May	366	23	59.50	60.60	59.50	60.55
July	46	2	58.50	58.70	58.50	58.60

	756					
June	307	19	45.75	46.00	45.60	46...
Aug	48	15	45.35	45.50	45.25	45.50

CHICKEN FUTURES

Chicago Board of Trade futures trading for previous day.

					Prev.
Deliv	Open	High	Low	Close	Close
July	41.20	41.47	41.15	41.40	41.25
Aug	40.30	40.65	40.30	40.65	40.25
Sept	39.15	39.60	39.15	39.45	39.20
Nov	38.25	39.00	38.25	38.65	38.15
Jan	39.40	40.05	39.40	40.05	39.40

POULTRY SITUATION

Turkeys rated full steady in moderate trading today. Offerings of hens are irregular, overall about adequate for current needs. Many lots are held off the market to higher prices. Demand at least seasonal but on the cautious side.

Consumer sizes of toms can be rated full firm and wanted. Many buyers press to accumulate stocks prior to school lunch purchase. The undertone is firm and asking prices have advanced in most quarters.

Toms over 22 lbs. are in rather limited stock and are held with a high degree of confidence. We find very limited stocks are available for sale.

THURSDAY, JULY 22, 1976

Skin.		Wi...th, Some Neck Skin		Ribs In, Some Neck Skin,
—	.90	.80	2-4 lbs	.83
.89	.79	4-6 lbs		.81
.92	.80	6-8 lbs		.80
		8-10 lbs		—

— — — Institutional Packaged — — —

				Back Out
.96	.91	10-12 lbs		.93
1.00	.93	12-14 lbs		.97
1.09	1.00	14-16 lbs		1.05
1.13	1.06	16 lbs &up		1.11

FURTHER PROCESSED TURKEY PRODUCTS
FROZEN L.C.L.

READY - TO - EAT

COOKED TURKEY ROLLS-	
White Meat	1 16-1 25
White & Dark Meat	98-1 09
Dark Meat	85- 92

COOKED & DICED TURKEY-	
White Meat	1 20-1 33
White & Dark Meat	1 02-1 15
Dark & White Meat	91-1 02
Dark Meat	88- 95

OVEN-ROASTED BREAST-	
Natural - With Skin	1 64-1 75
Skinless	1 62-1 75
Formed	1 31-1 43

OVEN ROASTED THIGH-	
Natural - With Skin	1 08-1 17

OVEN ROASTED ROLLS-	
Breast Meat	1 46-1 58
White...	49

READY - TO - COOK

PAN TURKEY ROASTS - BONED-	
Breast Meat	1 28-1 31
White Meat	1 14-1 25
Breast & Thigh Meat	1 15-1 18
Combination White & Dark	94-1 09
Thigh Meat	87- 90
Dark Meat	80- 87
Loaf	70- 79

BONED AND TIED RAW ROAST-	
Breast Meat	—
White Meat	—
Breast & Thigh Meat	1 05-1 08
White & Dark Meat	1 07-1 10
Thigh Meat	—
Dark Meat	—
White & Dark...	—

...E HOLDINGS

Both white and dark meat are on the strong side, offerings are limited and generally at some advance in price. Demand appears to be building slowly.

The iced chicken market continues to drift lower as offerings continue burdensome from many areas. Buyers show little interest as they concentrate on other items. Parts dull and freely offered with a good deal of pressure to sell noted on legs.

Iced fowl and roasters full steady as seasonally good demand readily clears present offerings.

POTATO FUTURES

On New York Mercantile Exchange Clearing House, the record of trading in Maine Potato Futures Contracts (Sale unit 1000 50-lb. bags) is as follows through last trading day:

Deliv	Comm.	Sales	Open	High	Low	Last
Nov	2,510	133	5.31	5.35	5.26	5.27
Mar	1,985	383	6.45	6.50	6.38	6.40
Apr	904	142	7.48	7.48	7.39	7.40
May	629	7	8.10	8.31	8.10	8.31

Contract Price Range to Date

	Open - Date		High	Low	Last
Nov	4.50	Nov 19	9.40	3.48	5.27
Mar '77	5.10	Jan 20	13.48	4.06	6.40
Apr '77	7.45	Mar 9	7.85	6.60	7.40
May '77	8.60	Mar 9	8.90	7.53	8.31

*NOTE- Daily price ranges subject to minor corrections.

BUTTER STORAGE HOLDINGS

	On hand Mon. A.M	Week Change	On hand Lst. yr.	Change Lst. yr.
4 mkts	15,331	- 273	13,998	- 261
6 mkts	2,471	- 27	2,457	- 65
10 mkts	17,802	- 300	16,455	- 326
Selected	47,761	- 63	44,420	+1,601

SHELL EGG STORAGE

	On hand Mon. A.M	Week Change	On hand Lst. yr.	Change Lst. yr.
4 mkts	900	+ 800	500	—
6 mkts	—	—	10,200	+1,900
10 mkts	900	+ 800	10,700	+1,900
Selected	8,000	- 200	16,600	-1,500

FROZEN EGG STORAGE HOLDINGS

	On hand Mon. A.M	Week Change	On hand Lst. yr.	Change Lst. yr.
4 mkts	2,441	+ 11	3,649	+ 197
6 mkts	2,625	- 155	2,734	+ 80
10 mkts	5,066	- 144	6,383	+ 277
Selected	11,141	+ 153	17,071	+ 514

TURKEY STORAGE HOLDINGS

	On hand Mon. A.M	Week Change	On hand Lst. yr.	Change Lst. yr.
4 mkts	10,359	+1,424	10,641	+1,081
6 mkts	8,256	+1,191	7,820	+ 577
10 mkts	18,615	+2,139	18,461	+1,658
Selected	101,089	+10,197	75,273	+5,701

OTHER POULTRY STORAGE HOLDINGS

	On hand Mon. A.M	Week Change	On hand Lst. yr.	Change Lst. yr.
4 mkts	6,323	+ 71	—	- 3,984
6 mkts	11,392	+1,168	—	- 6,655
10 mkts	17,715	+17,715	—	-10,639
Selected	49,549	+ 1,972	40,983	+1,332

[Cont.]

FIGURE 10—[Cont.]

Restaurant Buyers Guide

A complete report on Perishable Food prices designed for
Restaurants, Hotels, Motels, Country Clubs, Caterers, Schools and Institutions

Published every Friday by URNER BARRY PUBLICATIONS, INC.
34 Exchange Pl., Jersey City, N.J. 07302

Telephones: N.J. 201-432-7777; N.Y. 212-349-0240

Subscription Rate (including First Class postage):
One Year, $45.00

©

COPYRIGHT 1976 BY

Urner Barry Publications, Inc.

Editor
MICHAEL E. O'SHAUGHNESSY

IMPORTANT NOTE

This report is based on sales or prices by Purveyors to Restaurants, Hotels, Motels, Country Clubs, Caterers, Schools, Institutions and other dining places in the New York, New Jersey, Pennsylvania and Connecticut areas and may be used as a guide to the markets for the items listed. Prices are for delivery and for prompt payment; for shipment outside normal delivery area, extra freight charges may apply. Meat purveyors have the choice of making additional charges for aging, Cryovacing, individual packaging specifications, pinning and freezing. Price ranges vary according to quality, quantity, size, service needed and special preparation within each grade. Plus (+) or Minus (-) indicates change from previous week.

BEEF

IMPS		Good	Choice	Prime
103	Rib, (10 Inch, straight............	92- 94-	94- 97-	96- 99-
107	Rib (oven prepared, 3x4)..........	99-1 01-	1 02-1 05-	1 04-1 09-
109	Rib (oven-ready)................	1 42-1 45-	1 49-1 53-	1 52-1 55-
112	Rib eye rolls, boneless (lip on)......	2 40-2 43	2 67-2 69	2 71-2 74
114	Shoulder clods, boneless..........	1 20-1 23	1 25-1 27	-
115	Boneless chuck, whole............	86- 89	86- 89	-
123	Short ribs....................	82- 83	82- 84	-
135	Beef cubes (1 inch approx. cubes)......	1 25-1 28	1 25-1 29	-
158	Rounds.....................	89- 92	91- 93	92- 94
164	Rounds (no rump or shank, bone in).....	1 41-1 43	1 45-1 47	-
165	Rounds (no rump or shank, boneless)......	1 43-1 45	1 51-1 53	-
120	Boneless fresh brisket, deckle off......	-	1 04-1 08	-
	Top sirloin, bone in............	-	1 09-1 11	-
	Top round, bone in.............	-	1 28-1 30	-
	Bottom round, bone in...........	-	96- 99-	-
167	Knuckles, boneless (sirloin tip)......	1 25-1 30	1 28-1 31	-
168	Top round, boneless.............	1 42-1 47-	1 46-1 49-	-
170	Goose neck round, boneless........	1 08-1 12-	1 10-1 15-	-
173	Short loins (trimmed)............	1 29-1 34	1 40-1 45	1 85-1 90
175	Strip loin, bone in (10 inch cut)......	1 45-1 50	1 80-1 85	1 95-1 99
180	Strip loin, boneless (3x2).........	2 35-2 40	2 59-2 64	2 75-2 79
183	Boneless sirloin butt, trimmed.......	1 50-1 55	1 55-1 58	1 55-1 60
184	Top sirloin butt, boneless.........	1 67-1 69-	1 71-1 75-	1 73-1 77-
189	Whole tenderloins, trimmed........	2 45-2 49	2 55-2 59	2 45-2 49
190	Whole tenderloins, special trim......	3 30-3 35	3 35-3 40	-
1100	Cubed steaks, regular............	1 30-1 33	1 30-1 33	-
1101	Cubed steaks, special...........	1 40-1 42	1 49-1 51	-
1103	Swiss steaks..................	1 41-1 43	1 51-1 53	-
1112	Rib steaks, boneless............	3 50-3 60	4 10-4 20	-
1179	Strip steaks, bone in, (2 inch tail) center cut	3 00-3 15	3 40-3 50	-
1180	Strip steaks, boneless, (2 inch tail), center cut	3 90-4 05	5 20-5 35	-
1184B	Top sirloin butt steaks, boneless, (center cut)	3 45-3 55	3 75-3 85	-

Shell  Eggs

Fancy, Large, loose, doz........... 69.00-71.00+
Fancy, mediums, loose, doz....... 62.00-65.00+
Fancy, pullets, loose, doz.......... 45.00-46.00

Liquid Eggs

Whole, 4-8 lb, 4-10 lb, or 6-5 lb containers—
2-5 case drop..................... 57.00-60.00+

Butter

1 lb. solids.................... 1.22-1.27
Pats or cuts, lb.............. 1.27-1.31

Margarine

1 lb. solids.................... 45.00-48.00+
Pats or cuts, lb .... 51.00-53.00+
Reddies........................ 60.00-61.00+

Cheese

Cottage Cheese, lb —		
5 lb.....................	65-	77
10 lb....................	60-	70
35 lb....................	58-	68
Mozarella, lb., whole milk, 5 lb avg.	1 32-1	47
Mozarella, lb., part skim, 5 lb avg.	1 32-1	47
Muenster, lb., loaf, square 5 lb avg.	1 28-1	38
Swiss, lb - Domestic..................	1 63-1	75
Switzerland.....................	1 76-1	91
Denmark.......................	—	
Finland........................	1 56-1	76
Austria........................	1 56-1	76
Provolone, Domestic.............	1 52-1	62
Provolone, Imported.............	3 05-3	75
Pecorino, Romano, Imported.....	—	
Sardo.........................	2 20-2	55
Genuine......................	2 88-3	36

Richard F. Roethel & Sons, Inc.

Purveyors of Prime Meats

413 West 14th Street　(212) 675-2868　Federal Inspection
New York, N. Y. 10014　　　　　　　　　　Plant No. 5325

Beef Specialties

Calves liver, fancy........ 2 20-2 25
Pastrami................... 1 15-1 19

Lamb

233	Legs, (double).............	1 40-1 44
204	Hotel rack................	2 45-2 49-
206	Chuck...................	93- 96
231	Loin of lamb (whole)....	1 70-1 74
232	Loin lamb, trimmed......	2 49-2 54
1234AR	Lamb, leg boneless, tied	2 35-2 39
1295	Lamb for stewing, boneless	1 80-1 85-
1204	Rib lamb chops.............	4 20-4 35
1232	Loin lamb chops.............	2 90-3 10

Veal

334	Legs, (natures)..........	2 35-2 40
	Hotel..................	2 15-2 19

539	Sliced bacon, layers............	1 64-1 68
	Slab bacon..................	1 25-1 29
503	Ham, cured, skinned, smoked, 10 per cent water.............	1 19-1 23
	Smoked ham, fully cooked......	1 33-1 36
509	Ham, cured, skinned, smoked, cooked, tied..................	1 79-1 81
402	Fresh ham, std. skinned,17-20	1 04-1 09-
410	Pork loin, reg., 14 down.......	1 35-1 39-
	Pork butts, special trim.......	1 21-1 25+
415	Pork tenderloin, trimmed....	2 29-2 31
416	Spareribs, reg., side/sheet, 3 down....................	1 49-1 53
116C	Can. ham, pull., dom. 12-14..	1 70-1 73
116D	Can. ham, pear shap, dom12-14	1 73-1 76
	Imported canned hams 10-14	2 05-2 10

[Cont.]

Poultry
TURKEYS

Turkeys, frozen ready-to-cook, lb —
24 to 26 lbs.....................	69-	71
26 to 28 lbs.....................	71-	73
28 to 30 lbs.....................	73-	75

Turkey breasts, raw, wingmeat-portion of wing meat, back partially removed, ribs in, lb. —
10 to 12 lbs.....................	99-	1 03
12 to 14 lbs.....................	1 04-	1 07
14 to 16 lbs.....................	1 13-	1 17
16 lbs and up....................	1 27-	1 38

Turkey breasts, cooked, (boneless) —
Oven roasted 4/7-9...............	1 79-	2 15
Steamed, 4/7-9..................	1 49-	1 59

Turkey rolls, with broth, lb —
60 per cent white, 40 per cent dark	1 12-	1 17
white.....................	1 29-	1 36

Breast		
Thigh, 4/cs.....................	95-	1 00

CHICKENS

Chickens, iced —
2 lbs...........................	59-	62
2 1/4 lbs.......................	59-	62
2 1/2 lbs.......................	59-	62
3 lbs...........................	59-	62

Chickens, iced, shells, lb. —
2 lbs...........................	63-	66
2 1/4 lbs.......................	63-	66
2 1/2 lbs.......................	63-	66
Chicken breasts, fresh, lb......	95-	99
Chicken breasts, boneless, lb..	1 75-	1 80
Chicken legs, fresh, lb.........	75-	79
Chicken wings..................	62-	65
Chicken livers, lb..............	70-	75
Chicken meat, diced cooked, lb.	1 69-	1 90

ROASTERS

Roasters, iced —
4 lbs...........................	55-	59

FIGURE 10—[Cont.]

Fresh Vegetables

Price ranges shown below cover generally good quality to the best available.

ARTICHOKES, as to sz, ctn......	6 00-	6 15-
ASPARAGUS, Ca 30 lb cr jbo....	-	
BEANS, green, bu....................	10 75-	12 00+
Cranberry.....................	8 00-	8 15+
Pole.........................	-	
BEETS, topped, 1 1/2 bu cr ...		
BROCCOLI, 14s, cr......		
Cal, as to size................	8 10-	8 75-
Eastern, as to size.............	8 75-	8 85+
CORN, 4 1/2-5 dozen, cr.............	7 20-	7 75+
CUCUMBERS, med, wxd, cr or ctn	8 40-	9 60+
EGGPLANTS, lge, wrp, cr or ctn..	7 20-	7 75
Italian, 1/2 bu...............	12 00-	12 60+
ENDIVE (Chicory), 11/9 bu cr or ctn	5 00-	5 60+
ESCAROLE, 1 1/9 bu cr or ctn.....	5 00-	5 60-
GARLIC, as to size, lb.............	69-	75-
GREEN ONIONS, per bunch..........	13-	15
LEEKS, Per bunch..................	60-	69-
LETTUCE, iceberg, 24s, ctn........	9 25-	10 25+
Romaine, Eastern, 24s,ctn or cr.	8 75-	9 40+
Leaf, 24 qt. bskt................	3 75-	4 40-
MUSHROOMS, med-lge, 4 qt bkt...	5 00-	5 85+
Small-med, 4 qt bkt...........	4 40-	5 00+
ONIONS, 50 lb. bags — WESTERN		
Yellow large	5 45-	5 75+
Yellow, medium...............	-	
Red, 25 lb, bag.............	5 20-	5 75-
White Boilers, 25 lb.............	8 00-	9 20-

PARSLEY, curly, per bunch.......	18-	19+
PEAS, cr or bu.........................	-	
PEPPERS, grn, lg, cr, ctn or bu	3 60-	4 75-
Green, med, bu cr or ctn........	3 00-	3 60-
POTATOES, 1-A, 50 lb bag—		
Long White, ctn...............	4 30-	4 60-
Russet, 50 lb bag...............	-	
Long Wh, 10 oz min 100 lb bg	12 65-	12 75+
Russet, ctn....................	-	
Long White, 80-120s, Tis wrp	9 80-	10 35+
Long White, 80-120s, foil wrap	11 50-	11 75+
Round White, Eastern...........	4 30-	4 60+
Round Red....................	6 90-	7 00+
RADISHES, red, topped 30-6 oz bgs	5 75-	6 35+
SHALLOTS, dry, quart...........	2 00-	2 30-
SPINACH, 1 1/9 bu cr...........	8 40-	9 60+
SQUASH, grn, sm, bu or lug....		
Yellow, small, 1/2 bu or lug..	3 60-	4 20-
Acorn, cr.....................	5 20-	5 75+
TOMATOES, repacked, 25 lb ctn	7 00-	11 25-
Repacked, 20 lb ctn..........	5 50-	9 00-
Plum type, lugs...............	6 25-	6 90
Cherry, per pint...............	54-	57-
WATERCRESS, per bunch..........	29-	31
YAMS, 50 lb ctn...................	6 90-	8 00
Imported, 50 lb ctn............		

Fresh Fruit

AVOCADOS, Cal as to size, flat.....	12 00-	13 25
BANANAS, 150s, inst. pack.........	6 00-	6 50
CANTALOUPS, as to size, Jumbo cr	18 00-	19 20
HONEY DEWS, as to sz., ctn........	9 00-	9 60+
PINEAPPLES, 12's-15's cr..........	8 40-	9 00+
WATERMELONS, per lb..............	7-	9
LEMONS, 165s, ctn.................	7 50-	8 75
LIMES, as to size, 20 lb ctn.........	4 40-	5 00-
STRAWBERRIES Ca, med-lg per pt	81-	94+

5 1/2 lbs....................	70- 72
6 lbs. and up....................	71- 73
Roasters, trims, iced, 4-6 lbs.	55- 58

FOWLS

Fowls, Iced lb., 4 lbs................	45- 49
4 1/2 to 5 lbs................	49- 52
5 lbs and up................	51- 53
Fowl fat, 25 lb can................	54- 61

DUCKS

Ducklings, frozen, L.I.I., lb. —	
3 to 3 1/2 lbs....................	85- 89
3 1/2 to 4 lbs....................	85- 89
4 to 5 lbs....................	85- 89
5 1/2 lbs and up....................	85- 89

ROCK CORNISH

Rock Cornish Game Hens, frozen, lb. —	
16 oz. per head....................	1 05-1 10
16 to 20 oz. per head................	1 12-1 17

CAPONS

Capons, frozen, lb. —	
6 to 8 lbs........	1 11-1 21

Pheasant	
In feather, 5 bxs, to pair per lb	2 30-2 75
R.T.C. 1/2 to 3 1/2 lbs..........	2 30-2 75
Chukar Partridges —	
In feather, 1 to 1 1/4 lbs........	4 25-4 75
R.T.C. 1 lb each, per lb..........	4 25-4 75
Quail —	
In feather, 5 - 7 ozs............	--
R.T.C. 4-5 each................	1 75-1 85
R.T.C. 5-6 each................	1 95-2 05
Mallard Ducks —	
In feather, 2 to 3 lbs............	2 25-2 45
R.T.C. 1 1/2 to 3 lbs..........	2 25-2 45
Venison (Hide on hog-dressed)	
50 lbs and up per lb............	1 50-1 80
IMPORTED-Scotch Grouse - R.T.C. Frozen-	
3/4 lbs., each per lb............	5 50-7 00

YOUNG GUINEAS

R.T.C. Frozen —	
1 3/4 lbs., each per lb............	2 20-2 40
2 lbs. each per lb............	2 20-2 40
2 1/4 lbs....................	2 20-2 40

FROZEN FOODS

Vegetables

GRADE"A" or FANCY - ADVERTISED BRANDS
All Sizes 12/2 1/2 Except as Noted - per pound

ASPARAGUS, spears medium..........	1 25-1 30
Cut and tips....................	95-1 01
BROCCOLI, spears....................	48- 54
Chopped....................	41- 45
CARROTS, diced....................	24- 26
Sliced....................	26- 28
CAULIFLOWER....................	51- 55
COLLARD GREENS....................	26- 29
CORN, wh...................	42- 45
LIM............	

Potatoes

IDAHO

French fried, straight cut, 6/5 lb.....	33- 36
French fried, crinkle cut, 6/5 lb......	33- 36

Fruit

GRADE"A" or FANCY-ADVERTISED BRANDS
PER CAN

APPLES, Sliced, 1/30....................	10 40-11 30
BLUEBERRIES, Cultivated, 1/20...	13 30-14 50
Wild, 1/20....................	
CHERRIES, red sour, 1/30..........	15 50-16 60
MELON BALLS, 6/8..........	19 82-21 24
MIXED FRUITS, 6/8 1/2..........	29 40-31 40
PEACHES, Sliced 6/8 1/2..........	25 25-27 85
RASPBERRIES, 6/6 1/2..........	-
RHUBARB, 1/30..........	11 90-13 05
STRAWBERRIES, sliced, 6/6 1/2	23 00-25 00
Whole, 6/6 Mexican..........	20 80-22 00
GRAPEFRUIT SECTIONS, 4/1 gal, cs.	
per gal......	3 45-3 85

Seafood

FILLETS, Lb. —	
Cod, breaded....................	97-1 05
Plain....................	1 17-1 25
Flounder, breaded....................	1 21-1 33
Plain....................	1 18-1 30
Haddock, breaded....................	-
Plain....................	1 25-1 35
HALIBUT STEAKS, LB. —	
6-8-10 oz., 5 lb....................	2 05-2 10
CLAMS, Minced for chowder, lb. -	1 30-1 40
claws, (King), lb. -	
4/9 lb............	
LOBSTER MEAT, Ca	
24/12 oz. cans....................	10-3 40
LOBSTER TAILS, lb. — (Warm water)	
2-4 oz....................	7 10-7 20
4-6 oz....................	7 25-7 35
6-12 oz....................	7 10-7 20
SCALLOPS, Sea, lb....................	3 40-3 50
SHRIMP, peeled & deveined, lb. --	
Under 10 size....................	6 70-6 95
10-15 size....................	6 60-6 85
16-20 size....................	6 41-6 75
21-25 size....................	6 20-6 45
SHRIMP, raw, with shells, lb —	
Under 10 size....................	5 90-6 15
10-15 size....................	5 85-6 10
15-20 size....................	5 75-6 00
21-25 size....................	5 45-5 70
26-30 size....................	5 35-5 60
SHRIMP, uncooked, for salad, lb. —	
10/5 lb, "Tita", 100-200........	1 90-1 95
SHRIMP, cooked, for salad, lb., 6/3	2 35-2 50
BREADED OYSTERS, 4 dz/C......	8 50-9 40

[Cont.]

FIGURE 10—[Cont.]

Seafood Price-Current
DIVISION OF URNER BARRY PUBLICATIONS, INC.
ESTABLISHED 1858 - MORE THAN A CENTURY OF MARKET REPORTING SERVICE

Tuesday, June 22, 1976   Vol. 2 No. 22

EDITOR
PATRICK HARRINGTON
PUBLISHED TUESDAY & THURSDAY
By URNER BARRY PUBLICATIONS, INC.
4340 Redwood Hwy, Suite 237 — San Rafael, CA 94903
Phone 415/472-2090
SUBSCRIPTION RATES:
One Year's Subscription : $63.50 (postage included)
© Copyright 1976 by Urner Barry Publications, Inc.

IMPORTANT NOTE!

These quotations are based on sales and deliveries by Wholesalers and Distributors to Supermarkets, Fish and Poultry Stores, Restaurants and Institutions in the Northern and Southern California area including sections of Nevada and the New York metropolitan area. Other sources of information include Importers, Brokers and Seafood producers. Prices quoted are for normal delivery and prompt payment. For shipments outside of normal area extra charges may apply. Prices will vary with volume, size, quality, special service and preparation.

(+) OR (-) INDICATES CHANGE FROM LAST REPORT.

FRESH FISH

Fresh Fillets

(Premium of up to 15 cents per pound paid at various times due to shortages caused by bad weather)

	San Francisco	Los Angeles
Sole, Petrale	-1.90 - 2.00	-1.90 - 2.00
Sole, English	1.50 - 1.55	1.75 - 1.85
Sole, Dover	1.25 - 1.35	1.55 - 1.65
Rock Cod	1.05 - 1.10	1.30 - 1.35
Sea Bass (Baquetta) ...	-	2.10 - 2.20
Ling Cod	1.00 - 1.05	1.20 - 1.30
True Cod	1.00 - 1.05	1.25 - 1.30
Butter Fish	.50 - .55	-
Perch (skin on)	1.00 - 1.05	1.10 - 1.15
*Salmon Fillet	-	-

Fresh Whole

SALMON, King (Head off, plus 10 cents)

	San Francisco	Los Angeles
Small, Head on	1.90 - 1.95	2.20 - 2.25
Medium, Head on ...	2.10 - 2.15	2.35 - 2.40
Large, Head on	2.45 - 2.50	2.65 - 2.70
HALIBUT, Head off ..	2.05 - 2.10	
*Sea Bass, Dressed		

FROZEN FISH

	San Francisco	Los Angeles	New York
SOLE			
Petrale, IQF, Pac. Coast ..	2.00 - 2.05	2.10 - 2.15	
English, IQF, Pac. Coast .	1.50 - 1.55	1.60 - 1.70	
Dover, IQF, Pac. Coast ..	1.25 - 1.30	1.35 - 1.45	1.25 - 1.30
COD			
Rock, IQF, Pac. Coast ...	1.05 - 1.10	1.30 - 1.35	
Ling, IQF, Pac. Coast	1.00 - 1.05	1.10 - 1.20	
Icelandic, Inst. 5 lb.	1.25 - 1.35	1.25 - 1.35	1.30 - 1.35
Butter Fish, IQF, Pac. Coast	.50 - .55	-	
Salmon, IQF	2.40 -	-	
Sea Bass, IQF, Imported ..	1.80 - 1.85	1.75 - 1.80	
Turbot, IQF, Greenland ...	.76 - .84	.76 - .84	.77 - .80
Mahi Mahi, IQF	1.10 - 1.15	1.10 - 1.15	
HALIBUT			
Fletch, Japanese	3.25 - 3.30	3.25 - 3.30	
Fletch, Domestic	3.65 - 3.75	3.65 - 3.75	

SHATTER PACK: First Receiver, Truck Load or L.T.L.

FROZEN SHELLFISH

	San Francisco	Los Angeles	New York
ABALONE, (White)			
Small, Mexico (steak) ...	7.85 - 8.10	7.70 - 7.80	
Large, Mexico (steak) ...	7.95 - 8.10	7.85 - 7.95	
CRAB			
Dungeness, Brine frozen ..	1.10 - 1.20	1.20 - 1.30	
King, Leg & Claw	2.90 - 3.00	2.85 - 2.95	3.00 - 3.10
CRABMEAT			
Dungeness, 5 lb. tin ...	3.90 - 4.00	4.00 - 4.10	
Dungeness, legs	6.50 - 6.60	6.50 - 6.60	
King, 5 lb. block	+5.25 - 5.35	+5.30 - 5.40	+5.35 - 5.45
King, Salad Pk.	4.20 - 4.30	4.20 - 4.30	4.30 - 4.40
King, legs, Merus	+7.65 - 7.75	+7.50 - 7.60	7.75 - 7.85
Snow, 5 lb. tin Alaska .	3.90 - 3.95	3.95 - 4.00	-
Snow, 5 lb. blk. Alaska .	3.85 - 3.90	3.90 - 3.95	3.90 - 4.00
Snow, 5 lb. blk. Japan .	2.20 - 2.30	2.20 - 2.30	2.10 - 2.20
Snow, Salad Pk. Alaska .	2.90 - 3.00	2.90 - 3.00	-
Snow, legs, 5 lb. block .	4.65 - 4.75	4.60 - 4.70	4.50 - 4.60
SHRIMPMEAT (cooked & peeled)			
California 5 lb. tin	2.40 - 2.50	2.50 - 2.60	
Alaska, 5 lb. block	2.10 - 2.20	2.10 - 2.20	
Alaska, 5 lb. IQF	2.15 - 2.25	2.15 - 2.25	2.05 - 2.10
Asia, IQF	1.80 - 1.90	1.80 - 1.90	
SCALLOPS			
IQF 5 lb.	3.25 - 3.35	-	
5 lb. blk., Jumbo	3.20 - 3.30	3.15 - 3.25	2.75 - 2.85
5 lb. blk., medium	3.00 - 3.10	3.00 - 3.10	2.50 - 2.60
SCAMPI			
Iceland, 12-15	6.35 - 6.45	-	6.30 - 6.35
Iceland, 15-18	5.65 - 5.75	-	5.60 - 5.70
Iceland, 18-24	5.10 - 5.20		5.00 - 5.10

Local White	1.05 - 1.15	.90 - 1.00
Ling Cod, Dressed	.50 - .55	.60 - .65
Black Cod, Dressed ...	.40 - .45	-
Red Rock Cod	.45 - .50	-
Rex Sole	.55 - .60	.60 - .65
Sandabs	.55 - .60	.60 - .65
Rex Sole - Pan Ready .	.85 - .90	-
Sandabs - Pan Ready ..	.85 - .90	-
Rex Sole, Skin & Trim	1.30 - 1.35	1.40 - 1.50
Sandabs, Skin & Trim .	1.30 - 1.35	1.40 - 1.50
White Bait	.32 - .35	
Squid	.40 - .45	.40 - .50
Mackerel - Span.	.48 - .55	.50 - .55
Thresher Shark, Chunks ·	.80 - .90	.90 - 1.00
*Swordfish, Loins c/cut ..	-	-
(20c less for other than c/cut)		
*Sturgeon, Chunks	1.50 - 1.55	-
Skinned Rock Fish	.90 - .95	-
TROUT		
Idaho, Random wt. bags .	1.50 - 1.60	1.50 - 1.60
Idaho, 8 oz. box	1.65 - 1.70	1.65 - 1.70

FRESH SHELLFISH

*CRAB		
Whole Dungeness, Live	.80 - .95	-
Whole Dungeness, Cooked ..	.85 - 1.05	1.20 - 1.25
*Crabmeat, Dungeness	3.90 - 4.00	
Clams, Cherrystone, Shell ..	.79 - .83	.78 - .81
Clams, Littleneck, Shell ...	.88 - .92	.87 - .92
OYSTERS		
10 oz., Jar, Pacific	.98 - 1.02	1.00 - 1.05
East, Gal. X Select	+20.00 - 20.75	+21.00-23.00
East, Gal. Standard	18.50-19.00	20.00-20.50
Eastern Shell	.12 - .16	.12 - .16
Eastern, ½ Shell	.18 - .25	.18 - .22
Olympia, 4 oz. Jar	2.50 - 2.75	
LOBSTER, Live, Maine		
1-1½ lb.	+4.00 - 4.10	3.90 - 4.00
1¾-2 lb.	+4.30 - 4.40	4.20 - 4.30
Whole Cooked, Pacific....	3.65 - 3.75	3.50 - 3.60

* Seasonal

Dover, Pac. Coast	1.15 - 1.20	1.18 - 1.22	1.22 -1.26
English, Pac. Coast	1.30 - 1.35	1.33 - 1.37	
Rex Sole, P. Cst. Pan Ready	.90 - .95	.93 - .97	
Butter, Pac. Coast	.42 - .47	.45 - .50	
Perch, Skin on, Pac. Coast	.85 - .90	.88 - .92	.88 - .92
Red Snapper, Pac. Coast .	.75 - .80	.78 - .82	.83 - .86

PROCESSORS FISH BLOCKS
(Container Lots)

Pollock, Fillet, Japan ...	-	-
Cod, Fillet, Japan	-	-
Cod, Tails, Japan		
Salmon Meat, deboned (100% meat)		
Red	1.00 -	
Pale	-	-

Frozen Whole

SALMON, KING (Discounts available on Silver)

Small, Head off	2.00 - 2.05	2.30 - 2.40	-
Medium, Head off	2.20 - 2.25	2.45 - 2.55	2.50 - 2.55
Large, Head off	2.55 - 2.60	2.75 - 2.85	2.70 - 2.75
Mini Salmon, 8,10,12,14 oz.	1.80 - 1.85	1.85 - 1.90	1.65 - 1.70
Halibut, Northern	1.60 - 1.70	1.65 - 1.75	1.65 - 1.70
Sea Bass	-	-	
Imported Dover	3.25 - 3.35	3.25 - 3.35	3.20 - 3.30
Rex Sole	.45 - .50	.55 - .60	
Rex Sole, Pan ready ...	.85 - .90	-	
White Bait	.32 - .35		
Squid	.40 - .45	.50 - .60	.45 - .50
Sandabs	.55 - .60	.55 - .60	
Sandabs, Pan Ready ...	.85 - .90	-	
TROUT			
Idaho, Bone, in, Rd. wt.	.95 - 1.05	.95 - 1.05	1.15 - 1.25
Idaho, Bone in, 8 oz.	1.50 - 1.60	1.50 - 1.60	
Idaho, Boneless	1.80 - 1.85	1.80 - 1.85	
Japanese, Bone in	1.10 - 1.20	-	.89 - .95
STEAKS			
Halibut, Japan	2.10 - 2.20		1.85 - 1.90
Halibut, Domestic, Reg.	-	-	2.20 - 2.25
Halibut, Loin Cut Dom.	2.60 - 2.70	2.60 - 2.75	
Salmon	2.40 - 2.50	2.45 - 2.55	2.50 - 2.55
Turbot, 4 to 6 oz......	-	-	.80 - .83

Singapore, 12-15	5.70 - 5.80	-	5.60 - 5.70
Singapore, 15-18	5.55 - 5.65	-	5.50 - 5.60
Singapore, 18-24	5.00 - 5.10	4.95 - 5.00	5.20 - 5.30
Clam Meat, Minced ...	1.35 - 1.45	1.35 - 1.45	
Frog Legs, Small, Japan ..	3.80 - 3.90	3.70 - 3.80	-
Frog Legs, Med. Japan...	4.10 - 4.20	4.05 - 4.15	3.90 - 4.00
Frog Legs, Lge., Japan..	2.85 - 2.95	2.80 - 2.90	2.65 - 2.75
Frog Legs, Jumbo, Japan .	2.50 - 2.60	2.50 - 2.60	2.10 - 2.20
Lobsters, Whle. Ckd. Pac. .	3.35 - 3.45	3.30 - 3.40	

Lobster Tails

AUSTRALIAN –

5-6 oz.	7.90 - 8.00	7.85 - 7.95	8.00 - 8.10
6-8 oz.	7.75 - 7.85	7.70 - 7.80	7.85 - 7.95
8-10 oz.	7.70 - 7.80	7.70 - 7.80	7.85 - 7.95
10-12 oz.	7.60 - 7.70	7.55 - 7.65	7.75 - 7.85
12-16 oz.	7.60 - 7.70	7.55 - 7.65	7.75 - 7.85
16-20 oz.	7.40 - 7.50	7.35 - 7.45	7.50 - 7.60
20-24 oz.	7.40 - 7.50	7.35 - 7.45	7.50 - 7.60

FLORIDA – Bahama

4-6 oz.	-	-	7.20 - 7.30
6-8 oz.	-	-	7.20 - 7.30
8-10 oz.	-	-	6.90 - 7.00
10-12 oz.	-	-	6.90 - 7.00
12-14 oz.			
14-16 oz.			

SOUTH AFRICA

4-5 oz.	-	7.80 - 7.90	7.60 - 7.70
5-6 oz.	-	7.80 - 7.90	7.60 - 7.70
6-7 oz.	-	7.80 - 7.90	7.50 - 7.60
7-8 oz.	-	7.80 - 7.90	7.50 - 7.60
8-9 oz.	-	7.70 - 7.80	7.50 - 7.60
9-10 oz.	-	7.70 - 7.80	7.50 - 7.60

BRAZIL –

3 oz.	5.50 - 5.60	5.45 - 5.55	5.80 - 5.90
4 oz.	7.00 - 7.10	7.00 - 7.10	6.90 - 7.00
5 oz.	-	-	7.00 - 7.10

* Seasonal

MORE 👉

[Cont.]

FIGURE 10—Cont.]

Lobster Tails, Cont. (Brazil continued)	San Francisco	Los Angeles	New York
6 oz.	-	-	7.00 - 7.10
7 oz.	-	-	6.90 - 7.00
8 oz.	-	-	6.80 - 6.90
9 oz.	-	-	6.65 - 6.75
10 oz.	-	-	6.50 - 6.60
11 oz.	-	-	6.50 - 6.60
12 oz.	-	-	6.50 - 6.60

Slipper Lobsters

	San Francisco	Los Angeles	New York
SHELL ON			
1-2 ounces, China	-	-	3.75 - 3.85
2-4 ounces, Taiwan ...	4.40 - 4.50	4.30 - 4.40	4.20 - 4.30
4-6 ounces, China	4.85 - 4.95	4.80 - 4.90	5.00 - 5.10
MEAT - Shell off,			
Under 1 ounce, Taiwan	4.05 - 4.15	4.05 - 4.15	4.35 - 4.50
1-2 ounces, China	4.65 - 4.75	4.60 - 4.70	4.50 - 4.60
2-4 ounces, China	5.00 - 5.10	5.00 - 5.10	4.90 - 5.00

Shrimp

MEXICAN - No.1 White, shell on, headless (On certain sizes discount 5-10c for No. 2			(So.&Cent. America) White or Browns)
Under 10	5.95 - 6.05	5.90 - 6.00	6.00 - 6.10
Under 12	5.95 - 6.05	5.90 - 6.00	5.90 - 6.00
Under 15	5.95 - 6.05	5.90 - 6.00	5.80 - 5.90
16-20	5.85 - 5.95	5.80 - 5.90	5.70 - 5.80
21-25	5.50 - 5.60	5.45 - 5.55	5.50 - 5.60
26-30	4.95 - 5.05	4.90 - 5.00	4.90 - 5.00
31-35	4.45 - 4.55	4.40 - 4.50	4.25 - 4.35
31-40	4.25 - 4.30	4.20 - 4.25	
36-40	4.10 - 4.20	4.00 - 4.10	3.85 - 3.95
41-50	3.10 - 3.20	3.00 - 3.10	3.20 - 3.30
50 - 60	2.65 - 2.75	2.60 - 2.70	2.65 - 2.75
60-70	2.20 - 2.30	2.10 - 2.20	2.20 - 2.30
70-80	1.65 - 1.75	1.60 - 1.70	

SMOKED FISH

	San Francisco	Los Angeles	New York
Salmon Sides	4.75 - 4.85	4.70 - 4.80	3.69 - 3.75
Sliced Salmon, 5 lb. tray	5.85 - 5.95	5.80 - 5.90	4.70 - 4.80
Finnan Haddie	1.20 - 1.25	1.20 - 1.25	1.05 - 1.15
Kipper Cod, Rdm. Cut .	1.25 - 1.35	1.25 - 1.35	

SEAFOOD MARKET NEWS

FRESH FISH FILLET:
Market steady - Supplies adequate for fair demand.

FROZEN FISH FILLETS, I.Q.F. Shatter Pack:
Market steady. Processor inventories are building as fresh supply of certain species exceeds demand.

FRESH SALMON, KING & SILVER
Market unsettled and erratic — prices vary from one fishery to another as the market seeks a stable level of trading. Buyer interest good. Supply is light.

HALIBUT, NORTHERN
Market unsettled as new season opened in Kodiak, Alaska area. Ex-vessel prices are considered high by brokers and processors, and are expected to go down shortly.

DUNGENESS CRAB CALIFORNIA:
Market steady on whole cooked crab, dull on live. Demand fair. Supply is moderate on meat. Processors report cleaning up crab meat inventories as fishing season ends in July.

FROZEN ALASKA KING CRAB:
Market is steady on legs and claws. Supplies are adequate. Market firm on meat as demand exceeds a rapidly diminishing supply. Wholesalers report paying $5 for product.

FROZEN CALIFORNIA/OREGON SHRIMPMEAT:
Market steady — Demand good. Production remains poor. Some processors report a dim outlook with regards to this year's catch.

AUSTRALIAN LOBSTER TAIL:
Market steady with firm undertone. Supplies

SAN FRANCISCO WHOLESALE PRICE RECORD
SECOND WEEK OF JUNE

	1975	1976
Abalone, Mexico		
Small	6.90	7.85
Large	7.00	7.95
Crab Meat		
Dungeness, 5 lb. tin	5.50	3.90
King, 5 lb. block	3.35	5.10
King, Legs, Merus	5.50	7.40
Snow, 5 lb. block	2.25	3.85
King Crab, Legs & Claws	2.35	2.90
Shrimp Meat, C&P, Calif.	1.50	2.40
Clam Meat, Minced	.60	1.35
Lobster Tails, Australian		
5-6 oz.	5.80	7.90
6-8 oz.	5.70	7.75
8-10 oz.	5.90	7.70
Shrimp, Mexican		
Under 10	4.00	5.95
Under 12	3.60	5.95
Under 15	3.30	5.95

CHINESE, shell on, headless			
8-12	-	-	-
10-15	5.70 - 5.80	5.70 - 5.80	-
16-20	5.60 - 5.70	5.60 - 5.70	-
21-25	5.40 - 5.50	5.40 - 5.50	-

GULF, Texas/Louisana, shell on, headless, white			
Under 15	-	-	5.80 - 5.90
16-20	-	-	5.65 - 5.75
21-25	-	-	5.30 - 5.40
26-30	-	-	4.90 - 5.00

PEELED & DEVEINED			
100-200, Mexico			1.60 - 1.65
			Gulf
Under 15, Mexico	5.45 - 5.55	5.40 - 5.50	5.40 - 5.50
16-20, Mexico	5.35 - 5.45	5.30 - 5.40	5.20 - 5.30
16-20, China	-	-	5.00 - 5.10
Broken, Small Mexico . .	3.10 - 3.20	3.15 - 3.25	3.05 - 3.15
Broken, Medium Mexico .	3.35 - 3.45	3.30 - 3.40	3.30 - 3.40
Broken, Large Mexico . .	3.65 - 3.75	3.60 - 3.70	3.60 - 3.70

barely adequate for good demand. U.S. cold storage inventories on Spiny lobster are substantially lower this year than last. In storage May 31, 1975 — 5.301 million pounds. In storage May 31, 1976 — 3.601 million pounds. Consumption reported to be 30% higher than previous year, while production is said to be slightly improved.

GREENLAND TURBOT:

Market about steady — Supply adequate with fair demand. Buyers cautious as new season has begun.

MEXICAN SHRIMP:

Market steady on large and medium sizes, weak on small sizes. Supply is very light, particularly on large and medium whites. Under 10s and under 12s difficult to find. Buyer interest has waned and attitude is cautious.

GULF SHRIMP

Market steady on large and medium whites — supplies limited. Market steadier at lower price levels on small whites and browns. Trade advisors report stocks low on Caribbean No. 1 whites and No. 1 pinks.

Seafood Price-Current

URNER BARRY PUBLICATIONS, INC.

**4340 Redwood Hwy, Suite 237
San Rafael, CA 94903**

First Class Mail

AMERICA'S FIRST INDUSTRY

[Cont.]

Long Island Jewish-Hillside Medical Center   **FIGURE 10—[Cont.]**   To: David Fox
75-59 263 St.   52 Little West 12 St.
Glen Oaks, N.Y. 11004   New York, N.Y.
Hillside Division

order date:_____

for delivery on _____

QUANTITY	UNIT OF MEASURE	ITEMS	UNIT PRICE	TOTAL
		Chicken ready-to-cook, iced, crated no giblets included 2½# eviscerated Delaware, Maryland & Pennsylvania hens. Fresh only. U.S.D.A. Grade A	UB + .04½#	
		Chicken parts, ready-to-cook, iced, crated no giblets included 2½# eviscerated Delaware, Maryland & Pennsylvania hens. Fresh only. U.S.D.A. Quartered Grade A	UB + .06½#	
		Rock Cornish game hens, ready-to-cook, eviscerated frozen in printed bag, 24 oz per head. U.S.D.A. Grade A	UB + .08#	
		Cooked & diced chicken meat in natural proportions of white & dark meat	1.25#	
		Turkey wingmeat breast with portion of wingmeat; back out; ribs in; 14#-16# per head. Fresh or frozen. U.S.D.A. Grade A	UB + .06#	

TECHNIQUES FOR PURCHASING FOOD. Foodservice purchasing—whether food or equipment and supplies—is unique. Purchasing policies can affect food and labor costs, the sanitation and safety of the operation, nutritional dependability, the quality of the program, not to mention production, serving, and cleaning costs.

There are many pitfalls to be avoided in purchasing. Here are some erroneous practices the food buyer must avoid to perform well:

Overbuying. Most often an overbuyer is a "guesser." He guesses instead of plans. To be sure of having enough of everything on hand, he usually has far too much. As a result, overbuying is extremely wasteful and expensive.

The greatest waste occurs with perishable items, such as fruits, vegetables, meats and all grain products where overbuying results in a two fold waste—financial and nutritional. That which goes bad is lost and is sheer waste; that which can be utilized, even though it is comparatively old, has lost much of its nutritional value, so is practically useless. Because fresh produce deteriorates so quickly, it is good practice to pay a little more, if need be, for frequent deliveries than to load up at possible lower prices.

Underbuying. As with the overbuyer, the underbuyer does not know his average consumption, so he guesses. In addition, he is overcautious. As a result, he frequently runs out of items. This causes no end of confusion and brings on justifiable criticism.

It is better to have a little too much than not enough, and in large quantity foodservice waste cannot be prevented entirely. A little waste occasionally is normal procedure. The food buyer must study and know his operation's needs over a reasonable period and buy accordingly.

Price Buying. A price buyer bases his buying decision solely on price and usually purchases the cheapest products. The buyer can easily make this mistake unless he is familiar with correct buying principles. The lowest-priced item is not always the cheapest. With any food, but particularly with perishables, the institution usually gets only what it pays for and no more. Inferior merchandise consumes only initial savings, and the institution suffers in the "bargain."

Knowledge of merchandise is indispensable in evading this erroneous practice. The buyer must choose the quality best suited for his institution's needs and then shop for the best price.

Quality Buying. This person buys only the best of everything without considering price. He is a prime target for salesmen who might otherwise have to shade prices or offer inducements. The quality buyer also leaves himself open to the unscrupulous.

This type of "one track" buying is extravagant and expensive. Also, this buyer actually does not always get the high quality he thinks he is getting. Quality buying is frequently associated with "one house" buying. The buyer is completely sold on a distributor or label that has a reputation for high quality merchandise. He concludes, erroneously, that every item this company carries must be the best when he might, in fact, get a better quality at a lower price from a moderately priced house. The remedy for "quality buying" is to compare brands as well as prices.

Bargain Buying. A bargain buyer insists on a price reduction on every purchase. As long as he gets the cut rate, he thinks he has saved money. This buyer has fallen victim to first costs and is blind to the net, or overall, costs. Such a buyer is a fall guy for inferior merchandise and very often gets trimmed. In contrast, the smart buyer knows that there are few exceptional bargains, especially in food.

The bargain buyer frequently overbuys because he is captivated by seemingly getting something for nothing. Nothing is a bargain unless it will be used within a reasonably specified period.

Also, a price reduction means nothing in itself; there has to be a standard of comparison. The buyer must know the current market price.

Pressure Buying. This buyer cannot say no. He has no sales resistance whatsoever. He overstocks, duplicates items, and deals with too many concerns. The savvy food buyer is skeptical of fast talking pressure specialists with their "great bargains," particularly in perishables.

Cleaning supplies is another field in which the buyer can easily yield to pressure selling. Representatives of reputable houses usually avoid such practices. It is good practice never to make an on-the-spot decision to switch products of this kind; better to think it over and weigh all the considerations.

FIGURE 11

HOTEL • RESTAURANT • INSTITUTIONAL MEAT SERVICE REPORT

PUBLISHED BY THE NATIONAL PROVISIONER, INC. "SINCE 1891" • 15 WEST HURON STREET • CHICAGO, ILLINOIS 60610 • (312) 944-3380

Published each Thursday at Chicago, Ill. SUBSCRIPTION RATES: Yearly $58.50. Quarterly $17.50.
Thursday March 6th, 1975--Series No. H 10   Back issues $1.25 each.

(+) and (−) denotes prices up or down from previous week.

IMPS	BEEF CUTS	PRIME	CHOICE
103	Rib (primal)	95@98	.87@100+
107	Rib, oven prepared, short cut (4x3)	135@140	125@135
109	Rib (roast ready)(add 5¢ lb. if feather bone off)	140@150	132@145+
112	Rib eye rolls, boneless (lip off)	335@350--	285@310+
113	Chuck (square cut, shank off)	----	.60@65
114	Shoulder clods, boneless	----	105@120
116A	Boneless chuck roll		
115	Boneless chuck, regular	----	107@118
123	Short ribs, (two inch cut)	----	.79@86--
124	Corner pieces	----	.85@110--
135	Beef diced (1/2 or 1 in.)	----	.85@110+
1195	Beef for stewing	----	125@135
158	Rounds (primal)	----	130@149
164	Rounds (rump and shank off, bone in)	88@94-	.84@95+
165	Rounds (rump and shank off, boneless)	115@125-	115@125
		unq	125@135
167	Knuckles bnls. (sirloin tip) skinless, cap off	----	130@140
168	Top rounds, boneless	127@135	125@135--
169	Bottom rounds, boneless	----	120@135
170	Gooseneck round, boneless	----	115@125
172	Full loins (flank off, kidney out, trd.)	118@123	100@110
173	Short loins (trimmed)	170@180	140@150
181	Sirloin loin end	.98@114	.90@100
175	Strip loin, bone in, (regular)(10 inch cut)	185@210	150@160
180	Strip loin, boneless, (short cut)(3x2)	240@270	190@215
183	Full boneless sirloin butt, trimmed	----	115@130
184	Top sirloin butts, boneless	145@160	135@145+
186	Bottom sirloin butts, boneless, close trim	unq	.85@95
189	Full tenderloins 7/up	----	215@235--
189	Full tenderloins 7/down	----	205@225
190	Full tenderloins, special trimmed	----	365@400--
191	Butt tenders	----	205@220
1100	Cubed steaks, regular	----	135@160
1101	Cubed steaks, special	----	155@175
1102	Braising steaks, (swiss)	----	165@190
1103	Rib steaks, bone in.	----	. unq
1103A	Rib steaks, boneless	----	280@320
1112	Rib eye steaks, boneless	----	320@355--
1173	Porterhouse steaks (1-1/2 to 2 in. tail)	345@365	245@280--
1173A	T-Bone steaks (1-1/2 to 2 in. tail)	345@365	245@280--
1179	Strip steaks, bone in, (short cut)(2 in. tail)	340@360	250@285
1180	Strip steaks, boneless, (short cut 2 in. tail)	430@460	320@350--
1184	Top sirloin butt steaks, boneless	unq	260@290--
1184B	Top sirloin butt steaks, center cut, boneless	unq	290@360--
1189	Tenderloin steaks, close trim	unq	395@425--
1190	Tenderloin steaks, special (silver skin off)	unq	460@545--
---	Bottom sirloin butt ball tip (1-1/2@2 lb. avg.)	unq	165@180
---	Bottom sirloin butt triangle (1-1/2@2 lb. avg.)	unq	165@180
120	Boneless brisket, fresh, deckle off	----	100@110--
193	Flank steaks, trimmed and skinned	unq	160@180

FARM PRICES

Prices farmers receive for their crops and livestock dropped for the third consecutive month in mid-January. The Agriculture Department reported that one reason for the farm commodity price drops continued to be weakened demand in this country and abroad, due mostly to the recession. In addition, expectations are high for record crops this year, if last summer's poor weather does not recur.

For the month ended January 15, 1975, farm prices delcined 1.5 per cent. In December prices dropped 3 per cent after a 1.5 per cent decline in the previous month. Contributing most to the latest decrease were lower prices for wheat, soybeans corn and eggs. Prices were up for lettuce, tomatoes and broilers.

Dropping farm prices do not necessarily mean lower food prices at the retail level. Agriculture Department officials are still forecasting that retail food prices will increase at a 15 per cent annual rate during the first half of this year.

About 80 per cent of the retail food price rise has been coming after products leave the farm and costs of transporting, distributing and retailing food are expectaed to continue to rise this year at high rates.

SPECIFICATION NUMBERS

IMPS product numbers are according to "Institutional Meat Purchase Specifications" issued and approved by The United States Department of Agriculture, as also used by National Assn. of Meat Purveyors in their "Buyers Guide to Portion Control Meat Cuts" and "Meat Buyers Guide to Standardized Meat Cuts".

This service is a guide to current markets established by sales and offerings of the listed meats, delivered to hotels, restaurants, clubs, institutions and away-from-home eating places. Differentials for freight and in-transit shrinkage apply away from sellers regular delivery area. Sellers may charge extra for ageing, freezing, dry ice, or special packing. All products fresh unless otherwise stated. Quoted prices are for prompt payment. The sign @ denotes a range in price. Ranges in prices reflect quantities, service, size and quality within each grade. All prices are per pound.

IMPS	GOOD	UTILITY
103	No U.S.D.A. Graded Good Items Quoted	60@65
107		---
109		---
112		132@185-
113		---
114		65@70
116A		unq
115		62@68
123		---
124		---
135		---
1195		---
158		58@66
164		---
165		75@84
167		80@88
168		88@110
169		78@88
170		---
172		---
173		90@100
181		---
175		85@98
180		unq
183		76@89
184		94@97
186		---
189		180@190+
189		155@190+
190		185@195
191		120@125
1100		unq
1101		---
1102		unq
1103		unq
1103A		---
1112		---
1173		---
1173A		---
1179		---
1180		---
1184		unq
1184B		---
1189		unq
1190		295@309
---		---
---		---
120		---
193		110@112

MISCELLANEOUS PRODUCTS AND SPECIALTIES **PER POUND**

IMPS		
601	Boneless brisket corned beef, choice, deckle off, Hotel trim	105@115-
604	Boneless inside round, corned beef	120@140
606	Boneless outside round, corned beef	118@140
---	Cooked corned beef brisket, choice	195@210
---	Cooked corned beef round, choice	190@210
618	Sliced dried beef, individual packages	325@350-
618	Sliced dried beef, bulk packed	170@225-
136	Ground beef, regular, bulk	unq
1136	Ground beef patties, regular	unq
137	Ground beef 80% lean, special, bulk	70@78-
1137	Ground beef patties, 80% lean, special	72@79-
134	Beef bones (mixed)	14@18
---	Beef livers, No. 1 whole	58@65
---	Beef livers, No. 1 deveined, skd. sliced	.86@105-
716	Tongue, Beef - Fresh	66@77
613	Tongue, Beef - Cured	.95@112
614	Tongue, Beef - Smoked	125@140-
---	Oxtails, No. 1, fresh or frozen	58@68-
---	Oxtails cut up/disjointed	64@74

REPORT GOOD, BAD OF PRICE DROPS--Continuing decline in the price of beef, both on the hoof and on the rail, is attracting the attention of major urban media. Reports generally use a "good for the consumer bad for the producer" angle, pointing out the bargains now available to consumers at the meat counter, but warning of the impact on long-term supply if producers/feeders don't start making a profit. Pork producer problems are also often cited, with predictions for the decrease in hog production and the corresponding increase in retail prices.

Agriculture price/production stories are becoming regular items in the urban media. Events of past two years or so--and better media coverage of those events--have sharpened consumer awareness of the agriculture's importance in their lives. Expanding public/media relations programs of industry groups--including Meat Board--have helped bring this about.

Thursday March 6th, 1975--Series No. H 10

[Cont.]

FIGURE 11—[Cont.]

HOTEL · RESTAURANT · INSTITUTIONAL MEAT SERVICE REPORT

PUBLISHED BY THE NATIONAL PROVISIONER, INC. "SINCE 1891" · 15 WEST HURON STREET · CHICAGO, ILLINOIS 60610 · (312) 944-3380

Thursday March 6th, 1975--Series No. H 10

IMPS		PER POUND	IMPS
	LAMB		
233	Double leg, regular	125@136	233
1234AR	Lamb leg, boneless tied	180@205	1234AR
204	Hotel rack, trimmed	160@190	204
207	Shoulder, square cut, trimmed	85@95	207
1208R	Lamb shoulder, boneless tied	135@155–	1208R
232	Lamb loin, trimmed	190@205	232
1295	Lamb for stew, boneless, trimmed	135@165	1295
1207	Shoulder chops	140@160–	1207
1204A	Rib chops, fell off, frenched	375@415	1204A
1232	Loin chops, fell off	290@335	1232
.	Lamb shanks trimmed	.98@110–	.
	VEAL		
334	Double leg	170@205	334
1335R	Veal leg, boneless tied	185@235	1335R
1332	Loin chops	240@260	1332
.	Veal cutlet - chopped molded	110@175	.
1336A	Veal leg cutlets, special, regular or cubed	370@465	1336A
1395	Veal for stewing	160@175	1395
704	Calf liver	230@260–	704
707	Ground veal	125@140	707
	FRESH PORK		
402	Fresh ham, standard skinned, 14/18	.95@105	402
1402R	Fresh ham, skinless, boneless, tied 10/14	125@140–	1402R
410	Pork loin, regular 14/down	.93@110	410
412	Center cut pork loin from 14/down	135@150	412
413	Pork loin, boneless	135@155	413
414	Canadian back boneless pork loin, defatted	150@175	414
406	Boston butt, extra trimmed, 4/8	75@90	406
407	Boston butt, extra trimmed, boneless	.95@110	407
1412	Pork chops, center cut, loin or rib	145@165	1412
1412B	Pork chops, boneless center cut	170@195	1412B
1496	Diced pork	105@135	1496
1406	Boston butt steaks, bone in	105@116	1406
1407	Boston butt steaks, boneless, trimmed	unq	1407
415	Pork tenderloins, fresh/frozen	140@163–	415
416	Spareribs, 3/down weights	.90@100	416
.	St. Louis style spareribs, brisket bone off, skirt in	125@155	.
417	Loin back ribs, 1-1/2 and down weights	175@210	417
.	Pork shoulder hocks, 3/4 and down weights	60@75	.
.	Ground pork	.90@110	.
	PROCESSED and MFG.		
539	Sliced bacon, Hotel Pack Layers	120@140	539
539	Sliced bacon, Lay Out Packed	125@142	539
541	Sliced bacon, Grade "A" (irregular)	.95@115	541
503	Ham, skinned, cured and smoked, 10% water added	.95@120	503
503	Hams, skinned, cured and smoked, dry type	110@135	503
509	Ham, boneless, skinless, tied or in net or casing, smoked and cooked	165@195	509
530	Smoked butts, boneless	120@138	530
526	Shoulder picnic, smoked	70@80	526
.	Canned ham, pullman style, domestic 8/10	135@155	.
.	Canned ham, pear shape, domestic, 12/14	133@150	.
.	Canned ham, imported	160@180	.
550	Canadian style bacon, whole, smoked	180@210	550
.	Pure pork sausage, 16 links to lb. sheep casing, collagen or skinless	100@125	.
.	Pure pork sausage, rolls	83@100	.
.	Pure pork sausage, patties	.95@120+	.
.	Smoked liver sausage, braunschweiger AC	65@85	.
.	Smoked liver sausage, braunschweiger NC	.95@115	.
.	Frankfurters, skinless, fancy, 8/10 to lb. (high side of range is all beef)	85@105	.

ESSENTIAL MEDICINES FROM ANIMAL BY-PRODUCTS

A steer or hog represents more than food on the hoof. In addition to providing meat, livestock are a virtual "pharmaceutical factory," of medicines and other health aids.

Thus to de-emphasize animal agriculture in the U.S., as some have been suggesting, would not only mean a decrease in high quality meat protein but also a reduction in medicine production, according to the National Live Stock and Meat Board. Science has been able to manufacture artificially some of the pharmaceuticals originally obtained from livestock, but for many medications, cattle, hogs or sheep remain the best, and often the only sources, said H. Kenneth Johnson, the Board's Executive Director of Food Science.

One such medicine is insulin, needed by many diabetics to regulate their blood sugar level. It takes 6300 cattle to yield one pound of insulin. Some of the other animal source medications include heparin, estrogen, thyroid and adrenal extracts. Addison's disease, asthma, whooping cough, anemia and other blood ailments, certain mental disorders, rheumatoid arthritis, rheumatic fever and osteoporosis are some of the other diseases which have been treated with medicines obtained from livestock.

Mankind's health also benefits from livestock by-products used in research. Crystallized albumin, taken from cattle, is the "protein reference standard", for protein research work. Fibrinogen and gamma globulins are also used in medical research.

Animal intestines are the source for the sutures used to repair torn and damaged tissues.

Even the bones from livestock can be used to benefit health. Animals bones have been used to reconstruct the faces of persons disfigured in accidents. Temporary bone replacements are used in the treatment of certain human bone defects. Purified bone meal is a source for calcium and phosphorus, often used in pediatric foods.

OUR VIEW OF THE MARKET

It might be that Spring is starting to "sprung". Business in the Hotel, Restaurant and Institutional industry has picked up slightly. Foodservice operators as well as their suppliers look for another nudge upward next weekend with the advent of the annual celebration of a certain patron Saint's birthday. There will be increased consumption of the brine-cured boneless brisket of beef and cabbage. We predict that there will be some spirits served also and perhaps some singing. This celebration is a favorite of those of Hibernian decent. The foodservice operators appreciate that day as it usually means Erin Go "Moola". No foodservice person we know is adverse to a little more cash in the till, regardless of the reason. The wearin' of the "green" always looks better in the cash drawer.

All, however is not fun and frolic in the foodservice industry. We were told of some ominous demands in a large metropolitan city in the midwest, with a strike by butchers which might force some HRI suppliers out of business. Our reporting sources tell us of what they consider impossible demands by the unions. More more and more money and benefits. We make no speculations or opinions on this situation. We do however believe that outrageous demands, if met, can give "ammunition" to those highly vocal individuals who claim that the middleman is causing prices to go up. The unfortunate part of all this is that it is true that labor, shipping, packaging and delivery costs of the processed product each play a part of "middleman". It takes no genius to figure who is going to be asked to pay for this and we wonder what can happen to the entire trade if people reach the breaking point and begin to rebel.

The carcass beef market broke sharply early this week selling of 1-1/2¢ to 2¢ from last week's close. Better retail movement and reduced kills this week helped the market to respond today with selling advancing 1¢ to 1-1/2¢ over Monday's low point, with more interest for balance of week. Market will probably level off at Thursday's selling into next week unless the slaughter number increases.

The beef cut market strengthened, with interest switching to front meat and front meat showing some strength. FORES and CHUCKS sold down sharply at end of last week, but as of today have traded even with last week's quote. HINDS in weak position and offered at 1¢ to 1-1/2¢ under last quote. ROUNDS still under pressure and traded 4¢ under previous quotation. LOINS and RIBS in firm position and have traded 2¢ over last week.

Lambs selling steady with last week however shippers asking higher into next week. Lamb prices East this week was 89¢ to 90¢ on 55# down and 87¢ to 89¢ on heavier weight of 55#/65# GS lambs selling 91¢ East.

In the packer-wholesale market, fresh skinned HAMS 14/17 sold up 2¢ and fresh 4/8 PICNIC'S were 2-1/2¢ to 3¢ higher. BACON BELLIES were 2¢ lower than last week but fresh PORK LOINS 14 down sold up 3¢ to 3-1/2¢. BOSTON BUTTS 4/8 weak 1-1/2¢ higher and the export market continues strong for this item. With good buying interest from the fast food chains, fresh and frozen 3#/down SPARERIBS sold up 3¢ to 3-1/2¢ per lb. compared to last week.

From - U.S. Dept. of Commerce	Sales for week ended – (Millions of Dollars)				Sales compared to last year (Percent change)		
	Jan. 25 '75	Feb. 1 '75	Feb. 8 '75	Feb. 15 '75	Current week	Last 4 weeks	Year to date
Dollar Volume of Sales for Eating and Drinking Places	764	771	763	790	+11	+10	+12

The above weekly figures are estimates and are not adjusted for price differences for seasonal or holiday variations.

HOTEL, RESTAURANT AND INSTITUTIONAL
MEAT SERVICE REPORT
Thursday March 6th, 1975--Series No. H 10

FIGURE 12

Fresh Fruit and Vegetable

MARKET NEWS
FRUIT AND VEGETABLE DIVISION

U. S. DEPARTMENT OF AGRICULTURE. AMS
ROOM 3532 FEDERAL OFFICE BUILDING
550 MAIN STREET
CINCINNATI. OHIO 45202

TEL: 684-3194. 3195
AREA CODE 513

CINCINNATI
DAILY REPORT

VOL. LXII   NO. 134

MONDAY
JULY 12, 1976

Unless otherwise stated: Prices below cover sales by first receiver on available supplies to 9:30 a.m.. on this morning's terminal market in wholesale lots and are on stock of generally good merchantable quality and condition. Weather at 8:00 a.m.   PARTLY CLOUDY 66° - maximum yesterday 91°

/TELEPHONE RECORDER SERVICE/ - TAPED 11:30 a.m. - TEL. 621-2542 AREA CODE 513

VEGETABLES

ARTICHOKES: CA Ctns 30s 9.00-10.00
BEANS: ABOUT STEADY Rnd Grn IN Bu Crts 6.00 TN 6.50-7.25 mos 6.50-7.00
BROCCOLI: ABOUT STEADY CA Ctns bchd 14s 6.00-6.75 18s 6.75-7.00 few higher
CABBAGE: ABOUT STEADY Approx 50-lb Crts Green med-Lge. IN 2.50-2.75 MI 2.75-3.00 WI Ctns 3.50 Red NJ Crts 5.00 NOHIO Ctns 4.50-5.00
CARROTS: ABOUT STEADY Sks flm bgs unless otherwise stated CA 24-2 lb 7.00 48-1 lb wide range 6.50-7.50 few higher Ctns 24-2 lb & 48-1 lb 1 lot 7.50 Rpkd in MI 48-1 lb 7.25-7.50 50-lb Sks lse Lge 7.00. CA 50-lb Sks lse Lge 6.00-6.50 Ctns bchd 24s 5.50
CAULIFLOWER: CA Ctns flm wrpd 12s 7.75-8.50 mos 7.75-8.00
CELERY: ABOUT STEADY CA Crts & Ctns 2 doz 8.00 2½ doz 8.00-8.50 few higher NOHIO Crts 2 doz 7.00 2½ doz 7.50 3 doz 7.25 Hearts Ctns flm wrpd 24s MI 7.75-8.50 NOHIO 8.25 CA 12s 6.50
CHINESE CABBAGE: NOHIO 1-1/9 Bu Crt 4.50 16-qt bkts 2.50
CORN, SWEET: OFFERINGS LIGHT AL Crts approx 4½ doz White 1 lot 7.00
CUCUMBERS: LOWER Waxed NC 1-1/9 Bu Crts & Ctns med 8.50-9.00 some 8.00 fair qual 5.50 few higher sml 6.50

POTATOES: (Cont'd) 8.50 few higher fair cond 6.50-7.00 Bld Non SzA 5/10s 4.50-5.00 few higher fair qual 3.50-4.00 10/5s 5.50-6.00 few higher fair qual 4.00 New Crop Rnd Red AL 3.75-4.00 fair qual 3.25 100-lb sks 7.85 Bld 5/10s 5.00 fair cond 4.25 10/5s 5.50-5.60 mos 5.50 fair cond 5.00 Long White CA 4.00 fair cond 3.50 100-lb sks 7.50 10-oz min 100-lb sks 8.50 Bld 5/10s 1 lot 4.90 poor cond 2.00-2.50 10/5s 1 lot 5.50 Ctns Sz 80-100s 5.50-6.00 fair cond 5.00 poor cond 2.50-3.00 Russets CA 10-oz min 100-lb sks 12.00-13.00 Ctns Sz 80-100s 6.50-7.50 Bld 5/10s 4.75-5.00 Norgold Rpkd in OK Ctns Sz 80-100s 6.00-7.00 Bld 5/10s 4.50-4.75 fair cond 4.25
RADISHES: Red Ctns flm bgs NOHIO 30-6 oz & 12-1 lb 4.00 few higher MI 30-6 oz 3.50
SQUASH: FL fair qual Acorn 1-1/9 Bu Ctns 5.00 Butternut 1-1/9 Bu Crts 5.50 1-1/9 Bu Crts GA Acorn 5.50 Butternut 6.00 SC Acorn & Butternut 6.00 NJ Hlf Bu Ctns Yel St'nk & Zucch 4.00 TN 5/9 Bu Crts Zucch 4.00
SWEETPOTATOES: 50-lb Ctns Porto Rican Type US#1 AL 7.50-8.00 NC 7.50 poor cond 2.50
TOMATOES: ABOUT STEADY EXCEPT CA 2 LYR FLTS LOWER pink-red CA 2 lyr flts ExLge & MaxLge 5.25-6.00 3 lyr lugs Lge 8.00-8.50 AR 2 lyr Ctns Lge & ExLge 4.50-5.50 fair qual

APPLES: (Cont'd) & 100-113s 9.50-9.75 88s 8.75-9.75 125s 8.75-9.25 138s 8.75 WAFcy 80s & 100s 8.00 88s & 113-125s 8.00-8.25 Red Del WAExFcy 72-125s 9.25-9.50 138s 8.25-8.50 few higher WAFcy 72-125s 8.00-8.50 138s 7.25-7.50 Winesaps Reg-Stge WAExFcy 88-113s 8.00-8.50 125s 7.75-8.50 150s 7.50 ID IDFcy Red Del 125-138s 7.50 Loose Reg-Stge IL 1-1/9 Bu Ctns US#1 2½" & up Lodi 5.00 Bu Ctns Lodi & Williams Red 5.00 NOHIO Ctns aprox 40-lb Transparent US#1 2½" & up 6.00
AVOCADOS: CA 1 lyr Ctns Green Skin 24-30s 14.00 Hass 30s 13.50
BANANAS: Imports 40-lb Ctns 5.75-6.00 few higher
BERRIES: BLUEBERRIES: 12-pt flts flm wrpd MI 7.00 NJ 7.00-7.50 RED RASPBERRIES: MI 12-pt flts 14.00 STRAWBERRIES: CA 12-pt flts med-Lge 5.75-6.25 Lge-ExLge 6.75-7.00
CHERRIES: 20-lb lugs Bings 12-row & Lgr WA 8.00-9.00 mos 8.00-8.50 few higher ID 7.50-8.00 MI 8-qt flts sour 10.00
GRAPES: CA 22-lb lugs Exotic & Black Sdls 14.00 Cardinals 11.00 Thompson Sdls 12.50 few higher fair qual 10.50
MANGOES: FL Ctns 9s 3.00 14 & 18s 4.00 few 12s higher 16s 3.00-4.00
NECTARINES: CA 2 lyr lugs Early

Lge 4.50-5.00 some 5.50 Ctns 24s
3.00-3.40 mos 3.00-3.25 SC Bu Ctns
Lge 5.00 VA Ctns med ord qual 4.00
sml 5.00 Ctns 24s 2.75-3.00
EGGPLANT: GA 1-1/9 Bu Ctns 6.00 few
higher
ENDIVE: CA Ctns 24s 7.00 NOHIO 24-qt
bkts 2.50
ESCAROLE: CA Ctns 24s 6.50 NOHIO 24-
qt bkts 2.50
LETTUCE: HIGHER Ctns Iceberg 24s CA
7.25-8.00 mos 7.50-7.75 few 8.25-
8.50 1 label 9.00 poor cond 2.00-
3.00 WI 7.00-7.50 MI 6.75-7.00 30s
7.00 Romaine CA Ctns 24s 6.75 NOHIO
24-qt bkts 2.50 Big Bost CA Ctns
24s 7.50 NOHIO 16-qt bkts 16s 2.50
Leaf NOHIO 24-qt bkts 2.50 Bibb
NOHIO 12-qt bkts 2.50
MUSHROOMS: NOHIO 12-8 oz cups 6.25
1se 3-1b Ctns 2.75 10-1b Ctns 7.75
PA 12-8 oz cups 6.50 8-1 1b cups
7.90 10-1b Ctns 1se 8.75
ONIONS, DRY: ABOUT STEADY EXCEPT NM
YEL SLIGHTLY HIGHER & WHITE SLIGHTLY
LOWER 50-1b Sks unless otherwise
stated CA Yel Grano Lge wide range
3.50-4.50 mos 3.50-4.00 Med 3.50-
4.00 NM Yel Grano Lge & Lge med
4.25-4.75 Rpkr Sz 4.50-5.00 White
Lge 5.50-6.00 med 5.00-5.50 TX Yel
Grano Lge 4.00-4.50 poor-ord cond
1.00-2.50 med poor-ord cond 1.00-
2.50 Rpkr Sz 4.25 few higher White
Lge 5.50-5.75 Rpkr Sz 4.75 fair qual
3.50-4.00 Red 25-1b sks Lge 5.00
few higher med 5.00
ONIONS, GREEN: NOHIO Bchd 16-qt bkts
2 doz 2.50-2.75 mos 2.50 wirebound
Crts 4-doz 5.00
PARSLEY: NOHIO Bchd Curly 12-qt bkts
2 doz 2.50-2.60 1-1/9 Bu Crts 5-doz
6.50
PEAS, SOUTHERN: NC Bu Hprs Purple Hull
7.50
PEPPERS: LOWER Ca-Wdr Type GA 1-1/9 Bu
Ctns ExLge 6.75 NC ExLge 5.50-6.00
Lge 6.00 med 4.25-5.00
POTATOES: ABOUT STEADY 50-1b Sks US#1
SzA Washed unless otherwise stated
Russets ID 10-oz min 6.75 Ctns Sz 80-
90s 8.00-8.50 few higher 100s 8.00-

4.00-4.50 few higher ord qual &
cond 3.50 Cherry Type 12-pt flts
CA 5.00-5.50 some 6.00 few higher

FRUITS

MELONS: CANTALOUPS: Hlf Ctns AZ 12s
6.00 TX 12s 5.50 15s 6.50 18s 7.50
23s 7.00-7.25 CA 15s 7.00-7.25 18-23s
8.00-8.25 Jbo Crts 1 lot 27s 16.00
36s 18.00
WATERMELONS: ABOUT STEADY per melon
avg 1b FL Crimson Swt & Long Gray
22-1b 1.00-1.25 24½ 1b Jubilee 1.25
GA Crimson Swt 22-1b 1.00-1.25
Jubilee 24½ 1b 1.25 35-1b 2.25-2.50
Long Gray 22-1b 1.00-1.35 25-1b 1.75
28-1b 1.50
CITRUS: 4/5 Bu Crts & Ctns unless
otherwise stated:
GRAPEFRUITS: FL IND RVR 23-48s Pink
Sdls 5.25 Marsh Sdls 4.75 AZ Red
Sdls 27-48s 6.50-6.75 White Sdls
27s & 40s 6.00 32-36s 6.25 48s 5.50
CA Red Sdls 27-36s 6.25-6.75 40-48s
6.50-6.75 White Sdls 18-23s fair
qual 4.25-4.75 27s 6.00 fair qual
4.25-4.75 32s 5.50-6.25 fair qual
4.75-5.00 36s 6.25 40s 5.50-6.00
fair qual 4.75-5.00 48s 4.75-5.50
Best 5.50 56s fair qual 3.00-3.50
LEMONS: ;CA 95s 9.50 115-140s 9.25-
9.50 165s 9.25-10.00 200s 9.50
LIMES: FL 20-1b Ctns Persian Sdls
96 & 126s 5.00-5.50 fair appear 4.00
108s 5.00-6.00
ORANGES: CA Valencia 56s 5.25-5.50
72s 5.25-5.75 88-113s 5.75-6.00 few
higher FL Pope Summer 80-100s 5.00-
5.75 mos 5.00-5.50 125s 5.00

OTHER FRUITS

APPLES: ABOUT STEADY EXCEPT WA WINE-
SAPS LOWER Ctns CA-Stge USFcy 12-3
1b Flm bgs 2¼" or Lgr unless otherwise stated IL Reg-Stge US#1 Lodi
Duchess & Williams Red 6.00 MI Macs
6.00 Red Del 7.00 Romes 6.25 Winesap
6.50 WA Red Del WAExFcy 2½" 9.00-
9.50 Winesaps Reg-Stge WAExFcy 2½"
7.75 Traypack WA G Del WAExFcy 72-80s

Sun Grand 64s 7.00 70-72s 7.00-
7.25 80-88s 6.25-6.50 few higher
Mayfair 70s 7.50 25-1b lugs 1se
Early Sun Grand 80-84s 6.50-7.00
88s 7.00-7.50 mos 7.00 Independence
80-88s 7.00 96s 6.00 Star Grand
80-88s 7.00
PEACHES: 3/4 Bu Ctns USEx#1 GA Red
Globe 2" & up 1 lot 8.25 SC Loring
2-1/8" & up 8.00-8.50
PEARS: 4/5 Bu box WA CA-Stge
D'Anjous WAExFcy 110-135s 10.00-
10.50 AUSTRALIA Packham Triumph
90-135s 10.00-10.50
PLUMS: CA 28-1b lugs 1se Eldorado
3x4 14.00 4x4 12.50-12.75 July
Rosa 4x4 12.00-13.00 3x4x5 10.00-
10.50 Queen Rosa 3x3 3x4 & 3x4x4
13.00 4x4 12.50 Santa Rosa 3x3
3x4 & 3x4x4 13.00 4x4 12.50-13.50
mos 12.50-13.00 3x4x5 10.00-10.50
few 4x5 higher
PINEAPPLES: HI Flts via air 5s
5.75-6.00 6s 5.50-6.00 HONDURAS
40-1b Ctns 8s & 14s 6.00

NEARBY PRODUCE

BEANS: Bu Ctns 6.00
CABBAGE: Green Cant Crts 3.00 50-
1b sks Lge 2.00-2.25 Red wirebnd
Crts 4.00
CUCUMBERS: Grnhse Ctns 12s English
Type 3.50
GREENS: Bu Bkts Coll Kale Must &
TTops 2.50-3.00
LETTUCE: Bibb 5-1b Bkts & Leaf 24-
qt bkts 2.50
SQUASH: Hlf Bu Bkts Yel St'nk &
Zucch 4.00
TOMATOES: Grnhse 8-1b Ctns US#1 Lge
2.50-2.75 mos 2.75 med 2.50 sml
1.75 US#2 1.50

JAMES B. LAING,
LOCAL REPRESENTATIVE   11:50 a.m.
                         1/s

[Cont.]

VOLUME LXII   NO. 134   CINCINNATI, OHIO   DATE JULY 12, 1976 (MONDAY)

CARLOT SHIPMENTS: JULY 9-10-11, 1976
TRUCK SHIPMENTS: JULY 8, 1976
R-DENOTES RAIL   T-DENOTES TRUCK

COMMODITY	R	T	COMMODITY	R	T
APLS:	15	0	MANGO:	0	3
APR:	1	1	MXD CIT:	11	0
BANS:	0	1	MXD DEC:	13	0
BNS:	0	4	MXD HERB:	0	1
BLUBY:	0	33	MXD MELS:	4	2
BROC:	5	20	MXD VEGT:	24	2
CAB:	0	13	NECT:	56	88
CANTS:	101	128	OKRA:	0	7
CARR:	55	38	ONS, D:	26	161
CAUL:	2	18	ONS, G:	0	14
CEL:	20	87	ORGS:	48	0
CHER:	11	0	PCHS:	23	157
CORN:	0	37	PEARS:	2	1
CUX:	0	15	PEPS:	0	62
EGPLT:	0	4	PLUM:	27	74
GARLIC:	0	3	POTS:	258	546
GRPS:	2	117	RADS:	0	1
GRPFT:	4	0	STRBY:	21	55
HDEW:	8	9	SWPOTS:	0	3
LEM:	16	0	TOMS:	97	168
LETT:	209	240	WMELS:	0	156
LIM:	0	9			

SHIPPING POINT INFORMATION REPORTED JULY 9, 1976

/CANTALOUPS/ CALIFORNIA KERN: Demand very good, market steady. Jbo crts 36s 10.00, 27s 8.00
TEXAS PRESIDIO: Demand good, market higher. 12s 4.00-4.50, mos 4.50, 15s 4.00-5.00, mos 5.00, 18s 5.50, few 23s 4.00-5.00, mos 4.50-5.00

/ONIONS, DRY/ CALIFORNIA STOCKTON: Demand good, market slightly higher. 50 lb sks Stockton Yel lge 2.00-2.25, med 2.00-2.25, repkr few 2.50-2.75. Few shippers finishing season, others expecting to start direct seed fields. NEW MEXICO Demand Yel repkr good, market firm, others demand moderate, market steady. 50 lb sks Yel Grano repkr 2.75-3.00, med 2.00-2.25, lge 2.50-2.75, White offerings light repkr 2.25-2.50, med 2.50-2.75, mos 2.50, lge wide range 3.00-3.50

/PEACHES/ GEORGIA Demand good, market about steady, supplies light. Yel Flesh Vars USEx#1 3/4 bu ctns 2" & up 5.50-6.00, mos 5.50, 2-1/8" & up 6.00

CALIFORNIA
SALINAS-WATSONVILLE:
/BROCCOLI/ Demand very good, market slightly higher. Ctns 14s 4.50, 18s 4.75-5.00, mos 4.75 /CAULIFLOWER/ Demand good, market firm. Ctns flm wrpd 12s 4.00-5.00, mos 4.50, 16s 4.00-4.50 /CELERY/ Demand very good, market higher. Crts & Ctns 2s 4.50-5.00, 2½s 5.00, 3s 4.50-5.00, 4s 4.50
/CARROTS/ SALINAS -KING CITY: Demand good, market steady. 48-1 lb flm bgs in sks 4.25, 50 lb sks lse lge few 4.00
/GRAPES, TABLE/ COACHELLA VALLEY: Demand very good, market firm. 22 lb lug US#1 qual Thomp Sdls 9.00, few Exotics 10.00-11.00
/HONEYDEWS/ PALO VERDE: Demand light, market slightly lower. 2/3 crt 5s-6s & 8s 3.50. LAST REPORT.
/LETTUCE/ SANTA MARIA-GUADALUPE-OCEANO: Demand fairly good, market about steady. Iceberg Ctns 24s 4.00-4.50 SALINAS-WATSONVILLE: Demand moderate, market slightly lower. Iceberg Ctns 24s 4.00-4.50
CENTRAL & SOUTH SAN JOAQUIN VALLEY:
/NECTARINES/ Demand good, market steady. 2 lyr lug Tray Pack Early Sun Grand-Independence-Sun Grand 60-72s 4.50, few 64s & lgr 5.00, 80-88s 4.00, few includ straight 88s 3.50-3.75, 96s occ 3.00-3.50. 25 lb tight & volume fill Ctns 70s few 5.50-6.00, 80s 4.50, few includ straight 88s 4.00-4.25, 96s 3.50. 35 lb tight & volume fill ctns 70s 7.70-8.40, 80s 6.30-7.00, 96s few 4.90 /PLUMS/ Demand good, market steady. 28 lb tight & volume fill ctns US#1 Frontier 4x4s 10.00, 4x5s 8.00, Wickson 3x4s 8.00-10.00, 4x4s 8.00, Eldorado-Red Roy-Laroda 4x4s 10.00, 3x4x5s few Nubiana 3x4s 10.00 4x4s 8.00, few Santa Rosa July Santa Rosa 4x4s 10.00, 4x5s 8.00. 4 bkt crt all vars generally 1.00 higher all szs.
/STRAWBERRIES/ Demand good, market steady. 12 pt trays Var vars 4.00-4.75, mos 4.75

GEORGIA

CINCINNATI CARLOT ARRIVALS INCLUDING CHAIN STORES SINCE LAST REPORT & CARS ON TRACK BKN & UNBKN THIS MORNING BASED ON THE LOCAL RR REPORTS FOR MON., JULY 12, 1976

ARRIVALS		UNBKN	BKN
CANTS:	Az 3	-	-
CEL:	Ca 1	-	1
GRPFT:	Fl RT 1	-	-
LEM:	None	-	1
POTS:	Id 3	-	1

CINCINNATI WHOLESALE & CHAIN STORE WAREHOUSE TRUCK RECEIPTS TO THE NEAREST 1/10 RR CAR FOR JUL 12, '76
APLS: Il .5, Mi .6, Oh .5, Wa 1.9 BANS: Impts 9.8 BNS: In 1.0, Ky .2, NC .3, Oh .5, Tn 1.9 BLUBY: Mi .7, NJ .7 BROC: Ca .7 CAB: In .5, Ky 1.2, Mi 1.5, NC .7, Oh 1.8 CANTS: Ca 1.0, Tx 2.3 CARR: Ca .6 CAUL: Ca 1.6 CEL: Ca 2.1, Mi .8, Oh .4 CHER: Wa 2.5 CORN: In 1.7, Ga 4.9, Oh 9.7 CUX: In .2 NJ .6, NC 3.5, Oh .1, Va .5 EGPLT: Fl .2, Ga .2, NC .3 END-ESC: Ca .2 Oh .4 GRPFT: Ca .8 GRPS, TBL: Ca 2.8 GRNS: Oh .8 LEM: Ca .1 LETT: Ca 4.8, Oh .9, Wl 1.1 NECT: Ca 1.6 ONS, D: Ca 1.0, Mi 1.1, Oh 1.1, Tx 2.1 ONS, G: Oh .5 ORGS: Ca .9, Fl 1.6 PCHS: Ca .3, Ga 2.0, Il .2, Oh .2 PEARS: Australia .3 PEPS: Fl .7, Ga .4, NC 1.0, Oh .2 PLUM: Ca 1.4 POTS: Al 7.3, Ca 1.0, Id 1.0 RADS: Mi .5, Oh .5 SPIN: In .2, Oh .2 SQU: Ky .2, In .1, NC .4, Oh .4, NJ .2 STRBY: Ca 3.7 SWPOTS: NC .5 TOMS: Ar 3.2, Ca 3.5, Fl .3, Oh 2.9 TURNS: Ca .2 WMELS: Fl 7.1, Ga 4.1 ARTS: Ca .1 CKL-CAB: Oh .1 LIM: Fl .4 MANGO: Fl .1 MUSHRMS: Oh .2, Pa .9 OKRA: Mx .1 PARSL: Oh .2 PEAS, FLD: Fl .2 PINES: Hi 2.1 RASP: Mi .2 WCRESS: Fl .2 TOTAL: 122.3

MICHIGAN-Cont'd. early & late vars
/CELERY/ Demand good, market steady Crts 2-2½-3s 5.50, 4s & 6s 5.25, Hearts Ctns flm wrpd 24s 7.00
/RADISHES/ Offerings light, demand very good, market steady. Ctns flm bgs 30-6 oz Red 3.00, 24-8 oz Wh-

2¼" & up few 6.50
SOUTH CAROLINA Trading active, demand exceeds supply, market firm. Yel Flesh Vars USEx#1 3/4 bu ctns & crts 2" & up 5.50-6.00, mos 6.00, 2-1/8" & up 6.00-6.50, mos 6.50, few 2¼" & up 7.00

/POTATOES/ ALABAMA Demand good, market Rnd Rnd about steady, Rnd Whites higher. Wshd & sacked US#1A Rnd Reds 100 lb 5.00-5.50, mos 5.00, 50 lb 2.75-3.00, mos 2.75, 20 lb 1.20-1.30, 10 lb bld 70-75¢, 5 lb bld 40-43¢, Rnd White 100 lb 5.00, 50 lb 2.75, 20 lb 1.20-1.30, 10 lb bld 70-75¢, 5 lb bld 40-43¢
CALIFORNIA Demand very good, market firm. US#1A cwt basis mos mixed manifest Long White 100 lb sks 3.00, 50 lb ctns 4.00, 10 lb paper sks bld 4.50-5.00, 50 lb ctn 80-100s 6.00, US#1 10 oz min 4.00-4.50, US#2 2.25-2.50, Rnd Red offerings very light--insufficient to quote, Centennial Russets 50 lb ctn 80-90s 9.00-10.00, 100 lb sks Non SzA 3.00
NORTH CAROLINA Demand very good, market higher. US#1 SzA wshd Rnd White 100 lb sks 5.00, 50 lb sks 2.75

/WATERMELONS/ SOUTH GA-NORTH FL-SOUTH AL: Demand light, market steady but firm undertone. Var vars mos Long Grays-Crimson Sweets-Jubliees. Per cwt 18-24 lb avg 2.50, 25-30 lb avg 2.50-2.75, 15-17 lb avg few 2.00-2.25, 32-38 lb avg Jubliees 2.75-3.25, mos 3.00

NORTH CAROLINA
FAISON AUCTION SALES JULY 10 (SAT):
/CUCUMBERS/ Offerings light, market higher. Bu bkt & 1-1/9 bu crts unwxd med 85% US#1 5.65-8.05, mos 6.30-7.50 /PEPPERS/ Offerings heavy, market about steady. Bu bkt & 1-1/9 bu crt Ca-Wdr 85% US#1 lge 2.75-4.50 best mos 3.30-4.50, med-lge 2.50-3.45, mos around 3.00, Cubanelle 85% US#1 2.00-4.50, Long Hots 3.00-4.70, Hlf Bu bkts 2.00-2.30, Hung Wax Hlf bu bkt 4.55-5.60 /SQUASH/ Offerings light. Bu bkt & crts Acorn offerings insufficient to quote, Butternut 85% US#1 3.15-4.20

MICHIGAN
/BLUEBERRIES/ Offerings light, demand very good at lower prices, market slightly lower. Var vars mos Early Blue Crop 12 pt flt flm wrpd sml-med 5.75. Some growers between

ite 3.25-3.50 /STRAWBERRIES/ No offerings--most growers finished for the season. LAST REPORT.

TEXAS
HEREFORD-HI PLAINS: /ONIONS, DRY/ Demand repkr & lge good, market firm; Meds demand moderate, market steady. 50 lb sks Yel Grano lge 2.75, med 2.25, repkr 3.25-3.50, mos 3.50, White lge 3.50-3.75, med 2.50-2.75, mos 2.75, repkr 2.50
/POTATOES/ Demand good, market steady. Cwt basis Rnd Reds wshd US#1 2½-3½" 5.75-6.00, SzA 5.50 FIRST REPORT.

/TOMATOES/ CALIFORNIA CHULA VISTA: For lighter offerings demand very good, market steady. Breakers-Light Red no grade mark Place pack Flts 2 lyr 5x5-5x6s 4.00-4.50. Lugs 3 lyr 6x6s & 6x7s 5.00-6.00, 6x6s mos 6.00, 6x7s mos 5.00 CUTLER-OROSI: Demand inppoved fairly good, market about steady. Breakers-Light Red Place pack no grade mark wide range in qual 2 lyr flt 4x5-5x6s 3.50, 3 lyr lugs 6x6s & 6x7s 4.50-5.00. Cherry Type 12 pt flt 3.00-4.00, mos 3.50

U. S. DEPARTMENT OF AGRICULTURE
AGRICULTURAL MARKETING SERVICE
FRUIT AND VEGETABLE DIVISION
ROOM 3532 · 550 MAIN STREET
CINCINNATI, OHIO 45202
OFFICIAL BUSINESS
PENALTY FOR PRIVATE USE, $300

POSTAGE AND FEES PAID
U.S. DEPARTMENT OF
AGRICULTURE
AGR 101

FIRST CLASS

IMPORTANT
F & V MARKET REPORT NO. 134
12, JULY 1976.

R. B. Peddersen
Director Food Services
Jewish Hospital
3200 Burnett Avenue
Cincinnati, OH   45229

Panic Buying. An otherwise capable buyer can be panicked into buying more than he needs or paying prices that are too high. Emergencies—real or imaginary—are the basis for panic buying. Imaginary emergencies are those that sales representatives and periodicals tend to exaggerate beyond reality, such as droughts, frosts, strikes, shortages, or anything that might affect the flow of merchandise.

Unlike commercial restaurants, institutions need not stock certain items listed as scarce. Usually it is unwise to rush into buying quantities of an item because it is said to be in danger of becoming scarce or increasing in price. Frequently the prediction does not materialize. The food buyer must learn to avoid getting overly concerned about being short of certain items.

Extravagant Buying. The extravagant buyer does not appreciate the value of a dollar. He has no norm or guide; moderation is not in his vocabulary so costs mean little to him. Often he pays high prices for foods that are scarce or luxury items. This buyer wants almost everything he sees and cannot understand why a superior questions his judgment. He is easily captivated by what is new or a little different, even though what he has is perfectly satisfactory.

To avoid this problem the food buyer must thoroughly compare prices at all times. He must likewise be certain of the actual necessity of the purchase.

Miserly Buying. As stated earlier, the buyer does not always need to have the best. On the other hand, one should not buy inferior products just to save a few dollars or cut down expenses.

The food buyer must not descend to purchasing perishables, such as poultry, as an example, that could not be sold over the counter because it has started to deteriorate. It is a waste of money and time to invest in produce that has begun to decay with the intent of sorting out the good stuff.

The food buyer must try to avoid being tagged as "cheap." His responsibility is to provide for the normal needs of the institution, and he does not need to be overly concerned about the cost of ordinary operating expenses.

Personality Buying. Some buyers are influenced too much by the personality of sales representatives. To give most of the orders to one person simply because he is more likable than the others is contrary to good business practice.

Because this type of buying eliminates competition, it can be extremely costly. Showing favor in this way should prevail only when an individual's product measures up in every respect with that of his competitors. In other words, the quality, price, and service must be as good as that of other companies.

Friendship Buying. Friendship is a common sales approach. "I happen to know so-and-so," or "Your friend, so-and-so, sent me to see you," are typical. Sometimes the salesman has almost been assured of an order before he calls. A buyer has to be everlastingly on his guard lest he be unduly influenced in this manner. We usually want to give a friend—or a friend of a friend—a break, but sound business principles must be kept uppermost in mind.

What about developing friendships with sales representatives? The food buyer must beware of compromising himself or his institution. Buying can be dangerous for the buyer who allows friendship to insinuate itself into his work. Human nature being what it is, this mistake has even jeopardized careers.

Sentiment Buying. It is easy to let the heart rule the head. A buyer must be on his guard against any sales approach based upon sentiment. The answer to such approaches is simply, "I'd like to buy from you. I'd like to buy from everyone who calls but, of course, that's impossible. So, I must make my choice as I see it at the time. You are welcome to call back, but I cannot assure you of any business unless something unforeseen turns up."

The Satisfied Buyer. This buyer operates as though no possible improvements can be made under any circumstances. He puts unqualified trust in those with whom he deals, without even comparing quality or price. This dangerous procedure can lead to considerable monetary loss.

The term "satisfied" is absent from the vocabulary of the smart, progressive buyer who is on the alert to every possible saving or improvement. He sees as many sales representatives as possible and is constantly improving his ability. This effort pays big dividends in the long run. Likewise, it alerts sales representatives that they can take nothing for granted.

CONSTRUCTIVE PROCEDURES. In discussing the preceding buying mistakes some of the positive measures for correct buying have been pointed out. Following are some more constructive factors that should be part of a food buyer's policies.

Sales Representatives. It is usually a sign of ignorance of his tremendous responsibility if a buyer is inconsiderate, harsh, ungentlemanly, or suspicious of sales representatives in general. Most sales representatives are honest, hardworking, and know their products, as well as having many useful tips about purchasing. For the most part, they are educated, trained, and capable.

The food buyer should view these men as being in a position to help him in many ways. There is always the possibility that the salesman may have a money-saving proposition. Selling is highly competitive, and companies constantly generate new inducements to increase sales. Such advantages will never be realized unless the buyer's policy is to try to see every sales representative if at all possible.

Quality. Needless to say, the more the food buyer knows, the more he will get out of every dollar spent because price is directly related to quality and quantity.

Price. Likewise, the food buyer must keep abreast of current prices for specific grades and quality. It is impossible to study all the market reports and government and consumer bulletins, but at least he should keep some kind of a record so that he can readily compare prices when necessary, particularly for items that are purchased frequently. For purchases made at rare intervals, such as equipment, the buyer should "shop around," until he is satisfied he is getting the best combination of price and service.

Average Consumption. The food buyer should always strive to purchase in accordance with his needs. Before making any purchase he should compute the average consumption of the item over a definite period. The amount to order then follows logically.

Competitive Buying. If the food buyer fails to capitalize on the competition between companies, he loses financially. Instead of being a buyer, he is solely an "order giver." On the other hand, the buyer who capitalizes on competition will avoid such pitfalls as satisfied, one-house, sentiment, and friendship buying.

Quantity Buying. In general, buying in quantity means lower costs. Usually a distributor is willing to reduce the cost per unit if it can get volume business. The cost difference may amount to only 25 to 35 cents a case, but in lots of 10, 20, or more cases even small savings add up to a considerable amount. This is why it is so important for the buyer to know the average consumption of each item over a definite period.

Because there is the element of chance in most quantity buying, the food buyer must consider all factors before making such a purchase. What is the predicted supply of the item? If the supply is above normal, the price is likely to drop after a short time. Conversely, if there is a shortage, the price will no doubt rise as the supply dwindles. A normal supply means the price will remain stationary, barring something unforeseen.

In normal times, many food distributors contract for future delivery over a period of time. Suppose the food buyer wants 75 cases of an item. After getting the best price for the quality desired, he arranges to take delivery in 10-, 15- or 25-case lots and to pay as delivered. This procedure is called "futures"- order it now, take it out as needed.

Seasonal Buying. Even with modern transportation and frozen foods, seasonal buying has not been eliminated completely. In fact, the food buyer can make costly mistakes simply because many fresh foods can not be purchased year around, in or out of the regular season. Seasons directly affect canned and frozen foods, so the buyer must be alert and familiar with the terms "old" and "new" pack and all that they signify.

Supply and Demand. Fundamentally the price of all merchandise is controlled by the demand for it. Here a smart buyer's knowledge can pay high dividends. Some items are more affected than others, with perishables of all kinds heading the list.

At times, for instance, excellent buys of wholesale cuts of meat are available. And, the food buyer is far more likely to reap such an advantage from a jobber than directly from a packer. When a packer is overstocked on an item he calls the jobber to take it off his hands at a greatly reduced price. The jobber can pass this saving along because he wants a quick turnover.

Service. A buyer pays not only for merchandise but for service. To the experienced buyer, service includes such things as timely deliveries, an occasional emergency delivery, exactness in filling orders without padding or substitution, merchandise delivered in perfect condition, willingness to make adjustments or take back items for credit if necessary, procuring articles not in stock, efficient billing, and congenial relations.

In return, the buyer should be reasonable in his demands or complaints. A practical way of avoiding unreasonable demands is to obtain all the facts before pushing a complaint. Even though a vendor is obligated, patience pays higher dividends than a harsh or threatening attitude.

Deliveries. The responsibility of the food buyer does not end when the order has been placed. Unless the receiving clerk is vigilant, considerable loss is inevitable. Particularly in transporting foodstuffs, shortages, breakage, and the wrong merchandise are not rare exceptions. Certain merchandise ought to be weighed, so a large floor scale and a small table scale are indispensable.

To insure routine adjustments, deliverymen should list mistakes and sign the slip. The same applies to anything picked up for return and credit. Any faults on the part of the deliverymen must be brought to the attention of the main office; if the condition persists, more drastic action should be considered.

FOOD COSTS AND THE 40 THIEVES [1]

When you realize that foodservice products have two *perishable* time tables—*perishable* in the raw state, and *perishable* again in the processed state—you begin to understand some of the complexities. Here is a list of "40 Thieves" or causes of high food costs. There are many more, though some will not apply to all units because of operating differences.

[1]Robert C. Petrie, "Food Costs and the 40 Thieves," *Cooking for Profit*, November 1972. Reprinted with permission.

40 THIEVES

Purchasing
1. Purchasing too much.
2. Purchasing for too high a cost.
3. No detailed specifications—quality, weight, type.
4. No competitive purchasing policy.
5. No cost budget for purchasing.
6. No audit of invoices and payments.

Receiving
7. Theft by receiving man.
8. No system of credits for low quality, damaged merchandise, or goods not received.
9. Lack of facilities and/or scales.
10. Perishable foods left out of proper storage.

Storage
11. Foods improperly placed in storage (e.g., fats, eggs, milk near strong cheese and fish).
12. Storage at wrong temperature and humidity.
13. No daily inspection of stored goods.
14. Poor sanitation in dry and refrigerated storage areas.
15. Prices not marked in storeroom.
16. No physical or perpetual inventory policy.
17. Lack of single responsibility for food storage and issues.

Issuing
18. No control or record of foods issued from storeroom.
19. Permitting forced or automatic issues.

Preparation
20. Excessive trim of vegetables and meats.
21. No check on raw yields.
22. No use of end products for production of low cost meals.

Production
23. Overproduction, Overproduction, Overproduction!
24. Wrong methods of cooking.
25. Cooking at wrong temperatures.
26. Cooking too long.
27. No scheduling of foods to be processed (too early, too late).
28. Not using standard recipes.
29. Not cooking in small batches.

Service

30. No standard portion sizes.

31. No standard size utensils for serving.

32. No care of leftovers.

33. No record of food produced and leaving production area.

34. Carelessness (spillage, waste, cold food).

Sales

35. Food taken out of building.

36. Unrecorded sales and incorrect pricing; "not charges" or cash not turned in.

37. No food popularity index or comparison of sales and inventory consumption.

38. No sales records to detect trends.

39. Poor pricing of menu items.

40. Employee meal costs—overproduction or unauthorized meals.

AN UNCOMPLICATED ACCOUNTING SYSTEM

This section includes a simple-to-keep set of internal records. Though developed for a small hospital, this system is equally applicable to large and small hospitals, schools, colleges, in-plant and industrial foodservice, as well as most commercial operations. For more information on varied accounting systems, or in-depth study of financial records, accounting systems, and financial reports, refer to the sources listed in the bibliography. The purpose of this section is simply to present a method of following and controlling food by accounting methods.

A good system of record keeping is simple to keep while providing both control of foods and information for easy future utilization.

Invoices should be recorded for a standard accounting period. The example used here is for a calendar month. The length of the accounting period should be determined for each operation. The shorter the period, the more control the operator has. If manpower is available to provide one-week accounting periods, then that period is recommended. The earlier an out-of-control situation or a problem is identified, the earlier it can be resolved.

INVOICE RECORD. The system presented here shows invoices recorded on one continuous record (Figure No. 13). Each invoice is charged against the specific accounting areas the operator wishes to control. Figure No. 16 shows 12 categories that needed control at that particular operation. A shorter and perhaps more common grouping would be six to eight categories as follows:

1. Meat—beef, veal, lamb, pork, sausage and meat products, chicken, turkey and other fowl and products made from them. Fresh, frozen, canned, and dehydrated.

2. Seafood—all fish, crustaceans, etc., whether fresh, frozen, canned, or dehydrated.

3. Convenience Foods—frozen, canned, or dehydrated foods such as beef stroganoff, spaghetti and meat balls, and so on. If it is not desirable to keep these items as a separate category, then convenience items may be charged against the category which names their major ingredient. This is always the first ingredient on the label list of contents.

4. Dairy Products—butter, cheese, eggs, milk, ice cream, and such substitute dairy products as oleomargarine.

5. Groceries—canned, dried, and dehydrated fruits, vegetables, grain products, jams, jellies, etc.

6. Bakery Supplies and Baked Goods—items used in baking, such as flour and cake mixes, may be included here or under groceries. Baked goods purchased as a finished product such as bread, cake, and pie belong here.

7. Wines and Liquors—may be included in food accounting by the institutional operator, but should be kept as a wholly separate accounting category by restaurants and hotels.

8. Fresh and Frozen Fruits and Vegetables.

The purpose of these breakdowns is to establish percentage consumption guidelines which then can be used to determine over-expenditure or theft. These breakdowns also aid in predicting future expenses or the effect of menu changes on expenditures. Keeping these records forces close examination of invoices and a working knowledge of what goods are in the house at any given time.

FIGURE 13

MONTH OF June

PERPETUAL MONTHLY RECEIVING INVOICE FOR THE MONTH OF

PAGE 7 of 7   FROM June 2

INVOICE #	COMPANY NAME	DATE	INVOICE TOTAL	MEAT (1-6)	SEAFOOD (7)	SHTY & DAIRY (8-9)	FR & FRZ FR & VEG (10-12)
	Dairy Prod	1	7051			1485	
	"	2	5419			1460	
2641	"	3	2278			350	
	Oranges/Prod	2	566			516	
	Hurley	1	822				
	Hurley	3	1462				
509337	Armstrong	1	3030				
520619	"	2	4020				
521216	"	3	3410				
059	Cagiasrava	1	127.40	127.40			
153.39		2	114.70	114.70			
154		2	34.78	34.78			
182.77		1	93.75	93.75			
78.88	Pet. C.	1	105.94	105.94			
391		1	186.05	186.05			
1786		1	147.37			147.37	
293.13		1	72.1			72.1	
		2	110.05	55	5505		
		8	315801	315801			
		1	940	940			
		1	104.90				
		1	114.23			114.23	72.50
		2	92.28				3560
		1	501		501		2498
			132070				
		8	7488				
		8	13.1				
		8	30.90				
		1	1698				
		1	1825				
		1	3410				
		1	3640				
		1	131.19	131.19			
637117	Woodman Coffee		4449				
	PAGE TOTAL		253001	100679	10505	25423	5472
	TOTAL TODATE		253001	100679	10505	21823	36428

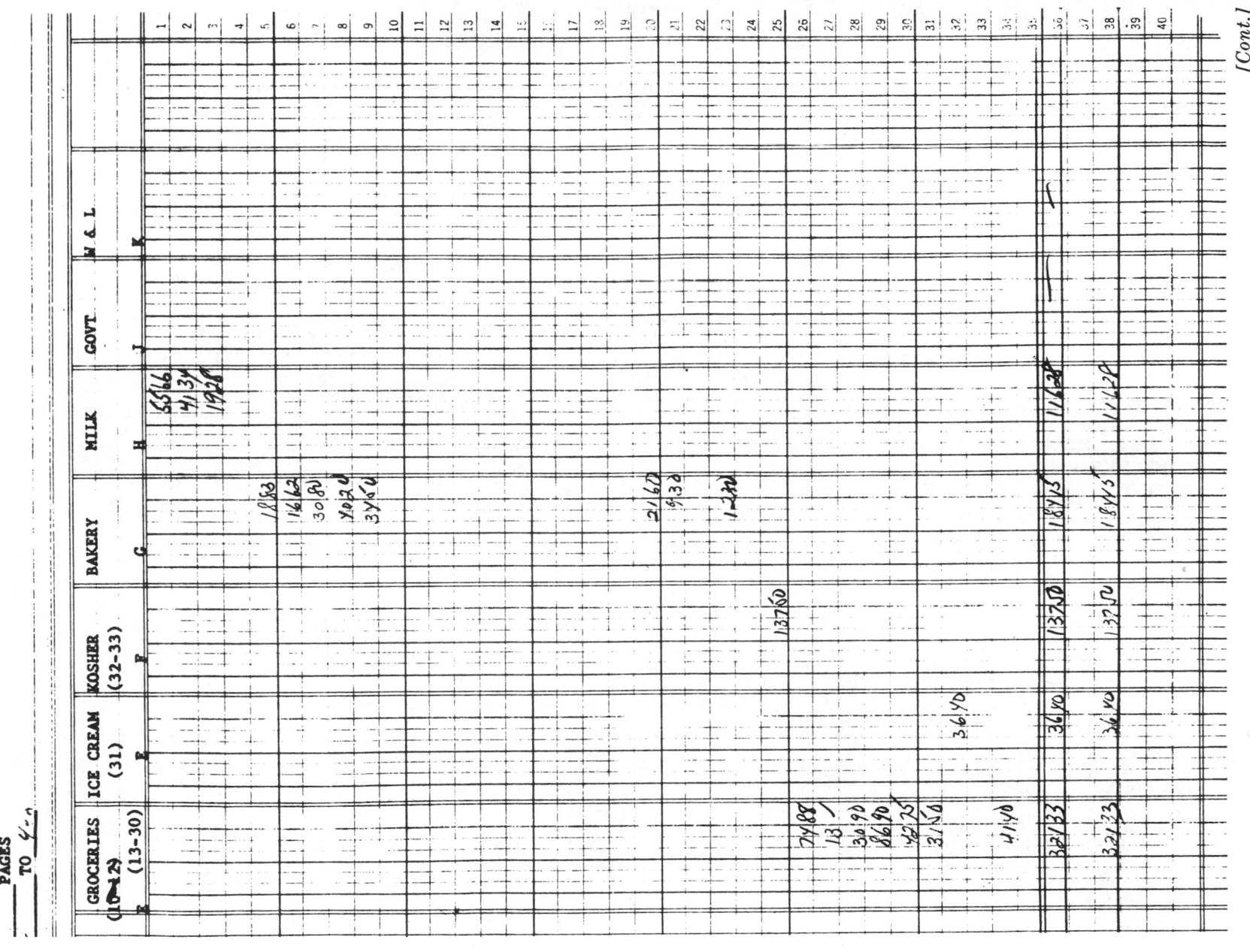

[Cont.]

FIGURE 13—[Cont.]
DAILY MILK, PIE, BREAD, INVENTORY ORDER SHEET

		MON.	TUES	WED	THURS	FRI	SAT	SUN
MILK ½ PT	L							
	O							
CHOC ½ PT	L							
	O							
BUT MILK ½ PT	L							
	O							
ORANGE ½ PT	L							
	O							
SKIM ½ PT	L							
	O							
COTT CHEESE 5# CONT	L							
	O							
WHITE BRD	L							
	O							
WHT BRD	L							
	O							
RYE BRD	L							
	O							
ROLLS	L							
	O							
BAGELS	L							
	O							
PIES	L							
	O							

ORDER/RECEIVING/INVENTORY RECORD (Figure No. 14).

Often the only record of receipt of food is a daily invoice record. It is desirable to have also a central record from which one can determine shortages and amount of product in the house, and from which one can refer to past consumption.

Inventories should be taken at least monthly. There are two different kinds of inventories. One is called a desk inventory and the other is called a physical inventory.

A desk inventory will tell an operator how much of any product (or all products) should be on hand at any time. A desk inventory is done by adding the amount of product received and subtracting the amount of product used since the last desk inventory. Thus, if there was 1 box of apples on hand on February 28, 6 boxes received during March, and 5 boxes issued before March 31, the desk inventory would be $1 + 6 = 7 - 5 = 2$ boxes.

A desk inventory is important because it tells what *should be* on hand at any given time. In order to know what *is* on hand, a physical inventory must be taken. To take a physical inventory, one must actually count the items in the storage areas.

If the physical inventory reveals, using the earlier example, only 1 box of apples on hand then the operator must decide whether:

    (a) 1 box of apples was stolen, or

    (b) 1 box of apples was never received, or

    (c) last month's physical inventory was wrong, or

    (d) an error has been made in bookkeeping.

Having been alerted, the operator can track down the cause and take corrective action.

Having an inventory also tells the operator the dollar value of the food on hand. Since there is commonly more than one price on food items in a weekly or monthly accounting period, the operator has a choice of dollar values to put on each product. He may choose to use the average price, the first price, or the last price paid. Since food prices fluctuate frequently, the most common and the easiest method is to use the last price paid.

A good inventory record will categorize all food items into the same groupings as used in the invoice record. Figure No. 14 is a page from an inventory/order/receiving book which allows an operator to keep a record of items received, disbursed, the desk inventory, the physical inventory, and consumption.

As orders are written, they are entered above a split line under the day of the month on which delivery is anticipated. On the day the goods are delivered, the actual quantity received is entered under the split line by the receiving clerk. This makes it easy to identify shortages immediately. The latest price paid is entered in the price column at the right side of the book.

At the end of the month, a physical inventory is taken directly into the "end inventory" column. This figure is then multiplied by the latest price and becomes the dollar inventory. The quantity consumed is determined by adding the beginning inventory (last month's ending inventory) to the quantities received and subtracting the end inventory. There is a column for this figure at the far right-hand side of the page.

The consumption figure is transferred to a master consumption book which holds the consumption figures for a three-year period. Thus, the operator can trace the long-term consumption of each item. This record is a tremendous aid in making future contract purchase commitments.

The Order/Receiving/Inventory Record has sections for food supplies which are the same categories as the Invoice Record. A second part of the Order/Receiving/Inventory Record is for supplies. At the back of the Order/Receiving/Inventory Record is a page which recaps the total dollar value of all goods by their respective categories.

BUDGET REPORTS. Every foodservice operator has an obligation to supply all relevant statistics that can be derived from his operation. (There are other more sophisticated statistics which are probably meaningful only to corporate or financial foodservice people.)

Figure No. 15 is typical of a form which might be used in an institutional operation. A commercial operation would expand the form to allow for such additional costs as rent, utilities, payroll taxes, and insurance.

FIGURE 14

HILLSIDE HOSPITAL FOOD SERVICE MONTHLY INVENTORY/ORDER/RECEIVING RECORD

#	ITEM	UNIT	INV. BEG.	M	T	W	TH	F	END	S/S	M	T	W	TH	F	END	S/S	M	T	W
	BEEF			4	5	6	7	8		9/10	11	12	13	14	15		16/17	18	19	20
1	Liver, Steer	lb.			60							25							27	
2	Round, MBG No. 158	lb.			20							92							99	
3	Round, MBG No. 170 Corned	lb.	10		40															
4	Round, MGB No. 1167r	lb.	32																	
5	Round, MBG No. 1168r	lb.																		
6	Round, diced 1 in. MBG No. 135	lb.	40																	
7	Round, ground 80/20	lb.			50							80							50	
8	Flk Stk MBG No. 193	lb.																		
9	Skt Stk 1-1/2 in.	lb.	57		100														50	
10	Strip Loin MBG 178	lb.																		
11	Strip Stks MBG 1178	lb.	248																61	
12	Bologna 100% Beef	lb.	133		14							61							23	
13	Salami 100% Beef	lb.	52									16							24	
14	Franks 8 to 100% Beef	lb.	34										50							
15	Pastrami, Pickled Roumanian	lb.																	45	
16	Patties, 4 oz. 80/20	lb.	40									45							75	
17	Salisbury Steak, 5 oz. 80/20	pc.	240					60											60	
18	Stuffed Cabbage	cs.						5												
19	Stuffed Peppers	cs.																		
20	Knockwurst, 4 to Skinless	lb.																	45	
21	Beef Burgundy	cs.																		
22	Beef Stew	cs.																		
23	Top Round—Cooked	lb.																		
24	Bttm Round—Cooked	lb.																		
25	Corned Beef—Cooked	lb.																		
26																				
27																				

PAGE 1   TOTAL 868.01

H	F	END	S/S	M	T	W	TH	F	END	S/S	M	T	W	TH	S/S	END INV	@		=	CON-SUMED	
	22		23/24	25	26	27	28	29		30/31		2			2/3						
												60					48			112	1
					390/376												74			733½	2
												30					84			50	3
																75	1 20	90	—	-43	4
																64	1 10	70	40	-64	5
				77												40	85	34	—	77	6
				2½ 59/50								39					64			256½	7
																					8
				59/60								120					67			267	9
																					10
																504	1 10	554	40	356	11
			15	2½/23								7				21	82	17	22	73½	12
			12	2½/25												43	82	36	98	86	13
				30/30								59				55	90	49	50	75	14
																	84			45	15
				60/60								50					70			250	16
																	33			840	17
												7				11/3	12 65	4	21	4 2/3	18
																					19
																	85			45	20
																					21
																					22
																					23
																					24
																					25
																10	1 20	12	—		26
																					27
																	868	01			

FIGURE 15
FOOD SERVICE BUDGET REPORT

June 1971

	This Month Actual Expenditures	This Month Budgeted Expenditures	This Year To Date Actual Expenditures	This Year To Date Budgeted Expenditures	Expenditures %	12 Month moving Average
Food Service Personnel	$ 14 211	$ 16 274	$ 85 719	$ 95 992	89.5	$
Clerical	716	713	4 401	4 214	104.4	
620.9 Total Salaries	$14 927	$17 057	$ 90 120	$100 206	89.9	$ 15 444
620.30 Equip. Repairs	124	150	933	1 000	93.3	190
620.51 Personnel Expenses	-	25	48	75	64.0	-
620.59 Food Supplies	14 892	14 250	86 485	86 750	99.7	13 953
620.60 Kitchen Supplies	2 195	1 500	14 021	10 640	131.8	2 035
620.75 Teaching & Training	250	400	799	850	94.0	76
Total Supplies & Expenses	$17 461	$16 325	$102 286	$ 99 315	103.0	$ 16 254
Sub Total Expenditures	$ 32 388	$ 33 382	$192 406	$199 521	96.4	$ 31 698
Cutback		(1 242)		(7 459)	(3.7)	
Total Expenditures	$ 32 388	$ 32 140	$192 406	$192 062	100.2	$ 31 698

This Month:	Patients	Staff	Total	12 Month Moving Aver.
Meals Served	13 142	7 104	20 246	xxxxxxxxxxx
Salary Expense	$ 12 098	$ 2 829	$ 14 927	xxxxxxxxxxx
Salaries per meal served	$ .92	$ .40	$ .71	$ .76
Food Expense	$ 9 183	$ 4 966	$ 14 149	xxxxxxxxxxx
Food Cost per meal served	$ .70	$ .70	$ .70	$ .71
Supplies Expense	$ 1 821	$ 427	$ 2 248	xxxxxxxxxxx
All other Expenses	$ 861	$ 203	$ 1 064	xxxxxxxxxxx
Food & Supplies Cost	$ 11 004	$ 5 393	$ 16 397	xxxxxxxxxxx
Food & Supplies Cost per meal served	$ .84	$ .76	$ .81	$ .80
Total Direct Costs	$ 23 102	$ 8 222	$ 31 324	xxxxxxxxxxx
Direct Costs per meal served	$ 1.76	$ 1.17	$ 1.55	1.57

This Year to date:	Patients	Staff	Total	12 Month Moving Aver.
Meals Served	77 353	43 036	120 389	xxxxxxxxxxx
Salary Expense	$72 851	$17 269	$ 90 120	xxxxxxxxxxx
Salaries per meal served	$ .94	$ .40	$ .75	$ .76
Food Expense	$55 061	$30 623	85 684	xxxxxxxxxxx
Food Cost per meal served	$ .71	$ .71	$ .71	$ .71
Supplies Expense	$11 007	$ 2 581	$ 13 588	xxxxxxxxxxx
All other Expenses	$ 2 000	$ 470	$ 2 470	xxxxxxxxxxx
Food & Supplies Cost	$66 068	$33 204	$99 272	xxxxxxxxxxx
Food & Supplies Cost per meal served	$ .86	$ .77	$ .83	$ .80
Total Direct Costs	$38 649	$50 473	$189 392	xxxxxxxxxxx
Direct Costs per meal served	$ 1.79	$ 1.17	1.57	1.57

COST ANALYSIS (Figure No. 16) **Top and left hand side.** This section of the form allows an analysis of where the food dollar was spent during the past month. An explanation of the categories and the reason for the 11-section breakdown were discussed in the section on the Monthly Invoice Record. Note that the column on the far left details the performance for the same month last year. This figure is used rather than a twelve-month average because the number of meals served in the same month of different years is comparable, and therefore a better comparison than a moving average of unlike months.

The current month's consumption in each category, as well as an average for the year-to-date (per month) is calculated to give a broad general measure of dollars being currently spent. The amount of money spent in each category should remain about the same. If there is a large difference, there should be a good explanation.

For example, in 1971 we were spending two to three per cent more of our food dollar on meat than in 1970. This was because of our increased use of convenience meats and a decrease in the amount of seafood used. Kosher had dropped because of a decrease in kosher patients. Bakery increased because we reduced our on-premise baking. Milk decreased both because of the availability of other beverages and because we converted to bulk milk dispensers from packaged half-pints.

Frequently these percentage changes represent a trade-off. Bakery costs increase with more buy-outs, but the cost of raw products used in baking, such as flour, eggs, and shortening, decreases. Only with these percentage calculations can one accurately measure how much new programs are costing.

Right-hand side (Figure No. 16). This section of the form contains the statistical analysis of the major phases of the operation. The record is meaningful because it gives a thumbnail sketch of everything going on during the particular month and year, as well as the long-term trend. To understand this section, and its figures and indications, a knowledge of industry-wide standards of performance is necessary.

"Number of patient days" is the total number of occupied beds for the month. In the hospital used as an example, there is a large group of day-care patients (44) who eat only one meal

per day at the hospital. To calculate the patient days for food-service purposes, the number of day-care patient days is divided by three. This is then added to the in-patient census to produce the total number of patient days. As explained later, this figure is essential in forecasting budget needs for the coming year.

"Cost per patient day" is achieved by dividing the total direct costs by the total number of patient days. Note from the example that the cost per patient day is less than three times the direct cost per patient meal. This is because not every patient eats every meal.

Here is an example of how these figures aided this operation. A closed ward was opened, the day-care program was expanded, and the policies governing weekend passes were changed. It was essential to know what the effect on the foodservice budget would be. With statistics on past cost per patient day, the operator could calculate cost per patient day for a full three-meal per day census. By interpolating these figures and using a percentage factor for the gain in census, he was able to calculate the increased costs in minutes. Without the ongoing figures on record, the increased costs might have taken days to forecast.

"Patient meals per patient day" is derived by dividing the total number of patient meals served by the total number of patient days. The "total meals per patient day" figure is arrived at by dividing the *total* meals served by the total number of patient days. The difference between the patient meals and total meals is the number of staff meals per patient day.

Knowing these three figures enables the operator to see the relationship between them, as well as the trend of patient and staff eating habits month-by-month, season-by-season, and year-by-year. Fluctuations in these figures signal such things as a changing program and a changing attitude towards menus.

"Number of man-hours worked" is the actual number from payroll records. Knowing this figure is important in controlling labor costs. Once the operator has done a labor analysis, it becomes possible to carefully regulate vacation

June 1971   Fig. 16 — COST ANALYSIS

	This Month	This Year	12 Mo. Avg.
No. of Patient Days	6 084	36 879	xxx
Cost per Patient Day	$ 3.80	3.76	xxx
Patient Meals per Patient Day	2.16	2.10	xxx
Total Meals per Patient Day	3.33	3.26	3.27
No. of Man-Hours Worked	3 421	20 797	3 538
No. of Meals Served	20 246	120 389	xxx
Meals served per Man-Hour Worked	5.9	5.8	5.6
Salary Expenses	$4 297	$90 120	xxx
Cost per Man-Hour Worked	$ 4.18	$ 4.33	$ 4.28
Cafeteria Income	$3 886	$23 218	$3 717
Check Avg.	$ .70	.68	n.a.
Income per Staff Meal	$ .48	.54	n.a.

This Month

Avg. Last Year	%	FOOD	totals	meat	sea.	dairy	veg.	groc.	ice cr.	kosh.	bake.	milk	govt.	liquor
12 866		Purchases	13 216	4 518	420	1 128	2 246	1 720	178	190	1 743	1 047	43	(17)
11 291		+ Beg. Inven.	11 182	1 682	83	435	352	8 314	53	65	33	12	—	153
24 157		= Sub Total	24 398	6 200	503	1 563	2 598	1 034	231	255	1 776	1 059	43	136
10 736		− End. Inven.	10 249	1 536	207	574	547	6 950	50	82	129	26	—	148
13 421		= Total Cons.	14 149	4 664	296	989	2 051	3 084	181	173	1 647	1 033	43	(12)

This Month Last Year	%	FOOD EXPENDITURE	$ this month	%	$ this year	avg.	%
4 691	35.0	Meat	4 664	33.0	28 120	4 687	32.9
497	3.7	Seafood	296	2.1	2 371	395	2.8
837	6.2	Shrtg & Dairy	989	7.0	6 360	1 060	7.4
1 535	11.4	Fr & Froz Veg.	2 051	14.5	10 519	1 753	12.3
3 065	22.8	Groceries	3 084	21.8	19 263	3 210	22.5
—	—	Ice Cream	181	1.2	793	132	0.9
341	2.5	Kosher	173	1.2	1 473	246	1.7
1 147	8.6	Bakery	1 647	11.6	8 423	1 404	9.8
1 171	8.9	Milk	1 033	7.3	7 470	1 245	8.7
77	0.6	Government	43	0.3	479	80	0.5
60	0.5	Wines & Liquor	(12)	(0.1)	413	69	0.5
13 421	100.0	Total	14 149	100.0	85 684	14 281	100.0

avg. This Month Last Year	%	SUPPLIES	Totals	paper	clng.	service
1 221		Purchases	1 907	580	848	479
4 184		+ Beg. Inven.	4 157	1 866	1 442	849
6 105		= Sub Total	6 064	2 446	2 298	1 328
4 005		− End. Inven.	3 816	1 367	1 562	887
2 100		= Total Cons.	2 248	1 079	728	441

This Month Last Year	%	SUPPLIES EXPENDITURES	$ this month	%	$ this year	avg.	%
980	46.7	Paper Goods	1 079	48.0	5 781	964	42.5
258	12.3	Cleaning Goods	728	32.4	3 363	561	24.8
862	41.0	Serviceware	441	19.6	4 444	741	32.7
2 100	100.0	Total	2 248	100.0	13 588	2 265	100.0

schedules according to work load needs and to keep the man-hours worked close to peak productivity.

Meals served per man-hour worked" is calculated by dividing the number of meals by the number of man-hours worked. This figure or its reciprocal, man-minutes worked per meal served, is the primary index of productivity. Knowledge of the average meals served per man-hour worked for similar operations would be useful in measuring cost effectiveness.

Cost per man-hour worked" is calculated by dividing total payroll expense by the number of man-hours worked. This figure does not indicate the average wage per hour paid to employees. That figure is relatively meaningless and the writer does not understand why government and industry use it in graphing labor indexes.

"The relevant figure is cost per man-hour worked. This figure takes into account the cost of such "free" fringe benefits as vacations and holidays. Seeing this brutal figure every month emphasizes the importance of finding new and better labor-saving work methods and equipment.

"Cafeteria income" is the amount of cash revenue derived from cafeteria sales to staff. The "check average" is the average amount paid for a meal if the staff pays for meals.

"Income per staff meal" is the average amount of cash revenue for all staff meals. This includes groups which eat free, such as resident physicians, foodservice staff, and official visitors. The income per staff meal figure deducted from the cost per staff meal (total cost divided by number of meals served) indicates the amount of subsidy for staff food.

BUDGET OR PRO-FORMA DEVELOPMENT. At Hillside Hospital, it is the responsibility of each department head to submit a proposed annual budget to the administration for approval. Justifications for present staff, present expenses, and any increases must also be presented. The intent is to provide an honest estimate of needs.

The administration is knowledgeable. Any padded requests or improper justifications to make the coming year's budget easier or to look good by having money left at the end can be shaken out quickly.

This system of budget development works well because the department head who must live with the budget plays a large role in its development, and because he is the person who has the expertise in that area. We use a cost accounting line budget because that format makes it easy to locate specific areas of overexpenditure.

In developing estimates on the funds to be needed, the operator must call upon many resources. General economic conditions reveal many trends. Knowledge of such things as corn blights, hog diseases, droughts, large union wage settlements, and more rigid federal controls on various foods all aid in making estimates.

Similarly, reading the *Wall Street Journal* reports on distant commodity futures, talking to middle managers of food contracting companies, and to buyers who work for purveyors, and reading trade magazines, the FDA papers and the daily USDA *Market Reports* will help in estimating.

If he has done these things all year, the operator has better than a guess about price trends for the coming year. In addition, he should keep records on the actual price trends for important items as well as for the 11 broad categories in my accounting system. From these records, he can see the average price rises of previous years.

He knows that menu changes are planned for the next year and now he can estimate what effect these will have on expenses in each category.

With all of the above factors in his head, the operator can make a final estimate of the anticipated price rises for the coming year. When these figures are multiplied by the per meal expenditures of the current year, he arrives at a per meal cost for the next year.

With his knowledge of the probable patient census for the next year, and using the "patient meals per patient day" and "total meals per patient day" calculations mentioned earlier, he can now simply multiply to get a food expenditure estimate. This figure, from past experience, will usually end up within two percentage points of the next year's actual expenses.

In "salaries and wages" estimates can be nearly exact because of knowledge of the next year's scheduled wage gains, vacation and holiday time due, and past records of sick time taken and overtime needs. And remember, if yours is a seven-day operation each station must still be covered on the regular employees days off.

For example, if a worker has Sunday and Monday off, his shifts must be covered those days. The "replacement" factor for this employee is 2/5, or 40 percent. The total time a worker is expected to be out in the next year should be multipled by his replacement factor. That product is then multiplied by his anticipated wage. That result, added to the like products of all the workers, is the total dollar cost of coverage for vacations, holidays, sick time, etc. This figure is used to calcuate the number of temporary replacements needed in the summer months.

SUMMARY

Figure No. 17 is a reprinting of the summary and conclusions of an Indiana State University study entitled *Food Purchasing Procedures of Small Food Service Operators* * which was published in December 1974. (Figure No. 17.) This figure is presented here as a summary to the work set forth thus far because this study pointed out just what level of buying sophistication is generally being used. It is hoped that this book will help remedy the situation.

*Reprinted with permission from *Food Purchasing Procedures of Small Food-service Operators* by Harry F. Krueckeberg and John F. Freshwater, published by School of Business, Indiana State University, December, 1974, pp. ix, x, xi.

FIGURE 17

Summary

and Conclusions

The small foodservice operator faces the challenges of growth and survival in the face of disadvantageous practices by himself and the supplier. Foodservice operators do not have the financial capability of conducting research with which to reduce the danger of potential problem areas such as the problems associated with food purchasing.

The research presented in this report was conducted in an effort to describe and analyze purchasing procedures of small foodservice operators. Hopefully, as a result, growth and survival will be more assured through the recommended improvements in purchasing procedures suggested at the end of each of the sections.

This project involved an analysis of 60 United States foodservice operators. Fifty-two operators were fullservice restaurants. These foodservice operators basically provided varied American menu items.

The average food cost as a percent of sales was 39 percent. Sixteen operators did not know the relationship of their food costs to sales. The average annual sales volume exceeded $500,000.

The typical foodservice operator placed 21.5 orders with an average of 11 suppliers per week. Approximately 7.6 hours were use to place the weekly orders. These orders were made up and placed by the same person in 47, or 78 percent, of the firms. It was originally hypothesized that the order maker (the person compiling the items needed) and the order placer (the person calling in the order or talking with salesmen) would be different persons in a firm with different responsibilities.

Two thirds of the orders were placed by telephone. The energy shortage may well have caused this percent to increase since the interviews. The extent of telephone orders was motivated by both suppliers trying to reduce costs of selling and by operators desiring to reduce time spent with salesmen and drivers.

The bulk of the orders were placed without the use of specifications or written ordering procedures. Sixteen of the operators had certain written policies dealing with ordering but many of these were authorized supplier lists only. Forty-four of the operators did not use product specifications but purchased by brand, label, or on the basis of supplier reputation or suggestion.

Control over food costs is enhanced by thoroughly checking merchandise upon receipt, not at the time of use by the cook or chef nor at the time of storing. The person responsible for checking was, in several cases, a person other than the order maker or order placer. In other words, the checker was a person not likely to know what merchandise to accept or reject, since the purchase was not made by the checker. There was an inadequate amount of thoroughly checking merchandise.

The extent to which inventories were taken left something to be desired. Annual or monthly

[Cont.]

FIGURE 17—[Cont.]

counts were the most common means of taking inventory. The frequency and methods were apparently satisfactory for accounting and tax purposes but did not enable the detection of shortages assoicated with small fluctuations in food costs as a percent of sales.

Employee pilferage was reportedly around one percent for those operators who had any knowledge of pilferage and shrink. Eighteen operators did not know the shrink or pilferage rate.

Failure to check and weigh everything upon each delivery was motivated by the fact that 57 of the restaurants indicated they seldom or never experienced shortages or losses due to pilferage or short deliveries.

The average supplier reported spending 1.4 hours per day checking and storing an average of five deliveries per day. This amounted to 17 minutes per delivery per day. The amount of time spent is not indicative of the "quality" of the check nor the idle time associated with storing. Very seldom was a thorough item check made except by the larger firms.

Receiving was done using basic equipment and facilities - off street parking, an over-sized receiving door, and a two-wheel hand truck. Scales were available in 50 operations but used mainly for meats, a high unit-price item and one subject to pilferage.

There was an average of three persons available for checking and receiving for an average of eight hours per day. The checkers used scales in 50 restaurants for weighing certain items upon receipt while 44 depended on counts as well as weights.

The majority of deliveries ranged from $46 to $120, averaging $107 per delivery.

Foodservice suppliers were selected on the basis of product quality, product price, and supplier service. "Service" appears to be defined as the "status quo," meaning that the supplier helps the operator maintain normal operating conditions over time.

The unfilled information needs of the operator include general operating information, new product information, and assistance in cost accounting practices.

Suppliers were normally selected by the owner or the manager. The average operator selected 11 suppliers and these suppliers normally delivered weekly or every other week.

Pick-ups were uncommon except for emergency order filling. One operator systematically picked up a particular meat order.

For the most part, the delivery man placed the merchandise into storage in addition to delivering the merchandise.

Storage space was utilized to the extent of 65 to 80 percent depending on type of space. Dry storage space was located on non-preparation levels of the operation while the freezer and refrigerators were located for the most part on the same level as the food preparation area.

Ten foodservice operators were studied in depth for one week each. The observations and analysis of these operators permitted the development of handling times and productivity rates associated with delivery receiving, checking, and storing of food merchandise.

Handling productivity increased with increased order size. As more cases were handled at one time, the labor cost was naturally spread over a larger quantity of merchandise and more merchandise was handled per man hour.

As a result of an analysis of handling times, several possible means of improving productivity were analyzed. These can be summarized as follows:

When the supplier transfers the storage of product entirely to the operator's labor, there is a possible 25 percent labor cost savings possible to the supply system. (Details on page 55).

When the operator reduces the deliveries by one-half, there is a possible man-hour savings of 8.25 hours; a possible man-hour reduction of 27 percent (Details on page 55).

When the foodservice operator goes to the one-stop concept, all cases delivered by one supplier, once per week, the potential man-hour reduction for the system amounted to 12.05 hours or a 39 percent reduction per 1,000 cases (Details on page 56).

The suggested improvements resulting from this analysis can be summarized as regarding the following:

In General

Spell out the description of the operation in order to better match present image and operating policy with expected image and expected operating results.

Ordering

1. Develop and document the buying procedures.

2. Know your food costs.

3. Delegate some of the ordering activities.

4. Develop product specifications on critical items in order to place

responsibility for product consistency and quality on the supplier.

Checking and Receiving

1. Equip receiving person with authority to reject a delivery or individual items.

2. Increase order size and reduce number of deliveries.

3. Be equipped to receive merchandise properly.

Supplier Selection

1. Develop sound procedures for supplier selection and objective criteria for continued evaluation of present suppliers.

2. Use alternative suppliers or "shop around" once in a while to verify that present suppliers are providing you with the best product quality, price, and service.

3. Eliminate unnecessary duplication of suppliers.

4. Know of alternative suppliers even though they are not used.

5. Gather new product information.

[Cont.]

FIGURE 17—[Cont.]

Storing

1. Utilize storage to the maximum extent by installing racks or shelves.

2. Storage space should allow proper product rotation.

Inventory Control

1. Know your inventory and the amounts on hand. Institute a perpetual inventory system.

2. Know what your shrink and loss rates are in order to be able to take steps to correct them.

3. Eliminate mental inventory records.

4. Develop an employee education system in order to increase their understanding of the business.

Impact of Order Size

1. Increase order size.

2. Handle more cases per man-hour.

3. Receive fewer deliveries.

4. Work on improving job performance.

5. Transfer costly labor functions to competent lower wage employees.

SOME IDEAL AND ACTUAL PURCHASING PROCEDURES

The Ideal Practices	Highlights of Actual Practices
1. One person purchasing control and authority.	1. Forty-seven operators (78 percent) had one person making up and placing all orders.
2. Thorough understanding of food cost control.	2. Sixteen operators (27 percent) did not have a food cost figure available. Eighteen operators (30 percent) did not know the extent of losses due to shortages or employee pilferage.
3. Discuss product requirements with staff and suppliers.	3. The impression gained from the research suggests that little communication was established among employees or between operator and suppliers.
4. Draft product specifications.	4. Forty-four operators (73 percent) did not use nor have written product specifications.
5. Consult with and depend on sources of information.	5. Little information on new products was sought and thus little was received by the operators.
6. Check all deliveries.	6. Six operators, mostly large, thoroughly checked merchandise. Little time was expended on checking orders.
7. Have simple inventory control system.	7. Thirty-seven operators made periodic inventory counts. Seven operators reported no inventory control methods.
8. Know your customers.	8. Two operators conducted consumer surveys and encouraged salesmen to discuss new products popular with customers.

BIBLIOGRAPHY

Berry, Harold A. *Purchasing Guide, Vol. 23.* Waterford, Connecticut: Prentice-Hall, Inc., 1970.

Bolton, Ralph A. *Systems Contracting, a New Purchasing Technique, 1966.* American Medical Association, 1966.

Cooking For Profit, (August 1973) pp. 5-50.

Dowst, Somerby R. *Basic For Buyers: A Practical Guide to Better Purchasing.* Boston: Cahners Publishing Company, Inc., 1971.

Dyer, Dewey A. *So You Want to Start A Restaurant?* Chicago: Institutions/Volume Feeding Books, 1971.

Eshbach, Charles E. *Food Service Management: A Consideration of Selected Problem Areas in the Management of Foodservice Operations.* Boston: Cahners Books International, Inc., 1974.

Feldman, Julian. *Church Purchasing Procedures.* Englewood Cliffs, New Jersey: Prentice-Hall, Inc., 1964.

Gardner, Jerry D. *Contract Foodservice/Vending.* Boston: Cahners Books International, Inc., 1973.

Gillian, Margiet. *The Master Food Purchasing Guide.* Chicago: The American Hospital Association, 1953.

Haines, Robert G. *Food Preparation For Hotels, Restaurants and Cafeterias.* Chicago: American Technical Society, 1973.

Hertzson, David, ed. *Food and Beverage Purchasing.* New York: ITT Educational Services, Inc., 1971.

Hodges, Henry. *The Modern Science of Purchasing.* New York: Harper, 1961.

"How To Use USDA Grades in Buying Food." Washington, D.C.: Government Printing Office, 1967.

Kahrl, W.L. *Foodservice on a Budget.* Boston: Cahners Books International, Inc., 1974.

Lifquist, Rosalind C. and BeTate, Edith. *Planning Food For Institutions.* Washington, D.C.: U.S. Department of Agriculture, 1951.

Nutrition and Technical Services Staff. *Food Buying Guide for Type A School Lunches,* Washington, D.C.: Food and Nutrition Service, 1972.

"Operating Budgets for Food Service Establishments." *Food Management,* Leaflet 12, pp. 2-10.

Purchases and Stores: School, Business, Management Handbook Number 5, New York: The University of the State of New York, 1964.

Rodgers, Richard K. "Procurement Programmed For Profit." *Foodservice Magazine,* February 1974, pp. 44-51.

Todoroff, Alexander. *Food Buying Today.* Chicago: The Grocery Trade Publishing House, 1934.

U.S. Department of Agriculture. "Food Purchasing Guide for Group Feeding." Agriculture Handbook No. 281, Washington, D.C.: Government Printing Office, 1965.

U.S. Department of Agriculture. *Shopper's Guide,* Washington D.C.: Government Printing Office, 1974.

Wenzel, George L. *How to Build Volume,* Austin, Texas: George Wenzel, Sr., 1971.

Zaccarelli, Brother Herman E., C.S.C. *Purchasing Techniques For Hospital Food Services.* North Easton, Massachusetts: The International Food Research and Educational Center.

Zaccarelli, Brother Herman E., C.S.C. and Maggiore, Josephine. *Nursing Home Menu Planning, Food Purchasing and Management.* Chicago: Cahners Books International, Inc., 1972.

MEAT

INTRODUCTION

MEAT HAS BEEN the basic item in mankind's diet since the beginning of his time. The earliest men started the development of more advanced cultures because of their quest for meat. It was the desire and need for meat which caused man to develop the first mare traps, a development which later led to the use of traps to capture animals for their fur. This sequence is encountered in the economic development of every region of the world.

It was the quest for meat that led man to the development of the first spears and arrows. It was the desire for a stable supply of meat which led men to abandon nomadic meat-hunting in favor of meat-raising and farming and to the eventual creation of stable cultures.

Pagan cultures did, and some still do, use certain meats in religious ceremonies. Some of this has carried over into modern culture. When did you last hear of a certain meat as being "brain food" or "food for strength"?

Wars have been fought in conquest of meat. Wars have been lost for lack of meat to feed the troops. Civilizations have been built on meat agriculture, and nations have been destroyed when their cattle succumbed to disease. Indeed, there is no chapter of history which has not been affected by the need, the desire, the uses of meat.

Do we really need meat in our diet? The answer to that question is no, if based on pure physical need. The nutrients we get from meat are all available from other sources. The protein which is so vital to the sustenance of life is available from the plant world, from indirect meat sources such as milk and eggs, and from the marine world of fish and crustaceans.

But, from a psychological point of view, meat is certainly a necessity. The aroma of a steak on the broiler, the succulence of a potted roast, the sight of a pig on the spit, the sound of a stew boiling are so enticing to us as to almost suggest an intuitive desire for meat. The economy of a nation and the well-being of its people are reflected by the supply and demand status of the meat industry. When a nation prospers, the price of the better cuts of meat rises sharply, as people can afford and, therefore, demand the expensive cuts.

Although we can get our nutrients from other sources, the minerals and proteins we need are most readily available from meat.

Importance in Foodservice Budget?

There is no single item in the foodservice budget which is as large or as important as meat. Of food purchases alone, meat may range from 30 percent of total food expenditures for an institution to 70 percent of food expenditures for a steak and chop house. Meat purchases may range from as much as 20 percent of all operating expenditure for the institutional foodservice to 40 percent for the commercial establishment. There is no way to overemphasize the importance of the proper purchasing and receiving of meat.

The purchase of the proper cut for the use intended is of paramount importance in the purchase of meat. Later on in this section you will note that each cut of meat is accompanied by cooking suggestions. As a general rule of thumb, one should buy the higher grades of meat for the dry methods of cooking (broiling, roasting), as such cuts have adequate marbling (fat) to retain the moist, juicy texture expected when eaten.

The lower grades of meat, which are not as well marbled, are good for the moist heat methods of cooking (braising, boiling, stewing) as the slow, moist cooking breaks down the tough meat fibers to an acceptable level for comfortable chewing. Thus, it is wise to purchase USDA Choice for roasts and steaks, but wasteful to use USDA Choice grades of meat for stews and pot roasts.

Composition and Structure

The meat we eat is the muscle of the animal. Muscles are of two types with two respective functions. The involuntary muscles are the smooth muscles of the blood vessels and digestive tract which do their jobs automatically and virtually continuously. These muscles are lacking in interspersed fat and are, therefore, very tough. The voluntary muscles are composed of many tiny fibers joined together by connective tissues in a fashion which is analogous to the wire cables used in building bridges. This type of formation is called striated. Muscles are composed of cells of sizes and shapes which vary according to the feed, age, sex, and type of animal.

The connective tissue cells are joined together into bundles by two types of connective tissue. White connective tissue, called collagen, is found in all the muscles of the animal; it is dominant in the more tender cuts of meat. Yellow connective tissue, called elastin, is predominant in the muscles which carry the heaviest load of constant strain and work.

The white connective tissue breaks up and becomes moist in cooking, whereas the yellow connective tissue requires mechanical means of tenderizing such as pounding, cubing, or grinding. The younger and less exercised an animal is, the less yellow connective tissue it will have and the more tender its meat will be.

Fat and Marbling

Of all the factors that go into the measurement of the quality of meat, fat is the most important. The amount, the distribution, and the condition of an animal's fat are essential ingredients in the mix of cost, cutability, and palatability of meats. The total amount of fat may range from as little as 5 percent on a very lean animal to as much as 35 percent on a very fat animal. The fat on the outside of an animal's muscles is called cover. The fat which lies between the bundles of muscle fibers is called marbling. The amount of marbling in the meat and between the connective tissues is a very important factor in meat since it creates the chewability looked for in cooked meat.

Meat in the United States is usually well marbled because the animals are finished on specialized grain feeds which convert rapidly to fat. This is in marked contrast to South American or Spanish meat which is usually raised only on grazing grasses and is, therefore, less fatty and much tougher to chew.

Fat accounts for much of the flavor of meat because a fat subcomponent, esters, imparts and enhances the typical "meat" flavors. The type of feed, again, reflects in the type of fat and the eventual flavor of the meat. Thus, the regional preference for "corn-fed" beef, for example.

The more fat on an animal, the less lean. This factor means that the more fat an animal has in ratio to its lean, the higher the cost of that lean. Prime Beef, (see Fig. No. 1) for example, is very well marbled and has a thick fat cover and thus costs much more than Choice, Good, or the lesser grades of meat.

The positive nutritive value of meat is in the lean tissue and not in the fat.

The food value of a pound of lean is the same whether it is from costly Prime or from inexpensive Commercial. As mentioned earlier, the means of cooking has much to do with the chewability and, therefore, the smart operator will buy according to need.

Prime meat should be purchased only for the "carriage trade" business of expensive steak and chop operations where the finest quality is called for and paid for by a clientele that can afford it. It is wasteful and foolish to use Prime meat in non-commercial applications.

Pigments, Extracts, and Water

The color of meat depends upon the animal's age at slaughter. The older an animal is the more of the red pigment (myoglobin) that is found in the meat. The range of color varies with the type of animal as well as the use of the particular muscles. Heavily exercised muscles, such as the muscles of the legs, and the involuntary muscles tend to be darker.

The connective tissue of meat contains extracts which contribute to the flavor of the meat. These extracts are water soluble; thus the meat which is cooked by the moist-heat method is less flavorful than meat cooked by dry-heat methods. The stock made of boiled meats is especially flavorful because it contains so much of these extracts.

The amount of water in meat increases as the percentage of fat decreases. Because meat may contain more than 60 percent water, the longer meat is cooked and the higher the temperature at which it is cooked, the greater the water loss and, therefore, the more "shrinkage" or loss of weight that occurs. Since fat is desirable, meat which is firm, as opposed to soft, is of preferred quality.

Aging or Dispensing

Aged meat is meat which has had the fibers broken down through material processes. Meat contains many fermenting agents which are called enzymes. These enzymes break down the cell structures of the lean and the connective tissue and so make the meat easier to chew. By storing meat at a controlled temperature and humidity, for a controlled period of time, the aging or ripening process will increase the tenderness and flavor of the meat. Generally speaking, it is not economical to age meat more than two weeks as water loss and discoloration may cause losses of 15 percent to 20 percent of the meat.

Beef may be aged as much as 45 days if held at $34°$F. and 88 percent humidity with at least 10 CFM air circulation. Lamb and mutton may be aged up to 10 days, but pork and veal are never aged.

All meat should be held at a temperature between $34°$ and $40°$F. for at least four days after slaughter. This period of time will allow the enzymes to combat the rigor mortis, or post-slaughter hardening, to a point where the meat has softened and is no longer considered "green."

REFRIGERATION

Fresh meat is best stored at a temperature of $32°$ to $34°$F. and a humidity of no less than 80 percent in a well-ventilated refrigerator. The meat should be allowed to "breathe" which means that it should be covered with material no more dense than a loose-net treated cheesecloth.

$32°$F. is the ambient state of liquid. It takes 160 BTU's to change a temperature from $32°$F., the *frozen state of water*, to $32°$F., the *liquid state of water*. The higher the temperature and the longer the fresh storage of meat, the greater the amount of weight which will be lost through evaporation, and the greater the amount of meat which will have to be trimmed off and, therefore, lost. A very important part of meat purchasing is keeping loss, due to storage time, to a minimum. Because of this potential for loss, it is often the wisest purchasing decision to specify delivery of fabricated meat in the frozen state.

FREEZING

When meat is frozen, the water in the meat expands. This is analogous to the expansion of tap water when frozen into ice cubes. If meat is frozen slowly, then the water in the meat will expand enough to form ice crystals, and the result will be broken cell walls in the meat. For this reason, it is important that meat be frozen very quickly in order to prevent formation of destructive ice crystals. Meat should be frozen at temperatures of at least $-25°$F. in an atmosphere with air circulating at 40 CFM. The center of the meat should be $0°$F. in a maximum of four hours. Do not accept frozen meat from a purveyor unless you are certain that this procedure has been followed.

When meat is frozen, a certain amount of evaporation takes place. This drying of the surface is commonly known as "freezer burn." Freezer burn may be prevented by wrapping the meat so that it is as airtight as possible before freezing. Many meat purveyors freeze their meats in vacuum (totally air free) bags. Some of these bags can be used to cook the meat in, saving the operator steps in handling and cutting down on pot washing.

FIGURE 1

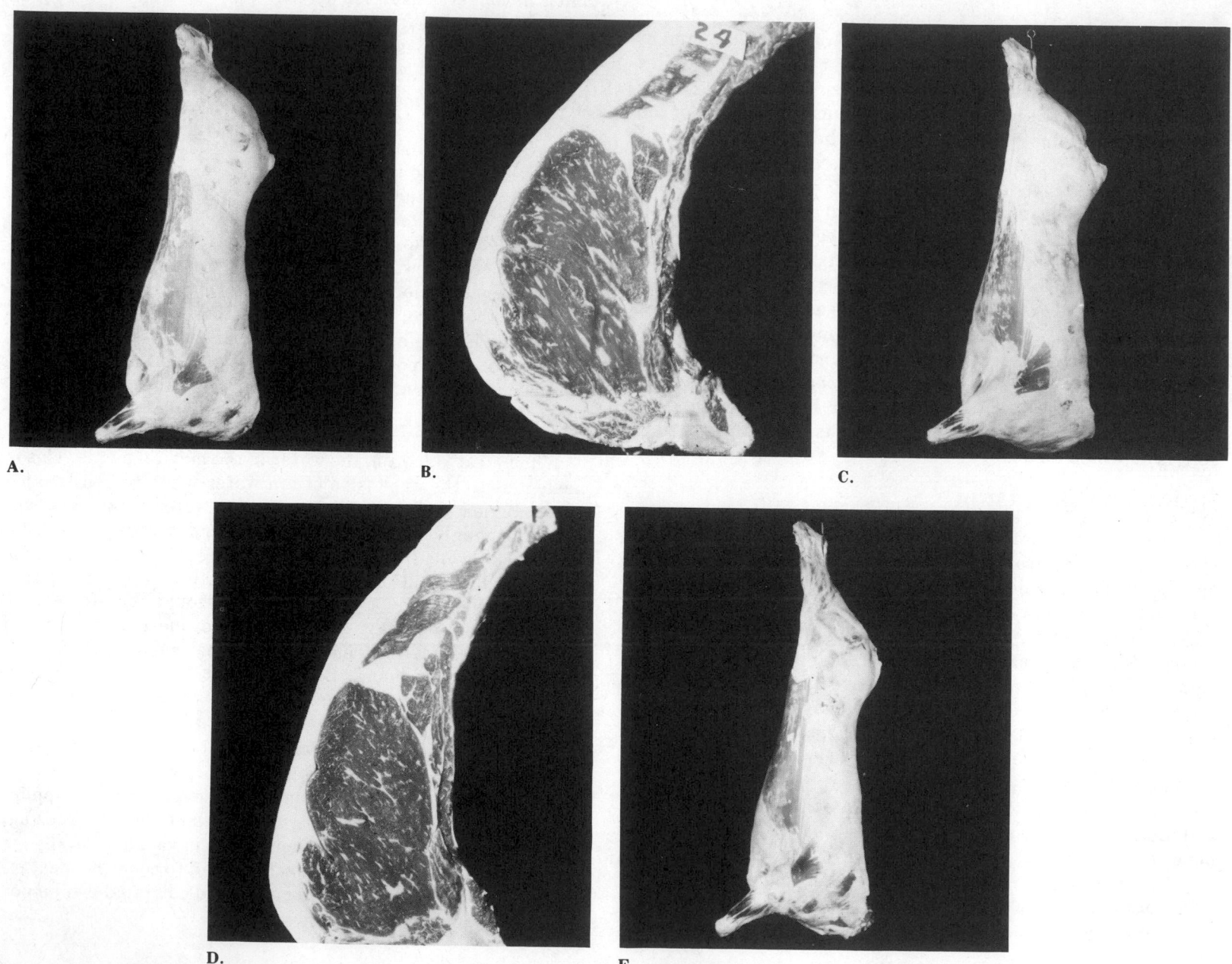

FIGURE 1 [Cont.]

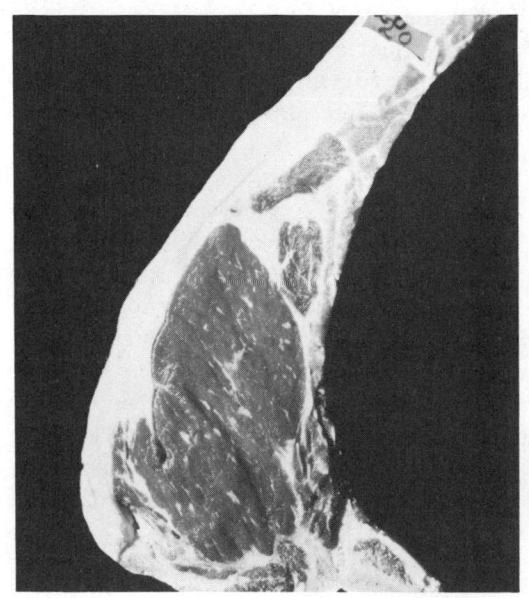

F.

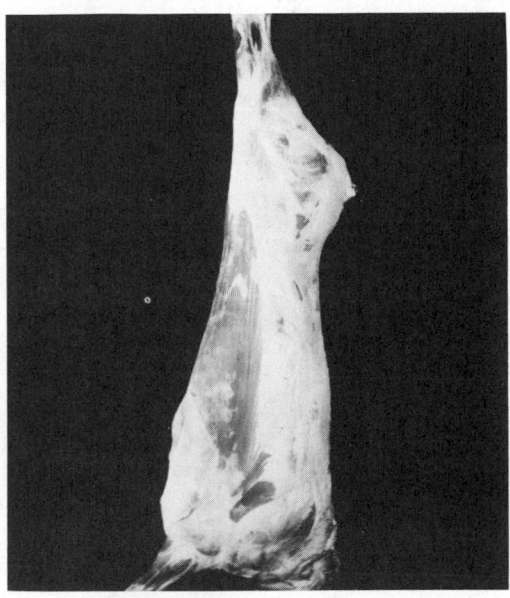

G.

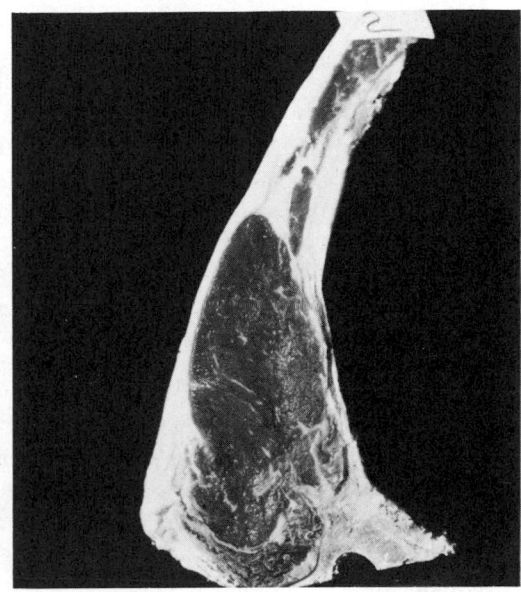

H.

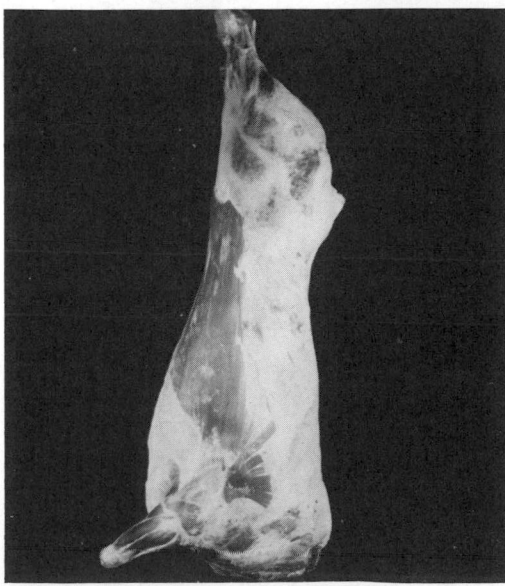

I.

A., B.—*U.S. Prime Beef;* **C., D.**—*U.S. Choice Beef;*
E., F.—*U.S. Good Beef;* **G., H.**—*U.S. Standard Beef;*
I.—*U.S. Commercial Beef. Courtesy of National
Live Stock and Meat Board.*

TEMPERING

Tempering is that process by which you defrost foods which are frozen. Frozen meat must be tempered under refrigeration only. If meat is tempered at room temperature (or any temperature between 50°F., and 140°F.), then an ideal medium for the growth of harmful bacteria will exist. It generally takes about 24 hours to completely defrost an 8-lb. roast at 34° to 40°F., 72 hours for a 24-lb. roast. Never, never put any kind of meat in a sink of water for any reason.

Meat may be roasted or potted from the frozen state only if done so at a carefully controlled low temperature. Many tests have shown that the difference in yield of roasts cooked at 250°F. as opposed to 350°F., may be as great as 10 percent.

MEAT BUYING KNOW-HOW

Meat buying is a complicated matter. It takes much experience in all phases of meat production, from slaughter to stew, to know all that is desirable for the wise purchasing and usage of meats. The purpose of this section is to present the *basic* facts about meat so that the buyer will know what is behind the terminology. It must be emphasized here that the rules set forth later in this section for the writing and the use of specifications must be *strictly* adhered to or else substantial money and/or quality loss will be suffered. The specifications which appear later in this section should be used *with* the pictures of the various meat cuts and with a ruler or meat-measuring device. Only after long experience can one be certain that a visual check, without the above mentioned aids, will be accurate. Few people have that ability. There is large a variety of ways in which meat can be cut; *caveat emptor* applies more to meat than to any other product used in the foodservice industry.

INSPECTIONS

There are many labels, stamps, and codes used in the meat industry. The ones most to be trusted are those of the United States Department of Agriculture. These federal certifications are standardized throughout the country. Some state and local governments maintain their own inspection programs. These programs vary widely from state to state and area to area and, consequently, generally cannot be relied upon to be of the quality of the USDA programs.

The military inspection programs are of the same quality as the USDA programs and are interchangeable so far as military meat purchasing is concerned. Religious inspections such as Kosher or Kasruth are certification that the meat has met certain religious codes as regards method of slaughter and butchering. These religious certifications carry no guarantee of quality.

Federal Inspection

The label shown in Fig. No. 2 certifies that the meat has met certain criteria of wholesomeness. The stamp must appear on all meat and meat products that are offered in interstate commerce. This label on the carcass of the meat or on the label attached to a further processed meat or meat product has met the following standards:

- The carcass has been thoroughly examined for disease and any unwholesome part has been removed and destroyed.
- The meat has been handled and prepared in a sanitary fashion in a meat plant which meets rigid federal standards of sanitation.
- No known harmful substances have been added to the meat.
- The federal stamp has been affixed. The number in the circle identifies the plant where the meat was prepared.
- Labels (Fig. No. 3) attached to further processed meats must meet certain federal criteria and must be approved before they can be used. The information on the label must include: the circular inspection stamp, the name and address of the plant, the net weight, and a list of ingredients in the order of their dominance.

If meat is packed in a container for shipping, then the container must be labeled. The Domestic Meat Label (Fig. No. 4) must be affixed to the outside of the container.

Imported Meat

Imported meats which meet USDA standards are stamped at the port of entry with the stamp shown in Fig. No. 5.

Exemption from Inspection

Although the cost of maintaining an on-premises USDA inspector is less than 50 cents per animal, there are some companies engaged in interstate commerce that are allowed an exemption from the requirement. These are the hotels or restaurants who raise their own meat. However, their plants

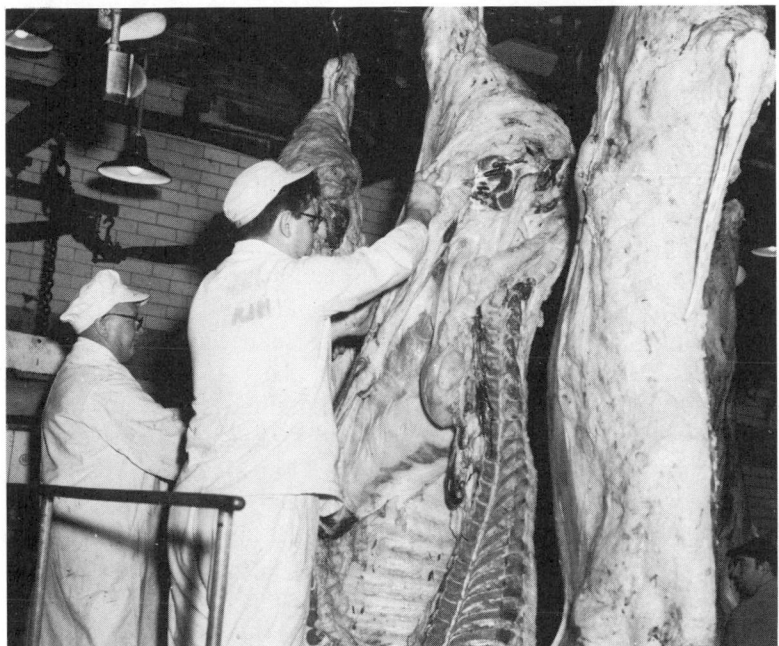

Inspection after slaughter is highly important. The federal inspector examines the head, glands, and organs of the animal for evidence of abnormalities. Then he carefully examines by sight and touch each half of the split carcass as it moves along the inspection line.

must undergo periodic inspection, and their exemption is revocable.

Other Inspection Programs

The state and local programs for inspection are varied in their standards. Some areas have no inspection. Before a buyer decides to purchase meat which has been inspected only by the state or local inspectors, it would be wise to make a personal comparison between those standards *and their enforcement* and the federal standards. The Utah State Inspection stamp and label are shown in Fig. No. 6.

The Kosher stamp (Fig. No. 7) is not a substitute for federal or state wholesomeness inspection. This is an additional label which indicates *religious* wholesomeness only.

The Military Inspection Program closely relates to the USDA Inspection Program. Meat is so inspected for the military service only. The military inspection stamps are shown in Fig. No. 8 and 9.

FIGURE 2

38 U.S. INSP'D & P'S'D

FIGURE 3

Aunt Hattie's BRAND
BREADED VEAL PATTIES
BEEF ADDED
INGREDIENTS: Veal, Beef, Water, Soya Flour, Precooked Corn and Wheat Flours, Salt, Hydrolyzed Vegetable Protein, Monosodium Glutamate, Sugar, Flavorings.
BATTER INGREDIENTS:
Water, Wheat and Rice Flours, Potato Starch, Salt, Monosodium Glutamate, Paprika, Flavoring, Vegetable Gum.
BREADING INGREDIENTS:
Wheat Flour, Paprika, Sweet Dairy Whey, Salt, Yeast, Leavening, Dextrose, and Flavoring.
BATTER and BREADING COLORED WITH PAPRIKA
KEEP FROZEN
Prepared by
COOK'S PROCESSED FOODS, INC., LOS ANGELES, CALIF. 90058

FIGURE 4

U.S. INSPECTED AND PASSED BY DEPARTMENT OF AGRICULTURE EST. 38

FIGURE 5

LA U.S. INSP'D & P'S'D

FIGURE 6

UTAH 214 INSPECTED & PASSED

FIGURE 7

כשר

FIGURE 8

0 031 4
5 34624
7032123

FIGURE 9

USDA 10 9 59 ACCEPTED FOR MILITARY 168

GRADING

The U.S. Dept. of Agriculture maintains a voluntary meat grading service. These federal grades are applied to meat as a means of giving the consumer a clear-cut guide as to the quality of the meat he buys. The grading standards are the same throughout the country. Since the grading standards are complicated, it is important that the meat buyer understand the meaning of the various grades and how they are determined. With this understanding, the buyer will be able to choose the grade of meat which is appropriate for the use intended.

Although a lot of the meat in the United States is graded by the Federal Grading Service, there are some meat packers who choose to apply their own grades instead of subscribing to federal grading.

The buyer should beware of such grading. The USDA grades are carefully worked out and consistent throughout the land. Private packer grading is capricious at best, and virtually fraudulent at worst. The professional meat buyer buys the measured, standardized, reliable federal grades and nothing else.

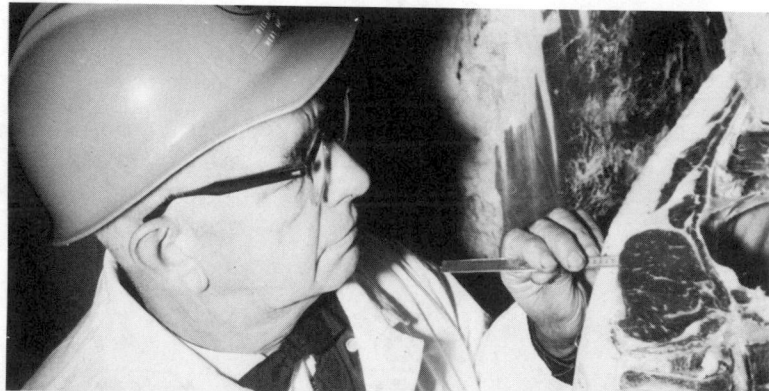

A federal meat grader measures the thickness of fat over the ribeye of a beef carcass—one step in determining its USDA yield grade. Since the amount of fat trimmed in making retail cuts affects the yield, fat thickness is the most important consideration. There are 5 USDA yield grades, numbered 1 through 5. Yield Grade 1 has the highest yield of retail cuts, and Yield Grade 5 has the lowest. In addition to fat thickness, three other factors are considered in determining yield grade—ribeye area, percent kidney, pelvic and heart fat, and carcass weight.

There are two types of federal grading. The first type, with which most people are familiar, is quality grading. Quality grading classifies meat according to a number of factors which contribute to how well the meat "eats" and "tastes."

The second type of grading is cutability grading or yield grading. The yield grade tells the buyer how much lean he can expect to obtain from the cut carcass.

The quality grade is determined by an examination of the kind (class) of animal, the sex, the shape (conformation), the amount of exterior fat (finish), the amount of interior fat (marbling), and the firmness of the lean and the fat. The specifics vary depending upon the class of animal. These specifics of grading quality are explained later on in the section where specifications are given for each separate class.

The 1975 Grading Changes: What Do They Mean?

Effective April 14, 1975, new standards took effect for the grading of meat. The changes affected the amount of grain that must be fed to cattle of a particular age. Essentially, this means that cattlemen will be able to save money by feeding their livestock less grain without taking the risk of having the meat from these grass-fed cattle fall into lower grades.

Before the grading change, approximately 4 percent of cattle were graded Prime; 50 percent, Choice; 35 percent, Good, and the rest below Good. Under the new grading standards, the ratio is said to be 4 percent Prime; 60 percent, Choice; 25 percent, Good, and the rest below Good. Before the 1975 change, to be graded Choice, cattle that were over 12 months, but less than 30 months, had to have more marbling than cattle under 12 months. Some experts argue that improved breeding has eliminated the need for older cattle to have more fat, as there is no relation between tenderness and maturity under 30 months.

The jury is still out on the change in grading. Some have noticed no perceptible change; others argue that they are now paying Choice prices for Good beef.

CLASS

The classes (kinds) of meat and the grades for which they are eligible are listed below. The stamps shown in Fig. No. 10 appear in red on all the major cuts of meat. Since the stamp is rolled down the uncut carcass, there are some interior cuts of meat which cannot bear the stamp.

FIGURE 10

Rolling on the grade marks.

Beef

Steer, Heifer, Bullock

USDA GRADES—Prime, Choice, Good, Standard, Commercial, Utility, Cutter, Canner.

Cow

USDA GRADES—Choice, Good, Standard, Commercial, Utility, Cutter, Canner.

Bull, Stag

USDA GRADES—Choice, Good, Commercial, Utility, Cutter, Canner.

Veal and Calf

USDA GRADES—Prime, Choice, Good, Standard, Utility, Cull.

Ovine

Lamb, Yearling, Mutton

USDA GRADES—Prime, Choice, Good, Utility, Cull.

Mutton

USDA GRADES—Choice, Good, Utility, Cull.

Pork [Hogs]

Barrows, Gilts

USDA GRADES—U.S. No. 1, U.S. No. 2, U.S. No. 3, U.S. No. 4, U.S. Utility.

Sows

USDA GRADES—U.S. No. 1, U.S. No. 2, U.S. No. 3, Medium, Cull.

The cuts of meat which have the greatest monetary value in the marketplace are from the back or hindquarter of the animal. The female animal usually has a heavier and, therefore, more valuable hindquarter than the male animal. When a male animal has its male hormones removed at an early age, the muscular development is then much like the female with the hindquarters being heavy.

Beef

STEER—a male animal which has had the male hormones removed at a very young age.

HEIFER—a female animal which has never borne a calf.

COW—a female animal which has borne one or more calves.

BULL—a male animal which has matured with male hormones intact.

BULLOCK—a young bull.

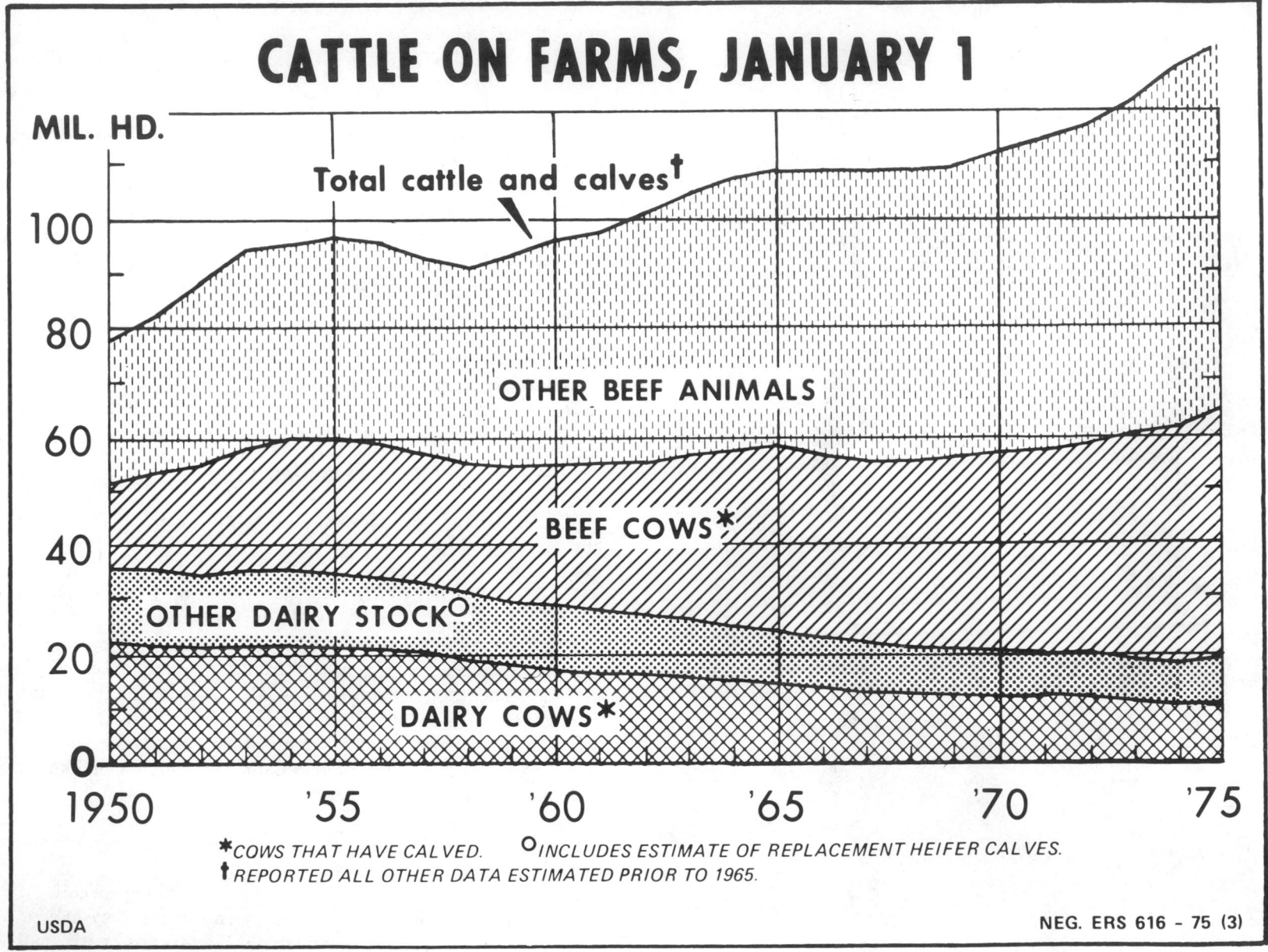

CATTLE ON FARMS, JANUARY 1

MIL. HD.

Total cattle and calves†

OTHER BEEF ANIMALS

BEEF COWS*

OTHER DAIRY STOCK○

DAIRY COWS*

*COWS THAT HAVE CALVED.   ○INCLUDES ESTIMATE OF REPLACEMENT HEIFER CALVES.
†REPORTED ALL OTHER DATA ESTIMATED PRIOR TO 1965.

USDA

NEG. ERS 616 – 75 (3)

STAG—a male animal which is heavier and fatter than a bull. Male hormones removed after a certain stage of maturity is reached.

When buying beef, the buyer will not know if he is buying steer, heifer, or cow except by examination of the pelvic area. The steer has rough fat in the cod area, a very small pelvic cavity, and a small "pizzle eye." The heifer has smooth cod fat and a larger pelvic cavity than the steer. A cow has a very large pelvic cavity and, usually being an old animal, the bones are hard and white as opposed to the softer, pink bones of a young animal.

Bulls and Stags are graded on a different set of standards than the Steer, Heifer, and Cow. A bull will have very heavy muscle development at the rounds, neck, shoulder, a large "pizzle eye," and coarse, dark meat.

The Stag will be less heavy and coarse than the bull, but not as light nor as finely fleshed as a steer.

VEAL AND CALF—a bovine of an age up to three months is classified as veal. Veal has a very light pink, actually almost gray colored, lean meat. The lean and fat are very soft, smooth, and flexible. The bones are very red, and the rib bones are very narrow.

A calf is a bovine which is older than three months. The calf has a pink to reddish-pink lean, which is soft and pliable to a degree not as great as veal, but is not nearly as firm as beef. The bones are pink and starting to harden. The rib bones are wider than on veal.

Ovine

Lamb is classified according to age. The very young, under weaning age, lamb is often called *Hothouse Lamb* or *Genuine Spring Lamb.* A lamb between two and five months of age may be called Spring Lamb or, sometimes, milk lamb or milk-fed lamb. Lamb has soft, porous bones, very light pink lean, and creamy white to pink fat which is soft and pliable. Perhaps the foremost indicator is the *break joint* of the foreleg. These joints break into four well-defined ridges which are smooth, soft, and blood-red.

Yearling Mutton has flesh which is light red to red; fat which is white and fairly firm; and graining in the flesh, which

is fine, but it does not have as little grain as lamb. The break joint in yearling mutton has four ridges as with lamb, but the edges are not smooth, and the bone is hard and white.

Mutton has flesh which is medium red to dark red with a grain which is similar to calf or young steer. The fat is quite white and has a brittle consistency. The foreleg of mutton will not break as with lamb and yearling mutton. Instead, a hard, shiny, smooth knuckle with two prominent ridges forms. Whereas sex has a bearing upon the classification of lamb and yearling mutton, mutton is classified according to sex.

Mutton

EWE—a female animal.

WETHER—a male animal which has had its male hormones removed at a young age.

BUCK—a mature male which has not been sexually altered.

Pork [Hogs]

BARROW—a male animal which has had the male hormones removed when very young.

GILT—a female animal which has never borne pigs.

SOW—a female animal which has borne pigs.

BOAR—a male animal which has matured with male hormones intact.

STAG—a male animal which has had its male hormones removed after reaching maturity.

It is very easy to remember hog classifications by equating the animals with their rough equivalent in bovines:

Barrow—Steer
Gilt—Heifer
Sow—Cow
Boar—Bull
Stag—Stag

Hogs are essentially graded in three categories. The grades U.S. No. 1, U.S. No. 2, and U.S. No. 3 are the Choice grades. The differences between these grades have to do with the ratio of lean to fat and the yield of the loin, the ham, the picnic, and the Boston Butt. The U.S. No. 4 (barrows, gilts) and U.S. Medium (sow) are the next level down in the grading and the bottom of the consumer grades. U.S. Utility (barrow, gilt) and U.S. Cull are not marketed for retail consumption. Sows are graded on a different set of standards than barrows and gilts.

Some 70 percent of the hog production is further processed before it reaches the retail marketplace. Hogs are raised for a variety of purposes. In the old days, they were referred to as Roasting (10 to 30 pigs), Shipping (large sows for barrel packing), Meat-Type (fairly lean for bacon and hams), and Fat-Type (hard and skinned hams). Today, hogs are marketed within a very narrow range of weights and carcass lengths. General well-defined grading of pork cuts on the basis of quality is not yet done, and pork is marketed mostly on the basis of weight and lean to fat ratio. When better control is possible over muscular development, amount of finish, evenness of marbling, and uniformity and texture of the lean, then accurate quality grading may be possible.

When buying carcass or packer style (split carcass) hogs, the following is a guideline to acceptable quality.

CUTS—muscles should not have more than a moderate amount of intramuscular fat.

BONES—should be porous with cartilage present. Brittle or flinty bones are not acceptable.

LEAN—should range from light pink to light red; smooth, fine texture similar to calf.

FAT—should be firm, creamy white, and fairly evenly distributed.

SKIN—thin, smooth, pliable.

Conformation

Conformation has nothing to do with the taste quality of an animal. The term refers to the animal's shape. The more meat in the higher priced regions of the body, the better the conformation. An animal with excellent conformation will have little meat in such areas as the neck, the shanks, but thick plump loins, ribs, rounds, and chucks.

Finish

Finish is the fat which covers the animal carcass and which is distributed inside the animal and between the muscles. As mentioned earlier, finish is an important determinant in grading all meats. White fat is desirable and is the result of careful breeding and grain-feeding. Heavy, rough fat is the result of too-fast, too-much or too-long feed lot feeding. Good fat is creamy white in appearance and occurs in increasing amounts according to age. Thus, bovine finish will be least on veal, more on calves, and heaviest on beef animals. Lambs are less well finished than yearling muttons; yearling muttons have less finish than muttons. Bovine and ovine have a firm to brittle texture, while hogs have a soft fat. Very soft hog fat is an indication of slop feeding and is quite undesirable as it is difficult to butcher a soft hog.

Marbling

The amount of finish which appears in the flesh itself is called marbling. The more numerous the flecks of fat in the meat, the more flavorful, juicy, and tender the meat will be. That is why marbling is such an important factor in grading. Fig. No. 11 shows the difference in amount of marbling in bovine species.

Although marbling is a very important factor in palatability and a prime determinant of grade, it should be pointed out again, that the positive food value is in the lean, and that an animal with lesser finish, or yellow finish, or lower grade will offer just as much nutritive value per pound as the "higher quality" meats.

Quality

Quality in meat is that combination of factors which contribute to the typical, excellent taste of a particular animal. This is called palatability. Besides finish and marbling, the factors for quality grading include the color of the flesh and the age of the animal.

In grading veal, calf, ovine, and hogs, the grader determines the grade on the whole carcass and without benefit of a cut surface of the lean. Finish is perhaps the most important of the grading factors. The grader depends not upon the amount of external finish, but rather on the fat streaking in the ribs (feathering) and the fat streaking in the inside flank muscles.

In beef cattle, the carcass is cut at the twelfth rib, and an evaluation can be made of the degree of ossification (hardening) of the bones and the firmness and marbling of the rib eye muscle.

The age or maturity of the animal has much to do with the quality. Age refers to the physiological age of the animal as indicated by the color and texture of the lean, condition of the

FIGURE 11

ILLUSTRATIONS OF THE LOWER LIMITS OF CERTAIN DEGREES OF TYPICAL MARBLING REFERRED TO IN THE OFFICIAL UNITED STATES STANDARDS FOR GRADES OF CARCASS BEEF

Illustrations adapted from negatives furnished by New York State College of Agriculture, Cornell University

1 – Very abundant
2 – Abundant
3 – Moderately abundant

4 – Slightly abundant
5 – Moderate
6 – Modest

7 – Small
8 – Slight
9 – Traces

(Practically devoid not shown)

UNITED STATES DEPARTMENT OF AGRICULTURE CONSUMER AND MARKETING SERVICE LIVESTOCK DIVISION

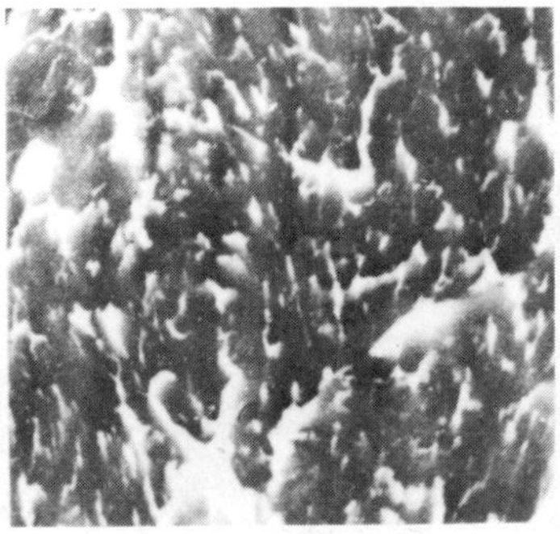

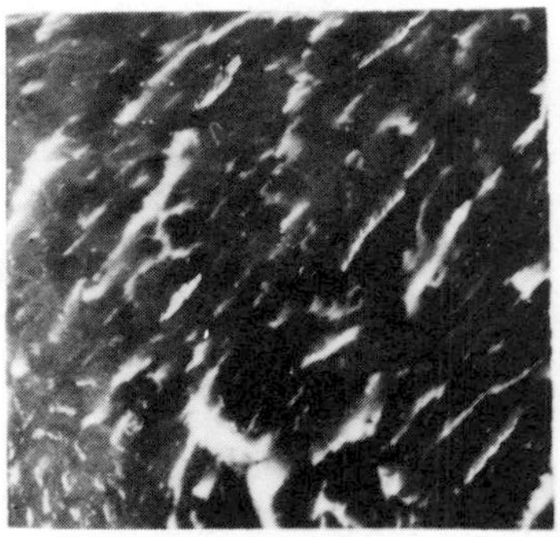

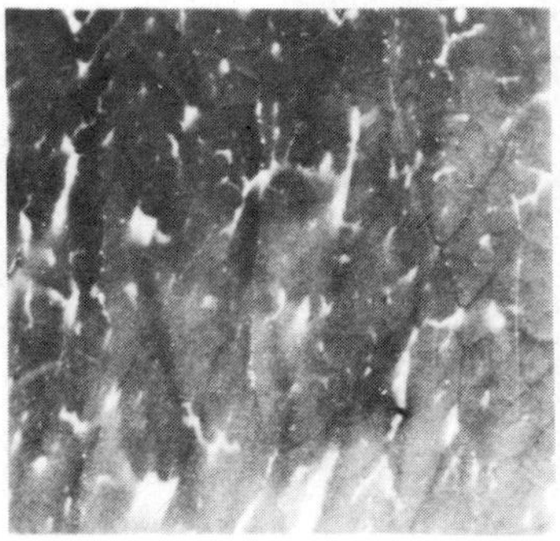

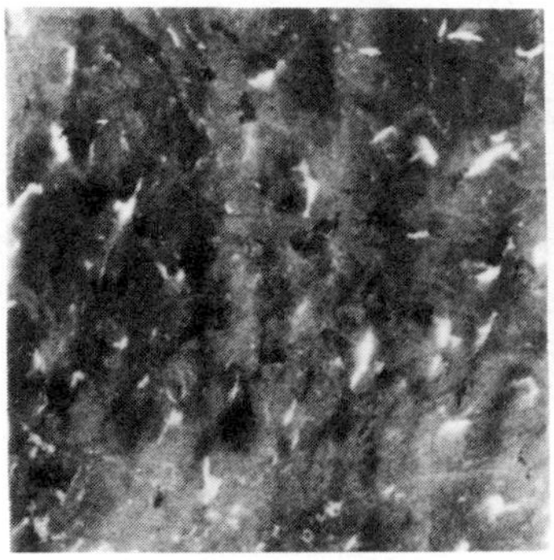

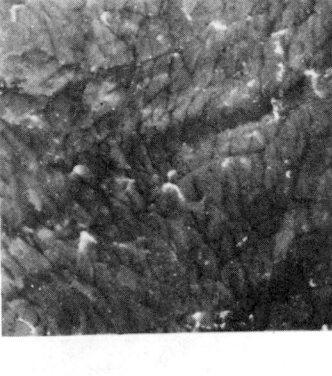

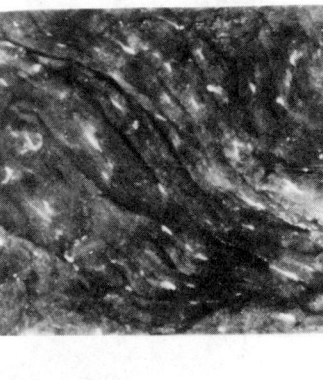

Courtesy National Live Stock and Meat Board.

FIGURE 12

RELATIONSHIP BETWEEN MARBLING, MATURITY, AND QUALITY*

Degrees of Marbling	Maturity*				
	A**	B	C	D	E
Abundant					
Moderately Abundant	PRIME			COMMERCIAL	
Slightly Abundant					
Moderate	CHOICE				
Modest					
Small					
Slight	GOOD			UTILITY	
Traces	STANDARD				
Practically Devoid				CUTTER	

*Maturity increases from left to right (A through E)
- - - - Represents midpoint of Prime and Commercial grades
**The A maturity portion of the figure is the only portion applicable to bullock carcasses.

Official U.S. Standards for Grades of Carcass Beef SRA 99.

U.S. Department of Agriculture, Consumer and Marketing Service, Livestock Division.

*Courtesy National Live Stock and Meat Board

bone, and hardening or ossification of the cartilage, and *not* the actual age of the animal. The physiological and actual age of an animal will be similar only in well-bred, properly raised animals.

There is a substantial overlap in the different quality factors and, therefore, the lack of some factors may be compensated for by the presence of others. Fig. No. 12 shows the relationship between marbling, maturity, and quality in beef, while Fig. No. 13 shows the relationship of age to grade in beef.

FIGURE 13

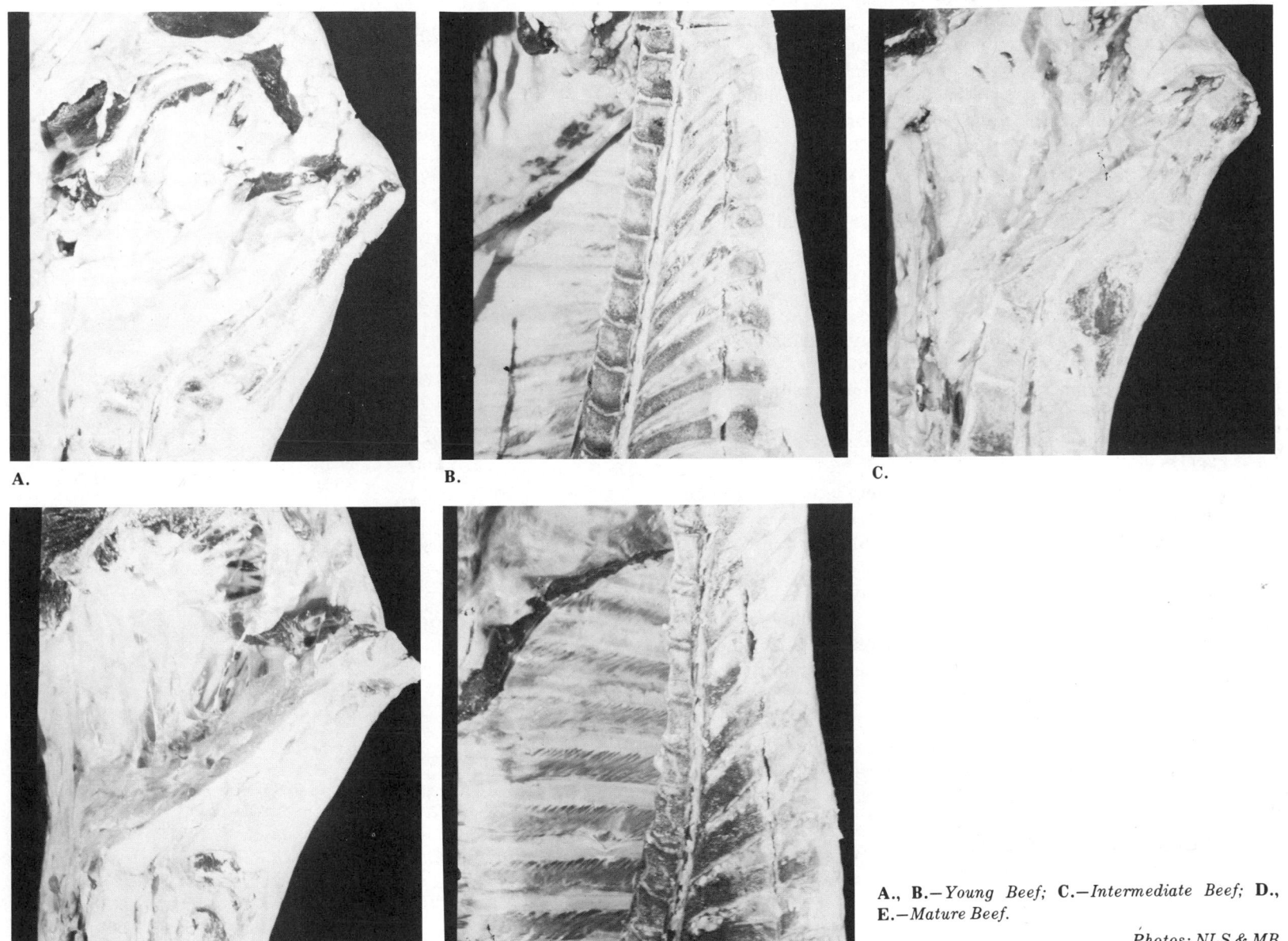

A.

B.

C.

D.

E.

A., B.—*Young Beef;* C.—*Intermediate Beef;* D., E.—*Mature Beef.*

Photos: NLS & MB

Cutability or Yield Grading

Above and beyond the grading for the quality of meat, there is a grading available on beef, lamb, and mutton which identifies the yield of trimmed retail cuts which will be achieved in cutting. These yield grades are Nos. 1, 2, 3, 4, and 5 and refer in declining order to the amount of yield. The method used for determining the yield grade is discussed more fully under the beef and lamb sections.

Since one objective of a meat purchasing program is to obtain the most value for the purchasing dollar, it is a wise meat buyer who understands and uses yield grades in meat purchasing.

CUT IT, OR BUY IT CUT?

The decision whether to buy carcasses, sides, or quarters and butcher them in the house, or to buy fabricated cuts of meat is not a difficult one to make. The procedures involved in making the decision are simple, but the time consumed may be substantial.

The information needed to make the decision is as follows:

(1) Do you have a butcher?

Not every operation has a butcher; a person who cuts meat is not necessarily a butcher as butchers must go through lengthy training and apprenticeship. If the butcher does not know exactly what he is doing, then a large amount of the meat dollar may be wasted due to cutting meat in a way which provides too few of the expensive cuts and too many of the cheap cuts. If an operation does not have a good butcher, then it should buy only fabricated and portion cut meats.

(2) Is your operation equipped to butcher meat?

Not every operation is. A butcher shop needs hard and mechanical saws, specialized cleavers and knives, special types of tables, proper refrigeration, and receiving facilities.

(3) Can you afford the butcher's salary?

If the butcher's salary, including taxes and fringe benefits, is $250 per week (or $13,000 per year), and if the operation saves an average of $.10 per lb. of meat through self-butchering, then the operation must use *more than* 2500 lb. of meat per week to break even with buying

Cost-Comparison Conversion Table

BASE	STEAKS		
Primal Cut	N.Y. Steak	Fillets	Top Sirloin
90	147	146	144
95	155	155	153
100	163	165	162
105	171	174	171
110	179	183	180
115	187	193	189
120	196	202	198
125	204	211	207
130	212	221	216
135	220	230	225
140	228	239	234
145	236	249	243
150	245	258	252
155	253	267	261
160	261	277	270
165	269	286	279
170	277	295	288
175	285	305	297
180	293	314	306
185	302	324	315
190	310	333	324
195	318	342	333
200	326	352	342
205	334	361	351
210	342	370	360
215	350	379	369
220	359	389	378
225	367	398	387
230	375	407	396
235	383	416	406
240	391	426	415
245	399	436	424
250	407	445	433

Reprinted with permission from *The Cornell Hotel and Restaurant Quarterly*, November, 1968, p. 87.

fabricated or portion controlled meat cuts. Since the butcher spends 20 percent of his time (8 hours per week) in set-up and clean up, this means he must be able to butcher almost 70 lb. of meat per hour. If the operation uses a lot of roasts, this will be possible, but if the operation uses mostly steaks, chops, ground meat, and diced meat, this level of productivity may well not be possible. Also, an institution which uses 2500 lb. of butchered meat per week must feed an average of over 700 people per meal.

(4) What is the cost per pound of meat butchered in the house?

This determination is made by using a Yield Test Card (fig. No. 14). In the example, a hindquarter has been broken down using the New York cutting method which yields a good institutional mixture of cuts. The $__.____ per pound for the hindquarter is the *actual price paid*.

The "market value per #" figures are obtained either from the National Provisioner "Yellow Sheet" or from market quotations on the date of fabrication.

Note that there is a figure called fabrication multiplier at the bottom of the card. This is the ratio of the in-house fabricated cost to the market value. When this figure is known, it may be used to calculate future costs of in-house fabrication as the price of hindquarters changes.

(5) What are the other implications of butchering at the operation?

The biggest drawback is the possible non-usage of the cuts which are obtained by butchering. In order for butchering to be beneficial, the menu must call for the use of *all* the cuts obtained and in the *amounts* obtained. Close co-ordination of menu and butchering plan is needed to make butchering pay off.

Another drawback is that all the cuts obtained by

FIGURE 14 – YIELD TEST CARD

Item: Hindquarter of Beef No. 155 **Pieces: 1** **Total Cost: $**   at   per 16.

Grade: Choice Y 6.2 **Weight: 150 lb.,**   oz.

Date:

Item	No.	Weight lb.	Weight oz.	% of Total Weight	Market Value per lb.	Total Market Value	Cost per
Knuckle	167	10	14		.98		
Round, Inside	168	19	11		1.24		
Round, Gooseneck, Bnls	170	23	14		1.07		
Strip Loin, bnls	180	10	15		1.92		
Top Sirloin Butt, bnls	184	9	12		1.65		
Bttm Sirloin Butt, bnls	185	5	2		.55		
Full Tenderloin, reglr	189	5	6		2.04		
Flank Steak	193	1	9		1.60		
Beef for Stewing	1195	21	14		.68		
Hanging Tender		1	9		N/V		
Fat and Bone		39	7		N/V		

Fabrication Multiplier

butchering will be of the same grade. It is generally accepted that an operation will need U.S. Choice for broiling and dry roasting, but that U.S. Good is sufficient for pot roasting and stewing.

(6) If I buy fabricated meat, how can I be sure it will be cut the way I want it?

The United States Department of Agriculture maintains an inspection service which verifies that the packer has prepared the meat to your specifications. This USDA Acceptance Service (stamp shown in Fig. No. 15) is available, for a fee, to any operator using substantial quantities of meat as an aid in the meat purchasing program.

FIGURE 15

HOW MUCH TO ORDER?

To know how much meat to order, an operator needs to know how much he uses. Knowing how much to use, means knowing both how much is used per serving and how many servings are needed.

The question of how much meat to use per serving is a matter of operational philosophy and type of institution. Our society places a large psychological value on meat. Nutritional adequacy calls for only 56 grams of protein per adult per day. If given their preference, people want as much meat as possible. This fact can be traced to the close correlation between our image of success and the meat we eat.

By far, the most popular meat in the United States is beef. In order to make a menu popular, the mix of meat dishes should take this preference into consideration. The means of

keeping the cost of meat on the menu down are varied.

1. Balance the menu entree offerings with popular, less expensive, extender items when offering the more expensive, solid entrees. A clientele which likes a relatively expensive, solid entree, like sauerbraten, may well choose a less expensive option such as stew or goulash.

2. Never buy a better grade of meat than needed for the use intended.

3. Buy meat on tight specifications. It is a costly mistake to pay for fat which is not needed or to fail to pay for fat when it is needed.

4. Cook meat at the temperatures at which it should be cooked. Cooking losses increase in proportion to the rise in oven temperature. A study, summarized below, of roasts cooked to identical internal temperatures shows just how great cooking loss may be.

Well-done	125°C	225°C
Ribs of Beef	23.0 percent	37.5 percent
Chuck of Beef	33.8 percent	34.6 percent
Rump of Beef	27.4 percent	29.8 percent
Half-ham of Pork	26.8 percent	36.1 percent
Leg of Lamb	16.4 percent	27.3 percent
Rare	125°	225°
Ribs of Beef	7.1 percent	20.2 percent
Chuck of Beef	11.6 percent	21.4 percent

Knowing how much meat to order means the keeping of accurate records. The first record needed is a file of Cooking Loss Cards (Fig. No. 16). This record needs to be computed only once for each menu item, as the loss should always be about the same for the same grade and cut of meat.

With the usable, after-cooking, weight as a base, one may calculate the number of portions per cooked pound and then the number of raw pounds needed for x number of cooked portions by determining a multiplier. The multiplier is simply the result of the following operation:

$$\frac{\text{raw pounds}}{\text{cooked pounds}} \quad X \quad \frac{\text{cooked pounds}}{\text{portion weight}}$$

The second necessary record is a card which records the

FIGURE 16

COOKING LOSS

ITEM _____

PORTION SIZE _____   COOKED_____ HOURS_____ MINUTES AT _____DEGREES

PORTION COST FACTOR _____   _____ HOURS_____ MINUTES AT _____DEGREES

BREAKDOWN	NO.	WEIGHT		RATIO TO TOTAL WEIGHT	VALUE PER POUND	TOTAL VALUE	READY TO EAT VALUE PER		READY TO EAT PORTION		COST FACTOR PER	
		LBS.	OZ.				LB.	OZ.	SIZE	VALUE	LB.	PORTION
ORIGINAL WEIGHT												
LOSS IN TRIMMING												
TRIMMED WEIGHT												
LOSS IN COOKING												
COOKED WEIGHT												
BONES AND TRIM												
LOSS IN SLICING												
SALABLE MEAT												
REMARKS												

$$\text{COST FACTOR PER LB. OR PORTION} = \frac{\text{READY TO EAT VALUE PER LB. OR PORTION}}{\text{PURCHASE PRICE PER LB.}}$$

To find ready to eat value of cuts at a new market price, multiply new price per lb. by the cost factor.

number of portions used in the past. (Fig. No. 17). Note that the percentage of items used, *in the same menu combination*, will stay within a narrow percentage range. Although the customer count in an individual operation may vary greatly from day to day, the percentage of the customers who favor a particular entree will remain very close to the same. Seasons of the year may have some bearing upon the ratio but, again, the ratio will remain true within that particular season.

Keeping such a record for a few months will be sufficient to start using it as an ordering guide; keeping the record over the years will help identify unpopular menu combinations, changing taste trends, and need for menu change.

The third record needed is some type of inventory/order/ and receiving record. Consideration should be given to the needs of the institution, i.e. volume, refrigeration, and freezing capacity, management time, purchasing plan (butch-

FIGURE 17

PRODUCTION HISTORY CARD							P.S.	P.C.		ITEM	
DATE	DAY	RAN QUAN	PORTIONS PREPARED	PORTIONS LEFT	PORTIONS SERVED	PORTIONS ALL ITEMS	%		OTHER ENTREE		NOTES

ering vs. fabricated and portion controlled product). These methods are:

(1) Operations which have a standing menu (restaurants, hotels) or a short cycle menu of 7 or 10 days will probably find a "par-stock" or a "minimum-maximum stock" inventory system best.

(a) Par-Stock (Fig. No. 18). Under this system, the operator determines a stock level which will cover the institution's needs for the period of the ordering cycle. For purposes of example, we will call it one week. If the maximum weekly need for Item No. 137 Ground Beef is 100 lb., then the par-stock is 100 lb. Each week the Ground Beef order will be the difference between the on-hand inventory and 100 lb. Thus, if the current inventory is 30 lb., the order will be for 70 lb., etc.

(b) Minimum-Maximum Stock. In this method the operator determines the maximum amount of the item which may be needed in the ordering cycle and the minimum quality which must be kept in inventory to prevent running out. This system is very good for operations which

FIGURE 18

| ITEM_____ **INVENTORY** |
| SIZE_____COST_____LOCATION_____ |
| WHEN STOCK REACHES_____REORDER_____QUANTITY |
| ORDER FROM_____ |
| DELIVERY TAKES_____DAYS |

DATE	Quantity Ordered	Quantity Received	Quantity Issued	ISSUED TO	BAL.

Am. Hotel Reg. Co., Chicago 60610   FORM 685

tend to have a week-to-week fluctuation which does not follow a set pattern. Whenever the inventory falls to the minimum level, an order is placed to bring the stock back up to a maximum. Again, using the 100 lb. of Ground Beef as a maximum inventory, then a minimum inventory of say, 20 lb., may be determined. Whenever the inventory falls to 20 lb., an automatic reorder of 80 lb. is placed.

(2) Operations which have a cyclical menu of some length (3 to 6 weeks), or operations which have high volume and/or limited refrigerated storage space often find it most convenient to order on an as-needed basis. The drawbacks of this system are twofold. The first is that, unlike the "par-stock" and "minimum-maximum stock" systems, management must review the stock and menu needs at regular intervals instead of placing standing orders or leaving the ordering in clerical hands. The second drawback is that there is no reserve stock to call upon in an emergency situation.

The advantages of this system are that no inventory is being carried on the books, and there is no excess stock in the house and, therefore, no chance of spoilage.

Simply stated, the procedure is to estimate, from the production history cards (Fig. No. 17), the number of portions (converted to raw pounds) that are needed, and then order just that quantity. Note, in the example inventory/order/receiving record (Fig. No. 19), that the amount ordered is entered above the diagonal line, and that the amount *actually* received is entered below that line. The "end" column provides for a weekly inventory, which precedes the ordering, so that any excess stock may be subtracted from the amount needed to order.

HOW MUCH TO PAY?

High quality and high price do not necessarily go hand-in-hand anymore than do low quality and low price. A full discussion of purchasing techniques is found in Chapter 1 "Purchasing Policies." When buying meat, the buyer must be aware of certain things.

(1) It costs the purveyor money to make deliveries. The

FIGURE 19

HILLSIDE HOSPITAL FOOD SERVICE MONTHLY INVENTORY/ORDER/RECEIVING RECORD

	ITEM	UNIT	INV. BEG.	M	T	W	TH	F	END	S/S	M	T	W	TH	F	END	S/S	M	T	W
	BEEF			4	5	6	7	8		9/10	11	12	13	14	15		16/17	18	19	20
1	Liver, Steer	lb.			60							25							27	
2	Round, MBG No. 158	lb.			20							90							69	
3	Round, MBG No. 170 Corned	lb.	10		40															
4	Round, MGB No. 1167r	lb.	32																	
5	Round, MBG No. 1168r	lb.																		
6	Round, diced 1 in. MBG No. 135	lb.	40																	
7	Round, ground 80/20	lb.			50							80							50	
8	Flk Stk MBG No. 193	lb.																		
9	Skt Stk 1-1/2 in.	lb.	57		100														50	
10	Strip Loin MBG 178	lb.																		
11	Strip Stks MBG 1178	lb.	248																612	
12	Bologna 100% Beef	lb.	133		14							61							23	
13	Salami 100% Beef	lb.	52									16							24	
14	Franks 8 to 100% Beef	lb.	34										50							
15	Pastrami, Pickled Roumanian	lb.																	45	
16	Patties, 4 oz. 80/20	lb.	40									45							75	
17	Salisbury Steak, 5 oz. 80/20	pc.	240					60											60	
18	Stuffed Cabbage	cs.						5												
19	Stuffed Peppers	cs.																		
20	Knockwurst, 4 to Skinless	lb.																	45	
21	Beef Burgundy	cs.																		
22	Beef Stew	cs.																		
23	Top Round—Cooked	lb.																		
24	Bttm Round—Cooked	lb.																		
25	Corned Beef—Cooked	lb.																		
26																				
27																				

PAGE 1   TOTAL 868.01

TH	F	END S/S	M	T	W	TH	F	END S/S	M	T	W	TH	5/5 S	END INV.	@	=	CON-SUMED	
21	22	23/24	25	26	27	28	29	30/31	2				2/3					
									60						48		112	1
				390/376											74		733½	2
									30						84		50	3
														75	1 20	90 —	-43	4
														64	1 10	70 40	-64	5
				77										40	85	34 —	77	6
			2½ 59/50						39						64		256½	7
																		8
				59/60					120						67		267	9
																		10
														504	1. 10	554 40	356	11
			15	2½/23					7					21	82	17 22	73½	12
			12	2½/25										43	82	36 98	86	13
				30/30					59					55	90	49 50	75	14
															84		45	15
				60/60					50						70		250	16
															33		840	17
									4					1/3	12 65	4 21	42⅔	18
																		19
															85		45	20
																		21
																		22
																		23
																		24
																		25
														10	1 20	12 —		26
																		27
																868 01		

larger the order and the less frequent the deliveries, the more likely it is that the price will be lower.

(2) Excessive "fill-in" orders, unclear specifications, and unreasonable demands put upon a purveyor will result in higher prices.

(3) If you deal with a purveyor who has an inefficient plant operation, the cost of his inefficiency will be passed on to you either in price, poor trim, or improperly cared-for product.

(4) Each grade of meat has a range of tolerance, thus there *is* such a thing as "high" Choice and "low" Choice meat. Beware of the purveyor who always claims his meat is "high" choice; appreciate the purveyor who tells you when the meat is "low," "middle range," or "high" in the grade.

(5) Beware of the "special" or the "lowball" price. Chances are that the meat is too fresh or has been either aged too long or aged improperly.

(6) Receiving controls must be *very tight*. Each piece of meat must be weighed and measured against the specifications. A simple ruler and the pictures later in this section are excellent receiving tools.

(7) Storage temperatures must be exact and storage time as brief as possible. Meat shrinks due to evaporation during storage.

(8) The buyer and the receiver must have complete loyalty to the operation. A system of checks and balances must be established in order to assure a high degree of honesty. Dishonesty, as discussed in Chapter 1, takes many forms and is often difficult to uncover.

(9) Meat buying must be conducted either on a bid basis or on a contract. Base contract prices should be arrived at by using one of the various USDA market reports or on the "Yellow Sheet" which is published by the National Provisioner.

HOW MUCH TO CHARGE?

What an operator must charge for his meat entrees is contingent both upon what the cost per portion is and upon the financial goals of the operation. The method for arriving at the charge is the same for all types of operation, but the goals may be very different.

A public establishment such as a hotel or restaurant is in business to make a profit. Here the price charged will have to contribute to a profit mixture. If the total profit from operations must be, for example, 12 percent, then every item must contribute to the profit to a degree of 12 percent. Some price-balancing may be done, but the average gain must be 12 percent over *all* costs involved. If the food cost of the operation is 40 percent of expenditures, then each item will have to sell at 2.5 times (100% ÷ 40%) its cost plus 12 percent.

Schools and colleges generally must run foodservice operations on a no profit-no loss basis. In this case, the price of food must be the amount which contributes to breaking even. Using the above example (40 percent food cost), the food in these institutions would be priced 2.5 times the raw cost.

Some institutions, such as industrial feeding operations and hospital employee cafeterias, operate on company subsidies in order to keep food charges low. The idea is to provide eating facilities for the employees which are close to the job. Prices in this situation are based either on what ceiling top management wants on food prices or on the amount of subsidy.

In the first case, the cost of raw food bears no relationship to the price charged. In the second case, it is necessary to estimate the total operating costs, subtract the subsidy, and charge prices for food which contribute proportionately to that expense figure. For example, if the total operating costs are $100,000, the food cost $40,000, and the subsidy $30,000, then the pricing calculation is as follows:

$$
\begin{array}{rl}
\$100,000 & \text{- operating costs} \\
30,000 & \text{- subsidy} \\
\hline
70,000 & \text{- income needed} \\
\div \ 40,000 & \text{- food cost}
\end{array}
$$

= 1.75 x raw food cost = price to be charged.

WHAT IS THE COST?

The steps to computing the cost per portion are as follows:

(1) Compute the raw ready-to-cash weight. (Meat either purchased that way *or* see Yield Test Card, Fig. No. 14, p. 85.)

(2) Cook, trim, and carve the meat. Subtract the combined weight of the carved *portions* from the cooked weight.

(3) Divide the total raw cost by the total weight of the carved portions.

Example: 100 lb. Inside Round - R.T.C. at $1.24 = $124.00

76 lb. Carved Weight

$$76\overline{)124.00} \quad 1.63x$$

$$\begin{array}{r} 76 \\ \hline 480 \\ 456 \\ \hline 240 \\ 228 \\ \hline 120 \end{array}$$

Cost per saleable pound $1.63
6 oz. Portion Weight

$1.63 ÷ 16 oz. = $.1078 per oz. x 6 = .612 per portion

or

76 lb. x 16 oz. = 1216 oz. ÷ 6 = 202.7 portions

.6117 or .612 per portion

$$202.7\overline{)124.00000}$$

$$\begin{array}{r} 121.62 \\ \hline 2380 \\ 2027 \\ \hline 3530 \\ 2027 \\ \hline 15030 \end{array}$$

The above calculation should be made for every menu item served. The carved weight percentage (76 percent in the above example) can be used to quickly recalculate the cost per portion when the raw product cost changes or portion size is changed. A comparison of the cost per portion on various cuts of meat will quickly reveal the most economical cut of meat to use for any given menu item.

WRITING MEAT SPECIFICATIONS

PURPOSE

The purpose of written specifications for meat and meat products is dual. The first purpose is to give the operator and his employees knowledge of which product should be used for what purpose. The second purpose is to tell the purveyor *exactly* what the expected product is. It is not possible *honestly* to take quotations on a meat item if the purveyor and the operator do not agree on the *exact* definition of the meat item.

Once written, a copy of the operation's specifications must be sent, for reference, to every purveyor that the operation buys from. The operator must insist that his deliveries meet the *exact* specifications he has set. Any variance from these standards is dishonest, costly to the operation, and, therefore, forbidden.

WHAT MUST BE INCLUDED:

The properly written meat specification should include the operation's exact requirements are regards:

1. Class of Animal
2. USDA Grade and Division of Grade
3. USDA Yield Grade
4. Acceptable Weight Range
5. State of Refrigeration
6. Fat Limitations

WHAT ARE THE IMPS?

IMPS, the Institutional Meat Purchase Specifications, are the official USDA requirements for the inspection, packaging, packing, and delivering of specific meats and meat products, and for the certification of those products by USDA meat graders. The IMPS are the most widely known and accepted meat specifications in our country. Formally, the IMPS are applied with the use of the Meat Acceptance Service of the USDA. In operations too small to use the Meat Acceptance Service, the IMPS can still be used as long as the person receiving the meat knows how to translate the written specification to the physical object.

WHAT IS *THE MEAT BUYERS GUIDE?*

The Meat Buyers' Guides contain the meat specifications agreed upon by the National Association of Meat Purveyors (NAMP), the largest and most powerful of all wholesale meat purveyor associations. The two publications, *The Meat Buyers Guide to Standardized Meat Cuts* and *The Meat Buyers Guide to Portion Control Meat Cuts*, were written as a means of simplifying the IMPS and to give pictoral definition to the most common meat cuts. There is no better set of meat specifications anywhere in the country than the *IMPS* and *Meat Buyer's Guides*. Since the *Meat Buyers Guides* are illustrated with photographs which show the proper dimensions of the cut product, they are the specifications that should be used by all operators. Every meat purveyor knows the MBG specifications and, therefore, should have no difficulty in delivering products that meet the MBG specifications.

The specifications set forth in the remainder of this chapter are both the IMPS and the MBG's. The MBG specifications are the specifications of first choice. Because the MBG's do not include all the IMPS, the IMPS are woven into the text. IMPS and MBG's have replaced the prevalent regional names for the various meat cuts. In order to help the reader identify cuts, the most common regional names are included, as well as the names used in the *Uniform Retail Meat Identity Standards*, published by the National Livestock and Meat Board.

Most common uses for each cut of meat are listed as a menu preparation aid to the reader.

INSTITUTIONAL MEAT PURCHASE SPECIFICATIONS
GENERAL REQUIREMENTS
(Effective August 1971 and January 1975)
BEEF SPECIFICATIONS:

USDA GRADE—To Be Specified by Purchaser

The purchaser must specify either (1) a quality grade, or (2) a combination of quality grade and yield grade. Yield grades 1 through 5 are applicable to all quality grades. However, those yield grades indicated by an "X" are in the largest supply

USDA GRADES

Quality	Yield[1]				
	1	2	3	4	5
U.S. Prime			x	x	x
U.S. Choice		x	x	x	x
U.S. Good		x	x		
U.S. Standard	x	x	x		
U.S. Commercial		x	x	x	x
U.S. Utility		x	x	x	
U.S. Cutter		x	x		
U.S. Canner		x	x		

1. The yield grades reflect differences in yields of boneless, closely trimmed retail cuts. Yield grade 1 represents the highest yield of cuts and yield grade 5, the lowest.

DIVISION OF QUALITY GRADE—To Be Specified by Purchaser (Not applicable to yield grade)

NOTE

If the upper half or lower half of a quality grade is desired, it must be so specified, otherwise the full range of the grade is acceptable.

WEIGHT RANGE—To Be Specified By Purchaser

Range A, B, C, D, or E, or actual weight range in pounds (8/10, 20/24, etc.)

STATE OF REFRIGERATION—To Be Specified by Purchaser

A. Chilled

B. Frozen

FAT LIMITATIONS—Carcasses, Sides or Quarters: (Not applicable if yield grade is specified)

Except when yield grade is specified by the purchaser, the thickness of external fat measured at the thinnest point over the rib or loin eye must not exceed that indicated for each quality grade in the following schedule:

GRADE	Maximum Thickness of Fat at Thinnest Point over Ribeye	
	WEIGHT RANGE A & B	WEIGHT RANGE C, D, & E
U.S. Prime	7/8 in.	1-1/4 in.
U.S. Choice	5/8 in.	1 in.
U.S. Good	3/8 in.	3/4 in.
U.S. Standard	1/4 in.	3/8 in.
U.S. Commercial	5/8 in.	7/8 in.
U.S. Utility	1/4 in.	1/2 in.
U.S. Cutter or Canner	1/8 in.	1/4 in.

In addition, carcasses, sides, or quarters are not acceptable if, because of an uneven distribution of external fat or large deposits of kidney and pelvic fat, they are wasty in relation to the maximum permitted thickness of fat over the ribeye.

FAT LIMITATIONS—Wholesale and Fabricated Cuts: To Be Specified by Purchaser (Not applicable if yield grade is specified)

Except when yield grade is specified, for all wholesale and fabricated beef products—except those for which definite fat limitations are indicated in the detailed specifications—the purchaser must specify one of the following maximum average thicknesses of surface fat:

MAXIMUM AVERAGE THICKNESS

1 in. (1-1/4 in. maximum at any point except for seam fat)
3/4 in. (1 in. maximum at any point except for seam fat)
1/2 in. (3/4 in. maximum at any point except for seam fat)
1/4 in. (1/2 in. maximum at any point except for seam fat)

Defatting must be done by smoothly removing the fat by following the contour of the underlying muscle surface. Beveling of the edges, only, is not acceptable.

NOTE

When string tying is required, roasts must be made firm and compact and held intact by individual loops of strong twine uniformly spaced at approx. 2-in. intervals girthwise. In addition, some roasts may require string tying lengthwise. In lieu of string tying, it is permissible to enclose roasts in a stretchable netting, provided it complies with the Regulations Governing the Meat Inspection of the USDA. Purchasers may specify that roasts be string tied when this requirement is not specified in the detailed roast item specifications.

MATERIAL—Beef products described must be derived from sound, well-dressed, split and quartered beef carcasses or from sound, well-trimmed, primal cuts from such carcasses. The beef must be prepared and handled in accordance with good commercial practice and must meet the type, grade, style of cut, weight range, and state of refrigeration specified.

Beef cuts which have been excessively trimmed in order to meet specified weights, or which are substandard according to the specifications for any reason, are excluded. The beef must be of good color normal to the grade, be practically free of residue remaining from sawing the meat and bones, and free of

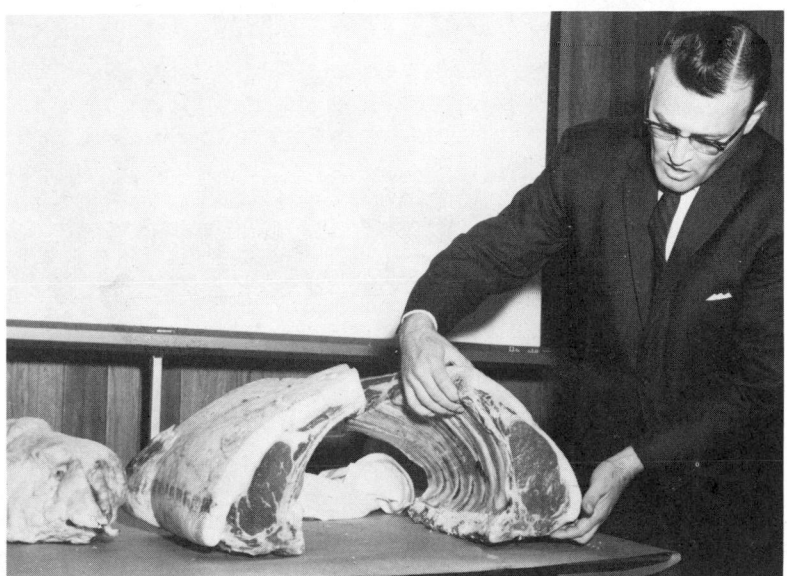

John C. Pierce, Agricultural Marketing Service, U.S. Department of Agriculture, illustrates the dual grading system for beef, which would provide separate grades for quality and for yield of trimmed retail cuts. This is one of the ways that AMS is striving to make federal grade standards more precise and descriptive to provide better measures of the merchantability and value of farm products.

blood clots, scores, odor foreign to strictly fresh beef (e.g. kerosene, putrid, stale, rancid, chemicals, etc.), mutilations (other than slight), ragged edges, superficial appendages, blemishes, discoloration, (e.g. green, black, blue, etc.), deterioration, damage, or mishandling. The spinal cord must be completely removed, and the beef also must be free from bruises, evidence of freezing or defrosting, and must be in excellent condition to the time of delivery. Stag and bull beef are not acceptable.

Portion-cut items described herein must be prepared from fresh-chilled carcasses or bone-in cuts which are in excellent condition, and they must be of the applicable kind and of the U.S. grade or selection specified. The meat must show no evidence of off-condition, including but not restricted to off-odor, slightly sticky, gassy, rancid, sour, discolored, and evidence of defrosting or mishandling. Also, the portion-cut items must be free of blood clots, scores (other than slight),

SLAUGHTER STEERS
U.S. GRADES
(QUALITY)

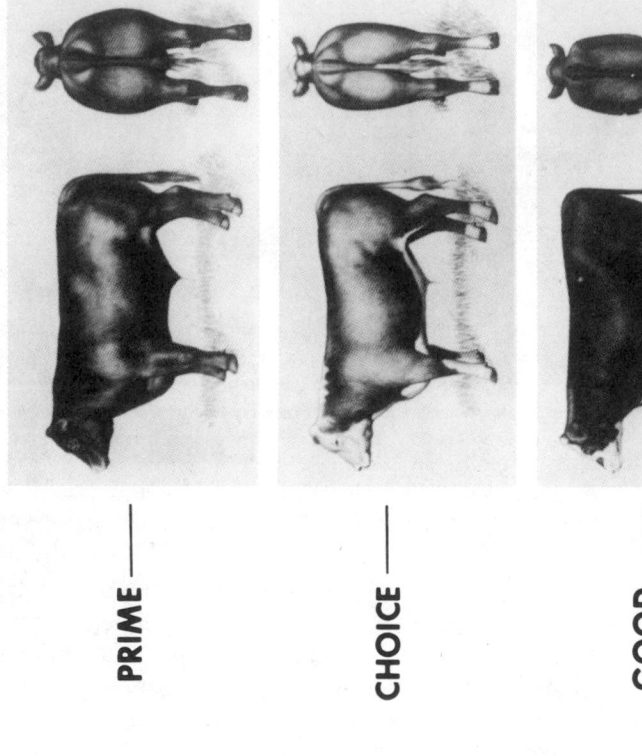

PRIME ——

CHOICE ——

GOOD ——

STANDARD ——

UTILITY ——

COMMERCIAL, CUTTER, AND
CANNER GRADES ARE OMITTED

COPIES OF THE OFFICIAL
UNITED STATES STANDARDS
FOR GRADES ARE AVAILABLE
ON REQUEST

UNITED STATES DEPARTMENT OF AGRICULTURE
CONSUMER AND MARKETING SERVICE
LIVESTOCK DIVISION
WASHINGTON, D.C.

AUGUST 1969

SLAUGHTER STEERS
U.S. GRADES
(YIELD)

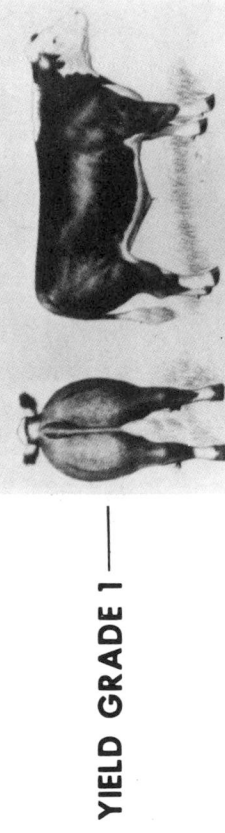
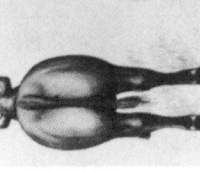
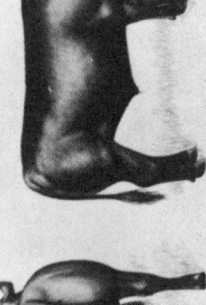

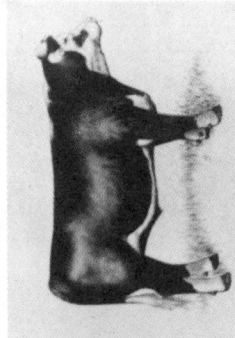

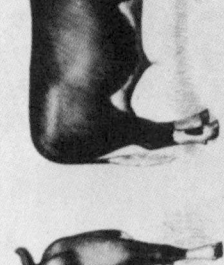
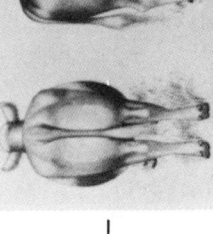
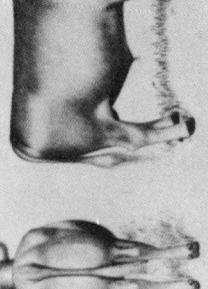

YIELD GRADE 1

YIELD GRADE 2

YIELD GRADE 3

YIELD GRADE 4

YIELD GRADE 5

UNITED STATES DEPARTMENT OF AGRICULTURE
CONSUMER AND MARKETING SERVICE
LIVESTOCK DIVISION
WASHINGTON, D.C.

AUGUST 1969

COPIES OF THE OFFICIAL
UNITED STATES STANDARDS
FOR GRADE ARE AVAILABLE
ON REQUEST

COMPARISON OF YIELDS* OF RETAIL CUTS AND RETAIL VALUES BETWEEN USDA YIELD GRADE 2 AND YIELD GRADE 4 CARCASSES

Closely Trimmed Retail Cuts	Percent Carcass Weight		Price per Pound**	Retail Value in Dollars per cwt.	
	USDA 2	USDA 4		USDA 2	USDA 4
Rump, boneless	3.5	3.1	$1.68	$5.88	$5.21
Inside round	4.5	3.7	1.81	8.15	6.70
Outside round	4.6	4.2	1.75	8.05	7.35
Round tip	2.6	2.4	1.77	4.60	4.25
Sirloin	8.7	7.9	1.69	14.71	13.35
Short loin	5.2	5.0	1.94	10.09	9.70
Rib, short cut (7 in.)	6.2	6.0	1.59	9.86	9.54
Blade chuck	9.4	8.4	.93	8.75	7.80
Chuck, arm, boneless	6.1	5.5	1.32	8.05	7.26
Brisket, boneless	2.3	1.9	1.48	3.41	2.81
Flank steak	.5	.5	2.01	1.01	1.01
Lean trim	11.3	9.3	1.21	13.67	11.25
Ground beef	12.2	10.0	1.01	12.30	10.10
Fat	12.7	22.9	.02	.25	.46
Bone	9.9	8.9	.01	.10	.09
Kidney	.3	.3	.66	.20	.20
TOTAL	100.0	100.0		$109.08	$97.08

Difference in retail value per cwt. between Yield Grade 2 and 4—$12.00

* Cuts trimmed to ½ inch of fat.

** Average retail prices for Choice beef for October 1973 (including sale priced items) as furnished by a large number of selected retailers throughout the country.

ragged edges, bruises, and spinal cord, and must be practically free of bone and meat dust. Portion-cut items supplied must be in compliance with applicable requirements specified herein and with other requirements specified by the purchaser.

PORTION WEIGHT OR THICKNESS OF STEAKS, CHOPS, CUTLETS

Purchasers must specify *either* the portion weight or thickness desired—*not both*. However, in order to control uniformity of portion sizes, the weight range of the trimmed meat cut from which the portions are to be produced may also be specified.

PORTION WEIGHT—If portion weight is specified, the actual portion weights desired (3 oz., 6 oz., 12 oz., etc.) must be indicated.

WEIGHT TOLERANCES—Unless otherwise specified by the purchaser, dependent upon the portion weight specified, the following tolerances over and under the weight specified will be permitted.

Weight Specified	Tolerances [over and under]
less than 6 oz.	1/4 oz.
6 oz. but less than 12 oz.	1/2 oz.
12 oz. but less than 18 oz.	3/4 oz.
18 oz. or more	1 oz.

Example: When 8-oz. steaks are specified, individual steaks weighing 7-1/2 to 8-1/2 oz. are applicable.

THICKNESS—If thickness is specified, the actual thickness desired must be indicated. (Cubed steaks, ground beef patties, and cubed cutlets excepted.)

THICKNESS TOLERANCE—Unless otherwise specified by the purchaser, dependent upon the thickness specified, the following tolerances over and under the thickness specified will be permitted:

Thickness Specified	Tolerances [over and under]
1 in. or less	3/16 in.
More than 1 in.	1/4 in.

Example: When 1-1/4 in. steaks are specified, individual steaks measuring 1 to 1-1/2 in. are acceptable.

WEIGHT RANGE FOR ROASTS

Purchasers must specify the actual weight range (4-6, 8-10, 17-19, etc.) desired. If purchasers want roasts further reduced in size, this must also be specified.

SURFACE FAT

STEAKS—Unless otherwise specified by the purchaser, or unless definite fat limitations are indicated in the detailed item specifications, on surfaces where fat is present, the fat must not exceed an average of 1/2 in. in thickness, and the thickness at any point must be not more than 3/4 in.

CHOPS, CUTLETS, AND FILETS—Unless otherwise specified by the purchaser, surface fat, where present, must not exceed an average of 1/4 in. in thickness, and the thickness at any one point must be not more than 3/8 in.

ROASTS—The purchaser must specify the maximum average surface fat thickness desired as expressed below, unless definite fat limitations are indicated in the detailed item specifications.

Maximum Average Surface Fat Thickness [seam fat excepted]
3/4 in. (1 in. maximum at any one point)
1/2 in. (3/4 in. maximum at any one point)

NOTE

Defatting must be done by smoothly removing the fat by following the contour of the underlying muscle surface. Beveling of the edges only is not acceptable. In determining the average thickness of surface fat or the thickness of fat at any one point on steaks and roasts which have an evident, natural depression into the lean, only the fat above the portion of the depression which is more than 3/4 in. in width will be considered.

INSPECTION

All meats, prepared meats, meat food products, and meat by-products (as defined in Rules and Regulations of the Department of Agriculture Governing the Grading and Certification of Meats, Prepared Meats, and Meat Products) covered by these specifications must originate from animals which were slaughtered or from product items which were manufactured or processed in establishments regularly operated under the supervision of the Meat and Poultry Inspection Program (MPIP) of the Consumer and Marketing Service (C&MS) of the United States Department of Agriculture (USDA) or under any other system of meat inspection approved by the Consumer and Marketing Service of the USDA.

ORDERING DATA

The purchaser will requisition product items by specifying the item number, name, and the desired options such as grade or selection, weight range, formula, state of refrigeration, etc., indicated in each specification, and products must be offered for delivery on such basis by the contractor, subject to official examination, acceptance, and certification by USDA meat graders or other designated personnel. The examination, acceptance, and certification of products by the USDA shall be in accordance with USDA Meat Grading instructions. (Copies of Meat Grading instructions may be obtained from the local Meat Grading Branch Main Station Office.)

CERTIFICATION

In connection with the issuance of meat grade certificates, one or more kinds of official USDA meat grade certificates will be involved depending on whether the product is for delivery chilled or frozen.

A. Products for Delivery Chilled.

When products are to be delivered chilled, an official final certificate will be issued by the responsible USDA meat grader to cover all factors and details of the products.

B. Products for Delivery Frozen.

When products are to be delivered frozen, the responsible

USDA meat grader will issue an official preliminary certificate, identified as such, to cover all factors and details of the chilled product prior to freezing. The responsible USDA meat grader will issue an official final certificate covering all factors and details of the frozen product prior to loading for delivery.

DISPOSITION OF CERTIFICATES

The original and up to two extra copies of all preliminary and final certificates are available to the contractor. The purchaser may request the contractor to supply copies of all final certificates.

THE COST OF THE EXAMINATION, ACCEPTANCE, AND CERTIFICATION SHALL BE PAID BY THE CONTRACTOR.

TIME LIMITATION

Products prepared for delivery under a purchase order shall not be offered to USDA meat graders for examination and acceptance more than 72 hours before shipment.

STATE OF REFRIGERATION

The detailed specifications for the various products indicate two different states of refrigeration. These are defined as follows:

A. Chilled.

Chilled products are those which, promptly after preparation and in accordance with good commercial practice, are thoroughly chilled (but not frozen or defrosted) to an internal temperature of not higher than 50°F. They must be held in suitable temperatures (32° to 38°F.) and must be in excellent condition to the time of delivery.

B. Frozen.

Products to be delivered frozen must be promptly and thoroughly frozen in suitable and reasonably uniform temperatures not higher than 0°F. Products thus frozen must be maintained and delivered in a solidly frozen state. The products must show no evidence of defrosting, refreezing, freezerburn, contamination, or mishandling.

When the state of refrigeration is not specified in the purchase order, the product must be maintained and delivered chilled.

PACKAGING AND PACKING

A. Packaging.

1. All carcass meat and wholesale cuts that are normally wrapped in commercial practice must be completely and properly packaged in suitable material (crinkled paper bags, grease and moisture-resistant paper, suitable plastic or metal foil covering, stockinettes, etc.) to insure sanitary delivery.

2. Fabricated and boneless cuts (including units of diced and ground meat); cured, smoked, and dried meat; and edible by-products that are normally wrapped in commercial practice must be separately and closely packaged with suitable grease and moisture-resistant paper or suitable plastic or metal foil covering, etc.

3. Portion-control products must be suitably packaged in accordance with good commercial practice and, unless otherwise specified in the purchase order, such packages must contain not more than 25 pounds net weight.

4. Unless otherwise specified in the purchase order, products such as frankfurters, sliced bacon, sliced dried beef, linked or bulk pork or breakfast sausage, etc., must be suitably packaged and placed in immediate containers of the kind conventionally used for such products as illustrated in the following:

   a. Frankfurters and linked sausage — One-pound retail-type individual packages packed not more than 10 pounds per unit in the outer container, or layer packed 1 link deep with parchment or waxed paper separators between layers in a 5- to 10-pound container.

   b. Sliced bacon — One-pound retail-type individual packages such as folded or sleeve-type cartons, cello covering, or flat hotel-style packets snugly packed in a substantial outer container not to exceed 50 pounds net packed weight.

   c. Sliced dried beef — Either ¼-pound, ½-pound, or 1-pound retail-type individual packages, snugly packed not more than 10 pounds net weight per outer container, or bulk or layer packed in a substantial inside-waxed or plastic or waxed paper-lined container not to exceed 10 pounds net packed weight.

d. Bulk pork or breakfast sausage — One-pound retail-type individual packages such as cello rolls, plastic bags, waxed paper cups, or folded or sleeve-type cartons, packed not more than 10 pounds net weight per container, or in waxed or plastic coated paper tubs of either 5 or 10 pounds net weight.

5. It is the contractor's responsibility to assure that products to be frozen are suitably wrapped and packaged in a material which is grease and moisture resistant and which will also prevent freezer deterioration.

B. Packing.

Unless otherwise specified in the purchase order, products customarily packed in shipping containers must not be packed in excess of 100 pounds, net weight, except that portion-control products are limited to units weighing not more than 25 pounds. Containers must be of a size and shape normally used and adapted to the product being packed. The shipping containers must be made from material which will impart no odor, flavor, or color to the product and must be packed to full capacity without slack-filling or overfilling.

Immediate containers used for packaging which meet the packing requirements may be used as shipping containers. Otherwise, immediate containers must be placed in a master container meeting the packing requirements except that part or whole shipments of not more than 5 packaged units may be shipped in their immediate containers.

Chilled products must be packed in wirebound wooden boxes or in fiberboard boxes. Products to be frozen must be packed in fiberboard boxes. Fiberboard used in making these boxes shall be as described in Federal Specification PPP-F-320 and must comply with the requirements listed below.

Products that are normally bulk packed (spareribs, oxtails, tongues, etc.) or those that are normally moist or subject to dripping moisture must be packed in either wax-resin impreg-nated fiberboard boxes or in boxes which are protected by one or both of the following methods:

1. Appropriate moisture-proof plastic or wax coated on the inside (not applicable to wirebound wood boxes). The quantity of wax applied to the interior must be sufficient to be visible when lightly scraped with the fingernail.

2. Completely lined on the inside (sides, ends, top, and bottom) with suitably waxed kraft or parchment paper or with appropriate moisture-proof plastic liners.

Cured products in pickle may be either put in plastic bags and then packed into fiberboard boxes of the type specified for use with products subject to dripping moisture or they may be packed directly into fiber, wooden, or metal drums. Drum interiors shall be suitably protected by a wax or plastic coating or lined with a plastic bag liner. When used, plastic bags and plastic bag liners must be securely closed. Drums shall have full opening tops with lock rim closures which permit sealing by USDA and opening and reclosure by the purchaser.

Unless otherwise specified in the purchase order, in lieu of the aforementioned shipping containers, new or reconditioned wooden slack barrels or fiber drums may be used for packing full ribs, oven-prepared ribs, roast-ready ribs, strip loins, lamb backs and similar cuts to be delivered in the fresh state. The wooden slack barrels must be protected from absorption and leakage by an inside lining of plastic or crinkled kraft paper. The fiber drums must be protected from absorption and leakage by a wax or plastic inside coating or by an inside lining of plastic or crinkled kraft paper. After packing, the barrels or drums must be properly headed and covered.

CLOSURE

Fiberboard boxes shall be securely closed using one or more of the following methods:

1. Strapping — Boxes may be strapped with one of the following:

a. Flat steel straps, at least ¼ inch in width, that are protected with an enameled or rust-resistant coating.

REQUIREMENTS FOR FIBERBOARD[1]

Weight of Product	State of Refrigeration of Product		
	Chilled	Frozen	
		Weather Resistant	Wax-Resin Impregnated
More than 25 pounds	200 p.s.i.	275 p.s.i.	200 p.s.i.
25 pounds or less	175 p.s.i.	175 p.s.i.	175 p.s.i.

1. Dry board bursting strength of fiberboard used in making boxes for products to be delivered either chilled or frozen.

b. Pressure-sensitive adhesive, filament reinforced tape at least 0.5 inch in width.
c. Non-metallic strapping at least 3/8 inch wide by 0.015 inch thick, or at least ¼ inch wide by 0.027 inch thick.
d. Substantial round or twist-tie galvanized, steel wire.

Containers with a net weight of more than 25 pounds must be strapped by placing one strap, wire, or tape girthwise at the approximate center around the top, sides, and bottom of the container and by a second strap, wire, or tape centrally located around the top, ends, and bottom of the container at a right angle to the first. For containers with a net weight of 25 pounds or less, the second strap may be omitted.

2. Stapling — Staples shall be sufficient in number and shall be properly distributed to insure a secure closure and to prevent lifting of edges and corners of outer flaps.
3. Gluing — The top and bottom flaps shall be firmly glued together over a sufficient area to insure a secure closure and to prevent lifting of edges and corners of outer flaps.

NOTE: USDA maintains the right to have the packing and closure materials determined by appropriate test procedures.

SEALING

When individual products are not stamped, the immediate or shipping containers in which the products are packed must be sealed in accordance with USDA meat grading instructions.

NOTE: If a tape or strap specified for sealing also qualifies as a strapping material under "Closure," it may be used as both a strap and the seal.

MARKING

A. Containers Packed to More Than 25 Pounds Net Weight.

1. The following markings must be legibly and conspicuously stenciled or printed on one end of the container in letters and numbers not less than ½ inch high:
   a. Upper left hand corner. The true name of the product and the code identification of these specifications (IMPS), together with the product item number (Roast Ready Ribs, IMPS No. 109; Bologna, IMPS No. 801, etc.).
   b. Upper right hand corner. The date of examination and acceptance by the USDA meat grader (month, day, and year).
   c. Lower left hand corner. The grade or selection of product (U.S. Prime, U.S. Choice, etc.; or Selection No. 1, Selection No. 2, as applicable).
   d. Lower right hand corner. The number of pieces or packages of product in the container and the net weight of the product. (This information may be applied with a felt tip pen, crayon, or pencil).
2. The following markings must be stenciled or printed on the top or side of the container in letters and numbers not less than ½ inch high:

a. The name and address of the contractor.
b. The name and address of the supplier if other than the contractor.
c. The name and address of the consignee (not applicable to stockpiled products).

In addition to the above markings, when product is prepared for stockpiling (not prepared under a purchase order) it shall have any deviations from specification requirements and all applicable options such as weight range, formula, portion-size, etc., stenciled or printed on the lower left hand corner of the same end on which the other markings appear.

NOTE: When lack of space precludes listing all the information required on the lower left hand corner of the end, it may be stenciled or printed on the opposite end or on a side panel.

The marking material must be flat, waterfast, non-smearing (take-on fiber) and black in color.

B. Containers Packed to 25 Pounds or Less Net Weight.

In lieu of stenciling, such containers may have a printed or typewritten label firmly attached by adhesive material on one end of the container which legibly and conspicuously bears the markings indicated in A above.

EXAMINATION FOR CONDITION OF CONTAINERS

Definitions and procedures contained in the United States Standards for Conditions of Food Containers shall apply for lots containing 50 or more shipping containers or 300 or more primary containers. (Copies of the Standard may be obtained from the Livestock Division, C&MS, USDA, Washington, D.C. 20250).

In lots that include less than 50 shipping containers or less than 300 primary containers, the containers shall be examined individually and all defective containers must be replaced or corrected, as applicable.

Examination for condition of containers shall be made in conjunction with the final examination and acceptance of the product. However, at the option of the contractor, on product to be delivered frozen, such an examination also may be made in conjunction with the preliminary examination and acceptance.

CONDITION OF PRODUCT AT TIME OF DELIVERY

Refrigerated trucks must be used when necessary to protect products during transport and these trucks must be clean and free from foreign odors. At destination, all products will be re-examined by the consignee for cleanliness and soundness.

SPECIAL NOTICE

Contractors furnishing products under these specifications are expected to furnish such assistance as may be necessary to expedite the grading, examination, and acceptance of these products. These specifications will be strictly enforced by the using agencies. The consignee may, by purchasing acceptable products in the open market, immediately replace any products which are not delivered or which he rejects. In such case, any increase in cost of these products will be charged against the defaulting contractor.

WAIVERS AND AMENDMENTS TO SPECIFICATIONS REQUIREMENTS

Waivers of a few specification requirements may be made provided: (1) the change can be indicated clearly and precisely, (2) there is agreement between purchaser and contractor on the changes, and (3) the purchaser furnishes the USDA meat grader who is to perform the examination and acceptance of the product with a written statement indicating the precise nature of the changes.

Examples of waivers that may be made:
1. Substitution of weight ranges for those specified.
2. Substitution of grade of meat specified.
3. Modification of fat content in ground or diced meat.
4. Slight variations in trim or style of cutting.
5. Slight variations in sausage formulas.

Changes involving extensive rephrasing of specification requirements must be considered as an amendment to the specification and may be placed in effect only after such changes have been submitted and approved by the Standardization Branch, Livestock Division, C&MS, United States Department of Agriculture.

Beef: Yield of wholesale cuts from the carcass and yield of boneless meat from wholesale cuts

Carcass and wholesale cuts	Yield of bone-in wholesale cuts		Yield of boneless meat from wholesale cuts[1]	
	Prime, Choice, and Good	Canner and Cutter	Prime, Choice, and Good	Canner and Cutter
	PERCENT	PERCENT	PERCENT	PERCENT
Carcass, whole	100.0	100.0	66.0	73.0
Forequarter	51.5	52.0	69.0	72.5
Rib	9.5	8.5	65.0	71.0
Chuck, square cut	26.5	28.5	73.5	76.0
Plate	8.5	7.5	63.5	74.0
Brisket	4.0	4.0	58.5	64.0
Foreshank	3.0	3.5	58.0	53.5
Hindquarter	48.5	48.0	63.0	73.0
Rump	5.5	6.0	63.0	65.5
Round, rump and shank off	14.0	16.0	79.5	87.0
Shank	3.0	3.5	46.0	44.5
Sirloin	9.0	10.0	72.5	76.0
Short loin	7.0	6.5	70.5	71.0
Flank	6.0	4.5	49.0	75.0
Kidney knob	4.0	1.5	—	—

1. All cuts trimmed of fat exceeding that amount normally left on retail cuts (1/4 in. to 1/2 in.).

INSTITUTION INSPECTION

Final acceptance of all products will be by the consignee at the point of delivery. Products that are not appropriately identified with the "USDA Accepted As Specified" stamp will be rejected. Products that are appropriately identified with that stamp but which have other obvious, major deviations from specification requirements also will be rejected. Products appropriately identified with the "USDA Accepted As Specified" stamp but which, in the opinion of the consignee, have minor deviations from the specification requirements which do not materially affect the usability of the product may be tentatively accepted subject to verification of such deviations by local USDA meat grading personnel. Disposition of products with such verified minor deviations will be at the option of the consignee. All deviations from the specifications noted at the point of delivery must be reported promptly to local USDA meat grading personnel who are instructed to investigate all such reports without delay.

MEAT AND MEAT PRODUCTS
Beef, cured, corned, pickled, dried or dehydrated: Relation between procurement and carcass weights

Product	Factors for determining equivalent carcass weight

Boneless beef:
  Cured, corned, or pickled:[1]
    Brisket, or corned beef unspecified
    Plate, or family beef
  Dried or chipped beef, sliced or unsliced
  Dehydrated beef
	
	1.08
	1.31
	2.08
	3.00

1. Based on 20% gain in pickling brisket from fresh weight, and 10% gain in pickling plate.

Beef: Conversion factors for determining equivalent carcass weight of boneless wholesale cuts and for converting boneless wholesale cuts to equivalent bone-in cuts of various U.S. grades.

Carcass and wholesale cuts	Factors for converting boneless wholesale cuts to equivalent carcass weight		Factors for converting boneless wholesale cuts to equivalent bone-in cuts	
	Prime, Choice, and Good	Canner and Cutter	Prime, Choice, and Good	Canner and Cutter
Carcass, whole	1.52	1.37	1.52	1.37
Forequarter	1.60	1.36	1.45	1.38
Rib	1.49	1.33	1.55	1.41
Chuck, square cut	1.69	1.42	1.37	1.32
Plate	1.46	1.38	1.58	1.36
Brisket	1.35	1.21	1.71	1.56
Foreshank	1.34	1.00	1.73	1.88
Hindquarter	1.44	1.37	1.60	1.37
Rump	1.44	1.23	1.60	1.52
Round, rump and shank off	1.84	1.63	1.26	1.15
Shank	1.06	.84	2.17	2.25
Sirloin	1.67	1.42	1.38	1.32
Short loin	1.63	1.33	1.42	1.41
Flank	1.12	1.41	2.05	1.33

BEEF

GRADE

Carcasses, Sides, or Quarters The purchaser must specify a quality grade and a yield grade.

Cuts and Roasts The purchaser must specify a quality grade, and may also specify a yield grade.

Portion Cuts and Diced Beef The purchaser must specify a quality grade.

Ground Beef The purchaser must specify a quality grade for Item Nos. 137 and 1137. However, a quality grade shall not be specified for other ground beef items. The upper half or lower half may be specified, otherwise the full range of the grade is acceptable.

When yield grade is specified for forequarters or forequarter cuts, any such item may not be derived from a carcass or side which was yield graded after the removal of more than minor amount of kidney and pelvic fat.

Yield grades 1 through 5 are applicable to all quality grades. However, those yield grades indicated by an "X" are in the largest supply.

USDA GRADES

QUALITY GRADES	YIELD GRADES[1]				
	1	2	3	4	5
U.S. Prime			X	X	X
U.S. Choice		X	X	X	
U.S. Good		X	X		
U.S. Standard	X	X	X		
U.S. Commercial		X	X	X	X
U.S. Utility		X	X	X	
U.S. Cutter		X	X		
U.S. Canner		X	X		

1. The yield grades reflect differences in yields of boneless, close trimmed, retail cuts. As such, they also reflect differences in the overall fatness of carcasses and cuts. Yield Grade 1 represents the highest yield of retail cuts and the least amount of fat trim. Yield Grade 5 represents the lowest yield of retail cuts and the highest amount of fat trim.

If desired, Bullock beef may be specified by the purchaser.

WEIGHT RANGE OR SIZE

Carcasses, Sides, Quarters, and Cuts See weight ranges.

Roasts See weight range table. If desired, purchasers may specify that roasts be further reduced in size.

Ground Beef Patties Either the individual patty weight or the number of patties per pound must be specified.

Ground Beef Patty Weight Tolerances

For patties with a specified weight of 3 oz. or less, a tolerance of +2 patties from the projected number in a 10-lb. unit will be permitted. For patients with diets having a specified weight of more than 3 oz., a tolerance of +1 patty from the projected number in a 10-lb. unit will be permitted. (When patties are specified by a number per pound, this shall be converted to patty weight to determine tolerances, i.e., 6 to the pound = 2.67 oz.)

EXAMPLE:

Specified Size		Number Per 10-Pound Unit	Tolerances [over and under]
Weight	No. Per Lb.		
1.6 oz.	10	100	2
2.0 oz.	8	80	2
3.2 oz.	5	50	1
4.0 oz.	4	40	1

EXAMPLE: When 2 oz. patties are specified, 10-lb. units containing 78 to 82 patties are acceptable.

Portion Cut Items Either the portion weight or thickness desired — not both — must be specified. If weight is specified, see the weight range tables. If thickness is specified, the actual thickness desired must be indicated. (Not applicable to cubed steaks.) Also, in order to control uniformity of portion sizes, the weight range of the IMPS cut from which the portions are to be produced may also be specified. In this case, the fat thickness of the referenced IMPS cut should be the fat thickness specified for the portion cut.

Portion Cut Weight Tolerances

If portion weight is specified, the following tolerances will be permitted:

Weight Specified	Tolerances [over and under]
Less than 6 oz.	1/4 oz.
6 oz. but less than 12 oz.	1/2 oz.
12 oz. but less than 18 oz.	3/4 oz.
18 oz. or more	1 oz.

EXAMPLE: When 8 oz. steaks are specified, individual steaks weighing 7-1/2 to 8-1/2 oz. are acceptable.

Portion Cut Tolerances

If thickness is specified, the following tolerances will be permitted.

Thickness Specified	Tolerances [over and under]
1 in. or less	3/16 in.
More than 1 in.	1/4 in.

EXAMPLE: When 1-1/4 in. steaks are specified, individual steaks measuring 1 to 1-1/2 in. are acceptable.

FAT LIMITATIONS

Cuts and Roasts Except when yield grade is specified, the purchaser must specify one of the following maximum average thicknesses of surface fat, unless definite fat limitations are indicated in the detailed specifications.

Maximum Average Thickness	Maximum at Any One Point
1 in.	1-1/4 in.
3/4 in.	1 in.
1/2 in.	3/4 in.
1/4 in.	1/2 in.

NOTE: When average fat thicknesses are specified in item descriptions, the appropriate "Maximum at Any One Point" limitations shall apply.

Steaks Unless otherwise specified by the purchaser, or unless definite fat limitations are indicated in the detailed item specifications, on surfaces where fat is present, the fat must not exceed 1/2 in. in thickness, and the thickness at any one point must be not more than 3/4 in.

Chops, Cutlets, and Filets Unless otherwise specified by the purchaser, surface fat, where present, must not exceed an average of 1/4 in. in thickness, and the thickness at any one point must not be more than 3/8 in.

NOTE: Defatting must be done by smoothly removing the fat by following the countour of the underlying muscle surface. Beveling of the edges only is not acceptable. In determining the average thickness of fat at any one point on steaks and roasts, which have an evident, natural depression of the lean, only the fat above the portion of the depression which is more than 3/4 in. in width will be considered.

STATE OF REFRIGERATION

A. Chilled

B. Frozen

When tieing is required, roasts must be made firm and compact, and held intact by individual loops of strong twine, uniformly spaced at approximately 2-in. intervals girthwise. In addition, some roasts may require tieing lengthwise. In lieu of string tieing, it is permissible to enclose roasts in stretchable netting, or by any other equivalent method. Purchasers may specify that roasts be tied, when this requirement is not specified in the detailed item specification.

AGED BEEF

The purchaser may specify aged beef. Unless otherwise specified, bone-in cuts may be dry aged, or aged in plastic bags. Boneless cuts must be aged in plastic bags. Meat which is dry aged must be trimmed to remove meat which is dry and discolored, and/or which has an odor foreign to fresh beef. When examining beef for compliance with these specifications, USDA meat graders will take into consideration the deviation of color from that of fresh-chilled meat that is normal for aged meat.

MATERIAL

Beef products described in these specifications must be derived from beef carcasses, or wholesale cuts. Cuts which have been excessively trimmed in order to meet specified weights, or which do not meet the specification requirements for any reason, are excluded. The beef shall be of good color normal to the grade; be practically free of bruises, blood clots,

BEEF CHART

RETAIL CUTS OF BEEF—WHERE THEY COME FROM AND HOW TO COOK THEM

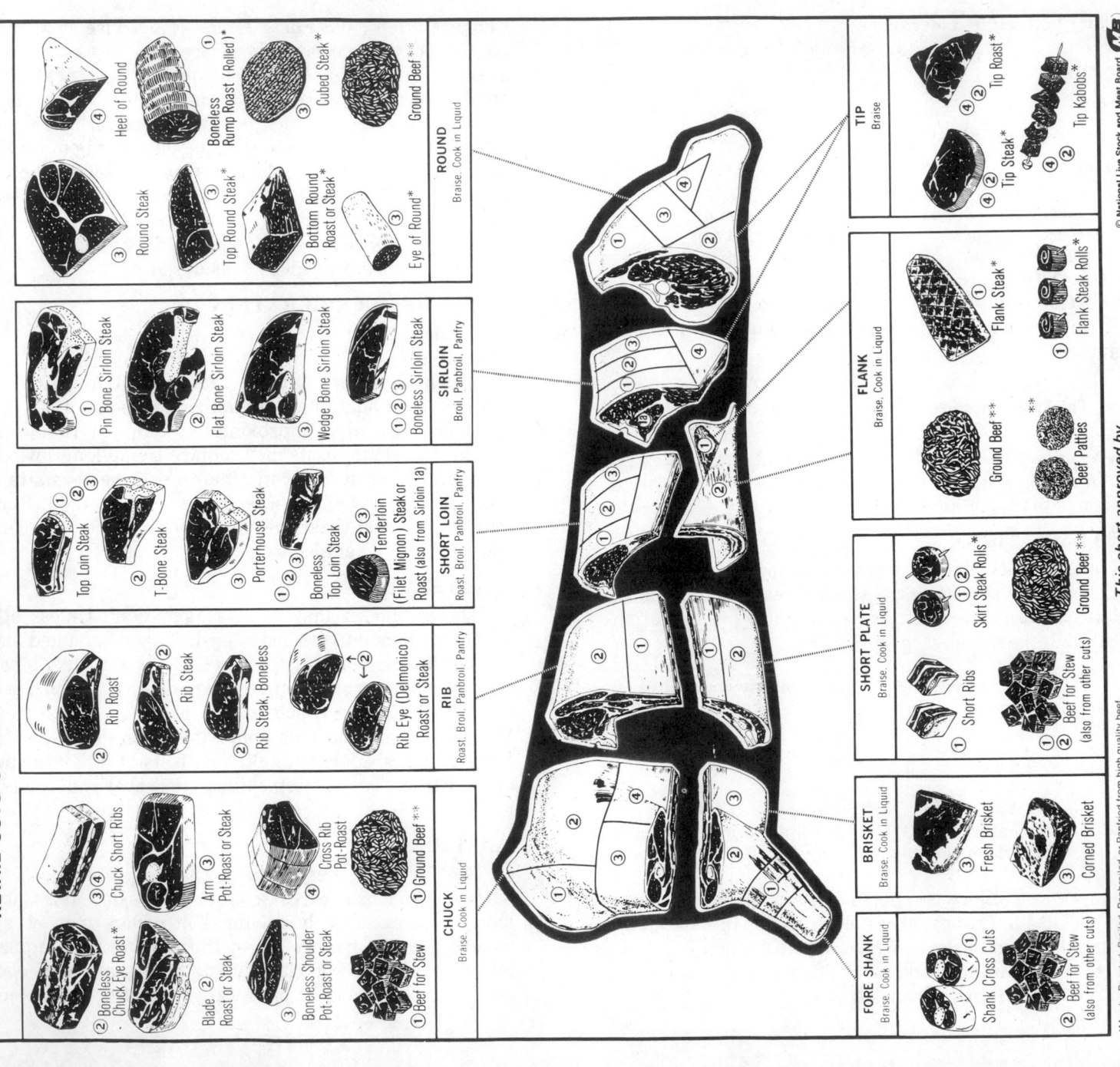

ROUND
Braise. Cook in Liquid

④ Heel of Round
③ Boneless Rump Roast (Rolled)*
③ Cubed Steak*
③ Ground Beef***
③ Round Steak
③ Top Round Steak*
③ Bottom Round Roast or Steak*
③ Eye of Round*

SIRLOIN
Broil, Panbroil, Panfry

① Pin Bone Sirloin Steak
② Flat Bone Sirloin Steak
Wedge Bone Sirloin Steak
①②③ Boneless Sirloin Steak

SHORT LOIN
Roast. Broil. Panbroil. Panfry

①②③ Top Loin Steak
② T-Bone Steak
③ Porterhouse Steak
①②③ Boneless Top Loin Steak
②③ Tenderloin (Filet Mignon) Steak or Roast (also from Sirloin 1a)

RIB
Roast. Broil. Panbroil. Panfry

② Rib Roast
② Rib Steak
② Rib Steak, Boneless
② Rib Eye (Delmonico) Roast or Steak

CHUCK
Braise. Cook in Liquid

③④ Chuck Short Ribs
③ Arm Pot-Roast or Steak
④ Cross Rib Pot-Roast
① Ground Beef***
② Boneless Chuck Eye Roast*
② Blade Roast or Steak
③ Boneless Shoulder Pot-Roast or Steak
① Beef for Stew

TIP
Braise

④② Tip Roast*
④② Tip Steak*
④② Tip Kabobs
④② Tip Steak*

FLANK
Braise. Cook in Liquid

① Flank Steak*
① Flank Steak Rolls*
Ground Beef**
Beef Patties

SHORT PLATE
Braise. Cook in Liquid

①② Skirt Steak Rolls*
① Short Ribs
①② Beef for Stew (also from other cuts)
Ground Beef***

BRISKET
Braise. Cook in Liquid

③ Fresh Brisket
③ Corned Brisket

FORE SHANK
Braise. Cook in Liquid

① Shank Cross Cuts
② Beef for Stew (also from other cuts)

*May be Roasted. Broiled. Panbroiled or Panfried from high quality beef.
**May be Roasted. (Baked). Broiled. Panbroiled or Panfried.

This chart approved by
National Live Stock and Meat Board

© National Live Stock and Meat Board

PRIMAL (WHOLESALE) CUTS AND BONE STRUCTURE OF BEEF

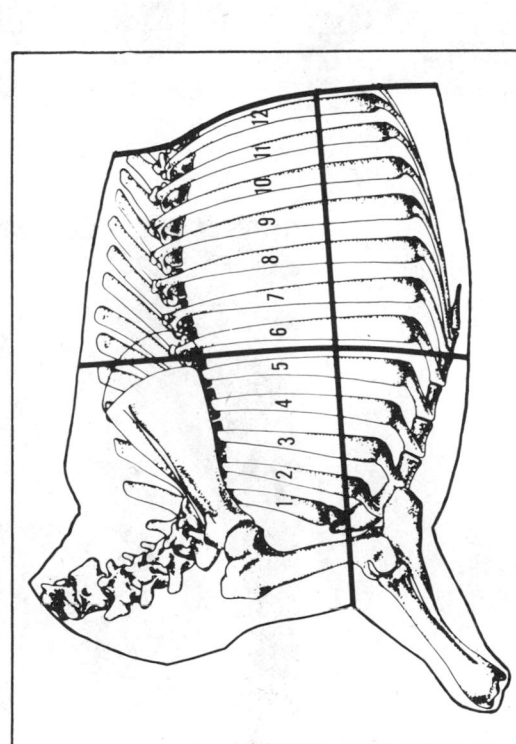

CHUCK
Chuck, Sq. Cut
Chuck, Blade Half
Chuck, Blade Portion
Chuck, Arm Half

RIB
Rib, Regular 10" × 10"
Ribs 3 × 4
Short Ribs

LOIN (SHORT LOIN)
Short Loin Regular 10"
Short Loin 3 × 4
Tenderloin

LOIN (SIRLOIN)
Sirloin Bl
Top Sirloin
Bottom Sirloin
Half Tip
Tenderloin

ROUND
Round
Rump
Shank
Half Tip

SHANK
Shank
Shank, Trmd.
Shank, Center

BRISKET
Brisket, Bl
Brisket, Bnls.

PLATE
Plate
Short Ribs

FLANK
Flank Meat
Flank Steak

TIP
Tip

National Live Stock and Meat Board

Figure 1

COUNTING RIBS IN A BEEF FOREQUARTER

In this manual, the method used to count ribs in the beef forequarter (Fig. 2) is to start at the front (chuck) and count toward the rear (1 to 12). The primal chuck contains five ribs (1–5). The primal rib contains seven ribs (6–12).

Some retailers reverse the counting process in the primal rib. They number ribs 6–12 instead by starting at the loin end, and numbering 1–7 from rear to front.

Figure 2

2

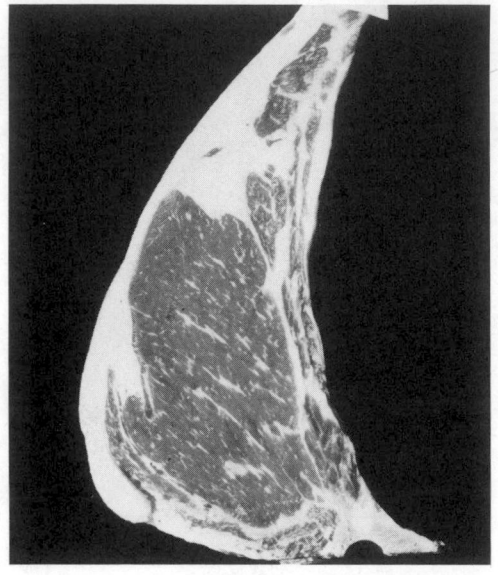

Yield Grade 1

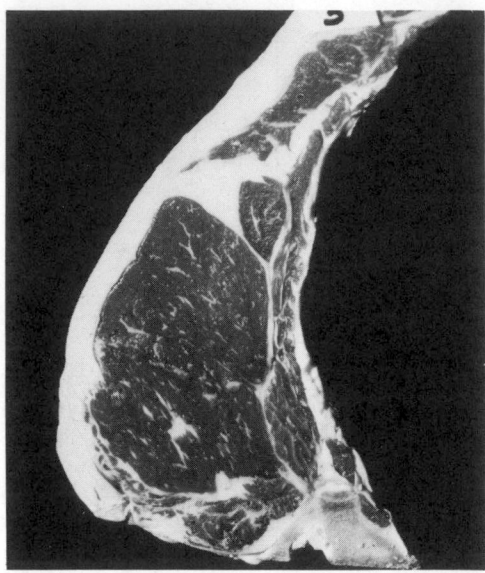

Yield Grade 2

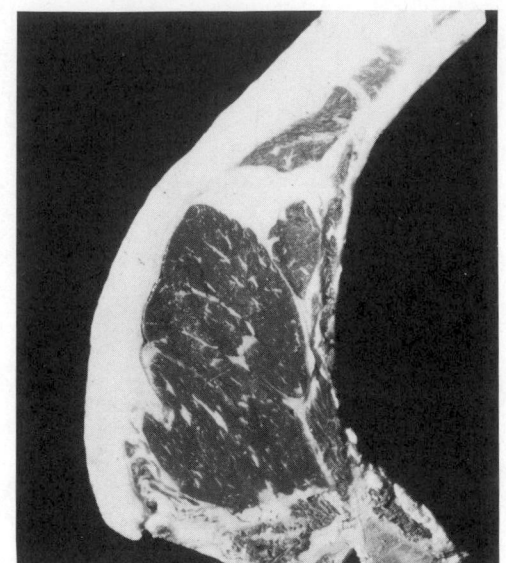

Yield Grade 3

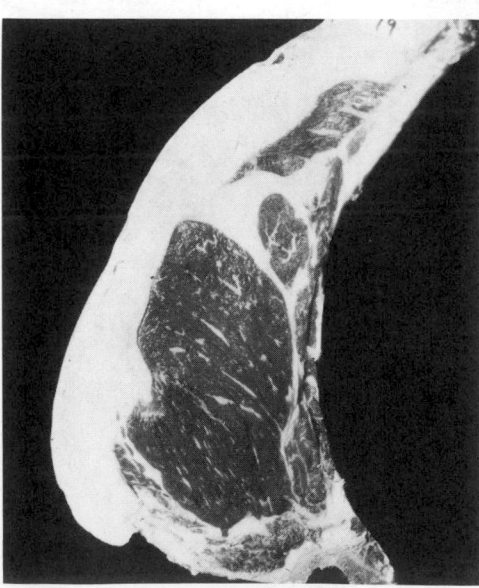

Yield Grade 4

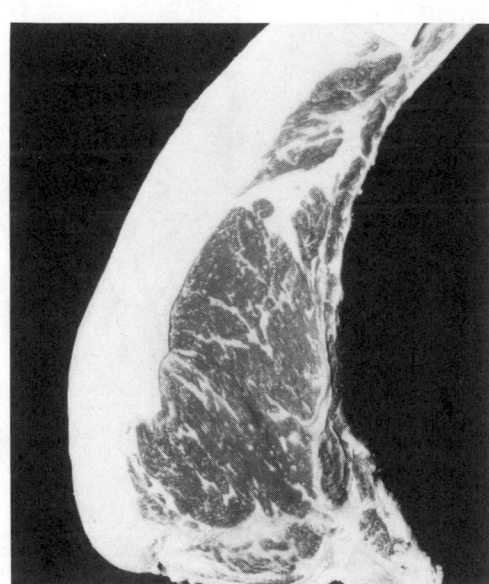

Yield Grade 5

Photos: NLS & MB

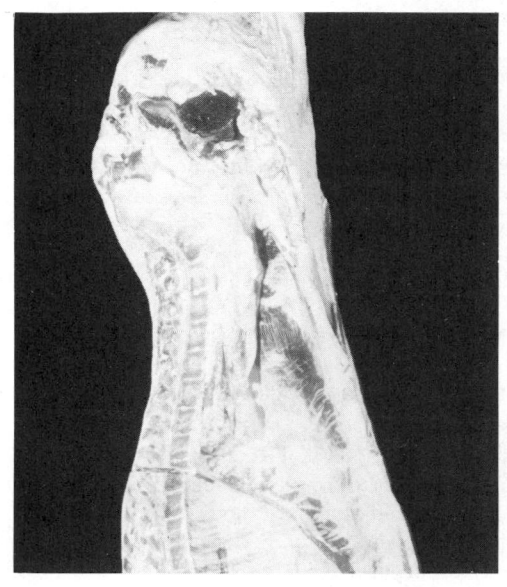

Yield Grade 1

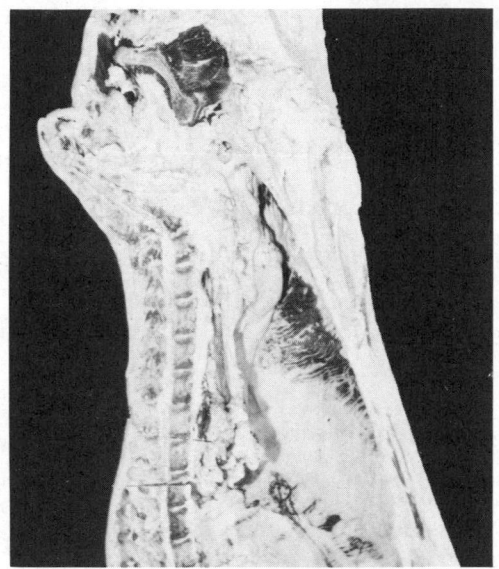

Yield Grade 2

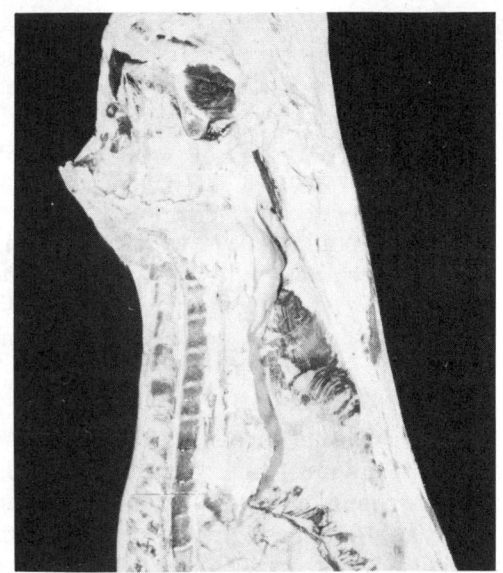

Yield Grade 3

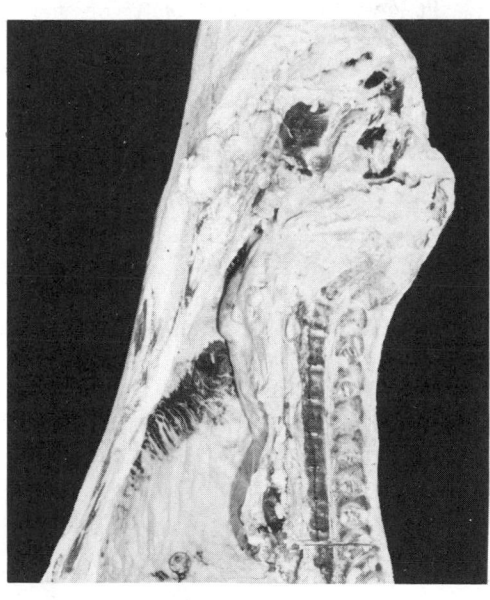

Yield Grade 4

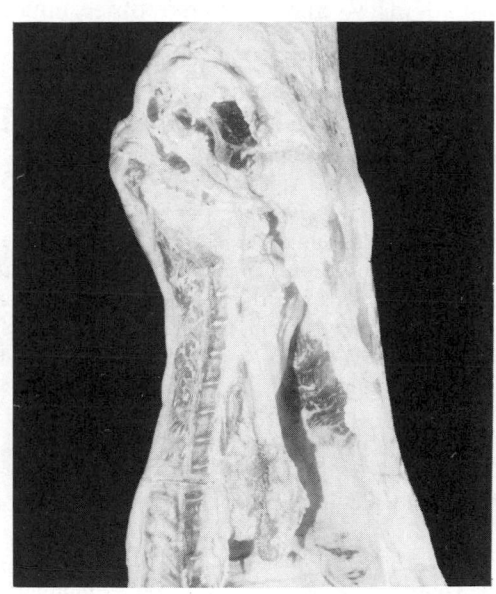

Yield Grade 5

Photos: NLS & MB

bone dust, ragged edges, and discoloration. The spinal cord, thymus glands, and heart fat must be removed. Except as otherwise provided herein, the meat shall show no evidence of freezing, or defrosting. Also, the product shall show no evidence of mishandling, and shall be in excellent condition to the time of delivery.

Portion-cut items to be delivered frozen may be produced from frozen meat cuts which have been previously accepted in the fresh-chilled state, provided such cuts are in excellent condition, and in their original shape. Products thus produced shall be packaged, packed, and promptly returned to the freezer.

CUTTING STEAKS

Unless otherwise specified in the individual item specification, steaks must be cut in full slices, in a straight line reasonably perpendicular to the outer surface, and at an approximate right angle to the length of the meat cut from which steaks are produced. Butterfly steaks are not acceptable.

BONING

Boning shall be accomplished with sufficient care to allow each cut to retain its identity, and to avoid objectionable scores in the meat.

IMPS NO. 100 Carcass
MBG NO. 100

Weight Range [in pounds]

RANGE A	RANGE B	RANGE C	RANGE D
500-600	600-700	700-800	800-up

A beef carcass is the four quarters from a single carcass. The quarters are produced by separating the forequarters from the hindquarters, cutting between the 12th and 13th ribs, the 13th rib remaining with the hindquarters. The diaphragm may be removed, but if not removed, the membranous portion shall be removed close to the lean. The thymus gland and heart fat shall be closely removed.

IMPS NO. 101 Side
MBG NO. 101

Weight Range [in pounds]

RANGE A	RANGE B	RANGE C	RANGE D
250-300	300-350	350-400	400-up

The side of beef consists of one matched forequarter and hindquarter from one-half the carcass prepared as described in Item No. 100.

IMPS NO. 102 Forequarter
MBG NO. 102

Weight Range [in pounds]

RANGE A	RANGE B	RANGE C	RANGE D
131-157	157-183	183-210	210-up

The forequarter is the front portion of the side, after severance from the hindquarter, as described in Item No. 100. The forequarter shall be trimmed as described in Item No. 100.

IMPS NO. 1100 Cubed Steaks, Regular
MBG NO. 1100
URMIS and COMMON NAMES: Cube Steak, Minute Steak, Swiss Steak.
COMMON USES: Braise; cook with moist heat; closed and open-faced sandwiches; swiss steak.
SUGGESTED PORTION SIZES: 3 oz., 4 oz., 6 oz., 8 oz.

Cubed steaks may be produced from any boneless meat from the beef carcass which is reasonably free of membranous tissue, tendons, and ligaments. The meat shall be made into cubed steaks through use of machines designed for this purpose. Knitting of two or more pieces, and folding of the meat when cubing, is permissible. Cubed steaks shall be reasonably uniform in shape, i.e., practically square, round or oval. After cubing, surface fat on the edge of the cubed steaks shall not exceed 1/2 in. in width at any one point, when measured from the edge of the lean. Surface and seam fat shall cover not more than 15 percent of the total area on either side of the steak. The cubed steak shall not break when suspended from any point 1/2 in. from the outer edge of the steak.

IMPS NO. 1101 Cubed Steak, Special
MBG NO. 1101
URMIS and COMMON NAMES: Cube Steak, Minute Steak, Swiss Steak.
COMMON USES: Braise; cook with moist heat; open-and closed-faced sandwiches; swiss steak.
SUGGESTED PORTION SIZES: 3 oz., 4 oz., 6 oz., 8 oz.

Special cubed steaks shall meet all the requirements for Item No. 1100, except that they shall be produced only from the muscles contained in the round, loin, rib, or square-cut chuck. Knitting of two or more pieces, or folding of the meat, is not acceptable.

IMPS NO. 102A **Forequarter, Boneless**
MBG NO. Not Included.
URMIS and COMMON NAMES: Beef Chuck Shoulder Pot-Roast Boneless, Forequarter.
COMMON USES: Cook in moist heat; center shoulder roast, chuck roast, pot roast, swiss steak.

Weight Range [in pounds]

RANGE A	RANGE B	RANGE C	RANGE D
104-125	125-146	146-168	168-up

The boneless forequarter is prepared from Item No. 102. Meat with dark discoloration, all bones, cartilage, backstrap, exposed large blood vessels, and the prescapular lymph gland shall be removed. The thick tendinous ends of the shank shall be removed by cutting back until a cross-sectional cut shows at least 75 percent lean. The clod shall be removed without undue scoring.

IMPS NO. 1102 **Braising Steaks, Swiss Steak**
MBG NO. 1102
URMIS and COMMON NAMES: Beef Chuck Shoulder Steak Boneless, Beef Chuck Arm Steak Boneless, Cube Steak, Potting Steak, Round Steak.
COMMON USES: Braise; panfry; potted swiss steak; country fried steak; stew meat.
SUGGESTED PORTION SIZES: 4 oz., 6 oz., 8 oz., 10 oz., 12 oz., 14 oz., 16 oz.

Braising steaks shall be produced from any part of any one, or any combination, of the following cuts of beef:
Item No. 112 — Ribeye Roll
Item No. 114 — Shoulder Clod
Item No. 167 — Knuckle
Item No. 168 — Top Round
Item No. 170A — Bottom Round, Heel Out
Item No. 180 — Strip Loin, Short Cut, Boneless
Item No. 184 — Top Sirloin Butt
Item No. 186 — Bottom Sirloin Butt, Trimmed

Each braising steak shall be practically free of fat on at least 1/2 the circumference, and the surface fat on the remaining half of the circumference shall not exceed 1/2 in. at any one point. If specified by the purchaser, each steak shall be mechanically tenderized, using machines designed for this purpose. Knitting of two or more pieces of meat, or folding of the meat, is unacceptable.

IMPS NO. 103 **Rib, Primal**
MBG NO. 103
URMIS and COMMON NAMES: Prime Rib of Beef, Standing Rib Roast, Rib Roast Oven-Ready, Oven-Ready Rib.
COMMON USES: Roast; prime rib of beef; standing rib roast.

Weight Range [in pounds]

RANGE A	RANGE B	RANGE C	RANGE D
24-28	28-33	33-38	38-up

The primal rib is that portion of the forequarter remaining after the removal of the cross-cut chuck and short plate, the skeletal part of which contains parts of seven ribs (6th to 12th inclusive), the section of the backbone attached to the ribs, and the rear tip of the blade bone (scapula).

The cross-cut chuck is removed by a straight cut, perpendicular to the split surface of the backbone between the 5th and 6th ribs. The short plate shall be removed by a straight cut across the ribs, from a point on the 12th rib which is not more than 10 in. from the center of the inside protruding edge of the 12th thoracic vertebra, through a point on the 6th rib which is not more than 10 in. from the center of the inside protruding edge of the 6th thoracic vertebra. The portion of the diaphragm, and practically all of the fat remaining on the side surface of the vertebrae, shall be removed.

IMPS NO. 1103 **Rib Steaks**
MBG NO. 1103
URMIS and COMMON NAMES: Beef Rib Steak, Beef Rib Steak Bone-In.
COMMON USES: Broil; panbroil; panfry; beef steak.
SUGGESTED PORTION SIZES: 8 oz., 10 oz., 12 oz., 14 oz., 16 oz.

Rib steaks shall be prepared from a Rib, Primal — Item No. 103. The short ribs on individual steaks shall be removed at a point which is not more than 3 in. from the outer tip of the ribeye muscle. All muscles above the major ribeye muscle; fat overlying these muscles; the blade bone and cartilage; the feather bones, and the backstrap shall be removed.

IMPS NO. 1103A **Rib Steaks [Boneless]**
MBG NO. 1103A
URMIS and COMMON NAMES: Beef Rib Steak, Rib Eye, Spencer, Delmonico Beauty Steak, Filet Steak.
COMMON USES: Broil; panbroil; panfry; beef rib steak.
SUGGESTED PORTION SIZES: 4 oz., 6 oz., 8 oz., 10 oz., 12 oz.

Boneless rib steaks shall be prepared as described in Item No. 1103, except that all bones and rib fingers (intercostal meat) shall be removed.

IMPS NO. 107 **Rib, Oven-Prepared**
MBG NO. 107
URMIS and COMMON NAMES: Beef Rib Roast, Prime Rib, Standing Rib Roast, Rib Roast Oven-Ready, Spencer Roll.
COMMON USES: Roast; standing rib roast; prime rib; roast beef.

Weight Range [in pounds]

RANGE A	RANGE B	RANGE C	RANGE D
17-19	19-23	23-26	26-up

The oven-prepared rib is prepared from Rib, Primal — Item No. 103. A straight cut is made across the ribs, from a point on the 12th rib which is not more than 3 in. from the outer tip of the ribeye muscle, through a point on the 6th rib which is not more than 4 in. from the outer tip of the ribeye muscle. The chine bone shall be removed by a straight cut, along a line at which the vertebrae joins the feather bones, exposing the lean but leaving the feather bones attached to the oven-prepared rib. The blade bone and related cartilage shall be removed.

IMPS NO. 108 **Rib, Oven-Prepared, Boneless and Tied**
MBG NO. 108
URMIS and COMMON NAMES: Beef Rib Roast, Spencer Roll, Beef Rib-Eye Roast.
COMMON USES: Roast; rolled roast; prime rib; beef rib roast; rib eye pot roast; delmonico pot roast; spencer roll.

Weight Range [in pounds]

RANGE A	RANGE B	RANGE C	RANGE D
15-17	17-21	21-24	24-27

The boneless and tied oven-prepared rib is the same as Item No. 107, except that the bones, backstrap and rib fingers (intercostal meat) shall be removed. The boneless rib shall be tied girthwise, and lengthwise.

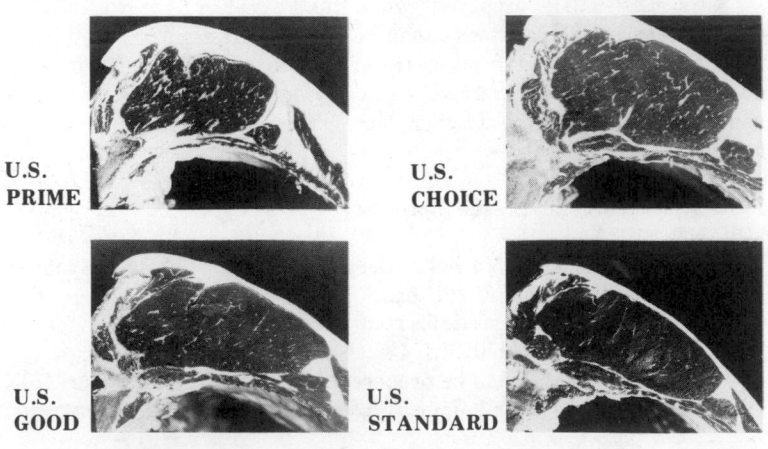

U.S. PRIME

U.S. CHOICE

U.S. GOOD

U.S. STANDARD

IMPS NO. 109 **Rib, Roast Ready**
MBG NO. 109
URMIS and COMMON NAMES: Beef Rib Roast, Prime Rib, Standing Rib, Spencer Roll.
COMMON USES: Roast; standing rib roast; prime rib, roast beef.

Weight Range [in pounds]

RANGE A	RANGE B	RANGE C	RANGE D
14-16	16-19	19-22	22-up

The roast-ready rib is prepared from a Rib, Primal — Item No. 103. A straight cut is made across the ribs, from a point on the 12th rib which is not more than 3 in. from the outer tip of the ribeye muscle, through a point on the 6th rib which is not more than 4 in. from the outer tip of the ribeye muscle. The chine bone shall be removed by a straight cut, along a line at which the vertebrae join the featherbones, exposing the lean meat, but leaving the featherbones attached to the roast-ready rib. The bladebone and related cartilage, the muscles lying firmly below and attached to the bladebone, and the backstrap shall be removed. The exterior fat covering and featherbones shall be held in their natural positions, by tying girthwise and lengthwise.

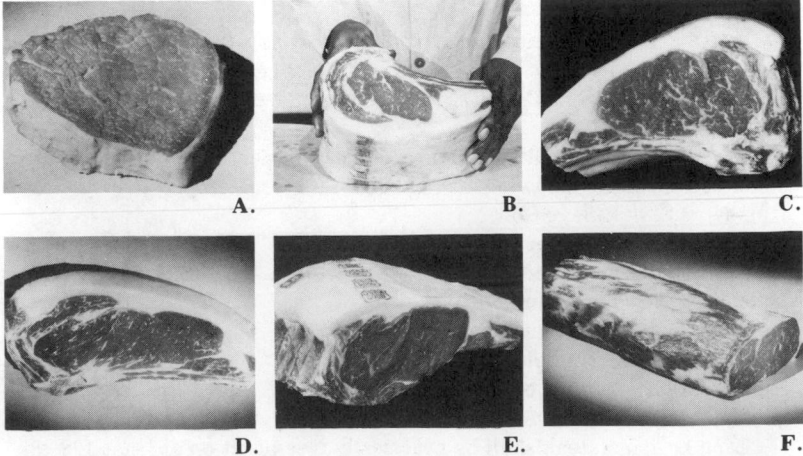

A.   B.   C.

D.   E.   F.

A. IMPS NO. 1102 Braising Steaks, Swiss Steak, P. 113; **B.** *IMPS NO. 103 Rib, Primal, p. 113;* **C.** *IMPS NO. 103 Rib, Primal. Rib roast: unexcelled for tenderness and flavor, easy to prepare, carve and serve, can be oven-roasted in the top four grades. For maximum tenderness, juiciness, and flavor select USDA Prime or Choice. Because it has a rather large proportion of bone and fat, you will need to allow at least one-half pound of rib roast per person. For company meals, you may wish to allow up to a pound per person. Buy it at least two ribs thick for proper cooking. This roast is often called a standing rib, or prime rib, even though it is not in that instance graded USDA Prime, p. 113;* **D.** *IMPS NO. 1103 Rib Steaks, p. 113;* **E.** *IMPS NO. 107 Rib, Oven-Prepared, p. 114;* **F.** *IMPS No. 112 Ribeye Roll, p. 115.*

IMPS NO. 109A **Rib, Roast-Ready, Special**
MBG NO. 109A
URMIS and COMMON NAMES: Beef Rib Roast, Prime Rib, Standing Rib Roast.
COMMON USES: Roast; beef rib steak; standing rib roast; rib roast oven-ready.

Weight Ranges [in pounds]

RANGE A	RANGE B	RANGE C	RANGE D
14-16	16-19	19-22	22-up

The special roast-ready rib is prepared from a Rib, Primal — Item No. 103. The chine bone shall be removed by a straight cut, along a line at which the vertebrae join the featherbones, exposing the lean meat. The featherbones shall be removed. Beginning at the sawed ends of the rib bones, the exterior fat covering over the entire rib shall be lifted intact from over the outermost muscles. All of the muscles lying above the level at the blade bone and cartilage, the small muscles below and firmly attached to the blade bone, and the backstrap shall be removed. The short ribs are then removed by a straight cut across the ribs, from a point on the 12th rib which is not more than 3 in. from the outer tip of the ribeye muscle, through a point on the 6th rib which is not more than 4 in. from the outer tip of the ribeye muscle. The fat overlying the ribeye muscle must be trimmed to a uniform level for the entire area of the seamed surface. The exterior fat shall be returned to its natural position, except that it shall extend from the ends of the rib bones, where the chine bone was removed, to the sawed ends of the rib bones. Fat cover extending beyond the sawed ends of the rib bones shall be removed even with the ends. The exterior fat covering shall be held in place by tieing girthwise and lengthwise.

IMPS NO. 109B **Blade Meat**
MBG NO. Not Included.
URMIS and COMMON NAMES: False Meat.
COMMON USES: Cube Steak

Weight Range [in pounds]

RANGE A
13-16

This item consists of the portions of the latissimus dorsi, trapezius, and serratus ventralis muscles contained in the primal rib. The lean surfaces shall be trimmed practically free of fat.

IMPS NO. 110 **Rib, Roast-Ready [Boneless and Tied]**
MBG NO. 110
URMIS and COMMON NAMES: Beef Rib Roast, Prime Rib, Standing Rib, Spencer Roll.
COMMON USES: Roast; standing rib roast; prime rib; roast beef.

Weight Range [in pounds]

RANGE A	RANGE B	RANGE C	RANGE D
11-13	13-16	16-19	19-up

The boneless and tied roast-ready rib is the same as Item No. 109 except that all bones and the rib fingers (intercostal meat) are removed. The boneless, roast-ready rib shall be tied, girthwise and lengthwise.

IMPS NO. 111 **Spencer Roll**
MBG NO. 111
URMIS and COMMON NAMES: Boneless Rib Roast, Lip-On Rib Eye Roll, Rib Roast Oven-Ready, Standing Rib, Prime Rib.
COMMON USES: Roast; roast beef.

Weight Range [in pounds]

RANGE A	RANGE B	RANGE C	RANGE D
10-12	12-15	15-17	17-up

The spencer roll is prepared from a Rib, Primal — Item No. 103. A straight cut is made from a point not more than 2 in. from the outer tip of the ribeye muscle on the loin end, to a point not more than 1 in. from the outer tip of the ribeye muscle on the chuck end. All bones, cartilages, the backstrap, rib fingers (intercostal meat) and the muscles and fat overlying the blade bone and cartilage shall be removed.

IMPS NO. 112 **Ribeye Roll**
MBG NO. 112
URMIS and COMMON NAMES: Beef Rib Eye Roast.
COMMON USES: Roast; delmonico pot roast; delmonico roast; beef ribeye pot roast; regular rolled roast.

Weight Range [in pounds]

RANGE A	RANGE B	RANGE C	RANGE D
5-6	6-8	8-10	10-up

The ribeye roll includes the longissimus dorsi, spinalis dorsi, multifidus dorsi and complexus muscles of a Rib, Primal — Item No. 103. All other muscles, bones, cartilage, backstrap and the exterior fat covering shall be removed.

IMPS NO. 112A **Ribeye Roll, Lip-On**
MBG NO. Not Included.
URMIS and COMMON NAMES: Boneless Rib Roast, Spencer, Delmonico.
COMMON USES: Roast; roast beef.

Weight Range [in pounds]

RANGE A	RANGE B	RANGE C	RANGE D
6-7	7-9	9-11	11-up

The lip-on ribeye roll is the same as Item No. 112, except that a "lip" (serratus dorsalis and longissimum costarum muscles and related intermuscular fat) remains firmly attached to the ribeye roll. The "lip" shall be removed by a straight cut, not more than 2 in. from the outer tip of the ribeye muscle.

IMPS NO. 1112 **Rib Eye Roll Steaks**
MBG NO. 1112
URMIS and COMMON NAMES: Beef Rib Eye Steak, Delmonico Steak, Beauty Steak, Filet Steak, Spencer Steak, Rib Eye Steak.
COMMON USES: Pan broil; panfry; broil; steaks.
SUGGESTED PORTION SIZES: 4 oz., 6 oz., 8 oz., 10 oz., 12 oz.

Rib eye roll steaks shall be prepared from a Rib Eye Roll — Item No. 112.

IMPS NO. 1112A **Ribeye Roll, Lip-On Steaks**
MBG NO. Not Included.
URMIS and COMMON NAMES: Rib Eye Roll, Lip-On Steaks, Delmonico Steak.
COMMON USES: Steak.
SUGGESTED PORTION SIZES: 4 oz., 6 oz., 8 oz., 10 oz., 12 oz.

This item shall be prepared from a Ribeye Roll, Lip-On — Item No. 112A. The "lip" shall be firmly attached.

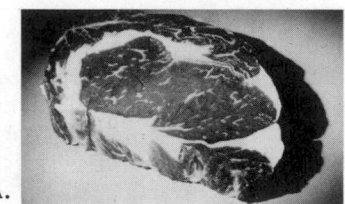 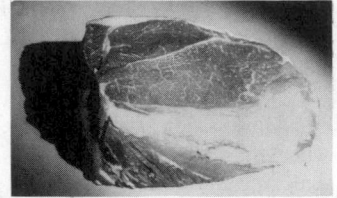

A. IMPS NO. 1112A Ribeye, Lip-On Steaks, p. 116; **B.** *IMPS NO. 114 Shoulder Clod, p. 116.*

IMPS NO. 113 **Square Cut Chuck**
MBG NO. 113
URMIS and COMMON NAMES: Beef Chuck Pot Roast, California Roast, Blade Roast, Chuck Roast.
COMMON USES: Cook in moist heat; chuck roast.

Weight Range [in pounds]

RANGE A	RANGE B	RANGE C	RANGE D
66-79	79-93	93-106	106-up

The square-cut chuck is that portion of the Forequarter — Item no. 102 — remaining after the foreshank, brisket, short plate, and rib is removed by making two straight cuts perpendicular to the split surface of the backbone. The first cut passes across the forequarter between the 5th and 6th ribs; this cut separates the cross-cut chuck from the rib and short plate. The second cut passes through the cartilagenous juncture of the first rib and the sternum, continuing in a straight line to the 5th rib perpendicular to the first described cut; this cut severs the foreshank and brisket from the square-cut chuck.

IMPS NO. 114 **Shoulder Clod**
MBG NO. 114
URMIS and COMMON NAMES: Beef Chuck Shoulder Pot-Roast Boneless, Beef Chuck Shoulder Steak Boneless, Center Shoulder Roast, Clod Roast, Chuck Roast.
COMMON USES: Cook in moist heat; stew meat; barbecuing; pot roast; swiss steak.

Weight Range [in Pounds]

RANGE A	RANGE B	RANGE C	RANGE D
13-15	15-18	18-21	21-up

The shoulder clod is the large outside muscle system which lies behind to the elbow joint and to the side of the medial ridge of the blade bone. The thick end of the clod includes all muscles overlying the first natural seam, and the thinner end includes all the muscles lying above the rear portion of the blade bone. The clod shall be removed without undue scoring.

IMPS NO. 114A **Shoulder Clod Roast**
MBG NO. 114A
URMIS and COMMON NAMES: Beef Chuck Shoulder Pot-Roast Boneless, Shoulder Roast, Clod Roast, Chuck Roast, Center Shoulder Roast.
COMMON USES: Cook in moist heat; pot roast; stew meat; barbecued beef; swiss steak.

Weight Range [in pounds]

RANGE A	RANGE B	RANGE C	RANGE D
under 15	15-18	18-21	21-up

The shoulder clod roast is the same as Item No. 114, except that the shoulder rose (cutaneous muscle) shall be removed when the underlying fat is in excess of the surface fat thickness specified. In this instance, the underlying fat must be trimmed to comply with the surface fat thickness requirements. The heavy tendons at the elbow end of the clod shall be trimmed even with the lean, and all sides shall be trimmed so that the clod is not less than 1 in. thick at any point. When smaller roasts are specified, the thick end of the clod shall be made into one roast, and the thin end shall be split lengthwise, the ends reversed, and the boned surfaces placed together to produce a uniformly thick roast. These roasts shall be held intact by tieing girthwise.

IMPS NO. 115 **Square-Cut Chuck, Boneless [Clod-In]**
MBG NO. 115
URMIS and COMMON NAMES: Beef Chuck, Pot Roast, California Roast, Blade Roast.
COMMON USES: Cook in moist heat; chuck roast.

Weight Range [in pounds]

RANGE A	RANGE B	RANGE C	RANGE D
54-65	65-77	77-88	88-up

The boneless square-cut chuck is prepared from Item No. 113. The shoulder clod shall be removed without undue scoring. (As an alternative, the shoulder clod may be removed before preparing the square-cut chuck, permitting full utilization of the clod.) Meat with dark discoloration, all bones, cartilage, backstrap, exposed large blood vessels, heavy connective tissue, and the prescapular lymph gland shall be removed. The remainder of the chuck may be separated by a straight cut, approximately parallel to the major back muscles, which is not less than 3 in. from the outer tip of the "chuck eye" muscle. Unless otherwise specified, each piece shall be individually wrapped, and packed in the same container.

IMPS NO. 116 **Square-Cut Chuck, Boneless [Clod Out]**
MBG NO. 116
URMIS and COMMON NAMES: Beef Chuck, Pot Roast, California Roast, Blade Roast.
COMMON USES: Cook in moist heat; chuck roast.

Weight Range [in pounds]

RANGE A	RANGE B	RANGE C	RANGE D
40-48	48-57	57-65	65-up

The boneless, square-cut chuck, clod out, is the same as Item No. 115, except that the shoulder clod is excluded.

IMPS NO. 116A **Chuck Roll**
MBG NO. Not Included
URMIS and COMMON NAMES: Beef Chuck Pot Roast, Boneless Chuck Roast, Chuck Pot Roast Boneless, Tied Roast.
COMMON USES: Cook in moist heat; pot roast.

Weight Range [in pounds]

RANGE A	RANGE B	RANGE C	RANGE D
13-15	15-18	18-21	21-up

The chuck roll is prepared from a boneless, clod out chuck. In addition, the chuck tender, the chuck cover, the thin muscle (subscapularis) underlying the blade bone, meat with dark discoloration, all cartilage, backstrap, exposed large blood vessels, and rib fingers (intercostal meat) shall be removed.

The chuck roll is then made by two cuts: (1) One cut is made perpendicular to the outer skin surface, parallel to the normal line of separation of the chuck and rib, and immediately behind the prescapular lymph gland (fat surrounding this gland shall be removed). This cut separates the neck portion from the major portion of the chuck. (2) A second cut is made perpendicular to the outer skin surface, through a point on the rib end which is 3 in. from the outer edge of the "chuck-eye" muscle, and continuing in a reasonably straight line, approximately parallel to the backbone side, to intersect the first cut, thus producing a chuck roll reasonably uniform in width, and thickness. The chuck roll shall be tied. When smaller roasts are specified, the chuck roll shall be separated by making a right angle cut to the length of the chuck roll through the meat.

IMPS NO. 117 Foreshank
MBG NO. 117
URMIS and COMMON NAMES: Beef Shank Cross Cut, Beef Shank Center Cut, Center Beef Shank, Cross Cut Shank, Leg Meat.
COMMON USES: Cook in liquid for soup stock.

Weight Range [in pounds]

RANGE A	RANGE B	RANGE C	RANGE D
7-8	8-10	10-12	12-up

The foreshank is the foreleg portion which remains intact with the brisket, after it has been removed from the cross-cut chuck, to make a Square-Cut Chuck — Item No. 113. The foreshank is separated from the brisket by a cut following the natural seam, except that part of the web muscle may remain on the foreshank.

IMPS NO. 118 Brisket
MBG NO. 118
URMIS and COMMON NAMES: Beef Brisket Whole Boneless, Beef Brisket Edge Cut Boneless, Beef Brisket Corned, Fresh Beef Brisket.
COMMON USES: Braise; cook in liquid; corned for corned beef brisket.

Weight Range [in pounds]

RANGE A	RANGE B	RANGE C	RANGE D
12-14	14-17	17-20	20-up

The brisket is separated from the foreshank as described in Item No. 117. Practically all heart fat shall be removed.

IMPS NO. 119 Brisket, Boneless, Deckle On
MBG NO. 119
URMIS and COMMON NAMES: Beef Brisket Whole Boneless, Fresh Beef Brisket, Brisket Boneless, Whole Brisket.
COMMON USES: Braise; cook in liquid; corned beef brisket.

Weight Range [in pounds]

RANGE A	RANGE B	RANGE C	RANGE D
9-10	10-12	12-14	14-up

The boneless brisket is that portion of Item No. 118 remaining after all bones and rib fingers (intercostal meat) have been removed.

IMPS NO. 120 Brisket, Boneless, Deckle Off
MBG NO. 120
URMIS and COMMON NAMES: Beef Brisket Edge Cut, Brisket Side Cut.
COMMON USES: Braise; cook in liquid; corned beef brisket.

Weight Range [in pounds]

RANGE A	RANGE B	RANGE C	RANGE D
6-8	8-10	10-12	12-up

The boneless, deckle off brisket is the same as Item No. 119, except that the deckle shall be removed at the natural seam, exposing the lean surface lying below. The hard fat along the sternum edge of the brisket shall be trimmed level with the boned surface of the brisket, and to within 1/2 in. of the lean lying between the hard fat and the border of the skin surface. The inside lean surface shall be trimmed practically free of fat, without undue scoring of the lean surface.

IMPS NO. 121 Short Plate
MBG NO. 121
URMIS and COMMON NAMES: Boston Roll, Beef Plate Skirt Steak Boneless, Beef Plate Skirt Steak Cubes Boneless, Skirt Steak, Boiling Beef, Plate Beef, London Grill Steak.
COMMON USES: Braise, broil, panfry, london broil, skirt steak.

Weight Range [in pounds]

RANGE A	RANGE B	RANGE C	RANGE D
16-23	23-27	27-31	31-up

The short plate is that portion of the forequarter immediately below the Rib, Primal — Item No. 103, and is separated from the primal rib as described therein.

IMPS NO. 121A Short Plate, Boneless
MBG NO. Not Included.
URMIS and COMMON NAMES: Navels, Skirt Steak Rolled Plate.
COMMON USES: Cook in moist heat; yankee pot roast.

Weight Range [in pounds]

RANGE A	RANGE B	RANGE C	RANGE D
16-23	23-27	27-31	31-up

The boneless short plate is the same as Item No. 121, except that the bones, cartilage, intercostal meat, diaphragm and serous membrane (peritoneum) shall be removed.

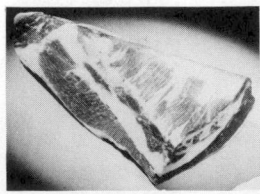 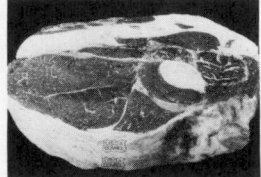 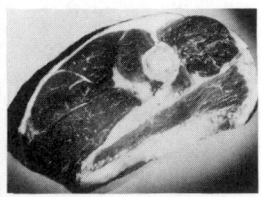

A.   B.   C.

A. IMPS NO. 119 Brisket, Boneless, Deckle On, p. 118; **B.** *IMPS NO. 125 Armbone Chuck, p. 119;* **C.** *IMPS No. 125 Armbone Chuck. Steak cut from Armbone Chuck is illustrated, p. 119.*

IMPS NO. 122 Full Plate
MBG NO. Not Included.
URMIS and COMMON NAMES: Rolled Plate, Plate Roll.
COMMON USES: Cook in moist heat; pot roast.

Weight Range [in pounds]

RANGE A	RANGE B	RANGE C	RANGE D
20-27	27-31	31-35	35-up

The full plate is the short plate and brisket intact. The short plate is separated from the rib as described in Rib, Primal — Item No. 103. The brisket is separated from the chuck as described in Square-Cut Chuck — Item No. 113, and from the foreshank as described in Foreshank — Item No. 117.

IMPS NO. 122A Full Plate, Boneless
MBG NO. 122A
URMIS and COMMON NAMES: Beef Plate Rolled Boneless, Plate Roll, Rolled Plate.
COMMON USES: Braise; cook in liquid; yankee pot roast.

Weight Range [in pounds]

RANGE A	RANGE B	RANGE C	RANGE D
21-27	27-29	29-32	32-35

The boneless full plate is the same as Item No. 122, except that all bones, cartilage, intercostal meat, diaphragm and serous membrane (peritoneum) shall be removed.

IMPS NO. 123 Short Ribs, Trimmed
MBG NO. 123
URMIS and COMMON NAMES: Beef Plate Short Ribs, Beef Plate Spareribs, Plate Beef, Plate Boiling Beef, Bone-In Stew Beef.
COMMON USES: Braise; cook in liquid; braised short ribs; barbecue spareribs.

Weight Range [in pounds]

RANGE A	RANGE B	RANGE C	RANGE D
2-3	3-4	4-5	5-up

Short ribs are prepared, from the 6th through the 10th ribs of the rib end of the primal rib and/or the short plate, by cutting across the rib **bones parallel to the cut which separates the rib and the short plate.** Short ribs produced from the short plate may not include the costal rib cartilage. The cutaneous muscle shall be removed. The surface fat shall not exceed 1/4 in. in thickness. The width of the short ribs shall be specified by the purchaser.

IMPS NO. 123A Short Ribs, Short Plate
MBG NO. Not Included.
URMIS and COMMON NAMES: Beef Plate Short Ribs.
COMMON USES: Cook in moist heat; short ribs.

Weight Range [in pounds]

RANGE A	RANGE B	RANGE C	RANGE D

Amount As Specified

This item is prepared from the 6th, 7th and 8th ribs of the Short Plate — Item No. 121, by cutting across the rib bones, parallel to the cut made when separating the short plate from the primal rib. Short ribs produced from the short plate may not include the costal rib cartilages. The cutaneous muscle, the exterior fat cover, and the first layer of lean shall be removed. Surface fat thickness shall not exceed 1/4 in. The width of the short ribs shall be specified by the purchaser.

IMPS NO. 123B Short Ribs, Special
MBG NO. Not Included.
URMIS and COMMON NAMES: Short Ribs.
COMMON USES: Braise; braised short ribs.

Weight Range [in pounds]

RANGE A	RANGE B	RANGE C	RANGE D

Amount As Specified

This item is prepared from the 6th, 7th and 8th ribs of the rib end of the Rib, Primal — Item No. 103, by cutting across the rib bones, parallel to the cut made when separating the primal rib from the short plate. The cutaneous muscle, the exterior fat cover, and the first layer of lean are removed. Surface fat thickness shall not exceed 1/4 in. The width of the short ribs shall be specified by the purchaser.

IMPS NO. 125 Armbone Chuck
MBG NO. 125
URMIS and COMMON NAMES: Beef Chuck Arm, Arm Chuck Roast, Round Bone Pot Roast, English Cut Roast.
COMMON USES: Braise; pot roast.

Weight Range [in Pounds]

RANGE A	RANGE B	RANGE C	RANGE D
77-88	88-103	103-118	118-up

The armbone chuck is the Square-Cut Chuck — Item No. 113, and Foreshank — Item No. 117 intact.

IMPS NO. 126 **Armbone Chuck, Boneless**
MBG NO. 126
URMIS and COMMON NAMES: Beef Chuck Arm Pot Roast Boneless, Round Bone Roast, Chuck Arm Roast, English Cut Roast.
COMMON USES: Braise; pot roast.

Weight Range [in pounds]

RANGE A	RANGE B	RANGE C	RANGE D
59-70	70-82	82-90	90-up

The boneless armbone chuck is prepared from Item No. 125. The clod shall be removed without undue scoring. Meat with dark discoloration, all bones, cartilage, backstrap, exposed large blood vessels, heavy connective tissue, and the prescapular lymph gland shall be removed. The thick tendinous ends of the shank shall be removed, by cutting back until a cross-sectional cut shows at least 75 percent lean. The remainder of the chuck may be separated into two portions by a straight cut, which is not less than 3 in. from the outer tip of the "chuck eye" muscle and approximately parallel to the major back muscles. Unless otherwise specified, each piece shall be individually wrapped and packed in the same container.

IMPS NO. 126A **Armbone Chuck, Boneless, Clod Out**
MBG NO. Not Included.
URMIS and COMMON NAMES: Arm Roast, English Roast, Armbone Chuck.
COMMON USES: Braise; roast beef.

Weight Range [in pounds]

RANGE A	RANGE B	RANGE C	RANGE D
46-57	57-69	69-77	77-up

The boneless, clod out, armbone chuck, is the same as Item No. 126, except that the shoulder clod is excluded.

IMPS NO. 127 **Cross-Cut Chuck**
MBG NO. 127
URMIS and COMMON NAMES: Beef Chuck Cross Rib Pot Roast, Boston Cut, Bread and Butter Cut, English Cut Roast, Cross Rib Roast, Thick Rib Roast.
COMMON USES: Braise; cook in moist heat; pot roast.

Weight Range [in pounds]

RANGE A	RANGE B	RANGE C	RANGE D
86-103	103-120	120-138	138-up

The cross-cut chuck is the Square-Cut Chuck — Item No. 113, Foreshank — Item No. 117, and Brisket — Item No. 118 intact.

IMPS NO. 128 **Cross-Cut Chuck, Boneless**
MBG NO. 128
URMIS and COMMON NAMES: Beef Chuck Cross Rib Pot Roast Boneless, Boneless Boston Cut, Boneless English Cut Roast.

Weight Range [in pounds]

RANGE A	RANGE B	RANGE C	RANGE D
68-81	81-95	95-109	109-up

The boneless, cross-cut chuck is prepared from Item No. 127. The clod shall be removed without undue scoring. Meat with dark discoloration, all bones, cartilage, backstrap, exposed large blood vessels, heavy connective tissue, and the prescapular lymph gland shall be removed. The thick tendinous ends of the shank shall be removed by cutting back, until a cross-sectional cut shows at least 75 percent lean. The remainder of the chuck may be separated into two portions by a straight cut, which is not less than 3 in. from the outer tip of the "chuck eye" muscle and approximately parallel to the major back muscles. Unless otherwise specified, each piece shall be individually wrapped and packed in the same container.

IMPS NO. 132 **Triangle**
MBG NO. 132
URMIS and COMMON NAMES: Triangle.
COMMON USES: Wholesale cut from which all other forequarter cuts are derived.

Weight Range [in pounds]

RANGE A	RANGE B	RANGE C	RANGE D
107-129	129-150	150-172	172-up

The triangle is that portion of the forequarter remaining after the removal of the Rib, Primal — Item No. 103. The rib is separated from the triangle by a straight cut across the ribs, perpendicular to the outer skin surface, to a point on the inside of the 5th rib which is not less than 10 in. from the center of the inside protruding edge of the 5th thoracic vertebra. A second cut is made perpendicular to the split surface of the backbone, between the 5th and 6th ribs through the bladebone and backbone, to remove the primal rib.

IMPS NO. 133 **Triangle, Boneless**
MBG NO. 133
URMIS and COMMON NAMES: Triangle.
COMMON USES: Wholesale cut from which all other forequarter cuts are derived.

Weight Range [in pounds]

RANGE A	RANGE B	RANGE C	RANGE D
83-101	101-117	117-134	134-up

The boneless triangle is prepared from Item No. 132. The clod is removed without undue scoring. Meat with dark discoloration, all bones, cartilage, backstrap, exposed large blood vessels, heavy connective tissue, and the prescapular lymph gland shall be removed. The thick tendinous ends of the shank shall be removed by cutting back, until a cross-sectional cut shows at least 75 percent lean.

IMPS NO. 134 **Beef Bones**
MBG NO. 134
URMIS and COMMON NAMES: Soup Bones.
COMMON USES: Preparation of beef stock.

Weight Range

RANGE A	RANGE B	RANGE C	RANGE D
	Amount As Specified		

Beef bones consist of any one, or any combination, of shank, femur, humerus bones sawed into lengths not to exceed 8 in. Marrow shall be exposed on at least one end. The bones shall be fresh, and show no evidence of rancidity, sourness, or other deterioration.

IMPS NO. 135 **Diced Beef**
MBG NO. 135
URMIS and COMMON NAMES: Beef Cubes, Beef for Stew.
COMMON USES: Beef ragout, beef goulash, beef stew.

Weight Range

RANGE A	RANGE B	RANGE C	RANGE D
	Amount As Specified		

This item may be prepared from any combination of carcasses, or cuts, which will produce diced beef complying with the end product requirements. Meat from shanks is not acceptable. Meat with dark discoloration, all bones, cartilage, backstrap, exposed large blood vessels, heavy connective tissue, and the prescapular, popliteal, and prefemoral lymph glands shall be removed. Prior to dicing, the meat shall be trimmed in such a manner that surface and seam fat shall not exceed 1/2 in. in thickness at any one point. In addition, the fat content of the boneless meat, determined visually, shall not exceed 25 percent.

After being prepared as described above, the boneless meat shall be either hand-diced, or processed through a dicing machine (grinding not permitted). Not more than 25 percent, by weight, of the resulting pieces shall be of a size which is less than a 3/4 in. cube, or more than a 1-1/2 in. cube, and no individual surface on these pieces shall exceed 2-1/2 in. in length.

For machine-diced product requiring one hour or more to produce, compliance with the piece-size requirement shall be determined as follows: The grader shall select and examine one sample weighing approximately 5 lb. during each 20 minutes of production. Failure of a sample to meet the piece-size requirement shall cause rejection of all product produced after the last acceptable sample has been drawn, until another acceptable sample is drawn. Following a rejection, more frequent samples may be taken at the request of the contractor, until an acceptable sample is drawn. Rejected product may be reworked and re-offered for acceptance.

For machine-diced product requiring less than 1 hour to produce, for hand-diced product, and for reworked product, the grader shall sample the amount of product he feels necessary to determine that the entire lot complies with the piece-size requirement.

IMPS NO. 135A **Beef for Stewing**
MBG NO. 135A
URMIS and COMMON NAMES: Stew Beef.
COMMON USES: Cook in moist heat; beef stew.

Weight Range [in pounds]

RANGE A	RANGE B	RANGE C	RANGE D
	Amount As Specified		

This item is the same as Item No. 135 — Diced Beef, except that the surface or seam fat of the boneless meat prior to dicing shall not exceed 1/4 in. in thickness at any one point. In addition, the fat content of the boneless meat determined visually shall not exceed 20 percent.

IMPS NO. 136 **Ground Beef, Regular**
MGB NO. 136
URMIS and COMMON NAMES: Ground Round, Ground Chuck, Ground Sirloin, Hamburger, Ground Beef, Chopped Meat.
COMMON USES: Broil; panbroil; bake; hamburger; chopped beef steak; meat loaf; sloppy joe; chili.

Weight Range
Amount As Specified

MATERIAL

Regular ground beef may be prepared from any beef (graded or ungraded), including trimmings. Meat from the head, tongue, heart, or esophagus or straight (added) fat is not acceptable. Meat with dark discoloration, all bones, cartilage, backstrap, exposed large blood vessels, heavy connective tissue, and the prescapular, popliteal, and prefemoral lymph glands shall be removed. The thick tendinous ends of shanks shall be removed by cutting back until a cross-sectional cut shows at least 75 percent lean.

PROCESSING

After being prepared as described above, the boneless meat shall be ground at least once through a plate having holes no larger than 3/4 in. in diameter (or it may be otherwise reduced in size provided the texture and appearance of the product after final grinding is typical of ground beef prepared by grinding only). Final grinding shall be through a plate having holes 1/8 in. in diameter.

The meat shall be thoroughly blended prior to and subsequent to each reduction in size, except that the ground beef shall not be mixed after the final grinding.

The boneless meat shall not exceed 50° F. during grinding and packaging. The ground beef shall be packaged in the amount specified by the purchaser and packed immediately upon completion of grinding.

FAT CONTENT

The visual fat content of the boneless meat, determined prior to grinding, shall not exceed 25 percent.

However, if specified for product to be delivered frozen, the fat content of the finished product shall be determined by chemical analysis. In such cases, compliance shall be based on the analyses of 4 samples from a lot of finished product. (A lot shall be not more than the amount of product produced in a single workshift.) Analyses shall be performed in an AMS laboratory in accordance with the Official Methods of Analyses of the Association of Official Analytical Chemists. Product shall be rejected (1) if the fat content analysis of one or more of the individual 4 sample units is more than 30.0 percent, and/or (2) if the arithmetic average of the fat content analyses of the 4 individual sample units exceeds 25.00 percent. When chemical analysis is specified, the ground beef shall be produced a sufficient number of days in advance of shipping to permit receipt of the fat content analysis results.

WITHDRAWING SAMPLES FOR CHEMICAL ANALYSIS

The grader shall randomly select four filled shipping containers from each lot. From each container he shall select (1) either one unit of bulk ground beef from which he shall cut 3 adjacent, approximately 1-lb. samples, or (2) 12 adjacent patties which shall be divided into 3 samples of 4 adjacent patties each. Each of the three samples shall be placed in an individual container that will prevent loss or gain of moisture or contamination. The three samples from each individual unit shall be assigned the same identification number, and one sample from each individual unit shall be submitted to an AMS laboratory for fat content analysis; one sample from each unit shall be solidly frozen and retained by the grader as a reserve sample; the remaining sample from each unit shall be offered to the contractor.

The reserve samples shall be used for analysis (1) when the original is lost, or (2) if requested by the purchaser or the contractor. When reserve samples are analyzed, all four samples shall be analyzed. Unused reserved samples shall be returned to the contractor after final acceptance or rejection of the involved product.

After withdrawal of samples, the contractor shall make correct fills of the boxes sampled by adding the necessary ground beef produced from the same lot.

IMPS NO. 1136 **Ground Beef Patties, Regular**
MBG NO. 1136
URMIS and COMMON NAMES: Hamburger, Sirloin Patty, Chopped Steak.
COMMON USES: Broil; panbroil; panfry; hamburger; chopped steak; swiss steak.
SUGGESTED PORTION SIZES: Amount as specified.

This item shall be prepared from Ground Beef, Regular — Item No. 136. The ground beef shall be mechanically formed into round patties of the size specified. They shall be arranged in stacks, with each patty separated from adjacent patties by two sheets of waxed patty paper, except that when patties are individually quick frozen, the patty paper may be excluded. When producing patties to be delivered frozen, frozen boneless beef previously accepted in the fresh state may be used.

IMPS NO. 136A **Ground Beef, Regular, TVP Added**
MBG NO. 136A
URMIS and COMMON NAMES: Ground Beef with TVP, Beef Patty Mix.
COMMON USES: Hamburgers; macaroni beef casserole.
Weight Range [in pounds]
RANGE A　　　RANGE B　　　RANGE C　　　RANGE D
Amount As Specified

This item is the same as Item No. 136 except that hydrated textured vegetable protein (TVP) shall be uniformly mixed with the coarsely ground beef, at a ratio of not more than 1 part hydrated TVP to not less than 4 parts beef, by weight. The TVP shall be hydrated at a ratio of 1 part TVP to not more than 1.5 parts water, by weight. Textured vegetable protein used shall be approved by the USDA Food and Nutrition Service, and shall be caramel colored with beef flavoring. The visual fat content of the boneless meat, determined prior to grinding, shall not exceed 30 percent.

IMPS NO. 1136A **Ground Beef Patties, Regular, TVP Added**
MBG NO. 1136A
URMIS and COMMON NAMES: Ground Beef Patties with TVP.
COMMON USES: Hamburgers, cheeseburgers.
Portion Sizes
Size As Specified

This item is the same as Item No. 1136, except that it shall be prepared from Ground Beef, TVP Added — Item No. 136A.

IMPS NO. 1137 **Ground Beef Patties, Special**
MBG NO. 1137
URMIS and COMMON NAMES: Hamburger, Chopped Steak, Sirloin Patties.
COMMON USES: Hamburgers; sirloin patties; chopped beef steak.
SUGGESTED PORTION SIZES: 3 oz., 4 oz., 6 oz., 8 oz.

This item is the same as Item No. 1136, except that it shall be prepared from Ground Beef, Special — Item No. 137.

IMPS NO. 137 **Ground Beef, Special**
MBG NO. 137
URMIS and COMMON NAMES: Ground Sirloin, Hamburger, Ground Chuck, Chopped Steak, Ground Round.
COMMON USES: Broil; panbroil; panfry; chopped beef steak; chili; meat loaf.
Weight Range
Amount As Specified

This item is the same as Item No. 136 except that not less than 50 percent, by weight, of any one or any combination of graded primal cuts (square-cut chucks, ribs, trimmed full loins, loin ends, or rounds) shall be used. Tenderloins may be excluded. Compliance with the formulation requirements shall be determined on a boneless basis. Primal cuts which have had more than a slight amount of lean removed may be used, provided that meat of similar character and amount is added from the above listed primal cuts.

IMPS NO. 155 **Hindquarter**
MBG NO. 155
URMIS and COMMON NAMES: Quarter of Beef, Hindquarter.
COMMON USES: Wholesale cut from which all other hindquarter cuts
are derived.

Weight Range [in pounds]

RANGE A	RANGE B	RANGE C	RANGE D
119-143	143-167	167-190	190-up

The hindquarter is the portion underneath the side after severance
from the forequarter, as described in Item No. 100.

IMPS NO. 155A **Hindquarter, Boneless**
MBG NO. 155A
URMIS and COMMON NAMES: Hindquarter.
COMMON USES: Wholesale cut from which all other hindquarter cuts
are derived.

Weight Range [in pounds]

RANGE A	RANGE B	RANGE C	RANGE D
90-108	108-126	126-143	143-up

This item is prepared from Item No. 155. Meat with dark discoloration, all bones, cartilage, exposed large blood vessels, the prefemoral and
popliteal lymph glands, kidney, mammary tissue, and the heavy
connective tissue surrounding the kneecap shall be removed. The thick
tendinous ends of the shank shall be removed by cutting back, until a
cross-sectional cut shows at least 75 percent lean. The tenderloin may be
withheld.

IMPS NO. 158 **Round, Primal**
MBG NO. 158
URMIS and COMMON NAMES: Chicago Round, Round of Beef.
COMMON USES: Panbroil; broil; cook in moist heat; roast beef; swiss
steak; chopped beef.

Weight Range [in pounds]

RANGE A	RANGE B	RANGE C	RANGE D
59-71	71-83	83-95	95-up

The primal round is that portion of the Hindquarter — Item No. 155,
remaining after the removal of the untrimmed loin. The untrimmed loin
is removed by a straight cut perpendicular to the outer skin surface,
beginning at the juncture of the last sacral vertebra, then passing
through a second point which is immediately in front of the protuberance
of the femur bone, and exposing the ball of the femur bone, then continuing in the same straight line to complete the cut. No more than two tail
vertebrae may remain on the round.

IMPS NO. 159 **Round**
MBG NO. 159
URMIS and COMMON NAMES: Chicago Round, Round Primal Bone-
less.
COMMON USES: Roast; panfry; cook in moist heat; roast beef; swiss
steak; chopped beef.

Weight Range [in pounds]

RANGE A	RANGE B	RANGE C	RANGE D
44-53	53-62	62-71	71-up

The boneless round is the same as Item No. 158, except that it shall
be made boneless. The round bone shall be removed, after a cut has been
made along the natural seam between the knuckle and the sartorius
muscle of the top round. All cartilage, heavy connective tissue, and the
thick opaque portion of the gracilis membrane shall be removed. The
thick tendinous ends of the shank shall be removed by cutting back, until
a cross-sectional cut shows at least 75 percent lean.

IMPS NO. 160 **Round, Shank Off, Partially Boneless**
MBG NO. 160
URMIS and COMMON NAMES: Beef Round Rump On — Shank Off
(Steamship Round).
COMMON USES: Braise; panfry; cook in moist heat; swiss steak; stew
beef; roast beef.

Weight Range [in pounds]

RANGE A	RANGE B	RANGE C	RANGE D
44-57	57-67	67-76	76-up

This item is prepared from Item No. 158. The shank shall be removed
along the natural seam between the shank meat and the heel (gastrocnemius muscle). The aitch bone, tail bones, and the thick, opaque portion of
the gracilis membrane shall be removed. The round bone shall be left in
the round.

IMPS NO. 161 **Round, Shank Off, Boneless**
MBG NO. 161
URMIS and COMMON NAMES: Boneless Round Shank Off.
COMMON USES: Braise; roast; steamship round; roast beef; swiss
steak; chopped beef.

Weight Range [in pounds]

RANGE A	RANGE B	RANGE C	RANGE D
44-53	53-62	62-71	71-up

This item is the same as Item No. 160, except that it shall be made
boneless. The round bone shall be removed as described in Item No. 159.

IMPS NO. 163 **Round, Shank Off, 3-Way Boneless**
MBG NO. 163
URMIS and COMMON NAMES: Top Bottom and Knuckle, Beef Set.
COMMON USES: Roast beef; swiss steak.

Weight Range [in pounds]

RANGE A	RANGE B	RANGE C	RANGE D
41-50	50-58	58-66	66-up

This item is the same as Item No. 161, except that it shall be separated into 3 pieces: Knuckle — Item No. 167; Top (Inside) Round — Item No. 168, and Bottom (Gooseneck Round — Item No. 170. The round bone shall be removed, as described in Item No. 159. The top round and the knuckle shall be separated from the bottom round along the natural seams between these sections. The top round, bottom round, and knuckle shall be individually wrapped, and packed in the same container.

IMPS NO. 164 **Round, Rump and Shank Off**
MBG NO. 164
URMIS and COMMON NAMES: Rump and Shank Off Round, Steamboat Round.
COMMON USES: Roast beef.

Weight Range [in pounds]

RANGE A	RANGE B	RANGE C	RANGE D
40-48	48-56	56-64	64-up

This item is the same as Item No. 161, except that it shall be separated into 3 pieces: Knuckle — Item No. 167; Top (Inside) Round — Item No. 168, and Bottom (Gooseneck) Round — Item No. 170. The round bone shall be removed, as described in Item No. 159. The top round and the knuckle shall be separated from the bottom round along the natural seams between these sections. The top round, bottom round, and knuckle shall be individually wrapped, and packed in the same container.

IMPS NO. 165 **Round [Rump and Shank Off] Boneless**
MBG NO. 165
URMIS and COMMON NAMES: Rump and Shank Off Round, Steamboat Round.
COMMON USES: Roast beef.

Weight Range [in pounds]

RANGE A	RANGE B	RANGE C	RANGE D
35-43	43-50	50-57	57-up

This item is the same as Item No. 164, except that it shall be made boneless. The round bone (femur) shall be removed, as described in Item No. 159. The kneecap (patella) and surrounding heavy connective tissue shall be removed. The thick, opaque portion of the gracilis membrane shall be removed.

IMPS NO. 165A **Round, Rump and Shank Off, Boneless, Special**
MBG NO. Not Included.
URMIS and COMMON NAMES: Rump and Shank Off Round, Steamboat Round.
COMMON USES: Roast beef.

Weight Range [in pounds]

RANGE A	RANGE B	RANGE C	RANGE D
38-46	46-54	54-60	60-up

This item is prepared from Item No. 161. The rump shall be removed by a straight cut through the bottom round, perpendicular to the outer skin surface starting along the inner, anterior edge of the top round.

IMPS NO. 165B **Round, Rump and Shank Off, Boneless, Tied, Special.**
MBG NO. Not Included.
URMIS and COMMON NAMES: Rump and Shank Off Round, Steamboat Round.
COMMON USES: Roast beef.

Weight Range [in pounds]

RANGE A	RANGE B	RANGE C	RANGE D
38-46	46-54	54-60	60-up

This item is the same as Item No. 165A, except that it shall be tied lengthwise and girthwise.

IMPS NO. 166 **Round, Rump and Shank Off, Boned, Tied**
MBG NO. 166
URMIS and COMMON NAMES: Rump and Shank Off Round, Steamboat Round.
COMMON USES: Roast beef.

Weight Range [in pounds]

RANGE A	RANGE B	RANGE C	RANGE D
35-43	43-50	50-57	57-up

This item is the same as Item No. 165, except that it shall be tied lengthwise and girthwise.

IMPS NO. 166A **Round, Rump Partially Removed, Shank Off**
MBG NO. Not Included.
URMIS and COMMON NAMES: Rump and Shank Off Round, Steamboat Round.
COMMON USES: Roast beef.

Weight Range [in pounds]

RANGE A	RANGE B	RANGE C	RANGE D
44-52	52-61	61-70	70-up

This item is the same as Item No. 164, except that part of the rump shall be removed as follows: The aitch bone and tail bones shall be removed. The rump shall be removed by a straight cut, beginning at the anterior end of the protuberance of the femur bone, which also is perpendicular to the outer skin surface and perpendicular to the length of the round bone.

IMPS NO. 167 **Knuckle**
MBG NO. 167
URMIS and COMMON NAMES: Knuckle, Veiny Sirloin Tip.
COMMON USES: Roast beef.

Weight Range [in pounds]

RANGE A	RANGE B	RANGE C	RANGE D
8-9	9-11	11-13	13-up

The knuckle is that portion of Item No. 158 that is at the side of the round bone, and is prepared as described in Item No. 163. When smaller roasts are specified, the knuckle shall be separated by a straight lengthwise cut which is reasonably perpendicular to the outer skin surface.

IMPS NO. 1167 **Knuckle Steaks**
MBG NO. 1167
URMIS and COMMON NAMES: Knuckle Steaks, Veiny Steaks.
COMMON USES: Roast; braise; swiss steak; steak; roast beef.
SUGGESTED PORTION SIZES: 3 oz., 4 oz., 6 oz., 8 oz., 10 oz.

Knuckle steaks shall be prepared from a Knuckle, Trimmed — Item No. 167A. The knuckle may be separated lengthwise into sections to accommodate the cutting of specified, portion-size steaks.

IMPS NO. 167A **Knuckle, Special**
MBG NO. 167A
URMIS and COMMON NAMES: Sirloin Tip, Knuckle.
COMMON USES: Braise; roast; roast beef; swiss steak.

Weight Range [in pounds]

RANGE A	RANGE B	RANGE C	RANGE D
8-9	9-11	11-13	13-up

This item is the same as Item No. 167, except that the outside "skin" tissue, fat, and overlying muscle (tensor fasciae latae) shall be removed along the natural seam separating them from the knuckle. When smaller roasts are specified, the knuckle shall be separated by a straight, lengthwise cut which is reasonably perpendicular to the outer skin surface.

IMPS NO. 168 **Top [Inside] Round**
MBG NO. 168
URMIS and COMMON NAMES: Top Round.
COMMON USES: Roast; braise; roast beef.

Weight Range [in pounds]

RANGE A	RANGE B	RANGE C	RANGE D
14-17	17-20	20-23	23-up

The top round is the inside portion of Item No. 158 that is behind the round bone, and is prepared as described in Item No. 163. When smaller roasts are specified, the top round shall be separated by not more than 2 lengthwise cuts, and subsequent cuts, if necessary, shall be made girthwise. All cuts shall be made reasonably perpendicular to the outer skin surface.

IMPS NO. 1168 **Top [Inside] Round Steaks**
MBG NO. 1168
URMIS and COMMON NAMES: Top Round Steaks.
COMMON USES: Braise; panfry; panbroil; beef top round steak, braciole steak.
SUGGESTED PORTION SIZES: 3 oz., 4 oz., 6 oz., 8 oz., 10 oz., 12 oz.

Top round steaks shall be prepared from a Top Round — Item No. 168. The top round may be separated lengthwise into sections to accommodate the cutting of specified, portion-size steaks.

IMPS NO. 170 **Bottom [Gooseneck] Round**
MBG NO. 170
URMIS and COMMON NAMES: Bottom Round, Outside Round.
COMMON USES: Roast beef; swiss steak.

Weight Range [in pounds]

RANGE A	RANGE B	RANGE C	RANGE D
18-21	21-25	25-29	29-up

The bottom round is the outside portion of Item No. 158 that is behind the round bone, and is prepared as described in Item No. 163. The heavy, connective tissue on the edge of the bottom round adjacent to the knuckle shall be removed.

IMPS NO. 1170 **Bottom [Gooseneck] Round Steaks**
MBG NO. 1170
URMIS and COMMON NAMES: Beef Bottom Round Steaks.
COMMON USES: Braise; panfry; swiss steak.
SUGGESTED PORTION SIZES: 3 oz., 4 oz., 6 oz., 8 oz., 10 oz., 12 oz., 14 oz., 16 oz., 18 oz., 20 oz., 24 oz.

Bottom round steaks shall be prepared from a Bottom Round, Heel Out — Item No. 170A. The bottom round may be separated lengthwise into sections to accommodate the cutting of specified, portion-size steaks.

IMPS NO. 170A **Bottom [Gooseneck] Round, Heel Out**
MBG NO. Not Included.
URMIS and COMMON NAMES: Outside Round, Bottom Round.
COMMON USES: Roast beef; swiss steak.

Weight Range [in pounds]

RANGE A	RANGE B	RANGE C	RANGE D
17-20	20-24	24-28	28-up

This item is the same as Item No. 170, except that the heel (gastrocnemius muscle) is removed along the natural seam separating it from the eye muscle (semitendinosus), and the outside muscle (biceps femoris). When smaller roasts are specified, the rump shall be removed by a cut approximately perpendicular to the length of the bottom round. The remaining portion shall be divided by a cut(s) approximately parallel with the bottom round length. All cuts shall be made reasonably perpendicular to the outer skin surface.

IMPS NO. 171 **Bottom [Gooseneck] Round, Untrimmed**
MBG NO. Not Included.
URMIS and COMMON NAMES: Bottom Round, Gooseneck Round, Outside Round, Army Bottom Round.
COMMON USES: Roast beef.

Weight Range [in pounds]

RANGE A	RANGE B	RANGE C	RANGE D
18-21	21-25	25-29	29-up

The bottom round is the outside portion of Item No. 158 that is behind the round bone, and is prepared as described in Item No. 163.

IMPS NO. 171A **Bottom [Gooseneck] Round, Untrimmed, Heel Out**
MBG NO. Not Included.
URMIS and COMMON NAMES: Prime Bottom Round with Heel Out.
COMMON USES: Roast beef.

Weight Range [in pounds]

RANGE A	RANGE B	RANGE C	RANGE D
17-20	20-24	24-28	28-up

This item is the same as Item No. 171, except that the heel (gastrocnemius muscle) is removed along the natural seam separating it from the eye muscle (semitendinosus) and the outside muscle (biceps femoris). When smaller roasts are specified, the rump shall be removed by a cut approximately perpendicular to the length of the bottom round. The remaining portion shall be divided by a cut(s) approximately parallel with the bottom round length. All cuts shall be made reasonably perpendicular to the outer skin surface.

IMPS NO. 171B **Outside Round**
MBG NO. Not Included
URMIS and COMMON NAMES: Gooseneck, Bottom Round.
COMMON USES: Roast beef.

Weight Range [in pounds]

RANGE A	RANGE B	RANGE C	RANGE D
8-10	10-13	13-16	16-up

This item is prepared from Item No. 171A, by removing the eye muscle along the natural seam separating it from the outside muscle.

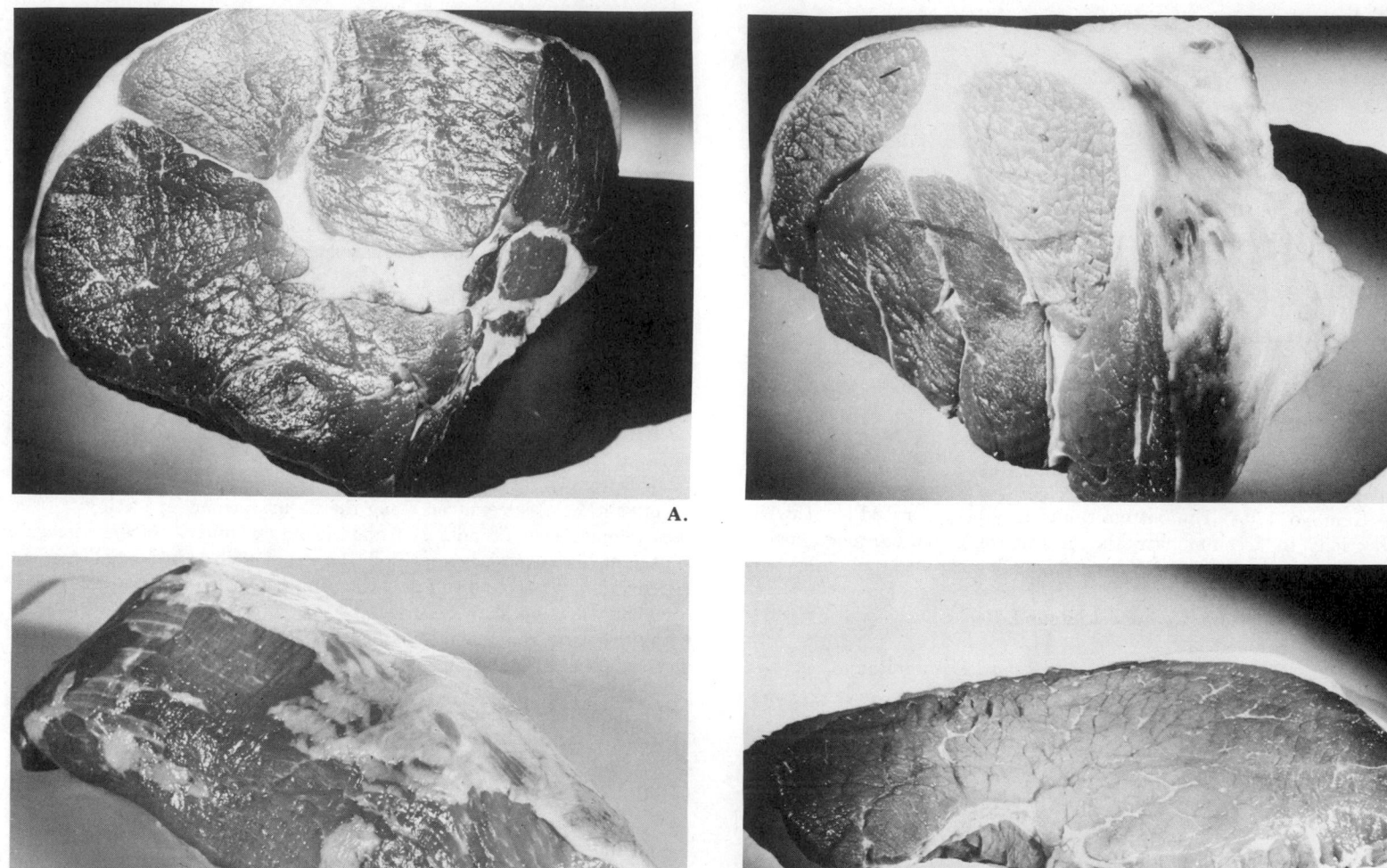

A.

B.

C.

D.

A. *IMPS NO. 167 Knuckle, p. 126;* B. *IMPS NO. 170 (Gooseneck) Round, p. 127;*
C. *IMPS NO. 171C Eye of Round, p. 130;* D. *IMPS NO. 168 Top (Inside) Round,*
p. 126; E. *IMPS NO. 1170 Bottom (Gooseneck) Round Steaks, p. 127;* F. *IMPS*

NO. 1174A T-Bone Steaks, Intermediate, p. 131; G. *IMPS NO. 1173B Porter-*
house Steaks, Short-Cut, p. 130; H. *IMPS NO. 1179 Strip Loin, Short Cut, p.*
132.

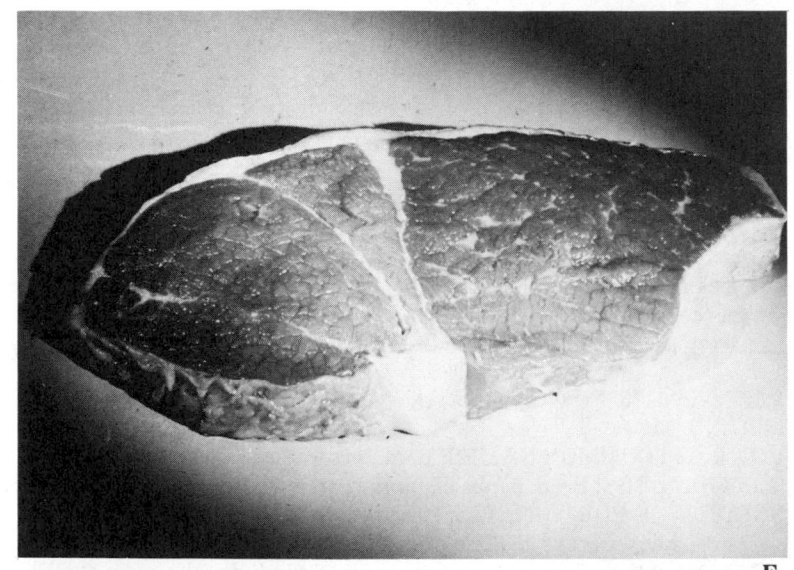

E.

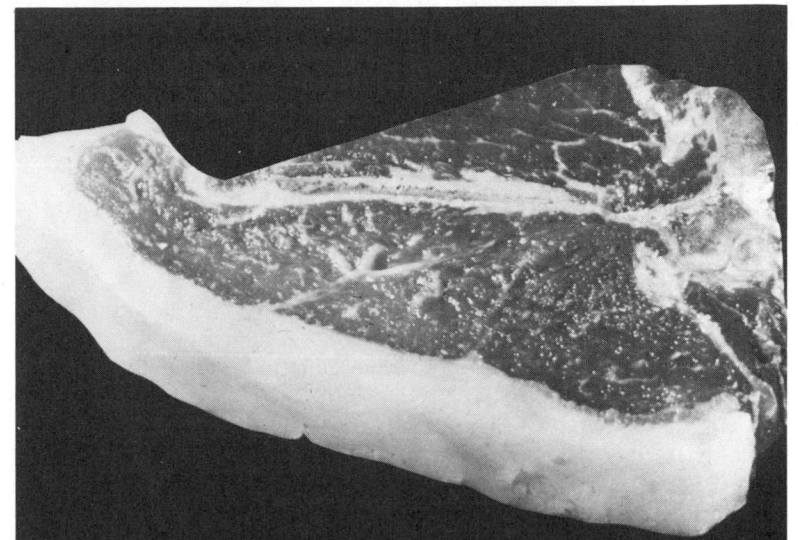

F.

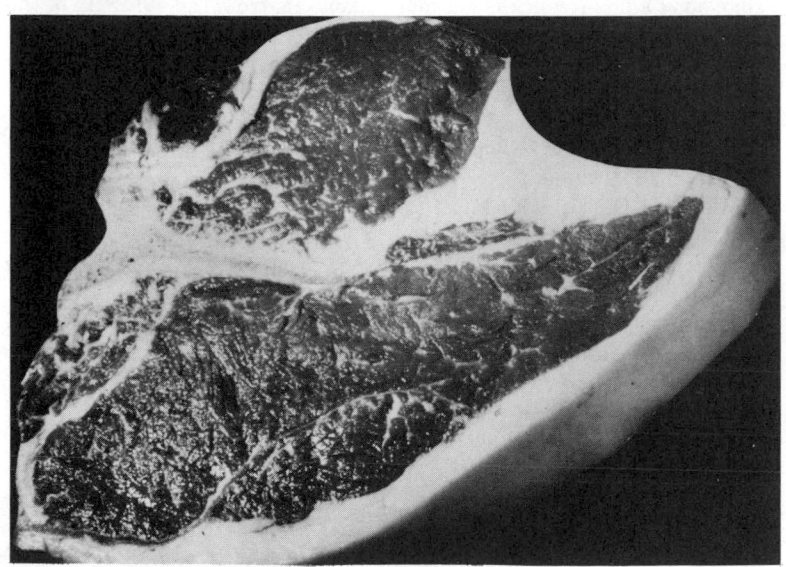

G.

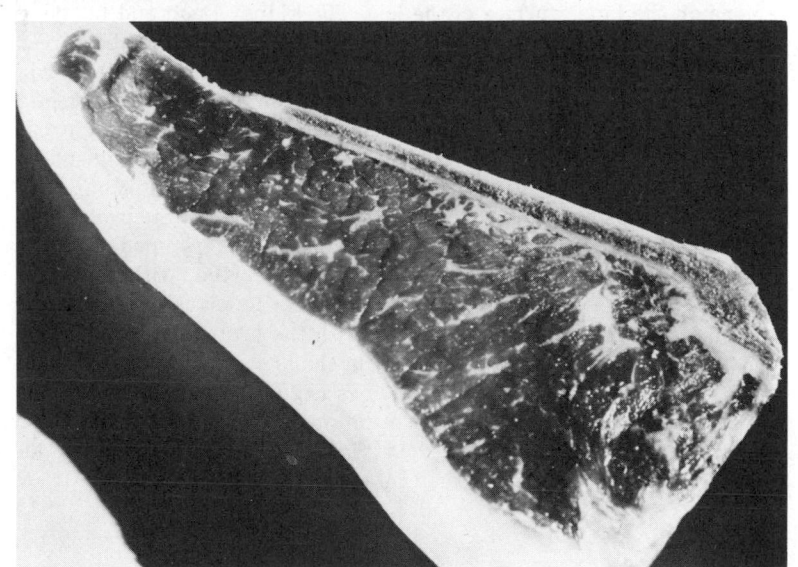

H.

IMPS NO. 171C **Eye of Round**
MBG NO. 171C
URMIS and COMMON NAMES: Eye.
COMMON USES: Corning beef.

Weight Range [in pounds]

RANGE A	RANGE B	RANGE C	RANGE D
under 3	3-5	5-up	- - -

The eye of round is prepared as described in Item No. 171B.

IMPS NO. 172 **Full Loin, Trimmed**
MBG NO. 172
URMIS and COMMON NAMES: Full-Loin.
COMMON USES: To be cut into sirloins, filets, tenderloins, top butt, steaks, or roasts.

Weight Range [in pounds]

RANGE A	RANGE B	RANGE C	RANGE D
35-42	42-50	50-57	57-up

The trimmed, full loin is that portion of the hindquarter remaining after the removal of the Round, Primal — Item No. 158, flank, hanging tender, kidney knob, and excess fat from both the lumbar and sacral regions on the inner surface of the loin. The kidney knob and fat lying closely around the kidney shall be removed by a cut starting at the rear end of the kidney, and slanting directly to the rear edge of the 13th rib, thus leaving the 13th rib practically free of lumbar fat. The hanging tender shall be removed. The flank shall be removed by a straight cut perpendicular to the outer skin surface, from a point on the round end no more than 1 in. from the ventral edge of the sirloin through a point on the 13th rib, which is not more than 10 in. from the center of the protruding edge of the 13th thoracic vertebra. The fat shall be trimmed from the internal, lumbar section of the loin lying unsupported, with the outer skin surface down on a flat surface. The fat above a plane parallel to the surface of the cutting bench, and level with the protruding edge of the chine bone, shall be removed. Another cut shall be made to remove all fat above a plane using the following two lines as guides for each edge of the plane: an imaginary line 1 in. above the protruding edge of the chine bone to a line on the inside of the loin 2 in. from the flank edge. The fat remaining in the sacral region shall not exceed 1 in. in thickness.

IMPS NO. 173 **Short Loin, Regular**
MBG NO. 173
URMIS and COMMON NAMES: Beef Short Loin.
COMMON USES: T-Bones; porterhouse; club steak; sirloin; filets.

Weight Range [in pounds]

RANGE A	RANGE B	RANGE C	RANGE D
17-21	21-25	25-28	28-up

The short loin is the anterior portion of Item No. 172. It is separated from the Sirloin — Item No. 181 — by a straight cut, perpendicular to the outer skin surface and perpendicular to the split surface of the lumbar vertebrae, through a point immediately in front of the hip bone, leaving no part of the hip bone and related cartilage in the short loin.

IMPS NO. 1173 **Porterhouse Steaks**
MBG NO. 1173
URMIS and COMMON NAMES: Beef Porterhouse Steak.
COMMON USES: Broil; panbroil; panfry; steak.
SUGGESTED PORTION SIZE: 10 oz., 12 oz.

Porterhouse steaks shall be prepared from a Short Loin — Item No. 173, or a portion thereof. The flank edge on individual steaks shall be removed at a point which is not more than 4 in. from the outer tip of the loin eye muscle. The diameter of the tenderloin muscle shall not be less than 1-1/4 in., when measured through the center of the tenderloin parallel to the backbone.

IMPS NO. 1173A **Porterhouse Steaks, Intermediate**
MBG NO. Not Included.
URMIS and COMMON NAMES: Porterhouse Steak.
COMMON USES: Broil; steak.
SUGGESTED PORTION SIZES: 10 oz., 12 oz., 14 oz., 16 oz., 18 oz., 20 oz., 24 oz.

This item is the same as Item No. 1173, except the flank edge on individual steaks shall be removed at a point which is not more than 3 in. from the outer tip of the loin eye muscle.

IMPS NO. 1173B **Porterhouse Steaks, Short-Cut**
MBG NO. Not Included.
URMIS and COMMON NAMES: Porterhouse Steak.
COMMON USES: Broil; steak.
SUGGESTED PORTION SIZES: 10 oz., 12 oz., 14 oz., 16 oz., 18 oz., 20 oz., 24 oz.

This item is the same as Item No. 1173, except the flank edge on individual steaks shall be removed at a point which is not more than 2 in. from the outer tip of the loin eye muscle.

IMPS NO. 174 **Short Loin, Short-Cut**
MBG NO. 174
URMIS and COMMON NAMES: Short Loin.
COMMON USES: T-Bones; porterhouse; club steak; sirloins; filets.

Weight Range [in pounds]

RANGE A	RANGE B	RANGE C	RANGE D
14-19	19-23	23-26	26-up

This item is the same as Item No. 173, except that the flank edge is removed by a straight cut, perpendicular to the outer skin surface, from a point on the rib end which is not more than 3 in. from the outer tip of the loin eye muscle, through a point on the sirloin end which is not more than 2 in. from the outer tip of the loin eye muscle.

IMPS NO. 1174 **T-Bone Steaks**
MBG NO. 1174
URMIS and COMMON NAMES: Beef Loin T-Bone Steak.
COMMON USES: Broil; panbroil; panfry; T-bone steak.
SUGGESTED PORTION SIZES: 8 oz., 10 oz., 12 oz., 14 oz., 16 oz., 18 oz., 20 oz., 24 oz., 28 oz.

T-Bone steaks shall be prepared from a Short-Loin — Item No. 173, or a Short Loin, Short-Cut — Item No. 174, or a portion thereof. The flank edge on individual steaks shall be removed at a point which is not more than 3 in. from the outer tip of the loin eye muscle. The diameter of the tenderloin muscle shall be not less than 1/2 in., when measured through the center of the tenderloin parallel with the backbone.

IMPS NO. 1174A **T-Bone Steaks, Intermediate**
MBG NO. Not Included.
URMIS and COMMON NAMES: T-Bone Steak.
COMMON USES: Broil; steak.
SUGGESTED PORTION SIZES: 10 oz., 12 oz., 14 oz., 16 oz., 18 oz., 20 oz., 24 oz.

IMPS NO. 1174B **T-Bone Steaks, Short Cut**
MBG NO. Not Included.
URMIS and COMMON NAMES: T-Bone Steak.
COMMON USES: Broil; steak.
SUGGESTED PORTION SIZES: 8 oz., 10 oz., 12 oz., 14 oz., 16 oz., 18 oz., 20 oz., 24 oz.

This item is the same as Item No. 1174, except the flank edge on individual steaks shall be removed at a point which is not more than 1 in. from the outer tip of the loin muscle.

IMPS NO. 175 **Strip Loin**
MBG NO. 175
URMIS and COMMON NAMES: Beef Strip Loin, Shell.
COMMON USES: Broil; panbroil; panfry; club steak; bone-in sirloin steak.

Weight Range [in pounds]

RANGE A	RANGE B	RANGE C	RANGE D
11-13	13-16	16-19	19-up

The strip loin is prepared from the Short Loin — Item No. 173. The short tenderloin is removed. (As an alternative, the tenderloin may be removed from the full loin before removing the sirloin.) The protruding edge of the chine bone shall be removed by sawing at an approximate 45 degree angle to the split thoracic vertebrae, beginning at the dorsal edge of the spinal cord groove. The flank edge shall be removed by a straight cut, perpendicular to the outer skin surface, from a point on the rib end which is not more than 6 in. from the outer tip of the loin eye muscle, through a point on the sirloin end which is not more than 4 in. from the outer tip of the loin eye muscle.

IMPS NO. 176 **Strip Loin, Boneless**
MBG NO. 176
URMIS and COMMON NAMES: Beef Sirloin Boneless, Untrimmed.
COMMON USES: Roast; roast beef.

Weight Range [in pounds]

RANGE A	RANGE B	RANGE C	RANGE D
8-10	10-12	12-14	14-up

The boneless strip loin is the same as Item No. 175, except that all bones and cartilage shall be removed.

IMPS NO. 177 **Strip Loin, Intermediate**
MBG NO. 177
URMIS and COMMON NAMES: Beef Sirloin, Trimmed.
COMMON USES: Roast; roast beef.

Weight Range [in pounds]

RANGE A	RANGE B	RANGE C	RANGE D
10-12	12-14	14-16	16-up

This item is the same as Item No. 175, except that the flank edge is removed by a straight cut, perpendicular to the outer skin surface, from a point on the rib end which is not more than 4 in. from the outer tip of the loin eye muscle, through a point on the sirloin end which is not more than 3 in. from the outer tip of the loin eye muscle.

IMPS NO. 1177 **Strip Loin Steaks, Bone-In, Intermediate**
MBG NO. 1177
URMIS and COMMON NAMES: Sirloin Steak, Strip Loin Steak, Shell.
COMMON USES: Broil; panbroil; panfry; club steaks; bone-in sirloin steaks.
SUGGESTED PORTION SIZES: 6 oz., 8 oz., 10 oz., 12 oz., 14 oz., 16 oz., 18 oz., 20 oz., 24 oz., 28 oz.

Intermediate strip loin steaks shall be prepared from a Strip Loin — Item No. 175. The flank edge on individual steaks shall be removed at a point which is not more than 3 in. from the outer tip of the loin eye muscle.

IMPS NO. 178 **Strip Loin, Intermediate, Boneless**
MBG NO. 178
URMIS and COMMON NAMES: Beef Sirloin, Trimmed, Sirloin Steak.
COMMON USES: Roast; roast beef.

Weight Range [in pounds]

RANGE A	RANGE B	RANGE C	RANGE D
8-9	9-11	11-13	13-up

This item is the same as Item No. 177, except that all bones and cartilage shall be removed.

IMPS NO. 1178 **Strip Loin Steaks, Boneless, Intermediate**
MBG NO. 1178
URMIS and COMMON NAMES: Beef Sirloin, Trimmed, Sirloin Steak.
COMMON USES: Roast; roast beef.
SUGGESTED PORTION SIZES: 8 oz., 10 oz., 12 oz., 14 oz., 16 oz., 18 oz., 20 oz., 24 oz., 28 oz.

Intermediate, boneless, strip loin steaks are prepared from a Strip Loin, Boneless — Item No. 176. The flank edge on individual steaks shall be removed at a point which is not more than 3 in. from the outer tip of the loin eye muscle.

IMPS NO. 179 **Strip Loin, Short Cut**
MBG NO. 179
URMIS and COMMON NAMES: Beef Strip Loin, Shell.
COMMON USES: Broil; panbroil; panfry; club steak; bone-in sirloin steak.

Weight Range [in pounds]

RANGE A	RANGE B	RANGE C	RANGE D
8-10	10-12	12-14	14-up

This item is the same as Item No. 175, except that the flank edge is removed by a straight cut, perpendicular to the outer skin surface, from a point on the rib end which is not more than 3 in. from the outer tip of the loin eye muscle, through a point on the sirloin end which is not more than 2 in. from the loin eye muscle.

IMPS NO. 1179 **Strip Loin Steaks, Bone-In, Short Cut**
MBG NO. 1179
URMIS and COMMON NAMES: Beef Strip Loin, Shell.
COMMON USES: Broil; panbroil; panfry; club steak; bone-in sirloin steak.
SUGGESTED PORTION SIZES: 8 oz., 10 oz., 12 oz., 14 oz., 16 oz., 18 oz., 20 oz., 24 oz.

This item is the same as Item No. 1177, except that the flank edge on individual steaks shall be removed at a point which is not more than 2 in. from the outer tip of the loin eye muscle.

IMPS NO. 1179A **Strip Loin Steaks, Bone-In, Extra Short Cut**
MBG NO. 1179A
URMIS and COMMON NAMES: Beef Strip Loin, Shell.
COMMON USES: Broil; panbroil; panfry; club steak; bone-in sirloin steak.
SUGGESTED PORTION SIZES: 8 oz., 10 oz., 12 oz., 14 oz., 16 oz., 18 oz., 20 oz., 24 oz.

This item is the same as Item No. 1177, except the flank edge on individual steaks shall be removed at a point which is not more than 1 in. from the outer tip of the loin eye muscle.

IMPS NO. 1179B **Strip Loin Steaks, Bone-In, Special**
MBG NO. 1179B
URMIS and COMMON NAMES: Beef Strip Loin, Shell.
COMMON USES: Broil; panbroil; panfry; club steak; bone-in sirloin steak.
SUGGESTED PORTION SIZES: 8 oz., 10 oz., 12 oz., 14 oz., 16 oz., 18 oz., 20 oz., 24 oz.

This item is the same as Item No. 1177, except the flank edge on individual steaks shall be removed at a point beyond the outer tip of the loin eye muscle which is not more than the specified thickness of surface fat.

IMPS NO. 180 **Strip Loin, Short Cut, Boneless**
MBG NO. 180
URMIS and COMMON NAMES: Short Cut Strip.
COMMON USES: Sirloin steak; roast sirloin.

Weight Range [in pounds]

RANGE A	RANGE B	RANGE C	RANGE D
7-8	8-10	10-12	12-up

This item is the same as Item No. 179, except that all bones and cartilage shall be removed.

IMPS NO. 1180 **Strip Loin Steaks, Boneless, Short Cut**
MBG NO. 1180
URMIS and COMMON NAMES: Short Cut Strip.
COMMON USES: Sirloin steak; sirloin roast.
SUGGESTED PORTION SIZES: 6 oz., 8 oz., 10 oz., 12 oz., 14 oz., 16 oz., 18 oz., 20 oz.

This item is the same as Item No. 1178, except the flank edge on individual steaks shall be removed at a point which is not more than 2 in. from the outer tip of the loin eye muscle.

IMPS NO. 1180A **Strip Loin Steaks, Boneless, Extra Short Cut**
MBG NO. 1180A
URMIS and COMMON NAMES: Short Cut Strip.
COMMON USES: Sirloin steak; sirloin roast.
SUGGESTED PORTION SIZES: 6 oz., 8 oz., 10 oz., 12 oz., 14 oz., 16 oz., 18 oz., 20 oz.

This item is the same as Item No. 1178, except the flank edge on individual steaks shall be removed at a point which is no more than 1 in. from the outer tip of the loin eye muscle.

IMPS NO. 1180B **Strip Loin Steaks, Boneless, Special**
MBG NO. 1180B
URMIS and COMMON NAMES: Short Cut Strip.
COMMON USES: Sirloin steak; roast sirloin.
SUGGESTED PORTION SIZES: 6 oz., 8 oz., 10 oz., 12 oz., 14 oz., 16 oz., 18 oz., 20 oz.

This item is the same as Item No. 1178, except the flank edge on individual steaks shall be removed at a point which is not more than the specified thickness of surface fat from the outer tip of the loin eye muscle.

IMPS NO. 181 **Sirloin**
MBG NO. 181
URMIS and COMMON NAMES: Sirloin Butt Bone-In.
COMMON USES: Roast; roast beef; sirloin steaks.

Weight Range [in pounds]

RANGE A	RANGE B	RANGE C	RANGE D
16-19	19-24	24-28	28-up

The sirloin is the underneath portion of the Full Loin, Trimmed — Item No. 172. It is separated from the Short Loin — Item No. 173, as described in that item.

IMPS NO. 182 **Sirloin Butt, Boneless**
MBG NO. 182
URMIS and COMMON NAMES: Sirloin Butt, Boneless.
COMMON USES: Roast; roast beef; sirloin steaks.

Weight Range [in pounds]

RANGE A	RANGE B	RANGE C	RANGE D
11-14	14-16	16-19	19-up

The boneless sirloin butt is the same as Item No. 181, except that all bones and the butt tenderloin shall be removed.

IMPS NO. 183 **Sirloin Butt, Boneless, Trimmed**
MBG NO. 183
URMIS and COMMON NAMES: Sirloin Butt, Boneless.
COMMON USES: Roast; roast beef; sirloin steaks.

Weight Range [in pounds]

RANGE A	RANGE B	RANGE C	RANGE D
9-10	10-13	13-15	15-up

This item is prepared from Item No. 182. The flap muscle (obliquus abdominis internus) and underlying membrane shall be removed. The fat on the left side and in front shall be trimmed to the specified surface fat thickness. However, the pocket of fat within the bottom sirloin, and adjacent to the top sirloin, need not be trimmed to the specified surface fat thickness, but shall be trimmed only to a smooth even surface. The heavy connective tissue adjacent to the sacral vertebrae shall be removed.

IMPS NO. 184 **Top Sirloin Butt, Boneless**
MBG NO. 184
URMIS and COMMON NAMES: Butt Loin, Top Butt, Sirloin Butt, Butt Sirloin.
COMMON USES: Roast; roast beef; top butt steaks.

Weight Range [in pounds]

RANGE A	RANGE B	RANGE C	RANGE D
6-7	7-9	9-11	11-up

The top sirloin butt is prepared from Item No. 182. The top and bottom sirloin butts shall be separated by a straight cut along the natural seam, and continuing in the same plane to the outside surface, completing the separation, and leaving a portion of the bottom sirloin butt attached to the top sirloin butt. The heavy connective tissue adjacent to the sacral vertebrae shall be removed. If specified, roasts shall be tied parallel to the cut surface made by separating the loin from the round.

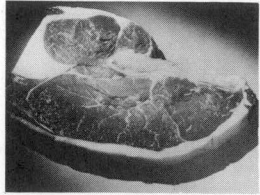 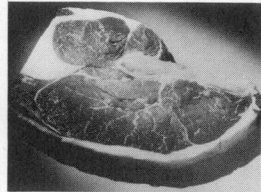 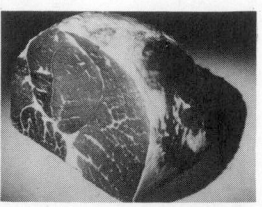

A.   **B.**   **C.**

IMPS NO. 1184 **Top Sirloin Butt Steaks**
MBG NO. 1184
URMIS and COMMON NAMES: Top Sirloin Steak.
COMMON USES: Broil; braise; steak; beef kabobs.
SUGGESTED PORTION SIZES: 4 oz., 6 oz., 8 oz., 10 oz., 12 oz., 14 oz., 16 oz., 18 oz., 20 oz., 24 oz., 28 oz.

Top sirloin butt steaks shall be prepared from a Top Sirloin Butt — Item No. 184. The last steak on the round end of the top sirloin butt, containing an excessive amount of ligaments and heavy connective tissue, shall be removed. The boneless top sirloin butt may be separated into sections, reasonably parallel to the backbone line, to accommodate the cutting of specified portion-size steaks. The sections shall be cut into steaks reasonably parallel to the cut surface resulting from separating the loin from the round.

IMPS NO. 1184A **Top Sirloin Butt Steaks, Semi-Center Cut**
MBG NO. 1184A
URMIS and COMMON NAMES: Butt Steak, Top Sirloin Steak, Top Sirloin Butt Steak.
COMMON USES: Broil; braise; panfry; steak.
SUGGESTED PORTION SIZES: 4 oz., 6 oz., 10 oz., 12 oz., 14 oz., 16 oz.

Semi-center cut, top sirloin steaks shall be prepared from a Top Sirloin Butt — Item No. 184. All muscles, except the longissimus dorsi, gluteus medius and the biceps femoris, shall be removed. All other cutting and trimming requirements are those specified in Item No. 1184.

IMPS NO. 1184B **Top Sirloin Butt Steaks, Center Cut**
MBG NO. 1184B
URMIS and COMMON NAMES: Top Sirloin, Butt Steak.
COMMON USES: Broil; braise; panfry; steak.
SUGGESTED PORTION SIZES: 4 oz., 6 oz., 8 oz., 10 oz., 12 oz., 14 oz., 16 oz.

Center cut, top sirloin butt steaks shall be prepared from a Top Sirloin Butt — Item No. 184. All muscles except the gluteus medius shall be removed. All other cutting and trimming requirements are those specified in Item No. 1184.

A. IMPS NO. 1184 Top Sirloin Butt Steaks, p. 134; **B.** *IMPS NO. 1184B Top Sirloin Butt Steaks, Center Cut, p. 134;* **C.** *IMPS No. 185B Bottom Sirloin, Ball Tip, p. 135.*

IMPS NO. 185 **Bottom Sirloin Butt**
MBG NO. 185
URMIS and COMMON NAMES: Bottom Sirloin, Bottom Butt.
COMMON USES: Roast beef; kabobs; stew.

Weight Range [in pounds]

RANGE A	RANGE B	RANGE C	RANGE D
4-5	5-6	6-7	7-up

The bottom sirloin butt is that portion of Item No. 182 remaining after the removal of the top sirloin butt, as described in Item No. 184.

IMPS NO. 185A **Bottom Sirloin Flap**
MBG NO. Not Included.
URMIS and COMMON NAMES: Flap.
COMMON USES: Broil; cook in moist heat; stew; stroganoff; cube steak; flat-iron steak.

Weight Range [in pounds]

RANGE A	RANGE B
1-3	3-up

This item is the loosely attached muscle (obliquus abdominis internus) on the inner surface of the bottom sirloin butt. Practically all of the surface fat and connective tissue shall be removed.

IMPS NO. 185B **Bottom Sirloin, Ball Tip**
MBG NO. Not Included.
URMIS and COMMON NAMES: Ball Steak, Mock Tenderloin.
COMMON USES: Broil; cube steak; beef tips.

Weight Range [in pounds]

RANGE A	RANGE B
1.5-3	3-up

This item is that portion of the knuckle muscles behind the bottom sirloin butt. The ball tip shall be removed from the bottom sirloin butt along the natural seam. Surface fat thickness shall not exceed an average of 1/4 in.

IMPS NO. 185C **Bottom Sirloin, Triangle**
MBG NO. Not Included.
URMIS and COMMON NAMES: Triangle, Triangle Steak.
COMMON USES: Broil; cook in moist heat; steak; swiss steak; cube steak; beef tips.

Weight Range [in pounds]

RANGE A	RANGE B
1.5-3	3-up

This item is the triangular shaped muscle (tensor fasciae latae) in the ventral end of the bottom sirloin butt. Surface fat thickness on the triangle shall not exceed an average of 1/2 in.

IMPS NO. 185D **Bottom Sirloin, Triangle, Defatted**
MBG NO. Not Included.
URMIS and COMMON NAMES: Triangle, Triangle Steak.
COMMON USES: Broil; cook in moist heat; steak; swiss steak; cube steak; beef tips.

Weight Range [in pounds]

RANGE A	RANGE B
1.5-3	3-up

This item is the same as Item No. 185C, except that practically all of the surface fat and membranous tissue shall be removed.

IMPS NO. 186 **Bottom Sirloin Butt, Trimmed**
MBG NO. 186
URMIS and COMMON NAMES: Bottom Sirloin, Bottom Butt.
COMMON USES: Roast beef; kabobs; stew.

Weight Range [in pounds]

RANGE A	RANGE B	RANGE C	RANGE D	RANGE E
2-3	3-4	4-5	5-6	6-up

The trimmed bottom sirloin butt is the same as Item No. 185, except that the flap muscle and the underlying membrane shall be removed. The fat on the ventral and front sides, and the pocket of fat on the inside, shall be trimmed to the specified surface fat thickness. If specified, roasts shall be tied parallel to the cut surface made by separating the loin from the round.

IMPS NO. 189 **Full Tenderloin, Regular**
MBG NO. 189
URMIS and COMMON NAMES: Beef Tenderloin, Filet Mignon Roast.
COMMON USES: Roast; broil; roast beef; to cut filet mignon steaks.

Weight Range [in pounds]

RANGE A	RANGE B	RANGE C	RANGE D
4-5	5-6	6-7	7-up

The tenderloin is removed from the full loin intact. Surface fat shall not exceed 3/4 in. in thickness on the butt end up to the point where the large lymph gland is exposed. The fat shall then be tapered down to the lean, at a point not beyond 3/4 of the length of the tenderloin, measured from the butt end. The tenderloin shall be trimmed free of ragged edges. Tenderloins with scores exceeding 1/2 in. in depth are not acceptable.

IMPS NO. 1189 Tenderloin Steaks, Close Trim
MBG NO. 1189
URMIS and COMMON NAMES: Beef Loin Tenderloin Steak, Filet Mignon, Beef Tender Steak.
COMMON USES: Broil; panbroil; panfry; tenderloin steak.
SUGGESTED PORTION SIZES: 4 oz., 6 oz., 8 oz., 10 oz., 12 oz., 14 oz.

Tenderloin steaks shall be prepared from a Full Tenderloin — Item No. 189, or a portion thereof. The cut surface of the major tenderloin muscle at the butt end shall not be less than 1-1/2 in. at its narrowest diameter. The narrowest diameter of other steaks shall be not less than 1 in., exclusive of surface fat. On individual steaks, when the side strip muscle and underlying fat are not firmly attached, these shall be removed. On surfaces where fat is present, the individual steaks shall have not more than an average of 1/4 in. surface fat (1/2 in. maximum) at any one point.

IMPS NO. 189A Full Tenderloin, Defatted
MBG NO. Not Included.
URMIS and COMMON NAMES: Beef Tenderloin Roast, Filet Mignon Roast.
COMMON USES: Roast; broil; roast beef; to cut filet mignon steaks.

Weight Range [in pounds]

RANGE A	RANGE B	RANGE C	RANGE D
3-4	4-5	5-6	6-up

The defatted tenderloin is prepared from Item No. 189 by removing all surface fat, including the fat lying between the main body of the tenderloin and the wing muscle (iliacus). The side strip muscle and underlying fat may remain, if firmly attached to the main body of the tenderloin. Tenderloins with score exceeding 1/2 in. in depth are not acceptable.

IMPS NO. 1189A Tenderloin Steaks, Defatted.
MBG NO. 1189A
URMIS and COMMON NAMES: Beef Loin Tenderloin Steak, Filet Mignon, Beef Tender Steak.
COMMON USES: Broil; panfry; panbroil; steak; filet mignon; tenderloin steak.
SUGGESTED PORTION SIZES: 3 oz., 4 oz., 6 oz., 8 oz., 10 oz., 12 oz., 14 oz.

Defatted tenderloin steaks shall be prepared from a Tenderloin, Defatted — Item No. 189A, or any portion thereof. The cut surface of the major tenderloin muscle at the butt end shall be not less than 1-1/2 in. at its narrowest diameter. The narrowest diameter of other steaks shall not be less than 1 in. On individual steaks, when the side strip muscle and underlying fat are not firmly attached, these shall be removed.

IMPS NO. 190 Full Tenderloin, Special
MBG NO. 190
URMIS and COMMON NAMES: Beef Tenderloin, Filet Mignon Roast.
COMMON USES: Roast broil; roast beef; to cut filet mignon steaks.

Weight Range [in pounds]

RANGE A	RANGE B	RANGE C
2-3	3-4	4-up

This item is the same as Item No. 189, except that the side strip muscle and all fat shall be removed. Other loose tissue shall be removed, but the principal membranous tissue over the tenderloin muscle shall remain intact. Tenderloins with scores exceeding 1/2 in. in depth are not acceptable.

IMPS NO. 1190 Tenderloin Steaks, Special
MBG NO. 1190
URMIS and COMMON NAMES: Beef Loin Tenderloin Steak, Filet Mignon, Beef Tender Steak.
COMMON USES: Broil; panbroil; panfry; tenderloin steak.
SUGGESTED PORTION SIZES: 3 oz., 4 oz., 6 oz., 8 oz., 10 oz., 12 oz., 14 oz.

Special tenderloin steaks shall be prepared from a Full Tenderloin, Special — Item No. 190, or a portion thereof. The cut surface of the major tenderloin muscle at the butt end shall not be less than 1-1/2 in. in its narrowest diameter. The narrowest diameter of other steaks shall be not less than 1 in.

IMPS NO. 190A Full Tenderloin, Skinned.
MBG NO. Not Included.
URMIS and COMMON NAMES: Tenderloin.
COMMON USES: Roast; tenderloin roast.

Weight Range [in pounds]

RANGE A	RANGE B	RANGE C
2-3	3-4	4-up

This item is the same as Item No. 190, except that practically all of the membranous tissue over the tenderloin muscle shall be removed. Tenderloins with scores exceeding 1/2 in. in depth are not acceptable.

IMPS NO. 1190A **Tenderloin Steaks, Skinned**
MBG NO. 1190A
URMIS and COMMON NAMES: Tenderloin Steaks.
COMMON USES: Broil; tenderloin steaks.
SUGGESTED PORTION SIZES: 3 oz., 4 oz., 6 oz., 8 oz., 10 oz., 12 oz., 14 oz.

Skinned tenderloin steaks shall be prepared from a Full Tenderloin, Skinned — Item No. 190A, or a portion thereof. The cut surface of the major tenderloin muscle at the butt end shall not be less than 1-1/2 in. in its narrowest diameter. The narrowest diameter of other steaks shall not be less than 1 in.

IMPS NO. 191 **Butt Tenderloin**
MBG NO. 191
URMIS and COMMON NAMES: Butt Tender, Butt Tenderloin.
COMMON USES: Broil; panbroil; panfry; to cut into steaks; roasts.

Weight Range [in pounds]

RANGE A	RANGE B	RANGE C	RANGE D
1-2	2-3	3-4	4-up

The butt tenderloin is that portion of the tenderloin muscle removed from a Sirloin — Item No. 181. The tenderloin shall be trimmed so that the fat does not exceed 3/4 in. in thickness at any one point. The large lymph gland shall be exposed. The tenderloin shall be trimmed free of all ragged and thin edges. Tenderloins with scores exceeding 1/2 in. in depth are not acceptable.

IMPS NO. 192 **Short Tenderloin**
MBG NO. 192
URMIS and COMMON NAMES: Beef Tenderloin Tip Roast, Filet Mignon Roast, Short Tender.
COMMON USES: Roast; broil; chateaubriand; beef tenderloin.

Weight Range [in pounds]

RANGE A	RANGE B	RANGE C
2-3	3-4	4-up

The short tenderloin is that portion of the tenderloin muscle removed from the Short Loin — Item No. 173. The fat on the short tenderloin shall not exceed 1/2 in. in thickness at the sirloin end, and shall be tapered down to the lean at a point not more than half the length of the short tenderloin, measured from the sirloin end. The short tenderloin shall be trimmed free of all ragged and thin edges. Tenderloins with scores exceeding 1/2 in. in depth are not acceptable.

IMPS NO. 193 **Flank Steak**
MBG NO. 193
URMIS and COMMON NAMES: Beef Flank Steak, Jiffy Steak, London Broil.
COMMON USES: Braise; broil; london broil.

Weight Range [in pounds]

RANGE A	RANGE B	RANGE C
under 1	1-2	2-up

The flank steak is the flat muscle (rectus abdominis) embedded in the inside of the clod or udder end of the flank, and is obtained by stripping the serous membrane from over the flank steak, loosening the narrow end of the muscle, and separating it from the thick membrane which lies underneath. The flank steak shall be practically free from fat and membranous tissue.

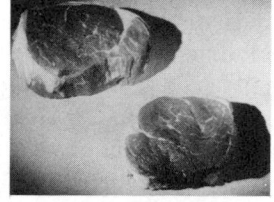
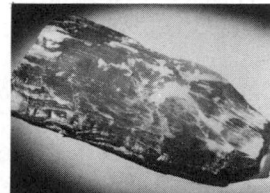

A.   B.

A. *IMPS NO. 1190A Tenderloin Steaks, Skinned, p. 137;* **B.** *IMPS NO. 193 Flank Steak, p. 137.*

CURED, DRIED AND SMOKED BEEF PRODUCTS

NOTE: Because it is impractical to list the weight ranges for all of the above products that purchasers may desire, only those included in this table are listed. Other weight ranges may be ordered if desired.

ORDERING DATA: TO BE SPECIFIED BY THE PURCHASER.

Selection [Not applicable to dried items.]
Selection No. 1
Selection No. 2

Style
A — Drained
B — Pickled

State of Refrigeration
A — Chilled
B — Frozen

FINISHED PRODUCT CHARACTERISTICS

The finished product must be sound and excellent in condition. Cured products must be mildly and thoroughly, but not excessively, cured. Smoked tongues must have the characteristic aroma and appearance of a well-smoked product, and must be fairly dry on the exterior, but not excessively dried or scorched. All products requiring drying shall be smoked and dried to a fairly uniform dryness and firmness throughout, without extreme hardness. Processed dried beef products must be thoroughly cooked and practically free from air holes, pockets of moisture, rendered fat, and gelatinous material. Any encrusted salt, extraneous matter, and smokehouse residue must be closely removed by careful light brushing or wiping (no washing), without damage to the product. Stockinettes, strings, and similar hanging devices must be completely removed and excluded.

The average surface fat thickness for all corned beef products, and for smoked beef tongues, shall not exceed 0.5 in. (maximum 0.8 in. at any one point). All dried beef products must be practically free of inter- and intra-muscular fat.

In accordance with the regulations of the applicable meat inspection agency, curing, smoking, cooking, and drying of all product items covered by these specifications must be normal to the particular kind of product produced.

DESCRIPTION OF SELECTIONS

Selection No. 1 Corned Beef

Selection No. 1 corned beef cuts shall be at least moderately thick fleshed, and moderately plump. The cut surface of the lean muscle shall be at least moderately firm, and fine-textured. Also, it shall be a uniform (slight two-toned or iridescent permissible) bright color, ranging from light pink to medium red. The fat shall be at least moderately firm and smooth. Cuts with scores which interfere with the making of satisfactory slices are not acceptable.

Selection No. 2 Corned Beef

Selection No. 2 corned beef cuts shall be not less than slightly thin-fleshed, and slightly flat. The cut surface of the lean muscle shall be at least moderately firm, and not more than moderately coarse-textured. Selection No. 2 cuts shall possess the color specified for Selection No. 1 cuts. The fat may be slightly soft or oily. Cuts with scores which interfere with the making of satisfactory slices are not acceptable.

Selection No. 1 Tongue, Cured or Smoked

A Selection No. 1 beef tongue shall be at least moderately short in relation to its length; shall be at least moderately thick and plump, and shall be firm and resilient. A selection No. 1 tongue may have 1 cut or score which measures less than 1 in. in any dimension. Tongues with the tip end removed are not acceptable.

Selection No. 2 Tongue, Cured or Smoked

A Selection No. 2 beef tongue shall be not less than slightly short in relation to its length; shall be at least slightly thick and plump, and shall be firm and resilient. A Selection No. 2 tongue may have 3 cuts or scores which measure less than 1 in. in any dimension. Tongues with a small portion of the tip end removed are acceptable.

IMPS NO. 600 Spencer Roll — Corned
MBG NO. Not Included.
URMIS and COMMON NAMES: Spencer Roll, Corned Chuck.
COMMON USES: Corned beef hash; cooked corned beef.

Weight Range [in pounds]

RANGE 1	RANGE 2	RANGE 3
under 15	15-22	22-up

The spencer roll is the boneless portion of a beef rib remaining after the rib ends have been removed by a straight cut, from a point not more than 2 in. from the extreme outer tip of the rib eye muscle on the loin end, to a point not more than 1 in. from the extreme outer tip of the rib eye muscle on the chuck end. The backstrap, intercostal meat (rib fingers), and the blade bone and attached cartilage and overlying flesh must be removed and excluded.

IMPS NO. 601 **Brisket, Boneless, Deckle-Off, Corned**
MBG NO. Not Included.
URMIS and COMMON NAMES: Corned Beef Brisket.
COMMON USES: Corned beef brisket.

Weight range [in pounds]

RANGE 1	RANGE 2	RANGE 3
under 9	9-12	12-up

The boneless brisket has the deckle removed at the natural seam, leaving the thick layer of fat attached to the deckle, and exposing the lean surface lying directly below. The inside surface must be practically free of fat. The thin tissue edge of the web muscle must be trimmed to expose the lean meat.

IMPS NO. 602 **Knuckle, Corned**
MBG NO. Not Included.
URMIS and COMMON NAMES: Corned Beef Round.
COMMON USES: Cooked corned beef; corned beef hash.

Weight Range [in pounds]

RANGE 1	RANGE 2	RANGE 3
under 8	8-15	15-up

The knuckle shall have the knuckle cover, kneecap (patella), and surrounding heavy connective tissue and periosteum, removed and excluded.

Refer to IMPS No. 167 on page number 126 for cutting specifications.

IMPS NO. 603 **Knuckle, Dried**
MBG NO. Not Included.
URMIS and COMMON NAMES: Dried Beef.
COMMON USES: Dried beef.

Weight Range [in pounds]

RANGE 1	RANGE 2	RANGE 3
under 5	5-8	8-up

The dried knuckle must be prepared from a Knuckle, Cured, Item No. 602.

Refer to IMPS No. 167 on page number 126 for cutting specifications.

IMPS NO. 604 **Inside Round, Corned**
MBG NO. Not Included.
URMIS and COMMON NAMES: Corned Beef Round.
COMMON USES: Sliced corned-beef; reuben sandwiches.

Weight Range [in pounds]

RANGE 1	RANGE 2	RANGE 3
under 14	14-20	20-up

The inside round must have the thick opaque portion of the gracilis membrane removed and excluded.

Refer to IMPS No. 167 on page number 126 for cutting specifications.

IMPS NO. 605 **Inside Round, Dried**
MBG NO. Not Included.
URMIS and COMMON NAMES: Dried Beef.
COMMON USES: Dried beef.

Weight Range [in pounds]

RANGE 1	RANGE 2	RANGE 3
under 9	9-12	12-up

The dried inside round must be prepared from an Inside Round, Corned, Item No. 604.

Refer to IMPS No. 167 on page number 126 for cutting specifications.

IMPS NO. 606 **Outside Round, Corned**
MBG NO. Not Included.
URMIS and COMMON NAMES: Corned Beef Round, Corned Beef Outside.
COMMON USES: Corned beef; corned beef hash; reuben sandwiches.

Weight Range [in pounds]

RANGE 1	RANGE 2	RANGE 3
under 11	11-18	18-up

The outside round must have the popliteal lymph gland and heavy connective tissue on the knuckle edge of the outside round removed, and excluded.

IMPS NO. 607 **Outside Round, Dried**
MBG NO. Not Included.
URMIS and COMMON NAMES: Dried Beef.
COMMON USES: Dried beef.

Weight Range [in pounds]

RANGE 1	RANGE 2	RANGE 3
under 8	8-14	14-up

The dried outside round must be prepared from an Outside Round, Corned, Item No. 606.

IMPS NO. 608 **Gooseneck Round, Corned**
MBG NO. Not Included.
URMIS and COMMON NAMES: Corned Gooseneck.
COMMON USES: Corned beef; corned beef hash.

Weight Range [in pounds]

RANGE 1	RANGE 2	RANGE 3
under 16	16-27	27-up

The gooseneck round shall have the popliteal lymph gland and heavy connective tissue on the knuckle side of the outside round removed, and excluded.

Refer to IMPS NO. 170 on page number 127 for cutting specifications.

IMPS NO. 609 **Rump Butt, Corned**
MBG NO. Not Included.
URMIS and COMMON NAMES: Corned Butt
COMMON USES: Corned beef hash; corned beef.

Weight Range [in pounds]

RANGE 1	RANGE 2	RANGE 3
under 8	8-12	12-up

The rump butt is the dorsal portion of a gooseneck round. This is made by a straight cut, approximately perpendicular to the skin surface, when preparing an outside round. In addition, it must be free of cartilage and exposed ligaments.

Refer to IMPS NO. 171 on page number 127 for cutting specifications.

IMPS NO. 613 **Tongue, Cured**
MBG NO. Not Included.
URMIS and COMMON NAMES: Pickled Tongue.
COMMON USES: Pickled tongue.

Weight Range [in pounds]

RANGE 1

3-5

The cured beef tongue must be well-trimmed, with the tongue root smoothly removed at the base (thick) end, immediately behind the hyoid (U-shaped) bones. Practically all major glandular tissue, and all of the trachea (windpipe), must be closely cut out and excluded. The hyoid bones and epiglottis (soft palate) may be left on the tongue. Major blood vessels at the base of the tongue, which have been used for pumping, may remain. Also, the cured tongue must be free from discoloration, other than natural pigmentation.

IMPS NO. 614 **Tongue, Smoked**
MBG NO. Not Included.
URMIS and COMMON NAMES: Smoked Tongue.
COMMON USES: Smoked tongue.

Weight Range [in pounds]

RANGE 1

3-5

The smoked tongue must be prepared from a Tongue, Cured, Item No. 613.

IMPS NO. 617 **Process Dried Beef**
MBG NO. Not Included.
URMIS and COMMON NAMES: Dried Beef Loaf.
COMMON USES: Chipped beef.

Weight Range [in pounds]

RANGE 1	RANGE 2	RANGE 3
under 8	8-14	14-up

Processed dried beef is a coarsely ground, cured, smoked, and fully cooked product which is stuffed into casings, then mechanically formed.

IMPS NO. 618 **Sliced, Process Dried Beef**
MBG NO. Not Included.
URMIS and COMMON NAMES: Sliced Dried Beef Loaf.
COMMON USES: Chipped beef.

Weight Range [in pounds]

1/4-lb., 1/2-lb., 1-lb., individual packages; bulk or layer packages.

Sliced process dried beef must be prepared from Process Dried Beef, Item No. 617. Slices shall be uniform in thickness, and must be 24 or more to the inch. Not less than 60 percent or more of the slices shall be fairly intact, but the remainder may be composed only of broken slices. No extremely frayed, shredded, small or scrap pieces, or product residue shall be included.

IMPS NO. 619 **Sliced Dried Beef.**
MBG NO. Not Included.
URMIS and COMMON NAMES: Sliced, Dried Beef, Chipped Beef Round.
COMMON USES: Chipped beef.

Weight Range [in pounds]

1/4-lb., 1/2-lb., 1-lb. individual packages; bulk or layer packed

Sliced dried beef must be produced from Knuckle, Dried, Item No. 603; Inside, Dried, Item No. 605, and Outside, Dried, Item No. 607 in approximately equal portions (by count), as evidenced in the sliced finished product. Slices must be uniform in thickness and must be 40 or more to the inch. No fewer than 75 percent of the slices must be intact. Slices from small end sections; extremely frayed or shredded slices; slices showing string or hanger marks; machine scrap pieces; or other product residue, must not be included.

IMPS NO. 620 **Sliced Dried Beef, Ends and Pieces**
MBG NO. Not Included.
URMIS and COMMON NAMES: Ends and Pieces.
COMMON USES: Chipped beef.

Weight Range [in pounds]

1/4-lb., 1/2-lb., 1-lb. individual packages; bulk or layer packed

Sliced dried beef ends and pieces must be obtained from the regular production of sliced, dried beef. The product may consist of frayed, shredded or broken slices; machine scrap sliced pieces, and slices showing string or hanger marks. Other product residue must not be included.

EDIBLE BY-PRODUCTS—BEEF

NOTE: Because it is impractical to list weight ranges for all of the edible by-products that purchasers may desire, only those included in this table are suggested. Other weight ranges may be ordered if desired.

ORDERING DATA: TO BE SPECIFIED BY THE PURCHASER.

Selection [Not applicable to beef hearts.]
Selection No. 1
Selection No. 2

Style [Applicable only to sliced beef and calf livers.]
A — Regular
B — Skinned

State of Refrigeration [Not applicable to sliced or portion-cut liver.]
A — Chilled
B — Frozen

Style of Packaging [Applicable only to sliced livers.]
A — Reassemble in natural sequence
B — Layer packed

DESCRIPTION OF SELECTIONS

Selection No. 1 Liver

Selection No. 1 livers shall be compact, thick, short, plump, and shall be practically free from blemishes. However, livers with cuts or scores not exceeding 1 in. in any dimension, or livers with small sections removed and excluded are acceptable, provided such defects do not interfere with making satisfactory slices that are intact. Selection No. 1 livers shall possess a bright, uniform color typical of the species.

Selection No. 2 Liver

Selection No. 2 livers shall be at least moderately compact, thick, short, plump, and shall be practically free of blemishes. However, livers with cuts or scores not exceeding 2 in. in any dimension, or livers with up to approximately 1/3 of the liver removed are acceptable, provided such defects do not interfere with making satisfactory slices that are intact. Selection No. 2 livers shall possess a bright, uniform color typical of the species.

Selection No. 1 Tongue

Selection No. 1 tongues shall be at least moderately short in relation to their width; shall be moderately thick and plump, and shall be firm and resilient. The fat covering the base of the tongues shall be firm and smooth, and must not exceed 1/2 in. at any one point. Selection No. 1 tongue may have 1 cut or score which measures less than 1 in. in any dimension. Tongues with the tip end removed are not acceptable.

Selection No. 2 Tongue

Selection No. 2 tongues shall be at least slightly short in relation to their width; shall be at least slightly thick and plump, and shall be at least moderately firm and resilient. The fat covering at the base of the tongues shall be moderately firm and smooth, and must not exceed 1/2 in. at any one point. Selection No. 2 tongues may have up to 3 cuts or scores which measure less than 1 in. in any dimension. Tongues with a small portion of the tip end removed are acceptable.

MATERIAL

The edible by-products described herein shall show no evidence of freezing or defrosting, and must be kept in excellent condition to the time of delivery.

All livers shall be trimmed free of ragged edges, and the gall bladder shall be removed. Whole livers shall have the heavy, connective tissue, the large blood vessel, and ducts lying along the liver wall trimmed even with the surface.

Livers to be sliced shall have the heavy connective tissue, the large blood vessel, and ducts lying along the liver wall removed, and excluded. Type B beef and calf livers shall have the outer connective tissue (capsula fibrosa), or "skin," removed, and excluded, except for small pieces remaining on the edges, and in the crease of the small (caudate) lobe.

Veal livers shall not be skinned. The liver may be molded, frozen, tempered (but not thawed), and/or pressed before slicing. Slices which are broken are not acceptable. Liver

slices shall be practically free from liver sawdust. As specified, they may be either (a) reassembled in natural sequence, or (b) layer packed, with plastic, parchment or waxed paper separators between layers. After slicing, the liver slices must be promptly packaged, and solidly frozen.

Livers to be portion-cut must be prepared in the manner described for livers to be sliced, except that the small (caudate) labe and the "skin" must be removed and excluded. Portion-cut liver shall be layer packed only.

IMPS NO. 701 **Beef Liver**
MBG NO. Not Included.
URMIS and COMMON NAMES: Steer Liver.
COMMON USES: Sauteed liver and onions; sweetbread casserole; liver loaf.

Weight Range [in pounds]

RANGE 1	RANGE 2
under 13	13-16

The color of beef liver may range from light brown, with reddish shades predominating, to dark brown.

IMPS NO. 702 **Beef Liver, Sliced, [Frozen]**
MBG NO. Not Included.
URMIS and COMMON NAMES: Sliced Liver.
COMMON USES: Sauteed liver and onions.

Weight Range [in pounds]

RANGE 1	RANGE 2
under 13	13-16

Sliced beef liver must be prepared from Beef Liver, Item No. 701. Liver slices shall be approximately 3/8 to 1/2 in. in thickness.

IMPS NO. 703 **Beef Liver, Portion-Cut, [Frozen]**
MBG NO. Not Included.
URMIS and COMMON NAMES: Portion-Cut Liver.
COMMON USES: Liver and onions.

Weight Range [in pounds]

RANGE 1	RANGE 2
5 to the pound	4 to the pound

Portion-cut liver must be sliced approximately 5/16 in. thick. Portions shall be at least moderately uniform in weight, and for portion sizes of 4 or less to the pound, the total number of individual portions per 10-lb. unit shall vary not more than plus or minus 2, from the number per pound specified multiplied by 10. (For example, if the number per pound specified is 4 to the pound, then 4x10 = 40 portions. Therefore, with the permitted tolerance of plus or minus 2 subtracted from 40, an acceptable 10-lb. unit could have from 38-42 individual portions.) For portion sizes of 5 or more to the pound, the total number of individual portions per 10-lb. unit shall vary not more than plus or minus 3 from the number per pound specified, multiplied by 10.

IMPS NO. 716 **Beef Tongue**
MBG NO. Not Included.
URMIS and COMMON NAMES: Tongue.
COMMON USES: Boil; tongue sandwiches.

Weight Range [in pounds]

RANGE 1
3-5

The beef tongue must be well-trimmed, with the tongue root smoothly removed at the base (thick) end, immediately behind the base of the hyoid (U-shaped) bones. Practically all glandular tissue, and all of the trachea (windpipe), must be removed, and excluded. The hyoid bones and the epiglottis (soft palate) may be left on the tongue. Major blood vessels at the base of the tongue may remain. Also, the tongue must be free from discoloration, other than natural pigmentation.

IMPS NO. 720 **Beef Heart**
MBG NO. Not Included.
URMIS and COMMON NAMES: Beef Heart.
COMMON USES: Beef pie.

Weight Range [in pounds]

RANGE 1
3-5

A beef heart shall have the "heart-cap" (auricles, arteries, and gristle) removed, and shall be trimmed practically free of fat. Hearts that have been excessively slashed are not acceptable.

LAMB

GRADE

Carcasses, Saddles and Cuts

The purchaser shall specify a quality grade and may also specify a yield grade, except that when surface fat thickness is included in the item description, yield grade shall not be specified.

Roasts

The purchaser shall specify a quality grade, and may also specify a yield grade.

Portion Cuts and Lamb for Stewing

The purchaser shall specify a quality grade.

Ground Lamb

The purchaser shall specify a quality grade.

YIELD GRADES[1] through 5 are applicable to all quality grades. However, those yield grades indicated by an "X" are in the largest supply.

USDA GRADES

QUALITY GRADES	Yield Grades[1]				
	1	2	3	4	5
U.S. Prime[2]			X	X	X
U.S. Choice		X	X	X	
U.S. Good	X	X	X		
U.S. Utility	X	X			
U.S. Cull	X	X			

1. The yield grades reflect differences in yields of boneless, closely trimmed, retail cuts. As such, they also reflect differences in the overall fatness of carcasses and cuts. Yield grade 1 represents the highest yield of retail cuts and the least amount of fat trim. Yield grade 5 represents the lowest yield of retail cuts and the highest amount of fat trim.
2. Prime does not apply to mutton.

CLASS

A — Lamb
B — Yearling Mutton
C — Mutton

LAMB CHART

RETAIL CUTS OF LAMB — WHERE THEY COME FROM AND HOW TO COOK THEM

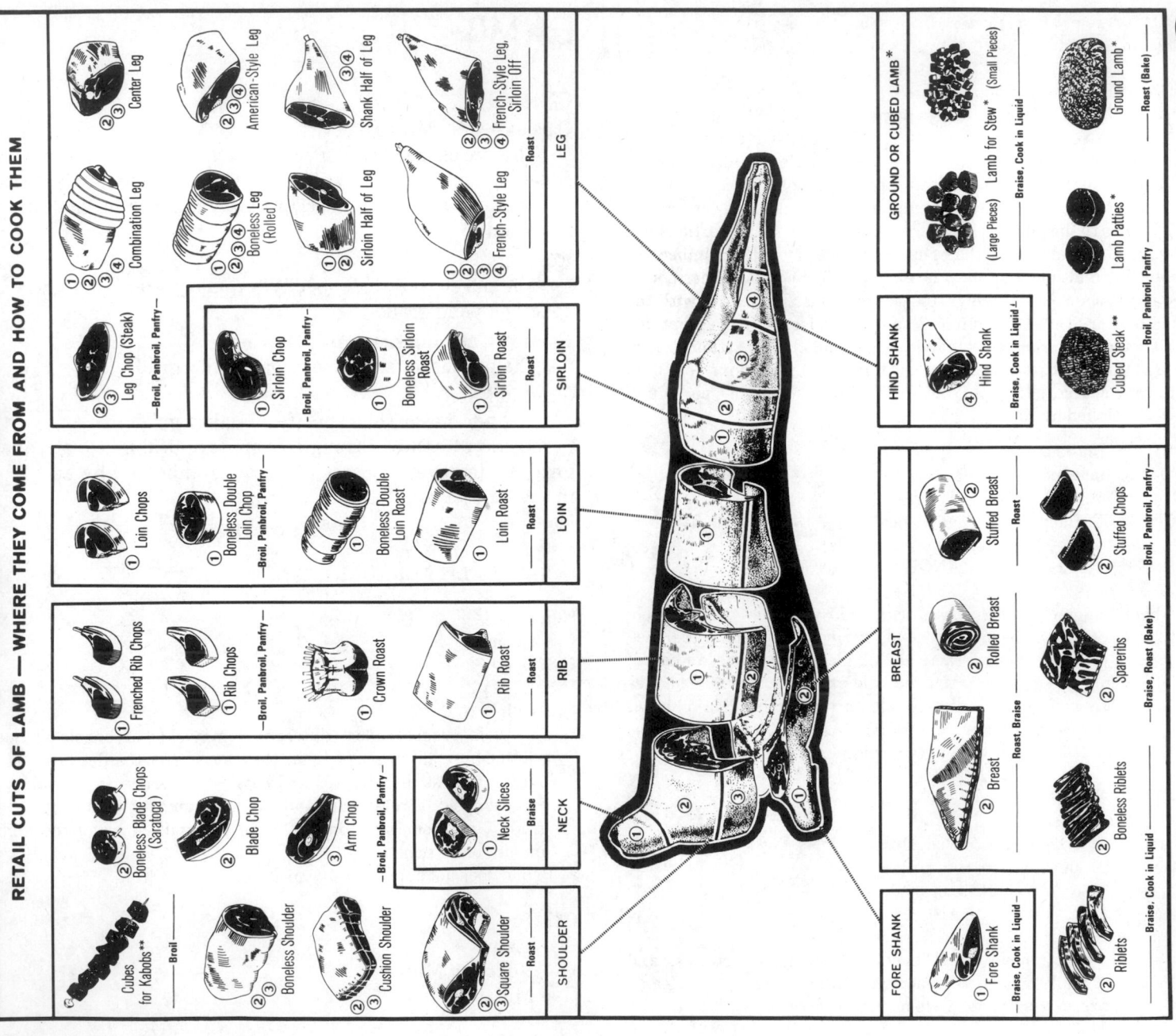

LEG

- ② ③ Center Leg
- ② ③ ④ American-Style Leg
- ③ ④ Shank Half of Leg
- ② ③ ④ French-Style Leg, Sirloin Off
- ① ② ④ Combination Leg
- ① ② ③ ④ Boneless Leg (Rolled)
- ② ③ ④ Sirloin Half of Leg
- ① ② ③ ④ French-Style Leg

SIRLOIN

- ② ③ Leg Chop (Steak) — Broil, Panbroil, Panfry —
- ① ③ Sirloin Chop — Broil, Panbroil, Panfry —
- ① Boneless Sirloin Roast
- ① Sirloin Roast — Roast —

LOIN

- ① Loin Chops
- ① Boneless Double Loin Chop — Broil, Panbroil, Panfry —
- ① Boneless Double Loin Roast
- ① Loin Roast — Roast —

RIB

- ① Frenched Rib Chops
- ① Rib Chops — Broil, Panbroil, Panfry —
- ① Crown Roast
- ① Rib Roast — Roast —

NECK

- ① Neck Slices — Braise —

SHOULDER

- ② Boneless Blade Chops (Saratoga)
- ② Blade Chop
- ② Arm Chop — Broil, Panbroil, Panfry —
- ② Cubes for Kabobs** — Broil
- ② ③ Boneless Shoulder
- ② ③ Cushion Shoulder
- ② ③ Square Shoulder — Roast —

GROUND OR CUBED LAMB*

- (Large Pieces) Lamb for Stew* (Small Pieces) — Braise, Cook in Liquid —
- Ground Lamb* — Roast (Bake)
- Lamb Patties*
- Cubed Steak** — Broil, Panbroil, Panfry

HIND SHANK

- ④ Hind Shank — Braise, Cook in Liquid ⊥

BREAST

- ② Stuffed Breast — Roast
- ② Stuffed Chops — Broil, Panbroil, Panfry
- ② Breast — Roast, Braise
- ② Rolled Breast
- ② Spareribs — Braise, Roast (Bake)
- ② Boneless Riblets — Braise, Cook in Liquid

FORE SHANK

- ① Fore Shank — Braise, Cook in Liquid
- ② Riblets — Braise, Cook in Liquid

© National Live Stock and Meat Board

This chart approved by
National Live Stock and Meat Board

* Lamb for stew or grinding may be made from any cut.
**Kabobs or cube steaks may be made from any thick solid piece of boneless Lamb.

MEAT AND MEAT PRODUCTS

Lamb: Yield of boneless meat from carcass and wholesale cuts of various U.S. grades, and conversion factors for determining carcass weight equivalent of boneless meat and bone-in cuts

Wholesale cuts	Percent of carcass weight	Percent of boneless meat[1]		Factors for determining equivalent carcass weight[3]
		Average above Cull[2]	Cull	
Boneless meat, all cuts:				
Average above Cull	—	—	—	1.39
Cull	—	—	—	1.60
Bone-in cuts:				
Carcass, whole[4]	100.0	72.0	62.5	1.00
Foresaddle, whole	50.0	67.9	58.5	.94
Breast, including shank	14.0	67.0	57.7	.93
Chuck	25.0	73.2	63.0	1.02
Hotel rack	11.0	72.7	62.6	1.01
Hindsaddle, whole	50.0	76.1	65.5	1.06
Leg	33.0	78.8	67.9	1.10
Loin, including flank and kidney	17.0	81.1	69.8	1.13

1. Commercial boning practice.
2. U.S. grades for lamb are Prime, Choice, Good, Utility, and Cull.
3. Edible offal items are excluded when converting to carcass weight. These include brains, casings, heart, liver, stomach or tripe, and tongue.
4. Pluck out.

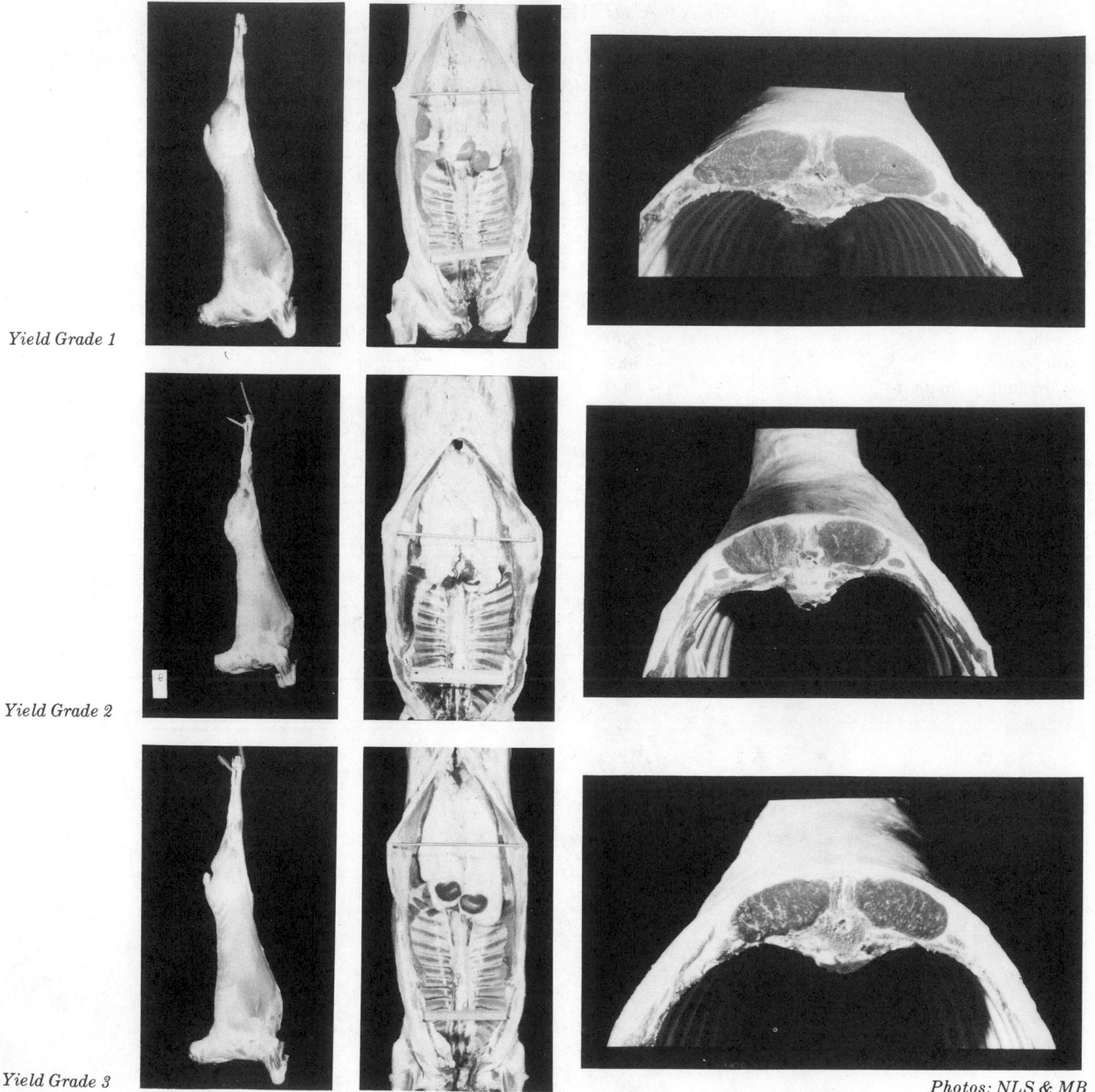

Yield Grade 1

Yield Grade 2

Yield Grade 3

Photos: NLS & MB

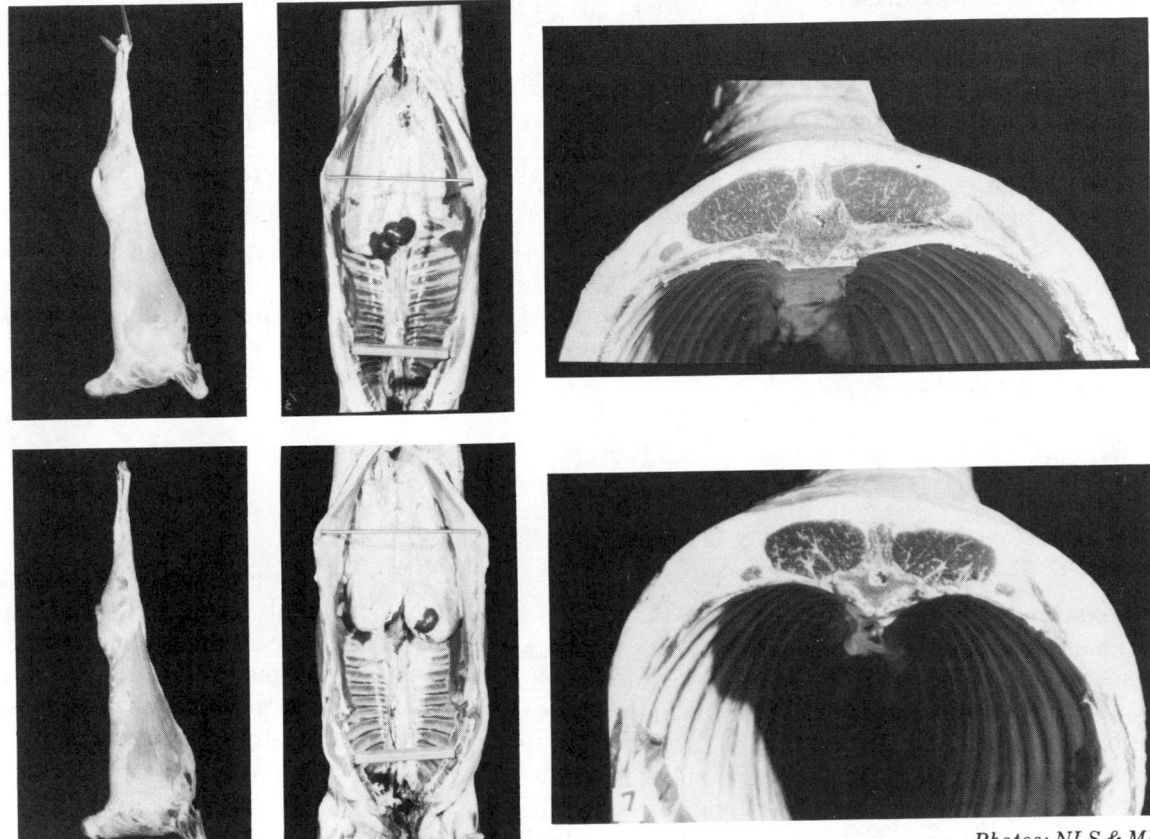

Yield Grade 4

Yield Grade 5

Photos: NLS & MB

Ground Lamb Patty Weight Tolerances

For patties with a specified weight of 3 oz. or less, a tolerance of plus/minus 2 patties from the projected number in a 10-lb. unit will be permitted. For patties with a specified weight of more than 3 oz., a tolerance of plus/minus 1 patty from the projected number in a 10-lb. unit will be permitted. (When patties are specified by a number per pound, this shall be converted to patty weight to determine tolerances, e.g., 6 to the lb. = 2.67 oz.) For example:

Specified Size	Number Per 10-lb. unit	Tolerances [over and under]	
Weight	No. per pound		
1.6 oz.	10	100	2
2.0 oz.	8	80	2
3.2 oz.	5	50	1
4.0 oz.	4	40	1

EXAMPLE: When 2 oz. patties are specified, 10-lb. units containing 78 to 82 patties are acceptable.

Portion Cut Items

Either the portion weight or thickness desired — not both — must be specified. If weight is specified, see the weight range table. If thickness is specified, the actual thickness desired must be indicated. Also, in order to control uniformity of portion sizes, the weight range of the IMPS cut from which the portions are to be produced may also be specified. In this case, the fat thickness of the IMPS cut should be approximately the same as the fat thickness specified for the portion cut.

Portion Cut Weight Tolerances

If portion weight is specified, the following tolerances will be permitted:

Weight Specified	Tolerances [over and under]
less than 6 oz.	1/4 oz.
6 oz. or more	1/2 oz.

EXAMPLE: When 4 oz. chops are specified, individual chops weighing 3-3/4 to 4-1/4 oz. are acceptable.

Portion Cut Thickness Tolerances

If thickness is specified, the following tolerances will be permitted:

Thickness Specified	Tolerances [over and under]
1 in. or less	
More than 1 in.	1/4 in.

Example: When 1-1/4 in. chops are specified, individual chops measuring from 1 to 1-1/2 in. are acceptable.

FAT LIMITATIONS

Chops

Unless otherwise specified by the purchaser, surface fat, where present, must not exceed an average of 1/4 in. thickness, and the thickness at any one point must not be more than 3/8 in.

STATE OF REFRIGERATION

A. Chilled
B. Frozen

TYING

When tying is required, roasts must be made firm and compact, and held intact by individual loops of strong twine, uniformly spaced at approximately 2-in. intervals girthwise. In addition, some roasts may require tying lengthwise. In lieu of string, it is permissible to enclose roasts in a stretchable netting, or by any other equivalent method.

Purchasers may specify that roasts be tied, when this requirement is not specified in the detailed roast item specification.

MATERIAL

Unless otherwise specified, the wholesale and fabricated cuts described in these specifications are double cuts. Single cuts are produced by cutting lengthwise centrally through the backbone. Cuts which have been excessively trimmed in order to meet specified weights, or which do not meet the specification requirements for any reason, are not acceptable. The meat shall be of good color, normal to the class, be practically free of bruises, blood clots, bone dust, ragged edges, and discoloration. Except as otherwise provided herein, the meat shall show no evidence of mishandling, and shall be in excellent condition to the time of delivery.

CUTTING CHOPS

Unless otherwise specified in the individual item specification, chops shall be cut in full slices in a straight line, reasonably perpendicular to the outer surface, and at an approximate right angle to the length of the meat cut from which chops are produced.

BONING

Boning shall be accomplished with sufficient care to allow each cut to retain its identity, and to avoid objectionable scores in the meat.

IMPS NO. 200 Carcass
MBG NO. 200
URMIS and COMMON NAMES: Carcass.
COMMON USES: Wholesale cuts from which all other cuts are derived.

Weight Range [in pounds]

RANGE A		RANGE B		RANGE C		RANGE D	
Lamb	Mutton	Lamb	Mutton	Lamb	Mutton	Lamb	Mutton
30-41	55-75	41-53	75-95	53-65	95-115	65-75	115-130

A lamb, yearling mutton, or mutton carcass, is the entire, unsplit carcass. The spleen, bloody tissue and frayed ends at the neck, and practically all heart fat, shall be removed. The diaphragm and the hanging tender may be removed.

IMPS NO. 202 Foresaddle
MBG NO. 202
URMIS and COMMON NAMES: Lamb Front, Lamb Forequarter.
COMMON USES: Roast; panfry; cook in moist heat; lamb stew; lamb chops; roast lamb.

Weight Range [in pounds]

RANGE A		RANGE B		RANGE C		RANGE D	
Lamb	Mutton	Lamb	Mutton	Lamb	Mutton	Lamb	Mutton
15-21	28-38	21-27	38-48	27-33	48-58	33-38	58-65

The foresaddle is the front portion of the carcass which is severed from the hindsaddle by cutting between the 12th and 13th ribs, the 13th rib remaining with the hindsaddle. Bloody tissue and frayed ends at the neck, and practically all heart fat shall be removed.

IMPS NO. 203 Bracelet
MBG NO. 203
URMIS and COMMON NAMES: Bracelet.
COMMON USES: Broil; panfry; lamb chops; ground lamb.

Weight Range [in pounds]

RANGE A		RANGE B		RANGE C		RANGE D	
Lamb	Mutton	Lamb	Mutton	Lamb	Mutton	Lamb	Mutton
5-6	8-11	6-8	11-14	8-10	14-17	10-12	17-19

The bracelet is prepared from Item No. 202, and consists of the rib rack and plates intact. The chucks shall be separated from the bracelet by a reasonably straight cut across the foresaddle, between the 4th and 5th ribs.

IMPS NO. 204 Rib Rack
MBG NO. 204
URMIS and COMMON NAMES: Double Rack.
COMMON USES: Broil; panfry; lamb chops.

Weight Range [in pounds]

RANGE A		RANGE B		RANGE C		RANGE D	
Lamb	Mutton	Lamb	Mutton	Lamb	Mutton	Lamb	Mutton
3-5	6-8	5-6	8-10	6-7	10-13	7-8	13-14

The rib rack is prepared from Item No. 203. The plates shall be separated from the rack by a straight cut, across the ribs, which is not more than 4 in. from the outer tip of the rib eye muscle.

IMPS NO. 1204 Rib Chops
MBG NO. 1204
URMIS and COMMON NAMES: Lamb Rib Chops.
COMMON USES: Broil; panfry; lamb chops.
SUGGESTED PORTION SIZES: 3 oz., 4 oz., 6 oz., 9 oz., 10 oz.

Rib chops shall be prepared from a single Rib Rack, Item No. 204. The plate portion on individual chops shall be removed at a point which is not more than 3 in. from the outer tip of the rib eye muscle. The protruding edge of the chine bone shall be removed by sawing, at an approximately 45 degree angle, to the split thoracic vertebrae beginning at the dorsal edge of the spinal cord groove. Chops cut from the blade bone section shall have the blade bone and related cartilage, and the muscles and the fat overlying the level of the blade bone and cartilage, removed. Rib chops shall have the fell removed.

IMPS NO. 1204A **Rib Chops, Frenched**
MBG NO. 1204A
URMIS and COMMON NAMES: Frenched Lamb Chops.
COMMON USES: Broil; panfry; lamb chops.
SUGGESTED PORTION SIZES: 3 oz., 4 oz., 5 oz., 6 oz., 7 oz., 8 oz.

Frenched rib chops shall be prepared as described in Item No. 1204. In addition, individual chops shall have the meat, including the rib fingers, removed (frenched) to expose at least 1-1/2 in. of the end of one rib bone. Chops having more than 1 rib bone shall have the rib bone nearest the center of the chop frenched, and the other rib bone shall be removed for the distance that the frenched rib bone is exposed. The frenched rib chops shall have the fell removed.

IMPS NO. 205 **Chucks and Plates**
MBG NO. 205
URMIS and COMMON NAMES: Lamb Slug.
COMMON USES: Cook in moist heat; stew; ground lamb.

Weight Range [in pounds]

RANGE A		RANGE B		RANGE C		RANGE D	
Lamb	Mutton	Lamb	Mutton	Lamb	Mutton	Lamb	Mutton
12-16	23-30	16-21	30-38	21-26	38-46	26-30	46-52

The chuck and plates are that portion of the foresaddle remaining after the removal of the Rib Rack — Item No. 204.

IMPS NO. 206 **Chucks**
MBG NO. 206
URMIS and COMMON NAMES: Chuck, Lamb Slug.
COMMON USES: Cook in moist heat; stew; roast lamb.

Weight Range [in pounds]

RANGE A		RANGE B		RANGE C		RANGE D	
Lamb	Mutton	Lamb	Mutton	Lamb	Mutton	Lamb	Mutton
11-14	19-26	14-19	26-33	19-23	33-40	23-27	40-46

The chucks are that portion of the foresaddle remaining after the removal of the Bracelet, Item No. 203.

IMPS NO. 207 **Square-Cut Shoulders**
MBG NO. 207
URMIS and COMMON NAMES: Chuck.
COMMON USES: Braise; broil; shoulder chops.

Weight Range [in pounds]

RANGE A		RANGE B		RANGE C		RANGE D	
Lamb	Mutton	Lamb	Mutton	Lamb	Mutton	Lamb	Mutton
8-10	14-19	10-13	19-24	13-16	24-29	16-19	29-33

The shoulders are prepared from Item No. 206, and are obtained by two straight cuts perpendicular to the outer skin surface. The first cut passes through the cartilagenous juncture on the first rib and the forward extremity of the sternum, continuing in a straight line to the 4th rib, perpendicular to the cut separating the chucks from the bracelet; this cut severs the foreshanks and briskets from the shoulders. The neck shall be removed by a second straight cut, perpendicular to the neck, which leaves not more than 1 in. of neck on the shoulders.

IMPS NO. 1207 **Shoulder Chops.**
MBG NO. 1207
URMIS and COMMON NAMES: Lamb Chops.
COMMON USES: Braise; broil; lamb chops.
SUGGESTED PORTION SIZES: 4 oz., 5 oz., 6 oz., 7 oz., 8 oz.

Shoulder chops shall be prepared from both the arm and blade bone sections of a single Shoulder, Item No. 207. Arm bone shoulder chops shall be cut first, and must be reasonably parallel to the normal line of separation of the shank from the shoulder up to the knuckle. Arm bone chops shall have the rib bones and intercostal meat removed. In addition, the underlying fat in excess of 1/4 in. also shall be removed. Blade chops shall be cut approximately parallel to the rib bones up to the knuckle.

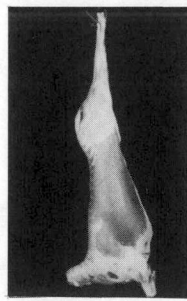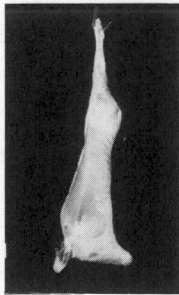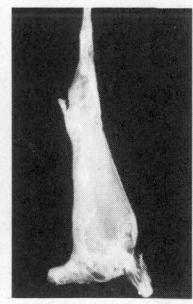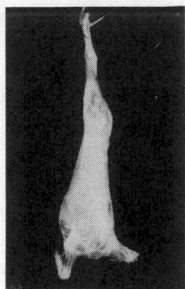

| *U.S. Prime* | *U.S. Choice* | *U.S. Good* | *U.S. Utility* |

Photos: NLS & MB

IMPS NO. 208 **Square-Cut Shoulders, Boneless and Tied.**
MBG NO. 208
URMIS and COMMON NAMES: Shoulder Roast.
COMMON USES: Roast; lamb roast.

Weight Range [in pounds]

RANGE A		RANGE B		RANGE C		RANGE D	
Lamb	Mutton	Lamb	Mutton	Lamb	Mutton	Lamb	Mutton
3-4	6-8	4-6	8-10	6-7	10-12	7-8	12-26

The boneless and tied shoulder is prepared from one-half of Item No. 207. Boning shall be done by scalping the rib and backbones. The blade bone shall be removed without cutting through the flesh at the ridge of the blade bone, so as to leave the shoulder meat, including the clod, intact. Meat with dark discoloration, all bones, cartilage, backstrap, exposed large blood vessels, and the prescapular lymph gland, and surrounding fat in excess of 1/2 in. in thickness, shall be removed. The boneless shoulder shall be rolled with the eye muscle lengthwise of the roll, and shall be tied girthwise and lengthwise.

IMPS NO. 209 **Breast, Flank-On**
MBG NO. 209
URMIS and COMMON NAMES: Breast.
COMMON USES: Cook in moist heat; stew; ground lamb.

Weight Range [in pounds]

RANGE A		RANGE B		RANGE C		RANGE D	
Lamb	Mutton	Lamb	Mutton	Lamb	Mutton	Lamb	Mutton
4-6	8-11	6-7	11-13	7-9	13-16	9-11	16-18

The breast shall include the flank, plate and brisket portions intact.

IMPS NO. 209A **Breast, Flank Off**
MBG NO. Not Included.
URMIS and COMMON NAMES: Breast.
COMMON USES: Cook in moist heat; stew; ground lamb.

Weight Range [in pounds]

RANGE A		RANGE B		RANGE C		RANGE D	
Lamb	Mutton	Lamb	Mutton	Lamb	Mutton	Lamb	Mutton
3-5	7-10	5-6	10-12	6-8	12-16	8-10	16-18

This item is the same as Item No. 209, except that the flank portion shall be removed.

IMPS NO. 210 **Foreshank**
MBG NO. Not Included.
URMIS and COMMON NAMES: Lamb Shank.
COMMON USES: Braising; roast.

Weight Range [in pounds]

RANGE A		RANGE B		RANGE C		RANGE D	
Lamb	Mutton	Lamb	Mutton	Lamb	Mutton	Lamb	Mutton
1-1.5	2-3	1.5-2	3-4	2-2.5	4-5	2.5-3	5 6

The foreshank is the foreleg portion, remaining intact with the brisket, after removal from the chucks in making Square-Cut Shoulders, Item No. 207. The foreshank is separated from the brisket by a cut following the natural seam, except that part of the web muscle may remain on the foreshank. The lower shank bones shall be removed at the knee.

IMPS NO. 230 **Hindsaddle**
MBG NO. 230
URMIS and COMMON NAMES: Hindquarter.
COMMON USES: Wholesale cut from which other cuts are derived.

Weight Range [in pounds]

RANGE A		RANGE B		RANGE C		RANGE D	
Lamb	Mutton	Lamb	Mutton	Lamb	Mutton	Lamb	Mutton
15-21	28-38	21-27	38-48	27-33	48-58	33-38	58-65

The hindsaddle is the back portion of the carcass remaining after the removal of the Foresaddle, Item No. 202.

IMPS NO. 231 **Loin**
MBG NO. 231
URMIS and COMMON NAMES: Lamb, Loin, Lamb Saddle.
COMMON USES: Braise; roast; lamb chops.

Weight Range [in pounds]

RANGE A		RANGE B		RANGE C		RANGE D	
Lamb	Mutton	Lamb	Mutton	Lamb	Mutton	Lamb	Mutton
5-6	8-11	6-8	11-14	8-10	14-17	10-11	17-20

This item is the forward portion of Item No. 230. It is separated from the legs by a straight cut, perpendicular to the outer skin surface, and perpendicular to the backbone, through a point immediately in front of the hipbone cartilage.

IMPS NO. 232 Loin, Trimmed
MBG NO. 232
URMIS and COMMON NAMES: Trimmed Hindquarter.
COMMON USES: Wholesale cut from which other cuts are derived.

Weight Range [in pounds]

RANGE A		RANGE B		RANGE C		RANGE D	
Lamb	Mutton	Lamb	Mutton	Lamb	Mutton	Lamb	Mutton
3-4	6-8	4-5	8-10	5-7	10-12	7-8	12-15

The trimmed loin is prepared from Item No. 231. The flank portions shall be removed by a straight cut which is not more than 4 in. from the outer tip of the loin eye muscle. The kidney knobs shall be removed, and the lumbar fat shall be trimmed so that it does not exceed 1/2 in. in thickness at the end. The fat must then be tapered down to the lean surface at a point not beyond 3/4 of the length of the loin.

IMPS NO. 1232 Loin Chops
MBG NO. 1232
URMIS and COMMON NAMES: Lamb Loin Chops, Lamb Chops.
COMMON USES: Panbroil; broil; lamb chops.
SUGGESTED PORTION SIZES: 4 oz., 5 oz., 6 oz., 7 oz., 8 oz., 9 oz., 10 oz.

Loin chops shall be prepared from a single Loin, Trimmed, Item No. 232. The flank edge on individual chops shall be removed at a point which is not more than 3 in. from the outer tip of the loin eye muscle. Loin chops shall contain no portion of the hip bone. However, a portion of the 13th rib may be present in chops cut from the rib end. Loin chops shall have the fell removed.

IMPS NO. 233 Legs
MBG NO. 233
URMIS and COMMON NAMES: Leg of Lamb.
COMMON USES: Roast; leg-o-lamb; lamb cutlets.

Weight Range [in pounds]

RANGE A		RANGE B		RANGE C		RANGE D	
Lamb	Mutton	Lamb	Mutton	Lamb	Mutton	Lamb	Mutton
11-14	19-26	14-19	26-33	19-23	33-40	23-27	40-46

The legs are that portion of the hindsaddle remaining after the removal of the Loin, Item No. 231.

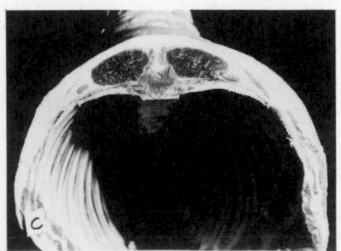

Cross section of a lamb carcass, Yield Grade 4, a grade with thin muscling, excess fat, and lesser retail value.

IMPS NO. 1233A Leg, Lower Shank Off [Single]
MBG NO. Not Included.
URMIS and COMMON NAMES: Leg of Lamb.
COMMON USES: Roast; leg-o-lamb; lamb cutlets.

Weight Range [in pounds]

RANGE A		RANGE B		RANGE C		RANGE D	
Lamb	Mutton	Lamb	Mutton	Lamb	Mutton	Lamb	Mutton
5-7	9-12	7-9	12-15	9-12	15-19	12-up	19-up

This item is prepared from one-half of Item No. 233. The lower hindshank bones shall be removed at the break joint and the gambrel cord shall be removed.

IMPS NO. 233B Leg, Lower Shank Off, Boneless
MBG NO. Not Included.
URMIS and COMMON NAMES: Leg of Lamb
COMMON USES: Roast; leg-o-lamb; lamb cutlets.

Weight Range [in pounds]

RANGE A		RANGE B		RANGE C		RANGE D	
Lamb	Mutton	Lamb	Mutton	Lamb	Mutton	Lamb	Mutton
4-6	8-11	6-8	11-13	8-11	13-17	11-up	17-up

This item is the same as Item No. 233A, except that it shall be made boneless. The round bone shall be removed after making a cut along the natural seam between the inside and the knuckle. The knee cap and the surrounding heavy connective tissue shall be removed. The boneless leg shall be tied lengthwise and girthwise.

IMPS NO. 233C Leg, Shank Off [Single]
MBG NO. Not Included.
URMIS and COMMON NAMES: Leg of Lamb.
COMMON USES: Roast; leg-o-lamb; lamb cutlets.

Weight Range [in pounds]

RANGE A		RANGE B		RANGE C		RANGE D	
Lamb	Mutton	Lamb	Mutton	Lamb	Mutton	Lamb	Mutton
5-7	8-10	7-9	10-12	9-12	12-15	12-up	15-up

This item is prepared from one-half of Item No. 233. The shank and heel portion of the leg shall be removed by a straight cut, approximately perpendicular to the outer skin surface and to the long axis of the shank bones, which passes through the stifle joint.

IMPS NO. 233D **Leg, Shank Off, Boneless**
MBG NO. Not Included.
URMIS and COMMON NAMES: Leg of Lamb.
COMMON USES: Roast; leg-o-lamb; lamb cutlets.

Weight Range [in pounds]

RANGE A		RANGE B		RANGE C		RANGE D	
Lamb	Mutton	Lamb	Mutton	Lamb	Mutton	Lamb	Mutton
4-6	7-9	6-8	9-11	8-11	11-14	11-up	14-up

This item is the same as Item No. 233C, except that it shall be made boneless. The round bone shall be removed after making a cut along the natural seam between the inside and knuckle. The knee cap and surrounding heavy connective tissue shall be removed. The boneless leg shall be tied girthwise and lengthwise.

IMPS NO. 233E **Hindshank, Heel Attached**
MBG NO. Not Included.
URMIS and COMMON NAMES: Leg of Lamb.
COMMON USES: Roast; leg-o-lamb; lamb cutlets.

Weight Range [in pounds]

RANGE A		RANGE B		RANGE C		RANGE D	
Lamb	Mutton	Lamb	Mutton	Lamb	Mutton	Lamb	Mutton
under 1	1-1.5	1-2	1.5-3	2-up	3-up	—	—

This item is the shank, with heel portion attached, that is removed from the leg in preparing Item No. 233C. The lower hindshank bones shall be removed at the break joint, and the gambrel cord shall be removed.

IMPS NO. 234 **Leg, Oven-Prepared, Partially Boneless**
MBG NO. 234
URMIS and COMMON NAMES: Oven-Prepared Leg of Lamb, Lamb Leg.
COMMON USES: Roast; roast lamb.

Weight Range [in pounds]

RANGE A		RANGE B		RANGE C		RANGE D	
Lamb	Mutton	Lamb	Mutton	Lamb	Mutton	Lamb	Mutton
4-6	8-10	6-8	10-13	8-9	13-16	9-11	16-18

The oven-prepared leg is prepared from one-half of Item No. 233. The pelvic, back, and tailbones shall be removed. The flank, practically all cod and udder fat, and surface fat in excess of 1/2 in. shall be removed. The shank shall be removed by a cut along the natural seam, between the shank meat and the heel (gastrocnemius muscle), and through the stifle joint.

IMPS NO. 234A **Leg, Oven-Prepared, Boneless and Tied**
MBG NO. Not Included.
URMIS and COMMON NAMES: Leg-o-Lamb, Lamb Leg Roast Boneless, Boneless Lamb Leg Roast.
COMMON USES: Roast lamb.

Weight Range [in pounds]

RANGE A	RANGE B	RANGE C	RANGE D
under 6	6-8	8-11	11-up

This item is the same as Item No. 234 except that it shall be made boneless. The round bone shall be removed after making a cut along the natural seam between the inside and knuckle. The knee cap and surrounding heavy connective tissue shall be removed. The boneless leg shall be tied girthwise and lengthwise.

IMPS NO. 235 **Back**
MBG NO. 235
URMIS and COMMON NAMES: Lamb Back.
COMMON USES: Braise; broil; chops.

Weight Range [in pounds]

RANGE A		RANGE B		RANGE C		RANGE D	
Lamb	Mutton	Lamb	Mutton	Lamb	Mutton	Lamb	Mutton
9-12	17-23	12-16	23-29	16-20	29-35	20-23	35-39

The back is that portion of the carcass remaining after the removal of Chucks, Item No. 206, and the Legs, Item No. 233.

IMPS NO. 236 **Back, Trimmed**
MBG NO. 236
URMIS and COMMON NAMES: Lamb Back.
COMMON USES: Braise; broil; chops.

Weight Range [in pounds]

RANGE A		RANGE B		RANGE C		RANGE D	
Lamb	Mutton	Lamb	Mutton	Lamb	Mutton	Lamb	Mutton
6-8	11-15	8-11	15-19	11-13	19-23	13-15	23-26

The trimmed back is prepared from Item No. 236. The plates and flanks are removed by a straight cut which is not more than 4 in. from the outer tip of the loin eye muscle. The kidney knobs must be removed, and the lumbar fat must be trimmed so that it does not exceed 1/2 in. in thickness at the leg end. The fat shall be tapered down to the lean surface at a point not beyond 3/4 of the length of the loin.

IMPS NO. 237 **Hindsaddle, Long Cut**
MBG NO. 237
URMIS and COMMON NAMES: Lamb Back.
COMMON USES: Wholesale cut from which other cuts are derived.

Weight Range [in pounds]

RANGE A		RANGE B		RANGE C		RANGE D	
Lamb	Mutton	Lamb	Mutton	Lamb	Mutton	Lamb	Mutton
20-27	36-49	27-34	49-62	34-42	62-75	42-49	75-85

The long cut hindsaddle is that portion of the carcass remaining after removal of the Chucks, Item No. 206.

IMPS NO. 238 **Hindsaddle, Long-Cut, Trimmed**
MBG NO. 238
URMIS and COMMON NAMES: Lamb Back.
COMMON USES: Wholesale cut from which other cuts are derived.

Weight Range [in pounds]

RANGE A		RANGE B		RANGE C		RANGE D	
Lamb	Mutton	Lamb	Mutton	Lamb	Mutton	Lamb	Mutton
17-23	33-41	23-29	41-52	29-36	52-63	36-41	63-72

The trimmed, long-cut hindsaddle contains the Legs, Item No. 233, and the Back, Trimmed, Item No. 236; portions of the carcass intact.

IMPS NO. 1295 **Lamb for Stewing**
MBG NO. 1295
URMIS and COMMON NAMES: Lamb Cubes, Lamb Stew Meat.
COMMON USES: Cook in moist heat; lamb stew.

Weight Range
Amount As Specified

This item may be prepared from any combination of carcasses or cuts which will produce lamb for stewing that complies with the end product requirements. Meat from shanks is not acceptable. Meat with dark discoloration as well as all bones, cartilage, backstrap, exposed large blood vessels, and the prescapular lymph gland shall be removed. Prior to dicing, the meat shall be trimmed in such a manner that surface and seam fat shall not exceed 1/4 in. in thickness at any point. In addition, the fat content of the meat, determined visually, shall not exceed 20 percent.

After being prepared as described above, the boneless meat shall be hand-diced, or processed through a dicing machine (grinding not permitted). Not less than 75 percent, by weight, of the resulting pieces shall be of a size which is the equivalent of not less than a 1/2 in. cube nor more than a 1-1/4 in. cube, and no individual surface on these pieces shall exceed 2-1/2 in. in length. (When specified, this item may be prepared from yearling mutton, or mutton; in that case, the name shall be changed to yearling mutton, or mutton, as applicable.)

U.S. Prime

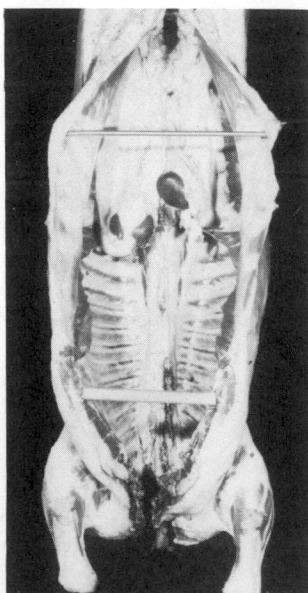

U.S. Choice

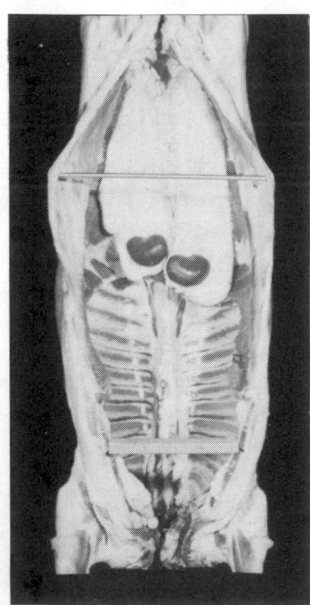

U.S. Good

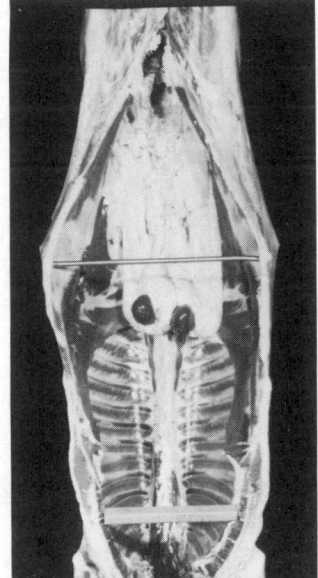

U.S. Utility

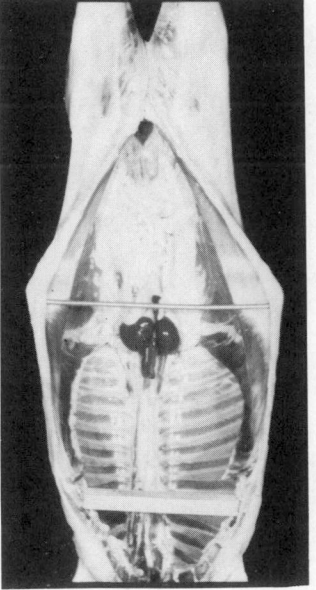

Photos: NLS & MB

IMPS NO. 1296 **Ground Lamb**
MBG NO. Not Included.
URMIS and COMMON NAMES: Ground Lamb.
COMMON USES: Broil; panfry; lamb patties.

Portion Sizes
Amount As Specified

Ground lamb may be prepared from any combination of carcasses or cuts. Meat with dark discoloration, all bones, cartilage, backstrap, exposed large blood vessels, and the prescapular lymph gland shall be removed. The visual fat content of the boneless meat, determined prior to grinding, shall not exceed 25 percent. After being prepared as described above, the boneless meat shall be ground, at least once, through a plate having holes no larger than 3/4 in. in diameter (or it may be otherwise reduced in size, provided the texture and the appearance of the product after final grinding are typical of ground lamb prepared by grinding only). Final grinding shall be through a plate having holes 1/8 in. in diameter.

The meat shall be thoroughly blended prior to, and subsequent to, each reduction in size, except that the ground lamb shall not be mixed after final grinding. The boneless meat shall not exceed 50°F. during grinding and packaging. The ground lamb shall be packaged and packed in the amount specified by the purchaser, and packed immediately upon completion of grinding. (When specified, this item may be prepared from yearling mutton, or mutton, in which case the name shall be changed to yearling mutton, or mutton, as applicable.)

IMPS NO. 1296A **Ground Lamb Patties**
MBG NO. Not Included.
URMIS and COMMON NAMES: Lamb Patties.
COMMON USES: Broil; panfry; lamb patties.

Portion Sizes
Size As Specified

This product shall be prepared from Item No. 1296. The ground meat shall be mechanically formed into round patties of the size specified. They shall be arranged in stacks, with each patty separated from adjacent patties by two sheets of waxed patty paper; except that, when patties are individually quick-frozen, the patty paper may be excluded. When producing patties to be delivered frozen, frozen boneless meat, previously accepted in the fresh state, may be used. (When specified, this item may be prepared from yearling mutton, or mutton, in which case, the name shall be changed to yearling mutton, or mutton, as applicable.)

EDIBLE BY-PRODUCTS — LAMB

MATERIAL

The edible by-products decribed herein shall show no evidence of freezing or defrosting, and must be in excellent condition up to the time of delivery.

All livers shall be trimmed free of ragged edges, and the gall bladder shall be removed. Whole livers shall have the heavy connective tissue, the large blood vessel, and ducts lying along the liver wall trimmed even with the surface.

Livers to be sliced shall have the heavy connective tissue, the large blood vessel, and ducts lying along the liver wall removed and excluded. Type B beef and calf livers shall have the outer connective tissue (capsula fibrosa), or "skin", removed and excluded, except for small pieces remaining on the edges and in the crease of the small (caudate) lobe. Veal livers shall not be skinned. The liver may be molded, frozen, tempered (but not thawed), and/or pressed before slicing. Slices which are broken are not acceptable. Liver slices shall be practically free from liver sawdust. As specified, they may be either (a) reassembled in natural sequence, or (b) layer-packed with plastic, parchment or waxed paper separaters between layers. After slicing, the liver slices shall be promptly packaged and solidly frozen.

Livers to be portion-cut must be prepared as described for livers to be sliced, except that the small (caudate) lobe and the "skin" must be removed and excluded. Portion-cut liver shall be layer packed only.

NOTE: Because it is impractical to list all weight ranges for edible by-products that purchasers may desire, those included in this table are suggested only. Other weight ranges may be ordered if desired.

ORDERING DATA: TO BE SPECIFIED BY THE PURCHASER

Selection
Selection No. 1
Selection No. 2

State of Refrigeration [Not applicable to sliced or portion-cut liver.]
A-Chilled
B-Frozen

Style of Packaging [Applicable only to sliced livers.]
A-Reassemble in natural sequence
B-Layer packed

DESCRIPTIONS OF SELECTIONS

Selection No. 1 Liver

Selection No. 1 livers shall be compact, thick, short, plump, and shall be practically free from blemishes. However, livers with cuts or scores not exceeding 1 in. in any dimension, or livers with small sections removed and excluded are acceptable, provided such defects do not interfere with making satisfactory, intact slices. Selection No. 1 livers shall possess a bright, uniform color typical of the species.

Selection No. 2 Liver

Selection No. 2 livers shall be at least moderately compact, thick, short, plump, and shall be practically free from blemishes. However, livers with cuts or scores not exceeding 2 in. in any dimension, or livers with up to approximately 1/3 of the liver removed are acceptable, provided such defects do not interfere with making satisfactory, intact slices. Selection No. 2 livers shall possess a bright, uniform color typical of the species.

IMPS NO. 713 **Lamb Liver**
MBG NO. Not Included.

Weight Range [in pounds]

RANGE 1	RANGE 2
under 1-1/2	none

VEAL AND CALF

When single fores, hotel racks, chucks and plates, square-cut chucks, hinds, loins, backs, legs, etc., are specified, their respective weight shall be 1/2 of that prescribed for double (i.e., in pairs) cuts.

The weights of the various wholesale, fabricated, and boneless cuts, as shown in weight range group in the above table, are those usually produced from carcasses of the weights indicated in the corresponding weight range groups. It should not be expected that all carcasses having weight within one of the indicated weight ranges will always produce cuts within the weight ranges shown. Nor should it be expected that cuts of the weights shown in each weight range will always originate from carcasses in the indicated weight range. Therefore, in ordering cuts, purchasing officials should order the specific weight range(s) desired, without regard to the carcass weights shown in the various ranges. Because it is impractical to list all weights that purchasers may desire, those identified are suggested only. Other weight ranges may be ordered, if desired.

GRADE

| U. S. Prime | U. S. Good | U. S. Utility |
| U. S. Choice | U. S. Standard | U. S. Cull |

CLASS
A—Veal
B—Calf

WEIGHT RANGE
Range 1
Range 2
Range 3

STATE OF REFRIGERATION
A.Chilled
B.Frozen

VEAL CHART

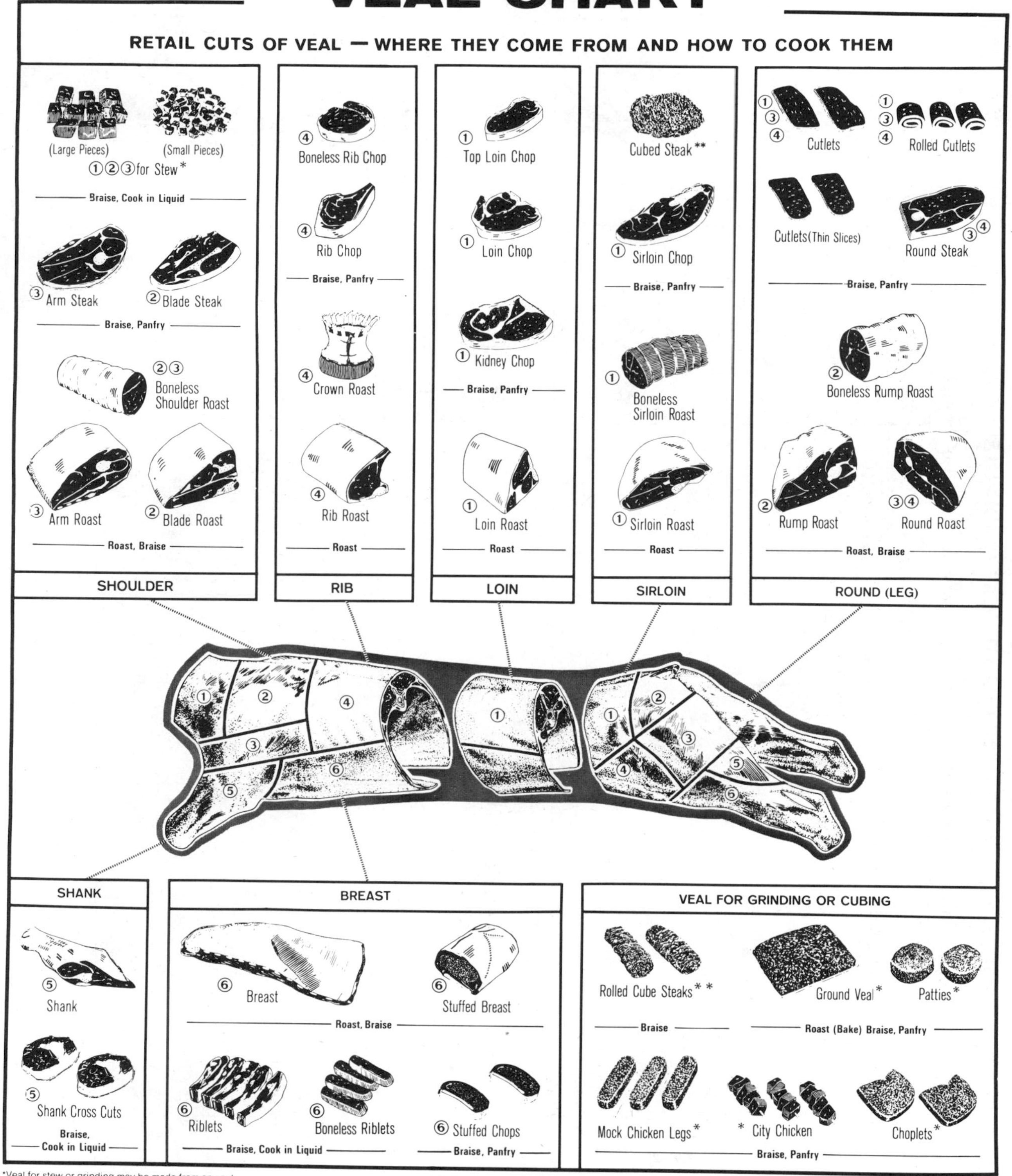

RETAIL CUTS OF VEAL — WHERE THEY COME FROM AND HOW TO COOK THEM

ROUND (LEG)

① ③ ④ Rolled Cutlets

③ ④ Round Steak

① ③ ④ Cutlets

① ④ Cutlets (Thin Slices)

② Boneless Rump Roast

③ ④ Round Roast

— Braise, Panfry —

② Rump Roast

— Roast, Braise —

SIRLOIN

Cubed Steak**

① Sirloin Chop

— Braise, Panfry —

① Boneless Sirloin Roast

① Sirloin Roast

— Roast —

LOIN

① Top Loin Chop

① Loin Chop

① Kidney Chop

— Braise, Panfry —

① Loin Roast

— Roast —

RIB

④ Boneless Rib Chop

④ Rib Chop

— Braise, Panfry —

④ Crown Roast

④ Rib Roast

— Roast —

SHOULDER

(Large Pieces) (Small Pieces)

① ② ③ for Stew*

— Braise, Cook in Liquid —

② Blade Steak

③ Arm Steak

— Braise, Panfry —

② ③ Boneless Shoulder Roast

② Blade Roast

③ Arm Roast

— Roast, Braise —

BREAST

⑥ Stuffed Breast

— Roast, Braise —

⑥ Breast

⑥ Stuffed Chops

— Braise, Panfry —

⑥ Boneless Riblets

⑥ Riblets

— Braise, Cook in Liquid —

SHANK

⑤ Shank

⑤ Shank Cross Cuts

— Braise, Cook in Liquid —

VEAL FOR GRINDING OR CUBING

Patties*

Ground Veal*

— Roast (Bake), Braise, Panfry —

Choplets*

Rolled Cube Steaks**

— Braise —

Mock Chicken Legs*

City Chicken

* City Chicken

— Braise, Panfry —

*Veal for stew or grinding may be made from any cut.

**Cube steaks may be made from any thick solid piece of boneless veal.

This chart approved by

National Live Stock and Meat Board

© National Live Stock and Meat Board

MEAT AND MEAT PRODUCTS

Veal and calf: Yield of wholesale cuts from the carcass and yield of boneless meat from wholesale cuts

Carcass and wholesale cuts	Yield of bone-in cuts		Yield of boneless meat from wholesale cuts[1]	
	Choice and Good	Standard, Utility, and Cull	Choice and Good	Standard, Utility, and Cull
	Percent	*Percent*	*Percent*	*Percent*
Carcass, whole	100.0	100.0	68.5	69.5
Foresaddle	48.6	49.7	70.4	69.3
Chuck	26.1	27.6	73.5	72.8
Breast	14.3	14.3	62.8	62.6
Hotel rack, 7 rib	8.2	7.8	73.8	69.3
Hindsaddle	51.4	50.3	66.6	70.1
Leg, includes sirloin	36.4	38.8	72.8	73.5
Loin	7.0	6.4	73.3	69.8
Flank	4.8	3.4	53.4	68.5
Kidney knob	3.2	1.7	—	—

1. All cuts trimmed of fat exceeding that amount normally left on retail cuts (1/4" to 1/2").

Veal and calf: Conversion factors for determining equivalent carcass weight of bone-in cuts and for converting boneless meat to the equivalent bone-in cuts of various U.S. grades

Carcass and wholesale cuts	Factors for converting bone-in cuts to equivalent carcass weight		Factors for converting boneless wholesale cuts to equivalent bone-in cuts	
	Choice and Good	Standard, Utility, and Cull	Choice and Good	Standard, Utility, and Cull
Carcass, whole	1.00	1.00	1.46	1.44
Foresaddle	1.03	.99	1.42	1.45
Chuck	1.07	1.04	1.36	1.38
Breast	.92	.89	1.59	1.62
Hotel rack, 7 rib	1.08	.99	1.35	1.45
Hindsaddle	.97	1.00	1.51	1.44
Leg, includes sirloin	1.06	1.05	1.38	1.37
Loin	1.07	.99	1.36	1.45
Flank	.78	.97	1.87	1.48

MATERIAL

The veal and calf product items described herein must be derived from sound, well-dressed, unsplit veal or calf carcasses without the hide and caul fat; from sound, split-sides; or from sound, well-trimmed, wholesale market cuts derived from such carcasses. Unless otherwise specified, the wholesale and fabricated cuts are double cuts. Single cuts are produced by splitting, or sawing and cutting through the median section of the long axis of the spinal processes, and related attachments of flesh and bone joining the pair of such cuts.

Veal or calf cuts which have been excessively trimmed in order to meet specified weights, or are substandard according to the specifications for any reason are excluded. The veal and calf must be free from any objectionable odors, blood clots, scores and mutilations (other than slight), discoloration, ragged edges, superficial appendages, blemishes, deterioration, damage, or signs of mishandling. The veal and calf also must be free from bruises, evidence of freezing or defrosting, and must be in excellent condition up to the time of delivery.

In ordering the various veal or calf portion-cut items covered by these specifications, purchasers must specify (1) the grade and class; (2) thickness **or** portion weight (chops), or actual weight range in pounds (roasts); and (3) state of refrigeration desired. Also, when ordering chops, purchasers may specify the weight range of the trimmed meat cut from which the portions are to be produced.

Veal and Calf Portion-Cut Chops, Steaks and Cutlets

Unless otherwise specified in the individual item specifications, chops, cutlets, and steaks must be cut in full slices, in a straight line reasonably perpendicular to the outer surface, and at an approximate right angle to the length of the meat cut from which chops, cutlets or steaks are produced.

Veal and Calf Roasts

When string tying is required, roasts may be made firm and compact and held intact by individual loops of strong twine, uniformly spaced at approximately 2 in. intervals girthwise. In addition, some roasts may require string tying lengthwise. In lieu of string tying, it is permissible to enclose roasts in a stretchable netting, provided it complies with the Regulations Governing the Meat Inspection of the U. S. Department of Agriculture. Purchasers may specify that roasts be string-tied, when this requirement is not specified in the detailed roast item specification.

IMPS NO. 300 **Carcass**
MBG NO. 300
COMMON USES: From which all other cuts are derived.

Weight Range [in pounds]

	RANGE 1	RANGE 2	RANGE 3
Veal:	60-100	100-140	140-175
Calf:	125-175	175-225	225-275

The veal or calf carcass consists of the entire unsplit, well-dressed carcass, with not-to-exceed 2 tail (caudal) vertebrae, and without the hide and caul fat. Practically all mediastinal tissue and heart fat usually present in the lower thorax (1st rib and sternum region), and bloody tissue and frayed ends, such as are usually at the neck, must be closely removed and excluded. The skirt (diaphragm) and the hanging tender may be removed in whole or in part.

IMPS NO. 301 **Carcass—Fabricated**
MBG NO. 301
COMMON USES: From which all other cuts are derived.

Weight Range [in pounds]

	RANGE 1	RANGE 2	RANGE 3
Veal:	57-95	95-133	133-165
Calf:	119-165	165-214	214-261

The carcass is separated into sides by neatly and uniformly splitting, or sawing and cutting lengthwise centrally through the spine of the carcass. Each side is devided into a forequarter and hindquarter by cutting between the 12th and 13th ribs, keeping the knife firmly against the 12th rib, following the curvature of the ribs, and continuing the cut through the cartilage and meat of the flank at an approximate right angle to the chine bone, then cutting through the chine bone between the 12th and 13th ribs.

The bones of the foreshank are completely removed by cutting on each side of the bone from the elbow to the knee joint, and on the inside of the shank, and cutting under the bone so as to leave the shank meat in one piece and attached to the forequarter. The cords at the knee are severed where they join the lean meat. The bones of the hindshank are completely removed by cutting on each side of the bone from the stifle to the hock joint on the inside of the shank, and cutting under the bone so as to leave the meat of the hindshank in one piece and attached to the hindquarter. The cords at the hock joint, including the gambrel cord, are severed where they join lean meat. Ragged or loose pieces of foreshank or hindshank meat must be removed and excluded.

IMPS NO. 302 **Carcass, Boneless**
MBG NO. 302
COMMON USES: From which all other cuts are derived.

Weight Range [in pounds]

	RANGE 1	RANGE 2	RANGE 3
Veal:	46-77	77-108	108-134
Calf:	96-135	135-173	173-212

All cuts of the carcass must be used in the proportion in which they exist in the carcass, except that tenderloins, flanks, navels, briskets, shanks, skirts, hanging tenders, necks, or rib fingers may be excluded at the contractor's option. Under no circumstances, can one of the above-mentioned cuts be substituted for another; that is, if flanks are excluded, a like quantity of navels cannot be substituted. Carcasses on which any appreciable amount of meat has been removed from the primal cuts (loins, ribs, rounds, or chucks) may not be used. Use of carcass with other cuts from which extensive amounts of lean have been removed is permissible.

All bones, bone slivers, kidney knobs, and cartilages must be removed and carcasses must be boned so as to leave all boneless cuts as nearly intact as possible. The *total fat content of the boneless veal must be determined visually, and must not exceed 10 percent.*

The forequarter is made into the following boneless cuts, in addition to such boneless trimmings as are normally produced in the boning operation: clod, chuck, shank, rib, navel, and brisket. In addition to removing all bones and cartilage, the following parts must also be removed and excluded:

1. The backstrap and all neck ligaments;
2. The prescapular lymph gland located in the shoulder;
3. The exposed large arteries and veins in the neck;
4. Neck meat with dark blood discoloration;
5. The serous membrane (peritoneum) over the inside of the abdominal section of the navel;
6. The strip of heavy connective tissue along the lower edge of the navel behind the brisket;
7. The tendon ends of the shank to a point at which the cross-section of the shank is at least 75 percent muscle;
8. The fibrous tissue (deckle) on the boned surface of the brisket;
9. All serous membrane and connective tissue from both sides of the skirts.

The hindquarter is made into the following boneless cuts, in addition to such boneless trimmings as are normally produced in the boning operation: strip loin, sir-butt, tenderloin, rump, flank, shank, and the inside, outside and knuckle of the round. In addition to all bones, bone slivers and cartilages, the following parts shall be removed and excluded:

1. The white tissue of the gracilis muscle on the inside round;
2. The white, fibrous sheet on the boned surface of the sir-butt and rump;
3. The heavy connective tissue on the edge of the outside round adjacent to the knuckle;
4. The popliteal and prefemoral lymph glands;
5. The fibrous tissue over the outside of the knuckle, and the white tissue (periosteum) remaining on the knuckle where removed from the femur (round bone);
6. The kneecap (patella) and surrounding heavy connective tissue;
7. The serous membrane (peritoneum) over the inside of the flank;
8. The heavy sheet of connective tissue (abdominal tunic) between the muscles of the flank;
9. The strip of heavy connective tissue along the lower edge of the flank;
10. The tendon ends of the shank to a point at which the cross-section is at least 75 percent muscle;
11. All udders, cod fat, pizzle ends, kidneys, kidney fat, and pelvic fat;
12. Blood vessels and all heavy external and internal connective tissue in the hanging tenders.

IMPS NO. 303 **Side**
MBG NO. 303
URMIS and COMMON NAMES: Side of Veal, Side of Calf, Half Veal-Half Calf.
COMMON USES: From which other cuts are derived.

Weight Range [in pounds]

	RANGE 1	RANGE 2	RANGE 3
Veal:	30-50	50-70	70-88
Calf:	63-88	88-113	113-138

A side consists of the approximate half portion of the carcass produced by neatly and uniformly splitting, or sawing and cutting lengthwise centrally through the spine of the carcass, thus separating the two sides.

The sides must be matched sides (right and left sides from the same carcass), insofar as practical. The sides may, at the contractor's option, be divided up into a forequarter and hindquarter by cutting between the 12th and 13th ribs, the 13th rib remaining with the hindquarter.

IMPS NO. 304 **Foresaddle**
MBG NO. 304
URMIS and COMMON NAMES: Foresaddle, Forequarter, Veal Front.
COMMON USES: From which all other cuts are derived.

Weight Range [in pounds]

	RANGE 1	RANGE 2	RANGE 3
Veal:	31-51	51-71	71-89
Calf:	64-89	89-115	115-140

The foresaddle is the unsplit front portion of the unsplit carcass remaining after the severance of the 1-rib hindsaddle made by "ribbing" the carcass, that is, separating the foresaddle from the hindsaddle by cutting between the 12th and 13th ribs, and continuing the cut between the flank and the plate portions at an approximate right angle to the spine. Practically all mediastinal tissue, heart fat, bloody neck meat, and the skirt must be removed and excluded.

IMPS NO. 305 **Bracelet [Double]**
MBG NO. 305 Hotel Rack, Regular (Double)
URMIS and COMMON NAMES: Veal Bracelet, Calf Bracelet, Full Bracelet.
COMMON USES: Roast; braise; panfry; veal rib chops; ground veal.

Weight Range [in pounds]

	RANGE 1	RANGE 2	RANGE 3
Veal:	6-10	10-13	13-17
Calf:	12-17	17-21	21-26

The bracelet is the double hotel rack and attached plates remaining all in one piece, after separating the same from the double chuck portion by cutting reasonably straight across and through the foresaddle at right angles to the spine, between the 5th and 6th ribs so that the 6th through the 12th ribs remain in the hotel rack. The Bracelet (Double) requires no further trimming.

IMPS NO. 306 **Hotel Rack, Trimmed [Double]**
MBG NO. 306
URMIS and COMMON NAMES: Trimmed Bracelet, Double Rack of Veal, Calf.
COMMON USES: Roast; veal rib roast; veal chops.

Weight Range [in pounds]

	RANGE 1	RANGE 2	RANGE 3
Veal:	5-8	8-11	11-13
Calf:	9-13	13-17	17-21

The trimmed hotel rack is that portion of the Bracelet (Double), Item No. 305, remaining after the breast portions have been removed. The breast portions must be removed from racks by starting a cut on the 12th rib, not more than 4 in. from the extreme outer tip of the rib eye muscle, and continuing in a straight line to a point on the 6th rib, not more than 4 in. (measured in a straight line) from the extreme outer tip of the rib eye muscle.

IMPS NO. 1306 **Rib Chops**
MBG NO. 1306
URMIS and COMMON NAMES: Veal Chops, Baby Beef Chops.
COMMON USES: Braise; panfry; veal chops.
SUGGESTED PORTION SIZES: 3 oz., 4 oz., 5 oz., 6 oz., 8 oz., 10 oz.

Rib Chops must be prepared from a Hotel Rack (Single), Item No. 306, Series 300; or may be a portion of a hotel rack, except that the breast portion must be removed by a cut starting on the 12th rib, not more than 3 in. from the extreme outer tip of the rib eye muscle, and continuing in a straight line to a point on the 6th rib, not more than 3 in. from the extreme outer tip of the rib eye muscle. The protruding edge of the chine bone must be removed at approximately a 45 degree angle to the split, thoracic vertebrae, beginning at the dorsal edge of the spinal cord groove. Chops produced from the blade bone section of the hotel rack must be free of blade bone and related cartilage, and all muscles and fat lying above the blade bone and cartilage.

IMPS NO. 307 **Chucks and Plates [Double]**
MBG NO. 307
URMIS and COMMON NAMES: Veal Slug.
COMMON USES: Braise; moist heat; veal stew; veal roasts.

Weight Range [in pounds]

	RANGE 1	RANGE 2	RANGE 3
Veal:	26-43	43-61	61-75
Calf:	54-75	75-97	97-118

The chucks and plates (double) are that portion of the foresaddle remaining after the removal of the Hotel Rack (Trimmed), Item No. 306.

IMPS NO. 308 **Chuck, Regular [Double]**
MBG NO. 308
URMIS and COMMON NAMES: Full chuck.
COMMON USES: Stew; roast; ground veal.

Weight Range [in pounds]

	RANGE 1	RANGE 2	RANGE 3
Veal:	25-42	42-58	58-73
Calf:	52-73	73-93	93-114

The regular chuck (double) is that portion of the foresaddle remaining after the removal of the Bracelet (Double), Item No. 305.

IMPS NO. 309 **Square-Cut Chucks [Double]**
MBG NO. 309
URMIS and COMMON NAMES: Veal Chuck.
COMMON USES: Braise; moist heat; stew; roast; ground.

Weight Range [in pounds]

	RANGE 1	RANGE 2	RANGE 3
Veal:	14-24	24-33	33-42
Calf:	29-42	42-53	53-65

The square-cut chucks (double) are that portion of the Chuck, Regular, Item No. 308, remaining after the removal of the foreshank and brisket, and each is obtained by a straight cut, perpendicular to the outer skin surface, which passes through the cartilagenous juncture of the first rib and the front extremity of the sternum (manubrium or breast bone cartilage), and is perpendicular to the long axis of the 5th rib.

IMPS NO. 1309 **Shoulder Chops**
MBG NO. 1309
URMIS and COMMON NAMES: Veal Chops.
COMMON USES: Braise; veal chops.
SUGGESTED PORTION SIZES: 3 oz., 4 oz., 5 oz., 6 oz., 8 oz., 10 oz.

Shoulder chops must be prepared from the arm and blade bone sections of one-half the Square-Cut Chuck (Double), Item No. 309, Series 300. Armbone chops must be removed first, and must be cut reasonably parallel to the normal line of separation of the shank from the shoulder, up to but not including the knuckle bone. The rib bones (riblets), and underlying fat in excess of 1/4 in., must be removed and excluded from the armbone chops. Blade chops must be cut approximately parallel to the rib bones, up to the juncture of the blade and knuckle bones.

IMPS NO. 1309R **Chuck, Square-Cut, Boneless, Tied**
MBG NO. 1309R
URMIS and COMMON NAMES: Veal chuck Roast.
COMMON USES: Braise; moist heat; veal stew; barbecued veal; ground veal.

Weight Range [in pounds]

RANGE 1	RANGE 2	RANGE 3	RANGE 4
under 10	10-15	15-22	22-up

The boneless, tied, square-cut chuck is prepared from one-half the Square-Cut Chuck, Double, Item No. 309, Series 300, after sawing and cutting lengthwise centrally through the spine, except that the neck must be removed, at a point where it joins the shoulder, by a straight cut reasonably perpendicular to the neck vertebrae. The square-cut chuck must be completely boned, by scalping, to produce a smooth-boned surface. The blade bone must be removed without cutting through the flesh at the ridge of the blade bone, so as to leave the chuck meat, including the clod, intact in one piece. All bones and cartilages, the backstrap, exposed major arteries and veins, neck meat with dark blood discoloration, and the prescapular lymph gland and surrounding fat in excess of 1/2 in. in thickness must be removed and excluded. The boneless, square-cut chuck must be rolled with the eye muscle lengthwise of the roll, and be string-tied girthwise and lengthwise. When smaller roasts are specified, the boneless roast must be cut at a right angle to the roast length.

IMPS NO. 310 **Shoulder Clod**
MBG NO. 310
URMIS and COMMON NAMES: Veal Shoulder Roast, Veal Blade Roast, Veal Shoulder Blade Roast.
COMMON USES: Braise; roast; shoulder roast; veal stew.

Weight Range [in pounds]

	RANGE 1	RANGE 2	RANGE 3
Veal:	2-3 1/2	3 1/2-4 1/2	4 1/2-6
Calf:	4-6	6-7 1/2	7 1/2-9

The shoulder clod is the large, outside muscle which lies behind the elbow joint (lower end of armbone) and to the side of the medial ridge of the blade bone. The thick end of the clod includes all muscles overlying the first natural seam, and the thinner end includes all the muscles lying above the rear edge of the shoulder blade. The clod must be removed in one piece without undue scoring, and all sides must be trimmed so that the clod is not less than 3/4-in. thick at any point. The heavy tendons at the elbow end of the clod must be removed and excluded.

IMPS NO. 1310R **Shoulder Clod, Roast Ready**
MBG NO. 1310R
URMIS and COMMON NAMES: Veal or Calf Chuck Roast, Clod Roast.
COMMON USES: Braise; moist heat; veal chuck roast; veal stew.

Weight Range [in pounds]

RANGE 1	RANGE 2	RANGE 3	RANGE 4
under 6	6-8	8-10	10-up

The roast ready, shoulder clod is the large outside muscle; it lies behind the elbow joint (lower end of armbone) and to the side of the ridge of the blade bone. The thick end of the clod includes all the muscles overlying the first natural seam, and the thinner end includes all the muscles lying above the rear edge of the shoulder blade. The clod must be removed in one piece, without undue scoring, and all sides must be trimmed so that the clod is not less than 1/2-in. thick at any point. The side edge must be trimmed approximately parallel with the edge lying adjacent to the medial ridge of the blade bone. The heavy elbow and knuckle joint tendons must be removed even with the surface of the meat. Also, the periosteum on the boned surface, remaining after removal of the blade bone, must be removed and excluded. If specified by the purchaser, roasts may be split lengthwise, the ends reversed and string-tied. Also, if specified by the purchaser, larger roasts may be produced by reversing the ends of two roasts and string tying girthwise.

IMPS NO. 1310 **Shoulder Clod Steaks**
MBG NO. 1310
URMIS and COMMON NAMES: Veal Shoulder Blade Steaks, Veal Cutlet, Veal Cubed Steaks.
COMMON USES: Braise; panfry; shoulder veal chops; veal cutlets.
SUGGESTED PORTION SIZES: 4 oz., 5 oz., 6 oz., 8 oz., 10 oz.

Clod steaks must be prepared from a shoulder Clod, Item No. 310, Series 300. The shoulder clod may be separated into sections to accommodate the cutting of specified portion-size steaks.

IMPS NO. 311 **Square-Cut Chuck, Boneless [Clod Out]**
MBG NO. 311
URMIS and COMMON NAMES: Chuck Roasts, Veal Shoulder Blade Roast.
COMMON USES: Braise; moist heat; chuck roast.

Weight Range [in pounds]

	RANGE 1	RANGE 2	RANGE 3
Veal:	10-19	19-26	26-33
Calf:	23-33	33-41	41-51

The square-cut chuck must be made entirely boneless. The shoulder clod is removed, as described in Shoulder Clod, Item No. 310, and excluded. The remaining meat of the chuck must be left intact and in one piece. In addition to all bones and cartilages, the backstrap, exposed major arteries, neck meat discolored with blood, and the prescapular lymph gland, located just in front of the shoulder joint, must be removed and excluded. Boning procedures must be accomplished with sufficient care to allow each single cut to retain its identity, and to avoid objectionable scores in the meat.

IMPS NO. 1311R **Chuck, Square-Cut, Clod-Out, Boneless, Tied**
MBG NO. 1311R
URMIS and COMMON NAMES: Veal Chuck Roast.
COMMON USES: Braise; moist heat; veal chuck roast; veal stew.

Weight Range [in pounds]

RANGE 1	RANGE 2	RANGE 3	RANGE 4
under 6	6-8	8-10	10-up

The boneless, tied, clod-out, square-cut chuck must be prepared from the Square-Cut Chuck, (Clod-Out), Item No. 311, Series 300, except that the neck must be removed as described in Item No. 1309R. The boneless chuck (clod-out) must be rolled with the eye muscle lengthwise of the roll, and be string-tied girthwise and lengthwise.

IMPS NO. 312 **Foreshank**
MBG NO. 312
URMIS and COMMON NAMES: Veal Shank, Foreshank, Ossobucci.
COMMON USES: Braise; cook in liquid; veal shank; cross-cut shank.

Weight Range [in pounds]

	RANGE 1	RANGE 2	RANGE 3
Veal:	1-2	2-3	3-3 1/2
Calf:	2 1/2-3 1/2	3 1/2-4 1/2	4 1/2-5 1/2

The foreshank is the foreleg portion remaining intact with the brisket, after removal from the regular chuck, in making the Square-Cut Chuck, Item No. 309. The foreshank must be separated from the brisket by a cut following the dividing or natural seam, and leaving the entire "lip" (web muscle) on the brisket.

IMPS NO. 313 **Breast**
MBG NO. 313
URMIS and COMMON NAMES: Breast of Veal/Calf, Veal Breast.
COMMON USES: Braise; roast; veal breast.

Weight Range [in pounds]

	RANGE 1	RANGE 2	RANGE 3
Veal:	3 1/2-6	6-7 1/2	7 1/2-9 1/2
Calf:	7-9 1/2	9 1/2-12	12 1/2-15

The breast is that portion of the forequarter remaining in one piece after the removal of the Foreshank, Item No. 312, Square-Cut Chuck, Item No. 309, and the Hotel Rack, Trimmed, Item No. 306.

IMPS NO. 330 **Hindsaddle**
MBG NO. 330
URMIS and COMMON NAMES: Hindquarter, Hind.
COMMON USES: Other cuts.

Weight Range [in pounds]

	RANGE 1	RANGE 2	RANGE 3
Veal:	29-49	49-69	69-86
Calf:	61-86	86-110	110-135

The hindsaddle is the rear portion of the unsplit carcass remaining after removal of the 12-rib Foresaddle, Item No. 304.

IMPS NO. 331 **Loin, Regular [Double]**
MBG NO. 331
URMIS and COMMON NAMES: Veal Loin Roast.
COMMON USES: Roast; veal loin roast; veal chops.

Weight Range [in pounds]

	RANGE 1	RANGE 2	RANGE 3
Veal:	5-9	9-13	13-16
Calf:	11-16	16-19	19-25

The regular loin is both loins (Double) remaining in one piece as a pair, after separation from the Hindsaddle, Item No. 330, at the front end of the hip bone in the leg. The cut must be perpendicular to the outer skin surface, and also perpendicular to the backbone. The regular loin requires no further trimming.

IMPS NO. 332 **Loin, Trimmed [Double]**
MBG NO. 332
URMIS and COMMON NAMES: Trimmed Loin, Loin, Veal Loin.
COMMON USES: Roast; veal loin roast; veal chops.

Weight Range [in pounds]

	RANGE 1	RANGE 2	RANGE 3
Veal:	4-7	7-10	10-12
Calf:	9-12	12-16	16-19

The trimmed loin is that portion of the Loin, Regular, Item No. 331, remaining after the flank portions have been removed. The flank portions must be removed by starting a cut on the 13th rib, not more than 4 in. from the extreme outer tip of the loin eye muscle, and continuing in a straight line to a point on the leg end which is not more than 4 in. from the extreme outer tip of the loin eye muscle. The kidney knobs must be removed, and, in addition, the lumbar fat must be trimmed from the loin so that the fat does not exceed 1/2 in. in thickness at the butt end. The fat must then be tapered down to the lean surface at a point not beyond 3/4 of the length of the entire loin.

IMPS NO. 1332 **Loin Chops**
MBG NO. 1332
URMIS and COMMON NAMES: Veal Chops, Veal Loin Chops, Veal Kidney Chops, Loin Veal Chops.
COMMON USES: Braise; panfry; veal chops; loin veal chops.
SUGGESTED PORTION SIZES: 3 oz., 4 oz., 5 oz., 6 oz., 8 oz., 10 oz., 12 oz., 16 oz.

Loin chops must be prepared from one-half the Loin, Trimmed (Double), Item No. 332, Series 300, except that the flank must be removed by a cut starting on the 13th rib, 3 in. from the extreme outer tip of the loin eye muscle, and continuing in a straight line to a point on the leg end which is not more than 3 in. from the extreme outer tip of the loin eye muscle. Loin chops must contain no portion of the hip bone. However, a portion of the 13th rib may be present in chops cut from the rib end.

IMPS NO. 333 **Full Loin, Trimmed [Single]**
MBG NO. Not Included.
URMIS and COMMON NAMES: Single Loin, Veal Loin Roast.
COMMON USES: Roast; veal loin roast; veal chops.

Weight Range [in pounds]

	RANGE 1	RANGE 2	RANGE 3
Veal:	6-9	9-12	12-15
Calf:	11-15	15-19	19-24

The trimmed, single, full loin is prepared from one-half the Hindsaddle, Item No. 330, after sawing and cutting lengthwise centrally through the spine, and is obtained as follows: the untrimmed full loin and flank is removed from the hindquarter by cutting in a straight line perpendicular to the contour of the outer skin surface. The cut is made on a straight line starting at a point on the backbone, which is the juncture of the last (5th) sacral vertebra and the first tail (caudal) vertebra, passes through a second point, which is immediately in front of the protuberance of the femur bone, and exposes the ball of the femur bone, and then continues in the same straight line beyond the second point to complete the cut.

The kidney knob and the fat lying closely around the kidney must be removed by a cut, starting at the rear end of the kidney and slanting directly to the rear edge of the 13th rib, thus leaving the 13th rib practically free of lumbar fat. The hanging tender must be entirely removed at a point opposite the juncture of the 1st and 2nd lumbar vertebrae.

The flank must be removed by a cut starting at a point on the leg end of the full loin, which leaves not more than 1/2 in. of fat and flank muscle on the side edge of the loin end (sirloin), and continuing in a straight line to a point on the 13th rib, not more than 4 in. measured in a straight line from the extreme outer tip of the rib eye muscle. The fat must be trimmed from the internal section of the loin, with the full loin lying unsupported with the outer skin surface down on a flat surface. The fat, which extends above a flat plane parallel to the flat surface of the cutting bench, and which is level with the protruding edge of the chine bone, must be removed. Another cut must be made trimming and removing all fat which extends above a flat plane, using the following two lines as guides for each edge of the plane: an imaginary line 1 in. above the protruding edge of the chine bone to a line on the inside of the loin 2 in. from the flank side cut edge. The fat remaining in the pelvic (sacral) region must not exceed 3/4 in. in depth.

IMPS NO. 334 **Legs [Double]**
MBG NO. 334
URMIS and COMMON NAMES: Leg of Veal, Veal Round.
COMMON USES: Roast; veal sirloin roast; veal cutlets.

Weight Range [in pounds]

	RANGE 1	RANGE 2	RANGE 3
Veal:	24-40	40-56	56-70
Calf:	50-70	70-90	90-110

The legs (double) are that portion of the hindsaddle remaining after the removal of the Loin, Regular (Double), Item No. 331.

IMPS NO. 335 **Leg, Oven-Prepared, Boneless [Single]**
MBG NO. 335
URMIS and COMMON NAMES: Leg of Veal/Calf, Veal Round.
COMMON USES: Roast; roast veal; cutlets.

Weight Range [in pounds]

	RANGE 1	RANGE 2	RANGE 3
Veal:	9-15	15-21	21-26
Calf:	18-26	26-33	33-40

The oven-prepared, single leg is prepared from one-half the Legs (Double), Item No. 334, after sawing and cutting lengthwise centrally through the spine. The pelvic bone, back bones, and tail bones must be closely removed from the rump and sirloin portions of the leg. The shank bone is removed by cuts starting at the muscular end of the gambrel cord (where the gambrel cord protrudes from the fleshy base of the leg), and going to the shank bone, following the bone to the stifle joint, passing through the joint and finally removing the shank bone from the leg.

The round bone (femur) is removed by cutting between the inside and knuckle in a straight line through the natural seam, and then closely removing the round bone, kneecap, and the adjacent heavy tendons. This leaves the boneless leg intact and in one piece. The boneless leg must be formed into a compact roast, and be held intact by individual loops of strong twine spaced uniformly around it.

IMPS NO. 1335 **Leg, Boneless, Tied, Roast Ready**
MBG NO. 1335
URMIS and COMMON NAMES: Veal Roast, Leg of Veal.
COMMON USES: Roast; roast veal; cutlets.

Weight Range [in pounds]

RANGE 1	RANGE 2	RANGE 3	RANGE 4
under 10	10-15	15-22	22-up

The boneless, tied, roast ready leg is prepared from the Leg, Oven-Prepared, Boneless (Single), Item No. 335, Series 300, except that the entire flank, all cod or udder fat, and exterior surface fat, in excess of 1/2-in. in thickness, must be removed and excluded. The pelvic, back, and tail bones must be removed. The shank bone is removed by a cut starting at the muscular end of the gambrel cord (where the gambrel cord protrudes from the fleshy base of the leg), following the natural seam which separates the shank meat and shank bone from the heel (gastrocnemius muscle) to the stifle joint, passing through the join to remove the shank bone with shank meat attached. The round bone (femur) is removed by cutting between the inside and knuckle in a straight line through the natural seam, and then closely removing the round bone, kneecap, and the adjacent heavy tendon. The boneless leg must be string-tied, girthwise and lengthwise.

IMPS NO. 336 **Leg, Shank-Off, Boneless [Single]**
MBG NO. 336
URMIS and COMMON NAMES: Boneless Leg of Veal.
COMMON USES: Roast; roast veal; cutlets.

Weight Range [in pounds]

	RANGE 1	RANGE 2	RANGE 3
Veal:	7-11	11-15	15-19
Calf:	13-19	19-24	24-29

The single leg, shank off, is prepared from one-half the Legs (Double), Item No. 334, after sawing and cutting lengthwise centrally through the spine. The shank meat and all bones must be removed and excluded. The boneless leg, shank off, is prepared as described in Leg, Oven-Prepared, Item No. 335, except that the shank meat and shank bone are removed by cutting through the muscular end of the gambrel cord to the natural seam between the heel (gastrocnemius) and the shank meat, then following this seam to the stifle joint, passing through the joint and flesh, thus severing the shank meat and shank bone from the boneless leg.

IMPS NO. 1336 **Cutlet, Regular**
MBG NO. 1336
URMIS and COMMON NAMES: Veal/Calf Cutlet, Cubed Veal/Calf Cutlet.
COMMON USES: Braise; panfry; breaded/unbreaded veal cutlets.
SUGGESTED PORTION SIZES: 3 oz., 4 oz., 5 oz., 6 oz.

Regular cutlets must be prepared from the Leg, Shank Off, Boneless (Single), Item No. 336, Series 300, except that the flank from the loin end and the heel (gastrocnemius muscle) must be removed. Major muscles of the leg must then be separated by cutting through the natural seams. All fat and membranous tissue must be removed from all surfaces of muscles. These muscles may be cut at any angle necessary to produce cutlets in the sizes specified. Cutlets must be cubed, but not more than twice, through a mechanical cubing machine, and must be of the same approximate shape. Cutlets may be folded during cubing.

IMPS NO. 1336A **Cutlet, Special**
MBG NO. 1336A
URMIS and COMMON NAMES: Veal/Calf Cutlet, Cubed Cutlet.
COMMON USES: Braise; panfry; breaded/unbreaded cutlet.
SUGGESTED PORTION SIZES: 3 oz., 4 oz., 5 oz., 6 oz.

Special cutlets must be prepared from the Leg, Shank Off, Boneless (Single), Item No. 336, Series 300, except that the flank from the sirloin end, the heel, popliteal lymph gland, and all heavy connective tissue must be removed, and excluded. The boneless leg may be separated by cutting into lengthwise sections, in a straight line reasonably perpendicular to the outer surface, to accommodate the cutting of the portion-size cutlets specified. The surface fat on the cutlets must not exceed 1/4-in. in thickness at any point, when measured from the edge of the lean. If specified by the purchaser that cutlets be cubed, the individual cutlets must be cubed twice through a mechanical cubing machine. However, knitting of two or more pieces of meat to produce a cutlet is not permissible.

IMPS NO. 337 **Leg, Rump and Shank Off [Single]**
MBG NO. 337
URMIS and COMMON NAMES: Boneless Veal Leg.
COMMON USES: Roast; roast veal; cutlets.

Weight Range [in pounds]

	RANGE 1	RANGE 2	RANGE 3
Veal:	4-8	8-10	10-13
Calf:	9-13	13-17	17-20

The single leg, rump and shank off, is prepared from one-half the Legs, (Double), Item No. 334, after sawing and cutting lengthwise centrally through the spine. The shank meat, shank bone, the sirloin (loin end), and the rough rump are removed as follows: The shank meat and shank bone are removed as described in Leg, Shank Off, Item No. 336. The rough rump and sirloin (loin end) are removed by a straight cut, perpendicular to the outer skin surface, immediately behind and parallel with the long axis of the exposed surface of the aitch bone, leaving no part of the aitch bone in the leg.

IMPS NO. 338 **Leg, Rump and Shank Off, Boneless [Single]**
MBG NO. 338
URMIS and COMMON NAMES: Boneless Veal Leg.
COMMON USES: Roast; roast veal; cutlets.

Weight Range [in pounds]

	RANGE 1	RANGE 2	RANGE 3
Veal:	3 1/2-7	7-9	9-12
Calf:	7-12	12-15	15-18

The boneless single leg, rump and shank off, is the same as Item No. 337, except that it must be made completely boneless. The round bone (femur) is removed by separating the inside and outside (with the heel attached) by a cut, starting at the muscular end of the gambrel cord between the inside and knuckle, and continuing through the natural seam and then closely removing the round bone. This leaves the boneless leg (rump, sirloin, and shank off), intact and in one piece. The flank, and the fat on any surface (including pelvic, cod or udder fat) in excess of 1/2 in., must be removed and excluded. The boneless leg must be formed into a compact roast, and held intact by individual loops of strong twine spaced uniformly around it.

IMPS NO. 339 **Leg, Short-Cut [Single]**
MBG NO. Not Included.
URMIS and COMMON NAMES: Leg of Veal Bone-In.
COMMON USES: Roast; roast veal; cutlets.

Weight Range [in pounds]

	RANGE 1	RANGE 2	RANGE 3
Veal:	9-16	16-23	23-28
Calf:	20-28	28-36	36-44

The short-cut leg (single) is that portion of the hindquarter remaining after the removal of the Full Loin, Trimmed (Single), Item No. 333. Not more than two tail (coccygeal) vertebrae may remain on the short-cut leg.

IMPS NO. 340 **Back, Regular**
MBG NO. 340
URMIS and COMMON NAMES: Back.
COMMON USES: Roasts; veal chops.

Weight Range [in pounds]

	RANGE 1	RANGE 2	RANGE 3
Veal:	11-19	19-26	26-31
Calf:	22-30	30-42	42-51

The regular back is that portion of the carcass remaining all in one piece after the removal of the Chucks, Regular, Item No. 308, and the Legs (Double), Item No. 334. The regular back requires no further trimming.

IMPS NO. 341 **Back, Trimmed**
MBG NO. 341
URMIS and COMMON NAMES: Back.
COMMON USES: Roasts; veal chops.

Weight Range [in pounds]

	RANGE 1	RANGE 2	RANGE 3
Veal:	9-15	15-20	20-25
Calf:	18-25	25-33	33-40

The trimmed back is that portion of the Back, Regular, Item No. 340, remaining after the breasts and flanks have been removed by a cut starting at a point on the 6th rib, which is not more than 4 in. measured in a straight line from the extreme outer tip of the rib eye muscle, and continuing in a reasonably straight line to a point on the leg end, which is not more than 4 in. measured in a straight line from the extreme outer tip of the loin eye muscle. The kidney knobs must be removed, and, in addition, the lumbar fat must be trimmed from the loin so that the fat does not exceed 1/2 in. in thickness at the loin end. The fat must then be tapered down to the lean surface at a point not beyond 3/4 of the length of the entire loin.

IMPS NO. 342 **Hindsaddle, Long-Cut, Regular**
MBG NO. 342
URMIS and COMMON NAMES: Veal Hind.
COMMON USES: Portion from which all other wholesale cuts are derived.

Weight Range [in pounds]

	RANGE 1	RANGE 2	RANGE 3
Veal:	35-58	58-81	81-100
Calf:	73-102	102-131	131-160

The long-cut, regular hindsaddle is that portion of the carcass remaining after the removal of the chucks, Regular, Item No. 308. The long-cut, regular hindsaddle requires no further trimming.

IMPS NO. 343 **Hindsaddle, Long-Cut, Trimmed**
MBG NO. 343
URMIS and COMMON NAMES: Veal Hind.
COMMON USES: Portion from which all other wholesale cuts are derived.

Weight Range [in pounds]

	RANGE 1	RANGE 2	RANGE 3
Veal:	33-55	55-77	77-96
Calf:	69-96	96-124	124-151

The long-cut, trimmed hindsaddle is the Legs, (Double), Item No. 334, and the Back, Trimmed, Item No. 341, portions of the carcass all in one piece.

IMPS NO. 1300 **Cubed Steaks, Regular**
MBG NO. 1300
URMIS and COMMON NAMES: Cubed Veal Steaks, Veal Cubed Steak.
COMMON USES: Braise; panfry; veal cubed steak.
SUGGESTED PORTION SIZES: 3 oz., 4 oz., 5 oz., 6 oz., 8 oz.

Regular cubed steaks may be produced from any boneless meat from the veal carcass which is reasonably free of membranous tissue, cartilage, tendons, and ligaments. The meat must be made into cubed steaks by machines designed for this purpose. Knitting of two or more pieces and folding of the meat when cubing is permissible. Also, cubed steaks must be reasonably uniform in shape, i.e., practically square, oval or round. After cubing, surface fat on the edge of the cubed steaks must not exceed 1/4 in. in width at any one point when measured from the edge of the lean. Surface and seam fat must cover not more than 15 percent of the total area on either side of the steak. The cubed steaks must not break when suspended from any point 1/2 in. from the outer edge of the steak.

IMPS NO. 1301 **Cubed Steaks, Special**
MBG NO. 1301
URMIS and COMMON NAMES: Veal Cubed Steak, Cubed Veal Steak.
COMMON USES: Braise; panfry; veal cubed steak.
SUGGESTED PORTION SIZES: 3 oz., 4 oz., 5 oz., 6 oz., 8 oz.

Special cubed steaks must meet all the requirements for Cubed Steaks, Regular, Item No. 1300, except that the special cubed steaks must be produced from any one, or any combination of, boneless muscles contained in the following cuts, as described in Series 300: Square-Cut Chucks, Item No. 309; Hotel Rack, Trimmed, Item No. 306; Loin, Trimmed, Item No. 332; or Leg, Item No. 334. Knitting of two or more pieces of meat to produce a special cubed steak is not permitted.

IMPS NO. 1395 **Veal for Stewing**
MBG NO. 1395
URMIS and COMMON NAMES: Stew Veal, Cubed Veal.
COMMON USES: Braise; cook in moist heat; veal kabobs; veal stew; veal city chicken.

Amount as Specified

Veal for stewing may be prepared from any boneless portion of the following cuts described in Series 300: Chuck, Regular, Item No. 308; Leg, Double, Item No. 334; and Breast, Item No. 313. However, when present, the following must be removed and excluded: bone, shank meat, cartilage, periostium, heavy connective tissue, major ligaments and tendons, and the tendinous ends of major boneless cuts. The boneless meat may be hand- or machine-cut (grinding not permitted) into uniform cubes of the approximate size specified by the purchaser. Surface or seam fat on any one piece must not exceed 1/4 in. The trimmable fat content for the total lot must not exceed 20 percent.

EDIBLE BY-PRODUCTS
VEAL and CALF

NOTE: Because it is impractical to list all weight ranges for edible by-products that purchasers may desire, those included in this table are suggested only. Other weight ranges may be ordered if desired.

ORDERING DATA: TO BE SPECIFIED BY THE PURCHASER.

Selection:
Selection No. 1
Selection No. 2

Style: [**Applicable only to calf livers.**]
A—Regular
B—Skinned

Weight Range: [**See weight range table.**]

State of Refrigeration: [**Not applicable to sliced or portion-cut liver.**]
A—Chilled
B—Frozen

Style of Packaging: [**Applicable only to sliced livers.**]
A—Reassembled in natural sequence
B—Layer packed

DESCRIPTION OF SELECTIONS

Selection No. 1 Liver

Selection No. 1 livers shall be compact, thick, short, plump, and shall be practically free from blemishes. However, livers with cuts or scores not exceeding 1 in. in any dimension, or livers with small sections removed and excluded are acceptable, provided such defects do not interfere with making satisfactory, intact slices. Selection No. 1 livers shall possess a bright, uniform color typical of the species.

Selection No. 2 Liver

Selection No. 2 livers shall be at least moderately compact, thick, short, plump, and shall be practcally free from blemishes. However, livers with cuts or scores not exceeding

2 in. in any dimension, or livers with up to approximately 1/3 of the liver removed are acceptable, provided such defects do not interfere with making satisfactory, intact slices. Selection No. 2 livers shall possess a bright, uniform color typical of the species.

MATERIAL

The edible by-products described herein shall show no evidence of freezing or defrosting, and must be in excellent condition to the time of delivery.

All livers shall be trimmed free of ragged edges and the gall bladder shall be removed. Whole livers shall have the heavy connective tissue, the large blood vessel, and ducts lying along the liver wall trimmed even with the surface.

Livers to be sliced shall have the heavy connective tissue, the large blood vessel, and ducts lying along the liver wall removed and excluded. Type B beef and calf livers shall have the outer connective tissue (capsula fibrosa), or "skin", removed, and excluded, except for small peices remaining on the edges and in the crease of the small (caudate) lobe. Veal livers shall not be skinned. The liver may be molded, frozen, tempered (but not thawed), and/or pressed before slicing. Slices which are broken are not acceptable. Liver slices shall be practically free from liver sawdust. As specified, they may be either (a) reassembled in natural sequence, or (b) layer-packed with plastic or parchment, or have waxed paper separators between layers. After slicing, the liver slices must be packaged and solidly frozen promptly.

Livers to be portion-cut must be prepared as described for livers to be sliced, except that the small (caudate) lobe and the "skin" must be removed and excluded. Portion-cut liver shall be layer-packed only.

IMPS NO. 704 **Calf Liver**
MBG NO. Not Included.
URMIS and COMMON NAMES: Calves' Liver, Baby Beef Liver.
COMMON USES: Fried; broiled; fried liver and onions.

Weight Range [in pounds]

RANGE 1	RANGE 2
under 6 1/2	6 1/2-8 1/2

The color of calf liver may range from tan to light brown, with reddish shades predominating.

IMPS NO. 705 **Calf Liver, Sliced [Frozen]**
MBG NO. Not Included.
URMIS and COMMON NAMES: Calves' Liver, Baby Beef Liver.
COMMON USES: Fried; broiled; fried liver.

Weight Range [in pounds]

RANGE 1	RANGE 2
under 6 1/2	6 1/2-8 1/2

Sliced calf liver must be prepared from Calf Liver, Item No. 704. Liver slices shall be approximately 3/8 to 1/2 in. in thickness.

IMPS NO. 707 **Veal Liver**
MBG NO. Not Included.
URMIS and COMMON NAMES: Calves' Liver, Baby Beef Liver.
COMMON USES: Fried; broiled; fried liver.

Weight Range [in pounds]

RANGE 1

under 3

The color of veal liver may range from light reddish tan to tan.

IMPS NO. 708 **Veal Liver, Sliced [Frozen]**
MBG NO. Not Included.
URMIS and COMMON NAMES: Calves' Liver, Baby Beef Liver.
COMMON USES: Fry; broil; fried liver.

Weight Range [in pounds]

RANGE 1

under 3

Sliced veal liver must be prepared from Veal Liver, Item No. 707. Liver slices shall be approximately 3/8 to 1/2 in. in thickness.

PORK

GRADE

Carcasses

U.S. No. 1	U.S. No. 3	U.S. Utility
U.S. No. 2	U.S. No. 4	

Wholesale and Fabricated Cut Selection: See Description of Selection Section

Selection No. 1

Selection No. 2

(Not applicable to spareribs, tenderloins, hocks, feet, trimmings, ground items, and neckbones.)

WEIGHT RANGE OR SIZE

Ground Pork Patty Weight Tolerances

For patties with a specified weight of 3 oz. or less, a tolerance of 2 patties from the projected number in a 10-lb. unit will be permitted. For patties with a specified weight of more than 3 oz., a tolerance of 1 patty from the projected number in a 10-lb. unit will be permitted. (When patties are specified by a number per pound, this shall be converted to patty weight to determine tolerances, i.e., 6 to the lb. = 2.67 oz.) For example:

Specified Size		Number Per 10-Pound Unit	Tolerance [over and under]
Weight	No. Per Lb.		
1.6 oz.	10	100	2
2.0 oz.	8	80	2
3.2 oz.	5	50	1
4.0 oz.	4	40	1

EXAMPLE: When 2-oz. patties are specified, 10-lb. units, having 78-82 patties are acceptable.

Portion Cut Items. Either the portion weight or thickness desired—not both—must be specified. If weight is to be specified, see the weight range table. If thickness is to be specified, the actual thickness desired must be indicated. (Not applicable to cubed filets.) Also, in order to control uniformity of portion sizes, the weight range of the IMPS cut from which the portions are to be produced may be specified. In this case, the fat thickness of the IMPS cut should be approximately the same as the fat thickness specified for the portion cut.

Portion Cut Weight Tolerances

If portion weight is specified, the following tolerances will be permitted:

Weight Specified	Tolerances [over and under]
Less than 6 oz.	1/4 oz.
6 oz. or more	1/2 oz.

EXAMPLE: When 4-oz. chops are specified, individual chops weighing 3-3/4 to 4-1/4 oz. are acceptable.

Portion Cut Thickness Tolerances

If thickness is specified, the following tolerances will be permitted:

Thickness Specified	Tolerances [over and under]
1 inch or less	3/16 inch
More than 1 inch	1/4 inch

EXAMPLE: When 1-1/4 in. chops are specified, individual chops measuring 1 to 1-1/2 in. are acceptable.

DESCRIPTION OF SELECTION

Selection No. 1

Hams, shoulders, shoulder picnics, loins, and Boston butts of Selection No. 1 are meaty, based on a composite evaluation of thickness of muscling and quantity of intermuscular and external fat. To meet the minimum requirements for meatiness, cuts usually are at least moderately thick and plump throughout; have at least moderately thick muscling, and not more than a small amount of intermuscular fat, nor more than a small amount of external fat on the unskinned portions of skinned hams and shoulders.

The bones must not be ossified to a degree that cartilage is not in evidence in the pelvic, spinal, and scapular sections of the pork cuts. The split chine bone, spinous processes, and cross-cut sections of bones must be porous and not appreciably brittle or flinty. The color of the bones must be in the range from red to deep pink. The exterior surfaces of the rib bones must show at least some redness. The lean must be at least slightly firm; possess a bright, reasonably uniform color (slightly two-toned is permissible), ranging from light pink to light red; and have a fine smooth texture. In addition, hams must have at the minimum two traces of marbling, and shoulders, shoulder picnics, loins and Boston butts must have at least a slight amount of marbling. (See NOTE at end of section.)

Selection No. 1 bellies must indicate a slightly high ratio of lean to fat, and have a uniform distribution of fat and lean layers. They may vary in thickness from slightly thick to moderately thick, and must be moderately uniform in thickness, moderately long in relation to width, and may show a slight amount of marbling.

The exterior fat on the fresh pork cuts must be at least slightly firm, white, and reasonably uniform in distribution. The skin must be thin, smooth and pliable. The pork cuts must be free from bruises, dislocated or enlarged joints or other malformation, or odor foreign to fresh pork. They must be practically free from scores, miscut, abrasions, hook marks, blemishes, hair roots, or other defects.

Selection No. 2

Hams, shoulders, shoulder picnics, loins and Boston butts of Selection No. 2 have a moderate degree of meatiness, based on a composite evaluation of thickness of muscling and quantity of intermuscular and external fat. Although various combinations of thickness of muscling and quantities of intermuscular and external fat will meet the minimum requirements for meatiness, cuts usually are at least slightly thick and plump throughout, with slightly thick muscling and a slightly high to high amount of intermuscular fat, with a somewhat high to high amount of external fat on the unskinned portions of skinned hams and shoulders.

The bones must not be ossified to a degree that cartilage is not in evidence in the pelvic, spinal, and scapular sections of the pork cuts. The split chine bone, spinous processes, and cross-cut sections of bones must be porous and not appreciably brittle or flinty. The color of the bones must be in the range from red to deep pink. The exterior surfaces of the rib bones must show at least some redness. The lean meat must indicate at the minimum a slight degree of firmness, possess a bright,

reasonably uniform color (slightly two-toned is permissible), ranging from light pink to light red, and have a fine, smooth texture. In addition, hams must have some traces of marbling, and shoulders, shoulder picnics, loins, and Boston butts must have at least a slight amount of marbling. (See NOTE at end of section.)

Selection No. 2 bellies must indicate a slightly low to moderately low ratio of lean to fat, except that bellies with a higher ratio of lean to fat, although not eligible for Selection No. 1 because of thickness, uniformity, or length-width proportions, may be included, provided they meet those requirements for Selection No. 2. They usually are moderately thick or thick, and usually have moderately thick fat deposits between the layers of lean. They may be uneven in thickness; may be slightly short in relation to width, and may have a slight amount of marbling.

The exterior fat on the fresh pork cuts must be at the minimum slightly firm, white, and fairly uniform in distribution. The skin must be thin, smooth, and pliable. The pork cuts must be free from bruises, dislocated or enlarged joints or other malformation, or odor foreign to fresh pork. However, pork cuts with slight scores, abrasions, hook marks, or other cuts, which do not interfere with the making of satisfactory slices, will be acceptable. Pork cuts showing only a slight amount of hair roots, or which are only slightly miscut, or misshapen, may be included.

TYING

When tying is required, roasts must be made firm and compact, and held intact by individual loops of strong twine uniformly spaced at approximately 2-in. intervals girthwise. In addition, some roasts may require tying lengthwise. In lieu of string tying, it is permissible to enclose roasts in a stretched netting, or by any other equivalent method. Purchasers may specify that roasts be tied, when this requirement is not specified in the detailed roast item specification.

PORK CHART

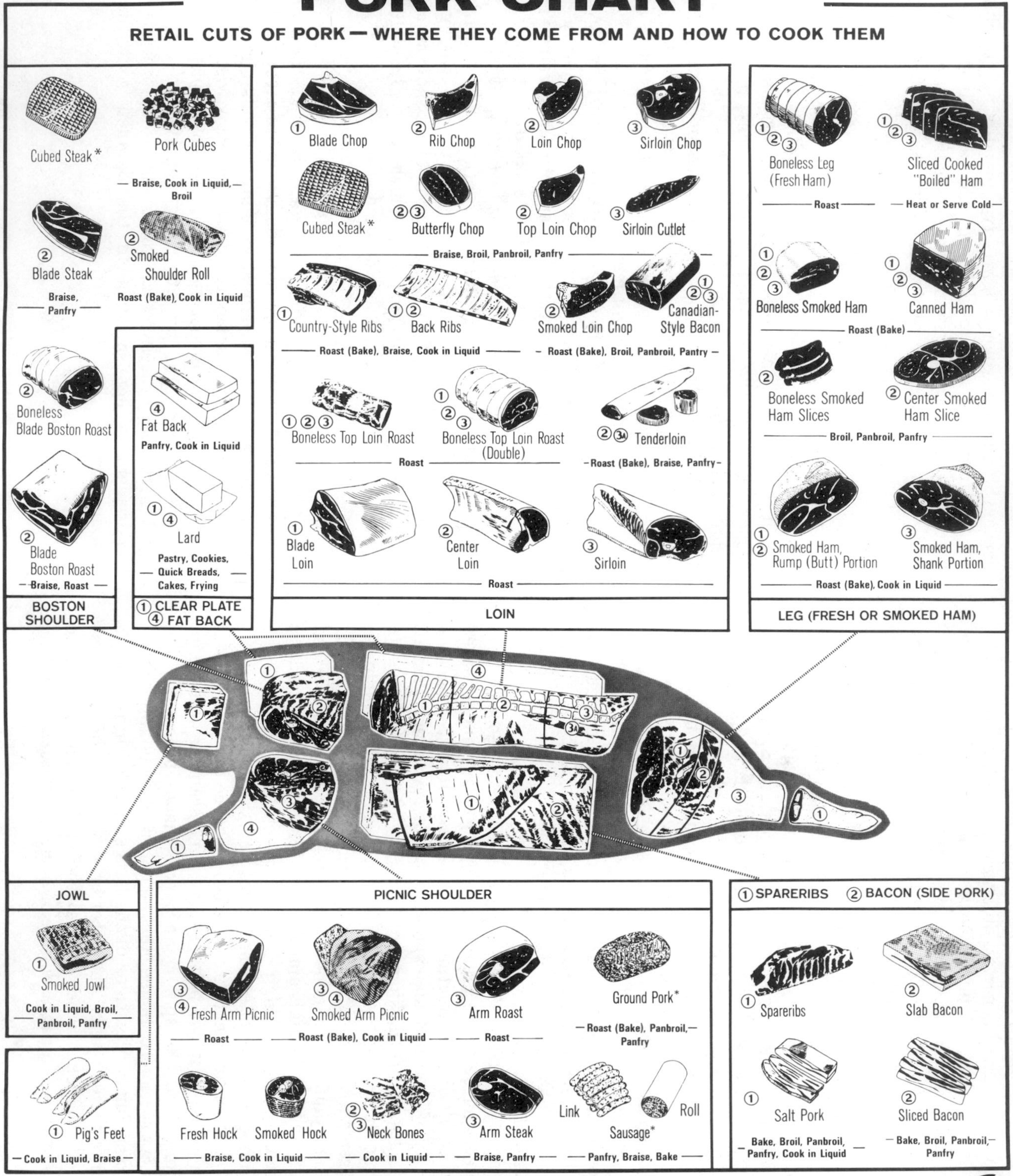

RETAIL CUTS OF PORK — WHERE THEY COME FROM AND HOW TO COOK THEM

LEG (FRESH OR SMOKED HAM)

- ①②③ Sliced Cooked "Boiled" Ham — Heat or Serve Cold
- ①②③ Boneless Leg (Fresh Ham) — Roast
- ①② Canned Ham — Heat or Serve Cold
- ① Boneless Smoked Ham — Roast (Bake)
- ② Center Smoked Ham Slice — Broil, Panbroil, Panfry
- ② Boneless Smoked Ham Slices
- ① Smoked Ham, Shank Portion — Roast (Bake), Cook in Liquid
- ① Smoked Ham, Rump (Butt) Portion — Roast (Bake), Cook in Liquid

LOIN

- ③ Sirloin Chop
- ③ Sirloin Cutlet
- ②③ Canadian-Style Bacon — Braise, Broil, Panbroil, Panfry
- ② Loin Chop
- ② Top Loin Chop
- ② Smoked Loin Chop — Roast (Bake), Broil, Panbroil, Panfry
- ②④ Tenderloin — Roast (Bake), Braise, Panfry
- ② Rib Chop
- ②③ Butterfly Chop — Braise, Broil, Panbroil, Panfry
- ①② Back Ribs
- ③ Sirloin — Roast
- ② Blade Chop
- ① Country-Style Ribs — Braise, Broil, Cook in Liquid
- ①②③ Boneless Top Loin Roast (Double)
- ②③ Boneless Top Loin Roast — Roast
- ③ Center Loin — Roast
- ①②③ Boneless Top Loin Roast
- ① Blade Loin

BOSTON SHOULDER

- ① Cubed Steak*
- ① Blade Steak — Braise, Panfry
- ② Smoked Shoulder Roll — Roast (Bake), Cook in Liquid
- ② Boneless Blade Boston Roast — Braise, Roast
- ② Blade Boston Roast — Braise, Roast
- ① Pork Cubes — Braise, Cook in Liquid, Broil

CLEAR PLATE / FAT BACK

- ④ Fat Back — Pantry, Cook in Liquid
- ④ Lard — Pastry, Cookies, Quick Breads, Cakes, Frying
- ① CLEAR PLATE
- ④ FAT BACK

PICNIC SHOULDER

- ③ Arm Roast — Roast
- ③ Ground Pork* — Roast (Bake), Panbroil, Panfry
- ③④ Smoked Arm Picnic — Roast (Bake), Cook in Liquid
- ③ Arm Steak — Braise, Cook in Liquid
- ②③ Neck Bones — Cook in Liquid
- ③④ Fresh Arm Picnic — Roast
- ③ Fresh Hock
- ③ Smoked Hock — Braise, Cook in Liquid
- Link / Sausage* — Pantry, Braise, Bake
- Roll

JOWL

- ① Smoked Jowl — Cook in Liquid, Broil, Panbroil, Panfry

Pig's Feet

- ① Pig's Feet — Cook in Liquid, Braise

SPARERIBS / BACON (SIDE PORK)

- ① SPARERIBS
- ② BACON (SIDE PORK)
- ① Spareribs — Bake, Broil, Panbroil, Panfry, Cook in Liquid
- ② Slab Bacon
- ② Sliced Bacon — Bake, Broil, Panbroil, Panfry
- ① Salt Pork

*May be made from Boston Shoulder, Picnic Shoulder, Loin or Leg.

This chart approved by
National Live Stock and Meat Board

© National Live Stock and Meat Board

MEAT AND MEAT PRODUCTS

Pork: Yield of boneless meat from carcass and wholesale cuts of pork, and conversion factors for determining weight of pork excluding lard

Carcass and wholesale cuts	Approximate percent of		Percent of boneless skinless meat, fresh	Factors for determining equivalent weight of pork excluding lard[1]			
	Live weight	Pork, excluding lard		Fresh or frozen	Cured	Smoked	Ready-to-eat
Total pork excluding lard[2, 3]	57.9	100.0	83.0	1.00	—	—	—
Packer-dressed carcass	69.1	—	—	.82	—	—	—
Shipper-dressed carcass	76.1	—	—	.74	—	—	—
Boneless skinless meat, all cuts	—	—	—	1.20	—	—	—
Hams:[4]							
Skinned, bone in	13.2	22.8	85.0	1.02	.94	1.02	1.15
Skinless, boneless	—	—	100.0	1.20	1.10	1.20	1.35
Shoulders:[5]							
Skinned, bone in	—	—	86.9	1.04	.98	1.06	—
Skinless, boneless	—	—	100.0	1.20	1.13	1.22	—
Picnics:[4]							
Skinned, bone in	6.1	10.5	81.9	.98	.90	.98	1.10
Skinless, boneless	—	—	100.0	1.20	1.10	1.20	1.35
Butts, skinless:							
Bone in (Boston)	4.8	8.3	93.3	1.12	1.08	1.17	1.31
Boneless	—	—	100.0	1.20	1.15	1.25	1.40[6]
Loins:							
Bone in	10.0	17.3	78.3	.94	.88	1.04	—
Semiboneless	—	—	87.0	1.04	.98	1.16	—
Boneless	—	—	100.0	1.20	1.13	1.33	—
Bellies:							
Bacon, slab, skin on	11.5	19.9	91.8	1.10	1.10	1.22	—
Bacon, sliced, skin off	—	—	100.0	1.20	1.20	1.33	—
Jowls (bacon squares)	1.8	3.1	88.0	1.06	1.06	1.12	—
Spareribs	1.5	2.6	58.0	.70	.67	.73	—

1. Edible offal items are excluded when converting to weight of pork excluding lard. These include brains, casings, heart, kidneys, liver, stomach or tripe, sweetbreads and tongue.
2. Pork excluding lard is computed by deducting the weight of fats rendered into lard or pork fat from the shipper-style carcass. Shipper-style carcass is computed by adding 7% to packer-style carcass, the 7% to include 4.5% head, 2.25% leaf fat, and 0.25% kidney, or the items normally on the shipper-style carcass.
3. 1954-63 average yield for federally inspected slaughter.
4. Skinned hams or picnics have about 50% of the skin removed. Skinless cuts have all of the skin removed.
5. Shoulder is picnic, butt, and plate, before cutting.
6. This factor may also be used for Capicola butts.

[Cont.]

MEAT AND MEAT PRODUCTS [Cont.]

Carcass and wholesale cuts	Aproximate percent of		Percent of boneless skinless meat, fresh	Factors for determining equivalent weight of pork excluding lard[1]			
	Live weight	Pork, ex-cluding lard		Fresh or frozen	Cured	Smoked	Ready-to-eat
Feet, front[7]	1.0	1.7	10.0	.12	.10	—	—
Tails.	.1	.2	20.0	.24	.23	—	—
Neckbones	1.0	1.7	37.4	.45	.43	.45	—
Trimmings, lean	2.7	4.7	87.2	1.05	—	—	—
Fat backs and plates, not rendered[8]	2.9	5.0	88.3	1.06	1.04	1.12	—
Head, snout, and cheek meat	.7	1.2	87.2	1.05	—	—	—
Snouts, ears, and lips	.6	1.0	10.0	.12	.12	—	—
Other cuts or items:							
Canadian-style bacon	—	—	100.0	1.20	1.15	1.41	—
Tenderloins	—	—	100.0	1.20	1.15	1.41	—
Briskets[9]	—	—	91.8	1.10	1.10	1.22	—
Hocks and knuckles	—	—	25.0	.30	.29	.30	—
Salt pork	—	—	90.0	1.08	1.08	—	—
Pork, dehydrated	—	—	—	—	2.18	—	—

7. Because of gambrel damage hind feet usually go to tankage.

8. Fat backs and plates amount to approximately 9% of live weight. During the three-year period 1947-49, however, only 2.9% were sold as such and the balance rendered into lard. The amount rendered and hence, the percentage of pork excluding lard represented by these items, will vary from month to month, and year to year, depending upon the price of lard and fat back or salt pork.

9. Brisket is shoulder end of belly.

PORK CARCASSES
U.S. GRADES

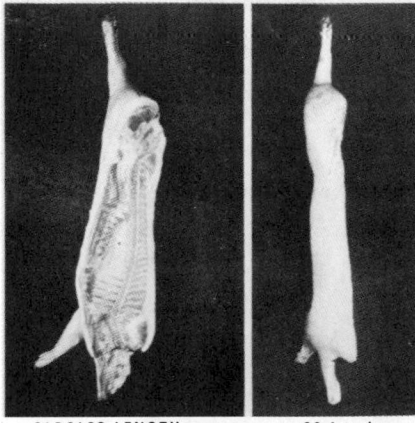

CARCASS LENGTH .... 30.4 inches
AVERAGE BACKFAT THICKNESS..... 1.3 inches
DEGREE OF MUSCLING .... thick

U.S. NO. 1

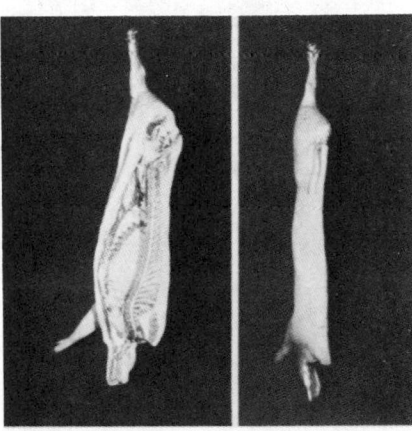

CARCASS LENGTH .... 29.5 inches
AVERAGE BACKFAT THICKNESS ..... 1.6 inches
DEGREE OF MUSCLING .... moderately thick

U.S. NO. 2

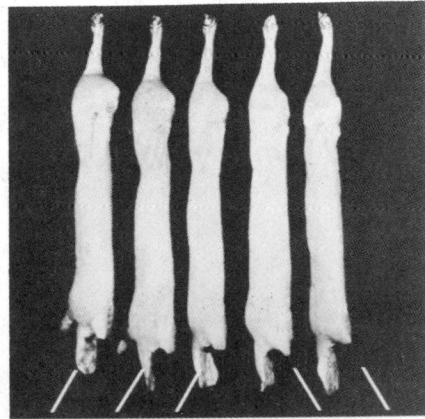

VERY   THICK MODERATELY SLIGHTLY THIN
THICK   THICK   THIN

DEGREES OF MUSCLING

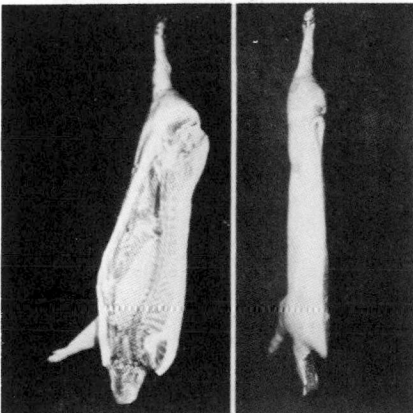

CARCASS LENGTH .... 30.0 inches
AVERAGE BACKFAT THICKNESS..... 1.9 inches
DEGREE OF MUSCLING .... slightly thin

U.S. NO. 3

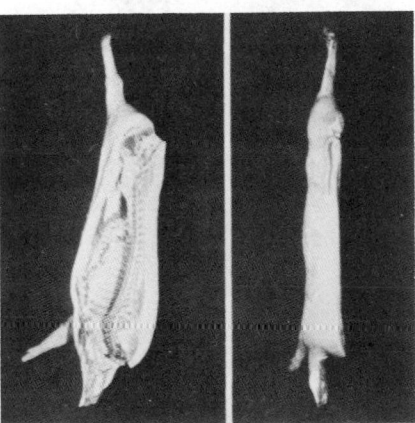

CARCASS LENGTH .... 28.5 inches
AVERAGE BACKFAT THICKNESS .. 2.2 inches
DEGREE OF MUSCLING .... thin

U.S. NO. 4

UTILITY GRADE
IS OMITTED

COPIES OF THE OFFICIAL
UNITED STATES STANDARDS
FOR GRADE ARE AVAILABLE
ON REQUEST

JANUARY 1969

UNITED STATES DEPARTMENT OF AGRICULTURE

CONSUMER AND MARKETING SERVICE

LIVESTOCK DIVISION

WASHINGTON, D.C.

SLAUGHTER SWINE
U.S. GRADES

   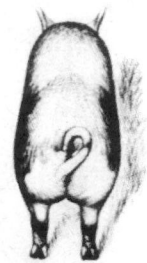  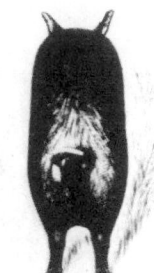

U.S. NO.1   **U.S. NO.2**   **U.S. NO.3**

U.S. NO.4   **U.S. UTILITY**

UNITED STATES DEPARTMENT OF AGRICULTURE

CONSUMER AND MARKETING SERVICE

LIVESTOCK DIVISION

WASHINGTON, D.C.

COPIES OF THE OFFICIAL
UNITED STATES STANDARDS
FOR GRADE ARE AVAILABLE
ON REQUEST

NOVEMBER 1969

MATERIAL

Items with coarse-textured dark meat, or other characteristics indicating that they were produced from aged sows, stags or boars, are not acceptable. Cuts which have been excessively trimmed in order to meet specified weights, or which do not meet the specification requirements for any reason are not acceptable. Except as otherwise provided herein, the meat shall show no evidence of freezing or defrosting. Also, the product shall show no evidence of mishandling, and shall be in excellent condition to the time of delivery.

Portion-cut items to be delivered frozen may be produced from frozen cuts which have been previously accepted in the fresh-chilled state, provided such cuts are in excellent condition, and in their original shape. Products thus produced shall be packaged, packed, and promptly returned to the freezer.

CUTTING CHOPS

Unless otherwise specified in the individual item specification, steaks and chops shall be cut in full slices, in a straight line reasonably perpendicular to the outer surface, and at an approximate right angle to the length of the cut from which they are produced.

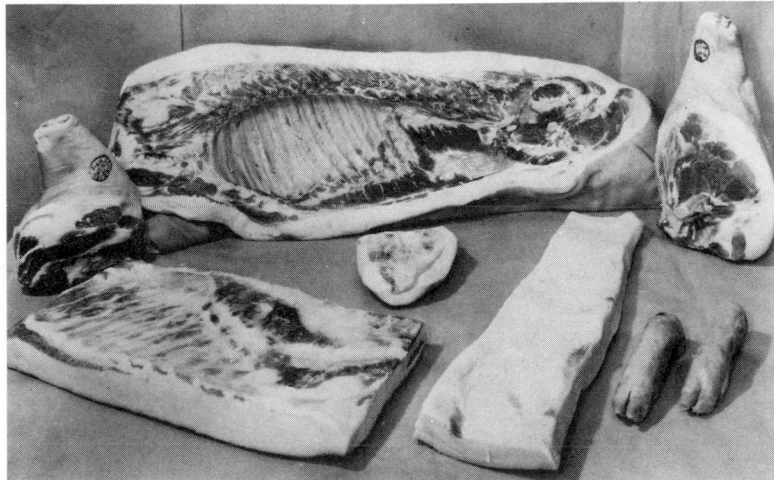

Chilled carcass showing parts derived, such as shoulder, ham, feet, jowl butt, fat back and belly.

BONING

Boning shall be accomplished with sufficient care to allow each cut to retain its identity, and to avoid objectionable scores in the meat.

IMPS NO. 400 Carcass
MBG NO. 400
URMIS and COMMON NAMES: Carcass.
COMMON USES: Portion from which all other wholesale cuts are derived.

Weight Range [in pounds]

RANGE A	RANGE B	RANGE C
120-150	150-180	180-210

The carcass shall be dressed "packer style", that is, without the head and with practically all internal fat removed. The major arteries of the ham essential for arterial pumping and curing shall be left intact. The diaphragm may be removed. The jowl shall remain intact on each carcass side, except for minor trimming and removal of bloody portions, lymph glands, etc. However, excessively trimmed or mutilated jowls not suitable for standard trimmed jowls or smoked jowl squares shall be removed by a reasonably straight cut, parallel to the body of the shoulder, behind the "ear dip," which shall remain on the jowl. Carcasses with "stuck" shoulders are not acceptable. Mutilated feet shall be removed at the hock or upper knee joint, as applicable. The carcasses shall be separated into reasonably uniform sides, by cutting lengthwise centrally through the backbone and the sternum. Pork carcasses shall be maintained and delivered in the form of matched sides.

IMPS NO. 1400 Pork Filets
MBG NO. 1400
URMIS and COMMON NAMES: Pork Filet, Cubed Pork Steaks, Pork Steak, Pork Tenderloin Steak.
COMMON USES: Pork tenderloin steak; pork filet.
SUGGESTED PORTION SIZES: 3 oz., 4 oz., 5 oz., 6 oz.

Filets shall be prepared from hams, shoulders, picnics, Boston butts, and/or loins (including shoulder and ham ends of loins). All bones, cartilages, skin, loosely attached lean or fat, tendons, ligaments and membranous tissue shall be removed. If specified, the filets may be cubed, once only, through machines designed for this purpose. Knitting of two or more pieces of meat is not acceptable. Surface and seam fat shall not exceed 1/4 in. in thickness at any one point. This measurement shall be made prior to cubing.

IMPS NO. 401 **Ham, Regular**
MBG NO. 401
URMIS and COMMON NAMES: Bone-In Fresh Ham.
COMMON USES: Roast; roast pork.

Weight Range [in pounds]

RANGE A	RANGE B	RANGE C
10-14	14-17	17-20

The ham is separated from the side by a straight cut approximately perpendicular to the outer skin surface and to a line parallel to the shank bones. This cut passes through a point which is not less than 1 1/2 in. and not more than 3 in. from the knob of the aitch bone. The foot shall be removed at, or slightly above, the hock joint. The tail bones and tail shall be removed. The fat on the face of the ham shall be removed, without any appreciable scoring or damage to the muscular portion. Practically all pelvic fat shall be removed. The ham shall be suitably faced with a smooth, well-rounded skin collar, extending not more than 2 1/2 in. inward from the center of the stifle joint; the lymph glands and fat in the flank area must be removed close to the muscles of the ham. The exterior fat thickness of the ham, measured directly under the bone at the butt edge, shall not exceed that indicated on the following schedule:

WEIGHT RANGE OF HAM	MAXIMUM FAT THICKNESS	
	Selection No. 1	Selection No. 2
10-14 lb.	1 1/4 in.	1 3/4 in.
14-17 lb.	1 1/2 in.	2 in.
17-20 lb.	2 in.	2 1/4 in.

IMPS NO. 401A **Ham, Regular, Short Shank**
MBG NO. Not Included.
URMIS and COMMON NAMES: Bone-In Fresh Ham.
COMMON USES: Roast; roast pork.

Weight Range [in pounds]

RANGE A	RANGE B	RANGE C
10-14	14-17	17-20

The short shank ham is the same as Item No. 401, except that approximately half or more of the shank (but not cut beyond the stifle joint) shall be removed by a straight cut made at an approximate right angle to the shank bones.

IMPS NO. 402 **Ham, Skinned**
MBG NO. 402
URMIS and COMMON NAMES: Fresh Ham.
COMMON USES: Roast; roast pork.

Weight Range [in pounds]

RANGE A	RANGE B	RANGE C
10-14	14-17	17-20

The skinned ham is prepared from Item No. 401. The ham shall be partially skinned, leaving a well-rounded skin collar not exceeding 20 percent of the distance from the stifle joint to the butt edge. The skin shall be removed so that the collar line is at a slant of at least 15 to 18 degrees toward the cushion side starting at the flank side, leaving the skin collar approximately 1 1/2 in. longer than the flank edge. Fat remaining on the skinned surface shall not exceed 1/2 in. in depth, measured from any point 1 1/2 in. or more from the edge of the skin collar, except that at the tail end of the pelvic area the fat thickness shall not exceed 1 in. The fat shall be neatly beveled so that it approximately meets the lean at the butt end.

IMPS NO. 402A **Ham, Skinned, short Shank**
MBG NO. Not Included.
URMIS and COMMON NAMES: Bone-In Fresh Ham.
COMMON USES: Roast; roast pork.

Weight Range [in pounds]

RANGE A	RANGE B	RANGE C
10-14	14-17	17-20

This item is the same as Item No. 402, except that approximately half or more of the shank (but not cut beyond the stifle joint) shall be removed by a straight cut, made at an approximate right angle to the shank bones.

RELATIONSHIP BETWEEN AVERAGE THICKNESS OF BACKFAT, CARCASS LENGTH OR WEIGHT, AND GRADE FOR CARCASSES WITH MUSCLING TYPICAL OF THEIR DEGREE OF FATNESS.

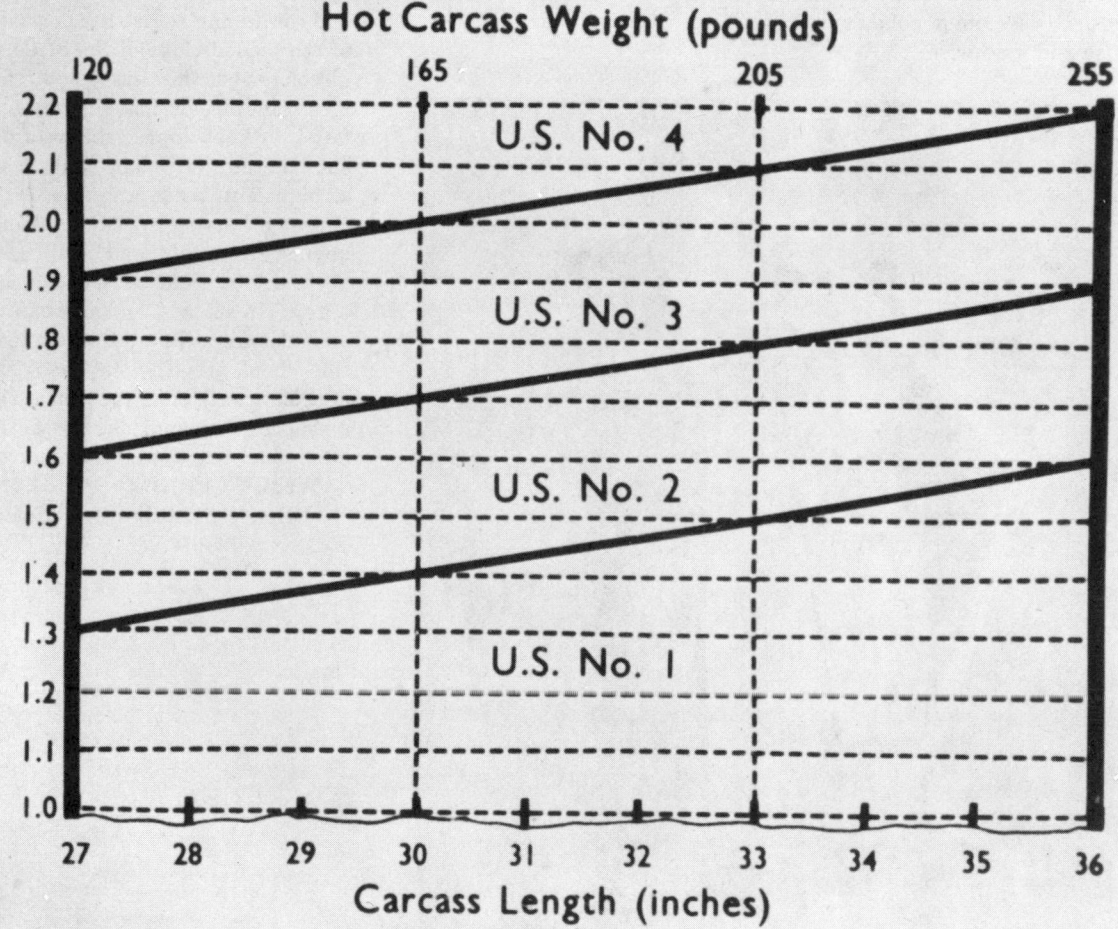

IMPS NO. 402B **Ham, Boned and Tied**
MBG NO. Not Included.
URMIS and COMMON NAMES: Fresh Ham.
COMMON USES: Roast; boneless pork roast.

Weight Range [in pounds]

RANGE A	RANGE B	RANGE C
6-8	8-10	10-12

This item is prepared from Item Nos. 401A or 402A. All bones, cartilages, skin and surface fat in excess of 1/2 in. shall be removed. Fat on the butt end shall be beveled back at least 1 in. from the edge of the lean. Shank meat which is naturally attached may be included, and shall be folded into the femur bone cavity as a plug. The ham shall be tied lengthwise and girthwise.

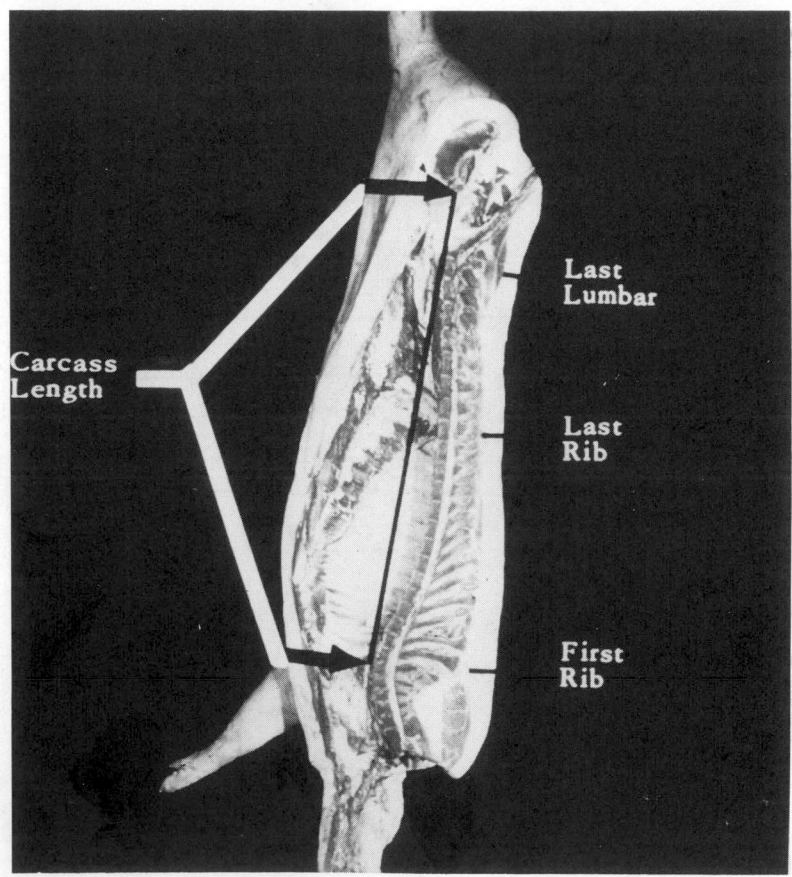

IMPS NO. 403 **Shoulder**
MBG NO. 403
URMIS and COMMON NAMES: New York Shoulder.
COMMON USES: Roast; Bar-b-que pork; pork sausage; economy pork roast.

Weight Range [in pounds]

RANGE A	RANGE B	RANGE C
8-12	12-16	16-20

The shoulder is separated from the side by a straight cut, approximately perpendicular to the outer skin surface, beginning not more than 1 in. behind the elbow joint but not exposing the elbow joint, and continuing across the hog side. Not more than a slight enlargement of the medial ridge of the blade bone shall be evident. Meat with dark discoloration, the neck bones, ribs, breast bones, cartilage, intercostal meat, and breast flap shall be removed. The shoulder shall be suitably faced without appreciable scoring or undue removal of lean. The foot shall be removed at, or slightly above, the upper joint of the knee by a straight cut, made at an approximate right angle to the shank bones. Unless otherwise specified, shoulders with shorter shanks (but not cut beyond the elbow joint) will be acceptable.

The jowl shall be removed by a straight cut perpendicular to the outer skin surface, and approximately parallel to the cut separating the shoulder from the side, which leaves not more than 1 in. of the jowl on the shoulder. The fat and skin shall be beveled so that they approximately meet the lean at the butt end. The exterior fat thickness, measured perpendicular to the skin at the approximate center of the butt, shall not exceed that indicated in the following schedule:

WEIGHT RANGE OF SHOULDER	MAXIMUM FAT THICKNESS	
	Selection No. 1	Selection No. 2
8-12 lb.	1 1/4 in.	1 3/4 in.
12-16 lb.	1 3/4 in.	2 1/4 in.
16-20 lb.	2 in.	2 1/2 in.

IMPS NO. 404 **Shoulder, Skinned**
MBG NO. 404
URMIS and COMMON NAMES: New York Shoulder.
COMMON USES: Roast; roast pork.

Weight Range [in pounds]

RANGE A	RANGE B	RANGE C
8-12	12-16	16-20

The skinned shoulder is prepared from Item No. 403. The shoulder shall be partially skinned, leaving a well-rounded skin collar not exceeding 25 percent of the distance from the elbow joint to the butt edge. The skin shall be removed so that the collar line slants at least 15 degrees from the elbow side toward the jowl side. Fat remaining on the skinned surface shall not exceed 1/2 in. in depth, measured at any point 1 1/2 in. or more from the edge of the skin collar, and shall be beveled so that it approximately meets the lean at the butt end, and on both sides. At least traces of false lean shall be evident on the skinned surface.

IMPS NO. 405 **Shoulder Picnic**
MBG NO. 405
URMIS and COMMON NAMES: Fresh Picnic.
COMMON USES: Roast; roast pork.

Weight Range [in pounds]

RANGE A	RANGE B	RANGE C
4-6	6-8	8-12

The shoulder picnic is prepared from Item No. 403. It is separated from the Boston butt by a reasonably straight cut perpendicular to the outer skin surface, and approximately parallel to the breast side of the shoulder, leaving not less than 1 nor more than 2 in. of the blade bone in the shoulder picnic. The skin and fat shall be beveled at least the equivalent of the thickness of the fat at the butt end. The exterior fat thickness, measured at the skin edge of the bevel directly under the blade bone at the butt edge, shall not exceed the following schedule:

WEIGHT RANGE OF PICNIC	MAXIMUM FAT THICKNESS	
	Selection No. 1	Selection No. 2
4-6 lb.	3/4 in.	1 1/4 in.
6-8 lb.	7/8 in.	1 3/8 in.
8-12 lb.	1 in.	1 1/2 in.

IMPS NO. 406 **Boston Butt**
MBG NO. 406
URMIS and COMMON NAMES: Pork Butt.
COMMON USES: Roast; diced pork; roast pork; sausage.

Weight Range [in pounds]

RANGE A	RANGE B	RANGE C
4-8	8-12	—

The Boston butt is separated from the shoulder as described in Item No. 405. The skin and underlying fat in excess of 1/4 in. thickness shall be removed. The false lean shall be exposed, and the fat shall be beveled so that it approximately meets the lean on all sides.

IMPS NO. 406A **Boston Butt, Boned and Tied**
MBG NO. Not Included.
URMIS and COMMON NAMES: Boneless Butt Roast, Boneless Shoulder Roast.
COMMON USES: Roast; pork roast.

Weight Range [in pounds]

RANGE A	RANGE B	RANGE C
4-6	6-8	—

The boned and tied Boston Butt is prepared from Item No. 406. The blade bone is removed without cutting through the flesh at the ridge of the blade bone so as to leave the blade meat firmly attached. The Boston Butt shall be tied girthwise.

IMPS NO. 1406 **Boston Butt Steaks**
MBG NO. 1406
URMIS and COMMON NAMES: Pork Steak.
COMMON USES: Broil; fry; bake; pork steak; rolled pork and dressing.
PORTION SIZES: 4 oz., 5 oz., 6 oz.

This item is prepared from Item No. 406.

IMPS NO. 407 **Shoulder Butt, Boneless**
MBG NO. 407
URMIS and COMMON NAMES: Pork Steak.
COMMON USES: Broil; fry; bake; pork steak; rolled pork and dressing.

Weight Range [in pounds]

RANGE A	RANGE B
1-1-2/3	3-5

The boneless shoulder butt is prepared from Item No. 406. The blade bone and overlying flesh shall be removed.

IMPS NO. 1407 **Shoulder Butt Steaks**
MBG NO. 1407
URMIS and COMMON NAMES: Boneless Pork Steak.
COMMON USES: Broil; fry; bake; pork steak; rolled pork and dressing.
PORTION SIZES: 3 oz., 4 oz., 5 oz., 6 oz., 8 oz., 10 oz.

Weight Range [in pounds]

RANGE A	RANGE B	RANGE C	RANGE D
4-6	6-8	8-10	10-12

This item is prepared from Item No. 407.

IMPS NO. 408 **Belly**
MBG NO. 408
URMIS and COMMON NAMES: Fresh Bacon.
COMMON USES: Panfry; broil; bacon.

Weight Range [in pounds]

RANGE A	RANGE B	RANGE C
10-12	12-14	14-16

The belly is prepared from that portion of the pork side middle remaining after removal of the loin, fat back, and the spareribs. The belly must be boneless, and be practically free of cartilages. Any remaining cartilages must be approximately level with, or slightly lower than, the surface lean, and the second longest diameter of any exposed cartilage must not exceed 3/8 in. Practically all leaf fat and other abdominable surface fat must be removed. The belly must be separated from the fat back, on a straight line not more than 1-1/2 in. beyond the outermost curvature of the scribe line. The sides of the belly must be reasonably straight and parallel, and approximately at right angles to the shoulder end. The ham end of the belly may be cut so that the flank side is approximately 1 in. longer than the fat back side. The belly shall be free of enlarged soft, porous, or seedy mammary tissue; the pizzle recess in barrow bellies; scores exceeding 1/4 in. in depth, and other damage affecting the end product. There shall be no area of exposed fat which exceeds 4 sq. in. on the face of the belly below the scribe line.

IMPS NO. 409 **Belly, Skinless**
MBG NO. 409
URMIS and COMMON NAMES: Bacon.
COMMON USES: Panfry; broil; bacon.

Weight Range [in pounds]

RANGE A	RANGE B	RANGE C
10-12	12-14	14-16

The skinless belly is the same as Item No. 408, except that it must have the skin removed, leaving a smooth-skinned surface free of hair roots.

IMPS NO. 410 **Loin**
MBG NO. 410
URMIS and COMMON NAMES: Pork Loin.
COMMON USES: Roast; roast pork loin; chops.

Weight Range [in pounds]

RANGE A	RANGE B	RANGE C
10-14	14-17	17-20

The loin is that portion of a side remaining after removal of the shoulder, ham, belly, and fat back, leaving the blade bone portion with its overlying flesh, and at least 2 sacral, but no caudal vertebrae in the loin. The lines of separation of the shoulder and ham from the loin shall be reasonably straight, and reasonably perpendicular to the split surface of the backbone. The medial ridge of the blade bone, when present, shall show no enlargement of the outer edge. The line of separation of the loin from the belly must be reasonably straight, extending from a point on the first rib of the loin, which is not more than 2-1/4 in. from the junction of the foremost rib and the foremost thoracic vertebra, to a point on the ham end which is immediately to the side of the major tenderloin muscle.

The fleshy side must be fairly smooth, with a well-arched, convex surface extending from a point close to the cut tip ends of the ribs to a point close to the outer extremities of the thoracic vertebrae. This smoothness and contour must continue over the rest of the loin. The false lean over the blade end must be exposed lengthwise with the loin, for a distance of at least 4 in. The fat shall not exceed 1/4 in. in thickness over the major loin muscles, except in the hip bone area. Lumbar and pelvic fat shall not exceed 1/2 in. in thickness at any one point. Loins with broken ribs and loins which have had more than a slight amount of lean removed from the major loin muscles are not acceptable. The diaphragm and hanging tender shall be removed from Selection No. 1 loins.

IMPS NO. 1410 **Chops**
MBG NO. 1410
URMIS and COMMON NAMES: Pork Chops.
COMMON USES: Broil; panfry; pork chops.
PORTION SIZES: 3 oz., 4 oz., 5 oz., 6 oz.

This item is prepared from Item No. 410. The diaphragm and hanging tender shall be removed prior to slicing. The loin must be cut from end to end into chops.

IMPS NO. 1410A **Chops with Pocket**
MBG NO. 1410A
URMIS and COMMON NAMES: Pork Chops with Pocket.
COMMON USES: Braise; bake; stuffed pork chops.
PORTION SIZES: 5 oz., 6 oz., 8 oz.

This item is prepared from Item Nos. 411 or 412. If prepared from Item No. 411, the ham end of the loin shall be removed immediately in front of the hip bone cartilage prior to slicing. On chops not containing tenderloin, the chine bone shall be removed by a cut which removes practically all the spinal cord groove. The pocket formed in the chop must be made by cutting into the meat from the rib bone side, or by cutting into the meat through the surface fat into the fleshy portion of the chop.

IMPS NO. 1410B **Rib Chops with Pocket.**
MBG NO. 1410B
URMIS and COMMON NAMES: Pork Chops with Pocket.
COMMON USES: Braise; bake; stuffed pork chops.
PORTION SIZES: 5 oz., 6 oz., 8 oz.

This item shall be prepared from the rib section only of Item No. 411 or 412. The chine bone shall be removed as described in Item No. 1410A. As specified, each chop shall contain one, or more than one, rib bone. (Chop thickness shall be specified.) Chops containing one rib shall include all the intercostal meat between that rib and an adjacent rib. The pocket shall be formed by cutting into the meat close to the rib on the side which includes the intercostal meat. Chops containing more than one rib shall have the pocket formed by cutting into the meat between the rib bones.

IMPS NO. 411 **Loin, Bladeless**
MBG NO. 411
URMIS and COMMON NAMES: Pork Loin Bladeless.
COMMON USES: For chops.

Weight Range [in pounds]

RANGE A	RANGE B	RANGE C
10-14	14-17	17-20

The bladeless loin is prepared from Item No. 410. The blade bone and related cartilage and overlying flesh shall be removed.

IMPS NO. 1411 **Chops, Bladeless**
MBG NO. 1411
URMIS and COMMON NAMES: Pork Loin Bladeless, Bladeless Pork Chop.
COMMON USES: Braise; pork chop.
PORTION SIZES: 3 oz., 4 oz., 5 oz., 6 oz., 8 oz.

This item is prepared from Item No. 411. The loin shall be sliced from end to end into chops.

IMPS NO. 412 **Loin, Center-cut**
MBG NO. 412
URMIS and COMMON NAMES: Pork Loin Center-Cut.
COMMON USES: Roast; roast pork loin; to cut center-cut chops.

Weight Range [in pounds]

RANGE A	RANGE B	RANGE C
4-6	6-8	8-10

The center-cut loin is prepared from Item No. 410. The shoulder end shall be removed by a straight cut, approximately perpendicular to the split surface of the back bone and to the length of the loin, which leaves not more than 8 ribs on the center-cut loin. The ham end of the loin is removed by a straight cut, approximately perpendicular to the split surface of the back bone and to the length of the loin, which passes through a point immediately in front of the hip bone cartilage.

IMPS NO. 1412 **Chops, Center-cut**
MBG NO. 1412
URMIS and COMMON NAMES: Boneless Center-Cut Pork Chop.
COMMON USES: Braise; bake; panfry; pork chops.
PORTION SIZES: 3 oz., 4 oz., 5 oz., 6 oz., 8 oz.

This item is prepared from Item No. 412. The center-cut loin shall be sliced from end to end into chops.

IMPS NO. 1412A **Chops, Center-Cut, Special**
MBG NO. 1412A
URMIS and COMMON NAMES: Center-Cut Pork Chops.
COMMON USES: Braise; bake; chops.
PORTION SIZES: 3 oz., 4 oz., 5 oz., 6 oz., 8 oz.

This item is prepared from Item No. 412. The tenderloin shall be removed, and the chine bone shall be removed by a cut which removes practically all the spinal cord groove.

IMPS NO. 1412B **Chops, Center-Cut, Boneless**
MBG NO. 1412B
URMIS and COMMON NAMES: Boneless Center-Cut Pork Chop.
COMMON USES: Panfry; braise; bake; chops.
PORTION SIZES: 3 oz., 4 oz., 5 oz., 6 oz., 8 oz.

This item is prepared from Item No. 412. The tenderloin and all bones and cartilage shall be removed.

IMPS NO. 413 **Loin, Boneless**
MBG NO. 413
URMIS and COMMON NAMES: Boneless Pork Loin.
COMMON USES: Roast; roast pork.

Weight Range [in pounds]

RANGE A	RANGE B	RANGE C
6-8	8-10	10-12

The boneless loin is prepared from Item No. 410. All bones, cartilage, flesh overlying the blade bone and related cartilage, intercostal meat, diaphragm, hanging tender and the tenderloin, and surrounding lumbar fat, shall be removed.

IMPS NO. 1413 **Chops, Boneless**
MBG NO. 1413
URMIS and COMMON NAMES: Boneless Pork Chops.
COMMON USES: Panfry; braise; pork chops.
PORTION SIZES: 3 oz., 4 oz., 5 oz., 6 oz., 8 oz.

This item is prepared from Item No. 413.

IMPS NO. 413A **Loin, Boned and Tied**
MBG NO. Not Included.
URMIS and COMMON NAMES: Pork Loin Roast.
COMMON USES: Roast; roast pork.

Weight Range [in pounds]

RANGE A	RANGE B	RANGE C
6-8	8-10	10-12

This item is prepared from Item No. 413. The boneless loin shall be separated into two approximately equal sections by a straight cut at an approximate right angle to the length of the loin. The loin halves shall be reversed, their boned surfaces shall be placed together, and shall be tied girthwise. The ends shall be trimmed so that their surfaces are straight, and approximately perpendicular to the length of the loin and to the outer skin surface.

IMPS NO. 414 **Canadian Back**
MBG NO. 414
URMIS and COMMON NAMES: Canadian Back Pork Loin.
COMMON USES: Roast; roast pork.

Weight Range [in pounds]

RANGE A	RANGE B	RANGE C
3-4	4-5	5-6

The Canadian Back includes the longissimus dorsi, spinalis dorsi, multifidus dorsi, complexus, and gluteus medius muscles of Item No. 410, after the ham end has been removed by a straight cut, approximately perpendicular to the split surface of the back bone and to the length of the loin, through a point immediately in front of the hip bone cartilage. All other muscles, bones, cartilage, and surface fat in excess of 1/4 in. shall be removed. The Canadian Back shall be reasonably square at both ends.

IMPS NO. 415 **Tenderloin**
MBG NO. 415
URMIS and COMMON NAMES: Pork Tenderloin.
COMMON USES: Roast; pork tenderloin; pork filet; pork tenderloin steak.

Weight Range [in pounds]

RANGE A	RANGE B	RANGE C
1/4-1/2	1/2-3/4	3/4-1

The tenderloin is removed from the loin intact. The side strip muscle and all glandular and bloody tissue shall be removed. Surface fat shall not exceed 1/8 in. in thickness.

IMPS NO. 416 **Spareribs**
MBG NO. 416
URMIS and COMMON NAMES: Spareribs.
COMMON USES: Braise; roast; bar-b-que spareribs.

Weight Range [in pounds]

RANGE A	RANGE B	RANGE C
1 - 1-2/3	3-5	5-up

Spareribs are the intact rib section removed from the belly, and may include portions of the costal cartilages, with or without portions of the breast bone and diaphragm.

IMPS NO. 416A **Spareribs, Breast Off**
MBG NO. Not Included.
URMIS and COMMON NAMES: Center-Cut Spareribs, St. Louis Rib.
COMMON USES: Roast; bar-b-que spareribs; sauerkraut and ribs.

Weight Range [in pounds]

RANGE A	RANGE B	RANGE C
1 - 2-1/2	2-1/2 - 4	4-up

This item is the same as Item No. 416, except that the sternum and costal cartilages shall be removed. When specified, the rib section shall be separated into two approximately equal portions by a lengthwise cut.

IMPS NO. 417 **Shoulder Hocks**
MBG NO. 417
URMIS and COMMON NAMES: Fresh Pork Hocks.
COMMON USES: Boil; braise; pork kunckles; pork hock.

Weight Range [in pounds]

RANGE A	RANGE B	RANGE C
1/2 - 1	1 - 1-1/2	1-1/2 - 2-1/2

Hocks are prepared from shoulders or picnics. They shall be cut through, or above, the knee joint towards the elbow, and shall be at least 2 in. in length.

IMPS NO. 418 **Pork Trimmings [90% Lean]**
MBG NO. 418
URMIS and COMMON NAMES: Pork Trimmings.
COMMON USES: Panfry; broil; sausage.

Weight Range [in pounds]
AMOUNT AS SPECIFIED

Trimmings shall not include jowls and diaphragms, and shall be practically free of bone, cartilages, seedy parts of bellies, wet mammary tissue, skin and lymph glands, except for those glands which normally form a part of the trimmings. The visually determined fat content of the trimmings shall not exceed 10 percent.

IMPS NO. 419 **Pork Trimmings [80% Lean]**
MBG NO. 419
URMIS and COMMON NAMES: Pork Trimmings.
COMMON USES: Panfry; broil; sausage.

Weight Range [in pounds)
AMOUNT AS SPECIFIED

This item is the same as Item No. 418, except that the visually determined fat content of the trimmings shall not exceed 20 percent.

IMPS NO. 420 **Front Feet**
MBG NO. 420
URMIS and COMMON NAMES: Pigs' Feet.
COMMON USES: Pigs' feet "dishes"; pickling; smoking; boiling.

Weight Range [in pounds]
RANGE A
3/4 - 1-1/2

Feet are removed from the shoulder at least slightly above the knee joint. They shall be practically free of hair and hair roots.

IMPS NO. 421 **Neck Bones**
MBG NO.421
URMIS and COMMON NAMES: Neck Bones.
COMMON USES: Steam; braise; pork bones.

Weight Range [in pounds]

RANGE A	RANGE B
3/4 - 1	1-1/2 - 2

The neck bones are cut in the conventional manner. A few, irregularly split neck bones are permissible in a lot. The bulk, however, shall consist of those including major portions of most of the cervical vertebrae, and not less than one nor more than three thoracic vertebrae and adjoining ribs, with or without portions of adjacent strenebrae or spinous extensions. The product shall carry the typical amount of lean as customarily produced from practicable cutting and/or trimming.

IMPS NO. 422 **Back Ribs**
MBG NO. Not Included.
URMIS and COMMON NAMES: Pork Back Ribs.
COMMON USES: Broil; roast; bar-b-que ribs.

Weight Range [in pounds]

RANGE A	RANGE B	RANGE C
under 1-1/2	1 - 1-2/3	3-up

Back ribs shall consist of the rib bones and related intercostal meat portion of a loin. The vertebrae shall be removed. Each back rib section shall be intact, and shall include portions of at least 11 ribs. If present, bloody portions along the inside of the ribs shall be removed.

IMPS NO. 423 **Country Style Ribs**
MBG NO. Not Included.
URMIS and COMMON NAMES: Pork Back Ribs.
COMMON USES: Roast; country style ribs.

Weight Range [in pounds]

RANGE A	RANGE B	RANGE C
1/2	2-3	3-up

Country style ribs shall be prepared from the shoulder end of a loin, and shall include at least 3 ribs. The blade bone and overlying flesh shall be removed. The chine bone, or bodies of the thoracic vertebrae, shall be removed by a straight cut along a line at which the vertebrae join the feather bones. The country style rib shall be separated into 2 approximately equal portions, by cutting through the flesh into the area where the chine bone was removed. This cut shall leave the featherbones in one portion, and the rib bones in the other. Both portions shall be packaged in the same container.

IMPS NO. 1496 **Pork for Chop Suey**
MBG NO. Not Included.
URMIS and COMMON NAMES: Diced Lean Pork.
COMMON USES: Cook in moist heat; chop suey; diced pork dishes.
PORTION SIZES: Amount As Specified.

Pork for chop suey may be prepared from any boneless meat from Ham, Skinned, Item No. 402, or Boston Butt, Item No. 406. Cuts used must be separated into their major muscles by cutting through the natural seams. Practically all surface and seam fat must be excluded. In addition, when present, the following must be removed and excluded: Bone, skin, opaque membranous tissue, cartilage, periostium, and major ligaments and tendons. The boneless meat shall be ground through a plate with 3/4 in. holes in a conventional grinder having a sharp, 3-bladed knife, or it may be machine-cut into pieces of an approximately comparable size as that produced by grinding. However, if specified by the purchaser, the meat must be hand-cut into pieces of the size desired.

IMPS NO. 1496 **Ground Pork**
MBG NO. Not Included.
URMIS and COMMON NAMES: Ground Pork.
COMMON USES: Roast; panfry; meat loaf; sausage.
PORTION SIZES: Amount As Specified.

Ground pork shall be prepared from Item Nos. 403, 404, 405, or 406. Meat with dark discoloration, all bones, cartilages, backstrap and exposed large blood vessels shall be removed. The visual fat content of the boneless meat, determined prior to grinding, shall not exceed 25 percent. After being prepared as described above, the boneless meat shall be ground at least once through a plate having holes no larger than 3/4 in. diameter (or it may be otherwise reduced in size, provided the texture and appearance of the product after final grinding is typical of ground pork prepared by grinding only). Final grinding shall be through a plate having holes 3/16 in. in diameter. The meat shall be thoroughly blended prior to, and subsequent to, each reduction in size, except that the ground pork shall not be mixed after the final grinding. The boneless meat shall not exceed 50°F. during grinding and packaging. The ground pork shall be packaged in the amount specified by the purchaser, and packed immediately upon completion of grinding.

IMPS NO. 1496A **Ground Pork Patties**
MBG NO. Not Included.
URMIS and COMMON NAMES: Ground Pork Patties.
COMMON USES: Broil; panfry; pork patties.
PORTION SIZES: Amount As Specified.

This item shall be prepared from Item No. 1496. The ground pork shall be mechanically formed into round patties of the size specified. They shall be arranged in stacks with each patty separated from adjacent patties by two sheets of waxed patty paper, except that when patties are individually quick frozen, the patty paper may be excluded. When producing patties to be delivered frozen, frozen boneless meat, previously accepted in the fresh state, may be used.

THE HISTORY OF SAUSAGE[1]

It is estimated that over 200 kinds of sausage are made in the U.S. by nearly 3000 meat processors. This sausage-making industry is by no means a 20th-century innovation for sausage was probably the world's first "convenience" food. Born of necessity centuries ago, as a means of preserving meats, sausage was pre-chopped or ground, pre-seasoned, stuffed into a serviceable "package" or casing, and pre-cooked, smoked or dried.

These services, developed because there was no refrigeration, met with approval not only because of their practicality, but also because of the flavors they produced.

The ancient art of sausage-making pre-dates recorded history. Homer in his "Odyssey" mentions sausage as a favorite food of the Greeks, and we learn from other writers that the Greeks liked sausage immensely. They served what we would now call wieners as an appetizer before meals.

By the time of Julius Caesar, who died in 44 B.C., the arts of seasoning and preserving meats had advanced to a high level. In his military campaigns, Caesar gained advantages over his barbarian enemies by issuing preserved meats to his legions. His enemies, meanwhile, lost precious hours hunting game in the forests, or seizing domestic animals and preparing them to eat.

The Romans' liking for sausage was so great that no festive occasion was considered complete without it. Sausage always accompanied manifestations of hilarity and joy, so much so that the early Church came to associate sausage with heathen and licentious behavior. A strong lobby of reformers put through a prohibition law against sausage. The Romans, as impatient of reformers then as today, smuggled sausage past the prohibition agents, and the odious law finally was stricken from the books.

The EPICIUS volume on cookery, one of the oldest in existence, listed a number of sausage recipes for dishes often served in the homes of Roman patricians: "Liver Kromeskis are made in this manner. Fry pork liver, remove skin and sinews. Crush pepper and rue in a mortar with broth. Add liver, pound and mix. This pulp shape to small sausages, wrap in cawl and laurel leaves, hang them up to be smoked. Whenever you want, when ready to enjoy them, take out of smoke, fry again and add gravy."

A small sausage named Botellum was made of pork, yolks of hard-boiled eggs, pignolia nuts, onions, leeks, rosemary and fine pepper, and then stuffed into casings. It usually was cooked in wine. Lucanian sausage was prepared in much the same way, except the seasonings were cumin, rue and laurel berries.

By the Middle Ages, "wurst" was popular throughout Europe, and served with beer and wine, was the symbol of conviviality and the joy of eating. The mighty medieval Butcher's Guilds did much to maintain the quality of their wares, and the honor of their craft during those long centuries of slow progress.

And just what IS sausage? The word is derived from the Latin "salus", meaning salted or preserved meat. While sausage was originally made of pork, during the last 700 years it has been made of mixed meats of all kinds, seasoned with spices gathered from around the world.

Modern sausage was developed mainly in the Germanic countries and in Italy. There the people, with their flair for the poetry of flavors, realized how enticing meat could be made by the skillful blending of different kinds of meats with various spices, and by curing and aging.

The warm Italian climate encouraged the development of the so-called "dry sausage". It was preserved with an abundance of salt and pungent spices, such as pepper and garlic, then thoroughly dried, generally without smoking. Treated in this way, the sausage could be kept for long periods, and stored against months of meat scarcity. Many a delectable sausage today bears the name of an Italian City, Milano, Romano, Genoa, Bologna.

In Germany, the much cooler climate and the cooler storage cellars accounted for the development of fresh and cooked sausage. These are the predecessors of our domestic

---

[1] Substantial portions of the material which appear in this chapter come from *Sausage And Smoked Meats*, 1966, a publication of Oscar Mayer Co. Reprinted with permission.

sausage today; included are frying sausages, "bratenwurst", many styles of liver sausage, head cheese, blood sausage, and various cooked, smoked sausages. Of all of these, the wiener and frankfurter, the "hot dog", has become the most popular sausage in the United States.

THE CURE THAT FLAVORS

Meats selected for most sausage-making acquire their first distinctive characteristics in the curing process. Until a century ago, curing was a principal method of preserving meat, but today it is used primarily to develop flavor and color in meats.

Although most curing agents are essentially the same, sausage-making companies use their own well-guarded techniques for applying them. Curing solutions vary depending on the meat to be cured, the flavor desired, and the length of cure. The solution is basically a brine mixture that has been blended with other preservatives and flavoring agents.

The curing solution is applied either by hand-operated equipment, or by automatic methods. For example, a side of pork, soon to become bacon, is cured by an "injecto-cure" machine. The meat passes under a row of descending needles, and the curing solution is pumped into the meat.

Ham curing is a vein-pumping operation in which a technician skillfully injects the solution into the natural circulatory system of the ham. This method assures that the curing solution penetrates every section of the ham for a thorough, even cure.

Meat that has been treated internally with the pickle solution, as it is sometimes called, and salted on the outside surface, then goes to a curing cooler to allow the solution to penetrate. Temperature control is used in the cooler to either speed up, or retard, the curing process, depending on product requirements for flavor. Time and temperature are most crucial in developing unique flavors in the curing process.

After meat has been cured, it is held at temperatures between 32° and 40°F. Cured meats are not frozen, as the brine solutions invite the development of rancidity, as well as texture changes in the meat, at lower temperatures.

A PINCH OF SPICE

One of the secrets of sausage flavor is the delicate blending of pure spices with fine meats. The old "wurstmacher" measured out spices with a well-trained eye, and an experienced hand. Today's exacting formulas call for precise quantities and strict quality to assure uniformity. This is not easy to acquire. Mere weight or volume measures are not enough.

Natural spices vary considerably in flavor effect, because of variance in crop conditions and soil conditions in different locations. The handling of spices from the time of harvest until the time of use is another important factor. When spices are extracted for their active flavor components, the extractives also will differ depending upon the methods used.

Pepper, therefore, is not merely pepper. The black pepper in Oscar Meyer Weiners is Tellicherry Pepper, grown on the Malabar coast of Southern India and named for the port of Tellicherry from which it is shipped. It is the most expensive of peppers because it is superior in flavor and pungency.

There have been times in history when pepper was worth its weight in silver and gold. After the Goths conquered Rome in the fifth century, they demanded a ransom of pepper as well as precious metals. Peppercorns were often employed as money. Adventurers such as Marco Polo, Christopher Columbus and Vasco da Gama, voyaged in search of shorter routes to the spice-laden East.

Countries controlling the spice trade became the richest and most powerful nations. Piracy and plundering between these major western powers marked nearly four centuries of struggle for the control of spice-producing lands in the Middle East and Orient.

Today, spices come from all over the world. Black pepper comes from India, white pepper from Borneo, nutmeg from the East Indies, marjoram and thyme from France, paprika from Spain, cloves from Zanzibar, cardamom from Guatemala, allspice from Jamaica and cinnamon from Java. Natural spice materials include herbs, seeds, and parts of aromatic plants, in addition to essential oils.

While spices are recognized principally as flavor

ingredients, some also have antibiotic properties which aid in preservation. Spices may also affect the color and aroma of sausages. Salt is almost universally used as a preservative for sausage. It also affects texture — a lack of salt results in a rubber-like product. Sugar has some use as a preservative, and has a minor effect upon color fixation.

Spice control is so essential in maintaining a uniform flavor standard that sausage processors often maintain a special spice department. They being by analyzing the basic materials even before purchase. Samples of natural spices and essential oils, as the liquid spice extracts are called, are tested thoroughly in the flavor laboratory.

Spice blends are prepared from basic spice materials in a centralized production unit. Blending spices in large lots — sometimes as much as 500-lb. batches — permits consistent seasoning of sausages even through they are made in different plants.

A WHIFF OF SMOKE

The aroma of smoke has haunted man through the ages, and the more civilized he pretends to be, the greater appears his delight in a fireplace, a grill, or an open fire with its pleasant smell of smoke.

The idea of smoking meat developed from the need to preserve meat, just as the curing process did, and smoking for flavor is by no means an innovation. Centuries ago, after curing meat with salt, people smoked it over a smoldering wood fire.

Smoking began as a very ordinary procedure, but today it is a technical, processing plant operation. Not all processed meat products are smoked, nor are all of them cured. However, with few exceptions, meats to be smoked must first be cured.

After the curing process is complete, meats and processed products are routed to the smokehouse on a conveyor system, or on a "smoking tree" assembly. Production employees transfer the meat to the smokehouse interior where the penetrating effect of time and temperature-controlled smoke determine the final flavor and appearance.

In "rotary" smokehouses, six or seven stories high, meat products hung on racks circulate through the smoke chambers on a moving frame resembling a ferris wheel. The products travel first in an upward direction and then downward for a thorough exposure to the permeating smoke. It requires almost 1-1/2 hours for 1 rack to complete a rotation. Hams and bacon sides usually are smoked in the large "rotary" houses.

In "stationary" smokehouses, meats are hung on standing frames or "treees", rather than on the rotating racks. These houses are smaller, have less capacity, but require much less floor space, and are easier to clean and maintain than the multi-story rotary smokehouses. They are used for smoking smaller sausages and specialties.

Hardwood sawdust, selected for its pleasant smoke aroma, is fed by stokers into a combustion chamber, and the resulting clouds of smoke are funneled into the smokehouse area. Large fans keep the air circulating so that the smoke reaches every corner of the smokehouse.

Smoking times vary according to product, some requiring 4 hours of smoke, and others requiring 24 hours. Temperature control is critical. Internal temperature of a pork product to be labelled "fully cooked" must reach at least 137°F., according to federal inspection regulations. Any trichinae would be destroyed at this temperature. Actually, many smoked meat products are processed to temperatures of 148°F. or higher to develop flavor and firmness. Other products which are to be cooked by the consumer may not require as high a temperature, but these products also depend on precise temperature controls to assure unique flavor qualities.

Smoking is said to give processed meat products their "second helping" of flavor, but according to research specialists, you don't taste the smoke — you smell it!

HANG IT UP TO DRY

One of the most interesting and exacting processes in sausage-making is drying. The practice probably originated centuries before Christ near the Mediterranean Sea as one of the earliest methods of preserving foods. Many names of dry sausages are taken from the city of origin, as each community developed its own particular style. There were differences in the kinds of meat and casing used, methods of chopping meat, seasonings, even in the wrapping of twine around the sausage for hanging to dry. Dried sausage may or may not be smoked after curing.

Sausage drying rooms have carefully controlled humidity, temperature, and air circulation. The drying process must be exact to produce even drying throughout the sausage, without too hard a crust and internal "soft" spots. The air is continuously washed and re-dried to eliminate air-borne spores and molds that could produce undesirable characteristics in the salami.

Drying may begin in the smokehouse, and some semi-dry sausages are processed entirely by smoking. Lebanon Bologna, for example, is smoked for as long as two weeks to develop its texture and flavor.

The distinctive tangy flavor typical of most dry sausages as well as the semi-dry varieties results from a bacterial fermentation. In addition to traditional methods, pure starter cultures have been developed to control and speed fermentation.

Dry and semi-dry sausages usually are eaten cold, although they have not been fully cooked in processing. There are various precautions taken to insure wholesomeness in this type of sausage. Either controlled refrigeration or controlled curing are effective treatments in destroying trichinae, as is heating to 137°F.

Although controlled freezing is an approved method of destroying trichinae, meats to be used in dry sausage are not generally certified this way. Frozen pork is not considered desirable for dry sausage-making.

Federal requirements for the refrigeration methods are specific for minimum temperatures and time in relation to the size of the meat pieces, to assure necessary penetration of freezing temperatures. For example, meat pieces requiring 20 days at 5°F. need only 10 days at -10°F. and 6 days at -20°F.

WHAT'S IN A NAME?

Sausages are usually classified according to processing procedures after stuffing. Although there are differences among sausages within a group, these differences are due primarily to meat combinations and seasonings used, and not to basic processing procedures. Also, they are basically alike, as far as preparation procedures and typical serving uses, are concerned.

The major sausage classifications, as recognized by the American Meat Institute and National Livestock and Meat Board, are:

Fresh Sausage
Uncooked, Smoked Sausage
Cooked, Smoked Sausage
Cooked Sausage
Cooked Meat Specialties
Dry and Semi-Dry Sausage

Fresh Sausage

As the name suggests, fresh sausage is made of meats that have not been cured — generally, selected cuts of fresh pork and sometimes beef. It is the most perishable of all sausage products. Its taste, texture, tenderness and color are directly related to the ratio of fat to lean.

Makers of quality fresh sausage use "trimmings" from primal cuts; that is, the pork loin, ham or shoulders. As with other sausage products, the spice formulation will vary with the meat processor. Expert wurstmachers say the product should be seasoned delicately, with a view toward enhancing the natural meat flavors, not masking them.

Fresh sausage must always be kept under refrigeration. It must be cooked thoroughly before serving, and is usually fried or grilled. Pork sausage and bratwurst are popular varieties in this classification.

Uncooked, Smoked Sausage

This class of sausage has all the characteristics of fresh sausage, with one major difference: it is smoked, producing a different flavor and color. Sometimes it contains fresh meat. These sausages, too, must be cooked thoroughly before serving. Smoked pork sausage and Kielbasa are two of the few examples of uncooked, smoked sausage.

Cooked, Smoked Sausage

Sausage in this category, usually made from cured meats, is chopped or ground, seasoned, stuffed into casings, smoked and cooked. The use of cured meats contributes to flavor, color and preservation of the product.

Cooked, smoked sausage comes in all shapes and sizes — short, thin, long, chubby — and is the largest and most popular of all the categories. The "skinless" varieties have been stripped of their casings after cooking. Wieners and Smokie Links are included in this grouping.

Within this category there are two basic classes: fine-cut sausage such as wieners and bologna, and course-cut sausage such as Berliner or New England.

Cooked Meat Specialties

As the name implies, the primary difference between this classification and cooked sausage is that specialty items, such as meat loaves, head cheese, souse, and scrapple, are included.

These prepared meat products are cooked or baked, and always ready to serve.

Cooked Sausage

Cooked sausage is usually prepared from fresh, uncured meats, although occasionally cured meats are used. Often variety meat or organ meat, such as liver, is included so that sausages in this classification may be especially nutritious. In many instances, the product is smoked; however, the essential difference between this class and cooked, smoked sausage is that the smoking is done after cooking has been completed. This product is always ready to serve.

Liver sausage is the most popular variety in this class, and has enjoyed increasing consumer acceptance in recent years.

Dry, Semi-dry Sausage

All dry sausages are characterized by a bacterial fermentation. This intentional encouragement of a lactic acid bacteria growth is useful as a meat preservative, as well as producing the typical, tangy flavor.

The meat ingredients, after being mixed with spices and curing materials, are generally held for several days in a curing cooler. Afterward, the meat is stuffed into casings, and is started on a carefully-controlled, air-drying process. Some dry sausage is given a light preliminary smoke, but the key production step is the relatively long, continuous, air-drying process.

Principal dry sausage products are salamis and cervelats.

Salamis are coarsely cut; cervelats, finely cut — with few exceptions. They may be smoked, unsmoked, or cooked. Italian and French dry sausages are rarely smoked; other varieties usually are.

Dry sausage requires more production time than other types of sausage, and results in a concentrated form of meat. Medium-dry sausage is about 70 percent its "green" weight when sold. Less-dry and fully-dried sausage range from 60-80 percent of original weight at completion. Logically, many varieties in this group are more expensive per pound than ones in other classifications.

Semi-dry sausages are usually heated in the smoke house to cook the product fully and partially dry it. Semi-dry sausages are semi-soft sausages, with good keeping qualities due to their lactic acid fermentation.

Although dry and semi-dry sausages originally were produced in the winter for use in the summer, and were considered summer sausage, the term "summer sausage" now refers to semi-dry sausages, especially Thuringer Cervelat.

Smoked Meats

Cuts of fresh meat, usually pork, may be cured with salt or brine, and then smoked to give a distinctive flavor and aroma. Current smoking techniques result in a product which is considerably less dry than the smoked products of the last century. The original drying-out in smoking meat contributed greatly to its keeping qualities. Modern refrigeration facilities have reduced the need for this effect of smoking, and methods have been developed which emphasize flavor and aroma rather than drying.

Kitchen preparation of today's fully cooked hams is quite different from the cooking methods necessary for heavily salted, slowly smoked hams which need to be simmered in water to reduce the salt content, and then slowly baked to an internal temperature of 160°F.

Fully cooked hams are heated in the oven without simmering to serving temperature (130°F.) in about half the baking time required for the cook-before-eating type ham. This is a time-saving factor of considerable importance.

Curing and smoking meat inhibit the development of bacterial growth, thus increasing the refrigerated storage life of the product. However, the smoke residues have no effect on mold growth.

Curing produces chemical changes in meat pigments; these are stabilized during the heat of smoking. This accounts for the characteristic deep pink color of the lean muscle of bacon, ham, and other smoked meats.

ALESSANDRIA See Milano Sausage.

APENNIO (dry sausage)
Coarsely chopped pork and beef are seasoned with garlic, then stuffed in the cap end of a hog middle. This Italian-style salami is air-dried, but not smoked. Serve without heating.
  • Ingredients: Beef, pork.
  • Seasonings: Garlic, salt, sugar, mustard, pepper.
  • Availability: Limited distribution.

ARLES, D'ARLES See Milano Salami.

BACON [smoked meat]
Pork "sides" are cured — "sugar-cured" is an often-heard term — and smoked, usually with hardwood chips. Nearly all bacon is now sold sliced, and packaged in 1 or 1/2-lb. units. Thick-sliced bacon is also packaged in 2-lb. units.

Bacon is packaged as "sliced bacon", "thick-sliced bacon", "thin-sliced bacon" and "ends and pieces." Typically, sliced bacon has 20 to 24 slices per lb.; thick slice, 14 to 18 slices per lb., and thin slice, 25 to 35 slices per lb. Actually, thin slice does not mean "thinner" but, rather, smaller slices. It is usually made from small pork "sides" which are shorter and narrower, thus yielding a higher slice count per pound.

The finest quality bacon is chosen from the center slices of selected bacon sides. These "sides" are cut from lean-type hogs, marketed at weights of 200 to 220 lb. The fat will be firm and white, evenly ribboned with lean. Too much lean may result in tough bacon.

Second grades of bacon may be sliced from the same sides as the processor's first quality, but slices will be less uniform in appearance. Other grades usually come from the larger bacon sides.

"Ends and pieces" are the irregular shaped pieces from either end of the bacon side (only the center slices will be uniform in length) and also part slices. This type of bacon may offer good value for flavoring, and use as cooked, crumbled bacon.

Bacon flavor and aroma is very elusive, and sliced bacon exposed to air and light loses quality rapidly. The innovation of vacuum-packing for sliced bacon was an important development for the consumer. Under refrigeration in an unopened vacuum package, bacon shows little or no loss of flavor and quality even after several days' storage.

Bacon should be cooked at low temperature in a skillet or griddle or baked on a rack in a shallow pan in a preheated 400°F. oven for 10 to 15 minutes.
  • Availability: Widespread distribution.

BAKED BLACK PUDDING [cooked sausage] See Blood Sausage.
A type of blood sausage. The mixture is baked in shallow pans, then cooled. To serve, it is sliced, then heated in a skillet or deep fat.

BEEF LOAF See Sliced Cold Meats.

BEEF SALAMI See Cotto Salami.

BEEF SUMMER SAUSAGE See Summer Sausage.

BEERWURST, BEER SALAMI [cooked, smoked sausage]
Meat is chopped and blended with curing ingredients and seasonings. After 48 hours, mixture is stuffed into beef bungs, and cooked at high temperatures in the smokehouse. When a round shape is desired for uniform slicing, large artificial casings are used.
Slice for sandwiches, cold meat platters, snacks.
  • Ingredients: Beef, pork.
  • Seasonings: Garlic, pepper, salt, sugar.
  • Availability: Packaged slices in supermarkets or bulk to slice in sausage shops, delicatessens.

BERLINER [**cooked, smoked sausage**] See New England Brand Sausage.

A coarsely cut sausage made of cured lean pork. May also include a small amount of beef. After curing, the meat is stuffed into large artificial casings, or beef casings. Berliner is smoked from 2 to 4 hours, and then cooked in water from 4 to 6 hours. Contains no spice.

Serve for sandwiches, cold meat platters, salads.

- Ingredients: Lean cured pork, or lean cured pork and small amount of beef.
- Seasonings: Salt, sugar.
- Availability: Generally sold as sliced cold meat. National distribution.

BERLINER BLOOD SAUSAGE [**cooked sausage**] See Blood Sausage.

A variety of blood sausage containing diced bacon instead of ham fat, snouts and lips. After cooking, the sausage is surface dried and smoked.

BLACK PUDDING [**cooked sausage**] See Blood Sausage.

English verion of blood sausage. Ingredients, which include cereal, are stuffed into large sheep casings and tied into 1-lb. rings. Typical seasonings are allspice, black pepper, coriander, ground mustard, celery seed, salt.

BLOOD SAUSAGE [**cooked sausage**]

This specialty sausage is undoubtedly of high food value, but its acceptance in this country is limited. The ingredients, except blood and ham fat, are cooked before grinding, then combined with seasonings, blood (and ham fat, if used), and ladled into casings, usually beef bungs or hog middles. After additional cooking in water, the casings are pricked to release any air, then chilled in cold water. Blood sausage is sometimes made into links 4 to 5 in. in length.

- Ingredients: Pork skins, pork jowls, blood (usually beef). May also include sweet pickled ham fat, snouts and lips.
- Seasonings: Allspice, black pepper, ground cloves, onion, salt.

- Availability: Chiefly consumed in Great Britain and Scotland.

BLOOD AND TONGUE SAUSAGE [**cooked sausage**]

Cooked and cured pork or lamb tongues are included with blood sausage mixture in beef casings 10 to 12 in. long. The tongues are so inserted that they will be in the center of the sausage when it is sliced. Tongues constitute about one-third of the finished weight of the sausage.

Slice for sandwiches, cold meat platters.

- Ingredients: Blood sausage mixture, cured pork, or lamb tongues.
- Seasonings: Allspice, black pepper, ginger, marjoram, salt, sugar.
- Availability: Sausage shops, delicatessens.

BOCKWURST [**fresh sausage**]

A very perishable, sausage-like delicacy, typically identified with Easter-time. Traditionally, it is made in the spring during the bock beer season, from which it acquires its name. The ingredients are finely chopped, and stuffed into wide, sheep rounds. The links, 5 in. in length, are light colored. Bockwurst is panboiled or scalded, then chilled. Constant refrigeration is essential.

Must be thoroughly cooked before serving.

- Ingredients: Freshly ground pork and veal, milk. May also include raw egg.
- Seasonings: Chopped green onions or chives, cloves, ground mace, parsley, sage, white pepper.
- Availability: Very limited distribution because of perishability.

BOHEMIAN PRESKY [**cooked, smoked sausage**]

Pork trimmings are cured only with salt, then ground, and seasoned. The meat is stuffed into beef weasands, and smoked. Baking is done in smokehouses, using high finishing temperatures.

- Ingredients: Cured pork.
- Seasonings: Garlic, pepper, salt, sugar.
- Availability: Specialty item in limited distribution.

BOLOGNA [cooked, smoked sausage]

A finely-cut sausage, generally stuffed into large casings, but other shapes are also made. This sausage, second only to wieners in popularity, originated in Bologna, Italy, during the Middle Ages.

Quality bologna is carefully mixed and stuffed to give a uniform color and even texture free of air bubbles. "Regular" bologna is always a blend of beef and pork, but an all-beef style is gaining in popularity. Garlic, a typical spice in either version, is a more prominant flavor in all beef bologna.

SLICED BOLOGNA Cut from large round "sticks". Usually 4 to 5 in. in diameter.

RING BOLOGNA Meat is stuffed into casings about 2 in. in diameter, and cut into pieces of about 1 lb. Ends are tied together forming horseshoe shape or "ring".

CHUB BOLOGNA A very smoothly blended bologna mixture of beef, pork and smoked bacon is processed in 1-lb. units in plastic wrap "tubes." An especially convenient style to slice for snacks.

Serve slices in sandwiches, with salads, cold meat platters. Heat ring bologna to serve with potato salad.

- Ingredients: Beef and pork, or all beef. Some processors may also use dry milk solids, cereals.
- Seasonings: Black pepper, cloves, coriander, garlic, ginger, nutmeg.
- Availability: Undoubtedly the most popular, cold, sliced meat. General distribution.

BONELESS HAM   See Ham.

BONELESS PORK LOIN   See Dewey Ham.

BOTERHAM WURST [cooked, smoked sausage]

This Dutch-style sausage is made of veal and pork which is coarsely chopped, cured, and then finely chopped. It is blended with coarsely chopped pork fat and seasonings, then stuffed into ox bungs, smoked, and cooked.

- Ingredeints: Pork, veal.
- Seasonings: White pepper, ginger, nutmeg, mace, salt, sugar.

- Availability: Specialty item in limited distribution.

BRATWURST [fresh sausage]

Bratwurst is German for "frying sausage". Originally a fresh sausage, made of coarsely ground beef and pork, zestily seasoned, some processors now make it in a pre-cooked version. Bratwurst is especially popular for grilling, so production is greatest during the cookout season. Links are large, typically about 1-3/8 in. in diameter. Usually 6 to 7 links per lb. Must be thoroughly cooked.* Very popular for charcoal broiling, especially in the Midwest. Grill and serve with buns or with German potato salad.

- Ingredients: Beef and pork, or pork and veal.
- Seasonings: Coriander, ginger, mustard, pepper, sage, salt, sugar, or thyme. Spice formulas vary greatly.
- Availability: Distribution greatest during the "outdoor grilling" season. Popular in the Midwest.
- * Exception: Fully cooked versions also available; check label carefully.

BRAUNSCHWEIGER LIVER SAUSAGE [cooked sausage]

A good grade of smoked liver sausage may be called Braunschweiger; it was in this town in Germany that the art of smoking liver sausage first originated. This desirable flavor may be developed either by careful smoking at low temperature of the cooked liver sausage, or by including proper amounts of smoked meat in the formulation.

Slice for sandwiches, spread on crackers for appetizers.

- Ingredients: Beef, pork livers, smoked bacon.
- Seasonings: Coriander, ginger, marjoram, onion, black pepper, salt.
- Availability: National distribution.

BRAUNSCHWEIGER METTWURST, "SMEARWURST" [cooked sausage]

An all-pork sausage made of finely ground meat, mildly cured, and smoked at low temperature. It is characterized by a soft spreading consistency similar to liver sausage. Hog or beef rounds are used for casings, and are tied in a ring, or into links 2 to 3 in. long. Certified pork is used, as processing temperatures are kept low.

To serve, spread on bread or crackers.
- Ingredients: Certified pork trimmings.
- Seasonings: Coriander, ground white pepper, salt, sugar.
- Availability: Delicatessen or specialty shop item.

BREAKFAST BEEF, BEEF BACON [smoked meat]

Beef brisket is cured, and smoked in similar fashion as pork sides. It is usually sliced and packaged. Consumer acceptance to this type of product has been limited.

BREAKFAST SAUSAGE See Smokie Links.

BUTIFARA CATALANE [cooked specialty] See Head Cheese.

A type of head cheese made of finely ground head meat and rinds, stuffed into hog casings, and cooked. It is seasoned with pepper, salt, and oregano.

CAMBRIDGE-TYPE PORK SAUSAGE [fresh sausage]

An English-style sausage of ground lean pork, pork fat cubes, cooked rice, and rusk. Mixture is stuffed into narrow or medium hog casings.

Must be thoroughly cooked before serving.
- Ingredients: Cooked rice, pork, pork fat, rusk.
- Seasonings: Allspice, cayenne, ginger, mace, mustard, salt, white pepper.
- Availability: Little distribution in the United States.

CANADIAN STYLE BACON [smoked meat]

The bone is carefully removed from 12- to 20-lb. pork loins, and then the loins are cured by dry curing or stitch pumping. This is followed by a brine pickle, then meat is stuffed into fibrous or stretch casings. The cured loins are slowly smoked at low temperatures. Canadian bacon may be fully cooked when purchased, or require additional cooking. Check labels carefully.

Serve fully cooked Canadian bacon slices for sandwiches, cold meat platters and with salads. May be fried or grilled.
- Availability: National distribution.

CANNED HAM See Ham.

CAPPICOLA [smoked meat]

This is a smoked meat of Italian origin. A mixture of paprika and ground red pepper pods is rubbed into cured pork butts, then each butt is stuffed into a beef bung, smoked, and airdried. Cappicola is made of certified pork, or heated in smokehouses to 137°F., and may be eaten without cooking.
- Ingredients: Pork butt.
- Seasonings: Paprika, red pepper pods, salt, sugar.
- Availability: Specialty shops, delicatessens.

CERVELAT [semi-dry sausage]

Meat is finely ground, and mixed with curing ingredients and seasonings. After curing, meat is stuffed into beef middles, 11 in. in length, or hog casings 25 in. long. After 48 hours in the curing cooler, it is warmed up, surface dried, and then smoked overnight.
- Ingredients: Beef, pork.
- Seasonings: Ground pepper, mustard, red pepper, salt, sugar.
- Availability: Sausage shops.

CHEESE SMOKIES [cooked, smoked] See Smokie Links.

Small cubes of cheese are added to Smokie Link batter. Stuffing, linking and processing is the same as for Smokie Links.

CHIPOLATA [fresh sausage]

Lean pork is chopped quite fine (fat pork more coarsely), and blended with seasonings. Rice and rusks are also typically included in the formula. Mixture is stuffed into sheep casings, and linked 16 to 20 to the pound in twos or threes.
- Ingredients: Pork, rice, rusks.
- Seasonings: Salt, white pepper, coriander, pimiento, nutmeg, thyme.

CHOPPED HAM See Sliced Cold Meats.

CHOPPED, PRESSED, SMOKED, SLICED BEEF [smoked meat]

Beef "hams" may be cured and smoked just as pork hams are, except both the curing and smoking process takes much longer. The smoked beef is sliced, usually very thin, and then packaged, or sealed, in sterilized jars.

CHORIZOS [dry sausage]

A Spanish sausage made from coarsely chopped prime pork cuts. It is seasoned with Spanish pimiento which gives the sausage a fine flavor, and a bright appetizing appearance. Seasonings may include garlic.

Chorizos are a lightly smoked and dried sausage popular in Spanish, Portuguese and Mexican areas. Mixture is stuffed into hog casings, and linked in 4-in. lengths. Links are not twisted, but tied off with string. Chorizos are also tied in 1-in. links, giving the appearance of a string of brightly colored balls.

Chorizos "sausage balls" are used in soups and stews.

CHUBBIES See Knackwurst.

COCKTAIL LOAF [cooked loaf]

A popular, American style, sliced cold meat characterized by colorfully diced sweet red peppers and pickles. Meats are finely chopped.

Use slices in sandwiches, for cold meat platters.
- Ingredients: Beef, pork, red sweet peppers, pickles.
- Seasonings: Cinnamon, coriander, dextrose, ginger, nutmeg, pepper, salt.
- Availability: General distribution.

COOKED HAM [sliced cold meat]

Cured hams are pressed into rectangular molds and fully cooked. After chilling, meat is sliced, usually quite thin.

Serve in sandwiches, on cold meat platters, with salads.
- Availability: General distribution.

COOKED SALAMI See Cotto Salami.

COTTO SALAMI, COOKED SALAMI [cooked, smoked, sausage]

A mildly flavored salami. Coarsely ground meats are mixed, and cured for 48 hours, then remixed, seasoned, and stuffed into large casings. The "sticks" are smoked, then cooked in dry heat.

Slice for sandwiches, cold meat platters. Also delicious in salads, casseroles.
- Ingredients: Beef, pork.
- Seasonings: Whole black peppercorns, dextrose, garlic, salt.
- Availability: Generally sold as sliced cold meat. National distribution.

D'ARLES See Milano Sausage.

DEVONSHIRE STYLE SAUSAGE [fresh sausage]

Dry, firm, fresh pork sausage is wrapped in hog caul fat, instead of being stuffed into casings. Originated in Scotland. The sausage, about an inch in diameter, is cut into 3- or 4-in. lengths for packing into cartons.

Must be thoroughly cooked before serving.
- Ingredients: Freshly ground pork, caul fat for casings.
- Seasonings: Mace, pepper, sage, salt, sugar.
- Availability: Limited to specialty shops.

DEWEY HAM, BONELESS PORK LOIN, LOIN ROLL [smoked meat]

Mildly cured, fresh pork loins are boned, matched, and tied tightly together in three or four places. Sixteen to 18-in. lengths are placed in beef casings, wrapped with loops of seine cord, then smoked and cooked.

DUTCH HEAD CHEESE [cooked specialty] See Head Cheese.

Meats are ground very fine, and include pigs' feet, occasionally calves' feet, too. Seasonings include bay leaves, dill pickles, and caraway.

DUTCH LOAF, OLD-FASHIONED LOAF, FAMILY BRAND [baked loaf]

A coarsely ground combination of pork and beef with a distinctive onion flavor. Baked in round pans, or, for uniform slicing to package, in long rectangular-shaped pans.

Slice for sandwiches, snacks, meat platters.
- Ingredients: Beef, pork.
- Seasonings: Dextrose, onion powder, pepper, salt.
- Availability: National distribution.

FAGGOTS [cooked, smoked sausage]

Cured meats are chopped and blended with spices. Medium sheep casings or small hog casings are stuffed with the chopped meat, and linked in pairs, each about 6 in. long. Links are then smoked and cooked.
- Ingredients: Beef, pork, veal.
- Seasonings: Cardamom, coriander, ginger, nutmeg, pepper, salt, sugar.
- Availability: Limited distribution.

FAMILY BRAND LOAF See Dutch Loaf.

FARMER SAUSAGE CERVELAT [dry sausage]

Beef, chopped medium fine, and pork, cut into 1/2-in. pieces, is mixed with curing ingredients and spices, and held for 2 or 3 days. It is then stuffed into beef middles which measure 2 - 2-1/4 in. in diameter, and 19 in. in length. The sausage is smoked for 60-84 hours, and dried from 25-60 days.
- Ingredients: Beef, pork.
- Seasonings: Mustard, pepper, salt, sugar.

FIESTA LOAF See Sliced Cold Meats.

FRANKS, FRANKFURTERS [cooked, smoked sausage]
Also see Wieners.

From Frankfurt, Germany, comes the frankfurter or frank. It was originally made of beef and pork, not too finely ground, and seasoned with more zest than the wiener, usually having a well-defined garlic flavor.

Pure beef franks have become increasingly popular, and in some areas outsell "hotdogs" made of blended meats. Ten links per lb. is a standard size.

Typically served warm, although it is not necessary to heat them.
- Ingredients: Beef and pork or beef.
- Seasonings: Coriander, garlic, ground mustard, nutmeg, salt, sugar, white pepper.
- Availability: National distribution.

FRESH POLISH SAUSAGE [fresh sausage]

Coarsely chopped pork shoulder is seasoned, stuffed into hog casings, and linked 10 to 14 in. long.

This style of Polish sausage is simmered or baked until crisp, and served with sauerkraut.
- Ingredients: Pork.
- Seasonings: Garlic, marjoram, salt, sugar, white pepper.

FRESH THURINGER [fresh sausage]

Made of all pork, or pork and veal, finely ground. The links are usually dipped briefly in hot water, then chilled. Fresh Thuringer is stuffed in large hog casings, and linked 3 to 5 to the lb. Dry milk solids are often included in the formula. Must be thoroughly cooked before serving.
- Ingredients: Pork, or pork and veal, and usually dry milk solids.
- Seasonings: Coriander, ginger, ground celery seed, mace, pepper, salt, sugar.
- Availability: Moderate distribution, mostly in sausage shops.

FRIZZES [dry sausage]

An Italian-style dry sausage, typically 10 to 12 in. long, 3 in. in diameter, and closely wrapped with Italian hemp. Pork and beef are chopped medium fine, seasoned, cured, and then stuffed into hog middles. The product is air-dried from 60 to 90 days. Frizzes are not smoked.

GALICIAN SAUSAGE [cooked, smoked sausage]

Cured meats are seasoned, and stuffed into beef rounds cut

to 36-in. lengths. Sausages are then smoked, with a very high, final temperature baking the sausage. Cooling is done in a draft of air, which produces the wrinkled appearance characteristic of Galician Sausage.

- Ingredients: Beef and pork.
- Seasonings: Corinader, garlic, pepper.

GENOA SALAMI [dry sausage]

A distinctive cording in a basket-weave style identifies Genoa Salami. This sausage is made of coarsely ground pork, lightly seasoned with garlic. Aged wine is sometimes used to give it additional flavor. Sewed hog casings 3 in. in diameter and 18 in. long are used for stuffing. Genoa Salami is air-dried, but not smoked.

Slice thin for snacks, sandwiches.

- Ingredients: Pork, sometimes wine.
- Seasonings: Garlic, pepper, salt, sugar.
- Availability: Sausage shops, delicatessens.

GERMAN SALAMI, HARD SALAMI [dry sausage]

This coarsely cut sausage is made of equal weights of beef and pork, seasoned with salt, white pepper, garlic, and sugar. After curing, the meat is stuffed into sewed beef middles that are 20 in. long and 3-1/2 in. in diameter, or hog casings. Loops of twine are drawn slightly into the casing every 2 in. to give a scalloped appearance. German salami is air-dried, and may also by lightly smoked.

Slice very thin to serve for snacks, sandwiches, chef's salads.

- Ingredients: Beef, pork.
- Seasonings: Garlic, black pepper, salt, sugar.
- Availability: General distribution.

GOTEBORG See Swedish Sausage.

HAM [smoked meat]

The cut of pork termed "ham" is the thigh of a hog, and is marketed as "fresh ham", "smoked ham", or "cooked ham."

The flavor acquired by curing and smoking is so popular that few hams are sold fresh, and usually we think of ham as cured, cooked, and probably smoked meat.

Smoked hams are divided into two groups by federal inspection: 'cook before serving' and 'fully cooked.' It is important to check labels before preparing ham, as baking times for these styles are quite different.

Cook-before-serving ham must be heated to an internal temperature of 160°F. before eating. This is best done at moderate temperature (325°F. in the oven or for simmering). Cooking time will depend on the size of the ham, and the amount of bone.

Fully cooked hams may be eaten without cooking, but generally are heated to develop flavor. An internal temperature of 130°F. is considered desirable for serving.

Fully cooked hams may be 'bone-in' or boneless. Quality of bone-in hams will vary, depending on the size, the amount of fat trimmed or removed, and amount of bone, as well as the quality of the cure, and smoking.

Terms used to describe processes which add to the quality of a bone-in ham and decrease waste are "skinless," "shankless," and "defatted." The skin, the shank bone, and excess fat may be removed to reduce the size of a ham, and create a more convenient, more attractive ham which yields more servings per pound.

Ham is sold as whole ham, half ham, center slices, butt end, and shank end. The center slices yield the highest portion of edible meat, and usually command the highest price per pound. The shank end yields the lowest, and costs the least per pound.

Fully cooked boneless hams are available to consumers as smoked ham or canned ham. (Some canned hams are also smoked.) Removal of the entire ham bone shortens heating time, simplifies slicing, and yields more servings per pound.

Canned hams are usually available in two shapes — "pear" and "pullman." After the bone and excess fat are removed, the meat is formed under pressure into the desired shape before further processing is done. Most canned hams are 3 lb. or larger, although pieces as small as 1-1/2 lb. are canned.

All hams should be refrigerated, including canned hams. Smoked hams may be stored in the refrigerator for 2 to 3 weeks; canned hams, unopened, indefinitely. Freezing ham is not recommended as flavor loss, even rancidity, may develop, and texture may be affected. Freezing canned ham may also cause damage to the seam of the can.

HAM AND CHEESE LOAF [cooked loaf]

Firm cheese is chopped into small cubes, then combined with finely ground ham. Mixture is stuffed into rectangular-shaped pans and cooked.

- Ingredients: Cheese, ham.
- Availability: Sliced and packaged, or sold in loaves to delicatessens and sausage shops to slice.

HARD SALAMI See German Salami.

HEAD CHEESE [cooked specialty]

Head cheese is made of edible portions of pork head, including cheek and temple meat, skins, snouts, and upperlips. Pork tongue may be included. After thorough cooking, materials are chopped and mixed with the jelly water in which they were cooked, and with spices. Pork hearts may be included, but original formulas included only "head" meats.

Slice and serve cold for sandwiches, cold meat platters.

- Ingredients: Cured pork tongue. Pork snouts.
- Seasonings: Caraway, coriander, dextrose, mustard, red pepper, salt, and sage, or thyme.
- Availability: National distribution.

HOLSTEINER CERVELAT [dry sausage] See Farmer Cervelat.

Varies from Farmer Cervelat only in size. Wide beef rounds are used for casings, forming a ring-shaped sausage.

HONEY LOAF See Sliced Cold Meats.

HUNGARIAN KOLBASE [cooked, smoked sausage]

Finely ground, cured meats are seasoned, stuffed into hog casings, and smoked.

- Ingredients: Cured beef, pork.
- Seasonings: Coriander, garlic, nutmeg, paprika, pepper, salt, sugar.

ITALIAN PORK SAUSAGE, SALSICCIA [fresh sausage]

A brightly colored, rope-style sausage made of finely cut pork trimmings. More highly spiced than fresh pork sausage. Stuffed into medium hog casings. Unlinked.

- Ingredients: Pork.
- Availability: Moderate distribution.

ITALIAN SALAMI (dry sausage)

There are many Italian salamis with similar characteristics. They are made of cured, lean pork, coarsely chopped, cured lean beef, finely chopped. Meats are seasoned with garlic and other spices, and typically are moistened with red wine or grape juice. Mixture is stuffed into large casings, and tied with flax twine wrapped at 1/2-in. intervals. Italian salamis are air-dried (never smoked) for nine to ten weeks.

- Ingredients: Beef, pork, red wine.
- Seasonings: Cinnamon, cloves, garlic, nutmeg, salt, sugar, white pepper, whole peppercorns.

JATERNICE (cooked sausage)

A sausage made of pork snouts which is seasoned with allspice, marjoram, garlic, salt, and pepper. Barley groats, softened by steam, and some well-trimmed livers and lean pork may be included in the formula. Large hog casings or beef rounds are stuffed with mixture, then cooked. This is a specialty item with limited distribution.

JELLIED BEEF LOAF (cooked loaf)

Cooked beef is chopped, and molded with gelatin.
Slice for sandwiches, cold meat platters.
- •Ingredients: Beef.
- •Seasonings: Celery, onion, pepper, salt, sugar.
- •Availability: Good distribution sliced in packages. Also available in loaves to be sliced, at delicatessens and sausage shops.

JELLIED CORNED BEEF LOAF (cooked loaf)

Cooked corned beef is chopped, and molded with gelatin.
Slice for sandwiches, cold meat platters.
- •Ingredients: Corned beef.
- •Seasonings: Pepper, salt, sugar.
- •Availability: Generally available sliced in packages.

JELLIED PORK AND TURKEY LOAF See Sliced Cold Meats.

JELLIED TONGUE (cooked specialty)

Sweet-pickle cured pork, lamb, or sheep tongues are skinned, and cooked until tender. After trimming and rinsing, they are placed in casings or loaf pans, and covered with clear gelatin that has been seasoned with bay leaves and lemon extract.
Slice and serve cold for sandwiches, snacks.
- •Ingredients: Lamb, pork, or sheep tongues, gelatin.
- •Seasonings: Bay leaves, lemon extract, salt, sugar, vinegar.
- •Availability: Moderate to limited distribution.

JUBILEE HAM See Ham.

KIELBASA, KOLBASSY (uncooked, smoked sausage)

A sausage of Polish origin. The links, made of coarsely ground lean pork and finely ground beef, are 1-1/2 in. in diameter and 4 to 5 in. long, or more typically, 8 to 10 in. long. Links are smoked for 4 to 6 hours.
Kolbassy is the Czechoslovakian name for this type of sausage.

Must be cooked before eating. If the label indicates the links are fully cooked, heat to serve.
- •Ingredients: Pork and Beef.
- •Seasonings: Highly seasoned with black pepper, garlic, salt, sugar, thyme.

KISKA (cooked sausage)

A type of heavy blood pudding with oat groats included in the ingredients. It is stuffed into a beef round, or large hog casings, and thoroughly cooked. Sections of the oat groat are apparent when the product is sliced.
Kiska is similar to Jaternice, except it is made with blood.

KNACKWURST, KNOCHBLAUCH (cooked, smoked sausage)

Similar in ingredients to frankfurters and bologna. Knackwurst is stuffed into beef rounds, and tied off in 4-in. lengths. It is usually flavored with garlic. Both natural casing and skinless styles are made.
Although fully cooked, Knackwurst is usually served hot. Simmer gently, or cover with boiling water and let stand ten minutes.
- •Ingredients: Beef, pork.
- •Seasonings: Coriander, garlic, nutmeg, salt, sugar, white pepper.
- •Availability: Both natural casing and skinless links are available.

KOSHER SALAMI (semi-dry sausage)

Kosher beef chucks are ground medium fine, and mixed with small cubes of brisket fat, salt, white pepper, paprika, and garlic. After curing, meat is stuffed, cooled, and then smoked.
- •Ingredients: Kosher beef.
- •Seasonings: Coriander, garlic, nutmeg, mustard, pepper, salt, sugar.

KRAKOW (cooked, smoked sausage)

Very lean pork, usually cut from the blade, is coarsely

ground, and mixed with finely chopped beef, seasoned, and stuffed into beef middles 3 in. in diameter and 20 in. long. It is then smoked, and cooked. Krakow resembles New England Brand Sausage.

Serve slices cold for sandwiches, snacks.
- Ingredients: Beef, pork.
- Seasonings: Black pepper, garlic, salt, sugar.
- Availability: Popular in Polish-German areas.

LACHSHINKEN (smoked meat)

Boneless, cured pork loins are sprinkled with pepper and paprika, and stuffed into a beef middle, two to each casing. They are smoked at low temperature to 137°F., or if made of certified pork, may be given a cold smoke.

In Germany, loins are wrapped with back fat, tied with string, and lightly smoked.

Usually sliced, and eaten without cooking.
- Ingredients: Pork loins.
- Seasonings: Paprika, pepper, salt, sugar.

LANDJAEGER CERVELAT (dry sausage)

A Swiss style sausage. Meat is stuffed and linked, then pressed to give a four-sided, stick-like link. Landjaeger is heavily smoked and dried, giving an almost black, wrinkled appearance.

Serve cold for snacks, sandwiches.
- Ingredients: Beef and pork.
- Seasonings: Mustard, pepper, salt, sugar.
- Availability: Specialty item available in ethnic areas.

LEBANON BOLOGNA (semi-dry sausage)

This sausage originated in Lebanon, Pa., and its manufacture is limited due to the special facilities required. Curing is similar to regular bologna, as is seasoning, but it is made entirely of lean beef chuck, and is not as finely chopped. It is smoked in a cool, wet, heavy smoke for 5 to 14 days, then dried for 24 hours to finish the surface and color. Typically sliced and served cold, especially for sandwiches, snacks. Distinctive tangy flavor combines best with hearty food and beverage.

- Ingredients: Beef.
- Seasonings: Cloves, coriander, ginger, pepper, salt, sugar.
- Availability: Distributed nationally.

LINGUISA, LONGANIZA (smoked sausage)

These Portuguese sausages are made from coarsely ground pork butts. The meat is cured in vinegar pickle before being stuffed into hog cases. The sausages are heavily smoked for about 12 hours.
- Ingredients: Pork butts.
- Seasonings: Cinnamon, cumin seed, garlic, red pepper, salt, sugar.

LITTLE SMOKIES See Smokie Links.

LITTLE WIENERS See Wieners.

LIVER LOAF (cooked sausage)

This sandwich-size form of liver sausage is characterized by square-shaped slices. The mixture is stuffed into a casing about 4 in. by 15 in. long, then pressed into a loaf, and cooked.

Another method of making liver loaf is to line pans with back fat, fill pans with liver sausage mixture, and fold fat over the top. After cooking and chilling, the loaves are removed from the pans, leaving the fat encasing the liver sausage.

Serve cold for sandwiches, cold meat platters.
- Ingredients: Pork.
- Seasonings: Coriander, ginger, marjoram, onion, pepper, salt, sugar.
- Availability: National distribution.

LIVER PUDDING (cooked specialty)

Finely chopped pork liver, meat by-products, and soya flour, or other binder are mixed, then stuffed into beef rounds, and tied off in rings. These are thoroughly cooked in hot water. The cooked sausage is pudding-like in consistency, hence its name. Typical seasonings are ginger, marjoram, pepper, sage, salt, sugar, and thyme.

Liver pudding is popular in Pennsylvania Dutch

communities, and typically is served for breakfast. It is sliced, dipped in cornmeal, and fried.

LIVER SAUSAGE (cooked specialty)
Also See Braunschweiger Liver Sausage

A very nutritious, distinctively flavored sausage which contains no less than 30 percent liver (typically pork liver) combined with pork, or pork and veal. Quality may vary greatly depending on ingredients used, and processing. Ingredients are chopped, and blended into a smooth, homogenous mass, and stuffed into natural or artificial casings in either "sticks" about 2 in. in diameter or tied in rings of about 1 lb. It is also packaged in plastic wrap in units of 1/2 lb., 1lb., or less. Liver sausage is fully cooked, and may also be smoked, or include smoked meat such as bacon.

Serve cold for sandwiches, snacks, meat platters.
- Ingredients: Pork jowls, pork liver.
- Seasonings: Cloves, mace, marjoram, onion, salt, sugar, white pepper.
- Availability: National distribution.

LOIN ROLL See Dewey Ham.

LOUKANIKA (fresh sausage)

This Greek style sausage is made of lamb and pork. Seasonings include orange, allspice, whole pepper, and salt. Loukanika must be cooked before eating.

LUNCHEON MEAT See Sliced Cold Meats.

LUNCHEON ROLL See Sliced Cold Meats.

LUXURY LOAF See Sliced Cold Meats.

LYONS SAUSAGE (dry sausage)

An all-pork sausage of French origin. Lean pork is chopped very fine, and combined with small diced fat and seasonings. It is stuffed into large casings, cured, and air-dried.

METTWURST (uncooked, smoked sausage)

Cured meats are ground and lightly seasoned. Links are 1-1/2 in. or more in diameter. Mettwurst has a smooth, "spreadable" consistency similar to Braunschweiger Mettwurst. To serve, spread on crackers, sandwiches.
- Ingredients: Beef and pork.
- Seasonings: Allspice, coriander, ginger, mustard, salt, sugar.

METZ (semi-dry sausage)

Cured lean beef and pork and well-cured bacon are finely chopped, seasoned, and stuffed into beef middles. It is air-dried for five days, then smoked in a cool smoke.
- Ingredients: Beef, pork, well-cured bacon.
- Seasonings: Black pepper, coriander, salt, sugar.

MILANO SALAMI (dry sausage)

Similar to Italian sausage, except Milano is fine cut, while the Italian is coarse cut. Lean beef, pork, and pork fat are finely chopped, then blended with curing agents and seasonings. After stuffing into hog bungs, it is wrapped at about 1/2-in. intervals with hemp twine and then air-dried for 9 to 10 weeks.
- Ingredients: Beef, pork, pork fat.
- Seasonings: Garlic, salt, sugar, white pepper, whole white peppercorns.

'D'ARLES' is similar to Milano, although it is made with more coarsely chopped meat. This salami of French origin is corded "criss-cross" style.

'ALESSANDRIS' is made of fresh, lean pork butts and enough beef chuck to bind the sausage together. It is seasoned with garlic, and stuffed into hog casings. This is an American version of an Italian-type salami.

MINCED HAM LOAF (cooked loaf)

Cured, lean, ham trimmings are ground, and mixed with spices, then packed tightly into molds. Loaves are cooked, cooled, and either sliced for packaging, or whole loaves are browned in a hot oven.

Serve cold for sandwiches, cold meat platters, in salads.

•Ingredients: Cured Ham.
•Seasonings: Allspice, caraway, nutmeg, pepper, salt, sugar.
• Availability: National distribution in slices, packaged, or in loaves to slice in sausage shops, delicatessens.

MINCED ROLL (cooked, smoked sausage)

A lean, finely ground sausage which is smoked and cooked much like Cotto Salami.

Slice and serve cold for sandwiches, cold meat platters.
•Ingredients: Beef, pork.
•Seasonings: Allspice, caraway seed, cinnamon, cloves, coriander, mace, pepper, salt, sugar.
•Availability: Moderate distribution.

MORTADELLA (dry sausage)

Finely chopped, lean ham is seasoned with garlic and anise to make this Italian style sausage. Cubes of white fat are mixed with lean ham before stuffing in beef casings. After a light smoking and drying, the sausage is wrapped in tin foil for exporting. May also be stuffed into beef bladders, and tied with string. This style will weight 8 lb. or more.

Mortadella looks like finely chopped bologna, but is much darker in color.

When the sausage is sliced, cubes of white fat, and occasionally pistachio nuts, are seen.

Serve slices in sandwiches, for snacks.
•Ingredients: Ham, pork fat.
•Seasonings: Anise, coriander, garlic, peppercorns, salt, sugar.

NEW ENGLAND BRAND SAUSAGE, NEW ENGLAND SAUSAGE, NEW ENGLAND HAM SAUSAGE (cooked, smoked sausage) See Berliner.

A Berliner-style sausage made of cured lean pork. As federal inspection requires that product names are not misleading, the name New England Ham Sausage cannot be used unless the product is made predominantly of ham. Likewise, federally inspected product cannot be labelled "New England Sausage" unless it is made in New England, so the title "New England Brand" is used for the product when made in other areas.

OLD-FASHIONED LOAF See Dutch Loaf.

OLIVE LOAF (cooked loaf)

Whole, green, stuffed olives and chopped, red sweet peppers are included with finely chopped beef and pork to make this colorful loaf for slicing.

Serve cold for sandwiches, cold meat platters.
•Ingredients: Beef, pork, red sweet peppers, stuffed olives.
•Seasonings: Allspice, sugar, nutmeg, pepper, salt.
•Availability: Packaged slices, or whole loaves for slicing. National distribution.

OXFORD STYLE SAUSAGE (cooked, smoked sausage)

Meat is cured, then chopped and stuffed into beef bungs 18 in. in length. It is wrapped with string before smoking and cooking.
•Ingredients: Lean pork trimmings.
•Seasonings: Salt, sugar.

PASTRAMI, PASTROMI, PASTROMA, PASTIRIMA (dry sausage)

Flat pieces of lean beef: shoulder clods, plate beef, briskets, or rounds of good quality beef are dried, then cured for about 20 days, rinsed well and then rubbed with a paste of garlic powder, ground cumin seed, red pepper, cinnamon, cloves, and allspice. They are then smoked and cooked.

Serve cold for sandwiches.
•Ingredients: Beef.
•Seasonings: Allspice, cinnamon, cloves, cumin seed, garlic, red pepper, salt, sugar.
•Availability: Metropolitan markets.

PEPPERED LOAF See Sliced Cold Meats.

PEPPERED BEEF LOAF See Sliced Cold Meats.

PEPPERONI (dry sausage)

Named for its pepper spicing, the meat is coarsely cut, mixed with seasonings, and cured before stuffing into pork casings about 1-1/2 in. in diameter and twin linked in pieces 10 to 12 in. long. Dried for 3 to 4 weeks at moderate temperatures.

This zesty sausage is popular for pizzas, other Italian style dishes.

- •Ingredients: Boneless beef chuck, lean pork trimmings.
- •Seasonings: Cayenne pepper, peeled garlic, pepperoni pepper, pimento, salt, sugar, whole anise.
- •Availability: National distribution.

PICKLE AND PIMENTO LOAF (cooked loaf)

Chopped pickles and pimento are combined with finely ground pork and beef to make this attractive loaf for slicing. Serve slices cold for sandwiches, cold meat platters.

- •Ingredients: Beef, pickles, pimento, pork, veal.
- •Seasonings: Allspice, nutmeg, pepper, salt, sugar.
- •Availability: Packaged slices, or loaves for slicing.

PICNICS (smoked meat)

Pork shoulder may be cured and smoked like ham, producing a very "ham-like" flavor. However, the picnic is quite unlike the ham in texture and amount of fat, and usually is priced lower per pound. Picnics are also available canned. Keep refrigerated.

May be simmered, baked, or sliced and panfried. Fully cooked picnics need only to be heated to serving temperature, other styles require longer cooking. Check labels carefully.

PICNIC LOAF See Sliced Cold Meats.

POLISH SAUSAGE (cooked, smoked meat)

Finely chopped beef and coarsely chopped pork are blended with seasonings, stuffed into casings 1/2 to 2 in. in diameter and linked at least 6 in. long: 10 to 14 in. is not unusual. Links are held 12 to 24 hours before smoking at high temperature which thoroughly cooks the product. Typically served hot, although cooking is not essential. Often served with sauerkraut.

- •Ingredients: Beef and pork.
- •Seasonings: Coriander, garlic, marjoram, pepper, salt, sugar.

PORK AND TURKEY LOAF See Sliced Cold Meats.

PORK SAUSAGE (fresh sausage)

Freshly ground pork is mixed with characteristic seasonings, and stuffed into a variety of shapes. In the South and Southwest, pork sausage is apt to be more highly seasoned than in other parts of the country.

LINKS: Links are about 5 in. long, 3/4 in. in diameter, with natural casings. Fresh link will have a bright pink color which fades with age to gray.

COUNTRY STYLE: Coarsely ground fresh pork is stuffed into casings 1-1/2 in. in diameter. Unlinked, the "rope" is coiled in 1-lb. lengths.

PORK SAUSAGE ROLL: Ground pork is stuffed into a polyethylene casing about 2 in. in diameter or into cloth bags.

Must be thoroughly cooked. Usually pan fried. Typically served for breakfast with eggs, pancakes, waffles. Patties made from pork sausage roll are served for supper in New England, with milk gravy and potatoes.

- •Ingredients: Freshly ground pork.
- •Seasonings: Black pepper, nutmeg, rubbed sage, salt, sugar.
- •Availability: National in popularity and distribution.

PORK SHOULDER BUTTS (smoked meat)

Pork shoulders are often cured, and smoked similar to hams. The flavor of smoked butts is much like that of ham processed in the same fashion. There is a greater proportion of fat to lean in pork butts, and the meat texture is somewhat stringy. Smoked butts are often an economical smoked meat, but they should not be compared pricewise with ham. There are many names for smoked butts, including Cottage Roll, Picnic Butt, and Sweet Morsel.

POTATO SAUSAGE (fresh sausage)

Meats and minced, cooked potatoes are blended with seasonings, stuffed into narrow hog casings, and linked about 10 to the lb. Potato sausage is also made in beef rounds, and tied in a ring 12 oz. to 1 lb. in size. It is highly perishable, and usually kept immersed in water before sale as it discolors quickly in air.

Potato sausage must be thoroughly cooked before serving.
- Ingredients: Beef, cooked potatoes, pork.
- Seasonings: Ginger, mace, onion, sage, salt, sugar, white pepper.
- Availability: Limited distribution.

ROUMANIAN SAUSAGE (uncooked, smoked sausage)

Cured lean meat is seasoned and stuffed into hog casings, and smoked.
- Ingredients: Cured lean pork.
- Seasonings: Coriander, garlic, ginger, pepper, salt, sugar.

RULTESPULSE (cooked specialty)

This Danish, cooked meat roll is made of beef flanks, built up in layers, and seasoned with chopped onion, pepper, and ginger. Units of about 6 lb. are bound together, cured, then cooked until tender.

SALAMI FOR BEER See Beerwurst.

SALSICCIA See Italian Pork Sausage.

SARNO (dry sausage)

A dry sausage of coarsely chopped beef and pork. Unlike many of the salamis, it is not spiced with garlic. After stuffing into beef middles in 7-in. lengths, it is smoked, and air-dried.

SAVELOY (cooked, smoked sausage)

An English sausage similar in formula to bologna. Finely ground meat is seasoned, and stuffed into hog casings (or beef middles). They are not linked, but twisted right, then left. Smoking is done in a warm, dense smoke for 1/2 hour, then sausage is cooked at 175°F. for 15 minutes.
- Ingredients: Beef, pork.
- Seasonings: Cinnamon, ginger, mace, salt, sugar, white pepper.

SCOTCH HAM (smoked meat)

A mildly cured, boned, rolled, and tied ham which has not been smoked. Hams are cured after skinning and boning, according to a Scotch formula, and method. This style of ham is more prevalent in the Eastern states.

SCRAPPLE (cooked specialty)

Thoroughly cooked pork, and pork by-products, are ground fine, and combined with cornmeal flour and seasonings, and cooked in tins, or forms. Rye or buckwheat flour may replace up to 1 percent of the cornmeal flour which produces scrapple which browns more easily.

To serve scrapple, dip in flour, and fry in melted fat.
- Ingredients: Cornmeal flour, pork trimmings.
- Seasonings: Pepper, sage, salt.
- Availability: Moderate distribution.

SERDELKI (cooked, smoked sausage)

Similar to Serdelowa, except that casings are linked into 3-in. lengths. Links are used like hot dogs. Often served with sauerkraut.

SERDELOWA (cooked, smoked sausage)

A sausage of Polish origin, made of medium ground, lean

pork, lightly seasoned. Meat is stuffed into hog casings, and shaped into rings of about 1 lb. Serdelowa is lightly smoked, and fully cooked.

To serve, simmer, until heat through.
- •Ingredients: Lean pork.
- •Seasonings: Coriander, nutmeg, salt, whole pepper.

SLICED COLD MEATS (cooked meat specialities)

There are many combinations of meats and seasonings cooked, or baked into loaves for slicing. Some of these have basic names and formulas typical throughout the industry, while others are titled individually by each sausage-maker. In all instances, federally inspected loaves will bear a label, with an ingredient statement, as well as a name that will not be misleading.

SMEARWURST See Braunschweiger Mettwurst.

SMOKED PORK SAUSAGE (uncooked, smoked sausage)

Similar to fresh pork sausage, except that lean pork is mildly cured and smoked. It is usually stuffed in medium casings. Smoked pork sausage is especially popular in the South. It is not as perishable as fresh pork sausage, but must be refrigerated.

Must be cooked before serving.
- •Ingredients: Cured lean pork.
- •Seasonings: Paprika, red pepper, sage, salt, sugar.
- •Availability: More typically available in the Southern states.

SMOKED COUNTRY STYLE PORK SAUSAGE

Coarsely ground pork is mixed with seasonings and mild curing agents, then stuffed into hog casings. It is typically twisted into links 12 in. long, and thoroughly smoked. It may be fully cooked in the smokehouse. If so, thorough cooking is not necessary to serve.
- •Ingredients: Pork.
- •Seasonings: Ground pepper, nutmeg, sage, salt, sugar.

SMOKED COUNTRY STYLE SAUSAGE

Includes beef as well as pork in the formula. Typical seasonings are ground pepper, salt, sage, nutmeg, sugar.

SMOKED THURINGER LINKS (cooked, smoked sausage)

A coarsely chopped sausage which is cured, smoked, and cooked. The formula for this large link sausage varies from fresh thuringer which is typically all pork. Seasoning blends are also less complicated. There are 5 to 6 links per lb. Typically served hot.
- •Ingredients: Beef, pork.
- •Seasonings: Mustard, garlic, salt, sugar, white pepper.
- •Availability: Moderate distribution.

SMOKED BEEF TONGUES (smoked meat)

Beef tongues are cured, trimmed, stuffed into casings, and slowly smoked. Some consider Black Angus tongue a delicacy.

SMOKED PORK CHOPS (smoked meat)

SMOKED PORK JOWLS (smoked meat)

Various names are used by packers to identify this product to consumers. A flavorful, inexpensive, smoked meat, used especially for seasoning.

SMOKIE LINKS—SMOKIES (cooked, smoked sausage)

A newcomer to the sausage family, Smokie Links are reported to have been developed in Wisconsin, in the late 1940's. Coarsely ground, cured meats are seasoned, then stuffed and linked like wieners. Links are heavily smoked and thoroughly cooked.

Typically served hot, although cooking is not essential.
- •Ingredients: Beef, pork.
- •Seasonings: Black pepper, dextrose, monosodium glutamate, mustard, salt.
- •Availability: National distribution.

SMOKY SNAX See Smoked Thuringer.

SOPPRESATA Another name for Frizzes.

SOUSE, SULZ (cooked specialty)

Souse is similar to head cheese, but vinegar is added. This gives Souse a mild sour taste. Originally, this product was made of pickled pigs' feet. Sometimes cubed pork shoulder is used. Seasonings vary, and may include caraway seed, or lemon and pimento, as well as pepper and salt. Slice and serve cold for sandwiches, cold meat platters.

SOUTHERN HOTS (cooked, smoked sausage)

A smoked and cooked sausage, made of beef, beef and pork fat, and cracklings. After grinding, curing agents, sugar, pork sausage seasonings and chili pods are added. Mixture is stuffed into hog casings and smoked, then cooked.

STRASSBURG SAUSAGE (cooked, smoked sausage)

A blended meat sausage. Meats are cured, lightly seasoned and stuffed into beef middles, smoked, then scalded in boiling water.
  • Ingredients: Beef, pork, veal.
  • Seasonings: Nutmeg, pepper, salt, sugar.

STRASSBURGER (cooked specialty)

A type of smoked liver sausage requiring goose livers in the formula. Diced back fat and cooked liver may also be included. Links are typically 4 in. long.

STUDZIENNA A Polish variety of Souse.

SUMMER SAUSAGE (semi-dry, dry sausage)

Properly refers to all dry sausage, however, generally used to refer to mildly seasoned soft cervelat. See Thuringer Cervelat.

"Summer sausages" were those made during the cooler months, when meat supplies were ample, to keep for use during the warm months, hence the name. The lactic acid fermentation and drying inhibited spoilage, a valuable factor in the absence of refrigeration. European meat markets (and occasionally American ones, too) still display this type of sausage unrefrigerated. However, refrigeration is recommended.

Serve slices for sandwiches, snacks, cold meat platters.

SWEDISH MEDWURST (semi-dry sausage)

Boneless beef chucks and medium-fat certified pork trimmings are finely ground, and mixed with curing ingredients and spices—salt, coriander, white pepper. After curing, meat is either stuffed into beef middles 14 in. in length, or sewed into beef rounds 16 to 18 in. in length, and tied in a ring. Sausage is dried for a day, smoked, and then dried two more days.

SWEDISH SAUSAGE, GOTEBORG (dry sausage)

Rather coarsely chopped pork and beef is combined with curing and seasonings ingredients, stuffed into wide beef middles, and cut into 18-in. lengths. After a heavy smoke, it is air-dried. Goteborg has a sweet flavor derived from the spice cardamom, the major seasoning used, and also tends to be salty.
  • Ingredients: Beef, pork.
  • Seasonings: Cardamom, pepper, salt, sugar.

SWISS CLUB SAUSAGE (cooked, smoked sausage)

A lightly smoked sausage, made mostly of pork and a little beef. Meats are ground, and stuffed into wide sheep, or small hog, casings.
  • Ingredients: Beef, pork.
  • Seasonings: Cardamom, mace and sage, pepper, salt, sugar.

SYLTA (cooked specialty) See Head Cheese.

Sylta is a Swedish variation of Head Cheese.

THURINGER CERVELAT (semi-dry sausage) See Summer Sausage.

A semi-soft summer sausage with a distinctive tangy, lactic acid flavor. Meat is ground, seasoned, and cured, then stuffed into hog casings 30 in. long and 2-1/2 to 2-3/4 in. in diameter. The stuffed sausage is cured for 2 to 4 days before smoking.

Serve slices cold for sandwiches, snacks.
- •Ingredients: Beef, beefheart, and ham, or pork fat.
- •Seasonings: Coriander, pepper, salt, sugar, whole mustard seeds.
- •Availability: General distribution.

TOMATO SAUSAGE (fresh sausage)

A sausage-like specialty made of pork, or pork and veal, canned tomatoes, or tomato puree, and dry rusk, or cracker meal. The seasonings are mild—salt, nutmeg, mace, ginger. Tomato sausage must be thoroughly cooked before serving.

TOULOUSE SAUSAGE (fresh sausage)

Seasoned ground meat is stuffed into small hog casings. This sausage must be thoroughly cooked before serving.
- •Ingredients: Fat pork.
- •Seasonings: Garlic, pepper, salt, sugar, white wine.

TURKEY LOAF See Sliced Cold Meats.

WEISSWURST (fresh sausage)

A very lightly colored, fresh sausage made of finely chopped pork and veal, mildly spiced. Of German origin, the name means "white sausage". Links are about 4 in. long and plump, similar to bratwurst.

Weisswurst must be thoroughly cooked before serving.
- •Ingredients: Pork and veal.
- •Seasonings: Lemon peel, mace, pepper, sage, salt, sugar, thyme.
- •Availability: Very perishable, and usually sold the same day it is made. Very limited distribution. A specialty at Christmas time.

WIENERS (cooked, smoked sausage) Also see Franks

Wieners are the version of the "hot dog" which is reported to have originated in Vienna. Beef, pork, and sometimes veal are finely chopped, and gently seasoned. The links are typically 5 in. long, 1 in. in diameter. Some processors include extenders such as dry milk solids, or cereals in the formulation, but federally inspected all-meat wieners are made entirely of skeletal meats. Links are smoked at high temperatures, and further processed either in the smokehouse, or hot water vats, to fully cook. Some wurstmachers believe that wieners made in sheep casings retain their flavor and juices better than skinless ones. The skinless ones are more tender. The limited number of casings available, and the labor involved in their cleaning and preparation, make sheep casing wieners more expensive than skinless ones.

Typically served hot. May be grilled, broiled, baked, or heated in hot water. It is best not to boil wieners. Instead, cover with boiling water, and let stand 8 to 10 minutes to heat through.
- •Ingredients: Beef, pork. May also include veal.
- •Seasonings: Allspice, cinnamon, coriander, dextrose, ginger, pepper, salt.
- •Availability: National distribution.

SAUSAGE

MATERIAL

Product items must contain only those kinds of meats specified. As applicable, curing, cooking, smoking (except for loaf items, smoke flavoring, or artificial smoke flavoring is permissible in lieu of smoking), and flavoring of the product must be normal to the particular kind of product produced. Amounts and kinds of all ingredients must be within the tolerance permitted by the applicable meat inspection regulations.

TABLE I—STICK ITEMS*

Applies to items: 801, 803, 804, 805, 806, 807, 808, 809, 812

SEVERE	MAJOR	MINOR	DEFECTS
			External Product Characteristics
101			Presence of foreign material.[1]
102			Product which is not in excellent condition (e.g., moldy, stale, slimy, oily, sticky, sour, or discolored).[2]
103			Product not of the formula, class, color, style, shape, or state of refrigeration specified by the purchaser.
104			Nonformula ingredients not as specified.
	151		Casing having a rupture or split 1 inch or more in length.
	152		Lacks good resiliency typical of the product.[3]
	153		Weight not within range specified.
	154		Diameter not within range specified.
	155		Casing not compactly stuffed with product.
		201	Casing having a rupture or split measuring 0.3 inch or more in length but less than 1 inch.
		202	Casing end extending more than 2.0 inches beyond fastening.
		203	Presence of rendered fat or smokehouse residue or combination of both.
		204	Moisture (water) on casing.
		205	Fat cap at either end deeper than 0.5 inch.[3]
		206	Gelatin cap at either end deeper than 0.5 inch.[3]

1. Acceptability of product with respect to the presence of foreign material shall be determined by the involved C&MS agent except that, for product produced in a plant operating under the Regulations Governing the Meat Inspection of the USDA, this determination shall be made by a USDA Meat Inspection Program employee.

2. Slight amount of surface mold permissible on Dry Salami, Item No. 808.

3. Not applicable to Dry Salami, Item No. 808, Cervelat, Item No. 809, and Liver Sausage, Item No. 803.

4. The fat measurement not applicable to Dry Salami, Item No. 808.

*Tables I-IV are referred to on p. 225.

[*Cont.*]

SEVERE	MAJOR	MINOR	TABLE I [Cont.]	DEFECTS
			Internal Product Characteristics	
105			Presence of foreign material.[1]	
106			Presence of a foreign flavor (e.g., musty, moldy, sour, or stale).	
107			Presence of a foreign odor (e.g., putrid, stale, sour or rancid).	
	156		Lacks good cohesion typical of the product.	
	157		Texture not as specified.	
	158		Any individual cut surface having more than 1 pocket of fat[4], gelatin, and/or air measuring 0.5 inch or more in length.	
	159		One or more pieces of material, other than bone, measuring 0.5 inch or more in any dimension which will not break up or disintegrate when subjected to pressure from the flat side of a knife or spatula.	
	160		Bone particle measuring 0.3 inch or more in any dimension.	
	161		Color not as specified.	
	162		Aroma not typical of the product.	
	163		Flavor not typical of the product.	
		207	Any individual cut surface having more than 3 pockets of fat[4], gelatin, and/or air that individually measures 0.3 inch or more but less than 0.5 inch in length.	
		208	One or more pieces of material, other than bone, measuring 0.3 inch or more but less than 0.5 inch in any dimension, which will not break up or disintegrate when subjected to the pressure from the flat side of a knife or spatula.	
		209	Bone particle measuring less than 0.3 inch in any dimension.	
		NOTE	In addition to the above, the following are also applicable to Dry Salami, Item No. 808.	
		210	Fat particles yellow in color.	
		211	Fat particles not evenly distributed.	
		212	Fat particle measuring 0.4 inch or more in length.	

1. Acceptability of product with respect to the presence of foreign material shall be determined by the involved C&MS agent except that, for product produced in a plant operating under the Regulations Governing the Meat Inspection of the USDA, this determination shall be made by a USDA Meat Inspection Program employee.

2. Slight amount of surface mold permissible on Dry Salami, Item No. 808.
3. Not applicable to Dry Salami, Item No. 808, Cervelat, Item No. 809, and Liver Sausage, Item No. 803.
4. The fat measurement not applicable to Dry Salami, Item No. 808.

TABLE II — LINK ITEMS
Applies to items: 800, 811, 813

SEVERE	MAJOR	MINOR	DEFECTS
			External Product Characteristics
101			Presence of foreign material.[1]
102			Product which is not in excellent condition (e.g., moldy, stale, slimy, sticky, oily, sour, or discolored).
103			Product not of the formula, color, style, or state of refrigeration specified by the purchaser.
104			Nonformula ingredients not as specified.
	151		Lacks good resiliency typical of the product.[2]
	152		Link is soft, mushy, or abnormally distended or shrunken after immersion in 160°F to 180°F. water for 10 minutes or more (slight curvature acceptable).[2]
	153		Number of links in one pound of product not as specified by the purchaser.[3]
	154		Uniformity of length not as specified.
	155		Uniformity of diameter not as specified.
	156		Length not as specified.
		201	Presence of all or part of artificial casing, other than collagen casing.
		202	Link having a split or rupture measuring more than 0.3 inch.
		203	Link which is broken.
		204	Link with fat cap or fat streak.
			Internal Product Characteristics
105			Presence of foreign material.[1]
106			Presence of foreign flavor (e.g., moldy, sour or stale).[4]
107			Presence of foreign odor (e.g., putrid, stale, sour or rancid).
	157		Lacks good cohesion typical of the product.
	158		Texture not as specified.
	159		Any individual cut surface having more than 1 pocket of fat, gelatin and/or air measuring 0.4 inch or more in any dimension.
	160		One or more pieces of material, other than bone, measuring 0.3 inch or more in any dimension which will not break up or disintegrate when subjected to pressure from the flat side of a knife or spatula.
	161		Bone particle measuring 0.3 inch or more in any dimension.

[*Cont.*]

SEVERE	MAJOR	MINOR	**TABLE II [Cont.]**	DEFECTS
	162		Color not as specified.	
	163		Aroma not typical of the product.[4]	
	164		Flavor not typical of the product.[4]	
		205	Any individual cut surface having more than 3 pockets of fat, gelatin, and/or air, that individually measures 0.2 inch or more but less than 0.4 inch in any dimension.	
		206	One or more pieces of material, other than bone, measuring less than 0.3 inch in any dimension which will not break up or disintegrate when subjected to pressure from the flat surface of a knife or spatula.	
		207	Bone particle measuring less than 0.3 inch in any dimension.	

1. Acceptability of product with respect to the presence of foreign material shall be determined by the involved C&MS agent except that, for product produced in a plant operating under the Regulations Governing the Meat Inspection of the USDA, this determination shall be made by a USDA Meat Inspection Program employee.

2. Applicable only to Frankfurters, Item No. 800.

3. Determined once per 10-pound unit drawn for sampling.

4. For Frankfurters, Item No. 800, this determination shall be made on samples heated to determine compliance with Defect No. 152.

TABLE III — LOAF ITEMS

Applies to items: 814, 815, 820

SEVERE	MAJOR	MINOR	DEFECTS
			External Product Characteristics
101			Presence of foreign material.[1]
102			Product which is not in excellent condition (e.g., moldy, stale, slimy, sticky, oily, sour, or discolored).
103			Product not of the formula, class, shape, type, or state of refrigeration specified by the purchaser.
104			Nonformula ingredients not as specified.
	151		Loaf not encased or wrapped.
	152		Unduly distorted loaves affecting their useability.
	153		Blackened and/or blistered surface area measuring 4 square inches or more.
	154		Loaf having a surface break measuring 2 inches or more in length.
	155		Lacks good resiliency typical of the product.
	156		Weight not within range specified.
		201	Blackened and/or blistered surface area measuring 2 square inches or more but less than 4 square inches.
		202	Loaf having a surface break measuring 1 inch or more but less than 2 inches in length.
		203	Presence of rendered fat on surface.
		204	Moisture on surface (including moisture between loaf and casing).
			Internal Product Characteristics
105			Presence of foreign material.[1]
106			Presence of a foreign flavor (e.g., musty, moldy, sour, or stale).
107			Presence of foreign odors (e.g., putrid, stale, sour, or rancid).
	157		Lacks good cohesion typical of the product.
	158		Texture not as specified.
	159		Any individual cut surface having more than 1 pocket of fat, gelatin, and/or air measuring 0.5 inch or more in any dimension.[2]
	160		One or more pieces of material, other than bone, measuring 0.3 inch or more in any dimension which will not break up or disintegrate when subjected to pressure from the flat side of a knife or spatula.
	161		Bone particle measuring 0.3 inch or more in any dimension.
	162		Color not as specified.

[Cont.]

SEVERE	MAJOR	MINOR	TABLE III [Cont.]	DEFECTS
	163		Aroma not typical of the product.	
	164		Flavor not typical of the product.	
		205	Any individual cut surface having more than 4 pockets of fat, gelatin, and/or air that individually measures 0.3 inch or more but less than 0.5 inch in any dimension.[2]	
		206	One or more pieces of material, other than bone, measuring 0.1 inch or more but less than 0.3 inch in any dimension which will not break up or disintegrate when subjected to the pressure from the flat side of a knife or spatula.	
		207	Bone particle measuring less than 0.3 inch in any dimension.	
		208	More than 3 pieces of pickle, pimento, etc., fall out upon cutting for examination.[3]	
		209	Very uneven distribution of components.[3]	

1. Acceptability of product with respect to the presence of foreign material shall be determined by the involved C&MS agent except that, for product produced in a plant operating under the Regulations Governing the Meat Inspection of the USDA, this determination shall be made by a USDA Meat Inspection Program employee.

2. Not applicable to Head Cheese, Item No. 820.

3. Scored on Meat Food Product loaf, Item No. 815 only.

TABLE IV — PORK SAUSAGE AND BREAKFAST SAUSAGE
Applies to Item 802, 810

SEVERE	MAJOR	MINOR	DEFECTS
			External Product Characteristics
101			Presence of foreign material.[1]
102			Product which is not in excellent condition (e.g., moldy, stale, slimy, sticky, oily, sour, or discolored).
103			Product not of the style, size[2], or state of refrigeration specified by the purchaser.
104			Nonformula ingredients not as specified.
	151		Difference in length between the longest and the shortest link in the sample is more than 0.5 inch.
	152		Uniformity of diameter not as specified.
	153		Presence of string.
		201	Casing or bag end more than 0.5 inch in length.
		202	Link having a split or rupture measuring 0.3 inch or more.
		203	Length not as specified.
			Internal Product Characteristics
105			Presence of foreign material.[1]
106			Presence of a foreign flavor (e.g., musty, moldy, sour or stale).
107			Presence of foreign odors (e.g., putrid, stale, sour or rancid).
	154		One or more pieces of material, other than bone, measuring 0.5 inch or more in any dimension which will not break up or disintegrate when subjected to pressure from the flat side of a knife or spatula.
	155		Bone particle measuring 0.3 inch or more in any dimension.
		204	Two or more pieces of material, other than bone, measuring 0.3 inch or more but less than 0.5 inch which will not break up or disintegrate when subjected to pressure from the flat side of a knife or spatula.
		205	Bone particle measuring less than 0.3 inch in any dimension.

1. Acceptability of product with respect to the presence of foreign material shall be determined by the involved C&MS agent except that, for product produced in a plant operating under the Regulations Governing the Meat Inspection of the USDA, this determination shall be made by a USDA Meat Inspection Program employee.

2. For links determine size once per 10-pound unit drawn for sampling.

IMPS NO. 800 **Frankfurters**
MBG NO. Not Included.
URMISand COMMON NAMES: Hot Dogs.
COMMON USES: Broil; boil; panfry; stuffed hot dogs; beans 'n' franks.

Frankfurters are a smoked, cooked link sausage. They are either skinless, stuffed in sheep casings, or stuffed in a collagen casing, and are uniform in length and diameter. Links shall be 5 to 6 in. in length. The meat components consist of very finely comminuted beef or beef and pork. The interior cut surface is a smooth, fine-textured, light to moderately dark pink in background color, and finely mottled, with evenly distributed light to dark red flecks.

End Item Examination—Table II
ORDERING DATA: OPTIONS DESIRED SHALL BE SPECIFIED BY THE PURCHASER
Formula (major ingredients only)
A —Beef and pork (in any combination)
A1—Formula A, plus nonfat dry milk
B —Beef, pork (beef is predominant)
B1—Formula B, plus nonfat dry milk)
C —Pork, beef (pork is predominant)
C1—Formula C, plus nonfat dry milk
D —Beef
Color
A—Natural (not artificially colored)
B—Artificially colored (red)

Style	*Size*
B3—Sheep casings)	
C —Skinless)	6, 8, 10, 12 links per pound
D —Collagen casings)	

State of Refrigeration
A—Chilled
B—Frozen

IMPS NO. 801 **Bologna**
MBG NO. Not Included.
URMIS and COMMON NAMES: Bologna.
COMMON USES: Broil; sandwiches; bologna roll-ups.

Bologna is a smoked, cooked sausage. The meat components consist of beef and pork very finely comminuted, and stuffed in artificial or natural casings. The interior cut surface is smooth, fine-textured, light pink in background color, and finely mottled, with evenly distributed light to dark red flecks. The 1 to 1.5-lb. size shall be ring style.

End Item Examination—Table I
ORDERING DATA: OPTIONS DESIRED SHALL BE SPECIFIED BY THE PURCHASER
Formula (major ingredients only)
A —Beef and pork (in any combination)
A1—Formula A, plus nonfat dry milk
B —Beef, pork (beef is predominant)
B1—Formula B, plus nonfat dry milk
C —Pork, beef (pork is predominant)
C1—Formula C, plus nonfat dry milk
Color
A—Natural (not artifically colored)
B—Artificially colored (red)

Style	*Size*	
	(1 to 1.5 lb.)	(1.3-1.5 in. in diameter)
A—Artificial casings	(4 to 7 lb.)	(2.5-3.5 in. in diameter)
	(7 to 12 lb.)	(3.5-5.0 in. in diameter)
B—Natural casings	(1 to 1.5 lb.)	(1.3-1.5 in. in diameter)

State of Refrigeration
A—Chilled
B—Frozen

IMPS NO. 802 **Pork Sausage**
MBG NO. Not Included.
URMIS and COMMON NAMES: Breakfast Sausage, Pork Sausage.
COMMON USES: Panfry; sausage.

Pork sausage is a fresh, all pork product. The meat is chopped or ground to a moderately coarse texture, and mixed with salt and spices. Pork sausage may be packed in bulk, formed mechanically, or stuffed in artificial or natural casings. The links, rolls, and bags are moderately uniform in length and diameter. For product in unlinked hog casings, no more than one piece shall be less than 12 in. in length in a primary container.

End Item Examination—Table IV
ORDERING DATA: OPTIONS DESIRED SHALL BE SPECIFIED BY THE PURCHASER

Style	*Size*
A —Artificial casings	1-, 2- or 3-lb. rolls
B1—Hog casings (linked)	6-8, 8-10 links per lb.
B2—Hog casings (unlinked)	
B3—Sheep casings	10-12, 12-14, 14-16 links per lb.
C —Skinless (mechanically formed)	8, 9, 10, 12, 16 links per lb.
D —Collagen casings	10-12, 12-14, 14-16 links per lb.
E —Cloth bags	2-, 3-, 5- or 7-lb. bags
F —Bulk	5-, 6-, 8- or 10-lb. units

State of Refrigeration
A—Chilled
B—Frozen

[*Cont.*]

Item No. 803 **Liver Sausage [Braunschweiger]**

Liver sausage is a cooked sausage with a smoked characteristic (a smoked characteristic may be imparted by smoking, by adding smoked meats to the formula, or a combination of both). The meat components consist of pork with smoked jowls and/or bacon ends; bacon ends included only in some formulas. These are combined with pork livers, finely comminuted, and stuffed in artificial or natural casings. Onion shall be included as a seasoning. Sticks measure from 2 to 3 in. in diameter, and shall weigh from 5 to 8 lb. The interior cut surface is fine-textured, and light reddish-brown in color.

End Item Examination—Table I

ORDERING DATA: OPTIONS DESIRED SHALL BE SPECIFIED BY THE PURCHASER

Formula (major ingredients only)

A —Pork livers, pork

A1—Formula A, plus nonfat dry milk

B —Pork livers, pork with smoked jowls and/or bacon ends and pieces

B1—Formula B, plus nonfat dry milk

Style

A—Artificial casings

B—Natural casings

State of Refrigeration

A—Chilled

B—Frozen

IMPS NO. 804 **Salami, Cooked**

MBG NO. Not Included.

URMIS and COMMON NAMES: Salami.

COMMON USES: Cold cut platter; cold cut sandwich.

Cooked salami is a smoked, cooked sausage. The meat components consist of moderately coarse cut pork and finely comminuted beef, with finely comminuted beefheart meat included in some formulas. Seasoning includes garlic and peppercorns. Salami is stuffed in artificial casings, and measures from 3.5 to 4.5 in. in diameter. Sticks shall weigh from 7 to 12 lb. The interior cut surface is moderately coarse in texture, and light to dark reddish-brown in color.

End Item Examination—Table I

ORDERING DATA: OPTIONS DESIRED SHALL BE SPECIFIED BY THE PURCHASER

Formula (major ingredients only)

A—Pork and beef

B—Pork and beef, beefheart meat

State of Refrigeration

A—Chilled

B—Frozen

Item No. 805 **Minced Luncheon Meat**

Minced luncheon meat is smoked, cooked sausage. The meat components consist of moderately coarse-cut pork and finely comminuted beef, with porkheart meat included in some formulas. The product is stuffed in artificial casings. Stuffed round casings shall measure from 3.5 to 4.5 in. in diameter. When the stuffed casings are formed into rectangular shapes by wire or metal molds, they shall measure from 3 to 4 in. in width and depth. Sticks shall weigh from 5 to 10 lb. The interior cut surface is moderately textured, fine, and light pink in color.

End Item Examination—Table I

ORDERING DATA: OPTIONS DESIRED SHALL BE SPECIFIED BY THE PURCHASER

Formula (Major ingredients only)

A —Pork, beef (pork is predominant)

A1—Formula A, plus nonfat dry milk

B —Pork, beef, porkheart meat

B1—Formula B, plus nonfat dry milk

Shape

A—Rectangular

B—Rounded

State of Refrigeration

A—Chilled

B—Frozen

IMPS NO. 806 **Lebanon Bologna**
MBG NO. Not Included.
URMIS and COMMON NAMES: Bologna.
COMMON USES: Sandwiches; cold platters.
Item No. 806 **Lebanon Bologna**

Lebanon bologna is a smoked, uncooked, all beef sausage. The meat component is finely comminuted beef stuffed in artificial casings. Sticks are from 3.5 to 4.5 in. in diameter, and shall weigh from 5 to 10 lb. The product has a characteristically sharp (fermented) flavor. The interior cut surface is fine-textured, and exhibits a uniform, dark reddish-brown background color with fine fat particles evenly distributed.

End Item Examination—Table I

ORDERING DATA: OPTION DESIRED SHALL BE SPECIFIED BY THE PURCHASER
State of Refrigeration
A—Chilled
B—Frozen

Item No. 807 **Thuringer**

Thuringer is a smoked, uncooked sausage. The meat components are moderately coarse-cut beef, or moderately coarse-cut beefheart meat and beef. Thuringer is stuffed in artificial casings, and measures from 2.5 to 3.5 in. in diameter. Sticks shall weigh from 6 to 8 lb. The product has a characteristically sharp (fermented) flavor. The interior cut surface is moderately coarse-textured, and a uniform, dark reddish-brown color.

End Item Examination—Table I

ORDERING DATA: OPTIONS DESIRED SHALL BE SPECIFIED BY THE PURCHASER
Formula (major ingredients only)
A—Beef
B—Beef, beefheart meat
State of Refrigeration
A—Chilled
B—Frozen

IMPS NO. 808 **Dry Salami**
MBG NO. Not Included.
URMIS and COMMON NAMES: Salami, Cold Cut.
COMMON USES: Sandwiches; cold plates.

Dry salami is a smoked, uncooked, dry sausage. The meat components consist of moderately coarse-cut beef, with moderately coarse-cut pork and/or beefheart meat included in some formulas. The product seasoning includes garlic. Dry Salami is stuffed in artificial or natural casings, measures from 2 to 3 in. in diameter, and is processed to produce a firm, hard product. Sticks shall weigh from 2 to 5 lb. The interior cut surface is firm, moderately coarse-textured, and exhibits a distinctive, uniform distribution of white fat particles. The background color is medium to dark reddish-brown meat.

End Item Examination—Table I

ORDERING DATA: OPTION DESIRED SHALL BE SPECIFIED BY THE PURCHASER
Formula (major ingredients only)
A—Beef
B—Beef, beefheart meat
C—Beef and pork (in any combination)
D—Beef and pork, beefheart meat
E—Beef, pork (beef is predominant)
F—Beef, pork, beefheart meat
Style
A—Artificial casings
B—Natural casings
State of Refrigeration
A—Chilled
B—Frozen
C—Unrefrigerated

IMPS NO. 809 **Cervelat**
MBG NO. Not Included.
URMIS and COMMON NAMES: Cold Cut, Cervelat.
COMMON USES: Sandwiches; cold plates.

Cervelat is a smoked, cooked, dry sausage. The meat components consist of finely comminuted beef and pork, stuffed in artificial or natural casings, and processed to produce a firm product. Sticks measure from 1.5 to 2 in. in diameter and shall weigh from 2 to 5 lb. The interior cut surface is fine-textured, and exhibits a uniform, medium to dark reddish-brown color.

End Item Examination—Table I
ORDERING DATA: OPTIONS DESIRED SHALL BE SPECIFIED BY THE PURCHASER
Formula (major ingredients only)
A—Beef, pork (beef is predominant)
B—Pork, beef (pork is predominant)
Style
A—Artificial casings
B—Natural casings
State of Refrigeration
A—Chilled
B—Frozen

IMPS NO. 810 **Breakfast Sausage**
MBG NO. Not Included.
URMIS and COMMON NAMES: Breakfast Sausage.
COMMON USES: Panfry; sausage and eggs.

Breakfast sausage is a fresh product. The meat components consist predominantly of pork, with smaller amount of beef and/or veal. The meat is chopped or ground to a moderately coarse texture. Breakfast sausage may be packed in bulk, or stuffed in artificial or hog casings. The links and rolls are moderately uniform in length and diameter. For product in unlinked hog casings, no more than 1 piece shall be less than 12 in. in length in a primary container.

End Item Examination—Table IV
ORDERING DATA: OPTIONS DESIRED SHALL BE SPECIFIED BY THE PURCHASER

Style	*Size*
A —Artificial casings	1-, 2-, or 3- lb. rolls
B1—Hog casings, linked	6-8, 8-10 links per lb.
B2—Hog casings, unlinked	
F —Bulk	5-, 6-, 8-, or 10-lb. units

State of Refrigeration
A—Chilled
B—Frozen

IMPS NO. 811 **Smoked Sausage**
MBG NO. Not Included.
URMIS and COMMON NAMES: Link Sausage.
COMMON USES: Panfry; broil; sausage and eggs.

Smoked sausage is a smoked, cooked, linked sausage. The meat components consist of all pork, or pork and beef with beef tripe, beef- and porkheart meat; beef and pork tongue meat are included in some formulas. The meat is chopped or ground to a moderately coarse texture. Smoked sausages are either skinless, or stuffed in hog casings, and are moderately uniform in length and diameter. The interior cut surface is moderately coarse in texture (formula D and D1 may be moderately fine-textured).

End Item Examination—Table II
ORDERING DATA: OPTIONS DESIRED SHALL BE SPECIFIED BY THE PURCHASER
Formula (major ingredients only)
A —Pork
B —Pork, beef (pork is predominant)
B1—Formula B, plus nonfat dry milk
C —Beef, pork (beef is predominant)
C1—Formula C, plus nonfat dry milk
D —Beef and pork, plus any one or any combination of beef tripe, beefheart meat, porkheart meat, beef tongue meat, and pork tongue meat
D1—Formula D, plus nonfat dry milk

Style	*Size*
B—Hog casings	6-8, 8-10 links per lb.
C—Skinless	6-8, 8-10 links per lb.

State of Refrigeration
A—Chilled
B—Frozen

IMPS NO. 812 **New England Brand Sausage**
MBG NO. Not Included.
URMIS and COMMON NAMES: Ham Sausage.
COMMON USES: Panfry; sausage and eggs.

New England brand sausage is a smoked, cooked sausage. The meat components consist predominantly of pork chunks, with a small amount of finely comminuted beef. The product is stuffed in artificial or natural casings, and measures from 3.5 to 4.5 in. in diameter. Individual sausages shall weigh from 5 to 10 lb. The texture of the interior cut surface is variable, 70 to 80 percent of the area consists of pork chunks, and the remaining portion is fine-textured.

End Item Examination—Table I
ORDERING DATA: OPTIONS DESIRED SHALL BE SPECIFIED BY THE PURCHASER
State of Refrigeration
A—Chilled
B—Frozen

IMPS NO. 813 **Polish Sausage**
MBG NO. Not Included.
URMIS and COMMON NAMES: Polish Sausage.
COMMON USES: Boil; broil; Polish sausage and sauerkraut.

Polish sausage is a smoked, cooked, linked sausage. The meat components consist of moderately coarse-cut pork, or moderately coarse-cut pork with fine comminuted beef. Seasoning includes garlic. The product is stuffed in hog casings, or equivalent diameter collagen casings. The links are moderately uniform in length and diameter. The interior cut surface is moderately coarse in texture, with a uniform distribution of white fat particles throughout the medium to dark reddish-brown meat.

End Item Examination—Table II
ORDERING DATA: OPTIONS DESIRED SHALL BE SPECIFIED BY THE PURCHASER
Formula (major ingredients only)
A—Pork
B—Pork, beef (pork is predominant)

Style	*Size*
B—Hog casings	3-5, 11-13 in. in length
D—Collagen casings	3-5, 11-13 in. in length

State of Refrigeration
A—Chilled
B—Frozen

IMPS NO. 814 **Meat Loaves**
MBG NO. Not Included.
URMIS and COMMON NAMES: Luncheon Meat for Slicing, Cold Cuts.
COMMON USES: Sandwiches; cold plates.

Meat loaves are baked (dry heat), or cooked (moist heat), products. The meat components are finely comminuted beef, pork, and veal. Meat loaves may be rectangular or rounded in shape, and shall weigh from 4 to 8 lb. The exterior surface may be smoked, unsmoked or browned in hot oil or fat. The interior cut surface is smooth, fine-textured, light pink in background color, and finely mottled with evenly distributed light to dark red flecks. The individual loaves are encased or wrapped in grease and moisture resistant paper, or plastic film.

End Item Examination — Table III
ORDERING DATA: OPTIONS DESIRED SHALL BE SPECIFIED BY THE PURCHASER
Formula (major ingredients only)
A —Pork, veal (pork is predominant)
A1—Formula A, plus nonfat dry milk
B —Pork , beef (pork is predominant)
B1—Formula B, plus nonfat dry milk
C —Pork, beef, veal
C1—Formula C, plus nonfat dry milk
D —Pork
D1—Formula D, plus nonfat dry milk
E —Veal
E1—Formula E, plus nonfat dry milk
F —Beef
F1—Formula F, plus nonfat dry milk
G —Ham
G1—Formula G, plus nonfat dry milk
Class
A—Smoked
B—Unsmoked
C—Browned in hot oil or fat
Shape
A—Rectangular
B—Rounded
Type
A—Baked (dry heat)
B—Cooked (moist heat)
State of Refrigeration
A—Chilled
B—Frozen

IMPS NO. 815 **Meat Food Product Loaves**
MBG NO. Not Included.
URMIS and COMMON NAMES: Luncheon Meat for Slicing, Cold Cuts.
COMMON USES: Cold plate; sandwiches.

Meat food product loaves are baked (dry heat), or cooked (moist heat), products. Beef, pork, and veal may be used singly, or in any combination. Other ingredients such as meat by-products, pickles, pimentos, cheese, nuts, etc., are added as applicable, except that lungs, spleens, tripe, udders, blood, skin, cracklings, brains, ears, lips, snouts, kidneys, tongue trimmings, and meat, and meat by-products from lamb, yearling mutton, mutton and goats, shall not be used in preparing the loaf. Nonfat dry milk may be added. Individual loaves shall weigh from 4 to 8 lb. The exterior surface may be smoked, unsmoked, or browned in hot fat or oil. The other ingredients shall be distributed uniformly throughout the entire surface. The individual loaves are encased, or wrapped, in grease and moisture resistant paper, or plastic film. Meat food product loaves must be specified by name. (For example: pickle loaf, ham and cheese loaf, etc.) Any meat food product loaf not listed below may be ordered. However, if the name is inadequate to identify the product appropriately, the purchaser may be requested to furnish additional information to establish a definite basis for identification.

End Item Examination — Table III
ORDERING DATA: OPTIONS DESIRED SHALL BE SPECIFIED BY THE PURCHASER
Formula (major condiment ingredients)
A—Pimento Loaf
B—Pickle and Pimento Loaf
C—Pickle Loaf
D—Olive Loaf
E—Pepper Loaf
F—Cheese Loaf
G—Macaroni and Cheese Loaf
H—Liver Loaf
Class
A—Smoked
B—Unsmoked
C—Browned in hot oil or fat
Shape
A—Rectangular
B—Rounded
Type
A—Baked (dry heat)
B—Cooked (moist heat)
State of Refrigeration
A—Chilled
B—Frozen

IMPS NO. 820 **Head Cheese**
MBG NO. Not Included.
URMIS and COMMON NAMES: Head Cheese
COMMON USES: Cold plate; sandwiches.

Head cheese is a cooked product. The meat components may consist of all pork head meats, or predominantly pork head meats, with pork, cured pork and/or other pork by-products included, except that ears, livers, and spleens are prohibited. The meat is coarse-cut to fine-cut. Onion shall be included as a seasoning. Head cheese may have gelatin added. The finished product is stuffed in artificial or natural casings, and shall weigh from 4 to 8 lb. The interior cut surface is resilient, and very coarse-textured, with an even distribution of ingredients.

End Item Examination—Table III
ORDERING DATA: OPTIONS DESIRED SHALL BE SPECIFIED BY THE PURCHASER
Style
A —Artificial casings
B4—Hog stomachs
B5—Beef bungs
State of Refrigeration
A—Chilled
B—Frozen

TABLE A—LOT AND SAMPLE SIZES FOR END PRODUCT EXAMINATIONS

Type of Item	Lot size and sample size expressed as[1]	Sample Unit
Linked Items	Number of 10-lb units	One link from each sampled 10-lb. unit[2]
Unlinked sausage in casing	Number of 10-lb. units	One approximately 4-in. section from each sampled 10-lb. unit.
Bag and roll packed sausage	Number of 10-lb. units	One bag or roll from each sampled 10-lb. unit.
Bulk-packaged pork sausage	Number of 10-lb. units	Contents of each sampled 10-lb. unit
Sticks and Loaves	Number of sticks or loaves	One stick or loaf

1. For product packed other than 10 lb. in a primary container, the lot size and sample size shall be the number of 10-lb. equivalents. This does not apply to sticks or loaves.
2. For Frankfurters, Item 800, additional samples must be drawn to determine compliance with Defect No. 152, Table II. See External and Internal Product Characteristics Examinations Section.

EXAMINATION OF END PRODUCT

All examinations prescribed herein shall be performed on the finished product. Lot size, sample size, and the sample unit shall be as shown in Table A. Sampling plans (sample size and acceptance [AC] and rejection [RE] numbers for different sizes) shall be as shown in Table B. All classification of defects shall be in accordance with Tables I through IV, as specified in the individual item descriptions. The tables are designed to apply to more than one product. Therefore, certain defects listed in Tables I through IV will not apply to all products examined according to a specific table. For example, Defect No. 104 in Table I would not be applicable when examining bologna, since this item description makes reference only to major ingredients which are examined under Defect No. 103. However, Defect No. 104 would be applicable when examining cooked salami, which requires that peppercorns and garlic be included.

EXTERNAL AND INTERNAL PRODUCT CHARACTERISTICS EXAMINATIONS

All sample units randomly selected for external product examinations also may be used for internal product examinations. On stick and loaf items, bulk-packed pork sausage, and bag and roll-packed sausage, internal product characteristics examinations shall be made on the right hand surface of one cross-section of each sample unit. The cut shall have been made by cutting through the sample unit at an approximate right angle to its length. On links or 4-in. section samples, the examination shall be made on the right-hand surface of the longitudinally bisected link or section.

For frankfurters, Item No. 800, an immersion test shall be performed to determine compliance with defects No. 152, 106, and 164 in Table II. For lot sizes of 50 or less, this examination shall be performed on 3 additional selected frankfurters. For larger lots, 5 frankfurters shall be selected. The frankfurters shall be immersed for approximately 10 minutes in 160°F. to 180°F. water.

TABLE B — SAMPLING PLANS FOR EXTERNAL AND INTERNAL PRODUCT EXAMINATION[1]

Lot Size	Sample Size[2]	Major Defects		Total Defects	
		AC	RE	AC	RE
20 or less	2	0	1	0	1
21-50	5	0	1	1	2
51-100	8	0	1	2	3
101-300	13	0	1	3	4
301-800	32	1	2	7	8
801-15,000	50	2	3	10	11
For larger lot size examinations, contact Standardization Branch, Washington, D.C.					

1. Finding of any Severe defect shall cause rejection of the lot.
2. If on stick, loaf, bag, and roll items the sample size equals or exceeds the lot size, do 100 percent inspection. For linked items if the sample size equals or exceeds the lot size, sample 2 links and for unlinked items, sample 2 approximately 4-inch sections.

SMOKED AND CURED PORK

DESCRIPTION OF SELECTIONS

Selection No. 1

Hams, shoulders, shoulder picnics, loins, and Canadian-style bacon of Selection No. 1 are meaty as a result of a combination of thick muscling and a minimum of intermuscular and external fat. The cuts are thick and plump throughout, with at least moderately thick muscling and have not more than a small amount of intermuscular fat. The lean meat must be firm and must possess a bright, reasonably uniform cured color (slightly two-toned permissible), and a fine, smooth texture. Selection No. 1 slab bacon must be slightly thick and moderately uniform in thickness, and be moderately long in relation to width. The bacon (slab or sliced) must indicate a moderately high ratio of lean to fat, and a uniform distribution of fat to lean layers. The exterior fat on Selection No. 1 pork cuts must be firm, white (except for the cured or well-penetrated smoke color), and reasonably uniform in distribution. The skin must be thin, smooth, and pliable. The pork cuts must be free from bruises, broken bones, dislocated or enlarged joints, or other malformation, odor, or flavor foreign to meat, and practically free from scores, miscuts, abrasions, hook marks, blemishes, hair roots, or other defects.

Selection No. 2

Hams, shoulders, shoulder picnics, loins, and Canadian-style bacon of Selection No. 2 lack meatiness, either because of thin muscling or thick intermuscular and external fat, or a combination of characteristics intermediate in both respects. The cuts are slightly thick and plump throughout, with slightly thick muscling. They have a slightly high to high amount of intermuscular fat. The lean meat must be firm and must possess a bright, reasonably uniform cured color (slightly two-toned permissible), and a fine, smooth texture. Selection No. 2 slab bacon must be not more than moderately thick, but it may be uneven in thickness, and slightly short in relation to width. The bacon (slab or sliced) may indicate a moderately low ratio of lean to fat, and have rather thick fat deposits between layers of lean. The exterior fat on Selection No. 2 pork cuts must be firm, white (except for the cured or well-penetrated smoke color), and fairly uniform in distribution. The skin must be at least moderately thin, smooth and pliable. Pork cuts, otherwise eligible for Selection No. 1 or Selection No. 2, but which have slight scores, abrasions, hook marks, or cuts not exceeding 1/2 in. in depth or more than 2 sq. in. in area on the surface of the pork cuts used for slicing, but which do not interfere with the making of satisfactory slices, will be acceptable. Pork cuts showing only a slight amount of hair roots, or which are only slightly miscut or mis-shaped may be included; however, pork cuts which have broken bones, dislocated or enlarged joints, or other malformation, bruises, abrasions, or odor, or flavor foreign to meat are not acceptable.

STATE OF REFRIGERATION:

A — Chilled

B — Frozen

PROCESSING:

Curing

In accordance with the regulations of the applicable meat inspection agency, all product items covered by these specifications must be mildly and thoroughly, but not excessively, cured, by an acceptable and recognized conventional method which will impart the typical, well-cured texture, cohesion, flavor, aroma, soundness, and appearance (including a bright, stable, cured color) to the finished product.

Smoking

In accordance with the regulations of the applicable meat inspection agency, all smoked products covered by these specifications must be smoked for a sufficient time, and with temperatures as necessary to appropriately dry the product, and to impart a uniform, bright, well-penetrated smoke color, and the characteristic aroma, flavor, firmness, bright sheen, and appearance of a well-smoked product. Any encrusted salt, extraneous matter, and smokehouse residue — other than the normal smoke color — must be closely removed (no washing), such as careful light brushing or wiping, without damage to the product. Stockinettes, strings, and similar hanging devices must be completely removed, and excluded, prior to wrapping, packing, and delivery of product.

Cooking

In accordance with the regulations of the applicable meat inspection agency, all product items covered by these specifications requiring cooking must be cooked by one of the following means as specified for the product item:

A. DRY HEAT

Dry-heat, fully cooked, smoked meat items should be smoked and cooked simultaneously without undue interruption, by an acceptable conventional method or means, for sufficient time to impart a uniform, bright, well-penetrated smoke color, and characteristic aroma and flavor to the product, and with temperatures as necessary to reflect the typical, fully-cooked characteristics in the finished product. The smoking and cooking procedure must be conducted in a fairly continuous manner, to appropriately dry the product without undue rendering of fat, undercooking, overcooking, or other damage. The fully-cooked items must be handled as necessary to remove rendered surface fat and extraneous matter.

B. MOIST HEAT

The cured pork items should be fully-cooked with moist (hot water, or hot water and steam) heat, in temperatures and for the time necessary to impart the typical, fully-cooked characteristics to the finished product. After cooking, the fully-cooked products must be lightly showered with tepid water to remove surface meat juices, jelly, or albumin, and then trimmed lightly and smoothly to conform them to the specification requirements.

FINISHED PRODUCT CHARACTERISTICS

The finished product as delivered must be sound and in excellent condition. The product must reflect appropriate selection, style, shape, weight range, curing, skinning, boning, defatting, smoking, cooking, packaging, packing, and state of refrigeration (as applicable). In addition, the product must meet other factors of conformance, without evidence of faulty workmanship and handling. The color of the lean meat must be fairly uniform and stable, characteristic of well-cured product, without evidence of greening, streaking, or other discoloration, (a slightly two-toned or iridescent color is permissible). The lean meat must possess a fine, smooth-texture, and be tender, cohesive, firm, or only slightly resilient, but not unduly hard.

Smoked products must have an acceptable flavor and aroma and a fairly uniform, bright, well-penetrated smoked color, and must be free from extraneous material, including encrusted salt and smokehouse residue (except the natural smoke color). The smoked product must be fairly dry on the exterior and the interior (including a well-sealed butt on hams not smoked in artificial casings), but not excessively dried or scorched. It must not have more than a very slight amount of dripping or exuding moisture upon appreciable careful hand pressure, although not such as will damage the product. Cooked products must be thoroughly cooked, and practically free from air holes, pockets of moisture, rendered fat, gelatinous matter, ragged edges, surface strings (except closely tied necessary stitching), and extraneous matter, and must be free from fermented, or other odor or flavor foreign to meat, rancidity, mold, or other deterioration or damage.

When string tying is required, roasts must be made firm and compact, and held intact by individual loops of strong twine, uniformly spaced at approximately 2-in. intervals girthwise. In addition, some roasts may require string tying lengthwise. In lieu of string, it is permissible to enclose roasts in a stretchable netting, provided it complies with the Regulation Governing the Meat Inspection of the USDA. Purchasers may specify that roasts be string-tied, when this requirement is not included in the detailed items specification.

MATERIAL

The curved and otherwise processed pork cuts described in these specifications must be derived from sound, well-trimmed wholesale market and fabricated cuts. The pork must show no evidence of freezer burn, mishandling, rancidity, or other detrimental blemish. Pork cuts which have been excessively trimmed in order to make specified weights, or which, for any reason, are substandard with these specifications must be excluded. They must be in excellent condition to the time of delivery.

IMPS NO. 500 **Ham, Short Shank, Regular [Cured]**
MBG NO. Not Included.
URMIS and COMMON NAMES: Pickled Ham.
COMMON USES: Roast; ham to be cut into other cuts of ham; baked ham; ground ham; ham salad; ham sandwiches.

Weight Range [in pounds]

RANGE A	RANGE B	RANGE C	RANGE D	RANGE E
10-12	12-14	14-16	16-18	18-20

The regular, cured, skin-on, short shank ham is produced by separating it from the side of a hog, at a point ranging from 2 to 3 in. in front of the exposed knob end of the aitch bone. The cut is made at an approximate right angle to a line parallel to the shank bones, with the knife held perpendicular to the outside skin surface of the side of the hog carcass to avoid undercutting in any direction on the butt end of the ham. Approximately half or more of the shank (but not beyond the stifle joint) must be cut off at an approximate right angle to the shank bone, and be excluded. The tail bone and the tail must be removed. Practically all pelvic fat (gut fat) and loose fat on the face of the ham must be removed, without any appreciable scoring on the muscular portion. The ham must be suitably faced without ragged edges, and with a smooth, well-rounded skin collar on the face side extending not more than 2-1/2 in. inward from the center of the stifle joint, on a line from that point to the bone on the butt end. The ham must be properly flanked to remove the lymph glands, fat, and tissue close to the major lean meat of the flank, and must be well-shaped and closely trimmed, being well-rounded at the cushion and butt end. The exterior fat thickness of the trimmed regular ham, measured directly under the bone at the edge of the butt, must not exceed that indicated on the following schedule:

WEIGHT RANGE OF REGULAR HAM	MAXIMUM FAT THICKNESS Selection No. 1	Selection No. 2
10-12 lb.	1 in.	1-1/2 in.
12-14 lb.	1-1/4 in.	1-3/4 in.
14-16 lb.	1-1/2 in.	2 in.
16-18 lb.	1-3/4 in.	2-1/4 in.
18-20 lb.	2 in.	2-1/2 in.

IMPS NO. 501 **Ham, Short Shank, Regular [Cured and Smoked]**
MBG NO. Not Included.
URMIS and COMMON NAMES: Smoked Ham.
COMMON USES: Roast; ham steaks; ham sandwiches; baked ham; ham salad; ground ham.

Weight Range [in pounds]

RANGE A	RANGE B	RANGE C	RANGE D	RANGE E
10-12	12-14	14-16	16-18	18-20

The regular (cured and smoked), short shank ham must conform with the requirements specified for Ham, Short Shank, Regular (Cured), Item No. 500, except that in addition to curing, the ham must be well-smoked.

IMPS NO. 502 **Ham, Short Shank, Partially Skinned [Cured]**
MBG NO. Not Included.
URMIS and COMMON NAMES: Short Shank Pickled Ham.
COMMON USES: Roast; ham sandwiches; baked ham; ham salad; ground ham.

Weight Range [in pounds]

RANGE A	RANGE B	RANGE C	RANGE D	RANGE E
10-12	12-14	14-16	16-18	18-20

The partially skinned, (cured) short shank ham must conform with the requirements specified for a Ham, Regular, Short Shank (Cured), Item No. 500, except that the ham must be partially skinned, leaving a well-rounded skin collar not exceeding 15 percent of the distance from the stifle joint to the edge of the butt. The skin must be removed so that the collar line is at a slant of at least 15 degrees toward the cushion side, starting at the flank side leaving the skin collar approximately 1 in. longer on the flank edge. Fat remaining on the skinned surface must be fairly smooth, and, except for beveling at the collar and butt ends, reasonably uniform in thickness, not exceeding 1/2 in. in depth measured at any point 1-1/2 in. or more from the edge of the skin collar. The fat must be neatly beveled on the back so it approximately meets the lean at the butt end.

IMPS NO. 503 **Ham, Short Shank, Partially Skinned [Cured and Smoked]**
MBG NO. Not Included.
URMIS and COMMON NAMES: Smoked Ham.
COMMON USES: Roast; ham steaks; ham sandwiches; baked ham; ham salad; ground ham.

Weight Range [in pounds]

RANGE A	RANGE B	RANGE C	RANGE D	RANGE E
10-12	12-14	14-16	16-18	18-20

The partially skinned (cured and smoked), short shank ham must conform with the requirements specified for Ham, Partially Skinned, Short Shank (Cured), Item No. 502, except that in addition to curing, the ham must be well-smoked.

IMPS NO. 504 **Ham, Skinless, Partially Boned [Cured and Smoked]**
MBG NO. Not Included.
URMIS and COMMON NAMES: Cured and Smoked, Partially Boned Ham, Semi-Boneless Ham.
COMMON USES: Roast; ham sandwiches; baked ham; ham salad; ground ham.

Weight Range [in pounds]

RANGE A	RANGE B	RANGE C	RANGE D	RANGE E
8-10	10-12	12-14	14-16	16-18

The skinless, partially boned ham (cured and smoked) must conform with the requirements specified for Ham, Regular (Cured and Smoked), Item No. 501, except that the ham must be made completely skinless, and be trimmed and defatted as necessary to produce a well-trimmed, skinless, cured, and smoked ham. Exterior fat, in excess of 3/8-in. average thickness as determined in the finished product, must be closely removed, and excluded. All trimming, skinning, and defatting may be accomplished either before or after curing, but must be done prior to smoking. The fat must be neatly beveled back, for at least 1 in. at the outer periphery of the butt end, from a point close to the lean meat edge of the butt. The aitch bone and overlying flesh and shank bones must be removed without excessive lacerations or other damage to the ham, leaving the femur bone intact in the ham. The lean meat of the shank, after proper trimming — removal of major tendons and practically all surface fat — may be left on the ham as a natural attachment, provided it is folded in and stitched. The ham must be encased in an artificial casing to produce a smooth, plump, elongated, oval-shaped, skinless, partially boned, cured, and smoked ham.

IMPS NO. 505 **Ham, Skinless, Completely Boneless [Cured and Smoked]**
MBG NO. Not Included.
URMIS and COMMON NAMES: Completely Boneless Ham, Boneless Ham Water Added.
COMMON USES: Panfry; roast; baked ham; ham steaks.

Weight Range [in pounds]

RANGE A	RANGE B	RANGE C	RANGE D	RANGE E
8-10	10-12	12-14	14-16	16-18

The skinless, completely boneless (cured and smoked) ham must conform with the specifications required for Ham, Skinless, Partially Boned (Cured and Smoked), Item No. 504, except that the ham must be made completely boneless. The femur bone must be removed closely without unduly lacerating or damaging the ham. The shank meat, if used, must be attached naturally, and after proper trimming — removal of major tendons and practically all surface fat—must be folded back into the adjacent femur bone cavity as a "plug" (preferably stitched). The prepared, cured ham must be encased in a close-fitting, artificial casing of sufficient transparency to reveal the exterior characteristics of the smoked ham. The casing must be of suitable size, strength, and quality to withstand conventional, careful handling of the product to the time of delivery. The ham must be handled and placed in the casing with the major muscle fibers running parallel (lengthwise) with the casing, so that customary slicing will be at approximate right angles thereto, and in a manner to result in an acceptable, smooth, compact, cohesive (properly sliceable) ham, of good symmetry, having a cylindrical, oval, or elliptical shape, and without detrimental recesses (pockets of air, moisture, rendered fat), in the finished product (close string stitching permissible). The encased ham may be smoked in stockinettes, or a similar hanging device.

IMPS NO. 505A **Ham, Skinless, Boned, Rolled, and Tied [Cured and Smoked]**
MBG NO. Not Included.
URMIS and COMMON NAMES: Boned, Rolled, and Tied Ham.
COMMON USES: Roast; panfry; baked ham; ham steaks.

Weight Range [in pounds]

RANGE A	RANGE B	RANGE C	RANGE D	RANGE E
8-10	10-12	12-14	14-16	16-18

The skinned, boned, rolled, and tied (cured and smoked) ham is the same as Ham, Skinless, Completely Boneless (Cured and Smoked), Item No. 505, except that the ham shall not be encased in an artificial casing. The boneless ham shall be rolled and string-tied.

IMPS NO. 506 **Ham, Partially Skinned [Cured and Smoked], Fully-Cooked, Dry Heat**
MBG NO. Not Included.
URMIS and COMMON NAMES: Boneless Cooked Ham.
COMMON USES: Roast; panfry; baked ham; ham steaks.

Weight Range [in pounds]

RANGE A	RANGE B	RANGE C
10-12	12-14	14-16

The partially skinned (cured and smoked), fully-cooked ham must conform with the requirements for Ham, Partially Skinned (Cured), Item No. 502, except that in addition to curing, the ham must be smoked, and cooked by the dry-heat method. All trimming, skinning, and defatting may be accomplished before or after curing, but must be done prior to smoking and cooking so that the finished product will be well trimmed, shapely, smooth and uniformly smoked over the entire surface. Promptly after smoking and cooking, the fully cooked ham must be handled as necessary to remove rendered surface fat and extraneous matter. After cooking, the fully-cooked ham must be properly chilled, prior to wrapping in suitable moisture- and grease-resistant paper of good quality.

IMPS NO. 507 **Ham, Boneless, Skinless [Cured and Smoked], Fully Cooked, Dry Heat**
MBG NO. Not Included.
URMIS and COMMON NAMES: Dried Cooked Ham.
COMMON USES: Roast; panfry; baked ham; ham steaks.

Weight Range [in pounds]

RANGE A	RANGE B	RANGE C
8-10	10-12	12-14

The boneless, skinless (cured and smoked), fully-cooked ham must conform with the requirements for Ham, Skinless (Cured and Smoked). Completely Boneless, Item No. 505, except that the ham must be fully-cooked by the dry-heat method. The dry-heat, fully-cooked ham must be stuffed into a close, smooth-fitting artificial casing, either prior to, or after, smoking and cooking. The ham may be dipped momentarily in dissolved, clear gelatin to facilitate putting it back in the casing.

IMPS NO. 508 **Ham, Boneless, Skinless [Cured], Pressed, Fully-Cooked, Moist Heat**
MBG NO. Not Included.
URMIS and COMMON NAMES: Boneless Cooked Ham.
COMMON USES: Roast; panfry; baked ham; ham steaks.
Weight Range [in pounds]

RANGE A	RANGE B	RANGE C	RANGE D
6-8	8-10	10-12	12-14

The boneless, skinless (cured), pressed, fully-cooked ham must conform with the requirements for Ham, Skinless (Cured and Smoked) Completely Boneless, Item No. 505, except that the ham must be cured only, and fully-cooked by the moist-heat method. The finished product may be rectangular, or pear-shaped, as specified by the purchaser. The moist-heat, fully-cooked ham may be stuffed intact into a close-fitting, artificial casing, or may be suitably wrapped — i.e., completely covered with paper, as specified by the purchaser. If artificial casings are specified, the exterior of the encased ham must be practically free of gelatinous material, rendered fat, extraneous matter, appendages, and strings, or mechanical fasteners, except as necessary to secure the ends of the tied casings. The external end or surface of the ham may be momentarily dipped in a gelatinous solution if it is necessary to facilitate stuffing in the casing.

IMPS NO. 509 **Ham, Boneless, Skinless [Cured and Smoked], Pressed, Fully-Cooked, Moist Heat**
MBG NO. Not Included.
URMIS and COMMON NAMES: Boneless Cooked Ham.
COMMON USES: Roast; panfry; baked ham; ham steaks.
Weight Range [in pounds]

RANGE A	RANGE B	RANGE C	RANGE D
6-8	8-10	10-12	12-14

The boneless, skinless (cured and smoked), pressed, fully-cooked ham must conform to the requirements for Ham, Boneless, Skinless (Cured), Pressed, Fully-Cooked, Moist Heat, Item No. 508, except that in addition to curing, the ham must be smoked in accordance with good commercial practice.

IMPS NO. 515 **Shoulder, Regular [Cured]**
MBG NO. Not Included.
URMIS and COMMON NAMES: Pickled Pork Shoulder.
COMMON USES: Ground Ham.
Weight Range [in pounds]

RANGE A	RANGE B	RANGE C	RANGE D
8-10	10-12	12-14	14-16
	RANGE E	RANGE F	
	16-18	18-20	

The cured, regular shoulder is produced by separation from the hog side by a cut starting at a point in the arm pit that is not more than 1 in. behind the elbow joint, but which does not expose the elbow joint, and which continues reasonably straight across the hog side, perpendicular to the outside skin surface. The neck bones, ribs and related cartilage, and breast bone, intercostal meat, breast flap, bloody discolorations, and loose ends must be closely and smoothly removed and excluded. The shoulder must be well-faced without undue removal of lean. The foot must be neatly sawed, and cut off in, or slightly above, the upper joint of the knee at an approximate right angle to the shank bone, and, unless otherwise specified, shoulders with shorter shanks (but not cut beyond the elbow joint) will be acceptable.

The jowl (neck portion) must be removed close to the body of the shoulder on a line approximately parallel to the opposite straight-cut side of the shoulder, starting behind the "ear-dip," which must remain on the jowls, and continuing the cut so as to remove the entire jowl section. Overhanging or protruding fat or skin at the butt must be removed closely, and on a slight bevel approximately meeting the major lean edge at the butt, to produce a shapely and closely trimmed regular shoulder. The exterior fat thickness of the trimmed regular shoulder, measured perpendicular to the skin at the approximate center of the butt, must not exceed that indicated in the following schedule:

WEIGHT RANGE OF REGULAR SHOULDERS	MAXIMUM FAT THICKNESS	
	Selection No. 1	Selection No. 2
8-10 lb.	1 in.	1-1/2 in.
10-12 lb.	1-1/4 in.	1-3/4 in.
12-14 lb.	1-1/2 in.	2 in.
14-16 lb.	1-3/4 in.	2-1/4 in.
16-18 lb.	2 in.	2-1/2 in.

IMPS NO. 516 **Shoulder, Regular [Cured and Smoked]**
MBG NO. Not Included.
URMIS and COMMON NAMES: Smoked Pork Shoulder.
COMMON USES: Ground Ham.

Weight Range [in pounds]

RANGE A	RANGE B	RANGE C	RANGE D
8-10	10-12	12-14	14-16

RANGE E	RANGE F
16-18	18-20

The regular (cured and smoked) shoulder must conform to the requirements specified for Shoulder, Regular (Cured), Item No. 515, except that in addition to curing, the shoulder must be well-smoked.

IMPS NO. 518 **Shoulder, Skinned [Cured and Smoked]**
MBG NO. Not Included.
URMIS and COMMON NAMES: Smoked Pork Shoulder.
COMMON USES: Ground Ham.

Weight Range [in pounds]

RANGE A	RANGE B	RANGE C	RANGE D	RANGE E
8-10	10-12	12-14	14-16	16-18

The skinned shoulder (cured and smoked) must conform with the requirements specified for Shoulder, Partially Skinned (Cured), Item No. 517, except that in addition to curing, the shoulder must be well-smoked.

IMPS NO. 517 **Shoulder, Partially Skinned [Cured]**
MBG NO. Not Included.
URMIS and COMMON NAMES: Pickled Pork Shoulder.
COMMON USES: Ground Ham.

Weight Range [in pounds]

RANGE A	RANGE B	RANGE C	RANGE D	RANGE E
8-10	10-12	12-14	14-16	16-18

The partially skinned shoulder (cured) must conform with the requirements specified for a Regular Shoulder (Cured), Item No. 515, except that the shoulder must be partially skinned, leaving a well-rounded skin collar at the shank end. The skin collar must not exceed 45 percent of the length of the entire back (skin-side) surface of the shoulder, measured lengthwise from the approximate center at the edge of the butt to the extreme outer tip of the shank end, when removed at, or near, the upper knee joint. For shoulders in which the foot is cut shorter, the skin collar must not exceed 25 percent of the length, measured centrally on the outside of the shoulder along a straight line which extends from below the elbow joint to the edge at the butt end. The skin must be removed so that the collar-line is at a slant of at least 15 degrees from the elbow side ventrally toward the jowl side. Fat remaining on the skinned surface must be fairly smooth, and, except for beveling at the collar and butt ends, reasonably uniform in thickness, not exceeding 1/2 in. in depth, measured at any point 1-1/2 in. or more from the edge of the skin collar. At least traces of false lean must be evident on the back (skinned side) surface of the shoulder. The fat must be neatly beveled to meet the lean meat approximately at the butt and sides.

IMPS NO. 525 **Shoulder Picnic [Cured]**
MBG NO. Not Included.
URMIS and COMMON NAMES: Picnic Ham, Pickled Shoulder.
COMMON USES: Ham sandwiches; ground cured pork.

Weight Range [in pounds]

RANGE A	RANGE B	RANGE C	RANGE D
4-6	6-8	8-10	10-12

The regular (skin on), cured shoulder picnic is that portion of the standard cut Shoulder, Regular, Item No. 515, remaining after the removal of the clear plate and the Boston butt. The shoulder picnic is separated from the Boston butt and clear plate by a cut which is reasonably straight, perpendicular to the outside skin surface (not slanted or undercut), and approximately parallel to the breast side of the shoulder, leaving all the major shoulder bone (humerus) and not less than 1 or more than 2 in. of the blade bone (scapula) in the shoulder picnic. The foot must be neatly sawed, and cut off in, or slightly above, the upper joint of the knee, at an approximate right angle to the shank bone. Unless otherwise specified, shoulder picnics with shorter shanks (but not cut beyond the elbow joint) will be acceptable. The shoulder picnic must be well-faced, including removal of practically all of the "lip" and breast flap, and must be well-rounded, with the skin and fat beveled at least the equivalent of the thickness of the fat at the butt end to produce a shapely and closely trimmed shoulder picnic. The exterior fat thickness at the butt end of the trimmed shoulder picnic, measured perpendicular to the skin at the skin edge of the bevel directly underneath the remaining portion of the scapular bone, must not exceed that indicated in the following schedule:

WEIGHT RANGE OF SHOULDER PICNICS	MAXIMUM FAT THICKNESS	
	Selection No. 1	Selection No. 2
4- 6 lb.	3/4 in.	1-1/4 in.
6- 8 lb.	7/8 in.	1-3/8 in.
8-10 lb.	1 in.	1-1/2 in.
10-12 lb.	1-1/4 in.	1-3/4 in.

IMPS NO. 526 **Shoulder Picnic [Cured and Smoked]**
MBG NO. Not Included.
URMIS and COMMON NAMES: Smoked Picnic Ham.
COMMON USES: Roast; steaks.

Weight Range [in pounds]

RANGE A	RANGE B	RANGE C	RANGE D
4-6	6-8	8-10	10-12

The shoulder picnic (cured and smoked) must conform with the requirements specified for Shoulder Picnic (Cured), Item No. 525, except that in addition to curing, the shoulder picnic must be well-smoked.

IMPS NO. 527 **Shoulder Picnic [Cured and Smoked]; Boneless, Skinless, Rolled and Tied**
MBG NO. Not Included.
URMIS and COMMON NAMES: Smoked Picnic Boneless, Boneless Picnic.
COMMON USES: Roasts; steaks.

Weight Range [in pounds]

RANGE A	RANGE B	RANGE C
6-8	8-10	10-12

The shoulder picnic (cured and smoked), boneless, skinless, rolled, and tied must conform with the requirements for Shoulder Picnic (Cured and Smoked), Item No. 526, except that the picnic must be made completely boneless and skinless. The arm bone and blade bone must be removed closely, without unduly lacerating or damaging the shoulder picnic. The shank meat, if used, must be attached naturally, and after proper trimming — removal of major tendons and practically all surface fat — must be folded back into the adjacent elbow bone cavity as a "plug" (preferably stitched). Exterior surface fat in excess of 3/8-in. average thickness, as determined in the finished product, must be closely removed, and excluded. All trimming, skinning, and defatting may be accomplished either before or after curing, but must be done prior to smoking. The boneless, skinless, cured, and smoked picnic must be rolled to produce a firm, compact, rolled roast, and must be held together by loops of strong twine uniformly spaced girthwise and lengthwise around the outside of the rolled roast.

IMPS NO. 530 **Shoulder Butt, Boneless [Cured and Smoked]**
MBG NO. Not Included.
URMIS and COMMON NAMES: Cottage Ham.
COMMON USES: Roast; boiled; cottage ham.

Weight Range [in pounds]

RANGE A
4-6

The boneless shoulder butt is the portion of the Boston butt on the flat (front) side of the blade bone. It must be removed intact, and must be closely trimmed by removing loose flesh, ragged edges, and surface fat in excess of 1/4 in. in thickness. The trimmed, boneless shoulder butt must be cured, and stuffed into a close and smooth-fitting artificial casing, either prior to, or subsequent to, smoking. Dissolved clear gelatin may be used as a momentary dip for the product to facilitate putting it in the casings. Promptly after smoking, the finished product must be handled as is necessary to remove grease and extraneous matter.

IMPS NO. 535 **Belly, Skin-On [Cured]**
MBG NO. Not Included.
URMIS and COMMON NAMES: Bacon, Slab Bacon, Pickled Pork.
COMMON USES: Broil; panfry; bacon.

Weight Range [in pounds]

RANGE A	RANGE B	RANGE C	RANGE D
8-10	10-12	12-14	14-16
	RANGE E	RANGE F	
	16-18	18-20	

The skin-on (cured) belly is that portion of the pork-side middle left after removal of the loin, fatback, and spareribs. The belly must be boneless, and the major cartilage of the sternum and the ribs must be removed closely and smoothly, without deep scoring. Any remaining embedded tips of the cartilage must be approximately level with, or slightly lower than, the surface lean. The longest diameter of any exposed cartilage must not exceed 3/8 in. Practically all leaf fat and other abdominal surface fat of similar character must be removed. The belly must be separated from the fatback on a straight line not more than 3/4 in. beyond the outermost curvature of the scribe line. The scribe line must not exceed 1/4 in. in depth. The inside surface area on the fatback side above the scribe line must not be unduly scalped (snowballed). The sides of the belly must be reasonably straight and parallel, and at approximate right angles to the shoulder end. The ham end of the belly may be cut on an angle, so that the flank side is about 1 in. longer than the fatback side. Any enlarged soft, porous, or seedy mammary tissue, and the pizzle recess of barrow bellies must be removed. No lean meat may be removed, except that necessary in appropriate squaring and trimming. Bellies showing any of the following objectionable characteristics detrimentally affecting the finished product will not be acceptable: severe or excessive trimming to make specified weights; undue removal of lean meat; poor workmanship; or any other damage or condition adversely affecting the end product.

IMPS NO. 536 **Bacon, Slab [Cured and Smoked] Skin-On**
MBG NO. Not Included.
URMIS and COMMON NAMES: Bacon, Slab Bacon.
COMMON USES: Broil; panfry; bacon.

Weight Range [in pounds]

RANGE A	RANGE B	RANGE C	RANGE D
8-10	10-12	12-14	14-16

The skin-on (cured and smoked) slab bacon must conform with the requirements specified for Belly, Skin-On (Cured), Item No. 535, except that the belly must be well-squared on all edges, and with approximately straight and parallel sides and ends (normal receding flesh at the brisket and ham ends, or slight distortion from smoking, is acceptable), and be well adapted to producing a high yield of full-cut, acceptable slices. In addition to curing, the belly must be well-smoked.

IMPS NO. 537 **Bacon, Slab [Cured and Smoked] Skinless, Formed**
MBG NO. Not Included.
URMIS and COMMON NAMES: Bacon, Slab Bacon, Derinded Bacon.
COMMON USES: Broil; panfry; bacon.

Weight Range [in pounds]

RANGE A	RANGE B	RANGE C	RANGE D
8-10	10-12	12-14	14-16

The skinless slab bacon must conform with the requirements specified for Bacon, Slab (Cured and Smoked) Skin-On, Item No. 536, except that the finished product must have the skin removed, and excluded, leaving a smooth-skinned surface, free of hair roots. The skin may be removed from the belly, or slab bacon, either before or after curing, but must be done prior to smoking. The skinless slab bacon must be well-formed (usually shaped mechanically) after smoking and cooling.

IMPS NO. 539 **Bacon, Sliced [Cured and Smoked] Skinless**
MBG NO. Not Included.
URMIS and COMMON NAMES: Sliced Bacon.
COMMON USES: Broil; panfry; bacon.
NUMBER OF SLICES PER POUND: 18-22; 22-26; 26-30.

The slices must be produced from skinless slab bacon. The bacon slices, as packaged in individual packages, must be at least moderately uniform in length, width, and thickness, ranging from 8 to 10 in. in length without underfolding. Unsliced pieces, or slices showing hanger comb marks, product residue, punctured or mutilated sections, cracked slices due to hard or granular fat, or those cut on an appreciable slant or bias, or from small or irregular pieces, or which have other serious damage, must be excluded. One part-slice may be used per package to make exact weight. The individual packages of sliced bacon must be of the number of slices per pound as specified.

IMPS NO. 541 **Bacon, Sliced [Cured and Smoked] Ends and Pieces**
MBG NO. Not Included.
URMIS and COMMON NAMES: Bacon Ends.
COMMON USES: Cook in moist heat.
Weight Range [in pounds]
5- and 10-lb. containers

The ends and pieces must be obtained from the regular production of sliced bacon. Frayed, shredded, broken, or otherwise damaged slices; small, unsliced pieces; slices showing string or hanger marks; or slices from small or extreme sections, and machine scrap pieces are acceptable.

How to Buy BACON

You have a better chance to choose the kind of bacon you like since a U.S. Department of Agriculture regulation on bacon packaging became effective. The regulation requires that all bacon packages have a transparent area at least 1½ inches wide revealing at least 70 percent of the length of a representative slice. To meet this requirement, many bacon packages added a new "back window"; some simply show a full slice in a "front" window.

Here are some basic factors to consider when you buy bacon:

Primarily, bacon differs in its amount of lean (lean-to-fat ratio), distribution of lean, and thickness of slice. These factors may vary considerably within a given brand.

LEAN-TO-FAT RATIO
Look at the slice in the window to see how much lean and fat it contains. These drawings show slices with different amounts of lean. Select according to your taste, but remember that most of the bacon produced looks like slices 2 and 3.

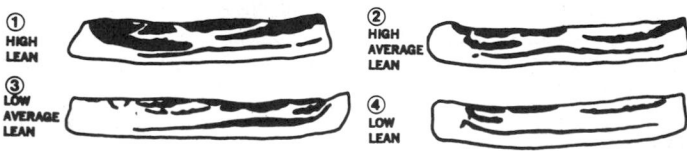

① HIGH LEAN ② HIGH AVERAGE LEAN ③ LOW AVERAGE LEAN ④ LOW LEAN

DISTRIBUTION OF LEAN
The distribution of lean within a slice of bacon affects its palatability. When fried, bacon with several strips of lean distributed throughout the slice will tend to be more crispy, while bacon with the same amount of lean concentrated in fewer but larger sections will tend to be more chewy. These drawings show slices with the same amount of lean distributed differently. Here again, select according to your taste.

 CRISPY    CHEWY

THICKNESS OF SLICE
Thick slices are chewier than thin or very thin slices—unless cooked longer. Very thinly sliced bacon and vacuum packed bacon is often hard to separate when cold. Warming it first helps. Regular one-pound sliced bacon packages contain about 20 to 22 slices, while a one-pound package of thick-sliced bacon usually contains about 12 slices.

Bacon is commonly sold in one-pound shingle packages. However, it is also available in a two-pound package, or the smaller 12-ounce or half-pound packages. When comparing prices, check the weight of the package.

IMPS NO. 545 **Loin, Regular [Cured and Smoked]**
MBG NO. Not Included.
URMIS and COMMON NAMES: Smoked Pork Loin.
COMMON USES: Broil; panfry; smoked pork chops.
Weight Range [in pounds]

RANGE A	RANGE B	RANGE C	RANGE D
8-10	10-12	12-14	14-16

The regular, cured and smoked pork loin is typical of a pork loin cut from a standard hog side, after the removal of the regular shoulder, ham, belly, and back fat, thus leaving the customary blade bone portion with its overlying flesh, 11 or more ribs and at least 3 sacral vertebrae in the loin. The line separating the loin from the belly is fairly straight, and reasonably parallel with the major loin muscles. It must extend from a point on the 1st rib of the loin, which is not more than 1-3/4 in. from the junction of the foremost rib and the foremost thoracic vertebra, to a point on the ham end, which is immediately adjacent to the major tenderloin muscle, which must remain practically intact in the loin. The fleshy side of the loin must be fairly smooth, with a well-arched, convex surface, extending from a point close to the cut tip ends of the ribs to a point fairly close to the outer extremities of the thoracic vertebrae (feather bone tips). This smoothness and contour must continue over the rest of the loin in a plane which is reasonably parallel with the major muscle of the loin. The outside muscle (false lean) over the blade must be exposed lengthwise with the loin for a distance of 4 or more inches. The fat on the loin over the major loin muscles must not exceed 1/4 in. in thickness. There must be no appreciable removal of the lean from the major loin muscles. Except for a thicker, shoulder end, the contour (width and thickness) of the loin must be fairly uniform and symmetrical. Lumbar and pelvic fat over 1/4 in. in thickness, and bloody portions (usually at the shoulder end) must be closely removed, and excluded. The skirt (diaphragm) and hanging tender must be removed, and excluded.

IMPS NO. 546 **Loin, Bladeless [Cured and Smoked]**
MBG NO. Not Included.
URMIS and COMMON NAMES: Smoked Pork Loin.
COMMON USES: Broil; panfry; smoked pork chops.
Weight Range [in pounds]

RANGE A	RANGE B	RANGE C	RANGE D
8-10	10-12	12-14	14-16

The bladeless (cured and smoked) loin must conform with the requirements specified for Loin, Regular (Cured and Smoked), Item No. 545, except that the blade bone and related cartilage and the overlying flesh must have been removed and excluded.

IMPS NO. 550 Canadian Style Bacon [Cured and Smoked] Unsliced
MBG NO. Not Included.
URMIS and COMMON NAMES: Canadian Bacon, Rolled Bacon.
COMMON USES: Breakfast meat; with Eggs Benedict.

Weight Range [in pounds]

RANGE A	RANGE B
3-5	5-9

Canadian style bacon must be produced from that portion of a regular pork loin, which is in front of the hip bone. All bones, cartilage, tenderloins, and accompanying lumbar fat and tissue, skirts, intercostal meat (rib fingers), glandular tissue, blade meat (includes the muscle lying directly beneath the blade bone), belly strip, and the thin layers of meat (whether exposed or covered with fat) lying over the major loin muscle must be closely removed, and excluded, leaving only the major loin muscle and closely adhering muscles on the inside thereof. The boneless, major loin muscle must be cut fairly square at both ends, and frayed and semi-loose pieces of flesh and fat in excess of 1/4 in. thickness of any exposed surface must be closely removed, and excluded. The finished product may be encased in artifical casings. Dissolved, clear gelatin may be used as a quick dip for the product to facilitate stuffing it in the casing.

IMPS NO. 551 Canadian Style Bacon [Cured and Smoked] Sliced
MBG NO. Not Included.
URMIS and COMMON NAMES: Canadian Bacon.
COMMON USES: Breakfast meat.

Weight Range [in pounds]

RANGE A	RANGE B	RANGE C	RANGE D
4-6	6-8	8-10	10-12
RANGE E	**RANGE F**	**RANGE G**	**RANGE H**
12-14	14-16	16-18	18-20

Sliced Canadian style bacon must be produced from cured and smoked Canadian Style Bacon, Item No. 550. The slices must be reasonably uniform in thickness, and they may range in thickness from 7 to 9 slices per linear inch. Slicing must be at approximate right angles to the major muscle. Insofar as practical, the slices must be maintained in conventional layers in the same order as produced. Slices showing string or hanger marks; slices from small or irregular end sections; mutilated slices; machine scrap pieces, or other product residue, must not be included.

IMPS NO. 555 Jowl Butts, Cellar Trim [Cured]
MBG NO. Not Included.
URMIS and COMMON NAMES: Pickled Jowl, Fat Cured Pork.
COMMON USES: Ham loaf; sausage.

Weight Range [in pounds]

RANGE A	RANGE B
1 - 2-1/2	2-1/2 - 4

Cured jowl butts must be of standard cellar trim, with boot jack points and ragged ends smoothly removed, and excluded. Slightly irregular trimming is permissible. The product must be free from dripping moisture, and must not exude moisture upon appreciable hand pressure. Individual pieces of the product delivered dry salted must be coated with clear granulated salt; however, loose and encrusted salt must be removed and excluded. The finished product must not exhibit evidence of over- or under-curing, or of improper storage.

IMPS NO. 556 Jowl Squares [Cured and Smoked]
MBG NO. Not Included.
URMIS and COMMON NAMES: Smoked Jowl, Fat Cured Pork.
COMMON USES: Broil; panfry; seasoning; bacon; sliced jowl bacon.

Weight Range [in pounds]

RANGE A	RANGE B
3/4 - 2	2-3

Jowl squares must be reasonably rectangular in shape, and at least reasonably well-squared on the sides and ends, being reasonably symmetrical and reasonably smooth on all surfaces. They must be well-faced by close removal, before smoking, of surface glandular and loose tissue, and bloody discoloration.

IMPS NO. 558 Spareribs [Cured]
MBG NO. Not Included.
URMIS and COMMON NAMES: Pickled Spareribs, Cured Spareribs.
COMMON USES: Ribs; spareribs; country style ribs.

Weight Range [in pounds]

RANGE A	RANGE B	RANGE C
3 or less	3-5	5 or more

Cured spareribs are the entire rib section intact, as removed by neatly "ribbing" the belly portion of the pork carcass midsection, extending from the scribe line at the fatback side of the belly to, and including portions of, the rib cartilage, with or without a portion of the split breast bone, and with or without the skirt (diaphragm) remaining.

IMPS NO. 559 **Spareribs [Cured and Smoked]**
MBG NO. Not Included.
URMIS and COMMON NAMES: Smoked Spareribs.
COMMON USES: Barbecue; broil; smoked spareribs.

Weight Range [in pounds]

RANGE A	RANGE B	RANGE C
3 or less	3-5	5 or more

The spareribs (cured and smoked) must conform with the requirements for Spareribs (Cured), Item No. 558, except that in addition to curing, the spareribs must be well-smoked.

IMPS NO. 560 **Hocks, Shoulder [Cured]**
MBG NO. Not Included.
URMIS and COMMON NAMES: Pickled Knuckles, Pickled Hocks.
COMMON USES: Soups; pork and beans; ham hocks.

Weight Range [in pounds]

RANGE A	RANGE B	RANGE C
1/2 - 1	1 - 1-1/2	1-1/2 - 2-1/2

Shoulder hocks are produced in making short shank shoulders or shoulder picnics. They must be cut in or above the upper joint of the knee and must include the fleshy portion of the shank as produced. They may not be less than 2 in. in length.

IMPS NO. 561 **Hocks, Shoulder [Cured and Smoked]**
MBG NO. Not Included.
URMIS and COMMON NAMES: Ham Hocks, Smoked Hocks.
COMMON USES: Soups; pork and beans; ham hocks.

Weight Range [in pounds]

RANGE A	RANGE B	RANGE C
1/2 - 1	1 - 1-1/2	1-1/2 - 2-1/2

The shoulder hocks (cured and smoked) must conform with the requirements specified for Hocks, Shoulder (Cured), Item No. 560, except that in addition to curing, the shoulder hocks must be well-smoked.

IMPS NO. 562 **Clear Fatback [Cured]**
MBG NO. Not Included.
URMIS and COMMON NAMES: Pickled Pork Fatback.
COMMON USES: Seasoning; sausage; larding meat.

Weight Range [in pounds]

RANGE A	RANGE B	RANGE C
6-8	8-10	10-12

The cured, clear fatbacks must be produced from the fatty portion of the back after the removal of the loin. They must be relatively short and thick, and the thickness must be relatively uniform throughout. All edges must be reasonably squared. The cured product must be well-drained, and reasonably free from loose and encrusted salt.

IMPS NO. 563 **Front Feet [Cured]**
MBG NO. Not Included.
URMIS and COMMON NAMES: Pigs' feet.
COMMON USES: Pickled pigs' feet; pigs' feet and greens; pigs' feet and beans.

Weight Range [in pounds]
3/4 to 1-1/2

Front feet are removed from the shoulder at least slightly above the knee joints. The feet must be properly scalded and cleaned, and be free from scurf. The feet must also be free from hair roots, and the nails must be removed. Extra-large, coarse feet are not acceptable.

BIBLIOGRAPHY

"All About Meat." *Food Service.* December 1964, pp. 4-56.

Bowes, Clifford G. *Complete Guide to Profitable Meat Management, Vol. 1, Meat Department Management.* Boston: Cahners Books International, Inc., 1971.

Brosington, Clayton F., Jr. "Marketing Research Report." *Hotel and Restaurant Meat Purveyors-Improved Methods and Facilities for Supplying Frozen Portion-Controlled Meat,* April 1971, pp. 1-44.

Buying Beef For the Eating-Out Business. Chicago: Armour and Company.

"Cashing in on Pork." National Live Stock and Meat Board, September 1971, pp. 3-78.

Committee on Preparation Factors National Cooperative Meat Investigations. *Meat and Meat Cookery.* Chicago: National Livestock and Meat Board, 1942.

Directory of Meat and Poultry Inspection Program Establishments and Officials. Washington, D.C.: U.S. Department of Agriculture, 1974.

Effects of Alternative Marketing Margins For Beef and Pork. Washington, D.C.: U.S. Department of Agriculture, 1973.

"How To Buy Beef Roasts." Washington, D.C.: U.S. Department of Agriculture, January 1968, pp. 3-15.

"How To Buy Beef Steaks." Washington, D.C.: U.S. Department of Agriculture, February 1973, pp. 3-15.

"How To Buy Meat for your Freezer." Washington, D.C.: U.S. Department of Agriculture, July 1974, pp. 3-27.

Kramlich, W.E., et al. *Processed Meats.* Westport, Connecticut: Avi Publishing Company, Inc., 1973.

Lamb Cutting and Purchasing Manual. Denver: American Sheep Products Council, 1957.

Lamb, How To Cut Today's New Lamb for Greater Sales and Profits. Chicago: National Livestock and Meat Board, 1971.

Lessons on Meat. Chicago: National Livestock and Meat Board, 1964.

Levie, Albert. *The Meat Handbook.* Westport, Connecticut: Avi Publishing Company, Inc., 1967.

Livestock and Meat Statistics. Washington, D.C.: U.S. Department of Agriculture, 1973.

Meat Buyers Guide To Portion Control Meat Cuts. Chicago: National Association of Meat Purveyors, 1967.

Meat Buyers Guide To Standardized Meat Cuts. Chicago: National Association of Meat Purveyors, 1961.

Meat Evaluation Handbook. Chicago: National Livestock and Meat Board, 1969.

"Meat Facts." *American Meat Institute.* July 1974, pp. 2-22.

"Merchandising Beef Loins." Chicago: National Livestock and Meat Board, pp.3-32.

"Merchandising Beef Ribs." Chicago: National Livestock and Meat Board, pp. 3-36.

"Merchandising Beef Rounds." Chicago: National Lifestock and Meat Board, pp. 3-24.

Miller, A.R., D.V.M. "To Assure Good Clean Meat, Food." *The Yearbook of Agriculture 1959.* Washington, D.C.: Government Printing Office, 1959, pp. 340-343. (Yearbook Separate No. 2970)

101 Meat Cuts ... a guide to meat selection and care. Chicago: National Livestock and Meat Board.

"Pork in the Foodservice Industry." *Pork Industry Committee,* pp. 2-47.

Price - Quantity Relationships For Selected Retail Cuts of Pork. Washington, D.C.: U.S. Department of Agriculture.

Putman, D.A., Northeastern Region, et. al. *Beef Cattle Breeds,* February 1975, pp. 1-33.

Rust, Robert E. and Olson, Dennis G. *Meat Curing Principles and Modern Practice.* Kansas City, Mo: Koch Supplies Inc., 1973.

U.S. Department of Agriculture. *Better Marketing for Beef with a New USDA Grading System,* (AMS-471), Washington, D.C.: Government Printing Office.

U.S. Department of Agriculture. *Consumer and Marketing Service.* Washington, D.C.: Government Printing Office, 1971.

U.S. Department of Agriculture. *Meat and Poultry Standards For You.* Home and Garden Bulletin No. 171, Washington, D.C.: Government Printing Office, 1969.

Wanderstock, J.J. "Meat Purchasing." *The Cornell Hotel & Restaurant Administration Quarterly,* II, No. 3, 1970, pp. 60-64.

Wrisley, Albert L., Buck, Ernest M., Eshbach, Charles E. *Purchasing Beef for Food Service Establishments.* Amherst, Mass.: University of Massachusetts.

3

POULTRY

STANDARDS AND GRADES

The difference between standards of quality and the grades assigned to poultry is sometimes misunderstood. The standards of quality cover the various factors that determine the grade. These factors, such as fat covering, fleshing, exposed flesh, discolorations, etc., when evaluated collectively, determine the grade of the bird.

The U.S. Consumer Grades for Poultry are used at the retail level. The U.S. Consumer Grades are: U.S. Grade A; U.S. Grade B; and U.S. Grade C.

The U.S. Procurement Grades are designed primarily for institutional use. These grades are: U.S. Procurement Grade 1 and U.S. Procurement Grade 2. The Procurement Grades place more emphasis on meat yield than on appearance.

OFFICIAL IDENTIFICATION BY GRADERS LICENSED BY THE U.S. DEPT. OF AGRICULTURE

Anyone having a financial interest in a lot of processed poultry may make application to the U.S. Dept. of Agriculture to have an official grade designation placed on the lot. This service, which is available throughout the country, is operated on a self-supporting basis. A nominal fee is charged which covers the time and travel expense of the grader, plus the cost of administering the program. The U.S. Dept. of Agriculture enters into cooperative agreements with state departments of agriculture, making it possible to license qualified state employees to grade and certify the quality of poultry.

Many processors utilize full-time resident graders in their plants. This enables the plant to apply the U.S. grade mark to each individual package, or each individual bird.

The Military and Federal, state, county, and city institutions, as well as other large-scale buyers such as steamship lines, independent and chain stores, and private hospitals, make use of the grading service by specifying U.S. grades in their contracts for poultry products.

Commercial firms often use the U.S. Standards and Grades as a basis for establishing specifications for their own product.

CLASSES

Some states provide a voluntary grading and inspection program. Such programs generally follow the U.S. Standards and Grades in whole, or in part. Producers, as well as processors, may use the standards of quality as a basis for sorting or selecting birds for market.

."Kind" refers to the different species of poultry, such as chickens, turkeys, ducks, geese, guineas, and pigeons. The kinds of poultry are divided into "classes" by groups which are essentially of the same physical characteristics, such as fryers or hens. These physical characteristics are associated with age and sex.

The kinds and classes of live, dressed, and ready-to-cook poultry listed in the U.S. Classes, Standards, and Grades are in general use in all segments of the poultry industry.

The following provisions apply to live poultry, dressed poultry, and individual carcasses of ready-to-cook poultry, in determining the kind of poultry and its class.

CHICKENS

ROCK CORNISH GAME HEN OR CORNISH GAME HEN. A Rock Cornish game hen or Cornish game hen is a young immature chicken (usually 5 to 7 weeks of age), weighing not more than 2 lb. ready-to-cook weight, which was prepared from a Cornish chicken, or the progeny of a Cornish chicken crossed with another breed of chicken.

BROILER OR FRYER. A broiler or fryer is a young chicken (usually 9 to 12 weeks of age), of either sex, that is tender-meated, with soft, pliable, smooth-textured skin and flexible breastbone cartilage.

ROASTER. A roaster is a young chicken (usually 3 to 5 months of age), of either sex, that is tender-meated, with soft, pliable, smooth-textured skin, and breastbone cartilage that may be somewhat less flexible than that of a broiler or fryer.

CAPON. A capon is a surgically unsexed, male chicken (usually under 8 months of age), that is tender-meated, with soft, pliable, smooth-textured skin.

STAG. A stag is a male chicken (usually under 10 months of age), with coarse skin, somewhat toughened and darkened flesh, and considerable hardening of the breastbone cartilage. Stags show a condition of fleshing and a degree of maturity intermediate between that of a roaster and a cock or rooster.

HEN OR STEWING CHICKEN OR FOWL. A hen, or stewing chicken or fowl, is a mature, female chicken usually more than 10 months of age), with meat less tender than that of a roaster, and nonflexible breastbone tip.

COCK OR ROOSTER. A cock or rooster is a mature, male chicken with coarse skin, toughened and darkened meat, and hardened breastbone tip.

TURKEYS

FRYER-ROASTER TURKEY. A fryer-roaster turkey is a young, immature turkey (usually under 16 weeks of age), of either sex, that is tender-meated with soft, pliable, smooth-textured skin and flexible breastbone cartilage.

YOUNG HEN TURKEY. A young hen turkey is a young, female turkey (usually 5 to 7 months of age), that is tender-meated, with soft-pliable, smooth-textured skin, and breastbone cartilage that is somewhat less flexible than in a fryer-roaster turkey.

YOUNG TOM TURKEY. A young tom turkey is a young, male turkey (usually 5 to 7 months of age), that is tender-meated, with soft, pliable, smooth-textured skin, and breastbone cartilage that is somewhat less flexible than a fryer-roaster turkey.

YEARLING HEN TURKEY. A yearling hen turkey is a fully matured, female turkey (usually under 15 months of age), that is reasonably tender-meated with reasonably smooth-textured skin.

YEARLING TOM TURKEY. A yearling tom turkey is a fully matured, male turkey (usually under 15 months of age), that is reasonably tender-meated, with reasonably smooth-textured skin.

MATURE TURKEY OR OLD TURKEY (HEN OR TOM). A mature or old turkey is an old turkey of either sex (usually in excess of 15 months of age), with a coarse skin and toughened flesh.

(For labeling purposes, the designation of sex within the class name is optional, and the three classes of young turkeys may be grouped and designated as "young turkeys.")

DUCKS

BROILER DUCKLING OR FRYER DUCKLING. A broiler duckling or fryer duckling is a young duck (usually under 8 weeks of age) of either sex, that is tender-meated and has a soft bill and soft windpipe.

ROASTER DUCKLING. A roaster duckling is a young duck (usually under 16 weeks of age), of either sex, that is tender-meated and has a bill that is not completely hardened and a windpipe that is easily dented.

MATURE DUCK OR OLD DUCK. A mature duck or an old duck is a duck (usually over 6 months of age) of either sex, with toughened flesh, hardened bill, and hardened windpipe.

GEESE

YOUNG GOOSE. A young goose may be of either sex, is tender-meated, and has a windpipe that is easily dented.

MATURE GOOSE OR OLD GOOSE. A mature goose or old goose may be of either sex and has toughened flesh and hardened windpipe.

GUINEAS

YOUNG GUINEA. A young guinea may be of either sex, is tender-meated and has a flexible breastbone cartilage.

MATURE GUINEA OR OLD GUINEA. A mature guinea or an old guinea may be of either sex, has toughened flesh and hardened breastbone.

PIGEONS

SQUAB. A squab is a young, immature pigeon of either sex and is extra tender-meated.

PIGEON. A pigeon is a mature pigeon of either sex, with coarse skin and toughened flesh.

Each class of poultry has one or more distinctive characteristics which enable the grader to properly classify an individual bird, or a lot of poultry. The list of characteristics shown below is not all-inclusive. A lot of poultry containing two or more classes would be described as a "mixed class."

The degree of maturity as used as a guide in cooking, and the names given to the classes are such that they are readily recognized. Processing into ready-to-cook poultry eliminates many of the definite indications which are seen in live and dressed poultry. Various indications which may be seen in live, dressed, and ready-to-cook poultry are listed on the following pages.

DRESSED POULTRY

"Dressed Poultry" refers to poultry slaughtered for human food, with head, feet, and viscera intact, and from which the blood and feathers have been removed. While the U.S. standards of quality apply to dressed poultry, and the USDA poultry grading regulations provide for the grading of dressed poultry, this product is practically nonexistent on today's poultry market.

The individual carcasses of dressed poultry may not be officially identified with the grade mark. Under certain conditions the grade mark may be applied to shipping containers of dressed poultry. No part other than wing tips may be removed from dressed poultry.

INDICATIONS OF AGE IN POULTRY

	Young Birds	Mature Birds
Comb Chickens	Pliable, resilient, not wrinkled, points sharp.	Wrinkled, coarser, thicker points, rounded.
Bill Ducks	Pliable — Not completely hardened.	Hardened.
Plumage	Fresh, glossy appearance.	Faded, worn except in birds which have recently molted.
Fat	Smooth layers with brighter color. Not lumpy over feather tracts.	Generally darker in color, inclined to lumpiness over heavy feather tracts.
Breastbone	Cartilage, if present, pliable and soft.	End of keel — hardened cartilage, bony.
Pinbones	Pliable.	Not pliable.
Shanks	Scales on shanks, smooth small.	Scales larger, rough, and slightly raised.
Oil Sac	Small, soft.	Enlarged, often hardened.
Spurs (Male chickens, turkeys, occasionally adult females)	Small, undeveloped. Corn-like.	Spurs gradually increase in length with age, becoming somewhat curved and sharper. Hens often have fine, sharp spurs after first year.
Wind pipe Ducks, Geese	Easily dented.	Hardened, almost bone-like to the touch.
Flesh	Tender-meated, translucent appearance. Fine texture.	Coarser texture, darker, hardened muscle fibers.
Drumsticks	Lacking in development, muscles easily dented.	Generally rounded, full, firm.

Sex does not become a factor in classing poultry until such time as the natural differences in the body conformation and distribution of flesh become quite evident. This never happens in such classes as geese and most breeds of ducks.

INDICATIONS OF SEX IN POULTRY

	Males	Females
Head	Usually larger, with larger and longer attachments, such as comb and wattles; coarser than that of females in appearance.	Smaller, rather fine and delicate in appearance compared with males. Hen turkeys have hair on center line of head.
Plumage	Feathers usually long and pointed at the ends. Tail feathers in chickens long and curved. Parti-colored varieties have more brilliant color than have the females. Most male ducks have a curl in the tail feathers.	Feathers inclined to be shorter and more blunt than those of the male. Tail feathers short and straight in comparison with the male. Modest colors in parti-colored varieties.
Body	Larger and generally more angular than the female. Depth from keel to back greater on same weight birds. Bones including shanks, longer, larger, and coarser.	Finer boned, body more rounded.

	Males	Females
Skin	Slightly coarser, particularly in old birds. Feather follicles larger. Less fat under skin between heavy feather tracts and over back.	Smoother, generally a better distribution of fat between feather tracts. Feather tracts narrower but carrying more fat.
Keel	Longer, with fleshing tending to taper at the base.	Shorter, with more rounded appearance over the breast.
Legs	Drumstick and thigh relatively long, with flesh tending to show less full until mature.	Drumstick and thigh relatively shorter, with drumstick more inclined to roundness, increasingly so with age.

There are three standards of quality for live poultry. They are: A Quality, or No. 1 Quality; B Quality, or No. 2 Quality; and C Quality, or No. 3 Quality.

SUMMARY OF STANDARDS OF QUALITY FOR LIVE POULTRY ON AN INDIVIDUAL BIRD BASIS
[Minimum Requirements and Maximum Defects Permitted]

FACTOR	A, OR NO. 1 QUALITY	B, OR NO.2 QUALITY	C, OR NO. 3 QUALITY
HEALTH AND VIGOR:	Alert, bright eyes, healthy, vigorous.	Good health and vigor.	Lacking vigor.
FEATHERING:	Well covered with feathers.	Fairly well covered with feathers.	Complete lack of plumage feathers on back.
CONFORMATION: Breastbone	Normal. Slight curve, 1/8" in. dent (Chickens) 1/4" dent (turkeys).	Practically normal. Slightly crooked.	Abnormal. Crooked.
Back	Normal (except slight curve).	Moderately crooked.	Crooked or hunched back.
Legs and Wings	Normal.	Slightly misshapen.	Misshapen.
FLESHING:	Well fleshed, moderately broad and long breast.	Fairly well fleshed.	Poorly developed, narrow breast, thin covering of flesh.
FAT COVERING:	Well covered, some fat under the skin over entire carcass. Chicken fryers, turkey fryers and young toms only moderate covering. No excess abdominal fat.	Enough fat on breast and legs to prevent a distinct appearance of flesh through skin. Hens or fowl may have excessive abdominal fat.	Lacking in fat covering on back and thighs, small amount in feather tracts.
DEFECTS: Tears and broken bones	Slight.	Moderate.	Serious.
Bruises, scratches and callouses	Free. Slight skin bruises, scratches and callouses.	Free. Moderate (except only slight flesh bruises).	Free. Unlimited to extent no part unfit for food.
Shanks	Slightly scaly.	Moderately scaly.	Seriously scaly.

The determination of whether dressed poultry carcasses are unwholesome or unsound is based only on external characteristics. The following conditions would exclude a dressed poultry carcass from a quality designation:

1. Decomposition (slippery or slimy condition, putrid or sour odor, greenish cast over the back and between thigh and rib).
2. Emaciation.
3. Bruises or mangling in excess of that permitted in C quality.
4. External evidence of disease, such as abnormally dark flesh or skin, external tumors, and abdominal accumulations.
5. Dirty head, carcass, feet, or vent; bloody head or carcass; green vent; feathers on the carcass; feed in the crop.

READY-TO-COOK POULTRY

The great majority of ready-to-cook birds are graded in processing plants following evisceration. Ready-to-cook poultry must have been inspected for wholesomeness in accordance with the regulations of the USDA before it can be officially graded. Relatively few birds are graded at points other than processing plants, and these birds must be in a form which makes it possible to examine the entire carcass. (For example, frozen poultry cannot be graded initally at a terminal market because the carcasses are not entirely visible.)

Ready-to-cook poultry, parts, or poultry products which are unsound or unwholesome are not eligible to be graded. Decomposition (slimy or slippery condition of the skin, or putrid or sour odor) would exclude ready-to-cook products from a grade.

In addition, ready-to-cook birds showing any of the following conditions cannot be graded. Such birds will be sent back for further processing, if grading is done at the processing plant.

a. Protruding pinfeathers
b. Bruises requiring trimming
c. Lungs or sex organs incompletely removed
d. Parts of the trachea
e. Vestigial feathers
f. Feathers
g. Extraneous material of any type inside or outside of carcass (for example, fecal material, blood, etc.)

CONFORMATION

The structure of the bird determines to a considerable degree the distribution and amount of meat. Certain defects in structure detract from the sales appeal of the carcass. Some of the defects that should be noted are: breasts that are dented, crooked, knobby, V-shaped, or slabsided; backs that are narrow, crooked, or hunched; legs and wings that are deformed; and bodies that are definitely wedge-shaped.

FLESHING

The drumsticks, thighs, and breast carry the bulk of the meat. There is, however, a definite correlation between the covering of the flesh over the back and the amount of flesh on the rest of the carcass. Females almost invariably carry more flesh over the back and will generally have a more rounded appearance to the breast, thighs, and legs. The common defects in fleshing are: breasts that are V-shaped or concave, rather than full and rounded; breasts that are full near the wishbone, but taper sharply to the rear; legs and drumsticks which are thin; and backs that have insufficient flesh to cover the vertebrae and hip bones.

FAT

The color of the fat is not a part of the fat factor in quality. As pointed out earlier, fat in poultry is judged entirely on the basis of accumulation under the skin. This is true even in the case of chicken parts. Accumulations occur first around the feather follicles in the heavy feather tracts. Poorly fatted birds may have some accumulation of fat in the skin along the heavy feather tracts on the breast. As the bird progresses in "finish," accumulations will be noted at the juncture of the wishbone and keel, and where the thigh skin joins the breast skin. At the same time, accumulations will be noted around the feather follicles, between the heavy feather tracts, and over the back and hips. Well-finished older birds will have sufficient fat in these areas and over the drumsticks and thighs so that the flesh is difficult to see. Fowl which have stopped laying have a tendency to take on excessive fat in the abdominal area. Well-finished young birds will have less fat under the skin between the heavy feather tracts on the breast and over the drumsticks and thighs, than mature birds. It should be noticeable, however.

FREEDOM FROM PINFEATHERS

There are two types of pinfeathers to be considered in grading. They are: (1) protruding, and (2) non-protruding. Protruding pinfeathers are those which have broken through the skin, and may or may not have formed a brush. Non-protruding pinfeathers are those which are in evidence, but which have not pushed their way through the outer layer of skin.

Ready-to-cook poultry must be free of protruding pinfeathers before a quality designation can be assigned. In this connection, the regulations define the words "free from protruding pinfeathers" to mean: The carcass is free from protruding pinfeathers which are visible to an inspector, or grader, during an examination of the carcass at normal operating speeds. However, a carcass may be considered as being free from protruding pinfeathers if it has a generally clean appearance (especially on the breast) and if not more than an occasional protruding pinfeather is in evidence during a more careful examination of the carcass.

Vestigial feathers, hair in the case of chickens, turkeys, guineas and pigeons, and down on ducks and geese, must also be considered.

FREEDOM FROM EXPOSED FLESH RESULTING FROM CUTS, TEARS, AND BROKEN BONES

Exposed flesh resulting from cuts, tears, missing skin, and broken, or disjointed bones detracts from the appearance of the bird, and, in addition, lowers the quality because of bruises and blood clots which occur frequently with broken bones. Tears and missing skin permit the flesh to dry out during the cooking process, thus lowering the eating quality of the bird. The number and extent of such defects that are permitted depend on their location, whether on the breast or elsewhere on the carcass.

FREEDOM FROM DISCOLORATION OF SKIN AND FROM FLESH BLEMISHES AND BRUISES

Today, most poultry is sold either ice-packed or wrapped in a water-resistant material. Either method prevents air from reaching and drying out the areas from which the outer cuticle

has been removed. The result has been that much of the poultry is scalded at temperatures around 140°F., and all of the cuticle is removed. This facilitates removal of pinfeathers and cuts down operating costs. Abrasions, as a consequence, do not become a problem unless the poultry has been exposed to the air, in which case the abrasions dry out and become discolorations. If this has occurred at the time of the examination, the size of the areas is taken into consideration under the heading of discolorations.

Bruises in the flesh or skin are permitted only to the extent that there is no coagulation or clotting (discernible clumps of red cells). Small clots in the skin or on the surface of the flesh may be cut to allow them to leach out in the chilling process. Such cuts would be taken into consideration in determining the quality. Blue or green bruises must be removed before grading.

Turkeys, most frequently older birds, may have discolored areas over the back and wings, and sometimes elsewhere. This condition, which is commonly called "blue back," may be caused by fluid, normally confined to the feather quills, moving into the skin, or it may be a condition known as "dermal melanosis" which is genetic in nature. A similar color, often found on the base of the keel, is associated with breast callouses. Certain varieties of chickens have a bluish or bluish-green color in the body lining. These discolorations detract from the appearance, and are included in the total aggregate areas permitted for discolorations.

FREEDOM FROM FREEZING DEFECTS

The discoloration and drying out of the skin of poultry carcasses during storage is called "freezer burn." This defect lowers the quality either in the case of moderate or of severe freezer burn.

The skin of frozen poultry often shows a condition known as "box burn." This shows up as a white area where the skin has come in contact with the lining of the box. The outer cuticle is the only part affected. This condition should not be confused with that of freezer burn. In grading, "box burns" would be included under discolorations. In addition to "freezer burn," there are other freezing defects of significance in establishing the grade of consumer-packaged poultry, parts, or specified poultry food products. These are: darkening of the carcass due to slow freeze or defrosting; and, in the case of consumer-packaged poultry or parts, seepage of moisture from the product, resulting in layers of clear, pinkish, or reddish-colored ice.

It is necessary to determine the class of the individual bird before evaluating the quality factors. It has been noted that the qualify factors of fat, fleshing, and conformation vary with the age and sex of the bird.

The tolerances for certain dressing defects vary with the weight of the ready-to-cook carcass. The tolerances also vary, depending upon whether they are on the breast and legs or elsewhere on the carcass.

A Quality

CONFORMATION. The carcass, or part, is free of deformities that detract from its appearance or that affect the normal distribution of flesh. Slight deformities, such as slightly curved or dented breastbones and slightly curved backs, may be present.

FLESHING. The carcass has a well-developed covering of flesh considering the kind, class, and part.

1. The breast is moderately long and deep and has sufficient flesh to give it a rounded appearance, with the flesh carrying well up to the crest of the breastbone along its entire length.

2. The leg is well-fleshed and moderately thick and wide at the knee and hip joint area, and has a well-rounded, plump appearance, with the flesh carrying well down toward the hock and upward to the hip joint area.

3. The drumstick is well-fleshed and moderately thick and wide at the knee joint, and has a plump-rounded appearance, with the flesh carrying well down toward the hock.

4. The thigh is well- to moderately-fleshed.

5. The wing is well- to moderately-fleshed.

FAT COVERING. The carcass, or part, considering the kind, class and part, has a well-developed layer of fat in the skin. The fat is well distributed so that there is a noticeable amount of fat in the skin in the areas between the heavy feather tracts.

DEFEATHERING. The carcass, or part, has a clean appearance, especially on the breast. The carcass, or part, is free of pinfeathers, diminutive feathers, and hair.

EXPOSED FLESH. Parts are free of exposed flesh resulting from cuts, tears, and missing skin (other than slight trimming on the edge). The carcass is free of these defects on the breast and legs. Elsewhere the carcass may have exposed flesh due to slight cuts, tears, and areas of missing skin, providing the aggregate of the areas of flesh exposed does not exceed the area of a circle of the diameter as specified in Table 3-1.

TABLE 3-1

Carcass Weight		Maximum Aggregate Area Permitted	
Minimum	Maximum	Breast & Legs	Elsewhere
None	1 lb. 8 oz.	None	3/4 in.
Over 1 lb. 8 oz.	6 lb.	None	1-1/2 in.
Over 6 lb.	16 lb.	None	2 in.
Over 6 lb.	None	None	3 in.

DISJOINTED AND BROKEN BONES AND MISSING PARTS. Parts are free of broken bones. The carcass is free of broken bones and has not more than one disjointed bone. The wing tips may be removed at the joint, and, in the case of geese, the parts of the wing beyond the second joint may be removed, if removed at the joint and both wings are so treated. The tail may be removed at the base. Cartilage separated from the breastbone is not considered as a disjointed or broken bone.

DISCOLORATIONS OF THE SKIN AND FLESH. The carcass, or part, is practically free of such defects. Discolorations due to bruising shall be free of clots (discernible clumps of red or dark cells). Evidence of incomplete bleeding, such as more than an occasional slightly reddened feather follicle, is not permitted. Flesh bruises and discolorations of the skin, such as "blue back," are not permitted on the breast or legs of the carcass, or on these individual parts, and only lightly shaded discolorations are permitted elsewhere. The total areas affected by flesh bruises, skin bruises, and discolorations, such as "blue back," singly or in any combination, shall not exceed one-half of the total aggregate area of permitted discoloration. The aggregate area of all discolorations for a carcass, or a part therefrom, shall not exceed the area of a circle of the diameter as specified in Table 3-2.

TABLE 3-2

Carcass Weight		Maximum Aggregate Area Permitted		
Minimum	Maximum	Breast & Legs	Elsewhere	Parts
None	1 lb. 8 oz.	1/2 in.	1 in.	1/4 in.
Over 1 lb. 8 oz.	6 lb.	1 in.	2 in.	1/4 in.
Over 6 lb.	16 lb.	1-1/2 in.	2-1/2 in.	1/2 in.
Over 16 lb.	None	2 in.	3 in.	1/2 in.

FREEZING DEFECTS. With respect to consumer-packaged poultry, parts, or specified poultry food products, the carcass, part, or specified poultry food product is practically free from defects which result from handling or occur during freezing or storage. The following defects are permitted if they, alone or in combination, detract only very slightly from the appearance of the carcass, part, or specified poultry food product:

1. Slight darkening over the back and drumsticks provided the frozen bird, or part, has a generally bright appearance.

2. Occasional pockmarks due to drying of the inner layer of skin (derma); however, none may exceed the area of a circle 1/8 in. in diameter for poultry weighing 6 lb. or less, and 1/4 in. in diameter for poultry weighing over 6 lb.

3. Occasional small areas showing a thin layer of clear or pinkish-colored ice.

B Quality

CONFORMATION. The carcass, or part, may have moderate deformities, such as a dented, curved, or crooked breast, or crooked back, or misshapen legs or wings, which do not materially affect the distribution of flesh or the appearance of the carcass or part.

FLESHING. The carcass has a moderate covering of flesh considering the kind, class, and part.

1. The breast has a substantial covering of flesh, with the flesh carrying up to the crest of the breastbone sufficiently to prevent a thin appearance.

2. The leg is fairly thick and wide at the knee and hip joint area, and has sufficient flesh to prevent a thin appearance.

3. The drumstick has a sufficient amount of flesh to prevent a thin appearance, with the flesh carrying fairly well down toward the hock.

4. The thigh has a sufficient amount of flesh to prevent a thin appearance.

5. The wing has a sufficient amount of flesh to prevent a thin appearance.

FAT COVERING. The carcass, or part, has sufficient fat in the skin to prevent a distinct appearance of the flesh through the skin, especially on the breast and legs.

DEFEATHERING. The carcass, or part, may have a few, non-protruding pinfeathers or vestigial feathers which are scattered sufficiently so as not to appear numerous. Not more than an occasional protruding pinfeather or diminutive feather shall be in evidence under a careful examination.

EXPOSED FLESH. Parts may have exposed flesh resulting from cuts, tears, and missing skin, provided that not more than a moderate amount of the flesh normally covered by skin is exposed. The carcass may have exposed flesh resulting from cuts, tears, and missing skin, provided that the aggregate of the areas of flesh exposed does not exceed the area of a circle of the diameter as specified in Table 3-3.

TABLE 3-3

Carcass Weight		Maximum Aggregate Area Permitted	
Minimum	Maximum	Breast & Legs	Elsewhere
None	1 lb. 8 oz.	3/4 in.	1-1/2 in.
Over 1 lb. 8 oz.	6 lb.	1-1/2 in.	3 in.
Over 6 lb.	16 lb.	2 in.	4 in.
Over 16 lb.	None	3 in.	5 in.

Notwithstanding the foregoing, a carcass meeting the requirements of A Quality for fleshing may be trimmed to remove skin and flesh defects, provided that no more than one-third of the flesh is exposed on any part, and the meat yield of any part is not appreciably affected.

DISJOINTED AND BROKEN BONES AND MISSING PARTS. Parts may be disjointed, but are free of broken bones. The carcass may have two disjointed bones, or one disjointed bone and one non-protruding, broken bone. Parts of the wing beyond the second joint may be removed at a joint. The tail may be removed at the base. The back may be trimmed in an area not wider than the base of the tail and extending from the tail to the area halfway between the base of the tail and the hip joints.

DISCOLORATIONS OF THE SKIN AND FLESH. The carcass, or part, is free of serious defects. Discoloration due to bruising shall be free of clots (discernible clumps of red or dark cells). Evidence of incomplete bleeding shall be no more than very slight. Moderate areas of discoloration, due to bruises in the skin or flesh, and moderately shaded discoloration of the skin, such as "blue back," are permitted, but the total areas affected by such discolorations singly, or in any combination, may not exceed one-half of the total aggregate area of permitted discoloration. The aggregate area of all discolorations for a carcass or a part therefrom shall not exceed the area of a circle of the diameter as specified in Table 3-4.

TABLE 3-4

Carcass Weight		Maximum Aggregate Area Permitted		
Minimum	Maximum	Breast & Legs	Elsewhere	Part
None	1 lb. 8 oz.	1 in.	2 in.	1/2 in.
Over 1 lb. 8 oz.	6 lb.	2 in.	3 in.	1 in.
Over 6 lb.	16 lb.	2-1/2 in.	4 in.	1-1/2 in.
Over 16 lb.	None	3 in.	5 in.	1-1/2 in.

FREEZING DEFECTS. With respect to consumer-packaged poultry, parts, or specified poultry food products, the carcass, part, or specified poultry food product may have moderate defects which result from handling or occur during freezing or storage. The skin and flesh shall have a sound appearance, but may lack brightness. The carcass, or part, may have a few pockmarks due to drying of the inner layer of skin (derma). However, no single area of overlapping pockmarks may exceed that of a circle 1/2 in. in diameter. Moderate areas showing layers of clear, pinkish, or reddish-colored ice are permitted.

C Quality

a. A part that does not meet the requirements for A or B Quality may be of C Quality if the flesh is substantially intact.

b. A carcass that does not meet the requirements for A or B Quality may be C Quality. Both wings may be removed or neatly trimmed. Trimming of the breast and legs is permitted, but not to the extent that the normal meat yield is materially affected. The back may be trimmed in an area not wider than the base of the tail and extending from the tail to the area between the hip joints.

POULTRY PARTS

Poultry parts have become increasingly popular with the consumer. Some people prefer all white meat, and the all breast pack serves this need. For those who prefer all dark meat, drumsticks, thighs, or whole leg packs serve the purpose. Parts are versatile. They are especially popular in specialty dishes and are ideal for barbecuing.

A ready-to-cook carcass which has a defect may be graded after the defective portion has been removed, and the fact that a portion of the carcass has been removed will not be considered in determining the quality of the balance of the carcass, if the remaining portion of the carcass is to be disjointed and packed as parts in the official plant where graded.

In 1969, specific grade standards were established for parts, and provision was made for parts after they have been cut from the carcass, providing the class is known, the parts are not misshapen and have nearly the same appearance as they had prior to cutting from the carcass. Specific requirements for parts are set forth in the preceding "Fleshing" categories for Grade A and Grade B ready-to-cook poultry.

The USDA standards of quality are applicable to poultry parts cut in the manner described in the following paragraphs, or in some other manner when approved by the Administrator. In addition, grade standards have been established for A, B, and C Quality poultry backs, depending upon the manner in which they are cut.

"BREASTS" are separated from the back at the shoulder joint, and by a cut running backward and downward from that point along the junction of the vertebral and sternal ribs. The ribs may be removed from the breast, and the breast may be cut along the breastbone to make two approximately equal halves; or the wishbone portion, as described under "wishbone" in this section, may be removed before cutting the remainder along the breastbone to make three parts. Pieces cut in this manner may be substituted for light or heavier pieces for exact weight-making purposes, and the package may contain two or more of such parts without affecting the appropriateness of its labeling as "chicken breasts." Neck skin is not included.

"BREAST WITH RIBS" are separated from the back at the junction of the vertebral ribs and back. Breasts with ribs may be cut along the breastbone to make approximately two halves; or the wishbone portion, as described under "wishbone" in this section, may be removed before cutting the remainder along the breastbone to make three parts. Pieces cut in this manner may be substituted for light or heavier pieces for exact weight-making purposes, and the package may contain two or more of such parts without affecting the appropriateness of its labeling as "breast with ribs." Neck skin is not included.

"WISHBONES" (Pulley Bones), with covering muscle and skin tissue, are severed from the breast approximately halfway between the end of the wishbone (hypocledium) and front point of the breastbone (cranial process of the sternal crest) to a point where the wishbone joins the shoulder. Neck skin is not included.

"LEGS" include the whole leg, i.e., the thigh and the drumstick, whether jointed or disjointed. Back skin is not included. Pelvic meat may be attached to the thigh, but shall not include the pelvic bones.

"WINGS" include the entire wing, with all muscle and skin tissue intact, except that the wing tip may be removed.

"DRUMSTICKS" are separated from the thigh by a cut through the knee joint (femorotibial and patellar joint) and from the hock (tarsal joint).

"THIGHS" are disjointed at the hip joint and may include the pelvic meat, but shall not include the pelvic bones. Back skin is not included.

"HALVES" are prepared by making a full-length back and breast split of the carcass, so as to produce approximately equal right and left sides.

"QUARTERS" are prepared by splitting the carcass as specified under "halves" in this section, with the resulting halves cut crosswise at almost right angles to the backbone to form quarters.

"BACKS" include the pelvic bones and all the vertebrae posterior to the shoulder joint. The meat may not be peeled from the pelvic bones. The vertebral ribs and/or scapula may be removed, or included. Skin shall be substantially intact.

A Quality backs shall meet all applicable provisions pertaining to parts, and shall include the meat contained on the ilium (oyster), pelvic meat and skin, and vertebral ribs and scapula with meat and skin.

B Quality backs shall meet all applicable provisions pertaining to parts, and shall include either the meat contained on the ilium (oyster), and meat and skin from the pelvic bones, or the vertebral ribs and scapula with meat and skin.

C Quality backs shall include the meat and skin from the pelvic bones, except that the meat contained on the ilium (oyster) may be removed. The vertebral ribs and scapula with meat and skin may also be removed, but the remaining portion must have the skin substantially intact.

POULTRY FOOD PRODUCTS

In the past few years, numerous frozen poultry pies and dinners have appeared on the market. Recently, other poultry food products, such as specialty dishes containing poultry, raw and cooked poultry rolls, and roasts have become available to the consumer.

A standard for Grade A poultry roasts is shown below. This is the first grade standard for a poultry food product.

POULTRY ROAST — A QUALITY

The standard of quality contained in this section is applicable to raw poultry products labeled in accordance with the poultry inspection regulations as ready-to-cook "Rolls," "Roasts," "Bars," or "Logs," or with words of similar import.

a. The deboned poultry meat used in the preparation of

the product shall be from young poultry of A Quality with respect to fleshing and fat covering.

b. All tendons, cartilage, large blood vessels, blood clots, and discolorations shall be trimmed from the meat.

c. All pinfeathers, bruises, hair, discolorations, and blemishes shall be removed from the skin, and where necessary, excess fat shall be removed from the skin covering the crop area or other areas.

d. Seventy-five percent or more of the outer surface of the product shall be covered with skin, whether attached to the meat or used as a wrap. The skin shall not appreciably overlap at any point. Product packaged in an oven-ready container need have only the entire exposed surface of the roast covered with skin. The combined weight of the skin and fat used to cover the outer surface and that used as a binder shall not exceed 15 percent of the total net weight of the product.

e. The product shall be fabricated in such a manner that each slice remains substantially intact (does not separate into more than three parts) when sliced warm after cooking. This may be accomplished by use of large pieces of poultry or by use of approved binders.

f. Seasoning or flavor enhancers, if used, shall be uniformly distributed.

g. Packaging shall be neat and attractive.

h. Product shall be practically free of weepage after packaging and/or freezing, and, if frozen, shall have a bright, desirable color.

Following are grade standards for boneless poultry breasts and thighs.

BONELESS POULTRY BREASTS AND THIGHS — A QUALITY

The standards of quality contained in this section are applicable to raw poultry products labeled as ready-to-cook boneless poultry breasts or thighs, or as ready-to-cook boneless poultry breast fillets or thigh fillets, or with words of similar import.

a. The breast or thigh shall be cut as specified.

b. Prior to deboning, the breast or thigh shall meet the A Quality requirements for ready-to-cook poultry parts, as specified.

c. The bone or bones shall be removed in a neat manner, without undue mutilation of adjacent muscle.

GRADES

U.S. CONSUMER GRADES FOR READY-TO-COOK POULTRY

U.S. Grade A

A lot of ready-to-cook poultry, or parts, consisting of one or more ready-to-cook carcasses, or parts, of the same kind and class, each of which conforms to the requirements for A Quality, may be designated as U.S. Grade A.

U.S. Grade B

A lot of ready-to-cook poultry, or parts, consisting of one or more ready-to-cook carcasses, or parts, of the same kind and class, each of which conforms to the requirements for B Quality or better, may be designated as U.S. Grade B.

U.S. Grade C

A lot of ready-to-cook poultry, or parts, consisting of one or more ready-to-cook carcasses, or parts, of the same kind and class, each of which conforms to the requirements for C Quality or better, may be designated as U.S. Grade C.

U.S. PROCUREMENT GRADES FOR READY-TO-COOK POULTRY

The U.S. Procurement Grades for ready-to-cook poultry are applicable to carcasses of ready-to-cook poultry of the kinds and classes when graded, as a lot, by a grader on the basis of an examination of each carcass in the lot, or each carcass in a representative sample thereof.

U.S. Procurement Grade I

Any lot of ready-to-cook poultry composed of one or more carcasses of the same kind and class may be designated and identified as U.S. Procurement Grade I when:

a. 90 percent or more of the carcasses in such lot meet the requirements of A Quality, with these exceptions:

1. Fat covering and conformation may be as described in this manual for B Quality.
2. Trimming of skin and flesh to remove defects is permitted to the extent that not more than one-third of the flesh is exposed on any part, and the meat yield of any part is not appreciably affected.

FORMS OF OFFICIAL IDENTIFICATION FOR READY-TO-COOK POULTRY

Inspection Mark

Grade Mark

Federal—State Graded

Grade Mark

EXAMPLES OF LABELS BEARING INSPECTION AND GRADE MARKS

WING TAGS

METAL WING CLIPS

Grade Mark for Fryers, Broilers, Stewing Chickens, Turkeys, Ducks, Geese, Guineas

SUMMARY OF SPECIFICATIONS FOR STANDARDS OF QUALITY FOR INDIVIDUAL CARCASSES OF READY-TO-COOK POULTRY AND PARTS THEREFROM
[Minimum Requirements and Maximum Defects Permitted]   September 1, 1965

FACTOR	A QUALITY			B QUALITY			C QUALITY
CONFORMATION: Breastbone Back Legs and Wings	Normal Slight curve or dent Normal (except slight curve) Normal			Moderate deformities Moderately dented, curved Moderately crooked Moderately misshapen			Abnormal Seriously curved or crooked Seriously crooked Misshapen
FLESHING:	Well-fleshed, moderately long, deep and rounded breast			Moderately fleshed, considering kind, class and part			Poorly fleshed
FAT COVERING:	Well-covered — especially between heavy feather tracts on breast, and considering kind, class, and part.			Sufficient fat on breast and legs to prevent distinct appearance of flesh through the skin.			Lacking in fat covering over all parts of carcass
PINFEATHERS: Nonprotruding pins and hair Protruding pins	Free Free			Few scattered Free			Scattering Free

EXPOSED FLESH:[1]		Breast and legs	Else-where	Part	Breast and legs	Else-where[2]	Part	No Limit
Carcass Weight:								
Minimum	**Maximum**	None	3/4 in.	(slight trim on edge)	3/4 in.	1-1/2 in.	(moderate amount of the flesh normally covered)	
None	1-1/2 lb.	None	3/4 in.		3/4 in.	1-1/2 in.		
Over 1-1/2 lb.	6 lb.	None	1-1/2 in.		1-1/2 in.	3 in.		
Over 6 lb.	16 lb.	None	2 in.		2 in.	4 in.		
Over 16 lb.	None	None	3 in.		3 in.	5 in.		

1. Total aggregate area of flesh exposed by all cuts and tears and missing skin.

2. A carcass meeting the requirements of A Quality for fleshing may be trimmed to remove skin and flesh defects, provided that no more than one-third of the flesh is exposed on any part, and the meat yield is not appreciably affected.

FACTOR	A QUALITY			B QUALITY			C QUALITY
DISCOLORATIONS:[3]							No Limit[4]
None — 1-1/2 lb.	1/2 in.	1 in.	1/4 in.	1 in.	2 in.	1/2 in.	
Over 1-1/2 lb. — 6 lb.	1 in.	2 in.	1/4 in.	2 in.	3 in.	1 in.	
Over 6 lb. — 16 lb.	1-1/2 in.	2-1/2 in.	1/2 in.	2-1/2 in.	4 in.	1-1/2 in.	
Over 16 lb. — None	2 in.	3 in.	1/2 in.	3 in.	5 in.	1-1/2 in.	
DISJOINTED BONES:	1			2 disjointed and no broken or 1 disjointed and 2 non-protruding broken			No Limit No Limit
Broken bones	None						
Missing parts	Wing tips and tail[5]			Wing tips, 2nd wing joint, and tail			Wing tips, wings and tail
FREEZING DEFECTS: (When consumer-packaged)	Slight darkening over the back and drumsticks. Few, small, 1/8 in. pockmarks for poultry weighing more than 6 lb. Occasional small areas showing layer of clear or pinkish ice.			Moderate dried areas not in excess of 1/2 in. in diameter. May lack brightness. Moderate areas showing layer of clear, pinkish, or reddish-colored ice.			Numerous pockmarks and large dried areas.

3. Flesh bruises and discolorations, such as "blue back," are not permitted on breast and legs of A Quality birds. Not more than one-half of total aggregate area of discolorations may be due to flesh bruises or "blue back" (when permitted) and skin bruises in any combination.

4. No limit on size and number of areas of discoloration and flesh bruises, if such areas do not render any part of the carcass unfit for food.

5. In geese, the parts of the wing beyond the second joint may be removed, if removed at the joint and both wings are so treated.

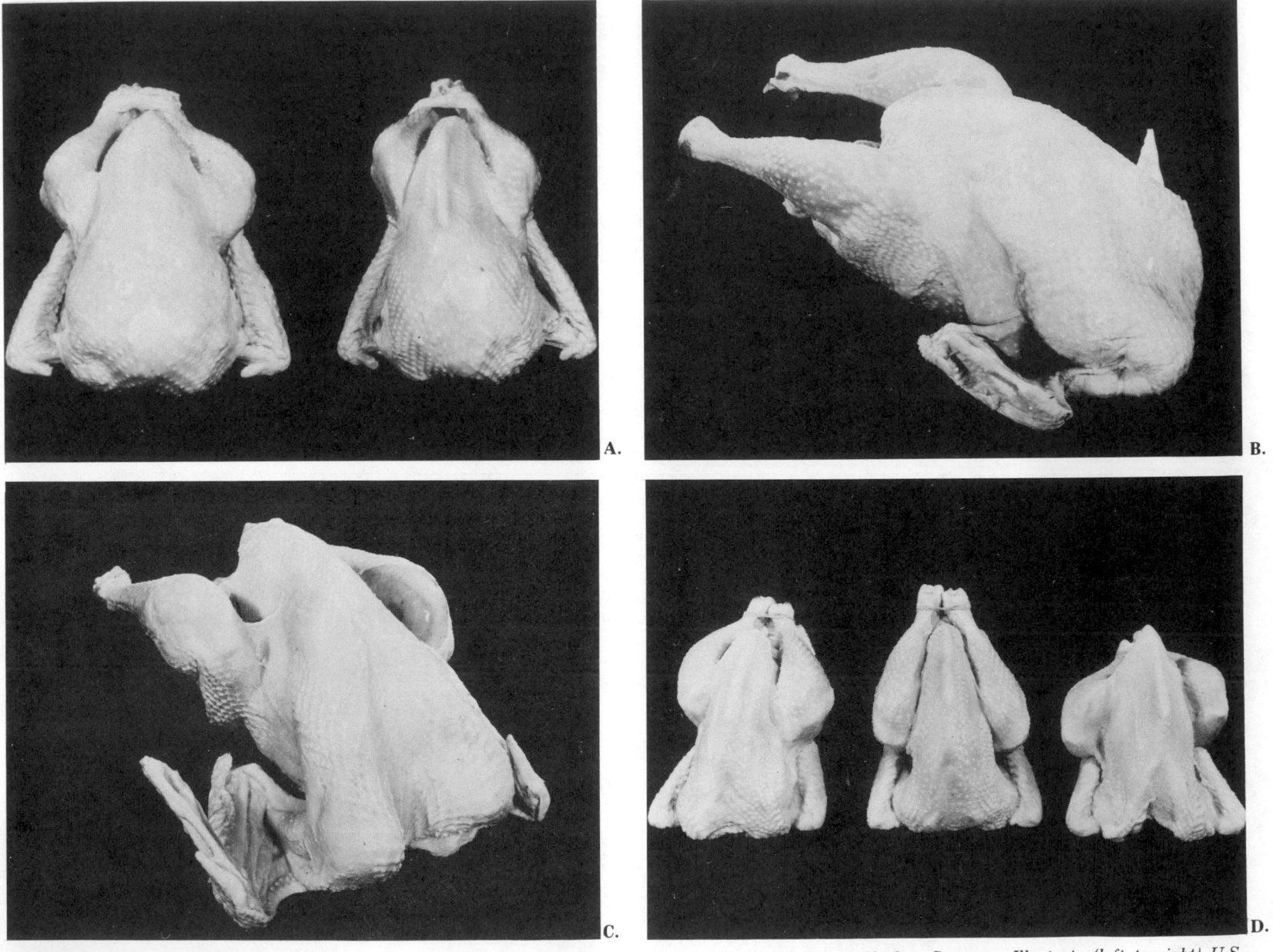

A. *Ready-to-Cook Young Turkeys. A Quality (left) B Quality (right);* **B.** *Young Tom Turkey Carcass, A Quality;* **C.** *Young Hen Turkey Carcass, C Quality;* **D.** *These Young Chicken Carcasses Illustrate (left to right) U.S. Grade A, U.S. Grade B and U.S. Grade C.*

3. Discoloration of the skin and flesh may be as described in this manual for B Quality.
4. One or both drumsticks may be removed if the part is severed at the joint.
5. The back may be trimmed in an area not wider than the base of the tail and extending to the area between the hip joints.
6. The wings or parts of wings may be removed if severed at a joint.

b. The balance of the carcasses meet the same requirements, except they may have only a moderate covering of flesh.

U.S. Procurement Grade II

Any lot of ready-to-cook poultry of the same kind and class which fails to meet the requirements of U.S. Procurement Grade I may be designated and identified as U.S. Procurement Grade II provided that:

a. Trimming of flesh from any part does not exceed 10 percent of the meat.

b. Portions of a carcass weighing not less than one-half of the whole carcass may be included, if the portion approximates in percentage the meat-to-bone yield of the whole carcass.

Voluntary Programs

For many years the USDA has offered the poultry industry official grading and inspection services on a voluntary basis. These services have been carried on under authority of Congressional Acts which have provided that fees shall be charged users of the service to cover costs.

Mandatory Program

Under the Poultry Products Inspection Act, enacted August 28, 1957, USDA provides compulsory Federal inspection of poultry and poultry products that are shipped in interstate or foreign commerce. The Wholesome Poultry Products Act, enacted August 18, 1968, amended the law to strengthen it and to open the way for vastly improved State poultry inspection systems. Each State was given from August 1968, two years (or three if progress is being made) to develop its own inspection system that is equal to the Federal inspection programs.

Administration of mandatory Federal inspection is assigned to the Meat and Poultry Inspection Program of USDA's Consumer and Marketing Service. All poultry slaughtered for human food which is destined for sale in commerce must be processed and handled in accordance with the Act and its regulations. Federal inspection service performed under the Act, except for overtime and holiday work, is paid for by the Government.

Poultry grading service is available to the industry on two bases: One is the *fee* basis and the other is the *resident* or *continuous grading* basis.

Fee grading is performed on the basis of request from applicants for the grading of a particular lot, or carload, of poultry. Requests for this type of service are usually made irregularly, and the charges for the service are based on the time consumed in performing the service. Most of the fee grading work is done at the terminal markets where impartial certification of quality or condition is desired. However, some service is rendered to shippers and processors on a fee basis, as required primarily in fulfilling purchase contract specifications.

Resident or *continuous grading* is performed by graders who are stationed in the applicant's processing plant, and are available at all times to perform grading service at the plant. Most of the resident grading is performed in processing plants at shipping points within the more concentrated areas of production, although some processors and distributors at terminal markets or major distribution centers also use resident, or continuous, grading service. The costs of resident grading service include an amount equal to the salary of the grader, plus an additional charge, based on the volume of product handled in the plant, to cover supervisory and administrative costs.

Grading generally involves the sorting of products according to quality and size, but it also includes the determination of the class and condition of products. For poultry, grading may be for determining class, quality, quantity, or condition, or for any combination of these factors.

Grading for quality can be accomplished by examining a representative sample of the lot of poultry to be graded. Only ready-to-cook poultry that is first inspected for wholesomeness, and then is graded on an individual-bird basis, may be individually marked with an official grade mark. Dressed poultry may not have individual grade labels applied.

Resident grading service is provided on the basis of written application on forms supplied by the Poultry Division of the Consumer and Marketing Service. The applicant agrees to comply with the regulations governing grading and, in addition, agrees to pay the full cost of the service requested. The government and cooperating agencies, in turn, agree to provide an adequate number of graders to perform the service. The conditions under which the service is performed are specified in the application and the regulations. The cost per pound for this service is generally very little more than in plants not using the grading service, but instead employing their own graders.

Inspection

Inspection refers to the condition of poultry and its healthfulness and fitness for food. It is not concerned with the quality or grade of poultry. The inspection mark on poultry or poultry products means that they have been examined during processing by a veterinarian, or by qualified inspectors under the supervision of a veterinarian. Plants which apply for inspection service and are approved are known as official plants or establishments.

Voluntary Inspection Service

The voluntary inspection service is provided for under the authority of the Agricultural Marketing Act of 1946. The cost of services rendered on this basis is paid for by the applicant for the service.

Processors who desire inspection for squab, game birds, and rabbits may apply for inspection under the voluntary program. These items are not covered under the mandatory program.

The requirements for the plant, operating procedures, inspection procedures, and packaging and labeling are the same for the voluntary program as those outlined for the mandatory program.

Grading service is conducted on the basis of cooperative agreements between the Consumer and Marketing Service and various state agencies.

OFFICIAL IDENTIFICATION MARKS FOR READY-TO-COOK POULTRY

The official, circular inspection mark (p. 251) is required on immediate containers and shipping containers for poultry that is inspected under the Poultry Products Inspection Act.

The grade mark must be one of the forms and designs illustrated on p. 251 and must be printed with light colored letters on a dark field.

Any wing tag, metal clip, insert label, or other label which bears either the inspection mark or grade mark, or both, must also show either the plant number or the firm name and address.

Wing tags and metal clips, bearing the grade mark, that are to be applied to poultry that is not consumer-packaged must show the class of the product. The class name can be the appropriate individual class, or the classes can be grouped according to the following system:

Name	Poultry to Be Packed Thereunder
Young poultry	Young birds of any of the kinds
Mature poultry	Any mature or old bird of any kind
Young chicken	Roasters and other young chickens
Stewing chicken	Fowl, baking hen, chicken hen
Young turkey	Young hen, young tom, and fryer-roaster turkeys
Yearling turkey	Yearling hen turkey, yearling tom turkey
Duckling	Broiler duckling, roaster duckling
Mature duck	Old duck

Indicating the *kind*, such as chicken, turkey or duck, without the qualifying term "young" or "mature" or "old," or the class name, is not permitted.

The figures on p. 251 are examples of wing tags. When both marks are shown on a tag, they must both appear on the same side of the tag. Both marks may appear on each side of the tag. Wing tags of shield design may not be used for showing the inspection mark only, but may be used to show both marks, or the grade mark singly.

In the case of multiple-bird ice pack, when the grade mark appears on a tag, or clip, without the inspection mark (p. 251), the inspection mark must be printed on the giblet wrapper and packed with the bird. If the tag or clip does not show the plant number (p. 251), then the plant number must be shown on the giblet wrapper.

RABBITS

FRYER OR YOUNG RABBIT. A fryer or young rabbit is a young, domestic rabbit carcass, weighing not less than 1-1/2 lb., and rarely more than 3-1/2 lb., processed from a rabbit usually less than 12 weeks of age. The flesh of a fryer or young rabbit is tender and fine-grained and of a bright, pearly pink color.

ROASTER OR MATURE RABBIT. A roaster or mature rabbit is a mature or old domestic rabbit carcass of any weight, but usually over 4 lb. processed from a rabbit usually 8 months of age or older. The flesh of a roaster or mature rabbit is more firm and coarse-grained, the muscle fiber is slightly darker in color and less tender, and the fat may be more creamy in color than that of a fryer or young rabbit.

Carcasses found to be unsound, unwholesome, or unfit for food shall not be included in any of the quality designations specified.

A Quality

To be of A Quality, the carcass:

a. Is short, thick, well-founded, and full-fleshed.

b. Has a broad back, broad hips, broad, deep-fleshed shoulders, and firm muscle texture.

c. Has a fair quantity of interior fat in the crotch and over the inner walls of the carcass, and a moderate amount of interior fat around the kidneys.

d. Is free of evidence of incomplete bleeding, such as more than occasional slight coagulation in a vein. Is free from any evidence of reddening of the flesh due to fluid in the connective tissues.

e. Is free from all foreign material (including, but not being limited to, hair, dirt, and bone particles) and from crushed bones caused by removing the head or the feet.

f. Is free from broken bones, flesh bruises, defects, and deformities. Ends of leg bones may be broken due to removing the feet.

B Quality

To be of B Quality, the carcass:

a. Is short, thick, fairly well-founded and fairly well-fleshed.

b. Has a fairly broad back, fairly broad hips, fairly broad and deep-fleshed shoulders, and fairly firm muscle texture.

c. Has at least a small amount of interior fat in the crotch and over the inner walls of the carcass, with a small amount of interior fat around the kidneys.

d. Is free of evidence of incomplete bleeding, such as more than an occasional slight coagulation in a vein. Is free from any evidence of reddening of the flesh due to fluid in the connective tissues.

e. Is free from all foreign material (including, but not being limited to, hair, dirt, and bone particles) and from crushed bones caused by removing the head or the feet.

f. Is free from broken bones, and practically free from bruises, defects, and deformities. Ends of leg bones may be broken due to removing the feet.

C Quality

A carcass that does not meet the requirements of A or B Quality may be of C Quality and such carcass:

a. May be long, rangy, and fairly well-fleshed.

b. May have thin, narrow back and hips, and soft, flabby muscle texture.

c. May show very little evidence of exterior fat.

d. May show very slight evidence of reddening of the flesh due to blood in the connective tissues.

e. Is free from all foreign material (including, but not being limited to, hair, dirt, and bone particles) and from crushed bones caused by removing the head or feet.

f. May have moderate bruises of the flesh, moderate defects, and moderate deformities; may have not more than one broken bone in addition to broken ends of leg bones due to removal of the feet; and may have a small portion of the carcass removed because of serious bruises. Discoloration due to bruising in the flesh shall be free of clots (discernible clumps of dark or red cells).

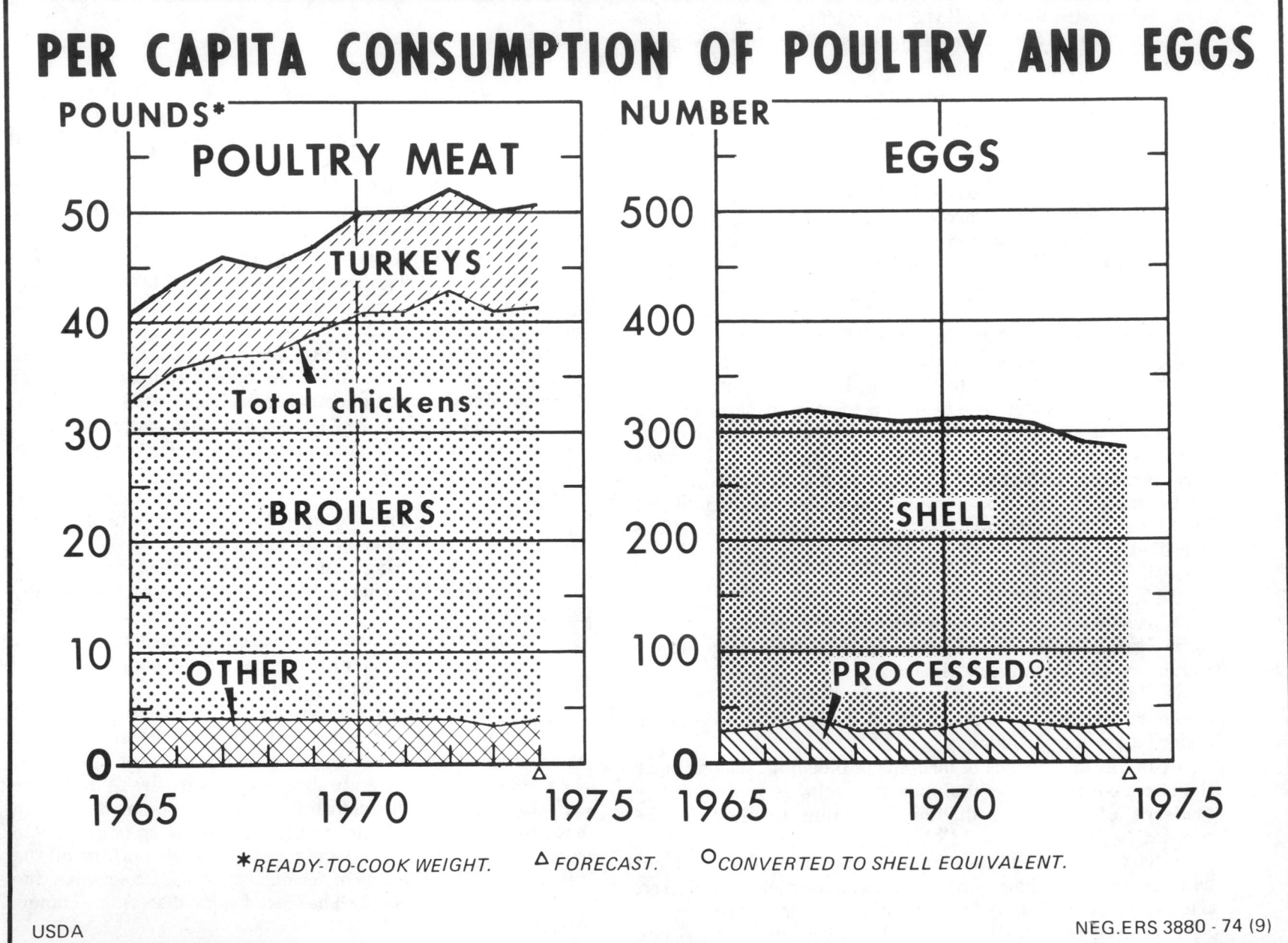

PER CAPITA CONSUMPTION OF POULTRY AND EGGS

POUNDS*

POULTRY MEAT

TURKEYS

Total chickens

BROILERS

OTHER

50
40
30
20
10
0

1965   1970   1975

NUMBER

EGGS

SHELL

PROCESSED°

500
400
300
200
100
0

1965   1970   1975

*READY-TO-COOK WEIGHT.   △ FORECAST.   °CONVERTED TO SHELL EQUIVALENT.

USDA

NEG. ERS 3880 - 74 (9)

POULTRY

Broilers: Weight of parts in relation to carcass weight[1]

Broiler parts	Unit	Weight of ready-to-cook broiler Carcass in ounces[2]				
		26	30	34	38	42
Wings:						
Calculated average	Ounces	1.9	2.1	2.4	2.7	2.9
Range for 95% of parts:	do.	1.6-2.1	1.9-2.4	2.1-2.7	2.4-2.9	2.7-3.2
Calculated percentage of carcass weight	Percent	6-8	6-8	6-8	6-8	6-8
Drumsticks:						
Calculated average	Ounces	2.1	2.5	2.8	3.1	3.5
Range for 95% of parts:	do.	1.8-2.5	2.1-2.8	2.4-3.2	2.8-3.5	3.1-3.8
Calculated percentage of carcass weight	Percent	7-10	7-9	7-9	7-9	7-9
Thighs:						
Calculated average	Ounces	2.8	3.2	3.6	4.1	4.5
Range for 95% fo parts:	do.	2.2-3.3	2.7-3.7	3.1-4.2	3.5-4.6	4.0-5.1
Calculated percentage of carcass weight	Percent	9-13	9-12	9-12	9-12	9-12
Backs:						
Calculated average	Ounces	3.6	4.1	4.6	5.2	5.7
Range for 95% of parts:	do.	2.8-4.4	3.3-4.9	3.8-5.4	4.4-6.0	4.9-6.5
Calculated percentage of carcass weight	Percent	11-17	11-16	11-16	12-16	12-16
Breasts:						
Calculated average	Ounces	8.4	9.7	10.9	12.2	13.5
Range for 95% of parts:	do.	7.2-9.6	8.4-10.9	9.7-12.2	11.0-13.4	12.2-14.7
Calculated percentage of carcass weight	Percent	28-37	28-36	29-36	29-35	29-35
Total weight of all parts[3]	Ounces	25.6	29.4	33.1	37.2	41.0

1. Table based on equations in table 3, page 28 of Marketing Research Report No. 604, *Relations for Weight and Sizes of Broiler Parts to Carcass Weights* U.S. Department of Agriculture, in cooperation with the University of Georgia.
2. Ice-packed carcass, weighed after giblets and neck were removed and free water was allowed to drain from carcass for about one minute.
3. Total of all parts adds to less than carcass weight due to loss from evaporation and weepage (dripping). Weight loss for all carcass in the above-mentioned study was 2.27%.

BIBLIOGRAPHY

Poultry Products Inspection Act, 71 Stat. 441, 21 U.S.C. 451-469.

U.S. Department of Agriculture. "Home Freezing of Poultry." Washington, D.C.: U.S. Department of Agriculture, February 1970, pp. 2-24.

U.S. Department of Agriculture. "Meat Poultry." Washington, D.C.: U.S. Department of Agriculture, October 1969, pp. 1-3.

U.S. Department of Agriculture. *Poultry Grading Manual*, Agriculture Handbook No. 31. Washington, D.C.: Government Printing Office, 1971.

U.S. Department of Agriculture. *Poultry Products Inspection Regulations*, Vol. 37, No. 95, Part II of Federal Register, Washington, D.C.: Government Printing Office, May 16, 1972.

U.S. Department of Agriculture. *Regulations Governing the Grading and Inspection of Poultry and Edible Products Thereof and U.S. Classes, Standards, and Grades with Respect Thereto*, 7CFR, Part 70. Washington, D.C.: Government Printing Office, July 1, 1971.

U.S. Department of Agriculture. *Regulations Governing the Grading and Inspection of Poultry and Edible Products Thereof and United States Classes, Standards, and Grades with Respect Thereto*, 7CFR, Part 70. Washington, D.C.: Government Printing Office, June 30, 1975.

4

EGGS

SHELL EGGS (FRESH EGGS)

Wholesomeness. All eggs and egg products processed for human consumption must be inspected for wholesomeness; all eggs which are inedible, leakers, checks, or dirties cannot be used for human consumption, even as processed eggs.

The Egg Products Inspection Act (1970) provides not only for wholesomeness inspection, but also for standards, grades, and weight classes.

Egg grading considers the following factors:

SHELL. Total lack of cracks, cleanliness, shape, and texture. An uncracked shell egg will give a tuning fork or bell tone when tapped against another shell egg; the shell exterior must be clean and have a normal egg shape with a smooth, fine texture. Brown-shelled eggs are no different than white-shelled eggs. Eggs with an irregular shape are lowered in grade.

AIR CELL. When held to a light (or "candled"), a pocket of air called an air cell will be seen in an egg. The depth of the air cell, as well as the consistency of that air cell, is a determinant of quality. A small air cell of less that 1/8 in. will be found in the highest quality eggs; an air cell of more than 3/8 in., with a bubbly consistency, will be found in the eggs which fail to meet the lowest grade.

WHITE. A fresh, high quality egg has a thick, white area which is milky in color. Eggs which are not properly refrigerated lose quality rapidly. As the egg gets older, the white becomes thinner in consistency and clearer in color.

YOLK. The yolk of a high quality egg is located in the middle of the egg, and is surrounded by a thin, barely visible membrane. As quality decreases, the yolk becomes flat due to the weakened membrane. No blood or meat spots are allowable.

There are two types of egg grades, Consumer Grades and Procurement Grades.

CONSUMER GRADES

Size is determined by weight per dozen, in the shell. Since eggs are generally packed in 30-doz., corrugated fiber cases, the buyer is concerned with case weight, as well as per-dozen weight. Two or more cases of 30-doz. eggs are known as a lot. When purchased by the lot, the lot is allowed to have a maximum of 3.3% of its eggs in the next lower weight range. Case weights, indicated below, include the 4-1/2 lb. weight of the standard, corrugated fiber case and the filler flats used to separate the individual eggs, and layers of eggs.

Size	Per Dozen	Per 30-Doz. Case
Jumbo	30 oz.	56 lb.
Extra Large	27 oz.	50-1/2 lb.
Large	24 oz.	45 lb.
Medium	21 oz.	39-1/2 lb.
Small	18 oz.	34 lb.
Peewee	15 oz.	28 lb.

Large and Medium eggs are most frequently used for fried, poached, hard-cooked, or soft-cooked eggs. If fresh eggs are to be used in cooking scrambled eggs, baked goods, etc., then the buyer will be concerned with comparative price per dozen. Using the price of Large eggs as a base, Medium eggs are a better buy when Medium eggs are 12% cheaper than

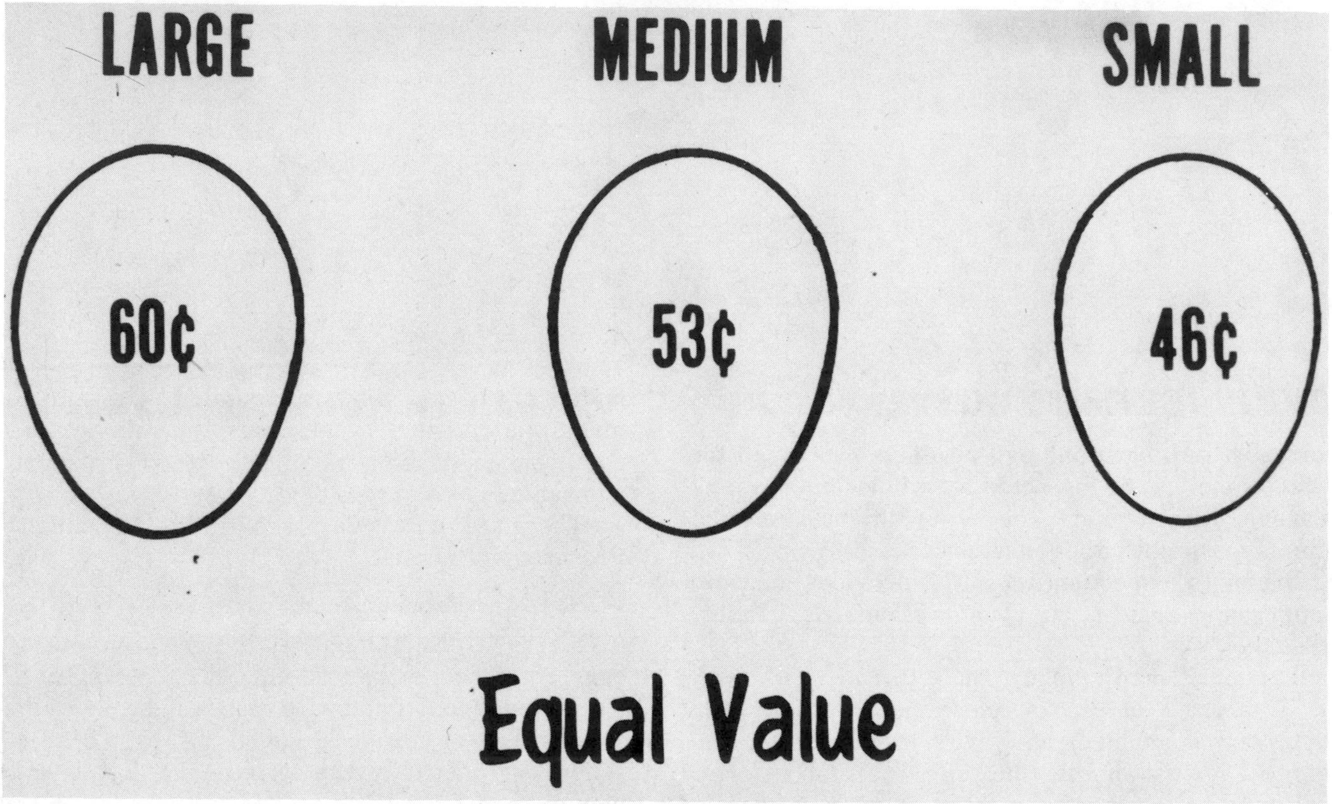

LARGE

MEDIUM

SMALL

60¢

53¢

46¢

Equal Value

Egg Values Per Dozen

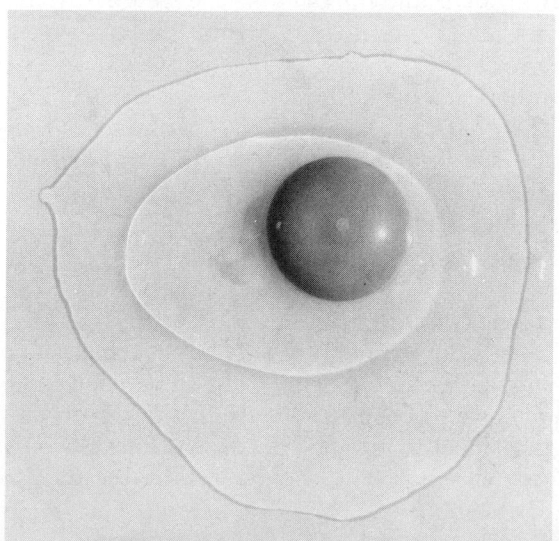

*This is a U.S. Grade A egg,
shown broken out of its shell.*

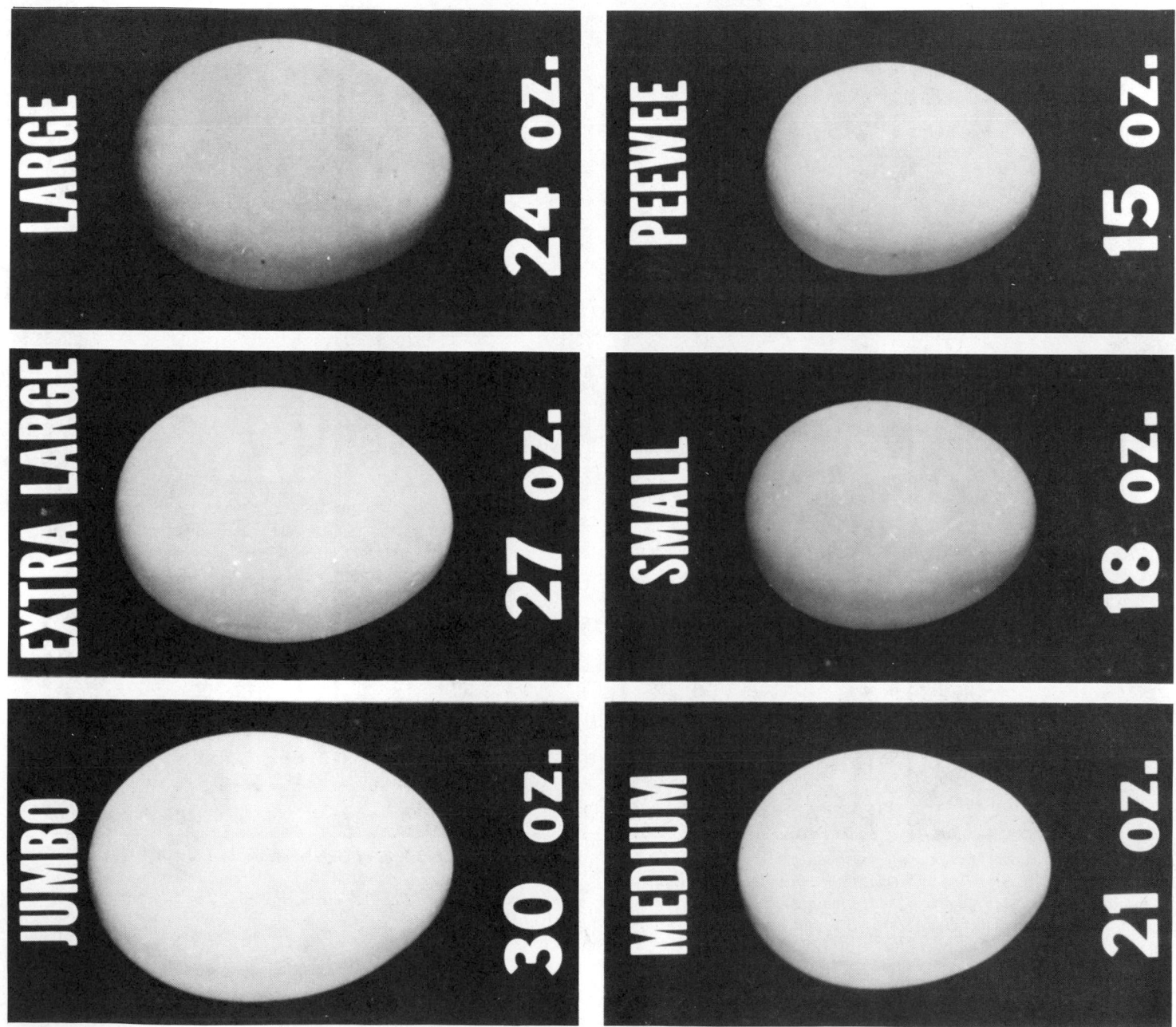

LARGE 24 oz.

PEEWEE 15 oz.

EXTRA-LARGE 27 oz.

SMALL 18 oz.

JUMBO 30 oz.

MEDIUM 21 oz.

Egg Weights Per Dozen

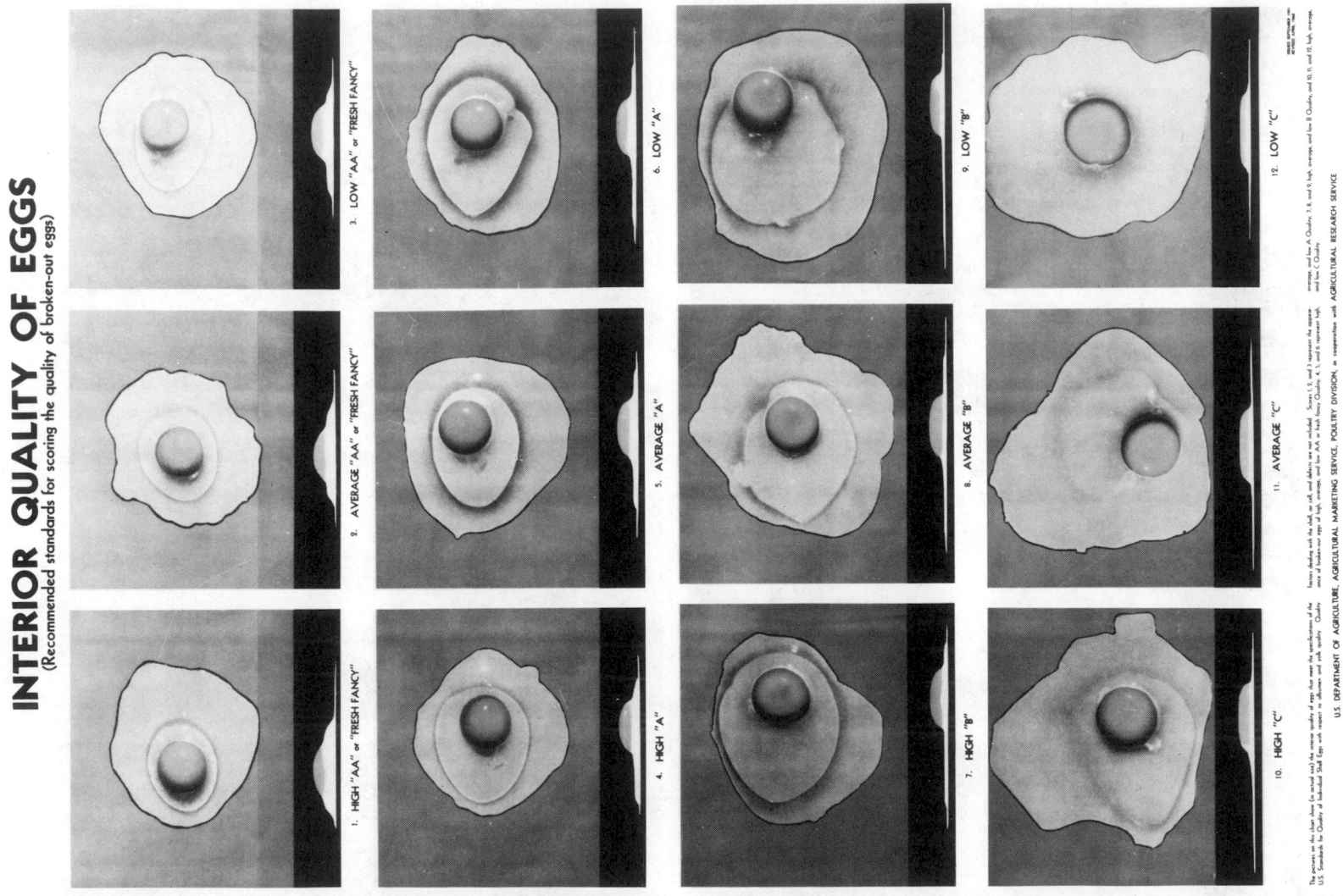

INTERIOR QUALITY OF EGGS
(Recommended standards for scoring the quality of broken-out eggs)

The pictures on this chart show the interior quality of eggs that meet the specifications of the U.S. Standards for Quality of Individual Shell Eggs with respect to albumen and yolk quality. Quality factors dealing with the shell, air cell, and defects are not included. Scores 1, 2, and 3 represent the appearance of broken-out eggs of high, average, and low AA Quality or Fresh Fancy Quality; 4, 5, and 6 represent high, average, and low A Quality; 7, 8, and 9, high, average, and low B Quality, and 10, 11 and 12 high, average, and low C Quality.

Egg Grade Marks

Large eggs. Small eggs are a better buy than Large eggs when 24% cheaper than Large eggs, or 12% cheaper than Medium eggs.

The Consumer Grades for shell eggs are U.S. Grade AA, U.S. Grade A and U.S. Grade B. The grade is shown inside the USDA shield on the case. The size is sometimes included in that shield, also. The quality standard for individual cases within a lot are lower than the quality standards for the lot as a whole. The quality standards for eggs at the grading point (time and place) is higher than at the point of receipt. This has to be so because eggs deteriorate in quality as they age. The grade of the individual eggs within the case or lot may be of the next lower grade (except in the case of U.S. Grade B) to the extent of a specified percentage.

U.S. GRADE AA

Clean, unbroken, and practically normal shells; practically regular air cell, no more than 1/8 in. deep, and practically regular in shape; clear and firm white; yolk practically free from defects with outline slightly defined. No less than 85% U.S. Grade AA at point of origin, and no less than 80% U.S. Grade AA at destination. Individual cases to be no less than 75% U.S. Grade AA, and no more than 15% U.S. Grade A and 10% U.S. Grade B at point of origin, and no less than 70% U.S. Grade AA, but no more than 20% U.S. Grade A and 10% U.S. Grade B at destination.

U.S. GRADE A

Clean, unbroken, and practically normal shell, practically regular air cell, 3/16 in. or less in depth; clear and reasonably firm white; yolk outline fairly well defined and practically free from defects. No less than 85% U.S. Grade A at point of origin, and no less than 80% U.S. Grade A at destination. Individual cases to be no less than 75% U.S. Grade A, and no more than 25% U.S. Grade B at point of origin, and no less than 70% U.S. Grade A, and no more than 30% U.S. Grade B at destination.

U.S. GRADE B

Clean to slightly stained shells, which may be slightly abnormal in shape; air cell may be free or bubbly, but not more than 3/8 in. in depth; the white must be clear, but may be slightly weak; yolk may be slightly enlarged, and have a well-defined outline. No less than 85% U.S. Grade B at point of origin, and no less than 80% U.S. Grade B at destination. Individual cases to be no less than 75% U.S. Grade B at point of origin, and no less than 70% U.S. Grade B at destination. No eggs that are less than Grade B can be included.

PROCUREMENT GRADES

The Procurement Grades are used mostly by large egg processors, repackers, and other middlemen. An individual foodservice operation would not use the Procurement Grades, especially since these grades include a Grade C which, by Federal Law, may not be used by foodservices. The Procurement Grades provide that the individual cases contain not more than 10% less than U.S. Grade A eggs in the entire lot; below U.S. Grade B, there may be up to 3% Checks, .3% Dirties, Leakers and Loss, of which the Loss cannot contain more than .15% at point of origin and .2% at destination of blood spots and meat.

Grade I

Not less than 85% U.S. Grade AA and U.S. Grade A at origin, nor less than 80% U.S. Grade AA and U.S. Grade A at destination. Origin allowed up to 15% U.S. Grade B, but not more than 5% U.S. Grade C*, Dirty, Leaker or Loss; destination allowed up to 20% U.S. Grade B, but not more than 5% U.S. Grade C, Dirty, Leaker or Loss.

Grade II

Not less than 65% at origin and 60% at destination of U.S. Grade AA and U.S. Grade A, with up to 35% U.S. Grade B and no more than 10% U.S. Grade C, Dirty, Check or Loss at origin, and up to 40% U.S. Grade B, but no more than 10% U.S. Grade C, Dirty, Check or Loss at destination.

HOW TO BUY SHELL EGGS

Specify the grade and size. U.S. Grade AA is best for visual appearance, as in fried eggs; U.S. Grade A is fine for hard-cooked and soft-cooked. Medium or Large size is best for

*Grade C: Shell is clean to moderately stained, unbroken, and may be abnormally shaped; air cell may be free, or bubbly, and more than 3/8 in. in depth; the white may be watery or weak, and small blood clots or spots may appear; the yolk may be flat and enlarged, with visible germ development, no blood, outline plainly visible, and may have other serious defects.

FORM PY - 210
(8-1-69)

U.S. DEPARTMENT OF AGRICULTURE
CONSUMER AND MARKETING SERVICE
POULTRY DIVISION

POULTRY PRODUCTS GRADING CERTIFICATE

PLACE ISSUED: Columbus, Ohio
DATE: 6-18-75
A 133066

TO: APPLICANT (Name and address. Include ZIP Code)
Hemmelgarn & Sons, Inc.
Box 82
Coldwater, Ohio 45828

NAME AND ADDRESS OF SHIPPER OR SELLER)
White Feather Farms
Muncie, Ind. 47303

NAME AND ADDRESS OF RECEIVER OR BUYER)
Jewish Hospital
Dietary Dept.
Cincinnati, Ohio

WHERE EXAMINED: Coldwater, Ohio 45828

PRODUCT GRADED (Check)
☐ POULTRY   ☐ EGG PRODUCTS

LOT NO.	NO. PKGS. PER LOT	NO. PKGS. EXAMINED	PRODUCT TYPE AND CLASS	MARKED WEIGHT OF LOT 1/	WHERE HELD AND TEMPERATURE	WAREHOUSE NO. OR CAR NO.	TEST SHORTAGE	TOTAL NET	CONTAINERS WERE STAMPED WITH:	OFFICIAL U.S. GRADE

TOTAL NO. OF CONTAINERS

TOTAL MARKED WEIGHT

☐ SAMPLE ☐ ALL
☐ SAMPLE ☐ ALL

TYPE AND CONDITION OF CONTAINERS

LOT NO.

REMARKS:

SHELL EGGS

LOT NO.	TOTAL CASES	CASES EXAMINED	NET WEIGHT 2/	PERCENTAGES									CASE QUALITY RANGE	CASE TEMP. RANGE	CHARACTER OF LOSS	OFFICIAL GRADE AND SIZE
				AA	A	B	C	DIRTIES/CHECKS	LOSS	SMALL END UP 3/	UNDER WEIGHT 3/	SHORT- AGE 4/				
1	(R)	4												52°F	°F °F	U.S. Grade AA Medium

DESCRIPTION OF:

EGGS: Fresh white/new fiber
Shell protector/scotch tapes

CASES: New filler flats

CASES WERE STAMPED WITH: U.S. Consumer grade AA + date
U.S.D.A. contract Compliance Stamp/Lot 133066

☒ SAMPLE ☒ ALL

WHERE HELD AND TEMPERATURE: Cooler 52°F

REMARKS: Product Processed under continuous supervision. Product meets
requirements of P.O.# 35107 per information Received by Telephone
(R) 459-15 Doz = 23½ doz   Del. Date 6-19-75

1/ As stated by applicant or contractor.   2/ Weights based on 30-dozen equivalent.   3/ Eggs reported as undersized and small end up are also reported under
other headings according to their quality.   4/ Percent reported as shortage was replaced to determine grade.

I CERTIFY THAT, in compliance with the regulations of the United States Department of Agriculture governing
the grading and inspection of poultry, eggs and/or egg products, issued pursuant to the Agricultural Marketing
Act of 1946, as amended, I examined the product(s) described above on the date shown, and the
class, quality, size, and/or condition thereof at the time were as stated.

Myrna Stehle
OFFICIAL GRADER

FEE.........
EXPENSE. President
TOTAL....

*This certificate is receivable in all courts of the United States as prima facie evidence of the truth of the statements therein contained
This certificate does not excuse failure to comply with any of the regulatory laws enforced by the United States Department of Agriculture.*

Factors relating to shell eggs

U.S. weight classes, consumer grades	Minimum net weight per		Minimum quantity of product approximating the amount in one dozen eggs						
	Case [30 doz.]	Dozen	Liquid or frozen			Dried			
			Whole	Yolk	Albumen	Whole	Yolk	Albumen	
	POUNDS	OUNCES	POUNDS	POUNDS	POUNDS	POUNDS	POUNDS	POUNDS	POUNDS
Shell eggs:									
Jumbo	56.0	30	1.88	1.64	0.71	0.93	0.42	0.32	0.12
Extra large	50.5	27	1.69	1.48	0.64	0.84	0.38	0.29	0.11
Large	45.0	24	1.50	1.32	0.57	0.75	0.34	0.26	0.10
Medium	39.5	21	1.31	1.16	0.50	0.66	0.30	0.23	0.09
Small	34.0	18	1.12	1.00	0.43	0.57	0.26	0.20	0.08
Peewee	28.0	15	0.94	0.80	0.35	0.47	0.21	0.16	0.06
Average weight Sold at retail	47.0[1]	25	1.57[1]	1.38	0.60	0.78	0.35	0.27	0.10

1. The approximate weight of eggs sold at retail is 1.57 pounds per dozen.

U S D A

OFFICIALLY GRADED

* 2 - 1 - 61 *

ACCEPTED FOR
ACE FOOD SHOPS
GRADER 151

Official mark to indicate acceptance under institutional purchase contracts.

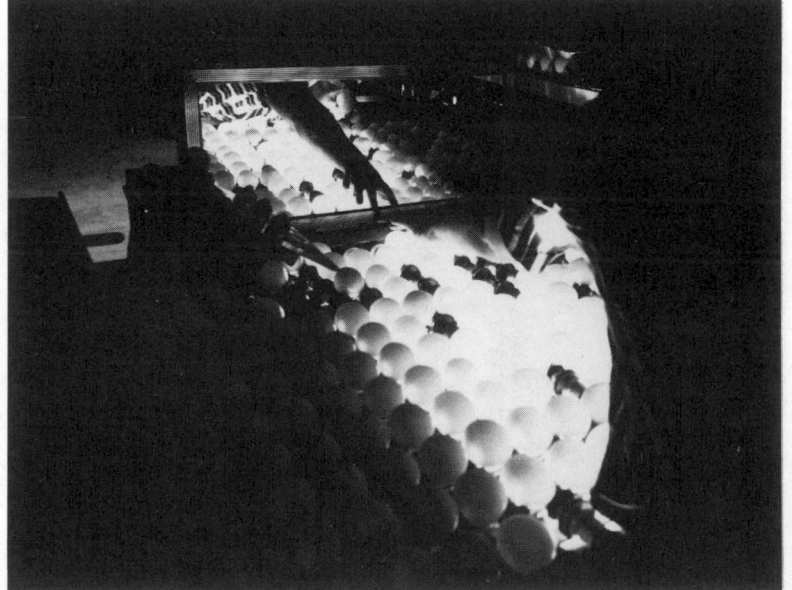

Eggs at a packing plant roll over a mass scanner, where undesirable eggs are weeded out. A special light allows workers to see both internal and external flaws.

Estimated conversion factors for yields of liquid eggs and dried eggs and the moisture content of dried eggs, by types of product, 1961[1]

Egg products	Liquid yield from 30 dozen shell eggs	Yield from one dozen shell eggs		Requirements for one pound of dried egg products		Yield of dried egg product from		Approximate moisture content content of egg product[2]
		Liquid egg	Dried egg	Liquid egg	Shell eggs	100 pounds of liquid egg	30 dozen shell eggs	
	POUNDS	POUNDS	POUNDS	POUNDS	POUNDS	POUNDS	POUNDS	PERCENT
Whole eggs	39.50	1.317	0.343	3.84	2.92	26.04	10.29	2-3
Albumen (flake)	22.55	.752	.099	7.58	10.10	13.19	2.97	12-14
Albumen (spray)	22.55	.752	.096	7.84	10.42	12.76	2.88	5-8
Yolk	16.95	.565	.257	2.20	3.89	45.45	7.70	3.5-5

1. The conversion factors were taken from table 16, page 36, *The Egg Products Industry of the United States*, Kansas Agricultural Experiment Station Bulletin 466, N. Cent. Reg. Res. Pub. No. 154.

2. Conversion factors were based on an average of the moisture content shown. It is recognized that moisture content may have ranged as high as 5% in some packs of dried whole egg.

those uses. U.S. Grade A eggs should be used for omelets and souffles; size is not important in this case. U.S. Grade B eggs are well-suited for general use, such as mixed-in for cooking or baking. Buy Medium size for these uses, unless Large or Small are better in price according to the formula stated earlier. Eggs should be delivered within 2 to 3 days of grading and kept at a temperature of no more than 42°F. in an area where they cannot absorb strong odors from other foods. U.S. Grade AA eggs will remain U.S. Grade AA for 10 days when held at 42°F.

Acceptance Service

Foodservice operators may have eggs graded to their own specifications by Federal graders. The inspection service which does this at the point of origin is the USDA Acceptance Service. In order to use this service, the operator must provide the purveyor with notice of inspection as a requirement, and provide both the purveyor and the grader with the specifications. Eggs so graded will have their cases on the invoices stamped with the USDA Acceptance Service Stamp. The cases may also bear the Federal stamps, and a grade letter designation.

A fresh egg is one that has been stored 29 days or less. Eggs that are held in storage for 30 or more days are called "storage eggs." Storage eggs must be held at a temperature of

To equal one shell egg, use 2½ tablespoons of sifted dried eggs, plus an equal amount of water. One cup of dried eggs and one cup of water equal six shell eggs. Water should be cold.

29°F. to 31°F., with a humidity of 90° to 92°. Storage eggs are sometimes oiled to prevent CO_2 loss; sometimes CO_2 is injected.

Processed Eggs

FROZEN. Frozen eggs must be pasteurized, just like milk, to prevent bacterial growth. The market forms are as follows:

Whole Eggs

This is the entire egg, without the shell, cracked, pasteurized, and packaged in 4 lb., 5 lb., 10 lb., or 30 lb. containers. Those with the best "eating" quality will have no additives or stabilizers. When comparing the price of shell eggs to whole frozen eggs, remember that 11% to 12% of the weight of shell eggs is in the shell. Pricing reciprocal: 1.12.

Egg Whites

This is the entire egg without shell and yolk. The white represents 58% of the whole egg. Pricing reciprocal: 1.72.

Egg Yolk

The whole egg without shell and white. The yolk represents 31% of the whole egg. Pricing reciprocal: 3.23.

Egg Yolk, Sugared

Egg yolk, as above, with about 11% sugar added, and as much as 5% glycerine added to prevent hardening of the yolks.

The frozen eggs are excellent for use in baking and in making souffles, scrambled eggs, and omelets as no labor need be expended in shelling eggs or in separating yolks and whites.

Frozen Egg Roll

The Ralston-Purina Company markets a frozen, processed roll of egg which gives the same number of center-cut slices as 17 hard-cooked eggs. Many operators have found this most practical for such uses as sliced egg salads and Eggs a la Russe. The "Gourm Egg" has food starch and stabilizers added, but this does not markedly affect the taste.

Hard-Cooked Refrigerated Eggs

In some areas of the country, hard-cooked eggs can be purchased already shelled, with a refrigerated shelf-life of up to 3 weeks.

The buyer should make sure that all frozen eggs have been Federally inspected, and should try to buy frozen eggs that are guaranteed to be salmonella-free.

Dried Eggs

Eggs are dried either by a roller process or a spray process. They are also treated with enzymes to remove glucose. The drying processes are explained in the Dairy section of this book. There is a high bacteria count in dried eggs, thus the buyer should attempt to buy dried eggs that are guaranteed salmonella-free, and the operator should refrigerate such products.

There are many dried egg-based egg-nog and custard bases on the market which are of high quality. There are no Federal quality standards in this area so the buyer must test them for preference.

BIBLIOGRAPHY

Econometric Models of Cash & Future Prices of Shell Eggs, No. 1502, August 1974, pp. 1-32.

Egg Grading Manual. Washington, D.C.: U.S. Department of Agriculture, 1972.

The Egg Product Industry: Structure, Practices and Costs. No. 917, February 1971, pp. 1-44.

U.S. Department of Agriculture. *Regulations Governing the Grading of Shell Eggs and U.S. Standards, Grades and Weight Classes for Shell Eggs*. 7 CFR, Part 56, Washington, D.C.: Agricultural Marketing Service, Poultry Division, July 1, 1971.

U.S. Department of Agriculture. *Regulations Governing the Inspection of Eggs and Egg Products*. 7CFR, Part 59, Washington, D.C.: Government Printing Office, June 30, 1975.

U.S. Department of Agriculture. *Regulations Governing the Inspection of Eggs and Egg Products*. 7CFR Part 59, Washington, D.C.: Government Printing Office, June 30, 1975.

5

DAIRY PRODUCTS

MILK

The responsibility for quality milk in a community is shared by the dairy industry, the medical profession, public health officials, and the consumers in that community, together with the public health officials of the Federal government.

Protecting the Quality of Milk through Cooperative Action

GRADE A PASTEURIZED MILK ORDINANCE. Every state, and most municipalities, operate a rigid milk regulation program. The Grade A Pasteurized Milk Ordinance recommended by the U.S. Public Health Service, first published in 1924 and revised periodically, sets forth in detail a type of regulation that is desirable. This Ordinance is formulated as a guide for state and local communities, and represents recommendations of Federal and state Departments of Agriculture; national, state, and local health authorities, and officials of the dairy industry. The milk supplies of much of the United States are covered by the Ordinance.

INDUSTRY AND GOVERNMENT COOPERATE. Legal responsibility for health protection of milk supplies for the market is exercised, for the most part, by state and local governments. The dairy industry works cooperatively with both state and municipalities to maintain the standards for the milk supply. The industry is continuously interested in technological advances, in procedures and equipment, and in research to make sure any technological change produces quality milk.

PASTEURIZATION AND SANITATION. Proper pasteurization is the only practical commercial measure today that destroys all disease organisms in fluid milk. Examination of cows and milk handlers can be done only at intervals. Disease organisms may enter milk accidentally from sources such as flies, contaminated water, and utensils. Pasteurization is by no means a substitute for sanitary dairy practices, but rather it is an additional safeguard for the consumer's health.

UNINTENTIONAL ADDITIVES. The dairy industry and public health officials have met a succession of technological problems, and today they are faced with the problem of unintentional additives to fluid milk. The chance that radioactive materials, insecticides, antibiotics, or carcinogens may appear in milk is occasion for much study and research. The Food and Drug Administration has set zero tolerance levels for a number of these substances. Both industry and government are dedicated to protecting the consumer from possible adulterants in the nation's milk supply.

RADIOACTIVE FALLOUT. Radioactivity from natural sources constitutes a part of man's normal environment. Nuclear explosions increase these radiation levels. Radioactive elements reach man directly through water and atmosphere, and indirectly through soil, plants and animals. The radioisotopes of three elements in particular, strontium, cesium, and iodine, have been the subject of study. Study has been made through surveys and experimental procedures, for the purpose of measuring current levels and of predicting equilibrium results.

Milk has probably been the most important single item for analysis because milk is convenient to handle and is produced on a year-round basis. The important parameter, however, is the level of contamination of the total human diet rather than concentration in any one food of any one kind.

Federal, state and local health officials monitor the American food supply for possible contamination from radio-activity. Responsible experts in the fields of medicine, nutri-tion, and radiation health concur that countermeasures against fallout are not presently needed. In the meantime, the successful completion of the research now in progress should provide suitable countermeasures should these become necessary.

PESTICIDES. Pesticides are needed to achieve maximum production of acceptable foodstuffs. Even the best farming practices cannot control pests without some of the pesticide remaining on the plant at harvest. For this reason, the USDA and the Food and Drug Administration have established toxicity tests that are as rigorous and thorough as current knowledge allows. The dairy farmer, who must have pest control, complies with the official policy of no pesticides in milk. As long as present regulations prevail, pesticides do not appear to present a public health problem. However, the pro-blem is under constant study and review. Industry and government continue to cooperate to protect the public health.

Supervision of Milk Supply

Principles that govern a quality milk supply can be briefed as follows:

1. Inspection and sanitary control of farms and milk plants.
2. Examination and testing of herds for the elimination of bovine diseases related to public health.
3. Regular instruction on desirable sanitary practices for persons engaged in production, processing, and dis-bution of milk.
4. Proper pasteurization of milk.
5. Laboratory examination of milk.
6. Monitoring of milk supplies by Federal, state, and local health officials to protect against unintentional additives.

Care of Milk in the Home

The cardinal rules for care of milk are these: Keep it clean, covered and cold, and consume it within a reasonable period of time. Milk should be protected from sunlight to preserve its riboflavin and its good flavor. Off-flavor in milk does not make it unsafe, merely unpleasant to the taste.

Milk should be stored promptly in the refrigerator or con-sumed quickly. After a milk container is opened, it should be covered before storage. Milk removed from the original container should not be returned to it.

Grades of Milk

Grade A designates quality fluid milk and is the grade purchased in retail stores and delivered to consumers. Milk used for manufacturing milk products — butter, cheese, and ice cream — is designated by the term Manufacturing Grade.

These grades are based on the conditions under which the milk is produced and handled, and on the bacterial count of the final product. The grades and their meanings vary only slight-ly, according to local regulations. Where the U.S. Public Health Service Grade A Pasteurized Milk Ordinance has been adopted, uniform standards are prescribed.

In different parts of the world, the milk of various species of animals is used for food. In the United States, however, the cow furnishes virtually all of the available market milk. There-fore, unless otherwise specified, the term "milk" as used in the book refers to cows' milk.

This centuries-old food is among the most perishable of all foods. Milk, as it comes from the cow, provides an excellent medium for bacterial growth and is subject to many possible flavor changes unless it is protected constantly from contamin-ation each step of the way from the cow to the consumer. Milk is relied upon as an important source of many of the nutrients known to be necessary for proper development and mainten-ance of the human body. Maximum retention of these nutrients must be assured as milk is stored, processed, trans-ported, and distributed in its many different forms.

The Attributes of Quality Milk

Quality milk has been described as milk that has low bacterial count, good flavor and appearance, satisfactory keep-ing quality, and high nutritive value. It is free from disease-producing bacteria, toxic substances, and foreign material.

Progress in dairy technology and public health results in milk that can be depended upon as a safe, nutritious, pleasing food, even though it may be produced hundreds or thousands of miles away. Vigilance is exercised continuously in maintain-ing this quality as new challenges arise in the environment. Pasteurization is a basic safeguard in the processing of all milk.

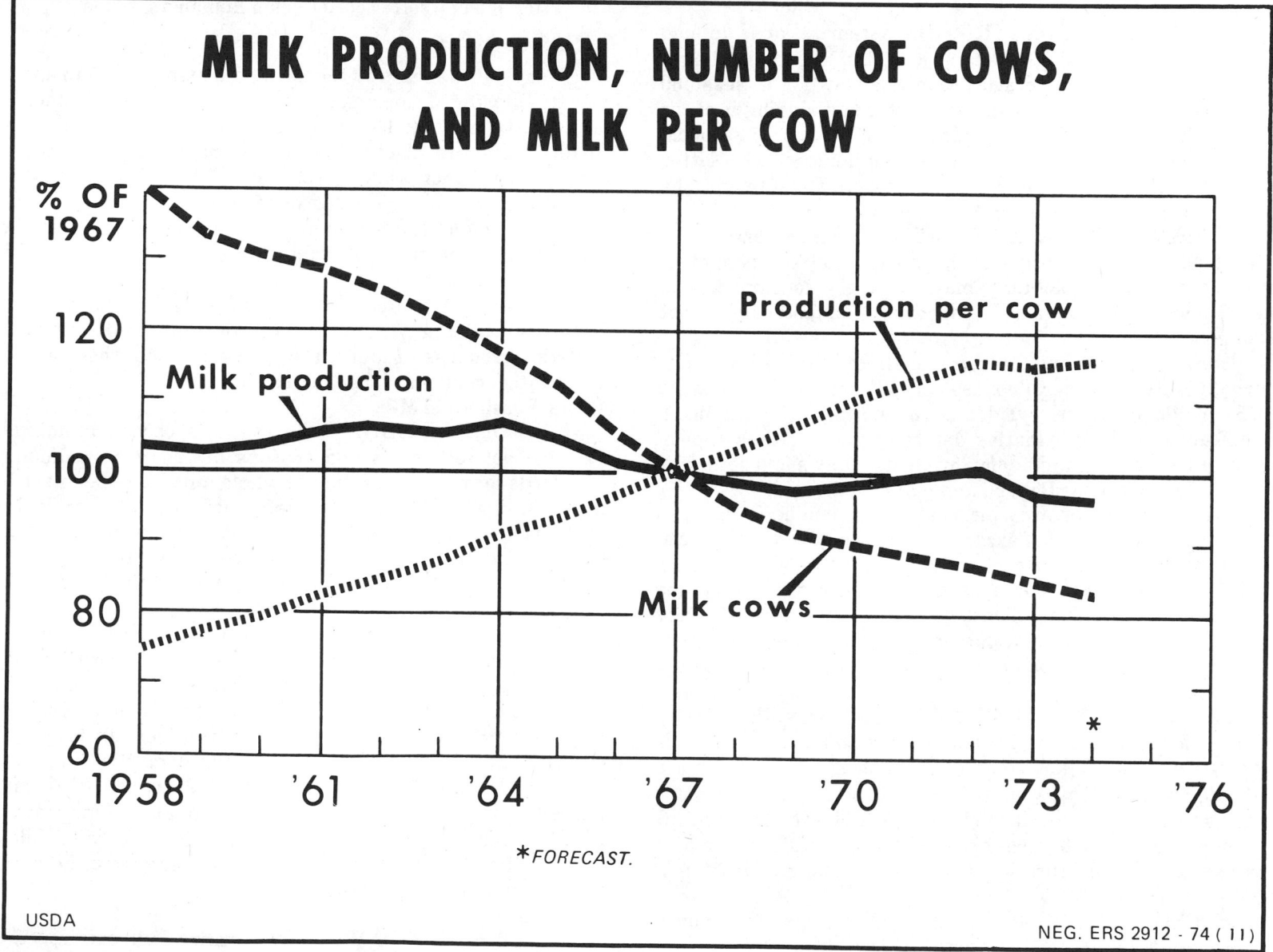

MILK PRODUCTION, NUMBER OF COWS, AND MILK PER COW

% OF 1967

Production per cow

Milk production

Milk cows

*FORECAST.

USDA

NEG. ERS 2912 - 74 (11)

Pasteurized Milk

HOW MILK IS PASTEURIZED. Pasteurization is defined as the process of heating milk to at least 145°F., and holding it at, or above, this temperature continuously for at least 30 minutes, or heating it to at least 161°F., and holding it at, or above, this temperature continuously for at least 15 seconds, in approved and properly operated equipment. The latter method is predominant today. Following this treatment, the milk is cooled promptly to 45°F., or lower.

EFFECTS OF PASTEURIZATION. Pasteurization destroys all pathogenic organisms, and most of the nonpathogenic bacteria, so that milk may be safely consumed. The keeping quality of milk also is improved. The food value is not changed significantly.

There is no apparent, undesirable effect on the protein, fat, carbohydrate, or mineral content of milk, nor on vitamins A, D, E, riboflavin, niacin, pyridoxine, or biotin. Both vitamins A and E are subject to oxidative deterioration, but they appear to be quite stable in fluid dairy products. Only slight losses, if any, occur in vitamins B_{12}, K, and pantothenic acid.

Greater losses of ascorbic acid and thiamine have been reported. But the level of ascorbic acid in milk is not of special importance. A varied American diet includes other sources rich in ascorbic acid. While pasteurization reduces thiamine somewhat, milk still supplies a significant amount in the daily diet. Carefully controlled, high-temperature-short-time pasteurization permits maximum retention of these two vitamins.

Homogenized Milk

PASTEURIZED MILK IS ALSO HOMOGENIZED. Today most whole milk is homogenized immediately after it is pasteurized. The milk is treated mechanically to break up the fat into smaller globules and then to disperse these permanently in a fine emulsion throughout the milk. The heated milk is channeled to the homogenizer where the milk, under high pressure, is forced through very tiny openings. Nothing is added or removed.

EFFECTS OF HOMOGENIZATION. Physically, homogenized milk differs from ordinary whole milk in that there is no separation of cream, and the product remains uniform throughout. Small differences in color and viscosity may be noted in the homogenized milk, and there is a slightly "richer" taste. Homogenization lowers the curd tension that results in

the formation of a softer curd during human digestion.

KINDS OF MILK

Today milk appears on the market in many forms to appeal to varied tastes of consumers and to satisfy their demands. A wide line of products has been developed to improve keeping quality, facilitate distribution and storage, make maximum use of by-products, and preserve surplus. The processing involved in producing each form of milk is designed and controlled to protect the health of the consumer. Some forms of milk are available in all communities; others may be found in only a few communities.

Standards of composition are generally established by state and local governments for all fluid milk products. Federal standards of identity have been established only on evaporated, condensed, and nonfat dry milk.

Whole Fresh Fluid Milk

ITS COMPOSITION. While the composition of milk is variable between cows and seasons of the year, minimum standards for the composition of whole milk have been set by individual states. Many states define whole milk as milk that contains not less than 3.25 percent milk fat and not less than 8.25 percent milk solids-not-fat. At the milk plant, the milk from different farms is pooled and "standardized" to meet or exceed the minimum legal requirements.

The standards of composition, however, vary with the different states. Even within the state, the milk composition may be well above the minimum standard. Milk of higher milk solids-not-fat and milk fat is available in most markets. This may be a premium product, or milk from certain breeds of cows that is sold by breed name in many communities.

BASIC PROCESSING. Most of the whole fluid milk marketed in this country is pasteurized and homogenized. Milk that receives no heat treatment is called raw milk. Unless it is Certified Milk, raw milk should be pasteurized at home, or boiled, before it is consumed.

Certified Milk

WHAT, WHY AND WHERE. Certified Milk originated in 1893 in response to a need for safe milk. Its certification on the container means that the conditions under which it was produced and distributed conform with the high standards for cleanliness set forth by the American Association of Medical Milk Commissions. These standards have been recognized in many state and local laws. The Grade A Pasteurized Milk Ordinance provides for the sale of certified pasteurized milk derived from certified raw milk.

Certified Milk continues to be available in only a few communities. Where it is available, it may be either raw or pasteurized, though most Certified Milk is now being pasteurized. It also may be homogenized. It may be fortified with vitamin D, too.

Soft Curd Milk

For certain uses, it is considered desirable to modify cows's milk so that the curd tension is considerably less, and the curd formed in digestion is softer. In digestion, the curd formed from soft curd milk tends to leave the stomach more quickly than does the curd of ordinary milk.

COMMERCIAL PREPARATION. Soft curd milk may be produced by homogenization, by enzymatic treatment, by sonic vibration, by ion-exchange, and by addition of various salts. Now that almost all fresh fluid milk sold is homogenized, and thus has a soft curd, the product labeled "soft curd milk," prepared by the other processes, is seldom seen.

HOME PREPARATION. For infant formulas, softening the curd may be accomplished, depending on the doctor's recommendation, by dilution, by heating, or by acidification. Boiling for one minute usually brings the curd tension of ordinary milk into the soft curd class.

Low Sodium Milk

WHAT IT IS. Ninety percent or more of the sodium that occurs naturally in milk can be removed by a process of ion-exchange. Fresh whole milk is passed through an ion-exchange resin to replace the sodium in milk with potassium. The milk is pasteurized and homogenized.

During the ion-exchange process, some B-vitamins and calcium are lost. Despite this loss, low-sodium milk has special use in certain sodium-restricted diets. It permits the inclusion of milk and other protein foods that may otherwise have to be severely limited because of their high sodium content. Low-sodium milk is available in various parts of the country as a dry, canned, or fresh product.

Fortified Milks

Fortified milks are those containing added amounts of one or more of the essential nutrients normally present in milk.

VITAMIN D MILK. The Council on Foods and Nutrition of the American Medical Association recognized the fortification of milk with vitamin D as being of public health significance.

Food in general does not contain appreciable quantities of vitamin D. Its primary source is the action of sunlight on the skin. A small but not physiologically significant amount occurs normally in milk. However, milk is the only food the Council on Foods and Nutrition of the American Medical Association has approved for fortification with vitamin D. Milk provides the proportion of calcium and phosphorus that must be present with vitamin D for normal calcification of bones and teeth.

To meet the requirements for acceptance by that Council, vitamin D milk must contain 400 International Units of vitamin D per quart, usually added in the form of a concentrate. The fortification of a large proportion of the fresh milk, and almost all evaporated milk, with vitamin D has contributed to the decline in the incidence of rickets, once a common scourge of infancy.

MULTIPLE FORTIFIED MILK. Milk can be fortified with substances such as vitamins A, D, multi-vitamin preparations, minerals, lactose, and nonfat dry milk. The substance added, and the amount of fortification, will vary depending on the dairy company. The dairy company, in turn, conforms to the state standards for multiple fortified milk, where these standards exist. Usually the products and amounts added must be declared on the label. Fortified milks will also vary in fat content. They can be made with whole, partially skimmed, or skim milk.

Concentrated Milks

Concentrated milks may be fresh, frozen, evaporated, condensed, or dried. Milks are concentrated by removal of varying amounts of water, under carefully controlled conditions of heat and vacuum. All may be reconstituted by the addition of appropriate quantities of water.

CONCENTRATED FRESH MILK. Fresh whole milk is concentrated by first pasteurizing and homogenizing, and then removing two-thirds of the water under vacuum. This 3:1 concentrate, standardized to about 10.5 percent milk fat, is rehomogenized, repasteurized, and packaged. Although perishable, concentrated fresh milk may retain its flavor and sweetness for as long as 6 weeks stored at near freezing temperature. This milk is available in only a few communities.

CONCENTRATED FROZEN MILK. To increase the

keeping quality of fresh concentrated milk, it may be quickly frozen and held at -10° to -20°F. for several months. Like other frozen foods, it must be used soon after defrosting. This milk, too, is available in only a few communities.

CONCENTRATED CANNED MILK. Considerable research is underway on the production of a concentrated, sterilized milk, aseptically packaged in cans. The product will keep 3 months on the shelf, or 6 months, if refrigerated.

EVAPORATED MILK. In the manufacture of evaporated milk, slightly more than half of the water is removed by heating pasteurized whole milk at 122° to 131°F. in vacuum pans. After evaporation, the milk is homogenized, and usually vitamin D is added to provide 400 I.U. per reconstituted quart. The evaporated milk is sealed in cans, and sterilized at about 239°F. for 15 minutes, thus preventing bacterial spoilage. A can of evaporated milk requires no refrigeration until opened.

CONDENSED MILK. In the preparation of condensed milk, sugar is added to the milk before the evaporation process is initiated. This milk contains not less than 28.0 percent milk solids and 8.3 percent milk fat. The sugar, which represents about 40 to 45 percent of the condensed milk, acts as a preservative. The milk, sealed in cans can be stored without further heat treatment and without refrigeration.

DRY MILK NONFAT. Nonfat dry milk is made of fresh whole milk from which both water and fat have been removed. After the fat has been removed, the skim milk is pasteurized and about two-thirds of the water removed under vacuum. This concentrated skim milk is dried by spraying it into a chamber of hot, filtered air. The resulting product is a fine-textured powder of very low moisture content.

A further step, the instantizing process, produces a dry milk that dissolves in water instantly. By one method, the dry milk is moistened with steam, then redried. Except for small losses in ascorbic acid, vitamin B_{12}, and biotin, the processing has no appreciable effect on the nutritive value. The presence of the milk fat does require special packaging to prevent oxidation during storage.

Skim Milk

Skim milk is milk from which fat has been removed by centrifugation to reduce its milk fat content to less than that of whole milk. In the skim milk ordinarily available, the fat content is 0.1 percent, although it may be lower or higher.

Various states have established standards ranging from 8.0 to 9.25 percent as the minimum for the total solids in skim milk. The product is pasteurized.

ITS FOOD VALUE. With the exception of milk fat and the vitamin A contained in the milk fat, the other nutrients of milk — the protein, lactose, minerals, and water-soluble vitamins — remain for the most part in the skim milk.

Because the vitamin A of whole milk is removed with the fat, a water-soluble vitamin A and D concentrate is frequently added to skim milk. Such fortified skim milk often contains 2000 I.U. of vitamin A and 400 I.U. of vitamin D per quart. However, the amounts may vary as discussed under *Fortified Milks*. Fortified skim milk may also contain additional milk solids-not-fat.

Two Percent Milk

As its name implies, two percent milk contains 2 percent milk fat. Made from fresh whole and skim milk, two percent milk is pasteurized and homogenized. It may be enriched by adding milk solids-not-fat and various vitamin and mineral preparations.

Cultured Milks

Cultured milks are prepared from pasteurized (or sterilized) milk. Certain desirable bacterial cultures, whose growth under controlled conditions of sanitation, inoculation, and temperature yield a variety of milks, have been added. These fermented milks may exert a favorable influence on the flora of the intestinal tract.

BUTTERMILK. Commercially produced buttermilk is a cultured product. Today it is not the by-product from churning cream into butter. Most of the cultured buttermilk marketed in the United States is made of fresh skim milk. However, cultured buttermilk may be made from fresh, fluid whole milk, concentrated fluid milk (whole or skim), or reconstituted, nonfat dry milk.

Pasteurized skim milk is cultured chiefly with *Streptococcus lactis* and incubated at 68° to 72°F. until the acidity is 0.8 to 0.9 percent, expressed as lactic acid. The result is a milk with characteristic tangy flavor and smooth, rich body. Butter granules are sometimes added in an amount to produce a buttermilk testing one or less-than-one percent milk fat. The concentration of milk solids-not-fat is similar to that of whole milk.

ACIDOPHILUS MILK. Pasteurized skim milk, cultured with *Lactobacillus acidophilus*, and incubated at 100°F, is called acidophilus milk. This tart milk, available in only a few communities, is sometimes used to combat excessive intestinal putrefaction by changing the bacterial flora of the intestine. As a therapeutic product, its use may be prescribed after antibiotic treatment to help reestablish a normal balance of bacterial flora in the intestine.

YOGURT. Possessing a consistency resembling custard, yogurt is usually manufactured from fresh, partially skimmed milk, enriched with added milk solids-not-fat. Fermentation is accomplished by a mixed culture of one or more strains of organisms, as *Streptococcus thermophilus, Bacterium bulgaricum*, and *Plocamo-bacterium yoghourtii*. The milk is pasteurized and homogenized, inoculated and incubated at 112° to 115°F. The final product has a tangy flavor, and contains between 11 and 12 percent milk solids. It is available in varied flavors.

EFFECTS OF FERMENTATION. In fermented milks, changes due to bacterial growth include formation of lactic acid from lactose, and coagulation of the milk protein, casein. Bacterial enzyme action on protein and fat constituents, plus the effect of the increased concentration of acid, changes the physical properties and chemical structure of the milk.

A thicker body and a pleasing flavor and aroma are developed in the finished product that varies with the type of culture and kind of milk used, the concentration of milk fat and milk solids-not-fat, the fermentation process, and the temperature at which it is carried out. Some alteration in the vitamin concentration may occur, but there is no evidence of major changes in these nutrients. These products are said to promote biological synthesis of vitamins within the small intestine.

Flavored Milks and Milk Drinks

WHAT THEY ARE. A flavored milk is whole milk with syrup or powder containing a wholesome flavoring agent, and sugar added. A flavored milk drink, or dairy drink, is skim or partially skimmed milk similarly flavored and sweetened. These milks are pasteurized, and usually homogenized.

CHOCOLATE MILK. Whole milk flavored with a chocolate syrup or powder is called chocolate milk. Usually its milk fat content is the same as for whole milk, and it contains 1 percent cocoa or 1-1/2 percent liquid chocolate, plus 5 percent sugar, and less than 1 percent stabilizers.

CHOCOLATE DAIRY DRINK. Skim or partially skimmed milk flavored with a chocolate syrup or powder is called chocolate dairy drink. Frequently its milk fat content is about 2.3 percent and its milk solids-not-fat about 90 percent of the amount in skim milk. Otherwise, it contains the same ingredients as chocolate milk and is processed in the same manner.

FOOD VALUE. Research indicates that the addition of normal quantities of good grade chocolate has no appreciable effect upon the availability of either the calcium or protein of milk to human beings. Therefore, the nutritive value of milk is not significantly altered by the addition of this flavoring, except in regard to the increased caloric value, chiefly from the added sugar. The sugar and chocolate content brings the caloric value of chocolate dairy drink made of skim milk to a slightly higher level than that of plain whole milk, but to a lower lever than the chocolate milk.

Canned Whole Milk

Whole milk that is homogenized, sterilized at 270° to 280°F. for 8 to 10 seconds, and canned aseptically, is available chiefly for use on ships or for export. It can be stored at room temperature until opened, after which it requires refrigeration.

Frozen Whole Milk

Homogenized, pasteurized, whole milk can be quickly frozen and kept below -10°F for six weeks to three months. Like concentrated frozen milk, it must be used soon after defrosting. This milk, used on ships and at overseas military installations, is not ordinarily available in retail markets.

EFFECT OF FREEZING. Freezing does not measurably change the nutritive value of milk. Freezing causes a destabilization of the protein, however, and particles of precipitated protein may be visible on the glass when the milk thaws. On thawing, there is also a tendency for the fat to separate. Milk that has been accidentally frozen (on the doorstep in winter, for example) is quite safe to use. It is a wise precaution to boil the milk for all uses, if during freezing the cap has been pushed out of the bottle.

NUTRIENT CONTENT OF ONE GRAM OF MILK FAT AND ONE GRAM OF MILK SOLIDS-NOT-FAT*

	Milk Fat	Milk Solids-Not-Fat
Food Energy, Cal**	8.79	3.76
Protein, gm		.39
Calcium, mg		12.97
Phosphorus, mg		10.22
Sodium, mg		5.49
Potassium, mg		15.83
Magnesium, mg		1.428
Thiamine, mg		.003
Riboflavin, mg		.019
Niacin Equiv., mg+		.101
Ascorbic Acid, mg		.109
Cholesterol, mg	3	
Vitamin A value, I.U.	40	

*Composition of Foods-raw, processed, prepared. Agriculture Handbook No. 8, U.S. Dept. of Agriculture, Washington, D.C. Revised December 1963. All values have been calculated, and do not appear as such in the reference.

**For rapid estimate of food energy, milk fat can be assumed to contribute 9 calories per gram and milk solids-not-fat 4 calories per gram.

+Calculated from Amino Acid Content of Foods. Home Economics Research Report No. 4, U.S. Dept. of Agriculture, Washington, D.C. December 1957.

Listed below are the excerpted regulations from Title 21 CFR on Milk and Cream. It is these regulations which should constitute the buyer's specifications for milk purchases. These regulations pertain except where state standards exceed the Federal standards:

"Cream" means the liquid milk product, high in fat and separated from milk, which may have been adjusted by adding thereto: Milk, concentrated milk, dry whole milk, skim milk, concentrated skim milk, or nonfat dry milk. Cream contains not less than 18 percent milkfat.

"Pasteurized," when used to describe a dairy product, means that every particle of such product shall have been heated in properly operated equipment to one of the temperatures specified in the table at the end of this paragraph, and held continuously at or above that temperature for the specified time (or other time/temperature relationship which has been demonstrated to be equivalent thereto in microbial destruction):

Temperature	Time
145°F.[1]	30 minutes
161°F.[1]	15 seconds
191°F.	1 second
204°F.	0.05 second
221°F.	0.01 second

1. If the dairy ingredient has a fat content of 10 percent or more, or if it contains added sweeteners, the specified temperature shall be increased by 5°F.

"Ultra-pasteurized," when used to describe a dairy product, means that the product shall have been thermally processed at or above 280°F for at least 2 seconds, either before or after packaging, so as to produce a product which has an extended shelf life under refrigerated conditions.

Milk

Milk is the lacteal secretion, practically free from colostrum, obtained by the complete milking of one or more healthy cows. Milk that is in final package form for beverage use shall have been pasteurized or ultra-pasteurized, and shall contain not less than 8-1/4 percent milk solids-not-fat and not less than 3-1/4 percent milkfat. Milk may have been adjusted by separating part of the milkfat therefrom, or by adding thereto cream, concentrated milk, dry whole milk, skim milk, concentrated skim milk, or nonfat dry milk. Milk may be homogenized.

VITAMIN ADDITION. 1. If added, vitamin A shall be present in such quantity that each quart of the food contains not less than 2000 International Units thereof, within limits of good manufacturing practice.

2. If added, vitamin D shall be present in such quantity that each quart of the food contains 400 International Units thereof, within limits of good manufacturing practice.

OPTIONAL INGREDIENTS. The following safe and suitable ingredients may be used: 1. Carriers for vitamins A and D. 2. Characterizing flavoring ingredients (with or without coloring, nutritive sweetener, emulsifiers, and stabilizers, as follows: a. Fruit and fruit juice (including concentrated fruit and fruit juice); b. Natural and artificial food flavorings.

The following terms shall accompany the name of the food wherever it appears on the principal display panel or panels of the label, in letters not less than one-half the height of the letters used in such name: 1. If vitamins are added, the phrase "vitamin A" or "vitamin A added" or "vitamin D" or "vitamin D added," or "vitamins A and D" or "vitamins A and D added," as is appropriate. The word "vitamin" may be abbreviated "vit." 2. The word "ultra-pasteurized," if the food has been ultra-pasteurized.

The following terms may appear on the label: 1. The word "pasteurized," if the food has been pasteurized. 2. The word "homogenized," if the food has been homogenized.

LABEL DECLARATION. When used in the food, each of the ingredients specified in paragraphs above of this section shall be declared on the label.

Lowfat milk

Lowfat milk is milk from which sufficient milkfat has been removed to produce a food having, within limits of good manufacturing practice, one of the following milkfat contents: 1/2, 1, 1-1/2, or 2 percent. Lowfat milk is pasteurized or ultra-pasteurized, contains added vitamin A as prescribed by paragraph above of this section, and contains not less than 8-1/4 percent milk solids-not-fat. Lowfat milk may be homogenized.

Vitamin A shall be present in such quantity that each quart of the food contains not less than 2000 International Units thereof, within limits of good manufacturing practice.

Addition of vitamin D is optional. If added, vitamin D shall be present in such quantity that each quart of the food contains 400 International Units thereof, within limits of good manufacturing practice.

OPTIONAL INGREDIENTS. The following safe and suitable ingredients may be used: 1. Carriers for vitamins A and D. 2. Concentrated skim milk, nonfat dry milk, or other milk-derived ingredients to increase the nonfat solids content of the food: Provided that the ratio of protein to total nonfat solids of the food and the protein efficiency ratio of all protein present shall not be decreased as a result of adding such ingredients. 3. When one or more of the optional milk-derived ingredients in the paragraph above of this section is used, emulsifiers, stabilizers, or both, it must be in an amount not more than 2 percent by weight of the solids in such ingredients. 4. Characterizing flavoring ingredients (with or without coloring, nutritive sweetener, emulsifiers, and stabilizers) as follows: a. Fruit and fruit juice (including concentrated fruit and fruit juice). b. Natural and artificial food flavorings.

The name of the food is "Lowfat milk." The name of the food shall appear on the label in type of uniform size, style and color. The name of the food shall be accompanied on the label by a declaration indicating the presence of any characterizing flavoring.

1. The following terms shall accompany the name of the food wherever it appears on the principal display panel or panels of the label in letters not less than one-half of the height of the letters used in such name: a. The phrase "   % milkfat," the blank to be filled in with the

fraction 1/2, or multiple thereof, to indicate the actual fat content of the food. b. The phrase "vitamin A" or "vitamin A added," or if vitamin D is added, the phrase "vitamins A and D added." The word "vitamin" may be abbreviated "vit." c. The word "ultra-pasteurized," if the food has been ultra-pasteurized. d. The phrase "protein fortified" or "fortified with protein" if the food contains not less than 10 percent milk-derived nonfat solids.

2. The following terms may appear on the label: a. The word "pasteurized," if the food has been pasteurized. b. The word "homogenized," if the food has been homogenized.

LABEL DECLARATION. When ingredients are used, such ingredients shall be declared on the label except that concentrated skim milk and nonfat dry milk may be declared as "nonfat milk solids."

Skim Milk

DESCRIPTION. Skim milk is milk from which sufficient milkfat has been removed to reduce its milkfat content to less than 0.5 percent. Skim milk that is in final package form for beverage use shall have been pasteurized or ultra-pasteurized, shall contain added vitamin A as prescribed by the paragraph of this section, and shall contain not less than 8-1/4 percent milk solids-not-fat. Skim milk may be homogenized.

Vitamin A shall be present in such quantity that each quart of the food contains not less than 2000 International Units thereof, within limits of good manufacturing practice.

Addition of vitamin D is optional. If added, vitamin D shall be present in such quantity that each quart of the food contains 400 International Units thereof, within limits of good manufacturing practice.

OPTIONAL INGREDIENTS. The following safe and suitable ingredients may be used: 1. Carriers for vitamins A and D. 2. Concentrated skim milk, nonfat dry milk, or other milk-derived ingredients to increase the nonfat solids content of the food: Provided that the ratio of protein to total nonfat solids of the food and the protein efficiency ratio of all protein present shall not be decreased as a result of adding such ingredients. 3. When one or more of the optional, milk-derived ingredients, emulsifiers, stabilizers, or a combination of both, is used in an amount not more than 2 percent by weight of the solids in such ingredients. 4. Characterizing flavoring ingredients (with or without coloring, nutritive sweetener, emulsifiers, and stabilizers) as follows: a. Fruit and fruit juice (including concentrated fruit and fruit juice). b. Natural and artifical food flavoring.

The name of the food is "Skim milk" or alternatively "Nonfat milk." The name of the food shall appear on the label in type of uniform size, style, and color. The name of the food shall be accompanied on the label by a declaration indicating the presence of any characterizing flavoring.

The following terms shall accompany the name of the food wherever it appears on the principal display panel or panels of the label, in letters not less than one-half of the height of the letters used in such name: 1. The phrase "vitamin A" or "vitamin A added," or if vitamin D is added, the phrase "vitamins A and D" or "vitamins A and D added." The word "vitamin" may be abbreviated "vit." 2. The word "ultra-pasteurized," if the food has been ultra-pasteurized. 3. The phrase "protein fortified" or "fortified with protein," if the food contains not less than 10 percent milk derived nonfat solids.

The following terms may appear on the label: 1. The word "pasteurized," if the food has been pasteurized. 2. The word "homogenized," if the food has been homogenized.

LABEL DECLARATION. When used in the food, each of the ingredients specified shall be declared on the label as required by the applicable sections of Part 1 of this chapter.

Half-and-Half

Half-and-half is the food consisting of a mixture of milk and cream which contains not less than 10.5 percent but less than 18 percent milkfat. It is pasteurized or ultra-pasteurized, and may be homogenized.

The following safe and suitable optional ingredients may be used: 1. Emulsifiers. 2. Stabilizers. 3. Nutritive sweeteners. 4. Characterizing flavoring ingredients (with or without coloring) as follows: a. Fruit and fruit juice (including concentrated fruit and fruit juice.) b. Natural and artificial food flavoring.

NOMENCLATURE. The name of the food is "Half-and-Half." The name of the food shall be accompanied on the label by a declaration indicating the presence of any characterizing flavoring.

The following terms shall accompany the name of the food wherever it appears on the principal display panel or panels of the label, in letters not less than one-half the height of the letters used in such name; 1. The word "ultra-pasteurized," if the food has been ultra-pasteurized. 2. The word "sweetened," if no characterizing flavor ingredients are used, but nutritive sweetener is added.

The following terms may appear on the label: 1. The word "pasteurized," if the food has been pasteurized. 2. The word "homogenized," if the food has been homogenized.

LABEL DECLARATION. When used in the food, each of the ingredients specified shall be declared on the label.

Light Cream

Light cream is cream which contains not less than 18 percent but less than 30 percent milkfat. It is pasteurized or ultra-pasteurized, and may be homogenized.

OPTIONAL INGREDIENTS. The following safe and suitable ingredients may be used: 1. Stabilizers. 2. Emulsifiers. 3. Nutritive sweeteners.

4. Characterizing flavoring ingredients (with or without coloring) as follows: a. Fruit and fruit juice (including concentrated fruit and fruit juice). b. Natural and artificial food flavoring.

NOMENCLATURE. The name of the food is "light cream," or alternatively "coffee cream," or "table cream." The name of the food shall be not less than one-half the height of the letters used in such name: 1. The word "ultra-pasteurized," if the food has been ultra-pasteurized. 2. The word "sweetened," if no characterizing flavoring ingredients are used, but nutritive sweetener is added. The following terms may also appear on the label: 1. The word "pasteurized," if the food has been pasteurized. 2. The word "homogenized," if the food has been homogenized.

LABEL DECLARATION. When used in the food, each of the ingredients specified shall be declared on the label.

Light Whipping Cream

Light whipping cream which contains not less than 30 percent, but less than 36 percent, milkfat. It is pasteurized or ultra-pasteurized, and may be homogenized.

The following safe and suitable optional ingredients may be used: 1. Emulsifiers. 2. Stabilizers. 3. Nutritive sweeteners. 4. Characterizing flavoring ingredients (with or without coloring) as follows: a. Fruit and fruit juice (including concentrated fruit and fruit juice). b. Natural and artificial food flavoring.

NOMENCLATURE. The name of the food is "light whipping cream" or alternatively "whipping cream." The name of the food shall be accompanied on the label by a declaration indicating the presence of any characterizing flavoring.

The following terms shall accompany the name of the food wherever it appears on the principal display panel or panels of the label, in letters not less than one-half the height of the letters used in such name. 1. The word "ultra-pasteurized," if the food has been ultra-pasteurized. 2. The word "sweetened," if no characterizing flavoring ingredients are used, but nutritive sweetener is added.

The following terms may appear on the label: 1. the word "pasteurized," if the food has been pasteurized. 2. The word "homogenized," if the food has been homogenized.

LABEL DECLARATION. When used in the food, each of the ingredients specified shall be declared on the label.

Heavy Cream

Heavy cream is cream which contains not less than 36 percent milkfat. It is pasteurized or ultra-pasteurized, and may be homogenized.

The following safe and suitable optional ingredients may be used: 1. Emulsifiers. 2. Stabilizers. 3. Nutritive sweeteners. 4. Characterizing flavoring ingredients (with or without coloring) as follows: a. Fruit and fruit juice (including concentrated fruit and fruit juice). b. Natural and artificial food flavoring.

The name of the food is "heavy cream," or alternatively "heavy whipping cream." The name of the food shall be accompanied on the label by a declaration indicating the presence of any characterizing flavoring. The following terms shall accompany the name of the food wherever it appears on the principal display panel or panels of the label, in letters not less than one-half of the height of the letters used in such name: 1. The word "ultra-pasteurized," if the food has been ultra-pasteurized. 2. The word "sweetened," if no characterizing flavoring ingredients are used, but nutritive sweetener is added.

The following terms may appear on the label: 1. The word "pasteurized," if the food has been pasteurized. 2. The word "homogenized," if the food has been homogenized.

When used in the food, each of the ingredients specified in the paragraph above of this section shall be declared on the label.

Evaporated Milk

Evaporated milk is the liquid food obtained by the partial removal of water from milk. The milkfat and total milk solids contents of the food are not less than 7.5 and 25.5 percent, respectively. Evaporated milk contains added vitamin D, as prescribed by the paragraph above of this section. It is homogenized. It is sealed in a container and so processed by heat, either before or after sealing, as to prevent spoilage.

Vitamin D shall be present in such quantity that each fluid ounce of the food contains 25 International Units thereof, within limits of good manufacturing practice.

Addition of vitamin A is optional. If added, vitamin A shall be present in such quantity that each fluid ounce of the food contains not less than 125 International Units thereof, within limits of good manufacturing practice.

OPTIONAL INGREDIENTS. The following safe and suitable ingredients may be used: 1. Carriers for vitamins A and D. 2. Emulsifiers. 3. Stabilizers with or without dioctyl sodium sulfosuccinate as a solubilizing agent.

The name of the food is "evaporated milk." The phrase "vitamin D" or "vitamin D added," or "vitamins A and D" or "vitamins A and D added," as is appropriate, shall immediately precede or follow the name of the food wherever it appears on the principal display panel or panels of the label, in letters not less than one-half the height of the letters used in such name.

When used in the food, the optional ingredients specified shall be declared on the label.

Concentrated Milk

Concentrated milk is the liquid food obtained by partial removal of water from milk. The milkfat and total milk solids contents of the food are not less than 7.5 and 25.5 percent, respectively. It is pasteurized, but is not processed by heat so as to prevent spoilage. It may be homogenized.

If added, vitamin D shall be present in such quantity that each fluid ounce of the food contains 25 International Units thereof, within limits of good manufacturing practice.

OPTIONAL INGREDIENTS. Safe and suitable carriers may be used for vitamin D.

The name of the food is "concentrated milk" or, alternatively, "condensed milk." If the food contains added vitamin D, the phrase "vitamin D" or "vitamin D added" shall accompany the name of the food wherever it appears on the principal display panel or panels of the label, in letters not less than one-half the height of the letters used in such name. The word "homogenized" may appear on the label, if the food has been homogenized.

When used in the food, the optional ingredients specified shall be declared on the label.

Sweetened Condensed Milk

Sweetened condensed milk is the food obtained by the partial removal of water only from a mixture of milk and safe and suitable nutritive sweetener. The finished food contains not less than 8.5 percent by weight of milkfat, and not less than 28 percent by weight of total milk solids. The quantity of nutritive sweetener used is sufficient to prevent spoilage. The food is pasteurized, and may be homogenized.

The name of the food is "sweetened condensed milk." The word "homogenized" may appear on the label if the food has been homogenized.

The optional sweetener used shall be declared on the label.

Nonfat Dry Milk

Nonfat dry milk is the product obtained by removal of water only from pasteurized skim milk. It contains not more than 5 percent by weight of moisture, and not more than 1-1/2 percent by weight of milkfat, unless otherwise indicated.

The name of the food is "nonfat dry milk." If the fat content is over 1-1/2 percent by weight, the name of the food on the principal display panel or panels shall be accompanied by the statement "contains   % milkfat," the blank to be filled in with the percentage to the nearest one-tenth of 1 percent of fat contained, within limits of good manufacturing practice.

NONFAT DRY MILK FORTIFIED WITH VITAMINS A AND D. Nonfat dry milk fortified with vitamins A and D conforms to the standard of identity for nonfat dry milk, except that vitamins A and D are added as prescribed by the paragraph above of this section.

VITAMIN ADDITION. 1. Vitamin A is added in such quantity that, when prepared according to the label directions, each quart of the reconstituted product contains 2000 International Units thereof. 2. Vitamin D is added in such quantity that, when prepared according to label directions, each quart of the reconstituted product contains 400 International Units thereof.

The requirements of this paragraph will be deemed to have been met if reasonable overages, within limits of good manufacturing practice, are present to insure that the required levels of vitamins are maintained throughout the shelf life of the food expected under customary conditions of distribution.

OPTIONAL INGREDIENTS. Safe and suitable carriers for vitamins A and D.

The name of the food is "nonfat dry milk fortified with vitamins A and D." If the fat content is over 1-1/2 percent by weight, the name of the food on the principal display panel or panels shall be accompanied by the statement, "Contains   % milkfat," the blank to be filled in to the nearest one-tenth of 1 percent with the percentage of fat contained, within limits of good manufacturing practice.

Cultured Buttermilk

Milk solids-not-fat: no standard. State standards may vary from 8.0% to 9.0% minimum where they exist.

Cultured Milk

Milk fat: no standard. State standards may be as high as 3.5% minimum where they exist.

Milk solids-not-fat: no standard. State standards may vary from 8.0% to 8.5% minimum where they exist.

Evaporated Milk

Milkfat: 7.5% minimum

Total milk solids: 25.5% minimum

Vitamin D: 25 USP units minimum

Filled Milk [dry]

Fat, animal or vegetable: May lawfully be shipped in interstate commerce, and is regulated under the provision of the Federal Food, Drug and Cosmetic Act.

Filled Milk [evaporated]

Fat, animal or vegetable: May lawfully be shipped in interstate commerce, and is regulated under the provision of the Federal Food, Drug and Cosmetic Act.

Total Solids: may lawfully be shipped in interstate commerce, and is regulated under the provision of the Federal Food, Drug and Cosmetic Act.

Vitamin D Per Ounce: may lawfully be shipped in interstate commerce and is regulated under the provision of the Federal Food, Drug and Cosmetic Act.

Flavored Milk

Milkfat: no standard. State standards may vary from 2.8% to 3.8% minimum.

Flavored Milk Drink

Milkfat: no standard. State standards may vary from 0.5% to 3.5% minimum, and .025% to 3.8% maximum, where they exist.

Milk solids-not-fat: no standard. State standards may vary from 7.5% to 10.0% minimum where they exist.

Total milk solids: no standard. State standards generally do not exist, but may be as high as 8.25% where they do exist.

Fluid Filled Milk

Fat: may lawfully be shipped in interstate commerce, and is regulated under the provision of the Federal Food, Drug and Cosmetic Act.

Milk solids-not-fat: may lawfully be shipped in interstate commerce, and is regulated under the provision of the Federal Food, Drug and Cosmetic Act.

Fortified Multiple Vitamin and/or Mineral Milk

Vitamin A per quart: 2000 USP units minimum

Vitamin D per quart: 400 USP units minimum

Vitamin B^1 per quart: no standard. State standards may vary from .6 to 1.0 mg. minimum where they exist.

Vitamin B^2 per quart: no standard. State standards may vary from .3 to 2.0 mg. minimum where they exist.

Niacin per quart: no standard. State standards may be as high as 10.0 mg. minimum where they exist.

Iron per quart: no standard. State standards may be as high as 10.0 minimum where they exist.

Iodine per quart: no standard. State standards are 0.1 mg. minimum where they exist.

Lowfat Milk

Milkfat: 0.5% minimum, 2.0% maximum

Added milk solids: 8.25% minimum, no standard for maximum. State standards generally do not exist but may vary from 2.0% to 12.0% maximum where they do exist.

Nonfat, Fat Free, Defatted Milk

Milkfat: no standard. State standards may vary from 0.1% to 9.25% maximum where they exist.

Milk solids-not-fat: no standard. State standards may vary from 8.0% to 9.0% minimum where they exist.

Skim Milk

Milkfat: less than 0.5% maximum

Milk solids-not-fat: no standard. State standards may vary from 8.25% to 9.3% minimum where they exist.

Total milk solids: 8.25% minimum

Added solids: no standard. State standards generally do not exist, but may vary from 1.0% to 9.0% minimum, and 2.0% to 12.0% maximum, where they do exist.

Vitamin A per quart: 2,000 USP units minimum
Vitamin D per quart: 400 USP units minimum

Vitamin D Milk

Vitamin D per quart: 400 USP units minimum

Whole Milk

Milkfat: 3.25% minimum

Milk solids-not-fat: 8.25% minimum

Total milk solids: no standard. State standards may vary from 11.0% to 12.3% minimum where they exist.

Half-and-Half

Milkfat: 10.5% minimum, 18.0% maximum

Milk solids-not-fat: no standard. State standards generally do not exist, but may be as high as 10.0% minimum and 12.0% maximum where they do exist.

Cream

Light:

Milkfat: 18.0% minimum

Medium:

Milkfat: no standard. State standards may vary from 25.0% to 30.0% minimum

Whipping:

Milkfat: 30.0% minimum

Heavy Whipping:

Milkfat: 36.0% minimum

Cultured Sour Cream

Milkfat: no standard. State standards may vary from 16.0% to 20.0% minimum

Milk solids-not-fat: no standards

GRADE and QUALITY SHIELD for consumer packages of dairy products manufactured under the grading and quality control service. *QUALITY APPROVED* shield for cultured buttermilk and cultured sour cream means these products were manufactured and packaged under USDA's grading and quality control service.

Stabilizer: no standard. State standards generally do not exist, but may be as high as 0.6% maximum where they do exist.

Acidified Sour Cream

Fat: no standard. State standards may vary from 8.0% to 20.0% minimum where they exist.

Milk solids-not-fat: no standard.

Stabilizer: no standard. State standards generally do not exist, but may vary from 0.6% to 1.0% maximum where they do exist.

Yogurt

Milkfat: no standard. State standards may vary from 0.5% to 3.8% minimum where they exist.

Milk solids-not-fat: no standard. State standards may vary from 8.25% to 8.5% minimum, and may be as high as 8.5% maximum where they do exist.

Frozen Yogurt

Milkfat: no standard. State standards generally do not exist, but may vary from 3.25% to 3.5% minimum where they do exist.

Weight per gallon: no standard. State standards generally do not exist, but may vary from 5.0 to 6.0 pounds minimum.

Whipped Cream

Milkfat: no standard. State standards may vary from 18.0% to 36.0% minimum where they exist.

Added solids-not-fat: no standard.

Stabilizer: no standard. State standards generally do not exist, but may be as high as 0.5% maximum where they do exist.

Sugar: no standard. Some state standards may follow U.S. Public Health Service Recommended Milk Ordinance and Code.

Flavoring: no standard.

Sweetened Condensed [whole] Milk

Milkfat: 8.5% minimum

Total milk solids: 28.0% minimum

Sugar: no standard. State standards generally do not exist, but may be as high as 18.0% minimum where they do exist.

Sweetened Condensed Skim Milk

Total milk solids: no standards. State standards may vary from 20.0% to 28.0% minimum where they exist.

Sugar: no standard. State standards generally do not exist, but follow the Federal Food and Drug standards when they do exist.

Plain Condensed Skim Milk

Total milk solids: no standards. State standards may vary from 18.0% to 27.0% minimum where they exist.

Dry Whole Milk

Milkfat: 26.0% minimum

Moisture: no standard. State standards may vary from 4.0% to 5.0% maximum where they exist.

Nonfat Dry Milk
Milkfat: 1.5% maximum

Moisture: 5.0% maximum

Egg Nog
Milkfat: no standard. State standards vary from 3.5% to 6.0% minimum where they exist.

Egg yolk solids: no standard. State standards may vary from 0.5% to 1.0% minimum where they exist.

Stabilizer: no standard. State standards are 0.5% to 0.6% maximum where they exist.

Dessert Topping [filled dairy product]
Fat, animal or vegetable: no standard. State standards generally do not exist, but may be as high as 18.0% minimum where they do exist. Illegal in some states.

Stabilizer: no standard. State standards generally do not exist, but are 0.5% or 1.0% maximum where they do exist. Illegal in some states.

Imitation Sour Cream
Fat: no standard. State standards may vary from 10.5% to 20.0% minimum where they do exist.

Milk solids-not-fat: no standard. State standards generally do not exist, but may be as high as 8.0% minimum where they do exist.

Non-Dairy Fluid Beverage
Fat: no standard. State standards generally do not exist, but may vary from 3.0% to 3.8% minimum where they do exist.

Solids-not-fat: no standard. State standards generally do not exist, but are 8.25% or 8.5% minimum where they do exist.

Non-Dairy Topping
Fat: no standard. State standards generally do not exist, but are 30.0% minimum where they do exist.

Solids-not-fat: no standard.

Non-Dairy Coffee Whiteners
Fat: no standard.

Solids-not-fat: no standard.

DRY WHOLE MILK December 1970

"Dry whole milk" (made by the spray process or the atmospheric roller process) is the product resulting from the removal of water from milk, and contains the lactose, milk proteins, milk fat and milk minerals in the same relative proportions as in the fresh milk from which made.

The term "milk" means milk produced by healthy cows and pasteurized at a temperature of 161°F. for 15 seconds, or its equivalent in bacterial destruction, before or during the manufacture of the dry whole milk.

U.S. Grade
The U.S. grades of dry whole milk are determined on the basis of flavor and odor, physical appearance, bacterial estimate, butterfat content, coliform estimate, copper content, iron content, moisture content, oxygen content, scorched particle content, solubility index, and titratable acidity.

U.S. Premium Grade
Dry whole milk manufactured by the spray process conforms to the following requirements:

a. Flavor and odor (applies equally to the reliquefied form): Sweet. It may have slight cooked flavors and odors, but is free from all other off-flavors and odors.

b. Physical appearance: Is white or light cream color; free from lumps that do not break up under slight pressure; and free from noticeable brown and black scorched particles.

c. Bacterial estimate: Not more than 30,000 per gram.

d. Butterfat content: not less than 26 percent.

e. Coliform estimate: Not more than 90 per gram.

f. Copper content: Not more than 1.5 p.p.m.*

g. Iron content: Not more than 10 p.p.m.

h. Moisture content: Not more than 2.25 percent.

i. Oxygen content: Not more than 2 percent.

j. Solubility index: Not more than 0.50 ml.

k. Scorched particle content: Not more than 7.5 mg.

l. Titratable acidity: Not more than 0.15 percent.

U.S. Extra Grade
a. Spray process. Dry whole milk manufactured by the spray process conforms to the following requirements:

1. Flavor and odor (applies equally to the reliquefied form): It may have definite cooked flavors and odors, and other off-flavors to a slight degree, but is free from objectionable flavors and odors.

2. Physical appearance: is white or light cream color; free from lumps that do not break up under moderate pressure; and practically free from brown and black, scorched particles.

3. Bacterial estimate: Not more than 50,000 per gram.

4. Butterfat content: Not less than 26 percent.

5. Coliform estimate: No requirement.

6. Copper content: Not more than 1.5 p.p.m.

7. Iron content: Not more than 10 p.p.m.

*parts per million

8. Moisture content: Not more than 2.5 percent.

9. Oxygen content: If gas packed, not more than 3 percent.

10. Scorched particle content: Not more than 15 mg.

11. Solubility index: Not more than 0.50 ml.

12. Titratable acidity: Not more than 0.15 percent.

b. Roller process. Dry whole milk manufactured by the roller process conforms to the requirements in paragraph a. of this section, except that the solubility index is not more than 15 ml., the scorched particle content is not more than 22.5 mg., and the moisture content is not more than 3 percent.

U.S. Standard Grade

a. Spray process. Dry whole milk manufactured by the spray process conforms to the following requirements:

1. Flavor and odor (applies equally to the reliquefied form): It may have definite scorched and storage flavors and odors, but has no other objectionable flavors and odors.

2. Physical appearance: Is white or light cream color; free from lumps that do not break up under moderate pressure; and may have moderate amount of brown and black, scorched particles.

3. Bacterial estimate: Not more than 100,000 per gram.

4. Butterfat content: Not less than 26 percent.

5. Coliform estimate: No requirement.

6. Copper content: No requirement.

7. Iron content: No requirement.

8. Moisture content: Not more than 3 percent.

9. Oxygen content: No requirement.

10. Scorched particle content: Not more than 22.5 mg.

11. Solubility index: Not more than 1 ml.

12. Titratable acidity: Not more than 0.17 percent.

b. Roller process. Dry whole milk manufactured by the roller process conforms to the requirements prescribed in paragraph a. of this section, except that the solubility index is not more than 15 ml., the scorched particle content is not more than 32.5 mg., and the moisture content is not more than 4 percent.

Explanation of Terms

Explanation of terms with respect to flavor and odor:

1. Slight. Detected only upon critical examination.

2. Definite. Not intense, but readily detectable.

3. Objectionable. Flavors and odors, such as fishy, cheesy, scorched, storage, oxidized, rancid, tallowy, soapy, utensil, or others equally objectionable.

NONFAT DRY MILK [ROLLER PROCESS] April 1, 1973

Basis for determination of U.S. grades of nonfat dry milk — roller process — are determined on the basis of flavor and odor, physical appearance, bacterial estimate on the basis of standard plate count, butterfat content, moisture content, scorched particle content, solubility index, and titratable acidity.

The final U.S. grade shall be established on the basis of the lowest rating of any one of the quality characteristics.

U.S. Extra

U.S. Extra grade must conform to the following requirements:

1. Flavor and odor (applies to reliquefied form): Shall be sweet and desirable, but may possess the following flavors to a slight degree: Chalky, feed, flat, and scorched. For detailed classification of flavor and odor characteristics, see Table 5-1.

2. Physical appearance: Shall possess a uniform white to light cream natural color; free from lumps except those that break up readily with very slight pressure, and reasonably free from visible, dark particles. The reliquefied product shall be reasonably free from graininess. For detailed classification of physical appearance characteristics, see Table 5-2.

3. Laboratory tests: Shall be used to determine classification of the following quality characteristics:

   a. Bacterial estimate: Not more than 50,000 per gram standard plate count.

   b. Butterfat content: Not more than 1.25 percent.

   c. Moisture content: Not more than 4.0 percent.

   d. Scorched particle content: Not more than 22.5 mg.

   e. Solubility index: Not more than 15.0 ml.

   f. Titratable acidity: Not more than 0.15 percent.

U.S. Standard

U.S. Standard grade shall conform to the following requirements:

1. Flavor and odor (applies to reliquefied form): Should

possess a fairly desirable flavor, but may possess the following to a slight degree: Bitter, oxidized, stale, storage and utensil; the following to a definite degree: Chalky, feed, flat, and scorched. For detailed classification of flavor and odor characteristics, see Table 5-1.

2. Physical appearance: May possess a slight unnatural color; free from lumps except those that break up readily under slight pressure, and moderately free from visible, dark particles. The reliquefied product shall be reasonably free from graininess. For detailed classification of physical appearance characteristics, see Table 5-2.

3. Laboratory tests: Shall be used to determine classification of the following quality characteristics:
   a. Bacterial estimate: Not more than 100,000 per gram standard plate count.
   b. Butterfat content: Not more than 1.50 percent.
   c. Moisture content: Not more than 5.0 percent.
   d. Scorched particle content: Not more than 32.5 mg.
   e. Solubility index: Not more than 15.0 ml.
   f. Titratable acidity: Not more than 0.17 percent.

For detailed classification of laboratory analyses, see Table 5-3.

TABLE 5-1
CLASSIFICATION OF FLAVOR AND ODOR CHARACTERISTICS FOR NONFAT DRY MILK — ROLLER PROCESS

Identified Flavors	Classification	
	Extra	Standard
Butter		Slight
Chalky	Slight	Definite
Feed	Slight	Definite
Flat	Slight	Definite
Oxidized		Slight
Scorched	Slight	Definite
Stale		Slight
Storage		Slight
Utensil		Slight

TABLE 5-2
CLASSIFICATION OF PHYSICAL APPEARANCE CHARACTERISTICS FOR NONFAT DRY MILK — ROLLER PROCESS

Physical Appearance	Classification	
	Extra	Standard
Dry Product:		
Lumps	Very Slight	Slight
Unnatural color		Slight
Visible dark particles	Slight	Definite
Reliquefied, grainy	Slight	Slight

TABLE 5-3
CLASSIFICATION ACCORDING TO LABORATORY ANALYSIS FOR NONFAT DRY MILK — ROLLER PROCESS

Laboratory Tests	Classification	
	Extra	Standard
(1) Bacterial estimate, standard plate count per gram	50,000	100,000
(2) Butterfat content; percent	1.25	1.50
(3) Moisture content; percent	4.0	5.0
(4) Scorched particle content; mg.	22.5	32.5
(5) Solubility index; ml	15.0	15.0
(6) Titratable acidity; percent	0.15	0.17

Nonfat dry milk which fails to meet the requirements for U.S. Standard Grade, and/or shows a direct microscopic clump count exceeding 100 million per gram, shall not be assigned a U.S. grade.

NONFAT DRY MILK [SPRAY PROCESS] April 1, 1973

"Nonfat dry milk" is the product resulting from the removal of fat and water from milk, and contains the lactose, milk proteins, and milk minerals in the same relative proportions as are in the fresh milk from which it is made. It contains not over 5 percent by weight of moisture. The fat content shall not exceed 1-1/2 percent by weight.

The term "milk" when used in this subpart means fresh, sweet milk produced by healthy cows, that has been pasteurized before, or during, the manufacture of the nonfat dry milk.

The U.S. grades of nonfat dry milk — spray process — are determined on the basis of flavor and odor, physical appearance, bacterial estimate on the basis of standard plate count, butterfat content, moisture content, scorched particle content, solubility index, and titratable acidity.

The final U.S. grade is established on the basis of the lowest rating of any one of the quality characteristics.

U.S. Extra

U.S. Extra grade must conform to the following requirements:

1. Flavor and odor (applies to reliquefied form): Shall be sweet, pleasing and desirable, but may possess the following flavors to a slight degree: Chalky, cooked, feed, and flat. For detailed classification of flavor and odor characteristics, see Table 5-1.
2. Physical appearance: Shall possess a uniform white to light cream natural color; free from lumps except those that readily break up with very slight pressure, and practically free from visible, dark particles. The reliquefied product shall be free from graininess. For detailed classification of physical appearance characteristics, see Table 5-2.
3. Laboratory tests: Shall be used to determine classification of the following quality characteristics:
   a. Bacterial estimate: Not more than 50,000 per gram standard plate count.
   b. Butterfat content: Not more than 1.25 percent.
   c. Moisture content: Not more than 4.0 percent.
   d. Scorched particle content: Not more than 15.00 mg.
   e. Solubility index: Not more than 1.2 ml., except that product classified as U.S. High Heat may have not more than 2.0 ml.
   f. Titratable acidity: Not more than 0.15 percent.

U.S. Standard

U.S. Standard grade must conform to the following requirements:

1. Flavor and odor (applies to reliquefied form): Should possess a fairly pleasing flavor but may possess the following flavors to a slight degree: Bitter, oxidized, stale, storage, utensil, and scorched; the following to a definite degree: Chalky, cooked, feed and flat. For detailed classification of flavor and odor characteristics, see Table 5-1.
   a. Feed: Characteristic of the feed flavors in milk carried through into the nonfat dry milk.
   b. Flat: Lacking characteristic sweetness or full flavor.
   c. Oxidized: A flavor resembling cardboard, and sometimes referred to as "cappy" or "tallowy."
   d. Scorched: A more intensified flavor than "cooked," and imparts a burnt aftertaste.
   e. Stale, storage: Lacking in freshness, and imparting a "roung" aftertaste.
   f. Utensil: A flavor suggestive of improper or inadequate washing and sterilization of milking machines, utensils, or factory equipment.
2. With respect to physical appearance:
   a. Practically free. Present only upon very critical examination.
   b. Reasonably free: Present only upon critical examination.
   c. Moderately free: Discernible upon careful examination.
   d. Very slight pressure: Lumps fall apart with only light touch.
   e. Slight pressure: Only sufficient pressure to disintegrate the lumps readily.
   f. Natural color: A color that is white or light cream.
   g. Grainy: Minute particles of undissolved powder appearing on the surface of a glass or tumbler in a thin film.
   h. Unnatural color: A color that is more intense than light cream, and is brownish, dull, or grey-like.
   i. Lumpy: Loss of powdery consistency but not caked hard chunks.
   j. Visible, dark particles: The presence of scorched or discolored specks.

Basis for Determination of U.S. Heat Treatment Classification

The whey protein nitrogen test shall be used in determining the heat treatment classification as follows:

United States Department of Agriculture
SCORCHED PARTICLE STANDARDS FOR DRY MILKS.

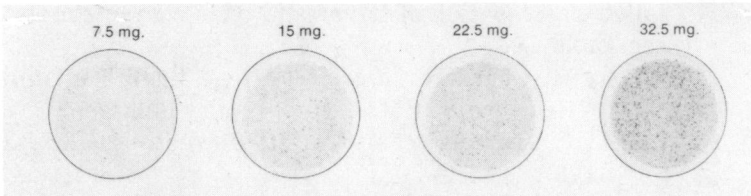

a. U.S. High-heat. The finished product shall not exceed 1.5 mg. undenatured, whey protein nitrogen per gram of nonfat dry milk.

b. U.S. Low-heat. The finished product shall show not less than 6.0 mg. undenatured, whey protein nitrogen per gram of nonfat dry milk.

c. U.S. Medium-heat. The finished product shall show undenatured, whey protein nitrogen between the levels of "high-heat" and "low-heat" (1.51 to 5.99 mg.).

INSTANT NONFAT DRY MILK October 1, 1970

Instant nonfat dry milk is nonfat dry milk which has been produced in such a manner as to improve substantially its dispersing and reliquefication characteristics over those produced by the conventional processes.

"Nonfat dry milk" is the product resulting from the removal of fat and water from milk, and contains the lactose, milk proteins, and milk minerals in the same relative proportion as in the fresh milk from which it is made. It contains not over 5 percent of moisture, by weight. The fat content is not over 1-1/2 percent by weight, unless otherwise indicated.

The term "milk" means fresh, sweet milk, produced by healthy cows, that has been pasteurized before, or during the manufacture of the instant nonfat dry milk.

U.S. Extra

The only U.S. grade is U.S. Extra.

The U.S. grade of instant nonfat dry milk is determined on the basis of flavor and odor, physical appearance, bacterial estimate on the basis of standard plate count, coliform count, milkfat content, moisture content, scorched particle content, solubility index, titratable acidity, and dispersibility.

The final U.S. grade is established on the basis of the lowest rating of any one of the quality characteristics.

USDA GRADE MARKS and the foods on which they are used.

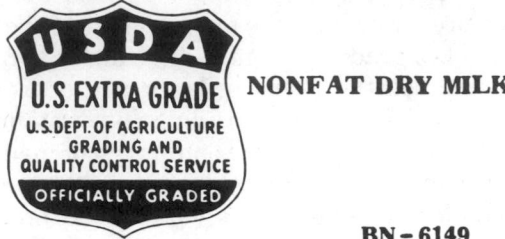

NONFAT DRY MILK

BN – 6149

These grade marks, under the law, are permitted only on foods officially graded under the supervision of The Agricultural Marketing Service, U.S. Department of Agriculture, Washington, D.C.

U.S. Extra grade conforms to the following requirements:
1. Flavor and odor (applies to reliquefied form): Shall be sweet, pleasing, and desirable, but may possess the following flavors to a slight degree: Chalky, cooked, feed, flat.
2. Physical appearance. Shall possess a uniform white to light cream natural color; shall be reasonably free-flowing, and free from lumps, except those that readily break up with very slight pressure.
3. Laboratory tests: Shall be used to determine classification of the following quality characteristics:
   a. Bacterial estimate: Not more than 30,000 per gram, standard plate count.
   b. Coliform count: Not more than 10 per gram.
   c. Milkfat content: Not more than 1.25 percent.
   d. Moisture content: Not more than 4.5 percent.
   e. Scorched particle content: Not more than 15.0 mg.
   f. Solubility index: Not more than 1.0 ml.
   g. Titratable acidity: Not more than 0.15 percent.
   h. Dispersibility: Not less than 85.0 percent.

Instant nonfat dry milk may not be assigned the U.S. grade for one or more of the following reasons:
   a. Fails to meet the requirements for U.S. Extra grade.
   b. Has direct microscopic clump count exceeding 75 million per gram.
   c. The phosphatase test, when run at the option of the USDA, or when requested by the buyer or seller, shows more than 4 micrograms of phenol per millileter

of reconstituted nonfat milk.

Explanation of terms:

a. With respect to flavor:

1. Slight: Detected only upon critical examination.
2. Chalky: A tactual type of flavor lacking in characteristic milk flavor.
3. Cooked: Similar to a custard flavor, and imparts a smooth aftertaste.
4. Feed: Characteristic of the feed flavors in milk.
5. Flat: Lacking characteristic flavor.

b. With respect to physical appearance:

1. Reasonably free-flowing: Pours in a fairly constant, uniform stream from the open end of a tilted container or scoop.
2. Very slight pressure: Lumps fall apart with only light touch.
3. Natural color: A color that is white or light cream.

DRY BUTTERMILK December 1970

"Dry buttermilk" (made by the spray process or the atmospheric roller process) is the product resulting from drying liquid buttermilk, derived from the manufacture of sweet cream butter to which no alkali or other chemical has been added, and which has been pasteurized either before or during the process of manufacture, at a temperature of 161°F. for 15 seconds, or its equivalent in bacterial destruction.

U.S. Extra grade.

The requirements of the U.S. Extra grade differ for dry buttermilk made by the spray process from that made by the *atmospheric* roller process.

a. Spray process: U.S. Extra grade dry buttermilk manufactured by the spray process conforms to the following requirements:

1. Flavor and odor (applies equally to the reliquefied form): Free from nonbuttermilk flavor and odors.
2. Physical appearance: Is cream to light brown color; free from lumps that do not break up under slight pressure; and practically free from black and brown, scorched particles.
3. Bacterial estimate: Not more than 50,000 per gram.
4. Butterfat content: Not less than 4.50 percent.
5. Moisture content: Not more than 4 percent.

6. Scorched particle content: Not more than 15 mg.
7. Solubility index: Not more than 1.25 ml.
8. Titratable acidity: Not less than 0.10 percent; not more than 0.18 percent.

b. Roller process. U.S. Extra grade dry buttermilk manufactured by the roller process conforms to the requirements in paragraph a. of this section, except that the solubility index is not more than 15 ml., and the scorched particle content is not more than 22.5 mg.

U.S. Standard Grade

The requirements of the U.S. Standard grade differ for dry buttermilk manufactured by the spray process from that manufactured by the atmospheric roller process:

a. Spray process. U.S. Standard grade dry buttermilk manufactured by the spray process conforms to the following requirements:

1. Flavor and odor (applies equally to the reliquefied form): Has not more than slight unnatural flavors and odors.
2. Physical appearance: Is cream to light brown color; free from lumps that do not break up under moderate pressure; and contains brown and black scorched particles to not more than a moderate degree.
3. Bacterial estimate: Not more than 200,000 per gram.
4. Butterfat content: Not less than 4.50 percent.
5. Moisture content: Not more than 5 percent.
6. Scorched particle content: Not more than 22.5 mg.
7. Solubility index: Not more than 2 ml.
8. Titratable acidity: Not less than 0.10 percent; not more than 0.20 percent.

b. Roller process. U.S. Standard grade dry buttermilk manufactured by the roller process conforms to the requirements prescribed in paragraph 1. of this section, except that the solubility index is not more than 15 ml., and the scorched particle content is not more than 32.5 mg.

Dry buttermilk shall not be assigned a U.S. Grade for one or more of the following reasons: 1. Fails to meet the requirements for U.S. Extra or U.S. Standard Grade; 2. the alkalinity of ash test, when run at the option of USDA, or when requested by the buyer or seller, shows a test result of more than 125 ml. of 0.1 N HCl per 100 grams.

CHEESE

There are two kinds of cheese. One is commonly called natural cheese. This is cheese that is made from the milk of one of several kinds of animals. The other kind of cheese is process cheese; it is made by combining or blending two or more natural cheeses.

Cheese is made by the modification of milk in the following steps:

a. Curdling: This is usually done by heating the milk to anywhere from 80°F. to 135°F. (depending on the type of cheese to be made); adding rennet, and waiting for the cheese to curdle into curds and whey. Farm cheese is sometimes made by waiting for the lactic acid in the milk to curdle the milk, instead of adding rennet.

b. Removal of Whey: The curdled mass is broken into small pieces, drained off.

c. Curing: Hard cheeses are kept in a cool environment for as long as three years. Salt, certain bacteria, and molds may be added to the cheese to help it develop its characteristic flavor.

There are Federal standards for many cheeses produced in America. Where these standards exist, the specification is listed below. The cheeses of other countries differ according to the producer, as many different types of milks and curing processes are used. The listings of cheeses presented here attempt to cover only the most common varieties. There are at least 600 different varieties on the market in the United States; obviously, space does not allow the classification of all of them.

American Cheese
Aging Period: 3 to 12 months
Color: Light yellow to orange
Texture: Hard, smooth
Flavor: Mild
Common Purchase Unit: Case of 5/1-lb. units

Appetitost Cheese
Aging Period: 2 to 3 months
Texture: Semihard

Apple Cheese
Aging Period: 3 to 12 months
Texture: Hard

Flavor: Sharp, smoked
In the shape of an apple

Asiago Cheese
Aging Period: 3 to 12 months
Texture: Hard, granular
Flavor: Piquant, sharp
Common Purchase Unit: Cylinders
Fresh:
    Milkfat in solids: 50.0% minimum
    Moisture: 45.0% maximum
Medium:
    Milkfat in solids: 45.0% minimum
    Moisture: 35.0% maximum
Old:
    Milkfat in solids: 42.0% minimum
    Moisture: 32.0% maximum

Bel Paese Cheese
Aging Period: 6 to 8 weeks
Color: Slightly gray surface with a creamy yellow interior
Texture: Smooth, soft, waxy body
Flavor: Mild to moderately robust
Common Purchase Unit: Small segments, wedges, and wheels

Blue Cheese
Aging Period: 2 to 6 months
Color: White inside, streaked with blue veins of mold
Texture: Pasty, semisoft, sometimes crumbly
Flavor: Spicy, tangy
Common Purchase Unit: 5-lb. wheels, cut portions, wedges, cylinders
Milkfat in solids: 50.0% minimum
Moisture: 46.0% maximum

Brick Cheese
Aging Period: 2 to 4 months
Color: Light yellow to orange inside and brown outside
Texture: Semisoft to medium firm, elastic. Has many round, small holes or eyes
Flavor: Mild
Common Purchase Unit: Brick slices and loaves
Milkfat in solids: 50.0% minimum
Moisture: 44.0% minimum

Brie Cheese
Aging Period: 4 to 8 weeks
Color: Thin, brown, edible crust with a creamy yellow interior
Texture: Smooth, soft
Flavor: Mild to pungent
Common Purchase Unit: 4-oz., pie-shaped wedges, 12 in a box

Cacciocavallo Cheese
Aging Period: 3 to 12 weeks
Color: White inside, tan outside
Texture: Hard, less moisture and milkfat than Provolone
Flavor: Sharp, piquant, similar to Provolone
Common Purchase Unit: 6/8 lb., spindle-shaped
Milkfat in solids: 42.0% minimum
Moisture: 40.0% maximum

Camembert Cheese
Aging Period: 4 to 8 weeks
Color: Thin, gray-white, edible crust with a creamy yellow interior
Texture: Smooth, soft
Flavor: Mild to pungent
Common Purchase Unit: 1-1/3 and 1-1/2 oz., pie-shaped, and circular portions, 6 in a box
Milkfat in solids: 50.0% minimum

Cheddar Cheese
Aging Period: 1 to 12 months or more
Color: Light yellow to orange
Texture: Hard, smooth, firm
Flavor: Mild to sharp
Common Purchase Unit: Cylinders, slices, cubes, pie-shaped wedges, grated, shredded
Milkfat in solids: 50.0% minimum
Moisture: 39.0% maximum

USDA GRADE MARKS and the foods on which they are used.

BUTTER
CHEDDAR
CHEESE

BN – 6149

These grade marks, under the law, are permitted only on foods officially graded under the supervision of The Agricultural Marketing Service, U.S. Department of Agriculture, Washington, D.C.

Cheshire Cheese
Aging Period: 12 to 16 months
Color: Yellow or carrot red

Texture: Hard, flaky, crumbly
Flavor: Sharp
Common Purchase Unit: 50/70-lb. cylinders

Colby Cheese
Aging Period: 1 to 3 months
Color: White to yellowish orange
Texture: Firm, but softer than cheddar
Flavor: Mild
Common Purchase Unit: Pie-shaped wedges, cylinders
Milkfat in solids: 50.0% minimum
Moisture: 40.0% maximum

Cook's Cheese
Moisture: 80.0% maximum

Dry Curd Cottage Cheese
Moisture: 80.0% maximum

Lowfat Cottage Cheese
Milkfat: 0.5% minimum, 2.0% maximum
Moisture: 82.5% maximum

USDA GRADE MARKS and the foods on which they are used.

COTTAGE CHEESE
PROCESS CHEESE

BN – 6149

These grade marks, under the law, are permitted only on foods officially graded under the supervision of The Agricultural Marketing Service, U.S. Department of Agriculture, Washington, D.C.

Cottage Cheese
Aging Period: Unripened
Color: White
Texture: Delicate, moist, large and small curd particles
Flavor: Acidic, mild
Common Purchase Unit: Cup-shaped containers
Milkfat: 4.0% minimum
Moisture: 80.0% maximum

Cream Cheese
Aging Period: Unripened

MEET THE FAVORITE AMERICAN-MADE CHEESES

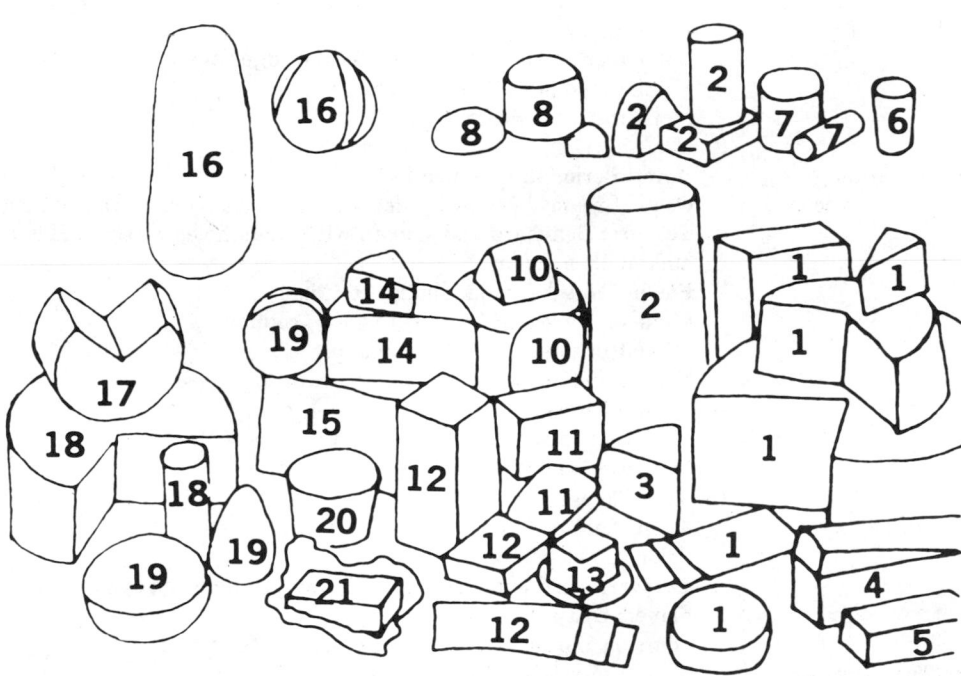

1. Cheddar
2. Colby
3. Monterey or Jack
4. Pasteurized Process Cheese
5. Cheese Foods
6. Cheese Spreads
7. Cold Pack Cheese Food or
   Club Cheese
8. Gouda and Edam
9. Camembert
10. Muenster
11. Brick
12. Swiss
13. Limburger
14. Blue
15. Gorgonzola
16. Provolone
17. Romano
18. Parmesan
19. Mozzarella and Scamorze
20. Cottage Cheese
21. Cream Cheese

Color: White
Texture: Buttery, smooth, and soft
Flavor: Mild, slightly acid
Common Purchase Unit: 2-lb., 3-lb., 5-lb. loaves; 3-oz., 6-oz., 8-oz. packages
Milkfat in solids: No standard. State standards are 65.0% minimum where they exist
Milkfat: 33.0% minimum
Moisture: 55.0% maximum

Derby Sage Cheese
Aging Period: 6 months
Color: Streaked with green
Texture: Creamy and soft
Flavor: Mild

Edam Cheese
Aging Period: 2 to 3 months
Color: Creamy yellow inside; sometimes has a red, wax coating
Texture: Semihard and smooth with small holes or eyes. Has less milkfat than Gouda
Flavor: Nutlike, mild
Common Purchase Unit: 1-lb. and up cannon balls
Milkfat in solids: 40.0% minimum
Moisture: 45.0% maximum

English Cheddar Cheese
Aging Period: 3 to 12 months
Color: Yellow or white
Texture: Hard
Flavor: Sharp
Common Purchase Unit: 11/14 lb. cheddar, 1/2- and 3-lb. packages

English Dairy Cheese
Texture: Hard, easy to grate
Common Purchase Unit: 18/23-lb. flats

Filled Cheese
Fat in solids: Regulated by Internal Revenue Service Tax Law, no composition standards

Fontina Cheese
Aging Period: 1 to 8 months
Color: Yellow with a brown rind
Texture: Firm with small yellow holes or eyes
Flavor: Buttery, rich

Gammelost Cheese
Aging Period: 1 to 8 months
Color: Brown
Texture: Hard
Flavor: Strong, pungent
Common Purchase Unit: 8-oz. unit

Moisture: 52.0% maximum

Gjedost Cheese
Aging Period: Unripened
Color: Golden brown
Texture: Hard, buttery
Flavor: Sweet, caramel
Common Purchase Unit: Cubes and rectangles

Gorgonzola Cheese
Aging Period: 3 to 12 months
Color: White inside streaked with blue-green mold; tan outside
Texture: Semisoft; may be crumbly, pasty; less moisture than blue
Flavor: Dry, spicy
Common Purchase Unit: 3- to 13-lb. wedges and cylinders, 20-lb. tub
Milkfat in solids: 50.0% minimum
Moisture: 42.0% maximum

Gouda
Aging Period: 2 to 6 months
Color: Creamy, yellow inside, sometimes has a red, wax coating
Texture: Semihard and smooth with small holes or eyes. Has more milkfat than Edam
Flavor: Nutlike, mild, similar to Edam
Common Purchase Unit: 7- to 40-lb. rounds
Milkfat in solids: 46.0% minimum
Moisture: 45.0% maximum

Granular Cheese
Milkfat in solids: 50.0% minimum
Moisture: 39.0% maximum

Gruyere Cheese
Aging Period: 6 to 9 months
Color: Light yellow
Texture: Hard and smooth, with tiny gas holes or eyes
Flavor: Salty, nutlike
Common Purchase Unit: Pieces, segments, wheels
Milkfat in solids: 45.0% minimum
Moisture: 39.0% maximum

Hand Cheese
Aging Period: 1 to 2 months
Texture: Soft
Flavor: Mild

Hard Cheese
Milkfat in solids: 32.0% minimum
Moisture: 39.0% maximum

Hard Grating Cheese
Milkfat in solids: 32.0% minimum
Moisture: 34.0% maximum

Lancaster Cheese
 Aging Period: 3 to 12 months
 Color: Yellowish white
 Texture: Spreadable
 Flavor: Sharp, mellows with age

Liederkranz Cheese
 Color: Red outside
 Texture: Soft, creamy
 Flavor: Similar to, but milder than Limburger
 Common Purchase Unit: 8-oz. packages

Limburger Cheese
 Aging Period: 4 to 8 weeks
 Color: Yellowish red surface with a creamy white interior
 Texture: Smooth, soft
 Flavor: Strong, aromatic
 Common Purchase Unit: 1/2 lb., 1 lb., 2 lb., rectangular shaped
 Milkfat in solids: 50.0% minimum
 Moisture: 50.0% maximum

Livarot Cheese
 Aging Period: 2 to 5 months
 Color: Yellow with a reddish crust
 Texture: Soft
 Flavor: Pungent
 Common Purchase Unit: Wheels

Monterey (Jack) Cheese
 Aging Period: 2 to 6 weeks for table use; 6 to 9 weeks for grating
 Color: Creamy white
 Texture: Smooth, semisoft
 Flavor: Mild
 Milkfat in solids: 50.0% minimum
 Moisture: 44.0% maximum

High Moisture Jack Cheese
 Milkfat in solids: 50.0% minimum
 Moisture: Greater than 44.0% minimum; 50.0% maximum

Mozzarella Cheese
 Aging Period: Unripened
 Color: Creamy white
 Texture: Plastic, semisoft
 Flavor: Mild, delicate
 Common Purchase Unit: Sliced, small round, or braided

Mozzarella, Scamorza Cheese
 Milkfat in solids: 45.0% minimum
 Moisture: 52.0% minimum, 60.0% maximum

Low Moisture Mozzarella, Scamorza Cheese
 Milkfat in solids: 45.0% minimum
 Moisture: 45.0% minimum, 52.0% maximum

Muenster Cheese
 Aging Period: 2 to 8 weeks
 Color: Creamy white inside and yellow, tan, or white outside
 Texture: Semisoft. Has many round, small holes, or eyes
 Flavor: Mild, between Brick and Limburger
 Common Purchase Unit: 4-lb., 5-lb., 6-lb. blocks
 Milkfat in solids: 50.0% minimum
 Moisture: 46.0% maximum

Neufchatel Cheese
 Aging Period: Unripened
 Color: White
 Texture: Creamy, smooth, and soft
 Flavor: Mild
 Common Purchase Unit: 2 1/2- to 3-oz. packages, 25 in a box
 Milkfat in solids: No standard. State standards generally do not exist
 Milkfat: 20.0% minimum, less than 33.0% maximum
 Moisture: 65.0% maximum

Noekkelost Cheese
 Aging Period: 2 to 3 months
 Texture: Semihard
 Flavor: Flavored with cumin and cloves

Parmesan Cheese (Reggiano Cheese)
 Aging Period: 14 to 24 months
 Color: Light yellow or white
 Texture: Hard, granular. Has less milkfat and moisture than Romano
 Flavor: Sharp, piquant
 Common Purchase Unit: 50-lb. cylinders, grated, shredded, wedges
 Milkfat in solids: 32.0% minimum
 Moisture: 32.0% maximum

Part Skim Spiced Cheese
 Milkfat in solids: 20.0% minimum, less than 50.0% maximum

Pimento Cheese
 A processed cheese made by mixing chopped pimentos with a smooth cheese, especially Neufchatel

Pineapple Cheese
 Texture: Hard
 Common Purchase Unit: 6 lb.
 Milkfat in solids: No standard. State standards generally do not exist but are 50.0% minimum where they do exist

Pont l'Eveque
 A soft cheddar cheese made of cream thickened by heat

Port du Salut Cheese (Oka Cheese)
 Aging Period: 6 to 8 weeks
 Color: Yellow inside and russet outside
 Texture: Semisoft, smooth, buttery, with small holes or eyes
 Flavor: Mellow to robust, between Cheddar and Limburger
 Common Purchase Unit: 7 to 10 in. diameter disk

Primost Cheese (Mysost Cheese)
Aging Period: Unripened
Color: Light brown
Texture: Buttery and firm
Flavor: Mild, sweet
Common Purchase Unit: Cylinders, cubes, pie-shaped wedges

Provolone
Aging Period: 2 to 12 months
Color: Yellowish white inside, and yellow or light brown outside
Texture: Smooth and firm
Flavor: Sharp
Common Purchase Unit: 4/7-lb., pear-shaped wedges, and slices
Milkfat in solids: 45.0% minimum
Moisture: 45.0% maximum

Reggiano Cheese
The best type of Parmesan

Ricotta Cheese
Aging Period: Unripened
Color: White
Texture: Soft, either moist or dry and grainy
Flavor: Bland, semisweet
Common Purchase Unit: Pint and quart containers; 3-lb. metal can

Romano Cheese
Aging Period: 5 to 12 months
Color: Light yellow inside and greenish black outside
Texture: Very hard and granular
Flavor: Sharp, salty
Common Purchase Unit: 2- to 25-lb. units, shredded, grated
Milkfat in solids: 38.0% minimum
Moisture: 34.0% maximum

Roquefort Cheese
Aging Period: 2 to 5 months
Color: White inside streaked with blue mold
Texture: Pasty, semisoft; may be crumbly
Flavor: Sharp, sweet
Common Purchase Unit: 3/4-oz. packages, 24 in a box; 1-1/4- and 1-1/2-oz. packages, 12 in a box; 5-lb. wheels
Milkfat in solids: 50.0% minimum
Moisture: 45.0% maximum

Samsoe Cheese
Color: Yellow
Texture: Smooth, but slightly harder than Bel Paese, with large holes or eyes
Flavor: Mild to moderately robust

Sap Sago Cheese
Aging Period: 5 months or more
Color: Light green due to the dried, powdered clover leaves which are added
Texture: Hard and granular
Flavor: Sweet
Common Purchase Unit: 4-oz. cones, 4 in. high, 2 in. at top, 2 in. diameter base
Moisture: 38.0% maximum

Sardo Cheese
Aging Period: 12 to 16 months
Color: Cream-colored with a yellow rind
Texture: Hard
Flavor: 2 types, mild and strong

Scamorza Cheese
Aging Period: Unripened
Color: Light yellow
Texture: Smooth, semisoft
Flavor: Mild

Semisoft Cheese
Milkfat in solids: 50.0% minimum
Moisture: Greater than 39.0% minimum; 50.0% maximum

Semisoft Part Skim Cheese
Milkfat in solids: 45.0% minimum, less than 50.0% maximum
Moisture: 50.0% maximum

Skim Milk Cheese
Milkfat in solids: No standard. State standards may be as high as 50.0% maximum where they exist

Soft Ripened Cheese
Milkfat in solids: 50.0% minimum

Spiced Cheese
Milkfat in solids: 50.0% minimum

Stilton Cheese
Aging Period: 2 to 6 months
Color: White inside streaked with blue-green mold
Texture: Flaky; semisoft; slightly more crumbly than blue
Flavor: Spicy, milder than Roquefort
Common Purchase Unit: 11- to 15-lb. wedges and circles

Swiss Cheese (Emmentaler Cheese)
Aging Period: 6 to 9 months
Color: Light yellow
Texture: Smooth and firm, with large, round holes, or eyes
Flavor: Sweet, nutlike
Common Purchase Unit: Domestic—125- to 175-lb. wheel; Imported—150- to 225-lb. wheels; slices
Milkfat in solids: 43.0% minimum
Moisture: 41.0% maximum

Washed Curd Cheese
Milkfat in solids: 50.0% minimum
Moisture: 42.0% maximum

Cheese comes in many different shapes and sizes—for use in sandwiches, salads, desserts, and main dishes.

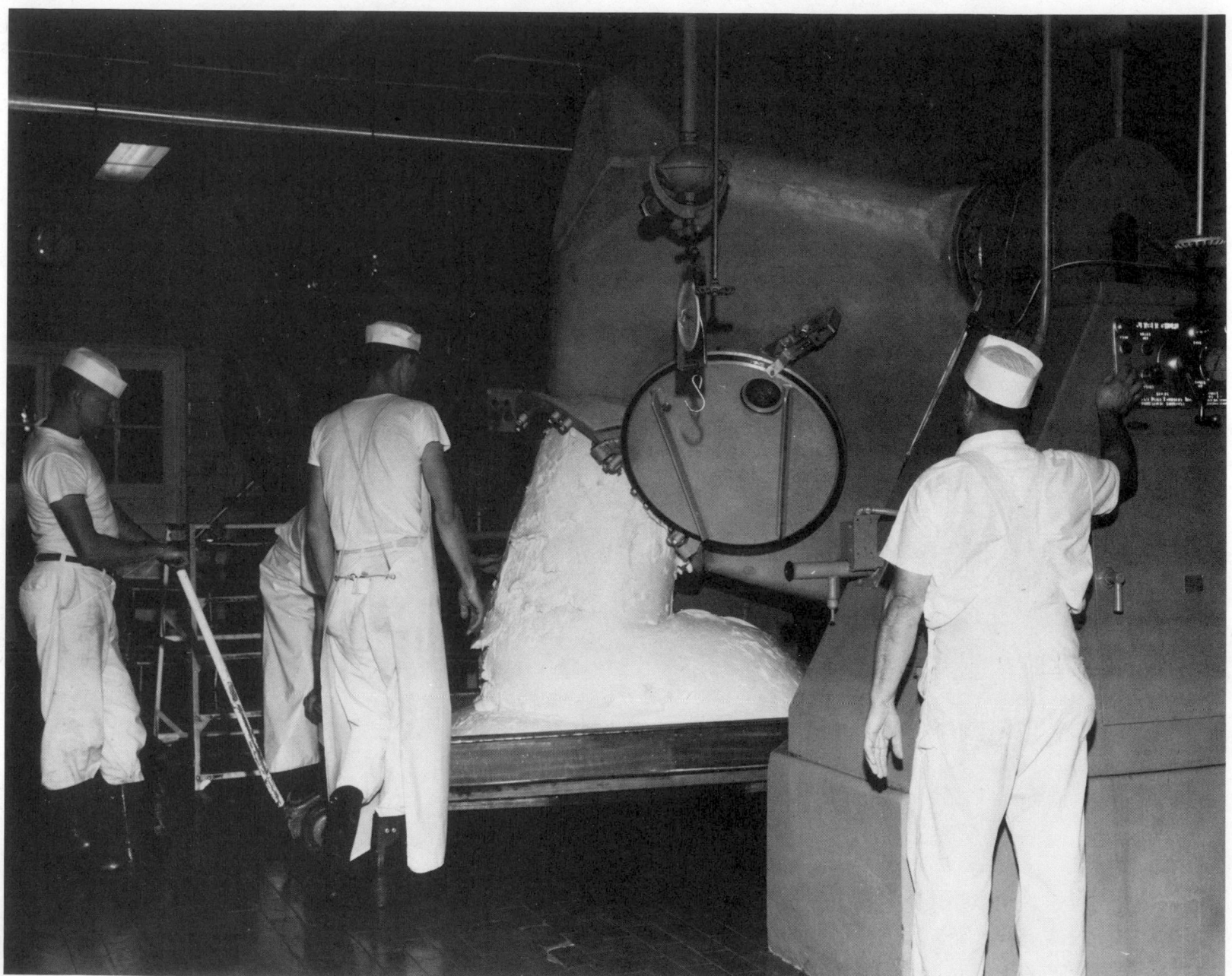

Butter unloaded from churn. Juneau, Wisconsin.

BUTTER

BUTTER April 1, 1960

Definitions

"Butter" means the food product usually known as butter, which is made exclusively from milk or cream, or both, with or without common salt, and with or without additional coloring matter, and containing not less than 80 percent by weight of milkfat, all tolerances having been allowed for.

Cream

The term "cream" means cream separated from milk produced by healthy cows. The cream shall be pasteurized at a temperature of not less than 165°F., and held continuously in a vat at such temperature for not less than 30 minutes; or pasteurized at a temperature of not less than 185°F., for not less than 15 seconds; or it shall be pasteurized by other approved methods giving equivalent results.

The U.S. grade of butter is determined on the basis of classifying first the flavor characteristics, and then the characteristics in body, color, and salt. Flavor is the basic quality factor in grading butter, and is determined organoleptically by taste and smell. The flavor characteristic is identified and, together with its relative intensity, is rated according to the applicable classification. When more than one flavor characteristic is discernible in a sample of butter, the flavor classification of the sample shall be established on the basis of the flavor that carries the lowest rating (see Table 5-4). Body, color, and salt characteristics are then noted, and any defects are disrated in accordance with the established classification, subject to disratings for body, color, and salt; when the disratings for body, color, and salt exceed the permitted amount for any flavor classification, the final U.S. grade shall be lowered accordingly (see Table 5-6).

The specifications for the U.S. grades of butter are as follows:

a. U.S. Grade AA or U.S. 93 Score butter conforms to the following: Possesses a fine and highly pleasing butter flavor. May posses a slight feed and a definite cooked (fine)

flavor. It is made from sweet cream of low natural acid to which a culture (starter) may or may not have been added. The permitted total disratings in body, color and salt characteristics are limited to one-half (1/2). For detailed specifications and classification of flavor characteristics, see Table 5-4, and for body, color, and salt characteristics, and disratings, see Table 5-5.

b. U.S. Grade A or U.S. 92 Score butter conforms to the following: Possesses a pleasing and desirable butter flavor. May possess any of the following flavors to a slight degree: Aged, bitter, coarse-acid, flat, smothered, and storage. May possess feed and cooked (coarse) flavors to a definite degree. The permitted total disratings in body, color, and salt characteristics are limited to one-half (1/2), except when the flavor classification is AA, a disrating total of one (1) is permitted. For detailed specifications and classification of flavor characteristics, see Table 5-4, and for body, color, and salt characteristics, and disratings, see Table 5-5.

c. U.S. Grade B or U.S. 90 Score butter conforms to the following: Possesses a fairly pleasing butter flavor. May possess any of the following flavors to a slight degree: Lipase, malty, musty, neutralizer, scorched, utensil, weed, whey, and woody. May possess any of the following flavors to a definite degree: Aged, bitter, coarse-acid, smothered, storage, and old cream; feed flavor to a pronounced degree. The permitted total disratings in body, color, and salt characteristics are limited to one-half (1/2), except when the flavor classification is AA, a disrating total of one and one-half (1-1/2) is permitted, and when the flavor classification is A, a disrating total of one (1) is permitted. For detailed specifications and classification of flavor characteristics, see Table 5-4, and for body, color, and salt characteristics, and disratings, see Table 5-5.

d. U.S. Grade C or U.S. 89 Score butter conforms to the following: May possess any of the following flavors to a slight degree: Barny, sour, wild onion or garlic, and yeasty. May possess any of the following flavors to a definite degree: Lipase, malty, musty, neutralizer, scorched, stale, utensil, weed, whey, and woody. The permitted total disratings in body, color, and salt characteristics are limited to one (1), except when the flavor classification is A, a disrating total of one and one-half (1-1/2) is permitted. For detailed specifications and classifications of flavor characteristics, see Table 5-4, and for body, color, and salt characteristics, and disrating, see Table 5-5.

e. General. Butter of all U.S. grades shall be free of foreign materials and visible mold. Butter possessing a flavor rating of AA or A and workmanship disratings in excess of one and one-half (1-1/2) shall be given a flavor rating only; butter possessing a flavor rating of B or C and workmanship disrating in excess of one (1) shall be given a flavor rating only.

Butter which fails to meet the requirements for U.S. Grade C or U.S. 89 Score shall not be given a U.S. grade.

Butter, when tested, which does not comply with the provisions of the Federal Food, Drug and Cosmetic Act, including minimum milkfat requirements of 80.0 percent, shall not be assigned a U.S. grade.

Butter produced in a plant found on inspection to be using unsatisfactory manufacturing practices, equipment, or facilities, or to be operating under insanitary plant conditions, shall not be assigned a U.S. grade.

GRADE and QUALITY SHIELDS for consumer packages of dairy products manufactured under the grading and quality control service. AA shield on top level quality for butter.

TABLE 5-4—CLASSIFICATION OF FLAVOR CHARACTERISTICS

Identified Flavors[1]	Flavor Classification			
	AA	A	B	C
Feed	S*	D*	P*	—
Cooked (fine)	D	—	—	—
Aged	—	S	D	—
Bitter	—	S	D	—
Coarse-acid	—	S	D	—
Flat	—	S	—	—
Smothered	—	S	D	—
Storage	—	S	D	—
Cooked (coarse)	—	D	—	—
Lipase	—	—	S	D
Malty	—	—	S	D
Musty	—	—	S	D
Neutralizer	—	—	S	D
Scorched	—	—	S	D
Utensil	—	—	S	D
Weed	—	—	S	D
Whey	—	—	S	D
Woody	—	—	S	D
Old cream	—	—	D	—
Barny	—	—	—	S
Metallic	—	—	—	S
Sour	—	—	—	S
Wild onion or garlic	—	—	—	S
Yeasty	—	—	—	S
Stale	—	—	—	D

*S—Slight; D—Definite; P—Pronounced.
1. When more than one flavor is discernible in a sample of butter, the flavor classification of the sample shall be established on the basis of the flavor that carries the lowest classification.

TABLE 5-5—CHARACTERISTICS AND DISRATINGS IN BODY, COLOR, AND SALT

BODY			
Characteristics	**Disratings**		
	S*	**D***	**P***
Crumbly	1/2	1	—
Gummy	1/2	1	—
Leaky	1/2	1	2
Mealy or grainy	1/2	1	—
Short	1/2	1	—
Weak	1/2	1	—
Sticky	1/2	1	—
Ragged boring	1	2	

COLOR			
Characteristics	**Disratings**		
	S	**D**	**P**
Wavy	1/2	1	—
Mottled	1	2	—
Streaked	1	2	—
Color specks	1	2	—

SALT			
Characteristics	**Disratings**		
	S	**D**	**P**
Sharp	1/2	1	—
Gritty	1	2	—

*S—Slight; D—Definite; P—Pronounced.

TABLE 5-6

Flavor Classification	**Total Disratings**	**U.S. Grade or U.S. Score**
AA	1/2	AA or 93
AA	1	A or 92
A	1/2	A or 92
AA	1 1/2	B or 90
A	1	B or 90
B	1/2	B or 90
A	1 1/2	C or 89
C	1	C or 89

TABLE 5-7

Example Number	Flavor Classification	Disratings			Total Disratings	Permitted Total Disratings	Disratings in Excess of Total Permitted	U.S. Grade or U.S. Score
		Body	Color	Salt				
1	AA	1/2	0	0	1/2	1/2	0	AA or 93
2	AA	1/2	1/2	0	1	1/2	1/2	A or 92
3	AA	0	1	0	1	1/2	1/2	A or 92
4	AA	1/2	1	0	1 1/2	1/2	1	B or 90
5	A	1/2	0	0	1/2	1/2	0	A or 92
6	A	0	1/2	1/2	1	1/2	1/2	B or 90
7	A	0	1	0	1	1/2	1/2	B or 90
8	A	1	1/2	0	1 1/2	1/2	1	C or 89
9	B	1/2	0	0	1/2	1/2	0	B or 90
10	B	1/2	1/2	0	1	1/2	1/2	C or 89
11	B	1	0	0	1	1/2	1/2	C or 89
12	C	1/2	1/2	0	1	1	0	C or 89
13	C	0	1	0	1	1	0	C or 89

Explanation of Terms

a. With respect to flavor intensity and characteristics
   1. Slight: Detected only upon critical examination.
   2. Definite: Detectable but not intense.
   3. Pronounced: Readily detectable and intense.
   4. Aged: Characterized by lack of freshness.
   5. Barny: A flavor associated with cow or stable odors.
   6. Bitter: Astringent, similar to taste of quinine, and produces a puckery sensation.
   7. Coarse-acid: Lacks a delicate flavor or aroma, and is associated with an acid condition, but there is no indication of sourness.
   8. Cooked (fine): Smooth, nuttylike character resembling a custard flavor.
   9. Cooked (coarse): Lacks a fine, delicate, smooth flavor.
   10. Feed: Aromatic flavor characteristic of the feeds eaten by cows.
   11. Flat: Lacks natural butter flavor.
   12. Lipase: Suggestive of butyric acid, sometimes associated with bitterness.
   13. Malty: A distinctive, harsh flavor suggestive of malt.
   14. Metallic: A flavor suggestive of metal, imparting a puckery sensation.
   15. Musty: Suggestive of the aroma of a damp vegetable cellar.
   16. Neutralizer: Suggestive of a bicarbonate of soda flavor, or the flavor of similar compounds.
   17. Old Cream: Aged cream, characterized by lack of freshness, imparts a rough aftertaste on the tongue.
   18. Scorched: A more intensified flavor than cooked (coarse); imparts a harsh aftertaste.
   19. Sour: Characterized by an acid flavor and aroma.
   20. Smothered: Suggestive of improperly cooled cream.
   21. Stale: Characterized by aged cream of poor quality.
   22. Storage: Characterized by a lack of freshness; more intensified than "aged" flavor.
   23. Utensil: A flavor suggestive of unclean cans, utensils, and equipment.

24. Weed: Aromatic flavor characteristic of the weeds eaten by cows.
25. Whey: A flavor and aroma characteristic of cheese whey.
26. Wild onion or garlic: A flavor and aroma characteristic of onion or garlic.
27. Woody: Resembles the odor of wood.
28. Yeasty: A flavor indicating yeast fermentation.

b. With respect to body
1. Crumbly. When a "crumbly" body is present, the particles lack cohesion. The intensity is described as "Slight" when the trier plug tends to break, and the butter lacks plasticity; and "Definite" when the butter breaks roughly or crumbles.
2. Gummy. Gummy-bodied butter does not melt readily, and is inclined to stick to the roof of the mouth. The intensity is described as "Slight" when the butter tends to become chewy, and "Definite" when it imparts a gum-like impression in the mouth.
3. Leaky. A "leaky" body is present when, on visual examination, there are beads of moisture on the surface of the trier plug and on the back of the trier, or when slight pressure is applied to the butter on the trier plug. The intensity is described as "Slight" when the droplets or beads of moisture are barely visible and about the size of a pinhead; "Definite" when the moisture drops are somewhat larger, or the droplets are more numerous, and tend to run together, and "Pronounced" when the leaky condition is so evident that drops of water drip from the trier plug.
4. Mealy or grainy. A "mealy" or "grainy" condition imparts a granular consistency when the butter is melted on the tongue. The intensity is described as "Slight" when the mealiness or graininess is barely detectable on the tongue, and "Definite" when the mealiness or graininess is readily detectable.
5. Ragged boring. A "ragged boring" body, in contrast to solid boring, is when a sticky-crumbly condition is present to such a degree that a full trier of butter cannot be drawn. The intensity is described as "Slight" when there is a considerable adherence of butter to the back of the trier, and "Definite" when it is practically impossible to draw a full plug of butter.
6. Short. The texture is shortgrained, lacks plasticity, and tends toward brittleness. The intensity is described as "Slight" when the butter lacks pliability and tends to be brittle, and "Definite" when sharp and distinct breaks form as pressure is applied against the plug.
7. Sticky. When a "sticky" condition is present, the butter adheres to the trier as a smear and possesses excessive adhesion. The intensity is described as "Slight" when the smear is present only on a portion of the back of the trier, and "Definite" when the trier becomes smeary throughout its length.
8. Weak. A "weak" body lacks firmness and tends to be spongy. The intensity is described as "Slight" when the plug of butter, under slight pressure, tends to depress, and is not firm and compact, and "Definite" when the plug of butter, under slight pressure, tends to depress easily, and definitely lacks firmness and compactness.

c. With respect to color
1. Mottled. "Mottles" appear as a dappled condition with spots of lighter and deeper shades of yellow. The intensity is described as "Slight" when the small spots of different shades of yellow, irregular in shape, are barely discernible on the plug of butter, and "Definite" when the mottles are readily discernible on the plug of butter.
2. Specks. "Specks" usually appear in butter as small white or yellow spots, however, the latter may be of variable size. The intensity is described as "Slight" when the spots are few in number, and "Definite" when they are noticeable in large numbers.

3. Streaked. "Streaked" color appears as light-colored portions surrounded by more highly colored portions. The intensity is described as "Slight" when only a few are present, and "Definite" when they are more numerous on the trier plug.

4. Wavy. "Wavy" color in butter is an unevenness in the color that appears as waves of different shades of yellow. The intensity is described as "Slight" when the waves are barely discernible, and "Definite" when they are readily noticeable on the trier plug.

d. With respect to salt

1. Sharp. "Sharp" salt is characterized by taste sensations suggestive of salt. The intensity is described as "Slight" when the salt taste predominates in flavor, and "Definite" when the salt taste is distinctly predominant in the flavor.

2. Gritty. A "gritty" salt condition is detected by the gritty feel of the grains of undissolved salt, imparting a sandlike feeling on the tongue. The intensity is described as "Slight" when only a few grains of undissolved salt are detected, and "Definite" when the condition is more readily noticeable.

PROBABLE CAUSES OF CERTAIN CHARACTERISTICS IN BUTTER

The material contained herein is a concise presentation of probable causes of certain characteristics in butter. It is intended to assist the buttermaker in avoiding deficiencies in manufacturing, particularly those over which he has primary control.

Basically, the quality of the finished butter can be no higher than the quality of the raw milk and cream from which it is made. Careful grading and segregation at the receiving platform is very important. However, poor workmanship can result in disratings that would cause the butter to be down-graded, and could detract from the flavor and stability of the finished product. Therefore, it is extremely important

that close attention be given to the workmanship factors, and especially to those conditions which influence spreadability and product stability. Every buttermaker should have a good butter trier, and should personally and carefully examine each churning of butter after the butter has been properly chilled for 48 hours.

FLAVOR

The flavor of butter in determined primarily by the senses of taste and smell. To register its full taste sensation, a substance must be soluble so that it can be carried quickly to the taste buds of the tongue.

The sense of smell supplements taste in determining flavor in butter. The warmth of the mouth melts the butter and frees it volatile aromas which then enter the olfactory chambers, coming forward into the nose. Moisture in the mouth and nasal passages enhances the transmission of flavor sensations.

There are only four primary taste sensations: sweet, sour, salt, and bitter. Sugar produces the sensation of sweetness; lactic acid or a tart apple produces a sour taste; common table salt produces a sensation of saltiness, and quinine produces a bitter sensation. When melted butter comes in direct contact with the taste buds, its sweet and salty characteristics are detected by the taste buds located at the tip of the tongue, its sour characteristics by those on the sides of the tongue, and its bitter characteristics by those at the back of the tongue.

The proper procedure in grading butter is first to use the sense of smell, and then the sense of taste to confirm and establish the character, probable origin, and degree of development of each flavor present. By discerning carefully the odor or aroma characteristics of the sample, the character, and degree of the flavor present, the grader is able to identify and classify the flavor properly.

Aroma in butter may be present to a greater or lesser degree. In the higher grades of butter, a pleasing aroma accentuates certain pleasing or desirable flavors. An objectionable aroma or odor is generally associated with flavors present in the lower grades of butter, and serves to accentuate the undesirable flavor characteristics. The aroma noted in butter before it is tasted reflects a general indication of its quality.

The temperature of the butter at the time of grading is important in determining the true characteristics of flavor and aroma. The temperature of the butter should preferably range from 40°F. to 50°F. A temperature of about 70°F. is preferable in the grading room; it should not be below 60°F.

a. Following is a listing of certain flavor characteristics and their probable causes:

1. Aged: Associated with short or extended holding periods of the butter above freezer temperature, depending upon the actual temperature level. May also occur if high quality raw material is not handled and processed promptly.

2. Barny: Attributable to absorption of barn odors or contamination during milking. May also result from an abnormal condition of cows.

3. Bitter: Attributable to the action of microorganisms in the cream before churning, certain types of feeds, and late lactation.

4. Coarse-acid: Associated with moderate acid development in the milk or cream or excessive ripening of the cream.

5. Cooked (fine): Associated with high-temperature pasteurization of sweet cream.

6. Cooked (coarse): Associated with high-temperature pasteurization of cream with slight acid development.

7. Feed: Attributable to feed flavors in milk carried through into the butter. Most dry feeds, like hay and many of the concentrates, silage, green alfalfa, and various grasses produce feed flavor in butter. Silage flavors may vary in degree and character, depending on the time of feeding, extent of fermentation, and the kind of silage.

8. Flat: Attributable to excessive washing of the butter or to a low percentage of fats of volatile acids and other volatile products that help to produce a pleasing butter flavor.

9. Lipase: Associated with the action of the enzyme lipase; may be accentuated by late lactation, excessive agitation of raw milk and cream at critical temperature of lipase activation (warming cold milk to 80° to 90°F. and then cooling again to 40° to 50°F.), or prolonged storage of raw cream at low temperatures which flavor the growth of lipolytic organisms. These conditions may cause splitting of the fat into fatty acids which are responsible for the particular flavor. The enzyme lipase is inactivated by adequate pasteurization.

10. Malty: Attributable to the growth of the organish streptococcus lactis var. maltigenses in milk or cream. It is often traced to improperly washed and sanitized cream cans or other utensils in which this organism has developed.

11. Metallic: Attributed to keeping milk or cream on the farm in poorly tinned containers. Contact of cream with iron or copper equipment in the plant may also cause the cream to develop a metallic flavor; the use of can steamings is also a contributing factor.

12. Musty: Attributable to cream held in a damp cellar; may also result from cows grazing on slough grass, eating musty or moldy feed (hay and silage), or drinking stagnant water.

13. Neutralizer: Attributed to the excessive or improper use of alkaline products to reduce the acidity of the cream before pasteurization.

14. Old cream: Attributable to aged cream; inadequate cooling of the cream on the farm. This flavor may be accentuated by unclean cans, utensils, and processing equipment.

15. Scorched: Associated with the pasteurization, at a relatively high temperature, of cream with developed acidity, pasteurization after holding cream in forewarming vats for long periods, or faulty pasteurization equipment.

16. Smothered: Attributable generally to improper handling and delayed cooling of the cream on the farm.

17. Sour: Attributable to the churning of high acid cream; cream not properly neutralized, or to acid development after pasteurization.

18. Stale: Attributable to holding cream for extended periods, usually without adequate cooling, and may be associated with partial oxidation of the fat. This flavor may be accentuated by faulty sanitation.
19. Storage: Associated with holding butter in storage at freezer temperatures for several months or longer.
20. Utensil: Attributable to a faulty physical condition of utensils and equipment, improper sanitary care of such items as milking machines, pails, farm bulk tanks, producer cans, or a possible lack of proper washing and bactericidal treatment of processing equipment.
21. Weed: Attributable to weed-infested pastures and weedy hay eaten by cows.
22. Whey: Attributable to use of whey cream, or a blend of whole milk cream and whey cream.
23. Wild onion or garlic: Attributable to cows grazing on wild onion- or garlic-infested pastures.
24. Woody: Attributable to new wooden churns or other wooden equipment which has not been properly treated before being used. May also be caused by action of microorganisms.
25. Yeasty: Usually attributable to cream held at high temperatures which cause yeast fermentation.

BODY

The factor of body in butter is considered from the standpoint of its characteristics or defects. Defects in body are disrated according to degree or intensity. Milkfat in butter is a mixture of various triglycerides of different melting points and appears in the form of fat globules and as free fat. In both of these forms, a part of the fat is crystalline and another part liquid. Some are solid at temperatures up to 100°F. or even higher; others are still liquid at temperatures far below the freezing point. Because of this, butter at the temperatures at which it is usually handled is always a mixture of solid (crystallized) and liquid fat. The variations in the composition of milkfat thus have a great influence upon the texture and spreadability of butter.

In summer, when milkfat contains more liquid fat, butter tends to be weak and leaky, and, in winter, when its solid fat content is high, butter tends to be hard and brittle, resulting in unsatisfactory spreadability. The ratio between the crystalline and the liquid particles depends upon the composition of the butterfat (varying with the season of the year), manufacturing methods, and the temperature of the butter.

There may be a wide range of variation in the percentage of globular fat, also due presumably to differences in the composition of fat and manufacturing practices. Close attention should be given to the proper relationship between the temperatures of heating and cooling, and rate of cooling, of the cream as well as temperature of churning, washing, and working of the butter, at different seasons of the year when there are different fat conditions. This is important in maintaining a uniformly firm, waxy body possessing good spreadibility.

The temperature of the cream after holding is a very important factor which determines the hardness of the butter. Butter with either a poor or excellent body may be made from cream containing either a hard or soft fat, depending upon the methods of processing. The state of the water droplets and air in butter also plays a vital role in the body of the butter.

Butter with a firm, waxy body has an attractive appearance, has granules that are close knit, and cuts clean when sliced, with good spreadability. The trier sample from such butter will show this clean-cut, smooth, waxy appearance.

The temperature of the butter at the time of grading is important in determining the true characteristics of body, and should be between 40° and 50°F.

a. Following is a listing of certain body defects and their probable causes:
1. Crumbly: Attributable to a high proportion of fat crystals in the free fat. Such a condition is associated with higher melting-point fats which result from feeding certain dry feeds like cottonseed meal, and also is associated with cows in late lactation. Cooling cream rapidly helps to form small globules of particles. If enough liquid fat is

available, the butter will not crumble. It will crumble if crystals are large and there is no liquid fat. Cooling cream too rapidly also may cause crumbliness. Lower wash water temperature (10° to 20°F. below the temperature of the buttermilk) will help to correct crumbliness. Butter with a normal body may appear to have a normal body at higher temperatures.

2. Gummy: Attributable to the presence of a high percentage of high-melting-point fats. Feeding cottonseed meal or whole cottonseed in quantities large enough to supply the bulk of the protein in a ration will result in a high proportion of high-melting-point fats and a hard-bodied butter. Such cream requires slower cooling, higher churning temperature, higher temperature wash water, and longer working time.

3. Leaky: Attributable generally to insufficient working, resulting in incomplete incorporation of the water. The water droplets are not reduced sufficiently in size to be well distributed throughout the mass of the butter. When the fat is soft and the granules are not sufficiently firm at the start of the working process, they mass together too quickly and do not offer enough resistance to break up the water droplets and obtain a minute and uniform distribution of the water in the butter. An uneven salt distribution may also cause a migration of moisture in the butter.

4. Mealy or grainy: Attributed to oiling-off of the butterfat at some stage of the buttermaking process, improper melting of frozen cream, or improper neutralization of sour cream. The oiled-off fat, upon being cooled, crystallizes into small particles which cannot be worked into a smooth texture.

5. Ragged boring: Attributable to certain types of dry feeds, especially when such feeds are not offset by succulent feeds. It is caused by a combination of the factors that are generally associated with crumbli-

ness and stickiness, particularly when the melting point of the continuous (non-globular) fat phase of butter is unusually high. Although this condition is related to crumbliness and stickiness, it differs in appearance as the butter tends to roll on the trier. It may be minimized by procedures which permit the fat in the cream to crystallize at relatively high temperatures, and by rapid chilling of the fat after the butter granules have formed.

6. Short: Attributable to predominance of high-melting-point fats with relatively small fat globules and comparatively low curd content of the butter. Certain types of manufacturing processes where partial melting of the fat takes place and normal granules are not produced, usually result in a short and brittle-bodied butter. Too rapid cooling to too low a temperature may also be a factor.

7. Sticky: Associated with dry feeds and late lactation period and predominance of high-melting-point fats. This defect may result from not having the correct proportion of liquid and solid fat in the butter, as well as the proper proportion of large and small crystals of fat. The condition may be accentuated by too rapid cooling, cooling of the cream to too low a temperature, or overworking the butter.

8. Weak: Attributable to churning cream which has not been cooled to a low enough temperature, or not held long enough at a low temperature following pasteurization to properly firm the granules. May also be caused by churning at too high a temperature and incorporating too much air into the butter churning and working.

COLOR

The natural color of butter varies according to seasonal and sectional conditions. The color of butter is considered defective when it is uneven, or lacks uniformity within the same churning or package.

a. Following is a listing of certain color defects and their probable causes:

1. Mottled: Attributable to insufficient working of the butter, resulting in an uneven distribution of salt and moisture. Diffusion of the moisture toward the undissolved salt, or areas of high salt concentration, causes the irregular color spots. Churning at too high a temperature, resulting in soft granules that do not have sufficient resistance to stand the necessary amount of working, may also cause a mottled condition.

2. Specks: Attributable to incorporation of small particles of coagulated casein or coloring. White specks present may be small particles of curd formed during heating of improperly neutralized sour cream or from partial coagulation caused by sweet-curdling organisms during pasteurization. The addition of a coarse-bodied starter may also be a contributing factor. Yellow specks may result from the use of butter color which has precipitated because of age or freezing.

3. Streaked: Attributable to insufficient working of the butter, faulty mechanical condition of churn causing uneven working of butter, and addition of remnants from previous churning.

4. Wavy: Attributable to insufficient working, resulting in an uneven distribution of the water and salt in the butter. May also be caused by faulty mechanical condition of the churn and addition of remnants from previous churnings.

SALT

In grading butter, the factor of salt is considered from the standpoint of the degree of salt taste, and whether it is completely dissolved. A range in the salt content or salty taste of butter is permitted without considering it a defect. This range provides for the various market preferences for salt taste in butter. Uniformity of salt content between churnings from the same factory is desirable.

a. Following is a listing of certain salt defects and their probable causes:

1. Sharp salt: Attributable to the use of too much salt or lack of sufficient working to obtain thorough distribution of salt and water.

2. Gritty: Attributable to the use of too much salt or insufficient working of the butter.

FROZEN DESSERTS

Ice Milk
Milkfat: 2.0% minimum, 7.0% maximum
Total milk solids: 11.0% minimum
Stabilizer: 0.5% maximum
Weight per gallon: 4.5 lb. minimum
Food solids per gallon: 1.3 lb. minimum

Fruit, Nut or Chocolate Ice Milk (and bulky flavors)
Milkfat: 2.0% minimum, 7.0% maximum
Total milk solids: 11.0% minimum
Stabilizer: 0.5% maximum
Weight per gallon: 4.5 lb. minimum
Food solids per gallon: 1.3 lb. minimum

Sherbet (milk)
Milkfat: 1.0% minimum, 2.0% maximum
Total milk solids: 2.0% minimum, 5.0% maximum
Acid: 0.35% minimum
Stabilizer: 0.5% maximum
Weight per gallon: 6.0 lb. minimum

Artifically Sweetened Ice Milk—plain
Milkfat: No standard. State standards may vary from 2.0% to 7.0% minimum and 4.99% to 8.0% maximum where they exist
Total milk solids: No standard. State standards may vary from 10.0% to 30.0% minimum where they exist
Stabilizer: No standard. State standards are 0.5% maximum where they exist
Artificial sweetener: No standard. Illegal in a few states
Edible carbohydrates: No standard. Illegal in a few states
Weight per gallon: No standard. State standards may vary from 4.2 to 4.5 lb minimum where they exist
Food solids per gallon: No standard. State standards are 1.0 or 1.3 lb. minimum where they exist

Artificially Sweetened Ice Milk—fruit, nuts, chocolate
Milkfat: No standard. State standards may vary from 2.0% to 7.0% minimum and 4.99% to 8.0% maximum where they exist
Total milk solids: No standard. State standards may vary from 10.8% to 30.0% minimum where they exist
Stabilizer: No standard. State standards are 0.5% maximum where they exist

Artificial sweetener: No standard. Illegal in a few states

Edible carbohydrates: No standard. Illegal in a few states

Weight per gallon: No standard. State standards may vary from 4.2 to 4.5 lb. minimum where they exist

Food solids per gallon: No standard. State standards are 1.3 lb. minimum where they exist

Plain Ice Cream

Milkfat: 10.0% minimum

Total milk solids: 20.0% minimum

Stabilizer: 0.5% maximum

Weight per gallon: 4.5 lb. minimum

Food solids per gallon: 1.6 lb. minimum

Fruit, Nut or Chocolate Ice Cream (and bulky flavors)

Milkfat: 8.0% minimum

Total milk solids: 16.0% minimum

Stabilizer: 0.5% maximum

Weight per gallon: 4.5 lb. minimum

Food solids per gallon: 1.6 lb. minimum

Artificially Sweetened Ice Cream—plain

Milkfat: No standard. State standards may vary from 6.0% to 12.0% minimum where they exist

Total milk solids: No standard. State standards may vary from 18.0% to 20.0% minimum where standards exist

Stabilizer: No standard. State standards are 0.5% or 0.6% minimum where they exist

Artificial sweetener: No standard. Illegal in some states

Edible Carbohydrates: No standard. Illegal in some states

Weight per gallon: No standard. State standards may vary from 4.2 to 4.5 lb. minimum where standards exist

Food solids per gallon: No standard. State standards may vary from 1.6 to 1.8 lb. minimum where standards exist

Artificially Sweetened Ice Cream — fruit, nuts or chocolate

Milkfat: No standard. State standards may vary from 7.0% to 10.0% minimum where they exist

Total milk solids: No standard. State standards may vary from 14.0% to 20.0% minimum where they exist

Stabilizer: No standard. State standards are 0.5% or 0.6% maximum where standards exist

Artificial sweetener: No standard. Illegal in some states

Edible carbohydrates: No standard. Illegal in some states

Weight per gallon: No standard. State standards may vary from 4.2 to 4.5 lb. minimum where they exist

Food solids per gallon: No standard. State standards are 1.6 lb. minimum where they exist

Frozen Custard

Milkfat: 10.0% minimum

Total milk solids: 20.0% minimum

Stabilizer: 0.5% maximum

Weight per gallon: 4.5 lb. minimum

Food solids per gallon: 1.6 lb. minimum

Egg yolks, per 90 lb.: No standard. State standards may vary from 1.5 to 5.0 dozen minimum where they exist

Solids: 1.4% minimum

Frozen Dessert—Mellorine type

Fat, animal or vegetable: No standard. State standards may vary from 6.0% to 10.0% minimum where they exist

Milk solids-not-fat: No standard. State standards may vary from 10.0% to 20.0% minimum where they exist

Stabilizer: No standard. State standards may vary from 0.5% to 1.0% maximum where they exist

Weight per gallon: No standard. State standards are 4.5 lb. minimum where they exist

Food solids per gallon: No standard. State standards may vary from 1.3 to 1.6 lb. minimum where they exist

Milk Shake Mix

Milkfat: No standard. State standards may vary from 2.0% to 4.0% minimum where they exist

Total milk solids: No standard. State standards may vary from 10.0% to 25.0% minimum where they exist

BIBLIOGRAPHY

"April Highlights." *Dairy Products*. May 31, 1974, pp. 2-14.

"August Highlights." *Dairy Products*. September 30, 1974, pp. 2-14.

Base Plans in U.S. Milk Markets: Development, Status, and Potential, No. 957, June 1972, pp. 1-35.

"Cheese in Family Meals." *Home and Garden Bulletin* 112, Washington, D.C.: U.S. Department of Agriculture, 1966.

"Cost of Dry Whole Milk Packaged For Household Use." Washington, D.C.: U.S. Department of Agriculture, September 1973, pp. 2-11.

"December Highlights." *Dairy Products*, January 30, 1975, pp. 2-11.

"February Highlights." *Dairy Products*, March 31, 1975, pp. 2-12.

Federal and State Standards For The Composition of Milk Products (and Certain Non-Milk Fat Products). Washington, D.C.: U.S. Department of Agriculture, 1974.

The Impact of Dairy Imports on the U.S. Dairy Industry, No. 278, January 1975, pp. 1-77.

"July Highlights." *Dairy Products*, August 30, 1974, pp. 2-14.

"June Highlights." *Dairy Products*, July 30, 1974, pp. 2-18.

"March Highlights." *Dairy Products*, April 30, 1974, pp. 2-14.

"May Highlights." *Dairy Products*, July 1, 1974, pp. 2-14.

Milk Ordinance and Code, 1953 Recommendations of the Public Health Service, 3rd Printing, Washington, D.C.: Department of Health, Education and Welfare.

Nelson, John and Trout, Malcomb. *Judging Dairy Products*, 4th ed. Milwaukee: Olsen Publishing Co., 1964.

Newer Knowledge of Milk. Chicago: National Dairy Council, 1965.

"November Highlights." *Dairy Products*, December 31, 1974, pp. 2-11.

Poultry Grading Manual. Washington, D.C.: U.S. Department of Agriculture, 1971.

"Production of Manufactured Dairy Products 1973." *Manufactured Dairy Products*, June 20, 1974, pp. 2-63.

"Salad Dressing, Mayonnaise, & Related Products 1969." Washington, D.C.: United States Department of Commerce, November 1970, pp. 1-12.

Sanders, G.B. *Cheese Varieties and Descriptions*, Agr. Handbook No. 54, Washington, D.C.: Government Printing Office, 1953.

"September Highlights." *Dairy Products*, October 31, 1974, pp. 2-16.

U.S. Department of Agriculture. *Federal and State Standards for the Composition of Milk Products*, Agr. Handbook No. 51, Washington, D.C.: U.S. Government Printing Office, May 1971.

U.S. Department of Agriculture. *Standards for Butter*, Washington, D.C.: Government Printing Office, 1960.

U.S. Department of Agriculture. *Standards for Frozen Desserts*, Washington, D.C.: Government Printing Office, 1968.

FISH AND SHELLFISH

Vertebrate, or fin fish. These are characterized by back-bone and fins, and are of two types: lean and fat. Fat fish, such as mackerel, salmon, and swordfish, are broiled or baked. Lean types, such as cod, flounder, and haddock, are best for frying.

Shellfish. These fish items have bodies partially or completely covered with a shell. Shellfish are further divided into two classes:

1. Crustaceans: These shellfish have hard shells over the back portions of the body and over the claws, and softer shells for protection of the underparts of the body and legs. Shrimp and lobster are examples.

2. Mollusks: Shellfish in this class have two shells of the same size and shape, usually hard, which are ordinarily held tightly closed. Clams, oysters, and scallops are examples.

Market Forms

Round (Whole): As it comes from the water.

Drawn: Eviscerated.

Dressed: Eviscerated, head, tail, and fins off.

Fillets: One-half the fish (backbone to belly) removed from the head, tail, fins, and skin.

Sticks: Blocks of fish meat of uniform size.

Steaks: A cross-section of one fish cut from a dressed fish with the skin off.

Fresh Fish

Evidence of Quality: Bright, shiny skin; no loose scales; bright, bulging, clean eyes; red inside the gills; firm flesh that bounces back when pressed; no strong odors; no slime.

Because fish deteriorates so very quickly, it is advisable to buy fresh fish, but only if it is to be used within 48 hours. All of the most popular varieties of fish are available frozen. There are approximately 200 varieties of fish marketed in the United States. The most popular are classified here in categories of fresh water fish, salt water fish and shellfish.

Frozen Fish

Cuts and Shapes of Prepared Fish

Aberdeen Cut	Rhombus shape, cut from block, sides squared, or tapered.
American Cut	Tapered or beveled edges of fish portions, or fillets.
Bits	Also known as bites, nuggets, cubes— small pieces of fish from blocks less than 1/2 to 1 oz., each in square, round, irregular shapes.
Cakes	Rounded, flat cakes of minced or ground fish, usually breaded.
Chunks	Large pieces, cross-section slices, similar to steaks.
Custom Cut	Same as Aberdeen Cut.
Diamond Cut	Same as Aberdeen Cut.
Fillet	Boneless piece of fish cut lengthwise from backbone. With/without skin. Butterflied fillets are two sides of fish held together by skin and flesh of back. Natural cut is cut from block.
Fish 'n' Cheese	Portion topped with cheese, or may be combined with fish.
French Cut	Same as Aberdeen Cut.
Portion	Usually a square or rectangle, cut from block, 1-1/2 to 6 oz., breaded, or unbreaded, raw/precooked. Grated fish portions is term used for portions made from mechanically separated fish flesh.

	NOTE: Many companies have identifying names for portions and cuts: Club, Imperial, Dover, etc.
Squares	Same as portions.
Steaks	Cross-section slices of dressed fish, with backbone section in center, 1/2 to 1-in. thick.
Sticks	Rectangles of fish cut from block, usually 1 by 3 in., 1 to 2 oz. ea., breaded. Also cut from mixed block.
Tails	One side of tail of fish, or portion which resembles fish tail. Boneless, usually breaded or battered, raw or precooked, from 3-1/2 to 8 oz. Entire tail, bone-in, also breaded, and sold as tail.
Tidbits	Same as Bits.

White Fleshed Ocean Fish

Cod (Scrod)
Flounder (Fluke, Sole)
Greenland Turbot
Haddock (Scrod)
Halibut
Ocean Catfish
Ocean Perch
Pollock
Sea Trout
Snapper (Red)
Sole (Grey, Lemon, Dover)
Whiting (Hake)
Whiting, Cape

These fish are usually available in these forms:

Fillets	1. Raw, breaded, or in batter, IQF	2 to 15 oz.
	2. Precooked, breaded, or in batter, IQF	
	3. Raw, unbreaded, skinless and boned, or skin on and boned; IQF or IQF glazed, bulk (cello wrap)	
Steaks	Usually raw, unbreaded, with or without skin, IQF (Cod, Halibut, Pollock)	2-1/2 to 6 oz.
Whole	Usually raw, unbreaded, with or without skin IQF (Sole, Snapper, Flounder, Whiting, Cape Whiting)	10 to 20 oz.
Bites	Very small cubes, raw, breaded, IQF	1/2 oz.
Portions	Raw or precooked, breaded or unbreaded, IQF, square, or rectangular, or shaped	1-1/2 to 6 oz.

Sticks	Usually 1 by 3 in., raw or precooked, breaded, IQF	1 to 2 oz.

Other Popular Species

Freshwater Catfish
Mackerel (Spanish, King)
Mullet
Salmon (Sockeye, Red, Coho)
Shad (and with roe)
Smelt
Trout (Rainbow, Brook, Speckled, Golden)
Yellow Perch

These fish are usually in these forms:

Fillets	1. Raw, breaded, or in batter, IQF	4 to 18 oz.
	2. Precooked, breaded, or in batter, IQF	
	3. Raw, unbreaded, skinless and boned, or skin on and boned; IQF or IQF glazed, bulk (cello wrap)	
	4. Butterflied and breaded	
	5. Stuffed	
Steaks	Raw, unbreaded, 1/2 to 1 in. thick (Catfish, Salmon)	2-1/2 to 6 oz.
Whole	With skin, with or without head, with or without tail, raw, or breaded, or unbreaded, dressed, boned, stuffed, butterflied (Catfish, Mackerel, Trout, Smelt, Shad, Perch)	2 to 9 oz.
Portions	Raw or cooked, breaded, or unbreaded, stuffed, shaped, square, or rectangular, tails	2 to 5 oz.

FRESH WATER

Blue Gill Also known as blue perch, blue sunfish, coppernose, gold perch, chainside. Peak season in summer months. Available whole or as fillets.

Brook Trout Salvelinus fontinalis. Caught in local streams from May to October.

New York Market	1/4 lb.	Round
	1/3 lb.	Round

Buffalo Fish Ictiobus cyprinella (bigmouth, gourdhead, or redmouth). Ictiobus bubalis (channel, razorback, smallmouth, suckermouth). Ictiobus niger (bugler, prairie, rooter). Caught in the Mississippi River and its tributaries, mostly in Louisiana from February to August.

Chicago Market	Medium	2 to 4 lb.	Round
	No. 1	4 to 8 lb.	Round
	Jumbo	8 lb. or more	Round
Gulf States Market		3 to 20 lb.	Drawn
New York Market	No. 1	4 to 7 lb.	Dressed, round, or skinned
	Jumbo	7 lbs. or more	Dressed, round, or skinned

Carp Cyprinus carpio. Also known as German carp. Caught in the Great Lakes, but mostly in the Mississippi. Sold in California, February through July; and in Chicago, in December and February through June, with April being the biggest month. Available in fillets, but mostly sold fresh.

Chicago Market	Medium	2 to 4 lb.	Round
	No. 1	4 to 8 lb.	Round
	Jumbo	More than 8 lb.	Round
New York Market	Medium	Less than 4 lb.	Round
	No. 1	4 to 7 lb.	Round
	Jumbo	7 lb. and more	Round

Catfish Ictalurus, Ameiurus, and Leptops olivaris are all known as bullheads or catfish. Also known as blue channel fish, yellow catfish, and fiddler or spotted fish. Caught along all coasts, Florida lakes, Great Lakes, and the Mississippi River; March through October. Available headless, round, skinned and dressed.

Chicago Market			
BULLHEADS	Large	1/2 lb.	Skinned and dressed
	Jumbo	Over 3/4 lb.	Skinned and dressed
CATFISH	No. 1	1-1/2 to 3 lbs.	Skinned and dressed
	Large	Over 3 lb.	Skinned and dressed
Gulf States Market	Large	1 to 40 lbs.	Drawn

Chub Leucichthys zenithicus. Also known as blackfin, bloater, bluefin, and tullibee. Caught in Lake Huron, Lake Michigan and Lake Superior in June through September, with November and December being the best months. Most are sold as smoked fish; only the blackfin is used as a fresh fish.

Chicago Market	Small	More than 7 per lb.	Drawn
	Medium	5 to 7 per lb.	Drawn
	Large	3 to 4 per lb.	Drawn

Eel Anguilla bostoniensis. Also known as Anguilla, Capitone, Sand Boy, and Shoestring. Can be bought all year.

Frogs Legs Bull frogs and common frogs found in the south, grass frogs mostly from the Mississippi River and its tributaries. Available all year but most are caught from April through October. The white-meated bull frog is the best grade.

New York Market	Small	9 to 12 pairs per lb.
	Medium	6 to 8 pairs per lb.
	Large	4 to 5 pairs per lb.
	Extra Large	2 to 3 pairs per lb.

Extra large is the best size.

Lake Herring Leucichthys artedi. Also known as blueback and cisco of Lake Erie. Caught in Lake Huron, Lake Michigan, Lake Ontario and Lake Superior. Available drawn and round, fresh and frozen, salted and smoked. Best Lake Herring is 1/2 lb., Lake Erie herring.

Chicago Market	Bluefin (Minnesota)	3 to 4 per lb.	Mostly drawn
	Regular	4 to 7 per lb.	Mostly drawn
New York Market	Regular	4 or more per lb.	Round
	Large	3 per lb.	Round

Lake Trout Cristivomer namaycush. Also known as gray trout, Great Lakes' trout, Mackinaw trout, and salmon trout. Caught in Lake Huron, Lake Michigan, Lake Superior and Lake Ontario, mostly from May to October. Available filleted, but most are sold drawn and fresh.

Chicago Market	No. 1	2 to 4 lb.	Drawn
	Medium	4 to 8 lb.	Drawn
	Large	8 to 10 lb.	Drawn
	Headless	over 8 lb.	Dressed
	Half breed and fat	all sizes	Drawn

Pickerel Pike Esox lucius (common pike); esox masquinongy (muskellunge); esox reticulatus and esox vermiculatus (pickerels). Also known as grass pike of Lake Erie, jack pike of Canada and lake pickerel. Caught mostly from the north Canadian lakes, especially Lake of the Woods. Can be bought all year, but the peak is in June. Available dressed, round and filleted; fresh and frozen.

Chicago Market	Medium	1-1/2 to 3 lb.	Round
	Large	over 3 lb.	Dressed

Pike Perch Includes blue pike, sauger, and yellow pike perch. Blue pike also known as blue pickerel, blues, grass pike, great northern pike, jack salmon, lake pickerel, and pike perch. Saugers also known as sand pike. Yellow pike also known as dore, pike perch, salmon jack, wall-eyed pike, and yellows. Blue pike caught mostly in Lake Erie, with some from Lake Ontario. Saugers caught in Lake Erie. Yellow pike caught in Canada with a few from Lake Erie, Lake Huron, Saginaw Bay, and other lakes. Available year round, with the blue pike peak from October to April, Sauger peak from October to February, and the yellow pike peak from April to June. Blue pike available round, and as fresh and frozen fillets; saugers available round, and as fresh and frozen fillets; saugers available fresh, round, and dressed, but most are filleted; yellow pike available dressed and filleted, but most are sold fresh.

BLUE PIKE:

Chicago Market	Pins	5 to 6 lb.	Round
		1/4 lb.	Round
New York Market	Regular	1/2 to 1-1/2 lb.	Round
	Jumbo	1-1/2 lb. or more	Round

SAUGER:

Chicago Market	Lake Erie	1/2 lb.	Round
	Winnipeg	1/2 to 3/4 lb.	Round
	Manitoba	3/4 to 1 lb.	Round
New York Market		1/2 to 1-1/2 lb.	Round

YELLOW PIKE:

Chicago Market	No. 2 hard	1 to 2-1/2 lb.	Most are round
	No. 1 hard	2-1/2 to 3-1/2 lb.	Most are round
	Large	2 to 4 lb.	Most are round
	Jumbo	over 4 lb.	Most are round
New York Market	No. 2	1 to 1-1/2 lb.	Round
	No. 1	1-1/2 to 3 lb.	Round
	Large	3-1/2 lb. or more	Round

Rock Bass Also known as goggle-eye bass, red eye, red eye perch, and sunfish. Peak season is the winter months. Available filleted and whole.

Sheepshead Aplodinotus grunniens. Also known as white perch, croaker, fresh water drum, gaspergou, and gray bass. Caught in Lake Erie, Lake Huron, and Lake Ontario, and in the Mississippi Valley to Texas and Louisiana. Peak falls in April through June. Available as fillets, but most are sold round. 3/4 to 3 lb. fish from the South are the best.

Chicago Market	Lake Erie	1 to 5 lb.	Round
	Small	3/4 to 1-1/2 lb.	Round
	Medium	1-1/2 to 5 lb.	Round
	Large	over 5 lb.	Round
Gulf States Market		3/4 to 10 lb.	Round

Smelts Osmerus mordax. Lake Michigan supplies most of the freshwater smelts, with the peak in mid-March.

Chicago Market	Medium	more than 10 per lb.	Round
	No. 1	7 to 10 per lb.	Round
	Jumbo	less than 7 per lb.	Round
Great Lakes	Medium	more than 10 per lb.	Round
	No. 1	7 to 10 per lb.	Round
	Jumbo	4 to 6 per lb.	Round

Sturgeon Acipenser oxyrhynchus. Also known as green, lake, sea and common sturgeon. Lake sturgeon is caught in large rivers and the Great Lakes, and common sturgeon is found in the North. In season all year. Available brined, canned, fresh, frozen, and smoked.

Terrapin Found in Minnesota, Missouri, Wisconsin, Iowa, Michigan, New York, Delaware, New Jersey, Maryland, Virginia, and Florida. In season from June through October. Available live.

Gulf States Market	Bulls	1/2 to 1 lb.	Live
	Heifers	1 lb.	Live
	Cows	1-1/2 to 2 lb.	Live

White Bass Also known as silver lake bass and striped lake bass. Peak season is the winter months. Available filleted or whole.

Whitefish Coregonus clupeaformis. Also known as Lake Champlain shad. Caught in the Great Lakes and Canadian lakes, mostly from May through August. Available drawn, dressed, filleted. The best, in order of desirability, are from Lake Superior, Lake Michigan, Lake Erie, and Lake Huron.

Chicago Market	No. 1	1 to 3 lb.	Most are drawn
	Medium-Large	3 to 4 lb.	Most are drawn
	Jumbo	over 4 lb.	Most are drawn
New York Market	Dressed	Mixed sizes	Dressed
	Medium	1 to 1-1/2 lb.	Round
	No. 1	1-1/2 to 3 lb.	Round
	Jumbo	3 lb. or more	Round

Yellow Perch Perca flavescens. Also known as red fin; jumbos or English perch (very large perch from Canada); Lake Erie perch (large sizes), and lake perch (small sizes). Caught in the Great Lakes and coastal streams and lakes from Maine to North Carolina. In season all year, but mostly from April through November. Available as fillets and rounds; fresh and frozen. The best are Lake Erie yellow perch, which are of two grades: pound net, which is best, and gill net, which is inferior.

Chicago Market

CANADIAN:	Large	about 1/2 lb.	Round
	Jumbo	3/4 lb.	Round
	Small	less than 1/4 lb.	Round
NATIVE:	Medium	1/4 lb.	Round
	Large	about 1/3 lb.	Round
	Jumbo	1/2 to 3/4 lb.	Round

SALT WATER

Abalone Haliotis cracherodi. Also known as aurora, black, green, grand ear shell, pink, rainbow, red, and rough abalone. Found along the Pacific Coast all year. Available canned, dried, fresh, and salted.

Barracuda Sphyraena barracude. Also known as Gauchanche. Found along the Atlantic Coast from the Carolinas to Florida and the West Indies. Can be bought all year.

Black Sea Bass Also known as channel bass and sea wolf. Peak season is during the summer months. Available whole and as fillets.

Black Fish Also known as bowfin, cottonfish, dog fish, grindle, lawyer, and speckled cat. Can be bought all year. Available whole and as fillets.

Bluefish Pomatomus saltatrix. Also known as blues, green fish, snapping mackerel, and tailors. Caught from Florida to Massachusetts and sometimes as far north as Maine. Caught in Florida, in mid-winter; in the Carolinas, in March and April; Long Island, in April, and Massachusetts, in May. Available as drawn, round, and smoked, but mostly fresh.

Gulf States Market		1 to 6 lb.	Drawn and round
New York Market	Snapper	less than 3/4 lb.	Round
	Small	3/4 to 1-1/2 lb.	Drawn and round
	Medium	1-1/2 lb. or more	Drawn and round
	Large	2-1/2 lb. or more	Drawn and round

Bonito Also known as Atlantic bonito, Chilean bonito, and Pacific Coast bonito. Peak season is summer and fall. Available whole or as fillets.

Butterfish Poronotus triacanthus. Also known as dollarfish and harvest fish. Caught along the Atlantic Coast in Chesapeake Bay, from May through November; in New England, in summer; in Rhode Island, in April; and north of Cape Cod, July through November. Available smoked, dressed or round, fresh, or frozen.

Boston Market	Small	less than 1/5 lb.	Round
	Mixed	1/5 lb. or more	Round
	Large	3/4 lb. or more	Round
New York Market	Small	less than 4-1/2 oz.	Round
	Medium	4-1/2 to 5-1/3 oz.	Round
	Large	5-1/3 to 8 oz.	Round
	Jumbo	1/2 lb. or more	Round

The U.S. Dept. of the Interior oversees the fishing industry in the United States. Grading of fish is not mandatory, but is available. The standards measured are appearance, uniformity, texture, and flavor. The grades are U.S. A, U.S. B, and U.S. Substandard.

Cod Gadus callarias. Caught in North Atlantic and Pacific Oceans, but landed mainly at Unga, Alaska; Portland, Me.; off coast of Maryland; at Gloucester, Boston, and Seattle. Caught all year, but mostly in March through September. Available dressed and drawn. Red specks on salted cod show deterioration.

Seattle Market		3 lb. or more	Dressed and round
Boston Market	Snapper	less than 1-1/2 lb.	A few drawn, most are round

	Scrod	1-1/2 to 2-1/2 lb.	Drawn
	Market	2-1/2 to 10 lb.	Drawn
	Large	10 to 25 lb.	Drawn
	Whole	over 25 lb.	Drawn
New York Market	Steak	5 lb. or more	Dressed
	Scrod	1-1/2 to 2-1/2 lb.	Drawn
	Market	2-1/2 to 8 lb.	Drawn
	Large	8 to 20 lb.	Drawn
	Whole	20 lb. or more	Drawn

COD FILLETS, FROZEN (10/1/72)

Grade A — Flavor and odor: Fish flesh has good flavor, and odor characteristic of cod (Gadus morhua or Gadus macrocephalus), and is free from staleness, off-flavor, and off-odors of any kind. Appearance: (Worth 25 points). Refer to Tables 6-1 and 6-2 for deduction points. Size: (Worth 20 points). Refer to Table 6-3 for deduction points. Defects: (Worth 40 points). Refer to Table 6-4 for deduction points. Character: (Worth 15 points). Refer to Table 6-5 for deduction points. Grade A may have no more than a total of 15 points deducted for variations in quality from Tables 6-1 through 6-5. The total of points deducted is subtracted from 100 to obtain the score, which may not be less than 85.

Grade B — Flavor and odor: Fish flesh may be somewhat lacking in good flavor and odor; and is free from objectionable off-flavors, and off-odors of any kind. Appearance, Size, Defects, and Character: Same as Grade A. Grade B may have no more than a total of 30 points deducted for variations in quality from Tables 6-1 through 6-5. The total of points deducted is subtracted from 100 to obtain the score, which may not be less than 70. Substandard: Fails to meet requirements. See score sheet.

TABLE 6-1
SCORE DEDUCTIONS FOR DISCOLORATION

Color of Frozen Product	Deduction Points	
	"Light" Colored Portion Comprising Main Portion of Fillet	"Dark" Colored Portion Occurring under Skin Mainly along Lateral Line
No discoloration	0	0
Slight yellowing	2	1
Moderate yellowing	4	2
Excessive yellowing and/or any rusting	13	12

TABLE 6-2
SCORE DEDUCTIONS FOR DEHYDRATION

Degree of Dehydration Frozen Product	Surface Area Affected [percent]		Deduction Points
	Over	Not Over	
Slight: Shallow and not color masking	0	1	0
	1	50	2
	50	100	5
	1	25	5
Moderate: Deep but just deep enough to easily scrape off with fingernail	25	50	8
	50	100	16
Excessive: Deep dehydration not easily scraped off	1	25	12
	25	100	25

TABLE 6-3
SCORE DEDUCTIONS FOR SIZE OF FILLET PIECES

Number of Fillet Pieces less than 2 Ounces per Pound		Deduction Points
Over	Not Over	
	0	0
0	1	1
1	2	10
2	3	15
3	4	20

TABLE 6-4
SCORE DEDUCTIONS FOR ABSENCE OF DEFECTS

Defects Subfactors	Method of Determining Subfactor Score	Deduction Points
Improper packing	Moderate defects, noticeably affecting the product's appearance.	2
	Excessive defects, seriously affecting product's appearance.	4
Blemishes	Number of blemishes per 1 lb. of fish flesh:	
	Over 0 not over 1	1
	Over 1 not over 2	3
	Over 2 not over 3	5
	Over 3 not over 4	8
	Over 4 not over 5	12
	Over 5 not over 6	16
	Over 6 not over 7	30
	Over 7	40
Bones	Number of instances per 1 lb. of fish flesh:	
	Over 0 not over 1	0
	Over 1 not over 2	2
	Over 2 not over 3	4
	Over 3 not over 4	6
	Over 4 not over 5	8
	Over 5 not over 6	14
	Over 6 not over 7	30
	Over 7	40
Cutting and trimming.	Slight defects, scarcely noticeable.	0
	Moderate defects, noticeable but not affecting the usability of any fillets.	4

Defects Subfactors	Method of Determining Subfactor Score	Deduction Points
	Excessive defects impairing:	
	a. the usability of up to 1/4 of the total number of fillets.	8
	b. the usability of over 1/4 but not more than 1/2 of the total number of fillets.	16
	c. the usability of over 1/2 of the total number of fillets.	40

TABLE 6-5
SCORE DEDUCTIONS FOR CHARACTER

Character Subfactors	Method of Determining Subfactor Score	Deduction Points
Texture	Texture of the cooked fish:	
	a. Firm, slightly resilient but not tough or rubbery; moist but not mushy.	0
	b. Moderately firm; only slightly tough or rubbery; does not form a fibrous mass in the mouth; moist but not mushy.	4
	c. Moderately tough or rubbery; has noticeable tendency to form a fibrous mass in the mouth; or is dry; or is mushy.	8
	d. Excessively tough or rubbery; has marked tendency to form a fibrous mass in the mouth; or is very dry; or is very mushy.	15
Drip	Percent of drip:	
	Over 0 not over 5	0
	Over 5 not over 6	1
	Over 6 not over 8	2
	Over 8 not over 10	4
	Over 10 not over 12	6
	Over 12 not over 14	9
	Over 14 not over 16	12
	Over 16	15

Score Sheet

Label:

Size and kind of container:

Container mark or identification:

Size of lot:

Number of packages per master carton:

Size of sample:

Type of overwrap:

Actual net weight: (lb.)   (kg.)

Factor	Score Points	Sample Score
Appearance	25	
Size	20	
Absence of defects	40	
Character	15	
Total	100	
Flavor and odor		
Final grade		

Croaker Micropogon undulatus. Also known as hardhead, king billy, and crocus. Caught in the North Carolina and New Jersey trail, but mostly in Virginia. May be from as far as Texas to Massachusetts. Available all year, but most are caught March through October. Available pan-dressed and round, fresh, and frozen.

Gulf States Market		1/4 to 1 lb.	Round
New York Market	Pins	less than 1/2 lb.	Round
	Small	1/2 to 3/4 lb.	Round
	Medium	3/4 to 1-1/2 lb.	Round
	Large	1-1/2 lb. or more	Round

Cusk Brosme brosme. Also known as deep sea whitefish. Caught in New England, usually north of New Jersey, in February through August. Available filleted and drawn, smoked, fresh, frozen, as steaks, sticks, boneless salted, and dried-salted.

Boston Market	Scrod	1-1/2 to 3 lb.	Drawn
		Over 3 lb.	Drawn

Drum Black drum: Pogonias cromis. Also known as sea drums. Red drum: Sciaenops ocellata. Also known as red fish, red bass, spotted bass, and channel bass. Caught from Texas to Massachusetts, but mostly in Texas. Caught from November to April in Florida, and February to June in Texas. Available drawn and filleted, but most are round.

Gulf States Market			
Black	Small	1/4 to 1 lb.	Round
	Medium	1 to 4 lb.	Drawn or round
	Large	4 to 15 lb.	Drawn or round
	Bulls	15 to 40 lb.	Drawn or round
Red	Rats	1-1/2 to 3 lb.	Round
	Medium	3 to 15 lb.	Drawn or round
	Bulls	15 to 40 lb.	Drawn or round

Eel Anguilla bostoniensis. Also known as Anguilla, Capitone, Sand Boy, Sea Eel, and Shoestring. Can be bought all year.

Fillets and Steaks Fillets are usually prepared from blue pike, cod, cusk, flounder, haddock, hake, and sole; but sometimes halibut, mackerel, perch, pollack (pollock), red snapper, salmon, and sea trout. Steaks are usually prepared from cod, grouper, salmon, and swordfish. Sticks are usually prepared from frozen whiting.

RAW BREADED FISH PORTIONS, FROZEN (10/1/72)

Grade A — Flavor and odor: The cooked product has the typical flavor and odor of the indicated species of fish, also of the breading, and is free from rancidity, bitterness, staleness, off-flavors and off-odors of any kind. Other factors, rated by score points: May have no more than 15 points deducted for variations in the quality of each factor in accordance with Table 6-6. The total points deducted are subtracted from 100 to obtain the score, which may not be less than 85.

Grade B — Flavor and odor: The cooked product is lacking in good flavor and odor, but is free from objectionable off-flavors and off-odors of any kind. Other factors are rated by score points: May have no more than 30 points deducted for variations in the quality of each factor in accordance with Table 6-6. The total of points deducted is subtracted from 100 to obtain the score, which may not be less than 70.

Substandard: Fails to meet requirements.

TABLE 6-6
SCHEDULE OF POINT DEDUCTIONS PER SAMPLE UNIT OF 10 PORTIONS

	Factors Scored		Method of Determining Score	Deduct
Frozen State	1. Condition of package		Small degree: Moderate loose breading and/or moderate frost	3
			Large degree: Excessive loose breading and/or excessive amount frost	6
	2. Ease of separation		Minor: Hand separated with difficulty. Each affected	1
			Major: Separated only by knife or other instrument. Each affected	2
	3. Broken portion		Break or cut greater than 1/2 width or length. Each affected	10
	4. Damaged portion		Mashed, mechanically and/or physically injured, misshaped or multilated[1]	
			Minor: 1 to 5 instances. Each affected	2
			Major: Over 5 instances. Each affected	4
	5. Uniformity	Size	Deviation in length or width between the 2 largest and 2 smallest portion is:	
			Up to 1/4 in.	0
			Over 1/4 in. and up to 1/2 in.	3
			Over 1/2 in.	10
	6.	Weight	Weight ratio of the 2 heaviest divided by the 2 lightest portions:	
			Over 1.0 but not over 1.2	0
			Over 1.2 but not over 1.3	2
			Over 1.3 but not over 1.4	5
			Over 1.4	10
Cooked State	7. Distortion		Minor: Bending, shrinking, twisting — 1/4 to 1/2 in. Each affected	1
			Major: Excessive bending, shrinking, twisting — over 1/2 in. Each affected	2
	8. Coating defects		Bare spots, blistering, ridges, breaks, curds:[1]	
			Minor: 1 to 6 instances. Each affected	1
			Major: Over 6 instances. Each affected	2
	9. Blemishes		Skin (except for style II), blood spots, bruises, and discolorations:[1]	
			Minor: 1 to 6 instances. Each affected	2
			Major: Over 6 instances. Each affected	4
	10. Bones		Portions containing bones (potentially harmful). Each affected	10
	11. Texture	Coating	Small degree: Moderately dry, soggy, doughy, or tough	5
			Large degree: Farinaceous (mealy), pasty, very tough	15
	12.	Fish flesh	Small degree: Moderately dry, soft, mushy	5
			Large degree: Dry to the point of fibrousness, very mushy, tough, or rubbery (skin for style II)	15

1. An instance = each 1/16 sq. in. (1/4-in. sq.).

FRIED FISH PORTIONS, FROZEN (10/1/72)

Grade A — Flavor and odor: Cooked product has the typical flavor and odor of the indicated species of fish and breading, and is free from rancidity, bitterness, staleness, off-flavors and off-odors of any kind. Factors rated by score points: May have no more than 15 points deducted for variations in the quality of each factor in accordance with Table 6-7. The total of points deducted is subtracted from 100 to obtain the score, which may not be less than 85.

Grade B — Flavor and odor: Cooked product is lacking in good flavor and odor, but is free from objectionable off-flavors and off-odors of any kind. Factors rated by score points: May have no more than 30 points deducted for variation in the quality of each factor in accordance with Table 6-7. The total of points deducted is subtracted from 100 to obtain the score, which must be between 70 and 84.

Substandard: Fails to meet requirements.

TABLE 6-7
SCHEDULE OF POINT DEDUCTIONS PER SAMPLE UNIT OF 10 PORTIONS
FROZEN STATE

Factors Scored	Method of Determining Score	Deduct
1. Condition of package	Small degree: Loose free oil, and/or moderate loose breading, and/or moderate frost.	3
	Large degree: Oil soaking through package, and/or excessive loose breading, and/or excessive amount frost.	6
2. Ease of separation	Minor: Hand separated with difficulty. Each affected	1
	Major: Separated only by knife or other instrument. Each affected	2
3. Broken portion	Break or cut greater than 1/2 length or width. Each affected	10
	Mashed, mechanically and/or physically injured, misshaped or mutilated[1]	
4. Damaged portion	Minor: 1 to 3 instances. Each affected	2
	Major: Over 3 instances. Each affected	4
5. Size	Deviation in length or width between the 2 largest and 2 smallest portions is:	
	Up to 1/4 in.	0
	Over 1/4 in. and up to 1/2 in.	3
	Over 1/2 in.	10
6. Weight	Weight ratio of the 2 heaviest divided by the 2 lightest portions:	
	Over 1.0 but not over 1.20	0
	Over 1.20 but not over 1.3	3
	Over 1.3 but not over 1.4	6
	Over 1.4	10

COOKED STATE

	Factors Scored	Method of Determining Score	Deduct
7.	Distortion	Minor: Bending, shrinking, twisting (1/4 to 1/2 in.). Each affected	1
		Major: Excessive bending, shrinking, twisting (over 1/2 in.). Each affected	2
8.	Color	Minor: Portions differing slightly from average color of portions in sample unit. Each affected	2
		Major: Portions excessively darker or lighter from average color of portions in sample unit. Each affected	4
		Bare spots, blistering, ridges, breaks, curds[1]	
9.	Coating defects	Minor: 1 to 3 instances. Each affected	1
		Major: Over 3 instances. Each affected	3
		Skin, blood spots, bruises, discolorations[1]	
10.	Blemishes	Minor: 1 to 6 instances. Each affected	1
		Major: Over 6 instances. Each affected	3
11.	Bones	Portions containing bones (potentially harmful). Each affected	10
	Texture		
12.	Coating	Small degree: Moderately dry, soggy, doughy, oily, and/or tough	5
		Large degree: Farinaceous (mealy), pasty, very tough, and/or oily	10
13.	Fish flesh	Small degree: Moderately dry, soft, mushy	5
		Large degree: Dry to the point of fibrousness, very mushy, tough, and/or rubbery	15

1. An instance = each 1/16 sq. in. (1/4-in. sq.).

RAW FISH PORTIONS, FROZEN (10/1/72)

Grade A — Flavor and odor: The cooked product has the typical flavor and odor of the indicated species and does not have rancidity, bitterness, staleness, and other off-flavors or off-odors of any kind. Factors rated by score points: May have no more than 15 points deducted for variations in the quality of each factor in accordance with Table 6-8. The total of points deducted is subtracted from 100 to obtain the score, which may not be less than 85.

Grade B — Flavor and odor: The cooked product does not have good flavor and odor, but is free from objectionable off-flavors and off-odors of any kind. Factors rated by score points: May have no more than 30 points deducted for variations in the quality of each factor in accordance with Table 6-8. The total of points deducted is subtracted from 100 to obtain the score, which must be between 70 and 84.

Substandard: Fails to meet requirements.

TABLE 6-8
SCHEDULE OF POINT DEDUCTIONS PER SAMPLE

FROZEN STATE

	Factors Scored	Method of Determining Score	Deduct
1.	Ease of separation	Minor: Hand separated with difficulty. Each affected	3
		Major: Separated only by knife or other instrument. Each affected	6
2.	Broken portion	Break or cut greater than 1/2 width or length. Each affected	10
3.	Damaged portion	Mashed, mechanically and/or physically injured, misshaped, or multilated.	
		Minor: 1 to 5 instances.[1] Each affected	2
		Major: Over 5 instances. Each affected	4
4.	Voids	Holes, spaces, or depressions:	
		Minor: 1 to 5 instances. Each affected	1
		Major: Over 5 instances. Each affected	2
5.	Discoloration (overall assessment)	Small degree: Slight yellowing or rusting	16
		Large degree: Excessive yellowing or rusting	31
6.	Dehydration (overall assessment)	Surface dehydration:	
		Small degree: Easily scraped off with fingernail. Each affected	5
		Large degree: Deep dehydration not easily scraped off, affecting over 10 percent of surface area. Each affected	10
7.	Uniformity of size	Deviation in length or width between the 2 largest and 2 smallest portions that are similarly shaped.	
		Up to 1/4 in.	0
		Over 1/4 in. and up to 1/2 in.	3
		Over 1/2 in.	10
8.	Uniformity of weight	Weight ratio of 2 heaviest divided by the 2 lightest.	
		Over 1.0 but not over 1.2	0
		Over 1.2 but not over 1.3	5
		Over 1.3 but not over 1.4	2
		Over 1.4	10
	COOKED STATE		
9.	Blemishes	Skin (except for Style II) blood spots, bruises and discolorations.	
		Minor: 1 to 6 instances.[1] Each affected	2
		Major: Over 6 instances. Each affected	4
10.	Bones	Portions containing bones (potentially harmful). Each affected	10
11.	Texture (overall assessment)	Small degree: Moderately dry, soggy, or tough	5
		Large degree: Dry to the point of fibrousness, very mushy, tough, or rubbery skin (Style II)	15

1. An instance = 1/4-in. sq.

FISH BLOCKS, FROZEN (10/1/72)

Grade A — Flavor and odor: The cooked product has the typical flavor and odor of the indicated species of fish, and is free from rancidity, bitterness, staleness, off-flavors, and off-odors of any kind. Other factors: May have no more than 15 points deducted for variations in the quality of each factor in accordance with Table 6-9. The total of points deducted is subtracted from 100 to obtain the score which may not be less than 85.

Grade B — Flavor and odor: The cooked product is lacking in good flavor and odor, but is free from objectionable off-flavors and off-odors of any kind. Other factors: May have 16 to 30 points deducted for variations in the quality of each factor in accordance with Table 6-9. The total of points deducted is subtracted from 100 to obtain the score, which may not be less than 70.

Substandard: Fails to meet requirements.

RAW BREADED FISH STICKS, FROZEN (10/1/72)

Grade A — Flavor and odor: Cooked product has the typical flavor and odor of the indicated species of fish and breeding, and is free from rancidity, bitterness, staleness, off-flavors and off-odors of any kind. Factors rated by score points: May have no more than 15 points deducted for variations in the quality of each factor in accordance with Table 6-10. The total of points deducted is subtracted from 100 to obtain the score, which may not be less than 85.

Grade B — Flavor and odor: Cooked product is lacking in good flavor and odor, but is free from objectionable off-flavors and off-odors of any kind. Factors rated by score points: May have no more than 30 points deducted for variations in the quality of each factor in accordance with Table 6-10. The total of points deducted is subtracted from 100 to obtain the score, which must be between 70 and 84.

Substandard: Fails to meet requirements.

TABLE 6-9
SCHEDULE OF POINT DEDUCTIONS PER SAMPLE UNIT

State	No.	Factors Scored	Aspects Determining Score	Deduct
Frozen	1.	Color	Small degree: Moderate yellowing Large degree: Excessive yellowing and/or rusting	4 16
	2.	Dehydration	Minor: Moderate dehydration for each 10 percent of surface area affected Major: Excessive dehydration for each 10 percent of surface area affected.	3 6
	3.	Uniformity of size	Minor: Each deviation from declared size in length, width, or thickness $\pm 1/8$ to 1/4 in. Major: Each deviation from declared size in length, width, or thickness over $\pm 1/4$ in.	3 6
	4.	Uniformity of weight	Minor: Any minus deviation from declared weight of more than 1 oz. but not more than 4 oz. Major: Any minus deviation from declared weight more than 4 oz.	3 8
	5.	Angles	Edge angle — 2 out of 3 readings deviating 3/8 in. Corner angle — each angle deviating 3/8 in.	2
	6.	Improper fill	For each 1-oz. unit cut from the block that would be adversely affected due to air spaces, ice spaces, depressions, ragged edges, damage, or imbedded packaging material	1
Thawed	7.	Blemishes	Each blemish in 5 lb. of fish block	2
	8.	Bones	Each instance of bones in 5 lb. of fish block	5
Cooked	9.	Texture	Small degree: Moderately tough, dry, rubbery, or mushy Large degree: Excessively tough, dry, rubber, or mushy	5 15

TABLE 6-10
SCHEDULE OF POINT DEDUCTIONS PER SAMPLE UNIT OF 10 STICKS
FROZEN STATE

Factors Scored	Method of Determining Score	Deduct
1. Condition of package	Small degree: Moderate loose breading and/or moderate frost	2
	Large degree: Excessive loose breading and/or excessive amount frost	5
2. Ease of separation	Minor: Hand separated with difficulty. Each affected	1
	Major: Separated only by knife or other instrument. Each affected	2
3. Broken stick	Break or cut greater than 1/2 length width. Each affected	10
	Mashed, mechanically and/or physically injured, misshaped or mutilated[1]	
4. Damaged stick	Minor: 1 to 3 instances. Each affected	2
	Major: Over 3 instances. Each affected	4
Uniformity:		
5. Size	Deviation in length or width between the 2 largest and 2 smallest sticks is:	
	Up to 1/4 in.	0
	Over 1/4 in. and up to 1/2 in.	3
	Over 1/2 in.	10
6. Weight	Weight ratio of the 2 heaviest divided by the 2 lightest sticks:	
	Over 1.0, not over 1.15	0
	Over 1.15, not over 1.3	2
	Over 1.3, not over 1.4	5
	Over 1.4	10
7. Distortion	Minor: Bending, shrinking, twisting (1/4 to 1/2 in.). Each affected	1
	Major: Excessive bending, shrinking, twisting (over 1/2 in.). Each affected.	2
	Bare spots, blistering, ridges, breaks, curds[1]	
8. Coating defects	Minor: 1 to 3 instances. Each affected	1
	Major: Over 3 instances. Each affected	2
	Skin, blood spots, bruises, discolorations[1]	
9. Blemishes	Minor: 1 to 6 instances. Each affected	2
	Major: Over 6 instances. Each affected	4
10. Bones	Sticks containing bones (potentially harmful). Each affected	10
Texture:		
11. Coating	Small degree: Moderately dry, soggy, doughy or tough	5
	Large degree: Farinaceous (mealy), pasty, very tough	15
12. Fish flesh	Small degree: Moderately dry, soft, mushy	5
	Large degree: Dry to the point of fibrousness, very mushy, tough, or rubbery.	15

1. An instance = each 1/16 sq. in. (1/4-in. sq.)

FISH STICKS, FROZEN FRIED (10/1/72)

Grade A — Flavor and odor: Has a typical flavor and odor of the indicated species of fish and of the breading, and is free from rancidity, bitterness, staleness, off-flavors, or off-odors of any kind. Other factors: May have no more than 15 points deducted for variations in the quality of each factor in accordance with Table 6-11. The total of points deducted is subtracted from 100 to obtain the score, which may not be less than 85.

Grade B — Flavor and odor: The cooked product is lacking in good flavor and odor, but is free from objectionable off-flavors and off-odors of any kind. Other factors: May have no more than 30 points deducted for variations in the quality of each factor in accordance with Table 6-11. The total of points deducted is subtracted from 100 to obtain the score, which may not be less than 70.

Substandard: Fails to meet requirements.

TABLE 6-11
SCHEDULE OF POINT DEDUCTIONS PER SAMPLE UNIT OF 10 STICKS
FROZEN STATE

Factors Scored	Method of Determining Score	Deduct
1. Condition of package	Small degree: Loose free oil and/or moderate loose breading and/or moderate frost.	2
	Large degree: Oil soaking through package and/or excessive loose breading and/or excessive amount frost.	5
2. Ease of separation	Minor: Hand separated with difficulty. Each affected	1/2
	Major: Separated only by knife or other instrument. Each affected	1
3. Broken stick	Break or cut greater than 1/2 length or width. Each affected	10
	Mashed, mechanically and/or physically injured, misshaped or mutilated[1]	
4. Damaged stick	Minor: 1 to 3 instances. Each affected	2
	Major: Over 3 instances. Each affected	4
Uniformity:		
5. Size	Deviation in length or width between the 2 largest and 2 smallest sticks is:	
	Up to 1/4 in.	0
	Over 1/4 in. and up to 1/2 in.	3
	Over 1/2 in.	10
6. Weight	Weight ratio of the 2 heaviest divided by the 2 lightest sticks:	
	Over 1.0, not over 1.15	0
	Over 1.15, not over 1.3	2
	Over 1.3, not over 1.4	5
	Over 1.4	10

[*Cont.*]

TABLE 6-11 [Cont.]
SCHEDULE OF POINT DEDUCTIONS PER SAMPLE OF 10 STICKS

COOKED STATE

Factors Scored	Method of Determining Score	Deduct
7. Distortion	Minor: Bending, shrinking, twisting (1/4 to 1/2 in.). Each affected	1
	Major: Excessive bending, shrinking, twisting (over 1/2 in.). Each affected	2
8. Color	Minor: Sticks differing slightly from average color of sticks in sample unit. Each affected	2
	Major: Sticks excessively dark or light from average color of sticks in sample unit. Each affected	4
	Bare spots, blistering, ridges, breaks, curds[1]	
9. Coating defects	Minor: 1 to 3 instances. Each affected	1
	Major: Over 3 instances. Each affected	3
	Skin, blood spots, bruises, discolorations[1]	
10. Blemishes	Minor: 1 to 6 instances. Each affected	1
	Major: Over 6 instances. Each affected	3
11. Bones	Sticks containing bones (potentially harmful). Each affected	10
Texture:		
12. Coating	Small degree: Moderately dry, soggy, doughy, oily, and tough	5
	Large degree: Farinaceous (mealy), pasty, very tough, and/or oily	15
13. Fish flesh	Small degree: Moderately dry, soft, mushy	5
	Large degree: Dry to the point of fibrousness, very mushy, tough, and rubbery.	15

1. An instance = each 1/16 sq. in. (1/4-in. sq.).

Flounder 5 species: Hippoglossoides platessoides (dab), Glyptocephalus cynoglossus (gray sole), Limanda Ferruginea (yellowtail), Pseudopleuronectes americanus (winter flounder). Also known as blackback, Pseudopleuronectes dignabilis (lemon sole).

Caught along the Atlantic Coast, especially from the Chesapeake Bay to Labrador. Yellowtail, most abundant in June, July, and December; gray sole, abundant from June through November; blackback and lemon sole, abundant May through November, with the blackback peak, June through November, and the lemon sole peak, June and July; and dabs, abundant May through December, with a peak from June through November. Available dressed, pan-dressed, filleted, and round, fresh and frozen. Gray sole is the best-flavored of the flounder, but of the smaller fish, the winter flounder is the meatiest, thickest, and best-flavored. The dab is a good pan fish.

Boston Market			
Blackback	Small	under 3/4 lb.	Round
	Large	3/4 lb. or more	Round
Dab		1 lb. or more	Round
Gray Sole	Small	2 lb. or more	Round
	Large	3 lb. or more	Round
Lemon Sole		3 lb. or more	Round
Yellowtail	Small	under 1 lb.	Round
	Large	1 lb. or more	Round
Gulf States Market	Small	1/2 to 1 lb.	Round
	Large	1 to 5 lb.	Drawn or Round
New York Market			
Blackback	Small	under 3/4 lb.	Round
	Medium	3/4 to 1-1/2 lb.	Round
	Large	1-1/2 lb. or more	Round

Fluke	Medium	1-1/2 to 2 lb.	Round
	Large	2 to 4 lb.	Round
	Jumbo	4 lb. or more	Round
Gray Sole	Small	under 2 lb.	Round
	Large	2 lb. or more	Round
Dab		1 lb. or more	Round
Lemon Sole		3 lb. or more	Round
Yellowtail	Mixed	1/2 to 2-1/2 lb.	Round
	Large	2-1/2 lb. or more	Round

Seattle Market

Dover	Small	10 in. to 23 in.	Round
	Large	24 in. to 30 in.	Round
English	Small	11-1/2 in. to 13 in.	Round
	Large	13 in. or more	Round
Petrale		16 in. to 18 in.	Round

Rex	11-1/2 in. or more	Round
Rock	11-1/2 in. or more	Round
Sand	11-1/2 in. or more	Round
Turbot	3 lb. or more	Round

FLOUNDER AND SOLE FILLETS, FROZEN (10/1/72)

Grade A: May have no more than 15 points deducted for variations in the quality of each factor in accordance with Table 6-12. The total of points deducted is subtracted from 100 to obtain the score, which may not be less than 85.

Grade B: May have no more than 30 points deducted for variations in the quality of each factor in accordance with Table 6-12. The total of points deducted is subtracted from 100 to obtain the score, which must be between 70 and 84.

Substandard: Fails to meet requirements.

TABLE 6-12
SCHEDULE OF POINT DEDUCTIONS PER POUND OF FLOUNDER OR SOLE FILLETS AND GRADING SCORE SHEET

	Scored Factors	Description of Quality Variation		Deduct	Deductions
Frozen	1. Appearance	Adversely affected by imbedded packaging material, voids, depressions, surface irregularity, and poor arrangements of fillets:	Slight / Moderate / Excessive		2 / 4 / 10
	2. Dehydration	For each inch square (determined by grid) of affected area	Color masking easily scraped off / Deep, not easily scraped off		1/2 / 1
Thawed	3. Weights	a. For each fillet or piece less than 1 oz., except first fillet or piece			5
		b. For sole only: For each fillet from 1 to 2 oz., except first fillet			2
		For flounder only: For each fillet from 1 to 2 oz., except first fillets			2
	4. Workmanship defects	For each inch square (determined by grid) of affected area.	a. Cutting and trimming (ragged edges holes, tears, improper, or unnecessary cuts and lace).		1/2
			b. Blemishes (belly lining, blood spots, bruises, extraneous material, fins, discolored pugh marks, scales, and skin)		2
			c. Bones normally removed.		3

[*Cont.*]

TABLE 6-12 [Cont.]
SCHEDULE POINT DEDUCTIONS PER POUND OF FLOUNDER OR SOLE
AND GRADING SCORE SHEET

	Scored Factors	Description of Quality Variation		Deduct	Deductions
	5. Color	a. Deteriorative discoloration (yellowing of fatty portion and/or darkening of light portion)	Slight	2	
			Moderate	5	
			Excessive	15	
		b. Nonuniformity of color (natural color differences within package due to packing fish of contrasting color)	Moderate	3	
			Excessive	5	
	6. Abnormal condition	Usability and/or desirability of fillets impaired by abnormal conditions (jellied, milky, chalky)	Moderate	16	
			Excessive	31	
Cooked	7. Texture	Tough, dry, fibrous, or watery for species involved	Slight	4	
			Moderate	8	
			Excessive	15	
	8. Odor and flavor	Very good: Full typical odor and flavor of fresh fish			
		Good: Noticeable decrease in typical odor and flavor of fresh fish		6	
		Reasonably good: Lacking typical odor and flavor of fresh fish, but not objectionable		16	
		Substandard: Objectionable odor and/or flavor		31	

Total deductions
Score (100 minus total deductions)
Grade (100 to 85 = Grade A; 84 to 70 = Grade B; 69 and below = Substandard)

Label	Actual net weight lb. oz.
Size of lot	Size and kind of container
Size of sample	Container mark or identification
Number of packages per master carton	Type of overwrap
Remarks	

Fluke Paralichthys dentatus. Caught from South Carolina north to Maine, but mostly in New England, from May through July. Available dressed, filleted, pan-dressed and round, fresh and frozen.
Boston and
New York Markets   3 lb. or more   Round

Grouper [Red] Epinephelus morio. Also known as black grouper, gag, nassau grouper, yellow fin grouper, and sea bass. Caught from Virginia to Rio de Janeiro, and mostly sold in Alabama, Louisiana, Mississippi, and Texas, from April to December. Available filleted, drawn, dressed, round, as steaks, fresh, and frozen.
Gulf States Market   5 to 15 lb.   Drawn

Haddock: Melanogrammus aeglefinus. Caught in the North Atlantic and shipped mostly to New York; Groton, Conn.; Boston; Portland, Me.; Gloucester, and Eastport, Me. Available all year, with June to October being the best months in Maine and March and April being the best months in the other markets. Available drawn, dressed, filleted, round, as fresh sticks, and smoked (finnan haddie), but all small sizes are sold round.
Boston Market
   Snapper   less than 1-1/2 lb.   Some drawn,
                                                          most are round

Scrod		1-1/2 to 2-1/2 lb.	Drawn
	Large	over 2-1/2 lb.	Drawn
New York Market			
Small scrod		less than 1 lb.	Drawn
Scrod		1 to 2 lb.	Drawn
Large		2 lb. or more	Drawn

HADDOCK FILLETS, FROZEN (10/1/72)

Grade A — Flavor and odor: The fish flesh has good flavor and odor characteristic of haddock (Melanogrammus aeglefinus) and is free from staleness, off-flavors, and off-odors of any kind. Appearance: (Worth 25 points). Refer to Tables 6-13 and 6-14 for deduction points. Size: (Worth 20 points). Refer to Table 6-15 for deduction points. Defects: (Worth 40 points). Refer to Table 6-16 for deduction points. Character: (Worth 15 points). Refer to Table 6-17 for deduction points. Grade A may have no more than a total of 15 points deducted for variations in quality from Tables 6-15 through 6-17. The total of points deducted is subtracted from 100 to obtain the score, which may not be less than 85.

Grade B — Flavor and odor: The fish flesh may be somewhat lacking in good flavor and odor, but is free of objectionable off-flavors and off-odors of any kind. Appearance, Size, Defects, and Character: Same as Grade A.

Grade B: May have no more than a total of 30 points deducted for variations in quality from Tables 6-13 through 6-17. The total of points deducted is subtracted from 100 to obtain the score, which may not be less than 70.

Substandard: Fails to meet requirements. See score sheet.

TABLE 6-13
SCORE DEDUCTIONS FOR COLOR SUBFACTOR

Color	Deduction Points	
	"Light" Colored Portion Comprising Main Portion of Fillet	"Dark" Colored Portion Occurring under Skin Mainly Along Lateral Line
No discoloration	0	0
Slight yellowing	2	1
Moderate yellowing	4	2
Excessive yellowing and/or any rusting	13	12

TABLE 6-14
SCORE DEDUCTIONS FOR DEHYDRATION SUBFACTOR

Degree of Dehydration	Surface Area Affected [percent]		Deduction Points
	Over	Not Over	
Slight: Shallow and not color masking	0	1	0
	1	50	2
	50	100	5
Moderate: Deep but just deep enough to easily scrape off with finger- nail	1	25	5
	25	50	8
	50	100	16
Excessive: Deep dehy- dration not easily scraped off	1	25	12
	25	100	25

TABLE 6-15
SCORE DEDUCTIONS FOR SIZE OF FILLET PIECES

Number of Fillet Pieces less than 2 Ounces per Pound		
Over	Not Over	Deduction Points
	0	0
0	1	1
1	2	10
2	3	15
3	4	20

TABLE 6-16
SCORE DEDUCTIONS FOR DEFECTS

Defects Subfactors	Method of Determining Subfactor Score	Deduction Points
Improper packing	Moderate defects: Noticeably affecting the product's appearance.	2
	Excessive defects: Seriously affecting product's appearance.	4
Blemishes	Number of blemishes per 1 lb. of fish flesh:	
	Over 0 not over 1	1
	Over 1 not over 2	3
	Over 2 not over 3	5
	Over 3 not over 4	8
	Over 4 not over 5	16
	Over 5 not over 6	30
	Over 6	40
Bones	Number of instances per 1 lb. of fish flesh:	
	Over 0 not over 1	0
	Over 1 not over 2	5
	Over 2 not over 3	10
	Over 3 not over 4	15
	Over 4 not over 5	30
	Over 5	40
Cutting and trimming	Slight defects, scarcely noticeable	0
	Moderate defects, noticeable but not affecting the useability of any fillets	4
	Excessive defects impairing:	
	a. the useability of up to 1/4 of the total number of fillets.	8
	b. the useability of over 1/4 but not more than 1/2 of the total number of fillets.	16
	c. the useability of over 1/2 of the total number of fillets.	40

TABLE 6-17
SCORE DEDUCTIONS FOR CHARACTER

Character Subfactors	Method of Determining Subfactor Score	Deduction Points
Texture	Texture of the cooked fish:	
	a. Firm, slightly resilient, but not tough or rubbery; moist, but not mushy	0
	b. Moderately firm; only slightly tough or rubbery; does not form a fibrous mass in the mouth; moist, but not mushy	4
	c. Moderately tough or rubbery; has noticeable tendency to form a fibrous mass in the mouth; or is dry; or is mushy	8
	d. Excessively tough or rubbery; has marked tendency to form a fibrous mass in the mouth; or is very dry; or is very mushy	15
Amount of drip	Percent of drip:	
	Over 0 not over 5	0
	Over 5 not over 6	1
	Over 6 not over 8	2
	Over 8 not over 10	4
	Over 10 not over 12	6
	Over 12 not over 14	9
	Over 14 not over 16	12
	Over 16	15

SCORE SHEET FOR FROZEN HADDOCK FILLETS

Label:
Size and kind of container:
Container mark or identification:
Size of lot:
Number of packages per master carton:
Size of sample:
Type of overwrap:
Actual net weight: (lb.)   (kg.)

Factor	Score Points	Sample Score
Appearance	25	
Uniformity	20	
Defects	40	
Character	15	
Total	100	

Flavor and odor
Final grade

Hake Urophycis chuss (white hake), Urophycis tenuis (squirrel hake). Also known as black hake, Boston hake, ling, mud hake, and white hake. Caught in the Middle Atlantic states in June through October, with a peak in September. Available drawn, dressed, round, and filleted, dry salted, boneless salted, as smoked fillets, and fresh and frozen sticks and fillets.

Boston Market

Red		1/2 to 1-1/2 lb.	Round
White	Small	2-1/2 to 6 lb.	Dressed
	Large	6 lb. or more	Dressed

New York Market

Red		1/2 to 2 lb.	Round
White	Medium	1 to 3 lb.	Drawn
	Large	3 lb. or more	Dressed

Halibut Hippoglossus vulgaris. Caught in the North Atlantic and Pacific Oceans all year, but most are sold in March through August. Available dressed, filleted, as steaks and center cuts. Most are sold fresh. Atlantic (Eastern) Halibut: Grade No. 1: firm, blue meat. Grade No. 2: white, mushy meat.

Boston Market

Eastern	Snapper	less than 7 lb.	Drawn
	Chicken	7 to 12 lb.	Drawn
	Medium	12 to 60 lb.	Drawn
	Large	60 to 125 lb.	Drawn
	Whole	over 125 lb.	Drawn

New York Market

Eastern: White	Snapper	less than 5 lb.	Drawn and dressed
	Chicken	5 to 10 lb.	Drawn and dressed
	Medium	10 to 50 lb.	Drawn and dressed
	Large	50 to 80 lb.	Drawn and dressed
	Whole	over 80 lb.	Drawn and dressed

Boston, New York, Seattle

Western	Chicken	5 to 10 lb.	Dressed
	Medium	10 to 60 lb.	Dressed
	Large	60 to 80 lb.	Dressed
	Whole	Over 80 lb.	Dressed

Chicago Market

	Chicken	5 to 10 lb.	Dressed
	Medium	10 to 60 lb.	Dressed
	Large and whole	over 60 lb.	Dressed

HALIBUT STEAKS, FROZEN (10/1/72)

Grade A — Flavor and odor: The fish flesh has the good flavor and odor characteristics of halibut, and is free from rancidity, off-flavors and off-odors. Other factors: May have no more than 15 points deducted for variations in the quality of each factor in accordance with Table 6-18. The total of points deducted is subtracted from 100 to obtain the score, which may not be less than 85.

Grade B — Flavor and odor: The fish flesh may be somewhat lacking in good flavor and odor characteristic of halibut; is reasonably free from rancidity and is free from objectionable off-flavors and off-odors. Other factors: May have no more than 30 points deducted for variations in the quality of each factor in accordance with Table 6-18. The total of points deducted is subtracted from 100 to obtain the score, which may not be less than 70.

Substandard: Fails to meet requirements. See score sheet.

TABLE 6-18
SCHEDULE OF POINT DEDUCTIONS FOR FACTORS RATED BY SCORE POINTS[1]

	Factor	Description of Quality Variation	Deduct
Frozen	1. Dehydration[2]	(Per Steak) Surface area affected: Less than 1 sq. in. but obvious 1 to 2 sq. in. Above 2 sq. in.	 1 2 3
	2. Percentage glaze	Over 0.0 not over 6.0 percent by weight of sample unit Over 6.0 not over 7.0 Over 7.0 not over 8.0 Over 8.0 not over 9.0 Over 9.0	0 1 2 3 4
	3. Uniformity of thickness	For each 1/16 in. above 1/8 in. variation in steak thickness (maximum total deduction permitted 6 points per sample unit).	2

	4. Uniformity of weight and minimum weight	Style I — Random weight. Use either (a) or (b), whichever gives a greater deduction.
		    a. For each steak less than 3.0 oz. in weight per sample package.
		    b. For each 0.1 oz. below 4.0 oz. in average steak weight per sample.
		Style II — Uniform weight or portions. For each full 1 percent of the steaks deviating by more than 0.6 oz. from the specified portion weight or the average of the specified portion range (per sample package).
			
			4
			1/2
			2

Thawed	5. Workmanship — Defects of: Cutting, collarbone, loose skin, fins, blood spots, bruises, foreign material, backbone, cartilage, sawdust.	Slight or moderate Excessive (For each defect, per occurrence, per sample package or per 2 lb. for packages over 2 lb. net weight.)	1 2

	Factor	Description of Quality Variation	Deduct
Cooked	6. Color defects: a. Discoloration of drip liquor	(Per Sample Unit) Slight Moderate Excessive	 1 2 3
	b. Discoloration of light meat[2]	(Per Steak) Slight Moderate Excessive	 1 2 3
	c. Discoloration of dark meat[2]	(Per Steak) Slight Moderate Excessive	 1 2 3
	d. Non-uniformity of color	(Per Sample Unit) Slight Moderate Excessive	 1 2 3

	7. Honeycombing[2]	(Per Steak)
		Surface area affected:
		  26 to 50 percent
		  51 to 75 percent
		  76 to 100 percent
			
			1/2
			1
			2

	8. Texture defect[2] (tough, dry, fibrous, or watery)	(Per Steak) Slight Moderate Excessive	 1 2 3

1. This schedule of point deductions is based on the examination of sample units composed of: (a) An entire sample package and its contents (for retail sized packages), or (b) a representative subsample consisting of three or more halibut steaks taken from each sample package (for institutional sized packages), except that the entire sample package shall be examined for factor 4.

2. Point deductions for these factors are based on a 3-steak sample unit. For samples containing other than 3 steaks per sample unit or per package, multiply the results by the correction factor 3/n where n equals the number of steaks.

SCORE SHEET FOR FROZEN HALIBUT STEAKS
GENERAL

Label
Size and kind of container
Container mark or identification
Size of lot
Number of samples
Actual net weight (ounces)
Number of steaks per container
Product style

Scored Factors [Table 6-18]	Deductions
Frozen:	
1. Dehydration	
2. Percentage glaze	
3. Uniformity of thickness	
4. Uniformity of weight	
Thawed:	
5. Workmanship	
6. Color defects	
7. Honeycombing	
Cooked:	
8. Texture	
Total deductions	
Rating for scored factors (100 — Total deductions)	

Unscored Factors	Rating
Cooked:	
a. Odor	
b. Flavor (light meat)	
(dark meat)	
Flavor and odor rating	
Final grade	

King Mackerel Scomberomorus cavallo. Also known as cero and king-fish. Caught in Texas, and from Florida to Massachusetts (but mostly in Florida) in November through March. Available dressed, drawn, as fillets and steaks, fresh, and frozen. Large fish are sold as steaks and small ones are sold whole.

New York Market	Small	less than 5 lb.	Drawn
	Medium	5 to 8 lb.	Drawn
	Large	8 to 12 lb.	Drawn
	Jumbo	12 lb. or more	Drawn

King Whiting Menticirrhus americanus. Also known as kingfish, northern whiting, round head, seaming, sea mink, sea mullet, surf whiting, and whiting. Caught in the South and Middle Atlantic and Chesapeake, in November through February. Available pan-dressed and round, but most are sold fresh.

Gulf States Market			
Mullet		1/2 to 2 lb.	Round
Ground Mullet		1/4 to 1 lb.	Round
New York Market	Small	less than 1 lb.	Round
	Large	over 1 lb.	Round

Lingood Found in the North Pacific all year. Available dressed and filleted.

Mackerel Scomber scombrus. Also known as Boston mackerel. Usually a fatty fish. Available as dressed, round, fillets, some smoked and salted. Best to buy dressed. Most preferable size is 1-1/2 to 2-1/4 lb.

SIZES:

Boston Market	Tack or Spike	Under 1/2 lb.	Round
	Tinker	1/2 to 1 lb.	Round
	Small	1 to 2-1/2 lb.	Round
	Medium	1-1/2 to 2-1/4 lb.	Round
	Large	2-1/4 lb. and up	Round
New York Market	Small	Under 1/2 lb.	Round
	Tinker	1/2 to 3/4 lb.	Round
	Medium	3/4 to 1-1/4 lb.	Round
	Large	1-1/4 lb. and up	Round
Chicago Market		1/2 to 2-1/2 lb.	Round
New York Market	Small	less than 1/2 lb.	Round
	Tinker	1/2 to 3/4 lb.	Round
	Medium	3/4 to 1-1/4 lb.	Round
	Large	1-1/4 lb. or more	Round

Marlin Makaira ampla. Also known as black marlin, blue marlin, striped marlin, and white marlin. Can be bought all year. Available fresh and frozen.

Mullet Mugil cephalus. Also known as common, jumping, silver, striped, white mullet. Caught in the Gulf and South Atlantic, from September to December. Available smoked or dry-salted, fresh or frozen, brine-cured, whole, round, dressed, and as fillets.

Gulf States Market		1/2 to 2 lb.	Round
New York Market	Small	under 3/4 lb.	Round
	Medium	3/4 to 1 lb.	Round
	Large	1 lb. or more	Round

Mussels Mytilus edulis. Also known as bouchets, horse, pleated horse, and mules. Found along the Atlantic Coast during the spring and summer. Available fresh, pickled, and smoked and packed in butter, wine, or olive oil.

Ocean Perch Sebastes marinus. Also known as brim, deep sea perch, red fish, red perch, and rose fish. Caught in deep waters from New Jersey to Greenland, during April through November, with the peak in May through July. Available round, but most are sold as frozen fillets.

| Boston Market | Mixed | 1/2 to 3 lb. | Round |

OCEAN-PERCH AND PACIFIC OCEAN-PERCH FILLETS, FROZEN (10/1/72)

Grade A — Flavor and odor: Fish flesh has good flavor and odor, characteristic of the species (either Sebastes marinus or Sebastodes alutus) and is free from staleness, off-flavors, and off-odors of any kind. Appearance: (Worth 15 points). Refer to Table 6-19 for deduction points. Size: (Worth 20 points). Refer to Table 6-20 for deduction points. Defects: (Worth 50 points). Refer to Table 6-21 for deduction points. Character: (Worth 15 points). Refer to Table 6-22 for deduction points. Grade A may have no more than a total of 15 points deducted for variations in quality from Tables 6-19 through 6-22. The total of points deducted is subtracted from 100 to obtain the score, which may not be less than 85.

Grade B — Flavor and odor: Fish flesh may be somewhat lacking in good flavor and odor and is free from objectionable off-flavors and off-odors of any kind. Appearance, Size, Defects, and Character: Same as Grade A. Grade B may have no more than a total of 30 points deducted for variations in quality from Table 6-19 through 6-22. The total of points deducted is subtracted from 100 to obtain the score, which may not be less than 70.

Substandard: Fails to meet requirements. See score sheet.

TABLE 6-19
SCORED DEDUCTIONS FOR APPEARANCE

Color of Frozen Product			Deduction Points
No discoloration			0
Slight yellowing			4
Moderate yellowing			9
Excessive yellowing and/or rusting			15
		Surface Area affected [percent]	
Degree of Dehydration of Frozen Product	Over	Not Over	
Slight — Shallow and not color masking	0	1	0
	1	50	2
	50	100	5
Moderate — Deep, but just deep enough to easily scrape with fingernail	0	25	5
	25	50	10
	50	100	15
Excessive — Deep dehydration not easily scraped off	0	5	10
	5	100	15

TABLE 6-20
SCORE DEDUCTIONS FOR SIZE OF FILLETS

	NUMBER OF SMALL FILLETS OR PIECES OF FILLETS											
Number of fillets per Pound	0	1	2	3	4	5	6	7	8	9	10	11
	Deduction Points	Deduction Points	Deduction Points	Deduction Points	Deduction Points	Deduction Points	Deduction Points	Deduction Points	Deduction Points	Deduction Points	Deduction Points	Deduction Points
UNDER TWO OUNCES IN WEIGHT												
2	0	5										
3	0	5	10									
4	0	4	7	10								
5	0	4	7	10	15							
6	0	3	6	9	15	20						
UNDER ONE OUNCE IN WEIGHT												
7	0	5	10	15	20	20	20					
8	0	5	10	15	20	20	20	20				
9	0	0	5	10	15	20	20	20	20			
10	0	0	5	10	15	20	20	20	20	20		
11	0	0	5	10	15	20	20	20	20	20	20	
12	0	0	4	7	10	15	15	20	20	20	20	20
13	0	0	0	4	7	10	15	15	15	20	20	20
14	0	0	0	1	4	7	10	15	15	15	20	20
15 or more	0	0	0	0	1	4	7	10	15	15	15	20

TABLE 6-21
SCORE DEDUCTIONS FOR ABSENCE OF DEFECTS

Subfactors	Method of Determining Subfactor Score	Deduction Points
Improper packing	Slight defects, not noticeably affecting the product's appearance	0
	Moderate defects, noticeably affecting the product's appearance	2
	Excessive defects, seriously affecting product's appearance	4
Blemishes	Number of blemishes per 1 lb. of product when there are 6 or less fillets per lb:	
	Over 0 not over 2	0
	Over 2 not over 4	2
	Over 4 not over 5	4
	Over 5 not over 6	7
	Over 6 not over 7	10
	Over 7 not over 8	15
	Over 8 not over 9	20
	Over 9 not over 10	30
	Over 10 not over 11	40
	Over 11	50
	Number of blemishes per 1 lb. of product when there are 7 to 12 (inclusive) fillets per lb.:	
	Over 0 not over 3	0
	Over 3 not over 5	2
	Over 5 not over 6	4
	Over 6 not over 7	7
	Over 7 not over 8	10
	Over 8 not over 9	15
	Over 9 not over 10	20
	Over 10 not over 11	30
	Over 11 not over 12	40
	Over 12	50
	Number of blemishes per 1 lb. of product when there are 13 or more fillets per lb.:	
	Over 0 not over 6	0
	Over 6 not over 8	2
	Over 8 not over 9	4
	Over 9 not over 10	7
	Over 10 not over 11	10
	Over 11 not over 12	15
	Over 12 not over 13	20
	Over 13 not over 14	30
	Over 14 not over 15	40
	Over 15	50
Bones	Number of instances per lb. of product when there are 6 or less fillets per lb.:	
	Over 0 not over 4	0
	Over 4 not over 5	1
	Over 5 not over 6	2
	Over 6 not over 7	5
	Over 7 not over 8	12
	Over 8 not over 9	20
	Over 9 not over 10	35
	Over 10	50
	Number of instances per lb. of product when there are 7 or more fillets per lb.:	
	Over 0 not over 3	0
	Over 3 not over 4	1
	Over 4 not over 5	2
	Over 5 not over 6	5
	Over 6 not over 7	12
	Over 7 not over 8	20
	Over 8 not over 9	35
	Over 9	50
Cutting and trimming	Slight defects, scarcely noticeable	0
	Moderate defects, noticeable but not affecting the usability of any fillets.	4
	Excessive defects impairing:	
	a. The useability of up to 1/4 of the total number of fillets.	
	b. The useability of over 1/4 but not more than 1/2 of the total number of fillets.	
	c. The useability of over 1/2 of the total number of fillets.	

TABLE 6-22
SCORE DEDUCTIONS FOR CHARACTER

Texture of the Cooked Fish	Point Deductions
1. Texture:	
a. Firm, but tender and moist	0
b. Slightly tough, dry, and/or fibrous, or mushy	4
c. Moderately tough, rubbery, and/or fibrous	8
d. Excessively tough, rubbery, and/or fibrous	15

SCORE SHEET

Label
Size and kind of container
Container mark or identification
Size of lot
Number of packages per master carton
Size of sample
Type of overwrap
Actual net weight   (lb.)   (kg.)

Factor	Score Points	Sample Score
Appearance	15	
Size	20	
Absence of defects	50	
Character	15	
Total	100	
Flavor and odor		
Final grade		

Pollock Pollachius virens. Also known as Boston bluefish. Sold September through January and again in May and June, in Maine and Boston. Available dressed, drawn, filleted, fresh, frozen, as dry salted, and fresh steaks.

Boston Market	Scrod	1-1/2 to 4 lb.	Drawn
	Large	4 lb. or more	Drawn
New York Market	Scrod	1 to 4 lb.	Drawn and round
		4 lb. or more	Drawn
	Steak	4 lb. or more	Dressed

Pompano Trachinotus carolinus. Also known as great pompano and Mexican pompano, but both of these fish are often inferior to the real pompano. Caught along the South Atlantic and Gulf coasts, and most is landed in Florida. Caught from January through April. Available round, filleted, fresh, and frozen.

Gulf States Market		1/2 to 3-1/2 lb.	Round
New York Market	Small	less than 3/4 lb.	Round
	Medium	3/4 to 1-1/4 lb.	Round
	Large	1-1/2 to 2-1/2 lb.	Round

Porgies Pagrus pagrus. Also known as common porgie, daughy, jolt head, little head, little mouth, saucer eye, and scuppang. Caught all year, but peak is in summer. Available whole, fresh, and as fillets.

Red Snapper Lutjanus blackfordia. Also known as red cod, red rock cod, red rockfish, and rockfish. Caught from Brazil to Long Island, but mostly in the Gulf of Mexico. The center of the red snapper industry is in Pensacola, Fla. The peak season is October through April. Available drawn, dressed, round, as fillets, and steaks.

Chicago Market		2 to 20 lb.	Drawn
Gulf States Market		2 to 20 lb.	Drawn
New York Market	Small	less than 2 lb.	Drawn
	Medium	2 to 5 lb.	Drawn
	Large	5 lb. or more	Drawn

Sablefish Also known as blackcod. Caught in the North Pacific, from April through November. Available dressed, round, smoked, and as steaks.

Chicago Market	Small	under 5 lb.
	Large	over 5 lb.
Seattle Market	Small	under 5 lb.
	Large	over 5 lb.

Salmon
FIVE VARIETIES:
CHINOOK Oncorhynchus tschawytscha. Finest variety. Also known as blackmouth, king, quinnat, spring, and tyee. Caught in the Pacific Ocean. Available fresh but mostly cured.
SOCKEYE Oncorhynchus nerka. Second best variety. Also known as blueback, quinault, and red salmon. Deep red meat that is rich in oil gives it an excellent quality. Most is canned.
COHO Oncorhynchus kisutch. Third best variety. Also known as medium red, silver, silver-side, and white salmon. Good flavor. Available as frozen, fresh, and canned.
HUMPBACK Oncorhynchus gorbuscha. Fourth best variety. Also known as pink salmon. Pale-pink, good-flavored, soft flesh. Available frozen and fresh, but most are canned.

CHUM Oncorhynchus keta. Also known as dog, fall, and keta. Light yellow, soft flesh with poor flavor. Available frozen and fresh, but most is canned.

Atlantic Salmon Salmo salar. Small importance. Available round and fresh. In season from May through September. Some salmon is sold frozen or fresh, but most is canned.

Chicago Market

Chinook	White	26 in. and over	Dressed
	Small red	Up to 12 lb.	Dressed
	Large red	12 lb. and up	Dressed
Chum		5 to 11 lb.	Dressed
Silver		6 to 12 lb.	Dressed

New York Market

Atlantic		5 lb. and over	Drawn, dressed, round
Chinook	Medium	5 to 10 lb.	Dressed
	Large	10 lb. and up	Dressed
Chum		7 to 10 lb.	Dressed
Silver	Medium	4 to 7 lb.	Dressed
	Large	7 to 10 lb.	Dressed

Seattle Market

Chinook	White	26 in. and up	Drawn
	Small red	Up to 12 lb.	Drawn
	Large red	12 lb. and up	Drawn
Chum		5 to 11 lb.	Round
Pink (Humpback)		4 to 6 lb.	Some drawn, most round
Silver		6 to 12 lb.	Drawn, round

SALMON STEAKS, FROZEN (10/1/72)

Grade A — Flavor and odor: Fish flesh has the good flavor and odor characteristic of the indicated species of salmon and is free from rancidity, off-flavors, and off-odors. Other factors, rated by score points: May have no more than 15 points deducted for variations in the quality of each factor in accordance with Table 6-23. The total of points deducted is subtracted from 100 to obtain the score, which may not be less than 85.

Grade B — Flavor and odor: Fish flesh may be lacking in the good flavor and odor characteristic of the indicated species of salmon, is reasonably free of rancidity, and is free from objectionable off-flavors and off-odors. Other factors, rated by score points: May have no more than 30 points deducted for variations in the quality of each factor in accordance with Table 6-23. The total of points deducted is subtracted from 100 to obtain the score, which may not be less than 70.

Substandard: Fails to meet requirements. See score sheet.

TABLE 6-23
SCHEDULE OF POINT DEDUCTIONS FOR FACTORS RATED BY SCORE POINTS[1]

Scored Factors	Description of Quality Variation	Deduct
FROZEN		
1. General appearance defects	Per occurrence:	
	Slight	1-2
	Moderate	3-4
	Excessive	5-10
2. Dehydration	(Per occurrence) for each 1 sq. in. of surface area	1
3. Uniformity of thickness	For each 1/16 in. above 1/8 in. variation tolerance in steak thickness (max. deduction: 6 points).	2
4. Uniformity of weight and minimum weight	Style I & II — Random weight. For each steak between 2.5 and 3.0 oz. in weight per package, or per lb. of product for packages over 1 lb. net wt.	4
	Style III — Uniform weight or portion. For each 0.1 oz. beyond the 0.1 tolerance of the specified portion weight range per 5 lb. of product.	1

TABLE 6-23 [Cont.]
SCHEDULE OF POINT DEDUCTIONS FOR FACTORS RATED BY SCORE POINTS[1] [Cont.]

Scored Factors	Description of Quality Variations	Deduct
THAWED		
5. Workmanship defects: Blood spots, bruises, cleaning, cutting, fins, foreign material, collarbone, girdle, loose skin, pugh marks, sawdust, scales.	Per occurrence:	
	Slight	1
	Moderate	2-5
	Excessive	5-8
6. Color defects:		
	Slight	1-5
a. Discoloration of fatty portion	Moderate	3-2
	Excessive	6-10
	Slight	1-2
b. Discoloration of lean portion	Moderate	3-5
	Excessive	6-10
	Slight	1-2
c. Non-uniformity of color	Moderate	3-4
	Excessive	5-6
7. Honeycombing	Percent sample area affected:	
	26 to 50	1
	51 to 75	2
	76 to 100	3
COOKED		
	Slight	1-2
8. Texture defect (tough, dry, fibrous, or watery)	Moderate	3-5
	Excessive	6-10
	Good (A)	0-2
9. Odor[2]	Reasonably good (B)	3-5
	Substandard (S)	6-15
10. Flavor:		
	Good (A)	0-2
a. Lean portion	Reasonably good (B)	3-5
	Substandard (S)	6-15
	Good (A)	0-2
b. Fatty portion	Reasonably good (B)	3-5
	Substandard (S)	6-15

1. This schedule of point deductions is based on the examination of sample units composed of: a. An entire sample package and its contents (for retail-sized packages) or b. A representative subsample consisting of about 1 lb. of salmon steaks taken from each sample package (for institutional sized packages), except that the entire sample package or its equivalent shall be examined for factor 4.

2. "Limiting rule" grade requirements of flavor and odor: Salmon steaks which received over 5 deduction points for odor or flavor of the lean or flavor of the fatty portion shall not be graded above substandard, and those which receive between 3 to 5 points shall not be graded above "U.S. Grade B," regardless of the total product socre. (This is a "limiting rule" based on flavor and odor as defined under definitions §268.21(g)(9) and (10)).

SCORE SHEET FOR FROZEN SALMON STEAKS.

Label
Size and kind of container
Container mark or identification
Size of lot
Number of packages per master carton
Size of sample
Number of steaks per container
Product style
Actual net weight   (oz.)   (lb.)

Scored Factors	Deductions
FROZEN	
1. General appearance defects	
2. Dehydration	
3. Uniformity of thickness	
4. Uniformity of weight	
THAWED	
5. Workmanship defects	
6. Color defects	
7. Honeycombing	
COOKED	
8. Texture	
9. Odor (Limiting rule — Table 6-23)	
10. Flavor (Limiting rule — Table 6-23)	
Total deductions	
Product score (100 — Total deductions)	
Flavor and odor rating	
Final grade	

Scup Stenotomus chrysops. Also known as silver bass, porgy, and white bass. Caught from Massachusetts to South Carolina, but mostly in New Jersey. Peak season from April through June in Rhode Island and New Jersey, and in October in Chesapeake Bay. Available fresh, frozen, round, filleted, and pan-dressed.

New York Market	Small	less than 1/2 lb.	Round
	Medium	1/2 to 1 lb.	Round
	Large	1 to 2 lb.	Round

Sea Bass Centropristes striatus. Also known as blackfish, grey bass, and weakfish. Caught from Florida to Massachusetts, but mostly near New Jersey. Peak months are January through April, in Virginia; March through October, in New Jersey; June, in New York; September through November, in California; and the winter months in North Carolina. Available drawn and round.

New York Market	Small	less than 1/2 lb.	Round
	Medium	3/4 to 1 lb.	Round
	Large	1-1/4 lb. or more	Round

Sea Squab Also known as blowfish, globefish, puffer, swellfish, and swell-toad. Caught December through October. Available dressed, fresh, and frozen.

Sea Trout Cynoscion arenarius (Gray squeteague, sand trout, white sea trout). Cynoscion nebulus (Salmon trout, speckled sea trout, spotted trout, spotted weakfish, squeteague). Cynoscion regalis (gray sea trout, salmon trout, speckled trout, weakfish squeteaque). Caught from Texas to North Carolina. Most of the spotted are found in Florida, North Carolina, and Texas, and most of the gray sea trout are found in New Jersey, North Carolina, and Virginia. Peak season is from April to September. Large are available drawn, dressed, and filleted, and small are available round.

Gulf States Market

Spotted	Small	1/2 to 3/4 lb.	Drawn or round
	Medium	3/4 to 1 lb.	Drawn or round
	Large	1 to 4 lb.	Drawn or round
White		1/2 to 1-1/2 lb.	Round

New York Market

Gray	Pin	Under 1/2 lb.	Drawn
	Small	3/4 to 1-1/4 lb.	Drawn
	Medium	1-1/4 to 1-1/2 lb.	Drawn
	Large-Medium	1-1/2 to 3-1/2 lb.	Drawn
	Large	3-1/2 lb. and up	Drawn
	Pin	Under 1/2 lb.	
	Small	3/4 to 1-1/4 lb.	Round
	Medium	1-1/4 to 3-1/2 lb.	Round
	Large	3-1/2 lb. and up	Round
Spotted	Small	Under 1-1/2 lb.	Drawn and round
	Medium	1-1/2 to 3-1/2 lb.	Drawn and round
	Large	3-1/2 lb. and up	Drawn and round

Shad Alosa sapidissima. Caught along Pacific Coast from San Diego, Calif., to British Columbia and along the Atlantic Coast from Long Island to North Carolina. Most are from Maryland and Virginia. Peak season in Maryland, Virginia, North Carolina, and New York is March through May; and peak season in California is April and

May. Available drawn, round, as boneless fillets, frozen, packed in ice.

New York Market	Skip	3/4 to 1-1/2 lb.	Round
	Buck	1-1/2 lb. or more	Round
	Cut	2 lb. or more	Drawn
	Roe	3 lb. or more	Round
Shad Roe	Small	less than 8 oz. per pair	
	Medium	8 to 10 oz. per pair	
	Large	10 to 14 oz. per pair	
	Jumbo	14 oz. or more per pair	

Sheepshead Archosargus probatocephalus. Caught along the Gulf and Atlantic Coasts from Texas to Cape Cod. The center of sheepshead industry is the Gulf of Mexico. Most are caught from April to November. Available filleted and round.

| Gulf States Market | | 1 to 5 lb. | Drawn |

Skates Raja erinaceus. Also known as Erenacca, Laevis, Raie, Rajahfish, Stingray, and Turbot. Caught along the Atlantic Coast year around. Available fresh, frozen, round, or drawn.

| Boston Market | Saddles | 1 to 10 lb. | Drawn or round |
| New York Market | Wings or Saddles | 1 to 10 lb. | Dressed |

Smelts Osmerus mordax. The Atlantic Coast, from Long Island to Canada (mostly Canada), supplies the sea smelt.

Boston Market

Canadian	Medium	less than 5-1/2 in. (15 or more per lb.)	Round
	No. 1	5-1/2 in. to 7 in. (12 to 14 per lb.)	Round
	Extra	more than 7 in. (8 to 10 per lb.)	Round
Native Green	Small	less than 5-1/2 in. (15 or more per lb.)	Round
	Medium	5-1/2 in. to 7 in. (12 to 14 per lb.)	Round
Sea	Large	more than 7 in. (10 or less per lb.)	Round
New Brunswick	Small	less than 4-1/2 in.	Round
	Medium	4-1/2 in. to 5-3/4 in.	Round

	No. 1	5-3/4 in. to 7 in.	Round
	Jumbo	7 in. and more	Round
Seattle Market	Silver	5 to 12 per lb.	Drawn, round
	Eulachon	5 to 8 per lb.	Drawn, round

Spanish Mackerel Scomberomorus maculatus. Caught along the Atlantic Coast from Massachusetts to Brazil, and in the Gulf of Mexico, especially near the Carolinas and the Florida Keys. In New York, from November through May and in North Carolina, from June through August. Available drawn, round, filleted, fresh, and frozen.

Gulf States Market		1 to 3 lb.	Drawn
New York Market	Small	less than 1/2 lb.	Drawn
	Large	1-1/2 lb. or more	Drawn

Spot Leiostomus xanthurus. Also known as goody, hard head, Lafayette, Norfolk spot, and silver gudgeon. Caught from Massachusetts to Texas, especially in North Carolina, New Jersey, and Virginia. Best season is May through October, in Hampton Roads; June through October, in the lower Northern Neck; July through November, in New York, Virginia, and along the Eastern Shore; and September through November, in North Carolina. Available pan dressed, but mostly round, fresh, and frozen. Virginia has the best fish.

New York Market	Small	less than 1/2 lb.	Round
	Medium	1/2 to 3/4 lb.	Round
	Large	3/4 lb. or more	Round

Squid Loligo pealeii. Also known as sea arrows. Found from Nova Scotia to Florida. Available fresh. A favorite food for the Chinese.

Striped Bass Roccus lineatus. Also known as rock, rock bass, and rockfish. Caught from the Gulf of St. Lawrence to Florida, especially in Maryland, North Carolina, and Virginia. Can be bought all year but are in the New York Market from February through April and in October and November. Available drawn and round.

Boston Market	Small	3 to 5 lb.	Round
	Medium	5 to 10 lb.	Round
	Large	10 to 15 lb.	Round
	Jumbo	over 15 lb.	Round
New York Market	Medium	2 to 5 lb.	Round
	Large	5 to 15 lb.	Round
	Jumbo	15 lb. or more	Round

Sturgeon Acipenser oxyrhynchus. Also known as green, sea, white, and common sturgeon. White sturgeon is caught in the Pacific Ocean, and common sturgeon is found in the North. In season all year. Available brined, canned, fresh, frozen, and smoked.

Swordfish Xiphias gladius. Caught in the North Atlantic off the Nova Scotia and New England Coasts. Foreign and domestic catch is shipped to Boston. Frozen swordfish can be bought all year, but fresh fish are in season from June through October, with the peak in August. Available fresh and frozen. Center cuts are best.

Boston Market	Pups	less than 110 lb.	Dressed
	Large	110 lb. or more	Dressed
New York Market			
Fresh	Pups	less than 100 lb.	Dressed
	Large	over 100 lb.	Dressed
Frozen	Chunk	40 to 100 lb.	Portion
	Fillet or Split	50 lb. or more	Sides
	Dressed	over 100 lb.	Dressed

Tuna Thunnus thynnus (bluefin tuna); Thunnus albacores (yellowfin tuna). Also known as bluefin, bonitus, horsemackerel, skipjack, striped albacore, tunny, and yellow fin. Bluefin tuna is caught along the East Coast; albacore is found along the Pacific Coast; and yellowfin is caught in the Gulf stream near Florida. Sold year round. Available fresh, dressed, whole, or as steaks, but most is canned: water or dry, packed in oils, and as chunk, flake, grated, or solid.

Turbot Scophthalmus maximus. Also known as Greenland, halibut, pane, sole, and English sole. Caught from Maine to the Carolinas all year, with peak season being January through March. Available dressed, fresh, frozen, whole, as steaks and fillets.

Turtles Found along the coast of Florida, in the Gulf of Mexico, and along the Nicaraguan coast. In season from June through October. Available live.

Gulf States Market	Fresh water	2 to 100 lb.	Dressed or live
	Sea	10 to 200 lb.	Dressed or live

Whiting Merluccius bilinearis. Also known as silver perch, silver hake, and silver trout. Caught from Newfoundland to the Bahama Islands, including New England and the Middle Atlantic states. Most are found between Cape Sable and Cape Cod. In season from May through August in Maine; May through October in Massachusetts; all year in Chicago and New York; but mostly from May to August in Chicago, and from May to December in New York. Available dressed, round, and as sticks.

Boston Market	Dressed	1/2 to 4 lb.	Drawn
	Round	1/2 to 4 lb.	Round
	Steak	1/2 to 4 lb.	Dressed
New York Market		1/4 lb. or more	Round

HEADLESS DRESSED WHITING, FROZEN (10/1/72)

Grade A — Flavor and odor: The cooked product has the typical flavor and odor of the species and is free from rancidity, bitterness, staleness, off-flavors, and off-odors of any kind. Factors rated by score points: May have no more than 15 points deducted for variations in the quality of each factor in accordance with Table 6-24. The total of points deducted is subtracted from 100 to obtain the score, which may not be less than 85.

Grade B — The cooked product is lacking in good flavor and odor, but is free from objectionable off-flavors and off-odors of any kind. Factors rated by score points: May have no more than 30 points deducted for variations in the quality of each factor in accordance with Table 6-24. The total of points deducted is subtracted from 100 to obtain the score, which may not be less than 70.

Substandard: Fails to meet requirements.

TABLE 6-24
SCHEDULE OF POINT DEDUCTIONS PER SAMPLE
FROZEN STATE [LOT INSPECTION ONLY]

	Factors Scored	Method of Determining Score	Deduct
1.	Arrangement of product[1]	Small degree: 10 percent of fish twisted, or bellies and backs not facing the same direction.	2
		Large degree: More than 10 percent of fish twisted, void present, or some fish cross packed.	5
2.	Condition of packaging (overall assessment)	Poor: Packaging material has been soaked, softened, or deteriorated.	2
3.	Dehydration	Small degree: Slight dehydration of the exposed surfaces	2
		Large degree: Deep dehydration of the exposed surfaces	5

TABLE 6-24 [Cont]
SCHEDULE OF POINT DEDUCTIONS PER SAMPLE

Factors Scored	Method for Determining Score	Deduct
THAWED STATE		

4. Minimum size: Fish 2 oz. or over are of acceptable size.	Number of fish less than 2 oz. per lb.
	   Over 0 not over 0.5
	   Over 0.5 not over 1.0
	   Over 1.0 not over 2.0
	   Over 2.0
		
		5
		10
		20
		30

5. Uniformity: Weight ratio of fish remaining. The 10 percent largest fish divided by the 10 percent smallest fish.[1]	Weight ratio 10 percent smallest and 10 percent largest:
	   Over 2.0 not over 2.4
	   Over 2.4 not over 2.8
	   Over 2.8 not over 3.2
	   Over 3.2 not over 3.6
	   Over 3.6
		
		2
		5
		10
		20
		30

6. Heading [1]	Small degree: 10 percent of fish carelessly cut Moderate degree: Over 10 percent of fish carelessly cut	5 15
7. Evisceration (overall assessment)	Small degree: Slight evidence of viscera Moderate degree: Moderate amounts of spawn, viscera, etc. Large degree: Large amounts of viscera, etc.	2 10 30
8. Scaling[1]	Small degree: 10 percent of fish not well scaled Large degree: Over 10 percent of fish not well scaled	2 5
9. Color of the exposed surfaces (overall assessment)	Small degree: Minor darkening, dulling Large degree: Objectionably dark, brown, dull	2 5

10. Bruises and split or broken skin	Presence of bruises and/or broken or split skin per pound:
	   Over 0 not over 0.5
	   Over 0.5 not over 1.0
	   Over 1.0 not over 1.5
	   Over 1.5 not over 2.0
	   Over 2.0
		
		1
		2
		4
		7
		10

11. Texture: (overall assessment)	Small degree: Moderately dry, tough, mushy, rubbery, watery, stringy Large degree: Excessively dry, tough, mushy, rubbery, watery, stringy	5 15

1. 10 percent of fish refers to 10 percent by count rounded to nearest whole fish.

SHELLFISH, FRESH

When purchasing shellfish, the buyer should be sure that the product is alive. The only exception to this is in the purchase of shrimp, which should be iced. Live shellfish will react to being touched or prodded.

Clams, hard or little-necked Venus mercenaria. Also known as quahaug, butter clam, and little neck. Found mainly in Alaska, Florida, Georgia, New Jersey, New York, Rhode Island, and Washington all year, but mostly in June through September. Sold alive in the shell. Should pull their necks in when tapped.

Boston Market	Little Neck in shell 1-1/2 in. to 2-1/2 in.	500 to 640 per bushel;
	Cherrystone in shell	325 to 360 per bushel; 2 in. to 4 in.
	Sharps in shell	160 to 200 per bushel; over 4 in.
	Sharps shucked	100 to 125 per gal.
New York Market	Little Neck in shell	450 to 650 per bushel
	Cherrystone in shell	300 to 325 per bushel
	Medium in shell	180 per bushel
	Large (chowder) in shell	125 per bushel
Seattle Market	Box in shell	80 lbs.
	Sack in shell	100 lbs.

1 bushel=80 lb.
80 lb. bushel=8 to 8-1/2 lb. of meat
1 gal.=8 lb. in tins
1 gal.=8-1/2 lb. in bulk

Clams, soft or long-necked Mya arenaria. Found from Boston to Arctic Ocean. Sold alive in the shell. Should pull their necks in when tapped.

Boston Market	March through September		
In shell		800 to 1000 per bu.	
Shucked	Small	500 to 700 per gal. (8 lb.)	
	Medium	350 to 500 per gal. (8 lb.)	
	Large	200 to 300 per gal. (8 lb.)	
New York Market	February through October		
In shell	Medium (steamers)	600 to 800 per bu. (60 lb.)	
	Large	400 per bu. (60 lb.)	
Shucked	Small	600 to 700 per gal. (8 lb.)	
	Medium	350 to 400 per gal. (8 lb.)	
	Large	200 to 250 per gal. (8 lb.)	

Crabs Blue crabs are caught along the Atlantic and Gulf Coasts, but most are caught in Chesapeake Bay; and Dungeness crabs are caught along the Pacific Coast, mainly off Grays and Willapa Harbors. Crisfield, Md. is the "crab capital" of the world. Crabs can be bought from April through December, but peak is from June through December. Available live as fresh, as frozen cooked meat, cooked in the shell, and as canned meat. Soft shell, blue crabs are also available live and frozen. Canned crabmeat grades are Fancy, Choice, Passed A, and Fair.

CRABS:

Gulf States Market			
Hard		1/3 to 2/3 lb.	Live
Soft		1/6 to 1/2 lb.	Live
Seattle Market			
Dungeness (Ocean & Puget Sound)		24 lb. per doz.	Live
New York Market			
Hard		all sizes	Live
Soft	Culls	all sizes	Live
	Medium	*less than 3-1/2 in.	Live
	Large		
	Medium	*3-1/2 to 4 in.	Live
	Hotel		
	Prime	*4 to 4-1/2 in.	Live
	Prime	*4-1/2 to 5 in.	Live
	Large		
	Prime	*5 to 5-1/2 in.	Live
	Jumbo	*5-1/2 in.	Live

CRABMEAT:

Boston Market	Broken	1 lb. can	Fresh cooked
	Flake	1/2 and 1 lb. can	Fresh cooked
Seattle Market	King and Dunge-ness	1 and 5 lb. can	Cooked

*Measurements taken across back

New York Market   Claw   claw meat   Cooked
Flake   all white flake meat   Cooked
Mixed, mostly flaked   topped with lump   Cooked
Mixed, mostly lump   Over 1/2 lump   Cooked
Lump   lump only   Cooked
Jumbo lump   all large lump   Cooked

King Crab Caught off the coast of Alaska, in the Bering Sea, and shipped to Seattle. Available frozen.

Seattle Market   Regular   1 and 5 lb. cans   Cooked

Crayfish Astacus fluviatilis. Also known as scampi and Dublin Bay prawns. Found along the Atlantic and Pacific Coasts.

Lobster Homarus americanus. Caught along the Atlantic Coast, mostly in New England, and the Middle Atlantic States. In season all year, with July through October being the peak months. Available boiled and canned, but mostly live.

LOBSTER MEAT: 6 to 14 oz. per can   Cooked

Boston Market
One claw   cull   all sizes   Live
Two claw   Weaks   all sizes   Live
Chicken   1 lb.   Live
Select   1-1/4 to 3 lb.   Live
Jumbo   3 lb. or more   Live
New York Market   Chicken   3/4 to 1 lb.   Live
Quarter   1-1/4 to 1-1/2 lb.   Live
Large   1-1/2 to 2-1/2 lb.   Live
Jumbo   over 3 lb.   Live

Lobster Tails From the spiny lobster (Panulirus argus). Also known as crayfish, rock lobster, and sea crawfish. Caught in subtropical and tropical waters. Most are shipped to California, but some go to Florida. In season all year, but the peak is December through May. Available boiled, canned, fresh, and frozen. The best are South African, second best Cuban, with Florida third best.

Boston Market   Rock Crab   1/3 to 1/2 lb.   Live
Chicago Market   Common   Live
Spiny   Tail

New York Market   Small   6 to 9 oz.   Tail
Medium   6 to 12 oz.   Tail
Large   12 to 16 oz.   Tail
Jumbo   16 oz. or more   Tail

Oysters [in shell] Found along the Atlantic Coast, especially near Virginia, New York, and Massachusetts. In season year round. Best are thin, broad, tough-shelled, Northern oysters.

Boston Market   September through April
Extra small   1050 to 2000 per bbl.
Small   900 to 1050 per bbl.
Medium   700 to 750 per bbl.
Large   500 per bbl.
New York Market   Bluepoint 400 per bu.
Half shell 325 per bu.
Medium 200 per bu.
Box 150 per bu.

Oysters [shucked] Found from Virginia to Rhode Island, and along the Gulf Coast, from September through April. Packed in cans. Northern oysters are best. Do not freeze oysters.

Boston Market   Standard 300 to 350 per gal.
Select 180 to 230 per gal.
Count 100 to 135 per gal.
New York Market   September through April
Standard 300 to 500 per gal.
Select 210 to 300 per gal.
Extra select 160 to 210 per gal.
Count under 160 per gal.
Seattle Market
Olympia   1500 to 1600 per gal.
Pacific   Large   64 or less per gal.
(Washington)   Medium   65 to 94 per gal.
(Olympic)   Extra small   over 144 per gal.
Small   97 to 144 per gal.
Breaded   16 per lb.   Frozen
Selects   2-1/2-lb. carton   Frozen

Scallops Pecten irradians. Mostly from the Atlantic Coast, with some from the Gulf of Mexico and Puget Sound. Caught all year, but the peak is from April to October. Most are sold fresh.

Boston Market   Bay   500 to 850 per gal.
(9 lb. gal.)   Shucked

	Sea	110 to 170 per gal.	Shucked
Chicago Market			Shucked
New York Market	Bay	small less than 1/2 in. diameter	Shucked
	Medium	1/2 in. to 3/4 in. diameter	Shucked
	Large	3/4 in. diameter	Shucked
	Sea	all sizes	Shucked
Seattle Market	Bay	Gal. 8-1/2 lb.	Shucked
		Sack	60 lb.

RAW SCALLOPS, FROZEN (10/1/72)

Grade A — Flavor and odor: Has the typical flavor and odor of the species, and is free from bitterness, staleness, off-flavors, and off-odors of any kind. Factors rated by score points: May have no more than 15 points deducted for variations in the quality of each factor in accordance with Table 6-25. The total of points deducted is subtracted from 100 to obtain the score, which may not be less than 85.

Grade B — Flavor and odor: Lacking in good flavor and odor, but is free from objectionable off-flavors and off-odors of any kind. Factors rated by score points: May have no more than 30 points deducted for variations in the quality of each factor in accordance with Table 6-25. The total of points deducted is subtracted from 100 to obtain the score, which may not be less than 70.

Substandard: Fails to meet requirements.

TABLE 6-25
SCHEDULE OF POINT DEDUCTIONS PER SAMPLE

FROZEN STATE

Factors Scored	Method of Determining Score	Deduct
1. Dehydration	Small degree: Easily scraped off of each 10 percent of top surface affected	2
	Large degree: Deep dehydration not easily scraped off, affecting each 10 percent of surface	4
FRESH OR THAWED STATE		
2. Undesirable pieces	Percent by weight:	
	Up to 5 percent	3
	Over 5 percent not over 10 percent	6
	Over 10 percent	16

Factors Scored	Method of Determining Score	Deduct
3. Uniformity	Weight ratio:	
	Over 2.5 not over 3.0	4
	Over 3.0 not over 3.3	6
	Over 3.3	10
4. Color	Each 10 percent by count of nonuniform colored scallops, in excess of the 10 percent of non-uniform colored scallops permitted	10
5. Extraneous material	Minor: Each instance of minor extraneous material in the sample unit per pound	1
	Major: Each instance of major extraneous material in the sample unit per pound	5
COOKED STATE		
6. Texture	Firm but tender and moist	0
	Small degree: Moderately tough, dry, and fibrous, or mushy	5
	Large degree: Excessively tough, dry and fibrous, or mushy	15

FRIED SCALLOPS, FROZEN (10/1/72)

Grade A — Flavor and odor: The cooked product has flavor and odor characteristic of good scallop meat and of the breading, and is free from staleness, off-flavors and off-odors of any kind. Appearance: (Worth 25 points). Refer to Table 6-26 for deduction points. Uniformity: (Worth 20 points). Refer to Table 6-27 for deduction points. Defects: (Worth 40 points). Refer to Table 6-28 and 6-29 for deduction points. Character: (Worth 15 points). Refer to Table 6-30 for deduction points. Grade A may have no more than a total of 15 points deducted for variations in quality from Tables 6-26 through 6-30. The total of points deducted is subtracted from 100 to obtain the score, which may not be less than 85.

Grade B — Flavor and odor: The cooked product is lacking in good flavor and odor, but is free from objectionable off-flavors and off-odors of any kind. Appearance, Uniformity, Defects, and Character: Same as Grade A. Grade B may have no more than a total of 30 points deducted for variations in quality from Tables 6-26 through 6-30. The total of points deducted is subtracted from 100 to obtain the score, which may not be less than 70.

Substandard: Fails to meet requirements.

TABLE 6-26

SCHEDULE OF POINT-DEDUCTIONS FOR VARIATIONS IN APPEARANCE

Appearance Subfactors	Method of determining Subfactor Score			Deduction Points
Condition of the package in the frozen state	**Degree of condition of the package**			
	a. Small (Moderate amount of free oil and/or loose breading and/or frost and/or packaging defects)			2
	b. Large (excessive amount of free oil and/or loose breading and/or frost and/or packaging defects)			5
		Percent of Scallops Affected		
	Degree of ease of separation	**Over**	**Not Over**	
Ease of separation of the scallops in frozen state	Moderate (scallops separated by hand with difficulty)	0	30	1
		30	70	2
		70		3
	Severe (scallops separated only by use of knife or other instrument)	0	30	4
		30	70	10
		70		15
Continuity of the scallops in the cooked state	Lack of continuity (breaks, ridges, and lumps)[1]	0	20	2
		20	50	4
		50	70	6
	Small (1 to 3 instances per scallop)	70		10
		0	20	4
	Large (over 3 instances per scallop)	20	50	8
		50	70	12
		70		25
Color of the scallops in the cooked state	**Deviation from predominating color of fried scallops in cooked state**			
	Small instance of deviation in color means that the scallop varies noticeably from the predominating color of the package after cooking.	0	10	0
		10	30	2
		30		4
	Large instance of deviation in color means that the scallop varies markedly from the predominating color of the package after cooking.	0	10	4
		10	30	10
		30		25

1. Each 1/16 sq. in. is considered an instance.

TABLE 6-27
SCHEDULE OF POINT-DEDUCTIONS FOR UNIFORMITY

Factor	Method of Determining Subfactor Score			Deduction Points
		Percent of scallops Affected		
	A. Style I [Random pack]	**Over**	**Not over**	
	a. Undesirable small pieces which pass through a sieve with 3/4 in. openings	0	10	3
		10	20	6
		20		10
		Ratio		
		Over	**Not over**	
Uniformity of size and weight of scallops in frozen state	b. Weight ratio of scallops remaining in the sieve. The 15 percent largest scallops (minimum 3) divided by the 15 percent smallest scallops (minimum 3). The 15 percent to be determined by count.		2.0	0
		2.0	2.5	1
		2.5	2.9	3
		2.9	3.3	6
		3.3		10
	B. Style II [Uniform pack]	**Percent of scallops Affected**		
	Deviation from average weight	**Over**	**Not Over**	
	a. Small (scallops deviating = 10 to 20 percent from average weight)	0	30	3
		30	70	5
		70		10
	b. Large (scallops deviating over = 20 percent from average weight)	0	30	6
		30	70	10
		70		20

TABLE 6-28

SCHEDULE OF POINT-DEDUCTIONS FOR ABSENCE OF DEFECTS, SUBFACTORS, MISSHAPED OR DOUBLED SCALLOPS, AND SHELL FRAGMENTS

Defect Subfactors	Method of Determining Subfactor Score	Percent of Scallops Affected		Deduction Points
		Over	Not Over	
Misshaped or doubled scallops in the frozen state	Misshaped scallops (elongated, flattened, mashed, or damaged scallop meats)	0	10	3
		10	20	7
	Doubled scallops (two or more scallops joined together during breading and/or frying operation)	20		15
Shell fragments in the cooked state	Each piece of shall fragment is considered an instance	0	5	15
		5	10	30
		10		40

TABLE 6-29

SCHEDULE OF POINT-DEDUCTIONS FOR ABSENCE OF DEFECTS SUBFACTOR OF EXTRANEOUS MATERIAL

Number of scallops per 7 oz.	Number of instances of extraneous material								
	0	1	2	3	4	5	6	7	8 or more
	Deduction Points								
10 or less	0	7	15	25	40				
11	0	6	15	25	40				
12	0	5	13	25	40				
13	0	5	11	25	40				
14	0	4	10	15	28	40			
15	0	4	9	15	25	40			
16	0	3	8	13	25	40			
17	0	3	8	12	20	30	40		
18	0	2	7	10	18	28	40		
19	0	2	6	9	15	25	40		
20 or more	0	2	5	8	12	20	30	40	

TABLE 6-30

SCHEDULE OF POINT-DEDUCTIONS FOR CHARACTER SUBFACTOR OF TEXTURE

Character Subfactors	Method of Determining Subfactor Score	Deduction Points
	Texture of the Coating	
Texture in the cooked state	Firm or crisp but not tough, pasty, mushy, or oily	0
	Moderately tough, pasty, mushy, or oily	5
	Excessively tough, pasty, mushy, or oily	15
	Texture of the Scallop Meat	
	Firm, but tender, and moist	0
	Moderately tough, dry, and/or fibrous, or mushy	5
	Excessively tough, dry, and/or fibrous, or mushy	15

Shrimp Penaeus setiferus. In season all year, with the peak season being January through April for frozen holdings; May through August, in the North Carolina Market; June through September, in the New York Market; July through September, in the California Market; and August through October, in the Gulf Market. Available beheaded and packed in ice.

Chicago Market	Very Small	66 or more per lb.	Headless
	Small	43 to 65 per lb.	Headless
	Medium	31 to 42 per lb.	Headless
	Large Medium	26 to 30 per lb.	Headless
	Large	21 to 25 per lb.	Headless
	Jumbo	15 to 20 per lb.	Headless
	Extra Jumbo	less than 15 per lb.	Headless
Gulf States Market	Small	over 35 per lb.	With heads on
	Medium	18 to 35 per lb.	With heads on
	Large	less than 18 per lb.	With heads on
New York Market			
	Small	more than 60 per lb.	Headless
		51 to 60 per lb.	Headless
		46 to 50 per lb.	Headless
		41 to 45 per lb.	Headless
	Medium	36 to 40 per lb.	Headless
		31 to 35 per lb.	Headless
Large	26 to 30 per lb.	Headless
	21 to 25 per lb.	Headless
Jumbo	15 to 20 per lb.	Headless
	less than 15 per lb.	Headless
Seattle Market	1 and 5 lb. cans	Fresh cooked

RAW HEADLESS SHRIMP, FROZEN (10/1/72)

Grade A — Flavor and odor: Has the good flavor and odor characteristic of freshly caught, chilled shrimp, and is free from off-flavors and off-odors of any kind. The presence of iodoform-like flavor and odor is not to be construed as off-flavor and off-odor. Factors rated by score points: May have no more than 10 points deducted for variations in the quality of each factor in accordance with Table 6-31. The total of points deducted is subtracted from 100 to obtain the score, which may not be less than 90.

Grade B — Flavor and odor: May be somewhat lacking in the good flavor and odor characteristic of freshly caught, chilled shrimp, but is free from objectionable off-flavors and off-odors of any kind. Factors rated by score points: May have no more than 20 points deducted for variations in the quality of each factor in accordance with Table 6-31. The total of points deducted is subtracted from 100 to obtain the score, which may be no less than 80.

Grade C — Flavor and odor: Same as Grade B. Factors rated by score points: May have no more than 30 points deducted for variations in the quality of each factor in accordance with Table 6-31. The total of points deducted is subtracted from 100 to obtain the score, which may not be less than 70.

Substandard: Fails to meet requirements. See score sheet.

TABLE 6-31
SCHEDULE OF DEDUCTIONS FOR FACTORS RATED BY SCORE POINTS[1]

State	Factor	Description of Quality Variation			Deduct
		Dehydrated — exposed ends		Desiccation of meat	
		Frozen State	Thawed State	Thawed State	
Frozen and thawed	Dehydration	Up to 5 percent	None	None	0
		5.1 - 15.0 percent	Up to 2.0 percent	Slight	3
			2.1 - 5.0 percent	Moderate	6
		Over 15.0 percent	Over 5.0 percent	Marked	11
		(Percent by count of total sample) Apply the one highest deduction only.			

[Cont.]

TABLE 6-31 [Cont.]
SCHEDULE OF DEDUCTIONS FOR FACTORS RATED BY SCORE POINTS[1]

State	Factor	Description of Quality Variation	Deduct

Thawed	Deterioration	Off-odor, overall sample:
		  Slight
		  Moderate
		  Marked
		  Any excessive, each 1 percent or fraction (percent by count)
			
			2
			6
			21
			5

	Black spot on shell or loose membrane only	Shell affected, but not meat:
		  Not over 5 percent
		  Each additional 5 percent or fraction (percent by count)
			
			0
			1

	Black spot on meat	None Not over 3 percent 3.1 to 5.0 percent Each additional 5 percent or fraction (percent by count)	0 1 2 2
	Broken, damaged, and pieces	Not over 1 percent 1.1 to 3.0 percent Each additional 3 percent or fraction (percent by weight)	0 2 2
	Legs, loose shell, and flippers	Not over 3 percent Each additional 3 percent or fraction (percent by count)	0 2
	Heads and unacceptable shrimp	Not over 1 percent Each additional 1 percent or fraction (percent by count)	2 3
	Extraneous material	1 piece 2 pieces Over 2 pieces	1 2 4
	Uniformity of size	Slightly large and slightly small: Each 3 percent or fraction Exceedingly large and exceedingly small: Each 3 percent or fraction (percent by count — based on actual count per pound of sample)	1 2

Cooked	Texture	Tough, dry, or mushy:
		  Slight
		  Moderate
		  Excessive
			
			2
			4
			11

1. This schedule of point deductions is based on the examination of sample unit composed of: a. The contents of an entire package or b. sufficient packages to provide a sample unit of 2 lb. or more declared net weight.

SCORE SHEET FOR FROZEN RAW HEADLESS SHRIMP.

GENERAL

Label
Size and kind of container
Container mark or identification
Size of lot
Number of samples
Declared count per pound
Actual net weight (ounces)
Actual count per pound
Descriptive size name

Scored factors [Table 6-30]	Deductions
Frozen and thawed:	
1. Dehydration	
Thawed:	
2. Deterioration	
3. Black spot on shell or loose membrane only	
4. Black spot on meat	
5. Broken, damaged, and pieces	
6. Legs, loose shell, and flippers	
7. Heads and unacceptable shrimp	
8. Extraneous material	
9. Uniformity of size	
Cooked:	
10. Texture	
Total deductions	
Rating for scored factors (100 minus total deductions)	
Flavor and odor	
Final grade	

SHRIMP, FROZEN, RAW, BREADED (3/30/73)

Grade A — Flavor and odor: The cooked product has flavor and odor characteristic of freshly caught or well-refrigerated shrimp, and the breading is free from staleness, off-flavors, and off-odors of any kind. Iodoform is not to be considered in evaluating the product for flavor and odor. Factors evaluated on breaded shrimp: Uniformity of size, condition of coating, extraneous material, and damaged, breaded shrimp, based on the examination of one complete individual package or sample unit, regardless of the net weight of the package. Ease of separation shall also be rated in addition to the above factors, when frozen, raw, breaded shrimp is inspected. (See Table 6-32.) Factors evaluated on unbreaded or thawed, debreaded shrimp: Degree of deterioration, dehydration, sand veins, black spots, extra shell, extraneous material, and swimmerets, based on the examination of 20 whole shrimp. (See Table 6-33.) General: May have no more than 15 points deducted for variations in the quality in accordance with Tables 6-32 and 6-33.

Grade B — Flavor and odor: The cooked product may be somewhat lacking in the good flavor and odor characteristic of freshly caught or well-refrigerated shrimp, but is free from objectionable off-flavors and off-odors of any kind. Factors evaluated on breaded shrimp: Same as Grade A. Factors evaluated on unbreaded or thawed debreaded shrimp: Same as Grade A. General: May have no more than 30 points deducted for variations in the quality in accordance with Tables 6-32 and 6-33.

Substandard: Fails to meet requirements.

TABLE 6-32
SCHEDULE OF POINT DEDUCTIONS FOR RATING IN BREADED STATE

Factor	Quality Description	Deductions Allowed
		Points
1. Ease of separation in the frozen state	Separate easily after being removed from carton and exposed to room temperature for not more than 4 minutes	3
	Separate easily after being removed from carton and exposed to room temperature for not more than 6 minutes	6
	Does not separate easily after being removed from carton and exposed to room temperature for 6 minutes	10
2. Uniformity	Ratio of weight of largest to smallest breaded shrimp in sample unit:	
	Up to 1.50	0
	1.51 to 1.60	1
	1.61 to 1.70	2
	1.71 to 1.80	3
	1.81 to 1.90	4
	1.91 to 2.00	5
	2.01 to 2.10	6
	2.11 to 2.20	7
	2.21 to 2.30	8
	2.31 to 2.40	9
	Over 2.40	10
3. Condition of coating	Degree of halo or balling up or holidays (identify type of defect by circling the proper word):	
	Slight — each 20 percent by count or fraction thereof	1
	Moderate — each 20 percent by count or fraction thereof	2
	Marked — each 20 percent by count or fraction thereof	4
	Excessive — each 20 percent by count or fraction thereof	16
4. Damaged breaded shrimp	For each 5 percent by count or fraction thereof	3
	Tail fin broken or missing, each 5 percent or fraction thereof (except in Type I, subtype C, and Type II, subtype C)	1
5. Extraneous material	If extraneous material, except filthy or deleterious substances, is found in more than one package per lot, the entire lot shall be declared substandard.[1]	

1. Filthy or deleterious substances in food products constitute a violation of the Food, Drug, and Cosmetic Act. Products containing such substances are ineligible for the purpose of applying this document.

TABLE 6-33
SCHEDULE FOR POINT DEDUCTIONS FOR EXAMINATIONS IN UNBREADED OR THAWED, DEBREADED; STATE DEDUCTIONS BASED ON 20 SHRIMP

[Subtotals brought forward]

Factor	Quality Description	Deductions Allowed
		Points
1. Degree of dehydration	Slight — each shrimp	1
	Moderate — each shrimp	2
	Marked — each shrimp	3
	Excessive — each shrimp	16
2. Deterioration	Slight — each shrimp	2
	Moderate — each shrimp	5
	Marked — each shrimp	10
	Excessive — each shrimp (provided that if excessive deterioration occurs in more than one sample unit per sample, the entire lot shall be declared substandard).	20
3. Sand veins where applicable[1]	For each dark vein present, deduct according to the following schedule:	
	Equivalent in length to two segments	1
	Equivalent in length to three segments	2
	Equivalent in length to four or more segments	3
4. Black spot	Slight but obvious, on average	3
	Moderate, on average	6
	Marked, each shrimp	3
5. Extra shell (see subtypes definition)	Beyond first segment adjacent to tail fin only for Type I, subtype A, and Type II, subtype A:	
	Less than one whole extra shell segment	1
	One extra segment or more	3
6. Swimmerets	For last pair only adjacent to tail fins	1
	For more than last pair	3
7. Extraneous material	If extraneous material, except filthy or deleterious substances, are found in more than one package per lot, the entire lot shall be declared substandard.[2]	

1. Deduction points for sand veins shall not be applied to shrimp smaller than 70 count per pound in the raw, headless state. The corresponding size in the breaded state is 40 count per pound and 80 count per pound in the peeled state.
2. Filthy or deleterious substances in food products constitute a violation of the Food, Drug, and Cosmetic Act. Products containing such substances are ineligible for the purpose of applying this document.

Product	Description	Pack
Clams	East Coast Quahog or steamer clams used for clam strips; breaded, sliced, raw, IQF	4 to 6 oz. bags
	Shucked clams sold by count:	6 lb. gal.
	Cherrystones — 131 to 188 to gal.	
	Medium — 82 to 131 to gal.	
	Cherrystones — 131 to 188 to gal.	
	Littlenecks — more than 188 to a gal.	
	Prepared, seasoned, littleneck or cherrystone clams on half shell available, IQF and in these combinations: Clams Oreganata; Clams Casino; Clams Bienville; Clams Mornay; Clams Rockefeller.	
	West Coast Clams available on regional basis	
Crabs	Alaska King Crab, frozen whole, or split legs, leg and body crabmeat.	6 to 24 lb.
	Blue Crab, soft shell, whole, plain, breaded	4 oz. to 1 lb.
	Blue Crab, hard shell, lump crabmeat picked, and packed.	1 lb. container
	Stone Crab — claws	10 to 25 per lb.
Lobster	Maine Lobster, whole, frozen in shell, lobster meat in brine	14 oz. tin, 1 lb. bag
	Rock lobster tails, from South Africa, New Zealand, Australia (cold water)	2 oz. to 12 oz.
	Warm water rock lobster tails also available.	2 oz. to 10 oz.
	Slipper lobster (shellfish of rock Lobster family) available with Oriental style crumb breading, precooked or raw	1-1/2 oz.
Oysters	Eastern (Blue Points, Long Island, Lynn Haven), shucked, packed in own liquor, sold by count:	1 gal. container
	Counts — less than 113	
	Ex. Selects — 114 to 148	
	Selects — 149 to 212	
	Small Standards — 213 to 352	
	Very small — more than 352	
	West Coast, (Olympia) by count:	
	Large — less than 45	
	Medium — 46 to 68	
	Small — 69 to 101	
	Extra Small — more than 102	
	Oysters also sold on half shell and flavored, as:	
	Oysters Rockefeller, Oysters Bienville, Oysters Mornay, Oysters Provencal.	

Product	Description	Pack
Scallops	Bay or Sea, available shucked plain or breaded, raw/precooked, IQF, or block frozen, glazed/unglazed, natural cubed, sized by number of pieces to pound. Breaded have 60 percent meat. Bay (smaller, more delicate)	40 to lb.
	Sea (larger, often cut into smaller pieces)	10, 15 to lb.
Shrimp	Frozen shrimp available in variety of forms and sizes	5 to 10 lb. boxes
	Headless queen shrimp, can be glazed and IQF, but usually bulk frozen.	
	Peeled, deveined (PD), usually IQF, glazed or bulk	5 lb. boxes
	Peeled, deveined, cooked (PDC), IQF	3,4,5, lb. boxes, bag
	Breaded shrimp, peeled, deveined, with/ without tails	2-1/2,3,4,5, lb. boxes
	Regular must contain 50 percent shrimp. Variety of breading and styles, including butterfly; may be raw, cooked, or pre-browned.	
	Shrimp, stuffed are breaded, butterfly shrimp filled with crabmeat and breadcrumb mixture.	3 to 6 oz.
	Shrimp Steaks — broken or imperfect PDC shrimp, block frozen, sliced in squares or rectangles, usually breaded.	
	Extruded Breaded Shrimp — minced or ground shrimp, shaped in sticks or shrimp shapes, usually mixed with breading, cooked or prebrowned.	1/3 to 1-1/2 oz.
	Size of shrimp based on count per pound.	
	Large: Extra colossal, colossal, extra jumbo, jumbo, extra large, large, from 10 to 30 per lb.	
	Medium: Medium large, medium, from 36 to 50 per lb.	
	Small: Small, extra small, tiny, from 50 to over 70 per lb.	
Snails	Prepared, heat and serve in shell or mushroom	poly bags, 72 per bag

FISH AND SHELLFISH

Factors relating to specified weights of fish and shellfish[1]

Specification	Factors for converting to			
	Round weight[2]	Reported weight[3]	Dressed weight[4]	Edible weight[5]
Fish, fresh and frozen:				
Not packaged, domestically produced:				
Round weight	1.000	1.000	0.700	0.450
Dressed weight	1.429	—	1.000	0.643
Edible weight	2.222	—	1.556	1.000
Packaged, domestically produced:				
Round weight	1.000	0.338	—	0.338
Packaged weight	2.959	1.000	—	1.000
Imports, reported weight	1.948	1.000	1.364	0.877
Shellfish, fresh and frozen:				
Not packaged:				
(shrimp, oysters, crab, lobster, etc.)				
Reported weight	—	1.000	—	0.450
Edible weight	—	2.222	—	1.000
Packaged: (including fresh shucked oysters, clams, shrimp, etc.)	—	1.000	—	1.000
Fish, cured, all types:				
(includes smoked, pickled, salted and dried fish):				
Reported weight (i.e., cured weight)	1.500	1.000	—	0.750
Edible weight	2.000	1.333	—	1.000

1. Factors are for specified groups and are not applicable to individual species.
2. Weight of the fish as removed from the water.
3. Production as reported to the Fish and Wildlife Service; imports as reported by the Bureau of the Census.
4. Weight of fin fish after removal of entrails, head, tail, and fins.
5. Weight of the edible portion of the fish or shellfish.

SHELLFISH

Net weight per gallon of specified shellfish

Product	Pounds per gallon
Clams	8.75
Oysters	8.75
Scallops	8.75

FISH, CANNED

Anchovies Part of the herring family. Anchovies in oil are produced in Portugal, Spain, and Italy. Salted anchovies, available beheaded, eviscerated, whole, and as fillets, are packed in bottles, kegs, and tins.

Containers	Amount in container
per oz.	5 to 6
2 oz.	10 to 12
13 oz.	75 to 90
29 oz.	165 to 180

Caviar Salted roe of fish, mostly made from the roe of sturgeon.

Four grades: 1. Sevruga
2. Osetrina
3. Beluga
4. Pressed

Clams [Canned]

Minced	12/51 oz.
	48/7 oz.
Whole	24/No. 2
	24/16 oz.
	48/16 oz.

Codfish, Dried [Canned] Can be bought in bits, threads, shredded, middles, cut pieces, medium, and large sizes. Available in 40, 20, 3 and 1 lb. containers.

Crabmeat (canned)	Pound
	12/2-1/2 lb.
	24/13 oz.
	48/7-1/2 oz.

Herring [Canned] Pacific Coast: Clupea pallasii. Atlantic Coast: Clupea harengus. Available fresh (round), but most are used for pickling, and sardines, such as Bismarck herring; Holland herring; Marinated herring; Rollmop, and Scotch; cured herring.

Containers			
	Bismarck	14 oz. jar	
		16 oz. jar	
	Holland	9 lb. keg	37/40 (3-1/2 oz. each
	Matjes	5 lb. pail	9 (9 oz. each)
		10 lb. pail	18 (9 oz. each)
	No. 1 can	15 oz.	5 pieces
	No. 2 can	20 oz.	15/17
	No. 4 can	60 oz.	30/34

Herring [Sardines] In season in California, from August to February, and in Maine, from April through November. Packed in cottonseed oil, mustard, olive oil, and tomato sauce. The best is Norwegian bristling; second best is "musse" from Norway, and the lowest class is from Maine, packed in cottonseed oil.

Container	Weight	Amount in container
1/16	1-1/2 oz.	8/10
		10/12
		10/14
1/8	2-1/2 oz.	6/8
		8/12
1/4	3-3/4 oz.	6/8
		8/12
		16/20
		20/24
		22/28
		30/35

Lobster [Canned]	48/6 oz.
Oysters [Canned]	24/4 2/3 oz.
Oyster Stew	24/8 oz.

Salmon Prepared from species of fishes deemed to be Salmon (See Types), properly cleaned, washed, and trimmed; free from extraneous tissue, and debris; and packed with added salt.

Chinook-Called Chinook on the Columbia River, this same species is called Spring Salmon on the Puget Sound, and in Alaska, is known as King Salmon. This salmon is recognized as the largest and most valuable of the salmon species. Some fish weighing as much as 100 lb. are caught but the average weight is about 22 lb. Chinook Salmon is graded Fancy, Choice and Standard according to color, which ranges from red to white. The large flakes and abundance of oil give this salmon a very tender texture so that it is more suitable for salads than for cooked dishes. Usually, Chinook Salmon commands a premium over the other varieties because it has a higher food value, and also because less of it is caught.

Sockeye-Known as Sockeye on Puget Sound, Alaska Red in Alaska, and called Blueback on the Columbia River because of the beautiful blue color on its back above the silver. This salmon possesses a deep red flesh and considerable oil. The flake is small and firm. Average weight of the fish is about 7 lb. Of this group, the Puget Sound Sockeye Salmon is especially attractive, and generally commands a premium. The sockeye is a great source of salmon for canning, and is especially valuable because of its attractiveness as well as from a nutritional point of view. Excellent eaten cold or in salads. Also delicious in cooked dishes.

Coho-Also known as Silver, or Medium Red Salmon. It usually weighs about 8 lb. but has been known to weigh 30 lb. The fish has a pleasing flavor but the paleness of the flesh (it is red in color but usually much lighter than the Sockeye) is a serious handicap to its commercial sale. Coho Salmon is very good eaten cold or in salads, and is especially nice in cooked dishes.

Pink The smallest and most numerous of the American species-average weight is about 4 lb. Half of the American pack consists of Pink Salmon. Its flesh is pale in color, and also a bit softer than the other species. The great abundance of this type brings the price very low.

Chum-Also called Keta Salmon. Average weight is about 8 lb. It is the chief salmon in Japan. Due principally to its lack of color, and because it is sometimes low in oil content, Chum Salmon is the cheapest of all the salmons. The red color is more pleasing to most people, and has become associated with fine salmon in this country. However, the light-meated varieties are just as palatable and nutritious as the more highly colored species, and as folks learn these facts, light meated varieties will become more valuable.

Common Available Can Sizes:

1/4-lb. Flat — 3-1/16 in. by 1-6/16 in. Label contents: 3-3/4 oz.
1/2-lb. Flat — 3-7/16 in. by 2-1/16 in. Label contents: 7-3/4 oz.
1-lb. Flat — 4-1/16 in. by 2-11/16 in. Label contents: 15-1/2 oz.
1-lb. Tall — 3-1/16 in. by 4-11/16 in. Label contents: 1 lb.
1-lb. Oval — Label contents: 15-1/2 oz.
1/2-lb. Oval — Label contents: 7-3/4 oz.
1/4-lb. Oval — Label contents: 3-3/4 oz.

Sardines Sardinella sagax (California sardines); Sardinia pilchardus (European sardine). Also known as Maine sardines or Spanish sardines. Spanish sardines caught from Cape Cod to the Gulf Stream; and the California sardine is caught from Puget Sound to Bay of Magdalena. Caught all year. Available brined, canned, fresh, and smoked.

Shrimp (Canned)　24/8Z　4-1/2 oz.
　　　　　　　24/No. 1　7 oz.
　　　　　　　Picnic
　　　　　　　48/5 oz.
　　　　　　　48/7 oz.

Snails Gastropoda Prosobranchiata. Caught along the Atlantic Coast during the winter months.

Tuna Fish Prepared from species of fish deemed to be "Tuna" (See Types), properly cleaned, washed, and trimmed; free from dark meat, bones, skin, extraneous tissue, and debris; and packed with added salt, cottonseed oil, vegetable oil, or olive oil.

TYPES:

Albacore Also known as Longfin. The only species that legally can be labeled "White Meat Tuna."

Yellowfin Color varies from almost white to pinkish. Usually labeled "Light Meat Tuna."

Bluefin Very similar to the Yellowfin in texture and color, and labeled the same way. Attains huge size — 1000 lb. and upward — and is famed among sportsmen as the "Leaping Tuna."

Striped Tuna, Skipjack or Aku This specie has a mild gamey flavor, and is pinkish with a buff tinge in color.

Oriental Tuna Not very well known in this market. Conforms to requirements for "Light Meat Tuna."

GRADES

Fancy Tuna Choice cuts of cooked tuna, from fish weighing not more than 60 lb. round weight, packed in cans with large pieces of solid meat, and with one or two small pieces of solid meat added, if necessary, to bring the contents up to required weight, but not including any flakes (or any grated or shredded tune) added at the time of packing.

　Fancy White Meat Tune — The descriptive term for choice cuts of Albacore packed in the same manner as "Fancy Tuna."

　Standard Tune — Wholesome, cooked tuna meat, not restricted as to size of fish, which when packed contains at least 75 percent large pieces of solid meat.

Grated or Shredded Tuna The descriptive term for small uniform pieces of wholesome, cooked tuna meat produced in grated or shredded form by a mechanical process. The tuna meat used for this type of pack shall be a kind and quality at least equal to that employed in packing "Standard Tuna."

Grated or Shredded White Meat Tuna The descriptive term for small, uniform pieces of wholesome, cooked Albacore prepared in the same manner as "Grated or Shredded Tuna." The tuna meat used shall be of a kind and quality at least equal to that employed in packing "Standard White Meat Tuna."

Tuna Flakes The descriptive term for small pieces of wholesome, cooked tuna meat from the whole tuna, or from parts of tuna not utilized in the packing of Fancy or Standard Grades of tuna.

White Meat Tuna Flakes The descriptive term for small pieces of wholesome, cooked Albacore from the whole tuna, or from parts of tuna not utilized in the packing of Fancy or Standard Grades of tuna.

Common Available Can Sizes

　No. 1/4 — 2-11/16 in. by 1-9/16 in. Label contents: 3-1/2 oz.
　No. 1/2 — 3-7/16 in. by 1-13/16 in. Label contents: 7 oz.
　No. 1 — 4-1/16 in. by 2-6/16 in. Label contents: 13 oz.
　4-lb.

CANNED FISH

Net weight per standard case of specified canned fish and shellfish

Product	Pounds per case
Alewives	45
Anchovies	31.25
Mackerel	45
Salmon	48
Sardines:	
Maine	23.4
Pacific	45
Shad	45
Tuna and tuna-like fish:	
Solid	21
Chunks	19.5
Flakes and grated	18
Crab meat, natural	19.5
Shrimp, wet pack[1]	15
Clam products:	
Whole and minced[1]	15
Juices, chowders, broth, etc.	30
Oysters, natural[1]	14
All other	48

1. "Cut out" or "drained" weights of can contents are given for shrimp, whole or minced clams, and oysters. Net can contents are given for other products.

BIBLIOGRAPHY

"How to Eye and Bye Seafoods." Washington, D.C.: U.S. Department of Commerce, 1970, pp. 3-19.

Kerr, R.G. "Savvy with Seafood." *U.S. Department of Agriculture Yearbook 1969*. Washington, D.C.: U.S. Government Printing Office, 1969, pp. 127-130.

Szathmary, Louis. "Fish—Food for Gourmets." *The Cornell Hotel and Restaurant Administration Quarterly*, 1965, pp. 1-13.

"Wildlife and Fisheries." *Code of Federal Regulations*, Part 261, October 1, 1972, pp. 1-5.

"Wildlife and Fisheries." *Code of Federal Regulations*, Part 262, March 30, 1973, pp. 1-3.

"Wildlife and Fisheries." *Code of Federal Regulations*, Part 263, October 1, 1972, pp. 1-30.

"Wildlife and Fisheries." *Code of Federal Regulations*, Part 264, October 1, 1972, pp. 1-5.

"Wildlife and Fisheries." *Code of Federal Regulations*, Part 265, October 1, 1972, pp. 1-2.

"Wildlife and Fisheries." *Code of Federal Regulations*, Part 266, October 1, 1972, pp. 1-5.

"Wildlife and Fisheries." *Code of Federal Regulations*, Part 267, October 1, 1972, pp. 1-5.

"Wildlife and Fisheries." *Code of Federal Regulations*, Part 268, October 1, 1972, pp. 1-4.

"Wildlife and Fisheries." *Code of Federal Regulations*, Part 269, October 1, 1972, pp. 1-4.

"Wildlife and Fisheries." *Code of Federal Regulations*, Part 270, October 1, 1972, pp. 1-5.

"Wildlife and Fisheries." *Code of Federal Regulations*, Part 271, October 1, 1972, pp. 1-3.

"Wildlife and Fisheries." *Code of Federal Regulations*, Part 272, October 1, 1972, pp. 1-5.

"Wildlife and Fisheries." *Code of Federal Regulations*, Part 273, October 1, 1972, pp. 1-3.

"Wildlife and Fisheries." *Code of Federal Regulations*, Part 274, October 1, 1972, pp. 1-3.

"Wildlife and Fisheries." *Federal Register*, Part 275, October 29, 1973, pp. 1-3.

"Wildlife and Fisheries." *Code of Federal Regulations*, Part 276, October 1, 1972, pp. 1-5.

"Wildlife and Fisheries." *Code of Federal Regulations*, Part 277, October 1, 1972, pp. 1-4.

"Wildlife and Fisheries." *Code of Federal Regulations*, Part 279, October 1, 1972, pp. 1-3.

CONVENIENCE FOODS

WORK SIMPLIFICATION is the key to most effective day-to-day operation for a foodservice organization.[1] The logic is simple: the more details to be handled and the more people there are, the greater are the opportunities for things to go wrong. Every job should be reduced to its basic components. Once reduced, tasks should be eliminated from the job, where possible, through the use of disposables, convenience foods, and automated equipment.

CONVENIENCE FOODS DEFINED

"Convenience Foods" is a relatively recent term in foodservice. As with all new broad-based terms, its meaning is not always precise. First, then a commonly accepted definition:

Convenience foods are those items to which some or all of the labor of preparation has been added at the time of purchase.

Clearly, while this definition is accurate, it is broad enough to cover almost every food item an operator purchases, whether canned, dried, fresh, or frozen, whether meat, poultry, fish, fruits, and vegetables, baked goods, dairy products, and the like.

For purposes of this chapter, I will use the term "convenience foods" generally to mean prepared entrees, customarily frozen, usually packed in multiple portions.

There is a vast range of such convenience food products now being packed for foodservice operations. Moreover, there is no longer a problem anywhere in the U.S. in acquiring them. There are, at this writing, in excess of 100 companies in national distribution of frozen foods.

The problem in setting up for use of convenience products comes with the short-term shelf-life refrigerated foods, such as prepared salads and desserts. However, a good convenience program will utilize prepared foods for all aspects of service.

Operators need convenience products for different reasons. Those in large cities have abundant potential labor, but it tends to be expensive. The small city and rural operator has the opposite problem, a lower wage scale, but a small pool of potential workers.

Thus, the metropolitan operator needs convenience foods to reduce his labor costs while the non-metropolitan operator needs them to fill the gap between his labor supply and production needs.

In evaluating a convenience food program, there are three options to consider. By far the most preferable, though it is practical only for a really high volume user, is the following:

OPTION 1: TAILORED CONVENIENCE FOODS

You begin by standardizing all recipe cards for premise-prepared items, not only as to products but also as to

1. Raymond B. Peddersen et al., *Increasing Productivity in Foodservice* (Chicago: Cahners Books, 1973), pp. 181-86.

procedures. Where possible, you specify quality and type of ingredients per USDA specifications.

Then calculate, from production records, the annual number of portions needed and the maximum number of portions for which storage is available. Take these requirements to the nearest 2 or 3 producers of convenience foods and ask for bids—using your processing method—for these products. This eliminates many problems that occur when convenience foods are purchased without reference to storage limitations.

One common problem is packaging size. Companies in national distribution package their products in different packages. Even foodservice operators disagree on standard packaging size. A commercial cafeteria or public restaurant may well prefer the few portions that can be packed in a quarter- or half-size steamtable plan because their individual orders come along slowly. But the non-commercial high volume operator—such as a hospital or college, or airline or in-plant caterer—may well want the added portions in a full-size pan.

By specifying his own package, the operator can tailor the best method and time of reheating for the specific product with his facilities, be they conventional or modern. A hospital with microwave ovens on the floor stations will find convenience products delivered in the frozen state perfectly acceptable (so long as the containers are not metallic, of course). However, where high volume must be served in a short period, a more shallow package would be required for a convection oven.

If there is enough refrigeration and conventional ovens are to be used, a bulk pack that can be reheated from the refrigerated state after a long defrost cycle may be preferred. Having the product packaged to your specification guarantees a product consistent with your tastes.

Among the minimum standards for user agreement for convenience products should be freedom from disease-producing organisms, nutritional content, shelf-life, and accuracy of the manufacturer's claims as to the number of portions per container. These standards should be applied also to the new frozen, dehydro-frozen, freeze-dried, chilled, or concentrated items that appear on the market almost daily.

Manufacturers and purveyors have special problems. For instance, chicken cordon bleu, veal marsala, stuffed cabbage, or codfish cakes are prepared differently in various regions of the country. What passes for good clam chowder in San Diego may not pass muster anywhere near the Charles River in Boston.

OPTION 2: GENERAL MARKETPLACE

When an operation is not big enough to have its own convenience food manufactured, the operator may enter the general marketplace.

The major shortcoming of convenience food packaging, besides varying sizes, is the failure of the container to communicate information about the contents and their use to the average unskilled kitchen employee. There are usually no receiving specifications on boxes to guide the receiver in examining the product for damage. There is no mention of dangerous temperature zones or shelf-life.

The advertising logo occupies the primary space although this space should be allocated to instructions. Sometimes instructions are on the bottom of the box—which means the worker may have to damage the product to read them. Instruction copy is confusing. Few companies provide line drawings. Those manufacturers who do publish product description sheets or merchandising brochures or, more importantly, nutritional data, generally make them available "upon request only." Such sheets should be included with each case.

Instructions should cover the following subjects: storage, including specific and numerical temperature figures, not simply the words "room temperature" or "freezing"; the method of removal from the master container; the number and size of portions; alternate uses of product and handling of leftovers; alternate preparation methods and service equipment that can be used; and any other appropriate warnings.

The instruction language should be clearly organized. It should be short and simple, with illustrated instructions. And, certainly today, it should be bilingual.

FIGURE 1

Within the form image:

REQUEST FOR QUOTATION
THIS IS ____ ORDER
RETURN ONE COPY TO
MAY 11 1973
UNIVERSITY OF CALIFORNIA
PURCHASING DEPARTMENT
DAVIS, CALIFORNIA 95616
DATE 4/30/73   NUMBER 1D 43073EE PS
IS YOUR ADDRESS INCLUDING ZIP CODE CORRECT?

CHEF'S ORCHID INFLIGHT SERVICE
1309 W. TEXAS ST
FAIRFIELD, CA.

TO BE CONSIDERED YOUR QUOTATION MUST BE RECEIVED BY ____ 5/10/73
IF FURTHER INFORMATION IS REQUIRED, PLEASE CONTACT
BOB RINKER (916) 752-0985

*1 [form] Please quote your lowest price for the material, and/or services, to be delivered, as specified below. Any deviation from the specifications must be identified and fully described. No charge for package, for drayage, or for any other purpose will be allowed over and above the prices quoted on this sheet. University of California standard purchase order terms and conditions apply. A copy of these conditions will be furnished on request. The right is reserved to accept or reject quotations on each item separately, or as a whole. If unable to quote, please return this form so marked.

ARTICLES SUPPLIED ON THIS FORM SHOULD BE PRODUCED OR MANUFACTURED IN THE UNITED STATES, IF OF FOREIGN MAKE, PLEASE SPECIFY ORIGIN.

UNLESS OTHERWISE SPECIFIED PRICES WILL BE F.O.B. UNIVERSITY OF CALIFORNIA WITH DELIVERY VARIOUS POINTS (FACULTY CLUB, STUDENT HEALTH CENTER AND SACRAMENTO MEDICAL CENTER.

UNIT PRICE MUST BE EXTENDED

CASH DISCOUNT ____ PER CENT FOR PAYMENT WITHIN ____ DAYS FROM RECEIPT OF GOODS OR INVOICE, WHICHEVER IS LATER.

PLEASE INDICATE YOUR WILLINGNESS TO PROVIDE AS NEEDED THE ITEMS DESCRIBED ON THE ATTACHED LIST TO THE UNIVERSITY OF CALIFORNIA WITH DELIVERY F.O.B. VARIOUS POINTS (FACULTY CLUB, STUDENT HEALTH CENTER, AND SACRAMENTO MEDICAL CENTER) FOR THE PERIOD JULY 1, 1973 THROUGH JUNE 30, 1974. PRICES SHALL BE EFFECTIVE FOR A THREE (3) MONTH PERIOD, STARTING ON THE FIRST DAY THROUGH THE LAST DAY OF THE THIRD MONTH. VENDORS SHALL BE REQUESTED TO SUBMIT PRICE QUOTATIONS EVERY THIRD MONTHS.

THE FOLLOWING CONDITIONS AND SPECIFICATIONS SHALL APPLY TO EACH QUOTATION (EVERY 90 DAYS).

COMMODITY CLASS: CONVENIENCE FOODS

A. ESTIMATED QUANTITIES: THE QUANTITY LISTED IS AN ESTIMATED REQUIREMENT PROJECTED FROM CURRENT USAGE. THE UNIVERSITY DOES NOT GUARANTEE TO PURCHASE A MINIMUM QUANTITY OR DOES NOT GUARANTEE TO PURCHASE VENDOR'S REMAINING STOCK.

B. PRICES: PRICES QUOTED MUST BE NET UNIT PRICE IN TERMS OF UNITS ASKED FOR IN REQUEST FOR QUOTE.

C. PREPARATION OF QUOTE: ALL BRAND NAMES, NUMBERS AND PRICE EXTENSIONS MUST BE SHOWN. CASE QUANTITIES AND SIZE OF PACKAGE MUST BE SHOWN IF DIFFERENT FROM SPECIFICATION. FAILURE TO DO SO MAY DISQUALIFY YOUR OFFER.

D. RESTRICTIONS: MINIMUM ORDER, DELIVERY CHARGES OR OTHER
(CONT PG. TWO)

DELIVERY WILL BE MADE IN ____ DAYS AFTER RECEIPT OF ORDER
SHIPPING WEIGHT ____ LBS. ____ METHOD OF SHIPMENT ____

*2 [form] As a supplier of goods or services to the University of California I/we certify that racially segregated facilities will not be maintained nor provided for employees at any establishment under my/our control, and that I/we adhere to the principles set forth in Executive Orders 11246 and 11375, and undertake specifically: to maintain employment policies and practices that affirmatively promote equality of opportunity for minority group persons and women; to take affirmative steps to hire and promote women and minority group persons at all job levels and in all aspects of employment; to communicate this policy in both English and Spanish to all persons concerned within the company, with outside recruiting services, and the minority community at large; to provide the University on request a breakdown of our total labor force by ethnic group, sex, and job category; and to discuss with the University our policies and practices relating to our affirmative action program.

DATE   TELEPHONE NO. (INCLUDING AREA CODE)   SIGNATURE OF FIRM REPRESENTATIVE

Fig. 1. An excellent example of a bid request and specification for convenience foods. The information included on the remaining pages appears on pp. 364-65.

*1

Please quote your lowest price for the material, and/or services, to be delivered, as specified below. Any deviation from the specifications must be identified and fully described. No charge for package, for drayage, or for any other purpose will be allowed over and above the prices quoted on this sheet. University of California standard purchard order terms and conditions apply. A copy of these conditions will be furnished on request. The right is reserved to accept or reject quotations on each item separately, or as a whole. If unable to quote, please return this form so marked.

DELIVERY WILL BE MADE IN ____ DAYS AFTER RECEIPT OF ORDER

SHIPPING WEIGHT _____ LBS. _____

METHOD OF SHIPMENT _____

*2

As a supplier of goods or services to the Univesity of California, I/we certify that racially segregated facilities will not be maintained nor provided for employees at any establishment under my/our control, and that I/we adhere to the principles set forch in Executive Orders 11246 and 11375, and undertake specifically: to maintain employment policies and practices that affirmatively promote equality of opportunity for minority group persons and women; to take affirmative steps to hire and promote women and minority group persons at all job levels and in all aspects of employment; to communicate this policy in both English and Spanish to all persons concerned within the company, with outside recruiting services, and the minority community at large; to provide the University on request a breakdown of our total labor force by ethnic group, sex, and job category; and to discuss with the University our policies and practices relating to our affirmative action program.

DATE   TELEPHONE NO. (INCLUDING AREA CODE)

SIGNATURE OF FIRM REPRESENTATIVE

Form 1 (top left):

ARTICLES SUPPLIED ON THIS FORM SHOULD BE PRODUCED OR MANUFAC... ...HE UNITED STATES, IF OF FOREIGN... ...IFY ORIGIN.

UNLESS OTHERWISE SPECIFIED PRICES WILL BE F.O.B. UNIVERSITY OF CALIFORNIA

UNIT PRICE MUST BE EXTENDED

CASH DISCOUNT _____ PER CENT FOR PAYMENT WITHIN _____ DAYS FROM RECEIPT OF GOODS OR INVOICE, WHICHEVER IS LATER.

RESTRICTIONS MUST BE SHOWN BELOW. IF NO RESTRICTIONS ARE SHOWN, IT WILL BE ASSUMED THAT NONE APPLY.

RESTRICTIONS: _____

_____

_____

E. BRAND NAME:

A. BRANDS AND NUMBERS WHEN USED ARE FOR REFERENCE TO INDICATE CHARACTER AND QUALITY DESIRED.

B. EQUAL ITEMS WILL BE CONSIDERED PROVIDING YOUR OFFER CLEARLY DESCRIBES THE ITEMS. OFFERS FOR EQUAL ITEMS SHALL STATE THE BRAND AND NUMBER OR LEVEL OF QUALITY.

C. WHEN BRAND, NUMBER OR LEVEL OF QUALITY IS NOT STATED BY THE BIDDER, IT IS UNDERSTOOD THE OFFER IS EXACTLY AS SPECIFIED.

F. ACCEPTABLE PRODUCTS: IN ORDER TO BE CONSIDERED ACCEPTABLE, AN ITEM QUOTED "AS EQUAL" TO THE BRAND CALLED OUT, MAY AT THE DECISION OF THE UNIVERSITY, BE REQUIRED TO PROVIDE ITS ACCEPTABILITY BY TEST SAMPLING AND EVALUATION PRIOR TO PLACEMENT ON AGREEMENT SHOULD TIME LIMITATIONS FAIL TO ALLOW FOR SUFFICIENT EVALUATION PRIOR TO AWARD OF THE AGREEMENT AS NOTED ON THE REQUEST FOR QUOTATION, THE ITEM, IF FOUND ACCEPTABLE, SHALL BE CONSIDERED

DELIVERY WILL BE MADE IN _____ DAYS AFTER RECEIPT OF ORDER

(CONT PG THREE)

Form 2 (top right):

ARTICLES SUPPLIED ON THIS FORM SHOULD BE PRODUCED OR MANUFACTURED IN THE UNITED STATES, IF OF FOREIGN MAKE, PLEASE SPECIFY ORIGIN.

UNLESS OTHERWISE SPECIFIED PRICES WILL BE F.O.B. UNIVERSITY OF CALIFORNIA

UNIT PRICE MUST BE EXTENDED

CASH DISCOUNT _____ PER CENT FOR PAYMENT WITHIN _____ DAYS FROM RECEIPT OF GOODS OR INVOICE, WHICHEVER IS LATER.

I. DELIVERIES: DELIVERIES SHALL BE MADE ON AN "AS REQUIRED" BASIS AS REQUESTED BY THE INDIVIDUAL USING FACILITIES BY MEANS OF A DEPARTMENTAL PURCHASE ORDER ISSUED AGAINST THEIR BASIC SUPPLY AGREEMENT.

J. SHOULD A SUPPLY AGREEMENT BE AWARDED AS A RESULT OF THIS REQUEST FOR QUOTE, CONTINUANCE OF SUCH AGREEMENT FOR THE FULL PERIOD SPECIFIED SHALL BE CONTINGENT UPON THE SATISFACTORY PERFORMANCE OF THE VENDOR AND PRODUCT. CONTINUING OR UNRECTIFIABLE PERFORMANCE DEFICIENCES MAY BE CAUSE FOR THE UNIVERSITY TO CANCEL ANY BALANCE OF THE AGREEMENT, WITHOUT PENALTY ON ANY PORTIONS PURCHASED PRIOR TO CANCELLATION.

K. PRICES AS QUOTED WILL BE CONSIDERED MAXIMUM AND FIRM. THE UNIVERSITY IS TO RECEIVE THE BENEFIT OF ANY PRICE DECLINE.

L. BASED ON EACH QUOTATION SOLICITED AN AWARD LETTER FOR THAT PERIOD WILL BE ISSUED BY THE PURCHASING DEPARTMENT TO THE SUCCESSFUL VENDOR CITING CURRENT PRICES.

M. INVOICES ARE TO BE RENDERED IN ARREARS, AND ONLY IF SERVICES OR SUPPLIES HAVE BEEN FURNISHED.

N. THE UNIVERSITY RESERVES THE RIGHT TO PERIODICALLY CHECK YOUR PRICING SCHEDULE COVERING THIS AGREEMENT.

O. VENDOR CERTIFIES THAT THE SUPPLIES COVERED BY THIS QUOTATION HAS NOT BEEN OFFERED IN LIKE QUANTITIES TO ANY OTHER CUSTOMER AT A LOWER PRICE.

DELIVERY WILL BE MADE IN _____ DAYS AFTER RECEIPT OF ORDER

METHOD OF SHIPMENT

(CONT PG. FIVE)

Form 3 (bottom left):

ARTICLES SUPPLIED ON THIS FORM ... ...ES, IF OF FOREIGN MAKE, PLEASE SPECIFY ORIGIN.

UNLESS OTHERWISE SPECIFIED ... ...WILL BE F.O.B. UNIVERSITY OF CALIFORNIA

UNIT PRICE MUST BE EXTENDED

CASH DISCOUNT _____ PER CENT FOR PAYMENT WITHIN _____ DAYS FROM RECEIPT OF GOODS OR INVOICE, WHICHEVER IS LATER.

FOR INCLUSION ON FUTURE REQUEST FOR QUOTATIONS. THE DECISION OF THE UNIVERSITY REGARDING ACCEPTABILITY SHALL BE FINAL.

ARRANGEMENTS FOR SAMPLING MAY BE MADE BY CONTACTING THE BUYER.

G. INTENT AND INTERPRETATION OF SPECIFICATIONS: ALL PRODUCTS DELIVERED SHALL:

1. HAVE BEEN PROCESSED AND PACKED IN ACCORDANCE WITH GOOD COMMERCIAL PRACTICE
2. BE MADE FROM THE LATEST AVAILABLE CROP
3. CONFORM IN ALL RESPECTS TO ALL APPLICABLE STANDARDS PROMULGATED UNDER THE FEDERAL FOOD, DRUG AND COSMETIC ACT IN EFFECT AT THE TIME OF DELIVERY.
4. WHEN APPLICABLE, BE LABELED SO THAT THEY MAY BE IDENTIFIED AS HAVING BEEN OFFICIALLY INSPECTED FOR WHOLESOMENESS.
5. WHERE APPLICABLE, MEET U.S. STANDARDS FOR FILL OF CONTAINER.

H. INSPECTION: UPON DELIVERY OF EACH ITEM TO THE SPECIFIED DELIVERY POINT, INSPECTION WILL BE MADE BY A REPRESENTATIVE OF THE UNIVERSITY AT THE POINT OF DELIVERY. ACCEPTANCE OF THE ITEM OR ITEMS WILL BE MADE AFTER INSPECTION DETERMINES THAT ALL REQUIREMENTS OF THE SPECIFICATIONS AND THE QUOTE CONDITIONS ARE MET.

(CONT PG. FOUR)

DELIVERY WILL BE MADE IN _____ DAYS AFTER RECEIPT OF ORDER

SHIPPING WEIGHT _____ LBS. METHOD OF SHIPMENT _____

Form 4 (bottom right):

ARTICLES SUPPLIED ON THIS FORM ... ...BE PRODUCED OR MANUFACTURED IN THE UNITED STATES, IF OF FOREIGN MAKE, PLEASE SPECIFY ORIGIN.

UNLESS OTHERWISE SPECIFIED PRICES WILL BE F.O.B. UNIVERSITY OF CALIFORNIA

UNIT PRICE MUST BE EXTENDED

CASH DISCOUNT _____ PER CENT FOR PAYMENT WITHIN _____ DAYS FROM RECEIPT OF GOODS OR INVOICE, WHICHEVER IS LATER.

P. "BY SUBMISSION OF THIS OFFER, OFFEROR CERTIFIES (1) THAT HE IS IN COMPLIANCE AND WILL CONTINUE TO COMPLY WITH THE REQUIREMENTS OF EXECUTIVE ORDER 11640, JANUARY 26, 1972, OR (2) THAT HE IS A SMALL BUSINESS CONCERN (AS DETERMINED IN ACCORDANCE WITH THE REGULATIONS OF THE COST OF LIVING COUNCIL IN 6 CFR 101.51, 37 F.R. 8939, MAY 3, 1972) AND AS SUCH IS EXEMPT FROM WAGE AND PRICE CONTROLS (EXCEPT WHERE HEALTH SERVICES OR CONSTRUCTION ARE INVOLVED)."

Q. "THE RIGHT IS RESERVED BY THE UNIVERSITY TO CANCEL ANY RESULTING AGREEMENT AT ANY TIME AT THE OPTION OF AND WITHOUT PENALTY TO THE UNIVERSITY."

DELIVERY WILL BE MADE IN _____ DAYS AFTER RECEIPT OF ORDER

ARTICLES SUPPLIED ON THIS FORM SHOULD BE PRODUCED OR MANUFACTURED IN THE UNITED STATES. IF OF FOREIGN MAKE, PLEASE SPECIFY ORIGIN.

UNLESS OTHERWISE SPECIFIED PRICES WILL BE F.O.B. UNIVERSITY OF CALIFORNIA WITH DELIVERY VARIOUS POINTS (FACULTY CLUB, STUDENT HEALTH CENTER AND SACRAMENTO MEDICAL CENTER.

UNIT PRICE MUST BE EXTENDED	
SHOW ANY APPLICABLE TAX SEPARATELY	
UNIT PRICE	TOTAL PRICE

CASH DISCOUNT _____ PER CENT FOR PAYMENT WITHIN _____ DAYS FROM RECEIPT OF GOODS OR INVOICE, WHICHEVER IS LATER.

PLEASE QUOTE PRICES IN ACCORDANCE WITH REQUEST FOR QUOTATION ID 430733EE DATED, 4/30/73 EFFECTIVE FOR THE PERIOD JULY 1, 1973 THROUGH SEPT. 30, 1973 TO PROVIDE AS NEEDED THE ITEMS DESCRIBED ON THE ATTACHED LIST TO THE UNIVERSITY OF CALIFORNIA WITH DELIVERY F.O.B. TO VARIOUS POINTS (FACULTY CLUB, STUDENT HEALTH CENTER AND SACRAMENTO MEDICAL CENTER.

COMMODITY CLASS: CONVENIENCE FOODS

IT IS UNDERSTOOD THAT UPON SIGNING THIS BID YOU, THE VENDOR, ARE WILLING TO TAKE ALL OR ANY PART OF THIS SUPPLY AGREEMENT, AND THAT YOU GUARANTEE TO DELIVER ALL ITEMS AS QUOTED. IT IS UNDERSTOOD THAT THE RIGHT IS RESERVED BY THE UNIVERSITY TO CANCEL THE AGREEMENT AT ANY TIME AT THE OPTION OF, AND WITHOUT PENALTY TO THE UNIVERSITY.

UPON DELIVERY OF EACH ITEM TO THE SPECIFIED DELIVERY POINT, INSPECTION WILL BE MADE BY A REPRESENTATIVE OF THE UNIVERSITY AT THE POINT OF DELIVERY. ACCEPTANCE OF THE ITEMS WILL BE MADE AFTER INSPECTION DETERMINES THAT ALL REQUIREMENTS OF THE SPECIFICATIONS AND THE QUOTE ARE MET.

F3-3

DELIVERY WILL BE MADE IN _____ DAYS AFTER RECEIPT OF ORDER

CONTINUATION SHEET   Page 2

			Document	
TYPE			NUMBER	
QUOTE			ID 43073EE PS	
FIRM/DEPARTMENT NAME				

CONVENIENCE FOODS -- FROZEN
MINIMUM MEAT CONTENT PER TRAY -33%
ACCEPTABLE BRANDS: THE FOLLOWING BRANDS ARE ACCEPTABLE - ARMOUR, CAMDEN, CARMENS, MARKES, REDS, SEABROOK FARMS, TOPMOST, VENEZIA, OR APPROVED EQUIVALENT

NOTE: WHERE APPLICABLE, UNIT PRICE MUST SHOW COST PER POUND OR PORTION AS WELL AS COST PER CASE.

ITEM	QUANTITY ESTIMATED MONTHLY QUANTITY	UNIT	DESCRIPTION	BRAND & NO.	UNIT PRICE	EXTENSION
				and standard pkg		
1.	AS REQUIRED	CS	BEEF, CUBE STEAKS, 4 OZ., 5/10#		portion / case	
2.	10	CS	SIRLOIN TIPS, IN MUSHROOM GRAVY 3/12#		lb / cs	
3.	10	CS	MEAT LOAF, WHOLE, UNSLICED, 8/5#		lb / cs	
4.	8	CS	MEAT BALLS IN BROWN GRAVY, 460/4 OZ.		portion / cs	
5.	8	CS	CHICKEN A'LA KING 2/10#		lb / cs	
6.	AS REQUIRED	CS	CHICKEN FRICASSE 6/5#		lb / cs	
7.	AS REQUIRED	CS	CHICKEN & NOODLES 2/10#		lb / cs	
8.	AS REQUIRED	CS	CHICKEN PIE FILLING, 2/10#		lb / cs	
9.	AS REQUIRED	CS	CHICKEN CHOW MEIN 2/10#		lb / cs	
10.	AS REQUIRED	CS	BEEF STROGANOFF 6/5#		lb / cs	
11.	14	CS	MANICOTTI, CHEESE FILLED, W/MEAT SAUCE - 36/4.5 OZ., 2/10#		portion / cs	
12.	8	CS	LASAGNA, WITH CHEESE & MEAT SAUCE 2/10#		lb / cs	
13.	AS REQUIRED	CS	SPAGHETTI & MEAT BALLS IN TOMATO SAUCE, 2/10# 188/.4 OZ. MEAT BALLS		portion / cs	
14.	8	CS	SPAGHETTI & MEAT SAUCE 2/10#		lb / cs	
15.	5	CS	MACARONI & CHEESE, 2/10#		lb / cs	
16.	11	CS	PEPPERS, GREEN, STUFFED W/BEEF & SAUCE 48/4.25 OZ., 2/10#		portion / cs	

FORM NO. PUR 0022 (A/C 224) (8/71)

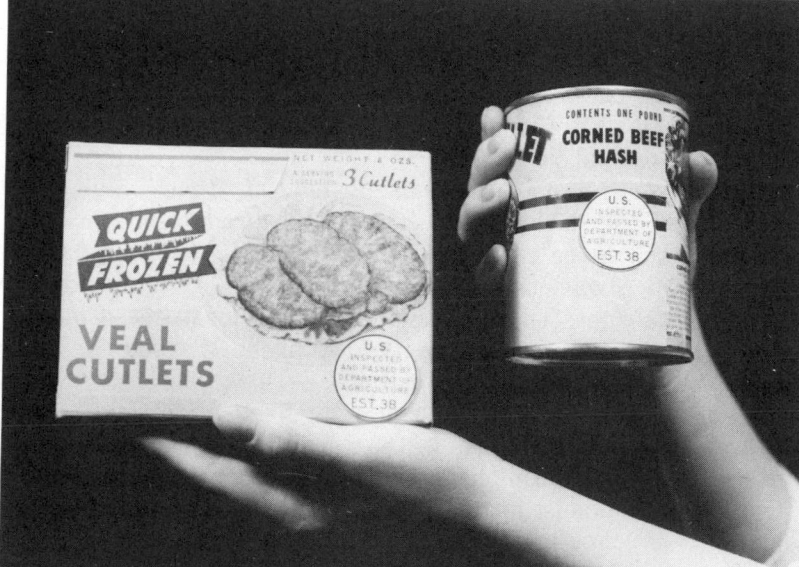

Meat inspection stamps on canned and frozen packages.

CONTINUATION SHEET					Page <u>3</u>	
				Document		
			TYPE	NUMBER		
			QUOTE	ID 43073EE PS		
			FIRM/DEPARTMENT NAME			

ITEM	QUANTITY	UNIT	DESCRIPTION	BRAND & NO.	UNIT PRICE	EXTENSION
	ESTIMATED MONTHLY QUANTITY			and standard pkg.		
17.	10	CS	SHRIMP CREOLE 6/5#		lb / cs	
18.	2	CS	SEA FOOD NUBERG 6/5#		lb / cs	
19.	AS REQUIRED	CS	TUNA & NOODLES 6/5#		lb / cs	
20.	5	CS	TAMALES, BEEF 72 /4 OZ.		portion / cs	
21.	2	CS	BURRITOS, BEEF & BEAN 144/3 OZ.		portion / cs	
22.	3	CS	ENCHILADAS, BEEF, IN CHILI SAUCE & MEAT 64/1.4 OZ.		portion / cs	
23.	3	CS	ENCHILADAS, BEEF, 144/CS		portion / cs	
24.	7	CS	TACOS - 2 1/4 OZ. 288/CS		portion / cs	
25.	10	CS	BEEF STEW, 2/10#		lb / cs	
26.	10	CS	MACARONI N' BEEF 2/10#		lb / cs	
27.	AS REQUIRED	CS	CANNELLONI CHEESE W/SAUCE 6/3#		lb / cs	
			RESTRICTED DIET ENTRES: PACKED 4/5# TRAYS PER CASE CHEF FRANCISCO, CHEF ORCHID, IDLEWILD FARMS OR APPROVED EQUIVALENT			
28.	AS REQUIRED	CS	BEEF STEW, SOFT; BLAND; LOW SALT		cs	
29.	AS REQUIRED	CS	SIRLOIN TIPS, IN MUSHROOM GRAVY, SOFT BLAND, LOW SALT		cs	
30.	AS REQUIRED	CS	TURKEY TETRAZZINI, SOFT, BLAND, LOW SALT		cs	
31.	AS REQUIRED	CS	BAKED MACARONI & CHEESE, SOFT, BLAND LOW SALT		cs	
32.	AS REQUIRED	CS	SPAGHETTI & MEAT BALLS, SOFT, BLAND LOW SALT		cs	
33.	AS REQUIRED	CS	SEA FOOD NUBERG, SOFT, BLAND, LOW SALT		cs	
34.	AS REQUIRED	CS	CHICKEN A-LA-KING SOFT, BLAND, LOW SALT		cs	
35.	AS REQUIRED	CS	SALISBURY STEAK, W/MUSHROOM GRAVY, SOFT BLAND, LOW SALT		cs	

FORM NO. PUR 0022 (A/C 224) (8/71)

OPTION 3: MAKE YOUR OWN

In this option, often termed a "ready-foods" system, an operation manufactures and freezes its own convenience products on premise. This system uses off-hour time periods to prepare, package and freeze bulk quantities of foods.

Regardless of the option chosen, every operator is left with the complicated business of reheating.

When food is removed from the freezer it must be carefully handled. Various types of food must be reheated differently. The only rule that always applies is, "Never defrost at room temperature." Instead, defrosting should be done under controlled conditions, either by heating or controlled refrigeration. If your volume is large enough to warrant it, several manufacturers now offer tempering refrigerators. These apply heat or refrigeration, as necessary, to maintain any size load within a limited, safe temperature range.

TEMPERING IS CRUCIAL

Whatever is done about tempering (bringing product from frozen to refrigerated) foods, it must be done carefully. Foods thawed slowly over 2 or 3 days generally retain more stability and "eat" better than those thawed quickly.

There is no doubt that, if the product permits, a properly adjusted, forced-air convection oven does an effective job in terms of load, efficiency, and cost in reheating frozen convenience foods.

If microwave ovens are used, heating times must be adjusted to the thickness or shape of the products. Improper timing can produce mushiness, and a steamed or ozone flavor in meat. Microwave ovens make their greatest contribution in bringing refrigerated foods to serving temperatures. Combination convection-microwave ovens, properly used, should offer an answer to many problems.

Ovens—deck, convection, revolving, and microwave—are referred to as dry heat. Steamers (high pressure, low pressure, and atmospheric) and conventional and pressure fryers provide moist heat. They are effective, even if slower, methods of reheating and/or cooking.

Here, too, serving temperature is crucial. What holds true for freshly prepared foods applies equally to convenience foods. Hot food must be served hot, and cold food must be served cold. Any variance from this rule may prove disastrous for the palatability, pathogenicity, and nutritional value of the food. While the facts of heat loss for liquids are generally known, new data is needed for most other foods on time requirements as related to specific states and mass in order to set standards for reheating and holding during service.

The possibilities convenience foods offer for increasing productivity are almost limitless. A kitchen planned for total convenience food use may take perhaps half as much space and capital as a conventional kitchen. Labor requirements m y be reduced by as much as 80 percent, although 40 percent to 60 percent is more common.

Today, almost any conceivable entree is available in a full convenience form. These items range in quality from unsatisfactory to the finest of haute cuisine. In addition, soups and sauces, sauced and seasoned vegetables, and cakes, pies, and fancy pastries abound in the marketplace.

While it is difficult to purchase pre-prepared salad plates, it is possible to buy fresh vegetables and fruits already peeled, chopped, diced, sliced, or in any form needed for salad preparation. Salad mixtures, including potato salad, coleslaw, macaroni salad, lobster salad, and tunafish salad are readily available. Puddings and gelatins of high quality are available.

GRADUAL MODIFICATION OFTEN BEST

Most foodservice operations are not in a position to adopt a total convenience system with requisite new equipment. Thus, it becomes advisable to gradually modify conventional systems when and where possible. If an operation still butchers meat, labor can be effectively reduced by purchasing cuts prefabricated to the specifications of the "Meat Buyer's Guides" of the National Association of Meat Purveyors. Instead of operating a bake shop, labor can be eliminated by purchasing commercial fresh or frozen goods.

Hillside Hospital (Queens, N.Y.) Foodservice devised a three-part objective scale for rating convenience food products on subjective values. Fig. 2 is a individual product rating chart. Commercial pre-prepared products are rated against an in-house prepared product on six inter-related, yet

individual quality factors. The closer to 0 a commercial product scores, the greater its potential for replacing the house-prepared product. The goal is to equal the house product, not necessarily replace it.

FIGURE 2 — OBJECTIVE RATING FORM

Convenience Product Rating against Hillside Hospital Product						Date: _____
Product _____ Packed by _____						
Portion Size _____ Cost per portion _____						
	-2 N.G.	-1 OK—	0 Same	+1 OK+	+2 Better	Comment
Color						
Sauce (Aroma)						
Sauce (Taste)						
Filler (Aroma)						
Filler (Taste)						
Seasoning (General)						
Total						
÷ 6=						

The third form, Fig. 3, measures the cost, in labor dollars, of the on-premise product as compared with the tested convenience product. These cards are kept for future reference. The important data on these cards is transferred to a card (Fig. 4, next page) which records similar data on various manufacturer's samples of a particular product. When an adequate number of samples have been tested, a decision based on comparative quality versus cost- and time-savings can be made. In this manner it is possible to test products over an extended period of time without a sophisticated research staff in the kitchen.

FIGURE 3 — MEASURING COST LABOR DOLLARS

Cost per 100 portions	Hillside Hospital Product	_____ Product
Man Minutes		
Rec. and Storage		
Preparation		
Garnish and Display		
Difference x $.10		
Food Cost	$	$
Recipe No. _____ as of / /		
Diff.		
+ or −		

A list of man-minutes saved by using a selected product should be kept by the labor task analyst. Such lists should be categorized into cold products used by salad girls and hot items prepared by cooks, and the minutes that can be saved through purchase rather than preparation of each product should be recorded. Then, when a position becomes vacant, and the time saved by using convenience foods in that work area is determined to be roughly equal in man-minutes to the output of the newly vacated position, the operator should leave the job empty and begin using the convenience products on the list.

These three simple forms can be quickly and easily filled in and maintained. Their use can prevent costly mistakes in customer satisfaction as well as money. This sytem, if used as outlined, can keep budget-oriented operations from cost overruns.

FIG. 4 — CONVENIENCE COMPARISON RATING CHART

Product _____

CO.	Qual. Points	100 Portion Cost	Man/Minute Savings	Test Date

Selection Date   **Comments** **New Recipe Card No.**

CODE OF RECOMMENDED PRACTICES FOR THE HANDLING OF FROZEN FOODS

To safeguard frozen food quality for the consumer, 11 related trade groups some years ago established a code of recommended handling practices. The subjects covered by these practices relate to merchandising aspects of frozen foods. The groups which joined in subscribing to these practices did so in an organized effort to insure that new technological developments will continually be made available and concurrently to up-date good practices for the care and handling of frozen foods.

These recommended practices are based upon extensive research in frozen food time-temperature-tolerance by the Western Utilization Research and Development Laboratory of the USDA which were concurred in by the Refrigeration Research Foundation. These practices do not replace more demanding company or industry practices which may be in effect. The industry's goal is to maintain reasonably uniform frozen food product temperatures of 0°F. or lower and to insure their proper care, from packer to consumer.

The development of these recommendations was based upon the principle that voluntary action by industry members would result in more rapid advancement and attention to good care and handling practice than would be produced by compulsion of laws and regulations.

I. FOODS FOR FREEZING

1. Raw products should be harvested at optimum maturity, then delivered promptly to the plant where they should be prepared for freezing, frozen, and packaged (or placed in proper bulk storage) with all reasonable speed. Similarly, frozen products to be used as ingredients in prepared frozen foods should be of best quality for the intended purpose, handled at temperatures of 0°F. or lower at all points and only permitted to thaw for the time and to the extent necessary for their incorporation into the end product.

2. Similar care should be used by processors without freezing facilities in moving prepared for packaging product to refrigerated warehouses for freezing.

3. Where processor has his own freezer and warehouse, product leaving the warehouse should be at 0°F. or lower.

4. In movement from processor, who freezes but does not have sufficient warehouse space to complete freezing, the product should leave the plant without delay, at 10°F. or lower, in an insulated and refrigerated vehicle. Such movement to the primary warehouse for reduction of temperature to 0°F. or lower should not exceed 8 hours.

5. Product temperatures should be reduced to 0°F. or lower promptly upon reaching the primary warehouse.

II. WAREHOUSE EQUIPMENT

1. Each warehouse should be of adequate capacity and should be equipped with suitable mechanical refrigeration to provide, under extreme conditions of outside temperature and peak load conditions, for maintaining an air temperature of 0°F. or lower, in all rooms in which frozen foods are stored.

2. Each storage room should be equipped with an accurate temperature measuring device so installed as to reflect correctly the average air temperature of the room. Each day the warehouse is open, temperatures of each room should be recorded, dated, and a file of such temperatures maintained for a period of at least 2 years.

III. WAREHOUSE HANDLING PRACTICES

1. The warehouse operator should record product temperature of each lot of frozen foods received and should accept custody in accordance with good commercial practice. He should retain lot arrival temperature records for a period of at least 1 year.

2. Whenever frozen foods are received with product temperatures of 15°F. or higher, the warehouseman should immediately notify the owner or consignee and request instructions for special handling. These procedures may consist of any available method for effectively lowering temperatures such as blast freezing, low temperature rooms with air circulation, and proper use of dunnage or separators in stacking.

3. Before a lot of frozen food is placed in storage, it should be code marked for effective identification.

4. Frozen foods should be moved over dock areas promptly to minimize exposure to elevated temperatures, rainfall, or other adverse weather conditions.

5. If frozen foods are purchased for resale directly to consumers, such products should be stored in the purchaser's own premises (regardless of whether such premises are owned or leased from a public warehouse or others) so that the purchaser would have complete control of all of the conditions for which he is responsible in adhering to the code. The

"first-in, first-out" method of inventory control is desirable.

6. During defrosting of overhead coils in storage rooms, stacks of frozen foods should be effectively protected by tarpaulins, or other protective covering, or by removal from beneath the coils.

7. Frozen foods going into a separate break-up room for order assembly must be moved out promptly unless break-up room is maintained uniformly at 0°F. or lower.

IV. TRANSPORTATION EQUIPMENT

1. All vehicles—railway cars, motor trucks, trailers, and ships—should be

(a.) so constructed and properly insulated that, when equipped with appropriate refrigeration units, they will be capable of maintaining product temperature of 0°F. or lower throughout the load in all movements; and

(b.) equipped with an appropriate temperature measurement device to indicate accurately air temperature inside the vehicle. The dial or reading element of the device should be mounted in a readily accessible position outside the vehicle; and

(c.) equipped with air leak-proof cargo spaces, including tight fitting doors and suitable closures for drain holes to prevent air leakage; and

(d.) racked, stripped, baffled, or otherwise so constructed as to provide clearance for air circulation around the load, unless of coldwall or envelope type construction. (Note: Floor racks will not be necessary when product is palletized or is loaded on extruded floors; however, such floors must be free from any dirt and debris. It is recommended that ceiling air circulation ducts extend from the air circulating fans to at least 3/4 the length of the load.) and

(e.) entirely free from any any dirt, debris, or offensive odors when placed for loading.

2. Route delivery trucks should comply with all the provisions of Section 1 above and, in addition, should be equipped with curtains or flaps in the doorway area or with port doors, to minimize loss of refrigeration during delivery stops.

3. Self-refrigerated containers and other self-contained units utilized in making small shipments of frozen food, such as those which might move in LCL or LTL lots via aircraft, pickup trucks, and other non-refrigerated vehicles should be so constructed as to give the product adequate protection against physical damage in transit, and be equipped with a refrigerant or refrigerating system capable of maintaining a product temperature of 0°F. or lower during the anticipated movement. All such containers should be free from dirt, debris, and offensive odors when offered for loading.

V. HANDLING PRACTICES FOR LINE-HAUL OR OVER-THE-ROAD TRANSPORTATION

1. All vehicles should be pre-cooled to an inside air temperature of 20°F. or lower prior to loading, and after completing pre-tripping procedures.

2. Frozen foods should be securely packaged before they are offered for transportation.

3. Product temperature should be 0°F. or lower when tendered to carrier for loading. Carrier should not accept product tendered at temperature higher than 0°F. Shipper, consignor, or warehouseman should not tender to a carrier any container which has been damaged or defaced to the extent that it is in an unsalable condition.

4. Carriers should provide their personnel with appropriate testing thermometers and instruction in proper procedure to determine that the product they receive is at 0°F. or lower. Arrival product temperatures should be taken inside the vehicle within a reasonable time after arrival and prior to any unloading. However, the carrier must continue to protect the product until such time as the consignee is ready to accept that which the carrier is ready to tender.

5. No product should be loaded in such manner in any vehicle that it will interfere with the free flow of air into or out of the refrigeration unit, or with the free flow of air around the load in vehicles of other than envelope or coldwall type construction, or those using Freon or liquid nitrogen as a refrigerant.

6. Vehicles should be loaded and unloaded within allowable free time as provided for in governing tariffs to prevent accrual of detention charges.

7. The vehicle's refrigeration unit should be turned on and

the doors kept closed during any period when loading and unloading operations cease.

8. The thermostat on the vehicle's refrigeration unit should be set at 0°F. or lower.

9. All frozen foods shall be held, tendered, and transported at an air temperature of 0°F., or lower, except for defrost cycles, loading and unloading, or other temporary conditions beyond the immediate control of the person under whose care and supervision the frozen food is held. The internal product temperature of frozen food shall be maintained at 0°F. as quickly as possible.

10. After loading has been completed and the vehicle doors closed, the carrier's equipment should be checked prior to departure to insure that the refrigeration system is in proper working order.

VI. HANDLING PRACTICES FOR ROUTE DELIVERY

1. All applicable sections under the part on over-the-road haul transportation above should be followed in the case of route delivery.

2. In addition, each lot for individual consignment should be refrigerated by means of mechanical refrigeration, or by any other method of maintaining product temperature.

3. Vehicles or containers should be precooled to a temperature of 20%F. or lower before being loaded with frozen foods.

4. Doors of route delivery trucks should be kept closed during any period when loading or unloading operations cease. In addition, door curtains or flaps should be used during actual unloading, if the vehicle is not equipped with port doors, to minimize loss of refrigeration.

VII. STORAGE FACILITIES FOR RETAIL STORES

1. Frozen food storage facilities should be capable of maintaining a product temperature of 0°F. or lower.

2. Cabinet type frozen food storage facilities should be defrosted as frequently as necessary to maintain refrigeration efficiency, and should be equipped with an accurate thermometer indicating a representative air temperature.

3. Frozen food storage facilities should have provision for circulation of refrigerated air and should be defrosted as frequently as necessary to maintain refrigeration efficiency. Such facilities should be equipped with an accurate thermometer, the sensing element of which should be located within the upper third of the distance between the floor and ceiling, but not placed in a direct blast of air from the cooling unit, cooling coils, heat exchange units, or near the entrance door.

VIII. RETAIL DISPLAY CASES

1. Display cases should be capable of maintaining an air temperature of 0°F. or lower.

2. Frost on the refrigerated coils and in air passages of the display cases should be removed as frequently as necessary to maintain refrigeration efficiency.

3. Each display case should be equipped with an accurate thermometer, the sensing element of which is located within the path of refrigerated air being returned to the evaporator coils.

4. The manufacturer of display refrigerators shall clearly mark on the walls of each refrigerator the proper food product load levels.

5. Each display case should be equipped with separators to provide false walls to insure free circulation of refrigerated air around the displayed product.

IX. RETAILER HANDLING PRACTICES

1. Frozen foods should not be accepted by a retail outlet when product temperature exceeds 0°F. Department or store manager should approve any product rejection.

2. All frozen foods at a retail outlet should not be held except in frozen food storage or display cases having the characteristics described above.

3. Each retail outlet should be equipped with frozen food storage facilities of sufficient cubic capacity to accommodate those frozen foods (except those to be sold in thawed or semi-thawed condition) that are not placed directly in display case at time of delivery.

4. Retailers should not place frozen food products outside the designated load limit lines.

5. Retail outlets should employ the "first-in, first-out" method of inventory control.

X. STORAGE FACILITIES FOR FOODSERVICE INSTALLATIONS

1. Frozen food storage facilities should be maintained at an air temperature of 0°F. or lower.

2. Total storage facilities should be of sufficient cubic capacity to easily accommodate frozen foods in quantities anticipated for operation of the installation, taking into account frequency of deliveries, probably peak requirements, ordering practices, and related factors.

3. Cabinet-type frozen food storage facilities should be equipped with an accurate thermometer indicating a representative air temperature and should be defrosted as frequently as necessary to maintain refrigeration efficiency.

4. Walk-in type storage facilities should have provision for circulation of refrigerated air and should be defrosted as frequently as necessary to maintain refrigeration efficiency. Such facilities should be equipped with an accurate thermometer, the sensing element of which should be located in the upper 1/3 of the distance between the floor and ceiling, and away from any entrance door or direct air blast from cooling unit or evaporator coil.

XI. FOODSERVICE INSTALLATION HANDLING PRACTICES

1. Frozen foods should not be accepted by a foodservice installation when product delivery temperature exceeds 0°F. Installation manager or his designee should approve rejection.

2. All frozen foods reeived at a foodservice installation should be placed promptly in storage facilities having the characteristics described above. Product should be removed from storage in quantities only sufficient for immediate use.

3. Foodservice installations should rotate frozen food inventories on a "first-in, first-out" basis.

XII. PRODUCT TEMPERATURE

1. Product temperature is that steady temperature that may be determined two ways. The first is by opening the top of the case, removing 2 corner packages, punching a hole through the case wall proceeding from the inside at a point coincident with the center of the first stack of packages and the first and second layer of packages, inserting the sensing element of an accurate dial thermometer or other appropriate means of temperature measurement about 3 in. from the outside so that it will fit snugly between the packages, replacing the 2 corner packages, closing the case, and placing a couple of cases on top to insure good contact with the sensing element of the thermometer.

The second way calls for using a sharp blade and partially cutting out a small section of the case wall in the approximate area of the first stack of packages and the first and second layer of packages, slitting the cut section to allow for insertion of the sensing element, and then proceeding as in the first method above.

2. Only when an accurate determination of temperature is impossible without sacrifice of packages of frozen foods should representative packages or units be opened to allow for insertion of the sensing element for temperature measurement to the approximate center of the packages in question.

3. All temperature measuring equipment should be of high quality and subject to periodic checking for accuracy, employing methods recommended by the manufacturer.

Note: It is recommended that frozen food handlers concerned with the taking of temperatures of frozen foods refer to Technical Service Bulletin No. 7, "Frozen Food Temperatures—Their Meaning and Measurement," by the American Frozen Food Institute. This outlines in detail correct methods for taking product temperatures, describes appropriate equipment for the purpose, discusses certain consideration for proper care and handling of frozen food, and cites certain pertinent provisions of the AFDOUS Model Frozen Food Code.

This code is endorsed and subscribed to by: American Frozen Food Institute, Frozen Potato Products Institute, International Foodservice Manufacturers Association, National Association of Food Chains, National Fisheries Institute, National Association of Refrigerated Warehouses, National Food Brokers Association, National Frozen Food Association, National Institute of Locker & Freezer Provisioners, National Prepared Frozen Food Processors Association, and the National Restaurant Association.

PRODUCTS FOR WHICH THERE ARE FEDERAL STANDARDS

MEAT PRODUCTS

(*All percentages of meat are on the basis of fresh uncooked weight unless otherwise indicated.*)

Baby Food. High Meat Dinner: at least 30% meat. Meat and Broth: at least 65% meat. Vegetable and Meat: at least 8% meat.

Bacon (cooked). Weight of cooked bacon cannot exceed 40% of cured, smoked bacon.

Bacon and Tomato Spread. At least 20% cooked bacon.

Bacon Dressing. At least 8% cured, smoked bacon.

Barbecued Meats. Weight of meat when barbecued cannot exceed 70% of the fresh uncooked meat. Must have barbecued (crusted) appearance, and be prepared over burning or smoldering hardwood or its sawdust. If cooked by other dry heat means, product name must mention the type of cookery.

Barbecue Sauce with Meat. At least 35% meat (cooked basis).

Beans and Meat in Sauce. At least 20% meat.

Beans in Sauce with Meat. At least 20% cooked, or cooked and smoked meat.

Beans with Bacon in Sauce. At least 12% bacon.

Beans with Frankfurters in Sauce. At least 20% frankfurters.

Beans with Meatballs in Sauce. At least 20% meatballs.

Beef and Dumplings with Gravy (or Beef and Gravy with Dumplings). At least 25% beef.

Beef and Pasta in Tomato Sauce. At least 17½% beef.

Beef Carbonade. At least 50% beef tenderloin.

Beef Burger Sandwich. At least 35% hamburger (cooked basis).

Beef Burgundy. At least 50% beef; enough wine to characterize the sauce.

Beef Sauce with Beef and Mushroom. At least 25% beef and 7% mushrooms.

Beef Sausage (raw). No more than 30% fat. No byproducts, no extenders.

MEAT PRODUCTS [Cont.]

Beef Stroganoff. At least 45% fresh uncooked beef or 30% cooked beef, and at least 10% sour cream or a "gourmet" combination of at least 7½% sour cream and 5% wine.

Beef with Barbecue Sauce. At least 50% beef (cooked basis).

Beef with Gravy. At least 50% beef (cooked basis). [**Gravy with Beef.** At least 35% beef (cooked basis).]

Breaded Steaks, Chops, etc. Breading cannot exceed 30% of finished product weight.

Breakfast (frozen product containing meat). At least 15% meat (cooked basis).

Breakfast Sausage. No more than 50% fat.

Brown and Serve Sausage. No more than 35% fat, and no more than 10% added water.

Brunswick Stew. At least 25% of at least two kinds of meat and/or poultry. Must contain corn as one of the vegetables.

Burgundy Sauce with Beef and Noodles. At least 25% beef (cooked basis); enough wine to characterize the sauce.

Burritos. At least 15% meat.

Cabbage Rolls with Meat. At least 12% meat.

Cannelloni with Meat and Sauce. At least 10% meat.

Cappelletti with Meat in Sauce. At least 12% meat.

Cheesfurter. At least 15% cheese.

Chili Con Carne. At least 40% meat.

Chili Con Carne with Beans. At least 40% meat in chili.

Chili Macaroni. At least 16% meat.

Chili Pie. At least 20% meat; filling must be at least 50% of the product.

Chili Sauce with Meat or Chili Hot Dog Sauce with Meat. At least 6% meat.

Chop Suey (American style) with Macaroni and Meat. At least 25% meat.

Chop Suey Vegetables with Meat. At least 12% meat.

Chopped Ham. Must be prepared from fresh, cured, or smoked ham, plus certain kinds of curing agents, and seasonings. May contain dehydrated onions, dehydrated garlic, corn syrup, and not more than 3% water to dissolve the curing agents.

Chorizos Empanadillos. At least 25% fresh chorizos, or 17% dry chorizos.

Chow Mein Vegetables with Meat. At least 12% meat.

MEAT PRODUCTS [Cont.]

Chow Mein Vegetables with Meat and Noodles. At least 8% meat, and the chow mein must equal 2/3 of the product.

Condensed, Creamed Dried Beef or Chipped Beef. At least 18% dried or chipped beef (figured on reconstituted total content).

Corned Beef and Cabbage. At least 25% corned beef (cooked basis).

Corned Beef Hash. At least 35% beef (cooked basis). Must contain potatoes, curing agents, and seasonings. May contain onions, garlic, beef broth, beef fat or others. No more than 15% fat; no more than 72% moisture.

Corn Dog. Must meet standards for frankfurters, and batter cannot exceed the weight of the frankfurter.

Country Ham. A dry-cured product frequently coated with spices.

Cracklin' Corn Bread. At least 10% cracklings (cooked basis).

Cream Cheese with Chipped Beef (**sandwich spread**). At least 12% chipped beef.

Crepes. At least 20% meat (cooked basis), or 10% meat (cooked basis) if the filling has other major characterizing ingredient, such as cheese.

Croquettes. At least 35% meat.

Curried Sauce with Meat and Rice (**casserole**). At least 35% meat (cooked basis) in the sauce and meat part; no more than 50% cooked rice.

Deviled Ham. No more than 35% fat.

Dinners (**frozen product containing meat**). At least 25% meat or meat food product (cooked basis) figured on total meal minus appetizer, bread, and dessert. Minimum weight of a consumer package is 10 oz.

Dumplings and Meat in Sauce. At least 18% meat.

Egg Foo Yong with Meat. At least 12% meat.

Egg Rolls with Meat. At least 10% meat.

Enchilada with Meat. At least 15% meat.

Entrees. Meat or Meat Food Product and One Vegetable must have at least 50% meat or meat food product (cooked basis). Meat or Meat Food Product, Gravy or Sauce, and One Vegetable must have at least 30% meat or meat food product (cooked basis).

MEAT PRODUCTS [Cont.]

Frankfurter, Bologna, and similar Cooked Sausage. May contain only skeletal meat. No more than 30% fat, 10% added water, and 2% corn syrup. No more than 15% poultry meat (exclusive of water in formula).

Frankfurter, Bologna and similar Cooked Sausage with Byproducts or Variety Meats. Same limitations as above on fat, added water, and corn syrup. Must contain at least 15% skeletal meat. Each byproduct or variety meat must be specifically named in the list of ingredients. These include hearts, tongue, spleen, tripe, stomachs, etc.

Frankfurter, Bologna and similar Cooked Sausage with Byproducts or Variety Meats and which also contain nonmeat binders. Product made with the above formulas and also containing up to 3½% nonmeat binder (or 2% isolated soy protein). These products must be distinctively labeled, such as "Frankfurters with byproducts, nonfat dry milk added." The binders must be named in their proper order in the list of ingredients.

Fried Rice with Meat. At least 10% meat.

Fritters. At least 35% meat. A breaded product.

German Style Potato Salad with Bacon. A least 14% bacon (cooked basis).

Goulash. At least 25% meat.

Gravies. At least 25% meat stock or broth, or at least 6% meat.

Ham, Canned. Limited to 8% total weight gain after processing.

Ham, Cooked or Cooked and Smoked (**not canned**). Must not weigh more after processing than the fresh ham weighs before curing and smoking; if contains up to 10% added weight, must be labeled "Ham, Water Added"; if more than 10%, must be labeled "Imitation Ham."

Ham a la King. At least 20% ham (cooked basis).

Ham and Cheese Spread. At least 25% ham (cooked basis).

Hamburger, Hamburg, Burger, Ground Beef, or Chopped Beef. No more than 30% fat; no extenders.

Ham Chowder. At least 10% ham (cooked basis).

Ham Croquettes. At least 35% ham (cooked basis).

Ham Salad. At least 35% ham (cooked basis).

MEAT PRODUCTS [Cont.]

Ham Spread. At least 50% ham.

Hash. At least 35% meat (cooked basis).

Hors d'Oeuvre. At least 15% meat (cooked basis), or 10% bacon (cooked basis).

Jambalaya with Meat. At least 25% meat (cooked basis).

Knishes. At least 15% meat (cooked basis), or 10% bacon (cooked basis).

Kreplach. At least 20% meat.

Lasagna with Meat and Sauce. At least 12% meat.

Lasagna with Sauce, Cheese and Dry Sausage. At least 8% dry sausage.

Liver Products (such as Liver Loaf, Liver Paste, Liver Pate, Liver Cheese, Liver Spread and Liver Sausage). At least 30% liver.

Macaroni and Beef in Tomato Sauce. At least 12% beef.

Macaroni and Meat. At least 25% meat.

Macaroni Salad with Ham or Beef. At least 12% meat (cooked basis).

Manicotti (containing meat filling). At least 10% meat.

Meat and Dumplings in Sauce. At least 25% meat.

Meat and Seafood Egg Roll. At least 5% meat.

Meat Shortcake. At least 25% meat (cooked basis).

Meat and Vegetables. At least 50% meat.

Meatballs. No more than 12% extenders. (cereal, etc., including textured vegetable protein). At least 65% meat.

Meatballs in Sauce. At least 50% meatballs (cooked basis).

Meat Casseroles. At least 25% fresh uncooked meat, or 18% cooked meat.

Meat Curry. At least 50% meat.

Meat Loaf (Baked or Oven-Ready). At least 65% meat, and no more than 12% extenders including textured vegetable protein.

Meat Pasty. At least 25% meat.

Meat Pies. At least 25% meat.

Meat Ravioli. At least 10% meat in ravioli.

Meat Ravioli in Sauce. At least 10% meat.

Meat Salads. At least 35% meat (cooked basis).

Meat Soups. Ready-to-Eat: at least 5% meat. Condensed: at least 10% meat.

MEAT PRODUCTS [Cont.]

Meat Spreads. At least 50% meat.

Meat Taco Filling. At least 40% meat.

Meat Tacos. At least 15% meat.

Meat Turnovers. At least 25% meat.

Meat Wellington. At least 50% cooked tenderloin spread with a liver pate or similar coating and covered with not more than 30% pastry.

Mincemeat. At least 12% meat.

Oleomargarine or Margarine. If product is entirely of animal fat, or contains some animal fat, it is processed under federal inspection. Must contain—individually or in combination—pasteurized cream, cow's milk, skim milk, a combination of nonfat dry milk and water, or finely ground soybeans and water. May contain butter, salt, artificial coloring, vitamins A and D, and permitted functional substances. Finished product must contain at least 80% fat. Labels must clearly state which types of fat are used.

Omelet with Bacon. At least 9% bacon (cooked basis).

Omelet with Dry Sausage or with Liver. At least 12% dry sausage or liver (cooked basis).

Omelet with Ham. At least 18% ham (cooked basis).

Pan Haus. At least 10% meat.

Pate de Foie. At least 30% liver.

Pepper Steak. At least 30% beef (cooked basis).

Peppers and Italian (type) Sausage in Sauce. At least 20% sausage (cooked basis).

Petcha. At least 50% calves feet.

Pizza Sauce with Sausage. At least 6% sausage.

Pizza with Meat. At least 15% meat.

Pizza with Sausage. At least 12% sausage (cooked basis), or 10% dry sausage, such as pepperoni.

Pork Sausage. No more than 50% fat; may contain no byproducts or extenders.

Pork with Barbecue Sauce. At least 50% pork (cooked basis).

Pork with Dressing and Gravy. At least 30% pork (cooked basis).

Prosciutto. A flat, dry-cured ham coated with spices.

Salisbury Steak. At least 65% meat, and no more than 12% extenders including textured vegetable protein.

MEAT PRODUCTS [Cont.]

Sandwiches (containing meat). At least 35% meat in total sandwich; filling must be at least 50% of the sandwich.

Sauce with Chipped Beef. At least 18% chipped beef.

Sauce with Meat, or Meat Sauce. At least 6% meat.

Sauerbraten. At least 50% meat (cooked basis).

Sauerkraut with Wieners and Juice. At least 20% wieners.

Scalloped Potatoes and Ham. At least 20% ham (cooked basis).

Scallopine. At least 35% meat (cooked basis).

Scrambled Eggs with Ham in a Pancake. At least 9% cooked ham.

Scrapple. At least 40% meat and/or meat byproducts.

Shepherd's Pie. At least 25% meat; no more than 50% mashed potatoes.

Sloppy Joe (sauce with meat). At least 35% meat (cooked basis).

Snacks. At least 15% meat (cooked basis), or 10% bacon (cooked basis).

Spaghetti with Sliced Frankfurters and Sauce. At least 12% frankfurters.

Spanish Rice with Beef or Ham. At least 20% beef or ham (cooked basis).

Stews (Beef, Lamb, and the like). At least 25% meat.

Stuffed Cabbage with Meat in Sauce. At least 12% meat.

Stuffed Peppers with Meat in Sauce. At least 12% meat.

Sukiyaki. At least 30% meat.

Sweet And Sour Pork or Beef. At least 25% meat and at least 16% fruit.

Sweet And Sour Spareribs. At least 50% bone-in spareribs (cooked basis).

Swiss Steak with Gravy. At least 50% meat (cooked basis). Gravy and Swiss Steak: at least 35% meat (cooked basis).

Tamale Pie. At least 20% meat; filling must be at least 40% of total product.

Tamales. At least 25% meat.

Tamales with Sauce (or with Gravy). At least 20% meat.

Taquitos. At least 15% meat.

Tongue Spread. At least 50% tongue.

Tortellini with Meat. At least 10% meat.

MEAT PRODUCTS [Cont.]

Veal Birds. At least 60% meat, and no more than 40% stuffing.

Veal Cordon Bleu. At least 60% veal, 5% ham, and containing Swiss, Gruyere, or Mozzarella cheese.

Veal Fricassee. At least 40% meat.

Veal Parmagiana. At least 40% breaded meat product in sauce.

Veal Steaks. Can be chopped, shaped, cubed, frozen. Beef can be added with product name shown as "Veal Steaks, Beef Added, Chopped, Shaped, and Cubed" if no more than 20% beef, or must be labeled "Veal and Beef Steak, Chopped, Shaped, and Cubed." No more than 30% fat.

Vegetable and Meat Casserole. At least 25% meat.

Vegetable and Meat Pie. At least 25% meat.

Vegetable Stew and Meat Balls. At least 12% meat in total product.

Won Ton Soup. At least 5% meat.

POULTRY PRODUCTS

(All percentages of poultry—chicken, turkey, or other kinds of poultry—are on cooked, deboned basis unless otherwise indicated. When standard indicates poultry meat, skin, and fat, the skin and fat are in proportions normal to poultry.)

Baby Food. High Poultry Dinner: at least 18-3/4% poultry meat, skin, fat, and giblets. Poultry with Broth: at least 43% poultry meat, skin, fat, and giblets.

Beans And Rice with Poultry. At least 6% poultry meat.

Breaded Poultry. No more than 30% breading.

Cabbage Stuffed with Poultry. At least 8% poultry meat.

Canned Boned Poultry. Boned (kind), Solid Pack: at least 95% poultry meat, skin and fat. Boned (kind): at least 90% poultry meat, skin and fat. Boned (kind), with Broth: at least 80% poultry meat, skin and fat. Boned (kind), with Specified Percentage of Broth: at least 50% poultry meat, skin, and fat.

Cannelloni with Poultry. At least 7% poultry meat.

Chicken Cordon Bleu. At least 60% boneless chicken breast (raw basis), 5% ham, and either Swiss, Gruyere, or Mozzarella cheese. (If breaded, no more than 30% breading.)

POULTRY PRODUCTS [Cont.]

Creamed Poultry. At least 20% poultry meat. Product must contain some cream.

Egg Roll with Poultry. At least 2% poultry meat.

Entree. Poultry or Poultry Food Product and One Vegetable: at least 37½% poultry meat or poultry food product. Poultry or Poultry Food Product with Gravy or Sauce and One Vegetable: at least 22% poultry meat.

Poultry a la Kiev. Must be breast meat (may have attached skin) stuffed with butter and chives.

Poultry a la King. At least 20% poultry meat.

Poultry Almondine. At least 50% poultry meat.

Poultry Barbecue. At least 40% poultry meat.

Poultry Blintz Filling. At least 40% poultry meat.

Poultry Brunswick Stew. At least 12% poultry meat. Must contain corn.

Poultry Burgers. 100% poultry meat, with skin and fat.

Poultry Burgundy. At least 50% poultry, enough wine to characterize the product.

Poultry Cacciatore. At least 20% poultry meat, or 40% with bone.

Poultry Casserole. At least 18% poultry meat.

Poultry Chili. At least 28% poultry meat.

Poultry Chili with Beans. At least 17% poultry meat.

Poultry Chop Suey. At least 4% poultry meat. Chop Suey with Poultry: at least 2% poultry meat.

Poultry Chow Mein (without noodles). At least 4% poultry meat.

Poultry Croquettes. At least 25% poultry meat.

Poultry Croquettes with Macaroni and Cheese. At least 29% croquettes.

Poultry Dinners (a frozen product). At least 18% poultry meat, figured on total meal minus appetizer, bread, and dessert.

Poultry Empanadillo. At least 25% poultry meat including skin and fat (raw basis).

Poultry Fricassee. At least 20% poultry meat.

Poultry Fricassee of Wings. At least 40% poultry wings (cooked basis, with bone).

Poultry Hash. At least 30% poultry meat.

POULTRY PRODUCTS [Cont.]

Poultry Lasagna. At least 8% poultry meat (raw basis).

Poultry Livers with Rice and Gravy. At least 30% livers in poultry and gravy portion, or 17½% in total product.

Poultry Paella. At least 35% poultry meat or 35% poultry meat and other meat (cooked basis); no more than 35% cooked rice; must contain seafood.

Poultry Pies. At least 14% poultry meat.

Poultry Ravioli. At least 2% poultry meat.

Poultry Roll. No more than 3% binding agents, such as gelatin, in the cooked product; no more than 2% natural cooked-out juices. Poultry Roll with Natural Juices: contains more than 2% natural cooked-out juices. Poultry Roll with Broth: contains more than 2% poultry broth in addition to natural cooked-out juices. Poultry Roll with Gelatin: gelatin exceeds 3% of cooked product.

Poultry Salad. At least 25% poultry meat (with normal amounts of skin and fat).

Poultry Scallopini. At least 35% poultry meat.

Poultry Soup. Ready-to-Eat: at least 2% poultry meat. Condensed: at least 4% poultry meat.

Poultry Stew. At least 12% poultry meat.

Poultry Stroganoff. At least 30% poultry meat and at least 10% sour cream, or a "gourmet" combination of at least 7½% sour cream and 5% wine.

Poultry Tamales. At least 6% poultry meat.

Poultry Tetrazzini. At least 15% poultry meat.

Poultry Wellington. At least 50% boneless poultry breast, spread with a liver or similar pate coating, and covered in not more than 30% pastry.

Poultry with Gravy. At least 35% poultry meat. Gravy with Poultry: at least 15% poultry meat.

Poultry with Noodles or Dumplings. At least 15% poultry meat, or 30% with bone. Noodles or Dumplings with Poultry: at least 6% poultry meat.

Poultry with Noodles Au Gratin. At least 18% poultry meat.

Poultry with Vegetables. At least 15% poultry meat.

Stuffed Cabbage with Poultry. At least 8% poultry meat.

Sauce with Poultry or Poultry Sauce. At least 6% poultry meat.

BASIC MEAT CUTS*

CUT	DESCRIPTION	WEIGHT/PACK	CUT	DESCRIPTION	WEIGHT/PACK
BEEF			**BEEF** [Cont.]		
Bottom Sirloin Butt Steak	Boneless piece of solid meat, cut from bottom sirloin butt.	3 to 16 oz.	**Fabricated Steak**	Chopped or flaked, in oval or in shape of strip steak, available raw, preserved with/without grill marks.	3 to 9 oz.
Braising Steak [Swiss Steak]	Boneless Piece of solid meat, from any primal cut; at least half circumference of steak must be trimmed almost free of fat.	3 to 16 oz.	**Flank Steak**	Boneless solid meat, oval-shape muscle on inside of flank, needs tenderizing.	1 to 3 lb.
Brisket	Thin layer of meat between the breast bone and portions of ribs with cartilage; available raw, cooked, smoked, corned, bone-in, or boneless.	5 to 14 lb.	**Knuckle Steak**	Boneless piece of solid meat, cut from round knuckle.	2½ to 12 oz.
			Liver [Steer]	May be cut across half the lobe or cut from squared off lobe, available plain or breaded.	3 to 12 oz.
Club Steak	Solid piece of meat, with bone; contains feather bone and may contain part of rib bone, cut from short loin.	4 to 20 oz.	**Porterhouse Steak**	Solid meat steak with bone in, fat around outer edge, diameter of tenderloin must be at least 1¼ in.	10 to 32 oz.
Corned Beef	Prepared from briskets, navels, clods, middle ribs, rounds, rumps, etc. Must be cured in pieces not less than 1 lb., raw or cooked, mild or garlic spice cure.	3 to 14 lb.	**Rib [Prime Rib]**	Sixth through 12th ribs with backbone and back tip of blade bone attached, available in various forms for roasting:	
				Rib, Bone-in, Short Cut	20 to 30 lb.
				Rib, Boneless, Tied, Short Cut	17 to 25 lb.
Cubed Steak	Rough surfaced, boneless piece of solid meat taken from anywhere on carcass, tenderized by machine. Can be single piece of solid meat (Special Cube Steak), or 2 pieces folded or "knitted" together.	2½ to 8 oz.		Rib, Bone-in, Tied, Roast Ready	17 to 25 lb.
				Rib, Bone-in, Tied, Roast Ready, Special	17 to 25 lb.
				Rib, Boneless, Tied, Roast Ready	14 to 22 lb.
				Rib Eye Roll	7 to 12 lb.
Eye of Round Steak	Boneless piece of solid meat, a crosswise cut of smallest muscle in round.	3 to 12 oz.	**Rib Eye Roll Roast**	Roast of solid meat, boneless, raw, or precooked.	5 to 12 lb.

*National Frozen Food Association.

CUT	DESCRIPTION	WEIGHT/ PACK	CUT	DESCRIPTION	WEIGHT/ PACK
BEEF [Cont.]			**BEEF [Cont.]**		
Rib Eye Roll Steak	(Delmonico Steak) Oval or rounded steak of solid meat, boneless.	4 to 12 oz.	**Top Sirloin Butt Steak**	Top Steak, boneless piece of solid meat cut from a top sirloin butt, boneless.	3 to 24 oz.
Rib Steak	Solid meat steak, bone-in or boneless, well streaked with fat.	6 to 18 oz. (bone) 4 to 14 oz. (boneless)	**Tongue**	Whole, cooked. Whole, smoked, pickled.	2 to 4 lb. 3 to 5 lb.
Short Ribs	Cut from rib end of the Primal rib, available bone-in or boneless.	3 to 10 oz.	**Kabobs**	Boneless chunks of sirloin for skewer cooking, some already on skewers with green and red peppers and mushrooms.	
Skirt Steak	Boneless piece of solid meat, diaphragm muscle, coarse texture, similar to flank steak.	2½ to 10 oz.	**LAMB**		
			Lambette	Scotch Chop or Lamb Ring. Breast of lamb stuffed with ground lamb shaped into oval.	4 to 6 oz.
Strip Loin Steak	(Kansas City or New York) long steak, bone-in on one side or boneless, fat covers outer edge, opposite bone.	8 to 20 oz. (bone-in) 5 to 16 oz. (boneless)	**Lamb Shoulder [Stewing]**	From boneless shoulder, neck may be attached, surface and seam fat cannot exceed 20% for total lot.	5 lb. cartons or bags
T-Bone Steak	Cut from short loin with flank edge removed, diameter of tenderloin muscle must be ½ in.	8 to 32 oz.	**Leg, Boneless, tied or netted**	One leg, all bones removed, raw or cooked.	6 to 11 lb. raw
Tenderloin Steak	Boneless steak cut as cross-section of the tenderloin muscle.	2½ to 14 oz.	**Loin Chop**	Trimmed or portion of trimmed loin, no hip bone.	3 to 11 oz.
Top Round Roast	Boneless piece of solid meat, cut from round muscle, available raw or cooked.	15 to 25 lb.	**Rib Chop**	Prepared from hotel rack or portion; frenched chops have meat removed from 1½ in. of rib bone.	3 to 10 oz.
Top Round Steak	Boneless piece of solid meat, cut from round muscle, usually 2 steaks cut from each slice of top round.	3 to 16 oz.	**PORK**		
			Bacon	Smoked side of carcass, skin off, precooked or raw, sliced thick or regular	
				Raw, thick slices	14 to 22 per lb.
				Cooked slices	45 to 55 per lb.
				Thin, raw slices	22 to 30 per lb.
				Cooked, slices	85 to 95 per lb.

VEAL*

CUT	DESCRIPTION	WEIGHT/ PACK
Calf's Liver	Sliced liver of calf, may be cut across the entire lobe.	3 to 10 oz.
Cubed Steak	Rough surfaced, boneless, solid meat from any part of carcass. Machine tenderized, available plain or breaded.	3 to 8 oz.
Cutlet	Regular-shaped, boneless slices from leg, available breaded or unbreaded.	2 to 6 oz.
Loin Chop	Also called T-Bone Steak. Cut from loin, trimmed, with flank edge removed.	6 to 12 oz.
Medallion	French name for small, round, flat cut of boneless veal.	
Scallops	Very thin, solid piece of boneless with little or no fat.	
Shoulder Clod Steak	From shoulder clod, in flat oval shape, boneless.	2 to 10 oz.
Stewing Veal	Boneless, solid meat, cut from leg, chuck, or breast by machine or hand into uniform cubes, fat trimmed.	5 or 10 lb. cartons
Leg, Boneless, Tied, Roast	Boneless, tied, solid meat roast from leg.	3 to 5 lb.
Steaks, Veal and Beef	Chopped, shaped and cubed from all veal or beef added, may have up to 30% fat, oval shape.	2½ to 8 oz.

* Veal is the meat of a beef when it is less than 3 months old. The meat is pale with very little fat. Calf is the meat of beef between 3 and 10 months old.

PATTIES AND COMBINATION MEAT PRODUCTS

PRODUCT	DESCRIPTION	WEIGHT/ PACK
Beef Pattie with Textured Vegetable Protein	Must have 3 to 10% textured vegetable protein, may have additional amounts of cereals, water, and vegetable and/or milk proteins; raw, precooked or preseared, IQF (Individually Quick Frozen).	2 to 6 oz. ea.
Beef & Textured Vegetable Protein Pattie	Must have more than 50% meat; must also contain significant amount of textured vegetable protein, may contain cereals, water, milk. Raw precooked, preseared, IQF.	2 to 6 oz. ea.
Beef Patties	Chopped beef, with/without added beef fat and/or seasonings. May have binders and/or extenders and/or beef by-products. (Many identifying names; see "Patties").	
Beef Stix, Sticks	Breaded product, similar to patties.	1 to 2 oz. ea.
Breakfast Sausage	From fresh or frozen meat or mixture, may have meat by-products added, seasoning added. May have binders or extenders added, available in bulk or links.	
	Links, raw or cooked	8 to 16 per lb.
	Bulk	6 to 10 lb. cartons
	Patties, raw or cooked	2 to 4 oz. ea.
Burger	Flat, round, square, rectangle, or oval of ground or chopped meat with 30% or less fat.	2 to 8 oz.

PRODUCT	DESCRIPTION	WEIGHT/ PACK
	May be made of beef, pork, lamb, veal, or combination. Cannot have any additives except seasonings. Available raw, precooked, preseared.	
Chopped Beef	See hamburger.	
Chopped Beef Pattie	See hamburger	
Dinner Balls	Mixture of ground meats and meat byproducts with extenders and/or milk proteins and flavorings; may be raw, fully cooked, or prebrowned, IQF.	½ to 3 oz.
Fritters	Breaded product from flaked, chopped, or thin slice of pork, chicken, beef, or combination. May contain 65% breading.	2 to 6 oz.
Fresh Pork Sausage	Made from fresh or frozen pork, with water and seasonings added.	
	Bulk packed	6 to 10 lb. cartons
	Links, raw or cooked	8 to 16 per lb.
	Raw or precooked patties	¾ to 2 oz. ea.
Ground Beef Patties	See hamburger.	
Hamburger	Ground beef with not more than 30% fat in raw product, up to 25% raw beef cheeks may be added.	10 lb. blocks 12½ lb. rolls
Meat Balls	Ground meat mixed with 12% or less binder, may be all beef or combination beef, veal and/ or pork; at least 65% meat must be used. Shapes in	½ to 2 oz. ea.

PRODUCT	DESCRIPTION	WEIGHT/ PACK
	rounds, IQF, raw, prefried, preseared, or precooked.	
Meat Loaf	Ground beef or beef with veal, lamb, and/or pork, at least 65% raw weight of meat, mixed with not more than 12% binders. May have seasonings and vegetables added. Precooked or raw. Frozen whole, or sliced, precooked meat loaf in dry pack with sauce, or sauce separate.	2 to 6 oz. loaves 2 to 7 lb. loaves 1 to 3 oz. slices
Partially Defatted Beef Fatty Tissue or Pork Fatty Tissue	Beef or pork byproduct derived from low temperature rendering of fresh fatty tissue (trimmings). Added to many ground or chopped meat products to lower costs.	
Patties	Made of ground or chopped turkey, or chicken, or beef, or veal, or lamb, or pork, and/or meat byproducts. May be one kind or mixture, plain or breaded, seasoned or bland, raw, precooked, or preseared. Includes BBQ patties, beef and bacon, chicken fried, Italian sausage & beef, Chuckwagon, Mushroom, Pepper, Taco flavor, Pizza, Hoagie, charbroiled, Pork choppettes, Salisbury, Cube. Poultry patties can be drumstick shaped.	2 to 8 oz.
Pizza Burger	Two thin beef burgers with pizza cheese between, or 1 burger topped with pizza	4 to 9 oz.

PRODUCT	DESCRIPTION	WEIGHT/ PACK	PRODUCT	DESCRIPTION	WEIGHT/ PACK
	cheese; may also have tomato sauces, available raw or pre-seared.			and mushrooms; at least 50% of product must be meat. Also called Beef Bourguignonne.	
Sausage	Farm or Country Style. Fresh pork, ground, flavored with natural spices and sugar. May not have more than 50% trimmable fat on meat before chopping.	3 to 6 lb. cubes	**Beef Crumbles**	Ground meat product, may contain partially defatted, beef fatty tissue, vegetable protein, or other extenders, bulk frozen.	5 lb. bags 20 lb. carton
	Bulk	5 or 10 lb. cartons	**Beef Goulash; Beef Goulash with Noodles**	Similar to Goulash, the meat is all beef, and cooked noodles are part of product.	4 to 6 lb. trays 10 to 12 lb. trays
	Patties	6 to 12 per lb.			
Steaks	Ground or chopped, shaped or molded and cubed product, made of all one kind of meat or combination, no extenders or water, may contain seasonings, plain or breaded, raw or precooked, plain, or sauced. Includes chicken-fried steak, Chuckwagon, pepper steak.	4 to 8 oz. ea.	**Beef Meat Pie**	Combination of diced, shredded, or ground beef, in brown sauce with vegetables, in 2-crust pastry shell in individual pie tins, raw or prebrowned. Must have at least 25% raw meat, before cooking. May be called Beef Pot Pie.	8 to 12 oz. pies
Whole Hog Sausage	Ground or chopped product from frozen or fresh meat with no more than 50% trimmable fat; spices added.		**Julienne Beef and Green Peppers**	Julienne strips of Beef in Red Wine Sauce with onions, mushrooms, and green pepper slices.	4 lb. tray

MEAT ENTREES

PRODUCT	DESCRIPTION	WEIGHT/ PACK	PRODUCT	DESCRIPTION	WEIGHT/ PACK
Barbequed Beef, Pork	Usually meat with barbecue sauce. (See Beef with BBQ Sauce.)		**Beef Pie Filling**	Cubes of beef in brown sauce or gravy, with vegetables such as peas, carrots, onions, and potatoes.	4 to 6 lb. trays
Beans & Wieners	Baked beans with chunks of frankfurters in tomato sauce; at least 20% must be wieners, also available as Beans and Smokie Sausages.	Full-sized trays	**Beef Stew**	Chunks or cubes of beef in brown sauce or gravy combined with vegetables.	4 to 6 lb. trays 10 to 12 lb. trays 5 lb. poly pouch
Beef Burgundy	Chunks or cubes of cooked or prepared beef in Burgundy wine, brown sauce, with onions	5 lb. trays 12 lb. trays	**Beef Tips in Sauce**	Chunks or cubes of beef cooked in brown sauce, plain or flavored with red wine, Burgundy, or Madeira, tomato, precooked. Can have mushrooms. Bulk frozen, may be called	4 to 6 lb. trays 10 to 12 lb. trays

PRODUCT	DESCRIPTION	WEIGHT/PACK	PRODUCT	DESCRIPTION	WEIGHT/PACK
	Beef Tips in Wine Sauce, Braised Beef Cubes, Beef Tips in Madeira, Braised Sirloin Tips.			frozen, must have 25% raw lamb.	
Beef with BBQ Sauce	Sliced, ground, chunk, or shredded cooked beef in tomato barbecue sauce, bulk frozen. Must be made with 50% cooked meat or 72% raw meat before cooking.	3 to 8 pouch 4 to 6 lb. trays 12 lb. trays. 4 lb. tubs	**Lamb Roasted with Gravy**	Slices of roasted lamb with gravy.	half size pan
Beef with Gravy	Sliced beef in brown gravy, unthickened. May have onions. Bulk frozen, must have at least 50% cooked meat. Gravy with Beef must have only 30% cooked beef. Up to 30% of beef may be fat in either product. May be called Braised, Sliced Pot Roast of Beef with Gravy. "Diet" style is salt free.	3 to 4 lb. trays 4 to 6 lb. trays 10 to 12 lb. trays	**Meat Balls with Sauce**	Ground meat mixed with binder such as soy flour; breading or dry milk, shaped into balls, ½ oz. to 2 oz. each, browned or fully cooked, bulk frozen in sauce. At least 65% raw meat is used. Sauce may be brown gravy, tomato, sweet and sour, Pineapple Polynesian, or BBQ. At least half must be meat, remainder can be sauce.	4 to 6 lb. trays
Creamed Chipped Beef	Dried, flaked or chipped beef in cream-style sauce, bulk frozen.	3 to 4 lb. tubs 4 to 6 lb. trays	**Meat Loaf, Sliced**	Ground beef or combination of veal and/or pork at least 65% raw weight, mixed with not more than 12% binders; vegetables may be added. Cooked, then sliced, and block frozen in tomato or BBQ sauce. At least 50% of total product must be meat.	4 to 6 lb. trays 10 to 12 lb. trays
Jambalaya	One or several seafoods, chicken, mixed with ham or sausage, tomatoes, onion, green pepper, in thick sauce, may be mixed with cooked rice. Block frozen, Ham Jambalaya has 25% ham. Can be called Seafood Jambalaya. Considered regional specialty.	3½ to 5 lb. trays	**Peppers, Stuffed**	Sweet green pepper halves stuffed with a mixture of ground meats, may have extension vegetables, IQF, and packed dry (without sauce).	4 to 9 oz. portions half & full trays 6 lb. tray
Lamb Stew	Mixture of lamb cubes or chunks, potatoes, carrots, onions, peas, and other vegetables in brown gravy, may be flavored with tomato. Bulk	4 to 6 lb. trays	**Peppers, Stuffed with Sauce**	Similar to Stuffed Peppers, may have a BBQ, sweet and sour, tomato sauce. Must have at least 12% meat.	5 lb. tray 6 lb. tray 12 oz. ind.
			Pot Roast	Yankee Pot Roast, Beef in Bordelaise sauce with vegetables.	5 lb. tray

PRODUCT	DESCRIPTION	WEIGHT/ PACK	PRODUCT	DESCRIPTION	WEIGHT/ PACK
Pot Roast with Cheese Dumplings	Beef slices in mushroom and tomato sauce with cheese dumplings in cheese cream sauce.	9 lb. 8 oz. tray	Sliced Ham with Raisin Sauce	Baked ham slices, in thickened stock with raisins. Usual portion is 2 or more slices with sauce.	3½ to 6 lb. trays
Pork Roast with Dressing	Sliced, precooked pork with bread-type dressing, dry packed and IQF, or packed with gravy or sauce.	5 to 8 oz. portions, dry 3½ to 6 lb. trays	Swiss Steak with Gravy	Tenderized beef pieces, or sectioned and formed meat, coated with flour, braised in brown gravy with onions. Can have tomatoes and mushrooms added. Must have 50% cooked meat. If label reads Gravy and Swiss Steak, must have 35% cooked meat.	3½ to 5 lb. trays 10 to 12 lb. trays
Pork Fritters	Chopped or tenderized loin or other thin cut portion, breaded, IQF, raw, or pre-cooked.	2 to 5 oz. ea.			
Pork with Sauce or Gravy	May be whole loin slices (less than 30% fat) or cut from shoulder or picnic, in brown gravy, or BBQ sauce.	3 to 5 oz. portions 4 to 6 lb. trays 10 to 12 lb. trays	Turnovers	Raw or precooked dough filled with beef, tamale filling, chicken, cheese pizza, Sloppy Joe filling, beef chili, egg omelet. Can be individually wrapped.	4 to 5 oz.
Salisbury Steak with Mushroom Sauce	Ground meat shaped into round or oval forms, pre-cooked. Must contain at least 65% meat (40% beef) and not more than 12% extenders, bulk frozen with brown sauce containing mushrooms and onions.	6 lb. trays 5 lb. boilable pouch half & full size	Veal Fritters	Chopped, breaded veal.	6 lb. boxes
			Veal, Roasted with Gravy	Veal, roasted, sliced, with gravy.	half size trays
			Western Ham loaf	Ground ham and beef seasoned with hickory flavor in sauce, raw.	half size trays
Sauces	Spicy sauces for frankfurters.	1 oz. tube 3 lb. 4 oz. tube			

PATTIES AND COMBINATION POULTRY PRODUCTS

PRODUCT	DESCRIPTION	WEIGHT/ PACK
Short Ribs with Sauce	Beef short ribs, bone in or boneless, braised in sauce, plain, wine, tomato, BBQ; must have 50% cooked meat. Also called Short Ribs with BBQ sauce, Braised Short Ribs with Gravy.	3 lb. tubs 4 to 6 lb. trays 10 to 12 lb. trays
Split Breast	Half breast, usually with tenderloin in, with/without skin, precooked.	2 to 4 lb.
Fillet	Skinless breast or thigh, large pieces of meat, shaped for portion control; no emulsion.	

PRODUCT	DESCRIPTION	WEIGHT/ PACK	PRODUCT	DESCRIPTION	WEIGHT/ PACK
Processed Oven Roasts (Fully-Cooked Specialties)	Portion control shape; breast or combination white-and-dark or thigh meat. Characterized by small pieces of meat; varying amounts of emulsion.	6 to 8 lb.		white, dark, or mixture, more than 3% cooked weight gelatin added, precooked, may have 15% raw weight skin.	
	Natural shape breast. Characterized by small pieces of meat; varying amounts of emulsion; when sliced will give natural appearing slices.	6 to 8 lb.		Slab, all white, or dark, or mixture pressed into oval cylinder, Cryovac wrapped.	8 lb.
	Breast or thigh or combination, usually not oven roast, round in shape, with smaller pieces of meat; contain varying amount of emulsion.		**Ground Thigh meat**	Ground, bulk frozen.	10 lb. poly bags
Rolls	Boneless cooked turkey meat formed into round or oval shapes with binders or extenders (nonfat dry milk, soy protein, isolate, soya protein concentrate, sodium caseinate, flours, etc.)		**Pulled Meat**	White, dark, or mixture, pulled from bone in irregular pieces, with/without skin, IQF.	5 or 10 lb. poly bags
			Diced Meat	All dark, all white or mixture, precooked, IQF, 1/4-, 3/8-, 1/2-, 3/4-in. dice.	5 lb. poly bags
	Boneless Breast Roll, may include 14% skin, less than 3% gelatin, 2% cooked-out juices, long cylinder or oval, Cryovac wrapped.	6 to 10 lb.	**Drumsticks**	Whole, raw, IQF, from turkeys weighing 10 to 22 lb.	
	Boneless Thigh Roll, may include 8% skin, less than 3% gelatin, 2% cooked-out juices, long cylinder or oval, Cryovac wrapped.	3 to 4 lb.	**Thighs**	Raw, IQF, from birds weighing 10 to 22 lb.	
			Wings	All three joints, from birds weighing 10 to 22 lb.	
	Roll with Broth Added, may be white, dark or mixture, has more than 2% added broth, precooked, may have 15% raw weight skin.	6 to 10 lb.	**Necks, Gizzards, Livers, Hearts, Tails**	Raw.	10 lb. poly bags
	Roll with Gelatin, may be	6 to 10 lb.	**Specialties**	Turkey on a Stick, breaded, precooked, ground meat cylinder on wooden skewer, IQF.	2¼ oz. ea.
				Turkey Bologna, cured meat and spices in sausage form.	5 to 7 lb.
				Turkey Pastrami, Thigh meat, seasoned, cured, and smoked, oval shape with pepper and spice on top.	5 to 6½ lb.

PRODUCT	DESCRIPTION	WEIGHT/PACK	PRODUCT	DESCRIPTION	WEIGHT/PACK
	Turkey Salami, dark meat, seasoned, cured, and smoked, oval shape.	5½ to 7 lb.	Chicken Pie Filling	Boned chicken pieces or cubes, sauce, and vegetables for pot pies, bulk frozen. Must have 14% cooked weight or 25% raw weight chicken.	4½ lb. trays
	Smoked and cured Turkey breast	3 to 7 lb.			

POULTRY ENTREES

PRODUCT	DESCRIPTION	WEIGHT/PACK
Barbecued Chicken	Similar to BBQ Beef, see Chicken in BBQ Sauce.	
Chicken Alfredo	Chicken Breasts or cutlets in sour cream sauce with noodles, block frozen, partially cooked.	5½ to 7 oz. portions 12 to 20 per carton 4 lb. tray
Chicken in BBQ Sauce	Chicken pieces (quarters or 8-cut), bone in, packed in BBQ sauce, bulk frozen.	4 to 6 lb. trays
Chicken in Cream Sauce	Boned chicken pieces in cream sauce, can include Chicken a la King, Chicken Fricassee, Creamed Chicken, Creamed Chicken Jardiniere (with vegetables), must have 20% cooked, boneless chicken.	4½ to 5 lb. tray 12 lb. trays
Chicken Fricassee	Pulled chicken blended in cream sauce with vegetables.	4 lb. tray
Chicken in Wine Sauce	Bone-in or boneless chicken breasts or legs in red or white wine sauce, can be with onions and mushrooms (Chicken Monmartre or Coq au Vin), block frozen.	4½ to 8 oz. portion in half and full trays
Chicken Paradise	Bone-in or boneless breast or leg in sauce with ham, vegetables, noodles, bulk frozen raw or partially cooked.	6 to 8 oz. portions, 12 portions per carton

For Chicken Pot Pie:

Chicken Pot Pie — Boned chicken chunks or cubes, sauce, and vegetables in 2-crust pastry shell, in pie pan, prebaked, or raw. Must have 14% cooked or 25% raw weight chicken. — 8 to 12 oz. ea.

The past few years has seen an expanded market for such poultry convenience foods as packaged and frozen poultry parts, poultry pot pies, and ready-to-heat-and-serve poultry dinners. The machine shown here removes bones from cooked poultry to be used in poultry pies and other prepared poultry foods.

PRODUCT	DESCRIPTION	WEIGHT/PACK
Chicken Stuffed with Rice	Boned-in or boneless chicken breast, filled with white or wild rice or mixture, IQF, available also in brown or tomato sauce, plain or with onions and mushrooms.	6 to 8 oz. portions IQF, 12, 18, 24 per carton
Chicken Turnovers	Diced or chunks of chicken in gravy or cream sauce, plain, with vegetables, in raw or pre-browned pastry case. Chicken filling is cooked, IQF.	2 to 6 oz. ea.
Chicken Whiskey	Similar to Chicken in Wine Sauce, with whiskey in sauce.	
Chicken with Apples and Almonds	Partially boned, or boneless breast or leg with filling of apples and almonds, IQF, raw, or precooked.	6 to 8 oz. portion. 12, 18, 24 per carton, half size tray
Chicken with Cheese and Mushrooms	Breast or leg in cheese sauce with mushrooms, bulk frozen; may also be chicken pieces with stuffing of cheese and mushrooms, IQF.	6 to 8 oz. portion, half size tray
Chicken with Dumplings	Chunks or cubes of boned chicken in sauce with round, oval biscuit-type dumplings, bulk frozen. Must have 15% cooked, boneless chicken. Dumplings with Chicken must have 6% boneless chicken.	4 to 6 lb. tray
Chicken with Noodles	Chunks or diced chicken in gravy or sauce with noodles, bulk frozen, may have vegetables added, or au gratin topping. Must have 15% cooked chicken, Noodles and Chicken must have 6% cooked chicken.	4 to 6 lb. tray

PRODUCT	DESCRIPTION	WEIGHT/PACK
Duckling	Half or quarter, precooked bone-in, or boneless, or partially boned, IQF plain, or IQF with bulk frozen sauce separate, or with sauce over Duckling. Sauces can be Cherry, Montmorency, Cerise or Sweet Cherry, or a la Orange.	varies with size of duck
Rock Cornish Game Hen Stuffed with Apples and Almonds	Bone-in, boneless or partially boned Cornish hen, whole or half, filled with stuffing of chopped apples and almonds, IQF, plain or block frozen, with glaze or au jus style sauce.	7 to 22 oz. portions
Rock Cornish Game Hen Stuffed with Rice or Bread Stuffing	Bone-in, boneless, or partially boned Cornish hen, whole or half, filled with stuffing of wild regular rice or combination, or New England style bread stuffing, IQF, plain or block frozen, with glaze or jus style sauce.	7 to 22 oz.
Turkey a la King	Chunks or pieces of white and dark turkey cooked in cream sauce with peas, mushrooms, and pimientos, at least 20% must be cooked, boneless turkey. Block frozen.	5 lb. pouch 3½ to 5 lb. tray 10 to 12 lb. tray
Turkey and Gravy	Sliced, cooked turkey, white and dark with gravy, must contain 35% cooked turkey; gravy plain or with chopped or ground giblets.	4 to 6 lb. tray 10 to 12 lb. tray
Turkey and Noodles	Similar to Chicken and Noodles.	

PRODUCT	DESCRIPTION	WEIGHT/PACK
Turkey Pie Filling	See Chicken Pie Filling.	
Turkey with Dressing and Gravy	Sliced, cooked meat, at least 25%, usually white and dark meat layered on dressing with gravy.	3½ to 6 lb. tray 12 lb. tray

STYLE	DESCRIPTION	WEIGHT/PACK
CHICKEN PARTS		
Halves	Split equally, full length along backbone and breast.	10 to 18 oz. ea.
Quarters	Four pieces of single bird, cut variously: Breast Quarter, half breast, wing, portion of back. Breast Quarter Without Wing, half breast, portion of back only. Leg Quarter, thigh and drumstick, portion of back. Thigh with Back Portion, similar to leg quarter, but with drumstick removed. Leg with Pelvic Bones, leg with adhering meat, skin and pelvic bone.	6 to 11 oz. ea.
Breast	Separated from back at shoulder joint cut through 2 sections of rib cage; ribs and/or keel bone may be removed, or breast may be completely boneless, with/without skin.	6 to 13 oz.
Two Cut Breast	Whole breast, cut lengthwise down breastbone, splitting the wishbone.	4½ to 7½ oz.
Leg	Thigh and drumstick, may in-	5 to 8 oz.

STYLE	DESCRIPTION	WEIGHT/PACK
	clude pelvic meat but not bone, no back skin.	
Wing	Entire wing with muscle and tissue, wing tip may be removed.	2 to 3½ oz.
Wing Drummette	Humerus of poultry wing—joint closest to body—with skin and meat attached.	1 to 2½ oz.
Wing Portion	Second and tip joints, or wing without drummette.	1½ to 2½ oz.
Back	Pelvic bone and entire backbone from tail to shoulder joint, with/without ribs and scapula.	approx. 10 oz.
Thigh	Disjointed at hip with drumstick removed, pelvic meat may be attached but no bone and back skin.	3 to 4 oz.
Drumstick	Disjointed at knee, no feet.	2½ to 4 oz.
Wishbone	Breast section closest to neck with covering meat and skin, cut halfway between ends and front point of breastbone, no neck skin.	3 to 5 oz.
Pulled, Cooked	White or dark meat or mixture, pulled from bone in various sized pieces, with/without skin, IQF.	5 or 10 lb. packages
Patties	See Patties section under Meat.	
CHICKEN SPECIALTIES		
Nuggets	Diced, cooked chicken, breaded, prebrowned; breading can be 30% raw weight of product.	

STYLE	DESCRIPTION	WEIGHT/ PACK
Franks	Ground chicken shaped into wiener, added spices.	8, 10, 12 to lb.
Bologna	Ground chicken and spices in sausage form.	20-lb. roll
Corn Dogs	Ground chicken in frankfurter style, cornmeal batter, may be on stick, breading can be 50% of raw weight.	2 to 3 oz. ea.
Rolls	Boneless cooked chicken of various sized pieces, all white, or all dark, or mixture, formed into roll. Butter, broth, stock, water, fats, or flavorings may be added.	
	Chicken Roll, may contain 25% skin in cooked product, but no more than 3% binders and 2% cooked-out juices.	4 to 6 lb.
	Boneless Chicken Breast Roll, may contain up to 20% skin, cooked weight, but no more than 3% binders and 2% cooked-out juices. Round or oval.	4 to 7 lb.

ETHNIC SPECIALTIES:

PRODUCT	DESCRIPTION	WEIGHT/ PACK
RUSSIAN, HUNGARIAN, GERMAN, DUTCH, SCANDINAVIAN		
Beef Stroganoff (Russian)	Cubes, slices, or chunks of beef or ground beef (30% cooked) in brown sauce, with 10% sour cream or 7½% sour cream, 5% wine. Tomato paste,	5-lb. pouches 4 to 6 lb. trays 10 to 12 lb. trays

ETHNIC SPECIALTIES [Cont.]

PRODUCT	DESCRIPTION	WEIGHT/ PACK
RUSSIAN, HUNGARIAN, GERMAN, DUTCH, SCANDINAVIAN [Cont.]		
	puree, or mushrooms, onions may be added. Stroganoff Sauce with Beef has more sauce than meat.	
Green Pepper Sauce and Beef Strips	Beef strips in wine sauce with vegetables garnished with green pepper strips.	4 lb. tray
Blintzes (Russian)	Thin, flat egg crepe with cheese or fruit filling, jelly roll fashion. Fillings include cottage or pot cheese, blueberries, cherries, or fruit in thickened sauce, IQF. Also considered Jewish specialty.	1½ to 4½ oz. ea.
Chicken Kiev (Russian)	Partly boned or boneless breast, with or without skin, filled with butter and herbs, coated with flour or breading, raw or prebrowned, IQF.	5 to 10 oz. portion 8 to 12 portions per carton
Cornish Hen Breast Kiev	Boned breast, wing bone attached, wrapped around finger of butter, egg-dipped, lightly breaded; ready to fry or prebrowned.	6 to 7 oz.
Chicken Bohemian (Hungarian)	Leg filled with forcemeat mixture containing spinach, cheese, spices, IQF.	6 to 8 oz. portion, 12 per carton half size tray
Cornish Breast Pojarsky	Boned breast, wing bone attached, contains diced breast meat, almonds, truffles, egg-	7 oz.

ETHNIC SPECIALTIES [Cont.]

PRODUCT	DESCRIPTION	WEIGHT/ PACK
RUSSIAN, HUNGARIAN, GERMAN, DUTCH, SCANDINAVIAN [Cont.]		
	dipped and lightly breaded, ready to fry.	
Goulash (Hungarian)	Stew of beef, veal cubes or chunks 25% raw weight with onions and tomatoes, seasoned with paprika; may also have sweet peppers and tomato-brown sauce, bulk frozen. Also Veal Goulash or Goulash with Noodles.	4 to 6 lb. tray 10 to 12 lb. tray
Chicken Scandia (Scandinavian)	Leg of chicken filled with cheddar cheese, apples, walnuts, IQF, wrapped individually or in layers.	9 to 12 lb. tray
Sauerbraten (German)	Sliced, cooked beef in tart brown gravy, tomato and/or wine may be added, may have spaetzle added, block frozen, 50% of product is cooked meat.	9 to 12 lb. trays
Stuffed Cabbage (Hungarian)	Cooked cabbage leaves filled with mixture of ground or chopped meat (beef or beef and pork) rice and tomato, usually in sweet sour tomato sauce. Bulk frozen. Also called Cabbage Rolls, Cabbage Rolls with Meat (12% meat), Stuffed Cabbage with Meat in Sauce (12% meat).	6 lb. trays
Stuffed Cornish Leg, (Dutch)	Boneless leg, skin on, stuffed with apple, almonds, bread, and spices.	8 oz.

ETHNIC SPECIALTIES [Cont.]

PRODUCT	DESCRIPTION	WEIGHT/ PACK
RUSSIAN, HUNGARIAN, GERMAN, DUTCH, SCANDINAVIAN [Cont.]		
Swedish Meat Balls (Swedish)	Ground meat mixed with binder in cream or brown sauce, generally flavored with nutmeg, prebrowned or fully cooked, bulk frozen.	4 to 6 lb. trays
BRITISH, WELSH, IRISH		
Beef Turnovers	Cooked filling of ground or diced beef, peas, other vegetables in brown sauce, in pastry case, raw or precooked, IQF, individually wrapped. May also be called Pasty. May also be made of ham or chicken.	2 to 6 oz.
Beef Wellington	Small filets or steaks from tenderloin and forcemeat or liver pate wrapped in pastry crust; must be 50% cooked tenderloin, 30% crust, IQF. Also called Filet de Boeuf Wellington.	6 to 12 oz.
Breast of Rock Cornish Game Hen Wellington	Breast filled with mushroom duxelle, Madeira wine, spices, wrapped in puff paste.	6 oz.
Welsh Rarebit	Savory cheese sauce, used over toast.	5 lb. tubs 3 to 5 lb. trays
Irish Stew	Mixture of lamb cubes or chunks, potatoes, onions, in brown gravy. Must have 25% raw lamb. Bulk frozen.	4 to 6 lb. trays

ETHNIC SPECIALTIES [Cont.]

PRODUCT	DESCRIPTION	WEIGHT/ PACK
PASTA [also see Italian Entrees]		
Macaroni and Beef	Mixture of cooked macaroni, elbow or short cut shape, and cooked ground beef, at least 25% raw meat. Bulk frozen. May be called Macaroni and Beef with Tomatoes if product has 12% beef and contains some tomatoes	4 to 6 lb. tray 10 to 12 lb. tray
Macaroni and Cheese	Cooked macaroni, elbow, short cut, or seashell, mixed with cheese sauce or cheese and cream-style sauce, bulk frozen. May also have ham added, up to 19% cooked.	3½ to 5 lb. tray 10 to 12 lb. tray
Tuna and Noodles	Casserole or cooked noodles and flakes of tuna fish; some have cheese or crumb topping, some cream-style sauce, bulk frozen. Also called Noodles and Tuna Casserole, more noodles and vegetables than tuna.	3½ to 5 lb. tray
FRENCH, CONTINENTAL		
Beef Bourguignonne	Chunks or cubes or cooked or preseared beef in Burgundy wine brown sauce with onions and mushrooms. 50% must be meat; bulk frozen.	5 lb. trays 12 lb. trays
Chicken Chasseur	Partially boned or boneless breast or leg in tomato-brown gravy, usually with mushrooms and onions, block frozen.	6 to 8 oz. portions half and full size trays

ETHNIC SPECIALTIES [Cont.]

PRODUCT	DESCRIPTION	WEIGHT/ PACK
FRENCH, CONTINENTAL [Cont.]		
Chicken Cordon Bleu	Boneless breast (with/without wing) or leg stuffed with cheese and cured pork, coated with seasoned breading, crumbs, or batter. Raw, browned, precooked. See Veal Cordon Bleu.	6 to 8 oz. portions 12, 15, 18 per tray, cartons, portion pouch
Chicken in Champagne	See Chicken in Wine Sauce.	
Coq Au Vin	See Chicken in Wine Sauce.	
Crepes a la Reine	Cream style veloute sauce with diced chicken and mushrooms used for filling, at least 10% chicken.	4½ oz. (2 per portion)
Crepes de la Mer	Diced seafood sauteed, wine seasoned, in French pancake.	5½ oz. (2 per portion)
Duckling Bigarade	Roasted, partially boned, half duck with orange based sauce.	10½ oz.
Fish Fillet Amandine	See Fish Fillet with Sauce.	
Quiche Lorraine	Cheese-bacon tart; can also be Lobster Quiche (lobster-cheese filling), Crab Quiche (king crab-cheese filling).	7 oz.
Coquille Saint-Jacques	Scallops in mushroom-cheese sauce, edging of fluted potato, served on shell.	7 oz.
Sole Nantua	Dover Sole fillet stuffed with sole/lobster mousse, garnished with Newburg sauce.	7½ oz.

ETHNIC SPECIALTIES [Cont.]

PRODUCT	DESCRIPTION	WEIGHT/ PACK
FRENCH CONTINENTAL [Cont.]		
Rock Cornish Game Hen, Stuffed	Boned hen, stuffed with wild rice, mushrooms, sauce, maison, cognac seasoned.	12 oz.
Cornish Game Hen Breast Cordon Bleu	Boned breast, with imported ham and blend of cheeses, egg-dipped and lightly breaded for frying, or prebrowned.	6 to 7 oz.
Stuffed Cornish Game Hen Leg Cordon Bleu or Parisian Style	Boneless leg filled with ham and cheese, egg-dipped and breaded, or can also be stuffed with wild rice, mushrooms, and cognac.	8 oz.
Veal Cordon Bleu	Scallop of Veal folded over thin slice of ham, Proscuitto, or bacon, and Swiss, Gruyere, or Mozzarella cheese; edges sealed, portion breaded, raw, or prebrowned, IQF, must be 60% raw veal, 5% ham and cheese, not more than 30% breading.	5 to 10 oz. ea.
ITALIAN		
Canneloni	Large, flat, square noodle with herbed Ricotta, or Ricotta mixed with other cheese, egg, or spinach. Other fillings may include veal, chicken, beef. IQF without sauce, bulk frozen with cream-style sauce, cheese sauce, tomato sauce. Also done in crepe style. Tomato sauce with meat must have 10% meat. Chicken filling must be 7% cooked, boneless chicken.	4 to 5½ oz.

ETHNIC SPECIALTIES [Cont.]

PRODUCT	DESCRIPTION	WEIGHT/ PACK
ITALIAN [Cont.]		
Chicken Cacciatore	Chunks of boned or bone-in chicken legs, or breasts in tomato sauce, tomato and wine sauce, Italian seasonings. Must have 20% cooked, boneless chicken; may have mushrooms and pearl onions, called Hunter Style. Bulk frozen, portion packed.	4 to 6 lb. trays 12 lb. trays pouches
Chicken Florentine	Bone-in or boneless breast or leg with spinach stuffing, IQF, bulk packed, plain or block frozen in sauce; chicken raw or partially cooked.	6 to 8 oz. portion 4 to 6 lb. tray 12 lb. tray
Chicken Parmigiana	Chicken in tomato sauce with Mozzarella, Parmesan cheese.	6 to 8 oz. portion 4 to 6 lb. tray 12 lb. tray
Chicken Tetrazzini	Sauteed chicken and sliced mushrooms in creamy cheese sauce over pasta.	4 lb. tray
Italian Sausage and Peppers	Italian hot or sweet sausage, short lengths, with sliced sweet peppers, block frozen.	3½ to 6 lb. tray
Lasagne	Casserole of wide macaroni layered with Ricotta or cottage cheese, ground or chopped beef, and/or pork, in herb flavored tomato sauce, topped with Mozzarella, Provolone, or Parmesan. Bulk frozen. Variations include All Cheese Lasagne; Lasagne with Meat and Sauce (12% meat); Lasagne Neopolitan; Lasagne with Sauce, Cheese and Dry Sausage (8% dry sausage).	5 to 6 lb. trays 10 to 12 lb. trays 85 oz. trays

ETHNIC SPECIALTIES [Cont.]

PRODUCT	DESCRIPTION	WEIGHT/ PACK
ITALIAN [Cont.]		
Lumache with Cheese Filling	Jumbo pasta shells stuffed with blend of cheeses topped with tomato sauce.	5 lb. tray
Manicotti	Large tubes of pasta stuffed with mixture of Ricotta or cottage cheese, herbs, and binder, IQF, plain, bulk frozen in cream-style sauce.	1 to 4 oz. ea. 4 to 6 lb. trays
Mostaccioli	Pasta with meaty Italian tomato sauce.	4 lb. tray
Meat Ravioli	Pillows of pasta filled with ground beef or beef-veal-pork combination, herb flavored, binder may be added. Packed with herbed tomato sauce. Meat Ravioli must have 10% meat. Dry pack IQF.	3½ to 6 lb. trays IQF 8 to 40 per lb.
Pizza	Yeast dough crust coated with herbed tomato sauce, Mozzarella cheese, or other toppings. Meat pizza must have 10% raw meat; sausage pizza, 12% cooked sausage or 10% dry sausage. Toppings may be hamburger, pepper, mushroom, pepperoni, textured vegetable protein, shrimp, onions. Can be cut in squares, rectangles, triangles.	2 to 6 oz. portions 6 to 32 oz. whole 4 to 16 oz. diam.
Ravioli in Sauce	Small pillows of pasta filled with ground meat or Ricotta or cottage cheese, block frozen in herbed tomato sauce. Meat Ravioli must have 10% meat.	4 to 6 lb. trays 10 to 12 lb. trays boilable bags

ETHNIC SPECIALTIES [Cont.]

PRODUCT	DESCRIPTION	WEIGHT/ PACK
ITALIAN [Cont.]		
Spaghetti with Meat Balls	Cooked spaghetti mixed with herbed tomato sauce and precooked meat balls, block frozen.	4 to 6 lb. trays 10 to 12 lb. trays
Spaghetti Sauce with Meat or Meatless	Herbed tomato sauce with 6% ground or chopped meat, cooked, block frozen; meatless with mushrooms.	3 lb. tubs 12 lb. trays
Turkey Tetrazzini	Similar to Chicken Tetrazzini.	5 lb. pouches
Veal Parmigiana	Chopped or ground veal patty or tenderized scallop, breaded with crumbs mixed with Parmesan, precooked, packed in herbed tomato sauce. May have Mozzarella topping. Must have 50% breaded meat, also called Veal Parmesan.	2 to 5 oz. portions 3½ to 5 lb. trays
Veal and Peppers	Cubes of veal with julienne strips of bell peppers, onions, in tomato sauce.	12 lb. trays
Veal Scallopini	Scallops of thin slices of boneless veal, tenderized, breaded, cooked, in tomato or wine flavored brown sauce, or with spinach (Florentine).	2 to 4 oz. portions 3 1/3 to 5 lb. tray 10 to 12 lb. trays
CHINESE, ORIENTAL, HAWAIIAN, POLYNESIAN		
Brochette of Cornish Hawaiian	Boneless breast of Cornish meat on skewer, alternated with pineapple, mushroom, kumquat, and pimiento.	9 oz.
Chicken Chop Suey	4% diced or chunks, cooked chicken with vegetables such	3½ to 6 lb. tray 10 to 12 lb. tray

ETHNIC SPECIALTIES [Cont.]

PRODUCT	DESCRIPTION	WEIGHT/PACK
CHINESE, ORIENTAL, HAWAIIAN, POLYNESIAN [Cont.]		
	as bean sprouts, mushrooms, celery, onions, bamboo shoots, water chestnuts.	
Chop Suey Vegetables with Meat	Combination of cooked pork, beef, or chicken with celery, bean sprouts, onion, pimienttos, mushrooms, water chestnuts; must contain 12% meat or 4% boneless chicken.	4 to 6 lb. tray 10 to 12 lb. tray 5 lb. pouches
Chicken Hawaiian	Bone-in or boneless leg or breast, or pieces in sweet and sour sauce, with fruits such as pineapple, maraschino cherries, tomatoes, green pepper, or onion. Also called Chicken Aloha, Sweet and Sour Chicken, Polynesian Chicken.	5 to 8 oz. portions in 4 to 6 lb. tray 10 to 12 lb. tray
Chicken Chow Mein	At least 4% chunks or cubes, cooked, in thickened sauce with oriental vegetables; bean sprouts, celery, sweet green and red pepper, water chestnuts, mushrooms, onion. Bulk frozen.	4 to 6 oz. pouches 5 lb. pouches half size trays 72 oz. pan
Chow Mein	Combination of cubes or chunks of beef, chicken, pork, or ground beef in thickened sauce with oriental vegetables. Bulk frozen. Also called Beef Chow Mein (more meat than vegetables) or Chow Mein Vegetables with Meat (12% raw meat or 4% cooked chicken).	4 to 6 lb. trays 10 to 12 lb. trays
Cornish Game Hen, Hawaiian	Partially boned and stuffed, leg and wing bone in, stuffed	12 oz.

ETHNIC SPECIALTIES [Cont.]

PRODUCT	DESCRIPTION	WEIGHT/PACK
CHINESE, ORIENTAL, HAWAIIAN, POLYNESIAN [Cont.]		
	with pineapple, walnuts; pimiento garnish.	
Polynesian Pork	Boneless pork loin in sauce with pineapple, raisins, and peppers. Also called Sweet and Sour Pork.	4 to 6 lb. tray
Stuffed Breast Hawaiian	Cornish game hen, breast, boned, stuffed with pineapple, walnuts and pimiento; skin on, wing bone attached.	8 oz.
Stuffed Leg Hawaiian	Cornish game hen, leg, boned, stuffed with pineapple, walnuts, pimiento.	8 oz.
Vegetable Chow Mein	Oriental style vegetables in soy-seasoned sauce, bulk frozen.	4 to 6 lb. trays
Egg Rolls Shrimp Rolls Meat Rolls	Usually pillow-shaped noodle type dough filled with chopped vegetables and shrimp, or meat (10% raw meat), or egg. Cocktail size, some hand rolled (shrimp) sold by count and weight, IQF.	7/16 to 2 oz. or 2 to 7 oz. ea.
Rumaki	Chicken livers wrapped with bacon and water chestnuts.	1/2 to 1 1/2 oz. ea.
Meat Balls Polynesian, Sweet and Sour, etc.	See Meat Entrees.	
MEXICAN		
Burritos	Tortilla filled with cooked, seasoned, ground or chopped meat, in spicy brown or tomato sauce. Other fillings are red	3 1/4 to 6 oz. some indiv., some bulk packed

ETHNIC SPECIALTIES [Cont.]

PRODUCT	DESCRIPTION	WEIGHT/ PACK
MEXICAN [Cont.]	chili with beef and beans; green chili with beef and beans.	
Chili Con Carne	Ground or chopped meat in highly seasoned tomato sauce, 40% raw meat; vegetable protein may be added; Chili Mac must have 17% meat, has macaroni. Chili con Carne with Beans must have 25% raw meat. Bulk frozen. Also available in concentrate in brick form.	3 to 5 lb. tubs 4 to 7 lb. trays 10 to 12 lb. trays 5 lb. brick
Enchiladas	Tortilla filled with bean, cheese, or chili-beef mixture; rolled up, covered with spicy tomato or brown sauce. IQF without sauce, bulk frozen with sauce.	2 to 3 oz. ind. 12 to 24 in 3 to 6 lb. tray
Pochito	Wiener with chili wrapped in tortilla.	2 doz. per bag
Refried Beans	Pinto beans, cooked, then refried.	5 lb. tubs
Tacos	Folded corn tortilla shell with meat filling.	12 per bag
Taco Filling	Beef cuts with seasoning.	3¼ lb. tub
Taquitos	Corn tortilla rolled around filling of sliced beef or ground beef, 6 in. by ½ in.	7 doz. to box 1 doz. to box
Tamales	Chunks of beef in corn husk-parchment wrap, ground beef in double parchment wrap.	5 oz. 4 oz.
Tamale Pie	Meat filling with corn meal topping.	4 lb. bag

SEAFOOD ENTREES

PRODUCT	DESCRIPTION	WEIGHT/ PACK
Alaskan King Crab Newburg	Chunks of King Crab in cream style sauce with eggs and sherry, bulk frozen.	4 to 6 lb. tray
Crab Cakes	Mixture of minced or shredded crabmeat with crumbs or breading, egg or binder, in patties, lightly breaded, IQF, raw or prebrowned.	1½ to 4½ oz. ea.
Crab Newburg	Similar to Alaskan King Crab Newburg, using crabmeat.	4 to 6 lb. tray
Deviled Crab	Shredded or chopped crabmeat mixed with highly spiced breading, can be in natural or foil shells, IQF.	2 to 5 oz. portion
Fish Cakes	Ground, minced, or shredded fish mixed with breading or binder, in patties of flat, rounded cakes, lightly breaded, pre-cooked, or raw, IQF.	1 to 4 oz.
Fish Fillet with Sauce	Square or natural shape fillet in sauce, often labeled by species name of fish and type of sauce; includes Amandine, Lemon, Tomato, Herbed butter, Cream style, Mornay.	2 to 8 oz.
Lobster Newburg	Similar to Crab Newburg, using Lobster meat.	
Seafood Cakes	Similar to Fish Cakes except a mixture of fish and shellfish is used. May be called Seafood Burger, Patty or Snack.	
Seafood Newburg	See Crab Newburg.	72 oz. pans
Seafood Turnovers	Similar to Beef or Chicken Turnovers, using seafood.	

SEAFOOD ENTREES [Cont.]

PRODUCT	DESCRIPTION	WEIGHT/PACK
Shrimp Creole	Shrimp in tomato sauce seasoned with okra, onion, pepper, celery, block frozen.	3½ to 6 lb. tray
Shrimp Newburg	See Crab Newburg.	
Stuffed Flounder	Large fillet, or small with bone in, stuffed with mixture of shredded crabmeat and breading, can have onions and celery, IQF, can be rolled with turban style filling, or envelope style.	4 to 12 oz. ea.
Stuffed Shrimp	Split or butterflied shrimp stuffed with shredded crabmeat breading, seasoning mixture. Breaded or battered and breaded, raw IQF.	1½ to 4 oz. ea.

FROZEN FRUITS

PRODUCT	DESCRIPTION	WEIGHT/PACK
Apples	Usually in sugar syrup or water pack; IQF dry pack sliced apples available.	5, 10, 15, 25 30-lb. tins or cans
Apricots	Peeled or unpeeled; halves, slices, diced, randon cut; machine or hand pitted; ascorbic acid added to prevent discoloration.	2½, 5, 6, 10, 15, 30-lb. containers
Berries, Misc.	Less common varieties are blackberries, boysenberries, dewberries, loganberries, nectarberries, youngberries, in sugar or in syrup, IQF with no sugar.	25, 28, 30-lb. containers
Blueberries	Cultivated or wild variety, dry pack.	20, 30-lb. polylined car-

FROZEN FRUITS [Cont.]

PRODUCT	DESCRIPTION	WEIGHT/PACK
		tons, 20-lb. tins, 500-lb. lugs, polylined.
Cranberries	Most are IQF without sugar.	5 lb. bags
Raspberries	Red, black, purple, IQF without sugar, block frozen in syrup or sugar.	6½, 28, 30-lb. containers
Strawberries	Whole (small, medium, large) IQF without sugar, whole in sugar syrup, block frozen; sliced in sugar syrup, block frozen.	30, 50 lb. cont. 6½, 30, 420-lb.
Cherries	Sweet, pitted or unpitted, IQF without sugar, block frozen with sugar, in syrup. Sour, mostly pitted, with sugar, in syrup.	30 lb. Retail pack of 1½ lb. available
Citrus Salad	Combination of grapefruit and orange sections, peeled, IQF.	4 oz. cup
Grapefruit	Peeled white or pink segments, IQF or bulk frozen in grapefruit juice or light syrup.	4 oz. indiv. cup
Melon Balls	1-in. spheres from cantaloup, or honeydew, or mixed, IQF or in light syrup.	8-lb. containers
Peaches	Block frozen with no sugar; with sugar and in syrup, halves, quarters, diced, slices, mixed pieces.	8½, 30, 32-lb. containers
Plums	Blue, red, yellow-green; pitted, whole, halved, crushed or broken, in sugar, block frozen.	30, 32-lb. containers

FROZEN FRUITS [Cont.]

PRODUCT	DESCRIPTION	WEIGHT/ PACK
Rhubarb	Cut (1 in. pieces) unsweetened, IQF, and in sugar mix.	2½, 6, 15, 30-lb. containers

FROZEN JUICE CONCENTRATES

PRODUCT	DESCRIPTION	WEIGHT/ PACK
Apple	Mixture of varieties, dispenser pack available.	25.6, 32, 46 oz. cans 5 gal. cont, dilution ratio: from 3-5 to 1
Grape	From one variety of mixture, unfermented, sweetened, dispenser pack available.	25.6, 32, 46 oz. cans dilution ratio: from 1-6 to 1
Grapefruit	White or pink, sweetened or unsweetened, must contain 3.47 lb. soluble grapefruit solids per gallon, dispenser packs available.	16, 32, 46 dilution dilution ratio: from 3-5 to 1
Grapefruit and Orange Blend	Not less than 50% orange juice, sweetened or unsweetened.	24, 32, 46 oz. dilution ratio: 3 to 1
Lemon	Unsweetened.	30 oz. can dilution ratio: 3 to 1
Orange	Single variety of mixture, sweetened or unsweetened. Dispenser packs available.	25.6, 32, 46, 96 oz. cans dilution ratio: from 3-4 to 1
Pineapple	Sweetened or unsweetened.	12, 32, 46 oz. cans dilution ratio: 3 to 1
Tomato	Mixture of varieties, dispenser packs available.	32, 46 oz. dilution ratio: 3 to 1

FROZEN JUICE BASED CONCENTRATES, DRINKS, AND ADES

PRODUCT	DESCRIPTION	WEIGHT/ PACK
Cranberry Juice Cocktail	Concentrate, with sweetener and water added to cranberry juice, dispenser pack available.	6, 12, 46 oz. cans dilution ratio: 4 to 1
Fruit Punch	Concentrate, blend of at least 3 kinds of juices, sweetener added, 10% of juice is full strength, dispenser pack available.	32 oz. cans dilution ratio: 5 to 1
Lemonade	Concentrate, white or pink, sweetened, may contain added lemon oil. Pink contains artificial color or other juice concentrate. Dispenser packs available.	16, 18, 18.5, 32, 46 oz. cans dilution ratio: from 3-5 to 1
Limeade	Concentrate, mixture of lime juice and lime oil, sweetened, dispenser packs available.	16, 18, 46 oz. cans dilution ratio: 2-4 to 1
Single Strength Juices	Apple, Apricot Nectar, Grape, Grapefruit, Orange, Orange-Grapefruit, Cranberry, Pineapple, Orange-Pineapple, Tomato, Prune, Lemon, unsweetened.	4 oz. individual cups, 24 to tray, 48 to case, 30 oz. can

OTHER JUICE BASE CONCENTRATES, DRINKS AND ADES

PRODUCT	DESCRIPTION	WEIGHT/ PACK
Orange Drink	Must contain 10% to 35% orange juice (less than single strength).	
Orange Juice Blend	Must contain at least 70% orange juice.	

OTHER JUICE BASE CONCENTRATES, DRINKS AND ADES [Cont.]

PRODUCT	DESCRIPTION	WEIGHT/ PACK
Orange Juice Drink	Must contain at least 35 to 70% orange juice.	
Orange Flavored Drink	Less than 10% orange juice.	

FROZEN TEA AND COFFEE

Iced Tea	Sweetened.	4 oz. indiv. cups 24 to tray
Coffee	Concentrate.	42.7 oz. can dilution ratio: 19 to 1

FROZEN BREADS AND ROLLS

Bagels	Partially or fully baked, plain water bagel; also egg, onion, poppy seed, raisin, and rye bagels.
Biscuits	Baking powder, buttermilk, ready to bake, partially baked; fully baked. Shape is round or square. Plain, buttermilk, and tea biscuits in several sizes, 1 to 2½ in.
Dinner Rolls	Ready to bake, fully or partially baked. Available in butterfly, clover leaf, sesame, round, finger, and Parkerhouse. Special rolls include malt rye, light rye, potato, egg, rye, sesame seed, and poppy seed. Hard rolls and croissants also available.

FROZEN BREADS AND ROLLS [Cont.]

Muffins	Baked, ready to heat and serve, available in regular and petite sizes. Varieties include bran, corn, orange, cherry, blueberry, and date muffins. English muffins are also available baked.
Bread Loaves (Unbaked)	Portioned dough for French or plain white bread, demi loaves and variety breads, ready to proof and bake. Sizes range from 5 to 6 oz. to 1 lb.
Roll Dough	Portioned dough for rolls to proof and bake.
Danish or Sweet Rolls	Baked, filled and iced or glazed available as petite (1 to 2 oz. ea.) or regular (2 to 4 oz. ea.) all one kind or assorted. Fillings include nuts, apple, apple cinnamon, apricot, almond, cheese, cherry, cinnamon, cinnamon raisin, pecan, raspberry, lemon, orange-pineapple, peach, pineapple, caramel pecan.
Sweet Dough, Danish Dough	See Dessert Listings.

FROZEN DESSERTS

PRODUCT	DESCRIPTION	WEIGHT/ PACK
Brownies	Chocolate nut cake style brownies, some with nuts.	3.75 lb. tray

FROZEN DESSERTS [Cont.]

PRODUCT	DESCRIPTION	WEIGHT/PACK
CAKES		
Cheese Cake	French style cheese cake, with creamy, light, uncooked cheese mixture, available plain, with rosettes around the outer edge to hold filling, and with fruit glaze. Fruit toppings include tart or sweet cherries, peaches, strawberries, pineapple, raspberries, French style has crumb crust or base. Regular cheese cake has creamy cooked cheese, cookie, or pastry crust, plain or with fruit glaze, or flavored with lemon, vanilla, pineapple, or custard.	9 or 10 in. 1¾ to 4 lb.
Layer Cake	Availabe in 2 or 3 layers, with frosting or filling between; flavors include carrot, German chocolate, devil's food, double chocolate fudge, Black Forest, yellow, walnut. Cream cakes include yellow cake with cream filling and frosting, chocolate cake with mocha filling and frosting, yellow or white cake with lemon or strawberry cream filling and frosting. Bavarian cream cakes also available in layer.	8 to 10 in. 2 to 3½ lb.
Pound Cake	Unfrosted in Pullman loaf or regular.	5½ by 14 in. 5½ by 9 in.
Sheet Cakes	Baked, plain with no frosting include yellow, white, chocolate, spice, banana, sponge, German chocolate. Frosted	12 by 16 in. 1½ to 5 lb.

FROZEN DESSERTS [Cont.]

PRODUCT	DESCRIPTION	WEIGHT/PACK
CAKES [Cont.]		
	sheet cakes iced with similar or different frostings including vanilla, buttercream, chocolate fudge, German, mocha, seafoam, butterscotch, lemon, orange. Cake flavors include yellow, white, spice, banana, orange, lemon, devil's food, chocolate, coconut.	
Shortcakes	Sponge cake base or yellow cake base, filled with whipped topping and fruit, including strawberry, peach, pineapple.	
Upside Down Cake	Pineapple upside down cake, bulk packed.	3.75 lb. tray
Cobbler	Fruit on cake base, sheet style.	
Cream Puffs	Baked, made of choux paste, with filling of cream style or custard type, vanilla flavored. Petite are 1 to 2 oz., regular, about 3 oz. round puffs, plain or glazed with vanilla icing.	
Crepes	Thin, flat pancakes, 4 to 8 in. in diameter, IQF, plain, flat, or folded in quarters. Fruit and sweet fillings.	1½ to 6 oz. ea.
Doughnuts	Cake type, regular style with hole, plain.	1½ to 3 oz.
Eclair	Baked and filled with custard or cream type filling, glazed with chocolate icing, made of choux paste in oblong shape.	2 to 3½ oz.

FROZEN DESSERTS [Cont.]

PRODUCT	DESCRIPTION	WEIGHT/ PACK
CAKES [Cont.]		
Mousse	Light, fluffy, rich pudding-type dessert frozen in portions, in chocolate, strawberry, and vanilla.	2 to 3 oz.
PIES		
Cream Pie	In plain pastry or crumb crust, vanilla wafer, or chocolate cookies, or graham crackers. Fillings include Dutch apple, banana, chocolate, chocolate chip, German chocolate, coconut, lemon, lime, Neapolitan, pecan, pumpkin, strawberry, rum. Some available in tray pack also.	8, 9, or 10 in.
Custard Pie	Baked, ready to thaw and serve, plain pastry crust; fillings are coconut custard, pumpkin, or plain.	8, 9, or 10 in.
Fried Pie	Plain pastry circle filled with fruit in sauce; or rectangle, folded and crimped. Raw or prebrowned crust with fruit fillings.	2½ to 5 oz.
Fruit Pie	Unbaked, 2-crust pie, with plain pastry. Single fruit fillings and combinations. Single crust pie with plain pastry crust includes Dutch apple, Dutch peach. Specialty fruit pies with fruit and/or cheese base.	8 to 10 in.
Meringue Pie	Meringue-topped pies with fil-	9 or 10 in.

FROZEN DESSERTS [Cont.]

PRODUCT	DESCRIPTION	WEIGHT/ PACK
PIES [Cont.]	lings of chocolate, coconut, lemon, crumb, or pastry crust.	
Pudding	Old-fashioned and Bavarian style (light), portion or bulk packed in various flavors. Rice pudding with raisins also available.	3½ to 5 oz. 3 to 5 lb. cans 3.75 lb. trays
Puff Pastries	Various types of puff pastry desserts, formed; patty shells with fruit or pudding, dumplings, turnovers, etc.	
Dessert Doughs	Cookie dough, ready to proof and bake	
	Danish pastry dough, ready to proof and bake	5 in. by 5 in. squares, 10 in by 15 in. sheets, 2 13½-lb. bulk pieces
	French Puff Pastry dough, to proof and bake.	5 in. by 5 in. squares, 10 in. by 15 in. sheets, 2 15-lb. bulk pieces
	Sweet dough, to proof and bake.	2 15-lb bulk pieces

(*Note: Doughs also listed in Bread and Rolls Section and in Specialty Section.*)

FROZEN HORS D'OEUVRES & APPETIZERS

Canapes. Kosher and non-Kosher assorted meat, fish, cheese, on rye, white, pumpernickel bread. Packed 50 per tray.

Hors d'Oeuvres. Kosher and non-Kosher assorted fillings in puff

FROZEN HORS D'OEUVRES AND APPETIZERS [Cont.]

pastry. Packed 96 to 100 per tray variety of miniature: meat balls, stuffed cabbage, knishes, eggroll, rumaki, franks, mushrooms, etc. Packed 30 to 120 per tray.

Quiche. Miniature or 4 oz. pastry shell with quiche filling, assorted seafood or cheese and bacon. Packed 30-4 oz.; 100 mini. per box.

Mousse. Seafood in Newburg sauce. Packed 4½ oz.; 48 per carton.

Crepes. Chicken, veal, seafood in a seasoned cream sauce. Packed: 4½ oz. to 5½ oz.; 42 to 96 per carton.

FROZEN SOUPS AND CHOWDERS

Chowder Concentrates. Thaw and mix with milk. Flavors: clam, haddock, seafood. Packed in ½ gal. tubs.

Soup Bases. Essence for chicken, beef, turkey. Packed 12.5 lb. per tub.

Soup Concentrates. Minestrone, clam and chicken chowder, vegetable beef. Packed ½ oz. trays.

Soup. Split pea, potato, minestrone, New England chowder, vegetable, won ton, chicken noodle, navy bean. Packed 8 oz. and 70 oz. tubs.

TEXTURED VEGETABLE PROTEIN ANALOGS

Links, Patties, Slices. Flavored to look and tast like sausage meat. Fortified with vitamins and minerals. Also available: beef type crumbles; chicken type chunks, dices, and rolls; ham type dices and roll; tuna flakes. Packed 4 to 5 lb. boxes; tuna in 3 lb. carton.

FROZEN FRUIT AND VEGETABLE CASSEROLES

Asparagus, Corn, Spinach Souffle. Packed half size trays.

Escalloped Apples, Yams and Apples. Packed half size trays.

Green Beans and Mushrooms, Mixed Vegetables or Zucchini in Curry Sauce. In half size trays. Variable weights.

Rice Pilaf or Fried Rice. In half size trays. Variable weights.

FROZEN EGG PRODUCTS

Hard Cooked Egg Roll. 17 oz. each.

Omelettes. Individual, precooked, plain or with flavor additions. 1 to 7 oz. each.

Liquid Whole Eggs. Pasteurized, homogenized, with/without milk. Some with seasonings and vegetables. Packed 4, 5, 8 lb. cartons; ½ gal.; 4 to 12 egg portion-pack.

Low-Cholesterol, Liquid. Combination of fresh egg whites and yolk substitute. In 8 oz. and 4 lb. cartons.

FROZEN PANCAKES, WAFFLES, FRENCH TOAST

Batter. Ready to use after thawing. In 30 oz. cartons.

Pancakes, Precooked. Thaw and heat. 4 and 6 in., IQF, 144 per case.

Waffles. Precooked, round, rectangle, IQF, 4 to 6 in. Packed 80 to 96 per case.

French Toast. Precooked, sliced white bread dipped in custard type mixture, IQF, packed 144 per case.

FROZEN NOODLES

Egg Noodles. 1/4 to 3/8 in. wide, bulk frozen. Packed in 10 to 12 oz. bags.

Green Noodles. Made with pureed spinach liquid, 1/4 to 3/8 in. wide. Packed in 10 to 12 oz. bags.

Noodles Romanoff. Combination of egg noodles and cream style sauce. Packed in 4 to 5 lb. trays.

FROZEN DRESSING OR STUFFING

Cornbread. Cornbread and seasonings; 5 lb. trays. Cornbread, croutons, and seasonings, 5 lb. bags.

Bread Dressing. Croutons with seasonings. 5 lb. bags.

FROZEN NON DAIRY PRODUCTS

Coffee Creamers. Packed ½ oz. cups, 400 to case; 4 oz. cup, 72 per case; 16, 32 oz. cartons; ½ gal. poly-containers.

Whipped Topping. Sweetened, whipped cream-type product, available whipped or ready to whip. Packed in 2 to 8 lb. tins; 12 to 16 oz. and ½ gal. aerosol cans.

Conclusion

From their role as an expensive, exotic specialty only a few years ago, frozen convenience foods have become commonplace in today's foodservice industry.

A decade ago it would have been possible to list those companies which produced and packed frozen convenience food items. Today, the list is not only nearly endless, it is volatile and changing.

While some magazines and associations do compile lists from time to time, of convenience food processors and the items they produce, I hesitate to recommend them in this book. Products are constantly being added and withdrawn from packers' lines; indeed, packers themselves come into and go out of the business regularly.

Such lists have begun to be obsolete in the month or two it takes for a magazine to be published and mailed. Imagine the possibility for error and exclusion a year or two later!

But this need not deter you from finding out what items are available and evaluating them, by brand, for possible inclusion in your operation. Both the food distributors and food brokers who call on you will be grateful for the opportunity to inform you as to the items they handle.

BIBLIOGRAPHY

Bird, K. *How Freeze-Drying Works*. Washington, D.C.: U.S. Department of Agriculture, 1965.

"Care and Handling of Prepared Frozen Foods in Food Service Establishments." *Cooperative Extension Service*, January 1965, pp. 1-8.

Chef, April/May 1974, pp. 5-74.

Cooking For Profit, January 1973, pp. 3-24.

The Directory of the Canning, Freezing, Preserving Industries, Westminster, Maryland: Edward E. Judge & Sons, 1974.

Dungan, Avalon and Lacey, Stephen E. "Convenience Foods—What Are They? How Are They Utilized," *The Cornell Hotel and Restaurant Administration Quarterly*, August 1969, pp. 2-15.

Focus on Frozen Foods. Restaurant Business and Industrial Distribution magazines, 1975.

Food Service Marketing, May 1973, pp. 16-30.

Food Service Marketing, May 1974, pp. 7-120.

Frosty Acres Buyers Guide. Atlanta, Georgia: The Frozen Food Forum Inc. National Headquarters, 1973.

"Home Care of Purchased Frozen Foods." Washington, D.C.: U.S.

Department of Agriculture, September 1967, pp. 1-6.

Institutions/Volume Feeding, December 15, 1971, pp. 8-37.

Institutions/Volume Feeding, Vol. 11, 1972-73, pp. 3-112.

Institutions/Volume Feeding, February 1, 1975.

Institutions/Volume Feeding, April 15, 1975.

Peddersen, Raymond B. et al. *Increasing Productivity in Foodservice*, Boston: Cahners Publishing Company, Inc., 1973.

Sayles, C. L. "The Application of Mass Production to a' la Carte Food Service Using Prepared-to-Order Food." *Ready Foods*, Chicago: Cahners Publishing Company, Inc., 1973, pp. 4-16.

"Storage and Shelf Life of Packaged Kale." Washington, D.C.: U.S Department of Agriculture, September 1971, pp. 1-19.

Thorner, Marvin Edward. *Convenience and Fast Food Handbook*, Westport, Connecticut: Avi Publishing Company, Inc., 1973.

Tressler, K. K., Van Arsdel, W. B., and Copley, M. J. *The Freezing Preservation of Foods*, 4th ed., Vol. 4., Westport, Connecticut: Avi Publishing Co., 1968.

Woodman, Julie. *The IFMA Encyclopedia of The Foodservice Industry*, Chicago: International Foodservice Manufacturer's Association, 1972.

8

KOSHER PRODUCTS

A RECENT PRESS release from Schreiber Caterers, of Brooklyn, specialists in Glatt kosher meat, poultry, and fish, home-style meals, so clearly explains kosher food, that we are glad to reproduce it below:

Put very simply, "kosher" or "kasher" means "fit." "Kosher" is also the popular name for the Jewish Kashruth (pronounced as spelled) dietary laws, which are the discipline of the Jewish faith set forth in the Bible.

'Glatt" kosher means that the meat used satisfies even the strictest of kosher standards.

The laws of Kashruth are concerned with the fitness of food for the Jewish table. However, in the traditional Jewish interpretation of the Bible, spiritual, not physical health is the sole reason for their observance. The Kashruth laws as part of Judaism help to keep the Jewish people aware of their obligations to God, to their fellow man, and to themselves.

Jewish dietary laws divide all food into 3 classifications:

(1.) Those which are inherently kosher (par-ve) and may be eaten in their natural state: grains, fruit, vegetables, tea, coffee, and so on.

(2.) Those which require some form of processing, to be kosher, such as meat, poultry.

(3.) Those which are inherently not kosher: pork products, shellfish, and fish without scales and fins. Kosher meat may come only from cloven-hooved creatures, such as cows, sheep, and goats—animals that graze and chew their cud. Only those fish that have fins and scales are permitted, such as halibut, sole, cod, tuna, and salmon.

It is not enough, however, for an animal to belong to the right family. It must be completely healthy and even then, some parts are not considered kosher. It must be quickly and painlessly slaughtered by an ordained "Shochet," and thoroughly cleaned (koshered) by soaking in water for 1/2 hr., then salted, and left to stand for 1 hr. to drain off the prohibited blood, and then completely rinsed—in preparation for cooking—to remove the salt which has soaked up the blood.

According to the rules, meat and milk products must not be cooked together, nor is one permitted to eat meat or meat products with milk or milk products. For example, butter may not be given with bread that is served with meat, nor is cream allowed with coffee served at the end of a meat meal.

No product that is processed should be considered kosher unless so certified by a reliable rabbinical authority whose name or insignia appears on the sealed package. Such an insignia is the Ⓤ which is the copyrighted symbol of the Union of Orthodox Jewish Congregations of America, who certify to the kosher nature of the product by the use of the Ⓤ symbol.

It is, therefore, important that in serving a kosher food package, it should be sealed and served, sealed, and presented to the user that way. It should be opened only by the user, or

Union of Orthodox Jewish Congregations of American, Harold M. Jacobs, President, 116 E. 27th St., New York, N.Y. 10016 —212-725-3415.

in his presence, or by one authorized by the religious authorities to do so.

KOSHER PRODUCTS and SERVICES DIRECTORY Ⓤ

Improved Service for Users of the Ⓤ Kosher Products Directory. The attention of users of this edition of the Ⓤ *Kosher Products and Services Directory* is called to a number of improvements in product listings aimed at maximum usefulness to consumers.

The designation (L) denotes a private label product. Firms offering such products contract to have their particular brands manufactured at Ⓤ supervised plants. Such contracts are sometimes terminated after a short period. For this reason, consumers are urged to check the label of such brands with special care to make sure the Ⓤ appears on the label.

The items listed in this Directory are divided into three categories: Parve, Dairy, and Meat.

PARVE: Unless otherwise indicated, the listed item is parve. Such items contain no dairy or meat ingredients and have been processed on parve equipment. They may be eaten with either meat or milk.

DAIRY: These items are listed under a DAIRY DESIGNATION. Items so designated are products which contain dairy ingredients, as well as products which do not contain milk ingredients but which have been prepared on dairy equipment.

MEAT: These items are listed under MEAT or POULTRY DESIGNATION.

All whole, frozen, kosher poultry must have the (a) metal seal (plumba) on the wing. The liver must be removed from the cavity and broiled separately.

In purchase of Ⓤ packaged meat or poultry parts, the consumer must be certain that both the sealed package and the inner cellophane wrapper have not been tampered with.

ITEMS APPEARING IN THIS DIRECTORY ARE CERTIFIED KOSHER ONLY WHEN BEARING THE Ⓤ EMBLEM ON THE LABEL.

This directory lists all Ⓤ consumer certified kosher products for the retail market. The Ⓤ Kashruth Division publishes two other directories.

An *Industrial and Institutional Directory* listing Ⓤ endorsed products and raw materials for the industrial and institutional markets.

A *Passover Products Directory* is published each year, with both consumer and industrial sections listing all products Ⓤ certified for Passover.

All directories are available free of charge upon written request.

Each new publication automatically outdates previous listings.

A *Consumer NEWS REPORTER*, serving as a supplement to the retail Consumer Directory, is published periodically and is available upon written request.

The Ⓤ *Kathruth Handbook for Home and School*, presenting a brief review of the principal laws of Kashruth and a ready source of guidelines, basic Kashruth information, and a complete fish list, can be obtained from the Ⓤ Kashruth Division at 50 cents per copy (25 cents for bulk orders of 10 or more).

ENDORSED AS KOSHER ONLY WHEN Ⓤ APPEARS ON LABEL OF PRODUCT

APPLESAUCE
IDEAL

FARMDALE

SUPERSAVER
Applesauce
(Acme Markets Inc., Philadelphia, Pa.)

LUCKY LEAF
Applesauce
(Knouse Foods Inc., Peach Glen, Pa.)

MUSSELMAN'S
Applesauce (Cinnamon, Raspberry, Pineapple, Blueberry, Chunky, Low Calorie)
(New England Prod. Co., Littleton, Mass.)

VERYFINE
Applesauce
(Cinnamon, Low Calorie, Strawberry, Raspberry, Banana, Peach)
(New England Prod. Co., Littleton, Mass.)

BABY FOOD & CEREAL
(Check label for milk, otherwise parve)

BEECH-NUT
Strained Apple Betty
Strained Apples and Apricots
Strained Applesauce
Strained Applesauce and Bananas with Mixed Cereal
Strained Applesauce and Bananas with Oatmeal
Strained Applesauce and Cherries
Strained Applesauce and Raspberries
Strained Apricot with Tapioca
Strained Bananas and Pineapple with Tapioca
Strained Bananas with Tapioca

Strained Beets
Strained Carrots
Strained Chocolate Custard Dessert
Strained Creamed Corn
Strained Custard Pudding
Strained Fruit Dessert with Tapioca
Strained Garden Vegetables
Strained Green Beans
Strained Mixed Fruit Juice
Strained Natural Cherry Apple Gel
Strained Orange Apple Juice
Strained Orange Pineapple Dessert
Strained Peaches
Strained Peach Melba
Strained Pears
Strained Pears and Pineapple
Strained Peas
Strained Pineapple Dessert
Strained Plums with Tapioca
Strained Prunes with Tapioca
Strained Squash
Strained Sweet Potatoes
Strained Vegetable Soup
Junior Apple Betty
Junior Apples and Apricots
Junior Applesauce
Junior Applesauce and Cherries
Junior Applesauce and Cranberries
Junior Applesauce and Pineapple
Junior Applesauce and Raspberries
Junior Apricots with Tapioca
Junior Banana Dessert
Junior Banana and Pineapple with Tapioca
Junior Carrots
Junior Creamed Spinach
Junior Custard Pudding
Junior Fruit Dessert with Tapioca
Junior Green Beans
Junior Natural Apple Gel
Junior Natural Orange Gel
Junior Natural Pineapple Gel
Junior Peaches
Junior Peach Melba
Junior Pears

Junior Pears and Pineapple
Junior Pineapple Dessert
Junior Plums with Tapioca
Junior Prunes with Tapioca
Junior Squash
Junior Sweet Potatoes
Junior Tropical Fruit Dessert
Junior Vegetable Soup
Apple Juice
Apple-Cherry Juice
Orange Juice
Orange Apricot Juice
Orange Banana Juice
Orange Pineapple Juice
Prune Orange Juice
High Protein Cereal
Maple Flavored Mixed Cereal
Maple Flavored Oatmeal Cereal
Maple Flavored Rice Cereal
Mixed Cereal
Oatmeal Cereal
Rice Cereal
Wheat Cereal

Dairy
Strained Carrots in Butter Sauce
Strained Squash in Butter Sauce
Strained Sweet Potatoes in Butter Sauce
Junior Carrots in Butter Sauce
Junior Squash in Butter Sauce
Junior Sweet Potatoes in Butter Sauce
(Beech-Nut Inc., Canajoharie, N. Y.)

BEANS
IDEAL
Butter Beans
Kidney Beans
Light Red Kidney Beans
Vegetarian Beans
SUPER SAVER
Kidney Beans
(Acme Mkts., Philadelphia, Pa.)

HEINZ
Beans in Molasses Sauce
Vegetarian Beans in Tomato Sauce
(H. J. Heinz Co., Pittsburgh, Pa.)

(L) WALDBAUM'S
Vegetarian Beans
(Waldbaum's Inc., Garden City, N.Y.)

BEVERAGES & DRINK MIXES

HOFFMAN QUALITY BEVERAGES

DR. BROWN QUALITY BEVERAGES

MYER 1890 QUALITY BEVERAGES
(American Beverage Co., College Point, N.Y.)

CORNELL BEVERAGES
Diet Flavors
Regular Flavors
(Cornell Beverages, Brooklyn, N.Y.)

COTT
Flavored Soda
Mixers
(Excluding Grape and Concord Punch)

ENERGADE

SPRING WATER
(Cott Corp., New Haven, Conn.)

CHEERI-AID DRINK MIXES
Black Cherry
Cherry
Grape
Lemon
Lemonade
Lemon/Lime
Orange
Raspberry
Rootbeer
(The Great Atlantic and Pacific Tea Co., A & P Stores)

FUNNY FACE DRINK MIXES
UNSWEETENED
Captain Black Cherry
Chilly Cherry Cola
Choo Choo Cherry

Freckle Face
Goofy Grape
Jolly Oily Orange
Lefty Lemon/Lime
Loud Mouth Punch
Rootin' Tootin' Raspberry

PRESWEETENED
Choo Choo Cherry
Freckle Face Strawberry
Goofy Grape
Jolly Oily Orange
Loud Mouth Punch
Rah Rah Root Beer
Rootin' Tootin' Raspberry
Watermelon
Tutti Fruitti
(The Pillsbury Co., Minneapolis, Minn.)

ROYAL CROWN COLA

DIET RITE COLA

UPPER-10

DIET LEMON LIME

FLAIR

NEHI
Ginger Ale
Orange
Sparkling Water

SHASTA
REGULAR/DIET
Cherry Cola
Cola
Ginger Ale
Grapefruit Soda
Lemon-Lime Soda
Orange Soda
Wild Raspberry Soda
Red Apple Soda
Root Beer
Strawberry Soda
Tiki
Club Soda
Creme Soda

Quinine Water
Collins Mix
Whiskey Sour
Chocolate Soda
(Shasta Beverages Inc., Hayward, Cal., Granite City, Ill.)

(L) KEY QUALITY BEVERAGES
(Key Food Stores, Inc., Brooklyn, N.Y.)

(L) STOP & SHOP
Sun Glory
(Stop & Shop, Inc., Boston, Mass.)

(L) WALDBAUM QUALITY BEVERAGES
(Waldbaum's Inc., Garden City, N.Y.)

Dairy
SECOND NATURE

QUIP

FLAVORED BEVERAGES
Vanilla, Chocolate, Strawberry
(Avoset Food Corp., Oakland, Cal.)

BREAD — ROLLS — MUFFINS — TOAST — BAGELS
BELLACICCO'S
Italian Bread
Heroes
Specials
French
Bostoni
Rolls
Garlic Bread
Onion Bread
Bread Sticks and Frissels
Kaiser Rolls
French Rolls
(Bellacicco & Sons, Inc., Corona, N.Y.)

DAMASCUS
Pita Bread
(Damascus Bakery, Brooklyn, N.Y.)

DEVONSHEER
Plain Devonsheer Melba
Rye Toast Devonsheer Melba
Whole Wheat Devonsheer Melba

Plain Toast Unsalted
Rye Toast Unsalted
Whole Wheat Unsalted
Plain Round Melba Regular
Large Plain Rounds
Large Salted Rye Rounds
Sesame Rounds
Garlic Rounds
Onion Rounds
Rice Wafers Salted
Rice Wafers Unsalted
Allgrane Wheat Wafers
Allgrane Wheat Wafers Unsalted
(Devonsheer Melba Corp., Carlstadt, N.J.)

ELGAWLY & RAZAK BAKERY
Pita Bread
(Elgawly & Razak Bakery, Brooklyn, N.Y.)

FT. LEE BAGELS/MISTER BAGEL
Bagels
(Ft. Lee Bagels Inc., Ft. Lee, N.J.)

IVERSEN
Slim Rye
Schwarz-Brot (black bread)
Rhine Valley-Rhine Brot
Mr. Pumpernickel
(Iversen Baking Co., Chicago, Ill.)

MASTER
Plain Zwieback Toast
Cinnamon Zwieback Toast
Orange Zwieback Toast
Dietetic Zwieback Toast
Honey Wheat Zwieback Toast
Old Country Hardtack
Old Style Crisp Bread
Hot-Ry Wafers
Cara-Ry Wafers
Onion-Garlic Wafers
Par-T-Ry Wafers
Dietetic Rye Wafers
Butter-Krust Toast
Cin-A-Mon Krust Toast
Rye Wafers

Onion/Garlic Wafers
(Zinnemaster Baking Co., Minneapolis, Minn.)

PALAGONIA
Italian Bread
French Bread
Spanish Bread
Toasted Crumbs
Garlic Bread
Egg Rolls
Club Rolls
Heroes
Italian Sliced
Italian Bread Sticks
Italian Fresgli
Onion Rolls
(Palagonia Bakery Co., Inc., Brooklyn, N.Y.)

RESTIVO
Italian Bread
Rolls
Bread Sticks
Sliced Bread
Heroes
Club Rolls
Garlic Bread
(Restivo Bros. Bakers, Inc., New York, N.Y.)

STELLA D'ORO
Bread Sticks
(Stella D'Oro Biscuit Co., Inc., Bronx, N.Y.)

T&E
Pita Bread
Sesame Seeded Rings
(T&E Baking Co., Inc., Brooklyn, N.Y.)

THOMAS'
Date-Nut Loaf
Whole Wheat Bread
White Bread
Protogen Protein Bread
Gluten Bread
Rye Bread
(S.B. Thomas, Inc., Totowa, N.J.)

WESTSIDE
Italian Bread (sliced and whole)

Seeded Italian Bread
Club Rolls
Hard Rolls
Rye Bread
Pumpernickel
French Bread
Submarine—Grinder—Wedgies Rolls
Round Bread
(Westside Baking, New Rochelle, N.Y.)

(L) MA-I BUD
Thin Rye
Pumpernickel
European Black Bread
(Purity Cheese Co., Mayville, Wis.)

Dairy
THOMAS'
Onion Muffins
English Muffins
Cinnamon-Raisin Loaf
Corn Muffins
Corn Toast-r-Cakes
Bran Toast-r-Cakes
Bran Muffins
Rite Diet Bread
Orange Toast-r-Cakes
Blueberry Muffins
Strawberry Muffins
(S.B. Thomas, Inc., Totowa, N.J.)

NEWLY WEDS WAYSIDE INN
English Muffins
(Casey's English Muffin Co., Chicago, Ill.)

BREAD CRUMBS AND MEAL
BELLACICCO'S
(Bellacicco & Sons, Inc., Corona, N.Y.)

HOROWITZ-MARGARETEN
Matzoh Meal
(Horowitz Bros. & Margareten, Long Island City, N.Y.)

JASON
Plain Bread Crumbs
Flavored Bread Crumbs
(Jason Dairy Prod. Co., Inc., Brooklyn, N.Y.)

PALAGONIA
TANTE'S
Flavored Bread Crumbs
Toasted Bread Crumbs
(Palagonia Bakery Co., Inc., Brooklyn, N.Y.)

RESTIVO
Bread Krums
(Restivo Bros. Bakers, Inc., New York, N.Y.)

WESTSIDE
(Westside Bakery, New Rochelle, N.Y.)

BUTTER

Dairy
ANN PAGE
Salted
Unsalted
(The Great Atlantic and Pacific Tea Co., A & P Stores)

DELLWOOD
Sweet Butter
(Dellwood Dairy Co., Inc., Yonkers, N.Y.)

FRIENDSHIP
Salted
Unsalted
Whipped
(Friendship Dairies, Inc., Maspeth, N.Y.)

RASKAS
Whipped Butter
(Raskas Dairy, Inc., St. Louis, Mo.)

BUTTERMILK

Dairy
ELMHURST
(Elmhurst Milk and Cream Co., Jamaica, N.Y.)

FRIENDSHIP
(Friendship Dairies, Inc., Maspeth, N.Y.)

CAKES, COOKIES, CRACKERS [Parve only when indicated on label]
BARTON'S BONBONNIERE
(Barton's Candy Corp., Brooklyn, N.Y.)

BAYBERRY FARMS
Honey Cake
Pound Cake
(Bayberry Farms, Inc., Los Angeles, Ca.)

CAKE STYLISTS
Cake Specialties
(Cake Stylists, Inc., Maspeth, N.Y.)

CARMEL BAKE SHOP
(Carmel Bakery, Miami Beach, Fla.)

COOKYLAND
Anisette Toast
Filled Goodies
Filled Goodies (Peach Apricot)
Anise Twist
Italian Style Assortment
Macaroons
Party Assortment
Fancy Goodies (Assorted)
Pignoli Cookies
Continental Goodies
Aunt Anne Assortment
Susie Sesame
Sprice Crops (Holiday Only)
Anisette Toast
Anisette Sponge
Vanilla Lemon Sponge
Vanilla Egg Ring
Cinnamon Breakfast Toast
Coconut Flip
Flip Chip
Sorrento
Spicy Treats
Goodie Delights
Bar Goodies
Almond Cookies
Fancy Shortbread
Rainbow
Little Snack
Kichel
Egg Twist
Continental Bars
Dietic Cookies
(Mazzola Bros. Biscuit Co., Inc., Brooklyn, N.Y.)

DEER PARK
Temptation
Danish Assortment
Elite
Royal Danish
Assortment Royale
Penn Dutch
Mambos (Coconut Macaroons)
County Fair
Family Treat
Coffee Break
Jelly Gems
Utility Pak
Star Dips
(Deer Park Baking Co., Hammonton, N.J.)

FROUMINE
Daf-Thinsies
Trio
Sextet
Poppy Snacks
Mandelach
Marie
Biscafe
Baron
Dutch Rusk
Dietetic Cookies and Crackers
(Froumine Ltd., Bnei Brak, Israel)

GOREN'S BAKERY
(Miami Beach, Fla.)

HADAR-MAGDONIAT
Assorted Cookies
Wafers
Crackers
(Hadar-Magdoniat, Tel Aviv, Israel)

HOROWITZ-MARGARETEN
Kosher-Crackers
(Horowitz Bros and Margareten, Long Island City, N.Y.)

HYGRADE
Vanilla Wafers
Chocolate Chip
Almond Chip

Oatmeal Raisin
Macaroons
Lemon
Sugar Cookies
Tea Cookies
Creme Filled Cookies
(Hygrade Bakeries, Pennsville, N.J.)

KUNGSHOLM
Magic Assortment
Home Style Cookies
Carnival Assortment
Old Amsterdam Assortment
(Kungsholm Baking Co., Hammonton, N.J.)

LADY CLAIR
Danish Assortment
(Lady Clair Baking Co., N.Y., N.Y.)

NOVELTY PASTRY
Cake, Cookies and Pastry Specialties
(Novelty Pastry Inc., Spring Valley, N.Y.)

SCHWARTZ KOSHER BAKERY
(Schwartz Bakery, Los Angeles, Ca.)

STELLA D'ORO
Almond Toast (Mandel)
Amaretti
Angelica Goodies
Anginetti
Anisette Sponge
Anisette Toast
Breakfast Treats
California Fruit Bars
Dutch Apple Pastry
Egg Biscuits—Plain—Sugared
Breakfast Treat
Egg Jumbo
Golden Bars
French Cookies
Lady Stella Assortment
Margherite
Old Country Treats (Kichel)
Onion Bread Sticks
Pastry Shells (Tarts)

Peach-Apricot Pastry
Pfefferneuse (Holiday Item)
Roman Egg Biscuits (Vanilla, Anise)
Sugared Egg Biscuits
Scotch Tarts
Sesame Cookies (Regina)
Bread Sticks—Salt Free
Dietetic Kichel
Dietetic Egg Biscuits
Dietetic Fig Pastry
Kichel (Dietetic)
Prune Pastry (Dietetic)
Apple Pastry (Dietetic)
Angel Puffs (Dietetic)
Continental Petits (Dietetic Assortment)
Have-A-Heart (Dietetic)
(Stella D'Oro Biscuit Co., Bronx, N.Y.)

PATHMARK
Danish Assortment
(Supermarket General, Woodbridge, N.J.)

SHOP-RITE
Danish Assortment
(Wakefern Food Corp., Elizabeth, N.J.)

(L) SWERSEY'S COOKIES
Deluxe Danish Assortment
Rumbas (Macaroons)
(Swersey's, Maspeth, N.Y.)

Dairy
AU NATURELLE
Date and Almond Nuggets
Carob Fudge Cookies
Molasses Cookies
Oatmeal Cookies
Prune and Almond Nuggets
(Au Naturelle, Inc., San Francisco, Ca.)

BURRY'S
Chocolate Chip
Butter Cookies
Mr. Chip
Girl Scout Mints
Shortbread

Scott Tea Cookies
(Burry Biscuit Co., Elizabeth, N.J.)

DEER PARK
Butter Cookies
Continental Assortment
Windmill
Vienna Waltz
Petits Fours
(Deer Park Baking Co., Hammonton, N.J.)

FROUMINE-ISRAEL
Petit Beurre
Shalom
(Froumine Ltd., Bnei Brak, Israel)

(L) HFS
Carob Fudge Cookies
Oatmeal Cookies
Granola Cream Cookies
(Health Fd. Store Co., Compton, Ca.)

CAKE FLOUR
PRESTO SELF RISING
(CPC Int., Best Foods Div., Englewood Cliffs, N.J.)

Dairy
ELAM'S
3-in-1 Mix (pancake, muffins, coffee cake)
Unbleached White Flour with Wheat Germ
Pastry Flour (graham flour) 100% Whole Wheat
(Elam's, Broadview, Ill.)

CAKE MIX

Dairy
PILLSBURY
Bundt Poundcake Supreme and Topping
(The Pillsbury Co., Minneapolis, Minn.)

CAKE FROSTING MIX
PILLSBURY
Fluffy White Frosting Mix
(The Pillsbury Co., Minneapolis, Minn.)

CAKE, PASTRY AND PIE FILLINGS

BAKER
Poppy, Apricot, Nut, Prune, Pecan, Almond, Cherry, Blueberry, Pineapple, Peach, Date, Apple Strudel, Lekvar (Prune Butter)
(Baker Brands, North Braddock, Pa.)

LUCKY LEAF
Apple, Apple Butter, Cherry, Peach, Blueberry, Strawberry, Blackberry, Red Raspberry, Strawberry-Rhubarb, Raisin, Apricot, Pineapple, Lemon, Bavarian Creme
(Krouse Foods, Inc., Peach Glen, Pa.)

MUSSELMAN'S
Apricot, Apple, Cherry, Blueberry, Peach, Raisin, Lemon, Apple Cranberry, Apple Butter, Pie Sliced Apples
(C.H. Musselman's, Div. of Pet Milk Co., Biglerville, Pa.)

PY-FIL
Apple, Apricot, Blueberry, Cherry, Lemon, Peach, Pineapple, Raisin, Strawberry

SIMON FISHER
Lekvar-Prune Butter, Golden Apricot Butter
(Globe Products Co., Clifton, N.J.)

Dairy

LIBBY
Pumpkin Pie Mix
(Libby, McNeil & Libby Co., Inc., Chicago, Ill.)

CANDY

ANN PAGE
Bittersweet Chocolate Mint Wafers, Dark-sweet Chocolate Mint Wafers, Chocolate Mint Wafers, Non-Pareils, Semi-Sweet Chocolate Bits, Lollypops, Hard Candies, Peppermint and Assorted Flavors, Gum Drop Candies Assorted Flavors
(The Great Atlantic and Pacific Tea Co., A & P Stores)

ANN RASKAS
(Parve must appear on label, otherwise dairy)
(Ann Raskas Candy Co., Englewood, N.J.)

ASTOR CHOCOLATES
(Parve must appear on label, otherwise dairy)
(Astor Chocolate Corp., Brooklyn, N.Y.)

BARTON'S BONBONNIERE
(Parve must appear on label, otherwise dairy)
(Barton's Candy Corp., Brooklyn, N.Y.)

CARLTON HOUSE
(Parve must appear on label, otherwise dairy)
Lollypops, Fruit Filled, Sour Balls, Assorted Drops
(Bloom Packing Co., Brooklyn, N.Y.)

COOK CHOCOLATES
(Parve must appear on label, otherwise dairy)
(Cook Chocolate Co., Chicago, Ill.)

CRESCENT CONFECTIONS
Rainbow Slice, Marzipan
(Multiflex Confections, Paterson, N.J.)

DATETREE
Rose Hip Chews, Fruit Nut Chews, Apricot Chews, Sesame Carob Chews, Sesame Sunflower Chews
(Organic Fds., Farmingdale, N.Y.)

HERSHEY
Special Dark Bars, Semi-Sweet Chocolate Chips
(Hershey Food Corp., Hershey, Pa.)

Dairy

ALOHA POPPYCOCK

ORIGINAL POPPYCOCK

MAPLE POPPYCOCK
(Ovaltine Div. of Sandoz Corp., Villa Park, Ill.)

ANN PAGE
Milk Chocolate, Imitation Rum Wafers, Milk Chocolate Assorted Nuts, Bridge Mix, Milk Chocolate Stars, Milk Chocolate Covered Raisins, Milk Chocolate Peanut Clusters, Milk Chocolate Honeycombed Molasses Chips, Chocolate Covered Peanuts, Chocolate Raisins and Peanuts, Chocolate Peanut Butter Chips, Solid Milk Chocolate, Chocolate Cream Hearts, Chocolate Covered Coconut Cream Eggs, Chocolate Covered Fudge Drops, Milk Chocolate Covered Orange Jellies, Milk Chocolate Covered Raspberry Jellies, Imitation Flavors, Assorted Chocolates Dark and Milk, Assorted Chocolate All Milk, Milk Chocolate Miniature Caramels, Milk Chocolate Caramel Pecans, Milk Chocolate Covered Modified Cherries, Chocolate Covered Fruit and Nut Egg, Decorated Chocolate Covered Coconut Cream, Chocolate Covered Cream Eggs, Milk Chocolate Caramel Peanut Clusters, Milk Chocolate Caramel Raisin Clusters, Milk Chocolate Maple Creams
(The Great Atlantic and Pacific Tea Co., A & P Stores)

FAMOUS GOURMET

AMERICAN GOURMET

OLD VIENNA
Peanut Crunch, Nutti-Kins, Chocolate Polly Doodles, Tyrolean Chocolates, Chocolate Doodley Doodles, Chocolate Moppets, Chocolate Crickets, Chocolate Crunch-a-Rixs, Chocolate Swirls, Rich Milk Chocolate Bars w/Almonds, Rich Milk Chocolate Bars w/Crunch, Chocolate Nut Fudge
(Chocolate Co. of America, Chicago, Ill.)

HERSHEY
Milk Chocolate Bars/without nuts, Rally Bars, Candy Coated Items, Milk Chocolate Chips, Kit-Kat Bars, Krackel Bars, Coconut Cream Eggs, Reese's Peanut Butter Cups and Eggs
(Hershey Food Corp., Hershey, Pa.)

MRS. LELANDS
Chocolate Pollywogs, Chocolate Crunch-a-Roos, Chocolate Mint Melt-Aways, Chocolate Puff'ns, Rich Milk Chocolate w/Almonds, Rich Milk Chocolate w/Crunch, Chocolate Nut Fudge
(Chesterton Candy Co., Chicago, Ill.)

MISS SAYLOR'S
Coffee-ets
(Miss Saylor's Unusual Candies, Los Angeles, Ca.)

PLANTATION

E.G. WHITMAN
Peanut Crunch, Cashew Crunch, Swiss Buttermints, Hard Filled Candies, Chocolate Straws, Peanut Butter Puffs, Mint Souffles, Buttermints, Mint Patties, Butter Creams, Cashew Patties, Coconut Delights, Dainties, Jinglebits, Golden Crunchies, Coffee Straws, Mint Straws, Sesame Crisps, Carmel Nut Cluster, Bitter Mints, Pecan Kisses, Pumpkin Kisses, Assorted Caramel, Hav-a-Banana, Fruitees Plantation Chocolate Co., Bridgeport, Pa.)

TURTLES
Pecan Nuts, Caramel, Pure Milk Chocolate
(De Mets Inc., Chicago. Ill.)

CASSEROLE MIXES
OSEM
Cholent Casserole Mix, Hungarian Casserole, Mix, Risi Bisi, Mushroom Risotto, Risotto Milanese
(Osem Nakid Ltd., Bnei Brak, Israel)

CATERERS

PAPILSKY
(Papilsky Caterers, New York City, N.Y.)

TAM TOV
(Tam Tov Caterers, Brooklyn, N.Y.; Cedarhurst, L.I.)

CEREAL
DATETREE
Granola Cereal, Farm Mix Granola, Touch o'Honey Granola
(Organic Food Corp., Farmingdle, L.I.)

ELAM'S
Cracked Wheat Cereal, Steel Cut Oat Meal, Stone Ground 100% Whole Yellow Corn Meal, Stone Ground 100% Whole Organically Grown Yellow Corn Meal, Stone Ground 100% Whole Scotch Style Oatmeal
(Elam's, Broadview, Ill.)

H-O
Enriched Farina, Oatmeal Cereals
(CPC International, Best Foods Div., Englewood Cliffs, N.J.)

HOROWITZ-MARGARETEN
Huber Grits-Cut Oats
(Horowitz Bros. & Margareten Co., Long Island City, N.Y.)

MALTEX

MAYPO WHEAT BARLEY CEREAL
Vermont Style, Maple Flavor, Banana and Chocolate
(Standard Milling Co., Kansas City, Mo.)

SKINNER'S
Raisin Bran
(Skinner Raisin Bran, Inc., Omaha, Neb.)

UNCLE SAM LAXATIVE CEREAL
(Uncle Sam Breakfast Food Co., Omaha, Neb.)

WHEATENA
Natural Wheat with Wheat Germ Cereal
(Standard Milling Co., Kansas City, Mo.)

VITA CRUNCH

GRANOLA
Granola with Almonds, Raisins, Dates
(Vita Crunch Foods, Inc., Div. of Specialty Brands, San Francisco, Ca.)

Dairy

ALPEN
(Mfg. by Weetabix Ltd, Kettering Northants U.K. Dist., Colgate Palmolive Co., New York, N.Y.)

AU NATURELLE
Granola Cereal
(Au Naturelle Foods, Inc., San Francisco, Ca.)

QUAKER
100% Natural Cereal, 100% Natural Cereal with Raisins and Dates
(The Quaker Oats Co., Chicago, Ill.)

CHAMPAGNE

CARMEL
(Bearing Halachic of Chief Rabbinate of Israel)
(Carmel Wine Co., Inc., N.Y., N.Y.)

STAR OF ABRAHAM-KEDEM
(Royal Wine Co., N.Y., N.Y.)

CHEESE

Dairy

ANN PAGE
Cream Cheese
(The Great Atlantic and Pacific Tea Co., A & P Stores)

FARMLEA
Creamed Cottage Cheese

DELLWOOD
Cream Cheese, Cottage Cheese
(Deltown Foods, Inc., Yonkers, N.Y.)

ELK BRAND
Cottage Cheese, Bakers Cheese
(Elk Brand Dairies, Inc., Philadelphia, Pa.)

FOREMOST

TUTTLE
Bakers Cheese, Cottage Cheese
(Tuttle Cheese Co., Div. of Foremost Foods, Glendale, Ca.)

FRIENDSHIP
Cottage Cheese, Pot Cheese, Pineapple Cheese, Calorie Meter Cheese, Farmer Cheese
(Friendship Dairies, Inc., Maspeth, N.Y.)

HOLYLAND CHEESE
(Kfir & Co. Ltd., Bnei Brak, Israel)
(Dist. by N. Dorman Co., Syosett, N.Y.)

JERSEY MAID
Cottage Cheese
(Jerseymaid Milk Prod. Co., Los Angeles, Ca.)

LADY LEE
Cottage Cheese
(Dairymen's Coop. Creamery Assoc., Tulare, Ca.)

MILLER'S
Mello-Gold, Smoked Baby Gouda, American, Diet Slices, Munster, Edam, Gouda, Swiss, Cheddar, Hickory Smoked, Baby Gouda, Baby Munster, Israeli Portion Spread
(Miller Cheese Co., N.Y., N.Y.)

RASKAS
Cream Cheese
(Raskas Dairy, Inc., St. Louis, Mo.)

REGENT
Cream Cheese, Cottage Cheese, Farmer Cheese

SANTE
Cottage Cheese, Cream Cheese, Farmer Cheese

BIG Z
Cream Cheese, Farmer Cheese, Neufchatel Spread

TUXEDO
Cottage Cheese, Cream Cheese

SUNNYBOY

LIBBY
Cream Cheese

NEW HOLLAND
Neufchatel Cheese, Cream Cheese
(Zausner Foods Corp., Mountainside, N.J.)

(L) BOHACK
Cottage Cheese
(Bohack Inc., Brooklyn, N.Y.)

(L) DAIRY BARN
Cottage Cheese

(L) GOLDEN KEY
Cottage Cheese, Cream Cheese
(Key Food Stores, Brooklyn, N.Y.)

(L) IDEAL
Cream Cheese
(Acme Mkts. Inc., Philadelphia, Pa.)

(L) LAND O'LAKES
Cream Cheese
(Land O'Lakes Inc., Spencer, Wis.)

(L) PATHMARK
Cream Cheese
(Supermarkets General Corp., Philadelphia, Pa.)

(L) ROYAL
(L) FOODTOWN
Cottage Cheese, Cream Cheese
(Royal Food Dist., Woodbridge, N.J.)

(L) SOUTH FLORIDA
Cream Cheese
(South Fla. Dairy Prod., Miami, Fla.)

(L) SUPER A
Cream Cheese
(Associated Food Stores, Inc., Jamaica, N.Y.)

(L) PANTRY PRIDE
Cream Cheese
(Food Fair Stores, Philadelphia, Pa.)

CHINESE VEGETABLES—CHOW MEIN
CHINESE MAID
Bean Sprouts, Chow Mein Vegetables, Chop Suey Vegetables
(Chinese Maid Fds., Chicago, Ill.)

HUNGS
Mushroom Chow Mein
(Hung's Food Prod., Brighton, Mass.)

Meat
BARNEY'S
Chow Mein Vegetables, Chow Mein Vegetables with Chicken
(Bernan Fds., Inc., Newark, N.J.)

COCOA
HERSHEY'S
(Hershey Food Corp., Hershey, Pa.)

SULTANA
(The Great Atlantic and Pacific Tea Co., A & P Stores)

COCONUT
DATE TREE
Coconut Shreds
(Organic Foods Corp. Farmingdale, L.I.)

COFFEE
ACME

IDEAL

SUPER SAVER

WINECREST
100% Colombian, Decaffeinated, Vacuum Packed
(Acme Mkts, Inc., Philadelphia, Pa.)

FOLGER'S COFFEE
(Folger's Div. of Procter & Gamble Co., Kansas City, Mo.)

A & P
97% Caffeine-Free, 100% Colombian, Electric Perk, Instant Coffee, Vacuum Packed
(The Great Atlantic and Pacific Tea Co., A & P Stores Coffee Div., Landover, Md.)

CORN CHIPS
DIPSEY DOODLES

CORN DOODELS
(Old London Foods, Inc., Bronx, N.Y.)

WISE CORN CHIPS
(Wise Foods Div. of Bordens, Berwick, Pa.)

CORNSTARCH
ARGO
DUREA'S
KINGFORD'S
(CPC Int. Best Foods Div., Englewood Cliffs, N.J.)

DERMA
MRS. ADLER'S
Stuffed Derma
(Mrs. Adler's Foods Corp., Brooklyn, N.Y.)

EGG SUBSTITUTE

Dairy

SECOND NATURE
(Avoset Food Corp., Oakland, Ca.)

MAZOLA SCRAMBLERS
(Best Foods Division, CPC Int., Englewood Cliffs, N.J.)

FISH PRODUCTS

BARBEY'S SALMON

RED BREAST SALMON
(Barbey Packing Corp., Astoria, Ore.)

BLUE RIBBON
Salmon Mild Cured (Lox), Nova Scotia Salmon (Smoked), Smoked
Whitefish, Smoked Chubs, Smoked Kippered Salmon, Smoked Sable,
Smoked Butterfish, Smoked Brook Trout
(Blue-Ribbon Smoked Fish Co., Brooklyn, N.Y.)

BREAST O'CHICKEN TUNA

CARNATION TUNA

PEACOCK TUNA
(Westgate Cal. Foods, San Diego, Ca.)

CARPION
Frozen Israeli Carp (Whole, Sliced, Ground)
(Gourmet Imports, Brooklyn, N.Y.)

CHICKEN OF THE SEA TUNA
(Ralston-Purina Co., St. Louis, Mo.)

DAGIM
Frozen Fish Fillets, Fish-Mish, Salmon, Tuna
(Dagim Tahorim Co., Brooklyn, N.Y.)

GOLD SEAL SALMON

RED SEAL SALMON

TEA ROSE SALMON

OCEAN SPRAY SALMON

GOLD STANDARD SALMON

HORSE SHOE SALMON

SEA WAVE SALMON
(Canadian Fishing Co., Vancouver, B.C., Canada)

ICY POINT SALMON

PILLAR ROCK SALMON

PINK BEAUTY SALMON

GOLD STANDARD SALMON

SUWANEE SALMON
(New England Fish Co., Seattle, Wash.)

KINERET
Frozen Fried Fish Cakes, Frozen Fried Fish Sticks
(Kineret Food Co., Bronx, N.Y.)

SEASON BRAND
Brisling Sardines, Skinless and Boneless Sardines, Sprats, Tuna in Oil
Water/Flakes, Salmon, Kippered Herring, Anchovies, Norwegian
Sardines in Tomato Sauce, Tomato Sardines, Kipper Snacks
(I. Epstein & Sons, Newark, N.J.)

STAR OF DAVID
Pickled Herring, Lox, Nova Lox

ROYAL TASTE
Pickled Herring
(R&D Food Prods., Inc., Chicago, Ill.)

VITA
Schmaltz Herring, Gefilte Fish, Salt Mackerel, Matjes Herring,
Iceland Matjes Herring, Headless Mikes, Fat Herring Fillets in Wine
Sauce, Fillets in Wine Sauce, Herring in Wine Sauce, Herring in
Cream Sauce, Roll Mops, Herring Salad, Spiced Anchovies, Bismark
Herring, Marine Herring, Marine Sardines, Anchovy Paste, White
Fish Roe-Caviar
(Vita Food Products, Inc., N.Y., N.Y.)

WELLWORTH
Pickled Schmaltz Herring, Herring in Wine Sauce
(Wellworth Pickle Co., Paterson, N.J.)

WINBORG'S
Herring Snacks with Onion, Herring Fillets with Onion, Herring
Fillets with Dill, Herring Fillets with Extra Spice
(CPC International Best Foods Div., Englewood Cliffs, N.J.)

SERV-A-GEN
Vanilla, Lemon and Imitation Extracts
(Serv-A-Gen Corp., Philadelphia, Pa.)

FLOUR

ELAM'S
Stone Ground 100% Whole Wheat Flour, 100% Whole Wheat Flour,
Stone Ground 100% Whole Rye Flour, Brown Rice Flour
(Elam's, Broadview, Ill.)

FROZEN AND FRESH PACKAGED MEALS

(Available on request from airlines, hospitals, and selected Holiday Inn motels.)

Parve

BORENSTEIN
Broiled Salmon, Fillet of Sole, Mushroom Omelette
(Borenstein Caterers Inc., Jamaica, N.Y.)

MADAN FROZEN DINNERS
Fish Dinners, Omelettes
(Madan Kosher Foods, Los Angeles, Ca.; Miami, Fla.)

SCHREIBER FROZEN DINNERS
Halibut Steak Dinner, Baked Haddock Dinner, Baked Fillet of Sole Dinner
(Schreiber Caterers, Brooklyn, N.Y.)

Meat

BORENSTEINS'S
Pot Roast of Beef, Cooked Brisket of Beef (Potted Brisket of Beef), Swiss Steak, Salisbury Steak, Roast Rock Cornish Game Hen, Roast Sliced Veal, Cooked Rock Cornish, Cooked Beef, Cooked Beef with Broth (Boiled Beef), Fillet of Beef Rib Steak, Roast Turkey, Roast Shoulder of Lamb, Corned Beef and Cabbage, Salt Free Dietetic Dinners
(Borenstein Caterers Inc., Jamaica, N.Y.)

MADAN FROZEN DINNERS
Chicken Dinners, Beef Dinners, Turkey Dinners, Salt Free Dinners
(Madan Kosher Food, Los Angeles, Ca.; Miami, Fla.)

SCHREIBER FROZEN DINNERS
Boiled Leg of Chicken Dinner, Boiled Breast of Chicken Dinner, Roast Leg of Chicken Dinner, Roast Breast of Chicken Dinner, Roast Breast of Chicken Dinner, Chicken Cacciatore Dinner, Roast Turkey Dinner, Braised Beef in Jardiniera Sauce Dinner, Boiled Beef Dinner, Pot Roast of Beef, Grilled Chopped Beefsteak Dinner, Braised Sliced Veal Dinner, Boiled Beef Tongue Dinner
(Schreiber Caterers, Inc., Brooklyn, N.Y.)

WILTON FROZEN DINNER
Dinners: Beef, Chicken, Turkey and Fish, and Omelettes
(Wilton Frozen Dinners, Inc., Spring Valley, N.Y.)

FRUITS, DRIED/CANNED

BORDO DATES

DANDI-DATE
(Borden Products, Chicago, Ill.)

CAL DATE

SUN GIANT
Dates (Chopped, pitted, whole), Raisins
(Cal-Date Co., California Agriculture Specialties, Indio, Ca.)

CALAVO
Dates
(Calavo Corp., Los Angeles, Ca.)

DEL MONTE
DRIED FRUITS: Apricots, Prunes, Raisins, Mixed Fruits, Apples, Peaches, Zante Currants
(Del Monte Corp., San Francisco, Ca.)

DROMEDARY
Dates, Fruits and Peels
(Dromedary Div. of National Biscuit Co., New York, N.Y.)

PUREED FRUIT
Bananas, Prunes, Applesauce, Peaches, Apricots with Tapioca
(H. J. Heinz Co., Pittsburgh, Pa.)

DRIED FRUITS
Apples, Apricots, Cherries, Currants, Dates, Natural-No Sugar Fruit Roll, Figs (Mission, Calmyrna), Mixed Fruits, Peaches, Prunes (Regular and Pitted), Raisins, Golden Raisins, Zante Currants
(Paul Mariani Co., Copertino, Ca.)

CANNED FRUITS
Cherries, Apple Rings, Spiced Crabapples, Sliced Apples, Dark Sweet Pitted Cherries, Blackberries, Blueberries, Raspberries, Purple Plums
(Musselman's Div. of Pet, Inc., Biglerville, Pa.)

SEASON
Dates, Prunes, Apricots, Pears, Mixed Fruits
(I. Epstein & Son, Irvington. N.J.)

SUN-RAY
DRIED FRUITS
Prunes, Dates, Pears
(Sun-Ray Orchards Co., Myrtle Creek, Ore.)

FRUIT ICES

BARTONS
Fruit Ices (Parve only when indicated on label)
(Barton's Candy Corp., Brooklyn, N.Y.)

CENTRONE'S
Italian Fruit Ices
(Centrone Italian Ices, Chesapeake, Va.)

GOLDSEAL—RIVIERA
Fruit Ices (Parve only when indicated on labels)
(Gold Star Ice Cream Co., Brooklyn, N.Y.)

COUNTRY CLUB (Parve only when bearing Parve label)
Ices and Desserts
(Country Club Frozen Desserts, Inc., Bronx, N.Y.)

MARINO'S
Italian Fruit Ices
(Olympic Ice Cream Co., Richmond Hill, N.Y.)

GEFILTE FISH PRODUCTS
HOROWITZ-MARGARETEN
Gefilte Fish Liquid Jell Sauce, Gefilte Pike and Whitefish-Jellied Sauce
(Horowitz Bros. and Margareten, Long Island City, N.Y.)

MOTHER'S
Gefilte Fish, Fish Hors d'Oeuvres, All Whitefish, Whitefish Hors d'Oeuvres
(Mrs. Schlorer's Inc., Philadelphia, Pa.)
White fish and Yellow Pike, Unsalted Gefilte Fish, Old World Gefilte Fish, Old World White Fish and Pike, White Fish Roe-Caviar
(Mother's Food Prod., Div. of Vita Foods, Newark, N.J.)

MRS. ADLER'S
Gefilte Fish (Liquid and Jell), Fish Bits, Pike and Whitefish, Fish Loaf
(Adler's Food Packing Co., Brooklyn, N.Y.)

ROKEACH
Gefilte Fish, Whitefish and Pike, Old Vienna, Premium Whitefish, Hors d'Oeuvres, Salt Free Gefilte Fish
(I. Rokeach & Son, Inc., New York, N.Y.)

GLAZE
MRS. SCHLORER'S
Chicken Glaze, Sugar N' Spice Glaze
(Mrs. Schlorer's Inc., Philadelphia, Pa.)

HONEY
ANN PAGE
(Gt. Atlantic & Pacific Tea Co., A & P Stores)

MRS. SCHLORER'S
(Mrs. Schlorer's Inc., Philadelphia, Pa.)

WALKER & SONS
(Walker & Sons Apiaries, Onstead, Mich.)

HORSERADISH
BEST FOODS MUSTARD WITH HORSERADISH
(CPC International, Best Foods Div., Englewood Cliffs, N.J.)

CAINS
Horseradish with Beets
(John E. Cain Co., Cambridge, Mass.)

GOLD'S
(Gold Pure Foods, Brooklyn, N.Y.)

MOTHER'S
(Mother's Food Products, Newark, N.J.)

TULKOFF'S
(Tulkoff's Horseradish Prod. Co., Baltimore, Md.)

VITA
(Vita Food Products, New York, N.Y.)

(L) ARROW
(Arrow Horseradish Co., Brooklyn, N.Y.)

(L) AXELROD
(A. M. Axelrod & Son, Inc., Paterson, N.J.)

(L) MRS. KATZ
(Mrs. Katz Food Co., Cleveland, Ohio)

(L) SHLOIMA'S
(Canter & Smolar Co., Pittsburgh, Pa.)

Dairy
CAIN'S—with (U) D
Horseradish (Contains cream)
(John E. Cain Co., Cambridge, Mass.)

ICE CREAM SHERBET
COUNTRY CLUB (Parve must appear on label)
Frozen Desserts
(Country Club Frozen Dessert, Inc., Bronx, N.Y.)

PARV-A-ZERT (Parve must appear on label)
Frozen Dessert
(Sugar-Lo Co., Atlantic City, N.J.)

Dairy

BARTON'S BONBONNIERE
Ice Cream, Sherbet
(Barton Candy Corp., Brooklyn, N.Y.)

GOLD SEAL

BORDEAU

MARCELL

WEIGH OF LIFE
Ice Cream, Sherbet, Ice Milk, Chocolate Ices
(Gold Star Ice Cream Co., Brooklyn, N.Y.)

JERSEYMAID
Ice Cream
(Jerseymaid Milk Prod. Co., Los Angeles, Ca.)

SWIFT'S

PIERRE'S

DIPPERDAN

GOLDMINE
Ice Cream, Ice Cream Novelties, Sherbet
(Swift Ice Cream Co., Woodridge, N.J.)

ICE CREAM CONES
LOV-E-LEE
Ice Cream Cones, Ice Cream Cups
(Cream Cone Co., Columbus, Ohio)

INFANT FORMULAS

Dairy

BAKER'S
Liquid, Powder, w/Iron, Ready to Feed, Concentrate
(Baker's Labs, Inc., East Troy, Wic.)

BREMIL

MULL SOY

NEO-MULL SOY

CHO-FREE

NUTRI-1000
(Special Formula Nutritional Supplement): Liquid, Powder, w/Iron,
Ready to Feed, Concentrate
(Syntex Laboratories, Palo Alto, Ca.)

ENFAMIL

BENIFLEX

PREMATURE FORMULA—RN

PREMATURE FORMULA BENIFLEX
Liquid, Powder, w/Iron, Ready to Feed, Concentrate
(Mead Johnson Inc., Evansville, Ind.)

SIMILAC
Liquid, Powder, w/Iron, Ready to Feed, Concentrate

PM 60/40

ISOMIL

ADVANCE
(Ross Labs., Div. of Abbot, Inc., Columbus, Ohio)

INSTANT BREAKFAST AND DIET DRINKS
ANN PAGE
Orange Flavored Instant Breakfast Drink
(Gt. Atlantic & Pacific, A & P Stores)

Dairy

ANN PAGE INSTANT BREAKFAST
Chocolate, Vanilla, Strawberry, Coffee, Chocolate Malt
(Gt. Atlantic & Pacific Tea Co., A & P Stores)

CARNATION INSTANT BREAKFAST
Chocolate, Chocolate Malt, Chocolate Marshmallow, Vanilla, Vanilla
Ice Cream, Strawberry, Coffee, Egg Nog, Butterscotch
(Carnation Co., Los Angeles, Ca.)

CARNATION SLENDER (DIET DRINK)
Liquid, Powder
(Carnation Co., Los Angeles, Ca.)

FIGURINE
Diet Flavors
(The Pillsbury Co., Minneapolis, Minn.)

KOSHER KAL
900 Calorie Diet
(Freeda Pharm., New York, N.Y.)

PILLSBURY INSTANT BREAKFAST
Chocolate, Chocolate Malt, Strawberry, Vanilla
(The Pillsbury Co., Minneapolis, Minn.)

JAMS, JELLIES, PRESERVES, AND MARMALADE
ANN PAGE
Jam: Blackberry, Cherry, Grape, Black Raspberry, Red Raspberry
Preserves: Apricot, Blackberry, Blueberry, Cherry, Damson Plum,

Peach, Pineapple, Red Plum, Red Raspberry, Strawberry
Jellies: Apple, Blackberry, Black Raspberry, Red Raspberry, Crabapple, Currant, Elderberry, Quince, Strawberry, Imitation Mint Flavor
Marmalade: Pure Orange

SULTANA

Strawberry Preserves, Apple Blackberry, Apple, Raspberry, Apple Strawberry
(The Great Atlantic & Pacific Tea Co., Inc., A & P Stores)

BARTON'S BONBONNIERE

Jam, Jelly, Marmalade
(Barton's Candy Corp., Brooklyn, N.Y.)

LOUIS SHERRY

Preserves: Strawberry, Red Raspberry, Cherry, Seedless Black Raspberry, Blackberry, Seedless Blackberry, Apricot, Peach, Pineapple, Pineapple-Cherry, Pineapple-Apricot, Plum-Damson, Blueberry, Orange Marmalade, English Morelio Cherry, Wild Strawberry, Irish Heart Orange, English Orange Marmalade
Jellies: Ruby Red Currant, Strawberry, Raspberry, Apple, Apple Mint, Cinnamon Apple, Guava
(Louis Sherry, Inc., Greenwich, Conn.)

MRS. ADLER'S

Preserves
Marmalde
Orange, Lemon, Grapefruit
(Mrs. Adler's Foods, Brooklyn, N.Y.)

POLANER

Jellies: Crabapple, Strawberry, Red Raspberry, Cherry, Quince, Mint, Red Currant, Florida Guava, Harvard Apple, Wild Elderberry, Blackberry, Cinnamon
Preserves: Better Grape Preserves, Sweet Orange Marmalade, Seedless Raspberry and Currant, Strawberry, Red Raspberry, Seedless Black Raspberry, Red Cherry, Seedless Blackberry, Hawaiian Pineapple, Purple Plum, Blenheim Apricot, Elberta Peach, Bing Cherry, Blueberry, Damson Plum, Apricot-Pineapple, Bitter Orange Marmalade, Orange-Cherry, 5 Fruits, Red Plum, Low Calorie Preserves
(M. Polaner & Son, Inc., Newark, N.J.)

REX JELLY

(Best Foods Div., CPC International, Englewood Cliffs, N.J.)

ROKEACH

Orange Marmalade
(I. Rokeach & Sons, Inc., Farmingdale, N.J.)

VITA

SHALOM

Jams, Jelly, Marmalade
(J. Plotkin & Son, Ramat Gan, Israel)

(L) AUNT NELLIES

Jelly and Preserves (excluding Grape)
(Harrisburg Grocery Co.)

(L) FOOD FAIR

Jams and Jellies
(Food Fair Stores Inc., Philadelphia, Pa.)

(L) IDEAL

Jam and Preserves: Apricot, Apricot-Pineapple, Crushed Cherry, Peach, Strawberry, Raspberry, Red Raspberry, Apple Blackberry, Apple Raspberry, Orange Marmalade, Seedless Red Raspberry, Blueberry, Seedless Blackberry
Jelly: Apple, Apple-Cherry, Apple-Strawberry, Blackberry, Raspberry, Cherry, Imitation Fruit, Jell-Mint, Currant, Wild Elderberry

SUPER SAVER

Apple-Blackberry, Apple-Raspberry, Apple-Strawberry
Jam, Preserves: Strawberry, Peach
Marmalade (Orange)
(Acme Markets, Inc., Philadelphia, Pa.)

(L) KEY

Jelly and Preserves (excluding Grape)
(Key Food Stores, Brooklyn, N.Y.)

(L) KING KULLEN

Jams and Preserves (excluding Grape)
(King Kullen Inc., Westbury, N.Y.)

(L) MET

(L) WHITE ROSE

Jelly and Preserves (excluding Grape)
(White Rose, Inc., Linden, N.J.)

(L) PREMIER

Jelly and Preserves (excluding Grape)
(Francis H. Legett Co.)

(L) WALDBAUM'S
Jelly and Preserves (excluding Grape)
(Waldbaum's Inc., Garden City, N.Y.)

(L) SEAWAY
Jelly and Preserves (excluding Grape)
(Seaway Foods, Bedford Heights, Ohio)

(L) SHOPMORE
Shopwell Jelly and Preserves (excluding Grape)
(Daitch Shopwell, N.Y., N.Y.)

JUICES
A&P
Apple Juice, Prune Juice
(The Great Atlantic and Pacific Tea Co., A & P Stores)

BENNETT'S
Prune Juice
(Doxsee Food Corp., Baltimore, Md.)

HEINZ
Tomato Juice
(H.J. Heinz Co., Pittsburgh, Pa.)

IDEAL

SUPER SAVER

FARMDALE
Tomato and Prune Juice
(Acme Markets Inc., Philadelphia, Pa.)

LIBBY'S
Tomato Juice
(Libby McNeil & Libby, Chicago, Ill.)

LUCKY LEAF
Apple Juice
(Krouse Foods, Inc., Peach Glen, Pa.)

MUSSELMAN'S
Apple and tomato juice
(C.H. Musselman Div. of Pet Milk Co., Biglerville, Pa.)

ROKEACH
Prune, Apple and Tomato Juices
(I. Rokeach & Sons Inc., Farmingdale, N.J.)

SILVER FLOSS
Kraut Juice
(Silver Floss Fds. Div. of Curtice Burns Inc., Phelps, N.Y.)

3 V PAPAYA JUICE CONCENTRATE
(Three Vee Co., Brooklyn, N.Y.)

VERY FINE
Apple and Prune Juice
(New England Apple Prod. Co., Littleton, Mass.)

WELCH'S
Tomato and Prune Juice
(Welch Foods Inc., Westfield, N.Y.)

JUICE DRINKS
A&P
Cranberry, Cranberry Apple, Cherry, Orange, Grapefruit, Pineapple, Tropical Fruit Punch
(The Great Atlantic and Pacific Tea Co., A & P Stores)

IDEAL
Cherry Drink, Honolulu Punch, Orange Drink, Apricot Nectar

SUPER SAVER

FARMDALE
Orange, Punch, Pineapple Grapefruit, and Apricot Nectar
(Acme Markets, Inc., Philadelphia, Pa.)

CATSUP, TOMATO SAUCE AND PUREE
ANN PAGE
Catsup, Chili Sauce, Hot Catsup, Barbecue Sauce
(The Great Atlantic and Pacific Tea Co., A & P Stores)

HEINZ
Tomato Ketchup, Hot Ketchup, Ketchup with Pickle Relish, Ketchup with Onions
(The H.J. Heinz Co., Pittsburgh, Pa.)

LIBBY'S
Tomato Catsup and Tomato Sauce
(Libby McNeill & Libby, Chicago, Ill.)

MUSSELMAN'S
Tomato Puree
(Musselman's Div., Pet Foods, Biglerville, Pa.)

VITA
(J. Plotkin & Sons, Ramat Gan, Israel)

(L) AUNT NELLIES
Chili Sauce
(Harrisburg Grocery Co.)

(L) KEY
Catsup
(Keyfood Stores, Brooklyn, N.Y.)

(L) KING KULLEN
Catsup, Chili Sauce
(King Kullen Corp., Westbury, N.Y.)

(L) MET

WHITE ROSE
(White Rose Tea Co., Linden, N.J.)

(L) PENNSYLVANIA DUTCH
Cocktail Sauce
(Pennsylvania Dutch Co.)

(L) SHOPMORE

SHOPWELL
Catsup, Chili Sauce
(Daitch Shopwell, Inc., N.Y., N.Y.)

(L) WALDBAUM'S
Ketchup, Chili Sauce
(Waldbaum's Inc., Garden City, N.Y.)

LIQUORS AND CORDIALS
LEROUX
Abisante (100°), Abisante (120°), Anesone, Anisette (Red), Anisette (White), Apple, Apricot Fl. Brandy, Apricot Liqueur, Acquavit, Banana Liqueur, Blackberry Fl. Brandy, Blackberry Liqueur, Cherry Fl. Brandy, Cherry Darise, Cherry Liqueur, Claristine, Creme de Cacao (Brown), Creme de Cacao (White), Creme de Cafe (Jugs), Creme de Cafe (Glass), Creme de Cassis, Creme de Menthe (Green), Creme de Menthe (White), Creme de Nova, Curacao, Ginger Fl. Brandy, Gold-O-Mint, Grenadine Liqueur, Kirschwasser, Kummel Maraschino, Peach Liqueur, Peach Fl. Brandy, Peppermint Schnapps, Polish Blackberry Brandy, Raspberry Liqueur, Rock & Rye (W/Crystals), Irish Moss, Rock & Rye (W/Fruits), Sloe Gin, Strawberry Liqueur, Triple Sec
(General Wine & Spirits Co., N.Y., N.Y.)

SABRA
(Park Ave. Imports, N.Y., N.Y.)

MACARONI, SPAGHETTI AND NOODLES
ANN PAGE
Alphabets, Macaroni, Perciatelli, Elbow Macaroni, Ditilni, Sea Shells
—Regular, Large, Mezzani, Rigatini, Lasagna, Spirelle, Spaghetti, Thin Spaghetti, Vermicelli, Linguine, Elbow Spaghetti, Fine Noodles, Broad Noodles, Extra Wide Noodles, Medium Noodles, Pastina, Egg Bows (Farfelle)
(The Great Atlantic & Pacific Tea Co., Inc., A&P Stores)

BUITONI
20% Protein Enriched Spaghetti, 20% Protein Enriched Macaroni, Enriched Egg Noodles and Noodle Nests, 20% Protein Pastina, Lasagna, Twists, Macaroni Specialties
(Buitoni Foods Corp., So. Hackensack, N.J.)

COLUMBIA

LIBERTY

ZEREGA

PATRIA
Macaroni, Spaghetti, and Egg Noodles
(A Zerega's Sons Inc., Fairlawn, N.J.)

CONTE LUNA
Spaghetti, Thin Spaghetti, Capellini, Elbow Macaroni, Large Shells, Twistetti, Egg Noodles, Egg Barley, Egg Flakes, Egg Alphabet, Egg Ringlets, Large Egg Bows, Small Egg Bows, Ruffled Edge Lasagne, **Egg Spaghetti**, Egg Baby Pastina
(Conte Luna Foods, Inc., Norristown, Pa.)

GREENFIELD
Egg Noodles
(Greenfield Noodle & Specialty Co., Detroit, Mich.)

HOME-WAY
Egg Noodles
(Homeway Real Egg Noodle Corp., Floral Park, N.Y.)

HOROWITZ-MARGARETEN
Egg Noodles; Egg Noddle: barley, flakes, bows, alphabets; Toasted Egg Noodles; Barley and Chow Mein Noodles
(Horowitz Bros & Margareten, Long Island City, N.Y.)

LA BELLANTE
Spaghetti and Egg Noodles
(Columbus Macaroni & Noodle Co., Cleveland, Ohio)

LA ROSA
Macaroni, Spaghetti, Egg Noodles
(V. La Rosa & Sons, Inc., Westbury, N.Y.)

MUELLER
Macaroni, Spaghetti, Egg Noodles
(C.F. Mueller Co., Jersey City, N.J.)

PARAMOUNT
Macaroni, Spaghetti, Noodles
(Paramount Macaroni Co., Brooklyn, N.Y.)

PENNSYLVANIA DUTCH CAVALIERE
Egg Noodles
(Pa. Dutch-Meg Co., Lawrence, Mass.)

PRINCE
Town Pride, Pasta Mia, Dutch Maid, Spaghetti, Egg Noodles, Macaroni, Pastina
(Prince Macaroni Mfg. Co., Lowell, Mass.)

REAMES
Frozen Egg Noodles and Flat Dumplings
(Reames Foods, Inc., Clive, Iowa)

SAN GIORGIO
Macaroni, Spaghetti, Egg Noodles
(San Giorgio Macaronie, Inc., Lebanon, Pa.)

SKINNER
Egg Noodles, Macaroni, Spaghetti
(Skinner Macaroni Co., Omaha, Neb.)

VIMCO
Macaroni, Spaghetti, Egg Noodles
(Vimco Macaroni Prod. Co., Carnegie, Pa.)

VIVA
Macaroni, Spaghetti, Noodles
(Viva Macaroni Mfg. Co., Lawrence, Mass.)

(L) BOHACK'S BEST
Macaroni, Spaghetti, Egg Noodles
(H.C. Bohack, Inc., Brooklyn, N.Y.)

(L) CO-OP
Macaroni, Spaghetti, Egg Noodles
(Mid-Eastern Cooperative, Inc., Lodi, N.J.)

(L) GRAND UNION
Macaroni, Spaghetti, Egg Noodles
(Grand Union Co., East Peterson, N.J.)

(L) KEY
Macaroni, Spaghetti, Noodles
(Key Food Stores, Inc., Brooklyn, N.Y.)

(L) MRS. ASIEN'S EGG NOODLES
(Asien Noodle Co., Wheeling, Ill.)

P & R
Macaroni, Spaghetti, Noodles
(Procino Rossi Corp., Auburn, N.Y.)

(L) SHOP RITE
Macaroni, Spaghetti, Egg Noodles
(Wakefern Food Corp. Elizabeth, N.J.)

(L) SHOPWELL
Macaroni, Egg Noodles
(Daitch Shopwell Inc., Bronx, N.Y.)

(L) SOPHIE TUCKER
Pure Egg Noodles
(Sophie Tucker Foods Inc., Baltimore, Md.)

(L) STAFF
Macaroni, Spaghetti, Noodles
(Staff Supermarkets Assoc., Jericho, N.Y.)

(L) STOP & SHOP
Spaghetti and Macaroni Products
(Stop & Shop Inc., Boston, Mass.)

(L) WALDBAUM'S
Macaroni, Egg Noodles
(Waldbaum's, Inc., Garden City, N.Y.)

(L) WHITE ROSE
Macaroni, Spaghetti, Noodles
(Met Food Stores)

MAYONNAISE AND SALAD DRESSINGS
ANN PAGE

SULTANA
Salad Dressings, Mayonnaise, 1000 Island Dressing, French Dressing, Sandwich Spread, Cole Slaw Dressing, Italian Dressing (Reg. & Creamy), Tartar Sauce, Russian Dressing, Low Calorie Dressing
(The Great Atlantic and Pacific Tea Co., A & P Stores)

CAIN'S
Mayonnaise, Sandwich Spread, Tartar Sauce, French Dressing, 1000 Island Dressing, Italian Island Dressing, Riviera Island Dressing
(John E. Cain Co., Cambridge, Mass.)

BENNETT'S

RED ROSE

GINGHAM GIRL

LUCKY LADY

SALAD TIME

MERIT

QUEEN ANN
Mayonnaise, Salad Dressing
(Doxsee Food Corp., Baltimore, Md.)

DUTCH PANTRY

HELLMAN'S

BEST FOOD'S
Mayonnaise, Mayonnaise with Relish, Tartar Sauce, Sandwich Spread,
Thousand Island Dressing, Italian Dressing, Old Homestead Dressing,
Spin Blend Dressing
(CPC International, Best Foods Div., Englewood Cliffs, N.J.)

HENRI'S
Mayonnaise, French Dressings, Italian Dressing, Garlic Dressing
(Henri's Food Prod. Inc., Milwaukee, Wis.)

HOSTESS
Dressings, Mayonnaise
(Hostess Products Corp., Brooklyn, N.Y.)

MRS. SCHLORER'S
Mayonnaise, Sandwich Spread, Salad Dressings
(Mrs. Schlorer's Inc., Philadelphia, Pa.)

PFEIFFER'S
Dressing: Russian, French, ColeSlaw, Italian, 1000 Island, Low
Calorie, Fruit, and Also Tartar Sauce
(Pfeiffer Foods, Inc., Buffalo, N.Y.)

(L) BOHACK
Mayonnaise, Dressings
(H.C. Bohack Co., Brooklyn, N.Y.)

(L) BUDDIE
Mayonnaise, Dressings
(Louis Lehrman & Son, Harrisburg, Pa.)

(L) CO-OP
Mayonnaise, Dressings
(Mid-Eastern Co-op, Carlstadt, N.J.)

(L) EDDIE'S
Mayonnaise, Dressings
(Indego, Inc., Baltimore, Md.)

(L) KEY
Mayonnaise, Salad Dressings
(Key Food Stores, Brooklyn, N.Y.)

(L) KING KULLEN
Mayonnaise, Dressings
(King Kullen Grocery, Inc., Westbury, N.Y.)

(L) FOOD CLUB

GAYLORD
Mayonnaise, Dressings
(Topco Associates, Inc., Skokie, Ill.)

(L) HILLS
Mayonnaise
(Hills Supermarkets, Brentwood, N.Y.)

(L) MAI-PAI
(Spice House Packing Co., Westbury, N.Y., N.Y.)

(L) MANOR HILL
Mayonnaise and Dressings
(Manor Hill Salad Co., Baltimore, Md.)

(L) MARSH
Salad Dressings
(Marsh Supermarkets, Yorktown, Ind.)

(L) PANTRY PRIDE
Mayonnaise and Dressings
(Pantry Pride Stores, Philadelphia, Pa.)

(L) PATHMARK
Mayonnaise and Salad Dressing
(Super-Market Gent Corp., Woodbridge, N.J.)

(L) PREMIER
Mayonnaise and Dressings
(Met Food Corp., Syosset, N.Y.)

(L) RICHFOOD
Mayonnaise and Dressings
(Richmond Food Stores, Richmond, Va.)

SHOP-RITE
Mayonnaise and Dressings
(Wakefern Food Products, Elizabeth, N.J.)

(L) SHOPWELL
Mayonnaise and Dressings
(Daitch Shopwell, Inc., N.Y., N.Y.)

(L) WALDBAUM'S
Mayonnaise and Dressings
(Waldbaum's, Inc., Garden City, N.Y.)

(L) WHITE ROSE
Mayonnaise and Dressings
(White Rose Co., Linden, N.J.)

MARGARINE (Parve only when indicated on label)
MAR-PARV
(Miami Margarine Co., Cincinnati, Ohio)

MOTHER'S
Salted and Unsalted; Soft Margarine—Stick Margarine
(Mother's Food Products, Newark, N.J.)

MAZOLA
(Parve only when indicated on label)
Unsalted; Diet Imitation Margarine
(CPC International, Best Foods Div., Englewood Cliffs, N.J.)

ROKEACH
(I. Rokeach & Sons, Inc., Farmingdale, N.J.)

Dairy
HOLIDAY

MAZOLA
Soft Margarine and Stick Margarine
(CPC Int., Best Foods Div., Englewood Cliffs, N.J.)

(L) SALLY SHOPWELL

(L) DAITCH-CRYSTAL
(Daitch Shopwell, Inc., N.Y., N.Y.)

(L) GOLDEN KEY
(Key Food Stores Inc., Brooklyn, N.Y.)

(L) WALDBAUM'S
(Waldbaum's, Inc., Garden City, N.Y.)

MARINADES
ADOLPH'S
Meat Marinade and Chicken Marinade
(Adolph's Ltd., Burbank, Ca.)

MARSHMALLOW TOPPING
MARSHMALLOW FLUFF
(Durkee Mower, Inc., East Lynn, Mass.)

MATZOH AND MATZOH PRODUCTS
HOROWITZ-MARGARETEN
Oven Crisp Unsalted Matzohs, Diet Crackers, Nu-Taste Matzohs, Onion-Flavored Matzohs, Whole-Wheat Matzohs, Egg-Onion Matzoh Crackers, Matzoh Meal, Matzoh Farfel
(Horowitz Bros. & Margareten, Long Island City, N.Y.)

MATZOH DUMPLINGS
MRS. ADLER'S
Matzoh Dumplings
(Mrs. Adler's Foods Corp., Brooklyn, N.Y.)

MEAT BALLS [CANNED]
Meat
BARNEY'S
Meat Balls and Ravioli
(Berman Food Prod. Co., Newark, N.J.)

ROKEACH
Meat Balls in Tomato Sauce
(I. Rokeach & Sons Inc., Farmingdale, N.J.)

MEATS AND PROVISIONS
Meat
DAVID ELLIOT
Beef Roasts and Steaks, Veal Chops, Boneless Veal Roasts, Lamb Chops, Steer Liver, Calves Liver
(David Elliot Poultry Farm, Lake Ariel, Pa.)

"999"
Salami, Bologna, Corned Beef, Frankfurters, Tongue, Smoked Beef, Pastrami
(Real Kosher Sausage Co., N.Y., N.Y.)

LOWY'S
Bologna, Salami, Corned Beef, Pastrami, Tongue, Frankfurters
(Lowy's Mehadrin Co., Brooklyn, N.Y.)

MEAL MART
Beef, Veal, Lamb, Salami, Bologna, Franfurters, Corn Beef, Pastrami, Tongue
(Alle Packing Co., Brooklyn, N.Y.)

SUPERVISED PRODUCTS

FROZEN MEAT PROVISIONS
Beef, Veal, Lamb, Roasts, Steaks, Chops, Liver
(Supervised Products, Inc., Denver, Colo.)

MEAT TENDERIZER

ADOLPH'S INSTANT MEAT TENDERIZER
Seasoned and Unseasoned
(Adolph's Ltd., Burbank, Ca.)

ANN PAGE
Meat Tenderizer
(The Great Atlantic and Pacific Tea Co., A & P Stores)

3 V
Meat Tenderizer
(Three Vee Co., Brooklyn, N.Y.)

MELBA TOAST

DEVONSHEER
Melba Toasts—Plain, Rye, Whole Wheat, Rounds—Plain, Salty, Rye—Garlic, Sesame, and Allgrane Wafers, Rice Wafers
(Devonsheer Melba Corp., Carlstadt, N.J.)

MASTER MELBETTS TOASTS
(Zinmaster Baking Co., Minneapolis, Minn.)

(L) NABISCO
(National Biscuit Co., N.Y., N.Y.)

OLD LONDON
Melba Toast, Rounds, Lady Melba
(Old London Foods, Inc., Bronx, N.Y.)

MILK, CREAM SUBSTITUTE

NO-LAC

CHOC-O-LUCK

FLAVOR PLUS
(Protein Products Corp., Bayonne, N.J.)

COFFEE RICH
(Rich Products Co., Buffalo, N.Y.)

KRIM

HELLER
(Heller Enterprises, Inc., E. Rockaway, N.Y.)

Dairy

AVOSET

DIET PLUS
(Dietetic—No-Cholestrol—Low Sodium)

SECOND NATURE

QUIP
(Avoset Food Corp., Oakland, Ca.)

(L) DITTO (Foremost)

(L) LUCERNE

CREAM WHITE
Powdered Coffee Creamer
(Humko Products, Memphis, Tenn.)

WEIGHT WATCHERS COFFEE LIGHT'NER
(Foodways National, Hawthorne, N.Y.)

MILK — [CHOLOV YISROEL]

Dairy
FARM FRESH
Milk: Homogenized and Skimmed
(Mason-Dixon Farms, Gettysburg, Pa.)

MILK [EVAPORATED]

Dairy
ANN PAGE
Evaporated and Evaporated Skim Milk
(The Great Atlantic and Pacific Tea Co., A & P Stores)

MILK [POWDER]

Dairy
ALBA
Instant Non-Fat Dry Milk, Chocolate Flavored Instant Non-Fat Dry Milk
(Weldon Foods, Inc., N.Y., N.Y.)

ANN PAGE
Instant Non-Fat Dry Milk; Chocolate Flavored (Instant Dry)
(The Great Atlantic and Pacific Tea Co., A & P Stores)

JERSEYMAID
Non-Fat Dry Milk
(Jerseymaid Milk Prod., Los Angeles, Ca.)

SANALAC
Instant Non-Fat Dry Milk
(Sanna Div., Beatrice Foods, Madison, Wis.)

(L) SHOPRITE
Instant Non-Fat Dry Milk
(Wakefern Food Corp., Elizabeth, N.J.)

(L) WALDBAUM'S
Instant Non-Fat Dry Milk
(Waldbaum's Inc., Garden City, N.Y.)

(L) WHITE ROSE
Instant Non-Fat Dry Milk
(Met Foods Corp., Elizabeth, N.J.)

MILK FLAVORINGS AND AMPLIFIERS

BOSCO
Chocolate Syrup
(Best Foods Div., CPC Int., Englewood Cliffs, N.J.)

OSEM
Chocolate Shake Mix
(Osem Ltd., Tel Aviv, Israel)

PDQ
Chocolate, Strawberry, Egg Nog
(Ovaltine Div. of Sandoz Warner Inc., Villa Park, Ill.)

Dairy

ALBA 66 (Hot Cocoa Mix)
ALBA 77 (Frosty Shake Mix)
ALBA 88 (Thick Shake Mix)
(Weldon Farm Prod., N.Y., N.Y.)

A & P
Chocolate Milk Mix
(The Great Atlantic and Pacific Tea Co., A & P Stores)

OVALTINE
Malt Flavor, Chocolate
(Ovaltine Prod. Div. of Sandoz Warner Inc., Villa Park, Ill.)

SERV AGEN
Instant Cocoa Mix
(Serv Agen Corp., Philadelphia, Pa.)

MUSTARD

ANN PAGE
Mustard, Hot and Horseradish
(The Great Atlantic and Pacific Tea Co., A & P Stores)

BEST FOODS
Mustard with Horseradish
(Best Foods Div., CPC Int., Englewood Cliffs, N.J.)

EVANGELINE
Mustard
(Evangeline Pepper & Food Prod. Inc., St. Martins, La.)

FRENCH'S
Salad Mustard, Brown and Spicy, with Onion Bits and with Horseradish
(The R. T. French Co., Rochester, N.Y.)

HEINZ
Sweet Mustard
(H.J. Heinz Co., Pittsburgh, Pa.)

OLD DUTCH
Mustard
(Old Dutch Inc., Brooklyn, N.Y.)

THELMA
Mustard
(Israel Edible Prod., Haifa, Israel)

(L) GIANT
Mustard
(Giant Foods, Inc., Washington, D.C.)

BENNETT'S
Salad King Mustard
(Doxsee Food Corp., Baltimore Md.)

NUT AND SEEDS

CARLTON HOUSE
Cashew Nuts, Salted, Indian and Pistachio
(Bloom Packing Co., Brooklyn, N.Y.)

COUNTRY FAIR
Oil and Dry Roasted Nuts
(Ace Pecan Co., Chicago, Ill.)

DATETREE
Seeds: Pumpkin, Sesame, Millet, Raw Sunflower, Roasted Sea Salted Sunflower, Roasted Unsalted Sunflower, Vegetable Sunflower; Raisin Nut Mix, Natural Almonds, Raw Almonds—Snack-ette, Raw Cashew—Snack-ette, Nat. Sea Salted Cashews—Snack-ette, Roasted Peanuts—Snack-ette
(Organic Foods Corp., Farmingdale, N.Y.)

FLAVOR HOUSE
Dry Roasted Nuts, Peanuts, Pecans, Cashews, Mixed Nuts, Dry Roasted Sunflower Seeds, Pistachios
(Flavor House Prod., Div. Borden Co., Des Plains, Ill.)

HYGRADE
Mixed Nuts, Peanuts, Cashews, Dry Roasted, Pistachios
(Hygrade Bakery Co., Pennsville, N.J.)

JIMBOS JUMBOS
Peanuts
(Jimbos Jumbos Inc., Edenton, N.C.)

SKIPPY (DRY ROASTED—OIL ROASTED)

DOUBLE KAY

KELLING
Mixed Nuts, Peanuts, Cashews
(CPC Int., Best Foods Div., Englewood Cliffs, N.J.)

SUN GIANT

TRI-GO
Almonds—Roasted and Salted
(Cal. Almond Orchards, Bakersfield, Ca.)

TEDDIE

RIVER QUEEN

AMERICANA

BURMA
Peanuts, Mixed Nuts, Cashews, Dry Roasted
(Leavitt Corp., Everett, Mass.)

(L) FARMER JACKS
Peanuts, Cashews, Dry Roasted Nuts
(Kingston Marketing Co., Skokie, Ill.)

(L) FINAST
Peanuts, Cashews, Mixed Nuts, Dry Roasted Nuts
(First National Stores Inc., Somerville, Mass.)

(L) FM
Peanuts, Cashews, Dry Roasted Nuts
(Fedmart Corp., San Diego, Ca.)

(L) FOOD CLUB
Nuts, Cashews, Dry Roasted Nuts
(Topco Assoc., Skokie, Ill.)

(L) GIANT
Peanuts, Cashews, Dry Roasted Nuts
(Giant Food Co., Washington, D.C.)

(L) GOLD CREST
Peanuts, Dry Roasted Nuts
(Gold Crest Cando Co., Springdale, Ohio)

(L) GRAND UNION
Nuts, Dry Roasted Nuts
(Grand Union Co., East Paterson, N.J.)

(L) IDEAL
Peanuts, Cashews, Dry Roasted Nuts
(Acme Mkts., Philadelphia, Pa.)

(L) PANTRY PRIDE
Mixed Nuts, Peanuts, Cashews, Dry Roasted, Pistachios
(Pantry Pride Fds., Philadelphia, Pa.)

(L) PATHMARK
Nuts, Cashews, Dry Roasted Nuts
(Supermarket General, Woodbridge, N.J.)

(L) SHOPWELL
Peanuts, Cashews, Dry Roasted Nuts
(Daitch Shopwell Dairies Inc., N.Y., N.Y.)

(L) STAFF
Peanuts, Cashews, Dry Roasted Nuts
(Staff Supermarkets Assoc., N.Y., N.Y.)

(L) UNITY
Peanuts, Cashews, Dry Roasted Nuts
(Kingston Marketing Co., Skokie, Ill.)

(L) YORK
Peanuts, Cashews, Dry Roasted Nuts
(Canada Packers Ltd., Toronto, Canada)

OLIVES
ANN PAGE
Plain and Stuffed with Red Sweet Peppers

ENCORE
Pitted Party Olives

SULTANA
Plain, Stuffed with Red Sweet Peppers
(The Great Atlantic & Pacific Tea Co., A & P Stores)

VITA
(J. Plotkin & Sons, Ramat Gan, Israel)

(L) WALDBAUM'S
Plain and Stuffed with Red Peppers
(Waldbaum's Inc., Garden City, N.Y.)

OVEN CLEANERS
JIFOAM
(Shelco Corp., Wellsley, Mass.)

PANCAKE MIXES
ELAM'S
Ground Buckwheat Flour
(Elam's, Broadview, Ill.)

PILLSBURY
Hungry Jack Extra Lights
(The Pillsbury Co., Minneapolis, Minn.)

Dairy
HUNGRY JACK
Pancake Mix: Complete, Buttermilk and Blueberry
(The Pillsbury Co., Minneapolis, Minn.)

ELAM'S
3 in 1 Mix
(Elam's, Broadview, Ill.)

PASTINA
Parve
BUITONI
20% Protein Pastina
(Buitoni Foods Corp., So. Hackensack, N.J.)

PRINCE
Pastina, Egg, Carrot, Spinach
(Prince Macaroni Mfg., Co., Lowell, Mass.)

PEANUT BUTTER
BIG TOP

JIF
(The Procter & Gamble Co., Cincinnati, Ohio)

DATETREE
Peanut Butter: Natural, Creamy, Sea Salted, Creamy, Sea Salted
Chunky, Chunky
(Organic Foods Corp., Farmingdale, N.Y.)

HYGRADE

BUDDY BOY
Smooth, Chunky
(Hygrade Bakery Co., Pennsville, N.J.)

JIMBO'S JUMBOS
Peanut Butter
(Jimbo's Jumbos Inc., Edenton, N.C.)

SKIPPY
Peanut Butter
(Best Foods Div. of CPC Int., Englewood Cliffs, N.Y.)

TEDDIE
(Leavitt Corp., Everett, Mass.)

(L) FOOD FAIR PEANUT BUTTER
Chunky and Smooth
(Food Fair Inc., Philadelphia, Pa.)

(L) GIANT
(Giant Foods, Washington, D.C.)

(L) KEY
(Key Foods, Brooklyn, N.Y.)

(L) KING KULLEN
(King Kullen Mkts., Westbury, N.Y.)

(L) PANTRY PRIDE
Chunk and Smooth
(Pantry Pride Stores, Inc., Philadelphia, Pa.)

(L) PATHMARK
Smooth and Chunky
(Supermarkets Gen. Corp., Woodbridge, N.J.)

(L) SHOP-RITE
Smooth and Chunky
(Wakefern Food Corp., Elizabeth, N.J.)

(L) SHOPWELL
(Daitch Shopwell Inc., N.Y., N.Y.)

(L) STOP & SHOP
Chunk and Smooth
(Stop & Shop Inc., Boston, Mass.)

(L) WALDBAUM'S
(Waldbaum's Inc., Garden City, N.Y.)

PICKLES, RELISHES, KRAUT
ALBRO
WISLA
Pickles, Peppers, Kraut
(Albro Packing Co., Springboro, Pa.)

ANN PAGE
Garden Relish and Mustard Relish
(The Great Atlantic & Pacific Tea Co., Inc, A & P Stores)

AUNT JANE'S
Fresh: Sweet Sandwich, Sticks, Kosher Iceberg, Hamburger Dill
Slices, Whole Dills, Diced Sweet Pickles, Sweet Relish, Sweet Chips,

Whole Sweet Pickles, Sweet Mixed Pickles, Mustard Pickles, Sweet Picallili, Corn Relish; Candied: Sweet Midgets, Sweet Chips, Orange Waffle Cut Chips, Sweet Dill Strips, Sweet Relish, Burr Gherkins, Dill Relish, Waffle Cut Dill Chips, Hamburger Dill Slices, Whole Dill Pickles, Whole Sour Pickles, Ol' Timer Kosher Dills, Spread Relish, (Aunt Jane's Food, Div. of Borden Co., Dearborn, Mich.)

BAN'G DELUXE
Cocktail Onions, Candied Tiny Treats, Appetizer Dills, Sweet Cauliflower, Candied: Sweet Dill Strips and Sweet Gherkins, Midget Candied Sweet Gherkins, Krinkle Krispies, Candied Sweet Mixed, Sweet Mustard Pickles, Senfgurken, Sweet Candied Watermelon Rind, Garden Salad, Kosher Dill: Baby Gherkins, Chips and Spears, Sweet-Sour Pickles

BAN'G DWARF
Gherkins: Dill, Sour, Sweet, Sweet Midget, Kosher Dill, Sweet Mixed, Hot Mixed, Cocktail Onions, Sweet Onions, Yellow Peperoncini, Sweet Pickle Relish, Other Relish: Hamburger, India, Barbecue, Hot Dog, Piccalilli, Hot, Emerald, Hot Cauliflower, Sweet Cucumber Pickles, Sweet Cucumber Sticks, Sweet Dainties, Kosher Dill Spears, Mixed Giardeniera, Savory Mixed, Sweet Pepper Rings, Hot Pepper Rings, Hot Cherry Peppers—Red/Green, Sweet Pimientos, Hamburger Dill Wafers, Genuine Dill Pickles, Pickled Cabbage, Ogorki Dills, Dill Pickles, Hot Dills, Kosher Dill Chips, Ogorki Spears, No Garlic Fresh Dills, Sweet Banana Peppers, Sweet Red Peppers, Sweet Peppers Red and Green, Hot Finger Peppers, Hot Hungarian Wax Peppers, Sour Pickles, Antipasto

BAN'G BRAND
Sweet Pickles, Sweet Mixed

BAN'G PICK PACK
Sweet Mixed, Sweet Pickle Relish

BAN'G PAK

SUPER PAK
Superkraut
(Bloch & Guggenheimer Div., Cons. Foods Corp., Long Island City, N.Y.)

BEST FOODS
Fanning's Bread and Butter Pickles, Sweet and Crisp Pickles
(Best Foods Div., CPC Int., Englewood Cliffs, N.J.)

BONDUEL

BONFIELD

MILWAUKEE ORIGINAL

WAUKESHA
Pickles, Relish, Relishes
(Bonduel Pickling Co., Bonduel Wis.)

CAIN'S

OXFORD

PIN MONEY

DEERFIELD

SILVER LANE

SUGAR LOAF
Cocktail Sauce, Relishes: Sweet, Sweet Pepper, Hamburg, Sweet Onion, Sweet Corn, Barbecue, Hot Dog; Pickles: Mustard, Cucumber, Sweet Pickle Chips, Sour and Sweet Onions, Dill Pickles, Sweet Gherkins, Sweet Mixed Pickles, Sweet Cauliflower, Kosher Spears, Fresh Kosher Chips and Dills; Peppers: Hot Cherry, Sweet and Finger, Dill and Sour Pickles, Sandwich Dill Slices, Cocktail Onion, Kosher Dills, Polish Ogorki, Kosher Gherkins, Sweet Cucumber Chips, Orange Flavored Watermelon, Sweet Tiny Tim Gherkins
(John E. Cain Co., Cambridge, Mass.)

EVANGELINE
Peppers: Italian, Hot, Cherry, Tabasco
(Evangeline Pepper & Food Prod., St. Martinville, Pa.)

GREEN BAY

DEAN

PETER PIPER

HEIFETZ

INDIAN TRAIL

FRESH PAK
Pickles, Relish, and Peppers
(Green Bay Foods, Green Bay, Wis.)

HEINZ
Processed Dills, Fresh Pack Kosher Dill Slices, Hamburger Dill Slices, Sour Gherkins, Sour Mixed, Fresh Pack Kosher Dills, Fresh Pack: Gherkins, Spears, and Polish Dills, Cured in Wood Genuine Dills, Fresh Pack Mild Dills, Cured in Wood Genuine Dill Gherkins, Processed Dill Gherkins; Fresh Pack: Hamburger Dill Slices, Mild Dill Slices, Polish Dill Spears, Hamburger Dill Pickle Slices, Spiced Pickle Chips, Fresh Pack Thin Kosher Dill Pickle Slices, Whole Kosher Dill Pickles, Fresh Pack Dill Pickle Slices, Genuine Dill Pickles, Fresh Pack Kosher Dill Pickle Spears, Fresh Pack Sweet Cucumber Spears,

Fresh Pack Mild 'N' Sweet Slices, Fresh Pack Sweet Cucumber Slices, Sweet Gherkins, Sweet Midget Gherkins, Sweet Mixed, Sweet Mustard Mixed, Sweet Sticks, Sweet Pickles, Sweet Slices, Sweet Cauliflower, Candied Dill Sticks, Candied Krinkle Chips, Fresh Pack Cucumber Slices, Sweet Pickle Spears, Sweet Pickle Chips, Fresh Pack Mild Sweet Cucumber Krinkles, India Relish, India, Hot Dog, Hamburger, Sweet Barbecue, Green Tomato Piccalilli, Sweet, Onion, Genuine Dill and Corn Relishes, Sweet and Spiced Onions
(H.J. Heinz, Co., Pittsburgh, Pa.)

LOHMAN'S
Pickled Beets
(Lohmann Food Corp., Gorham, N.Y.)

MOUNT OLIVE

LITTLE SISTER

WAY PACK

PICK OF CAROLINA
Pickles, Peppers, and Relish
(Mt. Olive Pickle Co., Mt. Olive, N.C.)

MOUNT ROSE
Kosher Gherkins, Sweet Gherkins, Sweet Pickles, Sweet Cucumbers, Kosher Pickles, Sweet Peppers, Sweet Mixed, Hot Mixed, Sweet Cauliflower, Sweet Relish
(Mount Rose Canning Co., King George, Va.)

PILGRIM FARM

WE PICK

HOOSIER PRIDE
Gherkins: Whole, Sweet, and Dills; Slices: Hamburger, Fresh Pack Sweet Sandwich, Italian Style Sweet; Dills: Crosscut, Medium, Fresh Pack Sliced, Fresh Pack Whole, Baby, Sweet Relish, Sweet Crosscuts, Fresh Pack Sliced Dills, Fresh Pack Whole Dills, Fresh Pack Sweet Sandwich Slices, Fresh Pack Dill Strips, Hot Banana Peppers, Sweet Banana Peppers, Sweet Cherry peppers, Hot Cherry Peppers, Italian Style Sweet Slices, Corn Relish, Sweet Sticks, Dill Gherkins, Baby Dills, Dill Chips, and Kraut.
(Pilgrim Farms Inc., Plymouth, Ind.)

PIC-O-PAC
Pickles, Tomatoes, Relish, Sauerkraut and Olives
(Pic-O-Pac Pickle Co., Chicago, Ill.)

PIKLE-RITE

MRS. WOODS

KING SOBIESKI

OUIKURE
Sauerkraut, Tomatoes, Peppers
(Pikle-Rite Co., Inc., Pulaskii, Wis.)

REESE
Pickles, Relish, Peppers
(Green Bay Foods, Green Bay, Wis.)

ROKEACH
Kosher New Pickles, New Spears, New Rings, New Gherkins, Sweet Peppers—All Red, Hot Peppers—All Red, Hot Peppers—Red and Green, Sweet Peppers—Red and Green, Kosher Tomatoes, New Kraut, Delux Mix, Picnic Garden Salad, Pepper 'N Kraut, Pickled Beets, Red Cabbage Kraut
(I. Rokeach & Sons, Inc., Farmingdale, N.J.)

SILVER FLOSS
Sauerkraut
(Silver Floss Foods, Div. of Curtice Burns, Phelps, N.Y.)

VLASIC
Fresh Pack: Kosher Baby Dills, Kosher Gherkins, Dill Chips, Polish Spears, Kosher Genuine Dills, Genuine Dills, Kosher Dills, Polish Dills, No Garlic Dills, Kosher Chips, Kosher Tomatoes, Kosher Icicles, Dill Gherkins, Sweet Butter Chips, Butter Stix, Garden Salad, Sweet Tomato Slices, Hot Chips, Gherkins, Midgets, Pickles, Slices, Mixed, Stix, Slices, Gherkins, Candied Watermelon, Hamburger Dill Chips, Hot Dog Dill Stix, Sour Pickles, Processed Dills, Kosher Dills, Hot Dog Relish, Hamburger Relish, Sweet Relish, India Relish, Corn Relish, Piccalilli, Hot Piccalilli, Sauerkraut, Polish Sauerkraut, Hungarian Mix, Pepperoncini, Tiny Hot, Hot Mexican, Sweet Red Peppers, Sweet Banquet Peppers, Hot Pepper Rings, Mild Pepper Rings, Medium Peppers, Hot Peppers, Mild Peppers, Sweet Cherry Peppers, Hot Cherry Peppers, Mild Sweet Peppers, Cocktail Onions, Candied Onions, Sweet Cauliflower, Hot Dill Caulilfower
(Vlasic Foods Inc., Lathrup Village, Mich.)

WELLWORTH
Pickles, Barrel Pickles, Tomatoes, Pickled Salad, Sauerkraut, Peppers
(Wellworth Pickle Co., Paterson. N.J.)

WISLA

ALBRO

DOLLY MADISON

MARY LOU

WARSAW-FALCON

MAYFAIR

BETTY LOU

NANETTE

PORTAGE

SMUCKERS
Pickles, Peppers, Relish, Sauerkraut
(H.W. Madison Co., Div., J.W. Smucker, Cleveland, Ohio)

(L) H&H
Pickles, Tomatoes, Salads
(Herbert Halpern Dist. Corp., Cheverly, Md.)

(L) KOHL'S
(Kohl's Food Stores, Milwaukee, Wis.)

(L(MITCHELL'S
Pickles, Tomatoes, Salads, Krau, Sweet Peppers
(Mitchell Foods, Feasterville, Pa.)

(L) PIC 'N PAY

MESMER

MONTCO
Pickles, Peppers, Relish, Sauerkraut
(Thriftway Foods, King of Prussia, Pa.)

PIE AND TART SHELLS
STELLA D'ORO
(Stella D'Oro Biscuit Co., Bronx, N.Y.)

PERFECT HOSTESS
(Perfect Hostess, Inc., Santa Monica, Ca.)

PIZZA

Dairy
EMPIRE
Pizza, 3-Pak, Medium Pizza, Jumbo Pizza, Bagel Pizza
(Empire Poultry, Mifintown, Pa.)

FESTIVE TIME
Pizza, Four Pak, Junior Pizza, Family Pizza, Bagel Pizza
(Festive Food Inc., Mount Vernon, N.Y.)

MACABEE
Pizza, 3-Pak, Medium Pizza, Jumbo Pizza, Bagel Pizza
(Macabee Foods, Inc., Hackensack, N.J.)

POPCORN
TV TIME

MERRY POPPIN
Hull-less Popcorn with Popping Oil
(TV Time Foods, Chicago, Ill.)

POPCORN TOPPING

Dairy
GOLDEN GLOW
Butter Flavored Popcorn Topping
(Butterful Inc., Richmond, Va.)

POTATO CHIPS
BON TON POTATO CHIPS
(Bon Ton Potato Chips, York, Pa.)

CAIN'S
Potato Chips
(John E. Cain Co., Cambridge, Mass.)

PRIZE

TREXLER PARK

VIRGINIA LEE
Potato Chips
(Crouthamel Potato Chip Co., Inc., Quakertown, Pa.)

SCHULER'S SUNSHINE
Potato Chips, Potato Frills, Bar-B-Q Flavored, Green Onion Flavored,
Potato Sticks, Vinegar Chips
(Schuler's Food, Rochester, N.Y.)

STATE FAIR

HYGRADE
Potato Chips, Bar-B-Q Chips, Dip 'N Chips
(Hygrade Bakery Co., Pennsville, N.J.)

SUNSHINE-MANN DIV.
Potato Chips
(Sunshine Inc., N.Y., N.Y.)

TREAT POTATO CHIPS
(The Treat Co., Jericho, N.Y.)

VALLEY MAID
Potato Chips
(Valley Maid, Inc., Phoenixville, Pa.)

WISE
Potato Chips, Ridgies, Barbecue-Flavored, Onion- and Garlic-Flavored, Juliennes
(Wise Foods, Div. of Borden Foods, Berwick, Pa.)

(L) ASSOCIATED
(Associated Food Stores, Inc., Jamaica, N.Y.)

(L) BOHACK
(H.C. Bohack & Co., Inc., Brooklyn, N.Y.)

(L) DART
Potato Chips
(Dart Drug, Landover, Md.)

(L) FINAST
(First National Stores, Somerville, N.J.)

(L) HIGH KING

LITTLE KING
(King Kullen Corp., Westbury, N.Y.)

(L) HILL'S
Potato Chips
(Hill's Supermarkets, Brentwood, N.Y.)

(L) PANTRY PRIDE
Potato Chips, Barbecue Chips, Dip 'N Chips
(Pantry Pride Stores, Philadelphia, Pa.)

(L) SHOPWELL
(Daitch Shopwell, N.Y., N.Y.)

(L) WALDBAUM'S
(Waldbaum's Inc., Brooklyn, N.Y.)

(L) WESTON'S
(I. Wachtel Biscuit Co., Brooklyn, N.Y.)

POTATO PRODUCTS
BETTY CROCKER HASH BROWNS
BETTY CROCKER POTATO BUDS
(General Mills, Inc., Minneapolis, Minn.)

CHEF'S CHOICE

CHEF'S BEST
Crinkle Cut French Fries, Shoestring Potatoes, Hashbrown Potatoes, French Fried Potatoes, Taters, Cottage Potatoes, Whole Potatoes
(Potato Service Inc., Great Neck, N.Y.)

BIRD'S EYE
Frozen French Fried Potatoes
(American Kitchen Fds., Caribou, Me.)

DORANN FROZEN

PRIDE O MAINE

MAINE SPECIAL

MAINE BEAUTY

FARMFARE

TEN PENNY TATERS

TATERHOUSE

TATERSTATE
Frozen French Fried Potoatoes
(Taterstate Frozen Foods, Rye, N.Y.)

EMPIRE
Potato: Knishes, Rolls, Pudding-Kugel
(Empire Kosher Poultry, Miffintown, Pa.)

FRENCH'S
(Check label for MILK ingredients. All others Parve)
Instant Mashed Potato with Vitamin C, Potato Pancakes
(The R.T. French Co., Rochester, N.Y.)

HOROWITZ-MARGARETEN
Potato Pancake Mix
(Horowitz Bros. & Margareten, Long Island City, N.Y.)

IDAHOAN
Instant Mashed Potatoes
(Idaho Fresh Pak, Louisville, Idaho)

INTERSTATE
Frozen French Fried Potatoes
(Chef Reddy Foods Corp., Othello, Wash.)

LOV-UM
Potato Pancakes
(Victory Spud Service, Inc., Chicago, Ill.)

MILADY
Potato Pancakes
(Milady Food Prod., Allentown, Pa.)

OSEM
Potato Pancake Mix
(Latkes)
(Osem Nakid Ltd., Bnei Brak, Israel)

PILLSBURY HUNGRY JACKS
Potatoes: Instant Mashed and Hash Brown
(Pillsbury Co., Minneapolis, Minn.)

ROGERS

PRIDE PAK

SNO SPUN
Mashed Potatoes, Hash Brown
(Rogers Bros., Co., Idaho Falls, Idaho)

TAMI
Potato Pancakes (Latkes), Potato Pudding (Kugel), Noodle Pudding (Kugel)
(Tami Foods Inc., Levitown, N.Y.)

(L) ARDSLEY FRIED POTATOES

(L) BOHACK
French Fried Potatoes
(Bohack Inc., Brooklyn, N.Y.)

(L) FLAGSTAFF FRIED POTATOES

(L) MONARCH
Instant Mashed Potatoes
(Consolidated Food Corp., River Grove, Ill.)

(L) SHOP RITE
Frozen French Fried Potatoes
(Wakefern Food Corp., Elizabeth, N.J.)

(L) SNOWKIST FRIED POTATOES

(L) SUN GLORY FRIED POTATOES

(L) WALDBAUM'S
French Fried Potatoes
(Waldbaum's Inc., Garden City, N.Y.)

(L) WHITE ROSE
French Fried Potatoes
(White Rose Tea Co., Linden, N.J.)

POULTRY AND POULTRY PRODUCTS

Meat
(Fresh and Frozen)

DAVID ELLIOT
Frozen Eviscerated Poultry, Boneless Chicken Steaks, Boneless Chicken Breasts, Boneless Rock Cornish Hens, Chicken Livers
(David Elliot Poultry Farms, Lake Ariel, Pa.)

DEAN

DAVID
Chicken, Turkey, Ducks, Poultry Parts, Cooked Turkey Breast, Turkey Rolls, Chicken Rolls, Turkey and Chicken Slices, Bar-B-Q Chicken and Turkey
(Dean Kosher Poultry, Bird-in-Hand, Pa.)

EMPIRE

NAOMI

ESSEX
Chicken, Turkey, Ducks, Poultry Parts, Cooked Turkey Breasts, Turkey Rolls, Cooked Rolls, Turkey and Chicken Slices, Bar-B-Q Chicken and Turkey
(Empire Kosher Poultry, Inc., Miffintown, Pa.)

"999"
Chicken, Turkey, Turkey Roll
(Real Kosher Sausage Co., N.Y., N.Y.)

MORIAH

(L) LAZY PAMPERED
Turkeys, Chickens, Turkey Rolls, Turkey Roast, Turkey Salami
(Moriah Kosher Poultry, N.Y., N.Y.)

QUEEN ESTHER

SIMCHA

BAZAAR
Chickens, Turkeys, Poultry Parts
(Levin Bros. Poultry Co., Inc., Wellston, Mo.)

PRETZELS
BACHMAN
Thin Pretzels, Pretzel Stix, Dietetic Pretzels, Bite Size Nutzels, Pretzel B's, Pretzel Logs, Pretzel Rods
(Bachman Foods, Inc., Reading, Pa.)

HYGRADE

KERR
Twist Pretzels, Old Dutch Pretzels, Salt Free Pretzels, Stixs, Rings, Buds, Shorties, Teething Pretzels.
(Hygrade Bakery, Inc., Philadelphia, Pa.)

JANE PARKER
(The Great Atlantic & Pacific Tea Co., Inc., A & P Stores)

NATIONAL
(National Pretzel Co., Inc., Scranton, Pa.)

SCHULER'S
Krun-Chee Pretzels, Thin Pretzels, Pretzel Stix, Pretz-O's, Pretzel
Logs, Pretzel Rods, Nutzels
(Bachman Foods Corp., Reading, Pa.)

QUINLAN (with Parve insignia only)
Old Fashioned (Hard), Nubs (Bite Size), TV Giants (Rods), TV Junior
(Logs), No Salt Pretzels
(Quinlan Pretzel Co., Denver, Pa.)

WEGE
Pretzels
(Wege Pretzel Co., Hanover, Pa.)

(L) DUTCHIE
Hard Pretzels

(L) WALDBAUM'S PRETZELS
(Waldbaum's Inc., Garden City, N.Y.)

Dairy
BACHMAN
Cheese Pretzels
(Bachman Foods Corp., Reading, Pa.)

QUINLAN
Butter Flavored Pretzels, Butter Flavored Sticks, Tiny Thin Pretzels,
Pretzel Q's (Rings)
(Quinlan Pretzel Co., Denver, Pa.)

(L) KEEBLER
Cheese Pretzels
(Keebler Inc., Cincinnati, Ohio)

RICE
BUITONI AMBRA RICE
(Buitoni Foods Corp., So. Hackensack, N.J.)

DATETREE
Brown Rice
(Organic Food Corp., Farmingdale, N.Y.)

ELAM'S
Short Grain Brown Rice
(Elam's, Broadview, Ill.)

P & S RICE
(P & S Rice Mills, Houston, Texas)

SALT
AMERICAN SALT
(American Salt Co., Kansas City, Mo.)

HARDY SALT
(Hardy Salt Co., St. Louis, Mo.)

MORTON
Coarse Kosher, Fine Table, Iodized
(Morton Salt Co., Chicago, Ill.)

PURITY
Table and Iodized Table

RED CROSS
Table and Iodized

STERLING
Plain Table, Iodized Table, Evaporated and Kosher
(International Salt Co., Clarks Summit, Pa.)

SALT SUBSTITUTES
ADOLPH'S
Salt Substitute, Seasoned Salt Substitute
(Adolph's Ltd., Burbank, Ca.)

FREE SALT
(Freeda Pharm., N.Y., N.Y.)

NU-SALT
(Cumberland Packing, Brooklyn, N.Y.)

SAUCES AND GRAVY MIXES
ANN PAGE
Chili Sauce, Barbecue, Tarter
(A & P Stores)

BUITONI
Sauces: Marinara, Mushroom, Meatless, Pizza, Diavolo, and Italiana
(Buitoni-Foods Corp., So. Hackensack, N.J.)

CAN'S
Cocktail and Tarter Sauce
(John E. Cain Co., Cambridge, Mass.)

EVANGELINE
Worcestershire and Condiment Sauces
(Evangeline Pepper & Good Prod., St. Martinville, La.)

FRENCH'S
Worcestershire Sauce, (contains less than 1% fish), Worcestershire
Sauce w/Hickory Smoke Flavor, Barbeque Sauce
(R.T. French Co., Rochester, N.Y.)

GOLD'S
Sauces: Barbecue, Duck, Kitchen, Spare-rib, Soy and Worcestershire
(Gold Pure Food Prod., Brooklyn, N.Y.)

GUIDO'S
Sauce: Pizza, Meatless Spaghetti, Marinara Spaghetti, Meat Flavor
Spaghetti, All Purpose Barbecue
(Supreme, Albany, N.Y.)

HEINZ
Chili and Barbecue Sauce
(H.J. Heinz Co., Pittsburgh, Pa.)

HELLMAN'S
BEST FOODS
Tartar Sauce
(Best Foods Div., Corn Prod. Co., New York, N.Y.)

HOROWITZ-MARGARETEN
Tomato and Mushroom Sauce
(Horowitz Bros. & Margareten, Long Island City, N.Y.)

HOUSE OF LORDS
Tartar Sauce
(Martin Gillet and Co., Baltimore, Md.)

LIBBY'S
Tomato Sauce
(Libby, McNeill & Libby, Chicago, Ill.)

MRS. SCHLORER'S
Barbecue Sauce
(Mrs. Schlorer's Inc., Philadelphia, Pa.)

MISSOURI HICKORY
Taco Sauce, Barbecue Sauce
(Missouri Hickory, Div. of Gibraltar Inc., Elmonte, Ca.)

NO-LAC
Brown Gravy, Ready to Use Gravy
(Protein Products Corp., Bayonne, N.J.)

OSEM
Sauce: Spaghetti, Champignon, and Tanoy Roast
(Osem Nakid Ltd., Bnei Braq, Israel)

PFEIFFER'S
Tartar Sauce, Tartar Sauce-Mayonnaise Type
(Pfeiffer's Food, Inc., Buffalo, N.Y.)

PILLSBURY
Home Style Gravy Mix, Dark Brown Gravy Mix
(Pillsbury Co., Minneapolis, Minn.)

PRINCE
Marinara and Cacciatore Sauces
(Prince Famous Foods of N.J., Inc., Pennsauken, N.J.)

ROKEACH
Tomato Sauce with Mushrooms, Brown Gravy
(I. Rokeach & Sons, Inc., Farmingdale, N.J.)

SERV-AGEN
Soy Sauce, Worcestershire, Liquid Gravy Maker

SERV-A-GRAVY
Brown Gravy Mix, Brown Gravy Mix w/Mushrooms, Imitation
Chicken Gravy Mix, Imitation Turkey, Onion Gravy Mix
(Serv-Agen Corp., Philadelphia, Pa.)

SPATINI
Spaghetti Sauce Mix, Brown Gravy Mix
(Spatini Co., Philadelphia, Pa.)

TELMA
Parsley Sauce Mix, Mushroom Sauce Mix, Onion Sauce Mix, Curry,
Tomato, Sesame Dip, Tehina Sauce
(Israel Edible Products Ltd., Haifa, Israel)

TULKOSS'S
Mild Horseradish Sauce, Tiger Sauce
(Tulkoss's Horseradish Prod. Co., Baltimore, Md.)

VITA
Sauce Mixes
(J. Plotkin & Sons, Ramat Gan, Israel)

(L) AUNT NELLIES
Chili Sauce
(Harrisburg Grocery Co., Harrisburg, Pa.)

(L) GIANT
Worcestershire Sauce
(Giant Food Stores, Washington, D.C.

(L) KEY
Barbecue
(Key Food Stores, Brooklyn, N.Y.)

(L) KING KULLEN
Chili Sauce
(King Kullen Stores, Westbury, N.Y.)

(L) PENNSYLVANIA DUTCH
Cocktail Sauce
(Pa. Dutch Co.)

(L) SHOPMORE
SHOPWELL
Chili Sauce
(Daitch-Shopwell Inc., New York, N.Y.)

(L) SHOP-RITE TARTAR SAUCE
(Wakefern Food Corp., Elizabeth, N.J.)

Dairy
FRENCH'S SPAGHETTI SAUCE MIX
(R. T. French Co., Rochester, N.Y.)

SHORTENINGS AND OILS
ANN PAGE
Olive, Corn Oil
(The Great Atlantic and Pacific Tea Co., A & P Stores)

ARGO

MAZOLA
Corn and Peanut Oils
(Best Foods Div., CPC International, Englewood Cliffs, N.J.)

CHEF-WAY

SAL-FRY
Vegetable Oil and Shortening
(Riceland Foods, Stuttgart, Ark.)

CRISCO OIL

CRISCO VEGETABLE SHORTENING

FLUFFO VEGETABLE SHORTENING
(The Procter & Gamble Co., Cincinnati, Ohio)

DYBER
Vegetable and Peanut Oil
(Dyber Oil Co., Brooklyn, N.Y.)

TEL AVIV

HOSTESS
Peanut and Soybean Oil
(Hostess Products Corp., Brooklyn, N.Y.)

HUMKO
Vegetable Oil
(Humko Products Co., Memphis, Tenn.)

NUT-OLA (Soybean Oil)
Cottonseed Oil, Vegetable Shortening
(Nut-Ola Food Prod., Brooklyn, N.Y.)

PAM
Dry-Fry Non-Fat Food Release
(Boyle-Midway, Div. of American Home Products, New York, N.Y.)

RICHTEX
Vegetable Oil
(Humko-Products, Memphis, Tenn.)

ROKEACH
Peanut and Vegetable Oils and Vegetable Shortening
(I. Rokeach & Sons, Inc., Farmingdale, N.J.)

(L) ACME

SUPERSAVER
Vegetable Shortening, Vegetable Oil
(Acme Markets, Inc., Philadelphia, Pa.)

(L) ALMACS (Salad Oil)
(Almacs, Inc., East Providence, R.I.)

(L) BOHACK
Vegetable Oil and Shortening
(Bohack Corp., Brooklyn, N.Y.)

(L) FOODTOWN
Vegetable Shortening and Oil
(Twin County Inc., Edison, N.Y.)

(L) GRAND UNION

FRESH PACK
Vegetable Shortening and Oil
(Grand Union Co., East Paterson, N.J.)

(L) HEINEN'S
Vegetable Shortening and Oil
(Heinen's Inc., Bedford, Ohio)

(L) HILLS
Vegetable Oils and Shortening
(Hills Supermarkets, Brentwood, N.Y.)

(L) KEY
Vegetable Shortening and Oil
(Key Foods Stores, Brooklyn, N.Y.)

(L) KOHL'S
Vegetable Oil and Shortening
(Kohl Fd. Stores, Milwaukee, Wis.)

(L) KRASDALE
Vegetable Shortening and Oil
(Krasdale Foods, N.Y., N.Y.)

(L) SHOPRITE
Vegetable Shortening and Oil
(Wakefern Foods, Inc., Elizabeth, N.J.)

(L) SHOPWELL
Salad Oils and Vegetable Shortening
(Daitch-Shopwell Inc., N.Y., N.Y.)

(L) STOP & SHOP
Vegetable Oil and Shortening
(Stop & Shop, Inc., Boston, Mass.)

(L) TWO GUYS
Vegetable Oil and Shortening
(Vornado, Inc., Garfield, N.J.)

(L) WALDBAUM'S
Salad Oils and Vegetable Shortening
(Waldbaum's, Inc., Garden City, N.Y.)

Dairy
COOKING EASE
Natural Vegetable Spray
(The Clorox Co., Oakland, Ca.)

SNACK FOODS
EMPIRE
Veg. Liver Knishes, Kasha Knishes, Potato Knishes, Rice Pudding,
Noodle Pudding
(Empire Kosher Poultry, Miffintown, Pa.)

OSEM
Snack Tidbits, Israeli Couscous
(Osem Nakid Ltd., Bnei Braq, Israel)

TELMA
Fallafel Mix
(Israeli Edible Products, Haifa, Israel)

Dairy
PILLSBURY ENERGY SPACE FOOD STICKS
Chocolate, Chocolate Malt, Caramel, Peanut Butter
(The Pillsbury Co., Minneapolis, Minn.)

SOUPS AND SOUP MIXES
GOLD'S
Borscht, Schav, Low Calorie Borscht, Onion Borscht
(Gold Pure Food Prod., Brooklyn, N.Y.)

GREAT AMERICAN HEINZ
Vegetarian Vegetable
(H.J. Heinz Co., Pittsburgh, Pa.)

HOROWITZ-MARGARETEN
Borscht, Kasha Soup, Kasha Gravy, Barley and Mushroom Soup,
Parve Soup, Soup Mix with Mushrooms (blend), Split Pea Soup Mix,
Lima Bean and Barley Soup Mix, Minestrone Mix
(Horowitz Bros. & Margareten, Long Island City, N.Y.)

MBT
Vegetable Broth Mix, Onion Mix, and Tomato Broth Mix
(Riviana Foods, Inc., Houston, Texas)

MOTHER'S
Borscht, Plain and Unsalted Schav (Egg Enriched)
(Mother's Foods Products, Newark, N.J.)

MRS. ADLER'S MODERN RECIPE
Barley Mushroom, Cabbage, Tomato, Vegetable, Mushroom, Onion,
Matzoh Ball, Fish Chowder, Celery, Potato, Split Pea, Rice, Kasha,
Noodle, Lentil, Bean, Borscht
(Mrs. Adler's Food Corp., Brooklyn, N.Y.)

NUTOLA
Noodle Soup Base
(Nutola Fat Products Co., Brooklyn, N.Y.)

OSEM-SOUP MIX & CUBES
Fruit Soup, Mushroom and Vegetable Soup, Clear Broth Bouillon,
Green Pea Soup, Alfebet, Asparagus, Noodle Soup, Country Style
Vegetable, Tomato with Rice, Continental Mushroom, Celery, Mush-
room Barley, Italian Veg. Soup Mix, and Garden Vegetable
(Osem Nakid Ltd., Bnei Braq, Israel)

ROKEACH
Borscht, Schav, Lemon Borscht, Barley Mushroom, Vegetable, Lima
Bean, Pea and Egg Barley, Tomato, Green Split Pea, Tomato Rice,
Lentil, Barley and Bean, New England Style Fish Chowder,
Manhattan Style Fish Chowder, Mushroom, Tomato Soup with Egg
Drops, Vegetable Soup with Mushrooms, Soup Greens
(I. Rokeach & Sons Inc., Farmingdale, N.J.)

SHALOM

VITA
Soup Mixes, Vegetable, Tomato, Mushroom Barley, Mushroom
Potato, Vegetable Cream, Noodle Soup, Onion Soup
(J. Plotkin & Sons, Ramat Gan, Israel)

TELMA

SOUP MIXES AND CUBES
Pea Soup, Asparagus, Mushroom Soups, Mushroom Barley,
Vegetable, Onion, Tomato, Tomato with Rice, Low Calorie Mushroom,
Low Calorie Consomme, Low Calorie Onion, Low Calorie Vegetable,
Consomme, Borscht, Instant Parve Broth, Golden Soup, Leek Soup
(Israel Edible Products Ltd., Haifa, Israel)

VICTOR VICTOR Soup Mix
Chicken Flavor Soup Base, Best Flavor Soup Base
(Victor Victor Corp., Brooklyn, N.Y.)

(L) ACME
Vegetarian Vegetable
(Acme Mkts, Philadelphia, Pa.)

(L) CENTRAL MARKETS
Vegetarian Vegetable
(Co-op Stores, Inc.)

(L) EDWARDS
Vegetarian Vegetable
(Edwards Supermarkets, Jarrat, Va.)

(L) FEDERATED FOODS
Vegetarian Vegetable
(Federated Fds., Inc.)

(L) FINAST
Vegetarian Vegetable
(First National Stores, Sommerville, Mass.)

(L) FOOD CLUB
Vegetarian Vegetable
(Topco Associates, Inc., Skokie, Ill.)

(L) FOOD FAIR
Vegetarian Vegetable
(Food Fair Stores Inc., Philadelphia, Pa.)

(L) FOODTOWN
Vegetarian Vegetable
(Foodtown, Bessemer, Ala.)

(L) GIANT FOOD
Vegetarian Vegetable
(Giant Foods, Inc., Washington, D.C.)

(L) HERITAGE HOUSE
Vegetarian Vegetable
(Heritage House, Inc.)

(L) HILLS
Vegetarian Vegetable
(Hills Supermarket, Brentwood, N.Y.)

(L) KEY
Vegetarian Vegetable
(Key Foods, Inc., Brooklyn, N.Y.)

(L) KOHL'S
Vegetarian Vegetable
(Kohl's Food Stores, Milwaukee, Wis.)

(L) KROGER
Vegetarian Vegetable
(Kroger's, Cincinnati, Ohio)

(L) MARKET BASKET
Vegetarian Vegetable
(Market Basket, Los Angeles, Ca.)

(L) PATHMARK
Vegetarian Vegetable
(Supermarket General Corp., Cranford, N.J.)

(L) SAFEWAY
Vegetarian Vegetable
(Safeway Stores, Inc., Oakland, Ca.)

(L) SHOP RITE
Vegetarian Vegetable
(Wakefern Food Corp., Elizabeth, N.J.)

(L) SHOPWELL
Vegetarian Vegetable
(Daitch-Shopwell, Inc., N.Y., N.Y.)

(L) STAFF
Vegetarian Vegetable
(Staff Supermarkets Assoc., Inc., Great Neck, N.Y.)

(L) STOP & SHOP
Vegetarian Vegetable
(Stop & Shop Inc., Boston, Mass.)

(L) SUPERFOODS
Vegetarian Vegetable
(Superfoods, Inc.)

(L) THOROFARE
Vegetarian Vegetable
(Thorofare Supermarkets, Pittsburgh, Pa.)

(L) TWO GUYS
Vegetarian Vegetable
(Vornado, Inc., Garfield, N.J.)

(L) WALDBAUM'S
Vegetarian Vegetable
(Waldbaum's, Inc., Garden City, N.Y.)

Dairy
GREAT AMERICAN HEINZ
Cream of: Mushroom, Pea, and Celery, Tomato with Rice, California Tomato, Cream of Tomato, Velvety Cream of Mushroom
(H.J. Heinz Co., Pittsburgh, Pa.)

ROKEACH
Cream of Mushroom, Pea, Celery, Potato
(I. Rokeach & Sons, Inc., Farmingdale, N.J.)

(L) CO-OP
Tomato and Cream of Mushroom
(Co-op Stores, Inc.)

(L) FAME
Cream of Mushroom and Tomato
(Superfood Services, Dayton, Ohio)

(L) FINAST
Cream of Mushroom and Tomato
(First National Stores, Sommerville, Mass.)

(L) FM
Tomato and Cream of Mushroom
(Fed. Mart Inc., San Diego, Ca.)

(L) FOOD FAIR
Tomato and Cream of Mushroom
(Food Fair Stores, Inc., Philadelphia, Pa.)

(L) FOOD CLUB
Cream of: Mushroom, Celery and Green Pea, Tomato with Rice, Tomato
(Topco Associates, Inc., Skokie, Ill.)

(L) FOODTOWN
Tomato, Tomato with Rice, Cream of Mushroom and Celery
(Twin County Inc., Edison, N.J.)

(L) GRAND UNION
Cream of Mushroom, Pea, Tomato
(Grand Union Inc., Paterson, N.J.)

(L) HERITAGE HOUSE
Tomato, Cream of Mushroom
(Fisher Fazio Costa, Cleveland, Ohio)

(L) HILLS
Cream of Pea, Tomato, Cream of Mushroom
(Hills Supermarkets, Brentwood, N.Y.)

(L) KEY
Cream of Pea, Mushroom, Potato
(Key Foods, Inc., Brooklyn, N.Y.)

(L) KOHLS
Tomato, Cream of Mushroom
(Kohl's Food Stores, Milwaukee, Wis.)

(L) KROGER
Cream of Celery
(Kroger Co., Cincinnati, Ohio)

(L) MARKET BASKET
Tomato, Cream of Mushroom, Celery
(Market Basket, Los Angeles, Ca.)

(L) PATHMARK
Cream of Pea, Celery, Mushroom, Tomato Rice
(Supermarkets General Corp., Woodbridge, N.J.)

(L) PURITY SUPREME
Tomato, Cream of Mushroom, Celery
(Purity Supreme, Inc., Billerca, Mass.)

(L) QUEEN OF SCOT
Cream of Mushroom, Celery, Tomato
(Scot Lad Foods, Inc., Chicago, Ill.)

(L) SHOPWELL
Tomato, Cream of: Pea, Mushroom, and Tomato Rice
(Daitch-Shopwell, Inc., New York, N.Y.)

(L) SHOP RITE
Tomato, Cream of Mushroom
(Wakefern Food Corp., Elizabeth, N.J.)

(L) STAFF
Tomato, Cream of Mushroom
(Staff Supermarket Associates, Inc., Great Neck, N.Y.)

(L) STOP & SHOP
Cream of Mushroom, Tomato
(Stop & Shop, Inc., Boston, Mass.)

(L) SUPER SAVER
Cream of Mushroom, Celery
(Acme Stores Inc., Philadelphia, Pa.)

(L) SWEET LIFE
Tomato, Cream of Mushroom
(Central Mkts. Inc., Schenectady, N.Y.)

(L) THOROFARE
Tomato, Cream of Mushroom
(Thorofare Supermarkets, Pittsburgh, Pa.)

(L) TWO GUYS
Cream of Mushroom, Tomato
(Vornado Inc., Garfield, N.J.)

(L) WALDBAUM'S
Tomato, Cream of Mushroom, Tomato Rice, Cream of Pea, Cream of Celery, Cream of Potato
(Waldbaum's, Inc., Garden City, N.Y.)

Meat
HOROWITZ-MARGARETEN
Chicken: Noodle Soup, with Rice, with Matzoh Balls, with Kreplach, Clear Chicken Soup, and Chicken Vegetable Soup
(Horowitz Bros. & Margareten, Long Island City, N.Y.)

ROKEACH
Chicken: Noodle, Rice, Clear, Kreplach, Matzoh Balls, Vegetable, and Onion Soup
(I. Rokeach & Sons, Inc., Farmingdale, N.J.)

TELMA
Chicken Consomme Cubes, Chicken Consomme with Egg Noodles Cubes
(Israel Edible Prod., Ltd., Haifa, Israel)

SOUP NUTS
OSEM
Soup Mandelach, Maxi Mandel, Mini Mandel Soup Tidbits, and Israeli Haimesha Farfel
(Osem Nakid Ltd., Bnei Braq, Israel)

SOUR CREAM-BUTTERMILK

Dairy
DELLWOOD
Auer Sour, Sour Cream

FARMLEA
(Dellwood Dairy Co., Inc., Yonkers, N.Y.)

ELK BRAND
Sour Cream
(Elk Brand Dairies, Philadelphia, Pa.)

ELMHURST
Sour Cream, Buttermilk
(Elmhurst Milk and Cream Co., Jamaica, N.Y.)

FRIENDSHIP
Sour Cream, Buttermilk
(Friendship Dairies, Friendship, N.Y.)

LADY LEE
Sour Cream, Buttermilk
(Dairyman's Coop. Assoc., Tulare, Ca.)

RASKAS
(Raskas Dairy, Inc., St. Louis, Mo.)

(L) DAIRY KING
Sour Cream, Half and Half
(Dairy King, Inc., Baltimore, Md.)

(L) KEY
Sour Cream
(Key Food Stores, Brooklyn, N.Y.)

(L) SUN CITY
Sour Cream
(Certified Poultry & Egg Co., Inc., Miami, Fla.)

(L) WALDBAUM'S
Sour Cream
(Waldbaum's, Inc., Garden City, N.Y.)

SOYBEANS
BAMBEANOS
Roasted Soybeans
(Colgate Palmolive Co., N.Y., N.Y.)

DATETREE
Cooking Soybeans
(Organic Foods Corp., Farmingdale, N.Y.)

SOY PROTEIN
BURGER BONUS
Textured Soy Protein
(A.E. Staley Co., Decatur, Ill.)

PLUSMEAT
Textured Protein
(Mrs. Filbert's Inc., Baltimore, Md.)

SPICES AND SEASONINGS
ACCENT
Monosodium Glutamate
(Stouffer Chemicals, San Jose, Ca.)

ADOLPH'S
Chicken Marinade
(Adolph's Ltd., Burbank, Ca.)

ANN PAGE SPICES
WHOLE
Allspice, Bay Leaves, Basil, Caraway Seed, Celery Seed and Celery Flakes, Cinnamon—Stick, Cloves, Ginger, Marjoram Leaves, Mustard Seed, Nutmeg, Oregano, Black Pepper, Leaf Sage, Savory Leaves, Thyme, Pickling Spices

GROUND

Allspice, Barbecue Spice, Cayenne Pepper, Crushed Pepper, Cinnamon, Cloves, Ginger, Italian Seasoning, Mace, Mustard Flour, Nutmeg, Paprika, Black and White Pepper, Sage, Turmeric, Cream of Tartar, Monosodium Glutamate, Black Pepper—Coarse Ground, Parsley Flakes, Celery Salt, Chili Powder, Curry Powder, Seasoned Salt, Poultry Seasoning, Onion Flakes, Minced Onion, Rosemary Leaves, Rubbed Sage, Pumpkin Pie Spiace, Instant Garlic Powder, Garlic Salt, Instant Onion Powder, Onion Salt, Dried Chives
(The Great Atlantic and Pacific Tea Co., A & P Stores)

EHLER'S
GROUND SPICES

Allspice, Apple Pie Spice, Black Pepper, Cardamom, Cayenne Red Pepper, Chili Powder, Cinnamon, Cloves, Cream of Tartar, Cumin, Curry Powder, Cinger, Mace, Marjoram Powder, Mustard, Nutmeg, Paprika, Poultry Seasoning, Pumpkin Pie Spice, Sage, Thyme, Turmeric, White Pepper, Barbecue Spice, Celery Salt, Garlic Pepper, Garlic Powder, Garlic Salt, Hamburger Spice, Seasoned Beef Tenderizer, Seasoned Lamb Tenderizer, Meat Tenderizer, Seasoned Meat Tenderizer, Mushroom Powder, Onion Powder, Onion Salt, Saute Onion, Seasoning Salt, Fish Seasoning, Sugar and Cinnamon, Toasted Chopped Onion, Vegetable Seasoning, Grated Lemon Peel, Grated Orange Peel

WHOLE SPICES

Allspice, Anise Seed, Annato Seed, Basil Leaves, Bay Leaves, Black Pepper, Caraway Seed, Celery Seed, Cinnamon, Cloves, Cumin Seed, Fennel Seed, Ginger, Marjoram Leaves, Mint Leaves, Mixed Pickling, Mustard Seed, Nutmeg, Poppy Seed, Pot Herbs, Rosemary Leaves, Sage Leaves, Sesame Seeds, Tarragon Leaves, Thyme, Bell Pepper Flakes, Celery, Mixed Onion and Parsley Flakes, Shallots, Leeks, Chives, Soursalt, Dillweed, Bacon Bits
(Brooke Bond Foods, Inc., Lake Success, N.Y.)

EVANGELINE

Pepper, Paprika, Garlic Salt, Onion Salt
(Evangeline Pepper & Food Prod., St. Martinville, La.)

FRENCH'S

Chill-O-Spice Mix
(R.T. French Co., Rochester, N.Y.)

GEL SPICE

Black Pepper, Paprika, Cinnamon, Assorted Spices
(Gel Spice Co., Inc., Brooklyn, N.Y.)

HUDSON

Allspice, Anise Seed, Annatto, Basil Leaves, Caraway Seed, Cayenne Pepper, Celery Flakes, Celery Salt, Celery Seed, Chili Powder, Cinnamon—Ground, Stick; Citric Acid (Sour Salt), Cloves—Whole, Ground; Cumin Seed—Whole, Ground; Curry Powder, Dill Seed, Fennel Seed, Garlic Powder (granulated), Garlic Salt, Ginger, Mace, Marjoram, MSG, Mint Leaves, Mustard, Nutmeg, Onion Flakes, Onion Salt, Onion (granulated), Oregano, Paprika, Pickling Spice, Poppy Seed, Poultry Seasoning, Pumpkin Pie Spice, Red Pepper, Rosemary, Savory Leaves, Sage, Sesame, Thyme, Turmeric, White Pepper, Black Pepper
(Hudson Tea & Spice Co., Brooklyn, N.Y.)

IDEAL

Black Pepper (Ground), Celery Seed, Cinnamon, Ground Chili Powder, Ground Nutmeg, Ground Paprika, Parsley Flakes, Minced Onion, Oregano, Garlic Salt, MSG
(Acme Markets Inc., Philadelphia, Pa.)

LAWRY'S

Seasoned Salt, Garlic Salt, Seasoned Pepper, Garlic Spread, Bac-Onion
(Lawry's Foods, Inc., Los Angeles, Ca.)

OSEM

Israeli Seasonings
(Hydrolized Protein)
(Osem Nakid, Ltd., Bnei Braq, Israel)

(L) SWEET LIFE

Oregano Leaves, Parsley Flakes, Minced Onions
(Sweet Life Prod. Corp., New Rochelle, N.Y.)

SUGAR

DATETREE

Turbinado Sugar
(Organic Foods Corp., Farmingdale, N.Y.)

JACK FROST

Granulated, Powdered Confectioners 10-X, Light and Dark Brown, Verifine, Free Pouring Brown, Pressed Tablets, Cubes, Poly Golden Brown, Poly Confectioners
(National Sugar Refining Co., Philadelphia, Pa.)

(L) WALDBAUM'S

Granulated Sugar
(Waldbaum's Inc., Garden City, N.Y.)

SWEETENERS—DIETETIC

ADOLPH'S SUGAR SUBSTITUTE

(Adolph's Ltd., Burbank, Ca.)

ANN PAGE
Low-Cal. Sweetener
(The Great Atlantic and Pacific Tea Co., A & P Stores)

FASWEET LIQUID SWEETENER
(The Fasweet Co., Jonesboro, Ark.)

SUGAR TWIN
(Sugar Twin Foods, Div. of Alberto Culver, Melrose Park, Ill.)

SWEET MAGIC
(Cumberland Packing Co., Brooklyn, N.Y.)

SWEET 10 SWEETENER-CUBES, LIQUID
(The Pillsbury Co., Minneapolis, Minn.)

Dairy
SUPEROSE POWDERED SWEETENER
(C.G. Whitlock Co., Springfield, Ill.)

SYRUPS
ANN PAGE
Pure Maple Syrup, Maple & Honey Blended Syrup, Pancake & Waffle
(The Great Atlantic and Pacific Tea Co., A & P Stores)

BARTON'S BONBONNIERE
(Barton's Candy Corp., Brooklyn, N.Y.)

CARY

HAPPY JACK
Maple & Pancake Syrup
(Doxsee Food Corp., Baltimore, Md.)

DATETREE
Blackstrap Molasses
(Organic Foods Corp., Farmingdale, N.Y.)

HERSHEY'S
Chocolate Flavored Syrup
(Hershey Food Corp., Hershey, Pa.)

KARO BLUE LABEL

KARO RED LABEL

KARO GREEN LABEL (Corn Syrup)

KARO IMITATION MAPLE SYRUP

OLD MANSE SYRUP

GOLDEN GRIDDLE (Pancake Syrup)
(CPC Int., Best Foods Div., Englewood Cliffs, N.J.)

PILGRIM FARMS
Imitation Pancake Syrup
(Weider Canning Co., Plymouth, Ind.)

MRS. SCHLORER'S
Pancake and Molasses Syrup
(Mrs. Schlorer's Inc., Philadelphia, Pa.)

POLANER PURE FRUIT SYRUPS
Strawberry, Red Raspberry, Blackberry, Whole Blueberry
(M. Polaner & Sons, Inc., Newark, N.J.)

(L) SEAWAY
Pancake Syrup
(Seaway Foods, Bedford Heights, Ohio)

THREE VEE PAPAYA
Fruit Syrup Concentrate
(Three Vee Co., Inc., Brooklyn, N.Y.)

(L) BOHACK SYRUP
Syrup
(H.C. Bohack Co., Brooklyn, N.Y.)

(L) FOOD FAIR
Syrup
(Food Fair Stores, Philadelphia, Pa.)

(L) GIANT
Syrup.
(Giant Foods, Inc., Washington, D.C.)

(L) GRAND UNION
Freshpak
(Grand Union Co., East Paterson, N.J.)

(L) HILLS
Syrup
(Hills Supermarket, Brentwood, N.Y.)

(L) KING KULLEN
Syrup
(King Kullen Grocery Co., Westbury, N.Y.)

(L) PANTRY PRIDE
Syrup
(Pantry Pride Stores, Philadelphia, Pa.)

(L) RICHFOOD SYRUP
Syrup
(Richmond Food Stores, Richmond, Va.)

Dairy
HERSHEY
Milk Chocolate Fudge Topping
(Hershey Food Corp., Hershey, Pa.)

TOMATO PUREE AND ASPIC
IDEAL

SUPERSAVE
(Acme Mkts., Inc., Philadelphia, Pa.)

SHRIVER'S
Tomato Aspic
(B.F. Shriver Co., Westminster, Md.)

TEA
ANN PAGE
Tea Bags, Instant Tea, Instant Tea with Sugar and Lemon, Instant
Tea with Lemon, Green, and Mixed

NECTAR
Tea Bags, Mixed and Green.

OUR OWN
Tea Bags, Instant Tea, Instant Tea with Sugar and Lemon, Instant
Tea with Lemon

MATINEE

MAYFAIR
(The Great Atlantic and Pacific Tea Co., A & P Stores)

WHITE ROSE
Tea Bags
(White Rose Tea Co., Linden, N.J.)

VEGETABLES
BUITONI
Italian Style Peeled Tomatoes
(Buitoni Foods Corp., So. Hackensack, N.J.)

CHINESE MAID
Chow Mein Vegetables, Bean Sprouts
(Chinese Maid Foods, Chicago, Ill.)

DROMEDARY
Pimientos
(Dromedary Div., National Biscuit Co., N.Y., N.Y.)

EVANGELINE
Yams, Cut Okra and Tomatoes, Okra
(Evangeline, St. Martinville, La.)

HEINZ
Pureed Vegetables—Beets, Carrots, Spinach, and Green Beans
(H.J. Heinz Co., Pittsburgh, Pa.)

HUNGS
Chow Mein Vegetables
(Hung's Food Products, Inc., Brighton, Mass.)

LOHMANN
Red Cabbage, Pickled Beets, Harvard Beets, Beet Balls, Beet 'N
   Onion Salad
(Lohman Div. of Pfeiffer Foods, Gorham, N.Y.)

MRS. ADLER'S CARROT TSIMMES
(Adler Food Packing Co., Brooklyn, N.Y.)

MUSSELMAN'S
Asparagus
(Musselman's, Div. of Pet Foods, Biglerville, Pa.)

ROKEACH
Mushroom Stems and Pieces
(I. Rokeach & Sons, Inc., Farmingdale, N.J.)

SHRIVER'S A NO. ONE TOMATO ASPIC
Jellied Tomato Salad
(B.F. Shriver Co., Westminster, Md.)

VITA
(J. Plotkin & Son, Ramat Gan, Israel)

VINEGAR
ANN PAGE
Cider and White Vinegar
(The Great Atlantic and Pacific Tea Co., A & P Stores)

EVANGELINE
Distilled Vinegar
(Evangeline, St. Martinville, La.)

HEINZ
Cider and Distilled White Vinegar
(H.J. Heinz, Pittsburgh, Pa.)

LUCKY LEAF
Cider Vinegar
(Knouse Foods, Inc., Peach Glen, Pa.)

MUSSELMAN'S
Cider Vinegar
(C.H. Musselman, Div. Pet Milk Co., Biglerville, Pa.)

ROKEACH
Cider Vinegar
(I. Rokeach & Sons, Inc., Farmingdale, N.J.)

VERYFINE
White Distilled Vinegar and Cider Vinegar
(New England Apple Prod. Co., Littleton, Mass.)

WHEAT GERM
APOLLO
(Apollo Wheat Germ, Flint, Mich.)

DATETREE
Raw Wheat Germ
(Organic Food Corp., Farmingdale, N.Y.)

ELAM'S
(Elam Mills, Broadview, Ill.)

KRETSCHMER
Wheat Germ, Caramel Apple Wheat Germ, Honey and Sugar Wheat
Germ, Cinnamon Raisin Wheat Germ
(Kretschmer Co., Minneapolis, Minn.)

WHIP AND DESSERT TOPPINGS
MIN-A-WHIP
(Protein Products Corp., Bayonne, N.J.)

RICH'S
Whip Topping
(Rich Prod. Corp. Buffalo, N.Y.)

WIRL WHIP
(Heller Enterprises, E. Rockaway, N.Y.)

Dairy
QUIP
(Avoset Foods Corp., Oakland, Ca.)

(L) ARDEN

(L) BLOSSOM TIME

(L) LUCERNE

(L) M.O.J.

A & P REAL CREAM TOPPING
(The Great Atlantic and Pacific Tea Co., A & P Stores)

(L) KROGER
(The Kroger Co., Cincinnati, Ohio)

(L) ARDEN

(L) ALBERTSONS

(L) ALPENROSE

(L) BROOKFIELD

(L) BERKELEY FARMS

(L) CLEVELAND

(L) CLOVER

(L) COUNTRY BELLE

(L) CRYSTAL

(L) DARIGOLD

(L) DARI-VALLEY

(L) FOREMOST

(L) GINAT

(L) GANDY'S

(L) GUILD

(L) HAWTHORN MELLODY

(L) HOLLAND

(L) KRAUSER

(L) LADY LEE

(L) LUCERNE

(L) LAWSONS

(L) MARKET BASKET

(L) MATANUSKA MAID

(L) MAYFRESH

(L) MEADOW GOLD

(L) MEADOWMOOR

(L) MENZIE

(L) MONARCH

(L) MOUNTAIN VIEW

(L) OLYMPIAN

(L) RALPHS

(L) SCHEPPS

(L) SHUR-FRESH

(L) SOUTHLAND

(L) STAFF

(L) ZIP WHIPT

WINE AND GRAPE JUICE
CARMEL—Bearing Halachi of Chief Rabbinate of Israel
(Carmel Wine Co., N.Y., N.Y.)

HERSH'S

KEDEM
Grape Juice, (Concord, Muscat), Sherry Wine, Concord Grape/Malaga, Cream Concord, Sparkling Wines/Cold Duck, Tokay/Rose, Sauterne (White Dry—Sugar Free), Burgundy (Red Dry—Sugar Free), Port, Muscatel, Honey (Mead Wine), Egg Nosh, Blackberry Wine, Cherry Wine, Wishniak
(Royal Wine Co., N.Y., N.Y.)

HOROWITZ-MARGARETEN
Grape Juice
(Horowitz Bros., & Margareten, Long Island City, N.Y.)

JERUSALEM WINES
(A.T.S. Wines, Israel)

LIPSCHITZ
Grape Juice
(Monterey Wine Co., Brooklyn, N.Y.)

SPECIAL SUPPLEMENT

BLINTZES [FROZEN] AND SUZETTES
Parve
GOLDEN

OLD FASHIONED
Potatoes, Blueberry, Cherry, Apple
(Milady Food Prod., Allentown, Pa.)

Dairy
GOLDEN

OLD FASHIONED
Cheese Blintzes
(Gee-Wiz Co., Lakewood, N.J.)

MILADY'S
Cheese Blintzes
(Milady Food Co., Allentown, Pa.)

CAKES, COOKIES, CRACKERS
(L) PANTRY PRIDE COOKIES
Vanilla Wafers, Chocolate Chip, Almond Chip, Oatmeal Raisin, Macaroons, Lemon, Sugar Cookies, Tea Cookies, Creme Filled Cookies
(Pantry Pride Co., Inc., Philadelphia, Pa.)

CANDY
Dairy
FALCON
Milk Chocolate Varieties
(Falcon Candies, Philadelphia, Pa.)

CLEANERS
PINESOL
(American Cyanamid, Con. Prod. Div., Wayne, N.J.)

FISH
FEATURE FOODS
Lunch Herring, Herring in Wine Sauce, Pickled Schmaltz Herring, Tasty Bits
(Feature Fds., Downsview, Ontario, Canada)

WM. UNDERWOOD
Brisling Sardines in Olive and Soy Oil, Sardines in Tomato Sauce/Mustard
(Wm. Underwood Co., Watertown, Mass.)

LASCCO
Herrings: Schmaltz, Bismarck, Roll Mop, Smoked Salmon, Herring Fillet, Kippered Salmon, Smoked Albacore, Smoked Whitefish, Smoked Shad, Kippered Sable
(Los Angeles Smoking & Curing Co., Los Angeles, Ca.)

FRUIT ICES
GREEN FARMS

D'ANGELOS
Twin Pops, Italian Ices
(Green Farms, Thompson Ridge, N.Y.)

ICE CREAM

Dairy

DAIRY GREEN FARMS
Ice Cream, Sherbet, Ice Cream Novelties
(Green Farms, Thompson Ridge, N.Y.)

INFANT & SPECIAL FORMULA DRINK

Dairy

SUSTACAL

STEP 2
(Mead Johnson, Inc., Evansville, Ind.)

MARGARINE

NUCOA
(Parve only when indicated on the label)
Soft and Stick Margarine
(CPC Int., Best Foods Div., Englewood Cliffs, N.J.)

MEAT PRODUCTS AND POULTRY

Poultry

CUSTOM POULTRY
Chickens and Turkeys
(Vineland Kosher Poultry, Vineland, N.J.)

Meat

LUNDY'S PACKAGED MEATS
Roasts, Briskets, Steaks, Chuck, Ground Beef, Beef Patties, Lamb
Chops, Veal, Breaded Veal
(S. Lundy's Sons, Vineland, N.J.)

I. GOLDBERG & SONS
Beef, Veal, Lamb, Delicatessen Products
(I. Goldberg & Sons, N.Y., N.Y.)

PUDDINGS AND DESSERTS

ANN PAGE PUDDINGS
Chocolate, Vanilla, Butterscotch, Tapioca, Banana Cream, Coconut
Cream, Imitation Custard, Toasted Coconut Cream, Chocolate
Tapioca, Vanilla
(The Great Atlantic and Pacific Tea Co., A & P Stores)

FLAVOR PLUS
Chocolate Pudding
(Protein Products, Bayonne, N.J.)

LIBBY'S FRUIT FLOAT
Cherry, Banana, Peach, Orange, Strawberry, Raspberry, Blueberry
(Libby, McNeill & Libby, Chicago, Ill.)

OSEM-JEL DESSERT
Cherry, Pineapple, Orange, Raspberry, Lemon, Apricot, Strawberry

OSEM PUDDING
Vanilla, Chocolate
(Osem Nakid Ltd., Bnei Braq, Israel)

VICTOR VICTOR
Chocolate, Vanilla
(Victor Victor Corp., Brooklyn, N.Y.)

VITA PUDDING
Chocolate, Vanilla
(J. Plotkin & Son, Ramat Gan, Israel)

Dairy

ANN PAGE INSTANT PUDDING
Chocolate, Vanilla, Butterscotch
(The Great Atlantic and Pacific Tea Co., A & P Stores)

ELAM'S
Vanilla Pudding and Vanilla Pie Filling
(Elam's, Broadview, Ill.)

SAUCE

CROSSE & BLACKWELL
Steak Sauce
(H.W. Madison Co., Medina, Ohio)

SOUP

KUBRO
Old World Vegetable Soup, Barley Mushroom Soup, Sweet and Sour
Cabbage Soup, Bavarian Lentil Soup, Roma Minestrone Soup, Old
Fashioned Potato Soup, Green Split Pea Soup
(Kubro Fds., Los Angeles, Ca.)

SOUR CREAM

Dairy

TUTTLE
Sour Cream
(Foremost Dairy, San Francisco, Ca.)

SPRAY SHORTENING

Dairy

MAZOLA NO-STIK
(CPC Int., Englewood Cliffs, N.J.)

SWEETENER—DIETETIC

WEIGHT WATCHERS SWEETENER
(Foodways National, Hawthorne, N.Y.)

WAFFLES AND PANCAKES

Parve

GOLDEN
Potato Pancakes, Pirogen
(Gee-Wiz Co., Lakewood, N.J.)

Dairy

DOWNYFLAKE
Waffles, Pancakes, Potato Pancakes
(Pet, Frozen Food Div., Allentown, Pa.)

KOSHER FOR PASSOVER

The Kashruth programs of the Union of Orthodox Jewish Congregations of America, operated in conjunction with the halachic authority of the Union, the Rabbinical Council of America, is the only national non-profit, public service program for kosher certification.

While the American Jewish Community has not been alerted sufficiently heretofore, please be informed that any matzoh that is made with fruit juices or eggs is permissible on Passover only for the elderly, sick, or infants.

The following matzohs fall into this category: Egg matzoh, whole wheat matzoh, and chocolate covered matzoh.

The items listed in this directory are divided into three categories: Parve, Dairy, and Meat.

Parve: Unless otherwise indicated, the listed item is parve.

Dairy: These items are listed under a **Dairy** designation.

Meat: These items are listed under **Meat** or **Poultry** designation.

All kosher raw poultry and meats bearing the Ⓤ seal are kosher for Passover.

The liver must be removed from the cavity and broiled separately.

In purchase or Ⓤ packaged poultry parts, the consumer must be certain that both the sealed package and the inner cellophane wrapper have not been tampered with.

Precooked and prepared provision and delicatessen require special Kosher for Passover certification.

APPLESAUCE

VERYFINE
(New England Apple Products Co., Littleton, Mass.)

MUSSELMAN'S
(C.H. Musselman Div., Pet Milk Co., Biglerville, Pa.)

SEASON BRAND
(I. Epstein & Sons, Inc., Irvington, N.J.)

ROKEACH
(I. Rokeach & Sons, Inc., N.Y., N.Y.)

HOROWITZ-MARGARETEN
(Horowitz Bros. & Margareten, Long Island City, N.Y.)

FESTIVE

TAMAR

ORA
(Festive Finer Fds., Brooklyn, N.Y.)

BEVERAGES
COTT
Black Raspberry, Cherry, Club Soda, Creme Soda, Orange Soda, Pale Dry Ginger Ale, Diet: Orange, Cream, and Cherry
(Cott Corp., New Haven, Conn.)

HOFFMAN QUALITY BEVERAGES

DR. BROWN QUALITY BEVERAGES

SNOW PEAK
(American Beverage Co., College Point, N.Y.)

WALDBAUM'S QUALITY BEVERAGES
(Waldbaum's Inc., Garden City, N.Y.)

KEY QUALITY BEVERAGES
(Key Food Stores, Inc., Brooklyn, N.Y.)

CORNELL BEVERAGES
Club, Pale Dry, Orange, Cream
(Cornell Beverage Co., Brooklyn, N.Y.)

OSEM
Chocolate Instant Shake
(Osem Nakid Ltd., Bnei Braq, Israel)

BORSCHT
GOLD'S
Borscht, Onion Borscht, Schav
(Gold Pure Food Prod., Brooklyn, N.Y.)

MOTHER'S
Egg Enriched Borscht, Schav, Borscht, Unsalted Borscht, Low Calorie Borscht
(Mother's Food Prod., Div. of Vita Foods, Newark, N.J.)

MRS. ADLER'S MODERN RECIPE
Borscht
(Adler's Food packing Co., Brooklyn, N.Y.)

ROKEACH
Borscht, Lemon Borscht, Diet Borscht
(I. Rokeach & Sons, Inc., N.Y., N.Y.)

HOROWITZ-MARGARETEN
Borscht
(Horowitz Bros. & Margareten, Long Island City, N.Y.)

BUTTER

Dairy
FRIENDSHIP
(Friendship Dairies, Inc., Maspeth, N.Y.)

BUTTERMILK

Dairy
FRIENDSHIP
(Friendship Dairies, Inc., Maspeth, N.Y.)

ELMHURST
(Elmhurst Milk & Cream, Jamaica, N.Y.)

CAKE MIXES
HOROWITZ—MARGARETEN
Cake Mixes: Sponge, Chocolate, Honey, Golden Yellow, Coffee, Chocolate Fudge Brownie Mix
(Horowitz Bros. & Margareten, Long Island City, N.Y.)

CAKES, COOKIES
BARTON'S BONBONNIERE
(Parve only when bearing Parve label, otherwise Dairy)
(Barton's Candy Corp., Brooklyn, N.Y.)

YOM TOV
(Parve only when bearing Parve label, otherwise Dairy)
Chocolate Covered Macaroons, Macaroons, Cakes
(Festival Dist. Co., Inc., Yonkers, N.Y.)

HOROWITZ—MARGARETEN
Egg Kichel, Dietetic Egg Kichel, Coconut Macaroons, Chocolate Flavored Macaroons, Chocolate Dipped Macaroons
(Horowitz Bros. & Margareten, Long Island City, N.Y.)

CANDY
BARTON'S BONBONNIERE
(Parve only when bearing Parve label, otherwise Dairy)
(Barton's Candy Corp., Brooklyn, N.Y.)

ASTOR CHOCOLATES
(Parve only when bearing Parve label, otherwise Dairy)
(Astor Chocolate Corp., Brooklyn, N.Y.)

CARLTON HOUSE
(Parve only when bearing Parve label, otherwise Dairy)
(Bloom Packing Co., Brooklyn, N.Y.)

CRESCENT CONFECTIONS
Marzipan Candies
(The Multiflex Co., Inc., Paterson, N.J.)

YOM TOV
(Parve only when bearing Parve label, otherwise Dairy)
Chocolate Bars, Assorted Chocolates, Hard Candies
(Festival Dist. Co., Inc., Yonkers, N.Y.)

HOROWITZ—MARGARETEN
Bittersweet Chocolate Bars, Chocolate Coated Egg Matzohs*
(Horowitz Bros. & Margareten, Long Island City, N.Y.)

Dairy
BARTON'S
(Barton Candy Corp., Brooklyn, N.Y.)
HOROWITZ—MARGARETEN
Milk Chocolate Bars
(Horowitz Bros. & Margareten, Long Island City, N.Y.)

*See Introduction Note on p. 448.

CARROT TZIMMES
MRS. ADLER'S CARROT TZIMMES
(Adler Food Packing Co., Brooklyn, N.Y.)

CHAMPAGNE
CARMEL—Bearing halachi of Chief Rabbinate
(Carmel Wine Co., Inc., N.Y., N.Y.)

STAR OF ABRAHAM
(Royal Wine Co., N.Y., N.Y.)

CHEESE
Dairy
FARMLEA

DELLWOOD
(Cream Cheese and Cottage Cheese
(Deltown Foods, Inc., Yonkers, N.Y.)

MILLER'S
Mello-Gold, Smoked, American, Muenster, Edam, Gouda, Swiss, Hickory Smoked, Baby Gouda, and Baby Muenster
(Miller Cheese Co., N.Y., N.Y.)

REGENT
Cream Cheese and Cottage Cheese

SANTE
Cream Cheese and Cottage Cheese

BIG Z
Cream Cheese, Farmer's Cheese, and Neufchatel Spread

TUXEDO
Cottage Cheese

SUNNYBOY CREAM CHEESE
Dairy
NEW HOLLAND
Neufchatel Cheese
(Zausner Food Corp., Mountainside, N.J.)

WALDBAUM'S
Cottage Cheese
(Waldbaum's Inc., Garden City, N.J.)

RASKAS
Cream Cheese
(Raskas Dairy Inc., St. Louis, Mo.)

KEY
Cottage Cheese
(Key Food Stores, Brooklyn, N.Y.)

FRIENDSHIP
Cottage Cheese, Pot Cheese, Pineapple Cheese, Calorie Meier Cheese, Farmer Cheese
(Friendship Dairies, Inc., Maspeth, N.Y.)

HOLYLAND CHEESE
(Frankenthal & Co. Ltd., Bnei Braq, Israel)

TUTTLE
Cottage Cheese, Sour Cream
(Foremost Dairies, San Francisco, Ca.)

COFFEE
FOOD FAIR
(Food Fair Stores, Philadelphia, Pa.)

ROKEACH
Instant Coffee
(I. Rokeach & Sons, Inc., N.Y., N.Y.)

HOROWITZ—MARGARETEN
Coffee, Instant Coffee
(Horowitz Bros. & Margareten, Long Island City, N.Y.)

CRANBERRY SAUCE
ROKEACH
(I. Rokeach & Sons, Inc., N.Y., N.Y.)

HOROWITZ—MARGARETEN
(Horowitz Bros. & Margareten, Long Island City, N.Y.)

EATMORE

APRIL ORCHARDS
(Morris April Bros., Eatmore Div., Inc., Millville, N.J.)

DESSERTS—PUDDINGS
COUNTRY CLUB FROZEN DESSERT
(Parve only when indicated on label)
(Country Club Frozen Dessert, Inc., Bronx, N.Y.)

HOROWITZ—MARGARETEN
Chocolate Pudding
(Horowitz Bros. & Margareten, Long Island City, N.Y.)

OSEM
Instant Vanilla Pudding, Instant Chocolate Pudding and Jel Dessert
(Assorted Flavors)
(Osem Nakid Ltd., Israel)

ROKEACH
Chocolate Pudding
(Ready to Eat)
(I. Rokeach & Sons, Inc., N.Y., N.Y.)

VITA
Strawberry, Raspberry, and Lemon Jel Dessert
(J. Plotkin & Son, Ramat Gan, Israel)

DAIRY DRESSINGS

Dairy
SMETINA BRAND
(Raskas Dairy, Inc., St. Louis, Mo.)

FISH PRODUCTS
MOTHER'S
Gefilte Fish, Fish d'Oeuvres, All Whitefish, Whitefish d'Oeuvres, Whitefish and Yellow Pike, Unsalted Gefilte Fish
(Mother's Food Prod., Div. of Vita Foods, Newark, N.J.)

MRS. ADLER'S
Gefilte Fish, Fish Bits, Pike and Whitefish, Fish Loaf
(Adler's Food Co., Brooklyn, N.Y.)

VITA
Gefilte Fish, Herring, Party Snacks in Wine Sauce
(Vita Food Prod., N.Y., N.Y.)

DAGIM
Salmon and Tuna
(Dagim Tahorim Co., Brooklyn, N.Y.)

MARSHALL'S
Kippered and Tomato Herring
(Adolph Goldmark & Sons Corp., N.Y., N.Y.)

NOVIE
Smoked Fish, Herring, Lox
(Nova Scotia Food Prod. Corp., Brooklyn, N.Y.)

SEASON BRAND
Norwegian Brisling Sardines, Danish Sprats, Tuna, Salmon, Portuguese Sardines
(I. Epstein & Sons, Irvington, N.J.)

ROKEACH
Gefilte Fish, Gefilte Fishbits, Whitefish and Pike, Premium Whitefish, Trumps
(I. Rokeach & Sons, Inc., N.Y., N.Y.)

MA COHEN'S
Herring
(City Smoked Fish Co., Detroit, Mich.)

HOROWITZ—MARGARETEN
Gefilte Fish—Liquid Broth, Gefilte Fish—Jellied Sauce, Gefilte Pike and Whitefish, Jelled Sauce
(Horowitz Bros. & Margareten, Long Island City, N.Y.)

NOVIE ICELAND
Smoked Fish/Lox
(Novie Iceland, Inc., Miami, Fla.)

BLUE RIBBON
Smoked Fish/Lox
(Blue Ribbon Fish Prod., Brooklyn, N.Y.)

FESTIVE

TAMAR

ORA
Tuna Fish
(Festive Finer Fds., Brooklyn, N.Y.)

Dairy

VITA HERRING IN CREAM SAUCE
(Vita Food Products, N.Y., N.Y.)

FROSTING

ROKEACH
Chocolate Frosting
(I. Rokeach & Sons, Inc., N.Y., N.Y.)

FROZEN DINNERS

Parve

SCHREIBER FROZEN DINNERS
(Available on request from airlines)
(Schreiber Caterers, Inc., Brooklyn, N.Y.)

MADAN FROZEN DINNERS
(Available on request from airlines)
(Madan Kosher Foods, Los Angeles, Ca. and Miami, Fla.)

BORENSTEIN'S
(Available on request from airlines)
Fresh and Frozen Dinners
(Borenstein Caterers, Inc., Jamaica, N.Y.)

Meat

SCHREIBER FROZEN DINNERS
(Available on request from airlines)
(Schreiber Caterers, Inc., Brooklyn, N.Y.)

MADAN FROZEN DINNERS
(Available on request from airlines)
(Madan Kosher Foods, Los Angeles, Ca. and Miami, Fla.)

BORENSTEIN'S
(Available on request from airlines)
Fresh and Frozen Dinners
(Borenstein Caterers, Inc., Jamaica, N.Y.)

WILTON FROZEN DINNERS
(Available on request from airlines)
(Wilton Frozen Dinners, Spring Valley, N.Y.)

FRUITS [CANNED]

FESTIVE

TAMAR

ORA
Pineapple, Fruit Compote
(Festive Fine Fds., Brooklyn, N.Y.)

VITA
Apricots, Peaches, Melons, Grapefruit Segments
(J. Plotkin & Sons Ltd., Ramat Gan, Israel)

ROKEACH
Peaches, Fruit Cocktail, Pears, Grapefruit Sections
(I. Rokeach & Sons, Inc., N.Y., N.Y.)

FRUITS [DRIED]

DEL MONTE
Prunes, Raisins
(Del Monte Corp., Berkeley, Ca.)

MARIANI
Apples, Apricots, Cherries, Currants, Dates, Figs, Mixed Fruits,
Peaches, Pears, Prunes, Raisins (Golden-natural)
(Paul A. Mariani Co., Cupertine, Ca.)

SEASON BRAND
Oregon Prunes, Sweet Prunes, Apricots, Pears, Mixed Fruits, Golden
Raisins, Pitted Dates
(I. Epstein & Sons, Inc., Irvington, N.J.)

SUN RAY
Prunes, Dates, Pears
(Sun Ray Orchards Co., Myrtle Creek, Oregon)

FRUIT BUTTER

Prune Lekvar, Golden Apricot
(Globe Preserves, Clifton, N.J.)

HONEY

ROKEACH
(I. Rokeach & Sons, Inc., N.Y., N.Y.)

HOROWITZ—MARGARETEN
(Horowitz Bros. & Margareten, Long Island City, N.Y.)

HORSERADISH

GOLD
(Gold Pure Foods, Brooklyn, N.Y.)

VITA
(Vita Food Prod., N.Y., N.Y.)

ROKEACH
(I. Rokeach & Sons, Inc., N.Y., N.Y.)

TULKOFF'S
(Tulkoff's Horseradish Prod. Co., Baltimore, Md.)

ARROW
(Arrow Horseradish Co., Brooklyn, N.Y.)

MRS. KATZ
(Mrs. Katz Food Co., Cleveland, Ohio)

AXELROD
(A.M. Azelrod & Sons, Inc., Englewood, N.J.)

STEIN'S
(Stein Food Product Co., Schenectady, N.Y.)

ICE CREAM, SHERBET
Dairy
BARTON'S BONBONNIERE
(Barton Candy Corp., Brooklyn, N.Y.)

GOLD SEAL

BORDEAU

MARCELL
(Gold Star Ice Cream Co., Brooklyn, N.Y.)

COUNTRY CLUB
(Parve only when bearing Parve label, otherwise Dairy)
Ices, Desserts
(Country Club Frozen Desserts, Inc., Bronx, N.Y.)

GOLD SEAL—RIVIERA FRUIT ICES
(Parve only when indicated on label, otherwise Dairy)
(Gold Star Ice Cream Co., Brooklyn, N.Y.)

BARTON'S FRUIT ICES
(Parve only when indicated on label, otherwise Dairy)
(Barton's Candy Corp., Brooklyn, N.Y.)

JAMS, JELLIES, MARMALADE
BARTON'S BONBONNIERE
(Barton's Candy Corp., Brooklyn, N.Y.)

POLANER
Preserves, Jellies, Marmalades
(M. Polaner & Sons, Inc., Newark, N.J.)

ROKEACH
Preserves, Marmalades
(I. Rokeach & Sons, Inc., N.Y., N.Y.)

HOROWITZ—MARGARETEN
Preserves
(Horowitz Bros. & Margareten, Long Island City, N.Y.)

SHALOM
Fruit Preserves, Marmalades
(I. Plotkin & Sons, Israel)

MRS. ADLER'S
Preserves, Marmalades
(Mrs. Adler's Food Corp., Brooklyn, N.Y.)

JUICE
VERYFINE
Apple and Prune Juice
(New England Apple Prod. Co., Littleton, Mass.)

ROKEACH
Juices: Prune, Apple, and Tomato
(I. Rokeach & Sons, Inc., N.Y., N.Y.)

HOROWITZ—MARGARETEN
Tomato and Apple Juice
(Horowitz Bros. & Margareten, Long Island City, N.Y.)

SEASON BRAND
Juices: Pineapple, Apple, Prune, Grapefruit
(I. Epstein & Sons, Inc., Irvington, N.J.)

SHALOM
Tomato
(I. Plotkin & Sons, Israel)

WELCH'S
Prune Juice
(Welch Foods, Inc., Westfield, N.Y.)

FESTIVE

TAMAR

ORA
Citrus and Pineapple Juices
(Festival Finer Fds., Brooklyn, N.Y.)

LOW CALORIE FOODS
MOTHER'S UNSALTED GEFILTE FISH
(Mother's Food Prod., Div. of Vita Foods, Newark, N.J.)

POLANER DIETETIC JAMS AND JELLIES
(M. Polaner & Sons, Inc., Newark, N.J.)

COTT LOW CALORIE BEVERAGES
(Cott Corp., New Haven, Conn.)

GOLD'S LOW CALORIE BORSCHT
(Gold Pure Foods, Brooklyn, N.Y.)

ROKEACH DIET BORSCHT
(I. Rokeach & Sons, Inc., N.Y., N.Y.)

MATZOH AND MATZOH PRODUCTS
HOROWITZ—MARGARETEN
Passover Matzohs, Passover Thin Tea Matzohs, Passover Shmurah Matzohs, Passover-Egg Matzohs*, Passover Whole Wheat Matzohs*, Passover Matzoh Meal, Passover Matzoh Farfel, Passover Matzoh Cake Meal, Passover Matzoh Cereal
(Horowitz Bros. & Margareten, Long Island City, N.Y.)

MAYONNAISE
MOTHER'S
(Mother's Food Prod., Div. of Vita Foods, Newark, N.J.)

SEASON BRAND
(I. Epstein & Sons, Irvington, N.J.)

TELMA
(Israel Edible Prod. Ltd., Haifa, Israel)

FESTIVE

TAMAR

ORA
Salad Dressings
(Festive Finer Fds., Brooklyn, N.Y.)

ROKEACH
Salad Dressing
(I. Rokeach & Sons, Inc., N.Y., N.Y.)

MEAT PROVISIONS
Meat
HILLS'S GLATT KOSHER
999, Salami, Knockwurst, Franks/Cocktail/Griddles, Bologna, Corned Beef, Tongue, Pastrami, Bake N' Fry, Smoked Shoulder Steaks, Shoulder Steaks, Briskets
(Real Kosher Sausage, N.Y., N.Y.)

MEDICINES
FREEDA
Effervescent Mineral Salt, Digestion Antacid Compound, Kam Anti-Diarrhea Mixture, Trophies Lozenges, Ko-Rub, Ko-Rub-MC, Dremi Tablets
(Freeda Pharmaceuticals Co., N.Y., N.Y.)

MILK-CHOLOV YISROEL
FARM FRESH

Homogenized, Skimmed
(Mason-Dixon Farms, Gettysburg, Pa.)

NUTS
CARLTON HOUSE
Indian Nuts, Pistachio Nuts
(Bloom Packing Co., Brooklyn, N.Y.)

BARTON'S BONBONNIERE
Assorted Nuts
(Barton's Candy Corp., Brooklyn, N.Y.)

PANCAKE MIX
HOROWITZ—MARGARETEN
Potato Pancake Mix and Griddle Pancake Mix
(Horowitz Bros. & Margareten, Long Island City, N.Y.)

ROKEACH
Potato Pancake Mix
(I. Rokeach & Sons, Inc., N.Y., N.Y.)

OSEM
Potato Pancake Mix
(Osem Nakid Ltd., Bnei Braq, Israel)

PASSOVER NOODLES
HOROWITZ—MARGARETEN
Passover Egg Noodles and Barley
(Horowitz Bros. & Margareten, Long Island City, N.Y.)

PICKLES
ROKEACH
New Pickles, Kosher New Gherkins, Deluxe Mix, Sweet Peppers, Hot Peppers, New Kraut, Cucumber Salad, Plum Tomatoes
(I. Rokeach & Sons, Inc., N.Y., N.Y.)

WELLWORTH
Half Sour Pickles, Pickled Tomatoes
(Wellworth Pickle Co., Paterson, N.J.)

FESTIVE

TAMAR

ORA
Pickle Products
(Festive Finer Fds., Brooklyn, N.Y.)

*See p. 448.

POTATO STARCH
HOROWITZ—MARGARETEN
Potato Starch
(Horowitz Bros. & Margareten, Long Island City, N.Y.)

POULTRY PRODUCTS
MORIAH
Turkey Rolls and Turkey Salami
(Moriah Kosher Poultry, N.Y., N.Y.)

EMPIRE
Turkey Rolls, Cooked Turkey Breast, Cooked Chicken Breast, and Turkey Slices
(Empire Kosher Poultry, Miffinton, Pa.)

DEAN
Turkey Rolls, Cooked Turkey Breast, Cooked Chicken Breast, Turkey Slices
(Dean Kosher Poultry, Bird-in-Hand, Pa.)

SALT
SEASONED BRAND
(I. Epstein & Sons, Inc., Irvington, N.J.)

FESTIVE
(Festive Finer Fds., Brooklyn, N.Y.)

FREEDA
Salt Substitute
(Free Salt)
(Freeda Pharmaceuticals, N.Y., N.Y.)

SAUCES
ROKEACH
Tomato Sauce with Mushrooms
(I. Rokeach & Sons, Inc., N.Y., N.Y.)

HOROWITZ—MARGARETEN
Tomato and Mushroom Sauce
(Horowitz Bros. & Margareten, Long Island City, N.Y.)

SHORTENING—OILS
NUT-OLA

ALOTUN

MRS. ZUPNIK

RO-DO

NUT-OLA VEGETABLE OIL
(Nut-Ola Fat Prod. Co., Brooklyn, N.Y.)

ROKEACH
Nyafat—Onion Flavored, Neutral Nyafat, Peanut Oil, Vegetable Oil (Poly-Unsaturated)
(I. Rokeach & Sons, Inc., N.Y., N.Y.)

SOUPS AND SOUP MIXES
MRS. ADLER'S MODERN RECIPE
Soups: Matzoh Ball, Onion, Mushroom, Celery, Potato, Vegetable, Tomato and Cabbage
(Adler Food Packing Co., Brooklyn, N.Y.)

MOTHER'S
Borscht, Low Calorie Borscht, Schav, Egg Enriched Borscht, and Unsalted Borscht
(Mother's Food Products, Newark, N.J.)

OSEM SOUP MIX
Tomato, Vegetable (Mix and Cube), Mushroom (Mix and Cube), Bouillon Cubes, Continental Mushroom, Country Style Vegetable
(Osem Nakid Ltd., Bnei Braq, Israel)

ROKEACH
Borscht, Lemon Borscht, Schav, Diet Borscht, Tomato Soup w/Egg Drops, Cabbage Soup, Mushroom, Stems and Pieces, Vegetable Soup, Soup Greens
(I. Rokeach & Sons, Inc., N.Y., N.Y.)

HOROWITZ—MARGARETEN
(Horowitz Bros. & Margareten, Long Island City, N.Y.)

SHALOM SOUP MIX
Vegetable, Consomme Mix, Mushroom
(I. Plotkin & Sons, Israel)

TELMA
Golden Broth; Soup: Vegetable, Mushroom, Onion, Tomato, Borscht
(Israel Edible Products Ltd., Haifa, Israel)

Meat
ROKEACH
Clear Chicken Soup, Chicken Matzoh Balls
(I. Rokeach & Sons, Inc., N.Y., N.Y.)

HOROWITZ—MARGARETEN
Clear Chicken Soup, Chicken Soup with Matzoh Balls
(Horowitz Bros. & Margareten, Long Island City, N.Y.)

TELMA
Consomme
(Israel Edible Products Ltd., Haifa, Israel)

SOUP NUTS
HOROWITZ—MARGARETEN
Soup Nuts
(Horowitz Bros. & Margareten, Long Island City, N.Y.)

SOUR CREAM

Dairy
DELLWOOD
(Deltown Fds., Inc., Yonkers, N.Y.)

RASKAS
(Raskas Dairy, Inc., St. Louis, Mo.)

BIG Z
(Zausner Fds. Corp., Mountainside, N.J.)

FRIENDSHIP
Sour and Sweet Cream
(Friendship Dairies, Inc., Maspeth, N.Y.)

ELK BRAND
(Elk Brand Dairies, Inc., Philadelphia, Pa.)

DAIRY KING
(Dairy King, Inc., Baltimore, Md.)

ELMHURST
(Elmhurst Milk & Cream Co., Jamaica, N.Y.)

WALDBAUM'S
(Waldbaum's Inc., Garden City, N.Y.)

A & P
(Available in Kings, Queens, Nassau and Suffolk Counties, N.Y.)
(The Great Atlantic and Pacific Tea Co., A & P Stores)

SOUR SALT
ROKEACH
(I. Rokeach & Sons, Inc., N.Y., N.Y.)

HOROWITZ—MARGARETEN
(Horowitz Bros. & Margareten, Long Island City, N.Y.)

EHLER'S
(Brooke Bond Fds., Lake Success, N.Y.)

HUDSON
(Hudson Tea & Spice Co., Inc., Brooklyn, N.Y.)

STUFFING AND COATING MIXES
HOROWITZ—MARGARETEN
Matzoh Farfel Stuffing Mix, Bake Chicken Coating Mix, Kote N' Bake
(Horowitz Bros. & Margareten, Long Island City, N.Y.)

MRS. ADLER
Stuffing and Stuffed Derma
(Mrs. Adler's Foods, Brooklyn, N.Y.)

SPICES—SEASONING
HOROWITZ—MARGARETEN
Black and White Pepper, Cinnamon, Ginger, Paprika, 100% Garlic
Powder, 100% Onion Powder
(Horowitz Bros. & Margareten, Long Island City, N.Y.)

EHLER'S
Cinnamon, Onion and Garlic Powders, Black and White Peppers,
Ginger, Paprika, Soup Greens and Parsley Flakes
(Brooke Bond Foods, Lake Success, N.Y.)

HUDSON
White and Black Pepper, Cinnamon, Ginger, Paprika, Garlic and
Onion Powders
(Hudson Tea and Spice Co., Brooklyn, N.Y.)

SUGAR
JACK FROST
Granulated and Sugar Cubes
(National Sugar Refining Co., Brooklyn, N.Y.)

WALDBAUM'S
(Waldbaum's Inc., Garden City, N.Y.)

TEA
HOROWITZ—MARGARETEN
Tea Bags
(Horowitz Bros. & Margareten, Long Island City, N.Y.)

FESTIVE

TAMAR

ORA
(Festive Finer Fds, Brooklyn, N.Y.)

VEGETABLES [CANNED]
FESTIVE

TAMAR

ORA
Beets, Mushrooms, Carrots, Irish Potatoes, Sweet Potatoes
(Festive Finer Fds. Brooklyn, N.Y.)

VINEGAR — CIDER
ROKEACH
Cider Vinegar
(I. Rokeach & Sons, Inc., N.Y., N.Y.)

VERYFINE
Cider Vinegar
(New England Apple Prod. Co. Inc., Littleton, Mass.)

VITAMINS
FREEDA
Passovite Tablets, Passovite Drops, Liquid Infant Vitamins
(Freeda Pharmaceuticals Co., N.Y., N.Y.)

WINES — GRAPE JUICE
KEDEM

HERSH'S KOSHER WINES
(Royal Wine Corp., Bronx, N.Y.)

CARMEL—Bearing halachi of Chief Rabbinate of Israel
(Carmel Wine Co., Inc., N.Y., N.Y.)

JERUSALEM WINES
(A.T.S. Wine, Israel)

LIPSCHUTZ
Grape Juice
(Lipschutz Kosher Food Prod. Co., N.Y., N.Y.)

HOROWITZ—MARGARETEN
Grape Juice
(Horowitz Bros. & Margareten, Long Island City, N.Y.)

FROZEN FISH
CARPION
Frozen Israeli Carp (whole, slices, ground)
(Gourmet Imports, Brooklyn, N.Y.)

DAGIM
Frozen: Fillets and Fish Mix
(Dagim Tahorim Co., Brooklyn, N.Y.)

MEATS
YITZCHOK GOLDBERG'S

(I. Goldberg & Sons, N.Y., N.Y.)

DAVID ELLIOT
(David Elliot Poultry Farm, Lake Ariel, Pa.)

SUPERVISED PRODUCTS [Packaged Meat Products]
Beef, Veal, Lamb, Roasts, Steaks, Chops, and Liver
(Supervised Products, Inc., Denver, Colo.)

LUNDY'S (Packaged Meat Products)
Beef Roast, Steaks, Chuck, Short Ribs, Ground Beef, Lamb Chops, and Beef Liver
(S. Lundy's Sons, Philadelphia, Pa.)

POULTRY
EMPIRE KOSHER POULTRY

NAOMI KOSHER POULTRY

ESSEX KOSHER POULTRY
(Empire Kosher Poultry, Miffintown, Pa.)

DEAN KOSHER POULTRY
(Dean Poultry Co., Bird-in-Hand, Pa.)

YITZCHOK GOLDBERG'S
(I. Yitzchok Goldberg & Sons, N.Y., N.Y.)

DAVID ELLIOT
(David Elliot Poultry Farm, Lake Ariel, Pa.)

QUEEN ESTHER

SIMCHA

BAZAAR
(Levin Bros. Poultry Co. Inc., Wellston, Mo.)

MORIAH KOSHER POULTRY
(Moriah Kosher Poultry, N.Y., N.Y.)

CUSTOM POULTRY
(Vineland Poultry, Vineland, N.J.)

TEA
WHITE ROSE
Tea Bags

ANN PAGE
NECTAR
OUR OWN
Tea Bags
(The Great Atlantic and Pacific Tea Co., A & P Stores)

SWEETENER—DIETETIC
PILLSBURY SWEET *10 LIQUID
PILLSBURY SWEET *10 GRANULAR
PILLSBURY SWEET *10 CUBES
(The Pillsbury Co., Minneapolis, Minn.)

ZEES TABLETS
(Freeda Pharmaceuticals, N.Y., N.Y.)

APPLESAUCE
VERYFINE
(New England Apple Prods., Inc., Littleton, Mass.)

MUSSELMAN'S
(C.H. Musselman, Div. Pet Food Prod., Biglerville, Pa.)

TAMAR

ORA

FESTIVE
(Festive Finer Fds., Brooklyn, N.Y.)

CANDY AND CHOCOLATES
ASTOR CHOCOLATE CORP.
(Parve only when indicated on label, otherwise Dairy)
(Astor Chocolate Corp., Brooklyn, N.Y.)

BARTON'S
(Parve only when indicated on label, otherwise Dairy)
(Barton's Candy Corp., Brooklyn, N.Y.)

BUTTER—CREAM
FRIENDSHIP
Butter, Sweet Cream
(Friendship Dairies Inc., Maspeth, N.Y.)

DELLWOOD
Sweet Butter
(Dellwood Fds., Inc., Yonkers, N.Y.)

BUTTERMILK
FRIENDSHIP
(Friendship Dairies, Inc., Maspeth, N.Y.)

ELMHURST
(Elmhurst Milk & Cream Co., Inc., Jamaica, N.Y.)

CHEESE

Dairy
MILLER'S
(Miller Cheese Co., N.Y., N.Y.)

RASKAS
Cream Cheese
(Raskas Dairy, Inc., St. Louis, Mo.)

DELLWOOD
Cream Cheese, Cottage Cheese
(Deltown Foods, Inc., Yonkers, N.Y.)

TUXEDO
Cottage Cheese

BIG Z
Cream and Farmer Cheeses, Neufchatel Spread

SANTE
Cottage and Cream Cheeses

REGENT
Cream and Cottage Cheeses
(Zausner Foods Corp., Mountainside, N.J.)

ELK
Cottage Cheese
(Elk Brand Dairies, Inc., Philadelphia, Pa.)

FRIENDSHIP
Bakers, Cottage, and Pot Cheeses
(Friendship Dairy, Inc., Maspeth, N.Y.)

DUMPLINGS—KNAIDEL
MOTHER'S MATZOH BALLS
(Mother's Food Prod., Div. of Vita Fds., Newark, N.J.)

MRS. ADLER'S
(Mrs. Adler's Food Corp., Brooklyn, N.Y.)

EGG PRODUCTS
QUALITY EGG
(Quality Egg Co., Inc., Dayton, N.J.)

OLSON BROS.
(Olson Bros., Philadelphia, Pa.)

NFA EGG PRODUCTS
(Pacific Growers, San Leandro, Ca.)

SCHNEIDER BROS. FROZEN EGGS
(Schneider Bros., Inc., Chicago, Ill.; Birmingham, Ala.)

TRAININ'S FROZEN EGG PRODUCTS
(Trainin Egg Prods. Co., Jackson, Miss.)

ALBEN BRAND EGGS
(Alexander Lewis, Inc., Allen, Inc., Frehold N.J.)

BALLAS EGG PRODUCTS (Ballas Egg Co., Zanesville, Ohio)

MARSHALL PRODUCE CO.
(Egg Prod. Div. of Marshall Foods, Inc., Marshall, Minn.)

EGGIT
(Eggit Inc., Interlaken, N.Y.)

ADAMS
(Adams Egg Prod., Jackson, Miss.)

GIBBER EGG CORP.
(Gibber Egg Corp., Kiamesha Lake, N.Y.)

BRASHER BROS.
(Brasher Bros., Inc., Burbank, Ca.)

WM. OLDACH
(William Oldah & Co., Flourtown, Pa.)

FISH PRODUCTS
MOTHER'S
Gefilte Fish
(Mother's Food Prod., Div. of Vita Foods, Newark, N.J.)

ROKEACH
Gefilte Fish
(I. Rokeach & Sons, Inc., N.Y., N.Y.)

VITA
Herring and Gefilte Fish
(Vita Food Products, N.Y., N.Y.)

HOROWITZ—MARGARETEN
Gefilte Fish
(Horowitz Bros. & Margareten, Long Island City, N.Y.)

NOVIE
Smoked Fish, Lox, Herring
(Nova Scotia Food Prod., Brooklyn, N.Y.)

MRS. ADLER'S
Gefilte Fish
(Mrs. Adler's Foods Corp., Brooklyn, N.Y.)

FESTIVE

TAMAR

ORA
Tuna Fish
(Festive Finer Fds., Brooklyn, N.Y.)

NOVIE ICELAND
Smoked Fish/Lox
(Novie Iceland Inc., Miami, Fla.)

BLUE RIBBON
Smoked Fish/Lox
(Blue Ribbon Fish Prod., Brooklyn, N.Y.)

DAGIM
Salmon and Tuna
(Dagim Tahorim Co., Brooklyn, N.Y.)

FLAVORS
AMERICAN FLAVORS AND FRAGRANCE CO.
(With letter of certification mentioning specific flavor)
(American Flavors & Fragrance Co., Mineola, N.Y.)

DRAGOCO
(With letter of certification mentioning specific flavor)
(Dragoco, Inc., Totowa, N.J.)

NORDA
(With letter of certification mentioning specific flavor)
(Norda Essential Oil & Chem. Co., N.Y., N.Y.)

STANGE
(With letter of certification mentioning specific flavor)
(Stange Co., Glen Rock, N.J.)

GENTRY
(With letter of certification mentioning specific flavor)
(Gentry International, Fairlawn, N.J.)

INTERNATIONAL BAKERS SERVICES
(With letter of certification mentioning specific flavor)
(International Bakers Services, South Bend, Ind.)

BUSCH, BOAKE & ALLEN
(With letter of certification mentioning specific flavor)
(Busch, Boake & Allen, Inc., Norwood, N.J.)

FOOD COLORING
KALAMAZOO
Vegetable Colors
(Kalamazoo Spice Extraction Co., Kalamazoo, Mich.)

FROZEN DINNERS

Meat and Parve (Parve only when indicated on label)

SCHREIBER FROZEN DINNERS
(Schreiber Caterers, Inc., Brooklyn, N.Y.)

MADAN FROZEN DINNERS
(Madan Frozen Dinners, Los Angeles, Ca.; Miami, Fla.)

BORENSTEIN'S
(Available on request from airlines)
Fresh and Frozen Dinners
(Borenstein Caterers Inc., Jamaica, N.Y.)

WILTON FROZEN DINNERS
(Wilton Frozen Dinners, Spring Valley, N.Y.)

FRUITS DRIED AND CANNED

PAUL A. MARIANI
Dates and Dried Fruits
(Paul A Mariani Co., Cupertino, Ca.)

SEASON BRAND
Dried Fruits and Canned Fruits
(I. Epstein & Sons, Inc., Irvington, N.J.)

DEL MONTE
Prunes
(Del Monte Corp., Berkeley, Ca.)

FESTIVE
Pineapple, Fruit Compote, Prepared Prunes
(Festive Finer Fds., Brooklyn, N.Y.)

GUMS [WATER SOLUBLE]

MEER
Agar Agar, Gum Arabic, Gum Karaye, Gum Tragacanth
(Meer Corp., N.Y., N.Y.)

TIC
Gum Arabic
Special AA USP Powder Gum
(Tragacanth Importing Co., N.Y., N.Y.)

NORDA
Gum Arabic
(Norda Essential Oils and Chem., N.Y., N.Y.)

HONEY

ROKEACH

(I. Rokeach & Sons, Inc., N.Y., N.Y.)

HUDSON
(Hudson Tea & Spice Co., Brooklyn, N.Y.)

S. WALKER & SONS APIARIES
(S. Walker & Sons, Milford, Mich.)

ICE CREAM—FRUIT ICES—FROZEN DESSERT

Dairy

BARTON'S
(Barton's Candy Corp., Brooklyn, N.Y.)

GOLD SEAL—RIVIERA
Ice Cream and Sherbet
(Gold Star Ice Cream Corp., Brooklyn, N.Y.)

GOLD SEAL FRUIT ICES
(Parve only when indicated on label)
(Gold Star Ice Cream Corp., Brooklyn, N.Y.)

COUNTRY CLUB
(Parve only when indicated on label)
(Country Club Frozen Desserts, Inc., Bronx, N.Y.)

BARTON'S FRUIT ICES
(Parve only when indicated on label, otherwise Dairy)
(Barton's Candy Corp., Brooklyn, N.Y.)

JAMS, JELLIES AND PRESERVES

GLOBE
Jams: Raspberry, Seedless Raspberry, Apricot and Evaporated Apricot; Apple Raspberry Jelly, Orange Marmalade, Orange Peel Paste, Orange Batter Paste
(Globe Preserves, Inc., Clifton, N.J.)

POLANER
Preserves, Marmalade
(M. Polaner & Sons, Inc., Newark, N.J.)

JUICES

VERYFINE
Apple and Prune Juices
(New England Apple Prod. Co., Littleton, Mass.)

FESTIVE

TAMAR

ORA

Citrus and Pineapple Juices
(Festive Finer Fds., Brooklyn, N.Y.)

MUSSELMAN'S
Apple Juice
(Musselman, Div. of Pet Milk, Biglerville, Pa.)

MATZOH PRODUCTS
HOROWITZ—MARGARETEN
Bulk Matzoh: Meal, Farfel, Cake Meal, Cereal
(Horowitz Bros. & Margareten, Long Island City, N.Y.)

MRS. ADLER'S
Matzoh Dumplings
(Mrs. Adler's Foods Corp., Brooklyn, N.Y.)

MAYONNAISE
MOTHER'S
(Mother's Food Prod., Newark, N.J.)

SEASON BRAND
(I. Epstein & Sons, Irvington, N.J.)

TELMA
(Israel Edible Prod. Ltd., Haifa, Israel)

FESTIVE

TAMAR

ORA
Salad Dressings
(Festive Finer Fds., Brooklyn, N.Y.)

MEAT AND PROVISIONS
HILL'S GLATT KOSHER
999, Salami, Knockwurst, Franks/Cocktail/Griddles, Bologna, Corned Beef, Tongue, Pastrami, Bake N' Fry, Smoked Shoulder Steaks, Shoulder Steaks and Briskets
(Real Kosher Sausage, N.Y., N.Y.)

MILK—CHOLOV YISROEL
FARM FRESH
Homogenized and Skimmed
(Mason-Dixon Farms, Gettysburg, Pa.)

MONOSODIUM GLUTAMATE [MSG]
GREAT WESTERN MSG
(Great Western Sugar Co., Denver, Colo.)

ACCENT
(Stauffer Chem. Corp., San Jose, Ca.)

HUDSON
(Hudson Tea & Spice Co., Inc., Brooklyn, N.Y.)

CONTINENTAL SEASONINGS
(Continental Seasonings, Teaneck, N.Y.)

PASSOVER NOODLES
HOROWITZ—MARGARETEN
Bulk Passover Egg Noodles
(Horowitz Bros. & Margareten, Long Island City, N.Y.)

PASTES [FRUIT-NUT]
GLOBE
Almond, Macaroon, Orange Peel, Orange Batter
(Globe Preserves, Inc., Clifton, N.J.)

PICKLES
ROKEACH
New Pickles, Kosher New Gherkins, Deluxe Mix, Sweet and Hot Peppers, New Kraut, Cucumber Salad, Plum Tomatoes
(I. Rokeach & Sons, N.Y., N.Y.)

WELLWORTH
Half Sour Pickles and Pickled Tomatoes
(Wellworth Pickle Co., Paterson, N.J.)

FESTIVE

TAMAR

ORA
Pickle Products
(Festive Finer Fds., Brooklyn, N.Y.)

POTATO PRODUCTS
HOROWITZ—MARGARETEN
Potato Starch
(Horowitz Bros. & Margareten, Long Island City, N.Y.)

ROGERS BROS.
Potato Flour and Potato Rice
(Rogers Bros., Idaho Falls, Idaho)

SHORTENING—VEGETABLE OIL
PRIMEX

PURITAN OIL
(The Procter & Gamble Co., Cincinnati, Ohio)

NUT-OLA
Shortening and Vegetable Oil
(Nut-Ola Food Prod., Brooklyn, N.Y.)

ROKEACH NYFAT
(I. Rokeach & Sons, Inc., N.Y., N.Y.)

TAMAR

ORA

FESTIVE
Vegetable Oil
(Festive Finer Fds., Brooklyn, N.Y.)

SOUR CREAM

Dairy
ELK BRAND
(Elk Dairy, Philadelphia, Pa.)

RASKAS
(Raskas Dairy, St. Louis, Mo.)

FRIENDSHIP
(Friendship Dairy, Maspeth, N.Y.)

DELLWOOD
(Deltown Foods, Inc., Yonkers, N.Y.)

SPICES AND SEASONING
GENTRY
(With letter of certification only)
Peppers: Cayenne, Red, Chili; Paprika, Chili Powder
(Gentry Corp., Oxnard, Ca.)

STANGE
Seasoning Compounds and Mixed Spice Blends
(Stange Co., Paterson, N.J.)

KALAMAZOO SPICE EXTRACTS
(Kalamazoo Spice Extraction Co., Kalamazoo, Mich.)

MEER CORPORATION
(Meer Corp., N.Y., N.Y.)

CONTINENTAL SEASONINGS
(Continental Seasonings, Teaneck, N.J.)

HUDSON
Ginger, Black and White Pepper, Paprika, Cinnamon, Basil, Oregano
(Hudson Tea & Spice Co., Brooklyn, N.Y.)

STABILIZER
HODAG SVO-9K POLYSORBATE 80
HODAG SVS-18K POLYSORBATE 60
(Hodag Chemical Corp., Skokie, Ill.)

T-MAZ
(R.R. Mazer Co., Chicago, Ill.)

SUGAR
FLO-SWEET
Liquid Sugar, Granulated Sugar
(Refined Syrups & Sugars, Inc., Yonkers, N.Y.)

JACK FROST
Liquid Sugars, Granulated Sugar
(National Refining Co., Philadelphia, Pa.)

SUCREST
Sugar
(Sucrest Corp., N.Y., N.Y.)

VEGETABLES [DEHYDRATED]—[POWDERED]
GENTRY
Onion (Powdered, Minced, Chopped), Garlic (Powdered, Minced, Chopped), Peppers
(Gentry Corp., Los Angeles, Ca.)

GOLDEN WEST
Onion (Powdered, Minced, Chopped), Garlic (Powdered, Minced, Chopped)
(Gilroy Foods, Inc., Gilroy, Ca.)

ROGERS
Onion (Powdered, Minced, Chopped), Garlic (Powdered, Minced, Chopped), Peppers
(Rogers Bros. Co., Idaho Falls, Idaho)

BASIC
Onion (Powdered, Minced, Chopped), Garlic (Powdered, Minced, Chopped), Peppers (Powdered, Minced, Chopped)
(Basic Vegetable Products, Inc., Vacaville, Ca.)

HUDSON
Onion and Garlic Powder
(Hudson Tea & Spice Co., Brooklyn, N.Y.)

VEGETABLES—CANNED
TAMAR

ORA

FESTIVE
Carrots, Irish Potatoes, Mushrooms, Sweet Potatoes
(Festive Finer Foods, Brooklyn, N.Y.)

VINEGAR—CIDER
MUSSELMAN'S
(C.H. Musselman, Div. Pet Foods, Biglerville, Pa.)

NEW ENGLAND APPLE PRODUCTS
(New England Apple Products Co., Littleton, Mass.)

ACIDULANTS
MONSANTO
Lactic Acid Food Grade, Fumaric Acid Food Grade
(Monsanto Co., St. Louis, Mo.)

ALCOHOL
SHELL
(Shell Chemical Co., Houston, Texas)

ANTI-OXIDANT
NEO-CEBITATE
(Merck, Inc., Rahway, N.J.)

FLAVORS
MONSANTO
Vanillin, Ethavan (Ethyl Vanillin)
(Monsanto Company, St. Louis, Mo.)

GLYCERINE
SHELL SYNTHETIC GLYCERINE
(Shell Chemical Corp., Houston, Texas)

DOW SYNTHETIC GLYCERINE
(Dow Chemical Corp., Midland, Mich.)

P&G GLYCERINE
(WITH Ⓤ ONLY)
(The Procter & Gamble Co., Cincinnati, Ohio)

ATLAS GLYCERINE
(Atlas Chemical Industries, Wilmington, Del.)

OLIN SYNTHETIC GLYCERINE
(Olin Chemical Corp., N.Y., N.Y.)

FMC CORP. GLYCERINE
(Organic Div., FMC Corp., N.Y., N.Y.)

HEXITOLS
MANNITOL NF
(Atlas Chemical Industries, Inc., Wilmington, Del.)

MEATS
LUNDY'S
Beef, Chuck, Roasts, Liver, Ground Beef, Veal, Lamb and Beef Tongue
(S. Lundy's Sons, Philadelphia, Pa.)

YITZCHOK GOLDBERG'S
(I. Goldberg & Sons, N.Y., N.Y.)

DAVID ELLIOT
(David Elliot Poultry Farm, Lake Ariel, Pa.)

SUPERVISED PRODUCTS
(Packaged Meat Products) Beef, Veal, Lamb, Roasts, Steaks, Chops, Liver
(Supervised Products, Inc., Denver, Colo.)

A. WEINSTOCK
Beef, Lamb, Veal
(Alle Packing, Brooklyn, N.Y.)

POULTRY
EMPIRE KOSHER POULTRY

NAOMI KOSHER POULTRY

ESSEX KOSHER POULTRY
(Empire Kosher Poultry, Miffintown, Pa.)

DEAN KOSHER POULTRY
(Dean Poultry Co., Bird-in-Hand, Pa.)

CUSTOM POULTRY
(Vineland Poultry, Vineland, N.J.)

YITZCHOK GOLDBERG'S
(I. Goldberg & Sons, N.Y., N.Y.)

DAVID ELLIOT
(David Elliot Poultry Farm, Lake Ariel, Pa.)

QUEEN ESTHER

SIMCHA

BAZAAR
(Levin Bros. Poultry Co., Inc., Wellston, Mo.)

MORIAH KOSHER POULTRY
(Moriah Kosher Poultry, N.Y., N.Y.)

PRESERVATIVES—FOOD
MONSANTO
Sodium-Benzoate USP
(Monsanto Co., St. Louis, Mo.)

MERCK
Neo-Cebitate
(Merck, Inc., Rahway, N.J.)

SALT
PURITY

RED CROSS SALT

STERLING SALT
(International Salt Co., Clark Summit, Pa.)

MORTON SALT
(Morton Salt Co., Chicago, Ill.)

HARDY SALT
(Hardy Salt Co., St. Louis, Mo.)

SWEETENERS—DIETETIC
SUGARINE LIQUID SWEETENER
(The Sugarine Co., Mt. Vernon, N.Y.)

PILLSBURY SWEET NO. 30 LIQUID SWEETENER
(The Pillsbury Co., Minneapolis, Minn.)

MONSANTO COMPANY
Sodium and Calcium
(Monsanto Co., St. Louis, Mo.)

The foregoing products marked with the Ⓤ are generally acceptable to all Orthodox Jews. Most, but not all, also accept products approved by the O.K. Laboratories, P. O. Box 218, Brooklyn, New York. The approval is noted on the food package by the symbol Ⓚ. These products are:

INSTITUTIONAL AND INDUSTRIAL PRODUCTS

ALMOND PASTE AND KERNEL PASTE
AMERICAN ALMOND PROD. CO., Brooklyn, N.Y. Kosher for Passover with Passover seal only.

BATTERS
MODERN MAID FOOD PRODUCTS, Garden City, N.Y. With Ⓚ seal only. **Dairy** unless otherwise specified.

BREAD CRUMBS AND BREADING
LAZZARA'S, Paterson, N.J.
Bread Crumbs

MODERN MAID FOOD PRODUCTS, Garden City, N.Y. With Ⓚ seal only. **Dairy** unless otherwise specified.

CANDY, CHOCOLATE, COCOA
BARRICINI CANDY CO., Long Island City, N.Y. With Ⓚ seal only. **Dairy** unless otherwise specified. Kosher for Passover with Passover seal only.

BLOMMER'S CHOCOLATE CO., Chicago, Ill. With Ⓚ seal only. **Dairy** unless otherwise specified.

CALLEBAUT CHOCOLATE, Wieze, Belgium. **Dairy** unless otherwise specified. Kosher for Passover with Passover seal only.

CARUTH CANDIES, Woodside, N.Y. **Dairy** unless otherwise specified. Kosher for Passover with Passover seal only.

COCOLINE CHOCOLATE CO., Brooklyn, N.Y. **Dairy** unless otherwise specified. Kosher for Passover with Passover seal only.

EDDYLEON, Garden City, N.Y. With Ⓚ seal only. **Dairy**, unless otherwise specified. Kosher for Passover with Passover seal only.

HOOTON CHOCOLATE, Newark, N.J. **Dairy** unless otherwise specified. Kosher for Passover with Passover seal only.

RENAUX CHOCOLAT, Stationsstraat, Belgium. **Dairy** unless otherwise specified.

WALTER BAKER CO., Dover, Del. All products parve only when so marked. Kosher for Passover with Passover seal only.

CAKE MIXES

MODERN MAID FOOD PRODUCTS, Garden City, N.Y. With Ⓚ seal only. **Dairy** unless otherwise specified.

CHEESES

KRAFT FOODS, Chicago, Ill. Kraft 50 lb. Cream Cheese, Kraft 30 lb. Bulk Cream Cheese, Kraft 3 lb. Cream Cheese.

COAGULATING AGENTS

DAIRYLAND FOOD LABORATORIES, Waukesha, Wis.
Emporase

MILES LABORATORIES, INC., Clinton, N.J.
Marzyme

NOVA ENZYME CORPORATION, Mamaroneck, N.Y., Copenhagen, Denmark
Renilaise

COFFEE

GENERAL FOODS CORP., Hoboken, N.J. Yuban, Maxwell House, Sanka, Maxim, Horizon, Brim, Freeze Dried Brim, Freeze Dried Sanka, Freeze Dried Yuban. Kosher for Passover—seal not necessary.

COLORING

H. KOHNSTAMM & CO., N.Y., N.Y. With Ⓚ seal only.

V & E KOHNSTAMM, Brooklyn, N.Y. With Ⓚ seal only.

CYSTEINE HYDROCHLORIDE

DIAMALT COMPANY, Munich, Germany

DAIRY—PROTEIN PRODUCTS

HUMKO SHEFFIELD CHEMICAL, Norwich, N.Y. Edible Casein, Caseinates, Lactose, Lactate

FOREMOST DAIRIES, San Francisco, Ca. Whey, Lactose, Casein and Sodium Caseinate. With Ⓚ seal only.

KRAFT FOODS, Chicago, Ill. Whey. With Ⓚ seal only.

VITAMINS, INC., Chicago, Ill. Casein, Sodium Caseinate

DETERGENTS

SPARTAN CHEMICAL CO., INC., Toledo, Ohio. SD-20 All Purpose Cleaner Sterigent. Spartan Golden-Glo Liquid Hand Dishwashing Compound

EGG PRODUCTS [DRIED AND FROZEN]

HURST PRODUCTS, INC., Newton, Kan. Eggs

KRAFT FOODS, Chicago, Ill. Kraft Dried and Frozen Eggs

STAUFFER CHEMICAL CO., Chicago, Ill. With Ⓚ seal only.

FILLINGS AND FILLERS

KRAFT FOODS, Chicago, Ill. Apricot Filling, Raspberry and Apple Filling, Prune Filling, Cherry Filling, Apple Filling, Pineapple Filling, Blueberry Filling, Strawberry Filling, Raspberry Filling.

FLAVORING EXTRACTS

AMERICAN FOOD LABORATORIES, Brooklyn, N.Y. With Ⓚ seal only.

AROMATICS INTERNATIONAL, Marietta, Ga. With Ⓚ seal only.

MONSANTO FLAVOR ESSENCE, N.Y., N.Y. With Ⓚ seal only.

FRIES & FRIES, Cincinnati, Ohio. With Ⓚ seal only

GIVAUDAN CORPORATION, Clifton, N.J. With Ⓚ seal only.

H. KOHNSTAMM & CO., N.Y., N.Y. With Ⓚ seal only.

V & E KOHNSTAMM, Brooklyn, N.Y. With Ⓚ seal only.

SALIENT FLAVORS, Brooklyn, N.Y. With Ⓚ seal only.

HUMKO SHEFFIELD CHEMICAL, Norwich, N.Y. With Ⓚ seal only.

SUNKIST GROWERS, Ontario, Ca. With Ⓚ seal only.

UNITED FLAVORS, Brooklyn, N.Y. With Ⓚ seal only.

VIRGINIA DARE, Brooklyn, N.Y. With Ⓚ seal only.

FRESH FRUIT PRODUCTS

KRAFT FOODS, Chicago, Ill. Fruit Salad, Ambrosia, Orange Juice, Red Grapefruit Segments, Pineapple Chunks, Grapefruit Segments, Orange Segments

ICE CREAM CONES

EAGLE CONE CO., Brooklyn, N.Y. With Ⓚ seal only.

EASTERN BAKING CO., Sommerville, Mass. With Ⓚ seal only.

KEYSTONE CONE CO., Pittsburgh, Pa. With Ⓚ seal only.

MARYLAND BAKING CO., Baltimore, Md. With Ⓚ seal only.

MARYLAND BAKING CO. OF GA., INC., Atlanta, Ga. With Ⓚ seal only.

NORTH WEST CONE OF CHICAGO, Chicago, Ill. Ice Cream cones, With Ⓚ seal only.

NORTH WEST CONE OF DETROIT, Detroit, Mich. Ice Cream cone. With Ⓚ seal only.

PACIFIC COAST BAKING CO., Los Angeles, Ca.

YOHAY BAKING CO., Brooklyn, N.Y.

ICE CREAM MIXES

HORSTMANN MIX & CREAM, INC., Long Island City, N.Y. Ice Cream Mix and Shake Mixes

IMITATION NUTS

THE PILLSBURY COMPANY, Minneapolis, Minn. Pecan Flavored Bitsyn, Butter Pecan Flavored Bitsyn, Bitsyn Confectionery Chip, Walnut Twin, Black Walnut Flavored Bitsyn

MARGARINE

CAPITAL CITY PRODUCTS, Columbus, Ohio. With Ⓚ seal only. All margarine **Dairy** unless otherwise specified.

KRAFT FOODS, Chicago, Ill. Bakers' Colored Margarine, Roll-in-Margarine—colored and uncolored, Colored Margarine, Special Margarine, 1 lb. Vegetable Print, 1 lb. Special Print (contains butter), 12 lb. Parkay Pats (72 & 90 count), 20 lb. Parkay Chiplets, 30 lb. Carton Vegetable Margarine, 30 lb. Tin Special Margarine, 30 lb. All Purpose Margarine, 20 lb. Tin Whipped Margarine, 30 lb. Tin Vegetable Margarine. All margarines **Dairy** unless otherwise specified.

MAYONNAISE

KRAFT FOODS, Chicago, Ill. Kraft Mayonnaise, Salad Bowl Mayonnaise, Kraft MDR Regular Mayonnaise, Kraft FDR Regular Mayonnaise, Kraft MDR Heavy Mayonnaise

NICKEL CATALYST

DREW CHEMICAL CO., Boonton, N.J. With Ⓚ seal only.

HARSHAW CHEMICAL CO., Cleveland, Ohio. With Ⓚ seal only

PIZZA CRUST

VIRGA PIZZA CRUST CO., Bronx, N.Y.

PORTION PAKS

AMSTAR CORP, Pitman, N.J. Mustard (parve), Ketchup (parve), Jellies and Jams EXCEPT GRAPE (parve), Pepper (parve), Salt (parve), Sugar (parve), Wee-Cal Sweetener (milchig)

KRAFT FOODS, Chicago, Ill. Kraft P.C. Products: Cranberry Sauce, Ketchup, Honey, Salad Dressing, Mayonnaise, French Dressing, Tartar Sauce, Mustard, Horseradish Sauce, Apple Jelly, Mint Apple Jelly, Jelly P.C.—4 Varieties, Strawberry Jam, Orange Marmalade, Orange Jam, Peach Preserves, Red Currant Jelly, Guava Jelly, Black Raspberry Preserves, Blackberry Preserves, Cherry Jelly, EXCEPT GRAPE JELLY.

RELEASE AGENTS

DALRIS CO., INC., Monmouth Junction, N.J.

INTERNATIONAL FOODCRAFT. With Ⓚ seal only.

RENNET

DAIRYLAND FOOD LABORATORIES, Waukesha, Wis. Kosher Beef Rennet with Ⓚ seal only

SALAD DRESSINGS

KRAFT FOODS, Chicago, Ill. Italian Dressing, Tartar Sauce, 1000 Island Dressing, Cuisine Salad Dressing, Miracle Whip Salad Dressing, French Dressing, Miracle French Dressing, Casino Dressing, Catalina Dressing, Sea Island Dressing, Oil & Vinegar Dressing, Russian, Coleslaw, Low Calorie Italian, Refrigerated 1000 Island, Refrigerated Green Goddess, Refrigerated Horseradish Sauce, Cuisine Coleslaw, MDR Miracle Whip Salad, MDR Cuisine Salad Dressings

SALT
DIAMOND CRYSTAL SALT CO., St. Clair, Mich. Diamond Crystal Kosher Coarse Salt, Diamond Weather Pruf Salt. Kosher for Passover with Passover seal only.

SOUP MIXES
ADMIRAL FOOD CO., White Plains, N.Y. Chicken Soup Base with Ⓚ seal only.

FARMLAND PRODUCTS, Brookland, N.Y. Garden Vegetable (parve), Red Tomato (parve), Yankee Bean (parve), Chicken Consomme (parve), French Onion Soup (parve), Chicken Noodle (parve), Minestrone (parve), Beef Consomme (parve), Mushroom Barley (parve), Beef Vegetable (parve), Beef Noodle (parve), Cream of Pea (milchig), Cream of Potato (milchig), Cream of Celery (milchig), Cream of Asparagus (milchig), Cream of Tomato (milchig), Cream of Mushroom (milchig). With Ⓚ seal only.

SPICES
CAL COMPAK FOODS, Santa Ana, Ca.

SCHILLING CO., Salinas, Ca. With Ⓚ seal only.

STABILIZERS AND EMULSIFIERS
AMERICAN FOOD LABORATORIES, Brooklyn, N.Y. With Ⓚ seal only.

SWIFT EDIBLE OIL COMPANY, Kearny, N.J. S-182K, S-184K, S-137K, S-146K, S-156K, S-119K, S-243K, S-244K, S-91K, S-26K, S-162K, S-175K. With Ⓚ seal only.

CONTROLLED FOOD SYSTEMS, Pittsburgh, Pa. With Ⓚ seal only.

DARI-TECH, Atlanta, Ga. With Ⓚ seal only.

DREW CHEMICAL CO., Boonton, N.J. With Ⓚ seal only.

HETERENE CHEMICAL CO., INC., Paterson, N.J. Sorbitan Mono Oleate Ethyl Oxylated, Sorbitan Mono Stearate Ethyl Oxylated. With Ⓚ seal only.

HUMKO SHEFFIELD CHEMICAL, Norwich, N.Y. With Ⓚ seal only.

STAUFFER CHEMICAL CO., Portland, Me. Carastay

WHITE STOKES PRODUCTS CO., Chicago, Ill. White Stokes Hanrol Creme, White Stokes Excello, White Stokes Coconut Paste, White Stokes California, Whisto-Gel, White Stokes Mallo Butterscotch, White Stokes Chocolate Flavor Syrup, White Stokes Creme Fondant

WRIGHT & WAGNER, Beloit, Wis. With Ⓚ seal only.

SUGAR AND SWEETENERS
AMERICAN SUGAR CO., Brooklyn, N.Y. Domino Granulated Sugars, Syrups No. 1 and 2, Med. Invert, Crystal 50 and 60, Amber Liquid Sugar, Brownulated, Amerfond, Amerose, Kosher for Passover with Passover seal only.

CUMBERLAND PACKING CO., Brooklyn, N.Y. Sweet 'N Low (milchig)

SYRUP
KRAFT FOODS, Chicago, Ill. Kraft Table Syrup

TEA
GENERAL FOODS CORP., Hoboken, N.J. Maxwell House Tea

TOMATO PRODUCTS, KETCHUP, VINEGAR
HUNT WESSON FOODS, INC., Fullerton, Ca. Solid Pack Tomatoes, Tomato Juice, Sauce, Hunt Manwich, Tomato Paste, Tomato Puree, Chili Sauce, Pizza Sauce, Tomato Ketchup, All Purpose Tomatoes, Kraft 100 Grain Vinegar

TOPPINGS
KRAFT FOODS, Chicago, Ill. No. 10 Tins of Toppings, Kraft Cherry Topping, Pineapple Topping, Strawberry Topping.

VEGETABLES
HUNT-WESSON FOODS, INC., Fullerton, Cal. Hunt's Spinach.

KRAFT FOODS, Chicago, Ill. 1 lb. Potato Flakes, 20 lb. Potato Flakes, 10 lb. Regular Instant Potatoes, 10 lb. Complete Instant Potatoes, 3 to 5 lb. Pear Potatoes, 2 to 5 lb. Hash Brown Potatoes

LA CHOY FOOD PRODUCTS CO., Archbold, Ohio. No. 10: Chop Suey, Bean Sprouts, Fancy Mixed Chinese Vegetables. With Ⓚ seal only

VEGETABLE GUMS

SWIFT EDIBLE OIL COMPANY, Kearny, N.J. Calcium Propionate, Sodium Propionate, Sodium Benzoate, Locust Bean Gum, Guar Gum, Gum Ghatti, Gum Karaya, Gum Tragacanth, Gum Arabic

VEGETABLE SHORTENINGS AND OILS

CAPITAL CITY PRODUCTS CO., Columbus, Ohio. With Ⓚ seal only.

DREW CHEMICAL CO., Boonton, N.J.

HUNT-WESSON FOODS, INC., Fullerton, Cal. Angela Mia Oil, 22 Oil, Midas, Key, Quiz, Gamma, Palm Oil, MFB, Quik-Blend, Golden Beem, Super Wesson, Lo-Melt, Crystal, Keap, Scoco, 77 Oil, Wesson Oil, Veltex. With Ⓚ seal only.

KRAFT FOODS, Chicago, Ill. 400 lb. Kraft Oil (bung-type drum)

THE THEOBALD COMPANY, Bayonne, N.J. With Ⓚ seal only

YOGURT FLAVORING

KRAFT FOODS, Chicago, Ill. Kraft Apricot Flavoring for Yogurt, Kraft Blueberry Flavoring for Yogurt, Kraft Raspberry Flavoring for Yogurt, Kraft Strawberry Flavoring for Yogurt, Kraft Peach Flavoring for Yogurt, Kraft Spiced Apple Flavoring for Yogurt, Kraft Rum Raisin Flavoring for Yogurt

9

PRODUCE SECTION

General

Fruits and vegetables may be purchased in many stages of processing. They are enumerated below.

Fresh[1] Fruits and vegetables which have been picked and packed for delivery in the fresh state. Generally, these have been freed of soil and insects and cooled before packing.

Processed Fruits and vegetables which have undergone some form of treatment to preserve them. These treatments are known as:

Canning: The process of putting food into a container to which enough heat is applied to kill all bacteria. In addition to using high heat to kill bacteria, there are processes used which apply a combination of pressure and lower heat to reduce the boiling point needed to sterilize the product.

Freezing: A process whereby fruits and vegetables are kept at a low enough temperature to prevent spoilage.

Dehydrating: A process by which fruits and vegetables have most of their water extracted.

Drying: A process by which fruits and vegetables, mostly peas, beans and cereal, are allowed to dry naturally or are machine-dried of most of their water content.

Freeze-Drying: A process in which fruits and vegetables are frozen and then dried in a vacuum so that the water content changes from ice to vapor, by-passing the liquid state. There is less damage to products that are freeze-dried than those that are dried or dehydrated.

Dehydro-Freezing: A process by which foods are dehydrated, then frozen.

Irradiation: A process by which the bacteria in foods is killed through exposure to radiation.

All of the above processes compromise the quality of fresh fruits and vegetables. However, it is usually not economically possible to use all fresh produce, and the various types of processing make it possible to serve almost any kind of fruit or vegetable out of its growing season.

There are USDA Standards for Fresh, Canned, Frozen, Dehydrated, and Dried Fruits and Vegetables. This book deals with those standards only, as the supply of Freeze-Dried, Dehydro-Frozen, and Irradiated foods is not a market factor of significance at this time.

Writing the Specifications

An attempt has been made to put together all the pertinent information on all states of processing for each type of fruit or vegetable. The essential grade information on each product in all of its processing states has been placed after the general information on each item. The grade selection may be gleaned from this abbreviated fact page, and the details of the specification will be covered in the pages immediately following.

---

1. *The author is grateful to Mr. R.A. Seelig and the United Fresh Fruit and Vegetable Association for permission to use in this book the data on Uses, Marketing Season, Varieties, Containers, Servings and Weights and Quality from the association's Fruit and Vegetable Facts and Pointers, Fresh Facts, Supply Guide, Serving Costs, Buying, Handling and Using Fresh Fruits and Buying, Handling and Using Fresh Vegetables.*

FRESH FRUITS AND VEGETABLES

A large variety of fresh fruits and vegetables is available at all seasons. It is not unusual for 70 or more distinctly different kinds of fresh produce (not counting the several varieties of each) to be on the market at the same time. During the year, more than 100 kinds of fresh produce are on sale, and if only the main varieties are counted, the number rises to 285.

AVAILABILITY AT ALL SEASONS

Even in mid-winter, a shopper in one of the big supermarkets probably can buy 47 different fresh fruits and vegetables, plus various varieties, and even more in some markets that have extensive produce departments.

The extension of the period of availability is due to such factors as increased production of truck crops in southern areas during the winter and early spring; planting of varieties that have been developed to produce earlier or later than previously; increased imports; improvement in storage methods; and improvements in transportation and terminal distribution which permit the transfer of tender produce for long distances during which they are maintained in good condition. The big change in all these factors has occurred in the last 10 years; further improvements are expected to occur in the future.

SPECIALIZED PRODUCTION

Because of the growing complexity of producing and marketing fresh fruits and vegetables, the trend is away from the very small market garden, or small home orchard, toward concentration in large tracts in areas where soil, climate, and water are most favorable. Big, specialized farms and orchards, run by well-trained operators, are able to take advantage of the most modern equipment, chemicals, and methods. Since costs of labor, material, and capital are rising, increased efficiency in production, packing, and marketing is essential.

While very small acreages far from market are no longer economical, there are still many truck farms of 40 to 60 acres, more or less, that are operated with much success. Orchards somewhat smaller than this are also successful. Many are located close to city markets.

The trend in fruit and vegetable growing is in line with the general trend in agriculture, i.e., toward fewer and larger farms in selected areas.

PACKING

In the last 15 years, a revolution in packing has taken place, and it is continuing. One trend is the elimination of waste parts, such as carrot tops, radish tops, cauliflower jacket leaves, celery tops, and inedible parts of greens. Transportation, material, and labor are so costly that it has become essential not to ship inedible parts when they can be removed at shipping point.

Another trend is toward automatic assembling, filling, and closing of shipping containers. This is coupled with mechanized washing, sorting, and conveying. Automatic checking of color by electronic means is used in some cases.

Almost all bagging of fruits and vegetables at the shipping point, and at repackaging houses at terminals, is done more or less automatically. Commodities are weighed by various mechanical means and are poured into the bag, which is then closed mechanically.

There is a trend toward packing fruits and vegetables in consumer units at the shipping point, then placing the consumer units in a master container for shipment. Not all commodities are suitable (with technology at its present stage) for packaging in small units at places distant from market, but many are.

Another trend apparent in the last few years is a shift from large, heavy shipping packages to smaller ones that are more easily handled. The size and weight of a package is an important consideration in restaurants and other institutions, and in retail stores where they may be lifted by hand.

A great deal of research and experimentation with various kinds of containers, liners, and trays is continuing.

The type of package used is important. It is intended to protect the packed commodity from crushing or bruising;

permit easy stacking and securing in a rail car or truck; permit refrigeration as required; and perform other functions, such as, in some cases, providing an atmosphere low in oxygen or providing chemical inhibition of development of molds. The container needs to be designed for easy assembling, filling, and closing; its weight should be as small as possible; and costs need to be as low as attainable, and still permit requirements to be met.

TRANSPORTATION

Rapid transportation is of major importance in the fresh fruit and vegetable industry. Fresh produce is perishable to highly perishable; it cannot stand long delays, wide variations in temperature, or rough handling. Smooth, rapid movement at well-controlled, suitable temperatures is necessary. Transportation has improved considerably since the turn of the century both as to speed and protection of products from damage. Equipment is much better than it used to be.

On the average, it takes about eight days to haul a carload of fresh produce by rail freight from the West Coast to the East Coast. Express is faster, but it costs more. Trucks are used widely for hauls up to 1500 miles or even farther.

Transportation is one of the major costs of marketing fresh produce and may range from a few percent of the consumer's dollar spent for these products to 20 percent or more. Transportation rates have gone up in line with prices of other services. Rail rates for fresh fruits and vegetables are, in general, about two-thirds higher now than they were in 1945. Truck rates are correspondingly higher.

One of the newer developments is "piggy-backing." A truck is loaded on a special flat car and unloaded at destination ready to roll to its delivery point. Or a truck body or other container, minus wheels, may be loaded in the same way, then placed on a wheeled chassis at the receiving terminal. The Interstate Commerce Commission says trailer-on-flat-car operations are continuing to grow.

Progress is also being made with air transport of fresh fruits and vegetables. Since air transport, in most cases, is more expensive than other types of carriage, it is applicable especially to commodities of relatively high value for their bulk and weight. Development of new jet transports designed for cargoes is expected to stimulate air shipment of highly perishable commodities.

TEMPERATURE CONTROL

The use of refrigeration or other methods of temperature control is on the increase at all stages of fresh fruit and vegetable marketing, from shortly after harvest right through to the consumer. While large quantities of produce are marketed near where they are grown and, as a rule, are not refrigerated en route, vast amounts are moved long distances and must be kept at a suitable temperature to keep them in good condition. This involves cooling or warming of the load, depending on outside temperatures. At the same time, high relative humidity, about 90 percent, is desirable for most commodities to prevent wilting or moisture loss. Humidity in both iced and mechanically refrigerated cars usually is high. Ice, on top of the load or in the package, is used for some commodities, especially the leafy vegetables, to provide added moisture and refrigeration. Evaporation also is reduced by use of film box liners and film bags for both fruits and vegetables.

Applications of Refrigeration

Important applications of refrigeration to fresh fruits and vegetables include pre-cooling before shipment; cooling in short or long storage; air-conditioning of wholesale produce warehouses and retail produce departments; refrigeration of retail displays; storing produce in retail stores; and refrigeration in the home.

PRE-COOLING. As the term implies, pre-cooling is the rapid, initial removal of field heat prior to shipment or storage. This is done as soon after harvest as possible. Tests show that pre-cooling slows the ripening process in fruit and the breakdown process in vegetables, checks development of molds and bacteria, and prolongs the market life of the produce. Various studies have shown that a reduction of 15-18 degrees F. in the temperature of deciduous fruits slows the ripening and the respiration rate by approximately one-half. While the ratio of reduction of temperature to slowing of respiration is not the same for all commodities, it is sufficient to justify pre-cooling of perishables before shipment.

METHODS. Methods of pre-cooling include: 1. placing

packages in an ordinary refrigerated storage room (a slow process and, therefore, not as effective in increasing market life as some other methods); 2. hydro-cooling by means of an ice-cold water spray or water bath (a rapid process); 3. forced-air cooling in a tunnel or specially built room (a fairly rapid means); 4. cooling in refrigerated rail cars or trucks (fast or slow, depending on the process used); 5. vacuum cooling (a rapid process).

HYDRO-COOLING. The most common form of hydro-cooler is a tunnel, constructed of metal sheets, through which the produce to be cooled is passed on a conveyor. Icy water is showered over the unlidded containers of produce. Often a chemical is put into the water as a sterilizing agent. A typical hydro-cooler 31 ft. long by 7 ft. wide, operating efficiently, can reduce the pulp temperature of peaches from 85°F. to 50°F. in 12 to 14 minutes. It cools from 350 to 450 bushels an hour. A well-refrigerated storage room would take about 48 hours to reduce the temperature to the same extent.

VACUUM COOLING. Vacuum cooling can reduce the temperature of lettuce from 73°F. to 33° to 35°F. in 30 minutes. This period of time will cover the entire cycle of operations from placing the lettuce cartons in the vacuum tank to removing them. One plant at Watsonville, Calif. has a cooling capacity of 75 carloads per day. In some plants, the tank will admit a railroad car. The lettuce is loaded ready to ship, and the entire load is cooled in one operation.

The vacuum cooling system is based on two facts: first, that water evaporating from a surface cools the surface; second, that as pressure is decreased, the boiling point of water is reduced. At the boiling point, evaporation is rapid. A vacuum cooler consists of a gas-tight chamber into which the produce is loaded. Pressure in the chamber is then reduced by exhausting air, resulting in rapid evaporation and cooling. A carton of lettuce (40 to 45 lb. net) loses about 2 percent to 2.5 percent of its weight.

Vacuum cooling can be applied to any of the leafy vegetables and also to some other commodities to which a little water can be applied for evaporation.

ICING. One of the common methods of refrigeration of fresh produce is with water ice, which provides both moisture and heat absorption. The ice may be placed in bunkers and air circulated through the load; or ice may be placed in the produce container or blown over the top of the load; or a combination of these methods may be used.

CONTINUOUS REFRIGERATION. Fruits and vegetables that have been refrigerated at shipping point and en route, for best results, should continue under refrigeration at the receiving point. Wholesalers generally have cold rooms which are insulated and mechanically refrigerated. These are known as "holding rooms." They also have special ripening rooms for such commodities as bananas and tomatoes which need to be kept relatively warm and humid until the correct stage of ripeness is reached.

LONG STORAGE. Items such as apples, pears or potatoes may be held for several months in specially built storages. Temperature and other conditions are controlled. The operators have the special knowledge and equipment needed. These storages usually are at shipping point.

DISTRIBUTION

No matter how plentiful and fine fresh fruits and vegetables are in the field or orchard, they would have little value if effective marketing channels did not exist. The function of placing foods where people who want them can buy them is carried out by distributors, the so-called "middle-men." The functions of the distributor are not as well understood by the public as the functions of the producer, leading to misunderstanding as to the value marketing adds to a product.

DISTRIBUTIVE LINKS. The distributive chain in a simple form is grower-to-shipper-to-transportation company-to-wholesaler-to-retailer-to-consumer. The variations, however, are very many and important.

The produce may be packed, shipped, and sold by a cooperative agency owned by the growers. A broker may buy at shipping point for a distant receiver; the commodities may be serviced by a packing and cooling agency; the produce may be stored for later sale either in a general storage warehouse or a specialized house; it may be packaged in consumer units at shipping point or shipped for repacking at the terminal.

It may be shipped directly to a buyer in a terminal market, or it may occasionally be shipped as a "roller," to be sold while en route and diverted to the buyer. It may be shipped on consignment to a receiver who sells it and then deducts a service charge or commission. It may be shipped to an auction house which sells it to the highest bidder. It may be handled through a broker at its destination.

Produce also may be shipped to a service wholesaler who buys for his own account and who warehouses, stores, ripens, repacks as necessary, and delivers to retail stores. The ultimate distributor, for example a retail chain, may buy commodities in the field or orchard, or at the packing house, and handle them all the way through the stores, even transporting them long distances in its own trucks.

Repackers may buy commodities by the carload for delivery to their warehouses, or buy at auction or at the terminal market, and then repack items in consumer-size packages for retailers.

According to a recent study, about 26 percent of fresh fruits and vegetables in 23 principal markets were shipped directly to central warehouses of retailers. Most of the remainder apparently were shipped to produce terminals, where many wholesalers are grouped in one area, or to individual wholesale warehouses outside the terminals.

These are only a few of the complex distribution channels which have developed.

LICENSED DEALERS. Wholesale distribution of fresh produce is largely carried on by about 25,000 licensed dealers. Under the Perishable Agricultural Commodities Act, all commission merchants, brokers and dealers, buying or selling fresh fruits and vegetables in wholesale or jobbing quantities in interstate commerce, must have a license from the U.S. Dept. of Agriculture. All licensed dealers must carry on their business under the requirements of the Act.

Those who violate this law, for example by failure to pay promptly for produce they have purchased and which has been delivered in accordance with the contract, can be called to account under the PAC Act. If necessary, the license of a dealer can be suspended or revoked by the Secretary of Agriculture. In the absence of a license, the dealer cannot continue in business.

TRADING RULES. Under the PAC Act, trading rules are laid down. Since dealers are operating under known rules enforceable by law, they can deal quickly at a distance. Marketing terms are defined under the Act so that a specific and binding agreement for sale of large quantities of fresh produce can be made with a few words. The rules and the enforcement machinery have helped to speed up buying and selling of fresh produce. This is important because delays can cause great loss of perishable products.

DEALERS APPROVE. Reliable firms in the trade express their approval of the PAC Act and the way it is administered by the USDA. The Act has helped raise business standards in the fresh fruit and vegetable industry to a relatively high level.

BROKERS. The broker is a middleman who does not take title to merchandise, rather his principal function is to bring buyer and seller together. He transacts business in the name of this principal function. He deals in large units, which in the case of fruits and vegetables is the carload or truckload. Brokers are generally classified as buying brokers and selling brokers.

The broker takes a commission, for instance $25 or $35 per car, or so much per package, depending on value.

AUCTIONS. Fresh fruits and vegetables are sold at auction at some shipping points and at some terminal markets. The auction operates at high speed and in a spectacular way. The auctioneers call for bids, each in his own special sing-song, almost hypnotic fashion. They know each buyer in the room and instantly recognize his bid signal, which may be a word or gesture. The hammer bangs down to sell the lot to the highest bidder. If bids are slow in coming on any lot, the auctioneer may pass it and go on to another, returning later to the slow lot. Everything possible is done to sell fast.

Onlookers unfamiliar with auctions usually cannot make head or tail of the proceedings. No merchandise is in sight.

The buyers work from lists of the merchandise which they have previously inspected. The seasoned buyers have no difficulty in following the rapid-fire offers.

New York City, Chicago, Philadelphia, Boston, Cleveland, St. Louis and Detroit have auctions that operate all year.

WHOLESALING. Wholesale trade in fresh fruits and vegetables is carried on by 9,554 establishments, including 6,291 merchant wholesalers, 986 merchandise agents and brokers, and 2,227 assemblers of farm products. These establishments had total sales of $6.4 billion in the census year.

The 6,291 classified as "merchant wholesalers" buy and sell largely for their own account, that is, they own the merchandise.

About 23 percent of the wholesale operators are packing houses, assemblers and buyers who buy from, or pack for, farmers, and ship to the wholesale markets or the warehouses of retailers.

Wholesaling (aside from packing and shipping) accounts for about 10 percent of the consumer's dollar spent for fresh fruits and vegetables.

In 1959, fresh fruit and vegetable wholesalers operated at a net profit on net sales of 1.2 percent as a median, according to a Dun and Bradstreet survey of records of 49 wholesalers.

The wholesaler's general function is to assemble merchandise in large lots, mostly carlots or trucklots, and then store, reassemble and sell to retailers, in accordance with their requirements. There is wide variation in service given by wholesalers. Some sell only to those who come to their stores and truck away the fruits and vegetables they buy. Others give a wide range of services.

SERVICE WHOLESALER. A merchant wholesaler whose functions are not too well understood is the service wholesaler. The word "service" indicates that he does more than just buy and sell. He also warehouses, delivers, extends credit, provides market information, may send out salesmen, and may, when necessary, aid retail customers with their merchandising.

The customers of service wholesalers are varied. They include independent retailers, voluntary and cooperative associations of retailers, chain stores, and institutions such as restaurants and hospitals.

Ordinarily a service wholesaler has both rail and truck docks; receives merchandise in carload or truckload lots; has common and refrigerated storage areas; banana ripening rooms; tomato ripening rooms; and often has facilities for packaging produce in consumer units. The service wholesaler maintains large and small trucks and may serve an area within a radius of 100 or more miles. A firm may serve several hundred stores and institutions.

RESTAURANTS AND MASS FEEDING INSTITUTIONS. According to the Bureau of Labor Statistics, about 17 percent of all food is consumed away from home, that is, in restaurants or other eating places, large scale feeding establishments such as in-plant cafeterias, and in public and private institutions such as hospitals.

Large restaurants and institutional eating places buy their fresh fruits and vegetables from service wholesalers specializing in these commodities or from restaurant and hotel supply houses that handle an extensive line of both fresh and processed commodities of all kinds. Smaller restaurants often buy from these retailers.

WASTE AND LOSS

Despite all the advances made in growing, harvesting, storing, and distributing fresh fruits and vegetables, a large amount of waste still occurs. Some waste is inevitable, as in eliminating culls and in trimming vegetables for marketing, but much waste can be prevented or reduced. Great strides have been made in combatting losses in growing due to pests, such as insects, weeds, rodents, nematodes, fungi, and bacterial and viral organisms. Losses in marketing also have been greatly reduced by improved temperature control, better packages, faster transportation, and use of chemicals to inhibit development of molds and bacteria. Waxing some items has cut down loss of moisture and preserved them longer.

Loss in the marketing process, aside from normal trimming of vegetables for display, still is heavy. USDA has estimated that of the fruit sent to market, 11 percent is lost during the marketing process. The loss figure given for vegetables is 8 percent. Such a loss would amount to $424 million worth of vegetables and $308 million worth of fruit, a total of $732 million a year.

While all general loss figures are necessarily estimates, various detailed studies of losses of particular items indicate these estimates are conservative.

STANDARD GRADES AND INSPECTION

A buyer can purchase a carload or many carloads of fresh fruits and vegetables in a few minutes from someone thousands of miles away and know what he is getting after a phone call or a brief message on the teletype. This can be done because there are federal standard grades and packs, as well as state standards, and federally approved trade terms and definitions that apply to these perishable products.

In addition, a system of federal and state inspection is provided both to protect the public and to avoid the innumerable disputes that might otherwise arise between buyer and seller as to grade, quality, and condition of fresh produce.

CONTRACT. Each time a buyer and a seller of fresh produce close a deal, they have made a binding and enforceable contract, even though no detailed contract has been written and signed. An exchange of short, confirmatory messages by telegram or teletype accomplishes the same purpose as a lengthy document.

This is possible because such a brief statement, for example, as "U.S. Extra Number 1 topped Carrots" has a definite and detailed meaning known to buyer and seller and stated in the standards published by the U.S. Dept. of Agriculture. A federal or state inspector, examining a shipment of carrots, can determine whether they actually are of the stated grade.

About 40 percent of all shipments of fresh fruits and vegetables are officially inspected, mostly at shipping point. In many cases, inspection is a regular routine procedure.

The fee for inspection is paid by the party ordering inspection. The fee is based on the quantity and number of kinds of commoditites to be inspected.

Arrangements are also made, if desired, for continuous inspection of fresh fruits and vegetables at the packing plant. Such packages may then be labeled with the U.S. shield with the wording "Packed under continuous inspection of the U.S. Department of Agriculture."

The inspection fees cover the government's costs for giving this service.

VOLUNTARY GRADING. Use of the U.S. Standards and use of the inspection service is generally voluntary, but may be compulsory under certain circumstances. Under provisions of the Marketing Agreement Act of 1937, authority is granted for restriction of shipments of produce by grade, size, or maturity where marketing agreements are in effect. These agreements are adopted by vote of those concerned. Grading and inspection of certain products has been made compulsory in areas which have adopted marketing agreements and orders.

COMPULSORY GRADING. Laws of some states require grading of various fresh fruits and vegetables in accordance with official U.S. standards or state grades. A few states also require inspection of some products.

The Export Apple and Pear Act makes it unlawful to ship apples or pears in the fresh state to foreign countries in carlot quantities, unless they meet certain minimum grades prescribed by the Secretary of Agriculture.

WHAT GRADES PROVIDE. The grades prescribe and define quality terms such as "U.S. Fancy," "U.S. Extra No. 1," "U.S. No. 1," "U.S. Combination," and "U.S. No. 2." Grades may specify size, maturity, color, cleanliness, shape, freedom from specified injuries or damage, interior structure of the fruit or vegetable, absence of seedstems, or any other factor of quality. The grades also set up tolerances, that is, percentages of permissible variations from any specification. Tolerances are necessary because in commercial practice it is impossible to pack fruits or vegetables to meet specifications 100 percent.

As a rule, U.S. No. 1 grade represents good, average

quality that is practicable to pack under commercial conditions. Usually, under normal growing conditions, more than half of a crop will be of U.S. No. 1 grade. The designation "U.S. No. 2" ordinarily represents the quality of the lowest grade that is deemed practicable to pack under normal conditions. Superior products are packed "U.S. Fancy" or "U.S. Extra No. 1."

Grades are worked out by USDA in response to requests of those interested. The policy of the department is not to issue standards for official use until they are considered practicable and workable.

Congressional action in 1913 paved the way for the promulgation in 1917 of the first standards for fruits and vegetables. Potatoes were the first product for which standards were adopted.

The inspection service started in 1918 when Congress provided for inspection at receiving markets. In 1922 Congress extended the service to shipping points. Inspection offices now are maintained in 78 of the larger cities throughout the continental U.S., 1 in Puerto Rico, 1 in Hawaii.

INSPECTION PROCEDURE. Inspectors are trained men thoroughly conversant with grades and with all fruits and vegetables. Some specialize in certain products, but all are licensed to inspect any fresh fruit or vegetable.

The inspector uses a random sampling procedure. He selects a number of boxes at random from the sorting line, or the car, or lot, and from each box examines a representative number of items, also selected at random. The sampling is large enough to make it reasonably certain that it reflects the quality of the entire lot.

The inspector notes findings as to each item inspected. If he finds the samples lack uniformity, he will inspect more of the merchandise than he would otherwise. Upon completion of his examination, he totals his scores of various defects and calculates percentages of defects. He makes up a worksheet and report, and from the report makes up an inspection certificate. He notes the condition of the car; how it is loaded; how it is iced; what the pack is, and the quality and condition of the merchandise.

Federal inspection certificates are prima facie evidence in any court of law.

GRADE, CONDITION, AND QUALITY. A distinction should be noted with regard to the terms "grade," "condition," and "quality." "Grade," as used by the USDA, is the sum of the characteristics of a commodity at the time it is graded, and includes both quality and condition. "Quality" denotes those characteristics that are relatively permanent, such as shape, solidity, color, maturity, and freedom from insect damage. "Condition" relates to factors that may change, such as decay and firmness. If a commodity grades, for example, "U.S. Extra Fancy" when packed, it means that it not only has the quality characteristics of the grade, but is in good condition within the meaning of the grade, that is, has no factor of poor condition outside the tolerances permitted.

A product that grades "U.S. Extra Fancy" when packed may, after a long journey or careless handling, be found out of grade due to its condition.

FRESH FRUITS

Here are important factors to specify for fresh fruits.

GRADE. When you specify a U.S. grade, such as "U.S. No. 1," it has definite, detailed meaning which makes it unnecessary to write out the details. A full set of U.S. grade standards for fresh fruits and vegetables can be obtained free by writing the Fresh Products Standardization Section, Agricultural

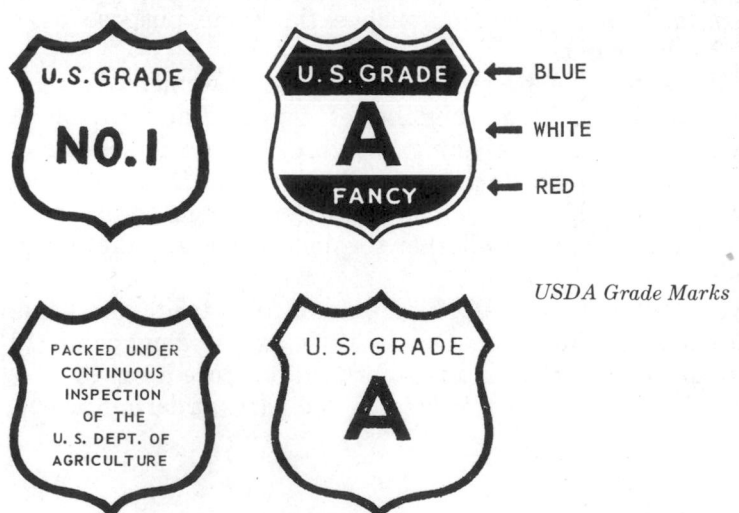

USDA Grade Marks

Marketing Service, Washington, D.C. 20250. In using grades, however, it should be noted that there can be quite a range of quality within the grade, due to tolerances provided in the grade. Also, U.S. No. 1, though it is the highest grade for some commodities, is a lower grade for others. Higher grades include U.S. Extra Fancy, U.S. Fancy, and U.S. Extra No. 1. The buyer should at all times specify that fruit must be up to the desirable grade at delivery, and not merely at the time it was shipped.

QUALITY. Grade alone does not necessarily define all the quality factors the restaurateur is interested in in buying a fruit for a certain purpose. The buyer should specify any additional factors as necessary.

VARIETY. In almost every instance it is necessary to specify variety because there are considerable differences which make one variety suitable for one purpose and another for a different purpose. Thus, Delicious apples might be wanted for table service or salads but would not be suitable for baking.

SIZE. In almost all instances it is important to indicate size. The end use will determine what size is needed. The medium sizes generally cost more per package than either the very small or very large, because mediums are more in demand. However, if a whole fruit is to be served, obviously a large fruit will cost more than a much smaller one. Size is usually indicated by the count in a standard container, the lowest counts meaning the largest sizes.

QUANTITY. Quantity should be stated in precise terms appropriate to the commodity. In the case of strawberries, it could be 30 12-pt. trays. In the case of watermelons, it could be 12 melons, average 30 lb. each. In the case of bananas, it could be 10 40-lb. cartons, also specifying the size of the bananas as small, medium, or large.

BRAND. It is advisable to specify brands when possible, because fruits packed under some labels are consistently good. Judging labels requires experience, but the suppliers can help on this.

GROWING AREA. Fruit from one area may be much different than fruit from another, so it is often desirable to specify the source from which the fruit is wanted. For example, because of climatic conditions, pears of the Far West are superior to those of the East.

WHAT ABOUT PRICE?

Price is important, but the buyer shopping on the basis of price only is likely to be a poor buyer. If he gets consistently low prices, he is also going to get consistently low quality and service. Fruit and vegetable dealers are as smart as the buyers, and they are not going to give something for nothing. Also, the price-only buyer tends to buy a little from one dealer and a little from another, splitting up his purchases so much that he may not be a profitable customer for anyone. Thus he does not merit the attention and co-operation that others may deserve and get. It is axiomatic in the trade that produce offered as a bargain is likely to be anything but.

INSPECTION

When fruit is delivered, it should be inspected at once to ensure that it is of the kind, quantity, variety, grade, size, pack, and of any special quality that has been ordered. It is not necessary to remove and check every piece to make an adequate inspection. Professional inspectors of the U.S. Dept. of Agriculture do not do that. A random spot check of a reasonable number of samples from a reasonable number of packages is all that is necessary. Over-inspection means over-handling and increases damage. If fruit has been ordered by brand, check the trademarks to see if they conform. Check for ripeness. What is found may make it necessary to change plans as to when certain items will be served. Some fruits, such as pears, bananas, cantaloup, and avocados, if too firm, as they usually are, will be much improved by holding at room temperature until they are at the best stage for eating.

ADEQUATE CARE

When good money has been spent to buy high quality fruits to serve discriminating customers, it is only good sense to spend some time and effort to give the fruits the right care. Here are the general rules:

INSIST ON GENTLE HANDLING. It is not unusual for those who deliver fruits, as well as those who handle the packages in the foodservice operation, to be rough. It takes supervision, explanation, and a rather firm policy and follow-up to induce all concerned to place rather than to drop fruit packages. They should never be thrown or pushed roughly across the floor. They should be handled the same as a crate of eggs. It will be easier to persuade workers to handle the fruit carefully if backbreaking labor is eliminated by provision of suitable materials-handling equipment, such as 2-wheel hand trucks, a 4-wheel, bar-handle truck, semi-live skids and jack, a conveyor, or whatever the particular situation and volume handled calls for.

HANDLE AS LITTLE AS POSSIBLE. Attention should be given to receiving and routing fruit efficiently so that it need not be removed repeatedly. This takes planning. No rule can be given, but certainly new fruit should not be stacked on top of older fruit or in such a way as to block efforts to reach and use the older fruit first. The rule should be first in, first out. Dating each package on receipt is a help.

AVOID LETTING FRUIT STAND IN DANGER AREAS. When fruit is received, it is sometimes allowed to stand almost any place before it is put in storage, and damage can result. A bad place, for example, is near a hot radiator, on a wet floor, or on a receiving platform in extreme cold, heat, or wind. If fruit is to be refrigerated, it should be moved into the cold room without delay.

STACK PACKAGES ACCORDING TO THEIR SHAPE AND WEIGHT. Stack so that the pressure comes on the structure of the package, not on the fruit. Some packages are properly stacked on their bottoms, some on their sides, and some on end. Bulge packs should not be stacked on the bulge because that brings crushing pressure on the fruit. In general, keep stacks low for ease of handling and to avoid excessive pressure on the lower layers.

TEMPERATURE, HUMIDITY, AND VENTILATION. Fresh fruits are alive. In a sense they "breathe," taking up oxygen and giving off carbon dioxide and other products such as ethylene. They generate heat which must be removed to maintain low temperatures. Fruits should be stacked so that air can circulate around the packages. No one rule as to temperature can be given.

It is recognized that most foodservice operations do not have facilities for keeping different kinds of produce at different temperatures and humidities. In most cases, the choice is simply between keeping a commodity refrigerated or at room temperature, and the refrigeration may be around 45°F. For brief periods, such as one or two days, neither exact temperature nor humidity is important, but for long periods proper control of both is essential. However, it should be noted that it is unwise to expose some fruits, such as bananas or avocados, to such low temperatures as 32°F. or thereabouts, for even a short time. Quality is adversely affected.

FRESH VEGETABLES

FRESHNESS

Specify and insist on freshness. If vegetables are wilted or stale, they should be rejected regardless of "bargain" prices. Check how well the original characteristics of the vegetable, such as bright, lovely color; crispness; good weight for size; good shape; lack of mechanical damage, and absence of decay have been preserved. Fresh vegetables are living, breathing organisms. Their life processes go on after harvest until death and decay. They use oxygen and give off heat. They gradually lose water. Retention of freshness requires lowering their temperature to retard the life processes and, in most cases — but not all, keeping humidity high to conserve moisture.

Vegetables that are warm on arrival should be considered suspect even if visible wilting has not yet occurred. The useful life of most vegetables is much shortened by allowing them to stay warm even for a few hours. (Exceptions include sweet potatoes, white potatoes, tomatoes, and others.)

SEASONALITY

Vegetables bought very early or very late in their season—except sweet corn which is often at its best in early and late periods—need to be bought with extra care. They will most certainly be high in price but will not necessarily on that account be of high quality. Generally, vegetables are lower in price and are likely to be of better quality and flavor when they are in season. Check the availability chart.

A precise, detailed guide to availability and sources of each commodity by months is the annual USDA report on Fresh Fruit and Vegetable Unload Totals for 41 cities. Any large scale buyer should have this at his fingertips. It is free from the USDA, Washington, D.C. 20250.

PRICE

The best buyer is not necessarily the one who gets everything for the least money. Instead, he is the one who buys vegetables best suited to the particular use to which they are to be put and which please customers. Experience shows the cheapest vegetables often may not be the best value. Price needs to be balanced against such factors as freshness, tenderness, shape and appearance, size, trim loss, and total waste.

GRADE

The U.S. and state standard grades are a handy tool for the buyer. Instead of detailing lengthy specifications, he can ask for U.S. No. 1 celery or U.S. 1 cauliflower. He should specify that it must meet the grade at time of delivery to his recieving room. A vegetable that met the grade at shipping point might be below grade later. The purchaser can add any special requirements, as for example, he may want pascal celery of a particular size from a preferred area; or he may want to specify film-wrapped cauliflower minus the jacket leaves and ribs. A set of the U.S. vegetable standards is available free from the Fruit and Vegetable Division, USDA, Washington, D.C. 20250.

VARIETY

For most vegetables, varietal distinctions are unimportant and are little used in institutional buying. Type but not variety is of considerable importance. Thus "pascal" is not a varietal name for celery but a type designation. "Danish" cabbage designates a type and so does "domestic round." Variety is more important for potatoes, but even so, type and origin is of more consequence. Even experts have trouble picking varieties out of a jumbled pile of many varieties of potatoes. In instances where variety is important, it is discussed under the vegetable subject heading.

SIZE

If size is important for a particular use, as it often is, it should be definitely specified. Such terms as "small" or "large" should only be used if these are defined in a standard grade specified in your order. Otherwise, size should be stated in terms such as length, or diameter, or in terms of the number of units in a standard pack, such as 24s in lettuce, or weight, such as 20 to 25 lb. watermelons.

PACKAGING

Vegetables are available in many kinds of containers and packs, with different net weights, as well as different degrees of protection. The buyer should specify a container suitable for his purpose. For example, an institution probably would want brussels sprouts in a 25-lb. drum or carton rather than in a crate or tray containing pint cups. Information on containers and net weights and other data on weights and measures for many products is available in Statistical Bulletin 362, Conversion Factors and Weights and Measures, U.S. Dept. of Agriculture, available from the Department.

PARTIALLY PREPARED VEGETABLES

Local produce suppliers, in many cases, are offering foodservice buyers a number of fresh vegetables in partially prepared form. Most universally available are pre-peeled potatoes, often marketed as peeled, whole; peeled and cut to various French fry sizes and styles; peeled and sliced for cottage fries; peeled, cut, and blanched for French fires. Other items offered by some suppliers include washed, cut, and mixed salad greens; coleslaw mixes; peeled, diced, sliced, or shredded carrots; washed and cut spinach; peeled, sliced, and chopped onions; peeled and sliced or diced turnips and parsnips.

These partially prepared vegetables are not available everywhere at present, but *they can be* if the produce dealers are made aware of the need.

INSPECTION

When vegetables are delivered, they should be inspected at once to make sure they are the kind, quantity, grade, size, pack, brand, or of any special quality that has been ordered. Inspection should be by random sampling. It is wasteful of time and harmful to the products to unpack and repack everything in order to check each item. Professional inspection services use the sampling method.

HANDLING CARE

While most vegetables need low temperature and high humidity during any holding period, there are exceptions, so

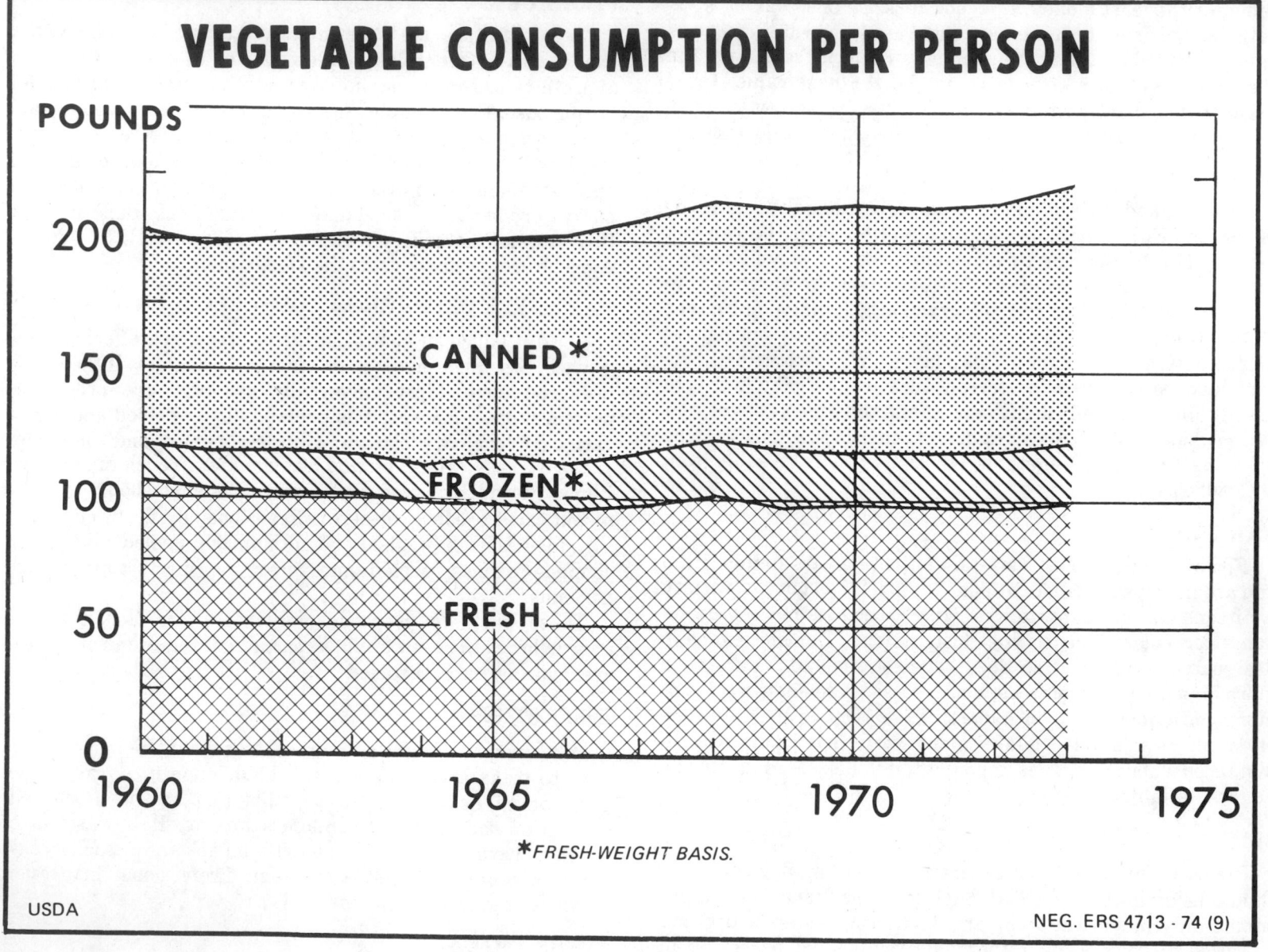

VEGETABLE CONSUMPTION PER PERSON

POUNDS

200

150

CANNED*

100

FROZEN*

50

FRESH

0

1960   1965   1970   1975

*FRESH-WEIGHT BASIS.

USDA   NEG. ERS 4713 - 74 (9)

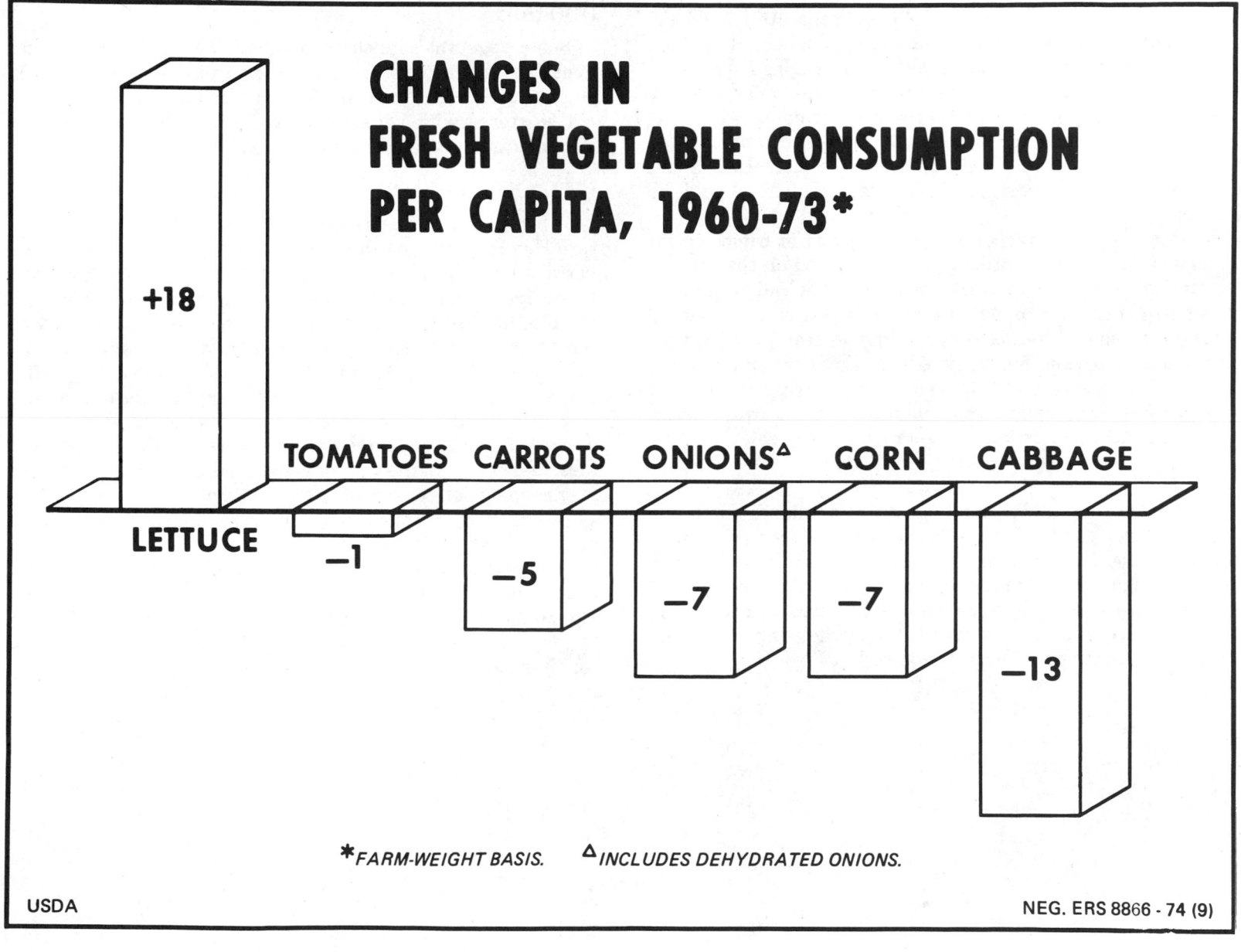

CHANGES IN FRESH VEGETABLE CONSUMPTION PER CAPITA, 1960-73*

+18

LETTUCE

TOMATOES   CARROTS   ONIONS△   CORN   CABBAGE

−1

−5

−7

−7

−13

*FARM-WEIGHT BASIS.   △INCLUDES DEHYDRATED ONIONS.

USDA

NEG. ERS 8866 - 74 (9)

each needs to be considered carefully and separately. All have in common the need for careful and knowledgeable handling. None should be banged around, thrown, or dropped. The term "hardware" is sometimes applied to such vegetables as potatoes and cabbage, but it is a false term. Much damage and loss results from the mistaken idea that some items can be handled roughly without harm. Handlers should be instructed about the need for gentleness, and this requirement should be enforced.

Vegetables should not be allowed to stand in frigid winter or high summer temperatures or in high wind on the loading dock or be placed temporarily next to a hot radiator or be allowed to stand in a puddle of water. Upon receipt and inspection, all should be placed promptly in storage with suitable temperature and humidity. All should have some ventilation space, not be tightly stacked, because fresh vegetables generate heat and need air movement to carry it away. Green leafy vegetables, in particular, generate a lot of heat.

STACKING

Crates, cartons, and other vegetable containers should be stacked properly to avoid pressure on the produce itself and to avoid toppling. Packages that have a bulge should be stacked to keep weight off the bulge. Height of stacks should be low enough to prevent crushing weight on the bottom packages. If vegetables are to be high stacked, then palletizing with suitable support for upper stacks is required.

ODORS

Some vegetables, such as onions, give off odors that can penetrate and incorporate with other products such as butter, eggs, and cheese. Products that pick up odors readily should not be stored with vegetables even if their temperature requirements happen to be compatible.

LIFE AND STORAGE

A booklet on storage temperatures (such as USDA Agriculture Handbook 66) gives data on the length of storage under certain conditions of temperature and humidity. However, these figures cannot be applied to vegetables as received at the foodservice operation. Their life has been shortened by their trip through the marketing process. Unless it is known that vegetables have been rapidly cooled immediately after harvest and have been kept at satisfactory temperatures, long storage is not desirable, except in the case of vegetables that do not have critical temperature requirements, such as potatoes; and except in the case of vegetables that naturally have a long keeping period, such as topped carrots.

It is recognized that foodservice operations, in most cases, cannot provide finely adjusted temperatures or humidity ranges required for different vegetables, and this is not necessary for brief periods. However, optimum temperature and humidity for commercial storage are quoted in this report to give the reader a yardstick for measuring the storage conditions he can provide.

CONTAINER NET WEIGHTS

Commodity	Containers	Net Weight [lb.] [Approximate]
Anise	Sturdee crt. and wbd.	40-50
	Crt. 24	35-40
Apples	Ctn. tray pk. or cell pk.	40-45
	Ctn. bulk	36-42
Apricots	Brentwood log	24-26
	LA lug tight fill	27-30
Artichokes	7 in. deep ctn.	20-25
Asparagus	Pyramid crt.	32
	Ctn. 16 1½-lb. pkgs.	24
	2-lyr. ctn.	28-30
	1-lyr. flat	14-18
Bananas	Ctn.	40
	Ctn.	20
Beans, Snap	Wbd. crt.	28-30
	Ctn.	28-30
	Bu. hmpr.	28-30
Beets, bchd.	Wbd. crt. 24 bchs.	36-40
Beets, topped	Film or mesh bag	50
	1-lb. bags in master	24
Berries (misc.) Raspberries Blackberries	12-½ pts. on tray	5½-7½
Blueberries	12-pt. tray	11-12
Broccoli	Pony crt.	40-42
	Ctn. or crt. 14 bchs.	20-23
Brussels Sprouts	Drum	25
	Flat 12 10-oz. cups	7½-8
	Ctn.	25

Commodity	Containers	Net Wegith [lb.] [Approximate]
Cabbage	Crt. or ctn.	50-55
	Bag, mesh, paper	50-60
	Wbd. crt.	50
Cantaloupe	Jumbo crt. 18-45	80-85
	Std. crt.	70-80
	Ctn. 9, 12, 18, 23	38-41
Carrots, bchd.	Ctn. 2-doz. bchs.	23-27
Carrots, topped	48 1-lb. film bags in ctn. or wbd. crt.	50
	Bulk in mesh film lined bag	50
Casabas	Ctn. 4, 5, 6	32-34
	Flat crt. 5, 6	48-51
Cauliflower	Ctn. 12-16 trimmed, wrpd.	18-24
	Catskill or LI wbd. crt.	45-50
Celeriac	24 1-lb. bags in master	24
	LA lug	30
	Sack	50
Celery, bchd.	Fla. wbd. crt.	55-60
	Calif. wbd. crate.	60-65
Celery, hearts	12 film bags in crt.	24-28
	Wbd. crts. 24	30
Cherries	Calex lug	18-20
	Campbell lug	15-16
	Lug, loose pack	12-14
Chinese Cabbage	Wbd. crt.	50

Abbreviations: * weight not available; bchd., bunched; bskt., basket; bu., bushel; crt., crate; ctn., carton; contr., container; hmpr., hamper; lb., pound; lyr., layer; oz., ounce; pk., pack; pkg., package; pt., pint; sk., sack; std., standard; var., various; wbd., wirebound; wrpd., wrapped.

[Cont.]

CONTAINER NET WEIGHTS [Cont.]

Commodity	Containers	Net Weight [lb.] [Approximate]
Coconuts	Burlap bag 40, 50	75-80
Cranberries	Ctn. 24 1-lb. bags or boxes	24
Cranshaws	Ctn. 4, 5, 6, 8	30-33
Cucumbers	1-1/9 bu. wbd. crt.	55
	Bu. bskt. or ctn.	47-55
	LA Lug	28-32
	Ctn.	26-30
Cucumbers, Greenhouse	Ctn.	8-10
Eggplant	Bu. bskt. or crt.	30-34
	1-1/9 bu. wbd. crt.	35
	LA lug 18-24	20-22
Endive - Escarole	Sturdee crt.	30-36
	Wbd. crt. and ctn.	30-36
	1-1/9 bu. wbd. crt.	25-30
Figs	1-lyr. tray	5-6
	1-lyr. tray	10-15
Garlic	Crt. and ctn.	30
	Sack	50
	LA lug	20-22
Grapefruit, Fla.	4/5 bu. ctn. or wbd. crt.	42½
	Bags, 4, 5, 8, 20 lb.	
Grapefruit, West	Ctn.	32-33½
	6-8 bags in master	48
Grapes, table	Lug or ctn.	24-28
	Lug 16, 22, 24, wrpd bchs.	22
Grapes, juice	Lug	36-44

Commodity	Containers	Net Weight [lb.] [Approximate]
Greens	Bu. bskt. or crt.	20-25
Mustard	Bu. bskt. or crt.	25
Turnip Tops	Bu. bskt. or crt.	25
Greens	1½ bu. wbd. crt.	30-35
Honeydews	Ctn. 4 or 5	29-32
	Flat crt.	40-45
	Jumbo flat crt. 6-8	45-50
Leeks	4/5 bu. wbd. crt.	25-30
Lemons	Ctn.	38
Lettuce, Bibb	12 qt. bskt.	5
Lettuce, Hot House	Bskt. (2 sizes)	5-10
Lettuce, Iceberg	Ctn.	40-45
Lettuce, Boston	Eastern crt. 1-1/9 bu. wbd.	20-25
Lettuce, Romaine	1-1/9 bu. wbd. crt.	30
	Ctn. 2-doz.	35
	Bu. bskt.	25-28
Lettuce, Looseleaf	Var. contrs. 2-doz.	20-25
Limes	Flat or ctn.	10-11
	Box or ctn.	40-41
Mangoes	Flat var. sizes	12-17
	Box or ctn.	32-36
Mushrooms	Flat 12 4½-oz. cups	4½-5
	Ctn. 4 2½-lb. bskts.	10
	Ctn. 8 2½-lb. contrs.	20-21
	4 qt. bskt.	3
	Var. contrs. of 1-lb. ctn.	*

[Cont.]

relevant

CONTAINER NET WEIGHTS [Cont.]

Commodity	Containers	Net Weight [lb.] [Approximate]	Commodity	Containers	Net Weight [lb.] [Approximate]
Nectarines	Sanger lug or 2-lyr. ctn. tray pack	19-22	Parsnips	Sack, film or mesh	50
	LA lug 2-lyr.	22-29		LA lug	30
	4-bskt. crt.	28-32		Bu. bskt	50
				Film bag	25
Okra	Bu. bskt. or crt.	30	Peaches	½ bu. wbd. crt. or ctn.	23-28
	LA lug	18		LA lug, 2-lyr.	22-29
	5/9 bu. wbd. flat	18		¾ bu. ctn. wbd. crt. or bsk.	35-42
Onions, dry	Sack	50		Sanger lug 2-lyr.	19-22
	Ctn.	48-50	Pears	Western box, lug and tight-filled ctn.	45-48
	Film bags 1½, 2, 3, 5, 10 lb. in master contr.	*		Ctn., tight-filled	36
				LA lug or 2-lyr. ctn.	21-26
Onions, green	Ctns. 4-doz. bchs.	15-18			
	Wbd. crt. 8-doz. bchs.	35-40	Peas, green	Bu. bskt. or hmpr.	28-30
				Wbd. bu. crt.	28-30
Oranges, Fla.	4/5 bu. ctn.	45			
			Peppers, Sweet	Ctn.	28-34
Oranges, Fla.	4/5 bu. ctn.	45		1-1/9 bu. crt.	28-33
	4/5 bu. wbd. box.	45		Bu. bskt. or crt.	28-30
	Also consumer bags 4, 5, 8, 20-lb.				
			Peppers, Chili	LA lug or ctn., loose pk	16-25
Oranges, West	Ctn.	37½			
	8 5-lb. film bags in mastr. contr.	40	Persians	Ctn. 4, 5, 6	*
				Flat crt.	35-50
Oriental vegetables	LA lug	26-28			
	Wbd. crt.	20-22	Persimmons	Lug 2-lyr. tray pk.	20-25
				Flat 1-lyr. tray pk.	9-12
Papayas	Ctn.	10			
			Pineapples	Crt. or ctn.	35
Parsley	Bu. bskt.	21		1-lyr. flat 4, 5, 6	18-20
	Ctn. 5-doz. bchs.	21		2-lyr. flat 8, 10, 12	36-40
	1-1/9 bu. wbd. crt. 5-doz.	21			
			Plums	4-bskt. crt.	24-32
Parsley Root	Sack, film or mesh	50		Sanger, 2-lyr. lug tray pack	18-22
	LA lug	30		LA lug	27-30
	Film bag	25		Ctn. loose	26-30
			Pomegranates	Lug 2-lyr. place pk.	23-26

[Cont.]

CONTAINER NET WEIGHTS [Cont.]

Commodity	Containers	Net Weight [lb.] [Approximate]
Potatoes	Sack	100
	Sack or ctn.	50
	5 10-lb. sks. baled	50
	10 5-lb. sks. baled	50
Prunes, Fresh	NW prune lug	15
	NW prune lug	12
	½ bu. bskt.	28-30
Radishes, Topped	Ctn. of 30 6-oz. bags	11¼-11½
	Film bag, bulk	25
	12-qt. bskt. 30 6-oz. bags	11¼-11½
	Film bag, bulk	40
Bchd.	Ctn. or crt. 4-5 doz. bchs.	30-40
Rhubarb	Case 10 5-lb. ctns.	50
	Ctn.	20
	Western apple box	35
Rutabagas	Sack	50
Spinach	Bu. bskt. or crt.	18-25
	Ctn. 2-doz. bchs.	20-22
	Wbd. crt.	20-22
Sweet Corn	Wbd. crt.	40-60
	Mesh or multiwall bag	45-50
Sweet Potatoes	Ctn.	40
	Bu. bskt. or crt.	50
Tangelos	Fla. 4/5 bu. ctn. or wbd. crt.	45
	Calif. ctn.	30

Commodity	Containers	Net Weight [lb.] [Approximate]
Tangerines	Fla. 4/5 bu. wbd. crt.	45
	Calif. ctn. and lug	23-30
	Fla. ctn.	30
Tomatoes	Ctn. or wbd. crt.	40
	LA lug	30-34
	Flats, ctns., 2-lyr.	20-23
	Lugs and ctns., 3-lyr.	30-33
	8-qt. bskt.	9-11
	12-qt. bskt.	18-20
Cherry	12 bskt. tray	16-18
Squash, small	Bu. bskt. or crt.	40-45
	1-1/9 bu. wbd. crt.	44
	½ bu. wbd. crt.	21
	Ctn. or LA lug	24
Squash, large	Bulk bins, var. sizes	900-2000
Strawberries	12 pt. cups in tray	11-12
Topped Root Vegetables	Sack or bu. bskt.	50
	Film or mesh bag	25
	LA lug	30
	1-lb. bags, 24 per master	24
Turnips, Topped	Sack	50
	Mesh or film bag	24
	LA lug	30
Bchd.	Bu. bskt. or crt.	29
Watercress	Ctn. 2-doz. bchs.	*
Watermelons	Var. bulk bins	800-2000
	Ctns. 3, 4, 5	55-80

A GLOSSARY OF FRUIT TERMS*

Blossom End—The opposite end from the stem end. The stem end will have a scar or remains of the stem to identify it. The blossom end is often more rounded than the stem end.

Breakdown of Tissue—Decomposition or breaking down of cells due to pressure (bruise) or age (internal breakdown).

Decay—Decomposition of the fruit due to bacteria or fungus infection.

Ground Color—The basic or background color of a fruit before the sun's rays cause the skin to redden. The ground color may be seen beneath and between the red blush of the fruit.

Hard—The terms "hard," "firm," and "soft" are subjective terms used to describe the degrees of maturity or ripeness of a fruit. A "hard" texture will not give when pressed; a firm texture will give slightly to pressure. A "soft" texture is, of course, soft to the touch. The term "mature green" is sometimes used instead of hard.

Mature—Describes a fruit that is ready to be picked, whether or not it is ripe at this time. If a fruit is picked when mature, it is capable of ripening properly, but if picked when immature, it will not ripen properly.

Netting—The vein-like network of lines running randomly across the rind of some melons.

Ripe—Describes a fruit that is ready to be eaten.

Russeting—A lacy, brownish, blemish-type coating on top of the skin.

Scald—A blemish or brownish discoloration, which develops occasionally in the skin of apples or other fruits in cold storage.

* Courtesy USDA

CANNED FRUITS AND VEGETABLES

Grades and standards of identity have been developed for a wide variety of canned fruits and vegetables and a number of related products such as peanut butter, jellies, etc. These grades are market classifications of quality. They classify products into groups according to established and generally accepted standards. The use of federal grades on the product is voluntary, but standards of identity, quality (wholesomeness), and fill are not.

Standards are measurements of quality, weight, or quantity. Minimum quality standards have been established for canned goods by the Federal Food, Drug, and Cosmetic Act. Provisions of this act prohibit the movement of adulterated and misbranded foods in interstate commerce. All canned foods covered by its provisions must conform to its general requirements under the threat of heavy penalty. Its provisions prescribe:

- A definition and standard of identity
- A standard of quality
- A standard of fill

A definition and standard of identity defines what a food is. For canned goods, it establishes the composition of the product in the can. This includes the name of, or synonym for, the product, specific mixture, and the ingredients used in canning. The ingredients need not be listed, unless the canner has added other ingredients, such as spices, herbs, artificial flavoring, or chemical preservatives. Definitions and standards of identity have been established for canned apricots, cherries, peaches, fruit cocktail, peas, corn, beans, tomatoes, and other fruits and vegetables.

A standard of quality defines a minimum level of quality for canned products. In the case of canned tomatoes, the minimum level of quality is based on drained weight, color, peel per pound, and blemishes per pound. For fruit cocktail, the product is defined by established mixtures of fruit and style of cut. If products do not meet these requirements, they must be labeled "below" standard in quality or "good food not high grade." The reason may also be listed, such as: "not well peeled," "poor color," "excessively trimmed."

A standard of fill defines the fill of the can. Standards of fill vary for products. The standard of fill for some products is based on maximum head space. Peas must be filled within 3/16 of an in. below the top of the double seam. For other products, such as tomatoes, corn, and potatoes, the standard of fill is based on the minimum percent of water capacity. They must be filled not less than 90 percent of total capacity. Other products such as apricots, cherries, peaches, and pears must be filled "the maximum quantity of . . . ingredients which can be sealed in the container and processed by heat to prevent spoilage, without crushing or breaking such ingredients." In other words, they must be filled as "full as commercially practical without impairment of the quality of the food product." If the products do not meet these requirements, they must be labeled "Below Standard in Fill" or "Slack Fill."

LABEL

As the old cliche goes, "the label is the window of the can." Provisions under the Food, Drug, and Cosmetic Act prescribe certain minimum requirements which must be adhered to by all packers and distributors. The provisions for labeling are mandatory for all canned food products shipped in interstate commerce. The law requires that the label contain the following information:

- The legal name of the product.
- The name and address of canner or distributor.
- The net contents in weight, measure, or numerical count.
- The variety, style, and packing medium when relevant.
- The dietary properties, if important.
- Any artificial color, flavor, or preservative.
- If the product falls below the quantity or standard of fill established by the Act, it must be so stated.
- All information must be in English, unless an imported product with foreign language is distributed solely in an area with a predominant language other than English.
- A statement of ingredients, unless a standard of identity has been established by the government.

SYRUP DENSITY

Federal law requires that the label state the type of packing medium. Fruits are packed in syrups consisting of water or juice, from plain syrup to extra-heavy syrup. Syrup density is not a factor in grading. However, as a general rule, the syrup with the greatest amount of sugar is used for the best grades. Syrup density for the same grades will differ according to the fruit canned because of the individual characteristics of fruit. This is illustrated in the following table.

DIFFERENCE IN SYRUP DENSITIES FOR FRUITS

Brix Measurements

Syrup	Apricots	Cherries	Grapes
Extra Heavy Syrup	25 - 40 degrees	24 - 35 degrees	22 - 35 degrees
Heavy	21 - 25 degrees	19 - 24 degrees	18 - 22 degrees
Light	16 - 21 degrees	14 - 19 degrees	14 - 18 degrees
Slightly Sweetened	Less than 16	Less than 14	Less than 14

The reason for the difference in the Brix or syrup density for the three products is that sweet cherries and grapes would break down, if packed in a heavier syrup than 35 degrees, because of their delicate nature.

The Brix is a measurement of the sugar content obtained by means of a reading in degrees taken on a Brix hydrometer or refractometer, 15 days or more after packing. Each degree of Brix may be estimated to have 1 percent sugar content.

GRADES

Grades are essentially market classifications of quality. Grading is simply a process of classifying units of commodity in groups according to established and generally accepted standards.

Grades have been developed for a wide variety of canned fruits and vegetables by the U.S. Dept. of Agriculture. The U.S. grades for canned fruits and vegetables are as follows:

- U.S. Fancy, or U.S. Grade A
- U.S. Choice for Fruits, or U.S. Grade B
- U.S. Extra Standard for Vegetables, or U.S. Grade B
- U.S. Standard, or U.S. Grade C

All canned foods not meeting the minimum quality standards for Grade C are graded substandard and must be prominently labeled as such.

For some products, there are grades A and C, but no grade B; for other products, grade C is omitted: For example, Tomato Puree is graded A and C. Fruit Cocktail is graded A, B, and Substandard. Canned clingstone peaches are graded A, B, C, D, or Substandard, Grade C, Solid Pack, and Substandard Solid Pack.

WHICH GRADES TO BUY

TOP GRADE NOT ALWAYS BEST

Each grade has its best use, but no one grade, even the top grade or most expensive product, is always the best for all purposes in a quantity foodservice program. It is important to remember that canned foods sold under the lower grades are perfectly wholesome and have essentially the same nutritional value. They differ mainly in appearance and, to a lesser degree, in taste and flavor.

In general, Grade A, or Fancy, consists of fruits and vegetables of the highest quality. They have been carefully selected for uniformity in size, color, maturity, and tenderness, and are practically free from defects or blemishes. When appearance and flavor are most important, Grade A, or Fancy, should be used.

Grade B (Choice for Fruits, Extra Standard Vegetables) is a fine quality but scores somewhat lower in one or more of the factors in grade than Grade A, or Fancy. Grade B products are not so uniform in color, size, or maturity and generally have larger tolerances to defects.

Grade C, or Standard, is a good quality product but fails to meet the more exacting standards of Grade B. It is just as nutritious and wholesome as the higher grades. The products are less uniform in size and color, slightly less tender, or have more blemishes. Where appearance or tenderness is not important, Grade C is of value. This grade is good for cooked fruit desserts, or in dishes where the product has to be cooked further, or when the product is one of several ingredients in a recipe.

Substandard does not mean that the food is unwholesome. All canned goods must be wholesome under the provisions of the Food, Drug, and Cosmetic Act. Substandard merely means that the food has some quality defect greater than allowed in the standard grade. It may be considerably broken up, off color, or it may contain more than the allowed amount of defects. When form and appearance are not important, substandard foods may be used. Substandard canned goods are usually sold as "seconds."

Grades give the buyer information on which to base his choice of quality as related to the planned use of the food in the menu. This is an advantage in the terms of cost, as the lower grades can be used in many forms of food preparation where appearance is of minor importance.

SCORING FACTORS

Grades are based on scoring factors. The total score determines the grade. The factors include color, uniformity of size, absence of defects, character, flavor, consistency, finish, size, and symmetry, liquor or clearness of liquor, maturity, texture, wholeness, and cut. There can be variations in any one of these items. In many cases, a variation will cause a product to be downgraded. This does not necessarily indicate low nutritional quality or edibility. It means that the product may contain more than the allowed amounts of defects, off color, or broken pieces established for a higher grade.

In addition to these factors, there are general requirements that must be met. Examples of these are the fill in the container, drained weight, and syrup density. The grading factors vary with individual canned fruits and vegetables, but the scoring range is the same. For some canned items there is no Grade B. Where canned foods are graded only A and C, the scoring range is greater. Following is a summary of the total scores for all grades.

A grader for the Consumer and Marketing Service examines models of peach halves here in the lab where they are made at the U.S. Department of Agriculture. The models are used by CMS graders and inspectors to determine quality of fruits and vegetables.

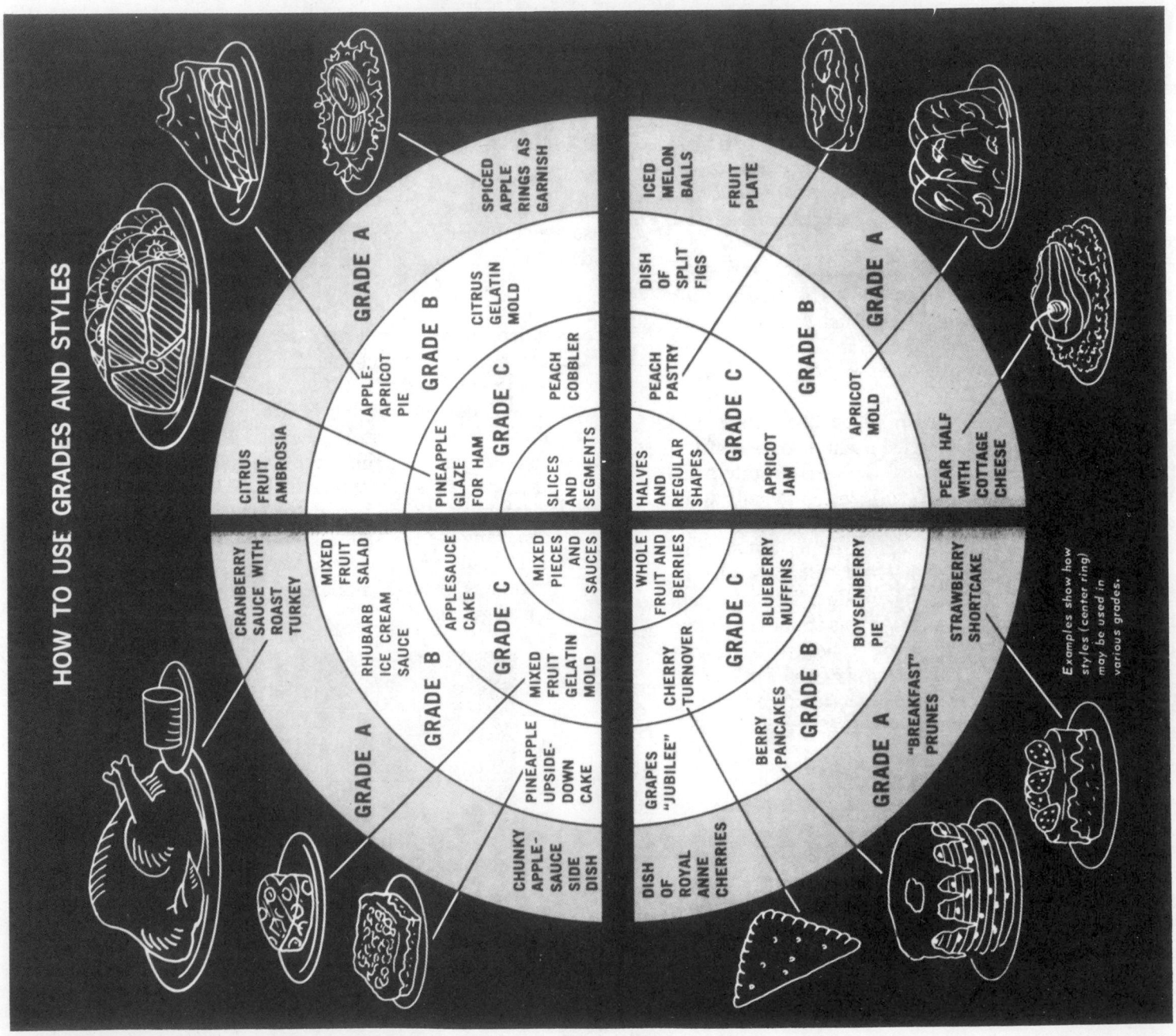

HOW TO USE GRADES AND STYLES

Examples show how styles (center ring) may be used in various grades.

SCORING RANGES FOR THE GRADES OF CANNED FOODS

GRADES	WHERE THERE IS A GRADE B	WHEN THERE IS NO GRADE B
A (Fancy)	90-100	85-100
B (Choice, Extra Standard)	75-89	--
C (Standard)	60-74	70-84
Substandard	0-59	0-69

Canned tomatoes must score 90 points or higher to be graded A, since there is a Grade B in the standards for canned tomatoes. Tomato juice needs to score only 85 or higher to be graded A, since there is no Grade B for tomato juice.

Occasionally, a product may not qualify for a high grade, even though its total score is above the minimum established for that grade. This is the result of a "limiting rule." Each grading factor is assigned a score range. Under the limiting rule, if the product fails to score above a certain scoring range on an important factor, it cannot be graded higher regardless of the total score.

SCORE CHART FOR CANNED PEAS

FACTOR	POINTS MAXIMUM	GRADE A FANCY	GRADE B EX. STD.	GRADE C STD.	SUB-STD.
Color	10	9-10	7-8	5-6**	0-4*
Liquor	10	9-10	8	7	0-6*
Defects	30	27-30	24-30	24-26*	0-20*
Maturity and Tenderness	50	45-50	41-44*	37-40*	0-36*
Minimum Score		90	80	70	

* Limiting rule: Peas receiving this score cannot be graded higher regardless of total score.
** Partial Limiting Rule: Peas receiving this score cannot be graded above U.S. Grade B, regardless of total score.

In light of the above information, if color is not an important factor to the buyer, peas that have been graded Grade B because of the partially limiting rule could be a good buy. Knowing the score of canned fruits and vegetables is of value to the buyer.

For example, let us take tomatoes. Tomatoes are graded on the basis of drained weight, wholeness, color, and absence of defects.

Grade A whole tomatoes must have a net drained weight of 54.7 to 67.9 oz.; Grade A tomatoes must have a net drained weight of 72.2 oz. to 76.6 oz.; Grade B tomatoes must have a net drained weight of 63.5 oz. to 67.9 oz., and Grade C tomatoes must have a net drained weight of 54.7 oz. to 59.1 oz.

The difference between 72.2 oz. and 76.6 oz. is 4.4 oz. This could mean the difference of one or two extra tomatoes. If you are quoted the same price for tomatoes at 72.2 oz. and 76.6 oz., you would be getting approximately 6 percent more tomatoes for the money by purchasing 76.6 oz.

So if you ask three purveyors, "What's your price on tomatoes today?" how are you going to receive comparable quotes if you do not specify grade and weight?

Buyers should be aware of the point spread that determines the various grades. For example, a lot of canned peas may score 88 or 89 points and be classified as Grade B. This lot may be closely related in quality to the lot of canned peas that just scored 99 points and is graded Grade A. The only major difference between the two major lots will be the prices because of grade classification. If the color factor were graded low and the other factors were graded high, and color was not an important factor to you, then the lot scoring 88 or 89 points would be a better buy.

It is difficult, if not impossible, for most buyers to determine the point spread because of the lack of time and equipment. However, buyers can obtain the scores by requesting a copy of the grader's certificate.

DRAINED WEIGHTS FOR CANNED TOMATOES, NO. 10 CAN

U.S. GRADE CLASSIFICATION	SCORE POINTS	DRAINED TOMATOES	OZ.
Grade A Whole	20	62%	67.9
Grade A Whole	19	60%	65.7
Grade A Whole	18	58%	63.5
Grade A Whole	17	54%	59.1
Grade A Whole	16	50%	54.7
Grade A	20	70%	76.6
Grade A	19	68%	74.4
Grade A	18	66%	72.2
Grade B	17	62%	67.9
Grade B	16	58%	63.5

[*Cont.*]

U.S. GRADE CLASSIFICATION	SCORE POINTS	DRAINED TOMATOES	OZ.
Grade C*	15	54%	59.1
Grade C	14	50%	54.1

Drained weight is a grading factor for tomatoes only. However, minimum drained weights are required for canned foods by the Food, Drug and Cosmetic Act.

* Limiting rule.

U.S. GRADE A

Fancy-Excellent high quality foods. Practically uniform in size and very symmetrical. Practically perfect in every respect, color, texture. Succulent, tender, represents the best of the crop.

Fruits are usually packed in extra heavy syrup.

U.S. GRADE B

Choice - Fruits

Extra Standard - Vegetables

High quality foods, reasonably uniform in size. Reasonably good color and texture. Reasonably free from defects.

Fruits are usually packed in heavy syrup.

U.S. GRADE C

Standard - Fairly good to quality foods. Fairly uniform in size, color, texture. Fairly free from defects. Fruits are usually packed in light syrup.

U.S. GRADE D

Substandard - Products which fail to meet the requirements of Grade C or the standard of quality outlined under the Pure Food and Drug Law.

Noticeable departure from these characteristics for any product is a good indication the product is of a lower quality. Among the key checks on quality include: color; texture; odor; absence of defects, such as cuts and bruises; uniformity of size and shape, and degree of firmness.

Careful review of quality checks covered in this manual will provide buyers added insurance that products delivered meet the standards specified in their purchasing order.

SCORING: Qualified experts employ a point scoring range to determine a product's quality bracket. The point factors vary somewhat from product to product.

The usual scoring point range is: 90-100 points, Grade A (Fancy); 80-89 points, Grade B (Choice) for fruits or (Extra Standard) for vegetables; 70-79 points, Grade C (Standard);

below 70 points is substandard. There are a few notable exceptions:

Applesauce

| Grade A (Fancy) | 85-100 points |
| Grade C (Standard) | 70-84 points |

Fruit Cocktail

| Grade A (Fancy) | 85-100 |
| Grade B (Choice) | 70-84 |

Tomato Puree and Tomato Paste

Grade A (Fancy)	90-100
Grade C (Standard)	80-89
Substandard	79 and under

All scoring factors are based upon the U.S. Dept. of Agriculture Consumer and Marketing Service standards. Experienced inspectors, either resident USDA personnel in canneries or trained inspectors employed by the companies, examine sample lots. The grade assigned to the lot represents an average score of the sampled products.

Inspectors do not always agree on grades of identical products. For example, the best of a crop of peaches might be scored Fancy by a local inspector. Yet an inspector from a preferred growing area might score them Choice in comparison to peaches from his region.

Because of the qualitative and geographical scoring differences, alert volume foodservice buyers prefer to use basic quality checks in determining grade and to select suppliers noted for purchasing the best products within each grade.

DRAINED WEIGHTS

Minimum drained weights designate the minimum amount of food per single can. The average drained weight of all the cans in one case should be greater than the minimum.

Ordinary kitchen equipment seldom will enable buyers to determine exact weight as defined by Food and Drug regulations. As a result, measuring headspace is a method often used for checking the percent of fill.

The usual method of checking contents or percent of fill is to measure the distance from the top of the opened can to the top of the contents. This is called headspace. Maximum gross headspace allowable in No. 10 or No. 3 cylinder cans is 27/32nds of an inch, which is greater than will be found in properly filled cans of most products.

In addition, solid contents of the can should usually be nearly level with the liquid surface level. If they seem unreasonably lower than the surface level, it would be best to request an official USDA certificate to fill weight from the packer.

Drained weights are not a factor on many foods, such as peas, Elberta peaches, cream-style corn, tomato puree, etc. On these products, the USDA uses a standard of fill of the container and a fill weight. For example, canned peas meet the fill standard when all contents (including liquid) are removed from the can and, when returned, completely fill the container —with or without the juice—after 15 seconds of settling.

Proper fill for fruits is determined by the maximum quantity that can be processed and sealed in the container without crushing or breaking the contents.

The Federal Food, Drug and Cosmetic Act permits variations from the stated weights, measure or numerical count on individual cans due to avoidable weighing, measuring or counting deviations that occasionally occur in even the best packaging circumstances.

Variation that results in the average of packs in a shipment falling below the stated individual quantity is not permitted.

Unreasonable shortages are never allowed, such as 20 peach halves in a can when it was specified that it should contain 30-35 count halves.

PACKING FRUITS AND VEGETABLES

Fruits and vegetables are grown and packed in nearly all sections of the United States, but certain areas consistently produce superior products. Time of harvest is also an important factor in product quality. These geographic and seasonal factors play important roles in food processors' guidelines for selecting raw products for canning. These guidelines are strictly followed except when nature fails to conform to normal moisture and warmth patterns.

GOOD TIMING LEADS TO GOOD BUYS

Prime harvest period for most fruits and vegetables used in volume feeding usually runs from July until late September or October.

Packers evaluate the products in October and November. As the season's canning activities progress, lot numbers are assigned to daily production runs and samples are re-checked against standards. When the harvest is in the cans, the "opening price" is computed using cost of materials, labor, and other price factors.

Prior to the firming up "opening prices," suppliers can only quote interim prices, based on the apparent harvest projected from the acreage planted and weather conditions. Interim prices are an educated guess at best because of the effect of heavy rainfall, hail, extreme dryness, and a host of other factors.

PREPARING ACCURATE BIDS
THE DO'S AND DON'TS

DO:

List products clearly.

A good bid sheet is an accurate bid sheet.

Any products listed on a bid sheet (see sample below) should be fully described by including the following factors:

BID DESCRIPTION	EXAMPLE
Product	Apples
Style of Product	Sliced
Count Range (or Sieve Size)	
Can Size and Pack	6/10
Source	Eastern
Variety	York Imperial
U.S. Grade	Grade A (Fancy)
Point Score	85 or better
Packing Medium	Solid-Pack—No Sugar Added
Minimum Drained Weight (or fill of container)	96 oz.

All of the information above is in accordance with canning industry and U.S. Government standards. Conformity with these standards makes it possible for bidders to quote on essentially the same product and, at the same time, permits the buyer to better evaluate the quotations and make the best possible purchase.

DO:

Make heading Sheets as clear as the specifications.

Heading sheets on bid forms can be as simple or detailed as the buyer desires. However, certain information should be included on every covering sheet.

1. Buyer's name and address
2. Closing date and hour for return of bids
3. Delivery address
4. Date or dates when deliveries are desired
5. Payment terms and dates

State and local regulations often require considerably more information than this minimum bid heading to avoid confusion among suppliers and to eliminate any questions about bidding procedures. The more extensive bid sheets generally include the following information:

Number of invoices required.

How to submit samples, if required.

Final adjustment of quantities shown on bid.

Prices quoted should or should not include prepaid transtation charges.

Products requiring grade certificates.

Method of price quoting - i.e., by the case; total quantity of each lot; any other method.

Identification of products by brand or trade name.

Method of quoting on a different size container and/or case.

Method and time of delivery.

Right to accept or reject any or all bids.

Penalties for non-performance.

Any other pertinent regulations or instructions.

DO:

Single out statements of intent.

Many misunderstandings may be avoided by clearly worded statements clarifying the buyer's intent or any special conditions of sale. For example, "the interpretation of descriptive terms of grade shall be in accordance with the U.S. Standards for grade in effect on the date of the invitation for bid."

One of the most common areas covered by amplifying statements concerns disposition of delivered products that are apparently not the grade specified. This problem can be avoided by including a clarifying statement in the bid heading to the effect:

"When delivered products appear to be below the grade of the products specified, the buyer reserves the right to submit items in doubt to the nearest local or regional USDA office for official inspection and grading. In such cases, it is agreed the party in error will pay the cost of the inspection."

Official inspection of processed fruits, vegetables, and other products is readily available nationally through regional offices of the U.S. Dept. of Agriculture. Inspection applications should be addressed to:

Processed Products Inspection
Fruit and Vegetable Division
Consumer and Marketing Service
U.S. Dept. of Agriculture

Simply consult the U.S. Government listing in your local telephone book for the inspection office nearest you, or write to the division's main office in Washington, D.C. 20250.

DON'T:

Use incorrect terminology in an effort to obtain special grades or items.

For example:

Extra Fancy Grade; the correct name is Fancy Grade. To indicate that you want the top range of the fancy grade, you can adjust your point score specifications to read "score 95 or better." You can similarly adjust your point score specification in any grade as long as you stay within the boundaries of the prescribed scoring range for the grade product.

Grade C (Standard) (fruit item) packed in extra heavy syrup. Grade C fruits are packed in light syrup only. Each grade of fruit is usually packed in its proper degree of syrup. Any grade of fruit may be packed in a lighter syrup, in water, or as "solid pack." You will not find any grade of fruit packed in a syrup heavier than that which is customarily used for the grade.

DON'T:

Be vague or general in your specifications. For example, the items listed below were abstracted from an actual bid request, exactly as they were written by the customer.

ITEM	SIZE CAN	AMOUNT
Peaches, halves	No. 10	200 cases
Pears, Bartlett, halves	No. 10	175 cases
Peas, Early June	No. 10	300 cases
Green Beans, Blue Lake, cut	No. 10	300 cases

This particular bid request contained a list of 25 items totaling 4500 cases, and each item was written like these examples.

You can readily see how impossible it would be for suppliers to submit quotations on identical items, and for the buyer to make an intelligent evaluation of the quotations submitted.

FROZEN

Frozen fruits and vegetables are graded identically, for the most part, with their canned equivalents. The grade standards for these items are shown in the text of their section only to the extent to which they differ from the canned product.

Frozen vegetables offer the advantage of having been frozen quite close to picking time, and thus offer the operator the advantage of not having been cooked in the canning process.

Frozen vegetables are purchased in a variety of packs and cases with the most common commercial sizes being 2-lb., 2½-lb., and 3-lb. packages, 12 packages to the case. There are also 10-oz., 12-oz., 1-lb., and 5-lb. packages available. Some items such as peas and corn are available, usually in the "B" grade, in 20-lb. bulk packages.

Frozen fruits are generally packed in either a sugar or syrup to preserve flavor, texture, and color. The fruit-sugar ratio of 4:1 or 5:1 should be part of the purchase specifications. Frozen fruits usually come in 6-lb., 6½-lb., 20-lb., 25-lb., and 30-lb. containers although there are some 10-oz., 12-oz., and 1-lb. packs available.

DEHYDRATED AND DRIED

These items are limited in their uses in foodservice. Some, such as potato flakes, buds, etc., are quite common, while others, like dehydrated pears or peaches, are not frequently seen. The buyer should require grading certificates on low moisture and dried fruits as the defects in these items become less evident than with their canned and frozen cousins.

Pack sizes range from 1 lb. to 50 lb. It is recommended that no more than a few weeks' supply be purchased at a time because insects prey upon dehydrated and dried foods.

COMMON COUNTS OF FRUITS

CHERRIES, SWEET—CANNED:

8 oz. — 20/25; 25/30; 30/35; 35/40

No. 2½ — 50/60; 60/65; 65/70; 70/80; 80/90; 90/105; 105/130; and 130/145

No. 10 — 210/235; 225/240; 240/260; 260/290; 290/335; 335/390; 390/480; and 480/540

FIGS, KADOTA—CANNED

No. 2½ — 12/17; 17/22; 22/28; and 28/35

No. 10 — 50/70; 70/90; 90/110; and 110/140

PEACHES, CANNED

8 oz. — 3/4; 5/6; and 6/7

No. 2½ — 5/6; 6/8; 8/10; 10/12; 13/15; 16/18; and 19/21

No. 10 — 18/22; 20/25; 25/30; 28/32; 30/35; 35/40; 40/45; and 45/55

PEARS, CANNED

8 oz. — 3/4; 4/5; 5/6; and 6/7

No. 2½ — 5/6; 6/8; 7/9; 9/12; 10/14; and 12/17

No. 10 — 18/22; 20/25; 25/30; 28/32; 30/35; 35/40; 40/45; 40/50; and 45/55

PINEAPPLE, CANNED

No. 2½ — 8 whole slices or 16 half slices

No. 10 — 50 whole slices (3/8 in. thick); 28 whole slices (1/2 in. thick); 44 whole slices; or 60 whole slices

PLUMS CANNED

No. 2½—Purple Plums: 12/18; 18/24, and 24/30
            Gage and Egg Plums: 10/15 and 15/20

No. 10—Purple Plums: 45/65; 65/90, and 90/110
            Gage and Egg Plums: 35/55 and 55/75

PRUNES, DRIED — CANNED

20/30 Size
    No. 2½ — 33/37 (Regular Pack)
    No. 10 — 120/140 (Regular Pack)
            190/210 (Nectarized Pack)

30/40 Size
    No. 2½ — 44/50 (Regular Pack)
    No. 10 — 160/180 (Regular Pack)
            240/260 (Nectarized Pack)

(Cont., p. 500)

FRUITS AND VEGETABLES, DEHYDRATED AND DRIED
Freeze-drying: Relation of freeze-dried product to frozen weight for selected fruits and vegetables[1]

Frozen food before freeze-drying		Weight of freeze-dried products as a percentage of frozen counterpart	Factors used to multiply freeze-dried weight to convert back to frozen weight
Items	Percentage moisture		
	PERCENT	PERCENT	
Apples, uncooked, sliced, sweetened	73.3	27.2	3.7
Apricots, non-cooked	85.4	14.9	6.7
Blueberries, non-cooked, unsweetened	85.0	15.3	6.5
Broccoli, cooked or non-cooked	90.6	9.6	10.4
Brussels sprouts, cooked or non-cooked	89.3	10.9	9.2
Cauliflower, cooked or non-cooked	92.9	7.2	13.9
Green peas, cooked	81.7	18.7	5.4
Green peppers, cooked	94.7	5.4	18.5
Mushrooms, non-cooked, whole, pieces or sliced	90.4	9.8	10.2
Pears, non-cooked pieces or slices	82.7	17.6	5.7
Pineapple, non-cooked slices or chunks, sweetened	77.1	23.4	4.3
Plums, Italian, non-cooked slices or pieces	78.7	21.7	4.6
Raspberries, red, non-cooked	74.3	26.2	3.8
Snap beans, cooked	91.6	8.6	11.6
Strawberries, whole, non-cooked	75.5	24.8	4.0

1. Freeze-dried products contain 2% moisture.

FRUITS AND VEGETABLES, DEHYDRATED AND DRIED
Fruits, Dehydrated [low-moisture]: Relation between farm and processed weights.

Items	Packaged weight of dehydrated product		Pounds of fresh weight to make one pound of dehydrated product
	No. 10 can	Gallon can	
	POUNDS	POUNDS	
Apples:			
Wedges	1.5	—)	
Slices	1.5	—)	
Dice	2.0	—)	11.0
Nuggets	2.5	—)	
Powder	—	5)	
Apricots:			
Slices	3.5	—)	
Dice	3.5	—)	
Nuggets	3.5	—)	7.1
Powder	—	6)	
Cherries:			
Sour-pitted	.7	—	7.0
Dates:			
Nuggets	3	—)	1.75[1]
Powder	—	6)	
Figs:			
Slices	3	—)	1.35[1]
Powder	—	6)	
Peaches:			
Slices	3	—)	
Dice	3	—)	7.1
Nuggets	3	—)	
Powder	—	6)	
Pears:			
Slices	1.5	—	11.0
Prunes:			
Whole pitted	3	—)	
Nuggets	3	—)	1.71[1]
Powder	—	6)	
Strawberries:			
(Freeze-dried)	.7	—	11.0

1. From commercially dried fruit.

FRUITS AND VEGETABLES, DEHYDRATED AND DRIED
Vegetables, dehydrated: Relations between farm and
processed weights and weight of product per 5-gallon container.

| Commodity | Percentage moisture content | | Average losses from sizing, trimming, peel-ing, blanching, sorting, and other [percent][1] | Factors for converting to[2] | | Weight of product per 5-gallon container | |
	Average for raw material	Product		Processed weight from farm weight	Equivalent farm weight from processed	Product	Pounds
Asparagus	93	4	55	.033	30	Dice	8
						Powder	17
Beans, green	89	4	30	.080	12.5	1/2-in. cut	7
Beets	88	5	33	.085	12	Powder	30
Cabbage	92	4	43	.048	21	Dice	9
						Powder	30
Carrots	88	4	33	.083	12	Dice	18-20
						Powder	35
Celery[3]							
Stalk and leaf flakes	—	—	20	.050	20	Flakes	3-6
Stalk dice	94	3.5	47	.033	30	Dice	8
Garlic	71	5	15	.260	4	Sliced	15
						Powder	30
Greens	92	4	20-50	.040-.067	15.25	Flakes	8
						Powder	18
Onion	88	4	11	.110	9	Flakes	10-15
						Powder	25
Parsley	84	5	15	.140	7	Flakes	4
						Powder	20
Peas, green	78	4	10	.200	5		18
Peppers:							
Green bell	93	3.5	38	.045	22	Dice	8
						Powder	20
Red bell	91	5.5	45	.053	19	Dice	10
						Powder	25
Potatoes:							
Dice	80	6	40	.125	8.0	—	17
Granules	78	6	33	.14	7.1	—	36
Flakes	80	4.5	33	.14	7.1	—	10
Turnips	91	5	33	.063	16	Dice	14
						Powder	25

FRUITS AND VEGETABLES, DEHYDRATED AND DRIED
Vegetables, dehydrated: Relations between farm and processed weights and weight of product per 5-gallon container [continued]

| Commodity | Percentage moisture content | | Average losses from sizing, trimming, peeling, blanching, sorting, and other [percent][1] | Factors for converting to[2] | | Weight of product per 5-gallon container | |
	Average for raw material	Product		Processed weight from farm weight	Equivalent farm weight from processed	Product	Pounds
Sweet potato flakes	69	3	23.5	.143	7		
Onions, green	88	4	43	.071	14	Flakes	6
						Minced	8
Tomato flakes	93	4	31	.050	20	Flakes	14
Horseradish	75	5	31	.180	5.5	Powder	20
Leek	88	4	27	.091	11	Powder	22
Okra	90	5	13	.091	11	Powder	22
Pimiento	88	4	70	.036	28	Powder	25
Pumpkin	91	5	13	.083	12	Powder	25

1. Includes fines and defects removed during final inspection of dried product and other process losses.
2. Successful dehydration of many of these vegetables depends upon the ability to divert undesirable sizes and/or grades to other kinds of processing. If such outlets are not available, shrinkage ratios will be greater than shown herein.
3. Celery tops (trimmings) may also be dehydrated.

40/50 Size
  No. 2½ — 52/57 (Regular Pack)
  No. 10 — 190/210 (Regular Pack)
          290/310 (Nectarized Pack)
50/60 Size
  No. 2½ — 60/68 (Regular Pack)
  No. 10 — 220/250 (Regular Pack)
          340/360 (Nectarized Pack)

APPLES*

MARKETING SEASON Apples are available nationwide throughout the year with heaviest movement September through March. October is the peak month, as both fall and winter varieties become available then. Most apples marketed from November through June are from refrigerated storage. Some apples require a storage period to reach prime quality, so that the apples from storage are generally highly desirable. The following table, taken from the United's Guide to Average Monthly Availability of 88 Fresh Fruits and Vegetables copyright 1964 shows monthly availability of apples expressed as a percentage of the total annual supply.

MONTHLY AVAILABILITY OF APPLES EXPRESSED AS A PERCENTAGE OF THE TOTAL ANNUAL SUPPLY

Jan. %	Feb. %	Mar. %	Apr. %	May %	June %	July %
11	10	10	8	6	3	2

Aug. %	Sept. %	Oct. %	Nov. %	Dec. %	ANNUAL TOTAL [million lbs.]
3	10	15	11	11	3,875

VARIETIES There are innumerable varieties of apples. More than 7,000 have been named. However, this figure is only of academic interest. Actually, only 17 clonal varieties, each with production of more than 1 million bushels annually, make up 91 percent of total production in the U.S. More Delicious are produced than any other variety. McIntosh is second. These two varieties are more than a third of the total. (A clonal variety is one which is produced directly from a portion of the plant, such as a bud or shoot, and not from seed. All standard Delicious trees, for example, have been propagated from a single tree which showed a deviation that was desirable.) There are a great number of sports.

A sport is a sudden spontaneous deviation or variation of an organism from type, beyond the usual limits of individual variation. Apple growers are on the lookout for tree limbs that show fruit with favorable variations, such as more red color or color that comes out earlier. Many new sports are announced every year; and now sports of sports (sometimes called super-sports) are coming out, and there are already sports of super-sports. It would take far more space than is available here to list and describe the sports. For example there is Starkrimson which is a super-sport of Red Delicious, and there are already many super-super-sports of Starkrimson. Some of the sports are spur-type trees on which fruit spurs are formed along scaffold limbs, and fruit is produced on practically all parts of the tree.

The rank of the varieties and the percentage that each variety is of total production is as follows: (1) Delicious 26 percent; (2) McIntosh 14 percent; (3) Golden Delicious 8 percent; (4) Rome Beauty 7 percent; (5) Johathan 7 percent; (6) Winesap 6 percent; (7) York 6 percent; (8) Stayman 5 percent; (9) Yellow Newtown 3 percent; (10) Cortland 3 percent; (11) Northern Spy 3 percent; (12) R.I. Greening 2 percent; all others 1 percent. Percentages are rounded to nearest whole unit. The first seven varieties are 74 percent of the total.

Following is data by varieties, including all four major varieties the harvesting and marketing season, the average crop, main growing areas, and description of the fruit.

SUMMER

Gravenstein Harvest July into September, with main marketing season July 15 to September 15; average crop 2.6 million bu.; grown mainly in California but also in New England and Appalachia; fruit above medium to large; skin thin, tender, slightly rough, greenish yellow to orange yellow overlaid with broken stripes of light and dark red; flesh whitish yellow, firm, moderately fine, crisp, moderately tender, juicy, sprightly, medium acid, aromatic; good for table use, cooking, and salads. Not a storage apple and must be sold

*Courtesy United Fresh Fruit and Vegetable Association.

quickly. The Gravenstein is said to have been found originally in the Duke of Augustinberg's garden at Gravenstein in Holstein, Germany. Another statement is that it derived its name from being found in the garden of the castle of Grafenstein in Schleswig. In any event, it is a common apple throughout Germany and Sweden and was received by English growers from those countries. The Gravenstein may have been received in the U.S. in the vicinity of Albany, N.Y., prior to 1826.

Others There are a great many summer apple varieties (average total production 2.4 million bu.) available from late June well into September. Among the more popular varieties are: **Lodi** From June on into early August; size medium to large; skin greenish yellow similar to the Yellow Transparent of which it is a relative and which it has largely replaced; flesh medium firm; flavor acid; good for sauce and pies. **Astrachan** (Red Astrachan) Size medium to sometimes large; very perishable; skin rather thin, moderately tender, smooth, pale yellow or greenish, often nearly or quite overspread with light and dark red, splashed and irregularly striped with deep crimson or carmine, and covered with rather heavy bluish booom, numerous small whitish dots; flesh white, often strongly tinged with red, rather fine, crisp, tender, juicy, brisk medium acid, aromatic, sometimes slightly astringent; good cooking apple before it becomes fully ripe; desirable for dessert when fully ripe and mellow. **Starr** Large to very large, skin rather thick, tough, nearly smooth, green becoming yellowish-green, sometimes with an indication of a faint blush, numerous small and large pale or russet dots, flesh tinged with yellow, moderately fine, very tender, crisp, very juicy, sprightly medium acid, aromatic; good for sauce and pies. **Summer Rambo** Large to very large; skin thick, smooth, attractive, clear bright yellow or greenish tinged with carmine striping; flesh yellowish green, firm, tender, very juicy, medium acid, aromatic; a distinctive "sauce" apple. **N.W. Greening** Large to very large; skin smooth, entirely green, turning to yellow with advanced ripeness; flesh greenish white, very firm, juicy, acid; generally used in the premature stage for "green apple" pies and other dishes calling for tartness and shape-retaining firmness. **Williams Red** Medium to large; skin moderately thick, rather tender, nearly smooth, pale yellow overlaid with bright deep red, indistinctly striped with dark red or crimson, numerous small grayish or russet inconspicuous dots; flesh sometimes tinged with red, firm, a little coarse, moderately crisp, tender, rather juicy, becoming dry when overripe, mildly acid, aromatic; good for dessert. **Yellow Transparent** Size medium to above medium, sometimes large; skin thin, tender, smooth, waxy, pale greenish yellow changing to attractive yellowish white, numerous greenish and light-colored dots, often submerged; flesh white, moderately firm, fine-grained, crisp, tender, juicy, sprightly medium acid with pleasant but not high flavor; good cooker. **Fenton** This is a red sport of Beacon. Ripens in August; size medium, shape oblate; skin fairly thick and tough and handles well; flesh crisp, juicy and sprightly to sub-acid; Miller Red is similar.

FALL

Grimes Golden Harvest September 1 to early October, but mainly in September; main marketing season September 10 to December 1; average crop 1.3 million bu.; grown mainly in Virginia, West Virginia, Pennsylvania and Ohio; fruit medium to large; skin tough, somewhat rough, clear deep yellow with scattering pale yellow or russet dots; flesh yellow, very firm, tender, crisp, moderately coarse, moderately juicy, medium acid, rich, aromatic, sprightly; food for cooking or dessert.

Jonathan Harvest generally September 1 to mid-October, but mainly September 15 to October 1; may be marketed until May; average crop 8.3 million bu.; grown mainly in Michigan, Washington, Illinois, Appalachian states, Ohio; fruit medium to small, rarely large; skin thin, tough, smooth, pale bright yellow overlaid with lively red faintly striped with carmine; well-colored fruit almost completely covered with red, which deepens to purplish on sunny side; less colored fruit has green to red toned appearance; prevailing effect attractive, lively, deep red; flesh whitish or somewhat yellow, sometimes tinged with red, firm, moderately fine, crisp, tender, juicy, very aromatic, sprightly medium acid; excellent for dessert or cooking; fine for baking.

Wealthy Harvest generally mid-August to early October, mainly late August into mid-September; main marketing

APPLES

FRESH (7/25/72   51.300)
GRADES: U.S. Extra Fancy; U.S. Fancy; U.S. No. 1; U.S. Utility; Combination Grades
CANNED (10/17/53   52.2161)

GRADES:	"A" or "FANCY"	"C" or "STANDARD"	"SUB-STANDARD"
Minimum Score:	85	70	less than 70

	NET WEIGHT OZ.	NET WEIGHT METRIC	DRAINED WEIGHT OZ.	DRAINED WEIGHT METRIC
No. 303	15.2	430.9 g	14	396.9 g
No. 2½	26.8	759.8 g	26	737.1 g
No. 10	98.5	2.8 kg	96	2.7 kg

FROZEN (5/17/54   52.361)

GRADES:	"A" or "FANCY"	"C" or "STANDARD"	"SUB-STANDARD"
Minimum Score:	85	70	less than 70

DEHYDRATED (7/1/57   52.2341)

GRADES:	"A" or "FANCY"	"B" or "CHOICE"	"SUB-STANDARD"
Minimum Score:	85	70	less than 70

DRIED (10/24/55   52.2481)

GRADE:	"A" or "FANCY"	"B" or "CHOICE"	"SUB-STANDARD"

season September to October; average crop 1.5 million bu.; grown mainly in New York, Michigan, Wisconsin; size above medium to large when well grown but often small on old trees; skin thin, tough, pale yellow or greenish, blushed and marked with narrow stripes and splashes of red, deepening in highly colored specimens to brilliant red, numerous small inconspicuous, pale or russet dots; prevailing effect bright red; flesh whitish, sometimes stained with red, moderately fine, crisp, tender, very juicy, agreeable medium acid, sprightly, somewhat aromatic; excellent for fresh eating; extra good for pies, sauce, and baking.

WINTER

Baldwin Harvest mid-September through October, mainly September 25 to October 25; marketing season mainly October through December, but some fruit marketed to June 1; average crop 3 million bu.; grown mainly in New York, New England, Michigan, and Ohio; size above medium and sometimes large to very large; skin tough, smooth, light yellow or greenish blushed and mottled with bright red, indistinctly striped with deep carmine, prevailing effect bright red; flesh yellowish, firm, moderately coarse, crisp, rather tender, juicy to very juicy, agreeably medium acid, sprightly, somewhat aromatic; good for dessert and salad; extra good for pie and sauce. About 75 percent are sold to processors.

Ben Davis Harvest generally September 25 through October, mainly October 10 to 25; marketing season mainly October to mid-November with some supplies to April 1 and later; average crop 1.3 million bu.; grown mostly in New York and Virginia; *production declining steadily*; size usually above medium to large; skin tough, waxy, bright, smooth, usually glossy, clear yellow or greenish, mottled and washed with bright red, striped and splashed with bright dark crimson, inconspicuous light, whitish or brown dots, prevailing effect deep, bright red or red striped; flesh whitish, slightly tinged with yellow, firm, moderately coarse, not very crisp, somewhat aromatic, juicy, mildly medium acid; usually used for cooking. Virtually all go to processors.

Cortland Harvest September 10 to October 20, mainly September 25 to October 10; marketing season mainly October to mid-January; average crop 3.5 million bu.; grown mostly in New York, New England, Ohio, Michigan, Pennsylvania, and Wisconsin; size medium to large; skin thin, moderately tender, smooth, shiny, red and striped indistinctly with deep dark carmine, prevailing effect red to deep red; size medium to large; flesh snow white, fairly firm, tender, delicate in texture, mildly medium acid, mildly aromatic, does not turn brown on exposure to air; excellent for eating out of hand, in salads, and fruit cocktails where flesh holds snowy white color; fine for all cooking purposes.

Delicious Harvest late August into November, depending on area, but mostly September 1 through October 25; marketing season mainly September 20 to May 20 with some available into June; average crop 26.5 million bu.; grown in substantial quantities in 19 states, mainly Washington, Virginia, California, Michigan, New York, Pennsylvania, Oregon; size

McIntosh Apple

medium to large; skin thin, tough, smooth, brilliant red over yellow with areas of lighter and darker color, striped red to solid red, prevailing effect deep red with lighter red areas, sometimes with small areas of yellowish green; calyx end has five characteristic low ridges or knobs; flesh white, fine-grained, tender, crisp, juicy, moderately low acid, mildly aromatic; excellent for eating raw in salads; not generally used for cooking; named accidentally by Lloyd C. Stark, governor of Missouri, who bit into one at a fair in 1894 and exclaimed, "That's delicious."

Golden Delicious Harvest late August to November 1, depending on area, but mostly September 10 to October 20; marketing season mostly September 25 to April and some into June; average crop 10 million bu.; grown mostly in Washington, Illinois, Virginia, Pennsylvania, West Virginia, Michigan, and also in 12 other states; size medium to large; skin bright yellow or golden, rather tough, and may be shiny, velvety or russeted; flesh white often with yellowish tinge, crisp, fine-grained, juicy, moderately low acid, mildly aromatic; fine for eating out of hand; especially good for salads because it does not turn brown; and excellent for cooking.

McIntosh Harvest August 20 to October 30, but mostly September 10 to October 10; marketing season mostly September 25 to May 1, but some may be available to June 30; average crop 16.6 million bu.; grown mostly in New York, New England and Michigan and 7 other states; size above medium, sometimes large; skin thin, moderately tender, smooth, readily separating from the flesh, clear whitish yellow or greenish washed and deeply blushed with bright red and faintly striped with carmine; highly colored specimens become dark, almost purplish red, with carmine stripes obscured or obliterated; prevailing effect bright red; flesh white or slightly tinged with yellow, sometimes veined with red, firm, fine, crisp, tender, very juicy, characteristically and agreeably aromatic; perfumed, sprightly, medium acid becoming mild and nearly sweet when ripe; excellent for

dessert and salad; good for cooking and baking but less cooking time is needed than for most other varieties.

Newtown (Yellow Newtown, Albermarle Pippin) Harvest September 10 to November 25, but mostly September 20 to October 20; marketing season mostly September 20 to January 30, but may extend to June 1; average crop 4 million bu.; grown mostly in California and Oregon, with some in Washington and Virginia; size medium to very large; skin rather tough, smooth, or slightly roughened with brownish russet dots; when fully mature the more highly colored apples are bright yellow, sometimes with distinct pinkish blush especially about the base; less highly colored fruit is greenish yellow shaded more or less with duller brownish pink; flesh slightly tinged with yellow, firm, crisp, moderately fine-grained, juicy, sprightly, medium acid, highly aromatic; excellent for dessert, good cooker, one of the best keepers.

Northern Spy Harvest October 1 to November 5, mostly October 15 to 31; marketing season mostly October 10 to May 1 with some available to June 30; average crop 2.9 million bu.; grown mostly in Michigan, New York, and New England; size usually large to very large; skin thin, tender, smooth, glossy; clear pale ground color is nearly concealed with bright pinkish red, mottled and splashed with carmine, and overspread with thin, delicate bloom, prevailing bright red or striped red; flesh yellowish, rather firm, moderately fine-grained, very tender, crisp, very juicy, sprightly, aromatic, medium acid; excellent for dessert or cooking.

Rhode Island Greening Harvest May 12 to October 25, mostly September 10 to October 10; marketing season mostly October 1 to February 1, extending sometimes to May 1; average crop 2.9 million bu.; grown mostly in New York with some in Michigan and New England, few in Ohio; size above medium to large or very large; skin moderately thick, tough, smooth, waxy, grass green varying to rather yellow, sometimes blushed with brownish red which rarely deepens to a distinct bright red, greenish white or russet dots often submerged, prevailing effect green or yellowish; flesh yellowish; firm, moderately fine-grained, crisp, tender, juicy, rich, sprightly, medium acid; not generally used for dessert or salad; extra good for pie, sauce, and good for baking.

Rome Beauty Harvest September 1 to November 10, mostly October 1 to October 30; marketing season mostly October 1 to April 1 with some supplies available to July 1; average crop 8.4 million bu.; grown mostly in New York, Pennsylvania, New Jersey, West Virginia, Washington, California, Virginia, Ohio, North Carolina, and 8 other states; size medium to very large; skin thick, tough, smooth, yellow or greenish more or less mottled with bright red which in highly colored specimens deepens to almost carmine, numerous small whitish or brown dots, prevailing effect red or red mingled with yellow; flesh nearly white with slight tinge of yellow or green, firm, moderately fine-grained to a little coarse, rather crisp, juicy, slightly aromatic, agreeably mild, medium acid; excellent for baking because it holds its shape; good for pie, sauce, and all cooking purposes; not generally used for eating raw but is rather good raw when fully ripe.

Stayman Harvest September 1 to November 1, mostly October 1 to November 1; marketing season mostly October 1 to April 30 and some supplies may be available later; average crop 6.6 million bu.; grown mostly in Virginia, Pennsylvania, West Virginia, New Jersey, Ohio, North Carolina, and 7 other states; size medium to large; skin smooth, rather thick, often nearly completely covered with rather dull mixed red or rather indistinctly striped with dull carmine, light russet dots often rather large and conspicuous, striped effect more noticeable in less highly colored specimens; flesh tinged with yellow or slightly greenish, firm, moderately fine-grained, tender, crisp, juicy to very juicy, aromatic, sprightly, pleasantly medium acid; fine all-purpose apple.

Winesap Harvest September 15 to November 15, mostly October 5 to November 1; marketing season mostly November 15 to June 30 with some supplies available as late as August; average crop 9.8 million bu.; grown mostly in Washington and Virginia, also in 12 other states; size medium to small; skin medium thick, tough, smooth, glossy, bright red indistinctly striped and blotched with very dark purplish red over a distinctly yellow ground color, or green if not fully mature, overspread with faint bloom; dots rather small, scattering, whitish; prevailing effect bright deep red; flesh tinged with yellow, veins sometimes red, very firm, rather coarse, moderately crisp, very juicy, sprightly, medium acid; fine all-purpose apple, good for eating fresh; one of best keepers.

York Imperial Harvest September 20 to October 30, mostly October 1 to October 25; marketing season mostly October 1 to March 30 but some supplies sometimes available to June 1; average crop 6.2 million bu.; grown mostly in Virginia, Pennsylvania, West Virginia; size medium to large; skin tough, bright, smooth, blushed to solid light red or pinkish red, with dots pale or russet, often conspicuous; flesh yellowish, firm, crisp, a little coarse, moderately juicy, at first sprightly medium acid but becomes mild medium acid or nearly sweet, somewhat aromatic; good for eating fresh and a fine cooking apple, holding its shape and flavor under heat. This fruit has peculiar oblique lines, as though each apple were leaning a little to one side.

DWARF ROOTSTOCKS: Thousands of trees of various varieties are now being planted on rootstocks that control the ultimate tree size. These are known as dwarfing stocks. The use of such stocks is not new, and in fact was familiar to Roman agriculturists. Recently, however, after 100 years of study and experiment in the U.S. and for centuries before that in Europe, interest of U.S. growers in these stocks has revived. There are many kinds of dwarf rootstocks, and they exert different degrees of dwarfing. Additionally, the effect depends to some extent on the variety that is grafted or budded onto the rootstock. The main object of dwarfing is to improve growing efficiency, since smaller apple trees cost less to prune, thin, spray, and harvest. More trees can be planted per acre; often they come into production earlier than regular trees, and it is said that better quality fruit is possible due to ease of spraying and harvesting and also because of greater exposure to light with consequent better color.

Such trees are generally on Malling or Malling Merton rootstocks. There are many kinds, identified by number, and each has its good and bad points and needs to be selected to fit individual needs. On the negative side of the ledger are the inability of the present standard dwarf stocks to stand extreme cold, their susceptibility to being blown over by a high wind, the requirement for strong bracing of many trees, and the requirement for more intensive horticultural practices than for regular trees.

SPUR TYPE TREES: The spur type tree is smaller than the standard tree because of the growth habit of the scion that is budded or grafted to the rootstock, rather than because of the rootstock itself. On this type of tree, fruit spurs are formed on the large limbs. The trees are narrower as well as shorter than the standard tree. They are reported to be highly productive. There is much controversy among experts as to the relative advantages of the dwarf rootstock and the spur-type scion. Both are being planted in large numbers. Many believe that the large apple tree is on its way out, to be replaced by some form of tailormade small tree. One advocate of the spur type tree has suggested it will replace the dwarf tree but this is vigorously denied by others.

CONTAINERS: There are five main types of wholesale containers for apples: (1) tray-pack cartons; (2) cell cartons; (3) bagmasters of many styles and sizes which hold a given number of consumer-sized bags; (4) bulk-fill cartons of various dimensions, and (5) tub baskets. The wooden box, which for many years was the standard container in the Pacific Northwest, has been replaced by fiberboard because of cost and market preference. Some wooden boxes are still in use in the East. Fiberboard cartons come in a wide array of dimensions. It is not possible to list all of them or even to say which dimensions are most generally used. About all that can be done is to give a few examples of container dimensions as published in the railroad container tariffs. Such publication in the tariffs does not imply that the listed containers are the most useful or the most generally used. *At least they are samples of dimensions that are in use.* The list can be obtained by writing to Chairman, Loading and Container Section, Uniform Classification Committee, Room 380, Union Station, 517 West Adams St., Chicago, Ill. 60606.

Among fiberboard apple boxes, bulk type, are the following: 11 x 13 x 17 (2431 cubic inches); 11 x 12-7/8 x 16-3/8 (2319

cu. in.); 11-3/8 x 12 x 19-3/4 in. (2695 cu. in.). There are a great many others of this approximate cubical content and many smaller ones for specialized purposes.

Among fiberboard boxes, cell type, in which each apple occupies its own cell, are the following: 11 x 14-1/2 x 18-1/4 (2910 cu. in.); 14-1/2 x 14-1/4 x 14-1/4 (2944 cu. in.); 10-1/2 x 17-1/2 x 17-1/2 (3216 cu. in.); and 14-1/8 x 14-3/8 x 18-1/8 (3689 cu. in.). There are, of course, a great many others.

Eastern box, 11 x 13 x 17 (2431 cu. in.); 11 x 12-1/2 x 16 (2200 cu. in.); and 10-1/2 x 11-1/2 x 18 (2173 cu. in.).

Fiberboard box, tray, bulk or bag pack, 11-3/4 x 12 x 19-3/4 (2785 cu. in.).

Among fiberboard boxes, bag pack, are the following: 12-1/2 x 11 x 21 (2888 cu. in.); 11-3/4 x 12 x 22 (3102 cu. in.) and 13-3/4 x 14-1/2 x 21-1/2 (4286 cu. in.).

Among figerboard boxes, tray-pack type, are the following: 11-3/4 x 12 x 19-3/4 (2785 cu. in.).

(*Reminder:* All containers are listed as *samples* of dimensions used and should not be interpreted as being more or less important than others not listed.)

As to net weights of apples in various packs, only an approximation can be given. The weight of a given volume of apples varies by variety, by size of the apples, by area in which grown, and by year, depending on climatic and other conditions.

Many of the states have checked apple weights, and a survey of some of these state figures shows the net weight of a bushel to be 42 to 46 lb. However, apples are no longer commonly sold by the bushel. The weight of a bushel, 2150 cu. in., can serve as a check against other bulk volumes used. Common units used for medium-sized fruit have weight ranges as follows: McIntosh, Cortland and early or summer varieties, 36 to 39 lb.; Golden Delicious, 37 to 40 lb.; Red Delicious and most winter varieties, 40 to 44 lb. per package.

To be sure what weight of apples they are getting, purchasers can check-weigh the fruit from typical containers. No rule or definite weight table for all containers can be given.

SERVINGS: The following information on fresh apples is from *Food Buying Guide for Type A School Lunches*, PA 270, USDA, revised January 1964:

Purchase Unit	Servings per Purchase Unit	Serving Size or Portion	Purchase Units for 100 Servings	Additional Yield Information
lb.	4.00	1 small raw apple (about 1/2 cup)	25	
lb.	5.60	1/2 cup raw, chopped, diced, or sliced	18	1 lb. as purchased - 0.76 lb. ready to cook or serve raw
	11.20	1/4 cup raw, chopped, diced, or sliced	9	
lb.	3.00	1 medium baked apple (about 1/2 cup cooked)	33-1/2	1 lb. as purchased - 0.63 lb. cooked
lb.	2.64	1/2 cup cooked, sliced	38	
	5.28	1/4 cup cooked, sliced	19	

QUALITY: The following is from Marketing Bulletin No. 13, USDA, "Firm, crisp, bright, clean, well-colored apples with good flavor are most desirable. Flavor is a varietal characteristic which is also greatly influenced by the stage of maturity at which the fruit is picked, and the conditions under which it is kept. Apples that are well colored for the variety usually have the full flavor of the particular variety, providing firmness and crispness of the flesh has not been impaired by age or other causes.

"Immature apples often lack color, are usually poor in flavor, and sometimes have a shriveled appearance after having been held in storage; overripe apples yield to slight pressure, and the flesh is usually soft, mealy, and lacking in flavor. Larger apples are more likely to be overripe than small or medium-sized fruits, particularly toward the end of the season for the variety.

"A defect known as 'scald' — a storage and transportation disorder caused by gases given off by the apples themselves — may occasionally be noted on apples during winter or spring months. It appears as brown-tinted, irregular surface areas. It affects green fruit more than that which is highly colored. In mild cases, scald merely causes light brown tinting of the skin and only slightly affects the quality of the fruit. In severe cases, the affected areas are dark brown, and the quality of the fruit is seriously affected. Other defects, such as decay, insect injury, or cuts affect the quality of apples in varying degrees. Since most apples now offered for sale are packed to comply with either a federal or state grade, it is unusual to find seriously defective, commercially packed apples, except as a result of natural deterioration from age and temperature."

GRADES: U.S. grade standards for apples are U.S. Extra Fancy, U.S. Fancy, U.S. No. 1, U.S. Utility, and Combination. "......*U.S. Extra Fancy* consists of apples of one variety which are mature but not overripe, carefully hand-picked, clean, fairly well formed; free from decay, internal browning, internal breakdown, scald, scab, bitter pit, jonathan spot, freezing injury, broken skins, bruises (except slight bruises which are incident to proper handling and packing), and visible watercore. The apples are also free from injury caused by russeting, sunburn, or sprayburn, limb rubs, hail, drought spots, scars, stem or calyx cracks, disease, insects, or other means; and free from damage by invisible watercore after January 31 of the year following the year of production. Each apple of this grade has the amount of color specified for the variety. (A table specifies color for each variety, and text further explains the color requirements, which cannot be reproduced here for lack of space.) ...In order to allow for *variations incident to proper grading and handling*, 10 percent of the apples in any lot may fail to meet the requirements of the grade, but not more than one-half of this amount, or 5 percent, shall be allowed for apples which are seriously damaged, including in the latter amount not more than 1 percent for apples affected by decay or internal breakdown. ...When size is designated by the numerical count for a container, not more than 5 percent of the apples in the lot may vary more than 1/4 inch in diameter. When size is designated by minimum or maximum diameter, not more than 5 percent of the apples in any lot may be smaller than the designated minimum and not more than 10 percent may be larger than the designated maximum. ...The *contents of individual packages* in the lot are subject to the following limitations: Provided, That the averages for the entire lot are within the tolerances specified for the grade: (a) Packages which contain more than 10 lb.: (1) Shall have not more than 1-1/2 times a specified tolerance of 10 percent or more and not more than double a tolerance of less than 10 percent, except that at least one apple which is seriously damaged by insects or affected by decay or internal breakdown may be permitted in any package. (b) Packages which contain 10 lb. or less: (1) Not over 10 percent of the packages may have more than three times the tolerance specified, except that at least one defective apple may be permitted in any package: Provided, That not more than one apple or more than 6 percent (whichever is the larger amount) may be seriously damaged by insects or affected by decay or internal breakdown.

"When the numerical count is marked on the container, percentages shall be calculated on the basis of count. When the minimum diameter or minimum and maximum diameters are marked on the container, percentages shall be calculated on the basis of weight.

"Packing Requirements. (a) Apples tray packed or cell packed in cartons shall be arranged according to approved and recognized methods. Packs shall be at least fairly tight or fairly well filled. "Fairly tight" means that apples are of the proper size for molds or cell compartments in which they are packed, and that molds or cells are filled in such a way that no more than slight movement of apples within molds or cells is possible. 'Fairly well filled' means that the net weight of apples in containers ranging from 2,100 to 2,900 cubic inch capacity is not less than 37 pounds for Cortland, Gravenstein, Jonathan, McIntosh and Golden Delicious varieties and not less than 40 pounds for all other varieties. (b) Closed cartons containing apples not tray packed or cell packed shall be fairly well filled, or the pack shall be sufficiently tight to prevent any appreciable movement of the apples. (c) Packs in wooden boxes or baskets shall be sufficiently tight to prevent any appreciable movement of apples within containers when the packages are closed. Each wrapped apple shall be completely enclosed by its individual wrapper. (d) Apples on the shown face of any container shall be reasonable representative in size, color and quality of the contents. (e) In order to allow for variations incident to proper packing, not more than 10

percent of the containers in any lot may fail to meet these requirements.

"Marking requirements. The numerical count or the minimum diameter of the apples packed in a closed container shall be indicated on the container. (a) When the numerical count is not shown the minimum diameter shall be plainly stamped, stenciled or otherwise marked on the container in terms of whole inches, or whole and not less than eighth inch fractions thereof, in accordance with the facts."

APPLES - Canned [10/17/53]

Grade A: Color: Internally or externally a reasonably uniform, bright color characteristic of similar varieties. **Uniformity of Size:** 90 percent of the drained weight of most uniform thickness, the thickness does not vary more than 1/4 in. **Absence of Defects:** Canned apples are practically free from defects. Extraneous matter present may not materially affect appearance or eating quality. For each 16 oz. of product, carpel tissue present does not exceed an area equal to 3/4 sq. in. Not more than 5 percent, by weight, of the units may be damaged, of which not more than 1 percent, by weight, may be seriously damaged. **Character:** Possess a reasonably tender texture, and not more than 5 percent of the drained weight consists of mushy apples.

USDA inspector weighs apple slices to be sure the minimum drained weight for the can size has been met. He also checks the color, flavor, and uniformity of size of the slices and looks for defects.

Grade C: Color: Characteristic of similar varieties, may vary noticeably, possess a slight, but not markedly brown, pink, or grey cast and are practically free from internal discoloration. **Uniformity of Size:** 75 percent of the drained weight consists of whole or practically whole slices 1-1/4 in. in length or longer. **Defects:** Fairly free from defects. Extraneous matter present may not seriously affect appearance or eating quality. For each 16 oz. of product, carpel tissue present does not exceed an area equal to 1-1/2 sq. in. Not more than 15 percent by weight of the units may be damaged, of which not more than 3 percent, by weight, may be seriously damaged. **Character:** May be variable in texture, with not more than 15 percent of the drained weight consisting of slices that are markedly hard, markedly soft, or mushy.

APPLES - Frozen [5/17/54]

Grade A: Same as canned, except in character, 3 percent of the drained weight consists of mushy apples.

Grade C: same as canned, except in character, not more than 12 percent of the drained weight consists of mushy apples.

APPLES - Dehydrated [Low Moisture] [7/1/57]

Grade A: Color: Have a good color that may be given a score of 17 to 20 points. "Good color" means a reasonably uniform, bright, light yellow to yellow white characteristic color, which upon cooking, is a reasonably bright color typical of cooked dehydrated apples that have been properly prepared and processed. **Uniformity of Size:** Reasonably uniform in size which may earn a score of 17 to 20 points. **Pie Pieces:** Not less than 75 percent are 3/4 in. or more in length; and of these, not less than 35 percent are 1 in. or more in length. Most of the units 3/4 in. or more in length are 3/16 in. or less thick. No more than 10 percent may be so fine as to pass through a U.S. Standard No. 4 sieve, and no more than 5 percent may pass through a No. 8 sieve. **Flakes:** Not less than 95 percent are less than 3/4 in. in length and 3/16 in. in thickness. Not more than

U. S. DEPARTMENT OF AGRICULTURE
AGRICULTURAL MARKETING SERVICE
FRUIT AND VEGETABLE DIVISION
PROCESSED PRODUCTS STANDARDIZATION AND INSPECTION BRANCH

INSPECTION AID No. 22
MAY 17, 1954

FROZEN APPLES—GUIDE FOR SCORING DEFECTS

KINDS OF DEFECT			DEFECTS PERMISSIBLE IN SCORE			
			20	19	18	17
Extraneous Material (Effect on appearance or eating quality)			None		Not material 2/	
Percent by Weight	Damaged units (as below) including seriously damaged	A	2	3	4 2/	5 2/
	Seriously damaged units		None		1 2/	1 2/
Carpel Tissue	Aggregating fraction of square inch per 16 ounces of product		1/8	1/4	1/2	3/4

[*Cont.*]

FROZEN APPLES—GUIDE FOR SCORING DEFECTS [Cont.]

Extraneous Material (May affect appearance or eating quality)		16 1/	15 1/	14 1/
		Materially	Not seriously 2/	
Percent by Weight	Damaged units (as below) including seriously damaged	8 2/	12 2/	15 2/
	Seriously damaged units	2 2/	3 2/	3 2/
Carpel Tissue	Aggregating in square inches per 16 ounces of product	1	1-1/4	1-1/2

C

DEFINITIONS:

Damaged unit - any unit which

Possesses area of green or light colored peel or
light brown bruise larger than 1/2 inch circle, or . . . .

Possesses light brown bruise more than 1/4 inch deep, or
Possesses area of red peel larger than 1/4 inch circle, or . . . .

Is materially affected as to appearance or eating quality
by blossom end material, dark brown bruise, or other internal
or external discoloration, or by other means.

Seriously damaged unit - Any unit which is damaged to such an extent that the appearance or eating
quality is seriously affected.

1/ Limiting rule.

2/ Provided extraneous matter, damaged and seriously damaged units singly or in combination, do not materially, or seriously affect
the appearance or eating quality. (As applicable)

AGRI-WASH

APPLES - Dried [10/24/55]

WORK SHEET

§ 52.2490 Work sheet for dried apples.

Size and kind of container _____
Container mark or identification _____
Label or brand _____
Net weight _____
Style _____
Moisture content _____
Varietal characteristics: ( ) Similar; ( ) Dissimilar _____
Flavor and odor: ( ) Normal; ( ) Other _____
Color: ( ) Good; ( ) Reasonably good; ( ) Fairly good _____

Uniformity of size	Grade A	Grade B	Grade C
Pie pieces:			
Approximate thickness	1/16 to 1/4 in.	1/16 to 1/4 in.	1/16 to 5/16 in.
Length, 1 in. or more (minimum)	85 percent	60 percent	40 percent
Pass through 5/16 in. square (maximum)	2 percent	6 percent	10 percent.
Slices (or rings):			
Approximate thickness (maximum)	1/4 in.	1/4 in.	5/16 in.
Whole and practically whole rings (minimum)	75 percent	60 percent	40 percent
Length, 1-1/4 in. or more (minimum)	75 percent	60 percent	40 percent.
Wedges:			
Variation in thickness (maximum)	1/4 in.	1/4 in.	5/16 in.
Length, 1-1/4 in. or more (minimum)	90 percent	75 percent	50 percent.
DEFECTS			
Slices (or rings): Small pieces (maximum)	5 percent	7 percent	10 percent.
All styles:			
Seeds (maximum)	4 per 16 oz.	6 per 16 oz.	10 per 16 oz.
Carpel tissue (maximum per 16 oz.)	3 sq. in.	6 sq. in.	9 sq. in.
Loose cores (maximum)	None	None	1 per 48 oz.
Damaged, total (maximum)	10 percent	15 percent	20 percent.
Includes calyxes and stems	1 percent	2 percent	3 percent.

Texture: ( ) Good; ( ) Reasonably good; ( ) Fairly good _____
Grade _____

(All percentages are "by weight" of dried apples)

10 percent may be so fine as to pass through a No. 8 sieve and almost none may pass through a No. 16 sieve. **Wedges:** Not less than 95 percent are 1 in. or shorter, and almost all are 5/8 in. or less thick. **Sauce Pieces:** Not less than 95 percent can pass through 0.466-in. square openings, not more than 10 percent can pass through a No. 8 sieve, and almost none can pass through a No. 16 sieve. **Defects:** Practically free from defects means practically free from carpel tissue and defects not specifically mentioned, and not more than 10 percent of pie pieces or wedges, or not more than 5 percent of flakes or sauce pieces may be damaged by pieces of peel, bitter pit or corky tissue, bruises or other discoloration, watercore, calyxes, and stems, provided that not more than 1 percent of pie pieces, or wedges, or .5 percent of flakes and sauce pieces may be damaged by calyxes and stems. **Texture:** Good texture means that the units are brittle and, upon cooking, are uniform in texture and tenderness, do not have tough units, and some of the pieces are disintegrated.

Grade B: Color: Dehydrated apples that fall into this class may not be graded above U.S. Grade B or U.S. Choice, regardless of the total score. "Reasonably good color" means a fairly uniform, bright, light yellow amber to yellow white color which, upon cooking, may be different in color, but is typical of properly prepared and processed, cooked dehydrated apples. **Size:** Fairly uniform in size which may earn a score of 14 to 16 points. **Pie Pieces:** At least 60 percent are 3/4 in. or more in length and 3/16 in. or less in thickness, and of these at least 25 percent are 1 in. or more in length. No more than 15 percent may be so fine as to pass through a No. 4 sieve and not more than 5 percent may pass through a No. 8 sieve. **Flakes:** At least 85 percent are less than 3/4 in. in length and 3/16 in. in thickness; and no more than 5 percent may pass through a No. 16 sieve. **Wedges:** At least 85 percent are 1 in. or more in length and 5/8 in. or less in thickness. **Sauce Pieces:** At least 85 percent can pass through 0.466-in. square openings, but no more than 5 percent can pass through a No. 16 sieve. **Defects:** "Reasonably free from defects" means reasonably free from carpel tissue and other defects not mentioned and that no more than 15 percent of pie pieces and wedges, or more than 8 percent of flakes and sauce pieces may be damaged by pieces of peel, bitter pit or corky tissue, bruises or other discolora-

tion, watercore, calyxes and stems, provided that no more than 2 percent of pie pieces and wedges or 1 percent of flakes and sauce pieces may be damaged by calyxes and stems. **Texture:** Brittle, and upon cooking are fairly uniform in texture and tenderness but moderately free from tough units. Pie pieces and wedges may have more than moderate disintegration, and flakes and sauce pieces may disintegrate to a grainy applesauce consistency. **Sstd:** Fails to meet requirements.

APRICOTS*

USES: Fresh apricots are eaten out of the hand; are fine stewed or baked, either by themselves, or with meat; are excellent in pies, puddings, cakes, and compotes; in or on ice cream and sherbet; and in molded deserts. Or try broiled apricots brushed before broiling with margarine and brown sugar. Rolling a thin strip of boiled ham around a fresh apricot wedge makes an interesting hors d'oeuvre. Apricots make excellent preserves. Commercially, great quantities of apricots are canned and some are dried, frozen, or made into preserves.

MARKETING SEASON: The marketing season for fresh apricots is May through August, but mostly June and July. The percentage of the annual total available each month is: May 2 percent; June 55 percent; July 37 percent; and August 5 percent.

The harvesting dates for apricots for fresh market in the three apricot states are as follows: California begins May 25, is most active June 1 to August 10, and ends August 15; Washington begins June 25, is most active July 10 to 30, and ends August 10; and Utah begins June 10, is most active June 15 - July 30, and ends August 5.

VARIETIES: Numerous apricot varieties have been grown in California. They can still be produced successfully, though not necessarily profitably, in several areas of the state. By about 1900, the list of acceptable varieties was greatly reduced. Since 1920 commercial production has been limited chiefly to two varieties, Royal and Tilton. The remainder is made up of Moorpark and minor varieties.

Royal and Blenheim These two varieties are so similar they

*Courtesy of United Fresh Fruit and Vegetable Association.

are considered together as Royal. Royal is supposed to have originated in France about 1830, and Blenheim in England a very few years later. "Royal is a firm, well-colored, highly flavored apricot of medium size. It is used widely for canning and drying and is also shipped fresh." When ripe the Royal is orange yellow, often with a red blush. The flesh is deep orange, rich, and sweet. It is medium to large in size, roundish in shape, with suture not too well defined. The stone is free.

Tilton This is orange to light yellow, often blushed. The fruit is medium-sized to small, oval and distinctly compressed, having a flat appearance, with the suture more noticeable than in the Royal. The flesh is somewhat lighter in color than Royal. It blooms and ripens somewhat later. The trees tend to bear alternate heavy and light crops but are prolific in the good years. Tilton was originated in King's County, Calif., by J.E. Tilton in 1885.

Moorpark A distinction should be made between the old English variety known as Moorpark and the Wenatchee Moorpark developed in Washington and now making up much of the Washington tonnage. The Moorpark as grown in California has fine quality with a rich plumlike taste. However, it ripens unevenly. The fruit matures and is marketed in California later than Royal and Tilton. The Wenatchee Moorpark is similar. Origin is not definitely known but is considered to be about 1880 in Washington or California. It has orange flesh and skin, unequal halves, large size, uneven ripening, fair texture and quality, may be used for fresh market or processing.

Derby Derby closely resembles Royal ... However, it tends to set somewhat lighter crops ... It is especially well suited for shipment to Eastern markets ... (it was) first planted near Winters, Calif. in about 1895. Derby Royals are the earliest commercial variety for fresh shipment.

Perfection This is an apricot grown both in Washington and California. It originated at Waterville, Wash. from seed planted in 1911 by John Goldbeck and was introduced in 1937. Orange skin and flesh, fruit somewhat flattened but usually with equal halves; skin pebbly; large (2-1/2 in.), medium suture, small pit, good flavor and quality, for fresh market, or processing. It is somewhat more acid than other important market varieties.

Chinese The "Chinese" apricot (actually not of Chinese origin, and not one variety, but a group of similar varieties) is important in Utah. There is a tendency to name seedling apricots with small early fruit "Chinese." Orange skin and flesh, small ripens unevenly, good quality, and texture.

The most commonly used container in California is the Brentwood lug box, measuring 16-1/8 x 12-1/2 x 4 to 7-1/8 in., net weight 25-1/2 lb. Others used in California to a lesser extent are the Los Angeles wooden lug box holding 27 to 30 lb., and 4-basket crates and cartons holding 26 lb. The Brentwood lug is used with a protective pad top and bottom and a liner. Its gross weight is about 29-1/2 lb.

In Washington, the most common container for out-of-state shipments is a corrugated carton holding 12 lb. and measuring 15-5/8 x 8-1/2 x 4-1/2 in. Four-basket wood crates and 4-basket cartons holding 20 lb. and measuring 16 x 16 x 4-3/4 in. were also used. A face-packed wood box holding 14 lb. and measuring 15 x 10-1/2 x 3-3/4 to 4-1/4 in. was used to a lesser extent. An unlidded 28-lb. loose-packed wood box measuring 18 x 11-1/2 x 7 in. is used for intrastate shipments.

Historically, apricots have been packed in rows, sized, and faced, and filled. In this method, the lug is made with the top in place and the bottom open. The top layer or two of fruit is packed on a regular arrangement before the remainder of the lug is loose-filled and the bottom is nailed on. In the face layers, the fruit is placed in a square pattern for the square pack and in a diamond pattern for the offset pack. The number of apricots per row in the face layers designates fruit size, with fractional counts denoting offset packs. Thus 6-row (or 7-row) means a straight pack of 6 (or 7) apricots per row while the 6-1/2-row count indicates an offset pack of 6 apricots per row with a half space at one end of each row.

High labor costs are sparking efforts to reduce the amount of labor in packing. One method of doing this is to volume-fill the lug and then settle it tight on a vibrator. However, this is little used for apricots.

The California Agricultural Code requires that apricots be packed in standard container numbers 1, 5, 22a, 22b or 24. *No. 1* is the standard basket approximately 8 in. square on top, 6-1/2 in. on bottom, and 4 to 5 in. deep, inside. *No. 5* is the standard crate 4 to 7-1/2 in. deep, 16 in. wide and 16-1/8 in. long inside. *No. 22a* is a special lug box 3-5/8 to 4-3/8 in. deep, 11 in. wide and 14-5/8 in. long. *No. 22b* is a special lug box 4 to 7-1/8

APRICOTS

FRESH (5/25/28   51.2925)
GRADES: U.S. NO. 1, U.S. No. 2
CANNED (4/1/74   52.2641)

GRADES:	"A" or "FANCY"	"B" or "CHOICE"	"C" or "STANDARD"	"SUBSTANDARD"
Minimum Score:	90	80	70	less than 70

Mixed pieces of irregular sizes & shapes	NET WT. OZ.	NET WT. METRIC	DRAINED WEIGHT OZ.		DRAINED WEIGHT METRIC	
			Extra heavy & heavy syrup	Other liquid mediums	Extra heavy & heavy syrup	Other liquid mediums
No. 8Z Tall	- -	- -	4.2	4.3	119.1 g	121.9 g
No. 303	- -	- -	8.7	8.9	246.6 g	252.3 g
No. 2½	18.7	530.1 g	15.5	16.0	439.4 g	453.6 g
No. 10	70.5	2.0 kg	59.7	61.7	1.7 kg	1.8 kg
Unpeeled or peeled halves						
No. 8Z Tall	5.3	150.3 g	4.2	4.3	119.1 g	121.9 g
No. 303	10.4	294.8 g	8.7	8.9	246.6 g	252.3 g
No. 2½	18.4	521.6 g	15.5	16.0	439.4 g	453.6 g
No. 10	69.5	1.97 kg	59.7	61.7	1.7 kg	1.8 kg
Peeled & unpeeled slices						
No. 8Z Tall	5.6	158.8 g	4.2	4.3	119.1 g	121.9 g
No. 303	11.0	311.8 g	8.7	8.9	246.6 g	252.3 g
No. 2½	19.4	550.0 g	15.5	16.0	439.4 g	453.6 g
No. 10	72.5	2.1 kg	59.7	61.7	1.7 kg	1.8 kg
Whole Unpeeled						
No. 8Z Tall	4.6	130.4 g	3.7	3.8	104.9 g	107.7 g
No. 303	9.2	260.1 g	7.6	7.8	215.5 g	221.1 g
No. 2½	16.5	467.8 g	13.8	14.2	391.2 g	402.6 g
No. 10	65.0	1.8 kg	57.5	59.0	1.6 kg	1.7 kg
Whole Peeled						
No. 8Z Tall	5.0	141.8 g	3.8	3.9	107.7 g	110.6 g
No. 303	9.9	280.7 g	8.0	8.2	226.8 g	232.5 g
No. 2½	17.5	496.1 g	14.4	14.8	408.2 g	419.6 g
No. 10	66.5	1.9 kg	57.9	59.5	1.6 kg	1.7 kg

CANNED APRICOTS

SYRUP	SPECIFIC GRAVITY (Brix Measurement)
"Extra heavy syrup" or "Extra heavily sweetened fruit juice(s) and water"; or "Extra heavily sweetened fruit juice(s)"	25° - 40°
"Heavy syrup" or "Heavily sweetened fruit juice(s) and water"; or "Heavily sweetened fruit juice(s)"	21° or more but less less than 25°
"Light syrup" or "Lightly sweetened fruit juice(s) and water" or "Lightly sweetened fruit juice(s)"	16° or more but less than 21°
"Slightly sweetened water" or "Extra light syrup" or "Slightly sweetened fruit juice(s) and water" or "Slightly sweetened fruit juice(s)"	10° or more but less than 16°
"In water"	N.A.
"In fruit juice and water"	N.A.
"In fruit juice"	N.A.
"Artificially sweetened"	N.A.

Canned Solid-Pack Apricots
(4/1/74   52.6241)

Grades:	"C" or "STANDARD"	"SUBSTANDARD"
Minimum Score:	70	Less than 70
	DRAINED WEIGHT OZ.	DRAINED WEIGHT METRIC
No. 10	89.5	2.5 kg

FROZEN (6/20/63   52.5521)
DEHYDRATED (6/30/74   52.3871)

Grades:	"A" or "FANCY"	"B" or "CHOICE"	"SUB-STANDARD"
Minimum Score:	85	70	less than 70

DRIED (5/24/67   52.5761)

Grades:	"A" or "FANCY"	"B" or "CHOICE"
	"C" or "STANDARD"	"D" or "SUBSTANDARD"

in. deep by 12-1/2 in. wide by 16-1/8 in. long. *No. 24* is a standard lug box 3-3/4 to 7-1/8 in. deep by 13-1/2 in. wide by 16-1/8

in. long. This is the Sanger lug, and is often packed with 25 lb. net.

Also authorized by California recently is standard container *No. 65A*, net weight 26 lb., 19-11/16 x 15-3/4 x 4 to 7 in.; container *No. 65B* 19-11/16 x 11-13/16 x 4 to 10 in. The depth is optional to accommodate any of a number of other commodities.

"The depth dimension of containers which are designated for apricots (in California) shall include in the measurement of the specified depth any cleats used, if any are used.

"Every container of apricots shall bear upon it in plain sight and in plain letters on one outside end all of the following information: (a) the name of the person that first authorized the packing of the apricots or the name under which such packer is engaged in business, together with a sufficiently explicit address to permit ready location of such packer; (b) the name of the variety, if known, or if not known, the words 'unknown variety' or 'seedlings'; (c) the size description, row count, or count, if the apricots are packed in any style container.

"In the case of the 4-basket crate, the numerical description of the pack in the top layer of the basket shall be used to designate size. If the numerical description is used to designate size on a lug of loose or packed apricots, it means that apricots of that size would tightly pack the top layer of the standard container number 1 as used in the 4-basket crate. Such size description shall be directly followed by the word 'size'. If row count is used to designate the size on any lug of packed apricots, the lug shall be marked with the number of rows of apricots packed laterally across the end of the container, directly followed by the word 'row' or 'rows'. If the count is used to designate the contents of the container, a variation of four apricots more or less than the number stated shall be allowed."

SERVINGS AND WEIGHTS: A pound of fresh apricots serves 6 with 2 medium raw apricots apiece, about half a cup. On this basis it takes 16-3/4 lb. for 100 servings. A pound of apricots provides 5.41 portions of 1/2 cup of raw halves and it takes 18-1/2 lb. to serve 100. A pound provides 10.82 servings of 1/4 cup of raw halves and it takes 9-1/4 lb. to serve 100. One pound as purchased equals 0.94 lb. ready to serve raw.

Grades: U.S. standards for apricots, effective May 1928, provide for two grades, U.S. 1 and U.S. 2. *"U.S. 1* shall consist of apricots of one variety which are mature but not soft, overripe, or shriveled and which are well formed, free from decay, cuts, skin breaks, worm holes, and from damage caused by limb-rubs, russeting, growth cracks, dirt, scab, scale, hail, disease, insects, or mechanical, or other means. In order to allow for variations incident to proper grading and handling, not more than 10 percent, by count, of any lot may be below the requirements of this grade, but not more than one-half of this tolerance, or 5 percent, shall be allowed for defects causing serious damage, and not more than one-fifth of this amount, or 1 percent, shall be allowed for decay."

MARKETING AND PACKAGING REQUIREMENTS: The minimum size, numerical count, or description of pack of the apricots in any package shall be plainly labeled, stenciled, or otherwise marked on the package. (a) *Numerical Count.* When the numerical count is used, the apricots in any container shall not vary more than 1/4 in. in diameter. (b) *Minimum Size.* "Minimum size" refers to the diameter of the smallest apricot in the package. It shall be stated in terms of whole and eighth inches, as 1-1/2 in. min., 1-5/8 in. min., etc., in accordance with the facts. (c) *Description of Pack.* "Description of pack" refers especially to apricots packed in 4-basket crates and shall be designated according to the arrangement of the apricots in the basket as 4-4, 4-5, 5-5, 5-6 or 6-6. These packs shall not be more than three layers deep. The figures given represent the number of rows of apricots each way in the basket. The bottom layer in any basket shall contain one row less than the two upper layers, that is in a 5-5 pack the apricots in the bottom layer must not be smaller than will pack 4-5. (d) *Tolerance.* In order to allow for variations incident to proper sizing, not more than 10 percent, by count, of the apricots in any package may be below the minimum size specified.

CALIFORNIA CODE. The Agricultural Code of California, applying to 68 percent or more of all fresh apricots shipped in the U.S., provides that "Fresh apricots shall be mature but not overripe and free from any of the following defects: (a) insect injury which has penetrated or damaged the flesh; (b) mold, brown rot, and decay; (c) serious damage caused by cuts, bruises, cracks, shot hole fungus, growth cracks, scab, hail, or other causes.

"With the exception of shot hole fungus, damage to any one apricot is not serious unless it causes a waste of 10 percent, by weight, of the individual apricot. Damage to any apricot caused by shot hole fungus is not serious unless the spots cover an aggregate area of more than 1/2 in. in diameter. *Not more than 10 percent, by count,* of the apricots in any one container or bulk lot may be below the requirements which are prescribed by this article, but not to exceed one-half of this tolerance shall be allowed for any one cause.

"Apricots shall be in standard container Numbers 1, 5, 22a, 22b, or 24.

"Packed apricots shall not vary in size between the fruits in any one container, more than 1/4 in. in diameter, if measured through the widest portion of the cross section of the fruit."

APRICOTS—Canned [9/18/70]

Grade A: Color: Unpeeled or peeled halves; unpeeled or peeled whole. All the units may possess pale yellow areas not exceeding 1/4 of a unit; not more than a total of 5 percent of the units, or 1 unit, may possess a reasonably good color including pale yellow areas, or may possess light greenish yellow area; but none of the units may possess a fairly good color including pale yellow areas, or light greenish yellow areas, or light green or light green areas on a unit.

Grade B: Color: Unpeeled or peeled halves; unpeeled or peeled whole. All of the units may possess pale yellow areas or may possess light greenish yellow areas; not more than a total of 10 percent by count of the units, or 1 unit, may possess a fairly good color, including pale yellow areas exceeding 1/2 on a unit, or light greenish yellow areas exceeding 1/4, but not more than 1/2 on a unit, or light green areas not exceeding 1/4 on a unit; and none may possess light greenish yellow areas exceeding 1/2 on a unit, or light green areas exceeding 1/4 on a unit.

Grade C & D: Color: Unpeeled or peeled halves; unpeeled or peeled whole. All units may possess pale yellow areas, may possess light greenish yellow areas, not exceeding 1/2 of a unit, or may possess light green areas not exceeding 1/4 of a unit; and not more than a total of 10 percent of the units, or 1 unit, may possess light greenish yellow areas exceeding 1/2 on a unit or may possess light green areas exceeding 1/4 on a unit.

Grade A: Color: Unpeeled or peeled slices; unpeeled or peeled, mixed pieces of irregular sizes and shape. Not more than 5 percent, by weight, of the drained fruit may possess a reasonably good color or may consist of units that possess predominating pale yellow or light greenish yellow areas, and none of the units may possess a fairly good color, including predominating light green area.

Grade B: Color: Unpeeled or peeled slices; unpeeled or peeled mixed pieces of irregular sizes and shapes. Not more than 10 percent, by weight, of the drained fruit may possess a fairly good color or may consist of units that possess predominating pale yellow or light greenish yellow areas or light green areas: Provided, that such light green areas do not affect materially the appearance of the product.

Grade C & D: Color: Unpeeled or peeled slices; unpeeled or peeled, mixed pieces of irregular sizes and shapes. Not more than 10 percent, by weight, of the drained fruit may consist of units that possess predominantly light greenish yellow areas, or light green areas, or shades of color not typical of fairly well-matured apricots: Provided, that such does not affect seriously the appearance of the product.

Canned Solid-Pack Apricots [C-SP]: Color: Not more than 15 percent, by weight, of the drained fruit may consist of units that possess light greenish yellow areas, or shades of color not typical of fairly well-matured apricots: Provided, see Color for Grades C & D.

Grade A: Uniformity of Size and Symmetry: Weight of largest full-size, halved or whole apricot does not exceed weight of smallest full-size unit by more than 50 percent. Weight of each half is not less than 2/5 oz., and not more than 5 percent, by count, of unpeeled halves may possess off-suture cuts. Unpeeled halves containing more than 10 percent and 15 percent off-suture cuts shall not be graded above U.S. Grade B and Grade C respectively, regardless of total score: see table.

Defects: All grades are practically free from pit material and are practically free from any defects not specifically

mentioned that affect materially the appearance or edibility.

Good Character: Unit possesses a practically uniform, tender, fleshy texture typical of well-ripened, properly prepared, and properly processed canned apricots; the units are uniformly intact and may be soft, but hold their original conformation and size without material disintegrating, and not more than 5 percent of the units or unit, if such unit exceeds 5 percent, may possess a reasonably good character: Provided, that the appearance or eating quality, or both, is not more than slightly affected by the character of such units.

Grade B: Uniformity of Size and Symmetry: see Grade A Size and Symmetry. All wording is the same, except for the percentages 75 percent; 2/5 oz.; 15 percent, 10 and 15 percent. **Defects:** All grades are reasonably free from any defects not specifically mentioned that affect materially the appearance or edibility. **Character:** Unit possesses a reasonably tender texture typical of properly ripened canned apricots that are properly processed; the texture is reasonably fleshy, and the units are reasonably thick, but the tenderness may be variable within the unit or among the units; the units may be soft to slightly firm or ragged but are not mushy; and not more than 10 percent of the units, or one unit if such unit exceeds the allowance of 10 percent, by count, may possess a fairly good character, except for units that are so firm as to be "not tender"; Provided, that in all containers comprising the sample, the units with fairly good character do not exceed an average of 10 percent of the total number of units.

Grade C: Uniformity of Size and Symmetry: see Grade A. All wording is the same except the percentages 100 percent, 2/5 oz., 30 percent. Apricots not meeting Standard S, Grade D and when not meeting minimum and variable weight requirements, are also "Below Standard in Quality." **Defects:** All grades are practically free from pit material and are fairly free from any defects not specifically mentioned that affect materially the appearance or edibility. **Character:** The units possess a texture of properly processed apricots which may be variable in fleshiness but the texture is fairly fleshy and the units are intact; the unit may be lacking uniformity of tenderness; may be markedly ragged with frayed edges or may be very soft; not more than 10 percent may be mushy or units that are so firm as to be "not tender."

Grade D: Uniformity of Size and Symmetry: "Below Standard in Quality." See Grade C. **Defects:** See Grade C. **Character:** May be canned apricots of any style that meet the requirements of Grade C with respect to units that are so firm as to be "not tender," but which otherwise possess a texture with not more than 25 percent by weight of the drained apricots that consist of mushy fruit.

Grade C-SP: Uniformity of Size and Symmetry: See Grade C. **Defects:** See Grade C. **Character:** Possess a "fairly good character for canned, 'solid pack' apricots"; a texture of properly processed apricots which may be variable in tenderness, consisting of very soft to fairly firm units and crushed or broken units.

APRICOTS—Canned[1975 Revisions]

The Food and Drug Administration amended the standards of identity for Canned Apricots, compliance with which may have begun on March 11, 1975, but mostly after December 31, 1975. The following amendment to the USDA standards for canned apricots was proposed to bring them into line with the amended FDA Standards of Identity.

Product description would be amended to include the Food and Drug citation for "artificially sweetened" canned apricots as follows: Product description.

"Canned apricots " is the product represented as defined in the Standards of Identity for canned apricots (21 CFR 27.10 and 27.14) issued pursuant to the Federal Food, Drug, and Cosmetic Act, and prepared in one of the styles specified in 52.2642; in one of the liquid media specified in 52.2644; and is sealed in a container and so processed by heat as to prevent spoilage.

The food may be seasoned with one or more of the optional ingredients permitted in the aforementioned standards of identity.

Canned Solid-Pack Apricots

Product description.

"Canned solid-pack apricots" is the product represented as defined in the Standards of Identity for canned apricots (21 CFR 27.10) issued pursuant to the Federal Food, Drug, and Cosmetic Act, and prepared in one of the styles specified in

52.6242 and is sealed in a container and so processed by heat as to prevent spoilage.

The food may be seasoned with one or more of the optional ingredients permitted in the aforementioned standards of identity.

APRICOTS—Dehydrated [Low Moisture] [6/30/74]

Grade A: Color: Overall color is characteristic for the product, with respective style ranging from bright reddish orange to bright orange amber among the units and within individual units, and is reasonably uniform; such characteristic color, upon cooking, is a reasonably bright color typical of cooked, low-moisture apricots that have been properly prepared and processed. **Size:** Nugget-type; pieces. Practically all of the units are of such size and shape as to pass through 0.625 in. (5/8 in.) square openings and not more than 10 percent may pass through meshes of U.S. Standard No. 8 sieve (0.0937 in. +3 percent, sq. openings). **Diced:** Practically all of the units except for fine pieces, are definite, partial cube-shaped and not less than 60 percent, approximate cube shapes of 1/4 in. to 1/2 in. square or 1 surface dimension; not more than 5 percent may pass through meshes of a U.S. Standard No. 8 sieve (0.0937 in., +3 percent sq. openings). **Slices:** Practically all of the units, except in small pieces, are definite parallel-cut strips and not less than 70 percent, approximate 1/4-in. to 1/2-in. in width and approximate 3/4 in. or more in length; and not more than 5 percent may pass through meshes of a U.S. Standard No. 8 sieve (0.0937 in. + 3 percent sq. openings). **Defects:** Practically free from defects that affect more than slightly the appearance or eating quality either in the low-moisture apricots or after cooking; and not more than a total of 5 percent may be damaged units: Provided, that not more than 2 percent may be seriously damaged. **Texture:** Nugget-type: The cooked mass has a reasonably uniform texture and finish that is coarse or grainy with practically no hard particles. **Pieces:** The cooked product is practically free from hard, firm, or tough units, and there is no more than moderate disintegration except for fine pieces that may have been present. **Diced:** Cooked product is practically free from hard or tough units and substantially retains the semblance of the strips of apricots, except for small pieces or odd-shaped pieces that may be present.

Grade B: Color: Overall color may vary considerably, ranging from slightly dull orange or dull amber; and such characteristic color, upon cooking, may be slightly dull but is typical of apricots that have been properly prepared and processed. **Size:** See Grade A: all wording is the same except as follows: Nugget-type; pieces: 25 percent. Diced: 40 percent ... 10 percent. **Slices:** 50 percent, approximately 1/4 in. to 1/2 in. in width; 10 percent. **Defects:** reasonably free from defects that affect materially the appearance or eating quality either in the low-moisture apricots or after cooking; and not more than a total of 10 percent may be damaged units: provided, that not more than 4 percent may be seriously damaged units. **Texture:** Nugget-type: The cooked mass has a fairly uniform texture and finish that may range from fine and grainy to coarse and grainy; and hard particles may be noticeable but not objectionable. **Pieces:** Cooked product is fairly free from hard, firm, or tough units, and may disintegrate generally into a coarse, saucelike consistency. **Diced:** Fairly free from hard or tough units and consists of substantial amounts of diced apricot pieces intermingled with a slight amount of mushiness from small pieces which may have been present. **Slices:** Fairly free from hard or tough units, and consisting of substantial amounts of strips of apricots intermingled with a slight amount of mushiness from small pieces which may have been present. sstd: Fails to meet requirements.

APRICOTS—Dried [5/24/67]

Grade A: Possess similar varietal characteristics; and possess a practically uniform, bright, typical color, characteristic of well-matured apricots. The fruit may possess pale yellow areas around the stem that do not exceed an area equivalent to 1/8 of the outer surface side of the unit; not more than 5 percent may be of a color described in U.S. Grade B, but none of the fruit may be of a color described in U.S. Grade C. Not more than a total tolerance of 10 percent may be slabs, immature, or may possess pits, or pieces of pits; may be damaged by discoloration, sunburn, hail marks, scab, disease, insect injury, or other similar defects; or may be affected by

mold, decay, insect infestation (no live insects are permitted); imbedded dirt, or other foreign material: Provided, that no more than 2/5 of the total tolerance, or 4 percent by weight, may be affected by mold, decay, insect infestation, etc. (see above): Further provided, that not more than 1/10 or 1 percent may be affected by decay.

Grade B: Possess a reasonably uniform, bright, typical color, characteristic of reasonably well-matured apricots. The fruit may possess pale yellow areas around the stem end that do not exceed an area of equivalent to 1/4 of the outer surface side of the units; not more than 10 percent of the fruit may be of a color described in U.S. Grade C, but none of the units may possess light green areas that exceed an area equivalent to 1/4 of the outer surface side of the unit. Not more than a total tolerance of 15 percent may be slabs, etc. See Grade A. Only changes are as follows: Provided, 5 percent; Further provided, 1/15.

Grade C: Possess similar varietal characteristics; and possess a fairly uniform, typical color, characteristic of fairly well-matured apricots. The fruit may be pale yellow in color and may possess light green areas around the stem end of the fruit that do not exceed an area equivalent to 1/25 of the outer surface side of the units, but not more than 15 percent may possess light green areas that exceed an area equivalent to 1/25 of the outer surface side of the unit. Not more than a total of 20 percent may be slabs, etc. See Grade A. All wording is the same except as follows: Provided, 5 percent: Further provided: 1/10 or 2 percent.

Grade D: Fails to meet requirements.

AVOCADOS*

USES: Devotees of the avocado claim its use as a food is limited only by the user's imagination. Beginning with breakfast, avocados are used to enhance the flavor and nourishment of scrambled eggs (cubed or mashed avocado is blended in just as the eggs begin to "set"). Mashed avocado spread on toast is another breakfast treat. For lunch, an avocado sandwich is attractive, filling, and good. Or, avocado cubes can be added to soup or made into a cream of avocado soup. The fruit also goes well in almost every salad. Some like just the thinly sliced

*Courtesy of United Fresh Fruit and Vegetable Association

AVOCADOS

FRESH (9/3/57   51.3050)
GRADES: U.S. No. 1; U.S. Combination;
U.S. No. 2; U.S. No. 3

avocado with a sprinkling of salt and pepper, and lemon or lime juice. Or it can be served with lettuce, watercress, bean sprouts, tomatoes, litchi nuts, cashew nuts, or as a mousse.

The avocado is the basic ingredient of a popular Mexican and American dish, guacamole. There are an infinite number of guacamole recipes governed mostly by the consumer's tolerance for highly seasoned food. Avocados are served with fish, they can be baked, they are made into souffles, sauces, cream pies, whips and even ice cream. Since 1964 there has been a growing market for frozen avocados in the form of guacamole. There has also been some experimentation with frozen, half-shell avocados, and the market is limited to institutional users.

MARKETING SEASON: Fresh avocados are available throughout the year, with varieties making the difference for any given month.

VARIETIES: Grouped within the three principal *races* described under *BOTANY* are about two dozen varieties of commercial value. Of the California varieties, the **Fuerte** is the production leader accounting for more than 75 percent (average) of the annual crop. It is almost ideally adapted to market requirements as to size, color, long season, or maturity, and hardiness. It is not adaptable to growing in Florida. The Fuerte is a Guatemalan/Mexican hybrid that was brought as budwood to California from Mexico in 1911. The fruit is green, pear-shaped, 8 to 16 oz., thin, pliable and leathery, somewhat pebbled skin. The flavor is very good.

Hass is the second leading variety from California, with production averaging about 50 percent of the Fuerte total. (Precise averages are rather meaningless due to the alternate bearing tendency discussed under *SUPPLY*. For example, during the 1963-64 season, Hass production was less than 40 percent of Fuerte. For the 1964-65 season it was almost 90 percent). The Hass is of the Guatemalan race but a seedling of California origin. It was introduced by R.G. Hass of LaHabra Heights. The fruit runs from 6 to 12 oz., has a leathery and somewhat rough skin of medium thickness, is green at maturity but gradually turns black.

Bacon and **Zutano** are the two other principal varieties which with Fuerte make up the "fall and winter" crop. **Rincon** and **MacArthur** are combined with Hass to make up the "spring and summer" supply. The season begins October 1 of each year. Fall and winter varieties are shipped during the first 6 months; spring and summer varieties during the second 6 month period.

Other California varieties of importance include the **Nabal** of the Guatemalan race; the **Anaheim**; the **Dickinson**; **Carlsbad**; **Itzamma** and **Edranol** all of the Guatemalan race. Mexican race varieties include the **Puebla** and previously mentioned Zutano.

Florida varieties, in order of commercial importance, are: **Booth 8**; **Lula**; **Booth 7**; and **Waldin**. Waldin appears on the market in late August followed by Booth 8 in early September, Booth 7 in early October and Lula in mid-October. **Fuchs** appears in late April, **Pollack** in mid-July and **Hickson** in mid-October, making up the next three varieties in order of importance.

Booth 8 and Booth 7 varieties both originated in Homestead, Fla., as seedlings of an unknown Guatemalan parent in mixed planting with West Indian avocados. Booth 8 is oblong-ovate, small to medium large, nine to 28 ounces, medium green, rather dull skin that is slightly roughened. Booth 7 fruit is rounded, obovate, medium size, 10 to 20 oz., bright green with slightly pebbled, glossy skin.

The Lula originated in Miami, Fla., from a seed reported to be from the original Taft tree at Orange, Calif. The fruit is pyriform or occasionally necked, medium large, 14 to 24 oz., light green with a nearly smooth skin. The Waldin is also from a seed, this one planted at Homestead, Fla. The fruit is oblong to oval with a characteristic flattening on one side of the blossom end, medium to large, 14 to 28 oz., pale green to greenish yellow in color and a smooth skin.

CONTAINERS: Both California and Florida ship avocados in corrugated cartons, with California using some wood. In California, either corrugated or wood flats contain 12-1/2 lb. of fruit net when packed. The state also ships quantities of doubles referred to in the trade as "lugs," which contain 25 lb. of fruit net when packed. California state law permits a tolerance of only 10 percent shrinkage in net weight of the fruit at any time after packing in the 12-1/2 or 25 lb. containers. The 4/5 bushel carton (fiberboard) holds 36 to 40 lb. of fruit.

BANANAS*

USES: Probably the most popular use of the banana is for eating out of hand; but it also has a wide variety of uses in the menu: as sliced in salads; for banana cream pie; banana cake; banana pudding; fried or baked banana slices; banana milk shakes; banana ice cream; and, of course, banana split sundae ... Try a chocolate banana cake with banana layers, mocha frosting and banana slices on top...A banana soda can make a teenager flip...And what about banana chunks with or without other fruit in a gelatin mold? ... Let us not overlook banana cookies or banana tea muffins...Try a sponge cake with bananas and lemon sauce; or a banana fresh fruit compote; and why not banana custard?...There are unlimited ways to serve bananas and these are only a few.

For example, a roast loin of pork takes on new glamour when ringed with broiled banana; and roast chicken is sparked by the addition of bananas that have been delicately sauteed in butter...A smart cook has come up with banana hotcakes, with banana pieces in the dough and bananas on the side. Another suggests banana wrapped in bacon and egg blanket...Then there is banana chutney; and one of the most obvious uses of bananas, not yet mentioned, sliced bananas in cream...A simple frosting for a plain white cake can be made by mashing ripe bananas, adding a teaspoon or so of fresh lemon juice, and sugar to taste...A favorite dessert of children is a banana whip. Just whip mashed ripe bananas into stiffly beaten, sweetened egg white, and sprinkle with cinnamon if you like.

Still another idea is home-made banana candles, involving no cooking. Just mash the bananas, mix in the sugar and mold the candles with your fingers. They can be dipped in coconut or chocolate shot...A banana omelet brings nothing but applause. And what is better than a banana in the school lunch? Nutritious, delicious, and so easy to eat ... Bananas combine deliciously with a sauce of strawberry puree and fresh orange juice for a dessert that looks and tastes like spring...West Indies Marmalade is made of banana, fresh pineapple, fresh orange, sugar and lemon or lime juice...And for fancy living, how about bananas in sherry?

For a tropical fruit medley, combine slices of bananas with wedges of papaya, mango, fresh pineapple, fresh orange sections, and sliced strawberries. Sprinkle with fresh lime juice and a little wine, chill, and serve in sherbet glasses... Banana shortcake should not be overlooked; nor sliced bananas on breakfast cereal; nor fresh banana eggnog...Bananas should not be overlooked by anyone on a low fat diet, since bananas have virtually no fat...And for a wind-up, there is a fine recipe for banana-orange nut bread.

There are many other uses of parts of the banana plant. Corms, shoots, and male buds are used in the Old World as food. The fleshy rhizomes are eaten in some places as a starchy food, resembling a yam in taste. Starch can be extracted from the pseudostems. Fiber is a common product of cultivated bananas. Green leaves of the banana are used throughout the tropics as umbrellas, plates, and wrapping material. Sometimes food is wrapped in banana leaves before baking. In Uganda the sheaths are sometimes used for thatching. Pads for carrying head loads are made from dried leaves twisted into the form of a ring. Sometimes this same material is used for bedding. Then, too, portions of certain kinds of bananas are used for love potions and for other magic, though documentation of the results is scarce. Banana plants have been used for stock feed. Some kinds are used as ornamentals.

MARKETING SEASON: Bananas are available in the United States in all months with no marked peaks or troughs, except in the event of severe blowdowns, revolution, or other catastrophes in the growing areas, or strikes involving shipping. Usually imports are a little less in July, August, and September than other months because of heavy competition from summer fruits. The following table shows average monthly availability of bananas as a percentage of the annual total.

MONTHLY AVAILABILITY OF BANANAS EXPRESSED AS A PERCENTAGE OF THE TOTAL ANNUAL SUPPLY

Jan.	Feb.	March	April	May	June
%	%	%	%	%	%
7.7	8.0	9.2	8.9	9.2	8.5

*Courtesy of United Fresh Fruit and Vegetable Association.

MONTHLY AVAILABILITY OF BANANAS [Cont.]

July %	Aug. %	Sept. %	Oct. %	Nov. %	Dec. %
7.6	7.4	7.6	8.6	8.4	8.8

VARIETIES: While there are innumerable varieties of cultivated bananas, the two main commercial varieties are **Cavendish** and **Gros Michel**. The scientific names are in dispute. Gros Michel in one classification is called **Musa sapientum** and the Cavendish is called **Musa cavendishii**. For the purposes of this report, the commercial names will be used. (Valery is a trademark name for Cavendish.) The Gros Michel formerly made up 73 percent of banana shipments and Cavendish 27 percent, but the proportions are now reversed with Gros Michel on the decline. The reasons are that the Cavendish variety is less subject to diseases that take a heavy toll of bananas, and more plants per acre can be grown.

The Gros Michel, according to Simmonds, is a big and a very vigorous plant that bears heavy, symmetrical bunches of large fruit; the fruits are bottlenecked; the plants have undersheaths of green or pale pink; the fruits are bright yellow when ripe and maintain this color; and the plants are susceptible to Panama disease. A further description by the Special Committee on Bananas of the Inter-American Economic and Social Council is: Tall variety with a stalk height of 15 to 20 ft. producing large bunches of 8 to 15 or more hands. The fruit may be distinguished from other commercial bananas by the tapered point...This variety has a pleasant flavor, ripens uniformly, and generally is highly resistant to bruising and discoloration.

Gros Michel was long the most abundantly produced banana clone. It has survived in the face of destruction by Panama disease by continual removal of plantations to new lands.

"Gros Michel appears to be 'native' (i.e., long established as a local cultivar) in Burma, Thailand, Malaya, Indonesia and Ceylon...In the New World, it appeared first in Martinique early in the 19th century. Kervegant (1935) suggests that it was introduced by one Baudin, a naval officer who introduced numerous Asian plants to the Botanic Garden at St. Pierre. It was known in the island as 'Figue Baudin' and was taken from there about 1835 to Jamaica by Jean Francois Pouyat.

"In Jamaica it became known first as the 'Pouyat' or 'martinique' banana, later as 'Gros Michel'. Pouyat was awarded a prize of one doubloon by the Jamaica Agricultural Society for 'introducing so valuable a variety into the Island'. Forty years later, Gros Michel had been widely distributed in the Caribbean area and was adopted for the banana trades that were then being developed. Introductions to the Pacific were made around the turn of the century from Jamaica to Fiji (1891), to Hawaii (by way of Nicaragua, 1903), and to Australia (1910)."

The Cavendish is a similar plant but the undersheaths, especially on young suckers, are bright red; the fruit is greenish at ripeness; the fruit tips are blunt (a primary distinguishing feature when the fruit only is being viewed), and the plant is immune to Panama disease.

In the case of both varieties, the fruit is 5 times or more as long as broad and markedly curved.

"The main advantages of the Cavendish forms," says the Special Committee on Bananas, "are their high resistance to Panama disease, their ability to withstand strong winds, and their high yield, due to the fact that many more plants can be grown per hectare. The chief disadvantages of this type of banana are that it requires a greater degree of care to prevent bruising in handling and shipping, and advanced techniques in obtaining uniform ripening results. The Cavendish has much the size and flavor of the Gros Michel" (some argue that they are dissimilar).

The main Cavendish clone is the Dwarf Cavendish, referring not to the fruit, but the height of the stalk. It bears under a wide range of conditions, says Simmonds, and seems to be better adapted to growth in cool climates than other clones. Its low stature makes it less susceptible to wind damage than most other bananas and also makes treatment of the bunches with insecticides, protective bags, etc., easy. But in winter in the subtropics, the stature permits chilling which a taller clone may avoid.

Another export type of banana, but one not much seen in the U.S., is the Lacatan, with numerous related forms. All produce bunches of blunt-fingered fruit similar to Cavendish and with much the same ripening characteristics. All are highly resistant to Panama disease.

Small quantities of the small-fingered red banana are also imported into the U.S.

SERVINGS AND WEIGHTS: The following table prepared by the U.S. Dept. of Agriculture gives information about purchasing and serving units. "A.P." means "As purchased."

Food as Purchased	Purchase Unit	Servings per Purchase Unit	Serving Size or Portion	Purchase Units for 100 Servings	Additional Yield Information
BANANAS					
Fresh	lb.	3.00	1 medium banana (about 2/3 cup)	33-1/2	1 lb. AP= 0.68 lb. ready-to-serve raw
	lb.	4.39	1/2 cup sliced	23	
		8.78	1/4 cup sliced	11-1/2	

On the basis of serving 1 medium banana as a portion, 1 lb. would serve three persons; for 25 portions, 8.5 lb. would be needed; for 100 portions, 33.5 lb. would be used; 25 lb. would serve 75 portions; and the usual 40-lb. box would serve 120. A pound sliced for 2-oz fruit cups provides 5.44 portions; 4.75 lb. are needed for 25 portions, and 18.5 lb. for 100 portions. For 3-oz. portions sliced, 1 lb. yields 3.63 portions; it takes 7 lb. for 25 portions, and 27.75 lb. for 100 portions. For 4-oz. mashed portions, 1 lb. provides 2.72 portions; and it takes 9.25 lb. for 25 portions, and 37 lb. for 100 portions. *Yield from fruit as purchased is 68 percent.*

QUALITY: Unlike some other fruits, bananas do not ripen satisfactorily on the plant and *can be ripened to optimum quality off the plant.* This means that fruit just as good as any harvested in the tropics where bananas are grown can be made available at distant points, such as in the United States. This is made possible by scientific techniques of determining maturity, harvesting, handling, packing, shipping, and ripening, followed by wholesale distribution and retailing.

Generally speaking, a good banana should be plump, unblemished, firm, and bright in appearance. Exact color is not a quality factor. A greenish banana may be of just as good quality as a fully yellow one, but not yet at the eating stage. It can be ripened at room temperature. However, bananas displayed at retail usually are mostly, if not all, yellow, and often are ready to eat, or required only very brief ripening. *When the banana is at the stage the consumer likes, it may be refrigerated.* Some persons like bananas fully ripe with brown-flecked skin; and some like them at the all-yellow stage; or even with a green tip. When the reach the desired stage, reserve supplies can be cooled and will keep for several days with continued good quality of the flesh, but the skin may turn brown.

On the other hand, the quality of a green banana will be damaged by ordinary household refrigeration. Once the ripening cycle of the banana has been interrupted by cold, it does not resume normal ripening when the temperature is raised. So keep it out of the refrigerator until it has reached the desired ripeness.

Avoid fruit that is soft, or otherwise shows bruising by considerable discoloration.

About the myth that "tree-ripened" bananas are the most desirable kind, the United Fruit Co. says, "The truth is that no resident of the tropics eats bananas directly from the tree. He gathers the bunch at the same stage of ripeness as the fruit which is harvested for export (fully developed but green), then he hangs it in a shady spot, and waits for it to ripen. He does this because experience has taught him that the majority of bananas, if left upon the tree until they ripen, split open and are attacked by insects which render the pulp unfit for eating, and that those which reach full ripeness without splitting have a pulp which has little flavor, is dry, and unpleasantly mealy in character."

GRADES OR SPECIFICATIONS: There are no standard U.S. grades for bananas. The major banana companies have their own grading systems.

There are no official international quality standards for bananas. The Study Group on Bananas of F.A.O., United Nations, while favoring international standards in theory, noted "the difficulties of developing meaningful standards were very great, due to varietal differences, and even different characteristics of the same varieties grown under different environmental conditions, the highly perishable nature of the fruit, and the long distances over which it had to be shipped. It was also pointed out that there were different grade standards which had been developed in accordance with the difference in taste, preferences, and requirements of different consumers."

"**Scope:** This specification covers the requirements for form, size, stage of ripeness, grade, and method of packing fresh bananas. **Classification:** Fresh bananas shall be of the following form, size, stage of ripeness, and grade, as specified. **Form:** Bananas shall be in individual 'fingers', 'clusters', 'hands', full 'stems', or in combinations of two or more of these forms, as specified. **Size:** (If other than required in the grade) shall be as specified. **Stage of Ripeness:** Bananas shall be of the stage or stages of ripeness specified. **Grade:** Bananas shall be No. 1 grade.

"**Description of Grades:** No. 1 consists of bananas of a yellow variety which have reached a stage of maturity which will insure satisfactory completion of the ripening process, and which are clean, bright, firm, well developed, and free from damage materially affecting appearance, shipping quality, or edible quality caused by scars or other discoloration, decay, disease, chilling, heat, sunburn, sprayburn, chemicals, mechanical, or other means ... When bananas are in 'hands' or 'clusters', the 'hands' or 'clusters' show a smooth cut where detached from the stalk and are free from portions of stalk. Each 'hand' has 8 or more 'fingers', each 'cluster' has 3 or more 'fingers'. Unless otherwise specified, the maximum diameter of each banana shall be not less than 1-1/8 in.; and the length of each banana shall not be less than 6 in., measured along the line of the outer curve from the blossom end of pulp.

"**Tolerances: For Defects:** Not more than 10 percent, by count, of individual bananas (fingers) in any lot may fail to meet grade requirements, including therein not more than 1 percent with defects which seriously affect edible quality. **For undersize fingers:** Not more than 15 percent by count may be smaller than required by the grade, or otherwise specified; but not more than 10 percent may be undersize for either diameter or length. **For 'clusters', 'hands', or 'stems':** Not more than 5 percent of either 'clusters', 'hands', or 'stems' may

fail to meet the requirements of the grade for trimming, or the specified size of 'cluster', 'hand', or 'stem'. **Application of Tolerances:** The contents of individual packages or individual 'stems' in the lot, based on sample inspection, are subject to the following limitations: (Provided, that the averages for the entire lot are within tolerances specified) For a tolerance of 10 percent or more, not more than 1-1/2 times the tolerance specified; and for a tolerance of less than 10 percent, not more than double the tolerance specified; except that in the case of 'clusters', 'hands', or 'stems' this variation applies to 'fingers' only, not to the tolerance of 5 percent for 'clusters', 'hands', or 'stems' as a whole.

Stages of Ripeness. Color No. 1, peel color green; No. 2, light green, breaking slightly toward yellow; No. 3, yellowish green; No. 4, greenish yellow, more yellow than green; No. 5, yellow with green tips; No. 6, yellow; No. 7, yellow, flecked with brown."

BLACKBERRIES — DEWBERRIES*

USE: Blackberries are used fresh eaten with cream, in pies, puddings, tarts, ice cream, muffins, stewed alone or with other fruits, as a sauce over desserts, and they are also canned in plain water or in syrup; frozen with sugar; and made into wines, cordials, and brandies.

VARIETIES: The blackberries of North America fall into five major groups, according to Dr. George M. Darrow, principal pomologist, USDA. They are: (1) The erect or nearly erect type of bush-like Early Harvest and Eldorado of the eastern United States, grown from Florida to Canada and from the Atlantic Coast to the prairie states; (2) the eastern trailing blackberries having about the same range as the erect ones; (3) the southeastern trailing blackberries, like the Manatee and Advance, ranging along the Atlantic and Gulf coasts from Delaware to Texas; (4) the trailing blackberries—from which the Logan is derived—of the Pacific Coast from Canada to Southern California; and (5) the semi-trailing Evergreen (Black Diamond) and Himalaya of Oregon, Washington, and California that have been naturalized from Europe.

Erect, semi-erect, and semi-trailing varieties include Alfred, Blowers, Brainerd, Crandall, Dallas, Early Harvest,

*Courtesy of United Fresh Fruit and Vegetable Association.

Early Wonder, Eldorado, Evergreen, Haupt, Himalaya, Iceberg, Lawton, McDonald, Mersereau, Nanticoke, Snyder, Thornless Evergreen, and Ward. *Trailing* varieties include Advance, Boysen, Cascade, Chehalem, Cory Thornless, Franklin D., Ideal Wild, Johnson, Logan, Lucretia, Mammoth, Mayes, Marion, Nectar, Ollalie, Pacific, Rogers, Thornless Boysen, Thornless Logan, Thornless Young, Young, and Zielinski. Above data on varieties is all from Farmers Bulletin No. 1995, except mention of Chelahem and Marion on which reference is made to "Blackberry Growing in Oregon", Extension Bulletin 768, Oregon State College.

Space does not permit describing a large number of varieties, so only a few kinds important for marketing fresh as well as for processing are described:

Boysenberry This is a moderately vigorous, dewberry (trailing) variety grown mainly in California but also to some extent in Oregon and Texas. California had 2,730 acres of Boysenberries and Youngberries in 1958. Production of these two berries in 1957 in California was 21,060,000 lb. of which 2,000,000 lb. were marketed fresh. The Boysenberry vines often make a growth of 10 ft. or more. Production of 5 tons per acre is common, and yields as high as 10 tons have been attained. The berries are large and long, 1-1/4 in. long by 1 in. thick, dark reddish black when fully ripe, and slightly more acid than the Youngberry. The Boysen is of unknown origin and is reported to have been developed by Rudolph Boysen of Anaheim, California and introduced commercially in 1926.

Eldorado (also called Stuart, Lowden, and Texas) is of Ohio origin. Berries are medium-sized to large, firm and sweet; season early to midseason and long. Bushes very vigorous, hardy, productive. One of the best varieties in most of the sections of eastern U.S. adapted to blackberries, except the extreme South.

Thornless Evergreen This is now the most important variety in Oregon, having largely replaced the Evergreen, of which it is a sport. The thornless sport was discovered near Stayton, Oregon in 1926. The origin of the thorny Evergreen is unknown but it was being grown in Europe at least as early as 1809. Berries are large, exceptionally firm, sweet; seeds large; season late to very late, and ripening continues after other blackberries are picked. Bushes vigorous, semi-hardy, deep-rooted, drought-resistant, productive; canes semi-

trailing; one of the best varieties in Oregon and Washington but not generally adapted to states east of Rocky Mountains, except New Jersey.

Lawton (also called New Rochelle). Of New York origin. Berries large, soft when fully ripe, sweet; ready for harvest in early mid-season. Bushes vigorous, nearly hardy, productive. Grown in Texas and Oklahoma. Thorns are long. Good yield is 5 tons per acre in California.

Logan (**Loganberry**) Has declined in importance in recent years. Of California origin; oldest trailing blackberry variety of Pacific coast. Berries are large, long, dark red, acid and high-flavored. Plants vigorous, not hardy in eastern U.S., very productive. Grown for fresh market, canning, freezing, juice, and wine.

Lucretia (**Bingleberry**) Of West Virginia origin. Oldest and most widely grown trailing blackberry variety. Found after Civil War and brought to general notice about 1886. Berries large, long, firm; picked for shipping as soon as black, but not very sweet unless left on plants a day or two longer; season about June 1 in North Carolina section. Hardy in protected location even in northern states.

Marion This is a recent introduction resulting from a cooperative breeding project of USDA and Oregon Agricultural Experiment Station. Marion is a cross of Chehalem and Olallie. Plants are vigorous, trailing, producing a few long canes of large diameter, productive, with berries medium to large, bright black, and of excellent flavor.

Olallie Grown extensively in California. Of Oregon origin, bred cooperatively by USDA and Oregon Agricultural Experiment Station. It is a cross between Black Logan and Young. Plants are vigorous, trailing, well adapted to California conditions, but not hardy under Oregon conditions. Berries are bright black, medium-sized, firm, excellent for local markets.

Young (**Youngberry**) The Young ripens about 10 days earlier than Boysen but since it only produces 50 to 70 percent as much fruit in the same locality as Boysen, and the fruit is not of as high quality, it is being supplanted by other varieties. The berries are larger than those of the Lucretia, an attractive deep wine color, much sweeter than the Logan, Boysen, or Lucretia when ripe. This is a trailing type.

WEIGHTS AND CONTAINERS: A quart of blackberries,

BLACKBERRIES

FRESH (2/13/28   51.4270)
GRADES: U.S. NO. 1, U.S. NO. 2
CANNED (12/1/56   52.551)

GRADES:	"A" or "FANCY"	"B" or "CHOICE"	"C" or "STAN-DARD"	"SUB-STAN-DARD"
Minimum Score:	90	80	70	Less than 70

Extra Heavy & Heavy Syrup	NET WEIGHT OZ.	NET WEIGHT METRIC	DRAINED WEIGHT OZ.	DRAINED WEIGHT METRIC
No. 8Z Tall	7.8	221.1 g	4-1/4	127.6 g
No. 303	15.2	430.9 g	8-1/2	241.0 g
No. 10	98.5	2.8 kg	62	1.8 kg
Light Syrup & Water				
No. 8Z Tall	7.8	221.1 g	4-3/4	134.7 g
No. 303	15.2	430.9 g	9-1/4	262.2 g
No. 10	98.5	2.8 kg	66	1.9 kg

FROZEN (5/24/67   52.5881)

GRADES:	"A" or "FANCY"	"B" or "CHOICE"	"D" or "SUB-STANDARD"
Minimum Score:	85	70	Less than 70

SYRUP	BRIX MEASUREMENTS
"Extra heavy syrup," or "Extra heavily sweetened fruit juice(s) and water," or "Extra heavily sweetened fruit juice(s)."	24° to 35°
"Heavy syrup," or "Heavily sweetened fruit juice(s) and water," or "heavily sweetened fruit juice(s)."	19° or more but less than 24°
"Light syrup," or "Lightly sweetened fruit juice(s) and water," or "lightly sweetened fruit juice(s)."	14°
"Slightly sweetened water", or "Extra light syrup," or "Slightly sweetened fruit juice(s) and water," or "Slightly sweetened fruit juice(s)."	14°
"In water"	N.A.
"In fruit juice(s) and water"	N.A.
"In fruit juice(s)"	N.A.

DEWBERRIES & OTHER SIMILAR BERRIES

FRESH (2/13/28   51.4270)
GRADES: U.S. No. 1, U.S. No. 2
CANNED (12/1/56   52.551)

GRADES:	"A" or "FANCY"	"B" or "CHOICE"	"C" or "STAN- DARD"	"SUB- Stan- DARD"
Minimum Score:	90	80	70	Less than 70
Extra Heavy & Heavy Syrup	NET WEIGHT OZ.	NET WEIGHT METRIC	DRAINED WEIGHT OZ.	DRAINED WEIGHT METRIC
No. 303	15.2	430.9 g	7-3/4	219.7 g
No. 10	98.5	2.8 kg	55	1.6 kg
Light Syrup & Water				
No. 303	15.2	430.9 g	8-1/4	233.9 g
No. 10	98.5	2.8 kg	60	1.7 kg

SYRUP	BRIX MEASUREMENTS
"Extra heavy syrup," or "extra heavily sweetened fruit juice(s) and water," or "extra heavily sweetened fruit juice(s)."	24° to 35°
"Heavy syrup," or "heavily sweetened fruit juice(s) and water," or "heavily sweetened fruit juice(s)."	19° or more but less than 24°
"Light syrup;" or "lightly sweetened fruit juice(s) and water," or "lightly sweetened fruit juice(s)."	14°
"Slightly sweetened water," or "extra light syrup," or "slightly sweetened fruit juice(s) and water," or "slightly sweetened fruit juice(s)."	14°
"In water"	N.A.
"In fruit juice(s) and water"	N.A.
"In fruit juice(s)"	N.A.

FROZEN (5/24/67   52.5881)

GRADES:	"A" or "FANCY"	"B" or "CHOICE"	"D" or "SUB- STANDARD"
Minimum Score:	85	70	Less than 70

Defect Table:

Classification	Score points	Harmless extraneous material		Undeveloped or damaged berries
		Sepal-like bracts	Leaves, stems, full caps	
		Maximum		
		Per 16 ounces net weight	Per 48 ounces net weight	(by count)
A	40	0	None	0%
	39	1	None	1%
	38	1	1	2%
	37	1	1	3%
	36	2	1	3%
	35	2	1	4%
	34	2	1	5%
			Per 16 ounces net weight	
B	33	3	None	6%
	32	3	1	6%
	31	4	1	7%
	30	4	1	8%
	29	5	1	9%
	28	5	1	10%
D	27 or less	More than allowances permitted in B Classification		

Color Table:

Classification	Score points	Marked variation from color of well-ripened berries	Marked variation from color of reasonably well-ripened berries	Definitely off color for any reason
		Maximum (by weight)		
A	30	None		None
	29	2% including not more than 1%		
	28	4% including not more than 2%		
	27	6% including not more than 3%		
	26	8% including not more than 4%		
	25	10% including not more than 5%		
B	24	——	6½ including not more than 1%	
	23	——	9% including not more than 2%	
	22	——	12% including not more than 3%	
	21	——	15% including not more than 5%	
D	20 or less	More than allowances permitted in (B) classification		

according to the U.S. Census Bureau, weighs 1.5 lb. farm weight. However, USDA gives the retail weight as 1.28 lb. per qt., i.e., 1 lb. 5 oz. For 1 lb. ready-to-serve raw, USDA suggests using 0.76 sq. (about 3/4 qt. basket) as purchased.

Fresh blackberries are marketed in a variety of pint and quart baskets and boxes. These, in turn, are packed in master containers of different sizes, such as the 24-pt., 16-qt., 24-qt., 12-basket, 32-qt., and 36-pt. The master container may be a crate, wirebound box, or fiberboard box. An idea of dimensions is obtainable from the following, taken from the National Container Committee publication entitled: "Containers for Fresh Fruits and Vegetables Published in Four Container Tariffs" (all dimensions quoted are inside measurements):

24-qt. crate, 11x11x21-1/4 in.; 24-pt. crate, 9x9x18 in.; 24-basket crate, 7-1/4x13-3/4x18-1/8 in.; 32-qt. crate, 14-3/4x11x22 in.; 36-pt. crate, 9x11x22 in.; 16-qt. crate, 7-1/2x11x21-15/16 in.; wirebound 24-pt crate, 9-1/2x9x18 in.; fiberboard boxes of dimensions similar to those above.

Maine states the weight of a *bushel of blackberries* to be 40 lb. but others, such as Alabama, North Carolina, and Tennessee, state the weight at 48 lb.

QUALITY: Good quality is indicated by a bright, clean, fresh appearance, combined with a solid, full color, and plumpness of the individual berry. Good berries should be free from dirt, trash, moisture, and adhering caps. Overripe berries usually are very dull in color, soft, and sometimes leaky. A leaky condition is indicated by stained containers and the general appearance of the fruit. Decay can easily be detected by presence of molds on the surface of the berries. Berries with the caps attached may be immature. A berry that has a number of cells or drupelets that are green or off-color—when the remainder are of the normal ripe color—will not have as good flavor as one of which all cells are ripe.

GRADES: U.S. standard grades for blackberries and dewberries are U.S. No. 1 and U.S. No. 2. "U.S. No. 1 shall consist of dewberries or blackberries of one variety which are firm, well-colored, well-developed, and not overripe; which are free from caps (calyxes), mold and decay, and from damage caused by dirt or other foreign matter, shriveling, moisture, disease, insects, mechanical, or other means. In order to allow for variations incident to proper grading and handling, not more than 10 percent by volume of the berries in any lot may be below the requirements of this grade, but not to exceed one-half of this tolerance, or 5 percent, shall be allowed for defects causing serious damage, and not more than one-fifth of this amount, or 1 percent, may be affected by mold or decay....." "Well-colored" means that the whole surface of the berry shall be a blue or black color. "Well-developed" means that the berries shall not be misshapen owing to anthracnose injury, lack of pollination, insect injury, or other causes. "Overripe" means dead ripe or soft, necessitating immediate consumption. "Damage" means any injury from the causes mentioned which materially affects the appearance, edibility, or shipping quality. "Seriously damaged" means berries which are badly deformed, crushed, leaky, moldy, decayed, or otherwise seriously injured. Berries which have less than one-half of the surface covered with black or blue color shall be considered as "seriously damaged."

BLACKBERRIES and Other Similar Berries Canned 12/1/56

Grade A: Color: Berries possess a color typical of well-ripened berries of their variety after proper processing; are practically uniform and bright in color. **Size:** Variation in size of berries does not materially affect appearance, and for blackberries not more than 15 percent may be less than 20/32 in. in diameter. **Defects:** "Practically Free" — Harmless, extraneous vegetable material may be present that does not more than slightly affect the appearance or edibility of the product; not more than 4 percent may be damaged. **Character:** Berries possess a firm, tender texture characteristic of well-ripened berries for the varietal type and are practically intact; berries and accompanying liquor are practically free from detached seed cells; and not more than 5 percent may be crushed and not more than 10 percent of dewberries, loganberries, or other similar types may be crushed.

Grade B: Color: Reasonably well-ripened berries of variety after proper processing. May be somewhat lacking in luster and may vary from lighter shades of reasonably well-ripened to darker hues of well-ripened. **Size:** Variation in size of berries does not seriously affect appearance, and for blackberries not more than 15 percent may be less than 18/32 in. in diameter. **Defects:** "Reasonably Free" — Harmless, extraneous vegetable material may be present that does not more than materially affect the appearance or edibility of the product; and not more than 8 percent may be damaged. **Character:** Berries may possess a reasonably tender texture, characteristic of reasonably well-ripened berries to slightly overripe berries for the varietal type, and are reasonably intact; the berries and accompanying liquor are reasonably free from detached seed cells; and not more than 10 percent may be crushed; and not more than 15 percent of dewberries, loganberries, boysenberries, or other similar types may be crushed.

Grade C: Color: Fairly well-ripened berries of variety after processing. May vary but not off color (Limiting Rule). See chart. **Size:** Berries may be variable in size, and for blackberries more than 15 percent may be less than 18/32 in. in diameter. **Defect:** "Fairly Free"—Harmless, extraneous vegetable material may be present that does not seriously affect the appearance or edibility of the product; and not more than 15 percent may be damaged. **Character:** Berries may possess a fairly tender texture, characteristic of fairly well-ripened berries to overripe berries for the varietal type, and are fairly intact; and not more than 20 percent of the berries may be crushed. **Substandard:** Fails to meet requirements, see chart.

SCORE CHART FOR CANNED BERRIES

	Points Maximum	Grade A Fancy	Grade B Choice	Grade C Standard	Sub-Standard
Color	20	18-20	16-17	14-15*	0-13*
Uniformity of Size	20	18-20	16-17	14-15*	——
Absence of Defects	30	27-30	24-26*	21-23*	0-20*
Character of Fruit	30	27-30	24-26*	21-23*	0-20*
Minimum Score	——	90	80	70	——

*Limiting Rule: Berries falling in this classification cannot receive higher grade regardless of Total Score.

BLACKBERRIES and Other Similar Berries — Canned (1975 Revisions)

The Food and Drug Administration amended the standards of identity for Canned Blackberries and Other Similar Berries, compliance with which may have begun on March 11, 1975, but mostly after December 31, 1975.

The following amendments to the USDA standards for Canned Blackberries and Other Similar Berries are proposed to bring them into line with the amended FDA Standards of Identity.

Product description.

"Canned blackberries", and other similar berries such as "boysenberries," "dewberries," "loganberries," and "young-berries," is the product represented as defined in the standards of identity (21 CFR 27.35) issued pursuant to the Food, Drug, and Cosmetic Act.

BERRIES — Frozen (5/24/67)

Grade A: Color: Not more than a total of 10 percent may vary markedly from the intensity and luster of the characteristic color of well-ripened berries, provided not more than 5 percent vary from the intensity and luster of reasonably well-ripened berries. **Defects:** There may be present not more than 2 sepal-like bracts per 16 oz. of net weight; and not more than one steam or one leaf or piece of leaf or the approximate equivalent of one full cap per 48 oz. of net weight; and not more than 5 percent may be undeveloped or damaged **Character:** Berries are mature and ripe but not overripe, are fleshy and tender, and are practically intact; that the berries and accompanying liquor are practically free from detached seed cells; and that not more than 5 percent of blackberries may be crushed and not more than 10 percent by weight of dewberries, boysenberries, loganberries, youngberries, or other similar types may be crushed.

Grade B: Color: Not more than 15 percent of the berries may vary markedly from the intensity and luster of the characteristic color of reasonably well-ripened berries, provided not more than 5 percent are definitely off color for any reason. **Defects:** There may be present not more than 5 sepal-like bracts; and not more than one stem or one leaf or piece of leaf or the approximate equivalent of one full cap per 16 oz. of net weight; and not more than 10 percent may be undeveloped or damaged. **Character:** Berries are reasonably mature, and may be not more than slightly immature, nor slightly overmature; berries may be not more than slightly lacking in fleshy texture; berries and any accompanying liquor are reasonably free from detached seed cells; and not more than 15 percent may be crushed, and not more than 20 percent of dewberries, loganberries, etc., or other similar types may be crushed.

Grade D: Color: Definitely off color for any reason, these berries fail to meet requirements. **Defects:** See Table. **Character:** Fail to meet requirements.

BLUEBERRIES*

USES: From morning to night, fresh blueberries in any form are a treat. At home, consumers serve them raw with sugar and milk or cream, or add them to dry cereal for breakfast. They go well when made a part of muffins, biscuits, pancakes, or waffles. Mix blueberries with other fruits such as strawberries, raspberries, melon balls, or banana for a fruit compote; they make fine jams and jellies; they give a fine fillip to puddings or gelatins. Fill meringue shells with the "blues" and top with whipped cream; heap fresh blueberries or blueberry sauce on ice cream. Bake them in cobblers, cream puffs, tarts, pies, and cakes. Commercially, the berries are canned in water or syrup for institutional and home use; are made into jams and jellies; and are frozen with or without sugar or syrup.

Blueberries are now widely available in cake, cookie, and waffle-pancake mixes, syrups, ice cream toppings, and pie fillings. They are found in a wide variety of convenience foods, such as toaster cakes and packaged ready-to-serve filled pastries, frozen waffles, and cheese cakes. They are also widely used in ice creams, sherbets, and yogurts, plus alcoholic beverages. There is now a commercially produced blueberry champagne, blueberry "cold duck," and several inexpensive blueberry wines. Blueberry soap and candles are promotional items available through the North American Blueberry Council.

MARKETING SEASON: Fresh blueberries are on the market from May through September. Peak months are June, July, and August. Early berries come from North Carolina and New Jersey; late berries from Michigan, New Jersey, and the West Coast. The following table shows availability by months expressed as a percentage of the annual total. The average fresh crop is 33 million pounds.

MONTHLY AVAILABILITY OF FRESH BLUEBERRIES AS A PERCENTAGE OF AVERAGE ANNUAL SUPPLY

Jan. %	Feb. %	Mar. %	Apr. %	May %	June %	July %	Aug. %	Sept. %	Oct. %	Nov. %	Dec. %
0	0	0	0	2	30	42	22	4	0	0	0

VARIETIES: The names "blueberry" and "huckleberry" are often used interchangeably. However, the huckleberry belongs to the genus Gaylussacia, while the blueberry belongs to the genus Vaccinium. The huckleberry has 10 large seeds, each of which is surrounded by a bony covering or pit. The blueberry has two or three times as many seeds as the huckleberry, but they are small and not noticeable when eaten. Also, the undersides of huckleberry leaves are sprinkled with resinous dots which are absent on blueberry foliage. Only blueberries are cultivated.

The lowbush blueberry is the only wild species commercially harvested today. It is native to the New England states, Quebec, and the Canadian Maritimes. Plants are usually 6 to 18 in. high and spread into large colonies by means of underground shoots called rhizomes. The fruit is harvested with rakes similar to cranberry scoops, but, owing to a growing scarcity of hand labor, much work is being done on developing a mechanical lowbush picking machine. One is now one the market which can be used successfully in fields cleared of stumps and large rocks, but it is not suited at this time for rough terrain.

The cultivated blueberry industry was developed through the cross-breeding of wild high-bush blueberry varieties which bore larger fruit or were prized for superior flavor. This cross-breeding resulted in today's superior varieties. Over the years, many of these superior varieties have been named, but through changing needs and horticultural practices, many of the "originals" have been eliminated from commercial

*Courtesy of United Fresh Fruit and Vegetable Association.

BLUEBERRIES

FRESH (6/1/66   51.3475)

Grades: U.S. NO. 1

CANNED (8/19/59   52.581)

Grades:	"A" or "FANCY"	"B" or "CHOICE"	"C" or "STAN- DARD"	"D" or "SUBSTAN- DARD"
Minimum Score:	90	80	70	Less than 70

	NET WEIGHT OZ.	NET WEIGHT METRIC	DRAINED WEIGHT OZ.	DRAINED WEIGHT METRIC
NO.10	98.5	2.8 kg	55	1.6 kg

SYRUP	SPECIFIC GRAVITY (BRIX MEASUREMENTS)
"Extra heavy syrup" or "Extra heavily sweetened fruit juice(s) and water," or	25° to 35°
"Extra heavily sweetened fruit juice(s)"	
"Heavy syrup" or "heavily sweetened fruit juice(s) and water" or "heavily sweetened fruit juice(s)."	20° or more but less than 25°
"Light syrup" or "lightly sweetened fruit juice(s) and water"; and "lightly sweetened fruit juice(s)."	15° or more but less than 20°
"Slightly sweetened water"; or "extra light syrup"; or "slightly sweetened fruit juice(s) and water"; or "slightly sweetened fruit juice(s)."	Less than 15°
"In water"	N.A.
"In fruit juice(s) and water"	N.A.
"In fruit juice(s)"	N.A.

FROZEN (5/7/55   52.611)

Grades:	"A" or "FANCY"	"B" or "CHOICE"	"C" or "STAN- DARD"	"D" or "SUBSTAN- DARD"
Minimum Score:	90	80	70	Less than 70

production. Names such as Coville, Herbert, Elizabeth, Dixie, and Darrow have been replaced by the following varieties, listed in order of commercial importance: Bluecrop, Jersey, Rubel, Weymouth, Blue Ray, Bluetta, Berkeley, Burlington, Collins.

The following descriptions of the leading varieties were prepared by the Blueberry-Cranberry Laboratory of the Extension Service, Rutgers College of Agriculture and Environmental Sciences, in cooperation with the Michigan Blueberry Growers Association Research Laboratory and the Coastal Plain Experimental Station in Alam, Ga.

Bluecrop (Jersey x Pioneer) x (Stanley x June). Introduced 1952. Bush vigorous, upright, very productive; fruit cluster loose; berry large, very light blue, firm, slightly aromatic; medium dessert quality; scar one of best, meaning it is small, smooth and dry; resistant to cracking; drops somewhat; early midseason; hardier than most others; drought resistant. Well like for consistent productiveness, hardiness, and light blue color. Picks well by machine. Resists red ring spot disease but is highly susceptible to stunt disease and anthracnose.

Jersey (Rubel x Grover). Introduced 1928. Bush vigorous, erect, productive; fruit cluster loose; berry medium to large, medium blue, firm, lacking in aroma, fair dessert quality, scar medium, resistant to cracking; season late. Liked for its vigorous, hardy bush and open fruit cluster. Most grown of any variety, but being replaced in New Jersey by Bluecrop. Picks well by machine. It is difficult to pollinate and requires a large concentration of honeybees where wild bees are not abundant. This variety resists red ring spot disease but is highly susceptible to stunt disease.

Rubel Selection from the wild in New Jersey. Bush vigorous, erect, productive; fruit cluster very loose; berry rather small, good blue, firm, slightly aromatic, fair dessert quality, scar medium; season late with Jersey. Liked for its hardiness and productiveness but is being replaced by Bluecrop. An excellent berry for processing.

Weymouth (June x Cabot). Introduced 1936. Bush small, open, spreading; fruit cluster medium loose; berry medium, dark blue, lacking in aroma, poor dessert quality; scar medium; berries drop; season early, crop ripens quickly. Picks

well mechanically, but because of its rather bland flavor, it is being replaced by Bluetta, another early variety.

Blue Ray (Jersey x Pioneer) x (Stanley x June). Introduced 1955. Bush vigorous, upright, spreading, productive; fruit clusters are tight; berry very large, light blue, firm, aromatic, high dessert quality, scar medium, resistant to cracking; early midseason. Liked for its open bush and very large high-flavored berries. Does not pick well mechanically. In New Jersey it is highly susceptible to red ring spot disease and anthracnose.

Bluetta No. 3 (North Sedgwich lowbush x Coville x Earliblue). Introduced in 1967. Bush short, compact, spreading, and medium vigorous. Fruit is medium sized, light blue, firm, broad stem scar. Early ripening with Weymouth but of better color and flavor. It is being planted in small blocks until proved to be worthy of more extensive planting.

Berkeley (Stanley x [Jersey x Pioneer]). Introduced 1949. Bush vigorous, open-spreading, productive; fruit cluster loose; berry very large, oblate, lightest blue, firm, slightly aromatic, medium dessert quality, scar above medium, resistant to cracking, drops somewhat; midseason, keeps well. Well liked for beauty of color, large size, firmness, and productiveness. Picks well mechanically.

Burlington (Rubel x Pioneer). Introduced 1939. Bush vigorous, upright-spreading, productive; fruit cluster medium tight; berry medium size, medium blue, firm, slightly aromatic, medium dessert quality, scar best of all, resistant to cracking; season late, lasting about a week after Jersey; stores well. Liked for its fine scar and good keeping in cold storage. Matures a large percentage of crop for one picking. Picks well mechanically. This variety appears to have good resistance to anthracnose, but it is highly susceptible to red ring spot.

Collins (Stanley x Weymouth). Introduced 1959. Very much like Earliblue but ripens 5 days later. This is the most underrated variety today. Its flavor is excellent. It ships well, has good size and color, picks well mechanically.

Blueberry varieties developed for the northern states are not adapted to North Carolina. One of the factors is susceptibility to cane canker disease. At present Wolcott is the principal North Carolina variety. Angola, Murphy and Croatan are being used but to much less extent than Wolcott. Morrow is the newest variety, but it is being used as a replacement for bushes suffering from stem canker. Wolcott is now susceptible to different races of stem canker and is being replaced by Croatan in North Carolina.

Wolcott Bush very vigorous, upright, productive; fruit cluster loose, berry large, round, dark blue, firm, medium dessert quality, scar small, very good; season early and short.

Morrow This is the coming variety in North Carolina. Slow growing, upright, highly productive, fruit cluster medium tight, berries hang very well, medium large, light blue, medium firm, mild, good dessert quality. Scar large, moist; season early and short. Resistant to stem canker. Picks well mechanically.

Croatan Bush vigorous, upright, highly productive; fruit cluster medium, loose; berry medium to large, dark blue, medium-firm, slightly aromatic, sweet, medium dessert quality; scar above average; resistant to cracking; season early. Resistant to bud mite and canker; picks well mechanically.

Murphy Bush vigorous, spreading, productive; fruit cluster loose; berry medium-large, medium to dark blue, firm, slightly aromatic, medium dessert quality; fair scar; early midseason, highly canker-resistant; picks well mechanically.

Rabbiteye This type of blueberry is native along many of the large streams in northern Florida, southeastern Georgia, and southeastern Alabama. This species can grow in more upland conditions than the highbush blueberry. It requires only a short rest period; is not so sensitive to soil acidity and is far more heat and drought resistant than the highbush blueberry. Since 1940, the USDA and Georgia Coastal Plain Experiment Station have engaged in a large-scale breeding and selection program, and the rabbiteye blueberry now has been developed to a point where certain varieties have excellent commercial possibilities. These varieties are being developed into an important blueberry industry for the deep South. More than one variety should be set in each planting to insure cross-pollination. Among the most desirable rabbiteye varieties are Tifblue, Briteblue, Woodard, Garden Blue and Blue Gem.

Tifblue The plants make vigorous upright growth and produce medium large, firm, highly flavorsome, light blue fruit.

Woodard The plants are lower and more spreading than Tifblue. Berries are large, medium firm, highly flavored, and light blue.

Briteblue This is one of the newer varieties. Plants are medium, vigorous with spreading growth. Berries are large, firm, light blue, and tart until fully ripe.

Garden Blue A vigorous, upright variety, producing berries of medium size, firm, light blue. It grows best in the Carolinas.

Blue Gem This is a Florida variety. The plants are vigorous, spreading, berries medium size, light blue. The only drawback is its rather mild flavor.

CONTAINERS: Most berries for the fresh market are packed in pint containers called "cups." These are filled rounding full, or "crowned," and covered with a sheet of cellophane called a "cello-cap." The cello-cap has the name and address of the grower, or the cooperative, or marketing organization to which the grower belongs printed across it together with information on how to freeze for future use, and where to write for free recipes. The cello-cap is fitted tightly around the pint cup and held in place by a rubber band. All berries are packaged at the shipping point. The Michigan Blueberry Growers Association also packages a 10-lb. freezer, family pack which is gaining consumer acceptance in several food chains.

The pints of fresh blueberries are packed in 12-pt. wooden containers or in fiberboard cartons called "trays" as the standard shipping containers. Due to costs, the carton is rapidly replacing the wooden container. Another advantage of the carton is that it is lighter than the wooden box and this is important, especially in connection with air shipments. A 12-pt. carton contains 11 lb. of fresh blueberries. The 12-pt. wirebound crate has been used experimentally.

SERVINGS AND WEIGHTS: One cup of blueberries weighs about 140 grams or 5 oz. One pt. of blueberries makes 4 to 5 half-cup servings; 22 pt. serve 100.

QUALITY: Blueberries should be plump, fresh in appearance, fairly uniform in size, clean, dry, free from leaves and stems, and with full color throughout the lot. Ripeness is indicated by the color, which may be light blue to dark blue to blue black. The berries may have a light-colored bloom which is a natural protective wax, depending on the variety. Freedom from moisture is essential to good quality. Moisture may be caused by natural breakdown, decay, or mechanical injury. Occasionally, moisture inside the package will be from condensation caused when the fruit is put on display at room temperature after being held in the cooler. Fruit should be neither green nor too ripe. Fruit that is overripe has a dull, lifeless appearance, and is often soft and watery. Berries held too long after picking take on an appearance similar to that of overripe fruit. They may be somewhat shriveled. Decay is usually indicated by the presence of molds. Blueberries are highly perishable and should be used as soon as possible. They should be cold when received and should be kept cold throughout marketing and until served. If properly cared for, good quality blueberries will last up to 2 weeks under home refrigeration, depending on how long they have been in marketing channels. Frozen blueberries held at 0°F. or lower will retain their taste and quality for more than 2 years.

Cultivated berries are generally sold according to size, the larger berries usually bringing the higher price. Size is based on the count of the number of berries required to fill a half-pint measure. The four main sizes are 90 or less, 90 to 130, 130 to 190, and 190 and over. In the 90 or less category, some varieties now count 70 or fewer to fill the half pint. USDA market news reporters generally classify the berries as large, medium, or small.

GRADES: U.S. standard grades for blueberries, effective June 1, 1966 provide for one grade, U.S. 1. "General. These standards apply only to selected and hybrid varieties of the highbush blueberry (Vaccinium australe and Vaccinium corymbosum) produced under cultivation, but not to other species of the genus Vaccinium, nor to the true huckleberries of the genus Gaylussacia.

"U.S. 1 consists of blueberries of similar varietal characteristics which are clean, well colored, not overripe, wet, or affected by decay: Provided, That defective berries are within the allowances specified . . . Count shall not exceed 250 berries per 2 gill cup.

"Size classifications. The following size classifications may be used . . .(a) Extra large. Less than 90 berries per standard 2 gill cup; (b) Large. 90 to 129 berries per standard 2 gill cup; (c) Medium. 130 to 189 berries per standard 2 gill cup; and (d) Small. 190 to 250 berries per standard 2 gill cup."

BLUEBERRIES — Canned (1/19/59)

Grade A: Color: A practically uniform, bright, dark blue-purple color typical of blueberries which have been properly processed from well-matured blueberries. **Defects:** Canned blueberries are reasonably free from cap stems, and for each 20 oz. of net weight, or the equivalent, there may be present: (1) not more than a total of 2 whole leaves or large stems, provided such whole leaves and any other portions of leafy materials do not exceed 1/2 sq. in.; not more than 5 berries that are undeveloped, or edible berries other than blueberries, **or berries that are damaged, and in native** (wild) type, not more than an average of 12 clusters in all containers comprising the sample, provided there are no more than blueberries, or berries that are damaged, and in native (wild) type, not more than an average of 20 clusters in all containers comprising the sample, provided there are no more than 28 clusters in any container or in cultivated type, not more than 8 clusters. **Character:** Blueberries may be lacking in firmness and fleshy texture but are reasonably whole and intact, with not more than 15 percent of the drained blueberries that may be crushed, mushy, or broken berries.

are reasonably free from cap stems, and for each 20 oz. there may be present: not more than a total of 4 whole leaves or large stems, provided such whole leaves and any other portions of leafy material do not exceed 3/4 sq. in.; not more than 8 berries that are undeveloped, or edible berries other than blueberries, or berries that are damaged, and in native type, not more than an average of 12 clusters in all containers comprising the sample, provided there are no more than 16 clusters in any single container or in cultivated type, not more than 4 clusters. **Character:** Blueberries are reasonably firm, fleshy, practically whole, and intact, with not more than 10 percent of the drained blueberries that may be crushed, mushy, or broken berries.

Grade C: Color: Blue-purple color typical of blueberries which have been properly processed and which are not off color for any reason. **Defects:** Fairly free from cap stems, and for each 20 oz. there may be present: not more than a total of 6 whole leaves or large stems, provided such whole leaves and any other portions of leafy material do not exceed 1 sq. in.; not more than 10 berries that are undeveloped, or edible berries other than blueberries or berries that are damaged, and in native (wild) type, not more than an average of 28 clusters in all containers, provided there are not more than 40 clusters in any single container; or in cultivated type, not more than 12 clusters. **Character:** Blueberries are fairly whole and intact with not more than 30 percent of the drained blueberries that may be crushed, mushy, or broken berries. **Sstd:** Fail to meet requirements, see chart.

BLUEBERRIES — Canned (1975 Revisions)

The Food and Drug Administration amended the standards of identity for Canned Blueberries, compliance with which may have begun on March 11, 1975, but mostly after December 31, 1975.

The following amendment to the USDA standards for Canned Blueverries is proposed to bring them into line with the amended FDA Standards of Identity.

Product description:

Canned blueberries is the product represented as defined in the standards of identity (21CFR 27.35) for canned berries issued pursuant to the Federal Food, Drug, and Cosmetic Act.

BLUEBERRIES — Frozen (5/7/55)

Grade A: Color: Bright, dark blue-purple color typical of properly matured berries for the variety, and there may be present not more than 5 percent of berries that possess a red-purple color. Frozen blueberries that are undercolored (not at least red-purple color) or that have a definite green cast are considered "green berries." **Defects:** Reasonably free from cap stems, and for each 16 oz. there may be present: (1) not more than a total of 2 whole leaves or large stems, provided such whole leaves and any other portions of leafy material do not exceed 1/2 sq. in.; not more than a total of 10 berries that are green, or undeveloped, or edible berries other than blueberries, or berries that are damaged, provided not more than 5 of these berries are undeveloped or edible berries

other than blueberries or berries that are damaged; and in native (wild) type, not more than an average of 12 clusters in all samples or containers comprising the sample, provided there are not more than 16 clusters in any single sample or in any single container, or in cultivated type, not more than 4 clusters. **Character:** Blueberries are reasonably firm, fleshy, practically whole and intact, with not more than 6 percent of berries that may be crushed, mushy, or broken.

Grade B: Color: Possess a reasonably uniform, dark blue-purple color typical of reasonably well-matured berries for the variety, and that there may be present not more than 10 percent that possess a red-purple color. Frozen berries that are under-colored (see Grade A). **Defects:** Reasonably free from cap stems, and for each 16 oz. there may be present: (1) Not more than a total of 4 whole leaves or large stems, provided such whole leaves and any other portions of leafy material do not exceed 3/4 sq. in.; not more than a total of 16 berries that are green, or undeveloped, or edible berries other than blueberries, or berries that are damaged, provided not more than 8 of these berries are undeveloped or edible berries other than blueberries or berries that are damaged; and in native (or wild) type, not more than an average of 20 clusters in all samples or containers comprising the sample, provided there are not more than 28 clusters in any single sample or in any single container, or in cultivated type, not ore than 8 clusters. **Character:** Blueberries may be lacking in firmness and fleshy texture but are whole and intact with not more than 10 percent of berries that may be crushed, mushy, or broken.

Grade C: Color: Blueberries may be moderately variable in color, and there may be not more than 20 percent that possess a red-purple color. For frozen blueberries that are under-colored (see Grade A: Color). **Defects:** Fairly free from defects, and for each 16 oz. there may be present: (1) Not more than 6 whole leaves or large stems, provided such whole leaves and any other portions of leafy material do not exceed 1 sq. in.; not more than a total of 20 berries that are green, or undeveloped, or edible berries other than blueberries, or berries that are damaged, provided not more than 10 of these berries are undeveloped or edible berries other than blueberries or berries that are damaged; and in native (or wild) type, not more than an anverage of 28 clusters in all samples or containers comprising the sample, provided there are no more than 40 clusters in any single sample or in any single container, or in cultivated type, not more than 12 clusters. **Character:** Are fairly whole and intact with not more than 20 percent of berries that may be crushed, mushy or broken. **Sstd:** Fails to meet requirements.

CANTALOUPES*

USES: With the exception of a very small amount of cantaloupes that go into frozen melon balls, cantaloupes are used almost exclusively fresh. Whether served chilled with salt or pepper, sugar, lemon or lime juice, or served in combination with any number of fruits, berries, or ice cream, cantaloupes fit admirably in any meal as an appetizer, salad, or dessert. A half cantaloupe makes a natural bowl for berries, ice cream, or custard. Slices of cantaloupe lend a decorative touch to salads.

SOME IDEAS: Cantaloupe chiffon cup, a half, filled with a light custard and topped with a mint leaf; cantaloupe divided into eighths, placed around the edge of a bowl and the center filled with strawberries; cantaloupe pickled with vinegar, water, sugar, cinnamon, and cloves; cantaloupe relish made with pickled cantaloupe plus lemon, fresh onion, and chopped nuts; cantaloupe a la mode with vanilla ice cream and fresh strawberry sauce; fresh cantaloupe balls in orange juice; cantaloupe chiffon tarts; cantaloupe stuffed with watermelon balls, fresh diced pineapple, fresh strawberries, sliced bananas, and blueberries; cantaloupe and grape cup; cantaloupe ice cream made with mashed fresh cantaloupes and other usual ice cream ingredients; cantaloupe and paprika sour cream salad; fresh cantaloupe and ham canapes; cantaloupe antipasto with chilled melon pieces on a tray filled in with celery stalks, rolled Italian salami slices or other meats, and tomato slices; cantaloupe rings filled with crab meat salad.

MARKETING SEASON: The main cantaloupe season is June, July, and August when huge quantities come to market, totaling in those three months 69 percent of the annual total. There are large quantities also in May and September; but only minor quantities in March, April, October, and November.

VARIETIES: "Development and release of variety PMR 45 refrigeration techniques have made it possible to harvest fully mature California-grown cantaloupes and deliver them in good edible condition not only to local markets, but to New York and other eastern seaboard markets. The important character here is firm flesh that does not soften or deteriorate rapidly after harvest and thus makes distance transportation feasible. All new varieties must have this character to be successful. In addition, the fruit in cross section should have a small, dry seed cavity, with thick, salmon-orange flesh, firm but not rubbery.

"Consumers in this country have come to expect cantaloupes of medium size, round to slightly oblong, nearly covered with net (not coarse), and with slight aroma.

"Almost all cantaloupes grown for market in California are of the Hale's Best group of varieties. Hale's Best originated in the Imperial Valley near Brawley, introduced in 1924 by I. D. Hale who obtained the seed from a nearby Japanese grower. Its origin is uncertain but probably comes from a chance hybridization of Pollock 10-25 and either the variety Emerald Gem or Perfecto. The original strain of Hale's Best was not very uniform for size, shape and other characters, but within a few years, by simple mass selection, seedsmen were able to introduce good uniform strains, each with a few distinct characteristics, but of the same general type."

At present Top Mark and PMR 45 are the two dominant varieties in California and Arizona.

Top Mark This variety, which is now grown on 30 percent of the entire California cantaloupe acreage and on 99 percent of the Imperial Valley acreage, was developed by Dr. Robert C. Tang, plant breeder of Dessert Seed Co. of El Centro, Calif. It is also used in Arizona and Mexico. Dr. Tang says that when he released this variety in 1963 it was because it is tolerant to crown blight. This disorder, which destroys the crop near the time of maturity, took a heavy toll in the Imperial Valley from 1958 to 1961. It has not been determined what pathogen causes crown blight. Dr. Tang took the parent material for Top Mark out of a badly infected field.

*Courtesy of United Fresh Fruit and Vegetable Association.

CANTALOUPES

FRESH (6/30/68   51.475)

Grades: U.S. Fancy   U.S. NO. 1
        U.S. Commercial   U.S. NO. 2

FROZEN (6/25/62   52.5361)

Grades:	"A" or "FANCY"	"B" or "CHOICE"	"SUB-STANDARD"
Minimum Score:	90	80	Less than 80

The variety is described as follows: "Originated Dessert Seed Co. Characteristic vigorous dark green vine and foliage. Very prolific and has excellent grown set. Fruits ribless, excellent netting, small seed cavity, and size of 5-1/2 to 6-1/2 in. Flesh salmon colored. Resembles **PMR 45,** or Hale's Best. Resistant to powdery mildew and sulphur. Tolerant to downy mildew. Adapted to southern and southwestern United States. American Vegetable Grower."

"**PMR 45** was introduced in 1936 by Jagger of the USDA and Scott of the University of California . . . PMR 45 is resistant to race 1 of powdery mildew, but not to race 2. For this reason it should not be planted where race 2 of the fungus is prevalent."

PMR 45 is a Hale's Best-type cantaloupe, but with firmer flesh. The fruits are slightly oblong, 6 x 5 in., weigh 3 to 5 lb., and are covered with moderately coarse net. The sutures are shallow and only partially netted. The flesh is firm, thick, salmon-orange; the seed cavity is small and dry. Under good growing conditions, the vines are vigorous enough to cover the entire bed and provide plentiful shade for the developing melons.

"The development of PMR 45 is one of the most interesting, important, and successful endeavors in the long history of plant breeding in this country. In 1925, powdery mildew (Erysiphe cichoracearum) suddenly widely infected cantaloupes and other muskmelons in the Imperial Valley. After an intensive search for muskmelon material resistant to powdery mildew, resistant material was obtained from India by J. T. Rosa of the University of California in 1928. This material had none of the desirable characteristics of modern cantaloupes. The melons were large, oblong, smooth, sutured, with thin skin and cracked at maturity. The flesh was whitish, dry, mushy and tasteless.

"It turned out that resistance was controlled by a single dominant gene. The problem was to transfer this gene for resistance to a Hale's Best background. A plant of the original resistant material was crossed with one from a good strain of Hale's Best. In the second generation a resistant selection was back-crossed to Hale's Best. In the third generation from this back-cross, a large resistant population was grown, mass selected, and the seed distributed as PMR 50. This variety was grown to a limited extent for several years, but the melons were variable in size, shape and quality. Selection in large populations of resistant plants for four additional generations produced a resistant population with melons of good appearance and quality, and of uniform size and shape. Mass selection in this population produced see of PMR 45, released to seedsmen in 1936.

"The release of PMR 45 revolutionized the cantaloupe industry in the western United States. It was the first variety of cantaloupe that could be harvested when mature (full-slip), yet arrive in eastern markets in good condition. Marketing of mature fruit of good quality created a vastly increased demand for the western product. PMR 45 proved to have a sufficient genetic variability to be adapted to a wide range of environmental conditions.

"PMR 450 originated as a selection from an inbred line of PMR 45. PMR 450 is similar to PMR 45 except that the vines are larger and more vigorous, and the fruit is larger and tends to be less uniform in size and shape. PMR 450 is planted on a limited scale in localities where PMR 45 does not mature fruits early enough or large enough to be desirable."

Variety Statistics. The best measure of what types are being planted is the amount of seed acreage and production of seed. This is shown in the Vegetable Seed Report of the U.S. Dept. of Agriculture published March 19, 1973.

The table shows the information for muskmelons and

cantaloupes, and clearly the Imperial and PMR types are dominant.

KIND AND VARIETY OR TYPE	ACREAGE		PRODUCTION	
	1972	1973	1972	1973
	ACRES		POUNDS	
Muskmelon and Cantaloupe	4	40	500	7,625
F1 Hybrids	223	305	68,677	86,600
Hales Best Strains				
Honey Dew Green Flesh	140	153	60,820	55,500
Imperial and PMR Types	637	855	198,585	261,000
Late Shippers	67	81	19,321	27,875
Rocky Ford	55	89	17,031	29,100
Other Varieties	475	610	155,606	193,050
TOTAL	1,601	2,133	520,540	660,750

CONTAINERS: There appears to be a trend away from wooden crates and toward cartons for shipment of cantaloupes. The main reason is cost of the container itself, and secondarily, economics in packing and in freight costs in favor of cartons. The smaller size and lighter weight of the cartons also makes them easier to handle at retail.

Western cantaloupes shipped in crates are now all shipped in WGA melon crates. This crate is packed with 18 to 45 melons, depending on their size, and contains net weight of 75 to 85 lb., according to the Calif. Dept. of Agriculture. The crate is 13 x 13 x 21-7/8 in. and is Container No. 1220 of the Uniform Classification Committee.

Cartons used by California shippers are the 1/2 crate size, net weight about 38 to 41 lb., mostly 41, and the 2/3 crate size, net weight 53 to 55 lb., mostly 54. These cartons may be either wet-strength corrugated board or wax treated for waterproofing. Which is used depends on whether the carton is to be exposed to ice and water. Packs are 12, 15, 18, and 23 melons for the 1/2 carton and 12, 13, 18, 24, or 30 for the 2/3 size. A few shippers pack in 2/3 TKV crates constructed of laminated wood and paper.

The following shows the containers authorized for cantaloupes by the Calif. Dept. of Agriculture by regulation effective July 10, 1973, pursuant to Division 17 of the Agricultural Code.

Subsection	Name	Description in Inches		
Cantaloupe Crates and Containers		Depth	Width	Length
39	Cantaloupe crate	12	12	21-1/8
40	Cantaloupe crate	11	11	22-1/8
41	Jumbo cantaloupe crate	13 or 13-1/2	13	21-7/8 or 22-1/8
42	Cantaloupe crate	13-1/2	13	22-1/2
43	Cantaloupe container	9 or 9-1/2	13	21-7/8 or 22
44	Cantaloupe container	9 to 10	13	22 or 22-3/8
44A	Cantaloupe container	10-1/2	13	22
44B	Cantaloupe 2-compartment container	5-1/2	9-1/8	21-3/8 or 21-5/8
44C	Cantaloupe container	15-1/2 to 16	12-7/8	12-7/8
44D	Cantaloupe container	9-3/4 to 10	12-3/4 to 13	16-3/4 to 17
44E	Cantaloupe container	10-1/4	14	16-1/2

The California code requires that the melons be packed in regular compact arrangement in standard containers numbers 41, 42, 43, 44, 44A, 44B, 44C, 44D, or 44E.

Conversion from wooden crates to cartons requires a heavy capital investment since crate packing plants usually are not convertible to cartons. An outlay of several hundred thousand to a million dollars is the current estimate for a carton plant. This includes large pre-cooling facilities and large cold rooms for holding melons after packing, since field heat must be removed before melons are placed in cartons. A disadvantage of the cartons is that their contents are more difficult to cool than contents of crates. However, cartons are being improved with larger holes for ventilation and more strength.

QUALITY: Sweetness, fine texture, flavor, and juiciness are factors that determine quality in cantaloupes. Such characteristics can only be found in melons that were mature at harvest. Cantaloupes do not increase their sugar content after picking, although they can soften and change their types of sugars. If a cantaloupe has been picked at right maturity, so it will ripen properly, it will be well netted or webbed and have a smoothly rounded, depressed scar at the stem end. This is called the "full-slip" condition, because the stem has come off fully and smoothly when the melon was given a slight lift by the picker. If the stem end is rough, with portions of the stem adhering, the cantaloupe was not fully mature when picked and will not be as satisfactory as the full-slip melon. As to ripeness, consumers in areas close to where melons are grown in large quantities are likely to find ripe melons on the retail stand because they are picked at advanced maturity and shipped with little or no refrigeration. However, consumers far from growing areas rarely find ready-to-eat melons at the store. If cantaloupes are shipped a long distance, as most are, they must be picked while firm. Yet at full slip they have developed their full sugar content and need only soften. This process may take 3 to 4 days. The retailer with melons shipped from a long distance almost always keeps them cold, and in any event does not keep melons that have been received cold long enough for ripening to occur even without refrigeration.

Cantaloupes should be of adequate size, such as 5 in. in diameter or more, not small, runty, or misshapen. They should not be mottled, have growth cracks, be shriveled, flabby, or badly bruised. Melons showing any degree of decay, such as mold or soft sunken spots on the surface, should be rejected.

Disappointment with potentially good cantaloupes often is due to eating them too soon. Give them time to take on a yellow background appearance, acquire an aroma and soften. This can be done by allowing them to "ripen" at room temperature in the home.

Unlike the consumer's eye view of quality, objective determination of quality is based on measurements. Davis, Baker, and Kasmire of the University of California at Davis published a report on muskmelon quality characteristics and their interrelationships. They report on 14 different characteristics that were measured in the case of samples from 24 sites. These characteristics are:

Ground-spot diameter, measured in centimeters; elevation of the net above the melon surface, judged visually; net tightness, that is, the lateral development of spread of net strands; melon color, both background color and color of the net; unnetted suture width; size as measured by melon cross diameter; ratio of melon length to cross diameter, which indicates shape; net toughness as indicated by resistance of the net to scraping by a knife blade held at a 60° angle; melon firmness, as measured by an instrument that makes a depression under a dead weight applied for a specified time at a point midway between stem and blossom ends and at about 90° from the groundspot center; cavity size; flesh thickness, that is, the difference between the cavity diameter and outside cross diameter; ratio of flesh thickness to cavity diameter; flesh firmness as measured by a Ballauf pressure fruit-tester; and concentration of soluble solids as measured by a hand refractometer.

GRADES: Federal cantaloupe grades as amended June 30, 1968 are U.S. Fancy, U.S. 1, U.S. Commercial, and U.S. 2. The grade used most is U.S. 1. This grade "consists of cantaloupes of one type which are mature and have good internal quality, but are not overripe or soft or wilted, which are well formed, well netted and free from decay, wet slip and sunscald, and free from damage caused by liquid in the seed cavity, sunburn, hail, dirt, surface mold or other disease, aphids or other insects, scars, cracks, sunken areas, ground spot, bruises or mechanical or other means."

SWEET CHERRIES*

USES: Cherries are eaten out-of-hand, in salads, cooked in pies, tarts, cakes, jellies, jams, preserves, sauces, pickles, and candies. They are used in ice cream, puddings and other desserts, and in fruit cups. Some varieties of both sweet and tart cherries are preserved and often added to drinks and ices, as much for ornament as to give flavor. Both sweet and tart cherries are canned. The bulk of Western sweet cherries are sold fresh, although some are sold for freezing and other types of processing. Most processed maraschino cherries are from California sweet varieties. Several liqueurs are made from cherries, especially in Europe. Large amounts of cherries are frozen for the bakery trade.

MARKETING SEASON: The marketing season for fresh sweet cherries is May into August, with the peak in June and

*Courtesy of United Fresh Fruit and Vegetable Association.

July. About 6 percent of the annual supply comes to market in May, 43 percent in June, 45 percent in July, and 6 percent in August.

VARIETIES: Big is the main fresh market variety in Washington and California, and therefore in the country. Acreage of Bing in California in 1972 was 10,124 while the next largest acreage was of Royal Ann (Napoleon) 2,251, but Royal Ann is largely processed. Other California sweet cherry varieties totaled 2,059 acres. Other varieties for fresh market include Chapman, Black Tartarian, Early Burlat, Lambert, Van, Jubilee, Larian, Mona, Moreau, Parkhill, Black Republican, Rosanna, and Sam. Only a few varieties can be described here.

Bing "Seth Lewelling of Milwaukee, Ore., the originator of several of our finest cherries, grew Bing from the seed of Republican in 1875. The variety was named after a Chinese workman. In 1899 the American Pomological Society placed the variety on its fruit list. Tree large, vigorous, erect, becoming upright-spreading, rather open, productive; trunk and branches thick, smooth; branches brownish with numerous small lenticels . . . Leaves abundant, large, folded upward, ovate to obovate, of medium thickness; upper surface dark green, smooth; lower surface light green, pubescent; apex abruptly pointed, or acute, base abrupt; margin slightly serrate, glandular; petiole (stem) long, pubescent, thickish, tinged red; . . . Fruit matures in mid-season or later; very large, 1 in. in diameter, broadly cordate (heart-shaped), somewhat compressed, slightly angular; cavity deep, of medium width, abrupt, regular; suture a dark line; apex roundish or slightly depressed; color very dark red almost black; dots small, russet, inconspicuous; stem variable in thickness, 1-1/4 in. long; skin of medium thickness, tough, adherent to the pulp; flesh purplish red with dark purple juice, rather coarse, firm, very meaty, brittle, sweet; of very good quality; stone semi-free, large, ovate to oval, blunt with smooth surfaces."

Lambert This variety originated as a seedling in Oregon under a Royal Ann (Napoleon) tree. It was planted by Henderson Lewelling about 1848 in the orchard of J. H. Lambert of Milwaukee, Ore. Mr. Lambert gave it his name, and in 1895 turned over his stock to the Oregon Horticultural Society with the exclusive right to propagate. The variety was placed on the fruit list of the American Pomological Society in 1899. Tree is medium to large in size, vigorous, very productive; branches smooth, dull reddish brown with numerous small lenticels; leaves 4-1/4 in. long, 2-1/2 in. wide, folded upward, oval to obovate, thin; upper surface medium green and smooth, lower surface light green, lightly pubescent; apex acute, base abrupt; margin doubly serrate, glandular; petiole 1-1/2 in. long, dull red; flowers 1-1/4 in. across, white, borne in twos; fruit matures in mid-season, 1 in. in diameter, roundish-cordate; color very dark red changing to reddish black, dots numerous, small, russet, obscure; skin thin; flesh dark red with scant dark red juice, meaty, firm, pleasant flavored, sweet; of very good quality. In California, Lambert matures late, following Bing by 15 to 20 days.

Black Tartarian This variety is grown primarily in the Eastern states. It came originally from Russia, was introduced into England in 1794 and was introduced in this country by William Prince of Flushing, L.I, N.Y. early in the 19th century. It was recognized as a standard U.S. variety in 1848. Its production has been reduced because it is too soft to handle well in harvesting and marketing. The fruit is heart-shaped, less than 1 in. in diameter, purplish black with purplish red flesh and dark colored juice.

Republican This variety, also known as Black Republican or Lewelling, originated about the middle of the 19th century in the orchard of Seth Lewelling of Milwaukee, Ore. The parentage is not known. The fruit matures late; is about 1 in. in diameter, heart-shaped or roundish, purplish black with numerous dots; flesh purplish red with dark colored juice.

Chapman This variety was grown by W.H. Chapman of Napa, Calif. and is supposed to be a seedling of Black Tartarian but surpasses that variety in size and earliness. The fruit is large, roundish, purplish black, the stem long and slender, and of good quality; stone small.

Early Burlat This is a newer California variety. It is large and sweet, and one of the first kinds shipped each year. It is red to dark red and has a medium-firm flesh that is semi-freestone. It has excellent shipping qualities, and with the Tartarian is used as a pollenizer in Bing orchards.

SWEET CHERRIES

Grades: Minimum Score:	"A" or "FANCY" 90		"B" or "CHOICE" 80		"C" or "STANDARD" 70	"SUBSTANDARD" Less than 70
Light syrup, slightly sweetened water or juice and "In water."	**NET WEIGHT OZ.**		**NET WEIGHT METRIC**		**DRAINED WEIGHT OZ.**	**DRAINED WEIGHT METRIC**
	Unpitted	**Pitted**	**Unpitted**	**Pitted**		
No. 8Z Tall	5.4	5.5	153.1 g	155.9 g	4.8	136.1 g
No. 303	10.7	10.9	303.3 g	309.0 g	9.5	269.3 g
No. 2-1/2	19.0	19.4	538.6 g	550.0 g	17.6	499.0 g
No. 10	71.5	73.0	2.0 kg	2.1 kg	68.2	1.9 kg
Extra heavy syrup and "dietetic packs," whether or not packed in water						
No. 8Z Tall	5.4	5.5	153.1 g	155.9 g	4.3	121.9 g
No. 303	10.7	10.9	303.3 g	309.0 g	9.0	255.2 g
No. 2-1/2	19.0	19.4	538.6 g	550.0 g	16.6	470.6 g
No. 10	71.5	73.0	2.0 kg	2.1 kg	61.7	1.75 kg
In heavy syrup						
No. 8Z Tall	5.4	5.5	153.1 g	155.9 g	4.6	130.4 g
No. 303	10.7	10.9	303.3 g	309.0 g	9.3	263.7 g
No. 2-1/2	19.0	19.4	538.6 g	550.0 g	17.1	484.8 g
No. 10	71.5	73.0	2.0 kg	2.1 kg	63.7	1.8 kg

SULFURED (6/12/51   52.741)

Grade: Minimum Score:	"A" or "FANCY" 85	"B" or "CHOICE" 70	"D" or "SECONDS" Less than 70	"COMBINATION" — —

CANNED SWEET CHERRIES

Syrup	Specific Gravity (Brix Measurements)
"Extra heavy syrup," or "extra heavily sweetened fruit juice(s) and water," or "extra heavily sweetened fruit juice(s)"	25° - 35°
"Heavy syrup," or "heavily sweetened fruit juice(s) and water," or "heavily sweetened fruit juice(s)"	20° or more but less than 25°
"Light syrup," or "lightly sweetened fruit juice(s) and water," or "lightly sweetened fruit juice(s)."	16° or more but less than 20°
"Slightly sweetened water," or "extra light syrup," or "slightly sweetened fruit juice(s) and water," or "slightly sweetened fruit juice(s)."	Less than 16°
"In water"	N.A.
"In fruit juice(s) and water"	N.A.
"In fruit juice(s)"	N.A.
"Artificially sweetened"	N.A.

CHERRIES

FROZEN (3/1/58   52.3161)

Grades: "A" or   "C" or   "SUB-
          "FANCY"   "STANDARD" STANDARD"

Larian This is a new variety released in 1964 by the California Agricultural Experiment Station, as a supplement or replacement for Tartarian or Bing. The fruit is larger, firmer, and has a better flavor than Tartarian. It is more resistant to cracking than Bing, and the fruit matures a week earlier than Bing. Larian resulted from a cross made in 1946 between Lambert and a University of California selection. The tree produces a lighter crop than Bing, but the average fruit diameter is larger. The cherry is round, heart-shaped, smooth and symmetrical, the flesh is red to dark red, meaty, fine-textured, and moderately juicy.

Jubilee This was introduced about 1964 by the California station as a supplement or replacement for Bing because it produces practically no fruit doubles. The fruit is larger and ripens several days before Bing. It maintains its high quality for a relatively long period at room temperature. It resulted from a cross made in 1940 between Lambert and Napa Long Stem Bing.

Mona This was introduced by the California station in 1964. It came from a 1940 cross between LaCima and Chapman by Guy L. Philp. This is a red to dark red cherry which is larger, firmer, and less tart than Tartarian which it is intended to replace. The fruit is sweet and averages 0.97 in. in diameter. It is satisfactorily cross-pollinated by Bing, Tartarian, Van, and some others.

Schmidt This is "the preferred cultivar in areas where Bing is not successfully grown because of excessive rain-cracking or lack of vigor. It is a main cultivar in eastern orchards, but is not considered productive enough in the West. Schmidt originated about 1841 as a seedling of an old German cultivar and was raised by a forester named Schmidt at Casekaw, Prussia, Germany. It was introduced into England by Thomas Rivers and then to America . . . The fruit is large, dark mahogany, roundish cordate, and flattened on the ventral side, with a slight swelling along the suture . . . The skin is thick and tough. The flesh is firm, wine red in color, and meaty. The flavor is sweet and rich but rather astringent . . . The tree is large, vigorous, and upright-spreading."

Windsor This "is the standard late-ripening dark cherry in eastern areas. Generally in the West this cultivar is not used because of its small size and also because it is softer and has more lightly colored flesh than Bing or Lambert. In the East its bud hardiness and regular, heavy productivity have generally outweighed the usual discount in the price of this cultivar in comparison to the larger firmer Bing . . . Windsor originated on the farm of James Dougall of Windsor, Ontario, Canada. It was first propagated in 1881."

CONTAINERS: "Most sweet cherries that are shipped for the fresh fruit market from the western states are packed in boxes or lugs that hold 10 to 20 lb. of fruit. The double-row, hand-faced pack, popular for many years, is little used now because of labor cost. The automatic sizer lends itself to the easy and less expensive method of jumble packing from the belts that carry the sized cherries. Consequently, most cherries are now jumble packed into wooden boxes or divided fiberboard boxes that hold 20 lb. of fruit.

"In the Pacific Northwest, sealed polyethylene liners are nearly always used with all types of boxes. Within the sealed 'poly' liner, which is usually 1.25 or 1.5 mills thick, the atmosphere becomes modified as oxygen is consumed and carbon dioxide is liberated by the respiring fruit. Levels of carbon dioxide and oxygen within the sealed liners at 31°F. become stabilized at about 6.5 and 9 percent respectively. Decay is retarded by the carbon dioxide which, together with the high moisture within the liner, preserves fruit brightness and freshness." Such liners are not used in California where there have been observations that they intensify fruit rotting. If liners are used, they must be opened before the fruit is warmed to avoid oxygen starvation and fermentation of the fruit.

"The standard shipping container for California cherries is the Calex lug-a wooden box 3-3/4 in. deep, 13-1/2 in. wide and 16-1/8 in. long, used for the 18 to 20 lb. cherry loose-pack. Face-packing is generally done in a Campbell lug which is 4 in. deep, 11-1/2 in. wide and 14-1/8 in. long. Corrugated containers are in limited use, especially for air shipments since their lighter weight is an advantage. (Ed. note: cost is also an advantage.) The wax coating used on some corrugated containers can help protect fruit from moisture loss. The wax coating can also slow the penetration of moisture into the corrugated board, and thus aid in maintaining the rigidity of the container. Corrugated containers must be constructed to provide sufficient stacking strength to protect the fruit during a normal marketing period under high humidity conditions.

"Although most cherries are packed to depths of 4 in. or less, recent studies indicate that a 6-in. depth could safely be used. Although there is considerable latitude in the depth for cherry containers, fruit damage does increase at depths greater than 6 in. Therefore a container could be designed with a greater depth and smaller horizontal dimensions to hold the same amount of fruit as the present lug. The smaller top surface would reduce top bulge and subsequent fruit loosening and damage."

Tests have been made of fiberboard and of expanded polystyrene foam boxes for cherries. It required 24 hours for cherries packed in fiberboard to cool from 72° to 56°; 13 hours for cherries packed in wood boxes; and 9 hours for cherries packed in polystyrene foam boxes. There was most bruising in the fiberboard box and least in the foam box.

GRADES: U.S. standards for grades of sweet cherries, effective May 7, 1971, are U.S. 1 and U.S. Commercial. "U.S. 1 consists of sweet cherries which meet the following requirements: (a) similar varietal characteristics; (b) mature; (c) fairly well colored; (d) well formed; (e) clean; (f) free from (1) decay; (2) insect larvae or holes caused by them; (3) soft, overripe, or shriveled; (4) undeveloped doubles; and (5) sunscald; (g) free from damage by any other cause; (h) size, unless otherwise specified the minimum diameter of each cherry shall be not less than 3/4 in. The maximum diameter of the cherries in any lot may be specified in accordance with the facts."

CHERRIES, Sweet—Canned (6/20/73)

Grade A: Color: (Light) Basic background color exclusive of blush is a pinkish yellow to pale amber color which may be no more than slightly dull. Blush appears as a surface color ranging from very light pinkish tan to tannish brown. (Dark) Basic background color is typical deep red to purple red or purple black. **Size:** The weight of each cherry is not less than 1/10 oz. (2.84 grams) and the weight of the largest cherry is not more than twice the weight of smallest. Pitted and unpitted: diameter of largest cherry may exceed diameter of smallest by not more than 3/16 in. and in 85 percent of the cherries with the most uniform diameter, the diameter of the largest cherries may exceed that of smallest by not more than 1/16 in. **Defects:** practically free. Maximum tolerance: 1 piece of harmless extraneous material for each 60 oz. of net contents; 1 portion of cherry stem for each 20 oz. of net contents; in pitted style, 1 pit for each 20 oz. of net contents and a total of 10 percent may be slightly damaged, damaged, seriously damaged, slightly misshapen, misshapen, blemished, seriously blemished, or any combination, but not more than 5 percent may be damaged, etc; Provided, That not more than 2 percent may be seriously blemished and seriously damaged. **Character:** Cherries are thick-fleshed, tender but not soft or noticeably flabby, and otherwise possess a good texture; not more than 10 may possess a reasonably good character; and in unpitted style, not more than 5 percent may possess serious processing cracks.

Grade B: Color: (Light) Pinkish yellow to amber which may be no more than slightly dull. Blush appears as a surface color ranging from tan to tannish brown. (Dark) The same (see Grade A Dark) and may be no more than slightly dull. **Size:** See size for Grade A, except the longest cherries may exceed the smallest by 1/8 in. **Defects:** reasonably free from defects. **Maximum Tolerance:** 1 piece of harmless extraneous material for each 40 oz. of net contents; a total of 5 portions of cherry stems, but not more than 1 portion of cherry stem may be longer than 1/4 in. but not longer than 1/2 in. for each 20 oz. of net content; in pitted style, 1 pit for each 20 oz. of contents and a total of 20 percent may be slightly damaged, damaged, seriously damaged, slightly misshapen; misshapen, blemished, seriously blemished, or any combination, but not more than 10 percent may be damaged; Provided, That not more than 4 percent may be seriously blemished and seriously damaged. **Character:** Reasonably thick-fleshed, reasonably tender but not more than slightly soft or markedly flabby; not more than 10 percent may possess a fairly good character provided in unpitted cherries, none are thin-fleshed; and in unpitted styles, not more than 10 percent may possess serious processing cracks.

Grade C: Color: (Light) Basic background color and blush may be variable or slightly dull but not off color. (Dark) May possess a slightly dull deep red to slightly dull purple red or purple black that may be variable but not off color. **Size:** Unpitted, see Grade A. Pitted and unpitted—may vary in diameter. **Defects:** Fairly free. Maximum Tolerance: 1 piece of harmless extraneous material for each 20 oz. of net content; a total of 10 portions of cherry stems but not more than 3 portions of cherry stems, each of which may be longer than

1/4 in. but not longer than 1/2 in. for each 20 oz. of net contents; and a total of 30 percent may be slightly damaged, etc; or any combination not more than 15 percent may be blemished, seriously blemished, and seriously damaged. **Character:** Cherries may be lacking in thickness of flesh but, in unpitted cherries, the total weight of pits is not more than 12 percent of the weight of drained cherries; may be variable in tenderness and texture; ranging from firm to soft but characteristic of canned sweet cherries that may have been processed from slightly immature to slightly over-mature cherries; not more than 10 percent may be markedly flabby; and in unpitted style, serious processing cracks may be present.

CHERRIES, Sweet—Canned (1975 Revisions)

The Food and Drug Administration amended the standards of identity for Canned Sweet Cherries, compliance with which may have begun on March 11, 1975, but mostly after December 31, 1975.

The following amendments to the USDA standards for Canned Sweet Cherries are proposed to bring them into line with the FDA Standards of Identity.

Product description.

"Canned Sweet Cherries" is the product represented as defined in the Standards of Identity for Canned Cherries (21CFR27.30 and 27.34); issued pursuant to the Federal Food, Drug, and Cosmetic Act.

CHERRIES, Sweet — Frozen (3/1/58)

Grade A: Color: Reasonably uniform color that is bright and typical of well-ripened sweet cherries, and not more than 10 percent may vary markedly from this color because of discoloration due to oxidation, improper processing, or other causes, or because of not well-ripened sweet cherries. **Size:** No unseparated doubles are present; 95 percent of the cherries are well formed and the diameter of the cherry with the greatest diameter may exceed the cherry with the smallest diameter by not more than 1/4 in.; and in 90 percent, all the cherries which are not uniform in diameter. The diameters do not vary by more than 1/4 in. **Defects:** For each 20 oz. net weight there may be present not more than 1 piece harmless extraneous material. 1 pit in pitted cherries. Not

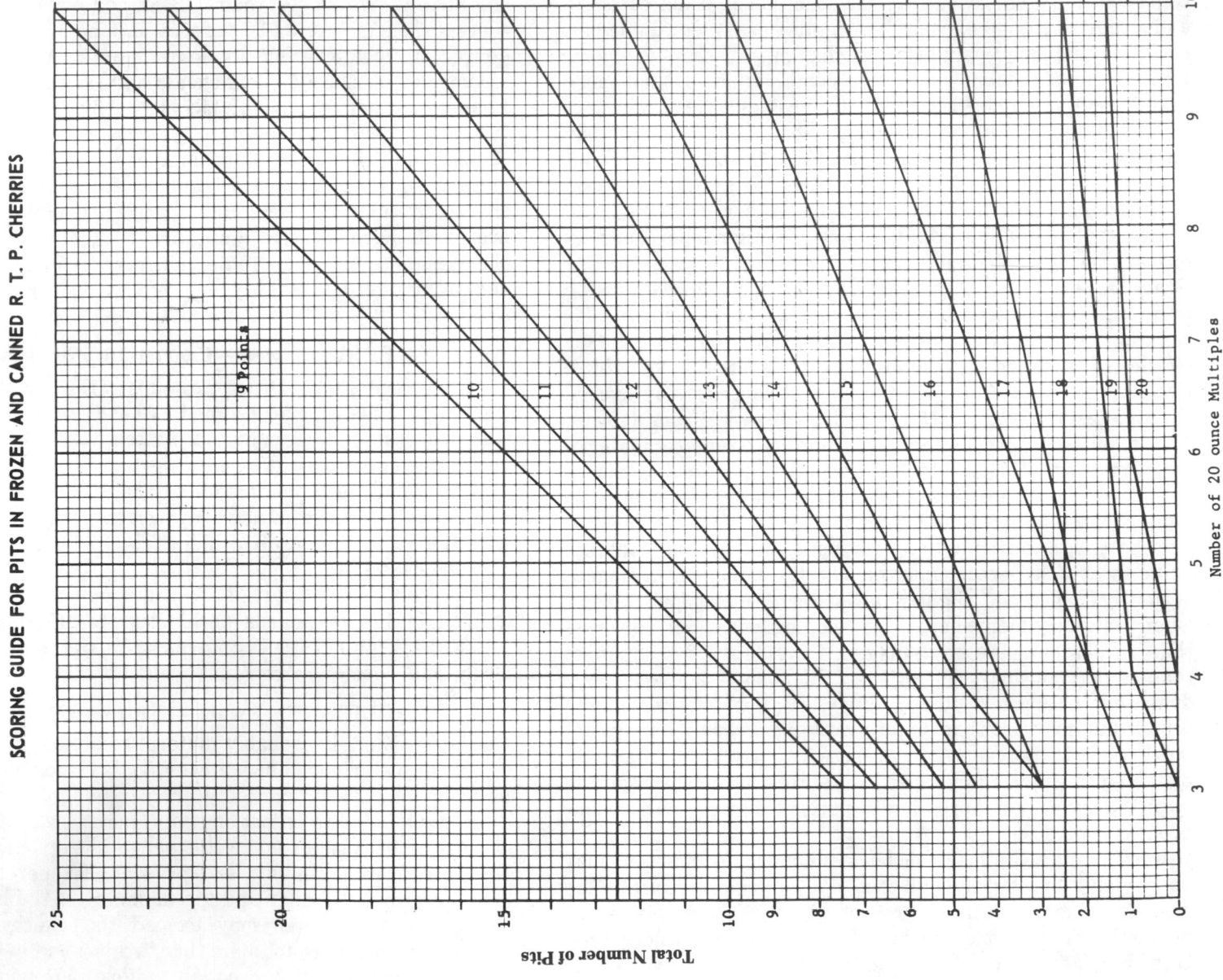

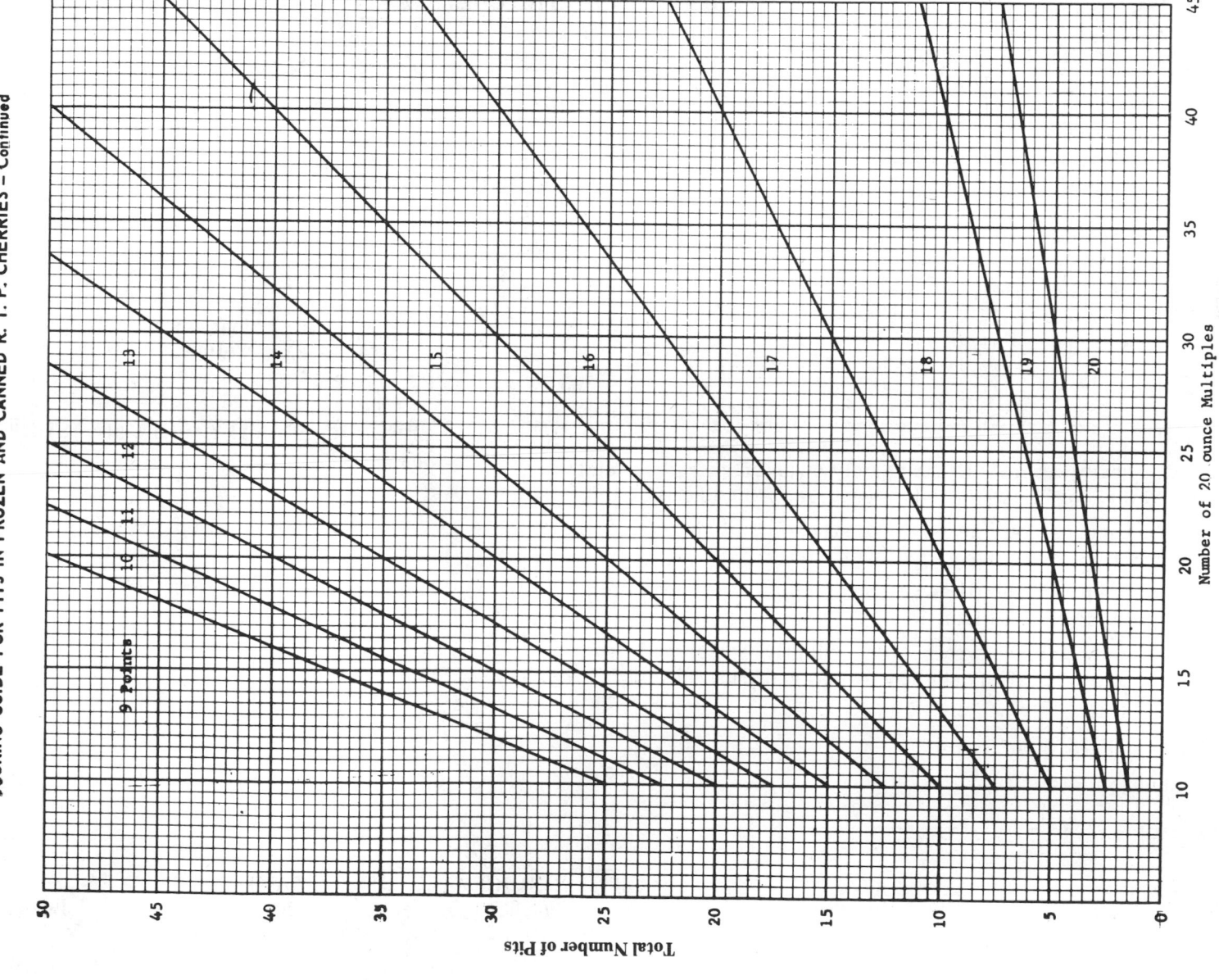

SCORING GUIDE FOR PITS IN FROZEN AND CANNED R. T. P. CHERRIES — Continued

INSPECTION AID NO. 58
AUGUST 1964
(Page 2)

RED TART PITTED CHERRIES

CANNED (5/15/74   52.771)

GRADES:	"A" or "FANCY"	"B" or "CHOICE"	"C" or "STANDARD"	"SUBSTANDARD"
Minimum score:	90	80	70	Less than 70

	NET WEIGHT OZ.	NET WEIGHT METRIC	DRAINED WEIGHT OZ.		DRAINED WEIGHT METRIC	
			Packed in water or cherry juice	Packed in syrup or slightly sweetened water	Packed in water or cherry juice	Packed in syrup or slightly sweetened water
No. 303	12.9	365.7 g	10.7	9.9	303.3 g	280.7 g
No. 10	86.7	2.46 kg	71.2	69.4		1.97 kg

SYRUP	SPECIFIC GRAVITY (BRIX MEASUREMENTS)
"Extra heavy syrup," "Extra heavily sweetened fruit juice(s) and water," or "Extra heavily sweetened fruit juice(s)."	28°-45°
"Heavy syrup," or "heavily sweetened fruit juice(s) and water," or "heavily sweetened fruit juice(s)."	22° or more but less than 28°
"Light syrup," or "lightly sweetened fruit juice(s) and water," or "lightly sweetened fruit juice(s)."	18° or more but less than 22°
"Slightly sweetened water," or "slightly sweetened fruit juice(s) and water," or "slightly sweetened fruit juice(s)."	less than 18°
"In water"	N.A.
"In fruit juice(s) and water"	N.A.
"In fruit juice(s)"	N.A.

FROZEN (6/28/74   52.801)

Grades:	"A" or "FANCY"	"B" or "CHOICE"	"C" or "STANDARD"	"SUBSTANDARD"
Minimum Score:	90	80	70	Less than 70

SULFURED (6/12/51   52.741)

Grades:	"A" or "FANCY"	"B" or "CHOICE"	"D" or "SECONDS"	"COMBINATION"
Minimum Score:	85	70	Less than 70	——

TABLE IV — ALLOWANCES FOR QUALITY FACTORS

Factor	Sample Unit Size	Maximum no. permissible for the respective grade					
		A		**B**		**C**	
Pits	20 oz.	Not more than 2 in any sample unit.	Sample average 1 per 40 oz.	Not more than 3 in any sample unit.	Sample average 1 per 30 oz.	4 or more in any sample unit.	Sample average 1 per 20 oz.
Defects: Total-mutilated, plus minor blemished plus blemished	100 cherries	10		15		20	
of which blemished limited to		3		7		15	
Harmless extraneous material....Total contents		Average 1 piece per 60 oz. net contents		Average 1.5 pieces per 60 oz. net contents		Average 3 pieces per 60 oz. net contents	

more than 7 percent may be damaged and seriously damaged: Provided, That not more than 3 percent of all of the cherries are seriously damaged. **Character:** Tender, fleshy texture, typical of well-ripened, properly processed frozen sweet cherries; and that not more than 10 percent of the cherries may possess a reasonably good character.

Grade B: Color: Possess a color that is reasonably bright and typical of well-ripened cherries and that not more than 20 percent may vary markedly from this color because of discoloration due to oxidation, improper processing or other causes, or because of sweet cherries that are not well-ripened. **Size:** Not more than 10 percent may be unseparated doubles; 85 percent of the cherries are well formed; in 90 percent, for all the cherries which are not uniform in diameter, the diameters do not vary more than 1/4 in. **Defects:** For each 20 oz. net weight, there may be present not more than: 2 pieces of harmless extraneous material; 1 pit in pitted cherries; not more than 15 percent may be damaged and seriously damaged: Provided, That not more than 5 percent of the cherries are seriously damaged. **Character:** Possess a texture of reasonably well-ripened, frozen sweet cherries that are properly processed; the texture is fleshy and the cherries

tender, or the tenderness may be variable from slightly soft to slightly firm; and that not more than 15 percent may be overripe or immature or otherwise fail to meet at least a reasonably good character. **Sstd:** Fails to meet requirements.

CHERRIES, Red Tart Pitted — Canned (5/18/74)

Grade A: Color: Practically uniform, bright, and typical. **Freedom from Pits:** Practically free from pits. Table IV. **Defects:** Practically free from defects. Table IV. **Character:** Thick fleshed and have a firm tender texture.

Grade B: Color: Reasonably uniform typical, may range from a slight yellowish red to a slightly mottled reddish brown. **Freedom from Pits:** Reasonably free from pits. See Table IV. **Defects:** Reasonably free from defects. See Table IV for maximum allowance. **Character:** May be reasonably thick fleshed and may be slightly soft.

Grade C: Color: May range from a brownish cast to mottled shades of brown. **Freedom from Pits:** Fairly free from pits. See Table IV. **Defects:** Fairly free from defects. See Table IV. **Character:** May be thin-fleshed, and may be soft, but not mushy, or slightly tough but not leathery.

CHERRIES, Red Tart Pitted — Frozen (6/28/74)

Grade A: Color: In addition to requirements in canned cherries, not more than 15 percent of frozen cherries may vary from a "good red color" for any reason. **Freedom from defects:** See Defects for Canned; also see Table IV. There is one exception; a unit measurement is applied to a "blemished cherry"—"aggregate area covered by the blemishes exceeds the area of a circle 9/32 in. in diameter."

Grade C: Color In addition to requirements in canned cherries, 25 percent may vary markedly from "reasonably good red color" for any reason. **Defects:** see Grade A.

CHERRIES, Red Tart Pitted — Frozen (6/28/74)

Grade A: Color: Have a color that is bright and typical of properly ripened cherries and is practically uniform in that the number of cherries that differ from this color, or that are under-colored, does not exceed 12 out of a sample size of 100 cherries. **Pits:** Not more than 2 pits in any sample unit of 20 oz. Sample average is 1 per 40 oz. **Defects:** Number of defects that may be present does not exceed the number specified for the applicable type of defect in Table I. **Character:** Cherries are thick-fleshed and have a firm, tender texture.

Grade B: Color: Have a color that is reasonably bright and typical of properly ripened cherries and that is reasonably uniform in that there are not more than 18 out of a sample unit size of 100 cherries that vary markedly in color or that are under-colored. **Pits:** Not more than 3 pits in any sample unit of 20 oz. Sample average is 1 per 30 oz. **Defects:** Number of defects that may be present does not exceed the number specified for the applicable type of defect in Table I. **Character:** Cherries may be reasonably thick-fleshed and slightly soft.

Grade C: Color: Have a color that is fairly bright and typical of properly ripened cherries and that is fairly uniform in that not more than 25 out of a sample unit size of 100 cherries vary markedly in color or are under-colored. **Pits:** Four pits or more in any sample of 20 oz. Sample average is 1 per 20 oz. **Defects:** Number of defects that may be present does not exceed the number specified for the applicable type of defect

in Table I. **Character:** Cherries may be thin-fleshed, and soft but not mushy, or slightly tough but not leathery. **Sstd:** Fails to meet requirements.

TABLE I

| Defects | Sample unit size | Maximum number permissible for the respective grade | | |
		A	B	C
Total-mutilated, minor blemished, and blemished of which	100 cherries	10	15	20
Blemished—limited to		3	7	15
Harmless extraneous material	20 oz.	Average 1 piece per 60 oz. net contents	Average 1 piece per 40 oz. net contents	Average 1 piece per 20 oz. net contents

COCONUTS*

USES: "Ranking among the 10 most useful tree species to mankind, coconut is the most important of cultivated palms. The fruits are eaten raw, prepared into candies, or shredded in pastries. When immature, the soft, jelly-like flesh can be eaten with a spoon. The watery liquids of green fruits and the milky juice of mature ones are pure, nutritious, cool, and refreshing drinks. Known as cocos de agua, these green fruits are sold on city streets. Under the name copra, the dried white oily part of the ripe fruits is marketed in large quantities for the manufacturer of soaps and coconut oil, the latter for preparing margarine and other foods and for cooking. It is also classed as a honey plant. The sugary sap collected from cut and unopened flower clusters is a fresh beverage known as toddy and a source of alcohol. The trunks serve for posts. Walking sticks have been made from the outer layer or ring of the trunk. The inner part is a very soft, light brown pith with scattered reddish brown bundles.

"The leaves furnish thatch for roofs and shelters and have

*Courtesy of United Fresh Fruit and Vegetable Association.

been made into lattice screens and fences. Various articles, such as novelties, souvenirs, cups, and flower pots are made from the husks and shells. The shells have also been used for kitchen implements and for high-grade charcoal. In other regions of the world different parts of the plant serve many purposes. Coconut fiber, or coir, is made into mats, ropes, brooms, and brushes." With regard to toddy, when distilled, it provides a powerful beverage, arrack. The sugar may be removed from toddy as jaggery, or the toddy may be used to produce vinegar . . . The terminal bud of the tree may be eaten as palm cabbage. (This is not a good idea, because palms have only one growing point, and when this bud is destroyed, the plant stops growing and its death is hastened.) The coconut palm makes a fine ornamental tree. There is a drawback; the nuts are heavy and when they drop or are blown off with extra force, they are a danger to man or animal below.

MARKETING SEASON: The following table shows the percentage of the annual total of fresh coconuts available each month in the U.S. The average annual supply is about 27 million lb. The figures are based on imports plus the quantity received from Puerto Rico. The average coconut weighs 1.5 lb. Due to rounding the total percentage comes to 101.

MONTHLY AVAILABILITY OF COCONUTS EXPRESSED AS A PERCENTAGE OF THE TOTAL ANNUAL SUPPLY

Jan.	Feb.	Mar.	Apr.	May	June	July	Aug.	Sept.	Oct.	Nov.	Dec.
%	%	%	%	%	%	%	%	%	%	%	%
7	8	9	9	4	4	4	5	9	13	16	17

VARIETIES: There are many varieties, varying in size, color, husk, and internal tissue. In the Philippines, there are strains that have very large nuts so that only 3,000 are required to produce a ton of copra instead of the usual 6,000. An interesting variety, says J. C. McCurrack, is the dwarf Malayan coconut which is much shorter than the usual tree, with fruits that are a golden yellow color. Another Philippine variety, known as Makapuno, has a fruit the interior of which is filled with soft, sweet tissue, used in the Philippines as a table delicacy. However, rather than a variety, this may be a variant fruit from the same trees that produce normal fruit. There is said to be a coconut in Sri Lanka called Nawasi which

has a soft, edible husk. The coconut of commerce is grouped under the name Cocos nucifera.

CONTAINERS: Coconuts are generally shipped in burlap sacks holding 40 to 50 nuts. The weight is around 75 to 80 lb. per sack. Some are also shipped in smaller plastic mesh sacks holding 12. Average weight per coconut is 1.5 lb.

QUALITY CRITERIA: There are no U.S. grade standards for coconuts. To check for quality, determine that the nut has milk by the slosh test; see that no mold is present, and that the eyes at the base are not wet or pierced. An unusual complaint from a coconut buyer to the Food and Drug Administration was that coconuts she bought contained water, not the natural coconut fluid. FDA advised her that replacement of the milk with water would be food adulteration in violation of the Food and Drug Act regardless of any signs or labelling that might advise the consumer that this had been done.

Puerto Rico has grade standards for dry husked coconuts. They are P.R. No. 1 and P.R. No. 2. P.R. No. 1 shall consist of coconuts of the same type which are mature, fresh, well husked, clean, well formed, fairly uniform in color, and free from sprouts, molds, decay, rancidity, cracks, broken shell, freezing injury, and free from damage caused by insects, diseases, or mechanical, or other means. Unless otherwise specified, the thickness of the meat of each coconut shall be not less than 3/8 in. **Tolerance for defects:** In order to allow for variations incident to proper grading and handling, other than for size, the following tolerances shall be permitted: 10 percent by count, for coconuts in any lot which fail to meet the requirements of this grade, but not more than 3/10 of this amount, or 3 percent, shall be allowed for defects causing serious damage; and 10 percent, by count, for coconuts in any lot having meat less than 3/8 in. thick.

Coconuts in the so-called half-sack are to be 30, 40, 50, 60, or 75. The size 30 coconut is to be 5 in. in diameter; the 40 is to be 4-1/2 to 5 in.; the 50 to be 4 to 4-1/2 in.; the 60 to be 3-1/2 to 4 in.; and the 75 to be 3 to 3-1/2 in. Diameter is to be measured at the largest dimension of the coconut at right angles to its length. Not more than 10 percent of the coconuts in any lot are permitted to be smaller or larger than the specified minimum and maximum diameters.

CRANBERRIES*

USES: Cranberries have a wide variety of uses, from an ingredient for turkey stuffing to a juice cocktail, spicy with cloves and cinnamon. Of course, cranberry sauce and jelly are old reliables. But cranberries are also used in relishes, ices, fruit salads, fruit molds, and in many combinations with apples, oranges, and other fruits. ...For a raw cranberry relish that is mighty good for serving with any kind of meat, poultry or fish, USDA's Food Facts gives the following ingredients: 1 lb. of fresh cranberries, 1 orange and 1 cup of sugar. Quarter the orange and take out the seeds, but use both pulp and skin. Grind the raw berries and orange peel, mix and place in covered jar in the refrigerator. It will keep for 2 or 3 weeks. ...Fresh cranberry nut bread is excellent. ...A baked fresh cranberry and apple compote is mouth watering. ...Cranberries make fine pies, pudding, and tarts. ...There is a recipe for fluffy cranberry custard. ...And a fresh cranberry and apple cobbler is deluxe.

MARKETING SEASON: Fresh cranberries are on the market from September through December, while processed products, such as cranberry jelly and cranberry juice are on the market all year. Cranberries have always been a festive item, and, as expected, the peak month for fresh cranberries is November, with large amounts used at Thanksgiving and also at Christmas. The following table shows monthly availability of fresh cranberries expressed as a percentage of the total annual supply.

MONTHLY AVAILABILITY EXPRESSED AS PERCENTAGE OF TOTAL ANNUAL SUPPLY

Commodity	Jan. %	Feb. %	Mar. %	Apr. %
Cranberries, All Massachusetts Wisconsin				

Commodity	May %	June %	July %	Aug. %
Cranberries, All Massachusetts Wisconsin				

Commodity	Sept. %	Oct. %	Nov. %	Dec. %
Cranberries, All	8	24	50	18
Massachusetts	12	18	45	24
Wisconsin	1	29	60	9

VARIETIES: "There are over a hundred different known varieties of cranberries, many with interesting names such as Potter's Favorite, Budd's Blues, Centennial, and Aviator, which conjure up fascinating pictures of earlier days. But four varieties account for most of the cranberries currently grown in North America."

Early Black The standard variety in Massachusetts and New Jersey. A small berry which is blackish red when ripe, usually during the first two weeks of September.

Howes A standard late variety named for its discoverer, Eli Howes, around 1843 and found principally in Massachusetts and New Jersey. Howes are oblong in shape, larger than Early Blacks, and ripen later. The fruit turns medium red when ripe.

Searles Predominant variety in Wisconsin, and perhaps the most productive of all cultivated cranberries. Berries are deep red when ripe, usually in late September.

McFarlin Named for Charles Dexter McFarlin of South Carver, Mass., who was the first commercial West Coast cranberry grower (in late 1800s). Now principal variety in Washington and Oregon, but also found in other areas. A nearly oblong berry which ripens late and produces a deep red color.

New varieties of cranberries have been developed by a selective breeding program sponsored by the U.S. Dept. of Agriculture and the state experiment stations. Three seedlings were named in 1950 based on New Jersey tests, namely Beckwith, Stevens, and Wilcox. Three other seedlings were named in 1961 based on tests conducted in Massachusetts, namely Franklin, Bergman, and Pilgrim. All of these hybrid varieties have various outstanding characteristics but have not been planted extensively due to limited amounts of planting stock.

CONTAINERS: Approximately 98 percent of cranberries for fresh market are packed at shipping point in 1-lb. consumer packages, either window boxes or film bags. However, the use of film bags is increasing and of window boxes declining, and it is likely the window box will be phased out. The major master container is a fiberboard carton holding 24 1-lb. packages. The master carton may be 7-3/4 x 14-3/8 x 16-3/8 or 8-1/2 x 14-3/4 x 16-5/8 in. or similar dimensions. There is also a 25-lb. bulk

*UFFVA

carton for the institutional trade, but only a few were shipped in 1973, and it may also be phased out.

In southern and eastern markets, window boxes are preferred; in western and midwestern markets, film bags are more in demand.

High speed mechanical filling equipment fills the boxes and bags which are then hand-packed into cartons.

GRADES: U.S. standard grades for fresh cranberries, effective Aug. 26, 1971, provide for one grade, U.S. 1. The standards apply only to the commonly cultivated cranberry, Vaccinium macrocarpon. In general, "compliance with these standards is determined by analyzing samples of 100 berries each, drawn at random from individual containers representative of the lot. The tolerances for off-size and defective berries apply to the lot, and there is no restriction on the percentage that may occur in individual samples or containers: Provided, That the averages for the entire lot are within the tolerances specified for the grade."

"U.S. 1 consists of cranberries which meet the following requirements: (a) Basic requirements: (1) one variety or similar varietal characteristics; (2) clean; (3) mature; (4) firm and (5) not soft or decayed. (b) Free from damage caused by: (1) moisture; (2) bruises; (3) freezing; (4) smothering; (5) scarring; (6) sunscald; (7) foreign material; (8) disease; (9) insects; or (10) mechanical or other means. (c) Color: individual cranberries shall be at least fairly well colored, and the cranberries in the container shall be fairly uniform in color; (d) Size: unless otherwise specified, the diameter of each cranberry shall be not less than 13/32 inch."

CRANBERRIES - Frozen [9/22/71]

Grade A, B, and C. See Table I. **Grade SStd.** fails to meet requirements. Defects of Grades A, B, C, see Table II. SStd fails to meet requirements. **Grade A: Character:** Cranberries may be slightly soft to moderately firm, but not more than 10 cranberries in the sample units may be mushy or hard.

Grade B: Character: Cranberries may be slightly soft to moderately firm, but not more than 20 cranberries in the sample unit may be mushy or hard.

Grade C: Character: Cranberries may be very soft to very firm, but not more than 60 cranberries in the sample unit may be hard or mushy. **SStd:** Fails to meet requirements.

TABLE I—COLOR ALLOWANCES FOR FROZEN CRANBERRIES

	Grade A Good Color	Grade B Reasonably Good Color	Grade C Fairly Good Color
Any condition affecting the overall color appearance of the sample unit.	Not more than slightly affected.	Not materially affected.	Not seriously affected.
	Maximum number of cranberries within each sample unit		
Fairly well-colored and/or poorly colored	15		
Fairly well-colored and/or poorly colored and/or uncolored.		30	
Poorly colored and/or uncolored			60
Poorly colored	3	10	
Uncolored	None	5	
Well colored	Remainder	Remainder	
Well colored and/or fairly well colored			Remainder

TABLE II—DEFECT ALLOWANCE FOR FROZEN CRANBERRIES

	Grade A	Grade B	Grade C
Defects affecting the overall appearance of the sample unit.	Not more than slightly affected.	Not materially affected.	Not seriously affected.
	Maximum in each sample unit		
Harmless extraneous plant material	1/8 sq. in.	1/4 sq. in.	1/2 sq. in.
Total - major & minor blemished cranberries	15 But no more than	25 But no more than	35 But no more than
Major blemished cranberries	7	10	15
Fine stems	4	4	No limit

CRANBERRIES

FRESH (8/26/71   51.2775)

Grades: U.S. NO. 1

FROZEN (9/22/71   52.6281)

Grades:	"A" or "FANCY"	"B" or "CHOICE"	"C" or "STAN-DARD"	"SUB-STAN-DARD"
Minimum Score:	90	80	70	Less than 70

CRANBERRY SAUCE — Canned [3/19/51]

Grade A: Color: Bright, dark red color typical of canned cranberries, which color is free from any dullness. **Consistency or texture:** Jelly or Strained: The gel is tender to slightly firm and there may be evidence of a reasonable separation of free liquid. **Defects: Jellied or Strained:** The product is free from foreign material and objectionable material, is free from any harmless extraneous particles that exceed the area of a circle 3/16 in. in diameter; and is practically free from harmless extraneous particles that are equivalent in area of a circle 3/16

in. or less in diameter. **Consistency and texture: Whole:** The skin particles and the semi-jellied portions are reasonably tender, and fruit, seed and skin particles are dispersed reasonably uniformly throughout the product. **Defects: Whole:** There may be present for each 12 oz. not more than 3 defective cranberries or foreign berries and not more than 4 fine stems 3/4 in. or more in length: the product is free from foreign material and is practically free from other defects which affect materially the appearance or edibility. **Flavor and Odor:** Possess a good, characteristic, slightly tart flavor typical of cooked cranberries, and the product is free from any trace of a caramelized flavor, abnormal flavor, or abnormal odor.

Grade C: Color: Red color typical of canned cranberries, which color may be slightly dull or may indiciate slight evidence of oxidation but is not off-color. **Consistency and Texture: Jellied or Strained:** The gel may lack firmness or may be stiff but is not tough or rubbery and there may be evidence of separation of free liquid which is not excessive. **Defects: Jelly or Strained:** The product is free from foreign material and objectionable material; is practically free from harmless extraneous particles that exceed the area of 3/16 in. in diameter; and is fairly free from harmless extraneous particles that are the equivalent in area of a circle 3/16 in. or less in diameter. **Consistency and Texture: Whole:** The skin portions are fairly tender, and the fruit, seed, and skin particles are dispersed fairly uniformly throughout the product, and there may be evidence of separation of free liquid which is not excessive. **Defects: Whole:** There may be present for each 12 oz. not more than 6 fine stems 3/4 in. or more in length; the product is free from foreign material and objectionable material and is fairly free from other defects which affect materially the appearance or edibility. **Flavor and Odor:** Possess a normal flavor typical of cooked cranberries and the product is free from objectionable flavors and objectionable odors of any kind. **Sstd:** Fails to meet requirements. See Table.

CURRANTS, Dried [10/11/65]

Grade A: Possess a good typical color; good characteristic flavor, that shows development characteristic of dried currants prepared from well-matured grapes; that contain not more than 20 percent of moisture; also see Table I: Not more than 1 piece of stem per 24 oz. of dried currants may be present; Not more than 12 seeds per 16 oz. may be present in seeded dried currants; not more than 1-1/2 percent of dried currants may possess capstems; not more than 1 percent, by weight, may be undeveloped, and not more than 2 percent be damaged; not more than 5 percent may be sugared; not more than 5 percent may be moldy. The appearance or edibility may not be affected by dried currants damaged by fermentation; and no grit, sand, or silt may be present that affects the appearance and edibility.

Grade B: Possess a good typical color, characteristic flavor; that show development characteristic of dried currants prepared from reasonably well-matured grapes; that contain not more than 20 percent of moisture; also see Table I. Not more than 1 piece of stem per 16 oz. of dried currants may be present; not more than 15 seeds per 16 oz.; not more than 2 percent may possess capstems; not more than 2 percent may be undeveloped; not more than 3 percent may be damaged; not more than 10 percent may be sugared; not more than 4 percent may be moldy. The appearance or edibility may not be more than slightly affected by dried currants damaged by fermentation, and no grit, sand, or silt may be present that affects the appearance or edibility of the dried currants.

Substandard: Fails to meet requirements.

CURRANTS

DRIED (10/11/65   52.981)

GRADES: "A" or   "B" or   "SUB-
               "FANCY"   "CHOICE"   STANDARD"

TABLE I—ALLOWANCES FOR DEFECTS IN DRIED CURRANTS

Defects	U.S. Grade A or U.S. Fancy	U.S. Grade B or U.S. Choice
	Maximum count	
Pieces of stem	1 per 24 oz.	1 per 16 oz.
Seeds (in Seeded style)	12 per 16 oz.	15 per 16 oz.
	Maximum (by weight) (percent)	
Currants with capstems	1-1/2	2
Undeveloped	1	2
Damaged	2	3
Sugared	5	10

Defects	U.S. Grade A or U.S. Fancy	U.S. Grade B or U.S. Choice
	Maximum (by count) (percent)	
Moldy currants	3	4
Damaged by fermentation	Appearance or edibility may not be affected.	Appearance or edibility may not be more than slightly affected.
Grit, sand, or silt	None of any consequence may be present that affects the appearance or edibility of the product.	

	A	B
Size of case or package		
Markings		
Label or brand		
Net weight		
Type		
Moisture content		
Similar varietal characteristics		
Color		
Flavor		
Development		

Defects	A	B
	Maximum	
Pieces of stem	1 per 24 oz.	1 per 16 oz.
Seeds (in Seeded style)	12 per 16 oz.	15 per 16 oz.
	Maximum (by weight) (percent)	
Currants with capstems	1-1/2	2
Undeveloped	1	2
Damaged	2	3
Sugared	5	10
	Maximum (by count) (percent)	
Moldy currants	3	4
Damaged by fermentation: Affecting appearance or edibility.	Not affected	No more than slightly affected.
Grit, sand, or silt: Affecting appearance or edibility	None of any consequence.	None of any consequence.
Grade		

DATES*

USES: Dates, especially the softer kinds and the excellent varieties, such as Deglet Noor and Khadrawy, are delicious when eaten out of hand. They may be bought with or without pits. They are tasty in cakes, puddings, breads, pies, fruit salad, muffins, and cookies. They also make fine candies, when, for example, stuffed with nuts and rolled in coconut or in a coconut and chocolate mixture. Good on cereals, too.

The trunk has served as timber, the leaves as thatch, and the fiber is woven into rope. In Europe, the leaves are used symbolically in the observance of Palm Sunday and the Passover. Less productive trees are tapped to yield a juice or toddy which when boiled down, forms a thick brown syrup, gur or sugar, jaggery. When fermented, the jaggery provides an alcoholic beverage, arrack, or may become vinegar. The pits have been roasted as a substitute for coffee.

Date products include date starch in honey, a rich syrup made from the juice of the fresh fruit; date palm flour made from the pith of the tree; an oil made from the seeds; date paste; baskets, bags, and pouches made from the leaves, and rope made from fibers near the bottom of the tree.

MARKETING SEASON: Dates are harvested in the U.S. September through December, but are available from storage all year. Their availability is highest October through December and lowest in May, August, and September. This may be more a matter of demand than of supply, since a storable food of this kind could be provided at any time.

VARIETIES: "Date varieties can be grouped into three types: soft, semi-soft, and dry or bread dates. The soft types have a soft flesh, a high moisture content, and consequently a relatively low sugar content. Dates of this type are highly perishable and must be kept in cold storage. Semi-soft varieties have a firm flesh, a fairly low moisture content, and a high sugar content. Most dates of this type may be stored in semi-moistureproof containers for months with little deterioration. Dry or bread dates have a high sugar content, a very low moisture content, and a dry, hard flesh. Very few palms of this type have been planted due to an unfavorable market reaction.

"In 1957, more than three-fourths of the imported palms in the U.S. were Deglet Noor. The three next most important varieties—Khadrawy, Zahidi and Halawy—together represented only about 10 percent. Medjool is another California date worth mentioning. It is very large. At present, there are about 500 acres planted, but not all are producing. However, Deglet Noor has been a commercial success thus far only in the Coachella Valley, although it has been tried to some extent in nearly all districts where dates are being grown. Outside the Coachella Valley, Khadrawy is the most widely grown variety."

Deglet Noor The words are Arabic and mean Date of the Light. The variety is said to have originated early in the 17th century near Touggourt in the Algerian Sahara. It was early recognized as a superior date and established in many other oases in Algeria and southern Tunisia by the end of the century. During the French colonial development, extensive plantings of Deglet Noor were made in the Saharan oases of Algeria and Tunisia, and the fruit is well known in the markets of Europe. The variety was introduced into the U.S. in 1900 by Swingle. The first offshoots were planted near Tempe, Ariz. in co-operation with the Arizona Agricultural Experiment Station. Four years later, a few of the young palms were transplanted to the new experiment station at Mecca in the lower Coachella Valley. From 1911 to 1921, several large importations of offshoots were made for planting in the valley. This palm did not ripen fruit properly in Arizona and is no longer planted there.

Deglet Noor palms have long, slightly arched leaves with relatively stiff pinnae. Foliage is olive green, and there are numerous spines for one-fourth to one-third of the blade length. The trunk is slender to medium heavy. The fruit stalks are greenish yellow to lemon colored. The fruit at the khalal stage (when it reaches maximum size and characteristic identifying color) is carnelian red or coral red, sometimes apricot orange to rufous. At the rutab stage (which covers the period from the time the fruit begins to soften at the tip until it is cured) it is amber brown or Sudan brown, while the dry fruit is light brown or straw-colored. At the tamar stage (fully cured or dried and not subject to fermenting or souring) it is a slightly deeper color. The fruit is 40 to 50 millimeters long by 20 to 25 mm diameter; skin medium thick, adhering to the flesh and forming rather coarse wrinkles and folds in curing; flesh 4 to 5 mm thick, firm, soft, amber except for paler inner zone; flavor excellent and distinctive; seed medium brown 23 to 30 mm. by 7 to 9 mm , narrowly elliptical.

*UFFVA

Of firm texture, the Deglet Noor shrinks less in curing and holds its shape better in packing, handling, and storage than the softer varieties. However, the fruit quality is very sensitive to environment, and unless the palms are planted under favorable conditions, inferior dates are likely to be grown. The Deglet Noor does not do well on soils either too heavy or too alkaline.

Khadrawy This word in Arabic means "green," referring either to the greenish cast of the fruit as it first begins to soften or to the foliage which has a bright green midrib and leaf base which is rather distinctive. Offshoots of this variety were first imported in 1902 from Basra, Iraq by Fairchild, the noted USDA plant explorer. More offshoots were imported in 1913 by Paul Popenoe of the West India Gardens. The Khadrawy plam is one of the most distinctive of all varieties. It makes a slow vertical growth, and among old palms it is conspicuously smaller than any other commercial variety. The moderately arched leaves are relatively few and have blades that appear more or less flattened. The pinnae are short, rather stiff, and closely and evenly set along the midrib. The fruit is yellow in the khalal stage and ripens early.

At rutab stage, the fruit is amber or near antique brown, sometimes with a greenish cast; size is 33 to 40 mm x 20 to 24 mm ; skin medium thick, tender, sometimes blistered but shrinking more or less with flesh in irregular undulations; flesh 3 to 4 mm thick, soft, melting, becoming caramel-like, rag slight or lacking; flavor pleasant, rich without being cloying; seed dark brown, oblong or oblong-elliptical, 20 to 25 mm x 7.7 to 9.8 mm. At the tamar stage, the fruit is reddish brown.

Zahidi The meaning is uncertain but one translation is said to be "nobility" and another "of a small quantity." Synonyms for this name are Zahdi, Zadie, Azydi, Zehedi and Zaheedy. The Zahidi was introduced into the U.S. in 1902 from Iraq by Fairchild, but most of the commercial plantings are traced to the Popenoe importations of 1913. This variety is the commonest one in northern Iraq.

The Zahidi palm as viewed from a distance has a characteristic compact crown. The closely set, even-angled pinnae and only slightly curved midrib give an appearance of solidity to the leaf blades and a stiff, formal aspect to the whole top. The foliage is green with a whitish bloom. The fruit is yellow in the khalal stage and has a distinctive obovate shape. The fruit is 34 to 40 mm x 23 to 25 mm , skin rather thick and tough, tending to adhere to the flesh, loosening but little in curing; flesh 4 to 5 mm thick, firm, and the drier part of the flesh is more or less fibrous and becomes rather hard; flavor not outstanding.

Halawy The word means "sweet." Synonyms are Halawi, Hallawi and Hellawi. The variety was introduced in 1902 from Basra, Iraq by Fairchild, but commercial plantings date from 1913 importations by Popenoe. The palm has a crown with an open center, foliage green with some bloom, leaves medium long with slight to moderate and rather uniform curvature and broad, stiff pinnae. The fruit is of a light amber color and has a wrinkled surface.

The khalal color of the fruit is buff yellow. The size of fruit is 35 to 45 mm x 17 to 20 mm ; skin is thin, shrinking with the flesh in irregular wrinkles with only slight blistering; flesh 3 to 4 mm thick, soft, caramel-like, translucent, with little or no rag; and the flavor is very rich, sweet and distinctive. It is early ripening.

Medjool The name comes from Majul; and it means "unknown," perhaps referring to its origin. This is the principal export date of Morocco. There are now about 500 acres of these dates in California, although not all are producing as yet. The Medjool is a large date, about 2 in. long by 1-1/4 in. diameter. The surface is deeply wrinkled and creased, of a bright bay to keep reddish brown in color. The skin is thin and tender; flesh firm, meaty, nearly 3/8 in. thick, brownish amber, translucent, with practically no fiber around the seed. The flavor is rich with a characteristic taste for the variety. It has been known commercially since the 17th century.

CONTAINERS: Containers for principal varieties of California dates are regulated by the California Date Administrative Committee operating under the Domestic Date Order. Plastic containers, other than bags, for U.S. and Canada shipments, are limited as follows: Whole Dates, net weight of contents must be either 8 oz., 12 oz., 1-1/2 lb. or over 2 lb.; Pitted Dates, net weight of contents must be either 10 oz., 16 oz., 1-1/2 lb. or over 2 lb. There are no other restrictions. Plastic cups are generally packed in 3 layers in a fiberboard box holding 24 cups.

The following table shows the contents of containers gener-

DATES

FRESH (8/26/55   52.1001)

GRADES:	"A" or	"B" or
	"FANCY"	"CHOICE"
Minimum Score:	90	80

GRADES:	"B (DRY)" or	
	"CHOICE (DRY)"	"C" or
		"STANDARD"
Minimum Score:	80	70

GRADES:	"C (DRY)" or	
	"STANDARD (DRY)"	"SUB- STANDARD"
	70	Less than 70

CONTAINERS—SHIPPING

Pack	Dates Whole or Pitted	Net Weight Pounds
24/7-1/4 oz. fiber	W	10.88
24/8 oz. fiber	W	12
24/10 oz. fiber	P	15
24/12 oz. fiber	W	18
24/16 oz. fiber	P	24
12/24 oz. fiber	P	18
15 lb. fiber	W-P	15
30 lb. fiber	W	30
24/8 oz. plastic cup	W	12
36/8 oz. plastic cup	W	18
24/10 oz. plastic cup	P	15
24/12 oz. plastic cup	W	18
18/16 oz. plastic cup	P	18
12/24 oz. plastic cup	W-P	18
24/250 grams plastic cup	W	13.25
24/500 grams plastic cup	W	26.5
24/10 oz. poly bag	W-P	15
24/12 oz. poly bag	W	18
24/16 oz. poly bag	W-P	24
12/24 oz. poly bag	W	18
12/3 lb. tin	W	36

ally used by packers, as determined by documents in the files of the California Date Administrative Committee. The master containers are almost entirely fiberboard.

QUALITY: Aside from grade, which means little to the consumer except in the most general way, quality refers to flavor, texture, and color. The sugar content is of little value in measuring quality since all dates that are acceptable in other respects have adequate sugar content. In general, dates should be soft and the texture smooth. But perception of flavor, texture and color all are subjective, and vary from person to person so that no certain criteria can be provided.

An inexpensive method of softening dates by activating a natural enzyme of the fruit was worked out by V.P. Maier and D.M. Metzler at the Fruit and Vegetable Chemistry Laboratory of USDA at Pasadena, Calif. and announced in 1962. The process increases the moisture content of the fruit and exposes it to moderately high temperature, activating the enzymes, which are later deactivated by drying dates to normal moisture level to prevent further change.

DATES—[8/26/55]

Grade A: Color: In units of dates that are predominantly light amber in color there may be not more than 5 percent that are dark amber in color; with respect to dates that are predominantly dark amber in color there may be not more than 5 percent that are light amber in color. **Size:** Not more than a total of 10 percent of the whole or pitted dates may be conspicuously larger or smaller than the approximate average size of the dates in the container. **Defects:** Practically free from defects, in pitted dates there may be present not more than 1 whole pit or 2 pit fragments for each 25 oz. of pitted dates; and that the whole or pitted dates do not exceed the total allowances. See Chart I. **Character:** Not less than 75 percent of the dates are well developed, well fleshed, and soft, or at the time of packing are in such a state of ripeness that within 15 days they will develop into such character; and the remainder may possess a reasonably good character including not more than a total of 2 percent that may possess semi-dry calyx ends, and none may possess dry calyx ends.

Grade B: Color: Color of the whole or pitted dates or whole dry dates for processing is reasonably uniform for the type; with dates that are predominantly light amber in color, there may be not more than 10 percent of dates that are dark amber; when dates are predominantly dark amber, there may be not more than 10 percent that are light amber. **Size:** Not more than 15 percent of the whole or pitted dates may be conspicuously larger or smaller than the approximate average size of the dates in the container. **Defects:** In pitted dates, there may be present not more than 1 whole pit or 2 pit fragments for each 25 oz. of pitted dates; and that the whole or pitted dates or whole dry dates for processing do not exceed the total allowance. See Chart II. **Character:** With respect to whole or pitted dates, other than whole dry dates for processing, means that the dates are pliable; not less than 75 percent are reasonably well developed, well fleshed, or at time of packing are in a state of ripeness that within 15 days will develop into such character, and the remainder may possess a fairly good character with not more than 10 percent of the dates having semi-dry calyx ends and dry calyx ends: Provided, that not more than 2 percent of the dates may possess dry calyx ends. With respect to whole dry dates for processing means that the dates may be firm and dry; not less than 75 percent are reasonably well developed and well fleshed, and that the remainder are fairly well developed and well fleshed.

Grade C: Color: Whole Pitted—With respect to dates that are predominantly light amber in color, there may be no more than 20 percent that are dark amber; with respect to dates that are predominantly dark amber, there may be no more than 20 percent that are light amber. **Defects:** Whole—The defects or defective units in whole dates or whole dry dates for processing do not exceed the total allowances; See Chart III. **Pitted:** Not more than 1 whole pit or 2 pit fragments for each 25 oz. of pitted dates may be present; and the defects or defective units in pitted dates do not exceed the total allowance. See Chart III. **Character:** Whole Pitted—In whole or pitted dates other than whole dry dates for processing, the dates may be firm but are pliable; may possess semi-dry calyx ends; and not less than 80 percent are fairly well developed, well fleshed or at time of packing are in a state of ripeness that within 15 days will develop into such character and the remainder may fail to possess such fairly good character or may possess dry calyx ends. In whole dates for processing, the dates may be firm and dry but are fairly well developed and well fleshed. **Color:** Pieces—macerated: The color may be variable throughout the units or mass, may be slightly dull but not off-color, and is typical of properly prepared dates of these styles. **Defects:** Not more than 1 whole pit or 2 pit fragments

CHART NO. I—ALLOWANCES AND LIMITATIONS FOR DEFECTS IN WHOLE AND PITTED DATES [OTHER THAN WHOLE DRY DATES FOR PROCESSING]; U.S. GRADE A OR U.S. FANCY

Total Allowance	Limitations
Not more than a total of 10 percent, by weight, of the dates may be the following:	Not more than 3/5 of the total allowance, or 2 percent, by weight, the dates may be the following:
Damaged by:	Damaged by:
Discoloration	Side spot
Broken skin	Black scald
Checking	Improper ripening
Deformity	Other defects
Puffiness	Affected by:
Scars	Souring
Sunburn	Mold
Insect injury	Dirt
Improper hydrating	Insect infestation
Mashing	Foreign material
Mechanical injury	Decay
Lack of pollination	Not more than 2/5 of the total allowance, or 4 percent, by weight, of the dates may be the following:
Blacknose	Damaged by:
Side spot	Improper ripening
Black scald	Other defects
Improper ripening	Affected by:
Other defects	Souring
Seriously damaged by checking	Mold
Seriously damaged by puffiness	Dirt
Affected by:	Insect infestation
Souring	Foreign material
Mold	Decay
Dirt	Not more than 1/10 of the total allowance, or 1 percent, by weight, of the dates may be:
Insect infestation	Affected by decay
Foreign material	
Decay	

CHART NO. II—ALLOWANCES AND LIMITATIONS FOR DEFECTS IN WHOLE AND PITTED DATES OR IN WHOLE DRY DATES FOR PROCESSING; U.S. GRADE B OR U.S. CHOICE AND U.S. GRADE B [DRY] OR U.S. CHOICE [DRY]

Not more than 15 percent, by weight, of the dates may be seriously damaged by checking.

Not more than 20 percent, by weight, of the dates may be damaged by broken skin.

Additional Allowance

Not more than a total of 15 percent, by weight, of the dates may be the following:

Damaged by:
  Deformity
  Puffiness
  Scars
  Sunburn
  Insect injury
  Improper hydrating
  Mashing
  Mechanical injury
  Lack of pollination
  Blacknose
  Side spot
  Black scald
  Improper ripening
  Other defects
Seriously damaged by puffiness
Affected by:
  Souring
  Mold
  Dirt
  Insect infestation
  Foreign material
  Decay

Limitations

Not more than 2/3 of the additional allowance, or 10 percent, by weight, of the dates may be the following:

Damaged by:
  Lack of pollination
  Blacknose
  Side spot
  Black scald
  Improper ripening
  Other defects
Affected by:
  Souring
  Mold
  Dirt
  Insect infestation
  Foreign material
  Decay

Not more than 1/3 of the additional allowance, or 5 percent, by weight, of the dates may be the following:

Damaged by:
  Improper ripening
  Other defects
Affected by:
  Souring
  Mold
  Dirt
  Insect infestation
  Foreign material
  Decay

Not more than 1/15 of the additional allowance, or 1 percent, by weight, of the dates may be:
  Affected by decay

CHART NO. III

Total Allowance

Not more than a total of 20 percent, by weight, of the dates may be the following:

Damaged by:
  Deformity
  Scars
  Sunburn
  Insect injury
  Improper hydrating
  Mashing
  Mechanical injury
  Lack of pollination
  Blacknose
  Side spot
  Black scald
  Improper ripening
  Other defects
Seriously damaged by puffiness
  Affected by:
    Souring
    Mold
    Dirt
    Insect infestation
    Foreign material
    Decay

Limitations

Not more than 1/2 of the total allowance, or 10 percent, by weight, of the dates may be the following:

Damaged by:
  Lack of pollination
  Blacknose
  Side spot
  Black scald
  Improper ripening
  Other defects
Affected by:
  Souring
  Mold
  Dirt
  Insect infestation
  Foreign material
  Decay

Not more than 1/4 of the total allowance, or 5 percent, by weight, of the dates may be the following:

Affected by:
  Souring. Dirt. Foreign material. Mold. Insect infestation. Decay.

Not more than 1/10 of the total allowance, or 2 percent, by weight, of the dates may be: Affected by decay.

for each 25 oz. of pitted dates may be present; and the units or mass consists of clean and sound date material, fairly free from defects that seriously affect the appearance, edibility, or keeping quality of the product. **Character:** The character may be variable throughout the units or mass but not seriously affected by dry calyx end material or inedible portions of dates. **Size:** Not more than a total of 20 percent of the whole or pitted dates may be conspicuously larger or smaller than the approximate average size of the dates in the container.

FIGS*

USE: The fruit can be eaten fresh, canned, preserved, and dried. Being easily digested, figs are palatable and healthful sweeteners. They are popular in salads, cakes, and candies.

MARKETING SEASON: Fresh figs are usually available June to October. Availability by months expressed as a total of average annual supply is: June 9 percent, July 9 percent, August 35 percent; September 28 percent; October 19 percent.

VARIETIES: Varieties include **Mission, Calimyrna, Adriatic**, and **Kadota**, all of which can be marketed fresh. These four leading types come from California. The Southeastern and Gulf states furnish such varieties as the **Brown Turkey**, the **Brunswick**, the **Celeste**, and the **Magnolia**.

"**Black Mission figs**," says the California Fig Institute, "are famous for their distinctive flavor and edibility, both in the fresh and dried state. The **Calimyrna**, originating in Smyrna, was first planted in California in 1882. It is a large, luscious, white fig, tender and excellent for eating fresh as well as dried. The dried Calimyrna is deliciously nut-like and sweet in flavor. Other varieties of figs well adapted to drying include the **Adriatic**, an Italian variety of white fig introduced into California in 1865. It holds its shape well in cooking and is produced in largest quantities of all. In its fresh state, the soft, heavy skin is light green, and the pulp is an appetizing dark pink. The **Kadota**, also an Italian importation, is less extensively used commercially in the dried state.

CONTAINERS: Fresh figs from California are shipped in one-layer boxes in which fillers are used to provide a separate cell for each fruit. The number of cells varies with the size of the fruit, but the boxes are uniformly 1-7/8 in. deep, 11 in. wide, and 16-1/8 in. long, inside. Shallow baskets with a top dimension of approximately 8 sq. in., bottom dimensions of 6-3/4 sq. in., and a depth of 1-1/4 in. are sometimes used. The baskets are packed with a single layer of fruit and shipped 4 to a crate. Weight is 5 lb. net in flats.

QUALITY: Fresh figs are highly perishable. They must be fully ripe to be of good quality. A ripe fig is rather soft and varies in color from greenish yellow to purplish or almost black according to the variety. Over-ripeness is detectable by a sour odor which is due to fermentation of the juice. Bruised or mechanically injured fruit should be avoided because such fruit breaks down very quickly. There are no U.S. standard grades.

FIGS, Kadota—Canned [6/20/73]

Grade A: Color: Practically uniform, and light amber or light greenish yellow color that is bright and typical of properly processed, canned Kadota figs; that not more than 5 percent of the figs may possess a reasonably good color; and that none of the figs possess a fairly good color. **Size:** In containers with less than 20 units, the weight of the largest whole fig does not exceed the weight of the smallest whole fig by more than 50 percent; or, that in containers with 20 units or more, 95 percent of the units are most uniform in weight, the weight of the largest whole fig does not exceed the weight of the smallest whole fig by more than 50 percent. **Defects:** Not more than 10 percent of the units may be split: Provided, that none are severed figs. Units possess insignificant, minor defects and major defects may be present which do not more than slightly affect the appearance of the product but that there may be present: Not more than 1 tough woody stem per 30 oz. of total contents and no other harmless extraneous material, and not more than a total of 10 percent may possess "minor" and "major" defects: Provided, that not more than 5 percent may possess major defects, 1 unit in a container is permitted to possess minor or major defects. If such unit exceeds the respective allowances of 10 percent, or 5 percent by count: Provided, that in all containers comprising the sample such units possessing minor and major defects do not exceed an average of 10 percent of the total number of units, including not more than an average of 5 percent of the total number of units that may possess "major" defects. **Character:** Are well matured and fleshy and have a practically uniform, tender texture; that not more than 5 percent may possess a reasonably good character; and none possess a fairly good character.

Grade B: Color: Reasonably uniform and reasonably bright light green color that may lack a definite yellow cast but is typical of properly prepared and processed figs; and that not more than 10 percent may possess a fairly good color. **Size:** With less than 20 units the weight of the largest whole fig odes not exceed the weight of the smallest whole fig by more than

*UFFVA

FIGS

CANNED (6/20/73   52.2821)

GRADES:	"A" or "FANCY"	"B" or "CHOICE"	"C" or "STANDARD"	"SUB-STANDARD"
Minimum Score:	90	80	70	Less than 70

		NET WEIGHT OZ.	NET WEIGHT METRIC	DRAINED WEIGHT OZ.	DRAINED WEIGHT METRIC
No. 8Z Tall		5.3	150.2 g	4.2	119.1 g
No. 303	whole	10.5	297.7 g	9.0	255.2 g
	other styles	10.8	306.2 g		
No. 2-1/2	whole	19.0	538.6 g	16.6	470.6 g
	other styles	19.2	544.3 g		
No. 10	whole other	69.0	1.96 g	70 whole figs & less 60.5	1.7 kg
	styles	71.0	2.0 kg	71 whole figs & more 63.5	1.8 kg

SYRUP	SPECIFIC GRAVITY (Brix Measurements)

"Extra heavy syrup," or "extra heavily sweetened fruit juice(s) and water," or "extra heavily sweetened fruit juice(s) " — 26° - 35°

"Heavy syrup," or "heavily sweetened fruit juice(s) and water," or "heavily sweetened fruit juice(s) " — 21° or more but less than 26°

"Light syrup," or "lightly sweetened fruit juice(s) and water," or "lightly sweetened fruit juice(s) " — 16° or more but less than 21°

"Slightly sweetened water," or "extra light syrup," or "slightly sweetened fruit juice(s) and water," or "slightly sweetened fruit juice(s) " — 11° or more but less than 16°

"In water" — N.A.

"In fruit juice(s) and water" — N.A.

"In fruit juice(s)" — N.A.

"Artificially sweetened" — N.A.

DRIED (2/27/67   52.1021)

GRADES:	"A" or "FANCY"	"B" or "CHOICE"	"C" or "STANDARD"	"SUB-STANDARD"

75 percent; or that in containers with 20 or more units, in 95 percent of the units that are most uniform in weight, the weight of the largest whole fig does not exceed the weight of the smallest whole fig by more than 75 percent. **Defects:** Not more than 15 percent may be split (or broken): Provided, that not more than 3 percent may be severed figs. 1 unit in a container is permitted to be severed if such units exceed the 3 percent allowance: Provided, that in all containers comprising the sample such units do not exceed the average of 3 percent of the total number of units. Insignificant, minor and major defects may be present which do not materially affect the appearance of the product but that there may be present: Not more than 2 tough woody stems per 30 oz. of total contents and not more than 1 piece of other harmless extraneous material per 10 oz. of total contents, and not more than a total of 20 percent may possess minor and major defects: Provided, that not more than 10 percent may possess major defects. 1 unit in a container is permitted to possess minor or major defects if such units exceed the respective allowance of 20 percent or 10 percent: Provided, that in all containers comprising the sample such units possessing minor and major defects do not exceed an average of 20 percent of the total number of units including not more than an average of 10 percent that may possess major defects. **Character:** reasonably uniform, reasonably tender texture; and that not more than 10 percent may possess a fairly good character.

Grade C: Color: Fairly good color that may possess a green, slightly milky, or a light brown color and that the figs may vary moderately in such typical color, but not more than 5 percent may be off-color, or 1 unit in a container is permitted to be off-color if such unit exceeds the 5 percent allowance. **Size:** In containers with less than 20 units, the weight of the largest whole fig may be not more than twice the weight of the smallest whole fig; in that in containers with 20 or more units in 95 percent of the units that are most uniform in weight, the weight of the largest whole fig may be not more than twice the weight of the smallest unit. **Defects:** See grade B. All wording is the same except as follows: 20 percent: Provided, 5 percent ...5 percent: Provided, 5 Percent. In the styles other than Style I Whole, not more than 10 percent may be severed figs. Fairly free from defects...seriously; 3 tough...per 30 oz.; 40 percent: Provided, 20 percent. **Character:** they be variable in texture from very soft to firm but are not excessively mushy or excessively firm. **SStd:** Fails to meet requirements.

CANNED FIGS [1975 Revisions]

The Food and Drug Administration recently amended the standards of identity for several canned fruits, compliance with which may begin on March 11, 1975, but mostly after December 31, 1975.

The following amendments to the USDA standards for these canned fruits are proposed to bring them into line with the amended FDA standards of identity.

Attention is drawn to areas where the USDA standards may differ from but do not conflict with the FDA standards.

Canned Figs

(a) 52.2821 paragraph (a) would be amended to read as follows: 52.2821 Product description.

(a) *Canned figs* —"Canned figs" is the product represented as defined in the Standard of Identity (21 CFR 27.70 and 27.73) for canned figs and artificially sweetened canned figs, respectively, issued pursuant to the Federal Food, Drug, and Cosmetic Act.

(b) 52.2821 paragraph (c) would be deleted in its entirety.

(c) 52.2824 would be amended to read as follows: 52.2824 Liquid media and Brix measurements.

Cut-out requirements for liquid media in Canned Kadota Figs are not incorporated in the grades of the product since syrup or any other liquid medium, as such, is not a factor of quality for the purpose of these grades. The cut-out Brix measurements, as applicable, for the respective designations are as follows:

DESIGNATION	BRIX MEASUREMENTS
"Extra heavy syrup," or "Extra heavily sweetened fruit juice(s) and water," or "Extra heavily sweetened fruit juice(s)"	26° or more but not more than 35°
"Heavy syrup," or "Heavily sweetened fruit juice(s) and water;" or "Heavily sweetened fruit juice(s)."	21° or more but less than 26°
"Light syrup," or "Lightly sweetened fruit juice(s) and water," or "Lightly sweetened fruit juice(s)"	16° or more but less than 21°
"Slightly sweetened water;" or "Extra light syrup;" or "Slightly sweetened fruit juice(s) and water," or "Slightly sweetened fruit juice(s)"	11° or more but less than 16°
"In water"	N.A.
"In fruit juice(s) and water"	N.A.
"In fruit juice(s)"	N.A.
"Artificially sweetened"	N.A.

No other changes are proposed.

FIGS—Canned (2/27/63)

Grades A, B, and C; see all charts.

TABLE I—MOISTURE ALLOWANCE

Grades	Color Types	Styles	Maximum Moisture Limits [by weight] Group I	Group II
			Percent	Percent
U.S. Grade A or	White	Whole	*24	
U.S. Fancy, and	White	Sliced	*23	30
U.S. Grade B or	Black	Whole	*23	30
U.S. Choice, and	Black	Sliced	*23	
U.S. Grade C or	Black and White (mixed)	Whole	*23	30
U.S. Standard				
	Black and White (mixed)	Sliced	*23	

U.S. Grade A; Styles I & II	U.S. Grade B	U.S. C Styles I & II.
Table II A-White Figs	Table III A-Whole Figs	Table IV A-White Figs
Table II B-Black Figs	Table III B-Black Figs	Table IV B-Black Figs

TABLE II A—DEFECTS IN WHITE FIGS
[STYLE I, Whole; Style II, Sliced]

Grade	Total allowance[1]—Not more than a total of 5 percent	Limited allowance—Not more than 3/5 of the total or 3 percent
U.S. Grade A	Damaged by: scars or disease, sunburn, mechanical injury, visible sugaring, other similar defects. Seriously damaged by: scars or diseases, sunburn, mechanical injury, other similar defects.	Seriously damaged by scar or disease, sunburn, mech. injury, or other similar defects.

TABLE IIB—ALLOWANCES FOR DEFECTS IN BLACK FIGS
[Style I, Whole; Style II, Sliced, except as indicated otherwise]

Grade	Total allowance—Not more than a total of 10 percent[2]	Limited allowance—Not more than 1/2 of the total or 5 percent[2]
U.S. Grade A or U.S. Fancy	Damaged by: scars or disease, sunburn, mechanical injury,[3] visible sugaring, other similar defects. Seriously damaged by: scars or disease, sunburn, mechanical injury,[3] other similar defects.	Seriously damaged by: scars or disease, sunburn, mechanical injury,[3] other similar defects.

1. Total maximum allowances: Provided, That the appearance or edibility of the product is not more than slightly affected by such defects or by the presence of otherwise defective units.
2. Percentages are by count.
3. Not applicable to Style II, Sliced figs.

TABLE III A—ALLOWANCES FOR DEFECTS IN WHITE FIGS
[Style I, Whole; Style II, Sliced, except as indicated otherwise]

Grade	Total allowance[1]—Not more than a total of 10 percent[2]	Limited allowance—Not more than 1/2 of the total or 5 percent[2]
U.S. Grade B or U.S. Choice	Damaged by: scars or disease, sunburn, mechanical injury,[3] visible sugaring, other similar defects. Seriously damaged by: scars or disease, sunburn, mechanical injury,[3] other similar defects.	Seriously damaged by: scars or disease, sunburn, mechanical injury,[3] other similar defects.

TABLE III B—ALLOWANCES FOR DEFECTS IN BLACK FIGS
[Style I, Whole; Style II, Sliced, except as indicated otherwise]

Grade	Total allowance[1]—Not more than a total of 15 percent[2]	Limited allowance—Not more than 7/15 of the total or 7 percent[2]
U.S. Grade B or U.S. Choice.	Damaged by: scars or disease, sunburn, mechanical injury,[3] visible sugaring, other similar defects. Seriously damaged by: scars or disease, sunburn, mechanical injury,[3] other similar defects.	Seriously damaged by: scars or disease, sunburn, mechanical injury,[3] other similar defects.

1. Total maximum allowances: Provided, That the appearance or edibility of the product is not materially affected by such defects or by the presence of otherwise defective units.
2. Percentages are by count.
3. Not applicable to Style II, Sliced figs.

TABLE IV A—ALLOWANCES FOR DEFECTS IN WHITE FIGS
[Style I, Whole; Style II, Sliced, except as indicated otherwise]

Grade	Total allowance[1]—Not more than a total of 15 percent[2]	Limited allowance—Not more than 7/15 of the total or 7 percent[2]
U.S. Grade C or U.S. Standard	Damaged by: scars or disease; sunburn; mechanical injury,[3] visible sugaring; other similar defects. Seriously damaged by: scars or disease; sunburn; mechanical injury,[3] other similar defects.	Seriously damaged by: scars or disease; sunburn, mechanical injury,[3] other similar defects.

FIGS, Canned [1975 Revisions]

The Food and Drug Administration amended the standards of identity for Canned Figs, compliance with which may begin on March 11, 1975, but mostly after December 31, 1975.

The following amendments to the USDA standards for Canned Figs are proposed to bring them into line with the amended FDA Standards of Identity.

Product description.

"Canned Figs" is the product represented as defined in the Standard of Identity (21 CFR 27.70 and 27.73) for canned figs and artificially sweetened canned figs, respectively, issued pursuant to the Federal Food, Drug, and Cosmetic Act.

52.2821 paragraph (c) would be deleted in its entirety.

FIGS, Canned Preserved [8/6/67]

Canned Preserved Figs
Promulgated May 29, 1967
Effective August 6, 1967
27.71 Canned preserved figs; identity; label statement of optional ingredients.

(a) Canned preserved figs is the food prepared from one of

TABLE IV B—ALLOWANCES FOR DEFECTS IN BLACK FIGS
[Style I, Whole; Style II, Sliced, except as indicated otherwise]

Grade	Total allowance[1]—Not more than a total of 20 percent[2]	Limited allowance—Not more than 2/5 of the total or 8 percent[2]
U.S. Grade C or U.S. Standard.	Damaged by: scars or disease, sunburn, mechanical injury,[3] visible sugaring, other similar defects. Seriously damaged by: scars or disease, sunburn, mechanical injury,[3] other similar defects.	Seriously damaged by: scars or disease, sunburn, mechanical injury,[3] other similar defects.

1. Total maximum allowances: Provided, That the appearance or edibility of the product is not seriously affected by such defects or by the presence of otherwise defective units.
2. Percentages are by count.
3. Not applicable to Style II, Sliced figs.

the optional fig ingredients specified in paragraph (b) of this section and the packing medium specified in paragraph (c) of this section, to which citric acid, or lemon juice, or concentrated lemon juice is added, if necessary, in such quantity as to reduce the pH of the finished product to 4.9 or below. The figs are precooked in the packing medium, sealed in a container, and so processed by heat, either before or after sealing, as to prevent spoilage.

(b) The optional fig ingredients referred to in paragraph (a) of this section are whole mature figs of the light or dark varieties that may be either peeled or unpeeled.

(c) (1) the packing medium referred to in paragraph (a) of this section is prepared from water and one of the following optional sweetening ingredients:

(i) Sugar.

(ii) Invert sugar syrup.

(iii) Any mixture of optional sweetening ingredients designated in subdivisions (i) and (ii) of this subparagraph.

(iv) Any of the optional sweetening ingredients designated in subdivisions (i), (ii), and (iii) of this subparagraph with dextrose: Provided, That the weight of the solids of dextrose does not exceed one-third of the total weight of the solids of the combined sweetening ingredients.

(v) Any of the optional sweetening ingredients designated in subdivisions (i), (ii), and (iii) of this subparagraph with corn syrup or with dried corn syrup or with glucose syrup or with dried glucose syrup, or with any two or more of these: Provided, That the weight of the solids of corn syrup, dried corn syrup, gluocse syrup, dried glucose syrup or the sum of the weights of the solids of corn syrup, dried corn syrup, glucose syrup, and dried glucose syrup in case two or more of these are used, does not exceed one-fourth of the total weight of the solids of the combined sweetening ingredients.

(vi) Any mixture of the optional ingredients designated in subdivisions (iv) and (v) of this subparagraph.

(2) The density of the packing medium described in subparagraph (1) of this paragraph, as measured on the Brix hydrometer 15 days or more after the figs are canned, is not less than 50° and not more than 55°.

(d) (1) The name of the food is "Preserved Figs—Precooked in Syrup." For the purpose of label declaration, the words "Precooked in Syrup" may appear immediately below the words "Preserved Figs," but there shall be no intervening written, printed, or graphic matter, and the letters used for the words "Precooked in Syrup" shall be of the same type style and not less than one-half of the height of the letters in the words "Preserved Figs."

(2) The label shall indicate which optional fig ingredients specified in paragraph (b) of this section is used.

(e) Wherever the name of the food appears on the label so conspicuously as to be easily seen under customary conditions of purchase, the words herein specified, showing the optional fig ingredient used, shall immediately and conspicuously precede or follow such name without intervening written, printed, or graphic matter, except that the varietal name of the figs may so intervene.

FIGS, Dried [2/27/67]

Grade A: Whole or sliced dried figs in which Style I, whole figs, are of one variety and in which Style II, sliced figs, are of one variety or similar varieties, that are well matured with not more than 5 percent of reasonably well-matured dried figs; that are practically uniform in size; except for Style I (a), whole, loose figs and Style II, sliced figs; that have a good flavor; are free from foreign material; and that do not exceed the maximum allowances and limitations as specified in Table I (Moisture), Table II A (Defects in White Figs) and Table II B (Defects in Black Figs).

Grade B: Whole or sliced dried fits in which Style I, whole figs, are of one variety and in which Style II, sliced figs, are of one variety or similar varieties; that are reasonably well-matured with not more than 10 percent of fairly well-matured dried figs; that are reasonably uniform in size, except for Style I (a), whole, loose figs and Style II, sliced figs; that have a reasonably uniform typical color, have a reasonably good flavor; are free from foreign material; and that do not exceed the maximum allowances and limitations as specified in Table I (Moisture), Table IIIA (Defects in White Figs), and Table III B (Defects in Black Figs).

Grade C: Whole or sliced dried figs that are of one variety or of similar varieties; that are fairly well matured with not more than 10 percent of figs that fail to meet the requirements for fairly well-matured dried figs; that are fairly uniform in size, except for Style I (a), whole, loose figs, and Style II, sliced figs; that have a fairly uniform typical color, have a typical and normal flavor, are free from foreign material; and that do not exceed the maximum allowances and limitations as specified in Table I (Moisture), Table IV A (Defects in White Figs), and Table IV B (Defects in Black Figs). **SStd:** Fails to meet requirements.

TABLE I—MOISTURE ALLOWANCES FOR DRIED FIGS

| Grades | Color Types | Styles | Maximum Moisture Limits | |
			Group I	Group II
			Percent	Percent
U.S. Grade A or	White	Whole	*24	30
U.S. Fancy, and	White	Sliced	*23	-
U.S. Grade B or	Black	Whole	*23	30
U.S. Choice, and	Black	Sliced	*23	-
U.S. Grade C or				
U.S. Standard	Black and White (Mixed)	Whole	*23	30
	Black and White (Mixed)	Sliced	*23	

*Except Dried Figs of this group may have a maximum moisture of 30 percent when a safe and suitable mold inhibitor is used.

TABLE II A—ALLOWANCES FOR DEFECTS IN WHITE FIGS

Grade	Total Allowance[1]—Not more than a total of 5 percent[2]	Limited allowance—Not more than 3/5 of the total or 3 percent[2]
U.S. Grade A or U.S. Fancy	Damaged by: scars or disease, sunburn, mechanical injury,[3] visible sugaring, other similar defects. Seriously damaged by: scars or disease, sunburn, mechanical injury, other similar defects.	Seriously damaged by: scars or disease, sunburn, mechanical injury,[3] other similar defects.

1. Total maximum allowances: Provided, that the appearance or edibility of the product is not more than slightly affected by such defects or by the presence of otherwise defective units.
2. Percentages are by count.
3. Not applicable to Style II, Sliced figs.

TABLE II B—ALLOWANCES FOR DEFECTS IN BLACK FIGS
[Style I, Whole; Style II, Sliced, except as indicated otherwise]

Grade	Total allowance[1]—Not more than a total of 10 percent[2]	Limited allowance—Not more than 1/2 of the total or 5 percent[2]
U.S. Grade A or U.S. Fancy	Damaged by: scars or disease, sunburn, mechanical injury,[3] visible sugaring, other similar defects. Seriously damaged by: scars or disease, sunburn, mechanical injury,[3] other similar defects.	Seriously damaged by: scars or disease, sunburn, mechanical injury,[3] other similar defects.

1. Total maximum allowances: Provided, that the appearance or edibility of the product is not more than slightly affected by such defects or by the presence of otherwise defective units.
2. Percentages are by count.
3. Not applicable to Style II, Sliced figs.

TABLE III A—ALLOWANCES FOR DEFECTS IN WHITE FIGS
[Style I, Whole; Style II, Sliced, except as indicated otherwise]

	Total allowance[1]—Not more than a total of 10 percent[2]	Limited allowance—Not more than 1/2 of the total or 5 percent[2]
U.S. Grade B or U.S. Choice	Damaged by: scars or disease, sunburn, mechanical injury,[3] visible sugaring, other similar defects. Seriously damaged by: scars or disease, sunburn, mechanical injury,[3] other similar defects.	Seriously damaged by: scars or disease, sunburn, mechanical injury,[3] other similar defects.

TABLE III B—ALLOWANCES FOR DEFECTS IN BLACK FIGS
[Style I, Whole; Style II, Sliced, except as indicated otherwise]

Grade	Total allowance[1]—Not more than a total of 15 percent[2]	Limited allowance—Not more than 7/15 of the total or 7 percent[2]
U.S. Grade B or U.S. Choice	Damaged by: scars or disease, sunburn, mechanical injury,[3] visible sugaring, other similar defects. Seriously damaged by: scars or disease, sunburn, mechanical injury,[3] other similar defects.	Seriously damaged by: scars or disease, sunburn, mechanical injury,[3] other similar defects.

1. Total maximum allowances: Provided, That the appearance or edibility of the product is not materially affected by such defects or by the presence of otherwise defective units.
2. Percentages are by count.
3. Not applicable to Style II, Sliced figs.

TABLE IV A—ALLOWANCES FOR DEFECTS IN WHITE FIGS
[Style I, Whole; Style II, Sliced, except as indicated otherwise]

Grade	Total allowance[1]—Not more than a total of 15 percent[2]	Limited allowance—Not more than 7/15 of the total or 7 percent[2]
U.S. Grade C or U.S. Standard	Damaged by: scars or disease; sunburn, mechanical injury,[3] visible sugaring; other similar defects. Seriously damaged by: scars or disease, sunburn, mechanical injury,[3] other similar defects.	Seriously damaged by: scars or disease, sunburn, mechanical injury,[3] other similar defects.

TABLE IV B—ALLOWANCES FOR DEFECTS IN BLACK FIGS
[Style I, Whole; Style II, Sliced, except as indicated otherwise]

Grade	Total allowance[1]—Not more than a total of 20 percent[2]	Limited allowance—Not more than 2/5 of the total or 8 percent[2]
U.S. Grade C or U.S. Standard	Damaged by: scars or disease, sunburn, mechanical injury,[3] visible sugaring, similar defects. Seriously damaged by: scars or disease, sunburn, mechanical injury,[3] other similar defects.	Seriously damaged by: scars or disease, sunburn, mechanical injury,[3] other similar defects.

1. Total maximum allowances: Provided, That the appearance or edibility of the product is not seriously affected by such defects or by the presence of otherwise defective units.
2. Percentages are by count.
3. Not applicable to Style II, Sliced figs.

FRUIT COCKTAIL, Canned [6/20/73]

Grade A: Liquid: Reasonably clear, reasonably bright without any tinge of pink or a dullness of color; may contain fine fruit particles which do not materially offset appearance. **Color:** Bright and characteristic of at least reasonably well-matured fruit, ingredients may be no more than slightly affected by pink staining; and no ingredients are dull or off-color for reasons other than being slightly affected by pink staining. **Size:** Not more than 10 percent of diced units of peaches, pears, and pineapple when diced are more than 3/8 in. in greatest edge dimension and will pass through the meshes of a sieve designated as 5/16 in. in Table I of "Standard Spec. for Sieves" published March 1, 1940, in L.C. 584 of the National Bureau of Standards, U.S. Dept. of Commerce; if pineapple is in sections, not more than 10 percent have outside arc of more than 3/4 in. or less than 3/8 in.; are more than 1/2 in. or less than 5/16 in. thick, are more than 1-1/4 in. or less than 3/4 in. long. If percentage is greater than 15 percent, product cannot be graded above B or Choice. Largest whole grape does not weigh more than 3 times weight of smallest whole grape. Longest dimension on cut surface of largest intact cherry half does not exceed such dimension on smallest cherry half by more than 33-1/3 percent. **Defects:** Practically free from defects. **Maximum Tolerance:** Practically free from harmless extraneous material; from pits or portions; from the presence of peel; from loose capstems and from any other defects not mentioned that more than slightly affect the appearance or edibility. "Blemish"—pear, peach: 5 percent; Pineapple—5 percent. Grape—1 blemished grape in a container containing less than 10 grapes; 10 percent in a container containing 10 grapes or more. Cherry—5 percent in a container containing 20 cherry halves or more, 1 cherry half in a container containing less than 20 cherry halves. Crushed Grape—see Cherry. Cherry—see Cherry above. **Character:** Reasonably uniform with no more than a slight disintegration. Peach—texture is typical of diced peaches prepared from at least reasonably well-matured fruit. Tenderness may range from slightly firm to slightly soft but possess fairly well-defined edges: Pear—texture is typical of diced pears prepared and processed from properly ripened pears or pears of Grade A moderate graininess. Unit may range in tenderness from slightly firm to slightly soft with slightly rounded edges. Pineapple—units are practically uniform in ripeness with fruitlets of Grade A compact; are reasonably free from porosity and practically free from hard core material. Grapes—units are reasonably plump and firm. Cherry—units are reasonably firm but not excessively flabby.

Grade B: Liquid: Liquid is fairly clear, may be slightly pink or dull but not off color; may contain fruit particles which materially affect but do not seriously affect appearance. **Color:** reasonably uniform and typical; reasonably bright and characteristic of at least fairly well-matured fruit; may be more than slightly affected by pink staining but not to extent that appearance is materially affected or may be slightly dull, but no fruit is off-color for reasons other than staining or dullness. **Size:** See Grade A, all wording is same except as follows: 20 percent of diced units of peaches, etc., 20 percent have outside core, etc., 4 times weight of smallest grape. Longest dimension of largest cherry half does not exceed smallest by 50 percent. **Defects:** Reasonably free. **Tolerances:** See Grade A.; all wording is the same except as follows: reasonably free; materially affects the appearance or edibility. Peach-Pear—10 percent. Pineapple—12-1/2 percent. Grape—20 percent all size containers. Cherry—15 percent by count all size containers. Crushed Grapes—10 percent in a container containing 10 grapes or more and 1 grape in a container containing less than 10 grapes. Cherry—15 percent in a container containing 6 cherry halves, and 1 cherry half in a container containing 6 cherry halves or less. **Character:** See Grade A. All wording is same except as follows: may range from firm to soft texture. Peaches—fairly firm to soft and may possess frayed edges. Pear—Marked graininess. Markedly firm to soft with rounded edges. Pineapple—reasonably compact structure; are fairly free and reasonably free. Units may vary in texture from firm to soft but not mushy or excessively flabby. Cherry—fairly firm to soft.

FRUIT COCKTAIL, Canned [1975 Revisions]

The Food and Drug Administration amended the standards of identity for Canned Fruit Cocktail, compliance with which may begin on Mar. 11, 1975, but mostly after Dec. 31, 1975.

FRUIT COCKTAIL

CANNED (6/20/73   52.1051)

GRADES: "A" or   "B" or   "SUB-
"FANCY"   "CHOICE"   STANDARD"

Minimum
Score: 85   70   Less than 70

	NET WEIGHT OZ.	NET WEIGHT METRIC	DRAINED WEIGHT OZ.	DRAINED WEIGHT METRIC
No. 8Z Tall	6.1	172.9 g	5.1	144.6 g
No. 303	11.7	331.7 g	10.3	292.0 g
No. 2½	20.7	586.8 g	18.3	518.8 g
No. 10	77.0	2.2 kg	69.4	1.97 kg

SYRUP	SPECIFIC GRAVITY (Brix Measurements)
"Extra heavy syrup," or "extra heavily sweetened fruit juice(s) and water," or "extra heavily sweetened fruit juice(s) "	22° - 35°
"Heavy syrup," or "heavily sweetened fruit juice(s) and water," or "Heavily sweetened fruit juice(s) "	18° but less than 22°
"Light syrup," or "lightly sweetened fruit juice(s) and water," or "lightly sweetened fruit juice(s) "	14° or more but less than 18°
"Slightly sweetened water," or "Extra light syrup," or "slightly sweetened fruit juice(s) and water," or "slightly sweetened fruit juice(s) "	10° or more but less than 14°
"In water"	N.A.
"In fruit juice(s) and water"	N.A.
"In fruit juice(s)"	N.A.
"Artificially sweetened"	N.A.

The following amendments to the USDA standards for Canned Fruit Cocktail are proposed to bring them into line with the amended FDA Standards of Identity.

Product description.

"Canned fruit cocktail" is the product represented as defined in the Standards of Identity (21 CFR 27.40 and 27.43) for canned fruit cocktail and canned artificially sweetened fruit cocktail, respectively, issued pursuant to the Federal Food, Drug, and Cosmetic Act.

LIQUID MEDIA AND BRIX MEASUREMENTS

Designations	Brix Measurements
"Extra heavy syrup," or "Extra heavily sweetened fruit juice(s) and water," or "Extra heavily sweetened fruit juice(s) "	22° or more but not more than 35°
"Heavy syrup," or "Heavily sweetened fruit juice(s) and water," or "Heavily sweetened fruit juice(s) "	18° but less than 22°
"Light syrup," or "Lightly sweetened fruit juice(s) and water," or "Lightly sweetened fruit juice(s) "	14° or more but less than 18°
"Slightly sweetened water," or "Extra light syrup," or "Slightly sweetened fruit juice(s) and water," or "Slightly sweetened fruit juice(s) "	10° or more but less than 14°
"In water"	N.A.
"In fruit juice(s) and water"	N.A.
"In fruit juice(s) "	N.A.
"Artificially sweetened"	N.A.

FRUITS FOR SALAD, Canned (6/20/73)

Grade A: Color: Each fruit reasonably uniform, typical, bright, and characteristic of at least reasonably well-matured fruit, properly prepared, and processed; not more than slightly affected by pink staining but none dull or off-color; 10 percent max. of all units may possess fairly good color, but no more than 20 percent of any single fruit may possess such color. **Size:** *Apricots.* Halves, Quarters: very symmetrical; weight largest half does not exceed smallest by more than 75 percent. *Pears or Peaches.* Quarters: very symmetrical; weight largest quarter does not exceed smallest by more than 60 percent.

CANNED FRUITS FOR SALAD

CANNED FRUITS FOR SALAD (6/20/73   52.3831)

GRADES:	"A" or "FANCY"	"B" or "CHOICE"	"SUB-STANDARD"
Minimum Score:	85	70	Less than 70

	NET WEIGHT OZ.	NET WEIGHT METRIC	DRAINED WEIGHT OZ.	DRAINED WEIGHT METRIC
No. 8Z Tall	5.4	153.1 g	4.7	133.2 g
No. 303	10.6	284.9 g	9.3	263.7 g
No. 2½	18.7	530.1 g	16.9	479.2 g
No. 10	70.5	2.0 kg	62.4	1.8 kg

SYRUP	BRIX MEASUREMENTS
"Extra heavy syrup or extra heavy fruit juice syrup"	22° - 35°
Heavy syrup or heavy fruit juice syrup	18° or more but less than 22°
Light syrup or light fruit juice syrup	14° or more but less than 18°
In water	No requirement
In fruit juice	No requirement

CANNED GRAPEFRUIT & ORANGE FOR SALAD (1/21/60   52.1251)

GRADES:	"A" or "FANCY"	"B" or "CHOICE"	"BROKEN"	"SUB-STANDARD"
Minimum Score:	90	80	70	Less than 70

GRADE A	NET WEIGHT	DRAINED WEIGHT OZ.	DRAINED WEIGHT METRIC
No. 8Z Tall	not less than 90 percent of volume of container	4.85	137.5 g
No. 303		9.5	269.3 g
GRADE B OR BROKEN			
No. 8Z Tall	not less than 90 percent of volume of container	4.60	130.4 g
No. 303		8.95	253.7 g

CANNED GRAPEFRUIT & ORANGE FOR SALAD:

GRADES: SSTD.	NET WEIGHT	DRAINED WEIGHT OZ.	DRAINED WEIGHT METRIC
No. 8Z Tall	not less than 90 percent of volume of container	4.35	123.3 g
No. 303		8.45	239.6 g

SYRUP	SPECIFIC GRAVITY (Brix Measurements)
Heavy	18° or more
Light	16° or more but less than 18°
Slightly sweetened water	12° or more but less than 16°

Sliced Peaches. 5 percent max. may be partial slices, slices, slabs; variation no more than a few may vary noticeably. *Sliced Pears.* 10 percent max. may vary noticeably from uniform shape. *Pineapple.* Wedges: 10 percent may vary noticeably in outside arc measurement, may be less than 5/16 in. thickness and 11/16 in. in length, or more than 1/2 in. thickness and 1-1/4 in. in length. **Defects:** Blemished include deformed, mechanical injury, surface discoloration, rough surfaced areas, checks, cracks, that materially affect appearance; seriously blemished cherries include same that seriously affect appearance or edibility. **Allowances:** Max Peel: 1/4 sq. in. Max. blemished and serious blemishes: 10 percent of all units, but not more than 5 percent serious; provided all defects individually or collectively do not materially affect appearance or edibility. **Character:** Requires, in general, same character as grade-standards A or B canned apricots, peaches, pears, and A pineapple, allowing 10 percent of all these fruits, that may not be such character; cherries or grapes, reasonably firm and of original conformation.

Grade B: Color: Reasonably good color; each fruit fairly uniform, fairly good, typical, and characteristic of at least fairly well-matured fruit, properly prepared and processed; fruits may be more than slightly affected by pink staining that does not materially affect appearance, but none may be off color for other reasons; not more than 10 percent may fail to have reasonably good color or be dull, and no more than 20 percent of any single fruit may be such color. **Size:** May be irregular in count, need not meet counts per table. Fairly uniform, in size for these fruits within containers: *Apricots.* Halves, Quarters: may vary; weight largest half does not exceed smallest by more than twice. *Pears or Peaches.* Quarters: see Apricots. *Sliced Peaches.* 20 percent max. may be partial slices, slivers, slabs; variation may vary noticeably. *Sliced Pears.* 20 percent may vary noticeably from uniform shape. *Pineapple.* Wedges: 15 percent max. may vary noticeably in outside arc measurements, may be less than 5/16 in. thickness and 11/16 in. in length or more than 1/2 in. thickness and 1-1/4 in. in length. **Defects:** See Grade A. **Allowances:** Max. Peel 1/2 sq. in. Max. blemished and serious blemishes—20 percent of all units, but no more than 10 percent serious; provided (See Grade A). **Character:** requires in general same character as grade-standards, at least Grade C canned apricots, peaches, pears, and B pineapple, allowing 10 percent of all these fruits that may not comply, provided appearance or edibility not materially affected; cherries or grapes may be only fairly firm.

GOOSEBERRIES*

USE: The English get a great deal of enjoyment from the ripened gooseberry, but the American taste tends toward the fully developed, but unripened fruit for use in pies, tarts, jams, jellies, conserves, preserves, and marmalades. They are also used in catsups, pastes, and spiced dishes. Combined with other fruits such as currants, pineapple, rhubarb, crabapples, they make an even better product than when used alone. Juice extracted from green gooseberries can be used alone or combined with other fruit juices to make jellies or beverages. Wine is also made from the fermented juice.

VARIETIES: Gooseberries developed in North America have been the result of crossing European cultivated varieties with native species and crossing the new hybrids with other wild species. This has brought about varieties with the quality of the European and the disease- and heat-resistant characteristic of the native stock. They are also more productive than the European varieties.

American: Carrie, small, red when ripe, chiefly in Minnesota, Wisconsin, and neighboring states; **Come**, fruit medium, yellow green, best for Minnesota; **Downing**, fruit large, pale green, most widely grown variety in the US.; **Glenndale**, fruit medium, dull red, stands heat best of all varieties, grown in Virginia, Tennessee and Arkansas; **Houghton**, fruit small, dark red, one of most widely grown and most productive; **Oregon** (Oregon Champion), fruit large, green, best variety for northwestern Rocky Mountain and Pacific Coast States, adaptable to all parts of the U.S.; **Poorman**, fruit the largest of American varieties, brilliant red, considered in New York and Utah the best of all, adaptable to all parts of the country; **Abundance, Perry, Pixwell**, three very productive varieties developed in North Dakota, large fruit and few thorns.

European: Chatauqua, Columbus, Portage, Triumph, similar thought not identical fruit, very large, pale green; **Industry**, fruit very large, dark red, somewhat hairy; **May Duke**, fruit large, dark red, season early, recommended by the New York Agriculture Experiment Station as the best early gooseberry of European parentage.

CONTAINERS: Gooseberries are generally marketed in quart baskets, rarely in pints. In harvesting, the pickers often use quart baskets, setting them in hand carriers, or in waist carriers attached to the belt or suspended from the shoulders. When picked green, they can be handled in bulk.

QUALITY AND GRADES: Gooseberries of good quality are fresh, plump, firm, well colored, and with unpunctured skin. There are no U.S. standards for this berry.

GRAPEFRUIT*

USES: About 40 percent of all grapefruit grown in the United States is marketed fresh. The fresh fruit is halved and eaten with a spoon or may be juiced; segments are used in salad combinations and are also good broiled with brown sugar, spices, and other toppings. The juice can be blended with other juices in punch; a grapefruit cake with grapefruit icing is unique and delicious; and grapefruit marinated in French dressing goes well with meat or poultry. Grapefruit pieces are

*UFFVA

GRAPEFRUIT

CALIFORNIA & ARIZONA:
FRESH (1/9/50   51.925)
  Grades: U.S. FANCY; U.S. NO. 1; U.S. NO. 2; U.S. COMBINATION GRADE; U.S. NO. 3.
FLORIDA: (1/31/73   51.750)
  Grades: U.S. FANCY; U.S. NO. 1; U.S. NO. 1 Bright; U.S. NO. 1 Golden; U.S. NO. 1 Bronze; U.S. NO. 1 Russet; U.S. NO. 2; U.S. NO. 2 Bright; U.S. NO. 2 Russet; U.S. NO. 3
TEXAS & STATES OTHER THAN FLORIDA, CALIFORNIA AND ARIZONA:
(10/1/69   51.620)
  Grades: U.S. FANCY; U.S. NO. 1; U.S. NO. 1 Bright; U.S. NO. 1 Bronze; U.S. COMBINATION; U.S. NO. 2; U.S. NO. 2 Russet

CANNED (10/25/73   52.1141)

Grades:	"A" OR "FANCY"	"B" OR "CHOICE"	"U.S. BROKEN"	"SUB-STAN-DARD"
Minimum Score:	90	80	70	Less than 70

	NET WEIGHT OZ.	NET WEIGHT METRIC	DRAINED WEIGHT OZ.	DRAINED WEIGHT METRIC
No. 8Z Tall	as full as practicable	as full as practicable	4.25	120.5
No. 303			8.50	241.0

SYRUP	BRIX MEASUREMENTS
Water	N.A.
Grapefruit juice	N.A.
Grapefruit juice and water	N.A.
Slightly sweetened water	12° or more, but less than 16°
Slightly sweetened grapefruit juice	12° or more, but less than 16°
Syrup	16° or more, but less than 18°
Grapefruit juice syrup	16° or more, but less than 18°
Heavy syrup	18° or more
Heavily sweetened grapefruit juice syrup	18° or more

FROZEN: (2/20/48   52.1171)

Grades:	"A" OR "FANCY"	"B" OR "CHOICE"	"U.S. BROKEN"	"D" OR "SUB-STAN-DARD"
Minimum Score:	90	80	70	Less than 70

a happy thought as a stuffing for poultry; and grapefruit juice with sugar and gelatin makes interesting jellied molds.

More than half the nation's grapefruit crop is processed into canned single strength, chilled and frozen concentrated juices, juice blends, and canned and chilled segments. Grapefruit peel is used in making candies. There are many by-products, such as chemicals for manufacturing dyes, soaps, paints, varnishes, artificial flavors, and antioxidants. Oil pressed from the seeds can be used in making margarine, and the pulp, peel, and seeds are treated and transformed into cattle feed.

VARIETIES: The principal varieties are Marsh seedless and its related kinds, including the red-fleshed sports, and the Duncan and its related kinds. There are several seeded grapefruit varieties similar to the Duncan, the differences being so slight that varietal names have been dropped; all now are known as Duncan. Grapefruit seeded varieties, selected and propagated from chance seedlings in most instances, are being displaced in the fresh fruit market by seedless varieties. **Duncan** This type, embracing **Duncan, Walters, Silver Cluster or Hall, McCarty, and Excelsior,** has rind of yellow color, is seedy, medium to large size (diameter 3-1/2 to 5 in., height 3-1/4 to 4-3/16 in.) and ranges in shape from oblate (flattened at the poles) to spherical, or almost spherical, or slightly obovate (egg-shaped with broader end at top). Rind medium thick, 3/16 to 1/4 in.; oil glands medium large; surface smooth; aroma pleasant and strong; glandular layer thick, one-third to one-half thickness of rind; segments 12 to 14; membranes medium tender; pulp flavor excellent; seeds 30 to 50; medium large; inner seed coat cinnamon colored; season early to mid-season.

The original seedling from which the Duncan was propagated was found in the old Snedicor or Davy grove near

Safety Harbor on Florida's Pinellas peninsula. It lived to be nearly 100 years old. The seed from which the Duncan was grown came from a tree planted by Count Phillippe about 1825. The variety was propagated and first named and distributed by A. L. Duncan of Dunedin, Fla. about 1892. It has been introduced into all countries where grapefruit is grown and is still an important early variety. It is favored for making canned grapefruit sections because of the firmness of the flesh.

Marsh (Seedless) Fruit light yellow; surface very smooth and even; shape similar to Duncan; size medium to large (diameter 3-1/2 to 4-11/16 in., height 3-3/8 to 4-1/2 in.); base evenly rounded or slightly collared; basal area small, usually slightly depressed, sometimes nearly even; calyx medium small, even, or slightly depressed, apex rounded or slightly flattened; oil medium abundant, aroma mild; segments 12 to 14; membranes tender; pulp colonial buff color, tender, melting; juice abundant; highly flavored; seeds few, 3 to 8 per fruit (best strains often seedless); season medium to late. It hangs late without dropping.

The variety probably originated from a seedling tree grown on the farm of William Hancock at Socrum near Lakeland, Fla. The farm was purchased in 1862 from a Mrs. Rushing who is credited with planting the seedling which became the parent of the Marsh. The commercial value of the seedless character of this grapefruit was first recognized by E. H. Tison, a nurseryman at Lakeland. In his price list of the Lakeland Nursery Co. issued in 1889, he listed "Budded seedless grapefruit (very choice)." Tison sold his nursery to C. M. Marsh, who later distributed the variety under the name of **Marsh's Seedless.** Today the variety is widely grown in Florida, Texas, California, and Arizona, as well as in South Africa, Palestine, Australia, and South America.

Marsh is of unusual horticultural interest also because of the pigmented varieties traced back to it. **Thompson (Pink Marsh)** originated as a limb sport of Marsh. **Redblush [Ruby]** or **Red Marsh** occurred as a bud mutation of Thompson.

Foster This is the first reddish colored grapefruit known to have originated as a bud sport. It is not an important variety. It came from a bud sport on a Walters (one of the Duncan type) in the Atwood grove of Ellenton near Manatee, Fla. It was discovered in the winter of 1906-07 by R. B. Foster. When grown in California, the Foster shows a light flush on the surface and in the middle section of the rind, and the pulp either has no color or is only slightly pinkish near the center of the fruit. When grown in Florida and Texas, it shows a pink color throughout, but this color is in the membranes only. The juice is colorless. It is seldom grown today except in old plantings.

Thompson (Pink Marsh) This grapefruit originated as a bud sport on a typical Marsh tree growing in the grove of W. B. Thompson at Oneco, Fla. The variety was named and introduced by Reasoner Brothers of the Royal Palm Nurseries, Oneco in 1924. Another pink-fleshed bud variation of the Marsh was described by A. D. Shamel in 1920 as occurring at Riverside, Calif. Both fruits are seedless and are similar to the Marsh except for color. The color is limited to the pulp, the membranes being white. When grown in California, some of the pink Marsh have little color except in the pulp near the axis, while others, grown in the Imperial Valley, show a fairly uniform pink color throughout the pulp.

Ruby This is a red-fleshed variety that originated as a bud sport from the Thompson. It was found by Albert E. Henninger of McAllen, Texas in 1929. The original tree was obtained by him in 1926. In the Marsh 1929 crop, Mr. Henninger noticed a fruit with a crimson flush on the rind and also colored flesh. The fruit is similar to the Marsh except for color. The pigment is uniformly distributed in the membranes and air pocket walls but is not in the juice. Buds taken from the sport branch were propagated and produced fruit like that of the branch. The variety was patented by Mr. Henninger in 1934, and may have been the first citrus fruit patented. It is grown extensively in Texas.

Redblush This is another variety that originated as a bud sport from the Thompson. The mother tree had been budded to the Thompson, or Pink Marsh, in May 1929 but had frozen back to within 2 in. of the bud union in Jan. 1930. Later a sprout was put out by the stump of the bud. In Sept. 1931, it bore fruit somewhat larger than that of the Thompson, the color showing as a flush on the rind. When cut, the fruit was found to be a much deeper red than the Thompson and to be seedless. Some observers feel that this variety is virtually identical with the Ruby.

Star Ruby This new variety, patented and released in 1970, was developed at the Texas A & I University Citrus Center, Weslaco, by Dr. Richard Hensz. Seeds of the seedy Hudson grapefruit, a little known Texas bud sport of the Foster Pink, were exposed to thermal neutrons, and a seedling from these developed a tree with distinct characteristics and fruit with redder peel and flesh than other varieties previously developed.

The tree has a somewhat bushy growth pattern, and the cambium cells (layer between bark and wood) are red. The fruit peel is yellow with a reddish tinge and distinct red blushes, with color development beginning in mid-summer on the small shaded fruit; peel is smooth and thin. Inside the fruit the albedo is red-tinged, and the flesh and juice are a deep red color, much more so than the Ruby. The flesh is firmer than the Ruby and suited for sectioning. The season of maturity is comparable to the Ruby. It has 0 to 9 seeds.

Others. Burgundy Red originated in Fort Pierce, Fla. by Oliver L. Peacock of Fort Pierce and Hudson J. McReynolds of Orlando; introduced commercially in 1956; patented in 1954; a bud mutation of Marsh discovered in 1944; rind thin, no blush; flesh deep red, high acidity; nearly seedless; juice content fairly low in early and mid-season; juice much deeper red than that of Ruby Red. **Frost Marsh** originated in Riverside, Calif. by Howard B. Frost, California Citrus Experiment Station; introduced in 1952. A nucellar seedling of Marsh from seed planted in 1916. Fruit resembles old-line Marsh but perhaps lower in acid. Tree has greater vigor and better yield than old-line Marsh.

CONTAINERS: In Florida, the principal containers are the 4/5 bu., fiberboard, telescope box and the fiberboard bag master, although some fruit is shipped in the 4/5 bu. wirebound box. Florida adopted a 4/5 bu. or half-box size as standard because of trade preference for smaller sizes that are easier to handle. (Formerly, the main package was twice as large).

The 4/5 bu., fiberboard, telescope box has inside dimensions of 17 x 10-5/8 x 9-5/8 in. with a minimum board weight of 42-33-42 for both body and cover. The 4/5 bu. wirebound box has inside dimensions of 16-1/8 x 10-5/8 x 10-5/8 in. The 4/5 bu. fiberboard box for shaker or volume fill packing only has inside dimensions of 17 x 11-1/4 or 12 x 9-3/4 in., with minimum board weight of 42-33-69 for the body and 42-33-42 for the cover. Most packers use a board weight of 69-33-69 in the body.

Citrus packs in Florida are regulated by the Florida Citrus Commission. The grapefruit pack rules were changed as of March 27, 1974 to provide only for the number and type of pack of grapefruit in a 4/5 bu. box without giving actual sizes of the fruit. Instead, the rule provides the fruit must be uniform in size within a diameter range expressed in 16ths of an inch. The main commercial packs are 23, 32, 40, and 48. The 18s are too large and the 56s too small for any large demand, but they are shipped to a limited extent. The following table expresses the pack rules for grapefruit, but they may be changed in the near future.

Size and Count	Pack	Rows	Layers	Diameter Range
18	2 x 2	3	3	9/16 in.
23	3 x 2	3	3	9/16 in.
32	4 x 3	3	3	7/16 in.
40	4 x 5	3	3	7/16 in.
48	3 x 3	4	4	5/16 in.
56	4 x 3	4	4	5/16 in.

The 4/5 bu. fiberboard bagmaster can be of any dimensions so long as the volume of the consumer units contained therein does not aggregate more than 4/5 bu. The specifications for the consumer size bags for grapefruit are as follows: 5-lb. plastic mesh, 11 x 20 in.; 5-lb. drawcord polyethylene, 10-1/2 x 15 in.; 5-lb. open mouth polyethylene, 10-1/2 x 19 in.; 8-lb. plastic mesh, 11 x 23 in.; 8-lb. drawcord polyethylene, 11-1/2 x 17 in.; 8-lb. open mouth polyethylene, 11-1/2 x 21 in.

The width of plastic mesh bags shall be determined by measuring at the top with material stretched to form 90° angles in all corners of the diamonds. The length of plastic mesh bags shall be determined by measuring from the inside of the bottom seam to the top of the bag.

All polyethylene bags shall have a minimum of 72 ventilation holes with a minimum diameter of 1/4 in. or the equivalent thereof. All 5-lb. polyethylene bags shall be made from material with minimum specification of 1.5 mils thickness and 2 mils for 8-lb. bags. The length of open mouth polyethylene bags shall be determined by measuring when flat from the inside of the bottom seam to the top of the bag; and for drawcord polyethylene bags by measuring from the bottom of the bag to the top of the bag. The width of polyethylene bags shall be determined by measuring, when flat, from side to side including the gusset, if any.

TEXAS "Texas. In Texas the principal containers used for fresh citrus are: 5-lb. bags; 8-lb. bags; 18-lb. woven or mesh bags; 7/20-bu. fiberboard cartons; 7/10-bu. fiberboard cartons; 1-2/5-bu. fiberboard cartons; 1-2/5-bu. wirebound boxes; and a wire crib. Fruit packed in 5- and 8-lb. bags must be shipped in one of the two authorized fiberboard master containers. Special purpose and gift fruit shipments may be also handled in 6-packs, 12-packs, and bushel baskets. The Texas citrus industry reports its orange and grapefruit crops in tons and fresh shipments in carlot equivalents (one carlot equals 1,000 7/10-bu. cartons). The USDA's Crop Reporting Board uses 90-lb. box equivalents in reporting Texas oranges, and 80-lb. box equivalents for Texas grapefruit."

"**Dimensions of Texas Containers.** The dimensions of the 7/20-bu. fiberboard carton are 12-1/4 x 10-1/2 x 7-1/4 in., and it holds 20 lb. of fruit, net weight. The 7/10-bu. fiberboard carton is 16-1/2 x 10-3/4 x 9-1/2 in., and it holds 40 lb. The 1-2/5-bu. fiberboard carton is 19-3/4 x 13-1/2 x 13 in., and it holds 80 lb. The 1-2/5-bu. wirebound box is 24-5/16 x 11-3/8 x 11-3/8 in., and it hold 80 lb. The wire crib is 46-1/2 x 37 x 30 in., and it holds 1,000 lb. One fiberboard master container is 19-3/4 x 13 in. and of depth from 12 to 13-1/2 in., and holds six 8-lb. bags of fruit. The other fiberboard master container is 20 x 13-1/4 in. and of a depth from 9-3/4 to 10-3/4 in., and holds either eight 5-lb. bags or five 8-lb. bags of fruit."

"**Standard Pack in Texas.** The pack sizes for 1-2/5-bu. containers range from 46 to 126 grapefruit. The pack sizes for 7/10-bu. containers are approximately one-half those for the 1-2/5-bu. containers. For grapefruit, the diameter range for size 46s is 4-5/16 to 5 in.; 54s or 56s is 4-2/15 to 4-12/16 in.; 64s is 3-15/16 to 4-8/16 in.; 70s or 72s is 3-13/16 to 4-5/16 in.; 80s is 3-10/16 to 4-2/16 in.; 96s is 3-6/16 to 3-14/16 in.; 112s or 113s is 3-2/16 to 3-10/16 in.; and 125s or 126s is 3 to 3-8/16 in."

QUALITY: "Grade" and "quality" are not synonymous. Fruit that was of high grade when packed at shipping point may have deteriorated in condition when received by the wholesaler or retailer. Quality is the measure of present goodness of the fruit. The following on quality is from *USDA Home and Garden Bulletin 21,* "A Fruit and Vegetable Buying Guide for Consumers."

"Grapefruit of good quality are firm, but springy to the touch; not soft, wilted, or flabby, but well-shaped and heavy for size. Fruits heavy for size are usually thin-skinned and contain more juice than those that have a coarse skin, or are puffy, or spongy. Generally speaking, most defects found on grapefruit in the markets (such as scale, scars, thorn scratches, and discoloration) are minor; they affect appearance only and not eating quality.

"Decay is sometimes evident and should be avoided, since it usually affects flavor, making the taste flat and somewhat bitter. (It also causes waste and spreads rapidly.) Decay sometimes appears as a soft, discolored area on the peel at the steam end or 'button' of the fruit; or may appear in the form of a water-soaked area, much of the natural yellow within the area being lost, and the peeling being so soft and tender that it breaks easily on pressure of the finger.

"Sometimes a fruit is somewhat pointed at the stem end and is likely to be thick-skinned, particularly if the skin is rough, ridged, or wrinkled. Judgment in selecting this kind of fruit should be based on texture and weight for size."

GRADES: U.S. grade standards have been established for Florida grapefruit, California and Arizona grapefruit, and for grapefruit of Texas and states other than Florida, California and Arizona. The Florida grades are U.S. Fancy, U.S No. 1, U.S. No. 1 Bright, U.S. No. 1 Golden, U.S. No. 1 Bronze, U.S. No. 1 Russet, U.S. No. 2, U.S. No. 2 Bright, U.S. No. 2 Russet and U.S. No. 3. The Texas grades and grades for states other than those previously mentioned are U.S. Fancy, U.S. No. 1 Bright, U.S. No. 1, U.S. No. 1 Bronze, U.S.

Combination, U.S. No. 2 Russet and U.S. No. 3. The California-Arizona grades are U.S. Fancy, U.S. No. 1, U.S. No. 2, U.S. Combination and U.S. No. 3.

Florida also has a state grade called Florida Special which is better than U.S. No. 2 but not quite as tight as U.S. No. 1. The official specifications say the grade shall be the same as U.S. No. 2 except for better shape and less thickness of skin. California-Arizona marketing organizations often have their own stringent grade specifications.

U.S. No. 1 grade for Florida grapefruit "consists of grapefruit which meet the following requirements: **[a] Basic requirements:** (1) Discoloration: (i) Not more than one-third of the surface, in the aggregate, may be affected by discoloration; (2) Fairly smooth texture; (3) Fairly well colored; (4) Firm; (5) Mature; (6) Similar varietal characteristics; and (7) Well formed. **[b] Free from:** (1) Bruises; (2) Cuts not healed; (3) Decay; (4) Growth cracks; (5) Wormy fruit. **[c] Free from damage caused by:** (1) Ammoniation; (2) Buckskin; (3) Caked melanose; (4) Dirt or other foreign material; (5) Disease; (6) Dryness or mushy condition; (7) Green spots; (8) Hail; (9) Insects; (10) Oil spots; (11) Scab; (12) Scale; (13) Scars; (14) Skin breakdown; (15) Sprayburn; (16) Sprouting; (17) Sunburn; (18) Thorn scratches; and (19) Other means."

Standard Pack. "(a) Fruits shall be fairly uniform in size unless specified as uniform in size, and when packed in boxes or cartons, shall be arranged according to the approved and recognized methods. Each wrapped fruit shall be fairly well enclosed by its individual wrapper.

"(b) All such containers shall be tightly packed and well filled but the contents shall not show excessive or unnecessary bruising because of overfilled packages. When packed in cartons or in wirebound boxes, each container shall be at least level full at time of packing."

Size of fruits in the various count packs are stated to be in the following ranges: 36s, minimum 5 in., maximum 5-9/16 in. in diameter; 45s or 46s, 4-11/16 to 5-4/16; 54s or 56s, 4-6/16 to 4-15/16; 64s, 4-3/16 to 4-12/16; 70s or 72s, 3-15/16 to 4-8/16; 80s, 3-12/16 or 4-15/16; 96s, 3-9/16 to 4-2/16; 112s, 3-7/16 to 4; 125s or 126s, 3-5/16 to 3-14/16.

U.S. No. 1 grade for Texas grapefruit (and states other than Florida, California, and Arizona) "consists of grapefruit which meet the following requirements: **[a] Basic requirements:** (1) Discoloration; (i) Nor more than one-half of the surface, in the aggregate, may be affected by discoloration; (2) Firm; (3) Mature; (4) Similar varietal characteristics; (5) Fairly well colored; (6) Fairly smooth texture; and (7) Fairly well formed. **[b] Free from:** (1) Bruises; (2) Cuts not healed; (3) Caked melanose; (4) Growth cracks; (5)sprayburn; (6) Decay; and (7) Wormy fruit. (8) Damage from any other cause." **Standard pack.** "(a) Fruits shall be fairly uniform in size, unless specified as uniform in size. When packed in boxes or cartons, fruit shall be arranged according to the approved and recognized methods. (b) All packages shall be tightly packed and well filled, but the contents shall not show excessive or unnecessary bruising because of overfilled packages. When grapefruits are packed in cartons or in wirebound boxes, each container shall be at least level full at time of packing."

U.S. No. 1 grade for California-Arizona "shall consist of grapefruit of similar varietal characteristics which are mature, fairly well colored, firm, well formed, of fairly smooth texture for the variety, and not excessively thick skinned; free from decay, broken skins which are not healed, hard or dry skins, bruises (except those incident to proper handling and packing), and from damage caused by dryness or mushy condition, sprayburn, fumigation, exanthema, scars, green spots, scale, sunburn, sprouting, dirt or other foreign material, disease, insects, or mechanical, or other means. Stems shall be properly clipped." (Tolerances are similar to those for Florida fruit.)

GRAPEFRUIT, Canned (10/25/73)

Grade A: Color: "Good"—practically uniform, bright, typical, free from noticeable tinge of amber. **Wholeness:** Not less than 65 percent of an individual sample unit, (50 percent average) by weight of the drained grapefruit are practically whole segments. U.S. Broken—Individual sample units contain less than 40 percent a sample, average less than 50 percent, practically whole segments. **Character:** Moderately firm and fleshy, the segments or portions possess a juicy, cellular structure free from dry cells, or "ricey" cells, or fibrous cells that materially affect appearance or eating quality.

For the drying step of dehydrofreezing, research has developed this belt-trough dryer, which dries large quantities of product rapidly and uniformly. This device, now in commercial use, also contributes to more efficient conventional drying of fruits and vegetables.

Grade B: Color: "Reasonably good"—fairly bright, may be variable but not off-color. **Wholeness:** Not less than 40 percent of an individual sample unit (50 percent average), by weight, of the drained grapefruit are practically whole segments. U.S. Broken—see Grade A. **Character:** Grapefruit may be affected but not seriously affected, by dry cells, "ricey" cells, or fibrous cells that detract from appearance or eating quality.

GRAPEFRUIT, Frozen (2/20/48)

Grade A: Color: May possess not more than a slight variation from the typical color of properly matured grapefruit or pink grapefruit from which prepared. **Wholeness:** Frozen grapefruit that consists of not less than 75 percent of dry weight of units that are whole or almost whole segments may be given a score of 18 to 20 points. **Defects:** No harmless extraneous material is present; that no more than 5 percent of the grapefruit may be damaged units; and that for each 16 oz. of net weight, there may be present: Not more than 6 seeds including not more than 1 large seed, and not more than an aggregate area of 1 sq. in. on the units covered by membrane. **Character:** Moderately firm and fleshy; segments possess a well-developed, juicy, cellular structure; that the product is fairly free from loose cell sacs; and that not more than 5 percent consists of soft, fibrous, or "ricey" segments.

Grade B: Color: Grapefruit may be variable in color, is fairly bright, and is not off-color. **Wholeness:** If the frozen grapefruit consists of at least 50 percent but less than 75 percent by weight of the units that are whole or almost whole segments, a score of 16 or 17 points may be given. Frozen grapefruit that falls into this classification shall not be graded above U.S. Grade B or Choice regardless of the total score for the product. **Defects:** Not more than 10 percent may be damaged units; and that for each 16 oz. of net weight there may be present: not more than 1 small piece of harmless extraneous material; not more than 12 seeds including not more than 3 large seeds, and not more than an aggregate area of 2 sq. in. in the units covered by membrane. **Character:** Grapefruit is firm and fleshy and that not more than 5 percent consists of soft, fibrous, or "ricey" segments. **Grade SStd:** Fails to meet requirements. See Chart. **Grade Broken:**

Wholeness: If the frozen grapefruit consists of less than 50 percent by weight of the units that are whole or almost whole segments, a score of 0 to 15 points may be given.

GRAPEFRUIT and ORANGE FOR SALAD, Canned (4/8/75)

Grade A: Drained Weight: see chart. Given a score of 18 to 20 pts. Whenever more than 1 container of the product is being graded and the average drained weight of the container indicates a score in this classification, the score point indicated by such average drained weight is assigned to each container; except that, if the drained weight of any individual container indicates a score of less than 16 points, each container will be assigned the score for its own drained weight. **Wholeness:** Canned grapefruit and orange for salad that consist of not less than 75 percent of each drained fruit ingredient in practically whole segments may be given a score of 18 to 20 points. **Color:** With respect to the grapefruit, practically uniform, bright, typical color, free from any noticeable tinge of amber, and with respect to the orange fruit, a practically uniform, bright, typical orange color. **Defects:** No harmless extraneous material; not more than 5 percent may be damaged and that for each 20 oz. of net weight there may be present: not more than 4 seeds including not more than 1 large seed, and not more than an aggregate area of 2 sq. in. on the units covered by tough membrane. **Character:** Moderately firm and fleshy; that the segments or portions thereof possess a juicy, cellular structure free from dry cells, or "ricey" cells, or fibrous cells that materially affect the appearance or eating quality; and that the product is reasonably free from loose floating cells.

Grade B: Drained Weight: Score of 16 to 17 pts; see Grade A. All wording is same except for one numeral: 14 points for each container. **Wholeness:** If less than 75 percent but not less than 50 percent of either or both of the drained fruit ingredients is in practically whole segments, a score of 16 or 17 points may be given. **Color:** With respect to grapefruit, a fairly bright color which may be variable but is not off-color, for any reason, and with respect to the orange fruit, at least a fairly bright, typical orange color which may be variable. **Defects:** Not more than 15 percent may be damaged and that for each

20 oz. there may be present: not more than 1 small piece of harmless extraneous material; not more than 12 seeds including not more than 3 large seeds; and not more than an aggregate area of 3 sq. in. on the units covered by tough membrane or albede. **Character:** Fruits may be affected, but not seriously so, by dry cells, "ricey" cells, or fibrous cells that detract from the appearance or eating quality of the product. **SStd:** Fails to meet requirements. **Broken: Wholeness:** If less than 50 percent of either or both of the drained fruit ingredients is practically whole segments, a score of 0 to 15 points is given.

GRAPES*

USES: Grapes for commerce are divided by use into 4 major groups and 1 minor group. These are: table grapes, raisin grapes, wine grapes, juice grapes, and the minor group—canning grapes. However, the same grape may be in more than one or even in all groups. Thompson Seedless, for example, is suitable for all 5 types of uses. The mature fruit of all grape varieties that have been named, some 8,000 or more, will ferment into a kind of wine when crushed, and most of them can be dried or eaten fresh. However, only a limited number of varieties produce wines of good quality, and the raisins of commerce are produced mainly from 3 varieties.

Fewer than a dozen varieties are grown extensively for table grapes. Most of the sweet juice produced in America is from 1 variety (Concord). Only 1 or 2 varieties are used for canning. Concord grapes are used extensively for juice and also for jams, jellies, puddings, and pies. Table grapes, such as Emperor, Thompson Seedless, Tokay, Cardinal, Ribier, and others, are mostly eaten out of hand but are also used in salads, fruit cups, pies, puddings, cakes, stewed fruit, and as meat accompaniments. Dried or raisin grapes are mainly Thompson Seedless, Black Corinth and Muscat of Alexandria. Wine grape varieties are numerous. Only seedless varieties are canned, usually Thompson Seedless and Canner.

MARKETING SEASON: Table grapes are available in the U.S. throughout the year, with the heaviest movement from July through November. September is the peak month. The following table, averaged from annual unloads for 41 cities, 1963 to 1967, shows availability of grapes expressed as a percentage of total annual supply. Figures are rounded, therefore do not total 100 percent.

MONTHLY AVAILABILITY OF GRAPES EXPRESSED AS PERCENTAGE OF ANNUAL TOTAL

Jan. %	Feb. %	Mar. %	Apr. %	May %	June %	July %
5	3	3	3	2	4	11

Aug. %	Sept. %	Oct. %	Nov. %	Dec. %	Annual Total [million lbs.]
17	19	15	10	7	1,124

VARIETIES: The present commercial grape industry in the United States has developed along two main lines. In California and Arizona the industry has imported and improved varieties of the species *Vitis vinifera L.*, while in the remainder of the country the industry has been based upon the development of the American species, indigenous to the regions, hybrids of these species, and, finally, hybrids of native species with *V. vinifera.* In general, the division is between European type (Old World) grapes in California and Arizona and the American types in other areas. More than 8,000 varieties of grapes have been named and described, but only 40 or 50 are commercially important.

Of *table* grapes, the following are important *European* types: Thompson Seedless, Emperor, Tokay, Ribier, Red Malaga, Cardinal, Almeria, Calmeria, and Perlette. Of lesser importance are Italia, Olivette, Muscat, and White Malaga (largely replaced by Thompson Seedless); and *American* types, Concord, Niagara, Catawba, and Delaware.

Other commercial American varieties are Moore's Early, Champion, and Worden. Grapes intended for use as fresh fruit, either for food or decorative purposes, are commonly designated as table grapes. They must be attractive in both appearance and eating quality, must have good shipping and keeping qualities, and must be produced and sold at a reasonable cost. The varieties that are grown as table grapes in a given area are determined by climate and the distance to preferred markets. Many of the choicest eating varieties are too soft or delicate to be shipped long distances. Tough skin, firm texture, and tough stems are usually associated with

*UFFVA

GRAPES

AMERICAN (EASTERN TYPE) BUNCH GRAPES:
FRESH (4/15/65   51.3610)
 Grades: U.S. FANCY TABLE GRAPES
    U.S. NO. 1 TABLE GRAPES
    U.S. NO. 1 JUICE GRAPES

EUROPEAN OR VINIFERA TYPE TABLE GRAPES:
FRESH (5/20/71   51.880)
 Grades: U.S EXTRA FANCY TABLE GRAPES
    U.S. EXTRA FANCY EXPORT
    U.S. FANCY TABLE
    U.S. FANCY EXPORT
    U.S. NO. 1 TABLE

CANNED (6/20/73   52.4021)

Grades:	"A" OR "FANCY"	"B" OR "CHOICE"	"SUB-STANDARD"
Minimum Score:	85	70	Less than 70

	NET WEIGHT OZ.	NET WEIGHT METRIC	DRAINED WEIGHT OZ.	DRAINED WEIGHT METRIC
No. 8Z Tall	6.0	170.1 g	4.7	133.2 g
No. 303	11.4	323.2 g	9.4	266.5 g
No. 2-1/2	20.3	575.5 g	16.1	456.4 g
No. 10	74.5	2.1 kg	60.3	1.71 kg

SYRUP	SPECIFIC GRAVITY (BRIX MEASUREMENTS)
"Extra heavy syrup," or "extra heavily sweetened fruit juice(s) and water," or "extra heavily sweetened fruit juice(s)."	22°-35°
"Heavy syrup," or "heavily sweetened fruit juice(s) and water," or "heavily sweetened fruit juice(s)."	18° or more, but less than 22°
"Light syrup," or "lightly sweetened fruit juice(s) and water," or "heavily sweetened fruit juice(s)."	14° or more, but less than 18°
"Slightly sweetened water," or "extra light syrup," or "slightly sweetened fruit juice(s)."	Less than 14°
"In water"	N.A.
"In fruit juice(s) and water"	N.A.
"In fruit juice(s)"	N.A.

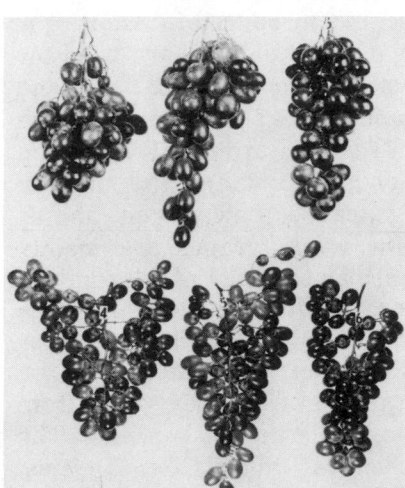

Table Grapes, Structure of Bunches —Emperor Nos. 4 and 5—Not straggly, not fairly well filled. (No. 5 not fairly well filled account upper laterals); No. 6—Minimum fairly well filled. (Upper row, bunches photographed hanging; lower row, same bunches spread out on flat surface)

table grape varieties so they can reach consumers in distant markets in an attractive condition.

Wine grapes for dry wines require grapes of high quality and moderate sugar content; sweet wines, high sugar and moderately low acidity. For making sweet, unfermented grape juice and jelly, it is desirable for grapes to retain their natural, fresh fruit flavor throughout the processing. Concord grapes (an American type) come through the usual processing almost unchanged; hence, most of the grape juice made in this country is of Concords alone or Concords blended with other varieties. Many grape varieties can be marketed interchangeably as fresh fruit, wine, or raisins. The following table describes the salient features of the leading varieties of commercial grapes which are used, at least in part, as table grapes.

EUROPEAN VINIFERA GRAPES

Variety	Description and Notes
Thompson Seedless [Sultana]	Medium size, green-white to light gold, firm, tender, sweet. Comprises 50 percent of total Calif. acreage. The No. 1 table grape; also used for dessert wines, and is main raisin grape.
Emperor	Large, light red to red-purple, normally seeded, moderately firm, skin thick and rough, neutral flavor. Ripens late; second in popularity as table grape; excellent shipping and storing properties; large quantities held in cold storage to extend season.
Tokay [Flame Tokay]	Large, brilliant to dark red, normally seeded, very firm, thick and fairly tough skin, neutral flavor. Good shipping and keeping qualities.
Ribier	Very large, purple-black, normally seeded, firm, somewhat tough skin, neutral flavor, low acid.
Cardinal	Very large, cherry red to red-purple. A cross of Flame Tokay and Ribier, adapted to hot areas. Early maturing.
Perlette	White with waxy appearance, seedless, firm flesh, crisp and juicy, skins thin and tender. Earliest maturing California white grape. Keeps and stores well.

Red Malaga	Medium-large, pink to reddish purple, normally seeded, very crisp and hard, neutral flavor, low acidity, skin tender. Fair shipping and keeping qualities.
Almeria	Medium-large, green-white, firm, normally seeded, neutral flavor, thick and tough skin. Excellent shipping and keeping qualities.
Calmeria	Large, cylindrical, green-white, firm pulp, thick and rough skin. A seedling selection of Almeria.
Italia Muscat	Very large, green, thick skin, heavy sweet flavor.

AMERICAN TYPE GRAPES

Concord	Large, round, purple, abundant bloom, seeded, aromatic, coarse, and sour flavor. Sometimes used as table grape, but mainly for juice, wines and jellies. Does not keep or ship well. Comprises 85 percent of all plantings in N.Y.
Niagara	Large, amber with heavy gray bloom, medium sugar content, coarse, and sour flavor. Leading American type white variety.
Catawba	Large, purplish red, distinctive flavor. Sometimes used as table grape, but mainly for wine, also for juice.
Delaware	Small, pink, tender skin. Used as table grape and for wine. Keeps comparatively well.

CONTAINERS: Grapes are still marketed mostly in wood lug boxes, some in combination with fiberboard and wood, though new developments in enhancing grape sizes have caused some changes in configuration. There are many types of lug boxes in common use, and lugs carry about 95 percent of the grape harvest to market. USDA Market News Service lists as the principal commercial containers for Western table grapes the *lug* or *carton* (24 to 28 lb.); *flat* (17 to 20 lb.); and the *sawdust chest* (20 to 22 and 32 to 34 lb.). The types, dimensions, and the conditions under which containers can be used are set forth in the Agricultural Code of California issued by the Department of Agriculture. Containers discussed here are a representative sample of dimensions used.

The *L.A. lug* is in widest use. Inside dimensions are 5-3/4 x 13-1/2 x 16-1/8 in. (1252 cu. in.), net weight 27 to 28 lb. There has been increasing use of special packs as low as 17 lb. due to the fact that making the 28-lb. weight limit required bulging the lid with resulting problems of damage and shatter. Early grapes from the desert regions commonly are packed in the *Desert lug*. It has the same dimensions as the L.A. lug, except for the depth which is 5-1/4 in. and a net weight of 24 lb. Another lug for early grapes measures 4-3/4 x 14-1/2 x 16-1/8 in. (1111 cu. in., net weight 24 lb.); in California the net weight must be stamped on the container. The depth of the lug is varied to facilitate packing of different varieties and to meet the wishes of growers and shippers.

In 1965, a new set of container sizes was written into law by the California legislature. The need for new standards arose from two concurrent developments. One was the widespread use of gibberrellic acid on Thompson Seedless grapes, which not only increases berry sizes but also creates bunches with wider shoulders. The other was general recognition by the grape industry that a flat pack was essential to good delivery at eastern markets. Among the newer, one-layer grape flats are the *square-end wood lug*, with top corners beveled, and the *TKV lug*. The latter was wooden ends, and a one-piece side and bottom wrap-around of laminated wood veneer and kraft paper. Inside dimensions are 4-3/4 x 14-3/4 x 16-1/8 in. (1098 cu. in., net weight 17 to 20 lb.)

Although a measure of standardization has been achieved, shippers still have a variety of choice based on three widths: 13-1/2 in., 14 and 14-3/4 in. The L.A. lug (13-1/2 in.) is used only with square corners on the ends. The 14 in. width may have square corners or 1-in. tapers at four corners. The 14-3/4 in. width is available square with either 1-1/2 in. tapers on the top 2 corners, or with 1-in. tapers on all 4 corners. According to a USDA specialist, "a large number of commercial shipments of grapes have been made recently to test the merits of various types of fiberboard boxes, usually was coated, and expanded polystyrene foam boxes."

The sawdust chest is the principal container used for grape exports. Inside dimensions are 7-3/4 x 14-7/8 to 15 x 18-5/6 in. (2155 to 2165 cu. in., net weight 32 to 34 lb. with 9 to 10 lb. of sawdust). The percentage of fruit packed in sawdust has declined in recent years as it has been found that by careful selection and the use of sulfur dioxide gas, plain packs will keep well. The *climax basket* is the principal container used for marketing American type grapes. The main containers are the eight 2-qt. baskets crate (24 to 25 lb.) and the 12-qt. basket (18 to 20 lb.).

Consumer units, or similar containers for small quantities of grapes, frequently appear on the market. They usually contain 2 lb.   Bags, window cartons, and overwrapped trays are used for preparing the grapes. One master container for consumer units has inside dimensions 6-5/8 x 15-5/8 x 16-1/8 in., holding twelve 2-lb. consumer units.

QUALITY: European type grapes, mostly grown in California, constitute the bulk of table grapes available in food stores. American type, grown in the East, are available only in small quantities.

The following is taken from USDA's "How to Buy Fresh Fruits": "European types are firm-fleshed and generally have high sugar content. American type grapes have softer flesh and are more juicy than European types.

"Look for: Well-colored, plump grapes that are firmly attached to the stem. White or green grapes are sweetest when the color has a yellowish cast or straw color, with a tinge of amber. Red varieties are better when good red predominates on all or most of the berries. Bunches are more likely to hold together if the stems are predominantly green and pliable.

"Avoid: Soft or wrinkled grapes (showing effects of freezing or drying), grapes with bleached areas around the stem end (indicating injury and poor quality), and leaking berries (a sign of decay)."

GRADES: U.S. grade standards for table grapes (European or Vinifera type) provide for three grades: U.S. Fancy, U.S. Extra No. 1, and U.S. No. 1. U.S. No. 1 is the chief trading grade used by the industry.

U.S. No. 1 consists of bunches of well developed grapes of one variety (except when designated as assorted varieties) which are mature and fairly well colored. The berries shall be firm, firmly attached to capstems, and shall not be weak, materially shriveled at capstems, shattered, split, crushed, or wet, and shall be free from decay, waterberry, and sunburn, and free from damage caused by scarring, discoloration, heat, Almeria Spot, mildew, other diseases, freezing, insects, or mechanical, or other means.

"Bunches shall not be straggly. They shall be free from damage caused by shot berries, dried berries, or other defective berries, or by the trimming away of defective berries, and each bunch shall weigh not less than one-fourth pound.

"*Stems* shall not be weak, or dry and brittle, and shall be free from mold, and free from damage caused by mildew or freezing. **Tolerances.** In order to allow for variations incident to proper grading and handling, the following tolerances, by weight, shall be permitted: (a) (i) 10 percent for bunches which fail to meet the color requirements; and, (ii) 10 percent for bunches which weigh less than 1/4 lb. and bunches and berries which fail to meet the remaining requirements of this grade, other than for maturity, including not more than 5 percent for shattered berries, and including not more than 2 percent for berries which are seriously damaged: *Provided,* That not more than one-fourth of the latter amount, or one-half of 1 percent, may be permitted for berries affected by decay: *And Provided further,* That when in packages containing 5 lb. or less, not more than 25 percent of the bunches may weigh less than 1/4 lb. There is no tolerance specified in this grade for grapes which fail to meet the maturity requirements. However, no lot shall be considered as failing to meet these requirements because the sample of grapes from one container tests below the required percentage of soluble solids."

GRAPES—Canned [6/20/73]
CANNED SEEDLESS GRAPES

STANDARD OF IDENTITY

Canned seedless grapes; identity; label statement of optional ingredients. (a) Canned seedless grapes is the food prepared from one of the optional grape ingredients specified in paragraph (b) of this section and one of the optional packing media specified in paragraph (c) of this section. Such food may also contain one or more of the following optional ingredients:

(1) Spice
(2) Flavoring, other than artificial flavoring
(3) A vinegar

Such food is sealed in a container. It is so processed by heat as to prevent spoilage.

(b) The optional grape ingredients referred to in paragraph (a) of this section are prepared from stemmed grapes of the light or dark seedless varieties or from unstemmed clusters of such grapes. For the purposes of paragraph (e) of this section, the names of such optional grape ingredients are "light seedless grapes" or "dark seedless grapes," as the case may be, preceded by the words "unstemmed clusters" where appropriate.

(c) (1) The optional packing media referred to in paragraph (a) of this section are: (i) Water (ii) Grape juice (iii) Slightly sweetened water (iv) Light syrup (v) Heavy syrup (vi) Extra heavy syrup. As used in this section, the term "grape juice" means the fresh or canned, expressed juice of mature grapes of the same variety as the optional fruit ingredient, and the term "water" means, in addition to water, any mixture of water and grape juice.

(2) Each of packing media in subparagraph (1) (iii) to (vi), inclusive, of this paragraph is prepared with water and one of the optional saccharine ingredients specified in paragraph (d) of this section.

(3) The respective densities of packing media in subparagraph (1) (iii) to (vi), inclusive, of this paragraph, as measured on the Brix hydrometer 15 days or more after the grapes are canned, are within the range prescribed after the name of each in the following list:

Name of packing medium	Brix measurement
Slightly sweetened water	Less than 14°
Light syrup	14° or more but less than 18°
Heavy syrup	18° or more but less than 22°
Extra heavy syrup	22° or more but not more than 35°

(d) The optional saccharine ingredients referred to in paragraph (c) are the same as in "Canned Prunes"—27.15 (c) (1), (2), (3), (4), (5), and (6).

LABEL STATEMENT OF OPTIONAL INGREDIENTS

(e) The label shall bear the name of the optional grape ingredient used, as specified in paragraph (b) of this section, and the name whereby the optional packing medium used is designated in paragraph (c) of this section, preceded by "in" or "packed in." When any of the optional ingredients permitted by one of the following specified subparagraphs of paragraph (a) of this section is used, the label shall bear the words set forth after the number of such subparagraph:

(a) (1) "Spiced" or "spice added" or "with added spice," or, in lieu of the word "spice," the common name of the spice.

(a) (2) "Flavoring added" or "with added flavoring," or, in lieu of the word "flavoring," the common name of the flavoring.

(a) (3) "Seasoned with vinegar" or "seasoned with . . . vinegar," the blank being filled in with the name of the vinegar used: When two or all of the optional ingredients specified in paragraph (a) (1), (2), and (3) of this section are used, such words may be combined as for example, "seasoned with cider vinegar, cloves, and cinnamon oil."

(f) Wherever the name of the food appears on the label so conspicuously as to be easily seen under customary conditions of purchase, the words specified in this section, showing the optional ingredients used, shall immediately and conspicuously precede or follow such name without intervening written, printed, or graphic matter, except that the varietal name of the grapes may so intervene.

GRAPES—Canned [1975 Revisions]

The Food and Drug Administration amended the standards of identity for Canned Grapes, compliance with which may begin on March 11, 1975, but mostly after December 31, 1975.

The following amendments to the USDA standards for Canned Grapes are proposed to bring them into line with the amended FDA Standards of Identity.

Product Description. "Canned grapes" is the product represented as defined in the Standards of Identity for canned grapes (21 CFR 27.25) issued pursuant to the Federal Food, Drug, and Cosmetic Act. For the purpose of these standards, canned grapes are prepared from the light, seedless varietal type and are stemmed.

LIQUID MEDIA AND BRIX MEASUREMENTS

Designations	Brix measurements
"Extra heavy syrup," or "Extra heavily sweetened fruit juice(s) and water," or "Extra heavily sweetened fruit juice(s) "	22° or more but not more than 35°
"Heavy syrup," or "Heavily sweetened fruit juice(s) and water," or "Heavily sweetened fruit juice(s) "	18° or more but less than 22°
"Light syrup," or "Lightly sweetened fruit juice(s) and water," or "Lightly sweetened fruit juice(s) "	14° or more but less than 18°
"Slightly sweetened water," or "Extra light syrup," or "Slightly sweetened fruit juice(s) and water," or "Slightly sweetened fruit juice(s) "	Less than 14°
"In water"	N.A.
"In fruit juice(s) and water"	N.A.
"In fruit juice(s)"	N.A.

HONEYDEWS*

USES: When you have before you a ripe, juicy melon, a knife, a spoon, and possibly a shaker of salt, it would seem most satisfying to set to work and polish it off right now. But it is also possible to do some very special and artistic things with honeydews. For example, make fresh honeydew boats, cutting the melon crosswise, in half, removing seeds and stringy portion; cutting each half into 3 wedges; placing each boat on a serving plate, and placing a mixture of grapes, orange sec-

Guava (Psidium guajava) fruit ripe on the tree, ready to harvest.

tions, fresh lemon juice, and sugar on each boat, garnishing with mint leaves. Or use fresh honeydew balls in a fruit sauce made of orange juice, lemon juice, currant jelly, and vanilla extract. Or how about honeydew rings, 1 to 1-1/2 in. thick, served on head lettuce beds, and filled with shrimp salad? Diced fresh honeydew with fresh blueberries and some lime ice or sherbet makes a mighty fine dessert. There are endless ways to serve honeydews with dressings, such as bleu cheese french dressing. The melon should be fragrant, creamy white, and springy to soft at the blossom end. But be sure to hold your melons at room temperature until well ripened.

For breakfast honeydews are quick and tasty. But here is a luncheon salad that is nice with hot rolls or cinnamon toast. Peel a chilled honeydew and slice the center in inch-thick slices. Dice the ends. Fill the rings with cottage cheese and sprinkle with the diced melon. Garnish with sliced peaches or other fruit. Serve with a favorite dressing.

MARKETING SEASON: Honeydews are available all year, but only in trace quantities in December and January and only a few in November. The period of major supply is June through October. The following table shows the percentage of the annual total marketed each month, on the average. The asterisks mean less than 0.5 percent. (Percentages are rounded and do not total 100 percent.)

PERCENTAGE OF TOTAL ANNUAL SUPPLY OF FRESH HONEYDEWS AVAILABLE

Jan. %	Feb. %	Mar. %	Apr. %	May %	June %
*	6	11	7	4	13

July %	Aug. %	Sept. %	Oct. %	Nov. %	Dec. %
9	18	21	11	1	*

The average supply in 1965 and 1966 was 247 million pounds a year, so that by using the percentages above, the approximate amount available each month can be calculated.

CONTAINERS: Honeydews are packed in the jumbo honeydew crate, holding 45 to 50 lb. net and loading 720 to a rail car; standard honeydew crate, 40 to 43 lb., 720 to a car; carton, 31-1/2 lb., 1040 to car; various flat crates, 40 to 45 lb., 720 to car, according to Market News Service, USDA.

Container numbers, railroad tariff numbers, and inside dimensions of containers are as follows: No. 1177, jumbo, tariff No. 1-H and 2-G, 7-3/4 x 16 x 22-1/8; No. 1175, standard, tariffs 1-H and 2-G, 6-3/4 x 16 x 22-1/8; No. 1176, pony, tariffs 1-H and 2-G, 5-3/4 x 14-1/2 x 22-1/8; No. 1178, pony, tariff 1-H, 5-3/4 x 13-1/2 x 22-1/8.

QUALITY: To be of the most desirable eating quality, honeydew melons should be fully ripe, with creamy outer color and waxy feel to the surface, and pale green flesh which is sweet, juicy, and fine-textured. In addition to color, ripeness may be indicated by a pleasant fruity aroma and by a slight softening at the blossom end. (However, in practice, honeydews in the retail store will rarely be found that have any aroma.) These melons are cut from the vine when harvested and, therefore, the condition of the stem does not indicate the stage of maturity.

Severe bruises, cuts, or other damaging defects can be readily detected if present. "Sugar cracks" and small wart-like proliferations or ridges of tissue do not detract from eating quality. Over-ripe (soft) melons should not be sold. They have a bitter flavor. Decay generally appears as sunken, water-soaked spots on which pink, black, or near-black fungal growths may be present. In advanced stages, such sunken spots may penetrate the rind and seriously affect the flesh. The decay mentioned here is not due to market decay in the usual sense but to chilling injury. The honeydew is quite resistant to the usual rots that afflict cantaloupes and other melons. However, if stored too long at too low a temperature, it becomes weakened and susceptible to decay. Though resistant to decay if held at the right temperature, it is still highly perishable from a flavor point of view. Immature melons offered for sale will keep almost indefinitely—but they will never be fit to eat.

HONEYDEW AND HONEYBALL TYPE MELONS

FRESH (4/1/67   51.3740)
GRADES: U.S. NO. 1
       U.S. Commercial
       U.S. NO. 2

FROZEN (6/25/62   52.5361)

GRADES:	"A" OR "FANCY"	"B" OR "CHOICE"	"SUB-STANDARD"
Minimum Score:	90	80	Less than 80

GRADES: U.S. grade standards for honeydews and honeyball type melons provide for three grades: U.S. No. 1, U.S. Commercial and U.S. No. 2.

"*U.S. 1* consists of honeydew or honeyball type melons which are mature, firm, well formed, which are free from decay, and free from damage caused by dirt, aphis stain, rust spots, bruises, cracks, broken skin, sunscald, sunburn, hail, moisture, insects, disease or other means. ... In order to allow for variations incident to proper grading and handling ..., the following tolerances, by count, are provided as specified: (a) 10 percent for melons in any lot which fail to meet the requirements of the grade: Provided, That not more than one-half of this amount, or 5 percent, shall be allowed for defects causing serious damage, including in this latter amount not more than 1 percent for melons affected by decay ..."

LEMONS*

USES: While fresh lemon garnishes add appetite appeal to all types of dishes, the principal use of lemons is in making drinks, the obvious one being lemonade. Yet large quantities are used in other ways. Lemon juice is a popular ingredient of salad dressings, or the juice may be used as the dressing. Lemon is excellent on meat and is a popular seasoning for fish and seafoods of all kinds. Fresh lemon is an accepted part of a vegetable or combination vegetable and meat or fish salad. No tall glass of ice tea is complete without a generous wedge of lemon. Lemon pies, tarts, cakes, and cookies are very popular. A squeeze of lemon accents the flavor of soups and juices such as tomato juice.

Lemon adds zest to many kinds of cooked vegetables, such as green beans, asparagus, or spinach. Lemon peel and juice added to ground beef is excellent for hamburgers, meat loaf, meat balls, or many of the packaged dinners. Lemon rubbed on lamb, fish, or poultry before cooking adds flavor. Lemon juice combined with spices, such as oregano, pepper, or dill, makes an excellent marinade for less expensive cuts of meats. Lemon juice keeps pears, apples, bananas, and avocados from turning brown quickly. Lemon is also a mild bleaching agent, useful for keeping white vegetables white. For example, when cooking potatoes, a little lemon can be used in the water to retain the natural coloring. Celery dipped in "lemonated" water is guarded against browning. Fresh lemon is almost sodium-free and may be used, according to the American Heart Association, in even the strict (500 mg./day) low sodium diet.

Oil, cold-pressed from the fruit, is used in flavoring for cooking and in bakery products. Such flavorings are also used in sherbets, candy, and icings, as well as jams, jellies, and preserves. Juice is used both from fresh lemons and from canned or canned and frozen juice.

There are many non-food uses. Distilled lemon oils are used in soaps and cleaners, in floor and shoe polishes, and in household fly sprays. Lemon oil is a favorite for polishing pianos and other fine furniture. Pectates help make paper coatings, stabilizers used in the manufacture of latex, printing inks, and a disintegrant for medicinal tablets. The oil is used in pharmaceuticals and in perfume and cosmetics.

Finally, after the last bit of juice has been extracted and the peel cut and firmly pressed, the remaining mass of pulp and peel is cooked and dried to become cattle feed. About the only factor in a lemon not used is the aroma from the crushed fruit, and this can be reproduced by using some of the lemon oil extracted from the peel.

MARKETING SEASON: Lemons are available all year in adequate quantities to meet the demand. Shipments are regulated under a marketing agreement pursuant to federal law. Harvesting goes on at all seasons. Fruit from the desert areas of California and Arizona is harvested during the fall and winter months, dovetailing with the main crop of California lemons which is produced in large supply from March to September. Since lemons of good vitality may also be stored 1 to 5 months, extreme shortages of lemons are unusual.

AVERAGE MONTHLY AVAILABILITY OF FRESH LEMONS, EXPRESSED AS A PERCENTAGE OF ANNUAL SUPPLY BASED ON LEMON ADMINISTRATIVE COMMITTEE FIGURES FOR 1972-73 INCLUSIVE

Jan. %	Feb. %	Mar. %	Apr. %	May %	June %
8	6	8	9	13	12

July %	Aug. %	Sept. %	Oct. %	Nov. %	Dec. %
9	10	6	6	7	6

*UFFVA

VARIETIES: Commercially, only the acid-type lemons are grown in the United States. The other type, sweet lemon, is grown only as a novelty. In California and Arizona the main varieties are **Eureka** and **Lisbon**. Eurekas predominate in the coastal areas about 2 to 1 over the Lisbon. The Eureka tends to mature a great deal of its fruit in the summer when demand is highest. In the desert areas and warmer inland regions, such as central California, the Lisbon variety has been most successful. In Florida, the varieties may best be categorized as Sicilian types, considered to be within the Lisbon group. Most widely grown variety is Bearss. Other varieties include Avon, Harney and Villafranco.

Insofar as fruit characteristics are concerned, the varieties grown in California are remarkably alike. The rind characteristics of the uncured fresh lemon may be modified during curing and storage. Consequently, for most varieties, it is difficult to identify accurately the variety of lemon by the fruit alone.

Eureka lemons are elliptical to oblong, sometimes egg-shaped, and commonly have a short neck. The blossom end or nipple is usually short, but sometimes long and often surrounded by an indentation or slight furrow. The medium thick rind has a rugose (corrugated) texture, often slightly ridged longitudinally. The surface may also be finely pitted with sunken oil glands. When mature, the fruit is lemon yellow. Juice is abundant, in about 10 segments, and seed count variable from usually a few to occasionally none. The quality of the juice is very acid but with a good fresh lemon flavor. In desert locations the Eureka lemon is rougher in texture with a more prominent, ribbed surface and smaller, flatter nipples.

The Eureka tree tends to be medium size, more open in growth habit and more sparsely foliated than the Lisbon tree. Also there are fewer and smaller thorns with some virtually thornless trees. The newer strains and rootstock combinations are producing a more vigorous tree. Compared to the Lisbon, the leaves are darker in color and less sharply pointed. Leaf margins are somewhat more scalloped or crenated. In coastal areas, the Eureka tends to be more everbearing and to produce fruit in terminal clusters.

The Eureka originated as a superior seedling among a group of seedlings grown from seed that was obtained from imported Sicilian lemons and planted by Dr. Halsey of Los Angeles in 1858. In 1860, Andrew Boyle bought some of the seedlings and when they fruited, 3 or 4 produced smooth thin-skinned fruits. In 1877, C.R. Workman, son-in-law of Boyle, gave bud woods from one of these seedlings to Thomas A. Garey, a prominent Los Angeles nurseryman. Mr. Garey propagated this wood and gave the tree the name of Garey Eureka. Because of its thornlessness and everbearing nature, it soon rivaled the Lisbon in popularity.

Lisbon The fruit is elliptical to oblong and tapering to an inconspicuous neck. From the apex it tapers to a prominent, symmetrical, often pointed nipple. The texture is generally smoother and less markedly ribbed than the Eureka. The rind is of medium thickness and the surface finely pitted. Color is yellow at maturity.

Juice content is of good flavor, very acid, and easily extracted. Seed content may be variable, but usually there are few to none. The tree is densely foliated, thorny, more vigorous, more upright growing, and more productive than the Eureka. It is also more resistant than Eureka to frost, heat, and wind. Lisbon has been accepted as the most desirable variety in the desert or very warm locations. It produces more of a one-bloom crop than Eureka, and has a shorter harvesting period. It tends to ripen in the fall in desert locations and in the winter and early spring in coastal areas.

The Lisbon is believed to be of Portuguese origin. In California, the first reference to it was in a catalog of Warren and Sons Nursery in Sacramento in 1853. Samuel P. Stow of Goleta, Calif. imported Lisbon trees from Australia in 1874. He shared the introduction with nurseryman Thomas A. Garey of Los Angeles who propagated and distributed the variety. Other importations were made later. Because of their hardiness and high yields, the Lisbon variety was popular, particularly in the California interior districts.

Over the years, the lemon industry of California has continued to develop and improve many strains of both Eureka and Lisbon varieties. A strain is an artificial variety only slightly differentiated, and originally budded from a single tree that shows outstanding characteristics. Bud trees are registered, certified to be free from virus and other diseases and outstanding in vigor and productivity, and considered to

LEMONS

FRESH (9/1/64   51.2795)
GRADES: U.S. NO. 1
U.S. EXPORT NO. 1
U.S. COMBINATION
U.S. NO. 2

be typical for the variety. The University of California Citrus Research Center at Riverside has been leading this development work. Nucellar bud strains have been developed, and new root stocks have been introduced. Factors influencing the use of new strains are: fruit quality, yield, resistance to disease, type of tree, e.g., being of suitable size for picking, spraying and pruning. Length of tree life is also important, since short-lived trees are uneconomic.

CONTAINERS: Lemons are now shipped in two-piece telescope fiberboard cartons. The inside dimensions are 10-1/4 in. depth, 10-11/16 in. width x 16-3/8 in. length. Lemon sizes or counts per carton are: 75, 95, 115, 140, 165, 200 and 235. The average diameters per size, from large to small, are: 75s-2.775 in., 95s-2.570 in., 115s-2.410 in., 140s-2.240 in., 165s-2.130 in., 200s-2.010 in. and 235s-1.880 in. The seasonal average weight per carton is 38 lb. net; however, individual cartons vary both above or below the average according to the size of the fruit. Large-sized fruit tends to be lighter in weight per carton and small-sized fruit heavier in weight per carton.

QUALITY: Almost all of the lemons that come to market are of high quality. Best lemons have a fine-textured skin and are heavy for their size. Those that are coarse, thick skinned, or light in weight have less juice. Lemons that are shriveled or hard skinned, or which are very soft or spongy, are not desirable. Some high-colored, soft fruit may be old, dried out, mechanically injured, or affected by a rot at the center of the fruit. If any internal decay is present, it generally appears as a mold, or as a discolored soft area at the stem, or sometimes the stylar end. Fruit that has a slightly greenish color is likely to have more vitality for keeping purposes. It also has a good flavor and is as desirable as a good-colored mature fruit.

GRADES: U.S. lemon standards have been in force since September 1, 1964. Grades are U.S. No. 1, U.S. Export No. 1, U.S. Combination, and U.S. No. 2.

"U.S. No. 1 consists of lemons which are firm, fairly well formed (unless specified as well formed), reasonably smooth (unless specified as smooth), which have stems which are properly clipped, and which are free from decay, contact spot, internal evidence of alternaria development, unhealed broken skins, hard or dry skins, exanthema, growth cracks, internal decline (endoxerosis), red blotch, membraneous stain or other internal discoloration, and free from damage caused by bruises, dryness or mushy condition, scars, oil spots, scale, sunburn, hollow core, peteca, scab, melanose, dirt or other foreign material, other disease, insects, or other means.

"(a) Color. The lemons are fairly well colored (unless specified as well colored), provided that any lot of lemons which meets all the requirements of this grade except those relating to color may be designated as 'U.S. No. 1 Green', if the lemons are of a full green color, or as 'U.S. No. 2 Mixed Color', if the lemons fail to meet the color requirements of either 'U.S. No. 1' or 'U.S. No. 1 Green'.

"(b) Lemons in the U.S. No. 1, U.S. Combination, and U.S. No. 2 grades shall have a juice content of not less than 30 percent by volume, except when designated at 'U.S. No. 1 Green for Export', 'U.S. Combination Green for Export', or 'U.S. No. 2 Green for Export'. When so designated, the lemons shall have a juice content of not less than 28 percent by volume."

LIMES*

USE: Fresh lime juice is used in the preparation of beverages such as limeade and lime rickey. It is used as flavoring for jellies, jams, and marmalades. Slices of fresh limes make attractive garnishes for meat and fish dishes. They dress up iced tea. The flavor peps up salad dressings, or the juice alone may be used on salads. Lime juice is popular in sherbets, ices, pies, and ice-box cakes. It is a natural base for fruit punches and supplies a spicy, fresh fruit flavor for beverages. It blends well with other citrus juices. Lime juice is frozen in a limeade concentrate, used in bottled soft drinks, and in canned, mixed citrus, single strength juices.

MARKETING SEASON: Fresh limes are available the year round. Peak supplies come in June, July, and August. Lime

*UFFVA

trees produce several "flushes" of bloom each season and are rarely without fruit in some stage or stages of maturity. In Florida, the early bloom which comes in January, February, and March is the heaviest. About 60 percent of the year's harvest matures in June, July, and August. The Mexican crop ripens between May and October so is at peak at the same time Florida limes are in heavy supply. Limes in California ripen principally from September to the beginning of January, with peak in the latter part of October or on the first of November. There is a secondary peak in March and April, but the supply is small.

AVERAGE MONTHLY AVAILABILITY OF FRESH LIMES EXPRESSED AS PERCENT OF AVERAGE TOTAL ANNUAL SUPPLY [1952-1956]

Million Lb.	Jan. %	Feb. %	Mar. %	Apr. %	May %
26	3	3	3	4	7

June %	July %	Aug. %	Sept. %	Oct. %	Nov. %	Dec. %
16	22	17	7	4	6	8

SOURCE: Guide to average monthly availability of 98 Fresh Fruits and Vegetables, United Fresh Fruit & Vegetable Association, 1958.

VARIETIES: Types Limes are divided into two distinct groups, acid and sweet. Acid limes are the only type grown in the U.S., while sweet limes are popular in many other citrus growing areas. Acid limes are further divided into *Tahiti* and *Mexican* types. The Tahiti group is characterized by large fruits, grown on larger, more spreading, and more cold-resistant trees than the Mexican group. Mexican limes are considered the true type of the species (Citrus aurantifolia). The fruits are small with very thin rinds.

Tahiti Group Varieties of the Tahiti type include Persian, Bearss, Idemore, and Pond. The *Persian* variety is the most extensively grown commercially. It was introduced into Florida in 1898 from Algeria by Dr. Walter Swingle, plant explorer for the USDA. This variety (commonly called Tahiti in California) was imported and sold in the California markets from early days. *Bearss*, which originated about 1895 on the place of T.J. Bearss, at Porterville, Calif., is so closely related to the Persian that it is believed it was developed from a se-

lected seedling grown from Persian seed. This is the principal lime variety in California.

Persian (Tahiti) fruit surface smooth, even or faintly lobed; oval to elliptical in shape; size, large, with average diameter when fully ripe 2-5/16 in., average length 2-3/4 in.; base evenly rounded, smooth, sometimes slightly ribbed and furrowed; rind 1/8- to 3/16-in. thick; oil glands small; axis small, diameter 3/16 to 5/16-in., solid, or in old fruits hollow; segments mainly 10; membranes tender; pulp fine grained, tender, light greenish yellow, very acid, highly flavored; seeds very few or none; fruit color when fully ripe light orange-yellow (marketed at green mature stage); fruit matures the year round.

Bearss (Bearss Seedless) fruit smaller than Persian, diameter averages 1-3/16 in. and length 2-1/4 in.; pulp very juicy, finely grained, color greenish yellow; flavor of true lime, very acid; quality excellent; seeds none; fruit color when fully ripe light lemon yellow (marketed at green mature stage); season winter to late spring, with fruit maturing more or less throughout the year.

Mexican Group There are only small differences in the fruits of so-called varieties in this group. In Florida the type is called **Key** because of the extensive plantings that existed on the Keys, until most of the acreage was destroyed during the storms of the late 1920s and mid-1930s. The variety is no longer commercially important for fresh fruit marketing, although as a dooryard tree it is very popular. It is estimated that as many trees exist for home use as there were at the height of its commercial importance in 1926. Most of the commercial production of this variety in Florida goes into locally frozen juice for "Key Lime Pie" (also made from Persian lime juice), or it is utilized in the manufacture of a fermented condiment known as "old sour" for use on fish and other seafood.

The same type lime is known as **Mexican** in Mexico, California, Texas, and Arizona; as **Dominican** when imported from the Dominican Republic or **West Indian** when imported from any of the West Indies. The fruit is larger than **Key** limes when the trees are grown in the deeper soils of the mainland, or under Mexican, or West Indies conditions.

PERSIAN [TAHITI] LIMES

FRESH (6/20/58   51.1000)
GRADES: U.S. NO. 1
U.S. Combination
U.S. NO. 2

Mexican (Key, Dominican, West Indian): fruit color light lemon yellow; surface smooth; shape round to obovate or oval; size small, diameter average 1-3/8 in., length average 1-1/2 in.; basal area smooth or commonly with a few light radiating ribs; rind smooth and leathery, very thin, 1/16- to 1/8-in.; oil glands small, surface depressed; oil abundant, highly aromatic; juice abundant; flavor strong, very acid; seeds few, 4 to 8, small; season late fall to spring, maturing more or less throughout year. (Marketed when fully ripe.)

The varieties **Rangpur** and **Kusaie**, which are commonly called limes and if used are used like limes, more properly belong to the mandarin orange (Citrus reticulata) species. The trees are hardy and frost resistant, but the fruits are not. Rangpur trees are attractive ornamentals. The so-called **Ogeechee Lime**, its name derived from the Ogeechee River, belongs to no citrus species and the fruit bears no resemblance to any citrus fruits. The fruit is like an olive in size and shape and of bright scarlet color. It has an acid flavor and is usually preserved in sugar.

CONTAINERS: Fiberboard containers are used almost exclusively for shipping limes from Florida. Two display cartons have been in general use, one measuring 12 in. x 9-5/8 in. x 3-3/4 in. inside, 2 layers, place pack. A third container measures inside 11 in. x 16-3/4 in. x 10 in., jumble pack, net weight 40 lb. The 40-lb. pack is used generally for shipments to large outlets, such as supermarkets, chains, and institutions.

No restrictions have been placed on the *type* of package for consumer-sized lots or on the master carton. The consumer pack, however, must hold *not more than 2 lb.* A popular pack is 5 or 6 limes in tubes with cello windows in display cartons holding 12 tubes. Overwrapped trays and polyethelene bags are also used for consumer packages.

Limes from Mexico are sized and graded at the Texas border and repacked in nailed wood boxes measuring 9-1/2 in. x 9-1/2 in. x 19-1/8 in. or 6 in. x 12 in. x 24 in., net weights 40 lb. Some are repacked in tubes or small display cartons. California limes are shipped in cartons similar to those used by Florida.

QUALITY: With reference to Persian type limes, those that are green in color and heavy for their size are the most desirable. Deep yellow fruits of this type do not have the desired acidity. When present, decay appears either as a mold or as a discolored soft area at the stem end. Fruits that have been mechanically injured are more or less subject to molds. (Limes suffering from harvesting injuries are generally detected before packing.) Sometimes limes may become spotted with purple-to brown-colored and irregularly shaped spots. The whole fruit may turn brown. This is the result of a defect known as scald. Such fruit has a poor appearance, but in many cases the flesh is unaffected. Pitting may occur as the result of freeze or too low temperatures in storage. This will occur rapidly after exposure to room temperatures. Immature limes have a tendency to become blackened, dry, and hard. The juice sacks in immature limes will not rupture readily. Under moderate pressure the sacks protrude without yielding the juice. This condition is called "riciness."

GRADES: Revised U.S. standards for Persian (Tahiti) limes became effective June 15, 1957. These standards provide for **U.S. No. 1, U.S. Combination and U.S. No. 2** grades. "U.S. No. 1 consists of Persian Limes which are firm, fairly well formed, of fairly smooth texture; which are free from decay, stylar end breakdown, or other internal discoloration, broken skins which are not healed, bruises (except those incident to proper handling and packing), hard or dry skins, and free from damage caused by freezing, dryness, or mushy condition, sprayburn, exanthema (ammoniation), scars, thorn scratches, scale, sunburn, scab, blanching, yellow color, discoloration, buckskin, dirt or other foreign material, disease, insects or mechanical or other means.

"Each fruit in this grade shall have not less than an aggregate area of three-fourths of the surface of the fruit which shows good green color characteristics of the Persian lime: *Provided*, That lots of limes which fail to meet the U.S. No. 1 grade requirements only because of blanching shall be designated as U.S. No. 1, Mixed Color; *And provided further*, That

designated as U.S. No. 1, Turning. The fruit shall have a juice content of not less than 42 percent, by volume.

"In order to allow for variations incident to proper grading and handling, not more than 10 percent, by count, of the fruit in any lot may fail to meet the color requirements. In addition, lots of limes which fail to meet the U.S. No. 1 or U.S. No. 1 Mixed Color grade requirements only because of turning yellow or yellow color, caused by the ripening process, shall be not more than 10 percent, by count, of the fruit in any lot may be below the remaining requirements of this grade, but not more than one-half of this amount, or 5 percent, shall be allowed for decay, stylar end breakdown, broken skins which are not healed, or defects causing serious damage, including not more than one-half of 1 percent for decay at shipping point; Provided, That an additional tolerance of 2-1/2 percent, or a total of not more than 3 percent, shall be allowed for decay en route or at destination.

"**Standard Pack** (a) Fruit shall be fairly uniform in size and when place-packed in crates or cartons, the fruit shall be arranged according to the approved and recognized methods. (b) All packages shall be well filled, but the contents shall not show excessive or unnecessary bruising because of over-filled packages. (c) Fairly uniform in size means that not more than 10 percent, by count, of the fruit in any container may vary more than 4/16th of an inch in diameter. (d) In order to allow for variations, other than sizing, incident to proper packing, not more than 5 percent of the packages in any lot may fail to meet the requirements of standard pack."

Florida regulations require that all Persian type limes must meet at least the minimum requirements of U.S. No. 2 Grade, Mixed Color, containing not less than 50 percent of U.S. No. 1 quality fruit, Mixed Color; and that all Key type limes must meet at least the minimum requirements of the U.S. No. 2 Grade for Persians, except for color.

LYCHEES*

USE: Due to the limited supply of lychees in the United States, most of the fruit is consumed fresh. The Chinese for many years have dried the fresh fruits which are then marketed throughout the world as lychee "nuts." In southern China,

some lychees are commercially canned in sugar syrup, honied, salted, and made into wine. Attention has recently been given in Florida and Hawaii to the preservation of lychees by freezing. Frozen lychees can be prepared either as a peeled or unpeeled product. Due both to the ease of preparation and the superior appearance of the brightly colored, unpeeled fruit, the latter method seems superior. Frozen, unpeeled fruit, if packaged in a suitable moisture-vapor-proof container, will retain their fresh fruit flavor for at least 2 years. Freezing of lychees offers considerable possibilities for extending the period of lychee availability throughout the year and expanding the market.

MARKETING SEASON: The bulk of the lychee crop in Florida usually matures between mid-June and early July. The size of the crop varies from year to year. The total crop marketed by the Florida Lychee Growers Association totals approximately 40,000 lb. Forty percent of this fruit is marketed in New York City and the remainder throughout the United States and Canada.

VARIETIES: The number of varieties of lychees which have been described in China indicates the popularity of these fruits in their native country. As early as 1492, a list of 40 varieties was published in China. Groff listed 49 varieties of which 15 were leading commercial ones in China about 40 years ago. The same author in 1951 listed 18 varieties which had been introduced into the U.S. Although numerous varieties of lychees are planted to some extent in Florida, the chief commercial variety is the **Brewster**. The Bengal, a seedling from India, has been under observation for several years, but has not yet been extensively planted.

MANGOS*

USES: The mango may be eaten as a fresh fruit when ripened to softness to suit the individual taste, and it can also be cooked, frozen, and dried. It can be used in various ways when green, half ripe, or fully ripe. "As a fresh fruit, ripe, chilled mangos can be peeled and sliced and served as a salad or dessert. Mango blends well with ice cream and there are many ways of serving it in this manner, the most popular being as a sundae. Slices also mix well with other fruit, such as oranges,

*UFFVA

grapefruit, and papaya. The unpeeled fruits can be cut lengthwise or crosswise and the two halves twisted to pull them apart from the stone; they are served on the half shell and eaten with a spoon. In some countries, a special mango fork is used in which the center prong pierces the stone. The fruit is held with the fork while it is peeled and eaten. A fresh puree can be made with sugar added to serve over ice cream.

"In cooking, green or half-ripe fruit as well as ripe fruit may be used. Such dishes, as pies, tarts, shortcakes, Brown Betty, and nutbread can be made. Mango chutney, jam, jelly, preserves, sauce, pickles, and butter also can be made. Mangos can be preserved by canning. They may also be home-frozen.

"In Jamaica, starch is made of the unripe fruit. In India, the unripe fruit is much used in conserves, tarts, and pickles, and the kernels of the seeds are boiled and eaten in times of scarcity."

MARKETING SEASON: As shown by the following table of unloads of mangos in carlot equivalents in 41 cities, by rail and truck, most of the fruit is marketed from May through August. Florida and Mexico are the main sources. The average carlot equivalents totals 289. A carlot is considered to be 2700 flats by the Market News Branch, Fruit and Vegetable Division, Agricultural Marketing Service which is the source of the table. There are various size flats, and they contain from 12 to 17 lb. On the basis of 15-lb. flats, the 41 cities received 11,705,000 lb. Other areas than the 41 also received some, but the amount is not known. The total annual supply may be around 15 million lb.

VARIETIES: "The mango is not native to Florida and production here had its origin from seed, seedlings, and graftwood introduced from other countries. Of the many varieties introduced, none has ever become a commercial factor in Florida, but they did serve as a basis for crossing, mixing, and integrating to bring about new improved variety selections suitable to Florida for commercial production. It is now generally recognized that Florida has contributed the best varieties for the humid tropics of the world. These new Florida varieties have been selected for attractive external appearance, excellent eating quality, and, above all, productivity. The most recent trend has been to grow varieties with a higher tolerance to anthracnose disease. Florida varieties, compared with old world varieties, are usually colorful and have tremendous eye appeal." (The information in this paragraph is from Dr. E. S. Malo of the University of Florida and Seymour Goldweber, associate county agent, both in Homestead, Fla.)

"For many years, Haden was the only variety planted commercially" [in Florida.] "But because of its irregular bearing in commercial plantings, it has lost favor and is being replaced by some of the newer varieties that have shown promise of bearing crops nearly every year." (Desirable mango varieties should not only bear regularly, but a high

UNLOADS IN 41 CITIES BY COMMODITIES, ORIGINS AND MONTHS														
Origin	Jan.	Feb.	Mar.	Apr.	May	June	July	Aug.	Sept.	Oct.	Nov.	Dec.	1971	1970
Mangoes - Rail														
P. Rico	-	-	-	1	1	1	2	-	-	-	-	-	5	50
W. Indies	3	5	-	-	2	1	1	1	-	-	-	-	13	38
Total	3	5	-	1	3	2	3	1	-	-	-	-	18	88
Mangoes - Truck														
Fla.	-	-	-	-	11	60	43	25	3	-	-	-	142	98
C. America	-	-	-	-	1	-	-	-	-	-	-	-	1	
Mexico	-	-	8	17	36	29	17	22	1	-	-	-	130	83
W. Indies	-	-	-	3	-	-	2	-	-	-	-	-	5	13
Total	-	-	8	20	48	89	62	47	4	-	-	-	278	194
Com. Total	3	5	8	21	51	91	65	48	4	-	-	-	296	282

percentage of flowers should be perfect so that there will be little tendency to produce embryoless fruit; the fruit should be attractively colored; it should ship well and ripen with good quality; it should have satisfactory flavor and pulp that is free from coarse fiber, and it should be resistant to anthracnose.)

Varieties that seem to meet most of these requirements, especially in bearing good crops, and that are being planted commercially include Tommy Atkins, Irwin, Kent, Palmer, and Keitt. Zill is no longer commercially important.

In dollar value, the Keitt is the most important, followed by Tommy Atkins, Irwin, and Kent in that order.

Tommy Atkins "The tree is a thrifty grower and good producer. The fruit is medium to large (16 to 25 oz.), somewhat oblong, base rounded, stout stem inserted obliquely in shallow cavity, nak (stigmatic point of the fruit) inconspicuous, beak small and lateral, dorsal shoulder sloping, ventral shoulder raised, surface slightly undulating, apex round. The skin has a heavy purplish bloom, ground color orange yellow, blush bright red, dots large, numerous, yellow green. The flesh is juicy and moderately fibrous. The quality is fair to good. The fruit matures early in the season (early June into July), usually along with the late Hadens, or slightly after.

Irwin "Fruit medium size, to 5-in. long, weighing up to 16 oz., averaging about 12; shape rather elongate or narrow-ovate; ground color orange yellow with a bright red blush, lenticels small and white. Flesh fiberless with mild flavor, and quality good to very good. Stone relatively small. Season June and July. Fruit holds up well in shipping. Tree somewhat dwarf; fruits produced in clusters."

Kent "Fruit large, becoming 5 in. or more in length, averaging about 24 oz. in weight; shape ovate and rather thick and plump; ground color greenish yellow with a dark red blush and gray bloom, lenticels numerous, small, and yellow. Flesh juicy and fiberless, rich and sweet, and quality very good to excellent. Stone makes up 9 percent of the weight of the fruit. Season is July and August and sometimes early September. Fruit ships well and is one of the better late mangos. Growth habit is upright with ascending branches."

Palmer "Fruit large, to 6 in. long and to 2 lb. in weight, orange yellow with a red blush and pale bloom, lenticels large averaging about 25 oz.; shape elongated but full; ground color

and numerous. Flesh firm and with only a small amount of fiber, quality fair to good. Stone long and of medium size. Season July and August. Tree of moderate vigor and open in growth."

Keitt "Fruit large, to 4-3/4 in. long and to 24 oz. in weight (some are 2 lb. or more); shape oval, plump and thick; ground color yellow with a light pink blush and with a lavender bloom, lenticels numerous, small, and yellow to red in color. Flesh juicy, fiberless, except near the seed, flavor rich and sweet, and quality very good. Stone small, 7 to 8.5 percent of the weight of the fruit. Season is August and September. Fruit ships well and is considered the best of the very late mangos. Tree has a very peculiar habit of growth, producing long, arching branches and a scraggly, open appearance."

Haden "Fruit large, to 5-1/2 in. long and to 24 oz. in weight; shape oval and plump; ground color yellow with a crimson blush and with numerous white lenticels and a heavy bloom, producing an attractive, variegated appearance. Flesh juicy, nearly fiberless with sub-acid flavor and good quality. Season June and early July. Tree becomes quite large and spreading. Formerly much planted in commercial groves and dooryards."

Manila type "The Mexican mangos (imported by some American firms) have been of the Manila type, which is the member of the Filipino race. As a group, this race of mangos is considered to be fiberless, sweet tasting, rich in flavor, and without the turpentine flavor which, to a certain extent, is found in Indian mangos. The Manila mango originally came from the Philippine Islands; its cultivation is centered mainly in Cordoba, Mexico, and it is available from April through May and June. In general, time of fruit maturity varies from year to year, weather conditions determining how early or late. Sometimes fruit matures from two separate blooms, which of course results in variations in the mango season."

Mexican plantings. Mexico is reported to be shifting from Manila type mangos to Florida varieties. Mexico is said to have less trouble with anthracnose on this fruit than Florida. One report is that Mexico may soon outstrip Florida in production.

Hawaiian varieties. "Dr. R. A. Hamilton of the University of Hawaii estimated that Hawaii had 250 acres of commercial mangos in 1960. The varieties grown in Hawaii are different from those grown in Florida." However, Hawaiian mangos rarely reach the mainland and are not considered here.

CONTAINERS: "Except for a few shipments in 4/5 bu. cartons, mainly of large fruit to New York City, Florida uses the 1-layer flat cartons. There are two sizes, the smaller with net weight of 10 to 12 lb., the larger, referred to as the 'Forum' flat with mostly 13 to 15 lb. net. The trend has been toward the larger flat, and it is estimated that in 1971 at least two-thirds of shipments were in this package."

QUALITY: "This tropical fruit normally has a smooth outer skin, usually green with yellowish to red areas. It is round to oval, varying considerably in size, weighing from half a pound to a pound as usually found on the market. The reds and yellows increase as the fruit ripens. The pulp, when fully ripe, in the varieties usually marketed, is yellow, delicate, juicy, and has a flavor that reminds one of apricot and pineapple."

GRADES: There are no U.S. standard grades for mangos.

MELON BALLS [6/25/62]

Grade A: Color: Any included garnish shall have a uniform and bright color that is typical for the garnish and that does not detract from the overall appearance of the melon units; and that the melon balls: Have a bright overall appearance; possess a reasonably uniform color which is typical for well-ripened melons of the variety or varieties used; may have present not more than 10 percent of units which may have a reasonably bright appearance or may possess color which is typical for reasonably well-ripened melon flesh, are free from exceptionally pale cantaloupe units, dark green honeydew units, and units that otherwise fail "reasonably good color."

Size and Shape: The percentages, by count, of "almost spherical units" and "misshapen units" do not exceed the allowances for classification in Table I, and—notwithstanding the applicable allowance in Table I—the "almost spherical units" or "misshapen" units, either individually or collectively, do not materially affect the appearance of the product. **Defects:** Not more than 20 percent of unit with rind spots: Provided, that not more than 5 percent may be major rind spots and that not more than 2-1/2 percent may be serious rind spots. (One unit in a container is permitted to possess a minor rind spot, major rind spot, or serious rind spot, if such unit exceeds the allowable percentage: Provided, that in all sample units comprising the sample such units do not, on the average, exceed the allowance percentage; not more than an average of 1 seed per 16 oz. net weight; Provided, that no individual container may contain more than 1 seed per 4 oz. net weight or fraction thereof; and no membrane material or other defects which detract more than slightly from the appearance.) **Character:** Possess a tender texture typical of mature, well-ripened, properly prepared, and properly processed melon units; and consist of not more than 10 percent which are excessively soft, mushy, frayed, fibrous, tough, or rubbery; provided, that not more than 5 percent are tough or rubbery. (One unit in a container is permitted to be excessively soft, mushy, etc., if such units exceed the allowable percentage: Provided, that in all sample units comprising the sample, such units of fruit do not, on the average, exceed the allowable percentages.)

Grade B: Color: Means that any included garnish has a reasonably uniform and reasonably bright color that is typical for the garnish and that does not materially detract from the overall appearance of the melon units; and that the melon balls: have a reasonably bright overall appearance; possess a color which is typical for reasonably well-ripened melon flesh; may have present not more than 10 percent which may lack a reasonably bright appearance or may possess color which is not typical of well-ripened or reasonably well-ripened melon flesh; in the case of "Cantaloupe Type," not more than 10 percent may be exceptionally pale; in the case of "Honeydew Type," not more than 10 percent may be dark green, and in the case of either "Mixed—Cantaloupe and Honeydew" or "Mixed Honeydew and Cantaloupe" not more than a total of 10 percent may be exceptionally pale cantaloupe units and/or dark green honeydew units.

Size and Shape: See Grade A. Do not seriously affect the appearance. **Defects:** See Grade A. All wording is the same except as follows: Not more than 40 percent; provided, 10 percent, 5 percent. Not more than an average of 2 seeds per 16 oz. provided, that no individual container may contain more than 1 seed per 2 oz. of weight or fraction thereof; and no membrane material or other defects which materially detract from the appearance. **Character:** Possess a reasonably tender texture typical of reasonably mature, well-ripened, properly prepared, and processed melon units; and see Grade A. All wording is same except the percentages; 20 percent provided: 10 percent. **SStd:** Fails to meet requirements.

TABLE I
Allowances for uniformity of size and shape in frozen melon balls

	[A] Classification	[B] Classification
Spherical units	80 percent or more (by count)	60 percent or more (by count)
Almost spherical units and misshapen units	Total—20 percent or less (by count) but no more than—	Total—40 percent or less (by count) but no more than—
Misshapen units	3 percent (by count)	20 percent (by count)

NECTARINES*

USES: The nectarine can be used in any recipe that calls for peaches. Obviously, a main use is eating out of hand. Other uses are in compotes blended with a variety of other fruits; in salads of many kinds; as a garnish with meat or poultry; a cereal topping; sliced and topped with cream or ice cream; for shortcake; in frozen desserts, such as ice cream, sherbets, and parfaits; in tarts; in a variety of puddings; and how about a deep-dish fresh nectarine pie? Fresh nectarine ambrosia calls for nectarines, orange sections, sliced bananas, sugar, fresh lemon juice, vanilla extract, and shredded coconut. The combinations are limitless. Nectarines are also canned.

MARKETING SEASON: Nectarines are on the market mainly June through September, with peak in July and August. Imports from Chile provide a fair amount in February, and some in January and March. The following table shows monthly availability of nectarines expressed as a percentage of the total annual supply. This is based on unloads in 41 cities for 5 years. (* means less than 0.5 percent.)

MONTHLY AVAILABILITY OF NECTARINES EXPRESSED AS A PERCENTAGE OF THE TOTAL ANNUAL SUPPLY

Jan. %	Feb. %	Mar. %	Apr. %	May %	June %
1	4	*			11

July %	Aug. %	Sept. %	Oct. %	Nov. %	Dec. %
33	38	13	*		

VARIETIES: There are scores of nectarine varieties, differing in ways such as in size, whether clingstone or freestone, color and quality of flesh, exterior color, tree vigor, and earliness or lateness of ripening. More are being registered yearly. Eight new ones were introduced in 1969; 3 in 1968, 3 in 1967 as listed by the American Society for Horticultural Science. Fifty-two varieties are listed by the Federal State Market News Service as being sold at auctions in 1969. The California Tree Fruit Agreement Report for 1970 lists 37 varieties. Efforts are being made to develop more. All of the California nectarines shipped in 1970 had been developed since World War II. All modern nectarines have yellow rather than the white flesh of the older varieties, and the flesh is firmer, permitting shipment to distant markets.

Leading varieties ranked in order of volume of shipments in 1970, with number of containers shipped, were: (1) Early Sun Grand—1,240,644; (2) Sun Grand—953,288; (3) Late Le Grand—840,894; (4) Le Grand—425,813; (5) Red Grand—412,893; (6) Gold King—399,392; (7) Red June—284,925; (8) September Grand—196,596; (9) Independence—156,629; and (10) Regal Grand—136,187.

Here are descriptions of a few varieties:

Early Sun Grand Size medium; shape rather elongated, irregular, sometimes has a small fleshy tip; skin has bright red blush, often with indistinct stripes, over amber yellow undercolor, often greenish at stem end; flesh light amber, often with slight greenish cast, fine texture, and somewhat softer than most varieties, slight aroma; freestone; moves to market third week in June.

Sun Grand Size medium; shape slightly elongated, regular and smooth, with suture deeply grooved at tip; skin with bright red blush, often with darker spots or streaks, with red covering up to two-thirds or more of otherwise creamy to greenish yellow skin; flesh clear amber yellow, slightly streaked along suture, attractive bright red on stone cavity surface, fine-grained, firm-melting texture, flavor slightly tart, little aroma; freestone; to market fourth week in June.

Late Le Grand Size large to very large; shape round to oval, fairly smooth, and regular; skin amber yellow with a red blush over one-half or more of the surface; flesh light yellow but dark red in stone cavity; texture firm-melting, good flavor,

*UFFVA

NECTARINES

FRESH (4/23/66   51.3145)

GRADES: U.S. FANCY
        U.S. EXTRA NO. 1
        U.S. NO. 1
        U.S. NO. 2

slight aroma; clingstone; to market fourth week in July.

Le Grand Size large; shape round to oval, fairly smooth, and regular; skin amber yellow with a delicate blush on about one-fourth of the surface; flesh clear, light yellow, but dark red in stone cavity, texture firm-melting, good flavor, slight aroma; clingstone; to market third week in July.

Red Grand Size large; shape nearly round, smooth, and regular, with suture slightly grooved; skin light amber yellow with greenish cast, medium red blush with prominent splashing and spotting of deeper red; flesh whitish yellow, stone cavity area intensely stained with red, some red along suture line, texture firm-melting; clingstone; to market third week in July.

Gold King Size large; shape nearly round, regular; skin deep red color over one-third to one-half of surface, undercolor light green yellow or amber yellow; flesh light amber yellow, deep red next to stone, reddish along suture, flavor pleasing, somewhat tart; clingstone; to market second week in August.

Red June Size small to medium; shape uniform, slightly elongated; skin bright red blush shading to maroon and covering most of amber yellow skin; flesh light amber yellow with fine firm texture; freestone when fully ripe; to market first week in June.

September Grand Size large to very large; shape round, uniform; skin amber, brownish with dark red blush on one-fourth to one-half of surface, marked with numerous russet dots; flesh light, whitish amber, but dark red in stone cavity, texture firm, meaty, slight aroma; clingstone; to market first week in September.

Independence This is a selection by USDA from open-pollinated progeny of Red King at the U.S. Horticultural Field Station, Fresno, Calif. The original seedling was selected in 1960 by Dr. John H. Weinberger. Independence ripens in late June or early July at Fresno; the fruit is medium-sized, ovate, with a brilliant cherry red surface; flesh yellow, firm, texture good but not exceptional, flavor good; freestone; trees moderately vigorous and more productive than Early Sun Grand.

Regal Grand Size large to very large; shape round to oval, uniform; skin red blush, sometimes with dark mottling, over one-quarter to one-half of amber yellow skin; flesh light amber yellow with firm texture; clingstone; to market third week in August.

Flamekist This is a new USDA release and is from a seed of Gold King self-pollinated in 1959, at Fresno, selected by Dr. John H. Weinberger. Flamekist ripens about 3 weeks after the Elberta peach, and a few days earlier than September Grand. The fruit is large, ovate, and clingstone; flesh yellow, firm, smooth-textured, and of excellent quality; exterior color yellow with a red blush, if tree is not heavily shaded; trees moderately vigorous and productive.

Fantasia This is one of the newest USDA releases. It has resulted from a cross of Gold King with a seedling Red King in 1961 at the Fresno field station and was selected by Dr. John H. Weinberger. The fruit is large, ovate, and freestone; exterior color bright red over a bright yellow undercolor; flesh yellow, firm, smooth-textured, and of good quality. It has been market-tested. The trees are vigorous and productive. Besides being freestone, it is larger than the clingstone Red Grand in the same ripening period; and it is more highly colored than the clingstone Le Grand. It was released Nov. 14, 1969.

Flavortop This also is one of the newest USDA releases, announced Nov. 14, 1969. It resulted from an open-pollinated seed of Fairtime peach, produced in 1961 at the Fresno field station, and has been market-tested. It ripens at the same time as the regular Sun Grand variety. The fruit is large, ovate, and freestone; the exterior color at maturity mostly red over an attractive undercolor; flesh yellow, firm, smooth-textured, and of excellent quality; trees vigorous and productive.

Private plant breeders often patent their nectarine introductions. It may be interesting to look at the claims made for one of these patented fruits. "Autumn Grand—Originated in Le Grand, Calif. by F.W. Anderson, Merced, Calif. Introduced in 1969. Plant patent 2,894, June 10, 1969, assigned to Reedley Nursery, Inc., Reedley, Calif. Late Le Grand x unnamed seedling of Gold King. Tested as Anderson 23H890. Fruit large; uniform, globose, skin yellow, partially overspread with red; flesh yellow, clingstone; resembles Gold King, but distinguished by the absence of the red suture line which ripens before the remainder of the fruit, has better shipping quality, and longer shelf life, ripening 1 week later. Tree: large to medium; vigorous and spreading; productive and regular bearer; flower large; leaf glands reniform." (The selection of this description, among many, in no way indicates any endorsement or preference.)

QUALITY: "Look for rich color and plumpness and a slight softening along the seam of the nectarine. Most varieties have an orange yellow color (ground color) between the red areas, but some varieties have a greenish ground color. Bright looking fruits which are firm to moderately hard will probably ripen normally within 2 to 3 days at room temperature. Avoid hard, dull fruits or slightly shriveled fruits (which may be immature—picked too soon—and of poor eating quality) and soft or overripe fruits, or those with cracked or punctured skin, or other signs of decay. Russeting or staining of the skin may affect the appearance but not detract from the internal quality of the nectarine."

GRADES: U.S. grade standards for nectarines, effective April 23, 1966, provide for four grades, U.S. Fancy, U.S. Extra No. 1, U.S. No. 1 and U.S. No. 2. The principal trading grade is U.S. 1, though in California, under their marketing order, there is emphasis on keeping toward the top of the grade or better, especially with regard to tolerance for scarring. The entire standards for nectarines are available without charge from Fruit and Vegetable Division, Consumer and Marketing Service, USDA, Washington, D.C. 20250. It is not practical, because of space limitations, to do more than quote extracts here.

"U.S. No. 1 consists of nectarines of one variety which are mature but not soft or overripe, which are well formed, clean and free from decay, broken skins which are not healed, worms, worm holes, and free from injury caused by split pit, and free from damage caused by bruises, growth cracks, hail, sunburn, sprayburn, scab, bacterial spot, scale, scars,

russeting, other disease, insects or mechanical, or other means. At least 75 percent of the nectarines in any lot shall show some blushed or red color, except that there are no color requirements for nectarines of the John Rivers variety in this grade."

"Standard Pack. (a) Nectarines shall be fairly uniform in size and shall be packed in boxes, lugs, crates, cartons or baskets and arranged according to the approved and recognized methods. All such containers shall be tightly packed and well filled, but the contents shall not show excessive or unnecessary bruising resulting from overfilling. The nectarines in the shown face shall be reasonably representative in size, color, and quality of the contents of the container. Each wrapped fruit shall be fairly well enclosed by its individual wrapper. (b) When packed in closed containers, the size shall be indicated by marking the container with the numerical count, the pack arrangement, or the minimum diameter or minimum and maximum diameters in terms of inches and not less than 1/8 fractions of inches. (c) Boxes, lugs, or cartons: (1) Nectarines packed in containers equipped with cell compartments, cardboard fillers, or molded trays shall be of the proper size for the cells, fillers, or molds in which they are packed, and the number of nectarines in the container shall correspond to the count marked on the container. (2) In order to allow for variations incident to proper packing, when packed in other types of packs in lugs, cartons, or boxes, the number of nectarines in the container may vary not more than 2 from the number marked on the container."

California standards. While the California code, Chapter 24, has a section on nectarines, the state standards are superseded by the regulations issued under the Federal Marketing Order in effect since 1958. The Order provides higher standards than the California code.

ORANGES*

USES: Fresh oranges are used for slicing; for juice; for eating out of hand; for flavoring, including use of the peel; in fruit cocktail; in cakes, pies, puddings, sauces, ices; in salads; and with meats, poultry, and seafoods. Fresh oranges also are

*UFFVA

ORANGES

FLORIDA:

FRESH (1/31/73   51.1140)

GRADES: U.S. FANCY; U.S. NO. 1 Bright; U.S. NO. 1; U.S. NO. 1 Golden;

U.S. NO. 1 Bronze; U.S. NO. 1 Russet; U.S. NO. 2 Bright; U.S. NO. 2;

U.S. NO. 2 Russet; U.S. NO. 3

CALIFORNIA & ARIZONA:

FRESH (9/23/57   51.1085)

GRADES: U.S. FANCY; U.S. NO. 1; U.S. Combination; U.S. NO. 2

TEXAS & STATES OTHER THAN FLORIDA, CALIFORNIA, & ARIZONA:

FRESH (10/1/69   51.680)

GRADES: U.S. FANCY; U.S. NO. 1; U.S. NO. 1 Bright; U.S. NO. 1 Bronze; U.S. Combination; U.S. NO. 2; U.S. NO. 2 Russet; U.S. NO. 3

made into products or used in products including frozen, concentrated orange juice; powered orange juice; candied peel, marmalade; molasses; canned segments; chilled and bottled, single-strength juice; canned, single-strength juice; bottler's base for carbonated drinks or non-carbonated drinks; fruit puree for use in baked goods; wine; bitters; flavoring extracts; oils; pectin; citric acid; stock feed; bioflavonoids; vinegar; industrial alcohol; and even an auto fuel for midget racers.

In general, no part of the orange need be wasted, except for economic reasons, not even the seeds. Useful oils are extracted from seeds. Much material left over from processing is converted to cattle feed. In practice, however, there is much waste, and disposal of these wastes is a serious problem.

MARKETING SEASON: Oranges are on the market all year, with largest quantities December through April and lowest July through September.

The table shows the percentage of annual total of oranges marketed each month, based on unloads in 41 cities as reported by USDA. Since percentages are averaged and rounded, they do not necessarily total 100. Such percentages are useful as a general guide. The "All Fruit" classification includes Texas and Louisiana fruit and imported fruit as well as Florida and California-Arizona oranges.

VARIETIES: Oranges are generally divided into sour oranges and sweet oranges. The sour orange (Citrus aurantium) is important in this country as a rootstock and is also grown in some countries, particularly Spain, for its bitter or sour fruits. However, the sweet orange (Citrus sinensis) is the species grown commercially for fruit in this country and in most others where oranges are cultivated. Mandarins or tangerines (Citrus reticulata) are considered distinct from the sweet orange. However, there are tangors which are interspecific hybrids between some type of mandarin and the sweet orange.

In turn, the sweet orange can be divided into four principal kinds, the *common* orange such as the Florida or California Valencia; the *blood* or pigmented orange such as Ruby; the *acidless* orange grown in some Mediterranean areas; and the *navel* orange such as the Washington navel of California. This is a general classification for convenience, not a botanical classification.

Only the sweet oranges (Citrus sinensis) and one tangor, the Temple, because it is marketed in large volume as the "Temple orange," are dealt with in this report. There are a

MONTHLY AVAILABILITY OF ORANGES EXPRESSED AS PERCENTAGE OF ANNUAL TOTAL

	Jan. %	Feb. %	Mar. %	Apr. %	May %	June %	July %	Aug. %	Sept. %	Oct. %	Nov. %	Dec. %
All Fruit	13	11	11	10	8	6	4	4	4	6	7	15
Florida	13	12	13	11	8	3	*			7	14	18
Calif.-Ariz.	12	10	10	9	9	7	6	6	6	6	4	14

*Less than 1/2 of 1 percent.

large number of varieties of sweet orange and many sub-varieties, but only a few are of large commercial importance in this country. These are the Valencia, Washington navel, Hamlin, Parson Brown, Pineapple, and Temple. The Lue Gim Gong is considered a form of Valencia.

Valencia This variety constitutes about half of the U.S. orange crop in most years. It is the main variety in both Florida and California, and the most important orange variety in the world. It is round or slightly oval; medium to large; rind deep golden orange; apex rounded, slightly flattened, scarred; base smooth, rounded; calyx small, sharp-pointed; rind thin, smooth (or slightly pebbled); sections—9 or more clearly marked; flesh orange, of medium grain; juice sacs spindle-shaped, of medium size; juice abundant, colored; acidity and sweetness well combined; pulp melting; flavor rich, sprightly and vinous; quality excellent; seeds few, about 6, large, oval, plump. (The Lue Gim Gong and Pope Summer oranges, discussed separately, are not separate varieties but probably nucellar seedlings of Valencia.

In California, Valencia harvest begins around March 10 and is most active April 15 to October 15, ending November 15. Marketing is most active April 20 to October 20 and ends about December 15. In Florida, harvest begins about February 1, is most active in April, and ends early in July. The marketing period is the same as the harvesting period. In Arizona, harvest of Valencias is carried on February through May with most activity in March, and the marketing period is the same. In Texas, the Valencia harvest is January 15 through May 15 with most active period in February and March.

"The Valencia orange produced in California and Florida originated from a similar source. Thomas Rivers, an English nurseryman, imported this variety from the Azores into English glass houses or 'orangeries' which were special houses devoted to the growing of oranges under glass in England and parts of the Continent. He first catalogued it in 1865 under the name 'Excelsior'. Rivers sold this variety about 1870 to S.B. Parsons, a Long Island nurseryman, who, in turn, transferred some of the trees to E.H. Hart of Federal Point, Fla. At about this time (1870-72) A.B. Chapman, San Gabriel,

Calif. received the variety direct from Thomas Rivers. The tree was called 'Hart's Late' or 'Hart's Tardiff' in Florida and 'Valencia Late' in California, but when it became evident that these varieties were the same, the name 'Valencia' was adopted. The Valencia is of distinct value because it ripens late in the season after other varieties are off the market."

A citrus grower from Valencia, Spain identified the orange as the same as one grown in Spain, resulting in the naming of the variety. Where it originated is not known. The Azores have been suggested as one possibility and China as another.

Washington Navels The Washington navel is an important and distinctive variety that constitutes about 9 percent of the U.S. orange crop. Because of its distinctiveness, however, it is of much more consequence than this percentage indicates. This orange is not only seedless, but has an easily removable skin and is readily divided into segments for eating out of hand or for use in other ways, such as salads. The Washington navel or Bahia or Riverside navel is a rounded orange somewhat tapering toward the apex which terminates in an umbilicus, the typical "navel" that gives the variety part of its name; size sometimes large, such as 3-5/8 x 3-1/2 in.; color orange or orange yellow; base rounded or somewhat flattened and frequently creased; calyx small; rind smooth, tough, leathery, 1/8 to 1/4 in. thick; flesh rather coarse, deep orange yellow; juice sacs large, spindle-shaped; juice plentiful in good specimens; pulp melting; acidity and sweetness well blended; flavor rich, vinous; seedless; quality excellent.

"The Washington navel orange, which was first imported from Brazil in 1870 by the U.S. Dept. of Agriculture, was sent out from Washington under the name of Bahia. It first fruited and first attracted attention at Riverside, Calif. For these reasons, the variety came to be referred to commonly as the Washington navel, or the Riverside navel, and was distributed under these incorrect names. Later, horticulturists attempted to introduce the correct name, Bahia, but to no avail; the markets had become so familiar with the designation Washington navel that it could not be supplanted. As the variety has spread to other citrus sections, mainly from California ... it has come to be known all over the world as the Washington navel." (Certain strains or variants of the Washington navel are grown to a limited extent in California and Arizona, including Thompson, Robertson, Atwood Early and Gillette.)

"Contrary to popular opinion, the navel type of sweet orange is not a modern product. It was described and pictured by John Baptisti Ferrarius in 1646 and is apparently of early origin. As early as 1820, the Bahia form of the navel orange had made its appearance in Brazil, where orange trees had been introduced by the Portuguese settlers. Its excellent qualities were soon recognized and the variety was extensively propagated in the vicinity of Bahia.

"The story of the Washington navel orange is a dramatic illustration of the value of superior varieties of economic plants. In 1870, the citrus industry had begun in California, but there was no outstanding early and midseason variety of sweet orange generally adapted to the climate. The early mission seedlings and varieties introduced after the middle of the 19th century were being tested out by various growers but there was a lack of standardization in quality. The value of alertness in using the plant material that has been produced as a result of centuries of selection is nowhere better illustrated than by the timely action of the late William Saunders, then superintendent of gardens and grounds of the U.S. Dept. of Agriculture, Washington, D.C.

"In 1870, through the assistance of a missionary stationed at Bahia, Saunders imported from Brazil 12 navel orange trees in tubs. These were housed in the Department greenhouse at Washington, and propagations were made for distribution to the regions adapted to citrus culture. The first propagations were sent largely to Florida and California ... Mr. and Mrs. Luther C. Tibbets were attracted to the settlement at Riverside, Calif. and early in 1873, before starting her journey, Mrs. Tibbets visited the Government propagation gardens at Washington; there Mr. Saunders gave her two Bahia navel trees. They were carried to California and planted beside the Tibbets' cottage in Riverside. In February 1879, the fruit was awarded first prize over other navels exhibited from Orange County, and these two trees were used as the source of extensive plantings. The variety was referred to as the Washington navel to distinguish it from the Australian importations ... It is now generally recognized that one of the outstanding events in the economic and social development of California was the introduction of this orange in 1873."

In California, the navel harvest generally starts about Nov. 1, is most active Nov. 15 to May 15, and ends about May 31. The marketing period begins Nov. 5, is most active Nov. 20 to May 20, and ends about June 20. In Arizona, navels are harvested beginning November through February, with the most active period in December; and the marketing period is the same.

Hamlin This is the most important early variety in Florida and has given good results in Texas. It ripens from October to January. The acidity and sweetness are well blended giving it excellent flavor; the rind is smooth and glossy, usually thin; seeds are none or few. Fruit color is orange to cadmium orange; shape oblate to globose; size medium, diameter 2-1/2 to 2-7/8 in., membranes tender; rag, little; juice abundant, light orange, and quality excellent. It is a heavy bearer, therefore sometimes small.

The Hamlin was discovered in a grove planted in 1879 near Glenwood, Fla. which later came into possession of A.G. Hamlin. The grove was planted by Isaac Stone for Mrs. Mary H. Payne. The value of the variety was recognized, and following the great freeze of 1894-95, it was extensively planted in the DeLand section ... It is generally considered the best of the early-maturing oranges.

Parson Brown This is another early orange of Florida. It ripens in October and November. It is rounded, somewhat oblong; medium to large; skin yellow orange to yellow; apex and base rounded; rind smooth and bright, 1/8 to 3/16 in. thick; flesh rather coarse-grained, yellow; juice sacs medium to large; juice abundant, colored; pulp melting; acidity and sweetness not well blended unless picked quite early; seeds 10 to 19.

The variety was introduced by C.L. Carney of Lake Weir about 1878, having originated at Webster, Fla. in a seedling grove owned by Parson Brown. It is recognized as one of the best early-maturing oranges. It is widely planted in Florida, and grown to some extent in Texas, Arizona, and Louisiana.

Pineapple This is a midseason variety of Florida, mainly available in January and February. It has a glossy rind of deep orange color, is vinous and sprightly in flavor; seeds rather large and numerous. Form of the fruit is variable, from nearly round to slightly oblate; size medium to large; full ripe, well-colored specimens show a reddish tinge; flesh medium grain, orange yellow; juice abundant, yellowish; pulp melting; acidity and sweetness well blended; seeds 13 to 23.

The Pineapple originated near Citra, Fla. and received its name from the fine aroma reminiscent of the pineapple. It is probably the most important midseason orange in Fla. The fruit was found in the grove of James B. Owens and was first marketed in quantity by Bishop, Hoyt & Co. It was originally called the Hickory orange, but in 1883, was given the name Pineapple by H.B. Stevens, then manager of the Bishop and Hoyt groves.

Temple The Temple, a popular Florida fruit, with easily removable skin and readily parted sections, is believed to be a hybrid of tangerine and sweet orange. It is oblate, tapering slightly to the stem; size medium to large; color deep orange red; rind smooth or pebbled, leathery, thin; flesh orange and melting, free from rag, very juicy; flavor spicy, rich, vinous, and distinctive; acidity and sweetness well blended; seeds about 20. (There are many new plantings of Temple in California and Arizona, and production is increasing in those states each year. California-Arizona Temples are harvested from February through April with peak in mid-March.

The original of the Temple, a budded tree, was on the old homestead of William Chase Temple at Winter Park, Fla. Its origin is unknown, but a similar fruit has been reported as occurring in Jamaica. It is believed to belong to the group of hybrids known as tangors. The variety was purchased and introduced by the Buckeye Nurseries of Tampa, Fla. in 1917. It is less frost-resistant than the tangerines and more susceptible to cold than the sweet orange.

The Temple is harvested in Florida starting December 1; harvest is most active in early February, ending about April 1.

Lue Gim Gong This is a medium large, oblong fruit; skin deep orange red, surface smooth and finely pitted; sections 10 to 11; flesh deep orange; juice abundant; flavor a blend of sweet and sub-acid; seeds 4 to 8; pulp orange-colored; texture fine and tender. Marketing period same as Valencia.

The fruit was originated in 1886 by a Chinese horticulturist, Lue Gim Gong. It was thought to be a hybrid of the Valencia and the Mediterranean Sweet, but it is suggested it is merely a nucellar seedling of the Valencia. It was introduced by the Glen St. Mary Nurseries in 1912. It is difficult to distinguish from the Valencia.

Pope Summer This is a late maturing orange considered to be a selection from Valencia. It is similar to Valencia in maturity, size, shape, and quality of fruit. Some advantages are claimed for it. However, production continues small.

Navels Navels are also grown in Florida but they continue to be a minor part of production. Florida navel varieties include Washington, Surprise, Summerfield, Dream, and others.

Selection There are a great number of selections of the main varieties, each supposedly differing in some small but possibly important way from the variety. Breeders seek to find individuals that have superior cold resistance, or that grow faster, or mature fruit earlier, or hold fruit on trees longer, etc. However, it is difficult to determine what the characteristics of a selection are. It takes a long time and exposure to different conditions before qualities attributed to a selection can be checked out. For example, what may be learned about a supposedly cold-resistant selection in one freeze may be upset in another. If evidence is found that a selection varies significantly from the original variety, it may then become a new variety. The term "strain," formerly applied to such selections, is not permissible under the international Rules of Botanical Nomenclature.

CONTAINERS: Orange containers for wholesale shipment are mainly the fiberboard box, wirebound box, mesh bag and film bag. The nailed wooden box is no longer used.

California oranges are shipped in fiberboard cartons and wirebound boxes of 1794 cu. in. capacity, that is, 0.83 bu. or about 4/5 bu. The California code (Section 796.2) requires that all oranges intended for shipment out of the state shall be packed in closed, standard containers No. 58 and shall be uniform in size. There are five No. 58 containers, 10-11/16 in. width and 16-3/8 in. length, 10-1/4 in. depth (inside dimensions). Of these, four are fiberboard containers with freight container tariff numbers 6490, 6491, 6498 and 6499; and one wirebound (also commonly known as the half Bruce box) tariff No. 3607.

The California code also provides that all oranges (with minor exceptions) within the state shall be packed in either container No. 58 (as detailed above) or 61 which is a corrugated box 9-5/8 x 10-1/2 x 16-7/8 in., holding 1705 cu. in. or 0.79 bus.

The required strength and construction of the containers is set forth in state regulations.

All containers of packed oranges holding more than 25 lb. must bear in plain sight and in plainly legible letters on one outside end the number of the packer, an explicit address, the number and average diameter of the fruit, and the variety. Oranges are to be packed as provided by the code (Sec. 796.6) so compactly that they will not readily move in the container; the container must be level full of fruit; and the count of fruit in each container must be not less than the count marked, with a permissible count in excess not exceeding 6 percent. Count is from 24 to 270, diameter ranging down from 4.37 in. to 1.92 in.

Florida oranges are shipped in wirebound and fiberboard boxes of 4/5 bu. capacity; in wirebound boxes of 1-3/5 bu. and a few fiberboard boxes of this capacity; and in mesh bags and film bags of various sizes with the 5-lb. size predominating. In the 1964-65 season, 45 percent of the Florida fresh orange tonnage was shipped in *wirebound* boxes; and 37 percent in *fiberboard*. Of the wirebound tonnage, 69 percent was in 4/5 bu. containers; the remainder in 1-3/5 bu. Virtually all of the tonnage shipped in fiberboard was in the 4/5 bu. size. Of *mesh* bag tonnage, 66 percent was in the 5-lb. size, 25 percent in 8-lb., and 8 percent in 20-lb. Of *film* bag tonnage, 80 percent was in the 5-lb. size, 15 percent in 4-lb., and 5 percent in 8-lb. Also about 5 percent of the fruit was shipped in bulk.

The 1-3/5 bu. wirebound box (container No. 5004 of the Uniform Classification Committee) has inside dimensions of 11-15/16 x 11-15/16 x 24-1/4 in. Counts of oranges in this container run from 100 to 324. A 1-3/5 bu. corrugated box for shipments to prepackers or terminal packers has inside dimensions of 19-3/4 x 13-1/2 x 13-1/2 in.

The 4/5 bu. wirebound box has inside dimensions of 16-1/8 x 10-5/8 x 10-5/8 in. and is Container No. 3673. The 4/5 bu. corrugated boxes have inside dimensions of 17 x 10-5/8 x 9-5/8 for Containers No. 6481 and 6494; 17 x 11 x 9-3/4 in. for Containers No. 6482 and 6495. The count in these containers ranges from 50 to 163 fruits, except that for navel oranges it is 48 to 162. Count for oranges, Temple oranges, and tangelos is 50, 64, 80, 100, 125, and 163.

SERVINGS AND WEIGHTS: USDA reports that a California winter navel, 2-4/5 in. in diameter, weighs 180 grams (6.3 oz.) and a Florida orange 3 in. in diameter weighs 210 grams or 7.35 oz. One cup of California Valencia (summer) orange juice weighs 249 grams; a cup of early and mid-season Florida juice, 247 grams; and a cup of Florida late season Valencia juice, 248 grams.

Small oranges, 3 to a lb., provide about a half cup of fruit and juice per orange; or 3 servings per lb.; and require 33-1/2 lb., as purchased, to serve 100 persons. A *medium orange,* 2 to the lb., provides about 2/3 cup of fruit and juice per orange, 2 servings per lb., and requires 50 lb. to serve 100.

A pound of oranges, any size, is considered to provide 2.82 servings of 1/2 cup sections *with membrane,* requiring 35-1/2 lb., as purchased, for 100 servings; or 5.64 1/4 cup sections with membrane, requiring 17-3/4 lb., as purchased, for 100 servings. One pound, as purchased, equals 0.7 lb. ready to serve.

A pound of oranges provides 2.26 servings of 1/2-cup sections *without membrane,* and requires 44-1/4 lb., as purchased, to serve 100; and 1 lb. provides 4.52 servings of 1/4 cup sections without membrane and requires 22-1/4 lb. to serve 100. With such servings, 1 lb., as purchased, provides 0.56 lb. ready to serve.

A pound of oranges provides 1.83 servings of 1/2 cup of juice, requiring 54-3/4 lb., as purchased, for 100 servings; and 1 lb. of oranges provides 3.66 servings of 1/4 cup of juice, requiring 27-1/2 lb., as purchased, for 100 servings. One pound, as purchased, yields 0.5 lb. (1 cup) of juice.

QUALITY: "Oranges of highest quality are firm, heavy for size, and have good color, and reasonably fine textured skin for the variety. Puffy or spongy oranges are apt to be light in weight, lacking in juice content, and poor in quality. Oranges are practically always sound when shipped, but occasionally decay may develop before the fruit reaches the consumer. Decay is indicated by soft surface areas which are water-soaked in appearance and may break under slight pressure. Frequently, decayed areas are covered by mold. Age or injury may cause fruit to be wilted, shriveled, or flabby. Such oranges are undesirable.

"Florida and Texas oranges are frequently russeted ... Such russeting or discoloration does not affect flavor. Oranges from these states are also frequently dyed on the outer peel to improve appearance. This coloring does not affect edible quality. Individual fruits so colored are stamped 'color added'." (California summer Valencias sometimes regreen on the tree after reaching full ripeness and color, while other oranges, some on the same branch, may keep their golden color. No color is added.)

GRADES: Grades may be either federal, state, or private. In the case of oranges, state law is the main factor governing minimum grades that can be shipped and covers such factors as juice content, sugar, and acid. *Federal grades are not generally quoted* in selling oranges at shipping point, but this does not mean they are not used. Actually, all Florida oranges are graded according to federal grades, although at times the state imposes some added requirements for short periods. Certain published private brands are specified as being of a certain grade. In Texas, oranges are shipped on the basis of federal grades. In California and Arizona, however, federal grades are not much used, although they are the basis for the numerous private grades that are used.

Even though oranges are not quoted by federal grade, the buyer in making a deal can specify the desired U.S. grade "or equivalent" to protect himself.

There are separate federal grades for oranges grown in California and Arizona; for Florida oranges; and for oranges from Texas and states other than those named. *California-Arizona* oranges can be graded U.S. Fancy, U.S. No. 1, U.S. Combination and U.S. No. 2; *Florida* oranges, U.S. Fancy, U.S. No. 1 Bright, U.S. No. 1, U.S. No. 1 Golden, U.S. No. 1 Bronze, U.S. No. 1 Russet, U.S. No. 2 Bright, U.S. No. 2, U.S. No. 2 Russet and U.S. No. 3; *Texas* oranges and those from states other than named, U.S. Fancy, U.S. No. 1, U.S. No. 1 Bright, U.S. No. 1 Bronze, U.S. Combination, U.S. No. 2, U.S. No. 2 Russet, U.S. No. 3. Following are quoted samples of information from the standards:

California-Arizona oranges. "*U.S. Fancy* consists of oranges of similar varietal characteristics which are mature, well colored, firm, well formed, of smooth texture, and which are free from decay, broken skins which are not healed, hard or dry skins, exanthema, growth cracks, bruises (except those incident to proper handling and packing), dryness or mushy condition,

and free from injury caused by split, rough, wide, or protruding navels, creasing, scars, oil spots, scale, sunburn, dirt, or other foreign material, disease, insects or mechanical, or other means ... In order to allow for variations ... not more than 10 percent, by count, of the oranges in any lot may fail to meet the requirements relating to color. In addition, not more than 10 percent, by count, of the oranges in any lot may fail to meet the remaining requirements of the specified grade, but not more than 1/20 of this amount or 0.5 percent shall be allowed for decay at shipping point: Provided, That an additional tolerance of 2.5 percent, or a total of not more than 3 percent, shall be allowed for decay en route or at destination.

"**Standard Pack.** (a) Oranges shall be fairly uniform in size, and shall be packed in boxes or cartons, and arranged according to the approved and recognized methods ... (b) All such containers shall be tightly packed and well filled, but the contents shall not show excessive or unnecessary bruising because of overfilled containers ... When packed in cartons or in wirebound boxes, each container shall be at least level full at time of packing. (c) 'Fairly uniform in size' means that when oranges are packed for 113 carton count or smaller size, or equivalent sizes when packed in other containers, not more than 10 percent, by count, of the oranges in any container may vary more than 5/16 in. in diameter; when packed for sizes larger than 113 carton count, ... not more than 10 percent, by count, of the oranges in any container may vary more than 7/16 in. in diameter. (d) ... Not more than 5 percent of the containers in any lot may fail to meet the requirements for standard pack. [Requirements under California law are somewhat different.]

"**Standard Sizing and Fill.** (a) Boxes or cartons in which oranges are not packed according to a definite pattern do not meet the requirements of standard pack, but may be certified as meeting the requirements of standard sizing and fill: Provided, That the oranges in the containers are fairly uniform in size as defined [in Standard Pack]: And provided further, That the contents have been properly shaken down, and the container is at least level full at time of packing. (b) Not more than 5 percent of the containers in any lot may fail to meet the requirements. "(Requirements under California law are somewhat different. In Florida, regulations of the Florida

Citrus Commission provide that "well-filled" means that containers should be "full and the fruit firmly in contact with the top of the container when closed.")

Terms are defined in detail in the standard. A sample is given here. "'Well colored' means that the fruit is at least light orange in color with not more than a trace of green at the stem end, and not more than 15 percent of the remainder of the surface of the fruit shows green color."

California count. While the U.S. standards do not specify per box count as related to diameter, the California agricultural code (Sec. 796.6) does. It specifies that for containers No. 58 or 60, which are standard California orange boxes, respectively 16-3/8 x 10-1/2 x 10-11/16 and 16-7/8 x 10-1/8 x 10-1/2 in. length, depth, and width, the counts as related to diameters are as follows: 24 count, 4.370 in.; 32-3.97 in.; 36-3.82 in.; 40-3.68 in.; 48-3.47 in.; 56-3.3 in.; 72-3.04 in.; 88-2.84 in.; 113-2.6 in.; 138-2.42 in.; 163-2.29 in.; 180-2.22 in.; 210-2.07 in.; 245-198. in.; and 270-1.92 in.

Florida oranges. *"U.S. Fancy* consists of oranges of similar varietal characteristics which are well colored, firm, well formed, mature, and of smooth texture, and which are free from ammoniation, bird pecks, bruises, buckskin, creasing, cuts which are not healed, decay, growth cracks, scab, split navels, sprayburn, and undeveloped or sunken segments, and are free from injury caused by green spots or oil spots, pitting, rough and excessively wide or protruding navels, scale, scars, thorn scratches, and from damage caused by dirt or other foreign materials, dryness or mushy condition, sprouting, sunburn, riciness or woodiness of the flesh, disease, insects, or mechanical, or other means. (a) In this grade not more than 1/10 of the surface, in the aggregate, may be affected by discoloration. (b) If any lot of U.S. Fancy fruit also meets the internal specifications of U.S. Grade AA juice or U.S. Grade A juice, it may be so specified. In order to allow for variations ... 10 percent of the fruit in any lot may fail to meet the requirements of this grade, but not more than one-half of this amount, or 5 percent, shall be allowed for very serious damage and not more than 1/20 of the tolerance, or 0.5 percent, shall be allowed for decay at shipping point: Provided, That an

additional tolerance of 2.5 percent, or a total of not more than 3 percent, shall be allowed for decay enroute or at destination. None of the foregoing tolerances shall apply to wormy fruit.

"Standard Sizing. (a) Boxes, cartons, bag packs, or bulk loads in which oranges are not packed according to a definite pattern do not meet the requirements of standard pack, but may be certified as meeting the requirements of standard sizing: Provided, that the oranges are fairly uniform in size as defined in this section: and provided further, that when packing. (b) 'Fairly uniform in size' ... means that not more shaken down, and the container is at least level full at time of packing. (b) "Fairly uniform in size" ... means that not more than 10 percent by count of the fruits are outside the range of diameters given for the following pack sizes: 100s, 3-6/16 in. to 3-12/16 in.; 125s, 3-3/16 in. to 3-9/16 in.; 163s, 2-15/16 in. to 3-4/16 in.; 200s, 2-11/16 in. to 3 in.; 252s, 2-8/16 in. to 2-12/16 in.; 342s, 2-4/16 in. to 2-8/16 in. (c) Not more than 5 percent of the containers in any lot may fail to meet the requirements of standard sizing."

PAPAYAS*

USES: "This esteemed, melonlike fruit is served at the breakfast table or as a dessert, often flavored with juice of limes (or lemons), but it is also made into preserves and sherbets. The juice is also extracted and canned. Green papayas can be cooked as a vegetable like squash." The ripe fruit may also be pulped and made into pies, nectars, purees, and juice; and firm fruit can be made into sweet pickles and into candied or crystallized fruit. It is good with seeds scooped out and ice cream placed in the hollow; and is a delightful addition to salads, fruit cups, and cocktails.

"The preparation of a papaya is simple ... cut lengthwise, scoop out the seeds. For salad, appetizer or dessert, pare as you would an apple, and then it can be sliced or cubed." It goes well with any citrus fruit, especially the more tangy kinds such as grapefruit and lemon or lime which set off the blandness and sweetness of the papaya.

The Florida Agricultural Extension Service has offered

*UFFVA

many ideas and recipes for use of papayas in its Circular 162 of May 1957. These include frosted papaya cocktail, papaya and orange cocktail, mixed fruit cocktail in grapefruit shells, papaya milk shake, papaya and apple scallop, papaya en cream, papaya sauce cake, golden papaya salad, papaya-coconut pie, papaya citrus salad, papaya-orange custard, papaya milk sherbet, papaya-pineapple marmalade, and others.

MARKETING SEASON: Papayas can be flowering and fruiting throughout the year, so the supply is not sharply seasonal. Supply depends more on the demand than on crop, which is usually adequate to satisfy consumer requirements. Following is a table of availability of Hawaiian papayas in the U.S., by months, shown as a percentage monthly of the annual total, which runs around 7 million lbs.

MONTHLY AVAILABILITY OF PAPAYAS AS A PERCENTAGE OF THE TOTAL ANNUAL SUPPLY

JAN. %	FEB. %	MAR. %	APR. %	MAY %	JUNE %
8	8	7	9	11	10

JULY %	AUG. %	SEPT. %	OCT. %	NOV. %	DEC. %
9	7	7	9	9	7

VARIETIES: "Most varieties of papayas are of indefinite types, with considerable variation exhibited in seedlings from a single fruit. The principal variety, and the one on which the industry is based in Hawaii, is called the **Solo**. It probably originated in Barbados, British West Indies, where G. P. Wilder of Honolulu purchased a single fruit and sent the seed to Hawaii. J.E. Higgins named it, implying that the fruit is adequate for one individual. The Solo is approximately 6 in. long and 4 in. wide, weighs from 14 to 16 oz., and is pear-shaped.

"Some of the (other) named hermaphroditic varieties are **Bluestem, Graham, Betty, Fairchild, Kissimee, and Hortus Gold.** [In growing] it is well to use varieties developed locally since papayas are sensitive to climatic changes.

"The '**Line 10**' Solo is a new, small-fruited, uniform, inbred strain of Solo papaya considered to be well suited to requirements of Hawaii for the mainland export trade. It is similar in many respects to the Kapoho purple-flowered strain common-ly grown in the Kapoho-Pahoa area for mainland export trade. Line 10, however, presents certain notable advantages over the Kapoho strain in size and uniformity of fruit. Because of these advantages, Line 10 is being named and released as a desirable commercial strain for trial by growers."

GRADES: Hawaii has 3 grades in its Wholesale-Standards for Hawaii-Grown Papayas, Hawaii Fancy, Hawaii No. 1, and Hawaii No. 2. "Hawaii No. 1 consists of Solo-type (a variety) papayas, which are mature but not overripe, clean, well trimmed, meet soluble solids requirements, fairly well formed, fairly smooth; and which are free from decay, breakdown, internal hard lumps, catfaces, brown spot, scars, disease, insects, mechanical, or other means. Unless otherwise specified or unless destined for export, the weight of each papaya shall be not less than 14 oz. nor more than 32 oz. in weight. Unless destined for export, papayas shall be pyriform in shape. (Note: Shipments to the U.S. are not exports but domestic, so that the detailed weight requirements of the grade apply.)

In order to allow for variations, other than size, incident to proper grading and handling, not more than a total of 10 percent, by count, of the fruit in any lot may fail to meet the requirements of this grade, but not more than 1/2 of this amount, or 5 percent, shall be allowed for serious damage by any cause, including not more than 1 percent for papayas affected by decay or breakdown.

"**Size Classification.** In lieu of specifying size by weight, the size of papayas in any lot may be specified in connection with the grades, as 'Hawaii No. 1 Small', 'Hawaii No. 1 Large', in accordance with the facts. The following classifications may be used for designating size of papayas: Small, 10 to 13 oz.; medium, 13 to 16 oz.; large 16 to 32 oz.; and extra large, over 32 oz. ... Papayas in any container shall be fairly uniform in size ... [meaning] that the difference in weight between the largest papaya and the smallest papaya in any container shall not be greater than 8 oz. ... In order to allow for variations incident to proper sizing, not more than a total of 10 percent, by count, of the papayas in any lot may vary from the size specified." (The grades give further details on application of tolerances.)

PEACHES*

USES: The peach is a popular fruit. Not only is it eaten fresh out of hand, but it is canned in great quantities and is used in appetizers, garnishes, salads, desserts and baked goods, jellies, preserves, nectar, and pickles. It is also marketed in a dried form; makes excellent cordials and brandies; and in recent years, has been marketed in frozen form.

As appetizer, used with other fruits, such as blueberries, for a compote. The hollowed, shell-like shape of the halved peach lends itself to a variety of fillings, from single jellies to flaming sugar cubes. Use finely diced peaches and chopped walnuts with chicken salad. *For other salads*, use fresh peaches with grapes and cottage cheese; halve and top with other fruit and sour cream; or combine with other fruit and serve plain or set in gelatin. *Use as garnish*, such as broiled with lamb chops, grilled with barbecued chicken, glazed with baked ham, or filled with cranberries to accompany turkey; and *sliced for cereal topping*.

For dessert, serve whole or sliced, plain or topped with sweet, sour, or whipped cream; in baked desserts, puddings, pies, cobblers, dumplings, or shortcake; or *in frozen desserts*, such as ice cream, sherbets and parfaits. Substitute peaches for cherries in Cherries Jubilee or for strawberries in Baked Alaska.

VARIETIES: According to the USDA's 1937 Yearbook of Agriculture, American pomologists in the past century tried to divide peaches into four groups or races: (1) the Persian race, brought to North America by the early settlers, best represented by varieties of the Crawford group; (2) the north China or Chinese Cling race, characterized by large fruits with tender skin and flesh, vigorous tree growth, abundant and regular bearing, and including such Chinese varieties as Chinese Cling, Chinese Free, and later descendants Belle and Elberta; (3) the south China race, sometimes called the Honey, represented by varieties that bear small, oval to pointed white-fleshed fruits with a peculiar honey-sweet flavor, and adapted to the U.S. only in some subtropical sections; (4) the Peeto race, warm-climate type with trees inclined to be evergreen and to bear fruits that are much flattened endwise, white-skinned and white-fleshed, and sweet to very sweet.

However, all varieties hybridize freely, and there has been so much crossing between the groups that is is practically impossible to classify many of our present yellow and white-fleshed varieties on this basis.

It is customary to classify peaches also as "clingstone" or "freestone." The flesh of the clingstone peach is firmly attached to the stone, while the flesh of the freestone peach is easily separated from the stone. There are also varieties that are semi-freestone. In general, freestone types go to fresh market, and the clingstones are processed. In 1961, of the California peach crop totalling 40 million bushels, 28 million bushels were clingstone and 12 million bushels were freestone. Within both the clingstone and freestone types are varieties that have white flesh and varieties that have yellow flesh. *In general, yellow-fleshed peaches are in greater demand than white.*

There are thousands of named varieties. As far back as 1916, Hedrick published a list of 2,818. However, only about 40 varieties are grown commercially in the United States, and few, if any, of them possess all of the desirable characteristics. In the past two decades or so, plant breeders have introduced many new varieties which they have selected because of some of the following qualities: excellent taste; profitable yield; uniform and desirable size; red color of the skin; flesh color with red streaks near the pit; firmness to allow shipping; resistance to or tolerance of bacterial leaf spot; hardiness for cold weather; season of harvest; and special adaptability for processing or fresh market. It would be difficult to find a new variety superior in all of these and other desirable characteristics. Nevertheless, considerable progress has been made, and at present most commercial peach growers plant several varieties which possess most of the desirable characteristics and furnish fruit for harvest over a period of about 2 months.

The present principal varieties for fresh market are: Dixired, Redhaven, Triogem, Redglobe, Sunhigh, Loring, Redskin, Elberta, J.H. Hale, and Rio Oso Gem. Other popular varieties are Cardinal, Coronet, Keystone, Blake, Hiland, and Sullivan Early Elberta. Some promising new varieties are Earlired, Sunhaven, and Earlihale.

*UFFVA

Following are descriptions of leading varieties, arranged according to season. The term "selfed" means self-pollinated, which is the transference of pollen from the anthers of a flower to its own stigmas or to those of another flower on the same plant. "Cross-pollinated," using the symbol X, pertains to a plant which has undergone transference of pollen from flower of one plant to a flower of another plant.

Dixired is a very early, medium-sized, round, highly colored clingstone with a light pubescence (down); yellow-fleshed, medium texture, firm, good quality; ships well. Tree is upright, vigorous, and productive. Originated by USDA and introduced in 1945. From Halehaven selfed. Ripens 6 weeks before Elberta.

Redhaven is an early, medium-sized, oval freestone to clingstone (the fruits tend to cling to stone some seasons) with very red skin which is tough; yellow-fleshed, non-browning, fine texture, very firm, good quality; ships well. Tree is large, spreading, productive, and hardy. The trees set heavy crops and require early and thorough thinning in order to size properly. Introduced in Michigan in 1940. Halehaven X Kalhaven. Ripens 4 weeks before Elberta.

Triogem is an early, medium to large, oval, highly colored freestone with light pubescence; yellow-fleshed, medium texture, firm, high quality; excellent shipper. Tree is spreading, vigorous, and productive. Requires thinning to size properly. Originated by New Jersey Ag. Exp. Station in 1923. J.H. Hale X Marigold. Ripens 3 weeks before Elberta.

Redglobe is a midseason, medium, round, highly colored freestone with light pubescence; yellow-fleshed, medium texture, firm, good quality; ships well. Tree spreading, vigorous, and productive. Introduced by USDA in 1954. (Admiral Dewey X St. John) X Fireglow. Ripens 2 weeks before Elberta.

Sunhigh is a large, midseason, oval, highly colored freestone with short pubescence; yellow-fleshed, medium texture, firm, excellent quality; packs and ships well. Tree is upright, productive although very susceptible to bacterial spot, and blossoms relatively early. It is an established variety in the East but often lacks attractiveness in California. Sunhigh is popular with the trade, and for the midseason remains one of the best varieties from the standpoint of the consumer.

Introduced in New Jersey in 1938. J.H. Hale X New Jersey 40 (Carmen X Slappy). Ripens 2 weeks before Elberta.

Loring is a midseason, medium-sized, lightly colored freestone; yellow-fleshed, medium texture, firm, good quality; handles well for commercial packing. Tree is upright, vigorous, and productive. Originated by Missouri State Fruit Exp. Station and introduced commercially in 1946. Frank X Halehaven. Ripens 1 to 1-1/2 weeks before Elberta or a few days after Sunhigh.

Redskin ripens with Elberta. It is a large, almost round, highly colored freestone; yellow-fleshed, medium texture, firm, good quality, although slightly astringent at times; ships well. Tree is spreading, moderately vigorous and productive, but it must be thinned well to attain good size. Quality slightly superior to Elberta, and it is earlier and more productive than Elberta. Released by Maryland Ag. Exp. Station in 1944. J.H. Hale X Elberta.

Elberta is a late-season, large, oval freestone, with a bright blush; yellow-fleshed, firm, juicy (called by scientists "melting"), medium quality; excellent shipper. Tree is large, upright, productive, but of medium hardiness. Though the tree is tender in bud and the fruit is of mediocre quality, the following qualities have combined to maintain it in its leading position, though it is gradually decreasing in popularity: large size, good appearance, excellent ability to withstand shipment, adaptability to many regions, and the fact that it is so well known in every market. Originated from an open pollinated tree of Chinese Cling grown by Samuel H. Rumph of Marshallville, Ga. in 1870.

J.H. Hale is a late, round, brightly colored freestone with almost no pubescence; yellow-fleshed, firm, good quality; excellent shipper—a standard for distant fresh-market shipping. Tree is upright, medium vigor, and lacks hardiness. Blossoms do not produce viable pollen and require cross-pollination. Chance seedling by J.H. Hale of Glastonbury, Conn. and introduced in 1912. Ripens with or about 1/2 week after Elberta.

Rio Oso Gem is a late, large round freestone with unusually well-colored skin; yellow-fleshed, medium texture, firm, excellent quality; ships well. Tree is small in most areas,

PEACHES

FRESH (6/15/52   51.1210)
GRADES: U.S. FANCY; U.S. EXTRA NO. 1; U.S. NO. 1; U.S. NO. 2
        CONTAINERS
        U.S. Standard bushel baskets) U.S. Standard half-bushel baskets; Standard western boxes; wire-bound &
        fiber board boxes; Cell compartments or molded trays
CLINGSTONE PEACHES:
CANNED (6/20/73   52.2561)

GRADES:	"A" OR "FANCY"	"B" OR "CHOICE"	"C" OR "STANDARD"			"D"	"SUB-STANDARD"		
Minimum Score:	90	80	70			60	Less than 60		
	NET WEIGHT OZ.	NET WEIGHT METRIC	DRAINED WEIGHT			DRAINED WEIGHT METRIC			
			OZ. Extra Heavy Syrup	OZ. Heavy Syrup	OZ. Other Liquid Med.	Extra Heavy Syrup	Heavy Syrup	Other Liquid Med.	
Sliced									
No. 8Z Tall	5.4	153.1 g	4.3	4.5	4.6	121.9 g	127.6 g	130.4 g	
No. 303	10.7	303.3 g	9.1	9.3	9.5	258.0 g	263.6 g	269.3 g	
No. 2½	19.0	538.6 g	16.3	16.7	17.1	462.1 g	473.4 g	484.8 g	
No. 10	72.0	2.0 kg	62.5	64.5	66.5	1.8 kg	1.8 kg	1.9 kg	
Diced in any liquid medium			DRAINED WEIGHT OZ.			DRAINED WEIGHT METRIC			
No. 8Z Tall	6.1	172.9 g	4.7			133.2 g			
No. 303	11.7	331.7 g	9.8			277.8 g			
No. 2½	20.7	586.8 g	17.5			496.1 g			
No. 10	77.0	2.2 kg	68.2			1.9 kg			
Heavy Pack									
No. 2½	—	—	18.6			527.3 g			
No. 10	86.0	2.4 kg	73.5			2.1 kg			
Solid Pack unsweetened									
No. 2½	—	—	24.1			683.2 g			
No. 10	—	—	89.5			2.5 kg			

CANNED CLINGSTONE PEACHES

	NET WEIGHT OZ.	NET WEIGHT METRIC	DRAINED WEIGHT			DRAINED WEIGHT METRIC		
			OZ. Extra Heavy Syrup	OZ. Heavy Syrup	OZ. Other Liquid Med.	Extra Heavy Syrup	Heavy Syrup	Other Liquid Med.
Halves								
No. 8Z Tall	5.4	153.1 g	4.3	4.5	4.6	121.9 g	127.6 g	130.4 g
No. 303	10.6	300.5 g	9.1	9.3	9.5	258.0 g	263.6 g	269.3 g
No. 2½								
7 count or more	18.7	530.1 g	16.2	16.6	17.0	459.3 g	470.6 g	482.0 g
6 count or less	18.0	510.3 g	15.6	16.0	16.4	442.3 g	453.6 g	464.9 g
No. 10								
24 count or more	70.5	2.0 kg	62.0	64.0	66.0	1.8 kg	1.8 kg	1.9 kg
23 count or less	69.0	2.0 kg	60.5	62.5	64.5	1.7 kg	1.8 kg	1.8 kg
Quarters								
No. 8Z Tall	5.5	155.9 g	4.3	4.5	4.6	121.9 g	127.6 g	130.4 g
No. 303	11.0	311.8 g	9.1	9.3	9.5	258.0 g	263.7 g	269.3 g
No. 2½	19.3	547.2 g	16.2	16.6	17.0	459.3 g	470.6 g	482.0 g
No. 10	74.0	2.1 kg	62.0	64.0	66.0	1.8 kg	1.8 kg	1.9 kg
Mixed pieces of ir-regular sizes & shapes								
No. 8Z Tall	—	—	4.3	4.5	4.6	121.9 g	127.6 g	130.4 g
No. 303	—	—	9.1	9.3	9.5	258.0 g	263.7 g	269.3 g
No. 2½	19.3	547.2 g	16.2	16.6	17.0	459.3 g	470.6 g	482.0 g
No. 10	74.0	2.1 kg	62.0	64.0	66.0	1.8 kg	1.8 kg	1.9 kg

SYRUP	SPECIFIC GRAVITY (BRIX MEASUREMENTS)
"Extra heavy syrup" or "Extra heavily sweetened fruit juice & water" or "Extra heavily sweetened fruit juice"	22° to 35°
"Heavy syrup" or "Heavily sweetened fruit juice and water" or "Heavily sweetened fruit juice"	18° or more but less than 22°
"Light syrup" or "Lightly sweetened fruit juice and water" or "Lightly sweetened fruit juice"	14° or more but less than 18°
"Slightly sweetened water" or "Extra light syrup" or "Slightly sweetened fruit juice and water" or "Slightly sweetened fruit juice"	10° or more but less than 14°
"In water"	N.A.
"In fruit juice and water"	N.A.
"In fruit juice"	N.A.
"Artificially sweetened"	N.A.

CANNED FREESTONE PEACHES

CANNED FREESTONE PEACHES (6/20/73   52.2601)

GRADES:	"A" OR "FANCY"	"B" OR "CHOICE"	"C" OR "STANDARD"	"D"	"SUB-STANDARD"
Minimum Score:	90	80	70	60	Less than 60

	NET WEIGHT OZ.	NET WEIGHT METRIC	DRAINED WEIGHT		DRAINED WEIGHT	
			OZ. Extra Heavy Syrup	OZ. Other Liquid Mediums	METRIC Extra Heavy Syrup	METRIC Other Liquid Mediums
Halves						
No. 8' Tall	5.6	158.8 g	4.1	4.3	116.2 g	121.9 g
No. 303	11.0	311.8 g	8.6	8.9	243.8 g	252.3 g
No. 2½						
7 count or more	19.4	550.0 g	15.2	15.7	430.9 g	445.1 g
6 count or less	19.0	538.6 g	14.8	15.3	419.6 g	433.8 g
No. 10						
24 count or more	73.0	2.1 kg	68.5	60.0	1.9 kg	1.7 kg
23 count or less	72.0	2.0 kg	57.5	59.0	1.6 kg	1.7 kg
Quarters & mixed pieces of irregular sizes & shapes						
No. 8Z Tall	5.7	161.6 g	4.2	4.4	119.1 g	124.7 g
No. 303	11.3	320.4 g	8.8	9.1	249.5 g	258.0 g
No. 2½	19.9	564.2 g	15.5	16.0	439.4 g	453.6 g
No. 10	76.0	2.2 kg	60.5	62.0	1.7 kg	1.8 kg
Sliced						
No. 8Z Tall	5.6	158.8 g	4.1	4.3	116.2 g	121.9 g
No. 303	11.1	314.7 g	8.6	8.9	243.8 g	252.3 g
No. 2½	19.6	555.7 g	15.2	15.2	430.9 g	445.1 g
No. 10	74.0	2.1 kg	58.0	59.0	1.6 kg	1.7 kg
Solid pack unsweetened			DRAINED WEIGHT OZ.		DRAINED WEIGHT METRIC	
No. 2½	—	—	22.6		640.7 g	
No. 10	—	—	87.5		2.5 kg	
Heavy pack						
No. 10	—	—	67.5		1.9 kg	

CANNED FREESTONE PEACHES

SYRUP

"Extra heavy syrup" or "Extra heavily sweetened fruit juice and water" or "Extra heavily sweetened fruit juice."

"Heavy syrup" or "Heavily sweetened fruit juice and water" or "Heavily sweetened fruit juice"

"Light syrup" or "Lightly sweetened fruit juice and water" or "Lightly sweetened fruit juice"

"Slightly sweetened water" or "Extra light syrup" or "Slightly sweetened fruit juice and water" or "Slightly sweetened fruit juice"

"In water"

"In fruit juice(s) and water"

"In fruit juice(s)"

"Artificially sweetened"

SPECIFIC GRAVITY (BRIX MEASUREMENTS)

22° to 35°

18° or more but less than 22°

14° or more but less than 18°

10° or more but less than 14°

N.A.
N.A.
N.A.
N.A.

FROZEN (7/3/61   52.3551)
DEHYDRATED (6/30/74   52.3911)

GRADES:	"A" OR "FANCY"	"B" OR "CHOICE"	"SUBSTANDARD"
Minimum Score:	85	70	Less than 70

DRIED (5/24/67   52.5801)

GRADES:	"A" OR "FANCY"	"B" OR "CHOICE"	"C" OR "STANDARD"	"D" OR "SUBSTANDARD"

lacking in vigor but moderately productive. Popular because of fruit size, firmness, attractiveness, and time of ripening. It is classed among the better varieties to follow Elberta. Originated in Rio Oso, Calif. by W.F. Yerkes. Parentage is unknown. Ripens 1 week after Elberta.

CONTAINERS: In the Eastern, Southern, and Central states, peaches for commercial shipment have been packed almost entirely in baskets which are faced and jumble filled. The tub-type basket with a flat, sawed-wood bottom was favored, and the 3/4- and 1/2-bu. has replaced the full bu. basket. In 1962, a 3/4-bu., wirebound, veneer crate with corrugated ends and a partial telescope corrugated cover was introduced. Indications are that it may be the major container for fresh peaches in all sections east of the Rockies. Also gaining in acceptance is a flat-top basket resembling the 3/4-bu. basket but with no handles, and so constructed that the face bulge of conventional baskets is almost eliminated.

Although baskets have far exceeded other containers in volume used throughout the United States, they have many disadvantages in shipping, such as lack of structural strength necessary to prevent buckling; tendency to cut and bruise the peaches, and difficulty in loading to prevent shifting in transit. In 10 test shipments conducted by USDA, the percent of bruising in various containers was as follows: 3/4 bu. basket-bulge cover, 15.7 percent; 3/4 bu. basket-flat cover, 11.9 percent; 3/4 bu. fiberboard box, 7.1 percent; 1-1/9 bu. wirebound crate, 8.8 percent; tray-pack wood box, 3.8 percent; and tray-back fiberboard box 2.3 percent.

The wirebound veneer crate has inside dimensions 17 x 10-7/8 x 10-7/8 in.; capacity 1987 cu. in. or .924 bu.; net weight 38 lb. The 3/4-bu. basket measures 15-3/4 in. minimum inside diameter at the top, maximum outside diameter at the top is 16-7/8 in.; capacity is 1612 cu. in.; net weight 36 to 39 lb., depending on bulge (Container No. 8055 of Tariff 823-D). A *bushel basket* has capacity of 2150 cu. in. and net weight of 47 to 52 lb. *Fiberboard peach box*, full telescope tray pack (No. 6615 of Tariff 823-D) measures 5 or 5-3/4 x 13-1/2 x 16-1/8 in. inside dimensions. An experimental fiberboard container used in testing 4-lb. consumer tills has inside dimensions 20-7/8 x 13-1/6 x 9-7/8 in.

In the western states, peaches are usually marketed in the western peach box, the Los Angeles lug, or Sanger lug. The Sanger lug differs in that it is not quite as deep as the L.A. lug. *The western peach box*, which is always lidded, generally offers good protection to peaches and makes an attractive display package. Peaches are sized, wrapped, and place-packed in 2 layers. Dimensions are 5-3/4 x 11-1/2 x 18-1/8 in. (Container 1310 of Tariff 1-G); weight 18 lb. The depth may vary from 4-1/2 to 5-3/4 in. to accommodate different sizes of fruit. *The Los Angeles lug* has inside dimensions 5-3/4 x 13-1/2 x 16-1/8 in.; capacity 1250 cu. in. and net weight 22 to 24 lb. (Container 1026 of Tariff 1-G).

SERVINGS AND WEIGHTS: One cup of sliced peaches weighs 168 gr. or 6 oz. ... One peach 2-1/2 x 2 in. in diameter weighs 114 gr. (4.1 oz.). The skin and pit is 12 percent of the weight of such a peach. (Agriculture Handbook No. 8, USDA).

One lb. of medium-sized peaches serves 4; and 25 lb. serve 100. A pound when sliced raw provides 3-1/2 servings of 1/2 cup and 29 lb. sliced serves 100. For 1 lb., ready-to-serve raw, use 1.32 lb. (about 1 lb. 5 oz.) as purchased. One quart of raw sliced peaches weighs 1.68 lb. (about 1 lb. 11 oz.). A bushel of peaches weights 47 to 52 lb.

QUALITY: Good quality peaches are bright and fresh in appearance. Other prime measures of quality of peaches are ripeness and soundness. The best indicator that a peach is ripe is that the "ground" (background) color of the skin is either yellowish or creamy. Red color or "blush" may also be present in differing degrees, depending on the variety, but red color alone is not a true sign of edible quality. A green ground color suggests that the peaches were immature when picked; such peaches do not ripen well. They will shrivel or become flabby, with the flesh tough, rubbery, and lacking in flavor. Sound peaches are firm, or fairly firm, and are free from bruise marks. Overmature peaches or soft peaches should be avoided unless they are for immediate use.

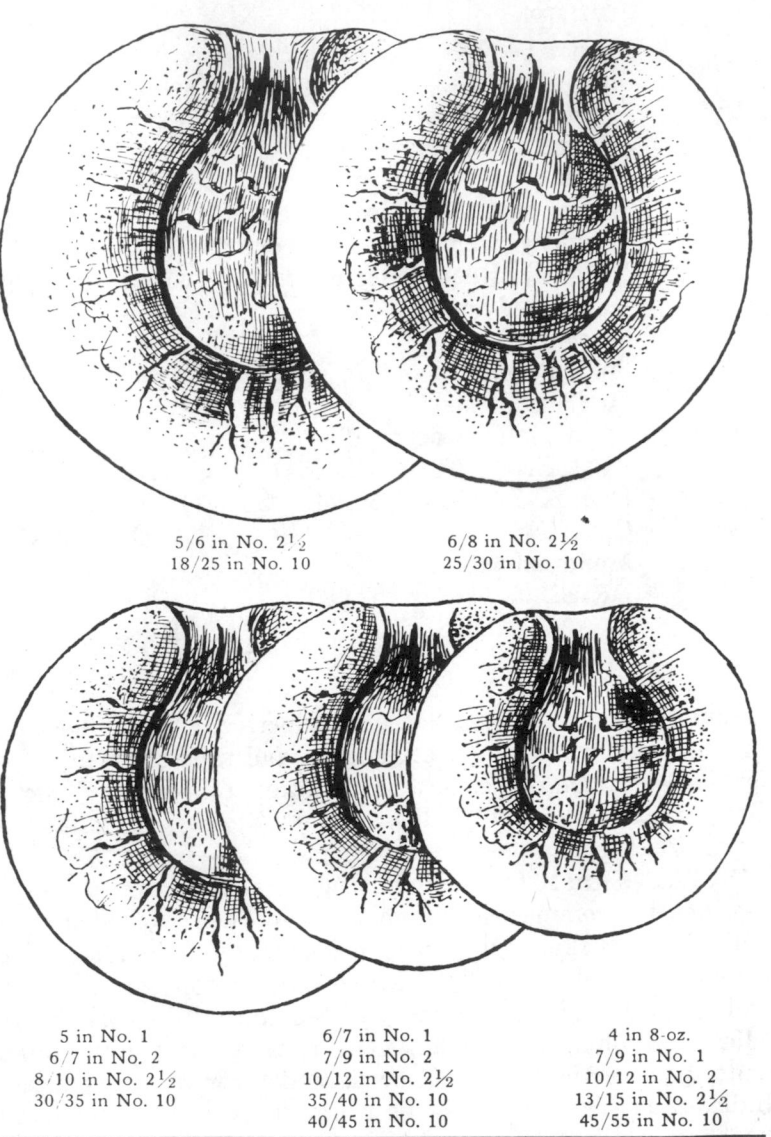

YELLOW CLING PEACH SIZES

5/6 in No. 2½
18/25 in No. 10

6/8 in No. 2½
25/30 in No. 10

5 in No. 1	6/7 in No. 1	4 in 8-oz.
6/7 in No. 2	7/9 in No. 2	7/9 in No. 1
8/10 in No. 2½	10/12 in No. 2½	10/12 in No. 2
30/35 in No. 10	35/40 in No. 10	13/15 in No. 2½
	40/45 in No. 10	45/55 in No. 10

Approximate sizes and counts per can. Note: Important variable factors are degrees of syrup used and lengths of cooks.

Due to their highly perishable nature, peaches are most frequently picked in a mature-hard stage for long distance shipment and may arrive on the market too firm for immediate use. This is because the riper the peach, the more difficult it is to ship. A tree-ripe peach is so tender that it bruises very easily and soon breaks down. Peachs on the tree increase in sugar content nearly up to the time they become mellow, too ripe for harvest, so that the riper they are at harvest, the more sugar they will contain. *Peaches do not gain in sugar after they are picked. The reason is that they have no reserve of starch which, in fruits such as pears, is converted to sugar in the ripening process.*

GRADES: U.S. standards for peaches are U.S. Fancy, U.S. Extra No. 1, U.S. No. 1, and U.S. No. 2. The standards may be obtained without charge from Agricultural Marketing Service, Washington, D.C. 20250. *Following are extracts from standards on peaches, effective June 15, 1962:*

"*U.S. Extra No. 1.* Any lot of peaches may be designated 'U.S. Extra No. 1' when the peaches meet the requirements of U.S. No. 1 grade: Provided, That in addition to these requirements, 50 percent, by count, of the peaches in any lot shall have not less than one-fourth of the surface showing blushed, pink or red color ... In order to allow for variations incident to proper grading and handling, not more than 10 percent by count of the peaches in any lot may fail to meet the requirements of U.S. No. 1 grade, but not more than 5 percent shall be allowed for defects causing serious damage, and not more than 1 percent shall be allowed for decay at shipping point: Provided, That an additional tolerance of 2 percent shall be allowed for soft, overripe, or decayed peaches, enroute or at destination. No part of any tolerance shall be used to reduce for the lot as a whole the 50 percent of peaches required to have not less than one-fourth of the surface showing blushed, pink or red color, but individual packages may contain not less than 40 percent of peaches having this amount of color: Provided, That the entire lot averages not less than 50 percent.

"*U.S. No. 1* consists of peaches of one variety which are mature, but not soft or overripe, well formed, and which are free from decay, growth cracks, cuts which are not healed, worms, worm holes, and free from damage caused by bruises, dirt or other foreign material, bacterial spot, scale, hail injury, other diseases, insects, or mechanical, or other means ... In order to allow for variation incident to proper grading and handling, not more than 10 percent may fail to meet the requirements of this grade, but not more than 5 percent shall be allowed for defects causing serious damage, and not more than 1 percent shall be allowed for decay at shipping point: Provided, That an additional tolerance of 2 percent shall be allowed for soft, overripe, or decayed peaches enroute or at destination.

"**Sizing.** The numerical count or the minimum diameter of the peaches packed in a closed container shall be indicated on the container. When the numerical count is not shown, the minimum diameter shall be plainly stamped, stenciled, or otherwise marked on the package in terms of whole, whole and half, whole and quarter, or whole and eighth inches. *Diameter or size* means the shortest distance measured through the center of the peach at right angles to a line running from the stem to the blossom end. Not more than 10 percent, by count, of peaches in any lot may be below the minimum and not more than 15 percent may be above the specified maximum size.

"**Packaging.** Each package shall be packed so that the peaches in the shown face shall be reasonably representative in size, color, and quality of the contents of the package. Peaches packed in bushel baskets or half-bushel baskets shall be ring faced and rightly packed with sufficient bulge to prevent any appreciable movement within the packages when lidded. Peaches packed in western boxes shall be reasonably uniform in size and arranged in the packages according to the approved methods. Each wrapped peach shall be fairly well enclosed by its individual wrapper. Not more than 10 percent of the packages in any lot may not meet these requirements.

"*Mature* means that the peach has reached the stage of growth which will insure a proper completion of the ripening process. *Well formed* means that the shape of the peach may be slightly irregular, but not to the extent that its appearance is materially affected. *Damage* means any injury or defect which materially affects the appearance or the edible or shipping quality of the peach."

PEACHES, CLINGSTONE—Canned [6/20/73]

Grade A: Color; Bright, ranging from yellowish-orange to orange yellow, but equal to or better than light orangish yellow. In whole, halves, quarters, slices, 10 percent may fall into B classification for color, provided that in the entire sample, such units do not exceed 10 percent. In diced or mixed pieces of irregular sizes and shapes, this tolerance is 10 percent, by weight.

Size and Symmetry: In "whole," "halves" or "quarters" weight of largest unit may not exceed smallest by more than: 40 percent and in "halves" or "quarters" each unit may weigh not less than 3/5 oz. and 3/10 oz., respectively: and not more than 10 percent, or 1 unit, may possess any combination of off suture cuts or partially detached or detached pieces, provided average of entire sample does not exceed permitted percentage. In "slices" not more than a total of 5 percent may be partial slices, slivers, and slabs, provided no more than 2-1/2 percent, by container is slabs; and excluding partial slices, slivers, and slabs, the variation in size and symmetry of the other units does not affect the appearance more than slightly. In "diced," not more than 10 percent by weight are more than 3/4 in. in greatest edge dimension or of size to pass through a 5/16-in. square opening.

Defects: All grades and styles are practically free from pit material: or practically free from harmless extraneous material and from any defects not specifically mentioned that affect appearance or edibility: and, in addition, there may be present, on an average, in all styles not more than 1/8-in. of peel for each pound of total contents. In "halves," "quarters," or "whole," maximum tolerance of crushed or broken is 5 percent by count or 1 unit, provided that in entire sample such crushed or broken units do not exceed an average of 5 percent of all units. Blemished units may not exceed in "halves," "quarters," or "whole" 35 percent by count of the units; or sliced and diced 3 percent by count; in halves, quarters, whole, and in slices, one unit in a container is permitted to be blemished, if such unit exceeds the respective percentage allowance: provided that in all containers comprising the sample, such blemished units do not exceed an average of the respective percentage of the total number of units. Tolerance of blemished units in "mixed pieces of irregular size and shapes" is 1 per 32 oz.

Character: Halves, quarters; slices; mixed pieces of irregular sizes and shape: Units are pliable and possess a tender, fleshy texture typical of mature, well-ripened, properly prepared and processed canned clingstone peaches; are intact and possess reasonably well-defined edges; and not more than 10 percent by count, or 1 unit, if such unit exceeds the 10 percent allowance, may possess a reasonably good character: Provided the appearance or eating quality, or both, is not more than slightly affected.

Grade B: Color: Reasonably bright, fails A but equal to or better than greenish yellow, may possess slight discoloration that does not materially affect appearance and/or edibility. In (whole, halves, quarters, slices) not more than 10 percent, or 1 unit, may fall into C classification, 10 percent for diced or mixed possess irregular size and shapes. **Size and Symmetry:** See Grade A. All wording is the same except as follows: For whole, halves, or quarters: 60 percent; 20 percent. In slices, 10 percent, 5 percent; materially. For diced: 15 percent. **Defects:** see Grade A. All wording is the same except as follows: reasonably. 1/2 in. Blemished units: halves, quarters; 10 percent; sliced and diced 6 percent. 1 per lb. **Character:** Texture is reasonably fleshy, and units are reasonably tender or tenderness may be variable within the unit: units are reasonably intact with not more than slight frayed edges and may be slightly firm or slightly soft but are not mushy; and not more than 10 percent by count, or 1 unit, if such unit exceeds the 10 percent allowance, may possess a fairly good character; Provided the appearance or eating quality, or both, is not affected materially.

Grade C: Color: Fails B but equal to or better than greenish-yellow, may possess slight discoloration that does not materially affect the appearance and/or edibility. 10 percent by count, 1 whole, halves, quarters, sliced, or 1 unit, may fail C. 10 percent for diced or mixed pieces of irregular sizes and shapes. **Size and Symmetry:** See Grade A. All wording is the same except as follows: 100 percent; 40 percent. The presence of such units does not give the appearance of "mixed pieces," or irregular size and shapes, or unevenly trimmed. In slices, 20 percent; 10 percent. The slices may vary noticeably in size, thickness, and symmetry. In diced 20 percent. **Defects:** See Grade A. All wording is the same except as follows: fairly free 1 sq. in. Blemished units: 20 percent, 20 percent, 20 percent of units by count. **Character:** May be variable in fleshiness, but the texture is fairly fleshy; the units may be lacking uniformity of tenderness; may be frayed but not excessively frayed, or may be soft; and not more than 10 percent of the drained peaches may be mushy, or units that are so firm as to be "not tender."

Grade D: Color; See Grade C. Defects: See Grade C. materially affect the appearance or edibility. Grade C-SP: Color: See Grade C. Defects: See Grade C. SStd: Fails to meet requirements.

PEACHES, Clingstone Canned [1975 Revisions]

The Food and Drug Administration amended the standards of identity for Canned Clingstone Peaches, compliance with which may have begun on March 11, 1975, but mostly after December 31, 1975.

The following amendments to the USDA standards for Clingstone Canned Peaches are proposed to bring them into line with the amended FDA Standards of Identity.

Product description.

"Canned clingstone peaches" means "canned yellow cling peaches" as such product is defined in the standard of identity for canned peaches (21 CFR 27.2 and 27.6) issued pursuant to the Federal Food, Drug, and Cosmetic Act. For the purposes of the standards in this subpart, and unless the text indicates otherwise, the terms "canned peaches" or "canned clingstone peaches" include "canned yellow clingstone peaches," "canned spiced yellow clingstone peaches," canned "solid-pack" clingstone peaches and "canned artificially sweetened yellow peaches" as defined in the aforesaid standards of identity.

The FDA standards of identity include yellow, white, red, and green color types. The USDA standards would continue to be restricted to the yellow color type, since to our knowledge the other color types are not canned in this country in any quantity of consequence, if at all.

Styles—would be amended to include a new style of "halves and pieces" and to delete the word "mixed" from the current style designation of "mixed pieces," or irregular sizes and shapes, as follows: Styles.

(a) "Halves" consist of peeled and pitted peaches, cut approximately in half along the suture from stem to apex.

(b) "Halves and pieces" consist of peeled and pitted peaches in which the halves will be more than 50 percent, by weight.

(c) "Quartered" consist of halved peaches cut into 2 approximately equal parts.

(d) "Sliced" consist of peeled and pitted peaches cut into sectors smaller than quarters.

(e) "Diced" consist of peeled and pitted peaches cut into approximate cubes.

(f) "Whole" consist of peeled, unpitted, whole peaches with or without stems removed.

(g) "Pieces of irregular sizes and shapes" consist of peeled, pitted, and cut units of canned peaches that are predominantly irregular in size and shape, which do not conform to a single style of halves, quarters, slices, or dice, and which may consist of:

(1) Units (commonly called "salad cuts" or "salad pieces") which may have been prepared originally as peach halves but which are irregular in size and shape in that more than 1/4 of the unit appears to have been removed at the outer curved surface and which have been cut further into pieces;

(2) Units which may have been prepared originally as peach slices but which are irregular in size and shape in that they have been cut further into pieces; or

(3) Mixtures of 2 or more of the following styles which may or may not be of normal shape; halves, quarters, slices, or diced.

PEACHES, Freestone—Canned [6/30/73]

Grade A: Color: Bright, ranging from pale yellowish orange to orange yellow. **Defects:** Only canned Freestone peaches (all styles) have a larger tolerance of peel—1/2 sq. in. for each pound of total contents. **Size and Symmetry:** Halves, Quarters, Whole. "Partially detached" or "detached pieces" are not considered in Canned Freestone Peaches; in largest unit may not exceed smallest by more than 50 percent. Slices—The tolerance of "slices," "slivers," and "slabs," is larger in Freestone Peaches—10 percent total, 5 max. slabs; Differing characteristics from Clings for Halves, Quarters, Slices, Mixed Pieces. Freestone peaches are: Free from any noticeable stringiness or toughness; may be soft or slightly frayed but not mushy; and halves may tend to flatten and be frayed.

Grade B: Color: Reasonably bright, fails A but equal to or better than pale yellow, may possess slight discoloration that not more than slightly affects appearance and for edibility. **Defects:** See Grade A. **Size and Symmetry:** Reasonably uniform in Size and Symmetry insofar as symmetry may be affected by presence of partial slices, slivers, slabs. Slices—15 percent total, 7-1/2 percent max. slabs; Units may abe soft or materially frayed but not mushy, or may be slightly firm or variable in tenderness within the unit; halves may be materially frayed; and not more than 10 percent, or 1 unit, if such unit exceeds the 10 percent allowance, may possess a fairly good characteristic, except for mushy units; Provided the appearance or eating quality, or both is not affected materially.

Grade C: Color: Fails B but equal to or better than dull greenish yellow, may possess slight discoloration that does not materially affect appearance and/or edibility. **Defects:** See Grade A. **Size and Symmetry:** Fairly uniform in Size and Symmetry whereby symmetry may be affected by presence of partial slices, slivers, and slabs. Slices—25 percent total, 12-1/2 percent max. slabs. Units may be variable in fleshiness, but texture is fairly fleshy; units may be lacking uniformity of tenderness, may be very soft but not frayed to the extent that the normal shape is destroyed, and not more than 10 percent may be mushy or units that are so firm as to be "not tender."

PEACHES, Freestone—Canned [1975 Revisions]

The Food and Drug Administration amended the standards of identity for Canned Freestone Peaches, compliance with which may have begun on March 11, 1975, but mostly after December 31, 1975.

The following amendments to the USDA standards for Canned Freestone Peaches are proposed to bring them into line with the amended FDA Standards of Identity.

Product description.

"Canned freestone peaches" means "canned yellow freestone peaches" or "canned yellow free peaches" as such product is purposed to be in the standard of identity for canned peaches. (21 CFR 27.2 and 27.6) issued pursuant to the Federal Food, Drug, and Cosmetic Act. For the purposes of the standards in this subpart, and unless the text indicates otherwise, the terms "canned peaches," or "canned freestone peaches" include "canned yellow freestone peaches," and "canned spiced yellow freestone peaches," canned "solid-pack" freestone peaches, and canned "artificially sweetened" freestone peaches, as defined in the aforesaid standard of identity.

The FDA standards of identity include yellow, white, red, and green color types. The USDA standards would continue to be restricted to the yellow color type, since to our knowledge the other color types are not canned in this country in any quantity of consequence, if at all.

Styles would be amended to include a new style of "halves and pieces" and to delete the word "mixed" from the current style designation of "mixed pieces of irregular sizes and shapes" as follows:

(a) "Halves" consist of peeled and pitted peaches cut approximately in half along the suture from stem to apex.

(b) "Halves and pieces" consist of peeled and pitted peaches in which the halves will be more than 50 percent, by weight.

(c) "Quartered" consist of halved peaches cut into 2 approximately equal parts.

(d) "Sliced" consist of peeled and pitted peaches cut into sectors smaller than quarters.

(e) "Diced" consist of peeled and pitted peaches cut into approximate cubes.

(f) "Whole" consist of peeled, unpitted, whole peaches with or without stems removed.

(g) "Pieces of irregular sizes and shapes" consist of peeled, pitted, and cut units of canned peaches that are predominantly irregular in size and shape, which do not conform to a single style of halves, quarters, slices, or dice, and which may consist of:

(1) Units (commonly called "salad cuts" or "salad pieces") which may have been prepared originally as peach halves but

which are irregular in size and shape, in that more than 1/4 of the unit appears to have been removed at the outer curved surface, and which have been cut further into pieces;

(2) Units which may have been prepared originally as peach slices but which are irregular in size and shape in that they have been cut further into pieces;

(3) Mixtures of two or more of the following styles which may or may not be of normal shape; halves, quarters, slices, or dice.

PEACHES—Frozen [7/3/61]

Grade A: Color: Frozen peaches possess a color that is bright, reasonably uniform, and typical of reasonably well-ripened to well-ripened peaches of the type and variety which have been properly prepared and processed; that not more than 10 percent of the drained, thawed peaches may possess more than a slight tinge of green, or slight tinge of brown due to oxidation, improper processing, or other causes, and none may possess a pronounced green or brown color. **Size:** Halves; quarters. In a 32-oz. sample unit of thawed drained peaches, or entire contents of smaller package, the weight of the largest normal-shaped unit does not exceed the weight of the smallest normal-shaped unit by more than 75 percent; and that not more than 10 percent may possess off-suture cuts or partially detached or detached pieces, or broken halves or quarters. Slices—Not more than 10 percent may consist of partial or broken slices, disintegrating fragments, or other than practically intact slices and slabs; not more than 5 percent of the thawed, drained peaches may be slabs, and the variation in size of the practically intact slice does not materially affect the appearance of the product. **Defects:** The frozen peaches are practically free from pit material, from harmless extraneous material, and from any defects not specifically mentioned that affect the appearance or edibility; any peel, blemished units, or seriously blemished units present do not exceed the allowance specified in Table I for the thawed drained peaches in the individual package, or other sample unit, and the average allowance for the entire sample. Although the maximum permitted in the individual sample unit may be as much as twice that of the average allowances, compliance of the entire sample with the average allowance is a prerequisite to scoring the sample unit with this classification, and, notwithstanding the allowances in Table I, the defects that may be present do not more than slightly affect the appearance or edibility.

Character: Unit possesses a tender texture characteristic of mature well-ripened peaches for the varietal type, and units after defrosting and proper handling retain good conformation and are reasonably uniform in texture within either of the following: Soft-ripe fruit. Units vary from soft to slightly firm, with not more than a total of 10 percent, in which the units may be very soft, mushy, firm, and rubbery or tough within the following futher limitations: Not more than 5 percent may be mushy, and not more than 2 percent may be rubbery or tough, and none may be hard. Firm-ripe fruit. Units vary from slightly firm to firm, with not more than a total of 10 percent in which the units may be soft, very soft, and rubbery or tough within the following further limitation: Not more than 2 percent may be very soft; and not more than 5 percent may be rubbery or tough, and none may be hard.

Grade B: Color: Frozen peaches possess a color that is reasonably bright, fairly uniform, and typical of reasonably well-ripened peaches of the type and variety which have been properly prepared and processed; that not more than a total of 20 percent may be affected by green or brown color of which not more than 5 percent may have a pronounced green or brown color and the remainder of this allowance (20 percent) may have no more than a slight tinge of green or of brown color: provided, that any such peaches do not materially affect the appearance. **Size:** Halves; quarters. See Grade A. All wording is the same except as follows: 100 percent; 20 percent. Slices. 20 percent; 10 percent. seriously affect appearance. **Defects:** Practically free from pit material; are reasonably free from harmless extraneous material and from any other defects not specifically mentioned that affect the appearance or edibility: See Grade A. All the following wording is the same except as follows: See Allowances in Table II; the allowances in Table II do not materially affect the appearance or edibility. **Character:** Units possess a reasonably tender texture characteristic of mature and at least reasonably well-ripened peaches for the varietal type, and which units, after defrosting and proper handling, retain reasonably good conformation and are fairly uniform in texture within either of the following categories: Soft-ripe fruit. See Grade A: all wording is the same except as follows: 20 percent. 10 percent; 5 percent. Firm-ripe fruit. Not more than 20 percent may be mushy etc.; not more than 5 percent may be mushy; not more than 5 percent may be hard.

Grade C: Color; Frozen peaches vary in color typical of fairly well-ripened peaches of the type and variety, including units that may possess slight tinge of green or brown color; and that not more than 15 percent may be materially affected by brown color due to oxidation, improper processing, or other causes, or may possess a pronounced green color; provided that any of such units individually or collectively do not seriously affect the appearance. **Size:** Halves; quarters. Not more than 40 percent may consist of off-suture cuts, or partially detached, or detached pieces, or broken halves or quarters. Slices. Not more than a total of 25 percent may consist of partial or broken slices, slivers, disintegrating fragments, or slabs; provided, that not more than 15 percent may consist of slabs. **Defects:** Fairly free from harmless extraneous material and from any defects not specifically mentioned that affect the

appearance or edibility; All wording is same, except as follows; Table III; Table III, defects do not seriously affect the appearance or edibility. **Character:** Possess a fairly tender texture characteristic of mature and fairly well-ripened peaches for the varietal type, and after defrosting and proper handling retain fairly good conformation, but may be variable in texture within any one of the following categories: Soft-ripe fruit. Not less than 50 percent vary from very soft to firm. The remainder may be mushy, firm, rubbery, or tough, and hard within the following limitations: Not more than 25 percent may be firm, rubbery, or tough and hard with the following further limitation: Not more than 10 percent may be hard. Firm-ripe fruit. See Grade B; all wording is the same except as follows: 50 percent; not more than 25 percent may be rubbery or tough and/or hard except that not more than 20 percent may be hard; and not more than 25 percent may be mushy, very soft, and soft within the following further limitations; not more than 10 percent may be mushy. Mixed soft-ripe and firm-ripe fruit. Not less than 50 percent vary from very soft to firm. The remainder may be mushy, tough, or rubbery, and hard within the following limitations; not more than 25 percent may

TABLE I—BASED ON THAWED DRAINED PEACHES OR INDIV. PACKAGE OR OTHER SAMPLE UNITS

Style	Defect	Individual container with 16 oz. or less	Individual container or sample units with more than 16 oz. to 32 oz. inclusive	Sample Units with more than 32 oz.	Average for entire sample
Halves and Quarters	Peel	1 sq. in.	2 sq. in.	1 sq. in. per 32 oz.	1 sq. in. per 32 oz.
	Blemished	1 unit	2 units; including no	1 per 32 oz. and 1	1 per 32 oz. and 1
	Seriously	or	more than	per 64 oz.	per 64 oz.
	blemished	1 serious	1 serious		
Sliced; diced	Peel	1 sq. in.	2 sq. in.	1 sq. in. per 32 oz.	1 sq. in. per 32 oz.
	Blemished				
and mixed pieces of irreg. sizes		2 units; including no more than	4 units; including no more than	2 per 32 oz.	2 per 32 oz.
and shapes	Seriously blemished	1 serious	2 serious	1 per 32 oz.	1 per 32 oz.

TABLE II

[B] Classification—maximum allowances for peel, blemished units and seriously blemished units.

Style	Defect	Based on thawed drained peaches in individual package or other sample unit[s]			
		Individual containers with 16 oz. or less	Individual containers or sample units with more than 16 oz. to 32 oz. inclusive	Sample units with more than 32 oz.	Average for entire sample
Halves and quarters.	Peel	1½ sq. in.	3 sq. in.	1½ sq. in. per 32 oz.	1½ sq. in. per 32 oz.
	Blemished units	2 units: including no more than—	4 units: including no more than—	2 per 32 oz. and	2 per 32 oz. and
	Seriously blemished units.	1 serious	2 serious	1 per 32 oz.	1 per 32 oz.
Sliced; diced; and mixed pieces of irregular sizes and shapes	Peel	1½ sq. in.	3 sq. in.	1½ sq. in. per 32 oz.	1½ sq. in. per 32 oz.
	Blemished units	4 units: including no more than—	8 units: including more than—	4 per 32 oz. and	4 per 32 oz. and
	Seriously blemished units	2 serious	4 serious	2 per 32 oz.	2 per 32 oz.

TABLE III

[C] Classification—maximum allowances for peel, blemished units and seriously blemished units.

Style	Defect	Based on thawed drained peaches in individual package or other sample unit[s]			
		Individual containers with 16 oz. or less	Individual containers or sample units with more than 16 oz. to 32 oz. inclusive	Sample units with more than 32 oz.	Average for entire sample
Halves and quarters.	Peel	2 sq. in.	4 sq. in.	2 sq. in. per 32 oz.	2 sq. in. per 32 oz.
	Blemished units	4 units: including no more than—	8 units: including no more than—	4 per 32 oz. and	4 per 32 oz. and
	Seriously blemished units.	2 serious	4 serious	2 per 32 oz.	2 per 32 oz.
Sliced; diced; and mixed pieces of irregular sizes and shapes.	Peel	2 sq. in.	4 sq. in.	2 sq. in. per 32 oz.	2 sq. in. per 32 oz.
	Blemished units	8 units: including no more than—	16 units: including no more than—	8 per 32 oz. and	8 per 32 oz. and
	Seriously blemished units.	4 serious	6 serious	3 per 32 oz.	3 per 32 oz.

be mushy and not more than 25 percent may be rubbery or tough and hard except that not more than 20 percent may be hard. SStd: Fails to meet requirements.

PEACHES, Low Moisture—Dehydrated [11/30/59]

Grade A: Color: Over all color is characteristic for the product and respective style, ranging from deep rich yellow or yellow-orange to deeper orange amber among the units and within individual units, and is reasonably uniform; and that such a characteristic color, upon cooking, is a reasonably bright color typical of cooked low-moisture peaches that have been properly prepared and processed. **Size:** Nugget-type, pieces: Practically all of the units are of such size and shape as to pass through 0.625 (5/8-in.) square openings and not more than 25 percent of the low moisture peaches may pass through meshes of a U.S. Standard No. 8 sieve (0.0937-in. = 3 percent, square openings). **Texture:** Nugget type; Pieces: The cooked mass has a reasonably uniform texture and finish that is coarse or grainy with practically no hard particles. 90 after Nugget-type texture. Pieces. The cooked product is practically free from hard, firm, or tough units, and there is no more than moderate disintegration except for fine pieces that may have been present. **Size:** Diced; Practically all of the units, except for fine pieces are definite partial cube-shapes, and not less than 40 percent of the dehydrated peaches approximate cube-shapes of 1/4 in. to 1/2 in. square on one surface dimension; and not more than 10 percent of the low-moisture peaches may pass through meshes of a U.S. Standard No. 8 sieve (0.0937-in. = 3 percent square openings). **Texture:** The cooked product is practically free from hard or tough units and substantially retains the semblance of diced peaches except for small pieces or odd-shaped pieces that may have been present. **Size:** Pieces: Practically all of the units, except for small pieces, are definite parallel-cut strips of varying lengths; and not less than 50 percent of the low moisture peaches approximate 1/4 in. to 1/2 in. in width; and not more than 10 percent of the low moisture peaches may pass through meshes of a U.S. Standard No. 8 sieve (0.0937-in. = 3 percent, square openings). **Texture:** The cooked product is practically free from hard or tough units and substantially retains the semblance of strips of peaches except for small pieces or odd-shaped pieces that may have been present. **Defects:** Practically free from any defects that affect more than slightly the appearance or eating quality within the low moisture peaches or after cooking; and that not more than a total of 5 percent of the low moisture peaches may be damaged units: Provided, that not more than 2 percent of the low moisture peaches may be seriously damaged units.

Grade B: Color: Over all color may vary considerably, ranging from slightly dull yellow or slightly dull yellow orange to darker orange and dark amber; and that such characteristic color, upon cooking, may be slightly dull but is typical of cooked, low moisture peaches that have been properly prepared and processed. **Size:** Nugget-type pieces: Practically all of the units are of such size and shape as to pass through 0.625 (5/8-in.) square opening and not more than 25 percent may pass through meshes of a U.S. Standard No. 8 sieve (0.0937-in. = 3 percent square openings). **Texture:** The cooked mass has a fairly uniform texture and finish that may range from fine and grainy to coarse and grainy; and hard particles may be noticeable but not objectionable. Pieces. The cooked product is fairly free from hard, firm, or tough units and may disintegrate generally into a coarse, saucelike consistency. **Size:** Diced: Practically all of the units, except for fine pieces, are definite, partial cube-shapes, and not less than 40 percent of the dehydrated peaches approximate cube-shapes of 1/4 in. to 1/2 in. square on one surface dimension; and not more than 10 percent may pass through meshes of a U.S. Standard No. 8 sieve (0.0937-in. = 3 percent sqaure openings). **Texture:** The cooked product is fairly free from hard or tough units and consists of substantial amounts of diced peach pieces intermingled with a slight amount of mushiness from small pieces which may have been present. **Size:** Slices: all wording is same except as follows: parallel cut strip, 50 percent. Texture: See texture for Diced Grade B. **Defects:** Reasonably free from any defects that affect materially the appearance or eating quality either in the low-moisture peaches or after cooking; and that not more than a total of 10 percent may be damaged units; provided that not more than 4 percent may be seriously damaged. SStd: Fails to meet requirements.

PEACHES—Dried [5/24/67]

Grade A: Not more than 5 percent may be of a color described in U.S. Grade B, and none of the fruit may be of a color described in Grade C; not more than a total tolerance of 10 percent may be slabs, immature, or may possess pits or pieces of pits; may be damaged by discoloration, sunburn, hail marks, scab, disease, insect injury, or other similar defects; or may be affected by mold, decay, insect infestation (no live insects are permitted) imbedded dirt, or other foreign material; provided, that not more than 3/10 may possess pits or pieces of pits; not more than 2/5 of the total tolerance, or 4 percent may be affected by mold, decay, insect infestation, etc.; (see above); further provided, that not more than 1/10 of the total tolerance, or 1 percent may be affected by decay.

Grade B: Not more than 10 percent of the fruit may be a color described in Grade C. Not more than a total tolerance of 15 percent may be slabs, immature, or may possess pits or pieces of pits; may be damaged by discoloration, etc. (see Grade A) provided, that, not more than 1/3 of the total tolerance, or 5 percent by weight may possess pits or pieces of pits; not more than 1/3 of the total tolerance or 5 percent may be affected by mold, etc.; (see Grade A): and further provided, that not more than 1/15 of the total tolerance or 1 percent may be affected by decay.

Grade C: Not more than a total tolerance of 20 percent may be slabs, etc. (see Grade A): Provided, that, not more than 1/2 of the total tolerance or 10 percent may possess pits or pieces of pits; not more than 1/4 of the total tolerance or 5 percent may be affected by mold, etc. (see Grade A) and further provided, that not more than 1/10 of the total tolerance or 2 percent may be affected by decay.

Grade D: Fails to meet requirements: provided that not more than 5 percent may be affected by mold, etc.; (see Grade A): And further provided, not more than 2 percent may be affected by decay.

WORK SHEET

§52.5810 Work sheet and summary of requirements for dried peaches.

Size of case or package				
Markings				
Label or brand				
Net weight				
Size or sizes				
Moisture content				

	A	B	C	D
COLOR	Minimum requirements			
Grade A color	95%			
Grade B color	5%	90%		
Grade C color			10%	100%
DEFECTS	Maximum tolerances			
Total defects	10%	15%	20%	
Slabs, and immature; damaged by discoloration, sunburn, hail marks, scab, disease, insect injury, or other similar defects; and	10%	15%	20%	
	But not more than			
Fruit possessing pits or pieces of pits; and	3%	5%	10%	
	But not more than			
Affected by mold, decay, insect infestation, imbedded dirt, or other foreign material	4%	5%	5%	5%
	But not more than			
Decay	1%	1%	2%	2%
Grade				

PEARS*

USES: Fresh pears may be eaten out of the hand; or in salads; are good stewed, baked, fried, pickled, glazed; are used in jellies, jams, marmalade, and baked goods; are canned in great quantities; and some are dried ... *To bake pears*, core and peel about 1-in. strip from the top, fill with fruit, and place in oven, serving hot ... For a sundae, place one scoop of mint chocolate ice cream in a sherbet glass, top with fresh pear slices, and garnish with fresh mint ... *Serve* whole pears in a bowl and let each guest select his own, cutting the pear as he likes, and eating it with selected cheeses and crackers ... For a pear salad, peel, halve, and core pears, fill center with cream

*UFFVA

PEARS

WINTER PEARS
FRESH (9/10/55   51.1300)
GRADES: U.S. Extra No. 1   U.S. NO. 1
         U.S. Combination   U.S. NO. 2
SUMMER AND FALL PEARS
FRESH (8/20/55   51.1260)
GRADES: U.S. NO. 1   U.S. Combination
         U.S. NO. 2
CANNED: (6/20/73   52.1611)

GRADES:	"A" OR "FANCY"	"B" OR "CHOICE"	"C" OR "STANDARD"	"SUBSTANDARD"
Minimum Score:	90	80	70	Less than 70
Styles of quarters, slices, mixed pieces of irregular sizes & shapes	NET WEIGHT OZ.	NET WEIGHT METRIC	DRAINED WEIGHT OZ.	DRAINED WEIGHT METRIC
No. 8Z Tall	5.2	147.4 g	4.5	127.6 g
No. 303	10.2	289.2 g	9.0	255.2 g
No. 2½	18.3	513.8 g	16.4	464.9 g
No. 10	70.0	2.0 kg	64.0	1.8 kg
Halves style				
No. 8Z Tall	5.1	144.6 g	4.2	119.1 g
No. 303 7 count or less	9.8	277.8 g	8.5	241.0 g
8 count or more	10.1	286.3 g	8.8	249.5 g
No. 2½ 8 count or less	17.2	487.6 g	15.3	433.8 g
9 count or more	17.7	501.8 g	15.8	447.9 g
No. 10 25 count or less	66.0	1.9 kg	60.8	1.7 kg
26 count or more	67.5	1.9 kg	62.2	1.8 kg
Diced Style				
No. 8Z Tall	6.0	170.1 g	5.3	150.2 g
No. 303	11.5	326.0 g	10.2	289.2 g
No. 2½	20.3	575.5 g	18.4	521.6 g
No. 10	74.5	2.1 kg	65.7	1.9 kg

SYRUP	BRIX MEASUREMENTS
"Extra heavy syrup," or "Extra heavily sweetened fruit juice(s) and water"; or "Extra heavily sweetened fruit juice(s)."	22° to 35°
"Heavy syrup"; or "Heavily sweetened fruit juice(s) and water"; or "Heavily sweetened fruit juice(s)."	18° or more but less than 22°
"Light syrup"; or "Lightly sweetened fruit juice(s) and water"; or "Lightly sweetened fruit juice(s)."	14° or more but less than 18°
"Slightly sweetened water" or "Extra light syrup"; or "Slightly sweetened fruit juice(s) and water" or "Slightly sweetened fruit juice(s)."	Less than 14°
"In water"	N.A.
"In fruit juice(s) and water"	N.A.
"In fruit juice(s)"	N.A.
"In clarified juice"	N.A.
"Artificially sweetened"	N.A.

DRIED (5/24/67   52.5841)

GRADES:	"A" OR "FANCY"	"B" OR "CHOICE"	"C" OR "STANDARD"	"D" OR "SUB-STANDARD"

cheese, place on a bed of lettuce ... *Fresh pears and apples poached* together in a syrup, made with equal parts of sugar and water with fresh lemon juice to taste, make a delightful dessert or meat accompaniment ... *Dip fresh pear cubes* in a mixture of 2 Tbsp. fresh orange and 2 Tbsp. fresh lemon juice, place on toothpices, alternating with cheese cubes ... *For fresh pear and shrimp appetizer*, toss diced fresh pears (unpeeled), cooked shrimp, and chopped celery with a lemony fresh dressing, and spoon into cocktail glasses lined with crisp greens ... *Try combining* diced pears with nuts and celery in a crunchy flavorful salad ... *Another salad* is fresh pear balls in clear aspic, ringed with fresh cucumber slices, and centered with cottage cheese ... *Fresh pears* make a delightful addition to Waldorf salad. Replace half of the diced apples called for with diced fresh pears. Add the usual amounts of diced celery and chopped walnuts. Season well and bind together with mayonnaise or salad dressing ... Try the French custom of serving a plump pear with a wedge of a fragrant cheese ... *Serve pears* cool but not icy. When they are too cold, they lack some of their bouquet, while if too warm, they are not as refreshing as

when cool. ... *A famous, easily prepared continental dessert* is poached fresh pear halves filled with vanilla ice cream and bathed in a warm, bittersweet chocolate sauce ... *For fresh pear ambrosia*, wash, core, and dice fresh pears, sprinkle with fresh orange juice, and arrange in sherbet glasses with shredded moist coconut.

MARKETING SEASON: Fresh pears are on the market in all months, but there are very few in June. The peak period is August through October. The following table shows availability by months.

MONTHLY AVAILABILITY OF PEARS EXPRESSED AS A PERCENTAGE OF TOTAL ANNUAL SUPPLY

Jan. %	Feb. %	Mar. %	Apr. %	May %	June %
7	6	7	7	4	2

July %	Aug. %	Sept. %	Oct. %	Nov. %	Dec. %
5	15	15	14	10	8

Calculated from unloads at Chicago, Los Angeles, New Orleans, New York and Portland, Ore.

VARIETIES: All of our important pear stock has been imported directly from Europe. The European varieties include Bartlett, Anjou, Bosc, Winter Nelis, Comice, and Easter. Only those pears selected primarily because of blight resistance have originated in the U.S. These include Seckel. European breeders have worked with pears to a far greater extent than with apples, and in all respects except resistance to fire blight their best varieties have proved superior to those that have developed as chance seedlings in the U.S. (Agriculture Yearbook, 1937, p. 618).

More than 3,000 varieties are known in the U.S., but less than a dozen are commercially important today. The Bartlett outranks all others in quantity of production and in value. Of pears grown in California, Oregon, and Washington in 1961, 78 percent were Bartletts. The Bartlett is the principal variety grown in the three Western states and is also the important commercial pear in Michigan and New York.

Bartlett "Fruit medium or larger in size, oblong-obtuse-pyriform (bell-like) in shape, somewhat irregular. Skin fairly thin, somewhat tender, clear yellow in color (when ripe), occasionally blushed, surface somewhat uneven, some inconspicuous

BARTLETT PEAR SIZES

5/6 in No. 2½
18/27 in No. 10

6/9 in No. 2½
27/37 in No. 10

6/8 in No. 2
9/12 in No. 2½
33/45 in No. 10

6/8 in No. 1
7/10 in No. 2
10/14 in No. 2½
40/50 in No. 10

4/5 in 8-oz.
7/9 in No. 1
9/12 in No. 2
12/17 in No. 2½
45/55 in No. 10

Approximate sizes and counts per can. Note: Important variable factors are degrees of syrup used and lengths of cooks.

dots, fairly attractive. Flesh white, fine, quite free of grit, melting, juicy. Sweet, vinous flavor with a grace of muskiness. Rates high in dessert quality. Fairly early in season. Tree medium or less in vigor, not well formed as an orchard tree, productive, susceptible to blight. In spite of blight susceptibility, Bartlett is quite cosmopolitan in adaptability and is now the world's leading commercial pear variety. It is highly prized for both dessert and processing qualities." (Catalog and Evaluation of the Pear Collection at the Oregon Agricultural Experiment Station, Technical Bulletin 41, Dec. 1957, Oregon State College, Corvallis, Ore., by Henry Hartman.) *On market in volume from July until mid-October* but available in small quantities in later months. (The description above applies to the main Bartlett variety, but there are various strains that depart from this description in color and other characteristics.)

The Bartlett (of which the English name is Williams' Bon Chretien) was found as a wild tree by a Mr. Stair, a schoolmaster at Aldermaston, Berkshire, England in 1770. It was acquired from him by Mr. Williams, a nurseryman at Turnham Green, Middlesex, who distributed it. The pear thus became known as the Williams and is still known by that name in England and France. It was brought to this country around 1797-99 by James Carter of Boston for the Brewer estate. In 1817, Enoch Bartlett of Dorchester, Mass. became the owner of the estate and, not knowing the true name of the pears being grown on it, distributed trees under his own name. The American Pomological Society accepted the name "Bartlett" in 1848 and listed the variety in its catalog. (Pears of New York, Hedrick, p. 124-5)

Anjou (full name Beurre d'Anjou) ("Beurre" means "butter") Fruit medium or larger in size with short stem; oval to globular with sides slightly unequal; short, obscure, thick neck; yellowish green skin, occasionally sprinkled with russet, sometimes shaded to dull crimson. Flesh yellowish white, fairly fine, buttery, juicy, some grit cells at center; aromatic, spicy, sweet flavor; stores well. The tree is vigorous, upright, spreading, somewhat temperamental as to production, and moderately susceptible to blight ... On market *October to May,* but with supplies tapering off after February. The Anjou is the principal winter pear, usually making up about three-fourths of the winter total.

This is supposed to be a French pear, but its origin is obscure. On the other hand, there is evidence it originated with Van Mons at Louvain, Belgium in 1819 and appeared in the Van Mons catalog in 1823 under the name of Nec Plus Meuris. The variety was introduced into this country by Col. Wilder of Boston about 1842. (Technical Bulletin 41, Oregon State College; and Pears of New York, Hedrick.)

Bosc (full name Beurre Bosc) The fruit is so uniquely shaped and colored as to be unmistakable. The Bosc has a long tapering neck. The skin color is dark yellow overlaid with cinnamon russet, which varies in intensity depending upon climatic and cultural conditions. The fruit is medium or larger in size. "Flesh yellowish white, some grit at the center, buttery but not melting, very juicy. Rich vinous, aromatic flavor, rates among the best in dessert quality when properly grown" ... Tree vigorous, upright, spreading, productive, difficult to shape during formative years but well shaped and stately at maturity. Quite susceptible to blight." (Quoted portion from Tech. Bul. 41, Oregon State College.) On market *October through March* with a very few in April. *October is peak month* with supplies tapering off after that and becoming small after February. Bosc is next to Anjou in quantity, considering only winter pears. It may amount to 19 or 20 percent of the winter pear crop.

The origin of this pear is in dispute. One view is it originated in Belgium, but Andre Leroy in his Dictionaire Pomologie of 1867 says it is of French origin, named in honor of Louis Bosc, an eminent French horticulturist. Scions were received in the U.S. in 1832 by Robert Manning and William Kenrich. It was cataloged by the American Pomological Society at its first meeting in 1848.

Comice (full name Doyenne du Comice) ("Doyenne" means "dean" and "comice" means "show" or freely translated, "Best in the show") "Fruit medium to large, sometimes very large; obovate-obtuse-pyriform; skin fairly thick, granular, susceptible to blemishes; sometimes russeted; greenish yellow in color, often blushed; flesh very fine, melting, extremely juicy, quite free of grit; sweet, rich, aromatic, vinous flavor. Regarded by many as the standard of dessert quality among pears. Fruit inclined to bruise easily in the ripe state. Tree large, stately, vigorous but slow in coming into bearing. Semi-dwarf on quince, moderately susceptible to blight. Doyenne du

Comice is a temperamental variety which reaches perfection only under limited conditions of soil, climate and location." (Quotation from Tech. Bul. 41, Oregon State College) Comice is on the market *October through March* with very few available after January.

The parent tree came from the first seed bed made in the fruit garden of the Comice Horticole at Angers, France. In November 1849, it produced its first fruit which at once became highly esteemed. It reached America about 1850.

Hardy (full name Beurre Hardy) Mainly for canning; no considerable quantity sold fresh. "Fruit medium or larger in size, obtuse-pyriform, symmetrical; skin usually granular, tender, dull greenish yellow, often with some russeting, dots numerous, and sometimes conspicuous; flesh somewhat granular, buttery, juicy; rich, aromatic flavor when properly grown and handled; inclined to be bitter in taste if picked too early, and susceptible to core breakdown if left on trees too long; fruit a little too soft to withstand commercial handling." Tree of good growth habits, vigorous and productive; often used as an intermediate trunk stock on quince; semi-dwarf on quince; fairly susceptible to blight. (Quotation from Tech. Bu. 41, Oregon State College).

The Hardy originated at Boulogne-sur-Mer, France in 1830.

Clapp Favorite "Fruit of this variety resembles Bartlett in size and form, but is somewhat smoother, and frequently has a clubbed stem; skin greenish yellow, quite free of blemish, often blushed, attractive; flesh fairly fine, melting, juicy, some grit at the center; sweet, pleasing, aromatic flavor; rates among the best of the early pears in dessert quality; a little too soft in texture to withstand commercial handling; high susceptibility to core breakdown if left on tree too long. Tree fairly vigorous, well formed, good foliage, productive; very susceptible to blight." (Quotation from Tech. Bu. No. 41, Oregon State College) *On market August through October.*

Clapp Favorite was raised by Thaddeus Clapp, Dorchester, Mass., but the date of its origin is uncertain. It was favorably mentioned as a promising new fruit at the 1860 meeting of the Massachusetts Horticultural Society. The American Pomological Society listed it in the catalog of 1867.

Winter Nelis "Fruit small to medium in size, roundish-obovate to obtuse-obovate-pyriform. Skin fairly thick, but tender, roughened with considerable russeting; dull green or yellowish in color; not attractive; flesh fairly fine except for grit at the center; buttery, moderately juicy; spicy, rich flavor; rates very high in dessert quality; late keeper. Tree fairly vigorous, willowy and spreading in habit, reasonably productive, moderately susceptible to blight. Winter Nelis is rapidly losing ground as a commercial variety because of small size, unattractive appearance, and a tendency to decay in storage." (Quotation from Tech. Bu. No. 41, Oregon State College) *On market October to May with peak in October.*

Winter Nelis was raised from seed by Jean Charles Nelis, Mechlin, Belgium, early in the 19th century. It was introduced into England by the London Horticultural Society. In 1823, the president of the Society sent scions to John Lowell of Roxbury, Mass. who shared them with Robert Manning of Salem, Mass. who sent some to various parts of the country. At the National Convention of Fruit Growers held in New York in 1848, Winter Nelis was included in a short list of pears recommended for general cultivation. (Pears of New York, Hedrick, p. 232-4).

Easter (full name Easter Beurre) "Fruit medium or larger in size; obovate-pyriform with thick neck; skin thick and somewhat tough, deep green in color, sometimes slightly russeted, occasionally blushed; flesh somewhat coarse, gritty; buttery, moderately juicy; fairly sweet, pleasing flavor when properly grown and handled; usually fails to ripen unless previously held under refrigeration for several months. Tree moderately vigorous, upright-spreading in habit, reasonably productive; fairly susceptible to blight. While many attempts have been made to grow Beurre Easter commercially, the variety has not become a popular market pear. It is sometimes used as a pollinizer for Anjou and other varieties." (Quotation from Tech. Bu. No. 41, Oregon State College)

The variety originated in the gardens of the Capucin Monastery at Louvain, Belgium, where about 1823 an old pear tree known to the monks as the Pastorale de Louvain attracted the attention of Dr. Jean Van Mons. By 1835, it was grown rather generally in the gardens of Belgium under the name of Pastorale. The name Easter was adopted in England and America. The Easter was brought to this country not later than 1837. Since 1862, Easter has appeared on the American Pomological Society list of pears recommended for general cultivation. (Pears of New York, Hedrick, p. 160)

Kieffer This pear has coarse, sandy flesh, and what one expert calls a "potato-like flavor." In fact, U. P. Hedrick in his Pears of New York says: "Dire necessity alone would compel their consumption uncooked." Some are canned, but the variety is going out of style. The best information obtainable is that there have not been any new plantings in recent years.

Seckel This American pear is distinct in type from any European variety. "Fruit very small unless heavily thinned and properly grown. Obovate-pyriform in shape; usually symmetrical; skin dull brownish yellow, usually overlaid with russet and blushed dull red; flesh somewhat granular, some grit at the centers; buttery and very juicy; noted for sweet, aromatic, spicy flavor; rates among the best in dessert quality; susceptible to core breakdown if held on the tree too long and does not ripen properly if harvested prematurely; does not respond well to cold storage. Tree moderately vigorous, sturdy, strong, very productive, with a tendency to overbear. Somewhat resistant to blight." (Quotation from Tech. Bu. No. 41, Oregon State College) A distinctive characteristic of the Seckel is that it does not lose much in quality by ripening on the tree. *On market late August to December.*

The Seckel apparently was first discovered on a tract south of Philadelphia by a Philadelphia sportsman and cattle dealer known as Dutch Jacob. He often distributed the pears to his friends but kept secret where he got them. In time, he bought the ground on which the secret pear tree stood on a neck of land near the Delaware river. Later this land became the property of a Mr. Seckel who gave the pear his name and introduced it. As early as 1819, Dr. Hossack of New York sent Seckel trees to the London Horticultural Society for distribution in England. At the first meeting of the American Pomological Society in 1848, the Seckel was recommended for general cultivation. (Pears of New York, Hedrick, p. 216)

CONTAINERS: Wooden boxes. The most common container for Western pears is the Northwestern pear box, wood, 8-1/2 x 11-1/2 x 18 in. inside, 1760 cu. in. capacity, holding 44 to 46 lb. net, with gross weight averaging around 52 lb. This is Container No. 1375 and 1376 in rail tariff 1-G. While the dimensions of the pear box are standard, there are variations in the thickness of shook, different types of covers and bottoms, and variations in use of cleats. Usually boxes for export shipments are constructed more heavily than for domestic shipments. The fruit is place-packed and usually is individually wrapped. Protective pads are used on top and bottom and protective liners around the sides and ends. A large proportion of the fruit is now also packed in a film liner to create a modified atmosphere to prolong storage and market life.

The wooden box, known as the L.A. lug, is 6-1/2 x 13-1/2 x 16 in. inside, 1404 cu. in. capacity, as used in the Hood River, Ore., Wenatchee, Wash., and Yakima, Wash. districts. As used in California, the L.A. lug is 5-3/4 x 13-1/2 x 16-1/8 in. inside, capacity 1252 cu. in. Another lug is 5-1/2 x 11-1/2 x 18 in.

The Lake County (Calif.) pear lug is 7-1/2 x 13-1/2 x 20-5/8 in. inside, capacity 1984 cu. in.

In the East, the Eastern wooden box, holding a little over a bushel, is used. There are a good many "Eastern" boxes of various dimensions. A typical set of dimensions is 11 x 13 x 17 in. inside, capacity 2435 cu. in. Another is 10-1/2 x 11-1/2 x 18, capacity 2175 cu. in.

Fiberboard boxes. There are various fiberboard boxes in use for pears, though none on a scale as yet approaching that of the standard wooden box or wooden L.A. lug. One fiberboard box used in the Northwest is Container No. 6146 (Tariff 1-G) which is 11-3/4 x 12 x 19-3/4 in. inside and holds a tray pack. This was originally designed for apples. About 100,000 boxes were packed last year in this container. There is also a corrugated box similar to the L.A. lug, and with the same dimensions, for a 2-layer wrapped pack. It may be either telescope type or have a folded top. ... Around Kelseyville, Calif., fiberboard box No. 6400 (Tariff 1-G) is used to some extent. It has a fully telescoping cover, and inside dimensions of 8-3/4 x 11 x 17-1/2 in.

Molded pulpboard trays in fiberboard boxes are now commonly used for apples. The pear industry is experimenting with them as a container for Bartletts and Anjous. In a study by the USDA, it was found that tray pack gave the fruit good protection.

Baskets. In the East and Midwest, bushel baskets are used to some extent for the larger varieties; and the half-bushel basket is used for smaller varieties such as Seckel. The bushel is 2150 cu. in. and a bushel of pears weighs 47 to 54 lb.

SERVINGS AND WEIGHTS: One cup of quartered pears weighs 192 gr (6.8 oz.) ... One pear 3 x 2-1/4 in. in diameter weighs 182 gr (6.4 oz.). Of such a pear, 17 percent is skin and core.

One pound of medium size pears (454 gr) serves 3; and 34 lb. serves 100. A pound when cut into raw cubed pears provides 4.5 servings of one-half cup, and 22 lb. serves 100. For such cubed pears, for 1 lb., ready-to-serve raw, use 1.28 lb. (about 1 lb., 5 oz.) as purchased. One quart of raw cubed pears weighs 1.36 lb. (1 lb., 6 oz.) ... A bushel of pears weighs 48 to 52 lb.

QUALITY: Pears normally develop to highest quality if picked unripe, but continue to mature, at a rate that can be determined by a pressure test. Flesh of pears ripened after picking is usually of fine texture, depending on the variety, while flesh of tree-ripened pears may be coarse, woody, or gritty. So the term "tree-ripened" as applied to pears is *not* an indication of good quality and should not be used in advertising.

Pears of good edible quality are clean, uninjured by cuts or bruises, firm or fairly firm, of characteristic color for the variety, and not wilted, shriveled, or materially misshapen. Bartlett pears normally reach a yellow color or yellow blushed with red when ripe; but Anjous reach ripeness when they are yellowish green. Boscs reach ripeness when they are a yellowish russet. However, the final test of whether a pear is ready to eat is whether it yields to gentle (and one should stress "gentle") pressure near the stem end and side surfaces. It is not suggested that customers press pears offered at retail, but buy them on the basis of general appearance and color, let them ripen at room temperature, and apply the pressure test at home. In general, all commercially grown pears are picked mature and will ripen satisfactorily, given the right conditions. Bartlett pears generally develop a delightful aroma when ready to eat.

Pears that show prominent bruises, any sizable blackened area, punctures, any decay at all, or any wilting or shriveling should be bypassed. Over-ripe fruit, characterized by obvious softness and accompanying discoloration, is undesirable.

GRADES: U.S. standards for summer and fall pears are U.S. No. 1, U.S. Combination and U.S. No. 2; and for winter pears, U.S. Extra No. 1, U.S. No. 1, U.S. Combination and U.S. No. 2.

Following are extracts from the standards applying to Bartletts:

"U.S. No. 1 consists of pears of one variety which are mature but not overripe, carefully handpicked, clean, fairly well formed, free from decay, internal breakdown, scald, freezing injury, worm holes, black end, and from damage caused by hard end, bruises, broken skins, russeting, limbrubs, hail, scars, drought spot, sunburn, sprayburn, stings or In order to allow for variations incident to proper grading and handling, not more than 1 percent shall be allowed for decay or internal breakdown. ... Decay, scald, or other deterioration which may have developed on pears after they have been in storage or transit shall be considered as affecting condition and not grade. (Editor's note: Condition is as important a factor in total quality as grade.)

"*Sizing.* The numerical count or the minimum size of the pears packed in closed containers shall be indicated on the package. The number of pears in the box shall not vary more than 3 from the number indicated on the box. When the numerical count is marked on western standard pear boxes, the pears shall not vary more than 3/8 in. in their transverse diameter for counts 120 or less; 1/4 in. for counts 135 to 180 inclusive; and 3/16 in. for counts 193 or more. When the numerical count is not shown, the minimum size shall be plainly stamped, stenciled, or otherwise marked on the container ... 'Size' means the greatest transverse diameter of the pear taken at right angles to a line running from the stem to the blossom end.

"*Packing.* Each package shall be packed so that the pears in the shown face shall be reasonably representative in size and quality of the contents of the package. Pears shall be tightly packed. All packages shall be well filled, but the contents shall not show excessive or unnecessary bruising because of overfilled packages. Pears packed in boxes shall be arranged in containers according to the approved and recognized methods, with the pears packed lengthwise. When wrapped, each pear shall be fairly well enclosed by its individual wrapper. Not more than 5 percent of the pears in any lot may fail to meet the size requirements.

"'Mature' means that the pear has reached the stage of maturity which will insure the proper completion of the ripening process ... 'Ripe' means that the flesh of the pear is at the stage where it is in its most desirable condition for eating ...

'Firm ripe', means that the flesh of the pear yields readily to moderate pressure."

PEARS—Canned [6/20/73]

Grade A: Color: Halves, quarters, slices, diced, or whole units, individually and collectively, are a typical light yellow white or light greenish white or light beige white; any skin pigment on the units may affect no more than slightly the overall color of the units or the product; there is otherwise no more than a slight variation from a typical translucent color; and in halves, quarters, slices, or whole, not more than 10 percent may possess Grade B color, provided none of such units are "dead white" (or chalky) in appearance; or 1 unit of halves, quarters, slices, or whole in a container is permitted to have Grade B color if such unit exceeds the allowance of 10 percent by count: Provided, that in all containers comprising the sample such units do not exceed an average of 10 percent of the total number of units. **Size and Symmetry:** Halves, quarters, whole—reasonable symmetry. And the weight of the largest full-size unit does not exceed the weight of the smallest full-size unit by more than 50 percent. In Grade A, the weight of each half is not less than 3/5 oz.; and the weight of each quarter is not less than 3/10 oz. **Slices**—not more than 10 percent by count may vary noticeably from uniform shape. Dices—fairly symmetrical; and not more than 10 percent by weight of the units may be of such size as to pass through 5/16 in. square opening. **Defects:** see defect chart. **Character:** The units possess a texture typical of properly and uniformly ripened pears that are properly processed; the texture is fleshy and free from noticeable graininess or toughness; the units are tender; the units are uniformly intact and pliable but firm enough to possess well-defined edges with no visible breaking down of the flesh; and not more than 10 percent (0r 1 unit) may fall into Grade B with respect to character.

Grade B: Color: Unit possesses a reasonably characteristic and reasonably uniform typical color; any skin pigment on the units may materially affect overall color of units or product; may show a very light tint of pink, or may be light tan (or beige) color, or may show a lack of uniformity, or may vary in translucency; and, in halves, quarters, slices, whole, or mixed pieces, not more than 10 percent may possess Grade C color,

U.S. GRADES CANNED PEARS
MAXIMUM ALLOWANCES FOR DEFECTS OR DEFECTIVE UNITS IN CANNED PEARS

All styles except as otherwise stated	Grade A	Grade B	Grade C
Peel	1/4 sq. in. per 16 oz. (average)	1/2 sq. in. per 16 oz. (average)	1 sq. in. per 16 oz. (average)
External stems[1]	1 per 100 oz.	1 per 100 oz.	1 per 100 oz.
Interior stems	1 per 60 oz.	1 per 30 oz.	1 per 15 oz.
Units of core material[2]	1 per 60 oz.	1 per 30 oz.	1 per 15 oz.
Loose seeds	1 per 30 oz. (Avg.)	1 per 15 oz. (Avg.)	1 per 10 oz. (Avg.)
Broken or crushed[3]	5 percent by count or 1 unit	10 percent by count or 1 unit	10 percent by count or 1 unit
Seriously trimmed[4]	None	None	10 percent by count or 1 unit
Moderately trimmed; and 4 Minor blemishes; and blemishes (combined)	Total: 10 percent by count	Total: 20 percent by count	No limit for moderately trimmed
	With further limitations of		
Minor blemishes; and blemished	10 percent by count but no more than 5 percent by count blemished or 1 unit (Avg.)	20 percent by count but no more than 10 percent by count blemished or 1 unit (Avg.)	Total: 30 percent by count but no more than 20 percent by count blemished or 1 unit (Avg.)

1 Does not apply to Whole uncored with stems. 2 Does not apply to Whole uncored. 3 Does not apply to Diced or mixed pieces. 4 Does not apply to Sliced, diced, or mixed pieces.

"1 unit" without further qualification means that an alternative allowance of one unit affected as described is permitted in a container when the percentage allowance by count would be exceeded by the one unit.

"1 unit (avg.)" means that an allowance of one unit affected as described is permitted in a container when the percentage allowance by count would be exceeded by the one unit: Provided, That in all containers comprising the sample such units affected as described do not exceed the allowance on an average based on the total number of units in the sample.

"Ounces" means avoirdupois weight based on total contents.

"Average" (or the abbreviation "Avg") means the average as ascertained from all sample units.

including units that may be "dead white" ("or chalky") in appearance; provided, that in all containers comprising the sample with "fairly good color," units do not exceed an average of 10 percent of the total number of units. **Size and Symmetry:** Halves, quarters, whole may vary in symmetry; and the weight of the largest full-size unit does not exceed the weight of the smallest full-size by more than 75 percent; see Grade A. Slices—not more than (no limit) of slices vary noticeably from uniform shape. Dices—20 percent of the units may be of such size as to pass through 5/16 in. square openings. **Defects:** See defect chart. **Character:** Units possess a texture of properly processed pears which may be variable; may possess a texture of marked graininess; may be lacking uniformity of tenderness; may be markedly firm or markedly ragged with frayed edges or may be soft; and not more than 10 percent by weight (by count, or 1 unit, in the can of whole) of the drained pears may be mushy, or consist of units with hard-calyx ends, or units that are not tender; not more than 20 percent by weight of drained sliced or diced canned pears may be disintegrated or mushy.

[1975 REVISIONS]

The Food and Drug Administration recently amended the standards of identity for several canned fruits, compliance with which may have begun on March 11, 1975, but mostly after December 31, 1975.

The following amendments to the USDA standards for these canned fruits are proposed to bring them into line with the amended FDA Standards of Identity.

Attention is drawn to areas where the USDA standards may differ from but do not conflict with the FDA standards.

Canned Pears

(a) 52.1612 Styles would be amended to read as follows: 52.1612 Styles.

(a) "Halves" are peeled pears, with cores and stems removed, cut longitudinally from stem to calyx into approximate halves.

(d) "Dice" or "diced" canned pears are peeled pears, with cores and stems removed, cut into approximate cubes.

(e) "Whole" canned pears are peeled, cored or uncored, whole pears, with or without stems removed.

U.S. DEPARTMENT OF AGRICULTURE
AGRICULTURAL MARKETING SERVICE
FRUIT AND VEGETABLE DIVISION

INSPECTION AID NO. 52
AUGUST 1963

UNIFORMITY OF SIZE AND SYMMETRY
REQUIREMENTS FOR CANNED PEARS

STYLES AND CRITERIA	GRADE CLASSIFICATION		
	A	B	C
HALVES; QUARTERS; WHOLE Symmetry of units	Reasonably symmetrical	May vary	May vary
Weight Variation (Smallest unit vs. largest unit)	50 percent maximum	75 percent maximum	100 percent maximum
Weight of individual unit: Halves Quarters	3/5 oz. minimum 3/10 oz. minimum	3/5 oz. minimum 3/10 oz. minimum	3/5 oz. minimum 3/10 oz. minimum
SLICES Variation from uniform shape	10 percent, by count, may vary noticeably	15 percent, by count, may vary noticeably	Any amount may vary noticeably
DICED Variation in symmetry	Fairly symmetrical	May vary	May vary
Size that pass through 5/16-in. square openings	10 percent, by weight, maximum	15 percent, by weight, maximum	20 percent, by weight, maximum

(f) "Pieces of irregular pieces" are peeled and cored, cut units of canned pears that are predominantly irregular in size and shape, which do not conform to a single style of halves, quarters, slices, or dice, and which may consist of:

(1) Units (commonly called "salad cuts" or "salad pieces" or "chunk style"), which may have been prepared originally as pear halves but which are irregular in size and shape in that more than 1/4 of the unit appears to have been removed at the outer curved surface, and which have been cut further into pieces; or

(2) Mixtures of 2 or more of the following styles which may or may not be of normal shape: Halves, quarters, slices, dice, or whole.

52.1614 Liquid media and Brix measurements.

The designation and Brix measurements would be amended as follows:

52.1614

Designations	Brix measurements
"Extra Heavy syrup;" or "Extra heavily sweetened fruit juice(s) and water;" or "Extra heavily sweetened fruit juice(s)"	22° or more but not more than 35°
"Heavy syrup;" or "Heavily sweetened fruit juice(s) and water;" or "Heavily sweetened fruit juice(s)"	18° or more but less than 22°
"Light syrup;" or "Lightly sweetened fruit juice(s) and water;" or "Lightly sweetened fruit juice(s)" "Slightly sweetened water;" or	14° or more but less than 18°
"Extra light syrup;" or "Slightly sweetened fruit juice(s) and water;" or "slightly sweetened fruit juice(s)"	less than 14°
"In water"	N.A.
"In fruit juice(s) and water"	N.A.
"In fruit juice(s)"	N.A.
"In clarified juice"	N.A.
"Artificially sweetened"	N.A.

PEARS—Dried [5/24/67]

Grade A: Dried pears possess similar varietal characteristics; possess a practically uniform, bright, typical color characteristic of well-matured pears; and are well shaped. Not more than 5 percent of the fruit may be of a color described in U.S. Grade B or U.S. Choice; and none of the fruit may be of a color described in U.S. Grade C or U.S. Standard. Not more than a total tolerance of 10 percent may be slabs, immature, or scraps; may be affected by russet or similar discoloration; may be damaged by discoloration, sunburn, hail marks, limb-runs, hard end, black end, external stems and calyx cups, scab, disease, insect injury, or other similar defects; or may be affected by mold, decay, insect infestation (no live insects are permitted), imbedded dirt or other foreign material: and further provided that not more than 1/10 of the total tolerance, or 1 percent by weight may be affected by decay.

Grade B: Possess similar varietal characteristics; possess a reasonably uniform, bright, typical color, characteristic of reasonably well-matured pears; and are reasonably well shaped. Not more than 10 percent by weight of the fruit may be a color described in U.S. Grade C. Not more than a total tolerance of 15 percent etc. for all the following wording, see Grade A. Provided, 1/3, 5 percent. Further provided; 1/15.

Grade C: Possess similar varietal characteristics; possess a fairly uniform color; characteristic of fairly well-matured pears; and are fairly well shaped. Not more than a total tolerance of 20 percent, etc. For the following wording, see Grade A. Provided, 1/4, 5 percent. Further provided, 1/10, 2 percent.

Grade D: U.S. D, or substandard, dried pears are wholesome and edible fruit that fails to meet the requirements of U.S. Grade C: Provided, that not more than 5 percent by weight of the total fruit may be affected by mold, decay, insect infestation (no live insects are permitted), imbedded dirt, or other foreign material: and further provided, that not more than 2 percent by weight of the total fruit may be affected by decay.

WORK SHEET

§52.5849 Work sheet and summary of requirements for dried pears.

Size of case or package
Markings
Label or brand
Net weight
Size or sizes
Moisture content

[*Cont.*]

WORK SHEET [Cont.]	A	B	C	D
COLOR	**Minimum requirements**			
Grade A color	95%			
Grade B color	5%	90%		
Grade C color		10%	100%	
DEFECTS	**Maximum tolerance**			
Total defects	10%	15%	20%	
Slabs, immature, or scraps; affected by russet or similar discoloration; damaged by discoloration; sunburn, hailmarks, limb-rub, hard end, black end, external stems, calyx cups, scab, disease, insect injury, or other similar defects; and	10%	15%	20%	
	But not more than			
Affected by mold, decay, insect infestation, imbedded dirt, or other foreign material	4%	5%	5%	5%
	But not more than			
Decay	1%	1%	2%	2%
Grade				

PERSIMMONS*

USES: "The persimmon, while delicious for eating out-of-hand, can also be used for fruit salads, ice cream, sherbet, custard, cake, pudding, and pie. It may be frozen whole, or pulped and then frozen."

"Satisfaction with which the fruit is eaten will depend in no small measure on its stage of maturity. Close attention to varietal characteristics is required. The 'sweet' varieties may be eaten when still hard; astringent sorts must become thoroughly ripe to avoid the 'pucker', which is of varying degrees of severity at different stages of maturity. In some varieties, it disappears when the fruit begins to soften; with others, the flesh must become almost jelly-like before it is really good to eat, and is then eaten with a spoon."

"In the Orient, especially China, great quantities of the Tamopan variety are frozen in the open air and held for transporting as frozen during the winter months. Large quantities of the fruit are also dried. ... Drying has been practiced to a limited extent in California, though it is not common."

MARKETING SEASON: Harvesting of persimmons starts in California about Sept. 25 and continues to Dec. 10 with most active period Oct. 10 to Nov. 20. Marketing usually begins about Sept. 25 and continues to Jan. 10, with most active period Oct. 10 to Nov. 20. Unloads of persimmons in 41 cities for 3 years show a few arrive in late September; and the following percentages of the annual total in other months as follows: Oct. 28 percent; Nov. 41 percent; Dec. 23 percent; Jan. 7 percent; and Feb. 1 percent.

VARIETIES: "Hachiya is by far the most popular variety grown in California; it accounts for about 90 percent of the total acreage in the state. The remaining acreage is mostly comprised of the Tanenashi, Hyakume, Fuyu, and Tamopan, plus a few of the so-called Maru varieties. Hachiya is an attractive, deep orange red color at maturity with a smooth glossy surface. The variety is large, sometimes weighing over a pound, and has a distinctive acorn shape, familiar to the trade and public. A fine shipping variety, it ripens uniformly and is ordinarily seedless, with clear yellow-colored flesh. When pollinated, black areas appear in the flesh around the seed. A large gelatinous membrane covers the seed, or occupies the seed cavity when no seed is present. The Hachiya is astringent until soft, when the flesh becomes pleasantly sweet and highly perfumed. It is very desirable as a table or dessert fruit and is also outstanding when dried or cooked in prepared foods."

CONTAINERS: The main containers are wooden, 1-layer flats holding 10 to 12 lb. net; and 2-layer flats, 20 to 24 lb. net. The smaller container is loaded 2000 to a carlot equivalent, the larger, 1000. Container No. 800 in Freight Container Tariff No. 1-H has inside dimensions of 3-1/2 x 13-1/2 x 16-1/8 in. with 762 cu. in. capacity. Container No. 801 has inside dimensions of 5 x 13-1/2 x 16-1/8 in. with 1088 cu. in. capacity. Currently, a new shipping container made out of expanded polystyrene foam is in use. This is a white box with a self-locking cover. Its inside dimensions are 16-1/8 in. by 13-1/2 in. by 6-3/8 in. deep. The fruits are packed in a semi-rigid, polyvinyl cell tray. Two trays are packed per box.

QUALITY: The fruit should be well-shaped, plump, smooth, highly colored, with unbroken skin, and with stem cap attached. While in theory it would be desirable to select fruits

*UFFVA

that are soft as jelly, scented and ready to eat, in practice such soft persimmons in a retail store probably would soon be too bruised to be acceptable. Certainly if offered unpackaged, they might be cut by customers' fingernails and severely damaged by pressure in handling. When buying, select firm, fully colored persimmons, and hold them at room temperature until they are soft, or ripen by placing them in a plastic bag with ripe apples.

GRADE: There are no U.S. standards for persimmons. However, California, which grows almost all the commercial persimmons, has standard requirements in Section 805 of the Agricultural Code. "Persimmons shall be mature but not over-ripe. Hachiya variety shall have 90 percent of surface at time of picking orange or reddish color. Other Oriental varieties shall have 75 percent of surface at time of picking orange or reddish, balance at least yellowish green color. Free from: mold, decay, serious damage wasting 10 percent by weight by: cuts, bruises, broken skin, hail, growth cracks, other causes. Total tolerance of defects 10 percent by count, only 5 percent of any one defect allowed. Packing requirements: variation in size of not over 1/2 in. allowed when packed or partially packed. Shall not be deceptively packed. No markings required but when any markings used shall not be false or misleading."

PINEAPPLES*

USES: Pineapples are used in salads and desserts, sliced, crushed, cubed, grated, eaten plain or dipped in sugar. They make a natural ingredient for cakes, cookies, pies, and sundaes. Pineapple makes tasty jam, garnish for beverages, is good pickled, and traditionally goes with ham. Special recipes include layers of pineapple sprinkled with sugar and alternated with vanilla ice cream; chicken salad with pineapple; seafood and pineapple, and fresh fruit salad. If pineapple is harvested sufficiently ripe, no sugar is needed. Such a stage would be with 1/8 of the shell yellow. Efforts should be made by shippers to provide pineapples with ample natural sweetness so no added sugar is required.

For slicing or dicing pineapple, wash it, and slice it crosswise with a large sharp knife into 1-in. thick slices. With a paring knife, peel each slice. Make the peeling thick enough to remove the eyes, or thinner, removing the eyes with the tip of a vegetable peeler, or apple corer. Then cut into desired shapes.

For serving in the shell, wash the pineapple, and with a large sharp knife start at the center of the crown, and saw gently down the spikes, cutting it in half lengthwise. Cut each half into 2 pieces. With a paring knife, cut about 1/4 in. from the skin, loosening the wedge completely. Cut the fruit into chunks and remove, leaving shell. The shell may then be used as an attractive container in which to serve the pineapple, or one of the many salads containing pineapple.

For serving in the shell, there is a special knife which cuts pineapple into 6 sections while coring it. This is similar to a pear cutter.

For serving luau style, there is a special barrel-type knife on the market which sections the fruit into spears and leaves the shell intact. The shell can be used for drinks or, in the case of small pineapples, as salad or appetizer cups.

For serving in the half shell, slice pineapple in half longitudinally through the crown. Using curved knife, scoop out core and flesh. Refill with fruit salad topped with sherbet or cottage cheese.

For pineapple snacks, wash the pineapple and then cut around each section with a sharp paring knife. Cut deeply enough to reach the core. Leave a row of uncut sections at the top and bottom. Guests may then serve themselves by pulling out a section at a time.

To prepare a pineapple luau style, cut a thick slice from the top and the bottom of a fresh, ripe pineapple, saving the bottom slice. Run a sharp, thin, long knife blade around the pineapple between the rind and the meat, leaving an intact shell 3/8 in. thick. To do this, cut the pineapple from either end to the half-way point, keeping the knife blade pointed toward the rind. Push the cylinder of pineapple out the big end by pressing from the small end. Cut the cylinder in half lengthwise, then cut each half into quarters. Cut away and discard the core adhering to the quarters. Cut the quarters into lengthwise strips, place the bottom slice on a plate, then place the pineapple shell on the slice. Fill with the pineapple strips.

*UFFVA

PINEAPPLES

FRESH (2/23/53   51.1485)
GRADES: U.S. FANCY   U.S. NO. 1   U.S. NO. 2
CANNED (3/16/57   52.1711)
GRADES: "A" OR   "B" OR   "C" OR   "SUB-
           "FANCY"   "CHOICE"   "STAN-   STAN-
                                   DARD"   DARD"

Minimum
Score   90   80   70   Less than 70

	NET WEIGHT OZ.	NET WEIGHT METRIC	DRAINED WEIGHT OZ.	DRAINED WEIGHT METRIC
Chunks				
No. 8Z Tall	7.8	221.1 g	5	141.8 g
No. 2½	26.8	759.8 g	18-1/4	517.4 g
No. 10	98.5	2.8 kg	65-3/4	1.9 kg
Cubes				
No. 8Z Tall	7.8	221.1 g	5	141.8 g
No. 2½	26.8	759.8 g	18-1/4	517.4 g
No. 10	98.5	2.8 kg	71-1/4	2.0 kg
Tidbits				
No. 8Z Tall	7.8	221.1 g	5	141.8 g
No. 2½	26.8	759.8 g	18-1/4	517.4 g
No. 10	98.5	2.8 kg	65-3/4	1.9 kg
Spears				
No. 2½	26.8	759.8 g	18-1/4	517.4 g
Slices				
No. 2½	26.8	759.8 g	18-1/4	517.4 g
No. 10	98.5	2.8 kg	61-1/2	1.7 kg
Half slices				
No. 2½	26.8	759.8 g	18	510.3 g

	NET WEIGHT OZ.	NET WEIGHT METRIC	DRAINED WEIGHT OZ.	DRAINED WEIGHT METRIC
Broken slices				
No. 2½	26.8	759.8 g	18	510.3 g
No. 10	98.5	2.8 kg	62-1/2	1.8 kg
Crushed: Any container size "Solid pack" crushed			not less than 78 percent by weight of contents	
"Heavy pack" crushed			73 percent to 78 percent by weight of contents	
Others			not less than 63 percent by weight of contents	

SYRUP

BRIX MEASUREMENTS

Crushed can pineapple

"Extra-heavy syrup" or
"Extra heavily sweetened"

22° to 35°

"Heavy syrup" or "Heavily
sweetened"

18° to less than 22°

"Light syrup" or "Lightly
sweetened"

14° to less than 18°

"Unsweetened" or "In pineapple juice"

Packed in pineapple juice

"In clarified juice"

Packed in clarified juice

Other styles other than
crushed

"Extra-heavy syrup" 22° to 35°
"Heavy syrup" 18° to less than 22°
"Light syrup" 14° to less than 18°
"In water" Packed in water
"In pineapple juice" or "In Packed in pineapple juice
unsweetened pineapple juice"
"In clarified juice" Packed in clarified juice

FROZEN (1/25/49   52.1741)

GRADES:	"A" OR "FANCY"	"B" OR "CHOICE"	"C" OR "STAN-DARD"	"D" OR "SUB-STAN-DARD"
Minimum Score:	90	80	70	Less than 70

WHAT BECOMES OF A PINEAPPLE

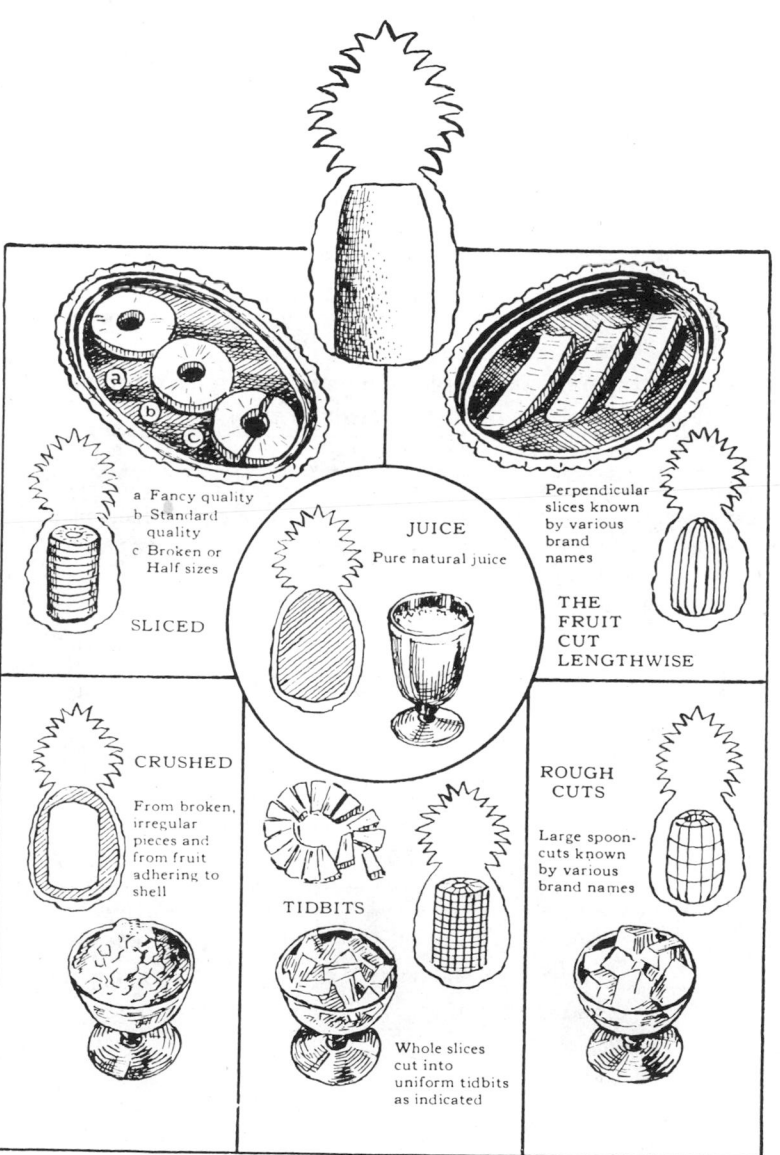

Courtesy of American Can Company

MARKETING SEASON: Pineapples are available on the fresh market in all months, but in much larger supply March through June.

MONTHLY AVAILABILITY EXPRESSED AS PERCENTAGE OF TOTAL ANNUAL SUPPLY

Jan.	Feb.	Mar.	Apr.	May	June
%	%	%	%	%	%
6	8	13	14	14	10
July	Aug.	Sept.	Oct.	Nov.	Dec.
%	%	%	%	%	%
6	5	4	5	7	6

VARIETIES: There are hundreds of varieties of pineapple, but only a few are commercially important. The following chart lists the main pineapples of commerce, with emphasis on varieties used at least partly in fresh form.

Name	Description	Growing Area	Use	Notes
Cayenne (Smooth Cayenne)	Abt. 3 to 5-1/2 lb., cylindrical; flesh yellow; high acid, high sugar content	Hawaii, Australia, Philippines, S. Africa	Fresh & Canning	"The most widely planted variety"
Red Spanish	Abt. 3 to 5 lb., squarish; flesh pale yellow, fibrous aromatic; spicy, acid flavor	Puerto Rico, Cuba, Florida	Mostly Fresh	Tough shell makes it a good shipper
Queen	2 to 3 lb.; flesh rich yellow; crisp, mild flavor, less acid and less juicy	S. Africa, Australia, Malaysia	Fresh & Canning	Durable, keeps well when mature

Name	Description	Growing Area	Use	Notes
Pernambuco (Pernambuca)	3 to 4 lb., cylindrical, slight tapering at top; flesh yellow-white, tender, juicy; flavor mild, sweet, less acid than Cayenne	Brazil	Fresh	Erratic ripening habits and appearance
Sugarloaf	Conical to globular; flesh yellow-white; flavor sweet and rich	Mexico, Cuba	Fresh	Name may apply to various varieties
Cabazoni (Cabezona)	5 to 10 lb., flesh yellow-white; flavor fairly good	Puerto Rico	Local Fresh	Notable mainly for size

Other varieties of local or regional importance are Abachi (Abakka or Abacaxi), Monte Lirio, Singapore Spanish, and Vermelho.

CONTAINERS: A fiberboard container is generally used for pineapple. A major container is a full-telescope style, fiberboard box, 12 x 10-1/2 x 16 in. inside, volume 2016 cu. in. This is Container No. 7482 in the railroad tariff. It holds 40 lb. net. Wirebound pineapple crates are also authorized in the railroad tariff, including Container No. 3980 which is 12 x 10-1/2 x 16-1/2 in. inside. Another pineapple fiberboard box authorized is No. 7480 which is 9 x 13 x 15., capacity 1755 cu. in. Another is No. 7485 which is 13-1/2 x 13-1/2 x 19-3/4 in., capacity 3599 cu. in. A much used fiberboard container is 5-1/4 x 13-1/4 x 19 in., authorized by the Uniform Classification Committee under a test permit which has been extended repeatedly at the request of shippers.

SERVINGS AND WEIGHTS: The following table, from USDA, gives the yield in percent and number of portions per purchase unit for pineapple; also the approximate number of purchase units necessary to yield 25 or 100 portions.

Unit of Purchase	Weight per unit [lb.]	Yield as served [percent]	Portion as served	Portions per purchase units [Number]	Approximate purchase units for	
					25 portions	100 portions
Pound	1.00	52	3 oz. cubed	2.77	9-1/4	36-1/4
1/2 crate	35.00	52	3 oz. cubed	97.07	less than 1	1-1/4
1/2 gal. jar (chunks)	4.36	100	4 oz.	17.44	1-1/2	5-3/4

QUALITY: Nobody doubts what good quality is when applied to a pineapple cut fully ripe from the plant. It is juicy and sweet if well grown. But there is some controversy about quality at the terminal market and retail level. There are suggestions that a pineapple "May be held for ripening." Really, there should be no controversy because the physiology of a pineapple is such that it cannot sweeten or ripen after harvest. The pineapple has no starch reserve, so there is no material to convert to sugar after cutting from the plant. It is the starch reserve that makes it possible for a banana or a pear to attain excellent texture and palatability by ripening after harvest. On the other hand, it is the lack of such reserve that makes it impossible for a grape or a pineapple to ripen after harvest. While a pineapple will never be any sweeter than when picked, it may be less acid than at harvest, because some acid can be lost through respiration. As time goes on after harvest, the shell color changes and the fruit finally becomes soft. This is a reflection of deterioration, not ripening. Pineapples need to be harvested as nearly ripe as possible and rushed to market. They should be eaten as soon as possible.

It must be accepted as a fact of life that a fully ripe pineapple cannot be shipped to any distant market with present marketing techniques. In this respect it is similar to the fully ripe apricot, plum, peach, or tomato. For a pineapple to be marketed fresh, it must be picked before full ripeness. The stage is sometimes called mature-green. In any event, the closer the pineapple comes to ripeness, the less market life it has, and the more difficult it is to get it to the consumer in edible condition. On the other hand, the greener it is when picked, the less palatable it will be upon reaching the consumer's table. The grower-shipper must compromise.

"For pineapple, ripening (on the plant) means an increase in sugar, an increase in acid, an increase in color, and an increase as well as a qualitative change in the volatile flavor constituents. Of these four quality factors, the only one usually observed by a consumer is the change in color, but in harvested fruit, the change in color of the shell does not mean that the other three factors have also improved. The sugar will never be any higher than it was at the time of harvest. The acids may go up or down depending on handling practices in marketing. Essentially nothing is known about the qualitative change in flavor volatiles during storage."

From all this, it appears there is nothing to be gained by holding a pineapple at home or in the restaurant in the hope it will improve. The sooner it is eaten, the better it will be.

In choosing a pineapple, select one that is plump and fresh looking and as large as possible. The larger the fruit, the greater the proportion of edible flesh. Thus, a 2- to 3-lb. pineapple has less than 30 percent edible flesh, while half of a 5-lb. pineapple has more flesh than a 3 to 3-1/2 lb. fruit. Fresh deep-green crown leaves are a good sign. A fruit that is old looking, dry, with brown leaves should be avoided. Fragrance is a good sign, but usually the fruit is kept too cold to be fragrant. Ease with which leaves can be pulled out is not a sign of good quality. The thump test is of no value. Shell color is not an indication of maturity. The grower himself can rely on a test of the sugar content, using an instrument called a refractometer. Probably the best criterion of selection is the brand of the shipper, if from experience the buyer knows it to be a good one.

GRADES: U.S. Standards for Pineapples provide for the following grades: U.S. Fancy, U.S. No. 1, and U.S. No. 2. U.S. No. 1 is the chief trading grade. Hawaii has its own wholesale grades, and these provide for Hawaii Fancy, Hawaii 1 and Hawaii Cocktail.

"U.S. No. 1 consists of pineapples of similar varietal characteristics which are mature, firm, dry, and well formed, which have well developed eyes, and which are free from decay and sunscald, and free from damage caused by bruising, sunburn, gummosis, disease, insects, rodents, or mechanical or other means. The butts shall be well trimmed, fairly well cured, and shall not be badly cracked. The tops shall be of characteristic color, single, reasonably straight, well attached to the fruit, and shall have not more than 5 crown slips, not more than 2 of which may be more than 2-3/4 in. in length. The length of the tops shall be not less than 4 in. nor more than twice the length of the fruit."

"In order to allow for variations incident to proper grading and handling, other than for size and marking, not more than a total of 10 percent by count of the pineapples in any lot may fail to meet the requirements of the grade: Provided, That no more than 1/2 of this amount, or 5 percent, shall be allowed for pineapples which are seriously damaged, including therein not more than 1 percent for pineapples affected by decay."

(See the complete grades, available from USDA, for definitions and further details. However, one point in the definitions should be challenged. "Mature" is defined as a stage that means "a proper completion of the ripening process." However, ripening does not occur after a pineapple is harvested.)

"Hawaii 1 consists of pineapples of similar varietal characteristics which are mature, but not overripe, fairly well formed, clean, well trimmed, which have no more than 2 crowns, and which have well-developed eyes firmly attached, characteristically colored, fresh tops, meets soluble solids requirements, and which are free from decay, yellow spot virus, spray burn, broken shells, bruises, crown slips, **gummosis, and from damage caused by sunburn, cracks,** knobs, trimming, disease, insects, or mechanical or other means. Single crown tops shall be no longer than twice the length of the fruit. Double crown tops shall be no longer than 1-1/2 times the length of the fruit. In order to allow for variations incident to proper grading and handling, not more than a total of 10 percent, by count, of the pineapples in any lot may fail to meet the requirements of this grade, but not more than 1/2 of this amount, or 5 percent shall be allowed for serious damage by any cause, including not more than 1 percent for pineapples affected by decay or breakdown."

PINEAPPLE—Canned [3/16/57]

Grade A: Color: Color of the pineapple units or mass is bright and is characteristic of properly ripened and matured pineapple of similar varietal characteristics; and that there may be slight variations in shades of such characteristic color in the units, with each unit or the mass, and that white radiating streaks may be present: Provided, that such variations do not materially affect the appearance of the product.

Size and Shape: Sliced. The diameter of the slice with the longest diameter does not exceed the diameter of the slice with the shortest diameter by more than 1/10 in. The thickness of the slice with the widest thickness at the circumference does not exceed the thickness of the slice with the most narrow thickness at the circumference by more than 3/22 in. The maximum radial axis of any slice does not exceed the minimum radial axis of the same slice by more than 1/8 in. The drained weight of the largest slice is not more than 1.4 times the weight of the smallest slice. Small Tidbits. Not more than 7-1/2 percent may consist of units which may fail to conform to any one or more of the following dimensions:

Length of outside arc	More than 3/4 in. but not more than 1-3/4 in.
Thickness	More than 5/16 in. but not more than 1/2 in.
Length	More than 11/16 in. but not more than 1-1/4 in.

Not more than 7-1/2 percent may consist of units each of which weighs less than 3/4 as much as the average weight of all the untrimmed tidbits. Chunks. None of the units may have a longest dimension greater than 1-1/2 in. Not more than 10 percent consists of pieces weighing less than 3/10 oz. each. Symmetrical Chunks. None of the units may have a longest dimension greater than 1-1/2 in. Not less than an aggregate of 90 percent consists of pieces weighing 5/16 oz. or more each nor exceeds at least one of the following dimensions.

Length of outside arc	3/16 in.
Thickness	1/2 in.
Length	11/16 in.

Cubes. Not more than an aggregate of 10 percent may consist of units of such size that they pass through meshes of a sieve with 5/16 sq. in. openings or pieces weighing more than 3/22 oz. each. Spears. The units are of substantially equal length. Not more than 10 percent of the units, or not more than 1 unit in a container or less than 10 units, may be less than 3/4 in. or more than 1-3/4 in. in the longest edge dimension other than the longitudinal measurement of the spear. The drained weight of the largest spear is not more than 1.4 times the weight of the smallest spear. Half sliced. The diameter of the half slice with the longest diameter does not exceed the diameter of the half slice with the shortest diameter by more than 1/10 in. The thickness of the half slice with the widest thickness at the circumference does not exceed the thickness of the half slice with the most narrow thickness at the circumference by more than 3/22 in. The drained weight of the largest half slice is more than 1.75 times the weight of the smallest half slice, except for an occasional broken piece due to splitting or an occasional whole slice not quite completely cut through. **Defects:** Sliced. Not more than an occasional unit may be insignificantly or slightly trimmed, but none may be excessively trimmed; not more than a total of 5 percent may be blemished or seriously blemished; or one unit in a container is permitted to be blemished or seriously blemished if such unit exceeds the allowance of 5 percent; Provided that in all containers comprising the sample such blemished units do not exceed an average of 5 percent of the total number of units; and not more than 1 unit in containers of 25 units or less, and not more than 3 units in containers of more than 25 units, may be mashed. Tidbits. Not more than 5 percent may consist of units that are excessively trimmed, not more than a total of 5 percent may be blemished or seriously blemished; but not more than 2-1/2 percent may be seriously blemished; and not more than 3 units in containers of less than 150 units, or not more than 2 percent in containers of 150 or more, may be mashed. Chunks. Not more than a total of 5 percent may be blemished or seriously blemished; but not more than 2-1/2 percent may be seriously blemished; and not more than 3 of units in a container of less than 70 units, or not more than 5 percent in containers of 70 units or more, may be mashed. Cubes. Not more than a total of 2 percent may be blemished or seriously blemished; but not more than 1 percent may be

seriously blemished. Spears. Not more than an occasional unit may be significantly or slightly trimmed; but none may be excessively trimmed; Not more than a total of 5 percent may be blemished or seriously blemished; or 1 unit in a container is permitted to be blemished or seriously blemished if such unit exceeds the allowance of 5 percent: Provided, that in all containers comprising the sample such blemished units do not exceed an average of 5 percent of the total number of units; and not more than 1 unit per container may be mashed. Crushed. Not more than 1/2 percent may consist of fragments becoming blemished, including seriously blemished fragments. Half Sliced. Not more than an occasional unit may be insignificantly or slightly trimmed, but none may be excessively trimmed; Not more than a total of 5 percent may be blemished or seriously blemished; or 1 unit in a container is permitted to be blemished or seriously blemished if such unit exceeds the allowance of 5 percent: Provided, that in all containers comprising the sample such blemished units do not exceed an average of 5 percent of the total units; and not more than 1 unit in containers of 25 units or less, and not more than 3 units in containers of more than 25 units, may be mashed. Broken Sliced. Not more than 5 percent may be excessively trimmed; Not more than a total of 5 percent may be blemished or seriously blemished; and not more than 5 percent may be mashed. **Character:** Sliced, half sliced; broken sliced—Units are of practically uniform ripeness, are at least reasonably firm with the fruitlets appearing as a compact structure, are reasonably free from porosity; and not more than 0.4 oz. of core is contained in 1 lb. of drained fruit. Tidbits; cubes; spears; crushed—See sliced, half sliced, etc. Chunks. Units are of practically uniform ripeness, the fruitlets appear as a compact structure; the units are reasonably free from porosity, and the units are practically free from any core material.

Grade B: Color: Color of the pineapple unit or mass may be no more than slightly dull but is characteristic of properly matured pineapple of similar varietal characteristics; and that there may be marked variations in shades of such characteristic color in the units, within each unit, within the mass, and that white radiating streaks may be present: Provided, that such variations do not seriously affect the appearance of the product. **Size:** See Grade A. All wording is the same except as follows: Slices: 1/8 in. 1/8 in. 1/4 in.

Small Tidbits: 12-1/2 percent

Length of outside arc	3/5 in.	3/4 in.
Thickness	5/16 in.	1/2 in.
Length	11/16 in.	1-1/4 in.

15 percent. Large Tidbits: 12-1/2 percent

Length of outside arc	3/4 in.	1-3/4 in.
Thickness	5/16 in.	1/2 in.
Length	11/16 in.	1-1/4 in.

15 percent. Chunks: 15 percent. Symmetrical chunks: 80 percent

Length of outside arc	9/16 in.
Thickness	1/2 in.
Length	11/16 in.

Not more than 15 percent consist of pieces weighing less than 3/16 oz. each.

Cubes. Not more than 15 percent may consist of pieces weighing more than 3/32 oz. each. Spears. 20 percent ... 5 units. Half Sliced. 1/8 in. 1/8 in. **Defects:** See Grade A. All wording is the same except as follows: reasonably free: sliced. 20 percent may be slightly or excessively trimmed. 7-1/2 percent may be excessively trimmed but, in any container having not more than 10 units, 1 unit may be excessively trimmed; and in any container having more than 10 units but not more than 27 units, 2 units may be excessively trimmed. 12-1/2 percent may be blemished ... 5 units but not more than 10 units, 2 units may be blemished; 10 units ... 32 units, 4 units may be blemished; and. Tidbits. 15 percent. 12-1/2 percent ... 6-1/4 percent. 70 units ... 5 percent ... 70 units ... Cubes. 12-1/2 percent ... 6-1/4 percent. Spears. Not more than a total of 20 percent may be insignificantly, slightly, or excessively trimmed; but not more than 15 percent may be excessively trimmed. Not more than 12-1/2 percent may be blemished, but in any container having not more than 5 units, 1 unit may be blemished; in 1 container having more than 5 units but not more than 10 units, 2 units may be blemished; and in containers having more than 10 units but not more than 32 units, may be blemished; Crushed. 1-1/4 percent. Half Sliced. Not more than 20 percent may be slightly or excessively trimmed; not more than 7-1/2 percent may be excessively trimmed, but in any container having not more than 10 units, 1 unit may be excessively trimmed; and in any container having more than 10 units but not more than 27 units, 2 units may be excessively trimmed. 8 percent ... 8 percent. 8 percent. Broken Sliced. 10 percent; 8 percent. **Character:** See Grade A. Wording is the same except as follows: Sliced, half sliced, broken sliced—reasonably uniform ... fairly free ... 1.1 oz. Tidbits, Cubes, Spears, Crushed—Reasonably uniform ... 1.1 oz. Chunks. See Grade B Tidbits, Cubes, etc.

Grade C: Color: Color may be dull but is characteristic of properly matured pineapple of similar varietal characteristics; and there may be marked variations in shades of such characteristic color in the units or within each unit, or white radiating streaks may be present which variations may seriously affect the appearance. **Size:** Half-sliced canned pineapple means that the units fail to meet the requirements; but the drained weight of the largest half slice is not more than 1.75 times the weight of the smallest. Not uniform for broken, sliced canned pineapple means: Not more than 10 percent may consist of pieces having an arc of less than 90°; not more than 5 percent may consist of: Pieces that measure in thickness less than 5/16 in. or more than 1 in.; or pieces that measure less than 3/4 in. in width as measured from the outer edge to the inner edge; and not more than 5 percent may consist of broken slices having an outside diameter differing by as much as 3/8 in. **Defects:** See Grade B. All wording is the same except as follows: Half Sliced. 12-1/2 percent may be blemished, not more than 5 units may be blemished; in containers having more than 5 units but not more than 10 units, 2 units may be blemished; and in containers having more than 10 units but not more than 32 units, 4 may be blemished. Broken Sliced. 15 percent; 12 percent ... but in any container having more than 10 units but not more than 32 units, 4 may be blemished; **Character:** Half sliced; broken sliced. See grade B, sliced; half sliced; etc. only changes in wording are: fairly uniform, fairly compact ... fairly free. **SStd:** Fails to meet necessary requirements.

PINEAPPLE—Frozen [1/25/49]

Grade A: Color: Yellow color typical of frozen pineapple, and there may be some variations of such color in the mass or of the units. **Size and Symmetry:** Whole Slices and Tidbits. All of the units with each style are the same apparent thickness, size, and shape, with not more than a slight deviation in actual dimensions. **Defects:** Whole Slices. No units are crushed; no units are excessively trimmed; not more than 5 percent may be blemished; and not more than 10 percent may be broken in 1 place only. 1 blemished unit and 1 broken unit are permitted if 1 unit exceeds the respective allowance of 5 percent and 10 percent by count. Tidbits and Chunks. Not more than 5 percent may be crushed, and not more than 5 percent may be blemished units. Crushed. Not more than 1/2 percent may be blemished units. In determining the weight of blemished material, the weight of the entire blemished piece is included, and the percentage is based on the net weight of the pineapple. **Character:** Whole Slices, Tidbits, and Crushed. The fruit is of practically uniform ripeness, and there may be present not more than 2-1/2 percent that is core material or fibrous stock; and, in the case of whole slices and tidbits, the fruit is reasonably firm, and the fruitlets appear as compact structure, reasonably free from porosity. Chunks. The fruit is of practically uniform ripeness and normally has had more of the fibrous portions around the core hold removed than is the case with other styles of pack; the fruit is reasonably firm, and the fruitlets appear as a compact structure, reasonably free from porosity.

Grade B: Color: Frozen pineapple may have considerable variation of such color in the mass or of the units. **Size and Symmetry:** See grade A. All wording is the same. **Defects:** See grade A. All wording is the same except as follows: Whole Slices. Not more than 3 percent may be excessively trimmed; not more than 5 percent may be crushed, not more than 12-1/2 percent may be blemished, not more than 25 percent may be broken in 1 place only. Tidbits and Chunks. 12-1/2 percent may be blemished. Crushed: 1 percent. **Character:** See grade A. All wording is the same except as follows: Whole Slices, Tidbits and Crushed—reasonably firm ... 5 percent ... fairly free. Chunks—reasonably uniform ... fairly free.

Grade C: Color: Individual units may vary markedly from a uniform, typical yellow color and may be slightly dull in color. **Size and Symmetry:** Frozen pineapple that falls into this classification shall not be graded above U.S. Grade C regardless of the total score for the product. **Defects:** Half Slices and Broken Slices. Not more than 5 percent may be crushed; and not more than 12-1/2 percent may be blemished. Since half slices and broken slices of frozen pineapple are whole slices broken in more than 1 place, these styles are scored in this classification and shall not be graded above U.S. Grade C, regardless of the total score. **Character:** Half slice and broken slices. Texture may be variable and there may be present not more than 5 percent that is core material or fibrous stick, and the fruitlets may be fleeced and loosely constructed. **SStd:** Fails to meet necessary requirements.

PLUMS—PRUNES*

USES: Plums and fresh prunes are excellent eaten out of hand. They make good pies, puddings, stewed fruit, preserves, jellies, and jams. Plums also go well in cakes, tarts, and other pastries. Stewed prunes and prune juice are well-known commodities. Plums may be stewed, scalloped, poached, or sliced into salads, served with ice cream, slaw, sherbet, Bavarian cream, or cake.

MARKETING SEASON: Domestic fresh plums and prunes are marketed from June through October. *Plums* start in late May and are available through September, while *prunes* are available July through October. In some other months, especially January through March, small quantities of fresh plums are imported from Chile and Argentina and marketed at fancy prices.

The following chart, derived from USDA data on unloads (representing about 60 percent of the national total) shows the monthly availability of fresh plums and prunes expressed as a percentage of the total annual supply, averaged for the 4-year period 1964-67.

Jan.	Feb.	Mar.	Apr.	May	June	July
%	%	%	%	%	%	%
*	*	*		*	16	30

Aug.	Sept.	Oct.	Nov.	Dec.	Annual Total Mill. lbs.
%	%	%	%	%	
31	19	2			293

VARIETIES: The principal commercial varieties of plums, in terms of California out-of-state shipments, are described in the following charts. Federal State Market News Service reports of sales indicate a trend toward more varieties, 59 now compared to 45 in 1958, that were important enough to be listed in sales statistics.

In recent years, sales have been divided over the larger number of varieties while per capita consumption has changed very little. Some varieties, such as Ace, Burbank, and Sharkey, have been on a declining trend in recent years. Other newer varieties, such as Casselman, Laroda, and Nubiana, have become increasingly important. However, Santa Rose and El Dorado have been consistent leaders.

become increasingly important. However, Santa Rosa and El Dorado have been consistent leaders.

The best known variety of P. institia (Damson plum) is Shropshire. In some locations, the Damsons and varieties of American species are of some importance to local food supplies. *P. americana* is native from the northeast states to Montana and southward to Colorado, Texas, and Florida. The fruit is yellow to pinkish, flesh golden yellow, flavor superior to other native species. Leading varieties include DeSota, Hawkeye, Terry, Weaver, and Wyant.

Variety	Description	Season	Notes
P. salicina			
Ace	med. to lge., oval, brown; red-fleshed	late	good shipper
Beauty	med., heart-shaped crimson; amber flesh streaked with scarlet	early	developed by Luther Burbank; intr. 1911
Burmosa	lge., semiheart-shaped, red, blushed; soft, light yellow flesh; mild flavor	early	Burbank x Formosa; intr. 1952
Casselman	similar to Santa Rosa but yellow-flecked and lighter red	late	considered bud mutation of Late Santa Rosa; intr. 1959
Duarte (early & late)	lge., dark red, heart-shaped; juicy, dark red flesh	— —	both early & late have declined in volume, 1964-67
El Dorado	med. sized, oblate; black; firm yellow flesh	mid	P. salicina x P. simonii x
Kelsey	lge., yellow-green splashed with red; firm yellow flesh	mid-late	intr. about 1870; tree is cold susceptible [Cont.]

*UFFVA

Variety	Description	Season	Notes
Laroda	lge., globular, reddish yellow; firm yellow flesh	mid-late	Gaviota x Santa Rosa; intr. 1954; large factor since 1963
Mariposa	round, red with gray bloom to dark red purple; red flesh; rich and aromatic	mid	chance seedling, patented in 1934
Nubiana	lge., oblate, black red; very firm amber flesh	late	Gaviota x El Dorado; intr. 1954; large factor since 1963
Queen Ann	lge., mahogany color; amber flesh, rich honey-like flavor	late	Gaviota x El Dorado; intr. 1954
Redroy	red; clear amber flesh, firm flesh, rich flavor	mid-late	Gaviota x Elephant Heart; intr. 1954
Santa Rosa (early & late)	med.-lge., conical, dark purple red; juicy, flesh yellow to dark red near skin	— —	developed by Luther Burbank; intr. 1967
Wickson	lge., heart-shaped, yellow red; flesh yellow, juicy	mid	a seedling of Kelsey, developed by Luther Burbank; intr. 1895

P. domestica

Variety	Description	Season	Notes
President (Imperatrice Subgroup)	lge., oval, dark purple; flesh yellow, late grained, sweet, juicy	late	intr. 1901; if Calif. winter is warm, next growth somewhat retarded
Diamond, Grand Duke, Tragedy (early & late)	other leading varieties of Imperatrice Subgroup		

[*Cont.*]

Variety	Description	Season	Notes
Italian, Giant, French (d'Agen), Sugar, German, Imperial	leading varieties of Prune Subgroup can be dried without removal of pit and without fermenting		
Reine Claude, Jefferson, Washington, Yellow Gage	leading varieties of Green Gage Subgroup, important canning varieties) fruits roundish, green yellow, sweet, tender, juicy		

CONTAINERS: For many years, the principal container used for shipment of plums and fresh prunes has been the 4-basket crate which holds approximately 27-30 lb. of fruit. However, the tightfill carton came into more general use because of its labor-saving characteristics. Others used to some extent are the L.A. lug, 1/2 bu. peach baskets, and Northwestern prune lugs, according to USDA's Market News Branch.

According to Donald R. Stokes, USDA expert on packaging, "more plums are now being place-packed in paperboard or plastic cell trays in the shipping containers. Both wood and fiberboard shipping containers are used. Some polystyrene foam boxes have been used experimentally. Substantially, more prunes and plums are being jumble-packed in 30-lb. fiberboard boxes. Some are also packed in wood and wire-bound boxes."

The California Agricultural Code specifies, "Plums and fresh prunes shall be in standard containers numbers 5, 9C, 10A, 12A, 12B, or 22D." These are described in the following chart:

No.	Description	Inside Dimensions [In.]
5	standard wooden crate	4 to 7-1/8 x 16 x 16-1/8
9C	special plum box	7 x 12-1/2 x 12-1/2
10A	standard fruit box	5 to 10 x 10-1/8 x 16-3/4
12A	standard cherry lug	3-3/4 x 11-1/2 x 14-1/8
12B	California fruit box	2-3/8 to 7-1/8 x 11-1/2 x 16-1/8
22B	special lug box	4 to 7-1/8 x 12-1/2 x 16-1/8
22D	standard lug box (L.A. lug)	2-7/8 to 7-1/8 x 13-1/2 x 16-1/8

PLUMS

FRESH (5/9/69   51.1520)
GRADES: U.S. FANCY   U.S. NO. 1
         U.S. COMBINATION   U.S. NO. 2
CANNED (12/15/72   52.1781)

GRADES:	"A" OR "FANCY"	"B" OR "CHOICE"	"C" OR "STAN-DARD"	"SUB-STAN-DARD"
Minimum Score:	90	80	70	Less than 70

Purple halves, unpeeled	NET WEIGHT OZ.	NET WEIGHT METRIC	DRAINED WEIGHT OZ.	DRAINED WEIGHT METRIC
No. 8Z Tall	5.2	147.4 g	4.2	119.1 g
No. 303	10.7	303.3 g	8.9	252.3 g
No. 2½	18.7	530.1 g	15.0	425.2 g
No. 10	70.0	1.98 kg	57.7	1.6 kg
Purple whole, unpeeled				
No. 8Z Tall	4.6	130.4 g	3.7	104.9 g
No. 303	9.8	277.8 g	7.5	212.6 g
No. 2½ less than				
17	17.0	482.0 g		
17-22	17.5	496.1 g	13.5	382.7 g
23 or more	18.0	510.3 g		
No. 10 less than				
70	66.0	1.9 kg	52.3	1.5 kg
70 or more	68.0	1.9 kg		
Green, yellow, whole, peeled				
No. 8Z Tall	5.3	150.2 g	3.7	104.9 g
No. 303	10.5	297.7 g	7.5	212.6 g
No. 2½	18.7	530.1 g	13.5	382.7 g
No. 10	68.8	1.95 kg	52.3	1.5 kg

Green, yellow, whole, unpeeled	NET WEIGHT OZ.	NET WEIGHT METRIC	DRAINED WEIGHT OZ.	DRAINED WEIGHT METRIC
No. 8Z Tall	5.1	144.6 g	3.7	104.9 g
No. 303	10.0	283.5 g	7.5	216.6 g
No. 2½	18.2	516.0 g	13.5	382.7 g
No. 10	67.0	1.9 kg	52.3	1.5 kg

SYRUP	SPECIFIC GRAVITY (Brix Measurements)
"Extra heavy syrup," or "Extra heavily sweetened fruit juice(s) and water," or "Extra heavily sweetened fruit juice(s)"	25° to 35°
"Heavy syrup," or "Heavily sweetened fruit juice(s) and water," or "Heavily sweetened fruit juice(s)"	19° or more but less than 25°
"Light syrup," or "Lightly sweetened fruit juice(s) and water" or "Lightly sweetened fruit juice(s)"	15° or more but less than 19°
"Slightly sweetened water," or "Extra light syrup," or "Slightly sweetened fruit juice(s) and water," or "Slightly sweetened fruit juice(s)"	11° or more but less than 15°
"In water"	N.A.
"In fruit juice(s) and water"	N.A.
"In fruit juice(s)"	N.A.

FROZEN (3/6/56   52.2911)

GRADES:	"A" OR "FANCY"	"B" OR "CHOICE"	"SUB-STANDARD"
Minimum Score:	85	70	Less than 70

PRUNES

FRESH (5/9/69   51.1520)
GRADES: U.S. FANCY; U.S. NO. 1; U.S. COMBINATION; U.S. NO. 2

CANNED DRIED (5/24/67   52.5601)

| GRADES: | "A" OR "FANCY" | "B" or CHOICE" | "C" OR "STANDARD" | "SUBSTANDARD" |

| Minimum Score: | 90 | 75 | 60 | Less than 60 |

	NET WEIGHT OZ.	NET WEIGHT METRIC	DRAINED WEIGHT (OZ.)			DRAINED WEIGHT METRIC		
			Metal Containers		Glass Containers	Metal Containers		Glass Containers
			Regular pack	Heavy pack	Regular pack	Regular pack	Heavy pack	Regular pack
No. 2½	26.8	759.8 g	19	29	18	538.6 g	822.2 g	510.3 g
No. 10	98.5	2.8 kg	70	110	—	2.0 kg	3.1 kg	—

SYRUP	SPECIFIC GRAVITY (Brix Measurements)
"Extra heavy syrup," or "Extra heavily sweetened fruit juice(s) and water," or "Extra heavily sweetened fruit juice(s)"	30° to 45°
"Heavy syrup," or "Heavily sweetened fruit juice(s) and water," or "Heavily sweetened fruit juice(s)"	24° or more but less than 30°
"Light syrup," or "Lightly sweetened fruit juice(s) and water," or "Lightly sweetened fruit juice(s)"	20° or more but less than 24°
"Slightly sweetened water," or "Extra light syrup" or "Slightly sweetened fruit juice(s) and water," or "Slightly sweetened fruit juice(s)"	less than 20°
"In water"	N.A.
"In fruit juice(s) and water"	N.A.
"In fruit juice(s)"	N.A.

DEHYDRATED (6/13/60   52.3231)

| GRADES: | "A" OR "FANCY" | "B" OR "CHOICE" | "SUBSTANDARD" |
| Minimum Score: | 85 | 70 | Less than 70 |

DRIED (10/11/65   52.3231)

| GRADES: | "A" OR "FANCY" | "B" OR "CHOICE" | "C" OR "STANDARD" | "SUBSTANDARD" |

WEIGHTS AND SERVINGS: The following table from USDA provides measures and equivalents useful in determining food quantities:

Food as Purchased	Purchase Unit	Servings per Purchase Unit	Serving Size or Portion	Purchase Units for 100 Servings	Additional Yield Information
PLUMS					
Fresh	lb.	4.00	2 medium raw plums (about 1/2 cup)	25	1 lb. AP= 0.94 lb. ready-to-cook or serve raw.
	lb.	4.67	1/2 cup raw halves	21-1/2	
		9.34	1/4 cup raw halves	10-3/4	
	lb.	4.20	1/2 cup raw sliced	24	
		8.40	1/4 cup raw sliced	12	
	lb.	3.27	1/2 cup cooked	30-3/4	
		6.54	1/4 cup cooked	15-1/2	

A pound of plums provides 2.67 portions of 3 medium plums each; and on the basis of such portions, it would take 9-1/2 lb. to provide 25 portions and 37-1/2 lb. to provide 100. ... If plums are to be served in portions of 3 oz. of pitted halves, each pound will yield 5.01 portions; and it will take 5 lb. to provide 25 portions; and 20 lb. to provide 100. The yield per pound after pitting is 94 percent. A 4-basket crate providing 28 lb. net will provide 140.37 portions of 3 oz. of pitted halves each.

QUALITY: USDA's "How to Buy Fresh Fruits" advises: "Quality characteristics for both (plums and prunes) are very similar and the same buying tips apply to both. *Plums* ... Varieties differ widely in appearance and flavor, so you should buy and taste one to see if that variety appeals to you. *Prunes*—Only a few varieties of prunes are commonly marketed, and they are all very similar. Prunes are purplish black or bluish black, with a moderately firm flesh which separates freely from the pit ... *Look for:* Plums and prunes with a good color for the variety, in a fairly firm to slightly soft stage of ripeness. *Avoid:* Fruits with skin breaks, punctures, or brownish discoloration. Also avoid immature fruits (relatively hard, poorly colored, very tart, sometimes shriveled) and overmature fruits (excessively soft, possibly leaking, or decaying)."

GRADES: U.S. grade standards for Fresh Plums and Prunes, effective April 23, 1966, provide for 4 grades, U.S. Fancy, U.S. No. 1, U.S. Combination and U.S. No. 2.

"U.S. No. 1 consists of plums or prunes of one variety which are well formed, clean, mature but not overripe, or soft, or shriveled; which are free from decay and sunscald, and free from damage caused by broken skins, heat injury, growth cracks, sunburn, split pits, hail marks, drought spots, gum spots, russeting, scars, other disease, insects, or mechanical or other means. Italian type prunes shall be fairly well colored and, unless otherwise specified, shall be not less than 1-1/8 in. in diameter."

PLUMS—Canned [12/15/72]

Grade A [Fancy]: Plums that are well colored and have a practically uniform color, and the number of reasonably well-colored plums does not exceed 2 in a whole sample unit size of 25 units, or 5 in a halves sample unit size of 50 units, may be given a score of 18 to 20 points. **Size:** No more than one unit of a whole sample unit size of 25 units, or 3 units of a halves sample unit size of 50 units, may exceed the maximum weight variation by 50 percent. **Defects:** There is no more than 1 small stem, 1 loose pit, or 2 damaged or seriously damaged, including 1 seriously damaged, units in a whole sample unit size of 25 units; or no more than 1 small stem, 1 loose pit, or 5 damaged or seriously damaged, including 1 seriously damaged, units in a halves sample size of 50 units. **Character:** No more than 2 units of a whole sample size of 25 units, or 5 units of a halves sample size of 50 units, may have reasonably good character. Reasonably good character means the units may be reasonably fleshy, variable in texture from soft to slightly firm, and otherwise have a reasonably good texture of skin and flesh. All other units must have good character and be thick fleshed and tender.

Grade B [Choice]: Color: Plums that are reasonably well colored and have a reasonably uniform color, and the number of fairly well-colored plums does not exceed 4 in a whole sample unit size of 25 units, or 7 in a halves sample unit size of 50 units, may be given a score of 16 or 17 points. **Size:** No more than 1 unit of a whole sample size of 25 units, or 3 units of halves sample size of 50 units, may exceed the maximum weight variation by 75 percent. **Defects:** There is no more than 1 piece of harmless extraneous material, 1 small stem, 1 crushed or broken unit, 2 loose pits, or 4 damaged or seriously damaged, including 1 seriously damaged, units in a whole sample size of 25 units; or 1 piece of harmless extraneous material, 1 small stem, 2 crushed or broken units, 1 pit, or 7 damaged or seriously damaged, including 2 seriously damaged, units in a halves sample size of 50 units. **Character:** All units must have at least a reasonably good character, except no more than 5 units of a whole sample size of 25 units, or no more than 10 units of a halves sample size of 50 units, may have a fairly good character. Fairly good character means the units may be thin fleshed, may be variable in texture from very soft to slightly tough, and otherwise have a fairly good texture of skin and flesh.

Grade C [Standard]: Color: Plums that are fairly well colored, have a markedly variable characteristic color, and have no more than 4 units with a poor color in a whole sample of 25 units, or halves sample size of 50 units, may be given a score of 14 or 15 points. **Size:** No more than 1 unit of a whole sample size of 25 units, or 3 units of a halves sample size of 50 units, may exceed the maximum weight variation by 100 percent. **Defects:** There is no more than 1 piece of extraneous material, 2 small stems, 3 crushed or broken units, 3 loose pits, or 5 damaged or seriously damaged, including 2 seriously damaged, units in a whole sample size of 25 units, or no more than 1 piece of extraneous material, 2 small stems, 5 crushed or broken units, 2 pits, or 10 damaged or seriously damaged, including 5 seriously damaged, units in a halves sample size of 50 units. **Character:** All units must have at least a fairly good character, except no more than 5 units of a whole sample size of 25 units, or 10 units of a halves sample size of 50 units, may have a poor character. Poor character means very thin fleshed, poor texture of skin and flesh, a mushy to slightly tough texture, and shriveled areas of the skin that seriously affect the appearance of the product. **SStd:** Fails to meet requirements.

CANNED PLUMS [1975 REVISIONS]

The Food and Drug Administration recently amended the standards of identity for several canned fruits, compliance with which may have begun on March 11, 1975, but mostly after December 31, 1975.

The following amendments to the USDA standards for these canned fruits are proposed to bring them into line with the amended FDA standards of identity.

Attention is drawn to areas where the USDA standards may differ from, but do not conflict with, the FDA standards.

(a) 52.1781 would be amended to read as follows:
52.1781 Product description.

"Canned plums" is the product represented as defined in the Standards of Identity (CFR 27.45) for canned plums issued pursuant to the Federal Food, Drug, and Cosmetic Act.

(b) 52.1785 Table I—Brix requirements would be amended to read as follows:
52.1785

TABLE I—Brix measurements

Designation	Brix measurements
"Extra heavy syrup," or "Extra heavily sweetened fruit juice(s) and water," or "Extra heavily sweetened fruit juice(s)"	25° or more but not more than 35°
"Heavy syrup," or "Heavily sweetened fruit juice(s) and water," or "Heavily sweetened fruit juice(s)"	19° or more but less than 25°
"Light syrup," or "Lightly sweetened fruit juice(s) and water," or "Lightly sweetened fruit juice(s)"	15° or more but less than 19°
"Slightly sweetened water," or "Extra light syrup," or "Slightly sweetened fruit juice(s) and water," or "Slightly sweetened fruit juice(s)"	11° or more but less than 15°
"In water"	N.A.
"In fruit juice(s) and water"	N.A.
"In fruit juice(s)"	N.A.

(c) 52.1787 would be amended in its entirety to read as follows:

52.1787 Minimum drained weight requirements.

(a) General. (1) The minimum drained weights specified in Table II are not incorporated in the grades of the finished product, since drained weight, as such, is not a factor of quality for the purpose of these grades.

(2) The minimum drained weights are based on equalization of the product 30 days or more after the product has been canned.

(b) Method for ascertaining drained weights. The drained weight is determined by emptying the contents of the container upon a U.S. Standard No. 8 circular sieve of proper diameter containing 8 meshes to the inch (0.0937-in. = 3 percent, square openings) so as to distribute the product evenly, turning the pit cavities down in halves, inclining the sieve to an angle of approximately 17 to 20 degrees to facilitate drainage, and allowing to drain for 2 minutes. The drained weight is the weight of the sieve and plums less the weight of the dry sieve. A sieve 8 in. in diameter is used for the equivalent of No. 3 size cans (404 x 414) and smaller, and a sieve 12 in. in diameter, is used for containers larger than the equivalent of the No. 3 size can.

(c) Compliance with drained weight requirements. A lot of canned plums is considered as meeting the minimum drained weights if the following criteria are met:

(1) The average of the drained weights from all the samples units in the sample meets the minimum average drained weight (designated as "X_d" in Table II): and

(2) The number of sample units which fail to meet the drained weight lower limit for individuals (designated as "LL" in Table II) does not exceed the applicable acceptance number specified in the single sampling plan contained in the Regulations Governing Inspection and Certification of Processed Fruits and Vegetables and Related Products.

(d) 52.1794 Paragraph (b) in sub-paragraph (6) the first word "Damaged" would be changed to "Blemished" and in sub-paragraph (7) "Seriously damaged" would be changed to read "Seriously blemished."

(e) 52.1796 Tables IV and V would be amended for the Grade C classification only to read as follows:

52.1796 Allowances for quality factors.

TABLE II—Minimum Drained Weight Requirements [Whole]

Container size [metal, unless otherwise stated]	water cap. [ounces-advp]	over-flow cap. [fl. oz]	3 LL	3 X_d	6 LL	6 X_d	13 LL	13 X_d	21 LL	21 X_d	29 LL	29 X_d	38 LL	38 X_d
8Z (211 x 304)	8.65	- -	3.7	4.1	3.7	4.2	3.7	4.3	3.7	4.4	3.7	4.4	3.7	4.4
8Z Glass	- -	8.1	3.6	3.9	3.6	4.1	3.6	4.2	3.6	4.3	3.6	4.3	3.6	4.3
No. 303 (303 x 406)	16.85	- -	7.5	8.0	7.5	8.2	7.5	8.4	7.5	8.5	7.5	8.5	7.5	8.6
No. 303 Glass	- -	17.0	7.9	8.4	7.9	8.6	7.9	8.8	7.9	8.9	7.9	8.9	7.9	9.0
No. 2 (307 x 409)	20.50	- -	9.2	9.8	9.2	10.1	9.2	10.3	9.2	10.4	9.2	10.4	9.2	10.5
No. 2-1/2 (401 x 411)	29.75	- -	13.5	14.3	13.5	14.6	13.5	14.9	13.5	15.0	13.5	15.0	13.5	15.1
No. 2-1/2 Glass	- -	28.35	13.4	14.2	13.4	14.5	13.4	14.7	13.4	14.9	13.4	14.9	13.4	15.0
No. 10 (603 x 700)	109.45	- -	52.3	53.7	52.3	54.3	52.3	54.7	52.3	55.0	52.3	55.1	52.3	55.2
HALVES—Minimum Drained Weight Requirements														
8Z (211 x 304)	8.65	- -	4.2	4.5	4.2	4.7	4.2	4.8	4.2	4.8	4.2	4.9	4.2	4.9
8Z Glass	- -	8.1	4.1	4.4	4.1	4.5	4.1	4.6	4.1	4.7	4.1	4.7	4.1	4.7
No. 303 (303 x 406)	16.85	- -	8.5	8.9	8.5	9.1	8.5	9.3	8.5	9.4	8.5	9.4	8.5	9.4
No. 303 Glass	- -	17.0	8.9	9.3	8.9	9.5	8.9	9.7	8.9	9.8	8.9	9.8	8.9	9.8
No. 2 (307 x 409)	20.50	- -	10.4	10.9	10.4	11.1	10.4	11.3	10.4	11.4	10.4	11.4	10.4	11.4
No. 2-1/2 (401 x 411)	29.75	- -	15.2	15.8	15.2	16.1	15.2	16.4	15.2	16.5	15.2	16.5	15.2	16.6
No. 2-1/2 Glass	- -	28.35	15.0	15.7	15.0	16.0	15.0	16.2	15.0	16.3	15.0	16.3	15.0	16.4
No. 10 (603 x 700)	109.45	- -	57.7	59.1	57.7	59.7	57.7	60.2	57.7	60.4	57.7	60.5	57.7	60.6

The column headers "In any liquid medium" and "Sample size" span the sample-size columns (3, 6, 13, 21, 29, 38), each subdivided into LL and X_d.

TABLE IV—STYLE-WHOLE SAMPLE UNIT SIZE-25 UNITS

Factors	Maximum number of units permissible for respective grade					
	A		B		C	
Color:						
Reasonably good	2		No limit		No limit	
Fairly good	0		4		No limit	
Poor	0		0		4	
Uniformity of size:						
Variation in weight	—		—		—	
Exceeds 50 percent	1		No limit		No limit	
Exceeds 75 percent	0		1		No limit	
Exceeds 100 percent	0		0		1	
	Ind[1]	Avg[2]	Ind	Avg	Ind	Avg
Absence of defects:						
Harmless extraneous material	0	0	1	0.2	1	0.4
Small stem	1	0.6	1	N/A[3]	2	N/A
Crushed or broken	0	0	1	N/A	6	N/A
Loose pits	1	N/A	2	N/A	3	N/A
Blemished and seriously blemished	2	N/A	4	N/A	7	N/A
	including		including		including	
Seriously blemished	1	N/A	1	N/A	3	N/A
Blemished, seriously blemished, and crushed or broken	—	—	—	—	8	N/A
Character:						
Reasonably good	2		No limit		No limit	
Fairly good	0		5		No limit	
Poor	0		0		5	

[1]Ind — Means individual sample unit

[2]Avg — Means average of all the sample units in the sample.

[3]N/A — Means not applicable.

TABLE V—STYLE-HALVES SAMPLE UNIT SIZE-50 UNITS

Factors	Maximum number of units permissible for respective grade					
	A		B		C	
Color:						
Reasonably good color	5		No limit		No limit	
Fairly good	0		7		No limit	
Poor color	0		0		4	
Uniformity of size:						
Variation in weight						
Exceeds 50 percent	3		No limit		No limit	
Exceeds 75 percent	0		3		No limit	
Exceeds 100 percent	0		0		3	
	Ind[1]	Avg[2]	Ind	Avg	Ind	Avg
Absence of defects:						
Harmless extraneous material	0	0	1	0.2	1	0.4
Small stem	1	0.6	1	N/A[3]	2	N/A
Crushed or broken	0	0	2	N/A	12	N/A
Pits	1	0.5	1	N/A	3	N/A
Blemished and seriously blemished	5	0	7	N/A	15	N/A
	including		including		including	
Seriously blemished	1	N/A	2	N/A	7	N/A
Blemished, seriously blemished, and crushed or broken					17	N/A
Character:						
Reasonably good	5		No limit		No limit	
Fairly good	0		10		No limit	
Poor	0		0		10	

[1]Ind — Means individual sample unit.

[2]Avg — Means average of all the sample units in the sample.

[3]N/A — Means not applicable.

No other changes are proposed.

PLUMS—Frozen [3/6/56]

Grade A: Color; Frozen plums, internally and externally possess a practically uniform, bright, typical color of well-ripened, properly prepared and processed frozen plums of similar varietal characteristics, and the frozen plums are practically free from any brown color due to oxidation, improper processing, or either cause, while color may affect no more than slightly the appearance or edibility. **Size:** In halves or whole pitted styles means that in 90 percent of the units which have the most uniform size, the weight of the largest does not exceed the weight of the smallest unit by more than 50 percent. **Defects:** Practically free from pit material and, individually and collectively, harmless extraneous matter, crushed and broken units with respect to halves and whole pitted styles, blemished and seriously blemished units, and other defects do not materially affect the appearance or eating quality; and there may be present: Not more than 5 percent of crushed or broken units in halved and whole pitted styles; Not more than 10 percent of blemished and seriously blemished units; Provided, that not more than 5 percent may be seriously blemished. **Character:** Possess a tender, fleshy texture, typical of well-ripened, properly processed frozen plums, and not more than 15 percent may possess a reasonably good character or possess shriveled areas that materially affect the appearance.

Grade B: Color; Frozen plums, internally and externally, possess a reasonably uniform, bright, typical color of reasonably well-ripened, properly prepared, and processed frozen plums of similar varietal characteristics, and the frozen plums are reasonably free from any brown color due to oxidation, improper processing, or other causes, which color may not materially affect the appearance or edibility. **Size:** In halved or whole pitted styles, in 90 percent of the units which have the most uniform size, the weight of the largest unit is not more than twice the weight of the smallest unit. **Defects:** See Grade A. All wording is the same except as follows: seriously affect. 10 percent; 20 percent; 10 percent. **Character:** Unit possesses the texture of reasonably well-ripened frozen plums that are properly processed; the texture is reasonably fleshy and the units reasonably tender, or tenderness may be variable from slightly soft to slightly firm, and not more than 30 percent may fail to meet at least a reasonably good character or possess shriveled areas that materially affect the appearance of the unit. **SStd:** Fails to meet requirements.

PRUNES—Dried Canned [5/24/67]

Grade A: Color: Color of the skins of the prunes is typical and may be black, blue black, or reddish brown, and not more than 5 percent may possess a dull, chocolate brown, surface color or abnormal darkening of the flesh due to caramelization or fermentation. **Size:** Weight of the largest may not exceed the weight of the smallest prune by 75 percent. **Defects:** There may be present not more than 5 percent of prunes affected by any defect or any combination of defects. 1 prune that is defective is permitted if it exceeds 5 percent by count. **Character:** Prunes are thick-fleshed; not more than 5 percent have fibrous or tough skins; and not more than 10 percent may be soft or hard in texture. 1 prune that possess a tough skin, is soft, or is hard, is permitted, if 1 prune exceeds 5 percent or 10 percent.

Grade B: Color: See Grade A. All wording is the same except as follows: 10 percent. **Size:** Weight of the largest prune may not be more than twice the weight of the smallest. **Defects:** See Grade A. All wording is the same except as follows: 10 percent. 10 percent. **Character:** Prunes are reasonably thick-fleshed, not more than 15 percent may be soft or hard in texture.

Grade C: Color: Prunes may vary in shade of typical colors, and not more than 15 percent may possess a dull, chocolate brown, surface color or abnormal darkening of the flesh due to caramelization or fermentation. **Size:** May vary in size. **Defects:** Not more than 15 percent or prunes may be affected by defect or any combination of defects. **Character:** May vary in thickness and texture of flesh or may possess fibrous or tough skins, and not more than 20 percent may be soft or hard in texture.

Grade D: Fails to meet requirements.

[1975 REVISIONS]

The Food and Drug Administration recently amended the standards of identity for several canned fruits, compliance with which may have begun on March 11, 1975, but mostly after December 31, 1975.

The following amendments to the USDA standards for these canned fruits are proposed to bring them into line with the FDA Standards of Identity.

Attention is drawn to areas where the USDA standards may differ from, but do not conflict with, the FDA standards.

Canned Prunes

(a) 52.5601 Product description would be amended to cite the Food and Drug Standard of Identity for canned prunes and to cover Pitted Prunes as follows:

Product description.

Canned prunes is the product represented as defined in the Standards of Identity for canned prunes (21 CFR 27.15), issued pursuant to the Federal Food, Drug, and Cosmetic Act, and can be either pitted or unpitted.

(b) 52.5604 Syrup density would be amended to read as follows:

52.5604 Liquid media and Brix measurements.

"Cut-out" requirements for liquid media in canned prunes are not incorporated in the grades of the finished product, since syrup or any other liquid medium, as such, is not a factor of quality for the purposes of these grades. The designations of liquid packing media and the Brix measurements, where applicable, are as follows:

Designation	Brix Measurements
"Extra heavy syrup"; or "Extra heavily sweetened fruit juice(s) and water"; or "Extra heavily sweetened fruit juice(s)"	30° or more but not more than 45°
"Heavy syrup"; or "Heavily sweetened fruit juice(s) and water"; or "Heavily sweetened fruit juice(s)"	24° or more but less than 30°
"Light syrup"; or "Lightly sweetened fruit juice(s) and water"; or "Heavily sweetened fruit juice(s)"	20° or more but less than 24°
"Slightly sweetened water"; or "Extra light syrup"; or "Slightly sweetened fruit juice(s) and water"; or "Slightly sweetened fruit juice(s)"	Less than 20°
"In water"	N.A.
"In fruit juice(s) and water"	N.A.
"In fruit juice(s)"	N.A.

(c) 52.5606 Recommended minimum drained weights would be amended in its entirety to read as follows:

52.5606 Recommended minimum drained weights.

(a) General. (1) The minimum drained weight recommendations for the various styles in Table II are not incorporated in the grades of the finished product, since drained weight, as such, is not a factor of quality for the purposes of these grades.

(2) The recommended minimum drained weights are based in equalization of the product 30 days or more after the product has been canned.

(b) Method for ascertaining drained weight. The drained weight is determined by emptying the contents of the container upon a U.S. Standard No. 8 circular sieve of proper diameter containing 8 meshes to the in. (0.0937-in. + 3 percent, square openings) so as to distribute the product evenly, inclining the sieve to approximately a 17 to 20 degree angle to facilitate drainage, and allowing the product to drain for 2 minutes.

The drained weight is the weight of the sieve and prunes less the weight of the dry sieve. A sieve 8 in. in diameter is used for No. 3 size cans (404 x 414) and smaller sizes, and a sieve 12 in. in diameter is used for containers larger than the No. 3 size can.

(c) Compliance with recommended minimum drained weights. A lot of canned prunes is considered as meeting the minimum drained weight recommendations if the following criteria are met:

(1) The average of the drained weights from all the sample units in the sample meet the recommended minimum drained weight specified in Table I; and

(2) Any sample unit(s) which fail to meet the recommended minimum drained weight is within the range of good commercial practice.

(e) Canned dried prunes that meet the recommended drained weight requirements for "Heavy Pack" will be certified as "Heavy Pack" in addition to the grade statement.

The name of the standard would be changed to United States Standards for Grades of Canned Prunes. The word dried would be deleted wherever it appears in the text.

No other amendments are proposed.

TABLE I

CONTAINER SIZE OR NAME	Recommended drained weight		
	Metal containers		Glass containers
	Regular Pack	Heavy Pack	Regular Pack
8 oz.	5-1/2 oz.		
No. 1 Tall	10-3/4 oz.		
No. 2	13 oz.		
No. 2-1/2	19 oz.	29 oz.	18 oz.
No. 10	70 oz.	110 oz.	

PRUNES—Dehydrated Low Moisture [6/13/60]

Grade A: Color: Color may range from characteristic light chocolate brown to darker brown, but the overall color impression is reasonably uniform, and in the style of "pieces" or "whole pitted" the units may vary from characteristic blue-black typical of the exterior skin color, and chocolate brown to darker brown typical of the interior color, of low-moisture prunes; and that such characteristic color of any style, after cooking, is a reasonably rich color, typical of cooked, low-moisture prunes that have been properly prepared and processed. **Size and Count:** Nugget-type; Pieces. Practically all of the units are of such size and shape to pass through 0.025 (5/8 in.) square openings, and not more than 10 percent may pass through meshes of a U.S. Standard No. 8 sieve (0.0937-in. + 3 percent, sq. openings), Whole Pitted. Not more than 3 percent may consist of small pieces that pass through meshes of U.S. Standard No. 4 sieve (9.187-in + 3 percent square openings), and the count of full-size units (after removal of small pieces and partial or inseparable units) is not more than 133 per lb., and the uniformity is such that in a sample of 100 oz. of full-size units: For prunes that average 83 prunes or less per lb., the count per lb. of 10 oz. of the smallest prune does not vary from the count per pound of 10 oz. of the largest prunes by more than 39 points; or for prunes that average 84 prunes or more per lb., the count per lb. of 10 oz. of the smallest prunes does not vary from the count per pound of 10 oz. of the largest prunes by more than 70 points. **Defects:** Whole Pitted. A total of 5 percent of the low-moisture prunes may be damaged: Provided, that not more than 2 percent may be seriously damaged; 7-1/2 percent may be partial and inseparable units, and a total of 5 percent may be slightly and seriously affected by pieces of pit: Provided, that not more than 3 percent may be affected by fragments which individually are 1/8 in. or more but no longer than 1/4 in. in the longest dimension: and further provided, that not more than 1 percent may be seriously affected by pieces of pit. **Texture:** Nugget type. The cooked mass has a reasonably uniform texture and finish that is coarse or grainy without practically any hard particles. Pieces. The cooked product is practically free from hard, firm, or tough units, and there is no more than moderate disintegration except for small pieces that may have been present. Whole Pitted. The cooked product is practically free from hard or tough units and substantially retains the semblance of whole pitted prunes except for small pieces that may have been present.

Grade B: Color: In style of "nugget-type," the color may vary noticeably in shade of brown color; and that in the style of "pieces" or "whole pitted," the units may possess a variable, dull blue-black to very dark brown color, and that in any style, after cooking, the color may be dull but is typical of cooked, low-moisture prunes that have been properly prepared and processed and are not off-color for any reason. **Size and Count:** Nugget-type; Pieces. Practically all of the units are of such size and shape as to pass through 0.625 (5/8 in.) sq. openings and not more than 25 percent may pass through meshes of a U.S. Standard No. 8 sieve (0.0937-in. + 3 percent sq. openings). Whole Pitted. Not more than 5 percent may consist of small pieces that pass through meshes of a U.S. Standard No. 4 sieve (0.187-in. + 3 percent sq. opening), and the count of full-size units, after removal of small pieces and partial or inseparable units, is not more than 140 per lb., and the uniformity of count is such that in a sample of 100 oz. of full-size units: see Grade A. **Defects:** Whole Pitted: A total of 10 percent may be damaged: Provided, that no more than 4 percent may be seriously damaged; 15 percent may be partial and inseparable units, and a total of 8 percent may be slightly and seriously affected by pieces of pit: Provided, that not more than 5 percent may be affected by fragments which individually are 1/8 in. or more but no longer than 1/4 in. in their longest dimension: And provided further, that not more than 2 percent may be seriously affected by pieces of pit. **Texture:** Nugget-type. The cooked mass has a fairly uniform texture and finish that may range from fine and grainy to coarse and grainy; and hard particles may be noticeable but not objectionable. Pieces. The cooked product is fairly free from hard, firm, or tough units and may disintegrate generally into a coarse, saucelike consistency. Whole Pitted. The cooked product is fairly free from hard or tough units and may consist of ragged or broken larger pieces and whole pitted units intermingled with slight amount of mushiness from small pieces which may have been present. **SStd:** Fails to meet requirements.

PRUNES—Dried [10/11/65]

Grade A: Fairly uniform in size, averaging 25 prunes or less per pound that meet the applicable moisture limits in Table IV but, regardless of size and kind of packaging, are reasonably uniform in moisture and do not exceed the total allowances and limitations for defects shown in Table I.

Grade B; Fairly uniform in size, meeting the applicable moisture limits in Table IV but, regardless of size and kind of packaging, are reasonably uniform in moisture and do not exceed the total allowances or limitations for defects shown in Table II.

Grade C: See Grade A. All wording is the same except as follows: ... defects shown in Table III.

Grade Sstd: See Grade A. All wording is the same except as follows: and that may fail to meet other requirements for Grade C, but not more than 5 percent may be affected by mold, dirt, foreign material, insect infestation, or decay: Provided, that not more than 10 percent may be affected by decay.

TABLE I—U.S. GRADE A OR U.S. FANCY; ALLOWANCES FOR DEFECTS

Total Allowance	Limitations		
Not more than a total of 10 percent, by weight, may be damaged or affected by:	Not more than 6 percent, by weight, may be damaged or affected by:	Not more than 3 percent, by weight, may be affected by:	Not more than 1 percent, by weight, may be affected by:
Off-color			
Poor texture	Poor texture		
End cracks	End cracks		
Skin or flesh damage[2]	Skin or flesh damage[2]		
Fermentation	Fermentation		
Scars	Scars		
Heat damage	Heat damage		
Insect injury	Insect injury		
Other means	Other means		
Mold	Mold	Mold	
Dirt	Dirt	Dirt	
Foreign material	Foreign material	Foreign material	
Insect infestation	Insect infestation	Insect infestation	
Decay	Decay	Decay	Decay

TABLE II—U.S. GRADE B OR U.S. CHOICE; ALLOWANCES FOR DEFECTS

Total Allowance	Limitations		
Not more than a total of 15 percent, by weight, may be damaged or affected by:	Not more than 8 percent, by weight, may be damaged or affected by:	Not more than 4 percent, by weight, may be affected by:	Not more than 1 percent, by weight, may be affected by:
Off-color			
Poor texture	Poor texture		
End cracks	End cracks		
Skin or flesh damage[2]	Skin or flesh damage[2]		
Fermentation	Fermentation		
Scars	Scars		
Heat damage	Heat damage		
Insect injury	Insect injury		
Other means	Other means		
Mold	Mold	Mold	
Dirt	Dirt	Dirt	
Foreign material	Foreign material	Foreign material	
Insect infestation	Insect infestation	Insect infestation	
Decay	Decay	Decay	Decay

TABLE III—U.S. GRADE C OR U.S. STANDARD; ALLOWANCES FOR DEFECTS

Total Allowance	Limitations		
Not more than a total of 20 percent, by weight, may be damaged or affected by:	Not more than 10 percent, by weight, may be damaged or affected by:	Not more than 8 percent, by weight, may be damaged or affected by:	Not more than 5 percent, by weight, may be affected by:
Off-color			
Poor texture			
End cracks[1]	End cracks[1]		
Skin or flesh damage[2]	Skin or flesh damage[2]	Skin or flesh damage[2]	
Fermentation	Fermentation	Fermentation	
Scars	Scars	Scars	
Heat damage	Heat damage	Heat damage	
Insect injury	Insect injury	Insect injury	
Other means	Other means	Other means	
Mold	Mold	Mold	Mold
Dirt	Dirt	Dirt	Dirt
Foreign material	Foreign material	Foreign material	Foreign material
Insect infestation	Insect infestation	Insect infestation	Insect infestation
Decay	Decay	Decay	Decay
			Provided, That not more than 1 percent, by weight, may be affected by decay.

1 Except that each 1 percent of end cracks to, and including, 8 percent, by weight, shall be considered as ½ percent damaged by end cracks; and any additional end cracks shall be calculated as true percentage, by weight.
2 Not applicable to "Whole Pitted" style.

TABLE IV—MOISTURE ALLOWANCES FOR DRIED PRUNES
[Non-hermetically sealed containers; 10 pounds or more]

Grades	Maximum moisture limits	
	Counts averaging 60 or less per pound	Counts averaging 61 or more per pound
	Percent	Percent
U.S. Grade A or U.S. Fancy	25	24
U.S. Grade B or U.S. Choice	25	24
U.S. Grade C or U.S. Standard	25	24
Substandard	25	24

POMEGRANATES*

USES: "When the fruit is eaten raw, it is broken open, the kernels are dislodged, usually with a nut pick, and the flesh is sucked from the pits. The kernels are also used as a garnish for desserts and salads. The juice may be used in beverages and ices. From the rind is made an ink that one writer described as 'unfading till the world's end'. From the rind, also, is brewed a bitter draught that many an adventurer and explorer has found valuable in combating dysentery ... Grenadine, for flavoring drinks, is made from pomegranate juice. The juice is also used in making gelatin desserts, icing for cakes, fruit drinks, and pudding sauces. For a pomegranate cocktail, boil the seeds of 1 large pomegranate with 2 slices of lemon in 3 cups of water until the water has absorbed the color and flavor from the seeds (about 15 min.). Add 1/2 cup of sugar and boil for 5 minutes more. Strain through a double thickness of cheesecloth, add 1 tablespoon of lemon juice, and chill. Serves 6."

As with any ancient fruit, there were many beliefs about its medical value. Mohammed is said once to have told his followers: "Eat the pomegranate, for it purges the system of envy and hatred."

MARKETING SEASON: Pomegranates are on the market from the latter part of September until the early part of December. In September, about 5 percent of the annual total comes to market; in October, the supply is at peak with 60 percent; in November, supplies are relatively plentiful at 33 percent; and, in December, the supply is very small, 2 percent. The total moving to market is about 6 million lb. annually, but an unknown part of this is used for juice and purposes other than for sale fresh.

VARIETIES: "The **Wonderful** or **Red Wonderful** is the principal commercial variety of pomegranate. ... The fruit of this variety is large, glossy, and of deep red or purple color. On well-cared-for trees, the fruit will range from 2 to 5 in. in diameter. The flesh and the juice is deep crimson in color, the seeds are tender, and the red arils, within which are contained the seeds, are used in salads, punches, and fancy dishes. ... Principal plantings are in the lower San Joaquin valley." This variety was said to have been started in California, near Porterville, in 1896 from cuttings from Florida. Varieties used in Florida are **Rhoda** and **Purple Seed**. Other recommended varieties are **Paper-Shell** which has a very thin rind and **Spanish Ruby** which is juicy with a sweet aromatic flavor.

CONTAINERS: Pomegranates are shipped place-packed in a wooden lug holding two layers with net weight of 23 to 26 lb.

QUALITY: Fruit should have unbroken rind with no sign of decay; be heavy for its size, and have a fresh, not dried-out appearance. There are no U.S. standards.

Quality of pomegranates for shipment fresh or for processing is regulated by the California Agricultural Code. The acid content of juice extracted from a sample of the pomegranates is limited to not more than 1.85 percent. The code also provides requirements for the color of juice. Methods of selecting the sample and for testing are prescribed. Color must be a shade of red equal to or darker than Munsell color chart 5R-512, Lot 8730.

RASPBERRIES*

USES: Raspberries are excellent served just with cream and sugar or featured in a wide variety of dessert dishes, such as bavarian cream, bombe, chiffon pie, jelly, ice or ice cream, mousse, preserves, pudding, punch, in cakes and tarts, and as syrup for pancakes.

MARKETING SEASON: Fresh raspberries are available in June and July, but mostly in July. The supply is small and uncertain.

VARIETIES: "Three main types of raspberries—red, black, and purple—are grown in the U.S. They differ in several ways other than the color of their fruit. Red raspberries have erect canes. They usually are propagated by suckers which grow from the roots of the parent plant. Red raspberries are grown most extensively in the West. Black raspberries (blackcaps) have arched canes that root at the tips of the canes. Blackcaps

*UFFVA

are grown mostly in the eastern half of the country and in Oregon. Purple raspberries are hybrids of red raspberries and blackcaps. They have the same growth characteristics as blackcaps and are propagated in the same way. They are grown extensively in western New York, though the area where they are adapted is about the same as the area where blackcaps are grown.

"Some raspberries have yellow fruit. Yellow raspberries are variations of red raspberries and, except for fruit color, have all the characteristics of red raspberries. They are grown chiefly in home gardens."

The most important cultivars, as listed by Dr. D.H. Scott, research horticulturist of Agricultural Research Service, are: red raspberries for western U.S.—**Canby, Puyallup, Willamette**; red for eastern U.S.—**Latham, Taylor**; black for western U.S.—**Munger, Plum Farmer**; black for eastern U.S.—**Bristol, Cumberland, New Logan**, and purple for eastern U.S.—**Clyde, Sodus.**

CONTAINERS: Most raspberries are shipped in fiberboard trays holding 12 half-pints, net weight 5-1/2 to 7-1/2 lb. Trays holding 12 pints are also used, with a net weight of 11 to 15 lb. The use of the larger container has been most often reported in Michigan.

QUALITY: The consumer, relying on inspection, should expect the raspberries to be fresh-looking, plump, cold, dry, and free of bruising and mold. To maintain quality until they are consumed, keep them cold and covered. Use as soon as possible.

GRADES: The U.S. standards for raspberries, adopted in 1931, provide for two grades, U.S. 1 and U.S. 2. Extracts of the standards are given here:

"U.S. 1 shall consist of raspberries of one variety which are well colored, well developed and not soft, overripe, or broken; which are free from cores, sunscald, mold, and decay, and from damage caused by dirt or other foreign matter, shriveling, moisture, disease, insects, mechanical, or other means. In order to allow for variations incident to proper grading and handling, not more than 10 percent, by volume, of the raspberries in any lot may be below the requirements of this grade, but not to exceed one-half of this tolerance, or 5 percent, shall be allowed for defects causing serious damage and not more than one-fifth of this amount, or 1 percent, may be affected by mold or decay." Any container is allowed 1-1/2 times the lot tolerance.

RASPBERRIES—Canned [3/1/58]

Grade A: Color: Possess bright and typical color of well-ripened raspberries for the varietal type that have been properly processed and are practically uniform in that not more than 5 percent may vary markedly from this typical color. **Size:** The variation in size of the raspberries does not materially affect the appearance, and not more than 10 percent may be less than 9/16 in. in diameter. **Defects:** The presence of harmless extraneous material does not more than slightly affect the appearance or edibility; not more than 5 percent may be undeveloped berries and damaged berries, and the presence of harmless extraneous material, undeveloped berries, and any other defects, individually and collectively, does not more than slightly affect the appearance or eating quality. **Character:** The raspberries are thick fleshed and well ripened; the presence of detached drupelets does not more than slightly affect the appearance, and not more than 10 percent may be broken or mashed.

Grade B: Color: Possess a reasonably bright and typical color of reasonably well-ripened raspberries for the varietal type that have been properly processed and are reasonably uniform in that not more than 15 percent may vary markedly from this typical color. **Size:** The variation in size does not materially affect the appearance and not more than 15 percent may be less than 1/2 in. in diameter. **Defects:** See Grade A. All wording is the same, except as follows: materially; 10 percent; materially. **Character:** See Grade A: all wording is exactly the same except as follows: reasonably; materially; 15 percent.

Grade C: Color: Possess a color typical of fairly well-ripened raspberries for the varietal type that have been properly processed and may or may not be variable, but not off-color. **Size:** May be variable in size, and not more than 25 percent

RASPBERRIES

FRESH (5/29/31   51.4320)
Grades: U.S. NO. 1   U.S. NO. 2

CANNED (3/1/58   52.3311)

Grades:	"A" OR "FANCY"	"B" OR "CHOICE"	"C" OR "STAN-DARD"	"SUB-STAN-DARD"
Minimum Score:	90	80	70	Less than 70

In syrup; artificially sweetened packing media; water (grades A & B) Black

	NET WEIGHT OZ.	NET WEIGHT METRIC	DRAINED WEIGHT OZ.	DRAINED WEIGHT METRIC
No. 8Z Tall	7.8	221.1 g	5	141.8 g
No. 303	15.2	430.9 g	8	226.8 g
No. 2½	26.8	759.8 g	14.5	411.1 g
No. 10	98.5	2.8 kg	55	1.6 kg

In syrup; artificially sweetened packing media; water (grades A & B) Red & Purple

No. 8Z Tall	7.8	221.1 g	4	113.4 g
No. 303	15.2	430.9 g	8	226.8 g
No. 2½	26.8	759.8 g	14.5	411.1 g
No. 10	98.5	2.8 kg	53	1.5 kg

In water (grades C & Sstd) Red & Purple

No. 8Z Tall	7.8	221.1 g	4.5	127.6 g
No. 303	15.2	430.9 g	8.25	233.9 g

	NET WEIGHT OZ.	NET WEIGHT METRIC	DRAINED WEIGHT OZ.	DRAINED WEIGHT METRIC
No. 2½	26.8	759.8 g	14.5	411.1 g
No. 10	98.5	2.8 kg	60	1.7 kg

In water (grades C & Sstd) Black

No. 8Z Tall	7.8	221.1 g	5.25	148.8 g
No. 303	15.2	430.9 g	8.25	233.9 g
No. 2½	26.8	759.8 g	14.5	411.1 g
No. 10	98.5	2.8 kg	65	1.8 kg

CANNED (3/1/58   52.3311)

SYRUP	SPECIFIC GRAVITY (BRIX MEASUREMENTS)
"Extra heavy syrup", or "Extra heavily sweetened fruit juice(s) and water", or "Extra heavily sweetened fruit juice(s)".	27° - 35°
"Heavy syrup", or "Heavily sweetened fruit juice(s) and water", or "Heavily sweetened fruit juice(s)".	20° or more but less than 27°
"Light syrup", or "Lightly sweetened fruit juice(s) and water", or "Lightly sweetened fruit juice(s)".	15° or more but less than 20°
"Slightly sweetened water", or "Extra light syrup", or "Slightly sweetened fruit juice(s) and water", "Slightly sweetened fruit juice(s)".	11° or more but less than 15°
"In water"	N.A.
"In fruit juice(s) and water"	N.A.
"In fruit juice(s)"	N.A.

FROZEN (8/16/48   52.1871)

Grades:	"A" OR "FANCY"	"B" OR "CHOICE"	"D" OR "SUB-STANDARD"
Minimum Score:	85	70	Less than 70

may be less than 7/16 in. in diameter. **Defects:** See Grade A; all wording is the same except as follows: seriously; 20 percent; seriously. **Character:** See Grade A; all wording is the same, except as follows: fairly; seriously; 20 percent. **Sstd:** Fails to meet requirements.

RASPBERRIES—Canned [1975 Revisions]

The Food and Drug Administration recently amended the standards of identity for several canned fruits, compliance with which may have begun on March 11, 1975, but mostly after December 31, 1975.

The following amendments to the USDA standards for those canned fruits are proposed to bring them into line with the amended FDA Standards of Identity.

Attention is drawn to areas where the USDA standards may differ from but do not conflict with the FDA standards.

Canned Raspberries

(a) 52.3311 Product description would be amended to read as follows:

52.3311 Product description

Canned raspberries is the product represented as defined in the Standards of Identity (21 CFR 27.35) for canned berries issued pursuant to the federal Food, Drug, and Cosmetic Act.

(b) 52.3311 would be amended in its entirety to read as follows:

52.3311 Liquid media and Brix measurements.

(a) Brix measurement requirements for the liquid media in canned raspberries are not incorporated in the grades of the finished product since syrup, or any other liquid medium, as such, is not a factor of quality for the purpose of these grades. The designations of liquid packing media and Brix measurements, where applicable, are as follows:

Designation	Brix measurements
"Extra heavy syrup;" or "Extra heavily sweetened fruit juice(s) and water; or "Extra heavily sweetened fruit juice(s)."	27° or more but not more than 35°
"Heavy syrup;" or "Heavily sweetened fruit juice(s) and water;" or "Heavily sweetened fruit juice(s)."	20° or more but less than 27°
"Light syrup;" or "Lightly sweetened fruit juice(s) and water;" or "Lightly sweetened fruit juice(s)."	15° or more but less than 20°
"Slightly sweetened water;" or "Extra light syrup;" or "Slightly sweetened fruit juice(s) and water;" or "Slightly sweetened fruit juice(s)."	11° or more but less than 15°
"In water"	N.A.
"In fruit juice(s) and water"	N.A.
"In fruit juice(s)"	N.A.

No other amendments are proposed.

RASPBERRIES—Frozen [8/15/48]

Grade A: Color: Possess a bright and good characteristic color and not more than 5 percent vary markedly from the intensity and luster of the characteristic color of well-ripened raspberries; and none of the raspberries possess a grey cast or darkening characteristic of oxidation or over-maturity. **Defects:** There may be present for each 16 oz. of net weight an area of not more than 1/4 sq. in. comprising harmless extraneous material (such as leaves and portions thereof), caps and portions thereof, and loose sepal-like bracts, and portions thereof; and not more than 2 stems; including not more than 1 stem which may exceed 1/2 in. in length, or 1 piece of harmless extraneous material that is not measurable by area (such as weeds and blades of grass), and there may be present not more than a total of 5 percent that are undeveloped raspberries and damaged raspberries. **Character:** Raspberries are mature, well developed, and practically intact, to the extent that not more than 5 percent may be slightly immature or slightly over-mature; raspberries are fleshy and tender; raspberries and accompanying liquor, if any, are practically free from detached seed cells; not more than 10 percent of red raspberries may be crushed, and not more than 5 percent of black raspberries may be crushed.

Grade B: Color: Possess a reasonably bright, reasonably good, characteristic color; not more than 10 percent vary markedly from the intensity and luster of the characteristic color of well-ripened raspberries, and that raspberries may possess a slight gray cast or slight darkening characteristic of oxidation or

TABLE NO. IV—BRIEF SUMMARY OF REQUIREMENTS FOR GRADES OF FROZEN RASPBERRIES FOR MANUFACTURING

Grades	Color	
	Typical Color	Marked variation from color of well-ripened raspberries
		Maximum (by weight) (percent)
U.S. Grade A for manufacturing or U.S. Fancy for manufacturing.	Bright, good characteristic color; none may possess a grey cast or darkening (oxidation or overmaturity).	5
U.S. Grade B for manufacturing or U.S. Choice for manufacturing.	Reasonably bright, reasonably good; may possess a slight grey cast or slight darkening (oxidation or overmaturity).	10

Grades	Absence of Defects		
	Harmless extraneous material (leaves, etc.), caps, sepal-like bracts and portions thereof	Harmless extraneous material (weeds, grass) and stems (including stems over ½ in.)	Undeveloped and damaged raspberries

Grades	Maximum		
	Per 16 oz. of Net Weight		By Weight
			Percent
U.S. Grade A for manufacturing or U.S. Fancy for manufacturing.	¼ sq. in.	2 stems, including 1 stem that may exceed ½ in., or 1 piece harmless material.	10
U.S. Grade B for manufacturing or U.S. Choice for manufacturing.	½ sq. in.	4 stems, including 1 stem that may exceed ½ in., or 1 piece harmless material.	20

Grades	Character		
	General description of texture and intactness	Slightly immature and slightly overmature	Crushed raspberries
		Maximum (by weight) (percent)	
U.S. Grade A for manufacturing or U.S. Fancy for manufacturing.	Good character for purposes of manufacturing: reasonably mature, reasonably well developed, reasonably intact, reasonably fleshy and reasonably tender, reasonably free from seed cells.	10	25
U.S. Grade B for manufacturing or U.S. Choice for manufacturing.	Reasonably good character for purposes of manufacturing: fairly mature, fairly well developed, fairly intact, fairly fleshy and fairly tender, fairly free from seed cells.	15	50

over-maturity. **Defects:** See Grade A; all wording is the same except as follows: 1/2 sq. in.; 4 stems; 10 percent. **Character:** See Grade A; all wording is the same except as follows: reasonably; 10 percent; 20 percent; 15 percent. **Sstd:** Fails to meet requirements.

RHUBARB*

USES: Only the leafstalk of rhubarb is suitable for human consumption. The leaf blade contains a high content of oxalic acid characterized by soluble salts and can be quite poisonous. In the stalks, however, the oxalic acid is present in smaller amounts and largely in insoluble form. It is, therefore, harmless. The stalks contain about the same amount of oxalic acid as spinach, beet greens, chard, and lambs-quarter.

Rhubarb is used as a fruit because of its high acidity and flavor. It has long been popular in pies and is frequently referred to as "pieplant." It is also used in tarts, sauces, puddings, punch, jams, and jellies. It is easily prepared and preserved and readily adapts to freezing. Rhubarb may be baked or stewed and eaten as a breakfast food, side dish with other meals, or as a dessert. The cooked juice, with a sweetener added, and chilled, makes a refreshing drink. Rhubarb has also been used for making home-made wines.

In Alaska, wild rhubarb (Polygonum alpinum) grows abundantly, and the oxalic acid-filled leaves are sometimes used for tanning hides, cleaning aluminum, and other processes utilizing the acid properties.

MARKETING SEASON: Fresh rhubarb is available throughout the year, with the heaviest supplies marketed January through August. The amount available from September through December is less than 0.5 percent per month, with most of it coming from California. California is the only state offering supplies nation-wide on a year-round basis. Michigan and Washington offer "forced" or hothouse-grown rhubarb from January through June over a wide territory. Most Michigan rhubarb goes to eastern markets and most of Washington's to western markets, though rhubarb from both states goes both East and West to some extent.

VARIETIES: There are more than 100 varieties of rhubarb, but few lend themselves to commercial growing. **Victoria** is an old variety and is the principal forcing variety. Victoria produces large yields of good sized stalks of good quality and color; is a good shipper. **Strawberry [or Linnaeus]**, another old variety, and **Early Mammoth** are grown in Michigan hothouses sometimes as the first crop because they can be forced rapidly. **German Wine** and **Crimson** are popular hothouse varieties in Washington. Among the newer varieties are **McDonald, Ruby, Valentine, Sunrise,** and **Cherry Red.**

CONTAINERS: Field grown rhubarb is most commonly packed in 20-lb. boxes. Hothouse rhubarb is most commonly packed in 50-lb. boxes or cases containing 10 5-lb. cartons. The Western Box, holding 15 lb., the Western Apple Box containing approximately 35 lb., and bundles containing a dozen bunches are also used in the commercial shipment of rhubarb. At one time, poultry crates were in common usage; however, they should never be used because of the danger of salmonella poisoning. In eastern markets, field grown rhubarb is often found in used crates from which one end has been removed. Full or partially trimmed leaves protrude through the open end.

The USDA Market News Service also lists the following types of containers as secondary but in use: lugs containing 19 to 20 lb.; 4/5 bushel crates containing 26 to 28 lb.; 1-3/5 bushel crates containing 51 to 52 lb.; cartons containing 15 to 20 lb.

Some consumer packaging is done at the wholesale and retail levels. This consists of cutting the rhubarb into 1-in. pieces and packaging them in 1-lb. units in perforated 10-oz. polyethylene bags. Experiments conducted by USDA show that rhubarb cut into 10-in. pieces, packaged in perforated polyvinyl chloride film, and heat shrunk had about the same market life as the 1-in. stalk cuts. Both had better market life than non-packaged controls.

QUALITY: Rhubarb of good quality is fresh, firm, crisp, tender, and either red or pink in color. The stalks should be fairly thick. This will provide a product which is tender and free from strings when cooked. Stalks of rhubarb that are well colored are usually well flavored, but some varieties on some soils show very little color. Forced rhubarb is usually lighter than field grown rhubarb. The younger stems on which the leaves are not fully grown are usually the most tender and

*UFFVA

RHUBARB

FRESH (2/1/66   51.3665)
Grades: U.S. FANCY   U.S. NO. 1   U.S. NO. 2
FROZEN (8/15/45   )
Grades: "A" OR   "B" OR   "D" OR "SUB-
               "FANCY"   "CHOICE"   STANDARD"
Minimum Score   85   70   Less than 70

delicate in flavor. Stale rhubarb usually has a wilted, flabby appearance. Old rhubarb or that which has grown too long before being pulled may be pithy, rough or stringy. Tenderness and crispness can be tested by puncturing or snapping the stalk.

Field grown rhubarb is rich, dark red in color, with coarse, green foliage, and a very tart flavor. It is sold with leaves attached or removed. Hothouse rhubarb is light pink with small leaves and is almost stringless. It is milder in flavor. Tops are usually trimmed before selling.

GRADES: Three U.S. grades are provided for rhubarb (field grown). U.S. Fancy, U.S. No. 1, and U.S. No. 2. U.S. Fancy consists of stalks of rhubarb of similar varietal characteristics which are very well colored, fresh, tender, straight, clean, well trimmed, and not pithy; which are free from decay and free from damage caused by scars, freezing, disease, insects, or mechanical, or other means. (a) The diameter of each stalk is not less than 1 in., and the length is not less than 10 in.

U.S. No. 1 and 2 are basically the same as U.S. Fancy, except for color, sizing, and shape.

The grade standards for field grown rhubarb became effective February 1, 1966. There are no published grade standards for "hothouse" rhubarb, but USDA has published grade standards for frozen rhubarb.

The State of Washington Dept. of Agriculture, has published grade standards for "Hothouse" or "Cellar Grown" rhubarb. It provides for two grades, "Extra Fancy" and "Fancy." A third category, "cull rhubarb," encompasses all rhubarb not included in the other two grades. Generally speaking, the Washington State grade standards are higher than the U.S. grade standards.

RHUBARB—Frozen [8/15/45]

Grade A: Color: Possesses a glossy appearance, and the color is characteristic of the variety and free from dull or grey color.

Defects: Not more than a total of 15 percent may be defective units (including "minor" and "major" defects), provided that not more than 5 percent are damaged by "major" defects. **Tenderness and Texture:** Rhubarb may contain not more than 5 percent that is tough, spongy, or stringy, and that differs noticeably in tenderness from the general texture.

Grade B: Color: Possesses a glossy appearance, and the color is characteristic of the variety and may possess a slightly dull or grey color that is not off color. **Defects:** Not more than a total of 20 percent may be defective units (including "minor" and "major" defects), provided that not more than 10 percent are damaged by "major" defects. **Tenderness and Texture:** Rhubarb may contain not more than 10 percent that is tough, spongy, or stringy, and that differs markedly in tenderness from the general texture of the product. **Sstd:** Fails to meet requirements.

STRAWBERRIES*

MARKETING SEASON: Prior to 1941, fresh strawberries were on the market from December through July, with 50 percent of the annual supply on the market in May. However, the growth of the strawberry industry in California after World War II made fresh strawberries available throughout the year. Peak supplies are still found in April, May and June, with substantial amounts on the market in March and July, but the strawberry has become a year-round rather than a seasonal fruit.

The table shows average monthly availability of fresh strawberries expressed as a percentage of the average total annual supply for the five years 1969-73 inclusive. The figures are based on the annual USDA report of unloads in 41 cities, and include both domestic and imported supplies.

PERCENTAGE OF TOTAL ANNUAL SUPPLY OF FRESH STRAWBERRIES AVAILABLE MONTHLY

Jan.	Feb.	Mar.	Apr.	May	June
%	%	%	%	%	%
4	4	8	18	48	18
July	Aug.	Sept.	Oct.	Nov.	Dec.
%	%	%	%	%	%
7	4	4	1	1	3

*UFFVA

VARIETIES: About 70 varieties are being planted commercially in the United States. Only a few can be described here, and they have been selected for their current or prospective importance by Dr. D.H. Scott, research horticulturist, Agricultural Research Service, Beltsville, Md. These are **Tioga, Fresno, Tufts, Hood, Florida Ninety, Headliner, Midway, Surecrop, Raritan,** and **Guardian.**

The strawberry plant grows from a central stem called a crown of which the terminal is a growing point. From this point leaves, flower buds, and runner develop. Runners are branches from the main stem. Branch crowns develop when the plants are growing vigorously. Buds in the axils of the leaves produce flower clusters when temperatures are cool and days are relatively short. Different varieties tend to produce clusters of a particular type. Thus some varieties produce clusters with many flowers, while others produce clusters with few flowers. Some varieties produce clusters that branch close to the crown while others branch far out on the stem. Clusters with many flowers may produce a large number of berries but the berries may be small.

Strawberry varieties grown commercially in many states, including the Pacific Coast states, are "short-day" types, commonly known as the spring or June bearing varieties. They produce flower buds in late summer or autumn and then flower and fruit the following spring.

Since 1920, federal and state agricultural experiment stations have carried on major breeding programs to produce strawberry varieties of better size, color, flavor, productiveness, and disease resistance, or which have better adaptability to a particular location or area, or to a special use such as local fresh market, distant shipping, or for processing. Some outstanding varieties have been produced while many others have been discarded.

Most commerical varieties are relatively limited in their area of productivity. Some are suitable for very restricted sections of the country and for particular conditions and uses in those sections. Others are more widely adapted and may be used for many purposes. The many active breeding programs have generated new varieties now important commercially which were unheard of 25 years ago. Important examples include the California cultivars, Tioga and Fresno, first fruited in 1955. More fruit of the Tioga is marketed in the United States today than of any other variety. Another is the Midway from Maryland (1951). Certain older varieties have persisted, however, notably Blakemore for Maryland (1930) and Northwest from Washington State (1941), but Northwest has been replaced by Hood in the last two years.

In general, newly released varieties are more productive than the varieties they have replaced, and the fruit is larger, firmer, and frequently of higher quality for fresh market and processing use. Often, the industry is literally revolutionized in a given area by new varieties. The best example of this is the 1945 introduction of Shasta and Lassen in California, giving origin to the dominant role of the California industry in the U.S. Each of these highly successful varieties has been replaced by more successful new ones, such as Tioga and Fresno. A new variety, Tufts, has been released by the University of California and patented basically for California use. Any use of it in other states must await approval from California.

Tioga originated in California in 1955 and was introduced in 1964. It has been grown successfully in all California producing areas. Berries are large and long conic in shape. They have firm flesh and tough skin; red to light-red flesh and yellow seeds, and attractive, light red skin. They also offer good appearance even when overripe, good dessert quality, cap easily and ship well to distant markets. Plants are vigorous and produce runners freely but are susceptible to leaf spot. Tioga is the leading variety in California and is recommended for summer and winter planting. In California, plants produce an exceptionally heavy crop for over 2 months beginning in March or April. Grown also in Florida for the winter crop.

Fresno originated in California in 1955 and was introduced in 1961. Berries are large, long conic, firm fleshed, and attractive with a bright-red skin. Caps are easily removed. Plants are productive with many runners; vigorous and resistant to viruses; recommended for summer planting only. Fresno is especially adapted to southern California where it follows a moderately heavy spring crop with a rather heavy midsummer bearing.

STRAWBERRIES

FRESH (7/1/65   51.3115)
Grades: U.S. NO. 1   U.S. COMBINATION   U.S. NO. 2
FROZEN (2/1/58   52.1981)

Grades:	"A" OR "FANCY"	"B" OR "CHOICE"	"C" OR "STAN-DARD"	"SUB-STAN-DARD"
Minimum Score:	90	80	70	Less than 70

Shasta introduced in 1945, having originated in California in 1935, has been very important. It is now obsolete having been replaced by Tioga and Tufts.

Tufts originated in California (by Bringhurst and Voth) and was introduced in 1972. The fruit is large, long, flat conic, skin bright red, tough; flesh orange red, firm; ripens earlier than Tioga but remains in production longer; productivity comparable to Tioga; plant medium size; erect, with a high canopy; vigorous; susceptible to Verticillium wilt; less susceptible to leaf spot than Tioga; recommended throughout California, including winter planting in southern California.

Hood in the last two years has replaced Northwest which was the most important processing strawberry in the north Pacific Coast states. Hood originated in Oregon and was introduced in 1965. Berries are large, round conic, uniform, and medium firm with bright medium red, glossy skin; of good dessert quality; very good for preserving; mildly subacid, and resistant to mildew and foliage diseases in Pacific Northwest. Not as tolerant of virus diseases as Northwest, but more resistant to red stele.

Florida Ninety originated in Florida in 1947. Berries are soft, irregular, and long conic. In Florida they are very large, early in season. Color is medium red, and flesh is light pink. They are of good to very good dessert quality; productive; grow unusually large number of runner plants, and are very susceptible to leaf spot and leaf scorch. This is a chief variety in Florida.

Headliner originated in Louisiana in 1957. Berries are large, blunt, conic, medium firm, and medium red; of good dessert quality and mildly subacid; appear in midseason. Plants are vigorous, productive, and make runners freely; are resistant to leaf spots and not adapted to Central or Northern states.

Midway originated in Maryland in 1951. Berries are long, conic, with firm flesh and a firm surface; medium to large; glossy, rich red in color; appear midseason; offer good dessert quality. They are subacid; very good for freezing. Plants produce runners freely; are resistant to some races of red stele; susceptible to leaf spots, leaf scorch, and verticillium wilt; and not as resistant to drought as some varieties. This is the leading variety in Michigan and very productive in all the Northeastern states south to Maryland.

Surecrop originated in Maryland in 1950. Berries are large, round, conic, and irregular, with glossy, firm surface, medium-red exterior, and light red interior; ripen early; offer good dessert quality, and are subacid. Plants are large and produce many runners; are productive when spaced 6 to 9 in. apart. Resistant to several races of red stele, to verticillium wilt, leaf spots, leaf scorch, and drought.

Raritan originated in New Jersey in 1968. Planting is on the increase. Berries are large, firm and glossy; bright red, with a good flavor. Plants are medium in size and very productive with moderate number of runners. Plants are susceptible to red stele and verticillium wilt, and not so drought-resistant as some varieties. Raritan ripens in midseason. Replaces Jerseybelle in some areas.

Guardian originated in Maryland and was introduced in 1969. Planting is on the increase. Fruit is large; primary berries have an irregular, conic shape; secondary and later berries are symmetrical and smooth; skin light red, glossy; flesh firm, light red; ripens 4 to 5 days later than Surecrop. Plant vigor is moderate, producing moderate number of runners. Resistant to 5 races of red stele, root rot, and verticillium wilt; leaves resistant to leaf scorch and mildew; moderate susceptibility to leaf spot; has yielded satisfactorily in narrow, matted rows in Maryland, New Jersey, Ohio, Michigan, southern Illinois, and Missouri.

Varietal resistance to diseases. Four major factors that have adversely affected the quality of strawberry varieties have been brought under control within the past few years through USDA and state agricultural experiment stations—red stele root rot and verticillium wilt (fungus diseases), virus-caused diseases, nematodes and cyclamen mites.

CONTAINERS: Strawberries for fresh market are packed directly in paper or plastic containers called boxes, cups, or baskets that hold 1 or 1-1/2 pt. These cups are packed 12 to a tray that requires a minimum weight in California of 9 lb. net for pints. To compensate for shrinkage during transit, most growers strive for a minimum of 11 to 12 lb. of fruit per tray.

The two legal sizes are, by dry measurement, either pint or quart. With a few exceptions, all areas use the pint, and it is mostly made of plastic, although a few are pulp or wood. Pint baskets fit the crate or container introduced in California in 1949. The open-work plastic baskets afford a more visual container than the pulp, but both pre-cool in approximately the same time. The so-called California tray is made of corrugated material, holds 12 pt. and is so constructed that it may be stacked 12 high for truck shipment.

SERVINGS: There is no agreement as to what constitutes a "portion" or serving of any fresh fruit or vegetable. However, there are some guidelines, including USDA's *Food Buying Guide for Type A School Lunches.* This suggests three possible servings: 1 cup, 1/2 cup, and 1/4 cup. If the serving is 1 cup, and the purchase unit is the pint, then 1 pt. provides 2.125 servings, and it would take 47.2 pt. for 100.

If the serving is 1/2 cup, there are 4.25 servings per pint, and it would take 23.6 pt. to serve 100. A 1/4 cup serving, which would be more a garnish than a serving, would run 8.5 servings per pint and would require 11.8 pt. for 100 servings.

One pint of strawberries, as purchased, is estimated to weigh 0.78 lb. and would provide 0.7 lb. ready-to-serve raw. It is also estimated that 1 lb. as purchased would provide 0.89 lb. ready-to-serve. One pound provides 5.41 servings of 1/2 cup raw whole berries; or 10.82 servings of 1/4 cup, or 2.7 servings of 1 cup.

QUALITY: Strawberries should be fresh, clean, bright, have solid red color or at least very little white or green, have caps in place, and be free of moisture and mold. There is no correlation between size of berries and flavor. Stained containers indicate leakage and spoilage. Strawberries are highly perishable. They must be kept cold and humid and should be used as soon as possible. The consumer should expect berries to be kept cold at retail as well as elsewhere.

GRADES: United States standards for grades of strawberries, effective July 1, 1965, are U.S. 1, U.S. Combination and U.S. 2. The principal grade is U.S. 1.

U.S. 1 consists of strawberries of one variety or similar varietal characteristics with the cap (calyx) attached, which are firm, not overripe or undeveloped, and which are free from mold or decay, and free from damage caused by dirt, moisture, foreign matter, disease, insects, or mechanical or other means. Each strawberry has not less than 3/4 of its surface showing a pink or red color.

(a) **Size.** Unless otherwise specified, the minimum diameter of each strawberry is not less than 3/4 in.

(b) **Tolerances.** In order to allow for variations incident to proper grading and handling the following tolerances, by volume, are provided as specified:

(1) For defects. Not more than 10 percent for strawberries in any lot which fail to meet the requirements of this grade, but not more than one-half of this tolerance, or 5 percent, shall be allowed for defects causing serious damage, including therein not more than 2/5 of this latter amount or 2 percent for strawberries affected by decay.

(2) For off-size. Not more than 5 percent for strawberries in any lot which are below the specified minimum size.

DEFINITIONS—"Overripe" means dead ripe, becoming soft, a condition unfit for shipment, and necessitating immediate consumption. "Undeveloped" means that the berry has not attained a normal shape and development due to frost injury, lack of pollination, insect injury, or other causes. "Button" berries are the most common type of this condition. "Damage" means any defect or any combination of defects which materially detract from the appearance or the edible or shipping quality of the strawberries. "Serious damage" means any specific defect described in this section; or an equally objectionable variation of any of these defects, any other defect, or any combination of defects, which seriously detract from the appearance, or the edible, or shipping quality of the strawberries. The following specific defects shall be considered as serious damage: (a) soft berries; (b) badly deformed berries; (c) badly bruised berries; (d) decayed or leaky berries; (e) berries badly caked with dirt, and (f) berries with less than half of the surface showing pink or red color.

STRAWBERRIES—Frozen [2/1/58]

Grade A: Color: Possess a reasonably uniform, good, characteristic pink to red color which is not more than slightly affected by a dull, gray, or reddish brown cast. In addition, with respect to whole style, 85 percent have at least a good characteristic pink to red color over practically the entire surface, and of the remainder not more than 5 percent may have less than 4/5 of the surface area of a good characteristic pink to red color, or are materially darkened. With respect to sliced style, 85 percent have at least a good characteristic pink to red color over practically the entire surface (not including cut surfaces), and of the remainder not more than 5 percent may have less than 1/2 of the outer surface (not including cut surfaces) of a good characteristic pink to red color, or are materially darkened. **Defects: Whole:** No grit, sand, or silt may be present that affects the appearance or eating quality, and for each 16 oz. there may be present an area of not more than 1/4 sq. in comprising harmless extraneous material, such as leaves and portions thereof, caps or portions, and loose sepal-like bracts and portions; not more than 2 stems, including not more than 1 stem may exceed 1/2 in. in length, or 1 small piece of harmless extraneous material that is not measurable by area such as weeds, weed seeds, and blades of grass, and not more than 16 short stems, and there may be present not more than a total of 5 percent that are damaged. **Sliced:** See Whole. All wording is the same except as follows: 2-1/2 percent that are damaged strawberries. **Character:** Strawberries are reasonably firm; the appearance and eating quality of the product are not materially affected by disintegration or seediness and that, with respect to whole style, not more than 10 percent may consist, in the aggregate, of partial strawberries or mushy strawberries or a combination thereof. With respect to sliced style, not more than 20 percent may consist of mushy strawberries.

Grade B: Color: See Grade A. All wording is the same except as follows: Fairly uniform ... 75 percent, 10 percent. 75 percent, 10 percent. **Defects:** See Grade A. All wording is the same, except as follows: Whole: 1/2 sq. in.; 4 stems; 32 short stems ... 10 percent. **Sliced:** 1/2 sq. in.; 4 stems. 32 short stems ... 5 percent. **Character:** Fairly firm, appearance and eating quality that is not seriously affected by seediness or disintegration. Whole style, See Grade A. Only changes are: 20 percent; sliced style, 30 percent.

Grade C: Color: Possess a predominant characteristic pink to red color and may show a dull, gray, or slightly dark color, but not to the extent that the eating quality or appearance is

seriously affected. See Grade A. All wording is the same except as follows: Whole style: 15 percent. Sliced: 15 percent. **Defects:** See Grade A. Only changes are as follows: Whole: materially affect ... 3/4 sq. in., 6 stems ... 3/4 in., 2 small pieces, 12 percent. Sliced: see Whole. Only change is: 6 percent are damaged. **Character:** See Grade A. Only changes are as follows: Whole style: 30 percent. Sliced style: 50 percent. **Sstd:** Fails to meet requirements.

TANGELOS*

USES: The tangelo combines the fine flavor of the orange and the grapefruit without the sharpness of the latter. Tangelos are especially good for eating out of hand and are excellent in fruit salads. Some of the tangelos have such a characteristic "tang" and are so juicy and highly flavored that they can be diluted with water or with other juices, such as orange or pomegranate, and still retain the characteristic tangelo flavor. Other varieties, such as the Sampson, make a marmalade of superior quality and flavor.

MARKETING SEASON: Tangelos are on the market from October through January, with the peak in November and December. *Florida is the sole producer of tangelos* for fresh market. The following table shows relative availability by months as calculated from unloads at Chicago, Los Angeles, Atlanta, New York, and Seattle:

PERCENTAGE OF TOTAL ANNUAL SUPPLY OF FRESH TANGELOS AVAILABLE MONTHLY

Jan.	Feb.	Mar.	Apr.	May	June
10	0	0	0	0	0
July	Aug.	Sept.	Oct.	Nov.	Dec.
%	%	%	%	%	%
0	0	0	7	46	37

VARIETIES: Tangelo varieties vary widely in tree and fruit characteristics. The different kinds of tangelo fruit vary considerably in size, shape, color of rind and flesh, flavor, and date of maturation. Following are descriptions of three leading commercial varieties, all of which originated at Eustis, Fla., and were introduced by the USDA in 1931. *All three varieties are crosses between the Bowen grapefruit and the Dancy tangerine, with the latter as pollen [male] parent. In regard to the*

*UFFVA

use of the variety named "Bowen," the female parent was a Duncan grapefruit tree growing on the property of Mr. Bowen.

Orlando [formerly Lake] Matures November, December; has little resemblance to either parent, and has come to be accepted on the market as "Orlando orange." Size and shape are tangerine-like but color and texture orange-like; fruit flavorful, attractive, highly colored; rind thin, deep orange to almost tangerine red, adheres firmly to pulp; size small to medium; averaging 10 seeds; shape slightly flat. It has been planted on a large commercial scale because of its sweetness and its resistance to scab. Requires cross-pollination by Temple or Dancy tangerine for satisfactory crop.

Minneola Matures January to March; shows evidence of tangerine parentage although not loose-skinned; delicious flavor and aroma when fully mature; dark reddish orange rind and dark orange flesh; very juicy; size medium large; averaging about 10 seeds; shape somewhat flattened at blossom end, and stem end is slightly raised. Requires cross-pollination, is subject to scab, and fruit shape does not lend itself to easy packing. Probably the most attractive variety.

Seminole Matures late (February to April); resembles Minneola but has more easily peeled rind, less susceptibliity to scab, and larger number of seeds; flavor, aroma, and juiciness good, though tart; size medium; fruit remains on tree longer than others without losing flavor. Replacing older Sampson variety; good shipping quality.

CONTAINERS: In Florida the 4/5 bushel container has replaced the larger containers previously used. Most tangelos are shipped in a 4/5 bu. wirebound container (4/5 bu. flat Bruce crate). Inside dimensions are 7-1/2 x 11-1/2 x 19-7/8 in.; capacity 1714 cu. in. This is Container No. 4016 of Tariff 823-D. Another container in use is a wirebound half citrus crate, with inside dimensions of 10-5/8 x 10-5/8 x 16-1/8 in.; capacity 1820 cu. in. (Container No. 3673 of Tariff 823-D). For rate making purposes, both containers have an estimated net weight of 45-1/2 lb.

SERVINGS AND WEIGHTS: The following servings and weights apply to oranges, but the figures are comparable for tangelos. One pound of tangelos provide 2.82 servings each of 1/2 cup sections with membranes. To serve 100, use 35-1/2 lb. of tangelos. One pound of tangelos, as purchased, equals 0.70 lb. ready-to-serve.

QUALITY: The maturing and ripening of citrus fruits is a slow process and is closely related to increase of diameter and weight. Unlike apples, pears, or bananas, citrus fruits contain little or no starch and will not ripen after they are harvested. Ripeness must be obtained while fruits are still on the tree.

"Quality is often associated with appearance, firmness, freedom from blemishes, thickness and color of rind. Actually the determination of quality should be based on texture of flesh, juiciness, content of total solids (principally sugars), total acid, aromatic constituents, vitamin and mineral content. The age of the fruit is also important, because immature fruit is usually coarse, very acid or tart, and the internal texture is ricey or coarse. Overripe fruit held on the tree too long may become insipid, develop off-flavors, and possess short transit, storage, and shelf life."

GRADES: U.S. standards for grades of Florida tangelos are U.S. Fancy, U.S. No. 1 Bright, U.S. No. 1, U.S. No. 1 Golden, U.S. No. 1 Bronze, U.S. No. 1 Russet, U.S. No. 2 Bright, U.S. No. 2, U.S. No. 2 Russet, U.S. No. 3. Grades for tangelos are contained in U.S. Standards for Grades of Florida Oranges and Tangelos, effective Sept. 15, 1960. (Grades apply only to the common or sweet orange group varieties of the Mandarin group, except tangerines.)

"U.S. No. 1 consists of oranges of similar varietal characteristics which are firm, well formed, mature, and of fairly smooth texture, and which are free from bruises, cuts which are not healed, buckskin or similar type of discoloration, decay, growth cracks, sprayburn, undeveloped or sunken segments, and free from damage caused by ammoniation, bird pecks, creasing, dirt or other foreign materials, dryness or mushy condition, green spots or oil spots, pitting, scab, scale, scars, split or rough or protruding navels, sprouting, sunburn, thorn scratches, riciness or woodiness of the flesh, disease, insects, or mechanical, or other means. Oranges of the early and midseason varieties shall be fairly well colored. In this grade not more than one-third of the surface, in the aggregate, may be affected by discoloration; 10 percent of the fruits in

TANGELOS

FLORIDA:

FRESH (1/31/73   51.1140)

    Grades: U.S. FANCY; U.S. No. 1 Bright; U.S. No. 1; U.S. No. 1 Golden; U.S. No. 1 Bronze; U.S. No. 1 Russet; U.S. No. 2 Bright; U.S. No. 2; U.S. No. 2 Russet; U.S. No. 3

any lot may fail to meet the requirements of this grade, other than for discoloration, but not more than 1/2 of this amount, or 5 percent, shall be allowed for very serious damage, and not more than 1/20th of the tolerance, or 0.5 percent, shall be allowed for decay at shipping point. 'Well colored' means that the fruit is yellow or orange in color with practically no trace of green color. 'Firm' as applied to tangelos means that the fruit is not soft, or noticeably wilted or flabby."

TANGERINES*

USES: "A tangerine is an orange with a sense of fair play. Loose-skinned for easy peeling, segmented for bite-sized convenience, it neither oozes, squashes, nor squirts at us. Even in the politest society, he who reaches for a tangerine reaches for a sure thing. And the tangerine's sense of timing is faultless. With a November-to-April season, reaching a peak supply precisely at Christmas, the tangerine has been the reward in every good American child's Yuletide stocking for generations. Obliging in all ways, it is a most accommodating citrus." This quote from *Gourmet* Magazine (December 1961) is an apt description of the tangerine.

Most tangerines are eaten fresh and out of hand. They are delicious as snacks anytime. They are often included in the school lunch box, served at breakfast, and included among other fruits to be presented as the finale to an elegant dinner. Tangerines are used in fruit salads and molded gelatin desserts. There are recipes for "Tangerine Shrimp Cocktail," "Low Calorie Fresh Fruit Pudding," "Fresh Tangerine and Turkey Salad," "Fresh Tangerine Bavarian," and "Stuffed Chicken Breast with Spiced Whole Tangerines." Many other recipes indicate uses in seafood cocktails, puddings, ambrosia, and sauces for cakes and puddings. Tangerine sherbet makes a light and refreshing dessert.

Tangerines are also processed. Tangerine juice, both canned and frozen concentrate, is marketed as are canned tangerine sections, but these processed forms are not generally well known to the consumer who continues to buy the fresh fruit.

MARKETING SEASON: Tangerines first become available in the fall; are in peak supply during November and December, and then taper off. 88 percent of the annual supply is available in a three-month period, November through January. The following table is derived from unloads of tangerines in 41 cities for four years, 1963-66:

MONTHLY AVAILABILITY OF TANGERINES EXPRESSED AS PERCENTAGE OF TOTAL ANNUAL SUPPLY

Jan.	Feb.	Mar.	Apr.	May	June
%	%	%	%	%	%
19	5	3	1	*	*
July	**Aug.**	**Sept.**	**Oct.**	**Nov.**	**Dec.**
%	%	%	%	%	%
*	*	*	1	22	48

* = less than 1 percent

VARIETIES: Although the names "mandarin" and "tangerine" are used interchangeably in some of the leading citrus-growing areas, "tangerine" is used herein to mean a sub-group of a larger group of C. reticulata varieties classified as "mandarins." The following list of "tangerine varieties," therefore, may include some fruits which others refer to as "mandarins."

"In Florida, the variety **Dancy** predominates, whereas in California, Texas, and Arizona, the **Algerian** tangerine (Clementine) is most comonly grown."

Experiments with mandarin hybridization in Florida have developed such hybrids as **Robinson, Osceola, Lee, Page, Nova, Fremont, Fortune,** and **Fairchild,** many of which are "commercially indistinguishable from the popular concept of 'tangerine' despite their hybrid background." By some classifications, such similar fruits as satsumas would be considered a variety of tangerine; by others, a variety of mandarin distinct from tangerines (based primarily on the lighter color).

Dancy "In the United States the Dancy is the best known and most highly priced of all ... because of their high color and rather small size (they) are prized for decorative purposes as well as for their quality and flavor ...

*UFFVA

The Dancy is to be commended because of its vigorous, strong growth, its cold-resistant quality, its abundant and regular fruiting habits, and its highly attractive, excellent-quality fruit. Moreover, it is resistant to disease, being only moderately susceptible to such diseases as gummosis, collar rot, and scaly bark. The factors that prevent it from becoming a great commercial fruit are its small size and its too numerous seeds.

"Fruit color deep orange red to scarlet; surface smooth and glossy, in age becoming bumpy and irregularly furrowed; shape oblate to pear-shaped; size medium, diam. 2-1/4 to 3 in., height 1-1/2 to 2-1/8 in.; base sometimes evenly rounded, but mainly slightly to markedly necked, more or less corrugated; stem slender ... rind thin, 1/8 to 3/16 in., leathery, tough, loose, and easily removed ... " About one-half of the tangerines grown in California (and the majority of those in Florida) are of this variety. Season: December through January, and in California January through April.

Kinnow Of increasing importance in the California industry is the Kinnow, a mandarin hybrid. "In the desert area it matures in December and lasts through February, while in others it is shipped during January through April. The Kinnow produces a medium to jumbo size (2-1/2 to 2-3/4 in.) fruit with a smooth rind and somewhat flat shape. It has an orange color, is of good flavor, has a long life, and should be a good shipper. It has a tight, thin rind, and has seeds."

Algerian Tangerine [Clementine] The Clementine, possibly a mandarin hybrid, originated in Algeria and was introduced into the U.S. in 1910. "Fruit color deep orange-red; surface smooth and glossy, slightly pitted; shape globose to elliptical, somewhat irregular; size medium, diam. 2 to 2-3/8 in., height 2 to 2-3/4 in.; base evenly rounded to slightly necked ... season early, November to December, but fruits remaining palatable and good into May or June."

Other similar fruits include the Satsuma, a cold-resistant citrus from Japan adaptable to a wide range of soils, almost totally seedless, but tending to remain green-colored even when mature "frequently causing difficulty and loss in marketing," and "retaining their good quality for so short a time." The Willow Leaf mandarin is a sweet, juicy, medium-sized fruit. "Its seediness and smaller size probably make it less desirable as a market fruit than the Satsuma, although it is in general of higher quality and less variable in type. If the variety does not exist in China, the recognized American name 'China' is misleading, and it would be better to designate it as Willow Leaf, a very appropriate name and one that is already in more common use in California than the name China."

CONTAINERS: Specifications for packing tangerines for Federal purchase are: "Unless otherwise specified, tangerines shall be packed in commercial cartons or crates which shall be clean, sound, well filled, and securely covered, and so constructed as to insure acceptance and safe delivery by common carriers for safe transportation to point of destination specified in shipping instructions at lowest transportation rates for such supplies. Each container shall be packed so that the tangerines on the shown face shall be reasonably representative in size, color, and quality of the contents of the container; each container shall be well filled, but the contents shall not show excessive or unnecessary bruising because of overfilled packages. Incident to packing, as herein defined, not more than 5 percent of the units may fail to meet the foregoing requirements: Provided, that no individual requirement shall be deliberately disregarded."

GRADES: U.S. Standards for Grades of Florida Tangerines provide for the following grades: U.S. Fancy; U.S. 1; U.S. 1 Bronze; U.S. 1 Russet; U.S. 2, U.S. 2 Russet, and U.S. 3. Tangerines produced in other states are covered by the U.S. Standards for Tangerines, an entirely separate set of standards.

U.S. 1 is the basic trading grade. Florida standards require that US.. 1 tangerines be: "fairly well colored; firm; mature; well formed; free from bruises, decay, unhealed skin breaks, and wormy fruit; and free from damage caused by ammoniation, buckskin, caked melanose, creasing, dirt or other foreign material, disease, dryness or mushy condition, green spots, hail, insects, oil spots, scab, scale, scars, skin breakdown, sprayburn, sunburn, unsightly discoloration, and other means. Not more than one-third of the surface, in the aggregate, may be affected by discoloration."

TANGERINES

FRESH (9/18/48   51.770)
  GRADES: U.S. Fancy; U.S. No. 1; U.S. No. 1 Bronze; U.S.
      No. 2; U.S. No. 2 Russet; U.S. No. 3
FLORIDA TANGERINES (1/31/73   51.1810)
  GRADES: U.S. Fancy; U.S. No. 1; U.S. No. 1 Bronze; U.S.
      No. 1 Russet; U.S. No. 2; U.S. No. 2 Russet;
      U.S. No. 3

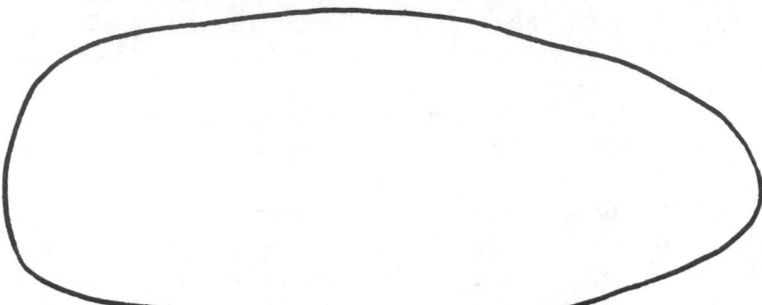

Permissible in U. S. No. 1 Grade

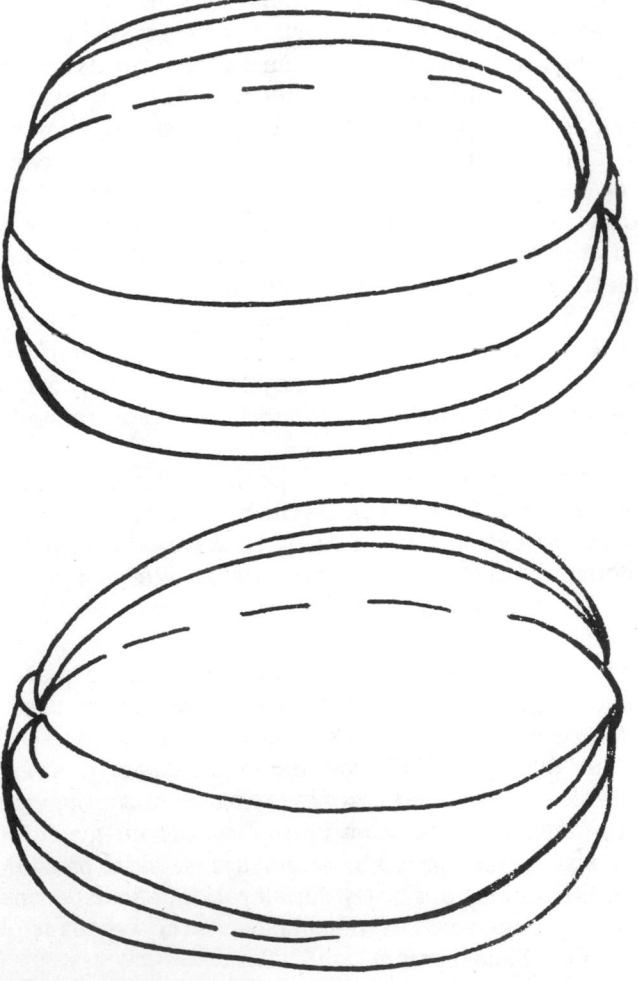

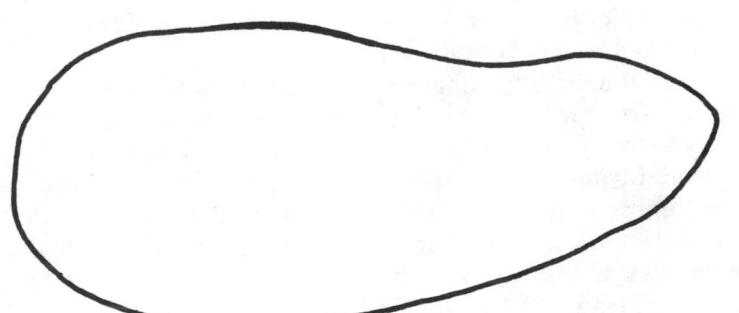

Permissible in U. S. No. 2 Grade

Two melons of round type illustrated
above are permitted in U. S. No. 1 grade

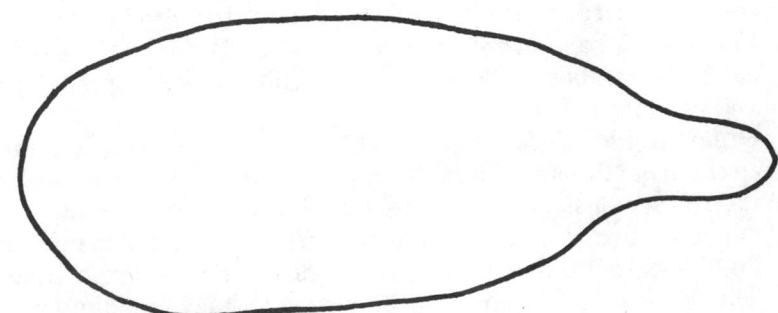

Cull. Not Permissible in U. S. No. 2 Grade

WATERMELONS*

USES: Watermelon is popular, especially in hot weather, for its sweet, cool juiciness. Cooled and eaten in slices, it makes a quick, no-cooking, delicious dessert or snack, perfect for a picnic, or it can be served as part of a mixed fruit salad. An eye-catching presentation can be made by cutting the melon in half lengthwise, scooping the fruit into balls, cleaning out the rind, and filling it with the watermelon balls, and adding cantaloupe and honeydew balls, coconut, and berries. The fruit can be juiced and used as a base for fruit punch, ices, or molded jellies. The watermelon can be used as a party centerpiece and portable bar by cutting a plug in it and filling it with vodka, gin, or rum. The juice is sipped out of the melon with straws. Watermelon pickles, made from the rind, are popular.

In other parts of the world, watermelon is eaten in different ways. "In southern Russia, a beer is made from watermelon juice, or the juice may be boiled down to a heavy syrup like molasses for its sugar. In Iraq, and in Egypt and elsewhere in Africa, the flesh of the melon is used as a staple food and animal feed, as well as a source of water in some dry districts. In the Old World, particularly Asia, the seeds are roasted, with or without salting, and eaten from the hand. Orientals also preserve watermelon by salting or brining large pieces or halves in barrels."

MARKETING SEASON: Watermelons are available March through October, but 80 percent are marketed in June, July, and August. The following table shows the monthly availability expressed as a percentage of the total annual supply of 2.69 billion pounds:

MONTHLY AVAILABILITY OF WATERMELONS AS PERCENTAGE OF TOTAL ANNUAL SUPPLY

Jan. %	Feb. %	Mar. %	Apr. %	May %	June %
*	*	1	2	10	29

July %	Aug. %	Sept. %	Oct. %	Nov. %	Dec. %
31	20	6	1	*	*

*less than .5 percent

VARIETIES: *The Descriptive List of Vegetable Varieties* (1972) reports 50 different watermelon varieties, many of which have been developed recently. One indication of the varieties commonly being produced currently is the *Seed Stock Report*. A second indicator of the current common varieties is the *Fresh Fruit and Vegetable Market News* for the New York City and Chicago wholesale markets, listing the daily prices and varieties on the market. Common varieties as indicated by both sources include Charleston Gray, which is by far the most prevalent, Crimson Sweet, Black Diamond (also called Cannonball or Florida Giant), Jubilee, Klondike, and Sugar Baby.

Charleston Gray was put on the market in 1954 and, since then, has assumed top rank, especially in states east of the Rockies. It takes about 85 days to maturity. The fruit is long and blocky, mostly weighing 28 to 35 lb.; rind is light grayish green with darker green veins. The flesh is bright red, crisp, sweet, of superior quality, and flavor; seeds are black. The Charleston Gray is very resistant to anthracnose; resistant but not immune to fusarium wilt, and resistant to sunburn. The rind is relatively thin, but very hard.

Crimson Sweet was introduced in 1964 and was developed from the Charleston Gray. It is light green with dark stripes. The fruit has fine texture, small dark seeds, and a high sugar content. It is resistant to anthracnose and fusarium wilt and is excellent for shipping.

Black Diamond [Cannonball or Florida Giant] has been on the market for many years. It is a standard shipping variety in the southeastern states and Texas. It takes about 90 days to maturity and is a high-yielding variety with good shipping quality, but inferior to some varieties in texture, flavor, and color of flesh. The fruit is large, commonly weighing 35 to 40 lb., or even up to 50 lb., and nearly round. The rind is very dark green, slightly ribbed, thick, tough, and hard. The flesh is red, rather coarse-grained, sweet, and crisp. The seeds are brownish black. In some strains it is relatively free from whiteheart. It is resistant to anthracnose and tolerant to fusarium wilt. The vines are vigorous and prolific.

Jubilee was a Garrison type originally, with moderate resistance to fusarium wilt, but many seed stocks are now susceptible. It takes 90 days to maturity. The fruit is oblong, weighs 30 to 35 lb., and is light with dark green stripes. The flesh is of excellent quality; it is bright red, firm, and sweet; seeds are black.

*UFFVA

WATERMELONS
FRESH (3/22/54   51.1970)
   Grades: U.S. No. 1; U.S. Commercial; U.S. No. 2

Klondike is a popular market and shipping melon, especially in California. Klondike types mature in 85 days. The striped Klondike is medium large, oblong, thick, 16 to 18 in. long and 8 to 10 in. in diameter. Its average weight is 27 lb. The rind is light green with irregular dark-green stripes, is medium thin and tough. The flesh is scarlet, very sweet, with excellent flavor. The seeds are small, black striped, and splotched with brown. The Striped, Blue Ribbon Klondike is wilt-resistant. The Peacock is a Klondike type.

Sugar Baby was introduced in 1956. It is an early variety, maturing in 75 to 80 days. It is small, weighing 8 to 10 lb., is 7 to 8 in. in diameter, and is, therefore, called an "icebox" melon. The rind is thin, hard, and tough, and can be either dark green with indistinct darker veining or medium green with indistinct darker veining. The flesh is medium red, firm, crisp, sweet, and of fine texture. There arc relatively few seeds; they are very small, dark tan mottled with black. The Sugar Baby is free of whiteheart.

Seedless varieties have been developed. They are round and weigh from 8 to 10 lb. The rind is thin, fairly tough, and striped. The deep-red flesh is sweet, crisp, and of excellent texture. The yield of melons is about equal to that of standard commercial varieties. Seedless melons have not shown resistance to any of the common watermelon diseases. The complex process involved in producing triploid seeds makes their cost very high. They usually are sprouted indoors at high temperatures; the seedlings are held in hotbeds or in greenhouses until they have 2 or 3 well-developed leaves.

Seedless watermelons are not generally available on the market due to the high cost and to their insufficient disease resistance. Research is being done in an effort to perfect these melons so they may become more available.

CONTAINERS: Traditionally, watermelons have not been shipped in containers, but have been loaded directly onto rail cars or trucks. They were stacked either lengthwise or crosswise, with straw on the floor of the car for padding and paper on the walls of the car to prevent abrasion of the melons touching the walls. The use of containers has gained popularity because they are more efficient and time-saving in unloading, and because they cut down on injuries related to rough handling in loading and unloading. In one study, conducted by the Florida Dept. of Agriculture and USDA, losses due to rough handling of watermelons shipped non-containerized in bulk from the field to the retail store were 11.3 percent, while losses of watermelons packed in cartons and shipped palletized were 0.2 percent. In addition, researchers found that for palletized loads the unloading time was cut greatly. Reduction of losses and unloading times offset the cost of the cartons. Bulk bins and cartons are presently in use.

Bulk bins are often collapsible and reusable. They can be made out of wood or wood slats, corrugated fiberboard, and wire. They generally hold from 800 to 2000 lb. of watermelon. Dimensions might be 42 in. x 47 in. x 36 in.

Watermelon cartons are generally made from double-wall, corrugated fiberboard with waterproof adhesive. The basic box size is 20 in. x 24 in. x 10 in., which holds 3 large melons. Other carton sizes hold 3, 4 or 5 melons, weighing from 55 to 80 lb. net. Cartons are often loaded onto pallets, usually 7 cartons high, although sometimes they are shipped floor loaded in cars or trucks.

STORAGE: Watermelons are not adapted to long storage. At low temperatures, (32 to 50° F.) they are subject to chilling injury. At 32°F. they tend to become pitted and have an objectionable flavor after one week. At 50°F. or lower, they lose color. At higher temperatures, watermelons are subject to decay. Holding watermelons for short periods (7 days) at room temperature can improve flavor and intensify color. However, after 6 weeks, melons held at room temperatures have very poor flavor.

If storage is necessary, watermelons will keep for 2 to 3 weeks at 40 to 50° F. Since watermelons do not store well, the marketing process generally is continuous from field to consumer.

QUALITY: "High quality in a watermelon is largely dependent upon high total sugar content. Other factors determining high quality are deep red color and pleasant texture of the edible flesh.

"Among essential factors of watermelon quality are maturity and size. The larger melons have more edible flesh, proportionately to weight, than the smaller ones. Maturity is difficult to determine without plugging and testing. Usually, ripe melons of good quality are firm, symmetrical, fresh, with good characteristic color for the variety. The lower side should be somewhat yellowish where the melon contacted the soil. If a melon is very hard and is white to very pale green on the under side, it is probably immature. If so, do not undertake to ripen it; in the watermelon, total sugar does not increase after it comes off the vine. Thumping a melon can provide exercise, but not much else for anyone other than a watermelon expert. Better look for a typical melon the retailer has cut, and then you can know what his melons look like inside."

Melons should have a good red flesh, that is crisp, and not mealy or water soaded (from bruising). Seeds, which can vary in color from white to black depending on the variety, should be fully mature and hard. At home, watermelons may be kept at room temperature until cut or may be refrigerated.

GRADES: U.S. standards for watermelons, effective March 22, 1954, provide for three grades: U.S. 1, U.S. Commercial and U.S. 2.

"U.S. 1 consists of watermelons of similar varietal characteristics which are mature but not overripe, fairly well formed, and which are free from anthracnose, decay, sunscald, and free from damage caused by other diseases, sunburn, hail, scars, insects, hollow heart, whiteheart, or mechanical or other means."

TOLERANCES—"In order to allow for variations incident to proper grading and handling, not more than a total of 10 percent, by count, of the watermelons in any lot may fail to meet the requirements of this grade: provided, that not more than one-half of this amount, or 5 percent, may be badly misshapen, or seriously damaged by any means, including therein not more than 1 percent for decay."

DEFINITIONS—"Mature" means that the melon has reached the stage of development at which the flesh is at least fairly sweet and shows characteristic color of a mature melon for the variety. "Fairly well formed" means having the characteristic shape but not necessarily the perfect type of the variety. "Damage" means any defect which materially affects the appearance or the edible or shipping quality of the melon. Any one of the following defects, or any combination of defects, the seriousness of which exceeds the maximum allowed for any one defect, shall be considered as damage: (a) Sunburn when affecting the appearance to a greater extent than 9 sq. in. of greenish yellow sunburn on a 30-lb. melon; (b) Hail, scars and other external defects, except anthracnose, when affecting the appearance to a greater extent than 9 sq. in. of greenish yellow sunburn on a 30-lb. melon; and (c) Hollow heart when the internal appearance is affected to a greater extent that than of a 30-lb., long type melon having cracks which aggregate 3/4 in. in width, or that of a 30-lb., round type melon having cracks which aggregate 1-1/2 in. in width. "Free from damage by anthracnose" means that each melon may have not more than 5 anthracnose spots which are not cracked or sunken below the contour of the surface of the melon. "Not badly misshapen" means that the melons are not bottlenecks or gourdnecks, but may be tapered at the ends or slightly constricted. "Serious damage" means any defect which seriously affects the appearance or the edible quality of the melon. Any one of the following defects, or any combination of defects, the seriousness of which exceeds the maximum allowed for any one defect, shall be considered as serious damage:

Anthracnose when there are more than 15 anthracnose spots, or when any spot is cracked or sunken below the contour of the surface of the melon; sunburn when affecting the appearance to a greater extent than 20 sq. in. of greenish yellow sunburn on a 30-lb. melon; Hail scars and other external defects, except anthracnose, when affecting the appearance to a greater extent than 20 sq. in. of greenish yellow sunburn on a 30-lb. melon; and Hollow heart when the internal appearance is affected to a greater extent than that of a 30-lb., long type melon having cracks which aggregate 1.5 in. in width, or that of a 30-lb., round type melon having cracks which aggregate 2.5 in. in width."

Apricots, Canned, Artificially Sweetened
[27.14 6/23/59]
Cherries, Canned, Artificially Sweetened
[27.34 6/23/59]
Figs, Canned, Artificially Sweetened
[27.73 6/23/59]
Peaches, Canned, Artificially Sweetened
[27.6 6/23/59]
Pears, Canned, Artificially Sweetened
[27.24 6/23/59]
Pineapple, Canned, Artificially Sweetened
[27.57 2/26/62]

Artificially sweetened canned fruits are the foods which conform to the definition and standards of identity prescribed for the above-mentioned canned fruits, except that the packing medium used is water artificially sweetened with saccharin, sodium saccharin, or a combination of both. Such packing medium may be thickened with pectin and may contain any mixture of any edible organic acid or acids as a flavor-enhancing agent, in a quantity not more than is reasonably required for this purpose.

The specified name of the food is "artificially sweetened _____," the blank being filled in with the name prescribed for the above-mentioned canned fruit having the same optional ingredient.

The artificially sweetened food is subject to the requirements for label statement of optional ingredients used, as prescribed for the above-mentioned canned fruits. If the packing medium is thickened with pectin, the label shall bear the statement "thickened with pectin." When any organic salt or acid or any mixture of two or more of these is added, the label shall bear the common or usual name of each such ingredient.

Canned Apricots with Rum [1/21/48]
Canned Cherries with Rum [1/21/48]
Canned Peaches with Rum [1/21/48]
Canned Pears with Rum [1/21/48]

The above-mentioned canned fruits with rum conform to the definitions and standards of identity and each is subject to the requirements for label statement of optional ingredients, prescribed for the above-mentioned canned fruits, except that it contains added rum in such amount that its alcoholic content is more than 3 percent but less than 5 percent by weight.

COMMON COUNTS OF VEGETABLES

ASPARAGUS, CANNED

No. 2½ Sq. Can—Small: 35/44
　　　　　　　　Large:25/34
　　　　　　　　Extra Large: 12/24

BEETS, CANNED

Midget (Petite): No. 2½—55/over
　　　　　　　No. 10—175/over
Tiny (Very Small): No. 2½—35/54
　　　　　　　No. 10—125/174
Baby (Small): No. 2½—22/34
　　　　　　　No. 75/124
Ruby (Medium): No. 2½—15/21
　　　　　　　No. 10—50/74
Large: No. 2½—8/14
　　　　No. 10—35/49

MUSHROOMS, CANNED

2 oz.—Midget: 55-60
　　　　Tiny: 30-35
4 oz.—Tiny: 60-70
　　　　Small: 40-50
　　　　Medium:30-40
8 oz.—Miniatures: 120-140
　　　　Medium: 60-70
16 oz.—Medium:110-120
　　　　Large: 70-80
　　　　Extra Large: 50-60
No. 10—Special Packs

ANISE*

USES: Anise bulbs may be quartered and eaten raw with salt or dressing. The inner stalks can be served raw with salt or dressing. Or cut the bulb and stalks in strips, crisp them in ice water, and serve as you would celery. Served hot, anise makes an enticing vegetable dish. Try it sauteed lightly in butter, then baked in a casserole with a rich cheese sauce. Or if you want to braise it, cut two stalks in quarters lengthwise, then saute in butter or olive oil until lightly browned, add salt and pepper, cover the pan and simmer until tender. Serve with the juice. Another idea is to chop the stalks and add them to tomato sauce or other sauces for fish or meat to give a delight-

fully different fragrance. Also, add anise to soup stock or to tossed green salads.

Irma Rombauer in the *Joy of Cooking* suggests cutting anise into slices, dropping the slices into boiling salted water, and simmering until tender, then serving with salt, paprika, hot olive oil, or melted butter or margarine.

MARKETING SEASON: Anise is scarce at all times, but is more likely to be available October through April, with the peak period in November and December. Monthly availability expressed as a percentage of total annual supply, based on periods when data on unloads of anise in five large cities was available, is as follows: (*means less than ½%)

MONTHLY AVAILABILITY OF ANISE AS PERCENTAGE OF TOTAL ANNUAL SUPPLY

Jan. %	Feb. %	Mar. %	Apr. %	May %	June %
7	1	4		*	

July %	Aug. %	Sept. %	Oct. %	Nov. %	Dec. %
		*	14	30	37

PACKING AND CONTAINERS: In California, where most of the anise is grown, the crop continues to be harvested by hand, hauled to a packing shed, cleaned, trimmed, cut to length, and packed. The container most used is the Sturdee nailed 15-1/2 in. crate or a wirebound holding 40 to 50 lb., but mostly 45, according to the California Department of Agriculture. The WGA crate, holding 80 to 85 lb., still is used to a small extent. Other crates are seen on the market from other areas, such as a 4/5 bu. crate from Virginia, and a 1-2/5 bu. crate from Arizona.

GRADES: The U.S. standards for so-called "sweet anise" (finocchio) adopted in 1930, provide one grade, U.S. 1. This "shall consist of stalks of sweet anise which are firm, tender, well trimmed, and fairly well blanched; which are free from decay and from damage caused by growth cracks, pithy branches, wilting, freezing, seed stems, dirt, discoloration, disease, insects, or mechanical or other means. Unless otherwise specified the minimum diameter of each bulb shall be not less than 2 in.

In order to allow for variations other than size incident to proper grading and handling, not more than 10 percent by

*UFFVA

SWEET ANISE

FRESH [3/15/73   51.2900]
Grades· U.S. No. 1

count of any lot may be below the requirements of this grade, but not to exceed 1/10 of this amount, or 1 percent, shall be allowed for decay. In addition, not more than 10 percent, by count, of any lot may be below the specified minimum diameter.

DEFINITIONS—"As used in these grades: 1. 'Stalk' means an individual plant. 2. 'Firm' means that the bulbs are not soft or wilted. 3. 'Tender' means that the bulbs are crisp and succulent. 4. 'Well trimmed' means that not more than one coarse outer branch is left on each side of the bulb to protect the tender inside portion, and the portion of the root remaining is not more than 1/2 in. in length. Tops may be either full length or cut back to not less than 10 in. except that not more than 5 of the outer branches may be cut back to less than 10 in. if necessary to facilitate proper packing, but not more than 3 of these may be on the same side of the bulb. 5. 'Fairly well blanched' means that the bulbs are of a light greenish to white color. 6. 'Damage' means any injury which materially affects the appearance, or the edible, or the shipping quality of the stalk. Any of the following defects shall be considered as damage: (a) growth cracks ... (b) pithy branches ... (c) wilting ... (d) freezing ... (e) seed stems ... (f) dirt ... (g) discoloration. 7. 'Diameter' means the smallest diameter measured through the center of the bulb at right angles to the longitudinal axis of the stalk."

ARTICHOKES*

USES AND PREPARATION: The artichoke has a delicate, nutty flavor causing it to be prized in salads or hors d'oeuvres. It can be eaten in its entirety or each leaf can be pulled off and dipped into a sauce. It can be served as a hot vegetable, with butter or special sauce, or serve cold.

HOW TO COOK—Wash artichokes, trim stems, and pull off and discard tough, outside leaves at the base. Cut off the top, and spread the leaves open. Remove the fuzzy thistle and tiny inner leaves with the tip of a teaspoon. This can be done before

ARTICHOKES

FRESH [5/15/69   51.3785]
Grades: U.S. No. 1, U.S. No. 2

or after cooking. Stand artichokes upright in a deep saucepan just big enough to hold them snugly, or tie them with a string so they will retain their shape. Add 1 tsp. salt, 1 Tbsp. fresh lemon juice, and boiling water to cover. Cook, covered, 45 to 60 min., or until base is soft. Lift out with 2 spoons, and let drain upside down.

HOW TO SERVE—If a whole artichoke is served to each person, place each on an individual salad plate. A half of an artichoke may be served on the dinner plate. Serve sauce, if thin, in small paper cups or in tiny bowls placed on the salad plates beside the artichoke. If sauce is thick, it may be served in lettuce cups.

HOW TO EAT—This is one vegetable that can be eaten properly with the fingers. Just pluck off each petal, and dip it in a savory sauce—a smooth hollandaise, spicy vinaigrette, bechamel, or melted butter with a dash of fresh lemon juice. When the prized heart is reached, after all the leaves have been removed, eat it with a fork.

MARKETING SEASON: As shown in the table below, from information calculated by the UFFVA, artichokes are available throughout the year, with the peak of supply occurring from March to May and the fewest available in July and August.

MONTHLY AVAILABILITY EXPRESSED AS PERCENTAGE OF TOTAL ANNUAL SUPPLY

Jan. %	Feb. %	Mar. %	Apr. %	May %	June %
6	7	12	23	15	5

July %	Aug. %	Sept. %	Oct. %	Nov. %	Dec. %
4	3	4	6	9	8

ANNUAL TOTAL 50 million lb.

(Percentages in the table are rounded to the nearest whole unit, therefore total more in this instance than 100.)

VARIETIES: The only variety of artichoke produced commercially in important quantities is the **Green Globe**, grown in California. This variety has deep green heads, 3 or 4 in. in

*UFFVA

diameter, round but slightly elongated. Other globular varieties, none of which are in commercial production, include the *White Globe, Red Dutch* and *Giant Bud*. A conical-bud

GLOBE ARTICHOKES

FRESH [5/15/69   51.3785]
Grades: U.S. No. 1, U.S. No. 2
type, more widely grown in Europe than in this country, is the *Thistle* or *Prickly Artichoke, Violet Artichoke,* and the *French* or *Green French Artichoke.*

Prevalent Terms	Bud Count per Box	Average Bud Diameter
Large	36 and larger	3-3/4 in.
Medium	42 to 63	3 in.
Small	72 to 96	2 in.
Heart and Baby	108 and smaller	1-3/4 in.

CONTAINERS: The main containers are the wooden box or fiberboard carton, 7 in. deep, 11 in. wide, and 20-5/8 in. long. The net weight of contents is 20 to 25 lb. A few shippers use a box 9-3/4 in. deep and of the same length and width as the more standard containers. Shipping tests were carried out by Western Wooden Box Assoc. on a reinforced container with splined instead of solid wooden ends. The 7-in. boxes and cartons are loaded 900 to an average rail car.

Some prepackaging is done at shipping point. One of the larger shippers packs about 25 percent of his production in consumer units. He packages 4 artichokes in a pulp tray overwrapped with heat-shrink film. Twelve trays are packed in a corrugated box 19-3/4 in. x 16-1/4 x 8.

QUALITY: "The most desirable artichokes are compact, plump, heavy in relation to size, somewhat globular, and with large, fresh, fleshy, tightly clinging, green leaf scales. Freshness is indicated by the green color. *Over-mature* artichokes have hard-tipped leaf scales which are opening or spreading; also the center formation may be fuzzy and dark pink or purple in color. Leaf scales on such overmature specimens are tough and woody when cooked and may be undesirably strong in flavor. Seriously discolored artichokes are usually bruised, or lacking in freshness. Bruises may appear as dark off-colored areas at the point of injury. They may also show mold growth. Bruised or seriously discolored artichokes usually turn gray-

ish-black or black when cooked. *Worm injury* is generally partially discernible at or near the base end of the bud. It may appear negligible from the outside but may extend deeply into the heart and cause excessive waste. The size of artichokes is not important in relation to quality and flavor."

WILTING—The effect of wilting on the flavor and tenderness of artichoke centers, and the effect of various storage conditions on flavor and tenderness were studied at the University of California at Davis. "During the study, artichokes were stored for periods of one, two and three weeks under three different temperature-relative humidity conditions. At the end of each period, the artichokes stored under each of the conditions were evaluated together, along with freshly picked artichokes, by a taste panel of 10 trained judges ... The study did not attempt to determine how much of the artichoke became inedible because of wilting ... The results of the test for tenderness (of centers only) ... show there was no great difference in the measure of tenderness after as long as three weeks of storage, even under the most undesirable storage conditions ... The conclusions of the study are that under the conditions most retailers are able to provide the edible portions of the artichoke suffer no loss of either tenderness or flavor."

GRADES: U.S. Grade Standards for artichokes provide two grades, U.S. No. 1 and U.S. No. 2. *"U.S. No. 1* shall consist of artichokes which are properly trimmed, fairly well formed, fairly compact, not overdeveloped; and which are free from damage caused by worms, snails, bruising, freezing, disease, insects, or other means. In order to allow for variations incident to proper grading and handling, not more than 10 percent, by count, of any lot may be below the requirements of this grade but no part of this tolerance shall be allowed for decay."

"U.S. No. 2 shall consist of artichokes which are not badly spread or over-developed: and which are free from serious damage caused by worms, bruising, freezing, disease, insects or other means. In order to allow for variations incident to proper grading and handling, not more than 10 percent, by count of any lot may be below the requirements of this grade but no part of this tolerance shall be allowed for decay."

Size. "Artichokes in any package shall not vary more than three-fourths of an inch in diameter. The size of the artichokes in any package shall be plainly stamped or otherwise marked on the package in terms of numerical count or minimum size. In order to allow for variations incident to proper sizing, not more than 5 percent, by count, of the artichokes in any package may be below the specified minimum size, or may vary from the 3/4 in. range in diameter permitted in any package."

ASPARAGUS*

USES: Asparagus is used in fresh form, or canned and frozen. Though principally used as a food, the plant has another use. The species *plumosus*, or asparagus fern, is widely used by florists for sprays in floral arrangements. As a food, asparagus is served in many forms—in salads, soups, hot dishes, and in combination with various sauces. The whole spears may be served, or only the green part, or just cuts or tips.

PREPARATION: "Fresh asparagus is a delight to the menu-maker; it goes with any meat, fish, or fowl. It adds crisp-tender consistency and delectable flavor to egg, cheese, or macaroni main dishes. Serve it hot with a luscious sauce. Or cook and chill asparagus spears and serve them with a well-seasoned french dressing, garnished with bright red tomato quarters, rice, cooked egg yolk, or strips of pimento.

"One! Two! Three! Quick! That is the way to cook asparagus. Fifteen minutes cooking time when spears lie full length in boiling water makes them crisp-tender. This allows 5 min. cooking time without lid, 10 additional minutes covered. When spears are cooked in an upright position in about 1-1/2 in. of boiling salted water, allow an additional 3 to 5 min. since the tips must steam while the lower parts cook in boiling water.

"The simplest thing to do with a platter of steaming, crisp-tender asparagus is to dress it with melted butter. Beyond that there are dozens and hundreds of delicious ways of preparing this spring-time delicacy," such as fresh asparagus with butter and egg sauce on toast, fresh asparagus oriental style, fresh asparagus and chicken a la king on toast, fresh asparagus au gratin, or asparagus with chive mayonnaise, with mustard butter, with caper butter sauce, with black butter sauce, or with dilly butter.

"TO PREPARE FOR COOKING—cut or break off each stalk as far down as it snaps easily. Remove scales with a knife. Then wash thoroughly, using a brush."

"TO COOK WHOLE STALKS IN UPRIGHT POSITION—Tie 5 to 6 stalks of asparagus in a bundle with string. Stand upright in the bottom part of a double boiler. Sprinkle with 1 tsp. salt. Pour in 1 to 1-1/2 in. boiling water. Cover with the top part of the double boiler, inverted. Boil 15 to 20 min. or until just crisp-tender. Lift out by catching tines of fork in string. Place on platter. Cut strings. The boiling water cooks the stalks while the rising steam cooks the tender heads. By this method, the whole stalk is uniformly cooked."

MARKETING SEASON: Ninety-six percent of fresh asparagus is available March through June. Peak months are April and May. The table below, based on unloads of asparagus in 41 cities, shows availability each month as a percentage of the annual supply.

MONTHLY AVAILABILITY OF ASPARAGUS AS PERCENTAGE OF TOTAL ANNUAL SUPPLY

Jan. %	Feb. %	Mar. %	Apr. %	May %	June %
*	2	20	33	28	15

July %	Aug. %	Sept. %	Oct. %	Nov. %	Dec. %
1	*	*	1	*	*

*indicates supply is less than 0.5% of annual total.

VARIETIES: "There are only a few varieties of asparagus, and the varietal differences between some of these are not well defined," says USDA Farmers' Bulletin No. 1646. "Male and female flowers are born on different plants, and this results in a constant mixing of strains in the field which makes it difficult to obtain seed that will produce plants uniform in type and true to varietal characteristics. Since the crowns are propagated almost wholly from seed, wide variation may appear in any lot of crowns unless special effort is made to isolate the seed-producing plants from the pollen producers. Where more than one variety is grown for seed, careless handling of seed stocks soon results in mixture and in less distinct varietal differences ..."

Asparagus varieties are of two general types based on the color of the spears. The more important group includes the

*UFFVA

ASPARAGUS

FRESH [3/5/72   51.3720]
Grades: U.S. No. 1, U.S. No. 2
Asparagus Plumosus (6/6/30   51.4455)
Grades: U.S. Fancy, U.S. No. 1, U.S. Commercial
CANNED [6/20/73   52.2541]

Grades:	"A" or "FANCY"	"C" or "STANDARD"	"SUB-STANDARD"
Minimum Score:	85	70	Less than 70

	NET WEIGHT OZ.	NET WEIGHT METRIC	DRAINED WEIGHT OZ.	DRAINED WEIGHT METRIC
Green tipped and white; small, medium or large sizes				
No. 8Z Tall	5.3	150.2 g	4.9	138.9 g
No. 303	10.9	309.0 g	10.1	286.3 g
No. 2½	19.3	547.2 g	18.0	510.3 g
Green and green tipped; small, medium, or large sizes and blends of these sizes				
No. 8Z Tall	5.1	144.6	4.7	133.2 g
No. 303	9.7	275.0 g	8.9	252.3 g
No. 2½	17.6	499.0 g	16.2	459.3 g
Extra large, colossal, giant sizes; or blends of these sizes Green tipped and white; white				
No. 8Z Tall	5.3	150.2 g	4.9	138.9 g
No. 303	10.3	292.0 g	9.5	269.3 g
No. 2½	18.3	518.8 g	17.0	482.0 g

	NET WEIGHT OZ.	NET WEIGHT METRIC	DRAINED WEIGHT OZ.	DRAINED WEIGHT METRIC
Extra large, colossal, giant sizes; or blends of these sizes Green and green-tipped				
No. 8Z Tall	5.1	144.6 g	4.7	133.2 g
No. 303	9.4	266.5 g	8.6	243.8 g
No. 2½	17.1	484.8 g	15.7	445.1 g
Cut spears, bottom cuts-tips removed Green-tipped and white				
No. 8Z Tall	5.4	153.1 g	4.7	133.2 g
No. 303	10.0	283.5 g	9.2	260.8 g
No. 2½	19.0	538.6 g	17.8	504.6 g
No. 10	71.0	2.0 kg	63.1	1.8 kg
Cut spears, bottom cuts-tips removed Green				
No. 8Z Tall	5.0	141.8 g	4.5	127.6 g
No. 303	9.5	269.3 g	8.7	246.6 g
No. 2½	17.5	496.1 g	16.2	459.3 g
No. 10	65.5	1.9 kg	58.8	1.7 kg

FROZEN [6/30/74   52.381]

Grades:	"A" or "FANCY"	"B" or "EXTRA STANDARD"	"SUB-STANDARD"

varieties **Mary Washington, Martha Washington, Reading Giant, Palmetto** and **Argenteuil**. Spears of this group become dark green in sunlight. The less important group includes such varieties as **Conover's Colossal** and **Mammoth White**. These produce light green or whitish spears. These light-colored varieties should not be confused with white (blanched) asparagus as grown for canning.

The older, light green varieties—Conover's Colossal and Mammoth White—and the dark green variety, Palmetto, have been largely replaced by the more rust-resistant Mary Washington and Martha Washington varieties. Reading Giant and Argenteuil are also largely replaced by the Washington varieties.

In the early 1900s asparagus rust threatened the U.S. asparagus industry. In response to this threat, Norton developed the Washington varieties. He crossed an unknown American male plant with a Reading Giant female from England. The male plant lent remarkable vigor and rust resistance to the resulting fruit, the plant of which was called Martha Washington. Since Norton's time a number of new selections from Mary Washington have been released. The newer improved selections replace the older strains. *None of these is immune to rust*, but some are more resistant than others. Recently, Waltham and Roberts have been planted widely in the East and 711 and 500 W in the West. Currently, two new strains—66 and 72—resistant to *Fusarium* wilt are being planted in the West.

Besides having rust resistance, the Washington varieties are of high commercial quality, fully equal or superior to the best other varieties on the market in earliness, vigor of growth, and size and quality of shoot. They are also more uniform in size, shape, and color than the old standard varieties and are very productive of large spears. The Martha Washington variety is the more rust resistant, but the Mary Washington variety is slightly earlier, more vigorous, and is resistant enough to make it more popular for general planting. Three new selections from the Washington varieties have been introduced. These are **Paradise, Mary Washington 500,** and **Mary Washington 499**. These are all reported to be rust resistant.

CONTAINERS: *Market News Service of USDA* lists the following containers as those used in the more important producing areas: pyramid crate holding 26 to 32 lb. net; fiberboard box or carton holding 24 1-1/2 lb. consumer packages, total of 36 lb.; pony crate 12 lb.; and 8 qt. basket, loose, 10 lb. Other packages listed by USDA are used in some areas are the bushel basket 30 to 35 lb. net; squares 12 lb.; 1/2 crate 12 lb.; used citrus crates or boxes, 48 to 50 lb.; crate holding 7 in. cut spears 23 to 25 lb.; and L.A. lug for tips, 17 to 18 lb.

Asparagus is shipped in different forms, that is, bunched, loose, or overwrapped. *USDA Market News* reports show Cal-

ifornia growers generally use pyramid crates containing 16 1-1/2 lb. bunches or 12 2-lb. bunches; New Jersey growers use the pyramid crate containing 12 2-1/4 lb. bunches.

The pyramid crate has two compartments. Its tapered shape and solid ends prevent shifting during handling and shipping. There are various forms and sizes of pyramid crates. The bottoms are usually lined with paper which is covered with a layer of damp moss or other material. The butts of the bunches are placed on the moss. When packed in this way and kept at a temperature just above freezing, asparagus can be shipped a long distance and arrive in good condition.

One package of special interest is a master container of wood and fiberboard which holds 16 consumer unit, open-face cartons each holding 1-1/2 lb. of asparagus. Each unit carton contains a water absorbent pad in the bottom. The package is suitable for going through a hydrocooler.

The drawing below shows a typical, nailed, wooden asparagus crate as shown in Freight Container Tariff 1-H. Asparagus crates listed in the July 11, 1966 issue of Containers for Fresh Fruits and Vegetables published in four Container Tariffs, as published by the Uniform Classification Committee, are No. 149, 150, 159, 160.

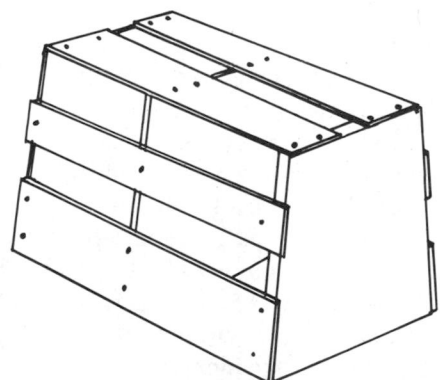

Crate No. 150 has inside dimensions of 10-1/2 in. depth, 17-9/16 in. length, and width at top of 9 to 9-1/2 in. and at bottom of 11 in. *Crate No. 149* has inside dimensions of 8-1/2 in. in depth, 12 in. length, and width at top 5 to 5-1/2 in. and at bottom 9-1/2 in. *Crate No. 160* has inside dimensions of 9-1/2 in. depth by 17-9/16 in. length by 9 to 9-1/2 in. width at top and 11 in. at bottom.

Increased air freight shipment of asparagus has brought the development of special containers for such shipment. These containers are composed of 45 percent wax and 55 percent cardboard, weigh 17 oz. and hold 15 lb. of asparagus. The carton can withstand the hydrocooling process.

Not much asparagus is prepackaged as yet, but the quantity is increasing. Predominantly it is shipped bunched or loose. Where it is prepackaged, the consumer unit can be a carton such as chipboard, or film bag, but the carton is more commonly used.

SERVINGS AND WEIGHTS: A pound of asparagus as purchased provides 3.38 portions of 4 medium cooked spears. For such portions for 25 persons, 7.5 lb. are required as purchased; and for 100 persons 29.75 lb. A pound as purchased provides 2.61 portions of 3 oz. of cut cooked spears. For such portions for 25 persons 9.75 lb. are required; and for 100 persons 38.5 lb. The yield in cooked, cut spears is 49 percent of the purchased asparagus. A crate of 28 lb. net at 49 percent yield gives 73.17 portions of 3 oz. of cooked cut spears and 1.5 crates are required for 100 portions.

QUALITY: "To be of best quality," says USDA, "asparagus should be fresh and firm with closed compact tips and the entire green portion tender. Asparagus ages rapidly after cutting; tips become partially open, spread, or wilted, and the stalks become tough and fibrous. Tender asparagus is brittle and easily punctured. Slightly wilted stalks may sometimes freshen in cold water, but are usually undesirable. Angular or flat stalks are apt to be tough and woody."

Further, USDA advises that, "Asparagus is cut a few inches below the surface of the ground when the spears have developed the desired length above ground. If growth is rapid, a green shoot 6 to 10 in. long may be obtained before any part of it has become tough. After a few inches of the tip are green, the white portion below the ground begins to toughen. Thus, the white portion of asparagus as commonly displayed in markets is generally tough, but can be used for flavoring or for soup.

"At the time of harvest, asparagus has some tough fibers toward the butt end, the extent of the fibrous portion depending upon the length and maturity of the spears. As time passes after harvest, more fibers toughen, and they extend farther and farther up the spear, which results in a corresponding reduction of the tender portion. Experimental lots of fresh spears which were 7 in. long had, on the average, a 'tender' portion of about 4 in. (The length of the 'tender' portion was determined with a fiberometer and is 1 to 2 inches shorter than the edible part) ... (There is) rapid loss of sugar after harvest. At 32°F., half the initial sugar is lost after about 2 weeks of holding; at 50°F. it takes one week; at 68°F., two days and at 86°F., only about a half day." This emphasizes the importance of adequate refrigeration of asparagus from immediately after harvest all the way to the consumer.

GRADES: The U.S. standards for asparagus provide two grades, U.S. No. 1 and U.S. No. 2. *U.S. No. 1* consists of: "Stalks of asparagus which are fresh, well-trimmed, and fairly straight; which are free from decay and free from damage caused by spreading or broken tips, dirt, disease, insects, or other means. (For definitions of such words as 'fresh' and 'damage' see below.) **Size.** Unless otherwise specified, the diameter of each stalk is not less than 1/2 in. **Color.** Unless otherwise specified, not less than 2/3 of the stalk length is of a green color.

"TOLERANCES. In order to allow for variations incident to proper grading and handling, the following tolerances, by count, are provided as specified: *For defects.* 10 percent for stalks in any lot which fail to meet the requirements of this grade other than for trimming, including therein not more than 5 percent for defects causing serious damage: Provided: That not more than 1/5 of this latter amount, or 1 percent, shall be allowed for stalks affected by decay. In addition, not more than 10 percent of the stalks in any lot may fail to meet the specified diameter or length requirements."

DEFINITIONS—"'Fresh' means that the stalk is not limp or flabby. 'Well trimmed' means that at least 2/3 of the butt of the stalk is smoothly trimmed in a plane approximately parallel to the bottom of the container and that the butt is not stringy or frayed. 'Damage' means any defect, or any combination of defects, which materially detracts from the appearance, or the edible, or marketing quality of the stalk.

'Diameter' means the greatest thickness of the stalk measured at a point approximately 1 in. from the butt. 'Fairly well trimmed' means that at least 1/3 of the butt of the stalk is smoothly trimmed in a plane approximately parallel to the bottom of the container, and that the butt is not badly stringy or frayed. 'Badly misshapen' means that the stalk is so badly flattened, crooked, or otherwise so badly deformed that its appearance is seriously affected. 'Serious damage' means any defect, or any combination of defects, which seriously detracts from the appearance, or the edible, or marketing quality of the stalk."

Most major asparagus-producing states have similar standards. NEW JERSEY has a grade called New Jersey No. 1. Among other things it provides that "Each stalk shall have a length of not less than 9 in.; and not less than 2/3 of the stalk length shall be of a green color, except that stalks less than 9 in. in length may be certified, provided that (such stalks) have not less than 6 in. of green, or if 6 in. or less in length shall be all green. Each stalk shall have a diameter of not less than 6/16 in., and in no case shall a minimum diameter of less than 6/16 in. be specified."

WASHINGTON adds to its general statement of grade a size classification: "Any lot of asparagus may be classified as *Small, Medium, or Large,* if 80 percent, by count of the stalks in any lot conform to the following requirements for such sizes: Small, 3/8 to 9/16 in.; Medium 9/16 to 3/4 in.; Large, over 3/4 in. The foregoing ... refers to the maximum diameter of the stalks measured at a point not more than 8 in. from the tip."

California asparagus must be packed according to the state agricultural code. CALIFORNIA makes an exception for "crooked" asparagus: "Asparagus which fails to meet these requirements (i.e. the California standards similar to federal standards) only because of being 'badly crooked' shall be considered as complying with this standard if the container in which it is packed is plainly marked on the outside of the end bearing other markings required by this section, in letters not less than 1/2 in. in height, with the word 'crooks'." California standards differentiate as to acceptable color between asparagus grown in different production areas: "In view of differences in climatic and other natural conditions prevailing south and east of San Gorgonio Pass, which cause fresh asparagus grown in the area to be satisfactory in quality only if a large portion of the stalk is green or colored, which asparagus must, therefore, be cut at a shorter length than asparagus grown in the area north and west of the San Gorgonio Pass, stalks of asparagus produced in the area south and east of San Gorgonio Pass shall have not more than 2 in. of white on the butt, except that not more than 20 percent of the stalks in any bunch, or when not packed in bunches, 20 percent of the stalks in any container, may have not to exceed 2-1/2 in. of white."

The California Agricultural Code defines other grades: "Bunches of asparagus classified according to the following designated grades shall contain the number of stalks indicated in each classification and shall weigh not less than 2 lb. net when packed: *Colossal,* not more than 14 stalks; *Jumbo,* 15-20; *Extra Select,* 21-28; *Select,* 29-42; *Extra Fancy,* 43-67; *Fancy,* 68-100." "... asparagus produced in the area south and east of San Gorgonio Pass with stalks which are less than 7-1/2 in. in length when marked with grade classification, shall be classified according to the following designated grades: *Mammoth,* not more than 17 stalks to a bunch; *Giant,* 18-24; *Fancy Regal,* 25-34; *Regal,* 35-52; *Fancy Standard,* 53-78; and *Standard,* 79-115."

The following box-marking requirement of Washington State is typical of those used by major asparagus-producing states: "The boxes shall be conspicuously and legibly stamped with the name and address of person, firm, or association shipping the asparagus, variety, grade, and net weight. The grade shall be stamped in letters of at least 3/8-in. type."

ASPARAGUS—Canned [6/20/73]

Grade A: Color: Spears, tips, and points possess good characteristic green, light green, or yellowish green color typical of well-developed asparagus, and the bottom portion of not more than 10 percent or 1 unit whichever is larger, may possess typical white or yellowish white color not to exceed 1/8 of the length of the unit. GREEN TIPPED—Unit possesses a good characteristic green, light green, or yellowish green color with typical white or yellowish white color at the base ends typical of well-developed asparagus; and not more than 20 percent by count may possess typical white or yellowish white color in excess of 1/2 of the length of the unit, or may be all green. GREEN TIPPED AND WHITE—Possess good characteristic

APPROXIMATE DIAMETER OF ASPARAGUS SPEARS

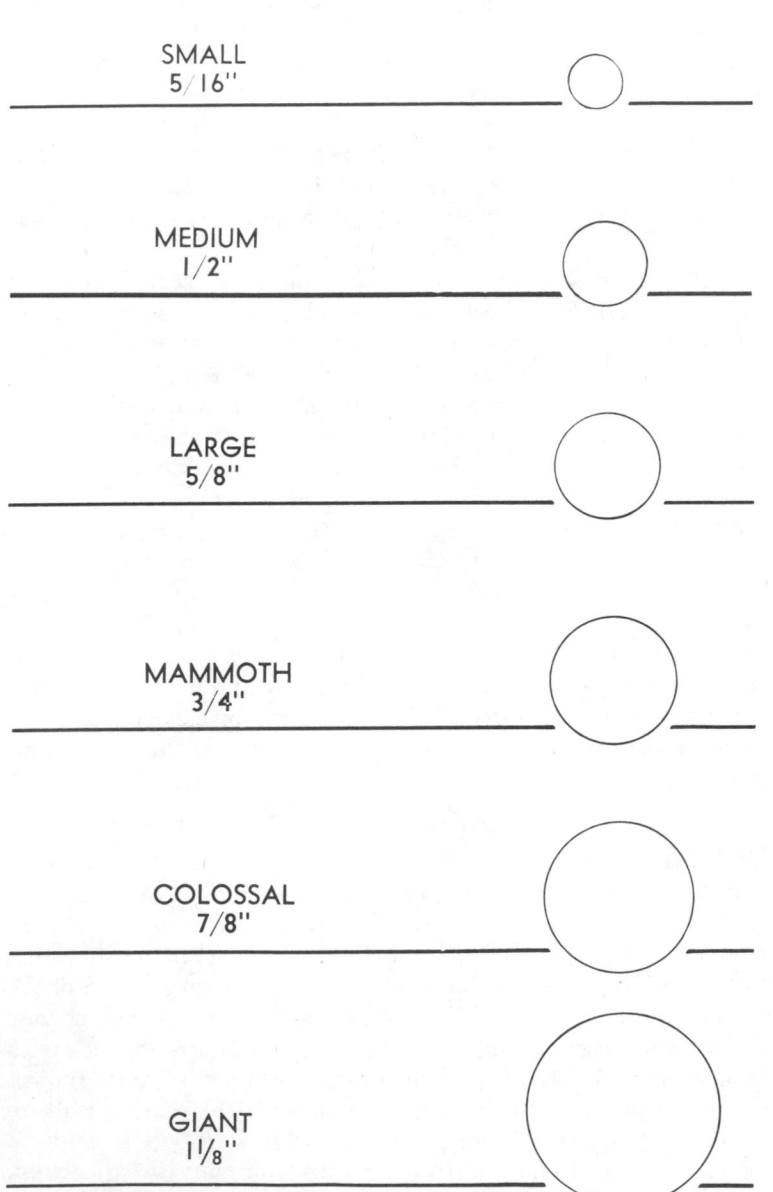

SMALL
5/16"

MEDIUM
1/2"

LARGE
5/8"

MAMMOTH
3/4"

COLOSSAL
7/8"

GIANT
1 1/8"

Source: Frosty Acres Buyers Guide—The Frozen Food Forum, Inc., Atlanta, Ga.

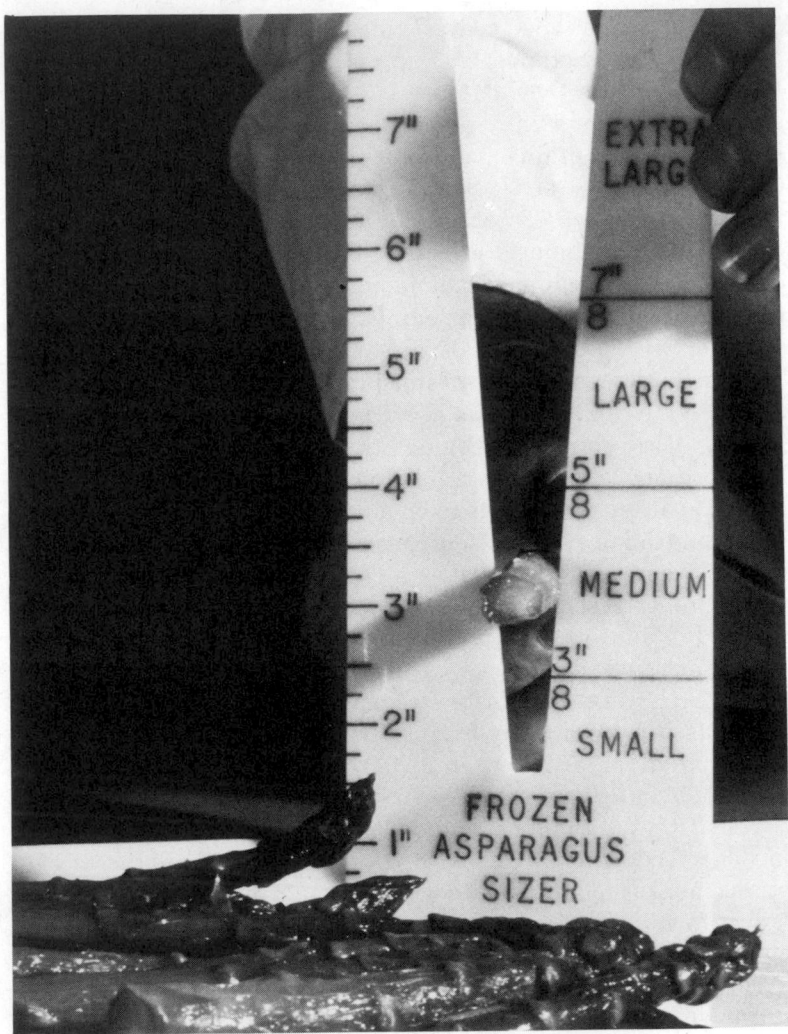

This simple plastic device, helps fruit and vegetable inspectors check the width and length of asparagus stalks. This is one of several devices used to help USDA inspectors enforce the standards for grades of processed fruits and vegetables.

white or yellowish white color and may possess green, light green, or yellowish green heads and adjacent areas typical of well-developed asparagus; and not more than 20 percent may possess green, light green, or yellowish green heads and adjacent areas not to exceed 1/2 of the length. WHITE—May possess good characteristic white or yellowish white color typical of well-developed asparagus; and not more than 10 percent or 1 unit, whichever is larger, may possess green, light green, or yellowish green heads and adjacent areas not to exceed 1/2 of the length. **Defects** SPEARS, TIPS, AND POINTS: GREEN AND GREEN TIPPED—Not more than 10 percent, and GREEN TIPPED AND WHITE and WHITE Not more than 15 percent, have shattered heads, misshapen, poorly cut, damaged, and seriously damaged units, provided that not more than 3 percent may be seriously damaged; or one unit in a single container may be seriously damaged if such unit exceeds the allowance of 3 percent, provided that in all of the containers comprising the sample such damaged units do not exceed an average of 3 percent of the total number of units. **Character** SPEARS, TIPS AND POINTS: Not less than 85 percent are well developed and the remainder at least fairly well developed. **Tough Units—Maximum tolerance** SPEARS, TIPS AND POINTS: GREEN and GREEN TIPPED 10 percent and WHITE 20 percent. One unit may be tough if it exceeds the percentage.

Grade A: Color: CUT SPEARS, BOTTOM CUTS, OR CUT-TIP REMOVED AND MIXED: GREEN—Units possess good characteristic green, light green, or yellowish green color typical of well-developed asparagus; and not more than 10 percent may be green and white or white; provided not more than 2 percent may be white. GREEN TIPPED AND WHITE OR WHITE—Possess good color typical of well-developed green tipped and white or white asparagus. **Defects:** Not more than 10 percent have shattered heads, are misshapen, poorly cut, damaged, and seriously damaged; provided not more than 2 percent may be seriously damaged, and provided that in all of the containers comprising the sample, or one unit in a single container if larger, such damaged units do not exceed an average of 2 percent by count of the total number of units. **Character:** Head development—not less than 50 percent are well developed and the remainder at least fairly well developed. **Tough Units—Maximum tolerance:** GREEN and GREEN TIPPED types not more than 10 percent. GREEN TIPPED AND WHITE and WHITE; not more than 33-1/3 percent.

Grade C: Color: SPEARS, TIPS AND POINTS: Fairly good characteristic color. See Grade A Color; fairly well-developed asparagus, bottom portion of not more than 20 percent may possess typical white or yellowish white color not to exceed 1/4 of the length of the unit. GREEN TIPPED—Fairly good characteristic. See Grade A Color. Fairly well-developed asparagus; and not more than 50 percent may possess typical white or yellowish white color in excess of 1/2 of the length of the unit, or may be all green. GREEN TIPPED AND WHITE—Fairly good characteristic. See Grade A Color. Fairly well-developed asparagus; and not more than 20 percent may possess green, light green, or yellowish green heads and adjacent areas not to exceed 1/2 of the length. **Defects:** See Grade A: Defects. GREEN AND GREEN TIPPED 20 percent, and GREEN TIPPED AND WHITE and WHITE not more than 30 percent have shattered heads, misshapen, poorly cut, damaged units; 10 percent may be seriously damaged. See Grade A: Defects; if such unit exceeds the allowance of 10 percent; provided that in all of the containers comprising the sample such damaged units do not exceed an average of 10 percent of the total number of units. **Character:** Applicable styles not less than 90 percent at least fairly well developed. **Tough Units—Maximum tolerance:** 25 percent; 50 percent. See Grade A: Defects.

Grade C: Color: CUT SPEARS, BOTTOM CUTS, OR CUT-TIP REMOVED AND MIXED: Fairly good characteristic green, light green, or yellowish green color typical of fairly well-developed asparagus; not more than 20 percent may be green and white or white; provided not more than 5 percent may be white. GREEN TIPPED AND WHITE or WHITE—Fairly good characteristic color, typical of fairly well-developed green tipped and white or white asparagus. **Defects:** Not more than 20 percent have shattered heads, are misshapen, poorly cut, damaged, and seriously damaged; provided that not more than 7 percent may be seriously damaged. See Grade A: Defects. **Character:** See Grade C Spears, Tips, etc. **Tough Units—Maximum tolerance:** 25 percent, 50 percent; 25 percent, 50 percent. See Grade A: Cut Spears and Mixed for interpretations of percentages. **Sstd:** Fails to meet requirements.

Liquor: Clear liquor may possess a typical yellow or green yellow and is fairly free from suspended material and sediment (typical for Grade A). Fairly clear liquor may be cloudy but not excessively cloudy or may possess an accumulation of sediment which may be slightly gray or brown (typical for Grade C).

ASPARAGUS SIZES

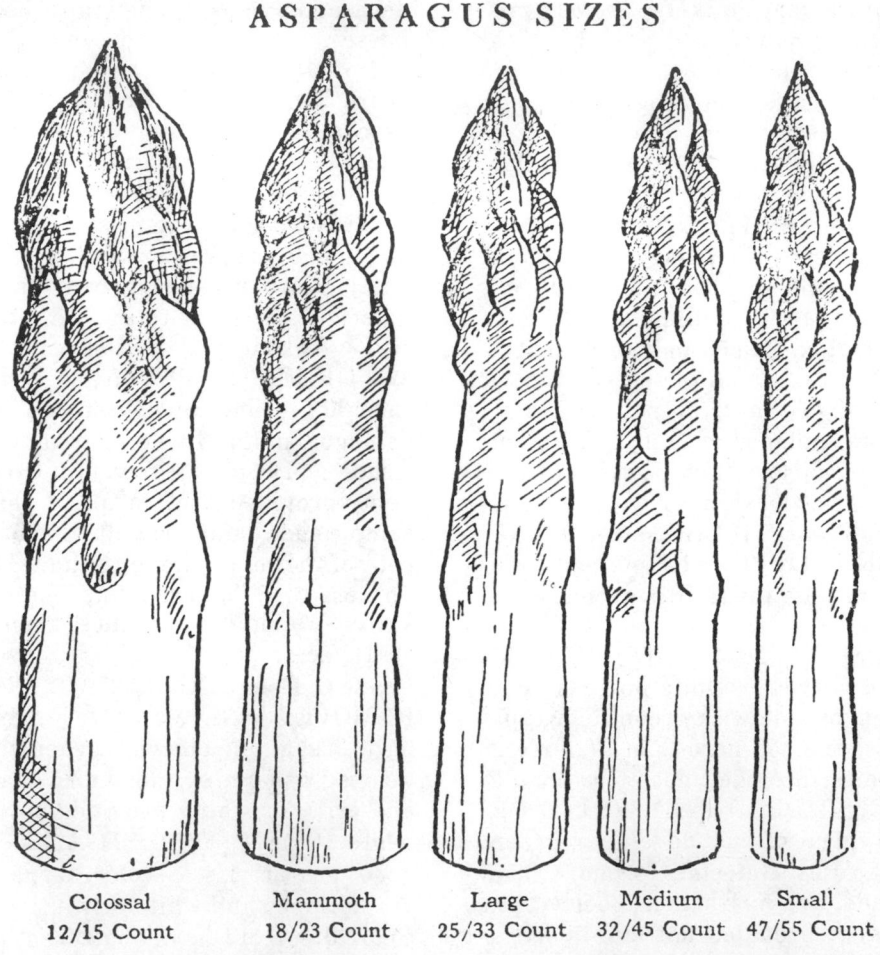

Colossal	Mammoth	Large	Medium	Small
12/15 Count	18/23 Count	25/33 Count	32/45 Count	47/55 Count

These illustrations show actual diameter. Counts and sizes are approximate for the No. 2 Can. Lengths will vary according to height of can.

ASPARAGUS—Frozen [6/30/74]

Grade A: Is of good similar varietal characteristics; has a good flavor and odor; has no grit or silt present that affects the appearance or edibility; in which no more than 5 percent, by weight, of loose material may be present; and has an attractive appearance and eating quality within the limits specified for the various quality factors.

Grade B: Is of similar varietal characteristics; has a good flavor and odor; has no more than a trace of grit or silt present that slightly affects the appearance or edibility; in which no more than 10 percent, by weight, of loose material may be present; and has a reasonably attractive appearance and eating quality, within the limits specified for the various quality factors. **Sstd:** Fails to meet requirements of Grade B. For Color and uniformity (Table IV); Character and damage (Table V); Harmless extraneous vegetable material (Table VI), defects are classified as minor, major, severe, or critical. Each "x" mark in Table IV, V, VI represents "one defect."

FROZEN ASPARAGUS CUT SPEARS (GREEN OR GREEN-WHITE TYPE)
Definition of Terms

Frozen Asparagus
June 1970

1.

(3/8 in. or more)
cut _ _ _ = **HEAD** (tip end)

= **HEAD** (possesses substantial amount head material)

cut _ _ _

= **CUT UNIT** (does not possess substantial amount head material)

cut _ _ _

= **CUT UNIT**

cut _ _ _
(less than 3/8 in.)
= **LOOSE MATERIAL**

(less than 3/8 in.)
cut == **LOOSE MATERIAL**

== **HEAD** (possesses substantial amount head material)

cut _ _ _

= **CUT UNIT** (does not possess substantial amount head material)

cut _ _ _

= **CUT UNIT** (over 2 in. is a "major" defect)

2.

In determining the percent, by count, of heads, a tip end that is 3/8 inch, or more, in length is counted as one head.

If a portion of a spear possesses a substantial amount of head material, it is counted as one head.

TABLE IV—CLASSIFICATION OF DEFECTS
Color—Length

Quality Factors	DEFECTS	Minor	Major	Severe
Color	*Green or all-green spears or tips:* White or yellowish white color exceeding 1/4 in. up to 1/3 the length of the stalk	X		
	White or yellowish white color over 1/3 of the length of the stalk		X	
	Green-white spears or tips: White or yellowish white color exceeding 1/3 of the length of the stalk	X		
	All Types—Cut Spears; Cuts and Tips; Cuts; Center Cuts: White or yellowish white; or partially of such color	X		
Uniformity of Length	*Spears; Tips:* Any unit which varies more than 1-1/2 in. from the predominant length of the sample unit	X		
	Cut Spears; Cuts and Tips; Cuts; Center Cuts: Any unit of cut asparagus less than 1/2 in. in length (excluding head material or loose material)	X		
	Any unit of cut asparagus, more than 2 in. in length.		X	

TABLE V—CLASSIFICATION OF DEFECTS
Character—Damage

Quality Factors	DEFECTS	Minor	Major	Severe
Character	*Spears and Tips:* *In Grade A only*—Reasonably well developed (worse than Plate 1 but not worse than Plate 2 or 3)	X		
	In all grades—Poorly developed (worse than Plate 2 or 3): Seedy		X	
	Flowered			X
	Cut Spears or Cuts and Tips: *In all grades*—Poorly developed (worse than Plate 2 or 3): Seedy	X		

Quality Factors	DEFECTS	Minor	Major	Severe
	Flowered		X	
	Tough fiber development: 2 in. or less		X	
	More than 2 in. or woody units of any length			X
Damage	Shattered heads—broken or shattered to the extent that it is definitely noticeable		X	
	Misshapen—badly crooked or affected in appearance by doubles or malformations		X	
	Poorly cut—angle of cut less than 45 degrees—cut is ragged or partially cut		X	
	Discoloration, mechanical injury, pathological, or damaged by other means to the extent that the appearance and eating quality of a unit is affected: Slightly	X		
	Materially		X	
	Seriously			X

For interpretative guides, see USDA illustrations of "Stages of Development in Frozen Asparagus," which are a part of this document.

TABLE VI—CLASSIFICATION OF DEFECTS
Extraneous Material

Quality Factors	DEFECTS	Minor	Major	Severe	Critical
Harmless extraneous vegetable material	Grass, weeds, leaves, stems, and dried stalks: 1 in. or less	X			
	More than 1 in. but not more than 2 in.		X		
	More than 2 in. but not more than 3 in.			X	
	More than 3 in.				X

GREEN OR WAX SNAP BEANS*

USES: Some forms of snap beans can be used as food at various stages of maturity. The beans may be just appearing in the pod; they may be plump in the pod, or they may be allowed
*UFFVA

to mature to the dry bean stage. In general "snap beans" means to most people the bean harvested when immature, at the stage when both seeds and pods are tender and edible. With today's stringless varieties, preparation is simple. Wash; snip off the stem end, or both ends if you like, and boil in a small amount of water until tender. Only the imagination of the cook limits the many ways of serving snap beans. The simplest method is to boil, flavor with salt and pepper, and serve hot. If it pleases the palate, add butter.

For a more sophisticated dish, beans may be served like asparagus with a hollandaise, cheese, or mushroom sauce. Some folks like to add bacon or fatback to the cooking water to give a special flavor.

Beans may be served in vegetable salads, either hot or chilled. Often beans are marinated and served cold, alone or with other salad vegetables. Snap beans are a good ingredient of stews and soups.

MARKETING SEASON: Fresh snap beans are on the market all year, with the peak in June, and relatively large quantities available also in all other months, May through October. The following table shows relative availability by months.

PERCENTAGE OF TOTAL ANNUAL SUPPLY OF FRESH SNAP BEANS AVAILABLE EACH MONTH

Jan.	Feb.	Mar.	Apr.	May	June
%	%	%	%	%	%
4	3	6	7	10	14

July	Aug.	Sept.	Oct.	Nov.	Dec.
%	%	%	%	%	%
11	11	10	10	8	6

VARIETIES: Remember the "string bean"? Until 1894, most varieties of snap beans were stringy and only of fair to medium quality. In 1894, the first conspicuously successful stringless bean was introduced as Burpee Stringless Green Pod. The majority of varieties introduced since have been stringless. All varieties now grown commercially are stringless, at least at the "snap" or "harvesting" stage.

Snap beans divide into two classes, bush and vining (or "pole") beans. Each of these in turn divides into green-podded and yellow wax-podded. The green-podded is the most important. In turn, the beans of either color may be classified by shape of the pod, i.e., oval, flat or round; or by the color of the seed. Bush beans are grown more widely than pole beans because of the cost of materials and labor in placing the poles. The pole type is grown in a few canning areas in the western United States where the cost is offset by yield and price. Some kinds of pole beans are also used for freezing, accounting for considerable acreage in California and Florida. In general, oval and round podded beans are more popular than the flat type which was prevalent some ten years ago.

Principal varieties of green snap beans for fresh market are **Contender, Resistant Asgrow Valentine, Tendergreen** (including other varieties of Tendergreen type such as **Tenderlong**), **Topcrop, Wade, Bountiful** and **Burpee** and **Landreth Stringless Greenpod.** This selection is based on 1959 acreage and production of seed and 1960 probable acreage and production as estimated by growers. This is the best index of the importance of varieties. All of the varieties named, and others, are described in the following paragraphs.

BUSH OR DWARF GREEN [Oval podded]
Resistant Asgrow Valentine Pods 6 in. to 7-1/2 in. long,

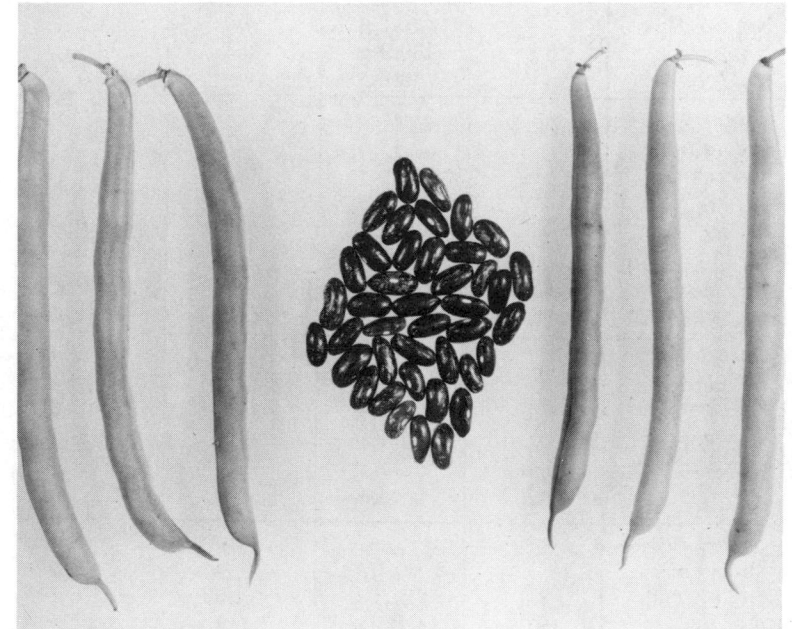

Pods and seeds of Topcrop.

GREEN BEANS & WAX BEANS

FRESH [8/1/36   51.3830]
Grades: U.S. Fancy, U.S. No. 1,
U.S. Combination, U.S. No. 2

CANNED [2/13/72   52.441]

Grades:	"A" or "FANCY"	"B" or "EXTRA STANDARD"	"C" or "STANDARD"	"SUB-STANDARD"
Minimum Score:	90	80	70	Less than 70

WHOLE	NET WEIGHT OZ.	NET WEIGHT METRIC	DRAINED WEIGHT OZ.	DRAINED WEIGHT METRIC
No. 8Z Tall	7.8	221.1 g	4.0	113.4 g
No. 303	15.2	430.9 g	8.5	241.0 g
No. 2½	26.8	759.8 g	6.0	453.6 g
No. 10	98.5	2.8 kg	57.5	1.6 kg
Whole vertical pack and whole asparagus style				
No. 8Z Tall	7.8	221.1 g	4.6	130.4 g
No. 303	15.2	430.9 g	9.5	269.3 g
No. 2½	26.8	759.8 g	17.0	482.0 g
Short cuts and cuts, less than 1½ in.				
No. 8Z Tall	7.8	221.1 g	4.5	127.6 g
No. 303	15.2	430.9 g	9.2	260.8 g
No. 2½	26.8	759.8 g	16.4	464.9 g
No. 10	98.5	2.8 kg	63.0	1.8 kg
Cuts 1½ in. & longer				
No. 8Z Tall	7.8	221.1 g	4.1	116.2 g
No. 303	15.2	430.9 g	8.7	246.6 g
No. 2½	26.8	759.8 g	16.2	459.3 g
No. 10	98.5	2.8 kg	60.0	1.7 kg
Mixed cuts & short cuts				
No. 8Z Tall	7.8	221.1 g	4.5	127.6 g
No. 303	15.2	430.9 g	9.2	260.8 g
No. 2½	26.8	759.8 g	16.4	464.9 g

	NET WEIGHT OZ.	NET WEIGHT METRIC	DRAINED WEIGHT OZ.	DRAINED WEIGHT METRIC
No. 10	98.5	2.8 kg	63.0	1.8 kg
Sliced lengthwise or French style				
No. 8Z Tall	7.8	221.1 g	4.1	116.2 g
No. 303	15.2	430.9 g	8.7	246.6 g
No. 2½	26.8	759.8 g	16.2	459.3 g
No. 10	98.5	2.8 kg	59.0	1.7 kg

FROZEN [5/8/74   52.2321]

Grades:	"A" or "FANCY"	"B" or "EXTRA STANDARD"	"C" or "STANDARD"	"SUB-STANDARD"
Minimum Score:	90	80	70	Less than 70

quite straight; medium to dark green; texture meaty and fine; seeds jet black, small oval to oblong, plump, abruptly rounded ends; growing period 52 days. Resistant to common bean mosaic and the New York 15 mosaic. **Contender** Originated by U.S. Vegetable Breeding Laboratory, Charleston, S.C. in 1949. Pods 6 in. to 7 in. long by 3/8 in. wide, often curved at tips; medium green; fiberless and tender; seeds buff or off-white, lightly mottled with brown, large and kidney shaped; very early and highly productive; growing period 48 days. Resistant to common bean mosaic and tolerant to powdery mildew.

BUSH OR DWARF GREEN [Flat podded]

Bountiful Introduced in 1898 by D.G. Burlingame of Genesee, N.Y.; said to be a selection from Long Yellow Six Weeks, named in 1899 through a contest. Pods 6 in. to 7 in. by 1/2 in., straight, broad, thick; light green; seeds fawn color when first harvested, changing to dark, dull, straw yellow or cinnamon with age; shape medium, oblong, plump with abruptly rounded ends; distinct, darker brown, narrow eye-ring always present; earliest of strictly stringless flat sorts; can be planted early or late, growing period 47 days. **Ferry's Plentiful [Black Seeded Bountiful]** Originated in 1938 as cross of Stringless Black Valentine and Bountiful; pods 7 in. by 1/2 in.; straight to slightly curved, narrower and longer than Bountiful; medium

GREEN AND WAX BEAN SIZES

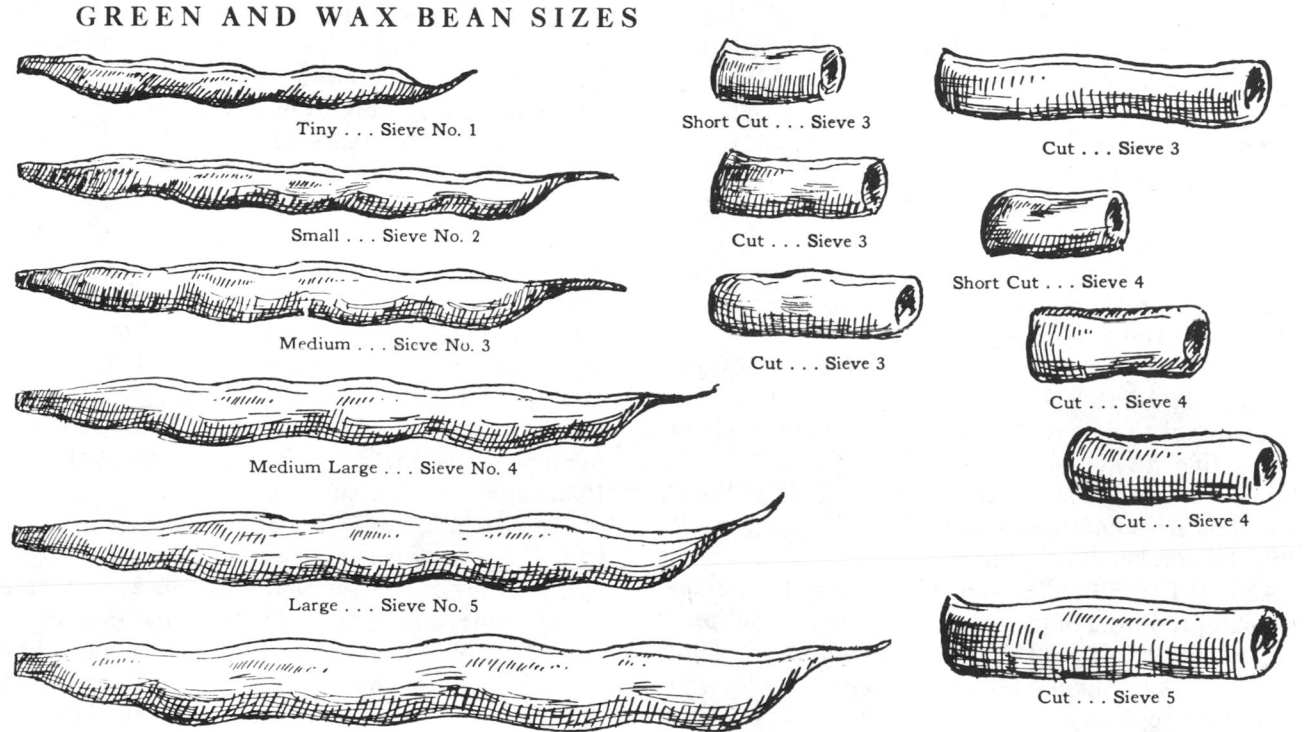

Tiny . . . Sieve No. 1

Small . . . Sieve No. 2

Medium . . . Sieve No. 3

Medium Large . . . Sieve No. 4

Large . . . Sieve No. 5

Extra Large . . . Sieve No. 6

Short Cut . . . Sieve 3

Cut . . . Sieve 3

Cut . . . Sieve 3

Cut . . . Sieve 3

Short Cut . . . Sieve 4

Cut . . . Sieve 4

Cut . . . Sieve 4

Cut . . . Sieve 5

Frosty Acres Buyers Guide—The Frozen Food Forum, Inc., Atlanta, Ga.

dark green; seeds large, flat-oval, jet black; about four days later than Bountiful; growing period 49 to 51 days; resistant to some forms of rust.

BUSH OR DWARF GREEN [Round podded]

Tendergreen Improved An improved and more productive Tendergreen type. Pods 6 in. by 3/8 in.; medium dark green; seeds dark purple mottled with tan; pods scattered and set well off the ground; growing period 54 days; resistant to common and N.Y. 14 mosaics. **Tenderlong 15** Pods 6-1/4 in. by 3/8 in.; straight, medium green color; fiberless; seeds purplish black, dull, mottled with buff; growing period 50 days. **Stringless Green Pod [Burpee and Landreth]** Pods 5 in. to 6 in. by 3/8 in.; cross section thick oval to heart-shaped and length slightly curved; medium green; seed dark brown; growing period 50 days; tolerant to heat. **Topcrop** Introduced by Dr. Wm. Zaumeyer of USDA, selection from a cross between

Refugee U.S. No. 5 and Full Measure. Pods 6 in. by 3/8 in., straight and smooth with slightly creased back; medium green; meaty; seed oblong, brown with buff mottling; pods set high on plant; growing period 48 days; resistant to common and New York 15 mosaics. **Wade** Developed by USDA at Charleston, S.C.; pods 6 in. by 3/8 in., slightly curved; dark green; good quality; pods set well off ground and scattered; growing period 53 to 62 days. Resistant to common and New York 15 mosaics and to pod mottle virus; tolerant to powdery mildew and some races of rust.

BUSH OR DWARF WAX [Oval]

Cherokee Wax Valentine type, developed for a shipping variety. Pods 6 in. to 6-1/2 in. by 7/16 in.; fairly straight with oval cross-section; uniform golden color; stringless; seeds oval and black; growing period 50 days. **Kinghorn Wax** Pods 6 in. by 3/8 in.; slightly curved; golden yellow; seeds pure white; growing period 53 days.

BUSH OR DWARF WAX [Flat]

Sure Crop Wax (Bountiful Wax) Pods 6 in. by 1/2 in.; slightly curved; butter yellow; growing period 54 days.

POLE OR TWINING [Green]

Kentucky Wonder Wax Pods 7 in. by 1/2 in.; curved; cross section flat oval; light golden yellow; somewhat stringy and fibrous; seeds broad, flattened-oval, and chocolate brown; growing period 68 days.

CONTAINERS: Bushel hampers, baskets, and crates are the most generally used containers for shipping snap beans. Net weight of beans is 28 to 30 lb. per bushel.

The wirebound bushel crate has inside dimensions of 11-15/16 in. x 11-15/16 in. by 16-3/4 in.

Snap beans are sent to nearby markets in a variety of other containers, including 12-qt. splint baskets in Ohio, 3/4 bu. baskets in Illinois, 1/2 bu. baskets in New York. On the West Coast local supplies are sometimes delivered in WGA crates or wirebounds of 40-lb. and 50-lb. capacity.

SERVINGS AND WEIGHTS: The usual serving is 1/2 cup of cooked snap beans. A pound of fresh beans, as purchased, provides 4-1/2 servings. It takes 22 lb. to serve 100. ... For 1 lb. ready-to-cook, use 1.14 lb. (about 1 lb., 2 oz.) as purchased. One quart of beans ready to cook equals 0.94 lb. (about 15 oz.). One bushel is 28 to 30 lb., as purchased.

QUALITY: Since grade is a meausre of quality at the time of grading, it is necessary in determining quality to check present condition. The principal factors in judging quality of snap beans are freshness, lack of stringiness, tenderness, color, shape, cleanness, and freedom from disease. Good snap beans should snap readily when broken. Pods in which the seeds are very immature are the most desirable. Length is unimportant if the beans are otherwise of good quality. Avoid beans that have a dull, dead, or wilted appearance and a wilted feel. Decay is shown by mold or a soft, watery condition.

GRADES: U.S. Standards for snap beans are U.S. Fancy, U.S. No. 1, U.S. Combination, and U.S. No. 2. *"U.S. Fancy* shall consist of beans of similar varietal characteristics which are of reasonable and fairly uniform size, well formed, bright, clean, fresh, young and tender, firm, and free from damage caused by leaves, leafstems, other foreign matter, hail, disease, insects, or mechanical or other means. In order to allow for variations incident to proper grading and handling, not more than a total of 10 percent, by weight, of the beans in any container may be below the requirements of this grade, but not more than 5 percent shall be allowed for defects causing serious damage, and not more than 1 percent shall be allowed for beans affected by soft rot. ... The tolerances are on a container basis. However, individual packages in any lot may vary from the specified tolerances as stated below, provided the averages for the entire lot, based on sample inspection, are within the tolerances specified. For a tolerance of 10 percent or more, individual packages in any lot may contain not more than 1-1/2 times the tolerance specified. For a tolerance of less than 10 percent, individual packages in any lot may contain not more than double the tolerance specified."

"DEFINITIONS—'Similar varietal characteristics' means that the beans are of the same color and general type ... 'reasonable size' means that the pods are not spindly or excessively short for the variety and have not been prematurely picked ... 'Well formed' means that the pods have the normal typical shape for the variety ... 'Firm' means that the pods are not wilted or flabby ... 'Damage' means any injury or defect which materially affects the appearance or the edible or shipping quality. Pods having spots due to blight or anthracnose and similar spots caused by other diseases shall be considered as damaged ... 'Fairly well formed' means that the pods are not badly crooked, curled, twisted, or otherwise badly misshapen for the variety. Excessively tapered pods caused by unfavorable pollinating or growing conditions shall not be considered as fairly well formed ... 'Overmature' means that the walls of the pods are distinctly woody or fibrous ... 'Serious damage' means any injury or defect which seriously affects the appearance or the edible or shipping quality."

BEANS, Green and Waxed, Canned [2/13/72]

Grade A: Color: Practically uniform and bright, typical of very young and tender beans, with no more than 5 percent that vary markedly. **Defects:** Practically free; provided defects individually and collectively do not materially affect appearance or edibility of products. **Character:** Good character with beans

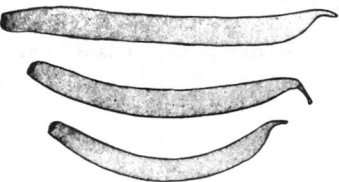

BROKEN ENDS—<u>NOT</u> AT THICK PORTION OF BEAN

BROKEN ENDS—AT THICK PORTION OF BEAN

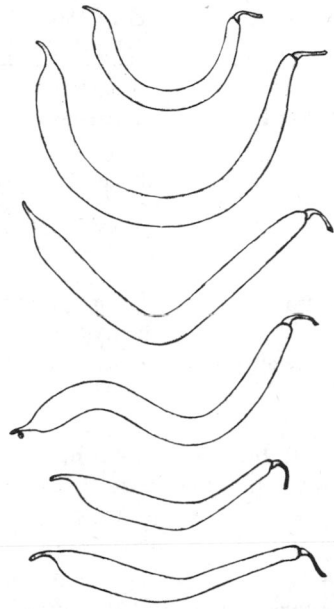

NOT SERIOUSLY MISSHAPEN
Poorest shapes permitted in U.S. No. 2 Grade

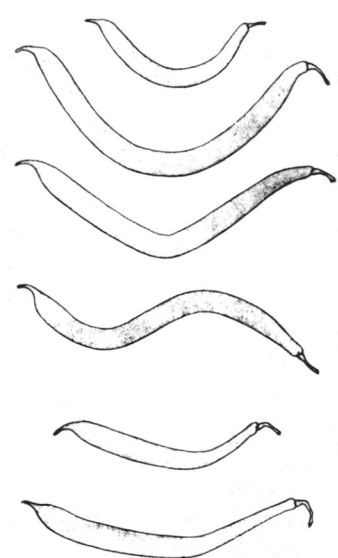

FAIRLY WELL FORMED
Poorest shapes permitted in U.S. No. 1 Grade.

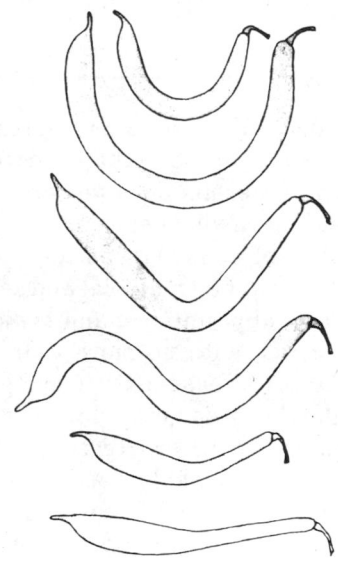

SERIOUSLY MISSHAPEN
Culls

MAXIMUM ALLOWANCES FOR DEFECTS OR DEFECTIVE UNITS

	[A] Classification	[B] Classification	[C] Classification
ALL STYLES Total—all defects other than loose seeds & seed pieces	10% of drained wt.	15% of drained wt.	20% of drained wt.
Blemished and Seriously Blemished	2% total, but no more than 1% by count, seriously	4% total, but no more than 2% by count, seriously	8% total, but no more than 4% by count, seriously
			Unstemmed units:
Unstemmed units and Detached stems	4 total, but no more than 2 long stems, per 12 oz. drained wt.	5 total but no more than 3 long stems, per 12 oz. drained wt.	6 total, but no more than 4 long stems, per 12 oz. drained wt.
Leaves and other extraneous vegetable matter	1 piece per 12 oz drained wt.	2 pieces per 12 oz. drained wt.	Including detached stems: 0.6 oz. per 60 oz. drained wt.
ALL STYLES except as indicated otherwise			

	[A] Classification	[B] Classification	[C] Classification
Loose seeds & pieces (except in Sliced Lengthwise style)	3% of drained wt.	4 % of drained wt.	5% of drained wt.
Small pieces of pod (in cuts; & mixed—cut & short cut styles only)			
(a) 240 count or less per 12 oz. drained wt.	40 pieces per 12 oz. drained wt. or	60 pieces per 12 oz. drained wt. or	60 pieces per 12 oz. drained wt. or
(b) More than 240 count per 12 oz. drained wt.	15% by count of all units	25% by count of all units	25% by count of all units
Ragged—cut units; and/or damage by mechanical injury (except in Sliced Lengthwise style)	5 total per 12 oz. drained wt.	10 total per 12 oz. drained wt.	no limits (but included in total allowance of 20% of drained wt.)

very young and tender, full fleshed and not fibrous; seeds in early stages of maturity; no more than 5 percent with tough strings, sloughing of epidermis does not materially affect appearance; and sliced lengthwise beans are well sliced. **Liquor:** May possess slight tint of yellow-green to green color and not more than a trace of suspended material and sediment.

Grade B: Color: Reasonably uniform and typical of young and reasonably tender beans, with no more than 10 percent that vary markedly. **Defects:** Reasonably free; provided defects individually and collectively do not seriously affect appearance or edibility of product. **Character:** Reasonably good character with beans young and reasonably tender with some loss of fleshy structure, practically free from fiber; seeds may have passed early stages, but not reached the late stages of maturity; no more than 10 percent with tough strings, with

sloughing of epidermis that does not materially affect appearance; and sliced lengthwise beans are reasonably well sliced. **Liquor:** May be cloudy with small quantity of sediment.

Grade C: Color: Fairly uniform and typical of nearly mature but fairly tender beans, with no more than 15 percent that vary markedly. **Defects:** Fairly free within limits of Defect Table. See Defect Table. **Character:** Fairly good character, beans may be nearly mature but fairly tender with considerable loss of fleshy texture; sloughing of epidermis does not seriously affect appearance; no more than 25 percent seeds and pieces in trimmed pods; no more than 0.15 percent fibrous material in seeded pods; no more than 20 percent units with tough strings, except when units are 27/64 in. or more in diameter; there may be no more than 12 strings or pieces thereof in 12 oz. drained weight which support a 1/2 lb. weight

MAXIMUM ALLOWANCES FOR DEFECTS

DEFECTS	WHOLE	CUT	SHORT CUTS & MIXED	SLICED LENGTH-WISE
	Per 10 oz.	*% by count*	*% by count*	*Per 10 oz.*
Blemished units	(A) 5, no more than 1 serious	(A) 3%, no more than 1% serious	(A) 3%, no more than 1% serious	serious
	*(B) 8, no more than 2 serious	(B) 5%, no more than 2% serious	(B) 5%, no more than 2% serious	(B) 8, no more than 2 serious
	(C) 12, no more than 4 serious	(C) 8%, no more than 3% serious	(C) 8%, no more than 3% serious	(C) 12, no more than 4 serious
Damaged units	(A) 2 (B) 4 (C) 6	See below for damaged	*Per 10 oz.* (A) 20, (B) 40, (C) 60	
Damaged units and small pieces,	See above for damaged	*Per 10 oz.* (A) 20 sm. pcs. or 20 damaged or 20		(A) well sliced (B) reason-

or slicing as applicable	combined (B) 40 sm. pcs. or 40 damaged or 40 combined (C) 60 sm. pcs. or 60 damaged or 60 combined	ably well sliced (C) fairly well sliced
Extraneous vegetable material, loose seeds and pieces	In all styles, including small pieces in Sliced Lengthwise: (A) do not more than slightly affect, (B) do not materially affect. (C) do not seriously affect appearance or eating quality	
Unstemmed units; Detached stems	In all styles: (A) *Per 10 oz.*: 2 unstemmed or 2 detached or 2 in combination; (B) 4 unstemmed or 4 detached or 4 in combination; (C) 5 unstemmed or 5 detached or 5 in combination.	

*May not be Grade A with this amount.

for not less than 5 seconds. **Liquor:** May be dull in color but not off color, cloudy, or possess noticeable accumulation of sediment. **Sstd:** Fails to meet requirements of Grade C in Color, Defects, and Character. See chart. **Liquor:** Definitely off color, excessively cloudy, seriously objectionable quantity of sediment.

BEANS, Green and Waxed—Frozen [5/8/75]

Grade A: Color: Bright, typical of young and tender beans of similar varietal characteristics, practically free from units that materially detract from appearance. **Defects:** See Defects Chart. **Character:** See in early development stage; units are tender not fibrous, full fleshed, no more than slightly affected by sloughing; no more than 4 units in 10 oz. with tough strings in Sliced Lengthwise, no more than 2 percent of units with tough strings in other styles.

Grade B: Color: Reasonably bright, typical of reasonably young, reasonably tender beans of similar varietal characteristics, free from units that materially detract from appearance.

Defects: See Grade A Defect. **Character:** Seeds may have passed early stage, not reached late stage of development; units are reasonably tender, not fibrous, may have lost to some extent their fleshy structure, not materially affected by sloughing; no more than 6 units in 10 oz. with tough strings in Sliced Lengthwise, no more than 4 percent of units with tough strings in other styles.

Grade C: Color: Typical of nearly mature and fairly tender beans of similar varietal characteristics, may be dull but not off color, variable but not seriously affect appearance. **Defects:** See Grade A. **Character:** Seed may be in late development stage; units are fairly tender, reasonably free from fiber, have not entirely lost their fleshy structure, not seriously affected by sloughing; no more than 8 units in 10 oz. with tough strings in Sliced Lengthwise, no more than 6 percent with tough strings in other styles. **Sstd:** Fails to meet any requirements.

LIMA BEANS, Canned [3/20/60]

Grade A: Color: Not less than 90 percent are "green" and not more than 10 percent lighter in color, provided that not more

LIMA BEANS

FRESH [1/5/38   51.3805]
    Grades: U.S. No. 1, U.S. Combination
            U.S. No. 2
CANNED [3/20/60   52.471]

Grades:	"A" or "FANCY"	"B" or "EXTRA STAN-DARD"	"C" or "STAN-DARD"	"SUB-STAN-DARD"
Minimum Score:	90	80	70	less than 70

	NET WEIGHT OZ.	NET WEIGHT METRIC	DRAINED WEIGHT OZ.	DRAINED WEIGHT METRIC
No. 8Z Tall	as full	as full	5.5	155.9 g
No. 303	as	as	11	311.8 g
No. 10	practicable	practicable	72	2.0 kg

Canned Dried Beans (10/24/47   52.411)

Grades:	"A" or "FANCY"	"C" or "STANDARD"	"D" or "SUB-STANDARD"
Minimum Score:	85	70	Less than 70

FROZEN: [4/16/57   52.501)

Grades:	"A" or "FANCY"	"B" or "EXTRA STAN-DARD"	"C" or "STAN-DARD"	"SUB-STAN-DARD"
Minimum Score:	90	80	70	Less than 70

FROZEN: Speckled Butter [Lima] Beans [7/21/62   52.56241]

Grades:	"A" OR "FANCY"	"B" or "EXTRA" STANDARD"	"SUB-STANDARD"
Minimum Score:	90	80	Less than 80

than 1 percent of all the lima beans of "Thin Seeded" or "Thick Seeded Baby Potato" and not more than 3 percent of "Thick Seeded" are "white", or the "Thin Seeded" or "Thick Seeded Baby Potato" may possess not less than 97 percent of "green" lima beans and not more than 3 percent lighter or "white" lima beans. **Defects:** Practically free from defects; see chart. **Character:** Young and tender. **Liquor:** May be slightly cloudy, small amount of sediment.
Grade B: Color: All types, not less than 50 percent are "green"

LIMA BEAN SIZES

	SIEVE SIZES	COMMER-CIAL NAMES
	No. 1	Tiny
	No. 2	Small
	No. 3	Medium
	No. 4	Large

and not more than 50 percent lighter, provided not more than 25 percent of all the limas are "white." **Defects:** Reasonably free from defects; see chart. **Character:** Reasonably young and tender. **Liquor:** Somewhat cloudy liquor; may contain considerable amount of sediment.
Grade C: Color: All types, less than 50 percent are "green", and all of the beans may be "white". **Defects:** Fairly free from defects; see chart. **Character:** May be nearly mature and possess a fairly tender texture, may be firm and mealy but not hard, or may be soft but not mushy. **Liquor:** May be dull in color but not to the extent that the appearance is seriously affected; may be rather viscous, cream-like, or starchy. **Sstd:** Fails to meet requirements.

LIMA BEANS—Frozen [4/16/57]

Grade A: Color: "Thin seeded" (skins off) and "Thick-seeded Baby Potato" (skins on)—Bright typical and either 93 percent or more "green", balance lighter but not more than 1 percent "white" or 97 percent or more "green," balance may be lighter or "white". THICK SEEDED—Bright typical and 85 percent or more "green", balance lighter but no more than 1 percent "white." **Defects:** Light discoloration, individually and collectively, that does not more than slightly affect appearance or eating quality of product. One piece or pieces of predominantly flat, extraneous vegetable matter aggregating 3/16 sq. in., and 1 predominantly cylindrical piece or pieces of extraneous vegetable material not exceeding 1/2 in. in length per 10 oz.; or per 30 oz.; not more than 1 spherical piece not more than 1/4 in. diameter.; pieces of beans 5 percent; shriveled and sprouted 1 percent; blemished and seriously blemished 2 percent including 1/2 percent seriously.

Grade B: Color: "Thin-seeded" (skins off) and "Thick-seeded Baby Potato" (skins on)—Typical and 65 percent or more "green," balance lighter or "white." THICK-SEEDED (SKINS ON)—Typical and 60 percent or more "green," balance lighter but no more than 5 percent "white." **Defects:** See defects for Grade A. All wording is same except the measurements and percentages are as follows: do not materially affect appearance or eating quality of product; 3/8 sq. in. and 3/4 in.; 2; spherical pieces not more than 1/4 in. diam. 10 percent; shriveled and sprouted 4 percent; blemished and seriously blemished 3 percent including 1 percent seriously.

Grade C: Color: "Thin-seeded" (skins off) and "Thick-seeded Baby Potato" (skins on)—Less than 65 percent "green", and all may be "white." "THICK-SEEDED (SKINS ON)—Less than 60 percent "green" but no more than 20 percent "white." **Defects:** See defects for Grade A. All wording is same except the measurements and percentages are as follows: do not seriously affect appearance or eating quality of product; 3/4 sq. in. and 1 in. in length per 10 oz., or per 30 oz.; not more than 3 spherical pieces not more than 1/4 in. diameter; pieces of beans 15 percent; shriveled and sprouted 8 percent. Blemished and seriously blemished 4 percent including 2 percent seriously. **Sstd:** Fails to meet any requirements; see chart.

BEANS, Speckled Butter [Lima]—Frozen [7/21/62]

Grade A: Color: The overall color is bright and typical for speckled types of similar color characteristics; not less than 15 percent of the beans possess at least a slight tinge of green in the cotyledons; not more than 20 percent of the beans may possess a light tan to tan color; there may be present no more

MAXIMUM ALLOWANCES FOR DEFECTS

Kind of Defect	Grade A	Grade B	
		When present as a single group	Combination of any two groups
Groups of harmless, extraneous vegetable material	*For each 30 oz. net weight, or average* [1]		
Flat material	1/4 sq. in. or 1 piece of any size	1 sq. in. or 1 piece of any size	1/2 sq. in. or 1 piece of any size
	or	or	or
Spherical material	1 unit	3 units	2 units
	or	or	or
Cylindrical material	1 piece (or pieces) not over 1/2 in. aggregate length	1 piece (or pieces) not over 2 in. aggregate length	1 piece (or pieces) not over 1 in. aggregate length
	Count per 10 oz. net weight		
Pieces of beans	20 pieces	40 pieces	
Shriveled beans; and sprouted beans.	2 beans	8 beans	
Blemished beans; and seriously blemished beans.	Total 10 beans, but no more than 5 seriously blemished of which no more than 1 may be accompanied by material discoloration.	Total 20 beans, but no more than 10 seriously blemished of which no more than 2 may be accompanied by material discoloration.	

than 4 beans per 10 oz. that are light brown to brown or a pronounced mottled brown; and the presence of abnormally colored beans does not materially affect the overall color. **Defects:** Frozen beans that are practically free from defects means: there may be present no more than the specified defects in Table I for the Grade A classification; and the presence of harmless, extraneous vegetable material, pieces of beans, shriveled and sprouted beans, and blemished and seriously blemished beans, or any other defects or defective units not specifically mentioned, individually and collectively, does

Dry Colored Beans: Principal Types

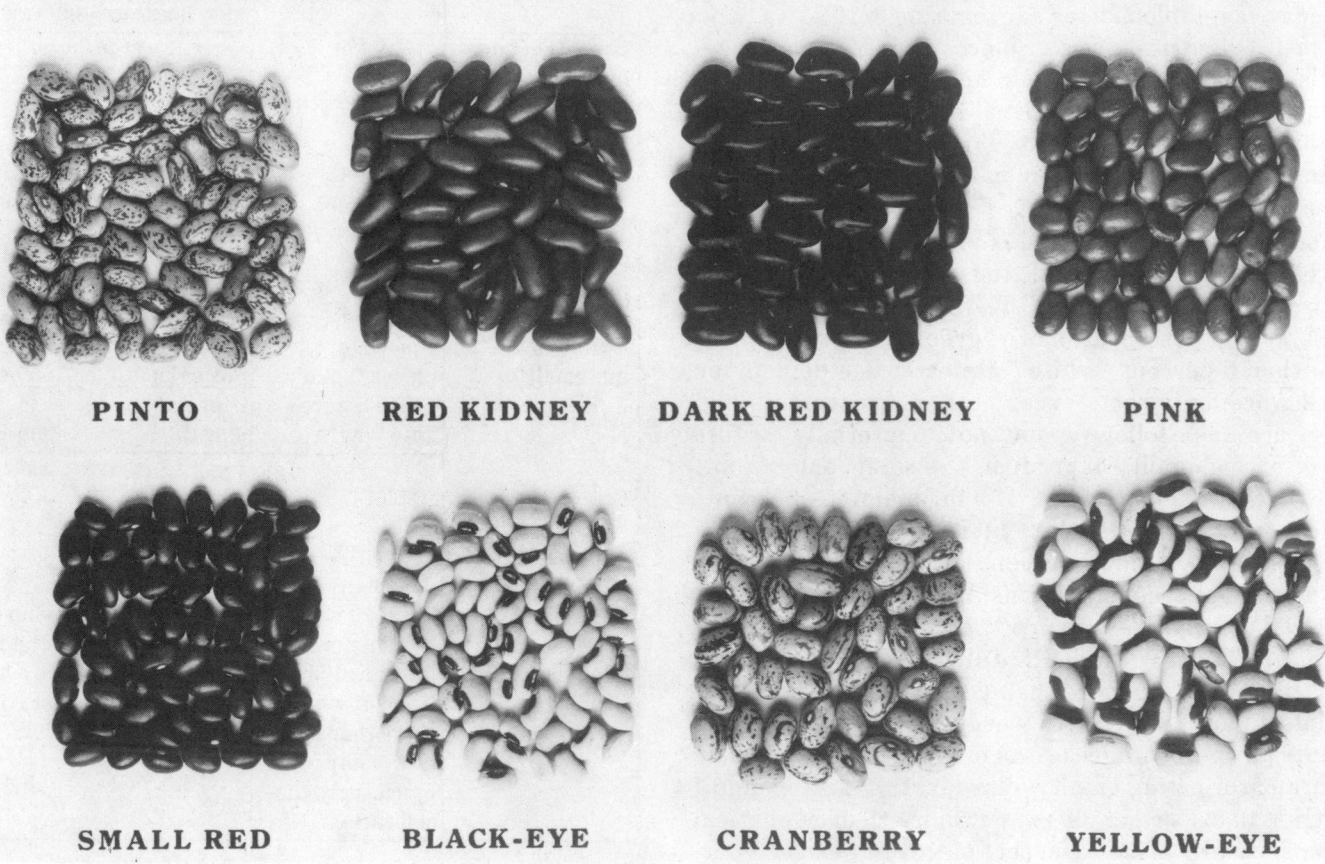

PINTO   RED KIDNEY   DARK RED KIDNEY   PINK

SMALL RED   BLACK-EYE   CRANBERRY   YELLOW-EYE

not materially affect the appearance or eating quality of the product. **Character:** Beans are reasonably tender and are practically uniform in texture and tenderness.

Grade B: Color: The overall color may be slightly dull, or the beans may possess a light tan to tan color but such colors are typical of speckled types of similar color characteristics; there may be present no more than 8 beans per 10 oz. that are light brown to brown or a pronounced mottled brown; and the pre-

sence of abnormally colored beans does not seriously affect the overall color. **Defects:** Reasonably free from defects. See Table I. Defects do not seriously affect the appearance or eating quality of the product. **Character:** The beans are fairly tender and may be variable in texture and tenderness, and the cotyledons may be mealy "but are not hard." **Sstd: Color:** Fails to meet requirements. See chart.

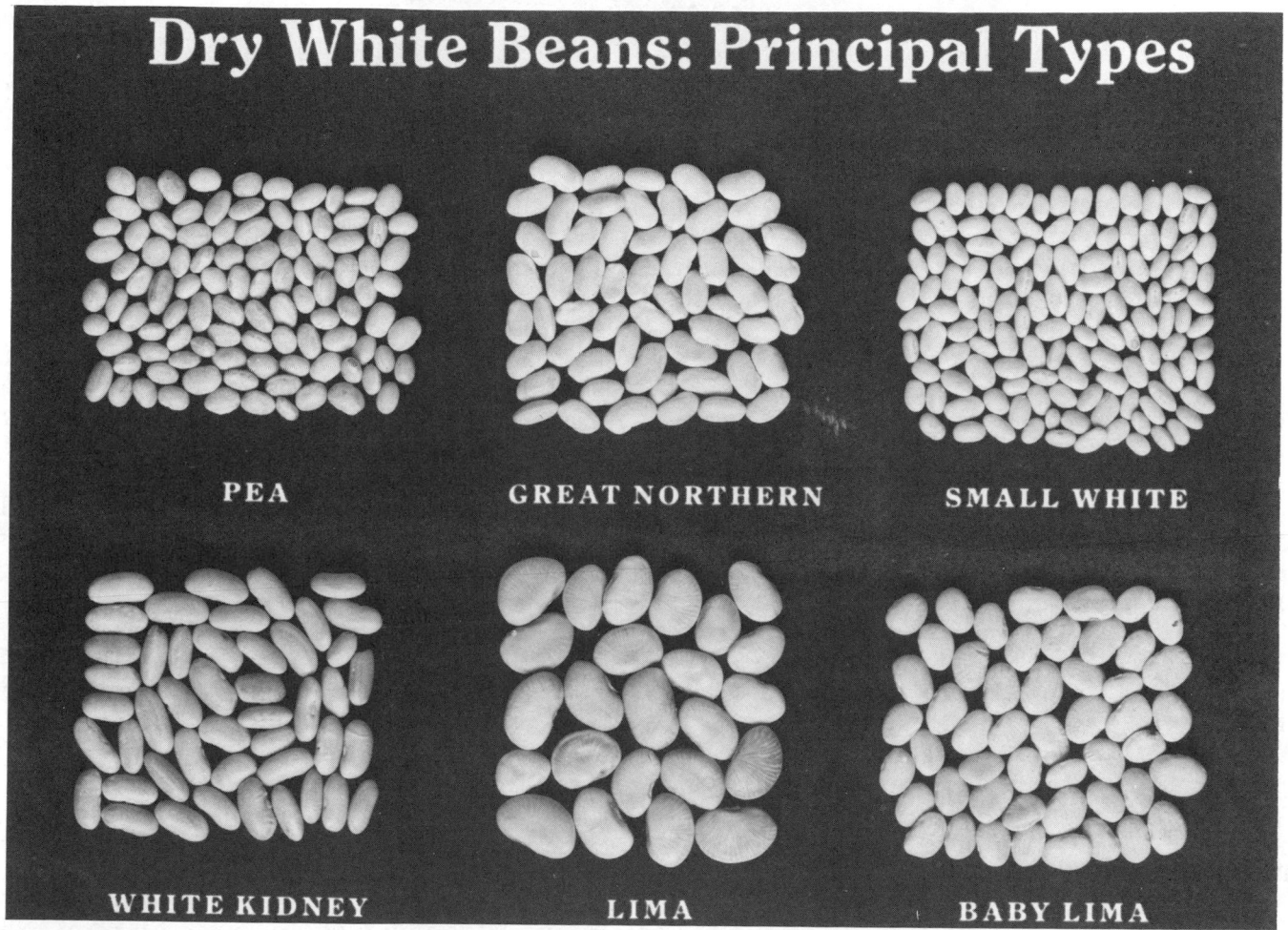

Dry White Beans: Principal Types

PEA   GREAT NORTHERN   SMALL WHITE

WHITE KIDNEY   LIMA   BABY LIMA

BEANS—Dried Canned [10/24/47]

Grade A: Color: Typical good color. **Consistency:** BEANS IN TOMATO SAUCE AND IN SWEETENED SAUCE—Sauce is smooth and is neither grainy nor lumpy, and product forms a slightly mounded mass with not more than a slight separation of liquid. BEANS IN BRINE—Packing medium is neither grainy nor lumpy, and the product may possess a thick consistency or there may be a separation of liquid. **Defects:** Practically free from defects. See chart. **Maximum Tolerance:** Not more than 5 percent by count of loose skins and broken and mashed units; and not more than 4 percent may be damaged units. **Character:** Possesses typical texture that may be slightly granular or slightly firm with skins that are tender.

Grade C: Color: Possesses a good typical color. **Consistency:** BEANS IN TOMATO SAUCE AND IN SWEETENED SAUCE—Sauce is fairly smooth and may be slightly grainy but not lumpy. Product possesses a thick consistency with moderate separation of liquid but not watery. BEANS IN BRINE—Packing medium is fairly smooth, may be slightly grainy but not lumpy. Product may show considerable separation of liquid or may be watery. **Defects:** Fairly free from defects. See chart. **Maximum Tolerance:** Not more than 1 small piece of harmless extraneous material for each 20 oz. of net weight; not more than 10 percent may be loose skins and broken and mashed units, and not more than 8 percent may be damaged units. **Character:** Beans may be firm but not hard, soft but not mushy, and the skins may be slightly tough. **Sstd:** Fails to meet any requirements of Grade C.

BEETS*

USES: Beets may be served boiled, pickled, and in salads. They can be steamed or cooked in a pressure cooker, as well as in an ordinary kettle without loss of color, as long as they are not pared or cut. Beet juice is a basic ingredient for the exotic Russian and Middle European borscht. Beet tops are prepared in the same manner as spinach. Sliced beets go well in salads; they are used molded in gelatin; as sweet and sour beets; they go well in soups, and can be baked or fried. A good dish is fresh beets with parmesan cheese; and another is fresh beets with sour cream, and there is a recipe for beets stuffed with a spicy egg mixture.

MARKETING SEASON: The following table shows the percentage of the annual total available in each month, based on average unloads of fresh beets in 41 cities.

MONTHLY AVAILABILITY OF BEETS EXPRESSED AS PERCENTAGE OF TOTAL ANNUAL SUPPLY

Jan.	Feb.	Mar.	Apr.	May	June
%	%	%	%	%	%
4	4	5	5	7	13

July	Aug.	Sept.	Oct.	Nov.	Dec.
%	%	%	%	%	%
15	13	12	11	7	4

VARIETIES: Production of vegetable seeds, as reported by USDA, shows that the leading varieties of garden beets are **Detroit** in tall top type, medium top type, and short top type; **Ruby Queen** type, and **Crosby**, or **Early Wonder** type. The seeds of these types accounted for 92 percent of production.

"*Globe-shaped* or only slightly flattened beets are the most popular in the United States. The old Flat Egyptian, formerly favored as a first-early beet is now little grown because it is not appreciably earlier than good strains having only slightly flattened to nearly globular roots. Crosby Egyptian and Early Wonder are generally recommended when rapid attainment of marketable size is important. Both are slightly flattened, and have alternate zones of purplish red and purplish pink flesh in warm weather. Plantings that reach the harvest stage in cool weather have darker flesh color with less prominent differences in color between the zones.

"Where quick maturity is not important and for processing purposes, Detroit Dark Red and strains developed from it such as Perfected Detroit are most commonly grown. The roots are nearly globular. The flesh color of these Detroit strains is a darker and less purplish red than in the early varieties named above. Although these will have light-colored zones when grown in hot weather, the zones are not so light as in the early varieties. When matured in cool weather, the interior is very dark red with inconspicuous zoning. Upon cooking, these color zones largely disappear."

HYBRIDS—"The release of a pollen sterile inbred table beet to the seed industry in 1964 paved the way for the commercial production of F_1 hybrids which at the same time carry a genetic characteristic called monogerm which limits the number of plants per seed ball to one. The first hybrid named with this new inbred factor is **Pacemaker**, released by the Wisconsin Agricultural Experiment Station in 1964 also. This hybrid is a large-topped variety. The roots are deeply pigmented, smooth and round. Commercial samples of this hybrid first became available in 1967."

CONTAINERS: For bunched beets the shipping containers most commonly used are the wirebound crate, holding about 45 lb. net; the 1/2 WGA crate, 40 to 45 lb., and the carton holding 18 bunches. Topped beets are generally shipped in the open mesh sack holding 50 lb. However, many other packages are used. According to *Market News Service of USDA*, they include 1-1/2 to 1-3/4 bushel crates, 50 lb. net; 4/5 bu. crate, 30 lb.; 16 in. celery crates, 45 lb.; 2/3 WGA crate 50 lb.; bushel boxes or crates 37-38 lb.; and other containers in which they are sold by the dozen bunches.

*UFFVA

The 1/2 WGA crate, 10 in. wirebound crate, and 16 in. celery crate load 640 to the car or carlot equivalent; the 1-1/2 to 1-3/4 bu. crate and 2/3 WGA crate load 570 to the car; 4/5 bu. crates, 920; bushel boxes or crates, 750; and a car holds 1000 to 1600 dozen bunches, depending on size. (A carlot is about 29,000 lb.)

When prepackaged in consumer units, topped beets are generally in film bags holding not more than 3 lb., and about 50 percent of beets are said to be prepackaged before reaching the retail store.

SERVINGS AND WEIGHTS: A pound of fresh, untrimmed beet greens provides 2.37 portions of 1/2 cup cooked; or 4.74 portions of 1/4 cup cooked. It takes 42-1/4 lb. as purchased for 100 servings of 1/2 cup; and 21-1/4 lb. for 100 servings of 1/4 cup. A pound, as purchased, provides 0.56 lb. ready to cook.

A pound of fresh beets without tops provides 3.76 servings of 1/2 cup cooked, diced or sliced; and 7.52 portions of 1/4 cup cooked, diced or sliced. It takes 26-3/4 lb. as purchased to provide 100 portions of 1/2 cup; and 13-1/2 lb. to provide 100 portions of 1/4 cup. One pound as purchased provides 0.76 lb. cooked.

A bushel of beets weighs 50 to 56 lb. A bunch weighs from 1 to 1-1/2 lb.

QUALITY: Early or new crop beets are usually marketed in small bunches with tops attached or partially cut back, or as topped beets in consumer size packages. The fresh, green tops of young bunched beets make excellent greens if the leaves are not discolored, turning yellow or ragged, and if leaf stems (petioles) are not tough. Late crop beets are usually sold as topped beets. Medium-sized beets of the late crop are less likely to be tough or woody than either large or very small ones. *Good quality beets* are relatively smooth and firm. Soft, flabby, rough, or shriveled beets may be tough, or woody, or involve excessive waste in preparation. In judging bunched beets, the condition of the tops or leaves alone does not indicate the quality of the beets, and any defects of the leaves may be disregarded when only the beets are to be utilized. Decay in beets usually appears as soft, wet areas. Beets showing any decay should be avoided.

"*Beet tops* are usually very young plants grown specially for leaf development. Occasionally the small undeveloped beets are attached. Good quality beet tops are young, clean, fresh, and tender. Slightly flabby or wilted tops can usually be restored to freshness in cold water if wilting is only in the initial stage. Beet tops showing any indications of a slimy or soft watery condition should be avoided."

GRADES: The federal grades are U.S. 1 and U.S. 2, and in each the styles are designated as bunched beets, beets with short-trimmed tops, and topped beets. Beets called bunched mean beets tied in bunches with tops full length or removed to not less than 6 in. Beets with short-trimmed tops are those showing leaf-stems ranging to not more than 4 in. long. Topped beets are those with tops removed to not more than 1/2 in. in length. Standard bunches shall be fairly uniform in size, and each bunch *shall weigh not less than 1 lb.* and contain at least 3 beets. Not more than 10 percent of the bunches in any lot may fail to meet the requirements.

U.S. 1 consists of beets of similar varietal characteristics, the roots of which are well trimmed, firm, fairly smooth, fairly well shaped, fairly clean, and free from soft rot, and free from damage caused by cuts, freezing, growth cracks, disease, rodents or insects, or mechanical or other means. Bunched beets or beets with short-trimmed tops shall have tops which are fresh and free from decay and free from damage caused by discoloration, freezing, disease, insects, or mechanical or other means. Unless otherwise specified, the diameter of each beet shall be not less than 1.5 in.

In order to allow for variations incident to proper grading and handling, tolerances are permitted. The tolerance for root defects is 10 percent, except that only 5 percent is allowed for serious damage including not more than 1 percent for soft rot. In bunched beets, 10 percent is allowed for defects of tops but including not more than 5 percent for decay. For off-size roots, 5 percent tolerance is allowed by count for roots smaller than the minimum and 10 percent for roots larger than any specified maximum diameter. For off-length tops, 5 percent tolerance is allowed by count for bunches that fail to meet the requirements of the style.

BEETS—Canned [2/4/55]

Grade A: Color: Possess a good color. **Uniformity of Size and Shape Factor:** WHOLE BEETS are not more than 2-1/4 in. in diameter. The maximum diameter variation is 50 percent.

BEETS

FRESH [8/1/55   51.375]
Grades: U.S. No. 1, U.S. No. 2
CANNED [2/4/55   52.521]

Grades:	"A" or "FANCY"	"C" or "STANDARD"	"SUB-STANDARD"
Minimum Score:	85	70	Less than 70

	NET WEIGHT OZ.	NET WEIGHT METRIC	DRAINED WEIGHT OZ.	DRAINED WEIGHT METRIC
Whole size No. 1-3, inclusive				
No. 8Z Tall	7.8	221.1 g	5.5	155.9 g
No. 303	15.2	430.9 g	10	283.5 g
No. 2½	26.8	759.8 g	19.5	552.8 g
No. 10	98.5	2.8 kg	69	1.96 kg
Whole Size No. 4-6, inclusive				
No. 8Z Tall	7.8	221.1 g	5	141.8 g
No. 303	15.2	430.9 g	9.5	269.3 g
No. 2½	26.8	759.8 g	19	538.6 g
No. 10	98.5	2.8 kg	68	1.93 kg
Sliced small				
No. 8Z Tall	7.8	221.1 g	5.5	155.9 g
No. 303	15.2	430.9 g	10.25	290.6 g
No. 2½	26.8	759.8 g	19	538.6 g
No. 10	98.5	2.8 kg	69	1.96 kg
Sliced medium & large				
No. 8Z Tall	7.8	221.1 g	5	141.8 g
No. 303	15.2	430.9 g	9.75	276.4 g
No. 2½	26.8	759.8 g	18.5	524.5 g
No. 10	98.5	2.8 kg	68	1.93 kg
Diced				
No. 8Z Tall	7.8	221.1 g	5.5	155.9 g
No. 303	15.2	430.9 g	10.5	297.7
No. 2Z½	26.8	759.8 g	19	538.6 g
No. 10	98.5	2.9 kg	72	2.0 kg
Quartered				
No. 8Z Tall	7.8	221.1 g	5.5	155.9 g
No. 303	15.2	430.9 g	10.5	297.7 g

	NET WEIGHT OZ.	NET WEIGHT METRIC	DRAINED WEIGHT OZ.	DRAINED WEIGHT METRIC
No. 2½	26.8	759.8 g	18.5	524.5 g
No. 10	98.5	2.8 kg	70	1.98 kg
Julienne				
No. 8Z Tall	7.8	221.1 g	5.25	148.8 g
No. 303	15.2	430.9 g	9	255.2 g
No. 2½	26.8	759.8 g	18.25	517.4 g
No. 10	98.5	2.8 kg	68	1.93 kg

Beets vary moderately in shape. **Defects:** WHOLE BEETS are not more than 15 percent defective units and not more than half of defective units or 1 beet, whichever weighs more, may consist of blemished units. **Size and Shape:** SLICED BEETS are not more than 5/16 in. in thickness nor more than 3-1/2 in. in diameter, and the maximum diameter variation does not exceed 50 percent. QUARTERED BEETS are cut from beets not more than 2-1/2 in. in diameter, weight variation 50 percent. CUT BEETS are pieces weighing not less than 1/4 oz. nor more than 2 oz., and the largest piece weighs not more than 4 times the smallest. **Defects:** SLICED, QUARTERED AND CUT BEETS—The aggregate weight of all blemished units and units damaged by mechanical injury does not exceed 15 percent of the weight of all the units, and of such 15 percent not more than 1/2 thereof or one slice, quarter or cut, whichever weighs more, may consist of blemished units, and with respect to sliced beets not more than 10 percent of all the units may consist of units that are slabs. **Size and Shape:** DICED BEETS are cubes not larger than 3/8 in. and not more than 15 percent of the pieces are smaller than 1/2 cubes or large and irregular in shape. JULIENNE, FRENCH STYLE OR SHOESTRING BEETS are strips with cross sections measuring not more than 3/16 in. square, the aggregate weight of all strips less than 1-1/2 in. long does not exceed 25 percent of the weight of all the strips. **Defects:** DICED AND SHOESTRING BEETS—not more than 10 percent are defective units, and no more than half the units of each grade may be blemished.

Grade C: Color: Fairly good. **Size and Shape:** WHOLE BEETS are not more than 2-1/2 in. in diameter. The maximum diameter variation is 100 percent. Grade C beets may vary con-

BEET SIZES

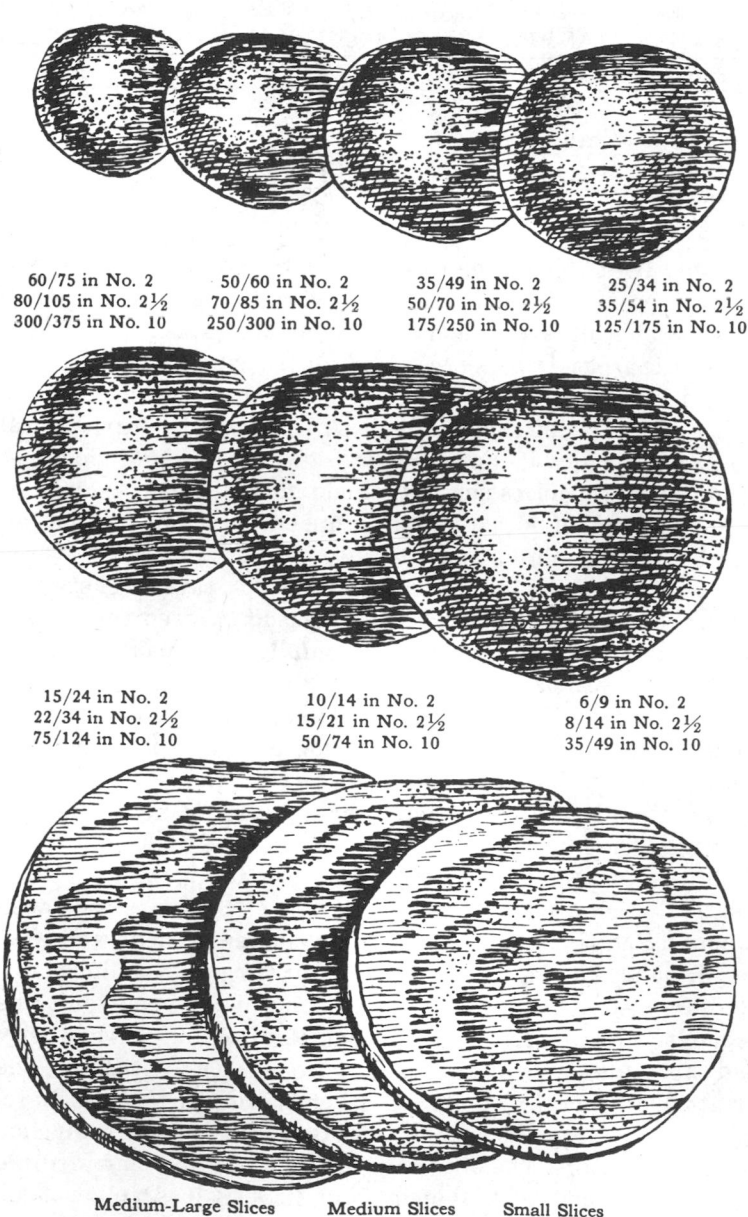

60/75 in No. 2	50/60 in No. 2	35/49 in No. 2	25/34 in No. 2
80/105 in No. 2½	70/85 in No. 2½	50/70 in No. 2½	35/54 in No. 2½
300/375 in No. 10	250/300 in No. 10	175/250 in No. 10	125/175 in No. 10

15/24 in No. 2	10/14 in No. 2	6/9 in No. 2
22/34 in No. 2½	15/21 in No. 2½	8/14 in No. 2½
75/124 in No. 10	50/74 in No. 10	35/49 in No. 10

Medium-Large Slices   Medium Slices   Small Slices

Frosty Acres Buyer's Guide — The Frozen Food Forum, Inc., Atlanta, Ga.

siderably in shape. **Defects:** WHOLE BEETS—not more than 30 percent are defective units; not more than half the defective units may be blemished. **Size and Shape:** SLICED BEETS—not more than 3/8 in. in thickness nor more than 3-1/2 in. in diameter, and the maximum diameter variation does not exceed 100 percent. QUARTERED BEETS are cut from beets no more than 3-1/2 in. in diameter; weight variation 100 percent. CUT BEETS—not less than 1/8 oz. nor more than 3 oz., and the largest piece weighs not more than 12 times the smallest. An occasional unit not representative is excluded in determining size variation. **Defects:** SLICED, QUARTERED AND CUT BEETS—The aggregate weight of all blemished units and units damaged by mechanical injury does not exceed 30 percent of the weight of all the units, and of such 30 percent not more than 1/2 thereof may consist of blemished units, and with respect to sliced beets not more than 25 percent of the weight of all the units may consist of units that are slabs. **Size and Shape:** DICED BEETS are cubes not larger than 1/2 in., and not more than 25 percent by weight of the pieces are smaller than 1/2 cube or large and irregular in shape. JULIENNE, FRENCH STYLE OR SHOESTRING BEETS are strips with cross sections measuring not over 3/16 in. and the aggregate weight of all strips less than 1-1/2 in. long does not exceed 40 percent of the weight of all the strips. **Defects:** DICED AND SHOESTRING—not more than 25 percent are defective units, and no more than half the units of each grade may be blemished. **Sstd:** Fails to meet the requirements of U.S. Grade C or U.S. Standard.

BROCCOLI*

USES: Broccoli is usually boiled, but after that simple operation, it can be a surprisingly versatile vegetable. This is demonstrated by the following listing of just some of its many uses: broccoli on toast with a cheese sauce; fresh raw broccoli as an hors d'oeuvre with a cocktail dip, or broken into small pieces and added to the tossed green salad; boiled broccoli with a creole sauce; left-over broccoli in tomato soup; broccoli with lemon sauce made of mayonnaise and fresh lemon juice; broccoli and ham casserole; broccoli au gratin; broccoli over slices of turkey or chicken; broccoli marinated in oil and vinegar and added to crisp greens; parboiled broccoli stalks sau-

*UFFVA

BUNCHED ITALIAN SPROUTING BROCCOLI

FRESH [7/12/43   51.3555]
Grades: U.S. Fancy, U.S. No. 1, U.S. NO. 2

GRADES:	"A" or "FANCY"	"B" or "EXTRA STANDARD"	"C" or "STANDARD"	"SUB-STANDARD"

BROCCOLI

FROZEN [4/14/62   52.631]

Grades:	"A" or "FANCY"	"C" or "STANDARD"	"SUB-STANDARD"

teed in olive oil with sliced onions and minced fresh garlic; broccoli with egg sauce or hard-boiled egg slices; broccoli with vinaigrette sauce; broccoli with tomato sauce and grated parmesan cheese; broccoli with sour cream sauce, and cream of broccoli soup.

To prepare for cooking, wash broccoli, and trim the main stem slightly. Do not remove the stem since the whole stalk is edible. Make lengthwise gashes in the stem, almost to the flowerettes if they are more than a half inch in diameter. UPRIGHT METHOD—Tie in a bunch; stand upright in the bottom part of a double boiler, containing about 1 in. of boiling water and 1/2 tsp. salt. Bring to the boiling point and cook 5 minutes. Cover with the inverted top of the double boiler, and cook 10 to 15 minutes or only until crisp-tender. SAUCEPAN METHOD—Place broccoli loose in a saucepan with 1 in. boiling water and 1/2 tsp. salt. Cook with cover off the first 5 minutes, and then cook covered 10 to 15 minutes or only until crisp-tender. Of if desired, leave cover on during the entire cooking period, but lift the lid three or four times to permit the gases to escape, and thus protect the green color of the vegetable. IN GENERAL—Cook as briefly as possible in a small amount of water, both to preserve the crisp texture and to conserve nutrients.

MARKETING SEASON: Fresh broccoli is on the market in all months but marketing is most active in March and April and October and November, with the low point in July and August. The following table shows the monthly availability of fresh broccoli expressed as a percentage of the total annual supply.

This supply, considering only the fresh, is 60 to 80 million lb.

MONTHLY AVAILABILITY OF FRESH BROCCOLI EXPRESSED AS PERCENTAGE OF TOTAL ANNUAL SUPPLY

Jan.	Feb.	Mar.	Apr.	May	June
%	%	%	%	%	%
10	10	12	11	9	5

July	Aug.	Sept.	Oct.	Nov.	Dec.
%	%	%	%	%	%
4	4	6	10	11	9

VARIETIES: "Most American grown broccoli is of the Italian green type called **Calabrese**. New varieties are being developed to meet different demands. Some are especially adapted to specific areas. Others are suited for freezing."

Varieties are coming and going so fast that it is not practical to list and describe them all here. A list given by Agricultural Research Service in *Farmers Bulletin 2239 of 1969* does not describe the varieties currently used in California. Andrew A. D'Arrigo comments that it is not unusual for a variety to be offered, widely adopted, and fade into obsolescence within three years. H.W. Mann of Mann Packing Co. says, "There are several new varieties just being released by seed companies, including some hybrids, which hopefully may lead to a once-over mechanical harvest."

Following are brief descriptions taken from seed catalogs of some of the varieties currently being grown commercially in California. Listings are alphabetical by name of the seed company, and the order of listing has no significance.

Medium Late 145 This is a variety, introduced by Asgrow Seed Co., to be planted in the fall for early spring harvest. "Plants relatively compact, producing a large central head, well rounded and tight, with little or no cluster division and with small, tight ... buds." Said to be a major variety in California.

Medium Late 423 This variety, by Asgrow, is reported to be replacing Medium Late 145 because of more uniform maturity and the tendency to be adaptable for one or two cuttings. "The plants are generally similar to other strains of Medium Late, producing a large, compact head with little or no division between clusters. The buds are somewhat larger than Medium Late 145; of good color, showing significantly less 'yellow head' than some other strains of Medium Late."

Gem [hybrid] This is for late spring and early summer plantings in the Salinas Valley. "A highly uniform, early-maturing hybrid, developed by Asgrow for shipping and processing. The plants are medium large, but relatively compact, showing early vigor and reaching cutting stage in about 75 days from direct seeding in late spring and early summer. The heads are medium large, with attractive, relatively small, uniform buds and a semi-divided head stem."

Topper 430 This is being used in the Oxnard and Santa Maria areas of California. "A refined and highly uniform variety for shipping and processing, developed by Asgrow from Topper 43. The plants are of medium size, with good vigor, producing a large, compact head, with small tight buds on a heavy central stem. Adapted primarily for coastal areas of California."

Atlantic This is said to be the main variety used in the San Joaquin Valley. From Asgrow, it is for late summer and fall harvest. "Plants dwarf and compact; well suited for relatively close spacing. Head medium large, rounded, compact, with segments borne on a divided stem. Atlantic develops rapidly."

Harvester This is a recent introduction of Asgrow, being used in the San Joaquin and Salinas valleys for mechanical harvesting on an experimental basis. There are many problems to solve before this can be used on large commercial acreages, Asgrow says. It was developed for growing an extra large number of plants per acre. Plants are very short, compact, adapted for 2 to 3 in. spacings in 12 in. rows. Heads small to medium with relatively slender stems. Very uniform in maturity."

Waltham 29 An Asgrow introduction for late summer and fall harvest. Plant is medium compact, the head is medium large with stems semi-divided. Widely adaptable.

No. 47 [hybrid] From Dessert Seed Co., "Matures about a week earlier than DeCicco. The large, compact, semi-globe heads, composed of very small beads, have an even, dark green color. Very uniform in habit, growth, and maturity, it produces excellent quality side shoots after central head is cut ... Recommended for fall harvest on Pacific Coast."

Green Umbrella [hybrid] From Dessert Seed Co., "Very early ... Outstanding for its uniformity and concentrated maturity, it is suitable for once-over mechanical harvesting. The central head is large, compact, with fine beads of an even, dark green color. The semi-globular head, borne on a solid central stem, averages more than 12 in. in diameter. Bearing many good side shoots after the central head is cut, it is an excellent variety for freezing and fresh market. The plant is very vigorous, with dark green foliage. Matures about 10 days earlier than DeCicco."

El Centro [open pollinated] From Dessert Seed Co., "Very uniform and concentrated maturity. Plants are medium sized and vigorous, producing uniform large compact heads with fine buds, dark green in color with a faint, purplish cast. Heads are borne on solid stems, with little or no secondary shoots ... Shows great possibilities as a mechanical harvester type for fresh market."

Green Mountain Ferry-Morse introduction; large head, compact; early dark green; fine buds; freezer type; widely adapted; concentrated maturity; plant medium tall, 2 to 3 ft., light green.

Morse's Medium Late Ferry-Morse introduction; primary heads large and compact; color, medium dark, bright green; for California only; late summer and late fall; plant tall, compact, vigorous.

Morse's 4638 Ferry-Morse introduction; large, compact, uniform heads; medium size buds; said to have performed well in Salinas Valley; is medium-early in California; for late spring and late summer; plant 24 to 26 in. tall.

Morse's Medium E Ferry-Morse introduction; compact, large, slightly flat head, small to medium buds; medium season in California; for summer and fall; plant medium large, medium dark green.

Pacifica Ferry-Morse introduction; for fall or early winter harvest on Pacific Coast; large heads, tight, slightly crowned; medium green; for freezing or fresh market; classed as medium in season; for spring or summer; plant tall and vigorous but compact, with large leaves, limited side shoots.

Rex [hybrid] Ferry-Morse introduction; heads elevated; consider this for mechanical harvesting; large heads, very uniform in size and season; dark green with slightly purplish cast; excellent in Pacific Coast trials; medium in season in California; plant 28 to 32 in. tall, vigorous.

Topper 43 Ferry-Morse introduction; large, compact; buds small, dark green; with a statement that this is "the most popular variety in California." In season it is medium; plant compact, 18 to 22 in. tall, big side shoots.

Bravo [hybrid] This is from Northrup King & Co. and was developed by T. Sakata Co. The plant is 14 in. in diameter; head shaped flat and dome-like. Bunching occurs at the later stages of maturity. Earlier than Crusader, which follows.

Crusader [hybrid] This is from Northrup King & Co. Plant 12 in. in diameter with tight beads. Heads are round and dinnerplate shaped with some branching. Uniform maturity, and low, even head height. This variety matures later than Bravo and Green Duke by several days. Developed by T. Sakata Co.

Green Duke [hybrid] From Northrup King, developed by T. Sakata Co. Plant is 14-1/2 in. in diameter, head has excellent uniformity with tight beads. Tends to branch out at the later stages of maturity. Matures at approximately the same time as Bravo.

There are many other varieties including: **Coastal, DeCicco, Green Sprouting Medium** and **Green Sprouting Late; Green Sprouting DeCicco, Improved Spartan Early, King Robert Purple, Cleopatra [hybrid]; Medium 4638; Green Comet [hybrid]; Green Sprouting; Green Mountain.**

CONTAINERS: Broccoli is placed-packed, usually either in a crate holding 40 to 42 lb., or a carton or crate holding 14 bunches with a net weight of 20 to 23 lb., or the same crate holding 18 smaller bunches with the same net weight. This 14 to 18 bunch crate is also stated to have a weight range up to 30 lb. The 14 to 18 bunch package is the one most used in California. If a crate, it is likely to be a wirebound. If a carton, it is usually treated with wax. The wax impregnation permits the carton to go through a hydrocooler like the wirebound. Ice is placed in either container with the broccoli. The heads are usually bunched with paper-covered wire—"Twistems"—and the bunches may be wrapped with paper, or plastic film, or left unwrapped. The packing is done in a packing shed rather than on the harvesting rig, but the shed may be close by in the field. Such field sheds sometimes include a hydrocooler.

All broccoli should be cooled before shipment to near 32°F. and preferably immediately after harvest. The trend is toward more packaging at shipping point. Usually a 1-1/2 lb. bunch is used as the packaging unit. An air-breathing, heat-shrink film such as polystyrene is used or a non-shrink type such as polyethylene with ample holes punched in it to permit ventilation. Packaging at shipping point reduces the amount of inedible material shipped. Ideally, there should be none, since consumers are demanding best quality and preferably a product ready to cook with no further preparation. Fresh broccoli is in competition with the frozen of which the entire content of a package is edible.

QUALITY: "Look for: A firm, compact cluster of small flower buds with none opened enough to show the bright yellow flower. Bud clusters should be dark green or sage green—or even green with a decidedly purplish cast. Stems should not be too thick or tough. Avoid: Broccoli with spread bud clusters, enlarged or open buds, yellowish green color, or wilted condition—signs of overmaturity and over-long display. Also avoid broccoli with soft, slippery, watersoaked spots on the bud cluster. These are signs of decay."

GRADES: U.S. grade standards effective July 12, 1943 for bunched Italian sprouting broccoli are U.S. Fancy, U.S. 1 and U.S. 2.

"U.S. 1 shall consist of bunched stalks of Italian sprouting broccoli. Each bunch shall be free from decay, and from damage caused by over-maturity, discoloration of bud clusters or leaves, freezing, wilting, dirt or other foreign material, disease, insects, mechanical or other means. The bud clusters in each bunch shall be generally fairly compact. Each bunch shall be neatly and fairly evenly cut off at the base, and well trimmed, unless otherwise specified as 'closely trimmed', 'fairly well trimmed', or 'leafy'. There are no requirements for diameter but diameter may be specified for any lot as shown under "Size Specification'. Unless otherwise specified, the length of each stalk shall be not less than 5 in. or more than 9 in."

BROCCOLI—Frozen [4/14/62]

Grade A: Color: Bright, reasonably uniform, characteristic green; may include lighter colored areas typical of young and tender broccoli that does not materially affect the appearance. Pieces not included. **Size:** SPEARS—All units 2 in.; 90 percent by count, most uniform length in Grade A is 1 in. SHORT

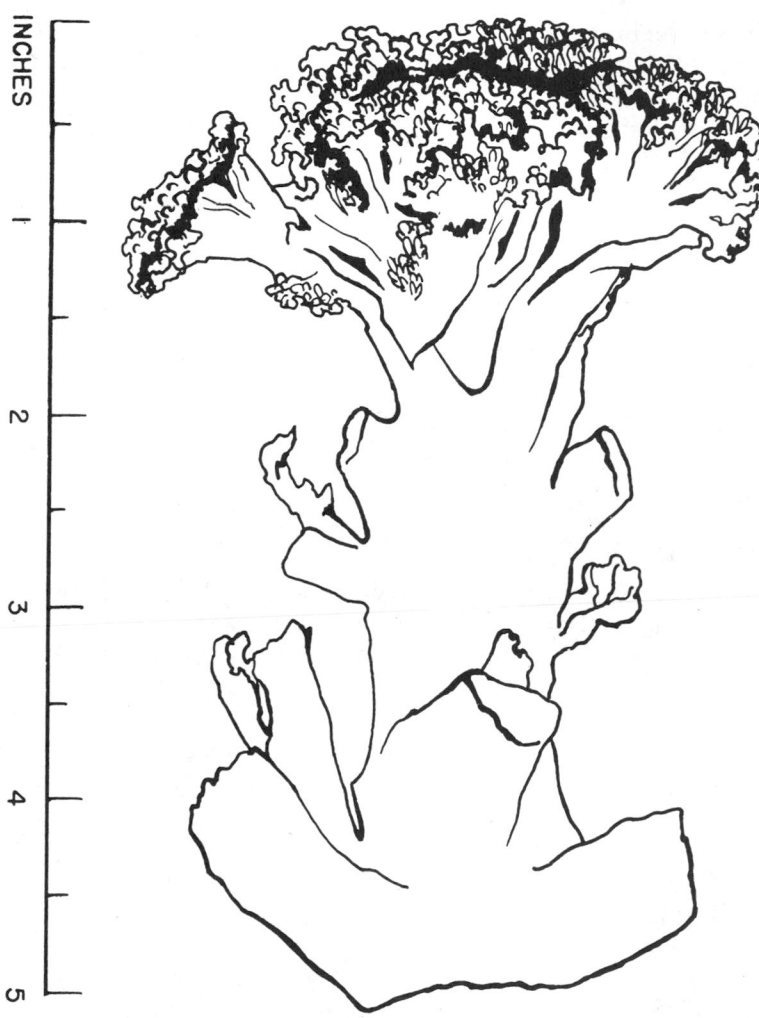

INCHES

FAIRLY WELL TRIMMED—LOWER LIMIT

SPEARS—95 percent by weight that are largest; largest does not exceed weight of smallest; 3 times. **Defects:** SPEARS AND SHORT SPEARS—Harmless, extraneous vegetable material: 1 piece per 30 oz. net weight. Detached fragments and

loose leaves or portions: 5 percent by weight, of which no more than 2 percent loose leaves or portions. Reasonably well and poorly trimmed units: 20 percent, but no more than 5 percent poorly trimmed. Broken, damaged, and seriously damaged units: 10 percent by count but no more than 5 percent seriously damaged. **Character:** SPEAR, SHORT SPEAR—Tender and free from tough fibers; 80 percent by count, well developed. **Size:** CUTS—1/2 in. or less in length. 10 percent, appearance not materially affected by variation. CHOPPED—3/4 in. or more in length; 5 percent by weight. PIECES—Grade A not included. **Defects:** CUT, CHOPPED AND PIECES—Harmless material not materially affecting appearance or eating quality in damaged and seriously damaged cuts, 6 percent by weight, but no more than 3 percent seriously. CHOPPED—4 percent by weight, but no more than 2 percent seriously. PIECES—Grade A not included. **Defects:** CHOPPED—Tender and free from tough fiber, buds are well or reasonably well developed. PIECES—Grade A, not included.

Grade B: Color: Characteristic green color which may be dull but not off color. **Size:** SPEARS—2 in. Maximum variation in diameter: most uniform diameter, 3/4 in. SHORT SPEARS—of the 95 percent, largest does not exceed weight of smallest 4 times. **Defects:** SPEARS AND SHORT SPEARS—Harmless, extraneous vegetable material: 2 pieces per each 30 oz. net weight. Detached fragments and loose leaves or portions: 10 percent by weight, of which no more than 5 percent loose leaves or portions. Reasonably well and poorly trimmed units: 100 percent by count, but no more than 20 percent poorly trimmed. Broken, damaged and seriously damaged units: 20 percent by count, but no more than 10 percent seriously damaged. **Character:** SPEARS AND SHORT SPEARS—Reasonably tender, 10 percent, by count, may possess tough fiber, 90 percent, at least reasonably well developed. **Size:** CUTS—20 percent, appearance not seriously affected by variation. CHOPPED—3/4 in. or more in length: 10 percent by weight. PIECES—Appearance not seriously affected by variation. **Defects:** CUT, CHOPPED AND PIECES—Harmless material not seriously affecting appearance or eating quality. Damaged and seriously damaged units: CUTS—12 percent by weight, but no more than 6 percent seriously. CHOPPED—8 percent by weight, but no more than 4 percent seriously. PIECES—10 percent by weight, but no more than 4 percent seriously. 10 percent by weight, but no more than 5 percent seriously. **Character:** CHOPPED—Reasonably tender, practically free from tough fiber; appearance or eating quality not materially affected by poorly developed buds. PIECES—Reasonably tender and practically free from tough fiber; appearance or eating quality not materially affected by poorly developed buds.

BRUSSELS SPROUTS*

USES: Brussels sprouts may be served boiled, baked, steamed, lyonnaise, french fried, au gratin, a la brigoule, buttered, creole, or almondine; also they may be served as casseroles, salads, or souffles, or with hollandaise, peanut butter, mustard cheese, bechamel, paprika and sour cream, tomato, or parmesan sauces. They may be prepared with chestnuts, grapes, mushrooms, celery, sweet potatoes, ham, squash, carrots, and tomatoes. To boil brussels sprouts, trim them as may be needed and cook in 1-in. depth of boiling, salted water or stock. Let sprouts cook without a cover for about 5 minutes; then cover and cook about 10 minutes longer, or until just crisp-tender.

VARIETIES: U.S. seed catalogs list 4 standard varieties of brussels sprouts: **Catskill, Long Island Improved, Fancy Most 50-A** (a form of the Half Dwarf) and **Jade Cross F1 Hybrid.** Two other varieties, **Half Dwarf** and **Paris Market**, are infrequently mentioned. Of the standard varieties, Catskill and Long Island Improved are the older, Fancy Most 50-A and Jade Cross the newer. Catskill and Fancy Most 50-A are, respectively, adapted to the Northeast and California. Long Island Improved appears to be grown widely as is Jade Cross, the only brussels sprouts hybrid. Two other varieties, Gravendeel and Sanda, originated in Holland, are being tried in California. Growers there planted several hundred acres of these varieties in 1964 and 1965.

Varietal features are: **Catskill,** big, firm sprouts that snap off easily; **Long Island Improved,** fall variety; **Fancy Most 50-A,** widely spaced leaves, easily picked sprouts and slow bolting; **Jade Cross,** performs well in warm conditions; is a generally heavier, earlier yielder, well adapted to freezing;

Gravandeel is good for late, fresh market planting; the sprouts are far apart along the stem, and there is little trouble with decay; **Sanda** is not a high yielder but has the advantage of holding small sizes for long periods between harvest, and the sprouts are compact, heavy, and of excellent quality for freezer or fresh market.

Varietal characteristics of main varieties are listed below:

Variety	Days*	Height	Plant	Color	Head	Sprout Size
Catskill	85-95	24 in.	dwarf, uniform	dark green	tight, firm	1-1/4 to 1-1/2 in.
Improved	90	20 to 24 in.	compact, uniform	medium green	small, firm	1-1/4 to 1-1/2 in.
Fancy	90	32 to 36 in.	tall, uniform	dark green	solid	
Jade Cross	85 to 90	24 to 24 in.	compact, uniform	bluish green	small, tight	1-1/2 in.

*Days from the setting of plants

CONTAINERS: Much of the crop in California is marketed by the Half Moon Bay Growers' Assn. This organization uses a 10-oz. wax cup packed 12 cups per tray. Each cup holds slightly more than 10 oz. The 12-cup tray holds about 7.5 lb. net. In addition, brussels sprouts are shipped in drums holding 25 lb. and bushel baskets holding 35 lb. either for institutional use or repacking. Other containers used include cartons of 25 lb. net; 16-qt. crates 17 to 18 lb.; small cartons, 15 lb.; apple boxes, 25 lb.; and a small broccoli crate 25 to 30 lb. Catskill, N.Y. growers tend to use the 16-qt. crate, while, for local shipment, California growers use lettuce or carrot crates or apple or artichoke boxes which hold 40 lb. The brussels sprouts drum, as authorized by Freight Container Tariff 1-H, has inside diameter of 13-1/4 in., and inside depth between heads of 14 in., and capacity of 1929 cu. in.

SERVINGS AND WEIGHTS: One pound of fresh brussels sprouts provides 4.42 portions of 1/2 cup cooked, or 8.84 portions of 1/4 cup cooked. It takes 22-3/4 lb. as purchased for 100 servings of 1/2 cup, and 11-1/2 lb. for 100 servings of 1/4 cup. A pound, as purchased, provides 0.74 lb. ready to cook.

QUALITY: "Brussels sprouts of good quality," according to
*UFFVA

USDA, "are hard or firm, compact, fresh, of bright appearance, and of good green color. Puffy sprouts, although edible, are usually of poor quality and flavor. Those that are wilted or have yellowed leaves are usually aged or stale, and because of their wastiness they should be avoided. Worm injury is indicated by riddled leaves. Much waste may be expected when worm injury is found. A smudgy, dirty appearance may indicate the presence of plant lice. Close examination is often necesary to detect the presence of these insects which sometimes make the sprouts unfit for food. Evidence of the presence of insects may be found on the inner surfaces of the leaves."

GRADES: The U.S. Standards for fresh brussels sprouts provide for two grades, U.S. No. 1 and U.S. No. 2. U.S. No. 1 consists of: "Brussels sprouts which are well colored, firm, not withered or burst, which are free from soft decay and seed stems, and free from damage caused by discoloration, dirt or other foreign material, freezing, disease, insects, or mechanical or other means. Unless otherwise specified, the diameter of each brussels sprout shall be not less than 1 in., and the length shall be not more than 2-3/4 in. In order to allow for variations incident to proper grading and handling other than for size, not more than a total of 10 percent, by weight, of the brussels sprouts in any lot may fail to meet the requirements of the grade: provided, that not more than 1/5 of this amount, or 2 percent, shall be allowed for soft decay. In addition, not more than a total of 5 percent, by weight, of the brussels sprouts in any lot may be smaller than the specified minimum diameter, and not more than 10 percent may be longer than the specified maximum length. 'Well colored' means that the brussels sprout has a light green or a darker shade of green color characteristic of well-grown brussels sprouts. 'Firm' means that the brussels sprout is of reasonable solidity and is fairly compact but may yield slightly to moderate pressure."

Besides these standards, which are primarily for wholesale trading, there are also U.S. Consumer Standards for brussels sprouts which provide for grades A and B. States, such as California, have also set grades for sprouts shipped out of state. *The Agricultural Code for California, Chapter 2, Section 810.7,* reads: "Brussels sprouts shall be free from mold, decay, burst heads, insect larvae, and from serious damage due to insects. Individual sprouts shall not be soft or spongy. Damage due to insects is not serious unless 50 percent, by weight, of the individual sprout is affected by insect injury or by the presence of insects. Not more than 10 percent, by weight, of the sprouts in any one container or bulk lot shall be below these requirements, and not to exceed one-half of this tolerance shall be allowed for any one cause, with the exception of serious damage due to insects for which not more than 10 percent tolerance shall be allowed. All containers of brussels sprouts shall bear upon them, in plain sight and in plain letters, on one side or one end, the name of the person who first placed or authorized the placing of the brussels sprouts in the containers, or the name under which such person is engaged in business, together with a sufficiently explicit address as to permit ready location of such person."

BRUSSELS SPROUTS—Frozen [5/11/51]

Grade A: Color: Not more than 5 percent of the units may be yellow with the remainder of the units yellow green or more green in color. One brussels sprout in a single container is permitted to be yellow if such unit exceeds the allowance of 5 percent. **Defects:** No grit or silt that affects the appearance or eating quality of the product is present; no harmless, extraneous material is present; loose leaves and loose small pieces that do not affect the appearance or eating quality of the product may be present; and the units that are damaged or seriously damaged to not exceed 10 percent of all the units, but of such 10 percent not more than 1/2 thereof or not more than 5 percent may be seriously damaged; and, in addition, not more than 10 percent of all the units may be poorly trimmed. **Character:** Not less than 80 percent of the units are well developed, and the remainder are reasonably well developed or fairly well developed, and not more than an occasional unit may be very loose-structured.

Grade B: Color: That more than 5 percent, but not more than 25 percent of the units are yellow, and that the remainder of the units are yellow green or more green in color. **Defects:** No grit or silt that affects the appearance or eating quality of the product is present; not more than one piece of harmless, ex-

BRUSSELS SPROUTS

FRESH [1/18/54   51.2250]
Grades: U.S. No. 1, U.S. No. 2
FROZEN [5/11/51   52.651]

GRADES:	"A" or "FANCY"	"B" or "EXTRA STAN-DARD"	"C" or "STAN-DARD"	"D" or "SUB-STAN-DARD"
Minimum Score:	90	80	70	Less than 70

traneous material may be present for each 20 oz. of net weight; loose leaves and loose small pieces that do not materially affect the appearance or eating quality of the product may be present; and that units that are damaged or seriously damaged do not exceed 20 percent, but of such 20 percent not more than 1/2 or 10 percent of all units may be seriously damaged; and, in addition, not more than 15 percent may be poorly trimmed. **Character:** Not less than 50 percent of the units are at least reasonably well developed; not more than 10 percent may be very loose structured units; and the remainder are fairly well developed.
Grade C: Color: 25 percent of the units are yellow, and the remainder, if any, are yellow-green or more green in color but are not off color for any reason. **Defects:** A slight trace of grit or silt that does not affect materially the appearance or eating quality of the product may be present; not more than 2 pieces of harmless, extraneous material may be present for each 20

oz. of net weight; loose leaves and loose small pieces that do not seriously affect the appearance or eating quality of the product may be present; and that units that are damaged, seriously damaged, or poorly trimmed do not exceed 50 percent, but of such 50 percent not more than 3/10, or 15 percent may be seriously damaged, and of such 50 percent, not more than 2/5 or 20 percent may have butt ends that are not trimmed smoothly and closely at the approximate points of attachment of the outer leaves. **Character:** Not less than 50 percent of the units are at least fairly well developed. **Grade Sstd or D:** Fail to meet requirements.

CABBAGE*

USES: Cabbage is a versatile, basic food rich in vitamin C. It is used raw in salads, such as coleslaw; made into sauerkraut (salted and fermented), and the red varieties may, in addition, be pickled. To avoid excessive loss of vitamin C, cutting with a knife is preferable to a chopper, followed by quick use within hours. For the same reason, cabbage should be boiled in an uncovered pan with a minimum of water and not over-cooked. Cabbage can be baked in casseroles, for example with tomatoes. For boiling, it can be stuffed whole, cut into wedges, or shredded. It combines with meats, such as corned beef or sausages, to provide tasty and nutritious meals. Numerous cabbage soup recipes exist, one combining cabbage with other vegetables and beef stock. Cabbage also mixes well with

*UFFVA

MONTHLY AVAILABILITY EXPRESSED AS PERCENTAGE OF TOTAL ANNUAL SUPPLY

Commodity	Jan. %	Feb. %	Mar. %	Apr. %	May %	June %	July %	Aug. %	Sept. %	Oct. %	Nov. %	Dec. %	ANNUAL TOTAL Million lb.
CABBAGE: ALL	9	8	10	9	9	9	8	7	8	8	8	8	1,860
CABBAGE: FLORIDA	18	16	22	24	11	1					1	8	326
CABBAGE: TEXAS	17	15	19	13	5	2	1	2	1	2	8	15	273
CABBAGE: CALIFORNIA	10	12	13	11	12	9	6	5	5	6	6	7	259
CABBAGE: NEW YORK	13	9	6	2		1	6	8	11	13	15	15	175
CABBAGE: NEW JERSEY*						19	25	17	14	14	9	2	126

*Figures for other months not available.

Round Head Type Cabbage showing no caterpillar injury.

CABBAGE

FRESH [9/1/45   51.450]
Grades: U.S. No. 1, U.S. Commercial

apples, pineapple, and raisins for combination salads. Some sample cabbage dishes are Stuffed Cabbage Russian Style; Pennsylvania Dutch Style Stuffed Cabbage Leaves; Cabbage and Cucumber Slaw; Baked Cabbage and Egg Casserole; and Cabbage with Sour Cream.

MARKETING SEASON: Cabbage is on the market quite uniformly throughout the year, with slightly more available in March than in other months. Following is a table showing percentage of annual total available each month, derived from USDA unload reports representing about 60 percent of the U.S. total.

VARIETIES: There are numerous cultivars of the variety *capitata* (cabbage) of *B. oleracea*, perhaps as many as 200 to 300, but few are more important commercially. For commercial purposes, cabbage may be classified into five types: **DANISH, DOMESTIC** (the most important), **POINTED, RED,** and **SAVOY. DANISH TYPE** is a late-maturing, solid-headed type used mainly for late fall market and storage. The leaves are usually closely compacted and smooth, the heads round or oval. Leading varieties include **Danish Ballhead**—about 6-1/2 lb., 7-1/2 in. in diameter, deep round, and compact, plant fairly large and sturdy; and **Wisconsin Hollander**—about 7 to 9 lb., globular to flattened globe, very firm, plant large and hardy.

DOMESTIC TYPE is largely produced as an early or mid-season crop and for sauerkraut, since most varieties mature earlier than Danish. Heads usually are less compact, and the leaf tissues more tender and brittle than Danish. There are both flat and round varieties. The leaves usually are crumpled or curled and do not overlap so far at the crown as the Danish. This type does not keep well and is seldom stored except for short periods. Some later maturing varieties are grown for sauerkraut as well as for fresh market.

DOMESTIC flat varieties include **Enkhuisen Glory, Flat Dutch,** and **Succession.**

POINTED TYPE, with pointed or conical heads, is marketed in the early spring as green cabbage. Heads tend to be somewhat smaller than Danish or Domestic. This is the leading type pro-

duced in some southeastern states, and is grown to some extent in the west. Leading varieties include **Charleston Wakefield**—about 4 to 5 lb., heart-shaped; and **Early Jersey Wakefield.**

Among the leading round varieties are:

Variety or Cultivar	Season	Description	Notes
Badger Market	early	About 3 lb., 5 to 6 in. diameter, dark, blue-green leaves, firm round heads	Yellows resistant (See Diseases)
Copenhagen Market	early	About 4 lb., 6 in. diameter, heads compact, plant vigorous	Used for early kraut as well as fresh
Golden Acre	early	About 3 lb., tightly folded, well-balanced	Includes a yellows resistant strain
Greenback	mid	About 5 lb., short-stemmed, dark green	Yellows resistant
Marion Market	mid	Plants larger and coarser than Copenhagen market	Yellows resistant
Round Dutch	mid	Medium small, green, smooth-leaved	
Wisconsin in All Seasons	late		Used most widely in north for late pack sauerkraut

RED TYPE is known for its distinctive reddish or purple color, and is used largely for pickling and salad purposes. It is grown as a market garden crop near many large cities, and to a limited extent as a field crop in Florida, New York, and Wisconsin. Two varieties in general use are **Danish Stonehead** and **Mammoth Red Rock.** Others include **Red Acre, Red Danish,** and **Round Red Dutch.**

SAVOY TYPE is readily identified by the crinkling of the leaf tissues throughout the leaves and head. Heads are loosely formed, usually flattened, sometimes round or pointed, and yellowish green. It is an important market garden crop in some areas, especially in the New York City area and on Long Island. Some well-known varieties are **Chieftain, Drumhead Savoy,** and **Vanguard.**

A large number of *hybrids* have been developed, most of which are yellows resistant. These are becoming increasingly important. In Florida **King Cole, Market Topper,** and **Market Prize,** among others, have been superior to regular varieties in yield and uniformity during trials.

CONTAINERS: Cabbage is most commonly packed either in the field or at the edge of the field in wirebound crates, mesh bags, or cartons. During the harvesting-packing operation in California, "A truck carrying assembling facilities for cartons or crates moves through the field with the harvesting crew. A man on the assembling truck and one on the ground to distribute the packages can assemble and distribute packages for about 8 pack-line crews. Packed cartons or crates are left in rows convenient for the loading crew to load them on the wide-

Container Number	Description	Dimensions	Tariff No.
408	cauliflower crate (also authorized for cabbage)	9 x 18-1/4 x 20-5/8	2-G
957	lettuce & vege- table crate	10-1/4 x 12-1/2 x 20-5/8	2-G
3803	wirebound let- tuce & vegetable crate	7-1/2 x 15-1/2 x 18-3/4	4-C, 823-D
3821	wirebound let- tuce & vegetable crate	9 x 14-1/4 x 21-1/2	2-G
3825	wirebound cab- bage crate	11 x 15-15/16 x 21-1/8	2-G
4016	wirebound fruit & vegetable crate	7-1/2 x 11-1/2 x 19-7/8	1-H, 2-G, 4-C
5004	wirebound citrus & vegetable crate	11-15/16 x 11-15/16 x 24-1/4	2-G, 823-D
5041	wirebound ve- getable crate	13 x 13 x 25	1-H, 2-G, 4-C
7303	fiberboard cab- bage box	10 x 14-1/4 x 21-5/16	1-H
7500	woven, waterproofed paper, fabric bags (open mesh)		1-H, 2-G, 823-D
7525	cotton fabric bags (mesh not larger than 1/2 in. sq.)		1-H, 2-G, 823-D
7550	burlap bags		1-H, 2-G, 823-D

gage, all-wheel drive trucks used for hauling lettuce and cabbage out of fields."

Over 30 different containers are authorized by the Uniform Classification Committee for shipping cabbage. A representative sample is shown in the following chart.

The most commonly used containers are 1-3/4 bushel crates or cartons holding about 50 to 60 lb. (some 65 lb.); 50 lb. sacks or mesh bags; WGA crates holding 75 to 80 lb.

Since most cabbage is sold in bulk, usually by the head, pre-packaging is not a factor except for coleslaw.

SERVINGS AND WEIGHTS: One pound of cabbage will yield 6.32 portions of coleslaw, 2 oz. each, for a yield of 79 percent as served. To obtain 25 portions, a buyer would need to order 4 lb.; 100 portions, 16 lb. One pound will yield about 4 portions of cooked slices or wedges, 3 oz. each, for a yield of 75 to 80 percent as served. To obtain 25 portions, a buyer would need to order 6 lb.; 100 portions, about 25 lb.

A 50-lb. crate or sack of cabbage will provide about 213 3-oz. portions of cooked slices or wedges, a yield of 80 percent.

QUALITY: The following advice on characteristics to look for in buying cabbage is taken from USDA's pamphlet, "How to Buy Fresh Vegetables."

"*Look for:* Firm or hard heads of cabbage that are heavy for their size. Outer leaves should be a good green or red color (depending on type), reasonably fresh, and free from serious blemishes. The outer leaves (called "wrapper" leaves) fit loosely on the head and are usually discarded, but too many loose wrapper leaves on a head cause extra waste.

"Some early-crop cabbage may be soft or only fairly firm—but is suitable for immediate use if the leaves are fresh and crisp. Cabbage out of storage is usually trimmed of all outer leaves and lacks green color, but is satisfactory if not wilted or discolored.

"*Avoid:* New cabbage with wilted or decayed outer leaves or with leaves turning decidely yellow. Worm-eaten outer leaves often indicate that the worm injury penetrates into the head. Storage cabbage with outer leaves badly discolored, dried, or decayed probably is over-aged. Separation of the stems of leaves from the central stem at the base of the head also indicates over-age."

GRADES: U.S. standards for cabbage, effective Sept. 1, 1945, provide for 2 grades: U.S. 1 and U.S. Commercial.

"*U.S. 1* shall consist of heads of cabbage of one variety, or similar varietal characteristics, which are of reasonable solidity, and are not withered, puffy, or burst, and which are free from soft rot, seedstems, and from damage caused by discoloration, freezing, disease, insects, or mechanical or other means. Stems shall be cut so that they do not extend more than 1/2 in. beyond the point of attachment of the outermost leaves. Unless otherwise specified, each head shall be well trimmed. However, cabbage which has fairly good green color and is specified as 'U.S. 1 Green', and red cabbage which is specified as 'U.S. 1 New Red' need be only fairly well trimmed.

"In order to allow for variations, other than excess number of wrapper leaves, incident to proper grading and handling, not more than a total of 10 percent, by weight, of the heads in any lot may fail to meet the requirements of this grade, but not more than 1/5 of this amount, or 2 percent, shall be allowed for soft decay. In addition, not more than 10 percent, by weight, may not meet the requirements as to the number of wrapper leaves."

Size. "The minimum size or minimum and maximum sizes may be specified in connection with the grades as 'U.S. 1, 1 lb. min.' or 'U.S. 1, 2 to 4 lb.' or any lot may be classified as Small, Medium, Large, Small to Medium, or Medium to Large in accordance with the facts.

"In order to allow for variations incident to proper sizing, not more than a total of 15 percent, by weight, of the heads in any lot may vary from the size specifications, but not more than 10 percent may be either above or below the size specified. This tolerance is in addition to the tolerance for grade defects."

	Small	**Medium**	**Large**
Pointed	under 1-1/2 lb.	1-1/2 to 3 lb.	over 3 lb.
Danish &			
Domestic	under 2 lb.	2 to 5 lb.	over 5 lb.

DEFINITIONS—See the U.S. Standards for Cabbage for the complete text of the definitions. Some samples are *"reasonable solidity* means fairly firm for pointed type cabbage and southern Domestic type cabbage. Northern Domestic type cabbage and Danish or Hollander type cabbage shall be firm ... as applied to Savoy cabbage means not soft or puffy; Savoy type is characteristically loosely formed and rather light in weight; *puffy* means that the heads are very light in weight in comparison to size, or have excessive air spaces in the central portion. They normally feel firm at time of harvesting but often soften quickly. They are known as 'Balloon Heads' in certain sections ... *damage* means any injury or defect which materially affects the appearance, or the edible or shipping quality. Worm injury on the outer head leaves or wrapper leaves which materially affects the appearance of the head, or worm holes which extend deeply into the compact portion of the head shall be considered as damage; *well trimmed* means that the head shall not have more than 4 wrapper leaves; *fairly well trimmed* means that the head shall not have more than 7 wrapper leaves; *wrapper leaves* means leaves which do not enfold the head fairly tightly more than 2/3 the distance from the base to the top."

CARROTS*

USES: Fresh carrots are truly an easy-to-prepare vegetable. One need not bother to peel them unless it is a lifelong habit. Just wash, trim off the little scar at the top and the tap root, if any, then slice, dice, or cut into "shoestrings." Cook quickly in just enough boiling water to keep them from sticking. Season with salt and other favorite seasonings. Onion, celery leaves, and parsley are excellent flavor companions with carrots. Black pepper often is used.

The carrot is a versatile vegetable and is good when served alone, raw or cooked, or in combination with meats or other vegetables. Carrots may be boiled as a main fresh vegetable dish and served with butter or white sauce; diced and creamed with peas and new potatoes; roasted with meats; baked, fried, sauteed, and pickled. ... They are used generally for lending body and seasoning to soups. Carrots are good sliced raw in hors d'oeuvre; grated, or sliced, and diced in salads, either alone or with other vegetables; sliced into thin sticks and refrigerated for between-meal snacks for junior dynamos... They are good cut in long strips and simmered with frenched or plain green beans, tiny onions, or cauliflower ... Try glazing them in honey or brown sugar for serving with pork or poultry. And do not let any of the wild-eyed faddists tell you the only way to consume carrots is when juiced. While juice is good, there is no valid nutritional reason for consuming them in that form rather than in the other forms noted. ... Carrots are often used to give color to soups.

MARKETING SEASON: Fresh carrots are on the market all year with no distinct peak and with large supplies at all times. The lowest supply is likely to be in the summer and the highest in the spring. The following table shows relative availability by months, as calculated from unloads at Chicago, Los Angeles, Atlanta, New York, and Seattle.

PERCENTAGE OF TOTAL ANNUAL SUPPLY OF FRESH CARROTS AVAILABLE EACH MONTH

Jan.	**Feb.**	**Mar.**	**Apr.**	**May**	**June**
%	%	%	%	%	%
9	9	10	9	10	9

July	**Aug.**	**Sept.**	**Oct.**	**Nov.**	**Dec.**
%	%	%	%	%	%
7	7	7	8	8	7

*UFFVA

CARROTS

FRESH [9/18/54   51.2455]
Grades: U.S. No. 1, U.S. Commercial
TOPPED [12/20/65   51.2360]
Grades: U.S. Extra No. 1, U.S. No. 1; U.S. No. 1 Jumbo; U.S. No. 2
Carrots with short trimmed tops (9/18/54   51.2485)
Grades: U.S. No. 1, U.S. Commercial
CANNED [7/2/59   52.671]

Grades:	"A" or "FANCY"	"C" or "STANDARD"	"SUB-STANDARD"
Minimum Score:	85	70	Less than 70

	NET WEIGHT OZ.	NET WEIGHT METRIC	DRAINED WEIGHT OZ.	DRAINED WEIGHT METRIC
Whole less than 1-1/2 in. in diameter				
No. 8Z Tall	7.8	221.1 g	5.5	155.9 g
No. 303	15.2	430.9 g	9.75	276.4 g
No. 2½	26.8	759.8 g	19.5	552.8 g
No. 10	98.5	2.8 kg	69	1.96 kg
Whole 1½ in. in diameter and over				
No. 8Z Tall	7.8	221.1 g	5	141.8 g
No. 303	15.2	430.9 g	9.25	262.2 g
No. 2½	26.8	759.8 g	19	538.6 g
No. 10	98.5	2.8 kg	68	1.93 kg
Sliced less than 1½ in. in diameter				
No. 8Z Tall	7.8	221.1 g	5.5	155.9 g
No. 303	15.2	430.9 g	10	283.5 g
No. 2½	26.8	759.8 g	19	538.6 g
No. 10	98.5	2.8 kg	69	1.96 kg
Sliced less than 1½ in. in diameter and over				
No. 8Z Tall	7.8	221.1 g	5	141.8 g
No. 303	15.2	430.9 g	9.5	269.3 g
No. 2½	26.8	759.8 g	18.5	524.5 g
No. 10	98.5	2.8 kg	68	1.93 kg

	NET WEIGHT OZ.	NET WEIGHT METRIC	DRAINED WEIGHT OZ.	DRAINED WEIGHT METRIC
Diced				
No. 8Z Tall	7.8	221.1 g	5.5	155.9 g
No. 303	15.2	430.9 g	10.5	297.7 g
No. 2½	26.8	759.8 g	19	538.6 g
No. 10	98.5	2.8 kg	72	2.0 kg
Quartered cut				
No. 8Z Tall	7.8	221.1 g	5.5	155.9 g
No. 303	15.2	430.9 g	10.5	297.7 g
No. 2½	26.8	759.8 g	18.5	524.5 g
No. 10	98.5	2.8 kg	70	1.98 kg
Julienne				
No. 8Z Tall	7.8	221.1 g	5.25	148.8 g
No. 303	15.2	430.9 g	9	255.2 g
No. 2½	26.8	759.8 g	18.25	517.4 g
No. 10	98.5	2.8 kg	68	1.93 kg

FROZEN [2/28/74   52.701]

Grades:	"A" or "FANCY"	"B" or "EXTRA STANDARD"	"SUB-STANDARD"
Minimum Score:	90	80	Less than 80

VARIETIES: The varieties of carrots being grown commercially are changing with the probability that hybrids will become important. However, as indicated by seed production, the types in order of quantity grown with percentage of total in each case are: Chantenay, 42 percent; Nantes, 28 percent; Imperator, including Gold Pak, 23 percent; Danvers, 4 percent; other varieties 3 percent.

There are hundreds of varieties of carrots although only a few are of commercial importance. USDA's "Synonymy of Orange-Fleshed Varieties of Carrots," 1950 (Circ. No. 833) lists 389 names of carrot varieties or strains, and there are more now.

The National Carrot Improvement Program of the USDA, states, and seed companies seek to develop carrot breeding stocks that resist diseases and nematodes; emerge earlier; are high in carotene; have uniformly high seed set; are even-colored, nonbitter, and of suitable sizes for the particular use—such as for sale fresh, or for freezing, or canning. The program includes basic genetic research.

Following are descriptions of roots only of principal commercial *types* of which there are numerous varieties and strains:

CHANTENAY NECK: short, medium-sized to large, averaging about 1/2 in. in diameter at point of attachment of the petiole (that is, leaf stalk) bases to the main root; *growth*—typically almost completely underground; *collar*—medium-sized to small, slightly to intermediately sunken; *shoulder*—usually of same color as main root, smooth, typically short-tapered; *surface*—typically smooth or free from deep depressions; *skin color*—a rather light reddish orange; *base*—typically rounded; *length*—4-1/2 to 5-1/2 in.; *diameter*—at shoulder 2 to 2-1/2 in.; at midlength 1-3/4 to 2-1/4 in., thus slightly tapering from the shoulder to well below the midlength point of the root or to the point where the well-rounded base commences; *flesh* (phloem) —medium thick, coarse-grained but for well-grown specimens tender and intermediately crisp; *flesh color*—medium-light, reddish color; *core* (xylem)—medium-sized, comprising on an average about 36 percent of the area of a cross section of the root at midlength; in old-type Chantenay usually tender but occasionally becoming woody in mature specimens, ranging in color from a very light yellow to a very light reddish orange; *growing time* 70 days.

NANTES NECK: short, small, averaging 5/16 in. in diameter at the point of attachment to the main root; *growth*—almost completely underground; *collar*—small, typically only very slightly sunken; *shoulder*—usually of same color as main root but occasionally tinged with purple, smooth, short-tapered; *surface*—smooth; *skin color*—bright orange; *base*—rounded; *length*—6 to 7 in.; *diameter*—at shoulder 1-1/4 to 1-1/2 in., practically the same throughout its entire length, or cylindrical in shape; *flesh* (phloem)—thick, fine-grained, tender, very crisp; *flesh color*—bright orange; *core* (xylem)—small, comprising on an average about 35 percent of the area of a cross section of the root at midlength, indistinct, or what is commonly called red-cored in other varieties, cylindrical, ap-

pearing circular in cross section, tender, crisp; *growing time*—68 days.

IMPERATOR NECK: typically rather short, medium-sized, averaging about 1/2 in. in diameter at the point of attachment to the main root; *growth*—typically completely underground; *collar*—medium-sized, typically not sunken; *shoulder*—usually of same color as main root, smooth, short-tapered to squared; *surface*—smooth on young roots but tending to become roughened or ridged as roots mature; *skin color*—orange; *base*—typically short-conic when mature but long-conic when immature or strain inferior; *length*—7 to 8 in.; *diameter*—at shoulder 1-1/2 to 1-3/4 in., at midlength 1-1/4 to 1-1/2 in.; *flesh* (phloem)—medium thick to thin, rather coarse-grained, tender at prime but often becoming woody in mature specimens; *flesh color*—deep orange; *core* (xylem)—large, comprising an average about 52 percent of the area of cross section of the root at midlength; color somewhat lighter than flesh; *growing time*—77 days.

DANVERS NECK: typically long, medium-sized to large, averaging 1/2 to 3/4 inch in diameter at the point of attachment to the main root; *growth*—typically almost completely underground; *collar*—medium-sized to large, occasionally slightly sunken; *shoulder*—usually of same color as main root but occasionally tinged with very light green, smooth, typically short-tapered; *surface*—typically smooth or free from deep depressions; *skin color*—deep red orange; *base*—typically short-conic, occasionally and on poor strains long-conic; *length*—6 to 7 in.; *diameter*—at shoulder 2 to 2-1/2 in., at midlength 1-1/4 to 1-1/2 in.; *flesh* (phloem)—medium-thick, coarse-grained, but for well-grown specimens tender and fairly crisp; *flesh color*—bright orange; *core* (xylem)—large, comprising on an average about 45 percent of the area of a cross section of the root at midlength, distinct, usually tender but occasionally rather fibrous in mature specimens, color, light yellowish orange; *growing time*—75 days.

CONTAINERS: As a general rule, carrots from the field are trucked to a packing house where they are washed and cooled. Usually cooling is done by hydrocooler, employing sprays or baths of icy water. Carrots packed warm in polyethylene bags cool too slowly in a refrigerator car; they deteriorate, especially in the middle layers of the load. Warm carrots at 72°F. can be cooled about 20 degrees by immersion for 5 minutes in 38°F. water. This takes about 6 tons of ice per carload of carrots, but it greatly reduces the ice requirement in transit. It would take 3 days or more to cool a carload of carrots that much by conventional transit icing.

After washing and cooling, carrots are usually sorted for size by mechanical devices. They may be conveyed to packers for grouping, weighing, and bagging by hand; or they may be conveyed to sorting stations where groups of roots are selected and placed (without weighing) on a conveyor that carries them to a bagging machine; or sorted carrots may be conveyed to stations where they are placed on a weighing device. The weighing scoop is then tilted, and the carrots slide into a film bag which is then sealed. (If not weighed before bagging, it is necessary for packers to be sure to select groups that will weigh more than the weight stated on the bag. Providing overweight is thought to be cheaper than the labor cost of weighing.) Weighed or not, it is customary to put more than a pound in each bag to insure that, as purchased, the carrots still weigh at least the required amount.

Carrots for sale to institutions are often packed loose, 50 lb. to a bag which may be film, paper, or mesh. These carrots usually are the larger sizes.

Topped carrots, with or without sizing, may also be packed loose in burlap bags for shipment to packagers.

As recently as 1951, it was estimated that only 1 percent of carrots retailed were prepackaged, yet by 1956 it was estimated that 85 percent were topped and packed in consumer-size bags prior to retail sale. It is safe to assume that the percentage packaged is higher now.

The 1-lb. film bags of carrots usually are packed 48 to a master container which may be a wood crate, fiberboard box, film bag, mesh bag, multiple-wall paper bag, or combination of these bag materials. Bunched carrots continue to be shipped to a limited extent in the 2/3 WGA crate, generally 4 dozen bunches to the crate.

SERVINGS AND WEIGHTS: One cup of grated fresh carrots weighs 110 grams (1 lb. is 454 grams); and 1 carrot (5-1/2 by 1 in., or 25 thin carrot strips) weighs 50 grams.

A pound of carrots, ready to cook, provides 1-1/4 servings of 1/2 cup each of cooked, diced or sliced vegetables. To serve 100, the requirement is 24 lb. of carrots ready to cook. For 1 lb. ready to cook or to serve raw, use 1.22 lb. (about 1 lb, 4 oz. as purchased). One qt. cooked, diced or sliced equals 1.23 lb., about 1 lb., 4 oz.

A pound of carrots grated or shredded gives 6-1/4 servings of 1/2 cup each; and it takes 16 lb. for 100 such servings. One quart raw, grated, or shredded equals 1.04 lb., about 1 lb., 1 oz.

A pound of carrots raw, diced, sliced or in strips, provides 5 servings of 1/2 cup each; and it takes 20 lb. for 100 such servings. One quart raw, diced, sliced or strips, equals 1.28 lb., about 1 lb., 5 oz.

A bushel of carrots (2150 cu. in.) weighs about 50 lb.

QUALITY: Carrots for fresh market are generally harvested before reaching full maturity and shipped immediately. Such carrots are smaller, more tender, milder in flavor, and brighter in external color than carrots which are harvested for storage ... Carrots of good quality are firm, fresh, smooth, well shaped, and generally well colored. Wilted, flabby, soft, or shriveled carrots are undesirable. Those which are excessively forked, rough, or cracked may cause considerable waste in preparation. Decay usually appears as soft or watersoaked areas which may be partially covered with mold.

Carrots from storage, although of good, marketable quality, usually are coarser than new stock. Often there are differences in flavor of carrots from different districts, and some consumers often show a preference for carrots from a certain area of production.

GRADES: There are U.S. wholesale standard grades for bunched, topped, and short-trimmed carrots. There are also consumer grades for fresh carrots as a whole, but they are little used and are, therefore, only mentioned here. The grades that are of most interest are for topped carrots. These are U.S. Extra No. 1, U.S. No. 1 and U.S. No. 2. Texts of all grades can be obtained by writing Agricultural Marketing Service, Washington 25, D.C. Space here permits giving a sample of only one of the grades.

TOPPED CARROTS—U.S. Extra No. 1 consists of carrots of similar varietal characteristics which are well trimmed, firm, clean, fairly well colored, fairly smooth, well formed, and which are free from damage caused by freezing, growth cracks, sunburn, pithiness, woodiness, internal discoloration, oil spray, dry rot, other disease, insects, or mechanical or other means.

Size. Unless otherwise specified, the diameter of each carrot shall be not less than 3/4 in. nor more than 1-1/2 in., and the length shall be not less than 5 in.

STANDARD SIZING—Carrots in packages of 2 lb. or less may be certified as "Standard Sizing," provided the variation in diameter of the carrots in any individual package is not more than 3/8 in., and the variation in length is not more than 2-1/2 in. Not more than 20 percent of the packages in any lot may contain carrots which fail to meet the requirements for "Standard Sizing."

Similar varietal characteristics means that the carrots in any lot are of the same general type. For example, carrots with a short, but blunt growth like the Oxheart variety shall not be mixed with long or half-long carrots like the Imperator or Danvers varieties.

The grades give definitions of all important words, such as "firm," "clean," "fairly well colored," "fairly smooth," "well formed," etc.

For bunched carrots and for carrots with short trimmed tops, there are two grades: U.S. No. 1 and U.S. Commercial.

CARROTS—Canned [7/2/59]

Grade A: Color: Canned carrots possess an orange yellow color that is bright and typical; green units do not more than slightly affect appearance or eating quality. **Size and Shape:** DICED—Not more than 12 percent of the weight of all units may be noticeably smaller than 1/2 the volume of an average size cube, or noticeably large, or, in large, irregular shapes. SHOESTRING—Cross section measures approx. 3/16 in. Aggregate weight of all strips less than 1/2 in. long does not exceed 12 percent of weight of all strips. CUT—Individual units weigh not less than 1/4 oz.; largest unit not more than 4 times weight of second smallest and whole carrot from which prepared not more than 2-1/2 in. in diameter, and weight of largest not more than 50 percent of weight of second smallest. **Defects:** Aggregate weight of all defective units in "whole," "sliced,"

"quartered" or "cut" does not exceed 15 percent, and in diced or shoestring, 10 percent of the weight of all units; and not more than 1/2 of defective units or 1 unit (whichever is greater) may be blemished or seriously blemished. However, not more than 1 percent may be seriously blemished. **Texture:** Carrots are tender and firm, but not fibrous, and possess a practically uniform texture.

Grade C: Color: May be slightly dull but not off color; green units do not materially affect appearance or eating quality. **Size and Shape:** DICED—Not more than 25 percent of the weight of all units may be noticeably smaller than 1/2 the volume of an average size cube, or noticeably large, or large irregular shapes. SHOESTRING—Cross section measures approx. 3/16 in. Aggregate weight of all strips less than 1/2 in. long does not exceed 25 percent of weight of all strips. CUT—Individual units weigh not less than 1/8 oz. largest unit. not more than 12 times weight of second smallest, and whole carrots from which prepared not more than 2-1/2 in. diameter, and weight of largest not more than 100 percent of weight of second smallest. **Defects:** Aggregate weight of all "whole," "sliced," "quartered," or "cut" does not exceed 25 percent, and in diced or shoestring 20 percent, of all the weight of all units; and not more than 1/2 of the defective units or 1 unit (whichever is greater) may be blemished or seriously blemished. However, not more than 2 percent may be seriously blemished. **Texture:** Carrots are fairly tender, may be variable in texture but not soft or mushy, tough or hard, and a few units may possess a coarse or fibrous texture.

Grade D: Fails to meet requirements.

CARROTS—Frozen [3/20/55]

Grade A: Color: Carrots possess a color that is bright and typical of young and tender, diced carrots, and the appearance of the product is not more than slightly affected by variations in the color of the carrots. **Defects:** Not more than one piece or pieces of extraneous carrot material having an aggregate area of 3/16 sq. in.; or one spherical or cylindrical piece of other harmless, extraneous vegetable material for each 40 oz. of the product. Not more than 10 damaged and seriously damaged units for each 10 oz. of the product of which not more than 2 units are seriously damaged: provided, that damaged and seriously damaged units, either singly or combination, no more than slightly affect the appearance or eating quality. Not more than 12 percent may consist of units markedly smaller than 1/2 the volume of, or markedly larger than, the predominating size of the dice: provided, that not more than twice this allowance of 24 percent may be present in any single sample. Other defects, individually or collectively, do not more than slightly affect the appearance. **Character:** The carrots are tender, not fibrous, and possess a practically uniform texture.

Grade B: Color: Possess a color that is reasonably bright and typical of young and tender diced carrots, and the appearance is not materially affected by variations in the color of the carrots. **Defects:** See defects for Grade A. All wording is the same except as follows: 3/8 sq. in. for each 40 oz. 14 for each 10 and 3; 17 percent, 34 percent. **Character:** See character for Grade A.

Grade C: Color: Possess a color that may be dull or off color, and the color of each ingredient may be variable but not to the extent to affect seriously the appearance. **Defects:** See Grade A defects. All wording is the same except as follows: 3/4 sq. in., for each 40 oz.; 17 for each 10 oz. and 5; 25 percent, 50 percent. **Character:** The carrots are at least reasonably tender, may be variable in texture but are not tough or hard, and there may be present a few units which possess a coarse fibrous texture.

Sstd: Fails to meet requirements.

CAULIFLOWER*

USES: Fresh cauliflower is one of the convenience vegetables. Almost all of it now comes to market stripped of ribs and leaves and ready for the pot.

A whole head of cauliflower needs not more than 25 minutes total cooking time. Set it in a 1-in. depth of boiling, salted water. Let cook for 5 minutes, without lid, then cover and cook another 15 to 20 minutes, depending on the size of the head. Cauliflower is one of those white vegetables that can pick up an unattractive yellowish cast if cooked in "hard" or alkaline water. Add a teaspoonful of fresh lemon juice to the water, and the cauliflower will stay nice and white. Cauliflower, like all other fresh vegetables, should not be over-cooked to a point of being very soft or mushy. (Nearly everyone except the Chinese over-cook vegetables).

There are many ways of serving cauliflower. Sprinkle it with fine breadcrumbs lightly browned in butter. Cheese, lemon, or tartar sauce is delicious over it. Cook it in chicken or beef stock, and garnish generously with chopped fresh parsley. Serve it with lemon butter or chopped almond butter. Raw, thinly sliced cauliflower is a nippy addition to a tossed green salad. Good, too, as a pick-up for dips on the hors d'oeuvre tray. Another excellent way to serve raw cauliflower is to chop it into small chunks and add mayonnaise, lemon juice, salt, pepper, and chopped green onion—to make an unusual salad low in calories and high in vitamin C.

VARIETIES: There is much confusion in the names given to cauliflower varieties and strains. The origin of some of these is obscure. Some varieties that are not well fixed as to type are sold under several names. There are many more names in the trade than there are varieties. The uniformity and heading ability of a strain are more important than its varietal designation.

"One of the most important differences in strains of cauliflower is the period required for a crop to reach maturity. Some early strains of the **Snowball** type become marketable in 50 to 55 days after being transplanted to the field. Some midseason strains of the **Danish Giant** type require 70 to 80 days. Late types, which are grown mostly in the Pacific Coast states, may require more than 150 days.

"Cauliflower varieties differ in plant size, in color, and size of head, and in other foliage characteristics, and in the manner in which the inner leaves enclose the developing curd protecting it from light. Such protection is very important in preventing discoloration of the curd as a result of exposure to light. Poor strains have an undesirable tendency to develop small leaves that extend out through the branches of the head, spoiling their salability. Some of the best of the cauliflower varieties are described below."

The best indicator of the general types of cauliflower planted are the annual reports of USDA on stocks of vegetable seeds as of June 30. For many years the **SNOWBALL** early types have been predominant. The report for 1966 showed that Snowball early seed on hand was 38,486 lb. against 8,604 for Snowball late types and 14,518 for winter types.

"**Early Snowball** is one of the earliest and probably the most
*UFFVA

important of the early strains; requires 50 to 60 days to mature. The plants are dwarf, compact, and quick-growing, with upright, medium-green leaves that turn outward at the tips. The heads are uniform, compact, solid, ivory white, and of excellent quality and flavor. It is especially desirable in districts having a short growing season."

"Super Snowball is one of the earliest maturing varieties, requiring 55 to 60 days to mature. The plants are of the short-leaved or dwarf type; leaves are somewhat spreading, longer than in **Early Snowball**, and blue-green. The heads are medium in size, solid, and clear white. It is a favorite for canning and freezing."

"Snowdrift requires 60 to 65 days to mature. The plants are larger and more vigorous than Early Snowball and produce a larger head, which is well protected by leaves during the early stages of development yet free of leaflets within the head."

"Danish Giant, also called Dry Weather, is a large, midseason cauliflower more adapted to dry, adverse weather than the smaller, less leafy Snowball types. The heads average about 7 in. in diameter and are a good white color. It is grown chiefly in the midwestern states."

"Veitch Autumn Giant is a large, tall-growing, very late variety with upright leaves, requiring 130 to 150 days to mature. The heads of Autumn Giant are the largest of the cauliflower varieties, averaging 8 in. or more in diameter. In eastern states it is recommended only as a fall crop."

CONTAINERS: Most commercially shipped cauliflower is now trimmed and overwrapped with transparent film. Such pre-packaged heads are shipped in fiberboard boxes (mostly 2-layer), nailed wooden boxes (1 layer), and wirebound crates, each holding 12 heads weighing between 21 and 25 lb. net, averaging 23 lb. A larger container sometimes used is the western pony crate holding 40 lb. net; and a still larger one for untrimmed cauliflower (but not used much any more), the WGA crate holding 60 lb. In the East, a popular container is the Catskill or L.I. crate holding 45 to 50 lb. Other containers sometimes used are the 1-3/5 bu. crate holding 37 to 40 lb.; 1-1/2 bu. or standard cantaloupe crate holding 35 lb.; various flat and 2-layer cartons holding 35 lb.; a carton holding 40 lb.; and a few in instances, bushel baskets holding 24 lb. or a 1/2-bu. box or crate holding 20 lb. trimmed.

One of the cartons in use, or being considered, is made of wax-impregnated board which resists moisture and is said to provide good insulating and cushioning qualities. If a board with enough wax impregnation is used, the carton can be run through a hydrocooler. Ice can also be packed in the box. The boxes are reported to stack well and retain their ridigity.

QUALITY: "Good quality in cauliflower is indicated by white or creamy-white, clean, firm, compact curd, with the jacket leaves (outer leaf portion remaining) fresh, turgid and green.

"Small leaves extending through the curd do not affect edible quality. Large or small heads, equally mature, are equally desirable. A slightly 'ricey' or granular appearance is not objectionable unless the flower clusters are spreading. Spreading occurs when the flower clusters have developed enough to cause a separation of the clusters which makes the curd open or loose.

"Spotted, speckled, or bruised curds should be avoided unless they can be trimmed without excessive waste. The appearance of aphids (plant lice) may be indicated by a smudgy or speckled appearance."

GRADES: There is only one U.S. grade for cauliflower, U.S. 1. This "consists of compact heads of cauliflower which are not discolored or overmature; and which are free from soft or wet decay and are free from damage caused by wilting, fuzziness, riciness, enlarged bracts, bruises, hollow stems, dirt, or other foreign matter, disease, insects, or mechanical or other means. Unless otherwise specified, the heads shall be not less than 4 in. in diameter. Jacket leaves shall be fresh, green, and free from damage caused by disease and free from serious damage by any other cause. Unless otherwise specified, jacket leaves shall be well trimmed. In order to allow for variations other than for size, incident to proper grading and handling, not more than a total of 10 percent, by count, of the cauliflower in any lot may fail to meet the requirements of this grade, but not more than 1/10 of this amount, or 1 percent may be affected by soft rot or wet decay affecting the curd. In addition, not more than 5 percent, by count, of the heads in any lot may be smaller than the specified minimum size."

CAULIFLOWER—Frozen [11/12/51]

Grade A: Color: Buds or buttons possess a white to light cream color over the tops, which color may be slightly variable, and the product may possess a green color or bluish tint on the

CAULIFLOWER

FRESH |3/15/68   51.540|
Grades: U.S. No. 1, U.S. Commercial
FROZEN [11/12/51   52.721|

Grades:	"A" or "FANCY"	"B" or "EXTRA STANDARD"	"SUB-STANDARD"
Minimum Score:	85	70	Less than 70

branches and greenish yellow to light green modified leaves or bracts: provided, that the buds or buttons may possess a color slightly darker than light cream which disappears upon cooking. **Defects:** Product is practically free from pieces and detached fragments and from any defects that affect materially the appearance or edibility; and in addition no seriously damaged clusters are present, and not more than 15 percent may be poorly trimmed clusters or small clusters, damaged clusters, or damaged small clusters, and seriously damaged small clusters. Provided, not more than 10 percent are damaged clusters, or damaged small clusters, and seriously damaged small clusters, further provided, not more than 5 percent are seriously damaged small clusters. **Character:** Not less than 80 percent are firm and compact clusters of buds or buttons; and the remainder of the clusters may be reasonably firm and compact or may be slightly soft, ricey, or fuzzy.

Grade B: Color: Buds or buttons may possess a color ranging from white or light cream to dull white or dark cream over the tops, and that the product may possess a characteristic green color or bluish tint on the branches, and greenish yellow to light green modified leaves on bracts: provided, that the buds or buttons may possess a color darker than dark cream but not seriously damaged, which color disappears upon cooking to the extent that the appearance is no more than slightly affected. **Defects:** Product is reasonably free from pieces, and detached fragments, and from any defects that affect seriously the appearance or edibility, and, in addition, not more than 30 percent may be poorly trimmed clusters, poorly trimmed small clusters, damaged clusters, damaged small clusters, seriously damaged clusters, and seriously damaged small clusters: provided not more than 15 percent are damaged clusters,

damaged small clusters; further provided not more than 10 percent are seriously damaged clusters and seriously damaged small clusters. **Character:** Not less than 60 percent are at least reasonably firm and compact clusters of buds or buttons; and that the remainder of the clusters may be soft, ricey, or fuzzy, but not more than 10 percent may be mushy. **Sstd:** Fails to meet requirements.

CELERY*

USES: Celery's principal use is as a pre-dinner appetizer, in salads, as a relish with meats and fish, and as a flavoring and a vegetable in soups and stews. Stuffed celery, too, is an old standby. The stuffing can be simply cream cheese or any of many interesting combinations of cheese and tomato paste or fish with parsley and seasonings. Chopped celery is good in sandwiches, too ... When cooking shellfish, throw in some celery leaves to improve the flavor and reduce the odor ... Then another use for celery—but no longer popular—was handing the winner of an athletic event in ancient Greece a bunch of celery, which he did not eat since celery was strictly for looks or medicine at that time ... Celery is excellent in fish chowder, and makes a good sauce in its own right ... Chopped celery, chopped onion, margarine, and seasoning sauteed to a golden brown makes a good sauce for vegetables or fish ... Sliced celery cooked in beef or chicken stock makes a tasty vegetable ... When preparing stuffed fish for Lenten menus, remember to add finely diced celery to the stuffing mixture ... And, of course, celery is good in poultry stuffing ... Celery is boiled and creamed and used as a vegetable; or it can be used in combination with other vegetables as in a celery and potato casserole. Aside from good eating, the volatile oil from ripe celery seeds has been used as a sedative.

MARKETING SEASON: Celery is on the market in all months, with no very large seasonal peaks or valleys in availability. The largest quantity usually is available in May and the least in September. The following table shows availability by months expressed as a percentage of the annual total. This annual total, on the basis of 6.8 lb. per capita annually and 180 million population is 1.2 billion lb. retail weight.

*UFFVA

AVERAGE MONTHLY AVAILABILITY OF CELERY SHOWN AS PERCENTAGE OF AVERAGE ANNUAL SUPPLY*

Jan.	Feb.	Mar.	Apr.	May	June
%	%	%	%	%	%
9	9	9	9	10	9

July	Aug.	Sept.	Oct.	Nov.	Dec.
%	%	%	%	%	%
7	7	6	7	9	9

Total Mil. Lb. 1,225

*Percentages based on unloads at Atlanta, Boston, Chicago, Cincinnati, Los Angeles, and New York for years 1955-59 inclusive. Total poundage calculated from USDA data.

VARIETIES: Celery varieties may be classified by color, *green* and *golden*, and by types within the color division. Types of *green* celery are the **Utah Type** which includes subtypes of ordinary **Utahs** and **Crystal Jumbo; Summer Pascal Type** with subtypes Summer Pascal (Waltham Strain), Emerson Pascal and FM D5; **Easy Blanching Type;** and **Slow Bolting Type.** The **Golden** varieties are divided into Golden Self Blanching, Golden Plume and "other" types. (Classification suggested by Dr. James E. Welch, associate olericulturist, University of California, and Phillip E. Hill, Research Dept., Ferry-Morse Seed Co.)

The trade generally calls all green celery "Pascal." However, the Utah varieties, especially the Crystal Jumbo subtype, are the most widely grown. The others are used only in areas where local conditions prevent Utah types from being grown successfully; or small plantings are made to meet local market requirements or for processing, for example, varieties that can be planted in certain temperate areas during the seasons that the temperature and day length factors promote premature seedstalk development in the Utah types.

Approximately 60 percent of the seed produced is of Utah types. (USDA Acreage and Seed Production reports.)

GREEN VARIETIES

UTAH TYPES: Ordinary Utah Subtype: Utah 16-11, a recent ASGROW development replacing Utah 16; plant 23 to 27 in. tall with good heart development, foliage dark green; stalks 9 to 11 in. long, rounded, thick; quality holds well after reaching cutting stage, considerable tolerance to frost when mature, used for fall and winter harvest on Pacific Coast; growing period 120 days ... **Utah ["short top", Golden Crisp],** strain of green celery of high quality, developed in the region of the Great Salt Lake, probably a hybrid of selection of Giant Pascal; plant 20 to 24 in. tall, compact, erect, full-hearted; stalk 8 in. in length, solid, stringless, with a distinct "nutty" flavor, blanches easily; original strain and source of several improved varieties; good shipper; particularly adapted for use on the Pacific Coast; growing period 125 days ... **Tall Utah 10-B,** originated and introduced by Ferry-Morse Seed Co., Mountain View, Ca., 1940; field cross on regular Utah; plants 26 to 28 in. tall, erect, compact, leaves moderately large, medium dark green; stalks 8 to 10-1/2 in. long, of uniform length, rounded, thick, waxy in appearance, blanches readily, tender, crisp, favorite for shipment from California; large, heavy and compact hearts; resistant to fusarium yellows; widely adapted; growing period 130 days.

CRYSTAL JUMBO SUBTYPE: Tall Utah 52-70, originated and introduced by Ferry-Morse Seed Co., 1953, similar to Tall Utah 10-B; plant 28 to 30 in. tall, good heart development, dark green foliage; stalks 9-1/2 to 11 in. in length, thick, smooth, waxy, medium green; rib count very high, makes large sizes; highly resistant to "Brown Check"; primarily for fall and winter harvest in the West; has bolting tendency when grown for early crop; growing period 130 days ... **Tall Utah 52-70 H,** originated and introduced by Ferry-Morse Seed Co., 1955, selection from 52-70 which is slightly taller and has longer ribs and rib count, less discoloration and longer standing than Utah 52-70; widely adapted; growing period 125 days ... **Utah No. 15,** originated and introduced by Ferry-Morse Seed Co., 1941, selection from Crystal White Jumbo; plant 26 to 28 in. tall, erect, compact, deeply cut, dark green leaves, full-hearted; stalks 9 to 10 in. in length, thick, rounded, and quite smooth and crisp, nutty flavor; a strain for Eastern and Northern growers; resistant to foliar discoloration and fusarium yellows; growing period 125 days ... **Compak No. 1** and **Compak No. 2,** introduced by Ferry-Morse Seed Co. in 1957,

CELERY

FRESH [4/7/59   51.560]

Grades: U.S. EXTRA No. 1, U.S. No. 1, U.S. No. 2

both derived from cross between Summer Pascal and Tall Utah 52-70; show the head conformity and size of Tall Utah 52-70, but have darker petiole color and better standing or holding ability; proven to be superior to Tall Utah 52-70 when grown in areas that have combination of relatively warm weather and shorter day-length, such as is found during the winter growing seasons in Southern California, and in South and Central Florida; Compak No. 1 performs best in Florida and Compak No. 2 performs best in the Chula Vista to Los Angeles area in California ... **Green Light**, originated and introduced by Joseph Harris Co., Rochester, N.Y., 1955; parentage unknown; plant full and compact with good hearts, and many extra-thick, well-rounded stems with the crispness and rich flavor of the Pascal types; not recommended for spring planting as it may produce seeders; excellent on deep muck or on rich mineral soils for later summer and fall crops; holds in prime condition and can be handled and packed with a minimum of breakage; growing period 122 days ... Green Light, taller strain, originated and introduced by Joseph Harris Co, 1959; plant habit same as original strain with compact, upright growth, well squared at the base; stalks numerous, taller and somewhat more slender than original; quality fine, and handles equally well; should be grown for late crops, as it bolts readily from early planting; growing period 125 days.

SUMMER PASCAL TYPE: Summer Pascal, Waltham Strain, originated by University of Massachusetts, Waltham Field Station, introduced by Boston Market Gardeners Assn., 1941, selection from material obtained from Groxx Bros. in Carlisle, Pa.; plant 23-in. tall, upright, full-hearted with dark green foliage; stalk 9 in. to first joint, thick, rounded, smooth, dark green, easy blanching; improved strain of Summer Pascal for the East and South, well adapted to home and market use in the North, and increasingly important since green celery has become so popular in the markets; adapted to both upland and muck soils; extra brittleness and somewhat flaring habit of growth make careful handling necessary; resists bolting well; growing period 120 days ... **Pascal 259-19**, originated and introduced by Ferry-Morse Seed Co., Detroit, Mich., single

plant selection from Summer Pascal; plants 25 to 27 in. tall, vigorous, compact; leaves darker than Summer Pascal; produces uniformly large sizes; stalks 9 to 10 in. long, smooth, rounded; color attractive, bright, excellent quality; growing period 120 days.

FM GREEN D5 SUBTYPE: FM D5, introduced by Ferry-Morse Seed Co. in 1957; cross between Tall Utah 52-70 and Summer Pascal Waltham Strain; intermediate in type between the two varieties but in appearance leans toward the Pascal; matures in 90 days from transplanting in South, East, and Midwest, and on the West Coast; matures in 150 days from direct seeding; shows size and petiole length of 52-70 combined with the sheen and smoothness of Pascal 259-19 and the Waltham Strain; darker in color than either; very resistant to Adaxial Crackstem and to a leaf chlorosis which affects Utah types when grown on soils deficient in magnesium; performs very well on much soils of Michigan, New York, and Florida ...

EMERSON PASCAL SUBTYPE: Emerson Pascal, originated by Cornell University, Everglades and Central Florida Experiment Stations at Ithaca, N.Y., Belle Glade, Fla. and Sanford, Fla., respectively, 1952 ...

Danish variety (White Plume) x Golden Self Blanching x Cornell 19 x Cornell 6; plant 22 in. tall, growth rather open and shows low heart development, distinctive deeply-cut foliage on large uniform plants; stalks 10 in. long, very thick and fleshy; flavor similar to Summer Pascal at maturity; growing period 135 days ... **Emerald** is a newer pascal celery highly resistant to Cercospora blight. It was developed by the Everglades Experiment Station in Florida and is gaining in popularity. The variety is more tolerant than many others to the high temperatures of late May and June in the Everglades area and has also shown considerable resistance to blackheart. It is more brittle than summer pascal varieties and has shown more node cracking than summer pascal. The plants mature a few days later than summer pascals. The color at market maturity is light to medium green. The flavor is good, and the petioles are free of "strings."

EASY BLANCHING TYPE: Earligreen, an excellent celery for use where early storage for hearts is desired; a slightly taller, heavier, and somewhat earlier Sweetheart strain; plants compact, well shingled with broad ribs; blanches to pale green; growing period 98 days.

SLOW BOLTING TYPE: Slow Bolting Green No. 12, originated and introduced by Ferry-Morse Seed Co., Mountain View, Ca., 1952; parentage Non-Bolting Golden Plume x Utah; distinct variety; plants erect, slower to bolt than other green types, vigorous, compact, and tightly shingled; stalks 10 to 11 in. long; widely adapted, particularly to California; resistant to yellows; growing period 120 days. **Slow Bolting Green No. 96** was developed by Ferry-Morse Seed Co. from a cross between Non-Bolting Golden Plume and Utah 15. It is said, when grown under adverse conditions, to be the slowest to bolt of any variety yet in commerical use. It is finding favor as a variety to be used for extra-early or "out of season" usage in the celery growing areas of California's central coast. Its growing period is the same as Slow Bolting Green No. 12.

GOLDEN VARIETIES

GOLDEN SELF BLANCHING TYPE: Golden Self Blanching, origin unknown, long a standard variety in France; plant 20 to 22 in. tall, compact, erect; foliage yellowish green; stalk 8 to 9 in. to first joint; blanches well to yellow color; wide, solid, excellent flavor, high quality, crisp, slightly ribbed; growing period 85 to 90 days ... **Golden Detroit,** uniform selection of Dwarf Golden Self Blanching; plant 24 to 25 in. tall, heavy, compact, full-hearted; stalks 7 to 8-1/2 in. to joint, fleshy, crisp and solid, easily blanched to a golden yellow; growing period 90 to 100 days ... **Supreme Golden** (Hadley 972), originated and introduced by Ferry-Morse Seed Co., Mountain View, Ca., 1937; plant 23 to 26 in. tall, compact, well formed and full-hearted; earlier and taller than Golden Detroit; very attractive member of the Golden Self Blanching group; stalk 8 to 10 inches to first joint; well adapted to Florida for winter crop and to Northern districts for main crop; resistant to fusarium yellows; growing period 85 days.

GOLDEN PLUME TYPE: Golden Plume [Wonderful], plant 19 in. tall, leafy, semi-dwarf in habit; stalk 7 in. in length, good firm stalks, blanching to golden yellow; slightly earlier and shorter than Golden Self Blanching; attractive appearance and fine quality; growing period 83 days ... **Golden Plume 4162,** originated and introduced by Ferry-Morse Seed Co., 1938; selection from Golden Plume, hardy for Golden type, bred for a taller, longer-stemmed Golden Plume; retains earliness and ease of blanching of original strain; plant 24 to 26 in. tall, more compact in form, straighter, and better "shingled" than

original strain; heavy producer; stalk 7-1/2 to 8-1/2 in. long and hearts full; growing period 83 days ... **Tall Slow-Bolting Golden Plume,** originated and introduced by Ferry-Morse Seed Co.; ability to withstand low temperatures without bolting make it the most satisfactory of the Golden Plume strains for growing under certain unfavorable conditions; plant 24 to 26 in. tall; stalks 8 to 9 in. to joint; growing period 90 days.

OTHER GOLDEN: Cornell No. 19, originated by Cornell University, Ithaca, N.Y., 1942 introduced by various seedsmen; developed from cross between Golden Self Blanching and Utah, combining good qualities of the Pascal type with the early blanching character and color of Golden Self Blanching; highly resistant to fusarium yellows; plant 24 to 25 in. tall, hearts long and comparatively full; stalks 9 in. to joint, thick, rounded, and smooth; growing period 100 days ... **Cornell 6.19,** originated by Cornell University, 1953, selected from a cross of Cornell 6 for petiole thickness and Cornell 19 for petiole length; has slightly better heart development and more open petiole; plant 23 to 25 in. tall, erect, with compact uniform growth, foliage yellow-green; stalk 10 in. in length, thick, and crisp; a long, full-hearted type of excellent quality, blanches easily.

CONTAINERS: Most containers for bunched celery are about 16 in. in one dimension, since most bunches are cut to about that length. Containers include wirebound cartes, nailed crates, and fiberboard cartons. Celery hearts are generally packed in containers of about half the capacity of the packages used for full size bunches.

The following table shows the containers used most generally for celery in the major shipping areas.

There are many other cartons in use, and also other nailed boxes, but these are the sizes most often used, according to present information from shipping points.

USDA states that Florida standard 16 in. crates are loaded 560 to the rail car, and that in other states the 16 in. crate is loaded 480 to the car. Smaller containers are loaded in proportionately larger number.

SERVINGS AND WEIGHTS: One quart of raw chopped celery is about a pound, according to USDA which also states that for 1 lb. ready-to-cook or serve raw, use 1.33 lb. (about 1 lb., 5 oz.) as purchased ... In the school lunch program, 1 lb. is

CELERY CONTAINERS SHOWING STANDARD CONTAINER NUMBER, DIMENSIONS, NET WEIGHT, CUBIC CONTENTS AND NUMBER OF THE APPLICABLE FREIGHT TARIFF.

Container: Number:	Type:	Inside Dimensions in Inches:			Capacity: Cu. In.	Net: Weight:	Freight Tariff
		Depth	Width	Length			
3601	Wirebound	9-3/4	16	20-1/4	3159	55-60	1-G, 2-F, 823-D, 4-B
516	Nailed	9-3/4	16	19-1/4	3003	52-57	1-F
7340	Carton	10	11	16	1760	31-33	1-G
7342	Carton	9-1/2	10-1/2	15-3/4	1571	27-30	1-G
7343	Carton	8-1/2	11	15	1361	24-26	1-G
477	Nailed	10	11	16	1760	31-33	823-D
482	Nailed	9-3/4	16	20	3120	54-59	823-D

figured as providing 5 servings; and 20 lb. provides 100 servings, these two figures relating to pounds ready to serve ... According to USDA 3 small inner stalks (5 in. long, 3/4 in. wide) weigh 50 grams. One large outer stalk (8 in. long, 1 in. wide, 1-1/2 in. at root end), 40 grams. One cup raw diced celery, 100 grams. One cup of diced cooked celery, however, weighs 130 grams.

QUALITY: If celery is bought by grade and then inspected to determine present condition, there should be no difficulty in obtaining the desired quality. Note the time it is graded, which indicates both quality and condition at that time. "Quality" denotes those characteristics that are relatively permanent, such as shape, solidity, color, maturity, and freedom from insect damage. "Condition" relates to factors that may change, such as decay and firmness. The condition of celery may change during transportation and marketing. Usually it is easy to determine the condition by inspection.

... Celery should be fresh, crisp, clean, of desirable length, thickness, and solidity, with good heart formation and branches that are brittle enough to snap easily. Pithy, woody, or stringy celery is undesirable. Soft, somewhat pliable branches indicate pithiness, and small, hard branches may be stringy or woody.

GRADES: U.S. standards for celery for use at shipping point and wholesale are U.S. Extra No. 1, U.S. No. 1, and U.S. No. 2. There are also U.S. Consumer Standards for Celery Stalks, for

Well Formed Lower Limit 'Bowing' U.S. Extra No. 1—Credit: USDA

use at retail, but these grades are little used. They are U.S. Grade AA, U.S. Grade A, and U.S. Grade B.

"*U.S. Extra No. 1* consists of stalks of celery of similar varietal characteristics which are well developed, well formed, clean, well trimmed, compact, and which are free from black-heart, brown stem, soft rot, doubles, and free from damage caused by freezing, growth cracks, horizontal cracks, pithy branches, seedstems, suckers, wilting, blight, other disease, insects, or mechanical or other means. Stalks shall be green unless specified as fairly well blanched or mixed blanch. (a) The average midrib length of the outer whorl of branches shall be not less than 7 in. (b) Unless otherwise specified in connection with the grade, stalks shall be of such length as to extend from one side, end, or bottom of the container to within 1-1/2 in. of the corresponding opposite side, end, or top of the container. Such measurement shall not include the bulge. In any container when stalk length is specified, it shall be the minimum length in terms of whole inches of even number, as 12 in., 14 in. etc., in accordance with the facts. (c) In order to allow for variations incident to proper grading and handling, the *following tolerances shall be permitted:* (1) *For defects*, 10 percent, by count, in any lot for stalks which fail to meet the requirements of the grade, including therein not more than 2 percent for soft rot; (2) *For off-length stalks*, 5 percent, by count, in any lot for stalks which fail to meet the minimum length required or specified; and (3) *for off-length midribs*, 5 percent, by count, in any lot for stalks which fail to meet the requirements as to average midrib length."

"Requirements as to count—The number of stalks of celery in the container may be specified by numerical count, or in terms of dozens, or half-dozens. Variations from the number specified shall be permitted as follows: provided that the average for the lot is not less than the number specified—24 stalks or less, 1 stalk variation; 25 to 50 stalks, inclusive, 3 stalk variation; 51 to 70 stalks, inclusive, 4 stalk variation; more than 70 stalks, 5 stalk variation."

CELERIAC*

USES: Wise's *Encyclopedia of Cookery* (copyright 1948, W.H. Wise & Co.) has the following to say about this little-known vegetable: "It may be served raw or cooked. Celeriac is one of the few vegetables *that must be peeled before cooking.* The skin is very tough and stringy. Raw celery knob may be peeled and cut into julienne strips. Marinate the strips in french dressing for an hour, then drain, squeezing slightly to remove any excess liquid. Mix with mayonnaise and serve well chilled on crisp lettuce leaves ... Peeled and diced, celery knob may be cooked in boiling salted water and will be tender in ten minutes or so. A little vinegar or lemon juice added to the water will keep the celeriac white. The cooked celery knob can be served with butter, or cream, or hollandaise sauce, or it may be mashed. Like celery, it may be braised in meat stock." Celeriac has a flavor similar to celery and may be used as flavoring in soups and stews.

MARKETING SEASON: Average monthly availability expressed as percent of average annual supply is shown below.

MONTHLY AVAILABILITY OF CELERIAC EXPRESSED AS PERCENT OF AVERAGE ANNUAL SUPPLY

Jan.	Feb.	Mar.	Apr.	May	June
%	%	%	%	%	%
12	15	11	8	4	3
July	Aug.	Sept.	Oct.	Nov.	Dec.
%	%	%	%	%	%
2	4	5	10	13	13

(Percentages based on unloads at New York, Chicago, Los Angeles, San Francisco, and Oakland)

VARIETY: Only one variety is currently listed in seed catalogs—**Large** or **Giant Smooth Prague**. The plant is spreading, celery-like in character, with dark green foliage and hollow stalks. Roots are 3 to 4 in. in diameter, bulbous and knobby, fairly smooth. Growing time 110 days.

CONTAINERS: *Celeriac may be marketed bunched or topped.* California uses an apple box which holds 40 to 45 lb., net. This is approximately a bushel. Half-bushel baskets are commonly used in Illinois, New York, and New Jersey. In addition, bushel baskets, used containers such as cantaloupe crates, 4/5 bushel boxes, or baskets are also used.

GRADE—QUALITY: No standards for celeriac have been established by the USDA. When grown properly, the roots should be solid and tender. Celeriac may come to market washed or unwashed.

*UFFVA

COLLARDS*

USES: Collard Greens have been a favorite in the South for generations. They are traditionally boiled with salt pork or hog jowls. Then the greens and "pot likker" are polished off with gusto, accompanied by wedges of corn bread or pone, and perhaps a glass of cold buttermilk. Also try frying pieces of bacon or salt pork in a skillet, then adding washed and shredded collard leaves. Cover and simmer until tender. Serve with lemon slices, vinegar, or other dressing. Cook the collards until just done, about 10 to 15 minutes. Some collards are finely chopped or sieved and canned for baby food.

VARIETIES: Among prominent varieties are Georgia (of which there are several forms), Vates, Morris Heading, and Louisiana Sweet.

Georgia Plants are 30 to 36 in. tall, upright, with large, blue-green, crumpled leaves. This is a non-heading plant that produces greens under adverse conditions of heat and in poor soil. It is grown chiefly in the South. It takes about 80 days from seed to harvest.

Vates This is a standard variety for over-winter cropping, holding color well in cold weather. It has relatively good resistance to bolting in early spring. The plants are low growing (1-1/2 to 2 ft.), erect, spreading, and relatively compact, producing good yields of large, thick, dark green leaves with short stems. The time from seed to harvest is about 75 days.

Morris Heading This is a plant 30 to 34 in. high, leaves broad, wavy, medium green, with short stems. The head is moderately tight. It is slow bolting and good for winter planting.

Louisiana Sweet This is an introduction by Louisiana State University Experiment Station, intended to supersede Georgia. It has a larger leaf area and less stem than Georgia, and has thick, tender leaves. Days from seed to harvest about 75.

In commenting on U.S. varieties, M. Nieuwhof, in his book *Cole Crops*, notes that Georgia is widely grown, and that it is an intermediate form between non-heading and heading cabbage.

CONTAINERS: The wirebound crate is a usual container for collards. The crate may be 1-2/5, 1-3/5 or rarely 1-3/4 bu., and they are sold at about the same price with little regard for the difference in contents. The 1-2/5 bu. crate holds about 30 to 35 lb. of greens. The *Federal-State Market News Service* estimates that 24 of the usual bunches run 20 to 25 lb., but the size of bunches varies. The bushel basket formerly used for collards and other greens is not much seen on the market.

A U.S. Department of Agriculture inspector examines collard greens being processed at the Winter Garden Freezer Company. This plant operates under the USDA Consumer and Marketing Service's voluntary continuous inspection program.

*UFFVA

GRADES: U.S. standards for collard greens or broccoli, effective April 1953, provide for one grade, U.S. 1. This "consists of collard greens ... of similar varietal characteristics which are fresh, fairly tender, fairly clean, well trimmed, and of characteristic color for the variety or type; which are free from decay, and free from damage caused by coarse stalks and seed-stems, discoloration, freezing, foreign material, disease, insects, or mechanical or other means.

"In order to allow for variations incident to proper grading and handling, not more than a total of 10 percent, by weight, of the units in any lot, may fail to meet the requirements of the grade: provided, that not more than 1/2 of this amount, or 5 percent, shall be allowed for serious damage by any cause, and including therein not more than 2 percent for decay."

SWEET CORN*

USES: At least since the days of the Pilgrims, corn-on-the-cob (boiled, steamed, or roasted) has been a popular American favorite. Sweet corn is used fresh, canned, and frozen. Kernels may be cut or scraped from the cob and used scalloped, in succotash (an American Indian dish), custards or puddings, in fritters, souffles, stuffed peppers, or made into soups and chowders. Corn may be used in relishes and, immature kernels, in mixed pickles. Corn meal and hominy are forms of ground corn kernels in wide usage.

MARKETING SEASON: Sweet corn is on the market every month of the year, but in peak supply May to September. It is least available December through March. The following table, derived from USDA unload statistics for 41 cities (representing about 60 percent of the national total) shows monthly availability of corn expressed as a percentage of total annual supply.

MONTHLY AVAILABILITY OF CORN EXPRESSED AS PERCENTAGE OF TOTAL ANNUAL SUPPLY

Jan.	Feb.	Mar.	Apr.	May	June
%	%	%	%	%	%
2	2	4	6	17	15

July	Aug.	Sept.	Oct.	Nov.	Dec.
%	%	%	%	%	%
13	19	10	5	4	3

VARIETIES: There are over 200 varieties of sweet corn being grown in the U.S., according to the National Sweet Corn Breeders Assn. The most important commercial varieties are yellow hybrids. As pollinization and hybridization experiments continue, new varieties are constantly being developed having characteristics especially suited for one region or climate.

"Some varieties and hybrids may be available for only a few years, being displaced by better ones ... Sweet corn variety tests are conducted every year in many states, and lists of recommended varieties may change annually."

According to a USDA geneticist, the following 54 varieties are "the main varieties that are being used commercially at this time."

Bonita	**Golden Nugget**	**Merit**
Calumet	**Golden Queen**	**Midway**
Carmel Cross	**Golden Rocket**	**Morning Sun**
Country Gentleman	**Golden Security**	**NK 195**
Defender	**Seneca Star**	**NK 199**
Dominator	**Silver Queen**	**North Star**
Duet	**Spancross**	**Northern Belle**
Earliking	**Tastyvee**	**Seneca Arrow**
Early Cogent	**Wintergarden**	**Seneca Beauty**
Florigold	**Golden Sensation**	**Seneca Chief**
Gold Cup	**Golden Valley**	**Seneca Explorer**
Golden Beauty	**Gourmet**	**Seneca Dawn**
Golden Bounty	**Illinois No. 13**	**Seneca Golden**
Golden Cross Bantam	**Illinichief**	**Seneca 60**
	Ioana	**Southern Belle**
Golden Delight	**Iobelle 104**	**Summit**
Golden Earlypack	**Marcross**	**Victory Golden**
Golden Fancy	**Mellogold**	**Wintergreen**
Golden Monarch		

Some seed catalogue descriptions of leading varieties are: "**Country Gentleman** germination 100 days: produces long, white, shoe peg kernels without rows ... Stalk 7 ft., ears 9 in.; **Earliking** 66 days. A first early high quality hybrid. Mostly 12 rowed. Plant 5-1/2 ft., ears 7 to 8 in., 1-3/4 in. diameter; **Golden Beauty** 73 days. Extra early variety. Superior in uniformity, ear shape, row appearance, rowing, and quality. *UFFVA

CORN

FRESH—GREEN [5/18/54   51.835]
Grades: U.S. FANCY, U.S. No. 1, U.S. No. 2
WHOLE KERNEL
CANNED [7/30/52   52.881]

Grades:	"A" or	"B" or	"C" or	"SUB-
	"FANCY"	"EXTRA	"STAN-	STAN-
		STAN-	DARD"	DARD"
		DARD"		

Minimum
Score: 90   80   70   Less than 70

	NET WT. OZ.	NET WT. METRIC	DRAINED WEIGHT OZ.		DRAINED WEIGHT METRIC	
			Grade A	Grades B, C, & Substandard	Grade A	Grades B, C, & Standard
No. 8Z Tall	as full as	as full as	5.25	5.50	148.8 g	155.9 g
No. 303	practi-	practi-	10.50	10.75	297.7 g	304.8 g
No. 10	cable	cable	70.00	72.00	1.98 kg	2.04 kg

CANNED CREAM STYLE [7/27/53   52.851]

Grades:	"A" or	"B" or	"C" or	"SUB-
	"FANCY"	"EXTRA	"STAN-	STAN-
		STAN-	DARD"	DARD"
		DARD"		

Minimum
Score: 90   80   70   Less than 70

FROZEN [8/1/52   52.911]

Grades:	"A" or	"B" or	"C"	"SUB-
	"FANCY"	"EXTRA	"STAN-	STAN-
		STAN-	DARD"	DARD"
		DARD"		

Minimum
Score: 90   80   70   Less than 70

FROZEN CORN-ON-THE-COB [7/27/70   52.931]

Grades:	"A" or	"B" or	"SUB-
	"FANCY"	"EXTRA	STANDARD"
		STANDARD"	

Minimum Score: 90   80   Less than 80

Tolerant to bacterial wilt. 12 to 14 rowed. Ears 7-3/4 in.; **Golden Cross Bantam** 85 days. Highly resistant to bacterial wilt and very prolific. Extremely uniform in plant and ear characteristics and in maturity. 10 to 14 rowed. Stalks 6 ft., sturdy. Ears 7-1/2 to 8 in.; **Golden Rocket** 67 days. Recommended for early planting. Primarily 12 rowed. Stalks 5-1/2 ft., ears 7 in. Kernels medium width and quality very good; **NK199** 84 days. High yield, narrow, very deep kernels, bright golden color, of excellent flavor; **Seneca Beauty** 65 days. A second early quality corn having size, appearance, and yield, fine flavor, and tender kernels. 12 rowed. Plant 5 ft., ears 8 in.; **Seneca Chief** 85 days. Yielded more marketable ears than any other hybrid tested in our trials. Highly resistant to wilt and Maize Dwarf Mosaic disease. Extra small cob and deep narrow kernels. 9 in. straight rowed ears; **Seneca Explorer** 64 days. Outstanding cold resistance and seeding vigor permitting early planting. Mostly 12 rowed, filled right to the tip. Plants 4 ft., ears 7-1/2 to 8 in.; **Seneca Golden** 72 days. Early midseason. Strong seedling vigor, high quality, outstanding cold resistance. Especially adapted for northeastern U.S. and Canada. Plant 5-1/2 ft., ears medium size."

In Florida, the leading sweet corn production state, some of the main varieties are *Iobelle, Florigold,* and *Illini Super-Sweet.* Tests in Florida in 1963-65, of spring plantings in organic soil, yielded the following average characteristics: **Iobelle [Florida 104]**, a highly productive midseason yellow hybrid, plant 6.6 ft., ears 7.5 in. long, 1.72 in. diameter, 14 to 16 rowed; **Florigold 107**, a highly productive yellow hybrid adapted for spring production, plant 6.6 ft., ears 7.7 in. long, 1.68 in. diameter, 14 rowed; **Illinichief Super-Sweet**, with unusually good retention of sugar content, plant 6.3 ft., ears 7.9 in. long, 1.81 in. diameter, 16 rowed.

CONTAINERS: Corn is shipped largely in wirebound crates, some in wet strength paper and polyethylene bags. Some typical inside dimensions of containers are given in the following table from data of the Uniform Classification Committee:

Container No.	Type	Inside Dimensions [inches]	Tariff No.
3726	Wirebound	7-3/4 x 14 x 21-1/8	1-H
3727	Wirebound	7-3/4 x 14 x 22-5/8	1-H
3728	Wirebound	9 x 14 x 22-9/16	1-H
3730	Wirebound	9 x 11 x 21-7/8	2-G, 4-C, 823-D
3731	Wirebound	9 x 11-15/16 x 21-7/8	823-D
3733	Wirebound	8 x 11 x 21-7/8	823-D
3734	Wirebound	9 x 11-15/16 x 23-5/8	823-D
7596	Polyethylene	Not specified	1-H, 2-G, 4-C, 823-D

SERVINGS AND WEIGHTS: In order to obtain 25 portions of sweet corn, a buyer for group feeding would need to purchase 1-3/4 doz. ears for 3 oz. portions of cooked kernels; for 25 portions of sweet corn cooked on the cob, he would need to purchase 25 ears; the usual 5-doz. crate or bag of sweet corn would provide 60 portions (1 ear each) of corn-on-the-cob.

The following table from USDA's *Food Buying Guide for Type A School Lunches*, January 1964, gives yields of sweet corn, with and without husks, by various size portions, and purchase units (in pounds) for 100 servings of each:

Food as Purchased	Purchase Unit	Servings per Purchase Unit	Serving Size or Portion	Purchase Units for 100 Servings	Additional Yield Information
With husks	lb.	2.00	1 medium ear (about 1/2 cup cooked)	50	1 lb. AP = 0.37 lb. edible portion cooked
	lb.	2.14	1/2 cup cooked	46-3/4	
		4.28	1/4 cup cooked	23-1/2	
Without husks	lb.	3.00	1 medium ear (about 1/2 cup cooked)	33-1/2	

Food as Purchased	Purchase Unit	Servings per Purchase Unit	Servings Size or Portion	Purchase Units for 100 Servings	Additional Yield Information
lb.		3.30	1/2 cup cooked	30-1/2	1 lb. AP = 0.55 lb. raw cut corn.
		6.60	1/4 cup cooked	15-1/4	

QUALITY: A recent USDA buying guide suggests, *"Look for:* fresh, succulent husks with good green color, silk-ends that are free from decay or worm injury, and stem ends (opposite from the silk) that are not too discolored or dried. Select ears that are well covered with plump, not-too-mature kernels; *Avoid:* ears with under-developed kernels which lack yellow color (in yellow corn), old ears with very large kernels, and ears with dark yellow kernels with depressed areas on the outer surface. Also avoid ears of corn with yellowed, wilted, or dried husks, or discolored and dried-out stem ends."

"Sweet corn may be either yellow or white, but is mostly yellow. Taste will tell. The white has virtually no vitamin A while the yellow is a fairly good source." Very little white corn is now marketed fresh.

Of prime importance to quality is rapid cooling after harvest. Studies have shown that the rate of sugar loss increases rapidly as temperature increases. As early as 1919, data was presented showing that sweet corn stored one day at 86°F. lost 50 percent of its total sugar. For the same period at 68°F., the loss was 26 percent; at 50°F., 17 percent; and at 32°F., only 8 percent. It was found that after about 62 percent loss of total sugar, an equilibrium was reached regardless of temperature. Raising or lowering the temperature, however, hastens or delays the attainment of the equilibrium.

GRADES: U.S. grade standards for green corn provide three grades, U.S. Fancy, U.S. 1, and U.S. 2. *"U.S. Fancy* consists of ears of green corn of similar varietal characteristics, which are well trimmed, well developed, and which are free from smut, decay, worms, or insect injury, and free from injury caused by rust, discoloration, birds, other disease, or mechanical or other means. Cobs shall be fairly well filled, with plump and milky kernels, and well covered with fresh husks. The length of each cob shall be not less than 6 in. and the ears shall not be clipped.

"*U.S. 1* consists of ears of green corn of similar varietal characteristics which are well trimmed, well developed, and which are free from smut and decay, and free from injury caused by rust, and free from damage caused by discoloration, birds, worms, other insects, other disease, or mechanical or other means. Cobs shall be fairly well filled, with plump and milky kernels, and fairly well covered with fresh husks. Each ear may be clipped, but each clipped ear shall be properly clipped. Unless otherwise specified, the length of each cob, clipped or unclipped, shall be not less than 5 in.

"*U.S. 2* consists of ears of green corn of similar varietal characteristics which are fairly well trimmed, fairly well developed, and which are free from smut and decay, and free from serious damage caused by birds, worms, other insects, other disease, or mechanical or other means. Cobs shall not be poorly filled, and kernels shall be plump and milky, and fairly well covered with fresh husks. Each ear may be clipped, but each ear shall be properly clipped. Unless otherwise specified, the length of each cob, clipped or unclipped, shall be not less than 4 in."

It should be noted that the standards specify green corn, not sweet corn. It would be advisable, therefore, for a buyer to specify "sweet corn" of a certain grade to avoid the chance of receiving field corn which otherwise meets the grade standards.

WHOLE KERNEL CORN—Canned [7/30/52]

Grade A: Color: Kernels possess a practically uniform color typical of tender sweet corn; product is bright and practically free from "off variety" kernels. CUT—The appearance of the product is not more than slightly affected by the presence of ragged cut kernels, torn kernels, irregular cut kernels, and kernels with attached cob tissue. **Defects:** Defects present do not more than slightly affect the appearance or eating quality. **Tenderness and Maturity:** Kernels are in the milk or early cream stage of maturity and have a tender texture. **Flavor:** Possess very good flavor including added seasoning ingredients; has a very good characteristic flavor and odor typical of tender, canned sweet corn.

Grade B: Color: Kernels possess a reasonably uniform color typical of reasonably tender sweet corn; product may lack brightness, but not to the extent that the appearance is materially affected, and is reasonably free from "off variety" kernels. CUT—The appearance is not materially affected by the presence of ragged cut kernels, torn kernels, irregular cut kernels, and kernels with attached cob tissue. **Defects:** Defects do not materially affect the appearance or eating quality of the product. **Tenderness and Maturity:** Reasonably tender meaning that the kernels are in the cream stage of maturity and have a reasonably tender texture. **Flavor:** Possess a good flavor including added seasoning ingredients; has a good characteristic flavor, etc. (see Grade A).

Grade C: Color: Kernels possess a fairly uniform color; the product may be dull, but not to the extent that the appearance is seriously affected, and is fairly free from "off variety" kernels. CUT—Appearance is not seriously affected by presence of ragged cut kernels, etc. (see Grade A). **Defects:** For each 14 oz. there may be present: not more than 1 cu. centimeter of pieces of cob; not more than 1 sq. in. of husk; and that for each 20 oz. there may be present not more than 1 brown or black discolored piece of kernel; and that for each 1 oz. there may be present: not more than 7 in. of silk; provided that pieces of cob, silk, or other harmless, extraneous vegetable matter, pulled kernels, ragged kernels, crushed kernels, loose skins, and damaged or seriously damaged kernels do not seriously affect the appearance or eating quality. **Tenderness and Maturity:** Kernels are in early dough and may be firm but not hard or tough. The weight of the alcohol or soluble solids shall not exceed 27 percent of the drained weight. **Flavor:** Fairly good flavor, product may be lacking in good flavor and odor, but is free from objectionable flavors and odors of any kind.

WHOLE KERNEL CORN—Frozen [8/1/52]

Grade A: Color: Practically uniform, typical of tender sweet corn; product bright, practically free from "off variety" kernels. **Defects:** Practically free from pieces of cob, husk, silk, other harmless, extraneous vegetable matter; pulled, ragged, crushed, damaged, seriously damaged kernels, loose skins that do not more than slightly affect the appearance or eating quality. **Tenderness and Maturity:** Kernels in milk or early cream stage of maturity, tender texture.

Grade B: Color: Reasonably uniform, typical of reasonably tender sweet corn; product reasonably bright, reasonably free from "off variety" kernels. **Defects:** Reasonably free from (that do not materially affect) etc. See Grade A. **Tenderness and Maturity:** Kernels in cream stage of maturity, reasonably tender texture.

Grade C: Color: Fairly uniform, typical of fairly tender sweet corn; product may be dull but appearance not seriously affected, fairly free from "off variety" kernels. **Defects:** Fairly free from (that do not seriously affect), etc., See Grade A. **Tenderness and Maturity:** Kernels in early dough or dough stage, fairly tender texture.

CORN, Cream Style—Canned [7/27/52]

Grade A: Color: Cut kernels possess a practically uniform color typical of tender sweet corn, and the product is bright and is practically free from "off variety" kernels. **Consistency:** Possess a heavy, cream-like consistency, with not more than a slight appearance of curdling; forms a slightly mounded mass, and at the end of 2 minutes after emptying there is practically no separation of free liquor. **Defects:** Practically free from defects, meaning all defects may be present that do not more than slightly affect appearance or eating quality of the product. **Tenderness and Maturity:** Kernels are in the milk, early cream, or middle cream stage of maturity; have a tender texture, and the pieces of the interior portions of corn kernels or ground kernels are characteristic of sweet corn in milk, early cream, or middle cream stage of maturity. **Flavor:** Product, including added seasoning ingredients, has a very good characteristic flavor and odor typical of tender canned sweet corn.

Grade B: Color: May lack brightness but not to the extent that the appearance is materially affected and is reasonably free from "off variety" kernels. **Consistency:** Reasonably good consistency, with not more than a moderate appearance of curdling; may flow just enough to level off to a nearly uniform depth; or may be moderately stiff and mounded, and at the end of 2 minutes after emptying there may be a slight separation of free liquor. **Defects:** Reasonably free from defects, meaning all defects may be present that do not materially affect the appearance, etc. of product. **Tenderness and Maturity:** Kernels are in the middle cream stage to late cream stage maturity; have a reasonably tender texture, and pieces of the interior

This special testing device was developed by FDA to check cream style corn. Corn is too "soupy" to meet the quality standard if a given quantity spreads too far on graduated plated.

portions of corn kernels or ground kernels are characteristic of sweet corn in the middle cream to late cream stage of maturity. **Flavor:** Has good characteristic flavor and odor typical of reasonably tender canned sweet corn.

Grade C: Color: Kernels possess a fairly uniform color typical of fairly tender sweet corn; the product may be dull, but not to the extent that the appearance is seriously affected, and is fairly free from "off variety" kernels. **Consistency:** May be thin but not excessively thin, or thick but not excessively curdled, and at the end of 2 minutes after emptying there may be a moderate but not excessive separation of free liquor. The approximate circular area over which the product spreads when emptied on a dry flat surface shall not exceed 12 in., except when the washed, drained residue of canned cream style corn contains more than 20 percent of alcohol insoluble solids, the average diameter of the area over which the product spreads shall not exceed 10 in. **Defects:** Fairly free from defects meaning that for each 20 oz. of net weight there may be present: not more than 1 cu. centimeter of pieces of cob; and not more than 1 sq. in. (1 in. x 1 in.) of husk; and that for each 2 oz. there may be present not more than 1 brown or black discolored kernel or discolored piece of kernel; and that for each 1 oz. there may be present: not more than 6 in. of silk; provided, that all defects do not seriously affect the appearance or eating quality. **Tenderness and Maturity:** Kernels are in the early dough or dough stage of maturity, may be firm but not hard or tough, and the pieces of the interior portions of corn kernels or ground kernels are characteristic of sweet corn in the dough stage of maturity. The weight of the alcohol insoluble solids of the washed, drained material does not exceed 27 percent of the weight of such material. **Flavor:** Product may be lacking in good flavors and odors but is free from objectionable flavors and odors of any kind.

CORN-ON-THE-COB—Frozen [7/27/70]

Grade A [or Fancy]: Flavor and Odor: "Good flavor and odor" means a good, characteristic, normal flavor and odor, and product is free from objectionable flavors and odors of any kind. **Color:** "Good color" means that the corn has a typical bright color and complies with the requirements for U.S. Grade A in Table I. **Size:** "Practically uniform in size" means

the differences in length and/or diameter of the ears do not exceed variations allowed for Grade A for the applicable style, in Table II. **Development:** "Well developed" means the ears are well filled with matured kernels, and the development defects present do not exceed the limits in Table III. **Defects:** Any combination of defects may slightly, but not materially, detract from the appearance or edibility of the product, but the defects may not exceed the limits in Table IV. **Tenderness and Maturity:** Tender means that the kernels are in the milk or early cream stage of maturity, the pericarp is tender, and none of the ears are in the blister stage.

Grade B [or Extra Standard]: "Reasonably good flavor and odor" means that the product may not have good flavor and odor but is free from objectionable flavors and odors. **Color:** Color may be slightly dull but product is not of abnormal color and must comply with requirements for U.S. Grade B in Table I. **Size:** Variations in the length and/or diameter of the ears may not exceed the variations allowed for U.S. Grade B in Table II. **Development:** Ears are well filled with kernels and the appearance of none of the ears is seriously affected by missing or undeveloped kernels; and developmental defects do not exceed the allowances in Table III. **Defects:** Defects present may not seriously detract from the edibility or appearance of the product nor exceed the limits in Table IV and V. **Tenderness and Maturity:** Kernels are in the cream stage or better stage of maturity, the pericarp is fairly tender, and none of the ears are in the blister stage. **Sstd:** Fails to meet requirements.

TABLE I—REQUIREMENTS FOR UNIFORMITY OF COLOR AND OFF-VARIETY KERNELS

	Uniformity of Color		Off-Variety Kernels	
	Each ear in the sample unit	All ears in the sample unit	Each ear in the sample unit	All ears in the sample unit
			Maximum number	
U.S. Grade A	Practically uniform	Reasonably uniform	3 kernels	6 kernels
U.S. Grade B	Reasonably uniform	Fairly uniform	15 kernels	30 kernels

TABLE II—VARIATION LIMITS FOR DIAMETER AND LENGTH

	Trimmed Style				Natural Style [untrimmed]	
	Regular Length Ears		Short Length Ears			
	Diameter	Length	Diameter	Length	Diameter	Length
	Maximum variation in sample unit					
U.S. Grade A	1/2 in.	3/4 in.	1/2 in.	1/2 in.	1/2 in.	1-1/2 in.
U.S. Grade B	3/4 in.	1 in.	3/4 in.	1/2 in.	3/4 in.	2 in.

TABLE III—DEFECTS AND DEFINITIONS

Type of Development Defect [applicable to each ear, regardless of length]	Classification	
	Minor	Major
Twisted ear: An ear twisted—more than the width of 4 rows of kernels or more than 1/4 of the circumference—from one end to the other	X	
Nonparallel kernels: (Not applicable to varieties which characteristically have staggered rows.) An ear having an area comprised of three (3) or more adjacent nonparallel rows extending more than two (2) in., lengthwise, of the ear	X	
Separation of rows exceeding 1/2 the length of the ear:		
One space showing cob more than 1/4, but not more than 1/2, the width of an average size kernel	X	
Two or more such spaces showing cob more than 1/4, but not more than 1/2, the width of an average size kernel		X
A space or spaces showing cob more than 1/2 the width of an average size kernel		X

TABLE III—DEVELOPMENT DEFECTS FOR EACH GRADE

Grade Classification	Total of Minor only [applicable only when there are no major]	Total of Minor and Major	Limit for Major
	Maximum in the sample unit		
U.S. Grade A	3	2	1
U.S. Grade B	6	4	2

TABLE IV—TYPES OF DEFECTS AND DEFINITIONS

	Classification		
	Minor	Major	Severe
Applicable to an individual ear, regardless of length			
Crushed or broken kernels (other than those at end of ears caused by trimming or cutting):			
Short length ears:			
7 to 15 kernels	X		
16 to 30 kernels		X	
More than 30 kernels			X
or			
16 or more kernels in one area materially affecting the appearance of the ear			X
Regular length ears:			
10 to 25 kernels	X		
26 to 50 kernels		X	
More than 50 kernels			X
or			
26 or more kernels in one area materially affecting the appearance of the ear			X
Blemished kernels (includes, but is not limited to, kernels affected by discoloration, blemishes, pathological injury, or other damage):			
Short length ears:			
1 or 2 kernels	X		
3 or 4 kernels		X	
More than 4 kernels			X
Regular length ears:			
2 or 3 kernels	X		
4, 5, or 6 kernels		X	
More than 6 kernels			X
Poorly trimmed ears:			
More than 30°, but not more than 45°, from a right-angle cut	X		
More than 45° from a right-angle cut		X	
Stalks:			
More than 1/4 in., but not more than 1/2 in. of attached stalk	X		
More than 1/2 in. of attached stalk		X	

(Cont.)

TABLE IV—TYPES OF DEFECTS AND DEFINITIONS [Cont.]	Classification		
	Minor	Major	Severe
Applicable to an individual ear, regardless of length			
The following are aggregated and apply to the entire sample unit			
Attached or loose husk:			
More than one (1) sq. in., but not more than two (2) sq. in.	X		
More than two (2) sq. in. but not more than three (3) sq. in.		X	
More than three (3) sq. in.			X
Dark or readily noticeable silk (strands one (1) in. long or longer):			
10 to 20 in.	X		
21 to 30 in.		X	
Over 30 in.			X

TABLE V—DEFECTS FOR EACH GRADE

Grade Classification	Total of Minor only [applicable only when there are no Major or Severe]	Total of Minor, Major, and Severe	Limit for Major and Severe	Limit for Severe
Maximum per sample unit				
U.S. Grade A	6	4	1	0
U.S. Grade B	12	9	3	1

CUCUMBERS*

USES: Sliced cucumbers blend delightfully into a wide variety of raw salads, as with tomatoes, green peppers and radishes used with any number of dressings and with or without meat, fish or cheese. They are excellent sliced, salted and peppered, and allowed to marinate in vinegar and water, and can be combined in this marinade with other vegetables. Usually they are peeled before slicing, but some eat peel and all, especially if the peel is not waxed. Most of the wax can be removed by placing the cucumber under a stream of very hot water, then wiping with a paper towel.

Here are some cucumber ideas: slice lengthwise into sticks with the skin left on to add color to a relish tray; use sliced in sandwiches; cut in bits and serve with condiments and sour cream; combine pineapple, cabbage, and cucumber in a molded salad; dice and add to any mixed salad; prepare a cucumber-fresh fruit salad with such fruits as pears, grapes, oranges, and lemons; cucumber slices go fine with lemonade; try a fresh cucumber lemon relish with chopped cucumber, some parsley, fresh lemon juice, and condiments; or a cucumber-seafood cocktail with chili sauce, chopped cucumber, lemon juice, horseradish and liquid hot pepper sauce.

Cucumber tartar sauce is chopped cucumber, mayonnaise, lemon juice, chopped green olives, minced fresh onions, capers, salt, and pepper. Cucumbers, thickly cut, are good as a hot vegetable sauteed 3 to 4 minutes in melted butter or margarine. Or spread cucumber slices with a cream cheese-anchovy spread, or curried egg spread, or deviled ham spread for cucumber canapes. Wilt cucumbers by cooking for 3 to 4 minute, slice and serve with dilly sour cream.

MARKETING SEASON: Fresh cucumbers are on the market all year, with the peak in August, September, and October and the least supply in January through March. The following table shows monthly availability of this vegetable expressed as a percentage of the total annual supply of around 620 million lb. average for the last 5 years. Percentages are rounded, therefore do not come out to exactly 100 percent.

MONTHLY AVAILABILITY OF CUCUMBERS EXPRESSED AS A PERCENTAGE OF TOTAL ANNUAL SUPPLY

Jan.	Feb.	Mar.	Apr.	May	June
%	%	%	%	%	%
5	5	5	7	11	14

July	Aug.	Sept.	Oct.	Nov.	Dec.
%	%	%	%	%	%
13	10	9	9	7	6

VARIETIES: "Most modern varieties have gradually evolved from the European sorts, either as selections from direct importations or as the result of planned or natural hybridization. Up to 1872, when Tailby's Hybrid was first exhibited, there had been little or no active interest shown toward new sorts."

There are a great number of varieties of slicing cucumbers but some of the open pollinated varieties are Ashley, Marketer, Polomar, Long Marketer, Marketmore, Poinsett, and Straight Eight. Some hybrid slicer types are Cherokee 7,

*UFFVA

Gemini 7, Hybrid Ashley, and High Mark II.

Ashley Developed by Clemson Truck Experiment Station; 8 to 9 in. long, 2-1/4 in. diameter, straight with taper toward the stem end, white spines, skin dark green, resistant to downy mildew, open pollinated, mid-season, about 70 days.

Marketer For many years, a standard shipping variety; 8 in. long, 2 to 2-1/4 in. in diameter, straight and slightly tapered toward both ends, white spines, skin dark green, heavy yielder, holds its color well, open pollinated, mid-season, about 70 days.

Palomar Favorite shipping variety in South because of earliness, 8 to 9 in. long, 2-1/4 in. diameter, tapered at ends, white spines, skin very dark green, resistant to downy mildew and powdery mildew, open pollinated, medium early, about 64 days.

Long Marketer Has been a popular shipping type, longer and slimmer than Marketer, 8 to 9 in. long, 2-1/4 in. diameter, slender and tapered at stem end, white spines, skin dark green, open pollinated, mid-season, about 70 days. (Long Marketer is susceptible to all the important cucumber diseases and is being rapidly replaced by disease-resistant hybrids.)

Marketmore A monoecious (with unisexual flowers, both sexes on same plant), vigorous grower, 8 in. long, 2 to 2-1/4 in. in diameter, straight with slight taper at both ends, white spines, skin dark green, field resistance to scab and mosaic, open pollinated, late season, about 76 days.

Poinsett Developed by Clemson Truck Experiment Station; vine vigor superior to Ashley and has out-produced Ashley and Polaris in Southern Co-op trials for three seasons; 8 to 8-1/2 in. long, 2-1/4 to 2-3/8 in. diameter, slight taper, spines white, skin dark green, high resistance to downy and powdery mildew, moderate resistance to anthracnose and angular leaf spot, open pollinated, mid-season about 70 days.

Straight Eight Introduced many years ago and now used mainly as a packet item for home gardens, 8 in. long, 2-1/4 in. diameter, straight with smooth rounded ends, white spines, skin medium dark green, open pollinated, early, about 62 days.

Cherokee 7 [hybrid] Developed by Clemson Truck Experiment Station, for Southern fresh market plantings; earlier than Ashley and produces a high percentage of its total crop within the first 7 to 10 days of bearing; 7-3/4 to 8-3/4 in. long, 2 to 2-1/4 in. diameter, straight with taper at the stem end, white spines, skin dark green, resistant to downy and powdery mildew, anthracnose and angular leafspot, earlier than mid-season Ashley, about 66 to 68 days.

Gemini [hybrid] Developed by Clemson Truck Experiment Station, gynoecious and prolific with female blossoms at almost every node, produces high percentage of crop within first 7 to 10 days of bearing, 7-1/2 to 8-1/2 in. long, 2 to 2-1/4 in. diameter, blocky, cylindrical, with white spines, skin very dark, resistant to scab and mosaic, moderately resistant to anthracnose and angular leafspot, downy and powdery mildew, medium early, about 70 days.

Hybrid Ashley Developed by Ferry-Morse, shows increased vigor in vines, is more productive and earlier than Ashley, 8-1/2 in. long, 2-1/4 in. diameter, straight with a tapered stem end, white spines, dark green skin, tolerant to downy mildew, medium early, about 66 days.

High Mark II Plants vigorous and highly productive, reaching maturity a few days after Ashley, 7 to 9 in. long, cylindrical and blocky at ends, white spines, skin very dark, resistant to mosaic, scab and downy mildew, medium as to season, suitable for field or greenhouse.

CONTAINERS: Field grown cucumbers are packed in wire-bound crates or cartons holding 50 to 55 lb. net; the bushel basket holding 50 to 55 lb.; the LA lug and a carton holding 30 to 32 lb. Greenhouse cucumbers may be packed in a carton holding 8 to 10 lb. or in larger cartons.

Packing may be done in a field shed or in a central packing house. Fruits are washed, often wax is applied to slow down evaporation and shriveling, and fruits are sorted by size and grade. Usually they are packed in layers.

QUALITY: Grade standards facilitate trading, but are not familiar to consumers, who must rely mainly on appearance. Cucumbers should be green, since a yellow color indicates old age and that the seeds are hard. Large cucumbers are generally more likely to have large seeds than small ones of similar color. Reject cucumbers that show any puffiness; also reject any that are withered or shriveled. Keep them cool (45 to 50°F.) and humid, and use within a few days.

GRADES: U.S. grade standards effective March 1, 1958 for field grown cucumbers provide for six grades, U.S. Fancy, U.S. Extra 1, U.S. 1, U.S. 1 Small, U.S. 1 Large and U.S. 2. It is practical to give only samples of these grades here.

CUCUMBERS

FRESH [3/1/58   51.2220]
Grades: U.S. Fancy; U.S. Extra No. 1; U.S. No. 1; U.S. No. 1 Small;
     U.S. No. 1 Large; U.S. No. 2
PICKLING CUCUMBERS [12/10/36   51.4170]
Grades: U.S. No. 1; U.S. No. 2; U.S. No. 3
GREENHOUSE CUCUMBERS [10/1/34   51.3855]
Grades: U.S. Fancy; U.S. No. 1; U.S. No. 2

MINIMUM SHAPES PERMISSIBLE IN U. S. FANCY GRADE
(About 1/3 actual size)

MINIMUM SHAPES PERMISSIBLE IN U. S. NO. 1 GRADE
(About 1/3 actual size)

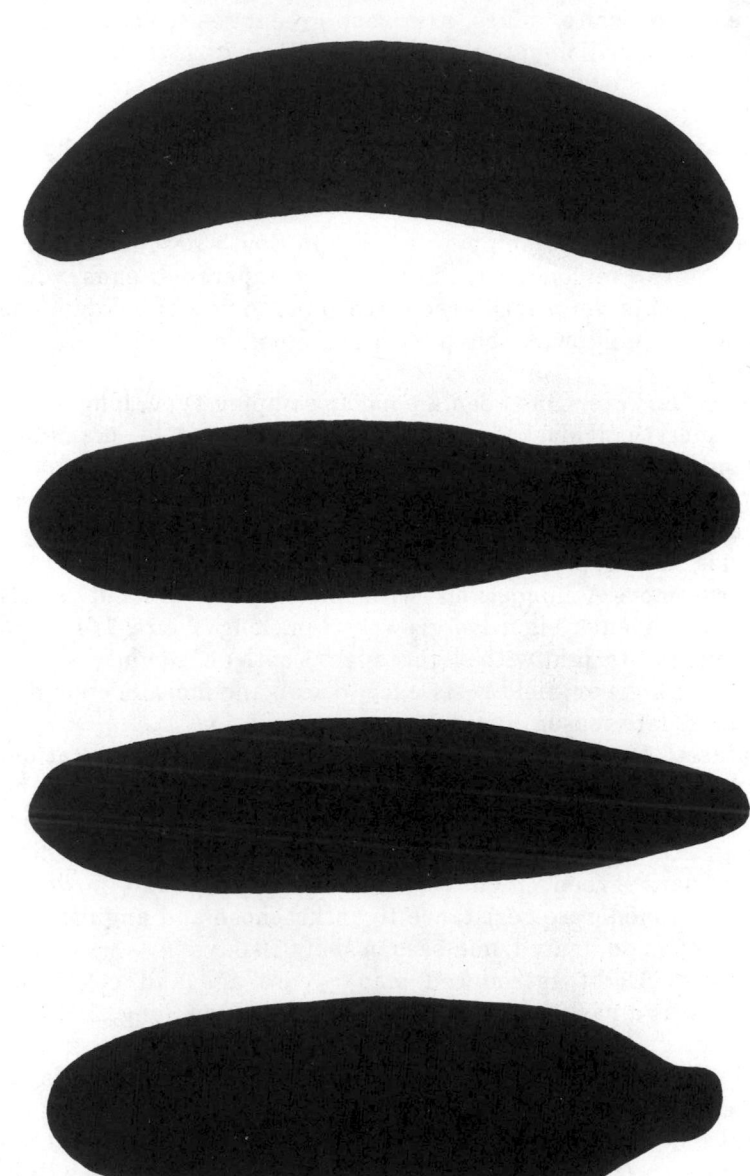

MINIMUM SHAPES PERMISSIBLE IN U. S. NO. 2 GRADE
(About 1/3 actual size)

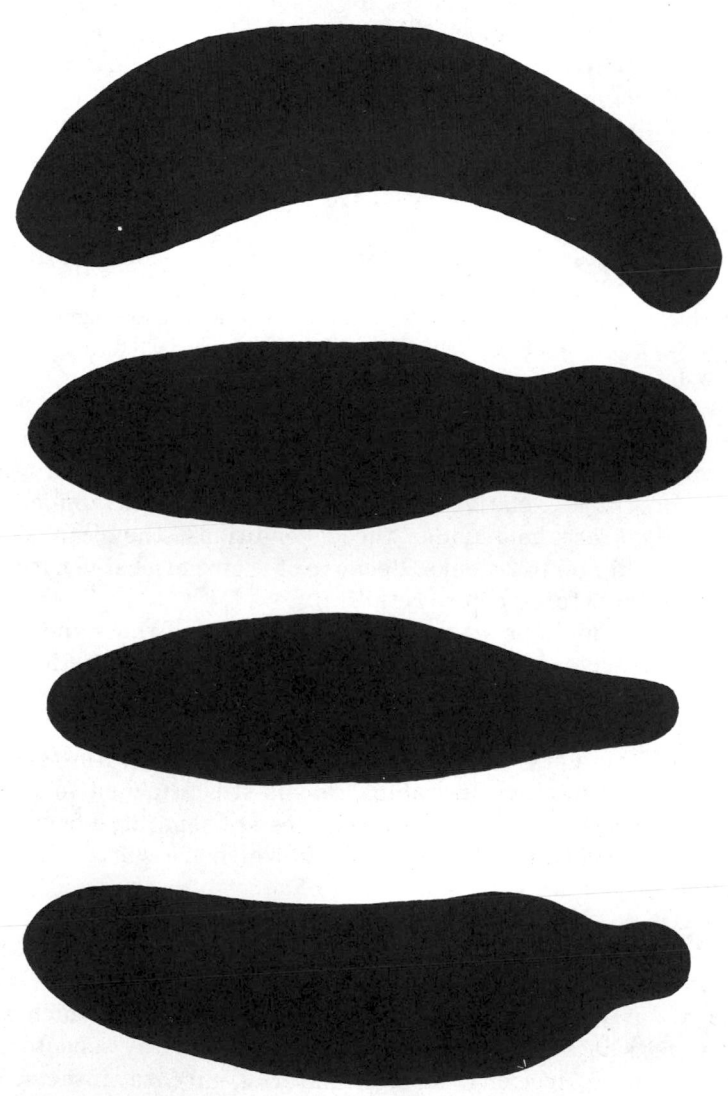

"*U.S. 1* consists of cucumbers which are fairly well colored, fairly well formed, not overgrown, and which are fresh, firm, and free from decay, sunscald, and from damage caused by scars, yellowing sunburn, dirt or other foreign material, freezing, mosaic or other disease, insects, cuts, bruises, mechanical or other means. (a) Unless otherwise specified, the maximum diameter of each cucumber shall be not more than 2-3/8 in. and the length of each cucumber shall be not less than 6 in.

"*U.S. 1 Small* consists of cucumbers which meet all requirements for the U.S. 1 grade except for size. (a) The diameter of each cucumber shall be not less than 1-1/2 in. or more than 2 in. There are no requirements for length.

"*U.S. 1 Large* consists of cucumbers which meet all requirements for U.S. 1 grade except for size. (a) The minimum diameter of each cucumber shall be not less than 2-1/4 in. and, unless otherwise specified, the length of each cucumber shall be not less than 6 in. There are no maximum diameter and length requirements."

DANDELIONS*

USES: The leaves of the dandelion plant are used as a green vegetable. They are gathered when young and tender and thoroughly cleaned. They can be eaten raw in a green salad or cooked, like spinach. To cook, put greens in a pan with a small amount of water, cover and steam 10 to 20 minutes. Serve with butter or vinegar. Bacon, fat salt pork, or sauteed onions can be added before cooking for complementary flavoring. For more elaborate dishes, dandelion greens can be substituted for spinach in recipes such as quiche, eggs florentine, and creamed spinach.

Dandelion wine is made from the flowers of the plant. The basic ingredients are the flower heads and water in equal amounts, sugar, yeast, and chopped oranges and lemons. Dandelion "coffee" is made from the tap root of a mature plant, which may be as long as 3 ft. The root is dug up, cleaned, roasted in an oven until brown, and then ground in a coffee mill.

A substance called Taraxacum can be extracted from dandelion roots. It has long been used in medicine and home
*UFFVA

remedies, although there is no convincing reason for believing it possesses any therapeutic virtues.

MARKETING SEASON: Dandelions are available on a year-round basis with the peak supply in April and May. The following table shows monthly availability expressed as percentage of the total annual supply. It was compiled in 1964 and although the total supply has probably decreased since then, the relative amount available each month has not changed appreciably.

MONTHLY AVAILABILITY OF DANDELIONS EXPRESSED AS PERCENTAGE OF TOTAL ANNUAL SUPPLY

Jan.	Feb.	Mar.	Apr.	May	June
%	%	%	%	%	%
3	4	10	18	12	10

July	Aug.	Sept.	Oct.	Nov.	Dec.
%	%	%	%	%	%
9	8	8	9	6	3

SOURCES OF SUPPLY: Dandelion greens being sold in New York and Chicago wholesale markets each month in 1974 were grown in the following states:

January	Texas, Florida
February	Texas, Florida
March	Texas, Florida, New Jersey
April	Texas, New Jersey
May	New Jersey
June	New Jersey
July	New Jersey, New York (Long Island), Illinois
August	New Jersey, New York (Long Island), Illinois
September	New Jersey, New York (Long Island), Illinois
October	New Jersey, New York (Long Island), Illinois
November	Florida, New York (Long Island), New Jersey
December	Texas, Florida

VARIETIES: Improved horticultural varieties, mostly of French origin, have been developed for commercial cultivation from the wild T. officinale. These generally have larger leaves which are more tender, less bitter, and of lighter green color than wild plants. Varieties being sold are:

Thick Leaf Matures in 95 days. "Plants are large with many thick leaves."

Improved Thick Leaf Leaves are large, partially toothed, thick in texture, prolific, dark green, blanch easily, and are fairly tender. Growth is compact. Plant spreads to 18 to 24 in. across.

Arlington Thick Leaf Leaves form a 14 to 18 in. rosette, are dark green, broad, thick, and tender. Plant is semi-erect.

PACKAGING AND CONTAINERS: Dandelions are shipped to terminal markets packed in a variety of containers, with the greens being either loose or in bunches. *The USDA Market News Service* for the Chicago and New York wholesale markets reports the following types of containers from each growing area:

Texas	wirebound crates and cartons holding 24 to 36 bunches each
Florida	bushel baskets or cartons containing loose greens
New York	cartons containing 15 to 20 bunches each
New Jersey	cartons containing 12 to 24 bunches each

TRANSPORTATION AND STORAGE CONDITIONS: Dandelion greens are shipped under conditions similar to those recommended for spinach. USDA recommendations are: temperature, 32°F., relative humidity, 90 to 95 percent, top-ice. If dandelions are held under these conditions, they can keep their quality up to 2 weeks. Because of their perishable nature, they are not stored before retailing.

Greens should be washed, dried, trimmed of roots and torn or wilted leaves, and stored in the refrigerator in a plastic bag. They will keep for at least 3 to 8 days, if not longer, if purchased when fresh.

QUALITY: Very young, fresh, green plants with tender leaves are the most desirable. Leaves still attached to roots are likely to be succulent; when leaves are separated from the base, they wilt rapidly. Avoid plants which are wilted, flabby, tough, or yellow as these are signs of age.

GRADES: U.S. standards for dandelion greens, effective Feb. 4, 1955, provide for one grade, U.S. 1. *U.S. 1* "consists of dandelion greens of similar varietal characteristics which are fresh, fairly tender, fairly clean, well trimmed, and which are free from decay, and free from damage caused by seedstems, discoloration, freezing, foreign material, disease, insects, or mechanical or other means."

"Tolerances for Defects In order to allow for variations incident to proper grading and handling, other than for mixtures of plants and cut leaves, not more than a total of 10 percent, by weight, of the units in any lot may fail to meet the requirements of the grade: provided that not more than one-half of this amount, or 5 percent, shall be allowed for serious damage by any cause, and including therein not more than 2 percent for decay."

"Tolerances for mixtures of plants and leaves Not more than 5 percent, by weight, of the dandelion greens packed as plants, in any lot, may consist of cut leaves or when packed as cut leaves may consist of plants."

"DEFINITIONS—'Similar varietal characteristics' means that the dandelion greens shall be of the same general color and character of the lot. 'Fresh' means that the greens are not more than slightly wilted. 'Fairly tender' means that the greens are not old, tough, or excessively fibrous. 'Fairly clean' means that the appearance of the greens is not materially affected by the presence of mud, dirt, or other foreign material. 'Well trimmed' as applied to plants means that they are cut at the crown of the root or cut so that the roots do not extend more than approximately 1-1/2 in. below the crown. 'Damage' means any defect which materially affects the appearance, or the edible or shipping quality, of the individual unit or the lot as a whole. Any one of the following defects, or any combination of defects, the seriousness of which exceeds the maximum allowed for any one defect, shall be considered as damage: (a) seedstems when more than 1/4 the length of the longest leaf, (b) discoloration when the appearance of the unit is materially affected by discoloration, (c) mechanical damage when the unit is badly crushed, torn, or broken."

EGGPLANT*

USES: Eggplant can be served as a substitute for or as an accompaniment to meat. In this country, it is usually sauteed or cut into strips and fried. In the Near and Far East, eggplant is stuffed with meat, and Italians usually saute slices in olive oil and cook it with plenty of tomato paste. Little eggplants may be cooked whole or stuffed for individual servings, while large ones are good for stuffing or making casserole dishes. Eggplant can be baked or broiled, scalloped, topped with cheese, creamed mushrooms, sour cream, hollandaise or tomato sauce ... marinated and sauteed as an hors d'oeuvre.

MARKETING SEASON: Fresh eggplant is on the market through the year, with relatively little variation in supply from month to month. Supplies are somewhat larger in August and September and lightest in February. The following table shows relative availability by months as calculated from unloads at Chicago, Los Angeles, Atlanta, New York, and Seattle.

PERCENTAGE OF TOTAL ANNUAL SUPPLY OF FRESH EGGPLANT AVAILABLE EACH MONTH

Jan.	Feb.	Mar.	Apr.	May	June
%	%	%	%	%	%
6	4	6	6	8	9

July	Aug.	Sept.	Oct.	Nov.	Dec.
%	%	%	%	%	%
10	12	12	11	9	7

VARIETIES: In the U.S. only large-fruited varieties of eggplant are grown commercially. Selection by growers and eating preferences of consumers have played a large part in reducing the numerous varieties to a few large, round, cylindrical, or bell-shaped types which are purple to dark purple in color, weighing from 1 to 5 lb.

According to the 1962 seed production, the leading varieties are listed in order of quantity grown, with percentage of total in each case: Black Beauty 44 percent; Florida Market 31 percent; and all other varieties 25 percent, including Fort Myers Market, Florida Beauty, New York Purple, and New Hampshire.

Black Beauty 23 to 30 in. tall, erect, compact, large-leaved, 4 to 6 fruits, produces well; *fruit:* very large, dark purple, smooth, glossy, globular to flattened egg shape, spineless, good quality, and flavor, has good retention of color after picking. Most popular variety in U.S. as it is fairly early and widely adapted. Originated in Swedesboro, N.J. about 1900. 85 days.

Florida Market 30 to 40 in. tall, very erect and heavy stemmed, productive over a long season, producing 8 to 10 fruits; late; *fruit:* rich deep purple, an elongated egg shape to tapered cylindrical, fruit produces high above ground for minimum losses

*UFFVA

EGGPLANT
FRESH [10/29/53   51.2190]
Grades: U.S. Fancy; U.S. No. 1; U.S. No. 2

from ground rots. Resistant to Phomopsis, etc. Not adapted to Northeast but well adapted to Florida. Originated by Florida AES in 1948. 85 days.

Fort Myers Market 30 to 36 in. tall, erect and strong stemmed, productive, 4 to 6 fruits, very vigorous; *fruit:* large, very dark purple, smooth, rarely lobed, elongated, and bell-shaped. 85 to 90 days.

Florida High Bush 30 to 40 in. tall (taller than most varieties), erect, heavy stemmed, holding fruit well above ground, 2 to 6 fruits; *fruit:* large, dark purple, elongated egg shape tapering gradually to stem end, smooth, moderately variable in color and size, good shipping quality. Introduced about 1905 by a Florida grower. 85 to 90 days.

New York Purple 30 to 36 in. tall, large, erect, branched, large-leaved, 5 to 8 fruits; *fruit:* deep purple, smooth, uniform, broad oval to blunt egg shape, very good quality. Developed by grower on Long Island about 1850. The modern strains of New York Improved are spineless and have been available since about 1900. 90 days.

New Hampshire 15 to 18 in. tall, spreading, heavily branched, medium sized leaves, 5 to 8 fruits, very productive; *fruits:* smaller than most American varieties, dark purple, nearly globular to blunt egg shape, smooth, glossy, uniform producer of high quality. Excellent northern variety. Developed by New Hampshire AES. 75 days.

Hybrid (F1) eggplant varieties are becoming popular with growers. **Black Magic Hybrid**, **Superhybrid**, and **Burpee Hybrid** are 3 which are rapidly being accepted. The hybrids are earlier than the standard varieties and are more vigorous than other commercial varieties.

CONTAINERS: The fruits of the eggplant are heavy, and care should be taken to avoid mechanical damage. Before packing, eggplants are usually graded somewhat to separate the sizes and to cull out inferior fruits. They are then washed, wrapped in individual papers, and carefully packed into containers to prevent the stems from puncturing the other fruits.

Eggplant is marketed in many types of containers, depending largely in each locality on the containers generally available for use with other commodities. The bushel basket has largely supplanted the pepper crate in Florida and the berry crate in Virginia. The bushel basket has a capacity of 2150 cu. in. and net weight of 33 to 35 lb. Other popular containers are the L.A. lug, capacity 1252 cu. in., net weight 19 to 21 lb.; and the 1-1/9 W/B crate or carton, capacity 2389 cu. in., net weight 37 to 39 lb.

SERVINGS AND WEIGHTS: An eggplant, weighing 1 lb., provides 5 servings of 1/2 cup each of cooked and sliced vegetable. To serve 100, the requirement is 20 lb. of eggplant ready to cook. For 1 lb. ready-to-cook, use 1.23 lb. (about 1 lb. 4 oz. as purchased). One bushel equals 33 lb.

QUALITY: A good quality eggplant is firm, heavy in relation to size, with a uniform, dark rich purple color, and free from scars or cuts. A wilted, shriveled, soft, or flabby eggplant will usually be bitter or otherwise poor in flavor. Worm injury can be seen on the surface and, if severe, will probably indicate excessive waste. Decay appears as dark brown spots on the surface and may progress very rapidly. Watch the size of the eggplants you buy. A good rule to follow is to choose pear shaped eggplants from 3 to 6 in. in diameter.

GRADES: U.S. standards for eggplant are U.S. Fancy, U.S. No. 1 and U.S. No. 2.

"U.S. No. 1 consists of eggplant of similar varietal characteristics, which are fairly well colored, firm, clean, fairly well shaped, and which are free from decay and worm holes, and free from damage caused by scars, freezing, disease, insects, or mechanical or other means. If count is specified, the eggplant shall be reasonable uniform in size in the containers. Not more than 10 percent by count of the eggplant in any container may be below the requirements, including not more than 1 percent for decay. 'Well colored' means that the eggplant has a uniform good color characteristic for that variety over practically the entire surface. 'Firm' means that the eggplant is not soft, flabby, or shriveled."

ENDIVE—ESCAROLE—CHICORY*

USES: The leafy forms of these vegetables are used raw as salad or cooked as greens. The witloof type is used raw as salad. Wash the greens well. When cooking, simmer them

*UFFVA

gently until tender in a tightly covered pan, with more or less water depending on your own taste. Use of large amounts of water tends to give a milder flavor in the final product, while use of less water gives stronger flavor and conserves more nutrients. Drain the greens and chop, if desired. Add a dab of margarine or butter, salt, and black pepper to taste, and reheat for a few minutes. These and other greens are good mixed with hard-boiled eggs. Mixing in some crisp bacon is another good way to tease the palate. Seasoning with lemon adds zip. Wilted endive is made by pouring hot bacon fat over the leaves. The greens can then be served with crumbled bits of bacon and maybe some grated onion. Avoid using soda in cooking any of the greens. It ruins texture, making the leaves soft and mushy, and destroys vitamin C. Endive, chicory, and escarole can be used in endless combinations with other greens in salad, with any of many dressings.

MARKETING SEASON: Endive—escarole—chicory are available all year in fairly even supply. Last year the supply each month, expressed as a percentage of the annual total was as follows:

MONTHLY AVAILABILITY OF ENDIVE—ESCAROLE—CHICORY EXPRESSED AS PERCENTAGE OF TOTAL ANNUAL SUPPLY

Jan.	Feb.	Mar.	Apr.	May	June
%	%	%	%	%	%
8	8	8	9	7	8

July	Aug.	Sept.	Oct.	Nov.	Dec.
%	%	%	%	%	%
9	9	8	10	8	8

VARIETIES: Seed dealers all list varieties of both broad-leaved endive (escarole) and a curly leaved endive. For escarole, almost all list Full Heart Batavian; and for endive (which commercially is always curly), they list several varieties, including Green Curled Ruffec or merely Ruffec, and Green Curled Pancalier, as well as some other variants.

"Endive *(Cichorium endivia)* is always marketed in the headed form, the larger heads weighing more than a pound. The heads are low, spreading, and loose-leaved. The leaves vary from deeply cut and deeply curled in some varieties to the broad, slightly cut, and curled leaf of escarole. The outer leaves are green, and the center leaves or heart and the midribs are pale green to creamy white.

Full Heart Batavian Most widely grown type of escarole; medium large, 12 to 15 in. across, upright to spreading growth, deep green, slightly crumpled, closely bunched with center leaves producing a well blanched heart; 80 to 90 days.

Ruffec 16 to 18 in. wide; curled and deeply cut; midribs white or green, thick; leaves can be tied up for blanching; 85 to 95 days.

Green Curled Pancalier 14 to 16 in. across; deeply cut, curly, dark green leaves like Ruffec, but midrib is rose tinted; 85 to 95 days.

There are 3 general forms of chicory, *(Cichorium intybus)* one grown for its large roots which are dried as a supplement for coffee; one that is used for greens, and one that is forced for production of a compact cluster of blanched leaves and known as Witloff.

Large-Rooted Magdeburg About 15 in. tall, medium green, with upright, dandelion-like foliage with fairly narrow leaves; root 12 to 14 in. long, tapered, white; young tender leaves can be used for greens at about 65 days; roots mature at about 120 days.

Cicoria San Pasquale Has compact growth of broader leaves than Magdeburg; light green color; used for greens; 70 days.

Cicoria Catalogna or Radichetta Has dandelion-like leaves useful for early greens; and flower shoots, which have a faint asparagus flavor, are also eaten; 65 days.

Witloof or French Endive 15 to 18 in. tall, foliage smooth, long, medium dark green; inner leaves and heart are used in salads; and, in fall, roots can be reset and forced indoors resulting in a second growth crown of self-blanching compact leaves. The blanched head of leaves is 4 to 5 in. long, tender, with a rich, mildly acrid flavor; 140 to 150 days.

CONTAINERS: Containers used include the bushel basket or tub holding 25 lb.; the 1-1/9 bu. wirebound crate holding 28 lb.; the WGA crate holding 60 to 62 lb., and the 2/3 WGA crate; the 24 qt. basket holding 18 to 19 lb.; and a wirebound crate holding 33 to 35 lb. Cartons holding 1-1/8 bu. are also used. Studies have been made on prepackaging endive and escarole in polyethylene bags in Florida, and shipping them to New York City. It was shown that dehydration losses could be reduced by such packaging in semi-moisture-proof film, with con-

ENDIVE, ESCAROLE, OR CHICORY
FRESH [10/1/64   51.3535]
Grades: U.S. No. 1

tinuous refrigeration. However, prepackaging may increase decay. Packaging is also being done at the terminal city where decay may be less of a problem because of the shorter time between packaging and sale.

SERVINGS AND WEIGHTS: One pound as purchased equals 0.74 lb. ready to serve raw. A pound as purchased 8.4 1/2 cup servings for salad or 16.8 1/4 cup servings. To serve 1/2 cup portions to 100 takes 12 lb. as purchased; and to serve 1/4 cup portions to 100 takes 6 lb.

QUALITY: "Best quality greens are fresh, young, tender, and green (other than deliberately blanched parts as in endive). Plants or leaves of any of the leafy vegetables to be used as greens, which show insect injury, coarse stems, dry or yellowing leaves, excessive dirt, or poor development are usually lacking in quality and may cause excessive waste. In any type of greens, the presence of seedstems indicates age and toughness. Flabby, wilted plants and leaves are generally undesirable.

GRADES: The U.S. standard grade for endive, escarole, or chicory (but not including so-called "French endive" or "Witloof" or chicory which is marketed for its roots) is *U.S. No. 1*. This "shall consist of plants of similar varietal characteristics, which are fresh, well trimmed, fairly well blanched, free from decay, and from damage caused by seedstems, broken, bruised, spotted or discolored leaves, wilting, dirt, disease, insects, or mechanical or other means. In order to allow for variations incident to proper grading and handling, not more than 10 percent by count of the plants in any container may be below the requirements of this grade, but not to exceed a total of 5 percent shall be allowed for defects causing serious damage, and not more than 2/5 of this amount, or 2 percent shall be allowed for decay."

GARLIC*

USES: Garlic is a flavor component in a wide variety of dishes, but usually in or on meats, vegetables, stews, soups, salads, dressings, tomato dishes, spaghetti, sauces, pickles, and sausages. Bread flavored with garlic and butter is much enjoyed. This vegetable is also extensively processed into dehydrated cloves, or slices, and into garlic powder. There is also a pureed garlic.

There are many claims of medicinal uses of garlic. Under the heading "Demons Beware," the Food and Drug Research Laboratories in New York in 1959 said: "Since ancient time, this lowly bulb has been credited with the power to drive away evil spirits. It was used as a preventive or cure for everything from the common cold to hydrophobia and was especially recommended in times of plague ... It is still used as an amulet and in the form of various preparations in many parts of the world, and certain garlic products are used in medicine even in this country. For some time, it has been known that compounds derived from garlic have a pronounced bactericidal effect which has been attributed to their reactivity for sufhydryl groups essential for the action of enzymes."

The Roman, Pliny, declared garlic to be a remedy for 61 ailments while Aristotle, Sotion, and Dioscorides praised its medicinal qualities. In India, garlic was touted for "improving the voice, intellect, and complexion, promoting the union of fractured bones, and helping to cure nearly all the ills that flesh is heir to." It was common in less scientific times to attribute virtually magical powers to a wide array of substances, edible or not.

MARKETING SEASON: Fresh garlic is on the market in all months. The following table shows monthly availability expressed as a percentage of the total annual supply which averages about 83 million lb., including imports.

MONTHLY AVAILABILITY OF GARLIC EXPRESSED AS PERCENTAGE OF TOTAL ANNUAL SUPPLY

Jan.	Feb.	Mar.	Apr.	May	June
%	%	%	%	%	%
6	9	10	9	7	7

July	Aug.	Sept.	Oct.	Nov.	Dec.
%	%	%	%	%	%
10	10	11	7	7	7

VARIETIES: "Garlic is an extremely variable species," says Jones and Mann. "Many strikingly distinct clones are known in cultivation and, as might be expected, some of these forms

*UFFVA

GARLIC

FRESH [9/4/44   51.3880]
Grades: U.S. No. 1

have been designated as botanical varieties of A. sativum ... Some 30 clones of garlic, collected from the U.S., South America, Europe, and Asia have been grown at Davis, Ca. ..." However, the authors find no adequate data on which to base recognition of varieties.

R. Ralph Clar, who wrote *Garlic Culture in Oregon* in 1955, recognized the varietal problem as follows: "There are many strains of garlic being grown, but for the most part, they are merely selections made by the various growers. This is a good way to improve the planting stock."

On the other hand, 3 "varieties" are recognized in Louisiana—the Creole, Italian, and Tahiti. The **Creole** is said to have a broader leaf than the Italian, greener tops, and generally larger cloves. The **Italian** has the strongest flavor and smallest cloves, which are pinkish. The **Tahiti** has large individual cloves, larger than those of either Italian and Creole, and the cloves are darker. (However, the Tahiti is not true garlic, but is probably Allium ampeloprasum, also called elephant garlic.)

"In California, three cultivars are grown: 'California Early' is high-yielding and early maturing but stores less well and has a lower content of solids than 'California Late'; 'Creole' does well in the hot southern interior, but is little grown elsewhere in the State."

CONTAINERS: The principal wholesale containers for garlic in California are the crate holding 30 lb. net and a carton holding the same amount. The weight range in these containers is 30 to 32 lb. The L.A. lug holding 21 lb. net with range of 20 to 22 is also used, as well as cartons containing 12 1-lb. display cartons; and also there are some 5-lb. cartons.

GRADES: U.S. standards for garlic, adopted in 1944, provide for one grade, U.S. No. 1. *"U.S. No. 1* consists of garlic of similar varietal characteristics which is mature and well cured, compact, with cloves well filled and fairly plump, free from mold, decay, shattered cloves, and from damage caused by dirt or staining, sunburn, sunscald, cuts, sprouts, tops, roots, disease, insects, or mechanical or other means. Each bulb shall be fairly well enclosed in its outer sheath. Unless otherwise specified, the minimum diameter of each bulb shall be not less than 1-1/2 in."

HOMINY—Canned [3/10/58]

Grade A: Color: Liquor is light in color, may be slightly cloudy, or slightly opaque, and may be slightly viscous, but is reasonably free from starchy globules and sediment. **Color:** Kernels possess a practically uniform, bright color, typical of white or golden (yellow) hominy, and the product contains not more than 2 percent "off-variety" kernels or pieces of kernels. **Defects:** Practically free from defects means practically free from harmless, extraneous material, kernels, or pieces of kernels with pericarp attached, and that not more than 2 percent of the kernels and pieces may be damaged and seriously damaged, and of such 2 percent, not more than 1 percent may be seriously damaged, and with respect to Style I, not more than 10 percent of the kernels may be broken; provided that the aforesaid defects, individually or collectively, do not more than slightly affect the appearance or eating quality. **Character:** Kernels or pieces of kernels may be reasonably firm and tender, and reasonably free from hard kernels, and from excessively soft kernels or pieces.

Grade C: Liquor: Liquor may be definitely cloudy, or opaque, and viscous, but not jellied, and is fairly free from starchy globules and sediment. **Color:** Kernels or pieces may possess a fairly uniform, typical color and may be slightly dull, and the product may contain not more than 3 percent "off-variety" kernels or pieces of kernels. **Defects:** Product is fairly free from harmless, extraneous material, from kernels or pieces of kernels with pericarp attached, and not more than 3 percent of the kernels or pieces of kernels may be damaged and seriously damaged, and of such 3 percent, not more than 1/3 or 1 percent may be seriously damaged; and with respect to Style I, not more than 20 percent of the kernels may be broken, provided: see Grade A, and substitute, do not seriously affect, in the wording. **Character:** Kernels or pieces of kernels may be fairly firm and tender, and fairly free from hard kernels, and excessively soft kernels, or pieces of kernels. **Sstd:** Fails to meet requirements.

HOMINY

CANNED [3/10/58   52.3281]

Grades:	"A" or "FANCY"	"C" or "STANDARD"	"SUB-STANDARD"
Minimum Score:	85	70	Less than 70

	NET WT. OZ.	NET WT. METRIC	DRAINED WEIGHT OZ. STYLE 1	STYLE 2	DRAINED WEIGHT METRIC STYLE 1	STYLE 2
No. 303	as full	as full	10	12	283.5 g	340.2 g
No. 2½	as	as	18	21.25	510.3 g	602.4 g
No. 10	practicable	practicable	72	76	2.0 kg	2.2 kg

HORSERADISH ROOTS

FRESH [7/27/36   51.3900]

Grades: U.S. Fancy, U.S. No. 1, U.S. No. 2

KALE*

USES: Kale's dark green leaves can add variety to meals. Young, tender kale should be cooked in a small amount of water. It is delicious served with a sprinkle of fresh lemon juice, butter, or crumbled bacon. The flavorful leaves can also be cooked in a heavy frying pan with a small amount of butter and boiling water. While cooked kale is always a little bitter, and many like this taste, raw tender kale as a salad green with oil and vinegar is sweet and distinctive, as demonstrated in tests made for the United Fresh Fruit & Vegetable Association.

To prepare kale, cut off and discard root ends, tough stems, and discolored leaves. Also cut out and discard midribs. Wash, lift out of the water, and shake the leaves well. Do not use soda. It makes kale mushy and destroys vitamin C.

MARKETING SEASON: Kale is on the market all year, but it is usually most abundant during the late fall and winter, and especially in December through February. Kale from Virginia is marketed principally from December to April. Long Island and New Jersey kale is marketed mostly from May to December. Some Virginia kale is shipped to Chicago and other middle western markets, but a large part of the production in Virginia and the Middle Atlantic states is marketed in Middle Atlantic cities. Approximate percentage of the annual total supply available each month (calculated by UFFVA from old data since later figures are not available) is as follows:

MONTHLY AVAILABILITY OF KALE EXPRESSED AS PERCENTAGE OF ANNUAL TOTAL SUPPLY

Jan. %	Feb. %	Mar. %	Apr. %	May %	June %
18	14	12	8	5	3

July %	Aug. %	Sept. %	Oct. %	Nov. %	Dec. %
3	3	5	6	8	15

VARIETIES: "There are several forms of kale, but only two are extensively grown for market—Scotch kale and blue kale. Scotch kale forms by far the greater bulk of the plantings in the Norfolk area, but because the blue kale is considered hardier, it is often used for late plantings and by those who have been delayed in seeding their crop." Vates is an important strain of blue kale.

"The Scotch kales tend to have extremely curled, wrinkled, and finely divided leaves, and most varieties have a bright green to yellowish green color. The Siberian kales have leaves usually flattened and smooth in the centers with curled and ruffled edges, and they are of a deep, bluish green color. The smooth-leafed kales have leaves with relatively little curl or crinkle ... and are usually marketed in the late spring and early summer."

THE SCOTCH KALES: Dwarf Green Curled Scotch is a dwarf, bright green kale. This variety has a 55-day growing season. The plant stands 12 to 14 in. tall; its leaves are large, bright green, finely curled, and plumed. It is a hardy plant, and its low-spreading habit of growth gives the stalk considerable production during cold weather. It is considered by some to be inferior in quality to the Siberian kale, but it is the most extensively grown for market. Large quantities are shipped from the South to northern markets during the fall and winter. The attractive appearance of the finely divided and curled leaves is doubtless responsible for much of its popularity.

Dwarf Blue Curled Scotch is very similar to the Dwarf Green Curled except that the leaves are of a deeper, rather bluish green instead of the bright or yellowish green. It will stand somewhat longer than the Dwarf Green in the late winter or spring without losing its deep green color.

The **Vates Strain** of Dwarf Blue Curled is a new strain developed by the Virginia Agricultural Station and is believed
*UFFVA

superior to the original. Vates has an upright plant habit. The growing season is from 55 to 60 days, and the plant stands 15 in. tall. Vates is a hardy plant with finely curled, blue green leaves that may spread nearly 2 ft. The strain is well adapted to Virginia and is also known as Vates Dwarf, Blue Curled Scotch, and Dwarf Scotch.

Tall Green Curled Scotch has a growing season of from 60 to 75 days. The leaves of the plant are essentially the same as those of the Dwarf Scotch, but the plant itself grows to a height of 2 to 3 ft., producing an abundance of leaves along the tall stem. It is a very hardy, upright plant, with large, deep yellowish green, finely curled, compact, plume-like leaves. As the stem increases in height, leaves may be harvested from time to time, leaving only a tuft of leaves at the top.

Siberian frequently called Dwarf Curled Siberian or Early Curled Siberian, is a very hardy type with broad thick leaves that are bisected and curled to a less extent than those of the Scotch varieties. Siberian has a growing season of from 65 to 70 days. Plants are vigorous, 12 to 15 in. tall, with a spread of 3 ft. or more. Leaves are large, numerous, thick, coarse, plume-like, with margins frilled and waved, and they are deep green, with bluish bloom.

CONTAINERS: The most common container for kale is the round-bottom bushel basket. Officially, it is supposed to hold an average of 18 to 25 lb. net, varying somewhat due to the tightness of the pack and the amount of bulge used. Other containers used include the following: the Jumbo cantaloupe crate, 40 to 45 lb.; WB corn crate, 30 to 35 lb.; 1-1/2 or 1-3/5 bu. crate, 30 to 32 lb.; 16-qt. basket, 10 lb.; 1-1/8 bu. carton, 22 lb.; a dozen bunches in various pkgs, at 10 to 12 lb.; 5/8 bu. hamper, 25 to 30 lb.; 1/2 bu. basket, 22 to 25 lb.; and the 3/4 bu. basket, 39 lb.

QUALITY: "Best quality kale is fresh, young, tender, and green. Plants or leaves which show insect injury, coarse stems, dry or yellowing leaves, excessive dirt, or poor development are usually lacking in quality and cause excessive waste. In buying, demand freshness and tenderness above all. Leaves should be crisp, green, and clean. Examine for yellow or brown leaves; bruising and crushing, or a large number of coarse stalks and stems. Check whether the kale has been shipped well iced. It should be cold and moist. In winter, however, also check for possible damage from freezing. Kale may be bought

KALE

FRESH [3/25/74   51.3930]
Grades: U.S. No. 1, U.S. Commercial

already washed and clipped. However, if there is any doubt about freedom from sand, rewashing is necessary."

GRADES: The U.S. standards for kale provide two grades, U.S. 1 and U.S. Commercial. The grade customarily used, *U.S. 1* "shall consist of plants of kale of one type which are well trimmed, not stunted, free from decay, and from damage caused by yellow or discolored leaves, seedstems, wilting, but burn, freezing, dirt, disease, insects, or mechanical or other means. In order to allow for variations incident to proper grading and handling, not more than 10 percent, by weight, of the plants in any container may be below the requirements of the grade, but not more than 1/10 of this tolerance, or 1 percent, shall be allowed for kale which is affected by wet decay."

KOHLRABI*

USES: "The young, small globes, not over 3 in. in diameter, are the best and have the most delicate flavor. The young leaves of kohlrabi may be cooked like spinach. The globes are best steamed without peeling, but if the vegetable is not as young and fresh as it might be, it should be peeled before cooking. This is most easily done by inserting a knife under the tough fiber at the base of the globe and stripping off the skin. Cut into quarters or slices and boil in very little, salted water. Kohlrabi is delicious steamed until tender, peeled, and cut into julienne strips. Marinate the strips in french dressing while they are still warm, and allow to cool in the marinade. Chill and serve as a salad with cold meat. A simple and very good vegetable is made by cooking peeled, sliced kohlrabi in boiling, salted water or bouillon until it is tender. Drain thoroughly and season with minced parsley, chives, a little lemon juice, and melted butter." —from *The Wise Encyclopedia of Cookery*, copyright 1948, by William H. Wise & Co., New York.

MARKETING SEASON: Kohlrabi is available May through November with a peak in June and July. Approximately 57 percent of the total annual supply is available in these two months.

*UFFVA

TABLE III—WHOLE LEAF; CUT LEAF; CHOPPED STYLES

Quality Factors	DEFECTS	Minor	Major	Severe
Color	Color appearance is:			
	adversely affected to a degree that is noticeable		X	
	adversely affected to a degree that is objectionable			X
Character	Appearance or eating quality, due to:			
	(1) A mushy texture, disintegration, ragged cutting, or shredded leaves and shredded stems, or portions thereof; and/or			
	(2) A tough texture, coarse, or fibrous stems or portions thereof; and/or			
	(3) Any other causes, as applicable for the style, is: adversely, but not seriously affected		X	
	Seriously affected			X
Extraneous	*Root crown:* Any significant portion of the solid area of the plant between the root and attached leaves		X	

Quality Factors	DEFECTS	Minor	Major	Severe
Plant	*Root stub;* Any portion of the root whether or not leaves are attached			X
Material	*Seed head—Whole Leaf; Cut Leaf Styles:*			
	Longer than one (1) in. or objectionable regardless of length		X	
	Seed head—Chopped Style: Pieces affecting appearance of eating quality			
	More than slightly but not materially	X		
	Materially		X	
	Seriously			X
Other Extraneous Material	*Grit, sand, silt, or other earthy material:*			
	A trace that no more than slightly affects appearance or eating quality	X		
	Presence materially affects appearance or eating quality			X

VARIETIES: The leading types in this country are the **White** and **Purple Vienna**. The White variety which is actually a light green is the most popular. Other varieties with fancy leaves are grown in Europe. These are used chiefly for ornamental purposes.

CONTAINERS: There are no standard containers for kohlrabi. Containers commonly used are bushel baskets and hampers.

QUALITY: The condition of the tops is a good indication of quality. The tops should be young and green. The thickened stem should be firm and crisp, and not over about 3 in. in diameter.

LEAFY GREENS—Canned [9/1/73]

Grade A [or Fancy]: Good flavor and odor characteristic of the type and has an attractive appearance and eating quality, within the limitations specified with respect to color, character, damage, and harmless, extraneous material. See Tables III through VI(c).

Grade B [or Extra Standard]: Good flavor and odor characteristic of the type and reasonably attractive appearance and eating quality, within the limitations specified with respect to color, character, damage, and harmless, extraneous material. See Table III through IV(c). **Sstd:** Fails to meet requirements.

PRODUCT CHARACTERISTICS

52.6090 Classification of defects.

(a) General. Scoreable defects in the factors of color, character, extraneous plant material, other extraneous material, and damaged leafy greens are outlined in Tables III, IV, and V.

(b) Extraneous plant material. Extraneous plant material includes root crowns, root stubs, and seed heads of the

TABLE IV—WHOLE LEAF; CUT LEAF; CHOPPED STYLES

Quality Factors	DEFECTS	Minor	Major	Severe
	WHOLE LEAF; CUT LEAF STYLES *Grass and Weeds* *(Aggregate Measurement)*			
Extraneous plant material	(1) Green, fine, tender, stringlike blades, and stems:			
	3 in. or less	X		
	More than 3 in. but not more than 8 in.		X	
	More than 8 in.			X
	(2) Green and coarse:			
	1/2 in. or less	X		
	More than 1/2 in. but not more than 2 in.		X	
	More than 2 in.			X
	CHOPPED STYLE *Grass and Weeds* *(Aggregate Measurement)*			
	(1) Green, fine, tender, stringlike blades, and stems:			
	3/4 in. or less	X		
	More than 3/4 in. but not more than 2 in.		X	
	More than 2 in.			X
	(2) Green and coarse:			
	3/4 in. or less	X		
	More than 3/4 in.			X
	(3) Other than green—of any texture or kind:			
	Any amount			X

TABLE V—WHOLE LEAF; CUT LEAF; CHOPPED STYLES

Quality Factors	DEFECTS	Minor	Major	Severe
	WHOLE LEAF; CUT LEAF STYLES *Discoloration or other injury* *(affecting the appearance or* *eating quality)*			
Damage	Less than 1 sq. in. that more than slightly but not materially affects	X		
	Less than 1 sq. in. that materially affects		X	
	1 sq. in. or more but less than 4 sq. in. that affects to any degree			X
	CHOPPED STYLE Any area that materially affects	X		

52.6091 Tolerances for Defects.

TABLE VI[a]—WHOLE LEAF; CUT LEAF STYLES

For container sizes: Less than No. 2-1/2; sample unit size—10 oz.		Number of defects permitted in a sample unit		
Grade Classification	Defect Classification	Upper Limit (UL)	Maximum Allowed for Deviants	Sample Average Value
U.S. Grade A	Severe	1	2	0.25
	Major	4	6	1.50
	Total 2	8	11	4.0
U.S. Grade B	Severe	2	3	0.50
	Major	8	11	4.0
	Total 2	18	23	12.0

2. Total—the sum of severe, major, and minor defects

applicable leafy green plant, and harmless grass, and weeds of various kinds and texture.

(c) Other extraneous material. Other harmless, extraneous material includes grit, sand, silt, or other earthy material.

(d) Damage. Damage includes discoloration or other similar injury on a leaf, or stem, or portion thereof, which damage affects, materially affects, or seriously affects the appearance or eating quality of the portion of leafy green and/or entire product.

(e) Degrees of defect classes. Defects are classified as to minor, major, or severe. Each "X" mark in Tables III, IV, and V represent "one (1) defect."

TABLE VI[b]—WHOLE LEAF; CUT LEAF STYLES

For container size: No. 2-1/2; sample unit size—15 oz.		Number of Defects Permitted in a Sample Unit		
Grade Classification	Defect Classification	Upper Limit (UL)	Maximum Allowed for Deviants	Sample Average Value
U.S. Grade A	Severe	1	3	0.375
	Major	5	8	2.25
	Total2	10	14	6.0
U.S. Grade B	Severe	2	4	0.75
	Major	10	14	6.0
	Total2	26	32	18.0

2. Total—the sum of severe, major, and minor defects

TABLE VI[c]—WHOLE LEAF; CUT LEAF STYLES

For container size: No. 10; sample unit size—30 oz.		Number of Defects Permitted in a Sample Unit		
Grade Classification	Defect Classification	Upper Limit (UL)	Maximum Allowed for Deviants	Sample Average Value
U.S. Grade A	Severe	2	4	0.75
	Major	8	12	4.5
	Total2	18	23	12.0
U.S. Grade B	Severe	4	6	1.5
	Major	18	23	12.0
	Total2	47	55	36.0

2. Total—the sum of severe, major, and minor defects

USDA, Agricultural Marketing Service, Inspection Aid No. 44

LEAFY GREENS [OTHER THAN SPINACH]—
Frozen [6/13/52]

Grade A: Color: Frozen leafy greens possess a nearly uniform light color characteristic of the variety. **Defects:** No grit, sand, or silt may be present that affects the edibility of the frozen leafy greens. Seedstems and roots may be present that do not more than slightly affect the appearance or edibility of the product, and for each 12 oz. of the product there may be present: damage affecting leaves and stems or portions of leaves and stems aggregating not more than 4 sq. in. (4 in. by 1 in.) in area: provided that the total damaged area, or any part, does not materially affect the appearance or edibility, and grass and weeds aggregating not more than 8 in. in length, provided that the total amount, or any part, does not materially affect the appearance or edibility. **Character:** Leafy greens are tender and practically free from coarse or tough leaves and stems, or coarse or tough portions of leaves and stems, and the appearance is not materially affected by ragged and torn leaves and stems or ragged and torn portions of leaves and stems.

Grade B: Color: Frozen leafy greens possess a reasonably uniform characteristic color which may be variable but not to the extent that the appearance of the frozen product is materially affected. **Defects:** Products may contain a trace of grit, sand, or silt that does not materially affect the edibility of the leafy greens; seedstems and roots may be present that do not materially affect the appearance or edibility of the product, and for each 12 oz. there may be present: damage affecting leaves and stems aggregating not more than 8 sq. in. (8 in. by 1 in.) in area: provided, that the total damaged areas, or any part, does not seriously affect the appearance or edibility and grass and weeds aggregating not more than 12 in. in length: provided, see Grade A. **Character:** Leafy greens shall be reasonably tender, and the appearance and eating quality shall not be materially affected by the presence of coarse or tough leaves and stems or coarse or tough portions of leaves and stems.

Sstd: Fails to meet requirements.

MEASUREMENT CHART FOR DEFECTS IN CUT OR CHOPPED FROZEN SPINACH

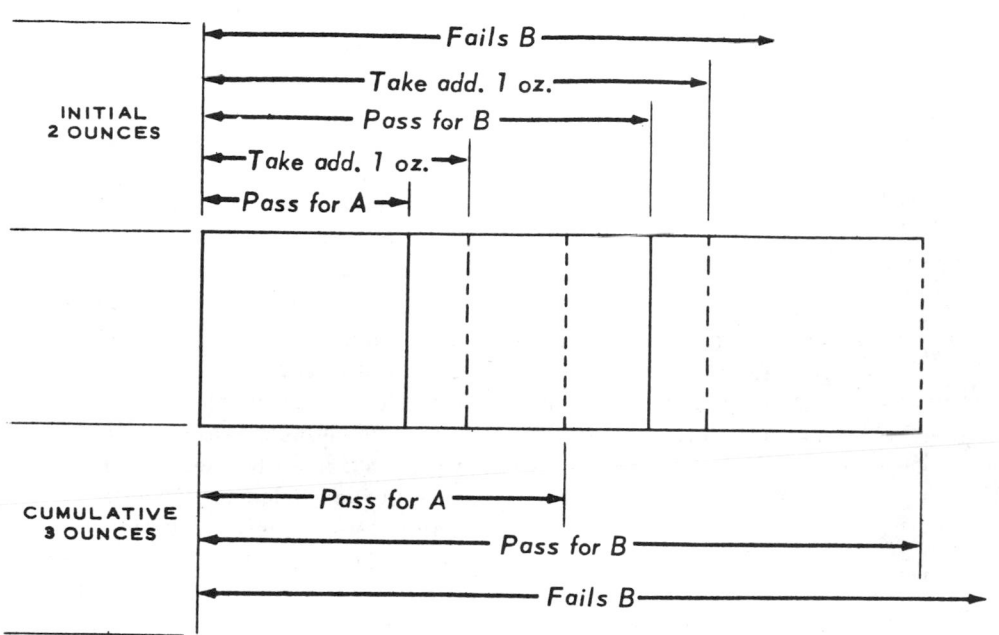

DIRECTIONS FOR USE

Lay inspection aid under sheet of clear plastic. Place damaged portions of leaves and stems on top surface of plastic sheet within the measuring rectangle. Classify sample unit for defects in accordance with the appropriate sample size.

SUMMARY OF ALLOWANCES FOR DAMAGE IN CUT OR CHOPPED STYLE FROZEN SPINACH

SAMPLE SIZE	AREA OF DAMAGED PORTIONS OF LEAVES				
INITIAL 2 OUNCES	17/16 square inches or less pass for grade A	18/16 to 22/16 square inches inclusive take additional 1 ounce	23/16 to 37/16 square inches inclusive pass for grade B	38/16 to 42/16 square inches inclusive take additional 1 ounce	More than 42/16 square inches fails grade B
CUMULATIVE 3 OUNCES	30/16 square inches or less pass for grade A		31/16 to 60/16 square inches inclusive pass for grade B		More than 60/16 square inches fails grade B

USDA, Agricultural Marketing Service, Inspection Aid No. 44

LEAFY GREENS OTHER THAN SPINACH
MUSTARD GREENS & TURNIP GREENS:
FRESH [3/8/53   51.1030]
Grades: U.S. No. 1
KALE:
FRESH [4/25/34   51.3930]
Grades: U.S. No. 1, U.S. Commercial
DANDELION GREENS:
FRESH [2/4/55   51.2585]
Grades: U.S. No. 1
COLLARD GREENS OR BROCCOLI GREENS:
FRESH [4/16/53   51.520]
Grades: U.S. No. 1
BEET GREENS:
FRESH [6/1/59   51.2860]
Grades: U.S. No. 1
CANNED [9/1/73   52.6081]

Grades:	"A" or "FANCY"	"B" or "EXTRA STANDARD"	"SUB-STANDARD"

	NET WEIGHT OZ.	NET WEIGHT METRIC	DRAINED WEIGHT OZ.	DRAINED WEIGHT METRIC
No. 8Z Tall	7.8	221.1 g	4.8	136.1 g
No. 303	15.2	430.9 g	10.2	289.2 g
No. 2½	26.8	759.8 g	17.6	499.0 g
No. 10	98.5	2.8 kg	54.7	1.55 kg

FROZEN [6/13/52   52.1371]

Grades:	"A" or "FANCY"	"B" or "EXTRA STANDARD"	"SUB-STANDARD"
Minimum Score:	85	70	Less than 70

LETTUCE*

USES: The word "lettuce" is virtually synonymous with "salad." All five types—crisphead, butterhead, romaine, leaf, and stem—are basic ingredients of a wide variety of salads that can include other vegetables, fruits, seafood, and meats, plus dressings. For chunky salads in which slices, quarters, or cubes are used, crisphead (Iceberg) is required because of its firm structure. Its characteristic crispness allows it to be the foundation for many other ingredients. This is also true of romaine. The softer types of lettuce usually are combined either with other greens or with somewhat dry ingredients, such as seafood or cheese.

Use of lettuce in sandwiches is universal. But use of this champion of the greens need not be limited to cold dishes. Lettuce may be braised or "wilted," and it makes a good soup when combined with a broth or bouillon and spices.

Here are some suggestions: head lettuce stuffed with a mixture of cream cheese, minced green pepper, minced chives, grated fresh carrots, and finely diced, fresh tomato, seasoned as desired; California salad bowl of lettuce, bread cubes, lemon juice, oil, crumbled bleu cheese and parmesan cheese, pepper, vinegar, and crumbled egg yolk; lettuce tossed with fresh orange and grapefruit sections, green seedless grapes, sliced fresh peaches, and sliced red plums, with a favorite dressing; head lettuce wedges with a dressing made from mayonnaise, chili sauce, and chopped, cooked shrimp; anchovy and cheese stuffed lettuce; bleu cheese dip with lettuce hearts; shrimp cocktail in lettuce cups; shrimp and lettuce saute; hors d'oeuvre of lettuce stuffed with seafood; head lettuce chunks and Roquefort cheese dressing; main dish salad of shredded crisp lettuce tossed with fresh orange and grapefruit sections, grapes, diced pears, and cubes of chicken; sliced lettuce over which is poured hot bacon drippings spiked with fresh lemon juice, seasoned with salt and pepper, and garnished with crumbled bacon; shredded lettuce floated on top of clear soup; steamed lettuce served as a vegetable with hollandaise sauce; bite-size lettuce pieces tossed with fresh fruit and served with cold sliced turkey or ham; aspic-studded lettuce salad; scalloped lettuce and tomatoes, alternating layers of shredded lettuce, tomatoes, and onions en casserole; cream of lettuce soup; Caesar salad; B.L.T. sandwich, that is, bacon, lettuce and tomato; tuna-lettuce bowl.

MARKETING SEASON: Lettuce is on the market in all months in large amounts, but there are considerable variations in supply from month to month, as can be seen in the table of unloads in 41 cities in the section on Sources of Supply by Months. These changes in supply, although not large as a percentage of the annual total, result in price variations much

*UFFVA

wider than the supply swings. The following chart shows the average monthly availability of lettuce each month as a percentage of the annual total which is given at the right in millions of pounds. The figures are based on unloads in 41 cities for the 5 years 1963-67 inclusive. The total poundage figures, however, are for the entire country.

MONTHLY AVAILABILITY OF LETTUCE EXPRESSED AS PERCENTAGE OF TOTAL ANNUAL SUPPLY

Commodity	Jan.	Feb.	Mar.	Apr.	May	June
	%	%	%	%	%	%
Lettuce, All	8	7	9	9	9	9
California	9	9	10	6	9	10
Arizona	9	6	10	23	12	3
New York					*	15
New Jersey					7	34

July	Aug.	Sept.	Oct.	Nov.	Dec.	ANNUAL TOTAL
%	%	%	%	%	%	Million lb.
9	9	8	8	8	8	4,214
10	10	10	9	5	5	2,596
			3	17	18	830
41	24	14	4	1		114
10	5	8	22	12	*	110

VARIETIES: Lettuce is generally grouped into five classes: (a) crisphead (usually but incorrectly called Iceberg); (b) butterhead; (c) cos or romaine; (d) looseleaf or bunching; and (e) stem.

CRISPHEAD "The crisphead varieties are distinguished by their firm heads and brittle texture. The leaves form a head by overlapping one another in a smooth, regular manner. The veins are coarse and the ribs are prominent. The head is usually 6 or more inches in diameter. Crisphead is the most important commercial type of lettuce in this country. There are numerous crisphead varieties, each with some specific character or set of characters that makes it desirable for culture in a particular region. Their firm, compact, solid heads make them popular. Such heads withstand long-distance transportation; they can be produced in areas best adapted to lettuce culture. Nearly all the lettuce harvested for market in the western region is of the crisphead type, and probably one-half or more of that produced in the other regions is of this type.

"Some common varieties of crisphead lettuce are **Great Lakes Regular, Premier Great Lakes, Imperial 101,** and **Imperial 615.** Most of the modern crisphead varieties have been derived by selection in progenies evolved from the old variety New York (synonymns - Los Angeles Market and Wonderful) crossed with various other varieties both foreign and domestic."

TWO CRISPHEAD TYPES—"The crisphead varieties of lettuce can be separated into two distinct types: (a) **Imperial** and (b) **Great Lakes** Varieties of the Imperial type are mostly large and normally medium green. The leaves are thin, entire margined (not distinctly toothed or lobed), savoyed, and crumpled. They form symmetrical, partly exposed heads, with many wrapper leaves. The quality is good to excellent. Great Lakes types are generally characterized by dark green, thick, crisp, tough, serrate leaves. They form extremely firm, heavy, mostly exposed heads. They are moderately slow bolting and resistant to tipburn. The quality is only fair to poor; the texture is generally coarse and tough."

(There are also crisphead varieties that do not fit into either the Imperial or Great Lakes types. These include **Vanguard** and **Valverde.**)

Butterhead "The butterhead varieties are distinguished by their soft, pliable leaves, and delicate buttery flavor. The leaves form a head by overlapping one another in a smooth regular manner. The veins are finer, and the ribs are less prominent than those of the crisphead varieties. The head is less firm and somewhat smaller than that of the crisphead type. Because of the soft, pliable texture of the leaves ... they bruise and tear easily. The damaged tissues become discolored, often blackened, and unsightly, before the lettuce arrives in the retail markets. Consequently, butterhead varieties are not adapted to long-distance transportation. Even for local markets, the produce must be handled with great care to place it before the consumer in good condition.

"The butterhead varieties are traditionally grown near the centers of population in the East, along the east coast of New York, New Jersey, Virginia, and North Carolina, and in the

LETTUCE
FRESH [6/16/70   51.2510]
Grades: U.S. FANCY, U.S. No. 1, U.S. Commercial, U.S. No. 2
GREENHOUSE LEAF LETTUCE
FRESH [9/1/64   51.3455]
Grades: U.S. FANCY, U.S. No. 1
Containers: Standard fiberboard lettuce containers, Net weight 40 to 48 lb.

Middle West. Prior to the development and expansion of the lettuce industry in the western region in the first and second decades of the century, the butterhead varieties were predominant in eastern markets. They rapidly lost favor, however, to the crisphead varieties, until it became imperative to develop crisphead varieties adapted to eastern conditions. During the 1950s, because of consumer dissatisfaction with the quality of some of the crisphead varieties, production of the butterhead varieties revived, especially for local and nearby markets. Principal varieties of butterhead lettuce are **Big Boston, White Boston, Bibb** and **May King.**"

Big Boston "Medium large; intermediate in season; young plant with upright twisted leaves; mature plant compact, with firm, well-defined broad, slightly pointed head; leaves broad, smooth, slightly savoyed, somewhat twisted, thick, stiff, hard, dull light green except for the borders of the outer leaves—which are tinged reddish brown; quality fair—not so sweet and tender as other butterhead varieties; bolts easily, and is very susceptible to tipburn damage; seeds whitish. It is widely adapted but grown mostly for local markets and short-distance shipping in the East and Southeast."

Bibb "Small, early to midseason; plant loose and spreading when young, compact when mature; leaves short, spatulate, closely clustered to form a compact globular head, not overlapping, dark green with some dark red pigment, thick, smooth, brittle; a rapid bolter; quality excellent—delicate buttery flavor, sweet, tender; seeds black. It is a good variety for the home garden, greenhouse, and local market. It was introduced into this county about 1890 as Half Century. It disappeared for a time from trade channels; later it returned under the names Bibb and, erroneously, Limestone."

COS OR ROMAINE "The cos, or romaine, varieties are easily recognized by the upright character of the plant, the long, loaf-shaped head, and the long, narrow leaves. The varieties of cos are divided into self-closing and loose-closing types. The leaves of the self-closing varieties curve inward at the tips and form a well-blanched closed head. The loose-closing varieties will not form a closed head. The leaves appear coarse, but they are tender, sweet, and tasty, and have less bitterness than other varieties. The table quality of the cos varieties is excellent. The growing popularity of the tossed salad has increased the demand for cos varieties. The dark green outer leaves and the golden-yellow inner ones are attractive and flavorsome ingredients of such salads.

"However, the cos varieties, like the butterhead varieties, are ill-adapted to long-distance transportation. The elongated heads with spatulate leaves are difficult to fit into conventional packages. The stiff, but tender, leaves are easily torn, punctured, and crushed. Therefore, the cos varieties are grown mostly for local and nearby markets, but there has also been a small but steady demand for these varieties in the winter-production areas of the western region for more distant shipping. From these areas, cos lettuce is shipped mainly in cars with other vegetables. Common varieties of cos lettuce are **Dark Green** and **White Paris.**"

White Paris "Large; self-closing; intermediate or late in season; leaves oval to spatulate or slightly spatulate, curving inward at the ends and overlapping to form a loaf-shaped, rather loose head; a slow bolter; quality excellent—firm, crisp, sweet; seeds whitish. It is an old variety of European origin; it has been listed by American seedsmen since 1860. This is one of the best varieties for the home garden."

LOOSELEAF, OR BUNCHING "The looseleaf, or bunching, varieties do not form heads. The leaves are clustered or pressed together, but only the young ones at the center of the plant overlap to any extent. The older leaves are arranged loosely around the stem. Looseleaf varieties are popular for the home garden and are the principal varieties grown in greenhouses. They are not adapted to long-distance transportation and have a short market life. Their soil, water, and temperature requirements are not so exacting as those of the three preceding classes; therefore, they are better adapted to the needs of the home gardener. Common varieties of looseleaf lettuce are **Black-Seeded Simpson, Prize Head, Grand Rapids**, and **Salad Bowl**."

Black-Seeded Simpson "Large; midseason; compact plant; leaves broad, savoyed, crumpled, twisted, thick, stiff, coarse, with serrate margins and prominent midribs, light green; easily grown, tolerant of high temperatures; a slow bolter; quality only fair; seeds black."

STEM "The edible part of stem lettuce is the enlarged stem, or seedstalk. It may be peeled and eaten raw or it may be boiled, stewed, or creamed. Stem lettuce is an ingredient of many Chinese dishes. It is little used in this country except by people of Chinese extraction. **Celtuce** is the only variety offered for sale in the U.S."

CONTAINERS: The usual, but not sole, container for head lettuce is the fiberboard box with inside dimensions of 9-3/4 x 14 x 21 in., 2867 cu. in., holding 40 to 45 lb. and up to 48 lb. This is a flat-pack carton, that is, it is intended to be packed so there will be little or no bulge at the top.

The non-bulge pack was agreed upon by growers and shippers, after long debate, to replace the old bulge pack which was so tight as to cause crushing of some of the heads. Unfortunately, the flat-pack carton is now also being overpacked by some shippers. The Bureau of Market News of the California Dept. of Agriculture cites 43 lb. as the most common weight of this pack.

The most usual container for Big Boston type lettuce is the Eastern wirebound crate of 1-1/9 bu. capacity holding 20 to 25 lb. net; for romaine lettuce, the 1-1/9 bu. wirebound crate holding 30 lb., the carton holding 24 heads, 35 lb.; and the bushel basket holding 25 to 28 lb.; for looseleaf lettuce, various containers holding 24 units, 20 to 25 lb.; for Bibb lettuce the 12-qt. basket holding 5 lb.; and for hothouse lettuce, baskets holding 5 or 10 lb.

The corrugated lettuce box, as provided in Freight Container Tariff 1-H "must be made of double-faced, corrugated fiberboard having proper bending qualities and possessing a Mullen or Cady test of not less than 300 lb. when dry and not less than 100 lb. after 24 hours immersion in water with no voluntary separation of the plies. The fiberboard must be constructed of 2 facings and a corrugated sheet, each facing to

weigh not less than 69 lb. per 1,000 sq. ft., and the corrugated sheet to weigh not less than 33 lb. per 1,000 sq. ft. The facings must be water-resistant and must each be firmly glued to the corrugated sheet with a water-resistant adhesive which cannot be dissolved in water after the film application has set."

Some fiberboard boxes are impregnated with wax and are substantially waterproof. Dimensions are the same for those not so treated.

Following are the containers authorized in the railroad freight tariffs for lettuce: Container 925, lettuce crate, 7-1/2 x 16 x 19; No. 935, lettuce and vegetable WGA crate, 14-1/4 x 18-1/4 x 20-5/8; No. 936, lettuce and vegetable S-W crate, 14-1/4 x 18-1/4 x 21-3/4; No. 957, lettuce and vegetable crate, 10-1/4 x 12-1/2 x 20-5/8; No. 3800, wirebound lettuce crate, 6-1/2 x 13 x 19-1/8; No. 3802, wirebound lettuce crate, 9 x 17 x 21-7/8; No. 3803, wirebound lettuce and vegetable crate, 7-1/2 x 15-1/2 x 18-3/4; No. 3815, wirebound lettuce and vegetable crate, 14 x 18 x 21-1/8; No. 3820, wirebound lettuce and vegetable crate, 9-1/4 x 13-3/16 x 21-1/4 or 21-1/2; No. 3822, wirebound lettuce and vegetable crate, 10 x 14-1/4 x 21-1/2 or 21-1/8; No. 7300, fiberboard lettuce and cabbage box, 9-1/2 x 13-1/2 x 20-1/2; No. 7301, 9 x 13 x 21-5/8; No. 7302, fiberboard lettuce and cabbage box, 9 x 14-1/4 x 21-5/16; No. 7304, fiberboard lettuce and cabbage box, 12-3/4 x 14 x 20-7/8; No. 7306, fiberboard lettuce box, 9-3/4 x 14 x 21; No. 7308, fiberboard lettuce and cabbage box, 10-1/4 to 11 x 16 x 22; No. 7310, fiberboard lettuce and cabbage box, 10-1/2 x 14-1/4 x 21-5/16; No. 7311, fiberboard lettuce box, 9-3/4 x 14 x 21; No. 7313, fiberboard lettuce box, 14 x 9-3/4 x 21; No. 7314, fiberboard lettuce box (wax impregnated), 14 x 9-3/4 x 21; No. 7315, fiberboard lettuce box, 8 x 12 x 18.

SERVINGS AND WEIGHTS: Yield of head lettuce is about 74 percent per pound purchased. One pound as purchased provides 5.92 portions of 2 oz. raw. The amount as purchased for such portions for 25 persons is 4.25 lb.; and for 100 is 17 lb.

A carton of Iceberg lettuce, 2 dozen heads, provides 144 portions of 1/6 head each. For 25 persons, such portions require 4-1/4 heads as purchased; and for 100, the total is 17 heads.

The yield of romaine is about 64 percent of the amount purchased. One pound yields 10.24 portions of 1 oz. each. For portions of this size for 25, about 2-1/2 lb. are required; and for 100, 10 lb.

QUALITY: Grades are trading standards. From the consumer's viewpoint, examination of a particular head of lettuce for quality is more useful than knowing the grade of the lot it came in. *"Look for:* Signs of freshness in lettuce. For Iceberg lettuce and romaine, the leaves should be crisp. Other lettuce types will have a softer texture, but leaves should not be wilted. Look for a good, bright color—in most varieties, medium to light green. *Avoid:* Heads of Iceberg type which are very hard and which lack green color (signs of over-maturity). Such heads sometimes develop discoloration in the center of the leaves (the midribs) and may have a less attractive flavor. Also avoid heads with irregular shapes and hard bumps on top, which indicates the presence of overgrown central stems. Check the lettuce for tipburn, a tan or brown area (dead tissue) around the margins of the leaves. Look for tipburn on the edges of the hard leaves. Slight discoloration of the outer or wrapper leaves will usually not hurt the quality of the lettuce, but serious discoloration or soft decay definitely should be avoided."

GRADES: U.S. grade standards for lettuce, effective June 16, 1970 provide four grades, U.S. Fancy, U.S. 1, U.S. Commercial, and U.S. 2. For full details, see the standard available from Consumer and Marketing Service, Washington, D.C. 20250.

Since U.S. 1 is the main trading grade, the information given here is for that grade, but is not complete.

"U.S. No. 1 consists of heads of lettuce of similar varietal characteristics which are fresh and green, which are not soft or burst, and which are free from decay and doubles, and from damage caused by tipburn, downy mildew, opening, seedstems, broken midribs, freezing, discoloration, dirt disease, insects, or mechanical or other means. Each head shall be fairly well trimmed, unless specified as closely trimmed. In any lot of Iceberg type lettuce, the percentages of hard and firm heads or the combined percentage of hard and firm heads shall be specified in connection with the grade.

"STANDARD PACK—Heads of lettuce shall be fairly uniform in size and tightly but not excessively tightly packed in uniform layers in the containers, according to the approved and regoznied methods, except that in standard fiberboard containers a 'bridge' of 6 heads may be used in a 2-1/2 doz. pack; and in standard wooden crates a 'bridge' may be used with sizes smaller than 5-doz. count.

"(1) Fairly uniform in size means that not more than 10 percent, by count, of the heads in any container may vary appreciably in size from the standard size head for the count pack. The standard size head for a 2-doz. pack is that size head, having four wrapper leaves, which will pack tightly but not excessively tightly in 3 rows, with 4 heads of uniform size in each row, in a layer in a standard fiberboard container. Heads having lesser or greater numbers of wrapper leaves which can be packed as specified herein are considered equivalent in size to a standard size head with 4 wrapper leaves.

"(2) Excessively tightly packed means that heads are packed so tightly as to cause distortion or crushing of the heads or breaking of the midribs. The packing of 24 heads of 18 size in a standard fiberboard lettuce container would result in an excessively tight pack.

"(3) Lettuce packed in standard fiberboard lettuce containers shall have a net weight of not less than 40 lb. and not more than 48 lb. In order to allow for variations incident to proper packing, not more than a total of 10 percent of the containers in any lot may fail to meet the requirements for standard pack.

"SOLIDITY CLASSIFICATION—(a) The following terms shall be used in describing the solidity of lettuce: (1) 'Hard' means that the head is compact and solid. This term represents the highest degree of solidity. (2) 'Firm' means that the head is compact, but may yield slightly to moderate pressure. (3) 'Fairly firm' means that although the head is not firm, it is not soft and spongy, and has good head formation, and edible content. (4) 'Soft' means that the head is easily compressed or spongy."

GOOD DELIVERY STANDARDS: In addition to grade standards, there is a regulation defining the meaning of "good delivery" as applied to lettuce. This is section 46.44 of the Regulations (other than rules of practice) Under the Perishable Agricultural Commodities Act, effective Jan. 1, 1969. The regulation provides that "unless otherwise agreed to between the contracting parties, 'Good Delivery', in connection with FOB contracts of purchase and sale, means that the commodity meets the requirements of the contract at time of loading or sale and, if the shipment is handled under normal transportation service and conditions, will meet the following additional requirements on delivery at the contract destination: destination:

(a) Lettuce. (1) If the contract specifies a U.S. grade, the lettuce may contain an average of not more than 3 percent condition defects, including not more than 2 percent decay affecting any portion of the head, exclusive of wrapper leaves, in excess of the destination tolerances provided for the applicable grade in the U.S. Standards for Grades of Lettuce ... (2) If the contract does not specify a U.S. grade or percentage of condition defects, the lettuce at destination may contain a maximum of 15 percent, by count, of the heads in any lot which are damaged by condition defects, including therein not more than 9 percent serious damage of which not more than 5 percent may be decay affecting any portion of the head exclusive of wrapping leaves." (There are other provisions in the Good Delivery Standards. See the complete regulations available from Consumer and Marketing Service, USDA, Washington, D.C. 20250.)

MUSHROOMS*

USES: Mushrooms serve many purposes on the menu, ranging from use as a garnish to a featured main dish. Sliced and added uncooked to a green salad, they make it a specialty dish. Served uncooked and whole, they are a delicious snack with an unusual texture. More commonly, they are added to gravies, sauces, soups, and casserole dishes. They can be used to garnish a thick steak by covering the top of the steak with mushroom slices before broiling. Mushroom slices in an omelet add a subtle flavor.

Mushrooms can also be served as a vegetable or main dish. Their delicate flavor is at its best when mushrooms are lightly sauteed. Large mushroom caps can be stuffed and baked for a delicious side dish or appetizer. Marinated mushrooms are considered a delicacy. Mushrooms should be cooked lightly since overcooking toughens them and deadens the flavor. If they are to be added to a gravy or sauce, it is sufficient to add them as a last step and to serve the gravy soon after.

In addition to being an important culinary item, mushrooms have several other potential uses. "Mushrooms are particularly important for reindeer. For cattle, they can be used as fresh food, or as 'lure' for the animals coming back from the pastures, or in salt bran, preserved for the winter. Several German authors during and after the first World War experimented successfully with wild mushrooms given to pigs, poultry, and fish. Dry mushrooms ground to powder are suitable as an addition to all kinds of fodder. In this form mushrooms can also serve as a substitute for fish meal." (These are usually mushrooms other than A. bisporus.) Cultivated mushrooms are also used by mycologists, microbiologists, and phytopathologists. "Certain media for the pure culture of fungi and other micro-organisms are extracted from carpophores (fruiting bodies) of fleshy Basidiomycetes."

MARKETING SEASON: Mushrooms, being grown in an artificially controlled atmosphere, do not have a harvest season which is dependent on the exterior climate. They are available all months of the year. The supply usually varies from a low in August to somewhat higher during winter months. Produce merchandisers, institutional and commercial foodservice operators can all plan and count on adequate supplies being available at the time they want them. The following table shows the estimated monthly availability of mushrooms expressed as a percentage of the total annual supply.

MONTHLY AVAILABILITY OF MUSHROOMS EXPRESSED AS A PERCENTAGE OF TOTAL ANNUAL SUPPLY

Jan.	Feb.	Mar.	Apr.	May	June
%	%	%	%	%	%
9	8	9	9	9	8

July	Aug.	Sept.	Oct.	Nov.	Dec.
%	%	%	%	%	%
7	7	7	8	9	9

VARIETIES: There are many species and varieties of mushrooms. Only one species (with one variety), A. bisporus, is cultivated in the U.S. and Europe. Three strains, or colors, of A. bisporus are cultivated—white, off-white, and tan. All three

*UFFVA

MUSHROOMS

FRESH [7/15/66   51.3385]
Grades: U.S. No. 1, U.S. No. 2
CANNED (4/7/62   52.1481)

Grades:	"A" or "FANCY"	"B" or "EXTRA STANDARD"	"SUB-STANDARD"
Minimum Score:	90	80	Less than 80

mushrooms are similar in keeping quality and shelf-life, although the darker strains show damage and bruises less readily. Generally, the darker mushrooms are canned. The white strains are sold fresh in the East, while tan mushrooms are sold fresh in California.

CONTAINERS: The trend in packaging has been away from shipping mushrooms in bulk to the seller. Mushrooms displayed in bulk bins often suffer from much handling. Also selling mushrooms from bulk bins is more time-consuming to the retailer. Mushrooms are generally packed by growers at harvest in 10-lb. containers, which are usually corrugated fiberboard, but sometimes are plastic. Mushrooms are sent to a repacking plant, and the 10-lb. containers are often returned to the grower for re-use. At the repacking plant, mushrooms are usually put into either 1-lb. or 8 oz. retailing cartons, or, less often, into 6-oz. retailing cartons. A pulpboard tray with shrink-film or stretch-film overwrap is the predominant consumer package. Consumer packages are packed for shipping into master containers which are corrugated fiberboard boxes holding either 8 1-lb. packages or 12 8-oz. packages. The boxes are put on pallets 40 in. by 40 in or 40 in. by 48 in. and strapped together with plastic strapping for shipping.

"Mushrooms are tightly packed without being forced. A loose pack leads to abrasion from movement and an excessively tight pack results in pressure bruises." Packages covered with film overwraps require film that is gas-permeable. If film is not, the atmosphere inside the package becomes depleted of oxygen, while carbon dioxide and water vapor increase. Respiration changes from aerobic to anaerobic, and mushrooms break down rapidly, become slimy, and produce odors. Overwrapping with moisture-permeable film aids in retarding wilting without causing accumulation of free moisture on the film and undesirable condensation on the mushrooms. A study of container types, chipboard, pulpboard box, and plastic, done at the University of Delaware, concluded: "There is little real difference in the effect on shelf-life among the three types of trays."

QUALITY: Freshness, color, and shape are the 3 points generally considered in buying mushrooms. Avoid mushrooms that are withered or have open veils around the base of the cap, as these are signs of old age. "Best quality mushrooms are clean, fresh in appearance, white, creamy white or tan (depending on strain), free from open caps, pitting, discoloration, wilting, or other injury. For most purposes, sizes ranging from 3/4 in. to 3 in. in diameter are usually preferred. If the mushroom caps are partially open, the gills (fluted formation between cap and stem) should be light in color. Brown or black gills indicate over-age mushrooms which should be avoided." The size of the mushroom is not a reliable indicator of tenderness. Since caps are more tender than stems, mushrooms with extra long stems should be cheaper.

GRADES: U.S. standards for Grades of Mushrooms, effective July 15, 1966, provide for two grades: U.S. 1 and U.S. 2.

U.S. No. 1 "consists of fresh mushrooms of similar varietal characteristics which are mature, at least fairly well shaped, well trimmed, free from open veils, disease, spots, insect injury, and decay, and from damage by any cause. Size is specified in terms of diameter and, unless otherwise specified, meets the requirements of one of the following size classifications: (1) small to medium—up to 1-5/8 in. in diameter; (2) large—over 1-5/8 in. in diameter.

TOLERANCES—"In order to allow for variations incident to proper grading and handling, the following tolerances, by weight, are provided as specified: (1) at shipping point: 5 percent for mushrooms in any lot which fail to meet the requirements of this grade, but not more than 1/5 of this amount, or 1 percent, shall be allowed for mushrooms affected by disease, spots, or decay; (2) en route or at destination: 10 percent for mushrooms in any lot which have open veils, 5 percent for mushrooms in any lot which fail to meet the remaining requirements of this grade, but not more than 1/5 of this latter amount, or 1 percent, shall be allowed for mushrooms affected by disease, spots or decay; (3) for off-size: 10 percent for mushrooms in any lot which fail to meet the specified size requirements."

DEFINITIONS—'Similar varietal characteristics' means that the mushrooms are of the same general color. For example, white and brown mushrooms shall not be mixed in the same container. 'Mature' means that the mushroom is firm and well developed; the veil area may be stretched but not broken. 'Fairly well shaped' means that the mushroom cap is not flattened, scalloped, indented, or otherwise deformed to an extent which materially detracts from the appearance or marketing quality. 'Well trimmed' means that the stems are smoothly cut, free from rough, fleshy butts, the flared portion of the butt is removed, and the remaining portion of the stem does not exceed the depth of the cap. 'Open veils' means that the cap has expanded to the extent that the protective covering or veils joining the margin of the cap to the stem have broken and exposed the gills or underside of the cap. 'Spots' means pitted or discolored areas. 'Damage' means any specific defect described in this section; or an equally objectionable variation of any one of these defects, any other defect, or any combination of defects which materially detract from the appearance, or the edible or marketing quality of the individual mushroom or of the mushrooms in the lot.

The following specific defects shall be considered as damage: Discoloration when the color of the cap or stem materially affects the appearance or marketing quality of the mushrooms. Dirt when any amount (of soil or compost material) is embedded in the cap or stem. 'Length of stem' means the greatest distance as measured from the point of attachment of the veils on the stem to the butt. 'Diameter' means the greatest dimension of the cap measured at right angles to the stem."

MUSHROOMS—Canned [3/7/62]

Grade A: Color: Color deviation and contrast may not more than slightly affect overall color appearance. Color is practically uniform and light and typical of canned mushrooms produced from mushrooms of similar characteristics. "White or Cream"—color of surface of individual cap or portion may be darker than medium cream and may possess a slight tannish cast. Color of gills of sliced units and/or stems and pieces is not darker than light tannish gray. "Brown"—color of surface of individual cap is not darker than light brown and may possess a slight grayish cast. Color of the gills of sliced units and/or stems and pieces is darker than medium brownish gray.

Size and Shape: "Whole" and "Buttons"—stems are cut transversely. Diameter of largest cap does not exceed diameter of smallest by more than 1/4 in.; and in the 85 percent, with the most uniform diameters, the diameter of largest cap does not exceed diameter of smallest cap by more than 1/8 in. "Sliced Whole" and Sliced Buttons"—presence of irregularly-shaped units does not materially affect appearance. Not more than 5 percent may be small side-slices, and diameter of largest center slice does not exceed diameter of smallest center slice by more than 3/8 in. "Random Slice"—not more than 5 percent may be small side-slices.

Defects: Total of crushed or broken units may not exceed 5 percent. Total of damaged and seriously damaged units may not exceed 5 percent, of which not more than 1 percent may be seriously damaged. 1 unit may be seriously damaged in either grade provided total number of seriously damaged units in the total sample is within the percentage permitted. Notwithstanding allowances, presence of defect may not materially affect appearance and eating quality. **Character:** Units are firm and tender; practically free from fibrous or rubbery units; and not less than 95 percent of all units possess closed veils. One unit which fails to meet requirements for closed veil is permitted in a container, provided the average in all containers comprising sample does not exceed 5 percent.

Grade B: Color: Color deviation and contrast may not seriously affect overall color appearance. Color is typical of canned mushrooms produced from mushrooms of similar varietal characteristics. Color may be dull. "White or Cream"—Color of surface of individual cap or portion may be dark cream; and may possess a gray or brown cast. Color of gills of sliced units and/or stems and pieces is not darker than tannish gray. "Brown"—Color of surface of individual caps is medium brown and may possess a grayish cast. Color of the gills of sliced units and/or stems and pieces may be dark brownish gray. **Size and Shape:** All wording is the same except as follows: "Whole and Buttons"—the diameter of largest cap does not exceed diameter of smallest cap by more than 1/4 in. "Sliced Whole" and "Sliced Buttons"—seriously affect the appearance; 10 percent; 5/8 in. "Random Sliced"—10 percent. **Defects:** All wording is the same except as follows: 10 percent; 2 percent; seriously affects appearance and eating quality. **Character:** Reasonably tender and may be slightly soft. Product is reasonably free from fibrous or rubbery units; and not less than 90 percent possess closed veil. One unit which fails to meet requirements for closed veils is permitted in a container provided the average in all containers comprising sample does not exceed 10 percent.

Sstd: Fails to meet requirements.

MUSTARD GREENS*

USES: The young, tender leaves of mustard greens can be used as salad, either alone or mixed with other salad greens and ingredients. The older, but tender, leaves are used for cooking and should be handled like other pot herbs. After washing, cook in a covered pan in a little water for 15 to 20 minutes. Season to taste. Salt, pepper, and butter, or salt, pepper, and lemon juice or vinegar enhance the pungency of the greens. In the South, mustard is cooked in water in which salt pork or ham has been simmered, but keep the water to a minimum and use it in sauce or gravy. Any water in which greens have been cooked will have its share of vitamins and minerals, as well as flavor. In addition to their uses as salad or side dish, the leaves can provide flavor in soups and stews. In buying, the smaller leaves, 6 to 12 in. long, are preferred.

MARKETING SEASON: Mustard greens are on the market all year with no high peak or extreme low. Somewhat more are available December through April than in other months, and the months when the least greens are available are July and August. While this is the general pattern of availability for shipped greens, considerable supplies are produced and marketed locally in July and August, especially in the South. Unloads of total greens and prices of mustard greens are reported daily in season by USDA Market News Offices in major cities.

VARIETIES: Principal varieties of B. juncea are Florida Broad Leaf, Southern Giant Curled, Fordhook Fancy, Large Smooth Leaf and Tendergreen. **Florida Broad Leaf** has leaves that are green, large, thick, broad-oval, with a distinct, whitish midrib, margin toothed, but not frilled. About 50 days. **Southern Giant Curled** Leaves large and wide, bright green, and yellow-tinged, very curly on the edges; upright in growth. About 40 days. **Fordhook Fancy** Leaves large, dark green, deeply curled, fringed, and recurved. Mild-flavored. Slow to bolt. About 40 days. **Large Smooth Leaf** Leaves large, broad-oval, deep green, margin toothed, but otherwise plain. About 50 days. **Tendergreen** Produces a large rosette of mild-flavored, thick, dark green leaves that are smooth, glossy, and not lobed. About 45 days. (From various seed catalogs.)

CONTAINERS: Mustard greens are usually shipped in a bushel basket or wirebound crate with net weight of 18 to 25 lb., not counting ice. At retail, they are sometimes offered washed and clipped, in film bags of various sizes, ranging from 10 oz. to 20 oz.

QUALITY: All kinds of greens should be fresh, young, tender, free from blemishes, and have a good green color. Some mustard greens show a slight bronze tint, and this is normal, and some are naturally light green. However, avoid mustard greens that are distinctly yellowed. Any that are wilted are not worth buying. Avoid greens that are coarse and fibrous, or that are soft, or decayed. Any with evidence of insects, especially aphids, should be rejected.

GRADES: U.S. grade standards for mustard greens and turnip greens, effective in 1953, provide for one grade, *U.S. 1.* This consists of greens of "similar varietal characteristics which are fresh, fairly tender, fairly clean, and which are free from decay, and free from damage caused by seedstems, discoloration, freezing, foreign material, disease, insects, or mechanical or other means. In order to allow for variations incident to proper grading and handling, other than for size of roots and mixtures of plants and leaves, not more than a total of 10 percent, by weight, of the units in any lot, may fail to meet the requirements of the grade: provided, that not more than 1/2 of this amount, or 5 percent, shall be allowed for serious damage by any cause, and including therein not more than 2 percent for decay ... Not more than 5 percent, by

*UFFVA

weight, of the mustard ... greens may consist of cut leaves in a lot consisting of plants or of plants in a lot consisting of cut leaves ..."

OKRA*

USES: Okra pods can be used in cooking in a variety of ways. Most commonly, okra is used in soups, stews, "gumbos," or "creole" dishes, in combination with other vegetables, especially tomatoes. It thickens and flavors soups and creoles in a unique way. It can be dipped in corn meal and fried. It may be boiled, but, "when cooked straight, its mucilaginous properties do not suit most people." "Pastiness will not occur if the whole pods are not broken or subjected to long cooking. Okra should preferably be cooked in agate, aluminum, porcelain, earthenware, or glass utensils. Copper, brass, iron, or tin will cause the okra to discolor, turning black, and unappetizing looking. No harm is done except to the appearance." "Okra may be preserved by drying, quick freezing, canning, or by being barreled in brine." Pickled okra is available.

MARKETING SEASON: Okra is available throughout the year, with the peak supply in June, July, and August. The following table shows the availability of okra by month expressed as a percent of the total annual supply.

MONTHLY AVAILABILITY OF OKRA EXPRESSED AS A PERCENT OF TOTAL ANNUAL SUPPLY

Jan.	Feb.	Mar.	Apr.	May	June
%	%	%	%	%	%
1	2	4	6	9	16

July	Aug.	Sept.	Oct.	Nov.	Dec.
%	%	%	%	%	%
20	18	12	7	3	2

VARIETIES: "Okra varieties vary in plant height, and in the length and color of their pods. Pods of some varieties have distinct lengthwise ridges, while those of other varieties are smooth." Currently popular varieties described by the USDA include the following:

Perkins Spineless, a dwarf; height 3 ft.; mature pods 7 in. long, ridged, and green.

Dwarf Long Pod, or **Dwarf Green Long Pod**, of the same type as Perkins Spineless; height about 3 ft.; mature pods 7 to 8 in. long, ridged, and green.

Clemson Spineless, of medium height, about 4-1/2 ft.; mature pods 6 in. long, moderately ridged, and green.

Louisiana Green, or **Green Velvet**, medium-tall, height 5 to 6 ft.; mature pods about 7 in. long, slender, slightly ridged, and green.

White Velvet, or **Ladyfinger**, medium-tall, height 5 to 6 ft.; mature pods 6 to 7 in. long, slender, tapered, cylindrical, not ridged, creamy white.

Perkins Mammoth Long Pod, very tall, height 6 to 7 ft.; mature pods 7 to 8 in. long, ridged, and green.

Other varieties are:

Emerald, which was developed by Campbell Soup Co. for use as a processing okra. Height is 5 ft., pods 8 in. long. The pods are smooth, round, very slender, and deep green. "The pod remains tender longer than the pods of many other varieties. This variety bruises rather easily when handled in too large containers."

Gold Coast, which was developed by the Louisiana Agricultural Experiment Station, is 3-1/2 to 4 ft. tall, pods are short, round, smooth, and dark green. Pod length is 3 to 4 in.

French Market is an old variety grown largely for the New Orleans market. Pods are 5 to 6 in. long, round, short, thick, and light green.

CONTAINERS AND WEIGHTS: Okra is shipped in bushel baskets or cartons, holding 30 lb. net; 1/2 bu. baskets, 15 lb.; LA lugs, net weight 18 lb., or 5/9 bu. wirebound flats, net weight 18 lb.

GRADES: The U.S. standards for okra were established in 1928 and codified in 1967. "*U.S. No. 1* shall consist of pods of okra of similar varietal characteristics which are fresh, tender, not badly misshapen, free from decay, and from damage caused by dirt or other foreign matter, disease, insects, mechanical or other means.

"In order to allow for variations incident to proper grading and handling, not more than 10 percent, by weight, of the okra in any lot may be below the requirements of this grade, but not to exceed a total of 5 percent shall be allowed for defects causing serious damage, and not more than 1/5 of this amount, or 1 percent, shall be allowed for decay."

*UFFVA

OKRA

FRESH [12/18/28   51.3945]
Grades: U.S. No. 1
CANNED [7/8/57   52.3331]

Grades:	"A" or "FANCY"	"C" or "STANDARD"	"SUB-STANDARD"
Minimum Score:	85	70	Less than 70

	NET WEIGHT OZ.	NET WEIGHT METRIC	DRAINED WEIGHT OZ.	DRAINED WEIGHT METRIC
Whole or Salad				
No. 8Z Tall	7.8	221.1 g	4.5	127.6 g
No. 303	15.2	430.9 g	10	283.5 g
No. 2½	26.8	759.8 g	17.8	504.6 g
No. 10	98.5	2.8 kg	60	1.7 kg
Cut:				
No. 8Z Tall	7.8	221.1 g	5	141.8 g
No. 303	15.2	430.9 g	10.5	297.7 g
No. 2½	26.8	759.8 g	18.8	533.0 g
No. 10	98.5	2.8 kg	60	1.7 kg

FROZEN [8/20/69   52.1511]

Grades:	"A" or "FANCY"	"B" or "EXTRA STANDARD"	"SUB-STANDARD"
Minimum Score:	90	80	Less than 80

OKRA—Canned [7/8/57]

Grade A: Color: Outer surface of the okra pods possesses a practically uniform color characteristic of the type and variety of young, tender, properly prepared, and properly processed canned okra. **Size:** WHOLE AND WHOLE SALAD—in 90 percent of the most uniform pods of okra, the longest units not more than twice the length of the shortest unit and that the overall length of the unit does not exceed 3-1/2 in. CUT—The appearance is not materially affected by the varieties in the size of the units. **Defects:** Extraneous vegetable matter, small pieces of canned okra, poorly trimmed units, misshapen units, and damaged, and seriously damaged units may be present for the applicable styles if they do not materially affect the appearance and eating quality of the product. **Character:** Units are tender and practically free from fibrous material which is objectionable upon eating; the seeds are in the early stages of development, and with respect to Type I canned okra, the appearance of the product is not more than slightly affected by the presence of broken, crushed, or mashed units, and with respect to Type II canned okra, the appearance is not materially affected by the presence of crushed, broken, and mashed units.

Grade C: Color: The outer surface of the okra pods possesses a fairly uniform color characteristic of the type and variety of fairly tender, properly prepared, and processed canned okra. **Size:** WHOLE AND WHOLE SALAD—in 90 percent of the most uniform pods of okra, the length of the longest unit is not more than 3 times the length of the shortest unit. CUT—The appearance of the product is not seriously affected by the variation in the size of the units. **Defects:** The extraneous vegetable matter, small pieces of canned okra, poorly trimmed units, misshapen units, and damaged or seriously damaged units may be present for the applicable styles if they do not seriously affect the appearance and eating quality of the product. **Character:** Units may be fairly tender; the seeds may have passed the early stages of development, and the product may contain not more than 0.20 percent of dried cellulose.
Sstd: Fails to meet requirements.

OKRA—Frozen [8/20/69]

Grade A: Color: The color of the frozen okra is bright, practically uniform, and typical of the varietal characteristic for young, tender okra. No more than 10 percent may possess a slightly dull color, or possess a slight yellowish green to brownish green coat, or vary materially from the overall general, uniform color; and none of the units in the sample unit may possess a noticeable yellow or brown color or be "off color." **Defects:** Any defects present, whether or not specifically defined or listed herein, should not materially detract from the appearance or edibility of the product; and the defects that may be present in the sample unit should not exceed the allowances in Table I. **Character:** Units are fleshy and tender; the seeds are in the early stages of maturity, and not more than 2 whole pods or 4 cut units per sample unit possess tough fibers.
Grade B: Color: Frozen okra possesses a color which may be slightly dull but which is typical of the natural characteristic

TABLE I—ALLOWANCES FOR DEFECTS IN FROZEN OKRA

	Whole Style		Cut Style	
	Grade A	Grade B	Grade A	Grade B
	Maximum—per 50 pods		*Maximum—per 10 oz.*	
Blemished units; and seriously blemished units	3 units, but not more than 1 unit seriously blemished	6 units, but not more more than 2 units seriously blemished	6 units, but not more more than 2 units seriously blemished	12 units, but not more more than 4 units seriously blemished
Insignificantly blemished units	Do not more than slightly detract from the appearance	Do not seriously detract from the appearance	Do not more than slightly detract from the appearance	Do not seriously detract from the appearance
Harmless extraneous material	2 pieces	3 pieces	1 piece	2 pieces
Poorly trimmed; excessively trimmed; small or damaged units; misshapen units; or any combination of these	10 units	15 units	12 units	18 units
Damaged by mechanical injury	5 units	10 units	Not applicable	Not applicable
Pathological or insect injury	None	1 unit	1 unit	2 units
Sand, grit, or silt	None	Trace	None	Trace
Total: All defects above and any other defects or including above	10 units, do not materially detract from the appearance	15 units, do not seriously detract from the appearance	12 units, do not materially detract from the appearance	18 units, do not seriously detract from the appearance

for reasonably young and reasonably tender okra. No more than 20 percent in the sample unit may possess a color that is typical of less than reasonably young and tender okra: provided, that not more than 6 percent may possess a noticeable yellow or brown color or vary markedly from the general overall color; and none may be "off-color." **Defects:** Any defects present, whether or not specifically defined or listed herein, do not seriously detract from the appearance or edibility of the product; and the defects that may be present do not exceed the allowances in Table I. **Character:** Units may have lost their fleshy texture to a considerable extent, the units are reasonably tender, the seeds may have passed the early stages of maturity, and that more than 4 whole pods or 8 cut units (as applicable) per sample unit possess tough fibers. **Sstd:** Fails to meet requirements.

OKRA AND TOMATOES, TOMATOES AND OKRA—Canned [12/24/57]

Grade A: Color: Tomato ingredient possesses a reasonably good, red color that is typical of reasonably well-ripened tomatoes, and the okra possesses the color of young, tender okra, which ingredients have been properly prepared and processed and meet the following additional requirements: TOMATOES—Not less than 50 percent of the drained tomato ingredient possesses as much or more red than USDA Tomato Red Color Standard: provided, that the color of not more than 10 percent of the remaining portion of the drained tomato ingredient may be yellow, and none is green in color. OKRA—The outer surface of the okra pods or pieces of pods, possesses a color, that is typical of young, tender okra.

Flavor: Means that the product has a characteristic flavor and odor typical of well-ripened tomatoes and young tender okra.

Defects: The presence of sand, grit, or silt; harmless, extraneous material; tomato peel; core material; and damaged, and seriously damaged ingredients, individually or collectively, does not materially affect the appearance and eating quality.

Character: Tomato ingredient is composed of whole, almost whole, or large pieces of tomato flesh, and the okra pods or pieces of pods are fleshy, tender, and practically intact, and the okra seed is in the early stages of development, and not more than 2 percent of the pods or pieces of pods may possess

TOMATOES & OKRA
&
OKRA & TOMATOES

CANNED [12/24/57   52.3421]

Grades:	"A" or	"C" or	"SUB-
	"FANCY"	"STANDARD"	STANDARD"
Minimum Score:	85	70	Less than 70

fibrous material which is materially objectionable upon eating.
Grade C: Color: Tomato ingredient possesses a fairly good, red color typical of fairly well-ripened tomaotes, and the okra possesses the color of reasonably tender okra, which ingredients have been properly prepared and processed. **Flavor:** Product may be lacking in good flavor and odor, but is free from objectionable flavors and odors of any kind. **Defects:** Fairly free from defects means that the presence of sand, grit, or silt; harmless, extraneous material; tomato peel; core material; and damaged, and seriously damaged ingredients, individually or collectively, does not seriously affect the appearance and eating quality. **Character:** Means the tomato ingredient may be predominantly in small pieces, and that the okra pods and pieces of pods may have lost to a considerable extent their fleshy texture; that the units may be fairly tender but not excessively mushy, that the seed may be in the later stages of maturity but are not hard; and that not more than 5 percent of the pods or pieces of pods may possess fibrous material which is materially objectionable upon eating.
Sstd: Fails to meet requirements.

GREEN ONIONS*

USES: Green onions are a savory morsel eaten raw with meat, cheese, or fish. Many like to munch on the tops as well as the small bulbs. The tops are more nutritious than the white parts. Sometimes the greens are chopped and mixed with cottage cheese. Often green onions are cut up and put in salad. They may also be boiled and served like asparagus. Hot green onions served on toast with a rich cheese are tasty. Green onions combine well into Chinese dishes. Serve them with meat loaf, with hash, hamburgers, even scrambled eggs. One good way of cooking green onions, according to the Western Growers Assn., is to boil in 1 in. of salted water until barely tender, 8 to 10 min.

MARKETING SEASON: Green onions are on the market all year with largest supplies May through July and smallest in January and February. The following table shows monthly availability of this vegetable expressed as a percentage of total annual supply.

MONTHLY AVAILABILITY OF GREEN ONIONS EXPRESSED AS PERCENTAGE OF TOTAL ANNUAL SUPPLY

Jan.	Feb.	Mar.	Apr.	May	June
%	%	%	%	%	%
6	6	8	9	10	11

July	Aug.	Sept.	Oct.	Nov.	Dec.
%	%	%	%	%	%
10	9	8	7	7	7

VARIETIES: "At times, almost any of the white varieties are used for green, or bunching onions. These include the short day types like **Crystal Wax** and **Eclipse,** and the long day types such as **White Sweet Spanish, Southport, White Globe** and **White Portugal.** For market, it is essential to choose the white varieties."

Many different varieties are used for green bunching onions, but Dr. Henry A. Jones of Dessert Seed Co., El Centro, Ca., an authority on onions, says that **White Lisbon** is "probably the most widely grown variety for green-bunch onions produced from seed. It is a long-day type and can be grown later than most varieties without getting bulb formation. The foliage is upright growing, dark green, and maintains a fresh look for a considerable time after harvest. The flesh is white, crisp and mild."

Other varieties suggested by the same source are: "**Perfecto Blanco,** an excellent selection of White Sweet Spanish widely used for green bunching. Leaves dark bluish green, with long, clear white stalks which are slow to bulb. **Beltsville Improved** "is winter hardy in the northern U.S. Over-wintered plants make a rapid growth in early spring and these white shoots are crisp and mild. Later in the season, they become more pungent." **He-Shi-Ko** (long white bunching) "A perennial bunching type that continues to divide at the base to from new shoots throughout the growing season. Plants are winter-hardy and are somewhat resistant to smut, pink root and yellow dwarf. Shoots are small, and the flesh is white and mildly pungent."
*UFFVA

CONTAINERS: The main containers used in California are the wax treated, waterproof carton, holding 4-doz. bunches with net weight of 15 to 25 lb. and most common weight of 18; and the 15-1/4 in. wooden crate holding 8-doz. bunches, with net weight of 35 to 40 lb. and most common weight of 35. A standard carlot equivalent is 1250 of the cartons.

QUALITY: Aside from grade at time of federal or state inspection, the consumer should expect green onions to have green, fresh tops, medium-sized necks, and be well blanched for 2 or 3 in. from the root, and that the onions are young, crisp, and tender. Wilted or discolored tops indicate poor quality.

GRADES: The U.S. standard grades for common green onions are U.S. 1 and U.S. 2. These standards do not apply to leeks, Welch or Japanese multiplier onions, or to shallots. *"U.S. 1 shall consist of green onions which are fairly well formed, firm, young and tender, fairly clean, free from decay, and from damage caused by seedstems, roots, foreign material, disease, insects, mechanical or other means. The bulbs shall be well trimmed. The tops shall be fresh, of good green color, free from damage caused by broken or bruised leaves, or by clipping. When all the tops of the onions have been evenly clipped back in accordance with good commercial practice, they shall be specified as 'Clipped Tops' in connection with the grade.*

"(a) OVERALL LENGTH—Unless otherwise specified, the overall length (roots excepted) of the onions shall be not more than 24 in. nor less than 8 in. and the onions shall be not less than 1/4 in. or more than 1 in. in diameter.

"(b) TOLERANCE FOR DEFECTS—In order to allow for variations, other than size, incident to proper grading and handling, not more than a total of 10 percent, by count, of the onions in any lot may fail to meet the requirements of this grade, but not more than 5 percent shall be allowed for defects causing serious damage, including not more than 2 percent for onions affected by decay.

"(c) TOLERANCE FOR SIZE—Not more than a total of 10 percent, by count, of the onions in any lot may fail to meet the requirements as to the specified length, minimum diameter, or maximum diameter, but not more than 5 percent shall be allowed for any one of the requirements for size."

"Size. 'Small' means less than 1/4 in. (in diameter). 'Medium' means 1/4 to 1 in. 'Large' means over 1 in."

ONIONS

CREOLE:
FRESH [4/10/43   51.3955]
Grades: U.S. No. 1, U.S. No. 2, U.S. Combination
BERMUDA-GRANEX-GRANO TYPE ONIONS (3/18/62   51.3195)
Grades: U.S. No. 1, U.S. Combination, U.S. No. 2
GREEN ONIONS (6/20/47   51.1055)
Grades: U.S. No. 1, U.S. No. 2
BUNCHED SHALLOTS (12/16/46   51.1630)
Grades: U.S. No. 1, U.S. No. 2
CANNED [11/2/57   52.3041]
ALL OTHER ONIONS:
FRESH [10/1/71   51.2830]
Grades: U.S. No. 1, U.S. Export No. 1, U.S. Commercial, U.S. No. 1 Boilers, U.S. No. 1 Picklers, U.S. No. 2

Grades:	"A" or "FANCY"	"C" or "STANDARD"	"SUB-STANDARD"
Minimum Score:	85	70	Less than 70

	NET WEIGHT OZ.	NET WEIGHT METRIC	DRAINED WEIGHT OZ.			DRAINED WEIGHT METRIC		
			Tiny	Small	Med.	Tiny	Small	Med.
No. 8Z Tall	7.8	221.1 g	4.5	4.5	4.5	127.6 g	127.6 g	127.6 g
No. 303	15.2	430.9 g	9.5	9	9	269.3 g	255.2 g	255.2 g
No. 10	98.5	2.8 kg	64	63	60	1.8 kg	1.8 kg	1.7 kg

SHALLOTS*

USES: Shallots are a gourmet's delight. Nearly every French or European recipe calls for their use in flavoring. Every part of the plant, from the fresh crisp green leaves to the white elongated bulb, is edible. They are chopped and added to salads, soups, stews, and other meat dishes. They have a characteristic alliaceous odor due to the presence of allyl sulphide, but they are milder and more aromatic than the onion. They also make excellent pickles. The bulbs of shallots are sometimes cured in the same manner as onions and marketed in dry form. These cloves are used in the same way as the green shallots.

MARKETING SEASON: Green shallots are available October through May with plentiful supplies in these months, except October and May. Monthly availability expressed as percentage of annual supply is: Oct., 1 percent; Nov., 10 percent; Dec., 17 percent; Jan., 15 percent; Feb., 15 percent; March, 20 percent; April, 20 percent; and May, 2 percent.
*UFFVA

VARIETIES: There are two commercially distinct types of shallots grown in Louisiana, distinguished broadly as stiff-leaf and broad-leaf or pin-leaf and flat-leaf. The principal commercial variety is the **Louisiana Pearl**, resistant to pink root. Two new varieties, **Bayou Pearl** for fall planting and **Wintergreen** for spring, were released in 1954 by Louisiana Agriculture Experiment Station. **Bayou Pearl** is very high yielding; somewhat pink root resistant; appears free of yellow dwarf disease; forms large-size sets for quick start. **Wintergreen** can outyield any present commercial varieties; starts slowly; seems to tolerate pink root and cold weather. **Wilmington**, especially adapted to North Carolina, matures in 8 to 10 weeks from September-October planting; 8 to 15 bulbs per clone; white skinned; uniform, free of virus, and bulb-born diseases.

CONTAINERS: The most common container for shipping shallots is 1-1/2 bu. wirebound crate, which holds 8 doz. bunches (15 shallots to a bunch), and weighs 40 lb. net. Inside dimensions are: depth, 8-7/8 in.; top 14 in. x 21-1/2 in.; bottom, 15 in. x 22-1/2 in. A similar crate, 1 bu. wirebound, is also used, holding 5 doz. bunches and weighing 25 lb. net.

QUALITY: Green shallots of good quality have green fresh tops, and medium-sized necks which are well blanched for at least 2 or 3 in. from the root and which are young, crisp, and tender. Bruised, yellowed, wilted, or otherwise damaged tops are not attractive and may indicate poor quality or damaged necks. The wilting and yellowing of the top may indicate age and flabby, tough, fibrous necks. This condition can be ascertained by puncturing with the thumbnail and twisting. Bruised tops are unimportant, if they can be trimmed without waste or without spoiling the appearance for table use.

GRADES: U.S. standards specify two grades for green shallots, U.S. No. 1 and U.S. No. 2. *"U.S. No. 1* shall consist of shallots of similar varietal characteristics, which are fairly well formed, firm, young and tender, well trimmed, fairly clean, free from decay, and from damage caused by seedstems, foreign material, disease, insects, mechanical or other means. The tops shall be fresh, of good green color, and free from damage caused by broken or bruised leaves. *Unless otherwise specified*, the overall length (roots excepted) of the shallots shall not exceed 22 in., and the shallots shall be not less than 1/4 in. or more than 3/4 in. in diameter. In order to allow for variations, other than size, incident to proper grading and handling, not more than a total of 10 percent, by count, of the shallots in any lot may fail to meet the requirements of this grade, but *not more than 5 percent shall be allowed for defects* causing serious damage, including not more than 2 percent for shallots affected by decay. Not more than a total of 10 percent, by count, of the shallots in any lot may fail to meet the requirements as to the specified length, minimum diameter, or maximum diameter, *but not more than 5 percent shall be allowed for any one of the requirements for size.* Bunches shall be fairly uniform in size, and the shallots in the individual bunches shall also be of fairly uniform size. The weight of the bunches shall be not less than 4 lb. per dozen bunches. The weight of the bunched shallots shall be determined after they have been wet and shaken or drained to remove excess water."

DRY ONIONS*

USES: Onions are used as a main vegetable dish or as a flavorful ingredient of main meat dishes. They are good boiled, broiled, baked, creamed, steamed, fried, french fried, roasted, pickled, in soups, and stews, for onion rings, sliced raw, and diced raw in salads. A glance through any good cookbook reveals few recipes, other than desserts, which do not include at least a suspicion of onion, says *Wise Encyclopedia of Cookery.*

There ae enough variations to keep the onion a popular repeater on the menu circuit. It develops different and interesting nuances without ever losing the distinctive individuality of its flavor. It contributes zip and nip even to such mild dishes as the souffle.

Here are some menu suggestions: cream of onion and celery soup; baked whole onions; creamy onion casserole; onions and peas aromatique; chili creamed onions and peppers; breast of veal with onion stuffing; beef liver creole; baked fresh onion and tomato casserole; onion and mushroom casserole; curry topped onion potpie; little onion pies with fresh mushroom sauce; shishkebab with onion; baked stuffed onions; stuffed onions with spinach and bacon crumbs; french fried onion

*UFFVA

rings; sage flavored onion stuffing for poultry; onion and potato au gratin; french onion soup; scalloped meat with eggplant and onion; open-faced onion and cheese sandwich; baked onion and beef casserole. The list is endless.

The onion is associated with memories of pleasant feasting; it arouses appetite for delights to come. "Without it there would be no gastronomic art," declares one 19th century epicure. "Banish it from the kitchen and all pleasure of eating flies with it. Its presence lends color and enchantment to the most modest dish; its absence reduces the rarest dainty to hopeless insipidity, and the diner to despair."

MARKETING SEASON: Onions are on the market all year in large amounts. Because of the good storability of the late summer crop, and also because there are crops in early spring, late spring and early summer, there is a relatively even flow of onions to market. There are few peaks or valleys in monthly marketing, and usually these are not steep. The following chart shows monthly availability expressed as a percentage of the total annual supply, with average annual total in millions of pounds at right. Percentages are rounded, do not necessarily total 100.

MONTHLY AVAILABILITY OF DRY ONIONS EXPRESSED AS PERCENTAGE OF TOTAL ANNUAL SUPPLY

	Jan.	Feb.	Mar.	Apr.	May	June
ALL STATES	8	7	8	9	9	10
TEXAS	*	*	6	30	31	13
NEW YORK	10	9	10	6	2	1
CALIFORNIA	2	1	1	1	11	22

July %	Aug. %	Sept. %	Oct. %	Nov. %	Dec. %	Total million lb.'
9	9	9	8	8	7	2,847
11	7	2	1	*	*	444
1	11	14	13	11	10	393
21	16	9	7	5	3	715

VARIETIES: "An important milestone in variety improvement was the discovery of cytoplasmic male-sterility, reported by H.A. Jones and S.L. Emsweller in 1937, and subsequent development of methods for utilizing male-sterility in producing hybrid seed, reported by Dr. Jones and A.E. Clarke

in 1943. The wide use of their methods by public and private plant breeders has resulted in the release of more than 50 commercial F1 hybrids adapted to all important U.S. onion producing areas. Recent development of hybrids adapted to specific areas and for specific purposes, such as dehydration and other processing, has resulted in a long list of improved hybrids being offered by seedsmen. It is impossible to discuss more than the principal types of standard, open-pollinated varieties and a few typical hybrids. Commercial seed firms and state experiment stations are conducting trials of new hybrids as they become available. These sources should be consulted for current recommendations and detailed descriptions of recent introductions." (This introductory statement to the difficult discussion of varieties is by Dr. C.E. Peterson, leader, Onion and Carrot Investigations, Vegetables and Ornamentals Research Branch, Crops Research Division, Agricultural Research Service, USDA, Madison, Wis.)

There are a large number of varieties of Allium cepa, with differences in shape, color, climatic adaptability, pungency, yield, size of bulb, firmness, storability, and resistance to one or another disease. A variety for planting needs to be chosen with regard to all these factors.

In general, on the American market there are three types of onions: (1) the **BERMUDA-GRANEX-GRANO TYPE** which are flat to top-shaped, mild, and early maturing; (2) the **LATE CROP ONIONS**, mostly globes, with yellow, white, or red skins, and mild flavor; and (3) the Creole type and other **VERY STRONG-FLAVORED ONIONS**, such as **Australian Brown, Ebenezer** and **White Portugal**. However, pungency is not entirely related to variety, since it has been found that the same variety can have considerably different flavor when grown in different locations and on different soils, according to Magruder and others. The general classification given in this paragraph is commercial, not at all botanical.

The Bermuda-Granex-Grano type is described by the Fresh Products Standardization and Inspection Branch of the Fruit and Vegetable Division, Consumer and Marketing Service, as onions that "are flat to top shaped, with varying amounts of intermediate shapes. These onions belong to the group which is considered by plant breeders as being the 'short day', or 'early maturing' types and are grown primarily below latitude 35°, which runs south of the following cities: Bakersfield, Ca., Flagstaff, Ariz., Albuquerque, N.M. and Amarillo, Tex. These onions are generally planted in late fall, winter or spring. As a general rule, these onions are usually only fairly well cured.

"The late or main crop onions are mostly of the globe type and have distinctly yellow, white, or red skins. Increasing quantities of hybrid strains are being developed and planted, and the old standard varieties are not as commonplace as they once were ... Yellow globe is a commercial term applied to several varieties and strains. **Sweet Spanish [Valencia]** onions are produced in large quantities in Idaho, Oregon, Utah and Colorado, and to some extent in Washington and California. The principal white globe variety is the **Southport White Globe**. Other white varieties are **White Portugal Silver Skin** and **White Silver King**. The **Southport** is also the leading red globe variety."

Dr. Henry Jones of Dessert Seed Co. separates varieties into short-day hybrids and standard kinds, and long-day hybrids and standard kinds. Following are sample statements by Dr. Jones on a few varieties. For the more complete list, see the booklet, available from Desert Seed Co.

"**Granex.** This short-day* hybrid was released by the USDA and the Texas Agricultural Experiment Station in 1952. Because of its attractiveness, low percentage of culls, and productiveness, it continues to grow in popularity, and today is probably the most widely grown, short-day onion. It will outyield Yellow Bermuda by about 50 percent and if grown where adapted, produces very few doubles and bolters (seeders). Granex has considerable resistance to the southern Texas strain of pink root, and increased resistance is being incorporated. Granex matures about a week earlier than Excel. The bulbs vary somewhat in shape with the method of growing from a thick-flat to almost globe. The thin yellow scales adhere fairly well during harvesting and transit. The flesh is medium firm, exceptionally mild in flavor, and crisp."

"**Texas Early Grano 502** This (standard short-day) variety was released by the Texas Agricultural Experiment Station in 1944, and is a selection out of Early Grano. It is adapted to the southernmost onion districts of the U.S. and matures at about the same time as Excel. The crops are usually grown from transplants, and the bulbs become very large when grown in productive soils. Most years the losses from bolting are rather light. The foliage is fairly upright, is light green in color, and has considerable thrips resistance. The dry, yellow scales are rather thin; the flesh is soft and mild in flavor. The bulbs will become soft if pulled when too immature. The storage life is short. A pink root resistant Texas Early Grano 502 has been developed and is presently being tested. If acceptable to the trade, it may replace the one now being used at least in those districts where pink root is a problem" (Robert S. DeBruyn of the DeBruyn Companies, Zeeland, Mi. notes that there is less of this variety being grown every year).

"**Excel [986]** This (standard short-day) variety was released by the USDA and the Texas and California agricultural experiment stations in 1945. It is an early selection out of Yellow Bermuda. The tops and necks of Excel are a little smaller than those of Yellow Bermuda, and the flat bulbs mature 10 to 14 days earlier. Because of its earliness, it makes a small bulb in the North even when grown from transplants. It is highly resistant to the southern Texas strain of pink root. The flesh is fairly firm, crisp, and very mild in flavor. The bulbs are usable for 3 to 4 months if provided good storage conditions. Excel has played an important role in the development of several short-day varieties." (This variety is considered not too important at present, says R.S. DeBruyn).

"**Yellow Bermuda** This short-day (standard) variety grown chiefly as a winter crop in the South. It was formerly the most extensively grown variety in southern Texas, but after about 1945 it was largely replaced by Excel. Since about 1952, when Granex was released, a considerable portion of the Bermuda acreage has been planted to Granex. The foliage development of Yellow Bermuda is usually more luxuriant than that of Excel, and the crop matures 10 to 14 days later. The bulbs are flat, and the flesh is soft and mild. The dry yellow scales are thin, soft, and silky. The storage life is short." Few are now being grown, notes R.S. DeBruyn.

*An excellent explanation of short-day, standard, and long-term onions, prepared by Dr. Henry Jones, is available from the Dessert Seed Co., El Centro,, Ca.

"**Abundance** This (long-day) hybrid was released by the USDA and the Iowa and Idaho agricultural experiment stations in 1953. It is grown as a summer crop in the North and is adapted to about the same districts as Early Yellow Globe and Downing Yellow Globe. As the name indicates, it is a good yielder and in many comparisons in the North has out-produced other early yellow globe types. In the West, it yields somewhat less than most Spanish onions, but keeps better in storage, and is more resistant to purple blotch. Abundance stores better than Early Yellow Globe, and its keeping quality has been improved since it was first introduced. It fits well into a program where some of the onion crop is sold from the field, or during the early part of the storage season. The bulbs are high-globe in shape, with medium yellow scales. The flesh is fairly firm and pungent."

"**Downing Yellow Globe** (standard long-day variety) This excellent, long-storage variety was developed by Kenneth Trapp of Michigan and is now being used rather extensively. It is adapted to most of the northern, onion-growing districts but does best in the North Central states. The bulbs are late maturing, medium in size, and globe-shaped with dark yellow tough scales that adhere well throughout a long storage period. The hard flesh and retentive scales make this onion suitable for machine handling and bulk storage. The flesh is pungent in flavor."

"**Yellow Sweet Spanish, Utah** (standard, long-day variety) This strain of Spanish was developed and released by the Utah Agricultural Experiment Station. It is strictly a long-day onion adapted to the more northern districts of the semi-arid irrigated regions of the western United States. It is a very late onion maturing at about the same time as Colorado No. 6. Most of the commercial crop is direct-seeded, but some transplants are grown in the South for shipping north in the spring, for home gardeners, and for an early commercial crop. The long growing season and vigor of this variety make it a heavy yielder. The large bulbs are globe-shaped; the dry scales are dark yellow, and adhere fairly well in handling and storage. The foliage is light green and somewhat resistant to thrips. The necks are fairly heavy, and these must be thoroughly dried if the bulbs are to be stored or held for any length of time. If well cured

and properly stored, bulbs can be held till February. The flesh is medium firm and mild."

"**Southport White Globe** (standard, long-day) This variety is adapted to most of the northern, onion-growing districts. It is used for the production of bulbs as well as for green-bunch onions. The bulbs are of medium size and globe to high-globe in shape. Like most white varieties, the bulbs are susceptible to most storage diseases, so if the bulbs are to be stored, curing should be rapid and thorough, and the storage room kept dry and well ventilated. The flesh is rather firm and pungent, but not so pungent as those strains that have been developed for dehydration purposes."

(The following information about Elite, Spartan Banner, Fiesta and El Capitan is from Dr. C.E. Peterson of Agricultural Research Service).

"**Elite** (long-day hybrid) Released in 1953 by the USDA and co-operating agricultural experiment stations in Indiana, Iowa and Idaho, this variety is adapted to north central and northeast producing areas. It is a high yield hybrid, with intermediate firmness and storage quality comparable to Abundance."

"**Epoch** (long-day hybrid) Released in 1953 by USDA and Iowa and Idaho agricultural experiment stations, this variety has the same range of adaptability as Abundance and Elite. It is a harder onion, better adapted to mechnical harvest and bulk storage, and will keep longer in storage. Similar hybrids in this class are **Autumn Spice, Hickory, Nugget** and **Spartan Era**."

"**Spartan Banner** A high-yielding, late-maturing hybrid released by the Michigan Agricultural Experiment Station in 1965, combines yielding capacity of Elite and Abundance with greater firmness for bulk handling and longer storage life. It is also suitable for the manufacture of frozen onion rings."

"**Fiesta** A hybrid involving parent lines derived from **Brigham Yellow Globe** and **Sweet Spanish**, released by the Idaho Agricultural Experiment Station, USDA, and Iowa in 1953, is adapted to Sweet Spanish production areas of the West. It is typical of hybrids made by crossing hard, storage onions of the Brigham or Downing Yellow Globe types with Sweet Spanish. Such combinations are generally harder, more pungent, and better keepers than the Sweet Spanish. Probably because of their greater pungency, hybrids of this type have not replaced the milder Spanish types. **Bronze Perfection, Golden Beauty** and **Treasure** are of the same general origin and type."

"**El Capitan** This mild, high-yielding hybrid released in 1963 by the Idaho Agricultural Experiment Station and the USDA is well adapted to areas where Sweet Spanish is grown. It combines the mildness of Sweet Spanish with greater uniformity and improved keeping quality."

CONTAINERS: The main wholesale container for dry onions is the mesh bag containing 50 lb. of bulk onions. Such a bag, if properly stacked, permits the ventilation essential in transport and storage of this commodity. Cartons holding 48 to 50 lb. are also used; and a variety of consumer size bags, including 1-1/2, 2, 3, 5 and 10-lb. bags, are shipped in a master container.

The material most used for 50-lb. onion bags is kraft paper spun into yarn which is then woven into open-mesh bags all in one piece. The yarn is moisture-resistant to the extent that after immersion in water for 24 hours and tested wringing wet, the material tests not less than 75 percent of the dry strength specified. A woven plastic film bag holding 50 lb. is now being used experimentally. The consumer-size bags are performated polyethylene film or polyethylene mesh.

Before packing, onions are sized, sorted to eliminate defects that would put them out of grade, and then conveyed to filling machines where bags are automatically filled to the desired weight. They are closed by sewing, by wire loops, draw strings, or draw tapes.

QUALITY: "Look for hard or firm onions which are dry and have small necks. They should be covered with papery outer scales and reasonably free from green sunburn spots and other blemishes. Avoid onions with wet of very soft necks, which usually are immature or affected by decay. Also avoid onions with thick, hollow, woody centers in the neck, or with fresh sprouts." Size has nothing to do with onion quality. Selection for size depends on the use to which the onions are to be put, that is, specify large onions for slicing; medium or small onions for roasting or boiling; small onions for boiling or pickling.

GRADES: U.S. grade standards effective Dec. 15, 1966 for dry onions other than Bermuda-Granex-Grano and Creole types provide 6 grades, U.S. 1, U.S. Export 1, U.S. Commercial, U.S. 1 Boilers, U.S. 1 Picklers, and U.S. 2. U.S. grade standards for Bermuda-Granex-Grano type onions effective Jan. 1, 1960, and amended March 18, 1962, provide for 3 grades, U.S. 1, U.S. Combination, and U.S. 2.

"Sec. 51.2830—*U.S. 1* onions (other than Bermuda-Granex-Grano-Creole) consist of onions of similar varietal characteristics which are mature, fairly firm, fairly well shaped, and which are free from decay, wet sunscald, doubles, bottlenecks, scallions, and free from damage caused by seedstems, splits, tops, roots, dry sunscald, sunburn, sprouts, freezing, peeling, cracked fleshy scales, watery scales, dirt or staining, foreign matter, disease, insects, or other means.

"(a) **Size.** Unless otherwise specified, the diameter shall be not less than 1-1/2 in. and yellow, brown, or red onions shall have 40 percent or more, and white onions shall have 30 percent or more, by weight, of the onions in any lot 2 in. or larger in diameter.

"(b) When a percentage of the onions is specified to be of any certain size or larger, no part of any tolerance shall be allowed to reduce the specified percentage, but individual packages in a lot may have as much as 25 percent points less than the percentage specified, except that individual packages containing 10 lb. or less shall have no requirements as to the percentage of a certain size or larger: provided, that any lot, regardless of package size, shall average within the percentage specified.

"Sec. 51.2837—**Size Classifications.** (a) The size of onions may be specified in accordance with one of the following classifications: (1) 'Small' shall be from 1 to 2-1/4 in. in diameter; (2) 'Medium' shall be from 2 to 3-1/4 in. in diameter, except that for onions grown in Minnesota, Iowa, and states east of the Mississippi River, 'Medium' shall be 1-1/2 to 3-1/4 in. in diameter, with percentage of onions 2 in. and larger in diameter as specified in Sec. 51.2830 (a); or, (3) 'Large' or 'Jumbo' shall be 3 in. or larger in diameter.

ONIONS—Canned [11/2/57]

Grade A: Color: Means that canned onions possess a reasonably bright, characteristic color which may include typical greenish areas in the surface of the balls; and that not more than 10 percent of the onions may individually possess such typical greenish areas, which, in the aggregate, exceed 1/2 of the surface area of the bulb. **Size and Shape:** In a container with a count of less than 21 onions, not more than 10 percent of the onions are poorly shaped, and the weight of the second largest onion is not more than 3 times the weight of the second smallest onion. In a container with a count of 21 or more onions, not more than 10 percent of the onions are poorly shaped, and with respect to 95 percent of all the onions, the weight of the largest onion is not more than 3 times the weight of the smallest onion. **Defects:** With repect to the onions in all containers, at least 95 percent of the onions are well trimmed, and for each 20 onions, there may be present not more than 2 loose scales or pieces of scales and 1 detached center, and with respect to the onions in the individual containers, not more than a total of 10 percent of the onions in the container are affected by mechanical damage, and not more than 3 percent of the onions in such container are blemished, including not more than 1 percent of the onions in such container, that are seriously blemished notwithstanding the requirements, 1 onion bulb in an individual container may be affected by one or more of the defects listed therein, although in excess of the percentages permitted for the particular defects: provided, that the percentages of each such defect completed on the basis of all of the onions in all containers is within the percentage permitted for such defect. **Character:** Onions are reasonably firm, tender, and not more than 10 percent are soft or spongy.

Grade C: Color: Canned onions possess a characteristic color which may include typical greenish areas on the surface of the bulbs; the product is not materially affected by oxidation, or dull, grayish-white casts, or watery-white casts, or other discoloration; and that not more than 20 percent of the onions may individually possess greenish areas, which in the aggregate, exceed 1/2 of the surface area of the bulbs. **Size:** In a container with a count of less than 21 onions, not more than 25 percent of the onions are poorly shaped, and the weight of the second largest onion is not more than 4 times the weight of the second smallest onion. In a container with a count of 21 or more onions, not more than 25 percent of the onions are poorly

BREADED ONION RINGS

FROZEN [10/17/59   52.4061]

Grades:	"A" or "Fancy"	"B" or "EXTRA STANDARD"	"SUB-STANDARD"
Minimum Score:	85	70	Less than 70

shaped, and with respect to 95 percent of all the onions, the weight of the largest onion is not more than 4 times the weight of the smallest onion. **Defects:** With respect to the onions in all of the containers, at least 90 percent of the onions are well trimmed and, for each 20 onions, there may be present not more than 4 loose scales or pieces of scales, and 2 detached centers, and for onions in individual containers not more than a total of 20 percent of the onions in the container are affected by mechanical damage, and not more than 5 percent of the onions in such containers, are blemished, with not more than 2 percent of the onions, in such container, seriously blemished. Notwithstanding, etc., see Grade A. **Character:** Onions are fairly firm, fairly tender, and not more than 20 percent are soft or spongy.

Sstd: Fail to meet requirements.

ONION RINGS, BREADED—Frozen [10/17/59]

Grade A: Color: Units possess a characteristic cream to golden color typical of properly prepared frozen onion rings; the product is light, practically uniform in color, and after heating in a suitable manner, is practically free from units which vary markedly from the predominating color. **Defects:** Means that the surface of the units are practically free from carbon specks; that not more than 25 percent of the units may be imperfect rings; and that for each 16 oz., on an average, in the frozen product there may be present not more than: 1 piece of harmless, extraneous vegetable material and 1 blemished unit: provided, that the harmless, extraneous vegetable material and blemished units in single packages of less than 16 oz. do not materially affect the appearance of the product, and that carbon specks, imperfect rings, harmless, extraneous vegetable material, blemished units, or any defects not specifically mentioned, individually or collectively, do not materially affect the appearance or edibility. **Character:** After heating in a suitable manner, the external surfaces of the units are at least moderately crisp; the appearance and eating quality is not materially affected by cracking or unbreaded areas; the units are not oily, soggy, or dry, and the main ingredient is succulent and tender.

Grade B: Units may possess a light cream to brown color typical of frozen onion rings and may be variable in such typical color; the product may be dull but not off color; and, after heating in a suitable manner, the variation in color of the units does not seriously affect the appearance of the product. **Defects:** Means that the surfaces of the units are reasonably free from carbon specks; that not more than 40 percent of the units may be imperfect rings; and that for each 16 oz., on an average, there may be present not more than 2 pieces of harmless, extraneous vegetable material and 2 blemished units: provided that the harmless extraneous vegetable material and blemished units in a single package of less than 16 oz. do not seriously affect the appearance of the product, and that any carbon specks, imperfect rings, harmless, extraneous vegetable material, blemished units, or any defects not specifically mentioned, individually or collectively, do not seriously affect the appearance or edibility. **Character:** After heating in a suitable manner, the external surfaces of the units are fairly crisp; the appearance and eating quality is not seriously affected by cracking, unbreaded areas; the units are not oily, soggy, or dry; and the onion ingredient is reasonably tender. **Sstd:** Fail to meet requirements.

PARSLEY*

USE: *The foliage parsleys* are used for garnishing and for flavoring soups, stews, gravy, and poultry stuffings. Parsley is usually an ingredient of *fine herbes*, a combination of several herbs, finely chopped and thoroughly mingled, used in omelets and sauces. Parsley may be chopped and mixed in salads, added to butter to make parsley butter, and may be made into a jelly. *Gourmet* Magazine suggests fried parsley. It says that "fried parsley is crisp, tasty and tasteful." A recipe for drying parsley is also given by *Gourmet*. "Strip the clusters of parsley leaves from the stalks and plunge them into boiling water for

PARSLEY

FRESH [7/30/30   51.4000]
Grades: U.S. No. 1

30 seconds. Drain, spread the leaves on a wire screen, and dry them in a slow oven (300°F.) until they are crisp. Leave the oven partially open. Store dried parsley—in clusters or powdered—in a tightly closed container." The *Wise Encyclopedia of Cookery*[1] says, "Parsley sprigs are probably the most popular of garnishes, and they are used largely with fish, meat, and poultry. Their ability to stimulate the appetite recommends their use with hors d'oeuvres and canapes. Parsley is very versatile. It seems to go well with everything but sweetmeats ..." Considerable quantities of *rooted parsley* are sold in Chicago and Eastern markets where there is a large foreign-born population. It is cooked and served as other root vegetables. It is also popular in stews.

MARKETING SEASON: Parsley is available all year. Average monthly availability expressed as percent of annual supply is shown in the table following:

MONTHLY AVAILABILITY EXPRESSED AS PERCENT OF TOTAL ANNUAL SUPPLY

Jan.	Feb.	Mar.	Apr.	May	June
%	%	%	%	%	%
6	6	7	7	10	10

July	Aug.	Sept.	Oct.	Nov.	Dec.
%	%	%	%	%	%
8	9	9	10	10	8

(Percentages based on unloads reported by USDA at Chicago, Cincinnati, Los Angeles, New Orleans, and New York for the 5-year period, 1955-59).

VARIETIES: Sturtevant *(Notes on Edible Plants)* describes five types of parsley—plain-leaves, celery-leaved or Neapolitan, curled, fern-leaved, and turnip-rooted. The types grown in this country are curled, plain leaved, and turnip-rooted. The relative importance of the types is indicated by the amount of seed produced over a period of time.

1. *Wise Encyclopedia of Cookery*, William H. Wise & Co. (1948) used with permission.

*UFFVA

CURLED-LEAVED: Evergreen, 12 to 13 in. tall, vigorous, large dark green leaves, compact; coarsely cut, and closely curled; widely adapted for market and home gardens; frost resistant; selection out of Double Curled; growing period 70 days. **Moss Curled** (double curled), 12 in. tall, vigorous, compact, and productive; leaves very dark green, finely cut, and deeply curled; excellent for garnishing, seasoning, and culinary decoration; growing period 70 days. There are other strains of Moss Curled called **Triple Curled** and **Extra Triple Curled. Paramount,** about 10 in. tall, very uniform, rather slow growing, and with stout stems for bunching; leaves triple curled, very dark green, developing a blue-green tint late in the season; some resistance to tip-burning; growing period 85 days. **Triple Curled,** about 11 in. tall, uniform; dark green, finely cut and closely curled leaves; slightly taller, earlier, and not as dark green as Paramount; growing period 75 days.
Extra Triple Curled, plant compact, leaves dark green, and so finely cut and closely curled as to resemble tufts of moss; aside from value for flavoring and garnishing, plant is decorative; taller than Paramount and lighter green; generally more productive; growing period 75 days.
PLAIN-LEAVED: Plain (single), vigorous, and spreading plant, leaves plain, deeply cut, flat, not curled; excellent for flavoring; growing period 72 days. **Dark Green Italian,** leaves flat, heavy, dark, glossy green; a more attractive variety of the plain type; used for flavoring; growing period 72 days.
TURNIP-ROOTED: Hamburg or **Turnip Rooted,** foliage similar to plain leaved, but plants are shorter, and lighter green; plant forms an edible root resembling a slender parsnip, 8 to 10 in. long; grown primarily for edible roots, although sometimes the tops are cut off and marketed separately in bunches; roots can be stored in sand for winter use. (References: See catalogs including *ASGROW Commercial Grower's Guide*; Northrup, King & Co., *Descriptive List of Vegetables and Flowers*; Ferry-Morse Seed Co., *Vegetable Varieties, Their Descriptions and Uses.*)
CONTAINERS AND WEIGHTS: There are no standard containers for parsley. Parsley brought to market from nearby areas may be packed in whatever used containers are on hand. During the past year, *Texas* shipped foliage parsley primarily in *1-2/5 bu. wirebounds* and *1 bu. nailed wooden crates.* Inside dimensions of the 1-2/5 bu. crate are 11-3/8" x 11-3/8" x 24-5/16"; the 1 bu. containers, 8-1/4" x 12-1/2" x 20-5/8". Both crates are packed with 5 doz. bunches, net weight 20 to 25 lb. *Florida and California* ship out-of-state mainly in wirebound 1-bu. containers, 8" x 16" x 20-1/2" packed with 5 doz. bunches. All 3 states occasionally use the 16 in. Howard celery crate, packed with 5 doz. bunches. In the East and Midwest, containers used include bushel baskets; tomato lugs packed 20 to 36 bunches; 8 qt., 12 qt., and 16 qt. baskets packed 2 to 4 doz. bunches; and used apple and pear boxes, packed with 15 to 24 bunches.
QUALITY: Parsely should be bright, green, fresh, and free from dirt and yellowed leaves. Wilting and yellowing of the leaves indicate age or damage. Slightly wilted stock can be revived by placing it in water. Badly wilted stock is worthless. *(A Fruit and Vegetable Buying Guide for Consumers,* Home and Garden Bulletin No. 21, USDA).
GRADE: U.S. standards were established in 1930 for *curly and plain parsley* (do not apply to parsley tops marketed with a part of the entire root attached.) There is one grade, *U.S. No. 1,* which "shall consist of parsley of similar varietal characteristics, and of good green color; which is free from decay, and from damage caused by seedstems, yellow or discolored leaves, wilting, freezing, dirt, or other foreign material, disease, insects, or mechanical or other means. In order to allow for variations incident to proper grading and handling, not more than 5 percent, by weight, of any lot may be below the requirements of this grade, but not more than 1/2 of 1 percent shall be allowed for parsley which is affected by decay."

PARSNIPS*

USE: "When properly cooked—and this means steamed, not boiled—parsnips have a sweet nutty flavor—To obtain the full flavor of parsnips, they should be steamed in their skins until tender. They then may be peeled and slit lengthwise. If the core is large, scoop it out with the point of a knife ... The parsnips are then ready to put through the ricer and served like

*UFFVA

PARSNIPS

FRESH [12/10/45   51.4010]
Grades: U.S. No. 1, U.S. No. 2

mashed potatoes. Or they may be sliced and glazed like sweet potatoes, pan-fried, creamed, or French fried."[1] Parsnips have been used to make wine, and there are recipes for parsnip pie. They are also good in stews.

MARKETING SEASON: Parsnips are available the year round with peak supply from October to January. Moderate supplies are on the market in August and September and February through April; very few are seen May, June, and July. Percentage of supplies by months is:

MONTHLY AVAILABILITY OF PARSNIPS EXPRESSED BY PERCENTAGE OF TOTAL ANNUAL SUPPLY

Jan.	Feb.	Mar.	Apr.	May	June
%	%	%	%	%	%
13	10	14	8	4	1

July	Aug.	Sept.	Oct.	Nov.	Dec.
%	%	%	%	%	%
1	5	8	13	12	11

VARIETIES: Hollow Crown (or **Guernsey, Ideal, Student**) is the principal variety. It matures in 130 to 135 days; has roots 9 to 11 in. long, 2-1/4 to 3 in. in diameter at shoulder, 1-3/4 in. at throat, creamy, crisp, brittle fleshed, hollow crown, medium collar, occasional ridges with few scattered side roots; tops 18 to 24 in. tall, strong, dark green, hardy. Other varieties include **Improved Half Long, Long Smooth, Short Thick, Smooth White, All American,** and **White Model.**

CONTAINERS AND WEIGHTS: Parsnips are marketed mainly in bushel and half-bushel baskets. A bushel of parsnips weighs about 50 lb.

QUALITY: Smooth, firm, well-shaped parsnips of small to medium size are generally of best quality. Soft, flabby, or shriveled roots are usually pithy or fibrous. Softness is sometimes an indication of decay, which may appear as a gray mold or watery soft rot. Woody cores are likely to be found in large, coarse roots. Misshapen roots are objectionable chiefly because of waste in preparation for table.

The parsnip is strictly a winter vegetable. Its flavor is not fully developed until it has been exposed to a temperature near freezing. Exposure to cold develops the sweet flavor. Scientists explain that at low temperatures, the starch in parsnips gradually changes to sugar. At least 2 weeks exposure to a temperature around freezing is necessary for best flavor.

GRADES: U.S. standard grades are U.S. No. 1 and U.S. No. 2. "*U.S. No. 1* shall consist of parsnips of similar varietal characteristics which are well trimmed, fairly well formed, fairly smooth, fairly clean, fairly firm, free from woodiness, soft rot, or wet breakdown, and from damage caused by discoloration, bruises, cuts, rodents, growth cracks, pithiness, disease, insects, mechanical or other means. Unless otherwise specified, the diameter of each parsnip shall be not less than 1-1/2 in. The maximum diameter of the parsnips in any lot may be specified in terms of inches and quarter inches, in accordance with the facts.

"In order to allow for variations incident to proper grading and handling, not more than 3 percent, by weight, of the parsnips in any lot may fail to meet the specified minimum diameter, and not more than 10 percent, by weight, may fail to meet any specified maximum diameter. In addition, not more than a total of 10 percent, by weight, of the parsnips in any lot may fail to meet the remaining requirements of this grade, but not more than 5 percent shall be allowed for defects causing serious damage, including not more than 1 percent for parsnips affected by soft rot or wet breakdown."

PEAS—Canned [5/13/55]

Grade A: Liquor: Good liquor is of typical color, may possess slight cloudiness or slight tint of green, not more than a slight quantity of suspended material or sediment; not viscous. **Color:** Color is good. May possess a color typical of tender peas of similar varietal characteristics; are light, and practically free from peas that materially detract from overall appearance. These latter in all grades include peas commonly referred to as "blond" or "cream colored" peas. **Tolerance for Defects:** For each 100 oz. of net contents, there may be present 1 piece, or pieces, of vegetable material, common to the pea

1. *Wise's Encyclopedia of Cookery,* copyrighted by Wm. H. Wise & Co., Inc. 1948.

PEA SIZES

Sizes	SIEV	COMMER-CIAL NAMES
	No. 1	Tiny
	No. 2	Small
	No. 3	Medium Small
	No. 4	Medium
	No. 5	Medium Large
	No. 6	Large
		Run of the Pod or Garden Run

Source: *Frosty Acres Buyers Guide*—The Frozen Food Forum, Inc., Atlanta, Ga.

plant having an aggregate area of 1/4 sq. in. (1/2 in by 1/2 in.); or 1 thistle bud, or nightshade berry, or other spherical piece of vegetable material, not exceeding the size of a No. 4 size pea; or one cylindrical piece or pieces of vegetable materialy from other plants, not exceeding 1/2 in. in length in the aggregate. Three percent by count may be pieces of peas in sizes larger than No. 2 or in blends of sizes, except that 3 percent by count of the peas may be pieces of peas in sizes No. 1 and No. 2, in blends of sizes No. 1 and No. 2. One-half of 1 percent may be spotted or otherwise discolored, provided defects individually or collectively do not more than slightly affect appearance and eating quality. **Maturity and Tenderness:** Not more than 12 percent of sweet peas will sink in a 11 percent salt solution; not more than 2 percent in a 13 percent salt solution. For early peas, not more than 20 percent in an 11 percent solution; and

not more than 2 percent in a 13-1/2 percent solution.

Grade B: Liquor: Reasonably good liquor, may be cloudy but not off color; not more than a moderate quantity of suspended material or sediment; not more than slightly viscous. **Color:** Reasonably good. May possess a color typical of reasonably tender peas of similar varietal characteristics; are reasonably light, and are reasonably free from peas that materially detract from overall color appearance. **Tolerance for Defects:** For each 50 oz. of net contents, there may be: 1 piece, or pieces of vegetable material, common to the pea plant having an aggregate area of 1/4 sq. in. (1/2 in. by 1/2 in.) on 1 surface of the piece; or 1 thistle bud, or nightshade berry, or other spherical piece of vegetable material, not exceeding size of a No. 4 size pea; or 1 cylinderal piece or pieces of vegetable material from other plants, not exceeding 1/2 in. in length in the aggregate; 7 percent may be pieces of peas; and 2 percent spotted or otherwise discolored, provided defects do not materially affect appearance or eating quality. **Maturity and Tenderness:** Skins of not more than 5 percent of the peas may be ruptured to a width 1/16 in. or more. In the test, not more than 15 percent of sweet peas sink in a 13 percent salt solution; not more than 4 percent in a 15 percent solution. For early peas, not more than 30 percent will sink in a 13-1/2 percent solution, and not more than 8 percent in a 15 percent solution.

Grade C: Liquor: Fairly good liquor may be very cloudy; possess a pronounced accumulation of sediment; may be dull, but not off color and viscous, but not so viscous that the liquor will not separate from the peas. **Color:** Fairly good. May possess a color typical of fairly tender peas of similar varietal characteristics; are fairly free from peas that materially detract from overall color appearance. **Tolerance for Defects:** 1/2 of 1 percent of the drained weight may be harmless, extraneous vegetable; 10 percent of the drained weight may be pieces of peas; 4 percent may be spotted or otherwise dis-colored, provided defects do not seriously affect appearance or eating quality. **Maturity and Tenderness:** Not more than 25 percent by count of the peas may be ruptured to a width of 1/16 in. or more; not less than 90 percent by count are crush-able by a weight of not more than 907.2 grams (2 pds.). The alcohol-insoluble solids of early type peas are not more than

PEAS

FRESH [6/1/42   51.1375]
Grades: U.S. No. 1, U.S. Fancy

CANNED [5/13/55   52.2281]

Grades:	"A" or "FANCY"	"B" or "EXTRA STAN- DARD"	"C" or "STAN- DARD"	"SUB- STAN- DARD"
Minimum Score:	90	80	70	Less than 70

FROZEN [5/28/59   52.3511]

Grades:	"A" or "FANCY"	"B" or "EXTRA STAN- DARD"	"C" or "STAN- DARD"	"SUB- STAN- DARD"
Minimum Score:	90	80	70	Less than 70

23.5 percent, and of sweet type peas not more than 21 percent. In the brine flotation test, which is the same for all sizes, not more than 10 percent of sweet peas will sink in a salt solution of 15 percent, and not more than 10 percent of early peas in a solution of 16 percent.

PEAS—Frozen [5/28/59]

Grade A: Color: Possess a bright, practically uniform, good, green color that is typical for the variety; that peas which vary markedly from such typical green color do not more than slightly affect the overall color appearance; and that not more than 1/2 of 1 percent of the peas may be blond, cream colored, or seriously detract from the overall color appearance. **Defects:** For each 30 oz. of net weight, there may be present not more than the following amounts of harmless, extraneous vegetable material; GROUP 1—flat material, pieces having an aggregate area of not more than 1/4 sq. in., equivalent to 1/2 in. by 1/2 in. on the surface; or 1 piece of any size, or GROUP 2—spherical material 1 unit; or GROUP 3—cylindrical material, a piece which singly or in the aggregate does not exceed 1/2 in. in length. Not more than 7 percent of the peas may be piece of peas; not more than 2 percent of the peas may be blemished, including not more than 1/2 of the 1 percent of all the peas that may be seriously blemished; the presence of harmless extraneous vegetable material, pieces of peas, blemished peas, seriously blemished peas, and other defects, individually or collectively, do not more than slightly affect the appearance or eating quality of the product. **Tenderness and Maturity:** Peas are in such a stage of maturity that not more than 10 percent of the peas may sink in solution containing 13 percent of salt; and that the frozen peas after cooking are very tender upon eating.

Grade B: Color: Possess a reasonably bright and reasonably uniform, green color typical for the variety; that peas which vary markedly from such typical, green color do not materially affect the overall color appearance; and that not more than 1-1/2 percent of the peas may be blond, cream-colored, or seriously detract from the overall color appearance. **Defects:** For each 30 oz. of net weight, there may be present not more than the following amounts of harmless, extraneous vegetable material: GROUP 1—flat material, pieces having an aggregate area of not more than 1/2 sq. in. (equivalent to 1/2 in. by 1/2 in.) on the surface; or one piece of any size; in GROUP 2—spherical material, 2 units; or GROUP 3—cylindrical material, a piece or pieces which singly or in the aggregate do not exceed 1 in. in length. When present in combination, not more than 2 of any of the following groups: GROUP 1—flat material, pieces having an aggregate area of not more than 1/4 sq. in. (equivalent to 1/2 in. by 1/2 in.) on the surface; or 1 piece of any size; GROUP 2—spherical material, 1 unit; GROUP 3—cylindrical material, a piece or pieces which singly, or in the aggregate, do not exceed 1/2 in. in length. Not more than 10 percent of the peas may be pieces of peas; not more than 4 percent may be blemished, including not more than 1 percent of all the peas may be seriously blemished. The presence of harmless, extraneous vegetable material, pieces of peas, blemished peas, seriously blemished peas, and other defects, individually or collectively, do not materially affect the appearance or eating quality of product. **Tenderness and Maturity:** Peas are in such a stage of maturity that not more than 12 percent may sink in a solution containing 15 percent, by weight, of salt; and that the frozen peas after cooking are reasonably tender upon eating.

Grade C: Color: Possess a fairly uniform, green color typical for the variety, which may be dull but not off-color; peas which vary markedly from such typical, green color do not seriously affect the overall color appearance; and not more than 2 percent may be blond, cream-colored, or seriously detract from the overall color appearance. **Defects:** For each 30 oz. of net weight, there may be present not more than the following amounts of harmless, extraneous material: When present at a single group: GROUP 1—flat material, pieces having an aggregate area not more than 1 sq. in. (equivalent to 1 in. by 1 in.) on the surface; or 1 piece of any size; or GROUP 2—spherical material, 3 units; or GROUP 3—cylindrical material, or pieces which singly or in the aggregate do not exceed 2 in. in length. When present in combination, not more than 2 of any of the following groups: GROUP 1—flat material, pieces having an aggregate area of not more than 1/4 sq. in. (equivalent to 1/2 in. by 1/2 in.) on the surface; or 1 piece of any size; GROUP 2—spherical material, 2 units; GROUP 3—cylindrical material, a piece or pieces which singly or in the aggregate do not exceed 1 in. in length: not more than 15 percent of the peas may be pieces of peas; not more than 6 percent of the peas may be blemished, including not more than 3 percent of harmless, extraneous vegetable material, pieces of peas, blemished peas, seriously blemished peas, and other defects, individually or collectively, do not seriously affect the appearance or eating quality. **Tenderness and Maturity:** Peas are in such a stage of maturity that not more than 16 percent of the peas may sink in a solution containing 16 percent of salt; and that the frozen peas after cooking are fairly tender upon eating.

Sstd: Fails to meet requirements.

FIELD PEAS AND BLACK-EYE PEAS—Canned [4/17/50]

Grade A: Color: Fairly uniform, typical of fairly young field or blackeye peas of similar varietal characteristics. **Defects:** Maximum tolerance, for each 12 oz. drained weight, Extraneous Vegetable Matter—2 pieces. Blemished Units—2 percent of drained weight; all other defects combined—5 percent of drained weight. **Character:** Units are tender and in a fairly early stage of maturity.

SOUTHERN PEAS [FIELD PEAS & BLACK-EYE PEAS]

FRESH [7/13/56   51.2670]
Grades: U.S. No. 1, U.S. Commercial

CANNED [4/17/50   52.1641]

Grades:	"A" or "FANCY"	"C" or "STANDARD"	"D" or "SUB-STANDARD"
Minimum Score:	85	70	Less than 70

	NET WEIGHT OZ.	NET WEIGHT METRIC	DRAINED WEIGHT OZ.	DRAINED WEIGHT METRIC
No. 303	15.2	430.9 g	11	311.8 g
No. 10	98.5	2.8 kg	72	2.0 kg

FROZEN [6/30/61   52.1661]

Grades:	"A" or "FANCY"	"B" or "EXTRA STANDARD"	"SUB-STANDARD"
Minimum Score:	90	80	Less than 80

Grade C: Color: May be variable and typical of nearly mature field or black-eye peas of similar varietal characteristics. **Defects:** Maximum tolerance for each 12 oz. drained weight, Extraneous Vegetable Matter—4 pieces. Blemished Units—6 percent of the drained weight; all other defects combined—10 percent of drained weight. **Character:** Units are fairly tender and may be mealy but not hard.

PEAS AND CARROTS—Canned [7/20/70]

Grade A: Color: Product possesses an overall color that is at least reasonably light, and each of the vegetables is not more than slightly affected by variations in color; carrots possess an orange-yellow color which is light and typical, and the presence of green, white, or orange-brown unit does not more than slightly affect the appearance or eating quality of the carrots; the color of the peas is normal and is typical of at least reasonably young and tender peas, with practically no "blond" or "cream"-colored peas. **Size and Shape:** Canned peas and carrots are practically uniform in size and shape; the carrots comply with the measurement, shape, and uniformity requirements for classification; and, in addition, the overall appearance of the product is not materially affected by variations or

PEAS & CARROTS

PEAS:
FRESH [6/1/42　51.1375]
Grades: U.S. No. 1, U.S. FANCY
CARROTS:
FRESH [7/17/54　51.495]
Grades: U.S. Grade A, U.S. Grade B
CANNED [7/20/70　52.6201]

Grades:	"A" or "FANCY"	"B" or "EXTRA STANDARD"	"SUB-STANDARD"
Minimum Score:	90	80	Less than 80

	NET WEIGHT OZ.	NET WEIGHT METRIC	DRAINED WEIGHT OZ.	DRAINED WEIGHT METRIC
Carrots sliced or in strips				
No. 8Z Tall	7.8	221.1 g	5.5	155.9 g
No. 303	15.2	430.9 g	10.6	300.5 g
No. 10	98.5	2.8 kg	70.0	1.98 kg
Carrots diced or double-diced				
No. 8Z Tall	7.8	221.1 g	5.5	155.9 g
No. 303	15.2	430.9 g	10.8	306.2 g
No. 10	98.5	2.8 kg	71.0	2.0 kg

FROZEN [3/20/55　52.2501]

Grades:	"A" or "FANCY"	"B" or "EXTRA STANDARD"	"C" or "STANDARD"	"SUB-STANDARD"
Minimum Score:	90	80	70	Less than 70

irregularities in size and shape of the units. **Defects:** Not more than 1 piece of harmless, extraneous material per 60 oz. of drained product; and not more than the following per sample unit of 10 oz.: a total of 8 damaged and seriously damaged units, of which not more than 1 may be severely damaged: provided, that damaged and seriously damaged units, either singly or in combination, may not more than slightly affect the appearance or eating quality, including harmless, extraneous

material and/or other defects, individually or collectively, which materially affect the appearance; and any combination of the foregoing which materially affect the appearance or eating quality. **Character:** Carrots are tender, are not fibrous, and possess a practically uniform texture. The peas are at least reasonably tender and comply with the requirements.

Grade B: Color: Product possesses an overall color which may be slightly dull, but is not off-color; the color of each of the vegetables may be variable but not to the extent that the appearance of the product is seriously affected; the presence of green, white, or orange-brown units does not seriously affect the appearance of the carrots; the color of the peas is typical of fairly young and tender peas. **Size and Shape:** The carrots comply with the measurements, shape, and uniformity requirements for (B) classification; and in addition the overall appearance of the product is not seriously affected by variations or irregularities in size and shape of the units. **Defects:** Not more than 1 piece of harmless extraneous material per 30 oz. of drained product; and not more than the following per sample unit of 10 oz.: a total of 15 damaged and seriously damaged units of which not more than 3 units may be seriously damaged: provided, that damaged and seriously damaged units, either singly or in combination, do not seriously affect the appearance or eating quality: including harmless, extraneous material and/or other defects, individually or collectively, which seriously affect the appearance or eating quality; and any combination of the foregoing which seriously affect the appearance or eating quality. **Character:** The carrot units are at least reasonably tender, may be variable in texture, but are not tough, hard, or mushy; and not more than 5 percent of the carrot ingredient may possess coarse, fibrous material. The peas are at least fairly tender; the skins of not more than 5 percent may be ruptured to a width of 1/16 in. or more; and the peas comply with the requirements.

PEAS AND CARROTS—Frozen [3/20/55]

Grade A [Fancy]: Color: The color is bright and typical of young and tender peas and tender diced carrots, and the appearance of the product is not more than slightly affected by variations in the color of the carrots and peas. **Defects:** Not more than 1 piece of extraneous pea or carrot material having an aggregate area of 3/16 sq. in., or 1 spherical or cylindrical piece for each 40 oz. of the product; not more than 10 damaged and seriously damaged units for each 10 oz., of which not more than 2 units are seriously damaged; provided that the appearance or eating quality is not more than slightly affected; and not more than 12 percent of the carrots are units smaller than 1/2 the volume of, or larger than, the predominating size of the dice, provided that 24 percent of such units may be present in any single sample. **Character:** Peas are reasonably tender and are equivalent to frozen peas that would not score less than 34 points for "tenderness and maturity" in the U.S. Standards for Grades of Frozen Peas; and carrots are tender and have an almost uniform texture. Both vegetables must be tender after cooking.

Grade B [Extra Standard]: Color: Color is reasonably bright and typical of reasonably young and tender peas and tender, diced carrots, and the appearance of the product is not affected by variations in color of the peas and carrots. **Defects:** Not more than 1 pea or carrot having an aggregate area of 3/8 sq. in., or 2 spherical or cylindrical pieces of other harmless, vegetable material for each 40 oz.; not more than 14 damaged and seriously damaged units for each 10 oz., of which not more than 3 units are seriously damaged, provided that the appearance or edibility of the product is not affected; not more than 17 percent of the carrots are smaller than one-half the volume of, or larger than the predominating size of the dice, provided that 34 percent of such units may be present in any single sample. **Character:** Peas are reasonably tender and are equivalent to frozen peas with a minimum score of 32 points for "Tenderness and Maturity" in the U.S. Standards for Grades of Frozen Peas; and carrots are tender and have an almost uniform texture. Both vegetables must be reasonably tender after cooking.

Grade C: [Standard]: Color: Color is typical of fairly young and tender peas and carrots, may be dull but not off color, and the color may be variable, but the appearance may not be seriously affected. **Defects:** Not more than 1 extraneous pea or carrot

material having an aggregate area of 3/4 sq. in., or 3 spherical or cylindrical pieces of other harmless vegetable material for each 40 oz.; not more than 17 damaged or seriously damaged units for each 10 oz. of which not more than 5 units are seriously damaged, provided they do not seriously affect the appearance or eating quality; and not more than 25 percent of the carrots are smaller than 1/2 the volume of, or larger than the predominant size of the dice, provided that not more than 50 percent of such units may be present in any single sample. **Character:** Peas are at least fairly tender, may be variable in texture, but not tough or hard, and may have a few units with a coarse, fibrous texture.

Sstd: Fails to meet requirements.

PEPPERS*

USES: Sweet peppers are good either raw or cooked, but do not overcook them. Brief parboiling is desirable if peppers are to be stuffed, but 3 to 5 minutes in boiling, salted water is long enough if they are to have additional cooking ... Stuffed peppers are easily prepared. Remove the "lid" of the pepper pod by cutting away a thin slice at the stem end. Remove seeds and membrane (placenta). Parboil in boiling, salted water to cover. Invert, drain, and fill with some well-seasoned mixture of cooked meat and vegetables ... Sweet peppers are delicious, too, cut in strips and sauteed briefly in garlic-flavored olive oil. Especially good with beef or fish ... In the hors d'oeuvre department, one quick-to-fix idea is stuffed pepper quarters. The stuffing can be cottage cheese which has been tossed with minced chives, carrot shreds, and crisp celery bits. For a final touch of color, sprinkle minced chives and paprika lightly over the top.

In the salad realm, the ways of stuffing green peppers seem to be never ending ... As a starter, try filling the cavity with a mixture of lightly cooked and marinated vegetables ... carrot cubes, snap beans, and tiny cauliflowerettes make a colorful trio. A gourmet alternative is a mixture of corn, potato cubes, and shreds of raw cabbage topped with a dollop of sour cream. To give menu offerings an extra flourish, fill peppers with a piquant Roquefort cheese and ham stuffing. And for a new look

*UFFVA

SWEET PEPPERS

FRESH [12/15/63   51.3270]
Grades: U.S. Fancy, U.S. No. 1, U.S. No. 2
FROZEN [3/13/59   52.3001]

Grades:	"A" or "FANCY"	"B" or "EXTRA STANDARD"	"SUB-STANDARD"
Minimum Score:	85	70	Less than 70

in side dish salads, chill these cheese-filled peppers thoroughly, and cut them into 1/4-in. slices ... It is especially important to use good sized, well shaped, and firm peppers for stuffing. Select those that are chunky and somewhat rounded at the base so that they will stand without tipping.

Additionally, sweet peppers are canned or are pickled in brine for use in salads or other foods. Diced green or red sweet peppers are sometimes mixed with sweet corn or other vegetables. Pimiento peppers, usually the Perfection variety, are canned extensively for use in preparing such foods as pimiento cheese and the red stuffing for olives. Paprika is the finely ground fruit walls of paprika peppers, a mild type.

MARKETING SEASON: Sweet peppers are available all year in good volume, with a slight peak from May through August. Percentages of total annual volume available each month, from data compiled by UFFVA, are as follows:

MONTHLY AVAILABILITY OF SWEET PEPPERS EXPRESSED AS PERCENTAGE OF TOTAL ANNUAL SUPPLY

Jan.	Feb.	Mar.	Apr.	May	June
%	%	%	%	%	%
7	6	7	7	10	10

July	Aug.	Sept.	Oct.	Nov.	Dec.
%	%	%	%	%	%
10	10	9	9	8	7

VARIETIES: "The varieties of garden peppers may be classified in two main kinds: (1) those with mild or sweet-fleshed fruits; (2) those with hot or pungent-fleshed fruits. Within each of these groups, is a remarkable range of sizes, shapes, and colors of fruits, and sizes and growth habits of plants. Most of the popular mild, or sweet, varieties have relatively large fruits, 2-1/2 to 4 in. in diameter and 4 to 5 in. long.

"The most popular, mild-fleshed pepper varieties for use as a fresh vegetable or for brining are 4 to 5 in. long and have maximum diameters nearly as great as their length. They are typically 3- or 4-lobed and taper only slightly toward the blossom end. Some of the longer, more tapering varieties are satisfactory for use in salads, but are losing in popularity because they are not so well suited for use in stuffed-pepper dishes.

"All the varieties, except Neapolitan, included in this group are dark green when immature and turn brilliant scarlet at maturity. They are generally used green (The Neapolitan, yellow) but sometimes they are used in the full-ripe stage because of the attractive red color."

Burlingon About 72 days. Resistant to tobacco mosaic virus. Fruits similar to World Beater, medium large, oblong, a strain of World Beater developed for use where tobacco mosaic is prevalent in the East.

California Wonder About 75 days. Fruits about 4-1/2 in. long, 3-3/4 in. in diameter, mostly 4-lobed, little or to taper, very smooth, and attractive. Slightly smaller and earlier (65 to 70 days), strains of this type are also available under the name of Early Calwonder.

Chinese Giant About 82 days. Fruits about 4-1/2 in. long, diameter nearly as great, 3- or 4-lobed, little taper, blossom ends tend to be crumpled and rough.

Florida Giant About 75 days. Fruits similar to California Wonder, but slightly larger, Florida Giant is a selection of California Wonder that is adapted to the South.

Harris Early Giant About 63 days. Fruits about 4-1/4 in. long, 3-1/4 in. in diameter, typically 3-lobed, large and block shaped, with little taper, smooth; one of the earlier peppers.

Keystone Resistant Giant About 74 days. Resistant to tobacco mosaic virus. Fruits about 4 to 4-1/2 in. long, 3 to 3-1/2 in. in diameter, block shaped, somewhat tapered, ridged, Similar to Florida Giant.

Neapolitan About 60 days. Fruits about 4 in. long, 2 in. in diameter, 3-lobed, tapered, yellowish green to greenish yellow when immature, bright red when mature.

Ruby King About 68 days. Fruits up to 5 in. long, 2-1/2 to 3 in. in diameter, typically 3-lobed, distinctly tapered, often irregular.

Windsor-A About 58 days. Fruits about 4-1/2 in. long, 2-1/4 in. in diameter, 3-lobed, tapered only slightly except near blossom end, tend to be slightly crumpled or irregular. The earliest pepper of this type. Developed for New England and other cool regions.

World Beater About 70 days. The fruits are up to 5 in. long, 3-3/4 in. in diameter, distinctly 4-lobed, little taper, but not crumpled or irregular.

Yolo Wonder About 74 days. Resistant to tobacco mosaic virus. Fruits about 4 in. long, 3 to 3-1/2 in. in diameter, block shaped, smooth. A strain of California Wonder.

"Harris Early Giant and Windsor-A are early varieties that are adapted to regions of relatively short, cool seasons. Ruby King is an old, well-established, widely adapted variety that has given way in popularity to the smoother, thicker, nontapered forms such as California Wonder and World Beater; Chinese Giant is productive and widely adapted, but it is a little later and a little rougher in form than generally desired. California Wonder and the earlier named strains of it are the most popular because of their highly desirable size, shape and smoothness. World Beater, the second in importance, is probably a little more widely adapted and a more dependable producer than California Wonder, except under the most favorable conditions. Mild varieties with tomato-shaped or yellow-colored fruits are relatively unimportant.

"*Mild varieties for processing.* The Perfection, a large variety of the pimiento type of pepper, is grown almost exclusively for canning; it is by far the main canning variety. It is not well adapted to the northern half of the country. A brief characterization follows:

"**Perfection** About 80 days to red ripe. Fruits are about 3-1/2 in. long, 3 to 3-1/4 in. in diameter, smooth and symmetrical, top shaped or short conical, sometimes described as heart-shaped, walls are unusually thick and firm, which suits the variety to canning.

"In the Maryland-Delaware-New Jersey area, a part of the pepper crop is grown for canning or for preservation in brine. California Wonder and similar varieties are also used."

CONTAINERS: Principal containers, as reported by *Market News Service* of USDA, with net weight and number of

SWEET PEPPERS—LOWER LIMIT "NOT SERIOUSLY MISSHAPEN" U.S. No. 2

packages to a carload are: bushel basket, hamper or crate, 28 to 30 lb., 775; 1-1/9 bu. crate, 28 to 33 lb., 775; fiberboard carton, 30 to 34 lb., 775; L.A. lug, 18 lb., 1280. Other containers often used are: 5/8 bu. hamper, 18 to 19 lb., 1205; 3/4 bu. basket 21 to 23 lb., 1035; 1/2 bu. basket, 15 lb., 1450; 1-1/8 bu. carton, 33 to 35 lb., 660; standard cantaloupe crate, 40 to 45 lb., 505; and 16-in. celery crate, 39 to 40 lb., 555.

Some typical inside dimensions of containers are given in the following table from data of the Uniform Classification Committee:

Container No.	Type	Inside Dimensions	Tariff No.
1420	Wood	13-3/8 x 11 x 21-7/8	1-H
1446	Laminated box	10-1/2 x 14-1/2 x 15-7/8	1-H
3952	Wirebound	11 x 13-3/8 x 21-1/4	1-H
5045	Wirebound	11-5/16 x 11-5/16 x 17-1/8	2-G; 823-D; 4-C
5670	Wired crate	13-3/8 x 11 x 22	823-D; 4-C
7450	Fiberboard	10-1/2 x 12 x 13 x 18-1/4	1-H
7455	Fiberboard	10-7/8 x 11-1/8 x 12 x 17-1/4	1-H
7460	Fiberboard	11 x 11-1/2 x 11-3/4 x 17-1/2	2-G

GRADES: U.S. grade standards for sweet peppers provide three grades, U.S. Fancy, U.S. 1 and U.S. 2. "*U.S. Fancy* consists of mature, green sweet peppers of similar varietal characteristics which are firm, well shaped, and free from sunscald, freezing injury, decay, and from injury caused by scars, hail, sunburn, disease, insects, mechanical or other means. **Size:** The diameter of each pepper shall not be less than 3 in. and the length of each pepper shall be not less than 3-1/2 in. **Color.** Any lot of peppers which meets all the requirements of this grade, except those relating to color, may be designated as 'U.S. Fancy Red' if at least 90 percent of the peppers show any amount of a shade of red color; or as 'U.S. Fancy Mixed Color' if the peppers fail to meet the color requirements of either 'U.S. Fancy' or 'U.S. Fancy Red'.

"*U.S. No. 1* consists of mature, green sweet peppers of similar varietal characteristics which are firm, fairly well shaped, and free from sunscald and decay, and free from damage caused by freezing injury, hail, scars, sunburn, disease, insects, mechanical or other means. **Size.** Unless otherwise specified, the diameter of each pepper shall be not less than 2-1/2 in. and the length of each pepper shall be not less than 2-1/2 in. **Color.** Any lot of peppers which meets all the requirements of this grade, except those relating to color, may be designated as 'U.S. No. 1 Red', if at least 90 percent of the peppers show any amount of red color; or as 'U.S. No. 1 Mixed Color' if the peppers fail to meet the color requirements of either 'U.S. No. 1' or 'U.S. No. 1 Red'."

PEPPERS, SWEET—Frozen [3/13/59]

Grade A: Color: A good characteristic light color for the type and, with respect to type I and type II, variations in color do not materially affect the appearance of the product. **Size and Symmetry:** WHOLE STEMMED—whole unstemmed; halved. Not less than 90 percent of the pods shall be at least 2-1/2 in. in length, exclusive of the stem, and 2-1/2 in. in diameter, and shall be practically uniform in size and symmetry. SLICED—The units are practically uniform in size, and the aggregate weight of all strips less than 1-1/4 in. in length does not exceed 30 percent by weight of all units. DICED: The units are practically uniform in size, and the aggregate weight of all the units which are noticeably smaller than 1/2 the area of an average sized unit, and of all markedly large and irregular shaped units, do not exceed 10 percent. **Defects:** Pods in whole unstemmed, whole stemmed, and halved styles are well trimmed; no grit, sand, and silt may be present that affects the appearance and eating quality, and seeds, undeveloped seeds, core and stem, naturally damaged, and seriously damaged units, individually or collectively, do not materially affect the appearance and eating quality. **Character:** Units are firm, full fleshed, and tender.

Grade B: Color: Reasonably light, characteristic color for the type, and, with respect to Type I and Type II, variations in color do not seriously affect the appearance of the product. **Size and Symmetry:** Whole stemmed; whole unstemmed; halved. Not less than 80 percent of the pods shall be at least 2-1/2 in. in length, exclusive of the stem, and 2-1/2 in. in diameter, and shall be reasonably uniform in size and symmetry. SLICED—The units are reasonably uniform in size, and the aggregate weight of all strips less than 1-1/4 in. in length does not exceed 40 percent of the units. DICED—The units are reasonably uniform in size, and the aggregate of all units which are noticeably smaller than 1/2 the area of an average sized unit, and of all markedly large and irregular-shaped units, does not exceed 20 percent of all the units. **Defects:** Pods in whole unstemmed, whole stemmed, and halved styles are reasonably well trimmed; no grit, sand, or silt may be present that affects the appearance and eating quality; and seeds, undeveloped seeds, core, and stem material, damaged and seriously damaged units, individually or collectively, do not seriously affect the appearance and eating quality. **Character:** Units are reasonably full fleshed, may lack firmness, but are not soft or mushy.

Sstd: Fails to meet requirements.

PIMENTOS—Canned [10/23/67]

Grade A: Color: Overall color is light, typical, practically uniform; exterior surfaces meet requirements. **Size and Shape:** Practically uniform, most of the whole pods are well trimmed, and any variation does not materially detract from overall appearance. **Defects:** Any combination of defects may not

more than slightly detract from the appearance or edibility. **Character:** Firm and full fleshed, and tender without apparent disintegration, and possess a practically uniform texture.
Grade C: Color: Color may be variable and slightly dull, but none of the units may be green, or of a greenish cast, or off color. **Size and Shape:** Fairly uniform, most of the whole pods are at least fairly well trimmed, and any variation does not seriously detract from overall appearance. **Defects:** Any combination of defects does not seriously detract from the appearance or edibility. **Character:** May be lacking in firmness and fleshiness, and may show some evidence of disintegration, but are not soft or mushy or tough.

PIMENTOS

CANNED [10/23/67   52.2681]

Grades:

	"A" or "FANCY"	"C" or "STANDARD"	"SUB-STANDARD"
Minimum Score:	90	80	Less than 80

	NET WEIGHT OZ.	NET WEIGHT METRIC	DRAINED WEIGHT OZ.	DRAINED WEIGHT METRIC
Whole; Halves				
No. 303	as full	as full	11.0	311.8 g
No. 2½	as	as	20.2	572.7 g
No. 10	practicable	practicable	70.7	2.0 kg
Whole and Pieces				
No. 303	as full	as fu	11.2	317.5 g
No. 2½	as	as	20.5	581.2 g
No. 10	practicable	practicable	72.2	2.0 kg
Pieces; Diced; Chopped				
No. 303	as full	as full	11.2	317.5 g
No. 2½	as	as	20.5	581.2 g
No. 10	practicable	practicable	74.0	2.1 kg
Sliced				
No. 303	as full	as full	11.0	311.8 g
No. 2½	as	as	20.2	572.7 g
No. 10	practicable	practicable	71.7	2.0 kg

POTATOES*

USES: Because of their bland, universally adaptable flavor, potatoes may be used frequently in meals without objectionable monotony. They are served baked, roasted, boiled, mashed, fried from raw strips, or pieces, or from boiled or baked pieces, french fried, creamed, hash browned, used in salads, stews, soups, in pancakes, and pastries; au gratin, curried, in souffles, in chowders, in croquettes, in dumplings, scalloped, and lyonnaise. The variety of potato salads is endless, either hot or cold, with various combiantions of added ingredients. Some hardy souls even eat them raw.

MARKETING SEASON: Fresh potatoes are on the market in large supply in all months with no distinct peak or trough. The following table shows availability of fresh potatoes from all sources (the first line) as a percentage of the annual supply by months. Data is also given for supplies from California, Maine, and Idaho. That data is an average of the situation in years as derived from *USDA Market News Service* unloads in 41 cities.

MONTHLY AVAILABILITY OF POTATOES EXPRESSED AS PERCENTAGE OF TOTAL ANNUAL SUPPLY

	Jan. %	Feb. %	Mar. %	Apr. %	May %	June %
POTATOES, ALL	9	8	9	9	9	9
IDAHO	12	11	13	13	13	6
CALIF.	5	4	4	4	8	23
MAINE	11	11	15	20	18	10

	July %	Aug. %	Sept. %	Oct. %	Nov. %	Dec. %
	8	8	8	8	8	8
	1	1	2	6	10	11
	25	10	5	4	4	4
	1	*	*	1	5	7

(*Less than 1/2 of 1 percent)

Fall harvested potatoes may be stored for 9 to 12 months which makes it possible to smooth out the marketing season. Additionally, potatoes are being grown and harvested somewhere in the U.S. in all months. While the winter, spring, and

*UFFVA

POTATOES

FRESH [2/5/72   51.1540]
Grades: U.S. Extra No. 1, U.S. No. 1, U.S. Commercial, U.S. No. 2
SEED POTATOES (4/29/72   51.3000)
Grades: U.. No. 1 Seed Potatoes
CANNED WHITE POTATOES [2/10/50   52.1811]

Grades:

	"A" or "FANCY"	"C" or "STANDARD"	"D" or "SUB-STANDARD"
Minimum Score:	85	70	Less than 70

	NET WEIGHT OZ.	NET WEIGHT METRIC	DRAINED WEIGHT OZ.	DRAINED WEIGHT METRIC
No. 2½	26.8	759.8 g	19	538.6 g
No. 10	98.5	2.8 kg	74	2.1 kg

PEELED POTATOES (6/8/54   52.2421)

	"A" or "FANCY"	"B" or "EXTRA STANDARD"	"SUB-STANDARD"
Minimum Score:	85	70	Less than 70

summer crops are much smaller than the fall storage crop, they make an important contribution.

The winter and early spring crops are from Florida, California, and Texas; the late spring crop from the South, plus Arizona, and California; and the summer crop comes from the South, Midwest, California, New York, and New Jersey. (To check in detail the planting, harvesting and marketing dates, see Agriculture Handbook 127, "Potatoes and Sweetpotatoes, Usual Dates For Planting, Harvesting, Marketing, by Seasons, In Principal Areas," USDA, 1967.)

VARIETIES: "The types of potatoes generally found on the market in the U.S. include long russet, long white, round russet, round white, and round red tubers. Such classification is arbitrary, since each category includes horticultural varieties which differ greatly in culinary or processing quality, storage life, and other important traits." As distinguished from these general types, varieties are difficult to recognize in the marketplace. Even experts have trouble in picking varieties out of a jumbled pile. For that reason, only brief descriptions of the principal varieties will be given here.

Varieties used in the U.S. are changing. Many varieties grown 40 to 50 years ago have been replaced by new ones. Nevertheless, the current leading variety by a large margin, the Russet Burbank, was developed many years ago, probably in the 19th century. The reasons for a variety's acceptance or rejection are complex. Among the factors are yield, cooking and processing characteristics, including percentage of dry matter, appearance, and resistance to diseases.

The USDA and the state experiment stations have a well-organized program of breeding new and improved potato varieties. Aside from disease resistance, varieties are tested before adoption for the amount of dry matter they contain. If the quantity is high under all growing conditions, a desirable, mealy potato is practically assured. Vitamin and mineral content ought to be considered more than they are. The problems of plant breeding are extremely complicated, and it takes many years to develop an improved variety.

Every current variety is resistant to one or another disease, or to more than one. However, as pointed out by Professor Elmer E. Ewing of Cornell University, "There are so many potato diseases that every variety is susceptible to more diseases than the number to which it is resistant." Consequently, in the following descriptions, resistance or susceptibility to disease is not stated, except resistance or susceptibility to scab. "This disease is very prevalent and is a serious problem in some soils where varietal resistance is the only practical control measure. Most varieties are tested for scab resistance before release."

The best measure of importance of a potato variety is how many acres of certified seed of that variety are grown. This figure indicates roughly how large the crop of that variety will be. Thirty-nine varieties in the U.S. in 1971 were listed as having 100 acres or more of seed passed as certified. The total acreage of seed potatoes of these 39 varieties was 191,120. However, only 18 of these, each with more than 1000 acres certified, accounted for 96.2 percent of the total.

These 18 in order of the certified seed acreage of each variety in 1971 were: (1) Russet Burbank 63,147; (2) Kennebec 29,318; (3) Katahdin 27,442; (4) Norchip 11,684; (5) Norland 10,298; (6) Norgold Russet 7,896; (7) Superior 6,928; (8) Red Pontiac 5,962; (9) Red La Soda 4,602; (10) White Rose 3,054;

(11) La Rouge 2,654; (12) Irish Cobbler 2,478; (13) Sebago 2,203; (14) Chippewa 1,620; (15) Chieftain 1,394; (16) Alamo 1,113; (17) Pungo 1,065; and (18) Monona 1,011.

The rank of potato varieties changes considerably from year to year. In 1961, Katahdin ranked first in certified seed acreage; Russet Burbank, second; Kennebec, third; and Red Pontiac, fourth. Note that in the current list, Red Pontiac has dropped to eighth. Cobbler was fifth on the list in 1961 but had dropped to 12th in 1971. The following descriptions are in order of production rank. (1) **Russet Burbank** Origin unknown. "Tubers are large, long, cylindrical or slightly flattened; skin russeted, heavily neeted; eyes numerous and well distributed, shallow, sometimes proturberant; eyebrows short, curved, inconspicuous; flesh white ... It is late and produces tubers that are very mealy when grown under favorable conditions, and thus is especially desirable for baking ... It is moderately good for potato chips from 55°F. storage or when conditioned at 70°F. from 40°F. storage, but the long tubers often give chips which are darker at one end than the other, and such uneven color is undesirable. However, the variety is very good for the manufacture of french fries, since its long shape and high specific gravity are desirable traits for that purpose. It is also used for dehydrating. It is somewhat resistant to scab."

(2) **Kennebec** It was originated by USDA from a cross between two unnamed seedlings. It was first grown in the fall of 1940 at the Plant Industry Station, Beltsville, Md., was tested under the National Potato Breeding Program, and released to growers in 1948. Tubers are elliptical to oblong, medium thick; skin smooth, self-colored, creamy buff; eyes, shallow of same color as skin; eyebrows medium long, curved, medium prominent; flesh white. This variety is a high yielder and requires close spacing of seed pieces to prevent development of over-size tubers. Quality is good to excellent. It is susceptible to scab. Kennebec is now grown almost exclusively for processing. It is good for potato chips at 55°F. storage and when conditioned at 70°F. from 40°F. storage.

(3) **Katahdin** This variety was originated by USDA from a cross between unnamed USDA seedlings; was first grown in 1923 at Presque Isle, Me.; was tested under the National Potato Breeding Program and released to growers in 1932 ... Tubers are large, short, elliptical to roundish, medium thick; skin smooth, dark, creamy buff; eyes shallow, of same color as skin; eyebrows medium long, curved, medium prominent, flesh white. Katahdin is a late-maturing variety adapted to a wide range of conditions. It is susceptible to scab. It produces tubers of good shape with shallow eyes and few culls, but the quality is generally medium, though good in some localities. It is good for potato chips at 55°F. storage, or when conditioned at 70°F. from 40°F. storage.

(4) **Norchip** This is a medium, early maturing variety, with good chip characteristics. Tubers are round to oblong, skin creamy white and smooth, tuber size medium, and shape uniform, eyes shallow, of same color as skin, flesh white. It is about the same in total solids in the Northeast as Kennebec, although reportedly higher in North Dakota. The variety was released in March 1968 by North Dakota State University. It was a selection from a cross made in 1960.

(5) **Norland** It was developed in North Dakota from a cross between Redkote and ND626; was released in 1957; and is grown mostly in the Midwest. Tubers are oblong, smooth, with smooth red skin, and shallow eyes; flesh white. It produces a high percentage of U.S. 1 tubers; is moderately resistant to scab.

(6) **Norgold Russet** This was developed in North Dakota and released in 1964. Both parents carry resistance to common scab. It is an early maturing variety; tubers, oblong to long; eyes, shallow; skin heavily netted with uniform russeting; flesh white.

(7) **Superior** Developed in Wisconsin from a cross between two unnamed lines, B96.56 and M59.44. It has early to medium maturity; tubers are oval, with rather shallow eyes, and a smooth to flaky skin; flesh white; high in total solids, and makes good chips; resistant to common scab.

(8) **Red Pontiac** This is a mutant variety of Pontiac and holds its skin color better. The tubers are large, and under favorable conditions become larger than desirable. Size can be controlled by closer spacing of seed pieces in the row. Tubers are oblong to round, blunt at the end; skin, smooth or sometimes netted, self-colored, red; eyes, medium deep and red; eyebrows, medium long, slightly curved, and inconspicuous; flesh, white.

FRUITS AND VEGETABLES, POTATO PRODUCTS
Potatoes: Estimated conversion factors for selected potato products

Products	Pounds, farm weight	Pounds of finished product	Percent recovery	To obtain farm weight equivalent, multiply product weight by —
	POUNDS	POUNDS	PERCENT	NUMBER
Starch				
Maine	100	9.3	9.3	10.75
Idaho	100	12.5	12.5	8.0
Average	100	11.1	11.1	9.0
Frozen	100	40	40	2.5
Chips	100	24.5[1]	24.5[1]	4.08

1. From potatoes with 1.075 specific gravity.

NOTE In commercial potato peeling plants, preparation loss including waste and shrinkage ranged from 5 to 48%, averaging approximately 25%. Source: Marketing Research Report No. 105, issued October, 1955.

(9) **Red LaSoda** This is a clonal mutation selected from LaSoda and released in 1954. It is like La Soda except for a more intense, red, skin color. It is medium early; has semi-round to slightly oblong tubers; smooth skin; eyes, medium to shallow in depth; flesh, white. The original LaSoda was derived from a cross between Triumph and Katahdin.

(10) **White Rose** Its pedigree is unknown. It is said that a variety known as American Giant (synonym for White Rose) was originated by Mrs. Rachel Campbell of Hebron, N.Y. in 1893 from a seed ball of the Jackson. Since 1871, the name White Rose has been applied to numerous introductions. It is now more generally referred to as the California long white. The tubers are large, long, elliptical, flattened, usually irregular; skin, smooth and very light tan; eyes, numerous, medium deep; eyebrows, medium long and curved; flesh, white.

(11) **LaRouge** "Medium to late-maturing; skin, smooth, attractive, red; flesh, white to cream. LaRouge has some scab resistance; matures 10 days earlier than LaSoda when grown in the North, and is well adapted to production in the north-central and southern potato-growing areas."

(12) **Irish Cobbler** The origin of Irish Cobbler is unknown. It was said that it was first grown by an Irish shoemaker of Marblehead, Mass. Tubers are large to medium sized, roundish with blunt ends, the stem end often notched rather deeply; skin, smooth, creamy white; eyes shallow to rather deep; eyebrows, long, slightly curved, medium prominent; flesh, white.

(13) **Sebago** This variety was originated by USDA from a cross between Chippewa and Katahdin. It was first grown in 1929 at Presque Isle, and was released to growers in 1938. Tubers are large, elliptical to round-elliptical, medium thick; skin, smooth and described as 'ivory yellow'; eyes, shallow and of same color as skin; eyebrows, short, curved, medium prominent; flesh, white. It is a late, high-yielding variety. Cooking quality variable, but usually good if tubers are allowed to mature fully before being dug.

(14) **Chippewa** Originated by USDA from a cross between unnamed USDA seedlings and was first grown in 1923 at Presque Isle, Me. It was released in 1933. Tubers large, elliptical to oblong, medium thick; skin, smooth, dark creamy buff; eyes, shallow, same color as skin; eyebrows, medium long, curved, medium prominent; flesh, white. It gives a high yield. Susceptible to scab.

CONTAINERS: Potatoes reach terminal markets mostly in

sacks of different kinds and sizes, but also in 50-lb. cartons which are growing in popularity, especially in Idaho. The carton gives better protection to potatoes than any sack and is suitable for premium packs of uniformly-sized tubers, often sold by count. Most potatoes, however, are still shipped in 100-lb. sacks, mostly burlap; but a vast number of 50-lb. sacks are also used. The 50s may be burlap or paper. There are also mesh, paper, and film bags of various sizes, mostly 5, 10, 15 and 25 lb. All must be of designated specifications as to material and strength to meet rail tariff specifications. Paper used must have designated wet strength. Types of closures are specified.

Multiple-wall, 50-lb. paper sacks are used as "balers," that is, to hold 5 10-lb. or 10 5-lb. bags or other suitable units.

The carton and the opaque paper bag have the advantage of protecting potatoes from greening which occurs when they are exposed to light. Solanine plus unknown compounds in green potatoes are toxic. Transparent plastic films allow as much greening as though the potatoes are in bulk under the light. The effect of light is cumulative, and therefore, potatoes should be protected from strong light—or any light—as much as possible.

In packing all bags—and other containers—it is necessary to pack overweight to allow for possible shrinkage. A study by this Association showed that the overweight runs from as much as 48 oz. in a 100-lb. bag to 2 to 6 oz. in a 5-lb. film or mesh bag.

One bushel (2150.42 cu. in.) of potatoes is presumed to weigh 60 lb. Actual weight of a given cubic quantity of potatoes is varied, depending on the specific gravity and the size of the tubers.

SERVINGS AND WEIGHTS: For potatoes to be pared by hand, 1 lb. provides 3 boiled potatoes of medium size; 8-1/2 lb. provides 25 portions; and 33-1/2 lb. provides 100.

For french fries, 1 lb. provides 4.32 portions of 1 oz. each; 6 lb. provides 25 portions; and 23-1/2 lb. provides 100.

For cubed and diced, cooked, 1 lb. provides 4.27 portions of 3 oz. each; 6 lb. provides 25 portions; and 23-1/2 lb. provides 100.

For mashed potatoes, 1 lb. provides 3.80 portions of 4 oz.

each; 6-3/4 lb. provides 25 portions; and 26-1/2 lb. provides 100.

To be pared by machine, 1 lb. provides 3 portions of 1 medium boiled; 8-1/2 lb. provides 25 portions; and 33-1/2 lb. provides 100.

For french fries, 1 lb. provides 4.16 portions of 2 oz. each, 6-1/4 lb. provides 25 portions; and 24-1/4 lb. provides 100.

For cubed, diced and cooked, 1 lb. provides 4.05 portions of 3 oz. each; 6-1/4 lb. provides 25 portions; and 24-3/4 lb. provides 100.

For mashed, 1 lb. provides 3.60 portions of 4 oz. each; 8-1/2 lb. provides 25 portions; and 33-1/2 lb. provides 100.

With ready-to-cook potatoes, 1 lb. provides 3 portions of medium boiled; 8-1/2 lb. provides 25 portions; and 33-1/2 lb. provides 100.

For french fries, 1 lb. provides 5.44 portions of 2 oz. each; 4-3/4 lb. provides 25 portions; and 18-1/2 lb. provides 100.

For mashed, 1 lb. provides 4.76 portions of 4 oz. each; 5-1/4 lb. provides 25 portions; and 21-1/4 lb. provides 100.

QUALITY: Grades help in the business of packing, shipping, and trading potatoes, but are only a fringe benefit to consumers who rely on visual inspection. Potatoes of any kind or size should be firm, relatively smooth, clean, reasonably well shaped, not badly cut, bruised or skinned, nor should they show any green from light-burn. They should not be wilted or show sprouts. Cooking quality varies by variety and production area. Aside from size, some types from some areas are known to be good bakers and french fryers. This is because they have a high content of dry matter. For boiling and salads, a potato of slightly higher moisture content is desirable. In general, the Russet Burbank potato, especially from the Pacific Northwest, tends to be high in dry matter and a good baker. Early or 'new' potatoes are good for boiling, frying, and salads; and this is also true of most of the late round varieties. Potatoes with high dry matter make especially good mashed potatoes.

SPECIFIC GRAVITY: Various studies, going back to 1950, have shown that consumers would like to be able to buy potatoes pre-sorted for a specific use, such as baking, mashing, boiling, or frying. Because it has been found that a

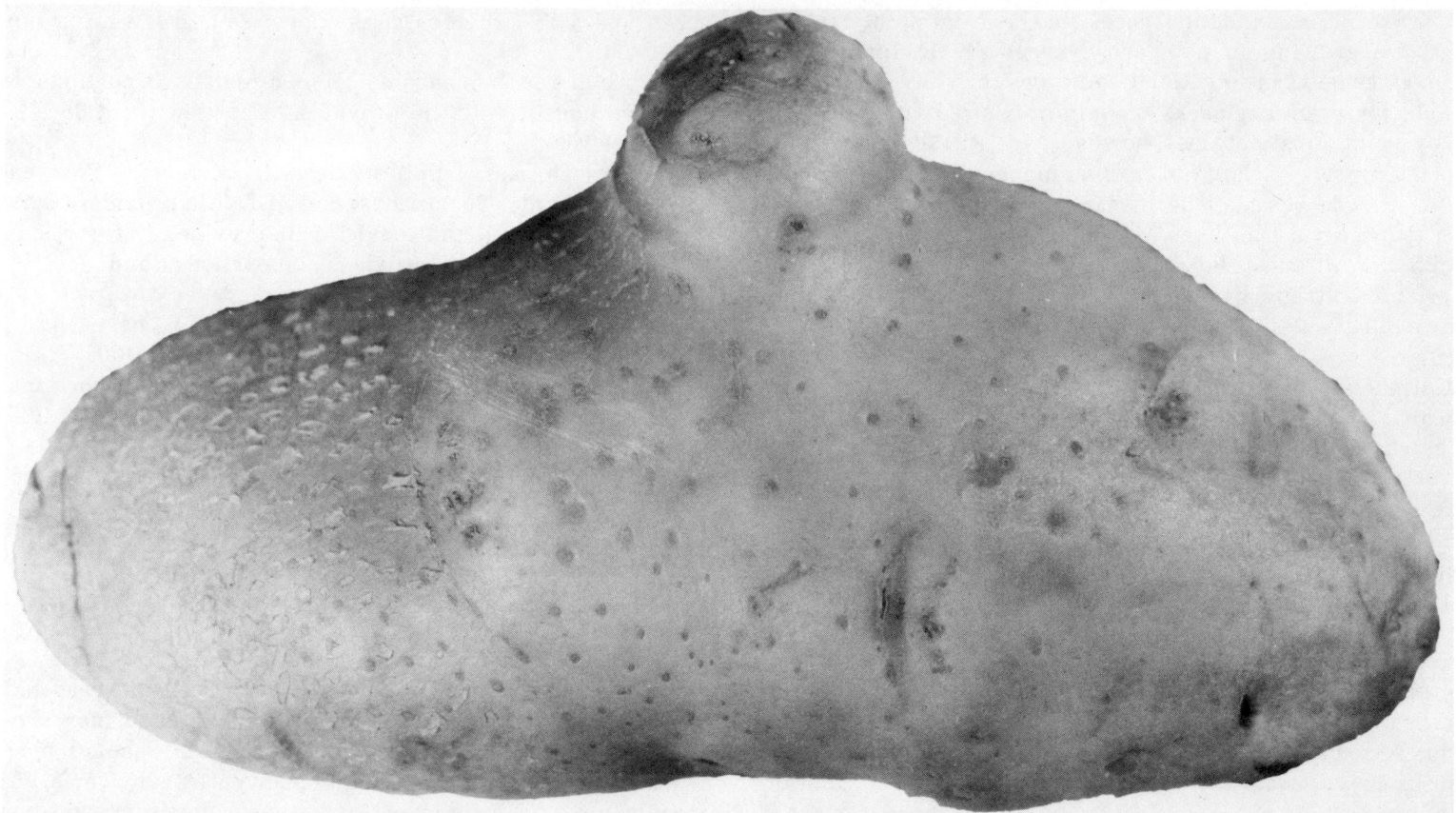

Irregularities pictured on these pages are permitted in U.S. No. 1 Grade to extent general appearance of lot not materially affected. Potato is actual size, weight 7 oz.

close relationship exists between specific gravity of a potato and its cooking characteristics, it is possible to separate potatoes to be sold for specific uses. The higher the specific gravity of a potato, the more mealy it usually is. Consequently a potato of high specific gravity is good for baking or mashing. A potato of a slightly lower specific gravity is better for boiling; and one of still lower specific gravity is preferred for frying. A high specific gravity in general means that the potato has a relatively large amount of dry matter, mainly starch. A satisfactory specific gravity (relationship of an object's weight to that of an equal volume of water under standard conditions) for baking or mashing is considered to be 1.08 or thereabout. Specific gravity for boilers is considered to be between 1.07 and 1.08; and for fryers below 1.07.

Specific gravity of a potato can be determined by placing it in one or another salt solution of known density. If a potato placed in a 1.08 solution sinks, its specific gravity is greater than 1.08, that is, it is more than 1.08 times as dense as a standard sample of water. If it floats, it may be placed in a 1.07 solution, and the test repeated. Mechanical separators have been designed and work satisfactorily. The potato hydrometer was designed by Ora Smith. This instrument is calibrated for determination of the specific gravity of an 8-lb. sample of potatoes. It is easy to use to determine the texture of potatoes before they are cooked for use fresh, or for processing. There is a method of determining the specific gravity of a sample by its weight-in-air and weight-in-water.

In Idaho, an increasing number of contracts between pro-

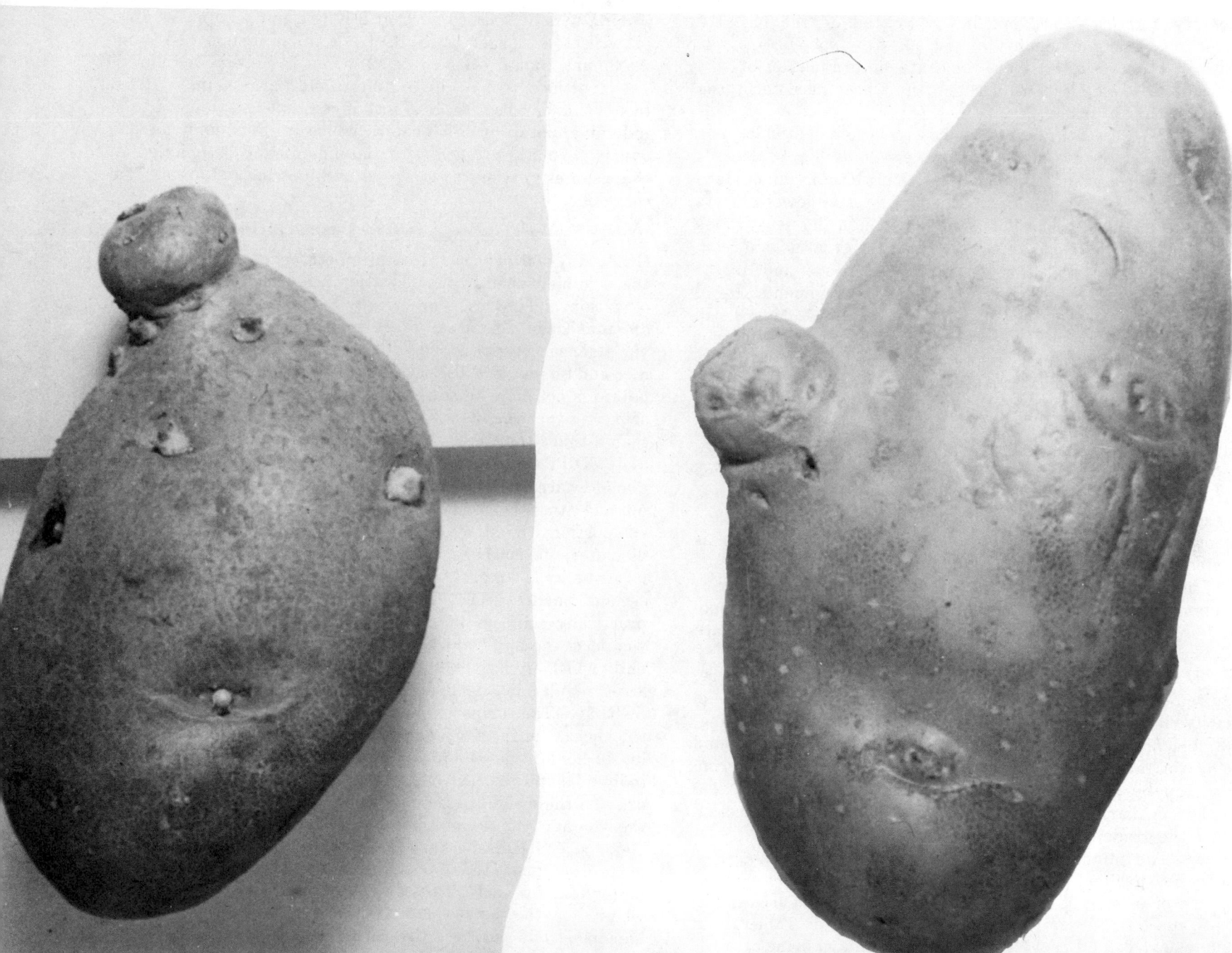

cessors and producers are being written on the basis of payment for higher quality as measured by specific gravity. This has necessitated more accurate determination of this parameter. Temperature of tuber and water need to be the same at time of test.

GRADES: Potato grade standards, as promulgated by the USDA, with approval of the trade, were revised as of Sept. 1, 1971. The new grades are "tighter" than those in effect since 1958, that is, potatoes must be cleaner and have fewer defects to make the grade than before. Even though the new grades are tighter than the old ones, there is still a great deal of room between potatoes at the top of U.S. 1 grade and at the bottom. It cannot be considered that two shipments are of similar quality merely because both grade U.S. 1. This is still a pretty loose grade, apparently because the trade has not been able to agree on stricter requirements.

Yet, the new grades provide total tolerance for defects in U.S. 1 of 8 percent, compared with 11 percent in the old grades; moderately shriveled, spongy, or flabby potatoes, formerly permitted in U.S. 1, are ruled out; artificial color, formerly not mentioned and, therefore, permitted, is scored as an external defect if it is unsightly, conceals other defects, or causes more than 5 percent waste when discolored flesh is removed; and scoring of sprouts or clusters of sprouts as defects is tightened.

The U.S. potato standards provide for U.S. extra 1, U.S. Commercial and U.S. 2 grades. Since U.S. 1 is the principal trading grade, only this grade will be outlined here, but space does not permit giving full details.

"*U.S. 1* consists of potatoes which meet the following requirements: (a) similar varietal characteristics; (b) firm; (c) fairly clean; (d) fairly well shaped; (e) free from (1) freezing, (2) blackheart, (3) late blight, southern bacterial wilt, and ring rot; and (4) soft rot and wet breakdown; (f) free from damage by any other cause; (g) size. Not less than 1-7/8 inches in diameter, unless otherwise specified in connection with the grade; (h) tolerances (as specified.)"

Size. "The minimum size or minimum and maximum sizes may be specified in connection with the grade in terms of diameter or weight of the individual potato, or in accordance with one of the size designations in Table I or Table II. In summary, Table I provides for size A minimum diameter of 1-

7/8 in., with at least 40 percent 2-1/2 in. in diameter, or 6 oz. in weight or larger; size B, 1-1/2 in. minimum, 2-1/4 in. maximum; Small, 1-3/4 to 2-1/2 in. in diameter; Medium, 2-1/4 in. or 5 oz. to 3-1/4 in. or 10 oz.; and Large, 3 in. or 10 oz. to 4-1/4 in. or 16 oz. Table II provides count and weight of the individual potato from 50 count, which is 15 oz. minimum, to over 140 count, which is 4 oz. minimum, to 8 oz. maximum, the size designations to apply to potatoes packed in any size container.

WHITE POTATOES—Canned [2/10/50]

Grade A: Color: The canned white potatoes, exclusive of units that are blemished by discoloration, are practically free from oxidation, and possess a practically uniform, light color typical of canned white potatoes processed from potatoes of similar varietal characteristics.

Size and Shape: WHOLE POTATOES—The size of each whole potato is not more than 2 in. in diameter, measured as aforesaid, and the weight of the largest whole potato is not more than 3 times the weight of the second smallest whole potato. SLICED POTATO—The diameter of any slice is the shortest diameter across the surface of the slice. The individual slice is not more than 3/4 in. in thickness when measured at the thickest portion; the size of each slice is not more than 2 in. in diameter, measured as aforesaid; and the diameter of the largest slice is not greater than 1-1/2 times the diameter of the second smallest slice. DICED POTATOES—The units are practically uniform in size and shape; and the aggregate weight of the units which are smaller than a 1/2-in. cube, the units which are larger than a 1/2-in. cube, and the units which are irregular in shape does not exceed 10 percent. SHOESTRING—The strips of potatoes are practically uniform in thickness, and the aggregate weight of all strips less than 1/2 in. in length does not exceed 10 percent. PIECES—The individual units each weigh not less than 1/2 oz. or more than 2 oz., and the weight of the largest unit is not more than twice the weight of the second smallest unit.

Defects: WHOLE—No harmless, extraneous material or grit is present; not more than 1/2 sq. in., in the aggregate of peel may be present for each 20 oz. of net weight, and the aggregate weight of the potatoes that are blemished or seriously blemished and potatoes that possess mechanical damage or

WHITE POTATOES

Approximate potato size found in various counts. Certain counts require blending of potato sizes. Illustrations therefore must be considered only as average diameter of potatoes in various counts.

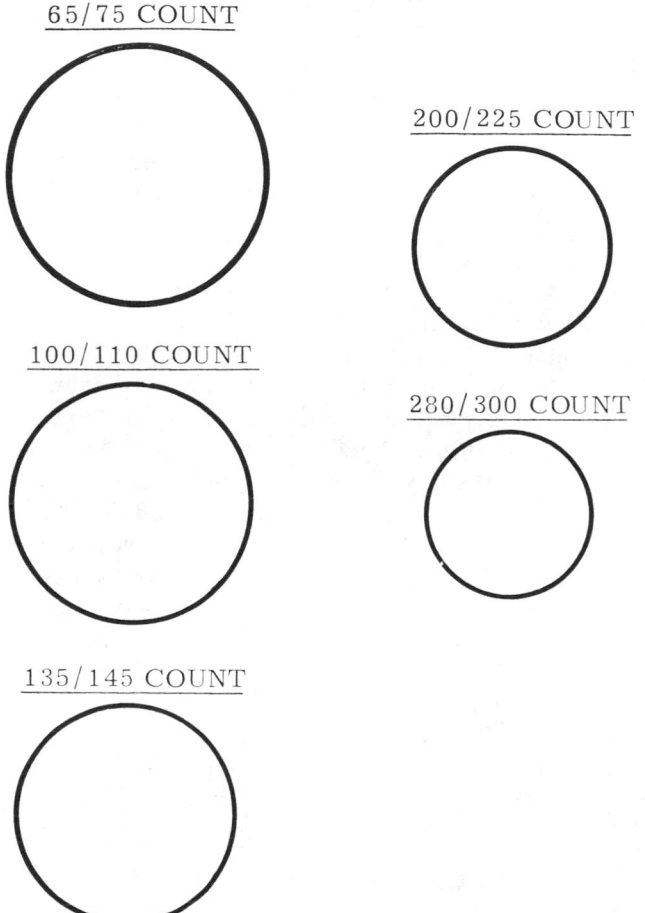

65/75 COUNT

100/110 COUNT

135/145 COUNT

200/225 COUNT

280/300 COUNT

Source: *Frosty Acres Buyers Guide*—The Frozen Food Forum, Inc., Atlanta, Ga.

serious mechanical damage does not exceed 20 percent of weight of all the units, but of such 20 percent, not more than 1/4 thereof, or one potato, whichever is the greater in weight, may be seriously blemished or possess serious mechanical damage. SLICED PIECES—No harmless, extraneous material or grit is present; not more than 1/2 sq. in., in the aggregate,

of peel may be present for each 20 oz. of net weight; and the aggregate weight of units that are blemished and units that are seriously blemished does not exceed 10 percent of all the units, but of such 10 percent not more than 1/4 thereof, or one unit, whichever is the greater in weight, may be seriously blemished. SLICED SHOESTRINGS—No harmless, extraneous material or grit is present; not more than 1/2 oz., in the aggregate, of peel may be present; for each 20 oz., the aggregate weight of units that are blemished and seriously blemished does not exceed 4 percent of all the units, but of such 4 percent, not more than 1/4 thereof may be seriously blemished. **Texture:** Texture of the potatoes is typical of properly prepared and processed potatoes, and the potatoes are firm and possess a fine and even grain, and may possess not more than a slight amount of sloughing that does not materially affect the appearance.

Grade C: Color: The canned white potatoes, exclusive of units that are blemished by discoloration, possess a fairly uniform color, typical of canned white potatoes, although the color of the potatoes, whether individually or in combination, may be variable, light, dull, grayish-white, yellow-white, or watery-white (semi-translucent), or indicative of slight oxidation, or slight discoloration, but not off-color. **Size and Shape:** See Grade A. All wording is the same, except as follows: WHOLE POTATOES: not more than 2-1/2 in. in diameter, 4 times. SLICED POTATOES—1 in.: 2-1/2 in. twice size. DICED POTATOES—Fairly uniform. 1/2 in.; 25 percent. PIECES—1/4 oz., 3 oz., 4 times. **Defects:** see Grade A: all wording is the same except as follows: not more than 1 small piece of harmless, extraneous material for each 20 oz.; not more than a trace of grit may be present; not more than 1 sq. in., 30 percent, 30 percent, 1/3. SLICED PIECES—Not more than 1 small piece of harmless, extraneous material for each 20 oz.; not more than a trace of grit may be present; 1 sq. in., 15 percent, 15 percent, 1/3. SLICED; SHOESTRING—See Grade A & C. 6 percent, 6 percent, 1/3. **Texture:** Potatoes may be variable in texture; may be slightly coarse-grained, may be slightly hard; may be slightly soft, or may possess more than a slight amount of sloughing, or more than a slight amount of disintegration, provided the amount of sloughing or disintegration does not seriously affect the appearance.

Sstd: Fails to meet requirements.

POTATOES—French Fried [2/8/67]

Grade A: Color: Bright, characteristic color of properly prepared, frozen, french fried potatoes. The fry color may be "extra light," "light," "medium light," or "medium." After heating, the product is practically free from units which vary markedly from the criterion for the fry color of the units. **Size:** STRIP STYLES—Any chips present and/or any variation in the size of the strips may no more than slightly detract from the appearance of the product, and of all the product units, except chips, not more than 15 percent may consist of small

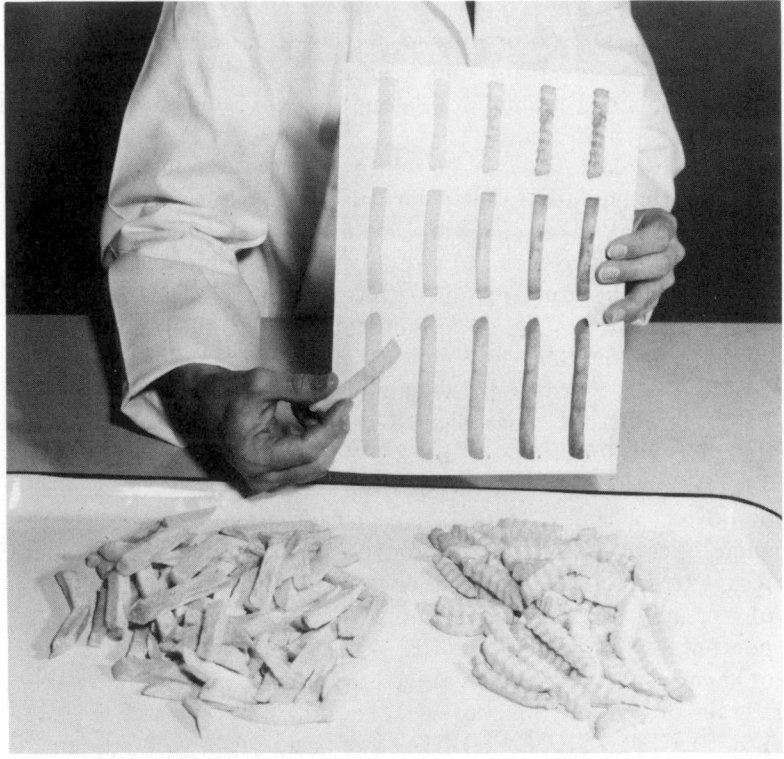

A USDA Consumer and Marketing Service specialist demonstrates the use of color standards for frozen French fried potatoes. The color standards, developed by C & MS with cooperation of leading industrial color experts, provide a practical means of designating the degrees of color attained by the frying process during manufacture. Color classification is useful for quality control, standardization, and for determining specifications in buying and selling.

pieces, slices, and/or irregular pieces. ALL STYLES EXCEPT STRIPS—Any chips present and/or any variation in the size and shape of the potato units may no more than slightly detract from the appearance. **Defects:** Any combination of defects present (including insignificant imperfections) may no more than slightly detract from the appearance or edibility; any carbon specks present may no more than slightly detract from the appearance. The minor and major defects that may be present in the sample unit do not exceed the allowances in Table I or Table II. **Texture:** External surfaces of the units are moderately crisp; show no noticeable separation from the inner portion, and are not excessively oily. The interior portions are well cooked, tender, and practically free from sogginess, except that shoestring style, strips, and dices may be moderately crisp throughout.

Grade B: Color: A characteristic, frozen french fry potato color which may be dull but not off color. The fry color may be variable, exceeding the uniformity criterion of "extra light," "light," "medium light," "medium," or "dark." After heating, the variation in the fry color of the unit does not seriously affect the appearance. **Size and Symmetry:** STRIP STYLES—Any chips present may not seriously detract from the appearance of the product, and of all the product units, except "chips," not more than 30 percent may consist of small pieces, slivers, and/or irregular pieces. ALL STYLES EXCEPT STRIPS—Any chips present and/or any variation in the size and shape of the potato units may not seriously detract from the appearance. **Defects:** Any combination of defects present (including insignificant imperfections) does not seriously detract from the appearance or edibility. Any carbon specks present do not seriously detract from the appearance of the

FRENCH FRIED POTATOES

FROZEN [2/8/67   52.2391]

Grades:	"A" or "FANCY"	"A" or "FANCY" SHORT	"B" or "EXTRA STANDARD"	"SUBSTANDARD"
Minimum Score:	90	90	80	Less than 80

TABLE I—MAXIMUM ALLOWANCES FOR DEFECTIVES IN ALL STYLES EXCEPT SHOESTRING STYLE STRIPS AND DICES

Grade Classification	Type of Defects	Institutional type Defectives in a 2-lb. Sample Unit
A and A short	Minor and major Limit for major	18 defectives 4 defectives
B	Minor and major Limit for major	28 defectives 8 defectives

TABLE II—MAXIMUM ALLOWANCES FOR DEFECTIVES IN SHOESTRING STYLE STRIPS AND DICES

Grade Classification	Type of Defects	Institutional type Defectives in a 2-lb Sample Unit
A and A short	Minor and major Limit for major	28 defectives 8 defectives
B	Minor and major Limit for major	36 defectives 12 defectives

product, and the minor and major defectives that may be present in the sample units do not exceed the allowances in Table I or Table II. **Texture:** External surfaces of the unit may be slightly hard or slightly tough with no more than a moderate separation from the interior portion, and are not excessively oily; the interior portions are well cooked, reasonably tender, and free from sogginess.
Sstd: Fails to meet requirements.

PUMPKINS*

USES: Aside from the artistry of making a scary jack-o-lantern, pumpkins provide the makings of spicy pumpkin pie; pumpkin bread or muffins; various puddings and custards; and a small pumpkin may be used for stuffing with meats and vegetables or meats and seafood for an interesting change. In some European countries, pumpkin is made into a delicious soup, sometimes mixed with pureed carrots or carrot pieces, sliced onion, and leeks, chopped celery, parsley, etc.

Here are basic cooking directions for pumpkin: halve or quarter the pumpkin; remove seeds and stringy portions; cut into small pieces; cut off rind. Cook, covered, in small amount of lightly salted, boiling water for 25 to 30 minutes. Since pumpkin is a watery vegetable, a large amount of cooking water is undesirable. When cooked, drain; mash well; place mashed pumpkin in strainer; let drain about 30 minutes to remove excess liquid. One 5-lb. pumpkin yields about 4-1/2 cups of mashed cooked pumpkin.

MARKETING SEASON: Most pumpkins for fresh market are sold in late October for Halloween use. Total fresh pumpkin supply may be about 46 million lb. a year. About 30 to 34 million lb. are accounted for by unloads in 41 cities in which *USDA's Market News Service* records supplies. Cities other than these 41 also receive supplies, and substantial quantities are marketed by roadside stands, and by stores dealing with local farmers.

The following table shows pumpkin availability as a percentage each month of the annual total. It is based on 5 years of reports of unloads in 41 cities.

MONTHLY AVAILABILITY OF PUMPKIN EXPRESSED AS PERCENTAGE OF TOTAL ANNUAL SUPPLY

Jan.	Feb.	Mar.	Apr.	May	June
%	%	%	%	%	%
1	1	2	2	3	1

July	Aug.	Sept.	Oct.	'Nov.	Dec.
%	%	%	%	%	%
1	1	4	79	3	2

CONTAINERS: There is no package especially made for pumpkins. Various types of crates are used, including cantaloupe crates, 13-1/2 x 13 x 21-7/8 in., and some 1-1/9 bu. crates. Often they are not lidded. Many are trucked in bulk. Just about any used container that will hold them is employed.

QUALITY: There are no grades specifically for pumpkins, but the same general criteria apply as to other winter squashes. They should be well matured, not broken or cracked, free from soft rot or wet breakdown, and from excessive scarring, free of indications of disease or freezing, and they should be clean. Generally, pumpkins are expected to have a rich, orange color.
*UFFVA

PUMPKIN

CANNED [3/9/56   52.2741]

Grades:	"A" or "FANCY"	"C" or "STANDARD"	"SUB-STANDARD"
Minimum Score:	85	70	Less than 70

NET WEIGHT—not less than 90 percent of volume of container

PUMPKIN & SQUASH—Canned [3/9/56]

Grade A: Color: Possess a practically uniform, light color. Typical of canned pumpkin or canned squash prepared from well-matured pumpkin or squash. **Consistency:** Canned pumpkin or squash often, after being emptied from the container to a dry-flat surface, retains the approximate shape of the container, and holds a high mound, and after being emptied on such surface, the highest point of the mound is not less than 60 percent of the length of the container; except with respect to H_2O 3 size can or larger, the highest point of the mound is not less than 50 percent of the length of the container, and irrespective of can size not more than 10 cu. centimeters of liquor separates for each 30 oz. of net content. **Finish:** Canned pumpkin and squash particles are evenly divided; the product is fine grained, smooth but not pasty, and the pumpkin or squash particles are not hard. **Defects:** No grit, sand, and silt may be present that affects the appearance or eating quality of the canned pumpkin or squash, and that the number, size and color of the aforesaid defects present, individually and collectively, do not more than slightly affect the appearance or eating quality.

Grade C: Color: Possess a color typical of fairly well-matured pumpkin or squash and may possess a slight tinge of gray or tan color, may be variable or slightly dull, but not to the extent that the appearance or eating quality is materially affected. **Consistency:** Canned pumpkin or squash, after emptying from the container to a dry-flat surface, may flow just enough to level off to a nearly uniform depth, or may be slightly mounded, and at the end of 2 minutes after emptying on such surface, not more than 30 cu. centimeters of liquor separates for each 30 oz. of net contents. **Finish:** The canned pumpkin or squash are evenly divided; the product may be slightly coarse; may be· slightly pasty but not decidedly pasty, and the pumpkin or squash particles are not hard. **Defects:** A trace of

sand or silt may be present that does not materially affect the appearance or eating quality of the canned pumpkin or squash, and any of the other aforesaid defects present, individually or collectively, may be noticeable but are not so large, so numerous, or of such contrasting color as to seriously affect the appearance or eating quality.

Sstd: Fails to meet requirements.

RADISHES*

USES: At first thought, it might seem that the uses of radishes could be expressed in one phrase; eaten raw out of hand or in salad. However, their uses are much more extensive than that. In Egypt, a radish is cultivated of which the leaves only are eaten. The Arabs are said to be very fond of radish tops. In India, a variety of radish (Raphanus caudatus) is grown for its fleshy edible seed pods which reach a length of 8 to 12 in. In the Orient, radishes are grown as stock feed and for a winter vegetable that can be stored. In China, one kind of radish, without an enlarged root, is grown for the oil in its seeds.

"In China and Japan," says Boswell, "most of the radish crop is pickled in brine in much the same way that we pickle cucumbers. Nearly a third of the tonnage of vegetables grown in Japan is radish (daikon). The radishes are pickled whole in large tubs, with rice hulls added to the brine ... This pickled radish ... adds savor and zest to the predominantly drab diet of rice."

Radishes may also be cooked and eaten with a cream sauce. The cooked radishes are reported to have a flavor like turnips.

MARKETING SEASON: Radishes are available in ample quantities all year, with peak supplies April through July. The following table shows the percentage of the annual total avail-

AVERAGE MONTHLY AVAILABILITY OF RADISHES EXPRESSED AS PERCENT OF AVERAGE ANNUAL TOTAL, BASED ON UNLOADS IN SIX CITIES*

Jan.	Feb.	Mar.	Apr.	May	June
%	%	%	%	%	%
6	6	8	10	11	10

July	Aug.	Sept.	Oct.	Nov.	Dec.
%	%	%	%	%	%
12	9	7	7	7	7

*Cities are Atlanta, Boston, Chicago, Cincinnati, Los Angeles, New York.

*UFFVA

able in each month, based on reports of unloads in 6 cities for 5 years.

VARIETIES: Radishes are sometimes grouped as spring, summer, and winter types, but such grouping is misleading, since any of the radishes will grow at any season if conditions are right, and, in fact, so-called "spring" radishes are grown all year. The most satisfactory grouping of American varieties is by shape, the general classes being globular (often called round), oval, turnip shaped, oblong, and long. The round varieties are the most important in the U.S., since they are the ones that are topped and packed in film bags. Quick-maturing round varieties grow from seed to harvestable size in about 22 to 27 days; some of the round varieties, often termed "summer" varieties, grow in about 30 days; the more rapid growing long radishes take about 30 days; and the large storage types of radishes, often called "winter" radishes, require 50 days or more to mature and are planted in late summer.

GLOBULAR (also called "round") **Cherry Belle** Skin, bright cherry red; flesh, solid and crisp; tops, 2-1/2 to 3 in.; growing period 22 to 23 days; suitable for forcing under glass ... **Comet** Skin, bright red; flesh, mild, white, unusually crisp, and firm; suitable for use when 5/8 to 3/4 in. in diameter, but becomes larger without growing pithy; tops 3-1/2 to 4 in.; growing period 23 to 25 days ... **Southern Market Globe** Skin, bright deep scarlet; flesh, white and crisp, and slow to become pithy; developed primarily for shipping; tops, medium; 24 days ... (The foregoing are typical. There are many others of this shape, either red, or red and white). There is also a round white radish and a round black.

OVAL Cavalier Skin, bright scarlet red; flesh, firm, crisp, and mild; bred for greenhouse forcing, and growing on muck or peat soil during summer; 22 to 23 days ... **Early Scarlet Globe, Short Top** Skin, red; flesh, white, mild, crisp; tops, 2-1/3 to 3 in.; bred for greenhouse forcing, and growing on peat or muck soils during summer; 23 days ... **Early Scarlet Globe, Medium Top** Skin, deep scarlet; flesh, white and mild; tops, medium; 24 days ... **Early Scarlet Globe, Vick's Strain** Skin, deep scarlet; flesh, white, firm, and crisp; tops 3-1/2 to 4-1/2 in.; recommended for upland planting; 24 days.

TURNIP Scarlet Turnip White Tipped Upper 2/3 of root bright scarlet, lower part white; tops, small; 25 days; replaced in some sections by Sparkler ... **Sparkler** Slightly flattened; top portion dull scarlet with white area at bottom taking up more than 1/3 of root; flesh, white, tender, crisp, tops, 5 to 6 in.; 25 days ... **Crimson Giant Forcing** (Crimson Giant, Crimson Giant Globe). Skin, crimson; flesh, white, crisp, mild, largest of early, turnip-rooted radishes, commonly reaching diameter of 1-1/2 in. before becoming pithy; tops, 4 to 5 in.; 28 to 30 days.

OBLONG (that is, somewhat longer than wide, but not in long class) **French Breakfast** Oblong and blunt; skin, rose-scarlet with white tip; flesh, white and tender, but texture coarser than most early radishes; tops, 5 to 6 in.; suitable for forcing under glass, but becomes pithy relatively soon; growing period 24 days.

LONG Cincinnati Market Skin, deep red with purplish tinge; flesh, white, mild, crisp; size 7 in. long, 5/8 in. thick, cylindrical, tapered near tip; tops, small; 28 to 29 days ... **Long Scarlet, Short Top** Skin, scarlet; flesh, white, mild, crisp; size, 6 to 7 in. long, tapered; tops, 6 in.; 30 days ... **White Icicle** Skin, smooth and white; flesh, white, tender, crisp, and mild; size 4-1/2 to 5-1/2 in. long, slender, tapering; tops, 5 to 6 in.; for out-of-door culture or forcing; 30 days ... **White Strasbourg** Skin, creamy white and smooth; flesh, white, firm, crisp, mildly pungent; size, up to 5 in. long, 1-1/2 in. in diameter at shoulder, tapering; classed as summer radish; 40 days ... **Chinese Rose Winter** (Scarlet China) Skin, deep rose; flesh, white, crisp, and pungent; size, 6 to 7 in. long by 2 in. in diameter at shoulder, becoming larger at base; tops, large; stores well; 52 days ... **Chinese White Winter** (Celestial) Skin, smooth and white; flesh, white, firm, crisp, mild; size about 8 in. long, 3 in. in diameter at mid-section, with square shoulder and blunt tip; 55 days ... **California Mammoth White** Skin, white and thick; flesh, white, solid, mildly pungent; size, 7 to 8 in. long by 2 to 3 in. thick; tops, large and coarse; largest of winter radishes; may be used at all stages of growth; good keeper; 55 days ... **Long Black Spanish** Skin, black; flesh, white, crisp, pungent; size 9 in. long by 2-1/2 in. thick, cylindrical, tapered at tip; tops, long and coarse; stores well; 60 days.

CONTAINERS: Bunched radishes are shipped in bushel

RADISHES

FRESH [10/1/68   51.2395]
Grades: U.S. No. 1; U.S. Commercial

baskets and boxes, 12 qt. and 16 qt. Climax baskets, and almost any vegetable crate on hand. Market reports often refer to bunched radishes in "various containers" and often they are quoted by the bunch or number of bunches because of the uncertainty about the quantity of miscellaneous containers.

The topped radishes, too, are packed in a wide range of containers, but if the radishes are packaged, the package is almost invariably the 6-oz. or 8-oz. film bag. The *16-qt. Climax basket*, holding 30 8-oz. film bags, is one of the favorite containers for topped radishes. The *12-qt. Climax basket* is also widely used, packed with 30 6-oz. bags. In any event, the price is quoted on a definite number of bags of a given weight. *Cartons* are being increasingly used for bagged radishes. One such container is 5-1/4 by 10 by 12 in. and holds 24 6-oz. bags. Cartons holding 48 bags are also used.

The usual package in the Lake Okeechobee section of Florida is the 16-qt. *Climax basket*, but others are also used. *A wirebound crate* holding 48 8-oz. bags is popular. This wirebound, listed in the railroad container tariff as W/B Radish crate No. 4126, is 7-1/2 by 7-1/2 by 18-3/4 in. Some bulk shipments from this area are in the 4/5 bu. wirebound crate (Container No. 3677 in the railroad tariff) with dimensions of 9-1/2 by 9-1/2 by 19-1/4 in. Bulk radishes are also shipped 40 or 50 lb. in a film bag.

A bushel of bunched radishes weighs about 35 lb. net. It takes about 1.6 lb. of bunched radishes, as purchased, to provide 1 lb. of ready-to-serve raw radishes. Also, 1 lb., as purchased, yields about two cups of sliced raw vegetable. One quart of raw, sliced radishes weighs about 1 lb., 10 oz.

QUALITY: *Grade and quality are not the same thing;* because grade is established at the time the radishes are packed and labeled, but the condition of the radishes may change with time. "Quality" describes both grade and condition at the time when the quality is noted. A high quality radish should be fresh, bright-looking, smooth, firm, well-formed, tender, crisp, of color characteristic of the variety, and with reasonably mild flavor. If tops are attached, they should be fresh, bright, and green. Radishes that are wilted, spongy, dry-looking, rough-skinned, cut, or broken are undesirable. Pithiness or sponginess can be detected by slight pressure.

In ordering radishes, it is necessary, as in ordering all other commodities, to be specific as to what is wanted. Name the type or variety of radish wanted, the grade, whether bunched or topped and packaged, size of the package, quality, quantity, master container, and agree on price. You may want to inquire whether the radishes were hydrocooled at the time of packing, and whether they have been kept under refrigeration. Are they waxed or unwaxed?

GRADES: Grades for topped or bunched radishes are U.S. No. 1 and U.S. Commercial. *"U.S. No. 1* consists of radishes of similar varietal characteristics, the roots of which are clean, well-formed, smooth, firm, tender, and free from decay, and which are free from damage caused by freezing, growth cracks or air cracks, cuts, pithiness, disease, insects, or mechanical or other means. Bunched radishes shall have tops which are fresh, and free from decay, and free from damage caused by freezing, seedstems, yellowing or other discoloration, disease, insects, or mechanical or other means.

"STYLES—'Bunched radishes' means radishes with full length tops which are tied in bunches. 'Topped radishes' means radishes with the tops clipped back to not more than 3/8 in. in length."

"Standard bunches of radishes shall be fairly uniform in size, and radishes in the individual bunches shall not vary more than 1/2 in. in diameter. Not more than 10 percent of the bunches in any lot may fail to meet the requirements for 'standard bunching.'

"SIZE TERMS—(1) 'Small' means less than 3/4 in. in diameter; (2) 'Medium' means 3/4 to 1 in. in diameter; (3) 'Large' means over 1 to 1-1/4 in. in diameter; and (4) 'Very large' means over 1-1/4 in. in diameter.

RUTABAGAS*

USES: Rutabagas, being large, are usually cut up before cooking. They may be boiled or roasted with meat and eaten in pieces; or boiled and mashed; or cut into julienne strips and boiled with other vegetables such as carrots; turnips, and

*UFFVA

celery and made into various savory combinations and even into puddings. For example, for rutabaga pudding, use 2 cups mashed, cooked rutabagas (about 1.25 lb.), 2 Tbsp. butter or margarine; 1 cup soft bread crumbs; 1/4 tsp. ground mace; 1/8 tsp. ground black pepper; 1 tsp. salt; 1 Tbsp. sugar; 1/8 tsp. ground ginger; 1/2 cup milk; 1 egg, beaten; 1 Tbsp. butter or margarine, melted. Combine first 9 ingredients, and beat until fluffy. Beat in egg. Turn into a buttered 1-qt. casserole. Brush top with melted butter or margarine. Bake in a preheated moderate oven (350°F.) 45 minutes or until brown. Yield: 6 servings ...

As another idea, try tossing diced, hot, cooked rutabagas with lemon butter seasoned with salt, ground black pepper, and crumbled basil leaves ... Other possibilities are rutabaga and potato salad; rutabaga parmesan; raw rutabaga and apple salad; french fried rutabagas; and rutabaga-chicken broth in which diced rutabagas are cooked in chicken broth instead of water, are appropriately spiced, and served with added green peas and mushrooms ... Or try Rutabagas Winnipeg as follows: Cook 6 cups diced rutabagas and 2 cups diced potatoes, with 2 cups boiling water, and 1 tsp. salt in a saucepan for about 15 minutes or until done. Drain and mash well. Add 1 tsp. sugar, 1/4 tsp. ground, black pepper, 1 cup grated cheddar or American cheese and 2 Tbsp. finely chopped onion. Beat until fluffy. Garnish with chopped parsley. Yield: 6 servings.

MARKETING SEASON: Rutabagas, being storable for long periods, are on the market all year, but more are available in the cold months. It is not possible to separate rutabagas and turnips in an availability chart, so the following is for both. Availability is given each month as a percentage of the total available all year. (Percentages are rounded, so do not total exactly 100.)

MONTHLY AVAILABILITY OF RUTABAGAS AND TURNIPS EXPRESSED AS PERCENTAGE OF TOTAL ANNUAL SUPPLY

	Jan.	Feb.	Mar.	Apr.	May	June
	%	%	%	%	%	%
ALL SOURCES	12	11	10	6	5	4
CANADA**	13	11	10	5	2	*

*Less than 0.5 percent of annual total
**Canada percentages apply to Canada total only.

	July	Aug.	Sept.	Oct.	Nov.	Dec.
	%	%	%	%	%	%
ALL SOURCES	4	5	9	12	13	11
CANADA**	*	4	11	15	18	13

VARIETIES: "Only two rutabaga varieties—**American Purple Top** and **Laurentian**—are commonly listed by seedsmen.

CONTAINERS: Canadian rutabagas are shipped mostly in sacks holding 50 lb. Large amounts are waxed before packing to prevent shriveling. In a survey of fruit and vegetable containers in New York and Los Angeles by USDA, it was found that domestic rutabagas coming into Los Angeles were packed mostly in polyethylene bags holding 25 lb.; while those coming into New York City were in 25- and 50-lb. textile bags.

QUALITY: Rutabagas should be firm, fresh looking, heavy for their size, generally smooth, not deeply cut or punchtured, and not showing any decay. Size is not a quality factor. Rutabagas stored for winter marketing often are coated with paraffin to prevent loss of moisture. Such a coated root is usually preferable.

GRADES: U.S. grade standards for turnips or rutabagas, effective Aug. 1, 1955, provide for two grades, U.S. 1 and U.S. 2. Information given here applies to topped turnips or rutabagas, with tops removed to not more than 3/4 in. in length. The following are excerpts:

"*U.S. 1* consists of turnips or rutabagas of similar varietal characteristics, the roots of which are well trimmed, firm, fairly smooth, fairly well shaped, fairly clean, and free from soft rot, and free from damage caused by cuts, discoloration, freezing, growth cracks, pithiness, woodiness, watercore, dry rot, other disease, insects, or rodents, or mechanical or other means. (a) Unless otherwise specified, the diameter of each turnip or rutabaga shall be not less than 1-3/4 in."

"**Tolerances.** In order to allow for variations incident to proper grading and handling, the following tolerances shall be permitted: (1) For defects of roots—10 percent, by weight, for roots in any lot which fail to meet the requirements of the grade: provided, that not more than 1/2 of this amount, or 5 percent, shall be allowed for defects causing serious damage, including therein not more than 1 percent for soft rot; ... (2)

TURNIPS OR RUTABAGAS

FRESH [8/1/55   51.2610]
Grades: U.S. No. 1; U.S. No. 2
FROZEN [8/19/58   52.3731]

Grades:	"A" or "FANCY"	"B" or "EXTRA STANDARD"	"SUB-STANDARD"
Minimum Score	85	70	Less than 70

For off-size roots—5 percent, by weight, for roots in any lot which are smaller than the specified minimum diameter, and 10 percent, by weight, for roots which are larger than any specified maximum diameter."

DEFINITIONS—"'Firm' means that the root is not soft, flabby or shriveled. 'Fairly smooth' means that the root is not rough or ridged to the extent that the appearance is materially affected. 'Fairly well shaped' means that the root is not mis-shapen to the extent that the appearance is materially affected. 'Fairly clean' means that the individual root is reasonably free from dirt or other foreign matter, and that the general appearance of the roots in the container is not more than slightly affected. 'Damage' means any defect which materially affects the appearance, or the edible or shipping quality of the individual turnip or rutabaga root, or the general appearance of the turnips or rutabagas in the container, or causes a loss of more than 5 percent, by weight, in ordinary preparation for use ..."

SPINACH*

USES: Spinach is both one of the most praised and most abused vegetables. It has been popularized in the comic strips by the Herculean feats of Popeye, the Sailor who needs only to gulp down a pound or so of spinach in any form to stop a freight train or flatten a dozen villains. On the other hand, Dr. Thurman B. Rice, of the Indiana State Board of Health, says: "If God had intended for us to each spinach, he would have flavored it with something." But flavoring is a job for cooks. The way spinach is thrown in a pot with a quart or so of water and boiled for a half hour or more, it is a wonder even Popeye relishes it.

Take a tip from the National Restaurant Assn.: cook spinach in a pressure cooker or steamer with very little or no added water other than what clings to the leaves after washing. In boiling, use only the water clinging to the leaves, and cook in a covered pan for not more than 10 minutes. Dr. Ida Bailey Allen, in her book *Solving the High Cost of Living*, suggests panning spinach and all greens by cooking in a heavy, wide saucepan. For 3 to 4 cups of the leaves, first brown slightly 1-1/2 tablespoons of butter or margarine, then pour in 1/3 in. of boiling water. Add seasoning, stir in the greens, cover, and boil for one minute. Then reduce the heat and boil until tender. (A similar method has been used by the Chinese for centuries.)

Some suggestions for serving: plain with melted butter and seasoned to taste; with hardboiled chopped eggs; escalloped; molded or creamed; in a spinach ring; a fondue; souffle, or served with cheese; Dutch style with bacon, vinegar, and sugar; cream of spinach soup; with broth sauce; with mushroom sauce; spinach roulade; spinach with eggs Florentine; spinach and herbs omelet; raw spinach salad with eggs and anchovies.

MARKETING SEASON: Fresh spinach is on the market in all months with peak availability March through June. The following table shows average availability each month based on unloads in Chicago, Los Angeles, New York, and Seattle.

MONTHLY AVAILABILITY OF SPINACH EXPRESSED AS PERCENTAGE OF TOTAL ANNUAL SUPPLY

Jan.	Feb.	Mar.	Apr.	May	June
%	%	%	%	%	%
9	8	11	11	11	10

July	Aug.	Sept.	Oct.	Nov.	Dec.
%	%	%	%	%	%
6	5	6	8	7	8

VARIETIES: Spinach is classified in two main types: the savoyed or cumpled leaf type for fresh market, and the flat or smooth leafed type for canning. Each of these is divided into plants that go to seed early and those that can stand relatively long in the field. In general, the long standing (called slow bolting) is preferred. Another classification is according to whether the seed is round and smooth or prickly, but this distinction is one that is mainly of interest to the grower.

*UFFVA

Some principal varieties for fresh market are:

Bloomsdale Dark Green A leading shipping variety. Leaves are large, blistered, and crumpled, and are a rich, glossy green. Grows in 40 days. Other types of Bloomsdale are Bloomsdale Savoy Long Standing and Bloomsdale Reselected.

Old Dominion Plants semi-erect, loose, resistant to cold, and suitable either for spring or fall planting. Leaves medium thick, dark green, moderately crumpled, medium broad, tapering to point. Grows in 40 to 42 days.

America A newer variety. Plants compact, slightly spread, vigorous; leaves, dark green, savoyed, and thick. Stands longer than other varieties without going to seed, but develops rather slowly. Growing period 44 days.

Viking (Northland, Heavy Pack) Plant large, spreading, vigorous, long standing, with large, thick medium dark, green, smooth leaves. Growing time 45 days.

The so-called "New Zealand spinach" is the plant Tetragonia expansa, and not true spinach, spinacea oleracea. The New Zealand "spinach" is a large, much branched, spreading plant that produces a succession of small, very thick and fleshy, pointed leaves on round, fleshy stems. The leaves and tips of branches are used like spinach.

Wild Spinach (so-called), or "Good King Henry," is a member of the goosefoot family that is native to Europe, was introduced into American gardens, and later escaped, and may now be found wild from Nova Scotia to Ontario and south to Maryland and Ohio. It is not abundant in this country. The plant is a perennial, grows 1 to 2 ft. tall, has triangular leaves that can be cooked and served like spinach.

CONTAINERS AND WEIGHTS: The weight of a bushel of spinach is stated variously by USDA as 18 to 25 lb. and an average of 20 lb. This great variation is due to the difference in tightness of pack, difference in the specific gravity of the leaves in different lots, and the presence or absence of moisture on the leaves.

Spinach is most often quoted by the bushel and is marketed either in bushel baskets, hampers, tubs, or boxes. Texas, the principal shipper, uses mostly bushel baskets. New Jersey uses bushel baskets and to some extent 1-3/5 bu. boxes. New York, Virginia, Michigan, Arkansas, Connecticut, South Carolina, Pennsylvania, and Maryland use bushel baskets or tubs. Colorado uses bushel baskets and wirebound crates; and Massachusetts uses a 1-bu. box.

USDA states that a Los Angeles type crate (13- by 18- by 21-5/8—in. approximately) contains 36 to 40 lb. of spinach, net.

QUALITY: The main requirements of quality, whether for spinach plants or for leaves in bulk or in packages, are freshness, crispness, cleanness, good color, and freedom from damage. Plants should be stocky and well developed, with no seedstems. Leaves should be tender and not wilted, crushed, or bruised. There should be no decay. Small heart leaves that are yellowish green because they have been shaded by other leaves are most tender and are desirable.

GRADES: There are U.S. standards for spinach plants, fresh spinach leaves, and fresh spinach for canning. The standards for *spinach plants* are U.S. No. 1 and U.S. Commercial; for *fresh spinach leaves*, U.S. Extra No. 1, U.S. No. 1, and U.S. Commercial; for *canning*, U.S. No. 1, U.S. No. 2, and U.S. 3. There are also U.S. *consumer standards* for fresh spinach leaves, that is, standards that can be applied to spinach placed in consumer size packages and sold to the consumer under a federal grade. The consumer standards are U.S. Grade A and U.S. Grade B.

As an example of the grades, *U.S. Extra No. 1* for fresh spinach leaves "shall consist of spinach leaves of similar varietal characteristics which are fairly clean, well trimmed, free from coarse stalks, seedstems, seedbuds, crowns and roots, sandburs or other kinds of burs, decay, and from damage caused by clusters of leaves, wilting, discoloration, freezing, foreign material, disease, insects, mechanical or other means ... Not more than 5 percent, by count, of any lot may fail to meet the requirements of this grade, including not more than 1 percent for spinach leaves which are affected by decay.

DEFINITIONS—'Well trimmed' means that the leafstems or petioles are not excessively long in relation to the size of the leafblades. 'Damage' means any defect which materially affects the appearance, or the edible, or shipping quality of the individual leaves or of the lot as a whole."

SPINACH

LEAVES:

FRESH [12/27/46   41.1730]

Grades: U.S. Extra No. 1; U.S. No. 1; U.S. Commercial

SPINACH PLANTS (11/19/56   51.2880)

Grades: U.S. No. 1; U.S. Commercial

CANNED [5/8/71   52.1901]

Grades: "A" or   "B" or   "SUB-
            "FANCY"   "EXTRA   STANDARD"
                          STANDARD"

	NET WEIGHT OZ.	NET WEIGHT METRIC	DRAINED WEIGHT OZ.	DRAINED WEIGHT METRIC
No. 8Z Tall	7.8	221.1 g	4.8	136.1 g
No. 303	15.2	430.9 g	9.6	272.2 g
No. 2½	26.8	759.8 g	17.6	499.0 g
No. 10	98.5	2.8 kg	54.7	1.6 kg

FROZEN [9/7/64   52.1921]

Grades: "A" or   "B" or   "SUB-
            "FANCY"   "EXTRA   STANDARD"
                          STANDARD"

Minimum Score   90   80   Less than 80

SPINACH—Canned [5/8/71]

Grade A and Grade B: Have a good flavor and odor and are (Grade A) attractive, (Grade B) reasonably attractive in appearance and eating quality within the limits set forth for color, character, stem material, damage, and harmless, extraneous material.

Sstd: Fails to meet requirements.

SPINACH—Frozen [9/7/64]

Grade A: Color: Possess a light, characteristic, good, green color; the yellow-green leaves, or portions thereof, or discolored leaves and stems, or portions therof, which may be present do not materially affect the color appearance of the product. **Defects:** No grit, sand, or silt may be present that affects the appearance or eating quality; and in addition: WHOLE LEAF STATE—The product does not exceed the applicable allowances prescribed for the respective type of defect in Table I and Table II. CHOPPED—The area of damage does not exceed the area prescribed for the applicable sample

TABLE I—RECOMMENDED MINIMUM DRAINED WEIGHTS FOR CANNED SPINACH

Container Designation (Metal, unless otherwise stated)	Container size Overall Dimensions Diameter (inches)	Height (inches)	Capacity Weight H$_2$O at 68°F.— ounces (avoirdupois)	Minimum Drained Weight —Ounces (avoirdupois) LL.[1]	Avg.[2]
8Z Tall	2-11/16	3-4/16	8.65	4.8	5.2
No. 1 picnic	2-11/16	4	10.90	6.3	6.8
No. 300	3	4-7/16	15.20	8.6	9.1
No. 1 tall	3-1/16	4-11/16	16.60	9.4	10.0
No. 303	3-3/16	4-6/16	16.85	9.6	10.2
No. 303 glass			17.70	9.4	10.0
No. 2 glass	3-7/16	4-9/16	20.50	11.9	12.6
No. 2½	4-1/16	4-11/16	29.75	17.6	18.6
No. 2½ glass			29.50	15.8	16.6
No. 10	6-3/16	7	109.45	54.7	58.4

1 LL. Lower limit for an individual drained weight.
2 Avg. Minimum sample average drained weight.

TABLE II—SAMPLE UNIT SIZE—DRAINED SPINACH

Style	Containers smaller than No. 2½	No. 2½ containers	No. 10 containers
Whole leaf; cut leaf	10 oz.	15 oz.	30 oz.
Chopped	2 oz.	3 oz.	6 oz.

TABLE III—WHOLE LEAF; CUT LEAF; CHOPPED STYLES

Quality Factors	Defects	Minor	Major	Severe
Color	Color appearance is —			
	Adversely affected to a degree that is noticeable		X	
	Adversely affected to a degree that is objectionable			X

Quality Factors	Defects	Minor	Major	Severe
Character	Appearance or eating quality, due to a mushy texture, disintegration, ragged cutting, or shredded leaves and shredded stems, or portions thereof, as applicable for the style, is—			
	Adversely, but not sriously, affected		X	
	Seriously affected			X
Extraneous plant material	Root crown:			
	Any significant portion of the solid area of the plant between the root and attached leaves.		X	
	Root Stub:			
	Any portion of the root whether or not leaves are attached			X
	Seed head—Whole Leaf; Cut Leaf Styles:			
	Longer than one (1) in. or objectionable regardless of length		X	
	Seed head—Chopped Style:			
	Pieces affecting appearance or eating quality—			
	More than slightly but not materially	X		
	Materially		X	
	Seriously			X
Other extraneous material	Grit, sand, silt, or other earthy material:			
	A trace that no more than slightly affects appearance or eating quality		X	
	Presence materially affects appearance or eating quality			X

TABLE IV

Quality Factors	DEFECTS	Minor	Major	Severe
Extraneous plant material	WHOLE LEAF; CUT LEAF STYLES *Grass and Weeds (Aggregate Measurement)*			
	(1) Green, fine, tender, stringlike blades, and stems:			
	3 in. or less	X		
	More than 3 in. but not more than 8 in.		X	
	More than 8 in.			X
	(2) Green and coarse:			
	1/2 in. or less	X		
	More than 1/2 in. but not more than 2 in.		X	
	More than 2 in.			X
	(3) Other than green—of any texture or kind:			
	1/2 in. or less		X	
	More than 1/2 in.			X
	CHOPPED STYLE *Grass and Weeds (Aggregate Measurement)*			
	(1) Green, fine, tender, stringlike blades, and stems:			
	3/4 in. or less	X		
	More than 3/4 in. but not more than 2 in.		X	
	More than 2 in.			X
	(2) Green and coarse:			
	3/4 in. or less		X	
	More than 3/4 in.			X
	(3) Other than green—of any texture or kind:			
	Any amount			X

size in Table III. CUT LEAF—See Table IV. ALL STYLES— The presence of harmless, extraneous vegetable material, root stubs, and heads, crowns, damaged leaves, and stems, or portions thereof, including insignificant damage or other injury, individually or collectively, does not materially affect the appearance or eating quality. **Character:** WHOLE LEAF STYLE—The spinach is tender; and there may be present: not more than 25 percent of the spinach may be stem material; and not more than 20 percent may be pieces of leaves. CUT LEAF; CHOPPED—The spinach is tender and the appearance and eating quality are not materially affected by the presence of stem material and the product does not present a pureed or stringy appearance.

Grade B: Color: Possess a characteristic, green color that may be dull but is not off color; that yellow-green leaves, or portions therof or discolored leaves and stems, or portions thereof, which may be present do not seriously affect the color appearance of the product. **Defects:** See Grade A. All wording is the same except as follows: seriously. **Character:** WHOLE LEAF STYLE—See Grade A. All wording is the same except as follows: reasonably tender; 30 percent; 30 percent. CUT LEAF; CHOPPED—reasonably tender; seriously affected. **Sstd:** Fails to meet requirements.

TABLE I—SUMMARY OF ALLOWANCES FOR CERTAIN DEFECTS IN WHOLE LEAF STYLE SPINACH

Grade Classification	Maximum Allowances Each 10 ounces net weight					Each 48 ounces net weight
	Damaged Leaves			Seed Heads	Crowns	Root Stubs
	Minor	Major	Severe			
A	6	0	0	1	1	1
	4	1	0			
	2	2	0			
	2	0	1			
B	12	0	0	3	3	3
	10	1	0			
	8	2	0			
	8	0	1			
	6	3	0			
	6	1	1			
	4	0	2			
	2	1	2			
	0	2	2			
SStd	Fails to meet foregoing requirements for Grade B classification					

TABLE II—SUMMARY OF ALLOWANCES FOR
HARMLESS EXTRANEOUS VEGETABLE MATERIAL
IN WHOLE LEAF STYLE SPINACH

Grade Classification	Group	Per sample unit—Provided, the average for all the sample units in the sample does not exceed the allowance for such average		Average for all sample units in the sample
		20 oz. net weight or less	More than 20 oz. net weight	
A	I or II or I and II combined.	Pieces aggregating 0.8 in. per 1 oz.; or 1 piece.		Total aggregate length of 0.4 in. per 1 oz. but no more than 0.1 in. per 1 oz. of Group II.
		Pieces aggregating 4 in., or 1 piece.	Pieces aggregating 0.2 in. per 1 oz.; or 1 piece.	
		Total aggregate of 0.8 in. per 1 oz.; but no more than 4 in. of Group II.	Total aggregate of 0.8 in. per 1 oz., but no more than 0.2 in. per 1 oz. of Group II.	
	III	None	None	None
B	I or II or III or I, II, and III combined.	Pieces aggregating 1.2 in. per 1 oz.; or 1 piece.		Total aggregate length of 0.6 in. per 1 oz. but no more than 0.2 in. per 1 oz. of Group II and Group III.
		Pieces aggregating 8 in.; or 1 piece.	Pieces aggregating 0.4 in. per 1 oz.; or 1 piece.	
		Pieces aggregating 8 in.; or 1 piece.	Pieces aggregating 0.4 in. per 1 oz.; or 1 piece.	
		Total aggregate of 1.2 in. per 1 oz. but no more than 8 in. of Group II and Group III.	Total aggregate of 1.2 in. per 1 oz. but no more than 0.4 in. per 1 oz. of Group II and Group III.	
Sstd	Fails to meet foregoing requirements for Grade B classification			

TABLE III—SUMMARY OF ALLOWANCES FOR
DAMAGE IN CHOPPED STYLE SPINACH

Sample Size	Area of Damaged Portions of Leaves				
Initial 2 oz.	17/16 sq. in. or less pass for A	18/16 to 22/16 sq. in. inclusive take additional 1 oz.	23/16 to 37/16 sq. in. inclusive pass for B	38/16 to 42/16 sq. in. inclusive take additional 1 oz.	More than 42/16 sq. in. fails grade B
Cumulative 3 oz.	30/16 sq. in. or less pass for A A	31/16 to 60/16 sq. in. pass for B	More than 60/16 sq. in. fails grade B		

TABLE IV—SUMMARY OF ALLOWANCES FOR
DAMAGE IN CUT LEAF STYLE SPINACH

Sample Size	Area of Damaged Portions of Leaves				
Initial 4 oz.	32/16 sq. in. or less pass for A	33/16 to 37/16 sq. in. inclusive—Take another 2 oz.	38/16 to 67/16 sq. in. inclusive—Pass for B	68/16 to 72/16 sq. in. inclusive—Take another 2 oz.	More than 12/16 sq. in.—Fails Grade B
Cumulative 6 oz.	30/16 sq. in. or less Pass for A	51/16 to 102/16 sq. in. inclusive-Pass for B	More than 102/16 sq. in.—Fails Grade B		

SQUASH*

USES: Summer squashes are picked at the immature stage when both skin and seeds are tender and edible. They may be prepared in any of the usual ways for boiling and baking vegetables, and may also be fried. Winter or hard-type squashes are cut in halves or pieces; seeds are removed, and the squash is then baked, steamed, or boiled. Where water is used in cooking, the quantity of water should be kept small to avoid taking flavor and nutrients out of the vegetable. In the case of the small delicate summer squashes especially, the flavor may be lost by cooking in a large volume of water. Squashes of the small, hard-type, such as Acorn and Butternut, frequently are cut in half and baked and served in the shell. When large squashes are cooked, pieces may be served in the shell or the pulp may be removed and mashed. Squash pulp is also used for pie, and may be served in casseroles, souffles, pancakes, and custards.

MARKETING SEASON: The so-called "summer" types are on the market all year; and so are some of the smaller so-called "winter" types. In general, the larger, hard-shelled, mature squashes with fully formed seeds are available from late August to March, peaking in October, November, and December. These include such varieties as Hubbard, Banana, Mammoth, Marblehead, Boston Marrow, Delicious, Warren Turban. On the other hand, some of the smaller, hard-shelled, mature squashes, such as Acorn and Butternut, are on the market all year; while a small, hard-shelled type, Buttercup, has a season corresponding to the larger hard-shell squashes.

The relatively small, immature, soft-shell squashes on the

MONTHLY AVAILABILITY OF SQUASH EXPRESSED AS PERCENTAGE OF TOTAL ANNUAL SUPPLY—AVERAGE FOR YEARS 1954-1958*

Jan.	Feb.	Mar.	Apr.	May	June
%	%	%	%	%	%
6	6	6	7	9	9

July	Aug.	Sept.	Oct.	Nov.	Dec.
%	%	%	%	%	%
9	8	10	13	10	7

*Based on unloads at Atlanta, Baltimore, Boston, Cincinnati, Chicago, Dallas, Ft. Worth, Kansas City, Los Angeles, Minneapolis-St. Paul, New York, Oakland, and San Francisco.

market all year include Yellow Straight neck, Yellow Crookneck, Zucchini, Scallop, Cocozelle.

VARIETIES: There are a great many varieties of squash, and they come in a wide range of sizes, shapes, and colors. Squashes are extremely difficult to classify and, in order to avoid numerous botanical complications, squash varieties are grouped here under three headings, based on marketing practice. It is hoped that using this system, identification will be relatively easy. The headings are: (1) soft-shelled, immature, small; (2) hard-shelled, mature, small; and (3) hard-shelled, mature, large. The terms "summer" and "winter" as applied to squash are deceptive and confusing, and so are not used here. Instead, under each variety, there is a statement of the general range of the marketing season. The soft-shelled, immature squash is harvested before the seeds harden. It is 100 percent edible.

(1) **SOFT-SHELLED, IMMATURE, SMALL Cocozelle** (Cucurbita pepo). This squash, of the Vegetable Marrow type, is widely grown and on the market all year. There are two general types, Long Cocozelle and Short Cocozelle, differing mainly in size. This is a bush squash. Fruits are straight, almost cylindrical when young, with very slight enlargement at apex; skin, smooth but ribbed widely and shallowy; skin, alternately striped in rather definite lines, with very dark green or dull greenish black and pale greenish yellow, both stripings appearing as a fine, lace-like pattern. This squash is in best edible condition when picked 6 to 8 in. long, and when it is 1-1/2 to 2 in. thick. When growth is allowed to continue, the long type becomes 14 to 18 in. long and 3-1/2 to 4-1/2 in. thick. The growing period is around 60 days to edible stage and satisfactory size.

Caserta This is one of the Cocozelle type, but earlier and reported to be more prolific. This also is widely grown and on the market all year. The plant is of the bush type. The fruits are cylindrical but thicker at the apex; are light glossy green with broken stripes of dark green; and fruits are 6 to 7 in. long by 1 to 1-1/4 in. thick at market stage. The growing period is 50 days.

Scallop [Pattypan] (C. pepo) Widely grown and on the market all year. Fruits disk or flared-bowl shape, with prominent ribbing on edge giving escalloped appearance, hence the name. (The term Pattypan derives from a crimped pan used for

*UFFVA

baking pies.) This is a bush squash. Fruits are generally harvested when about half grown, that is, 3 to 4 in. across. (If allowed to continue growing, they become up to 9 in. across.) In the white type, the fruits are pale green when young, become white later; skin, smooth or slightly warted; flesh, green tinged. Reaches marketable stage in around 54 days. The yellow Pattypan is similar to the white except for color.

Yellow Crookneck (C. pepo) A bush squash; one of the most widely grown squashes and available all year, though not storable. It is being grown somewhere in the country all the time. Fruits are curved at the neck, larger at the apex than at the base; moderately warted; skin, light yellow at early edible stage turning to deeper color in mature stage; flesh, creamy yellow, moderately fine though somewhat granular; fruits, 8 to 10 in. long, 2-1/2 to 3 in. at largest diameter; reaches harvesting stage at around 54 days from seeding. There are also larger Yellow Crooknecks (usually called Giant Yellow Crookneck) up to 20 in. long and 4-1/2 in. in diameter at apex.

Yellow Straightneck (C. pepo) Similar to Crookneck, but relatively straight. On market all year.

Zucchini (C. pepo) A bush squash. Widely grown and on market all year. Fruits are cylindrical, straight, with fairly square ends, the fruit being slightly enlarged at the apex; skin color, moderately dark green over a ground color of pale yellow, and surface is heavily marked with a greenish black, lace-like pattern over the entire fruit, which is concentrated to form narrow, distinct, nearly solid dark green stripes; fruits, 10 to 12 in. long and 2 to 3 in. in diameter at apex at edible stage; shell, soft and thin; flesh, pale greenish white, of moderately fine texture. There are variaations, such as Gray Zucchini, which is medium green with grayish mottling, and Black Zucchini, which has a solid dark greenish black color. Growing period to harvest, about 60 days.

(2) HARD-SHELLED, MATURE, SMALL Acorn [Table Queen, Des Moines] (C. pepo) Widely grown and available all year. This squash is acorn-shaped, hence the name. Fruits are 5 to 8 in. long, 4 to 5-1/2 in. thick; fruit turbinate, tapering abruptly from middle to apex; ribbed widely; skin, deep, dull blackish green during storage, changing to dull orange diffused with dull green; flesh, pale orange, tender, moderately dry, often rather fibrous; shell, hard and thin; surface has smooth feel except for ribbing; seed cavity, moderately large. There is also

a golden-skinned Table Queen and larger variations of the green variety. Growing period, 80 to 100 days.

Buttercup (C. maxima) One of the turban squashes, so named because of the turban-like cap at the blossom end; shape, somewhat drum-like, with sides slightly tapering near the apex; has a protuberant turban 2 to 3 inch. in diameter; squash size, 4 to 5 in. long, 6 to 8 in. in diameter; skin, dark ivy green to dull blackish green spotted with grayish pock marks and faintly striped with dull gray; turban is light gray or blue-gray; shell, moderately hard and thin; flesh, orange, dry, sweet, of fine texture; seed cavity, small. Growing period about 100 days. On market in late summer, fall, and winter.

Butternut (C. moschata) Available all year. Fruits, 9 to 12 in. long, 3-1/2 to 5 in. thick at largest diameter; nearly cylindrical but with slightly bulbous base; skin, light creamy brown or dark yellow; shell, smooth and hard; flesh, yellow or orange and fine grained; seed cavity, in the bulbous end. Growing period, 90 to 102 days.

(3) HARD-SHELLED, MATURE, LARGE Banana (C. maxima) On market, August through March. Fruit, nearly cylindrical and moderately tapering at base and apex; fruit, 18 to 24 in. long, 5 to 6-1/2 in. thick; skin, moderately smooth to obscurely wrinkled and pock-marked; skin color, pale olive gray changing to creamy pink in storage; shell of moderate thickness, medium hardness; flesh, thick, orange buff, moderately dry with fine texture; seed cavity, large. Growing period, 125 days. (Pink Jumbo Banana, used mostly for canning, normally runs 48 in. long and 12 in. thick.)

Boston Marrow (C. maxima) Primarily a canning variety. An early squash of the fall and winter group. Fruit 12 to 14 in. long, 10 to 11 in. thick; shape at the middle, nearly globular, tapering very abruptly to the apex, which is often nearly flattened, and tapering more gradually toward the base; surface, ribbed, furrowed, pock-marked; skin, orange, laced with an orange buff pattern; shell, moderately soft and medium thick; flesh, orange yellow, thick, with moderately fine texture, moderately moist, fair flavor. Growing period 97 to 100 days.

Delicious (C. maxima) On market from August through March. Fruits shaped like a top with the stem at the larger diameter; fruits, 8 to 12 in. long, about 8 to 10 in. in diameter; skin, dark green with light green stripes toward the blossom end, or

FALL AND WINTER TYPE SQUASH

FRESH [11/15/44   51.4030]
Grades: U.S. No. 1; U.S. No. 2

CANNED [3/9/56   52.2741]

Grades:	"A" or "FANCY"	"C" or "STANDARD"	"SUB-STANDARD"
Minimum Score:	85	70	Less than 70

	NET WEIGHT OZ.	NET WEIGHT METRIC	
No. 8Z Tall	7.8	221.1 g	
No. 303	15.2	430.9 g	
No. 2½	26.8	759.8 g	
No. 10	98.5	2.8 kg	

FROZEN [10/5/53   52.1941]

Grades:	"A" or "FANCY"	"B" or "EXTRA STANDARD"	"SUB-STANDARD"
Minimum Score:	85	70	Less than 70

SUMMER SQUASH

FRESH [3/26/45   51.4050]
Grades: U.S. No. 1; U.S. No. 2

CANNED [5/25/59   52.3581]

Grades:	"A" or "FANCY"	"C" or "STANDARD"	"SUB-STANDARD"
Minimum Score:	85	70	Less than 70

	NET WEIGHT OZ.	NET WEIGHT METRIC	DRAINED WEIGHT OZ.	DRAINED WEIGHT METRIC
Whole				
No. 8Z Tall	7.8	221.1 g	4.5	127.6 g
No. 303	15.2	430.9 g	10.8	306.2 g
No. 10	98.5	2.8 kg	70.0	2.0 kg
Sliced or Cut				
No. 8Z Tall	7.8	221.1 g	5.5	155.9 g
No. 303	15.2	430.9 g	11.0	311.8 g
No. 10	98.5	2.8 kg	70.0	2.0 kg

FROZEN [4/3/53   52.1961]

Grades:	"A" or "FANCY"	"B" or "EXTRA STANDARD"	"SUB-STANDARD"
Minimum Score:	85	70	Less than 70

bright reddish or tangerine with occasional green splotches at blossom end, or with cream stripes toward blossom end; slightly warted and ridged rind; rind, thin and hard; flesh, thick, yellow, dry; growing period, 100 to 105 days. (Variations of Delicious are called Green Delicious and Golden Delicious.)

Hubbard (C. maxima) Available from late August to March. Fruits, 10 to 16 in. long, 9 to 12 in. thick at largest diameter; globular, with fairly thick, tapered neck at stem end and somewhat smaller taper at blossom end; rind, very hard and strong; skin, warted, ridged, dark bronze green, or blue gray, or orange red; flesh, thick, orange yellow, and sweet. Growing period, 105 days. There are variations of Hubbard, hence the different colors and shapes. Variations include Blue Hubbard, Golden Hubbard, Warted Hubbard.

Marblehead (C. maxima) Available September through March. Fruits, 11 to 16 in. long, 9 to 10 in. thick at largest diameter; shape, nearly globular to short oval, abruptly tapering toward each end; surface, wavy and bumpy; skin, bluish gray to creamy gray or pinkish buff; rind, very hard and thick; flesh, light orange or yellow, medium thick, very firm, slightly tough, moderately dry, and of fair flavor; seed cavity, large. Growing period, 110 days.

Warren Turban (C. maxima) A winter squash noted here to represent the turban group, characterized by a turban-like formation at the blossom end. Warren Turban is drum-shaped, 8 to 10 in. long, 12 to 15 in. in diameter; skin, bright reddish orange with scattered striping at blossom end, blue turban; shell, very hard, thick, and heavily warted with fine warting; flesh, thick, bright orange, brittle, sweet, fairly dry, texture often rather stringy; seed cavity, medium large. Growing period, 115 to 125 days.

CONTAINERS: A bushel of small squashes (the only kind that would be offered by the bushel) is reported to weigh 48 to 50 lb. The Florida Crop Reporting Board estimates net weight of a bushel as 49 lb. Large winter squashes often are shipped in bulk. On the other hand, the smaller squashes, soft-shelled and hard-shelled, are shipped in a large variety of containers, including re-used containers in the East and Midwest.

The principal containers used in Florida for long distance shipments of small squashes are 1/2 bu. baskets, bu. hampers and baskets, 1-1/9 bu. wirebound crates, and 5/9 bu. wirebound crates. Others used by Florida shippers are 3/4 bu. hampers, baskets, and crates, 5/9 bu. cartons, 1-1/4 bu. wirebound crates, and bu. crates either nailed or wirebound.

California small squashes are generally packed in 2 sizes of lugs, one holding 20 lb., the other, 30. They are also packed in 40-lb. cartons ... In the New England area, the New England or Massachusetts box is popular. This holds approximately a bushel. In Ohio, Illinois, Michigan, and Pennsylvania, 8-qt., 16-qt., and 24-qt. baskets and cartons are used.

Although a very limited amount of squash is shipped by rail, Freight Container Tariffs have authorized the use of 45 different containers. Some of the representative, authorized containers are listed below. The weights are estimated billing weights, including weight of the container. Similar containers are used for motor truck shipments.

Container Number	Type of Container	Depth	Width	Length	Estimated Weights
935	Lettuce & Vegetable Crate	14-1/4 in.	18-1/4 in.	20-5/8 in.	57 lb.
952	Lettuce & Vegetable Crate	9	13	22	64
1236	1 Bushel Crate	12	12	15	49
5001	1 Bushel Wirebound Crate	12	12	15	49
5010 5045	W/B Crate (Winter Squash)	13	18	21-7/8	49
5045	W/B Vegetable Crate	11-15/16	11-15/16	16-3/4	77
8026	1 Bushel Basket				45-49
8028	1/2 Bushel Basket				29
8501	1 Bushel Hamper				49
8503	5 Peck Hamper (40 Qt.)				60
8504	3/4 Bushel Hamper (24 Qt.)				39

QUALITY: The soft-shell, immature squashes, such as Yellow Crookneck and Zucchini, should be obviously fresh, fairly heavy for size, and of characteristic color. Rind should be so tender it is easily punctured with the fingernail. Seeds should be soft and fully edible. *Hard-shelled, mature squashes* are not expected to be fresh in the same sense as immature squash. The shell should be intact and show no decay. In this type of squash, the seeds are expected to be hard and inedible and are scooped out before or after cooking.

Avoid squash that shows any soft or watery areas.

GRADES: U.S. standard grades were established in 1944 on fall and winter type squash and in 1945 on summer squash. In each case, the grades are U.S. No. 1 and U.S. No. 2. *The fall and winter grades* apply to such varieties as Hubbard, Turban, Table Queen (Acorn), Marrow, Delicious, Butternut, and others, eaten when seeds are mature, which have hard rinds. The *summer squash standards* apply to squash picked in the immature stage and eaten without the removal of seeds or seed cavity tissue. Such squashes include Yellow Crookneck, Yellow Straightneck, White Scallop (Pattypan), Zucchini, Cocozelle.

In the case of winter squash, "U.S. No. 1 shall consist of squash of one variety which are well matured, not broken or cracked, and which are free from soft rot or wet breakdown, and from damage caused by scars, dry rot, freezing, dirt, disease, insects, mechanical or other means ... In order to allow for variations other than size, incident to proper grading and handling, not more than a total of 10 percent, by weight, of the squash in any lot may fail to meet the requirements of the foregoing grades, including not more than 2 percent for squash which are affected by soft rot or wet breakdown, or are seriously damaged by dry rot. In addition, not more than 5 percent, by weight, of any lot may consist of squash smaller than any minimum weight specified, and not more than 15 percent, by weight, of any lot may consist of squash larger than any maximum weight specified ... In view of the size variations in different varieties, and because of market demands for squash of various sizes, it is not considered advisable to require a minimum size in the grade. It is therefore suggested that a minimum size or a range of sizes be specified in connection with the grade as, 'U.S. No. 1, 6 lb. min.,' 'U.S. No. 2, 4 lb. min.,' 'U.S. No. 1, 6 to 12 lb.,' in accordance with the facts."

In the case of fall and winter squash, "'Well Matured' means that the squash has completed its ripening process to a stage of development which is indicative of good handling and keeping quality for the variety" ... Damage that throws winter squash out of grade includes "scars (except stem scars) caused by rodents or other means which are not well healed and corked over, or which cover more than 10 percent of the surface, or which form depressions or pits that materially affect the appearance of the squash" ... Damage also means stem scars which are unhealed on Hubbard, Delicious, Marros, and other varieties which normally retain their stems after harvesting.

In the case of summer squash, "U.S. No. 1 shall consist of squash of one variety or similar varietal characteristics, with stems or portions of stems attached, *which are fairly young and fairly tender,* fairly well formed, firm, free from decay and breakdown, and from damage caused by discoloration, cuts, bruises and scars, freezing, dirt or other foreign material, disease, mechanical or other means ... In order to allow for variations incident to proper grading and handling, not more than 10 percent, by weight, of the squash in any lot may fail to meet the requirements of this grade, but not more than 1/2 of this tolerance, or 5 percent, shall be allowed for defects causing serious damage, and not more than 1/5 of this amount, or 1 percent, shall be allowed for squash affected by decay or breakdown ...

Because of the size differences between varieties and the difference in size preference in various markets, there are no size requirements in the grades. However, if so desired, size may be specified in connection with the grade, in terms of minimum or maximum diameter or both, or minimum length or both. When size is specified, it shall be stated in terms of inches and quarter inches. In order to allow for variations incident to proper sizing, not more than 5 percent, by weight, of any lot may consist of squash smaller than any minimum size specified; and not more than 10 percent, by weight, of any lot may consist of squash larger than any maximum size specified."

SQUASH [Summer Type]—Canned [5/25/59]

Grade A: Color: Squash is light and typical of young and tender squash of similar varietal characteristics which has been properly processed. **Defects:** Product contains no grit, sand, or silt that affects the eating quality or appearance of canned squash; for each 12 oz. there may be present not more than 1 piece of harmless, extraneous vegetable material. The combined weight of all of the defects and defective units shall not exceed 12 percent, provided that not more than 4 percent is of damaged units, and of such 4 percent not more than 1/4 thereof, or 1 percent, consists of units that are seriously damaged; or not more than 10 percent is of poorly cut units, or of units damaged by mechanical injury, or any combination thereof of not more than 10 percent, by weight provided that poorly cut units with attached stems or stem material do not exceed 2 percent. **Character:** Units are practically intact, are fleshy and tender, that the seeds are in the immature stage, and that not more than 5 percent may be of fairly good character.

Grade C: Color: All of the squash is typical of fairly young and tender squash of similar varietal characteristics which has been properly processed. **Defects:** See Grade A. All wording is the same except as follows: Fairly free from defects ... 20 percent; provided, 8 percent, 8 percent or 2 percent. 15 percent. 15 percent: provided 5 percent. **Character:** Units may show slight disintegration, may have lost to a considerable extent their fleshy textures, may be fairly tender, and that the seeds may have passed the immature stage of maturity, but are not hard, and that not more than 10 percent fail to meet the requirements for fairly good character.

Sstd: Fails to meet requirements.

SQUASH [Summer Type]—Frozen [3/3/53]

Grade A: Color: Squash is light, and typical of young and tender squash of similar varietal characteristics which have been properly processed. **Defects:** Product contains no grit, sand, silt that affects the eating quality or appearance; for each 12 oz. there may be present not more than 1 piece of harmless, extraneous vegetable material. The combined weight of all other defects and defective units must not exceed 8 percent, provided, that of such 4 percent, not more than 1/4 or 1 percent consists of units that are seriously damaged, or not more than 6 percent is of poorly cut units, or of units damaged by mechanical injury, or any combination thereof of not more than 6 percent. **Character:** Units are practically intact; are fleshy and tender; seeds are in the immature stage, and not more than 5 percent fails to meet the requirements for reasonably good character.

Grade B: Color: Color is typical of reasonably young and tender squash of similar varietal characteristics which has been properly processed. **Defects:** See Grade A. All wording is the same except as follows: Reasonably free from defects, 2 pieces ... 8 percent ... 8 percent, 2 percent, 10 percent, 10 percent. **Character:** Units may show slight disintegration, may have lost to a considerable extent their fleshy texture, may be reasonably tender, and that the seeds may have passed the immature stage of maturity, but are not hard and that not more than 10 percent fail to meet the requirements for reasonably good character.

Sstd: Fails to meet requirements.

Grade B: Consistency: The warmed, mixed squash, after emptying from the container to a dry flat surface, may be reasonably stiff, but not excessively stiff; forms a moderately mounded mass, and that at the end of 2 minutes, after emptying on such surface there may be a moderate, but not excessive separation of free liquor: **Color:** Possesses a reasonably uniform, light, typical color, and the color may be variable or slightly dull but is not off color. **Finish:** Has an even texture; may lack granular characteristic; may be slightly pasty, or slightly "salvy," but not decidely pasty or salvy, and the squash particles are not hard. **Defects:** A trace of grit, sand, or silt may be present that affects the appearance and eating quality, and the number, size, and color of the aforesaid defects present individually or collectively may be noticeable but are not so large, so numerous, or of such contrasting color as to seriously affect the appearance or eating quality.

Sstd: Fails to meet requirements.

SQUASH, [Cooked] Frozen [10/5/53]

Grade A: Consistency: The warmed, mixed squash, after emptying from a container to a dry surface, forms a well-mounded mass, and at the end of 2 minutes after emptying on such surface there is not more than a slight separation of free

USDA Inspector examines squash in a voluntary USDA continuous inspection program at a freezing company.

liquor. **Color:** Possesses a practically uniform, light, typical color; is free from discoloration due to oxidation, or other causes. **Finish:** Warmed, mixed squash has an even texture and is granular but not lumpy, pasty, or "salvy," and the squash particles are not hard. **Defects:** No grit, sand, or silt may be present that affects the appearance or eating quality of the frozen, cooked squash, and that the number, size, and color of the other aforesaid defects present individually or collectively do not more than slightly affect the appearance or eating quality.

SWEET POTATOES*

USES: The versatile sweet potato is boiled, baked, browned, fried, and candied. It can be used to make biscuits, bread, muffins, croquettes, pies, custards, cookies, or cakes.

"The greatest percentage of sweet potatoes used for food are prepared as needed from the fresh, raw product and stored, shipped, distributed, and purchased by the ultimate consumer in this form. Because of the bulk and perishability of sweet potatoes, many efforts have been made to process them into food products that can be stored and distributed without loss, and prepared for the table without waste, and with little time and effort." Frozen baked and candied sweetpotatoes, and sweetpotatoes in the form of chips and dehydrated powder are some of the newer commercial products, in addition to the more commonly known, canned sweet potato, "Sweet potato confections prepared by processes similar to those used in the preparation of candied or crystallized fruits are said to be popular in some South American countries." Other uses for the sweet potato and its plant parts, with varying degrees of importance, include flours or meals, puree, syrup, stock feed, and starch.

PREPARATION: Sweet potatoes are among the most easily prepared of all vegetables. They lend themselves to most of the cooking methods used for potatoes.

Baked sweet potatoes are especially good and very easy to prepare. Wash and scrub, then bake in a hot oven for 40 minutes to one hour, depending on size. Many sweet potato eaters like them skin and all, although others prefer to dig the sweet flesh from the shell.

"Candied sweets are ... popular ... in the country as a whole, but just because they are good that way is no reason to ignore the many other methods of preparation. Sauteed Sliced Sweet Potatoes are a slightly different approach. And when cool fall weather sparks appetites, try a Sweet potato, Carrot, and Apple Casserole. Or parboil them just until barely tender, then peel, and cut in thick slices, and brown slices in melted butter or margarine, being careful they do not burn since they are so high in sugar.

"You can whip the sweet potato into succulent softness, add some brown sugar, crunchy peanuts, and a nip of fresh lemon tartness, then bake to beautific goodness. (This rendition originated in New Orleans.) Or the sweet potato can step off into a smooth sophisticated rhumba with a nuance of nutmeg, orange rind, and rum extract—with total effect that is no less than lyrical.

"Notable for getting along congenially with other foods, sociable sweet potatoes have a special affinity for poultry. But do not serve them merely as a side dish with chicken. Combine leftover chicken and sweet potatoes in a savorily-seasoned casserole, creamed, and buttered with crisp bacon slices to add the punctuation of salty allure.

"Remember that to give their best nutriment and flavor, sweet potatoes should be cooked in their jackets, which slip off easily and promptly at a slight pressure of finger of knife."

MARKETING SEASON: Sweet potatoes are marketed all year, with period of greatest abundance September through December and lowest period May through July. The table below shows approximate availability each month expressed as a percentage of the total annual supply, based on average unloads of sweet potatoes in 41 cities. Percentages are rounded, so do not total exactly 100 percent.

APPROXIMATE MONTHLY AVAILABILITY OF SWEET POTATOES EXPRESSED AS PERCENTAGE OF TOTAL ANNUAL SUPPLY

Jan.	Feb.	Mar.	Apr.	May	June
%	%	%	%	%	%
9	8	9	7	4	2

July	Aug.	Sept.	Oct.	Nov.	Dec.
%	%	%	%	%	%
3	6	10	12	17	13

VARIETIES: Continued advances are being made in the development of new varieties. Many improvements in disease resistance, horticultural, and nutritional properties, and in production of varieties for fresh market and other uses are expected. Accompanying these improvements there will be further shifts in the importance of varieties.

Description of 6 top varieties. **Centennial** "Developed by Louisiana Station. Fresh market and canning. Soft-flesh type. Roots, variably tapered to cylindrical, medium to large, orange skin, and deep orange flesh. Good quality. Vines, vigorous, thick, long, trailing, reddish purple except green at terminal ends. Leaves, large, entirely to lightly toothed, light green. Very prolific, heavy yielder. Stores well. Only fair sprout producer. Moderately susceptible to fusarium wilt and internal cork; susceptible to black rot, soil rot, scurf, and root-knot nematode injury."

*UFFVA

Nemagold "Developed by Oklahoma Station. Fresh market and canning. Flesh, fairly soft when baked. Good quality. Root, medium size, short to long spindle, with russet golden orange skin and deep orange flesh. Skin, usually smooth, but sometimes veined. Vine type similar to that of Yellow Jersey. Leaves, distinctly shouldered, small but slightly larger than those of Yellow Jersey. Possesses certain other characteristics of Jersey-type varieties such as heavy root set, relatively uniform root size and shape, and relatively short storage life. Propagates well. Susceptible to fusarium wilt but resistant to root-knot nematode. Somewhat tolerant to soil rot and black rot. Best adapted in Jersey-variety production areas, especially the Eastern shore section of Maryland-Delaware-Virginia."

Goldrush "Developed by Louisiana Station. Excellent quality for market and canning. Soft-flesh type. Roots tapered-spindle, uniform, attractive bright orange skin, and deep orange flesh. (Strains with more copper-colored skin have largely replaced the original, lighter, orange-skinned form.) Skin smooth. Vines short to medium length, moderately vigorous, smooth, semi-bunch growth habit, vines and petioles deep reddish purple. Moderately heavy foliage density. Leaf blades sagittate with heart-shaped base. Stores and propagates well. Yields about same as Porto Rico. Very resistant to fusarium wilt under usual field conditions. Susceptible to black rot, soil rot, and internal cork."

Georgia Red Developed by Georgia Coastal Plain Station. Fresh market. Soft-flesh type. Roots slightly variable, taper-spindle, purplish red to copper red skin, and orange flesh. Excellent quality when baked. Heavy yielding. Stores and propagates well. Vines long, moderately vigorous, trailing. Foliage density, heavy. Leaves large, toothed to shouldered with heart-shaped base, green with light-bronzed tips. Susceptible to fusarium wilt, black rot, and internal cork. Somewhat tolerant to soil rot."

Porto Rico Light rose to rose skin color, with orange yellow flesh. Root is spindle-shaped to globular and irregular, but smooth. Vines are 5 to 10 ft. long, with coarse stems, and large green leaves. Porto Rico is below commercial acceptability for canning, but stores well, and has adequate sprout production."

Orange Little Stem, Orlis, Jersey Orange "Color-mutant selections from Yellow Jersey originally made at Kansas Station. Roots have orange tan skin and deep orange flesh. Flesh less 'firm' or 'dry' than Yellow Jersey. Other root and plant characteristics very similar to those of Yellow Jersey. All susceptible to fusarium wilt and black rot."

Julian (not one of the top six) is a new variety released by the Louisiana Agricultural Experiment Station. It has a copper to rose skin color with a deep orange flesh of a moist texture. It has a wide range of adaptability and is "recommended in all sweet potato growing areas as a fresh market and canning variety." It sets a large number of roots; requires a long growing season.

CONTAINERS: The main packages for sweet potatoes, according to *USDA Market News Service* are the bushel basket, hamper, crate, or fiberboard box holding 50 lb. net; the carton holding 40 lb. Other containers used are the 5/8 bu. hamper, 25 to 30 lb.; 1/2 bu. basket, 22 to 25 lb.; and 3/4 bu. basket, 39 lb. (Sacks are little used except for nearby markets in low-priced trade.)

"Growers should use the kind of package that is preferred in the area in which they expect their crop to be consumed," says Dr. Victor R. Boswell, of Agricultural Research Service. "Purchasers have been found to pay more for sweet potatoes that are packed as they prefer."

Container Numbers and Inside Dimensions of Containers Currently Provided in Each of the Governing Container Tariffs are listed in the table:

Container No.:	Container Name:	Inside Dimensions: D x W x L in inches:	Tariff No.:
4010	W/B Sweet potato Crate	11-7/16 in. deep x 14-5/8 (at top) x 13-5/8 x 16 (at bottom)	2-G
6905	F/B Sweet potato Box	9-1/2 to 10 x 11 x 16-3/4	1-H
6910	F/B Sweet potato Box	10 x 13 x 17-1/4	823-D

A study by the Transportation and Facilities Research Division A.R.S. showed that in four Los Angeles warehouses Container 6905 (40 lb. net) was the principal container used; and in four warehouses in the new York area, the bushel basket, wirebound crate, and fiberboard box (all 50 lb. net) were being used.

SWEET POTATOES

FRESH [7/1/63   51.1600]
Grades: U.S. EXTRA No. 1; U.S. No. 1; U.S. COMMERCIAL; U.S. No. 2

CANNED [7/9/51   52.2041]

Grades:	**"A" or "FANCY"**	**"C" or "STANDARD"**	**"SUB-STANDARD"**

FROZEN [9/4/62   52.5001]

Grades:	"A" or "FANCY"	"B" or "EXTRA STANDARD"	"SUB-STANDARD"
Minimum Score:	90	80	Less than 80

Wooden wirebound rectangular box. A "typical" box or crate might have inside dimensions of 18-3/4 in. in length, 12-7/8 in. in width, 10-13/16 in. in depth and hold 50 lb. of sweet potatoes at destination. Although the usual weight of. the quantity held by the box at harvest is about 55 lb., there is loss of weight in curing and drying. All surfaces of the wirebound box have openings, allowing ventilation. Most often, after the sweet potatoes have been graded and washed, these and washed, these same containers, first packed in the field, are used for shipping. Studies are being made to improve this box.

Corrugated cartons. These are being used in all sweet potato areas. The container is often a 2-piece (half-slotted) double side wall, telescope box holding the standard 50 lb.

RESEARCH—Wirebound boxes when compared to the bushel basket reduce root injury during harvesting and storage, and cut loss and damage by 13 percent, or an estimated 10 cents per bushel stored, according to USDA investigators.

"Injuries and decay serious enough to downgrade the roots were twice as prevalent among sweet potatoes in baskets as those in crates. Loss of weight and damage serious enough to downgrade the sweet potatoes from U.S. No. 1 grade were also greater among the sweet potatoes in baskets." In addition, the wirebound box allowed mechanical handling, thus becoming a factor in reducing labor costs and efficient use of storage area.

QUALITY: "Best quality sweet potatoes are clean, smooth, well shaped, firm, and bright in appearance. Selection of type and size is a matter of personal preference.

"There are two general types of sweet potatoes. One type has soft, moist flesh when cooked, and high sugar content (sweet potatoes of this type are commonly, but incorrectly, called 'yams'.) The second type, when cooked, has a firm, dry, somewhat mealy flesh, which is usually light yellow or pale orange in color, as contrasted to the usually deeper yellow or distinctly orange red colored flesh of the moist type.

"The skin of the dry type is usually light yellowish tan or fawn colored, while the skin of the moist-fleshed varieties may vary in color from whitish tan to brownish red.

"Varieties of each type vary considerably in shape, but moist-fleshed varieties are usually more plump in shape than most dry-fleshed varieties. A mixture of types or varieties within types is undesirable because of lack of uniformity in cooking, as well as differences in flavor and color of flesh.

"Seriously misshapen sweet potatoes, and those showing growth cracks, or wireworm injury are apt to be undesirable because of the waste entailed in preparation for use. Decay in sweet potatoes usually progresses and spreads very rapidly and generally imparts a disagreeable flavor to apparently unaffected flesh, even if the decayed portion is removed before cooking. Decay may appear as soft wet rot, frequently accompanied by mold groth, or as discolored, shriveled, or sunken areas of dry rot. A damp appearance may indicate decay in adjacent specimens. The ends of the tubers are most frequently affected, although decay often develops in other areas. Another type of decay occasionally appears as greenish black, variable-sized, circular spots. If occurring in bruised or injured areas, such spots may be irregular rather than circular in outline."

Some red-type sweet potatoes are also colored with a harmless red wax. Often this wax is objectionable to the buyer because in boiling sweet potatoes the red color comes off in the water. No physiological benefit from the coloring practice has yet been demonstrated. The Sweet Potato Council of the U.S. recommended that the full Council proceed to take necessary action to outlaw this practice. Of its 14-member state associations, the Council found that, with the exception of one state, all were in favor of the prohibitive action.

GRADES: U.S. grades for sweet potatoes are U.S. Extra No. 1, U.S. No. 1, U.S. Commercial, and U.S. No. 2. *U.S. No. 1 is the chief trading grade.*

"U.S. No. 1 shall consist of sweet potatoes of one type which are firm, fairly smooth, fairly clean, not more than slightly misshapen, which are free from freezing injury, internal breakdown, black rot, other decay, or wet breakdown, except soil rot, and from damage caused by secondary rootlets, sprouts, cuts, bruises, scars, growth cracks, scurf, soil rot, or other diseases, wireworms, weevils or other insects, mechanical or other means. *Unless otherwise specified,* each sweet potato shall be not less than 3 in. in length and 1-3/4 in. in diameter, and shall not exceed 10 in. in length. In no case shall the sweet potato be more than 3-3/4 in. in diameter or weigh more than 20 oz.

Tolerance for Defects: In order to allow for variations other than size, incident to proper grading and handling, not more than a total of 10 percent, by weight, of the sweet potatoes in any lot may fail to meet the requirements of this grade, but not to exceed a total of 5 percent shall be allowed for defects causing serious damage, including not more than 2 percent for sweet potatoes affected by soft rot or wet breakdown, except soil rot."

SWEET POTATOES—Canned [7/9/51]

Grade A: Color: Reasonably light, characteristic color (either yellow or golden) and there may be reasonable variations of such characteristic color in the units, in each unit, or in the moss. **Shape and Size and Consistency:** WHOLE AND PIECES (WHETHER PACKED SINGLY OR IN COMBINATION) IN A LIQUID PACKING MEDIUM OR VACUUM-PACK (WITHOUT PACKING MEDIUM)—Units of a single style may vary moderately in shape if the weight of the largest unit, irrespective of style, is not more than 8 times the weight of the 2 smallest units, and irrespective of state. WHOLE PROCESS AND MASHED (WHETHER PACKED SINGLY OR IN COMBINATION) PACKED AS "SOLID-PACK"—Possess a

SWEET POTATOES—SHAPE—FAIRLY WELL SHAPED
One usable piece available.

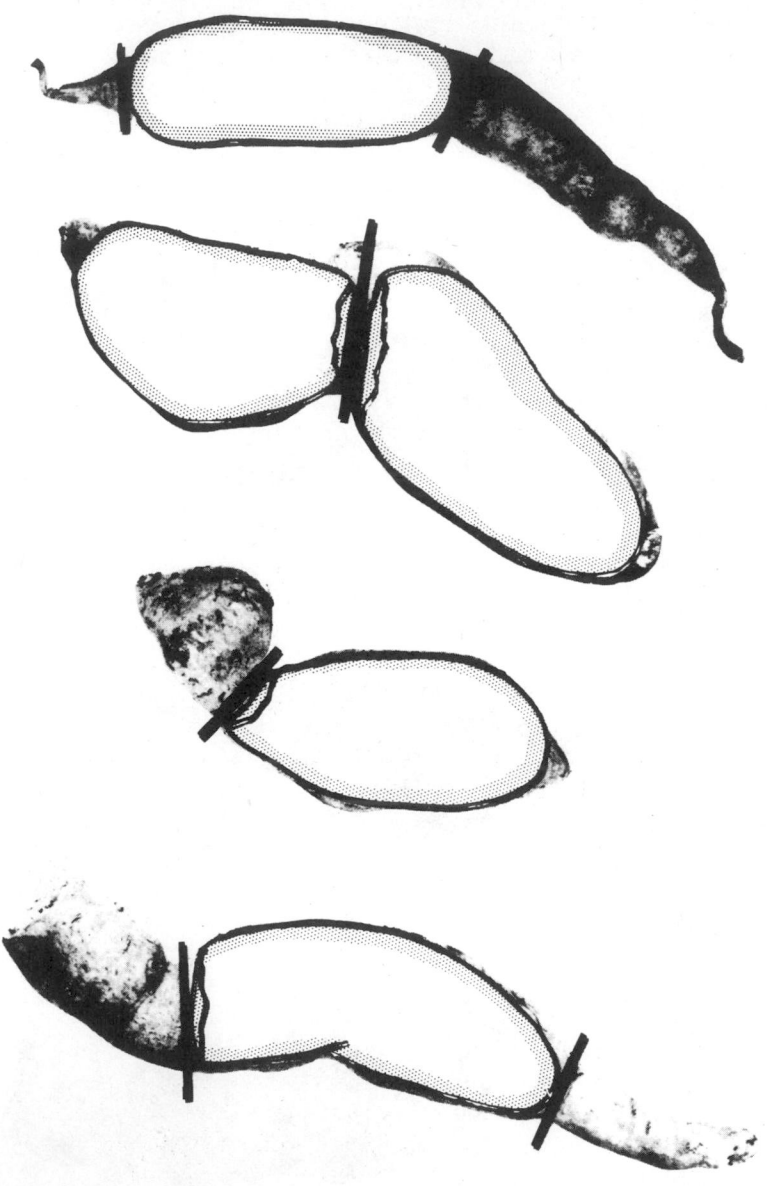

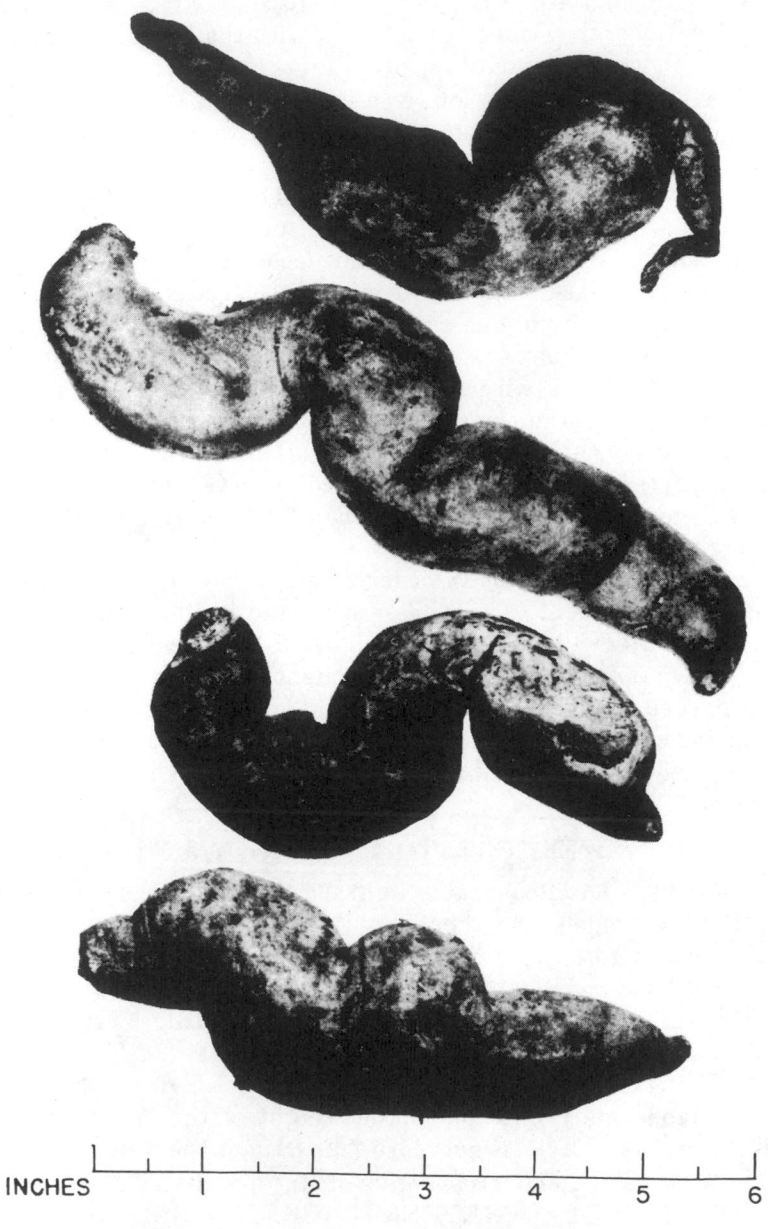

INCHES

SWEET POTATOES—SHAPE—FAIRLY WELL SHAPED
One or more usable pieces available.
[Pieces shown.]

SWEET POTATOES—SHAPE—NOT FAIRLY WELL SHAPED
No usable piece available.

stiff consistency which may show a slight separation of liquid. **Defects:** Contains not more than a slight amount of particle of peel, secondary rootlets, untrimmed ends, discolored areas, or other defects which do not affect materially the appearance or the edibility. **Character:** WHOLE AND PIECES, ETC. (See color)—Units possess a uniformly smooth texture; are practically free from tough or coarse fibers, and may be soft to firm but hold their apparent original confirmation and size without material disintegration. WHOLE PIECES AND MASHED, ETC.—Possess uniformly smooth texture; are practically free from tough or coarse fiber; may be soft to firm, and any mash sweet potatoes present possess a uniformly smooth texture, practically free from tough or coarse fibers.

Grade C: Color: Color may be variable in the units, in each unit, or in the mass, and color may be slightly dull but is not off-color. **Shape and Size:** WHOLE AND PIECES, ETC.—Units of a single style may vary considerably in shape, and the weight of the largest unit, irrespective of style, is not more than 4 times the weight of the 2 smallest units, irrespective of style. WHOLE, PIECES AND MASHED, ETC.—Sweet potatoes possess a thick consistency but may not be free flowing. **Defects:** The particles of peel, secondary rootlets, untrimmed fibrous ends, discolored areas, or other defects may be definitely noticeable, but are not so prominent as to affect seriously the appearance or edibility. **Character:** WHOLE AND PIECES, ETC.—Units possess a fairly uniform texture; may possess a few tough or coarse fibers; may be variable in tenderness but are not tough; may be very soft to very firm, and may possess a slight or partial disintegration of the units. WHOLE, PIECES AND MASHED, ETC.—See WHOLE AND PIECES. Only changes are as follows: ... only sweet potatoes present possess a fairly uniform texture; may be coarse but are practically free from lumps, and may possess a few tough or coarse fibers. MASHED,—May possess a fairly uniform texture; may be coarse but are free from lumps, and not more than a few tough or coarse fibers may be present.

Sstd: Fails to meet requirements.

SWEET POTATOES—Frozen [9/4/62]

Grade A: Color: Reasonably bright, characteristic color (either yellow or golden, but not mixed), and that there may be reasonable variations of such characteristic color among the units or in the mass. **Size:** The frozen sweet potatoes comply with the size and uniformity requirements in (A) classification in Table I, although the overall appearance of the product for the applicable style is not materially affected by units of abnormal size and shape. **Defects:** WHOLE BAKED; WHOLE STUFFED; HALVES STUFFED—The peel in shell is not broken nor the shell distorted to any noticeable extent, other than in the opening in whole stuffed style, and the units are practically free from primary and secondary rootlets, internal fibers, internal corky areas, and other defects which do not affect materially the appearance or the edibility. WHOLE PEELED; HALVES PEELED; MASHED—The product may contain not more than a slight amount of particles of peel, primary and secondary rootlets, untrimmed fibrous ends, discolored ends, tough areas, and any other defects which do not affect materially the appearance or the edibility. **All other defects:** The aggregate weight of all defective units does not exceed 5 percent of all the units; 1 unit in a container is permitted to be defective if such unit exceeds the allowance of 5 percent: provided, that in all containers comprising the sample such defective units do not exceed 5 percent and the overall appearance and edibility is not materially affected by the presence of defective units. **Character:** WHOLE BAKED:—Flesh is not soggy nor dry and is practically free from tough or coarse internal fibers. WHOLE STUFFED; HALVES STUFFED; MASHED—The mass or stuffing possesses a uniformly smooth texture and consistency, and is free from lumps and tough or coarse fibers. ALL OTHER STYLES—Units possess a uniformly smooth texture; are practically free from tough or coarse fibers, and may be firm to soft, but hold their apparent original conformation and size without material disintegration.

Grade B: Color: Yellow, golden, or mixed may be variable among the units, in each unit, or in the mass, and the color may be no more than slightly dull. Mixed color types shall not be graded above U.S. Grade B, regardless of the total score for the product. **Size:** The frozen sweet potatoes comply with the sizes and uniformity requirements for (B) classification in Table I: and the overall appearance of the product for the applicable style is not seriously affected by units of abnormal

TABLE I—UNIFORMITY OF SIZE REQUIREMENTS FOR CERTAIN STYLES OF FROZEN SWEET POTATOES

Styles, as applicable	(A) Classification Uniformity of Size	(B) Classification Uniformity of Size
Whole:		
(1) Peeled	May vary moderately in size.	May vary considerably in size.
(2) Baked (unpeeled) (3) Stuffed	The weight of the smallest unit is no less than 2/3 the weight of the largest unit.	The weight of the smallest unit is no less than 1/2 the weight of the largest unit.
Halves:		
(1) Peeled	May vary moderately in size.	May vary considerably in size.
(2) Stuffed	The weight of the smallest unit is no less than 2/3 the weight of the largest unit	The weight of the smallest unit is no less than 1/2 the weight of the largest unit

Styles, as applicable	(A) Classification Uniformity of Size		(B) Classification Uniformity of Size	
Sliced French-cut Cuts (or chunks)	May vary moderately in size except that the thickness of slices is reasonably uniform	Small units Composite weight does not exceed 5% by weight of all units	May vary considerably in size except that the thickness of slices is fairly uniform	Small units Composite weight does not exceed 10% by weight of all units
Diced	May vary moderately in size	No limits	May vary considerably in size.	No limits

size and shape. **Defects:** WHOLE BAKED; WHOLE STUFFED; HALVES STUFFED—See Grade A. Only changes are as follows: reasonably free ... seriously affect the appearance. WHOLE PEELED; HALVES PEELED; MASHED: only changes are as follows: moderate amount of particles ... seriously affect all items. **Styles:** Only changes are as follows: 10 percent: 10 percent ... seriously affected. **Character:** FOR ALL STYLES—See Grade A. The only changes are as follows: WHOLE BAKED—is not excessively dry, reasonably free. WHOLE STUFFED; HALVES STUFFED; MASHED—may be coarse ... practically free, and not more than a few tough or coarse fibers. ALL OTHER STYLES—reasonably uniform, reasonably free; 75 percent or more of the units hold their original conformation and size without material disintegration.
Sstd: Fails to meet requirements

SUCCOTASH—Canned [5/24/67]

Grade A: Consisting of cream style or whole-grain sweet corn and lima or snap beans which meet the requirements of U.S. Grade A for the respective canned or frozen commodities. If tomatoes are an ingredient, they must meet the requirements of U.S. Grade A canned tomatoes for color and absence of defects.
Grade B: See Grade A. All ingredients must meet requirements of U.S. Grade B.
Grade C: See Grade A. All ingredients must meet requirements of U.S. Grade C.
Grade D: Fails to meet requirements of U.S. Grade C.

TABLE NO. I

	Proportions by weight	
	Not less than	Not more than
	Percent	*Percent*
Corn	50	87-1/2
Snap Beans	25	50
Lima Beans, fresh	12-1/2	30
Lima Beans, dry "soaked"	12-1/2	30
Tomatoes	10	30

SUCCOTASH—Frozen [3/6/59]

Grade A: Color: Vegetables are bright and possess a color typical of young and tender vegetables that have been properly prepared and processed, and the frozen whole kernel

SUCCOTASH

CANNED [5/24/67   52.6001]

Grades:	"A" or "FANCY"	"B" or "EXTRA STAN- DARD"	"C" or "STAN- DARD"	"D" or "SUBSTAN- DARD"
	NET WEIGHT OZ.	NET WEIGHT METRIC		
No. 8Z Tall	7.8	221.1 g		
No. 303	15.2	430.9 g		
No. 2½	26.8	759.8 g		
N0. 10	98.5	2.8 kg		

FROZEN [3/6/59   52.2011]

Grades:	"A" or "FANCY"	"B" or "EXTRA STAN- DARD"	"C" or STAN- DARD"	"SUB- STAN- DARD"
Minimum Score:	90	80	70	Less than 70

(or whole grain) corn is practically free from "off-color" kernels. In addition, the lima beans shall meet the following color requirements: not less than 93 percent are green, and not more than 7 percent may be lighter in color; provided, that not more than 1 percent are white, or not less than 97 percent are green, and not more than 3 percent may be lighter in color in white beans. **Defects:** Defects, individually or collectively, do not more than slightly offset the appearance or eating quality. For each 10 oz., there may be present: 1 piece or pieces of extraneous vegetable matter, such as pieces of pod, huck, leaves, and stems having an aggregate area of not more than 3/10 sq. in. (1/2 in. by 3/8 in.) on 1 surface of the piece or pieces; and 1/4 cubic centimeter of pieces of cob. **Tenderness:** Vegetables are tender and, prior to cooking, meet the following requirements: CORN—whole kernel (or whole grain). The kernels are in the milk or early stage of maturity. LIMA BEANS—are young and tender. SOYBEANS—are young and tender. GREEN BEANS (OR WAX BEANS)—full-fleshed for the variety, and the seeds are in the early stage of maturity.

Grade B: Color: See Grade A: all wording is the same except as follows: reasonably good color; is reasonably free; 65 percent. 35 percent. **Defects:** See Grade A: all wording is the same except as follows: reasonably free from defects. 3/8 sq. in. (1/2 in. by 3/4 in.): 1/2 cu. centimeter. **Tenderness:** See Grade A: all wording is the same except as follows: CORN— reasonably tender: LIMA BEANS—reasonably young and tender. SOY BEANS—See lima beans. GREEN BEANS (or WAX BEANS)—The green beans or wax beans may have lost their fleshy texture to some extent, and the seeds may have passed the early stage of maturity or have not reached the early stage of maturity, and have not reached the late stage of maturity.

Grade C: Color: See Grade A: all wording is the same except as follows: vegetables possess a color that may be dull: 65 percent. **Defects:** See Grade A: changes in wording are as follows: seriously affect ... 3/4 sq. in. (1/2 in. by 1-1/2 in.); 1 cu. centimeter. **Tenderness:** See Grade A: only changes in wording are as follows: CORN, WHOLE KERNEL—Kernels are in tough stage of maturity. LIMA BEANS—Nearly mature. SOY BEANS—nearly mature. GREEN BEANS (OR WAX BEANS)—may have lost to a considerable extent their fleshy structure, and the seeds may be well developed and nearly mature.

Sstd: Fails to meet requirements.

SWISS CHARD*

USES: "In effect it is two vegetables in one, since the leaves may be cooked as greens, and the white stems may be cooked like celery. The flavor of chard is very delicate, rather like asparagus. It should always be steamed, never boiled, since boiling will remove the flavor. The leaves should be cooked like spinach, using only the water that clings to them from washing. A sliver of garlic or a dash of nutmeg adds a subtle flavor change to the greens. Cream of chard soup—made like cream of spinach—is a delicate and delicious luncheon or supper dish ... The white stems are prepared like asparagus or celery. Strip them carefully and cut into convenient pieces. Cook in very little boiling salted water until tender. Chilled, they are delicious, with French dressing or vinaigrette."[1]

*UFFVA

1. Reprinted with special permission of William H. Wise and Co. (New York City), from the *Wise Encyclopedia of Cookery*, copyright © 1948 by William H. Wise and Co.

MARKETING SEASON: Swiss chard begins to come on the market in April and is in heaviest supply June through October, tapering off in November. The percentage of the annual supply available each month is estimated as follows: April, 1 percent; May, 8 percent; June, 18 percent; July, 16 percent; August, 16 percent; Sept., 17 percent; Oct., 15 percent; Nov., 7 percent; Dec., 1 percent.

VARIETIES: "Lucullus is a leading yellowish green variety. There is also a Lucullus dark green." **Giant Lucullus** gives a plant 24 to 28 in. tall, upright, leaves yellowish green and heavily crumpled, with a cream-colored, slender midrib. It grown in 50 days.

"**Fordhood Giant** is a popular strain requiring 60 days to mature. the leaves are heavily crinkled and dark green. The stem and midrib are broad, thick, and white, and the plants are vigorous and sturdy." Plant 24 to 28 in. tall, upright. Said to be "probably the best, all-around variety for most areas."

Dark Green White Ribbed [White Silver Ribbed] Plant 18 to 24 in. tall, upright; leaves medium dark green, smooth with broad, prominent white ribs; liked by many gardeners for its crispness. 50 days.

Rhubarb Chard Plant 20 to 24 in. tall, upright; leaves crumpled, dark red to wine red with red veins. Stems and midribs are crimson. 55 days.

Burpee's Rhubarb Chard Crimson stalks look like rhubarb. Leaves are dark green and heavily crumpled. 60 days.

CONTAINERS: There is no standardized container for chard. Since it is marketed close to where it is produced, it may come to market in any of a variety of containers that are not damaged by water.

QUALITY: There are no U.S. standard grades for Swiss chard. Like all leafy greens, this vegetable should be fresh, crisp, not showing yellow or browned portions, and should be free of aphis or other insect infestation. It should be clean and *cold*. Unless it is under refrigeration, the quality is doubtful. Stalks that are wilted and rubbery will be tough and unsatisfactory. Coarse stalks indicate pithiness. This may be discovered by pressing or twisting the stalk.

TOMATOES*

USES: Fresh tomatoes are an ideal salad vegetable, served sliced or cut, in wedges, either alone or in combination with lettuce, asparagus, celery, cucumbers, onions, and greens. It is a standard item in sandwiches, a favorite flavor in soup, and the base for many delightful sauces and dressings. The tomato has a piquancy and succulent palatability that improves the flavor and edibility of whatever item with which it is combined. Tomatoes are served cooked in many delicious forms, stewed, fried, baked, and in conserves. Large green tomatoes are often used for frying, while small green ones are excellent for pickling. Tomatoes are processed commercially in many forms, including whole, pureed, solid pack, juice, catsup, pickles, chowder, chili sauce, soup, and tomato powder.

MARKETING SEASON: Fresh tomatoes are available all year in most markets in the U.S. Domestic production alone, including greenhouse crops, provides tomatoes every month, and imports swell the total noticeably in January through May. The following breakdown shows what percentage of the annual total of tomatoes is available each month. It is based on average annual unloads of fresh tomatoes by rail, boat and truck at 41 cities, as reported by USDA and summarized by UFFVA in its *Supply Guide:*

MONTHLY AVAILABILITY OF TOMATOES EXPRESSED AS PERCENTAGE OF TOTAL ANNUAL SUPPLY

Jan. %	Feb. %	Apr. %	Mar. %	May %	June %
6	6	8	8	11	12
July %	Aug. %	Sept. %	Oct. %	Nov. %	Dec. %
11	10	8	8	6	6

VARIETIES: Here are some of the varieties for major growing states.

FLORIDA—The most popular varieties for green-wrap, listed in order of importance: **Homestead-24** and several other strains, "Elite," "61" and "S & M 500": **Supermarket; Marion,** in limited spring production; **Tropi-Red,** in limited winter and

*UFFVA

spring production. In addition, there are a few scattered plantings in Grothens Globe, Rutgers and Immokalee. Pink harvest varieties in order of importance are: **Floradel, Manapal, Manalucie, Indian River** and **Tropic**. Florida expects significant changes to take place in the next year or so, changes brought about by the need for mechanization (new varieties are nearly ready) and by fusarium wilt (race 2), which is now spreading in Florida and several other areas of the U.S., and Mexico. **Walter** was released in 1969 and is resistant to this wilt.

CALIFORNIA—Varieties for fresh market are as follows: **Earlypak 7** and **Pearson A-1**, which are both principally ground (unstaked) grown; **Ferry-Morse 428 and H-11**, which are principally grown on stakes; and **Ace 55**, grown both ways. However, only 2 or 3 more years are expected with this lineup before the varieties change almost entirely as varieties being developed for machine harvest come into prominence.

NEW JERSEY—Early season recommendations for New Jersey growers are: **Starfire, Spring Giant, Moreton Hybrid, Kille 7,** and **Campbell 1327**. Midseason recommendations are: **Heinz 1439, Cardinal Hybrid, Superman, Rutgers Hybrid,** and **Tom-Tom**. Late season recommendations are: **Ace 55 VF** and **Manapal**. For staking or trellising, recommendations are: **Moreton Hybrid, Fantastic, Queen's Knight, Coronet, Rutgers Hybrid, Superman, Big Boy, Tom-Tom,** and **Manapal. Roma VF** is the recommended plum type. **Red Cherry** and **Basket Pak** are the recommended cherry types. Three varieties are listed for greenhouse forcing: **Michigan-Ohio Hybrid, Tuckcross O,** and **Veegan**.

SOUTH CAROLINA—**Homestead** comprises about 90 percent of the fresh market acreage. All it has is yield and earliness when grown in South Carolina. About 8 percent of the acreage is in **Marion** and **Supermarket**. The remaining 2 percent is supplied by **Floradel**. The last 3 varieties all have disease resistance that Homestead lacks, but do not yield as high or as early. For the future, in ground culture, the most promising varieties are **Sunburst** and **Tropi-Red**. Both have disease resistance and are earlier and yield more than Homestead. For fresh market trellis production, South Carolina uses only Manapal.

TEXAS—Generally throughout the state, Rutgers has passed out of the picture. Homestead replaced Rutgers, and now Homestead is being replaced rapidly by **El Monte** and some **La Pinta**. The variety picture in Texas is likely to change very rapidly during the next few years as there is a lot of promising material in breeding programs that will be released shortly. It is interesting to note that although **Chico** and **Chico Grande** are pear-shaped varieties intended for processing, a small but growing volume of these 2 varieties is being shipped vine ripe to the fresh market each year. Certain markets throughout the U.S. are now taking these in truckload lots.

CONTAINERS: In the continual search for greater efficiency and better product protection in handling tomatoes from packinghouse to terminal market, many companies have switched from container to container. The result is that an unbelievable number of sizes and types of containers are in use in the industry, and even their tops, for instance, may be part open, part telescope, full telescope, etc.

One effort to reduce the proliferation of fiberboard container sizes and types has resulted from cooperation between shippers and the Uniform Classification Committee, Trans-Continental Freight Bureau, and Fibrebox Association officials. Four containers were agreed upon to supply the industry:

85-269, Stak-Pak, No Divider, 275 lb. test board (69-33-69)
85-422, 3 in. cover, Bliss style, H Divider, 275 lb. (69-33-69) BTM, 200 lb. ends, 3 laminated, 200 lb. cover (42-33-43)
85-556, full telescope, No Divider, 275 lb. (69-33-69), 90 lb. facing BTM, 300 lb. (69-33-69) cover
85-557, 5 in. cover, 350 lb. (90-33-90), 350 lb. H Divider, 200 lb. cover

In particular, the Bliss container listed above has been gaining more acceptance, and the Fresno office of USDA reported recently that about 85 percent of the mature green tomatoes shipped out of the state were packed in that box. The LA lug is still widely used in California, particularly for intrastate shipments.

Popular for pink tomatoes are the 2-layer wooden flats (holding 20 lb.) and the 3-layer lugs (holding 30 lb.). These boxes are handpacked, with a chipboard pad between layers. Both boxes are 16-1/8 by 18-1/2 in. inside. the 2-layer flat is 5-

TOMATOES

FRESH [2/1/75   51.1855]
Grades: U.S. No. 1; U.S. No. 2; U.S. No. 3; U.S. Combination

GREENHOUSE TOMATOES (4/19/66   51.3345)
Grades: U.S. No. 1; U.S. No. 2

CANNED [7/24/64   52.5161]

Grades:	"A" or "FANCY"	"B" "EXTRA STAN-DARD"	"C" or "STAN-DARD"	"SUB-STAN-DARD"
Minimum Score:	90	80	70	Less than 70
	NET WEIGHT OZ.	NET WEIGHT METRIC	DRAINED WEIGHT OZ.	DRAINED WEIGHT METRIC
Whole				
No. 8Z Tall	7.8	221.1 g	4.3	121.9 g
No. 303	15.2	430.9 g	8.5	241.0 g
No. 2½	26.8	759.8 g	14.9	422.4 g
No. 10	98.5	2.8 kg	54.7	1.6 kg
Grade A				
No. 8Z Tall	7.8	221.1 g	5.7	161.6 g
No. 303	15.2	430.9 g	11.1	314.7 g
No. 2½	26.8	759.8 g	19.6	555.7 g
No. 10	98.5	2.8 kg	72.2	2.0 kg
Grade B				
No. 8Z Tall	7.8	221.1 g	5.0	141.8 g
No. 303	15.2	430.9 g	9.8	277.8 g
No. 2½	26.8	759.8 g	17.3	490.4 g
No. 10	98.5	2.8 kg	63.5	1.8 kg
Grade C				
No. 8Z Tall	7.8	221.1 g	4.3	121.9 g
No. 303	15.2	430.9 g	8.5	241.0 g
No. 2½	26.8	759.8 g	14.9	422.4 g
No. 10	98.5	2.8 kg	54.7	1.6 kg

3/4 in. deep, while the 3-layer lug is 7-1/8 in. deep. The 3-layer lug is used principally for 6 by 7 and 6 by 6 sixes, while the 2-layer flat is used more for the larger sizes, it is said.

In Florida about 1/3 of the mature green tomatoes are packed and shipped in the Bliss box. It measures 17-5/8 by 12 by 10-3/4 in. and holds 40 lb. of tomatoes. The remainder of the Florida mature greens are shipped in another H-divider fiberboard box also holding 40 lb. which is 17-5/8 by 11-7/8 by 10-3/8 in. Most Florida vine ripes are tissue wrapped and shipped in fiberboard boxes holding 20 lb. of tomatoes. This box measures 15-3/8 by 12-1/2 by 6-1/4 in. Some vine ripes are packed in fiberboard flats holding 8 lb. (About 1/4 of the Florida tomatoes are shipped as vine ripe, and 3/4 are shipped mature green.)

In eastern states, wide use is made of fiberboard boxes and lug boxes of various sizes, such as:

A part-telescope box measuring 17-1/2 x 11-3/8 x 10-7/8 in., holding 40 lb.

A part-telescope box measuring 15-3/4 x 12-5/8 x 6-3/4, holding 24 to 26 lb.

A shallower, part-telescope box measuring 15-3/4 x 9-5/8 x 2-7/8, holding 8 lb.

Many vine ripes are packed in 1-layer boxes, some in Panta-Pak trays, and some are individually tissue wrapped.

Weights of Containers. An idea of the principal containers in use for shipping tomatoes to wholesalers for repacking, and their respective weights, can be gained from the USDA. "Principal commercial shipping containers predominantly used in the more important producing areas shipping in volume by rail" are as follows. The figure in parenthesis indicates net weight in pounds.

Fiberboard carton or crate (60)
Carton (40)
Los Angeles lug (30 to 34)
2-layer flat (18 to 20)
8-quart climax basket (9 to 11)
12-quart climax basket (18 to 20)
16-quart climax basket (27)

Miscellaneous packages other than those listed above are as follows:

Bushel basket or hamper (55 to 60)
5/8 bushel hamper (35)
1/2-bushel basket (30)
11- or 12-quart basket, lidded (15 to 20)
12-pint flats—cherry (16 to 17)
2-layer carton (18 to 20)
8-quart basket—field run (10)
10-lb. basket (10)
Eight 2-quart baskets (30)

A recent development is the shipping container made both of corrugated and wood, like the 20-lb. WIBCO crate ... It holds 2 layers of vine ripes, separated by a chipboard liner. Two snap-in slats serve as a top for this container, which is also made in a 30-lb. (3-layer) size.

SERVINGS AND WEIGHTS: The following table prepared by USDA gives information about purchasing and serving units. "AP" means "As Purchased."

Food as Purchased	Purchase Unit	Servings per Purchase Unit	Serving Size or Portion	Purchase Units for 100 Servings	Additional Yield Information
TOMATOES					
Fresh	Pound	4.00	1 small tomato (about 1/2 cup)	25	1 lb. AP = 0.91 lb. ready-to-serve raw
	Pound	5.06	1/2 cup raw, diced or sliced	20	
		10.12	1/4 cup raw, diced or sliced	10	

Another guide states that for a 2-slice portion, a 1-lb. tomato results in 7-1/2 portions; and for 25 portions, 3.5 lb. would be needed; and for 100 portions, 13.5 pounds are needed. A pound cut into wedges provides 12 portions; and 2-1/4 lb. are needed for 25 portions, and 8-1/2 lb. are needed for 100 portions. Yield from tomatoes as purchased is 91 percent.

QUALITY: Dennison, Hall and Nettles in an article entitled, "Influence of Certain Factors on Tomato Quality," write as follows. "There are probably 4 basic, or general, factors on which the consumer evaluates the quality of tomatoes. These are color and general appearance, firmness of the fruit, internal appearance of the sliced fruit, and flavor.

FLAVOR—"The sugar and acid contents of the tomato fruit are 2 of the primary factors determining the flavor. The total amount of each and the ratio of sugar to acid is very important. If the ratio (percent sugar divided by percent acid) is too low, the fruit are sour and have an insipid flavor. An unnaturally sweet flavor is produced if the ratio is too high. The locular jelly is the most acid portion of the fruit and contains the lowest sugar content. The greater the percentage of locular jelly in the fruit, the lower the sugar/acid ratio will be ... The acid content of the fruit increases until the mature-green stage is reached and then decreases until the fruits are fully ripened. There is a rapid rise in the sugar/acid ratio from the mature-green fruit to the ripened fruit.

FIRMNESS—"A number of studies have been made of the pectic substances found in tomatoes. Most of these studies indicate that these materials have an important influence on the firmness of the fruit. During the development of the fruit the insoluble protopectin is laid down in the primary cell walls. With the onset of ripening the protopectin is gradually converted to soluble pectin. As ripening continues, the pectins decrease in concentration, and the fruit becomes softer.

"Hamson ("Factors Which Condition Firmness in Tomatoes," *Food Research* 17:370-9, 1952) studied factors which condition firmness in certain varieties and breeding lines of tomatoes. He found that the breeding lines with firm fruit accumulated more calcium in the fleshy portion of the fruit than the soft-fruited varieties ... Kertesz and his associates ("The Effect of Calcium on Plant Tissues," *The Canner* 88:26, 1939) observed that increasing the calcium content of plant tissues increased the firmness through the formation of a calcium pectate gel which provided additional support to the cell structure.

INTERNAL APPEARANCE—"The anatomy of the fruit has an important bearing on the internal appearance. The amount of locular contents (jelly and seeds) and flesh (locular and outer walls); in the fruit is important. The locular contents may be a small or fairly large proportion of the fruit. The locular contents of Florida fruit which have been studied varied from 15 percent to 32 percent of the fresh weight. The amount of pigment found in each portion of the fruit is very different. The outer wall has the highest lycopene (red) content and the lowest carotene (yellow) content; therefore, the outer wall has the highest lycopene/carotene ratio. Therefore, if the color of the sliced fruit is going to be good, the amount of locular jelly must be small in comparison with the amount of flesh."

SIZE—A tomato can be of good quality whether large or small. Size is a matter of preference. The view that large tomatoes are more easily injured in commercial handling than small tomatoes has not been sustained by research. "Tomatoes of small size were as often and as seriously damaged by bruising as those of larger size," says L.H. Halsey, of the Florida Agricultural Experiment Station.

Good quality tomatoes for use fresh are those that are mature but not over-ripe, firm, fairly well formed, plump, smooth, of good color, free from serious blemishes, good for slicing, and that have a good flavor, not sour, and not over-sweet. Catfaces or scars around the blossom end cause some waste but do not damage tomato flavor. Tomatoes with growth cracks are suitable only for immediate consumption, since they will spoil much sooner than unblemished fruit. Puffy or watery fruit is of poor flavor and wasty. The best-flavored tomatoes are those allowed to ripen on the vine. Tomatoes that have been damaged by chilling are never of good quality, but chill injury is difficult to recognize.

GRADES: "U.S. Standards for Fresh Tomatoes" were first issued in 1922, and have been revised many times.

BASIC TRADING GRADES—At present, the four grades for fresh tomatoes are U.S. No. 1, U.S. Combination, U.S. No. 2, and U.S. No. 3. *U.S. No. 1* consists of tomatoes of similar varietal characteristics which are mature but not overripe or soft, which are clean, well developed, fairly well formed, fairly smooth, and which are free from decay, freezing injury, and sunscald, and free from damage caused by bruises, from cuts and broken skins, internal discoloration, sunburn, puffiness, catfaces, other scars, growth cracks, hail, insects, disease, or mechanical or other means.

U.S. Combination consists of a combination of U.S. No. 1 and U.S. No. 2 tomatoes where at least 60 percent, by count, meet the requirements of the U.S. No. 1 grade. The reader should refer to the Standards for tolerances on U.S. Combination and for descriptions and tolerances on U.S. No. 2 and U.S. No. 3 grades. The term "unclassified" is not a grade, but means only that no grade has been applied to the lot.

DEFINITIONS—as used in the Standards include: "Similar Varietal Characteristics" means that the tomatoes are alike as to firmness of flesh and shade of color. "Mature" means that the contents of two or more seed cavities have developed a jelly-like consistency and the seeds are well developed. "Soft" means that the tomato yields readily to slight pressure. "Well Developed" means that the tomato shows normal growth. Tomatoes which are ridged and peaked at the stem end, contain dry tissue, and usually contain open spaces below the level of the stem scar are not considered well developed.

"Fairly Well Formed" means that the tomato is not more than moderately kidney-shaped lopsided, elongated, angular, or otherwise moderately deformed. "Fairly Smooth" means that the tomato is not conspicuously ridged or rough. "Damage" means any defect which materially affects the appearance, or the edible or shipping quality of the tomato. Any one of the following defects, or any combination of defects the seriousness of which exceeds the maximum allowed for any one defect, shall be considered as damage: (a) cuts; (b) puffiness; (c) catfaces; (d) scars (other than catfaces); (e) growth cracks; (f) hail injury; (g) insect injury. See the Standards for precise tolerances and descriptions of each of those seven conditions as well as for these additional terms: "Reasonably Well Formed," "Slightly Rough," "Serious Damage," "Misshapen," and "Very Serious Damage."

LOWER LIMIT U.S. NO. 1

PUFFINESS

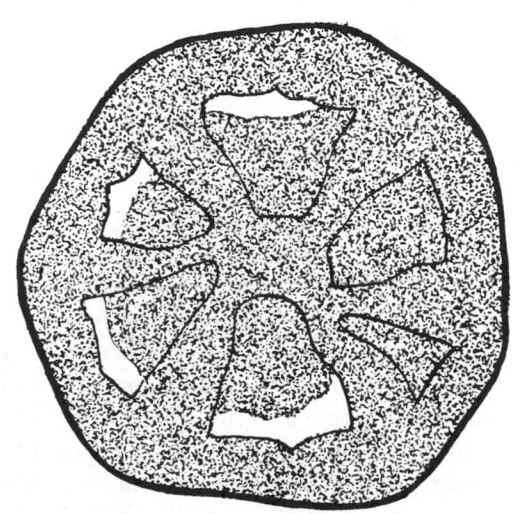
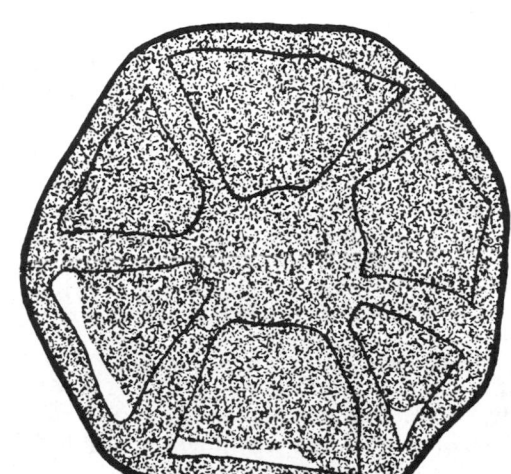

The proportion of open space permitted is dependent upon the thickness of walls. Tomatoes with thicker walls than those in the above illustrations may have proportionately greater amounts of open space. Tomatoes with thinner walls than illustrated shall have proportionately lesser amounts of open space.

Size Requirements: The big change in way of denoting size of tomatoes came in 1949. For years, tomatoes had been wrapped and packed in Los Angeles lugs, and size was described by showing the number of rows of tomatoes in the top layer. But packers and shippers were then beginning to ship tomatoes jumble-packed in several types of containers other than Los Angeles lugs. The USDA was urged to change the standards and use the diameter measurement of the tomatoes, rather than the descriptive sizes, when packed in lugs. This was intended to enable traders to have a measurable basis for trading in different sizes of tomatoes and in various containers. The following size requirements are now in effect:

Los Angeles Lug Size Arrangements[1]	Minimum Diameter	Maximum Diameter
	Inches	Inches
4 x 4	3-5/16	3-15/16

Los Angeles Lug Size Arrangements[1]	Minimum Diameter	Maximum Diameter
4 x 5	3	3-10/16
5 x 5	2-14/16	3-6/16
5 x 6	2-11/16	3-3/16
6 x 6	2-8/16	2-14/16
6 x 7	2-4/16	2-10/16
7 x 7	2	2-6/16
7 x 8	1-14/16	2-4/16

1. "In determining compliance with the above size arrangements, the measurement for minimum diameter shall be the largest diameter of the tomato measured at right angles to a line from the stem end to the blossom end. The measurement for maximum diameter shall be the smallest dimension of the tomato determined by passing the tomato through a round opening in any position ... In order to allow for variations incident to proper sizing, not more than a total of 10 percent, by count, of the tomatoes in any lot may be smaller than the specified maximum diameter."

Color Classification System: By 1961, the marketing of tomatoes with color was increasing, and there was demand for a change in the standards to reflect the importance of color separation. As a result, a new color classification system was added. These 6 colors are:

GREEN: Surface completely green; may vary from light to dark green.

BREAKERS: Definite break from green to tannish yellow, pink or red on not more than 10 percent of surface (normal break first occurs at blossom end).

TURNING: From 10 percent to 30 percent of surface in aggregate tannish yellow, pink, or red.

PINK: From 30 percent to 60 percent of surface in aggregate pink or red.

LIGHT RED: Over 60 percent of surface in aggregate pinkish red or red, but not over 90 percent red.

RED: Over 90 percent of surface in aggregate red.

This is intended to promote a more uniform method of describing the color of most lots of tomatoes. It is the practice of the USDA's inspection service to show color under the condition heading on all certificates of inspection at terminal markets. Color may be reported by showing the percentage of each of the six colors or by grouping the classification, such as: "green and breakers," or "turning and pink." The percentage of each color also is reported on shipping point certificates.

NOTE: A tomato color chart, based on USDA descriptions, has been developed by UFFVA's Tomato Division, as an industry service, for widespread, inexpensive distribution throughout the trade.

Greenhouse Grades. U.S. standards for grades of greenhouse tomatoes have also been established, effective April 19, 1966. The two grades are "U.S. No. 1." and "U.S. No. 2." These standards supersede the standards which had been in effect since April 15, 1962.

TOMATOES—Canned [7/24/64]

Grade A and [A Whole]: Color: Has a color that is typical of tomatoes of the red or reddish varieties, and of the total outer surfaces areas of the tomatoes, not less than 90 percent are as red as "USDA Tomato Red"; not more than 5 percent may be yellow, or may possess less red than minimum red for canned tomatoes, and none are a distinct vivid green. **Defects:** Any defects present, whether or not specifically defined or listed, no more than slightly detract from the appearance or edibility; practically no objectionable core material may be present; no more than a trace of harmless extraneous material may be present, and the defects present in the sample unit, and the entire sample, if applicable do not exceed the allowance specified in Table II.

Grade B: Color: Has a color that is typical of tomatoes of the red or reddish varieties, and of the total outer surface areas of the tomatoes not less than 50 percent are as red as "USDA Tomato Red"; not more than 10 percent are yellow, or are less than "minimum Red for canned tomatoes," and none are distinct, vivid green. **Defects:** Any defects present, whether or not specifically defined or listed, do not materially detract from the appearance or edibility; only a slight amount of objectionable core material may be present; no more than a slight amount of harmless extraneous material may be present; and the defects that may be present in the sample unit, and the entire sample if applicable, do not exceed the allowance specified in Table II.

Grade C: Color: The red predominates to the extent that the 50 percent of the drained tomatoes which possess the least redness are as red or redder than "minimum Red for canned tomatoes." **Defects:** Any defects present, whether or not specifically defined or listed, do not seriously detract from the appearance or edibility; only a moderate amount of objectionable core material may be present; only a moderate amount of harmless extraneous material may be present, and the defects that may be present in the sample unit, and the entire sample if applicable, do not exceed the allowances specified in Table II.

Sstd: Fails to meet requirements.

TURNIPS*

USES: Al Capp's Lil Abner has been eating "tarnips" since he was a baby if he ever was one, and his great strength and remarkable brain, it is reliably reported, are due to the diet rich in "tarnip presarves."

*UFFVA

TABLE II—MAXIMUM DEFECTS PERMITTED IN EACH GRADE

| Grades | Defect (aggregate area) | In a single container | | In total sample representing a lot; in cans of any size (per lb. of total of total contents of all containers (average)) |
		In cans of less than 2 lb. total contents (in any container)	In cans of 2 or more lb. total contents (equivalent amount per lb. of contents of any container)	
A and A Whole	Peel	2 sq. in.	1 sq. in.	1/2 sq. in.
	Blemished areas	1/8 sq. in.	1/16 sq. in.	1/16 sq. in.
	Discolored portions	1/2 sq. in.	1/4 sq. in.	1/4 sq. in.
B	Peel	3 sq. in.	2 sq. in.	1 sq. in.
	Blemished areas	1/4 sq. in.	1/8 sq. in.	1/8 sq. in.
	Discolored portions	1 sq. in.	1/2 sq. in.	1/2 sq. in.
C	Peel	No limit	No limit	1 sq. in.
	Blemished areas	1/2 sq. in.	1/4 sq. in.	1/4 sq. in.
	Discolored portions	1-1/2 sq. in.	3/4 sq. in.	3/4 sq. in.

Turnips are good in roasts, stews, soups, casseroles, as a boiled vegetable, and cut up raw in salads. They may be eaten in wholes or halves, or mashed, and served with a variety of sauces. Turnip slaw is excellent. It is made of finely shredded, raw turnips, some fresh parsley, vinegar and dressing, and, of course, other vegetables such as raw cabbage and carrots may be added. Turnips and potatoes may be cooked together and served with a savory sauce. The French serve turnips with a poulette sauce ... Try tossing diced, hot cooked turnips with lemon butter, seasoned with salt, ground black pepper, and crumbled basil leaves. It is delicious.

A popular method of preparation is to peel, cut in 1/2- to 3/4-in. cubes, place in a saucepan with 1 in. of boiling, salted water, bring to boiling point, and boil three minutes. Cover, and continue boiling 12 minutes, or until tender. Cooking turnips or rutabagas uncovered for several minutes, or lifting the lid several times during cooking, permits the escape of gases and gives roots a more delicate flavor.

When young and tender, turnip greens are excellent. Cook them only until crisp-tender, in as little boiling water as will keep them from sticking. Cooking time is 15 to 25 minutes. Salt to taste. The handsome green color can be preserved by a simple cooking trick; cover the boiling greens for about a minute, just long enough to wilt and compact them. Then remove the cover for a minute to let the vapors escape. Do this a time or two during cooking.

Here is a recipe for herbed turnip greens. 1/4 lb. salt pork; 1 cup water; 2-1/2 lb. of fresh turnip greens; 1-1/2 tsp. salt; 1 tsp. sugar, or this may be omitted; 1/2 tsp. marjoram leaves; 1/8 tsp. ground black pepper. Wash salt pork and cut into 4 pieces. Place in a large saucepan with water. Cover and cook 20 minutes or until pork is almost done. In the meantime, wash turnip greens thoroughly, and cut off coarse stems. Add to pork along with salt, sugar, marjoram, and black pepper. Cover and cook 15 minutes or until greens and pork are tender. Serve with corn bread and roast pork or pork chops. Yield: 6 servings.

The greens may be served, as in the South, with "pot likker," that is the thin broth obtained from boiling meat.

MARKETING SEASON: The table on the following page gives availability of turnips and rutabagas monthly as a percentage of the annual total. The Canada figures, given separately, but included in the percentages in the top line, are for rutabagas. The percentages in the two lines indicate that the supply May through August is virtually all turnips, while the supplies in other months are mixed. Turnips are on the market in all months.

VARIETIES: "The varieties may have white, green, or purplish red crowns, but crown color has no particular significance. The most common white-fleshed turnip varieties listed by seedmen are **Purple Top White Globe** and **White Egg.**

MONTHLY AVAILABILITY OF TURNIPS-RUTABAGAS
EXPRESSED AS PERCENTAGE OF ANNUAL TOTAL

	Jan. %	Feb. %	Mar. %	Apr. %	May %	June %
In United States	12	10	10	7	5	4
(All) From Canada	12	11	10	6	3	1

*Less than 0.5%

	July %	Aug. %	Sept. %	Oct. %	Nov. %	Dec. %
	4	5	9	11	13	11
	*	4	11	12	17	13

Shogoin, a white-skinned, white-fleshed Japanese variety, is widely used in the South for greens and salad because it is less subject to aphid damage than the other 2 mentioned. Early season, white-fleshed varieties such as Purple Top White Globe are favored in the South for the early spring market. Yellow-fleshed turnip varieties include **Golden Ball** or **Orange Jelly, Amber** or **Yellow Globe** and **Yellow Aberdeen.** The variety **Seven Top** is grown in the South for use as greens."

CONTAINERS: A wide variety of containers are used. Topped turnips are packed in 25 lb. and 50 lb. film or mesh bags; in cartons, loose, containing 50 lb.; in 1-lb. film bags packed 12 to a carton, or packed in larger amounts in larger cartons, and in the LA lug holding 30 lb. Turnips with tops are packed in wirebound crates, in bushel baskets (although the use of this container is declining for all commodities), and in other crates. Turnip greens are packed in bushel baskets or crates holding 25 lb.

QUALITY: Aside from grade, turnips should be smooth, firm, and with few leaf scars around the crown, or fibrous roots at the base. If tops are on, they should be fresh, green, young, and crisp. Yellowed or wilted tops indicate old age. Roots that are very large and coarse or are in any degree wilted should be rejected. If tops are on and good enough to eat, they should be removed and used as soon as possible. Turnips should be kept cold and humid until ready to use. The greens, like all greens, need to be fresh looking and tender as indicated by feel. They should be green, not yellow, and should not show insect injury, coarse stems, seedstems, dry or blackened areas. They need to be cold and moist at all times. Greens that are warm when sold are likely to be tough and, in general, should be avoided. After purchase, keep greens as nearly ice-cold as possible, and moist.

GRADES: U.S. grade standards for turnips or rutabagas, effective August 1, 1955, provide for two grades, U.S. No. 1 and U.S. No. 2, including bunched, topped, and short-trimmed turnips. U.S. Standards for mustard greens and turnip greens, effective March 8, 1953, provide for one grade, U.S. No. 1. It is not possible to reprint the entire standards here, but excerpts are given, and the complete text may be obtained free from Fruit and Vegetable Division, Agricultural Marketing Service, USDA, Washington, D.C. 20250.

TURNIPS-RUTABAGAS Styles: "Bunched turnips means turnips which are tied in bunches. The tops shall be full length or removed to not less than 6 in. Turnips with short-trimmed tops means, unless otherwise specified, turnips showing leafstems ranging to not more than 4 in. in length. Topped turnips ... means turnips with tops removed to not more than 3/4 in. in length.

"*U.S. 1* consists of turnips or rutabagas of similar varietal characteristics, the roots of which are well trimmed, firm, fairly smooth, fairly well shaped, fairly clean, and free from soft rot, and free from damage caused by cuts, discoloration, freezing, growth cracks, pithiness, woodiness, watercore, dry rot, other disease, insects or rodents, or mechanical or other means. Bunched turnips, or turnips with short-trimmed tops, shall have tops which are fresh and free from decay, and free from damage caused by discoloration, freezing, disease, insects, or mechanical or other means. Unless otherwise specified, the diameter of each turnip or rutabaga shall be not less than 1-3/4 in."

TURNIP GREENS "The standards are applicable to ... greens consisting of either plants (crown or root attached) or cut leaves, but they shall not be applicable to mixtures of plants and cut leaves ... in the same container ... U.S. 1 consists of ... turnip greens of similar varietal characteristics which are fresh, fairly tender, fairly clean, and which are free from decay, and free from damage caused by seedstems, discoloration, freezing, foreign material, disease, insects, or mechanical or other means. In the case of turnip greens with roots attached, the roots shall be firm and free from damage by any cause and, unless otherwise specified, the maximum diameter of the root shall be 1-1/2 in. In order to allow for variations incident to proper grading and handling, other than for size of roots and mixtures of plants and leaves, not more than a total of 10 percent by weight of the units in any lot may fail to meet the requirements of the grade, provided, that not more than 1/2 of this amount, or 5 percent, shall be allowed for serious damage by any cause, and including therein not more than 2 percent for decay. Not more than 5 percent by weight of the greens may consist of cut leaves, in a lot consisting of plants, or of plants, in a lot consisting of cut leaves. Turnip greens with roots attached shall have not more than 10 percent by weight of roots which are larger than the specified maximum size."

TURNIP GREENS WITH TURNIPS—Frozen [8/19/58]

Grade A: Color: Leaf ingredient possesses a bright, practically uniform, typical green color of young, tender turnip greens, and the turnip ingredients possess a practically uniform, light, color characteristic of the variety of young tender turnips, which ingredients have been properly prepared and processed. **Defects:** No grit, sand, or silt may be present that affects the appearance or edibility, and there may be present for each 10 oz. net weight, of turnip greens with turnips not more than, in whole leaf, an aggregate of 6 in. in length of grass and weeds, provided that the total amount does not materially affect the appearance or edibility; in other styles, no grass or weeds, or pieces of grass or weeds, that materially affect the appearance or edibility, and an aggregate area of damage affecting 3 sq. in. (3 in. by 1 in.) of leaves and stems or portions of leaves and stems, and 5 percent of units of turnip ingredients affected by damage, provided, that damaged units do not materially affect the appearance or edibility. **Character:** Leaf ingredient is tender and practically free from coarse or tough leaves and stems, and the turnip ingredient possesses a tender texture and is practically free from fibrous or pithy units.
Grade B: Color: The color of the leafy ingredient is reasonably light and typical of reasonably young and tender turnip greens, and the turnip ingredient possesses a characteristic color for the variety, which color is typical of reasonably young and tender turnips which have been properly prepared and processed. **Defects:** See Grade A, all wording is the same except as follows: seriously affect: whole leaf style: provided: seriously affect. In other styles ... seriously affect; 6 sq. in. (6 in. by 1 in.), 10 percent: provided, ... seriously affect.

Character: Leafy ingredient is reasonably tender and free from coarse and tough leaves and stems, and the turnip ingredient possesses a reasonably tender texture and is reasonably free from fibrous and pithy units.
Sstd: Fails to meet requirements.

VEGETABLES, MIXED—Frozen [5/24/54]

Grade A: Color: Combined basic vegetables, as a mass, and the individual basic vegetables are bright and characteristic of young or tender vegetables that have been properly prepared and processed; any pieces of vegetable material used for garnish are reasonably bright; and lima beans, if present, possess a light, typical color for the varietal type, and meet the following additional color requirements for the respective types: **THIN-SEEDED TYPES (WITH SKINS REMOVED); THICK-SEEDED BABY POTATOES (TYPE WITH SKINS ON).** 90 percent or more of all the lima beans are "green"; and the balance may be lighter in color or may be white or combinations thereof. Thick-seeded type (with skins on). 85 percent are "green"; and the balance may be lighter in color, but not more than 5 percent of all its lima beans may be white. **Defects:** No larger pieces of harmless extraneous vegetable material, but small piece of harmless extraneous vegetable material for each 16 oz. net weight, or for each package if the package is less than 16 oz. of frozen mixed vegetables: provided, that the combined weight of all the harmless extraneous material is not more than 1/2 of the 1 percent of the mixed vegetables, or a total of 3 moderately damaged units and seriously damaged units for each 30 oz. of frozen mixed vegetables of which 1 unit for each 4 oz. of frozen mixed vegetables may be seriously damaged: provided, that slightly damaged, moderately damaged, and seriously damaged units, either singly or in combination, do not affect materially the appearance or edibility; and other defects, individually or collectively, do not affect more than slightly the appearance of the frozen mixed vegetables. **Character:** The combined vegetables after cooking are tender, and the individual vegetables prior to cooking meet the following requirements: BEANS, GREEN OR WAX—The bean pods and seeds possess a good character. BEANS, LIMA—minimum of white beans;

MIXED VEGETABLES

FROZEN [5/24/54   52.2131]

Grades:	"A" or "FANCY"	"B" or EXTRA STAN-DARD"	"C" or "STAN-DARD"	"SUB-STAN-DARD"
Minimum Score:	90	80	70	Less than 70

are tender, and any white beans that may be present are tender or reasonably tender. CARROTS—Possess a tender texture. CORN—Kernels are no more advanced than the cream style of maturity. Have a reasonably tender texture, and are the equivalent of frozen whole grain corn that would score not less than 43 pt. for the factor of "Tenderness and Maturity." PEAS—reasonably tender and are equivalent of frozen peas that would score not less than 34 pt.

Grade B: Color: See Grade A. All wording is the same except as follows: reasonably light ... reasonably young and tender; ... fairly bright but are not off-color; reasonably light: **THIN-SEEDED TYPES [WITH SKINS REMOVED]: THICK SEEDED BABY POTATO TYPES [WITH SKINS ON]. 65 percent. THICK-SEEDED [WITH SKINS ON]: 65 PERCENT. Defects:** See Grade A: Only changes are as follows: 2 small pieces; 4 moderately damaged ... 3 oz.; ... do not affect materially. **Character:** See Grade A. only changes are as follows: reasonably tender and practically free from tough fibers. BEANS, GREEN OR WAX —reasonably. BEANS, LIMA—including white beans are reasonably tender. CORN—reasonably tender ... 40 pt. PEAS—reasonably tender ... 32 pt.

Grade C: See Grade B. The only changes are as follows: ... fairly bright ... may be only fairly bright but are not off-color for any reason; fairly light: **THIN-SEEDED TYPE [WITH SKINS REMOVED]: THICK-SEEDED BABY POTATO TYPES [WITH SKINS ON]. 55 percent ... including lima beans that may be white. THICK-SEEDED TYPE [WITH SKINS ON]. 40 percent ... 20 percent may be white. Defects:** See Grade B. Only changes are as follows: 5 moderately damaged ... 2 oz. of mixed

vegetable; provided, seriously offset; seriously affect. **Character:** All wording is same except as follows: fairly tender; BEANS, GREEN AND WAX—fairly good character. BEANS, LIMA—fairly tender. CARROTS—reasonably tender. CORN—fairly tender. PEAS—fairly tender.
Sstd: Fails to meet requirements.

WATERCRESS*

USES: Its most frequent use is as a garnish on meats or as a raw ingredient in salad, either in combination with other green or alone. Watercress lends an interesting zing to soups, vegetables and sauces. The watercress sandwich is as English as apple pie is American. The French have popularized a thick soup made of potatoes and watercress, potage cressoniere. Italians add the tangy cress to their minestrone and other soups, and the Chinese have long used it in their egg drop, won ton, and other soups. Hotels and restaurants are the big users of watercress.

MARKETING SEASON: Watercress is on the market all year. There are no details of monthly supply. However, when data were kept in New York City, the lowest supply was November to March and the highest May to October. In winter, supplies are mainly from Florida and California; and, in summer, from northern areas including scattered small growers.

QUALITY: Nobody knows more about watercress quality than the people who grow it. The following statements are made by Dennis Watercress, Inc. "Watercress must be young and fresh to be good. When you buy it, snap a leaf between your fingers to see if it is crisp. Be sure it has no yellow or wilted leaves. The color should be bright."

The same organization favors storage of watercress as follows: "Untie each bunch, inspect, wash thoroughly in cold water, drain, and dry on a towel or absorbent paper, then place in a container with a tight-fitting cover and refrigerate. Watercress stored in this manner will keep fresh for several days."

*UFFVA

FRUITS AND VEGETABLES, CONTAINERS

Shipping containers most commonly used for fresh fruits and vegetables

Commodity	Shipping container	Approximate net weight[1]
		POUNDS
Fresh fruits		
Apples	Bu. basket	40-50
	Fiberboard box, tray pack	37-48
	Fiberboard box, cell pack	37-44
	Fiberboard box, bulk pack	38-50
	Film bag 3, 4, 5, 10 lb.	
	(packed 4 to 15 bags to the master container)	36-48
Apricots	Lug, Brentwood	24-25
	Lug, L.A.	27-30
	Lug	12
	Lug	14
	4 basket crate	26
Avocados (California)	Lug	12-15
(Florida)	1-layer flat or 1/4 bu. wood or fiberboard box	13-14
(Florida)	4/5 bu. fiberboard box or carton	36-40
Bananas	Fiberboard folding box	25-50, mostly 40
All berries (California)	12 1-pt. tray or carton	11-12
All berries (other)	24 qt. crate	36
	24 pt. crate	18
	12 pt. crate	9
	16-qt. crate	24
Cherries	Lug, Calex	18-20
	Lug, Campbell	15-16
	Lug, wood	12-14
	Lug or carton	20
Cranberries	Box or fiberboard carton, 1/4 barrel	25
	1-lb. film bag or carton	
	(packed 24 to the master container)	24
Figs (California)	Flat, 2 layer	12-15
	9-basket crate	12-15
Grapefruit (Florida)	1-3/5 bu. wirebound box	85
	4/5 bu. wirebound or fiberboard box	42 1/2
	Film or mesh bags	4-5-8
	Mesh bags	20
Grapefruit (Texas)	1-2/5 bu. wirebound box	80
	7/10 wirebound or fiberboard box	40
	Bags	5-8
	Mesh bags	20

(continued)

FRUITS AND VEGETABLES, CONTAINERS

Shipping containers most commonly used for fresh fruits and vegetables
(continued)

Grapefruit (California Desert Valleys and Arizona)	7/10 bu. fiberboard box, carton	32
Grapefruit (California "other" areas)	7/10 bu. fiberboard box, carton	33 1/2
Grapes, table (California)	Lug	27-28
	Lug	24
	Flat	17-20
	Chest, sawdust pack	20-22
	Chest, sawdust pack	32-34
Grapes (Eastern)	8 2-qt. crates	24-25
	12-qt. basket	18-20
Grapes, juice (California)	Lug	26-28
	Lug	36-42
Lemons (California and Arizona)	7/10 bu. fiberboard carton	38
Limes (California and Florida)	Fiberboard box, carton 4/5 bu.	40
	Fiberboard box, carton 2/5 bu.	20
	Fiberboard box, carton 1/5 bu.	10
	Fiberboard master container	
	12 1-lb. pks.	12
	36 1-lb. pks, or 24 1-1/2-lb.	36
Mangoes (Florida)	1 layer flat	13
	Box or carton	40
Nectarines (California)	Flat	10
	Standard peach box	20-24
	Lug, Sanger	22-24
	Lug, L.A.	30
	4-basket crate	30-32
Oranges (Florida)	1 3/5 bu. wirebound box	90
	4/5 bu. wirebound or fiberboard box	45
	Film or mesh bags	4-5-8
	Mesh bags	20
Oranges (Texas)	1-2/5 bu. wirebound or fiberboard box	85
	7/10 bu. wirebound or fiberboard box	42 1/2
	Bags	5-8
	Mesh bags	20

FRUITS AND VEGETABLES, CONTAINERS

Shipping containers most commonly used for fresh fruits and vegetables
(continued)

Commodity	Shipping container	Approximate net weight[1]
		POUNDS
Oranges (California and Arizona)	7/10 bu. fiberboard carton	37 1/2
	Bags	2-8
Peaches (West)	Lug, L. A., wooden	22-28
	Western peach box	16-20
	Lug, Sanger	20
	Flat-1 layer	10
	Wood or fiberboard crate or carton	18-22
	4-basket crate	27
Peaches (all other States)	Bu. basket	46-52
	1 1/9 bu. crate	50-55
	3/4 bu. basket, carton or crate	35-42
	1/2 bu. basket	23-28
Pears (West)	Standard wood box or carton	40-54
	Lug, L. A. or 2-layer carton	22-28
	1/2 standard box	30
	3/4 bu. basket	38-41
Pears, prickly (California)	Lug	20
Persimmons (California)	Lug	20
Plums (California and Idaho)	Fiberboard box carton	25-30
Plums (California)	Standard peach box	20-24
	Lug, Sanger	24-28
	Lug, L. A.	32
	4-basket crate	28-34
Prunes (Northwest)	1/2 bu. basket, carton or lug	28-30
	4-basket crate	28-30
	Fiberboard carton	20
	Wooden box	15
	Wooden box	12
Pomegranates	Lug, L. A.	28
Tangerines (Florida)	4/5 bu. wirebound or fiberboard box	47 1/2
Tangerines (California)	Carton	25
Fresh vegetables		
Anise (California)	W.G.A. crate	75
Anise (Texas)	Wirebound crate	35-40
Artichokes (California)	1/2 box	20-26
	Fiberboard box, carton	22

(continued)

FRUITS AND VEGETABLES, CONTAINERS

Shipping containers most commonly used for fresh fruits and vegetables
(continued)

Commodity	Shipping container	Approximate net weight[1]
		POUNDS
Asparagus, all	Pyramid crate	26-32
	Pony crate	12
Asparagus (California)	Fiberboard box, carton containing	
	1-1/2 lb. consumer pkgs.	31
	3-qt. basket-loose	10
Beans, lima, all	Bu. hamper or basket	28-32
Beans, snap, all	Bu. hamper or basket	28-32
Beets, bunched	Wirebound crate	45
	1/2 W.G.A. crate	40-45
	Carton containing 18 bunches	15
Beets, topped, all	Open mesh sack	50
Broccoli	Wirebound crate	25
	Pony crate	40-42
	1/2 crate, wirebound	20-22
	Crate, 14 film-wrapped bunches	20-23
Brussels sprouts	Tray, 12-pt. cups	12-14
	Wirebound crate, 24 1-pt. cups	22-26
	Fiberboard box, carton	25
	Drums	25
Cabbage, all	Wirebound crate	50
	W.G.A. crate	70-100
	Mesh bag	50
	Paper bag	50-60
	Carton, fiberboard	44-70
Carrots, topped, all	Open mesh bags	50
	Wirebound crate	50
	Wirebound crate	80
	Burlap sack	70-85
	4 doz. 1-lb. film bags packed in mesh bag or carton	50
	2 doz. 2-lb. film bags packed in mesh bag or carton	50
	Bushel baskets	50
Carrots, bunched	2/3 crate	45-52
	S & W crate, 6 doz.	87

(continued)

FRUITS AND VEGETABLES, CONTAINERS

Shipping containers most commonly used for fresh fruits and vegetables
(continued)

Commodity	Shipping container	Approximate net weight[1]
		POUNDS
Cauliflower, all	Fiberboard box, 1 layer, wrapper leaves removed, film wrapped	16-23
	Fiberboard box, 2 layers, wrapper leaves removed, film wrapped	23-35
	Crate, lettuce	55-62
	L. A. crate	50-53
	W.G.A. crate	50-60
Celery, all	16" nailed or wirebound crate	55-70
	1/2 size carton	30-33
	2/3 carrot crate	72-75
	Pony crate	40
	Crate, lettuce	72-90
	Fiberboard box, 16" packed with 2 doz. film bags	50
	Fiberboard box, 16" packed with 1 doz. film bags	25
Chinese cabbage	1.45 bu. wirebound box	50-55
	1-1/8 or 1-1/9 bu. crate or carton	40
Corn, all	Wirebound crate	40-60
	Mesh or multi-wall bag	45-50
Corn (Texas)	Mesh bag-1/2 bu.	22-30
Cucumbers, all	Bu. basket, carton, hamper or crate	47-55
	Fiberboard carton	20-22
	1-1/9 bu. crate	55
	.57 bu. wirebound crate	27
	1/3 bu. fiberboard carton	19
	1/4 bu. fiberboard carton	14
	Lug, L.A.	28-32
Eggplant, all	Bu. basket or hamper	30-34
	1-1/9 bu. crate	35
Escarole, endive, and chicory	16" wirebound or nailed crate	36
	Bu. basket	25
	1-1/9 wirebound crate	25-28
Garlic	Open mesh sack	25
	Open mesh sack	50
	Fiberboard box, carton	30

(continued)

FRUITS AND VEGETABLES, CONTAINERS

Shipping containers most commonly used for fresh fruits and vegetables
(continued)

Commodity	Shipping container	Approximate net weight[1]
		POUNDS
Garlic-continued	Fiberboard box	25
	Nailed crate	50
	L.A. lug	28-30
Greens: Collards, mustard, turnip and spinach	Bu. basket, hamper, or crate	18-25
Lettuce and romaine, all	Fiberboard box, carton	38-55
	Wirebound crate	40
	1-1/9 bu. crate	26
Lettuce, hothouse	Basket	5
	Basket	10
Melons, cantalopes	Jumbo crate	80-89
	Standard crate	70-85
	Fiberboard carton, Eastern flat	15-18
	1/2 size carton	31 1/2
Melons, cantaloupes	Honeydew flat or crate	35-47
	Jumbo honeydew crate	52
	Standard honeydew crate	48
	Carton	31 1/2
Onions, dry, all	Open mesh sack	50
	do.	25
	do.	10
	do.	5
	Fiberboard carton	48-50
	Film bags, packed in master containers	1-1/2, 2, 3, 5, 10
Onions, green	Wirebound crate	15-20
	Wirebound crate	38
	16" fiberboard carton	25-30
	Carton, 4 doz. bunches	15-18
	Open lug	10-16
	Crate	60-65
Okra	Basket, 1/2 bushel	15
	Bushel basket or hamper	30
Parsley	16" crate	19
	Wirebound crate	26
	Nailed crate	18-20
	1/2 L.A. crate	24

(continued)

FRUITS AND VEGETABLES, CONTAINERS

Shipping containers most commonly used for fresh fruits and vegetables
(continued)

Commodity	Shipping container	Approximate net weight[1]
		POUNDS
Peas, green, unshelled	Bushel hamper or tub	28-30
Peppers, green, all	Bu. basket, hamper or crate	28-30
	1-1/9 bu. crate	28-33
	Fiberboard carton	30-34
Potatoes, all	Burlap sack	50 & 100
	Fiberboard carton	50-55
	Paper bag, with or without mesh window	5, 10, 15, 20, 25, 50
	2- and 3-lb. film-wrapped cardboard boats packed in master containers	50-55
	Mesh or film bag	3, 5, 8, 10, 15, 20, 25
Radishes, topped	12 qt. basket,	11 1/4
	30 6-oz. film bags	11 1/4
	25-lb. film bags	25
Radishes, bunched	Crate, 5 doz. bunches	30-40
	Carton, wax-treated, 4-5 doz. bunches	30-40
	W.G.A. crate, 8-10 doz. bunches	80-90
	W.G.A. crate, packed loose, unlidded, 6 doz. bunches	45-55
Rhubarb, field grown	Box	20
Rhubarb, hothouse	Box	15
	Case, 10 5-lb. carton	50
Squash, summer	Bu. basket, hamper or crate	40-45
	1/2 bu. wirebound crate	21
	Lub, L.A.	24-27
Squash, winter	Bu. basket, hamper or crate	50
Sweet potatoes[2]	Bu. basket, hamper or crate	50
	Fiberboard box carton	36-46
	Fiberboard box carton, uncurred	40-50
	1/2 bu. carton, hamper, or basket	22-25
Tomatoes	Lug, L.A.	30-34
	8-qt. climax basket	9-11
	12-qt. climax basket	18-20
	16-qt. climax basket	27
	Wirebound crate	58-62

2. The usual weight of sweet potatoes when harvested averages 55 pounds. Weight is lost in curing or drying.

(continued)

FRUITS AND VEGETABLES, CONTAINERS

Shipping containers most commonly used for fresh fruits and vegetables
(continued)

Commodity	Shipping container	Approximate net weight[1]
		POUNDS
Tomatoes-continued	1/2 bu. basket or hamper	30
	5/8 bu. hamper	33-35
	Wirebound crate	40
	Wooden flat or nailed box	15-25
	Fiberboard carton	8, 18, 20, 30, 40, 60
Turnips, bunched	Wirebound crate	42
	1/2 W.G.A. crate	35-40
	W.G.A. crate	70-80
Turnips, topped	Open mesh sack	50
	Film sack	25

1. Actual weights larger and smaller than the range shown may be found. It is suggested that the mid-point of the range be used where a single value is desired.

2. The usual weight of sweet potatoes when harvested averages 55 pounds. Weight is lost in curing or drying.

FRUITS AND VEGETABLES, FROZEN
Frozen fruits and vegetables: Estimated average relation between farm and processed weights

Commodity	Percentage recovery	Factors for converting to		Approximate fruit-to-sugar ratio
		Farm weight from frozen weight[1]	Frozen weight from farm weight[1]	
	PERCENT			
Frozen fruits:				
Apples	60	1.67	0.60	0 or 7 to 1
Apricots	78	1.10	.91	6 or 8 to 1
Berries:				
Blackberries	95	1.05	.95	0
Blueberries	97	1.03	.97	0
Boysenberries	88	1.14	.88	0
Gooseberries	97	1.03	.97	0
Loganberries	88	1.14	.88	0
Raspberries	95	1.05	.95	0
Strawberries	93	.89	.12	5 or 4 to 1
Cherries, sour	75	1.11	.90	5 to 1
Cherries, sweet	85	1.18	.85	0
Grapes	85	1.18	.85	0
Peaches	67	1.25	.80	5 to 1
Pineapples	50	1.60	.625	4 to 1
Prunes	85	1.18	.85	0
Frozen vegetables:				
Asparagus	52	1.92	.52	2*
Lima beans[3]	95	1.05	.95	2*
Snap beans	85	1.18	.85	2*
Broccoli	75	1.33	.75	2*
Brussels sprouts	75	1.33	.75	2*
Cauliflower	70	1.43	.70	2*
Corn, cut	27	3.70	.27	2*
Carrots	55	1.82	.55	2*
Okra	85	1.18	.85	2*
Peas, green[3]	92	1.09	.92	2*
Peas, southern	50	2.00	.50	2*
Potatoes, white	40	2.50	.40	2*
Peppers, sweet	70	1.43	.70	2*
Spinach	70	1.43	.70	2*
Other greens	75	1.33	.75	2*
Squash	55	1.82	.55	2*
Sweet potatoes	50	2.00	.50	2*

1. Frozen weight is weight of frozen fruit plus sugar content. Where more than one fruit-to-sugar ratio is shown, the first is used in this computation.
2*Fruit-to-sugar ratio does not apply to vegetables.
3. Shelled.

SERVING COSTS
OF SELECTED FRESH FRUITS & VEGETABLES

United Fresh Fruit & Vegetable Association   •   **777 14th St., N.W.**

Washington, D.C. 20005

In planning family menus, many customers like to consider the cost per serving. The tables on these pages, extracted from a USDA booklet, provide the serving costs of a number of the most popular fresh fruits and vegetables. Quantities used are the standard 4-oz. half-cup. A broad price range is provided enabling the user to calculate the per-serving-cost at any retail price. Retail produce managers can use the chart figures in making point-of-sale commodity promotion materials which will show the consumer the cost of serving fresh fruits and vegetables to each member of her family.

SERVING COSTS OF SELECTED FRESH VEGETABLES

Table 1. — Cost of a ½-cup serving of selected vegetables purchased fresh at specified prices per pound

Vegetables as served [cooked unless otherwise specified]	Price per pound [cents]																					
	8	10	12	14	16	18	20	22	24	26	28	30	32	34	36	38	40	42	44	46	48	50
	Cost of a ½-cup serving [cents]																					
Asparagus:																						
Spears (4 medium)	3	4	5	6	6	7	8	9	10	10	11	12	13	14	14	15	16	17	18	18	19	20
Cuts and tips (½ cup)	2	3	3	4	4	5	6	6	7	7	8	8	9	10	10	11	11	12	12	13	13	14
Beans:																						
Green or wax	1	2	2	3	3	3	4	4	4	5	5	5	6	6	6	7	7	8	8	8	9	9
Lima	4	5	6	7	8	8	9	10	11	12	13	14	15	16	17	18	19	20	21	22	23	24
Beets	2	3	3	4	4	5	5	6	6	7	8	8	9	9	10	10	11	11	12	12	13	14
Broccoli	3	3	4	4	5	6	6	7	8	8	9	10	10	11	12	12	13	13	14	15	15	16
Brussels sprouts	2	2	3	3	4	4	5	5	6	6	6	7	7	8	8	9	9	10	10	11	11	12
Cabbage:																						
Raw, chopped	1	1	2	2	2	3	3	3	3	4	4	4	4	5	5	5	6	6	6	6	7	7
Cooked, wedges	2	2	3	3	4	4	5	5	6	7	7	7	7	8	8	9	9	10	10	11	11	12
Carrots:																						
Raw, shredded	1	2	2	2	3	3	3	4	4	4	4	5	5	5	6	6	6	7	7	7	8	8
Cooked, diced	2	2	3	3	4	4	5	5	6	6	6	7	7	8	8	9	9	10	10	11	11	12
Cauliflower	3	4	4	5	6	6	7	8	8	9	10	10	11	12	13	13	14	15	15	16	17	18
Celery:																						
Raw, diced	1	2	2	3	3	3	4	4	4	5	5	5	6	6	6	7	7	8	8	8	9	9
Cooked, diced	2	2	3	3	4	4	5	5	6	6	7	7	8	8	9	9	10	10	11	11	12	12
Collards[1]	2	2	3	3	4	4	5	5	6	6	7	7	8	8	9	9	10	10	11	11	12	12
Cucumbers, raw, sliced	2	2	3	3	4	4	5	5	6	6	6	7	7	8	8	9	9	10	10	11	11	12
Eggplant, diced	2	3	4	4	5	6	6	7	7	8	9	9	10	11	11	12	12	13	14	14	15	16

Vegetables as served [cooked unless otherwise specified]	Price per pound [cents]																						
	8	10	12	14	16	18	20	22	24	26	28	30	32	34	36	38	40	42	44	46	48	50
Kale[2]	2	2	2	3	3	3	4	4	5	5	5	6	6	6	7	7	8	8	8	9	9	10
Kohlrabi	3	4	5	5	6	7	8	9	9	10	11	12	12	13	14	15	16	16	17	18	19	20
Lettuce, raw	1	1	1	1	1	1	2	2	2	2	2	2	3	3	3	3	3	3	4	4	4	4
Mustard greens[2]	3	4	5	6	7	8	8	9	10	11	12	13	13	14	15	16	17	18	18	19	20	21
Okra	2	2	3	3	4	4	4	5	5	6	6	7	7	7	8	8	9	9	10	10	11	11
Onion, pieces	2	3	3	4	4	5	6	6	7	7	8	8	9	10	10	11	11	12	12	13	13	14
Parsnips	2	2	3	4	4	4	5	6	6	6	7	8	8	8	9	10	10	10	11	12	12	12
Peas, green	4	5	6	7	8	9	10	11	12	13	14	15	16	17	18	19	20	21	22	23	24	26
Potatoes:																						
Mashed	2	3	3	4	5	5	6	6	7	8	8	9	9	10	10	11	12	12	13	13	14	14
Sliced	2	2	2	3	3	4	4	4	5	5	6	6	6	7	7	8	8	8	9	9	10	10
Rutabagas, mashed	3	3	4	5	5	6	7	7	8	9	10	10	11	12	12	13	14	14	15	16	16	17
Spinach[3]	2	2	3	4	4	4	5	6	6	6	7	8	8	8	9	10	10	10	11	12	12	12
Squash, summer:																						
Mashed	3	3	4	4	5	6	6	7	8	8	9	10	10	11	12	12	13	13	14	15	15	16
Sliced	2	2	3	3	4	4	5	5	6	6	7	7	8	8	9	9	10	10	11	11	12	12
Squash, winter:																						
Acorn, baked	4	5	6	7	8	9	10	11	12	13	14	15	16	17	18	19	20	21	22	23	24	25
Hubbard, mashed	4	5	6	7	8	8	9	10	11	12	13	14	15	16	17	18	19	20	21	22	23	24
Sweet potatoes, sliced	2	3	3	4	4	5	5	6	6	7	8	8	9	9	10	10	11	11	12	12	13	14
Tomatoes, raw, sliced	2	2	2	3	3	4	4	4	5	5	6	6	6	7	7	8	8	9	9	10	10	
Turnip greens[1]	4	5	6	7	8	9	10	11	12	13	14	15	16	17	18	19	20	21	22	23	24	25
Turnips, diced	2	3	3	4	4	5	6	6	7	7	8	8	9	10	10	11	11	12	12	13	13	14

1. Purchased untrimmed.   2. Purchased trimmed.   3. Purchased partly trimmed.

Fruits and vegetables are one of the BASIC FOUR food groups. The others are: Breads and cereals; meat, fish and poultry; milk and dairy products. Regular, balanced consumption of selections from all four groups is essential to adequate nutrition. While good nutrition does not guarantee good health, **good health is impossible without adequate nutrition.**

The 1969 national nutritional contribution of the fruit and vegetable group (fresh and processed) is:

- 94% of the vitamin C
- 51% of the vitamin A
- 43% of the folic acid
- 26% of the magnesium
- 20% of the iron
- 19% of the thiamine
- 10% of the riboflavin
- 9% of the calories (no sugar added)
- 7% of the protein
- less than 1% of the fat
- many trace minerals.

Nutritionists generally single out fruits and vegetables as the main food group which should be eaten in this country in considerably larger quantities than at present.

SERVING COSTS OF SELECTED FRESH FRUITS

Fruit as served [raw unless otherwise specified] and size of serving	Price per pound [cents]																									
	10	12	14	16	18	20	22	24	26	28	30	32	34	36	38	40	42	44	46	48	50	52	54	56	58	60
	Cost of a serving [cents]																									
Apples:																										
Whole .... 1 med.	3	4	5	5	6	7	7	8	9	9	10	11	11	12	13	13	14	15	15	16	16	17	18	18	19	20
Sliced or diced:																										
Raw .... ½ cup	2	2	3	3	3	4	4	4	5	5	5	6	6	6	7	7	8	8	8	9	9	9	10	10	10	11
Cooked .... ½ cup	4	5	5	6	7	8	8	9	10	11	11	12	13	14	14	15	16	17	17	18	19	20	21	21	22	23
Apricots:																										
Whole .... 2 med.	2	2	2	3	3	3	4	4	4	5	5	5	6	6	6	7	7	7	8	8	8	9	9	10	10	10
Halves, pitted .... ½ cup	2	2	3	3	3	4	4	4	5	5	5	6	6	6	7	7	8	8	8	9	9	9	10	10	10	11
Avocado, cubes.......... ½ cup	2	3	3	4	4	5	5	6	6	6	7	7	8	8	9	9	10	10	11	11	12	12	12	13	13	14
Bananas:																										
Whole .... 1 med.	3	4	5	5	6	7	7	8	9	9	10	11	11	12	13	13	14	15	15	16	16	17	18	18	19	20
Sliced .... ½ cup	2	3	3	4	4	5	5	6	6	6	7	7	8	8	9	9	10	10	11	11	12	12	12	13	13	14
Berries .... ½ cup	1	1	2	2	2	2	3	3	3	3	4	4	4	4	5	5	5	5	6	6	6	6	6	7	7	7
Cantaloup:																										
Wedge .... ¼ sm. melon	4	5	5	6	7	8	8	9	10	11	11	12	13	14	14	15	16	17	17	18	19	20	21	21	22	23
Diced .... ½ cup	4	5	5	6	7	8	8	9	10	11	11	12	13	14	14	15	16	17	17	18	19	20	21	21	22	23
Cherries, pitted .... ½ cup	2	2	3	3	3	4	4	5	5	5	6	6	6	7	7	8	8	9	9	10	10	10	11	11	11
Cranberries .... ½ cup	1	1	2	2	2	2	3	3	3	3	4	4	4	4	5	5	5	5	6	6	6	6	6	7	7	7
Grapefruit:																										
Half .... ½ large	6	7	9	10	11	12	14	15	16	17	19	20	21	22	24	25	26	27	29	30	31	32	33	35	36	37
Sections .... ½ cup	6	7	8	9	11	12	13	14	15	17	18	19	20	21	22	24	25	26	27	28	30	31	32	33	34	35
Grapes:																										
Seedless .... ½ cup	2	2	3	3	4	4	4	5	5	6	6	6	7	7	8	8	8	9	9	10	10	10	11	11	12	12
With seeds .... ½ cup	2	3	3	4	4	5	5	6	6	7	7	8	8	9	9	10	10	11	11	12	12	12	13	13	14	14
Honeydew melon, diced .. ½ cup	3	4	4	5	6	6	7	8	8	9	10	10	11	12	12	13	13	14	15	15	16	17	17	18	19	19
Mangoes .... ½ cup	3	3	4	5	5	6	6	7	8	8	9	9	10	10	11	12	12	13	13	14	14	15	16	16	17	17
Nectarines, whole .... 1 med.	2	3	4	4	4	5	6	6	6	7	8	8	8	9	10	10	10	11	12	12	12	13	14	14	14	15
Oranges:																										
Whole .... 1 small	3	4	5	5	6	7	7	8	9	9	10	11	11	12	13	13	14	15	15	16	16	17	18	18	19	20
Sections .... ½ cup	4	4	5	6	6	7	8	8	9	10	10	11	12	13	13	14	15	15	16	17	18	18	19	20	20	21
Peaches:																										
Whole .... 1 med.	2	3	4	4	4	5	6	6	6	7	8	8	8	9	10	10	10	11	12	12	12	13	14	14	14	15
Sliced .... ½ cup	3	3	4	4	5	5	6	6	7	7	8	8	9	9	10	10	11	11	12	12	13	14	14	15	15	16
Pears:																										
Whole .... 1 med.	3	4	5	5	6	7	7	8	9	9	10	11	11	12	13	13	14	15	15	16	16	17	18	18	19	20
Sliced .... ½ cup	2	3	3	4	4	5	5	6	6	6	7	7	8	8	9	9	10	10	11	11	12	12	12	13	13	14
Pineapple, diced .... ½ cup	3	4	5	5	6	7	7	8	9	10	10	11	12	12	13	14	14	15	16	16	17	18	18	19	20	20

Fruit as served [raw unless otherwise specified] and size of serving	Price per pound [cents]																									
	10	12	14	16	18	20	22	24	26	28	30	32	34	36	38	40	42	44	46	48	50	52	54	56	58	60
Plums:																										
Whole . . . . 2 med.	2	3	4	4	4	5	6	6	6	7	8	8	8	9	10	10	10	11	12	12	12	13	14	14	14	15
Halves . . . . ½ cup	2	3	3	3	4	4	5	5	5	6	6	7	7	8	8	8	9	9	10	10	10	11	11	12	12	13
Rhubarb . . . . ½ cup	3	3	4	4	5	5	6	6	7	8	8	9	9	10	10	11	11	12	12	13	14	14	15	15	16	16
Strawberries . . . . ½ cup	2	2	3	3	3	4	4	4	5	5	5	6	6	6	7	7	8	8	8	9	9	9	10	10	10	11
Tangerines:																										
Whole . . . . 1 large	2	3	4	4	4	5	6	6	6	7	8	8	8	9	10	10	10	11	12	12	12	13	14	14	14	15
Sections . . . . ½ cup	3	3	4	4	5	6	6	7	7	8	8	9	10	10	11	11	12	12	13	13	14	15	15	16	16	17

Yield data from U.S. Dept. AGr., HERR No. 37, **Family Food Buying: A Guide for Calculating Amounts to Buy and Comparing Costs.**

supply guide

AVERAGE MONTHLY AVAILABILITY OF FRESH FRUITS & VEGETABLES*

United Fresh Fruit & Vegetable Association, 777 14th St., N.W., Washington, D.C. 20005

The following chart shows the availability of 66 different fresh fruits and vegetables or groups, with information on major commodities by main states, making a total of 128 lines of entries. Availability is expressed as a monthly percentage of total annual supply, which is the right-hand column. The figures are based on five years of statistics of the U.S. Department of Agriculture or Department of Commerce. All percentages are rounded, so do not necessarily total 100.

MONTHLY AVAILABILITY EXPRESSED AS PERCENTAGE OF TOTAL ANNUAL SUPPLY

COMMODITY	Jan. %	Feb. %	Mar. %	Apr. %	May %	June %	July %	Aug. %	Sept. %	Oct. %	Nov. %	Dec. %	ANNUAL TOTAL million lbs.
APPLES, ALL	9	9	10	9	8	5	3	3	10	12	10	11	3,890
" WASHINGTON	10	11	12	12	12	8	4	2	5	7	8	11	1,643
" NEW YORK	10	10	11	10	8	5	2	2	8	12	11	10	483
" MICHIGAN	12	11	11	8	5	1	*	1	6	15	13	15	321
APRICOTS					6	60	32	2					20
ARTICHOKES	4	8	15	20	11	5	4	5	5	8	7	7	62
ASPARAGUS, ALL	*	5	23	34	23	13	1		*	1	*		104
" CALIFORNIA	*	6	31	45	12	4	*			*	*		75
" NEW JERSEY				7	54	38	1						17
AVOCADOS, ALL	9	8	9	8	9	7	7	8	7	8	9	10	166
" CALIFORNIA	9	9	11	10	11	10	8	8	6	6	6	7	132
" FLORIDA	12	3	*				4	7	10	17	24	23	31
BANANAS	8	8	9	9	9	9	8	7	7	8	8	9	3,623
BEANS, ALL	6	5	6	9	10	12	11	10	9	8	6	7	331
" FLORIDA	13	11	13	20	13	3	*		*	2	11	14	135
BEETS	4	4	6	7	6	12	14	13	12	11	6	4	83
BERRIES, MISC. (A)					2	31	43	13	4	4	2		4
BLUEBERRIES					2	31	38	26	3				36

MONTHLY AVAILABILITY EXPRESSED AS PERCENTAGE OF TOTAL ANNUAL SUPPLY

COMMODITY	Jan. %	Feb. %	Mar. %	Apr. %	May %	June %	July %	Aug. %	Sept. %	Oct. %	Nov. %	Dec. %	ANNUAL TOTAL million lbs.
BROCCOLI	11	10	12	10	7	6	4	4	6	9	10	10	62
BRUSSELS SPR.	15	14	9	6	4	1		1	6	12	17	14	20
CABBAGE, ALL	9	8	10	9	9	9	8	7	8	8	8	8	1,718
" FLORIDA	17	16	20	22	14	2	*				1	8	398
" TEXAS	15	15	18	14	6	2	2	2	2	2	7	16	245
" CALIFORNIA	10	11	11	10	11	10	7	5	5	6	7	7	229
" NEW YORK	12	8	6	3	1	1	7	9	12	14	14	14	153
" NEW JERSEY	*	*	*		*	19	27	16	14	14	7	2	106
CANTALOUPES, ALL		*	2	5	8	20	25	24	12	4	1		1,394
" CALIFORNIA					*	14	28	33	17	6	2		854
" MEXICO		*	12	35	43	9	*						174
" TEXAS					19	53	16	10	2	*			155
" ARIZONA					1	44	52	*		2	1		118
CARROTS, ALL	9	9	10	9	9	8	7	7	8	8	8	8	1,366
" CALIFORNIA	8	8	8	8	10	11	12	8	6	6	7	8	726
" TEXAS	13	14	17	15	10	4	2	3	3	4	6	9	346
CAULIFLOWER, ALL	9	7	8	7	5	5	4	5	10	17	13	9	145
" CALIFORNIA	12	10	11	11	8	7	5	5	5	6	9	12	90
" NEW YORK					*	2	7	19	43	26	3		27
CELERY, ALL	9	8	9	8	8	8	8	7	7	8	10	10	1,346
" CALIFORNIA	7	7	7	6	6	9	10	7	7	9	13	11	840
" FLORIDA	15	14	17	16	14	9	1			*	3	11	360
CHERRIES					6	43	45	6					124
CHINESE CABBAGE	9	9	8	8	7	7	7	7	8	9	10	9	41
COCONUTS	8	7	8	8	6	5	4	4	10	11	12	18	29
CORN, SWEET, ALL	2	2	3	6	14	18	17	16	10	5	4	3	1,470
" FLORIDA	4	3	5	12	27	27	5	*		4	7	6	724

MONTHLY AVAILABILITY EXPRESSED AS PERCENTAGE OF TOTAL ANNUAL SUPPLY

COMMODITY	Jan. %	Feb. %	Mar. %	Apr. %	May %	June %	July %	Aug. %	Sept. %	Oct. %	Nov. %	Dec. %	ANNUAL TOTAL million lbs.
" CALIFORNIA					6	21	28	20	12	7	4	2	150
CRANBERRIES, ALL									8	24	50	18	40
" MASSACHUSETTS									12	18	45	24	25
" WISCONSIN									1	29	60	9	13
CUCUMBERS	5	5	5	7	11	14	13	10	9	9	7	6	620
EGGPLANT	8	8	7	8	7	7	8	10	10	10	8	8	83
ENDIVE, BELGIAN	10	12	15	11	12	3			4	9	9	12	3
ESCAROLE-ENDIVE	9	8	9	9	8	8	8	8	8	8	8	8	145
GARLIC	6	9	10	9	7	7	10	10	11	7	7	7	83
GRAPEFRUIT, ALL	12	12	13	12	9	6	3	2	2	8	10	10	1,677
" FLORIDA	13	12	14	13	9	4	1	*	1	11	11	11	1,133
" WESTERN	7	6	7	8	13	16	13	13	8	2	3	4	292
GRAPES	5	3	4	4	3	6	10	15	18	15	10	8	497
GREENS	10	9	11	11	9	7	6	6	7	8	8	9	237
HONEYDEWS	1	3	7	6	5	12	12	20	21	11	2	1	315
LEMONS	7	6	8	8	9	11	11	10	8	7	7	7	373
LETTUCE, ALL	8	8	8	9	9	9	9	8	8	7	8		4,264
" CALIFORNIA	8	9	8	6	9	10	10	9	9	9	6	6	2,881
" ARIZONA	9	5	12	26	9	2	*			2	14	20	683
" NEW YORK					*	10	40	30	16	3	1		83
" NEW JERSEY					10	35	12	7	6	24	7		77
LIMES	5	5	5	5	7	14	15	12	9	7	7	8	40
MANGOES		1	6	11	17	23	22	14	5	1			19
MUSHROOMS	9	8	10	9	8	8	7	6	7	8	9	10	59
NECTARINES	2	3	1		*	11	35	34	13	1			124
OKRA	1	2	4	6	9	16	20	18	12	7	3	2	36
ONIONS, DRY, ALL	8	7	9	9	9	9	9	8	8	8	8	8	2,400
" TEXAS	*	*	5	27	31	13	11	8	3	1	*	*	494

MONTHLY AVAILABILITY EXPRESSED AS PERCENTAGE OF TOTAL ANNUAL SUPPLY

COMMODITY	Jan. %	Feb. %	Mar. %	Apr. %	May %	June %	July %	Aug. %	Sept. %	Oct. %	Nov. %	Dec. %	ANNUAL TOTAL million lbs.
" CALIFORNIA	3	1	1	2	11	20	23	17	9	6	4	3	387
" NEW YORK	11	9	11	6	2	1	1	8	14	12	12	11	358
ONIONS, GREEN	6	6	8	9	10	11	10	9	8	7	7	7	193
ORANGES, ALL	11	12	13	11	10	7	4	4	4	5	7	11	3,250
" WESTERN	9	10	12	12	10	7	5	6	6	6	6	10	1,900
" FLORIDA	16	15	14	10	10	6	3	1	*	3	9	13	1,155
PAPAYAS, HAWAII	7	8	8	8	9	9	10	8	7	9	9	8	20
PARSLEY & HERBS (B)	7	6	9	8	7	8	7	7	8	9	12	12	73
PARSNIPS	13	12	10	9	9	4	3	3	8	11	10	9	26
PEACHES, ALL	*	*	*		3	21	32	28	14	1			1,139
" CALIFORNIA					5	23	35	25	8	3			259
" SOUTH CAROLINA					2	20	49	28	1				235
" GEORGIA					4	45	42	8	*				207
PEARS, ALL	7	7	8	6	4	2	4	13	16	16	10	7	393
" OREGON	14	13	11	7	3	*		*	4	17	16	14	117
" CALIFORNIA	1	1	1	*			13	32	29	19	4	1	116
" WASHINGTON	9	9	7	5	3	*		10	17	16	14	11	99
PEAS, GREEN	8	13	12	13	13	13	10	9	6	1	1	2	40
PEPPERS, ALL	7	7	7	6	8	10	11	10	10	9	8	7	455
" FLORIDA	15	11	12	13	16	14	1			*	4	13	159
PERSIMMONS	4	1							1	29	46	19	4
PINEAPPLES, ALL	6	8	10	13	14	12	8	6	5	5	7	7	145
" PUERTO RICO	6	7	11	17	15	11	7	5	5	5	5	6	71
" HAWAII	7	8	8	8	12	10	9	10	5	5	10	8	53
PLANTAINS	7	7	8	9	9	10	9	12	10	7	6	7	109
PLUMS-PRUNES	1	1	1		*	13	29	31	20	3	*	*	290
POMEGRANATES									11	68	20	*	9
POTATOES, ALL	9	8	9	9	9	9	8	8	8	8	8	8	12,150

COMMODITY	Jan. %	Feb. %	Mar. %	Apr. %	May %	June %	July %	Aug. %	Sept. %	Oct. %	Nov. %	Dec. %	ANNUAL TOTAL million lbs.
" CALIFORNIA	5	4	4	4	8	23	25	10	5	4	4	4	2,162
" IDAHO	12	11	13	13	13	6	1	1	2	6	10	11	1,452
" MAINE	11	11	15	20	18	10	1	*	*	1	5	7	1,318
PUMPKINS	1	2	3	4	3	2	1	1	4	74	2	2	43
RADISHES	7	7	9	10	11	10	9	8	6	7	7	8	227
RHUBARB	6	13	16	19	26	12	3	1	1	1	*	1	17
SPINACH	10	10	12	10	9	8	6	5	6	8	8	8	83
SQUASH	7	7	6	7	8	9	9	9	10	11	9	8	339
STRAWBERRIES	3	5	8	19	26	19	8	4	3	1	1	3	352
" CALIFORNIA		*	4	22	33	18	10	6	4	2	*	*	237
" MEXICO	21	24	24	6						*	6	18	50
" FLORIDA	10	22	41	25	1							1	15
SWEETPOTATOES, ALL	9	8	9	7	5	2	3	5	9	12	18	13	766
" LOUISIANA	9	8	9	7	4	1	4	8	11	12	15	12	256
" N. CAROLINA	9	9	10	9	7	4	1	2	6	10	19	15	138
" CALIFORNIA	8	8	9	7	5	4	3	3	6	10	20	16	111
" NEW JERSEY	11	10	11	11	9	5	2	1	4	7	15	14	70
TANGELOS	16	3	*	*						1	10	30	40	125
TANGERINES	24	8	4	1	*					3	20	39	228
TOMATOES, ALL	7	6	7	8	10	12	11	10	8	8	6	6	2,153
" CALIFORNIA	1	*		*	1	7	17	17	16	23	14	4	643
" FLORIDA	13	10	11	13	19	14	1			*	5	14	577
" MEXICO	14	16	21	21	16	5	1	*	*	*	1	5	464
" OHIO	1	*	1	8	19	21	16	8	4	7	9	5	99
TURNIPS-RUTABAGAS	12	10	10	7	5	4	4	5	9	11	13	11	198
CANADA	12	11	10	6	3	1	*	4	11	12	17	13	78
WATERMELONS	*	*	1	2	10	29	31	20	6	1	*	*	2,690

NOTES: * Indicates supply is less than 0.5% of annual total.
(A) Mostly blackberries, dewberries, raspberries.
(B) Includes also parsley root, anise, basil, chives, dill, horseradish and others.

JUICES

Juices that are federally graded are presented here. There are some states which provide grading; for that information refer to the mother fruit in the preceding section covering produce.

Canned juices may be sweetened or unsweetened. The product should taste and look very much like the fresh product, allowing for some difference due to processing. The federal grades are U.S. Grade A (85 points); U.S. Grade C (70 points), and U.S. Grade D (less than 70 points). Purchase of U.S. Grade A is recommended.

Concentrate juices may or may not be purchased frozen. Both have grading levels of 85 and 70 points; U.S. Grade A and U.S. Grade C for canned, and U.S. Grade A and U.S. Grade B for frozen. The water/juice ratios for reconstitution vary from 2:1 to 18:1, an important factor in specifying for bids.

Only orange and grapefruit juice have federal grades in the dehydrated state, although some other dehydrated juices are marketed. The federal grades are U.S. Grade A (85) and U.S. Grade B (70); buy the former.

APPLE JUICE, Canned [7/1/71]

Grade A: Color: Bright and typical of freshly pressed juice; may vary from characteristic light non-amber shades to medium amber shades. Style I, Clear, is sparkling clear and transparent, and Style II, Cloudy, may range from a slight translucent appearance to a definitely hazy appearance. **Defects:** May have a slight amount of sediment or residue of an amorphous nature; may not have more than a trace of dark specks or of sediment or residue of a non-amorphous nature, and shall be free from particles of seed, coarse particles of pulp, or other defects. **Flavor:** Has a fine, distinct, fruity flavor that is free from astringent flavors, flavors due to overripe apples, oxidation, caramelization, ground or musty flavors, or any other undesirable flavor, and shall meet the following requirements: BRIX—Not less than 11.5°. ACID—Not less than 0.25g nor more than 0.70g, calculated as malic acid, per 100 ml. of juice.

APPLE JUICE

CANNED [7/1/71   52.301]

Grades:	"A" or "FANCY"	"B" or "CHOICE"	"SUBSTAN-DARD"
Minimum Score:	90	80	Less than 80

Syrup	Specific Gravity [Brix]
"A" Classification	not less than 11.5
"B" Classification	not less than 10.5

FROZEN CONCENTRATED [5/15/75   52.6321]

Grades:	"A" or "FANCY"	"B" or "CHOICE"	"SUBSTAN-DARD"
Minimum Score:	90	80	Less than 80

Dilution Factor	Minimum Brix Value of Concentrate
1 plus 1	22.9
2 plus 1	33.0
3 plus 1	42.2
4 plus 1	50.8
5 plus 1	58.8
6 plus 1	66.3
7 plus 1	73.3

Grade B: Color: Typical of canned apple juice, which color may be deep amber or other typical color but is not off-color for the respective style. **Defects:** May have a slight amount of sediment or residue of an amorphous or non-amorphous nature, of dark specks, of particles of seed, of coarse particles of pulp, or of any other defects, provided such defects do not seriously affect the appearance or palatability of the product. **Flavor:** Has a normal flavor which may be slightly astringent or affected by overripe apples, caramelization, or ground or musty flavors, but is free from objectionable flavors or odors of any kind; and meets the following requirements: BRIX—Not less than 10.5°. ACID—Not less than 0.20 g or more than 0.80g, calculated as malic acid, per 100 ml. of juice. **Sstd:** Fails to meet requirements.

APPLE JUICE, Frozen Concentrated [5/15/75]

Grade A: Color: Color, after reconstitution, is bright and transparent, and of a light, golden appearance, but not darker than USDA Honey Color Standards "White" designation.

Defects: After reconstitution the juice may have a slight amount of sediment or residue of an amorphous nature; may not have more than a trace of dark specks or sediment or residue of a non-amorphous nature, or any other defects: provided, that all defects present do not more than slightly affect the appearance or palatability of the product. **Flavor and Aroma:** After reconstitution the juice has a fine, distinct, fruity flavor and bouquet, is free from astringent flavors, flavors due to over-ripe apples, oxidation, caramelization, or ground or musty flavors, and is free from objectionable flavors or aromas of any kind; and has a Brix-Acid Ratio ranging from 21:1 to 53:1.

Grade B: Color: After reconstitution, the color is slightly dull or slightly turbid; may be light golden to light amber in appearance, but not darker than USDA Honey Color Standards "Light Amber" designation. **Defects:** After reconstitution, the juice may have a slight amount of sediment or residue of an amorphous or non-amorphous nature, of dark specks, or any other defects, provided, that all defects present do not materially affect the appearance or palatability of the product. **Flavor and Aroma:** After reconstitution, the juice has a normal flavor and bouquet, may be slightly astringent, or slightly affected by overripe apples, oxidation, caramelization, or ground or musty flavors, but is free from objectionable flavors or aromas of any kind; and has a Brix-Acid Ratio ranging from 18:1 to 60:1.

Sstd: Fails to meet requirements.

GRAPE JUICE—Canned [5/14/51]

Grade A: Color: Type I: A bright purple or bright reddish purple color, typical of properly prepared and processed juice from Concord type grapes. **Type II and III:** A bright color typical of properly prepared and processed juice characteristics of the varietal types from which prepared. **Defects:** Canned grape juice may possess a slight amount of sediment and residue of an amphorous nature; may possess not more than a trace of sediment and residue of a non-amphorous nature; is practically free from tartrate crystals; and is free from particles of skin, seed, and from other defects. **Flown:** Flown is distinct and normal flown, typical of well-matured

grapes, and the canned grape juice is free from any trace of senching, caramelization, and objectionable flowns, and odors of any kind. To score in this classification, the juice must meet the following requirements: BRIX—Style I, unsweetened and not less than 15.0°. BRIX—Style II, sweetened, not less than 17.0°. ACID—not less than 0.60 grams per 100 ml., or more than 1.20 grams per 100 ml. calculated as tartaric acid. BRIX-ACID RATIO—For both Style I and Style II, not less than 14 to 1 or more than 28 to 1.

Grade B: Color: See Grade A. All wording is the same except as follows: purple and reddish purple ... Color may be slightly dull purple, bluish purple, and reddish pruple, but is not off-color for any reason. **Types II and III:** ... color may be slightly dull, but is not off-color for any reason. **Defects:** See Grade A. All wording is the same except as follows: ... slight amount of tartrate crystals; trace of particles. **Flavor:** See Grade A. All wording is the same except as follows: reasonably well-matured grapes ... may be slightly astringent. BRIX—Style I: 14.0°. BRIX—Style II: 16.0°. ACID—0.45 grams per 100 ml. ... 1.40 grams per 100 ml. BRIX-ACID RATIO: 11.5 to 1.

Sstd: Fails to meet requirements.

GRAPE JUICE, Concentrate, Sweetened, Frozen [11/1/50]

Grade A: Color: Type I: A bright, reddish purple color characteristic of a grape juice beverage properly prepared from Concord type grape juice and, in addition, the grape juice beverage prepared conforms to the following requirements: Minimum absorbency at 520 millimicrons --- 4.0. Minimum absorbency ratio --- 1.5 **Type II:** A bright color, characteristic of a grape juice beverage properly prepared from Type I juice and from varietal types of juice other than Type I and, in addition, the grape juice beverage prepared conforms to the following requirements: Minimum absorbency at 520 millimicrons --- 4.0. Minimum absorbency ratio --- 1.5. **Defects:** There may be present not more than a slight amount of sediment and residue; juice is practically free from tartrate crystals; and is free from particles of skin, seed, and other defects. **Flavor:** Fine distinct and normal flavor, typical of well-matured grapes for the variety or varieties and free from any objectionable flavors and odors of any kind. To score in

GRAPE JUICE

JUICE GRAPES:

FRESH [7/20/39   51.4290]

Grades: U.S. No. 1 Juice Grapes; U.S. No. 1 Mixed Juice Grapes; U.S. No. 2 Juice Grapes; U.S. No. 2 Mixed Juice Grapes

CANNED [5/14/51   52.1341]

Grades:	"A" or "FANCY"	"B" or "CHOICE"	"D" or "SUB-STANDARD"
Minimum Score:	85	70	Less than 70

Syrup	Specific Gravity (Brix Measurements)
Grade A Unsweetened	15.0°
Sweetened	17.0°
Grade B Unsweetened	14.0°
Sweetened	16.0°

FROZEN CONCENTRATED SWEETENED [11/1/57   52.2451]

Grades:	"A" or "FANCY"	"B" or "CHOICE"	"SUB-STANDARD"
Minimum Score:	85	70	Less than 70

Dilution Factor	Brix Value
1 plus 1	24.8°
1 plus 2	35.5°
1 plus 3	45.4°
1 plus 4	54.5°
1 plus 5	62.8°
1 plus 6	70.7°

this classification the prepared grape juice beverage and concentrate shall meet the following requirements: **Type I:** BRIX—not less than 13.0°. ACID—not less than 0.40 grams per 100 ml., nor more than 0.65 grams per 100 ml. calculated as tartaric acid. BRIX-ACID RATIO—the ratio of Brix value to acid is not less than 20 to 1 nor more than 34 to 1. CONCEN-TRATE: methyl anthranilate (naturally occurring)—not less than the following for the respective dilution factor of frozen concentrated sweetened grape juice:

Dilution Factor	Minimum Methyl Anthranilate (naturally occurring) (mg./1.)	Dilution Factor	Minimum Methyl Anthranilate (naturally occurring) (mg./1.)
1 plus 1	0.4	1 plus 1	0.2
1 plus 2	.8	1 plus 2	.4
1 plus 3	1.2	1 plus 3	.6
1 plus 4	1.6	1 plus 4	.8
1 plus 5	1.6	1 plus 5	.8
1 plus 6	1.6	1 plus 6	.8

Grade B: Color: See Grade A. All wording is the same except as follows: **Type I:** color may be slightly dull, but is not off-color for any reason. **Type II:** color may be slightly dull, but not off-color for any reason. **Defects:** There may be present not more than a moderate amount of sediment and residue; may possess a slight amount of tartrate crystals; may possess not more than a trace of particles, of skin, seed, and other defects. **Flavor:** See Grade A. All wording is the same except as follows: reasonably typical flavor of reasonably well-matured. **Type I:** ACID—not less than 0.30 grams per 100 ml. or more than 0.65 gram per 100 ml. BRIX-ACID RATIO: 18 to 1 ... 36 to 1. **Type II:** ACID—See Type I (above). BRIX-ACID RATIO. See Type I (above).

Sstd: Fails to meet the necessary requirements of Grade B.

GRAPEFRUIT JUICE—Canned [12/7/68]

Grade A: Color: Bright, typical color of freshly extracted juice. It may be pale yellow to very slightly amber (if pink, clearly distinguishable). **Defects:** Not more than 10 percent free and suspended pulp, and no seeds, or seed particle, or other defects that more than slightly affect the appearance of the product. **Flavor:** "Good Flavor" substantially typical of freshly extracted grapefruit juice, may be only slightly affected by the process and complies with limits in Table I.

Grade B: Color: Reasonably good color, may be dull, or show evidence of slight browning, or characteristic dull mixtures of pink and white grapefruit juice, but can not be off-color. **Defects:** Not more than 15 percent free and suspended pulp, and does not contain seeds, or seed particle, or other defects that materially affect the appearance of the product. **Flavor:** Possesses a "good," reasonably good flavor, "less desirable than "good flavor" because of excess bitterness, terpene, processing, storage, and container flavors, but not seriously objectionable and complies with limits in Table I.

TABLE I—ANALYTICAL REQUIREMENTS

GRADE	U.S. GRADE A			
Type	Single Strength		Reconstituted	
Style	unsweetened	sweetened	unsweetened	sweetened
Brix—min.	9.0°	11.5°	10.0°	11.5°
Ratio—min.	8:1	9:1	8:1	9:1
—max.	14:1	14:1	14:1	14:1
Oil—max. (percent by volume)	0.020	0.020	0.020	0.020

GRADE	U.S. GRADE B			
Type	Single Strength		Reconstituted	
Style	unsweetened	sweetened	unsweetened	sweetened
Brix—min.	9.0°	11.5°	10.0°	11.5°
Ratio—min.	7:1	9:1	7:1	9:1
—max.	None	None	None	None
Oil—max. (percent by volume)	0.025	0.025	0.025	0.025

GRAPEFRUIT JUICE, Concentrated, Frozen [10/1/70]

Grade A: Color: Color that is bright and typical of freshly extracted grapefruit juice, may be either: pale yellow to very slightly amber, typical of the juice of properly ripened, white-fleshed grapefruit, or slightly red, typical of the juice of red-or deep pink-fleshed grapefruit. **Defects:** Practically free juice, cells only in such amounts as do not naturally detract from the appearance or drinking quality; not more than 10 percent free and suspended pulp; practically no seeds or portions that could not pass readily through round perforations of 1/8 in. in diameter; only such small seeds and portions that could pass through round perforations of 1/8 in. in diameter as do not materially detract from the appearance or drinking quality; other defects that are not more than slightly objectionable. **Flavor:** Flavor is free and distinct, and substantially typical of freshly extracted grapefruit juice with not more than a trace of bitterness. To score in this classification frozen concentrated grapefruit juice shall meet the following analytical requirements:

TABLE II—ANALYTICAL REQUIREMENTS— U.S. GRADE A

	Unsweetened Style	Sweetened Style
Ratio—Brix Value to Acid		
Minimum	9:1	10:1
Maximum	14:1	13:1
Recoverable oil—Percent by *volume* *(Reconstituted juice)*		
Minimum	0.008	0.008
Maximum	0.020	0.020

GRAPEFRUIT JUICE
CONCENTRATED GRAPEFRUIT JUICE
FOR MANUFACTURING [3/20/57   52.3481]

Grades:	"A" or "FANCY"	"C" or "STANDARD"	"SUB- STANDARD"
Minimum Score:	85	70	Less than 70

Dilution Factor	Brix Values
1 plus 3	37.5 to 40.1
1 plus 4	45.5 to 48.3
1 plus 5	52.7 to 56.0
1 plus 6	59.6 to 63.2

CANNED [12/7/68   52.6121]

Grades:	"A" or "FANCY"	"B" or "CHOICE"	"SUB- STANDARD"
Minimum Score:	90	80	Less than 80

SPECIFIC GRAVITY [BRIX MEASUREMENTS]

Single Strength	
Unsweetened	9.0°
Sweetened	11.5°
Reconstituted	
Unsweetened	10.0°
Sweetened	11.5°

FROZEN CONCENTRATED [10/1/70   52.1221]

Grades:	"A" or "FANCY"	"B" or "CHOICE"	"SUB- STANDARD"
Minimum Score:	90	80	Less than 80

DEHYDRATED [7/1/69   52.3021]

Grades:	"A" or "FANCY"	"B" or "CHOICE"	"SUB- STANDARD"
Minimum Score:	85	70	Less than 70

Grade B: Color: Color that is typical of freshly extracted grapefruit juice, but which may be slightly dull or slightly brown, as caused by scorching, oxidation, or caramelization. This color may be characteristic of the juice from red or pink grapefruit of advanced maturity, or of mixtures of the juice from white and colored varieties. **Defects:** Reasonably free; see Grade A. All wording is the same except as follows: seriously detract; materially objectionable. **Flavor:** Flavor is fairly typical of freshly extracted grapefruit juice and is free from abnormal flavors and off-flavors of any kind. To score in this classification, concentrated grapefruit juices shall meet the following analytical requirements:

TABLE III—ANALYTICAL REQUIREMENTS— U.S. GRADE B

	Unsweetened Style	Sweetened Style
Ratio—Brix Value to Acid		
Minimum	7:1	8:1
Maximum	16:1	13:1
Recoverable oil—Percent Volume		
(Reconstituted juice)		
Maximum	0.020	0.020

Sstd: Fails to meet requirements of Grade B.

GRAPEFRUIT JUICE, Dehydrated [7/1/69]

Grade A: Color: The color is bright and typical of fresh grapefruit juice. **Defects:** Appearance and drinking quality of the juice is not affected by defects. **Flavor:** Flavor is a fine, distinct grapefruit juice flavor, typical of properly processed, canned grapefruit juice; is definitely free from off-flavors; and the reconstituted juice meets the following requirements: recoverable oil not less than 0.011 nor more than 0.017 ml. per 100 ml. Acid—not less than 0.85 gram per 100 grams. Brix-acid ratio for the respective styles: Style I (unsweetened)—not less than 8 to 1 or more than 14 to 1; Style II (sweetened)—not less than 11 to 1 or more than 14 to 1.
Grade B: Color: Colors typical of fresh grapefruit juicy which may be slightly dull but is not off-color. **Defects:** Reasonably free; the appearance and drinking quality of the juice is not materially affected by the defects. **Flavor:** Flavor is reasonably typical of properly processed, canned grapefruit

juice which is free from abnormal and off-flavors of any kind; and the reconstituted juice meets the following requirements: recoverable oil—not less than 0.009 or more than 0.025 ml. per 100 ml. Acid—not less than 0.70 gram per 100 grams. Brix-acid ratio for the respective styles: Style I (unsweetened)—not less than 7 to 1, or more than 14 to 1; Style II (sweetened)—not less than 11 to 1, or more than 14 to 1.
Sstd: Fails to meet requirements of Grade B.

GRAPEFRUIT JUICE AND ORANGE JUICE, Canned [11/1/72]

Grade A: Color: Juice mixture has a yellow orange color that is bright and typical of freshly extracted juice of oranges and either white-fleshed grapefruit or red- or pink-fleshed grapefruit, and is free from flavors due to scorching, oxidation, caramelization, or other causes. **Defects:** Juice may not contain more than 12 percent free and suspended pulp, and that any other defects present may no more than slightly detract from the appearance or drinking quality. **Flavor:** Refrigerated juice or juice not subjected to high temperatures prior to refrigerating must have flavor that is fine, distinct, and substantially typical of freshly extracted grapefruit juice and orange juice which is free from off-flavors and off-odors of any kind. Canned juice or juice that has been subjected to high temperature: Fine, distinct grapefruit juice and orange juice flavor which is free from off-flavors and off-odors of any kind; and the flavor of all juices may be affected only slightly by the process, the packaging or storage conditions, and the juice complies with the analytical limits listed in Table I.
Grade B: Color: Juice has a fairly typical color that may range from light yellow to light amber, may be dull, or show evidence of slight browning, but is not off-color. **Defects:** Juice may not contain more than 18 percent free and suspended pulp, and that any other defects present may not materially detract from the appearance or drinking quality. **Flavor:** A flavor less desirable than "good flavor" because of excess bitterness, terpenic, processing, storage, or container flavors, but is not seriously objectionable, and is free from off-flavors and odors of any kind. Such juice complies with the analytical limits listed in Table II.
Sstd: Fails to meet any requirements of Grade B.

TABLE I—ANALYTICAL RQUIREMENTS—
U.S. GRADE A

Type	Single Strength		Reconstituted	
Style	Unsweetened	Sweetened	Unsweetened	Sweetened
Brix De-grees) Minimum	10.0°	11.5°	11.0°	12.5°
Brix-Acid Ratio If Brix is less than 11.5°				
Minimum	9.5:1		9.5:1	
Maximum	18.0:1		18.0:1	
If Brix is 11.5° or more				
Minimum	8.5:1	10.5:1	9.5:1	10.5:1
Maximum	18.0:1	18.0:1	18.0:1	18.0:1
Oil—Max-imum per-cent by volume	0.035	0.035	0.035	0.035

TABLE II—ANALYTICAL REQUIREMENTS—
U.S. GRADE B

Type	Single Strength		Reconstituted	
Style	Unsweetened	Sweetened	Unsweetened	Sweetened
Brix (De-grees) Minimum	9.5°	11.5°	11.0°	12.5°
Brix-Acid Ratio				
Minimum	8.0:1	10.5:1	9.0:1	10.5:1
Maximum	None	None	None	None
Oil—Maxi-mum per-cent by volume	0.055	0.055	0.055	0.055

GRAPEFRUIT JUICE AND ORANGE JUICE—
Concentrated, Blended, Frozen [9/21/68]

Grade A: Color: Color is bright, light yellow orange, and

BLENDED GRAPEFRUIT JUICE & ORANGE JUICE

FROZEN CONCENTRATED [9/21/68   52.1311]

Grades:	"A" or "FANCY"	"B" or "CHOICE"	"SUB-STANDARD"
Minimum Score:	85	70	Less than 70

typical of freshly extracted juices of such a blend, and is free from any trace of browning indicative of scorching, oxidation, caramelization, or other causes. **Defects:** Small seeds or portions thereof are of such size that they could pass through round perforations not exceeding 1/8 in. in diameter, provided such seeds or portions thereof do not materially affect the ap-pearance or drinking quality; juice cells that do not materially affect the appearance or drinking quality; other defects that are not more than slightly objectionable, and not more than 12 percent free and suspended pulp. To score in this classifica-tion, the frozen, concentrated, blended grapefruit juice and orange juice may contain not more than 0.097 ml. of recoverable oil per 10° grams in the concentrated product. **Flavor:** Flavor is fine, distinct, and substantially typical of freshly extracted juices of such a blend. The juice shall meet the following requirements: Style I, without sweetening ingredient added. The ratio of Brix value to acid is not less than 10 to 1 or more than 16 to 1 (see Table I). Style II with sweetening ingredient added: The ratio of Brix value to acid is not less than 11 to 1 or more than 123 to 1 (see Table II).

Grade B: Color: Color may range from light yellow to light amber, is fairly typical of freshly extracted juices of such a blend, and may be slightly dull, or may show traces of browning, but is not off-color for any reason. **Defects:** See Grade A. All wording is the same except as follows: Seriously affect; seriously affect; materially objectionable, 18 percent. 0.113 ml. **Flavor:** Flavor is fairly typical of freshly extracted juices of such a blend and is free from abnormal or off-flavors of any kind. The juices shall meet the following requirements: Style I, without sweetening ingredient added. The ratio of Brix value to acid is not less than 8 to 1 or more than 18 to 1 (see Table I). Style II, with sweetening ingredient added. The ratio of Brix value to acid is not less than 9 to 1 or more than 13 to 1 (see Table II).

Sstd: Fails to meet requirements.

TABLE I—MAXIMUM AND MINIMUM ACID FOR FROZEN CONCENTRATED BLENDED GRAPEFRUIT JUICE AND ORANGE JUICE
STYLE I. WITHOUT SWEETENING INGREDIENT ADDED

Brix value of the Concentrate in Degrees Brix	U.S. Grade or U.S. Fancy		U.S. Grade B or U.S. Choice	
	Ratio 10:1	Ratio 16:1	Ratio 8:1	Ratio 18:1
	Acid Percent by Weight		Acid Percent by Weight	
	Maximum	Minimum	Maximum	Minimum
40.0	4.00	2.50	5.00	2.22
40.1	4.01	2.51	5.01	2.23
40.2	4.02	2.51	5.03	2.23
40.3	4.03	2.52	5.04	2.24
40.4	4.04	2.53	5.05	2.24
40.5	4.05	2.53	5.06	2.25
40.6	4.06	2.54	5.08	2.26
40.7	4.07	2.54	5.09	2.26
40.8	4.08	2.55	5.10	2.27
40.9	4.09	2.56	5.11	2.27
41.0	4.10	2.56	5.13	2.28
41.1	4.11	2.57	5.14	2.28
41.2	4.12	2.58	5.15	2.29
41.3	4.13	2.58	5.16	2.29
41.4	4.14	2.59	5.18	2.30
41.5	4.15	2.59	5.19	2.31
41.6	4.16	2.60	5.20	2.31
41.7	4.17	2.61	5.21	2.32
41.8	4.18	2.61	5.23	2.32

TABLE I [Cont.]

Brix value of the Concentrate in Degrees Brix	U.S. Grade or U.S. Fancy		U.. Grade B or U.S. Choice	
	Ratio 10:1	Ratio 16:1	Ratio 8:1	Ratio 18:1
	Acid Percent by Weight		Acid Percent by Weight	
	Maximum	Minimum	Maximum	Minimum
41.9	4.19	2.62	5.24	2.33
42.0	4.20	2.63	5.25	2.33
42.1	4.21	2.63	5.26	2.34
42.2	4.22	2.64	5.28	2.34
42.3	4.23	2.64	5.29	2.35
42.4	4.24	2.65	5.30	2.35
42.5	4.25	2.66	5.31	2.36
42.6	4.26	2.66	5.33	2.37
42.7	4.27	2.67	5.34	2.37
42.8	4.28	2.68	5.35	2.38
42.9	4.29	2.68	5.36	2.38
43.0	4.30	2.69	5.38	2.39
43.1	4.31	2.69	5.39	2.39
43.2	4.32	2.70	5.40	2.40
43.3	4.33	2.71	5.41	2.41
43.4	4.34	2.71	5.43	2.41
43.5	4.35	2.72	5.44	2.42
43.6	4.36	2.73	5.45	2.42
43.7	4.37	2.73	5.46	2.43
43.8	4.38	2.74	5.48	2.43
43.9	4.39	2.74	5.49	2.44
44.0	4.40	2.75	5.50	2.44

[Cont.]

TABLE II—MAXIMUM AND MINIMUM ACID FOR FROZEN CONCENTRATED BLENDED GRAPEFRUIT JUICE AND ORANGE JUICE
STYLE II. WITH SWEETENING INGREDIENT ADDED

Brix Value of the Concentrate in Degrees Brix	U.S. Grade A or U.S. Fancy		U.S. Grade B or U.S. Choice	
	Ratio 11:1	Ratio 13:1	Ratio 9:1	Ratio 13:1
	Acid Percent by Weight		Acid Percent by Weight	
	Maximum	Minimum	Maximum	Minimum
40.0	3.64	3.08	4.44	3.08
40.1	3.65	3.08	4.46	3.08
40.2	3.65	3.09	4.47	3.09
40.3	3.66	3.10	4.48	3.10
40.4	3.67	3.11	4.49	3.11
40.5	3.68	3.12	4.50	3.12
40.6	3.69	3.12	4.51	3.12
40.7	3.70	3.13	4.52	3.13
40.8	3.71	3.14	4.53	3.14
40.9	3.72	3.15	4.54	3.15
41.0	3.73	3.15	4.56	3.15
41.1	3.74	3.16	4.57	3.16
41.2	3.75	3.17	4.58	3.17
41.3	3.75	3.18	4.59	3.18
41.4	3.76	3.18	4.60	3.18
41.5	3.77	3.19	4.61	3.19
41.6	3.78	3.20	4.62	3.20
41.7	3.79	3.21	4.63	3.21
41.8	3.80	3.22	4.64	3.22
41.9	3.81	3.22	4.66	3.22
42.0	3.82	3.23	4.67	3.23
42.1	3.83	3.24	4.68	3.24
42.2	3.84	3.25	4.69	3.25
42.3	3.85	3.25	4.70	3.25
42.4	3.85	3.26	4.71	3.26

TABLE II [Cont.]

Brix Value of the Concentrate in Degrees Brix	U.S. Grade A or U.S. Fancy		U.S. Grade B or U.S. Choice	
	Ratio 11:1	Ratio 13:1	Ratio 9:1	Ratio 13:1
	Acid Percent by Weight		Acid Percent by Weight	
	Maximum	Minimum	Maximum	Minimum
42.5	3.86	3.27	4.72	3.27
42.6	3.87	3.28	4.73	3.28
42.7	3.88	3.28	4.74	3.28
42.8	3.89	3.29	4.76	3.29
42.9	3.90	3.30	4.77	3.30
43.0	3.91	3.31	4.78	3.31
43.1	3.92	3.32	4.79	3.32
43.2	3.93	3.32	4.80	3.32
43.3	3.94	3.33	4.81	3.33
43.4	3.95	3.34	4.82	3.34
43.5	3.95	3.35	4.83	3.35
43.6	3.96	3.35	4.84	3.35
43.7	3.97	3.36	4.86	3.36
43.8	3.98	3.37	4.87	3.37
43.9	3.99	3.38	4.88	3.38
44.0	4.00	3.38	4.89	3.38
44.1	4.01	3.39	4.90	3.39
44.2	4.02	3.40	4.91	3.40
44.3	4.03	3.41	4.92	3.41
44.4	4.04	3.42	4.93	3.42
44.5	4.05	3.42	4.94	3.42
44.6	4.05	3.43	4.96	3.43
44.7	4.06	3.44	4.97	3.44
44.8	4.07	3.45	4.98	3.45
44.9	4.08	3.45	4.99	3.45
45.0	4.09	3.46	5.00	3.46
45.1	4.10	3.47	5.01	3.47
45.2	4.11	3.48	5.02	3.48

[Cont.]

TABLE II—[Cont.]

Brix Value of the Concentrate in Degrees Brix	U.S. Grade A or U.S. Fancy		U.S. Grade B or U.S. Choice	
	Ratio 11:1 Acid Percent Maximum	Ratio 13:1 by Weight Minimum	Ratio 9:1 Acid Percent Maximum	Ratio 13:1 by Weight Minimum
45.3	4.12	3.48	5.03	3.48
45.4	4.13	3.49	5.04	3.49
45.5	4.14	3.50	5.06	3.50
45.6	4.15	3.51	5.07	3.51
45.7	4.15	3.52	5.08	3.52
45.8	4.16	3.52	5.09	3.52
45.9	4.17	3.53	5.10	3.53
46.0	4.18	3.54	5.11	3.54
46.1	4.19	3.55	5.12	3.55
46.2	4.20	3.55	5.13	3.55
46.3	4.21	3.56	5.14	3.56
46.4	4.22	3.57	5.16	3.57
46.5	4.23	3.58	5.17	3.58
46.6	4.24	3.58	5.18	3.58
46.7	4.25	3.59	5.19	3.59
46.8	4.25	3.60	5.20	3.60
46.9	4.26	3.61	5.21	3.61
47.0	4.27	3.62	5.22	3.62
47.1	4.28	3.62	5.23	3.62
47.2	4.29	3.63	5.24	3.63
47.3	4.30	3.64	5.26	3.64
47.4	4.31	3.65	5.27	3.65
47.5	4.32	3.65	5.28	3.65
47.6	4.33	3.66	5.29	3.66
47.7	4.34	5.67	5.30	3.67
47.8	4.35	3.68	5.31	3.68
47.9	4.35	3.68	5.32	3.68
48.0	4.36	3.69	5.33	3.69

LEMON JUICE—Canned [12/8/62]

Grade A: Color: Color is bright and typical of fresh, properly processed lemon juice that is practically free of browning caused by scorching, oxidation, storage, storage combinations, or any other causes. **Defects:** There may be present: small seeds or portions thereof that are of such size that they could pass through round perforations not exceeding 1/8 in. in diameter, provided such seeds or portions do not affect the appearance or drinking quality of the juice; not more than 13 percent, by volume, of fine centrifuged pulp calculated; no coagulated pulp; and the juice does not contain peel, core, seeds, seed particles, or other defects that detract from the appearance or utility. **Flavor:** Product has the distinct flavor of properly prepared, freshly extracted, canned lemon juice that is free of any trace of terpenic, oxidized, scorched, or caramelized flavors, and is free of any other abnormal flavors. In addition, there are not less than 5.0 grams or more than 7.0 grams of acid per 100 ml. of juice.

Grade C: Color: Color may be only fairly bright, but is not off-color, and is typical of properly processed lemon juice that is reasonably free of browning, due to scorching, oxidation, improper storage, or any other causes. **Defects:** See Grade A. All wording is the same except as follows: "Fairly free from defects" ... juice does not contain coagulated pulp, etc. ... slightly detract. **Flavor:** Product has a normal flavor which may have a slightly caramelized or oxidized flavor, but is free of off-flavors of any kind. In addition, there are not less than grams or more than 7.5 grams of acid per 100 ml. of juice.

Sstd: Fails to meet requirements.

LEMONADE—Concentrated, Frozen [12/14/66]

Frozen concentrate for lemonade; identity. (a) Frozen concentrate for lemonade is the frozen food prepared from one or both of the lemon juice ingredients specified in paragraph (b) of this section, together with one of the sweetening ingredients specified in paragraph (c) of this section. Water may be added. The product contains not less than 48.0 percent by weight of soluble solids taken as the sucrose value determined by refractometer and corrected for acidity, as given in "Refractometric Determination of Soluble Solids in

LEMON JUICE

CANNED [12/8/62   52.5481]

Grades:	A or "FANCY"	"C" or "STANDARD"	"SUB-STANDARD"
Minimum Score:	90	80	Less than 80

CONCENTRATED LEMON JUICE FOR MANUFACTURING
[8/1/59   52.3951]

Grades:	"A" or "FANCY"	"C" or "STANDARD"	"SUB-STANDARD"
Minimum Score:	85	70	Less than 70

Citrus Juices," by Stevens and Baier.[1] *Industrial and Engineering Chemistry, Analytical Edition,* volume 11, page 447 (1939). When the product is diluted according to directions for making lemonade, which shall appear on the label, the acidity of the lemonade, calculated as anhydrous citric acid, shall be not less than 0.70 gram per 100 milliliters and the soluble solids, measured as described for the concentrate, shall be not less than 10.5 percent by weight.

(b) The lemon juice ingredients referred to in paragraph (a) of this section are: (1) Lemon juice, or a mixture of these. For the purposes of this section, lemon juice is the undiluted juice expressed from mature lemons of an acid variety; and concentrated lemon juice is lemon juice from which part of the water has been removed. In the preparation of the lemon juice ingredients, the lemon oil content may be adjusted by the addition of lemon oil, or concentrated lemon oil, in accordance with good manufacturing practice, and the lemon pulp in the juice as expressed may be left in the juice or may be separated. Lemon pulp that has been separated, which may have been preserved by freezing, may be added in preparing frozen concentrate for lemonade, provided that the amount of pulp added does not raise the proportion of pulp in the finished food to a level in excess of that which would be present by using lemon juice ingredients from which pulp has not been separated. The lemon juice ingredients may be treated by heat, either before or after the other ingredients are added, to reduce the enzymatic activity and the number of viable micro-organisms.

(c) The sweetened ingredients referred to in paragraph (a)

LEMONADE

FROZEN CONCENTRATE [9/21/68   52.1421]

Grades:	"A" or "FANCY"	"B" or "CHOICE"	"SUB-STANDARD"
Minimum Score:	85	70	Less than 70

Syrup	Brix Measurement
All syrups	10.5° or more

of this section are: (1) Sugar, or invert sugar syrup, or any mixture of these; (2) Any mixture consisting of sugar, or invert sugar syrup, or both, with dextrose, corn syrup, dried corn syrup, glucose syrup, dried glucose syrup, or any two or more of these: provided, that the solids of the sugar, or invert sugar syrup, or both amount to not less than two-thirds of the weight of the total solids of the mixture.

LEMONADE—Artificially Sweetened [11/13/66]

Frozen concentrate for artificially sweetened lemonade; identity; label statement of optional ingredients. (a) Frozen concentrate for artificially sweetened lemonade conforms to the definition and standard of identity prescribed for frozen concentrate for lemonade by 27.101, except that, in lieu of nutritive sweeteners, it is sweetened with one or more of the artificial sweetening ingredients listed in, and complying with the requirements of Part 121 of this chapter, and the soluble solids specifications prescribed in 27.101(a) do not apply.*

When the product is diluted according to directions which shall appear on the label, the acidity of the artificially sweetened lemonade, calculated as anhydrous citric acid, shall be not less than 0.70 gram per 100 ml. It may contain one or more safe and suitable dispersing ingredients serving the function of distributing the lemon oil throughout the food. It may also contain one or more safe and suitable thickening ingredients. Such dispersing and thickening ingredients are not food additives as defined in section 201 (s) of the Federal Food, Drug, and Cosmetic Act; or if they are food additives as

1. *Industrial and Engineering Chemistry, Analytical Edition,* volume 11, page 447 (1939).

*Numbers refer to the FDA Specs listed in the Bibliography at the end of this Chapter.

so defined, they are used in conformity with regulations established pursuant to section 409 of the act.

(b) Deleted.

(c) The name of the food is "frozen concentrate for artificially sweetened lemonade." The words "artificially sweetened" shall be of the same size and style of type as the word "lemonade."

(d) If an optional thickening or dispersing ingredient referred to in paragraph (a) of this section is used, the label shall bear the statement "_____ added" or "with added _____," the blank being filled in with the common name of the thickening or dispersing agent used. Such statement shall be set forth on the label with such prominence and conspicuousness as to render it likely to be read and understood by the ordinary individual under customary conditions of purchase.

(e) Frozen concentrate for artificially sweetened lemonade is labeled to conform to the labeling requirements prescribed for foods which purport to be, or are represented for, special dietary use by regulations promulgated pursuant to section 403(j) of the act.

LEMONADE, Colored

Frozen concentrate for colored lemonade conforms to the definition and standard of identity prescribed for frozen concentrate for lemonade, except that it is colored with a safe and suitable fruit juice, vegetable juice, or any such juice in concentrated form, or with any other color additive ingredient suitable for use in food, including artificial coloring, used in conformity with regulations established pursuant to section 706 of the Federal Food, Drug, and Cosmetic Act. The name of the food is "Frozen concentrate for _____ lemonade," the blank being filled in with the word describing the color, for example, "Frozen concentrate for pink lemonade." If artificial coloring is used, the label shall bear the statement "artificially colored." If the color additive ingredient used is not an artificial coloring, the label shall bear the statement "coloring added" or, in lieu of this statement, the label shall bear the statement "_____ added as coloring" or "colored with _____," the name of the color additive ingredient used; for example, "colored with grape juice."

LIMEADE

FROZEN CONCENTRATE [9/21/68   52.2521]

Grades:	"A" or "FANCY"	"B" or "CHOICE"	"SUB-STANDARD" Less than 70
Minimum Score:	85	70	Less than 70

Syrup	Brix Measurement
(A) Classification	10.5° or more
(B) Classification	10.5° or more

LIMEADE—Concentrate, Frozen [9/21/68]

Grade A: Color: A good, light, characteristic color that reflects the appearance of the limeade prepared from freshly expressed lime juice; or, if artificially colored, possesses a bright attractive light green color typical of artificially colored limeade. **Defects:** There may be present not more than an average of one seed or portion of seed for each quart of prepared limeade; and the appearance and drinking quality of the limeade is not materially affected by the presence of seeds, portions of seeds, objectionable material, harmless extraneous material, any other defects not specifically mentioned, or any combination thereof. **Flavor:** Fine, distinct, and substantially typical flavor of limeade prepared from freshly expressed lime juice, which flavor is free from terpenic, oxidized, rancid, or other off-flavors. To score in this classification, the limeade shall test not less than 10.5° Brix; shall contain not less than 0.7 gram of acid per 100 ml. of the limeade; may not contain more than 0.025 ml. or less than 0.008 ml. of recoverable oil per 100 ml. of the limeade; and the Brix-acid ratio shall not exceed 18:1.

Grade B: Color: A characteristic color that reflects to a reasonable extent the color of the limeade prepared from freshly expressed lime juice and is not dark, or otherwise discolored, for any reason; or, if artificially colored, possesses a reasonably bright color typical of artificially colored limeade. **Defects:** There may be present not more than an average of 2 seeds or portions of seeds for each quart of limeade; and the appearance and drinking quality of the limeade is not seriously affected by the presence of seeds, portions of seeds, etc. (See

Grade A). **Flavor:** Fairly typical flavor of limeade prepared from freshly expressed lime juice, which flavor is practically free from terpenic, oxidized, rancid or other off-flavors, and is free from abnormal flavors of any kind. The limeade shall test not less than 10.5° Brix; shall contain not less than 0.7 gram of acid per 100 ml. of the limeade; may not contain more than 0.035 ml. or less than 0.008 ml. of the recoverable oil per 100 ml. of the limeade; and the Brix-acid ratio shall not exceed 18:1.

Sstd: Fails to meet necessary requirements.

ORANGE JUICE [7/1/64]

Orange juice—identity. (a) Orange juice is the unfermented juice obtained from mature oranges of the species Citrus sinensis. Seeds (except embryonic seeds and small fragments of seeds that cannot be separated by good manufacturing practice) and excess pulp are removed. The juice may be chilled, but it is not frozen. (b) The name of the food is "orange juice." The name "orange juice" may be preceded on the label by the varietal name of the oranges used, and if the oranges grew in a single state, the name of such state may be included in the name, as for example, "California Valencia orange juice."

ORANGE JUICE—Canned [7/1/69]

Grade A: Color: Bright yellow to yellow orange color. As compared with USDA Orange Juice Color Standards may be scored as follows:

Equal to or better than USDA OJ 2	40 points
Equal to or better than USDA OJ 3	39 points
Equal to or better than USDA OJ 4	38 points
Equal to or better than USDA OJ 5	37 points
Equal to or better than USDA OJ 6	36 points

Defects: There may be present not more than 0.035 percent of recoverable oil, and juice does not contain particles of membrane, core, or skin, seeds or seed particles, or other defects that affect appearance more than slightly. **Flavor:** Fine, distinct, canned orange juice flavor, definitely free from traces of scorching, caramelization, oxidation, or terpene; is free from off-flavors of any kind; and meets the following re-

quirements: without sweetener: possesses a minimum of 10.5° Brix; a minimum acid per 100 grams of 0.70 grams, in California or Arizona oranges (0.60 grams outside of California or Arizona), and a maximum of 1.40 grams wherever grown; possesses a minimum Brix-acid ratio of 10.5 to 1 if Brix is less than 11.5° (9.5 to 1 if Brix is more than 11.5°), and a maximum of 20.5 to 1 in either case. With sweetener—Brix and acid same as unsweetened. Brix-acid ratio minimum of 12.5 to 1 if Brix less than 15° and a maximum of 20.5 to 1 in either case.

Grade C: Color: Fairly good color means a color not as good as USDA OJ 6; may be slightly amber, or very light in hue, or may show slight evidence of browning. **Defects:** See Grade A. All wording is same except as follows: 0.055 percent; materially. **Flavor:** Good, normal, canned orange juice flavor which may have a slightly caramelized or oxidized flavor, but is free from off-flavors of any kind and meets the following requirements: without sweetener—possesses a minimum of 10° Brix; a minimum of 1.55 grams acid per 100 grams; and possesses a minimum Brix-acid ratio of 9.5 to 1 and a maximum of 20.5 to 1. With sweetener—possesses a minimum of 10.5° Brix; minimum acid per 100 grams of 0.60 grams and a maximum of 1.60 grams wherever grown; possesses a minimum Brix-acid ratio of 12.5 to 1 if Brix is less than 15° (9.5 to 1 if Brix is more than 15°), and a maximum of 20.5 to 1 in either case.

ORANGE JUICE—Frozen [7/1/64]

Frozen orange juice is orange juice as defined in 27.105, except that it is frozen. The name of the food is "frozen orange juice." Such name may be preceded on the label by the varietal name of the oranges used, and if the oranges grew in a single state, the name of such state may be included in the name, as for example, "California Valencia frozen orange juice."

ORANGE JUICE—Canned Concentrated [7/1/64]

Canned concentrated orange juice, canned orange juice concentrate—identity; label statement of optional ingredients. (a) Canned concentrated orange juice complies with the requirements for composition, definition of dilution ratio, and labeling of optional ingredients prescribed for frozen concentrated orange juice, except that it is not frozen, and it is sealed in containers and so processed by heat, either before or after sealing, as to prevent spoilage. (b) The name of the food when concentrated to a dilution ratio of 3 plus 1 is "canned concentrated orange juice" or "canned orange juice concentrate." The name of the food when concentrated to a dilution ratio greater than 3 plus 1 is "canned concentrated orange juice, _____ plus 1" or "canned orange juice concentrate, _____ plus 1," the blank being filled in with the whole number showing the dilution ratio; for example, "canned orange juice concentrate, 4 plus 1." However, where the label bears directions for making 1 quart of the reconstituted article (or multiples of a quart), the blank in the name may be filled in with a mixed number; for example, "canned orange juice concentrate, 4-1/3 plus 1." For containers larger than 1 pint, the dilution ratio in the name may be replaced by the concentration of orange juice soluble solids in degrees Brix; for example, a 62° Brix concentrate in 1 gallon cans may be named on the label "canned concentrated orange juice, 62° Brix." If the food does not purport to be canned concentrated orange juice, the word "canned" may be omitted from the name.

ORANGE JUICE—Concentrated with Preservative [7/1/64]

Concentrated orange juice with preservative complies with the requirements for composition and labeling of optional ingredients prescribed for concentrated orange juice for manufacturing, except that a preservative is added to inhibit spoilage. The preservatives referred to in the above paragraph are sodium benzoate and sorbic acid. Sodium benzoate or sorbic acid may be used in an amount not exceeding 0.2 percent, by weight. The name of the food is "concentrated orange juice with preservative, _____," the blank being filled in with the figures showing the concentration of orange juice soluble solids in degrees Brix. The label shall bear the statement "_____ _____ added as a preservative," the first blank being filled in with the percent by weight of the preservative used, and the second blank by the name "sorbic acid" or "sodium benzoate" (or "benzoate of soda"), as appropriate. Wherever the name of the food appears on the label so conspicuously as to be easily seen under customary conditions

of purchase, the statement specified in the above paragraph for naming the preservative ingredient used shall immediately and conspicuously precede or follow the name of the food, without intervening written, printed, or graphic matter.

ORANGE JUICE—Concentrated, Frozen [9/21/68]

Grade A: Color: Very good color is bright yellow to yellow orange, typical of richly colored fresh juice. As compared with USDA OJ color standards, is scored as follows:

Equal to or better than USDA OJ 2	40 points
Equal to or better than USDA OJ 3	39 points
Much better than USDA OJ 4	38 points
Equal to or slightly better than USDA OJ4	37 points
Equal to or better than USDA OJ 5	36 points

Defects: Any combination of small seeds or portions that could pass readily through round holes 1/8 in. (3.2 mm) diameter, discolored specks, white flakes, harmless extraneous material, and similar defects: juice sacs, membrane, core, and peel may no more than slightly detract from appearance or drinking quality. Recoverable oil per 100 milliliters of reconstituted juice is not more than 0.035. **Flavor:** Very good flavor, is fine, distinct, and similar to fresh orange juice. Irrespective of style or area of production, it has a maximum Brix value to acid ratio of 19.5 to 1. The following minimums are applicable to style and area: Without Sweetener—California and Arizona 11.5 to 1, other areas 12.5 to 1. With sweetener—California and Arizona 12 to 1, other areas 13 to 1.

Grade B: Color: Good color is yellow to yellow orange, typical of fresh juice, may be dull, but not off-color. As compared with USDA color standards, may be scored as follows:

USDA OJ 5	35 points
Equal to USDA OJ 6	34 points
Not as good as USDA OJ 6	33 or 32 points

Defects: See Grade A. All wording is same as Grade A, except as follows: may not seriously detract from appearance or drinking quality. 0.040 milliliter. **Flavor:** Good flavor is similar to fresh orange juice and is free from abnormal or off-flavors. Irrespective of style or area of production, it shall have a Brix value to acid ratio of not less than 10 to 1.

Sstd: Fails to meet requirements.

ORANGE JUICE

PASTEURIZED [7/1/69   52.5641]

Grades:	"A" or "FANCY"	"B" or "CHOICE"	"SUB-STANDARD"
Minimum Score:	90	80	Less than 80

Syrup	Brix Measurement
Grade A without sweetener	11°
Grade B without sweetener	10.5°

CANNED [7/1/69   52.1551]

Grades:	"A" or "FANCY"	"C" or "STANDARD"	"SUB-STANDARD"
Minimum Score:	90	80	Less than 80

Syrup	Specific Gravity [Brix Measurements]
Grade A	10.5°
Grade C with sweetener	10.5°
Grade C without sweetener	10.0°

CONCENTRATED FROZEN [9/21/68   52.1581]

Grades:	"A" or "FANCY"	"B" or "CHOICE"	"SUB-STANDARD"
Minimum Score:	90	80	Less than 80

DEHYDRATED [9/21/68   52.2981]

Grades:	"A" or "FANCY"	"B" or "CHOICE"	"SUB-STANDARD"
Minimum Score:	85	70	Less than 70

CONCENTRATE [7/1/69   52.5681]

Grades:	"A" or "FANCY"	"B" or "CHOICE"	"SUB-STANDARD"
Minimum Score:	90	80	Less than 80

Syrup	Brix Measurements
without sweetener	11.8°

CONCENTRATED ORANGE JUICE FOR MANUFACTURING [11/17/64   52.2221]

Grades:	"A" or "FANCY"	"C" or "STANDARD"	"SUB-STANDARD"
Minimum Score:	90	80	Less than 80

ORANGE JUICE, From Concentrate [7/1/64]

Orange juice from concentrate; identity; label statement of optional ingredients—(a) Orange juice from concentrate is the food prepared by mixing water with frozen, concentrated orange juice as defined in 27.109, or with concentrated orange juice for manufacturing as defined in 27.114 (when made from mature oranges), or both. To such mixture may be added orange juice as defined in 27.105, frozen orange juice as defined in 27.106, pasteurized orange juice as defined in 27.107, orange juice for manufacturing as defined in 27.112 (when made from mature oranges and preserved by chilling or freezing but not by canning), orange oil, orange pulp, and one or more of the sweetening ingredients listed in paragraph (b) of this section. The finished orange juice from concentrate contains not less than 11.8 percent orange juice soluble solids, exclusive of solids of any added optional sweetening ingredients. It may be so treated by heat to reduce substantially the enzymatic activity and the number of viable micro-organisms. (b) The sweetening ingredients referred to in paragraph (a) of this section are sugar, sugar syrup, invert sugar, invert sugar syrup, dextrose, corn syrup, dried corn syrup, glucose syrup, dried glucose syrup. (c) The name of the food is "orange juice from concentrate." The words "from concentrate" shall be shown in letters not less than one-half the height of the letters in the words "orange juice." (d) When orange juice from concentrate contains any optional sweetening ingredient, as listed in paragraph (b) of this section, whether added directly as such or indirectly as an added ingredient of any orange juice product used, the label shall bear the statement "_____ added," the blank being filled in with the name, or an appropriate combination of the names of the sweetening ingredients added. However, for the purposes of this section, the name "sweetener" may be used in lieu of the specific name or names of the sweetening ingredients.

ORANGE JUICE, From Concentrate, ORANGE JUICE, Pasteurized [7/1/69]

Grade A: Style: No mention of Brix or soluble orange solids for these two products. **Grade Description:** No coagulation or no

material separation. **Defects:** None present. **Flavor:** Without sweetener—Brix not less than Grade A 11.8 degrees (pasteurized 11 degrees); Brix-acid ratio—not less than 12.5:1 (pasteurized 12.5:1), or more than 20.5:1 (pasteurized 20.5:1); California and Arizona not less than 11.5:1 (pasteurized 11.5:1), or more than 18:1 (pasteurized 18:1). With Sweetener Style: soluble orange juice solids, not less than 11.8 (pasteurized 11); Brix-acid ratio, not less than 12.5:1 (pasteurized 12.5:1), or more than 20.5:1 (pasteurized 20.5 to 1).
Grade B: Style: See Grade A. **Grade Description:** No coagulation but may show some separation. **Defects:** Percent by volume of recoverable oil of these two products, 0.045. **Flavor:** Without Sweetener Style: Brix, 11.8 degrees (pasteurized 10.5 degrees). Brix-acid ratio, (all areas) not less than 10.5:1 (pasteurized 10.5:1), or more than 22.1 (pasteurized 23.1). With Sweetener Style: Soluble orange juice solids, 11.8 (pasteurized 10:5) percent by weight of the sweetened product. Brix-acid ratio, not less than 11:1 (pasteurized 10.5:1) or more than 23:1 (pasteurized 23:1).

ORANGE JUICE—Dehydrated [9/21/68]

Grade A: Color: Very good yellow to yellow orange color that is bright and typical of fresh orange juice. **Defects:** Appearance and drinking quality of the juice are not affected by defects. **Flavor:** Fine, distinct orange juice flavor typical of properly processed, canned orange juice, which is definitely free from terpenic, caramelized, oxidized, rancid, or off-flavors. Ratio of the Brix to acid must range from 12:1 to 18:1; and the recoverable oil content should range from 0.011 to 0.017 ml. per 100 ml. of the reconstituted juice.
Grade B: Color: Yellow to yellow orange color typical of fresh orange juice, which may be slightly dull, but is not off-color. **Defects:** Appearance and drinking quality of the juice are not materially affected by defects. **Flavor:** Reasonably typical flavor of properly processed, canned orange juice which is free from abnormal and off-flavors of any kind. Ratio of the Brix to acid must be between 10.5:1 and 19:1; and the recoverable oil content must be between 0.009 and 0.025 ml. per 100 ml. of the reconstituted juice.
Sstd: Fails to meet requirements.

ORANGE JUICE, With Preservative [7/1/64]

Orange juice with preservative is the food prepared for further manufacturing use. It complies with the requirements for composition of orange juice for manufacturing as provided for in Par. 27.112, except that a preservative is added to inhibit spoilage. It may be heat-treated to reduce substantially the enzymatic activity and the number of viable microorganisms. The preservatives referred to in the above paragraph are sodium benzoate and sorbic acid. Sodium benzoate or sorbic acid may be used in an amount not exceeding 0.2 percent by weight. The name of the food is "orange juice with preservative." The label shall bear the statement "____ _____ added as a preservative," the first blank being filled in with the percent by weight of the preservative used, and the second blank by the name "sorbic acid" or "sodium benzoate" (or "benzoate of soda"), as appropriate. Wherever the name of the food appears on the label so conspicuously as to be easily seen under customary conditions of purchase, the statement specified in the above paragraph for naming the preservative ingredient used shall immediately and conspicuously precede or follow the name of the food, without intervening written, printed, or graphic matter.

PINEAPPLE JUICE—Canned [3/16/57]

Grade A: Color: Has a bright, typical color, characteristic of canned pineapple juice made from freshly pressed pineapple juice from properly matured and ripened pineapple, which pineapple juice has been properly processed. **Defects:** Does not contain specks or other objectionable particles that affect the appearance or palatability of the juice, and the canned pineapple juice may contain not less than 5 percent or more than 26 percent finely divided "insoluble solids." **Flavor:** Fine, distinct, canned pineapple juice flavor, characteristic of canned pineapple juice made from properly matured and ripened pineapple, which is free from any caramelized flavor. Must meet the following requirements: Not less than 12° Brix; not more than 1.10 grams of acid per 100 milliliters of juice; and not less than a 12 to 1 Brix-acid ratio.
Grade C: Color: Has a characteristic color which may be slightly dull or light amber, but is not off-color. **Defects:** May

PINEAPPLE JUICE

CANNED [3/16/57   52.1761]

Grades:	"A" or "FANCY"	"C" or "STANDARD"	"SUB-STANDARD"
Minimum Score:	85	70	Less than 70

Syrup	Brix Measurement
"A" classification	not less than 12.0°
"C" classification	not less than 10.5°

have specks or other objectionable particles that do not materially affect the appearance or palatability of the juice. The juice may contain not less than 5 percent or more than 30 percent finely divided "insoluble solids." **Flavor:** Good, normal, canned pineapple juice flavor that may be slightly caramelized, but is free from objectionable flavor or off-flavor of any kind. Must meet the following requirements: Not less than 15° Brix; not more than 1.35 grams of acid per 100 milliliters of the juice; and not less than a 12 to 1 Brix-acid ratio.

Sstd: Fails to meet requirements.

PRUNE JUICE—Canned [8/17/56]

Canned prune juice; identity; label statement of optional ingredients—(a) Canned prune juice is the food prepared from a water extract of dried prunes and contains not less than 18.5 percent by weight of water soluble solids extracted from dried prunes. The quantity of prune solids may be adjusted by the concentration, or dilution, or both, of the water extract or extracts made. Such food may contain one or more of the optional acidifying ingredients specified in paragraph (b) (1) of this section, in a quantity sufficient to render the food slightly tart; and it may contain honey added within the quantitative limits prescribed by paragraph (b) (2) of this section; and it may contain added Vitamin C in a quantity prescribed by paragraph (b) (3) of this section. Such food is sealed in a container and so processed by heat, before or after sealing, as to prevent spoilage. (b) The optional ingredients referred to in paragraph (a) of this section are: (1) One or any combination of 2 or more of the following acidifying ingredients: (i) Lemon juice, (ii) Lime juice, (iii) Citric acid. (2) Honey in a quantity not less than 2 percent and not more than 3 percent by weight

of the finished food. (3) Vitamin C, in a quantity such that the total Vitamin C in each 6 fluid oz. of the finished food amounts to not less than 30 milligrams and not more than 50 milligrams. Label statement of optional ingredients: (1) The name of the food is "Prune Juice—A water extract of dried prunes." For the purposes of the Federal Food, Drug, and Cosmetic Act concerning the label declaration of the name of the food, the explanatory statement "A water extract of dried prunes" may appear immediately below the words "prune juice," but there shall be no intervening written, printed, or graphic matter, and the type used for the words "A water extract of dried prunes" shall be of the same style and not less than half the point size of the type used for the words "Prune Juice." (2) (i) When one or more of the acidifying ingredients specified in paragraph (b) (1) of this section are used, the label shall bear the statement "_____ added" or "with added _____," the blank being filled in with the name or names of the optional ingredients used. (ii) When honey, as specified in paragraph (b) (2) of this section, is used, the label shall bear the statement "With _____ honey" or "_____ honey added," the blank to be filled in with the percent by weight of the honey in the finished food or with the statement "between 2 and 3 percent." (iii) When one or more of the ingredients designated in paragraph (b) (1) of this section and the ingredient designated in paragraph (b) (2) of this section are used, the statements specified in subdivisions (i) and (ii) of this subparagraph may be combined, as for example, "With lemon juice and between 2 and 3 percent honey added." (iv) When Vitamin C is added as provided in paragraph (b) (3) of this section, it shall be designated on the label as "Vitamin C added" or "with added Vitamin C." (3) Wherever the name of the food appears on the label so conspicuously as to be easily seen under customary conditions of purchase, the words specified in this paragraph, showing the optional ingredients used, shall immediately and conspicuously precede or follow such name, without intervening written, printed, or graphic matter.

TANGERINE JUICE—Canned [7/1/69]

Grade A: Defects: Not more than 7 percent free and suspended pulp and not more than 0.025 percent by volume of

TANGERINE JUICE

CANNED [7/1/69   52.2071]

Grades:	"A" or "FANCY"	"C" or "STANDARD"	"D" or "SUB-STANDARD"
Minimum Score:	85	70	Less than 70

Syrup	Specific Gravity (Brix Measurements)
"A" classification	
Regular	10.5°
Sweet	12.5°
"B" Classification	
Regular	10.0°
Sweet	12.5°

CONCENTRATED TANGERINE JUICE FOR MANUFACTURING [10/31/55   52.2931]

Grades:	"A" or "FANCY"	"C" or "STANDARD"	"STANDARD"
Minimum Score:	85	70	Less than 70

Dilution Factor	Brix Value
1 plus 3	38° to 41°
1 plus 4	46° to 49°
1 plus 5	53.3° to 56.3°
1 plus 6	60.3° to 63.3°

recoverable oil; no seeds or seed particles or other defects that more than slightly affect the appearance of the product. **Flavor:** Fine, distinct, canned tangerine juice flavor, free from traces of scorching, caramelization, oxidation, or terpene; Brix not less than 10.5°. Grade A sweet, 12.5°. Acid not less than 0.65 gram or more than 1.35 grams; Grade A sweet, 0.65 gram, not more than 1.35 grams. Brix-acid ratio—not less than 10.5 to 1 or more than 19 to 1; Grade A sweet, 11.5 to 1, not more than 19 to 1 provided that when the Brix is 16° or more, the Brix-acid ratio may be less than 11.5 to 1.

Grade C: Defects: Not more than 10 percent free and suspended pulp and not more than 0.035 percent by volume recoverable oil; no seeds or seed particles or other defects that materially affect the appearance of the product. **Flavor:** Good, normal, canned tangerine juice flavor which may have a slightly caramelized or oxidized flavor, but is free from off-flavors of any kind. Brix not less than 10.0°; Grade C sweet, 12.5°. Acid not less than 0.55 gram or more than 1.50 grams;

Grade C sweet, 0.60 gram or more than 1.50 grams (calculated as anhydrous citric acid) per 100 grams of juice. Brix-acid ratio—Grade C sweet, 11.5 to 1 provided that when the Brix of the juice is 16° or more, the Brix-acid ratio may be less than 11.5 to 1.

Grade D: Defects: Does not meet specifications of Grades A and C. **Flavor:** Juice that fails to meet requirements of Grades A and C, or is off-flavor, or unpalatable for any reason.

TOMATO JUICE—Canned [6/24/58]

Grade A: Color: Typical color of canned tomato juice, made from well-ripened red tomatoes, which has been properly prepared and processed. **Consistency:** Tomato juice flows readily and has a normal amount of insoluble tomato solids in suspension, with little tendency for such solids to settle out. **Defects:** Any defects present do not more than slightly affect the appearance or drinking quality of the product. **Flavor:** Has a distinct flavor and odor characteristic of good quality tomatoes and is not adversely affected by stems, leaves, crushed seeds, cores, immature tomatoes, or the effects of improper trimming or processing.

Grade C: Color: Typical color of canned tomato juice. **Consistency:** Product flows readily and has a normal amount of insoluble tomato solids in suspension, without a marked tendency for such solids to settle out. **Defects:** Defects present may be noticeable, but are not so large, numerous, or of such contrasting color as to affect seriously the appearance or drinking quality of the product. **Flavor:** Has a characteristic canned tomato juice flavor that may be affected adversely, but not seriously so, by stems, leaves, crushed seeds, cores, immature tomatoes, or the effects of improper trimming or processing.

Sstd: Fails to meet requirements.

TOMATO JUICE—Concentrated [2/25/70]

Grade A: Color: Typical color of canned tomato juice, made from well-ripened red tomatoes, which has been properly prepared and processed. **Consistency:** The reconstituted tomato juice flows readily and has a normal amount of insoluble tomato solids in suspension, with little tendency for such solids to settle out. **Defects:** Defects present in the re-

TOMATO JUICE

CANNED [6/24/58   52.3621]

Grades:	"A" or "FANCY"	"C" or "STANDARD"	"SUB-STANDARD"
Minimum Score:	85	70	Less than 70

CONCENTRATED [2/25/70   52.5201]

Grades:	"A" or "FANCY"	"C" or "STANDARD'	"SUB-STANDARD"
Minimum Score:	85	70	Less than 70

constituted juice do not more than slightly affect the appearance or drinking quality of the juice. **Flavor:** Distinct flavor and odor characteristic of good quality tomatoes. The flavor of the reconstituted juice may not be adversely affected by stems, leaves, crushed seeds, cores, immature tomatoes, or the effects of improper trimming or processing.

Grade C: Color: Typical color of canned tomato juice. **Consistency:** The reconstituted tomato juice flows readily and has a normal amount of insoluble tomato solids in suspension, without a marked tendency for such solids to settle out. **Defects:** Defects present in the reconstituted juice may be noticeable, but are not so large, numerous, or of such contrasting color as to seriously affect the appearance or drinking quality of the juice. **Flavor:** Has a characteristic canned tomato juice flavor which may be affected adversely, but not seriously so, by stems, leaves, crushed seeds, cores, immature tomatoes, or the effects of improper trimming or processing.

Sstd: Fails to meet requirements.

FRUITS and VEGETABLES, JUICES AND CONCENTRATES
Fruit juices and concentrates: Factors relating to farm and processed weights[1]

Item and specification	Approximate brix	Equivalent farm weight per gallon	Gallons per unit of farm weight		Net weight per gallon
	DEGREES	POUNDS	BOX[2]	TON	POUNDS
Apple:					
Single strength	13	12	—	170	8.7
Frozen 3 to 1 concentrate	45	47	—	43	10.0
Citrus fruits:[3]					
Orange					
Single strength juice	12	16	5.7	126	8.7
Frozen concentrate	42	60	1.5	34	9.9
Grapefruit					
Single strength juice	10	18	4.6	108	8.7
Frozen concentrate	40	76	1.1	26	9.8
Lemon					
Single strength juice	*	26	2.9	76	—
Non-frozen concentrate	*	148	0.5	13.5	—
Concentrate for lemonade	*	18	4.2	110	—
Grape:					
Single strength	16	11	—	175	8.9
Frozen concentrate	50	40	—	50	10.3
Pineapple:					
Single strength	14	15	—	133	8.8
4 to 1 concentrate	61	75	—	27	10.8
3 to 1 concentrate	50	60	—	33	10.3
Prune (from fresh prunes):					
Single strength	31	13	—	155	9.4
One & one-half to 1 concentrate	73	32	—	62	10.9

1. For additional information on concentration of fruit juices, see *Calculations of Volume and Weight Reduction in the Concentration of Fruit Juices*, Agricultural Research Service, U.S. Department of Agriculture, ARS 74-7, June 1956.
2. Oranges, 90 pounds; grapefruit, 85 pounds; lemons, 76 pounds.
3. Orange and grapefruit products based on Florida yields; lemons on California.
* Lemon product yields are based on a standard ton containing 36.5 pounds of anhydrous citric acid.

FRUITS AND VEGETABLES, JUICE POWDERS
Fruit and vegetable juice powders: Factors relating to farm and processed weights

Items	Approximate percentage solids content of juice	Yield of juice as a percentage of raw material	Factors for converting to —	
			Processed weight from farm weight	Equivalent farm weight from processed weight
	PERCENT	PERCENT		
Apple	14	75	0.107	9
Citrus:				
Grapefruit	11	49	.055	18
Lemon	9	40	.037	27
Orange	13	55	.072	14
Grape	17	75	.130	8
Pineapple[1]	15	58	.089	11
Prune	32	74	.250	4
Tomato	6-1/4	70	.044	23

1. Assuming juice is only product. In practice, however, juice is made only from edible grade peels, cores, trimmings, and sortouts.

JAMS AND JELLIES
FRUIT JELLY [12/21/55]

Jellies—Promulgated August 31, 1940, Amended March 20, 1952, December 21, 1955, and June 25, 1963.

Fruit jelly; identity; label statement of optional ingredients —(a) The jellies for which definitions and standards of identity are prescribed by this section are the jellied foods each of which is made from a mixture composed of not less than 45 parts by weight (as determined by the method prescribed in subsection (b)) of one or any combination of 2, 3, 4, or 5 of the fruit juice ingredients specified in subsection (c) to each 55 parts by weight (see subsection (e) (1)) of one of the optional saccharine ingredients specified in subsection (d). Such mixture may also contain one or more of the following optional ingredients:

(1) Spice

(2) A vinegar, lemon juice, lime juice, citric acid, lactic acid, malic acid, tartaric acid, fumaric acid, or any combination of two or more of these, in a quantity which reasonably compensates for deficiency, if any, of the natural acidity of the fruit juice ingredient

(3) Pectin, in a quantity which reasonably compensates for deficiency, if any, of the natural pectin content of the fruit juice ingredient

(4) Sodium citrate, sodium potassium tartrate, or any combination of these, in a quantity the proportion of which is not more than 3 oz. avoirdupois to each 100 lb. of the saccharine ingredient used

(5) Sodium benzoate or benzoic acid, or any combination of these, in a quantity reasonably necessary as a preservative

(6) Mint flavoring and harmless artificial green coloring, in case the fruit juice ingredient or combination of fruit juice ingredients is extracted from apple, crab apple, pineapple, or 2 or all of such fruits

(7) Cinnamon flavoring, other than artificial flavoring, and harmless artificial red coloring, in case the fruit juice ingredient or combination of fruit juice ingredients is extracted from apple or crab apple, or both such fruits

(8) The antifoaming agents, butter, oleomargarine, lard, corn oil, coconut oil, cottonseed oil, mono- and diglycerides of fat-forming fatty acids, in a quantity not greater than reasonably required to inhibit foaming

Such mixture is concentrated by heat to such point that the soluble solids content of the finished jelly is not less than 65 percent, as determined by the method prescribed in "Official Methods of Analysis of the Association of Official Agricultural Chemists."[1]

(b) Any requirements of this section with respect to the weight of any fruit juice ingredient, whether concentrated, unconcentrated, or diluted, means the weight determined by the following method: Determine the percent of soluble solids in such fruit juice ingredient by the method for soluble solids referred to in subsection (a); multiply the percent so found by the weight of such fruit juice ingredient; divide the result by 100; subtract from the quotient the weight of any added sugar or other added solids; and multiply the remainder by the factor for such fruit juice ingredient prescribed in subsection (c). The result is the weight of the fruit juice ingredient.

(c) Each of the fruit juice ingredients referred to in subsection (a) is the filtered or strained liquid extracted, with or without the application of heat and with or without the addition of water, from one of the following, mature, properly prepared fruits which are fresh, frozen and/or canned:

Name of Fruit	Factor Referred to in Subsection [b]
Apple	7.5
Apricot	7.0
Blackberry (other than dewberry)	10.0
Black Raspberry	9.0
Cherry	7.0
Crab Apple	6.5
Cranberry	9.5
Damson, Damson Plum	7.0
Dewberry (other than boysenberry, loganberry, and youngberry)	10.0
Fig	5.5

(Cont.)

1. "Solids by means of a Refractometer—Official" in *Official Methods of Analysis of the Association of Official Agricultural Chemists*, Seventh Edition, p. 495.

Name of Fruit (Cont.)	Factor Referred to in Subsection [b]
Gooseberry	12.0
Grape	7.0
Grapefruit	11.0
Greengage, Greengage Plum	7.0
Guava	13.0
Loganberry	9.5
Orange	8.0
Peach	8.5
Pineapple	7.0
Plum (other than damson, greengage, and prune)	7.0
Pomegranate	5.5
Prickly Pear	5.5
Quince	7.5
Raspberry, Red Raspberry	9.5
Red Currant, Currant (other than black currant)	9.5
Strawberry	12.5
Youngberry	10.0

In any combination of 2, 3, 4, or 5 of such fruit juice ingredients, the weight of each is not less than 1/5 of the weight of the combination. Each such fruit juice ingredient in any such combination is an optional ingredient.

(d) The optional saccharine ingredients referred to in subsection (a) are:

(1) Sugar

(2) Invert sugar syrup

(3) Any combination composed of optional saccharine ingredients (1) and (2)

(4) Any combination composed of dextrose and optional saccharine ingredient (1), (2), or (3)

(5) Any combination composed of corn syrup, dried corn syrup, glucose syrup, dried glucose syrup, or any 2 or more of the foregoing, with optional saccharine ingredient (1), (2), (3), or (4), in which the weight of the solids of corn syrup, dried corn syrup, glucose syrup, dried glucose syrup, or the sum of the weights of the solids of corn syrup, dried corn syrup, glucose syrup, and dried glucose syrup, in case 2 or more of these are used, does not exceed 1/4 of the total weight of the solids of the combined saccharine ingredients.

(6) Honey

(7) Any combination composed of honey and optional saccharine ingredient (1), (2), or (3), in which the weight of the solids of each component except honey is not less than 1/10 of the weight of the solids of such combination, and the weight of honey solids is not less than 2/5 of the weight of the solids of such combination

(e) For the purpose of this section:

(1) The weight of any optional saccharine ingredient means the weight of the solids of such ingredient.

(2) The term "sugar" means refined sugar (sucrose).

(3) The term "invert sugar syrup" means a syrup made by inverting or partly inverting sugar or partly refined sugar; its ash content is not more than 0.3 percent of its solids content, but if it is made from partly refined sugar, color and flavor other than sweetness are removed.

(4) The term "corn syrup" means a clarified, concentrated aqueous solution of the products obtained by the incomplete hydrolysis of cornstarch. The solids of the corn syrup contain not less than 40 percent by weight of reducing sugars calculated as anhydrous dextrose.

(5) The term "glucose syrup" means a clarified, concentrated, aqueous solution of the products obtained by the incomplete hydrolysis of any edible starch. The solids of glucose syrup contain not less than 40 percent by weight of reducing sugars calculated as anhydrous dextrose. "Dried glucose syrup" means the product obtained by drying "glucose syrup."

(6) The term "dextrose" means refined anhydrous or hydrated dextrose made from any starch.

(f) The name of each jelly for which a definition and standard of identity is prescribed by this section is as follows:

(1) In case the jelly is made with a single fruit juice ingredient, the name is "Jelly" preceded or followed by the name of synonym whereby the fruit from which such fruit juice ingredient was extracted is designated in subsection (c).

(2) In case the jelly is made with a combination of 2, 3, 4, or 5 fruit juice ingredients, the name is "Jelly" preceded or followed by the words "Mixed Fruit" or by the names or synonyms whereby the fruits from which the fruit juice ingredients were extracted are designated in subsection (c), in the order of predominance, if any, of the weights of such fruit juice ingredients in the combination.

Label Statements of Optional Ingredients

(g) (1) When optional ingredient (a) (1) is used, the label shall bear the word "Spiced," or the statement "Spice Added," or "With Added Spice"; but in lieu of the word "Spice" in such statements, the common name of the spice may be used.

(2) When optional ingredient (a) (5) is used, the label shall bear the words "Sodium Benzoate," or "Benzoic Acid," or "Sodium Benzoate and Benzoic Acid," as the case may be, followed by the words "Added as Preservative."

(3) When optional ingredient (a) (6) is used, the label shall bear the statement "Flavoring and Aritificial Coloring Added," or "With Added Flavoring and Artificial Coloring"; the word "Flavoring" in such statement may be preceded by the word "Mint."

(4) When optional saccharine ingredient (d) (7) is used, the label shall bear the names of the components of the combination whereby such components are designated in subsection (d), in the order of predominance, if any, of the weight of such components in the combination. Such names shall be preceded by the words "Prepared with."

(5) When optional saccharine ingredient (d) (6) is used, the label shall bear the statement "Prepared with Honey."

(6) When a combination of 2, 3, 4, or 5 fruit juice ingredients is used, and the jelly is designated on its label by the word "Jelly" preceded or followed by the words "Mixed Fruit," the label shall bear the names or synonyms whereby such fruits are designated in subsection (c), in the order of predominance, if any, of the weights of such fruit juice ingredients in the combination.

(7) When optional ingredient (a) (7) is used, the label shall bear the statement "flavoring and artificial coloring added," or "with added flavoring and artificial coloring." The word "flavoring" in such statement may be preceded by the word "cinnamon."

(h) Wherever the name specified in subsection (f) appears on the label of the jelly so conspicuously as to be easily seen under customary conditions of purchase, the words and statements herein specified showing the optional ingredients used shall immediately and conspicuously precede or follow such name, without intervening written, printed, or graphic matter, except that the varietal name of the fruit used in preparing such jelly may so intervene.

FRUIT JELLY [1/2/48]

Grade A: Consistency: Has a tendency to slightly firm texture and retains a compact shape without excessive "weeping." **Color:** Characteristic of the fruit jelly ingredient or ingredients, and the fruit jelly has a sparkling luster or may not be more than slightly cloudy, and is free from any dullness of color. **Flavor:** Has a good distinct flavor characteristic of the fruit ingredients after preserving and is free from any caramelized or objectionable flavor of any kind.

Grade B: Consistency: May lack firmness, but is not syrupy; may be more than slightly firm, but is not tough or rubbery. **Color:** Characteristic of the fruit jelly ingredients; and the fruit jelly may be slightly cloudy and have a slight dullness of color. **Flavor:** Has a reasonably good flavor characteristic of the fruit ingredients after preserving and may have a slightly caramelized flavor, but is free from any bitter flavor or objectionable or off-flavor of any kind.

Sstd: Fails to meet requirements.

FRUIT PRESERVES [or JAMS] [8/31/40]

Preserves or Jams—Promulgated August 31, 1940, as amended.

Preserves, Jams; identity; label statement of optional ingredients—(a) The preserves or jams for which definitions and standard of identity are prescribed by this section are the viscous or semi-solid foods, each of which is made from a mixture composed of not less than 45 parts by weight (see subsection (c)) of one of the fruit ingredients specified in subsection (b) to each 55 parts by weight (see subsection (e) (1)) of one of the optional saccharine ingredients specified in subsection (d). Such mixture may also contain one or more of the following optional ingredients:

(1) Spice

(2) A vinegar, lemon juice, lime juice, citric acid, lactic acid, malic acid, tartaric acid, fumaric acid, or any combination of 2 or more of these in a quantity which reasonably compensates for deficiency, if any, of the natural acidity of the fruit ingredient

(3) Pectin, in a quantity which reasonably compensates for deficiency, if any, of the natural pectin content of the fruit ingredient

(4) Sodium citrate, sodium potassium tartrate, or any combination of these, in a quantity the proportion of which is not more than 3 oz. avoirdupois to each 100 lb. of the saccharine ingredient used

(5) Sodium benzoate, or benzoic acid, or any combination of these, in a quantity reasonably necessary as a preservative

(6) The antifoaming agents, butter, oleomargarine, lard, corn oil, coconut oil, cottonseed oil, mono- and diglycerides of fat-forming fatty acids; in a quantity not greater than reasonably required to inhibit foaming

Such mixture, with or without added water, is concentrated by heat to such point that the soluble solids content of the finished preserve is not less than 68 percent of the fruit ingredient as specified in group I of subsection (b). The soluble solids content is determined by the method prescribed in "Official Methods of Analysis of the Association of Official Agricultural Chemists,"[1] except that no correction is made for water insoluble solids.

FRUIT PRESERVES [or JAMS] [10/29/74]

Grade A: Consistency: Fruit or fruit particles are dispersed uniformly throughout the product; the product is a tender gel, or may have no more than a very slight tendency to flow, except that a slightly less viscous consistency may be present when the fruit is chiefly in the form of whole or almost whole units; in the following kinds, the product does not have a macerated or pureed appearance, but in appearance and eating quality consists of whole units or pieces of fruit particles as indicated for the respective kinds, either singly or in combination with any other kind: Apricot—halves, pieces, or combination thereof. Cherry—whole, almost whole, or pieces of pitted cherries, or combinations thereof. Gooseberry—whole, almost whole, or combinations thereof. Peach—slices, pieces, or combinations thereof. Pineapple—crushed pieces, small pieces, or combinations thereof. Strawberry—whole or almost whole berries or combinations thereof. **Color:** Bright, practically uniform throughout, and characteristic of the variety of the fruit ingredients; the product is free from dullness of color due to any cause. **Defects:** Type I—Applicable defects do not exceed the allowance for Grade A as specified in Tables I, II, III, or IV, and any defects do not materially affect the appearance or edibility of the product. Type II (and any kinds with a macerated or pureed appearance, whether of Type I or II)—Defects do not materially affect the edibility or appearance of the product. **Flavor:** Has a good and distinct flavor characteristic of the applicable kinds of fruit ingredients.

Grade B: Consistency: Fruit or fruit particles are dispersed reasonably uniformly throughout the product; and the product may be firm, but not rubbery, or may be noticeably viscous, but not excessively thin. **Color:** Reasonably uniform throughout, and characteristic of the variety of fruit ingredients; however, the color may be slightly dull, but may not be off color. **Defects:** Type I—Applicable defects do not exceed the allowance for Grade B as specified in Tables I, II, III, or IV, and any defect does not seriously affect the appearance or edibility of the product. Type II (any any kinds with a macerated or pureed appearance, whether of Type I or II)—Defects do not seriously affect the appearance or edibility of the product. **Flavor:** Has a flavor reasonably characteristic of the applicable kind of fruit ingredients, and may have a slightly caramelized flavor, but is free from any bitter flavor or other objectionable or off flavor of any kind.

Sstd: Fails to meet requirements.

ORANGE MARMALADE [12/31/74]

Grade A: Color: Has a practically uniform, bright color, characteristic of properly prepared and processed orange marmalade for the respective kind; the product is practically free from green-colored peel; and the product is free from dullness of color due to any cause. **Consistency and Character:** Product is a firm but tender gel and may have no more than a very slight tendency to flow; contains a substantial, but not excessive, amount of peel; the peel is evenly distributed; the

1. *"Soluble Solids in Fresh and Canned Fruits, Jams, Marmalades, and Preserves—First Action."* From *Official Methods of Analysis of the Association of Official Agricultural Chemists*, Seventh Edition, p. 322.

peel is tender; in "sliced" style, the thin strips of peel are predominantly of strips approximately 1/32 in. to 1/16 in. in width; and in "chopped" style, the small pieces of peel are reasonably uniform in size. **Defects:** Not more than 1 seed or portion of seed, and not more than 6 pieces of blemished peel, may be present on an average for each 16 oz. net weight; and in a single container, the appearance and eating quality of the product is not materially affected by the presence of seeds, portions of seeds, blemished peel, objectionable material, harmless, extraneous material or any other defects. **Flavor and Odor:** Has a good and distinct flavor and aroma characteristic of properly processed orange marmalade; the flavor is neither excessively tart nor excessively sweet; and the product is free from any caramelized flavor or objectionable flavor or odor of any kind.

Grade B: Color: Has a reasonably uniform color; the product is reasonably free from green-colored peel; and the color of the product may be slightly dull, but is not off-color or excessively dark. **Consistency and Character:** Product may be definitely firm, but is not excessively gummy or rubbery; or product may be viscous, but is not excessively thin; the peel is fairly evenly distributed; peel is reasonably tender; in "sliced" style, the thin strips of peel are predominantly of strips approximating no more than 1/8 in. in width; and in "chopped" style, the small pieces of peel are fairly uniform in size. **Defects:** Not more than a total of 2 seeds or portions of seeds, and not more than 10 pieces of blemished peel, may be present on an average for each 16 oz. net weight; in a single container, the appearance and eating quality of the product is not seriously affected by the presence of seeds, portions of seeds, blemished peel, objectionable material, harmless, extraneous material, or any other defects. **Flavor and Odor:** Has a reasonably good flavor characteristic of the orange marmalade for the respective kind; flavor may be excessively tart or sweet or may have a slightly caramelized flavor, but the product is free from objectionable flavor or odor of any kind.

Sstd: Fails to meet requirements.

TABLE I—ALLOWANCES FOR DEFECTS

KINDS OF PRESERVES (OR JAMS) Type I Only	GRADE	STEMS	LEAVES	CAPS OR PORTIONS	OTHER EXTRANEOUS MATERIAL	LOOSE SEPAL-LIKE BRACTS	SEEDS, PITS, OR PORTIONS THEREOF	BLEMISHED, UNDERDEVELOPED OR OTHERWISE DAMAGED
		MAXIMUM ALLOWANCES						
BLACKBERRY BOYSENBERRY DEWBERRY LOGANBERRY YOUNGBERRY	U.S. Grade A	Total of 1 only per 96 oz.				1 per 8 oz.	10 per 8 oz. in "seedless"	2 per 8 oz.
	U.S. Grade B	Total of 1 only per 32 oz.				3 per 8 oz.	20 per 8 oz. in "seedless"	4 per 8 oz.
CHERRY	U.S. Grade A	Total of 1 only per 32 oz.					1 per 32 oz.	5 per 8 oz.
	U.S. Grade B	Total of 1 only per 16 oz.					1 per 32 oz.	8 per 8 oz.
BLUEBERRY ELDERBERRY HUCKLEBERRY	U.S. Grade A	Total of 1 large stem or 1 leaf per 8 oz.; and 1 cluster of cap stems per 8 oz.						3 per 8 oz.
	U.S. Grade B	Total of 3 large stems or 3 leaves per 16 oz.; and 3 clusters of cap stems per 16 oz.						5 per 8 oz.

TABLE II—ALLOWANCES FOR DEFECTS

KIND OF PRESERVES (OR JAMS) Type I Only	GRADE	STEMS SHORT 1/8 in. or less	SMALL Over 1/8 in. to 1/4 in. incl.	MEDIUM Over 1/4 in. to 1/2 in. incl.	LONG Longer than 1/2 in.	LEAVES	OTHER EXTRANEOUS MATERIAL	SEEDS, PITS, OR PORTIONS PIT OR PIECES OF PIT	SMALL PIECES OF PIT	PIT FRAGMENTS	PEEL	BLEMISHED, UNDERDEVELOPED OR OTHERWISE DAMAGED
						MAXIMUM ALLOWANCES						
APRICOT	U.S. Grade A	1 only per 16 oz.			None	1 only per 32 oz.	1 only per 200	1 only per 200	1 only per 128	1 only per 32 oz.	No limit	1 unit per 8 oz.
	U.S. Grade B	1 only per 8 oz.			None	1 only per per 16 oz.	1 only per 128 oz.	1 only per 200 oz.	1 only per 64 oz.	1 only per 16 oz.	No limit	4 units per 8 oz.
PEACH NECTARINE	U.S. Grade A					1 only per 32 oz.	1 only per 32 oz.	1 only per 96 oz.	1 only per 64 oz.	1 only per 16 oz.	1 sq. in. per 16 oz.	2 units per 8 oz.
	U.S. Grade B					1 only per 16 oz.	3 per 32 oz.	1 only per 48 oz.	1 only per 32 oz.	1 only per 8 oz.	1 sq. in. per 8 oz.	8 units per 8 oz.
DAMSON PLUM GREENGAGE PLUM (OTHERS)	U.S. Grade A	Total of 1 per 8 oz.					1 only per 128 oz.	1 only per 32 oz.			No limit	1 unit per 8 oz.
	U.S. Grade B	Total of 3 per 16 oz.					1 only per 32 oz.	1 only per 16 oz.			No limit	2 units per 8 oz.

TABLE III—ALLOWANCES FOR DEFECTS

KIND OF PRESERVES (OR JAMS) Type I Only	GRADE	STEMS LEAVES	OTHER EX-TRANEOUS MATERIAL	LOOSE SEPAL-LIKE BRACTS	SEEDS, PITS, OR PORTIONS THEREOF	PEEL	BLEMISHED, UNDERDE-VELOPED, OR OTHERWISE DAMAGED
		MAXIMUM ALLOWANCES					
CRANBERRY CURRANT (Other than Black) CURRANT, Red FIG GOOSEBERRY RHUBARB TOMATO TOMATO, Yellow	U.S. Grade A	Total of 1 per 32 oz.	1 only per 200 oz.	3 per 16 oz.		1 sq. in. per 16 oz. if prepared by peeling	2 units per 8 oz.
	U.S. Grade B	Total of 1 per 32 oz.	1 only per 128 oz.	5 per 16 oz.		1 sq. in. per 8 oz. if prepared by peeling	4 units per 8 oz.
PINEAPPLE	U.S. Grade A						2 units per 8 oz.
	U.S. Grade B						4 units per 8 oz.
GRAPEFRUIT ORANGE TANGERINE	U.S. Grade A	Total of 1 per 32 oz.	1 only per 200 oz.		1 per 16 oz.		3 units per 8 oz.
	U.S. Grade B	Total of 1 per 32 oz.	1 only per 128 oz.		1 per 8 oz.		5 units per 8 oz.

TABLE IV—ALLOWANCES FOR DEFECTS

KIND OF PRESERVES OR JAMS (Type I Only)	GRADE	STEMS SHORT 1/8 in. or less	SMALL Over 1/8 in. to 1/4 in. incl.	MEDIUM Over 1/4 in. to 1/2 in. incl.	LONG Longer than 1/2 in.	LEAVES	CAPS OR PORTIONS	OTHER EXTRANEOUS MATERIAL	LOOSE SEPAL-LIKE BRACTS	SEEDS	BLEMISHED, UNDERDEVELOPED, OR OTHERWISE DAMAGED
					MAXIMUM ALLOWANCES						
GRAPE	U.S. Grade A	3 short or small thin stems, including only 1 woody base stem per 16 oz.				1 only per 32 oz.		1 only per 200 oz.	3 per 16 oz.	3 seeds per 8 oz.	2 units per 8 oz.
	U.S. Grade B	3 short or small thin stems, including only 1 woody base stem per 8 oz.				1 only per 32 oz.		1 only per 128 oz.	5 per 16 oz.	6 seeds per 8 oz.	4 units per 8 oz.
STRAWBERRY	U.S. Grade A	4 per 8 oz.	2 small or medium or long stems, including only 1 long stem—or—1 piece harmless extraneous material ←——— such as weeds or grass per 32 oz. ———→			1/2 sq. in. if measurable by area					4 units per 8 oz.
	U.S. Grade B	8 per 8 oz.	4 small or medium or long stems, including only 1 long stem—or—1 piece harmless extraneous material ←——— such as weeds or grass per 32 oz. ———→			1/2 sq. in. if measurable by area					8 units per 8 oz.
RASPBERRY RASPBERRY, BLACK RASPBERRY, RED	U.S. Grade A	4 per 8 oz.	2 small or medium or long stems, including only 1 long stem—or—1 piece harmless extraneous material ←——— such as weeds or grass per 32 oz. ———→			1/2 sq. in. if measurable by area					4 units per 8 oz.
	U.S. Grade B	8 per 8 oz.	4 small or medium or long stems, including only 1 long stem—or—1 piece harmless extraneous material ←——— such as weeds or grass per 32 oz. ———→			1/2 sq. in. if measurable by area					8 units per 8 oz.

BIBLIOGRAPHY

The Almanac. Westminster, Maryland: Edward E. Judge & Sons, Inc., 1969-72, 1974-75.

"Buying, Handling and Using Fresh Fruits." Chicago: National Restaurant Association, 1973, pp. 2-19.

Canned Fruit and Vegetables, Chicago: American Hospital Association, 1958.

"Capabilities of U.S. and Mexican Production Areas." *Supplying U.S. Markets with Fresh Winter Produce*, No. 154, September 1971, pp. 1-25.

Castille, M.A., Dawson, E.H., and Thompson, E.R. "The Vegetable Round Up—From Buying to Cooking." *U.S. Department of Agriculture Yearbook* 1969. Washington, D.C.: Government Printing Office, 1969, pp. 174-195.

Eshbach, Charles E. *Food Service Trends.* Boston: Cahners Books International, Inc., 1974.

Facts and Pointers on Marketing Fresh Tomatoes. Washington, D.C.: United Fresh Fruit & Vegetable Association, 1972.

Food Purchasing Guide. Chicago: American Hospital Association, 1966.

"Home Freezing of Fruits and Vegetables." Washington, D.C.: Agriculture Research Service, November, 1971, pp. 3-48.

"How To Buy Canned and Frozen Vegetables." Washington, D.C.: U.S. Department of Agriculture, January 1975, pp. 3-23.

"How To Buy Fresh Fruits." Washington, D.C.: U.S. Department of Agriculture, pp. 3-21.

"How To Buy Fresh Vegetables." Washington, D.C.: U.S. Department of Agriculture, December 1967, pp. 3-23.

"Market Disease of Stone Fruit: Cherries, Peaches, Nectarines, Apricots and Plums." Washington, D.C.: U.S. Department of Agriculture, 1972.

"Market Diseases of Tomatoes, Peppers and Eggplants." Washington, D.C.: U.S. Department of Agriculture, 1968.

"Nutritive Value of Fruits and Vegetables." Washington, D.C.: United Fresh Fruit and Vegetable Association, pp. 1-12.

"Plant Hardiness Zone Map." Washington, D.C.: United States Department of Agriculture, 1972.

Reginald, Sister Mary. *Manual of Specifications for Canned Fruit and Vegetables*, Chicago: American Hospital Association, 1958.

Wood, Adeline. *Quantity Food Buying Guides*, Parts I and II. New York: Ahrens, 1957.

FRUIT AND VEGETABLE FACTS AND POINTERS UNITED FRESH FRUIT AND VEGETABLE ASSOCIATION

Anise, FVFP (2/74)
Apples, FVFP (1/65)
Apricots, FVFP (9/69)
Artichokes, FVFP (3/67)
Asparagus, FVFP (10/66)
Avocados, FVFP (1/70)
Bananas, FVFP (3/69)
Beans, Green or Wax Snap, FVFP (6/60)
Beets, FVFP (7/66)
Blackberries—Dewberries, FVFP (12/58)
Blueberries, FVFP (10/73)
Broccoli, FVFP (3/71)
Brussels Sprouts, FVFP (8/66)
Cabbage, FVFP (1/69)
Cantaloupes, FVFP (9/73)
Carrots, FVFP (7/63)
Cauliflower, FVFP (3/67)
Celeriac, FVFP
Celery, FVFP (8/61)
Cherries, Sweet, FVFP (6/74)
Coconuts, FVFP (6/70)
Collards, FVFP (3/74)
    Dandelions
Corn, Sweet, FVFP (8/68)
Cranberries, FVFP (10/74)
Cucumbers, FVFP (11/72)
Endive Escarole Choice
Dates, FVFP (8/74)
Eggplant
Garlic, FVFP (3/74)
Gooseberries, FVFP
Grapes, FVFP (10/74)
Grapefruits, FVFP (10/74)
Honeydew, FVFP (11/67)
Kale, FVFP (11/66)
Lemons, FVFP (10/74)
Lettuce, FVFP (11/56)

Limes, FVFP (2/58)
Lychees, FVFP (8/64)
Mangoes, FVFP (3/73)
Cultivated Mushrooms, FVFP (6/59)
Nectarines, FVFP (3/55)
Okra, FVFP (1/53)
Onions, Green, FVFP (2/74)
Mustard Greens
Parsley
Parsnips
Oranges, FVFP (3/66)
Papayas, FVFP (12/53)
Peaches, FVFP (4/53)
Pears, FVFP (5/62)
Peppers, FVFP (1/68)
Persimmons, FVFP (3/67)
Pineapple, FVFP
Plums & Prunes, FVFP (1952)
Pomegranates, FVFP (5/53)
Potatoes, FVFP (8/72)
Pumpkins, FVFP (3/70)
Radishes
Raspberries, FVFP (12/72)
Rhubarb, FVFP (8/69)
Rutabagas, FVFP (3/70)
Shallots
Spinach, FVFP (3/58)
Squash, FVFP (8/59)
Strawberries, FVFP (2/75)
Sweet Potatoes, FVFP (2/67)
Swiss Chard, FVFP (6/74)
Tangelos, FVFP (11/64)
Tangerines, FVFP (4/68)
Tomatoes, FVFP (12/69)
Turnips, FVFP (1/73)
Watercress, FVFP (2/74)
Watermelons, FVFP (6/75)
Wax Snap Beans, FVFP (6/70)

U.S. GOVERNMENT SPECIFICATIONS

Apples (7/25/72   51.300)
Apples, Canned (10/17/53   52.2161)
Apples, Frozen (5/17/54   52.361)
Apples, Dehydrated (7/1/57   52.2341)
Apples, Dried (10/24/55   52.2481)
Apricots (5/25/28   51.2925)
Apricots, Canned (4/1/74   52.2641)
Apricots, Frozen (6/20/63   52.5521)
Apricots, Dehydrated (6/30/74   52.3871)
Apricots, Dried (5/24/67   52.5761)
Avocados, Fresh (9/3/57   51.3050)
Blackberries, Fresh (2/13/28   51.4270)
Blackberries, Canned (12/1/56   52.551)
Blackberries, Frozen (5/24/67   52.5881)
Dewberries & Other Similar Berries, Fresh (2/13/28   51.4270)
Dewberries & Other Similar Berries, Canned (12/1/56   52.551)
Dewberries & Other Similar Berries, Frozen (5/24/67   52.5881)
Blueberries, Fresh (6/1/66   51.3475)
Blueberries, Canned (8/19/59   52.581)
Blueberries, Frozen (5/7/55   52.611)
Dewberries and Blackberries, USS, (2/13/28)
Cantaloupes, USS (6/30/68   51.475)
Cantaloupes, USS, Frozen (6/25/62   52.5361)
Sweet Cherries, USS (5/7/71)
Sweet Cherries, USS, Canned (6/20/73)
Sweet Cherries, USS, Frozen (3/1/58   52.3161)
Red Sour Cherries, USS For Manufacturing, (3/20/41)
Red Tart Pitted Cherries, USS, Frozen (6/28/74   52.801)
Red Tart Pitted Cherries, USS, Canned (5/15/74   52.771)
Sulfured Cherries, USS (6/12/51   52.741)
Cranberries, USS, (8/26/71   51.2775)
Fresh Cranberries, USS, For Processing (8/24/57)
Cranberries, USS, Frozen, (9/22/71   52.6281)
Cranberry Sauce, USS, Canned (3/19/51)
Currants, USS, Dried (10/11/65   52.981)
Dates, USS, (8/26/55   52.1001)
Figs, Kadota, USS, Canned, (6/20/73   52.2821)
Figs, USS, Canned (2/27/63)
Figs, USS, Canned Preserve, (8/6/67)
Figs, USS, Dried (2/27/67   52.1021)

Fruit Cocktail, USS, Canned (6/20/73   52.1051)

Orange Juice, USS, Concentrated For Manufacturing (11/17/64   52.2221)

Fruits for Salad, USS, Canned (6/20/73   52.3831)

Grapefruit, USS, California & Arizona (1/9/50   51.925)

Grapefruit, USS, Florida (1/31/73   51.750)

Grapefruit, USS, Texas & States other than Florida, California & Arizona (10/1/69   51.620)

Grapefruit, USS, Canned (10/25/73   52.1141)

Grapefruit, USS, Frozen (2/20/48   52.1171)

Grapefruit & Orange For Salad, USS, Canned (1/21/60   52.1251)

Grapes, USS, Table (5/20/71   51.880)

Grapes, USS, American Eastern Type Bunch (4/15/65   51.3610)

Juice Grapes, USS, (European or Vinifera Type) (7/20/39)

Grapes, USS, Canned (6/20/73   52.4021)

Lemons, USS (9/1/64   51.2795)

Limes, USS, Persian (6/20/58   51.1000)

Melons, USS, Honeydew and Honey Ball (4/1/67   51.3740)

Melon Balls, USS, Frozen (6/25/62   52.5361)

Nectarines, USS (4/23/66   51.3145)

Oranges, USS, California & Arizona (9/23/57   51.1085)

Oranges, USS, Texas & States (10/1/69   51.680)

Oranges & Tangelos, USS, Florida (1/31/73   51.1140)

Peaches, USS (6/15/52   51.1210)

Fresh Freestone Peaches, USS, For Canning, Freezing, or Pulping (6/1/66)

Freestone Peaches, USS, Canned (6/20/73   52.2601)

Freestone Peaches, USS, Frozen (7/3/61   52.3551)

Peaches (Low Moisture), USS, Dehydrated (6/30/74   52.3911)

Peaches, USS, Dried (5/24/67   52.5801)

Clingstone Peaches, USS, Canned (6/20/73   52.2561)

Pears, USS, Summer and Fall (8/20/55   51.1260)

Pears, USS, Winter (9/10/55   51.1300)

Pears, USS, For Processing (7/1/70)

Pears, USS, Canned (6/20/73   52.1611)

Pears, USS, Dried (5/24/67   52.5841)

Pineapples, USS (2/23/53   51.1485)

Pineapple, USS, Canned (3/16/57   52.1711)

Pineapple, USS, Frozen (1/25/49   52.1741)

Plums & Prunes, USS, Fresh (5/9/69   51.1520)

Plums & Prunes, USS, Canned (12/15/72   52.1781)

Plums, USS, Frozen (3/6/56   52.2911)

Dried Prunes, USS, Canned (5/24/67   52.5601)

Prunes (Low Moisture), USS, Dehydrated (6/13/60   52.3231)

Dried Prunes, USS, Canned (5/24/67   52.5601)

Prunes, USS, Dried (10/11/65   52.3181)

Raspberries, USS (5/29/31   51.4320)

Raspberries, USS, For Processing (5/18/52)

Raspberries, USS, Canned (3/1/58   52.3311)

Raspberries, USS, Frozen (8/16/48   52.1871)

Rhubarb, USS, Fresh (2/1/66   51.3665)

Rhubarb, USS, Frozen (8/15/45)

Strawberries, USS (7/1/65   51.3115)

Grauer's Stock Strawberries, USS, For Manufacture (6/1/35)

Strawberries, USS, Frozen (2/1/58   52.1981)

Tangerines, USS, Florida (1/31/73   51.1810)

Tangerines, USS (9/18/48   51.770)

Watermelons, USS (3/22/54   51.1970)

Sweet Anise, USS (3/15/73   51.2900)

Artichokes, USS (5/15/69   51.3785)

Green Asparagus, USS, For Processing (3/5/72   51.3720)

Asparagus, USS, Canned (6/20/73   52.2541)

Asparagus, USS, Frozen (6/30/74   52.381)

Asparagus Plumosis, USS (6/6/30   51.4455)

Lima Beans, USS (1/5/38   51.3805)

Fresh Shelled Lima Beans, USS, For Processing (6/6/53)

Lima Beans, USS, Canned (3/20/60   52.471)

Lima Beans, USS, Frozen (4/16/57   52.501)

Speckled Butter (Lima) Beans, USS, Frozen (7/21/62   52.5241)

Beets, USS (8/1/55   51.375)

Beet Greens, USS (6/1/59   51.2860)

Beets, USS, Canned (2/4/55   52.521)

Broccoli, USS, Bunched Italian Sprouting, (7/12/43   51.3555)

Broccoli, USS, For Processing (10/4/59)

Broccoli, USS, Frozen (4/14/62   52.631)

Brussels Sprouts, USS (1/18/54   51.2250)

Brussels Sprouts, USS, Frozen (5/11/50   52.651)

Bulk Sauerkraut, USS (5/24/67   52.3451)

Sauerkraut, USS, Canned (5/13/63   52.2951)

Cabbage, USS (9/1/45   51.450)

Cabbage, USS, For Processing (1/17/44)

Carrots, USS (7/17/54)

Carrots, USS, Bunched (9/18/54   51.2455)

Carrots, USS, Topped (12/20/65   51.2360)

Carrots, USS, Short Trimmed Top (9/18/54)

Carrots, USS, For Processing (7/1/44)

Carrots, USS, Canned (7/2/59   52.671)
Carrots, USS, Frozen (2/28/74   52.701)
Cauliflower, USS (3/15/68   51.540)
Cauliflower, USS, For Processing (9/4/59)
Cauliflower, USS, Frozen (11/12/51   52.721)
Celery, USS (4/7/59   51.560)
Corn, USS, Green (5/18/54   51.835)
Sweet Corn, USS, For Processing (5/15/62)
Whole Kernel or Whole Grain Corn, USS, Canned (7/30/52
     52.881)
Cream Style Corn, USS, Canned (7/27/53   52.851)
Whole Kernel or Whole Grain Corn, USS, Frozen (8/1/52   52.911)
Corn-on-the-Cob, USS, Frozen (7/27/70   52.931)
Cucumbers, USS (3/1/58   51.2220)
Cucumbers, USS, Greenhouse (10/1/34   51.3855)
Cucumbers, USS, Pickling (12/10/36   51.4170)
Dandelion Greens, USS (2/4/55   51.2585)
Dried Beans, USS, Canned (10/24/47   52.411)
Eggplant, USS (10/29/53   51.2190)
Endives, Escarole, or Chicory, USS (10/1/64   51.3535)
Garlic, USS (9/4/44   51.3880)
Hominy, USS, Canned (3/10/58   52.3281)
Kale, USS (3/25/74   51.3930)
Leafy Greens (other than spinach), USS, Frozen (6/13/52
     52.1371)
Lettuce, USS (6/16/70   51.2510)
Lettuce, USS, Greenhouse Leaf (9/1/64   51.3455)
Mushrooms, USS (7/15/66   51.3385)
Mushrooms, USS, For Processing (3/1/64)
Mushrooms, USS, Canned (4/7/62   52.1481)
Mixed Vegetables, USS, Frozen (5/24/54   52.2131)
Mustard & Turnip Greens, USS (3/8/53)
Okra, USS (12/18/28   51.3945)
Okra, USS, For Processing (12/15/65)
Okra, USS, Canned (7/8/57   52.3331)
Okra, USS, Frozen (8/20/69   52.1511)
Okra and Tomatoes, USS, Canned (12/24/57   52.3421)
Green Onions, USS, Common (6/20/47   51.1055)
     Onions, USS, Creole (4/10/43   51.3955)
     Onions, USS, Bermuda, Granex-Giardo Type (3/18/62
     51.3195)
     Onions, USS, (Other Than Bermuda, Granex, Grano) (10/1/71
     51.2830)
     Onion Sets, USS (21.140)
     Onions, USS, For Processing (1/17/44)
     Onions, USS, Canned (11/2/57   52.3041)

Breaded Onion Rings, USS, Frozen (10/17/59   52.4061)
Parsley, USS (7/30/30   51.4000)
Fresh Parsnips, USS (3/23/54)
Parsnips, USS (12/10/45   51.4010)
Peas, USS, Fresh (6/1/42   51.1375)
Peas, USS, Southern (7/13/56   51.2670)
Fresh Shelled Peas, USS, For Canning & Freezing (1/15/46)
Southern Peas, USS, For Processing (6/1/65)
Peas, USS, Canned (5/13/55   52.2281)
Peas, USS, Frozen (5/28/59   52.3511)
Peas and Carrots, USS, Canned (7/20/70   52.6201)
Field Peas & Black-eyed Peas, USS, Canned (4/17/50   52.1641)
Field Peas & Black-eyed Peas, USS, Frozen (6/30/60   52.1661)
Peppers, USS, Sweet (12/15/63   51.3270)
Sweet Peppers, USS, For Processing (3/22/48)
Sweet Peppers, USS, Frozen (3/13/59   52.3001)
Pimientos, USS, Canned (10/23/67   52.2681)
Peeled Potatoes, USS (6/8/54   52.2421)
Potatoes, USS (2/5/72)
Potatoes, USS, Seed (4/29/72   51.1540)
Potatoes, USS, For Processing (7/10/63)
White Potatoes, USS, Canned (2/10/50   52.1811)
French Fried Potatoes, USS, Frozen (2/8/67   52.2391)
Pumpkin & Squash, USS, Canned (3/9/56   52.2741)
Radishes, USS (10/1/68   51.2395)
Romaine, USS (8/10/60)
Shallots, USS, Bunched (12/16/46)
Rhubarb, USS, Fieldgrown (2/1/66)
Rhubarb, USS, Frozen (8/15/45)
Snap Beans, USS (8/1/36   51.3830)
Snap Beans, USS, For Processing (7/26/59)
Green Beans & Wax Beans, USS, Canned (2/13/72   52.441)
Green Beans & Wax Beans, USS, Frozen (5/8/75   52.2321)
Beans, Dried, USS, Canned (10/24/47)
Spinach Plants, USS (11/19/56   51.2880)
Spinach Leaves, USS, Fresh (12/27/46   41.1730)
Fresh Spinach Leaves, USS (5/19/49)
Spinach, USS, For Processing (7/10/56)
Spinach, USS, Canned (5/8/71   52.1901)
Spinach, USS, Frozen (9/7/64   52.1921)
Squash, USS, Summer (3/26/45   51.4050)
Squash, USS, Fall & Winter (11/15/44   51.4030)
Squash (Summer Type), USS, Canned (5/25/59   52.3581)
Squash (Summer Type), USS, Frozen (4/3/53   52.1961)
Cooked Squash, USS, Frozen (10/5/53   52.1941)

Sweet Potatoes, USS (7/1/63   51.1600)

Sweet Potatoes, USS, For Dicing or Pulping (7/23/51)

Sweet Potatoes, USS, For Canning or Freezing (7/24/59)

Sweet Potatoes, USS, Frozen (9/4/62   52.5001)

Succotash, USS, Canned (5/24/67   52.6001)

Succotash, USS, Frozen (3/6/59   52.2011)

Tomatoes, USS, Fresh (2/1/75   51.1855)

Tomato Plants, USS (1/3/44)

Tomatoes, USS, Greenhouse (4/19/66   51.3345)

Tomatoes, USS, For Processing (3/1/73)

Italian Tomatoes, USS, For Canning (5/7/57)

Green Tomatoes, USS, For Processing (3/15/50)

Tomatoes, USS, Canned (7/24/64   52.5161)

Tomatoes & Okra and Okra & Tomatoes, USS, Canned (12/24/57   52.3421)

Turnips or Rutabagas, USS (8/1/55   51.2610)

Turnip Greens with Turnips, USS, Frozen (8/19/58   52.3731)

Horseradish Roots, USS (7/27/36   51.3900)

Grapefruit and Orange Juice, USS, Frozen Concentrate (11/1/72   52.1311)

Lemonade, USS, Frozen Concentrate (9/21/68   52.1421)

Limeade, USS, Frozen Concentrate (9/21/68   52.2521)

Tomato Juice, USS, Concentrate (2/25/70   52.5201)

Tomato Juice, USS, Canned (6/24/58   52.3621)

Pineapple Juice, USS, Canned (3/16/57   52.1761)

Apple Juice, USS, Canned (7/1/71   52.301)

Apple Juice, USS, Frozen Concentrate (5/15/75   52.6321)

Sweetened Grape Juice, USS, Frozen Concentrate (11/1/57   52.2931)

Tangerine Juice, USS, Canned (7/1/69   52.2071)

Tangerine Juice, USS, Concentrated for Manufacturing 10/31/55   52.2931)

Lemon Juice, USS, Concentrated for Manufacturing (3/1/59   52.3951)

Grapefruit Juice, USS (12/7/68   52.6121)

Grapefruit Juice, USS, Frozen Concentrate (10/1/70   52.1221)

Orange Juice, USS, Concentrate (7/1/69   52.5681)

Orange Juice, USS, Canned (7/1/69   52.1551)

Orange Juice, USS, Frozen Concentrate (9/21/68   52.1581)

Orange Juice, USS, Dehydrated (9/21/68   52.2981)

Orange Juice, USS, Pasteurized (7/1/69   52.5641)

10

MISCELLANEOUS GROCERIES

MISCELLANEOUS GROCERIES takes up a sizeable amount, although it remains a minority, of the total time required for food purchasing. While a minority of the products in this classification have federal specifications, e.g., olives and pickles, some have just trade and industry specifications. We have tried to include in this section every miscellaneous grocery item that is available on the American market and all the information available about these products. In selecting products from this group, the same basic purchasing principles prevail. The buyer needs accurate knowledge as to the final use that will be made of the product to be purchased; information as to the products that are available, their description, and the range of quality offered for selection.

ALMOND PASTE: Also known as Marzipan. Made from ground almonds, sugar, and eggs. Used in baking.

ANCHOVY PASTE: Mixture of pounded anchovies, vinegar, water, and spices. **Pack:** Case of 24/2 oz. containers.

ANNONA: The tropical fruits cherimoza, soursop, custard apple, and bullock's heart. Canned. Imported. No grades.

APPLE BUTTER, Canned [8/5/57][See also, Fruit Butters]: Jam or sauce made by stewing apples in cider or water, with added flavoring and sugar.

Grade A: Color: "Good color" means a lustrous, practically uniform color, characteristic of properly prepared and properly processed apple butter. Color may be moderately reddish brown or moderately dark brown but is equal to or better than USDA Apple Butter Color Standard No. 1 or No. 2, whichever most nearly matches the color of the apple butter.

Consistency: "Good consistency" means that the apple butter after stirring and emptying from the container to a dry flat surface forms a moderately mounded mass and that at the end of 2 minutes there is practically no separation of free liquid. **Finish:** Apple butter is practically free from defects which means that any defects present do not more than slightly affect the appearance or edibility of the product. **Flavor:** Good and distinct flavor and aroma characteristic of properly prepared and properly processed apple butter prepared from good quality ingredients.

APPLE BUTTER

CANNED [8/5/57   52.2801]

Grades:	"A" or "FANCY"	"C" or "STANDARD"	"SUB-STANDARD"
Minimum Score:	85	70	Less than 70

NET WEIGHT: Not less than 90 percent of capacity of container

Grade C: Color: Apple butter color may be somewhat lacking in luster. Such color may be dark or light brown but is equal to or better than USDA Apple Butter Color Standard No. 3 or No. 4, whichever most nearly matches the color of the apple butter. **Consistency:** After stirring, the apple butter may possess a thick consistency so that it does not pour readily from the container or, after emptying from the container to a dry flat surface may form only a slightly mounded mass, and at the end of 2 minutes there is no more than a slight separation of free liquor. **Finish:** Apple particles are evenly divided; product may be slightly coarse, but the apple particles are neither hard or excessively grainy. **Defects:** Any defects

present may be noticeable but are not so large, so numerous, or of such contrasting color as to seriously affect the appearance or edibility of the product. **Flavor:** A characteristic apple butter flavor and odor may be excessively sweet, tart, and spiced, or lacking in proper spicing, or may be excessively caramelized, but is not seriously objectionable for any reason.
Sstd: Color: Apple butter fails to meet requirements and shall not be graded above Substandard. **Consistency:** See Color. **Finish:** See Color. **Defects:** See Color. **Flavor:** See Color.
APPLESAUCE, Canned [12/3/70] (See also Apples in chapter on "Produce."): Grade A: Color: Natural color is typical of the variety or varieties used; may range from white that may be slightly translucent to light golden. Artificially colored is bright and distinct but not saturated. All types are free from tinges of pink or gray and from discoloration due to oxidation, scorching, or other causes. **Consistency:** After stirring and emptying on a dry flat surface, forms a moderately mounded mass, and at the end of 2 minutes there is not more than a slight separation of liquor. **Finish:** Apple particles are evenly divided; product is granular but not lumpy, pasty, or "salvy," and the apple particles are not hard. **Absence of Defects:** Number, size, and color of defects do not materially affect the appearance or eating quality of product. **Flavor:** Distinct, desirable, characteristic normal flavor and odor, and free from objectionable odors of any kind, including but not limited to those caused by oxidation, fermentation, and caramelization.
Grade C: Color: Fairly uniform typical color that may be dull, slightly brown, slightly gray or pink, but not off-color. **Consistency:** May be more than moderately mounded, may be stiff but not excessively stiff, or may be slightly thin so that it levels itself, and at the end of 2 minutes there may be moderate but not excessive separation of free liquor. **Finish:** Apple particles are evenly divided; product may lack granular characteristics, may be slightly pasty, salvy, and the apple particles are not hard. **Defects:** Number, size, and color of defects do not seriously affect the appearance or eating quality of the product. **Flavor:** May be lacking in good flavor and odor; is practically free from flavor of overripe fruit, objectionable flavors, etc. See flavor for Grade A.
Sstd: Fails to meet the requirements of U.S. Grade C.

APPLESAUCE

CANNED [6/25/74   52.331]

Grades:	"A" or "FANCY"	"B" or "CHOICE"	"SUB-STANDARD"
Minimum Score:	90	80	Less than 80

NET WEIGHT: Not less than 90 percent of capacity of container; except in the case of glass containers having a total capacity of 6-1/2 fluid oz. or less, the fill is not less than 85 percent.

ARROWROOT: Used for thickening sauces, making pudding, etc., and flavoring biscuits. Made from the root of tropical plants. **Types:** 1) Arum maculatum: Portland arrowroot; 2) Brazilian: cassava; 3) British: a potato farina; 4) East India: curcuma; 5) Tacca: tacca pinnatifida; 6) Tulema: Indian. Excellent for bake shop use. Buy by the (expensive!) pound.

ASPERGE: Asparagus spears. U.S. products subject to grading as detailed in chapter on "Produce" under Asparagus, Canned. The white asparagus is often an ungraded import.

BAKING POWDER: Raising agent used in baking. Mixture of sodium bicarbonate, an acid substance, and a starchy base such as flour. When a mixture containing baking powder is wetted and heated, at least 12 percent carbon dioxide must be given off. **Types:** 1) Tartrate—contains cream of tartar. Quick acting. 2) Phosphate—contains sodium acid phosphate or calcium acid phosphate. Quick acting. 3) S.A.S. Phosphate—contains calcium acid phosphate and sodium aluminum phosphate. Slow acting. Double-action. 4) Combinations of above. **Sizes:** 1 lb. package, 5 lb. package, 10 lb. package.

BAKING SODA: Sodium Bicarbonate. Used in baking, cooking, and general cleaning. **Sizes:** 12 oz. package, 1 lb. package, 5 lb. package, 10 lb. package.

BEANS: See Legumes, dried.

BEEF EXTRACT: Made of beef juice and other soluble parts of beef meat. Used in sauces, stews, soups, etc. Very strong. Packs: 24/1 lb., 10 lb., 25 lb.

BENZOATE OF SODA: Food preservative. Benzoic acid dissolved in water and sodium carbonate. Illegal in some states.

BEVERAGES

COFFEE: The coffee beans that the foodservice operator buys are the product of roasting and, usually, grinding. Coffee is usually a blend of more than one coffee. Some of the important varieties are:

Armenia—full bodied (Colombia)
Aukola—light, sweet (Sumatra)
Blue Mountain—full bodied (Jamaica)
Bogota—full bodied (Colombia)
Cootepec—full bodied (Mexico)
Excelso—full bodied (Colombia)
Giradot—full bodied (Colombia)
Java—mild, good quality (Java)
Liberica—somewhat acrid (Venezuela)
Mandhelling—light, sweet (Sumatra)
Manizule—full bodied (Colombia)
Marciabo—light, rich (Venezuela)
Medellin—full bodied (Colombia)
Mocha—full bodied, rich (Arabia)
Oaxaca—low quality (Mexico)
Rio—low quality (Mexico)
Robusta—somewhat acrid (Kenya)
Sevilla—full bodied (Colombia)
Santo—somewhat acrid, high quality (Brazil)

It is possible to brew coffee from roasted whole beans, but this would take hours and the beverage would not taste very good.[1] It is also possible to make a beverage from pulverized coffee. Single cup vending machines, which are scientifically designed to use such coffee, can produce a good beverage from a very fine grind, but institutional and home-type brewing equipment are not designed for pulverized coffee, and its use in such equipment would result in a very bitter tasting brew. Consequently, beans for normal use should *not* be ground to a powder. This means that some intermediate grind size is required. To achieve this end there must be a method for accurately measuring sizes of particles. Such a method permits grinding to a desired degree of fineness and consistently provides the same balance of particle sizes.

Food operators should know whether their suppliers are actually making measurements of grinds, and whether consistency of grind is being provided.

Any grind contains particles of many sizes. Samples differ only in the proportion of each size of particles they contain. These proportions are measured by shaking the sample through a set of graded screens. A drip (or urn) grind, for example, should contain about 7 percent of particles that will

be held back by a 14 mesh screen, 73 percent that will be held back by a 28 mesh screen, and 20 percent that will pass through a 28 mesh screen.

	Regular	Drip	Fine
14 mesh screen	33 percent	7 percent	None
28 mesh screen	55 percent	73 percent	70 percent
Pan	12 percent	20 percent	30 percent

Any day-to-day or periodic variations in the consistency of the grind supplied can result in an inconsistent beverage. As the percentage of large particles increases, the brewed coffee will be weaker. As the fine particles increase, the resultant brew may become bitter.

A cautionary note should be added here on the use of coffee grinders on location. These grinders can and do vary in the type of grind they produce. This lack of control in the grind will be directly reflected in the beverage quality.

Accumulation of rancid oils and other materials in the grinder will offset the fine flavor of fresh coffee as well. Coffee that is ground in a roasting plant will be uniform day after day and will not adversely affect the quality of your beverage.

There are no federal grades for coffee, but there are grades maintained by the New York Coffee and Sugar Exchange. The grades limit the number of defects allowed in the coffee; the more defects the lower the grade.

Some things to look for:
COLORING—The coffee might be dyed. The color should be even throughout the bean.
ADDITIVES—Cereals and beans may have been ground into the coffee.
GLAZING—Adding of materials in the roasting to improve color. This adds weight but does not improve quality.

A specification for coffee should include: 1) roast, 2) grind, 3) percentage of types desired in blend, and 4) packaging. Since few foodservice operators have the purchasing power to specify the types, it is suggested that several brands be ordered "in the bean" and sent to the Coffee Brewing Center for quality evaluation. Customer testing must be part of the cost/quality evaluation.

DECAFFEINATED COFFEE [Sanka, DeCaf, etc.]: An in-

---

1. *Facts About Coffee*, The Coffee Brewing Center, New York, N.Y.

COFFEE AND TEA PRODUCTS
Factors for obtaining equivalents of green coffee beans and leaf tea from specified products

Product	Description	Factors
Coffee, green, bag[1]	Standard bag of 60 kilograms, number of pounds	132.276
Coffee, parchment	The green coffee bean contained in the parchment skin	.80
Coffee, roasted	Green coffee roasted to any degree and includes ground coffee	1.19
Coffee, soluble, pure (instant)	The water-soluble solids derived from roasted coffee	3.00
Coffee, decaffeinated	Green, roasted or soluble coffee from which caffein has been extracted:	
	Green	1.00
	Roasted	1.19
	Soluble (instant)	3.00
Tea, soluble (instant)	3 lb. of leaf tea yields 1 lb. of soluble tea	3.00

1. All coffee in the naked bean form before roasting.

stant coffee from which 97 percent to 99 percent of caffeine has been removed. **Pack:** Various size jars; individual packets.

FREEZE-DRIED COFFEE: A product which is the result of freezing brewed coffee and then drying in a vacuum without going through a liquid state. Higher quality and better aroma than soluble coffee.

FROZEN COFFEE: A concentrate coffee resulting from the partial extraction of the liquid from brewed coffee. Smooth, even high quality, but lacking in aroma.

SOLUBLE COFFEE: A powdered product resulting from vacuum drying brewed coffee. Often called "instant" coffee, it is of good quality but usually lacks aroma.

BREAKFAST COCOA: Breakfast cocoa is the product resulting from roasting, grinding, and defatting the nibs of the cocoa bean. Breakfast cocoa must have 22 percent cocoa butter but may have as much as 35 percent. The higher the cocoa butter content, the richer the product. Dutch process breakfast cocoa has been treated to make it richer and more easily soluble.

HOT CHOCOLATE: A beverage made from chocolate liquor, liquid or dried, which may contain up to 50 percent cocoa butter.

TEA: Tea varies in quality according to the altitude at which it is grown (the higher the better), the soil, and climate. There are three types of tea and many classes within those types. Quality and cost of tea can be affected by the amount of hand work that is done in the drying (fermenting) and rolling processes.

Green Tea is fired to stop fermentation shortly after it is picked. Green tea is classed as Basket Fired and Pan Fired when it is Japan Green. China Green is classed as Gunpowder, Imperial, Young Hyson, and Hyson. The Basket Fired variety is best as it is the result of a hand process which treats the tea gently. The best of the China Greens is **Gunpowder**, followed by **Young Hyson, Hyson,** and **Imperial**.

Oolong tea is allowed to oxidize for a few hours before it is fired.

Black tea oxidizes for many hours before it is fired. There are 2 kinds of black tea: China, and those from Sri Lank, India, Java, and Sumatra. The Tea Council of the U.S. grades black teas by Leaf Grades or Broken-Leaf Grades. These are **O.P. [Orange Pekoe]**, a pale tea; **P.E.K. [Pekoe]**, a medium colored tea; **S.O.U. [Souchong]**, a pale tea; **B.O.P. [Broken Orange Pekoe]**, a heavily colored tea; **B.P. [Broken Pekoe]**, a pale tea; **B.P.S. [Broken Pekoe Souchong]**, lighter than B.P.; **F.N.G.S. [Fannings]**, a heavily colored tea; **D. [Dust]**, strong. Teas are often marketed by the name of the area in which they were grown. **North China Congous** is a strong, full-bodied tea; **South China Congous** is a light tea; **Darjeeling** is generally thought to be the finest, most delicate tea; **Dovars** is a gentle tea; **Assam** is strong; **Trarancore** is another fine delicate tea, as is **Ceylon Black. Sumatra** and **Java Black** are heavier than **Darjeeling**, but lighter than the stronger teas.

POSTUM: A coffee-substitute product which is free of caffeine. **Pack:** Various size jars; individual packets.

BOLETUS [cepes]: A French mushroom. Market forms, dried or canned. Imported.

BOUQUET GARNI: Herbs held together in cheesecloth. Used in sauces, stews, soups, and stock. Consists of:

a few basil sprigs	1 marjoram sprig
1 bay leaf	3 parsley branches
1 celery rib top	1 tarragon leaf
1 kernel garlic	a few thyme sprigs

BOUILLON CUBES: Used to intensify flavor of soups and sauces. Beef flavor or chicken flavor. Usually contain salt. Quantity of beef or chicken flavor varies; buy according to flavor percentage. Packaged in tins of 12, 50, and 100 cubes.

BRABEN (fiddlehead): A fern. Fresh. Canned.

BREAD: Follow these guidelines:

STRAIGHT BREADS—Only flour, shortening, water, milk (or buttermilk), sugar, salt, and yeast are allowed.

NUT BREADS, RAISIN BREADS—Should have 50 percent by weight of the added product.

Additives: For softness, but tending to hold moisture, are used. White breads: Calcium propionate or Sodium propionate of 3.2 percent; other breads: 3.8 percent.

Quality: INTERIOR—good color, not crumbly, soft to the touch. EXTERIOR—even shape, even light brown, or typical color; no cuts or breaks.

Size: Varies from 1 lb. to 3 lb. loaves with slice size up to 4-1/2 in. square; slice thickness from 1/4 in. to 1/2 in.

BREAD CRUMBS: Crumbs of bread, fresh or browned, used in puddings, as a topping, or as a coating for foods before frying. Usually purchase in 10 lb. or 25 lb. cartons.

BREADFRUIT: A tropical fruit. Purchased fresh, ripe. Grown in the Caribbean. No grades.

CANTHARELLUS (Chanterelles): A mushroom. Canned. Imported.

CAPERS: Flower buds of a plant grown in the Mediterranean area. Pickled in salt and vinegar. Used as sauce flavoring, seasoning, and a condiment. **Sizes:** 2 oz., 4 oz., 6-1/2 oz., 9 oz., pint, 1/2 gal., gal.

CAROTTES: Very small Belgian or French carrots. Some at 350 + per No. 10 can. Domestic product graded according to Carrots, canned in chapter on "Produce."

CASSIA BUDS: Dried flower bud of Cinnamemum cassia. Used in mincemeat, stewed fruits, and in pickling.

CATSUP, TOMATO (7/31/53): Spiced sauce with tomatoes as the main ingredient. **Sizes:** 8 oz. bottle, 12 oz. bottle, 14 oz. bottle, No. 10 can, 1 gal. can.

Grades A and B: Color: Color is typical of tomato catsup made from well-ripened, red tomatoes which has been properly prepared and processed. Such color contains as much or more red than produced by spinning that specified Munsell cdn discs in the following combination: 65 percent of the area of Disc 1;

This device measures the flowing quality of catsup. High quality catsup should not be too thick or too thin. This is one of several devices used by USDA fruit and vegetable inspectors to help them enforce the standards for grades of processed fruits and vegetables.

21 percent of the area of Disc 2; 14 percent of the area of either Disc 3 or 4, or 7 percent of the area of Disc 3 and 7 percent of the area of Disc 4, whichever most nearly matches the reflectance of the tomato catsup. **Consistency:** Tomato catsup shows not more than a slight separation of free liquid when poured on a flat grading tray; is not excessively stiff; and flows not more than 9 centimeters in 30 seconds at 20 degrees Centigrade in the Bostwich Consistometer. **Defects:** Any defects present do not more than slightly affect the appearance or eating quality. **Flavor:** Good, distinct flavor characteristic of good quality ingredients. Such flavor is free from scorching or any objectionable flavor of any kind.

Grade C: Color: Color is typical of tomato catsup and contains as much or more red than that produced by spinning the specified Munsell cdn discs in the following combinations: 53 percent of the area of Disc 1; 28 percent of the area of Disc 2; 19 percent of the area of either Disc 3 or 4, or 9-1/2 percent of the area of Disc 3 and 9-1/2 percent of the area of Disc 4, whichever most nearly matches the reflectance of the tomato catsup. **Consistency:** Tomato catsup may show a noticeable, but not excessive, separation of free liquid when poured on a flat grading tray; is not excessively stiff and flows not more than 14 centimeters in 30 seconds at 20 degrees centigrade in the Bostwich consistometer. **Defects:** Any defects present may be noticeable but are not so large, so numerous, or of such contrasting color as to seriously affect the appearance or eating quality. **Flavor:** Flavor characteristic of the ingredients, in which there may be slight traces of undesirable flavor such as scorched, bitter, or astringent, but is free from objectionable or off-flavor of any kind.

Sstd: Fails to meet requirements.

TOMATO CATSUP

CANNED [8/31/53   52.2105]

Grades:	"A" or "FANCY" *	"B" or "EXTRA STAN-DARD"	"C" or "STAN-DARD"	"SUB-STAN-DARD"
Minimum Score:	85	85	70	Less than 70

NET WEIGHT: Not less than 90 percent of fill of container

*To be "A" grade it must have 33 percent solids.

CRANBERRY SAUCE

CANNED [3/19/51   52.951]

Grades:	"A" or "FANCY"	"C" or "STANDARD"	"D" or "SUB-STANDARD"
Minimum Score:	85	70	Less than 70

NET WEIGHT: Not less than 90 percent of capacity of container

DRY CEREALS, GRAINS, AND FLOURS

Wheat is the grain of common wheat, club wheat, and durum wheat which, before the removal of the dockage, consists of 50 percent or more of one or more wheats and not more than 10.0 percent of other grains for which standards have been established under the U.S. Grain Standards Act and which, after the removal of the dockage, contains 50 percent or more of whole kernels of one or more of these wheats.

Dockage is weed seeds, weed stems, chaff, straw, grain other than wheat, sand, dirt, and any other material other than wheat, which can be removed readily from the wheat by the use of appropriate sieves and cleaning devices; also underdeveloped, shriveled, and small pieces of wheat kernels removed in properly separating the material other than wheat and which cannot be recovered by properly rescreening or recleaning.

Foreign material is all matter other than wheat which is not separated from the wheat in the proper determination of dockage.

Other grains are rye, oats, corn, grain sorghum, barley, hull-less barley, flaxseed, emmer, spelt, einkorn, Polish wheat, poulard wheat, cultivated buckwheat, and soybeans.

Damaged kernels are kernels and pieces of kernels of wheat and other grains which are heat damaged, sprouted, frosted, badly ground damaged, badly weather damaged, moldy, diseased, or otherwise materially damaged.

WHEAT

Wheat is divided into the following seven classes: Hard Red Spring Wheat, Durum Wheat, Red Durum Wheat, Hard Red Winter Wheat, Soft Red Winter Wheat, White Wheat, and Mixed Wheat.

The class HARD RED SPRING WHEAT includes all

varieties of hard red spring wheat. This class is divided into the following three subclasses:

(a) **Dark Northern Spring Wheat:** Hard Red Spring Wheat with 75 percent or more of dark, hard, and vitreous kernels.

(b) **Northern Spring Wheat:** Hard Red Spring Wheat with 25.0 percent or more but less than 75 percent of dark, hard, and vitreous kernels.

(c) **Red Spring Wheat:** Hard Red Spring Wheat with less than 25.0 percent of dark, hard, and vitreous kernels.

The class DURUM WHEAT includes all varieties of white (amber) Durum Wheat. This class is divided into the following three subclasses:

(a) **Hard Amber Durum Wheat:** Durum Wheat with 75 percent or more of hard and vitreous kernels of amber color.

(b) **Amber Durum Wheat:** Durum Wheat with 60 percent or more but less than 75 percent of hard and vitreous kernels of amber color.

(c) **Durum Wheat:** Durum Wheat with less than 60 percent of hard and vitreous kernels of amber color.

The class RED DURUM WHEAT includes all varieties of of red durum wheat. There are no subclasses in this class.

The class HARD RED WINTER WHEAT includes all varieties of hard red winter wheat. This class is divided into the following three subclasses:

(a) **Dark Hard Winter Wheat:** Hard Red Winter Wheat with 75 percent or more of dark, hard, and vitreous kernels.

(b) **Hard Winter Wheat:** Hard Red Winter Wheat with 40 percent or more but less than 75 percent of dark, hard, and vitreous kernels.

(c) **Yellow Hard Winter Wheat:** Hard Red Winter Wheat with less than 40 percent of dark, hard, and vitreous kernels.

The class SOFT RED WINTER WHEAT includes all varieties of soft red winter wheat. There are no subclasses in this class.

The class WHITE WHEAT includes all varieties of white wheat. This class is divided into the following four subclasses:

(a) **Hard White Wheat:** White Wheat with 75 percent or more of hard kernels which may contain not more than 10.0 percent of wheat of the white club varieties.

(b) **Soft White Wheat:** White Wheat with less than 75 percent of hard kernels which may contain not more than 10.0 percent of wheat of the white club varieties.

(c) **White Club Wheat:** White Wheat consisting of wheat of the white club varieties which may contain not more than 10.0 percent of other white wheat.

(d) **Western White Wheat:** White Wheat containing more than 10.0 percent of wheat of the white club varieties and more than 10.0 percent of other white wheat.

The class MIXED WHEAT is any mixture of wheat which consists of one of the following:

(a) Two or more classes each of which constitutes more than 10.0 percent of the mixture; or

(b) One class that constitutes more than 10.0 percent and 2 or more other classes in combination that exceed 10.0 percent of the mixture; or

(c) Several classes none of which constitutes 10.0 percent or more of the mixture but which combined meet the definition for wheat.

Grades: Grades are the U.S. numerical grades, U.S. Sample grade, and special grades.

Mixed Wheat is graded according to the U.S. numerical and U.S. Sample grade requirements of the class of wheat which predominates in the mixture, except that the factor "wheat of other classes" is disregarded.

SPECIAL GRADES, SPECIAL GRADE REQUIREMENTS, AND SPECIAL GRADE DESIGNATIONS

(a) **Tough Wheat:** Wheat which contains more than 13.5 percent of moisture. Tough wheat is graded and designated according to the grade requirements of the standards applicable to such wheat if it were not tough, and there is added to and made a part of the grade designation the word "Tough."

(b) **Smutty Wheat:** Wheat which has an unmistakable odor of smut or which contains balls, portions of balls, or spores, of smut in a quantity equivalent to more than 14 balls of average size in 250 grams of wheat. Smutty wheat is graded and designated according to the grade requirements of the standards applicable to such wheat if it were not smutty; and

(i) In the case of smutty wheat which has an unmistakable odor of smut, or which contains balls, portions of balls, or spores, of smut, in excess of a quantity equal to 14 balls but not

GRADES AND GRADE REQUIREMENTS
WHEAT
[a] Grade and grade requirements for all classes of Wheat except Mixed Wheat

| Grade | Minimum Test Weight per Bushel | | Maximum Limits of— | | | | | | |
| | | | Defects | | | | | Wheat of other Classes[1] | |
	Hard Red Spring Wheat or White Club Wheat	All Other Classes and Sub-Classes	Heat-Damaged Kernels	Damaged Kernels [Total]	Foreign Material	Shrunken and Broken Kernels	Defects [Total]	Contrasting Classes	Wheat of Other Classes [Total]
	Pounds	*Pounds*	*Percent*	*Percent*	*Percent*	*Percent*	*Percent*	*Percent*	*Percent*
U.S. No. 1	58.0	60.0	0.1	2.0	0.5	3.0	3.0	1.0	3.0
U.S. No. 2	57.0	58.0	0.2	4.0	1.0	5.0	5.0	2.0	5.0
U.S. No. 3	55.0	56.0	0.5	7.0	2.0	8.0	8.0	3.0	10.0
U.S. No. 4	53.0	54.0	1.0	10.0	3.0	12.0	12.0	10.0	10.0
U.S. No. 5	50.0	51.0	3.0	15.0	5.0	20.0	20.0	10.0	10.0

U.S. Sample grade: U.S. Sample grade shall be wheat which does not meet the requirements for any of the grades from U.S. No. 1 to U.S. No. 5, inclusive; or which contains more than two crotalaria seeds (*Crotalaria spp.*) in 1,000 grams of grain, or contains castor beans (*Ricinus communis*), stones, broken glass, animal filth, an unknown foreign substance(s), or a commonly recognized harmful or toxic substance(s); or which is musty, sour, or heating; or which has any commercially objectionable foreign odor except of smut or garlic; or which contains a quantity of smut so great that any one or more of the grade requirements cannot be applied accurately; or which is otherwise of distinctly low quality.

1. Red Durum Wheat of any grade may contain not more than 10.0 percent of wheat of other classes.

in excess of a quantity equal to 30 balls of average size in 250 grams of wheat, there is added to and made a part of the grade designation the words "Light Smutty"; and

(ii) In the case of smutty wheat which contains balls, portions of balls, or spores, of smut, in excess of a quantity equal to 30 balls of average size in 250 grams of wheat, there is added to and made a part of the grade designation the word "Smutty."

(c) **Garlicky Wheat:** Wheat which contains 2 or more green garlic bulblets, or an equivalent quantity of dry or partly dry bulblets, in 1,000 grams of wheat. Garlicky wheat is graded and designated according to the grade requirements of the standards applicable to such wheat if it were not garlicky; and

(i) In the case of garlicky wheat which contains 2 or more but not more than 6 green garlic bulblets, or an equivalent quantity of dry or partly dry bulblets, in 1,000 grams of wheat,

there is added to and made a part of the grade designation the words "Lightly Garlicky"; and

(ii) In the case of garlicky wheat which contains more than 6 green garlic bulblets, or an equivalent quantity of dry or partly dry bulblets, in 1,000 grams of wheat, there is added to and made a part of the grade designation the word "Garlicky."

(d) **Weevily Wheat:** Wheat which is infested with live weevils or other insects injurious to stored grain. Weevily wheat is graded and designated according to the grade requirements of the standards applicable to such wheat if it were not weevily, and there is added to and made a part of the grade designation the word "Weevily."

(e) **Ergoty Wheat:** Wheat which contains more than 0.3 percent of ergot. Ergoty wheat is graded and designated according to the grade requirements of the standards applicable to such wheat if it were not ergoty, and there is added to and made a part of the grade designation the word "Ergoty."

(f) **Treated Wheat:** Wheat which has been scoured, limed, washed, sulfured, or treated in such a manner that the true quality is not reflected by either the U.S. numerical grade or the U.S. Sample grade designation alone. Treated wheat is graded and designated according to the grade requirements of the standards applicable to such wheat if it were not treated, and there shall be added to and made a part of the grade designation a statement indicating the kind of treatment.

(g) **Heavy Wheat:**

(i) Hard Red Spring Wheat of grade U.S. No. 1, U.S. No. 2, or U.S. No. 3 which has a test weight per bushel of 60 lb. or more, or

(ii) any other class of wheat of grade U.S. No. 1, U.S. No. 2, or U.S. No. 3 which has a test weight per bushel of 62 lb. or more. Heavy wheat is graded and designated according to the grade requirements of the standards applicable to such wheat if it were not heavy, and there is added to and made a part of the grade designation preceding the name of the class or subclass, as the case may be, the word "Heavy."

Grade Designations for Wheat: The grade designations for wheat include the letters "U.S."; the number of the grade or the words "Sample grade," as the case may be; the name of the applicable subclass, or in the case of Red Durum Wheat, Soft Red Winter Wheat, and Mixed Wheat, the name of the class; the name of each applicable special grade; and when applicable the word "dockage" together with the percentage thereof. In the case of Western White Wheat, the grade designation also includes, following the name of the subclass, the name and percentage of white club wheat and other white wheat in the mixture. In the case of Mixed Wheat, the grade designation also includes, following the name of the class, the name and percentage of Hard Red Spring, Durum, Red Durum, Hard Red Winter, Soft Red Winter, and White Wheat, if any, contained in the mixture.

Wheat Flours: The hard (spring) wheat flours are used for making breads and pastas. The flour that the operator buys depends upon the use to which it will be put. The rougher the handling the flour gets, the higher the protein value that the flour needs. Wheat is rolled and sifted many times, the flour

Grain inspectors with the Illinois Department of Agriculture fill bags with grain samples they have pulled from a barge on the Mississippi River. The grain will be carried with the inspectors by helicopter from the barge to a lab for analysis.

A grain grader for the USDA picks through a sample of grain to extract all foreign matter to determine the grade.

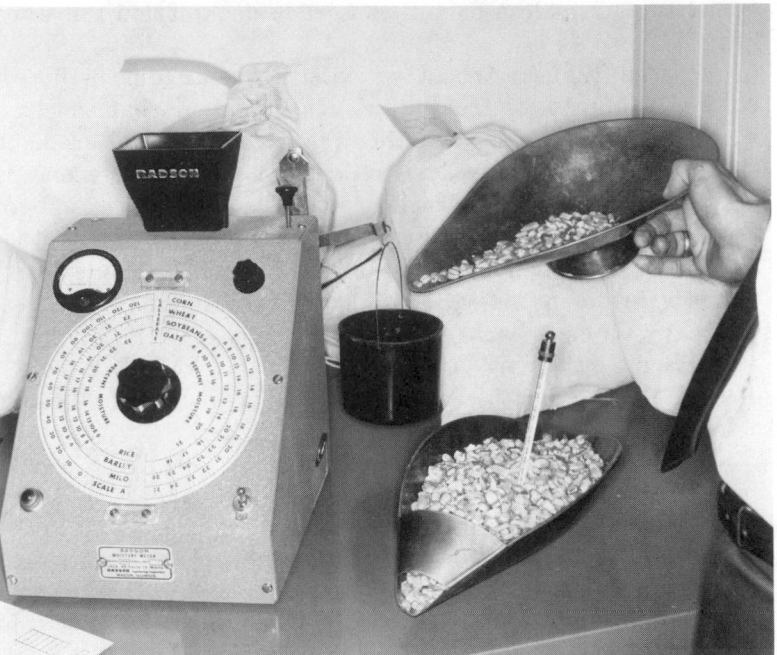

Special equipment, like this moisture tester that determines the moisture content of grain, and advanced mathematical practices help estimate production and yield in the objective yield surveys carried on by the Statistical Reporting Service of the USDA.

being separated each time until the stage is reached that is called a *patent*. The earlier the patent is reached, the higher the protein value of the wheat. The patents, in order of quality, are Extra Short (or Fancy), Short (or First), Medium, Long, and Straight. Besides the "Bran" and "Shorts" that are left in the milling of wheat, after the patent is out, there is a material called "clear." The best patent flours make a fancy clear flour. The characteristics of some flours are:

ALL-PURPOSE FLOUR—A mixture of hard and soft wheat flours.

CAKE FLOUR—Protein (gluten) of 8 percent.

DURUM FLOUR—Further refined to make pastas.

CLEAR FLOUR—Wheat meal left over when patent flour is made.

GRAHAM FLOUR—Contains the wheat germ and lots of the bran.

GLUTEN FLOUR—Has much of the starch removed. Ground gluten has virtually all the starch removed.

Here entomologist Geilen D. White takes a composite sample from grain, the surface of which has been treated with an experimental dust. Using a regular grain inspector's "trier," he obtains samples at different depths in the grain.

HARD FLOUR—Used for bread; high in gluten.

SELF-RISING FLOUR—A soft wheat flour with leavening added.

WHEAT GERM—Germ of the wheat usually marketed with bran added.

WHOLE WHEAT FLOUR—Straight wheat which has been ground into flour instead of being separated. Bran is added. Whole Wheat Flour with only a little bran is called "light."

Pastas are made from semolina, the inner part of durum wheat. Wheats other than durum make poor pastas and should be avoided.

Federal Standards:

13% maximum moisture

5-1/2% minimum egg solids if labeled "egg"

3.8% minimum milk solids if labeled "milk"

13% minimum protein

2% minimum, 5% maximum spinach or tomatoes if so labeled

1/2% to 2% egg white, bay leaf, celery, onions, and salt

There are several classes of pastas:

(a) ROPES OR STRINGS—**Spaghettini** (1/16 in. d.); **Spaghetti** (0.06 to 0.11 in. d.); **Vermicelli** (0.06 in. d. max.); **Fidellini.**

(b) TUBULAR—**Foratini** (3/32 in. d.); **Forati** (.125 in. d.); **Mezzarrelli** (5/32 in. d.); **Macaroni** (0.11 to 0.27 in. d.); **Zitoni** (1/2 in. d.); **Zifi, Perciatelli, Mezzani.**

(c) FLAT—**Lasagne** (1 to 2 in. w.); **Broad Noodles** (1/4 in. w., 0.03 in. thick); **Medium Noodles** (1/8 in. w., 0.033 in. thick); **Fine Noodles** (1/16 in. w., 0.035 in. thick); **Linguine, Fettucini.**

(d) TUBULAR, called ELBOWS—**Bonballati** (3/8 in. d.); **Ditali lisci** (1/4 in. to 7/10 in. d.); **Rigatoni** (9/16 in. d.); **Tochetti** (1/8 in. to 5/32 in. d.).

(e) ENVELOPES—**Ravioli, Manicotti, Canelloni.**

(f) FANCIES—In all shapes but generally small sizes. Made to look like stars, letters, shells, etc.

Good pastas are hard and yellow in color, almost translucent, and should break evenly.

BARLEY

Used by the foodservice operator principally in soups and as an entree accompaniment. Barley is also used to make malt.

PEARL—Has bran removed (brown)

DOT—Husk removed (white)

SCOTCH—Ground grains (brown)

24/1 lb., 10 lb., 25 lb., 100 lb. packs

BUCKWHEAT

The seed of the plant is ground into a flour which varies from brown to white in color with the amount of bran.

OATS

The endosperm of oats which is used to make oatmeal by cutting into small pieces and subjecting it to a steam treatment and dyeing.

STEEL-CUT—Very small pieces

STONE-GROUND—Buhr, old-fashioned or stone

QUICK-COOKING—Small pieces which have had extra steam treatment

QUALITY CHECKS—No off-flavors or odors. Off-white color, even.

RYE

The grain is ground to make rye meal (rye graham) for pumpernickel bread. A coarse flour. Rye flour—for rye bread. A fine flour which is mixed with wheat flour for baking. **Grades:** White, medium, dark.

SOY

Soybeans ground into a flour or a meal which is used with other products to enhance protein values.

RICE

Varieties:

PEARL—**American** and **California**

SHORT GRAIN—**Calora, Magnolia, Zenith**

MEDIUM GRAIN—**Blue Rose, Early Prolific**

LONG GRAIN—**Blue Bonnet, Edith, Fortuna, Lady Wright, Rexora**

WHITE—All bran removed

UNDERMILLED—Most bran removed

BROWN—Unpolished, bran on

CONVERTED—Steamed, dried, enriched

INSTANT—Cooked, dried

BEST VARIETIES—Long grain in Rexora or Calora. Buy Converted rice. **Grades:** WHITE RICE—U.S. No. 1, U.S. No. 2, U.S. No. 3, U.S. No. 4, U.S. No. 5, Sample Grade. BROWN RICE—U.S. No. 1, U.S. No. 2, U.S. No. 3, U.S. No. 4. Buy U.S. No. 1 or U.S. No. 2 as the defects in the lower grades are too great. Rice flour is made from rice and is used as a modified starch in some recipes.

WILD RICE

Not really rice but a grass seed (Zizania aquatica). **Varieties:** Short, small, large.

STYLES OF MACARONI

1 VERMICELLI

2 THIN SPAGHETTI

3 SPAGHETTI

5 PERCIATELLI

6 MACCARONCELLI

11 LINGUINE

11a LINGUINE FINI

13 FETTUCCINI

18 ALPHABETS

25 ELBOW

20 MACARONI FOR SOUP
(ACINI DI PEPE)

25 SQUARE ELBOW

21 MINI-MAC
(TUBETTINI)

24 CHILI-MAC
(DITALINI)

46 ORZO
(RICE MACARONI)

29 CUT MACARONI

30 READY-CUT MACARONI
(MEZZANI)

22 TUBETTI

27 DITALI

31 READY-CUT MACARONI WITH LINES
(MEZZANI WITH LINES)

32 ZITI

34 ZITI WITH LINES

36 RIGATONI

39 SMALL SHELLS

40 MEDIUM SHELLS

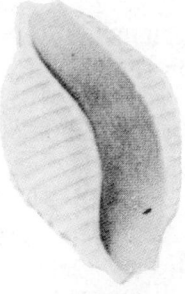

41 LARGE SHELLS

Source: Frosty Acres Buyers Guide—The Frozen Food Forum, Inc., Atlanta, Ga.

CORN

See Cornmeal, Cornstarch, Corn Flour, Hominy, Waxy Maize Starch on following pages.

TAPIOCA

Cassava root ground into a flour and processed into pellets. Used as a starch. **Varieties:** PEARL, SMALL PEARL, FLAKES (quick cooking), GRANULATED (minute, very quick cooking).

FLAKES [BRAN FLAKES, CORNFLAKES, WHEAT FLAKES]

Made from a paste of the parent product which is flaked and toasted. Available in bulk packages, but usually purchased in cases of 48, 50, or 100 individual serving packages or bowls.

PUFFS [PUFFED CORN, PUFFED RICE, PUFFED WHEAT

Made by cooking the parent product and then blowing or "shooting" the product into the air to force internal expansion, much like popcorn expansion. Purchased like flakes.

CHAGOTE: A South American squash.

CHESTNUTS [MARRONS]: MARRONS AU SIROP—Whole or pieces, used in sweet foods. MARRON ENTIERS AU NATUREL—Whole, in water, for use as a vegetable or in stuffing. PUREE DE MARRONS AU NATUREL—Unsweetened puree used with other vegetables. CREME DE MARRONS—Sweetened puree.

CHILI SAUCE, Canned [10/20/53]: Tomato sauce flavored with onions, red chili peppers, spices, sugar, and vinegar. **Sizes:** 8 oz. bottle, 12 oz. bottle, 14 oz. bottle, No. 10 can, 1 gal. can.

Grade A: Color: Color of the chili sauce is bright; the color of the tomato ingredient is predominant and characteristic of properly prepared, well-ripened, properly processed tomatoes, and the added seasoning ingredients do not materially detract from the appearance of the product. **Consistency:** Chili sauce is heavy-bodied and when emptied from the container to a flat surface forms a moderately mounded mass and shows not more than a slight separation of free liquid at the edges of the mass. **Character:** Product does not have a finely communited appearance, and the onion, celery, pickle relish, and other similar ingredients are tender, reasonably firm, and crisp in texture. **Defects:** Do not more than slightly affect the appearance or eating quality of the product. **Flavor:** A good, distinct flavor characteristic of chili sauce properly prepared from good quality ingredients, and free from scorching or any objectionable flavor of any kind.

Grade C: Color of the chili sauce may be slightly dull but not off-color; the color of the tomato ingredient is characteristic of properly prepared, fairly well-ripened, properly processed tomatoes, and the added seasoning ingredients do not seriously detract from appearance. **Consistency:** Chili sauce, when emptied from the container to a flat surface, may tend to level itself, or may show a moderate separation of free liquid at the edges of the mass, but is not excessively stiff or liquid. **Character:** Product may be finely comminuted, and the other vegetable ingredients may be only fairly tender. **Defects:** Defects may be noticeable but are not so large, so numerous, or so prominent as to seriously affect the appearance or eating quality of the product. **Flavor:** May be lacking in good characteristic flavor, but is free from objectionable or off-flavors of any kind.

CHILI SAUCE

CANNED [10/20/53   52.2191]

Grades:	"A" or "FANCY"	"C" or "STANDARD"	"SUB-STANDARD"
Minimum Score:	85	70	Less than 70

NET WEIGHT: Not less than 90 percent of volume of container

COCOA: [See Beverages.]

CHOCOLATE LIQUOR [See also, Cocoa]: BITTER—Ground, roasted cocoa beans. 45 to 50 percent cocoa butter. Generally 10 lb. cakes. In small cakes is called Premium Chocolate. SWEET—Bitter chocolate liquor with sugar added. Generally 10 lb. cakes. MILK CHOCOLATE—Sweet chocolate with a minimum of 12 percent whole milk solids.

CHOCOLATE SYRUP: Sweet syrup made with cocoa or chocolate, corn syrup, salt, sugar, and vanilla. **Pack:** Usually 6/No. 10 or in gallons.

CHUTNEY: Indian condiment made with fruits, spices, sugar, and vinegar. Served with cold meat. Packed in quarts.

COCONUT [See also Produce section]: Fruit of the coconut

This licensed inspector with the New Orleans Board of Trade is dividing a corn sample into a working sample. When the job of grading is completed, a prospective buyer will know the quality of the grain. He will bid accordingly.

palm. Shredded or grated and used in confectionery and baking. Available chip, sliced, shred, thread, or dessicated; sweetened or unsweetened; domestic or imported. **Packs:** 4 oz., 8 oz., 10 oz., 1 lb., 5 lb., 10 lb.

COFFEE: [See Beverages]

CORN FLOUR: Made from cornmeal.

CORNMEAL: Ground corn. **Varieties:** WHITE or YELLOW. **Grind:** Stone or machine; coarse or fine. Specify whether or not the bran and germ are included. **Pack:** 2 lb., 5 lb., 10 lb., 100 lb.

CORNSTARCH: A starch made from corn which is used to thicken food items. Gels at about 170°F.

CRACKERS: Crackers are baked from a dough that is made of flour, sugar, salt, and shortening. **Specifications:**

    2 in. by 2 in.—1/4 in. thick; 190 per lb.
    2 in. by 2 in.—3/16 in. thick; 120 per lb.
    2 in. by 1-1/3 in.—1/4 in. thick; 180 per lb.
    2 in. by 1-1/3 in.—3/16 in. thick; 235 per lb.

Saltines: 1 percent salt topping by weight; 5 percent maximum water; 10 percent minimum fat.

Graham: 30 percent whole wheat flour; 1/4 in. to 3/8 in. thick; 6 percent maximum water; 10 percent minimum fat.

Other varieties such as **Rye Crisp, Ritz, Oyster, Zwieback** are generally marketed by brand names and must be so specified according to the buyer's preference.

CRACKER CRUMBS AND CRACKER MEAL: Broken or ground crackers of various types. Packed in 1 lb., 5 lb., and 10 lb. containers.

CREAM OF TARTAR: Acid salt used in baking powders and self-rising flour. Used in icings. Found in wine vats. **Packs:** Oz., lb.

DRESSINGS

SALAD DRESSING: An emulsified, semisolid food prepared from edible vegetable oils, acidifying ingredients, and 1 or more egg-containing ingredients, and a cooked starchy paste prepared with food grade starches. May be seasoned or flavored with 1 or more of the following ingredients: salt, sugar, mustard, paprika, other spice or spice oil, except that no turmeric or saffron is used and no spice oil or spice extract is used which imparts to the salad dressing a color simulating the color imparted by egg yolk. Contains not less than 30 percent by weight of vegetable salad oil and not less than 4 percent by weight of liquid egg yolk.

MAYONNAISE: An emulsified, semisolid food prepared from edible vegetable oil, acidifying ingredients, and 1 or more of egg yolk-containing ingredients, and flavored with salt, sugar, spices, and any suitable harmless food flavoring other than imitations. Contains not less than 65 percent by weight of vegetable oil.

SANDWICH SPREAD: A preparation made from either mayonnaise or salad dressing base usually with the addition of pickle relish and may or may not contain cooked starch paste.

REFRIGERATED DRESSING: An emulsified, semisolid food of a perishable nature which requires refrigerated temperatures at all times. May contain ingredients such as blue cheese, Roquefort cheese, sour cream, pickle relish in combination with mayonnaise and salad dressing.

SPOON-TYPE: All other emulsified, semisolid types prepared with either a mayonnaise or salad dressing base in combination with other suitable food grade ingredients.

FRENCH DRESSING: A separable, liquid food or emulsified, viscous, fluid food prepared from vegetable oil, vinegar or a mixture of vinegar, and optional acidifying ingredient citric acid. May be seasoned or flavored with 1 or more of the following ingredients: Salt, sugar, mustard, paprika, spice or spice oils, monosodium glutamate, and any suitable harmless food seasoning other than imitations, tomato paste or tomato puree, emulsifying ingredients. Contains not less than 35 percent by weight of vegetable oil.

OIL AND VINEGAR: A separable, clear, liquid food meeting the requirements of a French type dressing, not emulsified or containing paprika, tomato paste, or tomato puree. Includes Italian garlic, herb and spice liquid dressing.

CHEESE: An emulsified, pourable, French dressing with cheese and egg yolk added.

LOW CALORIE AND DIETETIC: A separable, liquid food which may or may not be emulsified. Contains selected ingredients and is normally a product having low caloric content.

POURABLE-TYPE: All other separable, liquid food containing selected ingredients which may or may not be emulsified with a French type dressing base.

FATS AND OILS[1]

Crude fats and oils, as they are obtained from vegetable or animal sources, contain varying but relatively small amounts of naturally occurring, nonglyceride materials. Many of these substances such as free fatty acids, phosphatides, mucilagenous substances, and resins are undesirable elements in that they contribute color, flavor, odor, instability, foaming, and other unwanted characteristics to the fat. These materials are removed through a series of processing steps referred to as "refining, bleaching, and deodorization."

It should be pointed out, however, that not all of the non-glyceride materials are undesirable elements. *Tocopherols*, for example, perform the important function of protecting the oils from oxidation and provide vitamin E. Processing is usually carried out in such a way as to encourage retention of these substances.

Hydrogenation is frequently employed to improve the keeping qualities of fats and oils and to provide increased usefulness by imparting a semisolid consistency to the fat for many food applications.

It is generally agreed by most nutritionists and food technologists that the modern processing of edible fat and oils is the single factor most responsible for upgrading the quality of the fat consumed in the U.S. diet today.

The term *refining* generally refers to any purifying treatment that is intended to remove free fatty acids, phosphatides, proteinaceous and mucilagenous substances, or other gross impurities from the fat or oil.

By far the most important and widespread method of refining is by treatment of the fat or oil with an alkali—usually caustic soda or soda ash. This results in almost complete removal of free fatty acids through their conversion into oil-insoluble soaps.

The term *bleaching* refers to the treatment that is given to remove color producing substances and to further purify the fat or oil. It is normally accomplished after the oil has been refined.

The usual method of bleaching is by adsorption of the color producing substances on an adsorbent material. Bleaching earth or clay, sometimes referred to as fuller's or diatomaceous earth, is the adsorbent material that has been used most extensively. These substances consist primarily of hydrated aluminum silicate. Activated carbon is also used as a bleaching adsorbent to a limited extent.

Deodorization is the treatment of fats and oils for the purpose of removing trace constituents that give rise to undesirable flavors and odors. This is normally accomplished after refining and bleaching.

The deodorization of fats and oils is simply a removal of the

1. *Food Fats and Oils*, Technical Committee of Shortening and Edible Oils, Inc., Institute of Shortening and Edible Oils, Inc., Washington, D.C. 20006, 1968.

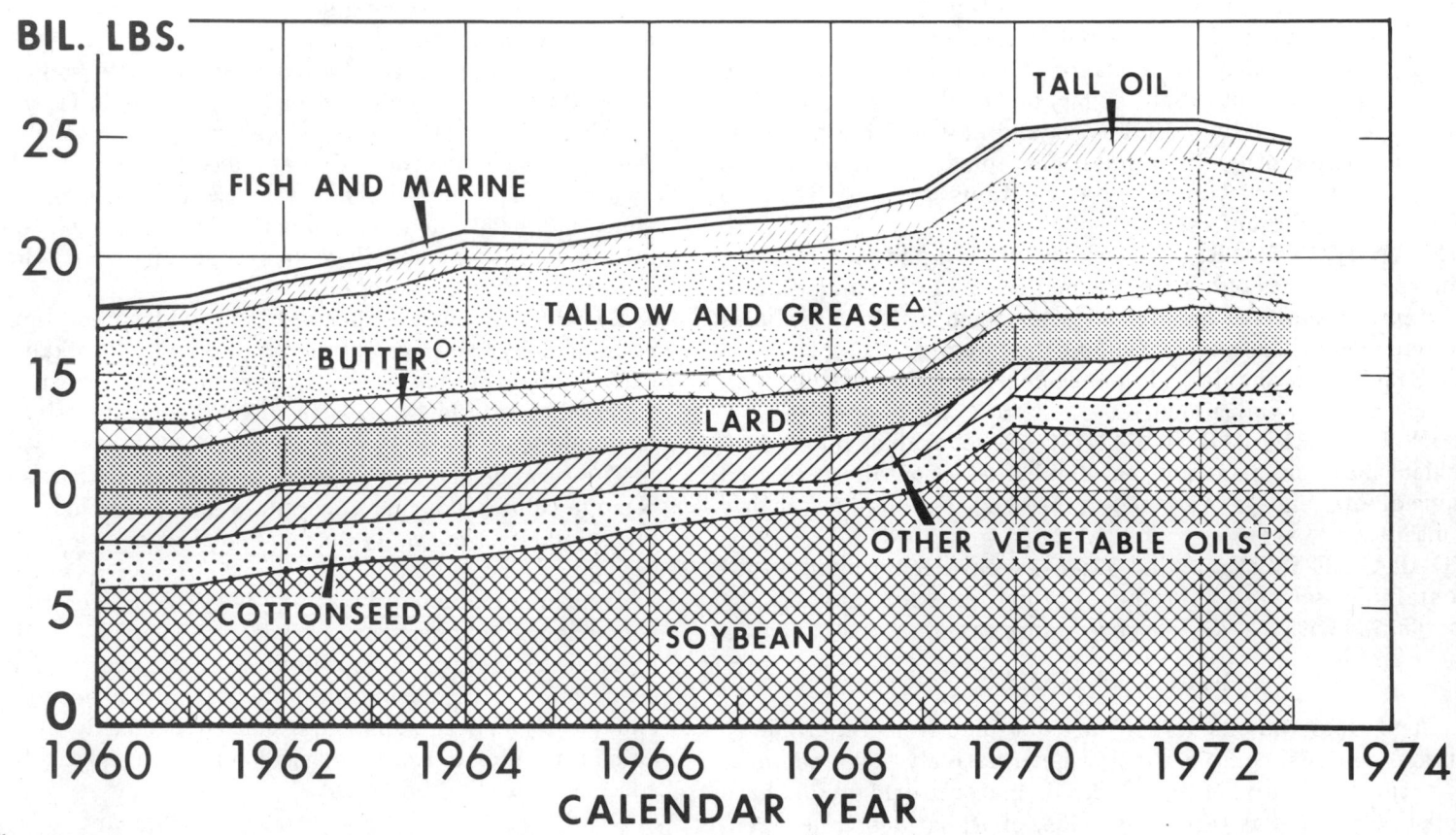

U.S. PRODUCTION OF FATS AND OILS*

(From Domestic and Imported Materials)

BIL. LBS.

TALL OIL

FISH AND MARINE

TALLOW AND GREASE△

BUTTER○

LARD

OTHER VEGETABLE OILS□

COTTONSEED

SOYBEAN

CALENDAR YEAR

* INCLUDES OIL EQUIVALENT OF EXPORTED DOMESTIC OILSEEDS.   □INCLUDES CORN, OLIVE, PEANUT, SAFFLOWER,
COCONUT, CASTOR, LINSEED, AND TUNG OILS.   ○ FAT CONTENT.   △ BOTH EDIBLE AND INEDIBLE KINDS.

USDA

NEG. ERS 602 - 74 (9)

relatively volatile components from the fat or oil using live steam. This is feasible because of the great differences in volatility between the substances that give flavors and odors to the fats and oils and the triglycerides.

Normally, deodorization is carried out under reduced pressures to facilitate the removal of the volatile substances, to avoid undue hydrolysis of the fat, and to make the most efficient use of the steam.

Deodorization, as it is usually accomplished by the industry, does not have any significant effect upon the fatty acid composition of the fat or oil. In the case of vegetable oils, most of the tocopherols remain in the finished oils after deodorization.

Hydrogenation is the process by which hydrogen is added directly to points of unsaturation in the fatty acids. Hydrogenation of fats has developed as a result of the need (1) to convert liquid oils to the semisolid form for greater utility in certain food uses, and (2) to increase the stability of the fat or oil to oxidative rancidity.

In the process of hydrogenation, oil is treated with hydrogen gas at a suitable temperature and pressure in the presence of a catalyst. The catalyst is frequently finely divided nickel which is, of course, removed from the food after the hydrogenation processing is completed. The hydrogenation process is easily controlled and can be stopped at any desired point. As hydrogenation progresses there is a gradual increase in the melting point of the fat or oil. If the hydrogenation of cottonseed or soybean oil, for example, is stopped after only a small amount of hydrogenation has taken place, the oils remain liquid. More hydrogenation produces soft, but solid appearing fats which still contain appreciable amounts of polyunsaturated fatty acids. This degree of hydrogenation is frequently employed in the preparation of vegetable oils for shortening and margarine. However, if hydrogenation is continued considerably beyond this point, a fat that is too hard to produce an acceptable shortening results. If an oil were completely hydrogenated the unsaturated double bonds would be entirely eliminated, and the resulting product would be a hard, brittle solid at room temperature, composed entirely of saturated triglycerides.

The hydrogenation conditions can be varied by the manufacturer to meet physical and chemical characteristics desired in the finished product. This is achieved through the selection of the proper temperature, pressure, time, catalyst, and starting oils. Both positional and geometric isomers are formed to some extent during hydrogenation, the amount depending on the conditions chosen.

WHAT HAPPENS AS YOU FRY?[1]

When fresh oil is heated in a deep fat fryer and the frying operation begins, 3 general chemical reactions occur simultaneously.

1. HYDROLYSIS—This is the reaction of the oil with moisture wherein the fatty acids are separated from the glycerol-forming free fatty acids. This change, when analyzed, is expressed as the percentage of free fatty acids.

A fresh oil will have a free fatty acids level of about 0.05 percent or less, but during the course of frying this value may go as high as 5 percent, if the oil is badly abused and broken down. Usually a value of 1 percent free fatty acids is considered maximum for most frying operations.

The smoke point of a fresh oil is usually in excess of 425°F. but as the free fatty acids rise, the smoke point correspondingly goes down so that at 0.8 percent free fatty acids, the smoke point is about 325°F.

Metals containing copper will cause an appreciable increase in the percentage of free fatty acids. Drip-back from the exhaust system will also cause increases in fatty acids.

2. OXIDATION—Frying oils have a bland flavor, but upon heating and frying become less bland and develop burned, scorched, or off-flavors through abuse.

During the frying operation, the surface of the oil is protected by a blanket of steam arising from the foods being fried. During slack periods, air comes in contact with the surface of the oil causing deterioration of the oil by oxidation. Reducing the temperature of the oil to 150° to 200°F. when it is not being used will reduce the rate of oxidation.

Aeration of the oil by allowing a pump to pull air or allowing the oil to cascade from one area to another results in rapid

---

1. *Frying Facts From Kraft*, Kraft Foods, Chicago, Illinois.

oxidation. It is best to have the oil enter the fryer or holding tank near the bottom to minimize the aeration. Holding tanks should be designed, if possible, to be vertical with a small surface area rather than horizontal or flat with a large surface area. Light catalyzes the development of off-flavors in oil and should be excluded wherever practical.

3. POLYMERIZATION—The union of 2 or more molecules of oil to form a larger molecule is known as polymerization. Thermal polymers cannot be detected by odor or flavor as can oxidative polymers. The decrease in iodine number, a measure of unsaturation or double bond, is an indication of polymer formation.

Polymer formations are visible on frying equipment that is not properly cleaned. This polymerized material should be removed at frequent intervals and the proper technique used in filtering the oil to remove as many of these polymers as possible.

PRODUCTS PREPARED FROM FATS AND OILS[1]

A wide variety of products based on edible fats and oils is offered the consuming public. Shortening, margarines, butter, salad and cooking oils, and other specialty salad dressings are some of the widely available products that are either based entirely on fats and oils or contain fat or oil as a principal ingredient. Many of these products are also sold in commercial quantities to food processors, bakeries, restaurants, and institutions.

SALAD AND COOKING OILS: Salad and cooking oils are prepared from vegetable oils that are usually refined, bleached, deodorized, and sometimes lightly hydrogenated. Cottonseed, corn, and soybean are the principal oils sold in this form, although peanut, safflower, and olive oils are also used. Due to the presence of substantial quantities of linolenic acid naturally occurring in soybean oil, it is frequently desirable to lightly hydrogenate this oil when it is to be used as a salad and cooking oil.

The fatty acid composition and iodine value of the principal vegetable oils used for food purposes in the U.S. are given in Table I.

TABLE I—TYPICAL FATTY ACID COMPOSITION AND IODINE VALUE OF SOME VEGETABLE OILS

Vegetable Oil	% of Total Fatty Acids				
	Unsaturated Fatty Acids			Saturated Fatty Acids	Iodine Value
	Oleic	Linoleic	Linolenic		
Soybean oil	24	54	7	15	132
Cottonseed oil	22	52	tr	26	110
Corn oil	29	56	tr-1	15	126
Peanut oil	49	30	tr	21	95
Olive oil	73	12	tr	15	85
Safflower oil	14	75	tr-1	10	144

SHORTENINGS: Shortenings are fats used in the preparation of many foods. Because they impart a "short" or tender quality to baked goods, they are called shortenings. For many years, lard and other animal fats were the principal edible fats used in this country, but during the last third of the 19th century large quantities of cottonseed oil became available as a by-product from the growing cotton.

The first semi-solid shortenings using vegetable oil were prepared by blending liquid cottonseed oil with certain animal fats. These were referred to as "compound" shortenings.

The introduction of the hydrogenation process in this country, in the early 1900s, initiated a new era in the manufacture of shortening. For the first time semi-solid shortenings could be prepared entirely from vegetable oils, and shortening manufacturers were no longer restricted by the availability of animal fats.

Many types of vegetable oils, including soybean, cottonseed, corn, and others, are now used in shortening products. Soybeans, not grown to any appreciable extent in this country until after 1930, are now by far our most important source of oil.

1. Technical Committee of Shortening and Edible Oils, Inc., *op. cit.*

Hydrogenated shortenings may be made from a single hydrogenated fat, but they are usually made from blends of 2 or more hydrogenated fats. The conditions and extent of hydrogenation may be varied for each to achieve the characteristics desired. Thus, in the manufacture of hydrogenated shortenings, considerable flexibility is possible, providing a wide choice of finished product characteristics.

Until 1961, most hydrogenated vegetable shortenings were processed under conditions that substantially reduced the polyunsaturate content of the fats to levels ranging from 5 to 12 percent and with iodine values ranging from 65 to 75. These products had excellent consumer acceptance and were noted for their high degree of stability.

Most manufacturers of vegetable shortenings are now producing these products with substantially higher levels of polyunsaturated fatty acids, in response to research findings which suggest the advisability of a greater intake of these fatty acids. These shortenings contain 22 to 33 percent polyunsaturated fatty acids and have iodine values with a range of 85 to 95. Some medical workers have referred to these products as "special" shortenings because, in addition to their use in normal diets, they are also suitable for use in "special" diets where an increased level of linoleic acid is desired.

Lard and other animal fats and mixtures of animal and vegetable fats are also used in shortening. Mixtures of animal and vegetable fats are frequently hydrogenated to some extent to obtain the physical characteristics desired. Lard is used extensively in some commercial applications such as pastry and bread.

In recent years, some shortening manufacturers have developed and marketed liquid shortening products that are based upon liquid or lightly hydrogenated liquid vegetable oils. These products have polyunsaturated fatty acid contents ranging from 30 to 50 percent and iodine values ranging from 95 to 125. These products have also had usage in some commercial bread and other baking applications.

MARGARINE: Margarines are fatty foods prepared by blending fats and oils with other ingredients such as milk solids, salt, flavoring materials, and vitamins A and D. By federal regulation, margarine must contain at least 80 percent fat. The fats used in margarines may be of either animal or vegetable origin although vegetable oils are by far the most widely used.

The fats may be prepared from single hydrogenated fats, from 2 or more hydrogenated fats or from a blend of hydrogenated fat and an unhydrogenated oil. Many manufacturers of margarines are now producing these products with substantially higher levels of polyunsaturated fatty acids, in response to medical research findings which suggest the advisability of higher levels of these fatty acids in the diet. These margarines contain fats having 22 to 60 percent polyunsaturated fatty acids and iodine values ranging from 92 to 130. In contrast, regular margarines contain 10 to 20 percent polyunsaturated fatty acids and have iodine values from 78 to 90. Some medical workers have referred to these products high in polyunsaturated fatty acids as "special" margarines because, in addition to their use in normal diets, they are also suitable for use in special diets where an increased level of linoleic acid is desired.

Table II gives the range in fatty acid composition and iodine value for the various types of margarine products made from vegetable oils.

TABLE II—FATTY ACID COMPOSITION AND IODINE VALUE OF FAT AND OILS IN MARGARINE PRODUCTS

| Type Margarine | % of Total Fatty Acids | | | | |
| | Unsaturated Fatty Acids | | | Saturated Fatty Acids | Iodine Value |
	Monoenoic	Dienoic	Trienoic		
Vegetable margarine —regular	42 to 63	10 to 20	0 to 0.5	16 to 25	78 to 90
Vegetable margarine —special	20 to 57	22 to 60	0 to 0.5	13 to 30	92 to 130

Although fried foods are generally cooked at 375°F. or less, it is important to specify a frying oil with a smoking point of no less than 426°F. Hydrogenated vegetable shortenings, peanut oil, and soybean oils meet this standard. Corn oil and animal fats smoke at lower temperatures. Some fats and oils are:

CORN OIL: Refined oil from corn germ. Used in salad oils and for deep frying. High smoking point.

COTTONSEED OIL: Refined oil from cottonseed. Used in making margarine, salad oils, and vegetable cooking fats. High smoking point.

HYDROGENATED FATS: Vegetable oils, usually cottonseed oil, solidified by hydrogen. Used as shortening. Smoking point is 440° to 460°F.

LARD: Melted pig fat. Best is from the abdomen or around the kidneys. The highest grade is kettle-rendered, leaf lard. Used for frying and baking. Should be firm when cold. Kettle-Rendered Lard: From back and leaf fat. Prime Stream Lard: From fats taken when preparing cuts for market. Most of lard.

OLIVE OIL: VIRGIN OLIVE OIL—Taken from ripe olives under low pressure.

SECOND GRADE OLIVE OIL—Most olive oil. Taken under pressure from remaining pulp after first press.

THIRD GRADE OLIVE OIL: Press cake remaining from second pressing is reheated in water and then pressed.

BLEACHED OLIVE OIL—Dark oil bleached to resemble better grade oils.

CLOUDY OLIVE OIL—May become thick and white when stored in refrigerator. Will melt if kept at room temperature.

FRENCH OLIVE OIL—Best. Fruity taste and golden color.

Used in mayonnaise, salad dressings, batters, marinades, and for frying foods.

Grade A: Color: Typical greenish to light yellow color. **Free Fatty Acid Content:** Not more than 1.4 percent calculated as oleic acid. **Defects:** Entirely free from cloudiness at 60°F. due to stearin, and from sediment. **Odor:** Has a typical olive oil odor and is practically free from off-odors of any kind. **Flavor:** Has a typical olive oil flavor and is practically free from off-flavors of any kind.

Grade B: Color: Typical greenish to light yellow color. **Free**

Fatty Acid Content: Between 1.4 percent and 2.5 percent, calculated as oleic acid. **Defects:** Reasonably free from cloudiness at 60°F. due to stearin, and from sediment; and no water or other liquid immiscible with the olive oil is present. **Odor:** Has a typical olive oil odor and is reasonably free from off-odors of any kind. **Flavor:** Has a typical olive oil flavor and is reasonably free from off-flavors of any kind.

Grade C: Color: Typical greenish to light yellow color. **Free Fatty Acid Content:** Between 2.5 percent and 3.0 percent calculated as oleic acid. **Defects:** May have cloudiness at 60°F. due to stearin and may have sediment, but they may not impair the quality of the product; and no water or other liquid immiscible with the olive oil may be present. **Odor:** Has a typical olive oil odor and is fairly free from off-odors of any kind. **Flavor:** Has a typical olive oil flavor and is fairly free from off-flavors of any kind.

Sstd: Fails to meet requirements.

OLIVE OIL

CANNED [3/22/48   52.1531]

Grades:	"A" or "FANCY"	"B" or "CHOICE"	"C" or "STAN-DARD"	"D" or "SUB-STAN-DARD"
Minimum Score:	90	80	70	Less than 70

NET WEIGHT: As full as practical

PEANUT OIL: Oil taken from peanuts and used in cooking and salad dressings.

SUET: Fat taken from around the kidneys and loins of sheep and bullocks. Bought in lumps or shreds. Used in mincemeat, steamed puddings, stuffings, and suet-crust pastry. Store in air-tight containers in refrigerator.

FILE GUMBO: Powdered sassafras leaves. Used in soups. **Pack:** Oz.; lb.

FINES HERBES: 1 spray chervil, 1 chive, 1 leek, 1 tsp. marjoram, 1 small onion, 2 parsley sprays, and 2 scallions mixed together. Used in stuffings, butter sauce for fish and omelets.

FLAGEOLETS: A very small bean which is used in fancy garnish work. Usually imported. Canned, various sizes.

FLAVORINGS AND EXTRACTS

Imitation: Synthetic chemical compounds which approximate the natural flavors extracted as oils from fruits and nuts. Available in oz., pints, quarts, gallons. **Natural:** The oils extracted from fruits and nuts (bark, leaves, sap, roots too) and emulsified (oil) or mixed with alcohol or water. **Strength:** Specify either 5:100 or 8:100 ratio of natural oil to the solvent (alcohol, water).

LEMON: Natural: 90 percent terpenes; 5 percent aldehyde, 5 percent alcohol esters. Pure: 5 percent lemon oil; 80 percent ethyl alcohol.

VANILLA: Pure: Specify Mexican, Bourbon, or Tahiti beans in that order of quality. Federal standards demand 10 g. soluble matter per 100 cc in extract. Pure vanilla is the best buy. Imitation: An artificial vanilla made from the oil of cloves.

Other extracts and flavorings available include: **almond, walnut, maple, clove, cinnamon, anise, tonka, peppermint, mint, spearmint, wintergreen, cheng, banana, orange, strawberry, raspberry, pineapple.**

FLOUR: [See Dry Cereals, Grains, and Flours]

FONDS D'ARTICHAUTS: Artichoke bottoms. Imported. Various can sizes. Not graded.

FRUIT JELLY*

CANNED [1/2/48   52.1081]

Grades:	"A" or "FANCY"	"B" or "CHOICE"	"SUB-STANDARD"
Minimum Score:	85	70	Less than 70

NET WEIGHT: Less than 90 percent of capacity of containers

*See Produce

FRUIT PRESERVES [OR JAMS]*

CANNED [10/29/74   52.1111]

Grades:	"A" or "FANCY"	"B" or "CHOICE"	"SUB-STANDARD"
Minimum Score:	85	70	Less than 70

NET WEIGHT: Not less than 90 percent of capacity of containers

*See Produce

FRUIT BUTTERS [3/20/52]: Identity: Smooth, semi-solid foods made from a mixture of not less than 5 parts of 1 or any combination of 2, 3, 4, or 5 of the optional fruit ingredients to each 2 parts of an optional saccharine ingredient, except a saccharine ingredient is not needed when fruit juice of at least 1/2 the weight of the optional ingredient is used. Mixtures may be seasoned with spice, flavoring, vinegar, lemon or lime juice, or citric, lactic, malic, or tartaric acid, and contain fruit juice, or sorbic acid, sodium sorbate, or potassium sorbate so long as the total of the last 3 ingredients does not exceed 0.1 percent of the finished food. Soluble solids content may not be less than 43 percent.

The optional fruit ingredients are prepared by cooking 1 of the following fresh, frozen, canned, and/or dried mature fruits, with or without added water, and screening out skins, seeds, pits, and cores: apple, apricot, grape, peach, pear, plum, prune, or quince. Optional saccharine ingredients are sugar, invert sugar syrup, brown sugar, invert brown sugar syrup, honey, dextrose, and 1 of the above-mentioned ingredients (except honey) and any combination of corn syrup, dried corn syrup, glucose syrup, or dried glucose syrup with 1 of the above mentioned ingredients (except honey). When the fruit butter is made from 1 fruit ingredient, the name is "Butter" preceded by the name of the fruit. When the fruit butter is made from more than 1 fruit ingredient, the name is "Butter" preceded by "Mixed Fruit" or the names of the fruits in the order of predominance of the weight of the fruit ingredients used.

Label Statement of Optional Ingredients: When spice is used, the label shall bear the word "Spiced" or the statement "Spice Added," but in lieu of the word "Spice" the name of the spice may be used. When flavoring is used, the label shall say "Flavoring Added"; the word "Flavoring" may be preceded by the name of the flavoring. When fruit juice is used, the label shall say "Prepared with _____ Juice," the blank to be filled in with the name of the fruit from which the juice is obtained; but if apple juice is used, the word "Cider" may be used in lieu of "Apple Juice." When honey is used, the label shall say "Prepared with honey." When optional saccharine ingredients are used, the label shall bear the names of the ingredients used. When the optional fruit ingredient is prepared from dried fruit, the label shall say "Prepared from Dried _____," the blank to be filled in by the name of the fruit. When sorbic acid, sodium sorbate, or potassium sorbate is used, the label shall bear the statement "_____ added as a preservative," with the name of the preservative filling in the blank. The label statements of different ingredients may be combined as for example, "Cinnamon Oil and Cloves Added" or "prepared with cider, apples, dried prunes, and honey." The names of the optional ingredients used must immediately precede or follow the name of the fruit butter on the label.

GELATIN: Transparent, tasteless, hard substance from animal connective tissue. Various flavors with sugar added. **Sizes:** 6/4-1/2 lb.; 2/20 lb.; 50 lb. packages of 12, 40, and 50 to a case (1 lb. each), 60 sheets per lb., 1 lb. packages of 1/4 oz. individual envelopes.

GUM TRAGACANTH: Gum from the tragacanth plant used in ice cream powders and for thickening jellies, creams, pastes, and icing. Primarily used in foodservice to coat culinary show pieces. **Pack:** By the pound, thin pieces.

HOMINY: Inside of the corn kernel. PEARLY—A coarse cornmeal used as a vegetable. FLAKES—Thin flakes of hominy made from a cornmeal paste. GRITS—Granulated hominy; coarse, medium, fine; a breakfast cereal served hot. **Pack:** No. 10 (105 oz.), 24 oz., 4 lb., 100 lb.

HONEY

Liquid sugar prepared from flow nectar. Used as a substitute for sugar in baking and as a preserve. **Packs:** 1 lb., 5 lb., 6/3 lb., 6/4 lb., 6/5 lb. Individuals.

COMB HONEY [5/24/67]: COMB-SECTION HONEY: U.S. FANCY: COMB: Has no uncapped cells except in row attached to wood section; is attached to 75 percent of adjacent area of wood section if outside row of cells is empty, or attached to 50 percent if the outside row is filled with honey; does not project beyond the edge of the wood section; does not have dry holes; not more than 2-1/2 in. of through holes, and is free from cells of pollen. **Cappings:** Dry and free from weeping and damage and have a uniformly even appearance except in the row attached to the wood section. **Color:** Conform to the requirements in the official color chart. HONEY—Uniform in color, and free from damage, and objectionable flavors and odors. WOOD SECTION—Free from excessive propolis and/or pronounced stains; is smooth and new in appearance, of white to light buff basswood, and does not contain excess knots and/or streaks. **Net weight:** 12 oz. or more.

U.S. NO. 1: COMB: Has no uncapped cells except in the row attached to the wood section and/or the row adjoining the outside row, in the corners, and along the lower edge, provided there are no more than 15 in a comb section; is attached to 50 percent of the adjacent area of wood section; does not project beyond the edge of the wood section; has no dry holes; not more than 4 in. of through holes; and is free from cells of pollen. **Cappings:** Dry and free from weeping and damage; have a uniformly even appearance except in the row attached to the wood section and except for slight irregularities which do not exceed 1/2 of the comb surface. **Color:** Conforms to the requirements in the official color chart. HONEY—Fairly uniform in color throughout, and free from damage, and objectionable flavor and odor. WOOD SECTION—Same as U.S. Fancy. **Net weight:** 11 oz. or more, unless otherwise specified.

U.S. NO. 1 MIXED COLOR: Different colors of U.S. No. 1 packed in the same container.

U.S. NO. 2: COMB: Has no uncapped cells except in the row attached to the wood section, the row adjoining the outside row, in the corners, and along the lower edge, provided there are no more than 30 in a comb section, and not more than 5 elsewhere in the comb with no more than 20 being empty; is attached to 50 percent of the adjacent area of the wood section; does not project beyond the edge of the wood section; has no dry holes larger than 3/8 in. across if more than 1-3/8 in. from the wood section; has no more than a total of 6 in. of through holes; and is free from serious damage due to cells of pollen. **Cappings:** Not badly bruised, marred, or leaking. **Color:** Conforms to the requirements in the official color chart. HONEY—Free from serious damage and objectionable flavors and odors. WOOD SECTION—Free from excessive propolis and/or pronounced stains as illustration A in the official color chart, and is new in appearance. **Net weight:** 10 oz. or more, unless specified.

SHALLOW-FRAME COMB HONEY: U.S. FANCY: COMB: Produced in shallow frame, spaced 1-3/8 in. from center to center, which will give a comb thickness of at least 1 in.; is drawn out on foundation which is light in color and is thin enough to produce a comb that is comparable in texture with the comb in comb-section honey; is well built out; has never contained brood; has no dry holes; has no uncapped cells except empty cells in the row attached to the frame and 150 uncapped cells filled with well-ripened honey in the adjoining row; and is free from cells of pollen. **Cappings:** Not broken or damaged; and have a uniformly even appearance. **Color:** Conforms to requirements for comb-section honey in the official color chart. HONEY—Uniform in color and free from damage and objectionable flavors or odors.

U.S. NO. 1: COMB: Same as U.S. Fancy except do not have to be well built out; may contain uncapped filled cells, provided they are confined to groups and do not cover more than 10 percent of the comb surface in any frame; and may have cells of pollen but must be free from damage caused by these cells. **Cappings:** Free from serious damage, and have a uniformly even appearance except for slight irregularities which do not exceed 1/2 of the comb surface. **Color:** Conforms to the requirements of comb-section honey in the official color chart. HONEY—Fairly uniform in color and free from objectionable flavors and odors.

Unclassified: Does not conform to the requirements for the foregoing grades.

WRAPPED CUT-COMB HONEY: U.S. FANCY: COMB: Drawn out on foundation that is light in color and is thin enough to produce a comb comparable in texture with the comb in comb-section honey; has no uncapped cells except on the cut edges; has never contained brood; has no dry holes; and is free from cells of pollen. **Cappings:** Free from weeping and damage and have a uniformly even appearance. **Color:** Conforms to the requirements for comb-section honey in the official color charts. HONEY—Uniform in color throughout the comb, and free from damage and objectionable flavors and odors. WRAPPER—Transparent, clean, and sealed to prevent leakage. **Minimum net weight:** 12 oz., unless otherwise specified.

U.S. NO. 1: COMB: Same as U.S. Fancy except may have uncapped cells on the cut edges and in the row adjoining the cut edge, provided there are no more than 15 in a cut comb. **Cappings:** Free from weeping and damage and has a uniformly even appearance except for slight irregularities affecting not more than 1/2 the comb surface. **Color:** Conforms to the requirements for U.S. No. 1 Comb-section honey in the official color chart. HONEY—Fairly uniform in color throughout the comb; and free from damage and objectionable flavors and odors. WRAPPER—Transparent, clean, and sealed to prevent leakage. **Minimum net weight:** 11 oz., unless otherwise specified.

Unclassified: Does not conform to the requirements for the foregoing grades.

CHUNK OR BULK COMB HONEY: U.S. FANCY: Packed in tin. Consists of not less than 50 percent, by volume, of honey, unless otherwise specified. **Comb:** Drawn out on foundation that is light in color and is thin enough to produce a comb that is comparable in texture with the comb in comb-section honey; has no more than one uncapped cell per sq. in. of comb surface; has never contained brood; has no dry holes; and is free from cells of pollen. **Cappings:** Free from damage and have a uniform even appearance. **Color:** Conforms to the requirements for U.S. Fancy comb-section honey in the official color chart, except that any amount of watery cappings is permitted. HONEY—Uniform in color throughout the comb and the color shall not be darker than the next darker color classification of the extracted honey used to make up the total weight and is free from damage and objectionable flavors and odors. **Weight:** Made up with U.S. Fancy extracted honey.

U.S. NO. 1: Packed in tin: Consists of not less than 50 percent by volume of honey, unless otherwise specified. **Comb:** Same as U.S. Fancy except may have not more than 2 uncapped cells per sq. in. of comb surface. **Cappings:** Free from damage and has a uniformly even appearance except for slight irregularities which do not exceed 1/2 of the comb surface. **Color:** Conforms to the requirements for U.S. No. 1 comb-section honey in the official color chart, except that any amount of watery cappings is permitted. HONEY—Fairly uniform in color throughout the comb, and the color shall not be darker than the next darker color classification of the extracted honey used to make up the total weight and is free from damage and objectionable flavors and odors. **Weight:** Made up with U.S. Fancy extracted honey.

Unclassified: Does not conform to the requirements of the foregoing grades.

Packs: U.S. FANCY: Packed in glass: Same as when packed in tin except no given volume of honey is required.

U.S. NO. 1: Packed in glass: Same as when packed in tin except no given volume of honey is required.

Unclassified: Packed in glass: Does not conform to the requirements of the foregoing grades.

EXTRACTED HONEY [4/16/51]: Grade A: Contains not less than 81.4 percent soluble solids. **Flavor:** Has a good normal flavor and aroma for the predominant floral source, or, when blended, a good flavor for the blend of floral sources and is free from caramelized flavor or other objectionable flavor due to any cause except the predominant floral source. **Defects:** Has no defects that affect the appearance or edibility of the product and must be at least as free from defects as honey that has been strained through a No. 80 sieve, at a temperature of not over 130°F. **Clarity:** "Clear" means that the honey may have air bubbles which do not materially affect the appearance of the product and may have a trace of pollen grains or other finely divided particles of suspended material which does not affect the appearance of the product.

Grade B: Contains not less than 81.4 percent soluble solids. **Flavor:** Has a reasonably good, normal flavor and aroma for the floral sources, and is practically free from caramelized flavor, and is free from objectionable flavor due to any cause except the floral source. **Defects:** May have defects which do not materially affect the appearance or edibility of the product and shall be at least as free from defects as honey that has been strained through a standard No. 50 sieve, at a temperature of not over 130°F. **Clarity:** May have air bubbles, pollen grains, or other finely divided particles of suspended material which do not materially affect the appearance of the product.

Grade C: Honey for reprocessing that contains not less than 80 percent soluble solids. **Flavor:** Has a fairly good, normal flavor and aroma for the floral sources, and may have a slightly caramelized flavor, but is free from objectionable flavor due to any cause except the floral source. **Defects:** Defects may be noticeable but shall be at least as free from defects as honey that has been strained through a standard No. 18 sieve, at a temperature of not over 130°F. **Clarity:** Appearance may be materially but not seriously affected by the presence of air bubbles, pollen grains, or other finely divided particles of suspended material.

Grade D or Sstd: Fails to meet requirements.

HONEY

COMB HONEY
FRESH [5/24/67   52.2861]
Grades:
    Comb-section Honey:
        U.S. Fancy comb-section honey
        U.S. No. 1 comb-section honey
        U.S. No. 1 mixed color comb-section honey
        U.S. No. 2 comb-section honey
        Unclassified comb-section honey
    Grades for Shallow-Frame Comb Honey
        U.S. Fancy shallow-frame comb honey
        U.S. No. 1 shallow-frame comb honey
        Unclassified shallow-frame comb honey
    Grades for Wrapped Cut-Comb Honey
        U.S. Fancy wrapped cut-comb honey
        U.S. No. 1 wrapped cut-comb honey
        Unclassified wrapped cut-comb honey
    Grades for Chunk or Bulk Comb Honey
        U.S. Fancy chunk or bulk comb honey—packed in tin
        U.S. No. 1 chunk or bulk comb honey—packed in tin
        Unclassified chunk or bulk comb honey—packed in tin
        U.S. Fancy chunk or bulk comb honey—packed in glass
        U.S. No. 2 chunk or bulk comb honey—packed in glass
        Unclassified chunk or bulk comb honey—packed in glass

EXTRACTED HONEY
CANNED [4/16/51   52.1391]

Grades:	"A" or "FANCY"	"B" or "CHOICE"	"C" or "STAN-DARD"	"D" or "SUB-STAN-DARD"
Minimum Score:	90	80	70	Less than 70

NET WEIGHT: Not less than 95 percent of capacity of container

HOT CHOCOLATE [See Beverages.]

KITCHEN BOUQUET: Seasoning and coloring for sauces and gravies. Blend of 13 vegetables, herbs, and spices. **Pack:** 12/quarts; 4/1-gallon.

LEGUMES, DRIED [Beans, Lentils, Peas] [See also Produce]

Grades to Buy: *U.S. No. 1* for dry whole or split peas, lentils, and black-eyed peas (beans). *U.S. No. 1 Choice Handpicked, or Handpicked* for Great Northern, pinto, and pea beans. *U.S. Extra No. 1* for lima beans, large or small. Instead of the federal grade on beans, you might find a state grade which is based on quality factors similar to those for federal grades.

QUALITY FACTORS: If you do not find packages of beans, peas, or lentils marked with federal or state grades, you can be your own grader in a way by looking for the same factors a federal grader considers.

Brightness of Color: Beans, peas, and lentils should have a bright uniform color. Loss of color usually indicates long storage, lack of freshness, and a product that will take longer to cook. Eating quality, however, is not affected. **Uniformity of Size:** Look for beans, peas, or lentils of uniform size. Mixed sizes will result in uneven cooking, since smaller beans cook faster than larger ones. **Visible Defects:** Cracked seed coats, foreign material, and pinholes caused by insect damage are signs of a low quality product.

BEANS: Beans undergo rather extensive processing before reaching the consumer. They are delivered to huge processing plants where they are cleaned to remove pods, stems, and other debris. Special machines separate debris by weight (gravity) and then screen the beans by size. Discolored beans are removed by machines equipped with photo-sensitive electric eyes.

Black Beans [or black turtle soup beans]: They are used in thick soups and in Oriental and Mediterranean dishes.

Black-eyed Peas [also called black-eyed beans or cowpeas]: These beans are small, oval-shaped, and creamish white with a black spot on one side. They are used primarily as a main dish vegetable. Black-eyed peas *are* beans. There is no difference in the product, but different names are used in some regions of the country.

Garbanzo Beans: Known as chick-peas, these beans are nut-flavored and commonly pickled in vinegar and oil for salads. They can also be used in the unpickled form as a main dish vegetable. Similar beans are cranberry and yellow-eyed beans.

Great Northern Beans: Larger than but similar to pea beans, these beans are used in soups, salads, casserole dishes, and home-baked beans.

Kidney Beans: These beans are large, and have a red color, and kidney shape. They are popular for chili con carne, and add zest to salads, and to many Mexican dishes.

Lima Beans: Not widely known as dry beans, lima beans make an excellent main dish vegetable and can be used in casseroles. They are broad and flat. Lima beans come in different sizes, but the size does not affect the quality.

Navy Beans: This is a broad term which includes Great Northern, pea, flat small white, and small white beans.

Pea Beans: Small, oval, and white, pea beans are a favorite for home-baked beans, soups, and casseroles. They hold their shape even when cooked tender.

Pinto Beans: These beans are of the same species as the kidney and red beans. Beige-colored and speckled, they are used mainly in salads and chili.

Red and Pink Beans: Pink beans have a more delicate flavor than red beans. Both are used in many Mexican dishes and chili. They are related to the kidney bean.

LENTILS: Types are **Chilean, Giant,** and **Russian.** Sizes are Jumbo and Regular.

PEAS: Green Dry Peas: This type of dry pea has a more distinct flavor than yellow dry peas. Green dry peas enjoy their greatest popularity in the U.S., England, and North European countries, and are gaining in popularity in Japan.

Yellow Dry Peas: This type of dry pea has a less pronounced flavor than other types of peas but is in popular demand in the southern and eastern parts of the country. They are also preferred in eastern Canada, the Caribbean, and South America.

Dry Split Peas: These peas have had their skins removed, and they are mainly used for split pea soup. Dry split peas also combine well with many different foods. How do split peas get split? Specially grown whole peas are dried, and their skins removed by a special machine. A second machine then breaks the peas in half.

Dry Whole Peas: These peas are used in making soups, casseroles, puddings, vegetable side dishes, dips, and hors d'oeuvres.

LENTILS: [See Legumes, dried.]

MARGARINE: [See Fats and Oils.]

MARSHMALLOWS: A soft, white, spongy candy, covered with powdered sugar and made from corn syrup, sugar, starch, and gelatin. **Pack:** 12 oz., 1 lb.

MINCEMEAT: Preserve used as a filling for tarts, pies, and in puddings. Made from dried fruits, sugar, spices, suet, peeled and cooked lean beef. **Pack:** Usually 6/No. 10.

MONOSODIUM GLUTAMATE: A wheat salt used to enhance meat, soups, stock, fish, cheese dishes, and poultry. **Pack:** 1 lb. can, 10-lb. can, 100-lb. drum.

MORELS: A French mushroom. Canned. Imported.

NOODLES, CHINESE: Pasta strings made from wheat and rice flour and served in soup, meat sauces, or fried. **Pack:** 6/No. 10 (64 oz.)

NUTS

ALMOND: Prunus amygdalus. Hard shell and soft shell. In season in September. Eaten plain and used in baking, cooking, and confectionery. **Sizes:** No. 10 cans (4 lb.), 5-lb. boxes, 25-lb. boxes, 100-lb. drum, 160-lb. bag, 200-lb. drum.

Almonds in the Shell [7/15/64]: U.S. No. 1: Almonds: Are similar in shape and degree of hardness of the shells, and bitter almonds are not mixed with sweet almonds; are free from loose, foreign material; have shells that are clean, fairly bright, fairly uniform in color, and free from damage due to discoloration, adhering hulls, broken shells, or other means; and have kernels that are well dried, free from decay, rancidity, and damage caused by insects, mold, gum, shriveling, discoloration, or other means; and are not less than 28/64 in. in thickness. **Tolerances:** Shell defects—10 percent; dissimilar varieties—5 percent, including not over 1 percent for bitter almonds mixed with sweet almonds; size—5 percent; foreign material—2 percent, including not over 1 percent that

can pass through a round opening 24/64 in. in diameter; kernel defects—10 percent.

U.S. No. 1 Mixed: Meet the requirements of U.S. No. 1 grade, except 2 or more varieties of sweet almonds are mixed. *U.S. No. 2:* Same as U.S. No. 1 except an additional tolerance of 20 percent is allowed for almonds with shells damaged by discoloration. *U.S. No. 2 Mixed:* Meet the requirements of U.S. No. 2 grade; except 2 or more varieties of sweet almonds are mixed.

Unclassified: No definite grade is applied.

Almonds, Shelled [8/15/60]: *U.S. Fancy:* Similar varietal characteristics which are whole, clean, and well dried, and which are free from decay, rancidity, insect injury, foreign material, doubles (shells containing 2 kernels), split or broken kernels, injury caused by chipped and scratched kernels, and damage caused by any means. See Table I for tolerances of defects. *U.S. Extra No. 1:* Same as U.S. Fancy except for increased tolerances (see Table I). *U.S. Select Sheller Run:* Same as U.S. Fancy except for increased tolerances (See Table I). *U.S. Standard Sheller Run:* Same as U.S. Fancy except for increased tolerances (See Table I).

U.S. No. 1 Whole and Broken: Similar varietal characteristics; are clean and well dried, and are free from decay, rancidity, insect injury, foreign material, doubles, particles, and dust, and damage caused by any means. Not less than 30 percent of the kernels are whole, and the minimum diameter shall not be less than 20/64 in. See Table I for tolerances of defects. *U.S. No. 1 Pieces:* Not bitter, clean and dried, and free from decay, randicity, insect injury, foreign material, particles, dust, and damage caused by any means. The minimum diameter shall not be less than 8/64 in. **Mixed Varieties:** A mixture of 2 or more dissimilar varieties which meet the other requirements of the grades shall be designated as "U.S. No. 1 Mixed"; "U.S. Select Sheller Run Mixed"; "U.S. Standard Sheller Run Mixed"; or "U.S. No. 1 Whole and Broken Mixed." No lot may contain over 1 percent of bitter almonds mixed with sweet almonds.

TABLE 1—TOLERANCES FOR DEFECTS [BY WEIGHT]

Defect:	Percent Allowed:						
	U.S. Fancy	U.S. Extra No. 1	U.S. No. 1	U.S. Sheller Run	U.S. Standard Sheller Run	U.S. No. 1 Whole & Brkn	U.S. No. 1 Pieces
Dissimilar varieties, including bitter almonds mixed with	5	5	5	5	5	5	
sweet almonds	1	1	1	1	1	1	1
Doubles	3	5	15	15	25	35	No Limit
Kernels damaged by chipping or scratching	5	5	10	20	20	No Limit	No Limit
Foreign material	0.2	0.2	0.2	0.2	0.2	0.3	0.3
Particles and dust	0.1	0.1	0.1	0.1	0.1	0.1	1
Split and broken kernels	1	1	1	5	15	—	—
Undersize	—	—	—	—	—	5	—
Other defects	2	4	5	3	3	5	5

ALMONDS

IN THE SHELL:
FRESH [7/15/64   51.2075]
Grades: U.S. Fancy; U.S. No. 1 Mixed; U.S. No. 2; U.S. No. 2 Mixed
SHELLED [8/15/60   51.2105]
Grades: U.S. Fancy; U.S. Extra No. 1; U.S. No. 1; U.S. Select Sheller Run; U.S. Standard Sheller Run; U.S. No. 1 Whole and Broken; U.S. No. 1 Pieces
BRAZIL NUT: Bertholletia incisa or Treculia africana. Also known as butternut and cream nut. Becomes rancid quickly.

BRAZIL NUTS IN THE SHELL

FRESH [8/25/66   51.3500]
Grades: U.S. No. 1
Brazil Nuts in the Shell [8/25/66]: U.S. No. 1 Grade: Well-cured whole Brazil nuts which are free from loose, foreign material and meet one of the size classifications below. The shells are clean and free from damage caused by splits, breaks, punctures, oil stain, mold, or other means, and contain kernels which are reasonably well developed, free from rancidity, mold, decay, and damage caused by insects, discoloration, or other means. **Permitted Tolerances:** FOR DEFECTS OF SHELL—10 percent may fail to meet the requirements of the grade, including not over 5 percent for serious damage. FOR DEFECTS OF THE KERNEL—10 percent may fail to meet the requirements of the grade, including not over 7 percent for serious damage provided that not over 5 percent is allowed for damage by insects, including not over 0.5 percent with live insects in the shell. FOR FOREIGN MATERIAL—1 percent.
Size Classifications: EXTRA LARGE—Not over 15 percent pass through a round opening 78/64 in. in diameter, or count does not exceed 45 nuts per pound. LARGE—Not over 15 percent pass through a round opening 73/64 in. in diameter, or count does not exceed 50 nuts per lb. MEDIUM—Not over 15 percent pass through a round opening 59/64 in. in diameter, or count is 51 to 65 nuts per lb.
CAROB: Ceratonia siliqua. Also known as St. John's bread. Can be eaten plain soon after harvesting but becomes brittle and acid after storage. Milled carob is used for baking as a filler.
CASHEW: Anacardium occidentale. Eaten plain and used in baking, confectionery, and cooking. Sometimes available in butter form or paste. **Size:** 25 lb. tins.
CHESTNUT: Castanea sativa. Usually available dried. In season in November. Used in cooking, baking, and confectionery.

TREE NUTS
Tree nuts: Relation between shelled and in-shell, and between farm and retail weights

| | | Factors for converting to — | | |
Commodity	Shelled weight from in-shell weight	In-shell equivalent from shelled weight	Retail weight from orchard-run	Orchard-run equivalent from retail weight[1]
Almonds:				
Domestic	0.52	1.92	0.95	1.05
Imported	.30	3.33	—	—
Brazil nuts	.50	2.00	—	—
Cashews	.22	4.55	—	—
Chestnuts	.84	1.19	—	—
Filberts:				
Domestic	.40	2.50	.95	1.05
Imported	.45	2.22	—	—
Macadamias (Hawaii)	.30	3.33	—	—
Pecans:				
Improved	.40	2.50	.91	1.10
Seedling	.36	2.78	.91	1.10
Walnuts, English:				
Domestic[2]	.37	2.67	.87	1.15
Imported	.35	2.86	—	—
Walnuts, black	.17	5.88	—	—

1. Orchard-run weight before culling. Both orchard-run and retail weight are in-shell basis.
2. Average for portion of crop shelled commercially. Equivalent shelled-in-shell ratio for graded walnuts sold in-shell is 0.45, and average for entire U.S. walnut crop is 0.41.

FILBERTS IN THE SHELL

FRESH [9/1/70   51.1995]
Grades: U.S. No. 1
FILBERT: Corylus. Round or oblong. In season in September. Eaten plain. **Sizes:** 5 lb. cartons, 100 lb. bags.
Filberts in the Shell [9/1/70]: U.S. No. 1 Grade: Filberts are of similar type and dry. The shells are well formed; clean and bright; free from broken or split shells, and kernels filling less than 1/4 the capacity of the shell, and free from damage caused by stains, adhering husks, or other means. The kernels are reasonably well developed; not badly misshapen; free from rancidity, decay, mold, and insect injury; and free from damage caused by shriveling, discoloration, or other means. The size is specified in connection with the grade, in accordance with Table I.

TABLE I

Size Classification	Maximum Size Will Pass Through a Round Opening of the Following Size	Minimum Size Will Not Pass Through a Round Opening of the Following Size
Round type varieties:		
Jumbo	No maximum	56/64 in.
Large	56/64 in.	49/64 in.
Medium	49/64 in.	45/64 in.
Small	45/64 in.	No minimum
Long type varieties:		
Jumbo	No maximum	47/64 in.
Large	48/64 in.	44/64 in.
Medium	45/64 in.	34/64 in.
Small	35/64 in.	No minimum

Permitted Tolerances: FOR MIXED TYPES—20 percent of which are of a different type. **Defects:** 10 percent for filberts below the requirements of this grade, provided that not over 5 percent are kernels filling less than 1/4 the shell, and not over 5 percent have rancid, decayed, moldy, or insect injured kernels, including not over 3 percent for insect injury. FOR OFF-SIZE—15 percent, but not over 10 percent are undersized filberts.

HICKORY NUT: Juglandacea carya. Also known as kingnut, mocker nut, pig nut, shagbark, and water hickory. Round to oblong in shape.

LOTUS SEED: Nelumba nucifera. Also known as rattle nut and water nut. Less delicate flavor, but firmer, than macadamia nuts. Available canned or dried.

MACADAMIA NUT: Macadamia turnifolia. Also known as Australian hazelnut and Queensland nut. Creamy white, round, tender kernel with a flavor similar to a filbert.

MIXED NUTS IN THE SHELL [9/18/70]: Mixed nuts in the shell which meet the requirements of a U.S. grade are required to conform to the applicable mixture, sizes, and grades set forth in one of the following grades.

GRADES

U.S. Extra Fancy

| Species of Nut | Allowable Mixture | | Minimum Size | Minimum Grade |
	Minimum Percent	Maximum Percent		
Almonds	10	40	28/64 in.	U.S. No. 1
Brazils	10	40	Large	U.S. No. 1
Filberts	10	40	Long type varieties 44/64 in. Round type varieties 49/64 in.	U.S. No. 1
Pecans	10	40	Extra Large	U.S. No. 1
Walnuts	10	40	Large	U.S. No. 1

§51.3522 U.S. Fancy

| Species of Nut | Allowable Mixture | | Minimum Size | Minimum Grade |
	Minimum Percent	Maximum Percent		
Almonds	10	40	28/64 in.	U.S. No. 1
Brazils	10	40	Medium	U.S. No. 1
Filberts	10	40	Long type varieties 44/64 in. Round type varieties 49/64 in.	U.S. No. 1
Pecans	10	40	Large	U.S. No. 1
Walnuts	10	40	Medium	U.S. No. 1

§51.3523 U.S. Commercial or U.S. Select

(Cont.)

GRADES [Cont.]

Species of Nut	Allowable Mixture		Minimum Size	Minimum Grade
	Minimum Percent	Maximum Percent		
Almonds	5	40	28/64 in.	U.S. No. 1
Brazils	5	40	Medium	U.S. No. 1
Filberts	5	40	Long type varieties 34/64 in. Round type varieties 45/64 in.	U.S. No. 1
Pecans	5	40	Medium	(a) External quality: U.S. No. 1. (b) Internal quality: 75 percent U.S. No. 1 quality with not more than 10 percent seriously damaged kernels, including therein not more than 6 percent which are rancid, moldy, decayed, or damaged by insects.
Walnuts	5	40	Baby	(a) External quality: 85 percent U.S. No. 1 quality. (b) Internal quality: 85 percent U.S. No. 1 quality, except that the lot need only meet the requirements for U.S. No. 2 grade for kernel color; with not more than 8 percent seriously damaged kernels, including therein not more than 5 percent which are damaged by insects.

MIXED NUTS IN THE SHELL

FRESH [9/18/70   51.3520]
Grades: U.S. Extra Fancy, U.S. Fancy, U.S. Commercial or U.S. Select
PEANUT: Arachis hypogaea (Spanish peanut). Also known as goober, groundnut, and monkey nut. In season in November. Eaten plain and used in cooking. Size: 85 lb. bag roasted.
Peanut, Cleaned Virginia Type in the Shell [9/18/48]: *U.S.*

Jumbo Hand Picked: Peanuts which are mature, dry and free from loose peanut kernels, dirt, or other foreign material, fully developed shells that contain almost no kernels (pops), peanuts that have very soft and/or very thin ends (paper ends), and from damage caused by cracked or broken shells, discoloration, or other means. The kernels are free from damage. The peanuts may not pass through a screen having 37/64 in. by 3 in. perforations and shall not average more than

176 count per lb. **Permitted Tolerances:** 10 percent for pops, paper ends, damaged shells, loose kernels, or other foreign material; 5 percent for peanuts that pass through the prescribed screen, but do not have pops or paper ends, and 3.5 percent for damaged kernels. *U.S. Fancy Hand Picked:* Mature, dry, and free from loose kernels, dirt, or other foreign material, pops, paper ends, and damage. The peanuts may not pass through a screen having 32/64 in. by 3 in. perforations and shall not average over 225 count per lb. **Permitted Tolerances:** 11 percent for pops, paper ends, or damaged shells and kernels, or other foreign material; 5 percent for peanuts that pass through the prescribed screen, but do not have pops, paper ends, or damaged shells; and 4.5 percent for damaged kernels. *Unclassified:* No definite grade.

Peanuts, Shelled Runner Type [7/31/56]: *U.S. No. 1 Runner:* Have similar varietal characteristics; are whole; are free from foreign material, damage, and minor defects due to discoloration, sprouts, and dirt, and will not pass through a screen having 16/64 in. by 3/4 in. openings. See Table I for tolerances permitted. *U.S. Runner Splits:* Have similar varietal characteristics; may be split or broken; but are free from foreign material, damage due to rancidity, decay, mold, or insects, and minor defects due to discoloration, sprouts, and dirt, and will not pass through a screen having 17/64 in. round openings. See Table I for tolerances permitted. *U.S. No. 2 Runner:* Have similar varietal characteristics; may be split or broken; but are free from foreign material, damage, and minor defects, and will not pass through a screen having 17/64 in. round openings. See Table I for tolerances permitted.

TABLE I—TOLERANCES [BY WEIGHT]

Percent Allowed:

Defect:	U.S. No. 1 Runner	U.S. Runner Splits	U.S. No. 2 Runner
Other varieties of peanuts	1 percent	2 percent	2 percent
Sound peanuts which are split or broken	3 percent	no limit	no limit
Damaged or unshelled peanuts and minor defects	2 percent	2 percent	2.5 percent
Foreign material	0.1 percent	0.2 percent	0.2 percent
Sound whole peanuts which pass through prescribed screen	3 percent	6 percent	6 percent

Peanuts, Shelled Spanish Type [7/15/65]: *U.S. No. 1 Spanish:* Whole and free from foreign material, damage, and minor defects, and will not pass through a screen having 15/64 in. by 3/4 in. openings. See Table II for tolerances permitted. *U.S. Spanish Splits:* Kernels may be split or broken, but are free from foreign material, damage due to decay, rancidity, mold, or insects, and minor defects due to discoloration, sprouting, and dirt. They will not pass through a screen having 16/64 in. round openings. See Table II for tolerances permitted. *U.S. No. 2 Spanish:* Same as U.S. Spanish Splits, except for tolerances. See Table II for tolerances permitted.

TABLE II—TOLERANCES [BY WEIGHT]

Percent Allowed:

Defect:	U.S. No. 1 Spanish	U.S. Spanish Splits	U.S. No. 2 Spanish
Other types of peanuts	1 percent	2 percent	2 percent
Sound peanuts which are split or broken	3 percent	no limit	no limit
Damaged or unshelled peanuts and minor defects	2 percent	2 percent	2.5 percent
Foreign material	0.1 percent	0.2 percent	0.2 percent
Sound whole peanuts which pass through the prescribed screen	2 percent	6 percent	6 percent

Peanuts, Shelled Virginia Type [8/31/59]: *U.S. Extra Large Virginia:* Kernels of similar varietal characteristics that are whole, and free from foreign material, damage due to rancidity, decay, mold, or insects, and minor defects due to discoloration, sprouts, and dirt, and which will not pass through a screen having 20/64 in. by 1 in. openings. There may not be more than 512 peanuts per lb. See Table III for tolerances permitted. *U.S. Medium Virginia:* Kernels of similar varietal characteristics which are whole, and free from foreign material, damage, and minor defects, and which will not pass through a screen having 18/64 in. by 1 in. openings. There may not be more than 640 peanuts per lb. See Table III for tolerances permitted. *U.S. No. 1 Virginia:* Same as U.S. Extra Large Virginia except the kernels will not pass through a screen having 15/64 in. by 1 in. openings, and there are not more than 864 peanuts per lb. See Table III for tolerances permitted. *U.S. Virginia Splits:* Kernels of similar varietal characteristics which are free from foreign material, damage, and minor defects, and which will not pass through a screen having 20/64 in. round openings. Not less than 90 percent, by weight, shall be splits. (Split means the separated half of a peanut kernel). See Table III for tolerances permitted. *U.S. No. 2 Virginia:* Kernels of similar varietal characteristics which may be split or broken, but which are free from foreign material, damage, and minor defects, and which will not pass through a screen having 17/64 in. round openings. See Table III for tolerances permitted.

TABLE III—TOLERANCES [BY WEIGHT]

Defect:	Percent Allowed:				
	U.S. Extra Large Virginia	U.S. Medium Virginia	U.S. No. 1 Virginia	U.S. Virginia Splits	U.S. No. 2 Virginia
Other varieties of peanuts	0.75%	1%	1%	2%	2%
Sound peanuts which are split or broken	3%	3%	3%	no limit	no limit
Damaged or un-shelled peanuts and minor defects	1.75%	2%	2%	2%	2.5%
Foreign material	0.1%	0.1%	0.1%	0.2%	0.2%
Sound whole peanuts that pass through the pre-scribed screen	3%	3%	3%	3%	6%

PEANUTS

CLEANED VIRGINIA TYPE PEANUTS IN THE SHELL
 [9/18/48   51.1235]
Grades: U.S. Jumbo Hand Picked; U.S. Fancy Hand Picked
SHELLED RUNNER TYPE PEANUTS
FRESH [7/31/56   51.2710]
Grades: U.S. No. 1 Runner; U.S. Runner Splits; U.S. No. 2 Runner
SHELLED VIRGINIA TYPE PEANUTS [8/31/59   51.2750]
Grades: U.S. Extra Large Virginia; U.S. Medium Virginia; U.S. Virginia Splits; U.S. No. 1 Virginia; U.S. No. 2 Virginia
SHELLED SPANISH TYPE PEANUTS [7/15/65   51.2730]
Grades: U.S. No. 1 Spanish, U.S. Spanish Splits, U.S. No. 2 Spanish

PECAN: Carya pecan, Carya olivaeformis, and Hicoria pecan. Most popular native nut. Hardshell or soft shell; small, medium, and large. In season in November and December. **Sizes:** SHELLED—3 oz. can, 8 oz. can, 5 lb. box, 25 lb. box, 50 lb. box, 180 lb. bushel; UNSHELLED—25 lb. box, 50 lb. box, 140 lb. bag, 175 lb. bushel.

Pecans in the Shell [9/15/72]: Size Classification: Specified in connection with the grade.

Size Classification	Number of Nuts per Pound	Minimum Weight of the 10 smallest Nuts in a 100-Nut Sample
Oversize	55 or less	In each classification, the 10 smallest nuts per 100 *must* weigh at least 7 percent of the total weight of the 100-nut sample.
Extra large	56 to 63	
Large	64 to 77	
Medium	78 to 95	
Small	96 to 120	

Kernel Color Classification:
 1) LIGHT—Outer surface is mostly golden brown or lighter, with not more than 25 percent darker than golden, none of which is darker than light brown.
 2) LIGHT AMBER—More than 25 percent of outer surface is light brown, with not more than 25 percent darker than light brown, none of which is darker than medium brown.
 3) AMBER—More than 25 percent of outer surface is medium brown, with not over 25 percent darker than medium brown, none of which is darker than dark brown.
 4) DARK AMBER—Over 25 percent of outer surface is dark brown, with not over 25 percent darker than dark brown. *Grade No. 1:* Free from loose hulls, empty broken shells and other foreign material. Shells are fairly uniform in color and free from damage; but 5 percent damaged shells, including not over 2 percent seriously damaged shells, are allowed. Kernels are free from damage; but 12 percent damaged kernels, including not over 5 percent seriously damaged, and 8 percent discolored kernels are allowed. *Grade U.S. Commercial:* Same as No. 1, except there is no requirement for uniformity of color; and 10 percent damaged shells, including 3 percent seriously damaged shells; and 30 percent damaged kernels, including 10 percent seriously damaged kernels, are allowed. 0.5 percent foreign material may be present in both grades.

CROSS SECTION ILLUSTRATION

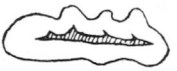   

1. WELL DEVELOPED

Lower limit. Kernels having less meat content than these are not considered well developed.

2. FAIRLY WELL DEVELOPED

Lower limit for U.S. No. 1 grade. Kernels having less meat content than these are not considered fairly well developed and are classed as damaged.

3. POORLY DEVELOPED

Lower limit, damaged, but not seriously damaged. Kernels having less meat content than these are considered undeveloped and are classed as seriously damaged.

Pecans, Shelled [7/15/69]: *U.S. No. 1 Halves:* **Quality:** Well dried; fairly well developed; fairly uniform in color; not darker than "amber"; free from damage or serious damage by any cause; free from pieces of shells, center wall, and foreign material, and comply with tolerances for defects (Table IV). **Sizes:** Halves are fairly uniform in size; conform to size classification or count specified, and comply with tolerances for pieces, particles, and dust (Table I). *U.S. No. 1 Halves and Pieces:* **Quality:** Same as U.S. No. 1 Halves. **Size:** Same as U.S. No. 1 Halves, except at least 50 percent are half-kernels; both halves and pieces will not pass through a 5/16 in. round opening, and comply with tolerances for undersize (Table III). *U.S. No. 1 Pieces:* **Quality:** Same as U.S. No. 1 Halves, except there is no requirement for uniformity of color. **Size:** Same as U.S. No. 1 Halves, except there is no requirement for percentage of half-kernels; they conform to any size classification, and comply with applicable tolerances for off-size (Table III). *U.S. Commercial Halves:* **Quality:** Same as U.S. No. 1 Halves, except no requirement for uniformity of color and increased tolerances for defects (Table IV). **Size:** Same as U.S. No. 1 Halves, except no requirement for uniformity of size. *U.S. Commercial Halves and Pieces:* **Quality:** Same as U.S. No. 1 Halves and Pieces, except no requirement for uniformity of color and increased tolerances for defects (Table IV). **Size:** Same as U.S. No. 1 Halves and Pieces. *U.S. Commercial Pieces:* Same as U.S. No. 1 Pieces, except for increased tolerances for defects (Table IV).

TABLE I

Size Classifications for Halves:	Number of Halves per Pound:
Mammoth	250 or less
Junior mammoth	251-300
Jumbo	301-350
Extra Large	351-450
Large	451-550
Medium	551-650
Small (topper)	651-750
Midget	751 or more

TABLE II

Size Classification	Total Tolerance for Offsize Pieces	Tolerance [included in total tolerance] for Pieces Smaller than	
		2/16 in.	1/16 in.
	Percent	*Percent*	*Percent*
Mammoth pieces	15	1	
Extra large pieces	15	1	
Halves and pieces	15	1	
Large pieces	15	1	
Medium pieces	15	2	
Small pieces	15	2	
Midget pieces	15		2
Granules	15		5
Other specified size	15	1	

TABLE III

Size Classification	Maximum Diameter [will pass through round opening of following diameter]	Minimum Diameter [will not pass through round opening of following diameter]
		In.
Mammoth pieces	No limitation	8/16
Extra large pieces	9/16 in.	7/16
Halves and pieces	No limitation	5/16
Large pieces	8/16 in.	5/16
Medium pieces	6/16 in.	3/16
Small pieces	4/16 in.	2/16
Midget pieces	3/16 in.	1/16
Granules	2/16 in.	1/16

TABLE IV—TOLERANCES [BY WEIGHT]

Defect:	Percent Allowed: No. 1 Halves; No. 1 Halves and Pieces; No. 1 Pieces	Commercial Halves; Commercial Halves and Pieces; Commercial Pieces
Shell, center wall, and foreign material	0.05 percent	0.15 percent
"Dark amber," or darker color, but are not otherwise defective	3 percent	25 percent
Fail to meet the remaining requirements	3 percent (not over .5 percent may cause serious damage)	8 percent (not over 1 percent may cause serious damage)

CROSS SECTION ILLUSTRATION

   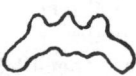

1. WELL DEVELOPED

Lower limit. Kernels having less meat content than these are not considered well developed.

   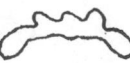

2. FAIRLY WELL DEVELOPED

Lower limit for U.S. No. 1 grade. Kernels having less meat content than these are not considered fairly well developed and are classed as damaged.

3. POORLY DEVELOPED

Lower limit, damaged, but not seriously damaged. Kernels having less meat content that these are considered undeveloped and are classed as seriously damaged.

PECANS

PECANS IN THE SHELL (9/15/72   51.1400)
Grades: U.S. No. 1, U.S. Commercial
SHELLED (7/15/69   51.1430)
Grades: U.S. No. 1 Halves; U.S. No. 1 Halves and Pieces; U.S. No. 1 Pieces; U.S. Commercial Halves; U.S. Commercial Halves and Pieces; U.S. Commercial Pieces

PINE NUT: Also known as Indian nut, pignolia, and pinon. Used in Levantine and barbecue dishes.
PISTACHIO: Pistacia vera. Has a green color. **Sizes:** 25 lb. tin, 27 lb. tin.
WALNUTS:
Walnut [English]: Juglans regia. Round to slightly elongated shape, medium light to hard shell, and small to large. Fresh nuts deteriorate a few months after harvesting but are good before this time. Meats are high in oil but quickly oxidize when exposed to air. In season in December. **Sizes:** 3 oz. can, 8 oz. can, 5 lb. carton, 25 lb. carton.
Walnut [Black]: Juglans nigra. Also known as American walnut. Hard shell which is hard to crack. **Sizes:** 50 lb. bushel, 100 lb. bag.
Walnuts [Juglans regia] in the Shell [9/1/68]: Size Specifications: Specified in connection with the grade. MAMMOTH SIZE—Not over 12 percent pass through a round opening 96/64 in. in diameter. JUMBO SIZE—Not over 12 percent pass

through a round opening 80/64 in. in diameter. LARGE SIZE —Not over 12 percent pass through a round opening 77/64 in. in diameter, except for the Eureka type, which limits the opening to 76/64 in. in diameter. MEDIUM SIZE—At least 88 percent pass through a round opening 77/64 in. in diameter, of which not over 12 percent pass through a round opening 73/64 in. in diameter. BABY SIZE—At least 88 percent pass through a round opening 74/64 in. in diameter, of which not over 10 percent pass through a round opening 60/64 in. in diameter. *U.S. No. 1:* Dry, practically clean, bright, and free from splits (walnuts with the seam opened completely around the nut so that the halves of the shell are held together only by the kernel), injury by discoloration, and free from damage due to broken shells, perforated shells, adhering hulls, or other means. Kernels are well dried, free from decay, discoloration, rancidity, and damage caused by mold, shriveling, insects, or other means. See Table I. At least 70 percent have kernels that are no darker than "light amber," provided that at least 40 percent have kernels that are not darker than "light" on the USDA Walnut Color Chart. *U.S. No. 2:* Same as U.S. No. 1, except at least 60 percent have kernels which are not darker than "light amber" on the USDA Walnut Color Chart. See Table I for tolerance of defects. *U.S. No. 3:* Dry, fairly clean, and free from splits, damage caused by broken shells, and serious damage caused by any means. The kernels are well dried, and free from decay, dark discoloration, rancidity, and damage caused by any means. See Table I for tolerance for defects. *Unclassified:* No grade has been applied.

TABLE I—TOLERANCE FOR GRADE DEFECTS

Grade	External [Shell] Defects	Internal [Kernel] Defects	Color of Kernel
U.S. No. 1	10 percent, by count, for splits, 5 percent, by count, for other shell defects, including not more than 3 percent seriously damaged	10 percent total, by count, including not more than 6 percent which are damaged by mold or insects or seriously damaged by other means, of which not more than 5/16 or 5 percent may be damaged by insects, but no part of any tolerance shall be allowed for walnuts containing live insects	No tolerance to reduce the required 70 percent of "light amber" kernels or the required 40 percent of "light" kernels or any larger percentage of "light amber" or "light" kernels specified
U.S. No. 2	10 percent, by count, for splits, 10 percent, by count, for other shell defects, including not more than 5 percent serious damage by adhering hulls	20 percent total, by count, including not more than 10 percent which are damaged by mold or insects or seriously damaged by other means, of which not more than 1/2 or 5 percent may be damaged by insects, but no part of any tolerance shall be allowed for walnuts containing live insects	No tolerance to reduce the required 60 percent or any specified larger percentage of "light amber" kernels, or any specified percentage of "light" kernels
U.S. No. 3	Same as above tolerance for U.S. No. 2	Same as above tolerance for U.S. No. 2	No tolerance to reduce any percentage of "light amber" or "light" kernels specified

Walnuts, Shelled [Juglans regia] [9/1/68]: *U.S. No. 1:* Portions of kernels that are well dried, clean, and free from shell, foreign material, insect injury, decay, rancidity, and damage due to shriveling, mold, and discoloration. **Tolerances for defects:** See Table I; **Color:** See Table II. **Size:** See Table III.

U.S. Commercial: Same as U.S. No. 1 except for increased tolerances. Color may not be darker than "amber." **Tolerance for Defects:** See Table I. **Color:** See Table II. **Size:** See Table III. *Unclassified:* No grade applied.

TABLE I

Grade	Tolerances for Grade Defects			
	Total Defects	Serious Damage	Very Serious Damage	Shell and Foreign Material
	Percent	*Percent*	*Percent*	*Percent*
U.S. No. 1	5	2 (included in 5 percent total defects)	1 (included in 2 percent serious damage)	0.05 (included in 1 percent very serious damage)
U.S. Commercial	8	4 (included in 8 percent total defects)	2 (included in 4 percent serious damage)	0.05 (included in 2 percent very serious damage)

TABLE II

Color Classification	Tolerances for Color			
	Darker than Extra Light[1]	Darker than Light[1]	Darker than Light Amber[1]	Darker than Amber[1]
Extra light	15 percent	2 percent (included in 15 percent darker than extra light)		
Light	—	15 percent	2 percent (included in 15 percent darker than light)	
Light amber	—	—	15 percent	2 percent (included in 15 percent darker than light amber)
Amber	—	—	—	10 percent

1. See illustration of this term on color chart.

TABLE III

Size Classification	Tolerances for Size				
	Smaller than three-fourths halves	Will not pass through 24/64 in. round hole	Pass through 24/64 in. hole	Pass through 16/64 in. hole	Pass through 8/64 in. hole
Halves	5 percent	—	—	1 percent (included in 5 percent)	—
Pieces and Halves[1]	—	—	18 percent	3 percent (included in 18 percent)	1 percent (included in 3 percent)
Pieces	—	—	25 percent	5 percent (included in 25 percent)	1 percent (included in 5 percent)
Small pieces[2]	—	10 percent	—	—	2 percent

1. No part of any tolerance shall be used to reduce the percentage of halves required or specified in a lot of "pieces and halves."
2. The tolerances of 10 percent and 2 percent for "small pieces" classification shall apply, respectively, to any smaller maximum or any larger minimum sizes specified.

WALNUTS

IN THE SHELL
FRESH [9/1/68   51.2945]
Grades: U.S. No. 1, U.S. No. 2, U.S. No. 3
SHELLED WALNUTS [9/1/68   51.2275]
Grades: U.S. No. 1, U.S. Commercial

OLIVES

GREEN [9/8/67   52.5444]

Grades:	"A" or "FANCY"	"B" or "CHOICE"	"C" or "STAN-DARD'"	"SUB-STAN-DARD"
Minimum Score:	90	80	70	Less than 70

	NET WEIGHT OZ.	NET WEIGHT METRIC	DRAINED WEIGHT OZ.		DRAINED WEIGHT METRIC	
				Pitted and		Pitted and
			Whole	Stuffed	Whole	Stuffed
Subpetite; Petite						
1/2 pt.			5-1/2	4	155.9 g	113.4 g
1 pt.			11	9	311.8 g	255.2 g
1 qt.			22	18	623.7 g	510.3 g
1 gal.			88	—	2.5 kg	—
Small; Select Standard; Medium						
1/2 pt.			5	3-3/4	141.8 g	106.3 g
1 pt.			10	8	283.5 g	226.8 g
1 qt.			21	17	595.4 g	482.0 g
1 gal.			88	—	2.5 kg	—
Large; Extra Large; Mixed Sizes						
1/2 pt.			5	4	141.8 g	113.4 g
1 pt.			10	8-1/2	283.5 g	241.0 g
1 qt.			21	18	595.4 g	510.3 g
1 gal.			88	—	2.5 kg	—
Mammoth						
1/2 pt.			4-3/4	4	134.7 g	113.4 g

	NET WEIGHT OZ.	NET WEIGHT METRIC	DRAINED WEIGHT OZ.	DRAINED WEIGHT METRIC
1 pt.			10	8-1/2	283.5 g	241.0 g
1 qt.			21	18	595.4 g	510.3 g
1 gal.			88	—	2.5 kg	—
Giant; Jumbo; Colossal				
1/2 pt.			4-1/2	3-3/4	127.6 g	106.3 g
1 pt.			9-1/2	8	269.3 g	226.8 g
1 qt.			20-1/2	17	581.2 g	482.0 g
1 gal.			86	—	2.4 kg	—
Super Colossal				
1/2 pt.			4-1/2	3-1/2	127.6 g	99.2 g
1 pt.			9	7-1/2	255.2 g	212.6 g
1 qt.			19	16-1/2	538.6 g	467.8 g
1 gal.			86	—	2.4 kg	—
Halves and Sliced				
4.4 oz.			2-1/4	63.8 g
1 pt.			7-1/2	212.6 g
1 qt.			15	425.2 g
1 gal.			72	2.0 kg
Chopped or Minced				
4.4 oz.			4-1/2	127.6 g
1 pt.			15-1/2	439.4 g
1 qt.			31	878.8 g
1 gal.			122	3.5 kg
Broken Pitted				
1 pt.			7-1/2	212.6 g
1 qt.			15	425.2 g
1 gal.			72	2.0 kg

CANNED RIPE OLIVES [9/1/71   52.3751]

Grades:	"A" or "FANCY"	"B" or "CHOICE"	"C" or "STAN-DARD"	"SUB-STAN-DARD"
Minimum Score:	90	80	70	Less than 70

TABLE I
SINGLE SIZES

ILLUSTRATION OF SIZES AND NUMERICAL DESIGNATION	SIZE DESIGNATION	OTHER SIZE DESIGNATIONS		ILLUSTRATION OF SIZES AND NUMERICAL DESIGNATION	SIZE DESIGNATION	OTHER SIZE DESIGNATIONS	
		COUNTS PER POUND	APPROXIMATE COUNTS PER KILO			COUNTS PER POUND	APPROXIMATE COUNTS PER KILO
Smaller than Sub-Petite		221 or more	more than 420				
00	Sub-Petite	Approximate 200 (181 to 220)	400/420	5	Mammoth	Approximate 70 (65 to 75)	150/160 140/150
0	Petite or Midget	Approximate 160 (141 to 180)	380/400 340/360 300/320	6	Giant	53 to 64	130/140 120/130
1	Small or Select or Standard	Approximate 135 (128 to 140)	280/300	7	Jumbo	42 to 52	110/120 100/110 90/100
2	Medium	Approximate 113 (106 to 127)	240/260	8	Colossal	33 to 41	80/90 70/80
3	Large	Approximate 98 (91 to 105)	200/220	9	Super Colossal	32 or less	60/70
4	Extra Large	Approximate 82 (76 to 90)	180/200 160/180				

GREEN OLIVE SIZES

(Count to Kilo)

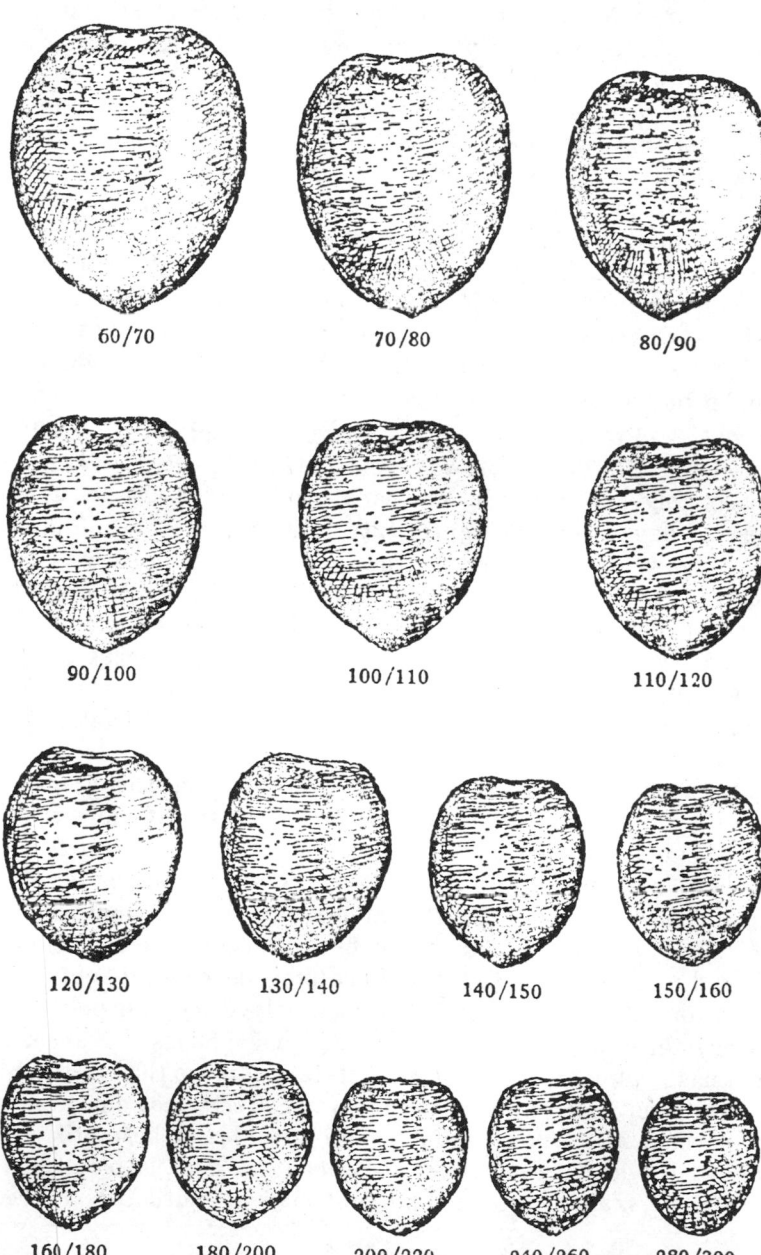

60/70   70/80   80/90

90/100   100/110   110/120

120/130   130/140   140/150   150/160

160/180   180/200   200/220   240/260   280/300

OATMEAL: (See Dry Cereals, Grains, and Flours.)

OLIVES, GREEN [9/8/67]: Grade A: Color: WHOLE, PITTED, STUFFED, AND HALVED—Practically uniform, bright, yellow green to green exterior, a light-colored flesh, and not over 5 percent may vary from the typical color, provided that, when applicable, the garnish and stuffing shall have a good color characteristic of the product used. SLICED —Have at least reasonably good color, and when garnish is added, it shall be of a good characteristic color. **Size:** Not more than a 1/8 in. variation in diameter; and in 90 percent that are most uniform in diameter, the largest diameter does not exceed the smallest diameter by over 1/16 in. **Defects:** Practically free from defects, and the defects may no more than slightly affect the appearance or edibility; packing medium is practically free of detached pieces of stuffing; the appearance is not materially affected by insignificant blemishes; and the defects do not exceed the allowances in Tables IV and V. **Character:** Have a uniform tender texture; and are practically free of slip skins.

Grade B: Color: WHOLE, PITTED, STUFFED, AND HALVED—Reasonably uniform, yellow green to green exterior, a light-colored flesh, and not over 10 percent may vary from the typical color, provided that, when applicable, the garnish and stuffing shall have a reasonably good color characteristic of the product used. SLICED, CHOPPED, OR MINCED—Normal and typical of olives having at least fairly good color, and when garnish is added it too has a reasonably good, characteristic color. **Size:** Not more than 3/16 in. variation in diameters; and in 80 percent that are most uniform in diameter, the largest diameter does not exceed the smallest diameter by more than 1/16 in. Subpetite size may not be graded above Grade B. **Defects:** Reasonably free of defects, and the defects may more than slightly, but not materially affect the appearance or edibility; packing medium is reasonably free of detached pieces of stuffing; appearance may be materially affected by insignificant blemishes; and the defects do not exceed the allowances in Tables IV and V. **Character:** Have a reasonably uniform texture, and are reasonably free of slip skins.

Grade C: Color: WHOLE, PITTED, STUFFED, AND HALVED—Fairly uniform, yellow-green to green exterior, a variable colored flesh, and not over 20 percent may vary from the typical color, provided that, when applicable, the garnish and stuffing shall have a fairly good characteristic color. SLICED, CHOPPED, AND MINCED—Normal, and varies more markedly than olives with fairly good color. BROKEN PITTED—Normal and may be variable but is typical of olives with good, reasonably good, or fairly good color. **Size:** In 60 percent that are most uniform in diameter, the largest diameter does not exceed the smallest diameter by over 1/16 in. Whole style olives with 221 to 275 per lb. may not be graded above Grade C. **Defects:** Fairly free of any defects, and defects may not seriously affect the appearance and edibility; packing medium is fairly free of detached pieces of stuffing, appearance may not be seriously affected by insignificant blemishes; and the defects do not exceed the allowances in Tables IV and V. **Character:** Have a fairly good texture and are fairly free of slip skins.

Sstd: Fails to meet requirements.

OLIVES, RIPE, Canned [9/1/71]: Grade A: Flavor: RIPE TYPE—Distinctive, nut-like flavor characteristic of properly prepared and processed ripe olives which are free from objectionable flavors. GREEN TYPE—Distinctive, sweet and mellow flavor characteristic of properly prepared and processed green ripe olives; and which are free from objectionable flavors. **Color:** RIPE TYPE (WHOLE, PITTED, HALVED, AND QUARTERED)—Have a practically uniform black color or dark rich brown color. Not less than 90 percent, by count, have a color no lighter than that produced by spinning the Munsell color discs in the following combinations: 3-1/2 percent Red (5R 4/14), 3-1/2 percent Yellow (2.5Y 8/12), and 93 percent Black (N/1 Glossy). RIPE TYPE (SLICED, CHOPPED OR MINCED)—Normal and typical of olives of at least reasonably good color. GREEN RIPE TYPE—Normal and practically uniform in such normal color for the type. **Size:** Variation in diameters is not over 1/8 in.; and of all the olives, in 90 percent, by count, that are most uniform in diameter, the largest diameter does not exceed the smallest diameter by more than 1/16 in. **Defects:** Practically free from any defects, and the defects present may not more than slightly affect the appearance or edibility; the appearance is not materially affected with insignificant blemishes; and in whole, pitted,

halved, and quartered styles there may be present, per 100 whole or pitted olives per 200 units in halved style, or per 9 oz. in quarter sytle, not more than 1 piece of harmless, extraneous material not more than 1 pit in pitted style and not more than 3 stems, of which not more than 1 may be a major stem; not more than 10 percent may have minor and major blemishes; minor, major, or serious wrinkles; and there may be mutilated olives, provided that not over 5 percent have major blemishes or wrinkles; and not over 2 percent may be mutilated, or 1 olive may be multilated if there are less than 50 olives in the container. SLICED, CHOPPED, OR MINCED OLIVES—May not be more than slightly affected in appearance or edibility by defects. **Character:** Have a characteristic fleshy texture, and at least 95 percent are practically uniform in texture, and are tender but not soft.

Grade B: Flavor: Same as Grade A. **Color:** RIPE TYPE (WHOLE, PITTED, HALVED, AND QUARTERED—Have a reasonably uniform black or dark brown color. At least 80 percent have a color no lighter than that produced by spinning the Munsell color discs in the following combinations: 6 percent Red (5R 4/14), 6 percent Yellow (2.5Y 8/12), and 88 percent Black (N/1 Glossy). RIPE TYPE (SLICED, CHOPPED OR MINCED—Normal and typical of olive of at least fairly good color. GREEN RIPE TYPE—Normal and reasonably uniform in such normal color for the type. **Size:** Variation in diameters is not over 1/16 in., and of all the olives of the 80 percent that are most uniform in diameter, the largest diameter does not exceed the smallest diameter by more than 1/16 in. **Defects:** Reasonably free from defects and the defects present may affect more than slightly, but not materially, the appearance or edibility; the appearance is not materially affected by insignificant blemishes; and in whole, pitted, halved, and quartered styles there may be present, per 100 whole or pitted olives, per 200 units in halved style, or per 9 oz. in quartered style, not over 2 pieces of harmless extraneous material, not over 2 pits in pitted style, not more than 6 stems, of which not more than 3 may be major stems; not more than 20 percent may have blemishes and wrinkles or be mutilated olives, provided that not over 10 percent have major blemishes or wrinkles, and not over 5 percent may be mutilated. There

TABLE IV—DEFECT ALLOWANCES GREEN OLIVES FOR
WHOLE—PITTED—STUFFED—HALVED STYLES

Defects	U.S. Grade A or U.S. Fancy	U.S. Grade B or U.S. Choice	U.S. Grade C or U.S. Standard
	Maximum [on an average] per 100 whole, pitted, or stuffed olives or per 200 halved olives		
Harmless extraneous material	1 piece	2 pieces	3 pieces
Pit material (pitted, stuffed, and halved styles)	1 pit or piece of pit	2 pits or pieces of pits	3 pits or pieces of pits
Stems: minor and major	Total of 6 but not more than 3 major stems	Total of 10 but not more than 5 major stems	Total of 20 but not more than 10 major stems
Darkened or blemished stuffing material (stuffed style)	5 olives	7 olives	10 olives
	Total and Limiting [maximum] Percentages by Count of Olives with Defects Stated		
	Total / **Provided These Limits are Not Exceeded**	**Total** / **Provided These Limits are not Exceeded**	**Total** / **Provided These Limits are Not Exceeded**
Blemishes: minor and major Wrinkles: minor and major Olives with internal gas pockets/mutilated olives	10 percent by count / 5 percent major blemishes or major wrinkles (combined) 3 percent with internal gas pockets and/or mutilated	15 percent by count / 10 percent major blemishes or major wrinkles (combined) 10 percent with internal gas pockets, 5 percent mutilated	25 percent by count / 15 percent major blemishes or major wrinkles (combined) 15 percent with internal gas pockets, 8 percent mutilated

TABLE V—DEFECT ALLOWANCES—GREEN OLIVES FOR
SLICED—CHOPPED—BROKEN PITTED STYLES

Defects	Broken Pitted Style U.S. Grade C or U.S. Standard	Sliced Style U.S. Grade A or U.S. Fancy	Sliced; Chopped Styles U.S. Grade B or U.S. Choice	Sliced; Chopped Styles U.S. Grade C or U.S. Standard
	Maximum [per pound of drained olives—average]			
Harmless extraneous material Pit material Stems: Minor and Major	2 pieces 2 pits or pieces of pit 4 stems	These or any other defects (including pieces of pits and fragments) do not more than slightly affect the appearance or edibility of the product	These or any other defects (including pieces of pits and fragments) do not materially affect the appearance or edibility of the product	These or any other defects (including pieces of pits and fragments) do not seriously affect the appearance or edibility of the product
Olives that are blemished by minor and/or major blemishes	*Maximum (by weight of drained olives)* 15 percent			

TABLE 1

DESIGNATION(S)	ILLUSTRATION	APPROXIMATE COUNT (Per pound)	AVERAGE COUNT (Per pound of drained olives)
	SINGLE SIZES		ALLOWANCES
Small (or) Select (or) Standard(s)		135	128 to 140 inclusive
Medium		113	106 to 121 inclusive
Large		98	91 to 105 inclusive
Extra Large		82	76 to 88 inclusive
Mammoth		70	65 to 75 inclusive
Giant		53 to 60 inclusive	53 to 60 inclusive
Jumbo		46 to 50 inclusive	46 to 50 inclusive
Colossal		36 to 40 inclusive	36 to 40 inclusive
Super Colossal		Not to exceed 32	32 or less
Special Super Colossal		28 or less	28 or less

may not be more than 15 percent of broken pieces in quartered olives. SLICED, CHOPPED, OR MINCED OLIVES—May not be materially affected in appearance or edibility by defects. **Character:** May vary moderately in texture in that not less than 90 percent are practically uniform in texture and of the remainder not more than 5 percent may be excessively soft.
Grade C: Flavor: May be slightly lacking in a distinctive, characteristic flavor for the respective type but the olives are free

CANNED OLIVES

	NET WEIGHT OZ.	NET WEIGHT METRIC	DRAINED WEIGHT OZ. Whole	DRAINED WEIGHT OZ. Pitted	DRAINED WEIGHT METRIC Whole	DRAINED WEIGHT METRIC Pitted
Family						
8Z Tall			4-1/2	3-1/2	127.6 g	99.2 g
No. 1 Tall			9	7-1/2	255.2 g	212.6 g
No. 300			7-3/4	6	219.7 g	170.1 g
No. 10			66	—	1.9 kg	—
King						
8Z Tall			4	3-1/4	113.4 g	92.1 g
No. 1 Tall			8-1/2	6-1/2	241.0 g	184.3 g
No. 300			7-1/4	5-3/4	205.5 g	163.0 g
No. 10			64	—	1.8 kg	—
Royal						
8Z Tall			4	3	113.4 g	85.05 g
No. 1 Tall			8	6-1/2	226.8 g	184.3 g
No. 300			7-1/4	5-1/2	205.5 g	155.9 g
No. 10			64	—	1.8 kg	—
Other Blends and Mixed Sizes						
8Z Tall			4-1/2	3-1/2	127.6 g	99.2 g
No. 1 Tall			9	7-1/2	255.2 g	212.6 g
No. 10			66	—	1.9 kg	—
Halved and Quartered						
8Z Tall			3-3/4		106.3 g	
No. 300			6-1/2		184.3 g	
No. 10			55		1.6 kg	
Chopped or Minced						
No. 10			100		2.8 kg	

	NET WEIGHT OZ.	NET WEIGHT METRIC	DRAINED WEIGHT OZ.	DRAINED WEIGHT METRIC
Sliced				
8Z Tall			3-3/4	106.3 g
No. 300			6-1/2	184.3 g
No. 10			55	1.6 kg
Broken Pitted				
No. 10			55	1.6 kg
Small, Select, Standard, and Medium				
8Z Tall	4-1/2	3-1/4	127.6 g	92.1 g
No. 1 Tall	9	7	255.2 g	198.4 g
No. 300	7-3/4	6	219.7 g	170.1 g
No. 10	66	—	1.9 kg	—
Large, Extra Large				
8Z Tall	4-1/2	3-1/2	127.6 g	99.2 g
No. 1 Tall	9	7-1/2	255.2 g	212.6 g
No. 300	7-3/4	6	219.7 g	170.1 g
No. 10	66	—	1.9 kg	—
Mammoth				
8Z Tall	4-1/2	3-1/2	127.6 g	99.2 g
No. 1 Tall	9	7-1/2	255.2 g	212.6 g
No. 300	7-1/2	6	212.6 g	170.1 g
No. 10	66	—	1.9 kg	—
Giant, Jumbo, Colossal				
8Z Tall	4	3-1/4	113.4 g	92.1 g
No. 1 Tall	8-1/2	7	241.0 g	198.4 g
No. 300	7-1/4	5-3/4	205.5 g	163.0 g
No. 10	64	—	1.8 kg	—
Super Colossal or Special Super Colossal				
8Z Tall	4	3-1/4	113.4 g	92.1 g
No. 1 Tall	8	6-1/2	226.8 g	184.3 g
No. 300	7-1/4	5-1/2	205.5 g	155.9 g
No. 10	64	—	1.8 kg	—

from objectionable flavors. **Color:** RIPE TYPE (WHOLE, PITTED, HALVED, AND QUARTERED)—May vary in color but not less than 60 percent have a black, dark brown, or reddish brown color not lighter than spinning the Munsell color discs in the following combinations: 6 percent Red (5R 4/14), 6 percent Yellow (2.5Y 8/12), and 88 percent Black (N/1 Glossy). RIPE TYPE (SLICED, CHOPPED, OR MINCED)—Normal and varies more markedly than these styles prepared from olives of fairly good color. RIPE TYPE (BROKEN PITTED)—Normal, and may be variable, but is typical for this style prepared from olives of good, reasonably good, or fairly good color. GREEN RIPE—Normal, but may vary markedly for the type. **Size:** Of all the olives, in 60 percent that are the most uniform in diameter, the largest diameter does not exceed the smallest diameter by more than 1/16 in. **Defects:** Fairly free from defects, but these defects may materially but not seriously affect the appearance and edibility; the appearance may not be seriously affected with insignificant blemishes; and in whole, pitted, halved, and quartered styles, there may be present per 100 whole or pitted olives, per 200 units in halved style, or per 9 oz. in quartered style, not over 2 pieces of harmless extraneous material, not over 2 pits in pitted style, not over 8 stems of which not more than 4 may be major stems; and not more than 30 percent may have major blemishes, and serious wrinkles, and may be mutilated olives, provided that not more than 25 percent may have major blemishes and serious wrinkles, and not more than 10 percent may be mutilated. There may not be more than 25 percent of broken pieces in quartered olives. SLICED, CHOPPED, OR MINCED OLIVES—May have defects that do not seriously affect the appearance or edibility. BROKEN PITTED OLIVES—May have, per 1 lb. of drained olives, not over 2 pieces of harmless extraneous material, not over 2 pits, not over 4 stems; and not over 20 percent may be pieces affected by major blemishes.

Sstd: Fails to meet requirements.

PEANUT BUTTER

CANNED [2/5/72   52.3061]

Grades:	"A" or "FANCY"	"B" or "CHOICE"	"SUB-STANDARD"
Minimum Score:	90	80	Less than 80

PEANUT BUTTER [2/5/72]: Grade A: Color: Rich color, typical of peanut butter prepared from properly roasted peanuts and otherwise properly processed peanut butter; such color is no less brown than USDA Color 1 or no more brown than USDA Color 4 and is without any tinge of a dull, grey, or other abnormal cast. **Consistency:** Spreads easily; is not thin or more than slightly stiff, and (1) in STABILIZED TYPE of peanut butter, there is no noticeable oil separation or (2) in NONSTABILIZED TYPE of peanut butter, there is no more than slight mixing required to disperse any separated oil. **Defects:** Presence of dark particles or other defects does not more than slightly affect the appearance or eating quality of the product; not more than 8 mg of water-soluble, inorganic residue per 100 grams of peanut butter provided that such residue does not affect the edibility or wholesomeness of the product. **Flavor and aroma:** Typical of freshly roasted and ground peanuts, or properly proportioned and blended ingredients; free from staleness, rancidity, and objectionable flavors and odors. Must have 1.0 percent to 1.8 percent, by weight, of salt in the peanut butter, provided that requirements for salt of an unsalted, "specialty pack" style are waived.

Grade B: Color: Color typical of peanut butter prepared from properly roasted peanuts and otherwise properly processed peanut butter; may be slightly dull and/or may have a slight grey cast; may be lighter brown in color than USDA Color 1 but is not excessively pale as indicative of insufficient roasting; or may be more brown than USDA Color 4 but is not excessively brown as indicative of excessive roasting. **Consistency:** Spreadable; moderately, but not excessively, thin or stiff; and (1) in STABILIZED TYPE, there may be no more than slightly noticeable oil separation or (2) in NONSTABILIZED TYPE, there may be no excessive oil separation that causes noticeable dryness or requires more than moderate mixing to disperse the oil. **Defects:** Presence of dark particles or other defects does not seriously detract from the appearance or eating quality of the product; not more than 20 mg of water-insoluble, inorganic residue per 100 grams of peanut butter, provided that such residue does not affect the edibility or wholesomeness of the product. **Flavor and Aroma:** Typical of properly prepared peanut butter which may be lacking good flavor and aroma, but is free of objectionable aromas. Must have 0.5 percent to 2.5 percent, by weight, of salt in the peanut butter provided that requirements for salt of an unsalted "specialty pack" style are waived.

Sstd: Fails to meet requirements.

PEAS: (See Legumes. Dried.)

PICKLES [9/1/66]: Grade A: Color: Typical of properly prepared, and preserved, or processed pickles; shall be free from ripe cucumbers or other off-color vegetable ingredients; and possess the following characteristics by type: CURED TYPE—Skin color ranges from a translucent light green to dark green; practically free from bleached areas. Not more than 10 percent may vary markedly from typical color. In mixed pickles, chow-chow pickles, and pickle relish, all of the pickle ingredients possess a good, practically uniform, typical color for the respective ingredients. FRESH-PACK TYPE—Skin color ranges from opaque yellow green to green; not more than 15 percent vary from typical color. In pickle relish, all of the pickle ingredients possess a good, reasonably uniform, typical color for the respective ingredient. **Size:** Units are practically uniform in size; may vary moderately in size but not to the extent that overall appearance is materially affected. Small odd size units in the top of the container, added to insure well-filled containers shall not be deemed as detracting from Grade A. Grade A meets Table VII. **Defects:** Possesses no more than a trace of grit, not seriously affecting edibility; and other defects individually or collectively do not materially affect appearance or edibility. **Texture:** Cucumber and other vegetable ingredient(s) are firm and crisp, practically free from units with large objectionable seeds, detached seeds and tough skins, and in cured pickles, there may be present not more than 5 percent that are shriveled, soft, or slippery (very slight shriveling permitted in sweet pickles); 5 percent by count of whole units with hollow centers; and 10 percent of count of whole, sliced, or cut units which chalky white areas. In the fresh-pack type, not more than 10 percent are shriveled, soft, or flabby; and not more than 15 percent are whole units with hollow centers.

Grade B: Color: See Grade A, all wording is the same, except as follows: reasonably, etc. CURED TYPE—Light green to

OFFICIAL PICKLE SIZES

3,000 to 45-gal. Cask (67 to gal.)

3,600 to 45-gal. Cask (80 to gal.)

4,500 to 45-gal. Cask (100 to gal.)

6,000 to 45-gal. Cask (133 to gal.)

10,000 to 45-gal. Cask (222 to gal.)

15,000 to 45-gal. Cask (333 to gal.)

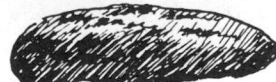

20,000 to 45-gal. Cask (444 to gal.)

Source: *Frosty Acres Buyers Guide*, The Frozen Food Forum, Inc., Atlanta, Ga.

OFFICIAL PICKLE SIZES
(two-thirds actual size)

800 to 45-gal. Cask (18 to gal.)

1,000 to 45-gal. Cask (22 to gal.)

1,200 to 45-gal. Cask (27 to gal.)

1,800 to 45-gal. Cask (40 to gal.)

2,400 to 45-gal. Cask (53 to gal.)

Courtesy of National Pickle Packers Association

dark green; reasonably free; 25 percent; reasonably good. FRESH-PACK TYPE—Yellow green to green; 30 percent; fairly uniform. **Size:** See Grade A, all wording is the same except as follows: reasonably uniform; considerably, seriously affected. May fail to meet criteria in Table VII. **Defects:** See Grade A, all wording is the same except as follows: a small amount of grit not seriously affecting edibility; seriously affect appearance or edibility. **Texture:** See Grade A, all wording is the same except as follows: reasonably firm and crisp; reasonably free; cured pickles: 10 percent shriveled, etc.; 10 percent; 20 percent. FRESH-PACK TYPE—15 percent; 25 percent.

PICKLES

CANNED [9/1/66   52.1681]

Grades:	"A" or "FANCY"	"B" or "EXTRA STANDARD"	"SUB-STANDARD"
Minimum Score:	90	80	Less than 80

NET WEIGHT: Not less than 90 percent of volume of container

POPCORN: Type of Indian corn whose kernels pop open when heated. **Pack:** Usually 24/1-lb.

POTATO CHIPS: Peeled potatoes cut into strips and deep fried. Some are prepared out of processed "paste." **Pack:** Various package sizes of quarts, 12 oz., 1 lb., 3 lb., 4 lb., 5 lb.

PURSLANE: Green, leafy plant for salads, mostly, fresh.

PROCESSED RAISINS [10/15/74]

THOMPSON SEEDLESS RAISINS: Grade A: Have similar varietal characteristics; have a good typical color in Unbleached and Soda-dipped raisins; have a good characteristic flavor; show development characteristics of raisins prepared from well-matured grapes with not less than 80 percent, by weight, of raisins that are well matured or reasonably well matured raisins; and not more than 1 percent, by weight, of select and mixed size raisins, and 2 percent, by weight, of small (midget) size raisins may have substandard development; contain not more than 18 percent, by weight, of moisture, and meet the requirements for absence of defects in Table I.

Grade B: Have similar varietal characteristics; have a reasonably good, typical color in Unbleached and Soda-dipped

TABLE VII—LIMITS IN [A] CLASSIFICATION FOR UNIFORMITY OF SIZE

	Length Variation		Diameter Variation		Thickness	
	In all Units [Maximum]	In 90 percent of units [Maximum]	In all Units [Maximum]	In 90 percent of Units [Maximum]	[Minimum]	[Maximum]
Whole styles:	*Inches*	*Inch*	*Inch*	*Inch*	*Inch*	*Inch*
Midget size	3/4	1/2	5/16	3/16		
Gherkin size						
Small size	1	3/4	3/8	1/4		
Medium size						
Large size	1-1/4	1	7/16	5/16		
Blend of sizes	Full range of 2 adjacent sizes		Full range of two adjacent sizes			
Mixed sizes	Range of more than 2 adjacent sizes		Range of more than 2 adjacent sizes			
Sliced lengthwise:						
Halves or triangular shapes	1-3/4	1				
With parallel surfaces	1-3/4	1			1/8	3/8
Sliced crosswise	Maximum diameter — 2-1/8 in.				1/8	3/8
Cut pickles	Weight variations—Not more than 5 percent, by weight, of all cucumber units may be smaller than 1/8 oz. each; and in the remainder, the largest unit is no more than 4 times the weight of the smallest unit.					
Relish	Size appearance—The pickle ingredients may vary moderately in size. The presence of oversized pieces does not affect overall appearance.					

TABLE VIII—MAXIMUM ALLOWANCES FOR DEFECTS, OR DEFECTIVE UNITS

Defects or defective units [in all styles and types unless stated otherwise]	Grade A	Grade B
Curved pickles (in whole style or whole units in other styles)	10 percent, by count, of whole units	20 percent, by count, of whole units
Misshapen pickles (in whole style or whole units in other styles)	5 percent, by count, of whole units	15 percent, by count, of whole units
Units with attached stems (longer than 3/8 in.)	10 percent, by count, of all cucumber units but no more than 1 percent, by count, of all cucumber units with "long stems"	20 percent, by count, of all cucumber units but no more than 4 percent, by count, of all cucumber units with "long stems"
End cuts (in sliced crosswise style or units sliced crosswise)	5 percent, by weight, of all cucumber units	15 percent, by weight, of all cucumber units
Damaged by mechanical injury	10 percent, by count, of all pickle units including vegetable ingredients other than cucumber	15 percent, by count, of all pickle units including vegetable ingredients other than cucumber
In cured type:		
Minor blemish	Reasonably free	
Major and serious blemish	10 percent, by count, but no more than 1 percent, by count, may be serious	20 percent, by count, but no more than 3 percent, by count, may be serious
In fresh-pack type:		
Minor blemish	Fairly free	
Major and serious blemish	20 percent, by count, but no more than 5 percent, by count, may be serious	30 percent, by count, but no more than 10 percent, by count, may be serious

raisins; have a good characteristic flavor; show development characteristics of raisins prepared from reasonably well-matured grapes with not less than 70 percent, by weight, of raisins that are well matured or reasonably well matured; and not more than 1-1/2 percent, by weight, of select size raisins, 2 percent, by weight, of mixed size raisins, and 3 percent, by weight, of small (midget) size raisins have substandard development; contain not more than 18 percent, by weight, of moisture; and meet the requirements for absence of defects in Table I.

Grade C: Have similar varietal characteristics; have a fairly good, typical color in Unbleached and Soda-dipped raisins; have a fairly good flavor; show development characteristics of raisins prepared from fairly well-matured grapes with not less than 55 percent, by weight, of raisins that are well matured or reasonably well matured, and not more than 2 percent, by weight, of select size raisins; 3 percent, by weight, of mixed size raisins; or 5 percent, by weight, of small (midget) raisins may have substandard development; contain not more than 18 percent, by weight, of moisture, and meet the requirements for absence of defects in Table I.

Sstd: Fail to meet requirements.

PROCESSED RAISINS

DRIED [10/15/74   52.1841]

THOMPSON SEEDLESS RAISINS

| Grades: | "A" or "FANCY" | "B" or "CHOICE" | "C" or "STAN-DARD" | "SUB-STAN-DARD" |

MUSCAT RAISINS

| Grades: | "A" or "FANCY" | "B" or "CHOICE" | | "SUB-STAN-DARD" |

SULTANA RAISINS

| Grades: | "A" or "FANCY" | "B" or "CHOICE" | "C" or "STAN-DARD" | "SUB-STAN-DARD" |

MIXED TYPES

| Grades: | "A" or "FANCY" | "B" or "CHOICE" | "C" or "STAN-DARD" | "SUB-STAN-DARD" |

TABLE I—ALLOWANCES FOR DEFECTS IN TYPE I, THOMPSON SEEDLESS RAISINS

Defects	U.S. Grade A or U.S. Fancy		U.S. Grade B or U.S. Choice		U.S. Grade C or U.S. Standard	
	Maximum Count [per 96 oz.]					
Pieces of stem	1		2		4	
	Maximum Count [per 16 oz.]					
Capstems	15		25		35	
	Maximum [percent by weight]					
Sugared	5		10		15	
Discolored, damaged or moldy raisins	4		6		9	
Provided these limits are not exceeded:						
Damaged	2		3		5	
Moldy	2		3		4	
Substandard and Undeveloped	Total	Maximum Undeveloped	Total	Maximum Undeveloped	Total	Maximum Undeveloped
Select size	1	1/2	1-1/2	1/2	2	1
Mixed size	1	1	2	1	3	1
Small (Midget) size	2	1	3	2	5	3
Slightly discolored or damaged by fermentation or any other defect not described above	Appearance or Edibility of Product					
	May not be affected		May not be more than slightly affected		May not be materially affected	
Grit, sand, or silt	None of any consequence may be present that affects the appearance or edibility of the product.				Not more than a trace may be present that affects the appearance or edibility of the product.	

MUSCAT RAISINS: Grade A: Have similar varietal characteristics; have a good, typical color with not more than 10 percent, by weight, of raisins that may be dark, reddish brown berries in Soda-dipped Unseeded or Seeded (Valencia) raisins; have a good characteristic flavor; show development characteristic of raisins prepared from well-matured grapes; contain not more than 18 percent, by weight, of moisture, except that Seeded or Soda-dipped Seeded raisins may contain not more than 19 percent, by weight, of moisture and meet the requirements for absence of defects in Table II.

Grade B: Have similar varietal characteristics; have a reasonably good, typical color with not more than 15 percent, by weight, of raisins that may be dark, reddish brown berries in Soda-dipped Unseeded or Seeded (valencia) raisins; have a good characteristic flavor; show development characteristic of raisins prepared from reasonably well-matured grapes; contain not more than 18 percent, by weight, of moisture, except that Seeded or Soda-dipped Seeded raisins may contain not more than 19 percent, by weight, of moisture, and meet the requirements for absence of defects in Table II.

Grade C; Have similar varietal characteristics; have a fairly good typical color with not more than 20 percent, by weight, of raisins that may be dark, reddish brown berries in Soda-dipped Unseeded or Seeded (Valencia) raisins; have a fairly good flavor; show development characteristic of raisins prepared from fairly well-matured grapes; contain not more than 18 percent, by weight, of moisture, except that Seeded or Soda-dipped Seeded raisins may contain not more than 19 percent, by weight, of moisture, and meet the requirements for absence of defects in Table II.

TABLE II—ALLOWANCES FOR DEFECTS IN TYPE II, MUSCAT RAISINS

Defects	U.S. Grade A or U.S. Fancy	U.S. Grade B or U.S. Choice	U.S. Grade C or U.S. Standard
	Maximum Count (per 32 oz.)		
Pieces of stem	1	2	3
	Maximum Count (per 16 oz.)		
Capstems in other than un-capstemmed types	10	15	20

Defects	U.S. Grade A or U.S. Fancy	U.S. Grade B or U.S. Choice	U.S. Grade C or U.S. Standard
Seeds in seeded types	12	15	20
Loose capstems in uncapstemmed types	20	20	20
	Maximum (percent by weight)		
Undeveloped	1	2	2
Sugared	5	10	15
Discolored, damaged, or moldy	5	7	9
Provided these limits are not exceeded:			
Damaged	3	4	5
Moldy	2	3	4
	Appearance or Edibility of Product		
Slightly discolored or damaged by fermentation or any other defect not described above	May not be affected	May not be more than slightly affected	May not be materially affected
Grit, sand, or silt	None of any consequence may be present that affects the appearance or edibility of the product.		Not more than a trace may be present that affects the appearance or edibility of the product.

LAYER [OR CLUSTER] MUSCAT RAISINS: Grade A: Have similar varietal characteristics; have a good typical color; have a good characteristic flavor; are uniformly cured and show development characteristic of raisins prepared from well-matured grapes; contain not more than 23 percent, by weight, of moisture; not less than 30 percent, by weight, of the raisins, exclusive of stems and branches, are 3-Crown size or larger, and meet the requirements for absence of defects in Table IIa.

Grade B: Have similar varietal characteristics; have a reasonably good, typical color; have a good characteristic flavor; are uniformly cured, and show development characteristic of raisins prepared from reasonably well-matured grapes; contain not more than 23 percent, by weight, of moisture; not less than 30 percent, by weight, of the raisins, exclusive of stems and branches, are 3-Crown size or larger, and meet the requirements for absence of defects in Table IIa.

Sstd: Fails to meet requirements.

TABLE IIa—ALLOWANCES FOR DEFECTS IN LAYER [OR CLUSTER] MUSCAT RAISINS

Defects	U.S. Grade A or U.S. Fancy	U.S. Grade B or U.S. Choice
	Maximum (by weight) (percent)	
Undeveloped	1	2
Damaged	3	4
Sugared	5	10
	Maximum (by count) (percent)	
Moldy raisins	2	3
Shattered (or loose) individual berries and small clusters of 2 or 3 berries each.	Practically free	Reasonably free
Damaged by fermentation	Appearance or edibility of product may not be affected	Appearance or edibility of product may not be more than slightly affected
Grit, sand, or silt	None of any consequence may be present that affects the appearance or edibility of the product	

SULTANA RAISINS: Grade A: Have similar varietal characteristics; have a good, typical color; have a good characteristic flavor; show development characteristic of raisins prepared from well-matured grapes; contain not more than 18 percent, by weight, of moisture, and meet the requirements for absence of defects in Table III.

Grade B: Have similar varietal characteristics; have a reasonably good typical color; have a good characteristic flavor; show development characteristic of raisins prepared from reasonably well-matured grapes; contain not more than 18 percent,

by weight, of moisture, and meet the requirements for absence of defects in Table III.

Grade C: Have similar varietal characteristics; have a fairly good, typical color; have a fairly good flavor; show development characteristic of raisins prepared from fairly well-matured grapes; contain not more than 18 percent, by weight, of moisture; and meet the requirements for absence of defects in Table III.

Sstd: Fails to meet requirements.

TABLE III—ALLOWANCES FOR DEFECTS IN TYPE III, SULTANA RAISINS

Defects	U.S. Grade A or U.S. Fancy	U.S. Grade B or U.S. Choice	U.S. Grade C or U.S. Standard
	Maximum Count (per 32 oz.)		
Pieces of stems	1	2	3
	Maximum count (per 16 oz.)		
Capstems	25	45	65
	Maximum (percent by weight)		
Undeveloped	1	2	2
Sugared	5	10	15
Discolored, damaged, or moldy	4	6	9
Provided these limits are not exceeded:			
Damaged	2	3	5
Moldy	2	3	4
	Appearance or Edibility of Product		
Slightly discolored or damaged by fermentation or any other defect not described above	May not be affected	May not be more than slightly affected	May not be materially affected
Grit, sand, or silt	None of any consequence may be present that affects the appearance or edibility of the product		Not more than a trace may be present that affects the appearance or edibility of the product

RELISH, PICKLE: Chopped pickles, peppers, etc. with slightly sweet seasoning. Specify:

  minimum 60 percent Immature cucumbers

  minimum 25 percent Cauliflower or

  minimum 10 percent Tomatoes

  3 to 5 percent Onions

  Cured in brine; then cured in vinegar

  Chopped fine and preserved in 15° Baume Vinegar/Sugar liquor.

Pack: 4/1 gal. 6/No. 10.

SAGO: Starchy, grain-like substance taken from the pith of the sago palm, used to thicken milk puddings, soups, and fruit molds.

SALSIFIS: Peeled oyster plant used in garnish work. Imported. Canned. **Specify:** Firm, crisp, well shaped.

SALAD DRESSINGS: (See Fats and Oils)

SALT SMOKE: Mixture of salt, propylene glycol, hardwood tar fractions, and tricalcium phosphate. Used in barbecued meats and barbecue sauce.

SANKA: (See Beverages)

SPICES AND HERBS[1]

Spices are easy to get to know, in part because most of them have distinctive flavor and aroma, but also because they come in just a few basic forms. Spices, herbs, and seeds are marketed whole or ground. Dehydrated vegetable seasonings are sold usually in a chopped or minced form, and as ground powders, and salts. Blends are combinations of spices, herbs, seeds, dehydrated vegetable seasonings, and salt.

The form in which the chef will use whole, ground, or blended spices, or seasoning salts will depend on the recipe. The flavor of spices, herbs, and seeds is derived largely from essential oils that are contained within their microscopic cell walls. In whole spices, the cell walls are intact. This means that they may be cooked for longer periods of time to release their full flavor.

In the grinding of spices, many cell walls are broken, the oils are more exposed, and release their flavor more readily than the whole spice.

Spices are added to foods early in the cooking process to give them ample time to mature to a desirable blending and delicate suspension. Whole spices require longer periods of time to produce their ultimate flavor, while ground spices require shorter time.

Whole spices are usually put in a small cheesecloth or muslin bag so that they may be removed easily when the desired level of flavor has been reached. The bag also prevents pieces of the whole spice from remaining in the finished dish. Ground spices are added directly to the food. Regardless of which form of spice is used, the dish should be tasted before it goes to the customer to see if last-minute spice correction is required.

Seasoning salts are usually added at the very end of the cooking, either just before or after the food is removed from the fire.

With this knowledge behind him, the chef is ready to work with the actual spices. First, examine them visually. Some have a distinctive color and shape, like bay leaf, allspice, rosemary, cloves. Then, smell them. Some spices are not aromatic, but others definitely are, and once sniffed, the aroma of ground cinnamon, pepper, nutmeg, or clove will tend to be remembered.

Tasting and chewing the spice itself comes next. Remember that spices are natural products, not chemicals. They do not affect the chemistry of cooking. Spices may be added to any recipe without fear that they will change the time of cooking or the relationship and behavior of the other ingredients.

In tasting spices, chew them or keep them on the tongue until the flavor develops. The last way, incidentally, is especially good since it permits development of the full flavor of the spice and makes the cook aware of how much flavor potential is in that spice. Chefs who learn to know spices in this way usually do not use a "heavy hand." They know the flavor power of various spices.

COMMONLY AVAILABLE SPICE PRODUCTS

Below is a listing of the commonly available spices from institutional supply houses. The name of the "true spice," herb, seed, or dehydrated vegetable seasoning, is given in the

---

1. The American Spice Trade Association, *Food Service Seasoning Guide*, (Empire State Building, N.Y., N.Y.). $1.25 per copy plus $.35 postage.

left column, while the next two columns indicate if the spice is usually available in whole or ground form. The spice blend section gives only a sampling of the blends that are available. Many spice blends are sold only regionally so it is best to check with your supplier to see what he has in stock. Also, new spice blends are being introduced frequently, and it is almost impossible to keep up with all of them.

A more detailed description of each spice and some of the blends on these pages will be found in the next few pages.

SPICE	FORMS AVAILABLE	
Allspice	Whole Allspice	Ground Allspice
Anise	Anise Seed	Ground Anise
Basil	Basil Leaves	
Bay Leaves	Bay Leaves	Ground Bay Leaves
Caraway	Caraway Seed	Ground Caraway Seed
Cardamom	Whole Cardamom	Ground Cardamom Seed
Celery	Celery Seed	Ground Celery Seed
Chervil	Chervil Leaves	
Chives	Chopped (Dehydrated or Freeze-dried)	
Cinnamon	Stick Cinnamon	Ground Cinnamon
Cloves	Whole Cloves	Ground Cloves
Cumin	Cumin Seed	Ground Cumin Seed
Dill	Dill Seed	Ground Dill Seed
Dill Weed	Dill Weed	
Fennel	Fennel Seed	Ground Fennel Seed
Garlic		Instant Minced Garlic Instant Garlic Powder
Ginger	Whole Ginger	Ground Ginger
Mace	Whole Mace	Ground Mace
Marjoram	Marjoram Leaves	Ground Marjoram
Mustard	Mustard Seed	Powdered Mustard
Nutmeg	Whole Nutmeg	Ground Nutmeg
Onion		Instant Minced Onion (or Chopped Onion) Instant Onion Powder (or Granulated Onion)
Oregano	Oregano Leaves	Ground Oregano
Paprika		Ground Paprika
Black Pepper	Whole Black Pepper	Ground Black Pepper, Coarse Ground Black Pepper
Red Pepper	Whole Red Pepper	Crushed Red Pepper Ground Red Pepper Ground Cayenne

SPICE	FORMS AVAILABLE	
White Pepper	Whole White Pepper	Ground White Pepper
Poppy	Poppy Seed	
Rosemary	Rosemary Leaves	Ground Rosemary
Saffron	Saffron	
Sage	Sage Leaves	Rubbed Sage, Ground Sage
Savory	Savory Leaves	Ground Savory
Sesame	Sesame Seed	
Shallots		Chopped (Freeze-dried)
Tarragon	Tarragon Leaves	
Thyme	Thyme Leaves	Ground Thyme
Turmeric		Ground Turmeric

SPICE BLENDS

Apple Pie Spice	Curry Powder	Onion Salt
Barbecue Spice	Garlic Salt	Poultry Seasoning
Celery Salt	Herb Seasoning	Pumpkin Pie Spice
Chili Powder	Italian Seasoning	Seasoned or Flavor Salt
Cinnamon Sugar	Mixed Pickling Spice	Shrimp Spice or Crab Boil

FLAKES
[All dehydrated]

Celery Flakes	Mixed Vegetable Flakes	Parsley Flakes
Mint Flakes	Onion Flakes	Sweet Pepper Flakes

ALLSPICE: Pimenta officinalis. **Origin and Description:** Jamaica, Honduras, Mexico. Allspice is a pea-sized fruit which grows in small clusters on a tree. Picked green, it is a shriveled brown berry after curing. As its name implies, allspice is reminiscent of several spices—cinnamon, nutmeg, and cloves. **Uses:** WHOLE—pickling, meats, gravies, boiling fish. GROUND—baking, puddings, relishes, fruit preserves. Try adding a dash to tomato sauce. **Available:** "Whole Allspice"; "Ground Allspice."

ANGELICA: Angelica archangelica or Archangelica officinalis. Grown in Europe where it is used as a vegetable and its root is used in cookery. **Available:** Glaceed stalks or packed in syrup.

ANISE: Pimpinella anisum. **Origin and Description:** Spain and Mexico. Anise is a dried, greenish brown seed of a foot-high annual shrub. It is used in flavoring licorice. **Uses:** Good in cookies, candies, sweet pickles, and as beverage flavoring. Sprinkle on coffee cakes, sweet rolls. For anise cookies, just add 1/4 tsp. ground anise to cookie batter. **Available:** "Anise seed"; "Ground Anise."

APPLE PIE SPICE: A ground blend of the sweet baking spices, with a predominance of cinnamon. Cloves, nutmeg or mace, allspice, and ginger are typical inclusions. Good for all fruit pies and pastries.

BALM OF GILEAD: Abies balsamea. Used as a pine aromatic in cookery.

BASIL: Ocimum basilicum. **Origin and Description:** United States, Hungary, and Indonesia. Also known as "Sweet Basil." Basil consists of cleaned and dried leaves and tender stems. Its aromatic flavor has a pleasing leafy note. **Uses:** An important seasoning in tomato paste and tomato dishes. Use in cooked peas, squash, and snap beans. Famed for use in turtle soup. Sprinkle chopped basil leaves over lamb chops before cooking. **Available:** "Basil Leaves."

BAY LEAVES: Lauris nobilis. **Origin and Description:** Turkey. Bay leaves are the dried leaves of an evergreen tree. These smooth oblong leaves are deep green on the upper surface and paler beneath. The flavor is sweet and herbaceous with a delicate floral spice note. **Uses:** For pickling, stews, sauces, and soups, Excellent for fish or chowder. Good with meats, such as fricassee of kidney, heart, or oxtail. Add bay leaf, with whole peppercorns, to tomato sauce for boiled cod. **Available:** "Bay Leaves."

BLENDS: Many mixtures, or blends, of spices have been developed by spice manufacturers to make the art of seasoning a quick and easy task. In some cases a specific blend may be unique with the company that produces it; in others, the blend may be one that has been adopted by most spice packagers. The following are the blends that are now sold by most spice firms and thus would be available to restaurants throughout the country.

BURNET: Sanguisorba canadensis. A perennial plant. **Uses:** For food garnishing and raw salad inclusions, especially with cucumbers.

CARAWAY: Carum carvi. **Origin and Description:** Nether-lands and Poland. The biennial plant grows 2 or 3 ft. high, and the seeds are somewhat curved, tapering toward both ends. The flavor is a combination of dill and anise with a slight fruitiness. Caraway is the important ingredient in the cordial Kummel. **Uses:** Widely used in baking, especially rye bread. Good in sauerkraut, new cabbage, noodles, and soft cheese spreads. Sprinkle over french fried potatoes; on pork, liver, kidneys before cooking. Sprinkle canned asparagus with caraway before heating. **Available:** "Caraway Seed"; "Ground Caraway Seed."

CARDAMOM: Elettaria cardamomum. **Origin and Description:** Guatemala and India. Tiny brown seeds which grow enclosed in a white or green pod varying from 1/4 to 1 in. in length. The flavor is sweet and spicy with a camphoraceous note. **Uses:** WHOLE—(in pod) used in Mixed Pickling Spice. SEED—(removed from pod) flavors demitasse. GROUND—flavors Danish pastry, bun breads, coffee cakes. Improves flavor of grape jelly. Sprinkle cardamom on iced melon for breakfast or dessert. **Available:** "Whole Cardamom"; "Ground Cardamom Seed."

CELERY: Apium graveolens. **Origin and Description:** India and France. Celery seed is a minute, olive brown seed, obtained from the celery plant. Celery Salt is made by combining ground celery seed with table salt. Celery seed has been described as having a parsley-nutmeg flavor. **Uses:** Excellent in pickling, salads, fish, salad dressing, and vegetables. For a different flavor, add celery seed to braised lettuce (about 1/2 tsp. to a head of lettuce). Ground celery seed is excellent in tomato juice cocktail. **Available:** "Celery Seed"; "Ground Celery Seed"; "Celery Salt."

CELERY FLAKES: Origin and Description: United States. Dehydrated, flaked leaves and stalks of vegetable celery. **Uses:** Soups, stews, sauces, stuffings. **Available:** "Celery Flakes."

CHERVIL: Anthriscus cerefolium. One of the 4 fines herbes. Lighter flavor than parsley, with a slight flavor of licorice.

CHILI POWDER: A ground blend of chili peppers, oregano, cumiun seed, garlic, salt, and sometimes such spices as cloves, red pepper, and allspice. Basic seasoning for Mexican-style cooking, including chili con carne. Good in shellfish and oyster cocktail sauces, or boiled and scrambled in eggs, gravy, and stew seasoning. Try it in ground meat or hamburgers.

CHISO: Perilla nankinensis. Red herb of the mint family. Good on cold foods or in cookery, especially in Oriental cookery. Flavor is similar to a combination of coriander, cumin, and parsley.

CHIVES: Allium schoenoprasum. **Origin and Description:** United States. Called the orchid of the lily family because of their purple flowers, chives are a perennial plant with slender, rush-like leaves, of a deep green color, that are chopped and used to give a subtle onion flavor to and enhance the appearance of many dishes. **Uses:** Excellent as garnishes for hot and cold dishes, chives make superb topping for soups, salads, dairy dishes, meat, fish, and egg dishes, and team beautifully with all green vegetables. Popular in sour cream dressing for baked potatoes. **Available:** "Dehydrated Chopped Chives"; "Freeze-dried Chopped Chives."

CHRYSANTHEMUM: Leaves are better than petals. Commonly used in Oriental foods.

CINNAMON: Cinnamomum cassia. **Origin and Description:** Indonesia. Cinnamon comes from the bark of an aromatic evergreen tree. Almost all cinnamon sold in the U.S. is of cassia cinnamon variety (the spice trade often refers to it merely as "cassia"). This has the reddish brown color and pungently sweet aroma and flavor we expect in cinnamon. We import true cinnamon, Cinnamomum zeylanicum (Ceylon cinnamon) from the Seychelles and Sri Lanka. This is more buff colored and milder flavored. **Uses:** WHOLE—Pickling, preserving, flavoring puddings, stewed fruits. Serve with clove-stuck lemon slices in hot tea. Used in hot wine drinks. GROUND—Baked goods, often in combination with allspice, nutmeg, and cloves. The principal mincemeat spice. Combine with mashed sweet potatoes; with sugar for cinnamon toast. Dust on fried bananas. **Available:** "Stick Cinnamon"; "Ground Cinnamon."

CINNAMON SUGAR: There are few if any times in cooking and baking when cinnamon is not accompanied by sugar, and this skillful blend of the two thus becomes a very convenient product. It is especially useful for cinnamon toast and as a quick topping for many other sweet goods.

CLOVES: Eugenia caryophyllata. **Origin and Description:** Madagascar. Cloves are the fruit (dried flower buds) of a tree belonging to the evergreen family and are dark brown and dusky red in color. The flavor is characterized by a sweet, pungent spiciness. **Uses:** WHOLE—For pork and ham roasts, pickling of fruits, spiced sweet syrups. GROUND—Baked goods, chocolate puddings, stews, vegetables. For a tastier meat stew, add a small onion studded with 2 or 3 whole cloves. **Available:** "Whole Cloves"; "Ground Cloves."

CORIANDER: Coriandrum sativum. **Origin and Description:** Mostly from Morocco and Rumania. Coriander is the dried fruit of a small plant. It is nearly globular and about 1/4 in. long. Externally the seed is a weak orange yellow to a moderate yellow brown, often with a purplish red blush. In flavor it has a sweet, dry, exotic spice character tending toward lavender and lemon. **Uses:** WHOLE—In mixed pickles, gingerbread batter, cookies, cakes, biscuits, poultry stuffings, mixed green salads. GROUND—In sausage making, to flavor buns. Rub ground coriander on fresh pork before roasting. **Available:** "Coriander Seed"; "Ground Coriander."

COSTMARY: Chrysanthemum balsamita or Balsamita vulgaris. Highly aromatic herb with a slightly bitter flavor.

CRAB BOIL OR SHRIMP SPICE: These products are similar or identical (depending on the manufacturer), both being mixtures of several whole spices that are to be added to the water when boiling seafood. Typically, the mixtures include whole peppercorns, bay leaves, red peppers, mustard seeds, ginger, and other spices in whole form.

CUMIN: Cuminum cyminum. **Origin and Description:** Iran. Cumin is a small, dried fruit, oblong in shape, and resembles caraway seed. The flavor is penetrating. Sometimes known as "Comino" seed. **Uses:** An important ingredient in curry and chili powder. Good for soups, cheese, meat pies, stuffed eggs. For canapes, mix chutney with snappy cheese and garnish with cumin seed. **Available:** "Cumin Seed"; "Ground Cumin Seed."

CURRY POWDER: A ground blend of as many as 16 to 20 spices, designed to give the characteristic flavor of Indian curry cookery. Ginger, turmeric, fenugreek seed, cloves, coriander, cumin seed, black pepper, and red pepper are typical, with others being used according to the manufacturer's individual formula. Used in curry sauces, for curry eggs, vegetables, fish, and meat. Try a dash in French dressing, scalloped tomatoes, clam and fish chowders, and split pea soup.

DILL SEED: Anethum graveolens. **Origin and Description:** India and Mexico. Dill is the small dark seed of the dill plant. It is brown, broadly oval in outline, and rounded at both ends. The flavor is clean, aromatic, reminiscent of caraway. **Uses:** Used for pickling, in cooking sauerkraut, salads, soups, fish and meat sauces, gravies, spiced vinegars, green apple pie. Sprinkle dill seed on potato salad, cooked macaroni, or when cooking sauerkraut. **Available:** "Dill Seed"; "Ground Dill Seed."

DILL WEED: Anethum graveoleus. **Origin and Description:** United States. Dill weed is the feathery leaf of the dill plant, an annual of the parsley family, and has a distinctive aromatic taste. **Uses:** Dill weed is particularly suited to uncooked mixtures, such as salads, sour cream sauces, and mayonnaise. It is delicious in baked potatoes, sandwich fillings, white sauce mixes, buttered green beans, and fish butter sauces. **Available:** "Dill Weed."

DITTANY: Origanum dictamnus. Also known as pepperwort. An aromatic herb with a light flavor.

ELDER: Sambucus nigra. S. caerulea, and S. canadensis. Used for beverages and cooking.

FENNEL: Foeniculum vulgare. **Origin and Description:** India and Bulgaria. Fennel is a small, seed-like fruit, with an agreeable odor and aromatic sweet taste somewhat like anise. **Uses:** Popular in sweet pickles and Italian sausage. Used in boiled fish, pastries, candies, and liqueurs. Add a dash to apple pie for an unusually good flavor. **Available:** "Fennel Seed"; "Ground Fennel Seed."

FENUGREEK: Trigonella foenumgraecum. Used in curry powders, salads, and salad dressings.

FITCHES: Nigella sativa. Used in soft cheeses and dips, and as a pepper substitute in sauces and seasonings.

GARLIC [DEHYDRATED]: Allium sativum. **Origin and Description:** United States. Dehydrated and processed. This is the most strongly flavored of the plants in the lily family and is used in a wide range of dishes. **Uses:** Very convenient way of adding garlic flavor to foods. **Available:** "Instant Garlic Powder"; Instant Minced Garlic"; "Garlic Salt."

GINGER: Zingiber officinale. **Origin and Description:** Nigeria, West Indies, Sierra Leone. Ginger is the rhizome (root) of a tuberous plant. Externally it is a weak yellow orange; internally, a yellow brown. The flavor is warm and fragrant with a pungent spiciness. **Uses:** WHOLE—Chutneys, conserves, pickling. Stew with dried fruits, applesauce. GROUND—Gingerbread, cakes, pumpkin pie, Indian pudding, canned fruits, pot roasts, and other meats. Rub chicken inside and out with mixture of ginger and butter before roasting. **Available:** "Whole Ginger"; "Ground Ginger."

GRAINS OF PARADISE: Amomum melegueta. A West African spice. Similar flavor to pepper, but less pungent.

HAWTHORN: Crataegus aestivalis and Crataegus mexicana. Berries are used for jellies and preserves.

HERB SEASONING: This is a savory blend of herbs, particularly suited to salad dressings. Actually, the blend varies somewhat according to the brand, but the end uses are essentially the same. Note that the term "herb" specifically refers to the milder flavored leafy products (i.e., marjoram, oregano, basil, chervil), as opposed to the stronger flavored tropical spices (i.e., pepper, cloves, cinnamon.)

HORSERADISH: Armoracia rusticana. Roots, dried or fresh, are used in cooking. Strong flavor. Grated, ground, minced, dried, or fresh.

ITALIAN SEASONING: Italian dishes have become so popular in this country that cooks asked for a simple way to achieve the characteristic flavoring of this cuisine. While no one blend could accomplish this completely, it is well known that such seasonings as oregano, basil, red pepper, and rosemary are certainly typical of many Italian creations—particularly the popular pastas and pizza. Italian Seasoning characteristically contains these and possibly garlic powder and others.

LEMON VERBENA: Lippia citriodora. Light lemon floral flavor.

LOVAGE: Levisticum officinale. Member of the carrot family. Seeds used in pastries and cakes; leaves used in salads and sweet cookery.

MACE: Myristica fragrans. **Origin and Description:** Indonesia, India, West Indies. Mace is the fleshy growth between the nutmeg shell and the outer husk, orange red in color. Flavor resembles nutmeg. **Uses:** WHOLE (called "Blade")—Excellent in fish sauces, pickling, preserving. Add a chopped blade to gingerbread batter. Good in stewed cherries. GROUND— Essential in fine pound cakes; contributes a golden tone and exotic flavor to all yellow cakes. Valuable in all chocolate dishes. Use 1/4 tsp. ground mace to 1 pt. of ready whipped cream. **Available:** "Whole Mace"; "Ground Mace."

MAGGI: Used to flavor gravies and sauces. Packed in pints and quarts.

MARIGOLD: Calendula officinalis. Buds and flowers are used. Petals are bitter and are used for appearance and flavor.

MARJORAM: Marjorana lorteusis. **Origin and Description:** France, Chile, Peru. Marjoram is an herb of the mint family. It has a peculiar, sweet-minty, herbaceous type flavor. **Uses:** Delicious combined with other herbs in stews, soups, sausage, poultry seasonings. Good in fish and sauce recipes. Sprinkle over lamb while cooking for an excellent flavor touch. **Available:** "Marjoram Leaves"; "Ground Marjoram."

MINT FLAKES: Mentha spicata or Mentha piperita. **Origin and Description:** United States and Europe. Dehydrated, flaked leaves of spearmint or peppermint. Strong flavor. **Uses:** Mint flakes are used for flavoring soups, stews, beverages, jellies, fish, sauces.

MIXED PICKLING SPICE: A mixture of several whole spices, usually including mustard seed, bay leaves, black and white peppercorns, dill seed, red peppers, ginger, cinnamon, mace, allspice, coriander seed. Useful for pickling and marinating meats, and to season vegetables, relishes, and sauces. Also good in stews and soups.

MIXED VEGETABLE FLAKES: Origin and Description: United States. Mixture of dehydrated, flaked vegetables, usually composed of celery, green peppers, carrots. **Uses:** Convenient means of seasoning soups, stews, sauces, stuffings.

MUSTARD: White—Brassica hirta; Brown—Brassica juncea. **Origin and Description:** Canada, Denmark, United States. Both varieties are herbs; widely cultivated. Mustard is a small seed, the brown or black being dark brown spheroidal seeds, while the yellow or white are subglobular seeds. The yellow or white is the milder flavored, whereas the brown or black is the pungent variety from which the mustard served in Chinese restaurants is made. Unlike other spices, mustard must be moistened with an equal amount of tepid water to start the enzyme action which releases the flavor. Let mixture stand 10 minutes for full aroma. **Uses:** SEED—Garnish salads, pickled meats, fish, and hamburgers. POWDERED—Meats, sauces, gravies. Add 1/2 tsp. powdered mustard for each 2 cups of cheese sauce for macaroni. **Available:** "Mustard Seed"; "Powdered Mustard."

NASTURTIUM: Tropaeolum majus. Used in salads; marinated, as substitute for capers. Peppery, but sour flavor.

NUTMEG: Myristica fragrans. **Origin and Description:** Indonesia, West Indies. Nutmeg is the kernel of the nutmeg fruit; it grows on a somewhat bushy tree which reaches a height of 40 ft. The fruit of the nutmeg tree is variable in shape—either globular, oval, or pear-shaped. The fleshy husk, grooved on one side, splits, releasing the deep-brown, aromatic nutmeg. (An orange red network of fleshy growth between the nut and outer husk is known as mace.) **Uses:** WHOLE—To be grated as needed. GROUND—Baked goods, sauces, puddings. Topping for eggnog, custards, whipped cream. Good on cauliflower, spinach. Sprinkle on fried bananas, on bananas and berries with cream. Excellent spice for flavoring doughnuts. A pinch of nutmeg adds flavor to the crust for meat pie. **Available:** "Whole Nutmeg"; "Ground Nutmeg."

ONIONS: [DEHYDRATED]: Allium capa. **Origin and Description:** United States. Dehydrated and processed. Now sold in several forms corresponding to the various sizes of onion cuts normally used in seasoning, i.e., sliced, chopped, minced, etc. Convenient labor savers wherever onion flavor is desired. **Uses:** Soups, chowders, stews, salads, dressings, sauces, steaks, hamburgers. **Available:** "Instant Chopped Onion"; "Instant Onion Powder"; "Granulated Onion"; "Onion Salt"; "Onion Flakes."

OREGANO: Lippia graveolens, Lippia origanum. **Origin and Description:** Greece and Mexico. Known also as "Wild Marjoram" and the "Pizza Herb," oregano leaves are about 5/8 in. long, and light green when dried. Oregano is strong and aromatic, with a tantalizing savor. It should be used with discretion. **Uses:** Any tomato dish tastes twice as good with a pinch of this herb. A quarter or half teaspoon can be sprinkled sparingly over pork, lamb, veal, and chicken. Add it to omelets, cheese dishes, soups, tossed green salads, cream sauce for quartered, hard-cooked eggs. Give zest to vegetables with a pinch of oregano in snap beans, spinach, creamed white onions, zucchini. **Available:** "Oregano Leaves"; "Ground Oregano."

OXALIS: Oxalidaceae. A sour herb used in South America.

PAPRIKA: Capsicum annum. **Origin and Description:** Spain, Central Europe, United States. A sweet red pepper, ground after seeds and membrane have been removed. Most paprika sold in U.S. is mild and sweet in flavor, slightly aromatic, and prized for brilliant red color. A type which has a slight pungency is also available. **Uses:** Used as colorful red garnish for any pale foods. Important ingredient in chicken paprika and Hungarian goulash. Used on fish, shellfish, salad dressings, vegetables, meats, gravies, canapes. For an excellent canape, mix paprika with cream cheese and celery seed and serve on crackers. **Available:** "Ground Paprika."

PARSLEY FLAKES: Petroselinum crispum. **Origin and Description:** United States. Dehydrated, flaked parsley leaf and stem material. **Uses:** Seasoning and garnish. Flavors soups, salads, meat, fish, sauces, and vegetable dishes. For spiced potato cakes made from leftover mashed potatoes, or to reheated mashed potatoes, try adding some parsley flakes, onion salt, and paprika. **Available:** "Parsley Flakes."

PEPPER, BLACK AND WHITE: Piper nigrum. **Origin and Description:** Indonesia, Brazil, India. Small dried berry of vine. Whole pepper is known as peppercorn. Pepper is the world's most popular spice. White pepper is the kernel of the black peppercorn with the outer cover removed before drying. Flavor is warm, pungent, aromatic. **Uses:** Adds a spicy tang to almost all foods. A "must" in the kitchen and on the table. WHOLE (black or white)—In pickling, soups, and meats. GROUND (black or white)—Meats, sauces, gravies, many vegetables, soups, salads, eggs. Dash fresh black pepper in tossed green salad. White pepper particularly useful in light colored sauces, soups, vegetables, where dark specks are not wanted. **Available:** "Whole Black Pepper"; "Ground Black Pepper"; "Coarse Ground Black Pepper"; "Whole White Pepper"; "Ground White Pepper."

PEPPER, CAYENNE: Capsicum minimum. Other name—red pepper. Small red pods that are ground. Used in gravies, on meats and seafoods, and sauces.

POPPY: Papaver somniferum. **Origin and Description:** The Netherlands, Romania, Poland. Tiny seeds of poppy plant; about 900,000 to the lb. Best is blue-colored seed from The Netherlands. Crunchy nut-like flavor. **Uses:** Excellent as topping for breads, rolls, cookies. Also delicious in salads and noodles. Filling for pastries. Add poppy seeds to buttered noodles and mix thoroughly. **Available:** "Poppy Seed."

POULTRY SEASONING: A ground blend of sage, thyme, marjoram, and savory, and sometimes rosemary and other spices. For poultry, veal, pork, and fish stuffings. Good with paprika for meat loaf. For a delightful combination, add to biscuit dough to serve with poultry.

PUMPKIN PIE SPICE: A ground blend of cinnamon, cloves, and ginger. Designed particularly for pumpkin pie, it is good also in spice cookies, gingerbread, and breakfast buns. French fry slices of raw pumpkin and dust lightly with pumpkin pie spice for a delicious "something new."

RAMPION: Campanula rapunculus. Also known as bellflower and ramp. Mild, but more penetrating flavor than garlic. Used in cookery and raw.

RED PEPPER: Capsicum frutescens. **Origin and Description:** United States, Mexico, Africa, Japan, Turkey, depending on type. There are dozens of types varying in degree of heat. A product sold as "Cayenne" or "Red Pepper" may contain several varieties in order to obtain desired strength. There are no heat standards for cayenne or red pepper, so it is better to consult your supplier as to the relative strength of his various products. **Uses:** WHOLE—Pickles, relishes, hot sauces. CRUSHED—Sauces, pickles, highly spiced meats, a prime ingredient for many Italian specialty dishes, including certain sausages. GROUND—With discretion, in meats, sauces, fish, egg dishes. A touch of ground red pepper (or cayenne) plus 1/4 tsp. paprika added to 2 or 3 tbsp. butter makes excellent sauce for vegetables. **Available:** "Whole Red Pepper"; "Crushed Red Pepper"; "Ground Red Pepper"; "Cayenne."

ROSE HIPS: Rosa canina. Slightly tangy and mildly sweet

flavor. Used for conserves and baking, but seldom used for cooking.

ROSEMARY: Rosmarinum officinalis. **Origin and Description:** France, Spain, Portugal. A spiked-leaved herb; looks like curved pine needle and is sweet and fresh-tasting. **Uses:** In lamb dishes, in soups, and stews. Sprinkle on beef before roasting. Flavors fish and meat stocks. Add a dash of rosemary to boiled potatoes in the early stages of cooking. **Available:** "Rosemary Leaves"; "Ground Rosemary."

RUE: Ruta graveolens. Known as "herb of grace." Has a strong odor and is used as a component of European liqueurs and bitters. Seldom used in cooking because of its bitterness.

SAFFRON: Crocus sativus. **Origin and Description:** Spain. The world's most expensive spice, yet a little goes a long way. Takes 225,000 stigma of a crocus-like flower to make a pound. Flavor is distinctive and aggreeable in character, but its ability to give food an appetizing yellow color is equally prized. **Uses:** In baked goods. Most highly esteemed in "Arroz Con Pollo," the rice-chicken dish of Spain. To add golden color and delicious flavor to rice, boil pinch of saffron in water for a moment before adding rice. **Available:** "Saffron."

SAGE: Salvia officinalis. **Origin and Description:** Yugoslavia, Albania, Greece. Sage is a perennial shrub about 2 ft. high. Flavor is camphoraceous, with a minty spiciness. **Uses:** Particularly good with pork and pork products. Used in sausages, meat stuffings, baked fish, and poultry. Excellent in salad greens. **Available:** "Sage Leaves"; "Rubbed Sage" (finer consistency than leaves); "Ground Sage."

SAVORY: Satureia hortensis. **Origin and Description:** France and Spain. Herb of the mint family, grown in many climates. Flavor is delicately sweet and herbaceous, resembling thyme. **Uses:** Combined with other herbs, makes an excellent flavoring for meats, meat dressings, chicken, fish sauces. A pinch of savory gives a lift to scrambled eggs. **Available:** "Savory Leaves"; "Ground Savory."

SHALLOT: Allium ascalonicum. **Origin and Description:** United States. Member of the lily family, ranging in size from walnut to small fig, shallots can easily be substituted for onion, although they are milder than onions. **Uses:** Sauces for delicate foods, such as chicken, fish, veal. Also in salad dressings, soups, stews, broiled meats, stuffings, eggs. **Available:** "Freeze-dried Chopped Shallots."

SEAFOOD SEASONING: A ground blend of approximately the same spices as used in Crab Boil and Shrimp Spice with the addition of salt. Especially good in seafood sauces because the ground seasoning blends into the sauce completely.

SEASONED OR FLAVOR SALT: This product goes by different names, according to the brand, but the idea is essentially the same. It is a mixture of spices, herbs, and salt which is designed to be an all-purpose seasoning. Many restaurants now place it next to the pepper on the table; others use it in preparation. It is especially suited to meats, vegetables, sauces, and dairy foods.

SESAME: Sesamum indicum. **Origin and Description:** Nicaragua, Mexico, Guatemala. Sesame is a small, honey-colored seed, with gentle nut-like flavor, and high oil content. **Uses:** A rich, toasted-nut flavor when baked on rolls, breads, and buns. Principal ingredient in Middle Eastern candy, halvah. Add to lightly cooked, cold spinach which has been blended with soy sauce. **Available:** "Sesame Seed." (It is a good idea to specify hulled also, since restaurants would not be satisified with "unhulled" sesame.)

SLOE: Prunus umbellata. Round, yellow or yellow orange, seedless fruits with red blotches. Lightly bitter and sour flavor. Gives a pink coloring to beverages.

SMOKE, LIQUID: An artificial flavor used on meats. Usually packed in quarts.

SUMAC: Rhus glabrum. Tart berry with a slightly sour, bitter, floral aroma. Should be bought commercially because many wild sumac berries are poisonous.

SWEET PEPPER FLAKES: Origin and Description: United States. Dehydrated, flaked sweet green or red peppers, or a mixture of both green and red (the red being sweet, not hot). **Uses:** A convenient way of adding green or red pepper flavor to sauces, salads, vegetables, casseroles, when a fine diced pepper is called for. **Available:** "Sweet Pepper Flakes."

TARRAGON: Artemisia dracunculus. **Origin and Description:** France and Spain. Tarragon is a small perennial plant which forms tall stalks, about 1-1/2 yards high. Minty, herbaceous, and anise-like in flavor. **Uses:** In sauces, salads, chicken, meats, egg, and tomato dishes. The important flavoring used in making tarragon vinegar. Just before taking broiled chicken out of oven, season and sprinkle with finely minced tarragon, and serve with pan gravy. **Available:** "Tarragon Leaves."

THYME: Thymus vulgaris. **Origin and Description:** Spain and France. Thyme is a low shrub about a foot high. The leaves and stems of this garden herb have a strong distinctive flavor. **Uses:** In stews, soups, and poultry stuffings. Excellent in clam and fish chowders, sauces, croquettes, chipped beef, fricassees. Thyme and fresh tomatoes go together like hand and glove. Sprinkle thyme over sliced tomatoes on bed of lettuce, use vinegar and olive oil dressing, with salt, and pepper. **Available:** "Thyme Leaves"; "Ground Thyme."

TURMERIC: Curcuma longa. **Origin and Description:** India and Jamaica. Root of the ginger family, orange yellow in color. Important ingredient of curry powder. Flavor has a mild, ginger-pepper note. **Uses:** Flavoring and coloring in prepared mustard, and is used in combination with mustards as flavoring for meats, dressings, and salads. Used in pickles, chow-chow, and other relishes. Try a little turmeric in creamed eggs, fish, seafood. **Available:** "Ground Turmeric."

VANILLA: Vanilla planifolia. Used as an extract or flavor in liquid form.

WOODRUFF: Asperula odorata. Known as waltmeister in Germany. One of the most delicate of herbs.

YARROW: Achillea millefolium. A bitter herb used for cooking and beverages.

SAUERKRAUT, Canned [5/13/63]

Grade A: Color: Possesses a light, practically uniform, typical white to light cream general appearance, characteristic of properly prepared and properly processed canned kraut equal to or better than kraut model No. 1. **Cut:** With respect to shredded kraut, the shreds are uniform in thickness, and the appearance of the product is not more than slightly affected by the presence of short or irregular cut pieces; and with respect to chopped kraut, the pieces are uniform in size, and the presence of pieces marked by smaller or larger than the predominant size of pieces does not more than slightly affect the appearance. **Defects:** Minor defects may be present that do not materially affect the appearance or eating quality, and

SAUERKRAUT

BULK [5/24/67   52.3451]

Grades:	"A" or "FIRST QUALITY"	"C" or "SECOND QUALITY"	"SUB-STANDARD"
Minimum Score:	85	70	Less than 70

CANNED [5/13/63   52.2951]

Grades:	"A" or "FANCY"	"B" or "EXTRA STAN-DARD"	"C" or "STAN-DARD"	"SUB-STAN-DARD"
Minimum Score:	90	80	70	Less than 70
	NET WEIGHT OZ.	NET WEIGHT METRIC	DRAINED WEIGHT OZ.	DRAINED WEIGHT METRIC
No. 8Z Tall	8.2	232.5 g	6.7	189.9 g
No. 303	16.0	453.6 g	13.2	374.2 g
No. 2½	28.3	802.3 g	23.0	652.0 g
No. 10	104.0	2.9 kg	80.0	2.3 kg

major defects may be present that do not more than slightly affect the appearance or eating quality. **Character:** Kraut is crisp and firm. **Flavor:** Possesses a good characteristic kraut flavor which is free from off-flavors and odors of any kind.

Grade B: Color: Possesses a reasonably light, reasonably uniform, typical cream to light straw general appearance, characteristic of properly prepared and processed kraut model No. 2. **Cut:** See Grade A. All wording is the same except as follows: materially affected; reasonably uniform ... materially affect. **Defects:** Minor and major defects may be present that do not materially affect the appearance or eating quality. **Character:** Kraut is reasonably crisp and firm. **Flavor:** Possesses a reasonably good, characteristic kraut flavor which is free from off-flavors and odors of any kind.

Grade C: Color: May possess a dark straw, slightly green, or yellowish general appearance and may be dull or slightly variable but is not off-color. **Cut:** Means, with respect to shredded kraut, that the presence of very short or very fine pieces or large and irregular pieces and, with respect to chopped kraut, that the presence of very fine pieces or large and irregular pieces, does not seriously affect the appearance.

Defects: Minor and major defects may be present that do not seriously affect the appearance or eating quality. **Character:** Kraut may lack crispness; may be soft or slightly tough, but is not necessarily tough, or excessively soft, or mushy. **Flavor:** Possesses a fairly good kraut flavor which is free from objectionable flavors and odors which may seriously affect the eating quality.

Sstd: Fails to meet requirements.

TEA: (See Beverages)

SHORTENING: (See Fats and Oils)

SYRUPS

CORN SYRUP: Made from corn flour and used as a table syrup or sweetening agent. Clear white to amber Color. Used in baking and is served hot on waffles. Specify:

   30% glucose

   30% dextrin

   20% maltose

   5% ash

   15% maximum moisture

REFINER'S SYRUP [6/15/67]: Grade A or Fancy: Has a flavor characteristic of refiner's syrup of fancy quality; contains no sediment; is free of foreign matter; has a Brix solids content of not less than 72 percent when corrected to 20°C. (68°F.); has a ratio of total sugars to Brix solids of at least 92 percent; has a ratio of sulfated ash to Brix solids of not more than 3.0 percent; and has a color no darker than RS Color Standard No. 1.

Grade B or Choice: Has a flavor characteristic of refiner's syrup of choice quality; has no sediment; is free of foreign matter; has a Brix solids content of at least 72 percent when corrected to 20°C. (68°F.); has a ratio of total sugars to Brix solids of at least 86 percent; has a ratio of sulfated ash to Brix solids of not more than 6 percent; and has a color no darker than RS Color Standard No. 2.

Grade C or Extra Standard: Has a flavor characteristic of refiner's syrup of standard quality; contains no excess of sediment; is practically free of foreign matter; has a Brix solids content of at least 76 percent when corrected to 20°C. (68°F.); has a ratio of total sugars to Brix solids of at least 76 percent; has a ratio of sulfated ash to Brix solids of not more

than 10 percent; and has a color no darker than RS Color Standard No. 3.

Grade D or Standard: Has a flavor characteristic of refiner's syrup of standard quality; contains no excess of sediment; is practically free of foreign matter; has a Brix solids content of at least 76 percent when corrected to 20°C. (68°F.); has a ratio of total sugars to Brix solids of not less than 70 percent; and has a ratio of sulfated ash to Brix solids of not more than 14 percent.

Grade E or Substandard: Fails to meet requirements.

REFINER'S SYRUP

CANNED [6/15/67   52.6041]

Grades:	"A" or "FANCY"	"B" or "CHOICE"	"C" or "EXTRA STAN-DARD"	"D" or "STAN-DARD"
	Refiner's syrup "E" or "SUB-STAN-DARD" Refiner's syrup	Refiner's syrup	Refiner's syrup	Refiner's syrup

	U.S. Grade A or Fancy	U.S. Grade C or Extra Standard
	U.S. Grade B or Choice	U.S. Grade D or Standard
Brix solids corrected to 20°C. (68°F.)	not less than 72%	not less than 70%

MAPLE SYRUP [5/24/67]: Sap from maple tree species boiled down to a syrup and used on waffles and pancakes and to flavor cakes, pudding, candy, and ice cream.

Grade AA: Color: No darker than light amber as represented by the color standards of the USDA. **Clarity:** No cloudier than light amber cloudy standard as represented by the standards of the USDA for cloudiness. **Weight:** Not less than 11 lb. per gal. of 231 cu. in. at 68°F. corresponding to 65.46°Brix or 35.27° Baume. **Flavor:** Has a characteristic maple flavor; is clean, and free from fermentation, damage caused by scorching, buddiness, and any objectionable flavor or odor.

Grade A: Color: No darker than medium amber as represented by the color standards of the USDA. **Clarity:** No cloudier than medium amber cloudy standard as represented by the standards of the USDA for cloudiness. **Weight:** Same as Grade AA. **Flavor:** Same as Grade AA.

Grade B: Color: No darker than dark amber as represented by the color standards of the USDA. **Clarity:** No cloudier than dark amber cloudy standard as represented by the standards of the USDA for cloudiness.

Unclassified: Not classified in accordance with the foregoing grades.

MAPLE SYRUP

TABLE SYRUP (5/24/67   52.5961)

Grades: "AA" or "FANCY"   "A"   "B"
                                                    "UNCLASSIFIED"

MAPLE SYRUP FOR REPROCESSING (5/24/67   52.5921)

Grades: "AA" or "FANCY"   "A"   "B"   "C"
                                                    "UNCLASSIFIED"

SUGARCANE MOLASSES [11/16/59]: Syrup taken from sugar during refinement. **Grade A: Flavor:** Has a flavor and odor characteristic of first centrifugal molasses of fancy quality. **Brix, Sugar, Ash, and Sulfites:** Refer to Table I. **Color:** Bright and typical of molasses properly prepared and processed from sound, well-matured sugarcane, and is no darker than USDA permanent, glass color standard No. 1 for sugarcane molasses. **Defects:** Appearance and edibility are not affected by the presence of harmless extraneous material which may be in suspension or deposited as sediment in the container.

Grade B: Flavor: Has a flavor and odor characteristic of second centrifugal molasses of choice quality. **Brix, Sugar, Ash, and Sulfites:** Refer to Table I. **Color:** Reasonably bright and is no darker than USDA permanent, glass color standard No. 2 for sugarcane molasses. **Defects:** Appearance and edibility are not materially affected by the presence of harmless extraneous material which may be in suspension or deposited as sediment in the container.

Grade C: Flavor: Has a flavor and odor characteristic of second centrifugal molasses of standard quality. **Brix, Sugar, Ash, and Sulfites:** Refer to Table I. **Color:** No darker than USDA permanent, glass color standard No. 3 for sugarcane molasses. **Defects:** Appearance and edibility are not seriously affected by the presence of harmless extraneous material which may be in suspension or deposited as sediment in the container. **Sstd:** Fails to meet requirements.

SUGARCANE MOLASSES

CANNED [11/16/59   52.3651]

Grades:	"A" or "FANCY"	"B" or "CHOICE"	"C" or "STANDARD"	"SUBSTANDARD"
Minimum Score:	90	80	70	Less than 70

NET WEIGHT: As full as practicable

REQUIRED MINIMUM BRIX SOLIDS AND TOTAL SUGAR AND MAXIMUM ASH AND TOTAL SULFITES

Grade Designation	Brix Solids [percent] [minimum]		Total Sugar [percent] [minimum]	
	Average from All Containers	Limit for Individual Container	Average from All Containers	Limit for Individual Containers
Grade A	79.0	78.5	63.5	63.0
Grade B	79.0	78.5	61.5	61.0
Grade C	79.0	78.5	58.0	57.0
Sstd.	Under 79.0	—	Under 58.0	—

	Ash [percent] [maximum]		Total Sulfites [ppm] [maximum]
	Average from All Containers	Limit for Individual Container	Average from All Containers
Grade A	5.00	5.25	200
Grade B	7.00	7.50	250
Grade C	9.00	10.00	250
Sstd.	Over 9.00	—	Over 250

SUGARCANE SYRUP [4/15/57]: Made by evaporation of sugarcane without removing any sugar.

Grade A: Color: Bright and typical of syrup properly prepared and processed from sound, well-matured sugarcane and is no darker than USDA permanent, glass color standard No. 1 for sugarcane syrup. **Flavor:** Has a good, characteristic flavor and is free from objectionable flavors of any kind. **Defects:** Appearance and edibility are not affected by the presence of harmless extraneous matter of other material. **Clarity:** May contain not more than a trace of finely divided particles of suspended material which does not affect the appearance or edibility of the product.

Grade B: Color: Reasonably bright and is no darker than USDA permanent, glass color standard No. 2 for sugarcane syrup. **Flavor:** Has a reasonably good, characteristic flavor and is free from objectionable flavors or odors of any kind. **Defects:** Appearance and edibility are not materially affected by the presence of harmless extraneous matter or other material. **Clarity:** May contain finely divided particles of suspended material which does not materially affect the appearance or edibility of the product.

Grade C: Color: Has a color that is no darker than USDA permanent, glass color standard No. 3 for sugarcane syrup. **Flavor:** Has a fairly good flavor and is free from objectionable flavors and odors of any kind. **Defects:** Appearance and edibility are not seriously affected by the presence of harmless extraneous matter or other material. **Clarity:** Appearance or edibility may be materially, but not seriously, affected by the presence of finely divided particles of suspended material.

Sstd: Fails to meet rquirements.

SUGARCANE SYRUP

CANNED [4/16/57   52.3101]

Grades:	"A" or "FANCY"	"B" or "CHOICE'"	"C" or "STAN-DARD"	"SUB-STAN-DARD"
Minimum Score:	90	80	70	Less than 70

NET WEIGHT: As full as practicable

SOY SAUCE: Dark brown, pungent sauce made from fermented soy beans. Used as a seasoning and flavoring agent. Genuine soy sauce is a fermented product and is not legal in the United States. **Pack:** 24/3 oz.; 24/5 oz.; gallons.

SUGARS: Sugar is almost pure sucrose when made by evaporating and crystallizing sugarcane or sugar beets. Corn sugar, made by the hydrolysis of the starch of corn, is dextrose. Glucose is dextrose in syrup form. Cellulose is crystallized dextrose.

Sugar's fineness is indicated by the number of "x's," with x being the most coarse and 10x being the most fine:

xx (2x)—Powdered sugar

xxxx (4x)—Confectioners' sugar. Has 3 percent starch added. For icing. (6x also)

Fine Granulated (also Beng)—For baking; dissolves quickly

Molasses—Uncrystallized sugar (See Syrups)

Brown Sugar (also called "Soft")—A mixture of granulated sugar and molasses. Grades are 1 through 15 with 15 being the darkest color. Buy No. 8 to No. 10 for light brown and No. 11 to No. 15 for dark brown.

Sugar Packaging: Granulated available in 100 lb., 50 lb., 25 lb., 10 lb., 5 lb., 2 lb., 1 lb. containers, as well as cases of 1000 to 3000 individual packets of 1/6 oz. and 1/4 oz. each. Powdered and brown sugars usually purchased in cases of 24/1-lb. boxes.

TOMATO PASTE [2/25/70]: Grade A: Color: Bright, typical, red tomato paste color. Such color, when the product is diluted and observed, is as red as or more red than that produced by spinning the specified Munsell color discs in the following combinations or is an equivalent of such composite color: 65 percent of the area of Disc 1; 21 percent of the area of Disc 2; and 14 percent of the area of Disc 3 or Disc 4, or 7 percent of the area of Disc 3 and 7 percent of the area of Disc 4, whichever most nearly matches the appearance of the diluted sample. **Defects:** Any defects present do not more than slightly affect the appearance or usability of the product.

Grade C: Color: Typical red tomato paste color which may be slightly dull or may have a slightly brownish cast. Such color, when the product is diluted and observed, is as red as, or more red than, that produced by spinning the Specified Munsell Color Discs in the following combinations, or is an equivalent of such composite color: 53 percent of the area of Disc 1; 28 percent of the area of Disc 2; and 19 percent of the area of either Disc 3 or Disc 4, or 9-1/2 percent of the area of Disc 3

and 9-1/2 percent of the area of Disc 4, whichever most nearly matches the appearance of the diluted sample. **Defects:** Any defects present may be noticeable but are not so large, so numerous, or of such contrasting color or nature as to seriously affect the appearance or usability of the product.
Sstd: Fails to meet requirements.

TOMATO PASTE

CANNED [2/25/70   52.5041]

Grades:	"A" or "FANCY"	"C" or "STANDARD"	"SUB-STANDARD"
Minimum Score:	90	80	Less than 80

NET WEIGHT: As full as practicable

TOMATO PUREE [PULP], Canned [2/25/70]: Grade A: Color: Bright, typical, red tomato puree color. Such color, when the product is of the proper concentration and observed, is as red as or more red than that produced by spinning the specified Munsell color discs in the following combinations, or is an equivalent of such composite color: 65 percent of the area of Disc 1; 21 percent of the area of Disc 2; and 14 percent of the area of either Disc 3 or Disc 4, or 7 percent of the area of Disc 3 and Disc 4, whichever most nearly matches the appearance of the sample. **Defects:** Any defects present do not more than slightly affect the appearance or usability of the product.
Grade C: Color: Typical red tomato puree which may be slightly dull or have a slight yellow, yellow orange, or brownish cast. Such color, etc. See Grade A; all wording is the same except as follows: 53 percent; 28 percent; and 19 percent; or 9-1/2 percent and 9-1/2 percent. **Defects:** Any defects present may be noticeable but are not so large, so numerous, or of such contrasting color or nature as to seriously affect the appearance or usability of the product.
Sstd: Fails to meet requirements.

TOMATO PUREE [PULP]

CANNED [2/25/70   52.5081]

Grades:	"A" or "FANCY"	"C" or "STANDARD"	"SUB-STANDARD"
Minimum Score:	90	80	Less than 80

NET WEIGHT: As full as practicable

TOMATO SAUCE, Canned [10/21/60]: Grade A: Color: Color is typical of tomato sauce made from well-ripened red tomatoes and which has been properly prepared and processed. Such color contains as much or more red than that produced by spinning the specified Munsell color discs in the following combinations: 65 percent of the area of Disc 1; 21 percent of the area of Disc 2; 14 percent of the area of Disc 3 or of Disc 4, or 7 percent of the area of Disc 3 and Disc 4, whichever most nearly matches the reflectance of the tomato sauce. **Consistency:** Tomato sauce shows not more than a slight separation of free liquid when poured on a flat grading tray; is not excessively stiff, and flows not more than 14 centimeters in 30 seconds at 20°C. in the Bostwick Consistometer. **Defects:** Any defects present may be noticeable but are not so large, so numerous, or of such contrasting color as to seriously affect the appearance or eating quality. **Flavor:** Good, distinct flavor characteristic of good quality ingredients. Such flavor is free from scorching or any objectionable flavor of any kind.
Grade C: Color: Color is typical of tomato sauce and contains as much or more red than that produced by spinning the Munsell color discs in the following combinations: 53 percent of the area of Disc 1; 28 percent of the area of Disc 2; 19 percent of the area of either Disc 3 or 4, or 9-1/2 percent of the area of Disc 3 or Disc 4, whichever most nearly matches the reflectance of the tomato sauce. **Consistency:** Tomato sauce may show a noticeable but not excessive separation of free liquid when poured on a flat grading tray; is not excessively stiff, and flows not more than 18 centimeters in 30 seconds at 20°C. in the Bostwick Consistometer. **Defects:** Fairly free from defects means: any defects present may be noticeable but are not so large, so numerous, or of such contrasting color as to seriously affect the appearance or eating quality. **Flavor:** A flavor characteristic of the ingredients in which there may be slight traces of undesirable flavor, such as scorched, bitter, or astringent, but is free from objectionable or off-flavors of any kind.
Sstd: Fails to meet requirements.

TOMATO SAUCE

CANNED [10/21/60   52.2371]

Grades:	"A" or "FANCY"	"C" or "STANDARD"	"SUB-STANDARD"
Minimum Score:	85	70	Less than 70

NET WEIGHT: Not less than 90 percent of capacity of container

TRUFFLES: A mushroom-like fungus. Black truffles are best. Available only from France; fresh in late winter, canned year round; 7/8 oz. upwards. Market forms: whole (extra or brushed), peelings, puree, paste.

VANILLA EXTRACT: (See Flavorings and Extracts; also see Spices and Herbs.)

VINEGAR: Diluted, impure acetic acid made from apples, beer, sugar, etc., and is used for pickling, preserving, sousing, and marinating. **Pack:** 5 gal. kit or jug, 10 gal. kit, 15 gal. keg, 30 gal. half-bushel, 50 gal. bushel. **Specify:** Clear, bright, free from sediment and floating particles, sterilized, 4 percent minimum and 5 percent maximum acetic acid.

WAXY MAIZE STARCH: A starch made from corn. Thickening power equal in hot food and cold food. Has a clear finish. Used in frozen goods because of its stability. Trade names: Colflo, Clearjel, Purity 69. Highly recommended replacement for cornstarch but not as good as arrowroot.

WORCESTERSHIRE SAUCE: Thin, dark, spicy sauce with a piquant flavor. Added to stews, soups, etc. **Specify:** Wood ripened minimum of 60 days; 20 percent minimum solids. **Pack:** 12 and 24/5 oz.; gallons.

YEAST

Table 65 — Relation between yeast solids of specified types of yeast and yeast products

Product	Factors for Converting to —	
	Compressed Yeast	Dry Active Yeast
Compressed yeast	1.00	0.305
Dry active yeast[1]	3.17	1.00

1. The functional relation between dry and compressed yeast differs from the weight relation. It requires about 40-45% of the weight of compressed yeast to give an equivalent activity of dried yeast. These factors are based upon the following average moisture levels: Compressed yeast, 70.5%; dry active yeast, 8.0%; nutritional yeast, 4.5%.

BIBLIOGRAPHY

Andersen, Alex L. *Dry Bean Production in the Lake and Northeastern States*, No. 285, August 1965, pp. 1-13.

Apple Butter, USS, August 5, 1957, 52.2801.

Applesauce, USS, Canned, June 25, 1974, 52.321.

Breads, Cakes, and Pies In Family Meals. No. 186, December 1971, pp. 1-30.

Chili Sauce, USS, October 20, 1953, 52.2191.

Cranberry Sauce, USS, Canned, March 19, 1951, 52.951.

A Glossary of Spices. New York: American Spice Trade Association, 1966.

Lews, Bernard L. *Food Service Seasoning Guide*. New York: American Spice Trade Association, 1969.

Maple Syrup, USS, For Reprocessing, May 24, 1967, 52.5921.

Official Grain Standards of the United States, Revised October 1961, SRA-AMS 177, Grain Division, AMS, U.S. Dept. of Agriculture, Washington, D.C.: Government Printing Office.

"The Official United States Standards For Grain." Washington, D.C.: Government Printing Office, 1974, pp. 11-96.

Orange Marmalade, USS, June 22, 1951, 52.1451.

Orange Marmalade, USS, December 31, 1974, 52.1451.

Pickles, USS September 1, 1966, 52.1681.

Reitz, L.P. and Lebsock, K.L. *Distribution of the Varieties and Classes of Wheat in the United States in 1969*. Washington, D.C.: U.S. Department of Agriculture, 1972.

Rice in the United States: Varieties and Production. No. 289, June 1973, pp. 1-154.

Tomato Catsup, USS, August 31, 1953, 52.2101.

Tomato Paste, USS February 25, 1970, 52.5041.

Tomato Puree (Tomato Pulp): USS, Canned February 25, 1970, 52.5081.

Tomato Sauce, USS, October 21, 1960, 52.2371.

11

QUALITY CONTROLS AND FEDERAL REGULATIONS

WHAT DO THOSE patient and customer complaints really mean? Many operators have had the experience of having someone tell them that some item is "lousy" or "garbage" or "no good." Some of those complaints are sensory. Maple syrup disrupts the flavor of coffee, so coffee with breakfast may have a bitter aftertaste. Menu combinations must be most carefully chosen to get the proper textures, flavors, and colors or these psychological complaints may be overwhelming.

In hospitals foodservice people most often receive complaints which are physiologicially based. The patient is ill, and his sensory illusions are distorted. The smells of a hospital ward often overpower the smells of the foods. These factors must be weighed carefully. In general, do not worry about patient complaints on a specific menu item unless they exceed 5 percent of the number of portions served; for the cafeteria, worry about it if the complaints exceed 1 percent.

Quality *is* measurable on objective grounds even though there are many varied subjective attributes. Quality is measured in terms of a product's chemical and physical attributes which are: flavor, texture, color, appearance, consistency, palatability, nutritional values, safety, ease of handling, convenience, storage stability, and packaging.

The five senses are invaluable. The average layman can identify about 2000 odors and tastes; the trained technician can identify some 5000.

Smell is not really a function of the nose. It is a function of the olfactory bulb which is located way, way back in the nasal cavity. The rest of your nose picks up only the sensations of touch: heat, pain and the like.

Taste is the most complex of the senses, because flavor is a combination of taste, smell, and feelings. The tongue is the receptor of flavor. It registers only four responses: sweet, salty, sour, and bitter. It is the taste buds which pick up three sensations and the intensity of these sensations is directly affected by the temperature of the food. Sweet tastes are picked up only at the front of the tongue; saltiness is determined at the sides of the back of the tongue, and bitterness is registered in the main body of the tongue.

The temperature of food tasted greatly affects the ability to judge flavor. Never, never, never sample food for taste that is below 40°F. or above 100°F. The tongue will not register accurate sensations of sourness or subtle flavor detections in any temperature range except 40°F. to 100°F. Those sensations of food being tough, mushy, gristly, or hard are really the qualities of firmness, softness, juiciness, chewiness, and grittiness.

How does one instruct a taste panel in order to get a valid judgment of the product? According to Marvin Thorner, Ch.E. and premier food technologist: "Prior to the actual testing, an inexperienced taster should perform a series of examinations using solutions of foods having the four basic tastes. Dilute solutions of pure substances exhibiting the effects of sweetness, sourness, bitterness, and saltiness should be prepared. As each solution is tested, a mental note should be made of the reaction and the location of the stimulus on the tongue.

"Before actual testing, the mouth should be rinsed with

warm water. This preliminary step will freshen the mouth cavity and the taste buds for sharper perception.

"The sample should be drawn into the mouth with a "slurp" or whirling action, so that all areas of the cavity are moistened. Immediately after the mouth is fully moistened and the sense registered, the liquid must be expelled. If the impression was not clear, a second or third test should be made. Between tests of the same or different substances, the mouth should be flushed with warm water.

"The sense of touch plays an important role in taste evaluation. The temperature of the material must be noted, and if not in the proper range, it must be adjusted to meet is physical character."

The tasting should be done early in the morning because people's tasting senses become dulled later in the day. Limit the number of samples to no more than 6 as the taster's perception is rarely accurate after that point. Use 2 identical samples and 1 different sample, all blind coded—to weed out faulty perception. Use definitive words for judging such as "like definitely," "like mildly," "neither like nor dislike, definitely."

Now what about the equipment that is used in the determination of quality? The first piece of equipment is the scale. Scales are needed to check the portion weights, not only as a receiving control but also as a cooking control.

Microwave ovens will cook or reheat properly only when the timings are set in accordance with the product weights.

Thermometers are essential in the receiving function of convenience foods as a minimal check against product damage. For testing the temperature of plated or plate-ready foods, one should use only the cup-type thermometer because it brings up some of the food with it and that prevents the temperature from changing before the reading is made.

Another valuable tool is the Abbe Refractometer. This tool measures the density of liquids through the refraction or bending of light. For most operations the operator will want a hand refractometer. Tables supplied with USDA Standards enable the operator to measure such things as the amount of sugar in fountain syrups, the amount of total solids in sauces,

gravies, and tomato products, and the purity of the fats and oils used in the operation.

Another helpful tool is the Brix Hydrometer. This instrument measures the sugar concentration in liquids; it is somewhat like the hydrometer which the fellow down at the gas station uses to measure the amount of anti-freeze in automobile radiators. All the syrups of canned goods have USDA Specified Brix points. Only a Brix Hydrometer or a Hand Refractometer will enable the buyer to know if he got what he ordered.

A fat analyzer is basic to a quality assurance program. This is a little machine about the size of a briefcase and just as portable. The fat analyzer will, in a 15-minute period, give you an accurate reading as to the percentage of fat in ground beef. Not only is this essential to measuring the quality of fresh meat, but it is invaluable in the determination of quality of frozen foods such as stuffed cabbage and stuffed peppers.

The United States Department of Agriculture has determined standards and specifications for virtually every food product on the market. It is important that buyers use these specifications in the purchase of all foodstuffs.

Buyers should purchase on quotations, and since the reading off of the detailed specifications is very involved, should try this method: Prepare a typewritten listing of all your specifications for your operation, and bind them into a booklet. Make divisions for the obvious purchase categories like milk, butter, eggs and cheese, fresh and frozen vegetables, meats, etc.; send each purveyor a copy of the appropriate section with the instructions that these are the detailed specifications on which future quotations will be taken. These specifications will mean *nothing* if the buyer does not have a receiving program which assures the quality of the goods received.

It is difficult to know just what quality level is needed in each product.

Wherever there is a USDA A, B, and C Grade on canned fruits and vegetables, most operations should find USDA Grade B quite satisfactory. Grade A is just too much extra money for the difference in quality. Grade C generally allows an excess of defects which will affect the plate-worthiness of the foods. If the choice is between Grade A and Grade C—as an example, with jams and jellies, where there is no USDA Grade B—then take Grade A. On canned goods the buyer must insist, at a minimum, that the cans or cases bear the mark of the Federal Inspector. If the operation was not large enough to take advantage of having the local USDA office run a grading inspection on a sample of the lot bought from, the buyer can, at least, cut his own cans and determine the appropriateness of the drained weight, sieve, or count, defects, and Brix of the syrup. The higher the Brix point, the more sugar in the syrup. For canned fruits which will be served in the juice, the buyer will want a heavy syrup of 21° or maybe extra heavy at 25°. Fruits for salads need only have a 16° Brix, which is called slightly sweetened water.

Frozen vegetables which are to be cooked need only be Grade B, but the buyer must assure that each bears the USDA shield and the grade.

Fresh vegetables and fruits, generally served in the raw state, should be Grade No. 1. On some products certification on the case is available. Local foodservice people should form a cartel of sorts to force the local fresh produce purveyors to keep a federal inspector on the premises to certify the grade of the products as shipped.

In meat, buyers should use the *Institutional Meat Purchase Specifications* (IMPS) or the *Meat Buyers Guides* (MBG) published by the National Association of Meat Purveyors. The MBG specs are the same as the IMPS but slightly shortened and accompanied by photographs which are a great aid in making receiving checks. The meat business can be very risky—the only way the buyer can assure that he is getting a fair deal is to insist on the specs being followed. For all meats which are cooked by dry heat methods—roasting, broiling, pan-frying—you should use USDA choice as the fat in the muscle walls is needed for tenderness. For moist heat cooking—boiling, stewing, etc.,—one can use USDA good or standard, as the slow cooking process will break down the long muscle tissues and create a tender product.

Note that in the case of all foods the buyer *must* require the Federal Grading. Not everything is graded.

During the fiscal year 1974 the following products were certified: 80 percent of the poultry; 69 percent of the butter; 67 percent of the lamb and mutton; 64 percent of the beef; 50 percent of the fresh fruits and vegetables, and 20 percent of the shell eggs. During the same period the following foods were certified for quality and/or wholesomeness: 87 percent of the dried eggs; 80 percent of the frozen fruits and vegetables; 77 percent of the processed liquid eggs; 46 percent of the nonfat dry milk, and 40 percent of the canned fruits and vegetables.

Standards for meat and poultry products are pertinent guidelines to assist in the task of quality interpretation and cost evaluation. To qualify for this classification, a food must contain a minimum amount of meat or poultry as prescribed by the USDA. For example, ready-to-serve chicken soup must contain at least 2 percent chicken. Condensed chicken soup must contain 4 percent or more, since it would then contain at least 2 percent when diluted with water. But chicken-flavored soup, which is not considered a poultry product, may contain less chicken.

The standards for meat ingredients usually are based on the fresh weight of the product, whereas those for poultry are measured on the weight of the cooked, deboned product. Since meat and poultry shrink during cooking, standards take this fact into account. For instance, beef pot pie must contain 14 percent or more cooked turkey. Chicken burgers must be 100 percent chicken; a product containing fillers must be called chicken patties.

At present there are about 150 standards for prepared convenience entrees. Some examples are: Beef Stroganoff, at least 45 percent fresh uncooked beef or 30 percent cooked beef, and at least 10 percent sour cream, or a "gourmet" combination of at least 7.5 percent sour cream and 5 percent wine; Chop Suey, at least 25 percent meat; Fritters, at least 50 percent cooked meat; Chicken or turkey a la king, at least 20 percent poultry meat.

We can look forward to such standards being developed for all convenience entree products.

Improper and careless storage techniques will downgrade

quality. Poor stock rotation and prolonged storing in any of the storage areas (dry, cooler, or freezer) may lead to flavor and texture changes. Positive storage control procedures will tend to eliminate these problems.

Haphazard food assembly methods, such as piling or stacking of food products, spillage, and mixing of liquids, such as sauces and gravies, so that they become contaminated with each other, will help to destroy the inherent character of the food. Spices, condiments, and herbs should be assembled in a neat, orderly fashion until needed for preparation. Sandwich spreads should be kept refrigerated and stored in tight containers during slack periods. Sandwich meats, fish, and other products that have a tendency to form a crust or hard surface when exposed to air should be mixed in small lots or covered. Improper thawing procedures for certain foods will affect quality. Items intended for microwave oven heating may require special thawing techniques to prevent uneven doneness. Foods that are to be cooked in the frozen state, like french fries, should not be allowed to thaw, but should be held in a freezer until used.

Although cooking refers to all modes of food heating (fully or partially), factors affecting quality, such as temperature, timing, formulations, and equipment maintenance, are all involved in the final outcome. For example, a faulty timer on a microwave oven will yield inconsistent quality; unfiltered fat for deep frying will produce low quality fried products; a loose door or a worn gasket on a steam pressure cooker may give unsatisfactory results.

Employment of proper utensils is essential for consistent quality. The use of a 10-gal. container to heat 1 gal. of a product will cause excessive shrinkage, texture changes, and flavor losses.

Salad dressings should be added just prior to serving tossed or mixed salads containing soft-textured components (tomato slices) since they should not be allowed to stand for long periods of time. Lettuce and other salad vegetables should be kept dry to prevent loss of crispness and browning. Tossed or mixed salad ingredients should be stored in coolers until used. Before storage they should be wrapped in plastic film or placed in a covered vessel.

Forcing or inducing heating by the use of high temperatures or exposed flames will reduce flavor, decrease tenderness, increase shrinkage, and may produce a burnt taste. Cooking should always be performed at the right temperature and within the prescribed time cycle.

Formulations or recipes should be written clearly and precisely. All quantity measurements should be listed, together with the size of the measuring device to be used, such as ladle or scoop size and number. Heating cycle and equipment should also be posted.

Holding food in a steam table, cabinet, or under infrared lamps for excessive periods of time will reduce quality, since it may affect food texture and flavor or increase shrinkage and loss of nutrients. Foods will become mealy, mushy, soggy, or dried out. Over-production should be held to a minimum. Coffee should not be held over 1 hour and only at temperatures of 185° to 190°F. Desserts like cream or custard pies require refrigerated storage to prevent spoilage.

Leftover foods should be properly refrigerated, and packed loosely in shallow, covered pans, labeled, and dated. Foods that will not be used should be thrown away. Fresh produce should always be washed before serving or use in salads or soup. Washing will remove excess soil, dust, insecticides, and surface bacteria.

The relative importance of each factor can be expressed numerically on a scale of 100 and the USDA has worked out a scoring system which is used in government grading. In commercial practice, while no particular attempt has been made to use a numerical scoring system, the factors emphasized do include:[1]

Flavor	Symmetry	Wholeness
General	Absence of	Cut
Appearance	Defects	Consistency
Color	Character	Finish
Type	Maturity	Clearness of
Style	Texture	Liquor
Count	Firmness	Clearness of
Uniformity of	Tenderness	Syrup
Size		Syrup Density
		Drained Weight

1. A.A. Frooman, *Five Steps to Institutional Food Buying;* Institutions, 1953.

There is no substitute for experience when it comes to determining the essential variations within each factor. Nevertheless, an effective job can be done if the buyer will keep in mind this general scoring and tolerance outline:

USDA Grade A must be practically perfect in every respect allowing a tolerance of from 15 percent to 18 percent within the grade which is scored between 85 to 100 points inclusive.

USDA Grade B must be reasonably perfect in every respect allowing a tolerance of from 16-2/3 percent to 20 percent within the grade which is scored between 75 to 89 points inclusive.

USDA Grade C must be fairly perfect in every respect allowing a tolerance of from 20 percent to 25 percent within the grade which is scored between 60 to 74 points inclusive.

The exceptions are those products where only 2 grades are commercially packed. In such instances the general scoring and tolerance outline is:

USDA Grade A must be practically perfect in every respect allowing a tolerance of from 15 percent to 18 percent within the grade which is scored between 85 to 100 points inclusive.

USDA Grade B must be fairly perfect in every respect allowing a tolerance of from 18 percent to 22 percent within the grade which is scored between 70 to 84 points inclusive.

FLAVOR—Because there is such a great variation in the individual's likes and dislikes, it is exceedingly difficult to score so elusive a factor as "Flavor." In most of the U.S. Standards for Grades of Foods, the term "Normal Flavor" is used. In commercial grading, however, "Flavor" is the prime factor. If what we eat tastes good, we somehow overlook minor deficiencies.

GENERAL APPEARANCE—My own judgment places the factor of "eat with their eyes" even before they taste of what they see. If a food does not look good, the prejudice may very well affect one's opinion of Flavor. For this reason, some food experts rate "General Appearance" every bit as important as "Flavor."

The relative importance of all other factors depends entirely upon the product being judged. While no attempt will be made here to score "Quality" or "Standard" factors for the available grades, the important factors by which to judge the quality of some of the more popular, everyday products are emphasized here to help food buyers make certain that deliveries conform to purchase specifications.

COLOR—The factor of "Color" is the chief subdivision of "General Appearance," and to receive proper rating, "Color" should by typical of the product. Many food experts score "Color" on a par with flavor for some items.

TYPE—By "Type," is meant distinctive classifications of a specific product. For example, Culturally Bleached Asparagus is one distinct type, and all Green Asparagus is a separate distinct type.

STYLE—When we refer to "Style" we think of prevalent approved ideas of form adaptable to popular food items which canners and processors make available to buyers. A good example is: PEACHES—Sliced or Halves.

COUNT—Actual number of pieces found upon opening and examination of container contents.

UNIFORMITY OF SIZE—The degree of consistency relative to freedom from variation or difference. Sameness or alikeness.

SYMMETRY—The degree of consistently harmonious proportions of units in container.

ABSENCE OF DEFECTS—By "Absence of Defects" we refer to the degree of freedom from grit, from harmless foreign or other extraneous material, and damage from poor or careless handling, or from mechanical, pathological, insect, or other similar injury.

GENERAL CHARACTER—Under the factor "General Character," consideration is given to degree of ripeness or maturity, the texture and condition of flesh, the firmness and tenderness of the product, its tendency to retain its apparent original conformation and size without material disintegration, the wholeness or cut, consistency or finish, and clearness of liquor or syrup.

MATURITY—This factor refers to the degree of development or ripeness of the product.

TEXTURE—By "Texture" we refer to structural composition or character of the product tissues.

FIRMNESS—The degree of soundness of product structure.

TENDERNESS—The degree of freedom from tough or hard fibers.

WHOLENESS—The state of completeness or entirety.

CUT—This refers to the character of cut; that is, the effect of the cut on the appearance of the product.

CONSISTENCY—In some products, such as Fruit Butters, this factor refers to viscosity, that is, stickiness or gumminess. In other products, such as Tomato Catsup and Tomato Puree, the term is applied to density or specific gravity.

FINISH—This factor especially refers to the size and texture of particles, the smoothness, evenness and uniformity of grain.

CLEARNESS OF LIQUOR—This factor requires no elaboration. The degree of sediment and cloudiness materially affects score for quality.

CLEARNESS OF SYRUP—Any degree of sediment or cloudiness materially affects grading score.

SYRUP DENSITY—The degree or percentage, by weight, of sugar going into the solution as measured by either the Brix or Balling Scale on hydrometers or saccharometers.

DRAINED WEIGHT—The weight of the product after draining of liquor or syrup according to method prescribed by the National Canners Assn. or the USDA.

IMPORTANT QUALITY "INSPECTION CHECK" FACTORS
CANNED FRUITS

APPLES

Flavor	Uniformity of Size	Texture
General Appearance	Absence of Defects	Cut
Color	General Character	Drained Weight
Style		

APPLESAUCE

Flavor	Consistency	Absence of Defects
General Appearance	Finish	Texture
Color		

APRICOTS

Flavor	Symmetry	Firmness
General Appearance	Absence of Defects	Tenderness
Color	General Character	Syrup Density
Style	Maturity	Clearness of Syrup
Uniformity of Size	Texture	Drained Weight
Count	Degree of Ripeness	

BLACKBERRIES

Flavor	Absence of Defects	Texture
General Appearance	General Character	Tenderness
Color	Maturity	Syrup Density
Uniformity of Size	Firmness	Drained Weight

BLUEBERRIES

Flavor	Absence of Defects	Texture
General Appearance	General Character	Syrup Density
Color	Firmness	Drained Weight

BOYSENBERRIES

Flavor	Absence of Defects	Texture
General Appearance	General Character	Tenderness
Color	Maturity	Syrup Density
Uniformity of Size	Firmness	Drained Weight

CHERRIES (BLACK SWEET)

Flavor	Symmetry	Firmness
General Appearance	Count	Tenderness
Color	Absence of Defects	Syrup Density
Style	General Character	Drained Weight
Uniformity of Size	Texture	

CHERRIES (ROYAL ANNE)

Flavor	Symmetry	Firmness
General Appearance	Count	Tenderness
Color	Absence of Defects	Syrup Density
Style	General Character	Drained Weight
Uniformity of Size	Texture	

CHERRIES (RED SOUR PITTED)

Flavor	Absence of Defects	Texture
General Appearance	General Character	Syrup Density
Color	Firmness	

CRANBERRY SAUCE

Flavor	Style	Texture
General Appearance	Absence of Defects	Finish
Color	General Character	Wholeness
		Consistency

FIGS (KODOTA)

Flavor	Symmetry	Texture
General Appearance	Count	Firmness
Color	Absence of Defects	Tenderness
Style	General Character	Syrup Density
Uniformity of Size	Maturity	Drained Weight

FIGS (TEXAS SKINLESS)

Flavor	Symmetry	Texture
General Appearance	Count	Firmness
Color	Absence of Defects	Tenderness
Style	General Character	Syrup Density
Uniformity of Size	Maturity	Drained Weight

FRUIT COCKTAIL

Flavor	Absence of Defects	Texture
General Appearance	General Character	Syrup Density
Color	Firmness	Clearness of Syrup
Uniformity of Size	Tenderness	Drained Weight
Percentage by Weight of Fruits in Combination		

FRUITS FOR SALAD

Flavor	Number of Portions	Texture
General Appearance	Absence of Defects	Syrup Density
Color	General Character	Clearness of Syrup
Uniformity by Weight of Fruits in Combination	Firmness	Drained Weight
	Tenderness	

GOOSEBERRIES

Flavor	Absence of Defects	Firmness
General Appearance	General Character	Maturity
Color	Texture	Syrup Density
Uniformity of Size	Tenderness	Drained Weight

GRAPEFRUIT

Flavor	Absence of Defects	Tenderness
General Appearance	General Character	Texture
Color	Maturity	Syrup Density
Wholeness	Firmness	Drained Weight

GRAPES

Flavor	Absence of Defects	Firmness
General Appearance	General Character	Tenderness
Color	Maturity	Syrup Density
Style	Texture	Drained Weight
Uniformity of Size		

ORANGE SEGMENTS

Flavor	Absence of Defects	Tenderness
General Appearance	General Character	Texture
Color	Maturity	Syrup Density
Wholeness	Firmness	Drained Weight

CANNED FRUITS (Cont.)

MIXED ORANGE AND GRAPEFRUIT SEGMENTS

Flavor	Absence of Defects	Tenderness
General Appearance	General Character	Texture
Color	Maturity	Syrup Density
Wholeness	Firmness	Drained Weight
Percentage by Weight of Each Fruit in Combination		

HUCKLEBERRIES

Flavor	Absence of Defects	Texture
General Appearance	General Character	Syrup Density
Color	Firmness	Drained Weight

LOGANBERRIES

Flavor	Absence of Defects	Texture
General Appearance	General Character	Tenderness
Color	Maturity	Syrup Density
Uniformity of Size	Firmness	Drained Weight

NECTARINES

Flavor	Symmetry	Firmness
General Appearance	Count	Tenderness
Color	Absence of Defects	Clearness of Syrup
Type	General Character	Syrup Density
Style	Maturity	Drained Weight
Uniformity of Size	Texture	

PEACHES

Flavor	Symmetry	Firmness
General Appearance	Count	Tenderness
Color	Absence of Defects	Clearness of Syrup
Type	General Character	Syrup Density
Style	Maturity	Drained Weight
Uniformity of Size	Texture	

PEARS

Flavor	Symmetry	Firmness
General Appearance	Count	Tenderness
Color	Absence of Defects	Clearness of Syrup
Type	General Character	Syrup Density
Style	Maturity	Drained Weight
Uniformity of Size	Texture	

PINEAPPLE

Flavor	Count	Firmness
General Appearance	Absence of Defects	Tenderness
Color	General Character	Consistency (if crushed)
Style	Maturity	Syrup Density
Uniformity of Size	Texture	Drained Weight
Symmetry		

PLUMS (GREENGAGE)

Flavor	Symmetry	Texture
General Appearance	Count	Tenderness
Color	Absence of Defects	Firmness
Style	General Character	Syrup Density
Uniformity of Size	Maturity	Drained Weight

PLUMS (YELLOW EGG)

Flavor	Symmetry	Texture
General Appearance	Count	Tenderness
Color	Absence of Defects	Firmness
Style	General Character	Syrup Density
Uniformity of Size	Maturity	Drained Weight

PLUMS (PURPLE or RED)

Flavor	Symmetry	Texture
General Appearance	Count	Tenderness
Color	Absence of Defects	Firmness
Style	General Character	Syrup Density
Uniformity of Size	Maturity	Drained Weight

PRUNES (CANNED DRIED)

Flavor	Symmetry	Texture
General Appearance	Count	Tenderness
Color	Absence of Defects	Firmness
Style	General Character	Syrup Density
Size	Maturity	Drained Weight
Uniformity of Size		

RASPBERRIES (BLACK)

Flavor	Absence of Defects	Firmness
General Appearance	General Character	Tenderness
Color	Maturity	Syrup Density
Uniformity of Size	Texture	Drained Weight

RASPBERRIES (RED)

Flavor	Absence of Defects	Firmness
General Appearance	General Character	Tenderness
Color	Maturity	Syrup Density
Uniformity of Size	Texture	Drained Weight

STRAWBERRIES

Flavor	Absence of Defects	Firmness
General Appearance	General Character	Tenderness
Color	Maturity	Syrup Density
Uniformity of Size	Texture	Drained Weight

YOUNGBERRIES

Flavor	Absence of Defects	Texture
General Appearance	General Character	Tenderness
Color	Maturity	Syrup Density
Uniformity of Size	Firmness	Drained Weight

CANNED VEGETABLES

ASPARAGUS

Flavor	Uniformity of Size	Firmness
General Appearance	Count	Tenderness
Color	Absence of Defects	Clearness of Liquor
Type	General Character	Cut
Style	Maturity	Drained Weight

BEANS (CANNED DRIED)

Flavor	Style	Firmness
General Appearance	Absence of Defects	Tenderness
Color	General Character	Consistency
Type	Texture	Wholeness

BEANS (GREEN)

Flavor	Sieve Size	Tenderness
General Appearance	Absence of Defects	Clearness of Liquor
Color	General Character	Cut
Types	Maturity	Wholeness
Style	Texture	Drained Weight
Uniformity of Size	Firmness	

BEANS (WAX)

Flavor	Sieve Size	Tenderness
General Appearance	Absence of Defects	Clearness of Liquor
Color	General Character	Cut
Type	Maturity	Wholeness
Style	Texture	Drained Weight
Uniformity of Size	Firmness	

BEANS (LIMA)

Flavor	Absence of Defects	Tenderness
General Appearance	General Character	Clearness of Liquor
Color	Maturity	Drained Weight
Uniformity of Size	Texture	
Sieve Size	Firmness	

BEETS

Flavor	Symmetry	Maturity
General Appearance	Count	Texture
Color	Absence of Defects	Tenderness
Style	General Character	Drained Weight
Uniformity of Size		

BRUSSELS SPROUTS

Flavor	Count	Texture
General Appearance	Absence of Defects	Tenderness
Color	General Character	Drained Weight
Uniformity of Size		

CABBAGE

Flavor	General Character	Crispness
General Appearance	Texture	Cut
Color	Firmness	Drained Weight
'Absence of Defects		

CANNED VEGETABLES (Cont.)

CARROTS

Flavor	Symmetry	Maturity
General Appearance	Count	Texture
Color	Cut	Tenderness
Style	Absence of Defects	Drained Weight
Uniformity of Size	General Character	

CORN (WHOLE KERNEL)

Flavor	Absence of Defects	Maturity
General Appearance	Cut	Tenderness
Color	General Character	Drained Weight

CORN (CREAM STYLE)

Flavor	Absence of Defects	Maturity
General Appearance	Cut	Tenderness
Color	General Character	Consistency

HOMINY

Flavor	Absence of Defects	Tenderness
General Appearance	General Character	Drained Weight
Color	Maturity	

OKRA

Flavor	Uniformity of Size	Tenderness
General Appearance	Absence of Defects	Clearness of Liquor
Color	General Character	Drained Weight
Style	Maturity	

PEAS

Flavor	Absence of Defects	Maturity
General Appearance	Sieve Size	Tenderness
Color	Uniformity of Size	Clearness of Liquor
Type	General Character	Drained Weight

PEAS (BLACK-EYED)

Flavor	Uniformity of Size	Tenderness
General Appearance	General Character	Clearness of Liquor
Color	Maturity	Drained Weight
Absence of Defects		

PUMPKIN

Flavor	Absence of Defects	Consistency
General Appearance	General Character	Finish
Color		

RHUBARB

Flavor	Absence of Defects	Tenderness
General Appearance	General Character	Syrup Density
Color	Maturity	Drained Weight

SAUERKRAUT

Flavor	Absence of Defects	Texture
General Appearance	Cut	Crispness
Color	General Character	Drained Weight

SPINACH

Flavor	Absence of Defects	Tenderness
General Appearance	General Character	Drained Weight
Color	Texture	

SQUASH

Flavor	Absence of Defects	Consistency
General Appearance	General Character	Finish
Color		

SUCCOTASH

Flavor	Proportion (by percentage) of each Vegetable in Combination	General Character
General Appearance		Texture
Color		Tenderness
		Consistency
Absence of Defects		Drained Weight

SWEET POTATOES

Flavor	Absence of Defects	General Character
General Appearance	Shape and Size	Texture
Color	Uniformity of Shape and Size	Syrup Density
Style	Consistency	Drained Weight

TOMATOES

Flavor	Absence of Defects	Wholeness
General Appearance	General Character	Drained Weight
Color		

TOMATO CATSUP

Flavor	Color	General Character
General Appearance	Absence of Defects	Consistency

TOMATO PASTE

Flavor	Absence of Defects	Percentage of Concentration
General Appearance	General Character	Texture
Color		Finish

CANNED VEGETABLES (Cont.)

TOMATO PUREE

Flavor	Absence of Defects	Specific Gravity
General Appearance	General Character	Texture
Color	Percentage of	Finish
	Concentration	

CANNED JUICES AND NECTARS

APPLE JUICE

Flavor	Style	Brix Test for
General Appearance	Absence of Defects	Sweetness
Color		Percentage of Free
		and Suspended
		Pulp

APRICOT NECTAR

| Flavor | Color Consistency | Brix Test for |
| General Appearance | Absence of Defects | Sweetness |

CHERRY JUICE

Flavor	Style	Brix Test for
General Appearance	Absence of Defects	Sweetness
Color		Percentage of Free
		and Suspended
		Pulp

CRANBERRY JUICE

Flavor	Style	Brix Test for
General Appearance	Absence of Defects	Sweetness
Color		Percentage of Free
		and Suspended
		Pulp

GRAPEFRUIT JUICE

Flavor	Style	Brix Test for
General Appearance	Absence of Defects	Sweetness
Color		Percentage of Free
		and Suspended
		Pulp

GRAPEFRUIT AND ORANGE JUICE (BLENDED)

Flavor	Style	Brix Test for
General Appearance	Absence of Defects	Sweetness
Color		Percentage of Free
		and Suspended
		Pulp

LEMON JUICE

Flavor	Style	Brix Test for
General Appearance	Absence of Defects	Sweetness
Color		Percentage of Free
		and Suspended
		Pulp

LOGANBERRY JUICE

Flavor	Style	Brix Test for
General Appearance	Absence of Defects	Sweetness
Color		Percentage of Free
		and Suspended
		Pulp

ORANGE JUICE

Flavor	Style	Brix Test for
General Appearance	Absence of Defects	Sweetness
Color		Percentage of Free
		and Suspended
		Pulp

PEACH NECTAR

Flavor	Color	Consistency
General Appearance	Absence of Defects	Percentage of Free
		and Suspended
		Pulp

PEAR NECTAR

Flavor	Color	Consistency
General Appearance	Absence of Defects	Brix Test for
		Sweetness

PINEAPPLE JUICE

Flavor	Style	Brix Test for
General Appearance	Absence of Defects	Sweetness
Color		Percentage of Free
		and Suspended
		Pulp

PLUM NECTAR

Flavor	Color	Consistency
General Appearance	Absence of Defects	Brix Test for
		Sweetness

PRUNE JUICE

Flavor	Color	Brix Test for
General Appearance	Absence of Defects	Sweetness
		Percentage for Free
		and Suspended
		Pulp

CANNED JUICES AND NECTARS [Cont.]

TANGERINE JUICE
Flavor	Style	Brix Test for
General Appearance	Absence of Defects	Sweetness

TOMATO JUICE
Flavor	Color	Consistency
General Appearance	Absence of Defects	

MISCELLANEOUS CANNED FOODS

CHILI SAUCE
Flavor	Color	General Character
General Appearance	Absence of Defects	Consistency

FRUIT BUTTERS
Flavor	Type	Consistency
General Appearance	Absence of Defects	Finish
Color	General Character	Percent Soluble Solids

JAMS
Flavor	Type	Consistency
General Appearance	Absence of Defects	Finish
Color	General Character	Percent Soluble Solids

JELLIES
Flavor	Type	Consistency
General Appearance	Absence of Defects	Finish
Color	General Character	

MARMALADE
Flavor	Type	Consistency
General Appearance	Absence of Defects	Finish
Color	General Character	

MUSHROOMS
Flavor	Absence of Defects	Symmetry
General Appearance	Count	General Character
Color	Size	Tenderness
Style	Uniformity of Size	

OLIVES (GREEN)
Flavor	Absence of Defects	General Character
General Appearance	Count	Firmness
Color	Size	Texture
Style	Uniformity of Size	Drained Weight
Type	Symmetry	

OLIVES (RIPE)
Flavor	Count	Texture
General Appearance	Size	Firmness
Color	Uniformity of Size	Tenderness
Type	Symmetry	Drained Weight
Absence of Defects	General Character	

PEANUT BUTTER
Flavor	Color	Absence of Defects
General Appearance	Type	Aroma

PICKLES
Flavor	Absence of Defects	General Character
General Appearance	Count	Texture
Color	Size	Firmness
Type	Uniformity of Size	Crispness
Style	Symmetry	Baume (Sweetness)

PIMIENTOS
Flavor	Absence of Defects	Texture
General Appearance	Uniformity of Size	Firmness
Color	Wholeness	Drained Weight
Type		

PRESERVES
Flavor	Type	Consistency
General Appearance	Absence of Defects	Finish
Color	General Character	Percent Soluble Solids

SALMON
Flavor	Color	General Character
General Appearance	Absence of Defects	Texture
		Tenderness

SHRIMP

Flavor	Absence of Defects	General Character
General Appearance	Count	Texture
Color	Size	Tenderness
	Uniformity of Size	

TUNA FISH

Flavor	Color	General Character
General Appearance	Absence of Defects	Texture
		Tenderness

DRIED FRUITS

APPLES

Flavor	Type	General Character
General Appearance	Style	Wholeness
Color	Uniformity	Cut
	Absence of Defects	

CURRANTS (ZANTE)

Flavor	Type	Maturity
General Appearance	Absence of Defects	Texture
Color	General Character	

DATES

Flavor	Type	General Character
General Appearance	Size	Maturity
Color	Uniformity	Texture
Style	Absence of Defects	

FIGS

Flavor	Style	General Character
General Appearance	Size	Maturity
Color	Uniformity	Texture
Type	Absence of Defects	Wholeness

PEACHES

Flavor	Size	General Character
General Appearance	Uniformity	Maturity
Color	Absence of Defects	Texture
Type		

PEARS

Flavor	Type	General Character
General Appearance	Size	Maturity
Color	Uniformity	Texture
	Absence of Defects	

PRUNES

Flavor	Size	General Character
General Appearance	Count	Maturity
Color	Uniformity	Texture
Type	Absence of Defects	

RAISINS

Flavor	Type	Absence of Defects
General Appearance	Style	General Character
Color	Size	Maturity

FROZEN FOODS

APPLES

Flavor	Uniformity of Size	Texture
General Appearance	Absence of Defects	Firmness
Color	General Character	Tenderness
Type	Maturity	Sugar or Syrup
Style		Ratio

APRICOTS

Flavor	Uniformity of Size	Maturity
General Appearance	Symmetry	Texture
Color	Absence of Defects	Cut
Type	General Character	Sugar or Syrup
Style		Ratio

ASPARAGUS

Flavor	Style	General Character
General Appearance	Size	Texture
Color	Uniformity	Tenderness
Type	Absence of Defects	Cut

BEANS (LIMA)

Flavor	Type	General Character
General Appearance	Size	Maturity
Color	Absence of Defects	Tenderness

BEANS (SNAP)

Flavor	Style	Maturity
General Appearance	Size	Tenderness
Color	Absence of Defects	Texture
Type	General Character	

FROZEN FOODS (Cont.)

BERRIES

Flavor	Size	Maturity
General Appearance	Uniformity	Texture
Color	Absence of Defects	Tenderness
Variety	General Character	Sugar or Syrup Ratio
Type		

BLUEBERRIES OR HUCKLEBERRIES

Flavor	Uniformity	Texture
General Appearance	Absence of Defects	Firmness
Color	General Character	Sugar or Syrup Ratio

BROCCOLI

Flavor	Uniformity of Size	Texture
General Appearance	Absence of Defects	Firmness
Color	General Character	

BRUSSELS SPROUTS

Flavor	Size	Texture
General Appearance	Absence of Defects	Firmness
Color	General Character	Tenderness
Count	Maturity	

CAULIFLOWER

Flavor	Absence of Defects	Texture
General Appearance	General Character	Firmness
Color	Maturity	Tenderness
Style		

CHERRIES (RED SOUR PITTED)

Flavor	Absence of Defects	Texture
General Appearance	General Character	Firmness
Color	Maturity	Tenderness
Style		

CHERRIES (SWEET)

Flavor	Count	General Character
General Appearance	Size	Maturity
Color	Uniformity	Texture
Type	Symmetry	Firmness
Style	Absence of Defects	Sugar or Syrup Ratio

CORN (WHOLE KERNEL)

Flavor	Type	Maturity
General Appearance	Absence of Defects	Firmness
Color	General Character	Cut

PEACHES

Flavor	Size	Maturity
General Appearance	Symmetry	Texture
Color	Count	Firmness
Type	Absence of Defects	Tenderness
Style	General Character	Sugar or Syrup Ratio

PEAS

Flavor	Sieve Size	Maturity
General Appearance	Absence of Defects	Texture
Color	General Character	Tenderness
Type		

RASPBERRIES

Flavor	Symmetry	Texture
General Appearance	Absence of Defects	Firmness
Color	General Character	Tenderness
Type	Maturity	Sugar or Syrup Ratio
Size		

RHUBARB

Flavor	Absence of Defects	Texture
General Appearance	General Character	Tenderness
Color	Maturity	Sugar or Syrup Ratio
Type		

SPINACH

Flavor	Absence of Defects	Tenderness
General Appearance	General Character	Drained Weight
Color		

STRAWBERRIES

Flavor	Symmetry	Texture
General Appearance	Absence of Defects	Firmness
Color	General Character	Tenderness
Style	Maturity	Sugar or Syrup Ratio
Size		

The U.S. Department of Agriculture (USDA) regulates food standards under the following divisions.

Dairy Products Division
Agricultural Marketing Service
U.S. Dept. of Agriculture
Washington, D.C. 20250

Fresh Products Standardization and Inspection Branch
Fruit and Vegetable Division
Agricultural Marketing Service
U.S. Dept. of Agriculture
Washington, D.C. 20250

Processed Products Standardization and Inspection Branch
Fruit and Vegetable Division
Agricultural Marketing Service
U.S. Dept. of Agriculture
Washington, D.C. 20250

Grain Division (includes soybeans, beans, peas, and rice)
Agricultural Marketing Services
U.S. Dept. of Agriculture
Washington, D.C. 20250

Livestock, Meat (and Wool) Division
Agricultural Marketing Service
U.S. Dept. of Agriculture
Washington, D.C. 20250

Poultry and Poultry Products Division (includes rabbits)
Agricultural Marketing Service
U.S. Dept. of Agriculture
Washington, D.C. 20250

Requests for Military Specifications used by the U.S. Department of Defense should be addressed to:

Commanding Officer
Naval Supply Depot
Attention: Code D.C.I.
5801 Tabor Avenue
Philadelphia, Pa. 19120

Legend to Abbreviations for the Department of Defense

AGR-AMS   Agricultural Research—Agricultural Marketing Service
BUSHIPS Dwg   Bureau of Ships

Fed   Federal Specification (as adopted and published by GSA in cooperation with appropriate other branches)
Ind #   Index Number is used (if no MIL, QM or Fed number is provided)
MIL   Military
QM Int. Pur. Des Quartermaster Interim Purchase Description
QM Lim. Prod. Pur. Des. Quartermaster Limited Production Purchase Description
QM Pur. Des.   Quartermaster Purchase Description
w/   with
w/a   without
abbreviation for number

The General Services Administration (GSA) regulates food standards under the following groups.

Group C: Animal Products
Group N: Cereal and Products
Group Y: Fruits
Group Z: Fruit Products
Group EE: Groceries
Group PP: Meats and Sea Foods
Group HHH: Vegetables
Group JJJ: Vegetable Products

Information may be obtained by writing:
General Services Administration
Washington 25, D.C.

There are also regional offices serving the areas listed below.

Region No. 1 General Services Administration Connecticut, Maine, Massachusetts, New Hampshire, Rhode Island, and Vermont
620 Post Office and Courthouse
Boston, Mass. 02109

Region No. 2 General Services Administration Delaware, New Jersey, New York, Pennsylvania, Puerto Rico, and Virgin Islands
26 Federal Plaza
New York, N.Y. 10007

Region No. 3 G.S.A. Regional Office Building District of Columbia, Maryland, Virginia, and West Virginia
Washington, D.C. 20407

Region No. 4 General Services Administration Alabama, Florida, Georgia, Mississippi, North Carolina, South Carolina, and Tennessee
1776 Peachtree St. N.W.
Atlanta, Ga. 30309

Region No. 5   General Services Administration   Illinois, Indiana, Kentucky, Michigan, Ohio, and Wisconsin
U.S. Courthouse
219 South Dearborn St.
Chicago, Ill. 60604

Region No. 6   General Services Administration   Iowa, Kansas, Minnesota, Missouri, Nebraska, North Dakota, and South Dakota
1500 E. Bannister Rd.
Kansas City, Mo. 64131

Region No. 7   General Services Administration   Arkansas, Louisiana, Oklahoma, and Texas
819 Taylor St.
Ft. Worth, Texas 76102

Region No. 8   General Services Administration   Arizona, Colorado, New Mexico, Utah, Wyoming
Building 41
Denver Federal Center
Denver, Colo. 80225

Region No. 9   General Services Administration   California, Hawaii, Nevada, American Samoa, Guam, and the Trust Territory of the Pacific Islands
525 Market St.
San Francisco, Ca. 94105

Region No. 10 General Services Administration   Alaska, Idaho, Montana, Oregon, and Washington
Auburn Depot Site
G.S.A. Center
Auburn, Wash. 98002

Information on food standards of the Food and Drug Administration is divided into the following parts:

21 CFR   Part 14—Cacao Products
21 CFR   Part 15—Cereal Flours and Related Products
21 CFR   Part 16—Alimentary Pastes
21 CFR   Part 17—Bakery Products
21 CFR   Part 18—Milk and Cream
21 CFR   Part 19—Cheeses; Processed Cheeses; Cheese Foods; and Related Foods
21 CFR   Part 20—Frozen Desserts
21 CFR   Part 25—Dressings for Food
21 CFR   Part 27—Canned Fruits and Canned Fruit Juices
21 CFR   Part 29—Fruit Butters, Fruit Jellies, Fruit Preserves, and Related Products

21 CFR   Part 36—Shellfish
21 CFR   Part 37—Fish
21 CFR   Part 42—Egg and Egg Products
21 CFR   Part 45—Oleomargarine, Margarine
21 CFR   Parts 51 and 53—Canned Vegetables
21 CFR   Part 281—Tea

Information may be obtained by writing:
Food and Drug Administration
5600 Fishers Lane
Rockville, Md. 20852

The Washington, D.C. FDA headquarters is assisted by the Field District Offices listed below:

Food and Drug Administration
60 Eighth St. N.E.
Atlanta, Ga. 30309

Food and Drug Administration
900 Madison Avenue
Baltimore, Md. 21201

Food and Drug Administration
Room 805
U.S. Appraiser's Stores
585 Commercial St.
Boston, Mass. 02109

Food and Drug Administration
599 Delaware Ave.
Buffalo, N.Y. 14202

Food and Drug Administration
Room 1222
433 West Van Buren St.
Chicago, Ill. 60607

Food and Drug Administration
1141 Central Parkway
Cincinnati, Ohio 45202

Food and Drug Administration
3032 Bryan St.
Dallas, Tex. 75204
(214) 749-3396

Food and Drug Administration
New Customhouse Building
Denver, Colo. 80202

Food and Drug Administration
1560 E. Jefferson Ave.
Detroit, Mich. 48207
(313) 962-7495

Food and Drug Administration
1009 Cherry St.
Kansas City, Mo. 64106
(816) 374-3436

Food and Drug Administration
1521 West Pico Blvd.
Los Angeles, Ca. 90015
(213) 749-4711

Food and Drug Administration
240 Hennepin Avenue
Minneapolis, Minn. 55401
(612) 332-3211

Food and Drug Administration
Room 831
970 Broad Street
Newark, N.J. 07102

Food and Drug Administration
Room 222
U.S. Customhouse
423 Canal St.
New Orleans, La. 70130
(504) 529-2411

Food and Drug Administration
850 Third Avenue
Brooklyn, N.Y. 11232

Food and Drug Administration
Room 1204
U.S. Customhouse
Second and Chestnut Streets
Philadelphia, Pa. 19106

Food and Drug Administration
Room 518
50 Fulton St.
San Francisco, Cal. 94102
(415) 556-6746

Food and Drug Administration
San Juan Office
P.O. Box 4427
San Juan Station
San Juan, Puerto Rico 00905

Food and Drug Administration
Room 5003
909 First Avenue
Seattle, Wash. 98104

TYPE	USDA[1]	DOD[2]	FDA[3]	GSA[4]
Bacon				
Canadian style				PP-B-5
Slab;chilled, frozen, or smoked		MIL-B-3503B		
Sliced, canned, pre-fried		MIL-B-35032		
Sliced, canned		MIL-B-3049		
Sliced and cured, chilled, or frozen		MIL-B-35030		
Smoked				PP-B-5
Barrow and Gilt				
Carcass	53.142			
Beef				
Boneless, frozen		QM Pur. Des. 244		
Boneless, frozen prefabricated		QM Pur. Des. CS-8-1		
Boneless, frozen, round		QM Pur. Des. 182		
Boneless, frozen 4-way		MIL-B-10017		
Boneless, frozen, 6-way		QM Int. Pur. Des. S-5-7		
Carcass, chilled or frozen	53.100	Fed PP-B-221		PP-B-221c
Chuck, frozen		Fed PP-B-221		PP-B-221c
Corned, bulk; chilled or frozen		Fed PP-B-196		PP-B-1966 PPB-00196c (Army-QMC)
Corned, canned		Fed PP-B-201		PP-B-201c
Dried, sliced; chilled or frozen		Fed PP-B-211		PP-B-211a
Ground, frozen hearts		MIL-B-3854		PP-H-201
Kidneys				PP-K-351
Liver, frozen		Fed-PP-L-351		
Liver, frozen, sliced		MIL-B-35047		
Patties, dehydrated, raw		Des. C-156-61		
Rib, frozen		Fed PP-B-221		PP-B-221c
Round, frozen		Fed PP-B-221		PP-B-221c

TYPE	USDA	DOD	FDA	GSA
Tenderloin, frozen		MIL-B-1040		
Tongue, canned				PP-T-571
Tongue, fresh, cured, or smoked				PP-T-576a
With gravy, canned		MIL-B-723		
With spiced sauce		MIL-B-3872		
Beefsteak				
Canned		MIL-B-1072		
Dehydrated, raw; ribeye and round		QM Lim. Prod. Pur. Des. C-149-61		
Flaked, dehydrated, raw		QM Lim. Prod. Pur. Des. C-163-61		
Bologna				
Chilled and frozen				PP-B-570
Chilled, Lebanon		Fed PP-L-160		PP-L-160
Chilled, 50 percent beef and 50 percent pork		Fed PP-B-570		
Frozen, Lebanon		Fed PP-L-160		PP-L-160
Frozen, 60% beef and 40% pork		Fed PP-B-570		
Frozen, 75% beef and 25% pork		Fed PP-B-570		
Cervelat				
Chilled, dry and soft (Thuringer)		Fed PP-S-74		PP-S-74a PP-S-0074b (Army-QMC)
Frozen, dry and soft (Thuringer)		Fed PP-S-74		PP-S-74a PP-S-0074b (Army-QMC)
Calf				
Carcass	53.107			PP-V-191c
Frankfurters				
Canned, whole		MIL-S-3069		
Chilled and frozen		Fed PP-F-660		PP-F-660

1. **Department of Agriculture**
2. **Department of Defense**
3. **Food and Drug Administration**
4. **General Services Administration**

TYPE	USDA	DOD	FDA	GSA	TYPE	USDA	DOD	FDA	GSA
Ham					**Luncheon Loaf**				
Canned, chunks		MIL-H-1021			Chilled or frozen		MIL-L-35066		
Canned, cured				PP-H-61a	**Luncheon Meat**				
Canned, pieces with gravy		MIL-H-3853			Canned, pork or pork and beef		MIL-L-1080		PP-P-578
Canned, sliced and fried		MIL-H-1071			**Meat Bar**				
Canned, whole		Fed PP-H-61			Dehydrated		MIL-M-3421		
Cooked, chilled, smoked		QM Lim. Prod. Pur. Des. C-128-60			**Meat Food Product**				PP-M-154
					Loaf (jellied)				PP-M-150
Cooked, frozen, smoked		QM Lim. Prod. Pur. Des. C-128-60			**Meat Loaf**				PP-M-170
Cured-cooked; chilled or frozen				PP-H-63	**Mincemeat**				
					Canned		Fed PP-M-351		PP-M-351a
Smoked, chilled or or frozen		MIL-H-1287							PP-M-00351b (Army-QMC)
Sweet-pickle-cured, smoked				PP-H-71	**Pepperoni**				
					Chilled, dry		Ind # 1140		
With gravy, canned		MIL-H-1048			**Pork**				
Hamburgers					Bellies, clear, dry-salt-cured				PP-P-586
Without gravy, canned, patties, deep-fat-fried		MIL-H-1048							PP-P-00586a (Army-QMC)
Hash					Butt, Boston; chilled and frozen		Fed PP-P-571		PP-P-571a
Canned, corned-beef				PP-H-91c	Chops, dehydrated, loin, boneless, raw		QM Lim. Prod. Pur. Des. C-147-61		
Hearts					Chops, frozen, loin, boned		QM Lim. Prod. Pur. Des. C-140-60		
Beef				PP-H-201					
Kidneys									
Beef				PP-K-351	Diced, frozen, Boston butt		QM Lim. Prod. Pur. Des. C-137-60		
Lamb									
Carcass, frozen	53.114	Fed PP-L-92		PP-L-92a					
Leg, frozen		Fed PP-L-92		PP-L-92a	Fat backs, dry-salt-cured				PP-F-81
Loin, frozen		Fed PP-L-92		PP-L-92a					
Telescope, frozen		MIL-L-1077			Fresh, chilled, or frozen				PP-P-571a
Liver									
				PP-L-351c	Ham, chilled, skinned		Fed PP-P-571		PP-P-571a
Liver Sausage									
Chilled and frozen		Fed PP-S-86							

TYPE	USDA	DOD	FDA	GSA	TYPE	USDA	DOD	FDA	GSA
Ham, frozen, bone-less		QM Lim. Prod. Pur. Des. C127-60			**Sausage**				
					Farmer (dry-type)				PP-S-78
Ham, frozen, skinned, short shank		Fed PP-P-571		PP-P-571a	Liver		PP-S-86a		PP-S-86a
					New England brand (chilled or frozen)				PP-S-88
Jowls, frozen, smoked, or cured		Fed PP-P-595		PP-P-595a	Pork				PP-S-916
Loin, bladeless, chilled, and frozen		Fed PP-P-571		PP-P-571a	canned, links		MIL-P-1104		
					chilled, uncooked		Fed PP-S-91		
Loin, frozen, boned, string-tied		QM Lim. Prod. Pur. Des. C-140-60			frozen, pre-cooked		QM Lim. Prod. Pur. Des. C-154-61		
Loin, frozen, boned, stringless in casing		QM Lim. Prod. Pur. Des. C-140-60			frozen, uncooked		Fed PP-S-91		
					Pork and beef, frozen, pre-cooked		QM Lim. Prod. Pur. Des. C-154-61		
Loin, frozen, par-tially boned		Fed PP-P-571		PP-P-571a	Salami				PP-S-0096a (Army-QMC)
Roll, chilled or frozen				PP-P-625a					PP-S-96
Spareribs, frozen		Fed PP-P-571			Vienna-style, canned		MIL-S-3069		PP-S-101
Steak, canned		MIL-P-1069			**Scrapple**				
Tenderloin, frozen		Fed PP-P-571		PP-P-571a					PP-S-141a
With gravy, canned		MIL-P-1044			**Sow**				
With gravy, canned chunks		QM Lim. Prod. Pur. Des. C-160-61			Carcass	53.144			
					Tongue				
Salami					Canned				PP-T-571
Chilled, cooked		Fed PP-S-96		PP-S-0076 (Army-QMC)	Fresh, cured, or smoked				PP-T-576a
Chilled, dry		Ind # 1460		PP-S-0077 (Army-QMC)	**Veal**				
					Boneless, frozen, prefabricated		QM Lim. Prod. Pur. Des. C-161-61		
Frozen, cooked		Fed PP-S-96		PP-S-0076 (Army-QMC)	Boneless, frozen		MIL-V-35036		
					Carcass	53.107			
Frozen, dry		Ind # 1480		PP-S-0077 (Army-QMC)	Diced, frozen, chuck		QM Lim. Prod. Pur. Des. C-161-61		
					Leg, chilled or frozen		Fed PP-V-191		PP-V-191c
					Loin, chilled or frozen		Fed PP-V-191		PP-V-191c

TYPE	USDA	DOD	FDA	GSA
Semi-boneless, frozen		MIL-V-3063		PP-V-191c
Sides, chilled or frozen		Fed PP-V-191		
Poultry	70.300			
Chicken				
Canned, boned, solid pack		MIL-C-1058		
Canned, boned, w/broth		MIL-C-1058		
Dehydrated, cooked, diced		QM Int. Pur. Des. CS-5-1		
Dehydrated, pre-cooked, boneless		QM Lim. Prod. Pur. Des. C-103-59		
Frozen, ready-to-cook, broiler-fryer, fowl (hen), roaster, breast, thigh		Fed PP-C-248		PP-C-248c
Duck				
Chilled, ready-to-cook				PP-D-7456 PP-D-00745c (AGR-AMS)
Frozen, ready-to-cook		Fed PP-D-745		PP-D-745b PP-D-00745c (AGR-AMS)
Goose				
Chilled and frozen, ready-to-cook				PP-D-745b PP-D-00745c (AGR-AMS)
Guinea				
Chilled and frozen, ready-to-cook				PP-D-745b PP-D-00745c (AGR-AMS)
Squab				
Chilled and frozen, ready-to-cook				PP-D-745b PP-D-00745c (AGR-AMS)

TYPE	USDA	DOD	FDA	GSA
Turkey				
Boneless, frozen, cooked		MIL-T-35006		
Canned, boned, solid pack		MIL-C-1058		
Canned, boned, with broth		MIL-C-1058		
Frozen, ready-to-cook		Fed PP-F-791		PP-T-791f
Turkey Loaf				
Canned		MIL-T-3899		
Rabbit	54.260			
Chilled or frozen ready-to-cook		Fed PP-R-21		PP-R-21a
Eggs			42.1	
Liquid or mixed			42.10	
Shell, fresh	56.200	Fed C-E-271		C-E-271d
White, frozen		MIL-E-1037		C-E-230a
Whole, dried, powdered		QM Int. Pur. Des. S-10-7 MIL-E-35062 or	42.30	
Whole, frozen			42.20	C-E-230a
bakery type		MIL-E-1037		
table type		MIL-E-35001		
Yolk, dried			42.60	
Yolk, frozen				
Sugared		MIL-E-1037		
Yolk, liquid			42.40	
Butter	58.2621			C-B-801e
Salted		Fed C-B-801		
Buttermilk				
Cultured				C-B-8166 C-B-00816c (AGR-AMS)
Dry	58.2651			
Fresh		Fed C-B-816		

TYPE	USDA	DOD	FDA	GSA	TYPE	USDA	DOD	FDA	GSA
Casein [Acid]					Grated		MIL-C-35057		
Dry, edible	58.2800				Parmesan and		QM Pur. Des.		
Cheese					Romano		101		
American,		MIL-C-10381			Gruyere			19.543	
processed		Fed C-C-291			Hard cheeses			19.650	
processed de-		MIL-C-35053			Hard grating			19.680	
hydrated					cheeses				
grated			19.790		Head cheese				PP-H-191
bulk, for manu-	58.2455				High-moisture jack			19.585	
facturing					cheese				
Asaigo			19.615		Limburger			19.575	
soft			19.615		Monterey (Jack)			19.580	
medium			19.620		Muenster			19.550	
old			19.625		Neufchatel			19.520	
Blue cheese			19.565		Nuworld			19.569	
Blue-veined,		Ind # 2030			Parmesan			19.595	
natural					Pasteurized			19.751	
Brick			19.545		blended cheese				
Caciocavallo			19.591		Pasteurized			19.763	
siciliano					blended cheese				
Cheddar					with fruits, vege-				
natural	58.2501	Fed C-C-271	19.500	C-C-271d	tables, or meats				
processed	58.2501	Fed C-C-291	19.500		Pastuerized cheese		MIL-C-595	19.776	
Cheese Bar, com-		MIL-C-3893			spread				
pressed					Pasteurized cheese			19.781	
Colby			19.510		spread with				
Cold pack cheese,					fruits, vege-				
club cheese, com-					tables, or meats				
minuted cheese					Pasteurized neu-			19.783	
Cook cheese			19.635		fchatel cheese				
Cottage		Fed C-C-281		C-C-281c	spread with				
plain			19.525		other foods				
creamed			19.530		Pasteurized process			19.750	C-C-291a
Cream			19.515		cheese				
Curd (washed)			19.505		Pasteurized process			19.755	
Edam			19.555		cheese with				
Emmantaler			19.540		fruits, vege-				
Gammelost			19.639		tables, or meats				
Gorgonzola			19.567		Pasteurized process			19.765	
Gouda			19.560		cheese food				
Granular cheese,			19.535						
stirred curd									
cheese									

TYPE	USDA	DOD	FDA	GSA
Pasteurized process cheese food with fruits, vegetables, or meats			19.770	
Pasteurized process cheese spread			19.775	
Pasteurized process cheese spread with fruits, vegetables, or meats			19.780	
Pasteurized process pimiento cheese		Fed C-C-291		19.760
Provolone		Ind # 2130	19.590	
Ricotta			19.532	
part skimmed			19.533	
Romano			19.610	
Roquefort			19.570	
Samsoe			19.544	
Sapsago			19.637	
Semisoft cheese			19.655	
part-skim			19.660	
Soft ripened			19.665	
Spiced			19.670	
part-skim			19.675	
Swiss	58.2570		19.540	
natural		Fed C-C-302		C-C-302a
processed		Fed C-C-305		C-C-305a
Chocolate Milk				
Pasteurized		MIL-M-3801		
Sterilized		MIL-C-35004		
Cream				
Dry, coffee or table type		MIL-C-35028	18.501	
Dry whipping type		QM Pur. Des. ~ 115a	18.510	
light			18.511	
heavy			18.515	
Fresh, pasteurized		Fed C-C-671	18.500	C-C-671d
Heavy			18.515	
Sour, cultured				C-C-00678 (AGR-AMS)
Stabilized, sterilized		MIL-C-688		

TYPE	USDA	DOD	FDA	GSA
Custard				
Frozen			20.2	
Half and Half				
Fresh		Fed C-C-671		C-C-671d
Ice Cream				
Plain, or with chocolate, fruit, nuts, or bulky flavors		Fed EE-I-116	20.1	EE-I-116b
Imitation, edible fat base (non-dairy origin)		MIL-D-35027		
Ice Cream Mix		MIL-I-705		
Ice Milk			20.3	
Malted Milk				
Powder, unflavored		Fed-C-M-341		C-M-341a
Margarine				
Vegetable oils, vitamin A added, colored		MIL-O-10958 Fed EE-0-451	41.5	EE-O-451b EE-0-00451c (DOD-QMC)
Milk				
Chocolate				C-C-00330
Concentrate, whole, fresh		MIL-M-3576	18.525	
Condensed, with corn syrup			18.535	
Condensed, sweetened			18.530	C-M-321a
Cultured				C-B-00816c
Dry nonfat, roller process	58.2550			
Dry, nonfat, spray process	58.2525	MIL-M-35052		C-M-350a
Evaporated, w/vitamin D		Fed C-M-371	18.520	C-M-371b
Filled (fluid)		QM Pur. Des. 246		
Instant, nonfat, dry	58.2750			
Reconstituted, pasteurized		MIL-M-1022		
Skimmed, dried			18.540	

TYPE	USDA	DOD	FDA	GSA
Skimmed, fresh, pasteurized, vitamin D increased		Fed C-M-390		C-M-390a
Sterilized		MIL-M-3722		
Whole, dry	58.2701	MIL-M-35039		C-M-355a
Whole, fresh, pasteurized, homogenized		Fed C-M-381		C-M-381g
Whole, frozen, pasteurized, homogenized		MIL-M-1050		
Fat, anhydrous		MIL-M-3233		
Milk Product				
Dry, cold water dispersible, spray process, sweetened				
Chocolate-coffee flavored		QM Lim. Prod. Pur. Des. C-139-60		
Cocoa flavored		MIL-M-35018		
Sherbet		Fed EE-I-116	20.4	EE-I-116b
Whey				
Dry	58.2601			
Clams				
Canned		Ind # 710		PP-C-00400 (Int.-F & WS)
Frozen, raw, shucked				PP-C-401a
Frozen, Raw, shucked		Fed PP-C-401		PP-C-401a
Cod				
Frozen, fillets		Fed PP-F-381		PP-F-00381e
Crabmeat				
Canned				PP-C-651a
Cooked, chilled and frozen				PP-C-656a
Crawfish				
Frozen, tail (Lobster tail)		Ind # 750		

TYPE	USDA	DOD	FDA	GSA
Fish				
Fresh (chilled) and frozen				PP-F-381d PP-F-00381e (Int.-F&WS)
Fish Squares				
Dehydrated, cod and haddock		QM Lim. Prod. Pur. Des. C-145-61		
Flounder				
Frozen, fillets		Fed PP-F-381		PP-F-00381e
Haddock				
Frozen, fillets		Fed PP-F-381		PP-F-381e
Halibut				
Frozen, steaks		Fed PP-F-381		PP-F-00381e
Mackerel				
Frozen, fillets		Fed PP-F-381		PP-F-00381e
Oysters				
Canned			36.5	PP-0-951
Fresh, raw, shucked			36.10	PP-0-956c
Extra large			36.11	
Large			36.12	
Medium			36.13	
Small			36.14	
Very small			36.15	
Olympia			36.16	
Large Pacific			36.17	
Medium Pacific			36.18	
Small Pacific			36.19	
Extra small Pacific			36.20	
Frozen, raw, shucked		Fed PP-0-956		PP-0-956c
Perch				
Frozen, fillets		Fed PP-F-381		PP-F-00381e
Rockfish				
Frozen, fillets		Fed PP-F-381		PP-F-00381e
Salmon				
Canned		Fed PP-S-31		PP-S-31c
Frozen		Fed PP-F-381		
Sardines				
Canned		Fed PP-S-51		PP-S-51d PP-S-0051e (Int.-F&WS)

TYPE	USDA	DOD	FDA	GSA
Scallops				
Frozen, sea		MIL-S-3642		
Shrimp				
Canned, deveined		Fed PP-S-311	36.3	PP-S-311a
Dehydrated, peel-ed, deveined		QM. Int. Pur. Des. CS-9-2		
Frozen, cooked				PP-S-316a
Frozen, raw, be-headed		Fed PP-S-316 QM. Int. Pur. Des. S-26-7		PP-S-361a
Frozen, raw, breaded				PP-S-315c PP-S-00351b (Int.-F&WS
Snapper				
Frozen, red, steaks		Fed PP-F-381		PP-F-00381e
Swordfish				
Frozen, steaks		Fed PP-F-381		PP-F-00381e
Tuna				
Canned		QM Int. Pur. Des. CS-5-9	37.1	PP-T-771 PP-T-00771a
Whiting				
Frozen, fillets		Fed PP-F-381		PP-F-00381c
Apples				
Fresh	51.300	Fed Y-A-606		Y-A-606d
Canned	52.2161	Fed Z-A-611		Z-A-611c(1)
Frozen	52.361			
Dehydrated	52.2341	Fed Z-A-612 MIL-A-1035		Z-A-612a(1)
Dried	52.2481			Z-A-613d(1)
Apricots				
Fresh	51.2925	Fed Ta-621		Y-A-621c
Canned	52.2641	Fed Z-A-631	27.10	Z-A-631c
Artificially sweetened			27.14	
Frozen	52.5521			Z-A-641a
Dehydrated	52.3871	Fed Z-A-00634		Z-A-634a
Dried	52.5761	Fed Z-A-636		Z-A-636b(1)
Aritchokes				
Fresh	51.3785		51.990	HHH-A-00696a
globe type				HHH-A-696

TYPE	USDA	DOD	FDA	GSA
Asparagus				
Fresh	51.3720	Fed HHH-A-731		HHH-A-731b
Canned	52.2541	Fed JJJ-A-711	51.990	JJJ-A-711d
Frozen	52.381	Fed HHH-A-735		HHH-A-735c
Avocado				
Fresh	51.3050	Fed Y-A-830		Y-A-830a
Bananas				
Fresh		Fed Y-B-91		Y-B-91b Y-B-0091a
Beans [Green & Wax]				
Fresh	51.3830	Fed HHH-B-130		HHH-B-130
Canned	52.441	Fed JJJ-B-151	51.10 (green) 51.15 (wax)	JJJ-B-151c JJJ-B-151d
Frozen	52.2321	Fed HHH-B-136		HHH-B-136
Dehydrated		MIL-B-35011		
Beans [Lima]				
Fresh	51.3805			HHH-B-141c
Canned	52.471	Fed JJJ-B-126 Fed JJJ-B-126d	51.990	JJJ-B-126f
Frozen	52.501	Fed HHH-B-145		HHH-B-145c
Dried	52.411	Fed JJJ-B-106		JJJ-B-106b
Bean Sprouts				
Canned		MIL-B-35012		
Green Bean Puree				
		MIL-V-815		
Beets				
Fresh	51.375	Fed HHH-B-166		HHH-B-166c
Canned	52.521	Fed JJJ-B-181	51.990	JJJ-B-181b JJJ-B-181c
Fresh beet greens	51.2860			
Beet Puree				
		MIL-V-815		
Blackberries				
Fresh	51.4270	Fed Y-B-426		Y-B-426b
Canned	52.551	Syrup pack Fed Z-B-421	27.35	Z-B-421a
		Water pack Fed Z-B-421		Z-B-00421b
Frozen	52.5881	Fed Z-B-211		Z-B-211a

TYPE	USDA	DOD	FDA	GSA
Blueberries				
Fresh	51.3475	Fed Y-B-496		Y-B-496b
Canned	52.581	Fed Z-B-491	27.35	Z-B-491b(2)
				Z-B-00491c
Frozen	52.611	52.611		Z-B-211a
Broccoli				
Fresh	51.3555	Fed HHH-B-691		HHH-B-691c
Frozen		Fed HHH-B-692		HHH-B-692b
Brussels Sprouts				
Fresh	51.2250	Fed HHH-B-725		HHH-B-725a
Frozen	52.651	Fed HHH-B-731		HHH-B-731
Cabbage				
Fresh	51.450	Fed HHH-C-26		HHH-C-266(1)
Dehydrated		MIL-C-826		
Cantaloupe				
Fresh	51.475	Fed Y-C-96		Y-C-966
				Y-C-0096c
Frozen	52.5361			
Carrots				
Fresh		Fed HHH-C-81		HHH-C-81c
bunched	51.2455			HHH-C-0081d
topped	51.2360			
short trimmed	51.2485			
tops				
Canned	52.671	Fed JJJ-C-76	51.990	JJJ-C-76b(2)
				JJJ-C-0076c
Frozen	52.701			
Carrot Puree				
		MIL-V-815		
Cauliflower				
Fresh	51.540	Fed HHH-C-101		HHH-C-1016
				HHH-C-00101c
Frozen	52.721	Fed HHH-C-102		HHH-C-102a
Celery				
Fresh	51.560	Fed HHH-C-191		HHH-C-191d
Cherries [Red Tart Pitted]				
Fresh		Fed Y-C-306		
Canned	52.771	Fed Z-C-00301	27.30	Z-C-301d
Frozen	52.801	Fed Z-C-315		Z-C-315b
Sulfured	52.741			
Cherries [Sweet]				
Fresh	51.2646	Fed Y-C-306		Y-C-306b
Canned	52.821	Fed Z-C-00301	27.30	Z-C-301d
Frozen	52.3161	Fed Z-C-315		Z-C-315b
Sulfured	52.741			
Collard or Broccoli Greens				
Fresh	51.520			HHH-G-620a
Corn				
Fresh		Fed HHH-C-591		HHH-C-591b
green	51.835			HHH-C-00591c
Canned				
whole kernel	52.881	Fed JJJ-C-542	51.20	JJJ-C-542
cream style	52.851	Fed JJJ-C-542	51.22	
Frozen				
whole kernel	52.911	Fed HHH-C-586		HHH-C-586a
				HHH-C-005866
				HHH-C-586c
Frozen				
on-the-cob	52.931			
Cranberries				
Fresh	51.2775	Fed Y-C-651		Y-C-651c
Frozen	52.6281			
Cranberry Sauce	52.951			
canned		Fed Z-C-656		Z-C-656
Cucumbers				
Fresh	51.2220	Fed HHH-C-751		Y-C-651c
Greenhouse	51.3855			
Pickling	51.4170			
Currants				
Dried	52.981	Fed Z-C-851		Z-C-8516(2)
				Z-C-00851c
Dandelion Greens				
Fresh	51.2585			
Dates				
Fresh	52.1001	Fed Y-D-126		Y-D-1266(1)
Dewberries and Other Similar Berries				
Fresh	51.4270			Y-B-4266
Canned	52.551		27.35	Z-B-421a(1)
				Z-B-00421b
Frozen	52.5881			Z-B-211a

TYPE	USDA	DOD	FDA	GSA
Eggplant				
Fresh	51.2190	Fed HHH-E-236		HHH-E-2366 HHH-E-00236c
Endive and Escarole and Chicory				
Fresh	51.3535	Fed HHH-E-516		HHH-E-516c
Figs				
Kadota canned	52.2821	Fed Z-F-351	27.70	Z-F-351d(1)
Dried	52.1021			Z-F-356a(1)
Fruit Cocktail				
Canned	52.1051	Fed Z-F-681	27.40	Z-F-681a
Canned Fruits for Salad				
Canned	52.3831			
grapefruit and orange for salad	52.1251			
Fruit Puree				
Apricot		Ind # 4030		
Peach		Ind # 4040		
Pear		Ind # 4050		
Prune		Ind # 4060		
Grapefruit				
Fresh		Fed Y-G-680 also		
California and Arizona	51.925	Y-G-682 and 683		Y-G-680a and Y-G-006806 Y-G-683(1) and Y-G-00683a Y-G-682c
Florida	51.750			
Texas and states other than California, Arizona and Florida	51.620			
Canned	52.1141	Fed Z-G-676	27.90	Z-G-676d(1)
Frozen	52.1171	Fed Z-G-678		Z-G-678
Grapes				
Fresh		Fed Y-G-671		Y-G-6716 and Y-G-00671c
Eastern type	51.3610			
Vinifera	51.880			
Juice	51.4290			
Canned	52.4021		27.25	

TYPE	USDA	DOD	FDA	GSA
Leafy Greens Other than Spinach				
Fresh				
Beet	51.2860			
Collard or Broccoli	51.520			HHH-G-620a
Dandelion	51.2585			
Mustard and Turnip	51.1030	Fed HHH-G-651		HHH-G-651a and HHH-G-00651b
Canned	52.6081		51.990	JJJ-T-806a
Frozen	52.1371	Fed HHH-G-640		HHH-G-640a
Hominy				
Canned	52.3281	Fed N-H-541		N-H-541a
Honeydew and Honey Ball Type Melons				
Fresh	51.3740	Fed Y-H-495		Y-H-495a
Frozen	52.5361			
Horseradish Roots				
Fresh	51.5361			
Kale				
Fresh	51.3930	Fed HHH-K-106		HHH-K-1066
Lemons				
Fresh	51.2795	Fed Y-L-231		Y-L-231c
Lettuce				
Fresh	51.2510	Fed HHH-L-226		HHH-L-226b HHH-L-00226c
Greenhouse	51.3455			
Limes				
Fresh	51.1000	Fed Y-L-369		Y-L-3966(1)
Mixed Vegetables				
Frozen	52.2131	Fed HHH-V-200		HHH-V-200
Mushrooms				
Fresh	51.3385			
Canned	52.1481	Fed JJJ-M-851	51.503	JJJ-M-8516
Mustard Greens and Turnip Greens				
Fresh	51.1030			
Nectarines				
Fresh	51.3145			

TYPE	USDA	DOD	FDA	GSA
Okra				
Fresh	51.3945			HHH-0-400a
Canned	52.3331	Fed JJJ-0-400	51.990	JJJ-0-400a
Frozen	52.1511	Fed HHH-0-402		HHH-0-402a
Onions				
Fresh				
Bermuda, Granex, Grano-type	51.3195			HHH-0-532(1)
Creole	51.3955			HHH-0-534(1)
Green	51.1055	Fed HHH-0-533		HHH-0-533b
Bunched	51.1630			HHH-S-256
Shallots				HHH-S-256b
All Others	51.2830			HHH-0-536(1)
Canned	52.3041		51.990	
Dehydrated		Fed JJJ-0-533		JJJ-0-533
				JJJ-0-00533a
				and
				JJJ-0-533b
Dry		Fed HHH-0-534		Dry (fresh)
		and		
		Fed HHH-0-536		Bermuda-
				Granex-
				HHH-0-535a
				HHH-0-00535
				Others —
				HHH-0-00539
Onion Rings				
Frozen Breaded	52.4061			
Oranges				
Fresh				
California and Arizona	51.1085			Y-0-660c
Florida	51.1140			Y-0-663(1)
				and
				Y-0-00663a
Texas and others	51.680			Y-0-662d
Temple		Fed Y-0-662, 663		
Any variety but Temple		Fed Y-0-660, 662, 663		

TYPE	USDA	DOD	FDA	GSA
Parsley				
Fresh	51.4000	Fed HHH-P-96		HHH-P-966
Dehydrated		QM Pur. Des. 152		
Parsnips				
Fresh	51.4010	Fed HHH-P-103		HHH-P-103a
				HHH-P-103b
Peaches				
Fresh	51.1210	Fed Y-P-151		Y-P-151d
				Y-P-00151c
Canned		Fed Z-P-191	27.2	Z-P-191c
Artificially sweetened			27.6	
Clingstone	52.2561			
Freestone	52.2601			
Frozen	52.3551	Fed Z-P-194		Z-P-194a
Dehydrated	52.3911	Fed Z-P-192		Z-P-192a
Dried	52.5801	Fed Z-P-193		Z-P-193b(1)
Pears				
Fresh		Fed Y-P-169		
Summer and Fall	51.1260			Y-P-1676
Winter	51.1300			Y-P-1696
Canned	52.1611	Fed Z-P-201	27.20	Z-P-201c(1)
Artificially sweetened			27.24	
Dried	52.5841			Z-P-206a(1)
Peas				
Fresh	51.1375			HHH-P-156c
Canned	52.2281	Fed JJJ-P-151	51.1	JJJ-P-151b
Frozen	52.3511	Fed HHH-P-160		HHH-P-106c
Dehydrated		CS-4-0		
Dried		Fed JJJ-P-156		
Dehydrofrozen		MIL-P-35031		
Pea Puree				
Fine		MIL-V-815		
Southern Peas [Field Peas and Black-eyed Peas]				
Fresh	51.2670			HHH-P-186a
Canned	52.1641	MIL-P-35034	51.990	JJJ-P-1516
Frozen	52.1661	Fed HHH-P-160		HHH-P-106c
Dehydrated		CS-4-0		
Dried		Fed JJJ-P-156		
Dehydrofrozen		MIL-P-35031		

TYPE	USDA	DOD	FDA	GSA
Peas and Carrots				
Canned	52.6201		51.990	
Frozen	52.2501			HHH-P-166a
Peppers [Sweet]				
Fresh	51.3270	Fed HHH-P-246		HHH-P-2466
Frozen	52.3001	Fed HHH-P-00250		HHH-P-00250
Green, dehydrated		MIL-P-35003		
Pimientos				
Canned	52.2681	Fed JJJ-P-400	51.990	JJJ-P-400
Pineapples				
Fresh	51.1485	Fed Y-P-381		Y-P-381c
Canned	52.1711	Fed Z-P-351	27.50	Z-P-351d(1)
Artificially sweetened			27.57	
Frozen	52.1741			Z-P-354a
Plums				
Fresh	51.1520	Fed Y-P-506		Y-P-506c
Canned	52.1781	Fed Z-P-491	27.45	Z-P-4916 / Z-P-00491c
Frozen	52.2911			
Potatoes [White]				
Fresh	51.1540	Fed HHH-P-622		HHH-P-622a
Seed potatoes	51.3000			
Canned	52.1811	Fed JJJ-P-621	51.990	JJJ-P-621a
Peeled	52.2421			
Dehydrated		MIL-P-1073		
French Fried	52.2391			
Frozen				
Prunes				
Fresh	51.1520			Y-P-506c(1)
Canned Dried	52.5601	Fed Z-P-671	27.15	Z-P-671c
Dehydrated	52.3231	Z-P-00665		Z-P-665a
Dried	52.3181	Fed Z-P-681		Z-P-681d(1)
Pumpkin				
Fresh				HHH-P-796b
Canned	52.2741	Fed JJJ-P-791	51.990	JJJ-P-791b
Radishes				
Fresh	51.2395	Fed HHH-R-86		HHH-R-86a / HHH-R-0086b

TYPE	USDA	DOD	FDA	GSA
Raspberries				
Fresh	51.4320			Y-R-1016
Canned	52.3311			Z-R-916(1)
Frozen	52.1871	Fed Y-R-104		Y-R-104
Rhubarb				
Fresh	51.3665	Fed HHH-R-301		HHH-R-3016
Canned		Fed HHH-R-303		HHH-R-303
Romaine				
Fresh	51.3295	Fed HHH-R-570		HHH-R-570a
Sauerkraut				
Bulk	52.3451			
Canned	52.2951	Fed JJJ-S-71	51.990	JJJ-S-71c
Shallots, Bunched				
Fresh	51.1630			
Spinach				
Fresh	51.1730	Fed HHH-S-616		
Spinach Plants	51.2880			HHH-S-616c
Canned	52.1901	Fed JJJ-S-611	51.990	JJJ-S-6116
Frozen	52.1921	Fed HHH-S-620		HHH-S-620a / HHH-S-0062b
Spinach Puree				
Canned		MIL-V-815		
Squash [Fall and Winter]				
Fresh	51.4030	Fed HHH-S-666		HHH-S-666a / HHH-S-00666b
Canned	52.2741		51.990	
Frozen	52.1941			HHH-S-668a
Squash [Summer]				
Fresh	51.4050	Fed HHH-S-666		HHH-S-666a / HHH-S-00666b
Canned	52.3581		51.990	
Frozen	52.1961	Fed HHH-S-668		HHH-S-668a
Squash Puree				
Fine		MIL-V-815		
Strawberries				
Fresh	51.3115	Fed Y-S-726		Y-S-726c
Frozen	52.1981	Fed Y-S-729		Y-S-729
Succotash				
Canned	52.6001		51.990	
Frozen	52.2011			HHH-S-782a

TYPE	USDA	DOD	FDA	GSA
Sweet Potatoes				
Fresh	51.1600	Fed HHH-P-621		HHH-P-621c
Canned	52.2041	Fed JJJ-P-611		JJJ-P-611c
				JJJ-P-00611d
Frozen	52.5001			JJJ-P-611c
Swiss Chard				
Fresh				HHH-S-900a
Tangelos				
Fresh	51.1140			
Tangerines				
Fresh	51.1770	Fed Y-T-96, 98		Y-T-966(1)
				Y-T-0996c
Florida	51.1835			Y-T-98
				Y-T-0098a
Tomatoes				
Fresh	51.1855	Fed HHH-T-576		HHH-T-576d
Greenhouse	51.3345			
Canned	52.5161	Fed JJJ-T-571	53.40	JJJ-T-5716
Tomatoes and Okra				
Canned	52.3421		51.990	JJJ-T-574a
Turnips or Rutabagas				
Fresh	51.2610	Fed HHH-T-851		HHH-T-8516
Frozen	52.3731			
Watermelon				
Fresh	51.1970	Fed Y-W-121		Y-W-121b
				Y-W-00121c
Apple Juice				
Canned	52.301	Fed Z-A-623		Z-A-623(2)
Frozen, concentrated	52.6321			
Beverage Base				
Cherry, grape, lemon, lemon-lime, lime, orange, raspberry, and strawberry-imitation base, liquid, w/o Ascorbic Acid, no fruit or fruit juices		MIL-B-35007		

TYPE	USDA	DOD	FDA	GSA
Lemon or orange, powdered, w/ ascorbic acid		MIL-L-1066		
Lemon, synthetic base, powder, w/ ascorbic acid		MIL-L-1066		
Grape Juice				
Canned, single strength	52.1341	Fed Z-G-661		Z-G-661b
Frozen, concentrated	52.2451	MIL-G-3791		Z-J-815
Grapefruit Juice				
Canned	52.6121	Fed Z-G-686		Z-G-6860(1)
				Z-J-00820
Frozen, concentrated	52.1221	MIL-G-11182		
Dehydrated	52.3021			
Instant				Z-J-00822
Sweetened		MIL-J-35050		
Unsweetened		QM Int. Pur. Des. S-12-7		
Concentrated for manufacturing-	52.3481			
Blended Grapefruit and Orange Juice				
Canned		Fed Z-G-691		Z-G-691a
Frozen, concentrated	52.1311			Z-J-00874
Lemon Juice				
Canned	52.5481			
Frozen, concentrated		MIL-L-11174		
Concentrated for manufacturing	52.3951			
Lemonade				
Frozen concentrate	52.1421	Z-L-199a	27.101	
Frozen concentrate for colored lemonade			27.102	
Lime Juice				
Frozen		Fed Z-L-351		Z-L-351a
Frozen concentrate	52.2521			

TYPE	USDA	DOD	FDA	GSA
Limeade				
Frozen concentrate	52.2521			
Orange Juice				
			27.106	
Canned	52.1551	Fed Z-0-661	27.108	Z-J-00875 (AGR-AMS) and Z-0-666a
Sweetened			27.110	
Concentrated, canned	52.2251		27.111	Z-0-670a
Sweetened			27.112	
Concentrated, frozen	52.1581			Z-0-671
From concentrate	52.5681			
Dehydrated	52.2981			
Frozen		Fed Z-0-671		
Instant		MIL-J-35049		Z-J-00890 (AGR-AMS)
Pasteurized	52.5641		27.107	
Sweetened			27.109	
Reconstituted			27.113	
Sweetened			27.114	
Concentrated for manufacturing	52.2221			
Pineapple Juice				
Canned	52.1761	Fed Z-P-356	27.54	Z-P-356(1)
Prune Juice				
Canned			27.60	
Tangerine Juice				
Canned	52.2071			
Concentrated for manufacturing	52.2931			
Tomato Juice				
Canned, concentrated	52.5201	MIL-T-3529		
Canned, single strength	52.3621	Fed JJJ-T-576	53.1	JJJ-J-00798 (AGR-AMS) JJJ-T-576a
Yellow			53.5	

TYPE	USDA	DOD	FDA	GSA
Vegetable Juice				
Canned		Ind # 4470		
Jelly				
		Fed Z-J-191		Z-J-1916
Jam [Preserves]				
		Fed Z-J-96		Z-J-96a
Almond Paste				
		MIL-A-35040		
Antioxidant Compound, foodservice				
		MIL-A-55043		
Apple Butter				
	52.2801	Fed Z-A-616	29.1	Z-A-616c
Applesauce				
Canned	52.331	Fed Z-A-621		Z-A-6216(1)
dietetic water pack		Ind # 10350		
Instant		MIL-A-35045		
Apricot Nectar				
Canned		MIL-A-35019		
Baby Food				
Junior				
Applesauce		Ind # 10370		
Beef		Ind # 10380		
Beets		Ind # 10390		
Carrots		Ind # 10400		
Green beans		Ind # 10410		
Liver		Ind # 10420		
Pork		Ind # 10430		
Spinach		Ind # 10440		
Veal		Ind # 10450		
Strained				
Applesauce		Ind # 10460		
Apricots		Ind # 10470		
Barley cereal		Ind # 10480		
Beef		Ind # 10490		
Beef broth, beef and barley		Ind # 10500		
Beets		Ind # 10510		
Carrots		Ind # 10520		
Chicken soup		Ind # 10530		
Custard pudding		Ind # 10540		

TYPE	USDA	DOD	FDA	GSA
Green beans		Ind # 10550		
Liver		Ind # 10560		
Mixed cereal		Ind # 10570		
		and # 10580		
Oatmeal cereal		Ind # 10590		
Peaches		Ind # 10600		
Pears		Ind # 10610		
Peas		Ind # 10620		
Pork		Ind # 10630		
Prunes		Ind # 10640		
Rice cereal		Ind # 10650		
Spinach		Ind # 10660		
Veal		Ind # 10670		
Vegetables, mixed		Ind # 10680		
Baby Formula Preparation				
Principal ingredients listed		Ind # 10690 10700, 10710, 10720		
Baking Powder				
		Fed EE-P-611		EE-B-0025 (Army-QMC) EE-P-611c
Baking Soda [Sodium Bicarbonate]				
		Fed EE-B-86		EE-B-86b
Barley				
Pearl, white	26.201	Fed N-B-121		N-B-121a
Beans and Meat with Tomato Sauce				
Canned		MIL-M-1106		
Beans with Frankfurter Chunks in Tomato Sauce				
		MIL-B-1065		
Beef and Corn				
Canned		MIL-M-1046		
Beef and Peas with Gravy				
Canned		MIL-B-3847		
Beef and Vegetables				
Canned		MIL-B-736		
Beefsteak and Potatoes with Gravy				
Canned		MIL-B-3877		

TYPE	USDA	DOD	FDA	GSA
Chocolate Drink				
2% or 1% minimum milk fat		MIL-M-3801		
Cocoa Beverage Powder				
Fortified and non-fortified		MIL-C-3031	14.3	
Cocoa				
10% or 22% minimum cocoa fat		Fed JJJ-C-501		JJJ-C-501b JJJ-C-00501c (Army-QMC)
High fat			14.3	
Low fat			14.5	
Medium fat			14.4	
Nibs, cracked cocoa			14.1	
Sweet cocoa and vegetable fat			14.12	
Coffee				
Instant, powdered, 100% coffee		Fed HHH-C-575		HHH-C-575
Roasted, ground, universal grind, blend		Fed HHH-C-571		HHH-C-571a
Tea				
Black		Fed HHH-T-191281.19		
Instant, powdered, 50% tea, w/ ascorbic acid		MIL-T-3527		
Instant, powdered, 100% tea, w/ ascorbic acid		MIL-T-352a		
Water				
Drinking, canned		MIL-W-15117		
Emergency drinking water, water-tight case		BUSH IPS Dwg S 3402-1250956		
Biscuit Mix				
Prepared				N-B-371
Wheat		MIL-B-3071		
Bouillon Cubes				
Beef		MIL-B-1112		

TYPE	USDA	DOD	FDA	GSA
Bread				
Canned, brown with raisins		Ind # 5920		EE-B-671c
Canned, white		MIL-B-1070		EE-B-671c
Fresh, French, hearth-baked		Fed EE-B-00671 QM Int. Pur. Des. S-39-7		EE-B-671c
Fresh, milk			17.3	
Fresh, part whole wheat		Fed EE-B-00671 QM Int. Pur. Des. S-39-7		EE-B-671c
Fresh, raisin		Fed EE-B-00671 QM Int. Pur. Des. S-39-7	17.4	EE-B-671c
Fresh, Vienna		Fed EE-B-00671		EE-B-671c
Fresh, white, enriched		Fed EE-B-00671 QM Int. Pur. Des. S-39-7	17.1— white 17.2— enriched	EE-B-671c
Fresh, whole wheat		Fed EE-B-00671 QM Int. Pur. Des. S-39-7	17.5	EE-B-671c
Bread and Roll Mix				
Shortbread, prepared				N-B-371
White		MIL-B-3071		
Cake				
Fresh coffee cake or loaf cake		Ind # 6090		
Cake Mix				
Devil's food, gingerbread, spice, white, yellow		MIL-B-3071		N-C-71b
5 lb. can or package		Fed N-C-71		N-C-71b
Universal, for altitude less than 3000 ft. above sea level		MIL-C-35009		
Cake Mix and Flavor Pack		MIL-C-35009		
Candy				
Sugar lozenge, peppermint square		MIL-C-10928 QM Int. Pur. Des. C-SL-1		EE-C-71
Catsup, Tomato				
	51.2101	Fed JJJ-C-91	53.10	JJJ-C-916 JJJ-C-0091c (AGR-AMS)
Cereal				
Pre-mixed, compressed, block shaped, enriched		MIL-C-3483		
Rolled oats, quick cooking		Fed N-0-41		
Wheat, farina, enriched		Fed N-C-201		N-C-2016
Whole wheat meal, quick cooking		Fed N-C-201		N-C-2016
Others		Fed N-C-196		N-C-196c N-C-00196d (AGR-AMS)
Chewing Gum				
Stick, flavors 1-7		MIL-C-10022a or QM Int. Pur. Des. CS-1-8		
Tablet, candy coated		MIL-C-10022		
Chicken and Noodles				
Canned		MIL-C-11076		
Chicken and Vegetables				
Canned		MIL-C-673		
Chili con Carne				
Canned				EE-C-281
without beans concentrated		MIL-C-1381		
without beans				PP-C-276
Chili Sauce				
Canned	52.2191	Fed EE-S-71		EE-S-71c(1)

TYPE	USDA	DOD	FDA	GSA
Chocolate				
Baking and cooking		Fed JJJ-C-271	14.2	JJJ-C-271a
				JJJ-C-00271b
				(Army-QMC)
Bitter and chocolate liquid			14.2	
Buttermilk chocolate			14.9	
Milk chocolate			14.7	
Mixed dairy product chocolate			14.10	
Skim milk chocolate			14.8	
Sweet			14.6	
Sweet chocolate and vegetable fat			14.11	
Chocolate Nut Roll				
Canned		MIL-C-35058		
Chocolate Syrup				
Beverage, stabilized		MIL-C-35041		
Beverage, stabilized or unstabilized		Ind # 8510		
Topping, unstabilized		MIL-C-35041		
Clam Chowder				
New England and New York, ready-to-serve and condensed		Fed JJJ-S-581		
Coconut				
Prepared Sweetened, long thread or fancy shred		Fed Z-C-571		Z-C-571b
Unsweetened, desiccated, macaroon		MIL-C-10928		

TYPE	USDA	DOD	FDA	GSA
Cookies				
Coconut macaroon		Fed EE-C-651		EE-651e(3)
Fig bar		Fed EE-C-651		EE-651e(3)
Gingersnap		Fed EE-C-651		EE-651e(3)
Oatmeal with chocolate chips		MIL-C-1029		EE-651e(3)
Sandwich, chocolate filling		MIL-C-1043		EE-651e(3)
Sandwich, cream filling		Fed EE-C-651		EE-651e(3)
Sandwich, vanilla filling		MIL-C-1043		EE-651e(3)
Shortbread		Fed EE-C-651		EE-651e(3)
Vanilla wafer		Fed EE-C-651		EE-651e(3)
Assortment		Fed EE-C-651		EE-651e(3)
Corn Meal				
White		Fed N-C-521	15.500	N-C-521c
bolted			15.502	
degerminated		Fed N-C-521	15.504	N-C-521c
self-rising			15.506	
Yellow		Fed N-C-521	15.501	N-C-521c
bolted			15.503	
degerminated		Fed N-C-521	15.505	N-C-521c
self-rising			15.507	
enriched			15.513	
Cornstarch				
Edible		Fed N-C-541		N-C-541a
Crackers				
Graham		Fed EE-C-651		EE-C-651e(3)
Oyster, salted		Fed EE-C-651		EE-C-651e(3)
Soda, salted, 10% minimum fat		Fed EE-C-651		EE-C-651e(3)
Soda, salted, 12% minimum fat		MIL-C-1324		EE-C-651e(3)
Cranberry Sauce				
Canned	52.951	Fed Z-C-656		Z-C-656
Dessert Powder				
Gelatin base cherry, lemon, lime, orange, raspberry, strawberry		Fed C-D-221		C-D-221c

TYPE	USDA	DOD	FDA	GSA
Starch base				
butterscotch		Fed C-D-221		
chocolate		Fed C-D-221 and Fed C-D-221a		
vanilla		Fed C-D-221		
Instant		MIL-D-35033		
butterscotch, chocolate, vanilla				
Doughnut				
Fresh		Ind # 6940		
Doughnut Mix		MIL-B-3071		N-D-591a
Dressing, Salad				
		Fed EE-M-131	25.3	EE-M-131(1) EE-M-00131a
French			25.2	
Extracts, Flavoring, and Flavors				
Imitation, maple		Fed EE-E-911		EE-E-911d(2)
Imitation, vanilla		Fed EE-E-911		EE-E-911d(2)
Lemon, nonalcoholic		Fed EE-E-911		EE-E-911d(2)
Orange, non-alcoholic		Fed EE-E-911		EE-E-911d(2)
Tablet, maple, imitation		MIL-F-805		
Tablet, vanilla, imitation		MIL-F-3040		
Flaxseed				
	26.501			
Flour				
Bromated			15.20	
enriched			15.30	
Corn				
white			15.508	
yellow			15.509	
Durum			15.40	
Enriched			15.10	
Farina			15.130	
enriched			15.140	
Graham (whole wheat meal)			15.80	N-F-461
Phosphated			15.70	
Rye				N-F-471a

TYPE	USDA	DOD	FDA	GSA
dark, not enriched		Ind # 6960		
medium, not enriched		Fed N-F-471		
Self-rising			15.50	
enriched			15.60	
Semolina			15.150	
Soy				JJJ-S-591
Wheat		Fed N-F-481	15.1	N-F-481f
cracked			15.120	
crushed			15.110	
Whole wheat			15.80	
bromated				
wheat			15.90	
Whole durum wheat			15.100	
White			15.1	
Food Coloring				
Liquid, egg-shade		QM Pur. Des. 255		
Liquid, red		QM Pur. Des. 255		
Assortment, liquid		Ind # 12190		
Fruit Butter				
			29.1	
Fruitcake				
Canned, light or		MIL-F-3233		
dark		MIL-P-1499		
Fresh, light		MIL-F-3232		
Bar		MIL-F-3897		
Fruit, Candied				
		MIL-F-35054		
Fruit Jelly				
	52.1081	Fed Z-J-191	29.2	Z-J-191b(1)
Artificially sweetened			29.4	
Fruit Preserves [or Jams]				
	52.1111	Fed Z-J-96	29.3	Z-J-96a(2)
Artificially sweetened			29.5	
Fry Mix				
Breading and batter		MIL-3501		

TYPE	USDA	DOD	FDA	GSA
Gelatine				
Plain, edible (unflavored), powdered		Fed C-D-221		C-D-221c
Ginger Ale				
				EE-G-391a
Grain				
Barley	26.201			
Corn	26.351			
Flaxseed	26.501			
Mixed	26.451			
Oats	26.251			
Rye	26.401			
Sorghum	26.551			
Soybeans	26.601			
Wheat	26.301			
Ham and Eggs				
Canned, chopped		MIL-H-1038		
Ham and Kidney Beans in Sauce				
Canned		MIL-B-3874		
Ham and Lima Beans				
Canned, pieces		MIL-H-619		
Ham and Potatoes with Gravy				
Canned		MIL-H-3830		
Hominy				
Grits			15.510	
enriched			15.514	
quick cooking			15.512	
White, plain or enriched		Fed N-C-516		N-C-516
Yellow			15.511	
Whole, canned	52.3281	Fed N-H-541		N-H-541a
Honey				
Comb	52.2861			
Extracted	52.1391	Fed C-H-571		C-H-571a
Horseradish				
Prepared		MIL-H-35044		
Hot Sauce				
		MIL-H-35021		
Ice				
Block or crushed, manufactured		Ind # 13690		

TYPE	USDA	DOD	FDA	GSA
Inhibitor, Mold, Bread and Rolls				
		Fed EE-B-00671		
Kitchen Sauce				
		QM Pur. Des. 154		
Lard				
		Fed EE-S-321		C-0-376a EE-S-00321a (QMC)
Macaroni				
Macaroni products			16.1	
enriched			16.9	
milk macaroni products			16.2	
vegetable macaroni products			16.5	
wheat and soy macaroni products			16.4	
whole wheat macaroni products			16.3	
Elbow		Fed N-M-51		N-M-51b N-M-0051c
Instant		MIL-M-35067		
Malted Cereal Syrup				
Dried or liquid, low diastatic		Fed N-M-96		
Malt Preparations				N-M-96a
Marmalade, Orange	52.1451	Fed Z-M-106		Z-M-106a
Marshmallows				
White		MIL-M-35068		
Mayonnaise		Fed EE-M-131	25.1	EE-M-131(1) EE-M-00131a (Army-QMC)
Meat Balls and Beans, in Tomato Sauce				
		MIL-M-3915		
Meat Sauce				
		MIL-M-35013		

TYPE	USDA	DOD	FDA	GSA
Meringue Powder				
		MIL-M-748		
Molasses [Sugarcane]				
	52.3651	Fed JJJ-M-576		JJJ-M-576d
Monosodium Glutamate				
				EE-M-591(1)
				EE-M-00591a
				(Army-QMC)
Mustard				
Ground		Fed EE-S-631		
Prepared, light		Fed EE-M-821		EE-M-821b(2)
				EE-M-00821c
				(Army-QMC)
Noodles				
Chow Mein		QM Pur. Des. 256		
Egg, fine to medium, ribbon-shaped		Fed N-N-591		N-N-591c
Noodle Products			16.6	
enriched			16.10	
vegetable noodle products			16.8	
Wheat and soy noodle products			16.7	
Oats				
	26.251			
Rolled				N-0-41b
Oil				
				C-0-376a
Peanut				Z-0-358
Olives				
Canned Ripe	52.3751	Fed Y-0-451		Y-0-451a(1)
				Y-0-00451c
Green	52.5447	Fed Y-0-451		Y-0-451a(1)
				Y-0-00451c
Olive Oil				
	52.1531			Z-0-351a

TYPE	USDA	DOD	FDA	GSA
Orange Marmalade				
	52.1451	Fed Z-M-106		Z-M-106a(1)
Orange Nut Roll				
Canned		MIL-0-35059		
Pancake Mix				
		Fed N-D-591		N-D-591a
Peanut Butter				
	52.3061	Fed Z-P-196		Z-P-196a
				Z-P-00196b
Pecan Cake Roll				
Canned		MIL-P-35000		
Peonies				
In the bud	51.4475			
Pie				
Fruit, fresh		Ind # 7250		
Pie Crust Mix				
		Fed N-P-361		
Pickles				
	52.1681	Fed JJJ-P-391		JJJ-P-391b
Pie Dough Mixes				
Prepared				N-P-361
				N-P-00361a
				(Army-QMC)
Pie Filling				
Prepared, fruit— apple, cherry, peach		MIL-P-35029		
Popcorn				
Unpopped, white or yellow		Ind # 11300		
Potato Chips				
		QM Pur. Des. 254		
Potato Sticks				
		MIL-P-35020		
Poundcake				
Canned		MIL-P-3234		
Pudding				
Canned—date and fig		MIL-P-1499		

TYPE	USDA	DOD	FDA	GSA
Raisin Cake				
Canned, baked and steamed		QM Lim. Prod. Pur. Des. C-148-61		
Raisin Nut Cake				
Canned, baked or steamed		QM Lim. Prod. Pur. Des. C-148-61		
Raisins				
Processed	52.1841	Fed Z-R-71		Z-R-71d(2)
Relish [Pickle]				
Sweet		Fed JJJ-P-391		
Rice				
Brown				N-R-346a
for processing	68.251			
Milled or par-boiled	68.301	Fed N-R-351	15.525	N-R-351c
Rough	68.201			
Rolls				
Brown-and-serve white or white enriched, pan-baked, Parker-house		Ind # 7390		EE-B-671c
Brown-and-serve white or white enriched, pan-baked, sandwich		Ind # 7400		EE-B-671c
Fresh, French, hearth-baked, hard		Fed EE-B-00671 QM Int. Pur. Des. S-39-7		EE-B-671c
Fresh, milk			17.3	EE-B-671c
Fresh, raisin			17.4	EE-B-671c
Fresh, sweet pan-baked		Ind # 7430		EE-B-671c
Fresh, white en-riched, pan-baked, finger (hot dog)		Fed EE-B-00671 QM Int. Pur. Des. S-39-7	17.1—white 17.2—enrich-ed	EE-B-671c
Fresh, white en-riched, pan-baked, Parker-house		Fed EE-B-00671 QM Int. Pur. Des. S-39-7	17.1Z—white 17.2Z—enrich-ed	EE-B-671c

TYPE	USDA	DOD	FDA	GSA
Fresh, white en-riched, pan-baked, sand-wich (hambur-ger)		Fed EE-B-00671 QM Int. Pur. Des. S-39-7	17.1—white 17.2—enrich-ed	EE-B-671c
Rye	26.401			
Salad Oil		Fed JJJ-S-30		
Vegetable				JJJ-S-30
Salt, Table				
Iodized		Fed SS-S-31		
Shortening Compound		Fed EE-S-321		EE-S-00321a (QMC) EE-S-321
Syrup				
All kinds		Fed JJJ-S-351		JJJ-S-351b JJJ-S-00351 (Army-QMC)
Maple	52.5961			
For reprocessing	52.5921			
Refiners	52.6041			
Sugarcane	52.3101			
Sorghum	26.551			
Soup and Gravy Base				
Dehydrated beef-flavored		MIL-S-3271		
chicken-flavored		MIL-S-35022		
Soup				
Condensed		Fed JJJ-S-581		JJJ-S-581a
Dehydrated chicken and chicken noodle		MIL-S-1049		
Green pea and pea		MIL-S-3059		
Onion		MIL-S-35046		
Tomato-vegetable w/noodles		MIL-S-35051		

TYPE	USDA	DOD	FDA	GSA
Instant				
cream of onion		MIL-S-35056		
and cream of po-				
tato, vitamin				
fortified				
green pea		MIL-S-3686		
Ready-to-serve		Fed JJJ-S-581		JJJ-S-581a
Soybeans				
	26.601			
Soy Sauce				
		Fed EE-S-610		EE-S-610
Spaghetti				
Solid		Fed N-M-51		N-M-51b
				N-M-0051c
				(AGR-AMS)
Spaghetti with Ground Meat				
Canned		MIL-M-1078		
Spaghetti with Meatballs				
Canned		MIL-S-682		
Stew Beef				
Canned		MIL-B-3045		
Sugar				
		Fed JJJ-S-791		JJJ-S-791d
Sweet Dough Mix				
		MIL-B-3071		
Tapioca				
Granulated		Fed N-T-101		N-T-101a
Tobacco, Naval Stores				
Burley	29.3001			
Connecticut Valley				
Cigar-Binder	29.5501			
Connecticut Valley				
Shade-green	29.6251			
Dark Air-Cured	29.3501			
Fire-Cured				
Type 21	29.2251			
Types 22 and 23	29.2501			
Flue-Cured	29.1001			
Georgia and Florida				
Shade-Grown	29.6501			
Maryland	29.3251			
Ohio Cigar-Leaf	29.4501			
Pennsylvania Seed				
Leaf	29.4251			
Puerto Rican Cigar-				
Filler	29.5251			
Wisconsin Cigar-				
Binder	29.6001			
Tomato Paste				
Canned	52.5041	Fed JJJ-T-579	53.30	JJJ-T-579c
				JJJ-T-00579b
				(AGR-AMS)
Tomato Puree [Pulp]				
Canned	52.5081	Fed JJJ-T-851	53.20	JJJ-T-581d
				JJJ-T-00581c
				(AGR-AMS)
Tomato Sauce				
Canned	52.2371			
Topping				
Dessert and bakery		MIL-T-35024		
products, frozen,				
w/nonfat milk				
solids				
Tuna and Noodles				
Canned		MIL-T-3906		
Vermicelli				
Solid		Fed N-M-51		M-N-51b
				N-M-0051c
				(AGR-AMS)
Vinegar				
Cider		Fed Z-V-401		Z-V-00401c
				(Army-QMC)
				Z-V-401b
Wine		Fed Z-V-401		Z-V-401b
Dry, synthetic,				Z-V-00401c
vinegar flavors				(Army-QMC)
Waffle Mix				
				N-D-591a
Water Ices				
			20.5	

TYPE	USDA	DOD	FDA	GSA
Wheat	26.301			
Wheat Base		MIL-W-3705		
Worcestershire Sauce		Fed EE-W-600		EE-W-600
Yeast, Baker's				
Active, dry, granular form and compressed, cake form		Fed EE-Y-131		EE-Y-131a EE-Y-00131b
Yeast Food				
Consisting of ammonium chloride, calcium sulfate, potassium bromate, sodium chloride, and wheat flour or cornstarch		MIL-M-3388		
Almonds				
In the shell	51.2075			
Shelled, roasted, salted	51.2105	MIL-N-10778		
Brazil Nuts				
In the shell	51.3500			
Cashew Nuts				
Shelled, roasted, salted, whole		MIL-N-10778		
Filberts				
In the shell	51.1995			
Nuts				
Assorted, unshelled		MIL-N-10778		Y-N-711c
Mixed, shelled, roasted, salted				Y-N-00725 (Army-QMC)
Mixed, unshelled	51.3520	Fed Y-N-711		Y-N-711c
Peanuts				
Shelled, blanched, roasted, salted		MIL-P-831		
Cleaned Virginia type in the shell	51.1235			

TYPE	USDA	DOD	FDA	GSA
Shelled				
Runner type	51.2710			
Spanish type	51.2730			
Virginia type	51.2750			
Pecans				
In the shell	51.1400			
Shelled, unsalted	51.1430	Fed Y-P-190		Y-P-190a
Walnuts				
In the shell	51.2945			
English, shelled		Fed Y-W-50		Y-W-50a
Shelled	51.2275			
Allspice				
Ground		Fed EE-S-631		EE-S-631d(1) EE-S-00631c (QMC)
Anise				
Sweet	51.2900			
Bay Leaves				
Whole		Fed EE-S-631		EE-S-631d EE-S-00631c (QMC)
Caraway Seed				
Whole		Fed EE-S-631		EE-S-631d EE-S-00631c (QMC)
Celery				
Salt		MIL-C-10023		
Seed, whole		Fed EE-S-631		EE-S-631d EE-S-00631c (QMC)
Chili Powder		MIL-C-3394		
Cinnamon				
Ground		Fed EE-S-631		EE-S-631d EE-S-00631c (QMC)

TYPE	USDA	DOD	FDA	GSA
Cloves				
Ground		Fed EE-S-631		EE-S-631d EE-S-00631c (QMC)
Whole		Fed EE-S-631		EE-S-631d EE-S-00631c (QMC)
Curry Powder		MIL-C-35042		
Garlic				
Dehydrated		MIL-G-35008		
Dry, white or red skinned		AG US Stds. for garlic		
Fresh	51.3880			
Salt		MIL-G-10024		
Ginger				
Ground		Fed EE-S-631		EE-S-631d EE-S-00631c (QMC)
Horseradish				
Dehydrated		QM Pur. Des. 155		
Roots	51.3900			
Mace				
Ground		Fed EE-S-631		EE-S-631d EE-S-00631c (QMC)
Marjoram				
Whole		Fed EE-S-631		EE-S-631d EE-S-00631c (QMC)
Mustard				
Ground		Fed EE-S-631		EE-S-631d EE-S-00631c (QMC)
Nutmeg				
Ground		Fed EE-S-631		EE-S-631d EE-S-00631c (QMC)
Onion Salt		MIL-0-35035		

TYPE	USDA	DOD	FDA	GSA
Oregano				
Ground		Fed EE-S-631		EE-S-631d EE-S-00631c (QMC)
Whole		Ind # 12540		EE-S-631d EE-S-00631c (QMC)
Paprika				
Ground		Fed EE-S-631		EE-S-631d EE-S0
Pepper				
Ground—black and cayenne		Fed EE-S-631		EE-S-631d EE-S-00631c (QMC)
Poppy Seed				
Whole		Fed EE-S-631		EE-S-631d EE-S-00631c (QMC)
Poultry Seasoning				
Ground		Fed EE-P-600		EE-P-600
Sage				
Ground		Fed EE-S-631		EE-S-631d EE-S-00631c (QMC)
Sesame Seed				
Whole		Fed EE-S-631		EE-S-631d EE-S-00631c (QMC)
Thyme				
Ground		Fed EE-S-631		EE-S-631d(1) EE-S-00631c (QMC)

COMPOSITE FOOD PACKAGES

TYPE	USDA	DOD	FDA	GSA
Cases, Watertight				
For Food Packet Carton		BUSHIPS Dwg S3402-1382602		
Food Packet				
Abandon aircraft, individual		MIL-F-35055		
Abandon ship, individual		MIL-F-16895		
In-flight, individual		QM Int. Pur. Des. CS1-1		

TYPE	USDA	DOD	FDA	GSA
Life raft, aircraft, individual		MIL-F-15381		
Survival, arctic, individual		MIL-F-2413		
Survival, tropic, individual		MIL-F-2409		
Meal, Combat				
Individual		MIL-M-35048		
Meal, Precooked				
Frozen, individual— Roast turkey dinner, Swiss steak dinner, Chopped beef dinner, Chicken dinner, Beef pot roast dinner, Tenderloin steak dinner, Waffles breakfast, Breakfast steak		MIL-M-13966		
Ration				
Combat, individual		MIL-R-1504		
Small detachment, 5 persons, menus 1 to 5, respectively		MIL-R-10754		
Ration Supplement				
Aid station		MIL-R-1041		
Sundries pack		MIL-R-3465		
Ration Food Packet				
Component unit		MIL-M-35048		
Component unit		MIL-R-10754		

TYPE	USDA	DOD	FDA	GSA
Component unit		MIL-R-35005		
Component unit		MIL-R-1504 Ind # 14310		
Ration—Food Packet Component Unit				
Dry-pack box, moisture-proof packet, or water-proof packet		MIL-R-10754 (QMC)		
Subassembly		QM Int. Pur. Des. CS 1-1 Ind # 14360		
Subassembly		MIL-R-1504 Ind # 14370		
Subassembly		MIL-R-35005 Ind # 14380		
Subassembly		MIL-M-35048 Ind # 24390		
Subassembly		MIL-R-1504 Ind # 14400		
Subassembly		MIL-M-35048 Ind # 14410		
Subassembly		MIL-M-35048 Ind # 14420		
Subassembly		MIL-R-1504 Ind # 14430		
Subassembly		MIL-M-35048 Ind # 14440		
Subassembly		MIL-R-1504 Ind # 14450		
Subassembly		QM Int. Pur. Des. CS 1-1 Ind # 14460		

12

STORAGE AND HANDLING

THE FLOW OF materials through a foodservice operation begins in the receiving and storage areas. Careful consideration should be given to receiving and storage procedures as well as to the construction and physical needs of both areas. In planning, there should be a straight line from receiving dock to the storeroom and/or refrigerators and preferably on the same level as the kitchen. A short distance between receiving and storage will reduce handling labor, lessen pilferage hazards, and cause the least amount of deterioration in food products. For these reasons, it is advisable from a cost standpoint.

This chapter is concerned with the following topics:

Quality Loss and Spoilage
Receiving Control
Storage Control—Dry and Frozen Items
Dry Storage
Frozen Food Storage
Refrigeration Storage

Quality Loss and Spoilage

Satisfactory methods of handling foods are designed to overcome the two major causes of food deterioration: (1) chemical changes within the food that result in loss of quality and reduction in nutrient value, and (2) spoilage organisms (mold, yeast, bacteria) that get into the food and produce undesirable or even dangerous effects. Changes in the surface of foods, such as softening, darkening, or discoloration, or losses of flavor and vitamins, are caused by chemical changes. As food travels from producer to consumer, deterioration begins. Chemical changes do not, however, affect the quality of the food to the point where it must be discarded, nor do they cause illness when the food is consumed. Chemical changes result primarily in a loss in vitamins and bring about obvious signs of quality loss such as the wilting of lettuce or the graying of meat.

True spoilage begins when food which is held to a certain holding point begins to develop off-odors, a condition that leads to food unfit for human consumption. This spoilage is caused by molds, yeasts and bacteria, all organisms which have a definite role in nature—that of decomposing plants and animals to the basic elements of the soil. These micro-organisms not only result in waste of food but can also cause illness. It is impossible to be completely protected from them as they are everywhere and are not visible to the naked eye. It is when they develop in large numbers that signs of their presence become apparent.

MOLDS

Molds require air and thus appear only on the surface of tart and bland foods. When massed, they grow in the form of odd colored patches—white, yellow, green, or black—and they also develop a "whiskery" appearance when allowed to grow. They are usually undesirable because of a characteristic musty odor and flavor except in foods such as Roquefort cheese where the flavor and odor are enhanced by this particular mold.

YEASTS

Yeasts grow best in tart foods which are liquid or semi-solid in consistency. Within this medium, yeasts form carbon dioxide gas which appears on the surface and throughout the food material. "Bulged" cans are examples of improper canning techniques in which yeasts have not been killed. Yeasts give off a typical odor and also change sugars to alcohol which adds a "fermented" flavor to the food. Although the fermentation process is useful in the making of wines, it is undesirable in most foods.

BACTERIA

Bacteria can grow and develop in all foods that are low-acid or bland, such as vegetables, meats, poultry, and dairy products, but not in tart foods, such as fruits, pickled products, etc. Unlike molds and yeasts, bacteria can cause varying degrees of illness. Since some bacteria are not harmful, it is difficult to distinguish between them, particularly since they grow in the same conditions. Bacteria are most obvious when massed on the surface of a food, as a glossy sheen is evident. The food may also have a "sulphury" odor, especially in meat or poultry. Low-acid canned foods may also be "bulged," thereby indicating bacteria spoilage. As bacteria grow, various acids are formed which cause an abnormally sour taste in usually bland food. This taste is a caution signal. The operator should be aware of changes caused by both chemical and micro-organism activity. Some signs which indicate quality loss but are not necessarily harmful include:

1. Changes in texture such as softening or shriveling
2. Discoloration
3. Loss of flavor
4. Yeast odor or flavor
5. Moldy odor or flavor
6. Mold formation

Those signs which indicate spoilage and may cause varying degrees of illness include:

1. Putrid, sulphury, or tainted color
2. Unnatural sourness
3. Gas bubbles
4. Bulged can or loose cover

Whether the food is merely unappealing because of deterioration or whether it is actually unsafe for human consumption, the operator must exercise caution in order to protect all consumers from hazardous foods.

Receiving Control

In both small and large foodservice operations, it is vitally important that meats, vegetables, and all other foods be carefully checked, weighed, and compared to the invoice accompanying the merchandise. Receiving personnel should be trained to weigh meats, fresh produce, eggs, etc., to verify quantity as well as quality. Scales capable of weighing large meat items should be available to assure the operator that he is paying only for the merchandise he has received.

Products which are spoiled or damaged should be reported to the operator so that the defective merchandise may be returned, and credit may be received from the vendor. When vendors are aware that all merchandise is being carefully inspected, there will be less chance of receiving inferior products. The operator should send a printed copy of quality specifications used in his operation to his vendors in order to inform them of his operation's quality standards.

If a receiving sheet is kept, the receiving clerk should also make certain that the unit price listed on the receiving sheet is the same as that on the invoice. Occasionally vendors will quote one price and charge another, a discrepancy which can easily be overlooked within the foodservice operation.

Dry Storage Control

Food is normally stored in dry or refrigerated areas. Both need to be carefully planned so that buying can be controlled and food can be stored efficiently which ultimately will save the operation many dollars. The storeroom should be well ventilated in order to remove odors; it should also be well lighted, dry, and clean.

Good lighting is achieved by the use of 2 or 3 watts for each sq. ft. of floor area. Control of temperature in storage areas is vitally important when planning storage spaces. Too often, dry storage space is given little attention, and whatever space remains after all other functions have been assigned is given over to it; frequently the dry storage space is fitted with water heaters, hot water pipes, and other heat-producing devices. Ideally, no equipment requiring on-going maintenance should be located in the dry storage area. Temperatures should be controlled in a range of 40°F. to 70°F. In no case should they exceed 80°F. as this may damage food products and later cause spoilage.

The floors of the storeroom should be of heavy concrete. Walls should be constructed of a material which may be easily washed. The room should be secured with a lock and opened only when receiving and storing or issuing items for use.

The storeroom should be kept neat and orderly at all times to ensure that items are not "lost," and that control is maintained. The area should look very much like a small supermarket. Stored items represent an investment and, in addition to the initial outlay of cash for these products, there are other cost factors which add to the original cost. These include: interest on the money invested; insurance; color; cost of storage; and possible losses due to shrinkage and deterioration. These factors influence the purchase quantities.

Some operators purchase according to a "par" stock level whereby each item in the storeroom has a set minimum and maximum level based on the usage of that item. As the quantity of an item reaches its minimum level, it is reordered up to its maximum level. In this way the operator seldom runs out of necessary items. This system of purchasing to par stock on every item used may, however, have its limitations by resulting in excessive inventories and overbuying. Some operators employ a combination of two methods of purchasing: (1) acquiring "par" stock levels for those items used daily which are not greatly affected by the menu, and (2) purchasing meats, vegetables and other more expensive and perishable items on an "as needed" basis. This system tends to control inventory costs more satisfactorily while providing the security of not running out of needed items.

In determining the amount of space required for dry storage, the operator needs to give thorough consideration to his menu, the type of operation, the volume of business, the purchasing policies, and the frequency of deliveries. There are varying procedures for calculating storage space requirements. A simple and effective method is to take the total meal load for the heaviest day expected and divide this number by 2, which results in the number of sq. ft. needed for a storeroom in an average operation for a 30-day supply of dry goods and supplies. For bi-monthly deliveries of supplies, the operator divides again by 2 or for weekly deliveries, by 4.

The 3 most common materials used for storeroom shelving are wood, formed steel, and wire. Metal is the ideal material for shelving because of its strength and durability, ease of maintenance, and versatility in adjusting shelf levels. Metal shelving is available in standard, prefabricated sizes and is easily assembled. The standard size is 7 shelves high and 36 in. wide.

Another type of shelving that many operators use, although more expensive, is made of heavy chrome-plated wire. Standard units come in sections 12 in. or 18 in. wide and 36 in. or 48 in. long. Sections are bolted together to achieve desired depth. Spacing is adjustable to a 7-ft. height.

Some typical sizes listed below may help the operator plan shelving requirements and arrangements:

No. 10 cans, 4 deep, 21 in. wide shelf
2 deep, 14 in. wide shelf
Dish and glass racks, 20 by 24 in., 21 in. wide shelf
Gallon jugs, 2 deep, 14 in. wide shelf
Cafeteria pans, 18 by 26-in. size, 21 in. wide shelf
12 by 20-in. size, 21 in. wide shelf
No. 2 cans, 6 deep, 21 in. wide shelf

Storage shelves should be labeled with the name of the item routinely found there, as well as its container size. Items should be placed in the same order as they appear on the inventory form in order to facilitate the taking of inventory. Some operators choose to arrange storeroom items alphabetically, while others arrange them according to product groups, such as fruits, vegetables, fats and oils, etc. Whatever the arrangement, storage on shelving should always be neat and orderly.

Within the storeroom, items should be rotated and issued so that items received first are used before new items. Commonly referred to as "first in and first out," this procedure generally insures that products will be of highest quality when served to the consumer.

Charts of practical storage suggestions for dry goods are presented on the following pages.[1] Food technologists, food processors, and storage experts have been consulted in the preparation of the charts. An operator should consider the limits listed as outside limits. By staying well within those limits, he should be able to get the most value from his purchasing dollar. In so doing, *you* will be able to serve *your* clientele nutritious and safe food.

1. Jule Wilkinson, *The Complete Book of Cooking Equipment*, rev. ed. Boston: Cahners Book International, Inc., pp. 175-183.

* DRY STORES CHART *

Products	Cool Storeroom	Refrig.	Humidity	Signs of Deterioration	Notes
BAKING STORES					
Baking Powder	8 to 12 mo.		Max. 60%	Caking	If stored too long, will lose leavening power.
Chocolate, baking	6 to 12 mo.	2 yr.	Max. 60%	Mold, mustiness, loss of flavor	Keep away from strong odored products.
Chocolate, sweetened	2 yr. (not over 65°F.)		Max. 60% (prefer. not over 50%)	Mold; sugar bloom on surface; stale flavor; webbing	Store off floor, away from walls; refrigerate in hot weather; more expensive grades keep longer due to better quality raw materials, higher fat coatings.
Chocolate Milk	6 to 12 mo.	1 yr.	Same as above.	Same as above	
Cornstarch	2 to 3 yr.	3 to 5 yr.	Max. 60%	Caking, foreign, musty odors	Same as above. Begins losing some flavor after one month.
Tapioca	1 yr.	2 yr.	Max. 70%		
Yeast, dry	18 mo.	3 yr.			Keep away from strong odored products.
Baking Soda	8 to 12 mo.		Max. 60%	Caking	
BEVERAGES					
Cocoa	1 yr.		Max. 85%	Caking, infestation (will occur if left uncovered for long)	Keep away from strong odored products. Will become rancid in high temperature.

Products	Cool Storeroom	Refrig.	Humidity	Signs of Deterioration	Notes
Coffee, ground (vacuum packed)	7 to 12 mo.	12 to 18 mo.	Max. 60%	Loss of flavor	Store off floor and away from walls and strong odored products.
Coffee, ground (not vacuum packed)	2 wk.	1 mo.	Max. 60%	Loss of flavor, foreign odors	
Coffee, instant	8 to 12 mo.	3 yr.	Max. 85%	Caking, loss of flavor	Caking tends to occur at high temperatures as well as in dampness if container leaks. Cakes are usually reclaimable.
Tea Leaves	12 to 18 mo.	3 to 4 yr.	Between 50% and 80%; 75% optimum	Loss of sweet aroma, absorption tion of foreign odors, mold, mustiness, dried out leaves, infestation	Store off floor away from direct sunlight and strong odored products. High temperatures and less than 50% humidity both tend to dry it out.
Tea, instant	8 to 12 mo.	3 yr.	Max. 85%	Loss of flavor, caking	Avoid high temperatures and excessive dampness as either condition will cause caking, particularly if container is not completely sealed. Gradual flavor loss over course of a year at room temperature.
Carbonated Beverages	Indefinitely				

DRY STORES CHART (cont.)

Products	Cool Storeroom	Refrig.	Humidity	Signs of Deterioration	Notes
CANNED GOODS					

NOTE: Following information is based on general Tolerances.

Products	Cool Storeroom	Refrig.	Humidity	Signs of Deterioration	Notes
Fruits (in gen.)	1 yr.	4 yr.	Max. 60%	Softening, fading color, loss of flavor, can bulge, leakage, pin holing	Good idea to specify "current pack only" or "last year's pack not acceptable" when buying canned fruits and vegetables. Keep away from direct sunlight, especially in warm climates as solar radiation can easily push temperature inside cans above 100°F. and considerably shorten storage life. Use well ventilated area. (See other suggestions in text.)
Fruits, acid-types, i.e., citrus, berries, sour cherries	6 to 12 mo.	3 yr.	Max. 60%	Same as above, but particularly pin holing due to acid action	Same as above. Acid factor reduces storage life.
Fruit Juices	6 to 9 mo.	3 yr.	Max. 60%		Same as above.
Meat, Poultry Seafood (in general)	1 yr.	2 to 4 yr.	Max. 60%	Same as above. Crystals may form in canned crabmeat. They are not harmful, but annoying and thus quality is reduced	Same as above. Temperatures above 90°F. hasten deterioration appreciably for these products. Freezing affects texture, particularly of those containing tomato, or other high acid sauces have slightly reduced storage life.
Pickled Fish Fish in Brine	4 mo.	12 mo.	Max. 60%	Mold and off-odor	If mold and off-odor develop, discard product.

Products	Cool Storeroom	Refrig.	Humidity	Signs of Deterioration	Notes
Smoked Fish, light smoking sauce	This is a highly perishable product.				
Smoked Fish, heavy smoking	1 mo.	2 to 3 mo.		Mold and off-odor	If mold and off-odor develop, discard product.
Dried Fish	1 mo.	2 to 3 mo.		Same as above	Same as above.
Soups (including bouillon cubes and dehydrated soup mixes)	1 yr.	3 to 4 yr.			Avoid freezing (most canned vegetables freeze at 25°F.) and all sudden changes in temperature (to minimize condensation). Keep away from direct sunlight (explained under fruits).
Vegetables (except high acid ones)	1 yr.	4 yr.		Softening, fading color, loss of flavor, can bulge, leakage, pin holing	
Vegetables, high acid, i.e., tomatoes and sauerkraut	7 to 12 mo.	2 to 3 yr.		Same as above, but particularly pin holing due to acid action	Same as above.

CONDIMENTS FLAVORS & SEASONINGS

Products	Cool Storeroom	Refrig.	Humidity	Signs of Deterioration	Notes
Mustard, prepared	2 to 6 mo.	1 yr.		Gas bubbles, brown surface color, sulfur-like odor	Affected by direct light as well as prolonged storage at high temperatures. Continual flavor loss to some degree from time of manufacture, so should be used as soon as possible.

(Cont.)

DRY STORES CHART (cont.)

Products	Cool Storeroom	Refrig.	Humidity	Signs of Deterioration	Notes
CONDIMENTS FLAVORS & SEASONINGS (cont.)					
Flavoring Extracts	Indefinite				Never refrigerate.
Monosodium Glutamate	Indefinite				
Salt	Indefinite		Max. 60%		Caking will occur in humid conditions, but has no lasting effect on quality.
Sauces (hot pepper, soy, steak, worcestershire)	2 yr.	2 to 3 yr.		Separation of ingredients, off-odors, color change	Affected by long exposure to light (color change), and should never be frozen.
Spices, Herbs, Seeds, whole	2 yr. to indefinite			Fading color in herbs, loss of aroma	In whole form, the flavor and aroma of spices are protected by cell structure. Bay leaves and other herbs lose bright color within a year.
Spices, Herbs, Seeds, ground (exc. paprika)	1 yr.	2 yr.	Max. 60%	Loss of aroma, faded colors, caking	Keep off floor, away from outside walls. Reseal containers quickly after each use. Purchase in moderate quantities, replace frequently.
Paprika, Chili Powder, Cayenne, Red Pepper	1 yr.	1 yr.	Max. 60%	Fading color, infestation	Keep away from direct light. During summer in hot climates, may be wise to refrigerate to guard against infestation.

Products	Cool Storeroom	Refrig.	Humidity	Signs of Deterioration	Notes
Seasoning Salts	1 yr.	2 yr.	Max. 60%	Caking	Very hygroscopic and once solidly caked, they are usually unredeemable.
Vinegar	2 yr.	3 yr.		Presence of "mother" or vinegar "eel," evaporation or infestation	Both "mother" and "eel" are signs of improper manufacturing; however, "mother" may also indicate storage troubles (usually loose caps) as may evaporation and infestation (fruit flies).

DAIRY FOODS & CHEESE

Products	Cool Storeroom	Refrig.	Humidity	Signs of Deterioration	Notes
Cheese, hard types (cheddar or American), particularly natural		1 mo. (32°F.) 2 wk. (45°F.)		Drying out, "oils off," moldiness	Needs tight wrapping. Store away from strong odored products.
Cheese, soft types, (cream, cottage, limburger, etc.)		1 to 2 wk.		Drying out, "oils off," moldiness	Needs tight wrapping. Store away from strong odored products. Soft cheeses tend to change body characteristics undesirably when stored at freezing temperatures. Storage life under refrigeration is shorter than for hard cheeses because texture allows spoilage agents to enter easily. Mild types in particular are potential sources of food poisoning if storage is prolonged or improperly handled.

(Cont.)

DRY STORES CHART (cont.)

Products	Cool Storeroom	Refrig.	Humidity	Signs of Deterioration	Notes
DAIRY FOODS & CHEESE (cont.) Cheese Spreads	1 yr.			Surface darkening, off-flavor, odor, mold	Those with wine have slightly longer storage life. All spreads become perishable once opened.
Cream, powdered	4 mo.	6 mo.		Stale or tallowy odor, separating of butterfat	Best refrigerated.
Milk, condensed	1 yr. (if av. temp. not more than 60°F. 2 mo. at 70°F.)	1 yr.	Max. 60%	Darkening, thickening, change in flavor, "sandiness," swelled cans (from fermentation)	Swelled cans should be discarded.
Milk, dry, nonfat (regular & instant)	1 yr.	2 yr.	Max. 35% containers not hermetically sealed	Flavor changes, lumping and darkening	Extra grade (moisture 4% in regular, 5% in instant) in hermetically sealed tins or glass keeps longer, but foil laminated or polyethylene bags are also good.
Milk, dry, whole	10 to 12 mo.	2 yr.		Darkening, stale flavor, rancidity	
Milk, evaporated	1 yr. (if aver. temp. not more than 60°F. 2 mo. at 70°F.)	1 yr.	Max. 60%	Darkening, separation of cream layer, gelling (due to changes in the protein)	Milk which has gelled should not be used because it could be due to a defective can as well as to protein changes.

Products	Cool Storeroom	Refrig.	Humidity	Signs of Deterioration	Notes
FATS & OILS					
Butter		1 mo. (35° to 45°F.) 6 to 9 mo. (0°F.)	Max. 55%	Absorption of foreign odors, rancidity	The sweeter the cream used in making the butter, the longer the product will keep. Use double the normal wrapping (or airtight moisture-proof containers) for freezer storage.
Margarine		1 mo. (35° to 45°F.) 3 mo. (0°F.)	Max. 55%	Stale flavors, rancidity, surface darkening, mold, foreign odors, oil separation	Keep away from strong odored products. Aluminum wrapping offers additional storage protection. Higher quality products keep longer.
Salad Dressings (inc. mayonnaise)	2 mo. (max. at 60°F.; opt. is 50°F.)	2 mo.	Not a factor	Rancidity, off-color, separation of oil from water	Avoid direct light or sunlight and sudden temperature changes.
Salad Oil	6 to 9 mo.		Not a factor	Rancidity (odor similar to old lard or grease	A light high grade oil will keep better.
Shortenings, vegetable	2 to 4 mo.	1 yr.	Not a factor	Rancidity, absorption of foreign odors	
Shortenings, animal fat (lard, etc.)		2 mo.	Not a factor	Rancidity, absorption of foreign odors	Should be refrigerated because they become very perishable at room temperature. More perishable than vegetable shortenings at room temperature because they are softer (harder the fat, the longer the storage life).

(Cont.)

DRY STORES CHART (cont.)

Products	Cool Storeroom	Refrig.	Humidity	Signs of Deterioration	Notes
GRAINS & GRAIN PRODUCTS					
Cereal Grains (for cooked cereal—any type)	8 mo.		Below 40%	Mold, webbing, infestation, musty stale or free fat odor	Store off floor away from walls. Be especially careful to keep them away from all strong odored products as they act like a sponge for odors around them; the same is true of dampness. As one expert put it, "Cereals are best when first made and thereafter deteriorate a little bit each day." In excessive heat or humidity they may last not more than a month.
Cereals (ready-to-eat)	6 mo.		Max. 60%	Loss of crispness and development of a toughness; mold; webbing, infestation, rancidity	Essentially the same as for cereal grains, above.
Cornmeal	8 to 12 mo.		Max. 60%	Rancidity, mold, infestation, caking	Essentially same as above.
Flour, bleached	9 to 12 mo.	2 yr.	Max. 60%	Infestation, caking, mustiness	Essentially same as above. Low temps. (32° to 43°F.) best protection against infestation. Refrigerating may be necessary in very hot climates.

Products	Cool Storeroom	Refrig.	Humidity	Signs of Deterioration	Notes
Flour, whole grain	2 to 4 mo.	4 to 6 mo.	Max. 60%	Rancidity, infestation, caking, mustiness	Essentially same as above. Since whole grain flours retain the oil bearing wheat "germ," they are more susceptible to rancidity than bleached flour.
Macaroni, Spaghetti, and all Pastas	3 mo.		Max. 60%	Mold, infestation, checking, mustiness	Essentially the same precautions as for other cereal grains, above. If pastas are subjected to sudden changes in temperature, they may check, that is, develop fine cracks that will cause disintegration in cooking.
Prepared Mixes	6 mo.	12 mo.	Max. 50%	Infestation, stale odor, discoloration, loss of baking performance	Temperature particularly important; level above 70°F. may reduce life to 2 to 3 mo.
Rice, parboiled	9 to 12 mo.			Infestation, color change (to yellowish), rancid odor	Same general precautions as for other grains.
Rice, brown or wild		6 to 9 mo.	Max. 50%	Rancid odor, infestation	Refrigeration is required because these products still have the dark outer covering which is more prone to rancidity and absorption of foreign odors than the rest of the kernel.

SWEETENERS

Products	Cool Storeroom	Refrig.	Humidity	Signs of Deterioration	Notes
Sugar, granulated	Indefinite		Max. 60%		Caking will occur in humid conditions, but has no lasting effect on quality.

(Cont.)

DRY STORES CHART (cont.)

Products	Cool Storeroom	Refrig.	Humidity	Signs of Deterioration	Notes
SWEETENERS (cont.)					
Sugar, confectioners'	Indefinite		Max. 60%		Same as above, but slightly less tendency to cake.
Sugar, brown		1 yr.	Max. 70% Min. 60%		Brown sugar should be refrigerated to give it the ratio of humidity it needs to keep soft.
Syrups, corn, honey, molasses, sugar	1 yr.			Mold	Susceptible to mold after container is opened. Refrigerate opened containers.
MISCELLANEOUS					
Beans, dried (also all lentils)	1 to 2 yr.	2 to 3 yr.	Max. 60% Min. 30%	Mold, musty appearance	More than 60% humidity will cause mold; less than 30% will dry out the product.
Candied Peel— Citron	18 mo.	3 yr.			
Cookies— Crackers	1 to 6 mo.	4 to 12 mo.	Max. 60%	Staling, infestation, rancidity, softening	Softening can be remedied by placing crackers in the oven to restore crispness.
Cracker Meal	1 yr.	3 yr.	Max. 60%	Same as above	Same as above.
Dried Fruits	6 to 8 mo.		About 75%	Sogginess or hardness, crystallization, infestation	Higher than 75% humidity will result in sogginess; less than that will dry the fruit out to the point of hardness.
Gelatin	2 to 3 yr.	3 to 4 yr.	Max. 70%	Caking	

Products	Cool Storeroom	Refrig.	Humidity	Signs of Deterioration	Notes
MISCELLANEOUS (cont.)					
Dried Prunes		15 mo. (see notes)	About 30%	Infestation, sweating, fermenting, molding, excessive dry out and sugaring	Best temperature is between 40° to 50°F. Store on skids away from walls and away from strong odored products.
Jams, Jellies	1 yr.	2 to 3 yr.	Max. 60%	Color change, crystallization, caramelization	Red colored jams and jellies lose color if stored at excessively high temperatures. All these products will caramelize at high temperatures.
Nuts	1 yr.			Mold, infestation, rancidity	If vacuum packed, they will keep better.
Pickles, Relishes	1 yr.	3 yr.	Max. 60%	Pickles soften, develop hollow centers, cloudy brine	Important to keep away from strong light, particularly dill pickles.
Potato Chips	1 mo.		Max. 50%	Staleness, rancidity	May be re-crisped by heating in oven.
Coconut, sweetened	4 to 6 mo.			Browning, mold, off-flavor, sogginess	If only soggy, may be reclaimed by heating in oven.
Dates, pasteurized	8 to 12 mo.	8 to 12 mo.	Max. 65%		
Dates, raw	1 to 2 mo.	8 to 12 mo.	Max. 65%		

(Cont.)

DRY STORES CHART (cont.)

Products	Cool Storeroom	Refrig.	Humidity	Signs of Deterioration	Notes
MISCELLANEOUS, (cont.)					
Dehydrated Vegetables	7 to 12 mo.	4 yr.	Max. 60%		
Eggs, powdered	4 mo.	1 yr		Caking, off-odors, mold	If moldy, discard.

Frozen Food Storage Control

The use of frozen foods within a foodservice operation has increased steadily in recent years. Frozen foods offer definite advantages to the operator:

1. Limited waste
2. Year around availability
3. Less preparation time
4. Long storage life
5. Many sources of supply
6. More menu variety

This increasing use of frozen foods requires the operator to have additional storage space. Frozen food storage requires lower temperature conditions than do other types of storage. Freezers provide storage space at 0°F. or lower at all times. Freezers should also be capable of freezing foods quickly, since the faster the process, the smaller the ice crystals that form within the food, thereby maintaining it at a higher quality. Food should be frozen in a 3-step process:

1. Refrigeration to cool
2. Sharp freezing
3. Holding at low temperature

Frozen foods are highly perishable and deteriorate quickly if not handled correctly. For this reason, the operator should check frozen items as they are received and store them as quickly as possible in a 0°F. freezer. Frozen foods never return to original quality once they begin to break down. Quality in frozen foods is judged by color, flavor, texture, appearance, and nutritive value of the product. Quantities ordered also affect the quality of the product as smaller inventories with more turnover generally result in higher quality products as compared with large inventories maintained over a long period of time.

It is advisable to store food items in the original shipping cartons. Foods should be packed in vapor-proof containers to prevent dehydration, oxidation, discoloration, odor absorption, and loss of volatile flavors. Operators should check the condition of the containers to verify that there are no breaks which will cause freezer burn on food items.

The following points should help the operator to improve the overall efficiency in the use of freezers:

1. When unloading food items in the freezer, move loaded cart directly into the freezer, if possible. If the cart is too large for the freezer, move it as close to the freezer as possible. This will reduce handling time and protect the frozen food against exposure to temperatures above 0°F.
2. Rotate stock by marking new frozen foods to show the date received so that the oldest dated food will be used first.
3. Arrange frozen foods in the freezer by product groups. Labels should be available so that foods can easily be identified. This reduces handling time and helps to keep the freezer arranged in an orderly manner.
4. Maintain optimum air circulation in the walk-in type freezer by keeping foods off the floors, away from ceilings and walls. To ensure proper air circulation, platform racks are often used for stacking boxes on floors.

5. Train employees to open freezers only when necessary. Remove as many items at one time as possible, in order to minimize door opening.

6. Install a thermometer to measure the average temperature of the freezer so that it will not be affected by the opening of the door, by the cooling coils, or by direct air from the cooling unit. The thermometer should be placed where it is easy to see. In walk-in freezers, the thermometer should be attached to the outside. An alarm system should also be installed to indicate mechanical failure. Occasionally, the temperature of the products should be checked with a calibrated, dial-type, hand thermometer.

7. Defrost freezers regularly to prevent excessive formation of ice. This will increase efficiency and also reduce operating costs, labor, and damage to the product.

8. Maintain a clean, orderly, and well-organized freezer. This requires daily clean-up but is well worth the time and effort since it will result in better utilization of products and reduction in damage to frozen foods.

9. Establish a regular service schedule to be followed regardless of the type of freezer being used.

The following tables indicate the length of time that frozen foods may be stored at 0°F. without noticeable loss of quality. If stored at 10°F., the foods have approximately 1/4 to 1/2 of the storage life listed. Those stored at -10°F. will retain their quality for periods longer than those shown in the tables. The times listed in these tables assume the food products are of high quality when placed into storage.

APPROXIMATE STORAGE LIFE OF VARIOUS FOODS AT ZERO DEGREES FAHRENHEIT (0°F.)[1]

Fruit	No. of Months at 0°F.
Apricots	12
Peaches	12
Raspberries	12
Strawberries	12

Vegetable	No. of Months at 0°F.
Asparagus	8 to 12
Beans, Snap	8 to 12
Beans, Lima	12
Broccoli	12
Brussels Sprouts	8 to 12
Cauliflower	12
Corn, on the cob	8 to 12
Corn, cut	12
Carrots	12
Mushrooms	8 to 12
Peas	12
Spinach	12
Squash	12

Meat	No. of Months at 0°F.
BEEF	
Roasts, Steaks	12
Ground	8
Cubed Pieces	10 to 12
VEAL	
Roasts, Chops	10 to 12
Cutlets, Cubes	8 to 10
LAMB	
Roasts, Chops	12
PORK	
Roasts, Chops	6 to 8
Ground, Sausage	4
Pork or Ham, Smoked	5 to 7
Bacon	3
Variety Meats	up to 4
Poultry	6 to 12

(Cont.)

1. Charles E. Eshbach, *Foodservice Management* (Boston: Cahners Books International, Inc., 1976), pp. 97-99.

APPROXIMATE STORAGE LIFE OF VARIOUS FOODS
AT ZERO DEGREES FAHRENHEIT (0°F.)　[Cont.]

Fish	No. of Months at 0°F.
Fatty Fish (Mackerel, Salmon, Swordfish, etc.)	3
Lean Fish (Haddock, Cod, Ocean Perch, etc.)	6

Shellfish	No. of Months at 0°F.
SHELLFISH	
Lobsters and Crabs	2
Shrimp	6
Oysters	3 to 4
Scallops	3 to 4
Clams	3 to 4

PRECOOKED FOODS

Item	No. of Months at 0°F.
BREAD	
Quick	2 to 4
Yeast	6 to 12
ROLLS	2 to 4
CAKE	
Angel	4 to 6
Gingerbread	4 to 6
Sponge	4 to 6
Chiffon	4 to 6
Cheese	4 to 6
Fruit	12
COOKIES	4 to 6
COMBINATION	4 to 8
PIES	
Fruit	12
Mince	4 to 8
Chiffon	1
Pumpkin	1
POTATOES	
French Fries	4 to 8
Scalloped	1
SOUPS	4 to 6
SANDWICHES	2

EQUIPMENT

There is a great deal the operator should know when planning the freezer equipment needed for his operation. First, the operator should be familiar with the correct terminology used when referring to various pieces of equipment.

Frozen Food Storage, also called "low temperature reach-in" or "walk-in space," is equipment designed to store frozen food usually at 10°F. to -10°F.

Processing freezer, the equipment designed to actually freeze food. It operates at -20°F. and is sometimes referred to as a "blast freezer," "plate freezer" or "tunnel freezer." After the freezing of food is completed, the food is transferred to frozen food storage. Based on current menu needs and projections of future changes, operators can determine their frozen food processing and storage requirements. The following facts should, however, also be determined:

1. Quality of off-premise prepared foods or ingredients specified during peak periods
2. Frequency of frozen food deliveries
3. Possibility of buying larger frozen quantities to reduce per pound or per serving costs
4. Maximum length of time on-premise that prepared frozen items are held.
5. Amount of on-premise frozen foods to be stored
6. Unusual consumption peaks
7. Short-term space needed for pre-dished foods
8. Anticipated use of government commodities
9. Time and equipment factors, if any, involved in proper defrosting

The 2 major types of storage facilities for frozen foods are reach-in and walk-in freezers. Reach-in units usually have less storage space. They may use either forced air or freezer plates to maintain temperatures. Those with plates cannot be defrosted automatically. Consider the following check points when purchasing reach-in equipment:

Construction—properly sealed, easily cleaned

Exterior—rust resistant; in keeping with decor if location makes this important

Adequate insulation

Doors—well constructed, easily opened, hinges easy to operate

Lights—adequate; consider automatic light switch on door

Shelves—easy to clean and adjust; maximum load provisions

Condensing Unit—sufficient horsepower; type; location; necessary ventilation

Temperature control—visible thermometer or temperature record; automatic alarm system

Defrosting system

Amount of floor space required

Reach-ins can be adapted to a wide variety of institutional requirements because of the optional accessories available, including tray and pan slides, roll-out shelves and drawers. One disadvantage of this type of storage is that it is more difficult to control the merchandise within the reach-in unit.

Walk-in freezer units provide more efficient use of storage space and make handling easier. Unlike reach-in units, walk-ins can function either as holding units or as processing units. They come in a wide range of standard ready-to-install models. Some of the popular walk-in models provide the following cubic content: 4- by 6-ft.—117 cu. ft.; 6- by 8-ft.—184 cu. ft.; 8- by 10-ft.—435 cu. ft.; 10- by 18-ft.—1022 cu. ft. Walk-ins provide a bulk storage capacity that enables operators to buy ahead. In many operations, frozen food walk-ins are located inside refrigeration walk-ins. These are called dual temperature walk-ins (part cooler, +35°F., and part freezer, 0°F. to -10°F.) As operators continue to use more frozen food products, pre-fabricated walk-ins are expected to best serve their space needs, as they may be added either inside or outside the building.

Insulation is important in food holding and processing equipment. The thickness of the insulation varies with different manufacturers. One manufacturer specifies 6 in. of insulation for -5°F. temperatures and 8 in. insulation for -20°F. A more recent development by manufacturers is 4 in. of polyurethane for either cooler (+35°F.) or freezer (0° to -20°F.) units. This material can be used for temperatures between -20°F. and 40°F. and gives the operator the flexibility of easily converting coolers to freezers by merely changing the refrigeration system.

Consider the following factors when planning walk-in space:

Exterior—material offering long life, easy cleaning

Interior—tight, easily maintained

Insulation—adequate for temperatures required

Assembly—easy, tight, minimum cost

Refrigeration system—sufficient capacity to maintain required temperature; conditions surrounding location where it is to be installed

Amount of cubic space needed for storage

Defrost System—how is it controlled, automatic

Door Construction

Floor Level—should provide easy movement of food

Transportation Cost

Alarm System

Accessories—shelving, racks, display doors, etc.

The importance of the above factors cannot be over-emphasized nor can the choice of the manufacturer from whom you purchase the equipment. In the long run, it will pay the operator to purchase from a reputable manufacturer.

When installing reach-in or walk-in frozen holding or processing equipment, locate the cabinets away from any heat-producing equipment. If the unit is self-contained, there should be necessary circulation of air around the equipment. Careful attention should be given to the amperage and voltage supply at the compressor locations to ensure proper electrical service. Floors should be checked for stability to ensure that they will be able to support the weight of freezers and their contents. Furthermore, floors should also be level to enable the cabinets to rest evenly on all 4 corners. Before the door is installed, the operator must determine satisfactory height and width dimensions based on the institution's food handling procedures. Some questions worth pondering when planning the efficient use of a walk-in unit are whether the door should swing right or left, whether it should open and close automatically, and whether glass panels should be installed in the door in order to check contents.

Because of the increasing quest for space, many operators are solving their frozen storage problem by installing a pre-fabricated walk-in unit outside. The units are designed for blast freezing or for holding frozen food, thereby permitting the purchase of larger quantities for maximum discounts while releasing expensive inside space for a more profitable use. An added advantage is that the equipment may be placed on a base, is delivered completely equipped and ready to use, and is designed to be easily expanded in size as the needs for frozen foods change.

Refrigeration Storage

In general, fresh and prepared foods are refrigerated between 30° to 45°F. to keep them safe from harmful bacteria. If separate refrigerators are used for each food, they should be kept at the following temperatures:

45° to 50°F.	Fruits
40° to 45°F.	Vegetables, Eggs, Processed Foods, Pastry
38° to 40°F.	Dairy Products
34° to 38°F.	Fresh Meats
32° to 36°F.	Fresh Poultry, Fish, and Seafood
-10° to 0°	Frozen Foods

For accurately checking these temperatures a thermometer should be located in the warmest place in each refrigerator.

The foodservice operator must carefully determine the best equipment and products to use in his establishment. In the case of refrigerated storage, the models to choose from are many:

1. Walk-in
2. Reach-in
3. Roll-in
4. Compartmentalized
5. Pass-thru
6. Counter Refrigeration
7. Display Refrigeration
8. Portable Refrigeration
9. Refrigerated Dispensers

All of the types listed above can be used to help "extend" the amount of refrigerated space in an operation. Operators are purchasing more and more foods which are partially or completely prepared and which, therefore, require immediate refrigeration. How does the operator decide which units can meet his needs most economically? Experts in this specialized area of refrigerated storage have suggested that the operator estimate what percentage of a typical meal will consist of fresh food. In addition, he should determine how many days' supply of each kind of food must be refrigerated according to delivery schedules. From these calculations, it is recommended that:

20 to 25% of the space be allocated for meat (if portion cuts are used, the space needed would be 10 to 15%)

30 to 35% for fruits and vegetables

20 to 25% for dairy products

5 to 10% for salads, sandwich material, bakery products, and leftovers.

The type of menu used and the type of establishment both influence the amount of refrigeration space required. For example, a school lunch kitchen with limited menu will require less refrigerated space than an expensive gourmet restaurant which serves many more fresh, refrigerated items.

The walk-in refrigerator is used extensively in the foodservice industry. One authority suggests that walk-ins are feasible in operations serving 300 to 400 meals per day. Some of the advantages of this type of storage include:

- The operator's ability to carry a greater variety of food to purchase in greater quantities with discount savings
- Decreases in the number of expensive deliveries
- The availability of more space for leftovers which reduces food loss

Walk-ins today usually are assembled from prefabricated sections. For this reason, they can be enlarged easily and/or relocated, if required. The metal walls are easily cleaned, protect against rodents, etc., and require little maintenance. As with frozen walk-in space discussed earlier, the operator should check the following points as summarized by Kotschevar and Terrell in *Food Service Planning*[1], in choosing a particular unit.

1. Proper insulation—at least 3 in. thick
2. Floor on level plane for walk-in
3. Vapor-proof walls, ceilings and floors
4. Sturdy, well-insulated door with heavy-duty lock
5. Opening device on the inside
6. Sturdy, durable, and adjustable shelving

1. L. Kotschevar and M. Terrell, *Food Service Planning*, New York: John Wiley and Sons, Inc., 1961

7. Outside thermometer
8. Adequate storage space—1-1/2 to 2 ft. on either side of aisle, 42-in. aisles preferrable, wide enough to accommodate whatever mobile equipment is used in the walk-in
9. Audio-visual alarm system to alert personnel when a change in holding temperature occurs

The operator has the option of leasing these prefab units from the manufacturer, thereby releasing available funds for other equipment, building projects, and related needs.

To be sure, there are many alternatives when choosing refrigerated storage. New innovations such as refrigerated drawers, refrigerated sandwich units, under-counter units, dispensers, display cases, and many more items give the operator a certain flexibility in planning. Manufacturers of modern refrigeration equipment can provide the operator with whatever units are needed to solve an organization's refrigerated storage problems.

The following guidelines, from *The Complete Book of Cooking Equipment*[1], may help the operator to attain optimum utilization, what type of refrigeration is used in an organization.

What You Do	Why You Do It
1. Pack food loosely	1. To get circulation
2. Hang van meats away from walls	2. Cold air needs to circulate to keep food from spoiling
3. Cover food (below) with wax, or other covering paper	3. Prevent dripping
4. Discard things not needed	4. To prevent crowding and increase circulation
5. Place new purchases at back	5. Use older things first
6. Wash refrigerator frequently	6. It must be kept clean
7. Defrost before 1/4 in. frost gathers	7. Frost slows cooling process
8. Open door only when necessary	8. Open door raises temperature

The following reference chart gives the operator information on how to store various foods and familiar food combinations. The all-important time limitations affecting the refrigeration of food should serve as a guide from which to start. Many factors actually affect the storage life of food; however, it is vitally important that the operator be able to distinguish between quality loss in food which would not ordinarily cause illness and danger signals in those foods which warn of potential health hazards.

STORAGE CHART

	How to Store	Approx. Time Limit for Storage		Evidence of Quality Loss
		Refrig.	Freezer	
SANDWICHES				
Meat, poultry, fish, and egg salad	Moisture-proof wrapper in refrig. or other cold place. Refrigerate 2 to 3 hr. before prolonged exposure to summer heat, e.g., if to be used for a picnic.	2 days	6 months	If merely dried out, reclaim by grilling, if practicable. Discard, if off-flavor.

(Cont.)

1. Jule Wilkinson, *The Complete Book of Cooking Equipment*, rev. ed. Boston: Cahners Books International, Inc., 1975, p. 210

STORAGE CHART [Cont.]

	How to Store	Approx. Time Limit for Storage		Evidence of Quality Loss
		Refrig.	Freezer	
SANDWICHES (Cont.)				
Other	Moisture-proof wrapper	5 to 6 days	6 months	If dried out or soggy, reclaim by grilling. If moldy, discard.
SOUPS, GRAVY, AND STUFFING				
Gravy	Allow to cool until just warm to the touch. Refrigerate in covered dish.	3 to 4 days	1 year	
Soups				
Left-over	Allow to cool until just warm to the touch. Refrigerate in original container or covered dish.	3 to 4 days	1 year	
Canned				
Unopened	Original container			
Opened	See left-over soups			
Frozen	Original container	7 days	1 year	
Stuffing	Remove from cavity. Refrigerate in covered container.	3 to 4 days	1 year	
FISH AND SHELLFISH				
Fresh	Moisture-proof wrapper or container. Refrigerate. Leave shellfish in shell. Plan to hold only briefly if to be eaten raw.	1 to 2 days	1 year	
Cooked Fish and Fish Salads	Covered container in refrigerator	3 to 4 days	1 year	
Bisques, Broths, Chowders, Stews and Soups	Original or other covered container in refrigerator	1 to 2 days	1 year	
Canned				
Unopened	Original container. Kitchen shelf			

	How to Store	Approx. Time Limit for Storage		Evidence of Quality Loss
		Refrig.	Freezer	
Opened	Original or other covered container	3 to 4 days	1 year	
Frozen	Original container. Freezer	3 days	1 year	
Smoked—Light	Orig. container. Refrigerator	1 to 2 days	1 year	If moldy and/or off-odors develop, not reclaimable. Discard.
Heavy	Original container. Cool place	2 to 3 months	1 year	Same as above
Dried	Orig. container. Cool place	2 to 3 months	1 year	Same as above
Pickled, with vinegar, wine, and/or sour cream	Orig. container. Refrigerator	2 to 3 months	1 year	Same as above

EGGS AND EGG DISHES

	How to Store	Refrig.	Freezer	Evidence of Quality Loss
Fresh				
In Shell	Clean if necessary. Covered container. Large end of egg up. Refrigerator	10 days		Slight off-odors can be masked by seasonings in cooking.
Separated Yolks	Covered container or cover with water. Refrigerator	1 to 2 days	1 year	If runny, or if shape has been lost, discard.
Separated Whites	Covered container. Refrigerator	1 to 2 days	1 year	If whites become water, discard.
Cooked				
In shell	Uncovered. Refrigerator	10 days		Useable if merely dried out, otherwise discard.
Shelled	Covered container. Refrigerator	10 days		Useable if merely dried out, otherwise discard.
Prepared Dishes, such as egg salads, stuffed, fondue, etc.	Covered dish. Refrigerator	3 to 4 days	3 to 4 months	
Frozen Yolks or Whites	Original container. Freezer	3 to 4 days	1 year	If not moldy, slight off-color can be masked by seasonings in cooking. If mold is present, discard.

(Cont.)

STORAGE CHART [Cont.]

	How to Store	Approx. Time Limit for Storage		Evidence of Quality Loss
		Refrig.	Freezer	
EGG AND EGG DISHES (Cont.)				
Pickled	Original container. Refrigerator	3 months		Useable if not moldy and if texture is acceptable. Otherwise discard.
Dried (powdered)	Original container. Kitchen shelf	1 year	1 year	If merely caked, slight off-odors and flavors can be masked by seasonings in cooking. If moldy, discard.
CHEESE AND CHEESE DISHES				
Hard Cheese, such as cheddar, swiss, grated, etc.	Original or other covered container in refrigerator	3 to 9 months	1 to 2 years	If dried, use as grated. If moldy, remove mold, and if flavor of remainder is acceptable, it is useable. Otherwise discard.
Soft Cheese, such as cream, cottage, limburger, and cheese spreads.	Original or other covered container in refrigerator	1 to 2 weeks	1 year	
Cheese and Cheese Spreads in cans or jars or in wine				
Unopened	Original container. Kitchen shelf			Remove surface discoloration. Remove mold. If the flavor of the remainder is acceptable, it is useable. Otherwise discard.
Opened	Original or other covered container in refrigerator	2 to 3 weeks		If surface darkens, remove discoloration and/or mold. Remains are useable if the flavor is acceptable. Otherwise discard.
Prepared Dishes, such as fondue, rarebit, etc.	Covered dish in refrigerator	2 to 3 days	1 year	

	How to Store	Approx. Time Limit for Storage		Evidence of Quality Loss
		Refrig.	Freezer	

POULTRY

Fresh				
Whole	Remove entrails of undressed poultry. Covered dish or original wrapping. If bloody, wipe with damp cloth and store in fresh wrapping material or covered dish. Refrigerator	6 to 8 days	6 months	If dried out, grease skin; if slightly moldy or of slightly tainted odor, wash with lightly salted water and scald body cavity.
Uncooked, stuffed	Cool dressing before stuffing the fowl. Moisture-proof wrapper. Refrigerator	1 day	6 months	
Cut-up	If bloody, wipe with damp cloth and store in fresh wrapping material or covered dish. Refrigerator	4 to 5 days	6 months	If slightly moldy or of slightly tainted odor, wash with lightly salted water.

POULTRY AND STUFFING

Left-over Cooked Poultry	Covered dish or moisture-proof wrapping. Refrigerator. Remove stuffing, refrigerate separately.	4 to 5 days	6 months	
Poultry Pies, Stews, a la King, etc.	Cool until just hot to the touch, then refrigerate	1 to 2 days	6 months	
Canned				
Unopened	Kitchen shelf			
Opened	Original or other covered container. Immerse in own liquid. Refrigerator	4 to 5 days	6 months	
Frozen	Original cointainer or moisture-proof wrapper. Refrigerator	10 days	6 months	If dried out, grease skin. If slightly moldy or of slightly tainted odor, wash with lightly salted water and scald body cavity.

(Cont.)

STORAGE CHART [Cont.]

	How to Store	Approx. Time Limit for Storage		Evidence of Quality Loss
		Refrig.	Freezer	
POULTRY (Cont.)				
Smoked	Original or other moisture-proof container. Cool place or refrigerator	10 to 20 days	6 months	If dried out, grease skin. If slightly moldy or of slightly tainted odor, wash with lightly salted water and scald body cavity.
MEAT [BEEF, LAMB, PORK, AND VEAL]				
Raw Roasts, Steaks, Chops, and Stew Meat	Covered dish or original wrapper. If bloody, wipe with damp cloth and store in fresh wrapping material or covered dish. Repeat if necessary during long storage. Refrigerator	6 to 8 days	6 months to 1 year	Darkening and drying out
Raw Boned and Rolled Roasts	Covered dish or original wrapper. If bloody, wipe with damp cloth and store in fresh wrapping material or covered dish. Repeat if necessary during long storage. Refrigerator	4 to 5 days	6 months to 1 year	Darkening and drying out
Raw Livers, Hearts, Kidneys, etc.	Covered dish or original wrapper. If bloody, wipe with damp cloth and store in fresh wrapping material or covered dish. Repeat if necessary during long storage. Refrigerator	3 to 4 days	6 months to 1 year	Darkening and drying out
Raw Ground Meats	Covered dish or wrapping material that will not stick to the meat. Refrigerator	1 to 2 days	6 months to 1 year	Graying and drying out
Smoked, Corned, Salt-Cured, Pickled, and Dried	Covered dish or original wrapper. If bloody, wipe with damp cloth and store in fresh wrapping material or covered dish.	10 to 20 days	1 year	Excessive drying

	How to Store	Approx. Time Limit for Storage		Evidence of Quality Loss
		Refrig.	Freezer	
	Repeat if necessary during long storage. Refrigerator			
Cold Cuts	Covered dish or original wrapper. Separate slices with waxed paper for longer storage life. Refrigerator	7 days	6 months to 1 year	Darkening and drying out
Left-over Broiled, Fried, or Roasted Meat	Cool to room temperature. Covered container. Refrigerator	5 to 6 days	6 months to 1 year	Darkening and drying out. Irridescence on cooked ham or lamb harmless
Left-over Casseroles, Meat Pies, and Stews	Cool until just hot to the touch. Covered container. Refrigerator	3 to 4 days	6 months to 1 year	
Canned				
Unopened	Original container. Kitchen shelf			
Opened	Original or other covered container. Immerse in own liquid if any is available. Refrigerator	4 to 5 days	6 months to 1 year	
Frozen	Original container or moisture-proof wrapper. Freezer	10 days	6 months to 1 year	Thawing, darkening and drying out

FRUITS AND VEGETABLES

	How to Store	Refrig.	Freezer	Evidence of Quality Loss
Fresh				
Soft-textured fruits and vegetables such as berries and tomatoes	Uncovered. Avoid bruising or crushing. Refrigerator	3 to 14 days	1 year*	If softening, discoloration, mold, and/or general decay is present, separate damaged produce for immediate use. Remove soft, moldy, and/or decayed parts. Partially cook for further storage.
Leafy Vegetables	Wash and remove undesirable parts. Cover or wrap to retain moisture. Refrigerator	3 to 8 days	1 year*	Discard decayed parts. Recrisp remainder by placing in cold water.

*Special preparation prior to freezing is required for most fruits and vegetables

(Cont.)

STORAGE CHART [Cont.]

	How to Store	Approx. Time Limit for Storage		Evidence of Quality Loss
		Refrig.	Freezer	

FRUITS AND VEGETABLES (Cont.)

	How to Store	Refrig.	Freezer	Evidence of Quality Loss
Firm or Hard Fruits and Vegetables, such as apples, oranges, carrots and potatoes	Uncovered. Cool place such as cold cellar or refrigerator. Do not refrigerate potatoes, because they become sweet.	1 to 4 months	1 year*	Separate damaged produce and use as soon as possible. Remove soft or bad parts. Some may be recrisped in cold water. Partially cook for further storage.
Cooked Fruits and Vegetables, including creamed vegetables	Cover with accompanying sauce or immerse in cooking liquid. Refrigerator	4 to 5 days	1 year	If curdled, or if mold and/or off-odor and flavor develop, is not reclaimable. Discard.
Canned Fruits and Vegetables Unopened	Original container. Kitchen shelf			If can is bulged or cover is loose, if bubbles appear on surface, and/or mold and off-odors develop, fruits may be used if flavor is acceptable. Vegetables, particularly home canned, should be brought to a boil and boiled for 15 minutes before tasting when spoilage is suspected. If moldy, curdled, and/or off-odor and flavor, not reclaimable. Discard.
Opened	Original or other covered container. Immerse in own liquid. Refrigerator	4 to 5 days	1 year	
Frozen Fruits and Vegetables	Original container. Freezer	7 days	1 year	If merely thawed, refreeze but expect some softening when thawed again for use. Useable if not moldy and if flavor is acceptable. Otherwise discard
Dried Fruits and Vegetables	Original or other covered container. Kitchen shelf	Not advisable because of moisture absorption		Remove mold if practicable; if the flavor of the remainder is acceptable, it may be used.
Pickled Fruits	Original containers. Refrigerator	2 to 3 weeks	1 year*	If food darkens or softens, or if mold develops, remove mold if practicable and if flavor is satisfactory, may be used.

*Special preparation prior to freezing is required for most fruits and vegetables.

	How to Store	Approx. Time Limit for Storage		Evidence of Quality Loss
		Refrig.	**Freezer**	
Vegetables, including pickles and relishes	Original container. Immerse in pickling liquid. Cool place or refrigerator	5 to 6 months		Remove mold if practicable, and if the flavor of the remainder is acceptable, use.

SPAGHETTI, MACARONI, NOODLES AND RICE

	How to Store	Refrig.	Freezer	Evidence of Quality Loss
Dry	Original or other covered container. Kitchen shelf			If odor and/or flavor are stale or rancid, slight off odor and/or flavor can be masked by seasonings.
Prepared Dishes, plain or with meat, fish, chicken, etc., added	Covered container. Refrigerator	4 to 5 days	1 year	

SALADS, DRESSINGS, AND SAUCES

	How to Store	Refrig.	Freezer	Evidence of Quality Loss
Salads				
Vegetable and fruit (raw, canned, cooked or frozen)	Plan to hold only briefly. Refrigerator	4 to 6 hours		If there is an excess of liquid and the garnish is limp, drain and replace garnish
Cooked meat, poultry, fish, and eggs	Plan to hold only briefly. Refrigerator	3 to 4 hours		
Left-over Salads	Discard garnish. Refrigerator	(See chart for particular ingredient in question)		
Thickened Salad Dressing	Original or other covered container. Cool place or refrigerator	1 week to 1 year		If liquid separates, stir or beat to reblend. If off-flavor, discard.
Oil and Vinegar Dressings	Original or other covered container. Cool place	1 week to 1 year		If off-flavor is evident, discard.
White Sauce and those sauces having a white sauce base	Covered container. Refrigerator	2 to 3 days	1 year. Frequently separates at these temperatures	If liquid separates, stir. If mold and/or off-flavors develop, discard.
Sweet or Sour Cream Sauces and their variations	Covered container. Refrigerator	2 to 3 days	1 year	If liquid separates, stir. If mold and/or off-flavors develop, discard.

(Cont.)

STORAGE CHART [Cont.]

		Approx. Time Limit for Storage		
	How to Store	**Refrig.**	**Freezer**	**Evidence of Quality Loss**
	SALADS, DRESSINGS, AND SAUCES (Cont.)			
Hard Sauce or Special Flavor Sauces, such as chocolate and butterscotch	Covered container. Refrigerator	1 to 6 months		If merely separated, stir or beat to reblend. If moldy and/or off-flavor, discard.
	FATS AND OILS			
Butter and Margarine	Covered or wrapped. Refrigerator	7 to 30 days	6 to 8 months	If off-odors and/or flavors are noticed, they can be masked by seasonings in cooking.
Lard	Covered or wrapped. Refrigerator	15 to 60 days	10 to 12 months	Slight off-odor and/or flavor can be masked by seasonings in cooking. If used for deep fat frying, some off-odors can be removed by frying a few pieces of potatoes first.
Firm Vegetable Shortenings	Original container, covered. Kitchen shelf	No definite limit		Mask slight off-odor and/or flavor by seasonings in cooking. If used for deep fat frying, fry few potatoes first to remove some off-odors.
Fat Drippings	Any covered container. Refrigerator	7 to 30 days	6 to 8 months	If off-odors and/or flavors develop, not reclaimable. Discard.
Cooking and Salad Oils	Original container, covered. Cool place or refrigerator, depending on the directions supplied with the material	No definite limits		If merely cloudy, warm to restore clarity. If off-odors and/or flavors occur, mask by seasonings in cooking.
	BREADS, BISCUITS, MUFFINS, AND ROLLS			
Breads, Biscuits, Muffins and Rolls, with or without fruit and/or nuts	Moisture-proof wrapper or container. Cool place	2 weeks	5 to 6 months	If moldy or dried out, or if yeasty odor or stale flavor develop, dry completely and use for bread crumbs, or discard if moldy or yeasty.
Rolls with Special Fillings	(See chart information for particular type of filling)			If mold, drying out, yeasty odor, or stale flavor develop,

	How to Store	Approx. Time Limit for Storage		Evidence of Quality Loss
		Refrig.	Freezer	
				use bread crumbs if reclaimable, but discard filling if moldy, yeasty, or sour.
Prepared Mixes				
Dry	Original or other covered container. Fold bag or liner to surface of contents. Kitchen shelf	5 to 6 months		If odor and/or flavor are stale or rancid, slight off-odor and/or flavor can be masked by adding flavoring or seasoning.
With added liquid	Covered dish. Refrigerator	3 to 4 days		If moldy, curled, or of sour or yeasty odor, not reclaimable. Discard.
"Ready-for-the-oven" Rolls (baked but not browned)	Original container. Refrigerator	2 weeks	5 to 6 months	If mold, drying out, yeasty odor or stale flavors, dry completely and use for bread crumbs, or discard if moldy or yeasty.
Refrigerator Doughs or Unbaked Doughs	Moisture-proof wrapper or container. Refrigerator	5 days	5 to 6 months	If moldy and/or soured, it is not reclaimable. Discard.
Dry Bread Crumbs	Original or other covered container. Kitchen shelf			Slight off-odor and/or flavor can be masked by using in highly seasoned food.

CEREALS, FLOUR, PANCAKE, AND WAFFLE MIXES

	How to Store	Refrig.	Freezer	Evidence of Quality Loss
Dry	Original or other covered container. Fold bag or liner to surface of contents. Kitchen shelf	5 to 6 months		If odor is stale or rancid, can be masked by adding flavoring or seasoning.
Uncooked Batter or Cooked Left-overs	Covered dish. Refrigerator	3 to 4 days		If batter thickens or there is a loss of leavening power in mixes, add liquid or leavening agent as needed. If moldy, curdled or soured, it is not reclaimable. Discard.

BAKING CHOCOLATE AND COCOA

	How to Store	Refrig.	Freezer	Evidence of Quality Loss
Bar Chocolate, Dry Cocoa, or Prepared Dry Cocoa Mix	Wrapped or in original covered container. Kitchen shelf	1 year		If an off-flavor is evident, discard.

(Cont.)

STORAGE CHART [Cont.]

		Approx. Time Limit for Storage		
	How to Store	Refrig.	Freezer	Evidence of Quality Loss

BAKING CHOCOLATE AND COCOA (Cont.)

Chocolate Beverage Prepared with Milk or Water	Covered container. Refrigerator	7 days		If curdled and/or off-flavor, discard.

SUGAR AND OTHER SWEETENING AGENTS

Sugar and Maple Sugar	Original or other covered container. Fold bag or liner to surface of contents. Kitchen shelf. Refrigerate brown sugar	(Brown Sugar) 1 year		If caked or hardened, dry out by brief heating in a very low oven.
Honey, Maple Syrup, Sugar Syrups and Corn Syrup Unopened	Original container. Cool place			If mold and/or off-flavor develop, remove mold. If flavor of remainder is satisfactory, it is useable. Otherwise discard.
Opened	Recover tightly. Original container. Refrigerator			If sugar crystals are present, or mold and/or off-flavors are evident, heat to dissolve crystals. Remove mold. If the flavor of the remains is satisfactory, it is useable. Otherwise discard.

CAKES, COOKIES, AND CRACKERS

Cakes and Cookies Containing No Fruit, with or without frosting	Covered container. Store with piece of apple or fresh bread. Kitchen shelf		6 months	If only stale and dried out, use for pudding. If moldy, discard.
Cakes and Cookies with Fruit and/or Nuts	Covered container. Store with piece of apple or fresh bread. Kitchen shelf	3 weeks to 6 months	1 year	If merely dried out, use for pudding. Otherwise, discard.
Cakes and Cookies with Custard Topping or Filling	Moisture-proof wrapper or container. Refrigerator	2 days		
Refrigerator Desserts Containing Cake or Cookies and Whipped Cream	Covered container for prolonged storage. Refrigerator	5 to 6 days	6 months	Useable if merely dried out. Otherwise discard.

	How to Store	Approx. Time Limit for Storage		Evidence of Quality Loss
		Refrig.	**Freezer**	
Crackers, Snacks, such as potato chips, cheese crackers, etc.	Moisture-proof wrapper or container. Kitchen shelf			If soggy or tough, recrisp in warm oven. Otherwise discard.
Canned Cakes, such as fruit cake				
Unopened	Original container. Kitchen shelf			If there is mold on the inside container, or if the food has a sour odor, discard.
Opened	Original or other covered container. Kitchen sehlf	3 weeks to 6 months	1 year	If moldy and/or sour in odor, or if cobwebs are noticed, discard.
Prepared Mixes				
Dry	Original or other covered container. Kitchen shelf	5 to 6 months		Slight off-odor and/or flavor may be masked by adding flavoring.
Batter	Covered container. Refrigerator	3 to 4 days		Useable if flavor is acceptable. More leavening may be added.
Raw Cookie Doughs	Covered container. Refrigerator	3 weeks	6 months	If moldy and/or sour in odor, discard.

PIES AND PUDDINGS

	How to Store	Refrig.	Freezer	Evidence of Quality Loss
Soft Custard and Cornstarch Pies and Puddings, with or without fruit	Refrigerator	2 to 3 days	6 to 8 months	
Baked Custard Pies and Puddings, with or without fruit. Squash and Pumpkin Pies	Refrigerator	2 to 7 days	6 to 8 months	If mold and/or sour odor develop, not reclaimable. Discard.
Gelatin and Tapioca Pies and Puddings, with or without fruit	Refrigerator	3 to 7 days	6 to 8 months	If moldy and/or soured, it is not reclaimable. Discard.
Fruit Pies and Puddings, such as apple pie, Brown Betty and mincemeat pie	Cool place or refrigerator	3 to 7 days	6 to 8 months	If mold and/or sour odor are evident, not reclaimable. Discard.
Other Baked Puddings, such as bread and rice puddings	Refrigerator	4 to 7 days	6 to 8 months	If mold and/or sour odor develop, not reclaimable. Discard.
Meringue and Whipped Cream Toppings	Refrigerator			If odor and/or flavor are sour, not reclaimable. Discard.

(Cont.)

STORAGE CHART [Cont.]

	How to Store	Approx. Time Limit for Storage		Evidence of Quality Loss
		Refrig.	Freezer	
PIES AND PUDDINGS (Cont.)				
Unbaked Pie Doughs	Covered container. Refrigerator	7 to 10 days	6 to 8 months	If moldy and/or rancid, discard.
Baked Pie Shells	Covered container. Kitchen shelf	3 to 7 days		If merely soggy, reclaim by heating in the oven. If moldy or rancid, discard.
ICE CREAM AND OTHER FROZEN DESSERTS				
Ice Cream Insulated bag	Unopened. Refrigerator	5 to 6 hours		If merely soft, refreeze. Useable if texture and flavor are acceptable.
Not in insulated bag	Original container. Surface should be covered to prevent ice crystals from forming. Refrigerator	3 to 4 hours	8 months	Refreeze to harden. Useable if texture and flavor are satisfactory.
Ices, Mousse and Sherbets Insulated bag	Unopened. Refrigerator	3 to 4 hours		If soft, refreeze.
Not in insulated bag	Original container. Surface should be covered to prevent ice crystals from forming. Refrigerator	1 hour	8 months	If softening has occurred, refreeze.
Frozen Combinations, with cake, cookies or pastry Insulated bag	Unopened. Refrigerator	3 to 4 hours		If frozen part has softened, but texture and flavor are acceptable, refreeze. If stale flavor and/or sogginess have developed in baked material, or if whipped cream garnish is sour, discard. Remove garnish if soured.
Not in insulated bag	Original container. Surface should be covered to prevent ice crystals from forming. Refrigerator	1 to 2 hours	4 months	If frozen part has softened, but texture and flavor are acceptable, refreeze. If stale flavor and/or sogginess have developed in baked material, or if whipped

	How to Store	Approx. Time Limit for Storage		Evidence of Quality Loss
		Refrig.	**Freezer**	
				cream garnish is sour, discard. Remove garnish if soured.
Ice Cream Powder	Original container. Kitchen shelf			If stale in flavor, discard.
Canned Ice Cream Mixes	Original container. Kitchen shelf			If can is bulged, discard.

JAMS, JELLIES, MARMALADES, AND PRESERVES

	How to Store	Refrig.	Freezer	Evidence of Quality Loss
Unopened Container	Original container. Kitchen shelf			If cover is loose or can is bulged, or if mold and/or fermented odor and flavor are evident, remove mold. If the flavor of the remainder is acceptable, it is useable, otherwise discard.
Opened Container	Original container. Keep covered. Refrigerate for long holding.	to 5 weeks	1 year	If mold and/or fermented odor and flavor are evident, remove mold. If the flavor of the remainder is acceptable, it is useable. Otherwise discard.

CANDY, GUM, AND NUTS

	How to Store	Refrig.	Freezer	Evidence of Quality Loss
Plain Chocolate Bars and Chocolate without fruit or nuts	Original container. Kitchen shelf. Refrigerate in hot weather.	1 year		If white spots appear, or softening and/or stale flavor are evident, useable if flavor is acceptable.
Hard Candy, such as lollipops and Christmas candy	Moisture-proof wrapper or container. Kitchen shelf			If softened, useable in sauces or frostings.
Candies and Chocolates containing fruit and/or nuts	Original container. Kitchen shelf. Refrigerate in hot weather.			Unless cobwebby, useable if flavor is acceptable. Otherwise discard.
All Other Candies, including those with caramel and nougat centers	Original container. Kitchen shelf	1 year		If dried out and/or stale in flavor, useable if the flavor is acceptable.

(Cont.)

STORAGE CHART [Cont.]

	How to Store	Approx. Time Limit for Storage Refrig.	Freezer	Evidence of Quality Loss
CANDY, GUM AND NUTS (Cont.)				
Gum	Original container. Kitchen shelf			If hardened, useable if desired.
Nuts				
In shell	Kitchen shelf			If moldy, or if worms, moths or cobwebs are evident, discard.
Shelled	Covered container. Kitchen shelf		6 months	If merely soggy, warm briefly in the oven or use in cooking.
Vacuum Packed, unopened	Original container. Kitchen shelf			If stale or rancid in flavor, useable if flavor is acceptable.
Vacuum Packed, opened	Covered container. Kitchen shelf	6 months		If moldy, stale, rancid in flavor, soggy, and/or cobwebby, warm briefly in oven or use in cooking. Otherwise discard.
FRUIT AND VEGETABLE JUICES				
Freshly Prepared	Non-metallic container. Refrigerator	5 to 6 days	1 year	If mold and off-odor and/or flavor develop, fruit juices can be tasted and, if the flavor is acceptable, are useable.
Canned				
Unopened	Original container. Cool place			Fruit juices: if can is bulged or cover is loose, or if mold, off-odor, and/or bubbles on the surface are evident, they can be used. Vegetable juices, particularly home canned, should be brought to a boil and boiled for 15 minutes before tasting, when spoilage is suspected.
Opened	Non-metallic container. Refrigerator	5 to 6 days	1 year	
Frozen				
Unopened	Original container. Freezer	7 days	1 year	

	How to Store	Approx. Time Limit for Storage		Evidence of Quality Loss
		Refrig.	Freezer	
Opened	Non-metallic container. Refrigerator	5 to 6 days	1 year	

MILK, MILK DRINKS, AND CREAM

	How to Store	Approx. Time Limit for Storage		Evidence of Quality Loss
		Refrig.	Freezer	
Cream, Flavored Milk Drinks and Plain Milk (whole or skimmed)	Original container. Refrigerator	3 to 4 days		If curdling, mold and/or sour odor are evident: if of acceptable flavor and not moldy, use for cooking.
Sour, Cultured or Buttermilk	Original container. Refrigerator	10 to 14 days		If curdled, moldy, and/or sour in odor, use for cooking, if free of mold and acceptable in flavor.
Condensed and Evaporated Unopened	Original container. Kitchen shelf. Invert can after 6 months storage.			If can is bulged, discard. If contents merely thickened, reclaim by adding water and use for cooking.
Opened	Original container, covered. Refrigerator	10 days		If moldy, discard. If curdled and/or sour in odor, but of acceptable flavor, use for cooking. If thickened, add water.

GENERAL BIBLIOGRAPHY

"Agricultural Prices and Parity." *Major Statistical Series of The U.S. Department of Agriculture*, Vol. 1, No. 365. Washington, D.C.: Government Printing Office, October 1970, pp. 1-44.

"Agricultural Production and Efficiency." *Major Statistical Series of The U.S. Department of Agriculture*, Vol. 2, No. 365. Washington, D.C.: Government Printing Office, April 1970, pp. 1-39.

American Hospital Association. *Food Service Manual For Health Care Institutions*. Chicago: American Hospital Association, 1972.

Beau, Francis N. *Quantity Food Purchasing Guide*. Boston: Cahners Books International, Inc., 1974.

Checklist of U.S. Standards for Farm Products. AMS-210, (rev.) January 1963. Washington D.C.: Marketing Information Division, AMS, U.S. Dept. of Agriculture.

Conversion Factors and Weight and Measures. Washington, D.C.: U.S. Department of Agriculture/Economic Research Service, May 1952.

Crawford, Hollie, and McDowell, Milton. *Mathematics for Food Service/Lodging*. Chicago: Cahners Books International, Inc., 1970.

Dahl, Crete. *Food and Menu Dictionary*. Chicago: Cahners Books International, Inc., 1972.

Escoffier, Auguste, and Gilbert, Phileas. *Larousse Gastronomique*. New York: Crown Publishers, Inc., 1961.

Food Consumption of Households in the North Central Region, Seasons and Year 1965-66. September 1972, pp. 1-214.

"Foreign Trade, Production and Consumption of Agriculture Products." *Major Statistical Series of the U.S. Department of Agriculture*, Vol. 2, No. 365, April 1972, pp. 1-29.

Goldbeck, Nikki and David. *The Supermarket Handbook*. New York: Harper & Row, Pub., Inc., 1973.

Grading America's Food. Consumer and Marketing Service. Washington, D.C.: U.S. Department of Agriculture, 1970.

"Gross and Net Form Income." *Major Statistical Series of the U.S. Department of Agriculture*, Vol. 3, No. 365, September 1969, pp. 1-17.

Handbook Agricultural Charts. Washington, D.C.: U..S. Department of Agriculture, 1974.

Handbook of Food Preparation. Washington, D.C.: American Home Economics Association, 1964.

"Home Economics." Washington, D.C.: Government Printing Office, April 1972, pp. 1-23.

Household Weights and Measures (Prepared by the National Bureau of Standards in cooperation with National Conference on Weights and Measures), National Bureau of Standards, Misc. Publication 234, November 15, 1960; Supt. of Documents, Washington, D.C.

"Knowing What's Good for You." Campbell Soup Company, pp. 1-21.

Kotschevar, Lendal H. *Management By Menu*. Chicago: National Institute For the Foodservice Industry, 1975.

Kotschevar, Lendal H. *Standards, Principles, and Techniques in Quantity Food Production*. Boston: Cahners Books International, Inc., 1974.

Kotschevar, Lendal H. *Quantity Food Purchasing*. New York: John Wiley & Sons, Inc., 1975.

Kramer, Amilhud. *Food and the Consumer*. Westport, Connecticut: Avi Publishing Company, Inc., 1973.

"Land Values and Farm Finance." *Major Statistical Series of the U.S. Department of Agriculture*, Vol. 6, No. 365, April 1971, pp. 1-35.

Lennartson, Roy W. "What Grades Mean, Food." *The Yearbook of Agriculture, 1959*, Yearbook Separate No. 2971. Washington D.C.: Supt. of Documents, pp. 344-352.

Maizel, Bruno. *Food and Beverage Purchasing*. New York: ITT Educational Services, Inc., 1971.

"Market News." *Major Statistical Series of the U.S. Department of Agriculture*, Vol. 10, No. 365, 1972, pp. 1-42.

Martin, Ruth. *International Directory of Food and Cooking*. New York: Hasting House, 1974.

Merrill, Annabel L., and Watt, Bernice K. *Energy Value of Foods ... Basic and Deviation*. Washington, D.C.: United States Department of Agriculture, 1973.

"Popular Publications for the Farmer, Suburbanite, Homemaker Consumer." Washington, D.C.: U.S. Department of Agriculture, November 1973, pp. 1-18.

"Protection Through Inspection." Washington, D.C.: U.S. Department of Commerce, May 1974, pp. 1-8.

"Publications Food and Nutrition Service." Washington, D.C.: U.S. Department of Agriculture, May 1974, pp. 3-18.

Rietz, Carl A. *A Guide to the Selection, Combination and Cooking of Foods, Vol. 1, Selection and Combination of Foods*. Westport, Connecticut: Avi Publishing Company, Inc., 1961.

Rietz, C.A., and Wanderstock, J.J. *A Guide to the Selection, Combination, and Cooking of Foods*, Vol. 2, Westport, Connecticut: Avi Publishing Co., Inc., 1965.

"A Selective List with Descriptive Annotations." *New Technical Books*, Vol. 59, No. 8, Reviews 1051-1247, October 1974, pp. 291-388.

Selected Research Abstracts of Published and Unpublished Reports Pertaining to the Food Service Industry. Washington, D.C.: U.S. Department of Agriculture, 1970.

Todd, Donald D., and O'Haver, JoAnne M. *Foodservice Vocabulary.* Boston: Cahners Books International, Inc., 1974.

Units of Weight and Measure (United States Customary and Metric), Definitions and Tables of Equivalents. National Bureau of Standards, Misc. Publication 233. Washington, D.C.: Government Printing Office, 1960.

"USDA Standards for Food and Farm Products." Washington, D.C.: U.S. Department of Agriculture, November 1974, pp. 1-15.

U.S. Department of Agriculture. *USDA Grade Marks and the Foods on Which They are Used*, AMS-242. Washington, D.C.: Agricultural Marketing Service.

U.S. Department of Agriculture, Marketing Economics Division. *Market Structure of The Food Industries*, Washington, D.C.: Government Printing Office, 1972.

U.S. Department of Agriculture. *The Yearbook of Agriculture 1959.* Washington, D.C.: The United States Government Printing Office, 1959.

"Using Financial Statements in Food Service Establishments." *Food Management*, Leaflet 11, pp. 2-16.

Watt, Bernice K., and Merrill, Annabel L. *Composition of Foods.* Washington, D.C.: U.S. Department of Agriculture, 1963.

Wenzel, George, Sr. *Wenzel's Menu Maker.* Austin, Texas: George L. Wenzel, Sr., 1972.

West, B.B., Wood, L., and Shugart, G. *Food Service in Institutions*, 5th ed. New York: John Wiley & Sons, Inc., 1970.

Wilkinson, Jule. *The Complete Book of Cooking Equipment.* Boston: Cahners Books International, Inc., 1972.

_____. *The Components of Communication.* Chicago: Cahners Books International, Inc., 1968.

_____. *The Finishing Kitchen.* Chicago: Medalist Publication, 1969.

"The World Food Situation." Washington, D.C.: U.S. Department of Agriculture, October 1974, pp. 1-5.

APPENDIXES

APPENDIX   I   1027

APPENDIX   II   1078

APPENDIX   III   1104

APPENDIX   IV   1152

APPENDIX I

FOOD PURCHASING GUIDE FOR GROUP FEEDING

Prepared by Betty Peterkin and Beatrice Evans, *Consumer and Food Economics Research Division, Agricultural Research Service, U.S. Department of Agriculture*

INTRODUCTION

This food purchasing guide contains information useful in estimating the number of purchase units of foods to buy to serve a specific number of portions.

Foods have been listed by major groups in tables 1 through 21. Within each group the individual foods are arranged alphabetically. For each purchase unit specified, these data are given: Weight of the unit of purchase, yield from weight "as purchased" to weight "as served," size and description of portion, number of portions from each purchase unit, and the approximate number of purchase units needed for 25 and 100 portions.

Table 22 presents an easy method for computing the number of purchase units needed for portions of sizes other than those given in tables 1 through 21. Table 23 gives an easy method for finding the cost of a portion of food.

The yields of edible meat from the carcass of wholesale cuts of beef, lamb, and pork given in tables 24 to 26 are useful to institutions that raise their own meat animals or purchase meat by the carcass or wholesale cuts. The yields of canned and frozen products from fresh vegetables and fruits given in table 27 are useful to institutions that produce and preserve their own vegetables and fruits.

Table 28 gives the common can and jar sizes, and on page 48 equivalents used frequently by food planners are given.

EXPLANATION OF TERMS USED

Food as purchased. — Foods are described in the forms as purchased — fresh, frozen, canned, dried. Further descriptive information that would affect the yield is also given, such as: for meats — bone in, bone out; for carrots — with tops, without tops; and for potatoes — to be pared, ready-to-cook.

Unit of purchase. — Sizes of cans, packages, or other containers and weights of units in common use in the wholesale and retail markets are given. Usually, data for the 1-pound unit are given; from these the yield of any weight purchase unit can be determined.

Weight per unit. — Weights given for purchase units refer to weights as purchased on the market. Legal weights for contents of such units as bushels, lugs, crates, and boxes may vary in different States. The lowest of these weights is used to insure that the specified portions can be obtained. Weights for canned goods are the same as those given as net weight on the label.

Yield as served. — Yield as served refers to the weight of food "as served" as a percentage of weight "as purchased." Absence of information in this column means a weight yield was not used to determine the number of portions per purchase unit.

The same item "as purchased" may have more than one yield, depending on the way it is served. For example, 1 pound of fresh carrots without tops will yield 0.75 pound cooked and 0.82 pound grated raw.

The yield does not always refer to a serving that is all edible. For example, because pork chops are usually served with bone, the yield given is the percentage of the "as purchased" weight represented by the cooked chop with the bone in. On the other hand, the yield of the chuck roast, usually served without bone, is the percentage of the chuck "as purchased" — that is, cooked and served without the bone. For meats, the yield of cooked lean is given in an additional column.

The amount of ready-to-serve food obtained from a given

amount of food "as purchased" may vary widely, depending on the size, grade, and general condition of the food, discards in preparation, and the method and time of cooking. For yields given in this Handbook, it is assumed that the food used is in good condition (free of rot, insect infestation, bruising), that only usual amounts are discarded in preparation, and that usual cooking methods and time of cooking for the food specified are used.

For yields given, discard of inedible material such as bones, pits, and shells, except where otherwise specified, is assumed. Also assumed as discard are some foods that could be eaten but are usually discarded, such as potato parings and outer leaves of vegetables.

The yields presented in these tables were obtained from Agriculture Handbook No. 102, "Food Yields Summarized by Different Stages of Preparation," and unpublished data from the Agricultural Research Service of the U.S. Department of Agriculture and from the Fish and Wildlife Service of the U.S. Department of the Interior. Yields for commercially prepared meat combinations (table 2) are based on minimum meat requirements for meat food products packed for interstate shipment under Federal inspection. Contents of cooked poultry meat in poultry products are based on regulations governing the inspection of poultry and poultry products, effective January 1, 1965.

Size and description of portion. — Weight or volume of portion commonly used is given. This portion for most foods refers to the amount served. For foods often used in combination with other foods, such as canned milk, nonfat dry milk, eggs, nuts, flour, and uncooked cereals, a portion refers to a measure commonly called for in institution recipes.

For meat, poultry, and fish, data for two sizes of portions are given. The larger portion may be appropriate for an adult serving; the smaller may be sufficient for a child's meal or a luncheon menu. The size of meat portions is given (1) in ounces of cooked meat as served including fat and, in some cases, bone; and (2) in ounces of cooked lean only.

For vegetables and fruits, the portion size is generally the weight of 1/2 cup rounded to the nearest ounce. It is assumed that canned, cooked fresh, and cooked dried fruits are served with sirup, and that heated canned vegetables and cooked fresh and frozen vegetables are served drained. It is assumed that solid-pack fruits are served without liquid.

Institutions that use a different portion size than those given may adjust the amount to purchase by the method given in table 22.

Portions per purchase unit. — In obtaining the portions per purchase unit or the yield of a purchase unit in portions, average quantities of refuse and usual weight losses in cooking are assumed. The number of portions may vary from that shown if the condition of the food purchased is poor or unusual waste occurs in preparation and cooking.

To obtain the number of units to purchase, the number of portions per purchase unit can be divided into the number of persons to be served. This may be the most practical method of computing the amount to purchase if the institution does not serve 25 or 100 persons or easy multiples of these numbers of persons.

For example, if 1 pound of meat will serve 2.57 portions of the size desired, the food manager of an institution serving 580 persons may divide 580 by 2.57 to get the amount of meat needed — 226 pounds. It is because of such use of these figures, and not because the figures represent this degree of accuracy, that they have been carried to the nearest one-hundredth of a portion. Had the portions per pound of meat been rounded to the nearest number of portions per pound (3), the food manager would purchase only 193 pounds of meat — 33 pounds short of the best estimate of his needs.

The number of portions per purchase unit can be used with the cost of the purchase unit and table 23 in obtaining the cost for one portion.

Approximate purchase units for 25 and 100 portions. — These columns represent 25 and 100 divided by the number of portions per purchase unit in the preceding column. The resulting number of purchase units is always carried to the next even one-quarter (1/4) unit. Thus, the number of purchase units specified is always sufficient if the yield and portion size are as shown in the table. If the purchase units serve many portions, such as a bushel of apples or a No. 10 can of vegetables, this 1/4 purchase unit may be very significant. If the purchase unit serves few portions as in the case of a pound of meat, the 1/4 purchase unit is relatively unimportant.

QUANTITIES TO PURCHASE FOR 25 AND 100 PORTIONS

Table 1.—MEAT

Meat as purchased	Unit of purchase	Yield, cooked As served	Yield, cooked Lean only	Description of portion as served	Size of portion As served	Size of portion Lean only	Portions per purchase unit	Approximate purchase units for— 25 portions	Approximate purchase units for— 100 portions
BEEF, FRESH OR FROZEN									
		Percent	*Percent*		*Ounces*	*Ounces*	*Number*	*Number*	*Number*
Brisket:									
Corned, bone out	Pound	60	41	Simmered	4	2.8	2.40	10½	41¾
					3	2.1	3.20	8	31¼
Fresh:									
Bone in	do	52	36	Simmered, bone out	4	2.8	2.08	12¼	48¼
					3	2.1	2.77	9¼	36¼
Bone out	do	67	46	Simmered	4	2.8	2.68	9½	37½
					3	2.1	3.57	7¼	28¼
Ground beef:									
Lean	do	75	75	Broiled	3	3.0	4.00	6¼	25
					2	2.0	6.00	4¼	16¾
Regular	do	72	72	Pan-fried	3	3.0	3.84	6¾	26¼
					2	2.0	5.76	4½	17½
Heart	do	39	39		2	2.0	3.12	8¼	32¼
Kidney	do	39	39		2	2.0	3.12	8¼	32¼
Liver	do	69	69	Braised	3	3.0	3.68	7	27¼
					2	2.0	5.52	4¾	18¼
Oxtails	do	29	29		(¹)	(¹)	(¹)	(¹)	(¹)
Roasts:									
Chuck:									
Bone in	do	52	42	Roasted, moist heat, bone out	4	3.2	2.08	12¼	48¼
					3	2.4	2.77	9¼	36¼
Bone out	do	67	54	Roasted, moist heat	4	3.2	2.68	9½	37½
					3	2.4	3.57	7¼	28¼
7-Rib (shortribs removed):									
Bone in	do	65	42	Roasted, dry heat, bone out	4	2.6	2.60	9¾	38½
					3	1.9	3.47	7¼	29
Bone out	do	73	47	Roasted, dry heat	4	2.6	2.92	8¾	34¼
					3	1.9	3.89	6½	25¾
Round:									
Bone in	do	69	56	Roasted, dry heat, medium, bone out	4	3.3	2.76	9¼	36¼
					3	2.5	3.68	7	27¼
Bone out	do	73	60	Roasted, dry heat, medium	4	3.3	2.92	8¾	34¼
					3	2.5	3.89	6½	25¾
Rump:									
Bone in	do	58	43	Roasted, dry heat, bone out	4	3.0	2.32	11	43¼
					3	2.2	3.09	8¼	32½
Bone out	do	73	55	Roasted, dry heat	4	3.0	2.92	8¾	34¼
					3	2.2	3.89	6½	25¾
Shortribs	do	67	32	Braised, bone in	6	2.9	1.79	14	56
					4	1.9	2.68	9½	37½

See footnotes at end of table.

Table 1.—MEAT—Cont.

Meat as purchased	Unit of purchase	Yield, cooked		Description of portion as served	Size of portion		Portions per purchase unit	Approximate purchase units for—	
		As served	Lean only		As served	Lean only		25 portions	100 portions
BEEF, FRESH OR FROZEN— Continued									
Steaks:		*Percent*	*Percent*		*Ounces*	*Ounces*	*Number*	*Number*	*Number*
Club:					6	2.7	1. 95	13	51½
Bone in	Pound	73	33	Broiled, bone in	4	1. 8	2. 92	8¾	34¼
					4	2.3	2. 92	8¾	34¼
Bone out	do	73	42	Broiled	3	1.7	3. 89	6½	25¾
					3	3. 0	3. 57	7¼	28¼
Flank	do	67	67	Braised	2	2. 0	5. 36	4¾	18¾
Hip:					6	2.6	1. 95	13	51½
Bone in	do	73	32	Broiled, bone in	4	1. 8	2. 92	8¾	34¼
					4	2.2	2. 92	8¾	34¼
Bone out	do	73	40	Broiled	3	1.6	3. 89	6½	25¾
					3	3. 0	4. 00	6¼	25
Minute, cubed	do	75	75	Pan-fried	2	2. 0	6. 00	4¼	16¾
Porterhouse:					8	4. 0	1. 46	17¼	68½
					6	3. 0	1. 95	13	51½
Bone in	do	73	36	Broiled, bone in	4	2. 0	2. 92	8¾	34¼
					4	2.3	2. 92	8¾	34¼
Bone out	do	73	42	Broiled	3	1.7	3. 89	6½	25¾
Round:					4	3. 1	2. 92	8¾	34¼
Bone in	do	73	56	Broiled, bone in	3	2.3	3. 89	6½	25¾
					4	3. 3	2. 92	8¾	34¼
Bone out	do	73	60	Broiled	3	2.5	3. 89	6½	25¾
Sirloin (wedge and round):					6	3.6	1. 95	13	51½
Bone in	do	73	44	Broiled, bone in	4	2.4	2. 92	8¾	34¼
					4	2.6	2. 92	8¾	34¼
Bone out	do	73	48	Broiled	3	2. 0	3. 89	6½	25¾
T-bone:					8	3.8	1. 46	17¼	68½
					6	2.8	1. 95	13	51½
Bone in	do	73	34	Broiled, bone in	4	1. 9	2. 92	8¾	34¼
					4	2.2	2. 92	8¾	34¼
Bone out	do	73	41	Broiled	3	1.7	3. 89	6½	25¾
					3	2.4	3. 57	7¼	28¼
Stew meat (chuck), bone out	do	67	54	Cooked, moist heat	2	1.6	5. 36	4¾	18¾
Tongue:					3	3. 0	3. 15	8	31¾
Fresh	do	59	59	do	2	2. 0	4. 72	5½	21¼
					3	3. 0	2. 72	9¼	37
Smoked	do	51	51	do	2	2. 0	4. 08	6¼	24¾
BEEF, CANNED [3]					3	3. 0	5. 33	4¾	19
Beef, corned	do	100	100	Heated	2	2. 0	8. 00	3¼	12½
	6-pound can	100	100	do	3	3. 0	32. 00	1	3¼

See footnotes at end of table.

Table 1.–MEAT–Cont.

BEEF, DRIED									
Beef, chipped	Pound	125	125	Cooked, moist heat	3	3.0	6.67	3¾	15
					2	2.0	10.00	2½	10
LAMB, FRESH OR FROZEN									
Chops:									
Loin	do	76	41	Broiled, bone in	5.0	2.7	2.43	10½	41¼
Rib	do	76	34	do	5.0	2.2	2.43	10½	41¼
Shoulder	do	70	41	do	5.0	2.9	2.24	11¼	44¾
Ground lamb	do	68	68	Broiled patties	3.0	3.0	3.63	7	27¾
					2.0	2.0	5.44	4¾	18½
Roasts:									
Leg:									
Bone in	do	54	45	Roasted, bone out	4.0	3.3	2.16	11¾	46½
					3.0	2.5	2.88	8¾	34¾
Bone out	do	70	58	Roasted	4.0	3.3	2.80	9	35¾
					3.0	2.5	3.73	6¾	27
Shoulder:									
Bone in	do	55	41	Roasted, bone out	4.0	3.0	2.20	11½	45½
					3.0	2.2	2.93	8¾	34¼
Bone out	do	70	52	Roasted	4.0	3.0	2.80	9	35¾
					3.0	2.2	3.73	6¾	27
Stew meat,[3] bone out	do	66	--------	Simmered	3.0	--------	3.52	7¼	28½
					2.0	--------	5.28	4¾	19
PORK, CURED (MILD)									
Bacon (24 slices per pound)	do	32	--------	Fried or broiled	2 slices	--------	12.00	2¼	8½
Canadian bacon	do	63	63	Broiled, sliced	2	2.0	5.04	5	20
					1	1.0	10.08	2½	10
Ham:									
Bone in	do	67	54	Roasted, slices and pieces	4	2.9	2.68	9½	37½
					3	2.2	3.57	7¼	28¼
	do	56	44	Roasted, slices	4	2.4	2.24	11¼	44¾
					3	1.8	2.99	8½	33½
Bone out	do	77	72	Roasted, slices and pieces	4	2.9	3.08	8¼	32½
					3	2.2	4.11	6¼	24½
	do	64	60	Roasted, slices	4	2.4	2.56	10	39¼
					3	1.8	3.41	7½	29½
Ground	do	77	77	Patties	3	3.0	4.11	6¼	24½
					2	2.0	6.16	4¼	16¼
Shoulder, Boston butt:									
Bone in	do	67	52	Roasted, bone out	4	3.1	2.68	9½	37½
					3	2.3	3.57	7¼	28¼
Bone out	do	74	58	Roasted	4	3.1	2.96	8½	34
					3	2.3	3.95	6½	25½
Shoulder, picnic:									
Bone in	do	56	41	Roasted, bone out	4	3.9	2.24	11¼	44¾
					3	2.2	2.99	8½	33½
Bone out	do	74	53	Roasted	4	3.9	2.96	8½	34
					3	2.2	3.95	6½	25½

See footnotes at end of table.

Table 1.—MEAT—Cont.

Meat as purchased	Unit of purchase	Yield, cooked		Description of portion as served	Size of portion		Portions per purchase unit	Approximate purchase units for—	
		As served	Lean only		As served	Lean only		25 portions	100 portions
PORK, FRESH		*Percent*	*Percent*		*Ounces*	*Ounces*	*Number*	*Number*	*Number*
Chops:									
Loin	Pound	69	42	Broiled, bone in	5	3. 0	2. 21	11½	45¼
					3	1. 8	3. 68	7	27¼
Rib	do	70	37	do	5	2. 6	2. 24	11¼	44¾
					3	1. 6	3. 73	6¾	27
Cutlet, tenderloin	do	75	75	Broiled	3	3. 0	4. 00	6¼	25
					2	2. 0	6. 00	4¼	16¾
Ground pork	do	57	57	do	3	3. 0	3. 04	8¼	33
					2	2. 0	4. 56	5½	22
Liver	do	60	60	Pan- or oven-fried	3	3. 0	3. 20	8	31¼
					2	2. 0	4. 80	5¼	21
Roasts:									
Ham:									
Bone in	do	54	40	Roasted, bone out	4	3. 0	2. 16	11¾	46½
					3	2. 2	2. 88	8¾	34¾
Bone out	do	68	50	Roasted	4	3. 0	2. 72	9¼	37
					3	2. 2	3. 63	7	27¾
Loin:									
Bone in	do	68	37	Roasted, bone in	5	2. 8	2. 18	11½	46
					4	2. 2	2. 72	9¼	37
	do	47	37	Roasted, bone out	4	3. 2	1. 88	13½	53¼
					3	2. 4	2. 51	10	40
Bone out	do	68	54	Roasted	4	3. 2	2. 72	9¼	37
					3	2. 4	3. 63	7	27¾
Shoulder, Boston butt:									
Bone in	do	62	49	Roasted, bone out	4	3. 2	2. 48	10¼	40½
					3	2. 4	3. 31	7¾	30¼
Bone out	do	68	54	Roasted	4	3. 2	2. 72	9¼	37
					3	2. 4	3. 63	7	27¾
Shoulder, picnic:									
Bone in	do	47	35	Simmered, bone out	4	3. 0	1. 88	13½	53¼
					3	2. 2	2. 51	10	40
Bone out	do	64	47	Simmered	4	3. 0	2. 56	10	39¼
					3	2. 2	3. 41	7½	29½
Sausage:									
Brown and serve	do	81	81	Heated	3	3. 0	4. 32	6	23¼
					2	2. 0	6. 48	4	15½
Bulk or link	do	48	48	Oven-fried	3	3. 0	2. 56	10	39¼
					2	2. 0	3. 84	6¾	26¼
Spareribs	do	66	26	Braised, bone in	6	[4] 2. 3	1. 76	14¼	57
					4	[4] 1. 6	2. 64	9½	38
PORK, CANNED [5]									
Ham, chopped	do	100	100	Sliced	3	3. 0	5. 33	4¾	19
					2	2. 0	8. 00	3¼	12½

See footnotes at end of table.

Table 1.–MEAT–Cont.

Ham, smoked	do	77	75	Slices and pieces	3	2.9	4.11	6¼	24½
					2	1.9	6.16	4¼	16¼
	do	73	71	Slices	3	2.9	3.89	6½	25¾
					2	1.9	5.84	4½	17¼
Pork luncheon meat (with natural juices).	do	89	89	Unheated	3	3.0	4 75	5½	21¼
					2	2.0	7.12	3¾	14¼
SAUSAGES									
Frankfurters:									
8 per pound	do	98	--------	2 frankfurters	--------	--------	4.00	6¼	25
				1 frankfurter	--------	--------	8.00	3¼	12½
10 per pound	do	98	--------	2 frankfurters	--------	--------	5.00	5	20
				1 frankfurter	--------	--------	10.00	2½	10
Luncheon meats (all meat varieties).	do	100	100	--------	3	3.0	5.33	4¾	19
					2	2.0	8.00	3¼	12½
Vienna sausage (all meat)	Pound (drained weight).	100	100	About 4 sausages	2	2.0	8.00	3¼	12½
				About 2 sausages	1	1.0	16.00	1¾	6¼
VEAL, FRESH OR FROZEN									
Chops:									
Loin	Pound	78	47	Broiled, bone in	5	3.0	2.50	10	40
					3	1.8	4.16	6	24¼
Rib	do	69	38	do	5	2.8	2.21	11½	45¼
					3	1.6	3.68	7	27¼
Shoulder	do	66	40	do	5	3.0	2.11	12	47½
					3	1.8	3.52	7¼	28½
Cutlet, bone out	do	75	75	Broiled	4	3.0	3.00	8½	33½
					3	2.2	4.00	6¼	25
Ground	do	64	64	Oven- or pan-fried	3	3.0	3.41	7½	29½
					2	2.0	5.12	5	19¾
Heart	do	35	35	Braised	2	2.0	2.80	9	35¾
Liver, calf	do	58	58	Fried or braised	3	3.0	3.09	8¼	32½
					2	2.0	4.64	5½	21¾
Roasts:									
Chuck (shoulder):									
Bone in	do	46	40	Braised, bone out	4	3.4	1.84	13¾	54½
					3	2.6	2.45	10¼	41
Bone out	do	66	56	Braised	4	3.4	2.64	9½	38
					3	2.6	3.52	7¼	28½
Leg:									
Bone in	do	44	36	Roasted, bone out	4	3.3	1.76	14¼	57
					3	2.5	2.35	10¾	42¾
Bone out	do	66	54	Roasted	4	3.3	2.64	9½	38
					3	2.5	3.52	7¼	28½
Plate (breast):									
Bone in	do	45	33	Stewed, bone out	4	2.9	1.80	14	55¾
					3	2.2	2.40	10½	41¾
Bone out	do	66	48	Stewed	4	2.9	2.64	9½	38
					3	2.2	3.52	7¼	28½
Stew meat	do	66	48	do	4	2.9	2.64	9½	38
					3	2.2	3.52	7¼	28½

[1] Size of portion and number of portions per purchase unit are determined by use.
[2] For combination foods including beef, see p. 8.
[3] Breast, flank.
[4] Fat and lean.
[5] For combination foods including pork, see p. 8.

Table 2.—COMBINATION FOODS CONTAINING MEAT

Meat combinations, canned or frozen, as purchased	Unit of purchase	Weight per unit [1]	Cooked meat	Size of portion	Meat in portion	Portions per purchase unit	Approximate purchase units for—	
							25 portions	100 portions
		Pounds	*Percent*	*Ounces*	*Ounces*	*Number*	*Number*	*Number*
Beans with frankfurters in sauce	Pound	1. 00	20	8	1. 6	2. 00	12½	50
	No. 3 cylinder	3. 12	20	8	1. 6	6. 24	4¼	16¼
	No. 10 can	6. 75	20	8	1. 6	13. 50	2	7½
Beans with ham in sauce	Pound	1. 00	12	8	1. 0	2. 00	12½	50
	No. 3 cylinder	3. 19	12	8	1. 0	6. 38	4	15¾
Beans with meat in chili sauce	Pound	1. 00	8	8	. 6	2. 00	12½	50
	No. 10 can	6. 50	8	8	. 6	13. 00	2	7¾
Beef goulash:								
Canned	Pound	1. 00	18	8	1. 4	2. 00	12½	50
	No. 3 cylinder	3. 12	18	8	1. 4	6. 24	4¼	16¼
Frozen	Carton	5. 00	18	8	1. 4	10. 00	2½	10
	do	6. 75	18	9	1. 6	12. 00	2¼	8½
	do	8. 25	18	11	2. 0	12. 00	2¼	8½
Beef stew	Pound	1. 00	18	8	1. 4	2. 00	12½	50
	No. 3 cylinder	3. 12	18	8	1. 4	6. 24	4¼	16¼
	No. 10 can	6. 62	18	8	1. 4	13. 24	2	7¾
Beef with barbecue sauce	Pound	1. 00	50	6	3. 0	2. 67	9½	37½
	No. 3 cylinder	3. 25	50	6	3. 0	8. 67	3	11¾
	No. 10 can	6. 50	50	6	3. 0	17. 33	1½	6
Beef with gravy	Pound	1. 00	50	6	3. 0	2. 67	9½	37½
	No. 3 cylinder	3. 00	50	6	3. 0	8. 00	3¼	12¾
	No. 10 can	6. 50	50	6	3. 0	17. 33	1½	6
Brunswick stew	Pound	1. 00	18	8	1. 4	2. 00	12½	50
	No. 10 can	6. 62	18	8	1. 4	13. 24	2	7¾
Chili con carne	Pound	1. 00	28	8	2. 2	2. 00	12½	50
	No. 3 cylinder	3. 19	28	8	2. 2	6. 38	4	15¾
	No. 10 can	6. 75	28	8	2. 2	13. 50	2	7½
Chili con carne with beans	Pound	1. 00	18	8	1. 4	2. 00	12½	50
	No. 3 cylinder	3. 19	18	8	1. 4	6. 38	4	15¾
	No. 10 can	6. 75	18	8	1. 4	13. 50	2	7½
Chili mac	Pound	1. 00	18	8	1. 4	2. 00	12½	50
	No. 3 cylinder	3. 19	18	8	1. 4	6. 38	4	15¾
	No. 10 can	6. 50	18	8	1. 4	13. 00	2	7¾

See footnotes at end of table.

Table 2.—COMBINATION FOODS CONTAINING MEAT—Cont.

Food	Unit							
Chop suey or chow mein vegetables with meat:								
Canned	Pound	1.00	8	8	.6	2.00	12½	50
Frozen	No. 3 cylinder	3.06	8	8	.6	6.12	4¼	16½
	Carton	5.00	8	8	.6	10.00	2½	10
Hash, corn beef, roast beef, beef	Pound	1.00	35	7	2.4	2.29	11¼	44¼
	No. 3 cylinder	3.19	35	7	2.4	7.29	3½	14
	No. 10 can	6.50	35	7	2.4	14.86	1¾	7
Lamb stew	Pound	1.00	18	8	1.4	2.00	12½	50
	No. 3 cylinder	3.19	18	8	1.4	6.38	4	15¾
	No. 10 can	6.62	18	8	1.4	13.24	2	7¾
Macaroni and beef in tomato sauce	Pound	1.00	8	8	.6	2.00	12½	50
	No. 10 can	6.50	8	8	.6	13.00	2	7¾
Meatballs with gravy:								
Canned	Pound	1.00 (10 count)	38	6	2.3 (4 count)	2.67	9½	37½
	No. 10 can	6.50 (70 count)	38	6	2.3 (4 count)	17.33	1½	6
Frozen	Carton	8.00 (160 count)	38	6	2.3 (7½ count)	21.33	1¼	5
	....do	10.00 (100 count)	38	6	2.3 (4 count)	26.67	1	4
Pork with barbecue sauce:								
Canned	Pound	1.00	50	6	3.0	2.67	9½	37½
	No. 3 cylinder	3.19	50	6	3.0	8.51	3	12
	No. 10 can	6.62	50	6	3.0	17.65	1½	5¾
In waxed tub (perishable)	4-pound tub	4.00	50	6	3.0	10.67	2½	9½
	5-pound tub	5.00	50	6	3.0	13.33	2	7¾
Pork with gravy	Pound	1.00	50	6	3.0	2.67	9½	37½
	No. 3 cylinder	3.12	50	6	3.0	8.32	3¼	12¼
	No. 10 can	6.50	50	6	3.0	17.33	1½	6
Ravioli with meat in sauce	Pound	1.00	7	8	.6	2.00	12½	50
	No. 3 cylinder	3.19	7	8	.6	6.38	4	15¾
		3.62	7	8	.6	7.24	3½	14
Spaghetti with meatballs and sauce	Pound	1.00	8	8	.6	2.00	12½	50
	No. 3 cylinder	3.19	8	8	.6	6.38	4	15¾
	No. 10 can	6.62	8	8	.6	13.24	2	7¾
Tamales, frozen	Pound	1.00 (4 tamales)	18	8 (2 tamales)	1.4	2.00	12½	50
	Carton	6.00 (24 tamales)	18	8 (2 tamales)	1.4	12.00	2¼	8½
	....do	18.00	18	8	1.4	36.00	(²)	3
Tamales with gravy or sauce (Packed in sizes from 1½ oz. to 6 oz. per tamale).	Pound	1.00	14	8	1.1	2.00	12½	50
	No. 10 can	6.50	14	8	1.1	13.00	2	7¾

[1] Net weights of containers are not standardized and may vary depending on establishment preparing the product.
[2] Number of purchase units needed is less than one.

Table 3.—POULTRY

Poultry as purchased	Unit of purchase	Yield, as served	Description of portion as served	Size of portion		Portions per purchase unit	Approximate purchase units for—	
				As served	Edible portion [1]		25 portions	100 portions
		Percent		*Ounces*	*Ounces*	*Number*	*Number*	*Number*
CHICKEN, FRESH OR FROZEN								
Live:								
Roasters	Pound	30	Boned, excludes neck and giblets.	3.0	3.0	1.60	15¾	62½
				2.0	2.0	2.40	10½	41¾
Stewers	----do	34	Boned, includes neck and giblets.	3.0	3.0	1.81	14	55¼
				2.0	2.0	2.72	9¼	37
Ready-to-cook:								
Broilers	1½-pound bird	70	½ bird	8.3	5.4	2.00	12½	50
Fryers	Pound [2]	43	Boned	3.0	3.0	2.29	11	43¾
				2.0	2.0	3.44	7½	29¼
	2½-pound bird	65	¼ bird	5.8	3.9	4.00	6¼	25
			⅙ bird	3.9	2.6	6.00	4¼	16¾
			⅛ bird	2.9	1.9	8.00	3¼	12½
Parts (from 2½-pound bird):								
Breast half	Pound	67	With bone	3.2	2.6	3.35	7½	30
Drumstick	----do	72	----do	2.1	1.4	5.49	4¾	18¼
Thigh	----do	68	----do	2.2	1.6	4.95	5¼	20¼
Drumstick and thigh	----do	70	----do	4.3	3.1	2.60	9¾	38½
Wing	----do	64	----do	1.6	0.8	6.40	4	15¾
Back	----do	49	----do	2.5	1.3	3.14	8	32
Rib	----do	65	----do	2.5	1.3	4.16	6¼	24¼
Giblets:								
Gizzards	----do	26		2	2	2.08	12¼	48¼
Hearts	----do	38		2	2	3.04	8¼	33
Livers	----do	65		2	2	5.20	5	19¼
Roasters	----do	42	Boned, excludes neck and giblets.	3	3	2.24	11¼	44¾
				2	2	3.36	7½	30
Stewers	----do	47	Boned, includes neck and giblets.	3	3	2.51	10	40
				2	2	3.76	6¾	26¾
CHICKEN, CANNED								
Boned	----do	90	Meat	3	3	4.80	5¼	21
				2	2	7.20	3½	14
	Can (35 ounces)	90	----do	3	3	10.50	2½	9¾
				2	2	15.75	1¾	6½
Boned, solid pack	Pound	95	----do	3	3	5.07	5	19¾
				2	2	7.60	3½	13¼

[1] Includes edible skin.

[2] Based on 2½-pound bird as purchased; neck and giblets not served.

Table 3.—POULTRY—Cont.

Commodity	Unit		Description					
Boned, with broth	do	80	do	3	3	4. 27	6	23½
				2	2	6. 40	4	15¾
Whole	do	32	do	3	3	1. 71	14¾	58½
				2	2	2. 56	10	39¼
TURKEY, FRESH OR FROZEN								
Live	do	36	Excludes neck and giblets	3	3	1. 92	13¼	52¼
				2	2	2. 88	8¾	34¾
Ready-to-cook: Roasters	do	47	do	3	3	2. 51	10	40
				2	2	3. 76	6¾	26¾
Parts: Breasts, whole	do	60		3	3	3. 20	8	31¼
				2	2	4. 80	5¼	21
Legs (thigh and drumstick)	do	48		3	3	2. 56	10	39¼
				2	2	3. 84	6¾	26¼
Giblets: Gizzards	do	34		2	2	2. 72	9¼	37
Hearts	do	38		2	2	3. 04	8¼	33
Livers	do	67		2	2	5. 36	4¾	18¾
TURKEY, FROZEN ONLY								
Stuffed, whole	do	33	Boned meat	3	3	1. 76	14¼	57
				2	2	2. 64	9½	38
Rolls, precooked	do	92	Meat	3	3	4. 91	5¼	20½
				2	2	7. 36	3½	13¾
Rolls, ready-to-cook	do	61	do	3	3	3. 25	7¾	31
				2	2	4. 88	5¼	20½
TURKEY, CANNED								
Boned	do	90	do	3	3	4. 80	5¼	21
				2	2	7. 20	3½	14
	Can (35 ounces)	90	do	3	3	10. 50	2½	9¾
				2	2	15. 75	1¾	6½
Boned, solid pack	Pound	95	do	3	3	5. 07	5	19¾
				2	2	7. 60	3½	13¼
Boned, with broth	do	80	do	3	3	4. 27	6	23½
				2	2	6. 40	4	15¾
OTHER POULTRY, FRESH OR FROZEN								
Duck, ready-to-cook	do	38	Boned, excludes neck and giblets.	3	3	2. 03	12½	49½
				2	2	3. 04	8¼	33
Goose, ready-to-cook	do	39	do	3	3	2. 08	12¼	48¼
				2	2	3. 12	8¼	32¼

Table 4.—COMBINATION FOODS CONTAINING POULTRY

Poultry combinations, canned or frozen, as purchased	Unit of purchase [1]	Weight per unit	Cooked meat	Size of portion	Meat in portion	Portions per purchase unit	Approximate purchase units for—	
							25 portions	100 portions
		Pounds	*Percent*	*Ounces*	*Ounces*	*Number*	*Number*	*Number*
Chicken a la king	Pound	1.00	20	8	1.60	2.00	12½	50
Chickenburgers	do	1.00	100	3	3.00	5.33	4¾	19
Chicken cacciatore	do	1.00	20	8	1.60	2.00	12½	50
Chicken chop suey	do	1.00	4	8	.32	2.00	12½	50
Chicken chow mein	do	1.00	4	8	.32	2.00	12½	50
Chicken fricassee	do	1.00	20	8	1.60	2.00	12½	50
Chicken noodles or dumplings	do	1.00	15	8	1.20	2.00	12½	50
Chicken potpie	do	1.00	14	8	1.12	2.00	12½	50
Chicken stew	do	1.00	12	8	.96	2.00	12½	50
Chicken tamales	do	1.00	6	8	.48	2.00	12½	50
Creamed chicken	do	1.00	20	8	1.60	2.00	12½	50
Creamed turkey	do	1.00	20	8	1.60	2.00	12½	50
Minced chicken barbecue	do	1.00	40	3	1.20	5.33	4¾	19
Noodles or dumplings with chicken	do	1.00	6	8	.48	2.00	12½	50
Sliced chicken with gravy	do	1.00	35	6	2.10	2.67	9½	37½
Sliced turkey with gravy	do	1.00	35	6	2.10	2.67	9½	37½
Turkey a la king	do	1.00	20	8	1.60	2.00	12½	50
Turkey fricassee	do	1.00	20	8	1.60	2.00	12½	50
Turkey potpie	do	1.00	14	8	1.12	2.00	12½	50

[1] There is no standardization of can or carton sizes for canned and frozen poultry products. Information given for a pound may be related to the weight of the contents of the can or carton.

Table 5.—FISH AND SHELLFISH

Fish and shellfish as purchased	Unit of purchase	Weight per unit	Yield, as served	Portion as served	Portions per purchase unit	Approximate purchase units for—	
						25 portions	100 portions
FISH, CANNED		*Pounds*	*Percent*		*Number*	*Number*	*Number*
Gefiltefish _____	16-ounce can (9¼ ounces drained).	1. 00	58	{3 ounces drained _____ {2 ounces drained _____	3. 08 4. 62	8¼ 5½	32½ 21¾
	32-ounce can (20½ ounces drained).	2. 00	64	{3 ounces drained _____ {2 ounces drained _____	6. 83 10. 25	3¾ 2½	14¾ 10
	51-ounce can (39 ounces drained).	3. 19	76	{3 ounces drained _____ {2 ounces drained _____	13. 00 19. 50	2 1½	7¾ 5¼
Mackerel _____	15-ounce can (12½ ounces drained).	. 94	83	{3 ounces drained _____ {2 ounces drained _____	4. 17 6. 25	6 4	24 16
Salmon _____	3¾-ounce can (2¼ ounces drained).	. 23	60	2¼ ounces drained _____	1. 00	25	100
	16-ounce can (13 ounces drained).	1. 00	81	{3 ounces drained _____ {2 ounces drained _____	4. 33 6. 50	6 4	23¼ 15½
	64-ounce can (50 ounces drained).	4. 00	78	{3 ounces drained _____ {2 ounces drained _____	16. 67 25. 00	1½ 1	6 4
Sardines:							
Maine _____	3¾- to 4-ounce can (3¾ ounces drained).	. 23 to . 25	100	{3 ounces drained _____ {2 ounces drained _____	1. 25 1. 87	20 13½	80 53½
	12-ounce can (10¼ ounces drained).	. 75	90	{3 ounces drained _____ {2 ounces drained _____	3. 58 5. 38	7 4¾	28 18¾
Pacific:							
In brine _____	15-ounce can (11½ ounces drained).	. 94	77	{3 ounces drained _____ {2 ounces drained _____	3. 83 5. 75	6¾ 4½	26¼ 17½
In mustard or tomato sauce _____	15-ounce can _____	. 94	100	{3 ounces _____ {2 ounces _____	5. 00 7. 50	5 3½	20 13½
Tuna _____	3½- to 4-ounce can (3¼ ounces drained).	. 22 to . 25	93	3¼ ounces drained _____	1. 00	25	100
	6- to 7-ounce can (6 ounces drained).	. 38 to . 44	100	{3 ounces drained _____ {2 ounces drained _____	2. 00 3. 00	12½ 8½	50 33½
	60- to 66½-ounce can (58 ounces drained).	3. 75 to 4. 16	97	{3 ounces drained _____ {2 ounces drained _____	19. 33 29. 00	1½ (¹)	5¼ 3½
FISH, DRIED							
Salt cod _____	Pound _____	1. 00	72	{3 ounces _____ {2 ounces _____	3. 84 5. 76	6¾ 4½	26¼ 17½
FISH, FRESH OR FROZEN							
Fillets _____	_____do_____	1. 00	64	{3 ounces _____ {2 ounces _____	3. 41 5. 12	7½ 5	29½ 19¾
Steaks (backbone in) _____	_____do_____	1. 00	²58	{3 ounces _____ {2 ounces _____	3. 09 4. 64	8¼ 5½	32½ 21¾
Dressed (scaled and eviscerated, usually head, tail, and fins removed).	_____do_____	1. 00	²45	{3 ounces _____ {2 ounces _____	2. 40 3. 60	10½ 7	41¾ 28
Drawn (entrails removed) _____	_____do_____	1. 00	²32	{3 ounces _____ {2 ounces _____	1. 71 2. 56	14¾ 10	58½ 39¼
Whole, or round (as caught) _____	_____do_____	1. 00	²27	{3 ounces _____ {2 ounces _____	1. 44 2. 16	17½ 11¾	69½ 46½

See footnotes at end of table.

Table 5.—FISH AND SHELLFISH—Cont.

Fish and shellfish as purchased	Unit of purchase	Weight per unit	Yield, as served	Portion as served	Portions per purchase unit	Approximate purchase units for— 25 portions	100 portions
FISH, FROZEN							
Portions:							
Breaded, fried or raw:		*Pounds*	*Percent*		*Number*	*Number*	*Number*
5⅓-ounce	Pound	1. 00	95	1 portion	3. 00	8½	33½
4-ounce	do	1. 00	95	do	4. 00	6¼	25
3-ounce	do	1. 00	95	do	5. 33	4¾	18¾
2-ounce	do	1. 00	95	do	8. 00	3¼	12½
Unbreaded:							
4-ounce	do	1. 00	69	do	4. 00	6¼	25
3-ounce	do	1. 00	69	do	5. 33	4¾	18¾
2-ounce	do	1. 00	68	do	8. 00	3¼	12½
Sticks, breaded, fried or raw, 1-ounce	do	1. 00	85	4 sticks	4. 00	6¼	25
				3 sticks	5. 33	4¾	18¾
				2 sticks	8. 00	3¼	12½
SHELLFISH, CANNED							
Clam chowder	8-ounce can, ready-to-serve.	. 50	100	8 ounces	1. 00	25	100
	10½-ounce can, condensed.	. 66	200	do	2. 62	9¾	38¼
	15-ounce can, condensed	. 94	200	do	3. 75	6¾	26¾
	50- to 51-ounce can, condensed.	3. 12 to 3. 19	200	do	12. 50	2	8
Clam juice	8-fluid-ounce can	----------	100	3 fluid ounces	2. 67	9½	37½
	12-fluid-ounce can	----------	100	do	4. 00	6¼	25
Clams, minced	7½-ounce can	. 47	100	3 ounces	2. 50	10	40
				2 ounces	3. 75	6¾	26¾
	51-ounce can	3. 19	100	3 ounces	17. 00	1½	6
				2 ounces	25. 50	1	4
Crabmeat	6½-ounce can (5½ ounces drained).	. 41	85	3 ounces drained	1. 83	13¾	54¾
				2 ounces drained	2. 75	9¼	36½
Oysters, whole	5-ounce can (5 ounces drained).	. 31	100	3 ounces drained	1. 67	15	60
				2 ounces drained	2. 50	10	40
Oyster stew	10½-ounce can, ready-to-serve.	. 66	100	8 ounces	1. 31	19¼	76½
Shrimp	4½-ounce can (4½ ounces drained).	. 28	100	3 ounces drained	1. 50	16¾	66¾
				2 ounces drained	2. 25	11¼	44½
SHELLFISH, FRESH, LIVE IN SHELL							
Clams:							
Hard	Dozen	----------	[2] 14	6 clams on half shell	2. 00	12½	50
Soft	do	----------	[2] 29	12 clams in the shell	1. 00	25	100
Crabs:							
Blue	Pound	1. 00	14	3 ounces cooked	. 75	33½	133½
				2 ounces cooked	1. 12	22½	89½
Dungeness	do	1. 00	24	3 ounces cooked	1. 28	19¾	78¼
				2 ounces cooked	1. 92	13¼	52¼

See footnotes at end of table.

Table 5.—FISH AND SHELLFISH—Cont.

Oysters	Dozen		²12	6 oysters on half shell	2.00	12½	50
SHELLFISH, FRESH OR FROZEN							
Clams, shucked	Pound	1.00	48	3 ounces meat	2.56	10	39¼
				2 ounces meat	3.82	6¾	26
Crabs, cooked in shell:							
Blue	do	1.00	14	3 ounces meat	.75	33½	133½
				2 ounces meat	1.12	22½	89½
Dungeness	do	1.00	24	3 ounces meat	1.28	19¾	78¼
				2 ounces meat	1.92	13¼	52¼
Crabmeat	do	1.00	97	3 ounces	5.17	5	19½
				2 ounces	7.76	3¼	13
Lobster, cooked in shell	do	1.00	²25	1 lobster	1.00	25	100
				½ lobster	2.00	12½	50
Lobster meat	do	1.00	91	3 ounces	4.85	5¼	20¾
				2 ounces	7.28	3½	13¾
Oysters, shucked	do	1.00	40	3 ounces	2.13	11¾	47
				2 ounces	3.20	8	31¼
Scallops, shucked	do	1.00	63	3 ounces	3.36	7½	30
				2 ounces	5.04	5	20
Shrimp:							
Cooked, peeled, cleaned	do	1.00	100	3 ounces	5.33	4¾	19
				2 ounces	8.00	3¼	12½
Raw, in shell	do	1.00	50	3 ounces meat	2.67	9½	37½
				2 ounces meat	4.00	6¼	25
Raw, peeled	do	1.00	62	3 ounces meat	3.30	7¾	30½
				2 ounces meat	4.96	5¼	20¼
SHELLFISH, FROZEN							
Clams, breaded:							
Fried	do	1.00	85	3 ounces	4.53	5¾	22¼
				2 ounces	6.80	3¾	14¾
Raw	do	1.00	83	3 ounces	4.43	5¾	22¾
				2 ounces	6.64	4	15¼
Crabcakes, fried	do	1.00	95	3 ounces	5.07	5	19¾
				2 ounces	7.60	3½	13¼
Lobster, spiny tails:							
8 ounce	do	1.00	²51	1 tail	2.00	12½	50
6 ounce	do	1.00	²51	do	2.67	9½	37½
4 ounce	do	1.00	²51	do	4.00	6¼	25
Oysters, breaded, raw	do	1.00	88	3 ounces	4.69	5½	21½
				2 ounces	7.04	3¾	14¼
Scallops, breaded:							
Fried	do	1.00	93	3 ounces	4.96	5¼	20¼
				2 ounces	7.44	3½	13½
Raw	do	1.00	81	3 ounces	4.32	6	23¼
				2 ounces	6.48	4	15½
Shrimp, breaded:							
Fried	do	1.00	88	3 ounces	4.69	5½	21½
				2 ounces	7.04	3¾	14¼
Raw	do	1.00	85	3 ounces	4.53	5¾	22¼
				2 ounces	6.80	3¾	14¾

¹ Number of purchase units needed is less than one.   ² Yield, edible portion.

Table 6.—EGGS

Eggs, in shell, frozen, and dried, as purchased	Unit of purchase	Weight per unit	Portion as served or used	Portions per purchase unit	Approximate purchase units for—	
					25 portions	100 portions
		Pounds		*Number*	*Number*	*Number*
In shell:						
Large	Dozen	1. 50	1 egg	12. 00	2¼	8½
	Case	45. 00	do	360. 00	(1)	(1)
Medium	Dozen	1. 31	do	12. 00	2¼	8½
	Case	39. 50	do	360. 00	(1)	(1)
Small	Dozen	1. 12	do	12. 00	2¼	8½
	Case	34. 00	do	360. 00	(1)	(1)
Frozen:						
Whole eggs	Pound	1. 00	1 egg (3 tablespoons thawed)	10. 00	(2)	(2)
			12 eggs (2¼ cups thawed)	. 83	(2)	(2)
	Can	10. 00	1 egg	100. 00	(2)	(2)
	do	30. 00	do	300. 00	(2)	(2)
Egg yolks	Pound	1. 00	1 yolk (1⅓ tablespoons thawed)	26. 00	(2)	(2)
			12 yolks (1 cup thawed)	2. 16	(2)	(2)
Egg whites	do	1. 00	1 white (2 tablespoons thawed)	16. 00	(2)	(2)
			12 whites (1½ cups thawed)	1. 33	(2)	(2)
Dried:						
Whole eggs	do	1. 00	1 large egg (½ ounce or 2½ tablespoons dried + 2½ tablespoons water).	32. 00	(2)	(2)
			12 large eggs (6 ounces or 2 cups dried + 2 cups water).	2. 67	(2)	(2)
	13-ounce package	. 81	1 large egg	26. 00	(2)	(2)
	No. 10 can	3. 00	do	96. 00	(2)	(2)
	Package	25. 00	do	800. 00	(2)	(2)
	do	50. 00	do	1, 600. 00	(2)	(2)
Egg yolks	Pound	1. 00	1 large yolk (2 tablespoons dried + 2 teaspoons water).	54. 00	(2)	(2)
			12 large yolks (1½ cups dried + ½ cup water)	4. 50	(2)	(2)
	Package	3. 00	1 large yolk	162. 00	(2)	(2)
Egg white, spray-dried	Pound	1. 00	1 large white (2 teaspoons dried + 2 tablespoons water).	100. 00	(2)	(2)
			12 large whites (½ cup dried + 1½ cups water)	8. 33	(2)	(2)
	Package	3. 00	1 large white	300. 00	(2)	(2)

[1] Number of purchase units needed is less than one.   [2] Number of purchase units needed is determined by use.

Table 7.—NUTS

Nuts in shell and peanut butter as purchased	Unit of purchase	Weight per unit	Yield, as served	Portion as used	Portions per purchase unit	Approximate purchase units for—	
						25 portions	100 portions
		Pounds	*Percent*		*Number*	*Number*	*Number*
Almonds;							
Nonpareil (softshell)	Pound	1.00	60	1 cup (0.31 pound)	1.94	(1)	(1)
Peerless (hardshell)	----do----	1.00	35	-----do-----	1.13	(1)	(1)
Brazil nuts	----do----	1.00	48	-----do-----	1.55	(1)	(1)
Cashew nuts	----do----	1.00	22	1 cup (0.30 pound)	.73	(1)	(1)
Chestnuts	----do----	1.00	84	8 large nuts (0.11 pound)	7.64	(1)	(1)
Coconut:							
Dried	----do----	1.00	100	1 cup (0.14 pound)	7.14	(1)	(1)
Fresh, in shell	----do----	1.00	52	1 cup (0.21 pound)	2.48	(1)	(1)
Filberts	----do----	1.00	39	1 cup (0.30 pound)	1.50	(1)	(1)
Peanuts, roasted	----do----	1.00	68	1 cup (0.32 pound)	2.12	(1)	(1)
Peanut butter	----do----	1.00	100	2 tablespoons (0.07 pound)	14.29	1¾	7
	No. 10 can	6.75	100	-----do-----	96.43	(2)	1¼
Pecans	Pound	1.00	52	1 cup halves (0.24 pound)	2.17	(1)	(1)
Walnuts:							
Black	----do----	1.00	22	1 cup (0.28 pound)	.79	(1)	(1)
English	----do----	1.00	45	1 cup (0.22 pound)	2.05	(1)	(1)

[1] Number of purchase units needed is determined by use.   [2] Number of purchase units needed is less than one.

Table 8.—DAIRY PRODUCTS

Dairy products as purchased	Unit of purchase	Weight per unit	Yield, as served	Portion as served or used	Portions per purchase unit	Approximate purchase units for—	
						25 portions	100 portions
		Pounds	*Percent*		*Number*	*Number*	*Number*
Cheese:							
Cheddar	Pound	1.00	100	4 ounces, grated, 1 cup	4.00	6¼	25
	do	1.00	100	2 ounces	8.00	3¼	12½
	do	1.00	100	1 ounce	16.00	1¾	6¼
	Longhorn	11 to 13	100	2 ounces	88–104	(1)	1¼
	Daisies	20 to 25	100	do	160–200	(1)	(1)
	Flats	32 to 37	100	do	256–296	(1)	(1)
	Cheddars	70 to 78	100	do	560–624	(1)	(1)
	Block	20	100	do	160.00	(1)	(1)
	do	40	100	do	320.00	(1)	(1)
Cottage, small or large curd, with pineapple or chive.	Pound	1.00	100	{4 ounces	4.00	6¼	25
				{2 ounces	8.00	3¼	12½
	32-ounce carton	2.00	100	4 ounces	8.00	3¼	12½
	Tin	30.00	100	do	120.00	(1)	(1)
Cream	8-ounce package	.50	100	1 ounce	8.00	3¼	12½
	12-ounce package	.75	100	do	12.00	2¼	8½
	16-ounce package	1.00	100	do	16.00	1¾	6¼
Processed, cheese food	Pound	1.00	100	{2 ounces	8.00	3¼	12½
				{1 ounce, 1 slice	16.00	1¾	6¼
	Package	2.00	100	2 ounces	16.00	1¾	6¼
	do	5.00	100	do	40.00	(1)	2½
Cream:							
Half and half	Pint	1.07	100	1½ tablespoons	21.33	1¼	4¾
	Quart	2.14	100	do	42.67	(1)	2½
Light	Pint	1.06	100	do	21.33	1¼	4¾
	Quart	2.13	100	do	42.67	(1)	2½
Sour	½ pint	.53	100	1 tablespoon	16.00	1¾	6¼
	¾ pint	.80	100	do	24.00	1¼	4¼
Whipping (volume doubles when whipped).	Pint	1.05	100	1¼ tablespoons	25.60	1	4
	Quart	2.10	100	do	51.20	(1)	2

See footnotes at end of table.

Table 8.—DAIRY PRODUCTS—Cont.

Ice cream:

Brick	Quart	1.25	100	1 slice (½ cup)	8.00	3¼	12½
				No. 12 scoop (sundae)	22–26	1	4
Bulk	Gallon	4.50	100	No. 16 scoop	31–35	(1)	3
				No. 20 scoop (a la mode)	38–42	(1)	2½
				No. 24 scoop	47–51	(1)	2
Cups	3-ounce	.19	100	1 cup	1.00	25	100
	5-ounce	.31	100	----do	1.00	25	100
				No. 12 scoop	25.00	1	4
Sherbet	Gallon	6.00	100	No. 16 scoop	35.00	(1)	3
				No. 20 scoop	42.00	(1)	2½
				No. 24 scoop	50.00	(1)	2

Milk:

Fluid [2]	Quart	2.15	100	1 cup	4.00	6¼	25
	Gallon	8.60	100	----do	16.00	1¼	6¼
	5-gallon	43.00	100	----do	80.00	(1)	1¼
Condensed	14-ounce can	.88	100	----do	1.24	(3)	(3)
	15-ounce can	.94	100	----do	1.33	(3)	(3)
Evaporated	14½-ounce can	.91	100	1 cup as is	1.67	(3)	(3)
		.91	200	1 cup reconstituted	3.33	(3)	(3)
	No. 10 can	8.00	100	1 cup as is	14.00	(3)	(3)
		8.00	200 (measure)	1 cup reconstituted	28.00	(3)	(3)

Dry:
Nonfat:

Instant	Pound (about 6½ cups)	1.00	100	1 cup as is	6.50	(3)	(3)
		1.00	267 (measure)	1 cup reconstituted	17.06	(3)	(3)
Regular (USDA)	Pound (about 3¼ cups)	1.00	100	1 cup as is	3.25	(3)	(3)
		1.00	533 (measure)	1 cup reconstituted	17.06	(3)	(3)
Whole	Pound (about 3½ cups)	1.00	100	1 cup as is	3.50	(3)	(3)
		1.00	400 (measure)	1 cup reconstituted	14.22	(3)	(3)

[1] Number of purchase units needed is less than one.
[2] Skim milk and buttermilk weigh slightly more than whole fluid milk.
[3] Number of purchase units needed is determined by use.

Table 9.—VEGETABLES—FRESH

Fresh vegetables as purchased	Unit of purchase	Weight per unit [1]	Yield, as served	Portion as served	Portions per purchase unit	Approximate purchase units for—	
						25 portions	100 portions
		Pounds	*Percent*		*Number*	*Number*	*Number*
Asparagus_____	Pound_____	1. 00	_____	4 medium spears, cooked_____	3. 38	7½	29¾
	-----do-----	1. 00	49	3 ounces cut spears, cooked_____	2. 61	9¾	38½
	Crate_____	28. 00	49	-----do-----	73. 17	(²)	1½
Beans, lima, green:							
In pod_____	Pound_____	1. 00	40	3 ounces cooked_____	2. 13	11¾	47
	Bushel_____	32. 00	40	-----do-----	68. 27	(²)	1½
Shelled_____	Pound_____	1. 00	102	-----do-----	5. 44	4¾	18½
Beans, snap, green or wax_____	-----do-----	1. 00	84	-----do-----	4. 48	5¾	22½
	Bushel_____	30. 00	84	-----do-----	134. 40	(²)	(²)
Beet greens, untrimmed_____	Pound_____	1. 00	44	-----do-----	2. 35	10¾	42¾
	Bushel_____	20. 00	44	-----do-----	46. 93	(²)	2¼
Beets:							
With tops_____	Pound_____	1. 00	43	3 ounces sliced or diced, cooked___	2. 29	11	43¾
Without tops_____	-----do-----	1. 00	76	-----do-----	4. 05	6¼	24¾
	Burlap bag_____	50. 00	76	-----do-----	202. 67	(²)	(²)
Blackeye peas, shelled_____	Pound_____	1. 00	93	3 ounces cooked_____	4. 96	5¼	20¼
Broccoli_____	-----do-----	1. 00	_____	2 medium spears, cooked_____	4. 57	5½	22
	-----do-----	1. 00	62	3 ounces cut spears, cooked_____	3. 31	7¾	30¼
	Crate_____	40. 00	62	-----do-----	132. 27	(²)	(²)
Brussels sprouts_____	Pound_____	1. 00	77	3 ounces cooked_____	4. 11	6¼	24½
Cabbage_____	Bulk_____	1. 00	79	2 ounces coleslaw_____	6. 32	4	16
	-----do-----	1. 00	75	3 ounces sliced, cooked_____	4. 00	6¼	25
	-----do-----	1. 00	80	3-ounce wedge, cooked_____	4. 27	6	23½
	Crate or sack_____	50. 00	80	-----do-----	213. 33	(²)	(²)
Cabbage, Chinese_____	Pound_____	1. 00	88	2 ounces raw_____	7. 04	3¾	14¼
Carrots, without tops_____	-----do-----	1. 00	82	2 ounces shredded or grated, strips or diced, raw.	6. 56	4	15¼
	-----do-----	1. 00	75	3 ounces sliced or diced, cooked___	4. 00	6¼	25
	Bushel_____	50. 00	75	-----do-----	200. 00	(²)	(²)
Cauliflower_____	Pound_____	1. 00	45	2 ounces sliced, raw_____	3. 60	7	28
	-----do-----	1. 00	44	3 ounces cooked_____	2. 35	10¾	42¾
	Crate_____	37. 00	44	-----do-----	86. 83	(²)	1¼
	Crate, large_____	50. 00	44	-----do-----	117. 33	(²)	(²)
Celery_____	Pound_____	1. 00	70	3 ounces chopped, cooked_____	3. 73	6¾	27
	-----do-----	1. 00	75	3 ounces sliced, raw_____	4. 00	6¼	25
	-----do-----	1. 00	75	2 ounces strips, raw_____	6. 00	4¼	16¾
	Crate_____	60. 00	75	3 ounces chopped, raw_____	240. 00	(²)	(²)
Celery hearts (24 pack)_____	Crate or box_____	30. 00	95	2 ounces strips, raw_____	228. 00	(²)	(²)
Chard, untrimmed_____	Pound_____	1. 00	56	3 ounces_____	2. 99	8½	33½
Collards_____	-----do-----	1. 00	81	3 ounces cooked_____	4. 32	6	23¼
	Bushel_____	20. 00	81	-----do-----	86. 40	(²)	1¼
Corn, in husks_____	Dozen_____	8. 00	37	3 ounces cooked kernels_____	15. 79	1¾	6½
	-----do-----	8. 00	_____	1 ear, cooked_____	12. 00	2¼	8½
	5-dozen crate or bag.	40. 00	_____	-----do-----	60. 00	(²)	1¾
Cucumber_____	Pound_____	1. 00	73	3 ounces sliced, peeled, raw_____	3. 89	6½	25¾
	-----do-----	1. 00	95	3 ounces sliced, unpeeled, raw_____	5. 07	5	19¾
	Bushel_____	48. 00	95	-----do-----	243. 20	(²)	(²)
Eggplant_____	Pound_____	1. 00	75	4 ounces cooked_____	3. 00	8½	33½
	Bushel_____	33. 00	75	-----do-----	100. 00	(²)	1

See footnotes at end of table.

Table 9.—VEGETABLES—FRESH—Cont.

Endive, escarole, chicory	Pound	1.00	75	1 ounce raw	12.00	2¼	8½
	Bushel	25.00	75	do	300.00	[2]	[2]
Kale, untrimmed	Pound	1.00	81	3 ounces cooked	4.32	6	23¼
	Bushel	18.00	81	do	77.76	[2]	1½
Kohlrabi	Pound	1.00	50	do	2.67	9½	37½
Lettuce:							
Head	do	1.00	74	2 ounces raw	5.92	4¼	17
Iceberg	Carton	2 doz. heads		⅙ head, raw	144.00	4¼ heads	17 heads
Romaine	Pound	1.00	64	1 ounce raw	10.24	2½	10
Mushrooms	do	1.00	67	1 ounce sliced, cooked	10.72	2½	9½
	Basket	3.00	67	3 ounces sliced, cooked	10.72	2½	9½
	do	9.00	67	do	32.16	[2]	3¼
Mustard greens	Pound	1.00	59	3 ounces cooked	3.15	8	31¾
	Bushel	20.00	59	do	62.93	[2]	1¾
Okra	Pound	1.00	96	do	5.12	5	19¾
	Bushel	30.00	96	do	153.60	[2]	[2]
Onions:							
Green, partly topped	Pound	1.00	60	3 ounces raw	3.20	8	31¼
	Wirebound crate	50.00	60	do	160.00	[2]	[2]
Mature	Pound	1.00	89	1 ounce chopped or grated, raw	14.24	2	7¼
	do	1.00	76	3 ounces small whole or pieces, cooked.	4.05	6¼	24¾
	Sack	50.00	76	do	202.67	[2]	[2]
Parsley	Pound	1.00		½ cup	16.00	[3]	[3]
	Crate	19.00		do	304.00	[3]	[3]
Parsnips	Pound	1.00	84	3 ounces cooked	4.48	5¾	22½
	Bushel	50.00	84	do	224.00	[2]	[2]
Peas, green:							
In pod	Pound	1.00	36	do	1.92	13¼	52¼
	Basket	15.00	36	do	28.80	[2]	3½
	Bushel	28.00	36	do	53.76	[2]	2
Shelled	Pound	1.00	96	do	5.12	5	19¾
Peppers, green	do	1.00	82	1 ounce diced or strips, raw	13.12	2	7¾
	Bushel	25.00	82	do	328.00	[2]	[2]
	Carton	30.00	82	do	393.60	[2]	[2]
	Pound	1.00	75	2 ounces strips, cooked	6.00	4¼	16¾
Potatoes:							
To be pared by hand	do	1.00		1 medium, boiled	3.00	8½	33½
	do	1.00	54	2 ounces french fried	4.32	6	23¼
	do	1.00	80	3 ounces cubed and diced, cooked	4.27	6	23½
	do	1.00	95	4 ounces mashed	3.80	6¾	26½
To be pared by machine	do	1.00		1 medium, boiled	3.00	8½	33½
	do	1.00	52	2 ounces french fried	4.16	6¼	24¼
	do	1.00	76	3 ounces cubed and diced, cooked	4.05	6¼	24¾
	do	1.00	90	4 ounces mashed	3.60	7	28
Ready-to-cook	do	1.00		1 medium, boiled	3.00	8½	33½
	do	1.00	68	2 ounces french fried	5.44	4¾	18½
	do	1.00	119	4 ounces mashed	4.76	5¼	21¼
To be cooked in jacket	do	1.00		1 medium, baked in jacket	3.00	8½	33½
	do	1.00		1 medium, boiled	3.00	8½	33½
	do	1.00	87	3 ounces cubed and diced	4.64	5½	21¾
	do	1.00	104	4 ounces mashed	4.16	6¼	24¼

See footnotes at end of table.

Table 9.—VEGETABLES—FRESH—Cont.

Fresh vegetables as purchased	Unit of purchase	Weight per unit [1]	Yield, as served	Portion as served	Portions per purchase unit	Approximate purchase units for—	
						25 portions	100 portions
		Pounds	*Percent*		*Number*	*Number*	*Number*
Pumpkin	Pound	1.00	63	4 ounces mashed, cooked	2.52	10	39¾
Radishes:							
With tops	do	1.00	63	1 ounce sliced, raw	10.08	2½	10
	do	1.00		4 small	11.34	2¼	9
Without tops	do	1.00	90	1 ounce sliced, raw	14.40	1¾	7
Rutabagas	do	1.00	79	3 ounces cubed, cooked	4.21	6	24
	do	1.00	77	4 ounces mashed	3.08	8¼	32½
	Bushel	56.00	77	do	172.48	(²)	(²)
Spinach:							
Partly trimmed	Pound	1.00	92	1 ounce raw for salad	14.72	1¾	7
Untrimmed	do	1.00	72	do	11.52	2¼	8¾
	do	1.00	67	3 ounces cooked	3.57	7¼	28¼
	Bushel	20.00	67	do	71.47	(²)	1½
Squash, summer	Pound	1.00	83	3 ounces diced or sliced, cooked	4.43	5¾	22¾
	Bushel	35.00	83	do	154.93	(²)	(²)
	Pound	1.00	83	4 ounces mashed	3.32	7¾	30¼
Squash, winter:							
Acorn	do	1.00		½ medium, baked	2.00	12½	50
Hubbard	do	1.00	58	4 ounces cubed, cooked	2.32	11	43¼
	do	1.00	57	4 ounces mashed	2.28	11	44
Sweetpotatoes	do	1.00		1 medium, cooked in jacket	2.00	12½	50
	do	1.00	83	3 ounces sliced	4.43	5¾	22¾
	do	1.00	81	4 ounces mashed	3.24	7¾	31
	Bushel	50.00		1 medium, cooked in jacket	100.00	(²)	1
Tomatoes (medium)	Pound	1.00	91	2 slices	7.50	3½	13½
	do	1.00		1 wedge	12.00	2¼	8½
	Lug	32.00		do	384.00	(²)	(²)
	Bushel	53.00		do	636.00	(²)	(²)
Turnip greens, untrimmed	Pound	1.00	48	3 ounces cooked	2.56	10	39¼
	Bushel	20.00	48	do	51.20	(²)	(²)
Turnips, without tops	Pound	1.00	74	3 ounces cubed, cooked	3.95	6½	25½
	do	1.00	73	4 ounces mashed	2.92	8¾	34¼
	Bushel	50.00	73	do	146.00	(²)	(²)
Watercress	Bunch	1.00	92	½ cup	27.77	(³)	(³)

[1] Legal weights for contents of bushels, lugs, crates, and boxes vary among States.

² Number of purchase units needed is less than one.

³ Number of purchase units needed is determined by use.

Table 10.–VEGETABLES–CANNED

Canned vegetables as purchased	Unit of purchase	Weight per unit	Yield, as served	Portion as served	Portions per purchase unit	Approximate purchase units for— 25 portions	100 portions
		Pounds	*Percent*		*Number*	*Number*	*Number*
Asparagus:							
Cuts and tips	No. 300 can	0.88	61	3 ounces	2.86	8¾	35
	No. 10 can	6.31	60	do	20.19	1¼	5
Spears	No. 300 can	.91		6 medium	2.57	9¾	39
	No. 10 can	6.44		do	18.53	1½	5½
Beans, lima, green	No. 303 can	1.00	69	3 ounces	3.68	7	27¼
	No. 10 can	6.56	69	do	24.14	1¼	4¼
Beans, snap, green or wax	No. 303 can	.97	59	do	3.05	8¼	33
	No. 2½ can	1.75	59	do	5.51	4¾	18¼
	No. 10 can	6.31	62	do	20.87	1¼	5
Beans, dry—kidney, lima, or navy	No. 303 can	1.00	80	6 ounces	2.13	11¾	47
	No. 10 can	6.75	80	do	14.40	1¾	6¾
Bean sprouts	do	6.62	52	3 ounces	18.37	1½	5½
Beets:							
Diced	No. 303 can	1.00	66	do	3.52	7¼	28½
	No. 10 can	6.50	69	do	23.92	1¼	4¼
Sliced	No. 303 can	1.00	61	do	3.25	7¾	31
	No. 10 can	6.50	65	do	22.53	1¼	4½
Whole baby beets	No. 303 can	1.00	62	do	3.31	7¾	30¼
	No. 10 can	6.50	66	do	22.88	1¼	4½
Carrots:							
Diced	No. 303 can	1.00	62	do	3.31	7¾	30¼
	No. 10 can	6.50	69	do	23.92	1¼	4¼
Sliced	No. 303 can	1.00	62	do	3.31	7¾	30¼
	No. 10 can	6.50	66	do	22.88	1¼	4½
Chop suey vegetables	do	6.38	100	do	34.00	(1)	3
Collards	No. 303 can	.94	72	4 ounces	2.71	9¼	37
	No. 2½ can	1.69	70	do	4.73	5½	21¼
	No. 10 can	6.12	61	do	14.93	1¾	6¾
Corn:							
Cream style	No. 303 can	1.00	100	do	4.00	6¼	25
	No. 10 can	6.62	100	do	26.48	1	4
Whole kernel	No. 303 can	1.00	66	3 ounces	3.52	7¼	28½
	No. 10 can	6.62	66	do	23.30	1¼	4½
Kale	No. 303 can	.94	72	4 ounces	2.71	9¼	37
	No. 2½ can	1.69	70	do	4.73	5½	21¼
	No. 10 can	6.12	61	do	14.93	1¾	6¾
Mushrooms	No. 8 Z	.78	64	3 ounces	2.66	9½	37¾
	No. 10 can	6.44	66	do	22.67	1¼	4½
Mustard greens	No. 303 can	.94	72	4 ounces	2.71	9¼	37
	No. 2½ can	1.69	70	do	4.73	5½	21¼
	No. 10 can	6.12	61	do	14.93	1¾	6¾
Okra	No. 303 can	.97	68	3 ounces	3.51	7¼	28½
	No. 10 can	6.19	61	do	20.14	1¼	5
Okra and tomatoes	No. 303 can	.94	100	do	5.01	5	20
	No. 10 can	6.31	100	do	33.65	(1)	3

See footnotes at end of table.

Table 10.—VEGETABLES—CANNED—Cont.

Canned vegetables as purchased	Unit of purchase	Weight per unit	Yield, as served	Portion as served	Portions per purchase unit	Approximate purchase units for—	
						25 portions	100 portions
		Pounds	*Percent*		*Number*	*Number*	*Number*
Olives, large:							
Ripe:							
Pitted	No. 1 tall	² 0. 47		2 olives	21. 33	1¼	4¾
Whole	do	². 56		do	25. 60	1	4
	No. 10	² 4. 12		do	187. 69	(¹)	(¹)
Green, whole	Gallon	² 5. 50		do	250. 25	(¹)	(¹)
Onions, small, whole	No. 303 can	1. 00	56	3 ounces	2. 99	8½	33½
	No. 10 can	6. 31	59	do	19. 86	1½	5¼
Peas, green	No. 303 can	1. 00	64	do	3. 41	7½	29½
	No. 10 can	6. 56	64	do	22. 39	1¼	4½
Peas and carrots	No. 303 can	1. 00	69	do	3. 68	7	27¼
	No. 10 can	6. 56	69	do	24. 14	1¼	4¼
Pickles:							
Dill or sour:							
Sliced or cut	Quart jar	² 1. 38	100	1 ounce	22. 00	1¼	4¾
	No. 10 jar	² 4. 50	100	do	72. 00	(¹)	1½
	Gallon jar	² 5. 62	100	do	90. 00	(¹)	1¼
Whole	No. 2½ jar	² 1. 19	100	do	19. 00	1½	5½
	Quart jar	² 1. 31	100	do	21. 00	1¼	5
Sweet:							
Sliced or cut	do	² 1. 50	100	do	24. 00	1¼	4¼
	No. 10 jar	² 4. 88	100	do	78. 00	(¹)	1½
	Gallon jar	² 5. 94	100	do	95. 00	(¹)	1¼
Whole	No. 2½ jar	² 1. 28	100	do	20. 50	1¼	5
	Quart jar	² 1. 38	100	do	22. 00	1¼	4¾
Pickle relish:							
Sour	Quart	² 1. 61	100	do	25. 75	1	4
	No. 10 jar	² 5. 73	100	do	91. 75	(¹)	1¼
	Gallon jar	² 7. 16	100	do	114. 50	(¹)	(¹)
Sweet	Quart	² 1. 75	100	do	28. 00	1	3¾
	No. 10 jar	² 6. 25	100	do	100. 00	(¹)	1
	Gallon jar	² 7. 81	100	do	125. 00	(¹)	(¹)
Pimientos, chopped	No. 2½ can	1. 75	73	½ cup	4. 80	(³)	(³)
	No. 10 can	6. 81	68	do	17. 39	(³)	(³)
Potatoes, small whole	No. 2 can	1. 25		2–3	4. 00	6¼	25
	No. 10 can	6. 38		2–3	25. 00	1	4
Pumpkin, mashed	No. 300 can	. 91	100	4 ounces	3. 64	7	27½
	No. 2½ can	1. 81	100	do	7. 24	3½	14
	No. 10 can	6. 62	100	do	26. 50	1	4
Sauerkraut	No. 303 can	1. 00	82	3 ounces	4. 37	5¾	23
	No. 2½ can	1. 69	85	do	7. 66	3½	13¼
	No. 10 can	6. 19	81	do	26. 74	1	3¾

See footnotes at end of table.

Table 10.—VEGETABLES—CANNED—Cont.

Soups:							
Condensed	No. 1 picnic	.66 to .75	200	1 cup diluted	2.50	10	40
	No. 3 cylinder	3.12	200	-----do-----	11.50	2¼	8¾
Ready-to-serve	12-fluid-ounce can	-----	100	1 cup	1.50	16¾	66¾
	25-fluid-ounce can (No. 2½)	-----	100	-----do-----	3.12	8¼	32¼
Spinach	No. 303 can	.94	72	4 ounces	2.71	9¼	37
	No. 2½ can	1.69	70	-----do-----	4.73	5½	21¼
	No. 10 can	6.12	61	-----do-----	14.93	1¾	6¾
Squash, summer	No. 303 can	1.00	69	-----do-----	2.75	9¼	36½
	No. 10 can	6.62	69	-----do-----	17.50	1½	5¾
Squash, winter	No. 300 can	.91	100	-----do-----	3.64	7	27½
	No. 2½ can	1.81	100	-----do-----	7.24	3½	14
	No. 10 can	6.62	100	-----do-----	26.48	1	4
Succotash	No. 303 can	1.00	65	3 ounces	3.47	7¼	29
	No. 10 can	6.75	65	-----do-----	23.40	1¼	4½
Sweetpotatoes	No. 3 vacuum or squat	1.44	65	4 ounces	3.74	6¾	26¾
	No. 2½ can, with sirup	1.81	66	-----do-----	4.78	5¼	21
	No. 10 can, with sirup	6.38	71	-----do-----	18.00	1½	5¾
Tomatoes	No. 303 can	1.00	100	-----do-----	4.00	6¼	25
	No. 2½ can	1.75	100	-----do-----	7.00	3¾	14½
	No. 10 can	6.38	100	-----do-----	25.52	1	4
Tomato products:							
Catsup	14-ounce bottle	.88	100	1 ounce	14.00	2	7¼
	No. 10 can	6.94	100	-----do-----	111.00	(1)	1
Chili sauce	12-ounce jar	.75	100	1 tablespoon	20.27	1¼	5
	No. 10 can	6.56	100	-----do-----	177.30	(1)	(1)
Juice, concentrate [4]	6-fluid-ounce can	.43	400	4 fluid ounces	6.00	4¼	16¾
Turnip greens	No. 303 can	.94	72	4 ounces	2.71	9¼	37
	No. 2½ can	1.69	70	-----do-----	4.73	5½	21¼
	No. 10 can	6.12	61	-----do-----	14.93	1¾	6¾
Vegetable juices	23-fluid-ounce can	1.54	100	4 fluid ounces	5.75	4½	17½
	46-fluid-ounce can	3.07	100	-----do-----	11.50	2¼	8¾
	96-fluid-ounce can	6.41	100	-----do-----	24.00	1¼	4¼
Vegetables, mixed	No. 303 can	1.00	68	3 ounces	3.63	7	27¾
	No. 10 can	6.50	68	-----do-----	23.57	1¼	4¼

[1] Number of purchase units needed is less than one.
[2] Drained weight.
[3] Number of purchase units needed is determined by use.
[4] See vegetable juices for canned tomato juice.

Table 11.—VEGETABLES—FROZEN

Frozen vegetables as purchased	Unit of purchase	Weight per unit	Yield, as served	Portion as served	Portions per purchase unit	Approximate purchase units for—	
						25 portions	100 portions
		Pounds	*Percent*		*Number*	*Number*	*Number*
Asparagus:							
Spears	Pound	1.00		4 medium, cooked	3.38	7½	29¾
	Package	2.50		do	8.44	3	12
Cuts and tips	Pound	1.00	80	3 ounces cooked	4.27	6	23½
	Package	2.50	80	do	10.67	2½	9½
Beans, butter (lima)	Pound	1.00	100	do	5.33	4¾	19
	Package	2.50	100	do	13.33	2	7½
	do	3.00	100	do	16.00	1¾	6¼
Beans, lima, green	Pound	1.00	100	do	5.33	4¾	19
	Package	2.50	100	do	13.33	2	7½
Beans, snap, green or wax	Pound	1.00	91	do	4.85	5¼	20¾
	Package	2.50	91	do	12.13	2¼	8¼
Blackeye peas	Pound	1.00	111	do	5.92	4¼	17
	Package	2.50	111	do	14.80	1¾	7
	do	3.00	111	do	17.76	1½	5¾
Broccoli:							
Spears	Pound	1.00		2 medium	4.57	5½	22
	Package	2.50	85	do	11.43	2¼	8¾
Cut or chopped	Pound	1.00	85	3 ounces cooked	4.53	5¾	22¼
	Package	2.50	85	do	11.33	2¼	9
Brussel sprouts	Pound	1.00	96	do	5.12	5	19¾
	Package	2.50	96	do	12.80	2	8
Carrots, sliced or diced	Pound	1.00	96	do	5.12	5	19¾
	Package	2.50	96	do	12.80	2	8
Cauliflower	Pound	1.00	90	do	4.80	5¼	21
	Package	2.50	90	do	12.00	2¼	8½
Collards	Pound	1.00	89	do	4.75	5½	21¼
	Package	2.50	89	do	11.87	2¼	8½
Corn:							
On cob	Pound (about three 5-inch ears).	1.00		1 ear, cooked	3.00	8½	33½
Whole kernel	Pound	1.00	97	3 ounces cooked	5.17	5	19½
	Package	2.50	97	do	12.93	2	7¾
Kale	Pound	1.00	77	do	4.11	6¼	24½
	Package	2.50	77	do	10.27	2½	9¾
	do	3.00	77	do	12.32	2¼	8¼

See footnotes at end of table.

Table 11.—VEGETABLES—FROZEN—Cont.

Mustard greens, leaf or chopped	Pound	1.00	80	----do	4.27	6	23½
	Package	2.50	80	----do	10.67	2½	9½
	----do	3.00	80	----do	12.80	2	8
Okra, whole	Pound	1.00	82	----do	4.37	5¾	23
	Package	2.50	82	----do	10.93	2½	9¼
	----do	3.00	82	----do	13.12	2	7¾
Peas, green	Pound	1.00	96	----do	5.12	5	19¾
	Package	2.50	96	----do	12.80	2	8
	----do	3.00	96	----do	15.36	1¾	6¾
Peas and carrots	Pound	1.00	98	----do	5.23	5	19¼
	Package	2.50	98	----do	13.07	2	7¾
Peppers, green:							
Whole	----do	1.00		½ pepper, cooked	12.00	2¼	8½
	----do	2.50		----do	30.00	(1)	3½
Diced or sliced	Pound	1.00	97	1 ounce cooked	15.52	1¾	6½
	Package	2.50	97	----do	38.80	(1)	2¾
Potatoes:							
French fried	----do	1.00		10 pieces	8.00	3¼	12½
	----do	5.00		----do	40.00	(1)	2½
Small whole	Container	5.00		3 cooked	16.67	1½	6
Spinach	Pound	1.00	80	3 ounces cooked	4.27	6	23½
	Package	2.50	80	----do	10.67	2½	9½
	----do	3.00	80	----do	12.80	2	8
Squash, summer, sliced	Pound	1.00	87	----do	4.64	5½	21¾
	Package	2.50	87	----do	11.60	2¼	8¾
	----do	3.00	87	----do	13.92	2	7¼
Squash, winter, mashed	Pound	1.00	92	4 ounces cooked	3.68	7	27¼
	Package	2.50	92	----do	9.20	2¾	11
Sweetpotatoes:							
Whole	Pound	1.00		1 whole, cooked	2.63	9¾	38¼
Sliced	----do	1.00	98	4 ounces cooked	3.92	6½	25¾
	Package	2.50	98	----do	9.80	2¾	10¼
	----do	3.00	98	----do	11.76	2¼	8¾
Succotash	Pound	1.00	106	3 ounces cooked	5.65	4½	17¾
	Package	2.50	106	----do	14.13	2	7¼
Turnip greens, leaf or chopped	Pound	1.00	80	----do	4.27	6	23½
	Package	2.50	80	----do	10.67	2½	9½
	----do	3.00	80	----do	12.80	2	8
Turnip greens with turnips	Pound	1.00	89	----do	4.75	5½	21¼
	Package	3.00	89	----do	14.24	2	7¼
Vegetables, mixed	Pound	1.00	95	----do	5.07	5	19¾
	Package	2.50	95	----do	12.67	2	8

[1] Number of purchase units needed is less than one.

Table 12.—VEGETABLES—DRIED

Vegetables, dried, regular and low-moisture, as purchased	Unit of purchase	Weight per unit	Yield, as served	Portion as served	Portions per purchase unit	Approximate purchase units for—	
						25 portions	100 portions
REGULAR		*Pounds*	*Percent*		*Number*	*Number*	*Number*
Beans (includes white beans, lima beans, kidney beans, blackeye beans or peas).	Pound_ _ _ _ _ _ _ _ _ _	1.00	232	3 ounces cooked_ _ _ _ _ _ _	12.37	2¼	8¼
Peas (includes any type, whole peas, split peas, or lentils).	_ _ _ _ _do_ _ _ _ _ _ _ _	1.00	223	_ _ _ _ _do_ _ _ _ _ _ _ _	11.89	2¼	8½
	Bushel_ _ _ _ _ _ _ _ _ _	60.00	223	_ _ _ _ _do_ _ _ _ _ _ _ _	713.60	(¹)	(¹)
LOW-MOISTURE							
Onions, sliced_ _ _ _ _ _ _ _ _ _ _ _ _ _ _ _	Pound_ _ _ _ _ _ _ _ _ _	1.00	417	_ _ _ _ _do_ _ _ _ _ _ _ _	22.24	1¼	4½
Potatoes, white:							
Flakes_ _ _ _ _ _ _ _ _ _ _ _ _ _ _ _ _ _ _	_ _ _ _ _do_ _ _ _ _ _ _ _	1.00	521	4 ounces cooked_ _ _ _ _ _ _	20.84	1¼	5
	Package_ _ _ _ _ _ _ _	2.50	521	_ _ _ _ _do_ _ _ _ _ _ _ _	52.10	(¹)	2
Granules_ _ _ _ _ _ _ _ _ _ _ _ _ _ _ _	Pound_ _ _ _ _ _ _ _ _ _	1.00	506	_ _ _ _ _do_ _ _ _ _ _ _ _	20.24	1¼	5
	Package_ _ _ _ _ _ _ _	2.50	506	_ _ _ _ _do_ _ _ _ _ _ _ _	50.60	(¹)	2
Sweetpotatoes, flakes_ _ _ _ _ _ _ _ _ _ _ _ _	Pound_ _ _ _ _ _ _ _ _ _	1.00	294	_ _ _ _ _do_ _ _ _ _ _ _ _	11.76	2¼	8¾

¹ Number of purchase units needed is less than one.

Table 13.—FRUITS—FRESH

Fresh fruits as purchased	Unit of purchase	Weight per unit [1]	Yield, as served	Portion as served	Portions per purchase unit	Approximate purchase units for— 25 portions	Approximate purchase units for— 100 portions
		Pounds	*Percent*		*Number*	*Number*	*Number*
Apples	Pound	1.00		1 medium, baked or raw	3.00	8½	33½
	Bushel	40.00		do	120.00	(2)	(2)
	Pound	1.00	76	2 ounces raw, chopped or diced	6.08	4¼	16½
	do	1.00	87	4 ounces applesauce	3.48	7¼	28¾
	do	1.00	63	4 ounces cooked, sliced or diced	2.52	10	39¾
	do	1.00		⅙ 9-inch pie (2.12 pounds of apples per pie).	2.83	9	35½
	do	1.00		⅛ 9-inch pie	3.77	6¾	26¾
Apricots	do	1.00		2 medium	6.00	4¼	16¾
	Lug	24.00		do	144.00	(2)	(2)
Avocados	Pound	1.00	75	2 ounces sliced, diced, or wedges	6.00	4¼	16¾
	Lug	12.00	75	do	72.00	(2)	1½
	Box (⅘ bushel)	36.00	75	do	216.00	(2)	(2)
Bananas	Pound	1.00		1 medium	3.00	8½	33½
	Box	25.00		do	75.00	(2)	1½
	Pound	1.00	68	2 ounces sliced for fruit cup	5.44	4¾	18½
	do	1.00	68	3 ounces sliced for dessert	3.63	7	27¾
	do	1.00	68	4 ounces mashed	2.72	9¼	37
Blackberries	Quart	1.42	95	1 ounce salad garnish	21.53	1¼	4¾
	do	1.42	95	3 ounces	7.18	3½	14
	Crate (24 quarts)	34.00	95	do	172.22	(2)	(2)
	Quart	1.42		⅙ 9-inch pie (0.92 quart per pie)	6.54	4	15½
	do	1.42		⅛ 9-inch pie	8.70	3	11½
Blueberries	do	1.97	92	1 ounce salad garnish	28.98	(2)	3½
	do	1.97	92	3 ounces	9.66	2¾	10½
	Crate (24 quarts)	47.25	92	do	231.84	(2)	(2)
	Quart	1.97		⅙ 9-inch pie (0.59 quart per pie)	10.20	2½	10
	do	1.97		⅛ 9-inch pie	13.51	2	7½
Cantaloup	Pound	1.00	50	3 ounces sliced or diced	2.67	9½	37½
	1 (No. 36 size)	2.50		½ medium	2.00	12½	50
	Crate (No. 36)	80.00		do	64.00	(2)	1¾
Cherries	Pound	1.00	89	3 ounces pitted, raw	4.75	5½	21¼
	Lug	16.00	89	do	75.95	(2)	1½
	Pound	1.00		⅙ 9-inch pie (1.60 pounds per pie)	3.75	6¾	26¾
	do	1.00		⅛ 9-inch pie	5.00	5	20
Cranberries	do	1.00	96	1 ounce raw, chopped, for relish	15.36	1¾	6¾
	do	1.00	182	2 ounces sauce, strained	14.56	1¾	7
	do	1.00	239	2 ounces cooked, whole	19.12	1½	5¼
	Box	25.00	239	do	478.00	(2)	(2)
Figs	Pound	1.00		3 medium	4.00	6¼	25
	Box	6.00		do	24.00	1¼	4¼

See footnotes at end of table.

Table 13.–FRUITS–FRESH–Cont.

Fresh fruits as purchased	Unit of purchase	Weight per unit [1]	Yield, as served	Portion as served	Portions per purchase unit	Approximate purchase units for— 25 portions	100 portions
		Pounds	*Percent*		*Number*	*Number*	*Number*
Grapefruit	Pound	1.00	44	4 fluid ounces juice	1.61	15¾	62¼
	Dozen (No. 64 size)	15.00	44	do	24.22	1¼	4¼
	Pound	1.00	47	4 ounces segments	1.88	13½	53¼
	Dozen	15.00	47	do	28.20	([2])	3¾
	do	15.00		½ medium	24.00	1¼	4¼
Grapefruit segments	½-gallon jar	4.22	100	4 ounces	16.88	1½	6
Grapes:							
With seeds	Pound	1.00	89	4 ounces, seeds removed	3.56	7¼	28¼
Seedless	do	1.00	94	4 ounces	3.76	6¾	26¾
	Lug	24.00	94	do	90.24	([2])	1¼
Honeydew melon	Pound	1.00	60	3 ounces sliced or diced	3.20	8	31¼
	1 melon	4.00		Wedge, ⅛ melon	8.00	3¼	12½
	do	4.00	60	3 ounces sliced or diced	12.80	2	8
Lemons	1 lemon (medium)	.23		1 slice	8.00	3¼	12½
	do	.23		1 wedge	6.00	4¼	16¾
	Pound (about 4 lemons)	1.00	43	2 fluid ounces juice	3.16	8	31¾
	Carton	36.00	43	do	113.76	([2])	([2])
Limes	1 lime (medium)	.15		Wedge, ¼ lime	4.00	6¼	25
	Pound	1.00	48	2 fluid ounces juice	3.52	7¼	28½
	Box (⅘ bushel)	40.00	48	do	140.80	([2])	([2])
Mangoes	Pound	1.00	67	3 ounces sliced or diced	3.57	7¼	28¼
	Lug	24.00	67	do	85.76	([2])	1¼
Oranges	Pound	1.00	50	4 fluid ounces juice	1.83	13¾	54¾
	do	1.00	56	4 ounces sections (no membrane)	2.24	11¼	44¾
	do	1.00	70	4 ounces sections (with membrane)	2.80	9	35¾
California	Carton	38.00	70	do	106.40	([2])	([2])
Florida	Box	85.00	50	4 fluid ounces juice	155.55	([2])	([2])
Medium No. 176	Pound	1.00		1 whole	2.00	12½	50
	Dozen	6.00	50	4 fluid ounces juice	11.01	2½	9¼
	do	6.00	56	4 ounces sections (no membrane)	13.44	2	7½
Small No. 250	Pound	1.00		1 whole	3.00	8½	33½
	Dozen	4.00	50	4 fluid ounces juice	7.34	3½	13¾
	do	4.00	56	4 ounces sections (no membrane)	8.96	3	11¼
Orange segments	½-gallon jar	4.28	100	4 ounces	17.12	1½	6
Peaches	Pound	1.00		1 medium	4.00	6¼	25
	do	1.00	76	3 ounces sliced or diced	4.05	6¼	24¾
	Bushel	48.00	76	do	194.56	([2])	([2])
	Pound	1.00		⅙ 9-inch pie (1.88 pound per pie)	3.19	8	31½
	do	1.00		⅛ 9-inch pie	4.26	6	23½
Pears	do	1.00		1 medium	3.00	8½	33½
	do	1.00	78	3 ounces sliced or diced	4.16	6¼	24¼
	Bushel	46.00	78	do	191.36	([2])	([2])

See footnotes at end of table.

Table 13.—FRUITS—FRESH—Cont.

Pineapples	Pound	1.00	52	3 ounces cubed	2.77	9¼	36¼
	½ crate	35.00	52	do	97.07	(2)	1¼
Pineapple chunks	½-gallon jar	4.36	100	4 ounces	17.44	1½	5¾
Plums	Pound	1.00		3 medium	2.67	9½	37½
	do	1.00	94	3 ounces halves pitted	5.01	5	20
	4-basket crate	28.00	94	do	140.37	(2)	(2)
Raspberries	Quart	1.47	97	1 ounce salad garnish	22.87	1¼	4½
	do	1.47	97	3 ounces	7.62	3½	13¼
	Crate (24 quarts)	35.00	97	do	181.07	(2)	(2)
	Quart	1.46		⅙ 9-inch pie (0.68 quart per pie)	8.85	3	11½
	do	1.46		⅛ 9-inch pie	11.76	2¼	8¾
Rhubarb, trimmed	Pound	1.00	103	3 ounces cooked	5.49	4¾	18¼
	do	1.00		⅙ 9-inch pie (1.44 pounds per pie)	4.17	6	24
	do	1.00		⅛ 9-inch pie	5.56	4½	18
Strawberries	Quart	1.48	87	1 ounce salad garnish	20.53	1¼	5
	do	1.48	87	3 ounces	6.84	3¾	14¾
	Crate (24 quarts)	35.00	87	do	162.40	(2)	(2)
	Quart	1.46		⅙ 9-inch pie (1 quart per pie)	6.00	4¼	16¾
	do	1.46		⅛ 9-inch pie	8.00	3¼	12½
Tangerines	Pound	1.00		1 medium	4.00	6¼	25
	Box	45.00		do	180.00	(2)	(2)
	Pound	1.00	74	3 ounces sections	3.95	6½	25½
Watermelon	do	1.00	46	3 ounces	2.45	10¼	41
	1 melon	18 to 30		1/16 melon	16.00	1¾	6¼

[1] Legal weights for contents of bushels, lugs, crates, and boxes vary among States.

[2] Number of purchase units needed is less than one.

Table 14.—FRUITS—CANNED

Canned fruits as purchased	Unit of purchase	Weight per unit	Yield, as served	Portion as served	Portions per purchase unit	Approximate purchase units for— 25 portions	100 portions
		Pounds	*Percent*		*Number*	*Number*	*Number*
Apples, solid pack	No. 2 can	1.12	100	4 ounces	4.48	5¾	22½
	No. 2½ can	1.62	100	do	6.48	4	15½
	No. 10 can	6.00	100	4 ounces	24.00	1¼	4¼
				⅙ 9-inch pie	24.00	1¼	4¼
Apple juice	23-fluid-ounce can	1.57	100	4 fluid ounces	5.75	4½	17½
	46-fluid-ounce can	3.14	100	do	11.50	2¼	8¾
	96-fluid-ounce can	6.56	100	do	24.00	1¼	4¼
Applesauce	No. 303 can	1.00	100	4 ounces	4.00	6¼	25
	No. 2½ can	1.81	100	do	7.24	3½	14
	No. 10 can	6.75	100	do	27.00	1	3¾
Apricots, halves	No. 303 can	1.00		3–5 medium	4.00	6¼	25
	No. 2½ can	1.88		do	7.00	3¾	14½
	No. 10 can	6.62		do	25.00	1	4
Blackberries	No. 303 can	1.00	100	4 ounces	4.00	6¼	25
	No. 10 can	6.62	100	do	26.48	1	4
Blueberries	No. 300 can	.91	100	do	3.64	7	27½
	No. 10 can	6.56	100	do	26.24	1	4
Boysenberries	No. 303 can	.94	100	do	3.76	6¾	26¾
	No. 10 can	6.62	100	do	26.48	1	4
Cherries:							
Red, sour, pitted	No. 303 can	1.00	100	do	4.00	6¼	25
	No. 10 can	6.56	100	4 ounces	26.24	1	4
				⅙ 9-inch pie	24.00	1¼	4¼
Sweet	No. 303 can	1.00	100	4 ounces	4.00	6¼	25
	No. 2½ can	1.81	100	do	7.24	3½	14
	No. 10 can	6.75	100	do	27.00	1	3¾
Cranberries, strained or whole	No. 300 can	1.00	100	2 ounces	8.00	3¼	12½
	No. 10 can	7.31	100	do	58.50	[1]	1¾
Cranberry juice	1 pint	1.11	100	4 fluid ounces	4.00	6¼	25
	1 quart	2.23	100	do	8.00	3¼	12½
	1 gallon	8.92	100	do	32.00	[1]	3¼
Figs	No. 303 can	1.06		3–4 figs	4.00	6¼	25
	No. 2½ can	1.88		do	7.00	3¾	14½
	No. 10 can	7.00		do	25.00	1	4

See footnotes at end of table.

Table 14.—FRUITS—CANNED—Cont.

Food	Purchase unit			Size of serving			
Fruit cocktail or salad	No. 303 can	1.06	100	4 ounces	4.24	6	23¾
	No. 2½ can	1.88	100	----do	7.52	3½	13½
	No. 10 can	6.75	100	----do	27.00	1	3¾
Grapefruit juice	18-fluid-ounce can	1.24	100	4 fluid ounces	4.50	5¾	22¼
	46-fluid-ounce can	3.14	100	----do	11.50	2¼	8¾
	96-fluid-ounce can	6.57	100	----do	24.00	1¼	4¼
Grapefruit sections	No. 303 can	1.00	100	4 ounces	4.00	6¼	25
	No. 3 cylinder	3.12	100	----do	12.48	2¼	8¼
Lemon juice	32 fluid-ounce can	2.16	100	2 fluid ounces	16.00	1¾	6¼
Lime juice	----do	2.17	100	----do	16.00	1¾	6¼
Orange juice	18-fluid-ounce can	1.24	100	4 fluid ounces	4.50	5¾	22¼
	46-fluid-ounce can	3.16	100	----do	11.50	2¼	8¾
	96-fluid-ounce can	6.59	100	----do	24.00	1¼	4¼
Oranges, mandarin	No. 10 can	6.38	100	4 ounces	25.50	1	4
Peaches:							
Halves or slices	No. 303 can	1.00	----------	2 medium	3.00	8½	33½
	No. 2½ can	1.81	----------	----do	7.00	3¾	14½
	No. 10 can	6.75	----------	{ 2 medium	25.00	1	4
				⅙ 9-inch pie	24.00	1¼	4¼
Whole, spiced	----do	6.88	----------	1 each	25.00	1	4
Pears, halves	No. 303 can	1.00	----------	2 medium	3.00	8½	33½
	No. 2½ can	1.81	----------	----do	7.00	3¾	14½
	No. 10 can	6.62	----------	----do	25.00	1	4
Pineapple:							
Chunks and cubes	No. 2½ can	1.88	100	4 ounces	7.52	3½	13½
	No. 10 can	6.75	100	----do	27.00	1	3¾
Crushed	No. 2½ can	1.88	100	----do	7.52	3½	13½
	No. 10 can	6.81	100	----do	27.24	1	3¾
Sliced	No. 2½ can	1.88	----------	1 large	8.00	3¼	12½
	No. 10 can	6.81	----------	1 large or 2 small	25.00	1	4
Pineapple juice	18-fluid-ounce can	1.24	100	4 fluid ounces	4.50	5¾	22¼
	46-fluid-ounce can	3.17	100	----do	11.50	2¼	8¾
	96-fluid-ounce can	6.62	100	----do	24.00	1¼	4¼
Plums	No. 2½ can	1.88	----------	2–3 plums	7.00	3¾	14½
	No. 10 can	6.75	----------	----do	25.00	1	4
Prunes	No. 2½ can	1.88	100	4 ounces	7.52	3½	13½
	No. 10 can	6.88	100	----do	27.52	1	3¾
Raspberries	No. 303 can	1.00	100	----do	4.00	6¼	25
	No. 10 can	6.75	100	----do	27.00	1	3¾
Strawberries	No. 303 can	1.00	100	----do	4.00	6¼	25
	No. 10 can	6.75	100	----do	27.00	1	3¾

[1] Number of purchase units needed is less than one.

Table 15.–FRUITS–FROZEN

Frozen fruits as purchased	Unit of purchase	Weight per unit	Yield, as served	Portion as served	Portions per purchase unit	Approximate purchase units for— 25 portions	Approximate purchase units for— 100 portions
		Pounds	*Percent*		*Number*	*Number*	*Number*
Apples, sliced	Pound	1.00	106	4 ounces	4.24	6	23¾
				⅙ 9-inch pie (1.50 pounds per pie).	4.00	6¼	25
	Package	2.50	106	4 ounces	10.60	2½	9½
	do	5.00	106	do	21.20	1¼	4¾
	Can	30.00	106	do	127.20	[1]	[1]
Apricots	Pound	1.00	95	do	3.80	6¾	26½
	Can	25.00	95	do	95.00	[1]	1¼
	do	30.00	95	do	114.00	[1]	[1]
Blackberries	Pound	1.00	103	do	4.12	6¼	24½
	Can	30.00	103	do	123.60	[1]	[1]
Blueberries	Pound	1.00	108	do	4.32	6	23¼
	Package	2.50	108	do	10.80	2½	9½
	Can	25.00	108	do	108.00	[1]	1
	do	30.00	108	do	129.60	[1]	[1]
Cherries, red, sour, pitted	Pound	1.00	100	4 ounces	4.00	6¼	25
				⅙ 9-inch pie (1.50 pounds per pie).	4.00	6¼	25
	Can	30.00	100	4 ounces	120.00	[1]	[1]
Grapefruit sections	Pound	1.00	100	do	4.00	6¼	25
	Package	3.00	100	do	12.00	2¼	8½
Grapefruit juice, concentrate	6-fluid-ounce can	.46	400	4 fluid ounces	6.00	4¼	16¾
	32-fluid-ounce can	2.46	400	do	32.00	[1]	3¼
Grape juice, concentrate	6-fluid-ounce can	.48	400	do	6.00	4¼	16¾
	32-fluid-ounce can	2.54	400	do	32.00	[1]	3¼
Lemon juice, concentrate	4-fluid-ounce can	.31	500	2 fluid ounces	10.00	2½	10
	6-fluid-ounce can	.47	500	do	15.00	1¾	6¾
Lemonade, concentrate	6-fluid-ounce can	.49	700	do	21.00	1¼	5
	18-fluid-ounce can	1.46	700	do	63.00	[1]	1¾
Melon scoops	Pound	1.00	100	3 ounces	5.33	4¾	19
	Package	6.50	100	do	34.67	[1]	3

See footnotes at end of table.

Table 15.—FRUITS—FROZEN—Cont.

Orange juice, concentrate	6-fluid-ounce can	.46	400	4 fluid ounces	6.00	4¼	16¾
	12-fluid-ounce can	.93	400	do	12.00	2¼	8½
	32-fluid-ounce can	2.48	400	do	32.00	[1]	3¼
Peaches, sliced	Pound	1.00	95	4 ounces	3.80	6¾	26½
				1/6 9-inch pie (1.33 pounds per pie).	4.50	5¾	22¼
	Can	6.50	95	4 ounces	24.70	1¼	4¼
	do	10.00	95	do	38.00	[1]	2¾
	do	30.00	95	do	114.00	[1]	[1]
Pineapple:							
Chunks	Pound	1.00	100	do	4.00	6¼	25
	Can	10.00	100	do	40.00	[1]	2½
Crushed	do	30.00	100	do	120.00	[1]	[1]
Pineapple juice, concentrate	6-fluid-ounce can	.47	400	4 fluid ounces	6.00	4¼	16¾
	32-fluid-ounce can	2.53	400	do	32.00	[1]	3¼
Raspberries	Pound	1.00	100	4 ounces	4.00	6¼	25
	Can	6.50	100	do	26.00	1	4
	do	10.00	100	do	40.00	[1]	2½
	do	30.00	100	do	120.00	[1]	[1]
Rhubarb	Pound	1.00	106	4 ounces	4.24	6	23¾
				1/6 9-inch pie (1.50 pounds per pie).	4.00	6¼	25
	Package	2.50	106	4 ounces	10.60	2½	9½
	Can	10.00	106	do	42.40	[1]	2½
	do	25.00	106	do	106.00	[1]	1
	do	30.00	106	do	127.20	[1]	[1]
Strawberries	Pound	1.00	100	do	4.00	6¼	25
	Can	6.50	100	do	26.00	1	4
	do	10.00	100	do	40.00	[1]	2½
	do	30.00	100	do	120.00	[1]	[1]
Tangerine juice, concentrate	6-fluid-ounce can	.47	400	4 fluid ounces	6.00	4¼	16¾
	32-fluid-ounce can	2.48	400	do	32.00	[1]	3¼

[1] Number of purchase units needed is less than one.

Table 16.—FRUITS—DRIED

Fruits, dried, regular and low-moisture, as purchased	Unit of purchase	Weight per unit	Yield, as served	Portion as served	Portions per purchase unit	Approximate purchase units for—	
						25 portions	100 portions
REGULAR		*Pounds*	*Percent*		*Number*	*Number*	*Number*
Apple slices	Pound	1.00	412	{4 ounces	16.48	1¾	6¼
				⅙ 9-inch pie (⅓ pound per pie)	18.00	1½	5¾
	Carton	5.00	412	4 ounces	82.40	(¹)	1¼
Apricots	11-ounce package	.69	344	___do	9.46	2¾	10¾
	Pound	1.00	344	___do	13.76	2	7½
	Carton	30.00	344	___do	412.80	(¹)	(¹)
Dates	12-ounce package	.75	100	3 ounces	4.00	6¼	25
	Pound	1.00	100	___do	5.33	4¾	19
	Carton	15.00	100	___do	80.00	(¹)	1¼
Peaches	11-ounce package	.69	422	4 ounces	11.60	2¼	8¾
	Pound	1.00	422	{4 ounces	16.88	1½	6
				⅙ 9-inch pie (⅓ pound per pie)	18.00	1½	5¾
	Carton	30.00	422	4 ounces	506.40	(¹)	(¹)
Prunes	Pound	1.00	253	___do	10.12	2½	10
	2-pound package	2.00	253	___do	20.24	1¼	5
	Carton	30.00	253	___do	303.60	(¹)	(¹)
Raisins	Pound	1.00	100	½ cup	6.00	4¼	16¾
LOW-MOISTURE							
Apples	Pound	1.00	584	{4 ounces	23.36	1¼	4½
				⅙ 9-inch pie (¼ pound per pie)	24.00	1¼	4¼
	No. 10 can	1.50	584	4 ounces	35.04	(¹)	3
Applesauce	Pound	1.00	911	___do	36.44	(¹)	2¾
	No. 10 can	2.50	911	___do	91.10	(¹)	1¼
Apricots	Pound	1.00	505	___do	20.20	1¼	5
	No. 10 can	3.50	505	___do	70.70	(¹)	1½
Fruit cocktail	Pound	1.00	558	___do	22.32	1¼	4½
	No. 10 can	2.75	558	___do	61.38	(¹)	1¾
Peaches	Pound	1.00	534	{4 ounces	21.36	1¼	4¾
				⅙ 9-inch pie (¼ pound per pie)	24.00	1¼	4¼
	No. 10 can	3.00	534	4 ounces	64.08	(¹)	1¾
Prunes, whole, pitted	Pound	1.00	462	___do	18.48	1½	5½
	No. 10 can	3.00	462	___do	55.44	(¹)	2

¹ Number of purchase units needed is less than one.

Table 17.—FLOUR, CEREALS, AND MIXES

Flour, cereals, and mixes as purchased	Unit of purchase	Weight per unit	Yield, as served	Portion as served or used	Portions per purchase unit	Approximate purchase units for—	
						25 portions	100 portions
		Pounds	*Percent*		*Number*	*Number*	*Number*
Flour	5-pound bag	5.00	---------	1 cup	20.00	(¹)	(¹)
	25-pound bag	25.00	---------	do	100.00	(¹)	(¹)
	100-pound sack	100.00	---------	do	400.00	(¹)	(¹)
Cereals, uncooked:							
Bulgur, cracked wheat (USDA)	Pound	1.00	401	¾ cup cooked	10.67	2½	9½
				1 cup uncooked	2.67	(¹)	(¹)
Cornmeal	1-pound box	1.00	628	¾ cup cooked	15.33	1¾	6¾
	5-pound bag	5.00	628	do	76.65	(²)	1½
	10-pound bag	10.00	628	do	153.30	(²)	(²)
	1-pound box	1.00	100	1 cup uncooked	3.00	(¹)	(¹)
Corn grits	do	1.00	628	¾ cup cooked	16.43	1¾	6¼
	do	1.00	100	1 cup uncooked	2.75	(¹)	(¹)
Farina	do	1.00	855	¾ cup cooked	21.92	1¼	4¾
	5-pound bag	5.00	855	do	109.60	(²)	1
Macaroni	1-pound box	1.00	311	do	12.00	2¼	8½
	20-pound box	20.00	311	do	240.00	(²)	(²)
	1-pound box	1.00	100	1 cup uncooked	3.75	(¹)	(¹)
Noodles	do	1.00	329	¾ cup cooked	10.67	2½	9½
	20-pound box	20.00	329	do	213.40	(²)	(²)
	1-pound box	1.00	100	1 cup uncooked	7.25	(¹)	(¹)
Rice	do	1.00	320	¾ cup cooked	11.27	2¼	9
	10-pound box	10.00	320	do	112.70	(²)	(²)
	100-pound sack	100.00	320	do	1,127.00	(²)	(²)
	1-pound box	1.00	100	1 cup uncooked	2.75	(¹)	(¹)
Rolled oats	do	1.00	610	¾ cup cooked	15.33	1¾	6¾
	3-pound box	3.00	610	do	46.00	(²)	2¼
	50-pound sack	50.00	610	do	766.50	(²)	(²)
	1-pound box	1.00	100	1 cup uncooked	4.50	(¹)	(¹)
Rolled wheat (USDA)	do	1.00	375	¾ cup cooked	8.89	3	11¼
	3-pound box	3.00	375	do	26.67	(²)	3¾
Spaghetti	1-pound box	1.00	359	do	12.12	2¼	8¼
	20-pound box	20.00	359	do	242.40	(²)	(²)
	1-pound box	1.00	100	1 cup uncooked	6.06	(¹)	(¹)
Whole wheat	do	1.00	608	¾ cup cooked	15.20	1¾	6¾
	4½-pound box	4.50	608	do	68.40	(²)	1½
	50-pound sack	50.00	608	do	760.00	(²)	(²)

See footnotes at end of table.

Table 17.—FLOUR, CEREALS, AND MIXES—Cont.

Flour, cereals, and mixes as purchased	Unit of purchase	Weight per unit	Yield, as served	Portion as served or used	Portions per purchase unit	Approximate purchase units for—	
						25 portions	100 portions
Cereals, ready-to-eat:		*Pounds*	*Percent*		*Number*	*Number*	*Number*
Bran flakes (25–40%)	Pound	1.00	100	1 ounce	16.00	1¾	6¼
	14½-ounce package	.91	100	do	14.50	1¾	7
	10-pound package	10.00	100	do	160.00	(²)	(²)
Bran flakes with raisins	Pound	1.00	100	1¼ ounces	12.80	2	8
	14-ounce package	.88	100	do	11.20	2¼	9
	200 individuals	15.62	100	do	200.00	(²)	(²)
Corn flakes	Pound	1.00	100	1 ounce	16.00	1¾	6¼
	12-ounce package	.75	100	do	12.00	2¼	8½
	10-pound package	10.00	100	do	160.00	(²)	(²)
Puffed rice	Pound	1.00	100	⅝ ounce	25.60	1	4
	8-ounce package	.50	100	do	12.80	2	8
	10-pound package	10.00	100	do	256.00	(²)	(²)
Puffed wheat	Pound	1.00	100	½ ounce	32.00	(²)	3¼
	8-ounce package	.50	100	do	16.00	1¾	6¼
	10-pound package	10.00	100	do	320.00	(²)	(²)
Puffed wheat, presweetened	Pound	1.00	100	⅞ ounce	18.29	1½	5½
	9-ounce package	.56	100	do	10.29	2½	9¾
	200 individuals	10.94	100	do	200.00	(²)	(²)
Rice flakes	Pound	1.00	100	do	18.29	1½	5½
	9½-ounce package	.59	100	do	10.86	2½	9¼
	10-pound package	10.00	100	do	182.86	(²)	(²)
Shredded wheat	Pound	1.00	100	1⅗ ounces	10.00	2½	10
	12-ounce package	.75	100	1⅗ ounces (2 small)	7.50	3½	13½
	200 individuals	20.00	100	1⅗ ounces	200.00	(²)	(²)
Wheat flakes	Pound	1.00	100	1 ounce	16.00	1¾	6¼
	10-ounce package	.62	100	do	10.00	2½	10
	10-pound package	10.00	100	do	160.00	(²)	(²)
Mixes: ³							
Cake:							
Angel food	Pound	1.00	----------	1/12 10-in. cake	12.00	2¼	8½
	12-cake case	12.00	----------	do	144.00	(²)	(²)
Other	Pound	1.00	----------	{ 2 in. x 3 in. cut	15–20	1¾	6¾
				{ Cupcake	20.00	1¼	5
	5-pound box	5.00	----------	{ 2 in. x 3 in. cut	75–100	(²)	1½
				{ Cupcake	100.00	(²)	1
Frosting	Pound	1.00	----------	{ 2 in. x 2 in.	38–39	(²)	2¾
				{ Cupcake	36–37	(²)	3
	5-pound box	5.00	----------	{ 2 in. x 2 in.	190–195	(²)	(²)
				{ Cupcake	180–185	(²)	(²)

See footnotes at end of table.

Table 17.–FLOUR, CEREALS, AND MIXES–Cont.

Cookie:							
Basic sugar	Pound	1.00		2½-ounce cookies	17–20	1½	6
	5-pound box	5.00		do	85–100	(2)	1¼
Brownie	Pound	1.00		2 in. x 2 in.	20–30	1¼	5
	5-pound box	5.00		do	100–150	(2)	1
Hot bread:							
Biscuit	Pound	1.00		2-inch biscuit	20.00	1¼	5
	5-pound box	5.00		do	100.00	(2)	1
Muffins	Pound	1.00		1½-ounce muffin	14–16	2	7¼
	5-pound box	5.00		do	70–80	(2)	1½
Rolls:							
Sweet	Pound	1.00		1¼-ounce roll	18–19	1½	5¾
	5-pound box	5.00		do	90–95	(2)	1¼
Yeast	Pound	1.00		1-ounce roll	23–25	1¼	4½
	5-pound box	5.00		do	115–120	(2)	(2)
Piecrust	Pound	1.00		9-inch shell	3.00	8½	33½
	5-pound box	5.00		do	16.00	1¾	6¼

[1] Number of purchase units needed is determined by use.
[2] Number of purchase units needed is less than one.

[3] Yields of mixes vary widely, depending on manufacturer, size of pan, and baking time and temperature. See instructions on package or box.

Table 18.—BAKERY FOODS

Bakery foods as purchased	Unit of purchase	Weight per unit	Portion as served	Portions per purchase unit	Approximate purchase units for—	
					25 portions	100 portions
		Pounds		*Number*	*Number*	*Number*
Bread: [1]						
Raisin	1-pound loaf	1.00	1 slice	18.00	1½	5¾
	2-pound loaf	2.00	----do	36.00	(²)	3
Rye	1-pound loaf	1.00	----do	23.00	1¼	4½
	1½-pound loaf	1.50	----do	28.00	1	3¾
	2-pound loaf	2.00	----do	33.00	(²)	3¼
White and whole wheat	1-pound loaf	1.00	⅝-inch slice	16.00	1¾	6¼
	1¼-pound loaf	1.25	----do	19.00	1½	5½
	1½-pound loaf	1.50	----do	24.00	1¼	4¼
	2-pound loaf	2.00	{ ½-inch slice	28.00	1	4
			{ ⅜-inch slice	36.00	(²)	3
	3-pound loaf	3.00	{ ½-inch slice	44.00	(²)	2½
			{ ⅜-inch slice	56.00	(²)	2
Cake:						
Layer	8-inch	--------	1/12 cake	12.00	2¼	8½
	9-inch	--------	1/16 cake	16.00	1¾	6¼
	12-inch	--------	1/30 cake	30.00	(²)	3½
	14-inch	--------	1/40 cake	40.00	(²)	2½
Loaf	Pound	1.00	{ ⅛ cake	8.00	3¼	12½
			1 cup soft cubes or crumbs	18.00	1½	5¾
			1 cup toasted cubes	13.50	2	7½
			{ 1 cup dry crumbs	6.00	4¼	16¾
Sheet	8-inch square	--------	2 in. x 2 in. (small)	16.00	1¾	6¼
	9 in. x 13 in	--------	3 in. x 3 in. (regular)	12.00	2¼	8½
	12 in. x 10 in	--------	{ 2 in. x 2 in	54.00	(²)	2
			{ 3 in. x 3 in	24.00	1¼	4¼
	16 in. x 24 in	--------	{ 2 in. x 2 in	96.00	(²)	1¼
			{ 3 in. x 3 in	40.00	(²)	2½
Cookies:						
Brownies	Pound	1.00	2 cookies	18.00	1½	5¾
Butter	----do	1.00	----do	46.50	(²)	2¼
Chocolate chip	----do	1.00	----do	21.50	1¼	4¾
Cream filled	----do	1.00	----do	19.50	1½	5¼
Fig bars	----do	1.00	----do	15.50	1¾	6½
Ginger snaps	----do	1.00	----do	30.00	(²)	3½
Shortbread	----do	1.00	----do	29.00	(²)	3½
Sugar	----do	1.00	----do	10.50	2½	9¾
Vanilla	----do	1.00	----do	46.50	(²)	2¼
Crackers:						
Graham	----do	1.00	2 crackers	32.50	(²)	3¼
Saltines	----do	1.00	----do	65–70	(²)	1¾
Soda	----do	1.00	----do	30–35	(²)	3½

See footnotes at end of table.

Table 18.—BAKERY FOODS—Cont.

Rolls:						
Frankfurter	do	1.00	1 roll (1⅓ ounces)	12.03	2¼	8½
Hamburger	do	1.00	1 roll (1¾ ounces)	9.14	2¾	11
Hard, round	do	1.00	1 roll (1⅚ ounces)	8.74	3	11½
Plain, pan	do	1.00	1 roll (1⅓ ounces)	12.03	2¼	8½
Sweet, pan	do	1.00	1 roll (1½ ounces)	10.67	2½	9½
Pie	8-inch		⅙ pie	6.00	4¼	16¾
	9-inch		⅐ pie	7.00	3¾	14½
	10-inch		⅛ pie	8.00	3¼	12½

[1] End crusts of bread were excluded in determining portions per purchase unit.

[2] Number of purchase units needed is less than one.

Table 19.—FATS AND OILS

Fats and oils as purchased	Unit of purchase	Weight per unit	Portion as served or used	Portions per purchase unit	Approximate purchase units for—	
					25 portions	100 portions
Butter or margarine:		*Pounds*		*Number*	*Number*	*Number*
Pound print	Carton	1.00	1 cup	2.00	([1])	([1])
			1 pat	72.00	([2])	1½
¼-pound print	do	1.00	1 pat	72.00	([2])	1½
Chips	Case	5.00	do	360.00	([2])	([2])
Lard	Carton	1.00	1 cup	2.00	([1])	([1])
	Can	50.00	do	100.00	([1])	([1])
Salad dressing (oil or mayonnaise type)	Pint	1.00	1 tablespoon	32.00	([2])	3¼
	Quart	2.00	do	64.00	([2])	1¾
	Gallon	8.00	do	256.00	([2])	([2])
Salad oil	Pint	.97	1 cup	2.00	([1])	([1])
	Quart	1.94	do	4.00	([1])	([1])
	Gallon	7.76	do	16.00	([1])	([1])
Shortening (Hydrogenated)	Can	1.00	do	2.50	([1])	([1])
	do	3.00	do	7.50	([1])	([1])
	do	50.00	do	125.00	([1])	([1])

[1] Number of purchase units needed is determined by use.

[2] Number of purchase units needed is less than one.

Table 20.—SUGAR AND SWEETS

Sugar and sweets as purchased	Unit of purchase	Weight per unit	Portion as served or used	Portions per purchase unit	Approximate purchase units for— 25 portions	100 portions
		Pounds		*Number*	*Number*	*Number*
Sugar:						
Brown, dark or light	Carton	1.00	1 cup	2.00	(1)	(1)
		25.00	do	50.00	(1)	(1)
Cubes	do	1.00	2 cubes	40.00	(2)	2½
	Bulk	25.00	do	1,000.00	(2)	(2)
Granulated:						
Bulk	Carton	1.00	2 level or 1 rounded teaspoon	54.00	(2)	2
			1 cup	2.25	(1)	(1)
	Bag	5.00	1 cup	11.25	(1)	(1)
	do	25.00	do	56.25	(1)	(1)
	Sack	100.00	do	225.00	(1)	(1)
Individuals	Package	1.50	1 packet	100.00	(2)	1
	Carton	45.00	do	3,000.00	(2)	(2)
Powdered (confectioners)	do	1.00	1 cup	3.50	(1)	(1)
	Sack	25.00	do	87.50	(1)	(1)
Sirup:						
Blends	12-fluid-ounce bottle	1.03	2 tablespoons	12.00	2¼	8½
	Quart	2.83	do	32.00	(2)	3¼
	No. 10 can	8.50	do	96.00	(2)	1¼
	Gallon	11.00	do	128.00	(2)	(2)
Corn	Pint	1.50	do	16.00	1¾	6¼
	5-pound can	5.00	do	53.33	(2)	2
	No. 10 can	8.79	2 tablespoons	93.76	(2)	1¼
			1 cup	11.72	(1)	(1)
Maple	Pint	1.38	2 tablespoons	16.00	1¾	6¼
	Gallon	11.00	do	128 00	(2)	(2)
Molasses	Pint	1.50	do	16.00	1¾	6¼
	Jar	2.00	do	21.00	1¼	5
	No. 10 can	9.31	do	99.00	(2)	1
Jam, jelly, marmalade:						
Bulk	Jar	1.00	1 tablespoon	23.00	1¼	4½
	No. 10 can	8.38	do	192.00	(2)	(2)
Individuals	Carton	----------	1 packet	200.00	(2)	(2)
Other sweets:						
Apple butter	Jar	1.00	do	11.00	2½	9¼
	No. 10 can	7.50	do	81.00	(2)	1¼
Honey	Jar	1.00	do	11.00	2½	9¼
	2-pound can	2.00	do	22.00	1¼	4¾
	5-pound can	5.00	do	54.00	(2)	2
Desserts, dry:						
Gelatin, flavored	3-ounce package	.19	½ cup	4.00	6¼	25
	6-ounce package	.38	do	8.00	3¼	12½
	Pound	1.00	do	21.33	1¼	4¾
Pudding, pie filling:						
Chocolate	4-ounce package	.25	do	4.00	6¼	25
	Pound	1.00	4 ounces	20.00	1¼	5
			Fill for ⅙ 9-inch pie	18.67	1½	5½
Lemon chiffon	do	1.00	Fill for ⅙ 9-inch pie	32.00	(2)	3¼

See footnotes at end of table.

Table 20.—SUGAR AND SWEETS—Cont.

Vanilla	3-ounce package	.19	½ cup	4.00	6¼	25
	Pound	1.00	4 ounces	25.60	1	4
			Fill for ⅙ 9-inch pie	24.00	1¼	4¼
Pudding, instant:						
Chocolate	4½-ounce package	.28	½ cup	4.00	6¼	25
	Pound	1.00	do	14.29	1¾	7
Vanilla	3¾-ounce package	.23	do	4.00	6¼	25
	Pound	1.00	do	17.39	1½	5¾

[1] Number of purchase units needed is determined by use.

[2] Number of purchase units needed is less than one.

Table 21.—BEVERAGES

Beverages as purchased	Unit of purchase	Weight per unit	Portion as served	Portions per purchase unit	Approximate purchase units [1] for—	
					25 portions	100 portions
		Pounds		*Number*	*Number*	*Number*
Carbonated drinks:						
6-ounce bottles	Case (24)		6 fluid ounces	24.00		
12-ounce bottles	do		do	48.00		
16-ounce bottles	do		do	64.00		
Cocoa:						
Regular, unsweetened	Pound	1.00	1 measuring cup, prepared	50.00	½	2
Instant, sweetened:						
Bulk	8-ounce carton	.50	1 cup	28.00	(1½ c.)	(6 c.).
	38-ounce carton	2.38	do	133.00	(1½ c.)	(6 c.).
Individuals	Carton (50)		1 packet	50.00	½	2
Sirup, sweetened	16-ounce can	1.00	1 cup	29.00	1	3½.
Coffee:						
Ground	Pound	1.00	1 measuring cup, prepared	[2] 37.00		
Instant:						
Bulk	6-ounce jar	.38	1 level teaspoon	180.00	(½ c.+1 t.)	(2 c.+4 t.).
			1 rounded teaspoon	90.00	(½ c.+1 t.)	(2 c.+4 t.).
	10-ounce jar	.62	1 level teaspoon	300.00	(½ c.+1 t.)	(2 c.+4 t.).
Individuals	Carton (72)		1 packet	72.00		
Tea:						
Bulk	Pound	1.00	1 measuring cup, prepared	256.00		(6¼ oz.).
Bags	Package (48)	.24	1 measuring cup or more	48.00		
	Carton (100)	.50	do	100.00	¼	1
Instant	1½-ounce jar	.09	1 cup hot tea	96.00	(½ c.+1 t.)	(2 c.+4 t.).
			1 cup iced tea	64.00	(¾ c.)	(3 c.).

[1] Numbers in parentheses refer to approximate measure to serve 25 and 100 portions: c., cup; t., teaspoon; oz., ounces.

[2] Varies depending on brand of coffee used and method of preparation.

TABLE 22.—*Conversion factors for computing the number of purchase units needed for portions of various sizes*

Portion size given in purchase tables (ounces)	Conversion factors for specified portion size, ounces									
	1	2	3	4	5	6	7	8	9	10
1	1. 00	2. 00	3. 00	4. 00	5. 00	6. 00	7. 00	8. 00	9. 00	10. 00
2	. 50	1. 00	1. 50	2. 00	2. 50	3. 00	3. 50	4. 00	4. 50	5. 00
3	. 33	. 67	1. 00	1. 33	1. 67	2. 00	2. 33	2. 67	3. 00	3. 33
4	. 25	. 50	. 75	1. 00	1. 25	1. 50	1. 75	2. 00	2. 25	2. 50
5	. 20	. 40	. 60	. 80	1. 00	1. 20	1. 40	1. 60	1. 80	2. 00
6	. 17	. 33	. 50	. 67	. 83	1. 00	1. 17	1. 33	1. 50	1. 67
7	. 14	. 29	. 43	. 57	. 71	. 86	1. 00	1. 14	1. 29	1. 43
8	. 12	. 25	. 38	. 50	. 62	. 75	. 88	1. 00	1. 12	1. 25

How To Use Table 22:

This table is to be used to help determine the number of purchase units if the size of portion is different from that specified in tables 1 to 21. For example, for 3-ounce portions of snap beans, five No. 10 cans are required (table 10); for other size portions, conversion factors in this table can be used to determine the number of No. 10 cans required.

The figures in the left-hand column of the conversion table represent the portion sizes given in tables 1 to 21. The figures across the top represent portion sizes that may be desired. If a 4-ounce instead of a 3-ounce portion of canned snap beans is to be used, for example, find the 3-ounce line in the left-hand column of the conversion table. Follow this line across to the factor in the 4-ounce column. Multiply this factor (1.33) by the number of purchase units (five No. 10 cans) given in table 10 for 100. Thus: 5 (No. 10 cans) $\times$ 1.33=6.65 No. 10 cans (round to 6¾ No. 10 cans) to serve 100 people each a 4-ounce portion.

Portion sizes in the purchase tables are sometimes given in terms of tablespoons, cups, slices, etc. Any of these measures can be substituted for ounces in this conversion table and the same computations performed.

Table 23—*Cost per portion for food priced from 10 cents to $2 per purchase unit.*

Price per purchase unit (cents)	Cost per portion for indicated portions per purchase unit							
	4	6	8	10	12	16	20	24
	Cents	Cents	Cents	Cents	Cents	Cents	Cents	Cents
10	2. 5	1. 7	1. 2	1. 0	0. 8	0. 6	0. 5	0. 4
15	3. 8	2. 5	1. 9	1. 5	1. 2	. 9	. 8	. 6
20	5. 0	3. 3	2. 5	2. 0	1. 7	1. 2	1. 0	. 8
25	6. 2	4. 2	3. 1	2. 5	2. 1	1. 6	1. 2	1. 0
30	7. 5	5. 0	3. 8	3. 0	2. 5	1. 9	1. 5	1. 2
35	8. 8	5. 8	4. 4	3. 5	2. 9	2. 2	1. 8	1. 5
40	10. 0	6. 7	5. 0	4. 0	3. 3	2. 5	2. 0	1. 7
45	11. 2	7. 5	5. 6	4. 5	3. 7	2. 8	2. 2	1. 9
50	12. 5	8. 3	6. 2	5. 0	4. 2	3. 1	2. 5	2. 1
60	15. 0	10. 0	7. 5	6. 0	5. 0	3. 8	3. 0	2. 5
70	17. 5	11. 7	8. 8	7. 0	5. 8	4. 4	3. 5	2. 9
80	20. 0	13. 3	10. 0	8. 0	6. 7	5. 0	4. 0	3. 3
90	22. 5	15. 0	11. 2	9. 0	7. 5	5. 6	4. 5	3. 7
100	25. 0	16. 7	12. 5	10. 0	8. 3	6. 2	5. 0	4. 2
110	27. 5	18. 3	13. 8	11. 0	9. 2	6. 9	5. 5	4. 6

Table 23— *Cost per portion for food priced from 10 cents to $2 per purchase unit*

120	30. 0	20. 0	15. 0	12. 0	10. 0	7. 5	6. 0	5. 0
130	32. 5	21. 7	16. 2	13. 0	10. 8	8. 1	6. 5	5. 4
140	35. 0	23. 3	17. 5	14. 0	11. 7	8. 8	7. 0	5. 8
150	37. 5	25. 0	18. 8	15. 0	12. 5	9. 4	7. 5	6. 2
160	40. 0	26. 7	20. 0	16. 0	13. 3	10. 0	8. 0	6. 7
170	42. 5	28. 3	21. 2	17. 0	14. 2	10. 6	8. 5	7. 1
180	45. 0	30. 0	22. 5	18. 0	15. 0	11. 2	9. 0	7. 5
190	47. 5	31. 7	23. 8	19. 0	15. 8	11. 9	9. 5	7. 9
200	50. 0	33. 3	25. 0	20. 0	16. 7	12. 5	10. 0	8. 3

How To Use Table 23:

Determine the number of portions per unit of purchase through use of the food item or from the column, "Portions per purchase unit," in appropriate table. Locate the column in the table above that is nearest to that number. Then locate in that column the number horizontal to the price paid for the purchase unit in the left-hand column. This number represents the approximate cost of a portion.

TABLE 24.—BEEF: *Approximate percentage of edible meat* [1] *from the carcass and wholesale cuts of Choice, Good, and Standard grades of beef*

[Steers ranging from 11 to 21 months in age]

Beef	Grade of carcass		
	Choice	Good	Standard
	Percent	*Percent*	*Percent*
Carcass	85	84	82
Wholesale cuts:			
Brisket	88	87	85
Chuck	86	85	83
Flank	100	100	100
Foreshank	58	58	56
Loin end	89	88	86
Round, with hindshank	85	84	82
Rump, knuckle out	87	86	84
Short loin	90	89	87
Standing rib	85	83	80
Short plate	90	89	86

[1] The remaining percentage of beef consists of bone, ligament, and tendon.

Table 25.—LAMB: *Approximate percentage of edible meat[1] from the carcass and wholesale cuts of Prime, Choice, and Good grades of lamb*

Lamb	Grade of carcass		
	Prime	Choice	Good
	Percent	*Percent*	*Percent*
Carcass	86	83	82
Wholesale cuts:			
Breast and flank	89	86	86
Leg	87	85	84
Loin	90	87	86
Neck	79	75	75
Rib cut (9 ribs)	86	82	80
Shoulder (3 ribs)	87	85	84

[1] The remaining percentage of lamb consists of bone and ligament.

Table 26.—PORK: *Approximate percentage of edible meat[1] from the carcass and wholesale trimmed cuts from hogs of 3 weight groups*

Pork	Weight of carcass [2]		
	200 pounds live, 158 pounds dressed	225 pounds live, 178 pounds dressed	250 pounds live, 197 pounds dressed
	Percent	*Percent*	*Percent*
Carcass	79	80	82
Wholesale cuts:			
Bacon	92	93	94
Ham	85	85	86
Head, full cut	47	50	53
Loin	78	79	79
Shoulder, full cut	84	85	86
Shoulder, ribs	40	42	45
Spareribs	58	61	63

[1] The remaining percentage consists of bone and skin.
[2] The average yield of lard per hog slaughtered is 14 percent per 100 pounds live weight. This percentage includes lard and rendered pork fat, and excludes bacon and salt pork.

Table 27.—VEGETABLES OR FRUITS: *Approximate amount of canned and frozen product obtained from specified quantities of fresh vegetables and fruits*

Vegetables or fruits	Home canning methods		Commercial canning methods		Frozen		
	Fresh	Yield, canned	Fresh	Yield of #10 cans, canned	Fresh	Yield, frozen	Fruit-to-sugar ratio
Vegetables:		*Quarts*		*Number*		*Pounds*	
Asparagus	2½ to 4½ pounds	1	8 to 9 pounds	1			
	1 crate	7–12	1 crate	3–4	1 crate	15	
Beans, lima	3 to 5 pounds [1]	1	5 pounds [2]	1			
	1 bushel [1]	6–11	1 bushel [2]	6	1 bushel [2]	29	
Beans, snap	1½ to 2½ pounds	1	4 to 5 pounds	1			
	1 bushel	12–20	1 bushel	6–8	1 bushel	24	
Beets, without tops	2 to 3½ pounds	1	8 pounds	1			
	1 bushel	15–26	1 bushel	6–7			
Broccoli					1 crate	23	
Carrots, without tops	2 to 3 pounds	1	8 pounds	1			
	1 bushel	17–25	1 bushel	6–7	1 bushel	25	
Corn, sweet, in husks	3 to 6 pounds	[3] 1	17 to 18 pounds	[3] 1			
	1 bushel	[3] 6–12	1 bushel	[3] 2	1 bushel	[3] 8	
Okra	1½ pounds	1	7 pounds	1			
Peas, green	3 to 6 pounds [1]	1	4 to 5 pounds [2]	1			
	1 bushel [1]	5–10	1 bushel [2]	6–8	1 bushel [2]	27	
Pumpkin and winter squash	1½ to 3 pounds	1	17 to 18 pounds	1			
	1 bushel	17–33	1 bushel	3	1 bushel	32	
Spinach, other greens	2 to 6 pounds	1	8 pounds	1			
	1 bushel	3–10	1 bushel	2–3	1 bushel	10–11	
Sweetpotatoes	2 to 3 pounds	1	7 pounds	1			
	1 bushel	17–25	1 bushel	7			
Tomatoes	2½ to 3½ pounds	1	12 pounds	1			
	1 bushel	15–21	1 bushel	4–5			
Tomato catsup			19 pounds	1			
			1 bushel	2–3			
Tomato paste			40 to 41 pounds	1			
			1 bushel	1–2			
Tomato sauce			21 pounds	1			
			1 bushel	3–4			
Fruits:							
Apples	2½ to 3 pounds	1	10 pounds	1			
	1 bushel	15–20	1 bushel	4–5	1 bushel	26–31	5 to 1
Berries, except strawberries	1¼ to 3 pounds	1	5 pounds	1			
	1 crate	12–24	1 crate	7	1 crate	34	4 to 1
Cherries, sour	2 to 2½ pounds	1	7 pounds	1			
	1 bushel	22–28	1 bushel	8	1 bushel	53	4 to 1
Peaches	2 to 3 pounds	1	7 pounds	1			
	1 bushel	15–25	1 bushel	6–7	1 bushel	41–44	3 to 1
Pears	2 to 3 pounds	1	8 pounds	1			
	1 bushel	15–24	1 bushel	5–6			
Plums	1½ to 2½ pounds	1	5 pounds	1			
	1 bushel	19–32	1 bushel	9–10			
Strawberries	1¼ to 3 pounds	1	6 pounds	1			
	1 crate	12–24	1 crate	6	1 crate	42	3 to 1

[1] In pods.   [2] Shelled basis.   [3] Whole kernel.

Table 28.—*Common can and jar sizes*

Container				Principal products
	Consumer description			
Can size (Industry term)	Average net weight or fluid measure per can [1] (check label)	Average cups per can	Cans per case	
		Number	*Number*	
8 ounces_____	8 ounces_____	1	48 and 72	Small cans—ready-to-serve soups, fruits, and vegetables.
No. 1 picnic_____	10½ to 12 ounces_____	1¼	48	Small cans—condensed soups, some fruits, vegetables, meat, and fish.
No. 300_____	14 to 16 ounces_____	1¾	24	Small cans—fruits, vegetables, some meat and poultry products, and ready-to-serve soups.
No. 303_____	16 to 17 ounces_____	2	24	Do.
No. 2_____	1 pound, 4 ounces (20 ounces) or 1 pint, 2 fluid ounces (18 fluid ounces).	2½	24	Family size—juices, ready-to-serve soups, and some fruits.
No. 2½_____	1 pound, 13 ounces (29 ounces)__	3½	24	Family size—fruits and some vegetables.
No. 3 cylinder_____	3 pounds, 3 ounces (51 ounces) or 1 quart, 14 fluid ounces (46 fluid ounces).	5¾	12	"Economy family size"—fruit and vegetable juices. Institutional size—condensed soups, some vegetables, and meat and poultry products.
No. 10_____	6 pounds, 8 ounces (104 ounces) to 7 pounds, 5 ounces (117 ounces).	12 to 13	6	Institutional size—fruits, vegetables, and some other foods.

[1] The label on one product may show net weight that differs slightly from the label on another product in cans or jars of identical size. (An example would be lima beans (1 pound) and blueberries (14 ounces) in the same size can.)

Source: National Canners Association.

Ounce equivalents in decimal parts of pound

Ounces	Pound	Ounces	Pound
1	0. 06	9	. 56
2	. 12	10	. 62
3	. 19	11	. 69
4	. 25	12	. 75
5	. 31	13	. 81
6	. 38	14	. 88
7	. 44	15	. 94
8	. 50	16	1. 00

Approximate scoop equivalents

Scoop No.[1]	Level measure	Scoop No.[1]	Level measure
6	⅔ cup	20	3⅕ tablespoons
8	½ cup	24	2⅔ tablespoons
10	⅖ cup	30	2⅕ tablespoons
12	⅓ cup	40	1⅗ tablespoons
16	¼ cup		

[1] A serving spoon may be used to replace a scoop. Since serving spoons are not identified by number, it is necessary to measure or weigh the quantity of food from sizes of spoons used to obtain the approximate serving size desired.

Common food-measure equivalents

3 teaspoons	1 tablespoon	16 tablespoons	1 cup
2 tablespoons	1 fluid ounce	1 cup	8 fluid ounces
4 tablespoons	¼ cup	2 cups	1 pint
6 tablespoons	⅜ cup	2 pints	1 quart
8 tablespoons	½ cup		

GOVERNMENT PUBLICATIONS AVAILABLE [1]

Food Preparation

Basic fish cookery.   USDI Test Kitchen Series 2, 26 pp.   1948.

Dry beans, peas, lentils . . . modern cookery. USDA Leaflet 326, 24 pp.   (Rev. 1957.)

Eggs in family meals—a guide for consumers. USDA Home and Garden Bulletin No. 103, 32 pp.   1965.

Green vegetables for good eating.   USDA Home and Garden Bulletin No. 41, 16 pp., illus.   (Rev. 1964.)

How to cook clams.   USDI Test Kitchen Series 8, 14 pp.   1953.

How to cook crabs.   USDI Test Kitchen Series 10, 14 pp.   1956.

How to cook lobster.   USDI Test Kitchen Series 11, 14 pp.   1957.

How to cook oysters.   USDI Test Kitchen Series 3, 12 pp.   1953.

How to cook scallops.   USDI Test Kitchen Series 13, 17 pp.   1959.

How to cook shrimp.   USDI Test Kitchen Series 7, 14 pp.   1952.

Meat for thrifty meals.   USDA Home and Garden Bulletin No. 27, 47 pp., illus.   (Rev. 1963.) 20 cents.

Potatoes in popular ways.   USDA Home and Garden Bulletin No. 55, 22 pp.   1957.

Root vegetables in everyday meals.   USDA Home and Garden Bulletin No. 33, 12 pp.   1961.

Tomatoes on your table.   USDA Leaflet 278, 15 pp.   (Rev. 1964.)

Food Purchasing

Fresh and frozen fish buying manual.   USDI Circular 20, 50 pp.   1954.

Shopper's guide to U.S. grades for food.   USDA Home and Garden Bulletin No. 58, 13 pp. (Slightly rev. 1964.)

Home Canning and Freezing

Home canning of fruits and vegetables.   USDA Home and Garden Bulletin No. 8, 48 pp., illus.   (Rev. 1964.)

Home canning of meat.   USDA Home and Garden Bulletin No. 6, 16 pp., illus.   (Rev. 1958.)

Home freezing of fruits and vegetables.   USDA Home and Garden Bulletin No. 10, 48 pp., illus.   (Rev. 1964.)

Home freezing of poultry.   USDA Home and Garden Bulletin No. 70, 24 pp.   (Sl. rev. 1964.)

Nutrition

Food for fitness . . . a daily food guide.   USDA Leaflet 424, 8 pp.   (Rev. 1964.)

Food for groups of young children cared for during the day.   U.S. Children's Bureau Pub. No. 386, 58 pp.   1960.   25 cents.

Foods your children need.   U.S. Children's Bureau Unnumbered, 15 pp.   1958.   10 cents.

Nutrition and healthy growth.   U.S. Children's Bureau Pub. No. 352, 35 pp.   1955.   20 cents.

Nutrition up to date . . . up to you.   Reprint from USDA Home and Garden Bulletin No. 1, Family Fare, Separate 1, 28 pp., illus.   (Rev. 1960.)

Nutritive value of foods.   USDA Home and Garden Bulletin No. 72, 30 pp.   (Rev. 1964.)

Quantity Food Service

A guide for planning and equipping school lunchrooms.   USDA Program Aid 292, 60 pp.   1956. 35 cents.

Fish cookery for one hundred.   USDI Test Kitchen Series 1, 44 pp.   1950.

Fish recipes for school lunches.   USDI Test Kitchen Series 5, 15 pp.   (Rev. 1959.)

Food buying guide for type A school lunches. USDA Program Aid 270, 75 pp.   1964. $1.25.

Quantity recipes for type A school lunches (card file).   USDA Program Aid 631.

Recipes for quantity service.   USDA Home Economics Research Report No. 5, 225 pp.   1958. $2.50.

---

[1] Publications indicated for sale may be obtained only from the Superintendent of Documents, U.S. Government Printing Office, Washington, D.C., 20402; USDI publications may be obtained from the Bureau of Commercial Fisheries, U.S. Department of the Interior, Washington, D.C., 20240; USDA publications may be obtained from the Office of Information, U.S. Department of Agriculture, Washington, D.C., 20250.

APPENDIX II

LONG ISLAND JEWISH/HILLSIDE MEDICAL CENTER
NEW HYDE PARK, NEW YORK 11040

SECTION —
PURCHASE SPECIFICATIONS
FOR
CANNED FRUITS

GENERAL SPECIFICATIONS

1. Goods must be of the latest pack.
2. Goods must be of the U.S.D.A. grade specified, U.S.D.A. verification of grade may be requested.
3. Swollen, rusted or dented cans are to be replaced at no charge or credited to us if vendor is notified within three (3) months of delivery date.
4. Products not covered by U.S.D.A. grades are to be of the best commercial quality.

PRODUCT	PACK	USDA GRADE MIN. SCORE	MIN. NET MIN. DRAINED WT.	SIZE OR COUNT	REMARKS
APPLESAUCE Sweetened	6/#10	Fancy 90	107 oz.		Course.
APRICOT Halves	6/#10	Choice 82	106 oz. 64 oz.	85/115	Unpeeled, 19° Brix, Heavy syrup.
CRANBERRY Sauce	6/#10 24/#303 200/½ oz	Fancy			Strained or Whole as specified. Kraft on individuals.
FIGS, Kadota	6/#10	Choice 82	106 oz. 66 oz.	70/90	Whole, 21° Brix, (Heavy Syrup.)
FRUIT Cocktail	6/#10	Fancy 90	110 oz. 71.1 oz.		18° Brix. (Heavy Syrup.)
ORANGE SECT Mandarin, Japanese	6/#10	Fancy			18° Brix. (Heavy Syrup.)
PEACH HALVES Cling	6/#10	Choice 84	108 oz. 66 oz.	30/35 35/40	19° Brix. (Heavy Syrup.)
PEAR HALVES Bartlett	6/#10	Choice 84	106 oz. 63 oz.	35/40 30/35 25/30	18° Brix. (Heavy Syrup.)

PRODUCT	PACK	USDA GRADE MIN. SCORE	MIN. NET MIN. DRAINED WT.	SIZE OR COUNT	REMARKS
PINEAPPLE, Sliced Hawaiian	6/#10	Fancy 90	104 oz. 61½ oz.	52	Heavy Syrup.
PINEAPPLE, TIDBITS, Hawaiian	6/#10	Fancy 90	107 oz. 65 ¾ oz.	512/960	Heavy Syrup.
PLUMS, Purple	6/#10	Choice 84	60 oz.	70/80	Brix 21°
PRUNES, Stewed, Whole	6/#10	Fancy 40/42	60 oz.		Brix 21°
APPLESAUCE, Dietetic	24/303	A 90			
APRICOTS, Dietetic	24/303	A 90	9¾ oz.	10/12	Brix 14° or water
CHERRIES, R.A. Dietetic	24/303	A 90	10¼ oz.		Brix 16° or water
FIGS, Dietetic, Kadota, Whole	24/303	A 90	10 oz.		16° Brix or water Tender, ripe flesh.
FRUIT COCKTAIL Dietetic	24/303	A			
PEACHES Sliced, Cling Dietetic	24/303	A 90	10 oz.		14° Brix or water.
PEAR HALVES Bartlett, Dietetic	24/303	A 90	11½ oz.	7/9	14° Brix or water.
PINEAPPLE Sliced Hawaiian, Diet.	24/303	A 90	12¾ oz.		Size 2 Brix 14° or water.
PLUMS Purple, whole, Dietetic	24/303	A 90	12 oz.		Brix 16° or water.

LONG ISLAND JEWISH/HILLSIDE MEDICAL CENTER
NEW HYDE PARK, NEW YORK 11040

SECTION —
PURCHASE SPECIFICATIONS
FOR
CANNED VEGETABLES

GENERAL SPECIFICATIONS

1. Goods must be of the latest pack.
2. Goods must be of the U.S.D.A. grade specified, U.S.D.A. verification of grade may be requested.
3. Swollen, rusted or dented cans are to be replaced at no charge or credited to us if vendor is notified within three (3) months of delivery date.
4. Products not covered by U.S.D.A. grades are to be of the best commercial quality.

PRODUCT	PACK	USDA GRADE MIN. SCORE	MIN. NET MIN. DRAINED WT.	SIZE OR COUNT	REMARKS
ASPARAGUS, Spears	6/#5	Fancy 92/103 oz. net	50½ oz.	54/80	All Green, Mammoth.
BEANS, BAKED Vegetarian	6/#10	Fancy 85			White beans, in tomato sauce.
BEANS, GREEN N. West Blue Lake	6/#10	XStd. 82/101 oz. net	61 oz.	4 or 5 sieve	Pound. variety.
BEETS Sliced	6/#10	Fancy 90/104 oz. net	68 oz.	2½" Max. Diam.	
BEETS Whole	6/#10	Fancy 90/104 oz. net	68 oz.	74/124	No softness, peel or black spots.
CARROTS, WHOLE "Belgian"	6/#10	Fancy 90/105 oz. net	69 oz.	290/350	Orange-Yellow; no green.
CORN, WHOLE Kernel	6/#10	Fancy 90/106 oz. net	70 oz.		Golden. Brine pack.
MUSHROOMS, Whole, Button	24/#8Z	Fancy 85/16 oz. net	8 oz.		Formosa; cream colored.
OKRA, CUT	6/#10	XSTD. 85/99 oz. net	60 oz.		½" to 1" pods.

PRODUCT	PACK	USDA GRADE MIN. SCORE	MIN. NET MIN. DRAINED WT.	SIZE OR COUNT	REMARKS
PEAS, Sweet	6/#10	XSTD. 82/105 oz. net	71 oz.	4 or 5 sieve	
PEPPERS, Green Diced	6/#10				
PEPPERS, Red Diced	6/#10				
POTATOES, DEHY. Pearls	6/#10				Without milk, vit. C added. Packed by Amer. Potato Comp. only. (whipped brand)
POTATOES, DEHY. Sliced	6/#4				
POTATOES, INST. w/o milk, vit. C added	6/#10				Packed by the Amer. Potato Comp. only.
POTATOES, Sweet Mashed	6/#10	A 85	72 oz.		Golden type Brix 25°
POTATOES, Sweet, Whole	6/#10	Fancy 85	72 oz.	25/35	Brix 25°, 2"-3" length.
RED CABBAGE, Sweet & Sour	6/#10	A 90	80 oz.		Shredded.
SAUERKRAUT	6/#10	Fancy 85	72 oz.		1/32" thick. No mold Max. 2.5% salt.
TOMATO Paste	6/#10 24/2½	Fancy 85/114 oz. net 85/31 oz. net			1.14 Specific Gravity 33% solids. Coarse Texture
TOMATO Puree	6/#10	Fancy 90/105 oz. net			California, 1.06 specific gravity 12% solids.
TOMATOES, Whole	6/#10	XSTD 80/102 oz. net	68 oz.		Solid Pack, 70% min. whole.
WATERCHESTNUTS, Sliced	6/#10				
ASPARAGUS Spears, Med. Dietetic A.G	24/303	A 85	93/4 oz.		Water pack.

[*Cont.*]

PRODUCT	PACK	USDA GRADE MIN. SCORE	MIN. NET MIN. DRAINED WT.	SIZE OR COUNT	REMARKS
BEANS, GREEN Snap, Blue Lake 1" cut Diet.	24/303	A 90	11¼ oz.		Water pack.
BEETS, Sliced, Diet.	24/303	A 85	12¼ oz.		3/8" max. Thickness Size #4
PEAS, Dietetic	24/303	A 90	none estab.		Water pack sieve #4 11/32" to 12/32"
TOMATOES, Dietetic	24/303	A 90	66% of can contents		Water pack max. .026% Calcium Chloride

LONG ISLAND JEWISH/HILLSIDE MEDICAL CENTER
NEW HYDE PARK, NEW YORK 11040

SECTION —
PURCHASE SPECIFICATIONS
FOR
CANNED JUICES

GENERAL SPECIFICATIONS

1. Goods must be of the latest pack.
2. Goods must be of the U.S.D.A. grade specified, U.S.D.A. verification of grade may be requested.
3. Swollen, rusted or dented cans are to be replaced at no charge or credited to us if vendor is notified within three (3) months of delivery date.
4. Products not covered by U.S.D.A. grades are to be of the best commercial quality.

PRODUCT	PACK	USDA GRADE MIN. SCORE	MIN. NET MIN. DRAINED WT.	SIZE OR COUNT	REMARKS
APPLE JUICE Unsweetened	12/46 oz. 12/qt.	Fancy			Brix 11.5° Clarified.
APRICOT Nectar	12/46 oz.	Fancy			Brix
CRANBERRY Juice	12/qt. 4/1 gal.				Ocean Spray
GRAPE JUICE Unsweetened	12/46 oz.	Fancy			Brix 14.0°
GRAPEFRUIT JUICE Unsweetened	12/46 oz.	Fancy			Brix 9.0°
ORANGE JUICE Unsweetened	12/46 oz.	Fancy			Brix 10.5° Florida
PEAR NECTAR	12/46 oz.	Fancy			Brix
PINEAPPLE JUICE, Unsweetened	12/46 oz.	Fancy			Brix 12.0° Hawaiian
PRUNE JUICE Unsweetened	12/46 oz. 12/qt.	Fancy			Brix
TANGERINE JUICE	12/46 oz.	Fancy			Brix 12.5°
TOMATO JUICE Dietetic	24/#2	Fancy			California, Homogenized

LONG ISLAND JEWISH/HILLSIDE MEDICAL CENTER
NEW HYDE PARK, NEW YORK 11040

SECTION —
PURCHASE SPECIFICATIONS
FOR
DRESSINGS, OIL, OLIVES, PICKLES,
RELISHES, & SHORTENINGS

PRODUCT	PACK	USDA GRADE MIN. SCORE	MIN. NET MIN. DRAINED WT.	SIZE OR COUNT	REMARKS
CATSUP	200/½ oz. 6/#10	Extra standard			29% solids, Heinz or Kraft.
DRESSING, Blue Cheese	4 gal/tub				Kraft.
DRESSING, French	4/1 gal. 200/Ind.				35% min. vegetable oil w/o emulsifier or artificial color
DRESSING, Russian	4/½ gal.				Kraft.
DRESSING, Salad	4/gal. (plastic)				Not less than 40% veg. oil, 5% egg yolks. Includes veg. oil, egg yolks, vinegar, water, lemon juice, salt, sugar, starch.
GHERKINS, Sweet	4/1 gal.				
MUSTARD	200/oz. 12/5 oz.				Guldens
MUSTARD, Prepared	4/1 gal. (plastic) 200/oz. 12/5 oz.				French or English style, No hulls, starch. min. 16.5% solids.
OIL, OLIVE	6/1 gal.				12% pure olive oil in blend. Clear refined, deodorized, not rancid.
OIL, SALAD	6/1 gal.				Pure cottonseed, clear, refined, not rancid, no smoking below 432°F.

PRODUCT	PACK	USDA GRADE MIN. SCORE	MIN. NET MIN. DRAINED WT.	SIZE OR COUNT	REMARKS
OLIVES, GREEN Stuffed	4/1 gal.				
PICKLES, DILL	25# Tin				George
PICKLES, SWEET MIXED	4/1 gal.				
PIMENTO	48/15 oz.				
RELISH, CORN	4/1 gal.				
RELISH, Red Pepper	4/1 gal.				
RELISH, Sweet Pickle Mixed.	4/ gal.				To consist of cucumbers (min. 60%), cauliflower (min. 25%), tomatoes, onions (min. 3%) all thoroughly cured in brine & vinegar. Fine chopped in uniform pieces 15% brine made of vinegar & sugar.
SHORTENING	50#/can				Min. smoking point: 426°F. Hydrogenated vegetable oils. No foreign odors, rancidity, suspended matter.
VINEGAR Cider	4/1 gal.				Min. 4 gr/Acetic acid per 100 cc. at 10°C. Bright, not cloudy, no floating particles.
VINEGAR, RED Wine.	4/1 gal.				
VINEGAR White Distilled.	4/1 gal. 12/qt.				Charcoal refined.

LONG ISLAND JEWISH/HILLSIDE MEDICAL CENTER
NEW HYDE PARK, NEW YORK 11040

SECTION —
PURCHASE SPECIFICATIONS
FOR
JAMS, JELLIES, & SYRUP

PRODUCT	PACK	USDA GRADE MIN. SCORE	MIN. NET MIN. DRAINED WT.	SIZE OR COUNT	REMARKS
APPLE BUTTER	6/#10	A 85			Dark brown with reddish shade. Free from defects, stems, seeds, etc. Fine grained, smooth with sweet apple flavor only.
JAM, type as specified	6/4# 200/½ oz.	Fancy 85			Pulpy, Min. 45% by weight of clean, sound mature fruits. Prefer Smuckers or Kraft.
JELLY, type as specified	6/4# 200/½ oz.	Fancy 85			Pulpy, Min. 45% by weight of clean, sound mature fruits. Prefer Smuckers or Kraft.
JELLIES, ASST. Dietetic	200/ind.				
MARMALADE, Orange, Sweet Type II	6/4# 200/½ oz.	Fancy 85			No seed, dark spots, gumminess. Translucent & of jelly-like consistency. Min. 30% orange fruit.
SYRUP, MAPLE, Light Amber	4/gal. 100/oz.	"AA"-11# per gal.			15% pure maple. No artificial flavoring. May have artificial coloring, 35% max. water content. 65.46° Brix.
SYRUP, REFINERS	gal. 24/16 oz.	Fancy — Refiners syrup			Light, Karo, sugar: Brix 70%

LONG ISLAND JEWISH/HILLSIDE MEDICAL CENTER
NEW HYDE PARK, NEW YORK 11040

SECTION —
PURCHASE SPECIFICATIONS
FOR
MISCELLANEOUS GROCERIES

PRODUCT	PACK	USDA GRADE MIN. SCORE	MIN. NET MIN. DRAINED WT.	SIZE OR COUNT	REMARKS
BEEF BASE	12/1#				
BEEF BASE Kosher	12/1#				Victors
BOUILLON CUBE Kosher (veg)	100/tin				
BUCKWHEAT Groats (Kasha)	24/1#				
CARAWAY Seeds	1#				
CAVIAR, BLACK	1#				
CHICKEN BASE	12/1#				
CHICKEN BASE (Kosher)	12/1#				Victors
CHOCOLATE, Hot, mix.	10/50's				Bakers. (General Foods)
CHOCOLATE Liquor, sweet	10#/slab				58% cocoa fat max. $\frac{1}{2}°$ weight emulsified
CHOCOLATE, Liquor, Unsweetened	10#/slab				58% cocoa fat.
CLAM JUICE	12/#5	net wt 46 oz			Pure.
COCOA	6/5#				35% choc. Liquor. Bakers (Gen. Foods)
COCONUT Shredded	10#/box 5#/box				short or long as specified.

[*Cont.*]

PRODUCT	PACK	USDA GRADE MIN. SCORE	MIN. NET MIN. DRAINED WT.	SIZE OR COUNT	REMARKS
COFFEE CREAM Imitation	12/1#				"N-Light"
CORN FLAKE Crumbs	6/5#				Kellogg's
CORNMEAL	8/5#				
CORNSTARCH	24/1#				
CROUTETTES	10#				Kellogg's
FLOUR, All Purpose	100#				
FLOUR Tortillas	75 each				Markers #F28T-1
FOOD COLOR, as specified	qt.	U.S. Cert.			
FRENCH TOAST	144/cas			Bulk	Downey Flake
FRENCH TOAST	1 oz each slice			160 each	Juno
GRAHAM Cracker Crumbs	30#/box				
HERRING Wine Sauce	4/1 gal				George
HORSERADISH Prepared	qt.				
LEKVAR	6/#10				
LEMON JUICE	12/qt.				Brix 8.0° Real Lemon
MARSHMALLOWS Large	24/12 oz.				
MATZOH MEAL	36/12 oz.				
MELBA TOAST	360 ind.				
MILK Evaporated	48/13 oz. A				
MILK Powdered skim	8/5#				Alba

PRODUCT	PACK	USDA GRADE MIN. SCORE	MIN. NET MIN. DRAINED WT.	SIZE OR COUNT	REMARKS
MINTS, WHITE Small pillow	6/5#				
MOLASSES	6/#10				Dark
NUT MEAT, SLI Almond	5#	U.S. No. 1			
NUT MEAT, Walnut Broken	5#	U.S. No. 1			
NUTS, MIXED	10#	Fancy			
NUTS, PEANUT Whole shelled	5#	Fancy Hand Picked			Unsalted
PANCAKE MIX	6/5#				Hungry Jack only (Pillsbury)
PEANUT BUTTER	12/1#				
POP TARTS	100/cas				Kellogg's
POTATO CHIPS	4#/box 100/packs 4/1# box				Treat
PRETZELS	4½#/box 12/9 oz.				Treat
RALSTON	18/22 oz.				
ROLLS, Parker House	12/24's			24 each	Morton
SANKA	24/6 oz. 10/100's				General Foods
SPROUTS, BEAN	6/#10				
TACO SHELLS	200/cas				Foam Pack. Lawry's
TEABAGS	10/100 ind.				Tetley
TOMATO	12/#5				California
WAFFLE, Round	8/12's			12" dia each	Eggo

LONG ISLAND JEWISH/HILLSIDE MEDICAL CENTER
NEW HYDE PARK, NEW YORK 11040

SECTION —
PURCHASE SPECIFICATIONS
FOR
GELATIN & PUDDINGS

PRODUCT	PACK	USDA GRADE MIN. SCORE	MIN. NET MIN. DRAINED WT.	SIZE OR COUNT	REMARKS
GELATIN Flavor as specified	2/20# 12/34 oz				Pure leaf Belgium. Jello or Gumperts
GELATIN Assorted Reds & Citrus	24/24 oz.				
GELATIN, Kosher, Diet Reds & Citrus	24/2½ oz.				Kitchen Kraft
GELATIN, Kosher, Reg. Assorted Reds & Citrus	24/24 oz.				Kitchen Kraft
GELATIN, DIET	24/3 oz				Dzerta
GELATIN Unflavored	24/1#				
JUNKET Assorted Flav.	12/1#				
PUDDING, Flavor as specified	12/4½# 24/20 oz.				Regular, w/o milk, Jello - (General Foods)
PUDDING Prepared, Flav. as specified					Rich's

LONG ISLAND JEWISH/HILLSIDE MEDICAL CENTER
NEW HYDE PARK, NEW YORK 11040

SECTION —
PURCHASE SPECIFICATIONS
FOR
NOODLES

PRODUCT	PACK	USDA GRADE MIN. SCORE	MIN. NET MIN. DRAINED WT.	SIZE OR COUNT	REMARKS
SHELLS	10#/box				Goodmans
SPAGHETTI	20#/box				Goodmans, #1 fine
SPAGHETTI Reg. & Linguini	20#/box				
SPIRALS	20#/box				Goodmans
MACARONI, Elbow	10#/box				Goodmans
NOODLES, Alphabet	10#/box				Goodmans
NOODLES, Bow Ties	10#/box				Goodmans
NOODLES, EGG Fine, Broad, or med. as specified	10#/box				Goodmans
NOODLES, Lasagna, Ribbed					LaRosa
NOODLES, Chow Mein	6/#10				

LONG ISLAND JEWISH/HILLSIDE MEDICAL CENTER
NEW HYDE PARK, NEW YORK 11040

SECTION —
PURCHASE SPECIFICATIONS
FOR
DRIED FRUITS & LEGUMES,
RICE

GENERAL SPECIFICATIONS

1. Must be of the latest crop, prepared from clean, sound, properly matured fruit.

PRODUCT	PACK	USDA GRADE MIN. SCORE	MIN. NET MIN. DRAINED WT.	SIZE OR COUNT	REMARKS
BARLEY, PEARL	24/1# 24/18 oz.	U.S. #1			
BEANS, BLACK Turtle	25#/sack	U.S. #1			
BEANS, GREAT Northern Navy	25#/sack 24/1#	U.S. #1			White, small, dried
BEANS, Kidney	25#/sack 24/1#	U.S. #1			Red, dried
BEANS, LIMA Baby	25#/sack 24/1#	U.S. #1			Recleaned
DATES, PITTED Whole	10#/box	Choice			"Sair," firm
LENTILS	24/1#	U.S. #1			Yellow, dried.
MIXED FRUITS	25#/cas	X Fancy			Dried, no apples or cherries.
PEAS, GREEN Split	25#/sack 24/1#	U.S. #1			Green, no whites
PRUNES, ROBE	30#/box	Fancy			75% Free of colors other than black, splits, scabs, insect injury or cracks.

PRODUCT	PACK	USDA GRADE MIN. SCORE	MIN. NET MIN. DRAINED WT.	SIZE OR COUNT	REMARKS
RAISINS, Black or Bleached	24/15 oz.	Choice			Thompson seedless: uniform size: 19/64" to 24/64".
RICE, MILLED Converted	100#/sack	U.S. #1			Uncle Ben's or Kraft only.

LONG ISLAND JEWISH/HILLSIDE MEDICAL CENTER
NEW HYDE PARK, NEW YORK 11040

SECTION —
PURCHASE SPECIFICATIONS
FOR
CANNED FISH

GENERAL SPECIFICATIONS

1. Goods must be of the latest pack.
2. Goods must be of the U.S.D.A. grade specified, U.S.D.A. verification of grade may be requested.
3. Swollen, rusted or dented cans are to be replaced at no charge or credited to us if vendor is notified within three (3) months of delivery date.
4. Products not covered by U.S.D.A. grades are to be of the best commercial quality.

PRODUCT	PACK	USDA GRADE MIN. SCORE	MIN. NET MIN. DRAINED WT.	SIZE OR COUNT	REMARKS
ANCHOVIES	100/2 oz. 13 oz.	Portuguese Fancy	2 oz.		12 count. Packed in olive oil.
CLAMS, Chopped	12/51 oz.	Fancy	51 oz.		Doxee only.
GEFILTE FISH	16/½ gal. 6/3#3 oz.				Mother's, in jellied broth
GEFILTE FISH Unsalted	24/15 oz.		15 oz. 6 pieces		Mother's only
SALMON, Bluefack	48/3¾ oz.	3¾ oz.			Gilnetter's only. Soft bones, no gills or fins. In oil.
SALMON, PINK Med., Red	12/4# 24/1#				No checks or tail pieces.
SARDINES, Brisling	50/3¾ oz.	Norwegian Fancy	3¾ oz.		Sea Herring or Pilchard. Firm, Unbroken, cleaned. In oil.
TUNAFISH, Light meat Chunk	6/66½ oz.	Fancy	66½ oz.		Bonita or Albacore, no skin, bones, dark meat, artificial coloring. Prefer Japanese. In oil or oil & brine.
SALMON Dietetic	48/3¾ oz. 48/7¾ oz.		3¾ oz.		Med. red in water.
TUNAFISH, Dietetic	48/3¾ oz.	Fancy	3¾ oz.		In water. Chunk style.

LONG ISLAND JEWISH/HILLSIDE MEDICAL CENTER
NEW HYDE PARK, NEW YORK 11040

SECTION —
PURCHASE SPECIFICATIONS
FOR
BABY & JUNIOR FOODS

PRODUCT	PACK	USDA GRADE MIN. SCORE	MIN. NET MIN. DRAINED WT.	SIZE OR COUNT	REMARKS
APPLESAUCE	24/4½ oz.				Baby
APRICOT Puree	12/1#				
BANANAS	24/4½ oz.				Baby
BARLEY Cereal	12/8 oz.				Baby
BEEF	24/4½ oz.				Kosher Baby
BEEF NOODLE Dinner	24/7½ oz.				Junior Foods
CARROTS	24/4½ oz.				Baby
CHICKEN	24/4½ oz.				Kosher Baby
COTTAGE CHEESE and Pineapple	24/7½ oz.				Junior Foods
HIGH PROTEIN Cereal	12/8 oz.				Baby
LAMB	24/4½ oz.				Kosher Baby
OATMEAL	12/8 oz.				Baby
PEACHES	24/4½ oz.				Baby
PEACH PUREE	12/#1				
PEARS	24/4½ oz.				Baby
PEAR PUREE	12/1#				
PEAS	24/4½ oz.				Baby

[*Cont.*]

PRODUCT	PACK	USDA GRADE MIN. SCORE	MIN. NET MIN. DRAINED WT.	SIZE OR COUNT	REMARKS
PRUNES	24/4½ oz.				Baby
RICE CEREAL	12/8 oz.				Baby
SPINACH	24/4½ oz.				Baby
STRING BEANS	24/4½ oz.				Baby
TURKEY & RICE Dinner	24/7½ oz.				Junior Foods
VEAL	24/4½ oz.				Kosher Baby

LONG ISLAND JEWISH/HILLSIDE MEDICAL CENTER
NEW HYDE PARK, NEW YORK 11040

SECTION —
PURCHASE SPECIFICATIONS
FOR
SODA

PRODUCT	PACK	USDA GRADE MIN. SCORE	MIN. NET MIN. DRAINED WT.	SIZE OR COUNT	REMARKS
BLACK CHERRY	24/12 oz.				
CLUB SODA	12/28 oz.				
COLA	24/12 oz.				
CREAM	24/12 oz.				
CO2	50# Tank				
GINGERALE	12/28 oz. 24/12 oz.				
GRAPE	24/12 oz.				
ORANGE	24/12 oz.				
PEPSI-COLA	5 gal. Tank				
QUININE WATER	24/6 oz.				
ROOT BEER	24/12 oz				

LONG ISLAND JEWISH/HILLSIDE MEDICAL CENTER
NEW HYDE PARK, NEW YORK 11040

SECTION —
PURCHASE SPECIFICATIONS
FOR
SEASONINGS & SPICES

PRODUCT	PACK	USDA GRADE MIN. SCORE	MIN. NET MIN. DRAINED WT.	SIZE OR OR COUNT	REMARKS
ALLSPICE, Ground	6# 1#				#5217 Ehlers #5212 Ehlers
ALMOND Paste	6/#10				
BAKING POWDER	5#/can 6/1#can				Double-acting type.
BAKING SODA	24/1#				Arm & Hammer
BASIL, SWEET Whole	5# 1#				#7048 Ehlers #7044
CHILI POWDER	6# 1#				#5264 Ehlers #5261 Ehlers
CINNAMON, Ground	10# 1#				#5257 Ehlers #5252
CINNAMON, Whole	5# 1#				#7087 Ehlers #7083 Ehlers
CLOVES, Ground	6# 1#				#5274 Ehlers #5274 Ehlers
CLOVES, WHOLE	6# 1#				#7107 Ehlers #7102 Ehlers
CREAM OF TARTAR	1#				#5291 Ehlers
CURRY POWDER	6# 1#				#5314 Ehlers #5312 Ehlers
DILL WEED	1#				#7273 Ehlers
EXTRACT Almond	qt.		5:1:00 oil		Pure not Imitation.

PRODUCT	PACK	USDA GRADE MIN. SCORE	MIN. NET MIN. DRAINED WT.	SIZE OR COUNT	REMARKS
EXTRACT Honey, liquid Light Amber	6/5# 200/oz.	Fancy 90			81.4% min. soluble solids. 1.4129 specific gravity. 18.6% moisture.
EXTRACT Orange	qt.		5:1:00 oil		Pure.
EXTRACT Vanilla, Bourbon	Gal. qt.				Pure, 10% vanilla bean.
FENNEL SEED	1#				#7282 Ehlers
GARLIC Powder	6# 1#				#5347 Ehlers #5342 Ehlers
GINGER	1#				#5372 Ehlers
LAUREL, BAY LEAVES CRUSHED	1#				#7323 Ehlers
LAUREL, BAY LEAVES, WHOLE	1#				#7307 Ehlers
MACE	1#				#5391 Ehlers
MARJORAM	6# 1#				#5407 Ehlers #5402 Ehlers
MIXED SPICES	6# 1#				#5884 Ehlers #5882 Ehlers
MONOSODIUM GLUTAMATE	25# 1#				#5808 Ehlers #5801 Ehlers
MUSTARD, A.E.	6# 1#				#5437 Ehlers #5432 Ehlers
NUTMEG, GROUND	1#				#5451 Ehlers
OMELET HERBS	1#				#5913 Ehlers
ONIONS, Flaked, dehy.	75#/barrel				Kraft, dried.
OREGANO, Leaf	10#				#7398 Ehlers #7394 Ehlers
PAPRIKA	10# 1#				#5467 Ehlers #5461 Ehlers

[Cont.]

PRODUCT	PACK	USDA GRADE MIN. SCORE	MIN. NET MIN. DRAINED WT.	SIZE OR COUNT	REMARKS
PARSLEY Flakes	5# 1#				#7208 Ehlers #7202 Ehlers
PEPPER BLACK Ground	10# 1#				#5507 Ehlers #5501 Ehlers
PEPPER, RED	1#				#7424 Ehlers
PEPPER, WHITE	10#. 1#				#5567 Ehlers #5561 Ehlers
POULTRY SEASONING	20# 1#				#5768 Ehlers #5762 Ehlers
ROSEMARY, Leaf	1#				#7474 Ehlers
SAGE, POWDERED	6# 1#				#5627 Ehlers #5622 Ehlers
SALAD HERBS	15#				#5928 Ehlers
SALT, COOKING	100#				Not iodized, coarse.
SALT SUB. Potassium	3/1000's				Ind. Packets
SALT, TABLE	24/26 oz. 5/1000 ind.				Not iodized and iodized
SAUCE, CHILI	6/#10	A 85			Bright color. No free liquid. No scorched flavor.
SAUCE, HOT	24/2 oz.				Tabasco
SAUCE, SOY Light	24/6 oz. 4/1 gal				LaChoy
SAUCE, STEAK	12/5 oz.				A-1
SAUCE, TACO	4/1 gal				Marker st-4
SAUCE, WORCHESTERSHIRE	4/1 gal 24/5 oz.				Lea & Perrins only. Min. 20% solids. 60 days wood ripened
SESAME SEED	1#				#7521 Ehlers
SEASONING, Kitchen Bouquet	Gal.				

PRODUCT	PACK	USDA GRADE MIN. SCORE	MIN. NET MIN. DRAINED WT.	SIZE OR COUNT	REMARKS
SEASONING, Maggi	Gal				
SUGAR & CINNAMON	10#				#5837 Ehlers
SUGAR, BROWN, Dark or Light as specified	24/1#				
SUGAR, DOTS	24/1#				
SUGAR, Granulated	100# bag				
SUGAR, PACKET Granulated	30/100's 10,000/cas				
SUGAR, 6x	100# bag 24/1#				
TACO Seasoning					Lawry's
TARRAGON Leaf	1#				#7544 Ehlers
THYME Powdered	6# 1#				#5857 Ehlers #5852 Ehlers

LONG ISLAND JEWISH/HILLSIDE MEDICAL CENTER
NEW HYDE PARK, NEW YORK 11040

SECTION —
PURCHASE SPECIFICATIONS
FOR
CEREALS, COOKIES, & CRACKERS

PRODUCT	PACK	MIN. GRADE MIN. SCORE	MIN. NET MIN. DRAINED WT.	SIZE OR COUNT	REMARKS
CEREALS					
CEREALS, TYPE As specified	48/7/8 oz. 50/1 oz.				Kellogg's
CREAM OF RICE	12/1#				
CREAM OF WHEAT	12/28 oz.				
FARINA	12/28 oz.				
OATS, QUICK	12/42 oz.				
WHEATENA	12/22 oz.				
COOKIES & CRACKERS					
COOKIES Butter cake	6#/cas				Sunshine
COOKIES, CHOC. Nuggets	6½/cas				Sunshine
COOKIES Ginger Snaps	6/14 oz				Sunshine
COOKIES, Golden Fruit	Cas				Sunshine
COOKIES, HYDROX	7¼#/cas				Sunshine
COOKIES, Orbit, Creme	7½#/cas				Sunshine
COOKIES, VIENNA	6½#/cas				Sunshine

PRODUCT	PACK	USDA GRADE MIN. SCORE	MIN. NET MIN. DRAINED WT.	SIZE OR COUNT	REMARKS
CRACKERS, Saltfree	300/2				Burry's
CRACKERS, Graham	6/4# 6/1#				
MATZO'S REG. OR EGG as specified	24/1#				Manischewitz
SALTINES	360/ 280/				
VANILLA WAFERS	5#box				
ZWEIBACK	12/6 oz				

APPENDIX III

MONTEFIORE HOSPITAL & MEDICAL CENTER
BRONX, N.Y. 10467
MANUAL OF PURCHASE SPECIFICATIONS
FOR
FOOD PRODUCTS

Date of Latest Revision:
January, 1972

NOTICE TO VENDORS

The following specifications are intended to serve as a uniform basis for the information of vendors when quoting prices and to be a standard for inspection when these foods are received by Montefiore Hospital & Medical Center.

Upon delivery, products not meeting these specifications will be returned at vendor's expense. This emphasizes the importance of retaining the specifications in your file to be referred to at all times when quoting prices or filling our orders.

Please destroy all previous specifications.

The specifications were prepared by:

Jacques W. Bloch,
Director of Food Service
of Montefiore Hospital & Medical Center

TABLE OF CONTENT

CATEGORY: **SECTION:**

Meats (Fresh, Cured and Smoked)
Poultry ....
Fish (Fresh, Frozen Salted, Smoked) ....   A
Shell Fish ....
Fresh Vegetables and Fruits ....   B
Dairy Products and Eggs   C
Canned Goods (Fruits, Juices, Vegetables,   D
Tomato Products, Fish) ....
Dried Fruits & Legumes, Rice,   E
Frozen Fruits and Vegetables,
Other Frozen Products
Miscellaneous Products (Dressings, Seasonings,   F
Oil, Spices, Olives, Pickles, Relishes, Shortening) ....   G

SECTION - A
PURCHASE SPECIFICATIONS
FOR
FRESH, CURED AND SMOKED MEATS,
POULTRY
MANUFACTURED MEATS AND MEAT PRODUCTS

Date of Latest Revision:
January 1972

PURCHASE SPECIFICATIONS FOR BEEF
WHOLESALE & FABRICATED CUTS
WHOLESALE CUTS MUST BE FEDERALLY QUALITY GRADED "USDA CHOICE",
YIELD GRADED NO. 3
STATE OF REFRIGERATION: CHILLED

FOR DETAILED DESCRIPTION — WHERE APPLICABLE*—
REFER TO USDA "INSTITUTIONAL MEAT PURCHASE SPECIFICATIONS" FOR FRESH BEEF
SERIES 100, ISSUED MARCH 1970

FABRICATED CUTS MUST BE PRODUCED FROM SAME QUALITY AS WHOLESALE CUTS
IN ACCORDANCE WITH USDA INSTITUTIONAL MEAT PURCHASE SPECIFICATIONS
FOR PORTION-CUT MEAT PRODUCTS — SERIES 1000, REVISED MARCH 1969

EVIDENCE OF QUALITY FOR FRESH BEEF:

COLOR: BRIGHT CHERRY RED;
TEXTURE: SMOOTH, MODERATELY FIRM;

BONES: REDDISH AND **POROUS**;
FATS: MOTTLED EVENLY
(MARBLED), CREAMY WHITE.

PURCHASE SPECIFICATIONS FOR BEEF   —   WHOLESALE & FABRICATED CUTS

PRODUCT	WEIGHT RANGE	REQUIREMENTS
BRISKET, BONELESS, CURED*	9 - 12#	NO. 1, DECKEL OFF, CLOSELY TRIMMED, BRIGHT APPEARANCE, NO INDICATION OF RUST OR OTHER DISCOLORATION. (SEE USDA IMPS. SERIES 600)
BRISKET, BONELESS, FRESH*	10 - 12#	CLOSELY TRIMMED: DECKEL OFF.
CHUCK, SQUARE CUT, BONE-IN*	93 - 106#	TO BE CUT BETWEEN 5TH AND 6TH RIB. FORESHANK, BRISKET, SHORT PLATE AND RIB OFF. 1/2" MAXIMUM COVERING SUET.
CHUCK, ARMBONE*	103 - 118#	TO BE CUT BETWEEN 5TH AND 6TH RIB. FORESHANK, BRISKET, SHORT PLATE AND RIB OFF. 1/2" MAXIMUM COVERING SUET.
CROSSCUT CHUCK*	120 - 138#	TO INCLUDE 5 RIBS, SQUARE CUT CHUCK, FORESHANK AND BRISKET. 1/2" MAXIMUM COVERING SUET.
FOREQUARTER*	183 - 210#	TO INCLUDE 12 RIBS, CUT INTO MATCHED WHOLESALE MARKET CUTS. 1/2" MAXIMUM COVERING SUET.
GROUND BEEF, REGULAR*	10# CONTAINER	PACKED COMPACTLY, NOT MORE THAN 25% FAT. SHALL BE WELL MIXED, SO THAT FAT AND LEAN MEAT ARE EVENLY DISTRIBUTED.
HINDQUARTER*	167 - 190#	TO INCLUDE 1 RIB, CUT INTO MATCHED WHOLESALE MARKET CUTS. 1/2" MAXIMUM COVERING SUET.
INSIDES, DRIED, SLICED	10# CONTAINERS	BRIGHT APPEARANCE, SLICES TO BE A MINIMUM OF 3" LONG AND 2" WIDE.
LIVER, WHOLE	8 - 10#	SELECTION NO. 1, UNBLEMISHED, FRESH CHILLED OR FROZEN; LIGHT BROWN COLOR.
OXTAILS	1-1/2 - 2#	STEER, NO. 1, COLOR OF FAT: WHITE TO SLIGHTLY YELLOW.
PASTRAMI, PLATE; RED	3-1/2 - 4#	NO CORNER PIECES—ALL BONES AND FAT TO BE REMOVED. MILDLY CURED WITH SPICES ADDED. SMOKED 6-8 HOURS.
RIB, FULL*	33 - 38#	SEVEN RIBS, 8" CHUCK END, 10" RIB END. 1/2" MAXIMUM COVERING SUET.
RIB, BONELESS, TIED, ROAST-READY*	12 - 16#	SAME AS ABOVE, WITH RIBS, FEATHER-BONES AND INTERCOSTAL MEAT REMOVED. STRING-TIED GIRTHWISE EVERY 2", ALSO TIED LENGTHWISE. 1/2" MAXIMUM COVERING SUET.

PURCHASE SPECIFICATIONS FOR BEEF — WHOLESALE & FABRICATED CUTS (CONTINUED)

PRODUCT	WEIGHT RANGE	REQUIREMENTS
ROUND, BONE-IN, FULL CUT*	83 - 95#	RUMP AND SHANK ON; FLANK OFF; CUT CHICAGO STYLE.
ROUND, INSIDE, BONELESS*	18 - 20#	INSIDE PORTION OF ABOVE, WITH ALL BONES REMOVED.
ROUND, OUTSIDE, BONELESS*	11 - 13#	OUTSIDE PORTION OF BONE-IN ROUND, WITH ALL BONES REMOVED.
SHOULDER, CLOD, ROAST-READY*	16 - 18#	MUST BE ONE PIECE WITHOUT UNDUE SCORING. NOT LESS THAN 1" THICK AT ANY ONE POINT. STRING-TIED GIRTHWISE.
SHORTLOIN, TRIMMED*	26 - 30#	10" RIB END, DIAMOND-BONE CUT.
SHORTRIBS, TRIMMED*	4 - 5#	BONE-IN, TO INCLUDE 4 RIBS, CLOSELY TRIMMED, APPROXIMATELY 3" WIDE. DECKEL AND ALL COVERING FAT REMOVED.
SIDE OF BEEF*	350 - 400#	CUT INTO 5 MATCHED PRIMAL CUTS. LOIN TO BE WHOLE.
STEWING BEEF (CUBES)	AMOUNT AS SPECIFIED	UNIFORM CUBES, APPROXIMATELY 1". SURFACE FAT NOT TO EXCEED 1/4" AT ANY ONE POINT. MAXIMUM FAT CONTENT: 20%.
STRIP-LOIN, BONE-IN*	16 - 19#	10" WIDE.
STRIP-LOIN, BONELESS*	12 - 14#	10" WIDE.
TONGUE, FRESH	4 - 5#	SHORT CUT; SELECTION NO. 1. FAT COVERING NOT TO EXCEED 1/2" AT ANY ONE POINT.
TONGUE, SMOKED*	3 - 5#	SHORT CUT, NO. 1. (SEE USDA IMPS. SERIES 600)
TONGUE, CURED*	3 - 5#	DRY-PACK, NO. 1, SHORT-CUT. (SEE USDA IMPS. SERIES 600)
TRIPE, HONEYCOMB		FRESH FROZEN OR FRESH, NO. 1, SCALDED AND THOROUGHLY SCRAPED; RESILIENT.
TRIPE, PLAIN		FRESH FROZEN OR FRESH, NO. 1, SCALDED AND THOROUGHLY SCRAPED; RESILIENT.
TENDERLOIN, FULL*	6 - 7#	NOT MORE THAN 1/2" COVERING SUET.
TENDERLOIN, BUTT*	4# UP	NOT MORE THAN 1/2" COVERING SUET.

PURCHASE SPECIFICATIONS FOR BEEF — PORTION CUTS
MUST BE PRODUCED FROM FEDERALLY QUALITY GRADED "USDA CHOICE", YIELD GRADED NO. 3
STATE OF REFRIGERATION: FROZEN

FOR DETAILED DESCRIPTION—WHERE APPLICABLE*—
REFER TO USDA "INSTITUTIONAL MEAT PURCHASE SPECIFICATIONS" FOR PORTION-CUT MEAT PRODUCTS—
SERIES 1000 ISSUED MARCH 1969.

PRODUCT	SIZE	WEIGHT RANGE	REQUIREMENTS
BRAISING STEAKS (SWISS), BONELESS*	5 OZ.	4-3/4 OZ-5-1/4 OZ	TRIMMED, FREE OF FAT ON AT LEAST 1/2 OF CIRCUMFERENCE; 3/4" MAXIMUM EXTERIOR FAT AT ANY ONE POINT. KNITTING OF TWO OR MORE PIECES NOT PERMITTED. 1/2" AVERAGE EXTERIOR FAT.
RIB-EYE ROLL STEAKS, BONELESS*	8 OZ	7-1/2 OZ-8-1/2 OZ	BUTTERFLY STEAKS NOT ACCEPTABLE.
STRIP-LOIN STEAKS, BONELESS*	9 OZ	8-1/2 OZ-9-1/2 OZ	SHORT CUT, FLANK EDGE NOT TO EXCEED 2" FROM EXTREME OUTER TIP OF LOIN EYE MUSCLE.
TENDERLOIN STEAKS*	5 OZ	4-3/4 OZ-5-1/4 OZ	CLOSE TRIM. NARROWEST DIAMETER NOT LESS THAN 1", EXCLUSIVE OF SURFACE FAT. NOT MORE THAN 1/2" SURFACE FAT AT ANY ONE POINT. BUTTERFLY STEAKS NOT ACCEPTABLE. 1/4" AVERAGE EXTERIOR FAT.
LIVER (STEER)*	4 OZ	3-3/4 OZ-4-1/4 OZ (38 TO 42 PORTION PER 10 LB CARTON)	UNIFORM SLICES, APPROXIMATELY 5/16" THICK. SELECTION NO. 1. UNBLEMISHED. SKINNED. LAYER PACKED.

PURCHASE SPECIFICATIONS FOR VEAL
WHOLESALE & FABRICATED CUTS
WHOLESALE CUTS MUST BE FEDERALLY QUALITY GRADED "USDA CHOICE".
STATE OF REFRIGERATION: CHILLED
FOR DETAILED DESCRIPTION—WHERE APPLICABLE*—
REFER TO USDA "INSTITUTIONAL MEAT PURCHASE SPECIFICATIONS" FOR FRESH VEAL AND CALF
SERIES 300, ISSUED MAY 1969.

FABRICATED CUTS MUST BE PRODUCED FROM SAME QUALITY AS WHOLESALE CUTS
IN ACCORDANCE WITH USDA INSTITUTIONAL MEAT PURCHASING SPECIFICATIONS
FOR PORTION-CUT MEAT PRODUCTS*—SERIES 1000, REVISED MARCH, 1969.

PURCHASE SPECIFICATIONS FOR VEAL   —   WHOLESALE & FABRICATED CUTS
EVIDENCE OF QUALITY

COLOR: LIGHT GRAYISH PINK;   *FAT:* EVENLY DISTRIBUTED AROUND
TEXTURE: FIRM;   RIBS AND LOIN, BUT NOT
                                               EXCESSIVE;
                                    SURFACE: FREE FROM SLIMINESS.

PRODUCT	WEIGHT RANGE	REQUIREMENTS
BREAST*	6 - 7-1/2#	WELL TRIMMED.
CHUCK, SQUARE CUT, SINGLE*	12 - 16-1/2#	FOREQUARTER LESS RACK, FORESHANK AND BRISKET OFF.
CHUCK, SQUARE CUT, CLOD OUT, BONELESS*	6 - 8#	SAME AS ABOVE WITH NECK REMOVED. ROLLED WITH EYE MUSCLE LENGTHWISE AND STRING-TIED GIRTHWISE EVERY 2", ALSO TIED LENGTHWISE.
FORESADDLE*	51 - 71#	CUT BETWEEN 12TH and 13TH RIB.
HINDSADDLE*	49 - 69#	TO INCLUDE 1 OR NO RIB.
LEG, SINGLE, BONE-IN*	20 - 28#	SMALL SHANK, KNUCKLE AND BONES.
LEG, BONELESS, ROAST-READY*	10 - 15#	SAME AS ABOVE WITH ALL BONES REMOVED; NOT MORE THAN 1/2" SURFACE FAT AT ANY ONE PLACE. STRING-TIED GIRTHWISE EVERY 2", ALSO TIED LENGTHWISE.
LIVER, CALF'S	2-1/2 - 4#	NO. 1, UNBLEMISHED, FRESH OR FRESH FROZEN. COLOR: REDDISH BROWN TO DARK BROWN. (SEE USDA IMPS - SERIES 700)
LOIN, SINGLE*	4-1/2 - 6-1/2#	FLANK OFF, KIDNEY OUT.
RACK, HOTEL, DOUBLE* TRIMMED	8 - 11#	7 RIB CUT, (6TH THROUGH 12TH RIB). FULL EYE, FRESH CUT.

PURCHASE SPECIFICATIONS FOR VEAL — WHOLESALE & FABRICATED CUTS (CONT'D)

PRODUCT	WEIGHT RANGE	REQUIREMENTS
SHOULDER CLOD, ROAST-READY*	6 - 8#	MUST BE ONE PIECE. NOT LESS THAN 3/4" THICK AT ANY POINT. STRING-TIED GIRTHWISE, IF SO SPECIFIED.
SIDES OF VEAL*	50 - 70#	FRESH CUT, TO BE MATCHED, INSOFAR AS PRACTICABLE.
STEWING VEAL (CUBES)*	AMOUNT AS SPECIFIED	UNIFORM CUBES, APPROXIMATELY 1". SURFACE OR SEAM FAT OF ANY ONE PIECE MAY NOT EXCEED 1/4" MAXIMUM TRIMMABLE FAT CONTENT OF LOT: 20%.
SWEETBREAD, PAIR	1/2 - 3/4#	NO. 1, TRIMMED, SELECTED, FRESH.

PURCHASE SPECIFICATIONS FOR VEAL — PORTION CUTS

MUST BE PRODUCED FROM FEDERALLY QUALITY GRADED "USDA CHOICE"

STATE OF REFRIGERATION: FROZEN

FOR DETAILED DESCRIPTION — WHERE APPLICABLE*—

REFER TO USDA "INSTITUTIONAL MEAT PURCHASE SPECIFICATIONS" FOR PORTION-CUT MEAT PRODUCTS*—

SERIES 1000, ISSUED MAY, 1969

PRODUCT	SIZE	WEIGHT RANGE	REQUIREMENTS
RIB CHOPS*	5 OZ	4-3/4 OZ-5-1/4 OZ	CUT FROM SINGLE HOTEL RACK; RIB-BONE NOT TO EXCEED 3" FROM EXTREME OUTER TIP OF RIB EYE MUSCLE. NOT MORE THAN 1/4" SURFACE FAT AT ANY POINT. PART OF CHINE-BONE REMOVED.
	— OR —		
	6 OZ	5-1/2 OZ-6-1/2 OZ	
	(AS SPECIFIED)		
CUTLETS, REGULAR*	3 OZ	2-3/4 OZ-3-1/4 OZ	CUT FROM SINGLE LEG, BONELESS, WITH SHANK, FLANK & HEEL REMOVED. CUTLETS MUST BE CUBED, BUT NOT MORE THAN TWICE. MUST BE OF SAME APPROXIMATE SHAPE. NOT MORE THAN 1/4" SURFACE FAT AT ANY ONE POINT.
	— OR —		
	4 OZ	3-3/4 OZ-4-1/4 OZ	
	(AS SPECIFIED)		

PURCHASE SPECIFICATIONS FOR LAMB — WHOLESALE & FABRICATED CUTS
WHOLESALE CUTS MUST BE FEDERALLY QUALITY GRADED "USDA CHOICE"
YIELD GRADED NO. 3
STATE OF REFRIGERATION: CHILLED

FOR DETAILED DESCRIPTION — WHERE APPLICABLE*—
REFER TO USDA "INSTITUTIONAL MEAT PURCHASE SPECIFICATIONS" FOR FRESH LAMB AND MUTTON
SERIES 200, ISSUED OCTOBER 1961, AS AMENDED APRIL, 1969.

FABRICATED CUTS MUST BE PRODUCED FROM SAME QUALITY AS WHOLESALE CUTS
IN ACCORDANCE WITH USDA INSTITUTIONAL MEAT PURCHASING SPECIFICATIONS
FOR PORTION-CUT MEAT PRODUCTS — SERIES 1000, REVISED MARCH, 1969.

EVIDENCE OF QUALITY

COLOR: DULL PINKISH;
TEXTURE: FINE, YET FIRM;
AGE: MUST BE YOUNG, THE JOINT AT WHICH THE
FORE-FEET ARE REMOVED MUST BE SMOOTH,
MOIST & RED, WITH 4 NOTICEABLE RIDGES;

BONES: PINKISH WHERE CUT;
FAT: PINKISH WHITE, WELL DISTRIBUTED,
NOT EXCESSIVE.

PRODUCT	WEIGHT RANGE	REQUIREMENTS
CHUCK, DOUBLE*	19 - 23#	TO INCLUDE 4 RIBS.
FORESADDLE*	27 - 33#	TO INCLUDE THE 1ST THRU 12TH RIBS.
HINDSADDLE*	27 - 33#	TO INCLUDE 1 (THE 13TH) RIB.
LEG, DOUBLE*	19 - 23#	FRESH CUT.
LEG, BONELESS*	8 - 11#	ALL BONES REMOVED. NOT MORE THAN 1/2" COVERING SURFACE FAT. STRING-TIED EVERY 2" GIRTHWISE, ALSO TIED LENGTHWISE.
LOIN, DOUBLE, REGULAR*	8 - 10#	KIDNEYS ON, FLANK OFF. TO INCLUDE 1 OR NO RIB.
RACKS, HOTEL, TRIMMED, DOUBLE*	6 - 7#	LARGE "EYE" SHORT RIBS, WELL TRIMMED. (INCL. 5TH TO 12TH RIB) 5" CUT FROM CHINE BONE TO RIB BONE.
STEWING LAMB (CUBES)	AMOUNT AS SPECIFIED	MUST BE PREPARED FROM BONELESS SHOULDER. FREE FROM BONES & CARTILAGES. UNIFORM CUBES APPROXIMATELY 1". SURFACE OR SEAM FAT OF ANY ONE PIECE MAY NOT EXCEED 1/4". MAXIMUM TRIMMABLE FAT CONTENT OF LOT: 20%.
WHOLE LAMB CARCASS*	54 - 65#	SEE "EVIDENCE OF QUALITY" ABOVE.

PURCHASE SPECIFICATIONS FOR LAMB   —   PORTION-CUTS
MUST BE FEDERALLY QUALITY GRADED "USDA CHOICE" & YIELD GRADED NO. 3
STATE OF REFRIGERATION: FROZEN

FOR DETAILED DESCRIPTION—WHERE APPLICABLE*—
REFER TO USDA "INSTITUTIONAL MEAT PURCHASE SPECIFICATIONS" FOR PORTION-CUT MEAT PRODUCTS
SERIES 1000, ISSUED MARCH 1969.

PRODUCT	SIZE	WEIGHT RANGE	REQUIREMENTS
RIB CHOPS	6 OZ	5-1/2 OZ-6-1/2 OZ	PREPARED FROM TRIMMED HOTEL RACK RIB-BONE NOT TO EXCEED 3" FROM EXTREME OUTER TIP OF RIB EYE MUSCLE.
	— OR — 7 OZ (AS SPECIFIED)	6-1/2-7-1/2 OZ	FELL COMPLETELY REMOVED. NOT MORE THAN 1/4" SURFACE FAT AT ANY ONE POINT. PART OF CHINE BONE REMOVED.
SHOULDER CHOPS	6 OZ	5-1/2 OZ-6-1/2 OZ	PREPARED FROM ARM & BLADE BONE SECTIONS OF SHOULDER. RIBLETS & UNDERLYING FAT IN EXCESS OF 1/4" MUST BE REMOVED.
LOIN CHOPS	5 OZ	4-3/4 OZ-5-1/4 OZ	PREPARED FROM TRIMMED LOINS. FLANK NOT TO EXCEED 3" FROM EXTREME OUTER TIP OF LOIN EYE MUSCLE. FELL COMPLETELY REMOVED. NOT MORE THAN 1/4" SURFACE FAT AT ANY ONE POINT:

PURCHASE SPECIFICATIONS FOR PORK
MUST BE QUALITY GRADED "U.S. NO. 1"
FOR DETAILED DESCRIPTION—WHERE APPLICABLE*—
REFER TO USDA "INSTITUTIONAL MEAT PURCHASE SPECIFICATIONS" FOR FRESH PORK—
SERIES 400, ISSUED MAY 1969 AND CURED OR CURED & SMOKED PORK PRODUCTS—
SERIES 500, REVISED MARCH 1969.

FABRICATED CUTS AND PORTION CUTS MUST BE PRODUCED FROM SAME QUALITY AS WHOLESALE CUTS
IN ACCORDANCE WITH USDA INSTITUTIONAL MEAT PURCHASING SPECIFICATIONS
FOR PORTION-CUT MEAT PRODUCTS—SERIES 1000, REVISED MARCH, 1969.

PRODUCT	WEIGHT RANGE	REQUIREMENTS
BACON, CANADIAN STYLE,* CURED & SMOKED (UNSLICED)	3 - 5#	NOT MORE THAN 1/4" FAT AT ANY POINT.
BACON, SLICED, SKINLESS* CURED & SMOKED	26 - 30SLI/LB OR 24 - 28SLI/LB	DRY CURE; LEAN STREAKS SHOULD PREDOMINATE, 8-10" LONG SLICES.
BUTTS, FRESH, BOSTON STYLE*	4 - 6#	REGULAR SHOULDER WITH PICNICS AND PLATE REMOVED. WELL TRIMMED.
BUTTS, SHOULDER, CURED AND SMOKED, BONELESS	4 - 6#	FREE FROM SOURNESS & DISCOLORATION CLOSELY TRIMMED; EXCESS FAT AND THE LEAN MEAT OVERLYING THE LARGE "FAT SEAM" TO BE REMOVED.
CHOPS, REGULAR	5 OZ 4-3/4 to 5-1/4 OZ OR 6 OZ 5-1/4 to 6-1/2 OZ (AS SPECIFIED)	CUT FROM ENTIRE LOIN, WEIGHING 10-12 LBS. CHOPS TO BE REASONABLY UNIFORM. NOT MORE THAN 1/4" SURFACE FAT AT ANY ONE POINT.
FATBACK, DRY SALT		NOT LESS THAN 1-1/2" THICK AT ANY ONE POINT. TRIMMED SQUARE ON ALL EDGES. WEIGHED ON THE BASIS OF "REASONABLY FREE OF SALT."
HAM, BONELESS, COOKED* SKINNED	8 - 10#	FAT NOT TO EXCEED 1/2" AT ANY ONE POINT. GELATINE NOT TO EXCEED 12-1/2% OF TOTAL WEIGHT.
HAM, FRESH, SKINNED*	14 - 16#	FAT NOT TO EXCEED 1/2" AT ANY POINT. NOT MORE THAN 40% OF ENTIRE LENGTH TO BE COVERED BY FAT.
HAM, CURED AND SMOKED SKINNED*	14 - 16#	SHORT SHANK; FAT NOT TO EXCEED 1/2" AT ANY EXPOSED POINT. NO "BURNT OUT" MARROWS; NOT EXCESSIVELY PUMPED.

PURCHASE SPECIFICATIONS FOR PORK (CONT'D)

WHOLESALE CUT	WEIGHT RANGE	REQUIREMENTS
HAM, CURED AND SMOKED (MORRELL)	10 - 12#	BLUE PACKAGE
HAM, CURED AND SMOKED READY-TO-EAT*	14 - 16#	SAME AS SKINNED SMOKED HAM, STAMPED BY USDA: "READY-TO-EAT"; FIRM AND DRY.
LOIN, (REGULAR), FRESH, WHOLE*	10 - 12#	UNIFORMLY TRIMMED: FAT NOT TO EXCEED A DEPTH OF 1/4".
LOIN, -ROASTS (PREPARED)	2 - 3#	3 LB. LOIN-END PIECES AND 2-2-1/2 LB. SHOULDER END PIECES. SUITABLE PREPARED FOR ROASTING BY CUTTING THRU THE CHINE & BACK BONE TO THE FLESH WITH CUTS SPACED 1" APART.
PICNIC, SHOULDER, FRESH*	6 - 8#	AT LEAST 1" OF BLADE BONE TO BE PRESENT. CLOSELY TRIMMED WITH "LIP" OR BREAST FLAP REMOVED. WELL TRIMMED.
PICNIC, SHOULDER CURED AND SMOKED*	6 - 8#	SAME AS FOR "FRESH PICNIC". MUST BE FREE FROM SOURNESS.
PORK HOCKS, FRESH (SHOULDER)*	1/2 - 1#	UNIFORM SIZE, NOT LESS THAN 2" IN LENGTH.
SALT BELLIES, DRY SALT CURED*, SKIN-ON	14 - 18#	SQUARE CUT. BONELESS AND FREE FROM CARTILAGE. UNIFORM IN THICKNESS. FREE FROM DISCOLORATION AND BRUISES.
SHOULDER, CURED AND SMOKED, FULL CUT, SKINNED	14 - 16#	SQUARE CUT, N.Y. STYLE. FAT NOT TO EXCEED 1-3/4" IN DEPTH AT ANY EXPOSED POINT.
SPARERIBS, FRESH*	3# OR UNDER	NEATLY TRIMMED. SEMI-LOOSE PIECES TO BE REMOVED.

PURCHASE SPECIFICATIONS FOR POULTRY
MUST BE GRADED "U.S. GRADE A" AND SO IDENTIFIED
U.S.D.A. GRADING CERTIFICATE MUST BE FURNISHED WITH DELIVERY FOR FRESH POULTRY AND BE DATED NO MORE THAN (2) BUSINESS DAYS PRIOR TO DELIVERY.

PRODUCT	WEIGHT RANGE PLUS OR MINUS 5%	REQUIREMENTS
BROILERS, EVISCERATED	1-3/4 - 2# (21-27# TO DZ.)	FRESH OR FROZEN
DUCKS, YOUNG, EVISCERATED	3 - 4# (36-48# TO DZ.)	FROZEN
FOWLS, EVISCERATED	3-3/4 - 4-1/4# (45-51# TO DZ.)	FRESH OR FRESH FROZEN
FRYERS, EVISCERATED	2-1/4 - 2-3/4# (27-33# TO DZ.)	FRESH
SQUABS, EVISCERATED	10 - 14 OZ. (7-1/2-10-1/2# TO DZ.)	FROZEN
TURKEYS, HEN, EVISCERATED	8 - 10# (96-120# TO DZ.)	FRESH OR FROZEN
TURKEYS, YOUNG TOM, EVISCERATED	22 - 24# (264-288# TO DZ.)	FRESH OR FROZEN BROADBREASTED, MEAT TYPE.
TURKEY, BONELESS ROLL,* UNCOOKED, FROZEN	9#	ALL WHITE MEAT, NO SEASONING OR CHEMICAL PRESERVATIVE ADDED, GRADED FOR CONDITION, IF REQUESTED.
TURKEY-BREAST, DOUBLE, RAW WITH WING & RIB CAGE	14 - 16# EA	FRESH OR FROZEN
TURKEY, BONELESS ROLL, PULLMAN, COOKED	6# OR 9#	SOLID, ALL WHITE MEAT
ROCK CORNISH GAME HEN, FROZEN	12/10-12OZ PER CASE	BONED & STUFFED WITH WILD RICE

*U.S. GRADING NOT ALWAYS AVAILABLE.

PURCHASE SPECIFICATIONS
FOR
MANUFACTURED MEATS AND MEAT PRODUCTS
MUST BE GRADED NO. 1 (UNLESS OTHERWISE SPECIFIED)
AND FEDERALLY INSPECTED.
STATE OF REFRIGERATION: CHILLED
FOR DETAILED DESCRIPTION—WHERE APPLICABLE*—
REFER TO USDA "INSTITUTIONAL MEAT PURCHASE SPECIFICATIONS FOR SAUSAGE PRODUCTS—
SERIES 800, EFFECTIVE MARCH 1970

PRODUCT	WEIGHT RANGE	REQUIREMENTS
BOLOGNA, LARGE, SHORT*	5 - 6" DIAMETER (7 to 12 LB)	BEEF OR ARTIFICIAL CASINGS. FREE FROM WRINKLES, BREAKS, JELLY OR WATER POCKETS. ALL BEEF.
BRAUNSCHWEIGER OR LIVERWURST*	3" DIAMETER (5 TO 8 LB)	NATURAL OR ARTIFICIAL CASINGS, BEEF OR VEAL, NO PORK. MUST BE FRESH AND "DRY". NO TRIMMINGS TO BE USED.
FRANKFURTERS, FRESH*	10 PER LB. (NOT OVER 10# CONTAINER)	SKINLESS, FREE FROM WRINKLES AND BREAKS; HIGHLY RESILIENT. FREE FROM JELLY POCKETS AND DISCOLORATION. ALL BEEF.
KNOCKWURST	4 PER LB.	FREE FROM WRINKLES AND BREAKS; HIGHLY RESILIENT. FREE FROM JELLY POCKETS AND DISCOLORATION. ALL BEEF. ARTIFICIAL CASINGS.
LUNCHEON MEAT,* SPICED (CANNED)	9/6-1/2# RECTANGULAR CANS PER CASE	FREE FROM WRINKLES, BREAKS, JELLY, WATER POCKETS AND DISCOLORATION. BEEF OR VEAL-50-40%— (95% LEAN) PORK CHUNKS-50-60%-(80% LEAN).
PORK SAUSAGE, PURE	16 LINKS PER LB. (NOT OVER 10# CONTAINER)	SHEEP CASING. FRESH. NOT LESS THAN 60% LEAN, NOT OVER 40% FAT. FREE FROM BREAKS AND AIR POCKETS; REASONABLY DRY.
PORK SAUSAGE, PURE ALL PORK*	8 - 10 LINKS PER LB.	HOG CASING. FRESH, NOT LESS THAN 60% LEAN, NOT OVER 40% FAT. FREE FROM BREAKS AND AIR POCKETS, REASONABLY DRY.
BRATWURST	4 PER LB.	
POLISH SAUSAGE	1 - LB RING	
HAM, TAYLOR	6 - LB CAN	
WEISSWURST	4 PER LB.	
PORK SAUSAGE, BULK.	10 - LB UNIT	FRESH, NOT LESS THAN 60% LEAN, NOT MORE THAN 40% FAT.

PURCHASE SPECIFICATIONS FOR MANUFACTURED MEATS, ETC. (CONT')

PRODUCT	WEIGHT RANGE	REQUIREMENTS
SALAMI* COOKED	3-1/2 - 4-1/2" DIAMETER (7 TO 12 LB)	ARTIFICIAL OR BEEF CASINGS; FREE FROM WRINKLES, BREAKS, POCKET AND DISCOLORATION. HIGHLY RESILIENT. ALL BEEF.
SCRAPPLE	5 - 6# LOAVES	FIRM ENOUGH TO SLICE, NOT DRY & HARD. NO CARTILAGE OR BONE. 75% PORK HEAD MEAT; 4% SKIN; 4% PORK LIVERS; 16% CORN MEAL; 1% RYE FLOUR.
THURINGER	3" DIAMETER	ARTIFICIAL CASINGS; FIRM AND DRY; FREE FROM MOLD, BREAKS, WRINKLES, SOURNESS AND RANCIDITY. BEEF 65-75% (95% LEAN), PORK TRIMMINGS 25-35% (50% LEAN).

SECTION - B
SPECIFICATIONS
FOR
FISH & SHELLFISH

Date of Latest Revision:
January 1972

PURCHASE SPECIFICATIONS
FOR
FRESH FISH

WHOLE FISH—Must be "Dressed" (Scaled, Eviscerated, Head, Tail, Fins and Blood Clots Removed).
No Salt Added. Tail On.

ITEM:	AVERAGE WEIGHT + or -5%
Whiting Or Other "Pan-size" Fish	8 - 10 Oz Each
Codfish	5 Lbs. Or Over
Halibut, Dressed	10 - 12 Lbs.
Salmon, Dressed, Pink Or Silver	10 - 12 Lbs.

Fillets must be of fish weighing 1-1/2 Lbs. or more, 3/8 - 5/8" in thickness. End fillets are to be kept to a minimum. Must be practically boneless. Skin, with scales removed, may be on or off, as specified. Individual fillets to weigh no less than 1 Lb., nor more than 2 Lbs.
Steaks are to be cut 4 Oz. each of fish weighing 10 - 12 Lbs. "US Grade A".

EVIDENCE OF FRESHNESS:

Odor is fresh - not stale or tainted.
Fresh fish usually sinks in water.
Flesh adheres strongly to the backbone of a fresh fish and difficulty is experienced in boning the fish.
Flesh is firm and elastic and will not retain the imprint of the fingers.
Eyes are clear, not sunken. Gills are red.

FROZEN FISH
THOSE PRODUCTS MUST BE "US GRADE A" FOR WHICH U.S. GOVT. PROVIDES GRADING SERVICE.

Same specifications as for fresh fish, with due allowance for having been frozen.
Must be delivered frozen solid, free from contamination, deterioration and freezer burns and show no evidence of re-freezing. Net weight as specified.
Brook Trout Eviscerated, Unbreaded, 8 oz. each. 9 - 8 Oz. Fish Per Case, or 20 - 8 OZ Fish Per Case.
Fish Sticks (Cod) Breaded, Precooked, 64/1 Oz Sticks Per Box.

SALTED OR SMOKED FISH

Must be free from artificial coloring, preservatives and impurities. Weight to be ascertained by shaking the fish free from salt and draining for 10 minutes before weight is taken.
White Fish, smoked, whole, dressed, head and tail on, 1-1/2 - 2 Lbs. each.

PURCHASE SPECIFICATIONS
FOR
SHELLFISH

PRODUCT	AVERAGE WEIGHT	COUNT	REQUIREMENTS
CLAMS, IN SHELL, HARD MEDIUM: CHERRYSTONES		BUSHEL 300 - 350	SHELLS MUST BE TIGHTLY CLOSED. TEST BY KNOCKING SHELLS TOGETHER. DISCARD THOSE WITH A HOLLOW SOUND.
CLAMS, SOFT-SHELL SMALL, MEDIUM OR LARGE			MUST CLOSE WHEN SHELL IS TOUCHED. SHALL NOT HAVE BEEN PLACED IN DIRECT CONTACT WITH ICE.
CRABS, HARD- OR SOFT-SHELL, MEDIUM PRIME, JUMBOS		SOLD INDIVIDUALLY	MUST BE ALIVE.
CRABMEAT, BACKFIN	LB.		LUMP MEAT FROM BACKFIN, WHITE IN COLOR. STRICTLY FRESH FROM HARD-SHELL CRABS. PROPERLY COOKED. FREE FROM PARTICLES OR SHELL AND OTHER SUBSTANCES. MAY NOT HAVE ANY DIRECT CONTACT WITH WATER OR ICE.
CRABMEAT, REGULAR FLAKE	LB.		SAME SPECIFICATIONS AS FOR BACKFIN, EXCEPT IT IS FROM OTHER PORTIONS OF BODY, ALSO WHITE IN COLOR.
CRABMEAT, SPECIAL (LUMPS & FLAKE)	LB.		LUMP AND FLAKE PACKED TOGETHER.
CRABMEAT, CLAW	LB.		MEAT FROM CLAWS, BROWNISH IN COLOR. OTHERWISE SAME SPECIFICATIONS AS FOR BACKFIN.
LOBSTERS, LIVE	3/4 - 1 LB.		MUST BE ALIVE; COLOR TO VARY FROM DARK BLUISH GREEN TO BROWNISH OLIVE; MUST HAVE 2 CLAWS.
LOBSTER MEAT	14 OZ. CAN		MEAT PICKED FROM COOKED LOBSTER & CHILLED. MUST BE OF EXCELLENT QUALITY FREE FROM SHELL PARTICLES AND OTHER SUBSTANCES.

PURCHASE SPECIFICATIONS
FOR
SHELLFISH (CONT'D)

PRODUCT	AVERAGE WEIGHT	COUNT	REQUIREMENTS
OYSTERS, IN SHELL, BLUEPOINTS	75#	900-1000/BU. BARREL: DZ.	MUST BE ALIVE. SHELLS TO BE CLOSED TIGHTLY. GAPING SHELLS THAT DO NOT CLOSE WHEN HANDLED ARE NOT ACCEPTABLE.
OYSTERS, SHUCKED, COUNTS OYSTERS, SHUCKED, SELECTS OYSTERS, SHUCKED, STANDARDS	8/8-1/2#/GAL. 8/8-1/2#/GAL. 8/8-1/2#/GAL.	GAL: 125-150 GAL: 175-200 GAL: 250-300	MUST BE PACKED IN METAL CANS SURROUNDED BY ICE OR REFRIGERATED; BE BRIGHT IN COLOR AND OF PLEASING FLAVOR. UNIFORM SIZE WITHIN SPECIFIED TYPE. LIQUOR SHALL BE OF GOOD COLOR AND OF A CONSISTENCY NATURAL TO THE PRODUCT. REJECT THOSE WHICH HAVE BEEN "FLOATED" IN FRESH WATER. EASTERN.
OYSTERS, BREADED UNCOOKED, EXTRA LARGE	2 LB. PACKAGE	12 EA/LB	FROZEN.
SCALLOPS, BAY, MED.	9#/GAL. OR BY LB.	GAL: 680	PINKISH-WHITE IN COLOR; 3/4" CUBES. U.S. GRADE "A".
SCALLOPS, DEEP SEA, MED.	9/# GAL. OR BY LB.	GAL: 152	2" CUBES TO BE SPLIT ACROSS THE GRAIN TO AN APPROXIMATE THICKNESS OF 5/8". U.S. GRADE "A".
SHRIMPS: FRESH OR FROZEN JUMBO EXTRA LARGE LARGE MED. LARGE SHRIMPS, FANTAIL, BREADED, UNCOOKED JUMBO MED.	 LB. LB. LB. LB. 2-LB PACKAGE 2-LB PACKAGE	 21 - 25 26 - 30 31 - 35 36 - 42 16/20 21/25	HEAD AND THORAX TO BE REMOVED, UNIFORM IN SIZE. NO MASHED SHRIMPS SHALL BE INCLUDED. MUST BE THOROUGHLY WASHED AND 95% MUST CONSIST OF UNBROKEN SHRIMPS. U.S. GRADE "A". FROZEN, U.S. GRADE "A". FROZEN, U.S. GRADE "A".
SHRIMPS, FROZEN TINY BROKEN	5-LB PACKAGE		COOKED, PEELED & DE-VEINED.

SECTION-C
PURCHASE SPECIFICATIONS
FOR
FRESH VEGETABLES AND FRUITS

Date of Latest Revision:
January 1972

PURCHASE SPECIFICATIONS FOR FRESH VEGETABLES

All vegetables must be *U.S. Grade No. 1*, unless otherwise specified.
There will be tolerance allowed for size only, but goods must be sound,
free from decay and of good quality.
When prices are requested, they must be given on a net *"Per Lb."* Basis

PRODUCT	MIN./MAX. SIZE	REQUIREMENTS	PURCHASE UNIT (COUNT)	APPROX. WEIGHT		
				NET	TARE	GROSS
CABBAGE, GREEN DOMESTIC TYPE	1-1/2 LBS. MIN.	FIRM, SOLID AND HEAVY FOR SIZE; FREE FROM DISCOL-ORATION. (4 LEAVES WRAPPER).	BAG (MESH) CRATE	50 LBS. 50 LBS.	1/4 LB. 6 LBS.	50-1/4 LBS. 56 LBS.
CABBAGE, WHITE	2 LBS. MIN. 5 LBS. MAX.	FIRM, SOLID AND HEAVY FOR SIZE; FREE FROM DISCOLORATION.	BAG, CRATE	50 LBS. 50 LBS.	1 LB. 7 LBS.	51 LBS. 57 LBS.
CABBAGE, RED	1 LB. MIN 4 LBS. MAX.	FIRM, SOLID AND HEAVY FOR SIZE.	BAG, CRATE	50 LBS. 50 LBS.	1 LB. 7 LBS.	51 LBS. 57 LBS.
CARROTS, TOPPED UN-PEELED, "LOCAL" OR "WESTERN" AS SPECI-FIED.	4" MIN. LENGTH. 1-1/2" MAX. DIA. AT TOP.	FIRM, SMOOTH, UNI-FORM AND FAIRLY WELL COLORED.	ROUND STAVE BASKET; BAG (MESH)	50 LBS. 50 LBS.	3-1/2 LBS. 1/4 LB.	53-1/2 LBS. 50-1/4 LBS.
CARROTS, WHOLE, PEELED	4" MIN. LENGTH. 1-1/2" MAX. DIA. AT TOP.	FIRM, SMOOTH, UNI-FORM AND FAIRLY WELL COLORED.	BAG	30 LBS.	1/4 LB.	30-1/4 LBS.
CELERY, PASCAL	——	ORIGINAL CRATES, CRISP, BRITTLE, FREE FROM PITHYNESS AND BLACK HEARTS. WELL DEVELOPED AND WELL FORMED.	CRATE EASTERN (4 DOZ.) WESTERN (3 DOZ.)	50 LBS. 60 LBS.	5 LBS. 5 LBS.	55 LBS. 65 LBS.

PURCHASE SPECIFICATIONS FOR FRESH VEGETABLES (CON'T)

PRODUCT	MIN./MAX. SIZE	REQUIREMENTS	PURCHASE UNIT(COUNT)	APPROX. WEIGHT		
				NET	TARE	GROSS
CHICORY	—	SMALL LEAVES, TENDER MIDRIB. FRESH, FREE FROM BLEMISH AND WELL BLANCHED.	CRATE (36-72HDS.) HAMPER BASKET (18-24HDS.) DOZEN	8-10 LBS. PER DOZ.	—	—
CHIVES	—	FRESH CUT, TENDER, GOOD GREEN COLOR	LB.	LB.	—	—
CORN, GOLDEN	6" MIN. LENGTH	EARS WELL FORMED AND WELL DEVELOPED. MILKY KERNELS.	CRATE OR BAG (4 OR 5 DOZ.)	33 OR 45 LBS.	—	—
CUCUMBERS	6"-9" LONG 2-3/8" MAX. DIA.	REG. SHAPE, AVOID THOSE CONICAL IN SHAPE. FAIRLY WELL COLORED.	BUSHEL (75 EA.) DOZEN	50 LBS 8 LBS.	3-1/2 LBS. —	53-1/2 LBS. —
EGGPLANT	4" MIN. 6" MAX. DIA.	FIRM, GLOSSY SURFACE, CHARACTERISTIC COLOR, AND WELL SHAPED.	BUSHEL	30 LBS.	3-1/2 LBS.	33-1/2 LBS.
ESCAROLE	—	CRISP, WELL BLANCHED	HAMPER (18 OR 24 HDS) CRATE, BASKET, DOZ.	22 LBS.	5 LBS.	27 LBS.
GARLIC	1-1/2" MIN DIA.	FIRM, WELL CURED, FREE FROM DECAY.	LB.	—	—	—
HORSERADISH ROOT	1-1/2" MIN. DIA. 8" MIN. LENGTH	FIRM AND WELL SHAPED.	LB.	—	—	—

PURCHASE SPECIFICATIONS FOR FRESH VEGETABLES (CONT'D)

PRODUCT	MIN./MAX. SIZE	REQUIREMENTS	PURCHASE UNIT (COUNT)	APPROX. WEIGHT		
				NET	TARE	GROSS
LEEKS	12" MAX. LENGTH	GOOD QUALITY AND GOOD GREEN TOPS.	LB.	LB.	—	—
LETTUCE, BOSTON	—	SMOOTH, TENDER LEAF, MEDIUM GREEN COLOR.	CRATE (24 HDS) BASKET (36 HDS)	18 LBS.	3-1/2 LBS.	21-1/2 LBS.
LETTUCE, ICEBERG	—	CRISP, COMPACT HEADS, LIGHT GREEN COLOR. FULL ORIGINAL CARTON. WESTERN	BOX OR CARTON (2 DOZ.)	45 LBS.	3 LBS.	48 LBS.
LETTUCE, ROMAINE	3/4-1 LB.	LOOSE HEADS, ELONGATED LEAVES	HAMPER (18, 20 OR 24 HDS.) DOZEN	—	—	—
MINT	—	FRESH, GREEN, FRAGRANT.	LB.	LB.	—	—
MUSHROOMS	CAPS, 1" - 1-5/8" DIA. STEMS 1-1/4" MAX. LENGTH	CLOSED AROUND STEM, CREAMY WHITE TO WHITE.	BASKET,	3LBS.	1LB.	4LBS
ONIONS, YELLOW, NORTHERN GROWN	2" MIN. DIA.	FREE FROM SPROUTS ROT & BRUISES, UNIFORM SIZE.	BAG	50LBS	1/4LB	50-1/4LB
ONIONS, GREEN (SHALLOTS)	(NO BULB)	IN WINTER FROM L.A. TOPS GREEN & FRESH	LB.	LB	—	—
(SPRING ONIONS)	BULB, 3/8"-3/4" DIA.	TOPS GREEN & FRESH	LB.	LB	—	—
ONIONS, WHITE BOILERS	1" - 1-5/8" DIA.	SHINY WHITE SKIN, DRY & WELL CURED.	BAG	25LBS	1/4LB	25-1/4LB

PURCHASE SPECIFICATIONS FOR FRESH VEGETABLES (CONT'D)

PRODUCT	MIN./MAX. SIZE	REQUIREMENTS	PURCHASE UNIT (COUNT)	APPROX. WEIGHT		
				NET	TARE	GROSS
PARSLEY	—	CURLY, TRIMMED OF ROOTS, TENDER, FREE FROM DIRT & DAMAGE. GOOD. GREEN COLOR.	LB.	LB.	—	—
PARSNIPS	1-1/2"-3" DIA.	YOUNG ROOTS, FIRM, FAIRLY WELL FORMED AND FAIRLY SMOOTH.	1/2 BUSHEL	23 LBS	3 LBS	26 LBS
PEPPERS, GREEN	2-1/2"MIN.DIA. 2-1/2"MIN. LENGTH	HARD, BULLNOSE TYPE, SHINY GREEN SKIN, NO WRINKLES FLESHY WALLS, WELL SHAPED. FULL BUSHEL.	ROUND STAVE BASKET, (APPR. 125EA.) DOZEN	25 LBS	3-1/2 LBS	28-1/2 LBS
POTATOES, UNPEELED WHITE "NEW" OR "OLD" AS SPECIFIED. MAINE OR L.I. AS SPECIFIED.	2"MIN. SIZE "A"	MED. UNIFORM SIZE. SHALLOW EYES, NO SPROUTS, FIRM, FREE FROM BLEMISH.	100LB. BURLAP BAG. 50LB. PAPER BAG.	100 LBS 50 LBS	1 LB 1/4 LB	101 LBS 50-1/4 LBS
POTATOES, WHOLE, PEELED	2" MIN. SIZE "A"	—	50 LB. PAPER BAG.	50 LBS	1/4 LB	50-1/4 LBS
POTATOES, BAKING, LONG, WHITE, IDAHO OR CALIFORNIA AS SPECIFIED.	2" MIN. AVERAGE 6OZ. PER POTATO	MED. UNIFORM SIZE. SHALLOW EYES, FREE FROM BLEMISH.	(140 PER BOX)	50 LBS	2-1/4 LBS	50-1/4 LBS
POTATOES, SWEET	10" MAX. LENGTH. 1-3/4" MIN. 3-3/4" MAX. DIA.	FIRM, FAIRLY SMOOTH. DRY TYPE. FREE FROM DECAY & GROWTH CRACKS.	BUSHEL, HAMPER, BASKET OR CRATE	50 LBS	3 LBS	53 LBS
PUMPKIN	5LB. MIN. WEIGHT.	REG. SHAPE, FREE FROM DECAY.	EACH	5 LB. OR MORE	—	—

PURCHASE SPECIFICATIONS FOR FRESH VEGETABLES (CONT')

PRODUCT	MIN./MAX. SIZE	REQUIREMENTS	PURCHASE UNIT (COUNT)	APPROX. WEIGHT		
				NET	TARE	GROSS
RADISHES, RED, ROUND	3/4" MIN. DIA.	WELL FORMED, FIRM & TENDER FREE FROM DAMAGE, UNI-FORM SIZE.	CELLO-PACK	6 OZ	—	—
RUTABAGAS, EASTERN OR CANADIAN	3-1/2"-7" DIA.	CLEAN, FAIRLY WELL SHAPED MED. SIZE, SMOOTH SKIN, UNDAMAGED	BUSHEL, BAG	50 LBS. 50 LBS	5 LBS 1 LB	55 LBS 51 LBS
SQUASH, ACORN	3-1/2"-5" DIA.	YELLOWISH GREEN, DARK GREEN, HARD RIND.	ROUND STAVE BASKET	40 LBS	3-1/2 LBS	43-1/2 LBS
SQUASH, BUTTERNUT	3" MIN. 6" MAX.	MED. SIZE, WELL SHAPED.	BUSHEL CRATE	40 LBS	5 LBS	45 LBS
SQUASH, HUBBARD	7 LB. MIN.	UNIFORM SHAPE. JUDGE RIPENESS BY SOUND WHEN KNOCKING ON SHELL.	BUSHEL CRATE OR BAG	50 LBS 50 LBS	5 LBS 1 LB	55 LBS 51 LBS
TOMATOES, HARD, RED RIPE (REPACKED)	6x6 ROWS 2-4/8" MIN. DIA. 2-7/8" MAX. DIA.	SMOOTH, RED SKIN. REG. UNIFORM SHAPE, MIN. OF SEEDS. FIRM.	CARTON (108 EA)	25 LBS	1-1/2 LBS	26-1/2 LBS
TOMATOES, HARD, RIPE (NEARBY)	2-1/2"-3" DIA.	SMOOTH RED SKIN. REG. UNIFORM SHAPE. MIN. OF SEEDS. FIRM	1/2 BUSHEL	18 LBS	3 LBS	21 LBS
TURNIPS, WHITE	2"-3-1/2" DIA.	NEW CROP, MED. SIZE, SMOOTH SKIN, FREE FROM DAMAGE. CLEAN, FAIRLY WELL SHAPED.	BUSHEL BAG	50 LBS 50 LBS	5 LBS 1 LB	55 LBS 51 LBS

PURCHASE SPECIFICATIONS FOR FRESH VEGETABLES (CONT')

PRODUCT	MIN./MAX. SIZE	REQUIREMENTS	PURCHASE UNIT (COUNT)	APPROX. WEIGHT		
				TARE	NET	GROSS
TURNIPS, YELLOW	SEE "RUTABAGAS"	—	—	—	—	—
WATERCRESS	—	DARK GREEN, FREE FROM DISCOLOR-ATION, PUNGENT FLAVOR	LB	LB	—	—

PURCHASE SPECIFICATIONS
FOR FRESH FRUIT

All fresh fruits must be *U.S. Grade No. 1*, unless otherwise specified.
There will be tolerance allowed for size only, but goods must be sound,
free from decay and of good quality.
When prices are requested, they must be given on a *"UNIT"* or *"LB."*
basis, as indicated in the last column, headed "Price Per".
The following will be purchased on a *"Per LB."* basis: apricots,
bananas, cherries, cranberries, grapes, peaches, plums, rhubarb, melons.

PRODUCT	MIN./MAX. SIZE	REQUIREMENTS	PURCHASE UNIT (COUNT)	APPROX. WEIGHT			PRICE PER:
				NET	TARE	GROSS	
APPLES, TABLE (EASTERN OR WESTERN, WINESAP McINTOSH, CORTLANDT OR DELICIOUS) AS SPECIFIED.	2-1/4" MIN. DIA.	FIRM FLESH, BRIGHT SKIN, GOOD AROMA	CARTON, (120's OR 125's)	42LBS	5LBS	47LBS	CARTON
APPLES, BAKING (ROME BEAUTY)	2-3/4" MIN. DIA.	SMOOTH SKIN; REGULAR SHAPE.	CARTON (100's OR 120's)	42LBS	5LBS	47LBS	CARTON
APRICOTS, WESTERN	1-1/2" MIN.	GOLDEN COLOR, UNBRUISED SKIN, JUICY FLESH.	LUG (192) (8 ROWS-8/12 PER LB.)	24LBS	3LBS	27LBS	LB.
AVOCADO	3"-4" DIA.	LARGE GREEN FRUIT, YIELDING GENTLY WHEN PRESSED. SEED RATTLES.	FLAT (16-28) (8-12 OZ. EA.)	13LBS	3LBS	16LBS	FLAT
BANANAS "RIPE", "ON TURN" OR "ALL GREEN" AS SPECIFIED	6" MIN. 7" MAX. LENGTH	CUT HANDS, PRACTICALLY FREE FROM SCARS, BRUISES & UNBROKEN SKIN.	CARTON (3 PER LB)	40LBS	5LBS	45LBS	LB.
BLACK-BERRIES	—	BLACK, GLOSSY BERRIES, SMALL SEEDS, FIRM & FREE FROM MOLD. NO "CAPS"	QUART PINT	1-1/4LBS 3/4LBS	—	—	QT. PT.

PURCHASE SPECIFICATIONS FOR FRESH FRUIT (CONT'D)

PRODUCT	MIN./MAX. SIZE	REQUIREMENTS	PURCHASE UNIT (COUNT)	APPROX. WEIGHT			PRICE PER:
				NET	TARE	GROSS	
BLUE OR HUCKLE-BERRIES	90-130 PER PINT	RIPE & DRY, FREE FROM STICKS LEAVES & STEMS.	PINT (90-130)	—	—	—	PINT
CHERRIES, TABLE	—	UNBRUISED SKIN STEM ON, FREE FROM MOLD, WORMS, AND BROWN SPOTS.	LUG, BOX LB. (13 ROW)	15LBS 1LB	5LBS —	20LBS —	LB. LB.
GRAPES, RED, TABLE OR WHITE SEEDLESS, AS SPECIFIED.	—	COMPACT BUNCHES, WELL FORMED GRAPES WHICH DO NOT FALL OFF STEMS. NO SOFT OR MOLDY FRUIT. FIRM & BRIGHT.	LUG, BOX	28LBS	3LBS	31LBS	LB
GRAPEFRUITS, "DUNCAN" OR "MARSH SEEDLESS" AS SPECIFIED.	3-3/4" MIN. DIA.	UNIFORM SIZE. HEAVY FOR THEIR SIZE; THIN AND OILY SKIN. ROUND OR FLATTENED END. NOT PEAR SHAPED.	CARTON (40's) FLORIDA CALIF.	37LBS 33LBS	4LBS 3LBS	41LBS 36LBS	CARTON
LEMONS	2.01" MIN. DIA.	US COMB. (NO. 1 & 2 MIXED) TIGHT PACK. HEAVY FOR THEIR SIZE; OILY AND ELASTIC THIN SKINS; NO SHARPLY POINTED ENDS. FIRM	CARTON, (195's OR 200's) OR 165's)	38LBS	3LBS	41LBS	CARTON
LIMES	1-1/2" MIN. DIA. 2" MAX. DIA.	GREEN IN COLOR. HEAVY FOR THEIR SIZE.	DOZEN	—	—	—	EACH
MELONS, CANTALOUPE	5" MIN. DIA.	UNIFORM SIZE, WELL DEVELOPED "NETTING" COVERING YELLOWISH SKIN INDICATES RIPENESS. SHOULD BE HEAVY FOR THEIR SIZE, FIRM	CRATE (36) LUG FLAT	80LBS	10LBS	90LBS	LB

PURCHASE SPECIFICATIONS FOR FRESH FRUIT (CONT')

PRODUCT	MIN./MAX. SIZE	REQUIREMENTS	PURCHASE UNIT (COUNT)	APPROX. WEIGHT			PRICE PER:
				NET	TARE	GROSS	
MELONS, HONEYDEW (JUMBO)	6" MIN. DIA.	OVAL. CHARACTER-ISTIC FRAGRANCE. UNDERSIDE IS CREAM OR PALE YELLOW COLOR.	CRATE: 12's CARTON: 6 OR 8's (AS SPECI-FIED)	40LBS 26LBS	8LBS 3LBS	48LBS 29LBS	LB. LB
MELONS, WATERMELONS (LONG TYPE)	30LBS MIN. WEIGHT	MATURE FRUIT WILL GIVE A DULL SOUND WHEN THUMPED. DARK GREEN WITH YELLOW MOTTLING. OVAL SHAPE. EXAMINE INSIDE.	EACH	30LBS	—	—	LB
ORANGES, CALIF., ARIZONA	2-7/8" MIN. DIA. (FOR 88's) 2-3/4" MIN. DIA. (FOR 100's) 2-5/8" MIN. DIA. (FOR 113's)	SKIN BRIGHT YELLOW ORANGE, NO CREASES IN IT, HEAVY FOR THEIR SIZE, NO SOFT SPOTS; MAY HAVE RUSSET SKIN OR SHOW GREEN SPOT EVEN WHEN RIPE. FIRM.	CARTON, (88, OR 113 OR 125)	38LBS	7-1/2LBS	45-1/2LBS	CARTON
ORANGES, FLORIDA	2-7/8" MIN. DIA. (FOR 88's) 2-3/4" MIN. DIA. (FOR 100's) 2-5/8" MIN. DIA. (FOR 113's)	SKIN BRIGHT YELLOW ORANGE, NO CREASES IN IT, HEAVY FOR THEIR SIZE, NO SOFT SPOTS, MAY HAVE RUSSET SKIN OR SHOW GREEN SPOT EVEN WHEN RIPE. FIRM.	CARTON, (80, OR 1)	45LBS	5-1/2LBS	50-1/2LBS	CARTON
ORANGES, TEXAS & STATES OTHER THAN FLA. CALIF. & ARIZONA	2-7/8" MIN. DIA. (FOR 88's) 2-3/4" MIN. DIA. (FOR 100's) 2-5/8" MIN. (113's)	SKIN BRIGHT YELLOW ORANGE, NO CREASES IN IT. HEAVY FOR THEIR SIZE, NO SOFT SPOTS, MAY HAVE RUSSET SKIN OR SHOW GREEN SPOT EVEN WHEN RIPE. FIRM.	CARTON, COUNT AS SPECIFIED	35LBS	5-1/2LBS	40-1/2LBS	CARTON

PURCHASE SPECIFICATIONS FOR FRESH FRUIT (CONT'D)

PRODUCT	MIN/MAX. SIZE	REQUIREMENTS	PURCHASE UNIT (COUNT)	APPROX. WEIGHT			PRICE PER:
				NET	TARE	GROSS	
PEACHES, RIPE FREESTONE	2" MIN. DIA.	UNIFORM SIZE. RED FLESH, TREE RIPENED, FRAGRANT ODOR; ROUND, PLUMP. REG. SHAPE, FLESH YIELDS WHEN GENTLY PRESSED	BUSHEL, 1/2 BUSHEL, BOX	47LBS 23-1/2LBS 20LBS	5LBS 3LBS 3LBS	52LBS 26-1/2LBS 23LBS	LB
PEARS. RIPE D'ANJOU, BARTLETT OR BOSC, AS SPECIFIED.		UNIFORM SIZE; NO SOFT SPOTS OR BRUISES. FIRM FRUITS.	BOX (135)	45LBS	7LBS	52LBS	BOX
PINEAPPLES, RIPE	TOP TO BE NO LESS THAN 4" NOR MORE THAN TWICE THE LENGTH OF THE FRUIT.	FIRM, CHARACTERISTIC "PINEY AROMA". SQUARE SHOULDER. NO BROWN DISCOLORATION AT STEM.	1/2 CRATE (12) OR CRATE (24)	—	—	—	1/2 CRATE OR CRATE
PLUMS, RED, YELLOW OR BLUE AS SPECIFIED.	—	FULLY RIPE, UNBROKEN SKINS, FREE FROM BRUISES. FIRM.	BOX (4 TILLS) 4X5 OR 5X5	24LBS	—	—	LB
STRAWBERRIES	—	FIRM. "CAPS" OR "HULLS" ARE ON. BERRIES SHOULD NOT HAVE GREEN OR WHITE TOPS. NO SAND. AROMA, COLOR AND FRAGRANCE FREE FROM SOFT AND MOLDED BERRIES.	QUART OR PINT	1-1/2LBS 3/4 LB.	— —	— —	QT PT
TANGERINES	2-11/16" MIN. DIA.	SKIN BRIGHT YELLOW ORANGE. HEAVY FOR THEIR SIZE. NO SOFT SPOTS. FAIRLY FIRM.	CRATE OR BOX (120 OR 150's)	—	—	—	CRATE OR BOX
TEMPLE ORANGES	2-11/16" MIN. DIA.	SKIN BRIGHT YELLOW ORANGE. HEAVY FOR THEIR SIZE. NO SOFT SPOTS.	CRATE OR BOX (80 OR 100's)	—	—	—	CRATE OR BOX

SECTION - D
PURCHASE SPECIFICATIONS
FOR
DAIRY PRODUCTS & EGGS

Date of Latest Revision:
January, 1972

PURCHASE SPECIFICATIONS
FOR
DAIRY PRODUCTS AND EGGS

PRODUCT	U. S. GRADE	UNIT	REQUIREMENTS
BUTTER, SWEET (UNSALTED) PRINTS OR 90 REDI-PATS (AS SPECIFIED)	"U.S." 92-A	LB., 24, 30 OR 36 LBS PER BOX	
BUTTER, SALTED PRINTS OR 90 REDI-PATS (AS SPECIFIED)	"U.S." 92-A	LB., 24, 30 OR 32 LBS PER BOX.	
CHEESE, PROCESSED YELLOW AMERICAN, OR WHITE AMERICAN (AS SPECIFIED)	"U.S.D.A.- QUALITY APPROVED"	LB. OR 6/5 LBS PER CARTON OR 12/3 LBS PER BOX (SLICED OR UNSLICED)	TO BE FREE FROM MOLD. NO OPENINGS OR PINHOLES. MUST SLICE WITHOUT BREAKING OR STICKING TO KNIFE.
CHEESE, COTTAGE, ("REGULAR" OR "SALT POOR"). (AS SPECIFIED)	"U.S.D.A.- QUALITY APPROVED"	LB., 5, 10, 30 OR 33 LBS CONTAINERS	SHALL BE FREE FROM IMPURITIES, OBJECTIONABLE FLAVORS, AND EXCESSIVE MOISTURE. MEDIUM SIZE CURDS. MUST BE CERTIFIED AS TO KASHRUTH SUPERVISION.
CHEESE, CREAM LOAF	"U.S.D.A.- QUALITY APPROVED"	3 LB LOAF OR 10/3 LBS PER CASE	MUST BE CERTIFIED AS TO KASHRUTH SUPERVISION.
CHEESE, FARMER	"U.S.D.A.- QUALITY APPROVED"	3 LB LOAF (15/3 LBS PER BOX)	MUST BE CERTIFIED AS TO KASHRUTH SUPERVISION.
CHEESE, MUENSTER	"U.S.D.A.- QUALITY APPROVED"	LB. (6/5 LBS PER BOX)	SEMI-HARD; MADE OF COW'S AND GOAT'S MILK. MUST BE CERTIFIED AS TO KASHRUTH SUPERVISION.

PURCHASE SPECIFICATIONS
FOR
DAIRY PRODUCTS AND EGGS (CONT'D)

PRODUCT	U.S. GRADE	UNIT	REQUIREMENTS
CHEESE, GRATED	"U.S.D.A. QUALITY APPROVED"	LB (24/1 LB. PER BOX)	PARMESAN, MADE OF PARTLY DEFATTED COW'S MILK; HARD; SHARP FLAVOR.
CHEESE, SWISS OR SWEITZER, DOMESTIC	U.S. GRADE "A"	LB. (8/10 LBS. PER BOX)	CENTER CUT OR PIECES TO BE CUT WEDGE-WISE FROM WHEELS WEIGHING 125 - 175 LBS., OR RINDLESS BLOCK, AS SPECIFIED.
CHEESE, SHARP (AMERICAN)	U.S. GRADE "A"	"MIDGETS," 10-12 LBS., "DAISIE" 20-26 LBS: "FLATS" 32-34 LBS.	NEW YORK, AGED, NATURAL AMERICAN CHEDDAR, SHARP CURE
MARGARINE, 90 REDI-PATS KOSHER AND PAREVE, OR 72 REDI-PATS, KOSHER AND PAREVE	—	LB. OR 10 LBS. PER CARTON	100% PURE VEGETABLE OIL
MARGARINE, PRINTS KOSHER AND PAREVE	—	LB. OR 30-1/4 LBS. PER CARTON	100% PURE VEGETABLE OIL
MARGARINE, REGULAR PRINTS	—	LB., OR 30 LBS. PER CARTON	100% PURE VEGETABLE OIL
MARGARINE, LOW SODIUM 90 REDI-PATS	—	LB., 10, 40 LBS. PER CARTON	100% PURE VEGETABLE OIL

PURCHASE SPECIFICATIONS
FOR
SHELL EGGS

PRODUCT	U.S. GRADE	UNIT	REQUIREMENTS
EGGS, FRESH, "MEDIUM", "LARGE", OR "SMALL" (AS SPECIFIED)	MUST BE U.S. GRADE "A" AND SO IDENTIFIED	30 DZ./CS. OR, 15 DZ./ 1/2 CS.	MINIMUM NET WEIGHT: LARGE: 46 LBS. MEDIUM: 40 LBS. SMALL: 34 LBS. TARE WEIGHT: APPROX. 6 LBS. 20% MUST BE "AA", 70% MUST BE GRADE "A" WITHIN THE MAXIMUM TOLERANCE OF 5% WHICH MAY BE BELOW "A" QUALITY NOT MORE THAN 5% MAY BE "C" QUALITY OR 'CHECKS' IN ANY COMBINATION. CASES TO BE NEW, SEALED, STAMPED AND DATED BY U.S.D.A. DELIVERY TO BE NO LATER THAN (2) BUSINESS DAYS FOLLOWING DATE SHOWN AND MUST BE ACCOMPANIED BY GRADING CERTIFICATE.
FROZEN EGGS			
EGGS, FROZEN, WHOLE	MUST BE U.S. GRADE "A" QUALITY AND SO IDENTIFIED	10-LB. DIS-POSABLE FIBRE CARTON, WITH POLYETHYLENE LINER OR 8/5 LBS. CARTONS	MUST BE DELIVERED COMPLETELY FROZEN & SHOW NO EVIDENCE OF RE-FREEZING. CONTAINERS MUST BE SOUND & CLEAN.

SECTION - E
PURCHASE SPECIFICATIONS
FOR
CANNED GOODS
AND
JAMS, JELLIES & SYRUP

Date of Latest Revision:
January, 1972

PURCHASE SPECIFICATIONS
FOR
CANNED FRUITS

Canned goods must be of the latest pack and U.S.D.A. grade as specified. All cans must be free from rust and dents, ends to be flat, or curved inward. Cans with "swells" are to be replaced at no charge to us or are to be credited in full, if vendor is notified within 6 months from date of delivery.* Products not covered by U.S.D.A. grades shall be of best commercial quality.

PRODUCT	UNIT PER CASE	U.S.D.A.	MINIMUM U.S.D.A. SCORE	APPROX. SIZE OR COUNT	REQUIREMENTS
APPLES	6/#10	FANCY	—	1/8 OR 1/4's AS SPECIFIED	YORK IMP. HEAVYPACK
APPLESAUCE, SWEETENED	6/#10	FANCY	90	—	MIN. 16° BRIX. COARSE FINISH
APRICOT HALVES	6/#10	CHOICE	82	85/115	UNPEELED, HEAVY SYRUP
BLUEBERRIES	6/#10	FANCY	—	—	WATER PACK
CHERRIES, LIGHT, SWEET	6/#10	CHOICE	84	270/330	UNPITTED, HEAVY SYRUP
CHERRIES, MARASCH. WHOLE OR BROKEN, AS SPECIFIED.	48/8 OZ. 24/8 OZ. OR 4/1 GAL.	*	—	—	PITTED, WITHOUT STEMS
CHERRIES, RSP	6/#10	FANCY OR STAND.	—	—	WATER PACK MONTMORENCY TYPE
CRANBERRY SCE.	6/#10	FANCY	—	—	STRAINED
FIGS, KADOTA	6/#10	CHOICE	84	70/90	HEAVY SYRUP STYLE:WHOLE

PURCHASE SPECIFICATIONS
FOR
CANNED FRUITS (CONT'D)

PRODUCT	UNIT PER CASE	U.S.D.A. GRADE	MINIMUM U.S.D.A. SCORE	APPROX. SIZE OR COUNT	REQUIREMENTS
FRUIT COCKTAIL	6/#10	FANCY	90	—	HEAVY SYRUP
GRAPEFRUIT, WHOLE SECTIONS.	12/#5	FANCY	—	—	LIGHT SYRUP
PEACHES, HALVES, YELLOW CLING	6/#10	CHOICE	84	30/35	HEAVY SYRUP
PEACHES, SLICED, YELLOW CLING	6/#10	CHOICE	84	—	THICK SLICES, HEAVY SYRUP
PEAR HALVES, BARTLETT	6/#10	CHOICE	84	25/30	HEAVY SYRUP
PINEAPPLE, HAWAIIAN,	6/#10	FANCY			HEAVY SYRUP
PINEAPPLE, HAWAIIAN CRUSHED	6/#10	FANCY	90	52	EXTRA HEAVY SYRUP
PLUMS, PURPLE	6/#10	CHOICE	84	70/80	HEAVY SYRUP

PURCHASE SPECIFICATIONS
FOR
CANNED JUICES

PRODUCT	U.S.D.A. GRADE	UNIT PER CASE	REQUIREMENTS
APPLE JUICE	FANCY	12/46 FL. OZ.	CLARIFIED
APRICOT NECTAR	*	12/46 FL. OZ.	CALIFORNIA
GRAPE JUICE	FANCY	12/24 FL. OZ.	UNSWEETENED
GRAPEFRUIT JUICE	FANCY	12/QT.	UNSWEETENED, SINGLE STRENGTH
PEACH NECTAR	*	12/46 FL. OZ.	—
PEAR NECTAR	*	12/46 FL. OZ.	—
PINEAPPLE JUICE	FANCY	12/46 FL. OZ.	UNSWEETENED, HAWAIIAN
PRUNE JUICE	FANCY	12/QT.	UNSWEETENED
TOMATO JUICE	FANCY	12/46 Fl.OZ.	EASTERN OR CALIFORNIA
TOMATO JUICE DIETETIC	FANCY	24/NO. 303 OR 24/NO. 2	HOMOGENIZED, AS SPECIFIED

PURCHASE SPECIFICATIONS
FOR
CANNED VEGETABLES AND TOMATO PRODUCTS

PRODUCT	UNIT PER CASE	U.S.D.A. GRADE	MIN. U.S.D.A. SCORE	SIZE OR COUNT	REQUIREMENTS
ASPARAGUS, CUT	6/#10	STAND.	—	—	ALL GREEN
ASPARAGUS, WHOLE SPEARS	6/#5 SQUAT OR 24/#2 OR 24/#300 (14 OZ)	FANCY	92	4/80 17/24	ALL GREEN MAMMOTH, CALIFORNIA
BEANS, BAKED VEGETARIAN	6/#10	FANCY	—	—	WHITE BEANS IN TOMATO SAUCE
BEANS, GREEN, CUT	6/#10	EX. STAND.	82	4 OR 5 SIEVE	"BLUELAKE", ROUND, 1-1/2" CUT.
BEANS, LIMA	6/#10	EX. STAND.	—	#3 SIZE	GREEN & WHITE MIXED
BEANS, RED KIDNEY	6/#10	FANCY	—	—	DARK RED IN SAUCE
BEANS, WAX, CUT	6/#10	FANCY	—	SIZE #3 OR 4 OR 3 & 4 MIXED	ROUND OR FLAT
BEETS, SLICED	6/#10	FANCY	90	2-1/2" DIA. OR UNDER	MEDIUM
BEETS, DICED	6/#10	FANCY	90	—	—
CARROTS, SLICED	6/#10	FANCY	90	—	SMALL
CARROTS, DICED	6/#10	FANCY	90	—	—
CORN, CRM, STYLE	6/#10	FANCY	—	—	GOLDEN, EXTRA HEAVY CONSISTENCY
CORN, WHOLE KERNEL	6/#10	FANCY	90	—	GOLDEN, SMALL KERNEL
MUSHROOMS	48/#1 OR 24/#1 (8 OZ) OR 24/#2-1/2 (16 OZ)	STAND.	—	—	STEMS & PIECES, DOMESTIC OR IMPORTED. CREAM COLOR.

PURCHASE SPECIFICATIONS
FOR
CANNED VEGETABLES AND TOMATO PRODUCTS (CONT')

PRODUCT	UNIT PER CASE	U.S.D.A. GRADE	MIN. U.S.D.A SCORE	SIZE OR COUNT	REQUIREMENTS
OKRA, CUT	6/#10	STAND.	—	1/2 - 1" PIECES	—
PEAS, SWEET	6/#10	EXTRA STAND.	85	#4 OR #5 SIEVE OR #4 & 5 MIXED	SWEET
PIMIENTOS, WHOLE OR CHOPPED (AS SPECIFIED)	24/#2-1/2	FANCY	—	—	FLESH OF SOUND SMOOTH SKINNED RED, RIPE, LARGE SWEET PEPPERS, PROPERLY PEELED, TRIMMED, CORED & FREE FROM SEEDS & SEED CELLS. UNIFORM RED COLOR. NO GREEN TINGE, CAST OR SPOT.
SAUERKRAUT	6/#10	FANCY	—	—	SHREDDED. FIRST QUALITY.
TOMATOES, WHOLE	6/#10	EX. STAND	80	—	SOLID PACK. MIN. DRAINED WEIGHT 68 OZ
TOMATO CATSUP	6/#10 OR 24/14 OZ. BOTTLES	FANCY	—	—	SP. GR. 1.15 (33% SOLIDS) TO BE OF GOOD CONSISTENCY AND SHOW NOT MORE THAN A SLIGHT SEPARATION OF FREE LIQUID: UNIFORM & SMOOTH FINISH.
TOMATO PUREE	6/#10	FANCY	90	—	HEAVY CONC. 12% SOLIDS. SP. GR. 1.06, CALIF.
CHILI SAUCE	6/#10	FANCY	—	—	SHALL BE HEAVY BODIED OF BRIGHT RED COLOR, PREPARED FROM CLEAN, SOUND, RIPE TOMATOES. SHALL NOT SHOW MOLDS IN OVER 12% OF MICROFIELDS.

PURCHASE SPECIFICATIONS FOR CANNED FISH

PRODUCT	UNIT	REQUIREMENTS
SALMON (A) CHINOOK (B) RED (C) COHO (D) PINK (AS SPECIFIED)	12/4#	FREE FROM GILLS, FINS AND EXTRANEOUS MATTER. BONES TO BE SOFT AND YIELDING. PACKED IN OIL OR WATER, AS SPECIFIED.
SALMON, DIETETIC	48/7-3/4 OZ. OR 48/3-3/4 OZ.	MED. RED.
SARDINES: DOMESTIC OR IMPORTED	"QUARTER OIL" 3-3/4 OZ OR 4 OZ. (100 CANS/CASE)	SEA HERRING OR PILCHARD, NOT LESS THAN 8 OR 16 SARDINES TO A CAN. WELL CLEANED FIRM AND UNBROKEN. NOT TOUGH OR FIBROUS. PACKED IN EDIBLE VEGETABLE OIL.
SARDINES/TOMATO SAUCE	24/15 OZ.	5 TO 7 FISH PER CAN.

TUNAFISH: LIGHT MEAT
    1. FANCY: LARGE PIECES OF SOLID MEAT
    2. STANDARD: 75% LARGE PIECES. 25% FLAKES.
    3. TUNA FLAKES: SMALL PIECES (AS SPECIFIED)
	12/4# 2 1/2 OZ. OR 6/4# 2 1/2 OZ.	YELLOW OR BLUE FIN, SKIPJACK, BONITA OR ALBACORE SPECIES. PROPERLY COOKED, LIGHT MEAT TO BE SEPARATED FROM SKIN, BONES AND DARK MEAT. NO ARTIFICIAL COLORING. PACKED IN WATER AS SPECIFIED.

TUNAFISH, DIETETIC	48/6 1/2 OZ.	CHUNK STYLE.
GEFILTE FISH, REGULAR	12/1 LB 11 OZ. CANS PER CASE (4 PCES PER CAN)	IN JELLIED BROTH (MANISCHEWITZ)
GEFILTE FISH, UNSALTED	24/15 OZ. JARS PER CASE (6 PCES PER JAR)	(MOTHER'S)

PURCHASE SPECIFICATIONS FOR JAMS, JELLIES & SYRUP

PRODUCT	U.S.D.A GRADE	UNIT	REQUIREMENTS
JAM, APRICOT	FANCY	6/NO. 10 CANS	MUST BE OF PULPY CONSISTENCY, AND PREPARED FROM CLEAN, SOUND, MATURE FROZEN, FRESH AND/OR CANNED FRUITS. DRIED FRUITS ARE NOT TO BE INCLUDED. MIN. 45% BY WEIGHT OF FRUIT INGREDIENTS TO EACH 55% OF SWEETENING INGREDIENT SOLIDS.
JAM, GRAPE	FANCY	6/NO. 10 CANS	
JAM, PEACH	FANCY	6/NO. 10 CANS	
JELLY, APPLE	FANCY	6/NO. 10 CANS	THE FRUIT JUICE INGREDIENT SHALL BE THE STRAINED PRODUCT OBTAINED FROM CLEAN, SOUND, PROPERLY MATURED AND PREPARED FRUITS. EITHER FRESH, FROZEN AND/OR CANNED. MIN. 45% BY WEIGHT OF FRUIT JUICE INGREDIENTS TO EACH 55% OF SWEETENING INGREDIENT SOLID.
JELLY, APPLEMINT	FANCY	6/NO. 10 CANS	
JELLY, CURRANT	FANCY	6/NO. 10 CANS	
JELLY, GRAPE	FANCY	6/NO. 10 CANS	
ORANGE MARMALADE, SWEET	FANCY	6/NO. 10 CANS OR 24/1LB.	TO BE CLEAR TRANSLUCENT, OF JELLY-LIKE BODY AND GOOD FINISH. FREE FROM DARK SPOTS, SEEDS, BITTERNESS, GUMMINESS AND EXCESS SUGAR. MIN. 35% FRUIT (CONTENT) MAX. 65% SUGAR (CONTENT).
HONEY, EXTRACTED	FANCY	5 LB. CAN	DOMESTIC, AMBER COLOR. MAX. 18.6% WATER CONTENT, 81.4% MIN. SOLUBLE SOLIDS.
PEANUT BUTTER	FANCY	1 LB. JAR	SALT ADDED; PLEASING ODOR AND FLAVOR, SMOOTH CONSISTENCY. STABILIZED.
MOLASSES	FANCY	6/NO. 10 CANS	SULPHUR DIOXIDE MAY BE ADDED. MAX. 25% WATER.
SYRUP, PANCAKE		4/1 GAL. CANS	MADE OF SUGAR, CANE AND MAPLE FLAVORED. MAY HAVE ARTIFICIAL FLAVORING AND/OR COLORING ADDED; MAX. 30% WATER CONTENT.

SECTION—F
PURCHASE SPECIFICATIONS FOR DRIED FRUITS & LEGUMES, RICE, FROZEN
FRUITS & VEGETABLES, OTHER FROZEN PRODUCTS

DATE OF LATEST REVISION:

PURCHASE SPECIFICATIONS FOR FRUITS, DRIED

JANUARY 1972

MUST BE OF THE LATEST CROP, PREPARED FROM CLEAN, SOUND, PROPERLY MATURED FRUIT.

PRODUCT	USDA GRADE	UNIT PER/CASE	REQUIREMENTS
APRICOTS, DRIED	CHOICE	25 OR 30 LBS.	"BLENHEIM"—13/16" TO 1". REASONABLY UNIFORM, BRIGHT TYPICAL COLOR CHARACTERISTIC OF WELL MATURED FRUIT.
DATES, PITTED, WHOLE	USDA GRADE B	10 LBS., 35 LBS., 70 LBS. OR 24/7 1/4 OZ., 24/16 OZ., 24/8 OZ. PACKAGES	"SAIR" GOLDEN BROWN, UNIFORM SIZE, FIRM AND RIPE.
PRUNES, DRIED, WHOLE	CHOICE	30#	FRENCH OR ITALIAN TYPE. 30-40 PER LB. NOT MORE THAN 15% MAY BE OF A COLOR DIFFERENT FROM BLACK OR MAY HAVE DAMAGES SUCH AS SPLITS, CRACKS, SCABS, OR INSECT INJURY.
RAISINS, DRIED	CHOICE	30 LBS. OR 24/15 OZ. PACKAGES	THOMPSON SEEDLESS: UNIFORM IN SIZE, 19/64" TO 24/64" IN DIAMETER. GENERALLY AMBER OR GREENISH AMBER, WITH NOT MORE THAN 20% OF DEFINITELY DARK BERRIES.
MIXED FRUITS, DRIED	EXT. FANCY	25 LBS.	TO CONTAIN NO APPLES, NOR CHERRIES. OTHER FRUITS SHOULD BE PROPORTIONED AS CONTAINED IN GOOD COMMERCIAL PRACTICE.

LEGUMES, DRIED, & RICE

PRODUCT	USDA GRADE	UNIT PER/CASE	REQUIREMENTS
BEANS, NAVY, DRIED	US#1	25 LB. SACK	SMALL WHITE PEA BEANS, HAND PICKED.
BEANS, LIMA, DRIED	US#1	25 LB. SACK	THIN-SEEDED, RE-CLEANED.
LENTILS, DRIED	FANCY	25 LB. SACK OR CS. 24/1 LB.	YELLOW TO BROWN IN COLOR.
PEAS, GREEN, SPLIT	US#1	25 LB. SACK	SOUND SPLIT HALVES OF A DISTINCTLY GREEN COLOR.
PEAS, YELLOW, SPLIT	US#1	25 LB. SACK	SOUND SPLIT HALVES OF A GOOD YELLOW COLOR.
RICE, MILLED	US#1	100 LB. SACK	LONG GRAIN; WHITE; SHALL NOT INCLUDE WEEVILY RICE.

PURCHASE SPECIFICATIONS FOR FROZEN FRUITS & FROZEN JUICES

U.S. GRADE "A". SUGAR ADDED AS SPECIFIED. ALL FRUITS ARE TO BE REASONABLY FREE FROM PATHOLOGICAL, OR MECHANICAL INJURY AND HARMLESS EXTRANEOUS MATERIAL. FREE FROM INSECTS. MUST BE DELIVERED COMPLETELY FROZEN AND SHOW NO EVIDENCE OF REFREEZING. CONTAINERS MUST BE SOUND AND CLEAN. LATEST PACK.

PRODUCT	UNIT	REQUIREMENTS
APPLES, SLICED	30#	PRACTICALLY FREE FROM DARK BRUISES. SUGAR RATIO: 6 X 1 OR 7 X 1 AS SPECIFIED.
APRICOTS, HALVES	30#	UNPEELED, PITTED. PRACTICALLY UNIFORM BRIGHT YELLOW COLOR, THICK AND FLESHY. MINIMUM WEIGHT OF HALF: 2/5 OZ. SUGAR RATIO: 3 X 1 OR 4 X 1 AS SPECIFIED.
BLUEBERRIES, CULTIVATED	30#, 20#, 10#, 5# OR 2 1/2#	MUST BE BRIGHT DARK BLUE-PURPLE IN COLOR, FIRM FLESHY. SUGAR RATIO: 5 X 1 OR "DRY PACK" AS SPECIFIED.
BOYSENBERRIES	30# OR 10#	MUST BE FLESHY AND TENDER, BUT NOT OVER-RIPE, PRACTICALLY FREE FROM DETACHED SEEDS. SUGAR RATIO: 5 X 1 OR "DRY PACK" AS SPECIFIED.
CHERRIES, RED, SOUR	30#, 10# OR 6 1/2#	PITTED. GOOD BRIGHT RED COLOR. FIRM, FLESHY TEXTURE. SUGAR RATIO: 5 X 1.
CHERRIES, LIGHT OR DARK AS SPECIFIED	6# OR 10# 30#	PITTED OR UNPITTED, AS SPECIFIED. UNPITTED VARIETY: WEIGHT OF EACH CHERRY MUST NOT BE LESS THAN 1/10 OZ. OR IMMATURE. SUGAR RATIO: 5 X 1.
GRAPEFRUIT SECTIONS, WHOLE	3#	MUST NOT WEIGH LESS THAN 3/8 OZ. PER SECTION. NOT MORE THAN 25% MAY BE BROKEN.
MELON BALLS	6 1/2#, 8 1/2# OR 8#	TRI-COLOR OR BI-COLOR AS SPECIFIED. PERCENTAGE OF INDIVIDUAL SPECIES OF MELONS SHOULD BE PROPORTIONED AS CONTAINED IN GOOD COMMERCIAL PRACTICE.
PEACHES, SLICED	32#, 30#, 8 1/2# OR 6 1/2#	PEELED AND PITTED. MUST BE FIRM BUT TENDER; NOT MUSHY. FREE FROM BROWN COLOR RESULTING FROM OXIDATION; SUGAR RATIO: 3 X 1.
PINEAPPLE, WHOLE, HALF OR BROKEN SLICES, CHUNKS, TIDBITS OR CRUSHED	30#, 10# OR 6 1/2#	PRACTICALLY BRIGHT YELLOW COLOR.
RASPBERRIES, RED	6#, 6 1/2# OR 10#	BRIGHT GOOD TYPICAL COLOR. NO GREY CAST OR DARKENING. MUST BE FLESHY AND TENDER. SUGAR RATIO: 4 X 1 OR "DRY PACK" AS SPECIFIED.

PURCHASE SPECIFICATIONS FOR FROZEN FRUITS & FROZEN JUICES (Cont.)

PRODUCT	UNIT	REQUIREMENTS
STRAWBERRIES, WHOLE, IQF	30#, 10#, 6 1/2#, 2 1/2# OR 1 LB.	95% MUST BE MEDIUM SIZE, 5/8" TO 1" IN DIAMETER AND FULLY DEVELOPED. 10% MAY BE CRUSHED FOR "WHOLE" 20% FOR "SLICED". MUST BE FLESHY AND REASONABLY FIRM. SUGAR RATIO: 4 X 1 OR "DRY PACK" AS SPECIFIED.
FROZEN JUICES		
LEMON JUICE, FROZEN	12/30 FL. OZ. PER CASE	RECONSTITUTED, SINGLE STRENGTH; NO SUGAR ADDED.
ORANGE JUICE, FROZEN CONCENTRATE	12/32 OZ. PER CASE	"U.S. GRADE A"; MIN. SCORE: 85; MUST RECONSTITUTE PROPERLY; NO SUGAR ADDED. WATER JUICE RATIO: 3 X 1.

PURCHASE SPECIFICATIONS FOR FROZEN VEGETABLES

U.S. GRADE "A". LATEST PACK. ALL VEGETABLES ARE TO BE REASONABLY FREE FROM PATHOLOGICAL OR MECHANICAL INJURY AND HARMLESS MATERIAL. FREE FROM INSECTS. MUST BE DELIVERED COMPLETELY FROZEN AND SHOW NO EVIDENCE OF RE-FREEZING. CONTAINERS MUST BE SOUND AND CLEAN.

PRODUCT	UNIT	REQUIREMENTS
ASPARAGUS, WHOLE SPEARS GREEN	12/2 1/2#	MEDIUM SIZE, 3/8" TO 5/8" DIAMETER. JUMBO SIZE 7/8" OR LARGER. TENDER. NO GRIT OR "FLOWERED" HEADS. NOT LESS THAN 3 1/3" IN LENGTH.
ASPARAGUS, CUT SPEARS OR CUTS AND TIPS	12/2 1/2#	CUT IN LENGTH OF 1 1/4" OR LESS. NOT LESS THAN 18% OF HEADS. NO GRIT OR "FLOWERED" HEADS.
BEANS, LIMA, GREEN, BABY	12/2 1/2#	THIN-SEEDED. PRACTICALLY FREE FROM BROKEN AND SHRIVELED BEANS AND LOOSE SKINS.
BEANS, GREEN, REG. CUT (1") OR CUT FRENCH STYLE BEANS, WAX, CUT (1") BEANS, ITALIAN	12/2 1/2#	"ROUND" OR "FLAT" TYPE. WELL CUT CROSSWISE OR LENGTHWISE AS SPECIFIED. FULL FLESHED, YOUNG AND TENDER. PRACTICALLY FREE FROM TOUGH STRINGS.
BROCCOLI, STALKS, WHOLE	12/2# OR 12/2 1/2#	LONGEST UNIT NOT TO EXCEED THE LENGTH OF SHORTEST UNIT BY MORE THAN 1". APPROXIMATELY 5" STALKS. UNIFORM GREEN COLOR; NO YELLOW OR "GREY" STALKS. NO GRIT OR "FLOWERED" HEADS.
BROCCOLI, CUT	12/2# OR 12/2 1/2#	UNIFORM CUTS OF GOOD GREEN COLOR. NO YELLOW OR "GREY" PIECES. NO GRIT.
BRUSSELS SPROUTS	12/2# OR 12/2 1/2#	SMALL UNIFORM, FIRM HEADS, FREE FROM MUD AND CLAY. UNIFORM LIGHT GREEN COLOR.
CARROTS, DICED	20#	TYPICAL ORANGE-YELLOW COLOR WITH ONLY SLIGHT EVIDENCE OF GREEN; UNIFORM CUBES MEASURING 1/4" TO 1/2".
CARROTS, SLICED	1212# OR 20#	TYPICAL ORANGE-YELLOW COLOR WITH ONLY SLIGHT EVIDENCE OF GREEN. UNIFORM SLICES, LARGEST SLICE NOT TO EXCEED SMALLEST BY MORE THAN 3/8". MAXIMUM THICKNESS: 1/4". MAXIMUM WIDTH: 1 3/4".
CARROTS, WHOLE, BABY	20#	TYPICAL ORANGE-YELLOW COLOR. UNIFORM IN SIZE AND SYMMETRY; LARGEST CARROT NOT TO EXCEED SMALLEST BY MORE THAN 3/16" IN DIAMETER AND 5/8" IN LENGTH. MAXIMUM DIAMETER: 1 1/4".
CARROTS AND PEAS	12/2 1/2# OR 12/2#	NOT LESS THAN 25% BY WEIGHT OF DICED CARROTS 1/4" TO 3/8". NOT LESS THAN 50% BY WEIGHT OF "EARLY" OR "SWEET" TYPE PEAS.

PURCHASE SPECIFICATIONS FOR FROZEN VEGETABLES (Cont.)

CAULIFLOWER	12/2#	MUST BE WHITE TO LIGHT CREAM IN COLOR; MAY POSSESS A SLIGHT TINGE OF DARKER COLOR WHICH DISAPPEARS UPON COOKING.
CORN, WHOLE GRAIN, YELLOW	12/2 1/2#	MUST BE IN THE EARLY-MILK TO MILK STAGE OF MATURITY. UNIFORM BRIGHT YELLOW COLOR CHARACTERISTIC OF THE GOLDEN VARIETIES. PRACTICALLY FREE FROM INEDIBLE HUSK AND SILK.
CORN-ON-COB	42 EACH/BOX OR 48 EACH/BOX	GOLDEN; EVENLY FILLED COBS; FREE OF SILK AND HUSKS.
KALE, CHOPPED	12/2#	UNIFORM TYPICAL GREEN COLOR; FREE FROM COARSE OR TOUGH STEMS OR LEAVES, OR INSECT INJURY.
PEAS, GREEN	12/2 1/2#	NOT LESS THAN 95% OF UNIFORM TYPICAL GREEN COLOR. FOR EACH 1 LB. NET NOT MORE THAN 2 PIECES OF EXTRANEOUS MATERIAL SUCH AS THISTLE, BUD, PEA POD OR STEM.
PEAS AND ONIONS	12/2# OR 12/2 1/2#	
POTATOES, FRENCH FRIED	6/5#	KRINKLE-CUT.
RHUBARB, CUT, SPLIT GREEN CRIMSON	10#	UNIFORM GLOSSY APPEARANCE; NO DULL OR GREY COLOR. NO SUGAR ADDED.
SPINACH, BROAD LEAF, OR SPINACH, CUT (AS SPECIFIED)	12/2 1/2# OR 12/3#	UNIFORM TYPICAL GREEN COLOR, FREE FROM SHREDDED AND RAGGED LEAVES AND STEMS, "GRIT", AND SAND.
SQUASH, WINTER (COOKED)	12/4# OR 12/2 1/2#	YELLOW, MASHED; UNIFORM COLOR, EVEN TEXTURE WHICH IS NOT LUMPY, PASTY AND DOES NOT INCLUDE HARD PARTICLES.
SQUASH, SUMMER	12/3#	SLICED INTO TRANSVERSE CUTS. BRIGHT COLOR, TENDER TEXTURE; FLESHY, FULL PLUMP UNITS. SOFT SEEDS.
SQUASH, ZUCCHINI	12/3#	SLICED INTO TRANSVERSE CUTS. BRIGHT COLOR, TENDER TEXTURE; FLESHY, FULL PLUMP UNITS. SOFT SEEDS.
SUCCOTASH	12/2 1/2# OR 12/2#	COLOR TO BE BRIGHT, TYPICAL OF YOUNG TENDER VEGETABLES. PRACTICALLY FREE FROM LEAVES, STEMS, PODS, HUSK, SILK.

| VEGETABLES, MIXED | 12/2 1/2#, 5#
10# OR 20# | PERCENTAGE OF INDIVIDUAL VEGETABLES SHOULD BE PROPORTIONED AS CONTAINED IN GOOD COMMERCIAL PRACTICE. SUCH 5-WAY MIX, 20% EACH DICED CARROTS, CORN, PEAS, CUT GREEN BEANS, BABY LIMA BEANS. |
| YAMS, WHOLE | 12/2# OR 6/5# | FAIRLY UNIFORM SHAPE. COARSE VEINING SHOULD IN-DICATE NO EXCESSIVE STRINGINESS. |

OTHER FROZEN PRODUCTS

| PIZZA, FROZEN | 48/5" ROUND PER CASE
OR 50/3 1/2 OZ. (4" X 2" RECT.)
PER CASE | |
| PATTY SHELLS, UNBAKED | 12 DOZ. 3" DIAMETER
PER CASE | |

SECTION G
PURCHASE SPECIFICATIONS
FOR
MISCELLANEOUS PRODUCTS
(DRESSING, SEASONINGS, OIL, SPICES, OLIVES
PICKLES, RELISHES, SHORTENING)

DATE OF LATEST REVISION:
JANUARY 1972

PURCHASE SPECIFICATIONS FOR DRESSINGS, SEASONINGS & OIL

PRODUCT	UNIT	REQUIREMENTS
DRESSING, SALAD	CASE: 4/1 GAL.	SHALL BE PREPARED FROM WHOLE OR PARTIALLY COOKED OR BOILED SEMI-SOLID EMULSION OF EDIBLE VEGETABLE OIL, EGG YOLKS, VINEGAR, WATER, LEMON JUICE, SALT, SEASONINGS, SUGAR, STARCH; NOT LESS THAN 30% VEGETABLE OIL, NOT LESS THAN 4% BY WEIGHT OF LIQUID EGG YOLK.
DRESSING, FRENCH	CASE: 4/1 GAL.	TO BE FREE FROM ARTIFICIAL COLORING, PRESERVATIVES, ADULTERANTS, AND IMPURITIES, BE CLEAN, SOUND AND OF FINE FLAVOR, MADE FROM EDIBLE VEGETABLE OIL. NOT LESS THAN 35% BY WEIGHT OF EDIBLE VEGETABLE OIL, WITH OR WITHOUT EMULSIFIER ADDED.
MAYONNAISE	CASE: 4/1 GAL.	SHALL BE A SEMI-SOLID EMULSION OF EDIBLE VEGETABLE OIL, EGG YOLKS, VINEGAR, LEMON JUICE, SALT, SWEETENING AND SEASONINGS. SHALL BE CLEAN, SOUND, SMOOTH, OF FINE FLAVOR, SHOW NO EVIDENCE OF SEPARATION & CONTAIN NOT LESS THAN 65% BY WEIGHT OF VEGETABLE OIL.
MUSTARD, PREPARED	48/8 OZ, 48/8-1/2 OZ., 48/9 OZ. OR 4/1 GAL.	ENGLISH (YELLOW) OR FRENCH STYLE; SHALL CONTAIN NO ADDED FOREIGN STARCH-BEARING MATERIALS AND BE FREE FROM EXCESS HULLS. NOT LESS THAN 16.5% TOTAL SOLIDS. MUST BE OF SMOOTH, HEAVY CONSISTENCY.
OIL, SALAD	5 GAL. CN.	PURE EDIBLE VEGETABLE OIL MADE FROM CORN, SOYA OR COTTONSEED. SHALL BE CLEAR, THOROUGHLY REFINED, DEODORIZED, FREE FROM RANCIDITY AND STAND 5 HOUR COLD TEST IN CRACKED ICE. "SMOKING POINT" TO BE ABOVE 432°F.

PRODUCT	UNIT	REQUIREMENTS
VINEGAR, CIDER	CASE: 4/1 GAL. (GLASS)	SHALL BE CLEAR, BRIGHT, BROWN YELLOWISH COLOR, FREE FROM CLOUDINESS, SEDIMENT AND FLOATING PARTICLES AND HAVE A CLEAN FRUIT ODOR. SHALL HAVE BEEN STERILIZED, SO THAT IT IS FREE FROM ACETOBACTERIA WHICH CAUSE "MOTHER OF VINEGAR". NOT LESS THAN 4 GR. OF ACETIC ACID PER 100 CUBIC CENTIMETERS AT 20°C.
WORCESTERSHIRE SAUCE	CASE: 4/1 GAL.	TO BE WELL COOKED, AND RIPENED IN WOOD FOR NOT LESS THAN 60 DAYS, AND CONTAIN NOT LESS THAN 20% TOTAL SOLIDS. SHALL BE PREPARED FROM SOY-BEAN SAUCE, TO WHICH SALT, VINEGAR, PICKLED FISH, MUSHROOMS, AND/OR ONIONS & OTHER SEASONINGS WERE ADDED.

PURCHASE SPECIFICATIONS FOR SPICES (GROUND & WHOLE)

SHALL BE PREPARED IN ACCORDANCE WITH BEST COMMERCIAL PRACTICE, UNDER STRICTLY SANITARY CONDITIONS FROM CLEAN, SOUND, PURE PRODUCTS AND MADE FROM TRUE AROMATIC VEGETABLE SUBSTANCES FROM WHICH NO PORTION OF ANY VOLATILE OR OTHER FLAVORING PRINCIPLE HAS BEEN REMOVED, AND SHALL BE FREE FROM ARTIFICIAL COLORING, ADULTERANTS AND IMPURITIES; THE AROMA AND CHARACTERISTIC QUALITIES SHALL BE TRUE TO NAME, AND WHERE INDICATED, MILLED SPICES SHALL BE UNIFORMLY GROUND.

PRODUCT	UNIT	REQUIREMENTS
CLOVES, WHOLE	LB.	TO CONTAIN NOT MORE THAN 5 % OF STEMS.
PEPPER, BLACK, GROUND PURE	LB.	TO CONTAIN THE SEVERAL PARTS OF THE BERRY IN THEIR NORMAL PROPORTIONS; NOT LESS THAN 30% STARCH.
PEPPER, WHITE GROUND PURE	LB.	VERY BRIGHT LIGHT COLOR, NOT LESS THAN 52% STARCH.
OLIVES, PICKLES & RELISHES		
OLIVES, GREEN CHOPPED	4/1 GAL.	U.S. CHOICE SHALL BE CLEAN, SOUND, CHOPPED OLIVES, FREE FROM IMPURITIES AND OF FINE FLAVOR.
OLIVES, GREEN WHOLE	4/1 GAL.	U.S. CHOICE 90-110'S SIZE-275/GAL. SOUND, GREEN OLIVES, UNIFORM SIZE, PREPARED IN ACCORDANCE WITH BEST COMMERCIAL PRACTICE.
PICKLES, WHOLE (SOUR) DILL	4/1 GAL. OR 16 GAL. KEG, OR 6/10# CNS.	U.S. FANCY 40 PICKLES PER GAL. GREEN AND FIRM CUCUMBERS, FREE FROM CRACKS, NUBS, ROUGH AND SEEDY STOCK. UNIFORM SHAPE, NO HOLLOW OR SPONGY STOCK. BRINE AND/OR VINEGAR TO FULLY COVER PICKLES.
PICKLES, SWEET, CROSSCUT	6/10'S OR 4/1 GAL.	SLICED CUCUMBER PICKLES, PRESERVED IN SWEET LIQUOR WHICH SHALL FULLY COVER THE PICKLES; NOT LESS THAN 15% BAUME FOR SUGAR CONTENT, NOT MORE THAN 2.5% FOR SALT CONTENT.
RELISH, SWEET, MIXED	6/10'S OR 4/1 GAL.	TO CONSIST OF: 60-70% IMMATURE CUCUMBERS, 25-30% CAULIFLOWER OR 10% TOMATOES, 3-5% ONIONS, ALL THOROUGHLY CURED IN BRINE AND SUBSEQUENTLY IN VINEGAR, CHOPPED INTO FINE AND UNIFORM SIZE PIECES, PRESERVED IN SUFFICIENT QUANTITY (WITHOUT EXCESS) OF SWEET LIQUOR (15% BAUME) MADE OF VINEGAR & SUGAR.

PRODUCT	UNIT	REQUIREMENTS
SHORTENING		
SHORTENING	50# CAN OR CARTON	HYDROGENATED VEGETABLE FATS OR OILS. SHALL BE PRACTICALLY FREE OF SUSPENDED MATTER, RANCIDITY, SOURNESS AND FOREIGN ODOR OR FLAVORS. "SMOKING POINT" TO BE ABOVE 426°F.

APPENDIX IV
COMMON AND SCIENTIFIC NAMES OF ANIMALS
AND PLANTS USED FOR FOODS[1]

Common Name	Scientific Name	Common Name	Scientific Name
Abalone	Haliotis species	Breadfruit	Artocarpus altilis
Acerola	Malpighia punicifolia	Broad bean	Vicia faba
Albacore (A, P)	Thunnus alalunga	Broccoli	Brassica oleracea var. botrytis
Alewife (A, F)	Alosa pseudoharengus	Brussels sprout	Brassica coleracea var. gemmifera
Almond	Prunus amygdalus	Buckwheat	Fagopyrum esculentum
Amaranth	Amaranthus species	Buffalo fish (F)	Ictiobus species
Anchovy (A, P)	Engraulidae	Bullhead, black (F)	Ictalurus melas
Apple	Malus sylvestris	Burbot (F)	Lota lota
Apricot	Prunus armeniaca	Butterfish (A)	Poronotus triacanthus
Artichoke, globe or French	Cynara scolymus	Butternut	Juglans cinerea
Asparagus	Asparagus officinalis	Cabbage, common, red and savoy	Brassica oleracea var. capitata
Avocado	Persea species	Cabbage, celery or Chinese	Brassica pekinensis
Bamboo	Bambusa species and Phyllostachys species	Cabbage, spoon or pakchoy (white mustard cabbage)	Brassica chinensis
Banana, common	Musa X paradisiaca	Carambola	Averrhoa carambola
Banana, red	Musa X paradisiaca	Carissa, or natal plum	Carissa grandiflora
Barley	Hordeum vulgare	Carob	Certania siliqua
Barracuda, Pacific (P)	Sphyranena argentea	Carp (F)	Cyprinus carpio
Bass, black sea (A)	Centropristes straitus	Carrot	Daucus carota var. sativa
Bass, smallmouth and largemouth (F)	Micropterus dolomieui and M. salmoides	Cashew	Anacardium accidentale
Bass, striped (A, F, P)	Roccus saxatilis	Catfish (F)	Ictalurus species
Bass, white (F)	Roccus chrysops	Cauliflower	Brassica oleracea var. botrytis
Bean, common	Phaseolus vulgaris	Celeriac	Apium graveolens var. rapaceum
Bean, lima	Phaseolus limensis	Celery	Apium graveolens
Bean, mung	Phaseolus aureus	Chard	Beta vulgaris var. cicla
Bean, snap	Phaseolus vulgaris	Chayote	Sechium edule
Beaver	Castor canadensis	Cherimoya	Annona cherimola
Beechnut	Fagus species	Cherry	Prunus species
Beef	Bos taurus	Chervil	Anthriscus cerefolium
Beet, common red	Beta vulgaris	Chestnut	Castanea species
Blackberry (including dewberry, boysenberry, and youngberry)	Rubus species	Chicken	Galus domesticus
		Chickpea	Cicer arietinum
Blueberry	Vaccinium species	Chicory	Cichorium intybus
Bluefish (A)	Pomatomus saltatrix	Chive	Allium schoenoprasum
Bonito (including Atlantic, Pacific, and striped) (A, P)	Sarda sarda, S. chiliensis, and S. orientalis	Chocolate	Theobroma cacao
Boysenberry	Rubus ursinus var. loganobaccus		
Brazil nut	Bertholletia excelsa		

[Cont.]

Letters in parentheses following the common names of fish refer to area of occurrence: [A] Atlantic Ocean; [P] Pacific Ocean; [F] Fresh Water.

COMMON AND SCIENTIFIC NAMES OF ANIMALS
AND PLANTS USED FOR FOODS [Cont.]

Common Name	Scientific Name
Chub (F)	Coregonus species
Citron	Citrus medica
Clam, soft (A, P)	Mya arenaria
Clam, hard or round (quahog) (A, P)	Mercenaria mercenaria
Clam, razor (F)	Siliqua patula
Coconut	Cocos nucifera
Cod (A, P)	Gadus morhua and G. macrocephalus
Coffee	Cofea species
Collard	Brassica oleracea var. acephala
Corn	Zea mays
Cornsalad	Valerianella olitoria
Cottonseed	Gossypium species
Cowpea (including blackeye pea)	Vigna sinensis
Crab (including blue, Dungeness, rock and king) (A, P)	Callinectes sapidus, Cancer species, and Paralithodes camschatica
Crab apple	Malus species
Cranberry	Vaccinium macrocarpon
Crappie, white (F)	Pomaxis annularis
Crayfish, freshwater (F) and spiny lobster (A, P)	Cambarus species, Astacus species, and Panulirus species
Cress, garden (peppergrass)	Lepidium sativum
Croaker, Atlantic (A)	Micropagon undulatus
Croaker, yellowfin (P)	Umbrina roncador
Croaker, white (P)	Genyonemus lineatus
Cucumber	Cucumis sativus
Currant (black, European, red, white)	Ribes species
Cusk (A)	Brosme brosme
Custard apple, bullockheart	Annona reticulata
Dandelion	Taraxacum officinale
Date	Phoenix dactylifera
Dock, curly or narrowleaf, broadleaf, and sheep sorrel	Rumex species
Dogfish, spiny (grayfish) (A, P)	Squalus acanthias
Dolly Varden (P, F)	Salvelinus malma
Drum, freshwater (F)	Aplodinotus grunniens
Drum, red (redfish) (A)	Sciaenops ocellata
Duck, domesticated	Anas platyrhynchos

Common Name	Scientific Name
Duck, wild	Anas boschas
Eel, American (A, F)	Anguilla rastrata
Eggplant	Solanum melongena
Elderberry	Sambucus species
Endive (curly endive and escarole)	Chichorium endivia
Eulachon (smelt) (P, F)	Thaleichthys pacificus
Fennel, common	Foeniculum vulgare
Fig	Ficus carica
Filbert or hazelnut	Corylus species
Finnan haddie (smoked haddock) (A)	Melanogrammus aeglefinus
Flatfish (flounder, sole, and sand dab) (A, P)	Pseudapleuronectes americanus, Paralichthys dentatus, P. lethostigma, Platichthys stellatus, Limanda ferruginea, Atheresthes stomias, Parophrys vetulus, Microstomus pacificus, Eopsetta jordani, Hippoglossoides elassodon, Glyptocephalus zachirus, Lepidopsetta bilineata, Citharichthys sordidus, Psettichthys melanostictus
Frog (F)	Rana species
Garlic	Allium sativum
Ginger, common	Zingiber officinale
Goose, domesticated	Anser anser
Gooseberry	Ribes species
Granadilla, purple (passionfruit)	Passiflora edulis
Grapefruit	Citrus paradisi
Grape (American and European type)	Vitis species
Groundcherry	Physalis species
Grouper (including red, black, and speckled hind) (A)	Epinephelus morio, Mycteroperea bonaci and Epinephelus drummondhayi
Guava, common	Psidium guajava
Guava, strawberry	Psidium littorale
Guinea	Numida meleagris
Haddock (A)	Melanogrammus aeglefinus

Common Name	Scientific Name	Common Name	Scientific Name
Hake (including Pacific hake, squirrel hake, and silver hake or whiting) (A, P)	Merluccius productus, Urophyeis chuss, and Merluccius bilinearis	Mamey or mammee apple	Mammea americana
		Mango	Mangifera indica
		Menhaden, Atlantic (A)	Brevoortia tyrannus
Halibut, Atlantic and Pacific (A, P)	Hippoglossus hippoglossus and H. stenolepis	Millet, proso	Panicum miliaceum
		Mullet, striped (A, F, P)	Mugil cephalus
Halibut, California (A)	Paralichthys californicus	Mushroom, cultivated	Agaricus campestris
Halibut, Greenland (A)	Reinhardtius hippoglossoides	Muskellunge (F)	Esox masquinongy
Haw (hawthorn), scarlet	Cataegus species	Muskmelon, cantaloupe	Cucumis melo var. cantalupensis
Herring, Atlantic (A)	Clupea harengus harengus	Muskmelon, other netted varieties	Cucumis melo var. reticulatus
Herring, Pacific (P)	Clupea harengus pallasi	Muskmelon, casaba (Golden Beauty)	Cucumis melo var. inodorus
Hickory nut	Carya species		
Horseradish	Armoracia rusticana	Muskmelon, Honeydew	Cucumis melo
Hyacinth-bean	Dolichos lablab	Muskrat	Ondatra zibethica
Inconnu (or sheefish) (F)	Stenodus leucichthys	Mussel, Atlantic and Pacific (A, P)	Mytilus edulis and M. californianus
Jackfruit	Artocarpus integra	Mustard	Brassica juncea
Jack mackerel (P)	Trachurus symmetricus	Mustard spinach	Brassica perviridis
Jerusalem artichoke	Helianthus tuberosus	Nectarine	Prunus persica var. nectarina
Jujube, common (Chinese date)	Ziziphus jujuba	New Zealand spinach	Tetragonia expansa
Kale	Brassica oleracea var. acephala	Oat	Avena sativa
Kingfish; southern, gulf, and northern whiting) (A)	Menticirrhus americanus, M. littoralis, and M. saxatilis	Ocean perch, Atlantic (or rosefish) (A)	Sebastes marinus
Kohlrabi	Brassica oleracea var. gongylodes	Ocean perch, Pacific (P)	Sebastodes alutus
Kumquat	Fortunella species	Octopus (P)	Octopus bimaculatus
Lake herring or cisco (F)	Coregonus artedii	Okra	Hibiscus esculentus
Lake trout (F)	Salvelinus namaycush	Olive	Olea europaea
Lake trout (siscowet) (F)	Salvelinus namaycush	Onion	Allium cepa
Lamb	Ovis aries	Onion, Welsh	Allium fistulosum
Lambsquarters	Chenopodium album	Opossum	Didelphis virginiana
Leek	Allium porrum	Orange, sweet (except Temple)	Citrus sinensis
Lemon	Citrus limon	Orange, Temple (hybrid-tangor)	Citrus sinensis X C. reticulata
Lentil	Lens culinaris	Oyster, Eastern (A, P)	Cassostrea virginica
Lettuce	Lactuca sativa	Oyster, Pacific and Western (Olympia)	Cassostrea gigas and Ostrea lurida
Lime	Citrus aurantifolia		
Lingcod (P)	Ophiodon elongatus	Papaw	Asimina triloba
Lobster, northern (A)	Homarus americanus	Papaya	Carica papaya
Loganberry	Rubus ursinus var. loganobaccus	Parsley, common garden and curly	Petroselinum crispum and P. crispum var. latifolium
Longan	Euphoria longan		
Loquat	Eriobotrya japonica	Parsnip	Pastinaca sativa
Lychee	Litchi chinensis	Peach	Prunus persica
Macadamia nut	Macadamia ternifolia	Peanut	Arachis hypogaea
Mackerel, Atlantic (A)	Scomber scombrus	Pear	Pyrus communis
Mackerel, Pacific (P)	Scomber japonicus	Pea, edible-podded	Pisum sativum var. macrocarpum

[Cont.]

COMMON AND SCIENTIFIC NAMES OF ANIMALS
AND PLANTS USED FOR FOODS [Cont.]

Common Name	Scientific Name
Pea, green immature and mature seeds	Pisum sativum
Pecan	Carya illinoensis
Pepper, hot, chili	Capsicum annuum
Pepper, sweet, garden varieties	Capsicum annuum
Perch, white (A, F)	Roccus americanus
Perch, yellow (F)	Perca flavescens
Persimmon, Japanese or kaki	Diospyros kaki
Persimmon, native	Diospyros virginiana
Pheasant	Phasianus colchicus
Pickerel, chain (F)	Esox niger
Pigeonpea	Cajanus cajan
Pike, blue (F)	Stizostedion vitreum glaucum
Pike, northern (F)	Esox lucius
Pike, walleye (F)	Stizostedion vitreum vitreum
Pili nut	Canarium ovatum
Pimiento	Capsicum annuum
Pineapple	Ananas comosus
Pinenut, pignolia	Pinus pinea
Pinenut, pifion	Pinus cembroides var. edulis
Pistachio nut	Pistacia vera
Pitanga (Surinam-cherry)	Eugenia uniflora
Plantain, or baking banana	Musa X paradisiaca
Plum (including damsons, Japanese and hybrids, prune type, and greengage)	Prunus species
Pokeberry or poke	Phytolacca americana
Pollock (A)	Pollachius virens
Pomegranate	Punica granatum
Pompano (A)	Trachinotus carolinus
Popcorn	Zea mays var. everta
Porgy and scup (A)	Calamus sp., Stenotomus caprinus and S. chrysops
Pork	Sus scrofa
Potato	Solanum tuberosum
Prickly pear	Opuntia species
Prune	Prunus species
Pumpkin	Cucurbita pepo

Common Name	Scientific Name
Purslane	Portulaca species
Quail	Bonasa unbellus and Colinus virginianus
Quince	Cydonia oblonga
Rabbit, domesticated	Oryetolagus euniculus
Rabbit, wild	Sylvilagus floridanus
Raccoon	Procyon lotor
Radish	Raphanus sativus
Radish, oriental (including daikon or Japanese and Chinese)	Raphanus sativus var. longipinnatus
Raisin	Vitis species
Raspberry (black and red)	Rubus species
Red and gray snapper (A)	Lutjanus blackfordi and L. griseus
Redhorse, silver (F)	Moxostoma anisurum
Reindeer	Rangifer species
Rhubarb	Rheum thaponticum
Rice	Oryza sativa
Rice, glutinous	Oryza glutinosa
Rockfish (including black, canacy, yellowtail, rasphead, and boccaccio) (P)	Sebastodes pinniger, S. melanops, S. flavidus, S. ruberrimus, and Sebastodes species
Rose apple	Eugenia jambos
Rutabaga	Brassica napobrassica
Rye	Secale cereale
Sablefish (P)	Anoplopoma fimbria
Safflower	Carthamus tinctorius
Salmon, Atlantic (A, F)	Salmo salar
Salmon, chinook (or king) (F, P)	Oncorhynchus ishawytscha
Salmon, chum (P, F)	Oncorhynchus keta
Salmon, Coho (or silver) (A, F, P)	Oncorhynchus kisutch
Salmon, pink (or humpback) (A, F, P)	Oncorhynchus gorbuscha
Salmon, sockeye (or red) (P, F)	Oncorhynchus nerka
Salsify or vegetable-oyster	Tragopogon porrifolius
Sapodilla or sapota	Achras zapota
Sapote, or marmalade plum	Calocarpum sapota
Sardine, Atlantic (A)	Clupeidae
Sardine, Pacific (P)	Sardinops sagax

Common Name	Scientific Name	Common Name	Scientific Name
Sauger (F)	Stizostedion canadense	Sucker, carp (F)	Carpiodes forbesi and C. cyprinus
Scallop, bay and sea (A)	Pecten species and Placopectens magellanicus	Sugar apple (sweetsop)	Annona squamosa
		Sunflower	Helianthus annuus
Seabass, white (P)	Cynoscion nobilis	Swamp cabbage	Ipomoea reptans
Seaweed, agar	Gelidium species	Sweet potato	Ipomoea batatas
Seaweed, dulse	Dilsea edulis	Swordfish (A, P)	Xiphias gladius
Seaweed, Irish moss	Chondrus crispus	Tamarind	Tamarindus indica
Seaweed, kelp	Laminaria species	Tangelo	Citrus paradisi X C. reticulata
Seaweed, laver	Porphyra laciniata	Tapioca	Manihot esculenta
Sesame	Sesamum indicum	Tangerine	Citrus reticulata
Shad or American shad (A, F, P)	Alosa sapidissima	Taro	Colocasia species
Shad, gizzard (A, F)	Dorosoma cepedianum	Tautog or blackfish (A)	Tautoga onitis
Shallot	Allium ascolonicum	Tea	Camellia sinensis
Sheepshead, Atlantic (A)	Archosargus probatocephalus	Terrapin (diamondback)	Malaciemys species
Shrimp (A, P)	Penaceus and Pandalus species, and other	Tilefish (A)	Lopholatilus chamaeleonticips
		Tomato	Lycopersicon esculentum
Skate (or raja fish) (A, P)	Raja species	Tomcod, Atlantic (A)	Microgadus tomcod
Smelt, Atlantic, jack, and bay (A, F, P)	Osmerus mordax, Atherinopsis californiensis, and Atherinops affinis	Towel gourd	Luffa acutangula
		Trout, brook (A, F)	Salvelinus fontinalis
Snail	Helix pomatia	Trout, rainbow or steelhead (A, F, P)	Salmo gairdneri
Snail, Giant African	Achatina fulica		
Sorghum	Sorghum vulgare	Tuna, Bluefin (A, P)	Thunnus thynnus
Soursop	Annona muricata	Tuna, Yellowfin (A, P)	Thunnus albacares
Soybean	Glycine max	Turkey	Meleagris gallopavo
Spanish mackerel (A)	Scomberomorus maculatus	Turnip	Brassica rapa
Spinach	Spinacia oleracea	Turtle, green	Chelonia mydas
Spot (A)	Leiostomus xanthurus	Veal	Bos taurus
Squab (pigeon)	Columba livia	Venison (deer)	Odocileus species
Squash, summer (Crookneck, Straightneck, and Scallop varieties)	Cucurbita pepo var. melopepo	Vine spinach	Basella species
		Walnut, black	Juglans nigra
		Walnut, Persian, English	Juglans regia
Squash, summer; Italian marrow group (including Zucchini and Cocozelle)	Cucurbita pepo var. medullosa	Waterchestnut, Chinese (matai, waternut)	Eleocharis dulcis
		Watercress	Nasturtium officinale
Squash, winter (Acorn, Butternut, and Hubbard)	Cucurbita maxima	Watermelon	Citrullus vulgaris
		Wax gourd or Chinese preserving melon	Benincasa hispida
Squid (A, P)	Ommastrephes species and Loligo species		
		Weakfish (A)	Cynoscion regalis
Strawberry	Fragaria species	Whale (A, P)	Balaena glacialis, Balenoptera borealis, B. physalus, B. musculus, and Physeter catadon
Sturgeon (A, F)	Acipenser oxyrhynchus		
Sucker (including white sucker and mullet sucker) (F)	Catostomus commersoni and Catostomidae species	Wheat	Triticum aestivum

[*Cont.*]

COMMON AND SCIENTIFIC NAMES FOR ANIMALS
AND PLANTS USED FOR FOODS [Cont.]

Common Name	Scientific Name	Common Name	Scientific Name
Wheat, Durum	Triticum durum	Yeast, baker's	Saccharomyces cerevisiae
Whitefish, lake (A, F)	Coregonus clupeaformis	Yeast, brewer's	Saccharomyces cerevisiae
Wild rice	Zizania aquatica	Yeast, torula	Torulalopsis utilis
Wreckfish (A)	Polyprion americanus	Yellowtail (Pacific coast) (P)	Seriola dorsalis
Yam (true yam of tropical areas)	Disocorea species		
Yam bean	Pachyrhizus species		

Source: USDA Handbook No. 8

Allspice 932
  Federal specifications 984
Almond Paste 881
  Federal specifications 975
Almonds 906-07
  Federal specifications 984
Anchovy Paste 881
Angelica 932
Anise 932-33
  Federal specifications 984
Antioxidant Compound,
  Foodservice
  Federal specifications 975
Apple Butter 881-82
  Federal specifications 975
Apple Pie Spice 933
Applesauce 882
  Federal specifications 975
Apricot Nectar
  Federal specifications 975
Arrowroot 882
Asperge 882
Baby Food
  Federal specifications 975-76
Baby Formula Preparation
  Federal specifications 976
Baking Powder 882
  Federal specifications 976
  Storage, dry 990
Baking Soda (Sodium Bicarbonate) 882
  Federal specifications 976
  Storage, dry 990
Balm of Gilead 933
Barley 891
  Federal specifications 976
Basil 933
Batter
  Storage, refrigerated 1017
Bay Leaves 933
  Federal specifications 984
Beans and Meat with
  Tomato Sauce
  Federal specifications 976
Beans with Frankfurter Chunks
  in Tomato Sauce
  Federal specifications 976
Beef 106-43
  Aged 107
  Blade meat 115
    Common name:
    False meat 115
    Common use:
    Cube steak 115
  Bones 121
    Common name:
    Soup bones 121
    Common use:
    Beef stock 121
  Brisket 118

Beef (cont.)
  Brisket
    Common names:
    Beef brisket corned 118
    Beef brisket edge cut boneless 118
    Beef brisket whole boneless 118
    Fresh beef brisket 118
  Brisket, boneless, deckle off 139
    Common name:
    Corned beef brisket 139
  Brisket, boneless, deckle on 118
    Common names:
    Beef brisket whole boneless 118
    Brisket boneless 118
    Fresh beef brisket 118
    Whole brisket 118
  Carcass 112
  Chuck 116-20
    Armbone 119
    Common names:
    Arm chuck roast 119
    Beef chuck arm 119
    English cut roast 119
    Round bone pot roast 119
    Common use:
    Pot roast 119
    Armbone, boneless 120
    Common names:
    Beef chuck arm pot roast
      boneless 120
    Chuck arm roast 120
    English cut roast 120
    Round bone roast 120
    Armbone, boneless, clod out 120
    Common names:
    Arm roast 120
    Armbone chuck 120
    English roast 120
    Common use:
    Roast beef 120
    Cross-cut 120
    Common names:
    Beef chuck cross rib pot roast 120
    Boston cut 120
    Bread and butter cut 120
    Cross rib roast 120
    English cut roast 120
    Thick rib roast 120
    Cross-cut, boneless 120
    Common names:
    Beef chuck cross rib pot roast
      boneless 120
    Boneless Boston cut 120
    Boneless English cut roast 120
    Roll 117
    Common names:
    Beef chuck pot roast 117
    Boneless chuck roast 117
    Chuck pot roast boneless 117

Beef (cont.)
  Chuck
    Roll
    Common names:
    Tied roast 117
    Square cut 116
    Common names:
    Beef chuck pot roast 116
    Blade roast 116
    California roast 116
    Chuck roast 116
    Square-cut, boneless (clod in) 117
    Common names:
    Beef chuck 117
    Blade roast 117
    California roast 117
    Pot roast 117
    Square-cut, boneless (clod out) 117
    Common names:
    Beef chuck 117
    Blade roast 117
    California roast 117
    Pot roast 117
  Cured, dried and smoked
    products 137-41
    Corned beef 138-40
    Brisket, boneless, deckle-off,
      corned 139
    Common name:
    Corned beef brisket 139
    Gooseneck round 140
    Common use:
    Corned beef 140
    Inside round 139
    Common name:
    Corned beef round 139
    Knuckle 139
    Common name:
    Corned beef round 139
    Outside round 139
    Common names:
    Corned beef outside 139
    Corned beef round 139
    Rump butt 140
    Spencer roll 139
    Surface fat thickness 138
    Dried beef products 138-41
    Inside round 139
    Knuckle 139
    Outside round 139
    Process 140
    Common name:
    Dried beef loaf 140
    Sliced 141
    Common use:
    Chipped beef 141
    Sliced ends and pieces 141
    Common use:
    Chipped beef 141

Beef (cont.)
  Cured, dried and smoked products
    Dried beef products
    Sliced, process 140
    Common use:
    Chipped beef 140
    Tongue 138, 140
    Cured 138, 140
    Common name:
    Pickled tongue 140
    Smoked 138, 140
  Diced 121
    Common names:
    Beef cubes 121
    Beef for stew 121
    Common uses:
    Beef goulash 121
    Beef ragout 121
    Beef stew 121
  Edible by-products 141-43
    Heart 143
    Liver 141-43
    Beef 142
    Common name:
    Steer liver 142
    Common uses:
    Liver loaf 142
    Sweetbread casserole 142
    Tongue 142, 143
    Beef 143
  Fat limitations 107
    Chops, cutlets, and filets 107
    Roasts 107
    Steaks 107
  Federal specifications 962
  Forequarter 112
  Forequarter, boneless 113
    Common name:
    Beef chuck shoulder pot roast,
      boneless 113
  Foreshank 118
    Common names:
    Beef shank center cut 118
    Beef shank cross cut 118
    Center beef shank 118
    Cross cut shank 118
    Leg meat 118
    Common use:
    Soup stock 118
  Grades 106
    Ground beef 106
    Portion cuts and diced beef 106
    Roasts 106
    USDA 106
    Quality 106
    Yield 106
  Ground beef patties, regular 123
    Common names:
    Chopped steak 123

Beef *(cont.)*
Ground beef patties, regular
Common name :
Hamburger 123
Sirloin patty 123
Common uses:
Chopped steak 123
Hamburger 123
Swiss steak 123
Ground beef patties, regular,
TVP added 123
Common uses:
Cheeseburgers 123
Hamburgers 123
Ground beef patties, special 123
Common names:
Chopped steak 123
Hamburger 123
Sirloin patties 123
Common uses:
Chopped beef steak 123
Hamburgers 123
Sirloin patties 123
Ground beef, regular 122
Common names:
Chopped meat 122
Ground beef 122
Ground chuck 122
Ground round 122
Ground sirloin 122
Hamburger 122
Common uses:
Chili 122
Chopped beef steak 122
Hamburger 122
Meat loaf 122
Sloppy Joe 122
Ground beef, regular,
TVP added 123
Common name:
Beef patty mix 123
Common uses:
Hamburgers 123
Macaroni beef casserole 123
Ground beef, special 123
Common names:
Chopped steak 123
Ground chuck 123
Ground round 123
Ground sirloin 123
Hamburger 123
Common uses:
Chopped beef steak 123
Meat loaf 123
Hamburgers
Federal specifications 963
Hash
Federal specifications 963
Hearts
Federal specifications 963
Storage, refrigerated 1012
Hindquarter 124

Beef *(cont.)*
Hindquarter
Common name:
Quarter of beef 124
Hindquarter, boneless 124
Kidneys
Federal specifications 963
Storage, refrigerated 1012
Knuckle 126
Common name:
Veiny sirloin tip 126
Common use:
Roast beef 126
Knuckle, special 126
Common names:
Knuckle 126
Sirloin tip 126
Common uses:
Roast beef 126
Swiss steak 126
Knuckle steaks 126
Common name:
Veiny steaks 126
Common uses:
Roast beef 126
Steak 126
Swiss steak 126
Liver
Federal specifications 963
Storage, refrigerated 1012
Loin 130-33
Full, trimmed 130
Common name:
Full loin 130
Short loin, short-cut 131
Common name:
Short loin 131
Common uses:
Club steak 131
Filets 131
Porterhouse 131
Sirloin 131
T-bone 131
Short, regular 130
Common name:
Beef short loin 130
Common uses:
Club steaks 130
Filets 130
Porterhouse 130
Sirloin 130
T-bones 130
Strip 131
Common names:
Beef strip loin 131
Shell 131
Common uses:
Bone-in sirloin 131
Club 131
Strip, boneless 131
Common names:
Beef sirloin boneless 131

Beef *(cont.)*
Loin
Strip boneless
Common names:
Untrimmed 131
Common use:
Roast beef 131
Strip, intermediate 131
Common names:
Beef sirloin 131
Trimmed 131
Common use:
Roast beef 131
Strip, intermediate, boneless 132
Common names:
Beef sirloin 132
Sirloin steak 132
Trimmed 132
Common use:
Roast beef 132
Strip, short cut 132
Common names:
Beef strip loin 132
Shell 132
Common uses:
Bone-in sirloin 132
Club steak 132
Strip, short cut, boneless 133
Common name:
Short cut strip 133
Common uses:
Roast sirloin 133
Sirloin steak 133
Plate 118-19
Full 119
Common names:
Plate roll 119
Rolled plate 119
Common use:
Pot roast 119
Full, boneless 119
Common names:
Beef plate rolled boneless 119
Plate roll 119
Rolled plate 119
Common use:
Yankee pot roast 119
Short 118
Common names:
Beef plate skirt cubes
boneless 118
Beef plate skirt steak
boneless 118
Boiling beef 118
Boston roll 118
London grill steak 118
Plate beef 118
Skirt steak 118
Common uses:
London broil 118
Skirt steak 118
Short plate, boneless 118

Beef *(cont.)*
Plate
Short plate, boneless
Common names:
Navels 118
Skirt steak rolled plate 118
Common use:
Yankee pot roast 118
Rib 114-15
Oven-prepared 114
Common names:
Beef rib roast 114
Rib roast oven-ready 114
Spencer roll 114
Standing rib roast 114
Oven-prepared, boneless, tied 114
Common names:
Beef rib-eye roast 114
Beef rib roast 114
Spencer roll 114
Common uses:
Delmonico pot roast 114
Rib-eye pot roast 114
Rolled roast 114
Spencer roll 114
Primal 113
Common names:
Oven-ready rib 113
Prime rib of beef 113
Rib roast oven-ready 113
Standing rib roast 113
Roast ready 114
Common names:
Beef rib roast 114
Prime rib 114
Spencer roll 114
Standing rib 114
Roast-ready (boneless, tied) 115
Common names:
Beef rib roast 115
Prime rib 115
Spencer roll 115
Standing rib roast 115
Common uses:
Prime rib 115
Roast beef 115
Roast-ready, special 115
Common names:
Beef rib roast 115
Prime rib 115
Standing rib roast 115
Rib eye roll 115
Common name:
Beef rib-eye roast 115
Common uses:
Beef rib-eye pot roast 115
Delmonico pot roast 115
Delmonico roast 115
Regular rolled roast 115
Rib eye roll, lip-on 116
Common names:
Boneless rib roast 116

Beef *(cont.)*
Rib eye roll, lip on
  Common names:
    Delmonico 116
    Spencer 116
Rib-eye roll, lip-on steaks 116
  Common names:
    Delmonico steak 116
    Lip-on steak 116
    Rib-eye roll 116
Round 124-27, 130
  Bottom (gooseneck) round 127
    Common names:
      Bottom round 127
      Outside round 127
    Common uses:
      Roast beef 127
      Swiss steak 127
  Bottom (gooseneck) round,
  heel out 127
    Common names:
      Bottom round 127
      Outside round 127
    Common uses:
      Roast beef 127
      Swiss steak 127
  Bottom (gooseneck) round
  steaks 127
    Common name:
      Beef bottom round steaks 127
    Common use:
      Swiss steak 127
  Bottom (gooseneck) round,
  untrimmed 127
    Common names:
      Army bottom round 127
      Bottom round 127
      Gooseneck round 127
      Outside round 127
  Bottom (gooseneck) round,
  untrimmed, heel out 127
    Common names:
      Prime bottom round with
      heel out 127
    Common use:
      Roast beef 127
  Eye of round 130
    Common name:
      Eye 130
    Common use:
      Corning beef 130
  Outside round 127
    Common names:
      Bottom round 127
      Gooseneck 127
  Primal 124
    Common name:
      Chicago round 124
    Common uses:
      Chopped beef 124
      Roast beef 124
      Swiss steak 124
  Round 124

Beef *(cont.)*
Round
  Common names:
    Chicago round 124
    Round primal boneless 124
  Common uses:
    Chopped beef 124
    Roast beef 124
    Swiss steak 124
  Rump and shank off 125
    Common names:
      Rump and shank off round 125
      Steamboat round 125
  Rump and shank off, boned,
  tied 126
    Common names:
      Rump and shank off round 126
      Steamboat round 126
    Common use:
      Roast beef 126
  Rump and shank off, boneless 125
    Common names:
      Rump and shank off round 125
      Steamboat round 125
    Common use:
      Roast beef 125
  Rump and shank off, boneless,
  special 125
    Common names:
      Rump and shank off round 125
      Steamboat round 125
    Common use:
      Roast beef 125
  Rump and shank off, boneless,
  tied, special 125
    Common names:
      Rump and shank off round 125
      Steamboat round 125
    Common use:
      Roast beef 125
  Rump, partially removed, shank
  off 126
    Common names:
      Rump and shank off round 126
      Steamboat round 126
    Common use:
      Roast beef 126
  Shank off, boneless 124
    Common name:
      Boneless round, shank off 124
    Common uses:
      Chopped beef 124
      Roast beef 124
      Steamship round 124
      Swiss steak 124
  Shank off, partially boneless 124
    Common names:
      Beef round rump on 124
      Shank off (steamship round) 124
    Common uses:
      Roast beef 124
      Stew beef 124
      Swiss steak 124

Beef *(cont.)*
Round
  Shank off, 3-way boneless 125
    Common names:
      Beef set 125
      Top bottom and knuckle 125
    Common uses:
      Roast beef 125
      Swiss steak 125
  Top (inside) 126
    Common name:
      Top round 126
    Common name:
      Roast beef 126
  Top (inside) round steaks 126
    Common name:
      Top round steak 126
    Common uses:
      Beef top round steak 126
      Braciole steak 126
Short ribs 119
Short plate 119
  Common name:
    Beef plate short ribs 119
  Common use:
    Short ribs 119
Special 119
  Common name:
    Short ribs 119
  Common use:
    Braised short ribs 119
Trimmed 119
  Common names:
    Beef plate short ribs 119
    Beef plate spareribs 119
    Bone-in stew beef 119
    Plate beef 119
    Plate boiling beef 119
  Common uses:
    Barbecued spareribs 119
    Braised short ribs 119
Shoulder clod 116
  Common names:
    Beef chuck shoulder pot roast
    boneless 116
    Beef chuck shoulder steak
    boneless 116
    Center shoulder roast 116
    Chuck roast 116
    Clod roast 116
  Common uses:
    Pot roast 116
    Swiss steak 116
Shoulder clod roast 117
  Common names:
    Beef chuck shoulder pot-roast
    boneless 117
    Center shoulder roast 117
    Chuck roast 117
    Clod roast 117
    Shoulder roast 117
  Common uses:
    Stew meat 117

Beef *(cont.)*
Shoulder clod roast
  Common uses:
    Swiss steak 117
    Side 112
Specifications. *See* entries for
  specific cuts of meat
Spencer roll 115
  Common names:
    Boneless rib roast 115
    Lip-on rib eye roll 115
    Prime rib 115
    Rib roast oven-ready 115
    Standing rib 115
  Common use:
    Roast beef 115
Steaks
  Beefsteak
    Federal specifications 962
  Braising, Swiss 113
    Common names:
      Beef chuck arm steak
      boneless 113
      Beef chuck shoulder steak
      boneless 113
      Cube steak 113
      Potting steak 113
      Round steak 113
    Common uses:
      Country fried steak 113
      Swiss steak 113
  Cubed, regular 112
    Common names:
      Minute steak 112
      Swiss steak 112
  Cubed, special 112
    Common names:
      Minute steak 112
      Swiss steak 112
  Cutting 112
  Flank 137
    Common names:
      Beef flank steak 137
      Jiffy steak 137
      London broil 137
    Common use:
      London broil 137
  Porterhouse 130
    Common name:
      Beef porterhouse steak 130
    Common use:
      Steak 130
  Porterhouse,
  intermediate 130
    Common name:
      Porterhouse steak 130
  Porterhouse, short-cut 130
    Common name:
      Porterhouse steak 130
  Rib 113
    Common name:
      Beef rib steak 113
  Rib, boneless 113

Beef *(cont.)*
  Steaks
    Rib, boneless
      Common names:
        Delmonico beauty steak   113
        Filet steak   113
        Rib eye   113
        Spencer   113
    Rib-eye roll   116
      Common names:
        Beauty steak   116
        Beef rib eye steak   116
        Delmonico steak   116
        Filet steak   116
        Rib-eye steak   116
        Spencer steak   116
    Ribeye roll, lip-on   116
      Common names:
        Delmonico   116
        Lip-on steak   116
        Rib eye roll   116
    Sirloin
      Bottom sirloin, ball tip   135
        Common names:
          Ball steak   135
          Mock tenderloin   135
        Common uses:
          Beef tips   135
          Cube steak   135
      Bottom sirloin butt   135
        Common names:
          Bottom butt   135
          Bottom sirloin   135
        Common uses:
          Kabobs   135
          Roast beef   135
          Stew   135
      Bottom sirloin butt,
      trimmed   135
        Common names:
          Bottom butt   135
          Bottom sirloin   135
        Common uses:
          Kabobs   135
          Roast beef   135
          Stew   135
      Bottom sirloin flap   135
      Bottom sirloin, triangle   135
        Common names:
          Triangle   135
          Triangle steak   135
        Common uses:
          Beef tips   135
          Cube steak   135
          Steak   135
          Swiss steak   135
      Bottom sirloin, triangle,
      defatted   135
        Common names:
          Triangle   135
          Triangle steak   135
        Common uses:
          Beef tips   135

Beef *(cont.)*
  Steaks
    Sirloin
      Bottom sirloin, triangle, defatted
        Common uses:
          Cube steak   135
          Steak   135
          Swiss steak   135
      Butt, boneless   133
        Common names:
          Boneless   133
          Sirloin butt   133
        Common uses:
          Roast beef   133
          Sirloin steaks   133
      Butt, boneless, trimmed   134
        Common names:
          Boneless   134
          Sirloin butt   134
        Common uses:
          Roast beef   134
          Sirloin steaks   134
      Sirloin   133
        Common name:
          Sirloin butt bone-in   133
        Common uses:
          Roast beef   133
          Sirloin steaks   133
      Top sirloin butt   134
        Common name:
          Top sirloin steak   134
        Common uses:
          Beef kabobs   134
          Steaks   134
      Top sirloin butt, boneless   134
        Common names:
          Butt loin   134
          Butt sirloin   134
          Sirloin butt   134
          Top butt   134
        Common uses:
          Roast beef   134
          Top butt steaks   134
      Top sirloin butt, center cut   134
        Common names:
          Butt steak   134
          Top sirloin   134
        Common use:
          Steak   134
      Top sirloin butt, semi-center
      cut   134
        Common names:
          Butt steak   134
          Top sirloin butt steak   134
          Top sirloin steak   134
        Common use:
          Steak   134
    Storage
      Frozen   1003
      Refrigerated   1012
    Strip loin, bone-in, short cut   132
      Common names:
        Beef strip loin   132

Beef *(cont.)*
  Steaks
    Strip loin, bone-in, short cut
      Common names:
        Shell   132
      Common uses:
        Bone-in sirloin steak   132
        Club steak   132
    Strip, bone-in, special   133
      Common names:
        Beef strip loin   133
        Shell   133
      Common uses:
        Bone-in sirloin steak   133
        Club steak   133
    Strip loin, bone-in, extra
    short cut   132
      Common names:
        Beef strip loin   132
        Shell   132
      Common uses:
        Bone-in sirloin steak   132
        Club steak   132
    Strip loin, bone-in,
    intermediate   132
      Common names:
        Shell   132
        Sirloin steak   132
        Strip loin steak   132
      Common uses:
        Bone-in sirloin steak   132
        Club steak   132
    Strip loin, boneless, extra
    short cut   133
      Common name:
        Short cut strip   133
      Common uses:
        Sirloin steak   133
        Sirloin roast   133
        Sirloin steak   133
    Strip loin, boneless,
    intermediate   132
      Common names:
        Beef sirloin   132
        Sirloin steak   132
        Trimmed   132
      Common use:
        Roast beef   132
    Strip loin, boneless, short cut   133
      Common name:
        Short cut strip   133
      Common uses:
        Sirloin roast   133
        Sirloin steak   133
    Strip loin, boneless, special   133
      Common name:
        Short cut strip   133
      Common uses:
        Roast sirloin   133
        Sirloin steak   133
    T-bone   131
      Common name:
        Beef loin T-bone   131

Beef *(cont.)*
  Steaks
    T-bone
      Common use:
        T-bone steak   131
        T-bone, intermediate   131
      Common name:
        T-bone steak   131
    T-bone, short cut   131
      Common name:
        T-bone steak   131
    Tenderloin
      Butt   137
        Common names:
          Butt tender   137
          Butt tenderloin   137
        Common use:
          Roasts   137
      Close trim   136
        Common names:
          Beef loin tenderloin steak   136
          Beef tender steak   136
          Filet mignon   136
        Common use:
          Tenderloin steak   136
      Defatted   136
        Common names:
          Beef loin tenderloin
          steak   136
          Beef tender steak   136
          Filet mignon   136
        Common uses:
          Filet mignon   136
          Steak   136
          Tenderloin steak   136
      Full tenderloin, defatted   136
        Common names:
          Beef tenderloin roast   136
          Filet mignon roast   136
        Common uses:
          Filet mignon steaks   136
          Roast beef   136
      Full tenderloin, regular   135
        Common names:
          Beef tenderloin   135
          Filet mignon roast   135
        Common uses:
          Filet mignon steak   135
          Roast beef   135
      Full tenderloin, skinned   136
        Common name:
          Tenderloin   136
        Common uses:
          Roast   136
          Tenderloin roast   136
      Full tenderloin, special   136
        Common names:
          Beef loin tenderloin   136
          Filet mignon roast   136
        Common uses:
          Filet mignon steak   136
          Roast beef   136
    Short   137

Beef (cont.)
  Steaks
    Tenderloin
      Short
        Common names:
          Beef tenderloin tip roast   137
          Filet mignon roast   137
          Short tender   137
        Common uses:
          Beef tenderloin   137
          Chateaubriand   137
      Skinned   137
        Common name:
          Tenderloin steaks   137
        Common use:
          Tenderloin steaks   137
      Special   136
        Common names:
          Beef tenderloin steak   136
          Beef tender steak   136
          Filet mignon   136
        Common use:
          Tenderloin steak   136
    Stewing   122
    Tongue
      Federal specifications   964
    Triangle   120
    Triangle, boneless   121
    Weight range   106-07
      Ground beef patties   106
      Ground beef patty weight
        tolerances   106
      Portion cut   106-07
        Items   106
        Weight tolerances   107
    See also Appendixes; Meats
Beef and Corn
  Federal specifications   976
Beef and Peas with Gravy
  Federal specifications   976
Beef and Vegetables
  Federal specifications   976
Beef extract   882
Beefsteak and Potatoes with
  Gravy
  Federal specifications   976
Benzoate of Soda   882
Beverage Base
  Federal specifications   974
Beverages   882-84
Biscuit Mix
  Federal specifications   976
Biscuits
  Storage, refrigerated   1016
Bisques
  Storage, refrigerated   1008
Boletus   885
Bouillon Cubes
  Federal specifications   976
Bouquet Garni   885
Braben   885
Brazil Nuts   907
  Federal specifications   984

Bread   885
  Federal specifications   977
  Storage, refrigerated   1016
Bread and Rice Puddings
  Storage, refrigerated   1019
Bread and Roll Mix
  Federal specifications   977
Bread Crumbs   885
Breadfruit   885
Broths
  Storage, refrigerated   1008
Brown Betty
  Storage, refrigerated   1019
Buckwheat   891
Burnet   933
Butter   298-308
  Characteristics   304-08
    Body   306-07
    Color   307-08
    Flavor   300, 304-06
      Characteristics classified   300
    Salt   308
  Cream   299
  Federal specifications   965
  Grades - U.S.   299
    A   299
    AA   299
    B   299
    C   299-300
  Storage
    Dry   977
    Refrigerated   1016
  See also Appendixes;
    Dairy Products
Cake
  Federal specifications   977
  Storage, refrigerated   1018
Cake Mix
  Federal specifications   977
Calf
  Federal specifications   962
  See also Veal and Calf
Candied Peel
  Storage, dry   1000
Candy
  Federal specifications   977
Cantharellus   885
Capers   885
Caraway   933
Caraway Seed
  Federal specifications   984
Carbonated Beverages
  Storage, dry   991
Cardamom   933
Carottes   885
Cases, Watertight
  Federal specifications   985
Cashew Nuts
  Federal specifications   984
Cassia Buds   885
Catsup, Tomato   885-86
  Federal specifications   977
  Quality factors, canned   954

Cayenne
  Storage, dry   994
Celery Flakes   933
Cereal
  Federal specifications   977
Cereal Grains
  Storage, dry   998
Cereals (ready-to-eat)
  Storage, dry   998
Chagote   893
Cheese   290-97
  Federal specifications   966
  Standards, federal   290-97
    American   290
    Appetitost   290
    Apple   290
    Asiago   290
    Bel Paese   290
    Blue   290
    Brick   290
    Brie   290
    Cacciocavallo   291
    Camembert   291
    Cheddar   291
      English   294
    Cheshire   291
    Colby   291
    Cook's   291
    Cottage   291
      Dry curd   291
      Lowfat   291
    Cream   291-92
    Derby sage   294
    Edam   294
    English dairy   294
    Filled   294
    Fontina   294
    Gammelost   294
    Gjedost   294
    Gorgonzola   294
    Gouda   294
    Granular   294
    Gruyere   294
    Hand   294
    Hard   294
    Hard grating   294
    Lancaster   295
    Liederkranz   295
    Limburger   295
    Livarot   295
    Monterey (Jack)   295
      High moisture jack   295
    Mozzarella   295
      Low moisture, scamorza   295
      Scamorza   295
    Muenster   295
    Neufchatel   295
    Noekkelost   295
    Parmesan (Reggiano)   295
    Pimento   295
    Pineapple   295
    Pont l' Eveque   295
    Port du Salut (Oka)   295

Cheese (cont.)
  Standards, federal
    Primost (Mysost)   296
    Provolone   296
    Reggiano   296
    Ricotta   296
    Romano   296
    Roquefort   296
    Samsoe   296
    Sap sago   296
    Sardo   296
    Scamorza   296
    Semisoft   296
    Skim milk   296
      Part skim spiced   296
      Semisoft   296
    Soft ripened   296
    Spiced   296
    Stilton   296
    Swiss (Emmentaler)   296
    Washed curd   297
  Storage
    Dry   995
    Refrigerated   1010
    Hard
      Cheddar   1010
      Grated   1010
      Swiss   1010
    Soft
      Cottage   1010
      Cream   1010
      Limburger   1010
  Whey
    Federal specifications   968
  See also Appendixes; Dairy Products
Cheese Crackers
  Storage, refrigerated   1019
Cheese Spreads
  Storage, dry   1010
Chervil   933
Chestnuts   893
Chewing Gum
  Federal specifications   977
Chicken and Noodles
  Federal specifications   977
Chicken and Vegetables
  Federal specifications   977
Chickens   240
  Broiler or fryer   240
  Capon   240
  Cock or rooster   240
  Federal specifications   965
  Hen or stewing chicken or fowl   240
  Roaster   240
  Rock cornish game hen or
    cornish game hen   240
  Stag   240
  See also Appendixes; Poultry
Chili Con Carne
  Federal specifications   977
Chili Powder   933-34
  Federal specifications   984
  Storage, dry   994

Chili Sauce 893
  Federal specifications 977
Chiso 934
Chives 934
Chocolate
  Baking
    Federal specifications 978
    Storage, dry 990
  Bar
    Storage, refrigerated 1017
  Drink
    Federal specifications 976
  Liquor 895
  Milk
    Storage, dry 990
  Sweetened
    Storage, dry 990
  Syrup 893
    Federal specifications 978
Chocolate Nut Roll
  Federal specifications 978
Chops
  Storage, refrigerated 1012
  See also Meat
Chowders
  Storage, refrigerated 1008
Chrysanthemum 934
Chutney 893
Cinnamon 934
  Federal specifications 984
Cinnamon Sugar 934
Citron
  Storage, dry 1000
Clam
  Federal specifications 968
  Storage, frozen 1004
  See also Shellfish
Clam Chowder
  Federal specifications 978
Cloves 934
  Federal specifications 985
Cocoa 893
  Federal specifications 976
  Storage, dry 990
Cocoa Beverage Powder
  Federal specifications 976
Cocoa, Breakfast 884
Coffee 882-83, 894
  Federal specifications 976
  Storage, dry 991
Cold Cuts
  Storage, refrigerated 1013
  See also Meat
*Complete Book of Cooking
  Equipment, The* 989-1002, 1007
Convenience Foods 361-402
  Chicken 388-89
    Parts 388
      Back 388
      Breast 388
      Drumstick 388
      Halves 388
      Leg 388

Convenience foods (*cont.*)
Chicken
  Parts
    Patties 388
    Pulled, cooked 388
    Quarters 388
    Thigh 388
    Two cut breast 388
    Wing 388
    Wing drummette 388
    Wing portion 388
    Wishbone 388
  Specialties 388-89
    Bologna 389
    Corn dogs 389
    Franks 389
    Nuggets 388
    Rolls 389
  Comparison rating chart 368
  Cost overruns 368
  Display cases 371
  Entrees
    Meat 382-84
      Barbequed beef, pork 382
      Beans and wieners 382
      Beef burgundy 382
      Beef crumbles 382
      Beef goulash; beef goulash
        with noodles 382
      Beef meat pie 382
      Beef pie filling 382
      Beef stew 382
      Beef tips in sauce 382
      Beef with BBQ sauce 383
      Beef with gravy 383
      Creamed chipped beef 383
      Jambalaya 383
      Julienne beef and green
        peppers 382
      Lamb roasted with gravy 383
      Lamb stew 383
      Meat balls with sauce 383
      Meat loaf, sliced 383
      Peppers, stuffed 383
      Peppers, stuffed with sauce 383
      Pork fritters 384
      Pork roast with dressing 384
      Pork with sauce or gravy 384
      Pot roast 383
      Pot roast with cheese
        dumpling 384
      Salisbury steak with
        mushrooms 384
      Sauces 384
      Short ribs with sauce 384
      Sliced ham with raisin sauce 384
      Swiss steak with gravy 384
      Turnovers 384
      Veal fritters 384
      Veal, roasted with gravy 384
      Western ham loaf 384
    Poultry 386-89
      Barbecued chicken 386

Convenience foods (*cont.*)
Entrees
  Poultry
    Chicken Alfredo 386
    Chicken fricassee 386
    Chicken in BBQ sauce 386
    Chicken in cream sauce 386
    Chicken in wine sauce 386
    Chicken paradise 386
    Chicken pie filling 386
    Chicken pot pie 386
    Chicken stuffed with rice 387
    Chicken turnovers 387
    Chicken whiskey 387
    Chicken with apples and
      almonds 387
    Chicken with cheese and
      mushrooms 387
    Chicken with dumplings 387
    Chicken with noodles 387
    Duckling 387
    Rock cornish game hen
      stuffed with apples and
      almonds 387
    Rock cornish game hen
      stuffed with rice or bread
      stuffing 387
    Turkey a la king 387
    Turkey and gravy 387
    Turkey and noodles 387
    Turkey pie filling 388
    Turkey with dressing and
      gravy 388
  Seafood 395-96
    Alaskan king crab newburg 395
    Crab cakes 395
    Crab newburg 395
    Deviled crab 395
    Fish cakes 395
    Fish fillet with sauce 395
    Lobster newburg 395
    Seafood cakes 395
    Seafood newburg 395
    Seafood turnovers 395
    Shrimp creole 396
    Shrimp newburg 396
    Stuffed flounder 396
    Stuffed shrimp 396
  Ethnic specialties 389-95
    British, Welsh, Irish 390-91
      Beef turnovers 390
      Beef Wellington 390
      Breast of rock cornish game
        hen wellington 390
      Irish stew 390
      Macaroni and beef 391
      Macaroni and cheese 391
      Tuna and noodles 391
      Welsh rarebit 390
    Chinese, Oriental, Hawaiian,
      Polynesian 393-94
      Brochette of Cornish
        Hawaiian 393

Convenience foods (*cont.*)
Ethnic specialties
  Chinese, Oriental,
    Hawaiian, Polynesian
    Chicken chop suey 393
    Chicken chow mein 394
    Chicken Hawaiian 394
    Chop suey vegetables with
      meat 394
    Chow mein 394
    Cornish game hen, Hawaiian 394
    Egg rolls, shrimp rolls,
      meat rolls 394
    Meat balls 394
    Polynesian pork 394
    Rumaki 394
    Stuffed breast Hawaiian 394
    Stuffed leg, Hawaiian 394
    Vegetable chow mein 394
  French, continental 391-92
    Beef bourguignonne 391
    Chicken chasseur 391
    Chicken cordon bleu 391
    Chicken in champagne 391
    Coq au vin 391
    Coquille Saint-Jacques 391
    Cornish game hen breast
      cordon bleu 392
    Crepes a la reine 391
    Crepes de la mer 391
    Duckling bigarade 391
    Fish fillet amandine 391
    Quiche lorraine 391
    Rock cornish game hen,
      stuffed 392
    Sole nantua 391
    Stuffed cornish game hen leg
      cordon bleu or Parisian style 392
    Veal cordon bleu 392
  Italian 392-93
    Canneloni 392
    Chicken cacciatore 392
    Chicken florentine 392
    Chicken parmigiana 392
    Chicken tetrazzini 392
    Italian sausage and peppers 392
    Lasagne 392
    Lumache with cheese filling 393
    Manicotti 393
    Meat ravioli 393
    Mostaccioli 393
    Pizza 393
    Ravioli in sauce 393
    Spaghetti sauce with meat
      or meatless 393
    Spaghetti with meat balls 393
    Turkey tetrazzini 393
    Veal and peppers 393
    Veal parmigiana 393
    Veal scallopini 393
  Mexican 394-95
    Burritos 394-95
    Chili con carne 395

Convenience foods *(cont.)*
Ethnic specialties
  Mexican
    Enchiladas   395
    Pochito   395
    Refried beans   395
    Tacos   395
    Tamale pie   395
    Tamales   395
    Taquitos   395
  Russian, Hungarian, German,
    Dutch, Scandinavian   389-90
    Beef stroganoff (Russian)   389
    Blintzes (Russian)   389
    Chicken Bohemian
      (Hungarian)   389
    Chicken kiev (Russian)   389
    Chicken scandia
      (Scandinavian)   390
    Cornish breast pojarsky   389-90
    Cornish hen breast kiev   389
    Goulash (Hungarian)   390
    Green pepper sauce and
      beef strips   389
    Sauerbraten (German)   390
    Stuffed cabbage (Hungarian)   390
    Stuffed cornish leg (Dutch)   390
    Swedish meat balls   390
Federal standards for meat
  and poultry products   373-77
  Meat products   373-76
    Baby food   373
    Bacon and tomato spread   373
    Bacon (cooked)   373
    Bacon dressing   373
    Barbecue sauce with meat   373
    Barbecued meats   373
    Beans and meat in sauce   373
    Beans in sauce with meat   373
    Beans with bacon in sauce   373
    Beans with frankfurters in
      sauce   373
    Beans with meatballs in
      sauce   373
    Beef and dumplings with
      gravy   373
    Beef and pasta in tomato
      sauce   373
    Beef carbonade   373
    Beef burger sandwich   373
    Beef burgundy   373
    Beef sauce with beef and
      mushroom   373
    Beef sausage (raw)   373
    Beef stroganoff   373
    Beef with barbecue sauce   373
    Beef with gravy   373
    Breaded steaks, chops, etc.   373
    Breakfast (frozen product
      containing meat)   373
    Breakfast sausage   373
    Brown and serve sausage   373
    Brunswick stew   373

Convenience foods *(cont.)*
Federal standards for meat
  and poultry products
  Meat products
    Burgundy sauce with beef
      and noodles   373
    Burritos   373
    Cabbage rolls with meat   373
    Cannelloni with meat and
      sauce   373
    Cappelletta with meat in sauce   373
    Cheesfurter   373
    Chili con carne   373
    Chili con carne with beans   373
    Chili macaroni   373
    Chili pie   373
    Chili sauce with meat or chili
      hot dog sauce with meat   373
    Chop suey (American style)
      with macaroni and meat   373
    Chop suey vegetables with
      meat   373
    Chopped ham   373
    Chorizos empanadillos   373
    Chow mein vegetables
      with meat   373
    Chow mein vegetables with
      meat and noodles   374
    Condensed, creamed dried
      beef or chipped beef   374
    Corn dog   374
    Corned beef and cabbage   374
    Corned beef hash   374
    Country ham   374
    Cracklin' corn bread   374
    Cream cheese with
      chipped beef   374
    Crepes   374
    Croquettes   374
    Curried sauce with meat
      and rice (casserole)   374
    Deviled ham   374
    Dinners   374
    Dumplings and meat in sauce   374
    Egg foo yong with meat   374
    Egg rolls with meat   374
    Enchilada with meat   374
    Entrees   374
    Frankfurter, bologna,
      cooked sausage   374
    Fried rice with meat   374
    Fritters   374
    German style potato
      salad with bacon   374
    Goulash   374
    Gravies   374
    Ham   374
    Ham a la king   374
    Ham and cheese spread   374
    Ham chowder   374
    Ham croquettes   374
    Ham salad   374
    Ham spread   375

Convenience foods *(cont.)*
Federal standards for meat
  and poultry
  Meat products
    Hamburger, hamburg, burger,
      ground beef or chopped beef   374
    Hash   375
    Hors d'oeuvre   375
    Jambalaya with meat   375
    Knishes   375
    Kreplach   375
    Lasagna with meat and sauce   375
    Lasagna with sauce, cheese
      and dry sausage   375
    Liver products (liver loaf, liver
      paste, liver pate, liver cheese,
      liver spread, liver sausage)   375
    Macaroni and beef in
      tomato sauce   375
    Macaroni and meat   375
    Macaroni salad with ham
      or beef   375
    Manicotti   375
    Meat and dumplings in sauce   375
    Meat and seafood egg roll   375
    Meat and vegetables   375
    Meat casseroles   375
    Meat curry   375
    Meat loaf (baked or
      oven-ready)   375
    Meat pasty   375
    Meat pies   375
    Meat ravioli   375
    Meat ravioli in sauce   375
    Meat salads   375
    Meat shortcake   375
    Meat soups   375
    Meat spreads   375
    Meat taco filling   375
    Meat tacos   375
    Meat turnovers   375
    Meat wellington   375
    Meatballs   375
    Meatballs in sauce   375
    Mincemeat   375
    Oleomargarine or margarine   375
    Omelet   375
    Pan haus   375
    Pate de foie   375
    Pepper steak   375
    Peppers and Italian (type)
      sausage in sauce   375
    Petcha   375
    Pizza   375
    Pork   375
    Pork sausage   375
    Prosciutto   375
    Salisbury steak   375
    Sandwiches   376
    Sauce with chipped beef   376
    Sauce with meat or meat sauce 376
    Sauerbraten   376
    Sauerkraut with wieners   376

Convenience foods *(cont.)*
Federal standards for meat
  and poultry
  Meat products
    Scalloped potatoes and ham   376
    Scallopine   376
    Scrambled eggs with ham
      in a pancake   376
    Scrapple   376
    Shepherd's pie   376
    Sloppy joe   376
    Snacks   376
    Spaghetti with sliced
      frankfurters   376
    Spanish rice with beef or ham   376
    Stews   376
    Stuffed cabbage with meat
      in sauce   376
    Stuffed peppers with meat
      in sauce   376
    Sukiyaki   376
    Sweet and sour pork or beef   376
    Sweet and sour spareribs   376
    Swiss steak with gravy   376
    Tamale pie   376
    Tamales   376
    Tamales with sauce
      (or with gravy)   376
    Taquitos   376
    Tongue spread   376
    Tortellini with meat   376
    Veal birds   376
    Veal cordon bleu   376
    Veal fricassee   376
    Veal parmagiana   376
    Veal steaks   376
    Vegetable and meat casserole   376
    Vegetable and meat pie   376
    Vegetable stew and meat balls   376
    Won ton soup   376
  Poultry products   376-77
    Baby food   376
    Beans and rice with poultry   376
    Breaded poultry   376
    Cabbage stuffed with poultry   376
    Canned boned poultry   376
    Cannelloni with poultry   376
    Chicken cordon bleu   376
    Creamed poultry   377
    Egg roll with poultry   377
    Entree   377
    Poultry a la Kiev   377
    Poultry a la king   377
    Poultry almondine   377
    Poultry barbecue   377
    Poultry blintz filling   377
    Poultry brunswick stew   377
    Poultry burgers   377
    Poultry burgundy   377
    Poultry cacciatore   377
    Poultry casserole   377
    Poultry chili   377
    Poultry chili with beans   377

Convenience foods *(cont.)*
Federal standards for meat
and poultry
Poultry products
Poultry chop suey 377
Poultry chow mein 377
Poultry croquettes 377
Poultry croquettes with
macaroni and cheese 377
Poultry dinners 377
Poultry empanadillo 377
Poultry fricassee 377
Poultry fricassee of wings 377
Poultry hash 377
Poultry lasagna 377
Poultry livers with rice gravy 377
Poultry paella 377
Poultry pies 377
Poultry ravioli 377
Poultry roll 377
Poultry salad 377
Poultry scallopini 377
Poultry soup 377
Poultry stew 377
Poultry stroganoff 377
Poultry tamales 377
Poultry tetrazzini 377
Poultry wellington 377
Poultry with gravy 377
Poultry with noodles
au gratin 377
Poultry with noodles
or dumplings 377
Poultry with vegetables 377
Sauce with poultry or
poultry sauce 377
Stuffed cabbage with poultry
or poultry sauce 377
Foodservice installation
handling practices 372
Frozen foods 396-401
Breads and rolls 398
Bagels 398
Biscuits 398
Bread loaves 398
Danish or sweet rolls 398
Dinner rolls 398
Muffins 398
Roll dough 398
Sweet dough, Danish dough 398
Desserts 398-400
Brownies 398
Cheese cake 399
Cobbler 399
Cream puffs 399
Crepes 399
Dessert doughs 400
Doughnuts 399
Eclair 399
Layer cake 399
Mousse 400
Pies 400
Cream 400

Convenience foods *(cont.)*
Frozen foods
Desserts
Pies
Custard 400
Fried 400
Fruit 400
Meringue 400
Pound cake 399
Pudding 400
Puff pastries 400
Sheet cakes 399
Shortcakes 399
Upside down cake 399
Dressing or stuffing 401
Bread 401
Cornbread 401
Egg products 401
Hard cooked egg roll 401
Liquid whole eggs 401
Low-cholesterol liquid 401
Frozen foods, code of
recommended practices
for handling 368-72
Foodservice installation
handling 372
Line-haul or over-the-road
transportation 370-71
Product temperatures 372
Retail display cases 371
Retailer handling practices 371-72
Storage facilities 371
Storage facilities for food-
service installations 372
Transportation equipment 370
Warehouse equipment 369
Warehouse handling
practices 369-70
Frozen fruits 396-97
Apples 396
Apricots 396
Berries, misc. 396
Blueberries 396
Cherries 396
Citrus salad 396
Cranberries 396
Grapefruit 396
Melon balls 396
Peaches 396
Plums 396
Raspberries 396
Rhubarb 397
Strawberries 396
Frozen juice based concentrates,
drinks, and ades 397-98
Cranberry juice cocktail 397
Fruit punch 397
Lemonade 397
Limeade 397
Orange drink 397
Orange flavored drink 398
Orange juice blend 397
Orange juice drink 398

Convenience foods *(cont.)*
Frozen foods
Frozen juice based concentrates,
drinks and ades
Single strength juices 397
Frozen juice concentrates 397
Apple 397
Grape 397
Grapefruit 397
Grapefruit and orange blend 397
Lemon 397
Orange 397
Pineapple 397
Tomato 397
Frozen tea and coffee 398
Coffee 398
Iced tea 398
Fruit and vegetable casseroles 401
Asparagus, corn, spinach
souffle 401
Escalloped apples, yams and
apples 401
Green beans and mushrooms,
mixed vegetables, or zucchini
in curry sauce 401
Rice pilaf or fried rice 401
Hors d'oeuvres and
appetizers 400-01
Canapes 400
Crepes 401
Hors d'oeuvres 400-01
Mousse 401
Quiche 401
Non dairy products 401
Coffee creamers 401
Whipped topping 401
Noodles 401
Egg 401
Green 401
Romanoff 401
Pancakes, waffles, french toast 401
Batter 401
French toast 401
Pancakes 401
Waffles 401
Soups and chowders 401
Chowder concentrates 401
Soup 401
Soup bases 401
Soup concentrates 401
Instructions 362
*Meat Buyers' Guides of
the National Association
of Meat Purveyors* 367
Meat cuts, basic 378-80
Beef 378-79
Bottom sirloin 378
Braising steak (swiss) 378
Brisket 378
Butt steak 378
Club steak 378
Corned beef 378
Cubed steak 378

Convenience foods *(cont.)*
Meat cuts, basic
Beef
Eye of round steak 378
Fabricated steak 378
Flank steak 378
Kabobs 379
Knuckle steak 378
Liver (steer) 378
Porterhouse steak 378
Rib (prime rib) 378
Rib eye roll roast 378
Rib eye roll steak 379
Rib steak 379
Short ribs 379
Skirt steak 379
Strip loin steak 379
T-bone steak 379
Tenderloin steak 379
Tongue 379
Top round roast 379
Top round steak 379
Top sirloin butt steak 379
Lamb 379
Lambette 379
Leg, boneless, tied or netted 379
Loin chop 379
Rib chop 379
Shoulder 379
Pork 379
Bacon 379
Veal 380
Calf's liver 380
Cubed steak 380
Cutlet 380
Leg, boneless, tied, roast 380
Loin chop 380
Medallion 380
Scallops 380
Shoulder clod steak 380
Steaks, veal and beef 380
Stewing veal 380
Packaging 362
Patties and combination
meat products 380-82
Beef and textured
vegetable protein 380
Beef patties 380
Beef stix, sticks 380
Breakfast sausage 380
Burger 380-81
Chopped beef 381
Chopped beef pattie 381
Dinner balls 381
Fresh pork sausage 381
Fritters 381
Ground beef patties 381
Hamburger 381
Meat balls 381
Meat loaf 381
Patties 381
Pizza burger 381-82
Sausage 382

Convenience foods (cont.)
Patties and combination
  meat products
    Steaks   382
    Whole hog sausage   382
  Patties and combination
  poultry products   384-86
    Breast, split   384
    Diced meat   385
    Drumsticks   385
    Fillet   384
    Ground thigh meat   385
    Necks, gizzards, livers,
      hearts, tails   385
    Processed oven roasts   385
    Pulled meat   385
    Rolls   385
    Thighs   385
    Wings   385
  See also Appendixes
Cookie Doughs
  Storage, refrigerated   1019
Cookies
  Federal specifications   978
  Storage
    Dry   1000
    Refrigerated   1018
Coriander   934
Corn Flour   894
Corn Meal   894
  Federal specifications   978
  Storage, dry   998
Corn Syrup   940
  Storage
    Dry   1000
    Refrigerated   1018
Cornstarch   894
  Federal specifications   978
  Storage, dry   990
Costmary   934
Crab Boil or Shrimp Spice   934
Crabmeat
  Federal specifications   968
  See also Shellfish
Cracker Crumbs   894
Cracker Meal   894
  Storage, dry   1000
Crackers   894
  Federal specifications   978
  Storage   1000
    Dry   1019
    Refrigerated
Cranberry Sauce   886
  Federal specifications   978
Crawfish
  Federal specifications   968
  See also Shellfish
Cream   278, 280-84
  Federal specifications   967
  Half and half   280
    Federal specifications   967
  Heavy   280-81
  Light   280

Cream (cont.)
  Sour
    Acidified   283
    Cultured   283
    Imitation   284
  Storage
    Dry   996
    Refrigerated   1023
  Whipped   283
  Whipping, light   280
    Storage, refrigerated   1018
  See also Appendixes; Dairy
    Products
Cream of Tartar   894
Cumin   934
Curry Powder   934-35
  Federal specifications   985
Custard
  Federal specifications   967
  Storage, refrigerated   1019
Custard Pies
  Storage, refrigerated   1019
Custard Topping or Filling
  Storage, refrigerated   1018
Dairy Products   271-310
  See also Appendixes; Butter;
    Cheese; Cream; Desserts
    (Frozen); Milk
Dessert Powder
  Federal specifications   978-79
Desserts (Frozen)   308-09
  Custard   309
  Ice cream   309
    Artificially sweetened   309
      Chocolate   309
      Fruit   309
      Nuts   309
      Plain   309
    Chocolate   309
    Federal specifications   967
    Fruit   309
    Mix
      Federal specifications   967
    Nut   309
    Plain   309
    Storage   1020
  Ice milk   308
    Artificially sweetened   308-09
      Chocolate   308-09
      Fruit   308-09
      Nuts   308-09
      Plain   308
    Chocolate   308
    Federal specifications   967
    Fruit   308
    Nut   308
  Mellorine type   309
  Milk shake mix   309
  Sherbet   308
    Federal specifications   968
    Storage, refrigerated   1021
  Storage, refrigerated   1020
  See also Appendixes; Dairy Products

Dill Seed   935
Dill Weed   935
Dittany   935
Dough Mix, Sweet
  Federal specifications   983
Doughnut
  Federal specifications   979
Doughs, Refrigerator
  Storage, refrigerated   1017
Dressing, Salad
  Federal specifications   979
Dressings   894-95
Dry Bread Crumbs
  Storage, refrigerated   1017
Dry Cereals, Grains and Flour   886-93
Dry Cocoa
  Storage, refrigerated   1017
Ducks   241
  Broiler duckling or fryer
    duckling   241
  Federal specifications   965
  Mature duck or old duck   241
  Roaster duckling   241
  See also Appendixes; Poultry
Eggs   261-70
  Federal specifications   965
  Fresh   261-69
    Buying guidelines   266, 269
    Grades
      A   266
      AA   266
      Acceptance service (USDA)   269
      B   266
      Consumer grades   261
      Factors considered   261
        Air cell   261
        Shell   261
        White   261
        Yolk   261
      Procurement   266
  Powdered   270
    Storage, dry   1002
  Processed   270
    Dried   270
    Frozen egg roll   270
    Hard-cooked refrigerated   270
    Whites   270
    Whole   270
    Yolk   270
    Yolk, sugared   270
  Shell. See Fresh
    Storage, refrigerated   1009-10
  See also Appendixes
Elder   935
Encyclopedia of Cookery   46
Epicus   134
Extracts, Flavoring, and Flavors   901
  Federal specifications   979
Fast Foods. See Convenience Foods
Federal Regulations. See Quality
  Control and Federal Regulations
Fennel   935
Fenugreek   935

Filberts   909-10
  Federal specifications   984
File Gumbo   900
Fines Herbes   900
Fish   311-44
  Canned   358-60
    Anchovies   358
    Caviar   358
    Codfish, dried   358
    Herring   358
    Herring (Sardines)   358
    Salmon   358-59
      Chinook   358
      Chum   359
      Coho   358-59
      Pink   359
      Sockeye   358
    Sardines   359
      Federal specifications   968
    Tuna Fish   359
      Albacore   359
      Bluefin   359
      Striped, skipjack or aku   359
      Yellowfin   359
  Categories   311
    Vertebrate or fin fish   311
  Cooked
    Storage
      Refrigerated   1008
  Dried
    Storage, dry   993
  Federal specifications   968
  Fresh   311
  Fresh water   312-15
    Blue gill   312
    Blue perch   312
    Blue sunfish   312
    Chainside   312
    Coppernose   312
    Gold perch   312
    Brook trout   312
    Buffalo fish   313
      Bigmouth   313
      Bugler   313
      Channel   313
      Gourdhead   313
      Prairie   313
      Razorback   313
      Redmouth   313
      Rooter   313
      Smallmouth   313
      Suckermouth   313
    Carp   313
      German   313
    Catfish   313
      Blue channel   313
      Bullhead   313
      Fiddler   313
      Spotted fish   313
      Yellow   313
    Chub   313
      Blackfin   313
      Bloater   313

Fish *(cont.)*
Fresh water
Chub
Bluefin 313
Tullibee 313
Eel 313
Anguilla 313
Capitone 313
Sand boy 313
Shoestring 313
Frog's legs 313
Herring, lake 313
Blueback 313
Cisco 313
Pike, perch 314
Blue pike 314
Blue pickerel 314
Blues 314
Grass 314
Great northern 314
Jack salmon 314
Lake pickerel 314
Pike perch 314
Saugers 314
Sand pike 314
Yellow pike 314
Dore 314
Pike perch 314
Salmon jack 314
Wall-eyed 314
Yellows 314
Pike, pickerel 314
Grass 314
Jack 314
Lake 314
Rock bass 314
Goggle-eye 314
Red eye 314
Red eye perch 314
Sunfish 314
Sheepshead 314
Croaker 314
Fresh water drum 314
Gas pergou 314
Gray bass 314
White perch 314
Smelts 314
Sturgeon 314
Common 314
Green 314
Lake 314
Sea 314
Terrapin 314
Trout, brook 312
Trout, lake 313
Gray 313
Great Lakes' 313
Mackinaw 313
Salmon 313
White bass 314
Silver lake 314
Striped lake 314
Whitefish 314-15

Fish *(cont.)*
Fresh water
White fish
Lake Champlain shad 314
Yellow perch 315
English perch 315
Jumbos 315
Lake 315
Lake Erie 315
Red fin 315
Frozen 311
Blocks 323
Cuts and shapes of prepared
fish 311-12
Fillets
Cod 316
Flounder and sole 327
Haddock 329
Ocean perch 335
Pacific Ocean perch 335
Popular species
Catfish, freshwater 312
Cod (scrod) 312
Flounder (fluke, sole) 312
Greenland turbot 312
Haddock (scrod) 312
Halibut 312
Mackerel (Spanish, king) 312
Mullet 312
Ocean catfish 312
Ocean perch 312
Pollock 312
Salmon (sockeye, red, coho) 312
Sea trout 312
Shad (and with roe) 312
Smelt 312
Snapper (red) 312
Sole (grey, lemon, Dover 312
Trout (rainbow, brook,
speckled, golden) 312
Whiting, cape 312
Whiting (hake) 312
Yellow perch 312
Portions
Fried 320
Raw 318, 321
Breaded 318
Steaks
Halibut 331-34
Salmon 339-41
Sticks 323
Fried 325
Raw, breaded 323
Whiting, headless, dressed 343
Market forms 311
Prepared, cuts and shapes 311-12
Salt water 315-44
Abalone 315
Aurora 315
Black 315
Grand ear shell 315
Green 315
Pink 315

Fish *(cont.)*
Salt water
Abalone
Rainbow 315
Red 315
Rough 315
Barracuda 315
Gauchanche 315
Black fish 315
Bowfin 315
Cottonfish 315
Dog fish 315
Grindle 315
Lawyer 315
Speckled cat 315
Black sea bass 315
Channel bass 315
Sea wolf 315
Bluefish 315
Blues 315
Green fish 315
Snapping mackerel 315
Tailors 315
Bonito 315
Atlantic 315
Chilean 315
Pacific Coast 315
Butterfish 315
Dollarfish 315
Harvest fish 315
Cod 315-18
Federal specifications 968
Fillets, frozen 316-18
Storage, frozen 1004
Croaker 318
Crocus 318
Hardhead 318
King billy 318
Cusk 318
Deep sea whitefish 318
Drum 318
Channel bass 318
Red 318
Red bass 318
Red fish 318
Sea 318
Spotted bass 318
Eel 318
Anguilla 318
Capitone 318
Sand boy 318
Sea 318
Shoestring 318
Flounder 326-28
Blackback 326
Federal specifications 968
Gray sole 326
Lemon sole 326
Winter 326
Yellowtail 326
Flounder and sole fillets 327
Fluke 328
Grouper 328

Fish *(cont.)*
Salt water
Grouper
Black 328
Gag 328
Nassau 328
Sea bass 328
Yellow fin 328
Haddock 328-31
Federal specifications 968
Fillets, frozen 329
Storage, frozen 1004
Hake 331
Black 331
Boston 331
Ling 331
Mud 331
White 331
Halibut 331-34
Federal specifications 968
Steaks, frozen 331-34
King mackerel 334
Cero 334
Kingfish 334
King whiting 334
Kingfish 334
Northern 334
Round head 334
Sea mink 334
Sea mullet 334
Seaming 334
Surf 334
Whiting 334
Lingood 334
Mackerel 334
Boston 334
Federal specifications 968
Storage, frozen 1004
Marlin 334
Black 334
Blue 334
Striped 334
White 334
Mullet 334-35
Common 334
Jumping 334
Silver 334
Stripped 334
White 334
Mussels 335
Bouchets 335
Horse 335
Mules 335
Pleated horse 335
Perch, ocean 335-38
Red 335
Red fish 335
Rose fish 335
Perch, ocean and Pacific Ocean
fillets 335-38
Pollock 338
Boston blue fish 338
Pompano 338

Fish (cont.)
Salt water
Pompano
Great 338
Mexican 338
Porgies 338
Common 338
Daughy 338
Jolt head 338
Little head 338
Little mouth 338
Saucer eye 338
Scuppang 338
Red snapper 338
Red cod 338
Red rock cod 338
Red rockfish 338
Rockfish 338
Sablefish 338
Black cod 338
Salmon 338-41
Atlantic 339
Chinook 338
Blackmouth 338
King 338
Quinnat 338
Spring 338
Chum 339
Dog 339
Fall 339
Keta 339
Coho 338
Medium red 338
Silver 338
Silver-side 338
White 338
Humpback 338
Pink 338
Sockeye 338
Blueback 338
Quinault 338
Red 338
Steaks, frozen 339-41
Scup 341
Porgy 341
Silver bass 341
White bass 341
Sea bass 341
Blackfish 341
Grey bass 341
Weakfish 341
Sea squab 341
Blowfish 341
Globefish 341
Puffer 341
Swellfish 341
Swell-toad 341
Sea trout 341
Gray sea 341
Salmon 341
Sand 341
Speckled 341
Spotted 341

Fish (cont.)
Salt water
Sea trout
Spotted weakfish 341
Weakfish 341
White 341
Shad 341-42
Sheepshead 342
Skates 342
Erenacca 342
Laevis 342
Raie 342
Rajahfish 342
Stingray 342
Turbot 342
Smelts 342
Spanish mackerel 342
Spot 342
Goody 342
Hard head 342
Lafayette 342
Norfolk 342
Silver gudgeon 342
Squid 342
Sea arrows 342
Striped bass 342
Rock 342
Rock bass 342
Rockfish 342
Sturgeon 342
Common 342
Green 342
Sea 342
White 342
Swordfish 342-43
Federal specifications 969
Storage, frozen 1004
Tuna 343
Bluefin 343
Bonitus 343
Horsemackerel 343
Skipjack 343
Striped albacore 343
Tunny 343
Yellow fin 343
Turbot 343
English sole 343
Greenland 343
Halibut 343
Pane 343
Sole 343
Turtles 343
White fleshed ocean 312
Whiting 343
Silver hake 343
Silver perch 343
Silver trout 343
Whiting, headless, dressed,
frozen 343-44
See also Appendixes
Fish Squares
Federal specifications 968
Storage

Fish Squares (cont.)
Storage
Dry 992-93
Frozen 1004
Fitches 935
Flageolets 900
Flakes 893
Bran 893
Corn 893
Wheat 893
Flavoring Extracts
Storage, dry 994
Flavorings 901
Flaxseed
Federal
specifications 979
Flour 891, 901
Buckwheat 891
Federal
specifications 979
Rice 891
Rye 891
Soy 891
Storage, dry 998
Wheat 886
Fonds d'Artichauts 901
Fondue
Storage, refrigerated 1010
Food Buying Guide for Type A
School Lunches 51
Food Coloring
Federal
specifications 979
Food Packet
Federal
specifications 985-86
Fruit Butter
Federal
specifications 979
Fruit, Candied
Federal
specifications 979
Fruitcake
Federal
specifications 979
Storage, refrigerated 1019
Fruits 495-674
Apples 500-12
Canned 502, 508-09
Quality factors 969
Dehydrated 509
Dried
Quality factors 957
Federal
specifications 969
Food Buying Guide for Type A
School Lunch 506-07
Fresh 502
Frozen 509-10
Quality factors 957
Rootstocks, dwarf 505
Spur-type trees 506

Fruits (cont.)
Apples
Varieties
Fall 501
Grimes golden 501
Jonathan 501
Wealthy 501
Summer 500-01
Astrachan 501
Fenton 501
Gravenstein 500
Lodi 501
N.W. greening 501
Starr 501
Summer rambo 501
Williams red 501
Yellow transparent 501
Winter 502
Baldwin 502
Ben Davis 502
Cortland 502
Delicious 502, 504
Golden delicious 504
McIntosh 504
Newtown 504
Northern spy 504
Rhode Island greening 504-05
Rome beauty 505
Stayman 505
Winesap 505
York imperial 505
Apricots 512-19
California Agricultural Code 513
Sanger lug 515
Canned 515-16
Artificially sweetened 674
1975 revisions 518
Quality factors 950
With rum 674
Dehydrated 518-19
Dried 519
Federal specifications 969
Frozen
Quality factors 957
Storage 1003
Marketing season 512
Varieties
Chinese 513
Derby 513
Moorpark 512-13
Perfection 513
Royal and Blenheim 512
Tilton 513
Avocados 520-21
Federal specifications 969
Marketing season 520
Varieties
Anaheim 520
Bacon 520
Booth 520
Carlsbad 520
Dickinson 520
Edranol 520

Fruits (cont.)
  Avocados
    Varieties
      Fuchs   520
      Fuerte   520
      Hass   520
      Hickson   520
      Itzamma   520
      Lula   520
      Pollack   520
      Mac Arthur   520
      Nabal   520
      Puebla   520
      Rincon   520
      Waldin   520
      Zutano   520
  Bananas   521-24
    Federal specifications   969
    Marketing season   521
    Varieties
      Cavendish   522
      Gros Michel   522
      Lacatan   522-23
      Musa cavendishii   522
      Musa sapientum   522
  Berries
    Blackberries—Dewberries
      Canned   529
        1975 revisions   530
        Quality factors   950
      Federal specifications   969-70
      Fresh   526
      Grades   526
      Varieties
        Boysenberry   525
        Eldorado   525
        Lawton   525
        Loganberry   525
          Quality factors, canned   952
        Lucretia (Bingleberry)   525
        Marion   525
        Olallie   525
        Thornless evergreen   525
    Blueberries—Huckleberry   531-37
      Canned   532, 535-36
        1975 revisions   536
        Quality factors   950, 952
      Federal specifications   970
      Fresh   532
      Frozen   536
        Quality factors   958
      Varieties
        Berkeley   533
        Blue gem   534
        Blue ray   533
        Bluecrop   533
        Bluetta   533
        Briteblue   534
        Burlington   533
        Collins   533-34
        Croaton   534
        Garden blue   534
        Jersey   533

Fruits (cont.)
  Berries
    Blueberries-Huckleberry
      Varieties   533
        Morrow   533
        Murphy   534
        Rabbiteye   534
        Rubel   533
        Tifblue   534
        Weymouth   533
        Wolcott   533
        Woodard   534
    Boysenberries
      Quality factors, canned   950
      Frozen   530-31
        Quality factors   958
      Storage, refrigerated   1013
    Youngberries
      Quality factor, canned   953
  Cantaloupes   537-40
    Federal specifications   970
    Varieties
      PMR 45   538
        Hale's best-type   538
  Cherries
    Canned
      Artificially sweetened   674
        Quality factors   950-51
      With rum   674
      Quality factors, frozen   958
    Red tart pitted   548-50
      Canned   549
      Federal specifications   970
      Frozen   550
      Sulphured   550
    Sweet   540-47
      Canned   544-45
        1975 revision   544
      Federal specifications   970
      Frozen   545
      Varieties
        Bing   541
        Black tartarian   541
        Chapman   541
        Early burlat   541
        Jubilee   543
        Lambert   541
        Larian   543
        Mona   543
        Republican   541
        Schmidt   543
        Windsor   543
  Coconuts   550-51
    Federal specifications   978
    Storage, dry   1001
    Varieties   551
  Cranberries   552
    Federal specifications   970
    Frozen   553
    Sauce-canned   554
      Quality factors   951
    Varieties
      Beckwith   552

Fruits (cont.)
  Cranberries
    Varieties
      Bergman   552
      Early black   552
      Franklin   552
      Howes   552
      McFarlin   552
      Pilgrim   552
      Searles   552
      Stevens   552
      Wilcox   552
  Currants, dried   554-55
    Federal specifications   970
    Quality factors, canned   957
  Dates   556-60
    Federal specifications   970
    Quality factors, dried   957
    Storage, dry   1001
    Varieties
      Deglet noor   556
      Halawy   557
      Khadrawy   557
      Medjool   557
      Zahidi   557
  Figs   561-68
    Canned   561-64
      Artificially sweetened   674
      Kadota   561-62
        1975 revisions   563
      Preserved   564
        Quality factors   951
    Dried   565-67
      Quality factors   957
    Federal specifications   971
    Varieties
      Adriatic   561
      Black mission   561
      Brown turkey   561
      Brunswick   561
      Calimyrna   561
      Kadota   561
      Mission   561
  Fruit Cocktail   568-69
    Canned   568
      1975 revisions   568-69
      Quality factors   951
    Federal specifications   971
  Fruit puree
    Federal specifications   971
  Fruits, dried
    Storage, dry   1000
  Fruits for salads   569-70
    Canned   568-69
      Quality factors   951
    Federal specifications   971
  Gooseberries
    Quality factors, canned   951
    Varieties
      Abundance   571
      Carrie   571
      Chatauqua   571
      Columbus   571

Fruits (cont.)
  Gooseberries
    Varieties
      Come   571
      Downing   571
      Glenndale   571
      Houghton   571
      Oregon   571
      Perry   571
      Pixwell   571
      Poorman   571
      Portage   571
      Triumph   571
  Grapefruit   571-79
    Canned   572, 576
      Quality factors   951
    Federal specifications   971
    Fresh   572
    Frozen   578
    Varieties
      Burgundy red   574
      Cluster   572
      Duncan   572
      Excelsior   572
      Frost marsh   574
      Hall   572
      McCarty   572
      Marsh   572-73
      Redblush   573
      Silver cluster   572
      Star ruby   574
      Thompson (pink marsh)   573
      Walters   572
  Grapefruit and orange for salad   578
  Grapes   579-84
    Canned   583
      1975 revision   584
      Quality factors   951
    Federal specifications   971
    Varieties
      American type
        Catawba   581
        Concord   581
        Delaware   581
        Niagara   581
      European vinifera
        Almeria   581
        Calmeria   581
        Cardinal   581
        Emperor   581
        Italia muscat   581
        Perlette   581
        Red malaga   581
        Ribier   581
        Thompson seedless (sultana)   581
        Tokay   581
  Honeydew and honey ball
    type melons   585-86
      Federal specifications   971
  Honeydews   584-85
  Lemons   586-88
    Federal specifications   971
    Fresh   588

Fruits *(cont.)*
Lemons
  Varieties
    Eureka 587
    Lisbon 587
Limes 588-89
  Federal specifications 971
  Fresh 588
  Varieties
    Bearss 589
    Dominican 589
    Key 589
    Kusaie 589
    Ogeechee 590
    Persian 589
    Rangpur 590
    Tahiti group 589
    West Indian 591
Lychee 591
  Varieties
    Bengal 591
    Brewster 591
Mangos 591-94
  Containers
    Forum flat 594
  Varieties
    Haden 593
    Irwin 593
    Keitt 593
    Kent 593
    Manila type 593
    Palmer 593
    Tommy Atkins 593
Melon balls 594-95
Nectarines 595-97
  Canned
    Quality factors 952
  Federal specifications 971
  Fresh 596
  U.S. grade
    standards 597
  Varieties
    Early sun grand 595
    Fantasia 596
    Flamekist 596
    Flavortop 596
    Gold king 596
    Independence 596
    Le grand 596
    Late le grande 595
    Red grand 596
    Red June 596
    Regal grand 596
    September grand 596
    Sun grand 595
Orange and grapefruit segments,
mixed
  Canned
    Quality factors 952
Orange segments
  Canned
    Quality factors 951
Oranges 597-604

Fruits *(cont.)*
Oranges
  Containers
    California 601
    California-Arizona 603
    Florida 602, 604
    Standard sizing 604
  Federal specifications 972
  Fresh 598
  Storage, refrigerated 1014
  Varieties
    Navels 601
    Hamlin 600
    Parson Brown 600
    Pineapple 600-01
    Temple 601
    Washington 599-600
    Sour (citrus aurantium) 598
    Sweet (citrus sinensis) 598
    Lue gim gong 601
    Pope Summer 601
    Valencia 599
    Excelsior 599
    Hart's late 599
Papayas 604-05
  Varieties
    Betty 605
    Bluestem 605
    Fairchild 605
    Gold 605
    Graham 605
    Hortus 605
    Kissimee 605
    Solo 605
    Line 10 605
Peaches 606-21
  Canned
    Artificially sweetened 674
    Clingstone 609, 614-615
    Freestone 610-11, 615-17
    1975 revisions 615-16
    Quality factors 952
    With rum 674
  Containers
    Los Angeles lug 612
    Sanger lug 612
    Western peach box 612
  Dried 612
    Quality factors 957
  Federal specifications 972
  Freestone 606, 610
    1975 revisions 615-16
  Fresh 608
  Frozen 617
    Quality factors 958
    Storage 1003
  Low-moisture-dehydrated 620
  Quality
    Blush 612
    Ground 612
  Varieties
    Dixired 606-07
    Elberta 607

Fruits *(cont.)*
Peaches
  Varieties
    J.H. Hale 607
    Loring 607
    Redglobe 607
    Redhaven 607
    Redskin 607
    Rio oso gem 607
    Sunhigh 607
    Triogem 607
Pears 621-32
  Canned 628-29
    Artificially sweetened 674
    1975 revisions 629
    Quality factors 952
    With rum 674
  Containers 626-27
    Eastern wooden box 627
    L.A. lug 627
    Lake county (Calif.) lug 627
    Trays for bartletts, anjous 627
  Dried 631-32
    Quality factors 952
  Federal specifications 972
  Grades 622, 627-28
    For bartletts 627-28
    U.S. standards for summer
     and fall 627-28
  Quality 627
    Anjou 627
    Bartlett 627
    Boscs 627
  Varieties
    Anjou (beurre d'anjou) 624-25
    Bartlett (Williams' Bon
     Chretien) 624
     American Pomological
      Society 624
    Bosc (beurre bosc) 625
    Clapp favorite 625
    Comice (doyenne du comice) 625
    Easter (Easter beurre) 626
    Hardy (beurre hardy) 625
    Kieffer 626
    Seckel 626
    Winter nelis 625-26
Persimmons 632-33
  Varieties
    Hachiya 632
Pineapples 633-41
  Canned 638-40
    Artificially sweetened 674
    Quality factors 952
  Federal specifications 973
  Fresh 634
  Frozen 640-41
  Grades 637-38
    Hawaii 638
    U.S. standards 637-38
  Varieties
    Cabazoni 636
    Cayenne 636

Fruits *(cont.)*
Pineapples
  Varieties
    Pernambuco 636
    Queen 636
    Red spanish 636
    Sugarloaf 636
Plums—Prunes 642-55
  Canned 646-47
    1975 revisions 647
    Quality factors 952
  Containers 643
  Federal specifications 973
  Fresh 644-45
  Frozen 651
  U.S. grade standards 646
  Varieties
    Ace 642
    Beauty 642
    Burmosa 642
    Casselman 642
    Duarte 642
    Duke, tragedy 643
    El Dorado 642
    French 643
    Italian 643
    Kelsey 642
    Laroda 643
    Mariposa 643
    Nubiana 643
    President 643
    Queen Ann 643
    Redroy 643
    Reine Claude 643
    Santa Rosa 643
    Wickson 643
Pomegranates 656
Prunes 651-55
  Canned
    Dried 651
    1975 revisions 651-52
    Quality factors 953
  Containers
    California Agricultural Code 643
    1/2 bu. baskets 643
    L.A.lug 643
    Northwestern lugs 643
  Dehydrated low moisture 653-54
  Dried 654-55
    Quality factors 957
    Storage,dry 1001
  Federal specifications 973
  Quality factors, canned 953
Raisins, dried
  Quality factors 957
Raspberries 656-60
  Canned 657
    1975 revisions 659
    Quality factors 953
  Federal specifications 973
  Frozen 659-60
    Quality factors 958
    Storage 1003

Fruits *(cont.)*
Raspberries
  Varieties
    Bristol 657
    Canby 657
    Clyde 657
    Cumberland 657
    Latham 657
    Munger 657
    New Logan 657
    Plum farmer 657
    Puyallup 657
    Sodus 657
    Taylor 657
    Williamette 657
Rhubarb 661-62
  Canned
    Quality factors 954
    Federal specifications 973
  Frozen 662
    Quality factors 958
  Oxalic acid 661
    Polygonum alpinum 661
  Varieties
    Cherry red 661
    Crimson 661
    Earl Mammoth 661
    German wine 661
    McDonald 661
    Ruby 661
    Strawberry or linnaeus 661
    Sunrise 661
    Valentine 661
    Victoria 661
  Storage
    Dry 992
    Refrigerated 1013
Strawberries 662-66
  Canned
    Quality factors 953
    Federal specifications 973
  Frozen 665-66
    Quality factors 958
    Storage 1003
  Varietal resistance to disease
    Factors affecting quality
      Nematodes 664
      Red stele root rot 664
      Verticillium wilt 664
  Varieties
    Florida ninety 663-64
    Fresno 663
    Guardian 663-64
    Headliner 663-64
    Hood 663-64
    Midway 663-64
    Raritan 663-64
    Shasta 664
    Surecrop 663-64
    Tioga 663
    Tufts 663-64
Tangelos 666-68
  Federal specifications 974

Fruits *(cont.)*
Tangelos
  Use
    Sampson for marmalade 666
  Varieties
    Minneola 667
    Orlando (formerly Lake) 667
    Seminole 667
Tangerines 668-70
  Federal specifications 974
  Varieties
    Algerian (Clementine) 668-69
    Dancy 668
    Kinnow 669
    Satsuma 669
    Willow leaf mandarin 669
Watermelons 671-73
  Federal specifications 974
  Varieties
    Black diamond (Cannonball
      or Florida giant) 671
    Charleston gray 671
    Crimson sweet 671
    Jubilee 671
    Klondike 672
    Sugar baby 672
  See also Appendixes; Produce
    Section
Fry Mix
  Federal specifications 979
Geese 241
  Federal specifications 965
  Mature or old 241
  Young 244
  See also Appendixes, Poultry
Gelatin 902
  Storage
    Dry 1000
    Refrigerated 1019
Gelatine
  Federal specifications 980
Ginger 935
  Federal specifications 985
Ginger Ale
  Federal specifications 980
Grain
  Federal specifications 980
Grains of Paradise 935
Gravy
  Storage, refrigerated 1008
Ground Meats
  Storage, refrigerated 1012
  See also Meats Ground
Guineas 241
  Mature 241
  Young 241
  See also Poultry
Gum Tragacanth 902
  Storage, refrigerated 1022
Ham
  See Pork
Ham and Eggs
  Federal specifications 980

Ham and Kidney Beans in Sauce
  Federal specifications 980
Ham and Lima Beans
  Federal specifications 980
Ham and Potatoes with Gravy
  Federal specifications 980
Hard Sauce
  Storage, refrigerated 1016
Hawthorn 935
Herb Seasoning 935
Herbs
  Storage, dry 994
Honey 902
  Federal specifications 980
  Storage
    Dry 1000
    Refrigerated 1018
Horseradish 935
  Dehydrated
    Federal specifications 985
  Prepared
    Federal specifications 980
Hot Sauce
  Federal specifications 980
Ice
  Federal specifications 980
Ices
  Storage, refrigerated 1020
Inhibitor, Mold, Bread and Rolls
  Federal specifications 980
Italian Seasoning 935
Jams (Preserves) 867-71, 901-02
  Federal specifications 975, 979
  Fruit preserves or jams 869-71
  Quality factors, canned 956
  Storage, dry 1001
  See also Appendixes;
    Produce Section
Jelly
  Federal specifications 975, 979
  Quality factors, canned 956
  Storage, dry 1001
  See also Appendixes;
    Produce Section
Joy of Cooking 676
Juices 847-66
  Apple
    Canned 847
      Quality factors 955
    Federal specifications 974
    Frozen 847-48
  Apricot nectar
    Quality factors, canned 955
  Cranberry
    Quality factors, canned 955
  Fruit
    Storage, refrigerated 1022-23
  Grape
    Canned 848
    Concentrate 848-49
    Federal specifications 974
  Grapefruit
    Canned 849-50

Juices *(cont.)*
  Grapefruit
    Canned
      Quality factors 955
      Federal specifications 974
    Grapefruit and orange, blended 852
      Federal specifications 974
      Quality factors, canned 955
  Lemon 855
    Federal specifications 974
    Quality factors, canned 955
  Lemonade 855
    Artificially sweetened 856-57
    Colored 857
    Federal specifications 974
  Lime
    Federal specifications 974
  Limeade 857-58
    Federal specifications 975
  Loganberry
    Quality factors, canned 955
  Orange
    Concentrated, frozen 859
    Concentrated with preservative 859
    Dehydrated 860
    Federal specifications 975
    From concentrate 860
    From concentrate, orange
      juice, pasteurized 860
    Quality factors, canned 955
    With preservative 861
  Peach nectar
    Quality factors, canned 955
  Pear nectar
    Quality factors, canned 955
  Pineapple
    Canned 861-62
      Quality factors 955
      Federal specifications 975
  Plum nectar
    Quality factors, canned 955
  Prune
    Canned 862
      Quality factors 955
      Federal specifications 975
  Tangerine 862-63
    Federal specifications 975
    Quality factors, canned 956
  Tomato
    Canned 863
      Quality factors 956
    Concentrated 863-64
    Federal specifications 975
  Vegetable
    Federal specifications 975
    Storage, refrigerated 975
  See also Appendixes; Produce
    Section
Kitchen Bouquet 905
Kitchen Sauce
  Federal specifications 980
Kosher Products 403-68
  Introduction 403-04

Kosher products *(cont.)*
Introduction
Bible   403
Dairy   404
"Glatt"   403
Glatt kosher   403
Kasher   403
Meat   404
Parve   404
Slaughtered   403
Institutional and industrial
  products   464-68
  Almond paste and
    kernel paste   464
  Batters   464
  Bread crumbs and breading   464
  Cake mixes   465
  Candy, chocolate, cocoa   464
  Cheeses   465
  Coagulating agents   465
  Coffee   465
  Coloring   465
  Cysteine hydrochloride   465
  Dairy-protein products   465
  Detergents   465
  Egg products   465
  Fillings and fillers   465
  Flavoring extracts   465
  Fresh fruit products   465
  Ice cream cones   466
  Ice cream mixes   466
  Margarine   466
  Mayonnaise   466
  Nickel catalyst   466
  Nuts   466
  Pizza crust   466
  Portion paks   466
  Release agents   466
  Rennet   466
  Salad dressings   466
  Salt   467
  Soup mixes   467
  Spices   467
  Stabilizers and emulsifiers   467
  Sugar and sweeteners   467
  Syrup   467
  Tea   467
  Tomato products, ketchup,
    vinegar   467
  Toppings   467
  Vegetable gums   468
  Vegetable oils   468
  Vegetables   467
  Yogurt flavoring   468
Kosher Ⓤ Products and
  Services Directory   404-48
  Applesauce   404
  Baby food and cereal   404-05
  Beans   405-06
  Beverages and drink
    mixes   406-07
  Blintzes and suzettes   446
  Bread crumbs and meal   408-09

Kosher products *(cont.)*
Kosher Ⓤ Products and
  Service Directory
  Bread, rolls, muffins, toast,
    bagels   407-08
  Butter   409
  Buttermilk   409
  Cake frosting mix   411
  Cake mix   411
  Cake, pastry and pie filling   412
  Cakes, cookies,
    crackers   409-10, 446
  Candy   412-13, 446
  Casserole mixes   413
  Catsup, tomato sauce and
    puree   421-22
  Cereal   413-14
  Champagne   414
  Cheese   414-15
  Chinese vegetables—chow mein   415
  Cleaners   446
  Cocoa   415
  Coconut   415
  Coffee   415
  Corn chips   415
  Cornstarch   415
  Derma   415
  Diet drinks   419
  Dumplings   425
  Egg substitute   416
  Fish   446
  Fish products   416
  Flour   411
  Frozen and fresh packaged
    meals   417
  Fruits   417
  Gefilte fish   418
  Glaze   418
  Honey   418
  Horseradish   418
  Ice cream   419, 447
  Ices   417-18, 446
  Infant and special formula
    drink   419, 447
  Jams, jellies, preserves and
    marmalades   419-21
  Juice drinks   421
  Juices   421
  Liquors and cordials   422
  Macaroni, spaghetti and
    noodles   422-23
  Margarine   425, 447
  Marinades   425
  Marshmallow topping   425
  Matzoh   425
  Mayonnaise and salad
    dressings   423-25
  Meat products and poultry   447
  Meat tenderizer   426
  Meats and provisions   425
  Melba toast   426
  Milk   426
    Evaporated   426

Kosher products *(cont.)*
Kosher Ⓤ Products and
  Service Directory
  Milk
    Flavorings and amplifiers   427
    Powder   426-27
  Milk, cream substitute   426
  Mustard   427
  Nuts and seeds   427-28
  Olives   428
  Oven cleaners   428-29
  Pancake mixes   429
  Pastina   429
  Pastry   410-11
  Peanut butter   429
  Pickles, relishes, kraut   429-32
  Pie and tart shells   432
  Pizza   432
  Popcorn   432
  Popcorn topping   432
  Potato chips   432-33
  Potato products   433-34
  Poultry and poultry products   434
  Pretzels   434-35
  Puddings and desserts   447
  Rice   435
  Salt   435
  Salt substitutes   435
  Sauce   447
  Sauces and gravy mixes   435-37
  Sherbet   418
  Shortenings and oils   437-38
  Snack food   438
  Soup   447
  Soup nuts   441
  Soups and soup mixes   438
  Sour cream—buttermilk   441, 447-48
  Soy protein   441
  Soybeans   441
  Spices and seasonings   441-42
  Spray shortening   448
  Sugar   442
  Sweeteners   442-43, 448
  Syrups   443-44
  Tea   444
  Tomato puree and aspic   444
  Vegetables   444
  Vinegar   444-45
  Waffles   448
  Wheat germ   445
  Whip and dessert toppings   445-46
  Wine and grape juice   446
Passover, Kosher for, " Ⓤ P"
  Acidulants   463
  Alcohol   463
  Anti-oxidant   463
  Applesauce   448, 458
  Beverages   449
  Borscht   449
  Butter   449, 458
  Buttermilk   449, 458
  Cake mixes   449
  Cakes, cookies   449

Kosher products *(cont.)*
Passover, Kosher for, " Ⓤ P"
  Candy   449-50
  Candy and chocolates   458
  Champagne   450
  Cheese   450
  Coffee   450
  Cranberry sauce   450
  Desserts—puddings   451
  Dressings   451
  Dumplings—Knaidel   458
  Egg products   458-59
  Fish, frozen   457
  Fish products   451-52, 459
  Flavors   459, 463
  Food coloring   459
  Frosting   452
  Frozen desserts   460
  Frozen dinners   452, 460
  Fruit butter   452
  Fruit ices   460
  Fruits   452, 460
  Glycerine   463
  Hexitols   463
  Honey   452
  Horseradish   452-53
  Ice cream, sherbet   453, 460
  Jams, jellies, marmalade   453, 460
  Juice   453, 460-61
  Low calorie foods   453-54
  Matzoh   454, 461
  Mayonnaise   454, 461
  Meat and provisions   454, 461
  Meats   457, 463
  Medicines   454
  Milk   461
  Monosodium glutamate   454
  Nuts   454
  Pancake mix   454
  Passover noodles   454, 461
  Pastes   461
  Pickles   454, 461
  Potato   461
  Potato starch   455
  Poultry   457, 463
  Poultry products   455
  Preservatives   464
  Salt   455, 464
  Sauces   455
  Shortening—oils   455, 461-62
  Soup nuts   456
  Soups and soup mixes   455-56
  Sour cream   456, 462
  Sour salt   456
  Spices and seasonings   456, 462
  Stabilizer   462
  Stuffing and coating mixes   456
  Sugar   456, 462
  Sweetener   458, 464
  Tea   456, 457
  Tzimmes   450
  Vegetables   456-57
    Canned   463

Kosher products *(cont.)*
  Passover, Kosher for, " Ⓤ P "
    Vegetables
      Dehydrated—powdered . . . 462
      Vinegar, cider . . . 457, 463
      Vitamins . . . 457
      Wines—grape juice . . . 457
  See also Appendixes
Lamb . . . 143-56
  Back . . . 153
    Common name:
      Lamb back . . . 153
    Common use:
      Chops . . . 153
  Boning . . . 149
  Bracelet . . . 149
    Common name:
      Double rack . . . 149
  Breast . . . 151
  Carcass . . . 149
  Chops . . . 148
  Chucks . . . 150
    Common name:
      Lamb slug . . . 150
  Chucks and plates . . . 150
    Common name:
      Lamb slug . . . 150
  Class . . . 143
    Lamb . . . 143
    Mutton . . . 143
    Yearling mutton . . . 143
  Edible by-products . . . 155-56
    Liver . . . 155, 156
  Federal specifications . . . 963
  Foresaddle . . . 149
  Foreshank . . . 151
    Common name:
      Lamb shank . . . 151
  Ground . . . 155
    Common use:
      Lamb patties . . . 155
  Ground patties . . . 148
    Common name:
      Lamb patties . . . 155
  Hindsaddle . . . 151, 154
    Common names:
      Hindquarter . . . 151
      Lamb back . . . 154
  Hindshank . . . 153
    Common name:
      Leg of lamb . . . 153
  Leg . . . 152-53
    Common names:
      Boneless lamb leg roast . . . 153
      Leg of lamb . . . 152
      Oven-prepared leg of lamb . . . 153
    Common use:
      Lamb cutlets . . . 152
  Loin . . . 151
    Common names:
      Lamb . . . 151
      Lamb saddle . . . 151
      Loin . . . 151

Lamb *(cont.)*
  Loin
    Common use:
      Lamb chops . . . 151
    Loin chops . . . 152
      Common name:
        Lamb chops . . . 152
    Loin, trimmed . . . 152
    Material . . . 148-49
    Rib chops . . . 149, 150
      Frenched . . . 150
    Rib rack . . . 149
      Common name:
        Double rack . . . 149
    Shoulder . . . 150-51
      Chops . . . 150
        Common name:
          Lamb chops . . . 150
      Square-cut . . . 150
        Common name:
          Chuck . . . 150
      Square-cut, boneless and tied . . . 151
        Common name:
          Shoulder roast . . . 151
    Stewing . . . 154
      Common names:
        Lamb cubes . . . 154
        Lamb stew meat . . . 154
      Common use:
        Lamb stew . . . 154
    Storage
      Frozen . . . 1003
      Refrigerated . . . 1012
    Tying . . . 148
    See also Appendixes; Meat
Lard
  Federal specifications . . . 980
Lemon Verbena . . . 935
Liquid Smoke . . . 938
Liver. *See* Beef; Lamb; Pork; Veal
  and Calf
Lovage . . . 935
Macaroni
  Federal specifications . . . 980
  Storage, dry . . . 999
Mace . . . 935-36
  Federal specifications . . . 985
Maggi . . . 936
Malt Preparations
  Federal specifications . . . 980
Maple Sugar
  Storage, refrigerated . . . 1018
Maple Syrup . . . 940-41
  Storage, refrigerated . . . 1018
Margarine . . . 906
  Federal specifications . . . 967
  Storage
    Dry . . . 997
    Refrigerated . . . 1016
Marigold . . . 936
Marjoram . . . 906, 936
  Federal
    specifications . . . 985

Marmalade
  Quality factors . . . 956
Marmalade, Orange
  Federal specifications . . . 980
Marshmallows . . . 906
  Federal specifications . . . 980
Marzipan . . . 881
Mayonnaise
  Federal specifications . . . 980
  Storage, dry . . . 997
Meal, Combat
  Federal specifications . . . 986
Meal, Precooked
  Federal specifications . . . 986
Meat . . . 69-238
  Aging or dispensing . . . 71
    Discoloration . . . 71
    Enzymes . . . 71
    Ripening . . . 71
  Budget, foodservice . . . 69-70
  Butchering . . . 84-86
    Butcher . . . 84
    Fabricated multiplier . . . 85
    Yield test card . . . 85
  Buyers' guides . . . 94
    MBG . . . 94
    The Meat Buyers' Guide to Portion
      Control Meat Cuts . . . 94
    The Meat Buyers' Guide to
      Standardized Meat Cuts . . . 94
    National Association of Meat
      Purveyors (NAMP) . . . 94
    National Livestock and Meat
      Board . . . 94
    Uniform Retail Meat Identity
      Standards . . . 94
  Buying know-how . . . 74
    Caveat emptor . . . 74
    Specifications . . . 74
  Charging . . . 92
    Profit . . . 92
    Subsidies . . . 92
  Class of meat . . . 76-77, 79-80
    Beef . . . 77, 79
      Bull . . . 77
      Bullock . . . 77
      Cow . . . 77
      Heifer . . . 77
      Stag . . . 77, 79
      Steer . . . 77
        Cod . . . 79
        Pizzle eye . . . 79
      Bovine . . . 79
      Ovine . . . 77, 79
        Lamb . . . 77, 79
          Breck joint . . . 79
          Hothouse . . . 79
          Spring . . . 79
        Mutton . . . 77, 79
          Buck . . . 79
          Ewe . . . 79
          Wether . . . 79
          Yearling . . . 77

Meat *(cont.)*
  Class of meat
    Pork . . . 77, 79
      Barrow . . . 77, 79
      Boar . . . 79
      Gilt . . . 77, 79
      Sow . . . 79
      Stag . . . 79
  Composition and structure . . . 70
    Collagen . . . 70
    Connective tissues . . . 70
    Elastin . . . 70
    Muscle . . . 70
  Cooking loss. *See* Ordering
  Cost . . . 92-93
    Carved weight percentage . . . 93
    Yield test card . . . 92
  Federal specifications . . . 963
  Freezing . . . 71
    Evaporation . . . 71
    Vacuum . . . 71
  Grading . . . 76-84
    Conformation . . . 80
    Cutability or yield grading . . . 84
    Federal grading service . . . 76
    Finish . . . 80
    Marbling . . . 80
      Palatability . . . 80
    1975 grading changes . . . 76
    See also Classes of meat
  Ground meat
    Storage, refrigerated . . . 1012
  Inspections . . . 74-75
    Domestic meat label . . . 74
    Imported . . . 74
    Military . . . 74
    Religious . . . 74
      Kasruth . . . 74
      Kosher . . . 74
    Wholesomeness . . . 74
  Loaf
    Federal specifications . . . 964
  Marbling . . . 70
    Esters . . . 70
    Lean . . . 70
    Nutritive value . . . 70
  Ordering . . . 86-89
    Cooking loss . . . 86-87
    Inventory (order) receiving
      record . . . 89
    Menu balance . . . 86
    Minimum-maximum stock . . . 88-89
    Par-stock . . . 88
    Production history cards . . . 89
    Specifications . . . 86
  Pigments, extracts and water . . . 71
    Color . . . 71
    Myoglobin . . . 71
    Shrinkage . . . 71
    Stock . . . 71
  Refrigeration . . . 71
  Specifications . . . 93-104
    Certification . . . 100

Meat *(cont.)*
Specifications
General requirements, beef   94-100
IMPS (Institutional Meat Purchase
Specifications)   93
Inspection   100
Institution   104
Meat acceptance service   93
Ordering data   100
Package and packaging   100-03
Closure   102-03
Marking   103
Refrigeration   100
Time limitation   100
Waivers and amendments   103
Storage
Dry   992
Refrigerated   1012-13
Tempering   74
Roasted or potted   74
Yield   74
See also Appendixes
See also Beef; Lamb; Pork; Veal
and Calf
**Meat Balls and Beans in Tomato
Sauce**
Federal specifications   980
Meat Sauce
Federal specifications   980
Meringue
Storage, refrigerated   1019
Meringue Powder
Federal specifications   981
271-89
Milk
Drinks
Storage, refrigerated   1021, 1023
Federal specifications   967-68
Homogenized   274
Kinds   274-89
Canned whole   277
Certified   274-75
Concentrated   275-76, 281
Canned   276
Condensed   276, 281
Evaporated   276, 281, 282
Cultured   276-77, 282
Acidophilus   277
Buttermilk   276, 282
Dry   97
Federal specifications   965
Storage, refrigerated   1021, 1023
Storage, refrigerated   1021
Yogurt   277, 283
Frozen   283
Dry   284-89
Buttermilk   289
Nonfat   285-89
Storage, dry   996
Whole   284-85
Grades, U.S.   284-85
Extra   284-85
Premium   284
Standard   285

Milk *(cont.)*
Kinds
Dry
Whole
Storage, dry   996
Eggnog   284
Evaporated   276, 281, 282
Storage, dry   996
Filled   282
Dessert topping   284
Dry   282
Evaporated   282
Flavored   277, 282
Chocolate   277
Chocolate milk
Federal specifications   967
Chocolate dairy drink   277
Flavored drink   282
Fluid filled   282
Fortified   275, 282
Frozen whole   277
Half-and-half   280, 283
Low sodium   275
Low fat   279, 282
Malted milk
Federal specifications   967
Mineral   282
Nonfat
Dry   281-82, 284
Roller process   285-86
Spray process   286-88
Fat free, defatted   282
Instant, dry   288-89
Skim   276, 279-80, 282-83
Condensed, plain   283
Condensed, sweetened   281, 283
Soft curd   275
Sour
Storage, refrigerated   1021
2 percent   276
Vitamin D   283
Whole   283
Canned   277
Condensed, sweetened   281, 283
Storage, dry   996
Dry   283
Grades   284-85
Fresh, fluid   274
Frozen   277
Label declaration   279
Non-dairy
Coffee whiteners   284
Fluid beverages   284
Topping   284
Ordinance, grade A, pasteurized   271
Pasteurized   271, 274, 278
Ultra   278
Products
Federal specifications   968
Storage, refrigerated   1021, 1023
Storage, refrigerated   1021, 1023
See also Appendixes; Dairy Products
Mincemeat   906

Mincemeat *(cont.)*
Federal specifications   963
Storage, refrigerated   1019
Mint Flakes   936
Miscellaneous Groceries   881-944
Almond paste   881
Marzipan   881
Anchovy paste   881
Apple butter   881-82
Applesauce   882
Arrowroot   882
Cassava   882
Curcuma   882
Asperge (asparagus)   882
Baking powder   882
Baking soda   882
Beans   882
Beef extract   882
Benzoate of soda   882
Beverages   882-84
Chocolate, hot   884
Cocoa, breakfast   884
Coffee   882-83
Decaffeinated   883
Freeze-dried   883
Frozen   884
Postum   883
Soluble   884-85
Tea   884
Boletus (french mushroom)   885
Bouquet garni   885
Braben   885
Bread   885
Bread crumbs   885
Breadfruit   885
Cantharellus   885
Capers   885
Carottes   885
Cassia buds   885
Catsup, tomato   885-86
Chagote   893
Chestnuts   893
Chili sauce   893
Chocolate liquor   895
Chocolate syrup   893
Chutney   893
Cocoa   893
Coconut   893
Coffee   893
Corn   894
Corn flour   894
Corn meal   894
Cornstarch   894
Cracker crumbs   894
Cracker meal   894
Crackers   886
Cranberry sauce   894
Cream of tartar   894-95
Dressings   895
Cheese   895
French   895
Oil and vinegar   895
Refrigerated   894-95

Miscellaneous Groceries *(cont.)*
Dressings
Salad   894
Sandwich spread   894
Spoon-type   895
Dry cereals, grains and flour   886-93
Barley
Pearl   891
Scotch   891
Buckwheat   891
Corn   893
Flakes   893
Bran   893
Corn flakes   893
Wheat   893
Flour
Buckwheat   891
Rice   891
Rye   891
Soy   891
Wheat   886
Classes
Durum   887
Amber durum   887
Hard amber durum   887
Red durum   887
Hard red winter   887
Dark hard winter   887
Hard winter   887
Hard red spring   886-87
Dark northern spring   887
Northern spring   887
Red spring   887
Grades   887-90
Ergoty   888-89
Garlicky   888
Heavy   889
Smutty   887
Tough   887
Treated   889
Weevily   888
Pasta classes
Bonballati   891
Canelloni   891
Ditali lisci   891
Fidellini   891
Forati   891
Foratini   891
Lasagne   891
Linguine   891
Macaroni   891
Manicotti   891
Mezzani   891
Mezzarrelli   891
Noodles   891
Broad   891
Fine   891
Medium   891
Perciatelli   891
Ravioli   891
Rigatoni   891
Spaghetti   891
Spaghettini   891

Miscellaneous Groceries *(cont.)*
  Dry cereals, grains and flour
   Pasta classes
    Tochetti   891
    Vermicelli   891
    Zifi   891
    Zitoni   891
   Puffs
    Puffed corn   893
    Puffed rice   893
    Puffed wheat   893
   Rice   891
    Wild   891
   Rye   891
   Soy   891
   Tapioca   893
  Fats and oils   895-900
   Bleaching   895
   Chemical reactions in frying
    Hydrolysis   897
    Oxidation   897
    Polymerization   898
   Corn oil   900
   Cottonseed   900
   Hydrogenation   895, 897, 900
   Lard   900
   Margarine   899
   Nonglyceride materials
    Free fatty acids   895
    Phosphatides   895
   Olive oil   900
   Peanut oil   900
   Phosphatides   895
   Refining   895
   Salad and cooking oils   898
   Shortenings   898-99
    Hydrogenated   899
    Polyunsaturated   899
   Suet   900
   Tocopherols   895
  File gumbo   900
  Fines herbes   900
  Flageolets   900
  Flavorings and extracts   901
   Lemon   901
   Vanilla   901
  Flour   901
  Fonds d'artichauts   901
  Fruit preserves
   (or jams)   901-02
   Fruit butters   901-02
  Gelatin   902
  Gum tragacanth   902
  Hominy   902
  Honey   902-04
   Comb
    Chunk or bulk   903-04
    Comb-section   902
    Shallow frame   903
   Extracted   904
  Hot chocolate   905
  Kitchen bouquet   905
  Legumes (beans, lentils, peas) 905-06

Miscellaneous Groceries *(cont.)*
  Legumes (beans, lentils, peas)
   Beans
    Black (or turtle soup beans)   905
    Black-eyed peas or cowpeas   905
    Garbanzo   905
    Great northern   905
    Kidney   905
    Lima   905
    Navy   905
    Pea   905
    Pinto   905
    Red and pink   905
   Lentils   905
   Peas   905-06
    Dry split   905
    Dry whole   906
    Dry yellow   905
   Margarine   906
   Marshmallows   906
   Mincemeat   906
   Monosodium glutamate   906
   Morels   906
   Noodles, Chinese   906
   Nuts
    Almond   906-07
    Brazil   907
     In the shell   907-08
    Filberts   909-10
    Mixed   910
    Peanuts   910-12
    Pecans   913-14
    Pine   914
    Pistachio   914
    Walnuts   914-17
   Oatmeal   919
   Olives   917-24
   Peanut butter   924
   Pickles   925
   Raisins   926-30
    Processed   928
    Sultana   930
    Thompson seedless   926
   Relish   931
   Salsifis   931
   Salt smoke   931
   Sanka   931
   Sauerkraut   939
   Shortening   940
   Soy sauce   942
   Spices and herbs   931
    Allspice   932
    Angelica   932
    Anise   932-33
    Apple pie spice   933
    Balm of Gilead   933
    Basil   933
    Bay leaves   933
    Blends   933
    Burnet   933
    Caraway   933
    Cardamom   933
    Celery   933

Miscellaneous Groceries *(cont.)*
  Spices and herbs
    Celery flakes   933
    Chervil   933
    Chili powder   933-34
    Chiso   934
    Chives   934
    Chrysanthemum   934
    Cinnamon   934
    Cinnamon sugar   934
    Cloves   934
    Coriander   934
    Costmary   934
    Crab boil or shrimp spice   934
    Cumin   934
    Curry powder   934-35
    Dill seed   935
    Dill weed   935
    Dittany   935
    Elder   935
    Fennel   935
    Fenugreek   935
    Fitches   935
    Ginger   935
    Grains of paradise   935
    Hawthorn   935
    Herb seasoning   935
    Horseradish   935
    Italian seasoning   935
    Lemon verbena   935
    Lovage   935
    Mace   935-36
    Maggi   936
    Marigold   936
    Marjoram   936
    Mint flakes   936
    Mixed pickling spice   936
    Mixed vegetable flakes   936
    Mustard   936
    Nutmeg   936
    Onions   936
    Oregano   936-37
    Oxalis   937
    Paprika   937
    Parsley flakes   937
    Pepper   937
    Pepper, cayenne   937
    Poppy   937
    Poultry seasoning   937
    Pumpkin pie spice   937
    Rampion   937
    Red pepper   937
    Rose hips   937-38
    Rosemary   938
    Rue   938
    Saffron   938
    Sage   938
    Savory   938
    Seafood seasoning   938
    Seasoned or flavor salt   938
    Sesame   938
    Shallot   938
    Sloe   938

Miscellaneous Groceries *(cont.)*
  Spices and herbs
    Smoke, liquid   938
    Sweet pepper flakes   938
    Tarragon   938
    Thyme   939
    Turmeric   939
    Vanilla   939
    Woodruff   939
    Yarrow   939
   Syrups   940-42
    Corn   940
    Maple   940-41
    Refiner's   940
    Sugarcane   942
    Sugarcane molasses   941
   Tomato paste   942-43
   Tomato puree   943
   Tomato sauce   943
   Truffles   944
   Vanilla extract   944
   Vinegar   944
   Waxy maize starch   944
   Worcestershire sauce   944
   Yeast   944
   See also Appendix
  Mixed Pickling Spice   936
  Mixed Vegetable Flakes   936
  Molasses   941
   Storage, dry   1000
   Sugarcane
    Federal specifications   981
  Monosodium Glutamate   906
   Federal specifications   981
   Storage, dry   994
  Morels   906
   See also Vegetables, mushrooms
  Mousse
   Storage, refrigerated   1020
  Muffins
   Storage, refrigerated   1016
  Mustard   936
   Federal specifications   981, 985
   Storage, dry   993
  Noodles
   Chinese   906
   Federal specifications   981
  Nutmeg   936
   Ground
    Federal specifications   985
  Nuts   906-17
   Federal specifications   984
   Storage
    Dry   1001
    Refrigerated   1022
  Oatmeal   919
  Oats
   Federal specifications   981
  Oil, Peanut
   Federal specifications   981
  Oils   895-900
  Olive Oil
   Federal specifications   981

Olives | 917-24
  Federal specifications | 981
  Quality factors
    Green | 956
    Ripe | 956
Onion Salt
  Federal specifications | 985
Orange Marmalade
  Federal specifications | 981
Orange Nut Roll
  Federal specifications | 981
Oregano | 936-37
  Federal specifications | 985
Oxalis | 937
Oysters
  Federal specifications | 968
  See also Shellfish
Pancake Mix
  Federal specifications | 981
Paprika | 937
  Federal specifications | 985
  Storage, dry | 994
Parsley Flakes | 937
Pastas | 891-92
  Storage, dry | 999
Peanut Butter | 924
  Federal specifications | 981
Peanuts | 910-12
  Federal specifications | 984
Pecan Cake Roll
  Federal specifications | 981
Pecans | 913-14
  Federal specifications | 984
Peonies
  Federal specifications | 981
Pepper | 937
  Black
    Federal specifications | 985
  Cayenne | 937
    Federal specifications | 985
Perch
  Federal specifications | 968
  Storage, frozen | 1004
  See also Fish
Pickles | 925
  Federal specifications | 981
  Quality factors, canned | 956
  Storage, dry | 1001
Pie
  Federal specifications | 981
Pie Crust Mix
  Federal specifications | 981
Pie Dough Mixes
  Federal specifications | 981
Pie Filling
  Federal specifications | 981
Pie Shells
  Storage, refrigerated | 1020
Pigeons | 241
  Squab | 241
    Federal specifications | 965
  See also Poultry
Pine | 914

Pistachio | 914
Popcorn
  Federal specifications | 981
Poppy Seed | 937
  Federal specifications | 985
Pork | 172-88
  Back, Canadian | 186
  Barrow and gilt
    Federal specifications | 962
  Belly | 184
    Common name:
      Fresh bacon | 184
  Belly, skinless | 184
    Common name:
      Bacon | 184
  Boston butt | 183
    Common name:
      Pork butt | 183
    Common use:
      Diced pork | 183
  Boston butt, boned and tied | 183
  Boston butt steaks | 183
    Common name:
      Pork steak | 183
  Carcass | 179
  Chop suey pork | 188
    Common name:
      Diced lean pork | 188
  Chops | 184-86
    Bladeless | 185
      Common name:
        Bladeless pork chop | 185
    Boneless | 131
    Center cut | 185-86
    Center cut special | 185
    Rib chops with pocket | 185
    With pocket | 185
      Common name:
        Stuffed pork chop | 185
    Federal specifications | 963-64
  Feet, front | 187
    Common name:
      Pigs' feet | 187
  Filets | 179
    Common names:
      Cubed pork steaks | 179
      Pork tenderloin steak | 179
  Ground | 188
    Common use:
      Meat loaf | 188
    Ground patties | 172, 188
  Ham | 180, 181
    Boned and tied | 182
      Common name:
        Fresh ham | 182
      Common use:
        Boneless pork
          roast | 182
    Federal specifications | 963
    Regular short shank | 180
      Common name:
        Fresh ham | 180
    Skinned | 180

Pork *(cont.)*
  Ham
    Skinned
      Common name:
        Fresh ham | 180
    Skinned, short shank | 180
      Common name:
        Bone-in fresh ham | 180
  Loin | 184-86
    Boned and tied | 186
      Common name:
        Pork loin roast | 186
    Boneless | 186
    Center cut | 185-86
  Neckbones | 187
    Common name:
      Pork bones | 187
  Ribs
    Back | 187
      Common use:
        Bar-b-que ribs | 187
    Country style | 188
  Shoulder | 182-83
    Common name:
      New York shoulder | 182
    Common uses:
      Bar-b-que pork | 182
      Economy pork roast | 182
  Shoulder butt | 183
  Shoulder butt steaks | 184
    Common name:
      Boneless pork steak | 184
  Shoulder hocks | 187
  Shoulder picnic | 183
  Smoked and cured | 226-37
    Bacon | 234-35, 236
      Canadian style (cured and
        smoked) sliced | 236
        Common name:
          Canadian bacon | 236
      Canadian style (cured and
        smoked) unsliced | 236
        Common names:
          Canadian bacon | 236
          Rolled bacon | 236
      Federal specifications | 962
      Slab (cured and smoked)
        skinless, formed | 234
        Common names:
          Bacon | 234
          Derinded bacon | 234
          Slab bacon | 234
      Slab (cured and smoked) skin-
        on | 234
      Sliced (cured and smoked) ends
        and pieces | 235
      Sliced (cured and smoked)
        skinless | 235
    Belly, skin-on (cured) | 234
      Common names:
        Bacon | 234
        Pickled pork | 234
        Slab bacon | 234

Pork *(cont.)*
  Smoked and cured
    Fatback, clear (cured) | 237
      Common name:
        Pickled pork fatback | 237
    Feet, front (cured) | 237
      Common name:
        Pigs' feet | 237
    Finished product
      characteristics | 227-28
    Ham | 228-31
      Boneless, skinless (cured and
        smoked) fully-cooked,
        dry heat | 230
        Common name:
          Dried cooked ham | 230
      Boneless, skinless (cured), pressed,
        fully-cooked, moist heat | 231
      Boneless, skinless (cured and
        smoked), pressed, fully-cooked,
        moist heat | 231
      Partially skinned (cured and
        smoked), fully-cooked,
        dry heat | 230
        Common name:
          Boneless cooked ham | 230
      Short shank, partially skinned
        (cured) | 229
        Common name:
          Short shank pickled ham | 229
        Common uses:
          Baked ham | 229
          Ham salad | 229
          Roast | 229
      Short shank, partially skinned
        (cured and smoked) | 229
        Common name:
          Smoked ham | 229
        Common uses:
          Baked ham | 229
          Ham salad | 229
          Ham steaks | 229
          Roast | 229
      Short shank, regular (cured) | 228
        Common name:
          Pickled ham | 228
        Common uses:
          Baked ham | 228
          Ham salad | 228
      Short shank, regular (cured
        and smoked) | 229
        Common name:
          Smoked ham | 229
        Common uses:
          Baked ham | 229
          Ham salad | 229
          Ham steaks | 229
          Roast | 229
      Skinless
        Boned, rolled, tied (cured
          and smoked) | 230
          Common names:
            Boned | 230

Pork *(cont.)*
Smoked and cured
Ham
Skinless
Boned, rolled, tied
(cured and smoked)
Common names:
Rolled   230
Tied   230
Boneless, completely (cured
and smoked)   230
Common names:
Boneless ham with water
added   230
Completely boneless ham   230
Partially boned (cured and
smoked)   229
Common names:
Cured and smoked   229
Partially boned ham   229
Semi-boneless ham   229
Common uses:
Baked ham   229
Roast   229
Hocks, shoulder (cured)   237
Common names:
Pickled hocks   237
Pickled knuckles   237
Hocks, shoulder (cured and
smoked)   237
Common names:
Ham hocks   237
Smoked hocks   237
Jowl butts, cellar trim
(cured)   236
Common names:
Fat cured pork   236
Pickled jowl   236
Jowl squares (cured and
smoked)   236
Loin, bladeless (cured and
smoked)   235
Common name:
Smoked pork loin   235
Loin, regular (cured and
smoked)   235
Common name:
Smoked pork loin   235
Processing   227
Cooking   227
Curing   227
Smoking   227
Selections, description of   226-27
No. 1   226
No. 2   226-27
Shoulder   231-33
Butt, boneless (cured and
smoked)   233
Common name:
Cottage ham   233
Partially skinned (cured)   232
Picnic (cured)   233
Picnic (cured and smoked)   233

Pork *(cont.)*
Smoked and cured
Shoulder
Picnic (cured and smoked),
boneless, skinless, rolled and
tied   233
Regular (cured)   231
Regular (cured and smoked)   232
Skinned (cured and smoked)   232
Spareribs (cured)   236
Common names:
Cured spareribs   236
Pickled spareribs   236
Common use:
Country style ribs   236
Spareribs (cured and smoked)   237
Common name:
Smoked spareribs   237
Sow
Federal specifications   964
Spareribs   186
Common name:
Bar-b-que spareribs   186
Spareribs, breast off   187
Common names:
Center cut spareribs   187
St. Louis ribs   187
Storage
Frozen   1003
Refrigerated   1012
Tenderloin   186
Common name:
Pork tenderloin   186
Common uses:
Pork filet   186
Tenderloin steak   186
Trimmings   187
See also Appendixes
Postum   883
Potato Chips
Federal specifications   981
Storage
Dry   1001
Refrigerated   1019
Potato Sticks
Federal specifications   981
Poultry   239-59
Classes—"kind"   239
Chickens   239
Ducks   239
Geese   239
Guineas   239
Pigeons   239
Turkeys   239
Conformation   244
Dressed poultry   241-44
Federal
specifications   965
Fleshing   244
Food products   249-50
Boneless poultry breasts and
thighs—A   250
Poultry roast—A   249

Poultry *(cont.)*
Graders   239
Grading service   255-56
Fee grading   255
Resident or continuous   255-56
Indications of age in poultry   242
Bill ducks   242
Breastbone   242
Comb chickens   242
Drumsticks   242
Fat   242
Flesh   242
Oil sac   242
Pinbones   242
Plumage   242
Shanks   242
Spurs   242
Wind pipe   242
Indications of sex in poultry   242-43
Body   242
Head   242
Keel   243
Legs   243
Plumage   242
Skin   243
Inspection   255, 256
Poultry Products Inspection
Act   255
Wholesome Poultry Products
Act   255
Parts   248-49
Backs   249
Breasts   248
Breast with ribs   249
Drumsticks   249
Halves   249
Legs   249
Quarters   249
Thighs   249
Wings   249
Wishbones   249
Quality standards   243-45
Live poultry   243
Ready-to-cook   244-57
A quality   246
B quality   247
C quality   248
Conformation   244
Discoloration from flesh
blemishes and bruises   245
Exposed flesh resulting from
cuts, tears and broken bones   245
Fat   244
Fleshing   244
Freezing defects   245
"Box burn"   245
"Freezer burn"   245
Grades   250-57
Consumer grades   250
Official identification marks   256
Wing tag   256
Pinfeathers   245
Standards and grades   239

Poultry *(cont.)*
Storage
Dry   992
Refrigerated   1011
Voluntary inspection
service   256
See also Appendixes
See also Chickens; Ducks; Geese;
Guineas; Pigeons; Rabbits; Turkeys
Poultry Pies
Storage, refrigerated   1011
Poultry Seasoning   937
Federal specifications   985
Poundcake
Federal specifications   981
Prepared Dry Cocoa Mix
Storage, refrigerated   1017
Prepared Mixes
Storage
Dry   999
Refrigerated   1017
Produce Section   469-880
Availability   470
Canned   487-99, 674
Bids   493-94
Bid sheet   493
Heading sheet   493
Statement of intent   494
Common counts of
fruits   495, 500
Cherries, sweet   495
Figs, Kadota   495
Peaches   495
Pears   495
Pineapple   495
Plums   495
Prunes, dried   495
Grades   488-90
Substandard   489
Label   488
Food, Drug and Cosmetic Act   488
Scoring factors   489
Standard of:
Fill   487-88
Identity   487
Quality   487
Syrup density   488
Brix   488
Weight, drained   492-93
Federal Food and Cosmetic
Act   493
Headspace allowable   492
Container net weights   483
Anise   483
Apples   483
Apricots   483
Artichokes   483
Asparagus   483
Bananas   483
Beans   483
Beets   483
Berries   483
Blackberries   483

Produce Section (cont.)

Container net weights

Berries
Blueberries 483
Raspberries 483
Broccoli 483
Brussels sprouts 483
Cabbage 483
Canteloupe 483
Carrots 483
Casabas 483
Cauliflower 483
Celeriac 483
Celery 483
Cherries 483
Chinese cabbage 483
Coconuts 484
Corn 484
Cranberries 484
Cranshaws 484
Cucumbers 484
Eggplant 484
Endive 484
Escarole 484
Figs 484
Garlic 484
Grapefruit 484
Grapes 484
Greens 484
Honeydews 484
Leeks 484
Lemons 484
Lettuce 484
Bibb 484
Boston 484
Hothouse 484
Iceberg 484
Looseleaf 484
Romaine 484
Limes 484
Mangos 484
Mushrooms 484
Nectarines 485
Okra 485
Onions, dry 485
Oranges 485
Oriental vegetables 485
Papayas 485
Parsley 485
Parsnips 485
Peaches 485
Pears 485
Peas 485
Peppers 485
Persians 485
Persimmons 485
Pineapple 485
Plums 485
Pomegranates 485
Potatoes 486
Prunes 486
Radishes 486
Rhubarb 486

Produce Section (cont.)

Container net weight

Rutabagas 486
Spinach 486
Squash 486
Strawberries 486
Sweet corn 486
Sweet potatoes 486
Tangelos 486
Tangerines 486
Tomatoes 486
Cherry 486
Topped root vegetables 486
Turnips 486
Watercress 486
Watermelons 486
Dehydrated and dried 495-99
Distribution 472-74
Auctions 473-74
Brokers 473
PAC Act 473
Service wholesaler 474
Trading rules under PAC 473
Wholesaling 474
Fresh fruits 476-78
Glossary of terms 487
Blossom end 487
Breakdown of tissue 487
Decay 487
Ground color 487
Hard 487
Mature 487
Netting 487
Ripe 487
Russeting 487
Scald 487
U. S. grade standards 476
Fresh vegetables 478-82
U. S. vegetable standards 479
Frozen fruits and vegetables 495
Life and storage 482
U. S. Agriculture Handbook 482
Packing 470-71
Preserves. See Jams
Preserving treatments for
processing 469
Canning 469
Dehydrating 469
Dehydro-freezing 469
Drying 469
Freeze-drying 469
Freezing 469
Irradiation 469
Standard grades and
inspection 475-76
Contract 475
Inspection procedures 476
Marketing Agreement Act of
1937 475
Temperature control methods 471-72
Continuous refrigeration 472
Hydro-cooling 472
Icing 472

Produce Section (cont.)

Temperature control methods
Long storage 472
Pre-cooling 471-72
Vacuum cooling 472
Transportation 471
Waste and loss 474-75
See also Appendixes
See also Fruits; Vegetables
Protein, Availability of 69
Eggs 69
Fish and crustaceans 69
Meat 69
Milk 69
Puddings
Federal specifications 981
Storage, refrigerated 1019
Puffed Corn 893
Puffed Rice 893
Puffed Wheat 893
Pumpkin Pie Spice 937
Purchasing Policies 1-67
Accounting 53, 57, 60
Budget reports 57
Cost analysis 60
Invoice record 53
Order/receiving/inventory
record 57
Desk inventory 57
Physical inventory 57
Records 53
Book use for 2-3
Buyer 2
Middlemen 2
Operator 2
Photocopying 3
Purveyor 2-3
Budget 61
FDA papers 61
USDA Market Reports 61
Cooperative buying 21
Central agency 21
Ethics-morality 8-9
Bribes 8
Discount prices 8
Donations 8
Premium offer 8
Presents 8
Dishonesty 8
Kickbacks 8
Price fixing 8
Theft 8
Food costs 6-7, 52-53
Issuing 52
Preparation 52
Production 52
Purchasing 52
Receiving 52
Sales 53
Service 53
Storage 52
Food Purchasing Procedures of
Small Food Service Operators 62

Purchasing Policies (cont.)

Forecasting 3
Manual 3-4
National Association of
Purchasing Management 3
Policies 4
Procedures 4
One-stop shopping 20
Policy 4-5
Code of ethics 4
Competitive buying 51
Deliveries 5
Gifts 4
Objectives 4
Organization chart 4
Price 7
Purchasing manager 4
Price increases 8
Wholesale Food Price Index 8
Prices 7
Procedures 5-6
Job descriptions 5
Procedures, constructive 51-52
Competitive buying 51
Deliveries 51
Price 51
Quality 51
Quantity 51
Sales representatives 51
Seasonal buying 51
Service 51
Supply and demand 51
Profit, fair 11
Purchasing systems 9-11
Meat Buyer's Guide 9
Specifications 9
Role of purchasing 1, 6
Objectives 6
Relations with suppliers 6
Sales analysis 6-7
Systems contracting 12
Market Guide by Urner Barry 12
Meat Service Report 12
Techniques for purchasing
food 41, 50
Bargain buying 41
Extravagant buying 50
Friendship buying 50
Miserly buying 50
Overbuying 41
Personality buying 50
Price buying 41
Quality buying 41
Panic buying 50
Pressure buying 41
Price buying 41
Sentiment buying 50
Underbuying 41
Yield grade 2
Quality Control and Federal
Regulations 945-86
Complaints 945
Cafeterias 945

Quality Control and Federal
Regulations *(cont.)*
Complaints
  Hospitals 945
Department of Defense
  abbreviations 959
Federal specifications 962-86
Food and Drug
  Administration 960-61
General Services
  Administration 959-60
Menu combinations 945
  Color 945
  Flavor 945
  Texture 945
Purchasing specifications for buyers
  Canned fruits 947
  Fresh fruits 947
  Fresh vegetables 947
  Frozen vegetables 947
  Meat
    Entree standards 947
      Beef stroganoff 947
      Chicken or turkey a la king 947
      Chop suey 947
      Fritters 947
    Institutional Meat Purchase
     Specifications 947
    Meat Buyers' Guide 947
  Quality factors 948
    Absence of defects 949
    Clearness of liquor 950
    Clearness of syrup 950
    Color 949
    Consistency 950
    Count 949
    Cut 950
    Drained weight 950
      National Canners' Assn. 950
    Finish 950
    Firmness 949
    Flavor 949
    General appearance 949
    General character 949
    Maturity 949
    Style 949
    Symmetry 949
    Syrup density 950
    Tenderness 949
    Texture 949
    Type 949
    Uniformity of size 949
    Wholeness 950
  Quality determining equipment 946
  Brix hydrometer 946
  Fat analyzer 946
  Microwave ovens 946
  Refractometer 946
  Scales 946
  Thermometers 946
  Quotations 946
Smell
  Olfactory bulb 945

Quality Control and Federal
Regulations *(cont.)*
  Taste responses 945
    Butter 945
    Salty 945
    Sour 945
    Sweet 945
  Thorner, Marvin, Ch. E. 945
  United States Department of
    Agriculture Divisions of 959
Rabbit 257
  A quality 257
  B quality 257
  C quality 257
  Federal specifications 965
  Fryer or young 257
  Roaster or mature 257
  See also Poultry
Raisin Cake 931
  Federal specifications 982
Raisin Nut Cake
  Federal specifications 982
Raisins 926-30
  Federal specifications 982
Rampion 937
Rarebit
  Storage, refrigerated 1010
Ration
  Federal specifications 986
Ration Food Packet
  Federal specifications 986
Ration-Food Packet Component Unit
  Federal specifications 986
Ration Supplement
  Federal specifications 986
Red Pepper 937
  Storage, dry 994
Relish (Pickle)
  Federal specifications 982
Relishes 931
  Storage, dry 1001
Rice 891
  Brown
    Storage, dry 999
  Parboiled
    Federal specifications 982
    Storage, dry 999
  Wild 891
    Storage, dry 999
Roasts
  Storage, refrigerated 1012
Rockfish
  Federal specifications 968
  See also Fish
Rolls
  Federal specifications 982
  Storage, refrigerated 1016
Rose Hips 937-38
Rosemary 938
Rue 938
Rye
  Federal specifications 982
Saffron 938

Sage 938
  Federal specifications 985
Salad Dressings
  Storage
    Dry 997
    Refrigerated 1015
Salad Oil
  Federal specifications 982
  Storage
    Dry 997
    Refrigerated 1016
Salads
  Storage, refrigerated 1015
Salmon
  Federal specifications 968
  Quality factors 956
  Storage, frozen 1004
  See also Fish
Salsifis 931
Salt, Seasoned or Flavor 938
Salt, Table
  Federal specifications 982
  Storage, dry 994
Salt Smoke 931
Sandwiches
  Storage, refrigerated 1007-08
  Egg salad 1007
  Fish 1007
  Meat 1007
  Poultry 1007
Sanka 931
Sauces (Hot Pepper, Soy, Steak,
Worcestershire)
  Storage, dry 994
Sauerkraut 939
Sausage 189-216
  American Meat Institute 192
  Classifications 192-94
    Cooked meat specialties 193
      Head cheese 193
      Meat loaves 193
      Scrapple 193
      Souse 193
    Cooked sausage 193
    Cooked, smoked sausage 192-93
      Berliner 193
      Bologna 193
      New England 193
      Smokie links 193
      Wieners 193
    Dry, semi-dry sausage 193
      Bacterial fermentation 193
      Cervelats 193
      Salamis 193
      Thuringer cervelat 193
    Fresh sausage 192
    Smoked meats 193-94
    Uncooked, smoked sausage 192
  Drying 191-92
  Federal specifications 964
  Ham 190
  History 189-90
    Blood sausage 190

Sausage *(cont.)*
  History
    Botellum 189
    Bratenwurst 190
    Dry sausage 189
    Frankfurter 190
    Head cheese 190
    Hot dog 190
    Liver Kromeskis 189
    Liver sausage 190
    Lucanian 189
    Salus 189
    Wiener 190
    Wurst 189
    Wurstmacher 189
  Kinds
    Alessandria 194, 204
    Apennio 194
    Arles, d'arles 194
    Bacon 194
      Sugar-cured 194
    Beef loaf 194
    Beef salami 194
    Beef summer sausage 194
    Beerwurst, beer salami 194
    Berliner 195
    Black pudding 195
      Baked 194
    Blood sausage 195
    Blood and tongue sausage 195
    Bockwurst 195
    Bohemian presky 195
    Bologna 196
      Federal specifications 962
      Specifications for 219
    Boneless ham 196
    Boneless pork loin 196
    Boterham wurst 196
    Bratwurst 196
    Braunschweiger liver sausage 196
      Specifications 220
    Braunschweiger, mettwurst,
     "smearwurst" 196-97
    Breakfast beef, beef bacon 197
    Breakfast sausage 197, 217, 219
      Specifications 222
    Butifara catalane 197
    Cambridge-type pork sausage 197
    Canadian style bacon 197
    Canned ham 197
    Cappicola 197
    Cervelat 197
      Federal specifications 962
      Specifications 222
    Cheese smokies 197
    Chikolata 197
    Chopped ham 198
    Chopped, pressed, smoked,
     sliced beef 198
    Chorizos 198
    Chubbies 198
    Cocktail loaf 198
    Cooked ham 198

Sausage (cont.)
Kinds
Cooked salami 198
Cotto salami, cooked salami 198
D'arles 198, 204
Devonshire style sausage 198
Dewey ham, boneless pork loin, loin roll 198
Dutch head cheese 198
Dutch loaf, old-fashioned loaf, family brand 199
Faggots 199
Family brand loaf 199
Farmer sausage cervelat 199
Fiesta loaf 199
Franks, frankfurters 199
 Federal specifications 962
 Specifications 218
Frizzes 199
Galician 199-200
Genoa salami 200
German salami, hard salami 200
Goteborg 200
Ham 200-01
Ham and cheese loaf 201
Hard salami 201
Head cheese 201
 Specifications 224
Holsteiner cervelat 201
Honey loaf 201
Hungarian kolbase 201
Italian pork sausage, salsiccia 201
Italian salami 201
Jaternice 201
Jellied beef loaf 202
Jellied corned beef loaf 202
Jellied pork and turkey loaf 202
Jellied tongue 202
Jubilee ham 202
Kielbasa, Kolbassy 202
Kiska 202
Knackwurst, knochblauch 202
Kosher salami 202
Krakow 202-03
 New England brand sausage 203
Lachshinken 203
Landjaeger cervelat 203
 Swiss style 203
Lebanon bologna 203
 Specifications 221
Linguisa, longaniza 203
Liver loaf 203
Liver pudding 203-04
Liver sausage 204
 Federal specifications 963
 Specifications 220
Loin roll 204
Loukanika 204
Luncheon loaf
 Federal specifications 963
Luncheon meat 204
 Federal specifications 963
Luncheon roll 204

Sausage (cont.)
Kinds
Luxury loaf 204
Lyons sausage 204
Meat bar
 Federal specifications 963
Meat food product loaves 224
 Specifications 224
Meat loaves 224
 Specifications 224
Mettwurst 204
Metz 204
Milano salami 204
Minced ham loaf 204-05
Minced luncheon meat 220
 Specifications 220
Minced roll 205
Mortadella 205
New England brand, New England sausage, New England ham sausage 205
 Specifications 223
Old-fashioned loaf 205
Olive loaf 205
Oxford style sausage 205
Pastrami, pastromi, pastroma, pastirima 205
Peppered loaf 205
Peppered beef loaf 205
Pepperoni 206
 Federal specifications 963
Pickle and pimento loaf 206
Picnic loaf 206
Picnics 206
Polish sausage 199, 206
 Specifications 223
Pork and turkey loaf 206
Pork sausage 206, 217
 Country style 206
 Links 206
 Pork sausage roll 206
 Specifications 219
Pork shoulder butts 207
Potato sausage 207
Roumanian sausage 207
Rultespulse 207
Salami 220
 Federal specifications 964
 Specifications 220
Salami, dry 221
 Specifications 221
Salsiccia 207
Sarno 207
Saveloy 207
Scotch ham 207
Scrapple 207
 Federal specifications 964
Serdelki 207
Serdelowa 207-08
Sliced cold meat 208
Smearwurst 208
Smoked beef
 tongues 208

Sausage (cont.)
Kinds
Smoked country style pork sausage 208
Smoked country style sausage 208
Smoked pork chops 208
Smoked pork jowls 208
Smoked pork sausage 208
Smoked sausage 223
 Specifications 223
Smoked thuringer links 208
Smokie links—smokies 208
Smokie snax 208
Soppresata 209
Souse, sulz 209
Southern hots 209
Strassburg 209
Strassburger 209
Studzienna 209
Summer sausage 209
Swedish medwurst 209
Swedish sausage, goteborg 209
Swiss club sausage 209
Sylta 209
Thuringer 199, 209-10
 Specifications 221
Tomato sausage 210
Toulouse sausage 210
Turkey loaf 210
Weisswurst 210
Wieners, "hot dog" 210
Link items 213-14
Loaf items 215-16
Making 189
National Livestock and Meat Board 192
Smoked meats 193-94
 Bacterial growth 193
 Meat pigments 194
Smoking 191
 Sawdust 191
 Smokehouses 191
Spice 190-91
 Tellicherry pepper 190
 Wurstmacher 190
Stick items 211-12
See also Appendixes; Meat
Savory 938
Scallops
 Federal specifications 969
See also Shellfish
Seafood
 Storage, dry 992
See also Fish; Shellfish
Seafood Seasoning 938
Seasoning Salt
 Storage, dry 995
Seeds
 Storage, dry 994
Sesame Seed 938
 Federal specifications 985
Shallots 938
Shellfish 311, 345-60

Shellfish (cont.)
Canned
 Clams 358
 Lobster 358
 Oyster stew 358
 Oysters 358
 Snails 359
Categories 311
 Crustaceans 311
 Mollusks 311
Fresh 345-57
 Clams, hard or little-necked 345, 356
 Butter 345
 Little neck 345
 Quahaug 345
 Clams, soft or long-necked 345
 Crabs 345-46, 356
 Crayfish 346
 King crab 346
 Lobster 346, 356
 Lobster tails 346
 Crayfish 346
 Rock 346
 Sea crawfish 346
 Oysters (in shell) 346
 Oysters (shucked) 346, 356
 Scallops 346-50, 356
 Fried, frozen 347-50
 Raw, frozen 347
 Shrimp 351-55, 356
 Raw, breaded, frozen 353-55
 Raw, headless, frozen 351-52
 Snails 356
Frozen
 Crabs
 Storage 1004
 Lobsters
 Storage 1004
 Oysters
 Storage 968
 Scallops
 Fried 347
 Raw 347
 Storage 1004
 Shrimp
 Raw breaded 353
 Raw headless 351
 Storage 1004
See also Appendixes; Fish
Shortenings 940
Vegetable
 Storage, dry 997
Shrimp
 Federal specifications 969
 Quality factors, canned 957
 Storage 1004
See also Shellfish
Sloe 938
Smoke, Liquid. See Liquid Smoke
Snacks
 Storage, refrigerated 1019

Snapper
  Federal specifications 969
  See also Fish
Soup and Gravy Base
  Federal specifications 982
Soups
  Federal specifications 982-83
  Storage, dry 993, 1008
Sour Cream Sauces
  Storage, refrigerated 1015
Soy Sauce 942
  Federal specifications 983
  Storage, dry 994
Soybeans
  Federal specifications 983
Spaghetti
  Federal specifications 983
  Storage, dry 999
Spaghetti with Ground Meat
  Federal specifications 983
Spaghetti with Meatballs
  Federal specifications 982
Spices, Whole
  Storage, dry 994
Squash and Pumpkin Pies
  Storage, refrigerated 1019
Steaks
  Storage, refrigerated 1012
  See also Beef
Stew Beef
  Federal specifications 983
Stews
  Storage, refrigerated 1008
Storage and Handling 987-1023
  Complete Book of Cooking
    Equipment 1007
  Dry storage 988
    Calculating space requirements 989
    Floors 989
    Lighting 988
    "Par" stock 988
    Shelving 989
    Walls 989
  Equipment
    Processing freezer 1004
      Insulation 1005
      Reach-in 1004-05
      Walk-in 1004-05
    Terminology 1004
  Food Service Planning 1006
  Frozen food storage control
    Air circulation 1002
    Defrost 1003
    Product group 1002
    Rotate 1002
    Thermometer 1003
    Unloading 1002
  Quality loss and spoilage
    Bacteria 987-88
    Mold 987
    Yeast 987
  Receiving 987-88
    Pilferage 987

Storage and Handling *(cont.)*
  Refrigeration storage
    Dairy products 1006
    Eggs 1006
    Fish and seafood 1006
    Fresh meats 1006
    Fresh poultry 1006
    Frozen foods 1006
    Fruits 1006
    Pastry 1006
    Processed foods 1006
    Vegetables 1006
  Storage chart 1007-23
Stuffing
  Storage, refrigerated 1008
Sugar
  Federal specifications 983
  Storage
    Dry 999
    Refrigerated 1018
Sugarcane 942
Sweet Pepper Flakes 938
Syrups 940-42
  Federal specifications 982
  Malted cereal
    Federal specifications 980
  Refiner's 940
  Storage, dry 1000
Tapioca 893
  Federal specifications 983
  Storage
    Dry 990
    Refrigerated 1019
Tarragon 938
Tea 884
  Federal specifications 976
  Leaves
    Storage, dry 991
Thyme 939
  Federal specifications 985
Tobacco, Naval Stores
  Federal specifications 983
Tomato Paste 942-43
  Federal specifications 983
  Quality factors, canned 954
Tomato Puree (pulp) 943
  Federal specifications 983
  Quality factors, canned 956
Tomato Sauce 943
  Federal specifications 983
Topping
  Federal specifications 983
Topping, Whipped Cream
  Storage, refrigerated 1019
Truffles 944
  Federal specifications 969
  Quality factors 957
  See also Fish
Tuna and Noodles
  Federal specifications 983
Turkeys 240
  Federal specifications 965
  Fryer-roaster 240

Turkeys *(cont.)*
  Mature or old (hen or tom) 240
  Turkey Loaf
    Federal specifications 965
  Yearling hen 240
  Yearling tom 240
  Young hen 240
  Young tom 240
  See also Poultry
Turmeric 939
Vanilla 939
  Extract 944
Veal and Calf 156-71
  Back 156, 168-69
  Bracelet 162
    Common names:
      Calf bracelet 162
      Full bracelet 162
      Veal bracelet 162
  Breast 165
    Common names:
      Breast of veal/calf 165
      Veal breast 165
  Carcass 159-60
  Chops, portion-cut 159
  Chuck 162-64
    Regular 162
      Common name:
        Full chuck 162
    Square-cut 156, 163
      Common name:
        Veal chuck 163
    Square-cut, boneless 164
      Common names:
        Chuck roast 164
        Veal shoulder blade roast 164
    Square-cut, clod out, boneless, tied 164
      Common name:
        Veal chuck roast 164
    Square-cut, tied 163
      Common name:
        Veal chuck roast 163
      Common use:
        Barbecued veal 163
  Chucks and plates 156, 162
    Common name:
      Veal slug 162
    Common use:
      Veal roasts 162
  Cutlet 159, 167
    Regular 167
      Common name:
        Cubed veal/calf cutlet 167
    Special 167
  Edible by-products 170-71
    Liver 170-71
      Calf 171
        Common names:
          Baby beef liver 171
          Calves liver 171
        Veal 171
  Federal specifications 964

Veal and Calf *(cont.)*
  Forequarter 160
  Fores, single 156
  Foresaddle 161
    Common names:
      Foresaddle 161
      Forequarter 161
      Veal front 161
  Foreshank 164
    Common names:
      Foreshank 164
      Ossobucci 164
      Veal shank 164
    Common names:
      Cross-cut shank 164
  Hinds 156
  Hindsaddle 165, 169
    Common name:
      Veal hind 169
  Hotel rack 156, 162
    Common names:
      Double rack of veal, calf 162
      Trimmed bracelet 162
  Leg 156, 166-168
    Boneless, tied, roast ready 167
      Common names:
        Leg of veal 167
        Veal roast 167
      Common uses:
        Cutlets 167
        Roast veal 167
    (Double) 166
      Common names:
        Leg of veal 166
        Veal round 166
      Common uses:
        Veal cutlets 166
        Veal sirloin roast 166
    Oven-prepared, boneless 166
      Common names:
        Leg of veal 166
        Veal round 166
      Common uses:
        Cutlets 166
        Roast veal 166
        Roast veal 168
    Rump and shank off, boneless (single) 168
      Common name:
        Boneless veal leg 168
      Common uses:
        Cutlets 168
        Roast veal 168
    Rump and shank off (single) 168
      Common name:
        Boneless veal leg 168
      Common names:
        Cutlets 168
    Shank-off, boneless (single) 167
      Common name:
        Boneless leg of veal 167
      Common uses:
        Cutlets 167

Veal and Calf (cont.)
Leg
 Shank-off, boneless (single)
  Roast veal 167
 Short-cut (single) 168
  Common name:
   Leg of veal bone-in 168
  Common uses:
   Cutlets 168
   Roast veal 168
Loin 156
 Chops 165
  Common names:
   Loin veal chops 165
   Veal chops 165
   Veal kidney chops 165
   Veal loin chops 165
 Full loin, trimmed (single) 166
  Common names:
   Single loin 166
   Veal loin roast 166
 Regular (double) 165
  Common name:
   Veal loin roast 165
  Common use:
   Veal chops 165
 Trimmed (double) 165
  Common name:
   Veal loin 165
  Common uses:
   Veal chops 165
   Veal loin roast 165
Rib chops 162
 Common names:
  Baby beef chops 162
  Veal chops 162
Shoulder chops 163
Shoulder clod 163
 Common names:
  Veal blade roast 163
  Veal shoulder blade roast 163
  Veal shoulder roast 163
Shoulder clod, roast ready 164
 Common names:
  Clod roast 164
  Veal or calf chuck roast 164
Shoulder clod steaks 164
 Common names:
  Veal cubed steaks 164
  Veal cutlet 164
  Veal shoulder blade steaks 164
Side 161
Steaks, cubed 159, 169
 Common name:
  Veal cubed steaks 169
Stewing veal 170
 Common name:
  Stew veal 170
Storage
 Frozen 1003
 Refrigerated 1012
 See also Appendixes; Meat
Vegetables 676-846

Vegetables (cont.)
Anise 676
 Grades 676
 Joy of Cooking 676
Artichokes 677
 Federal specifications 969
 Varieties
  French or green french 677
  Giant bud 677
  Green globe 677
  Red dutch 677
  Thistle or prickly 677
  Violet 677
  White globe 677
Asparagus 679
 Canned 676, 680, 683-85
  Quality factors 953
 Federal specifications 969
 Frozen 680, 686
  Quality factors 957
  Storage 1003
 Uses
  Plumosus 679
 Varieties
  Argenteuil 680
  Conover's colossal 680
  Mammoth white 680
  Martha Washington 680
  Mary Washington 680
  Palmetto 680
  Reading giant 680
Beans 682, 905
 Dried canned 699
 Green 688
  Canned 692-93
   Quality factors 953
  Federal specifications 969
  Flat podded 690
   Bountiful 690
   Ferry's plentiful 690
  Frozen 695
  Oval podded 689
   Resistant Asgrow Valentine 689
  Pole or twining 692
   Kentucky wonder 692
  Puree
   Federal specifications 969
  Round pod 691
  Stringless (Burpee & Landreth) 691
   Tendergreen improved 691
   Tenderlong 691
   Topcrop 691
   Wade 691
  Snap 689
  String 689
 Lima 695-96
  Canned 695-96
  Federal specifications 969
  Frozen 696-97
   Storage 1003
  Quality factors, frozen 957
 Snap 689
  Storage, frozen 1003

Vegetables (cont.)
Beans
 Speckled butter (lima) 697
  Frozen 697
 Sprouts
  Federal specifications 969
 Storage, dry 1000
 String 689
 Wax snap 691-92
  Bush or dwarf 692
  Flat 692
   Sure crop 692
  Oval 691
   Cherokee 691
   Kinghorn 691
 Canned 692-93
  Quality factors 953
 Federal specifications 969
 Frozen 695
Beets 676, 700
 Borscht 700
 Canned 701-02
  Quality factors 953
 Federal specifications 969
 Puree
  Federal specifications 969
 Tops 701
 Varieties
  Crosby 700
  Crosby Egyptian 700
  Detroit 700
   Dark red 700
   Perfected 700
  Early wonder 700
  Flat Egyptian 700
  Pacemaker 700
  Ruby queen 700
Broccoli 703
 Bunched Italian sprouting 704
 Farmers Bulletin 2239 704
 Federal specifications 970
 Frozen
  Quality factors 958
  Storage 1003
 Varieties
  Atlantic 705
  Bravo 706
  Cleopatra 706
  Coastal 706
  Crusader 706
  DeCicco 706
  El Centro 705
  Gem 705
  Green comet 706
  Green duke 706
  Green mountain 705, 706
  Green sprouting 706
  Green sprouting DeCicco 706
  Green sprouting late 706
  Green sprouting medium 706
  Green umbrella 705
  Harvester 705
  Improved spartan early 706

Vegetables (cont.)
Broccoli
 Varieties
  King Robert purple 706
  Medium late 423 704
  Medium late 145 704
  Morse's 4638 705, 706
  Morse's medium E 705
  Morse's medium late 705
  No. 47 705
  Pacifica 705
  Rex 705
  Topper 43 706
  Topper 430 705
  Waltham 29 705
Brussels sprouts 710
 Canned
  Quality factors 953
 Federal specifications 970
 Fresh 710
 Frozen 709
  Quality factors 958
  Storage 1003
 Varieties
  Catskill 708
  Fancy most 50-A 708
  Half dwarf 708
  Jade cross F, hybrid 708
  Long Island improved 708
  Paris market 708
Cabbage 710-15
 Federal specifications 970
 Fresh 712
 Quality factors, canned 953
 Varieties
  Danish 712
   Ballhead 712
   Wisconsin Hollander 712
  Domestic 712
   Enkhuisen glory 712
   Flat dutch 712
   Succession 712
  Pointed 712
   Charleston Wakefield 712
   Early Jersey Wakefield 712
  Red 712
   Danish stonehead 712
   Mammoth red rock 712
   Red acre 712
   Red danish 712
   Round red dutch 712
  Savoy 712-14
   Chieftain 713
   Drumhead savoy 713
   King Cole 713
   Market prize 713
   Market topper 713
   Vanguard 713
Carrots 715-20
 Canned 716, 719
  Quality factors 954
 Container 717-18
 Federal specifications 970

Vegetables *(cont.)*
Carrots
Fresh   715
Frozen   719-20
Puree
   Federal specifications   970
Storage
   frozen   1003
   refrigerated   1014
Topped   715, 718
Varieties
   Chantenay neck   717
   Danvers neck   717
   Imperator neck   717
   Nantes neck   717
Cauliflower   720-22
Federal specifications   970
Frozen   721
   Quality factors   958
   Storage   1003
Varieties
   Danish giant   720-21
   Snowball   720
   Early   720
   Super   721
   Snowdrift   721
   Veitch autumn giant   721
Celery   722-27, 933
Federal specifications   970, 984
Varieties
   Crystal jumbo   723
   Compak No. 1   723
   Easy blanching   723-24
   Emerson pascal   724
   Danish variety   724
   Emerald   724
   FM green   724
   Golden   723
   Slow bolting   723, 725
   Summer pascal   723
   Utah   723
   "Short top"   723
   Waltham strain   724
Celeriac   727-28
Variety
   Giant Smooth Prague   727
Collards   728-29
Federal specifications   970
Varieties
   Georgia   728
   Louisiana sweet   728
   Morris heading   728
   Vates   728
Corn   729-36
Canned   730
   Cream style   730, 733
   Quality factors   954
Cut
   Storage, frozen   1003
Federal specifications   970
Food Buying Guide for Type
   A School Lunches   731
Fresh   730

Vegetables *(cont.)*
Corn
Frozen   730
   Corn-on-the-cob   734
   Storage   1003
Quality factors, frozen   958
Sweet corn   729
Varieties
   Country gentleman   729
   Earliking   729
   Florigold   730
   Golden beauty   729
   Golden corn bantam   730
   Golden rocket   730
   Illinichief super-sweet   730
   Iobelle   730
   NK 199   730
   Seneca beauty   730
   Seneca explorer   730
   Seneca golden   730
Whole kernel   730, 732
   Canned   732
   Frozen   732-33
Cucumbers   736-39
Federal specifications   970
Fresh   738
Greenhouse   738
Pickling   738
Varieties
   Ashley   737
   Cherokee   737
   Gemini   737
   High Mark II   737
   Hybrid Ashley   737
   Long marketer   737
   Marketer   737
   Marketmore   737
   Palomar   737
   Poinsett   737
   Straight eight   737
Dandelions   739-41
   Taraxacum   739
Dehydrated
   Storage, dry   1002
Eggplant   741-42
Federal specifications   971
Fresh   742
Varieties
   Black beauty   741
   Black magic hybrid   742
   Florida high bush   742
   Florida market   741
   Fort Meyers market   742
   New Hampshire   742
   New York purple   742
   Superhybrid   742
Endive—Escarole—Chicory   742-44
Federal specifications   971
Varieties
   Cicoria   743
   Full heart Batavian   743
   Green curled pancalier   743
   Large-rooted Magdeburg   743

Vegetables *(cont.)*
Endive—Escarole—Chicory
Varieties
   Ruffec   743
   Witloof or French endive   743
Garlic   744-45
Federal specifications   985
Fresh   745
Varieties
   Creole   745
   Italian   745
   Tahiti   745
Hominy   745-46, 902
Federal specifications   971, 980
Quality factors, canned   954
Horseradish roots   746
Federal specifications   971
Kale   746-47
Federal specifications   971
Fresh   747
Varieties
   Dwarf blue curled scotch   746
   Dwarf curled Siberian   747
   Dwarf green curled scotch   746
   Siberian   747
   Tall green curled scotch   747
   Vates strain   746
Kohlrabi   747-48
Varieties
   Purple Vienna   748
   White   748
Leafy Greens   748-50
   Canned   748
Leafy Greens (other than spinach)   750
   Beet greens   752
   Collard greens or broccoli greens   752
   Dandelion greens   752
   Federal specifications   970
   Kale   752
   Federal specifications   971
   Mustard greens or turnip greens   752
Legumes   905-06
Lentils   905
Lettuce   752-56
Federal specifications   971
Fresh   754
Greenhouse leaf   754
Varieties
   Bibb   754
   Big Boston   754
   Butterhead   753-54
   Cos or romaine   754
   Green   754
   White Paris   754
   Crisp, head   753
   Great Lakes   753
   Imperial   753
   Looseleaf or bunching   754
   Black-seeded Simpson   755
   Grand Rapids   755
   Prize head   755
   Salad bowl   755
May king   754

Vegetables *(cont.)*
Lettuce
Varieties
   Stem   755
   Celtuce   755
   Valverde   753
   Vanguard   753
   White Boston   754
Mushrooms   757-60
   Canned   676, 759
   Quality factors   956
   Federal specifications   971
   Fresh   758
   Storage, frozen   1003
Mustard Greens   760-61
   Federal specifications   971
   Varieties
     Florida broad leaf   760
     Fordhook fancy   760
     Large smooth leaf   760
     Southern giant curled   760
     Tendergreen   760
Okra   761-63
   Canned   762
   Quality factors   954
   Federal specifications   972
   Fresh   762
   Frozen   762
   Varieties
     Clemson spineless   761
     Dwarf green long pod   761
     Dwarf long pod   761
     Emerald   761
     French market   761
     Gold coast   761
     Green velvet   761
     Louisiana green   761
     Perkins mammoth long pod   761
     Perkins spineless   761
     White velvet   761
Okra and tomatoes, tomatoes
   and okra   763-64
   Canned   763-64
Onions   764-72, 936
   Bermuda-granex-grano type   765
   Bunched shallots   765
   Canned   770-71
   Creole   765
   Dry
     Abundance   769
     Australian brown   767, 769
     Autumn spice   769
     Bronze perfection   770
     Downing yellow globe   769
     Ebenezer   767
     El capitan   770
     Elite   769
     Epoch   769
     Excel (986)   768
     Fiesta   769
     Golden beauty   770
     Granex   768
     Hickory   769

Vegetables (cont.)
Onions
Dry
Nugget   769
Southport white globe   768, 769
Spartan banner   769
Spartan era   769
Sweet spanish   768
Texas early grano (502)   768
Treasure   770
White Portugal silver skin   768
White silver king   768
Yellow Bermuda   768
Federal specifications   972
Green
Varieties
Beltsville improved   764
Crystal wax   764
Eclipse   764
He-Shi-Ko   764
Perfecto blanco   764
Southport   764
White globe   764
White Lisbon   764
White Portugal   764
White sweet spanish   764
Rings
Breaded   771-72
Federal specifications   972
Shallots   765-66
Varieties
Bayou   766
Louisiana pearl   766
Wilmington   766
Wintergreen   766
Parsley   772-73
Federal specifications   972
Varieties
Curled-leaved   773
Plain-leaved   773
Turnip-rooted   773
Parsnips   773-74
Federal specifications   972
Fresh   774
Varieties
All American   774
Guernsey   774
Hollow crown   774
Ideal   774
Improved half long   774
Long smooth   774
Short thick   774
Smooth white   774
Student   774
White model   774
Peas   774-77, 905
Canned   774
Quality factors   954
Federal specifications   972
Field and black-eye   777
Canned   777
Fresh   777
Fresh   774

Vegetables (cont.)
Peas
Frozen   774
Quality factors   958
Storage   1003
Puree
Federal specifications   972
Southern peas (field peas or
black-eyed peas)
Federal specifications   972
Peas and Carrots   777-79
Canned   777
Federal specifications   973
Frozen   778
Peppers   779-82
Fresh   780
Frozen   780, 782
Sweet   780-82
Federal specifications   973
Frozen   782
Varieties
Burlington   780
California wonder   780
Chinese giant   780
Florida giant   780
Harris early giant   780
Keystone resistant giant   780
Neapolitan   780
Perfection   781
Ruby king   780
Windsor-A   781
World beater   781
Yolo wonder   781
Pimentos   782-83
Canned   782-83
Quality factors   956
Federal specifications   973
Potatoes   783-93
French fried   792-93
Strip styles   792
Fresh   784
Peeled   784
Seed   784
Varieties
Chippewa   786
Irish cobbler   786
Katahdin   785
Kennebec   785
La rouge   786
Norchip   785
Norgold russet   785
Norland   785
Red la soda   786
Red pontiac   785
Russet Burbank   785
Sebago   786
Superior   785
White rose   786
White
Canned   784, 790-91
Diced   790
Pieces   790
Shoestring   790

Vegetables (cont.)
Potatoes
White
Canned
Sliced   790
Whole   790
Federal specifications   973
Storage
Frozen   1004
Refrigerated   1014
Pumpkins   793-94
Canned   794
Quality factors   954
Federal specifications   973
Pumpkin and Squash
Canned   794
Radishes   794-96
Federal specifications   973
Fresh   796
Varieties
Globular   795
Long   795
Oblong   795
Oval   795
Turnip   795
Romaine
Federal specifications   973
Rutabagas or Turnips   796-98
Federal specifications   974
Fresh   798
Frozen   798
Varieties
American purple   797
Laurentian   797
Sauerkraut
Federal specifications   973
Quality factors, canned   954
Shallots, bunched
Federal specifications   973
Spinach   798-803
Canned   800
Quality factors   954
Federal specifications   973
Fresh   800
Frozen   800
Quality factors   958
Storage   1003
Puree
Federal specifications   973
Varieties
America   799
Bloomsdale dark green   799
Old dominion   799
Viking   799
Wild spinach   799
Squash   804-09
Fall and winter
Federal specifications   973
Puree
Federal specifications   973
Quality factors,
canned   954
Storage, frozen   1003

Vegetables (cont.)
Squash
Summer
Federal specifications   973
Varieties
Banana   805
Boston marrow   805
Buttercup   805
Caserta   804
Cocozelle   804
Delicious   805-06
Hubbard   806
Marblehead   806
Warren turban   806
Yellow crookneck   805
Yellow straightneck   805
Zucchini   805
Storage
Dry   993
Refrigerated   1013-15
Succotash   816-17
Federal specifications   973
Quality factors, canned   954
Sweet Potatoes   810-15
Federal specifications   974
Quality factors, canned   954
Varieties
Centennial   810
Georgia red   811
Goldrush   811
Nemagold   811
Orange little stem   811
Porto Rico   811
Swiss Chard   817-18
Federal specifications   974
Varieties
Burpee's rhubarb chard   818
Dark green white ribbed   818
Fordhook giant   818
Giant Lucullus   818
Lucullus   818
Rhubarb chard   818
Tomatoes   818-24
Federal specifications   974
Quality factors, canned   954
Storage, refrigerated   1013
Varieties
Ace (55)   819
Basket pack   819
Big boy   819
Campbell (1327)   819
Cardinal hybrid   819
Chico   819
Chico grande   819
Coronet   819
Early pack (7)   819
El Monte   819
Fantastic   819
Ferry-Morse (428) and (H-11)   819
Floradel   819
Grande   819
Heinz (1439)   819
Homestead-24   818

Vegetables *(cont.)*
  Tomatoes
    Varieties
      Indian river   819
      Kille (7)   819
      La Pinta   819
      Manalucie   819
      Manapal   819
      Marion   818
      Michigan-Ohio hybrid   819
      Moreton hybrid   819
      Pearson A-1   819
      Queen's knight   819
      Red cherry   819
      Roma VF   819
      Rutgers hybrid   819
      Spring giant   819
      Starfire   819
      Sunburst   819
      Superman   819
      Supermarket   819
      Tom-tom   819
      Tropic   819

Vegetables *(cont.)*
  Tomatoes
    Varieties
      Tropic-red   819
      Tuckcross O   819
      Veegan   819
    Tomatoes and Okra
      Federal specifications   974
    Turnips   824-27
      Federal specifications   974
      Greens   826-27
    Turnips-rutabagas   826
      Varieties
        Amber   826
        Golden ball   826
        Orange jelly   826
        Purple top white globe   825
        White egg shogoin   825-26
        Yellow Aberdeen   826
        Yellow globe   826
  Vegetables, mixed   827-28
    Beans, green or wax   827
    Beans, lima   827-28

Vegetables *(cont.)*
  Vegetables, mixed
    Carrots   828
    Corn   828
      Federal specifications   971
    Peas   828
    Watercress   828
  See also Appendixes; Produce
  Section
Vermicelli
  Federal specifications   983
Vinegar   944
  Federal specifications   983
  Storage, dry   995
Waffle Mix
  Federal specifications   983
Walnuts   914-17
  Federal specifications   984
Water
  Federal specifications   976
Water Ices
  Federal specifications   983
Waxy Maize Starch   944

Wheat
  Federal specifications   984
Wheat Base
  Federal specifications   984
White Sauce
  Storage, refrigerated   1015
Whiting
  Federal specifications   969
  See also Fish
Woodruff   939
Worcestershire Sauce   944
  Federal specifications   984
  Storage, dry   994
Yarrow   939
Yeast   944
  Baker's
    Federal
      specifications   984
  Dry
    Storage, dry   990
  Food
    Federal
      specifications   984

NOTES